T5-BYJ-098

St. James Encyclopedia of Popular Culture

Second Edition

St. James Encyclopedia of Popular Culture

Second Edition

VOLUME 3
1–NEW

Thomas Riggs
EDITOR

ST. JAMES PRESS
A part of Gale, Cengage Learning

GALE
CENGAGE Learning®

Detroit • New York • San Francisco • New Haven, Conn • Waterville, Maine • London

St. James Encyclopedia of Popular Culture

Thomas J. Riggs, Editor

Product Manager: Douglas Dentino

Project Editor: Carol A. Schwartz

Editorial: Laura Avery; Dana Barnes; Erin Bealmear; Shawn Corridor; Matthew Derda; Jason Everett; Dana Ferguson; Jennifer Greve; Kristy Harper; Kristin Hart; Alan Hedblad; Andrea Henderson; Monica Hubbard; Jeff Hunter; Victor Ibarra; Reed Kalso; Kristin Key; Debra Kirby; Laurie Malashanko; Kim McGrath; Chelsea Merchan; Kathy Nemeh; Scot Peacock; Jennifer Wisinski

Rights Acquisition and Management: Christine Myaskovsky

Composition: Gary Leach

Manufacturing: Wendy Blurton

Imaging: John Watkins

Product Design: Kristine Julien

LIBRARY OF CONGRESS CATALOGING-IN-PUBLICATION DATA

St. James encyclopedia of popular culture / Thomas Riggs, editor ; with an introduction by Jim Cullen. -- 2nd edition.
p. cm. --
Includes bibliographical references and index.
ISBN 978-1-55862-847-2 (set) -- ISBN 978-1-55862-848-9 (vol. 1) -- ISBN 978-1-55862-849-6 (vol. 2) -- ISBN 978-1-55862-850-2 (vol. 3) -- ISBN 978-1-55862-851-9 (vol. 4) -- ISBN 978-1-55862-852-6 (vol. 5) -- ISBN 978-1-55862-853-3 (ebook)
1. United States--Civilization--20th century--Encyclopedias. 2. United States--Civilization--21st century--Encyclopedias. 3. Popular culture--United States--History--20th century--Encyclopedias. 4. Popular culture--United States--History--21st century--Encyclopedias. I. Riggs, Thomas, 1963- II. Title: Saint James encyclopedia of popular culture.

E169.1.J3 2013
973.9--dc23 2012049921

Gale, a part of Cengage Learning
27500 Drake Rd.
Farmington Hills, MI, 48331-3535

ISBN-13: 978-1-55862-847-2 (set) ISBN-10: 1-55862-847-9 (set)
ISBN-13: 978-1-55862-848-9 (vol. 1) ISBN-10: 1-55862-848-7 (vol. 1)
ISBN-13: 978-1-55862-849-6 (vol. 2) ISBN-10: 1-55862-849-5 (vol. 2)
ISBN-13: 978-1-55862-850-2 (vol. 3) ISBN-10: 1-55862-850-9 (vol. 3)
ISBN-13: 978-1-55862-851-9 (vol. 4) ISBN-10: 1-55862-851-7 (vol. 4)
ISBN-13: 978-1-55862-852-6 (vol. 5) ISBN-10: 1-55862-852-5 (vol. 5)

This title is also available as an e-book.
ISBN-13: 978-1-55862-853-3 ISBN-10: 55862-853-3
Contact your Gale, a part of Cengage Learning, sales representative for ordering information.

Printed in China
1 2 3 4 5 6 7 17 16 15 14 13

Contents

List of Entries

C

VOLUME 2

C *continued*

D

VOLUME 3

I

J

M

VOLUME 5

S *continued*

T

U

V

W

I

I Dream of Jeannie

I Dream of Jeannie appeared on the NBC airwaves from 1965 to 1970, debuting with a handsome young air force astronaut parachuting down onto a deserted island after aborting a mission. While waiting for the rescue team, he finds a groovy purple bottle and uncorks it. In a puff of smoke, a curvaceous genie in a harem outfit appears, calls him Master, and instantly falls in love with him. Coming hot on the heels of the television sitcom *Bewitched*, about a good witch married to a mortal, *Jeannie* featured another magical blond who was denied use of her powers by the misguided man in her life. A glaring difference, however, was that Jeannie called her roommate (and the man she loved) Master, although in many ways Jeannie was really the one in charge in the relationship.

Barbara Eden, who played Jeannie (and occasionally her naughty sister), told *Entertainment Weekly*, "'Master' didn't mean she was a slave. 'Master' was the master because he got the bottle." Nevertheless, Jeannie did stop calling him Master once they got married, which was toward the end of the series run. The long-suffering Master was actually Anthony (Tony) Nelson, played by Larry Hagman.

The only other character who knew of Jeannie's existence at first was Tony's girl-crazy best friend and fellow astronaut, Roger Healey, played by Bill Daily. The supporting characters included Dr. Bellows, the base psychiatrist and perpetually dour straight man (Hayden Rorke); his overbearing wife, Amanda (Emmaline Henry); and an assortment of commanding officers. The first year it was General Stone (Philip Ober), to whose daughter Tony was engaged, although a jealous Jeannie made sure that relationship failed. By the second season father and daughter were both gone, the series went to color, and General Peterson (Barton MacLane) came in as the authority figure for most of the series after that, replaced only in the last season by General Schaeffer (Vinton Hayworth). Originally captains, Nelson and Healey were promoted to majors during the course of the series.

THE WEEKLY STORY

When Captain Nelson is first rescued from the deserted island, he tries to tell everyone about his magic discovery, but no one believes him. Dr. Bellows even diagnoses him as delusional. In addition, Jeannie disappears if anyone but Tony and Roger are around, often leaving them fumbling to get out of unexplainable situations. And that was the premise week after week: well-meaning, mischievous Jeannie "blinks" Tony into trouble, leaving him to find a way to explain it to Dr. Bellows. Sometimes Roger adds to the mix, putting Tony into situations that make Jeannie jealous; one of her favorite punishments is "blinking" someone into the tenuous position of hanging by a rope over a pit of alligators. The show's magical element gave the writers carte blanche with historical figures and situations; Tony was either "blinked" back in time, or they were "blinked" to him. Viewers also got to learn some unsubstantiated history of the Fertile Crescent—after all, Jeannie was originally from Baghdad.

I Dream of Jeannie could only have existed where and when it did on the cusp of the women's movement. Notwithstanding the whole master-slave issue, the arc of the show from beginning to end could also be interpreted as a metaphor for an old-fashioned view of the "power" that women have over men. She knows she will get him to fall in love with her by using her

I Dream of Jeannie. *Barbara Eden starred as the title character in* I Dream of Jeannie. SIDNEY SHELDON PRODS/THE KOBAL COLLECTION.

"magic" on him; he tries to deny the power and remain a bachelor but finally succumbs. In subsequent unsuccessful attempts at featuring genies in sitcoms, the genies were male. In one especially misguided 1983 attempt called *Just Our Luck*, the genie was an African American male . . . with a white master.

The show also captured the mid- to late-1960s fascination with the post-Kennedy space program. After all, the genie could just as well have been found by a tire salesman, but Nelson was an astronaut, frequently sent on missions. The moon landing seemed as magical as Jeannie's powers back then. It was somehow fitting that the series ended soon after the actual moon landing and as the more jaded 1970s began.

AFTER THE SERIES

In 1973 an animated *Jeannie* appeared on Saturday mornings. This Jeannie was not discovered by an astronaut but by a high school student named Corey Anders. In 1985 the dream heroine returned to television in the TV movie *I Dream of Jeannie Fifteen Years Later*. Eden and Daily rejoined the cast, but Hagman, by then again a household name as the ruthless J. R. Ewing on the prime-time drama *Dallas*, would have seemed quite out of place, so Wayne Rogers (Trapper John from TV's *M*A*S*H*) signed on as Nelson. This movie had a special significance: viewers were finally treated to the sight of Jeannie's belly button. Although Eden had spent much of the original series in a low-cut harem outfit, the pants were high-waisted enough to cover her navel, by order of NBC (they did not seem to have a problem with showing cleavage). Another network rule the series had to follow was that Jeannie's bottle could never be seen in Tony's bedroom.

Eden and Daily reunited again in the TV movie *I Still Dream of Jeannie* in 1991. The original series, created by best-selling novelist Sidney Sheldon and presumably named after the old Stephen Foster tune, enjoyed rerun success on Nick at Nite in the 1990s. "It's timeless," relates Eden in *Entertainment Weekly*. "A genie is always in a costume, and the guys in the show are in uniform, so it doesn't become dated."

Karen Lurie

SEE ALSO: Bewitched*;* Dallas*;* M*A*S*H*; Sheldon, Sidney; Sitcom; Television.*

BIBLIOGRAPHY

Baldwin, Kristen. "Dream Team." *Entertainment Weekly*, January 24, 1997, 11.

Brooks, Tim, and Earle Marsh. *The Complete Directory to Prime Time Network and Cable TV Shows 1946–Present*, 6th ed. New York: Ballantine Books, 1995.

McNeil, Alex. *Total Television*. New York: Penguin, 1996.

Mukherjee, Tiarra. "Still Dreaming of 'Jeannie.'" *Entertainment Weekly*, September 20, 1996, 91.

I Love a Mystery

The Golden Age of Radio produced many successful adventure series, but none is recalled with quite the same mixture of devotion and awe as Carlton E. Morse's *I Love a Mystery (ILAM)*. Radio historian John Dunning says that the program "weaves a spell over its fans that is all but inexplicable." While nostalgia often filters the static of creaky plots and wheezing gags characteristic of much of old-time radio, the few extant recordings of *ILAM* prove it to be worthy of its extravagant reputation and have made it the "most sought of all radio shows," according to Dunning. *ILAM* is to the world of radio mystery what *Amos 'n' Andy* is to radio comedy and *One Man's Family* is to radio soap opera—the peak achievement of its particular form. The bizarre adventures of the trio forming the A-1 Detective Agency ("No job too tough, no mystery too baffling") may have been too outrageous to be especially influential in the world of popular entertainment, and the series was not successful in its few forays into books and movies (although Indiana Jones would have fit right in as a fourth partner), but the program still bears examination for the way in which it exhibits, and yet transcends, many of the qualities that defined the classic era of radio drama.

ILAM's opening train whistle, followed by the haunting strains of Jean Sibelius's *Valse triste* and the eerie chiming of a clock, first sounded in 1939, heralding an initial string of fifteen-minute and half-hour serial adventures that would come to the end of the line in 1944. Reappearing in 1948 in a curiously muted form as *I Love Adventure*, the series finally got back on track in 1949, with a new cast reprising the scripts from the initial run, until the last chime sounded in 1952. Regardless of the format, Carlton Morse wrote the series at a feverish pitch, with a globe right next to him to help locate the next exotic setting to which he would zip his peripatetic heroes and rapt listeners. Whether holed up in a gloomy mansion with "The Thing That Cries in the Night" or facing down the mad Holy Joe on "The Island of Skulls," *ILAM*'s intrepid trio would be certain to encounter enough baffling mysteries, beautiful women, and howling terrors to outrage parents and delight their offspring.

The leader of the group was Jack Packard, a tough-talking rationalist who could find a logical explanation for anything he couldn't punch, but never found a dame he could trust. Texas cowboy Doc Long, Jack's loyal assistant (whose catchphrase was "Honest to my grandma!"), spent most of his time making certain that the many damsels in distress rejected by Jack were well taken care of. The trio was rounded out occasionally by spunky secretary Jerri Booker but most famously by the Englishman Reggie Yorke, who was voiced by a young Tony Randall in the show's later years and could be counted on to lend a more gentlemanly air to the proceedings. Plunging headlong into whatever harebrained escapade Morse could conjure up, the three comrades lived a life so outlandish as to make the *The Shadow* or *The Green Hornet* seem positively sedate in comparison.

While the series was most notable for its creative exaggeration of adventure genre trappings, it was innovative in at least three other ways as well. Although Jack, Doc, and Reggie encountered only the most remarkable mysteries and terrible villains, the three men themselves were satisfyingly ordinary. Lacking any special abilities beyond their love of a good scrap and grim determination, they were often puzzled, incorrect, or just plain scared out of their wits, lending to the otherwise fantastical goings-on a realism that listeners could identify with and share. The prosaic nature of the program's heroes was another key ingredient in *ILAM*'s unique formula, which combined elements from the private eye and adventure genres to create a new form capable of encompassing both traditional "whodunits" and blood-and-thunder terrors. Listeners never knew from one case to the next which would get a greater workout, thinking caps or fists. Finally, Morse was innovative in his storytelling style. While most radio dramas switched settings several times an episode, Morse liked to open and close each installment in the same location and to approximate "real time" as closely as possible. Such adherence to Aristotelian unity not only bolstered the show's verisimilitude but also heightened the suspense and allowed Morse to give each of his varied settings a powerful and individual atmosphere.

While the crazed characters and bizarre plots made the most immediate impact, it is the peculiar mood associated with each adventure that remains in the memory—the sound of a phantom baby crying before each murder in Grandma Martin's gloomy mansion, for example; or the howling winds of the Western ghost town with the unlikely name of Bury Your Dead, Arizona; or the "roar with lights and shades in it" that conjured the image of the giant waterfall hiding the magical "Stairway to the Sun." It is, finally, this almost dreamlike evocation of an otherworldly reality that enables *I Love a Mystery* to haunt listeners long after the final train whistle vanished in the distance.

Kevin Lause

SEE ALSO: The Amos 'n' Andy Show*;* The CBS Radio Mystery Theater*; Morse, Carlton E.; Radio; Radio Drama.*

BIBLIOGRAPHY

Dunning, John. *On the Air: The Encyclopedia of Old-Time Radio*. New York: Oxford University Press, 1998.

Harmon, Jim. *Radio Mystery and Adventure and Its Appearances in Film, Television and Other Media*. Jefferson, NC: McFarland, 1992.

Harmon, Jim. *The Great Radio Heroes*. Rev. and expanded ed. Jefferson, NC: McFarland, 2001.

Maltin, Leonard. *The Great American Broadcast: A Celebration of Radio's Golden Age*. New York: Dutton, 1997.

Nachman, Gerald. *Raised on Radio*. New York: Pantheon, 1998.

I Love Lucy

I Love Lucy, starring Lucille Ball and Desi Arnaz, is perhaps the most popular and influential television comedy of all time.

I Love Lucy. *Left to right, William Frawley, Vivian Vance, Lucille Ball, and Desi Arnaz play golf in an episode of* I Love Lucy *in 1951.* CBS/GETTY IMAGES.

Since its debut on CBS on October 15, 1951, the show has been translated into almost every language in the world and has run continuously in international syndication in U.S. markets and virtually every country in the world for more than a half century. When the show first began to rerun episodes in 1959, its ratings outperformed most of CBS's new programming that year. Such is the continuing popularity of the show that each episode is available in Spanish, Japanese, Italian, Portuguese, and French. The program also has become a popular cultural phenomenon, inspiring worldwide fan clubs, websites, retrospective screenings, and memorabilia for avid collectors. Postcards featuring classic scenes from the show, CDs of music from the series, dolls, lunch boxes, T-shirts, pajamas, aprons, and DVDs of episodes continue to sell at a phenomenal rate.

In 1983 a Los Angeles television station honored Ball on her seventy-second birthday by airing a thirteen-hour *I Love Lucy* marathon running from 9 a.m. until 10 p.m. The station vaulted to number one in the ratings and stayed there for the entire day, with each half hour winning its time period. The show also has been honored by the Academy of Television Arts and Sciences and by the Museum of Television and Radio.

The secret of the show's continuing popularity beyond the fact that it was incredibly funny and unceasingly creative is that it held up a mirror to every married couple in the United States. Although the mirror was more of the fun house than the cosmetic type, it was still unstintingly honest in its depiction. "We just took ordinary situations and exaggerated them," Ball admitted.

Additionally, the unpretentious family-oriented situation comedy virtually revolutionized the production and distribution of television shows, setting the standard for all the TV series to follow. The show was one of the first comedies performed before a live audience. It also originated the concept of producing a program on film instead of broadcasting it live. Shot with three cameras, the show could be fully edited before it was shown. Using film permitted the rebroadcast of high-quality prints of the show at a time when most of its competitors were rerunning their programming on poor-quality kinescopes of live shows photographed off the TV screen. The use of film hastened the move of the television industry from New York to Los Angeles, which, during the 1950s, became the hub of filmed programming. It also popularized the concept of reruns and proved that recycled programming could have renewed life on local stations once its network prime-time days had ended.

SHOW BEGINNINGS

Despite the later success of *I Love Lucy*, the show was viewed by many as a long shot when it began. In the late 1940s Ball had been playing opposite actor Richard Denning on a popular radio show *My Favorite Husband*. CBS-TV became impressed with the program and wanted to bring it to television, but Ball would agree only if her real husband, Desi Arnaz, could play opposite her in the Denning role. According to a number of sources, this demand was a ploy on her part to save her marriage, which had been gradually deteriorating. Although Ball and Arnaz had been married since 1940, they had been separated by the demands of their work, with him touring with his band while she was confined to Hollywood making films. According to Ball, if they both stayed in one place and did a television show, the process of working together would help their relationship. Unfortunately, CBS executives and the program's potential advertisers did not agree with the idea, feeling that casting a thick-accented Latino as the husband of a typical American wife would not sit well with U.S. viewers.

To convince them otherwise, the two performers formed Desilu Productions, put together a twenty-minute skit, and took it on a cross-country barnstorming tour. When the TV show did not immediately materialize, however, Ball went back to radio and Arnaz returned to his band. By the end of 1950, CBS relented somewhat, agreeing to let them do a pilot of the proposed show but declining to finance its production or the air time. Undeterred, Ball and Arnaz raised the money themselves and came up with a script about a successful bandleader and his movie-star wife. Yet, they could not find a sponsor willing to put the show on the air. The basic problem was that the pilot relied too much on vaudeville traits with an overemphasis on rapid repartee and one-liners.

At this point, composer Oscar Hammerstein Jr., who had toured with Arnaz, stepped in and suggested that the show be rewritten. He lobbied to keep the comedic sense of the show but to shed the movie-star trappings and to make the characters appear more like an ordinary couple. Arnaz remained a bandleader but would be a struggling one; like many people in the United States, he would occupy his time trying to get his big break. When the show began, his character was leading the house band at New York's Tropicana nightclub. Ball's character would be an ordinary housewife harboring visions of breaking into show business that she would act upon almost weekly with inevitably comic results.

Another stumbling point for the show was the title. Arnaz was an unknown quantity, while Ball had a popular following from her motion pictures and radio work, so CBS wanted to call the program *The Lucille Ball Show*. Ball objected because Arnaz's name was not in the title, so an advertising agency executive working on the show suggested the "off-the-wall" title *I Love Lucy*. Since the *I* stood for Arnaz, Ball quickly agreed, feeling that the almost equal billing would help her marriage: not only was her husband's name in the title, but also with this format he was actually listed first.

FILMING THE SHOW

The show's production location became yet another source of contention. CBS wanted to broadcast from New York City, the center of the fledgling television industry in 1950, but Ball and Arnaz were reluctant to leave Los Angeles and their show business connections in case the show failed. CBS objected because broadcasting from Los Angeles would mean that the rest of the country would be able to view the show only through the use of kinescopes. Arnaz suggested that if the show were shot on 35-millimeter film, as motion pictures were, CBS could distribute high-quality prints to network affiliates throughout the country in a manner similar to the distribution systems employed by most movie studios. The production costs would be higher, but the overall product would be much better.

The network agreed but was still faced with the never-before-attempted problem of actually filming a thirty-minute TV show. To overcome this hurdle, CBS hired Oscar-winning cinematographer Karl Freund (*The Good Earth*, 1937), who collaborated with Ball and Arnaz on treating the show like a stage play and filming it before a live audience, a rare occurrence in 1950. It also was decided to film with three cameras, each shooting from a different angle, and then edit the best shots into the finished product. Director Marc Daniels, one of the few directors to have experience with three cameras, was hired to direct the show. He also had a background in the theater working with live audiences.

To provide a counterpoint for the married Ball and Arnaz characters, another couple who lived upstairs joined the cast. After a number of actors and actresses were considered, the parts went to Vivian Vance and William Frawley. However, both were considered risky choices at the time. Vance was coming off a string of stage successes but was not nationally known (in fact, Ball and Arnaz had never heard of her when her name was proposed); Frawley was rumored to be an alcoholic and unreliable.

The show's four lead characters of Lucy and Ricky Ricardo and Fred and Ethel Mertz (Frawley and Vance) relate to each other amazingly well. The combination of the younger, more affluent Ricardos and the older, fixed-income Mertzes gave the writers a number of opportunities to take the show in different directions without covering the same themes week after week. One episode might find Lucy and Ethel involving themselves in a crazy scheme, with Ricky and Fred attempting to teach them a lesson. The next might feature the two men planning a secret outing, while the women try to crash the party. The Mertzes provided a mainstream older couple to offset the always volatile mixed marriage of the Ricardos.

The Ricardos portray a recognizable American family. Together, they explored the dynamics of their relationship in a manner that was new to television sitcoms. They are able to convey the fact that while they are adversaries in many of Lucy's "break into show business" shenanigans, they are also deeply in love with each other at the same time. Though bonded as a couple, each character maintains his or her own unique individuality.

CHARACTER ATTRIBUTES

Lucy, with her natural clownlike features, reflects a combination of Yankee bravura and touching vulnerability. Although, true to the times, she was cast as a housewife, she displays a striking independence and is unafraid to speak her mind to her macho Latin husband. For his part, Ricky represents a spectrum of familiar characters. Beginning with the macho hubris of a Latin lover, his expressive face and brown eyes run the gamut from childlike vulnerability to fiery Latin anger that expresses itself through a hilarious accent that mangles the English language beyond repair.

Lucy is a stage-struck schemer, possessed with a hyperactive imagination. The character relies on an arsenal of visual and vocal tricks in her effort to execute her wild schemes to crash the world of show business or to outsmart her husband when she gets caught. The first is her tendency to drop her jaw in an open-mouthed stance to express her disbelief at what is occurring. When this does not work, she holds both arms straight out in front of her and then drops her forearms to indicate that something has gone wrong. Vocally, she adopts a high-pitched voice that erupts in a shriek when she is caught in an embarrassing moment. Then comes the cry, monumental in nature, which rises from her gut and then slowly wails its way up the register to the pitch of a police siren. This is followed by a blubbering whimper that constitutes her final plea for sympathy and understanding. If her adversary happens to be Ricky, as was most often the case, she then throws his mangled English language back at him as he attempts to scold her.

The writers used the characters' differing ethnic backgrounds to great comedic effect. Ricky's accent and nationality formed the nucleus of some of the show's more popular running gags. In addition to his mispronunciation of words, which was a real occurrence for Arnaz as well as Ricky, the Cuban actor also erupts in a string of Latin epithets whenever he gets mad. As Arnaz admitted in an interview, he had to walk a fine line in his use of the language to make sure that it came across as humor instead of rage. "It was the most difficult problem I faced while playing Ricky," he said. "It helped when I overemphasized the acceptable Latin use of hands and arms when I was excited. Most of all, the rat-tat-tat-tat parade of Spanish words helped me tread that thin line between funny mad and mad mad." He augmented this with an ability to pop out his eyes in an inimitable expression of incredulity in reaction to Lucy's antics.

The Mertzes, on the other hand, provide a calmer counterpart to the fiery Ricardos. Ethel and Fred are, first and foremost, older than their downstairs neighbors and somewhat more passive. The Vance character provides a "girlfriend" for Lucy and a partner in crime. Fred is a pal of Ricky's and someone who helps him in his schemes to thwart Lucy. He also provides one of the series' recurring gags, with many jokes and episodes being built on his miserly actions. He simply does not like to spend money—a fact that sends the other three characters into a tizzy.

CRITICAL ACCLAIM

The show premiere won unanimous critical approval. It achieved the sixteenth position in the ratings within eight weeks and climbed to number three by the end of the season with an average of twenty-nine million viewers watching the show each week. The premise is established in the pilot show when Lucy disguises herself as a clown to sneak into Ricky's nightclub act. Throughout the rest of the season, she continues to rebel against the confines of her life as a housewife and the unfair restrictions of a male-dominated society that seemingly conspire to thwart her dreams of breaking into show business. Each of her attempts to enter into the entertainment world ends in a spectacular mess, and she is inevitably forced to backtrack into the shackles of home and hearth.

The show was so popular that department stores, doctors, and dentists canceled their Monday night hours because viewers would not leave their TV sets. During the presidential elections, candidate Adlai Stevenson's office was flooded with hate mail when he cut in on *I Love Lucy* for a five-minute campaign spiel. This mistake was not repeated a decade later when CBS was tempted to preempt morning reruns of the show to televise the Senate Vietnam War hearings but backed away because of fears that viewers would be outraged.

LATER PLOTS

In succeeding seasons the show continued to build on the basic premise as Lucy and Ricky's on-screen married life evolved. In the second and third seasons the show centers on the birth of Little Ricky, which was the most popular episode in television history for many years (interestingly, more people watched the birth of Little Ricky than watched the inauguration of Dwight D. Eisenhower as thirty-fourth president of the United States and the coronation of Queen Elizabeth II of England, all in 1953). Predictably, the biggest adjustment for Lucy lay in the impact of motherhood on her dreams of crashing into show business. The fourth season finds Ricky landing a screen test with a Hollywood studio and devotes a number of episodes to a cross-country trip from New York to Hollywood, where Lucy becomes involved in adventures with celebrity guest stars, including a now famous encounter with William Holden in a comedy of mistaken identities.

The fifth season has the family returning to New York but quickly taking off on a laugh-filled adventure tour of Europe. The final season revolves around the exploits of now five-year-old Little Ricky and the couple's move to the suburbs. Ricky purchases the Tropicana and renames it the Club Babalu, and the family grows in affluence and begins to tackle a variety of family issues.

One of the prime secrets of the show's success in addition to the chemistry among the four regulars was that the production team stayed relatively intact over the full run of the show. The writer/producer Jess Oppenheimer and the two regular writers Madelyn Pugh and Bob Carroll Jr. came over with Ball from the *My Favorite Husband* radio show, and only three directors were employed during the show's original production: Marc Daniels (1951–1952), William Asher (1952–1956), and James V. Kern (1955–1956).

THE SHOW ENDS

By 1957, however, Ball and Arnaz had grown tired of the weekly grind of series TV and ceased production of the program. But that was not the end of the characters. They were featured over the next three years in a series of thirteen one-hour episodes airing as specials and as episodes of the *Westinghouse-Desilu Playhouse*, which ran from 1958 to 1960. Their production company, Desilu, which was started primarily to produce *I Love Lucy*, grew from twelve employees in 1951 to 800 in 1957 and branched out into producing a number of well-regarded programs, including *The Danny Thomas Show*, for other networks and producers. In 1957 the company purchased the old RKO Studios and continued to be one of the most influential producers of the 1950s and 1960s.

The Arnazes divorced in 1960, and Ball went to New York to appear in the Broadway show *Wildcat*. She married comedian Gary Morton and returned to network TV in 1962 with *The Lucy Show*, which also featured Vance and Gale Gordon. The show ran until 1968, when it was retitled *Here's Lucy* and featured Ball's real-life children, Lucie and Desi Jr. Vance made only sporadic appearances between 1968 and 1971, but the show continued until 1974 as part of the CBS Monday night comedy bloc that dominated the ratings for the entire period that Ball's show ran.

Steve Hanson
Sandra Garcia-Myers

SEE ALSO: *Arnaz, Desi; Ball, Lucille; Frawley, William; Holden, William; Hollywood; Screwball Comedies; Sitcom; Television; Vance, Vivian.*

BIBLIOGRAPHY

Andrews, Bart. *Lucy & Ricky & Fred & Ethel: The Story of "I Love Lucy."* New York: Dutton, 1976.

Andrews, Bart. *The* I Love Lucy *Book*. New York: Doubleday, 1985.

Brooks, Tim, and Earle Marsh. *The Complete Directory to Prime Time Network and Cable TV Shows 1946–Present*, 6th ed. New York: Ballantine Books, 1995.

Edwards, Elisabeth. I Love Lucy: *Celebrating Fifty Years of Love and Laughter*. Philadelphia: Running Press, 2003.

Hill, Tom. *Nick at Nite's Classic TV Companion*. New York: Simon & Schuster, 1966.

Horowitz, Susan. *Queens of Comedy*. Amsterdam: Gordon and Breach Publishers, 1997.

Krohn, Katherine E. *Lucille Ball: Pioneer of Comedy*. Minneapolis, MN: Lerner Publications, 1992.

McClay, Michael. I Love Lucy: *The Complete Picture History of the Most Popular TV Show Ever*. New York: Warner Books, 1995.

Mitz, Rick. *The Great TV Sitcom Book*. New York: Perigee Book, 1983.

Oppenheimer, Jess. *Laughs, Luck and Lucy: How I Came to Create the Most Popular Sitcom of All Time*. New York: Syracuse University Press, 1996.

Waldron, Vince. *Classic Sitcoms*. New York: Macmillan, 1987.

Warner Bros. *Warner Bros. Presents Television Favorites*. Miami, FL: Warner Bros., 1995.

I Spy

The popular NBC network television program *I Spy* ran for three years from 1965 to 1968. Arriving in the wake of the James Bond phenomenon in the mid-1960s, it was one of several American television series of the period whose fantastic plots revolved around matters of espionage. It was the alchemical partnership of actors Robert Culp and Bill Cosby, however, that elevated *I Spy* to the pantheon of well-loved and well-remembered escapist entertainment, although the duo was supported by scripts that were consistently witty. The stars played secret agents who roamed the world masquerading as a professional tennis player (Culp) and his manager/trainer (Cosby). Cosby thus became the first black actor in American television to star in a prime-time drama as a hero character on an equal footing with his white fellow actors. Noteworthy, too, for its foreign locations, *I Spy* was filmed almost entirely outside the United States, frequently in Mexico, the Mediterranean areas of Europe, and Asia.

In 1994 the *I Spy* duo returned in a television movie called *I Spy Returns*. The plot visited Scott and Robinson some years after their spy days, with Scott working as a college professor and Robinson in management at the spy organization. In 2002 a feature film version was released. It starred Eddie Murphy and Owen Wilson in the leading roles.

David Lonergan

SEE ALSO: *Cosby, Bill; James Bond Films; Murphy, Eddie; Television.*

BIBLIOGRAPHY

Brooks, Tim, and Earle Marsh. *The Complete Directory to Prime Time Network and Cable TV Shows*, 6th ed. New York: Ballantine Books, 1995.

Cushman, Marc, and Linda J. LaRosa. *I Spy: A History and*

Episode Guide to the Groundbreaking Television Series. Jefferson, NC: McFarland, 2007.

I Was a Teenage Werewolf

I Was a Teenage Werewolf is generally considered the first of a genre of horror films targeting teenage audiences. The birth of this genre can be attributed to television, drive-in theaters, and the rise of suburbia. Because adults in the 1950s were content to stay home and watch television, teenagers became the marketing targets of the motion picture industry.

The film was the brainchild of twenty-nine-year-old producer Herman Cohen. American International Pictures (AIP) released the film to much notoriety. In this conservative and frightened era, parents and even the federal government felt the delinquency depicted in the film would promote the same type of behavior offscreen—there were even government investigations that attempted to prove this. All this negative publicity brought teenagers to see the film in droves, making it AIP's biggest moneymaker of 1957. *I Was a Teenage Werewolf* also spawned a series of films that put a spin on the original title.

Jill A. Gregg

SEE ALSO: *American International Pictures; "B" Movies; Horror Movies; Landon, Michael; Teenagers.*

BIBLIOGRAPHY

Arkoff, Sam, and Richard Trubo. *Flying through Hollywood by the Seat of My Pants: From the Man Who Brought You* I Was a Teenage Werewolf *and* Muscle Beach Party. Secaucus, NJ: Carol Publishing Group, 1992.

Kessler, Lauren. *My Teenage Werewolf: A Mother, a Daughter, a Journey through the Thicket of Adolescence*. New York: Penguin, 2011.

McGee, Mark Thomas. *Fast and Furious: The Story of American International Pictures*. Jefferson, NC: McFarland, 1984.

Iacocca, Lee *(1924–)*

Lee Iacocca grew up as a blunt-spoken, patriotic son of immigrants and rose to become president of the Ford Motor Company and, later, chief executive officer of the Chrysler Corporation.

Born Lido Anthony Iacocca in Allentown, Pennsylvania, in 1924, Iacocca earned an engineering degree from Lehigh University and a master's degree from Princeton University before joining Ford as a student engineer in 1946. After less than a year, he talked his way into a sales job and, at the age of thirty-three, became the head of all national car marketing at the company's Detroit, Michigan, headquarters. He became vice president and general manager of the Ford Division in 1960.

THE MUSTANG

In his new position, Iacocca recognized the growing power of the youth market (the average age of car buyers at the time was thirty-one) and organized a team to design a car for it. He repackaged the engine and platform from the moderately successful Ford Falcon and placed it within a European-inspired, stylish shell, designed to capture the excitement of youth. The result was the Mustang, a small car that could seat four people and weighed less than most cars on the road. At $2,300 each, Ford sold more than 400,000 Mustangs in 1964, its first model year. Soon Mustang clubs and paraphernalia such as key chains and hats sprang up around the country. A picture of the car ran simultaneously on the covers of both *Time* and *Newsweek*, and Iacocca also appeared inside the magazines.

In 1970 Iacocca was named president of Ford, second in the company only to Chairman Henry Ford II. Iacocca soon released another successful car, the Cougar, as well as a large failure, the Pinto. When his aggressive ambition and showboating drew the ire of Ford, a power struggle developed between the two men. As each attempted to outmaneuver the other, Ford promoted other executives above his former number two man. Despite the company's profits of $1.8 billion in both 1976 and 1977, Iacocca was fired in 1978.

THE MOVE TO CHRYSLER

In 1978, Iacocca accepted the position of CEO at the unprofitable and debt-ridden Chrysler Corporation across town. He was famous when working at Ford, but at Chrysler, Iacocca built himself into a celebrity. The car industry in America traditionally represented the best successes of American capitalism. But by the 1970s, it had come to signify inefficiency and the abdication of America's economic leadership role to international, or "foreign," competition. When Iacocca took over Chrysler, it was the smallest of the Big Three American automakers and was rapidly losing money and market share.

Iacocca made a number of radical, public steps to turn the company around. In an unprecedented move, in 1979 he lobbied the American government to bail Chrysler out of its financial problems. After a protracted public debate in the media and on Capitol Hill, both houses of Congress approved $1.5 billion of loan guarantees for the company. Iacocca won discounts from his suppliers, wage concessions from his workers, and loan payment reschedulings from Chrysler's creditors. Prior to these bold steps, the auto industry had traditionally fought government interference and proudly recalled the day Henry Ford shocked the country by doubling his workers' wages. Its executives had boasted of how America's prosperity was tied to its successful auto industry.

As part of his aggressive salvage effort, Iacocca put a face on America's tenth-largest corporation, appending his signature to Chrysler print ads and personally appearing in its television ads. He played the role of the blunt, tough-talking, honest businessman by challenging the public, "If you can find a better car—buy it!" He not only personalized the fight to save Chrysler as *his* fight but represented it as America's fight to save itself. In Chrysler's television ads he appeared surrounded by red, white, and blue, entreating viewers, "Let's make America mean something again." Iacocca's public persona was the right image at the right time. When Ronald Reagan came to occupy the White House in 1981, a wave of patriotism was sweeping the country, and the American carmaker's challenge to be proud of America and its products was met with a warm response.

NEW MODELS

In 1980 Chrysler released its line of utilitarian K-cars, similar in build to Iacocca's beloved Mustang but its polar opposite in terms of character and style. Boxy, plain, and functional, the K-cars were spare, restrained cars for a time of diminished economic expectations. Iacocca, ever the patriot, boasted that, though they were small and light, they were still "roomy enough to hold 'six Americans.'" His next move was to introduce the nation's first minivan. It was wildly successful, and other automakers soon released their own versions.

By 1983 Chrysler had paid back its loans seven years early and was a remarkable success story by any measure. Iacocca was treated as a national hero and was considered a possible presidential candidate. In the mid-1980s he published a best-selling autobiography and served as chairman of the commission that renovated the Statue of Liberty.

Iacocca retired from Chrysler in 1992. After his departure, he publicly criticized the new management's efforts to improve quality and, in 1996, joined an investment group seeking to acquire the automaker. The effort failed and, ironically, earned him such enmity from within Chrysler that it canceled plans to name its new headquarters after him. In 2007 Iacocca published a book called *Where Have All the Leaders Gone?* in which he vented his outrage over what he perceived as a lack of leadership in both American government and the auto industry.

As the father of the Mustang, Iacocca considers himself a "car man" who disdained the bean counters at Ford and understood what made automobiles magical and exhilarating to Americans. Though he depended on the government, his workers, his creditors, and his suppliers to help Chrysler out of trouble, his unabashed challenge to be proud of America and its products won him the image of a self-reliant patriot out to redeem the country. Throughout, Iacocca was a master creator of products, profits, and his own image.

Steven Kotok

SEE ALSO: *Advertising; Automobile; Ford Motor Company; Minivans;* Newsweek; *Reagan, Ronald;* Time.

BIBLIOGRAPHY

Collier, Peter, and Chris Horowitz. *The Fords: An American Epic*. New York: Summit Books, 1987.

Iacocca, Lee, and William Novak. *Iacocca: An Autobiography*. New York: Bantam Books, 1984.

Iacocca, Lee, and Catherine Whitney. *Where Have All the Leaders Gone?* New York: Scribner, 2007.

Ingrassia, Paul J., and Joseph B. White. *Comeback: The Rise and Fall of the American Automobile Industry*. New York: Simon & Schuster, 1994.

Levin, Doron P. *Behind the Wheel at Chrysler: The Iacocca Legacy*. New York: Harcourt Brace, 1995.

IBM (International Business Machines)

According to the *Washington Post*, "IBM didn't invent the computer . . . it invented the computer industry." Eventually expanding to become the largest company in the world, International Business Machines (IBM) came to represent, at different points in its history, the best and the worst of big business and American corporate culture.

IBM Computer, 1944. *Operators tend to IBM's Harvard Mark I Automatic Sequence Controlled Calculator (ASCC) on the campus of Harvard University in 1944.* **PHOTOQUEST/GETTY IMAGES.**

COMPANY FOUNDERS

Charles Ranlett Flint founded the Computing-Tabulating-Recording Company in 1911 after acquiring three companies that manufactured products including shopkeepers' scales, punch clocks, and the large tabulating machines used by the census bureau. Flint hired Thomas J. Watson Sr. to run his new company. Watson was a star salesman and business executive at National Cash Register before joining what would become IBM. Upon his arrival he implemented a system of territories, quotas, and commissions for his salesmen. The motto "THINK" was posted in all branch offices, and salesmen were required to dress in sharp blue suits and white shirts. Those who met their quota joined the Hundred Percent Club.

His methods were successful, and by 1920 the company had tripled its revenues to $15.9 million. Watson renamed the firm International Business Machines in 1924. The sales focus and buttoned-up image Watson honed during the company's early days came to define IBM through the remainder of the twentieth century.

Beyond his sales focus, Watson was evangelical in his company pride and instilled his brand of optimism in his employees. He offered perks such as company sports teams, bands, and family outings. In the 1930s IBM became one of the first companies to offer life insurance, survivor benefits, and paid vacations to its staff, and during World War II it used profits from its government weapons manufacturing to start a fund for widows and orphans of IBM war casualties.

From its origins as a manufacturer of tabulating machines hawked by impeccably dressed salesmen, IBM came to dominate the computer mainframe market in the 1950s, 1960s, and 1970s, earning the moniker Big Blue. Fueled by the personal computer boom of the early 1980s, the company became the largest and most profitable corporation the world had yet known. Ranked as America's most admired company year after year in surveys of U.S. businesses, IBM astonished the business community and consumers alike with its consistent growth and profitability; its lifetime employment policy; and its famed management methods, crack sales force, and technological leadership. It represented to many the ideal of what American corporate culture and big business could achieve.

By the early 1990s, however, IBM had come to represent just the opposite. In a very public fall from grace, it recorded the largest-ever financial loss in corporate history, abandoned its lifetime employment guarantee, and shed tens of thousands of workers. The company, it seemed, had become the epitome of an overgrown, anonymous, monopolistic, bureaucratic monster—outmatched in marketing and technology by swifter, nimbler competitors. Seemingly too big to change, it appeared destined to collapse under its own ungainly weight. By the end of the twentieth century, though, IBM staged a turnaround and reemerged as a profitable corporate giant once more.

SUCCESS THROUGH COMPUTERS

From the beginning IBM grew rapidly. Through the 1920s and 1930s the company profited by renting electric punched-card accounting machines to large companies. During the Great Depression, famously holding to its optimism and faith that the economy would improve, it continued production at full capacity, even as sales declined. By 1936 IBM held 85 percent of the office machine market, with sales of more than $26 million. New Deal programs such as the Social Security Act of 1935 required businesses and government alike to keep more records, thus increasing the demand for IBM's punched-card tabulating systems. By 1940 IBM had revenues of $46 million and a workforce of nearly 13,000 employees. *Fortune* magazine proclaimed, "The International Business Machines Corporation has beheld no past so golden as the present. The face of Providence is shining upon it . . . it has skirted the slough of the Depression . . . its growth has been strong and steady."

The mainframe computer business propelled IBM's explosive growth in the postwar era. After World War II, Watson greatly increased the firm's research and development budget, and his son, Thomas Watson Jr., championed computer development. In 1948 IBM installed one of its first computers—abuzz with thousands of neon lamps, relays, switches, tape readers, and punches—on the ground floor of its New York headquarters for passersby to gawk at through the window. By 1960 there were 5,000 computers in the United States, most of them made by IBM, whose annual revenues had ballooned to $1.6 billion.

During this period, IBM was legendary as a fair and generous employer. Watson Sr. had not resorted to mass layoffs during the Depression and continued to pay salaries to absent employees serving in World War II. The firm generously paid moving expenses for transferred employees, guaranteeing a minimum resale price for their homes and retraining spouses for jobs in their new cities. Most famous of all was IBM's guarantee of lifetime employment for all workers.

Through its introduction of large-scale public goods, the company became an institution. IBM created FORTRAN in 1957, the world's first widely accepted computer language. In 1964 it implemented the largest civilian computerization task ever undertaken, the revolutionary SABRE reservation system used by American Airlines, and then implemented similar systems for the other major airlines. In 1973 IBM created and launched the ubiquitous Universal Product Code and bar code systems used in supermarkets.

But IBM's core business was mainframe computers, holding a 70 percent market share in this area through the 1960s. Its competitors, left to split up the remainder of the industry, were often referred to in the business press as the "seven dwarfs." IBM's investment in research and development was unmatched. In the 1960s the company undertook its largest-ever development project up to that point, a $5 billion push to create the next generation of mainframe computers, an effort larger than the Manhattan Project.

As technology advanced, computing power became less concentrated in large mainframes and, by the mid-1970s personal computers were possible in the home, each as powerful as the early mainframes of decades before. IBM's next challenge was to sell these computers, not directly to other businesses via its sales network as in the past but to consumers through the retail market. In the early 1980s the company unveiled its line of personal computers, which propelled its growth ever higher, even as new competitors such as Apple Computer and Microsoft began to stake out claims in the growing market.

CHALLENGES TO BIG BLUE

Dubbed "America's most beloved stock" by *Barron's* and "long the bluest of the blue-chip performers" by the *Washington Post*, the reliability and size of IBM stock and dividend growth was renowned. According to *Barron's*, "just about everyone and his dog owns IBM." Watson Jr. was labeled "the greatest capitalist in history" by *Fortune* magazine, and IBM was featured in the 1982 business book *In Search of Excellence*. It grew to be the most valuable company in the world in 1984, worth $72 billion and earning the largest profit ever to that point, $6.6 billion.

But as IBM's reputation as a wildly successful and innovative company was growing, it was coming to represent something else too. In 1969 the government began a thirteen-year, ultimately unsuccessful antitrust case against the company. In 1975 IBM pulled the plug on its five-year Future Systems development project for the next generation of mainframe computers, effectively wasting more than $100 million and many millions of staff hours. The impression was spreading that IBM was just too big—involved in too many businesses and too bureaucratic to execute or innovate—and that as a monopoly it didn't even have to try.

In 1984, the year of IBM's record profits and valuation, a comparatively small upstart, Apple Computer, ran a historic television advertisement during the Super Bowl. In the ad, an endless regiment of identical gray drones stared at a large screen, listening to a speech by an authoritarian leader—only to be freed by a colorful interloper who shatters the screen. This portrayal of Big Blue as Big Brother was an explicit reference to the dystopian totalitarian vision in George Orwell's novel *1984*.

The final blows came in the early 1990s, when the company suffered its first loss in history and its stock market value fell by more than half. In 1993 the company took a loss of $8.5 billion. Said *Barron's* in late 1992, "The old saw that IBM is always a safe stock pick, handed down through the generations . . . finally bit the dust last week." In 1992 *Fortune* wrote about IBM's "bulging, lethargic bureaucracy," noting that "employee morale is in the dumps," labeling the company a "humbled American corporate behemoth" with an "inward-looking culture" that had "lost touch with consumers." According to the *Wall Street Journal*, by 1993 the company had "unraveled." IBM ran nearly 100 different voluntary buyout and early retirement programs to reduce staff while trying to maintain its no-layoff policy.

IBM'S RECOVERY

By the late 1990s IBM had largely recovered. By hiring its first CEO from outside the company, acquiring other firms, and selling off some of its businesses, it was able to regain profitability but not its unquestioned dominance in what had become a much larger industry. Even so, it held an enviable position. Its move toward placing more emphasis on software and services—combined with an ad campaign that touted IBM as helping to build a "smarter planet"—helped the company regain a healthy profit margin. *Fortune* magazine listed it as number seven on the list of the twenty most profitable companies of 2010. In 2011, the hundredth anniversary of IBM's founding, *Fortune* reported that it had nearly 427,000 employees and nearly a trillion dollars in sales. Those figures caused IBM to be ranked as the thirty-first largest company in the world.

For many Americans, IBM—strong, paternalistic, and rapidly growing—was emblematic of the triumph of American corporate culture for most of the twentieth century. This made the company's dramatic failures in the early 1990s all the more astonishing, as observers watched the company rapidly became a symbol for all that was wrong, not right, with corporate America. Its reemergence in the late 1990s saved the company but not the rarefied ideal that large, benevolent corporations could represent the best of an ingenious, industrious, and compassionate American business culture. That was an American myth that IBM helped to create and ultimately helped to dispel.

Steven Kotok

SEE ALSO: *Apple Computer; Consumerism; The Fifties;* Fortune; *Industrial Design; The Internet; Microsoft; New Deal; Stock Market Crashes; Super Bowl; World War II.*

BIBLIOGRAPHY

Campbell-Kelly, Martin, and William Aspray. *Computer: A History of the Information Machine*. New York: HarperCollins, 1997.

Carrol, Paul. *Big Blues: The Unmaking of IBM*. New York: Crown Publishers, 1993.

Maney, Kevin. *The Maverick and His Machine: Thomas Watson, Sr. and the Making of IBM*. Hoboken, NJ: John Wiley & Sons, 2003.

Mills, Daniel Quinn, and G. Bruce Friesen. *Broken Promises: An Unconventional View of What Went Wrong at IBM*. Boston: Harvard Business School Press, 1996.

Pugh, Emerson W. *Building IBM: Shaping an Industry and Its Technology*. Cambridge, MA: MIT Press, 1995.

Rodgers, William H. *Think: A Biography of the Watsons and IBM*. New York: Stein and Day, 1969.

Watson, Thomas J., and Peter Petre. *Father, Son and Co.* New York: Bantam Books, 1990.

iCarly

A children's comedy aired on Nickelodeon, *iCarly* centers on Carly Shay (Miranda Cosgrove), an Internet-savvy teenager from Seattle, Washington, who produces a webcast with best friends Sam Puckett (Jennette McCurdy) and Freddie Benson (Nathan Kress). Although Carly is ostensibly raised by her older brother, Spencer, an eccentric twenty-something artist who is her legal guardian, the show does not often focus on family dynamics and the challenges of growing up without parents, as many shows featuring characters with similar family backgrounds do. Instead, *iCarly* concentrates on the ups and downs of digital life. Since it first aired in 2007, episodes have examined the challenges of securing advertising for a webcast; the pressure of providing content to insatiable fans; the way cyberspace imposes on one's privacy; the sense of isolation engendered by social media; cyber-bullying; and, somewhat more whimsically, the perils a teen encounters when coping with world fame.

iCarly is arguably one of the first teen shows to prioritize Internet life over home life, although several episodes do stress the importance of having loved ones in proximity and other issues important to tweens, including relationships and environmental activism. Carly's father, though he rarely appears on screen, is in the military. Her mother is neither seen nor mentioned. The show examines some of the complications arising from Carly's home life when First Lady Michelle Obama joins Carly in the eighth episode of season five ("iMeet the First Lady") as part of Obama's Joining Forces initiative—a program that provides services and opportunities for military members and their families.

Many aspects of the show parody the digital life of twenty-first century teens. The title itself is a play on Internet-based media products such as the iPod. Within the show, references to the computer company Pear are a parody of real-life computer company Apple, and the show's social networking website Splashface is a mashup of MySpace and Facebook. *iCarly* also includes a unique audience participation element in which viewer-submitted video clips are written into the script.

Though it has not garnered much critical acclaim, *iCarly* remains tremendously popular with its target market and has won the Kids Choice Award for Favorite Kids Show each year from 2008 to 2011. *iCarly* has also been nominated for three Emmys for Outstanding Children's Program, and the "iCarly Saves TV" special won the most-viewed entertainment show on cable TV in June 2008. In addition to the popular television series itself, *iCarly* has spawned a successful franchise that includes made-for-television movies, a music soundtrack, an interactive website, several video games for the Nintendo DS and the Wii systems, an app sold through Apple's iTunes store, a Twitter feed, a Facebook fan site, books, and ongoing concert tours. Much like the tech-savvy teens on the show, the *iCarly* franchise keeps pace with ever-changing online media formats. As of 2012, this constant evolution and wide media presence helped to propel *iCarly* into its sixth season.

Dayna Goldstein

SEE ALSO: *Apple Computer; Cable TV; Facebook; The Internet; iPad; iPod / iTunes; Sitcom; Social Media; Teenagers; Television; Tweens; Twitter; Wii.*

BIBLIOGRAPHY

Gleason, Lindsay. "iTalk with iCarly." *Current Events*, November 2009, 6.

Rogers, John. "'iCarly' Combines the Internet with TV." Fox News. Accessed June 2012. Available from http://www.foxnews.com/printer_friendly_wires/2007Sep18/0,4675,APonTViCarly,00.html

Ross, Robin. "*iCarly* Coming to an End, Cast to Film Together for Final Time in June." *TV Guide*, May 17, 2012.

Starr, Michael. "Kid $tar: iCarly." *New York Post*, March 19, 2010.

Ice Cream Cone

The ice cream cone is a familiar feature of the American leisure landscape, carrying with it associations of fairgrounds, ice cream parlors, drugstore soda fountains, and all-American kids (and adults) enjoying a treat in the sunshine. Since its invention early in the twentieth century, the cone has spread to become a common confection all over the developed world. Ice cream itself was a popular treat in America as early as the 1800s but was only placed in an edible container 100 years later. The first patent for an ice cream cone maker was granted to New York City ice cream vendor Italo Marchiony in 1903, but aficionados continue to debate the true inventor of the cone. The popularity of the ice cream cone dates to the 1904 St. Louis Exposition, when Ernest Hamwi, a Syrian who sold waffles next to an ice cream concessionaire, thought to combine the two treats, creating the "World's Fair Cornucopia"—a portable way to eat ice cream.

During the 1920s and 1930s new cone designs came out almost every year, resembling real or fanciful objects such as skyscrapers and rocket ships, but by the 1940s two main types dominated the cone market—the flat-bottomed "waffle" cone cast from batter and the pointed "sugar" cone, made from a large waffle-patterned wafer. Along with the rise of specialist ice cream shops such as Ben & Jerry's in the 1980s came a new interest in homemade cones. Sometimes costing as much as the ice cream itself, these new waffle cones, hand-baked and hand-rolled, are offered in a variety of flavors, including chocolate, chocolate chip, oat bran, and honey.

In 2003, to commemorate the 100th anniversary of Marchiony's patent, Dairy Queen gave away 5-ounce ice cream cones. The fast-food chain refused to take sides on the question of the cone's inventor, however, so it repeated the giveaway in 2004 on the 100th anniversary of the World's Fair.

Wendy Woloson

SEE ALSO: *Soda Fountains; State Fairs; World's Fairs.*

BIBLIOGRAPHY

Ball, Jacqueline A. *Food Creations: From Hot Dogs to Ice Cream Cones (Which Came First?)*. New York: Bearport Publishing, 2006.

Damerov, Gail. *Ice Cream! The Whole Scoop*. Lakewood, CO: Glenbridge Publishing, 1995.

Dickson, Paul. *The Great American Ice Cream Book*. New York: Atheneum, 1972.

Funderburg, Anne. *Vanilla, Chocolate, and Strawberry: A History of American Ice Cream*. Bowling Green, OH: Bowling Green State University Popular Press, 1995.

Gustaitis, John. "Who Invented the Ice Cream Cone?" *American History Illustrated* 22, no. 4 (1988): 42–44.

Ice Shows

No sport grew as phenomenally during the last two decades of the twentieth century as figure skating. Having been a favorite sport among women, its popularity was bolstered by Olympic gold medal winners Peggy Fleming (1968), Janet Lynn (1972), Dorothy Hamill (1976), Scott Hamilton (1984), Brian Boitano (1988), and Kristi Yamaguchi (1992). While diehard fans followed the sport through various ice shows, competitions, and television performances, it was the bumbling fiasco of the attack on Nancy Kerrigan in 1994 by the cohorts of an envious Tonya Harding that propelled figure skating into the news headlines. By the end of the twentieth century, it ranked second behind pro football in television ratings. It is particularly significant that the sport came so far after suffering the devastating loss of its entire roster of top U.S. skaters and coaches in an airplane crash on the way to the World Championships in Prague, Czechoslovakia, on February 5, 1961.

While the popularity of ice skating has declined somewhat in the twenty-first century, ice shows continue to draw large audiences. The Stars on Ice tour has expanded to include shows in Canada and Japan. Ice shows symbolize the melting pot of American culture by bringing Olympic medalists from all over the world together to perform for American audiences while continuing to provide exhibition venues for American skaters. The 2011 Stars on Ice tour, for instance, featured American medalists Evan Lysacek and Sasha Cohen, Canadian winners

Disney on Ice. *Skaters perform in the Disney on Ice production of* Beauty and the Beast *in 2004.* WILLIAM WEST/AFP/GETTY IMAGES.

Jamie Salé and David Pelletier, Russian skaters Ekaterina Gordeeva and Ilia Kulik, Japanese skater Yuka Sato, and Chinese pair skaters Xue Shen and Hongbo Zhao.

EARLY HISTORY

Though ice shows benefited greatly from a new surge in popularity with increased exposure and million-dollar incomes for top skaters, ice shows have been an American tradition since the early twentieth century. The first show was held at the Hippodrome in New York City in 1915. It was followed by an ice ballet imported from Berlin, *Flirting in St. Moritz*, which ran for an unprecedented 300 days and inspired the movie *The Frozen Warning* in 1916. The Ice Follies began in 1936 and continued to entertain audiences for thirty years. Ice skating had its superstars even in its early days. Norwegian skating sensation Sonja Henie enticed fans to ice shows by the thousands in the 1930s and 1940s and eventually skated her way into Hollywood films.

ICE CAPADES

The Ice Capades was the most venerable of ice shows. From its founding in 1940 in Hershey, Pennsylvania, to its last performances in 1995, it featured some of the greatest names in ice skating, including Dick Button, Hamilton, Jayne Torvill, Christopher Dean, and Hamill, who bought the show in 1991. Hamill believed that the focus of the show should be on telling a story rather than on the disjointed vaudevillian skits of the past. *Cinderella Frozen in Time*, for example, turned the classic fairy tale into a skating spectacular. Unfortunately, the Ice Capades foundered under her stewardship.

STARS ON ICE

In 1986, after Hamilton won the 1984 gold medal for men's figure skating, he determined that skaters should have more opportunities for participating in the sport they loved. The result was Stars on Ice, sponsored chiefly by Discover Stars of America. Each year, roughly a dozen top skaters spend December through April touring the country, providing fans with performances that are elegant, breathtaking, or funny. A number of other ice shows, including Campbell's Tour of World Champions and Disney's World on Ice (later renamed Disney on Ice), have followed suit. Before the establishment of these modern ice shows, skaters often performed in ten to twelve shows a week, a grueling schedule that sapped both their energies and their talents. While the shows appear glamorous, they require hard work from skaters who spend much of the year traveling from city to city, rarely staying long enough to enjoy the local sights. They frequently spend holidays away from their families and friends, and members of the professional skating world often fall victim to broken relationships that cannot survive the strain.

For fans, though, ice shows are memorable events. No other sport offers the diversity of so much talent. Whether it be the spectacular jumps of Boitano, the crazy antics of Hamilton, the sheer beauty of Kristi Yamaguchi, the elegance of Gordeeva, the awesomeness of Isabelle Brasseur and Lloyd Eisler, the innovativeness of Torvill and Dean, the athleticism of Surya Bonaly, or the unexpectedness of Gary Beacom, ice shows are sheer magic.

ICE SHOWS ON TELEVISION

In addition to the traveling shows, television has become a smorgasbord of skating talent. Virtually every major skater has had at least one television show devoted to his or her talents. In 1988 Boitano became the first male athlete to have his own television special with *Canvas on Ice*. In addition, his *Skating Romance* specials were featured annually on American television. In December 1998 the USA network aired *Skate against Hate*, one of a number of theme-related shows with Boitano as both producer and star. Fleming, a frequent star of skating specials after bringing home the gold in 1968, joined cohost Button in serving as commentator for ice skating competitions. Hamilton frequently joins them, along with appearing in specials of his own, such as *Disney's Scott Hamilton Upside Down*. Both Kerrigan and Yamaguchi also became regular hosts for skating events. Canadian skater Elvis Stojko appeared in *Elvis on Ice*. Russian skater Gordeeva starred in the Christmas specials featuring Snowden the snowman. Boitano joined Ukrainian skaters Oksana Baiul and Viktor Petrenko in an ice show version of *The Nutcracker Suite*.

With its phenomenal success, ice skating has become a gold mine for skaters and promoters alike. Yamaguchi reportedly earned $2 million to $3 million a year in the late 1990s. Other millionaire skaters include Boitano, Hamilton, Kerrigan, and Baiul. Michelle Kwan and Tara Lipinski, who won the Olympic silver and gold, respectively, in the 1998 Olympics, were well on the way to joining that elite group by the end of the century. Paul Wylie, 1992 silver medalist, chose to continue skating over entering Harvard Law School, declaring that he would be foolish to give up the income of a high-profile professional skater. Kwan, on the other hand, chose to forsake her dreams of Olympic gold to pursue a degree in international studies and to serve as a diplomatic envoy for the Department of State. Given their enormous popularity and ability to rake in huge revenues, ice shows will continue to entertain a besotted American public and inspire young skaters to reach for the gold.

Elizabeth Rholetter Purdy

SEE ALSO: *Fleming, Peggy; Hamill, Dorothy; Harding, Tonya; Kerrigan, Nancy; Kwan, Michelle; Olympics; Skating.*

BIBLIOGRAPHY

Boitano, Brian, and Suzanne Harper. *Boitano's Edge: Inside the Real World of Figure Skating.* New York: Simon & Schuster, 1997.

Brennan, Christine. *Inside Edge: A Revealing Journey into the Secret World of Figure Skating.* New York: Anchor, 1997.

Brennan, Christine. *Edge of Glory: The Inside Story of the Quest for Figure Skating's Olympic Gold Medals.* New York: Penguin, 1999.

Gordeeva, Ekaterina, with E. M. Swift. *My Sergei: A Love Story.* New York: Warner Books, 1996.

Hines, James R. *Figure Skating: A History.* Urbana: University of Illinois Press, 2006.

Lawrence, Kelli. *Skating on Air: The Broadcast History of an Olympic Marquee Sport.* Jefferson, NC: McFarland, 2011.

Swift, E. M. "The Day the Music Stopped. " *Sports Illustrated,* February 21, 2011, 70–75.

Torvill, Jayne, and Christopher Dean, with John Man. *The Autobiography of Ice Dancing's Greatest Stars.* New York: Carol Publishing Group, 1996.

Ice-T *(1958–)*

Over the course of his career as a musician, an actor, and a reality television star, Ice-T has earned a reputation for being outspoken. He has been unafraid to identify himself as a social outsider and former criminal; indeed, in many songs, he boasts about his violent past and claims to have been shot on two occasions. Ice-T first achieved musical fame in 1983 with the release of his debut single, "The Coldest Rapper."

Ice-T quickly became known for his raw, uncensored lyrics and was the first rap artist to have warning stickers placed on his album sleeves. His gangster persona was later copied and perfected by many other West Coast "gangsta" rappers, notably Snoop Dogg and Dr. Dre. In spite of his notoriety within the mainstream media, Ice-T's brutal honesty has made him a vital voice for the dispossessed black youth of America. As he rose to the top of the music profession, Ice-T formed his own record company, Rhyme Syndicate, and has enjoyed success as a film and television actor.

Ice-T was born Tracy Marrow in Newark, New Jersey. Following his parents' deaths he moved to California and attended Crenshaw High School in South Central Los Angeles. His journey to the big time was anything but smooth. He made several records and appeared in three hip-hop films, *Breakin'* (1984), *Breakin' II* (1984), and *Rappin'* (1985), without any notable success. A few years later he signed a record deal with Sire Records and released his debut album, *Rhyme Pays* (1987).

While most of the tracks on *Rhyme Pays* deal with the familiar topics of sex and women (for example, "I Love Ladies" and "Sex"), two stand out in particular: "6 'N the Mornin'" and "Squeeze the Trigger." These tracks defined the subject matter of Ice-T's later hard-core rapping: living in the ghetto, street violence, criminal activity, and survival. He stated, "I try to walk the edge. I'm going to tell you what you need to hear, not what you want to hear." Indeed, the latter track inspired actor/director Dennis Hopper to ask Ice-T to contribute the title song to his movie *Colors* (1988), a brutal depiction of gang culture in Los Angeles.

Following the success of the track "Colors," Ice-T released his second album, *Power* (1988). The record depicts a Los Angeles cityscape that would not be out of place on the set of a blaxploitation movie: pimps, hookers, hit men, cars, and drugs. This was backed up by wah-wah guitar riffs and samples borrowed from Curtis Mayfield, giving the album the sound of 1970s funk. On "I'm Your Pusher," Ice-T lifted a track wholesale from Mayfield's *Superfly* (1972).

Ice-T's third album, *Freedom of Speech* (1989), seemed to demarcate a shift to an even more militant stance. The track "Lethal Weapon" recalls Public Enemy's "Miuzi Weighs a Ton" (1987), adopting a violent persona with lines such as "I'm a nigger on the trigger / Madder than a pit bull." Ice-T had not discarded his pimp/player image, which is evidenced in his fourth album, *Original Gangster (O.G.)* (1991). The title of the album coined a new phrase that entered the rap lexicon, and the album as a whole was placed alongside some of rap's best recordings.

During these years Ice-T recorded two more albums, *Home Invasion* (1993) and *Born Dead* (1994), and appeared in several films, the most notable being his part as a cop in *New Jack City* (1991). In addition to his solo performances, Ice-T formed a spin-off metal/hard-core band, *Body Count,* that released an eponymous album in 1992. The inclusion of the notorious track "Cop Killer" ensured further headlines and earned Ice-T the number two slot on the FBI National Threat list.

As Ice-T continued to appear in films and on television throughout the 1990s, the controversy he incited receded. In 2000 he landed the role of detective Odafin Tutuola on the TV crime series *Law & Order: SVU,* a part he continued to play into the next decade. In 2011 Ice-T starred alongside his wife, Coco, on the reality series *Ice Loves Coco.* During this period he also became involved in projects that revealed his continued dedication to the music and social issues that defined his early career. He published a book exploring his difficult rise to fame, *Ice: A Memoir of Gangster Life and Redemption—From South Central to Hollywood* (2011). He appeared in the documentary *Uprising: Hip Hop and the L.A. Riots* (2012) and made his directorial debut with *Something from Nothing: The Art of Rap* (2012), a film that explored the genre's explosion into a worldwide phenomenon, told from Ice-T's deeply personal perspective.

Nathan Abrams

SEE ALSO: *Blaxploitation Films; Funk; Gangsta Rap; Hip-Hop; Hopper, Dennis;* Law & Order: SVU*; Mayfield, Curtis; Public Enemy; Rap; Reality Television; Snoop Dogg.*

BIBLIOGRAPHY

Collins, Hattie. "Me Get into Politics? Nah, I've Left Crime Behind." *Guardian* (London), May 28, 2004.

Fernando, S. H., Jr. *The New Beats: Exploring the Music Culture and Attitudes of Hip-Hop.* Edinburgh: Payback Press, 1995.

Ice-T, as told to Heidi Siegmund. *The Ice Opinion: Who Gives a Fuck?* New York: St. Martin's Press, 1994.

Ice-T, and Douglas Century. *Ice: A Memoir of Gangster Life and Redemption—From South Central to Hollywood.* New York: One World/Ballantine, 2011.

Nelson, Havelock, and Michael A. Gonzales. *Bring the Noise: A Guide to Rap Music and Hip-Hop Culture.* New York: Harmony Books, 1991.

IKEA

IKEA is a global retailer that offers housewares and fashionable, ready-to-assemble furniture at affordable prices. It was founded in 1943 by seventeen-year-old Swede Ingvar Kamprad. The name of the company is derived from Kamprad's initials (*IK*); his childhood farm, Elmtaryd (*E*); and his native village of Agunnaryd (*A*). Kamprad initially sold small items, such as pens, watches, and jewelry, before expanding into furniture in 1948.

During the latter half of the twentieth century, IKEA grew from a regional Scandinavian company to a major European brand, opening stores throughout Western Europe during the 1970s. The first North American IKEA store opened outside of Philadelphia in 1985, by which time the company had more than 10,000 employees and sixty stores worldwide. By the beginning of the twenty-first century, IKEA had become the largest furniture retailer in the world, earning over $23 billion in annual revenues. As of 2012, in addition to millions of catalog subscribers and a website offering thousands of products, IKEA had physical stores in thirty-eight countries, including Russia and China.

Since its inception, IKEA has focused on keeping costs down, a priority that has driven innovation throughout the company's history. Most IKEA furniture is made of medium-density fiberboard (MDF), a synthetic wood product composed of wood fibers, wax, and resin. Although it is less durable than

IKEA Grand Opening. *Thousands of people wait outside a new IKEA store in Canton, Michigan, in 2006, to be part of its grand opening.* BRETT MOUNTAIN/BLOOMBERG/GETTY IMAGES.

solid wood furniture, MDF is nonetheless an economical and reasonably strong alternative to expensive hardwoods, such as teak and mahogany, and softwoods, such as pine. While high-end furniture retailers scoffed at Kamprad's bargain-rate merchandise, consumers liked the look of IKEA furniture and appreciated the savings. MDF has since been widely adopted by other furniture makers.

In 1956 Gillis Lundgren, an IKEA store employee, introduced the concept of self-assembled furniture, which became the signature feature of IKEA. Another of Kamprad's cost-effective ideas was flat packing, a method of packing the pieces of furniture so that air does not take up space in the box. Such strategies allowed the company to amass a loyal customer base.

Kamprad also developed an ingenious one-way layout in his stores that showcased IKEA's most attractive merchandise, while also steering customers to areas offering smaller items where they were likely to make a few impulse purchases as they meandered up and down the aisles. Instead of entering the store on the ground floor, the traditional location for a store entrance, customers enter IKEA stores on the highest level, where vast showrooms boasting the latest IKEA products are located. On lower levels, customers find the marketplace, which offers smaller items that complement the furniture in the showrooms. Ultimately, customers end up on the bottom level at the warehouse, where large items that may have caught their eye in the showroom can be picked up and purchased. This type of store design requires shoppers to pass through the entire store, greatly increasing the likelihood that they will buy more than they originally intended.

In addition, Kamprad introduced a number of diversions to keep the nonshoppers in the building occupied. Many stores have a children's play spot called Småland and an area replete with video games, televisions, and snacks. IKEA stores also feature restaurants, which primarily serve Swedish staples but occasionally offer regional specialties as well.

A large part of IKEA's success springs from Kamprad's knack for making quirky choices that strike a chord with buyers. For example, he had the exterior of IKEA's large outlets stores painted the striking blue and yellow of the Swedish flag, making IKEA buildings the most easily recognizable and inviting structures in the otherwise drab environment of the suburban strip mall. IKEA product names, with their odd arrangements of vowels that invoke Scandinavian culture, are unfailingly catchy. Several of the unusual names spring from Swedish and Danish cities, men's names, and a play on Swedish words. Among the most well-known are the Poäng chair and the Karlstad sofa.

Not every attempt to promote the store has worked, however. For example, IKEA made headlines in the mid-1990s when it aired what is believed to be the first commercial depicting a homosexual couple. The spot was quickly pulled after threats of violence were made against IKEA stores.

IKEA has also been criticized for selling wares that lack character and sacrifice style for function. The 1999 movie *Fight Club*, directed by David Fincher, includes a famous diatribe against the brand for its perceived contribution to the blandness of modern society. Despite the criticism, IKEA has been lauded for being an environmentally responsible corporation. In 2011 the company purchased a wind farm in northern Scotland, taking a step toward its stated goal of operating on 100 percent renewable energy.

Jill Gregg Clever

SEE ALSO: *Consumerism;* Fight Club.

BIBLIOGRAPHY

Dahlvig, Anders. *The IKEA Edge: Building Global Growth and Social Good at the World's Most Iconic Home Store.* New York: McGraw-Hill, 2012.

Kamprad, Ingvar, and Bertil Torekull. *Leading by Design: The IKEA Story.* New York: Harper's Business, 1999.

Stenebo, Johan. *Truth about IKEA: The Secret behind the World's Fifth Richest Man and the Success of the Flatpack Giant.* London: Gibson Square, 2010.

IMDb.com

SEE: *Amazon.com.*

In Living Color

Airing on Fox Television from 1990 to 1994, the series *In Living Color* was the first sketch comedy to feature a majority African American cast. Keenen Ivory Wayans was the creative force behind the show, which included his brother Damon and a smattering of other comic actors such as David Alan Grier, Tommy Davidson, Chris Rock, Jamie Foxx, and Jim Carrey. *In Living Color* brought to the screen lasting characters like Homey the Clown, gay film critics Blaine and Antoine in "Men on Film" (with their ratings system of "two snaps up" or "*hated* it!"), Wanda the Ugly Woman, and the oblivious Fire Marshal Bill, in addition to a troupe of well-choreographed female dancers ("Fly Girls") that appeared after skits. Though the show was sometimes criticized for its stereotypes and objectionable material, it was nevertheless respected for being the first to address urban themes in such a context.

The star-making effect of the show is hard to ignore. Carrey went on to critically acclaimed success with films such as *Ace Ventura: Pet Detective*, *The Mask*, *The Truman Show*, and *Dumb and Dumber*. Foxx won an Oscar in 2004 for his portrayal of Ray Charles in the movie *Ray*. As a family, the Wayans Brothers proved to be immensely successful. Brothers Shawn and Marlon Wayans followed with the situational comedy *The Wayans Brothers* that ran on the WB Network between 1995 and 1999. Keenen directed the comedies *Scary Movie* and *White Chicks*, and Damon starred in ABC's *My Wife and Kids*. Fly Girl Jennifer Lopez went on to a lucrative singing and acting career and returned to TV as one of the judges for *American Idol*. The once controversial cast became fixtures on television and movie screens. In 2012 TV Land awarded *In Living Color* the Groundbreaking Award for its predominately African American cast and its irreverent format.

Geri Speace

SEE ALSO: *Academy Awards;* American Idol*; Charles, Ray; Foxx, Jamie; Lopez, Jennifer; Television; The Wayans Family.*

BIBLIOGRAPHY

Brumley, Al. "'In Living Color' Brightens with Age." *Dallas Morning News*, October 7, 1997, 1C.

Justin, Neal. "The Wonderful World of 'Color.'" *Minneapolis Star Tribune*, August 26, 1997, 1E.

MacDonald, J. Fred. *Blacks and White TV: African Americans in Television since 1948*. Chicago: Nelson-Hall, 1992.

An Inconvenient Truth

The debate over global climate change took a dramatic turn in 2006 with the release of the Academy Award–winning film *An Inconvenient Truth*. In addition to bringing this environmental issue to an immense audience, the film created the twenty-first century's first environmental celebrity: former Vice President Al Gore, who earned a Nobel Peace Prize in 2007 for his efforts to combat one of the world's most pressing concerns.

Directed by Davis Guggenheim, the film began its journey as an artistic hit at the well-known Sundance Film Festival. Organized around Gore's crusade to expose the myths and misconceptions that surround global warming, the film is pitched as a last-ditch, all-out effort to help save the planet from irrevocable change. The bulk of the film records Gore giving a slide lecture that he has offered around the world. Its success is at least partly attributable to the power of Gore's slideshow and his careful, intricate explanation of the science behind it. The movie grossed almost $50 million at the box office and as of July 2012 had more than $31 million in DVD sales.

David Roberts described *An Inconvenient Truth* for the online magazine *GRIST* in this way:

> It's something of a miracle that *An Inconvenient Truth*, the chronicle of Al Gore's quest to raise alarm about "climate chaos," exists at all. A movie with a scantily clad Jessica Alba presenting a computer slideshow on climate science is implausible enough. Al Gore doing it, well . . . even C-SPAN could be forgiven for having second thoughts.

Only a few years prior, a fictional account of possible outcomes of global warming had been released as the feature film *The Day after Tomorrow* (2004), but public response was minimal. *An Inconvenient Truth* at once moved the issue into a progressive, hip, mainstream portion of American popular culture and also resurrected the fortunes of Gore, who had been largely out of the public eye since losing the 2000 election.

In 2007, shortly after the movie's release, Gore made his first visit to Congress since the 2000 presidential election. He came to Capitol Hill to educate Congress about the implications of global climate change. He forecasted what lawmakers would hear from their grandchildren in a few decades, as they would ask: "What in God's name were [you] doing? Didn't [you] see the evidence? Didn't [you] realize that four times in fifteen years the entire scientific community of this world issued unanimous reports calling upon [you] to act?" To further motivate legislators, Gore referred to the determination it took previous generations to fight Nazism and communism and claimed that the same level of commitment was needed to halt climate change. "What we're facing now is a crisis that is by far the most serious we've ever faced," he said.

Gore has a long history of trying to warn Congress about the threat of global warming. Shortly after arriving as a freshman congressman in 1976, he held a hearing on the topic and gained the respect of another representative who cared about the issue—Representative Ed Markey (D-MA). Markey now believes that Gore was ahead of his time in issuing those warnings. "What you were saying about information technologies, what you were saying about environmental issues back then, now retrospectively really do make you look like a prophet," Markey has told Gore. "And I think that it would be wise for the Congress to listen to your warnings, because I think that history now has borne you out."

Although Gore's appearance before Congress on behalf of the issue of climate change was remarkable, the oddest by-product of this initiative was a series of rock concerts called Live Earth. Surrounded by many global rock stars, Gore, a policy wonk, became a rock star himself. Live Earth, which was held on seven continents (in Sydney, Tokyo, Shanghai, Johannesburg, Hamburg, London, New York, and Rio de Janeiro) during a span of twenty-four hours, attempted to bring the issue of climate change to a global audience. Although most ticket buyers came for the music, they were also treated to lessons—by rock stars and speakers—about how to reduce their own carbon emissions and campaign for serious political action.

Everyone watching (in person or on live television broadcasts) was urged to sign up by text or online for a sevenfold pledge: to plant trees, protect forests, buy from eco-friendly businesses, vote for green-minded politicians, and make "a dramatic increase" in energy savings. The pledge also involved promising to fight for new laws and policies, to demand that their country sign a new treaty—and the very specific demand that any new coal power station be able to trap and store the carbon dioxide it produces. The featured speaker was Gore himself. In an era of multimedia information technology, Gore had positioned himself as the Rachel Carson of the twenty-first century, and despite reluctance on the part of the U.S. government to take drastic actions to combat climate change, *An Inconvenient Truth* can be credited with reinvigorating environmentalism at the grassroots level around the globe.

Brian Black

SEE ALSO: *Academy Awards; Best Sellers;* Bush v. Gore *(2000); Celebrity; Environmentalism; Global Warming; Live Television; Rock and Roll; Sundance Film Festival.*

BIBLIOGRAPHY

Black, Brian, and Gary Weisel. *Global Warming*. New York: Greenwood, 2010.

Gore, Albert. *Earth in the Balance*. New York: Simon & Schuster, 1992.

Gore, Albert. *An Inconvenient Truth: The Planetary Emergency of Global Warming and What We Can Do about It*. New York: Rodale, 2006.

Gore, Albert. *Our Choice: A Plan to Solve the Climate Crisis*. New York: Rodale, 2009.

The Incredible Hulk

The Incredible Hulk is one of Marvel Comics' most popular superheroes. Created in 1962 by Stan Lee and Jack Kirby, the

Hulk is a green-skinned brute with enormous physical strength, dull wits, and a hot temper. He is the alterego of Dr. Bruce Banner, a nuclear physicist accidentally exposed to gamma radiation. Banner transforms into the Hulk during times of stress.

Along with Spider-Man, the Hulk established Marvel's definitive formula of troubled superheroes alienated from the society that they fight to protect. Constantly misunderstood by the public and persecuted by the authorities, the Hulk, during the 1960s and 1970s, became a natural favorite among young people who identified themselves with antiestablishment trends, and he reemerged in the early twenty-first century as a hero to a new generation of youth, who were introduced to the sensitive behemoth in animated television series, three major motion pictures, and a number of video games.

The Hulk's popularity peaked in the late 1970s when the comic book was adapted into a successful prime-time CBS TV series and again in the early twenty-first century with the release of the Ang Lee–directed *Hulk* (2003); the 2008 film *The Incredible Hulk*, starring Edward Norton as Bruce Banner/the Hulk; and 2012's *The Avengers*, which features a wide array of superheroes from the Marvel universe. These later films spawned a range of Hulk-branded merchandise, including clothing, action figures, and several video games, once again making the Hulk a household name. Despite frequent revisions in the Hulk's appearance and character during the late twentieth and early twenty-first centuries, he remains one of the most recognizable superheroes ever produced by the comic-book industry, and Marvel continues to add to his legacy, having introduced an entirely new series and story line as recently as 2011.

Bradford Wright

SEE ALSO: *Comic Books; Kirby, Jack; Lee, Stan; Marvel Comics; Spider-Man.*

BIBLIOGRAPHY

Daniels, Les. *Marvel: Five Fabulous Decades of the World's Greatest Comics*. New York: Harry N. Abrams, 1991.

Fein, Eric. *The Creation of the Incredible Hulk*. New York: Rosen Publishing Group, 2006.

Lee, Stan. *Origins of Marvel Comics*. New York: Simon & Schuster, 1974.

The Incredibles

The twentieth century can be seen as a kind of golden period for superheroes in cinema. The X-Men, Spider-Man, the Hulk, Iron Man, Batman, Superman, the Watchmen, and others routinely brought record audiences into theaters. But in the midst of these characters licensed by the major comic-book publishers came an entirely new team of heroes created specifically for the big screen: the Incredibles.

The Incredibles (2004) was the sixth computer-animated feature produced by Pixar Animation Studios. Directed by Brad Bird, the film depicts a world in which superheroes (called "Supers"), once commonplace, have been forced underground due to very real-world concerns about vigilante justice, civil liberties, collateral damage, and the like. The story of the Parr family, very loosely modeled on Marvel Comic's Fantastic Four, develops against this backdrop. Former Supers, Bob, or Mr. Incredible (voiced by Craig T. Nelson), and Helen, or Elastigirl (Holly Hunter), are not only forced to live mundane suburban lives but also must raise three Super children in a society that shuns those with powers. Daughter Violet (Sarah Vowell) has the power to turn invisible and create force fields, reflective of her paralyzing shyness and lack of confidence. Son Dash (Spencer Fox) possesses super speed but is constantly frustrated by the fact that he must keep the ability secret. Jack-Jack, the baby of the family, demonstrates no special powers until the end of the film. *The Incredibles* also features the ice-powered Frozone (Samuel L. Jackson) as Bob's best friend and Syndrome (Jason Lee), who once idolized Mr. Incredible and later becomes his nemesis, the villain who drags the heroes back into the public spotlight.

The most action-oriented film in Pixar's canon, *The Incredibles* works as both a straight superhero adventure and as a parody of the genre, having fun with common tropes such as capes and sidekicks. Not surprisingly, the film thematically emphasizes the importance of working together as a family unit. As an individual Mr. Incredible is defeated by Syndrome, but when joined by his wife and children, who are initially perceived as a vulnerability or handicap, he is able to save the day once again. The film also explores the threat of mediocrity. When Dash, barred from engaging in school sports because he is "special," is told by Helen that everyone is special, he replies, "which is another way of saying no one is." Indeed, the surname "Parr" itself suggests the detriments of trying to fit into a society by pretending to be less than one is.

As with all Pixar-produced films *The Incredibles* pushed the limits of what computer animation was capable of, all the more since Bird, coming from a background in traditional animation, had very specific expectations of how he wanted the movie to look. The challenges paid off however, as *The Incredibles* grossed more than $70 million in its opening weekend in 2004. It also won critical raves and an Oscar for Best Animated Feature, among other awards. It has continued to profit from video releases and extensive licensing and is to be rereleased in 3-D in 2014.

Marc Oxoby

SEE ALSO: *Academy Awards; Animated Films; Batman; CGI; Comic Books;* The Fantastic Four*; The Incredible Hulk; Marvel Comics; Spider-Man; Suburbia; Superman; The X-Men.*

BIBLIOGRAPHY

Anton, Audrey. "The Nietzschean Influence in "The Incredibles" and the Sidekick Revolt." In *The Amazing Transforming Superhero!*, ed. Terrence R. Wandtke. Jefferson, NC: McFarland, 2007.

Paik, Karen. *To Infinity and Beyond!: The Story of Pixar Animation Studios*. San Francisco: Chronicle, 2007.

Independence Day

Directed by Roland Emmerich and written by Dean Devlin, *Independence Day* is an epic film about an apocalyptic invasion of the earth by extraterrestrials. The film opened in July 1996 to enormous box-office profits. It benefited from a canny advertising campaign featuring as its centerpiece a shot of the destruction of the White House and set a new record for collecting $100 million in six days. *Independence Day* ultimately went on to earn more than $800 million worldwide, placing it as one of the top thirty highest-grossing films ever.

Most critics were less kind to *Independence Day*, pointing to its stereotypical ethnic characters, an implausible deus ex machina ending, and a rather nationalistic subtext disingenuously cloaked behind its multicultural pretensions. Others pointed to the extremely derivative nature of the film, including not-so-subtle science fiction borrowings from movies and television shows such as *The War of the Worlds* (1953), *The Day the Earth Stood Still* (1951), and *The X-Files* (1993–2002). Nevertheless, audiences flocked to *Independence Day*, making it the cinematic success story of 1996 and initiating a revival of Hollywood mega-disaster movies.

THE PREMISE

Set in a July of the near future, *Independence Day* opens ominously with a shot of a gigantic shadow, accompanied by rumbles and tremors, passing over the site of humankind's first lunar landing. Scientific and military organizations quickly detect that an immense object one-fourth the size of the moon, apparently under intelligent control, is taking up a position in near-earth orbit. The object, which turns out to be a mother ship, releases fifteen smaller, but still miles across, disk-shaped craft that enter the earth's atmosphere in clouds of fire to hover silently over major world cities.

The film then introduces its major characters, all of whom will transcend personal failure to become heroes in the upcoming battle: Thomas Whitmore (Bill Pullman), the politically embattled U.S. president and veteran Gulf War pilot; Steven Hiller (Will Smith), an F-16 pilot and failed NASA applicant; Jasmine Dubrow (Viveca A. Fox), Hiller's exotic-dancer girlfriend; David Levinson (Jeff Goldblum), a New York cable-television scientist who has failed at his marriage and his career; Constance Spano (Margaret Colin), Levinson's ex-wife and aide to President Whitmore; and Russell Casse (Randy Quaid), an alcoholic crop duster and Vietnam War veteran pilot.

As a panicked civilization becomes ever more destabilized, Levinson discovers that the disks are using the earth's satellites to synchronize a countdown to a simultaneous worldwide attack. Accompanied by his father, Levinson convinces Spano to tell the president about the imminent attack. Though the news comes too late for any effective evacuation, the president, some of his staff, and the Levinsons are able to escape Washington just as the disks, acting in concert, fire their primary weapons to create firestorms that engulf and utterly destroy the world's major cities, including New York and Los Angeles.

SECOND HALF

The second part of the film focuses on humankind's counterattack against the alien invaders. The president, who has lost his wife in the invasion, personally commands the national, and eventually worldwide, effort. Hiller not only survives a massive but futile F-16 attack on one of the disks and its hordes of fighters but also manages to shoot down and capture alive one of the aliens. During the counteroffensive Whitmore learns to his anger that a covert branch of the government, kept secret even from the president, has been studying an alien fighter, captured in the late 1950s, at the infamous Area 51 in the Nevada desert. Through close inspection of the captured ship, Levinson finds that he will be able to introduce a disabling computer virus into the alien computer network, provided someone can dock the smaller fighter with the mother ship. Hiller volunteers to fly the alien fighter.

Meanwhile, the president and Casse, among other volunteers, suit up to fly a coordinated F-16 attack against all the disks as soon as the virus paralyzes the alien craft and lowers their shields. Whitmore proves himself to be of presidential caliber by delivering an inspirational speech to the amassed volunteers shortly before the attack. Even with the virus successfully introduced and the shields down, however, the disks prove too hardy for missiles until Casse's suicide plunge into a disk's primary weapon shows the other pilots how to bring the disks down. Hiller and Levinson, barely escaping the destruction of the mother ship, fly back to earth to find that the smaller disks have all been destroyed as well. The victory, which takes place on July 4, ensures that Independence Day will no longer be only an American holiday.

BEHIND THE SCENES

German-born Emmerich and American Devlin, the creative duo behind *Independence Day*, first teamed up in the United States for *Universal Soldier* (1992), featuring action star Jean-Claude Van Damme. Emmerich and Devlin achieved name recognition and a more modest commercial success with *Stargate* (1994), a film about aliens, time travel, the modern military, and ancient Egypt. For *Stargate*, Emmerich directed, cowrote, and coproduced; Devlin cowrote and coproduced, as would be the case with their next project. According to its creators, *Independence Day* was conceived to be an homage to war and adventure movies but most specifically to the 1970s epic-scale and multicharacter disaster movie. The chairman of Twentieth Century Fox, Peter Chernin, agreed to back Emmerich and Devlin's project. Solid, recognizable supporting actors such as Mary McDonnell (the First Lady), Judd Hirsch (doting Jewish father Julius Levinson), Harvey Fierstein (David Levinson's boss Marty Gilbert), and Brent Spiner (in a brief but unforgettable cameo as the outlandish Dr. Brakkish Okun, scientific leader at the Area 51 research facility) were cast.

Location shooting began in 1995. Manhattan provided an urban background for crowd reaction shots to the awe-inspiring arrival of the interstellar visitors. The Bonneville Salt Flats in Utah served as a panoramic backdrop for the scene where Hiller leads an enormous caravan of refugees to the Area 51 facility. The hangars of the old Hughes aircraft facility in Los Angeles housed the special effects facilities involving the film's extensive pyrotechnic and miniatures (aircraft, cities, alien ships) work. In postproduction, dozens of computer-generated images were combined with existing special effects shots to create an intricately layered, visually spectacular depiction of the alien invasion. (The special effects won the 1997 Academy Award in that category.) The film ultimately cost $71 million—not an extravagant amount by cinematic budgetary standards in the 1990s.

The resultant financial success of *Independence Day* placed enormous pressure on Emmerich and Devlin to produce a follow-up film of similar spectacle and profitability. Their subsequent movie, *Godzilla* (1998), while profitable, was (perhaps inevitably) considered to be one of the big-budget flops of 1998. The duo's next collaboration was *The Patriot* (2000), a

Revolutionary War epic tale of revenge starring Mel Gibson, which was released to respectable critical notice. Emmerich subsequently directed two other notable mega-disaster movies: *The Day after Tomorrow* (2004), about global warming, and *2012* (2009), about the end of the world as supposedly forecast by the ancient Mayan calendar.

Stephen Molstad, author of the film's tie-in novelization, published a prequel titled *Independence Day: Silent Zone* (1998) and another story with the action happening simultaneously with the movie *Independence Day: War in the Desert* (1999). The original film also generated a Marvel comic and video game.

Philip L. Simpson

SEE ALSO: *Academy Awards; Blockbusters; CGI; Disaster Movies; Fourth of July Celebrations; Gibson, Mel; Godzilla; Marvel Comics; Movie Stars; Science Fiction Publishing; Smith, Will; War Movies;* War of the Worlds; The X-Files.

BIBLIOGRAPHY

Aberly, Rachel, and Volker Engel. *The Making of Independence Day*. New York: Harper, 1996.

Molstad, Stephen. *Independence Day: Silent Zone*. New York: HarperEntertainment, 1998.

Molstad, Stephen. *Independence Day: War in the Desert*. New York: HarperEntertainment, 1999.

Rogin, Michael. *Independence Day*. London: British Film Institute, 1998.

The Indian

Numerous tribes of Native Americans, or Indians, populated the Americas for thousands of years before the arrival of Europeans. As Jack Weatherford writes in his book *Indian Givers* (1988), these peoples created great architectural monuments, made intelligent use of natural resources, created new plant species through selective breeding, made great discoveries in mathematical and astronomical knowledge, and reshaped the physical landscape. As impressive as the achievements of Indian peoples have been, however, the image of the Indian—in literature, in the visual arts, in advertising, in entertainment, and elsewhere—has cast a far longer shadow upon the consciousness of the Euro-American society than the living individuals. This deficient image has been true since the earliest days of European contact.

CAPTIVITY NARRATIVES

One of the earliest outlets for disseminating the image of the Indian was the outpouring of Indian captivity narratives, which began in the early eighteenth century. These popular writings record hair-raising tales—both true and fictional—of settlers captured by Indians. Bearing titles such as *The Redeemed Captive Returning to Zion* (1707) by Massachusetts minister John Williams, they follow a predictable formula. In these narratives, a white hero or heroine is abducted, undergoes sufferings and even torture, is initiated into Indian society, and is finally and miraculously delivered once again to his or her own people through the grace of God. The Indian who emerges out of these narratives is typically a savage beast: primitive, sadistic, cunning, filthy, villainous, and altogether terrifying. Especially in the Puritan era, he is often revealed as a direct tool of Satan, and he shrinks not even from such vile acts as human mutilation, dismemberment, and cannibalism.

The captivity narratives were more than just a well-loved form of American entertainment, although they were certainly that; virtually no first edition copies of these narratives exist in the twenty-first century because people actually read them until the pages disintegrated. Besides diverting their audience, however, the captivity narratives also instructed. Their wide circulation made them an influential source of information about Indians in both America and Europe and allowed the Puritans to think through their place and mission in the New World. In them, America became the new, biblical promised land to be given over to them, the children of God, after the occupying hordes of pagans, the children of Satan, had been driven out.

THE NOBLE SAVAGE

It is hardly the case, however, that all the images of the Indian in America have been negative. To stand alongside the bad Indian of the captivity narratives, Americans also invented a good Indian, or noble savage. The good Indian was handsome, strong, gentle, kind, brave, intelligent, and unfettered by the artificiality and corruptions of civilized life. One powerful version of the good Indian appeared in the early nineteenth century. This was the image of the Indian as wise healer. By this time Euro-Americans had discovered that American Indians had a sophisticated knowledge of a great many medical procedures and preparations, including bone setting, febrifuges, and painkillers.

Whereas the bad Indian had been ideologically useful to the dominant society, the Indian healer turned out to be commercially useful. White purveyors of patent medicine began capitalizing on widespread respect for Indian medical knowledge by associating their products with Indians, and traveling medicine shows such as the Kiowa Indian Medicine and Vaudeville Company often featured Indian performers. Unfortunately, however, the main ingredients in patent medicines commonly consisted of alcohol, cocaine, or opium rather than any of the more useful therapeutic substances known to Indian healers. The increasing sensationalization of medicine shows, along with the professionalization and increasing social power of white physicians, eventually caused Indian medicine to fall into disrepute.

THE WARRIOR

Nevertheless, the Indian did not disappear from public consciousness with the eclipse of the healer image. In 1883 William F. Cody—commonly known as Buffalo Bill—introduced a new kind of traveling entertainment. His Wild West shows also featured Indian performers, but in this case they appeared as ferocious warriors. In staged battles they assaulted wagon trains, fired off volleys of arrows, and displayed impressive equestrian skills. Many Indian people—including even the great Lakota Sioux chief Sitting Bull—acted in these shows.

The same warrior image had been featured in the cheap paperbacks of the mid-nineteenth century known as dime novels, and it was eventually transferred with little alteration into Western movies, the first and most famous of which was *The Great Train Robbery* (1903). Like the captivity narratives that were their literary forebears, the Western movies frequently thematized the savage horrors awaiting whites who fell into Indian hands. "Save the last bullet for yourself" was Hollywood's oft-repeated advice to anyone fending off an Indian attack.

THE ECOLOGIST

The Western shows, books, and movies defined the war-bonneted Plains tribesman as the prototypical, or real, Indian. This image has remained the standard against which "Indianness" is commonly measured even into the twenty-first century. Yet the intervening years have also introduced some new roles for this standardized Indian to play. One of the more important is the role of the gentle ecologist. American boys' and girls' clubs such as the Scouts, Woodcraft Indians, and Campfire Girls have played a significant role in the dissemination of this additional good Indian image ever since the early years of the twentieth century. The clubs packed young people off to summer camps with Indian-sounding names where they were to enjoy outdoor sports and natural living after the supposed fashion of native peoples, who were imagined as innocent children of nature with deep knowledge of its secrets. American youths progressed within the hierarchy of the clubs by acquiring knowledge of such things as woodsmanship, nature lore, and the production of rustically imagined Indian crafts such as buckskin clothing and birch bark models.

Commercial advertising has also made free use of the ecologist image. Its best-known representative was the late Iron Eyes Cody, an actor who starred in an educational campaign in the 1970s for the nonprofit organization called Keep America Beautiful. The television advertisement in which Cody rides a horse down a garbage-strewn beach, silently surveys the desecration of the land, and finally allows a single tear to slip down his weathered cheek burned itself into the minds of an entire generation of Americans.

The Keep America Beautiful advertisement is interesting for at least two reasons. For one thing, it reveals a great deal about how Americans conceptualize the Indian. Its remarkable symbolic efficacy depends upon some of the most powerful modern racial stereotypes: that Indians are typically stoic and unemotional (what depth of suffering can move an Indian to tears?) and that they are bound to the natural world in a romanticized and inexpressible union. For another thing, although Iron Eyes Cody is still one of the most recognized Indian figures in America, controversy following his death suggested that he was not of Indian ancestry but the son of two Italian immigrants. In this, Cody is a typical Hollywood figure. Whereas many of the performers in the early Wild West shows were actually Indians, many of the best-known actors who later played them in films and on television have not been.

THE MYSTIC

If Americans in the 1970s used the imagery of the Indian to address developing ecological values, they had other uses for it as well. This was a period in which the hopefulness with which the post–World War II generation had once viewed science and technology had begun to fade, as Americans became increasingly discontented with the visions for human fulfillment that these held out. People expressed a renewed interest in spirituality, but many found the faiths of their parents unsatisfying. They turned in increasing numbers to non-Western traditions, including those of American Indians. Out of this burgeoning spiritual discontent was born the image of the mystical ceremonialist.

Americans were widely introduced to this impressive personage by Peruvian-born anthropologist Carlos Castaneda. In his long series of fictionalized books, starting with *Journey to Ixtlan* (1972), which was once considered accurate ethnography, Castaneda relates the story of his supposed tutelage by Don Juan, a Yaqui *brujo*, or possessor of traditional Indian sacred knowledge. The articulation of Castaneda's immensely popular works with the counterculture's interest in mind-altering drugs is evident. He describes many revelatory experiences under the influence of peyote; officially classified in the United States as a hallucinogenic drug, this spineless cactus is ingested by some tribal peoples as a sacrament.

The mystical Indian ceremonialist did not disappear when other preoccupations of the counterculture fell by the wayside. Instead, he was reinvented in the 1980s and 1990s by adherents of that loose set of movements that collect together under the rubric of New Age spirituality. The New Age includes spiritual believers who may call themselves Wiccans, goddess worshippers, Druids, ecofeminists, and many other names. Its followers have replaced their predecessors' fascination with hallucinogens with an equally intense interest in a variety of esoteric subjects such as reincarnation, crystals, alternative healing, astral projection, and extrasensory perception. Accompanying all these various preoccupations is a frequent attraction to (more or less accurately reproduced) versions of traditional, American Indian ceremonial practices.

Many of the New Age faithful ravenously consume how-to manuals penned by Indian shamans (often self-proclaimed). Such putative spiritual teachers have purported to reveal everything from the sacred beliefs and rituals of Indian medicine people to their secret sexual practices. Inquirers also crowd seminars, workshops, and spiritual retreats claiming to offer the experience of Indian rituals, and they flock to reservations and sacred sites to participate in Indian ceremonies. Some non-Indians have associated themselves so closely with this recent image of the mystical Indian as to assert that they were Indian in a past life, even though they currently exist in a non-Indian body.

The upsurge of interest in Indian sacred rituals created by the image of the mystical Indian has created a great deal of tension in Indian communities, which rarely appreciate the reinterpretation of their sacred traditions. In some cases non-Indian efforts to appropriate and market versions of Indian ceremonial practice have turned deadly, including the 2009 Spiritual Warriors Retreat held at an Arizona spa by New Age motivational speaker James Arthur Ray. Promising to assist seekers along the road to "harmonic wealth in all areas" of their lives, Ray assessed aspirants about $10,000 apiece and then conducted them to a rather different terminus. In a 2011 trial, a jury concluded that Ray's extreme version of an American Indian sweat lodge ceremony had precipitated the deaths of three participants; they convicted him on multiple counts of negligent homicide.

SPORTS MASCOTS

Of all the many images of Indians that have remained with Americans into the twenty-first century, perhaps the most vulgarly stereotyped appears in the sports mascot. Professional and college teams include the Kansas City Chiefs, the Atlanta Braves, and the Florida State Seminoles. Innumerable high schools similarly name themselves the Indians, Injuns, Redskins, and Savages. Indian mascots range from the Cleveland Indians' clownishly grinning Chief Wahoo to the Washington Redskins' dignified silhouette of a warrior. Fans for all these teams frequently sport feathers and war paint at games; give war whoops; beat tom-toms; and perform the tomahawk chop, a slicing gesture intended to encourage players to scalp the other team.

Some non-Indian as well as Indian commentators contend that sports mascots are intended to honor American Indians and their historic record of bravery in battle. Many others, however, including representatives of the American Indian movement, protest. They complain that the use of Indian names and imagery suggests a blind spot involving this specific racial group. Brian Barnard, in his article "Would You Cheer for the Denver Darkies?" wonders if anyone would fail to see the offensive implications of a team that honored African Americans by christening itself as the title of his piece suggests. And what if the same team sponsored half-time shows featuring mascots in blackface and Afro wigs, who danced around grunting their own version of supposed African chants?

Some Indian leaders have brought lawsuits against particular sports teams, alleging racial discrimination or human rights violations. So far, these suits have not succeeded, but protests against mascots have made some headway. For instance, in 1994 the University of Iowa announced that it would no longer play nonconference athletic events against teams employing Indian names or symbols. Several universities have banned from their campuses the buffoonish Chief Illiniwek, a white University of Illinois student dressed as an Indian who performs at halftime. And some newspapers, including the *Minneapolis (Minnesota) Star Tribune* and the Portland *Oregonian*, have decided not to print the names of specific teams with Indian names or mascots. Instead, they simply refer to the Washington team, the Atlanta team, and so on. Teams themselves have sometimes opened discussions on the question of whether they should change their names or their mascots, but the suggestions are frequently met with angry resistance from fans.

CONSTANTS IN POPULAR CULTURE

American popular culture has played host to a diversity of images of the Indian over a period of several hundred years. Through all the changes, however, certain things have remained fairly constant. One is the tendency of the Indian to function as a magnifying mirror of Euro-American values and concerns. Non-Indians have persistently made and remade their ideas about Indians to serve the social goals of every historic period. Indians have functioned sometimes as a vehicle for social criticism; this is clear in the ecology movement's exploitation of associations between Indians and nature that reproved American irresponsibility toward the land. They have served, at other times, as a foil against which non-Indians have displayed all that is right with America and its European settlement. This is nowhere more evident than in the Wild West shows that boldly dramatized the juggernaut of conquest: the inevitable and laudable progress of civilization over all that was savage, primitive, and untamed.

A second constant in the popular imagery of Indians is the assumption that their cultures and peoples are vanishing—that they have died out or will soon do so. James Fenimore Cooper's much-loved novel *The Last of the Mohicans* (1826)—as well as a great many romanticized, popular artworks of a related theme—depend for their poignant appeal upon this motif. Frederic Remington's easily recognized bronze sculpture titled *The End of the Trail*, for instance, falls into this category. Remington describes his piece as depicting the hapless, homeless, and helpless Indian discovering himself driven to the final, Western rim of the American continent by European expansion. A corollary of the vanishing Indian theme is the belief that there are no more real Indians: that those who may claim an Indian identity have lost the culture that once distinguished them from other Americans—and their racial authenticity along with it.

Finally, throughout American popular culture runs an unremitting fascination with the idea that non-Indians can become Indians. The fantasy is tirelessly replayed from the earliest captivity narratives through modern movies. Blockbusters such as *Little Big Man* (1970) and *Dances with Wolves* (1990) reliably feature protagonists who not only traverse the great racial divide between red and white but also somehow actually transform themselves mentally and emotionally into the other race. The New Age sensibility, which allows overburdened, modern executives briefly to exchange their corporate responsibilities for a weekend spent seeking a vision—with the able assistance of a shaman-for-hire—is a culmination of this journey of the non-Indian imagination.

Clearly, the use of the Indian in popular culture betrays complex psychological and sociological dynamics that have manifested on a national scale. No doubt the ability of the Indian to serve as a projection screen against which the dominant society has played out both its greatest aspirations and anxieties—whatever those implied at the moment—derives in large part from the essential emptiness of the image. As Robert Berkhofer suggests in his book *The White Man's Indian* (1978), at no time has the Indian in popular culture ever been developed into an actual person. Instead, he invariably lacks complexity, motive, personality, or other individualizing features. The result is an infinite possibility, a metaphor that can be employed to give substance to the most starkly diverse ideas. Because the Indian is simply a container to be filled, he can be used interchangeably as, for instance, the symbol of savagery and as the symbol of primal innocence.

THE VANISHING INDIAN

The persistent themes of the vanishing Indian and of the non-Indian who becomes an Indian are a bit harder to explain. Jack Forbes addresses this problem in his essay "The Manipulation of Race, Caste, and Identity: Classifying AfroAmericans, Native Americans, and Red-Black People." He suggests that the aforementioned themes originate in Americans' persisting knowledge of themselves as aliens in a New World wrested from its first inhabitants only through unspeakable violence. From the beginning of the European occupation of America, Indians "had to vanish because they were a threat or an impediment to the colonial settlers. That is, the colonial settlers could not truly become 'native' until the real natives were gone." Moreover, "this is the most compelling reason why 'Indians' must still vanish. Their continued existence as a separate population is a constant reminder of the foreignness" of American immigrants. Forbes's theory addresses not only the enduring American fascination with the vanishing Indian but also with the idea of becoming Indian. Changing one's racial identification is a way to complete the symbolic journey from conqueror to conquered and to achieve vindication for national sins.

NATIVE AMERICAN VIEWS

The decades since the 1950s have produced many important contributions to popular culture that speak in the voice of individuals who have most certainly not vanished. These works honestly express and address the concerns and values common to Indian people themselves rather than those of the larger society, and they have no need to explore the notion of becoming Indian because their authors have been Indian all along. Into this category belong novels such as N. Scott Momaday's *House Made of Dawn* (1968), a familial and tribal recollection of Kiowa migration; Louise Erdrich's *Tracks* (1988), the story of an Ojibwe family struggling to retain its tribal allotment; and Leslie Marmon Silko's *Ceremony* (1977), a poetic and profound excursion into the tormented world of a Vietnam veteran who returns to his childhood home in Laguna Pueblo.

To the same grouping belong works from around the turn of the twenty-first century, including Debra Magpie Earling's *Perma Red* (2002), a story of a girl desired by three men on the Flathead Reservation; Thomas King's *Truth and Bright Water* (1999), a tale of magical events along the Canadian-American border; and James Welch's *The Heartsong of Charging Elk* (2000), which relates the life of a young Lakota recruited by Buffalo Bill's Wild West Show. One might seek a similar place for the numerous literary products of Sherman Alexie, Gerald Vizenor, Louis Owens, Simon Ortiz, LeAnne Howe, and many others.

That the carefully elaborated themes and characters created by such authors have proven popular with both Indian and non-Indian audiences suggests a hopeful conclusion: perhaps America in the twenty-first century is ready to encounter Indian people in their individual and tribal particularity and real-life complexity. It has taken 500 years, but perhaps America is becoming willing to think about Indian people as more than a series of interchangeable representatives of the generic category of the Indian.

Eva Marie Garroutte

SEE ALSO: *Castaneda, Carlos; Cody, Buffalo Bill, and His Wild West Show; Dime Novels; Medicine Shows; New Age Spirituality;* Stagecoach; *The Western.*

BIBLIOGRAPHY

Barnard, Brian. "Would You Cheer for the Denver Darkies?" *Indian Country Today*, August 17, 1994, A5.

Berkhofer, Robert, Jr. *The White Man's Indian: Images of the American Indian from Columbus to the Present.* New York: Vintage, 1979.

Castaneda, Carlos. *Journey to Ixtlan: The Lessons of Don Juan.* New York: Simon & Schuster, 1972.

Cooper, James Fenimore. *The Last of the Mohicans*. New York: Oxford University Press, 1998.

Deloria, Philip J. *Playing Indian.* New Haven, CT: Yale University Press, 1998.

Derounian-Stodola, Kathryn. *The Indian Captivity Narrative, 1550–1900.* New York: Twayne, 1993.

Forbes, Jack D. "The Manipulation of Race, Caste, and Identity: Classifying AfroAmericans, Native Americans and Red-Black People." *Journal of Ethnic Studies* 17, no. 4 (1990): 1–51.

"James Arthur Ray." *New York Times.* Accessed January 2012. Available from http://topics.nytimes.com/topics/reference/timestopics/people/r/james_arthur_ray/index.html

Lacey, Marc. "New Age Guru Guilty in Sweat Lodge Deaths." *New York Times*, June 23, 2011. Accessed December 2011. Available from http://www.nytimes.com/2011/06/23/us/23sweat.html

Van Der Beets, Richard. "The Indian Captivity Narrative as Ritual." *American Literature* 43 (1972): 548–562.

Weatherford, Jack. *Indian Givers: How the Indians of the Americas Transformed the World.* New York: Ballantine, 1988.

Williams, John. *The Redeemed Captive Returning to Zion; or, A Faithful History of Remarkable Occurrences in the Captivity and Deliverance of Mr. John Williams.* Ann Arbor, MI: University Microfilms, 1966.

Indianapolis 500

For most of the twentieth century, the Borg-Warner Trophy, awarded to the winner of the Indianapolis 500 Motor Speedway race, has been the most coveted prize in auto racing. Known as "the greatest spectacle in racing," the Memorial Day event—which since the late 1960s has actually been run on the Sunday before Memorial Day to permit the scheduling of a rain delay—has featured the best drivers and the fastest speeds in the sport.

The Indianapolis 500 consists of 200 laps around the Indianapolis Motor Speedway's 2.5-mile oval. The first race took place in 1911 and lasted most of the day; the 1997 race was won by Arie Luyendyk in less than three-and-a-half hours. The first race averaged a then-staggering 74.602 miles per hour, but by the end of the twentieth century the course speed record was held by Rick Mears, who won the 1991 race with an average speed of more than 176 miles per hour. One other difference is notable: Ray Harroun took home a hefty $14,250 for winning the first Indianapolis 500, whereas 2011 winner Dan Wheldon pocketed a whopping $2.5 million.

Like most nonteam sports, the history of auto racing is chronicled in the personalities who defined its various eras. With one notable exception (NASCAR's Richard Petty), racing's dominant personalities gravitated to Indianapolis. In the early years, when the Speedway was paved with more than three million bricks (a 36-inch strip of which is still visible at the finish line), it was the home of barnstormers such as Harroun, Ralph DePalma, and Howdy Wilcox. In those days drivers would carry mechanics in the car with them, and repairs would be undertaken on the track.

The next great Indianapolis legend was Wilbur Shaw, who won the race three times in four years (1937 to 1940). In 1945 Shaw convinced Anton "Tony" Hulman to buy the Speedway from an ownership group that included the legendary Captain Eddie Rickenbacker; Shaw became its president. It was under the guidance of Shaw (who died in a plane crash in 1954) and Hulman that the Indianapolis 500 became the premier auto-racing event in the world. The 1950s and 1960s saw Indianapolis become the unofficial home of racing greats such as Maury Rose, Bill Vukovich, Johnnie Parsons, and Parnelli Jones, who drove the first turbine-powered race car to within four laps of a win before gearbox failure cost him the race.

The personality that most defines the Indianapolis 500, though, is A. J. Foyt Jr. Foyt first raced in Indianapolis in 1958 and continued to be an integral part of the facility's lore for the next forty years. His records include most career starts (35), most consecutive starts (35), most competitive miles during a career (12,273), and most races led (13). Foyt's record of four wins is matched by his contemporary Al Unser and was later tied by Mears. Another reason Foyt has cast such a long shadow over Indy racing is that he stands as a nostalgic contrast to the reality that championship racing has now become the province of only the best-financed teams. The names of drivers such Johnny Rutherford, Mario Andretti, and Jim Clark have been overshadowed by the names of owners such as Penske and Newman/Haas. Because so much money is now at stake in championship Indy-car racing, the complexion of the sport is changing, and the preeminence of the Indianapolis 500 is in danger. In 1994 Speedway president Tony George inaugurated the Indianapolis Racing League, a circuit meant to compete with the Championship Auto Racing Teams League (CART) established by Roger Penske. The friction between the rivals has caused many of the sport's most popular drivers to skip the Indianapolis 500 in order to boost CART's leverage in the marketplace.

In 2011 the Indianapolis 500 celebrated the centennial anniversary of its first race. Over the Speedway's 100-year history, Indy racing has endured significant transformations. Although speeds and prize money have risen precipitously, Indy racing fell out of favor with motorsport enthusiasts in the 1980s when stock-car racing initiated a dramatic rise from a regional southern sport to the highest-grossing national pastime. NACSAR has become a significant competitor and often attracts younger drivers and fans. Indy racing has been criticized for ineffective marketing of its new generation of budding stars, and in 2012 many of the best-known Indy racers were older than forty.

Around the time of NASCAR's rise, women began attempts to qualify for the Indy 500. In total eight women have qualified, and in 2010 a record number of four women competed. Danica Patrick is perhaps the most recognized female Indy racer. She also holds the title for best finish for a woman, coming in third place in the 2009 race. But even Indy racing's most famous woman has transitioned to NASCAR. Patrick follows a steady trend that includes Indy legends such as Foyt, who owns a NASCAR team, and Mears's nephew, driver Casey Mears. In spite of this ongoing contention, the Indy 500 continues to thrive: it remains, for many, "the greatest spectacle in racing." Although many of the other Indy-style races are largely disregarded by the racing community, the 500 remains a marquee event.

Barry Morris

SEE ALSO: *Andretti, Mario; Automobile; Foyt, A. J.; Patrick, Danica; Petty, Richard; Stock-Car Racing; Unser, Al; Unser, Bobby.*

BIBLIOGRAPHY

Binford, Tom. *A Checkered Past: My Twenty Years as Indy 500 Chief Steward.* Chicago: Cornerstone, 1998.

Reed, Terry. *Indy: The Race and Ritual of the Indianapolis 500.* Washington, DC: Potomac Books, 2005.

Taylor, Rich. *Indy: 75 Years of Auto Racing's Greatest Spectacle.* New York: St. Martin's Press, 1991.

Indie Music

The term *indie* (short for "independent") has at least three different meanings when applied to music. Although these meanings overlap to some extent, they came about separately and are related to different groups of fans and musicians. The most fundamental definition pertains to music that is produced and distributed outside the traditional system of the record industry. Indie music does not depend on the corporate-owned major labels, and indie musicians do not start their careers by looking for a recording contract. In this sense, any musician who takes a do-it-yourself approach to making and selling music is indie, regardless of whether the genre is jazz, country, pop, folk, rock, or even classical.

Nevertheless, certain styles of music are often referred to as indie, and that has created a second meaning of the term. There is no single indie sound, but there are distinctive indie versions across the musical spectrum. Originally, the indie sound differed from mainstream music in part because it had a more basic, or raw, sound with few production effects. As computer technology developed, however, relatively inexpensive software and hardware made it possible for almost anyone to create high-quality audio and add complex effects. Consequently, it became difficult to distinguish indie from mainstream music just by production values.

In the same way, the Internet has made it easy for musicians to market and deliver their work directly to consumers. At the most basic level, musicians can use free social media such as Facebook and Twitter to promote their work. They can also create low-cost websites where visitors can hear and buy their music, or even download it for free. Many local groups and aspiring singer-songwriters start off this way, then utilize digital services such as CDBaby and TuneCore, which will not only sell their music online but also manage the process of placing it in high-profile outlets such as iTunes and Amazon. By this means, independently produced songs and albums can be present in the marketplace right alongside music that has been made in state-of-the-art studios and promoted by major record companies.

A CULTURAL MOVEMENT

If indie music cannot be effectively categorized by style, production quality, marketing, or distribution, what remains? It can perhaps best be described as a kind of culture with certain characteristics and values. So-called indie culture takes in not only music but also literature, visual art, and other forms of artistic expression that reject commercialization and mainstream values. Indie artists in every medium favor handicraft over manufacturing and niche appeal over mass approval. However, when indie music is viewed as a value system, the whole picture becomes even more complicated. Do indie musicians stop being such if they sign major-label contracts? What happens when indie groups attract large audiences?

In this respect, indie culture falls into two distinct camps. For one camp, the indie scene is a starting point; for the other, it is a core commitment. The first group does not necessarily intentionally use the indie format as a stepping-stone, but it might be more concerned with becoming successful than with maintaining a confrontational stance toward the music industry. If these musicians are discovered by enthusiastic audiences, they are likely to pursue wider distribution and take advantage of financial opportunities. Such musicians might have difficulty, however, maintaining the indie qualities that made them interesting in the first place.

For the second group, indie culture is an end in itself. In its subversive or countercultural aspects, indie is the direct descendant of other movements that have opposed the prevailing values of popular music. Punk, the best-known example of early indie music, developed in the mid-1970s as a reaction to the commercialization of rock and roll. The punk sound features a fast beat, minimal instrumentation, and unsentimental, often political lyrics. Punk also established the do-it-yourself ethos that became a key aspect of indie music. In retrospect, punk can be seen as a further development of the garage rock movement of the mid-1960s, which was driven by young upstarts who borrowed elements from a variety of musical genres to create their own sounds. Many garage groups made and distributed their recordings themselves, and some achieved local or regional success, but the movement's lasting influence came from its introduction of an independent approach to music production.

INDIE EVOLUTION

Beginning in the 1980s, punk-inspired music splintered into a number of different styles and subcultures. In the United Kingdom, post-punk, or indie pop, groups gained popularity, and the Official Charts Company launched a separate listing of the best-selling independently produced singles. In the United States, major variants included the influential punk and heavy metal mixture known as grunge, along with a more pop-inflected style so widely played on campus radio stations that it became known as college rock. During this period, "alternative" became a general American term for non-mainstream musical genres and subcultures, and "underground" became widely used to describe music that resisted commercial assimilation.

By the 1990s, "indie" was frequently used to describe not only alternative rock but also fusion forms such as indie electronic and indie folk. The National Academy of Recording Arts and Sciences added a Grammy Award category for Best Alternative Music Album in 1991, but it was not until 2000 that the influential industry publication *Billboard* added a chart for independent albums.

Although indie music cannot be defined in a simple way, there is no doubt that it has become an enduring part of popular culture. A number of musicians and groups that started out in the indie scenes of the 1980s and 1990s went on to achieve mainstream success, including R.E.M., Nirvana, and Pearl Jam. In the first decade of the 2000s, indie folk gained widespread popularity, represented by groups such as Iron & Wine, the Decemberists, and Bon Iver. However, the essence of indie remains focused on musical experimentation and freedom from corporate control, as each new generation reinvents the indie sound to reflect emerging social and artistic trends.

Cynthia Giles

SEE ALSO: *Alternative Country Music; Alternative Rock; Amazon .com; Apple Computer; Facebook; Folk Music; Grunge; Nirvana; Pearl Jam; Pop Music; Punk; R.E.M.; Rock and Roll; Twitter.*

BIBLIOGRAPHY

King, Richard. *How Soon Is Now?: The Madmen and Mavericks Who Made Independent Music 1975–2005*. London: Faber and Faber, 2012.

Kruse, Holly. *Site and Sound: Understanding Independent Music Scenes*. New York: P. Lang, 2003.

Oakes, Kaya. *Slanted and Enchanted: The Evolution of Indie Culture*. New York: Henry Holt, 2009.

Smith, Kerry L. *Encyclopedia of Indie Rock*. Westport, CT: Greenwood Press, 2008.

Industrial Design

The "American system" of mass production, successfully implemented during the mid-1800s, was characterized by the large-scale manufacture of standardized products with interchangeable parts. Different from the individualized handcraftsmanship that preceded it, this production method required artificially powered machine tools and simplified operations, endowing products made from machine production with a certain aesthetic—an industrial design. At first used for the manufacture of revolvers, clocks, pocket watches, and agricultural machinery, the American system eventually produced most consumer goods.

Sewing machines and typewriters were the first products consciously designed with different contexts of use in mind—an early implementation of industrial design. In order to sell his sewing machines, Isaac Singer created two different models: the first, an ornamented machine for the domestic market, and the second, a plain black model for a factory setting. Early typewriters shared the same aesthetic variations as their sewing machine counterparts.

FUNCTIONALISM VS. AESTHETICS

In 1908 Henry Ford improved upon assembly line production by making an automobile, the Model T, specifically for a mass market. Ford believed in the design philosophy called "functionalism," a system also touted by architect Louis Sullivan (1856–1924). As one of the first self-conscious modern design movements, functionalism stressed that an "honest" design did not hide what an object did, a belief summed up most eloquently by Sullivan's famous phrase "form follows function." Architect and Sullivan protégé Frank Lloyd Wright (1867–1959) was a well-known proponent of the functionalist aesthetic, but he designed only for an exclusive clientele.

The rise of business in the 1910s and 1920s, which required the mass manufacture of office equipment and furniture, brought functionalism to the masses. During the 1910s the fine arts, especially from Europe, still remained influential in popular design, overshadowing the sheer power of machinery and industry that would prevail in the following decades. For example, Art Nouveau, expressed most clearly in the work of Belgian designer Henry van de Velde, was based on organic forms and the insistence that production occur in small craft workshops—a reaction against the forces of machine-driven mass production. Although meant for the elite, his designs were easily and readily appropriated for the mass market.

It was not until the crash of 1929, however, that industrial design in America became professionalized and considered a valid pursuit in its own right. Many designers who were previously involved in the theater or in advertising were recruited to develop viable and useful product designs in a small yet very competitive market. These American designers were highly influenced by the modernist aesthetic of the Bauhaus, which celebrated industrial materials such as metal and elevated machines to works of art. This method was used in the production of appliances, furniture, and architecture.

Norman Bel Geddes (1893–1958), a former stage designer, put his talents to work designing more substantial objects such as airplanes. Although he did not invent streamlining, he did democratize it. Popular between 1927 and the beginning of World War II, streamlining was characterized by smooth metal surfaces, long, sweeping, horizontal curves; rounded edges; and the elimination of extraneous detail. It was based on scientific principles and produced shapes with the least resistance in water and air. Streamlining was a wildly popular design aesthetic that appeared in a wide range of objects, from railroads and camping trailers to toasters and juicers, and symbolized speed and efficiency. Examples of streamlining included the Boeing 247 of 1933, the Douglas DC1 (an all-metal structure with an aluminum skin), and Carl Breer's 1934 Chrysler Airflow automobile.

MODERNIZATION

Industrial design styles did not change much during the decades immediately following World War II. Sullivan's "form follows function" credo had become the accepted canon in the design world. The exceptions to the functionalist design aesthetic appeared in the automobile industry owing to economic growth and prosperity in the United States following World War II. The Cadillacs and Buicks of the 1950s and early 1960s were known for their outlandish colors—pink, turquoise, yellow—and for their extravagant body styles, complete with jutting tail fins that resembled something from outer space. At that time cars such as the Jaguar E-type were considered art by many designers and manufacturers as well as in the art world in general. In the early twenty-first century, the cars of the 1960s were still considered to be some of the most beautiful, aesthetically appealing vehicles ever made.

By the late 1970s and early 1980s, technology addressed the miniaturization of electronic equipment, radically changing Americans' material universe. Although designers from the 1940s and 1950s had designed functional objects in attractive packages, they could not get rid of their bulk. The impact of computers was revolutionary, both in terms of how people communicated and in the nature of design itself. Computers used on the production line allowed for more flexibility, shorter production runs, and more differentiation in design—a return to the nature of production a hundred years earlier.

Automobile designers were able to make cars that were not only smaller but also safer. The introduction of antilock brakes, traction control, and airbags during the 1970s was in part a result of federal safety standards and regulations that became effective March 1, 1967. The hatchback, sedan, and sport utility vehicle all became popular models that have continued to dominate the market in the twenty-first century. In the 1980s, cars were designed to be aggressive and powerful, but little attention was paid to aesthetic. The Range Rover was built to be tough and rugged, and the form of the vehicle was boxy and utilitarian. The only vehicle to be displayed in the Louvre in France as a symbol of industrial design, the Range Rover was one of the first cars during the late twentieth century to proudly adopt Sullivan's mantra of "form over function."

At the same time that microprocessing was allowing objects to become smaller, thinner, and more portable, postmodern design also changed the outward appearance of industrially produced objects. Architect Robert Venturi (1925–) became one of the first American proponents of postmodern design with his 1972 book *Learning from Las Vegas*. Formally established in Italy in 1981 and called "Memphis," the school of postmodernism embraced exuberant styles and colors. Memphis, referring to both Elvis and Egypt, reacted against the cultural supremacy assumed by modern design, which its proponents saw as a constant restatement of the power of technology and the triumph of large American corporations.

In contrast, postmodern design attempted to be more egalitarian, incorporating stylistic elements from both high and low art—from marble to Formica, from Greek columns to polka dots. Michael Graves (1934–) was another American architect and designer who embraced the postmodern aesthetic and began designing toasters, picture frames, and other housewares for Target stores near the end of the 1990s, indicating a downward trend of taste in the selling of what had formerly been high style to the masses. The appearance of postmodernism to some, however, marked the triumph of surface over substance. Influenced more by the information age than the industrial age, postmodernism perhaps signaled the end of the reign of industrial design and the beginning of a new design ethic based on and in the hyperreality of cyberspace rather than the materiality of tangible objects.

By the twenty-first century, industrial design marked a transition from its aesthetic focus into an increasingly consumer-driven model. Perhaps the most significant influence on popular culture is Jonathan Ive. Apart from designers such as Graves, who became better known for his housewares; Massimo Vignelli, whose designs for corporate entities include American Airlines and the map of the New York Metro System; and Niels Diffrient's omnipresent ergonomic chairs that anonymously entered daily life, Ive's mark can be seen in the variety of handheld devices that populated the marketplace. His first project was the iMac, which laid the groundwork for his other notable designs, such as the iPod, iPhone, and iPad. The focus on design led to sleek, functional, and immensely popular products that provided the maximum amount of content without drawing attention to the device.

Car manufacturers began designing cars such as the Smart car that looked similar to popular gadgets such as iPods and smartphones. Car designers also became more aware of the balance between form and function. A car might be completely safe but if it does not look attractive, consumers will not purchase the model. Another focus of the automobile industry has been fuel efficiency and the reduction of emissions, resulting in a challenge to create a car that still has the power that Americans demand while still minimizing the vehicle's effect on to the environment. The Toyota Prius, a gasoline-electric hybrid hatchback, become popular beginning in the late 1990s. One of the environmentally cleanest cars available for purchase, according to the U.S. Environmental Protection Agency (EPA), the Prius blended the elements of safety, functionality, and sleekness. Other vehicles like the Prius continued to be developed, helping indicate the future of industrial design.

Wendy Woloson

SEE ALSO: *Apple Computer; Cadillac; Cell Phones; Consumerism; Ford, Henry; Ford Motor Company; The Great Depression; IBM (International Business Machines); iPad; iPod / iTunes; Kodak; Minimalism; Skyscrapers; Smartphones; Walkman.*

BIBLIOGRAPHY

Bayley, Stephen; Philippe Garner; and Deyan Sudjic. *Twentieth-*

Century Style and Design. New York: Van Nostrand Reinhold, 1986.

Bush, Donald J. *The Streamlined Decade.* New York: George Braziller, 1975.

Dormer, Peter. *Design since 1945.* New York: Thames and Hudson, 1993.

Forty, Adrian. *Objects of Desire: Design and Society since 1750.* New York: Thames and Hudson, 1986.

Gantz, Carroll. *The Industrialization of Design: A History from the Steam Age to Today.* Jefferson, NC: McFarland, 2011.

Gorman, Carma R. *The Industrial Design Reader.* New York: Allworth Press, 2003.

Heskett, John. *Industrial Design.* New York: Thames and Hudson, 1987.

Horn, Richard. *Memphis: Objects, Furniture, and Patterns.* Philadelphia: Running Press, 1985.

Lesko, Jim. *Industrial Design Materials and Manufacturing.* New York: John Wiley, 1999.

Lupton, Ellen. *Mechanical Brides: Women and Machines from Home to Office.* New York: Princeton Architectural Press and Cooper-Hewitt National Museum of Design, 1993.

Pulos, Arthur J. *American Design Ethic: A History of Industrial Design to 1940.* Cambridge, MA: MIT Press, 1983.

Sexton, Richard. *American Style: Classic Product Design from Airstream to Zippo.* San Francisco: Chronicle Books, 1987.

Votolato, Gregory. *American Design in the Twentieth Century: Personality and Performance.* New York: Manchester University Press, 1998.

Wilson, Richard Guy; Dianne H. Pilgrim; Dickran Tashjian; et al. *The Machine Age in America, 1918–1941.* New York: Harry N. Abrams and the Brooklyn Museum, 1986.

The Ink Spots

With their wistful, plangent, sentimental love songs, the Ink Spots are redolent of the 1940s, when their music provided a romantic backdrop to lovers throughout the years of World War II and beyond. They had their first and greatest hit, the million-seller "If I Didn't Care," in 1939, while among the best and most enduring of the many that followed were "My Prayer," "I Don't Want to Set the World on Fire," "To Each His Own," "Maybe," "Java Jive," "Prisoner of Love," "It's a Sin to Tell a Lie," and "I'll Never Smile Again."

The group was formed in Indianapolis in 1932, initially calling themselves the Riff Brothers, then the Percolating Puppies. The original members were tenor and lead vocalist Jerry Daniels, who also played the guitar and the ukulele; Ivory "Deek" Watson, baritone vocals and guitar; Charles Fuqua, tenor vocals, guitar, and ukulele; and Orville "Hoppy" Jones, bass vocals and cello. In 1934 the quartet settled on calling themselves the Ink Spots, and Bill Kenny eventually replaced Daniels. It was Jones who conjured up their trademark "talking chorus" in which the lead singer speaks, rather than sings, for added dramatic effect. Across the decades, the Ink Spots underwent numerous personnel changes. Perhaps the most significant came in 1945, when Kenny was replaced by Jim Nabbie, who led the group until his death in 1992.

All the popular black vocal "doo-wop" groups of the early rock-and-roll years owed a supreme debt to the Ink Spots. Their soft, smooth, group harmonizing, backing the steady, silky-throated vocalizing of their lead singers, inspired a generation of adolescents who started out singing on urban street corners in the early 1950s, some of whom went on to score some of rock and roll's earliest hits. Nobody, however, quite succeeded in emulating the unique sound of the Ink Spots, whose high delicate tenors seemed almost to have originated from classical music's countertenor tradition. The Ink Spots were inducted into the Rock and Roll Hall of Fame in 1989. Although they had long been superseded in the charts, and their original members were no more, the Ink Spots were still touring the country in the 1990s, a nostalgic throwback to a gentler past.

Rob Edelman

SEE ALSO: *Doo-wop Music.*

BIBLIOGRAPHY

Goldberg, Marv. *More Than Words Can Say: The Ink Spots and Their Music.* Lanham, MD: Scarecrow Press, 1998.

Warner, Jay. *American Singing Groups: A History from 1940s to Today.* Milwaukee, WI: Hal Leonard Corp., 2006.

Watson, Deek, with Lee Stephenson. *The Story of the "Ink Spots."* New York: Vantage Press, 1967.

Inner Sanctum Mysteries

From 1941 to 1952, years that spanned the golden era of radio, the macabre anthology series *Inner Sanctum* invited listeners each week to pass through its famous opening creaking door into a world that provided a unique mixture of horror and the darkest of comedy. In its day, *Inner Sanctum* was perhaps the quintessential radio program, using sound to produce effects that wove a spell unique to the medium. In a larger sense, the show's peculiar combination of chills and chuckles has influenced the American horror genre ever since and has found expression in everything from EC Comics in the 1950s to the self-referential works of Stephen King and Wes Craven in the 1990s. A listener today who has the nerve to step through the *Inner Sanctum* doorway (being careful not to bump into that corpse "just hanging around over there") will discover a world both historically distant and entertainingly familiar.

Inner Sanctum used sound in three principal ways to horrify and amuse its listeners. First among these was, of course, the creaking door, an effect that radio historian John Dunning has said "may have been the greatest opening signature device ever achieved." The door was the idea of the program's creator Himan Brown, who once claimed that it was one of only two sounds in radio to be trademarked (the other being the NBC chimes). Regardless of its legal status, there is no doubt that the ominous squeak of the *Inner Sanctum* portal takes its place alongside Fibber McGee's overcrowded closet, the menacing chuckle of the Shadow, and the sputtering of Jack Benny's car as the best-remembered sounds of old-time radio. King may have put it best, recalling years later that "nothing could have looked as horrible as that door *sounded.*"

Brown's second achievement in sound was *Inner Sanctum*'s innovative use of the organ. While other suspense programs used the instrument in its musical guise, Jim Harmon reports in *Great Radio Heroes* (1967) that Brown "warned his organist never to play a recognizable song . . . or even an original snatch of melody." The man at the somber Hammond organ was to play sharp "stings"—high musical notes struck to emphasize an important piece of dialogue—and "doom chords" designed to produce a sense of unease and foreboding in listeners. Dunning goes so far as to claim that "the organ became one of the star players . . . brooding, ever-present, worrying, fretting . . . the epitome of radio melodrama."

Finally, Brown was grimly innovative in his creation of realistic sound effects to lend believability to the outlandish goings-on and render them truly terrifying. Only on *Inner Sanctum*, for example, would the soft *thunk* of a man's skull being crushed be so deliciously captured with the act of a small metal hammer striking a melon, a Brown favorite.

Presiding over this dark world of sound is the show's famous host, Raymond. Played most notably by Raymond Edward Johnson (1941–1945), Raymond is the source of much of the program's black humor, as he ushers listeners in and out of the creaking door with a series of ghoulish puns ("Quiet now—no 'coffin.' We have 'grave' matters to uncover") and doubtful morals ("Careful the next time you ask your wife to 'pass' the knife. She may do it—right through you. Good Niiiiiight!"). The tradition of the sardonic host to horror would find equally memorable expression years later in American popular culture with figures such as the Cryptkeeper in EC Comics and Rod Serling in television's *The Twilight Zone*, but the stories introduced by Raymond are unique in their ability to arouse and exploit audience fears of the supernatural before ultimately providing a "realistic" explanation.

As otherworldly as the universe of the *Inner Sanctum* sometimes seems for most of the tale, events are always finally shown to be the result of a very human combination of folly and foible—of greed, ambition, and just plain bad luck. The show's self-imposed need to create situations that are outlandish yet capable of "rational" explanations in the final moments leads to some of the most wildly improbable twists and turns imaginable, and it is this element that makes the series both memorable and campish. It is also for this reason that the creative peak of the program is usually regarded as the early series of episodes performed by Boris Karloff and Peter Lorre and based upon classic works by Edgar Allan Poe and Guy de Maupassant, skilled practitioners of the peculiar art of "realistic horror."

In its unique mixture of horror and humor, classics and camp, the supernatural with the everyday, *Inner Sanctum* helped shape the face of popular horror in all media—even in its own time by spawning a set of *Inner Sanctum* novels and occasional movies. *Inner Sanctum* can also be fondly recalled as a program that exploited the basic elements of radio perhaps more than any other show, taking an entire generation of listeners deep into the "inner sanctums" of their own imaginations.

Kevin Lause

SEE ALSO: The CBS Radio Mystery Theater*; EC Comics; Karloff, Boris; King, Stephen; Lorre, Peter; Radio; Serling, Rod.*

BIBLIOGRAPHY

Dunning, John. *On the Air: The Encyclopedia of Old-Time Radio*. New York: Oxford University Press, 1998.

Harmon, Jim. *The Great Radio Heroes*. Garden City, NY: Doubleday, 1967.

Nachman, Gerald. *Raised on Radio*. New York: Pantheon Books, 1998.

Sterling, Christopher H., and Michael C. Keith. *The Museum of Broadcast Communications Encyclopedia of Radio*. New York: Fitzroy Dearborn, 2004.

International Business Machines

SEE: *IBM (International Business Machines).*

International Exhibition of Modern Art

SEE: *Armory Show.*

The International Male Catalog

With its bold, offbeat fashions and subtly suggestive, all-male photography layouts, the International Male catalog gained popularity and renown among trendy twenty- and thirty-somethings looking for unique and stylish clothes in the late twentieth century. One of the originators of the mail-order boom, International Male began operations in the early 1970s. The company's focus on colorful and daring styles from around the world, including pants in bright prints, mesh shirts, and a vast selection of unique men's underwear, gave it a special appeal to gay men. Lesbians, too, were drawn to the clothes, which often transcend gender with kaleidoscopic élan.

Part of Hanover Direct, a subsidiary of Pennsylvania-based Brawn LLC of California, International Male consolidated with its swimwear and underwear line, Undergear, in 2009. The merger brought all of the company's products into a single catalog and website and expanded Undergear's marketing strategies. The website and catalog have incorporated more accessories such as jewelry and cologne and have targeted younger audiences with aggressive social media and Internet campaigns. The company has gained notoriety through its risqué YouTube advertisements and by enlisting soccer star David Beckham in 2012 to design and model an underwear line.

Tina Gianoulis

SEE ALSO: *Catalog Houses; Gay Men; The Internet; Lesbianism; Online Shopping; Social Media; YouTube.*

BIBLIOGRAPHY

Brubach, Holly. "Mail Order America." *New York Times Magazine*, November, 21, 1993, 54.

Undergear.com. Accessed May 2012. Available from http://www.internationalmale.com/

The Internet

The Internet is the most powerful individual electronic communications network in the world's history. From a 140-

Internet Shopping. *An Internet user checks out a website for purchasing prescription drugs.* TIM BOYLE/GETTY IMAGES.

character post on Twitter to the World Digital Library, the Internet makes instant communication possible for anyone with a computing device, software, and an appropriate connection. The Internet has spawned new terms and given new meanings to existing words and phrases—such as *e-book, cyberspace, geek, domain, hacker*, and *spam*, to name just a few—and revolutionized popular culture. As it has transformed communication, it has also affected the ways that information is used and shared, how human society is organized, and how humans value and relate to each other.

The telegraph was the direct antecedent of the Internet. The earliest scheme for using electricity to send messages appeared in a British magazine in 1753, and two French brothers transmitted the first electronic message in 1791. But it was American inventor Samuel F. B. Morse who gave the U.S. Congress an opportunity to buy outright his patent to the telegraph technology in 1844. The government failed to see the advantage of a single, standardized electronic communications network, however, and the result was the formation of thousands of privately owned telegraph companies that were gradually purchased or put out of business by Western Union, which became a telegraph monopoly. In turn the monopoly provided everything from the first professional baseball scores in 1876 to breaking the news of the bombing of Pearl Harbor in 1941 to the delivery of love notes, all at a low, nearly universal cost. The original American Telephone and Telegraph (AT&T) system, developed in the wake of Alexander Bell's patent of the telephone in 1876, became the standardized telephone monopoly, controlling long-distance and most short-distance communication for radio and television networks and interpersonal information consumers.

One factor common to the telegraph and telephone was that neither could work without interconnection. A telephone is useless without there being someone else to call. It took some time, however, for people to recognize the advantages of computer networks; the first cumbersome, room-sized electronic computer, developed by Iowa State University physicist John V. Atanasoff between 1939 and 1942, could function alone, as could its descendants. In 1964 a group of researchers at the Rand Corporation conceived of a configuration of computers interconnected by pathways similar to telephone lines employing "packets," small electronic groups of data, as a means for military personnel to communicate following a nuclear war. Such an occurrence would have disrupted standard military communication channels, preventing surviving military from coordinating a response. The proposed network would not have a central station and thus could continue operating even if major portions were destroyed.

ARPANET

In 1969 the Advanced Research Projects Agency Network (ARPANET) was created as a system of twenty individual computer stations, or nodes, located at various distances from one another. The first electronic message—part of the word *login*—was transmitted October 29, 1969, between scientists at the University of California at Los Angeles and Stanford University. Each station used a common language, or control protocol, that allowed it to communicate electronically and a transmission protocol that made all nodes equal, as opposed to using a central station hierarchy. Even if several nodes were destroyed in an attack, messages could still be transmitted as long as at least one pathway remained. The original AT&T and Western Union each had block-long manual switchboards in central locations vulnerable to attack. ARPANET, however, could reroute critical messages between nodes and around interruptions instantaneously without any human intervention.

Three years later forty-six university and research organization networks were added to the system, and ARPANET began to grow, as the Internet would, by chance rather than by design. Perhaps one of its strongest appeals was that no one could predict accurately its future. Unix was developed as a common operating system around 1970. By 1972 the "@" symbol was first used in an e-mail address. The following year, sociologist Daniel Bell predicted that computers would define the late twentieth century in the same way that automobiles had done in the first half of the century. In particular, rapid computer communication characteristics enabled the spread of e-mail and group e-mails, messages sent simultaneously at the touch of a key that eliminated the age-old need for duplicate messages.

Discussion areas, called news groups, allowed users to meet with others interested in specifically designated topics. File transfer protocol (FTP) and Telnet, which allowed computer users to log in to a remote computer, allowed greater numbers of nontechnical people to use the Internet. The decentralized Jeffersonian democracy of the Internet held an appeal for independent-minded Americans at the time, and the demise of Western Union and the court-ordered breakup of the original AT&T in 1982 only added to the attraction of a communications system without a central station or control.

In spite of the Internet's wider advantages, its growth remained tightly controlled by the military during its initial years. While the Department of Defense permitted university nodes to share supercomputing resources, news groups and university research-oriented networks such as CSNET (Computer Science Network) and NSFNET (National Science Foundation Network) began overtaxing the system in the 1980s, necessitating a new addressing system that allowed users to distinguish between government or educationally endorsed content and content generated by individuals or groups without sanction or authority. The new addressing system also allowed the Internet to evolve from a medium for simple back-and-forth messages to one capable of providing complex mass-audience content, similar to publishing or broadcasting.

Eventually the glut of the new network traffic inspired the military to develop a new network for itself, and the original ARPANET ceased to exist in June 1990. The military left an impression on the Internet before it departed, however. Beyond its decentralized structure and the teaching of three generations of computer scientists in the difficult art of computer networking, the military helped spawn early startup computer network companies such as 3Com and the manufacturer of Ethernet.

EMERGENCE OF PERSONAL COMPUTING

Meanwhile, major developments were taking place in computer hardware and software that would broaden the appeal of a network such as the Internet. Marcian Hoff Jr. of Intel Corporation combined several integrated electronic circuits into a tiny piece of electronics called a microprocessor in 1968. The new chips performed arithmetic and logic functions and could be programmed like more expensive wired circuits. The availability of the new Intel microprocessor attracted the attention of computer hobbyists and home experimenters such as Steve Wozniak and Steve Jobs, who began marketing their Apple I computer from Wozniak's garage in 1976. In 1980 Apple started to develop the Macintosh computer. Mainframe computer manufacturer IBM unveiled its own microcomputer in 1981, employing an operating system provided by college dropouts Paul Allen and Bill Gates.

Within a few years Apple and IBM had created a market for a previously unknown product, the personal computer. Other manufacturers joined the fad, selling inexpensive "clones" of the IBM PC, and software writers developed thousands of programs to use on the new machines, from spreadsheets and word processors to games. Digital subscriber line, or DSL, first suggested in 1948, gradually replaced standard telephone lines beginning in the late 1980s, decreasing the cost of higher-speed Internet connections. But until the arrival of the Internet, one of the greatest strengths of personal computers—communication—remained largely untapped. As late as 1995, Gates, by then a software baron, actively opposed the Internet.

As the military backed away from the Internet, the network's content evolved from computer-related uses to content more representative of popular culture. By the 1980s the telephonic backbone of the Internet enabled it to spread from the United States to other countries that had political systems that allowed at least some form of free speech. The growing Internet audience attracted new application developers providing uses in such areas as education, reference, and entertainment. Businesses also began logging onto the Internet to conduct research and share information. The National Science Foundation accepted the task of managing the Internet's backbone in 1987, but its task was just that—to manage, rather than control, the growth. Computerized organizational systems became the first search engines, providing databases of various Internet resources broken down by categories, subjects, and locations. These included Archie, named after the word *archive*; Wide Area Information Servers, or WAIS; and Gopher, named after the mascot of the University of Minnesota, where it was created.

Wireless technology—popularly known as Wi-Fi, a play on the older term *hi-fi*, meaning high fidelity—became possible in 1985 when the U.S. Federal Communications Commission released the appropriate bandwidth. Wi-Fi eventually became associated with the Internet as wireless routers hooked up to high-speed connections began replacing noisy dial-up telephone modems in the late 1990s and the first decade of the 2000s. By 1990 the Internet had most of the hardware technology it needed, but it lacked visual appeal or any demonstrable superiority other than speed. That would be solved by the development of three related technologies: the World Wide Web, hypertext markup language (HTML), and the Web browser.

THE WEB

The World Wide Web, introduced in 1989, allowed vast amounts of information, including graphics and print-style typefaces, to be delivered over the Internet. HTML provided a way to structure and display Web content, including hyperlinks. A hyperlink, which is a highlighted or underlined passage in Web text, could speed a reader to related information instantaneously with the click of a mouse. The process of hyperlinking between all of the files and directories of the Internet, as if it were one large computer, was simplified in 1992 when the National Center for Supercomputing at the University of Illinois wrote and released an application called Mosaic, which was the first Web browser. Mosaic allowed computer users to view and switch between websites more easily. The Illinois program evolved into the Netscape Corporation in 1994 and produced Netscape Navigator, a popular early Web browser.

The proliferation of personal computers accelerated the growth of the Internet during the 1990s. The number of host computers climbed from 313,000 in 1990 to 56,218,000 in 1999. The first computer radio station went online in 1994. Libraries began offering Web versions of books along with OCLC, an early computerized library database. Newspapers and magazines began putting their contents online for free, helping to stimulate advertising on the Internet beginning in 1991. The growing commercial character of the Internet was acknowledged in 1995 when the National Science Foundation backbone became commercially supported. The Internet Activities Board (IAB), founded in 1983, guided the evolution of the Internet; the Internet Assigned Numbers Authority (IANA) assigned Internet protocol (IP) addresses or network numbers; and a hired private company, Network Solutions Inc., began registering website domain names in 1993.

Meanwhile, the growing popularity of the Internet instigated a late twentieth-century technological "gold rush" as entrepreneurs and venture capitalists sought to emulate the successes of personal computing pioneers Wozniak, Jobs, Allen, and Gates. CompuServe went from a mainframe computer timesharing business in 1969 to become one of the first online service providers in the 1980s, later to be joined by America Online (AOL), founded in the early 1980s as a gaming provider. AOL purchased Netscape, making Netscape founder Jim Clark an instant billionaire. AOL then purchased CompuServe in 1998, and the resulting firm merged with Time Warner in 2001 to form AOL Time Warner, the first large-scale Internet content provider. The term *AOL* was dropped from the corporate name in 2003, and the AOL component of the business was spun off in 2009.

Gates's Microsoft Corporation finally embraced the Internet in the mid-1990s in its Windows 95 operating system. It included the first versions of Internet Explorer, which would become the world's most widely used Web browser. Two Stanford University students, Jerry Yang and David Filo, became millionaires when their Internet search engine company Yahoo! went public in 1996. The stock of online auction house eBay, one of a growing number of Internet companies nicknamed "dot-coms," increased 2,000 percent in value in less than a year when it went public in 1998.

THE DOT-COM BUBBLE

The market value of the first Internet-inspired companies peaked in March 2000, but many never made a profit before they ran out of venture capital. By 2003 so many dot-coms had failed that analysts were calling the era the "dot-com bubble." Among the casualties was WorldCom, an Internet-service and long-distance-telephone provider that used fraudulent accounting practices to inflate its market value. CEO Bernard Ebbers was convicted of fraud and conspiracy and sentenced to twenty-five years in prison in 2005 in what was at the time the largest bankruptcy in U.S. history. A few Internet entrepreneurs continued to make spectacular profits in the wake of the dot-com bubble, obscuring the fact that most of the rest failed. They were motivated in part by Moore's law, which holds that the speed and capacity of computers increases exponentially over time. Advances in computer technology were creating new and expanded Internet opportunities.

Abandoned by Apple Computer in 1985, cofounder Jobs returned in 1997, and under his leadership the company went on to develop successful Internet-inspired products and services, including the iPod, iTunes software and the iTunes music store, the iPhone, and the iPad. When he died in 2011, Jobs was worth an estimated $7 billion, and Apple was one of the most valuable companies in the world. Using hypertext and other Internet data-mining technologies, Sergey Brin and Larry Page created the Google search engine in 1998. Their company went public in 2004 and raised $1.66 billion. By 2011 Google was handling more than eleven billion searches per month—nearly two-thirds of all searches conducted on the Internet.

Mark Zuckerberg used a program he created at Harvard University called Facemash, in which students rated the pictures of other students, as the inspiration for the social network service Facebook in 2004. Inspired in part by AOL's popular Instant Messenger program, Jack Dorsey created Twitter in 2007, one of the first successful Internet companies to capitalize on smartphone technology. Groupon, an online coupon marketer founded by Andrew Mason in 2008, had an initial public stock offering in 2011 of $700 million, the most for an Internet company since Google in 2004.

SOCIOPOLITICAL RAMIFICATIONS

The political impact of the Internet has expanded greatly since Bill Clinton became the first president to establish a White House website in 1994. The nature of political discourse in the United States and other countries was altered by social networking; citizen journalism; the availability of raw, unprocessed information on the Internet in contrast to traditional print and broadcast journalism; and crowdsourcing, Internet-based information provided by volunteer groups or communities. This led to what some observers characterized as a period of close or disputed elections, recalls, and political incivility. In turn, the disruptive nature of the Internet itself—displacing existing technologies and services from mainframe computing and postal services to newspapers, bookstores, and libraries—made supervision or regulation on local, national, and international levels difficult, if not impossible, to achieve. Providing Internet bandwidth to the developing world and the equitable sharing of existing bandwidth in more developed societies, an issue known as net neutrality, remained politically and technologically challenging.

An Internet-delivered computer virus attack on a uranium-enrichment center in Iran in 2010 by at least two Western nations revealed another political aspect of the Internet: its use as an offensive military weapon. The so-called Stuxnet virus broached the possibility of wider Internet attacks against the information systems and infrastructures of larger, more technologically advanced nations. Access to the Internet through smartphone, notebook, and computer tablet technologies, in conjunction with social networking, was often credited with facilitating large-scale populist movements, including the 2009 Iran election protests, the 2011 Arab Spring uprisings, and the so-called Occupy movements in the United States and other nations. Group-sourced websites such as WikiLeaks revealed that intelligence contractors as well as countries were using the Internet to implement mass interception systems to spy on political opponents as well as invade personal privacy.

GOING MAINSTREAM

The Internet transformed popular culture in the early twenty-first century. Perhaps the most dramatic change was in the redefining of the Internet itself from a highly technical, less user-friendly, and more masculine entity to one that was less competitive, more connective, and therefore more feminized. Some of the most profitable uses of the Internet in the 1990s were computer games, pornography, and equities trading. With the development of encrypted data transference procedures in 1994, Amazon.com began online retailing in 1995, eBay was conceived that same year, and the Internet-based PayPal e-commerce service began in 1998. By 2010 U.S. e-commerce was at $142.5 billion, or about 8 percent of all retail product sales.

More than two-thirds of American females age eighteen and over compared to just 54 percent of men of the same age range used social network services to connect with friends in 2011, a phenomenon that began with the introduction of the first large-scale social network service, MySpace, in 2003. Blogs—websites with personal information and reflections typically written in the style of old-fashioned print diaries and journals—evolved from the Internet interest groups and forums of the 1980s and 1990s. With the help of services such as WordPress, began in 2003 as a means of improving the appearance and accessibility of blogs, and Tumblr, started in 2007, blogging became an acceptable pastime for celebrities as well as the unknown, much as Tweeting did in the first decade of the 2000s. Pop stars Lady Gaga and Justin Bieber had more than fifteen million Twitter followers each in 2011. Visual sites such as Flickr, introduced in 2004, and YouTube, started in 2005, allowed computer and smartphone users to share photographs and videos. By restricting copyrighted material, such visual sites avoided the legal problems experienced by audio crowdsourcing site Napster, which was found guilty of copyright infringement and was shut down in 2001.

The prevalence of the Internet in the early twenty-first century also led to new cultural, health, and legal problems, such as Internet addiction disorder, spam, and a host of privacy concerns. Child cyber-porn and cyber-bullying, Internet-enabled forms of harm, threats, or intimidations, were facilitated by the anonymity of social networking sites and contributed to emotional damage and suicides among children and teenagers. Internet cafés, started in San Francisco in 1991, provided wireless Internet service to customers in safe public settings. Twenty-first-century commentators lauded the Internet, personal computers, e-mail, social networking services, and smartphones as American inventions, but those same technologies were used for undermining the values, economy, and creativity of society.

Impending Internet innovations or challenges include wider use of cloud computing, the delivery of computing services over a network such as the Internet; WiMax, long-range Wi-Fi transmission; a shortage of IP addresses; greater use of the Internet for public purposes such as delivering court testimony and voting; providing more and improved video content in lieu of older broadcast and cable technologies; and the accessing of the Internet through biological rather than mechanical pathways. Arguments will also continue over whether the word *Internet* is a proper noun or common noun, with a lowercase *i*, in the English language. The Internet remains a story of hard work by many and good luck for a few, but it continues to fulfill at least one elemental human need: as an unknown e-mailer paraphrased French philosopher René Descartes, "I post, therefore I am."

Richard Junger

SEE ALSO: *Amazon.com; Apple Computer; AT&T; Bieber, Justin; Blogging; Cable TV; Cell Phones; Computer Games; Craigslist; Drudge, Matt; eBay; E-mail; Facebook; File Sharing; Google; Hulu; IBM (International Business Machines); iPad; iPod / iTunes; Lady Gaga; Microsoft; MP3; Napster; Netbooks; Netflix; Online Dating; Online Gaming; Online Shopping; Pornography; Sexting; Smartphones; Telephone; Twitter; Viral Videos; Wii; WikiLeaks; Wikipedia;* Wired *Magazine; Xbox Kinect; YouTube; Y2K.*

BIBLIOGRAPHY

Auletta, Ken. *Googled: The End of the World as We Know It.* New York: Penguin Books, 2010.

Carr, Nicholas G. *The Big Switch: Rewiring the World, from Edison to Google.* New York: W. W. Norton, 2008.

Goldsmith, Jack L., and Tim Wu. *Who Controls the Internet: Illusions of a Borderless World.* New York: Oxford University Press, 2006.

Keen, Andrew. *The Cult of the Amateur: How Today's Internet Is Killing Our Culture.* New York: Doubleday/Currency, 2007.

Kiesler, Sara, ed. *Culture of the Internet.* Mahwah, NJ: Lawrence Erlbaum Associates, 1997.

Porter, David, ed. *Internet Culture.* New York: Routledge, 1997.

Rensberger, Boyce. "Networks Are Conduits for the 'Infection': 50,000 Terminals Affected by Outbreak." *Washington Post,* November 4, 1988, A4.

Segaller, Stephen. *Nerds 2.0.1: A Brief History of the Internet.* New York: TV Books, 1998.

Shirky, Clay. *Here Comes Everybody: The Power of Organizing without Organizations.* New York: Penguin Press, 2008.

Standage, Tom. *The Victorian Internet: The Remarkable Story of the Telegraph and the Nineteenth Century's On-Line Pioneers.* New York: Walker, 1998.

Surratt, Carla G. *Netlife: Internet Citizens and Their Communities.* Commack, NY: Nova Science Publishers, 1998.

Wellman, Barry, and Caroline Haythornthwaite, eds. *The Internet in Everyday Life.* Malden, MA: Blackwell Publications, 2002.

Young, Gray, ed. *The Internet.* New York: H.W. Wilson, 1998.

Internet Dating

SEE: *Online Dating.*

Intervention

Intervention is a reality television program on the A&E Network sponsored by the Partnership for a Drug Free America. The show, which began in 2005, deals with multiple forms of addiction and treatment. Some topics covered in the series include alcoholism, drug addictions, eating disorders, gambling problems, and oniomania (impulse shopping). The program's format follows one or two addicts per episode who believe that they are being filmed for a documentary about their respective addictions. The show centers on a surprise confrontation, or intervention, in which the addict's friends and family members offer him or her a chance at treatment. *Intervention* features everyday people as well as celebrities such as musician and meth addict Travis Meeks, actress and compulsive shopper Vanessa Marquez, and professional cyclist and crack addict Chad Gerlach.

The concept of intervening in an addicted person's life was pioneered in the 1960s by Episcopal priest and recovered alcoholic Dr. Vernon Johnson. At his Minnesota institute, Dr. Johnson developed a unique method for intervention based on confrontation, after which the show is modeled. Each episode includes a preintervention, during which family members discuss plans to confront their loved one and the steps they will follow if the person chooses not to seek the help provided. The program uses three main interventionists, who are all recovering addicts: former priest Jeff VanVonderen; counselor Candy Finnigan; and Ken Seeley, who founded Intervention-911, a group that pairs addicts with proper treatment centers.

At each episode's end the subject or subjects of the show arrive thinking that they are debriefing for their documentary, only to be confronted with a surprise intervention and offered a ninety-day, all-expenses-paid treatment program at a rehabilitation facility, the catch being that they must leave immediately. Although most subjects initially reject the offer of treatment, almost every person participating in the series eventually accepts the help. While some fail to complete treatment and a handful refuse it entirely, the majority of the program's subjects have been successful in their recovery.

Critics feel that the show often fuels the addicts' problems in order to heighten the drama of seeing them at their lowest point, but the program has raised overall awareness of these various addictions and treatment programs. Critics have also pointed out that such filmed interventions take advantage of individuals in compromised circumstances by offering free treatment in exchange for making their intimate problems public entertainment, which some consider unethical or coercive given that many addicts are not well equipped to give consent. *Intervention* does follow-ups on its subjects and strives to ensure that those who went through treatment remain sober. As of 2012, the show's official website boasts having conducted more than 211 interventions in eleven seasons, with 161 of its participants remaining sober. Since first airing in March 2005, *Intervention* has won five PRISM awards (bestowed in honor of accurately portraying social problems) and an Emmy Award in 2009 for Outstanding Reality Series.

Intervention paved the way for later television shows dealing with addiction such as Dr. Drew Pinsky's *Celebrity Rehab* (2008–) and *Sober House* (2009–2010). There have also been several parodies of the show by the Funny or Die Network, including actress Kristin Chenoweth staging a Broadway-style musical intervention. Another comedic spin-off depicts Fred Armisen of *Saturday Night Live* fame undergoing an *Intervention* intervention for watching too much of the show and neglecting his friends, life, and work. Other more minor tributes include characters undergoing interventions in the television shows *30 Rock* (2006–), *The Cleveland Show* (2009–), *South Park* (1997–), and *True Blood* (2008–).

Ron Horton

SEE ALSO: *Cable TV; Cocaine/Crack; Emmy Awards; Hollywood; Pinsky, Dr. Drew; Reality Television;* Saturday Night Live*;* South Park*; Television;* 30 Rock*; Twelve-Step Programs; War on Drugs.*

BIBLIOGRAPHY

Finnigan, Candy, and Sean Finnigan. *When Enough Is Enough: A Comprehensive Guide to Successful Intervention.* New York: Avery, 2008.

Seeley, Ken, and Myatt Murphy. *Face It and Fix It: A Three-Step Plan to Break Free from Denial and Discover the Life You Deserve.* New York: HarperOne, 2009.

VanVonderen, Jeffrey. *Good News for the Chemically Dependent and Those Who Love Them.* Minneapolis, MN: Bethany House, 2004.

Intolerance

D. W. Griffith, the director of the motion-picture epic *Intolerance* (1916), has been called the father of the American cinema. He was not only one of America's first great movie showmen but also the first director who saw moviemaking not merely as entertainment but as an important art form. Stung by charges of racism leveled at him by the critics for his first important feature, *Birth of a Nation* (1915), Griffith responded by making *Intolerance*, a film of a complexity and scale never seen before this time. It is a motion picture so grand in its conception that the original rough cut was, according to film historian David Cook in *A History of Narrative Film*, eight hours long. Although the movie was a critical success and is considered a masterpiece of the silent cinema, the rather preachy, melodramatic work was not a success at the box office.

Intolerance is, however, one of the first great American epic films. At nearly three and a half hours, it has a complex narrative that consists of four separate plots carefully interwoven to create a critique of cruelty and intolerance throughout history. Each segment takes place in a different era. Three historical stories—one set in ancient Babylon dealing with religious intolerance, another set in ancient Judea with the injustice of religious authorities in the time of Jesus Christ, and the last set in Paris in 1572 with the Massacre of St. Bartholomew's Day—are intermingled within the context of a modern-day story about a young couple caught up in labor unrest, widespread crime, and injustice. All the stories concentrate on the effects of historical events upon ordinary people.

Jeannette Sloniowski

SEE ALSO: *Griffith, D. W.; Hollywood; Silent Movies.*

BIBLIOGRAPHY

Cook, David A. *A History of Narrative Film.* New York: Norton, 1990.

Drew, William M. *D. W. Griffith's Intolerance: Its Genesis and Its Vision.* Jefferson, NC: McFarland, 1986.

Merritt, Russell. "D. W. Griffith's *Intolerance*: Reconstructing an Unattainable Text." *Film History* 4, no. 4 (1990): 337–375.

Simmon, Scott. *The Films of D. W. Griffith.* New York: Cambridge University Press, 1993.

Invisible Man

First published in 1952, Ralph Ellison's (1914–1994) novel *Invisible Man* revolutionized the literary and cultural world by examining the near-total lack of awareness of African Americans that pervaded mainstream, white society. One of the most widely read novels in American literature, *Invisible Man* has been translated into at least fifteen languages and has undergone numerous printings and special editions. It has been called the *Moby Dick* of the twentieth century—epic in scope, mythic in subject, and classic in structure. Part of its appeal lies in its quintessentially American theme: the quest for identity. What distinguishes Ellison's treatment of this theme is his bold creation of a central character who is black and unnamed, everyman and no one.

CULTURAL IMPLICATIONS OF *INVISIBLE MAN*

Foregrounding black identity while universalizing the central character on his quest for self-realization, the text expands the horizons of the American hero to include racial difference. By naming the invisible condition of his central character, Ellison broke barriers of silence and challenged traditional representations of African Americans, anticipating the movement for racial equality of the 1960s.

The book's central metaphor of the "invisible man," however, raises many questions, as Susan Parr and Pancho Savery point out. Particularly important is the question of how best to view the novel: should it "be valued primarily as a work with universal implications, as an example of the best that the American literary tradition offers, or as a representative of black American fiction?" To what extent do the social and political issues represented in the text contribute to its power? Given the nonfictional parameters of these social issues, should the novel be judged by aesthetic or sociological terms? That this novel has opened up these questions points to its importance in helping to shape a continually evolving American identity.

THE NOVEL

Built on a classical three-part structure consisting of a prologue, a twenty-five–chapter narrative, and an epilogue, the story is told in first person by an unnamed narrator and follows a circular rather than linear trajectory. The prologue begins with the narrator's announcement of the book's major interrelated themes of identity and race, innocence and experience, and rebirth and transformation. "I am an invisible man," he says, and the reader enters into the world of the narrator after the series of events about to be told have already taken place. Elaborating on his condition of invisibility, the narrator goes on to say, "That invisibility to which I refer occurs because of a peculiar disposition of the eyes of those with whom I come in contact. A matter of the construction of their inner eyes, those eyes with which they look through their physical eyes upon reality." Thus stated, Ellison's narrator brings to light unspoken tensions generated by divisions of race and class.

Much like a bildungsroman, the novel traces the development of the narrator as a young man who believes in the possibility that hard work will reward him with success, through a number of painfully illuminating episodes. Although he retains his innocence through disillusioning experiences, he does mature and undergoes rebirth. From his southern hometown of Greenwood, he travels to Harlem and passes through a series of initiations into adulthood. These adventures are often represented as surreal and dreamlike, narrated in an energetic and intense voice, often punctuated with humor as he makes observations about white culture and learns more about black history.

Among his most pivotal early experiences is the death of his grandfather, who first opens the young boy's eyes to the fact that appearances do not always represent reality. Following this are his humiliating experiences at a "battle royal" and public speaking contest, which results in an award that sends him to college. Ultimately expelled, he finds his way to Harlem, where he works in a paint factory that blows up, joins "The Brotherhood" of the Communist Party, and eventually returns to the basement where the reader first met him in the prologue. Pondering his condition, he is matter-of-fact: "So there you have all of it that's important," he says, "Or at least you almost have it. I'm an invisible man and it placed me in a hole—or showed me the hole I was in." Devoid of anger or self pity, the narrator remains philosophical, recognizing that "the world is just as concrete, ornery, vile and sublimely wonderful as before, only now I better understand my relation to it and it to me."

INFLUENCES

Invisible Man is thick with allusions to other texts, literary, philosophical, political, and psychological. Ellison draws from sources as diverse as classical European texts, major American works of literature, African American literature and folklore, Native American mythology, children's games, sermons, blues and gospel music, as well as his own experience. Music plays a major role illuminating some of the book's major themes. Ellison himself identified five novels as essential background reading to *Invisible Man*: Herman Melville's *Moby Dick*, André Malraux's *Man's Fate*, Stendhal's *The Red and the Black*, Mark Twain's *Huckleberry Finn*, and Fyodor Dostoyevsky's *The Brothers Karamazov*. In short, as Mark Busby writes, "Ellison uses everything he knows, not to prove anything to anybody but to exploit as fully as possible the artistic materials he is conjuring—to render Harlem with enough accuracy that Harlemites who read the book would recognize the place."

OTHER WORKS

Ellison was awarded the National Book Award for *Invisible Man* (his only novel) in 1953. His work was largely ignored after this. However, two collections of Ellison's essays, *Shadow and Arts* (1964) and *Going to the Territory* (1986), were republished posthumously in 1995 under one title, *The Collected Essays of Ralph Ellison*. In 2002 Avon Kirkland's documentary *Ralph Ellison: An American Journey* was shown on PBS (Public Broadcasting Service) as part of the *American Masters* series. A collection of Ellison's short stories, *Flying Home and Other Stories*, was published posthumously in 1996.

In an interview on PBS about his documentary, Kirkland noted that Ellison "was a true man of letters whose reflections on race, literature, American and African American identity were visionary, enlightening, and most of all, enduring. . . . He was among the first to point out that much that is distinctive and vibrant in American culture grew (and still grows) out of the African American experience." Anne Seidlitz wrote, "In writing *Invisible Man* in the late 1940s, Ralph Ellison brought . . . a new kind of black protagonist," one that was "far from the downtrodden, unsophisticated picture presented by writers, sociologists and politicians, both black and white" of the period. Ellison was, she said, "ahead of his time."

Lolly Ockerstrom

SEE ALSO: *Blues; Gospel Music; Harlem Renaissance; Public Television (PBS); Twain, Mark.*

BIBLIOGRAPHY

Busby, Mark. *Ralph Ellison.* Boston: Twayne, 1991.

Ellison, Ralph. *Invisible Man.* New York: Random House, 1952.

Ellison, Ralph. *The Collected Essays of Ralph Ellison.* New York: Modern Library, 1995.

Ellison, Ralph. *Flying Home and Other Stories.* New York: Random House, 1996.

Graham, Maryemma, and Amritjit Singh, eds. *Conversations with Ralph Ellison.* Jackson: University of Mississippi, 1995.

Kirkland, Avon. "Ralph Ellison Filmmaker Interview: Avon Kirkland." PBS. Accessed January 3, 2012. Available from http://www.pbs.org/wnet/americanmasters/episodes/ralph-ellison/filmmaker-interview-avon-kirkland/589/

O'Meally, Robert, ed. *New Essays on Invisible Man.* New York: Cambridge University Press, 1988.

Pierce, Susan Resneck, and Pancho Savery, eds. *Approaches to Teaching Ellison's "Invisible Man."* New York: Modern Language Association of America, 1989.

Reilly, John M., ed. *Invisible Man; A Collection of Critical Essays.* Englewood Cliffs, NJ: Prentice-Hall, 1970.

Seidlitz, Anne. "Ralph Ellison: An American Journey." PBS. Accessed January 3, 2012. Available from http://www.pbs.org/wnet/americanmasters/episodes/ralph-ellison/an-american-journey/587/

Sisco, Dolores V. "Invisible Man." In *Icons of African American Literature: The Black Literary World,* ed. Yolanda Williams Page. Santa Barbara, CA: Greenwood, 2011.

Sundquist, Eric J., ed. *Cultural Contexts for Ralph Ellison's "Invisible Man."* Boston: Bedford Books of St. Martin's Press, 1995.

iPad

Unveiled on January 27, 2010, the iPad is a line of tablet computers that revolutionized the personal computer and entertainment markets. The touch-screen devices are used to run apps, or programs, that can be purchased only through Apple Inc.'s App Store. When Apple began selling the iPad in April 2010, demand was much greater than predicted. Consumers purchased three million of the tablets within the first eighty days, and by the end of 2010 Apple had sold 14.8 million. The iPad dominated the nascent tablet computer market, capturing 75 percent of the market share in 2010.

As early as the 1960s, researchers had envisioned tablet computers. Computer scientist Alan Kay in 1968 described the idea for the DynaBook tablet, which was backed by the U.S. military to replace bulky maintenance and repair manuals. Kay's vision expanded to creating a tablet computer that children and adults could easily use for learning and creating. Like the iPad, the DynaBook would have the capability of acquiring data and information from remote sources, such as the Internet.

But consumer versions of the DynaBook would not be available until Apple released its Newton MessagePad, which required the use of a stylus, in 1993. The pad had limited functionality, and Apple discontinued the product in 1998. In 2003 Microsoft's Windows XP Tablet PC Edition operating system entered the marketplace on machines made by Hewlett-Packard, Toshiba, and other hardware manufacturers. Although tablets running Windows software continue to be sold, they have not gained wide popularity. Some critics believed that the Windows operating system was not designed for tablet computers, since of the system's functions were not easily performed without a keyboard and mouse.

In a *New York Times* review of the iPad, tech writer David Pogue called the device "basically a gigantic iPod Touch"—a smaller multimedia device that Apple had unveiled in 2007. But, Pogue wrote, "The simple act of making the multitouch screen bigger changes the whole experience." Board games such as Scrabble, which had been adapted for the iPod Touch, became much easier to play on the iPad. Electronic books, magazines, and newspapers could be viewed at nearly full size. And digital video subscription services, such as Hulu and Netflix, offered apps for streaming television shows and movies in high definition.

Advancements such as these led analysts to predict that the iPad and other tablets would eventually replace laptop computers. The first-edition iPad came in models with 16, 32, or 64 gigabytes of memory. Apple also offered two options for network connectivity—one that allowed Internet access via Wi-Fi only and another that offered 3G connectivity through services such as AT&T and Verizon. (The latter added about $130 to the cost of each model.)

In less than three years, the iPad had a remarkable impact on Apple as a company, catapulting it from the fifty-fourth largest in the world at the end of 2008 to the second largest at the end of 2011. Laptop sales fell dramatically after tablets like the iPad came on the market, and as its users become increasingly more mobile many critics believe the laptop will suffer the same fate as the desktop computer. Some schools have adopted the technology in their classrooms, and many publishers have adapted their media, including television shows, websites, films, and books, to fit the dimensions of the iPad's screen. Like Band-Aids and Kleenex, iPads have become so ubiquitous that many Americans use the brand name iPad to refer to any tablet computer.

Jeff Merron

SEE ALSO: *Apple Computer; Computer Games; High Definition TV; Hulu; The Internet; iPod / iTunes; Laptops; Netflix.*

BIBLIOGRAPHY

Arthur, Charles, and Killian Fox. "How the iPad Revolution Has Transformed Working Lives." *Guardian* (London), March 26, 2011, 18.

Kay, Alan. "A Personal Computer for Children of All Ages." In *Proceedings of the ACM Annual Conference, Vol. 1.* New York: Association for Computing Machinery, 1972.

Lyons, Daniel. "Think Really Different." *Newsweek,* April 5, 2010, 47–51.

Sherman, Erik. "Apple's iPad Re-ignites the Great Technology Culture War." *CBS News,* April 5, 2010.

iPod / iTunes

Since Apple Inc. released the iTunes software in January 2001, coupled with the introduction of the iPod in November 2001, the company has altered the digital media landscape. Launched as part of a strategy to make Apple computers, especially the popular iMac, the center of a digital hub, iTunes and the iPod were several avenues CEO Steve Jobs explored to help consumers easily manage and manipulate photos, videos, audio, and other forms of media. During the 1990s audio files encoded in MP3 format had become ubiquitous on the Internet. But Apple saw two major problems: no company had yet produced good software for managing music, and digital music players had failed to gain much of a market because, as Apple vice president Greg Joswiak put it, "The products stank."

In 2003 Apple launched the iTunes store, which allowed consumers to purchase and download single songs, and sold thirty million songs, helping revive the struggling music industry. Less than three years after Apple debuted its digital music player, however, *Newsweek*'s Steven Levy in 2004 dubbed America "iPod Nation" and the iPod a "life-changing cultural icon." By the end of 2011 the company had sold more than 300 million iPods, and more than sixteen billion songs had been purchased through iTunes, making it the largest music retailer in the United States.

EVOLUTION OF THE IPOD

The first iPod, with a 1.5-inch black-and-white screen and mechanical scroll wheel for navigating playlists and songs, had a small hard drive with a capacity of 5 gigabytes. The palm-sized player had enough space, Jobs said, to put 1,000 songs in the user's pocket. The device retailed for $399, and by mid-2004 the company had sold more than three million. In 2004 Apple also released a click-wheel model of the iPod, which was lower in price and could be purchased with either 20 or 40 gigabytes of storage space. Only months earlier, Apple had introduced the iPod Mini, a smaller, lighter version that had less storage space but appealed to the many users who carried music players while exercising.

As demand remained strong, Apple added other models to the iPod line. The 2005 iPod Shuffle was smaller than a pack of gum but had no screen. The 2005 iPod Nano, the next generation of the iPod Mini, was little more than a quarter-inch thick. The iPod Touch, introduced in 2007, allowed users to run apps, and its 3.5-inch color screen could display videos, e-mail, word processing apps, and games. Because Apple offered thousands of games and applications for free or for ninety-nine cents, the iPod Touch quickly dominated the handheld gaming market, usurping stalwarts such as the Nintendo DS and Sony's PSP. Staying true to its roots, Apple in 2007 introduced the iPod Classic, which closely resembled the original model with its small screen and click wheel, in capacities of 80 or 160 gigabytes, much more than the other models.

As of November 2011, Apple had sold more than 300 million iPods, dominating the digital music player industry with a market share of 78 percent in the United States. Overall sales of digital music players declined late in the first decade of the 2000s and into the 2010s, but the iPod continued to fare better than its competitors. Still, iPod sales dropped for eleven consecutive quarters as industry analysts speculated that competition from two other Apple products, the iPhone and the iPad, was responsible for changing demand. Both the iPhone and iPad can run the same apps as the iPod Touch and can be used to play and manage music collections.

iTUNES AND THE MUSIC INDUSTRY

The software Apple designed for managing the iPod, as well as the iPhone and iPad, was dubbed iTunes to fit with the naming scheme the company had for its other media management software: iMovie, iDVD, and iPhoto. The iTunes software was built off SoundJam MP, a program Apple purchased and rebuilt while retaining key features such as custom playlists and retrieval of song, album, and artist data from the Internet. Apple released the first version of the software on January 9, 2001, for users to freely download. The version, which was for Macintosh systems only, allowed users to import and encode compact discs and create music CDs.

Within months of its debut, one million copies of iTunes had been downloaded. The second version, released in October 2001, added functionality for loading songs, playlists, and albums onto an iPod. The third version could run on Microsoft Windows, allowing non-Mac users, who comprised the vast majority of PC owners, to purchase and use iPods in much the same fashion as Mac users.

On April 28, 2003, when Apple released iTunes 4, the company also unveiled the iTunes music store, which Michael Simon for *Mac|Life* in 2009 called "a first-of-its kind shopping experience that blew the roof off the industry." Hundreds of thousands of high-quality digital tracks from labels such as BMG, EMI, and Sony became available for legal and convenient purchase. Although a few other websites had made nascent attempts to license and sell music online, the iTunes store far exceeded their scope. Within five months the store had sold ten million tracks.

Later Apple added a podcast feature, which allowed users to produce and distribute a series of free audio or video programs via the iTunes store. Many mainstream media sources created podcasts composed of complete or partial versions of broadcast programs. The new medium also became popular among amateur, small-scale producers. Often producers added new episodes on a daily or weekly basis. Users had the option to subscribe to podcasts in order to automatically download episodes as they became available.

Offerings in the iTunes store continued to grow, with books, apps, TV shows, and movies available for use on the iPod Touch, iPhone, and Apple TV (introduced in 2007). The debut of iTunes U allowed universities and other institutions to upload audio or video lectures. Apple's media library and user-friendly devices have helped it to not only dominate the digital media market but also become a technological juggernaut. Through the iPod, and later iTunes, Apple altered the way consumers listen to and purchase music. The introduction of additional forms of media has helped Apple extend its influence far beyond that of its competitors.

Jeff Merron

SEE ALSO: *Apple Computer; Compact Discs; Computer Games; E-mail; The Internet; iPad; MP3; Online Shopping; Video Games; Videos.*

BIBLIOGRAPHY

Apple Inc. "iPod + iTunes Timeline." Apple Inc. Accessed May 2012. Available from http://www.apple.com/pr/products/ipodhistory/

Levy, Steven. "iPod Nation." *Newsweek*, July 26, 2004, 42.

Levy, Steven. *The Perfect Thing: How the iPod Shuffles Commerce, Culture, and Coolness.* New York: Simon & Schuster, 2006.

Rojek, Chris. *Pop Music, Pop Culture.* Cambridge, UK: Polity Press, 2011.

Simon, Michael. "The Complete iTunes History—SoundJam MP to iTunes 9." *Mac|Life*, September 11, 2009.

Wittkower, D. E., ed. *iPod and Philosophy: iCon of an ePoch.* Peru, IL: Open Court, 2008.

Iran Contra

No other scandal in American history has had such far-reaching complexities with so few consequences as the Iran-Contra scandal that plagued Presidents Ronald Reagan and George H. W. Bush in the 1980s. Comparisons with other well-known scandals illustrate the political consequences of most presidential scandals.

PAST PRESIDENTIAL CORRUPTION

During the presidency of Ulysses S. Grant, corruption was the order of the day, and cabinet members and federal judges were forced to resign to avoid impeachment. Grant prudently decided not to seek a third term. Warren G. Harding, considered by most scholars to be the worst president of all time, was spared removal from office only by his death. His wife then burned his papers to spare what was left of his reputation. Richard Nixon was not so fortunate. Once he was ordered to release tapes of conversations conducted in the Oval Office that revealed a cover-up of the Watergate hotel break-in, Nixon reluctantly resigned. Bill Clinton was dogged by opponents as soon as he became the front-runner in the 1992 presidential campaign. While he survived the Whitewater scandal in 1998, he became only the second president to be impeached—after he was accused of lying under oath about having an affair with a White House intern. Both Reagan and Bush, however, survived their presidencies with few scars. Unlike the Watergate defendants, the Iran-Contra defendants escaped prison terms.

DETAILS OF THE SCANDAL

On the surface Iran Contra was an arms-for-hostage exchange. Upon closer examination, it was much more. President Reagan and his advisers chose to sell arms to Iran, a designated enemy of the United States, in order to finance the activities of the Nicaraguan anticommunist insurgents known as the Contras. While noted scholar Theodore Draper writes in his extensive study of the Iran Contra affair, *A Very Thin Line: The Iran-Contra Affairs*, that selling arms to Iran and funding the Contras were two separate operations, they were inherently connected because the Reagan administration could not have financed the Contras without the proceeds from the arms sale.

In November 1986 a Beirut magazine broke the story that the United States had sold arms to Iran despite an embargo against such activities that had been in effect since 1979. The American public later learned that after arms were shipped to Iran through Israel, American hostages were released. While still reeling from the repercussions of this story, the Reagan administration was forced to admit that it had used from \$10 million to \$30 million of the money from the arms sale to finance the Contras' battle against the Sandinista-led government in Nicaragua, even though both groups had been charged with human rights violations. Reagan later wrote in his memoirs that he believed that dealing with the moderates in Iran would

Iran Contra Affair. *Lt. Col. Oliver North, right, and his lawyer Brendan Sullivan Jr. appear before the House Foreign Affairs Committee where North invoked the Fifth Amendment constitutional right to refuse to answer questions on the grounds of possible self-incrimination.* © BETTMANN/CORBIS.

open up channels of communication. Critics argued that the action took place simply because it was a pet project of the president's, and Reagan was forced to look elsewhere for funds when Congress refused to appropriate the money.

THE REPERCUSSIONS

Other than Reagan and Vice President Bush, the chief players in the Iran-Contra scandal were Bud McFarlane and John Poindexter, both national security advisers, and Oliver North, a midlevel member of the National Security Council (NSC) staff. A subsequent congressional investigation determined that the three were the ringleaders of a "cabal of zealots" who were headquartered in the NSC. The common consensus was that the three believed their superiors, who told them that selling arms to Iran was a way of easing existing hostilities.

While North and Poindexter took advantage of the Fifth Amendment's protection from self-incrimination during the investigations, McFarlane talked to members of Congress. He later attempted suicide when faced with the repercussions of the scandal. North, who was considered by many to be the fall guy for the entire affair, became a cult hero and avoided prison when a federal judge handed down his judgment: three suspended sentences, two years on probation, $150,000 in fines, and 1,200 hours of community service. In 1992 Poindexter was found guilty on five separate charges, and Caspar Weinberger was indicted on charges of perjury and making false statements during the inquiry. Nevertheless, in 1992 outgoing President Bush quietly pardoned McFarlane and the others who had been found guilty on Iran-Contra charges. Both the Tower Commission appointed by Reagan and a subsequent investigation by Special Prosecutor Lawrence Walsh revealed serious misconduct throughout Iran-Contra activities.

In his autobiography, North admitted that Reagan knew everything that was going on from the beginning. Whether or not Nixon had known what was going on from the beginning was instrumental in his eventual resignation. Robert Timberg argued that there were inherent similarities with the Watergate scandal: abuses of authority, a bunker mentality, presidential cover-ups, Oval Office tapes, televised hearings, and world-class irresponsibility permeated both scandals. Nixon, he wrote, was smart but paranoid. Reagan was not nearly so smart, yet he was charming and made a slicker getaway. Whatever his reasons for engaging in the activities of the Iranian hostage deal and funding the Nicaraguan Contras, Reagan admittedly did both. Later investigations revealed that Bush had been privy to the activities from the beginning. Both finished their terms while retaining the respect of the American people. It will be left to future scholars with the benefit of hindsight to understand why.

Elizabeth Rholetter Purdy

SEE ALSO: *Reagan, Ronald; Watergate.*

BIBLIOGRAPHY

Draper, Theodore. *A Very Thin Line: The Iran-Contra Affairs.* New York: Hill and Way, 1991.

North, Oliver L., and William Novak. *Under Fire: An American Story.* New York: HarperCollins, 1991.

Reagan, Ronald. *An American Life.* New York: Simon & Schuster, 1990.

Timberg, Robert. *The Nightingale's Song.* New York: Simon & Schuster, 1995.

Tyler, Patrick. *A World of Trouble: The White House and the Middle East—from the Cold War to the War on Terror.* New York: Farrar, Straus & Giroux, 2009.

Wilentz, Sean. *The Age of Reagan: A History.* New York: Harper, 2008.

Iron Maiden

Perhaps the quintessential heavy metal band, Iron Maiden has sold more than eighty-five million records worldwide, remaining the object of a faithful international fan base since the early 1980s. Numerous hit singles and platinum albums have also attested to the consistency of the listening habits of metal fans long after the much-maligned genre had ceased to make headlines in the music press. Ditching the more bluesy grooves of hard rock bands from the 1970s, such as Deep Purple and UFO, Iron Maiden came up with a faster, riff-laden yet melodious song structure that set the standards for what most listeners came to understand to be heavy metal. A marked preference for lyrics grounded on horror, mythology, wars, and history became another of the genre's key reference points, not to mention gargantuan onstage production values and globetrotting concert tours.

EARLY FAME

Iron Maiden was formed in London in 1976 by bassist Steve Harris. At the height of the so-called punk revolution spearheaded by the Sex Pistols and the Clash, Harris persisted with heavy metal through constant lineup changes and difficulties in finding performing venues. By the time both punk and disco were on the decline, however, he had managed to recruit more reliable group members, including singer Paul Di'Anno and lead guitarist Dave Murray. After playing the club circuit, the band began to generate some minor attention in the press and produced an independent three-song record in 1979. The single pressing of 5,000 copies flew off the shelves, and record label EMI offered them an album deal.

The early 1980s marked what the British press dubbed the "New Wave of British Heavy Metal": Iron Maiden, Def Leppard, Saxon, and other bands began to storm onto the domestic charts and soon enjoyed international success. Heralded by the hit single "Running Free," the band's debut album, *Iron Maiden* (1980), reached an impressive fourth place on the UK charts. This allowed the band to enlist the services of producer Martin Birch for their second album, *Killers* (1981). Birch had been at the helm of some classic Deep Purple albums in the 1970s and proved himself capable of bringing out the best in Iron Maiden. Elaborate introductions and solos and an overall "cleanness" of sound became trademarks that countless musicians soon attempted to emulate. Harris always remained at the creative center, writing most of the songs, but the lineup now also featured a second lead guitarist, Murray's longtime friend Adrian Smith, who would write and cowrite some of the band's greatest hits, including "2 Minutes to Midnight" (1984) and "Wasted Years" (1986).

Early on, Maiden began to be identified with its fictitious mascot, "Eddie," a mummified zombie designed by artist Derek Riggs and featured on all their album covers. The band began playing larger venues in Europe and the United States, touring in support of KISS and Judas Priest, and discovered the fanatical enthusiasm of their Japanese fans after a number of headline appearances in Japan. Surprisingly, at the end of the tour, Di'Anno departed, citing stress and exhaustion.

GLOBAL SUCCESS

Former Samson singer Bruce Dickinson joined the band in 1981. The energetic and charismatic front man became an immediate favorite with fans and indelibly embodied Iron Maiden's mainstream success in the 1980s. An accomplished songwriter with powerful, semioperatic vocal skills and manic stage antics, Dickinson is also one of rock's most imitated singers. *The Number of the Beast* topped the UK charts in 1982, and the album's satanic-themed cover and title song generated considerable outrage among conservative groups in numerous countries. Iron Maiden soon became a household name, alongside those of Black Sabbath, Ozzy Osbourne, and AC/DC whenever the topic of the supposedly harmful influence of heavy metal on young listeners became an issue of heated debates.

The album *Powerslave* (1984) probably saw the band at its peak in the studio, with exemplary instrumental passages that culminated in the thirteen-minute epic "The Rime of the Ancient Mariner," based on the Samuel Taylor Coleridge poem. *Powerslave* led to a mammoth-scale, yearlong world tour—ambitiously labeled the "World Slavery Tour"—with sell-out crowds on four continents. A tradition of sorts was also inaugurated in 1984 when Maiden played a pioneering tour of Poland at a time when, amid renewed international fear of nuclear war, virtually no other Western European or American artists ventured beyond the Iron Curtain. Over the years, the band would constantly make an effort to "brave" new territories previously ignored by other bands, such as Moscow, Istanbul, and even war-torn Sarajevo. Another high point of their 1984–1985 tour was an appearance at the megalomaniac "Rock in Rio" festival in Brazil, in front of an estimated crowd of 200,000 people.

MAIDEN WITHOUT DICKINSON

After five consecutive platinum albums in the United States, Iron Maiden saw local musical tastes shift toward the more commercial sounds and glamorized looks of groups such as Bon Jovi and Cinderella. The band's popularity dwindled in North America during the late 1980s and early 1990s, but its international following remained strong, as evidenced by two headline appearances at the annual Monsters of Rock festival in Donington, England (1989 and 1992) in front of 100,000-plus crowds. In 1993 Dickinson announced his departure after eleven successful years, leaving for a more low-profile solo career. The search for his replacement began, with the band sponsoring an international contest that resulted in thousands of tapes being sent in by would-be rock stars. Blaze Bayley, formerly of the group Wolfsbane, was ultimately announced as the new singer. With the retirement of Martin Birch, bassist Harris himself was now at the helm producing the band's records and videos.

Apart from Birch, another backstage personality who played a key role in the lasting success of Iron Maiden was manager Rod Smallwood, the man who, from the beginning, ran the band's financial and commercial arm, Sanctuary Music. In the late 1990s Sanctuary was also managing a number of other bands—whose records were sometimes produced by Harris—and even entered London's stock market in an ambitious (and successful) move.

DICKINSON RETURNS

Bayley left the band in 1999, at which time Maiden reconnected with Dickinson and guitarist Adrian Smith. They embarked on a reunion tour that featured a three-guitar lineup. The tour coincided with the release of a greatest hits album, *Ed Hunter*, which included a state-of-the-art video game featuring the band's mascot, Eddie. Returning to the studio, they enlisted Kevin Shirley as their producer to record the 2000 release *Brave New World*, and they took off on a world tour that included nearly 100 dates, ending at Brazil's Rock in Rio festival.

In 2003 Maiden recorded their thirteenth studio album *Dance of Death*. The album was heralded by critics as a return to their earlier sound. Riding their success, the band went on a retrospective tour in 2004 and released a DVD titled *The Early Days*. During their 2005 tour, the band was inducted into the Hollywood RockWalk on Sunset Boulevard and followed up with 2006's critically and commercially successful *A Matter of Life and Death*, which climbed to the Billboard Top 10.

Maiden achieved more than merely revitalizing their career. Akin to their mascot Eddie, Iron Maiden is a ubiquitous presence in the worlds of heavy metal and rock and roll, influencing countless bands—from Slayer and Anthrax to Weezer and Lady Gaga. Maiden released their most commercially successful record, *The Final Frontier*, in 2010, and, as of 2011, they had played more than 2,000 live shows.

Alex Medeiros

SEE ALSO: *AC/DC; Black Sabbath; Bon Jovi; Heavy Metal; Judas Priest; KISS; Lady Gaga; Osbourne, Ozzy; Punk; Rock and Roll; The Sex Pistols.*

BIBLIOGRAPHY

Arnett, Jeffrey Jensen. *Metalheads: Heavy Metal Music and Adolescent Alienation.* Boulder, CO: Westview Press, 1996.

Harris, Steve, and Rod Smallwood, eds. *Visions of the Beast: A Pictorial History of Iron Maiden—and Eddie 1979–1997.* London: Omnibus Press, 1999.

Stenning, Paul. *Iron Maiden: 30 Years of the Beast: The Complete Unauthorised Biography.* Surrey, UK: Chrome Dreams, 2006.

Wall, Mick. *Iron Maiden: Run to the Hills: The Official Biography.* London: Santuary, 1998.

Walser, Robert. *Running with the Devil: Power, Gender, and Madness in Heavy Metal Music.* Hanover, NH: University Press of New England, 1993.

Weinstein, Deena. *Heavy Metal: A Cultural Sociology.* New York: Lexington Books, 1991.

Ironman Triathlon

The Ironman Triathlon, arguably the world's toughest endurance competition, has come a long way from humble origins. In 1977 a group of recreational athletes and naval officers in an Oahu bar got into a dispute over who was the better athlete—the runner, the swimmer, or the cyclist. Trying to resolve the argument, Naval Commander John Collins proposed a one-day race combining the courses for the 2.4-mile Waikiki Roughwater Swim; the two-day, 112-mile Around Oahu Bike Race; and the 26.2-mile Honolulu Marathon. A year later fifteen bold

Ironman Triathlon. *Participants in the 1990 Ironman Triathlon take to the water at the start of the competition.* JOHN KELLY/GETTY IMAGES.

adventurers gathered on a Waikiki beach to attempt the first Ironman Triathlon, unaware they were to become a part of sports history. The competition grew quickly. By the 1980s the annual Hawaii Ironman had become an internationally televised professional competition and had helped inspire countless other multi-sport endurance events. Its popularity lives on: Competing in the Ironman remains the Holy Grail for hundreds of thousands of triathletes worldwide.

GAINING POPULARITY

Triathlons first gained recognition in 1979, when *Sports Illustrated* published an article on the second annual Hawaii Ironman. The next year a highlight package was aired on ABC's *Wide World of Sports*. Although the Ironman was presented as an obscure competition for only the most obsessed athletes, the telecast still helped launch hundreds of other multi-sport challenges.

In 1981 the Hawaii competition was moved from Waikiki to the Kailua-Kona on the Big Island to take advantage of the spectacular backdrop of open shores and lava fields. This photogenic locale made for good television, but it was the telecast of the dramatic finish of the 1982 Hawaii Ironman that truly placed triathlons in the public consciousness. Toward the end of the race, women's leader Julie Moss collapsed in severe glycogen debt. She refused to accept any medical attention and staggered on. She ultimately crumpled to the ground and literally finished the race crawling to the finish line, watching as Kathleen McCartney passed her for the victory. Viewers around the world watched in awe, wondering not only whether Moss would finish the race but whether she would survive. Interest in the race by would-be participants as well as TV viewers immediately soared.

The popularity of triathlons skyrocketed throughout the 1980s, resulting in the establishment of other major Ironman races around the world, a World Cup Circuit of shorter races, and thousands of multi-sport events for more recreational athletes. The multi-sport craze swept the world, inspiring other "extreme" adventure races in the 1990s, such as the Eco-Challenge and the Raid Gauloises, both multi-day, terrain-crossing challenges that combined sports such as trail running, cycling, mountaineering, paddling, and even skydiving. More recently, the Tough Mudder races, 10- or 12-mile extreme obstacle course events designed by British Special Forces, have soared in popularity.

THE COMPETITION HEATS UP

By the late 1980s triathlons had become the ultimate challenge for amateur athletes as well as professional competitions where full-time athletes competed for prize money and sponsorship. The World Triathlon Corporation was founded in 1990 to organize competitions and further the sport. The Hawaii Ironman race (later called the Ironman World Championship), with its *ho'omumuku* headwinds and searing temperatures on the black lava flats, continues to be the premier event. Just to enter, competitors must either qualify at a national competition or hope for one of the coveted lottery spots. The competition has also expanded to include athletes with physical challenges or handicaps, although these racers must meet qualifying times as well.

Throughout the 1980s and early 1990s, the competitive men's field was dominated by six-time winners Dave Scott and Mark Allen. In the dramatic 1989 Hawaii Ironman, Allen narrowly edged Scott after racing for more than eight hours. The competition increased throughout the 1990s, and the winning times dropped accordingly. Craig Alexander's record 8:03:56 time in 2011 is more than three hours faster than Gordon Haller's 1978 winning time. The improvement in the women's field is even more remarkable. In 1992, eight-time winner Paula Newby-Fraser finished in just under nine hours, an astonishing four hours faster than Lyn Lemair, the first female winner in 1979.

CONTINUING POPULARITY

In 1998 the Hawaii Ironman celebrated its twentieth anniversary. In just two decades it had evolved into the world's most recognized endurance race, with 1,500 competitors, including 140 professional triathletes, competing for pride and prize money. It also transformed the world of exercise, introducing the concept of cross-training and capturing the imagination of both recreational and professional athletes around the world. The competition received its ultimate compliment when a shorter version became an official medal sport for the 2000 Olympics in Sydney, Australia. The sport now even has its own magazine: In 2010 the World Triathlon Corporation launched *LAVA* magazine to keep participants and hopefuls informed of Ironman news and to provide tips for gear and training.

As of 2012 there were twenty-eight Ironman competitions worldwide through which racers could qualify for the Hawaiian championship. As the competition grew, being a triathlete came to require more than a large lung capacity and a large threshold for pain; it required a large wallet. A week in Hawaii plus all the equipment—including titanium bicycles, wetsuits, shoes, accessories like heart-rate monitors, and enough food to replace the 5,000 calories a triathlete might burn in a day of training—could cost thousands of dollars. The Ironman slowly became a sport for the rich, a status symbol for business executives and athletes in other disciplines.

What started as simply a bar bet has become a worldwide phenomenon and an internationally recognized moniker. Once a 50-person scramble, the Ironman had to cap competitors at 1,800 in the 2010s. As tens of thousands compete in qualifying races around the world or enter the highly selective lottery for a chance to compete on the famed Hawaiian course, the popularity of Ironman continues to grow. Most races limit registrants to 2,000, and many sell out in only a few days. Triathlon competitions were even introduced at the high school level in 2011. New sports enthusiasts discover triathlons each day, and for such individuals, the Hawaiian Ironman triathlon remains the sport's culminating event and greatest achievement. In spite of its arduous nature, this ultimate challenge for the athlete holds an enduring allure for participant and spectator alike.

Simon Donner

SEE ALSO: *Extreme Sports; Jogging;* Sports Illustrated.

BIBLIOGRAPHY

Cook, Jeff S. *The Triathletes.* New York: St. Martin's Press, 1992.

Edwards, Sally. *Triathlon: A Triple Fitness Sport.* Chicago: Contemporary Books, 1983.

Levin, Dan. "Gall Divided into Three Parts." *Sports Illustrated,* October 10, 1983, 86–100.

McCormack, Chris, and Tim Vandehey. *I'm Here to Win: A World Champion's Advice for Peak Performance.* New York: Center Street, 2011.

Moore, Kenny. "Big Splash in Hawaii." *Sports Illustrated,* October 23, 1989, 62–73.

Scott, Dave. *Dave Scott's Triathlon Training Guide.* New York: Simon & Schuster, 1986.

Irving, John *(1942–)*

The novels of John Irving have been perennial best sellers ever since *The World According to Garp* won international acclaim in 1978. Irving's first novel, *Setting Free the Bears* (1968), established many of the fictional characteristics that would earn him critical and popular favor in works such as *The Hotel New Hampshire* (1981), *The Cider House Rules* (1985), *A Prayer for Owen Meany* (1989), *A Son of the Circus* (1994), *A Widow for One Year* (1998), *The Fourth Hand* (2001), *Until I Find You* (2005), *Last Night in Twisted River* (2009), and *In One Person* (2012). He has also published two memoirs, *Imaginary Girlfriend* (1995) and *My Movie Business* (1999), as well as a children's book, *A Sound Like Something Trying Not to Make a Sound* (2004).

Believing that "exquisitely developed characters and heartbreaking stories were the obligations of any novel worth remembering," Irving is a comedic writer whose books are distinguished by engaging heroes and detailed plots. Thematically, many of his novels probe the issues of parenthood, children, relationships between men and women, and sexual entanglements. Critics voiced vexed feelings over 2009's *Twisted River.* Although the novel remained steeped in the author's traditional themes as it self-reflexively explored the profession of the writer, the thinly veiled autobiographical content and metafictional tropes detracted from the plot. Irving's novels have sold in the millions, with *The World According to Garp, The Hotel New Hampshire, The Cider House Rules,* and *A Widow for One Year* made into films. He won the Academy Award for Best Adapted Screenplay for *Cider House Rules* in 1999. In 2001 Irving was elected into the elite honor society the American Academy of Arts and Letters.

Paul Grainge

SEE ALSO: *Academy Awards; Best Sellers.*

BIBLIOGRAPHY

Freeland, Alison. "A Conversation with John Irving." *New England Review* 18, no. 2 (1997): 135–142.

Irving, John. *My Movie Business.* New York: Ballantine, 2000.

Irving, John. *The Imaginary Girlfriend.* New York: Ballantine, 2002.

Reilly, Edward C. *Understanding John Irving.* Columbia: University of South Carolina Press, 1991.

It Gets Better Project

SEE: *Savage, Dan.*

It Happened One Night

A spoiled and willful young heiress, cocooned from reality by bodyguards and her father's trillions, jumps ship off the Florida coast when her father wishes to have her recent unconsummated marriage to a gold-digging roué annulled. Her worried father hires detectives to comb the land for his runaway daughter, offers a hefty reward for news of her, and has headlines blazon her disappearance while she sets off to reach New York by cross-country bus—her first foray into the real world of ordinary people. She runs into difficulties and a broke, straight-talking journalist who has just been fired. He recognizes her, spots a scoop, and escorts her through a series of adventures to the obligatory climax of temporary misunderstandings and true love.

Such are the bones of "Night Bus," a short story by Samuel Hopkins Adams that, retitled *It Happened One Night*, became not only one of the most successful, enduring, and best-loved romantic comedies of all time but also arguably the most influential contribution to screwball comedy. Written for the screen by the accomplished Robert Riskin, the movie was directed by Frank Capra with a sure sense of its characters, its comedy, and its humanity and was played with irresistible charm and polish by Clark Gable and Claudette Colbert.

Screwball was a genre born of the troubled times of the Depression to provide a perfect escape from the humdrum into a celluloid world teeming with glamour, wealth, romance, and laughter. Curmudgeonly or eccentric but never dangerous, characters supplied a thread of reality. The films satirized the rich in an era of poverty but did so with affection, often creating a happy alliance between the idle rich and the ordinary working person. Heroines were spirited, independent-minded women, a liberating departure from the sweet-natured and compliant wives or girlfriends, hard-bitten molls, or fallen women who were the staple characters of pre-1930s cinema. The feel-good plot resolutions were always arrived at via comedy, often so screwy as to give the genre its name, but the best of them were constructed with infallible logic and sincere conviction.

PERFECT CHEMISTRY

It Happened One Night conformed gloriously to the rules and did so with seamless panache. Gable's middle-class journalist—virile, opportunistic, and commanding—gets more than he bargains for from Colbert's heiress, whom he addresses as "Brat" throughout but who turns out to have unexpected wit and intelligence. In a series of inspired sequences that have become justly famous anthology pieces, the pair constantly turn the tables on each other. The best known of these are the "walls of Jericho" and hitchhiking scenes. In the first, he turns the tables on her apprehensive suspicions by lending her his pajamas and stringing a blanket between two beds in a room they're forced to share (Gable's removal of his shirt to reveal a bare chest famously sent the sales of undershirts plummeting). In the second, she triumphs, seductively hitching her skirts to get them a ride after his self-proclaimed expertise with his thumb has failed to stop a succession of vehicles.

The chemistry between Gable and Colbert is potent, a battle of the sexes in which acid insults give way to warm wisecracking and then to a beguiling sweetness and vulnerability in both of them. Aside from the major set pieces, the film offers a cornucopia of treasurable lunacies—Alan Hale's singing crackpot who gives them a ride; Colbert's unsuitable suitor clad in top hat and tails piloting himself to their wedding in a gyroplane; and Gable and Colbert fooling detectives by faking a blue-collar marital row—to mention but three. Amid the comedy, Capra, always a devoted chronicler of the common man, introduces an episode on the bus when a group of passengers play and sing popular songs. Colbert's childlike glee and amazement as she listens to "That Daring Young Man on the Flying Trapeze" serves to highlight with some poignancy her previously cosseted isolation—a moment of truth in the fantasy.

HAPPY ACCIDENTS BRING SUCCESS

Arguably the first, and certainly the greatest, of the screwball comedies of the 1930s, the tale of *It Happened One Night*'s success is a tale of alchemy: all the right ingredients combined and perfectly controlled to create a concoction of pure magic. It is also, like so many Hollywood success stories, a tale of happy accidents. In 1934 little Columbia, run on a relative shoestring by the foul-mouthed autocratic Harry Cohn, was considered a Poverty Row studio and struggled to compete with giants such as Metro-Goldwyn-Mayer (MGM). One of its few assets was Capra, who, having fallen on hard times after his first early successes with silent comedy, accepted a contract with Columbia in the late 1920s, which later proved to have been the turning point in the fortunes of both studio and director.

Capra read "Night Bus" in *Cosmopolitan* magazine and persuaded an unenthusiastic Cohn to buy it for $5,000. Capra wanted MGM's Robert Montgomery for the role of journalist Peter Warne, but Louis B. Mayer refused to lend him out. He proved amenable, however, to the idea of lending Gable to Columbia, viewing a spell on Poverty Row as suitable punishment for his rising star who, in a rebellion against his tough-guy typecasting, had checked himself into a hospital on grounds of overwork.

After several actresses rejected the role of heiress Ellen Andrews, Columbia turned to Colbert. (Her debut film, *For the Love of Mike* [1927], directed by Capra, had been a failure.) By now desperate to fill the role, Columbia agreed to Colbert's punishing demands: double her contract salary at Paramount and a shooting schedule guaranteed not to exceed four weeks. The auguries were not of the best.

At the 1935 Academy Awards, *It Happened One Night* made a grand slam, winning Oscars for Best Picture, Director, Screenplay Adaptation, Actor, and Actress—an unprecedented feat not equaled until *One Flew over the Cuckoo's Nest* forty-one years later. Its success elevated Capra's status, made Colbert a star, brought Gable superstardom and his desired freedom of choice, and transformed Columbia into a major studio.

The film set the tone for a certain style of romantic comedy officially defined as "Capraesque" and, like all true works of art, defied time to give pleasure to successive generations of viewers.

Robyn Karney

SEE ALSO: *Academy Awards; Capra, Frank; Colbert, Claudette; Gable, Clark; The Great Depression; Mayer, Louis B.; Screwball Comedies; Studio System.*

BIBLIOGRAPHY

Capra, Frank, and Leland A. Poague. *Frank Capra: Interviews*. Jackson: University Press of Mississippi, 2004.

Carney, Raymond. *American Vision: The Films of Frank Capra.* Cambridge, UK: Cambridge University Press, 1986.

McBride, Joseph. *Frank Capra: The Catastrophe of Success.* New York: Simon & Schuster, 1992.

Pogue, Leland A. *The Cinema of Frank Capra: An Approach to Film Comedy.* South Brunswick, NJ: A. S. Barnes, 1973.

It's a Wonderful Life

Although a box-office failure in 1946, Frank Capra's *It's a Wonderful Life* today is a well-loved Christmas classic for many Americans. Combining sentimental nostalgia and tough realism to deliver a popular message of faith in God and faith in basic human decency, the film tells the story of everyman George Bailey (Jimmy Stewart) and his desire to escape what he considers the everyday boredom of his hometown, Bedford Falls. Despite his efforts, events conspire against him, forcing him to give up his dreams of travel and begrudgingly stay home to run the family business, the Building and Loan. In the meantime, without realizing it, George becomes a pillar of his community, helping to protect the people of Bedford Falls from Mr. Potter (Lionel Barrymore), a mean, frustrated millionaire. Finally, on Christmas Eve 1946, Potter threatens George with financial ruin. George considers suicide but is rescued by an elderly angel, Clarence Oddbody (Henry Travers). Clarence shows George how much poorer the world would be if he had never been born, teaching him that each life touches another and that no one is a failure as long as one has a friend. The film ends on an exhilarating note as grateful friends bring George all the cash they can scrape together and help him defeat Potter.

It's a Wonderful Life began life as "The Greatest Gift," a short story by Philip Van Doren Stern. Stern had sent it as a Christmas card to his friends, and the story was later published in *Good Housekeeping*. Charles Koerner, head of production at RKO, purchased the rights to "The Greatest Gift" and hired three writers—Dalton Trumbo, Marc Connelly, and Clifford Odets—to make it into a screenplay. They were, however, unable to produce a solid script. Odets's main contribution, it seemed, was to name one of George's children Zuzu. Knowing that Capra (just out of the army and trying to establish his own production company, Liberty Films) was looking for good material for his first postwar film, Koerner offered it to him. Delighted with the story, Capra bought the film rights and developed a script with writers Frances Goodrich and Albert Hackett (Jo Swerling and Dorothy Parker also contributed, although they received no screen credit).

The film Capra crafted from this final script is an artful mixture of nostalgia, light sentimentality, and film noir. Capra makes clear links between George's personal life and national events (for example, the influenza epidemic of 1918–1919, the Roaring Twenties, the Great Depression, and World War II) that would profoundly and wistfully resonate with his audience. Although many of these milestones were moments of great trial for the country, Capra sentimentalized them by depicting his small-town characters as facing these difficulties with courage, pluck, and warmth. For example, during the Depression, we see George and his new bride, Mary (Donna Reed), successfully

It's a Wonderful Life. *James Stewart and Donna Reed star as George and Mary Bailey in the 1946 film* It's a Wonderful Life, *which has become a Christmas classic.* RKO PICTURES/ARCHIVE PHOTOS/ GETTY IMAGES.

fend off Potter's attempted takeover of the Building and Loan. In a remarkable example of American virtue, the couple sacrifice their own honeymoon money so they can lend it to their worried customers. Later that night, in a warm and endearing scene, Mary arranges a simple, homespun honeymoon complete with a roaring fire, a homemade dinner, and local townspeople crooning "I Love You Truly" outside. By contrast, Capra depicts the world without George as a dark, cold, and pitiless place. Borrowing shooting techniques from the popular film noir genre, he used deep shadows and uncomfortably odd close-ups and camera angles to produce the paranoia, distrust, and heartlessness that reigns in a George-less Pottersville.

Considering the film's immense popularity today, it may be hard to believe that it was not a hit with the audiences or critics of 1946, who were not quite ready to accept a dark Christmas story. Furthermore, it was simply too naive in the wake of World War II. The film's heartwarming conclusion could not expunge the dark cruelties of Pottersville. Although the film was nominated for a Best Picture Academy Award (with Capra and Stewart also receiving nominations), it could not draw enough box office to cover its production costs. Liberty Films went under, and the rights to *It's a Wonderful Life* reverted to Capra's distributor, RKO. Capra went on to make other films, including *State of the Union* (1948) and *Pocketful of Miracles* (1961), but his career never recovered.

Eventually, RKO sold *It's a Wonderful Life* to television, where it began to develop a following each Christmas season. By the late 1970s the film was enormously popular among holiday audiences. With the advent of cable, it could be seen on various networks for practically twenty-four hours a day, generating thousands of dollars in advertising revenue. (Ironically, however, Capra received no royalties, having lost them to RKO with the collapse of Liberty. The situation was later rectified when grateful broadcasters paid him a large sum of money.)

Capra himself called *It's a Wonderful Life* his favorite of all his films. Most critics also have come to recognize the film as Capra's best and most typical work, although not always without reservations. The *New Yorker*, for example, grudgingly admitted that "in its own icky, bittersweet way, it's terribly effective."

Scott W. Hoffman

SEE ALSO: *Academy Awards; Capra, Frank; Christmas; Cult Films; Film Noir;* Good Housekeeping*; The Great Depression; Parker, Dorothy; Reed, Donna; Stewart, Jimmy; World War II.*

BIBLIOGRAPHY

Basinger, Jeanine; Leonard Maltin; and Frank Capra. *The "It's a Wonderful Life" Book*. London: Pavilion, 1986.

McBride, Joseph. *Frank Capra: The Catastrophe of Success*. New York: Simon & Schuster, 1992.

Schickel, Richard. *The Men Who Made the Movies*. New York: Atheneum, 1975.

Umphlett, Wiley Lee. *Mythmakers of the American Dream: The Nostalgic Vision in Popular Culture*. Lewisburg, PA: Bucknell University Press, 1983.

Willis, Donald C. *The Films of Frank Capra*. Metuchen, NJ: Scarecrow Press, 1974.

It's Garry Shandling's Show

It's Garry Shandling's Show was the beginning of comedian and sometime 1980s *Tonight Show* guest host Garry Shandling's ongoing exploration of lives led in front of the camera, while parodying the world of television. His magnum opus, the fruits of these years, is *The Larry Sanders Show* (1992–1998).

Shandling, with former *Saturday Night Live* writer Alan Zweibel, created *It's Garry Shandling's Show*, which was on Showtime from 1986 to 1988 and Fox from 1988 to 1990. The gimmick of the show was inspired by a device that hadn't often been used since the 1958 end of *Burns and Allen*'s run: breaking the fourth wall. Shandling played himself, a neurotic comedian, and regularly talked to the camera, making observations, updating the plot, or interjecting a joke. The difference was that everyone else in the cast knew they were on television too; sometimes other characters criticized Shandling for paying too much attention to the camera or to his appearance or complained about not being featured in an episode. And, of course, the live audience was in on it as well. If Shandling was leaving, he'd tell the audience they could use his living room while he was gone, and they would. He would also go into the audience to get reactions or "take a call from a viewer."

The sitcom took place in Shandling's Sherman Oaks condominium. The supporting cast included Garry's platonic friend Nancy (Molly Cheek); his mother, Ruth (Barbara Cason); his married friend Pete (Michael Tucci); Pete's wife, Jackie (Bernadette Birkett); their intellectual son, Grant (Scott Nemes); and nosy condo manager Leonard (Paul Wilson). In the 1989–1990 season, both Garry and Nancy acquired steady love interests: Nancy's was Ian (soap opera actor Ian Buchanan) and Garry's was Phoebe (Jessica Harper), whom he married before the show ended.

The format and premise allowed guest stars to drop by and play themselves, among them Tom Petty, Zsa Zsa Gabor, and the late Gilda Radner in one of her last television appearances. There was also a 1988 election special with *Soul Train*'s Don Cornelius providing political analysis. Garry's "wedding" was attended by Bert Convy, Connie Stevens, and Ned Beatty. Besides covering Shandling's trials and tribulations with girlfriends, his mom, and his friends, *It's Garry Shandling's Show* lovingly spoofed television conventions and sitcom "rules" with parodies of *Lassie* (1954–1974) and *The Fugitive* (1963–1967). Even the show's theme song winked at tradition: "This is the theme to Garry's show, the opening theme to Garry's show, Garry called me up and asked if I would write his theme song."

The idea for the show originated in a sketch on NBC's *Michael Nesmith in Television Parts* (1985) that featured Shandling narrating a date with Miss Maryland to the camera. The sitcom was pitched to the three networks, which all turned it down. Showtime, where Shandling had done two successful comedy specials, *Garry Shandling: Alone in Vegas* (1984) and *The Garry Shandling Show 25th Anniversary Special* (1986), picked it up. Though other shows (such as *Moonlighting*, 1985–1989, and *Saved by the Bell*, 1989–1993) came to break the fourth wall occasionally during the 1980s, the use of the device in *It's Garry Shandling's Show* was fresh and innovative, providing the creators with an effective outlet to skewer their own industry.

Karen Lurie

SEE ALSO: *Burns, George, and Gracie Allen;* The Fugitive*;* The Larry Sanders Show*; Lassie;* Moonlighting*; Radner, Gilda;* Saturday Night Live*; Sitcom; Standup Comedy; Television.*

BIBLIOGRAPHY

Brooks, Tim, and Earle Marsh. *The Complete Directory to Prime Time Network and Cable TV Shows 1946–Present,* 6th ed. New York: Ballantine Books, 1995.

Jarvis, Jeff. "It's Garry Shandling's Show." *People Weekly,* September 15, 1986.

McNeil, Alex. *Total Television.* New York: Penguin, 1996.

Newcomb, Horace. *Encyclopedia of Television, Volume 1.* New York: Fitzroy Dearborn, 2004.

Ives, Burl *(1909–1995)*

Perhaps the most versatile entertainer of the twentieth century, Burl Ives did it all. He sang; acted on stage, screen, and television; wrote songs and prose; compiled books of traditional music—which he often arranged—and taught music in a series of popular guitar manuals. Once described by Carl Sandburg as "the mightiest ballad singer of this or any other century," Ives was quintessentially American. A man of strong populist leanings (as evidenced by his 1948 autobiography *The Wayfaring Stranger*), Ives always saw himself as a grassroots folksinger. His musical legacy remains his most significant contribution, preserving for future generations an enormous wealth of material—a musical portrait of the America he had known.

Born to a farm family of modest means in Jasper County, Illinois, Ives was raised on music. His whole family sang. His maternal grandmother taught him the ballads of her Scottish-Irish-English forefathers. By the time he was four, Ives was performing in public as a child entertainer and evangelical singer. Pressured to pursue a more conventional career than minstrel, he entered Illinois State Teachers College in 1927 with a mind toward becoming a football coach, but he left a year shy of attaining a degree, preferring to live the life of a vagabond to the static life of a teacher. Recalling his college career, Ives said, "I never did take to studies."

Ives had several innate talents, which kept him afloat during his early professional years and would eventually prove his most distinctive features as an entertainer. He was a friendly man, of abundant natural charm, with an innate gift for storytelling. He was also a singer who labored for years to perfect his voice. And at a time when folk music was looked down upon as a musical form, Ives's faith in the ballads he had learned at his grandmother's knee—and while traversing the country—preserved him through the lean years prior to his meteoric rise to fame.

While wandering throughout forty-six of the forty-eight states, Ives supported himself by playing music in bars or doing odd jobs; he slept rough and hitchhiked from town to town. In 1931 he was living at the International House in Manhattan, a cheap hotel catering to foreign students, working in its cafeteria while he continued the formal musical training he had begun in Terre Haute, Indiana. An avid music student, Ives absorbed the classical canon, finding work singing in churches and in madrigal groups. But his ambitions were hampered by a sinus problem, which affected his voice, as well as by his lingering doubts about singing classical music: at heart he was still a folk balladeer. He credits one Ella Toedt, a well-known voice instructor of the day, with curing his sinus problem (he endured a year of falsetto exercises before he was rid of the blockage) and with encouraging his folk music. Soon Ives was singing ballads at charity events and parties, sharing his vast repertoire of folk songs with appreciative audiences that often included some of the leading lights of New York's leftist intelligentsia.

Burl Ives. *Burl Ives's talent as a singer and a musician paved the way for his stage, film, and television appearances.* MICHAEL OCHS ARCHIVES/GETTY IMAGES.

He was encouraged by his show business friends to try his hand at acting. Ives won a small part in an out-of-town production, then charmed his way into a nonsinging part in the Rodgers and Hart musical *The Boys from Syracuse* (1938). The duo then cast him in a traveling production of *I Married an Angel,* which Ives followed with a four-month engagement at the Village Vanguard. By 1940 he had his own radio show, *The Wayfaring Stranger,* on which he sang and told stories from his years of traveling. Suddenly folk songs were in vogue.

By 1945 Ives was starring in *Sing Out Sweet Land,* a musical revue based on the folk songs he had popularized on his radio broadcasts. The following year he made his film debut, playing a singing cowboy in *Smoky.* He went on to appear in numerous Broadway productions and in films, and he began a recording career that would eventually number more than 100 releases. His visibility was further enhanced by his appearance as Big Daddy in the 1958 film *Cat on a Hot Tin Roof,* a role he had already popularized on Broadway. That year he won an Oscar for his performance opposite Gregory Peck in *The Big Country.*

Throughout the 1960s, 1970s, and 1980s, Ives continued to appear in theater and film and in such television productions as the *Roots* miniseries (1977). He portrayed a mean-spirited racist in noted filmmaker Samuel Fuller's last film, *White Dog* (1982). He also kept abreast of the times, expanding his repertoire to include standards such as "Little Green Apples" and going so far as to cover Bob Dylan's "The Times They Are A-Changing," though his fling with the counterculture was brief.

By the time of his death in 1995, Ives was best remembered as a singer of children's songs and as a narrator of animated Christmas specials for television—the kindly, avuncular man with the hefty girth.

Michael J. Baers

SEE ALSO: *Academy Awards; Broadway; Christmas; Dylan, Bob; Minstrel Shows; The Musical; Peck, Gregory; Radio; Rodgers and Hart;* Roots*;* Rudolph the Red-Nosed Reindeer*; Sandburg, Carl; Television.*

BIBLIOGRAPHY

Dicaire, David. *The Early Years of Folk Music.* Jefferson, NC: McFarland, 2010.

Ives, Burl. *Wayfaring Stranger.* New York: Whittelsey House, 1948.

Ives, Burl. *Tales of America.* Cleveland, OH: World Publishing, 1954.

Ives, Burl. *A Wayfaring Stranger's Notebook.* Indianapolis, IN: Bobbs-Merrill, 1962.

Locher, Frances C., ed. *Contemporary Authors, Vol. 103.* Detroit, MI: Gale Research, 1982.

Ivy League

The term *Ivy League* describes eight East Coast universities—Brown, Cornell, Columbia, Dartmouth, Harvard, Princeton, the University of Pennsylvania, and Yale—which are acknowledged as among the most prestigious postsecondary schools in the United States. The moniker alludes to the schools' ivy-covered buildings and historic campuses, which predate most of the country's other collegiate institutions. Originally all-male institutions, Ivy League schools are now coed, with women slightly outnumbering men at seven among the eight universities. Racial diversity among Ivy League admissions has also increased manifold over the past half century, but a lack of socioeconomic diversity among students remains controversial. Because of highly selective admissions criteria, popular belief holds that an Ivy League degree represents a near guarantee of success in the professional world.

The term was coined in the late 1930s by Caswell Adams, a *New York Herald-Tribune* reporter who noticed that buildings on all eight campuses were covered in vines. Although the designation was limited to these eights schools, "planting the ivy" was a ceremony performed on many college campuses in the late nineteenth century. Adams's coinage did not connote the academic excellence it does today and was used primarily in reference to older northeastern schools with established intercollegiate athletics programs. Before the 1880s, when intercollegiate athletic teams began to develop, the institutions had little contact with each other. By the turn of the twentieth century, the eight universities dominated the sport of college football, which Walter Camp, a Yale student in the 1870s, had helped to standardize.

Applications to most Ivy League universities averaged between 20,000 and 40,000 a year in the early 2010s. With acceptance rates hovering around 10 percent, the Ivy League sets the standard for exclusivity. Many high school seniors and their parents heavily invest in applying to Ivy League schools—from SAT preparation classes to costly counselors—overlooking colleges that do not have elite names, which is perhaps one reason for the economic disparity in these university populations compared with other schools. Loren Pope, in *Looking beyond the Ivy League*, writes about myths of an Ivy League education: "An Ivy League school will absolutely guarantee the rich, full, and successful life." However, critics question whether this is a result of the quality of an Ivy League education or a result of the privilege already enjoyed by many students. In *The Cultivation of Ivy*, Joseph Thelin writes that the mystique of the Ivy League reflects "the process by which the collegiate ideal has been . . . associated with trade marks, and brand-name imagery." In the 2010s the value of an Ivy League diploma remained high, despite persistent criticism about inequalities perpetuated by a culture of elitism, nepotistic legacy policies, and a sense of social conditioning long associated with these institutions.

Even among Ivy League institutions, large differences in endowments have created an uneven playing field for students and faculty alike; the richest schools—Harvard, Yale, and Princeton—can provide the best research facilities, woo big-name professors, and spend more on student amenities. In 1990 Brown received $441 million a year from endowments, a fraction of Harvard's $4.683 billion. Although endowments for the Ivy League grew 261 percent between 1990 and 2000, the increase did not close the gap. In 2011 Brown recorded $2.5 billion in comparison to $32 billion for Harvard.

Daryna M. McKeand

SEE ALSO: *College Football.*

BIBLIOGRAPHY

Barreca, Regina. *Babes in Boyland: A Personal History of Co-Education in the Ivy Leagues.* Hanover, NH: University Press of New England, 2005.

Ehrenberg, Ronald G., and Christopher L. Smith. *What a Difference a Decade Makes: Growing Wealth Inequality among Ivy League Institutions.* New York: Andrew W. Mellon Foundation, 2001.

Goldstein, Richard. *Ivy League Autumns.* New York: St. Martin's Press, 1996.

Pope, Loren. *Looking beyond the Ivy League.* New York: Penguin, 1995.

Thelin, John. *The Cultivation of Ivy: A Saga of the College in America.* Cambridge, MA: Schenkman Publishing, 1976.

J. Walter Thompson

The J. Walter Thompson Company, known since 2005 as JWT, is an advertising agency that transformed the business of media in the United States. Founded in New York City as Carlton and Smith in 1864, the agency was originally a broker of advertising space in religious journals. In 1868 it hired James Walter Thompson, who purchased the agency from William James Carlton in 1877, renamed it after himself, and rapidly positioned it as the exclusive seller of advertising space in many leading U.S. magazines.

Until the late nineteenth century, most large magazines survived on subscription and newsstand revenue. To create a market for print advertisements, Thompson persuaded reluctant publishers to accept advertising in their pages. The publishers initially feared that advertisements would tarnish their publication's image. Thereafter, America's largest magazines relied on advertising as their largest source of revenue, increasing the importance of the composition of a publication's readership and its appeal to advertisers.

In 1908 Stanley Resor joined J. Walter Thompson Company and soon hired copywriter Helen Lansdowne. In 1916 he purchased the agency, and the next year he and Lansdowne married. Together they remade the agency and developed it from a mere broker of advertising space into a full-service shop that conceived and executed major national advertising campaigns.

Print advertising of the previous era emphasized brand identity, iconic images, and simple slogans. In the early twentieth century J. Walter Thompson pioneered a new strategy aimed at delivering a "hard-sell" print ad, known as the "reason-why" approach. These advertisements typically captured the reader's attention with a bold, capitalized statement accompanied by an artistic or arresting image. The ad copy methodically outlined each selling point of the product and ended with a free or reduced-price product offer.

Since women made most household purchasing decisions in the early twentieth century, Helen, as she once explained, "added the feminine point of view" to the company's advertising to ensure that it was "effective for women." Her wing of the offices was known as the Women's Copy Group. Among the most famous advertisements produced under Helen were campaigns for Lux soap, Maxwell House coffee, and Crisco shortening. Her "A skin you love to touch" ad for Woodbury's Facial Soap featured a man seductively caressing a woman's arm and kissing her hand. While the overt sexuality caused a number of *Ladies' Home Journal* magazine readers to cancel their subscriptions, the ad launched one of the most successful selling techniques of all time.

In 1912 Stanley commissioned the market research study, "Population and Its Distribution." The study detailed both the composition of the American population and the distribution of retail and wholesale stores across the cities and rural areas. In 1915 Stanley established a research department, inaugurating the massive efforts of corporate America to determine consumer desires. As part of this effort, Stanley hired Johns Hopkins University behavioral psychologist John B. Watson in 1920. Watson theorized that humans are capable of only three basic emotions—love, fear, and rage—and sought to tap these feelings with advertising. Watson's application of psychology to advertising was a precursor to later use of psychological and subliminal selling techniques.

RAPID EXPANSION

Watson's employment with the company coincided with the trend toward "whisper" advertising that sowed insecurity in the reader. One such J. Walter Thompson ad, for Odorono deodorant in 1919, read, in part, "It is a physiological fact that persons troubled with perspiration odor seldom can detect it themselves." The use of testimonials from stars, such as Joan Crawford's 1927 endorsement of Lux soap, was another of the agency's firsts.

As with magazine publishers, early radio operators initially resisted commercial advertising. But by 1933 J. Walter Thompson's clients sponsored nine weekly shows, including *The Kraft Music Hall* and the *Fleischmann Yeast Hour*. Products were promoted in short "spots" that lasted from fifteen seconds to a couple of minutes and were often live minidramas in their own right complete with original jingles. Television advertising adopted the same model in the 1940s and 1950s.

As a result of J. Walter Thompson's innovations, most media now depend upon advertising as their primary source of revenue. Advertising is so culturally ubiquitous and established that advertisements themselves are considered an art form worthy of serious critique. Numerous awards annually honor outstanding work.

Americans are bombarded with thousands of advertising messages each year, and most can recite slogans and jingles from their most, or least, favorite advertisements. The "Where's the beef?" television ad for Wendy's restaurants in the 1980s was embraced so eagerly by the public that former U.S. vice president Walter Mondale used it as a rejoinder in a presidential campaign debate. The machinations and untruths of U.S. president Richard M. Nixon's administration once led consumer advocate and political activist Ralph Nader to label it a "J. Walter Thompson production" and, in fact, five of Nixon's top aides were former employees of the agency. The creative pressure and client dependency that is the recognizable perpetual state of agencies was captured in television programs, such as *Bewitched* in the 1960s and *thirtysomething* in the 1980s.

In the 1950s J. Walter Thompson was one of the first agencies to aggressively expand internationally, eventually growing into a global corporation. In 1980 it became a subsidiary of JWT Group Inc., a Delaware, Maryland–based holding company that was in turn purchased by the British marketing firm WPP Group in 1987. Starting in 1985, the agency experienced a great deal of turnover, losing top executives to either resignation or dismissal. Over the next few years clients abandoned the agency as J. Walter Thompson failed to show a profit and lingered in legal battles. The company's troubles continued throughout the 1990s, and by 1998 it had lost accounts for Kodak, Dell, Citibank, and Sprint. Part of J. Walter Thompson's success had been its stability, but in the increasingly interactive advertisement age, it found itself unable to adapt.

RESURRECTING AND REBRANDING

In 1998 J. Walter Thompson hired Bob Jeffrey. A veritable outsider, Jeffrey was charged with resurrecting and rebranding the New York office. He resuscitated the ad agency and created a content and entertainment division, which quickly paid dividends. In 2000 the company targeted college students with its successful "Breakfast Is Back" campaign for Kellogg's Raisin Bran. Focusing on the possibilities of incorporating narrative elements with digital technology, the company enlisted its digital group in all of its ad campaigns. Online campaigns included De Beers "Design Your Own Engagement Ring" and a coordinated effort between the *Onion*, an online newspaper, and Schieffelin & Somerset, a liquor distributor, to create a multimedia Web store called Liquorfairy.com to promote Schieffelin & Somerset's J&B Scotch.

The J. Walter Thompson agency's influence on the multibillion-dollar advertising industry and the media it supports was profound. Informative, persuasive, seductive, and intrusive, advertising became omnipresent in the national media and the national consciousness. As the industry leader for decades, both creatively and financially, J. Walter Thompson defined the advertising agency to a public inundated with its product. By the early twenty-first century, it was one of the largest advertising agencies in the world, headquartered in New York. In 2005 it dropped the name J. Walter Thompson for JWT. It went on to design a branding model that helped companies such as Stride gum take on Wrigley gum. JWT also created the Bing search engine campaign for Microsoft and the "Because It Counts" campaign for Canon. In 2009 JWT was named *Adweek* magazine's Global Agency of the Year. Although the agency lost the majority of its Microsoft accounts in 2011, it continued to lead the way in innovative digital campaigns for companies such as Smirnoff, Bayer, and Macy's.

Steven Kotok

SEE ALSO: *Advertising;* Bewitched*; Consumerism; Crawford, Joan; Kodak; Macy's; Nader, Ralph; Radio; Television.*

BIBLIOGRAPHY

Berger, Warren. "J. Walter Thompson: Wired Case Studies in Radical Upgrade Attempts." *Wired*, April 2000.

Fox, Stephen R. *The Mirror Makers: A History of American Advertising and Its Creators.* New York: Morrow, 1997.

Meyers, William. *The Image Makers: Power and Persuasion on Madison Avenue.* New York: Times Books, 1984.

Prescott, Eileen. "How Don Johnston Lost JWT." *New York Times*, August 9, 1987.

Sivulka, Juliann. *Soap, Sex, and Cigarettes: A Cultural History of American Advertising.* Belmont, CA: Wadsworth Publishing, 1998.

Strasser, Susan. *Satisfaction Guaranteed: The Making of the American Mass Market.* New York: Pantheon Books, 1989.

Jack Armstrong

For the greater part of its radio life, *Jack Armstrong, the All-American Boy* was a fifteen-minute children's serial that aired daily. The show began in the summer of 1933 and didn't leave the air until the summer of 1951—though it was considerably modified by then. The sponsor for all those years was Wheaties, the Breakfast of Champions. The show originated in Chicago, long the center for soap operas and the adventure serials that filled the 5 to 6 p.m. children's hour on radio. The *Jack Armstrong* show was produced by an advertising agency headed by Frank Hummert, who with his wife, Anne, would later produce such long-lasting programs as *Ma Perkins, Just Plain Bill, Our Gal Sunday*, and *Mr. Keen, Tracer of Lost Persons.* Writer Robert Hardy Andrews, a prolific and supremely self-confident man, developed the idea and turned out the initial scripts; Jim Ameche was the first actor to portray the clean-cut and adventure-prone Jack.

INTRODUCING THE ALL-AMERICAN BOY

Jack, who attended high school in the midwestern town of Hudson, excelled as both an athlete and a student. He was clearly inspired by the dime novel hero Frank Merriwell. Every show opened with a vocal quintet singing the school fight song—"Wave the flag for Hudson High, boys, show them how we stand"—but Jack spent relatively little time behind a desk or even on the gym floor. Instead, accompanied by his teen friends Billy and Betty Fairfield, he traveled to the four corners of the world and got entangled in an endless series of intriguing adventures. During the early years of the program, Jack, Betty, and Billy journeyed to the Northwest to work with the Royal Canadian Mounted Police, found a lost tribe of Eskimos in the Arctic, outwitted cattle rustlers in Arizona, hunted for a lost city in the jungles of Brazil, and returned to Hudson to round up a gang of counterfeiters. A character named Captain Hughes served as a mentor and an adult companion on many of the adventures. Don Ameche, Jim's brother, was the first actor to play that role.

In the spring of 1936, Talbot Mundy, who'd written such successful adventure novels as *King of the Khyber Rifles* (1916), *Jimgrim* (1931), and *Tros of Samothrace* (1925), was having financial difficulties. He accepted the job of writing for *Jack Armstrong* and stayed with the show until his death in 1940. He took Jack and his companions to such locations as Egypt, Easter Island, India, Africa, and Tibet. Most of these spots had been favored settings for Mundy's novels and stories in the 1920s and 1930s.

According to Jim Harmon in *Radio Mystery and Adventure*, it was Mundy who introduced Billy and Betty's Uncle Jim to the show in the fall of 1936. Actor James Goss had a distinctive radio voice that fit "the commanding but warm father figure" he played. Uncle Jim traveled with the young trio on their adventures, many of which stretched across several months. Mundy was able to recycle not just settings but plots from his novels. In an early 1937 story, for instance, Jack and the gang end up in Africa hunting for the ivory treasure to be found in an elephants' graveyard. The plot, with considerable changes, was earlier used in Mundy's 1919 novel *The Ivory Trail*.

PLUGGING PREMIUMS

The program was a great promoter of premiums. Whenever a portable gadget was introduced into a continuity, listeners could be certain it would eventually be offered for sale. But first its utility and desirability—emphasized in many instances by the fact that the current villains would do almost anything to get hold of the object in question—were romanced for several weeks. Typically all kids had to do to get their copy of the gadget was to send a Wheaties box top and a dime. There were dozen of premiums from 1933 to 1948, including a Torpedo Flashlight, a Pedometer, an Explorer Telescope, a Secret Bombsight, a Dragon's Eye Ring, a Rocket Chute, an Egyptian Whistling Ring, and Tru-Flite model planes. The more popular items sold in the millions.

The only outside merchandising in the 1930s involved two Big Little Books issued by the Whitman Publishing Company. Both *Jack Armstrong and the Ivory Treasure* (1937), which once again used the elephants' graveyard story line, and *Jack Armstrong and the Mystery of the Iron Key* (1939) were based on Mundy scripts. These small, fat illustrated novels included pictures by the gifted Henry E. Vallely. His Jack was a handsome fellow in polo shirt, jodhpurs, and riding boots who looked to be in his early twenties.

EXPLORING OTHER MEDIA OPPORTUNITIES

The Jack Armstrong property didn't seriously branch out into other media again until after World War II. Several things happened in 1947: a movie serial was developed, along with a comic strip and a comic book. Columbia Pictures produced the fifteen-chapter serial, with John Hart (later to play the Lone Ranger on television for two seasons) as a somewhat older Jack. In the spring of that year, the Register and Tribune Syndicate introduced a *Jack Armstrong* newspaper strip, illustrated by Bob Schoenke. The strip was dropped in 1949. The *Parents' Magazine* outfit started a comic book late in 1947. Like their *True Comics*, it was rather dull and polite, never capturing the fun and gee-whiz spirit of the radio show. It, too, folded in 1949, after just thirteen issues.

Charles Flynn inherited the role of Jack in 1939 and, with the exception of a year out for military service, stayed with it to the end. In 1947, with the popularity of daily serials waning, Wheaties transformed *Jack Armstrong* into a half-hour program that aired two or three times a week. Then in 1950 the title was changed to *Armstrong of the SBI*. Jack had started working for the Scientific Bureau of Investigation (SBI) some years earlier and also had acquired a new mentor, Vic Hardy, a reformed crook who headed up the SBI. Uncle Jim had long since been phased out; Billy went next, and only Betty remained of the old gang in the final days. Through all those adventurous years she and Jack had never been more than just good friends.

Ron Goulart

SEE ALSO: *Advertising; Big Little Books; Comic Books; Comics; Dime Novels; The Lone Ranger; Radio; Radio Drama; Soap Operas; Teenagers; Television; Toys; World War II.*

BIBLIOGRAPHY

Dunning, John. *On the Air*. New York: Oxford University Press, 1998.

Goulart, Ron, ed. *The Encyclopedia of American Comics*. New York: Facts On File, 1990.

Harmon, Jim. *Radio Mystery and Adventure*. Jefferson, NC: McFarland, 1992.

Harmon, Jim. *The Great Radio Heroes*. Jefferson, NC: McFarland, 2001.

Jackass

Jackass (2000–2002) was an MTV reality show that originated from actor/writer Johnny Knoxville's idea for a magazine article about testing the effects of various self-defense devices—such as tasers and mace—on himself. Encouraged by Jeff Tremaine, editor of *Big Brother* skateboarding magazine, to actually videotape his experiments, the two joined forces with eclectic film director Spike Jonze (*Being John Malkovich*), pro-skateboarder Bam Margera, and an extended "crew" of family and friends to film the stunts and practical jokes that would later become the basis of *Jackass*.

Debuting in 2000, the show's mix of crude humor, outlandish pranks, and death-defying stunts rendered it an immediate hit. Antics often involved the cast attacking each other with weaponry but also dressing up in costume—or taking off their clothes—as they rode skateboards, shopping carts, and skis into things and people. However, they were equally adept at practical jokes—such as Chris Pontius stripping down to a thong and bow-tie to prance about shocked citizens as his alter-ego "Party Boy," and Margera's constant surprise attacks on his very normal and forgiving family. Beyond the often life-threatening fun of the outrageous and imaginative stunts was the simple pleasure of watching these good-natured friends simply having a good time together—sans drugs or alcohol.

However, the show's portrayal of dangerous "fun" also rendered it an immediate source of controversy. Though each show began with the signature *Jackass* logo—a skull with crossed crutches—and disclaimers for people to refrain from emulating their behavior between each gag, this warning did not deter Connecticut teenager Eric Lind from setting himself on fire in attempting a stunt in 2001. This and other reported incidents spurred Senator Joe Lieberman to denounce *Jackass* and MTV. In 2002, at the height of its popularity, the show ended after just three seasons due to censorship issues. The *Jackass* phenomenon was far from over, though, as it shifted format from television to the big screen, where censorship was no longer a factor.

Costing less than $5 million, the film grossed in excess of $60 million, causing the *New York Times* to describe *Jackass: The*

Movie (2002) as "the most successful plotless movie in American film history." Some memorable movie clips include Ryan Dunn being X-rayed with a toy car in his rectum, Steve-O putting a fish hook through his cheek and swimming with sharks, and Knoxville being gored by a bull. Despite the dangerous nature of their stunts, as of 2012, only one participant, Dunn, has died in an unrelated car accident.

Since the end of the series, there have been five *Jackass* movies, six video collections, and multiple series spin-offs including Margera's *Viva La Bam* (2003–2006), Dunn's *Homewrecker* (2005), and Pontius and Steve-O's *Wildboyz* (2003–2006), although none has achieved the recognition or success achieved by the original *Jackass* program. The *Jackass* phenomenon continues to live on through video gaming; in 2007 PlayStation and Nintendo released *Jackass: The Game*, where players act as director, picking stunts to complete and use in the show's next season.

Ron Horton

SEE ALSO: Being John Malkovich*; MTV; Reality Television; Television; Video Games.*

BIBLIOGRAPHY

Cliver, Sean. *Jackass: The Movie: The Official Companion Book.* New York: Pocket Books, 2002.

Cliver, Sean. *Jackass: 10 Years of Stupid.* New York: MTV Press, 2010.

Margera, Bam. *Serious as Dog Dirt!* New York: Pocket Books, 2009.

Steve-O, and David Peisner. *Professional Idiot: A Memoir.* New York: Hyperion, 2011.

Jackie O

SEE: *Onassis, Jacqueline Lee Bouvier Kennedy.*

Jackson, Janet *(1966–)*

Janet Damita Jo Jackson is the youngest member of the musical family of Joseph and Katherine Jackson. Growing up in the shadow of her male siblings, who became famous as the Jackson Five, Jackson would get her first taste of fame as an actress before making her mark in music with *Janet Jackson's Rhythm Nation 1814* (1989) and *The Velvet Rope* (1997). In a career spanning four decades, Jackson has become one of the most accomplished and respected singers in music history, releasing eight platinum or multiplatinum albums and garnering thirty-three Billboard Music Awards and six Grammy Awards. In recent years she has primarily been recognized for her infamous performance and "wardrobe malfunction" at Super Bowl XXXVIII, which led the Federal Communications Commission (FCC) to impose new decency standards.

Born on May 16, 1966, Jackson was exposed to the entertainment business from an early age, performing both with her family and as a solo act. After being discovered in 1974 while appearing onstage with her family in Las Vegas, Nevada, Jackson appeared on television, playing Penny in *Good Times* (1977–1979). Roles in *A New Kind of Family* (1979), *Diff'rent Strokes* (1980–1984), and *Fame* (1984–1985) followed. While in New York working on *Fame*, Jackson began to develop her musical inclinations. With the help of her family, she recorded her self-titled debut album in 1982 and began to create a strong, defiant stage persona reminiscent of her older brother Michael's aggressive, dance-oriented performances.

After her second album, *Dream Street* (1984), became a modest success, Jackson started to distance herself from her domineering father/manager, and her third album, *Control* (1986), emphasized her newfound independence with songs such as "Nasty" and "Control." Recognized as one of the most influential albums of the 1980s, *Control* was a huge success, with more than fourteen million records sold around the world. She followed with the equally successful, though stylistically and thematically different, *Janet Jackson's Rhythm Nation 1814* (1989), which produced an astounding seven top-five singles. Later albums such as *The Velvet Rope* (1997) and *Damita Jo* (2004) documented Jackson's increasing comfort with her status as a fashion icon and sex symbol. Her evolution as a performer has been cited as a driving force in the mainstream crossover of African American performers and was an inspiration for singers such as Beyoncé Knowles, Toni Braxton, and Jennifer Lopez.

Jackson returned to acting in 1993, starring in John Singleton's *Poetic Justice* and contributing the closing song "Again," which originally appeared on her album *janet* (1993). She went on to star in several films, including *Nutty Professor II: The Klumps* (2000) and the Tyler Perry films *Why Did I Get Married* (2007) and *For Colored Girls* (2010). She won an MTV Movie Award for her performance in *Poetic Justice* and an Image Award for *Why Did I Get Married.*

Jackson's personal life has been marred with family trials, stalking, and divorce. After cutting ties with her father, whom her sister La Toya claimed sexually abused her and her siblings, Jackson found herself being stalked and threatened by a group of men, an experience detailed in the songs "Nasty" and "What Have You Done for Me Lately." Her marriages, which she kept private, ended in divorce. Jackson stood by her brother, Michael, when he was the subject of child molestation charges and co-wrote the song "Scream" (1995) with him to express the frustration and anger Michael felt over the situation. Upon her brother's death in 2009, Jackson assumed the role of family spokesperson and delivered the tribute for her brother at the 2009 BET Awards. She also performed "Scream" as a tribute to him during the 2009 MTV Video Awards.

Jackson's performance with pop singer Justin Timberlake at Super Bowl XXXVIII (2004) was one of the most controversial and well-known pop culture moments of the first decade of the 2000s. During their performance, Timberlake sang the song "Rock Your Body" from his debut album while Jackson danced and provided backing vocals. When he sang the line, "bet I'll have you naked by the end of this song," he reached across and pulled her costume back, supposedly expecting to reveal a red bra. Instead, television audiences got a brief glimpse of Jackson's right breast and an elaborate nipple ring. The performers, CBS, MTV, and the National Football League claimed no knowledge that this was going to happen, but the conservative Parents Television Council issued complaints, which the FCC acted upon. Their investigation led to the Broadcast Decency Enforcement Act (2005), which established the FCC as the arbitrator of indecent and profane behavior and allowed it to levy fines ranging from $27,500 to $500,000. The law, which some consider a form of censorship, has significantly impacted live television performances and remains a topic of fierce debate.

Linda Martindale

SEE ALSO: *Bra; Celebrity;* Diff'rent Strokes; *Divorce;* Good Times; *Grammy Awards; Jackson, Michael; The Jackson Five; Knowles, Beyoncé; Las Vegas; Live Television; Lopez, Jennifer; MTV; National Football League (NFL); Pop Music; Sex Scandals; Sex Symbol; Super Bowl; Television; Timberlake, Justin.*

BIBLIOGRAPHY

Cornwell, Jane. *Janet Jackson.* London: Carlton, 2002.

Jackson, Janet, and David Ritz. *True You: A Journey to Finding and Loving Yourself.* New York: Gallery Books, 2011.

Jackson, La Toya, and Patricia R. Bashe. *La Toya: Growing Up in the Jackson Family.* New York: Dutton, 1991.

Jackson, Jesse *(1941–)*

Baptist minister and civil rights leader Jesse Jackson had become the leading advocate for racial equality in the United States by the 1980s. His initial bid for the presidency in 1983–1984 marked the first serious attempt by an African American for a nationwide office in the history of the United States and provided a great stimulus to black registration and voting.

Jackson was born to a single mother in Greenville, South Carolina, on October 8, 1941. Raised by his mother and stepfather in modest surroundings, he also lived near his affluent father, witnessing and resenting the material well-being of his half-brother. These tensions fueled a lifelong determination in him to transcend his initial surroundings. Ambitious, charismatic, and intelligent, he achieved success as a student and as an athlete in segregated Greensboro, earning a scholarship to the University of Illinois in 1959. When his dream of playing quarterback failed to materialize, he left Illinois and transferred to North Carolina Agricultural and Technical College, where he met his future wife, Jacqueline Davis. He later attended the Chicago Theological Seminary and was ordained as a Baptist minister in 1968.

BECOMING AN ACTIVIST

At first hesitant to engage in direct action, Jackson was increasingly drawn away from his studies by the mushrooming southern civil rights movement. After an initial stint with the Congress of Racial Equality, he began in 1965 to work with Martin Luther King Jr. as a young staffer at the Southern Christian Leadership Conference (SCLC). While not especially close to King personally, Jackson's effective organizational skills led King to appoint him to head up efforts to expand SCLC operations in Chicago. Jackson's work there formed the basis for King's unsuccessful 1966 Chicago Campaign for Freedom. Following the Chicago campaign, Jackson was placed in charge of Operation Breadbasket, the economic arm of the SCLC.

On April 4, 1968, Jackson stood beside King on the balcony of the Lorraine Motel in Memphis, Tennessee, when an assassin's bullet ended King's life. In a controversial episode following the murder, Jackson appeared on national television and before a rally the next morning still wearing his bloodstained olive turtleneck. Some perceived his actions as a disrespectful attempt to manipulate King's death for personal gain.

Following King's assassination, Jackson sought to counter growing white reaction to civil rights gains nationally by focusing on economic empowerment rather than traditional civil rights issues. After breaking with the SCLC in 1971, he founded Operation PUSH (People United to Save Humanity [later changed to Serve Humanity]) to press the business and financial community for jobs and increased economic opportunity for African Americans and other people of color. As director of PUSH and self-appointed black ambassador to the white business community, Jackson gently threatened to boycott selected firms that did not move toward greater racial equality. In 1981 the Coca-Cola Company became the first corporation to sign an agreement to increase business with African American vendors and expand management opportunities for blacks. Similar agreements were negotiated with Kentucky Fried Chicken, Anheuser-Busch, Seven-Up, and Burger King. Operation PUSH ultimately grew to include seventy chapters and more than 80,000 members.

Jackson also began his foray into international politics at this time. In 1979, despite substantial criticism and pressure

Jesse Jackson. *Jesse Jackson, the leading advocate for racial equality in the late twentieth century, delivers a speech in 1995.* CYNTHIA JOHNSON/GETTY IMAGES.

from the U.S. government, he met with Yasir Arafat, head of the Palestine Liberation Organization (PLO), to discuss the prospects for a peaceful settlement to the PLO/Israeli conflict in the Middle East. Similarly, in 1983, again to considerable negative press at home, Jackson met with the head of Syria and came away with the release of captured U.S. Navy pilot Lieutenant Robert Goodman.

POLITICAL AMBITIONS

By the early 1980s Jackson had become the black leader most capable of mounting a presidential bid. In November 1983 he announced his candidacy for president, emphasizing economic empowerment for minorities and increased voter registration among black citizens. He sought to stir a grassroots opposition movement and confront both the Republican and Democratic establishments as a populist insurgent. His rousing oratory, combining elements of uplift ("I am somebody!") and militancy ("It's Nationtime!"), began to attract a large popular following. In the antiphonal style he had learned from Afro-Christianity, Jackson chanted, "There is a freedom train a comin'. But you got to register to ride, so get on board and get on with it." In response, his audience would yell, "Run, Jesse run! Run, Jesse run!"

Jackson's presidential bid was hurt, though, after a journalist reported an off-the-record derogatory reference to New York City as Hymietown (*hymie* is an offensive term to denote Jewish people). Despite denials and numerous apologies, the incident continued to dog Jackson throughout the campaign. His candidacy was also damaged by the fact that he lacked experience as an elected official. Nevertheless, he ran a surprisingly strong third in the Democratic primaries, polling more than three million votes.

In the 1988 presidential race Jackson recast himself from a race leader to a multiracial, progressive populist. He sought to "Keep Hope Alive" with an alliance between people of color and white workers, appealing to inner-city churchgoers, the urban poor, midwestern farmers, Rust Belt auto workers, and even some of the former constituency of segregationist politician George Wallace. In the end Jackson garnered 6.7 million votes in the primaries and produced a full third of the convention delegates, forcing significant concessions in the platform from the eventual nominee, Michael Dukakis. While he did not capture the Democratic nomination, Jackson's successful showing made him one of the country's most prominent African American leaders as well as a significant force on the Democratic Left.

CHANGING DIRECTIONS

Following the 1988 election, though, Jackson struggled to define a coherent new course of action. He hoped to build on his electoral successes by forming the Rainbow Coalition, a multiracial, progressive countermovement emphasizing economic and racial justice for all U.S. citizens and an end to the sexual exploitation of women. Some members hoped the Rainbow Coalition would serve as the foundation for a new third party, while others envisioned the coalition as a liberal Left pressure group working from within the Democratic Party.

In 1989, however, Jackson undercut the potential of the new group when he demanded that he alone make appointments for state chapter chairs. By centralizing control at the national level and, thus, curtailing local independence and autonomy, he severely crippled the Rainbow Coalition as a mass membership and activist organization. In addition to his attempts to build an effective progressive political coalition, he served as shadow senator for Washington, D.C., in the early 1990s and hosted a national television talk show, *Both Sides*, on CNN (Cable News Network).

The mid-1990s found Jackson more at ease with the Democratic Party and the presidency of Bill Clinton. Initially a gadfly, hoping to cajole the administration toward more progressive positions, Jackson settled into an established political role as adviser and minister to the president. In what many considered to be the precursor to a third presidential bid in 2000, Jackson began to reorient himself in the late 1990s toward issues of economic justice, appearing with poor white workers and their families in Appalachia as well as with poor people of color in cities across the country. In 1996 he founded the Wall Street Project, aimed at bringing capital into the inner city and more minorities into brokerages.

During Barack Obama's run for the presidency in 2008, Jackson caused a minor scandal by making what he later termed as "crude and hurtful" remarks about the future president. Not knowing that his mike was open, Jackson criticized Obama's speeches at African American churches, contending that Obama's comments about absent black fathers and family responsibility was being construed as talking down to blacks. He apologized, and Obama stated that his apology was accepted. In January 2012 Jackson celebrated his fifteenth year of holding the Rainbow PUSH Wall Street Project Economic Summit. The theme for the summit was "We Are One World—Bringing Everyone to the Table: Celebrating Fifteen Years of Access to Capital, Industry, and Technology."

Patrick D. Jones

SEE ALSO: *Burger King; Civil Rights Movement; CNN; Coca-Cola; Kentucky Fried Chicken; King, Martin Luther, Jr.; Obama, Barack.*

BIBLIOGRAPHY

Barker, Lucius. *Our Time Has Come: A Delegate's Diary of Jesse Jackson's 1984 Presidential Campaign.* Urbana: University of Illinois Press, 1988.

Barkley, Charles. *Who's Afraid of a Large Black Man?* New York: Penguin Press, 2005.

Clemente, Frank. *Keep Hope Alive: Jesse Jackson's 1988 Presidential Campaign.* Boston: South End Press, 1989.

Frady, Marshall. *Jesse: The Life and Pilgrimage of Jesse Jackson.* New York: Random House, 1996.

Ifill, Gwen. *The Breakthrough: Politics and Race in the Age of Obama.* New York: Doubleday, 2009.

Marable, Manning, ed. *Freedom on My Mind: The Columbia Documentary History of the African American Experience.* New York: Columbia University, 2003.

Jackson, Mahalia *(1911–1972)*

With her magnificently powerful contralto voice, superb rhythmic control, and passionate commitment to her music, Mahalia Jackson is widely considered the best of all gospel singers. She added a dimension to American cultural life in reaching a wide white audience, entering territory previously crossed by black artists only in the fields of jazz and blues, and achieved the highest accolade for any performing artist: the universal reference to her by her first name only. The daughter of a preacher, she secretly listened to and was influenced by the records of American blues singer Bessie Smith but steadfastly eschewed the genre in her own performance, dedicating herself to gospel music. These lines from the Thomas A. Dorsey composition "I've Got to Live the Life I Sing about in My Song" became Jackson's credo: "I can't sing one thing and then live another, / be a saint by day and a devil undercover, / I've got to live the life that I sing about in my song."

GOSPEL ROOTS

Jackson's allegiance to gospel music brought her the rewards of wealth and fame and earned her the undisputed title of "the world's greatest gospel singer," paving the way for the acceptance and integration of gospel music into the wider American culture. In 1948 she and Theodore Frey established the National Baptist Music Convention as an auxiliary to the National Baptist Convention, and that year her recording of "Move on up a Little Higher" was the first gospel song to sell a million copies, largely to a black record-buying public. Jackson was one of the first gospel singers to use the Hammond organ and the piano as accompaniment, as well as one of the first to introduce gospel music into more familiar contexts. She performed for programs in support of the civil rights movement and, as a confidante of Martin Luther King Jr., sang at the March on Washington as a prologue to his famous "I Have a Dream" speech.

Jackson was born on October 26, 1911, in New Orleans. Her mother died when she was five years old, and she was raised within the Baptist religion, absorbing the church music that would prove to be the major influence on her life and her music. At the age of sixteen, she moved to Chicago to stay with an aunt and supported herself in a variety of humble domestic jobs. At the same time, she joined the Greater Salem Baptist Church and sang with the Johnson Singers, a quintet that toured local churches. She turned down an offer to work with bandleader Earl Hines but subsequently met Dorsey, with whom she forged a mutually beneficial relationship. (Some of Dorsey's songs were dedicated to Jackson.) By 1938 Jackson had married, opened a beauty and floral shop, and acquired real estate. Her early performances in Chicago were in diverse venues. Not accepted in the established black churches, she had to perform at storefronts and in basement halls, and it was Studs Terkel, author and radio host, who first presented her to his largely white radio audience.

EARLY RECORDINGS

Few of Jackson's early performances were recorded, but she signed with Decca, for whom she recorded "God Shall Wipe Away All Tears" (1937) and "God's Gonna Separate the Wheat . . . " (1937). These early recordings were artistically but not commercially successful, and her refusal to record blues music led Decca to drop her. In 1946 she signed with Apollo Records and recorded her million-plus best seller, the Reverend W. Herbert Brewster's composition, "Move on up a Little Higher," and cut a long-playing album, *No Matter How You Pray*. Her early recording repertoire is mixed and the artistic quality variable—the Apollo recordings suffer from technical problems and undistinguished accompaniment, but her voice is in fine form.

In 1954 Jackson signed with Columbia Records. The Columbia sessions, consisting of early compositions previously recorded on Apollo as well as new material, generally excelled in both technical and artistic quality, and she made several albums for the label. By the 1950s she had engaged Mildred Falls, a gospel pianist, who received neither the recognition nor the remuneration that she deserved, and organist Ralph Jones as her accompanists. The duo was called the Falls-Jones Ensemble.

JACKSON'S STYLE

When in her finest form, Jackson's contralto swoops, dives, and easily vacillates from high declamatory shouts to low lyrical melodies, couched in the style of black preachers and executed within a single breath. She confounded musicologists by breaking all the rules while holding her audiences spellbound. Jackson and Falls also made liberal use of blues phrasing, together with the rhythmic vitality of the sanctified church. Notable and memorable recordings in her repertoire of congregational-style chants, hymns, and African American spirituals include "Amazing Grace," "Nobody Knows the Trouble I've Seen," "Didn't It Rain," and "Deep River," as well as Dorsey compositions such as "Precious Lord." She recorded a small number of secular songs such as "I Believe." Jackson frequently sang parts of a song without meter and preferred songs heavily infused with the scale, chords, and modified structure of blues. "Walk over God's Heaven," "Move on up a Little Higher," "Jesus Met the Woman at the Well," and "I'm Going to Live the Life I Sing About" fall into this category.

FILM WORK

Jackson performed at Rhode Island's Newport Jazz Festival in 1957 and is featured singing "The Lord's Prayer" at the end of the film *Jazz on a Summer's Day*. She sang, too, with Duke Ellington's band, both at the festival and in the studio, explaining away her participation by saying that she considered Ellington's band "a sacred institution." The same year she appeared in the film *St. Louis Blues*, the biopic of composer W. C. Handy that starred Nat King Cole, and then provided the emotional climax to director Douglas Sirk's remake of *Imitation of Life* (1959), singing "Trouble of the World" at the tear-sodden funeral of actress Lana Turner's black maid (Juanita Moore). By then, Jackson had given many international concert tours and was world famous. During the 1950s and 1960s she appeared frequently on television and sang at the presidential inauguration of John F. Kennedy.

By the late 1960s Jackson commanded mostly large, white audiences in Europe and America, but by then her voice and her health were in decline. Her favorite pastime was cooking, and she continued to consume the rich soul food of her home, New Orleans, including red beans, rice, and ham hocks. Her grueling touring schedule, entrepreneurial ventures, two failed marriages, and other personal problems also had exacted a heavy toll on her health. Jackson suffered heart failure and died in the Chicago area at the age of sixty. Her body lay in state as thousands of mourners filed past to pay their respects to the unique performer. At her funeral her good friend Aretha Franklin sang "Precious Lord," just as the great gospel singer herself had done at the funeral of King.

Willie Collins

SEE ALSO: *Blues; Civil Rights Movement; Cole, Nat King; Ellington, Duke; Franklin, Aretha; Gospel Music; Handy, W. C.; King, Martin Luther, Jr.; March on Washington; Newport*

Jazz and Folk Festivals; Sirk, Douglas; Smith, Bessie; Terkel, Studs; Turner, Lana.

BIBLIOGRAPHY

Dunham, Montrew, and Cathy Morrison. *Mahalia Jackson: Gospel Singer and Civil Rights Champion.* Carmel, IN: Patria Press, 2003.

Goreau, Laurraine. *Just Mahalia, Baby: The Mahalia Jackson Story.* Gretna, LA: Pelican, 1984.

Jackson, Mahalia, and Evan McLeod Wylie. *Movin' on Up: Mahalia Jackson.* New York: Hawthorn Books, 1966.

Schwerin, Jules Victor. *Got to Tell It: Mahalia Jackson, Queen of Gospel.* New York: Oxford University Press. 1992.

Jackson, Michael *(1958–2009)*

Singer and dancer Michael Jackson was among the most beloved performers in the history of modern music. Known as the King of Pop, he absorbed the most influential African American musical traditions from his formative years, infused them with his own musical eccentricity and the popular trends and technology of the moment, and created a musical explosion of nearly unprecedented proportions. Between 1982 and 1984 Jackson's acclaimed album *Thriller* (1982) shattered all music industry records by selling more than forty million copies; in the late 1980s Jackson again established new standards with his album *Bad* and its accompanying worldwide concert tour.

Michael Jackson. *Michael Jackson performs in concert in 1988.* DAVID MCGOUGH/DMI/TIME LIFE PICTURES/GETTY IMAGES.

As his fame grew to epic proportions, however, Jackson eventually became the nucleus of his own mammoth sideshow, earning headlines for his face-altering plastic surgery; his increasingly eccentric public behavior; and, on repeated occasions, allegations that the singer had engaged in the sexual abuse of minors. By the early 1990s and first decade of the 2000s Jackson's inscrutable offstage antics had transformed him into one of the most idiosyncratic, and in many ways tragic, cultural figures in modern history. While his death from a drug overdose in June 2009 shocked legions of fans worldwide, for many it seemed the sad but predictable end for a man who had become consumed by the enormity of his own stardom.

PUSHED TO SUCCEED

Before the madness of *Thriller* and the subsequent publicity stunts and notorious allegations regarding his personal life, Jackson was a member of a family singing group from Gary, Indiana, called the Jackson Five. In addition to Jackson, the group originally included four of his five brothers. A child-performing sensation from the age of five, Jackson was one of the nation's finest 1960s rhythm-and-blues vocalists long before his grade school graduation. An acolyte of James Brown and Jackie Wilson, the young Jackson was also a dancer of nearly unmatched ferocity and versatility. His singing skill far surpassed any other child recording artist. The eleven-year-old boy sang of desire, joy, anguish, and loss with all the sophistication and embittered knowledge of a man in his forties. His presence on the radio in the early 1970s stunned and impressed listeners. Very quickly, the group amassed a vast collection of gold records and was able to move to a California mansion.

Although clearly gifted, Jackson did not come by his success naturally. Instead, he was trained by a fierce, brutal, and unforgiving group leader: his father, Joseph. Joseph was a crane operator at a Gary steel mill who left a music career behind in the early 1950s to support his rapidly growing family. He put his guitar away in a closet as a memory piece and warned his children never to touch it. When nine-year-old Tito was caught playing the guitar in 1962, he was, by his own account, "torn up" by his father. This was the founding event of the Jackson Five; after the incident with Tito, Joseph began to organize the youngsters into a singing group. At first the group did not include the three-and-a-half-year-old Jackson; he made his entrance when his parents caught him imitating older brother Jermaine's singing. They were alarmed and delighted, and Jackson was immediately installed as the group's tiny new figurehead.

ABUSE CHARGES

Jackson and his siblings reported being beaten and terrorized by their father during their childhood. Joseph ran long daily rehearsal sessions armed with belts and switches, which he used with frequency and severity. Sister La Toya said that the beatings the siblings endured were bloody and often involved the use of fists, while Jackson reported in his autobiography that he fought back with his own small fists. "I would fight back and my father would kill me, just tear me up. Mother told me I'd fight back even when I was very little, but I don't remember that. I do remember running under tables to get away from him, and making him angrier."

Joseph denied the abuse charges to the Associated Press with telling succinctness: "Maybe I should've punched La Toya, like any other normal parent would do . . . but La Toya stayed quiet and never did get into any trouble or nothing." La Toya also made charges of sexual abuse against her father, which he repeatedly denied. At the age of thirty-four, Jackson said he was still frightened of his father and that on meeting him, he often "would get sick; I would start to regurgitate." Joseph responded to this too. "If he regurgitated," he told Michel McQueen on ABC TV's *Day One* program in 1993, "he regurgitated all the way to the bank."

Joseph kept a grueling rehearsal schedule and groomed his sons to be polished professionals in a very short time. By the age of nine, Jackson was singing in nightclubs, working side by side with strippers and drag queens, and getting an education in the process. "This one girl with gorgeous eyelashes and long hair came out and did her routine," he later wrote, "She put on a *great* performance. All of a sudden, at the end, she took off her wig, pulled a pair of big oranges out of her bra, and revealed that she was a hard-faced guy under all that make-up. That blew me away."

CAREER WITH HIS BROTHERS

In late 1968 Jackson and his brothers were on their way to New York for a taping of their first television appearance on *David Frost* when they received a call from Motown Records. The group handily passed their audition for Berry Gordy, owner and founder of Motown, then the largest black-owned business in the United States. He told the boys that they would have three number one records in a row and become stars. The success engendered by Jackson's singing and dancing prowess went beyond even Gordy's confident estimates. The young brothers became the first black teen idols, and Jackson made his first teen dream solo album at the age of thirteen. Rock critic Vince Aletti expressed amazement at the ability of so young a boy to convey such subtle emotions as "anguish and doubt" with startling authenticity.

During the winter of 1972–1973, Jackson's voice broke, leaving both his career and that of the group in question. The music business has been generally unkind to former boy sopranos, and Gordy seemed ready to move on to other projects. It looked as though Jackson was destined to be a pubescent golden oldie. The group began to think seriously of breaking their contract. According to his memoirs, it was fifteen-year-old Jackson who presented Gordy with the ultimatum: "Let us have creative control or we're gone." In 1975 the family held a press conference to announce that they would sign a new record contract with Epic Records, a division of the CBS Records conglomerate.

After two lukewarm CBS albums with the group and one big success, Jackson made good on CBS's plan for him to record a solo album, though he later remarked that he felt they were merely securing their investment. He had his own, more grandiose plans for a solo career. His first tentative step in this direction involved his acceptance of Gordy's offer to costar in an all-African American version of *The Wizard of Oz*, renamed *The Wiz* (1978). Oscar-winning producer Quincy Jones was the musical director of the movie. He got on well with Jackson during the shoot, and when Jackson suggested that Jones produce his next solo album, he agreed.

The collaboration worked both musically and artistically: the *Off the Wall* album turned out to be smooth as silk, with Jones applying sandpaper to Jackson's audible and exciting rough edges. The tracks conformed to a soft, cascading beat underneath the rich, erotic yearning of Jackson's voice. This new voice, full and mature with low moans and floating falsetto wails, was entirely unrecognizable. The child sensation was gone—in more ways than one.

INDIVIDUAL STARDOM

It was during this period that Jackson began to display, for the first time, some of the odd personal characteristics for which he would later gain notoriety. During the filming of *The Wiz*, he gave several promotional interviews. Timothy White of the rock magazine *Crawdaddy* was assigned to interview Jackson and found him quite amusing. He said Jackson appeared "to be in some sort of daze" as he ate food with his fingers at a glitzy French restaurant in Manhattan.

During this transitional time, Jackson began to hone his skills as a songwriter. On the Jacksons' album *Triumph*, he unveiled the idiosyncratic and disquieting songwriting style that would drive the success of the *Thriller* album. One song, called "This Place Hotel," "came from a dream I had. I dream a lot," he told a reporter. "Live and sin," the song begins, making the narrator's guilt an overwhelming and permanent condition. Set in a haunted hotel run by "wicked women" who appear suddenly in groups of two or three, the singer is trapped by "faces staring, glaring, tearing through me." Probably inspired by the unstable nature of public fame, Jackson's legendary paranoia makes its first appearance: "Every smile's a trial thought in beguile to hurt me." At one point the singer declares bluntly, "hope is dead." The singing is pained, open-throated, and raw.

In 1982 Jackson was completing work on his second Jones collaboration, *Thriller*. Determined that the new album must match or exceed *Off the Wall*'s popularity, Jones and Jackson sought more powerful music. When Jackson brought in a tape of a new song, "Beat It," Jones began to realize that Jackson could become a powerful phenomenon—a crossover to the white rock market. Jackson's hard-rocking song about backing away from a fight fit perfectly in the rock style. Jones brought in metal guitarist Eddie Van Halen to do a solo, and the pounding beat coupled with the song's accompanying visual representation of a rhythm-and-blues singer performing white rock began literally to change the face of the music industry.

As the album neared the end of production, Jones still needed one more solid hit and asked Jackson to write another song. For reasons that are unclear, Jackson wrote a fierce song denying paternity of a little boy whose "eyes were like mine." "Billie Jean" is now considered a rock classic. There are times during the song when it seems that the arrangement just cannot keep up with the singer's passion, and Jackson's frenzy seems barricaded by the cool, solid majesty of the arrangement, singing as if lives really did depend on listeners believing his story. The magic of the song is, of course, that the singer is not really sure if he believes himself.

KING OF POP

The new album quickly jumped to number five on its release. This time, reluctantly, Jackson did a great number of promotional interviews. He spoke to reporters from *Ebony*, *Newsweek*, *Interview*, and *Rolling Stone* and filled out written questionnaires for other publications such as *Creem*. He did television shots for *Entertainment Tonight*, *Ebony/Jet Showcase*, and *America's Top Ten*. The interview that everyone talked about, however, was the February 17, 1983, cover story for *Rolling Stone*.

"I'm the type of person who will tell it all, even though it's a secret. And I *know* that things should be kept private," Jackson explained to interviewer Gerri Hirshey, neatly encapsulating the secret of his success as well. Hirshey described him as extremely nervous and flighty; he suffered the interview as if he were getting stitches. He said he liked to watch cartoons and explained why: "It's like everything's all right. . . . It's like the world is happening now in a faraway city. Everything's fine." Hirshey says the interview remained tense until Jackson relaxed when talking about his animals; he even forced Hirshey to play with his boa constrictor. Then, unbidden by Hirshey, he asked, "Know what I also love? Mannequins. . . . I guess I want to bring them to life," he went on. "I like to imagine talking to them." It may have been with those lines that *Thriller* mania really began. It was not just that Jackson sounded or even looked peculiar; he had marked himself as irrefutably different, a stranger in a strange land.

By the early spring of 1983, "Billie Jean" had skyrocketed to number one on the Billboard charts and remained there for seven weeks. This song was followed almost immediately by "Beat It," which stayed on top for three weeks. The album *Thriller* also reached number one and stayed there. At one point in early 1983, Jackson had an unprecedented number one record on four charts: pop singles and albums and black singles and albums. To promote "Billie Jean," CBS had meanwhile financed an expensive music video, a little film set to the tune. The chief outlet for airing these videos was the cable channel founded in 1981 called Music Television, or MTV. According to a September 22, 1986, *TV Guide* story, the cable channel refused to air the video because they said it was not "rock and roll" enough for their format. When CBS threatened to pull all its videos from the cable channel, "Billie Jean" became a rock-and-roll song.

In 1983 Jackson participated in the *Motown 25* televised reunion and stole the show with his innovative and breathtaking dancing. He unveiled his famous moonwalk for the first time, spun as if on ice skates, and perched precariously on his toes for the briefest moment. He pursued his dance in a sort of calamitous rage. Jackson seemed to sense that this was his chance to escape the confines of mere stardom and become something quite different: not the star he had been for years, but an iconic signifier on the order of Marilyn Monroe or Elvis Presley. The show aired in May, with "Beat It" and *Thriller* already skyrocketing on the charts. After this success there was a buzz of excitement surrounding Jackson, as if each new gesture brought with it a revelation.

PRESSURES OF FAME

As time went on, the revelations Jackson's gestures brought were increasingly disturbing. The shadowy transformation revealed itself quickly; in 1984 he reluctantly submitted to his father's pressure to go on a concert tour with the Jacksons. This Victory Tour turned into an unmitigated disaster: high ticket prices created a backlash; the tour was mismanaged; and the infighting became unmerciful. In the end Jackson decided to give away all his proceeds to charity.

After the tour Jackson disappeared from the limelight for a while in an attempt to cope with an onslaught of unprecedented pop pressure. He severed many ties with his family and finally moved out of the family home to a new ranch in Santa Barbara County, California, that he called Neverland. When he did appear in public, he often wore a surgical mask over his face, which served to hide the cosmetic changes he was making to his appearance. His skin became lighter (due, he said later, to a skin disease); his nose was thinned after several surgeries; and he added a cleft to his chin. During this time Jackson engaged in a variety of eerie publicity stunts. His manager announced Jackson's wishes to sleep in a hyperbaric chamber and purchase the skeleton of Joseph Merrick, England's disfigured Elephant Man.

In 1991 Jackson released a new album, *Dangerous*, which went on to sell more than twenty million copies worldwide. Although his music still sold alarmingly well (and was alarmingly good), and though he was perhaps more famous than ever, by the early 1990s he was a figure of extreme curiosity, arousing as much pity as fascination. His career took an unexpectedly dark turn in August 1993, however, after a Los Angeles County Child Protective Services (CPS) caseworker took a report alleging that Jackson had molested a young Beverly Hills boy. In November of that year, the underage son of one of Jackson's former employees also made a claim of impropriety to Los Angeles County's CPS. After Jackson settled the civil case and the investigation closed, he attempted to resume his career, while also establishing some stability in his life. In 1994 he married Presley's daughter, Lisa Marie; however, the union ended in divorce after only eighteen months. Jackson subsequently married Debbie Rowe, a Los Angeles nurse with whom he had two children, but they divorced after three years.

STRUGGLES CONTINUE

Still, allegations of sexual impropriety continued to hound Jackson's career well into the late 1990s, and his reputation never fully recovered. He also suffered financial setbacks during this time; while his albums still sold well in Europe, they did not fare as well in the United States. Jackson also had not recorded an album of new material since the early 1990s. Instead of focusing on music, he concentrated on arranging his personal financial matters, while announcing plans to create theme parks in places such as Poland, Brazil, Japan, and the United States.

In 1996–1997 Jackson embarked on his HIStory world tour. HIStory proved an enormous success, generating $83 million in ticket sales, as Jackson played to a string of sold-out shows in Europe. He finally returned to the studio in 2001, with the release of *Invincible*, his first new studio album in nearly a decade. With tracks such as the Top 10 hit "You Rock My World," *Invincible* was warmly welcomed by Jackson's fan base; however, it received mixed reviews from critics, many of whom considered the effort tame compared to such seminal titles as *Thriller* and *Bad*. In the end *Invincible* sold only 2.1 million copies.

As the decade progressed, Jackson's struggles continued to mount. In 2002 he shocked the world after he was videotaped dangling his infant son over a hotel balcony in Berlin. While he later apologized for the incident, the bizarre gesture upset many child-welfare experts, who questioned Jackson's fitness as a parent. A year later the singer once again found himself facing child molestation charges; although he was ultimately acquitted, the allegations damaged his public persona even further. Throughout this period Jackson also struggled with significant financial woes and was forced to sell off partial control of his Neverland ranch in order to cover his mounting debts.

Jackson's painful personal odyssey came to a tragic end on June 25, 2009, when the singer died in Los Angeles of a drug overdose. He was fifty years old. Following his death, Jackson's personal physician, Conrad Murray, found himself on trial for criminal negligence, amid allegations he had contributed to his patient's fatal decline. In November 2011 Murray was found guilty of involuntary manslaughter. In the streets outside the Los Angeles courtroom, hundreds of Jackson's fans were on hand to cheer the verdict. Reporting on the trial and its aftermath, *Times* writer Annie Nightingale struck a note of sympathy, both for Jackson and his doctor. Concentrating on the "incredible pressure to deliver" that Jackson endured in his later years, Nightingale reflected on the singer's desperate attempts to "cope with the circling wolves and demanding fans" that plagued him until the end of his life, concluding: "It was a tragedy, and it was almost inevitable."

Robin Markowitz

SEE ALSO: *Brown, James; Drag;* Ebony*;* Entertainment Tonight*; Gordy, Berry; Grammy Awards; The Jackson Five;* Jet*; Monroe, Marilyn; Motown; MTV;* Newsweek*; Plastic Surgery; Pop Music; Presley, Elvis; Rhythm and Blues; Rock and Roll;* Rolling Stone*; Taylor, Elizabeth; Teen Idols; Top 40;* TV Guide*; Van Halen;* The Wizard of Oz.

BIBLIOGRAPHY

Andersen, Christopher P. *Michael Jackson: Unauthorized.* New York: Simon & Schuster, 1994.

Brooks, Barnes. "A Star Idolized and Haunted, Michael Jackson Dies at 50." *New York Times*, June 25, 2009.

Campbell, Lisa D. *Michael Jackson: The King of Pop.* Boston: Branden Books, 1993.

Cascio, Frank, and Hilary Liftin. *My Friend Michael: An Ordinary Friendship with an Extraordinary Man.* New York: Morrow, 2011.

George, Nelson. *The Michael Jackson Story.* New York: Dell, 1984.

Gundersen, Edna. "Pop Icons at 50: Michael Jackson." *USA Today*, August 14, 2008.

Hirshey, Gerri. *Nowhere to Run: The Story of Soul Music.* New York: Times Books, 1984.

Jackson, Katherine, and Rich Wiseman. *My Family: The Jacksons.* New York: St. Martin's Paperbacks, 1990.

Jackson, La Toya, and Patricia Romanowski. *La Toya: Growing Up in the Jackson Family.* New York: Dutton, 1991.

Jackson, Michael. *Moonwalk.* New York: Doubleday, 1988.

Matthews, Gordon R. *Michael Jackson.* New York: Messner, 1984.

Nightingale, Annie. "The Loneliness of the Long-Playing Superstar." *Times* (London), November 12, 2011.

Taraborrelli, J. Randy. *Michael Jackson: The Magic and the Madness.* New York: Birch Lane Press, 1991.

Jackson, Reggie *(1946–)*

Reggie Jackson was a professional baseball player whose award-winning career spanned twenty-one years. He was the first player in Major League Baseball history to hit 100 or more home runs for three different teams: the Oakland A's, the New York Yankees, and the California Angels. Nicknamed "Mr. October" for his amazing play during World Series games, Jackson was inducted into the National Baseball Hall of Fame in 1993.

Jackson was born Reginald Martinez Jackson in Wyncote, Pennsylvania, on May 18, 1946. In 1967 he was chosen second in the amateur draft by the Oakland Athletics. He quickly established himself as a powerful home-run hitter who struck balls out of the park at a near-record pace. He first grabbed national headlines when he swatted a home run over the roof at Tiger Stadium during the 1971 All-Star Game in Detroit, Michigan, and the Oakland A's domination of the World Series from 1972 to 1974 kept him firmly planted in the public eye. Although a knee injury kept Jackson out of the Fall Classic in 1972, he returned the following season with a stellar performance, and the American League named him its Most Valuable Player with a .293 average and a league-leading thirty-two home runs. He was also named the World Series Most Valuable Player, establishing a postseason reputation that he would solidify in the following years. Proclaiming "Reginald Martinez Jackson is the best player on the best team in the sport," *Time* magazine put Jackson on the cover of its June 3, 1974, issue.

The new world of free agency gave the rising superstar the chance to test his value on the open market. In 1976 the New York Yankees responded with a lucrative five-year contract offer. Jackson leapt at the chance to play in the world's largest media market. The marriage of convenience between the swaggering Jackson and the club's dictatorial owner, Cleveland shipbuilder George M. Steinbrenner III, was to prove an eventful one.

Arriving in New York, Jackson almost immediately proclaimed himself "the straw who stirs the drink," alienating the Yankees' team captain, Thurman Munson, along with almost everyone else in town. Sportswriters found Jackson made for great copy, but Yankee manager Billy Martin could not stand him. Martin looked for every opportunity to humiliate his star slugger, benching him for no reason at one point and pulling him off the field midgame at another. Their feud came perilously close to blows on more than one occasion. Nevertheless, the Yankees steamed over the American League teams on their way to the pennant.

The 1977 World Series proved to be the high point of Jackson's career. Mr. October became the first player ever to hit five home runs in one World Series. He clouted three in the sixth game alone, on three consecutive pitches, off three different Los Angeles Dodger pitchers. That feat, never accomplished before, helped earn Jackson Most Valuable Player honors as the Yankees took the championship four games to two.

REGGIE!

That off-season, Jackson became the toast of New York. While still with the Oakland A's, he once boasted, "If I played in New York, they'd name a candy bar after me." Someone at Standard Brands Confectionery must have been listening, because in 1978 Jackson got his candy bar. The Reggie! bar was a crumbly lump of chocolate, peanuts, and corn syrup sculpted to the approximate diameter of a major-league baseball. It came packaged in an orange wrapper bearing the slugger's likeness.

Sportswriters had a field day with the unpalatable confection. One wrote that once unwrapped, the Reggie! bar told you how good it was. Another derided it as the only candy bar that tasted like a hot dog. But the ultimate verdict came from Yankee fans, 44,667 of whom were given free samples on April 13, 1978, when the Yankees opened their home campaign against the Chicago White Sox. In typical Jackson fashion, the slugger clouted a home run in his first at-bat. The raucous crowd then showered the field with Reggie! bars as Jackson made his trip around the bases. Orange wrappers quickly carpeted the green field. The only detractor from the prevailing air of absurdist resignation was White Sox manager Bob Lemon, who groused, "[There are] people starving all over the world and 30 billion calories are laying on the field."

In June 1978 the White Sox fired Lemon, and in July he replaced Martin as Yankee manager. The volatile Martin had finally worn out his welcome with a drunken screed against Jackson and Steinbrenner in which he famously declared, "One's a born liar, the other's convicted," an apparent reference to Steinbrenner's conviction for making illegal contributions to President Richard M. Nixon's reelection campaign. Undeterred, Lemon, Jackson, and the Yankees stormed to a second straight World Series championship.

Jackson soon wore out his own welcome with the team, and in 1982 Steinbrenner refused to renew his contract. Jackson then played a few seasons with the California Angels before returning to the Oakland A's for his final season in 1987. After retiring, Jackson served as a coach for several teams before accepting a front office position with the Yankees in 1996. In 1998 Steinbrenner fired him for charging thousands of dollars in unapproved expenses on his team credit card. In 2002 Jackson was rehabilitated as a Yankee when a plaque created in his honor was dedicated in Monument Park at Yankee Stadium. It reads, in part, "One of the most colorful and exciting players of his era . . . a prolific hitter who thrived in pressure situations." However, Jackson got in trouble with the team again in the summer of 2012 when he told *Sports Illustrated* that in his opinion Yankee third baseman Alex Rodriguez's career accomplishments were tainted because Rodriguez had admitted to using performance-enhancing drugs. In response the Yankees asked Jackson to stay away from all team functions for the remainder of the season.

OTHER INTERESTS

One of Jackson's interests is classic cars, and over the decades he built a personal collection of more than 100 vehicles. He has also owned automobile dealerships. Jackson has done a small amount of acting, including in the movies *The Naked Gun: From the Files of Police Squad!* (1988) and *Richie Rich* (1994). In 2007 ESPN aired the dramatic miniseries *The Bronx Is Burning*, which focuses on the contentious relationships among Steinbrenner, Martin, and Jackson. In 2009 Jackson spoke out against the steroid-fueled players who jumped past him on the all-time list of home run hitters: "It bothers me. A lot of Hall of Famers are very offended by this. I am starting to get affected, and I am hoping that those guys that get caught don't get into the Hall of Fame."

Robert E. Schnakenberg

SEE ALSO: *Baseball; ESPN; The New York Yankees; Sports Heroes; Steinbrenner, George;* Time; *World Series; Yankee Stadium.*

BIBLIOGRAPHY

Baker, Kevin. "Backtalk: The Day It Rained Candy Bars." *New York Times*, April 12, 1998. Accessed May 13, 2012. Available from http://www.nytimes.com/1998/04/12/sports/backtalk-the-day-it-rained-candy-bars.html?src=pm

Gallagher, Mark. *The Yankee Encyclopedia*, 6th ed. Champaign, IL: Sports Publishing, 2003.

Jackson, Reggie, and Mike Lupica. *Reggie: The Autobiography.* New York: Villard Books, 1984.

Miller, Stuart. *The 100 Greatest Days in New York Sports.* Boston: Houghton Mifflin, 2006.

"The Muscle and Soul of the A's Dynasty." *Time*, June 3, 1974.

Perry, Dayn. *Reggie Jackson: The Life and Thunderous Career of Baseball's Mr. October*. New York: HarperCollins, 2010.

Shatzkin, Mike, ed. *The Ballplayers: Baseball's Ultimate Biographical Reference*. New York: Morrow, 1990.

Shea, John. "Baseball Hall of Fame Agonizing Begins in Earnest Now." *San Francisco Chronicle*, January 11, 2012. Accessed May 13, 2012. Available from http://scrippsnews.com/content/shea-baseball-hall-fame-agonizing-begins-earnest-now

Ward, Robert. *Renegades*. Blue Ash, OH: Tyrus Books, 2012.

Jackson, Shirley *(1916–1965)*

About her short story "The Lottery," Shirley Jackson writes, "It was not my first published story, nor would it be my last, but I have been assured over and over that if it had been the only story I ever wrote or published, there would be people who would not forget my name." First printed in the *New Yorker* magazine in June 1948, the chilling story of ritual violence generated more mail to the magazine than any piece of fiction before or since, and hundreds of shocked readers canceled their subscriptions. Since then, "The Lottery" has been translated into hundreds of languages and made into a radio play, two television plays, a ballet, and even an opera. It is ubiquitous in short-story anthologies and part of the required curriculum of many high school English programs.

The story concerns a ceremonial custom in a small, unnamed town. With masterful strokes, Jackson builds a sense of trepidation and horror, describing a perfectly normal village making preparations for their annual lottery. Children gather piles of stones as the villagers arrive, excited and nervous, in the town square. The ritual is performed with the utmost seriousness and formality, with a few murmurs about other towns giving up their lotteries. Finally, Mrs. Hutchinson's name is chosen, and the villagers stone her to death.

Jackson avoids graphic violence or gross-out horror at all times. Her no-words-wasted style is especially evident in the last line of "The Lottery": "'It isn't fair, it isn't right,' Mrs. Hutchinson screamed, and then they were upon her." The ugly flow of blood that must accompany her appalling end is left to the imagination of the reader.

The torrent of mail that descended on the *New Yorker* offices could broadly be divided into three categories. Some readers wrote to demand an explanation for the story; others wrote abusive letters, venting their anger against Jackson for her "sick" surprise ending. The most bizarre and disturbing response came from those who inquired where these lotteries took place and whether they could go and watch.

Jackson generally refused to explain the meaning of the story but suggested in private to at least one friend that anti-

Semitism in North Bennington, Vermont, was at its heart. (Her husband, literary critic Stanley Edgar Hyman, was Jewish.) On another occasion she told a journalist, "I suppose I hoped, by setting a particularly brutal rite in the present and in my own village, to shock the readers with a graphic demonstration of the pointless violence and general inhumanity of their own lives [but] I gather that in some cases the mind just rebels. The number of people who expected Mrs. Hutchinson to win a Bendix washer at the end would amaze you."

Jackson was born in San Francisco on December 14, 1916, and grew up in California and in Rochester, New York. She graduated from Syracuse University in 1940 and married Hyman. They settled in North Bennington in 1945, where they owned an enormous library and hosted dinner parties for guests who included literary luminaries Bernard Malamud, Ralph Ellison, and Dylan Thomas. They also raised four children.

Jackson wrote dozens of short stories, most of which, like "The Lottery," concerned gothic terrors lurking just beneath the surface of everyday life. In addition, she authored a series of darkly funny stories about her family's bustling home life, collected in *Life among the Savages* (1953) and *Raising Demons* (1957). Unlike many horror writers, she had an elegant way with the English language. Famously, one critic notes, "Miss Jackson seemingly cannot write a poor sentence."

Jackson's novels *The Haunting of Hill House* (1959) and *We Have Always Lived in the Castle* (1962) are classics of the horror genre. Her understated yet intensely powerful brand of horror inspired even Stephen King, who dedicates his novel *Firestarter* "In memory of Shirley Jackson, who never had to raise her voice." King also writes that Eleanor Vance, the heroine of *The Haunting of Hill House*, "is surely the finest character to come out of the new [identity-centered] American gothic tradition," and, coupling her with Henry James, asserts that this novel and *The Turn of the Screw* are "the only two great novels of the supernatural in the last hundred years." In 1963 *The Haunting of Hill House* was made into a horror film, *The Haunting*. Directed in Britain by Robert Wise, it failed to live up to the standard of the book, but, in keeping with Jackson's literary style, no violence is shown directly, and an aura of fear pervades the film from start to finish.

A sometime witch, Jackson claimed that she could bring kitchen implements to the top of a drawer by "calling" them. She was an excessive smoker, drinker, and eater, as well as a workaholic writer prone to debilitating anxiety. After intense periods of productivity, she would endure periods of serious depression and also suffered on and off from asthma. She died of heart failure in North Bennington on August 8, 1965.

Jessy Randall

SEE ALSO: American Gothic; *Best Sellers; Horror Movies; King, Stephen; The* New Yorker.

BIBLIOGRAPHY

Hall, Joan Wylie. *Shirley Jackson: A Study of the Short Fiction.* New York: Twayne, 1993.

King, Stephen. *Danse Macabre.* New York: Everest House, 1981.

Murphy, Bernice M. *Shirley Jackson: Essays on the Literary Legacy.* Jefferson, NC: McFarland, 2005.

Oppenheimer, Judy. *Private Demons: The Life of Shirley Jackson.* New York: Putnam, 1988.

Jackson, "Shoeless" Joe *(1887–1951)*

"Shoeless" Joe Jackson endures in baseball lore as the game's tragic hero, a naive country boy in over his head. He became embroiled with big-time gamblers in the infamous "Black Sox" scandal of 1919 and was subsequently banned for life from the sport—cutting short an otherwise brilliant career.

The illiterate son of a southern miller, Jackson grew up near Greenville, South Carolina. He acquired his famous nickname while playing baseball with the local mill teams as a teenager. After buying new baseball cleats, Jackson found himself with blistered feet. Desperate to play and too sore to wear his old shoes, Jackson lumbered out to right field in stocking feet. The crowd picked up on Jackson's lack of footwear, and henceforth he became known as "Shoeless" Joe.

Jackson's stellar play in the mill leagues attracted major league scouts, and in 1908 he signed with the Philadelphia Athletics. Frightened by big cities and wary of leaving his family behind, Jackson initially refused to show up. He finally made his debut with the Athletics in 1909 but endured intense taunting from teammates and fans for his alleged ignorance and naïveté. A disheartened Jackson failed to live up to his promise with the Athletics, and manager Connie Mack shipped the young outfielder to the Cleveland Indians. In Cleveland Jackson developed into a star. In 1911, his first full season, Jackson batted .408; the following year, he batted .395. His stellar defense in the outfield and fearless base running made Jackson a complete ballplayer and launched him into the baseball stratosphere.

Strapped for cash, the Indians traded Jackson to Chicago in 1915 in exchange for three undistinguished players and $31,500. Jackson hit an uncharacteristically low .301 for the championship-winning 1917 White Sox but rebounded with a more typical .351 for the 1919 team (which lost that season's World Series to the Cincinnati Reds).

In September 1920, in the midst of one of Jackson's greatest seasons (batting .382 with 121 RBI), a shocking revelation rocked the country: eight White Sox players, including Jackson, had conspired with gamblers to fix the 1919 World Series. Jackson admitted his complicity in the scheme shortly after journalists had uncovered the story. According to baseball lore, as Jackson emerged from the Chicago courtroom where he and his teammates were standing trial, he stumbled upon a teary-eyed youngster whose only words to him were: "Say it ain't so, Joe." The grand jury ultimately acquitted all the players, but new baseball commissioner Judge Kenesaw Mountain Landis subsequently banned them from the sport for life. Jackson returned to his native South Carolina and started a dry-cleaning business, occasionally playing in sandlot and outlaw games.

A groundswell of support for Jackson's reinstatement to baseball developed after his death in 1951. Supporters of Jackson pushed for his reinstatement and admission to the Hall of Fame, pointing to his naïveté and to his .375 batting average in the World Series as evidence that he had not deliberately tanked the series. Writers romanticized Jackson's tragic story; the Chicago outfielder was the subject of W. P. Kinsella's wistful novel *Shoeless Joe* (1982), which was later adapted into the major motion picture *Field of Dreams* (1989). The 1988 movie *Eight Men Out* also attempted to exculpate Jackson and the others from their

"Shoeless" Joe Jackson. *"Shoeless" Joe Jackson, center, of the Cleveland Naps (later Indians), talks with Detroit Tiger stars Ty Cobb, left, and Sam Crawford before a game in 1913.* MARK RUCKER/ TRANSCENDENTAL GRAPHICS/GETTY IMAGES.

misdeeds, suggesting that the gambling fix represented the players' only escape from Chicago owner Charles Comiskey's penury.

Scott Tribble

SEE ALSO: *Baseball; Black Sox Scandal;* Field of Dreams*; World Series.*

BIBLIOGRAPHY

Asinof, Eliot. *Eight Men Out: The Black Sox and the 1919 World Series.* New York: Henry Holt, 1963.

Frommer, Harvey. *Shoeless Joe and Ragtime Baseball.* Reno: University of Nevada Press, 2008.

Gropman, Donald. *Say It Ain't So, Joe: The Story of Shoeless Joe Jackson.* Boston: Little, Brown, 1979.

Kinsella, W. P. *Shoeless Joe.* New York: Ballantine Books, 1982.

Rader, Benjamin G. *Baseball: A History of America's Game.* Urbana: University of Illinois Press, 1992.

Shatzkin, Mike, ed. *The Ballplayers: Baseball's Ultimate Biographical Reference.* New York: Arbor House, 1990.

The Jackson Five

When Motown recording artists the Jackson Five burst upon the music scene in 1969, the group of five brothers followed an extremely successful career trajectory that launched the youngest brother, Michael Jackson, into superstardom. But as a group, the Jackson Five was more than the sum of its parts, or even the sum total of Michael's charisma: all the brothers were talented singers and songwriters in their own right. During the 1970s they enjoyed a lengthy string of hit singles, becoming the most popular black soul vocal group of all time.

The Jackson Five comprised Jackie (born May 4, 1951), Tito (born October 15, 1953), Jermaine (born December 11, 1954), Marlon (born March 12, 1957), and Michael (August 29, 1958–June 25, 2009)—all of whom sang. The five brothers were born into a large family run by authoritative patriarch Joseph, an aspiring amateur musician who occasionally played around their hometown of Gary, Indiana. In addition to those five brothers, there were three sisters (Rebbie, La Toya, and Janet) and another brother, Randy, who joined the group when they moved to Columbia Records and were redubbed the Jacksons.

The Jacksons were a musical family. Joseph and his wife, Katherine, often led the brothers in singing harmony-rich songs in the family's living room during their childhood. As the result of constant practice overseen by Joseph, the boys—soon dubbed the Jackson Five—evolved into a popular regional act that eventually came to the attention of Motown president and founder Berry Gordy. In 1969 Motown signed the group, and their first single, "I Want You Back," went to number one on the Billboard pop charts in January 1970.

This breakthrough began a string of thirteen Top 20 pop singles, including "ABC," "I'll Be There," "Never Can Say Goodbye," "Mama's Pearl," and "Dancing Machine." The Jackson Five were among the last groups to produce hits following Motown's tradition of using in-house songwriting and recording teams, a practice that had become increasingly infrequent once Motown artists Marvin Gaye and Stevie Wonder had begun to break out on their own. And soon, the assembly-line Motown production techniques began to displease the

The Jackson Five. *The Jackson Five included, clockwise from bottom left, brothers Michael, Tito, Jackie, Jermaine, and Marlon.* MICHAEL OCHS RCHIVES/GETTY IMAGES.

maturing Jackson brothers, who also demanded more artistic control. It was this issue that led to their departure from Motown, prompting both a $20 million lawsuit by Motown for breach of contract and the family's first major split, when Jermaine stayed with Motown while his brothers signed with Epic Records in 1976. Randy filled Jermaine's shoes, and the group was renamed the Jacksons.

During the 1970s the Jackson Five virtually formed a franchise, with regular tours, an animated cartoon featuring the brothers, and a 1976 variety show hosted by the brothers. The Jacksons continued to record sporadically throughout the 1980s, but they could not match the success they achieved during their Motown years. The group's last album, *2300 Jackson Street*, was released in 1989 and did not include Michael, who had already left to pursue a solo career. The Jacksons were inducted into the Rock and Roll Hall of Fame in 1997 and came together for a reunion at Madison Square Garden on September 7, 2001, marking the last time that the group would play together.

Although all the Jacksons eventually struck out on their own as solo artists, Michael became the most successful of the family. His fame reached its apex with *Thriller* (1982), which sold more than 40 million copies worldwide, charted at number one in every European and North American country, generated an unprecedented seven Top 10 singles, and won eight Grammy Awards. Even though none of the other brothers came close to rivaling Michael's commercial sales, they remained a near constant, though not overwhelming, presence on the R&B charts.

In the twenty-first century Michael's career began to decline as his life became overwhelmed by sex scandals and drugs, ending in his death in 2009 of a drug overdose. More than a billion people are estimated to have watched the televised memorial service. In contrast, Janet, who also pursued a solo music career, remained strong through this period, selling more than 100 million records and ranking as one of the richest women in entertainment by *Forbes* magazine. After the death of Michael, the Jacksons made efforts to reunite but suffered discord in relation to Michael's legacy. Through all this turmoil the Jackson family's omnipresence in popular culture guaranteed their status as a de facto musical dynasty.

Kembrew McLeod

SEE ALSO: *Gordy, Berry; Grammy Awards; Jackson, Janet; Jackson, Michael; Motown; Pop Music; Rhythm and Blues; Soul Music; Wonder, Stevie.*

BIBLIOGRAPHY

Henning, Shawn. *Michael Jackson: The Book the Media Doesn't Want You to Read.* Bloomington, IN: AuthorHouse, 2009.

Jackson, Katherine, with Richard Wiseman. *My Family, the Jacksons.* New York: St. Martin's, 1990.

Taylor, Paula. *On Stage with the Jackson Five.* New York: Creative Company, 1975.

Jakes, John *(1932–)*

John Jakes was born in Chicago on March 31, 1932. His parents fostered a love of libraries in him, and his association with books has followed him throughout his life. Jakes has enjoyed a long and distinguished writing career but has worked hard for his success. He is the prolific author of more than seventy books and 200 short stories in such diverse categories as mystery and suspense, science fiction, Western, and children's literature. He is, however, best known for his best-selling historical fiction and intergenerational family sagas.

Jakes was so prolific in the mid- to late twentieth century that one rumor stated that John Jakes was actually the pen name for a group of writers, historical researchers, and publishers. His works have sold millions of copies each, and several have had the distinction of being on the *New York Times* best-seller list. His historical novels have been so influential that he is often referred to as the "godfather of the historical novel" and "the people's author."

Jakes's early plans to be an actor lasted until he sold his first short story and felt the exhilaration of publication. He graduated from DePauw University in 1953 with a degree in creative writing and went on to earn a master's degree in American literature from Ohio State University. He also has been awarded several honorary degrees and has served as a writer in residence and research fellow at several universities. Such recognition shows his dedication to the historical accuracy of his works and his influence as a popular historian.

Jakes worked at several advertising agencies as a copywriter after graduation while devoting his spare time to the pursuit of his writing career. In *John Jakes: A Critical Companion*, Mary Ellen Jones quotes him as remarking that his inspiration came from "the swashbuckling adventure films of the 1930s and 1940s" that offered adventure and romance within a framework of loosely based historical events. His most famous works include the eight-volume *Kent Family Chronicles* (1974–1979), the *North and South* trilogy (1982, 1984, and 1987), *California Gold* (1989), *Homeland* (1993), and the *Homeland* sequel *American Dreams* (1998). Six of his novels have been made into television miniseries, with the *North and South* saga being one of the highest-rated miniseries of all times. Despite his advancing age, Jakes continued to put out new material into the twenty-first century, including 2002's *Charleston*, and many of his older titles have found new readers through reprinting.

Jakes has enjoyed a wide following as a writer of American historical fiction. He traditionally places his fictional characters into a background of real historical events and personages based on extensive research. Aware that he is often the reader's only source of history, he pays a remarkable amount of attention to detail, which makes his works dominate in the important field of public history. Jakes also understands that the author must entertain the reader in order to educate them. Jones characterizes his works as promoting "an optimistic affirmation of America and its principles." Jakes's popularity will ensure his lasting reputation as "America's History Teacher."

Marcella Bush Treviño

SEE ALSO: *Best Sellers; Made-for-Television Movies; The* New York Times*; Television.*

BIBLIOGRAPHY

Budick, Emily Miller. *Fiction and Historical Consciousness: The American Romance Tradition.* New Haven, CT: Yale University Press, 1989.

Hamilton, Geoff, and Brian Jones. *Encyclopedia of American Popular Fiction.* New York: Facts On File, 2009.

Jones, Mary Ellen. *John Jakes: A Critical Companion.* Westport, CT: Greenwood, 1996.

James, Elmore *(1918–1963)*

Undeniably the most influential electric slide guitarist of all time, Elmore James revolutionized the blues with his raw, sharp sound. Born in Richland, Mississippi, in 1918, James first learned to play on a homemade instrument fashioned from a broom handle and a lard can. He became an itinerant musician in his teens, frequently meeting up with other players, including the legendary Robert Johnson and Howlin' Wolf. After serving in the navy during World War II, James moved to Memphis and became a frequent guest on local radio stations.

James's first solo recording, "Dust My Broom," became the biggest rhythm-and-blues hit of 1951. Not long after the session, he moved to Chicago, assembling his all-star band the Broomdusters and recording for the Chess label. Over the next ten years he shuttled back and forth between Chicago and Mississippi before suffering a fatal heart attack in 1963. In 1980 James was elected to the Blues Foundation's Hall of Fame, and in 1992 he was inducted into the Rock and Roll Hall of Fame.

Marc R. Sykes

SEE ALSO: *Blues; Electric Guitar; Howlin' Wolf; Johnson, Robert; Rhythm and Blues.*

BIBLIOGRAPHY

Franz, Steve. *The Amazing Secret History of Elmore James.* St. Louis, MO: BlueSource Publications, 2003.

Oakley, Giles. *The Devil's Music: A History of the Blues.* New York: Taplinger, 1976.

Palmer, Robert. *Deep Blues.* New York: Viking, 1981.

James, Harry *(1916–1983)*

Reared in a circus atmosphere by parents who toured with the Big Top, Harry James was one of the star trumpet players of the swing era. As a child he studied trumpet with his father and won the Texas State Championship with a solo at age fourteen. James made his recording debut with the Ben Pollack Band in September 1936. Three months later he was a featured sideman with the Benny Goodman Band, a springboard to forming his own swinging, Basie-style band in January 1939. Ironically, James's biggest hits with his own band were not his upbeat numbers like "Two O'clock Jump," but his dulcet-tone, non-jazz solos like "You Made Me Love You." The band remained widely popular into the late 1950s.

Benjamin Griffith

SEE ALSO: *Basie, Count; Big Bands; Blues; Goodman, Benny; Rock and Roll.*

BIBLIOGRAPHY

Balliett, Whitney. *American Musician.* New York: Oxford University Press, 1986.

Collier, James Lincoln. *Benny Goodman and the Swing Era.* New York: Oxford University Press, 1989.

Levinson, Peter J. *Trumpet Blues: The Life of Harry James.* New York: Oxford University Press, 2001.

Simon, George T. *The Big Bands.* New York: Macmillan, 1967.

LeBron, James *(1984–)*

LeBron James is among the most gifted players in the history of the National Basketball Association (NBA). At 6 feet, 8 inches tall and 250 pounds, "King" James is an intimidating presence on the court. He uses his rare combination of speed, agility, and raw strength to dominate opposing players and to dictate the flow of a game—whether by driving the length of the court for an emphatic slam dunk or by hitting a fall-away baseline jumper over a swarm of defenders. James is among the league's most creative passers, and his athleticism and tenacity as a defender have earned him repeated NBA All-Defensive honors. Although his basketball talent remains unquestioned, his polarizing public persona has sometimes alienated fans. Among his most controversial actions was appearing in a July 2010 ESPN network special to announce his departure from his home state's beloved Cleveland Cavaliers for the Miami Heat.

CHILDHOOD

James overcame tremendous obstacles to reach the heights of NBA stardom. He was born on December 30, 1984, in Akron,

Ohio. Raised by a single mother, he moved frequently during his early childhood and at one point spent two years in a foster home. A turning point came around the time he entered middle school, when he began competitively playing basketball. He quickly established himself as one of the top players in his age group, leading his Amateur Athletic Union team to the national championship game when he was in eighth grade.

By the time he entered high school, James had already begun to earn widespread attention as one of the most promising basketball prospects in the country. As a freshman at St. Vincent–St. Mary High School, he averaged eighteen points per game and led the Fighting Irish to an undefeated season and the state title. A year later, he raised his scoring average to 25.2 points per game while earning praise for his rebounding, passing, and defense. During his senior year, he scored 31.6 points per game and took St. Vincent–St. Mary to its third state championship in four years.

CLEVELAND CAVALIERS

As the 2003 NBA draft approached, there was little doubt that he would be the number one overall pick even though he had never played college ball. The first-round selection belonged to the Cleveland Cavaliers, which snatched him up, allowing him to launch his professional career in his home state. Immediately appearing in the starting lineup, he averaged 20.9 points and 5.9 assists per game during the 2003–2004 season and won the NBA Rookie of the Year Award.

As his NBA career took off, James quickly emerged as one of the league's most marketable players, signing lucrative endorsement deals with Nike, McDonald's, Coca-Cola, and other major brands. In his second season, he established himself as a perennial all-star, finishing second among NBA scorers with 2,175 total points and leading the league in minutes played (3,388). By 2005–2006 he had helped transform the Cavaliers into a legitimate championship contender, leading the team to its first postseason appearance since the 1997–1998 season. James averaged 31.4 points per game during the season and was named the Most Valuable Player (MVP) of the NBA All-Star game.

A year later, he led Cleveland to the NBA Finals for the first time in franchise history. Although the Cavs were ultimately swept by an overpowering San Antonio Spurs team in the championship series, James left his mark on the postseason, scoring 25.1 points per game. He also averaged 8.1 rebounds and eight assists. In 2007–2008 he led NBA scorers with an average of 27 points per game and won his second All-Star MVP Award. In the playoffs he averaged 28.2 points per game, and the Cavs pushed the heavily favored Boston Celtics to Game Seven of the Eastern Conference semifinals. In the final game James engaged in a memorable scoring duel with Celtics forward Paul Pierce. Although Pierce and the Celtics won the game, 97–92, James won the individual matchup, leading all scorers with 45 points.

By the 2008–2009 season, there was little doubt that James had emerged as one of the league's most dominant players. That season he led the Cavaliers to a league-best mark of 66–16 while earning his first league MVP Award. He elevated his game in the playoffs, averaging 35.3 points, 9.1 rebounds, and 7.3 assists per game; however, the Cavaliers were ultimately upset by the Orlando Magic in the Eastern Conference Finals. A year later, after James again was named the NBA's MVP, the Cavs seemed poised to make a run at the NBA title. But the year again ended in disappointment when Cleveland lost to the Celtics in the Eastern Conference semifinals.

DEPARTURE FOR THE MIAMI HEAT

With James poised to become a free agent, many in the media wondered whether he had played his last game in Cleveland. The answer came on July 8, 2010, when ESPN aired *The Decision*, a live broadcast during which James famously announced that he was going to take his "talents to South Beach and join the Miami Heat." His choice was a crushing blow to Cleveland fans. The press harshly criticized him, and many commentators questioned his decision to transform his free agency into a media spectacle.

Unfazed by the negative attention, James thrived in his first season in Miami, Florida. Playing alongside teammates Dwyane Wade and Chris Bosh, James averaged 26.7 points per game in 2010–2011 as the Heat decimated the Eastern Conference en route to the NBA Finals. But James again fell short in his quest for a title as the Heat lost to the Dallas Mavericks in six games. At the conclusion of the series, many writers began to question James's ability to perform in the clutch; during the series, he had averaged only 17.8 points per game and had failed to make an offensive impact late in games. Commenting on the series, *New York Times* writer William C. Rhoden referred to James's "fourth-quarter disappearing acts."

James further raised eyebrows in his final press conference after the series, when he appeared to become defensive in the face of critics. "At the end of the day, all the people that was rooting on me to fail, they have to wake up tomorrow and have the same life that they had before they woke up today," he told the media. In spite of the disappointing end to his first year with Miami, he remained one of the top players in the league. At only twenty-seven, James became one of the Top 50 NBA scorers of all time, and his career average of 27.6 points per game was the third highest in NBA history (behind superstars Michael Jordan and Wilt Chamberlain). In 2012, things were looking up again when James and the Heat won the NBA Finals.

Steve Meyer

SEE ALSO: *Basketball; Chamberlain, Wilt; Coca-Cola; ESPN; Jordan, Michael; McDonald's; National Basketball Association (NBA); Nike; Sports Heroes.*

BIBLIOGRAPHY

Gonzales, John, "LeBron James Cements His Status as an Antihero." *Philadelphia Inquirer*, June 16, 2011, E2.

Raab, Scott. *The Whore of Akron: One Man's Search for the Soul of LeBron James*. New York: HarperCollins, 2011.

Rhoden, William C. "James Is Still Seeking His Moment, but Time Is on His Side." *New York Times*, June 12, 2011, 5.

Zillgit, Jeff. "LeBron Must Take Disillusionment to South Beach." *USA Today*, June 14, 2011, 8C.

James Bond Films

The James Bond films, concerning the adventures of the debonair British secret agent, constitute one of the most success-

Sean Connery as James Bond. *Sean Connery played James Bond in the 1963 film* From Russia with Love, *one of the seven films in which he starred as the secret agent.* UNITED ARTIST/GETTY IMAGES.

ful series of films in cinema history, with twenty-two official films released between 1962 and 2011. Collectively they are known for a number of elements, including spectacular stunts, outrageous villains, and beautiful women. The films have survived multiple changes in the actors playing Bond and changing times as well, to captivate the public imagination the way few other series have.

FROM PRINT TO FILM

The roots of the Bond character begin with British author Ian Fleming, who served in World War II as a member of British Intelligence. In the early 1950s he began a career as a writer with the publication of *Casino Royale*, a hard-boiled adventure about British Intelligence agent James Bond. The book contained many elements for which the films would eventually be renowned: an exotic location (the casinos of Monaco), an outrageous villain (Soviet agent Le Chiffre), and a beautiful woman (the doomed Vesper Lynd).

Fleming's books were an instant sensation, with their mixture of high living, violence, and sex proving irresistible to readers. Inevitably, film and television producers courted Fleming for the rights to his creation, but found little success. One such failed deal, with Irish film producer Kevin McClory in 1959, would come back to haunt Fleming.

In 1961 Fleming closed a deal with producers Harry Saltzman and Albert "Cubby" Broccoli to make the first Bond film, *Dr. No*. While its pace and style may seem slow and old-fashioned to contemporary audiences, the film's casual violence and even more casual sex shocked and excited movie audiences of the 1960s. Scottish actor Sean Connery, who played Bond, became a star for his tough, ruthless portrayal of the secret agent. The image of the film's love interest, actress Ursula Andress, rising from the ocean in a white bikini with a knife strapped to her side has become an indelible commentary on female sex appeal.

Fleming died in 1964, but his most famous creation was destined to outlive him. A second film was soon in production, and when *From Russia with Love* was released in 1963, it found more success than *Dr. No*. With the release of *Goldfinger* in 1964 the series reached its highest pinnacle yet. The film, concerning Bond's efforts to stop a madman's attempt to detonate a nuclear warhead in the Fort Knox gold depository, became one of highest-grossing movies of its time. It captured the public's imagination with its fantastic imagery and set a standard future Bond films would have to work hard to match: the body of a nude woman covered in gold paint; production designer Ken Adam's spectacular stainless steel Fort Knox; Bond's Aston Martin DB-5, a classic automobile equipped with a number of deadly gadgets; the most famous Bond woman of all, Honor Blackman (fresh from her role of Mrs. Cathy Gale on the British TV spy series *The Avengers*) playing pilot and martial arts expert Pussy Galore; mad villain Auric Goldfinger and his lust for gold; and Goldfinger's lethal henchman, Oddjob, and his razor-edged bowler hat. Connery was never more appealing to audiences. His blend of ruthlessness and humor defined the part of Bond for a generation.

EVOLUTION OF THE FRANCHISE

Connery starred in the next two Bond films: *Thunderball* (1965) and *You Only Live Twice* (1967). When the novel *Thunderball* was published in 1961, it became the source of litigation from McClory, who accused Fleming of using material they had developed together in 1959. McClory won the lawsuit and was involved in the 1965 production of the film, which concerned the terrorist hijacking of a pair of nuclear warheads by Bond's archenemies, the forces of SPECTRE. The Bond series reached fantastic heights in *You Only Live Twice*, with its gorgeous Japanese scenery and incredible technology of sleek space rockets, along with SPECTRE's glimmering headquarters in the heart of a dormant volcano. It also marked the first on-screen appearance of one of Bond's more sinister foils, Ernst Stavro Blofeld, played by Donald Pleasence.

On Her Majesty's Secret Service (1969) was the first Bond film to feature an actor other than Connery in the role of the deadly agent. George Lazenby, an Australian actor, took over the role. While competent, he lacked Connery's appeal, and conflicts with producers and agents prevented him from taking the role again. *On Her Majesty's Secret Service* is considered by some purists to be one of the better Bond films; it hews closely to its source novel and features former *Avengers* star Diana Rigg as Bond's doomed wife, Tracy. Box-office results did not reach the heights they had for the first three films, however, and Connery was coaxed back for a farewell performance in *Diamonds Are Forever* (1971). The baton was passed again when Roger Moore took over the part in *Live and Let Die* (1973). Moore's portrayal differed considerably from Connery's; Moore lacked Connery's sense of menace, but compensated with his own sophistication and sense of humor, creating a lighter kind of Bond film, which was perfect for the jaded 1970s.

Moore returned in *The Man with the Golden Gun* to face off against Christopher Lee's villain, Scaramanga, but box-office receipts were disappointing. Broccoli bought out his partner Saltzman, and came back in 1977 with *The Spy Who Loved Me*, Moore's third turn as Bond and the most lavish to date. It found tremendous success with audiences. The film was laden with expensive sets and elaborate stunts, including a sleek sports car that transformed into a submersible vehicle. It also included the steel-toothed villain Jaws, played by the imposing Richard Kiel. Moore returned again in the successful *Moonraker* (1979), which took advantage of the science fiction craze spawned by the blockbuster *Star Wars* (1977). It had Bond in an outer space adventure centered on the *Moonraker* space shuttle.

For Your Eyes Only (1981) marked a return to more realistic espionage adventure that continued in Moore's next two efforts as Bond, *Octopussy* (1983) and *A View to a Kill* (1985). *A View to a Kill* was Moore's last film as Bond, and respected stage and film actor Timothy Dalton assumed the role. His first outing, *The Living Daylights* (1987), was a moderate success. His next effort, *License to Kill* (1989), was poorly received by critics and fans alike. While Dalton was a superb actor who stayed true to Fleming's characterization of Bond as a dark, driven man, his grim performances simply came as too much of a change after the lighthearted Moore. The Bond saga then endured a six-year hiatus, owing to protracted legal and financial troubles involving the films' producers and studio, Metro-Goldwyn-Mayer/United Artists. When Bond returned, however, it was with a bang.

A MORE MODERN BOND

Goldeneye (named for Ian Fleming's Jamaica estate) was released in 1995 to excellent reviews and the highest ticket sales in the series' history. Irish actor Pierce Brosnan assumed the role at last (after briefly having the part and then losing it to Dalton due to his commitment to the television series *Remington Steele*) to great acclaim. His mixture of Connery's toughness, Moore's humor, and his own good looks and skills as an actor made him a suitable candidate for the role. His next effort, *Tomorrow Never Dies* (1997) was another huge box-office and critical success. Brosnan also starred in *The World Is Not Enough* (1999) and ended his run as Bond with *Die Another Day* in 2002.

For a time, it seemed as though the series might have finally run its course. The formulaic nature of the films and what many perceived as the overuse of special effects turned away some moviegoers. However, it was announced in 2005 that British actor Daniel Craig would be the new Bond, and the series was rejuvenated. Craig's approach to Bond is much darker, and his movies have reflected that tone. *Casino Royale* was released in 2006 and was a box-office and critical success. The follow-up film, *Quantum of Solace* (2008) also performed well and has helped solidify the franchise.

Certain unofficial Bond productions have seen the light of day through the years. Eon Productions did not obtain the rights to *Casino Royale* in 1961—they had already been sold for an October 21, 1954, black-and-white episode of the CBS television series *Climax!* starring American actor Barry Nelson as an American agent named "Jimmy" Bond. These rights were then bought for a late 1960s spoof of the Bond phenomenon starring David Niven, Orson Welles, and Woody Allen. McClory's *Thunderball* rights led to *Never Say Never Again* (1983), which featured one last encore by Sean Connery as Bond.

More than just a series of massively successful films, Bond has worked his way into the fabric of American culture. His name and certain other phrases—license to kill, Agent 007—have become synonymous with action, adventure, and a glamorous lifestyle, as well as the gadgets and top-secret equipment Bond uses under the direction of the professorial "Q" character, played by several actors over the years but most notably by Desmond Llewelyn. The Bond series has spawned uncounted spoofs and imitators, from the 1960s spy craze that included the Matt Helm films, the Flint movies, and the television series *Mission: Impossible*, *The Man from U.N.C.L.E.*, and *The Wild, Wild West*, to such 1990s productions as the spectacular *True Lies* (1994) and the affectionate series of spoofs that began with *Austin Powers: International Man of Mystery* (1997). Bond theme songs have frequently become Top 40 hits. Moreover, the Bond films have in large part set the bar for the action film genre with their incredible stunts and high production values.

Bond also reflects the changing times. The Bond of Connery—sexist, violent, and cruel—that was so popular in the 1960s changed with the attitudes of the times, especially concerning women, into the more gentle and funny Bond of Moore in the late 1970s and 1980s. As the Cold War ended, Dalton's Bond found himself facing a maniacal drug dealer in *License to Kill*, and the AIDS crisis prompted a monogamous (!) Bond in *The Living Daylights*. In the 1990s Brosnan's Bond faced ex-Soviet agents in *Goldeneye* and a crazed media baron in *Tomorrow Never Dies*. Reflecting contemporary health trends, Bond even quit smoking.

Jay Parrent

SEE ALSO: *Allen, Woody;* The Avengers*; Cold War; Fleming, Ian;* Get Smart*;* The Man from U.N.C.L.E.*; MGM (Metro-Goldwyn-Mayer);* Mission: Impossible*;* Star Wars*; Top 40; Welles, Orson; World War II.*

BIBLIOGRAPHY

Benson, Raymond. *The James Bond Bedside Companion*. New York: Dodd, Mead, 1984.

Cork, John. *James Bond Encyclopedia*. London: Dorling Kindersley, 2009.

Rubin, Steven Jay. *The Complete James Bond Movie Encyclopedia*. Chicago: Contemporary Books, 1995.

Japanese American Internment Camps

Between February and November 1942, nearly 120,000 residents of Japanese descent were evacuated from their homes on the West Coast of the United States and sent to government War Relocation Authority camps. Many of these Japanese and Japanese Americans would spend the remainder of World War II in the camps, which were located in Gila River, Arizona; Granada, Colorado; Heart Mountain, Wyoming; Jerome, Arkansas; Manzanar, California; Minidoka, Idaho; Poston, Arizona; Rohwer, Arkansas; Topaz, Utah; and Tule Lake, California. The largest camp, the one at Tule Lake, housed nearly 19,000 internees, while the one at Granada held about 7,000.

The internees lived in crudely built barracks and ate, bathed, and washed clothes in communal facilities. Each camp was surrounded by barbed wire and guarded by armed soldiers. The first camp, in Manzanar, opened in March 1942. Nearly two years later the government began closing the camps, starting with the one in Jerome in June 1944 and ending with the one in Tule Lake in March 1946.

Internment of the Japanese was authorized by President Franklin D. Roosevelt in Executive Order 9066 (February 19, 1942), which sanctioned the evacuation of any and all persons from military zones established along the western coastline of the United States. Although the federal government also viewed persons of German and Italian descent with suspicion, only residents of Japanese ancestry were forced to move to the camps.

President Roosevelt authorized the order because Japan attacked Pearl Harbor, Hawaii, on December 7, 1941, drawing the country into World War II. Following the attack, government officials—including U.S. Attorney General Francis Biddle, Los Angeles Congressman Leland Ford, and California Attorney General Earl Warren—called for securing the Japanese population of the West Coast. They believed that these Japanese had helped plan the attack on Pearl Harbor and hoped the internment would prevent further acts of disloyalty.

In fact, studies indicate that anti-Japanese sentiment, which had been building on the West Coast since the late nineteenth century, played a role in the forced evacuation. These studies point to the fact that only Japanese living on the West Coast were forced to live in camps—not those living in Hawaii or on the East Coast—and that the people calling for the action were California nativists, laborers, and farmers, who had long viewed Japanese immigrants as social and economic threats. The 1982 report issued by the Commission on Wartime Relocation and Internment of Civilians concluded that the removal of Japanese residents was not a military necessity and that it occurred because of racism, wartime hysteria, and poor political leadership.

Under the direction of Lieutenant General John L. DeWitt, the government first evacuated the Japanese to assembly centers at county fairgrounds and racetracks and then to the camps. In some locations, such as Terminal Island in San Pedro, California, Japanese residents were given as few as two days to dispose of, or store, their belongings before departing. In other areas, the Japanese had several weeks to prepare. Although the Federal Reserve Bank and the Farm Security Administration helped make arrangements for the sale or storage of property and belongings, many Japanese lost hundreds of thousands of dollars through the quick sales of their homes and land at below-market prices. While in camp the internees suffered additional losses through vandalism, arson, and neglect of the belongings that had been stored.

Life in the camps was difficult. Internees had lost their jobs, social networks, and educational opportunities and were isolated from the rest of society. Angered by the loss of their rights and freedom and bitter toward the U.S. government, internees sometimes directed their hostility toward one another. In some camps riots broke out during clashes between pro-Japanese and pro-American factions. A loyalty test administered by the War Relocation Administration also helped to factionalize the internees.

As a result of the turbulence and the living conditions, hundreds of young Japanese left the camps when the opportunity arose. Colleges, such as Oberlin College in Ohio, sponsored Japanese students, allowing them to relocate and resume their education. Christian churches arranged for Japanese internees to work in homes and offices located in the South and Midwest. In addition, more than 1,000 Japanese men joined the U.S. military forces and served in the all-Japanese 442nd Regimental Combat Team.

Although many Japanese protested the relocation, four individuals—Fred T. Korematsu, Mitsuye Endo, Minoru Yasui, and Gordon K. Hirabayashi—challenged the constitutionality of the relocation order through the courts. Initially all four petitions were denied. But in December 1944 the U.S. Supreme Court decided that Endo's detention in the camps violated her civil rights. Following this decision, in January 1945, the War Department rescinded the evacuation orders and arranged for the internees to leave the camps.

It was not until the 1970s that branches of the U.S. government acknowledged any wrongdoing. In 1976 President Gerald R. Ford proclaimed that the evacuation was wrong. The 1982 commission report and its condemnation of the relocation sent an even stronger message. In 1983 Korematsu, Hirabayashi, and Minoru refiled their petitions, which the court granted. The change in political tenor encouraged the Japanese to seek redress and reparations for the forced relocation. Their organizing efforts culminated in September 1987, when the U.S. House of Representatives formally apologized to the former internees and provided $1.2 billion as compensation.

Midori Takagi

SEE ALSO: *World War II.*

BIBLIOGRAPHY

Commission on Wartime Relocation and Internment of Civilians. *Personal Justice Denied.* Washington, DC: Government Printing Office, 1982.

Daniels, Roger; Sandra C. Taylor; and Harry H. L. Kitano; et al., eds. *Japanese Americans from Relocation to Redress*, rev. ed. Seattle: University of Washington Press, 1991.

Girdner, Audrie, and Anne Loftis. *The Great Betrayal: The Evacuation of the Japanese-Americans during World War II.* New York: Macmillan, 1969.

Houston, Jeanne Wakatsuki, and James D. Houston. *Farewell to Manzanar: A True Story of Japanese American Experience during and after the World War II Internment.* Boston: Houghton-Mifflin, 1973.

Irons, Peter H. *Justice at War.* Berkeley: University of California Press, 1993.

Jaws

Arguably the first of what is now a familiar Hollywood staple, the "summer blockbuster," the film *Jaws* was released to an eager public in June 1975. The film's plot centered on a series of fatal shark attacks at the beaches of a New England resort town and the efforts of an ill-matched trio of men to kill the 25-foot-long great white shark responsible for the deaths. Promoted through a massive advertising campaign and given unprecedentedly widespread distribution by Universal Studios, *Jaws* quickly became the first film in cinematic history to gross more than $100 million during its initial release.

With its rousing adventure and horror elements and its crowd-pleasing finale, the film became a worldwide phenomenon and for at least one summer made millions of people very

***Robert Shaw in* Jaws.** *Robert Shaw stands over the fearsome mechanical shark that played the title role in the 1975 horror film* Jaws. UNIVERSAL PICTURES/GETTY IMAGES.

nervous about swimming in the ocean. *Jaws* received three Academy Awards in 1976 and continues to appear on many "best of" lists, including several of the American Film Institute's Top 100. *Jaws* also established its unknown twenty-seven-year-old director, Steven Spielberg, as a powerful creative force, destined to achieve financial and critical success consistently in the "new Hollywood" with popular films such as *Close Encounters of the Third Kind* (1977), *Raiders of the Lost Ark* (1981), *E.T. The Extra-Terrestrial* (1982), *Schindler's List* (1993), *Jurassic Park* (1993), *Amistad* (1997), and *Saving Private Ryan* (1998). In 2001 the Library of Congress placed *Jaws* in the National Film Registry.

JAWS THE NOVEL

However remarkable the success of *Jaws* the film, the novel upon which it was based was a literary phenomenon in its own right. In January 1973 author Peter Benchley submitted to New York publishing house Doubleday the final draft of a novel inspired by Benchley's memory of a monstrous great white shark caught off the coast of Montauk, New York, in 1964. In a documentary accompanying the laser-disc release of the film, Benchley remembers that several titles, such as *Stillness in the Water*, were considered and rejected for the novel before the simple, visceral *Jaws* was chosen. Very quickly, Bantam paid for paperback rights to the novel, and Hollywood producers David Brown and Richard Zanuck bought not only the film rights but also the services of Benchley for a first-draft screenplay. All of this early interest in the novel, combined with book-club deals and an aggressive promotional strategy by Doubleday and Bantam, ensured *Jaws*'s climb to the top of the *New York Times* best-seller list, where it stayed for months.

The book is divided into three sections. The first section opens with a nighttime shark attack upon a skinny-dipping young woman named Christine Watkins. When her mutilated body is discovered on the Amity town beach the next morning, police chief Martin Brody urges Mayor Larry Vaughan to close the beaches for a few days. Vaughan refuses, and the shark then kills a six-year-old boy and an elderly man in two separate attacks in full view of horrified beachgoers. Forced to close the beaches, the town selectmen hire a local fisherman, Ben Gardner, to catch the shark, but Brody and his deputy Hendricks later discover Gardner's empty, drifting boat and realize that the shark has killed yet another person. At this point, an ichthyologist from Wood's Hole, Matt Hooper, arrives at the invitation of the town's newspaper editor.

Hooper's arrival leads into the novel's second section, which focuses on the domestic tensions between Brody and his wife, Ellen. Ellen's discontent with her married life, based in part on class differences between herself and local-born Brody, leads her to embark on a brief affair with the handsome and rich Hooper, who is the younger brother of one of Ellen's old boyfriends. Brody begins to suspect the affair just as his battle to keep the beaches closed for the lucrative Fourth of July weekend reaches its highest pitch with Vaughan and the town selectmen. Brody learns from the newspaper editor that Vaughan is fighting so hard to reopen the beaches because Vaughan is in debt to the New England mob. When Brody reluctantly agrees to open the beaches again, the shark nearly kills a teenage boy. In desperation, the town hires another shark fisherman, Quint. Out of a sense of duty and guilt, Brody accompanies Quint and Hooper on Quint's boat, the *Orca*.

The shark hunt occupies the final third of the novel. Blue-collar fisherman Quint takes an immediate dislike to the collegial Hooper. The hostility between Hooper and Quint/Brody forms a human counterpoint to the ensuing struggle between man and fish. The shark proves to be larger and fiercer than anyone could have guessed, and Quint's repeated failures to harpoon the shark compel Hooper to descend beneath the surface in a shark cage in an effort to kill the shark with a "bang stick." The shark tears the cage apart and devours Hooper. On the last day of the hunt, Quint finally manages to harpoon the shark and weigh him down with three barrels. The shark sinks the *Orca*, and Quint drowns. Brody, expecting to be eaten, is unexpectedly saved as the shark finally succumbs to Quint's harpoons and dies.

MOVIE PRODUCTION

The film that grew out of this narrative kept the main characters and the basic three-act structure but radically changed the characterizations and deleted the Hooper/Ellen subplot, much to the benefit of the story. Also gone were Vaughan's links to the mob. Brody was transformed from a local to a New York outsider, eager to escape urban violence and in his uncertain first summer as Amity's police chief. Hooper became a much more humorous and sympathetic character, to the extent that later drafts of the script spared him from the jaws of the shark as it attacks Hooper's cage. Quint remained a blue-collar antagonist for preppie Hooper, but Quint's mania for shark hunting was explained in the film as a result of his surviving a shark feeding frenzy that followed the sinking of the heavy cruiser USS *Indianapolis* during World War II. Instead of drowning as he does in the novel, Quint is eaten in the movie during the shark's final frenzied assault upon the *Orca*.

Spielberg and Benchley reportedly argued over many of the changes, including Spielberg's suggested new ending. He wanted a much more cathartic resolution and came up with the idea that one of Hooper's oxygen cylinders should explode in the shark's mouth. Benchley scoffed at the idea, insisting that no one would believe it. Spielberg's vision prevailed, and Benchley himself now admits that Spielberg was correct. Various writers, including Benchley, John Milius, Howard Sackler, Carl Gottlieb, and Spielberg himself, contributed to the script at different stages in its development, right through location shooting at Martha's Vineyard. By all accounts, much of the dialogue and many of the most memorable moments were improvised by the actors and/or crew, often on set as the cameras rolled.

Early troubles with the script foreshadowed the tortuous production to come. Some early casting choices, such as Sterling Hayden for Quint, also fell through for a variety of reasons. Finally, in the crucial three leading roles, Roy Scheider was cast as Brody, Richard Dreyfuss as Hooper, and Robert Shaw as Quint. After an extensive scouting expedition, production designer Joe Alves selected Martha's Vineyard as the fictional Amity, and Robert Mattey built three full-size mechanical sharks collectively dubbed "Bruce," allegedly after Spielberg's lawyer. The producers hoped that the mechanical sharks, when intercut with second-unit footage of real great white sharks shot off the coast of Australia by famed underwater team Ron and Valerie Taylor, would prove convincing enough to scare audiences.

Eventually, the producers' hopes were realized, but during production the mechanical sharks, each one built for $150,000, barely worked and caused much anguish for the producers and film crew. One shark sank during a test run, and the complex hydraulic system exploded during another. The recalcitrance of the mechanical sharks prevented Spielberg from showing them on-screen as completely as he had intended and may actually have helped the film's suspense by keeping the shark's appearances brief and startling. Other troubles, such as changing weather conditions, shifting ocean currents, and labor disputes, interfered with the production logistics. Very worried studio executives even briefly considered shutting down the production. All of these combined difficulties extended the original fifty-two-day shooting schedule to more than 150 days. By some estimates, the $3.5 million initial budget ballooned more than 200 percent.

BOX-OFFICE SUCCESS

In the end, what saved *Jaws* from its industry-anticipated disaster was the brilliance of Spielberg's unifying vision, which somehow managed to impose order on the chaotic and improvised shoot, and his close collaboration with film editor Verna Fields. In postproduction, the two managed a near impossibility by matching scenes that were often shot months apart in completely different weather and ocean conditions. Even at that, however, rough-cut screenings to studio executives produced a lukewarm response. Spielberg has also said that what made *Jaws* so gripping was the contribution of composer John Williams, whose Oscar-winning score for the film introduced the famous four-note motif for the shark scenes.

Finally, in March 1975, a sneak preview for the public was scheduled in Dallas. By all accounts, the audience loved the film, screaming the loudest when the shark surprises Brody as he ladles chum off the stern of the *Orca*. Eager to get one more terrified shriek out of future audiences, Spielberg reshot one scene (where Hooper discovers the body of Gardner) in Fields's swimming pool, and the film was ready for more sneak previews and exhibitor screenings. Stars Scheider and Dreyfuss were mobbed as heroes after one New York preview.

Favorable word of mouth spread quickly, and by the time the movie was released in 490 theaters in June 1975, the stage was set for the first worldwide blockbuster. *Jaws* was the most financially successful motion picture of all time until the summer of 1977, when George Lucas's film *Star Wars* surpassed its record. Nearly every summer since 1975 has seen the major Hollywood studios competing with one another to gross as many hundreds of millions of dollars as possible.

Though many films have surpassed *Jaws*'s box-office success since then, and three inferior sequels have somewhat diluted the impact of the original, the movie about a man-eating shark is often praised (or blamed) as the beginning of the Hollywood blockbuster era; the film remains one of the highest-grossing movies in history. Ironically, another of the highest-grossing films of all time also focuses on the terrors of the ocean and suffered many problems while in production: James Cameron's 1997 *Titanic.*

Philip L. Simpson

SEE ALSO: *Academy Awards; Best Sellers; Blockbusters;* Close Encounters of the Third Kind*;* E.T. The Extra-Terrestrial*; Horror Movies;* Jurassic Park*; Lucas, George;* Raiders of the Lost Ark*;* Schindler's List*; Spielberg, Steven;* Star Trek*; World War II.*

BIBLIOGRAPHY

Andrews, Nigel. *Nigel Andrews on "Jaws."* London: Bloomsbury, 1999.

Benchley, Peter. *Jaws.* Garden City, NY: Doubleday, 1974.

Blake, Edith. *On Location on Martha's Vineyard: The Making of the Movie "Jaws."* New York: Ballantine, 1975.

Brode, Douglas. *The Films of Steven Spielberg.* New York: Carol, 1995.

Buckland, Warren. *Directed by Steven Spielberg: Poetics of the Contemporary Hollywood Blockbuster.* New York: Continuum International Publishing Group, 2006.

Gottlieb, Carl. *The "Jaws" Log.* New York: Dell, 1975.

Mott, Donald R., and Cheryl McAllister Saunders. *Steven Spielberg.* Boston: Twayne, 1986.

Taylor, Philip M. *Steven Spielberg: The Man, His Movies, and Their Meaning.* New York: Continuum, 1992.

Jay-Z *(1969–)*

One of the wealthiest hip-hop superstars of the late 1990s and the first decade of the 2000s, Jay-Z has never been content to be just a rapper. In addition to achieving the most number one albums by a solo artist on the Billboard 200, he has proven to be an innovative and successful businessman. As president of Def Jam Records, he has signed many successful artists, including rappers Kanye West and Beanie Sigel, singer Rihanna, and hip-hop group State Property. Through his successful music

Jay-Z. Jay-Z performs in Los Angeles, California, in 2009. DR. BILLY INGRAM/WIREIMAGE/GETTY IMAGE.

career and diverse business ventures, Jay-Z has accrued a net worth of more than $450 million and has cemented a prominent place in hip-hop history.

His rise to stardom is a classic rags-to-riches tale. Born Shawn Carter, he grew up in Marcy Projects, a public housing complex in the Bedford-Stuyvesant section of Brooklyn, New York, where he experienced firsthand the pervasive violence of the crack cocaine epidemic. When he was eleven, his father left the family. His childhood dream was to become a rap star. In grade school he began tapping on the kitchen table to improvised rhymes, displaying an intuitive gift as a rhymester and wordsmith. At an early age he received a boom box from his mother, who encouraged his pursuit of music. "I would sit at my table for hours and hours 'til my mother made me go to bed," he recalled in 2011 on the radio show *Fresh Air.*

But despite his musical passion and talent, he could not escape the drug epidemic that had swept many urban neighborhoods. He dropped out of high school and moved to Trenton, New Jersey, with a friend who taught him the lucrative drug business. Still he continued to pursue music. He refined his lyrical content and delivery by working with mentors such as Jaz-O (Big Jaz), a small-time New York rapper who had a record deal with a major label, and Big Daddy Kane, who invited the young rapper to join his tour and perform during intermission. Jay-Z also gained practice as an MC at parties. But without a record contract, he continued to deal drugs in order to finance his fledging music career.

As he gained exposure, he left the drug business to concentrate solely on music. "I sold Kilos of coke, so I'm guessin' I could sell CDs / I'm not a businessman, I'm a business, man," he raps in West's "Diamonds from Sierra Leone (Remix)." DJ Clark Kent, an A&R employee of Atlantic Records, introduced the rapper to producer Damon Dash, who soon became Jay-Z's partner. Along with mogul Kareem "Biggs" Burke, Dash and Jay-Z founded Roc-A-Fella Records, an independent label that proved to be an incredibly successful entrepreneurial model. Instead of signing an artist deal, Jay-Z signed a distribution deal, thus retaining far more profits.

Jay-Z's rise as a hip-hop artist came in the wake of the violent deaths of fellow East Coast rapper Notorious B.I.G. and West Coast rapper Tupac Shakur. Both artists influenced Jay-Z, though he offered a mellower brand of hip-hop. His style came to be defined by seemingly effortless rhymes that flow over catchy pop beats. His lyrics are witty, with allusive, metaphorical phrases derived from urban black vernacular and street culture.

His single "Ain't No Nigga" (also called "Ain't No Playa") was released in 1996 and catapulted him into the national spotlight. The song featured a duet with sultry female rapper Foxy Brown and sampled "Ain't No Woman (Like the One I've Got)" by classic soul group the Four Tops. In 1998 Jay-Z garnered crossover appeal with "Hard Knock Life (Ghetto Anthem)," a track that featured a sampled snippet from the musical *Annie* (1976) and remained number one for five weeks. Since then he has received more than a dozen Grammy Awards and has racked up album sales of more than $50 million.

Known for projecting a hustler image, Jay-Z often raps about an opulent lifestyle, which his fans can experience through him. By referencing specific brands and expensive products in his songs, such as Cristal champagne, platinum jewelry, Motorola pagers, Bentleys, and an "all-black everything" look, he has set trends, built brand identity, and influenced perceptions of hip-hop style. His entrepreneurial endeavors include the urban clothing line Roca Wear (he also has a signature sneaker, the S. Carter by Reebok) and a sports bar and lounge chain, the 40/40 Club. He is part owner of the New Jersey Nets professional basketball team.

Jay-Z's influence as a tastemaker has extended to his work as a businessman and as an activist. His philanthropic work has included creating the Shawn Carter Scholarship Foundation and donating $1 million to Hurricane Katrina relief efforts. He also aided Barack Obama's bid for the presidency in 2008 by urging young citizens to vote.

Willie R. Collins

SEE ALSO: Annie*; Atlantic Records; Cocaine/Crack; Compact Discs; Grammy Awards; Hip-Hop; Hurricane Katrina; Obama, Barack; Rap; Rihanna; Shakur, Tupac; West, Kanye.*

BIBLIOGRAPHY

Greenburg, Zack O'Malley. *Empire State of Mind: How Jay-Z Went from Street Corner to Corner Office.* London: Penguin, 2011.

Jay-Z. *Decoded.* New York: Spiegel & Grau, 2010.

Jay-Z. "Jay-Z 'Decoded': The Fresh Air Interview." By Terry Gross. *Fresh Air*, November 25, 2011.

Keyes, Cheryl L. *Rap Music and Street Consciousness.* Urbana: University of Illinois Press, 2004.

Jazz

Of all the great American musical forms—blues, rock and roll, country, and jazz—jazz has proven to be the most subtle, the most flexible, the most capable of growth and change, the one that has developed from folk art and popular art to fine art. The wide range of artistic possibilities available to jazz are inherent in the form itself: a music that is structured enough to permit intricate compositions for ensemble play but loose enough to allow for individual improvisation, individual style and voicing, and considerable virtuosity.

ORIGINS OF JAZZ

Jazz developed around the turn of the twentieth century in the South and Southwest, particularly in New Orleans, Louisiana. It built on a number of earlier African American musical forms, including blues and ragtime, and on European-influenced popular music and dances. The first great New Orleans jazz innovators, such as Buddy Bolden (who never recorded), Louis Armstrong, Bunk Johnson, Jelly Roll Morton, Freddie Keppard, King Oliver, and Sidney Bechet, added a number of key African American musical techniques to conventional popular and dance music styles. The two most important were the blue note, a microtonal variation on conventional pitch, and the complex rhythmic variations developed from the polyrhythmic heritage of African drumming. These additions gave jazz the rhythmic flexibility that came to be called *swing*—an almost indefinable quality that has been summed up best in the Duke Ellington song, "It Don't Mean a Thing if It Ain't Got That Swing."

Miles Davis and John Coltrane. *Miles Davis, left, and John Coltrane perform together in Chicago, Illinois, in 1960.* TED WILLIAMS/MICHAEL OCHS ARCHIVES/GETTY IMAGES.

Although there are reports of jazz being played in the first few years of the twentieth century, the early musicians were not recorded. The first recorded jazz album came in 1917 when a white group, the Original Dixieland Jass (Jazz) Band, recorded for both Columbia and RCA Victor, with million-selling results. It took longer for record companies to take a chance on black jazz musicians. Mamie Smith's recording of "Crazy Blues," in 1920, began a blues craze, and many of the early appearances on record by the great African American jazz masters, such as Armstrong, were as accompanists to blues singers.

THE JAZZ AGE

Meanwhile, as the recording industry grew throughout the 1920s, the post–World War I generation found itself restless, dissatisfied, and looking for expressions of its own identity. The era was called the Jazz Age, but the Jazz Age was basically a white, middle-class phenomenon, and the music that became popular was mostly by white groups such as the Original Dixieland Jass Band. Some of them were excellent musicians—in particular Iowa-born cornetist Bix Beiderbecke.

The African American musicians of New Orleans continued to be the artistic vanguard of jazz, although the scene had shifted. Oliver was one of many who moved to Chicago. Arriving in 1918, he formed his first band in 1920 and was joined by Armstrong in 1922. Oliver's New Orleans–style ensemble jazz influenced many musicians, both black and white, but it was Armstrong who became jazz's seminal influence. He left Oliver in 1924 to join Fletcher Henderson's orchestra in New York, then returned to Chicago to record with his own groups, the Hot Five and the Hot Seven. Armstrong's extraordinary technique and his artistic intensity and innovation dominated jazz, and as a result, the role of the soloist became predominant. Armstrong in the 1920s not only created one of the greatest artistic legacies of any American artist, but he also established the importance of individual creativity in jazz.

During this same era, however, ensemble jazz was developing into orchestral jazz—the big bands, featuring section arrangements and tight organization. Armstrong, through his work with Henderson, was important in integrating the concept of fiery, original jazz solo work into the large ensemble framework. Equally important in Henderson's band was the work of Coleman Hawkins, a great soloist who, more than any other musician, introduced the tenor saxophone as an important jazz solo instrument.

Just as jazz experienced its first great wave of popularity in the 1920s, the era of the phonograph record, Prohibition, and the speakeasy, big-band jazz was also a product of its time. As newly legal nightclubs closed and musical groups disbanded due to the hardships of the Great Depression, jazz continued to find audiences in major supper clubs, such as the Cotton Club (located in New York's Harlem but open only to white audiences), and ventured into the increasingly important medium of radio. With fewer venues, the bigger, richer sound of big-band jazz become more popular. At the same time, the glut on the market of talented musicians drove salaries down and made it cheaper for a successful bandleader to hire a large group.

The single most successful band of the Big Band Era, or Swing Era, was led by Benny Goodman. Goodman's success was because of his brilliant musicianship and his organizational and promotional skills, but it was also due to the fact that he was white. Goodman used his preeminence to advance the mainstream acceptance of black jazz musicians. He not only hired Henderson as an arranger, which was a behind-the-scenes job, but he also integrated his band, hiring great black musicians such as Teddy Wilson, Lionel Hampton, and Charlie Christian. There had been a few other integrated jazz groups before, but none as successful as Goodman's group.

Artistically, the Ellington and Count Basie bands represented the pinnacle of the big-band style. Ellington, who began as a bandleader in the mid-1920s and continued to lead a band far beyond the Swing Era until his death in 1974, may have been the first jazz musician to gain an international reputation as a serious artist—the first to draw attention to jazz as a serious art form, although this battle was not to be won for a long time. By the end of the 1970s, jazz was being taught in universities, and major grants and awards were going to jazz musicians and composers. But in 1965 Ellington was passed over for the Pulitzer Prize for music because of a stubborn insistence by older conservatives on the committee that jazz was not really art.

Basie, who came from the Kansas City tradition of blues-influenced jazz, was arguably the most important figure in developing the concept of *swing* in the big-band idiom. J. Bradford Robinson, in *The New Grove Dictionary of Jazz*, says that Basie's rhythm section "altered the ideal of jazz accompaniment, making it more supple and responsive to the wind instruments." Basie's approach to rhythm, and the musical innovations of his leading soloists, particularly tenor saxophonist Lester Young, provided an important basis for the revolutionary changes that were to come.

1930s–1950s

Throughout the 1930s, jazz was primarily popular music. Goodman, Ellington, and Basie played for dances, just like the "sweet" big bands led by Sammy Kaye, the Dorsey Brothers, and others. But in the 1940s, jazz enjoyed the fruits of the steady growth of the previous decade. After the end of Prohibition, a new generation of jazz clubs had begun to grow throughout the 1930s. They tended to be small, which meant they created a demand for small-group jazz, generally a rhythm section and two lead instruments. The most important of these clubs were on 52nd Street in New York, making the city more than ever before the center of jazz creativity.

New jazz musicians, primarily black, gravitated to New York, where they represented an urban, sophisticated generation. Impatient with what they perceived as the "Uncle Tom" image of many black showmen, such as Armstrong and Cab Calloway, they presented themselves as cool, cerebral, and introspective. They were artists more than entertainers.

These new musicians investigated the possibilities of improvisational music, trying more complex rhythms and harmonies and improvisations built on melodic and chordal substitutions that went far beyond conventional melodies. The two most important figures in the modern jazz, or bebop, movement were alto saxophonist Charlie Parker and trumpeter Dizzy Gillespie. Their experiments galvanized an entire generation of musicians, who began to hear music in a whole new way. Experimentation became the new wave of jazz. In 1941 Minton's, a small club in Harlem, became the center for a series of after-hours jam sessions that soon attracted all the best players who were interested in the new music.

Modern jazz attracted a fiercely dedicated audience, though it was never as large as the audience for the big bands. It created a style: the hipster, who wore a beret, sunglasses, and a goatee and listened to unintelligible music and spoke in an unintelligible slang. Jazz, and the jazz subculture, filled an important role in the post–World War II era as mainstream America plunged headlong into the conformity of prosperity and a small vanguard was left to search for more elusive artistic and social values. The artistic legacy of the bebop and cool jazz years, the 1940s and 1950s, is extraordinary. Besides Parker and Gillespie, other important figures include Thelonious Monk, Max Roach, Gerry Mulligan, the Modern Jazz Quartet, Sonny Rollins, Dave Brubeck, and Miles Davis, who was to play an increasingly important role in the next decades of jazz. In addition to the achievements of individual musicians, the modern jazz era also drew attention to the aesthetic importance of jazz. It began to be described, for the first time, as "America's classical music." Widespread acceptance of jazz as an art form was slow in coming to America, however; European intellectuals embraced it much more quickly.

During the 1950s, the jazz audience became more communal. The 1940s prototype had been the night-owl, club-hopping hipster; in the 1950s the jazz festival became a fixture. The first jazz festival was held in Nice, France, in 1948; the first in America was the Newport (Rhode Island) Jazz Festival in 1954. By the 1990s there were estimated to be close to 1,000 significant jazz festivals held annually around the world.

As the experimental sounds of modern jazz entered the mainstream and became accepted by mass audiences (TV shows such as *Peter Gunn* used jazz soundtracks), young jazz musicians were finding a new avant-garde. A historic 1959 engagement at New York's Five Spot Cafe by alto saxophonist Ornette Coleman became a milestone in the emergence of free jazz. While bebop had explored unusual possibilities and inversions in conventional chord and harmonic structures, free jazz virtually dispensed with them. Coleman, Don Cherry, and Cecil Taylor were among the young iconoclasts who pioneered free jazz. At first rejected by the 1950s jazzmen, they proved impossible to ignore, and soon major jazz figures such as John Coltrane, Eric Dolphy, and even Davis were exploring the possibilities of free jazz.

Free jazz was the artistic vanguard of the antiestablishment 1960s. Like bebop before it, it made previous styles sound tired and a little formulaic. Unlike bebop, though, it never established itself beyond a small, avant-garde audience. Nevertheless, it remained an important alternative musical direction.

CONTEMPORARY JAZZ

The indigenous music of the 1960s was rock, and by the end of the decade, some jazz musicians were becoming intrigued by the artistic possibilities of this phenomenally popular form—most importantly, Davis. Davis had been listening to Jimi Hendrix and other rock innovators, and he realized there was musical promise in a fusion between the improvisational freedom of jazz and the simple beat of rock. At the same time, rock musicians such as John McLaughlin and Jack Bruce were being drawn to the creative possibilities of jazz. Purists refused to accept jazz-rock fusion as real jazz. Its rhythmic regularity deadened the swing of jazz. But many noted jazz musicians, particularly Davis alumni Herbie Hancock and Chick Corea, embraced the new form. A number of young musicians, such as the members of the group Spiro Gyra, made their entire careers playing fusion.

Fusion was essentially an artistic dead end. The next generation of jazz musicians was not much interested in pursuing its leads. Jazz in the late 1970s, 1980s, and 1990s became in many ways a retro music. With no new dominant style, many young musicians looked to the past—all eras of the past. The most dominant young musician of the 1980s and 1990s, trumpeter Wynton Marsalis, demonstrated on his early albums that he could play in all styles, from the free jazz of Coleman to the classic jazz of Armstrong.

A salient symbol of this era is the jazz repertory company, a jazz orchestra made up of young musicians devoted to playing the jazz classics. The National Jazz Ensemble, founded by bassist Chuck Israels, was the first of these, and the Lincoln Center Jazz Orchestra, led by Marsalis, was probably the best known. This was the era during which jazz studies courses entered the universities, when the Smithsonian Institution issued its Classic Jazz collection, when grants for jazz studies, composition, and performance burgeoned in both government and private sectors. Equally important to this period was the CD explosion, which created a new listener interest in jazz of all periods.

The 1980s and 1990s, even without developing a new sound, have their own importance in the history of jazz for precisely this recombinant quality. Jazz developed so fast—no other art form in human history has moved from folk to popular to fine art in such a short amount of time—that its revolutionary vanguard frequently eclipsed earlier styles. Players not in the vanguard were too often dismissed as "moldy figs," in the slang of the beboppers. That changed in the 1980s and 1990s. The artistry—and the modernity and innovation—of artists such as Armstrong, Hawkins, and Basie became fully recognized. Jazz will probably never again be as popular as it was in the 1930s, but it remains something other than art music that is played alongside classical music in the concert halls and the academy. It retains that mystique of something hip, something adventurous, and continues to be a music for the vanguard of young audiences to graduate to, after rock begins to lose its immediate appeal.

By the twenty-first century, jazz enthusiasts were debating the issue of whether or not jazz could survive the technological age. Davis had recognized the advantage of being labeled pop rather than jazz in the late 1960s. When his *Bitches Brew* was geared toward the rock crowd rather than jazz purists, it went gold in 1969. Forty years later, a survey conducted by the National Endowment for the Arts revealed that the number of Americans attending live jazz concerts had been declining precipitously for twenty-six years. That survey set off a storm of protests and began a new discussion of whether jazz was alive or dead. Despite this, jazz musicians continue to sell.

In 2009 Columbia Records released a seventy-two-disc box set, *Miles Davis: The Complete Columbia Album Collection*, covering the music of the jazz legend from 1955 to 1985. Box sets of the music of Ella Fitzgerald and Stan Getz were also released. Most of the great jazz artists of the past are also selling in digital form for iPods, MP3 players, and other electronic devices. It may be that the future of contemporary jazz can be found in the blending of jazz and pop that is seen in the music of entertainers such as Harry Connick Jr., who grew up in New Orleans, studied with James Booker and Ellis Marsalis before making his first jazz recording at the age of ten. His score for the Rob Reiner romantic comedy *When Harry Met Sally* (1989) went multiplatinum and started him on his way to introducing jazz to new generations.

Tad Richards

SEE ALSO: *Armstrong, Louis; Basie, Count; Beiderbecke, Bix; Big Bands; Brubeck, Dave; Calloway, Cab; Chicago Jazz; Coltrane, John; The Cotton Club; Davis, Miles; Dixieland; Dorsey, Jimmy; Dorsey, Tommy; Ellington, Duke; Fitzgerald, Ella; Gillespie, Dizzy; Goodman, Benny; The Great Depression; Hancock, Herbie; Harlem Renaissance; Hawkins, Coleman; Henderson, Fletcher; Kansas City Jazz; Latin Jazz; Morton, Jelly Roll; New Orleans Rhythm and Blues; Newport Jazz and Folk Festivals; Original Dixieland Jass (Jazz) Band; Parker, Charlie; Prohibition; Rhythm and Blues; Savoy Ballroom.*

BIBLIOGRAPHY

Balliett, Whitney. *American Musicians: 56 Portraits in Jazz.* New York: Oxford University Press, 1986.

Blesh, Rudi, and Harriet Janis. *They All Played Ragtime.* New York: Knopf, 1950.

Collier, James Lincoln. *The Making of Jazz: A Comprehensive History.* Boston: Houghton Mifflin, 1978.

Giddins, Gary. *Riding on a Blue Note.* New York: Oxford University Press, 1981.

Giddins, Gary. *Rhythm-a-Ning.* New York: Oxford University Press, 1986.

Giddins, Gary. *Visions of Jazz.* New York: Oxford University Press, 1998.

Gioia, Ted. *The Imperfect Art: Reflections on Jazz and Modern Culture.* New York: Oxford University Press, 1988.

Gioia, Ted. *The History of Jazz.* New York: Oxford University Press, 1997.

Gitler, Ira. *Jazz Masters of the Forties.* New York: Macmillan, 1966.

Hentoff, Nat, and Nat Shapiro. *Hear Me Talkin' to Ya: An Oral History of Jazz.* New York: Dover, 1966.

Hodeir, André. *Jazz: Its Evolution and Essence.* New York: Grove Press, 1956.

Kernfeld, Barry, ed. *The New Grove Dictionary of Jazz.* New York: St. Martin's Press, 1988.

Prouty, Ken. *Knowing Jazz: Community, Pedagogy, and Canon in the Information Age.* Jackson: University Press of Mississippi, 2012.

Sales, Grover. *Jazz: America's Classical Music.* Englewood Cliffs, NJ: Prentice-Hall, 1984.

Snitzer, Herb. *Glorious Days and Nights: A Jazz Memoir.* Jackson: University Press of Mississippi, 2011.

Walls, Seth. "Jazz Is Dead. Long Live Jazz. " *Newsweek,* December 9, 2009, 25.

Whitehead, Kevin. *Why Jazz? A Concise Guide.* New York: Oxford University Press, 2011.

Williams, Martin. *The Jazz Tradition*. New York: Oxford University Press, 1983.

The Jazz Singer

Produced in 1927, *The Jazz Singer* brought sound film to Hollywood. Directed by Alan Crosland and starring Al Jolson, the film was based on Samson Raphaelson's 1922 short story "The Day of Atonement." This story of Jewish assimilation to American culture through popular music has been adapted as a Broadway play (starring George Jessel in 1925), two radio plays (both starring Al Jolson in 1936 and 1947), a televised production (starring Jerry Lewis in 1959), and two subsequent film versions (starring Danny Thomas in 1953 and Neil Diamond in 1980). *The Jazz Singer* not only illustrates the emergent sound technology of the 1920s but also demonstrates the mainstream acceptance of jazz music and comments on the acculturation process of immigrants to the United States.

The Jazz Singer recounts the story of Jakie Rabinowitz, the son of immigrants living in New York. He is expected to succeed his father, as well as many ancestors, as the cantor in their synagogue. Young Jakie, however, has ambitions of fame and fortune as a jazz singer, expressing himself in American popular music instead of Jewish religious music. Jakie's intention to sing popular music leads to his father's denunciation and sends Jakie (now Jack Robin) to a career on the vaudeville circuit.

As Jack's career progresses, he falls in love with Mary Dale, a star dancer and Gentile. Jack's two worlds collide when he accepts a part in a Broadway revue (starring Mary) and returns to New York upon his father's sixtieth birthday. Jack's father has still not accepted his son, but seeing him results in his father falling ill. In the film's climactic scene, Jack must decide between the show's opening on Broadway and filling in for his dying father at the synagogue singing "Kol Nidre" for Yom Kippur, the day of atonement. Jack fulfills his father's dying wish and still manages to make it big on Broadway, bringing a sense of balance between his parents' old-world immigrant ways and his new Americanized life.

The Jazz Singer is often referred to as the first sound film, yet this is only partially true. The idea of synchronized sound and motion picture is as old as the movies themselves, but it was not until the early 1920s that a workable method of recording both image and sound came into use. Warner Brothers was the first to undertake sound film production, primarily as a last-ditch effort to battle the larger studios that had, by the 1920s, solidified their hold on the movie industry.

Warner's first efforts at sound film were variety programs with talking shorts, musical numbers, and staged productions using a sound-on-disc recording technology. Fox studios also entered the sound film market with its Movietone newsreels, which presented news stories with a sound-on-film technology. Different studios could use different sound formats since each studio primarily exhibited at their own theaters. Warner's *The Jazz Singer*, however, was the first feature film to integrate the use of sound, both music and dialogue, into the story itself. The film is primarily a silent film with a musical soundtrack, but in several scenes synchronized singing and dialogue are presented. This is most notable in the sequence where Jack sings to his mother: after finishing one song, he says to her, "You ain't heard nothin' yet."

The film's significance goes beyond its historical role in film technology to illustrate the mainstream acceptance of jazz music as an American art form. Even though the music in the film is not, strictly speaking, jazz music, it does contain elements of jazz style, such as increased syncopation and a blues tonality. More important, the film expresses the belief that jazz music is an Americanizing force since it is a uniquely American form of music.

Raphaelson, the original author of the story, writes in the introduction to the published stage play that "in seeking a symbol of the vital chaos of America's soul, I find no more adequate one than jazz." Ironically, in order to perform jazz music onstage, Jack dons the costume of a minstrel performer, including blackface. Jack "becomes" black in order to become an American and in the process reinforces nineteenth-century stereotypes of African Americans in popular culture. The film promotes both acculturation and the maintenance of ethnic identity as significant parts of economic prosperity and success—the American dream.

Charles J. Shindo

SEE ALSO: *Blackface Minstrelsy; Broadway; Diamond, Neil; Hollywood; Jazz; Jolson, Al; Lewis, Jerry; Silent Movies; Thomas, Danny.*

BIBLIOGRAPHY

Alexander, Michael. *Jazz Age Jews*. Princeton, NJ: Princeton University Press, 2001.

Carringer, Robert L., ed. *The Jazz Singer*. Madison: University of Wisconsin Press, 1979.

Raphaelson, Samson. *The Jazz Singer*. New York: Brentano's, 1925.

Jeans

Jeans, or blue jeans, are casual trousers made most often of indigo-blue cotton denim with reinforced stitching at the seams and metal rivets placed at stress points. Though introduced as durable work clothing, jeans have become an almost universal part of modern culture, worn by people all over the world for all manner of occasions.

Blue jeans, or dungarees, were originally associated with the hardworking miners during the California gold rush in the mid-1800s and are most directly descended from the "waist overalls" developed by Levi Strauss and Jacob Davis in 1873. Featured in Western movies in the 1930s and 1940s, jeans began to attain cult status. Military servicemen during World War II gave jeans further exposure by regularly wearing them while engaging in leisure activities. It was, however, the children of these servicemen who brought jeans to the forefront of popular culture. Banned from many public schools, hard to find in stores outside of the United States, and worn by rebellious movie characters in the 1950s, jeans emerged as a symbol of restless American youth in the 1960s. Eventually jeans became popular worldwide through U.S. servicemen stationed overseas and the international influence of American cinema and other mass media.

Levi's blue jeans were first sold in Europe in 1959. Now jeans can be found in virtually every country on the globe. The manufacture of jeans is a worldwide industry, encompassing a wide variety of styles, colors, designers, fashions, and accessories. In 2008 Levi Strauss & Co. reported that it had sold 3.5 billion pairs of jeans since 1873.

ORIGINS

Jean fabric, originally a tough and durable twill weave, can be traced to twelfth-century Genoa, Italy. Beginning in about the seventeenth century in Europe, the term *jeans* generally described a working man's outerwear. Modern blue jeans, however, are most often manufactured from denim and not jean fabric. The word *denim*, derived from the term *serge de Nimes*, refers to a finer-grade serge fabric, also a twill, which appears to have originated in Nimes, France.

Denim was originally a woven blend of wool and silk, but U.S. textile mills began using cotton as early as the mid-nineteenth century as a substitute for the more expensive imported wools and linens and as a means of gaining independence from foreign suppliers. This trend gained popularity and resulted in the continued use of cotton in both denim and jean fabrics. Denim tends to wear better than jean fabric, becoming softer with each successive wash, and it became the preferred material for the manufacture of work jeans.

Today jeans are generally associated with a line of denim trousers developed by Strauss in San Francisco in the 1870s. Popular myth credits him with the invention of blue jeans. He is imagined somewhat romantically as a figure who rose to the occasion of innovation during the California gold rush by using surplus tent canvas and surplus indigo for dye to create much-needed overalls for miners. In actuality, Levi Strauss & Co. archives attribute the invention of modern jeans to Davis, a Latvian tailor who immigrated to Reno, Nevada. According to company records, Davis invented a process whereby copper rivets were added to stress points in the seams, greatly enhancing their durability.

Davis's overalls were an immediate hit with the miners. Wanting to establish a patent for his process of riveting overalls but not having the money to do so, Davis reportedly approached Strauss, a successful dry goods merchant in San Francisco, and offered to share the profits with Strauss in exchange for his funding of the patent. Strauss agreed, and a patent was issued in 1873. Trousers made using this process were known as "waist overalls" until 1960, when the common term *jeans* was inserted into Levi Strauss & Co. advertising and literature. Initially a uniquely "working man's" garment, the first jeans developed exclusively for women were not introduced until 1934. Before that, women wore men's jeans.

BECOMING ICONIC

Western movie stars of the 1940s and early 1950s such as John Wayne started the popular association of jeans with the myth of rugged individuals who helped build the American West while braving harsh elements and savage attacks. In 1947 *Life* printed pictures depicting a California conflict in which denim-clad rioters challenged police officers in California. These rioters became the model for Marlon Brando's performance in *The Wild One* (1953) and James Dean's in *Rebel without a Cause* (1955). The clothing worn in both movies was adopted by youths as a symbol of the carefree lifestyle they wished to emulate.

Jeans gained notoriety in American schools in part because of their association with rebelliousness. In the 1950s and 1960s, types of leisure wear such as jeans were thought to give students the wrong impression about the serious nature of school. There were also practical concerns: the original complaint against wearing jeans in schoolrooms seems to have stemmed from the copper rivets damaging wooden desks and chairs. Jeans were banned from many schools until the early 1980s, and this outlaw quality only fueled their popularity.

Jeans became a symbol of the antiestablishment movement of the 1960s. Certain people sought out clothing that would link them to the societal fringes, and jeans fit the bill. Jeans were elevated to the level of art in this era, as they were decorated, modified, and painted. This was when jeans truly became iconic. In fact, a pair of blue jeans was added to the permanent collection of the Smithsonian Institution in 1964.

STYLE EVOLUTION

Eventually jeans gained acceptance as casual wear and became fully integrated into mainstream American fashion, which led to an array of styles. The first big shift came when retailers began selling jeans that had already been broken in. Later, this would evolve through the process of stone washing, in which jeans were pretreated with stones or chemicals in order to create a worn-in look and to soften the denim fabric. Manufacturers also mimicked the 1960s-era practice of adding patches, paint, or other ornamentation to jeans. Companies began making jeans in increasingly varied styles, creating trend after trend. In 1976, for example, a Ramones album cover pictured the band wearing slim, ripped jeans, and a new style was born: pre-ripped jeans hit the market. In the 1980s acid-washed denim that was almost white became popular, as did bleach-splattered jeans. In 1991 Kurt Cobain and his bandmates in Nirvana helped to launch the "grunge look" when they appeared in concert clad in shabby jeans.

In addition to the condition, the fit and form of jeans have also undergone many transformations. Bellbottom jeans, which are fitted to the knee and then flare out, were patterned after naval uniforms and popular throughout the 1960s and 1970s. Fitted, tapered, or skinny jeans appeared in the 1970s on the legs of punk rockers who wanted to counter the hippie bellbottom fashion. This became a leading trend throughout the 1980s and again in the first decade of the 2000s. During the 1990s, in contrast, the dominant shape was baggy (differentiated from bellbottoms because the entire pant leg is wide). This style originated in impoverished communities where children often had to wear oversized hand-me-down clothes from their older siblings. Often associated with rap music, the style entered mainstream American fashion in the late 1990s. Each jeans style has endured its own transformations in fit, as well as ebbs and flows in popularity.

DESIGNER JEANS

Once jeans arrived in the cultural mainstream, it was inevitable that designer styles would follow. Designer jeans are marked by their expensive prices, quality workmanship, and haute couture associations. Among the first designer brands were Calvin Klein, Jordache, and Guess, and now hundreds of labels exist. Levi Strauss & Co. even entered the fray: by 2012, it was producing more than fifty different fits. A risqué Calvin Klein advertisement in the 1980s featuring a teenage Brooke Shields gave jeans their sex appeal. Since then, upscale retailers have kept pace with and inaugurated jean fashions. Whereas a pair of basic Levi's cost about $45 in 2012, a pair of designer jeans could go for upward of $150.

Despite, or perhaps because of, their constantly evolving look and fit, jeans have become ubiquitous in American culture. Jeans are no longer relegated to the weekend or casual Friday—instead, they are a versatile part of daily life. Throughout the garment's history, it has been associated with any number of social movements—from the biker rebelliousness of Brando in the 1950s to the hippie counterculture of the 1960s to the urban angst of rap in the 1990s. While trends have come and gone, blue jeans have remained a staple.

Ethan Hay

SEE ALSO: *Bellbottoms; Brando, Marlon; Casual Friday; Dean, James; The Gap; Grunge; Hippies; Klein, Calvin; Levi's; Low-Rise Jeans; Nirvana; Punk; The Ramones; Rap;* Rebel without a Cause*; Retro Fashion; Teenagers; The Western;* The Wild One*; Wrangler Jeans.*

BIBLIOGRAPHY

"Denim through the Ages." *Men's Health*, October 2008.

Downey, Lynn; Jill Novack Lynch; and Kathleen McDonough. *501: This Is a Pair of Levi's Jeans: The Official History of the Levi's Brand.* San Francisco: Levi Strauss & Co., 1995.

Owens, Richard, and Tony Lane. *American Denim: A New Folk Art.* New York: Harry N. Abrams, 1975.

Sullivan, James. *Jeans: A Cultural History of an American Icon.* New York: Gotham Books, 2006.

Weidt, Maryann N. *Mr. Blue Jeans: A Story about Levi Strauss.* Minneapolis, MN: Carolrhoda Books, 1990.

Jeep

The Jeep is a multipurpose, light motor vehicle developed by the U.S. Army Quartermaster Corps for Allied military forces in World War II. Designed by Colonel Arthur William Sidney Herrington (1891–1970) at the Marmon Motor Company in Indianapolis, Indiana, more than 360,000 jeeps were manufactured by the Willys-Overland Motor Company in Toledo, Ohio, and, under license, by American Bantam Car Company and the Ford Motor Company, from 1941 to 1945. The small, sturdy, versatile Jeep had the ruggedness of a truck and the maneuverability of an automobile. It carried four passengers or .25 ton of cargo over difficult terrain at speeds up to 65 miles per hour.

The origin of its name is unclear. It may have derived from its military nomenclature, *general purpose vehicle* (g.p.), or it might have come from Eugene the Jeep, a 1936 *Popeye* comic strip character drawn by E. C. Segar. In any case, American newspapers were using the name Jeep by 1941. The fast, all-terrain reconnaissance vehicle was used in World War II by all U.S. military forces, as well as by British, French, Russian, Australian, and New Zealand armed forces. The war correspondent Ernie Pyle recalled that the army jeep was "as faithful as a dog, as strong as a mule and as agile as a goat." The U.S. military was still using M38A1 jeeps for various purposes at the end of the twentieth century.

Following World War II, army surplus jeeps were used for a variety of agricultural, construction, and commercial purposes by American veterans familiar with the jeep's practicality. By 1945 Willys-Overland had designed the first model intended for civilian use. The CJ-2A jeep was an all-steel sedan or station wagon used as a two-wheel drive, seven-passenger or delivery vehicle. By 1949 a four-wheel-drive, six-cylinder jeep was produced for the growing number of drivers who used it for fishing, hunting, skiing, and other recreational off-road activities.

In 1953 the Kaiser-Frazer Company acquired the Willys-Overland Company and began producing the larger, wider CJ-5 Willys Jeep Station Wagon, a functional four-wheel-drive utility vehicle. This civilian jeep, based on the army's M38A1 jeep that had been used in the Korean War, became a milestone in postwar American automotive history. It was manufactured for thirty years in thirty countries and was sold in 150 nations. By 1963 the new Jeep Wagoneer marked the end of the classic Willys Wagon, which ceased production in 1965. The Wagoneer was the first sport utility vehicle (SUV), and by 1970 it had tripled annual jeep production and was being imitated by Ford, Chevrolet, and Chrysler.

EXPANDING MARKET SHARE

In 1970 the American Motors Corporation (AMC) took over the Kaiser-Jeep Corporation, thus gaining the Wagoneer's

Jeep Dealership. *New Jeep vehicles line the lot of a dealership in Peoria, Illinois, in 2012.* DANIEL ACKER/BLOOMBERG/GETTY IMAGES.

expanding baby boomer market. Throughout the 1970s, more comfortable models derived from the jeep were seen on highways around the world, as Plymouth, Toyota, and Isuzu introduced similar off-road vehicles. In the 1980s, when fuel conservation was no longer the concern it had been in the 1970s, larger, heavier, more expensive SUV models became popular with suburban motorists. Although not replacing the jeep, the most popular SUV models, with names evocative of the outdoors and the western frontier (such as Navigator, Explorer, Renegade, and Blazer), combined the rough-and-tough jeep reputation with the appealing features of the station or ranch wagon and the pickup truck.

When Chrysler absorbed AMC in 1987, it was largely to gain the jeep's increasing share of the market. A right-hand drive Jeep Cherokee model was produced for the U.S. Postal Service. In Britain, Australia, and Japan, the Grand Cherokee replaced the Wagoneer in 1993. Chrysler, having merged in 1998 with Daimler-Benz, continued to produce a variety of DaimlerChrysler jeep models for civilian, military, and government drivers.

Since World War II, when soldiers drove the American jeep around the world, it has proven to be a ubiquitous warhorse and workhorse, and the most popular vehicle ever manufactured. One indication of the jeep's popularity with GIs during World War II was the Glenn Miller Army Air Force Band recording of "Jeep Jockey Jump" in 1943 and Spike Jones's song "Little Bo Peep Has Lost Her Jeep." The 1944 movie *Four Jills in a Jeep* portrayed a USO troupe entertaining soldiers during the war. Television featured the jeep in two popular programs: *The Roy Rogers Show* (NBC, 1951–1957) had a jeep named Nellybelle and *The Rat Patrol* (ABC, 1966–1968) showed a U.S. Army jeep squad harassing Erwin Rommel's Afrika Korps during the war. Perhaps the most unusual legacy of the jeep may be Manila's jeepney. These brightly colored, elaborately decorated jeep taxis carry one-third of the city's commuter and tourist traffic daily. Many other tourist and resort centers used jeeps for off-road recreation by the end of the twentieth century, as did millions of dedicated jeep motorists around the world.

In the early twenty-first century, Chrysler continued to modernize the jeep for popular use and to enhance its appeal as a desirable vehicle. In 2008 the company introduced the apple-green Jeep Renegade at Detroit's North American International Auto Show, calling it the wave of the future. Special features included a waterproof exterior and a drain plug to allow for easy cleaning after off-road experiences. Optional features included Wi-Fi, e-mail, Web access, and updates for automatic wireless maps. In 2012 Chrysler attempted to cash in on the enormous popularity of the *Call of Duty* video game series by introducing the Jeep Wrangler Call of Duty: MW3 Special Edition Vehicle. The MW3 included Call of Duty graphics on the front fender and spare-tire cover and the game logo on seats, dashboard, and floor mats.

Peter C. Holloran

SEE ALSO: *Automobile; Sport Utility Vehicles (SUVs); World War II.*

BIBLIOGRAPHY

Bailey, Ronald H. "The Incredible Jeep." *World War II* 24, no. 3 (2009).

Cattanach, John. *The Jeep Track.* London: Regency Press, 1990.

Fetherston, David. *Jeep: Warhorse, Workhorse and Boulevard Cruiser.* Osceola, WI: Motorbooks International, 1996.

Fowler, Will. *Jeep Goes to War.* Philadelphia: Courage Books, 1993.

Guttmacher, Peter. *Jeep.* New York: Crestwood House, 1994.

Torres, Emmanuel. *Jeepney.* Manila: GCF Books, 1979.

Jefferson Airplane/Starship

Formed in 1965, Jefferson Airplane was the most commercially successful band to come out of San Francisco in the mid- to late 1960s. Along with contemporaries such as the Grateful Dead, it pioneered a blend of folk, blues, and psychedelia to play what became known as West Coast Rock. The band's presence at some of the defining cultural moments of the 1960s attests to its status as one of the key bands of this era.

COUNTERCULTURE

While Jefferson Airplane's eclectic sound could be traced to folk music and the blues, it also signaled significant departures from such generic origins, with its distorted, extended guitar improvisations and lyrics that referred to altered states of consciousness and countercultural concerns. As *Time* pointed out in June 1967, what became known as the San Francisco sound "encompasses everything from bluegrass to Indian ragas, from Bach to jug-band music—often within the framework of a single song."

Bay Area artists such as Jefferson Airplane could only have flourished in historically tolerant San Francisco and in close proximity to the University of California campus at Berkeley. Living communally in the hippie epicenter of Haight-Ashbury, the band drew much of its support and attitude from this politically active and culturally experimental milieu. Sharing its audience's background, values, and choice of chemical stimulants, the band developed a symbiosis between itself and its fans that was typical of an initially democratic musical scene. As Airplane guitarist Paul Kantner himself acknowledged, "it was like a party. The audience often far overshadowed any of the bands, and the distance between the two was not that great. Grace [Slick] used to say that the stage was just the least crowded place to stand."

Jefferson Airplane was the first of the San Francisco bands to sign with a major record label. The debut album *Jefferson Airplane Takes Off* (1966) was moderately successful. However, it was not until original vocalist Signe Anderson departed and was replaced by Slick that the band achieved wider acclaim and commercial success. Slick left rival band the Great Society to join the Airplane and significantly brought two songs with her—the antiromantic love song "Somebody to Love" and the trippy "White Rabbit." These tracks subsequently became the first of the group's Top 10 hits and were featured on the breakthrough album *Surrealistic Pillow* (1967), which stayed in the *Billboard* Top 10 for most of what became known as the "summer of love."

The counterculture was built around rock music, which expressed its values and acted as a powerful recruiting vehicle for the movement. In January 1967 Jefferson Airplane had played at a countercultural gathering christened the "Human Be-In" alongside the poets Allen Ginsberg and Gary Snyder in San

Francisco's Golden Gate Park. Later in the same year the band appeared at the nation's first national rock festival in Monterey, California, that drew an audience in excess of 200,000. While this event also was billed as a countercultural happening—"three days of music, love, and flowers"—it was also undeniably a shop window for profit-making talent. As Jon Landau wrote, Monterey witnessed an "underground culture at [the] point of transformation into mass culture."

COMMERCIAL APPEAL

Subsequent late-1960s recordings consolidated the band's commercial appeal. In 1969 it appeared at Woodstock, an event that confirmed that rock music was now big business and that any countercultural politics it might espouse had taken a backseat to hippie chic. In December of that same year Jefferson Airplane performed at Altamont—an event mythologized as symbolic of the death of the decade's youthful optimism. While the Rolling Stones played "Sympathy for the Devil," a number of members of the motorcycle gang Hells Angels murdered a black spectator, Meredith Hunter, and later attacked Airplane member Marty Balin when he tried to help another black youth. For Landau "Altamont showed that something had been lost that could not be regained."

In recognition of this shift in mood, the band released the angrier, more explicitly political album *Volunteers* (1969). Its lyrical and musical aggression channeled the frustration and outbursts of violence that characterized the tail end of the 1960s. In "We Can Be Together" the group called on listeners to unite and overthrow the "dangerous, dirty and dumb" policies of the establishment and screamed, "Up against the wall, motherfuckers." *Volunteers* was a powerful statement about post-Chicago 1968, Vietnam-embroiled America.

By the early 1970s any lingering idealism in the Bay Area music scene and the countercultural movement that it fed and served had evaporated. During this period founding member Balin left the band, which released two more studio albums and a live set, the last release to bear the Jefferson Airplane name.

The 1970s and 1980s were marked by personnel changes and shifts in musical style. Under the creative control of Kantner and Slick, the band evolved into Jefferson Starship. Balin's return in 1975 coincided with a revival in the band's commercial fortunes. However, Slick and Balin (again) left in 1978, and the 1979 album *Freedom from Point Zero* saw the band move toward a hard rock formula suited to the lucrative stadium market. Detoxed and dried out, Slick returned to the lineup in the early 1980s. Subsequently the band, minus Kantner and with its name shortened to Starship, emerged with a series of MTV-friendly hits such as the self-mythologizing "We Built This City" and the anodyne "Nothing's Gonna Stop Us Now." Things turned full circle in 1989 when Slick left Starship and joined up with the rest of the original lineup to resurrect Jefferson Airplane, but this lasted for only a short time. Jefferson Starship is the incarnation that lived on into the twenty-first century, playing through multiple personnel changes. The original Jefferson Airplane was inducted into the Rock and Roll Hall of Fame in 1996 and was the subject of a documentary film, *Fly Jefferson Airplane*, in 2004.

It has become impossible to separate West Coast Rock from the counterculture. This was ably demonstrated when "White Rabbit" was memorably featured in Oliver Stone's Vietnam movie *Platoon* (1986), in which it functioned as audio shorthand for a specific cultural moment. The 1960s is depicted as an era of peace movements and flower children, yet it was also characterized by widespread conflict and violence. The story of Jefferson Airplane demonstrates the tension between these two images of the period.

Simon Philo

SEE ALSO: *Altamont; Ginsberg, Allen; The Grateful Dead; Haight-Ashbury; Hells Angels; Hippies; MTV; Rock and Roll; The Rolling Stones; Vietnam; Woodstock.*

BIBLIOGRAPHY

Fenton, Craig. *Take Me to a Circus Tent: The Jefferson Airplane Flight Manual.* West Conshohocken, PA: Infinity Publishing, 2006.

Friedlander, Paul. *Rock and Roll: A Social History.* Boulder, CO: Westview, 1996.

Gillett, Charlie. *The Sound of the City: The Rise of Rock and Roll.* London: Souvenir Press, 1983.

Gleason, Ralph. *The Jefferson Airplane and the San Francisco Sound.* New York: Ballantine, 1969.

Landau, Jon. "It's Too Late to Stop Now." In *The Penguin Book of Rock and Roll Writing*, ed. Clinton Heylin. London: Viking/Penguin, 1992.

Palmer, Robert. *Dancing in the Street: A Rock and Roll History.* London: BBC Books, 1996.

Slick, Grace, and Andrea Cagan. *Somebody to Love? A Rock-and-Roll Memoir.* New York: Warner Books, 1998.

Storey, John. "Rockin' Hegemony: West Coast Rock and Amerika's War in Vietnam." In *Tell Me Lies about Vietnam*, ed. Alf Louvre and Jeffrey Walsh. Philadelphia: Open University Press, 1988.

Tamarkin, Jeff. *Got a Revolution!: The Turbulent Flight of Jefferson Airplane.* New York: Atria Books, 2005.

The Jeffersons

The Jeffersons, an American television sitcom, featured the comic antics of George Jefferson and his wife Louise, an African American couple who find themselves part of the nouveau riche. The show was a spin-off of the series *All in the Family*, which was created by veteran television writer and producer Norman Lear.

All in the Family, which debuted in 1968, was one of the most controversial television programs of the 1970s. The show starred Carroll O'Connor as Archie Bunker, a loud-mouthed, right-leaning, pigheaded bigot who lives in Queens, New York, with his ditzy wife, Edith (Jean Stapleton). Joining the couple are their childish grown daughter, Gloria (Sally Struthers), and their left-leaning ex-hippie son-in-law, Michael (Rob Reiner). One of the many occasional characters to appear on the show is Bunker's irascible African American neighbor, George Jefferson (Sherman Hemsley). Jefferson never backs down from a fight; he often jousts with the narrow-minded, dim-witted Bunker, trouncing him with clever repartee. Hemsley began the role of Jefferson in 1973, and two years later he was cast as the lead in the show *The Jeffersons*, which debuted on CBS television in January 1975.

Each episode of *The Jeffersons* opens with the up-tempo, gospel music-infused theme song, "Movin' on Up." George and Louise (Isabel Sanford) materialize as they move into their "dee-luxe apartment in the sky," a ritzy penthouse on Manhattan's fashionable and moneyed East Side. They live there with their grown son, Lionel (played at various times by Damon Evans and Mike Evans). By now, George is a successful businessman and millionaire—he owns seven dry-cleaning stores. His wife's job is to rein in her sometimes blockheaded husband and learn to adjust to the life of a woman of means. George is rude and headstrong and refers to white people as "honkies." An article in *Ebony* magazine describes him as "bombastic, frenetic, boastful, ill-mannered, prejudiced, and scheming." Referred to by George as "Weezy," Louise spends most of her time apologizing for him.

A unique supporting cast adds high jinks and panache to the show. Paul Benedict played Harry Bentley, an eccentric upper-class British neighbor. Ned Wetimer played the ever-obsequious Ralph the Doorman. Other neighbors include Helen and Tom Willis (Roxie Roker and Franklin Cover, respectively), an interracial couple with two adult children—one black, one white—very likely the first such racial pairing to be featured on prime-time American television. George's elderly mother, the quietly cantankerous but seriously comical Mother Jefferson, was played by Zara Cully until the actress's death in 1978. In addition, the Jeffersons have their own housekeeper, a wise-cracking maid named Florence (Marla Gibbs).

Indeed, some of the show's funniest moments are the scenes between George and Florence. She refers to him as Shorty and never misses a chance to put him in his place, fully contemptuous of the expected etiquette between employee and employer. George, though a millionaire businessman, is often positioned as a buffoon or the butt of someone's joke. As the *Ebony* article notes, "He was often the victim of his own acts: a put-down that backfires, a contrivance that goes astray, an ego-filled balloon suddenly deflated." No one, not even the hired help, takes him seriously.

The Jeffersons was an enormously popular and highly rated program that lasted ten years on prime-time television. Even so, the show endured its share of criticism. After a time, some members of the black community began to question whether audiences were laughing with George and his contempt for convention or at George as he made a fool of himself. Anthony W. Jackson noted that the character is "presented as a successful Black businessman . . . . Yet rarely, at best, is the viewing audience made aware of the intelligence and business savvy which allowed his success and affluence, even in a comical way. Rather we are endlessly bombarded with his narrow-mindedness, pomposity, meanness of spirit, and penchant for buffoonery. The image is one of a lucky clown who somehow made it big" (Jackson, p. 98). As with the controversial program *The Amos 'n' Andy Show*, which aired some twenty years prior (1951–1953), America's black community remains divided in their assessment of the program—even as the conservatism of the Ronald Reagan years brought a slight change in tone to the scripts.

Along with two other Lear products (*Good Times* and *Sanford and Son*), *The Jeffersons* features a predominantly African American cast, the first such programming since *The Amos 'n' Andy Show*. With biting humor and daring scenarios, *The Jeffersons* helped set a new tone in prime-time television, proving that such programming could be successful and profitable. Hemsley, a March 2012 inductee of the Academy of Television Arts & Sciences Hall of Fame who died later that year on July 24 in El Paso, Texas, talked extensively about the development of his Jefferson character and offerred his opinion on the popularity of the sitcom on the academy's foundation website. The show continues its run in syndication and is available on DVD.

Pamala S. Deane

SEE ALSO: All in the Family*;* The Amos 'n' Andy Show*;* Good Times*; Lear, Norman;* Sanford and Son*; Sitcom; Television.*

BIBLIOGRAPHY

Barnouw, Erik. *Tube of Plenty: The Evolution of American Television*, 2nd rev. ed. New York: Oxford University Press, 1990.

Brooks, Tim, and Earle Marsh. *The Complete Directory to Prime Time Network and Cable TV Shows, 1946–Present*, 9th ed. New York: Ballantine Books, 2007.

Jackson, Anthony, ed. *Black Families and the Medium of Television*. Ann Arbor: Bush Program in Child Development and Social Policy, University of Michigan, 1982.

MacDonald, J. Fred. *Blacks and White TV: African Americans in Television since 1948*, 2nd ed. Chicago: Nelson-Hall Publishers, 1992.

Marc, David, and Robert J. Thompson. *Prime Time, Prime Movers: From "I Love Lucy" to "L.A. Law," America's Greatest TV Shows and the People Who Created Them*. Boston: Little, Brown, 1992.

Robinson, Louie. "*The Jeffersons*: A Look at Life on Black America's New 'Striver's Row.'" *Ebony*, January 1976.

"Sherman Hemsley." Academy of Television Arts & Sciences Foundation, Archive of American Television. Accessed December 2011. Available from http://www.emmytvlegends.org/interviews/people/sherman-hemsley

Taylor, Ella. *Prime Time Families: Television Culture in Postwar America*. Berkeley: University of California Press, 1989.

Jell-O

Once given its trademarked name, Jell-O gelatin quickly became "America's Most Famous Dessert," with more than one million boxes sold every day by the late 1990s. Even more than apple pie or hot dogs, Jell-O epitomizes not just American cuisine but America itself and has been one of its most enduring icons. Powdered gelatin, invented in 1845 by Peter Cooper, was one of the first convenience foods in America, making the arduous task of preparing gelatin from scratch—boiling calves' hooves for hours—merely a matter of adding water to powder and leaving in a cool place to set. Not until the end of the nineteenth century, however, did the concept of granulated gelatin catch on.

In 1897 Pearl B. Wait invented a fruit-flavored gelatin, named Jell-O by his wife. Because of low sales, he sold the patent to Orator Francis Woodward in 1899 for $450. Woodward began his first advertising campaign in 1902, making Jell-O, manufactured by the Genesee Pure Food Company of Le Roy, New York, a worthy contender with Knox, Cox, Plymouth Rock, and other instant gelatins on the market at the time. In 1909 Jell-O's profits were recorded as more than $1 million. Within four years, profits had quadrupled. By the early twenty-first century, the company was owned by Kraft/General Foods, and Jell-O was manufactured in Dover, Delaware. Kraft recorded profits of more than $1 billion in 2011.

THE GENESIS OF JELL-O

Although gelatin was an important ingredient in aspics and desserts, its rigorous preparation requirements meant that before the turn of the nineteenth century it graced only the tables of the wealthy, who had the time, money, equipment, and paid labor to prepare such dishes. Preparations like powdered gelatins helped to democratize desserts in America. Jell-O, the most popular brand, was inexpensive, initially selling for ten cents a box, and simple to make. Further, Jell-O instituted a premium system that allowed one to send away for free "melon" molds with the purchase of so many boxes of Jell-O products.

Even in its early years, Jell-O came in a variety of flavors that allowed cooks to create many bright, fanciful dishes. Strawberry, raspberry, orange, and lemon were the first flavors, and they continued to be the most popular. Lime was introduced in 1930. Jell-O also offered an Ice Cream Powder, which, something like a frozen pudding, brought a variation of the frozen confection to the homes of the masses. Genesee also began producing D-Zerta, the first sugar-free gelatin, in 1923. Later that same year the company changed its name to the Jell-O Company and was then acquired by the Postum Company in 1925, forming the foundation for what became General Foods. Rounding out its product line, the Jell-O Company introduced its pudding powder in 1929, eventually making fifty-one different flavors.

Advertising played a key role in Jell-O's popularity over other gelatins and made it the quintessential "American" dessert.

Jell-O. *Since its early years at the turn of the 20th century, Jell-O gelatin has come in a variety of flavors and colors that make bright desserts.* BILL HOGAN/CHICAGO TRIBUNE/MCT VIA GETTY IMAGES.

From the beginning, brightly colored promotional recipe booklets touted the Jell-O product line and also educated Americans about how to use this new foodstuff. The Jell-O Girl appeared in 1903 as the personification of Jell-O's purity and ease of preparation. In later years the talents of well-known people were instituted to promote Jell-O. Rose O'Neil, creator of Kewpie dolls, refashioned the Jell-O Girl in 1908. In the 1920s such familiar artists as Norman Rockwell and Maxfield Parrish illustrated Jell-O's print material. Even L. Frank Baum, author of the *Wizard of Oz* series, published a set of his books in conjunction with Jell-O. The connection with the series has remained an important element in Jell-O's history, and Jell-O-Brick Road is maintained in Le Roy as a way of preserving that history.

In later years, as advertising media expanded, so did Jell-O's use of popular talents, including famous celebrities. Jack Benny and Mary Livingston promoted it on radio, coming up with the catchy "J-E-L-L-O" tune. Kate Smith sang the praises of Jell-O in magazine advertisements during World War II. In the 1950s such luminaries as Roy Rogers, Andy Griffith, and Ethel Barrymore became spokespeople. Since the 1970s actor and comedian Bill Cosby has been the chief spokesperson for Jell-O and Jell-O Pudding.

The history of Jell-O has traditionally reflected transformations in eating patterns and ethnic and regional variations in American foodways. In *The Encyclopedia of Bad Taste*, Jane and Michael Stern write, "More than any other food, Jell-O symbolizes how America really eats. . . . Jell-O is Americana in a mold." At the beginning of the twentieth century, Jell-O proved to be an affordable and accessible version of a previously upper-class food, hence its great appeal. In later years it reflected events in American history and changes in food fads. During World War I Jell-O still sold for ten cents a box and helped families to live within their budgets during the war years. During World War II it answered the needs brought on by food rationing because it could be used as either a low-sugar dessert or as a salad.

Because Jell-O by nature is a colorful and moldable substance, the things made from it have embodied America's aesthetic sensibilities of the time, from daring dishes such as Egg Slices en Gelée in the Roaring Twenties to modern Jell-O cheesecake in the convenience-driven 1950s to postmodern creations like Pistachio Pineapple Delight—also known as Watergate Salad—in the 1980s. Jell-O not only manifested adult preoccupations but also appealed to the younger set. Ever since the days of the Jell-O Girl, Jell-O was associated with children, who have constituted a large group of Jell-O's consumers. Cosby's 1970s "Kids Love Pudding" campaign was followed by the advent of multicolored, multishaped Jell-O Jigglers for children of the 1980s and increased the popularity of gelatin-based candies like Gummy Bears in the 1980s and Gummy Worms in the 1990s.

Jell-O's versatility was a large factor in its enduring nature as an icon of American culture during the twentieth century. It has frequently appeared as a palliative dessert on hospital meal trays, accompanied families to potluck dinners as a side dish, and shown up in the lunch boxes of schoolchildren. It has also been used in ways not officially approved of by the General Foods Corporation. Jell-O "shooters," made of Jell-O gelatin powder mixed with vodka or grain alcohol, became popular in the 1980s and 1990s as college novelty cocktails. Once congealed, they were eaten with spoons out of cups or by the cube from trays. Jell-O shots using vodka, rum, or tequila are still popular, and their use is no longer limited to college students. Enterprising cooks are also substituting other liquids such as root beer for added twists. Novelty wrestling, a popular bar entertainment during the 1980s, involved body-to-body combat of typically scantily-clad women; when not wrestling in mud, they wrestled in Jell-O, with lime being the most popular color/flavor.

Wendy Woloson

SEE ALSO: *Advertising; Benny, Jack; Cosby, Bill; The Great Depression; Rockwell, Norman; Rogers, Roy; The Twenties;* The Wizard of Oz; *World War I; World War II.*

BIBLIOGRAPHY

Celebrating 100 Years of Jell-O. Lincolnwood, IL: Publications International, 1997.

Inness, Sherrie, ed. *Cooking Lessons: The Politics of Gender and Food.* Lanham, MD: Rowman & Littlefield, 2001.

LeBesco, Kathleen, and Peter Naccarato, eds. *Edible Ideologies: Representing Food and Meaning.* Albany: State University of New York, 2008.

Stern, Jane, and Michael Stern. *The Encyclopedia of Bad Taste.* New York: HarperCollins, 1990.

Jennings, Peter *(1938–2005)*

Peter Jennings was among the most respected newscasters and TV journalists of the late twentieth and early twenty-first centuries. Remembered as the man who helped usher in the age of the super-anchor, Jennings got an early start to his broadcast career. At age nine he was the host of *Peter's People*, a short-lived Saturday morning children's radio show on the Canadian Broadcasting Corporation network. For the precocious Jennings, journalism qualified as a family business. When the Canadian Broadcasting Corporation was established in the mid-1930s, his father Charles Jennings became its first voice, and he was known as the "Edward R. Murrow of Canada." After serving as American Broadcasting Companies (ABC) bureau chief in Lebanon for most of the 1970s, Peter Jennings became coanchor of the network's evening news channel, a position he held until his death in 2005.

Jennings was born in Toronto. A high school dropout, he never finished tenth grade. Initially discouraged by his father from choosing journalism as a career, Jennings worked as a bank teller for three years before joining a small private radio station in Brockville, Ontario. In 1961 Jennings made the transition to television, joining one of Canada's first private television stations. There his duties included everything from reporting news to hosting a Canadian version of *American Bandstand.* When his television station became part of CTV, Canada's first national private chain, Jennings was appointed coanchor of the national newscast. His work in this role caught the attention of ABC news executives in New York.

MOVE TO ABC

Hired by ABC's *World News Tonight* in 1964, Jennings and his first wife, Canadian Valerie Godsoe, moved to New York City. Within a year, the twenty-six-year-old Jennings became America's youngest national network anchor ever, an appointment that failed because Jennings lacked journalistic experience and in-depth knowledge of the United States. After three years of poor ratings, he resigned and was replaced by Frank Reynolds. The network made Jennings a traveling correspondent, and he quickly headed overseas. In 1969 he opened a permanent ABC bureau in Beirut, Lebanon, the first time a U.S.-based television reporter held a full-time post in the Arab world. Jennings spent seven years in Lebanon as Beirut bureau chief.

In 1975 Jennings returned to Washington, D.C., to anchor *A.M. America*, the predecessor to *Good Morning America.* Disliking both the job and the city, however, he arranged a transfer to London by 1977. In 1978, while still posted in London, Jennings was named coanchor of the ABC evening news as part of an innovative three-anchor system that included Reynolds in Washington and Max Robinson in Chicago. Referring to his time in London as his "dream job" because the triumvirate system gave him both the flexibility to travel and the status to cover major news stories, he stayed in the position for six years.

THE LONE ANCHOR

In 1983 one of the anchoring triumvirate, Reynolds, became ill with cancer, and Jennings reluctantly returned to the United States to fill in during his illness. In an interview he explained his problem with being sole anchor: "Anchorpeople are slaves to the daily broadcast. Very high-priced slaves, I grant you. But slaves." Instead, Jennings preferred field reporting, and he was known to speak with a "little regret about not being in the trenches covering stories." When Reynolds died, however, Jennings was reappointed to the sole anchor position he had held sixteen years earlier.

Jennings and his peers Dan Rather (at CBS) and Tom Brokaw (and NBC) transformed the role of network news anchor into superstar journalist. In their book *Anchors*, authors Robert and Gerald Goldberg explain that while Walter Cronkite was "the original 800-pound gorilla," Jennings, Rather, and Brokaw "acquired a different order of magnitude." These super-anchors commanded huge salaries and had their trustworthiness figures measured just like the president. Acting as the "living logos" of the network news divisions, they provided news to more Americans than any other source.

Some analysts point to Jennings's coverage of the 1986 *Challenger* space shuttle explosion as a career milestone, from which point his "credibility, both internally at ABC and with the American public, has continued to grow." Once described as a "natural anchor" who had to work hard "to turn himself into a reporter," Jennings grew into his role as star journalist. Acclaimed for his ability to ad-lib in live broadcasts, Jennings said that he considered that skill to be a critical function of anchors. Despite the fact that the majority of Jennings's editorial work involved rewriting rather than writing, colleagues described his writing style as "distinctive" and "cooler" than that of Rather or Brokaw. Analysts noted a tendency for Jennings to reverse the traditional order of a news story, for example, putting the punch line before a joke.

Described as "perhaps the most hands-on of any of the anchors," Jennings reportedly spent a great deal of time working with correspondents on the phone and editing their stories. While coworkers often lauded his willingness to spend time working with people and sharing ideas, contacts, and opinions, some complained about a tendency toward micromanaging and perfectionism. Most of all, however, observers noted that Jennings applies those stringent standards to himself. Reportedly never satisfied with his performance, he was frequently quoted as saying, "I always tend to look at the program in terms of how many nights I can be proud of. The top score is rarely more than two and a half a week. Never close to four."

REPUTATION FOR EXCELLENCE

Into the early twenty-first century, Jennings remained one of the most trusted voices in American news reporting. On New Year's Eve, 1999, the anchor helmed the news special *ABC 2000* for twenty-five consecutive hours, a singular achievement among the major network news programs. More than 175 million Americans watched Jennings usher in the 2000s, the largest audience for a live television event in history. His indefatigable coverage helped earn the network a Peabody Award. Jennings also became a published author, collaborating with Todd Brewster in producing the best-selling history books *The Century* (1998) and *In Search of America* (2002); both works were companion pieces to TV news miniseries.

One of the high points in Jennings's career came in the aftermath of the terrorist attacks of September 11, 2001. In the days following the event, Jennings was widely hailed for his calm, reassuring demeanor in the face of tragedy, devoting more than sixty hours to anchoring the network's coverage. His 9/11 reporting garnered both a Peabody and a duPont Award. In 2004 Jennings was the only major news anchor to report live from the court proceedings against deposed Iraqi dictator Saddam Hussein. That same year, he won an Edward R. Murrow Award for his documentary *The Kennedy Assassination: Beyond Conspiracy*.

In early 2005 Jennings shocked the nation when he revealed that he had been diagnosed with lung cancer. He died on August 7 of that year. A month later, the anchor's colleagues, friends, and fans gathered at a ceremony in New York to pay respect to his career. Speaking before a crowd of roughly 2,200 guests, fellow news anchor Ted Koppel spoke of Jennings's unique personal charm and grace. "Not many people had that genuine charisma," Koppel told the gathering, "that sort of animal magnetism that makes it difficult to focus on anyone else in the room." In the months following Jennings's death, many of his former colleagues at ABC News wore blue bracelets reading "What Would Peter Do?" in his honor.

Courtney Bennett

SEE ALSO: *Brokaw, Tom;* Challenger *Disaster; Cronkite, Walter; Murrow, Edward R.; 9/11; Rather, Dan; Television; Television Anchors.*

BIBLIOGRAPHY

Goldberg, Robert, and Gerald Jay Goldberg. *Anchors: Brokaw, Jennings, Rather and the Evening News*. Secaucus, NJ: Carol Publishing Group, 1990.

Jennings, Peter, and Todd Brewster. *The Century*. New York: Doubleday, 1998.

Kurtz, Howard. "Peter Jennings's Fans Remember an Anchor of Their Lives." *Washington Post*, September 21, 2005.

Steinberg, Jacques. "ABC News Remembers Peter Jennings as It Moves on without Him. *New York Times*, January 9, 2006.

Jennings, Waylon *(1937–2002)*

A professional musician since the 1950s, Waylon Jennings is known for his contribution to the country-and-western "Outlaw Movement" of the 1970s. Along with Willie Nelson, Billy Joe

Waylon Jennings. *Waylon Jennings is known as a force behind country music's "Outlaw Movement" in the 1970s.* STEPHANIE CHERNIKOWSKI/MICHAEL OCHS ARCHIVES/GETTY IMAGES.

Shaver, Kris Kristofferson, Tompall Glaser, and wife Jessi Colter, Jennings bucked the Nashville system in a big way. His 1973 release *Honky Tonk Heroes*, with all but one song penned by Shaver, defined the movement and the era. Recorded with his road band and not the slick studio musicians that most Nashville labels preferred, Jennings created a sound that was edgy and most certainly of the traditional honky-tonk variety.

EARLY CAREER

Born Waylon Arnold Jennings in Littlefield, Texas, Jennings learned to play guitar, formed his own band, and was a disc jockey (DJ) on a local radio station by the time he was twelve. Leaving school several years later, he ended up in Lubbock, where he became friends with future rock-and-roll legend Buddy Holly. A mentor of sorts, Holly produced Jennings's first recording, a single on Brunswick released in 1958 called "Jole Blon." Later that same year Jennings joined Holly's band, the Crickets, playing bass during the course of Holly's final tour. It was Jennings who gave up his seat to the Big Bopper on the ill-fated airplane that crashed in Mason City, Iowa, on February 3, 1959. Along with Holly and the Big Bopper, a young Los Angeles rocker, Ritchie Valens, lost his life. Jennings was devastated and returned to Lubbock, where he worked as a DJ.

A move to Phoenix in 1960 and the formation of a rockabilly band, the Waylors, gave Jennings another shot at success. Signing with the independent Trend label, the Waylors cut a number of singles. Although the records failed to create a buzz, Jennings did get his first shot as a record producer at Audio Recorders. A move to Los Angeles followed, as did a contract with Herb Alpert's A&M Records. Alpert looked at Jennings as a pop artist, but Jennings was already hip-deep in country music. His only single for A&M was "Sing the Girl a Song, Bill." By 1965 he made the move to Nashville, Tennessee, where he worked with Chet Atkins and Bobby Bare for RCA. At this time Jennings met Johnny Cash and they formed a strong bond.

OUTLAW MOVEMENT

Releasing hits such as "That's the Chance I'll Have to Take," Jennings quickly moved into the Top 10 by 1968 with tunes such as "Only Daddy That'll Walk the Line." Jennings, who was working with session players, wanted to move his sound more toward the hard-core side of country music. During the 1970s he began recording songs by a songwriter named Kris Kristofferson and working with Willie Nelson. Releasing *Singer of Sad Songs* and *Ladies Love Outlaws* provided the foundation for the "Outlaw Movement" that was to come. Just as significant, in 1972 Jennings successfully renegotiated his RCA contract demanding total control over the production of his next project. This project was *Honky Tonk Heroes.*

Gaining momentum, Jennings had his first number one single in 1974, "This Time." He followed up with another number one single, "I'm a Ramblin' Man" and a number two hit, "Rainy Day Woman." By 1975 he also was crossing over to the pop charts with "Are You Sure Hank Done It This Way." Awarded the Country Music Association's Male Vocalist of the Year Award, Jennings found himself entering mainstream popular culture. This was underscored by the release in 1976 of *Wanted! The Outlaws*, recorded with his wife, Nelson, and Glaser. It hit number one on the pop charts and made Jennings a superstar.

POP SUCCESS

The next decade would secure Jennings's place in the collective consciousness of popular culture. Working with Nelson, a series of duets resulted in hits such as "Mammas Don't Let Your Babies Grow Up to Be Cowboys" and the multiplatinum 1978 album *Waylon & Willie.* As a solo artist, Jennings scored big on both the country and pop charts with "Luckenbach, Texas (Back to the Basics of Love)." He also became part of the cast of the successful hit TV series *The Dukes of Hazzard*, for which he also wrote the theme song. Jennings appeared in several television movies and had a cameo in the big-screen release *Maverick* in 1994. A guest spot on the Fox series *Married . . . with Children* also brought Jennings popular attention.

By the mid-1980s Jennings's musical career was suffering from a lack of radio airplay. The pop-tinged "hot, young country" fad made it nearly impossible for Jennings and his peers, including country crooner George Jones, to be heard. Radio-driven, country-and-western music had always appealed to a grassroots fan base that depended upon radio for entertainment. This shift made it difficult for Jennings to remain at the top of his profession by industry standards. Still, joining up with old friends Nelson, Cash, and Kristofferson, Jennings forged ahead and formed the super group, the Highwaymen in 1985. Releasing three projects over the next decade, the group had a number one hit with their first single, "The Highwayman."

LATER CAREER

After twenty years with RCA, Jennings moved to MCA in 1986. He had several hits with MCA, most notably "Rose in Paradise," but found he was stifled by age discrimination within the country-music industry. In 1990 he went over to Epic and had two more Top 40 hits with "Wrong" and "The Eagle." Back with RCA, he released *Waymore Blues (Part II)* in 1994. By 1996 Jennings had signed with Texas independent label Justice Records and released the critically acclaimed *Right for the Time.* That same year, RCA put together a twentieth-anniversary edition of *Wanted! The Outlaws.*

In 1998 Jennings overcame major health problems, much as he had done earlier when he had been forced to deal with drug and alcohol abuse, and he joined a new band, the Old Dogs. Together with Mel Tillis, Jerry Reed, and Bare, Jennings created a strong country sound that defied the youth-oriented country music business. With songs penned by Shel Silverstein, the topic of the Old Dogs projects was "getting old." With humor and irreverence, the country-music foursome gleaned strength from their unity and shared history as they came to terms with the process of aging. Released on Atlantic Records, *Old Dogs, Vol. I* and *Vol. II*, gave notice that Jennings was once again a working artist. Nothing would keep him down—not old age, ill health, or an ungrateful music industry.

During the course of his career, Jennings maintained a high level of individuality and always remained true to his own vision. Musically, he set in motion a precedent that upholds the traditional tenets of country-and-western music. Younger artists who refuse to kowtow to the Nashville system cite Jennings as a strong influence. He also made his presence felt in music beyond the bounds of country, performing in 1996 on the Lollapalooza Tour with heavy-metal stars Metallica. Gritty and honest, Jennings's distinctive baritone and sense of self made him a towering influence within country-and-western music.

In 2000 Jennings underwent procedures to treat the lack of circulation in his legs caused by diabetes. The diabetes continued to worsen, however, and his left foot was amputated. Always the outlaw, he declined to attend his induction into the Country

Music Hall of Fame in 2001. Jennings died on February 13, 2002, from complications of diabetes. Since his death, he has been posthumously awarded the Cliffie Stone Pioneer Award by the Academy of Country Music as well as the Lifetime Achievement Award by the Nashville Songwriters' Festival.

Jana Pendragon

SEE ALSO: *Atkins, Chet; Big Bopper; Cash, Johnny; Country Music; Diamond, Neil; Disc Jockeys;* Dukes of Hazzard*; Holly, Buddy; Jones, George; Lollapalooza;* Married . . . with Children*; Nelson, Willie; Radio; Top 40; Valens, Ritchie.*

BIBLIOGRAPHY

Cash, Johnny, and Patrick Carr. *Cash: The Autobiography*. San Francisco: Harper, 1997.

Denisoff, Serge. *Waylon: A Biography*. Knoxville: University of Tennessee Press, 1983.

Jennings, Waylon, and Lenny Kaye. *Waylon: An Autobiography*. New York: Warner Books, 1996.

Jeopardy!

The popular television game show *Jeopardy!* reversed the "question and answer" format typical of most trivia shows, to the delight of fans who have followed the show either on NBC or in syndication since its debut in March 1964. The unique format of *Jeopardy!* was established in response to the quiz show scandals of 1958, giving contestants the answers up front and requiring them to provide the correct questions. Three contestants vie for cash by supplying correct questions to answers revealed on a board of thirty squares containing five answers in each of six categories. The show, originally hosted by Art Fleming, consists of three rounds: Jeopardy, Double Jeopardy, and Final Jeopardy.

After a five-year hiatus *Jeopardy!* returned to the air in 1984 hosted by game-show veteran Alex Trebek. With his erudite manner and textbook pronunciation of foreign words and phrases, Trebek became the object of admiration and scorn, gaining a wide viewership of fans who were riveted by the show and critics who were eager to see his rare blunders. By the end of the 1980s *Jeopardy!* had become one of the most popular first-run syndicated series, packaged by King World Entertainment with the perennial primetime favorite *Wheel of Fortune*. A lucrative merchandising vehicle as well, *Jeopardy!* spawned home versions of the game and computerized scoring devices that viewers could use to play along at home.

Jeopardy! was the leading game show during the 1990s, and Trebek earned a star on the Hollywood Walk of Fame in 1999, but the future of the show appeared to be tenuous due to an aging and limited demographic. Then came a revival of *Hollywood Squares* in 1998 and the advent of *Who Wants to Be a Millionaire*, which topped television ratings charts almost instantly in 1999. That was followed by *Survivor* and *American Idol*, ushering in the era of reality television.

Jeopardy! had helped launch the reality television wave, and now it rode that wave into the twenty-first century by introducing new ideas to keep the show fresh. The five-episode limit on a returning champion was lifted in 2003, enabling Ken Jennings to set a record of seventy-four consecutive wins during the 2004–2005 season, earning him more than $2.5 million. Five-time *Jeopardy!* winner and stand-up comedian Bob Harris published a creative nonfiction book titled *Prisoner of Trebekistan: A Decade in Jeopardy!* in 2006. In 2011 *Jeopardy!* celebrated its 6,000th episode with its first Teachers Tournament, and IBM's "Watson" supercomputer won a man-versus-machine *Jeopardy!* showdown against two former champions, Jennings and Brad Rutter, representing a milestone for computer developers in their quest to create a computer that can communicate more naturally with human beings.

Trebek received a Lifetime Achievement Award from the National Academy of Television Arts & Sciences in 2011, his 27th year hosting *Jeopardy!*, and the show earned a Peabody Award in 2012.

Tilney Marsh

SEE ALSO: American Idol*; Game Shows; Griffin, Merv; Hollywood;* Hollywood Squares*; IBM (International Business Machines); Milton Bradley; Quiz Show Scandals; Reality Television;* Survivor*; Syndication; Television;* Wheel of Fortune*;* Who Wants to Be a Millionaire.

BIBLIOGRAPHY

McNeil, Alex. *Total Television: A Comprehensive Guide to Programming from 1948 to the Present*, 4th ed. New York: Penguin, 1996.

Trebek, Alex, and Peter Barsocchini. *The Jeopardy! Book: The Answers, the Questions, the Facts, and the Stories of the Greatest Game Show in History*. New York: HarperPerennial, 1990.

Jessel, George *(1898–1981)*

American comedian, actor, and producer George Jessel lived his life in show business, and he toiled with boundless energy to adapt to the changing modes of the entertainment world. His professional career spanned three-quarters of a century, from 1907 to just before his death. Primarily, he was a live-audience entertainer, with his show-business persona evolving from the cocky but lovable Jewish American immigrant boy to the middle-aged professional emcee and purveyor of nostalgia and then on to the pompous, self-proclaimed Toastmaster General of the United States.

With an unfailingly brash personality, good looks, a nasal voice, and quick-tongued wit, Jessel began performing in children's musical comedy at the age of nine, shortly after the death of his father. Before long he was a featured performer with other youthful talents such as Eddie Cantor and Walter Winchell in vaudeville acts produced and written by Gus Edwards. By the time he reached his twenties, Jessel had developed into a successful vaudeville monologist, with a specialty routine of speaking on the telephone to his immigrant Jewish Momma. Each of his dozens of comical telephone routines similarly began, "Hello, Operator! Fentingtrass 3522. Hello, Momma? Georgie!"

In spite of his prosperity in vaudeville, Jessel strived to conquer New York's legitimate stage. He received his break in 1925 when he was awarded the role of Jack Robin/Jakie Rabinowitz in Samson Raphaelson's *The Jazz Singer*, a melodrama about a young man torn between the confining world of his Jewish roots and the exhilarating American culture of the Jazz Age. Jessel successfully performed the role in New York and around the country for two years and was negotiating with Warner Brothers to star in the film version. Yet the role was not to be his, due in part to his extraordinary demands for remuneration and the fact that Al Jolson (who had been Raphaelson's inspiration for writing *The Jazz Singer*) had become interested in playing the screen role. Jessel may have been a headliner in vaudeville and a success in the play, but Jolson was the king of their profession, a nationally known top draw who would garner a much larger audience. Jessel never forgave Jolson for usurping the role and publicly griped about the circumstances of the loss for decades.

Jessel's own career as a film star was quite short-lived, in part because his ethnicity limited his opportunities for lead roles. Also, the few feature films he made in the late 1920s demonstrated that his guileless acting style was more suited to the stage than to the close scrutiny of the motion picture camera. He fared better in radio and onstage as a nightclub and variety show emcee/singer/comedian.

By 1945, as American soldiers were returning home from World War II, Twentieth Century Fox recognized a desire among moviegoers to look backward with longing to the lifestyle of the early years of the century. Acknowledging in the middle-aged Jessel an expertise in selling nostalgia to audiences, Fox signed him to produce musicals that featured warm memories of show business and home life. Among the charming and heartwarming films he produced in the immediate postwar years are *The Dolly Sisters* (1945), *When My Baby Smiles at Me* (1948), and *Oh, You Beautiful Doll* (1949). Yet Jessel's personal life was fraught with scandal. He was married four times, claimed numerous love affairs, and was involved in a $200,000 paternity suit.

As Jessel aged, he became more effusive in his onstage monologues. As a popular emcee, he made elaborate after-dinner speeches at testimonials to leading performers. This style of monologue evolved into Jessel's becoming the self-proclaimed Toastmaster General of the United States. By the Vietnam War years, he had become an aging self-parody as he appeared on television talk shows in military regalia. In that capacity, he endlessly pontificated on the state of the world and shamelessly name-dropped as he cited his association with politicians and royalty. As more years passed and many of his colleagues and friends died, he put his talent for speechmaking to work as a eulogizer at many celebrity funerals.

Even when his own health was fading, Jessel refused to quit show business. Although his audience had dwindled and he was considered—by those who remembered him at all—the ghost of vaudeville past, Jessel still performed, telling jokes in restaurants and obtaining an occasional club date.

Audrey E. Kupferberg

SEE ALSO: *Cantor, Eddie;* The Jazz Singer*; Jolson, Al; Vaudeville; Winchell, Walter.*

BIBLIOGRAPHY

Cullen, Frank; Florence Hackman; and Donald McNeilly. *Vaudeville Old & New*, Vol. 1. New York: Routledge, 2004.

Jessel, George. *"Hello, Momma."* Cleveland, OH: World Publishing, 1946.

Jessel, George. *This Way Miss.* New York: Holt, 1955.

Jessel, George. *Elegy in Manhattan.* New York: Holt, 1961.

Jessel, George. *The World I Lived In.* New York: Regnery, 1975.

Jesus Christ Superstar

Few musical forms have fallen into lower repute than the rock opera. Through the bombastic efforts of a handful of well-meaning composers, the whole enterprise has become almost synonymous with egotism in the minds of pop music consumers. Yet the form still has its adherents. A stage revival of the Who's trailblazing *Tommy* (1969) opened to packed houses on Broadway in 1995, and *Jesus Christ Superstar*, the mind-blowing 1970 rock opera about the last days of Christ, continues to work its magic on theatergoers the world over in countless touring company and summer stock productions.

CONTROVERSIAL SUBJECT MATTER

Originally conceived as a stage musical, *Jesus Christ Superstar* was the brainchild of two enterprising English whiz kids, composer Andrew Lloyd Webber, who was twenty-three at the time, and lyricist Tim Rice, who was twenty-six. The pair's 1968 collaboration *Joseph and the Amazing Technicolor Dreamcoat* had set the Old Testament story of Jacob's feuding sons to a throbbing backbeat, to the consternation of many in the rabbinate. With *Superstar*, the composers took the even more audacious step of setting the sufferings of Jesus to music. Not surprisingly, they had difficulty finding financial support for such a venture. They were forced to give up their stage plans and settle instead for a double album. Dubbed a "concept album" in the hipster parlance of the times, the recording was released in late 1970 with a drab brown cover featuring almost no religious iconography.

The question of blasphemy aside, few could dispute the quality of the recording. A tight backing band provides muscular support for vocalists Murray Head, Ian Gillian, and Yvonne Elliman. The work's twenty-four songs chronicle the final days of Jesus, from his entry into Jerusalem through his trial and Crucifixion by the Roman authorities. A number of songs are cast in the form of dialogues, with various New Testament figures hurling accusations and invectives at one another. The balladeering chores were assigned to the Hawaiian-born Elliman, whose mellifluous renditions of "Everything's Alright" and "I Don't Know How to Love Him" became FM radio staples.

A mass-market rock-and-roll composition on so hallowed a subject could not pass public scrutiny without generating some religious controversy. However, negative reaction to *Superstar* was muted and with good reason. While hardly the stuff of a theological dissertation, *Superstar* is no less scripturally sound than the average Catholic missal. Other than the arguably tasteless references to Christ as "J.C.," there is little in the work to offend Christian traditionalists. The issue of Jesus's Resurrection is bypassed entirely, consistent with the entire opera's depiction of Jesus as an imperfect mortal struggling with a divine commission he does not fully understand. "If you knew the path we're riding," sings Gillian's Jesus in one number, "you'd understand it less than I." Among traditionalists, perhaps the most galling part of the musical is the central role afforded to Judas Iscariot, voiced with quivering urgency by Murray Head. Questioning both the political message and personal behavior of his master in such songs as "Heaven on Their Minds," this Judas is no treacherous asp but rather a conflicted, doubting Thomas.

***Crucifixion Scene in* Jesus Christ Superstar.** *Ted Neeley as Jesus is crucified by Roman soldiers in a scene from* Jesus Christ Superstar *in 1973.* UNIVERSAL/GETTY IMAGES.

A SMASH HIT

Jesus Christ Superstar sold more than two million copies in twelve months and became 1971's top-selling album. In July 1971, 13,000 people packed Pittsburgh's Civic Arena to see the opera performed in concert. That performance was the precursor to a full-blown Broadway production—the realization of Rice and Lloyd Webber's original dream—that opened at the Mark Hellinger Theater in New York on October 12, 1971. Newcomer Jeff Fenholt assumed the role of Jesus, while a youthful Ben Vereen played Judas. Surprisingly, Lloyd Webber would later renounce this production, which lasted twenty months on Broadway.

More to the composer's liking was the 1973 film version, directed by Norman Jewison. Today the film seems dated, with its army of scraggly hippies disembarking from a psychedelic bus. However, it benefits from a number of strong performances. African American actor Carl Anderson makes a dynamic Judas, while Texas rock drummer Ted Neeley, an understudy in the Broadway production, brings a wild-eyed passion to the title role. Derided by some as "the screaming Jesus" for his piercing tremolo, Neeley was given the part only after Gillian turned it down because he could make more money touring with his band Deep Purple. Neeley has since turned playing Jesus Christ into a career, calling himself "a palette on which people project the Jesus they came to see."

REVIVALS

Spurred on by a wave of 1970s-era nostalgia, *Superstar* was revived in the 1990s. A twenty-five-month, 116-city tour, starring Styx's Dennis DeYoung, was mounted in 1994. A made-for-TV adaptation of the musical aired in 2000, starring Glen Carter as Jesus and directed by Gale Edwards and Nick Morris. It won an Emmy in 2001 for Best Performing Arts Film. Many of the actors in the film went on to perform in a Tony Award–winning musical revival that same year.

Jesus Christ Superstar was resurrected yet again in 2011, premiering at the Stratford Shakespeare Festival in Canada before a run at the La Jolla Playhouse in California. Directed by Des McAnuff, who won Tony Awards for *Jersey Boys* and the Who's *Tommy*, the modernized remake moved to Broadway in 2012. Though reviews were mixed, the revival was nominated for two Tony Awards.

Certainly *Jesus Christ Superstar* turned its composers, Lloyd Webber and Rice, into major celebrities. After they ended their professional relationship in 1978, Rice went on to cowrite the songs for Disney's *The Lion King* and Lloyd Webber created smash hits such as *Cats* and *Phantom of the Opera*.

Jesus Christ Superstar continues to meet with some localized pockets of resistance from those who disagree with its portrayal of a flawed, all-too-human Jesus. For the most part, however, it has legions of devoted fans who were acknowledged in a comment by Vereen: "What the people up in arms failed to look at is that as long as people were rockin' to Jesus, everything was gonna be all right for humanity."

Robert E. Schnakenberg

SEE ALSO: *Broadway;* Cats; *Disney (Walt Disney Company); Hippies;* The Lion King; *Lloyd Webber, Andrew; The Musi-*

cal; The Phantom of the Opera*; Pop Music; Rock and Roll; The Who.*

BIBLIOGRAPHY

Daly, Steve. "A Hit of Biblical Proportions." *Entertainment Weekly*, July 19, 1996, 88.

Isherwood, Charles. "A Glitzy Execution in a Religious Revival." *New York Times*, March 22, 2012.

Kelly, Christina. "A Superstar Is Reborn." *Entertainment Weekly*, December 23, 1994, 65.

Sella, Marshall. "Is God Ted?" *New York*, January 23, 1995, 46.

Jet

Jet is a weekly magazine, offering a synopsis of important news and events for African Americans. Introduced on November 1, 1951, by Chicago magazine publisher John H. Johnson, it is a pocket-size digest rather than the traditional magazine size. After its debut, *Jet* quickly gained acceptance among African Americans for providing understandable, accurate information, and they came to view it as the definitive word on current events. In the process of achieving that fame, *Jet* was the first national publication to print the photograph of the corpse of a fourteen-year-old boy who was lynched for whistling at a white woman in Mississippi in 1955. That picture alerted African Americans, especially those in the news media, to the growing civil rights movement in the South.

Johnson created *Jet* as the black version of *Quick*, a vest-pocket-size magazine featuring capsulized news that Americans could read "on the bus or in the beauty parlor." Introduced in 1949 by Gardner Cowles Jr., the publisher of *Look* magazine, *Quick* presented a problem for advertisers because its small size, 4 by 6 inches, required special advertising copy, and Cowles discontinued the publication in 1953 due to a lack of advertising. Johnson, who also published *Ebony*, the African American version of *Life* magazine, used the profits of *Ebony* to support his new pocket-size publication until advertisers adjusted. "In the world today everything is moving along at a faster clip," Johnson wrote in the first issue. "Each week we will bring to you complete news coverage on happenings among Negroes all over the U.S.—in entertainment, politics, sports, social events as well as features on unusual personalities, places and events." The first issue sold out and garnered a circulation of 300,000 within six months, making it the largest circulating black news magazine in the world.

In the 1950s lynching of African Americans, which dated back to slavery, still occurred in the South, and the U.S. Supreme Court decision in favor of Brown in the 1954 case *Brown v. Board of Education* desegregated public schools, making the South an even more dangerous place for blacks, a fact that visiting northern blacks did not always recognize. In August 1955, when fourteen-year-old Emmett Till, a Chicago boy visiting relatives in Money, Mississippi, allegedly whistled at a white woman, he was lynched and his corpse mutilated. His mother asked photographers to take pictures of his mangled body when it was returned to Chicago for burial.

Johnson and his editors agonized over the gruesome photographs but finally decided to publish them in the September 15, 1955, issue of *Jet*, providing the first national coverage of the murder. The issue sold out, traumatizing and angering African Americans and preparing "the way for the Freedom Movement of the sixties," as Johnson recalled. An interracial team of *Jet* and *Ebony* reporters and photographers covered the resulting trial in Mississippi, alerting other northern journalists to the deteriorating situation in the South. The historic Montgomery bus boycott, which was organized in response to the arrest and conviction of African American Rosa Parks for refusing to move to the back of a segregated bus, began in Montgomery, Alabama, just three months later, on December 1, 1955.

In the following years *Jet* reported on a wide variety of subjects, including the civil rights movement, business, education, religion, health, medicine, journalism, politics, labor, and crime. In the 1990s it offered features such as "Census," a weekly digest of births and deaths; "Ticker Tape U.S.A.," a discussion of news and news personalities written by Washington, D.C., bureau chief Simeon Booker; "This Week in Black History," a recap of traditional and more recent historical events; "People Are Talking About," gossip about personalities; "Sports," an overview of black athletes and predominantly black teams; and "Jet Beauty of the Week," featuring a young African American woman in a swimsuit.

Starting in 1999, *Jet* published its issues in full color, and in 2009 it added a monthly double issue. The magazine offers no editorial comment, although the stories and images of African Americans are positive and upbeat, reflecting Johnson's traditionalist beliefs in free markets and working within the system. Circulation peaked at close to one million in the 1990s but declined after the end of the twentieth century. It rebounded to around 700,000 in 2010 with a new editor and as a new generation of readers discovered *Jet*'s upbeat Afro-centric perspective.

Richard Junger

SEE ALSO: *African American Press; Civil Rights Movement;* Ebony*;* Life*; Parks, Rosa.*

BIBLIOGRAPHY

Dates, Jannette L., and William Barlow. *Split Image: African Americans in the Mass Media*. Washington, DC: Howard University Press, 1990, 374.

Johnson, John H., and Lerone Bennett Jr. *Succeeding against the Odds*. New York: Warner Books, 1989.

Marek, Lynne. "40 under 40—Mitzi Miller." *Crain's Chicago Business*, December 5, 2011.

Pride, Armistead S., and Clint C. Wilson. *A History of the Black Press*. Washington, DC: Howard University Press, 1997.

Wolseley, Roland E. *The Black Press, U.S.A*, 2nd ed. Ames: Iowa State University Press, 1990.

Jet Skis

In 1974 Kawasaki introduced the Jet Ski, a revolutionary jet-propelled, single-person watercraft capable of speeds up to 40 miles per hour. Based on the concept of a motorized water ski, the original Jet Ski required the rider to stand and use considerable strength and balance for control. It was not until 1986, when Yamaha introduced the WaveRunner, a more manageable sit-down version, that "personal watercraft" gained widespread appeal. Within ten years it blossomed into a $300-million-a-year industry, with annual sales of more than 200,000 in the United States alone, and led to the creation of two competitive Jet Ski racing circuits. But in the late 1990s, increased complaints about safety, fuel emissions, and noise resulted in a public backlash. Several states enforced mandatory driver's education and minimum age restrictions, and some areas, including Lake Tahoe, the San Juan Islands, and the majority of the national parks, banned the craft outright.

In spite of negative publicity, the personal watercraft remains a solid commodity. Bombardier and Polaris entered the market with their own models of watercraft, and Silveira Customs has most recently entered the fray with a sporting design called the Samba, which looks like a stingray and is ridden in a motorcycle-like crouch. Industry experts agree that the continued popularity of personal watercraft depends on improved driver education and cleaner, quieter engines, particularly as the power of the vehicles increases with each new version.

Simon Donner

SEE ALSO: *Leisure Time.*

Jewish Defense League

In 1968 Rabbi Meir Kahane started the Jewish Defense League (JDL) in the Orthodox Jewish neighborhoods of Brooklyn, New York. The JDL was initially a vigilante organization dedicated to the protection of Jews, but, fueled by the fanaticism of its founder, it swiftly grew to become one of America's highest-profile terrorist organizations. Between 1968 and 1987 members of the JDL committed fifty terrorist acts against the Palestine Liberation Organization, Soviet officials, and one Nazi war criminal. The organization forged close links with the conservative extremist Kach party in Israel. Rabbi Kahane was murdered by an Egyptian fundamentalist on November 5, 1990, and on February 25, 1994, Baruch Goldstein, a former JDL member, opened fire on Palestinians praying at a mosque on the West Bank, killing thirty people. The massacre resulted in the banning of the Kach party by the Israeli government.

In 2001 the FBI described the JDL as a "right-wing terror group," and it has been categorized as a "hate group" by the Southern Poverty Law Center. In the twenty-first century, various factions and splinter groups have vied for control of the JDL and its name.

S. Naomi Finkelstein

SEE ALSO: *FBI (Federal Bureau of Investigation); Fundaentalism.*

BIBLIOGRAPHY

Dolgin, Janet. *Jewish Identity and the JDL.* Princeton, NJ: Princeton University Press, 1977.

Gaines, Larry K. *Policing in America.* Amsterdam: Elsevier, 2011.

Kahane, Meir. *The Story of the Jewish Defense League.* Radnor, PA: Chilton Book, 1975.

JFK

After the 1991 release of *JFK,* director Oliver Stone's controversial film about the 1963 assassination of President John F. Kennedy (JFK), many Americans insisted that the U.S. government make the confidential files of the Warren Commission, the government body that investigated the assassination, available to the public. That the government released some (but not all) of the files following the film's popular success not only reflects the power of Stone's film but also the overall power of film as a pop culture medium.

With *JFK,* Stone challenged the U.S. government by providing an alternative theory to the one reached by the Warren Commission. Stone not only consulted texts by popular historians, such as Jim Garrison and Jim Marrs, and historical records, but he also posited his own interpretation of events concerning JFK's assassination. Although many individuals and groups had challenged the Warren Commission Report since its release, the American public had not responded to the report with a collective fervor until Stone presented his film. In response to viewer outcry, President George H. W. Bush "signed into law the President John F. Kennedy Assassination Records Collection Act of 1992. The bill provided for the establishment of an independent commission charged with releasing all government records related to Kennedy's assassination except those that clearly jeopardized personal privacy or national security."

JFK chronicles the events propelled into motion by New Orleans district attorney Garrison in 1969, when Garrison brought New Orleans businessman Clay Shaw to trial, accusing him of conspiring to assassinate JFK. The technical achievements of *JFK* add a dimension of realism to the film, but this realism makes it difficult for viewers to distinguish fact from fiction. For example, Stone blends actual film footage of the assassination with his fabricated footage, editing them together in a seamless fashion. And finally, there is Stone's theory about what really happened: The U.S. government; the military; the Mafia; Cuban nationalists; the military-industrial complex; Vice President Lyndon B. Johnson; and, of course, Shaw and Lee Harvey Oswald all conspired to assassinate JFK.

The response to *JFK* by the general public and the media was both positive and negative. Positive responses mostly came from those viewers whom Stone enlightened, such as younger Americans who knew little about the details of the assassination. The negative responses to the film came (and still come) from those whom Stone attacks, mainly the press, the government, and historians. Interestingly, to promote further reading on the topic and to appease his harshest critics, Stone released a fully documented screenplay to the film, replete with some ninety critical articles dealing with the film as well as the assassination itself and actual historical records.

Stone included the phrase "The Story That Won't Go Away" in his title for *JFK.* If the overall response to the film is any indication, this story certainly will not go away. If anything, Stone brought it back into the public consciousness. *JFK* is a film whose power relies not upon its accuracy in portraying certain events but upon its ability to reopen one of the darkest chapters in American history.

Jason T. McEntee

SEE ALSO: *Conspiracy Theories; Kennedy Assassination; Mafia/ Organized Crime; Onassis, Jacqueline Lee Bouvier Kennedy; Stone, Oliver.*

BIBLIOGRAPHY

Garrison, Jim. *On the Trail of the Assassins.* New York: Warner Books, 1988.

JFK. DVD. Directed by Oliver Stone. Burbank, CA: Warner Brothers, 1991.

Mackey-Kallis, Susan. *Oliver Stone's America: Dreaming the Myth Outward.* Boulder, CO: Westview Press, 1996.

Marrs, Jim. *Crossfire: The Plot That Killed Kennedy.* New York: Carroll & Graf Publishers, 1989.

Prouty, Fletcher L.; Jesse Ventura; and Oliver Stone. *JFK: The CIA, Vietnam, and the Plot to Assassinate John F. Kennedy.* New York: Skyhorse Publishing, 2011.

Stone, Oliver, and Zachary Sklar. *JFK: The Book of the Film, a Documented Screenplay.* New York: Applause Books, 1992.

Jimenez, Jose

SEE: *Dana, Bill.*

Jogging

Jogging became one of the most popular forms of physical exercise during the last decades of the twentieth century. Running and sprinting, which have been around since ancient times, have generally been associated with competitive running. Jogging, on the other hand, achieved currency when individuals took up deliberately paced trotting as part of fitness regimes. At some point, when the briskness or doggedness of noncompetitive jogging reached a certain level, the more impressive word *running* came to be more or less interchangeable with *jogging.* The interest in jogging continued into the twenty-first century, and more Americans are entering marathons than ever before. In 2010 marathon winners were predominately male (59 percent), but the number of female runners continues to climb.

The interest in jogging that began in the late twentieth century was partly a result of interest aroused by James (Jim) Fixx, who in 1977 triggered a revolution in physical activity with his book *The Complete Book of Running.* He made getting out of bed early to put on sweat clothes and sneakers the stylish thing to do. Panting and sweating became fashionable. Although Fixx popularized the movement, four years earlier Dr. Kenneth Cooper was already advocating jogging as a healthful activity in his book *Aerobics.* Athletes such as runner Bill Rodgers had also promoted physical activity as being good for one's health, and Rodgers continued to be a strong advocate for the activity. Most runners credit Fixx with universalizing the sport through his book, which sold almost a million copies in hardback. Fixx helped to get overweight people off couches and onto the roads of America. He advocated jogging or running as good for everything, from weight loss to better sex. He said that joggers digested food better, felt better, and had more energy. A number of studies have also shown that jogging can promote more productive brain activity.

Would-be converts to running were able to identify with Fixx as an average guy, relating to his description of how running changed his life. He had been an overweight New York magazine editor and was smoking two packs of cigarettes a day before hitting the road at age thirty-five. After pulling a calf muscle while playing tennis, he began jogging regularly in order to strengthen the injured muscle. He became hooked on the activity and ultimately competed eight times in the famed Boston Marathon.

HEALTH BENEFITS OF JOGGING

Fitness experts urge people to get physical examinations before starting rigorous running programs. This includes stress tests, where the heart can be tested by cardiologists during a fast walk on a treadmill. The purpose of jogging is to improve the heart and lungs by improving the delivery of oxygen through the body. Speed is not the main goal, according to fitness experts, who insist that the time spent performing an aerobic activity that strengthens muscles and overall cardiovascular system is more important. Trainers suggest that running no more than three or four times a week allows muscles to receive necessary rest between runs. The experts believe that, during runs, an individual's pulse rate should rise to about 70 or 80 percent of his or her maximum rate. The rule of thumb for calculating the maximum rate is 220 minus the individual's age. Thus a forty-year-old runner's rate should rise to a level somewhere between 125 and 145 beats a minute. To test the level of strain, runners are urged to take the talk test. If they cannot talk easily while running, they are straining and should slow down. While knee, leg, and muscle injuries are common among runners, experts advise stretching after a jog to avoid such injuries.

Fixx stressed that running could lower cholesterol and blood pressure, thus improving the cardiovascular system and otherwise giving people better lives. However, he could not outrun his own genes. His father had suffered a heart attack at the age of thirty-five and died eight years later. At the age of fifty-two, while running on a country road in Vermont in 1984, Fixx fell and died of a heart attack, shocking America, particularly the running world. As it turned out, he had not paid enough attention to earlier signs of heart problems, including chest pains he experienced only weeks before he died. Critics of the jogging craze tried to use Fixx's death as a rationale that running could "kill you." Physicians countered that claim with evidence to show that running could add years to a person's life and delay the onset of disabilities that usually accompany the aging process. The key, they insisted, was in building up intensity and duration of jogging slowly. Out-of-shape individuals, particularly those over the age of thirty-five, were advised to get a medical examination before attempting to start a jogging program.

Fixx's death stunned runners but did not stop them. U.S. presidents had already taken up the jogging craze, and others continued it. A famous picture of Jimmy Carter shows him exhausted after a jog. George H. W. Bush was also a jogger, combining a form of jogging and golf. He was known as a speed golfer who would dash through an eighteen-hole course as fast as he could. President Bill Clinton was often photographed while jogging and had run daily through the streets of Little Rock when he was governor of Arkansas. When he went to Washington as president, he caused a brief furor by having a jogging track built around part of the South Lawn of the White House to shield his running form from the prying lenses of photographers. In addition to presidents, senators, congressmen, and celebrities are runners, as are homemakers, businesspeople, and students, all of whom are determined to use jogging to maintain physical fitness.

Stanford University began a longitudinal study of the health impact of jogging during the jogging craze of the 1980s, following 538 middle-aged runners over the following decades. A report issued in 2008 revealed that, contrary to popular belief, runners did not develop higher rates of osteoarthritis and had not required knee replacement surgery in higher numbers. What they did find was that there had been half as many deaths among runners as nonrunners and that disabilities associated with aging had been delayed by twelve to sixteen years. Individuals who engaged in brisk walking or who regularly used an elliptical machine also demonstrated some of the same benefits as those evidenced by joggers.

Michael L. Posner

SEE ALSO: *Aerobics; Boston Marathon; Tennis Shoes/Sneakers.*

BIBLIOGRAPHY

Burfoot, Amby. "Like Father, Like Son (John Fixx, Son of Jim Fixx)." *Runner's World*, August 1, 1994, 45.

Fixx, James F. *The Complete Book of Running*. New York: Random House, 1977.

Glover, Bob, and Jack Shepherd. *The Runner's Handbook*. New York: Penguin, 1985.

Gupta, Sanjay Danielle. "Run for Your Life." *Time*, January 17, 2008.

"Jogging Can Kill You." *New Scientist*, January 6, 2010.

John, Elton *(1947–)*

A flamboyant superstar during the early 1970s, Elton John has become one of the music industry's most consistently successful artists, fielding a Top 40 single every year from 1970 to 1996. John's penchant for outrageous costumes and zany eyeglasses put him among rock and roll's most recognizable icons during the 1970s. He is also a tremendously gifted songwriter, whose versatility and ability to churn out memorable melodies has guaranteed him longevity in a field where so many of his fellow performers quickly faded into obscurity.

BREAKING INTO THE BUSINESS

Born Reginald Kenneth Dwight on March 25, 1947, in a London suburb, he showed prodigious talent as a pianist at a young age and, at eleven, won a scholarship to the prestigious Royal Academy of Music, where he attended classes for gifted children. Although classically trained, Reginald loved rock and roll, particularly performers such as Buddy Holly, Chuck Berry,

Elton John. *Elton John performs in Los Angeles, California, in 1975.* TERRY O'NEILL/GETTY IMAGES.

and Ray Charles. He joined his first band in 1961: Bluesology, a blues-soul-rock combo that had moderate success opening for American acts in England throughout the 1960s. But as other bands rose to stardom, the teenage musician grew frustrated and quit the band. Changing his name to Elton John, he auditioned for lead singer in a number of bands before hooking up with lyricist Bernie Taupin in the mid-1960s. The duo would become one of the top songwriting teams in England and eventually the world.

After the release of their moderately successful first album in 1969 (*Empty Sky*), Taupin and John collaborated on a lushly orchestrated eponymous second effort, which quickly climbed the charts in America and England on the strength of the Top 10 single "Your Song." Following up with three albums in less than two years—*Tumbleweed Connection* (1970), *Madman across the Water* (1971), and *Honky Chateau* (1972)—John soon became one of the most prolific and popular rock-and-roll musicians of the 1970s.

POP CULTURE PHENOMENON

Although Taupin and John produced hit after hit throughout the decade, it was John's flamboyant onstage persona that made him a star. Taking his cue from the early-1970s glam rock movement in Britain, he was a peerless live performer, wearing anything from ostrich feathers to $5,000 eyeglasses that spelled out his name in lights to a Donald Duck costume. John's sartorial splendor became his trademark, as his singles such as "Crocodile Rock" (1972), "Daniel," and "Bennie and the Jets" (both 1973) became global Top 10 hits.

In 1976 John revealed his bisexuality in an interview in *Rolling Stone.* His confession was said to have put off many of his fans, and his popularity gradually began to wane. In truth, though his sexual orientation may have deterred some of the American public from buying his records, it was more the case that John's prolific output (sixteen Top 20 singles in four years and fifteen albums in seven years) had left him exhausted. He took a hiatus from performing, cut back on his recording schedule, and even stopped working with Taupin.

In 1981 John signed with Geffen Records and throughout the decade continued to produce gold albums, each of which contained at least one Top 40 single. However, while his career remained successful, his personal life was in a state of turmoil. He had become addicted to cocaine and alcohol, and he struggled with substance abuse throughout the 1980s. After announcing his bisexuality in 1976, John was afraid to reveal his homosexuality, and in 1984 he married Renate Blauel. Four years later he was divorced, and, after a playing a record-breaking five nights at Madison Square Garden in 1988, John auctioned off all of his costumes and memorabilia, effectively breaking with his past.

PHILANTHROPIC AND PHENOMENAL

Since the early 1990s, John has continued to release successful albums and singles on a yearly basis, reestablishing himself as one of pop music's most consistent performers, even as he devoted more and more time to his philanthropic efforts. In 1992 John announced his sobriety and his homosexuality, and he also established the Elton John AIDS Foundation. After publicly befriending Ryan White, the American teenager living with AIDS, John has tirelessly given his time and energy in contributing to the fight against AIDS. His foundation has raised more than $150 million for research, prevention, and support since its founding, and its annual White Tie & Tiara Ball and Lunch around the World events continue to contribute large sums of money toward such efforts.

In 1994 John collaborated with Tim Rice to create the music for Disney's *The Lion King*, which earned him an Academy Award for Best Original Song and was later adapted into a hit musical. Three years later, John once again came to global attention, with the deaths of two close friends in less than two months of each other. Shortly after attending the funeral of murdered fashion designer Gianni Versace with Princess Diana, John performed at the internationally televised memorial service for the princess herself, playing a revised version of his hit single, "Candle in the Wind." His recording of the single, with all proceeds going to charity, became the fastest-selling single of all time. Several months later, Queen Elizabeth II named the fifty-year-old John a Knight of the British Empire.

The subject of an unsparing 1997 documentary, *Elton John: Tantrums & Tiaras*, made by his partner David Furnish (with whom he entered into a civil union in 2005), John has made peace with both himself and his persona, becoming a perfect role model for millennial pop culture. After winning a Grammy Legend Award in 1999, he helped write the music for several award-winning musicals, including *Elton John and Tim Rice's Aida* (1999), *Billy Elliot the Musical* (2005), and *Lestat* (2006). He received Kennedy Center Honors in 2004, was inducted into the Rock and Roll Hall of Fame in 1994, and was named a Fellow of the British Academy of Songwriters and Composers in 2004, and he continues to tour the globe in support of his singles, albums, and greatest hits compilations.

Flamboyant yet sober, the philanthropic celebrity remains a pop music phenomenon, even as he embraces his new spiritual ethos. The metamorphosis of John through the decades has seemed to mirror the popular mood, even as the talented singer continues to help define what the world likes to hear.

Victoria Price

SEE ALSO: *Academy Awards; AIDS; Berry, Chuck; Broadway; Charles, Ray; Diana, Princess of Wales; Disney (Walt Disney Company); Gay Men; Glitter Rock; Grammy Awards; Holly, Buddy;* The Lion King*; Pop Music; Rock and Roll;* Rolling Stone*; Tony Awards; Top 40; Versace, Gianni.*

BIBLIOGRAPHY

Bernardin, Claude, and Tom Stanton. *Rocket Man: Elton John from A–Z.* Westport, CT: Praeger, 1996.

Buckley, David. *Elton: The Biography*. Chicago: Chicago Review Press, 2007.

Cagle, Jess. "Elton John." *Entertainment Weekly,* December 26, 1997, 36–37.

Eden, Dawn. "Elton John." *Good Housekeeping,* February 1998, 29–30.

Rosenthal, Elizabeth J. *His Song: The Musical Journey of Elton John.* New York: Billboard Books, 2001.

Walters, Barry. "A Triumph of Love."*Advocate,* January 20, 1998, 95.

John Birch Society

The death in 1957 of Joseph McCarthy, a Republican senator from Wisconsin, left a vacuum in the conspiracy-minded wing of the American conservative movement. In 1958 a retired candy manufacturer, Robert Welch, who believed that the senator had been murdered by a Communist conspiracy, formed the John Birch Society to continue McCarthy's mission. The society took its name from Captain John Birch, a young American soldier who had been killed by Chinese communists in 1945 and who was regarded by Welch as the first American martyr of the Cold War.

EARLY DOCTRINES AND HISTORY

Like McCarthy, the John Birch Society promoted an ideology that combined anticommunism with antiliberalism and populism. For the society communism included not just the external threat of the Soviet Union but also the more pernicious danger of internal subversion by what it called the "creeping socialism" of the New Deal. Liberals and moderate conservatives are regarded by the society as being either communist agents or unwitting dupes. Especially dangerous, it believed, were elitist liberal intellectuals, allegedly in control of universities, the mass media, and the government. At various times Welch estimated that from 60 to 80 percent of the United States was under communist control.

In developing the John Birch Society, Welch drew on his considerable managerial expertise as a successful businessman, but he also deliberately imitated what he perceived as the tactics of the communist enemy. He created a tightly organized and well-disciplined movement that allowed little room for debate. Not a political party but rather a movement, the society sought to control the Republican Party at the grassroots level. It also sought to influence public opinion by sponsoring magazines—the *American Opinion*, the *New American*—and books—*Global Tyranny . . . Step by Step*. A special issue of the *New American* devoted to conspiracies sold more than half a million copies in 1996.

As the Cold War intensified in the early 1960s, the John Birch Society gained tens of thousands of members, and it became a powerful force in the Republican Party in such states as California, Texas, and Indiana. The society played an important role in securing the nomination of Barry Goldwater, a senator from Arizona, as the Republican candidate for president in 1964. In the early 1960s the young George H. W. Bush, later president of the United States, actively invited society members to fill key offices in the Texas Republican Party.

At its moment of greatest political influence, however, the John Birch Society came under increasing scrutiny and criticism. The Anti-Defamation League denounced the extremism of the society, while cartoonist Walt Kelly mocked members' paranoia in his comic strip *Pogo*. In 1961 Welch described former president Dwight D. Eisenhower as a "dedicated, conscious agent of the Communist conspiracy." In response, mainstream conservatives such as William F. Buckley Jr. felt that they had to distance themselves from the society. In the pages of the *National Review*, Buckley denounced "the drivel of Robert Welch." In 1965 Goldwater called upon all Republicans to "resign from the society."

LATER DEVELOPMENTS

After the mid-1960s the John Birch Society underwent a steep decline in membership and also changed its orientation. Unwilling to support the war in Vietnam, which he saw as being sabotaged by communists in the American government, Welch turned his attention to domestic issues such as the civil rights movement, which he opposed with the slogan "Impeach Earl Warren." African Americans who fought for civil rights were seen by the society as pawns of an anti-American conspiracy and were described as "indigenous animals" and "gorillas."

In addition to the focus on racial politics there was a radical extension of the society's conspiracy theories. In 1966 Welch declared that "the Communist movement is only a tool of the total conspiracy" controlled by the "Bavarian Illuminati," which he believed had masterminded the French and Russian revolutions, the two World Wars, the creation of the United Nations (UN), and other world events. The UN, as the alleged center of a world conspiracy, became a particular bête noir for the society, which adopted the slogan "U.S. out of the U.N.!" Welch's elaborate conspiracy theories about the Bavarian Illuminati and the UN alienated some members and further marginalized the society. Even in its low point during the 1970s, however, the John Birch Society had prominent and influential supporters, including Congressman Larry McDonald, Democrat of Georgia, who was briefly head of the society in 1983. Later, with the death of Welch in 1985 and the accession of G. Vance Smith as leader, the society began to revitalize itself.

In the 1990s the John Birch Society gained new prominence and popularity. In the post–Cold War period many other right-wingers, especially those belonging to militia groups, came to share the society's fear of the UN. Among right-wing militias, the society was respected as an organization of scholars who had uncovered the secret agenda of the UN, even though, unlike some of the militias, the society did not advocate overthrow of the government by violence. "There is a plethora of newsletters, tabloids, magazines, and radio shows out there mimicking us," Smith complained in 1996. He also criticized the fact that more organs of the mainstream media were spreading the society's gospel to the unconverted. For example, Pat Buchanan, a conservative political commentator, author, and sometime presidential candidate, praised the society's *New American* magazine for "its advocacy, its insights, its information, [and] its unique point of view."

The John Birch Society also gained notice in popular culture. Its ideas were frequently parodied, notably in the movie *Dr. Strangelove* (1964), in which the character Jack D. Ripper mouths the conspiracy theories of the society. In 1965 *MAD* magazine mocked the society along the same lines. In the 1997 movie *Conspiracy Theory*, the main character has a copy of the *New American* in his apartment. Thus, despite its small numbers and eccentric ideas, the society clearly had become a force in American life. Although the John Birch Society continued its activities into the twenty-first century, it found itself competing with a number of other right-wing groups for the attention of the public and of politicians.

Jeet Heer

SEE ALSO: *Buckley, William F., Jr.; Cold War; Communism; Conspiracy Theories;* Dr. Strangelove or: How I Learned to Stop Worrying and Love the Bomb*;* MAD Magazine*; McCarthyism;* Pogo*; White Supremacists.*

BIBLIOGRAPHY

Carter, Gregg Lee. *Guns in American Society: An Encyclopedia of History, Politics, Culture, and the Law*. Santa Barbara, CA: ABC-CLIO, 2002.

Hofstadter, Richard. *The Paranoid Style in American Politics and Other Essays*. New York: Knopf, 1965.

Judis, John B. *William F. Buckley, Jr.: Patron Saint of the Conservatives*. New York: Simon & Schuster, 1988.

Lipset, Seymour Martin, and Earl Raab. *The Politics of Unreason: Right-Wing Extremism in America, 1790–1977*. Chicago: University of Chicago Press, 1978.

Johns, Jasper *(1930–)*

After attending the University of South Carolina for only a short time, Jasper Johns moved to New York City at the age of twenty-four. A southerner, Johns was born in Augusta, Georgia, and brought up in the Carolinas. He supported himself as a window decorator and a salesman in a bookstore while painting during his spare time. Johns painted objects that were familiar to both him and his audience. He once stated, "Using the design of the American flag took care of a great deal for me because I didn't have to design it. So I went on to similar things like the targets—things the mind already knows. That gave me room to work on other levels." The innovative way that Johns approached common subjects attracted the attention of art dealer Leo Castelli.

Castelli was visiting Johns's upstairs neighbor and friend, the artist Robert Rauschenberg, in 1957, when the art dealer asked for an introduction to Johns. Castelli was immediately taken with the paintings of flags and targets, including *White Flag* (1955) and *Target with Plaster Casts* (1955). He added Johns to his stable of gallery artists, beginning a relationship that lasted more than thirty-five years. In 1958 Johns had his first solo exhibition at the Castelli gallery; it was an unqualified critical success for both artist and dealer, establishing both of their reputations. The show sold out, and the Museum of Modern Art bought a total of three pieces, an unprecedented amount from an artist's first show.

Signaling the end of abstract expressionism, Johns's paintings, prints, and sculptures helped usher in the era of American pop art in the late 1950s; additionally, his artwork became instrumental to the tenets of minimalism and conceptual art. Beginning in the 1950s Johns's appropriated images of flags, targets, maps, the alphabet, numbers, and text contrasted sharply with the abstracted, emotion-filled paintings that exemplified abstract expressionism. His use of commonplace symbols focused the attention onto the surface of the canvas. His chosen media—encaustic, oil, or acrylic paints—were as important, if not more important, than his subject matter. His artwork inspired several generations of artists, and his adaptation of cultural icons and mass-media signage have become almost as familiar as the images they mimic.

Johns's early work in the 1950s and 1960s reflected the influences of Marcel Duchamp and the found object. He collected items such as ceramic pieces, brooms, and rulers and attached them to his canvases. Several actual-sized, cast sculptures of everyday items such as beer cans, lightbulbs, and flashlights, together with Johns's painted repetition of flags, numbers, and letters, became abstracted and ceased to exist as powerful objects. The representations become tools of the medium and exert their power only as an artwork.

Johns's artwork challenges the line between art and reality. His concern was with questioning the basic nature of art, with the process as the significant core of the works. The process, to Johns, was of utmost importance, and his images were often the result of chance or accident. Variations in letters and numbers were consequently a result of the types of stencils available. Decisions on placement did not necessarily stem from aesthetics but from necessity. For example, the bronze-cast elements of a lightbulb, *Bronze* (1960–1961), came back to Johns in pieces—the bulb, the socket, and the cord. He left them unassembled, feeling that the pieces issued a provocative statement in that form.

In the early 1970s, Johns's work became increasingly abstract, and he adopted a method of cross-hatched painting as seen in *The Dutch Wives* (1975). The wide brush strokes covered the entire canvas, highlighting the process and technical aspects of his medium. Johns remarked that he was "trying to make paintings about painting." This abstract period soon gave way, however, to a more representational era in the 1980s. He began to pay homage to his artistic inspirations—Pablo Picasso, Paul Cézanne, and Edvard Munch—in a body of work that contains some of his most revealing personal and psychological matter. Johns's contemplation on the cycle of life and death in *The Seasons* (1986) incorporates a shadowy figure of his body; this imagery refers to Picasso's *The Shadow* (1953). In the early decades of the twenty-first century, Johns continues to produce paintings and sculpture on themes similar to those that have permeated his body of work. His new pieces are shown frequently around the New York gallery art scene, and many American museums have hosted exhibits of both his new and older works.

The paintings, sculpture, prints, and drawings by Johns all contain either biographical elements or iconographical components from the second half of the twentieth century. He changed the direction of American painting with his adaptation of common icons and his emphasis on the technique of painting. His later works, filled with psychological dramatics, continue to have the impact of earlier pieces that redefined the common symbols and icons of American culture. Often reproduced, Johns's *Flags* and *Targets* have become popular greeting card and poster images, introducing new generations to his work. In recognition of Johns's lasting contributions to the arts, he was awarded the Presidential Medal of Freedom in 2011.

Jennifer Jankauskas

SEE ALSO: *Abstract Expressionism; Conceptual Art; Minimalism; Picasso, Pablo; Pop Art.*

BIBLIOGRAPHY

Brundage, Susan, ed. *Jasper Johns—35 Years—Leo Castelli*. New York: Harry N. Abrams, 1993.

Crichton, Michael. *Jasper Johns*. New York: Harry N. Abrams, 1994.

Lanchner, Carolyn. *Jasper Johns*. New York: Museum of Modern Art, 2010.

Varnedoe, Kirk, ed. *Jasper Johns: Writing, Sketchbook Notes, Interviews*. New York: Museum of Modern Art, 1996.

Varnedoe, Kirk; Jasper Johns; and Roberta Bernstein. *Jasper Johns: A Retrospective*. New York: Harry N. Abrams, 1996.

Johnson, Blind Willie *(1900?–1947)*

Blind Willie Johnson was an itinerant Texas street singer who made his last record in 1930 and died in poverty in 1947. Yet such was the force and individuality of his guitar playing and singing that all thirty of the gospel songs he recorded during his brief professional career are easily available today. His versions of "If I Had My Way I'd Tear This Building Down," "Keep Your Lamp Trimmed and Burning," and "Bye and Bye I'm Going to See the King" are now considered classics and have attracted admirers in many fields of popular music.

Johnson dropped back into obscurity after his fifth and final recording session for Columbia Records in the spring of 1930, and for many years his strong, highly personal renditions of gospel songs could be heard only on bootleg records. Eventually, through the efforts of jazz historians such as Samuel Charters, more and more people became aware of his work. Eventually Columbia reissued Johnson's entire output in both cassette and CD formats.

An intensely religious man, Johnson nevertheless used many of the techniques of the rowdy, secular blues in his performances. On most of his recordings, he'd shift from his normal tenor to a gruff, growling bass. His slide guitar playing, done with the blade of a pocket knife, was harsh, intense, and impressive. "He had few equals as a slide guitarist," notes Francis Davis in *The History of the Blues*. Although Johnson's faith underlies all of his performances, there is a grimness to many of his songs. Many are of such stark intensity that one can imagine his causing his sidewalk listeners' hair to stand on end.

Johnson was not born blind but lost his sight as a child after his angry stepmother threw lye in his face. He eventually took to the streets of his native Marlin, Texas, and sang on corners, begging with a tin cup. He played in other Texas towns and eventually in neighboring states. It is uncertain who discovered him and persuaded him to record for Columbia. The company had a fairly ambitious program of issuing what were then called race records, employing scouts to work throughout the South. Blind Willie Johnson cut his first six 78-rpm sides in a makeshift studio in Dallas in early December 1927. According to Charters, the first record, issued on Columbia's 140000 Race series, sold extremely well—more than 15,000 copies, better than the popular Bessie Smith was doing—and Johnson from the start "was one of the strongest selling artists in the Columbia series."

Only one picture of Johnson is known to exist. It comes from a small ad that was run in black newspapers to promote the first record. "I Know His Blood Can Make Me Whole" appeared on one side, with "Jesus Make Up My Dying Bed" on the other. The company assured potential buyers that Blind Willie Johnson "sings sacred selections in a way that you have never heard before."

In December 1928 Johnson cut four more sides, again in Dallas. This time a woman named Willie B. Harris, whom Charters says was Johnson's first wife, recorded as a sort of backup singer. It was another year before Johnson, accompanied by a different woman singer, recorded again. These third and fourth sessions took place in New Orleans, Louisiana, in a studio set up above Werlein's Music Store, on the French Quarter side of Canal Street. The last session was in Atlanta, Georgia, where Johnson, again working with Harris, recorded ten songs.

The Great Depression ended his recording career, as it did that of many other folk artists. Johnson, with a new wife, continued his wanderings, singing and begging on street corners in Texas and Louisiana. The two eventually settled in Beaumont, Texas, and he died there of pneumonia in 1947. He'd slept in their shack after a fire had gutted it and the dampness caused his sickness. Many years later Charters tracked down his widow and when he asked her if she'd brought her sick husband to a hospital, she answered that she had but "they wouldn't accept him."

Johnson's influence on American folk and rock music has been extensive. Two delta blues musicians, Son House and Fred McDowell covered, respectively, "John the Revelator" and "Keep Your Lamp Trimmed and Burning." His songs have also been covered by folk artists such as Bob Dylan and Peter, Paul, and Mary; 1970s rock bands Led Zeppelin and the Grateful Dead; 1990s rockers Beck and Eric Clapton; and contemporary bands the White Stripes and Ben Harper. The song "Dark Was the Night" is included on the *Voyager Golden Record*, the selection of phonograph recordings chosen by physicist Carl Sagan to represent the variety of life and culture on Earth, which was launched into space on both of the Voyager spacecrafts in the early 1970s.

Ron Goulart

SEE ALSO: *Blues; Clapton, Eric; Dylan, Bob; Folk Music; Gospel Music; The Grateful Dead; The Great Depression; Led Zeppelin; Peter, Paul, and Mary; Rock and Roll; Sagan, Carl; Smith, Bessie.*

BIBLIOGRAPHY

Charters, Samuel. Liner notes for *The Complete Blind Willie Johnson*. New York: Sony Music Entertainment, 1993.

Corcoran, Michael Joseph. *All over the Map: True Heroes of Texas Music*. Austin: University of Texas Press, 2005.

Davis, Francis. *The History of the Blues*. New York: Hyperion, 1995.

Johnson, Earvin "Magic" *(1959–)*

Earvin "Magic" Johnson was one of the marquee basketball players of his era. He began his National Basketball Association (NBA) career in 1979. During the following decade, he and Larry Bird helped to elevate the popularity of professional basketball to previously unscaled heights. Johnson's wall-to-wall smile and ingratiating manner made him a favorite of hoops and nonhoops fans alike. Nonetheless, he will be remembered for much more than his exploits on the hardwood. On November 7, 1991, he shocked America—and the sporting world in particular—by announcing his retirement from basketball because he was HIV-positive. This admission, in such a public forum, forever altered the face of the AIDS plague. AIDS no longer could be ghettoized and trivialized as a disease whose sufferers were promiscuous gays and intravenous drug abusers or lived far away on another continent.

Earvin Johnson Jr., the sixth of ten children, grew up in Lansing, Michigan, and was dubbed "Magic" by a sportswriter after amassing sterling statistics—36 points, 18 rebounds, and 16 assists—in a high school game. Wherever he played, Johnson helped to pilot a winner. For four straight years he made the

Earvin "Magic" Johnson. *Earvin "Magic" Johnson won five world championships as a member of the Los Angeles Lakers.* ANTHONY BARBOZA/GETTY IMAGES.

Michigan all-state high school team. In his senior year he tallied 28.8 points and 16.8 rebounds per game and led Lansing's Everett High School to a 27–1 record and the state championship. He attended Michigan State University, where as a freshman he guided the Spartans to a 25–5 record and their first Big Ten championship in nineteen years. He capped his college career in 1979, when he was a sophomore. That season Michigan State won the National Collegiate Athletic Association (NCAA) title, and Johnson, who averaged 17.1 points per game, was named the tournament's most outstanding player.

The six-foot-nine point guard decided to turn pro after his second year at Michigan State and was selected by the Los Angeles Lakers as the first overall pick in the 1979 NBA draft. In his first year with the team he maintained his status as a winner by helping the Lakers win the NBA title. He capped off his season by being the first rookie cited as the Most Valuable Player (MVP) of the NBA Finals. In the deciding game against the Philadelphia 76ers, he replaced an ailing Kareem Abdul-Jabbar at center and went on to score 42 points, adding 15 rebounds and seven assists in a 123–107 victory. However, Johnson lost Rookie of the Year honors to Larry Bird, who became one of his chief on-court adversaries during the 1980s.

In his thirteen seasons with the Lakers, Johnson astounded fans and players alike with his no-look passes, clutch baskets, and "showtime" style of offense. He led the team to five NBA titles, with the Lakers' 1987 victory against Bird and the Boston Celtics especially sweet. In the deciding minutes of game four, with the Celtics holding a one-point lead, Johnson won the contest with an Abdul-Jabbar-like sky hook. The Lakers went on to beat their rivals in six games.

In 1987, 1989, and 1990, Johnson was the league's MVP; he also earned two additional MVP citations for starring in the NBA Finals. Prior to his retirement he played in twelve All-Star games, and in 1990 he was the contest's MVP. He was a first-team, all-NBA selection from 1983 through 1991. He led the NBA in assists on four occasions. During the 1990–1991 season he broke the all-time NBA assists record, and he completed his career with 10,141.

Johnson came out of retirement to score 25 points and make 9 assists in the 1992 NBA All-Star game, helping the West earn a 153–113 victory and winning a second All-Star MVP trophy. Near the end of the contest, he inspired the crowd by making successive three-point shots while being defended by Michael Jordan and Isiah Thomas. Johnson joined Jordan, Bird, and other NBA stars as a member of the U.S. Olympic Dream Team, which drubbed opponents by an average of 43.8 points per game, earned a gold medal at the 1992 Barcelona Olympics, and helped to escalate the sport's popularity across the globe. He then announced that he was returning to the Lakers, but he withdrew prior to the beginning of the 1992–1993 season. In March 1994 Johnson became head coach of the Lakers, but quit with a 5–11 record after the team completed the season. He also became a minority owner of the team—a position he held before selling his share in 2010—and came out of retirement one last time during the 1995–1996 season, in which he played in thirty-two Lakers games. Also in 1996 he was cited as one of the fifty greatest players in NBA history. He entered the Naismith Memorial Basketball Hall of Fame in 2002; four years later ESPN rated him the all-time-greatest NBA point guard.

In his post-NBA career, Johnson has been a frequent guest on TV talk shows. His own venture into late-night television, *The Magic Hour*, flopped soon after its 1998 premiere, but in 2002 he signed a six-year contract to serve as announcer-commentator on Turner Network Television basketball-related programming. Then in 2008 he became a studio analyst on ESPN's *NBA Countdown*. More important, however, Johnson has regularly accepted motivational speaking engagements and is a celebrity who has eagerly donated his services to an array of charitable organizations. He is an ambassador of peace for the United Nations and has been active as a fund-raiser for the Starlight Foundation, the American Heart Association, the Muscular Dystrophy Association, the American Cancer Society, the United Negro College Fund, and the Urban League. He has offered his name and his presence to a host of HIV/AIDS awareness programs. He established the Magic Johnson Foundation, which bestows grants to community-based, youth-oriented organizations.

He became chairman and chief executive officer of Magic Johnson Enterprises, whose projects include the Johnson Development Corporation, Magic Johnson All-Star Camps, Magic Johnson Productions, and Magic Johnson Theaters. He believes that all business endeavors must benefit society, and so his theater chain, developed in conjunction with Sony Entertainment, consists of state-of-the-art multiplex cinemas located in economically depressed urban neighborhoods. The first opened in Baldwin Hills, a run-down area of Los Angeles.

Rob Edelman

SEE ALSO: *Abdul-Jabbar, Kareem; AIDS; Basketball; Bird, Larry; Dream Team; Jordan, Michael; The Los Angeles Lakers; National Basketball Association (NBA); National Collegiate Athletic Association (NCAA); Olympics; Sports Heroes.*

BIBLIOGRAPHY

Gutman, Bill. *Magic, More than a Legend.* New York: Harper Paperbacks, 1992.

Haskins, James. *"Magic": A Biography of Earvin Johnson.* Hillside, NJ: Enslow Publishers, 1982.

Johnson, Earvin. *32 Ways to Be a Champion in Business.* New York: Crown Business, 2008.

Johnson, Earvin, with William Novak. *My Life.* New York: Random House, 1992.

Johnson, Earvin, and Larry Bird, with Jackie MacMullen. *When the Game Was Ours.* New York: Houghton Mifflin Harcourt, 2009.

Johnson, Earvin, and Roy S. Johnson. *Magic's Touch.* Reading, MA: Addison-Wesley Publishing, 1989.

Johnson, Earvin, and Richard Levin. *Magic.* New York: Viking Press, 1983.

Pascarelli, Peter. *The Courage of Magic Johnson: From Boyhood Dreams to Superstar to His Toughest Challenge.* New York: Bantam Books, 1992.

Johnson, Jack *(1878–1946)*

Jack Johnson, the first modern African American heavyweight boxing champion of the world, served as a lightning rod for the racial turmoil of the early twentieth century. Johnson won the heavyweight title in 1906 and then defeated a series of "Great White Hopes," culminating in his epic match with ex-champion Jim Jeffries. The bout was billed as a battle between the "The Hope of the White Race vs. The Deliverer of the Negroes." The implications of Johnson's ensuing easy victory frightened many white Americans, inspired many black Americans, and upset the understood racial hierarchy of Victorian America.

One of six children, Johnson was born Arthur John Johnson in Galveston, Texas, in 1878. He lived a tough childhood and dropped out of school after receiving five or six years of elementary education. By the mid-1890s Johnson was working a variety of jobs around the port of Galveston and participating in battle royals. Organized by all-white athletic and social clubs for the entertainment of their members, battle royals featured groups of young black men fighting in a ring until only one man was left standing. These "exhibitions" had no rules, and the last fighter standing received a small purse of a few dollars for his efforts. A frequent winner of these matches, Johnson was gradually matched one-on-one against the best local fighters, both black and white, in traditional boxing matches. By the turn of the twentieth century, he had beaten all challengers in eastern Texas, and he took to the road to find new competition.

Over the next few years, Johnson traveled all over the United States, from Philadelphia to Chicago to San Francisco, learning the "manly art" and slowly building a national reputation. By 1903 he had defeated the best black heavyweights in the country and claimed the mythic "Negro Heavyweight Championship." A separate title for black boxers was necessary, because the white champion, Jeffries, following a tradition established in the 1890s by America's first boxing superstar, John "The Boston Strongboy" Sullivan, refused to cross the color line and box against African American fighters.

HISTORIC MATCHES

In 1905, with only a lackluster group of white fighters to challenge him, Jeffries tired of boxing and retired without ever being beaten. In the ensuing scramble for the now-vacated championship, a mediocre Canadian boxer named Tommy Burns claimed the title. Over three years of mounting disinterest, Burns defended his championship for smaller and smaller purses against an increasingly weak selection of white boxers. Finally in 1908, in order to generate interest (and a larger payday), Burns agreed to fight Johnson, still a leading contender for the championship. Although Burns was the heavy favorite of both the gambling community and the crowd—which showered Johnson with racial epithets throughout the fight—he was no match for the stronger and quicker black fighter. Johnson dominated the fight for thirteen rounds, punching the overmatched white boxer at will until police stopped the match and saved the bloody and battered Burns the indignity of being knocked out.

After more than five years of fruitless challenges, Johnson had finally gotten his day in the ring and had proven himself against the best white boxer in the world. While white America struggled to come to grips with the fact that an African American had been crowned the heavyweight champion, Johnson returned to Chicago to celebrate his victory. Much to the chagrin of mainstream America, he refused to follow the prevailing racial rules of the day. Instead of being humble and respectful as African Americans were expected to act, Johnson flaunted his newfound wealth, buying fast cars and throwing lavish parties. More threatening to many white Americans, though, Johnson broke the ultimate taboo and publicly romanced white women.

In response to the new champion's behavior, Jack London, writing in the *New York Herald*, echoed the popular sentiment and appealed to the last great white champion: "But one thing now remains. Jim Jeffries must now emerge from his alfalfa farm and remove that golden smile from Jack Johnson's face. Jeff it's up to you. The White Man must be rescued." After Johnson defeated several mediocre white challengers, Jeffries bowed to the public pressure and, though overweight and out of shape, agreed to come out of retirement to fight for the title. Scheduled for July 4, 1910, in Reno, Nevada, the fight was front-page news across the country. White America expected the smart, quick, and scientific Anglo-Saxon to easily win the match, even though the black boxer was emotional, strong, and violent. These expectations were shattered. The old and tired ex-champion was simply no match for Johnson. Again, the black fighter controlled the action in the ring, toying with his opponent and delivering a savage beating for fifteen rounds, until Jeffries's corner men stopped the fight.

VICTORY SPARKS RACE RIOTS

White America reacted with disbelief and anger after Johnson's victory. The nearly all-white crowd filed out of the Reno arena in silence, as social critics wondered how an African American could be so successful. More ominously, white Americans began to take out their frustrations on their black neighbors. In cities around the country, race riots broke out in response to the fight, as gangs of whites descended violently on innocent blacks to forcefully remind them of their position in society despite Johnson's victory.

In 1912 Johnson was arrested and convicted of violating the Mann Act. Known popularly as the White Slave Traffic Act, the Mann Act made it illegal to transport women across state lines "for the purpose of prostitution or debauchery, or for any other immoral purpose." The law was intended to target organized prostitution rings, and, although Johnson was technically guilty for traveling around the country with several of his white girlfriends, he was one of only a handful of people ever tried under the Mann Act for anything other than participation in prostitution. Before he could be sentenced, Johnson fled the country and remained abroad for the next seven years.

Although Johnson left the United States, he did not leave boxing. He successfully defended his heavyweight title until April 5, 1915. On that day Johnson lost the title in a match against Jess Willard in Havana, Cuba. Willard, a white, 250-pound boxer from Kansas, knocked out Johnson in the twenty-sixth round. Having lost his title and squandered his winnings, Johnson returned to the United States in 1920 and was sentenced to one year in jail. Although he would fight a few times in the 1920s, his serious boxing days were over, and Johnson drifted into the relative obscurity of an ex-champion.

On June 10, 1946, outside of Raleigh, North Carolina, Johnson was killed in a car accident. He was eulogized as a good fighter, but no representatives from the boxing community attended his funeral. By the time of his death, he had become a shell of the person who forty years earlier had terrified white Americans and upset the racial sensibilities of white America.

Gregory Bond

SEE ALSO: *Boxing; London, Jack; Race Riots; Sullivan, John L.*

BIBLIOGRAPHY

Batchelor, Denzil. *Jack Johnson and His Times.* London: Weidenfeld and Nicolson, 1990.

Gilmore, Al-Tony. *Bad Nigger! The National Impact of Jack Johnson.* Port Washington, NY: Kennikat Press, 1975.

Johnson, Jack, and Christopher Rivers. *My Life and Battles.* Westport, CT: Praeger, 2007.

Naison, Mark. "America Views Jack Johnson, Joe Louis, and Muhammad Ali." In *Sport in America: New Historical Perspectives*, ed. Donald Spivey. Westport, CT: Greenwood Press, 1985.

Roberts, Randy. *Papa Jack: Jack Johnson and the Era of White Hopes.* New York: Free Press, 1983.

Johnson, James Weldon *(1871–1938)*

James Weldon Johnson enjoyed success as a novelist, a poet, a songwriter, an educator, a diplomat, and a lawyer. He was also an official of the National Association for the Advancement of Colored People (NAACP). A celebrated writer and active leader, Johnson was a venerated figure of the Harlem Renaissance. He believed that artistic achievement was a key to racial uplift, and he urged fellow African American artists to assimilate black folk culture into their work. His novel *The Autobiography of an Ex-Colored Man* (1912) explores the dilemmas faced by a light-skinned black man who turns away from his cultural heritage and decides to "pass" for white. Johnson's ideas and themes had a marked influence on the African American literary tradition, as shown in works by Jean Toomer and Ralph Ellison. Johnson was also a talented musician and songwriter who penned the lyrics to "Lift Every Voice and Sing" (1900), which has become the official song of the NAACP and is widely known as the "Black National Anthem."

Adam Golub

SEE ALSO: *African American Press; Harlem Renaissance;* Invisible Man.

BIBLIOGRAPHY

Johnson, James Weldon. *Along This Way.* New York: Penguin, 1990.

Johnson, James Weldon. *The Autobiography of an Ex-Colored Man.* New York: Penguin, 1990.

Oliver, Lawrence, and Kenneth Price, eds. *Critical Essays on James Weldon Johnson.* New York: G.K. Hall, 1997.

Johnson, Michael *(1967–)*

The unique convergence of spectacular achievement, special time and place, and creative image allows certain athletes to make indelible impressions on the popular mind. Michael Johnson exemplifies this phenomenon—his name evokes memories of an unprecedented accomplishment in track and field; the 1996 Olympic Summer Games at Atlanta, Georgia; and golden running shoes. Few athletes have more consciously planned their moment of greatest triumph than did Johnson. Deprived of individual achievement in the 1992 Summer Olympics in Barcelona because of illness and aware of the American public's relative disinterest in track and field, he relentlessly determined that he would make the Atlanta Olympics uniquely his own. He resolved to win both the 200- and the 400-meter races in Atlanta, something that had never been attempted in the Olympics, and to do so while wearing golden shoes.

The pre-Olympic pressure on Johnson was enormous, with the media nominating him in advance as the star of the Atlanta games. Spectacularly fulfilling his own and others' expectations, he first won the 400 meters easily, literally running away from the rest of the field. Three days later he won the 200 meters in the astonishing world-record time of 19.32 seconds. At the age of twenty-nine, Johnson was unquestionably the dominant figure in international track and field.

EARLY CAREER

Even before Atlanta, Johnson had established an impressive record as a sprinter. In the 1995 World Championship meet held in Göteborg, Sweden, he previewed his Atlanta performance by completing the 200-400 double and won a third gold medal by anchoring the winning United States 4×400-meter relay team. He had previously won three World Championship gold metals (individually he won the 200 meters in 1991 and the 400 meters in 1993, and he won as anchor of the U.S. 4×400-meter relay team in 1992). Nevertheless, in a sport that traditionally valorizes youth, Johnson had been something of a slow starter. A native of Dallas, he never won a Texas state high school running championship.

Born on September 13, 1967, Johnson is the son of a truck driver and an elementary school teacher. His father, Paul Johnson Sr., determined that his five children would obtain college degrees and began teaching them early the virtues of planning and dedication. All five children did in fact earn degrees, and son Michael proved to be especially receptive of his father's lessons. As an adult Michael leads a rigidly compartmentalized life and has been described by friends and rivals as being virtually inhuman in his concentration and dedication to immediate tasks and challenges. He attended Skyline High School in Dallas, where, an obviously gifted athlete, he surprised people by participating in track rather than football. Upon graduation he was recruited by Baylor University's track-and-field coach Clyde Hart, primarily to fill out Hart's successful relay teams. Under Hart's tutelage, Johnson's potential as a sprinter began to manifest itself quickly, though injuries kept him from recording the collegiate record that he might have (he did win the National Collegiate Athletic Association [NCAA] 200-meter championship in 1989 and 1990 and the NCAA outdoor 200-meter title in 1990).

After graduation from Baylor, Johnson's running achievements became more and more spectacular until they culminated in the Atlanta Olympics. In between though, there was Barcelona. Going into the 1992 Olympics, Johnson was viewed as the meet's most certain individual winner, but he contracted food poisoning and failed to qualify for the finals in either of his events. He did, however, win his first Olympic gold medal as a member of the U.S. 4×400 relay team. After Barcelona his determination began to pay off even before Atlanta. Between 1992 and 1996 he was virtually unbeatable, and between 1989 and 1997 he won an amazing fifty-eight consecutive 400-meter finals. Beginning in 1993 awards began to pour in for Johnson, climaxing in 1996 when he received the Sullivan Award as U.S. amateur athlete of the year and the Associated Press Male Athlete of the Year Award.

WORLD'S FASTEST HUMAN

Since Atlanta, Johnson's career, because of recurring injuries, has been less than spectacular. The biggest damage to his golden image was truly unnecessary. Johnson agreed to an exhibition race on June 1, 1997, with Olympic 100-meter champion Donovan Bailey of Canada to determine the mythical title of "world's fastest human." From the beginning, the event took on a carnival atmosphere, and with 50 meters left in the race, Johnson, who was trailing Bailey, pulled a muscle in his left thigh and dropped out. Afterward Bailey ridiculed Johnson on Canadian television, calling him a "chicken" and a "coward." Responding to criticism, Bailey subsequently apologized for his harsh comments. The entire episode proved a black eye for track and field rather than the boost anticipated by the two competitors and their sponsors. However, the Bailey race fiasco seems not to have seriously damaged Johnson's image.

Still plagued by the thigh injury, Johnson went on have a mediocre 1997 season. Still, the golden touch had not entirely deserted him, and when he could not otherwise qualify, Johnson was granted a waiver to compete in the World Championships in Athens, where he won the 400-meter finals. This win represented his seventh World Championship title, second only to Carl Lewis's eight.

In 1998 he won the 400-meter championship in the Goodwill Games at Uniondale, New York, and anchored the U.S. 4×400-meter relay team to victory in world record time. In 2000 he injured himself in the qualifying trial for the 200 meter and so was unable to defend his title; he did run and win—again—the 400 meter, earning his fourth gold medal. Johnson ended his career with the 2000 Olympics and went on to a lucrative series of endorsements for sports products; he also worked as a television commentator. He eventually founded a training facility for young athletes in Texas along with a sports management company. Johnson was elected to the U.S. Track and Field Hall of Fame in 2004, where his 200-meter performance was cited as "the greatest track and field moment of the last twenty-five years."

In spite of his many achievements, Johnson will always be the man who achieved the "impossible double" and who ran the "astonishing" 19.32 in the 200 meters in the Atlanta Olympics while wearing his golden shoes. If he hasn't reawakened U.S. interest in track and field, he remains a nationally and internationally admired athletic figure: he will always be America's "golden boy of running."

James R. Giles

SEE ALSO: *Advertising; Olympics; Sports Heroes; Television.*

BIBLIOGRAPHY

Battema, Doug. "'The Danger Zone': Michael Johnson, Blackness, and Masculinity." *Journal of African-American*

Studies 3, no. 4 (1998): 23–52.

Griffith-Roberts, C. "The Road to Atlanta." *Southern Living*, May 31, 1996.

Miller, David. *Atlanta 1996: Official Commemorative Book of the Centennial Olympic Games*. San Francisco: Woodford Press, 1996.

Ribowsky, Mark. *Twice Golden: The Story of Michael Johnson and His Triumphs in Atlanta*. Secaucus, NJ: Carol Publishing, 1997.

Smith, G. "The Tortoise and the Hare." *Sports Illustrated Olympics Preview Issue*, July 22, 1996.

The "Sports Illustrated" 1997 Sports Almanac. Boston: Little, Brown, 1997.

Johnson, Robert *(1911–1938)*

Arguably the most influential figure in the history of the blues, Robert Leroy Johnson was at once a virtuoso guitarist, a gifted poet, and a skilled vocalist. Johnson, who emerged out of the Mississippi delta in the early 1930s as one of the premier practitioners of the blues form, left a recorded legacy of just forty-one songs. However, the tracks he laid down over two sessions in 1936 and 1937 became fundamental to the repertoires of other blues players and, after the "rediscovery" of the blues by white musicians in the 1960s, to blues-influenced rock artists everywhere. (Among the most covered and recorded Johnson compositions are "Crossroads Blues," "Sweet Home Chicago," and "Love in Vain.")

So prodigious were Johnson's skills on the six-string guitar, a legend (fostered by Johnson himself) grew up around him that he had sold his soul to the devil in exchange for this particular gift. His violent and untimely demise, allegedly at the hands of the jealous husband of one of his many lovers, combines with the romance of his shadowy, itinerant life to make him one of the most celebrated folk legends of the twentieth century. His enormous talent and the dark reputation he self-consciously promoted help explain his enduring place in the popular imagination. The fact that Johnson, unlike many other talented blues musicians of the early part of the twentieth century, was recorded has further cemented his reputation as one of the all-time greats of the genre.

HUMBLE BEGINNINGS

Born in Hazlehurst, Mississippi, to Julia Dobbs and Noah Johnson, "Little Robert" was fascinated with making music from an early age. As sharecroppers in the fertile but dirt poor Yazoo basin, his parents had neither the inclination nor the means to give Johnson a formal musical education, and certain of his contemporaries have suggested that the young Johnson, although wildly enthusiastic about music, was not much of a musician. Eddie James "Son" House Jr., one of the most respected blues performers of the generation before Johnson's, remembered the youngster as an eager apprentice but one who did not at first show much promise. Johnson would show up at the juke joints and house parties, where House was a Saturday night fixture, and beg the older man to teach him to play. Rebuffed and mocked by the older musicians he worshipped, Johnson eventually took to the road in search of a willing mentor.

A reluctant maestro, House nevertheless made a large impression on Johnson. House's sometime traveling partner Willie Brown, later immortalized in a Johnson song, also affected the youngster profoundly. ("You can run, you can run," Johnson sings in the last verse of "Crossroads Blues," hinting at the cost of his infernal bargain, "Tell my friend Willie Brown. / Lord, I'm standing at the crossroads / I believe I'm sinking down.") Johnson's style, however startlingly unprecedented it seems in retrospect, was in fact fashioned from elements taken from such players as 1920s Texas great Blind Lemon Jefferson; Mississippi delta legend Charley Patton; and, of course, House.

Johnson's brand of the blues emphasizes an intricate interplay between guitar and voice. In many of his recordings, he highlights sung lines with rhythmic bursts of guitar playing, typically playing a bass line with his thumb while picking out chords and riffs with his fingers. A major innovator of slide-guitar technique—in which the player frets the instrument with a glass or metal object—Johnson routinely makes his guitar sound like a human voice, his voice like a guitar. On such numbers as "If I Had Possession over Judgment Day," he creates a drumlike beat with slide fingerings. He pushes his plangent alto across the verses, often dropping into a speaking voice at the end of lines (as in "Stones in My Passway").

CREATING A MYTH

His early travels account in part for the mystery in which Johnson's life would always be shrouded. He traveled under his natural father's name or either his stepfather's original or changed names (Dodds and Spencer), and on returning to his home was coy about where he had been. He further bolstered his mysterious reputation by bragging that he had made a Faustian pact to become the best guitar player alive—a publicity strategy that had been used to great effect by older bluesmen such as Skip James, whose "Devil Got My Woman" Johnson refashioned as "Hellhound on My Trail." Johnson's wanderlust remained unsatisfied throughout his brief life, as evidenced by his two-year ramble with Johnny Shines and Walter Horton from 1933 to 1935. Two widely reproduced photographs of Johnson exist: one seems to have been taken in a coin-operated photo booth; the other, a studio portrait, features a giddy-looking Johnson in a new suit and hat.

More crucial to the continuation of the legend than the photographs, though, are the sound recordings Johnson cut. These were made during a boom period for so-called race records—78-rpm recordings of African American blues and jazz singers, aimed at the nonwhite market. Race records were a big business in the 1920s and 1930s, and music scouts from the white-owned record companies were commonly sent into the American South in search of new talent. Jefferson (one of the musicians who influenced Johnson artistically) was one of the top-selling artists of his day and thus a model of both aesthetic and business success for Johnson. In 1936 Don Law, an American Recording Company (ARC) engineer tasked to find the next Blind Lemon, recorded Johnson in San Antonio, Texas.

Law famously reported that Johnson suffered so badly from stage fright that the young singer recorded his songs facing the back wall of the hotel room in which the session was held. His shyness has entered somewhat too easily into the historical record. The story of an enormously talented but bashful country boy overwhelmed and intimidated by the big city has, of course, a certain charm. However, a more convincing explanation might be found in his general reluctance to show other musicians his riffs. He was, it seems, somewhat notorious among musicians in the South for his refusal to reveal his unconventional fingerings to potential competitors, and he was known to conceal his hands from audiences as he played. This secrecy, of course, had the collateral advantage of enhancing his satanic reputation.

A LEGACY RECORDED

Whatever his motives for turning away from the team from ARC, Johnson managed to lay down a bona fide hit during the San Antonio session, the sly "Terraplane Blues." The song, which playfully confuses a complaint about a lover's infidelities with a car owner's frustration over a rough-running jalopy (anticipating by decades smashes such as Chuck Berry's "Mabeline" and Prince's "Little Red Corvette"), sold around 5,000 copies and established Johnson's reputation as a leading performer of the blues. Sings Johnson: "Now you know the coils ain't even buzzin' / Little generator won't get the spark / Motors in a bad condition / You gotta have these batteries charged. / But I'm cryin' please, please don't do me wrong / Who been driving my Terraplane / Now for you since I been gone."

Law recorded Johnson again the following year, this time for Vocalion Records, in Dallas. In the second session, Johnson recorded what would become some of his best-loved, most enduring sides, including "Dust My Broom" and "Love in Vain." The two sessions together yielded twenty-nine songs that Columbia eventually brought out on two albums, issued in 1961 and 1970. Johnson's recordings had previously been little known, despite the 1930s juke-box popularity of "Terraplane Blues." In 1990 the twenty-nine songs from the two albums plus twelve alternate takes were released on CD, again by Columbia, and garnered Johnson a posthumous 1990 Grammy Award for Best Historical Album. The same set of recordings was released on May 8, 2011, with one additional alternate take and new packaging and supplemental materials to commemorate the 100th anniversary of Johnson's birth.

Johnson has the dubious distinction of being one of the only blues musicians to have had a movie made about his legend (*Crossroads*, 1986). The film is significant in that it suggests the longevity and seemingly universal appeal of the Johnson legend. For better or worse, Johnson's songs have been recorded by such British rock heavyweights as Led Zeppelin, the Rolling Stones, and Cream, groups whose work continues to have a considerable influence on rock musicians on both sides of the Atlantic. Johnson's legacy has also been recognized by the Rock and Roll Hall of Fame, which honored the musician as an "Early Influence," as well as the Library of Congress, which included his complete recordings in the National Recording Registry for their cultural and historical significance.

The mysterious circumstances of Johnson's death—some say he was knifed while others claim that he was poisoned—have further enhanced the romance of his story. A particularly provocative rumor that has circulated about Johnson is that just prior to his death he had been in Chicago, where he put together an electric-guitar-based combo. Whether Johnson was in Chicago or not, his influence there shines through clearly in the work of, among others, Muddy Waters, viewed by many critics as the next link in the chain connecting traditional country blues to electrified blues-based urban forms such as rhythm and blues, soul, and rock and roll.

Matthew Mulligan Goldstein

SEE ALSO: *Berry, Chuck; Blues; Grammy Awards; Led Zeppelin; Long-Playing Record; Prince; Rhythm and Blues; Rock and Roll; The Rolling Stones; Soul Music; Waters, Muddy.*

BIBLIOGRAPHY

Guralnick, Peter. *Searching for Robert Johnson.* New York: Dutton, 1989.

Komara, Edward. *The Road to Robert Johnson: The Genesis and Evolution of the Blues in the Delta from the Late 1800s through 1938.* Milwaukee, WI: Hal Leonard Publishing, 2007.

Lomax, Alan. *The Land Where the Blues Began.* New York: Pantheon, 1993.

Schroeder, Patricia. *Robert Johnson, Mythmaking, and Contemporary American Culture.* Urbana: University of Illinois Press, 2004.

Wald, Elijah. *Escaping the Delta: Robert Johnson and the Invention of the Blues.* Amistad Publishing, 2004.

Welding, Pete, and Toby Byron. *Bluesland: Portraits of Twelve Major American Blues Masters.* New York: Dutton, 1991.

Johnson, Virginia

SEE: *Masters and Johnson.*

Jolie, Angelina *(1975–)*

Though actress Angelina Jolie is a popular and successful film star, it is her intensely dramatic persona, her passionate relationships, and her career as a philanthropist and United Nations goodwill ambassador that has captivated the public throughout her career. The daughter of a less than idyllic Hollywood marriage, Jolie learned early to mistrust the superficial glamour of celebrity, approaching both her conspicuous good looks and her fascination for the press and public with wariness and a cynicism that bordered on outright hostility. Despising hypocrisy, Jolie was always bluntly honest about the controversial aspects of her life, which resulted in a dark and dangerous bad-girl image during the first part of her career. This image has been tempered somewhat by her socially conscientious philanthropic work and her long-term relationship with Brad Pitt, as well as by their family of six children. Still a high-profile celebrity in the twenty-first century, Jolie has learned to remain philosophical in the face of both adulation and vilification.

Angelina Jolie Voigt was born on June 4, 1975, in Los Angeles, one of two children of actors Marcheline Bertrand and Jon Voigt. Her parents divorced when she was only a year old, and though she had the name of her famous father, she had very little of his presence in her life. Bertrand moved to New York, where she raised Jolie and her brother, James, as a single mother with very little support from her successful ex-husband. Raised on the edge of poverty, estranged from a wealthy and famous father, Jolie began to develop a rebellious personality and a fascination with danger and death. One of her early ambitions was to be a mortician, of which she later said, "There's something about death that is comforting. The thought you could die tomorrow frees you to appreciate your life now." When the family moved back to Los Angeles in 1986, the eleven-year-old Jolie began modeling and attending acting classes at the Lee Strasberg Theatre Institute. She soon dropped her last name and began using Angelina Jolie professionally.

BREAKING INTO FILMS

Though she had small roles in several films, including *Lookin' to Get Out* (1982) when she was only seven years old, her acting career began to take off in earnest in the mid-1990s with such films as *Hackers* (1995). Her first subversive bad-girl role was Legs Sadovsky, the charismatic center of a girl gang, in *Foxfire* (1996). Though she won a Golden Globe for her work in John Frankenheimer's biopic *George Wallace* (1997), it was Jolie's smoldering screen presence and her comfort with the lesbian scenes in *Foxfire* that led to her breakthrough role in the HBO film *Gia* (1998), directed by Michael Cristofer. With her full lips, prominent cheekbones, and thin but voluptuous figure, Jolie not only looked like the reckless and ill-fated supermodel Gia but also seemed to live the same high-risk lifestyle. Her performance was highly praised and earned another Golden Globe.

Jolie's next major success came in 1999 with James Mangold's adaptation of Susanna Kaysen's novel *Girl, Interrupted.* Playing Lisa Rowe, an incorrigibly rebellious mental patient, Jolie was taken back into the darkly defiant territory of *Gia*, and she once again wowed both audiences and critics. She received a Golden Globe and an Academy Award for her performance. Along with her antisocial rebel roles, Jolie became known for playing tough action heroes. Her first major film in this genre was the Simon West movie *Lara Croft: Tomb Raider* (2001), based on a popular video game. Two *Lara Croft* movies were followed by *Mr. & Mrs. Smith* (2005), about rival assassins unwittingly married to each other, and *Salt* (2011), where Jolie portrays a rogue CIA agent, a role originally written for a man.

In 2011 Jolie stepped to the other side of the camera to write and direct the feature film *In the Land of Blood and Honey*, a dramatic love story set in the war-torn Bosnia of the 1990s. The film was controversial in the Balkans, drawing protest from the group Women Victims of War, and critical reviews were mixed, though it won the Cinema Award for Peace in 2012.

CONTROVERSIAL RELATIONSHIPS

The public and the press found Jolie's personal life to be at least as compelling as her professional career, and the actor has obliged her public with shocking frankness about such topics as her fascination with knives, tattoos, and kinky sex. Openly bisexual, she had a public relationship with Jenny Shimizu, one of her *Foxfire* costars, and other relationships with women were rumored. In 1996 she married *Hackers* costar Jonny Lee Miller, wearing a T-shirt on which she had written his name in her blood. After the two divorced in 1999, Jolie became involved with actor and filmmaker Billy Bob Thornton, twenty years her senior. Famous for getting matching tattoos and wearing vials of each other's blood, the two wed in 2000 and divorced three years later. In 2005 she began a relationship with Pitt, her *Mr. & Mrs. Smith* costar, and the two remained together into the 2010s.

While in Cambodia filming *Lara Croft* in 2000, Jolie was moved to see the devastating effects of war on the people of that nation. Her sympathy with the victims would change her life forever. She volunteered to become a goodwill ambassador for the United Nations High Commissioner for Refugees and began visiting victims of violence in Cambodia, Africa, and Pakistan. She not only worked to publicize the terrible personal consequences of war and donated millions of dollars of her own money to relief efforts but also adopted a Cambodian war orphan as her first child, Maddox. After she became involved with Pitt, the couple continued to fund massive relief projects worldwide and adopted two more children, Zahara from Ethiopia and Pax from Vietnam. The couple had three more biological children, Shiloh, Knox, and Vivienne.

In the twenty-first century Jolie shed much of her sociopathic rebel image in favor of one of concerned social activist and caring wife and mother. Her large family owned several homes and moved frequently to accommodate Pitt's and Jolie's film careers and vast philanthropic efforts. While caring for her family, Jolie continued to make movies and received Golden Globe and Oscar nominations for her work in director Clint Eastwood's *Changeling* in 2008 and a Golden Globe nomination starring opposite Johnny Depp in *The Tourist* in 2010.

Tina Gianoulis

SEE ALSO: *Academy Awards; Celebrity; Celebrity Couples; Depp, Johnny; Eastwood, Clint; Hollywood; Movie Stars; Pitt, Brad; Sex Symbol; Tattoos; T-Shirts; War Movies.*

BIBLIOGRAPHY

Christenson, Randy. "The Ultimate Badass: Angelina Jolie." *Cosmopolitan*, June 2001, 248.

Connelly, Chris. "Angelina Unstoppable." *Marie Claire*, January 2012, 56.

Essex, Andrew. "Girl Uncorrupted." *Entertainment Weekly*, November 5, 1999, 40.

Jolie, Angelina. *Angelina Jolie: Notes from My Travels*. New York: Gallery Books, 2003.

Ressner, Jeffrey. "Rebel without a Pause." *Time*, January 24, 2000, 72.

Sessums, Kevin. "Wild at Heart." *Allure*, November 1, 2004, 208.

Tracy, Kathleen. *Angelina Jolie: A Biography*. Westport, CT: Greenwood, 2008.

Jolson, Al *(1883?–1950)*

Al Jolson lived the American dream. Born in Lithuania, he rose through the ranks of vaudeville as a comedian and a blackface "Mammy" singer. By 1920 he had become the biggest star on Broadway, but he is probably best remembered for his film career. Jolson starred in *The Jazz Singer* (1927), the first talking movie ever made, and his legend was ensured in 1946 with the release of the successful biography of his life, *The Jolson Story*. Jolson was the first openly Jewish man to become an entertainment star in America. His marginal status as a Jew informed his blackface portrayal of southern blacks. Almost singlehandedly, Jolson helped introduce African American musical innovations such as jazz, ragtime, and the blues to white audiences.

The brightest star of the first half of the twentieth century, Jolson was eternally grateful for the opportunities America had given him. He tirelessly entertained American troops in World War II and the Korean War, and he contributed time and money to the March of Dimes and other philanthropic causes. While some of his colleagues in show business complained about his inflated ego, he certainly deserved his moniker: "The World's Greatest Entertainer."

MAMMA'S BOY

Perhaps it should come as no surprise that the man who made his mark singing "My Mammy" in blackface was himself a "mamma's boy." Jolson was born Asa Yoelson in Seredzius, Lithuania, sometime between 1883 and 1886. He was the youngest of four children—the baby of the family and the favorite of his mother, Naomi. When Asa was four, his father, Rabbi Moshe Reuben Yoelson, left Lithuania to put down roots for the family in the United States. From age four to eight, Asa was raised by his mother. She introduced him to the violin and told him that if he practiced hard he could become a star performer in America someday.

When Asa was eight Rabbi Yeolson brought his family to Washington, D.C., where he had found work as a rabbi and a cantor at a Jewish congregation. Later that same year Naomi died. Seeing his mother in her death throes impacted young Asa, and he spent much of his life struggling with that trauma. After her death he remained withdrawn for several months until he met Al Reeves, who played the banjo, sang, and introduced him to show business. At age nine Asa and his older brother, Hirsch, changed their names to Al and Harry Jolson, and by age eleven Jolson was singing in the streets for nickels and dimes that he used to buy tickets to shows at the National Theater.

After running away from home to New York City and doing a stint with a circus, Jolson joined Harry on the vaudeville circuit. In 1904 the brothers teamed up with a disabled man named Joe Palmer to form a comedy troupe. A friend of Joe's wrote them a comedy skit, but Jolson was uncomfortable with it until he took fellow performer James Dooley's advice to try it in blackface. He would remain in blackface for the rest of his stage and screen career. His blackface routine was a hit on the vaudeville circuit, and Jolson came to New York to perform it in 1906. His trademarks included vocal scales, dramatic facial expressions, and a whistling trick that approximated a frenetic birdcall. He billed himself as "The Blackface with the Grand Opera Voice." After his New York debut, he had success as a blackface comedian and singer in California. In 1911 he returned to New York to star in *La Belle Paree*, a vaudeville revue. There, Jolson quickly established himself as the biggest star on Broadway.

THE MOVE TO FILM

Jolson's film career began inauspiciously with a short film for the Vitagraph Company in 1916. In 1923 he agreed to star in a film by D. W. Griffith, but he backed out of his contract after filming had begun because Griffith had assigned an assistant to direct Jolson's scenes. In 1926 he made another short film for Warner Brothers, and in 1927 he was signed to star in a screen version of Samson Raphaelson's play *The Jazz Singer*. This was the role that Jolson had waited his whole life to play. It is the story of a Jewish boy, Jakie Rabinowitz, who runs away from his father, a cantor from the old world, because Jakie wants to be in show business. Jakie returns home to chant the Kol Nidre service as his father lies on his deathbed. The film was incredibly popular because it combined old silent film technology (words printed on the screen) with four dramatically innovative vitaphone "talking" sequences.

Jolson quickly became the first movie star in the modern sense. He went on to make *The Singing Fool* (1928), *Say It with Songs* (1929), *Mammy* (1930), and *Big Boy* (1930) before returning to Broadway in 1931. His star dimmed a bit in the late 1930s and early 1940s until the highly acclaimed biographical film *The Jolson Story*, starring Larry Parks, was released in 1946. Parks mouthed the songs that Jolson himself sang for the film, and the soundtrack of the film sold several million copies.

A LASTING LEGACY

Jolson was to jazz, blues, and ragtime what Elvis Presley was to rock and roll. He had first heard African American music in New Orleans in 1905, and he performed it for the rest of his life. Like Elvis, Jolson gyrated his lower body as he danced. In *The Jazz Singer*, white viewers saw Jolson moving his hips and waist in ways that they had never seen before. Historian and performer Stephen Hanan wrote in *Tikkun* magazine in 1998 that Jolson's "funky rhythm and below-the-waist gyrations (not seen again from any white male till the advent of Elvis) were harbingers of the sexual liberation of the new urban era. Jolson was a rock star before the dawn of rock music." Jolson paved the way for such African American performers as Louis Armstrong, Duke Ellington, Fats Waller, and Ethel Waters. It is remarkable that a Jewish mamma's boy from Lithuania could do so much to bridge the cultural gap between black and white America.

Adam Max Cohen

SEE ALSO: *Armstrong, Louis; Blackface Minstrelsy; Broadway; Ellington, Duke; Griffith, D. W.;* The Jazz Singer; *Movie Stars; Presley, Elvis; Silent Movies; Vaudeville; Waters, Ethel.*

BIBLIOGRAPHY

Freedland, Michael. *Jolson*. New York: Stein and Day, 1972.

Goldman, Herbert. *Jolson: The Legend Comes to Life*. New York: Oxford University Press, 1988.

Hanan, Stephen Mo. "Al Jolson: The Soul beneath the Mask." *Tikkun*, September 1998, 21–22.

Leonard, William Torbert. *Masquerade in Black*. Metuchen, NJ: Scarecrow Press, 1986.

Peterson, Bernard L. *Profiles of African American Stage Performers and Theatre People, 1816–1960*. Westport, CT: Greenwood Press, 2001.

Jon & Kate Plus 8

The first episode of the reality television series *Jon & Kate Plus 8* (2007–2009) begins with the words, "Jon and I both always knew we wanted to have kids but never imagined we'd have this many." First airing in 2007, the show heralded a glut of shows highlighting the joys and challenges of unusually large families in the first decade of the 2000s and the 2010s. Even as it began a new trend in reality television, however, the series soon became a cautionary tale about the ways that the camera's gaze, not to mention millions of viewers, paparazzi, and tabloid reporters, can affect those under the scrutiny of the lens. Although many viewers were enchanted by watching two ordinary people deal with the challenges of multiple births, others tuned in to critique the public breakdown of the couple's marriage.

When Jon Gosselin, an information technology analyst, and his wife, Kate, a nurse, used fertility drugs to conceive, they were not surprised when Kate delivered twins in 2000. However, they were less composed three years later when, trying for another child, they had sextuplets, three girls and three boys. The multiple births attracted media attention, and in 2006 the Discovery Health channel filmed two specials about the young family. The following year the Gosselins agreed to do a reality series, making cameras a part of their daily lives. The series soon moved to Discovery's TLC network and became the anchor of a line of large-family reality programs, including such shows as *Table for 12* (2009–) and *17 Kids and Counting* (2008–) (the title of the latter increases in number as the family increases in size).

Jon & Kate Plus 8 was a hit with audiences who were charmed by the children's engaging spontaneity and their parents' good-natured struggles to cope with the sheer volume of parenting they were required to do. However, as the show progressed through five seasons, revealing everything from Kate's short temper to Jon's hair implants, the strain of constant observation began to show. Exasperated by the constant intrusions of curious fans, the Gosselins left their home in Elizabethtown, Pennsylvania, to move to a gated mansion on 24 acres of land in rural Berks County. Propelled into celebrity status by the success of their show, Jon and Kate began to have problems in their marriage. Each flaw was magnified as tabloids printed pictures of Jon with other women and fan websites such as Gosselins without Pity ridiculed Kate's hairstyle and personality.

Discord proved even more popular than lovability: almost ten million viewers, more than twice the usual audience, tuned in to the fifth season premiere of the show to see the truth behind rumors of marital trouble. Even more watched the June 22, 2009, episode in which the couple announced their separation. *Jon & Kate Plus 8* was replaced by *Kate Plus 8* in 2009, which ran until 2011.

Tina Gianoulis

SEE ALSO: *Celebrity; Celebrity Couples; Divorce; Reality Television; Tabloids; Television.*

BIBLIOGRAPHY

Gosselin, Jon; Kate Gosselin; and Beth Carson. *Multiple Bles8ings: Surviving to Thriving with Twins and Sextuplets.* Grand Rapids, MI: Zondervan, 2008.

Rice, Lynette. "'Jon & Kate': Kids, Cameras, and Controversy." *Entertainment Weekly*, May 25, 2009. Accessed May 2012. Available from http://www.ew.com/ew/article/0,,20278901,00.html

Weinman, Jaime J. "What's So Great about 'Jon & Kate'?" *Maclean's*, June 16, 2009, 64.

The Jonas Brothers

As pop singers and Disney Channel stars, the Jonas Brothers became one of the most popular teenage bands in U.S. history with the release of their eponymous 2007 album. They channeled their energy into creating uplifting songs—either as a band or as solo artists—while creating a clean-cut image that appealed to a preteen and young adult audience.

Kevin (1987–), Joe (1989–), and Nick (1992–) grew up in New Jersey, the sons of a pastor and Christian musician father and a musician mother. All three brothers have credited Christianity and music as two of their strongest influences. Nick, the youngest of the trio and the acknowledged leader, began performing on Broadway at the age of six. After appearing in shows such as *Les Misérables*, *Beauty and the Beast*, *A Christmas Carol*, and *Annie Get Your Gun*, he released his first solo album, *Nicholas Jonas*, in 2004. Soon after, the three brothers began rehearsing together and officially became the boy band known as the Jonas Brothers.

The Jonas Brothers signed with Columbia Records in 2005 and released their first album a year later. The album, *It's about Time*, eventually sold exceedingly well, but Columbia decided not to release a second one and dropped them from the label. It did not take long for Disney executives to offer the group a contract and exposure on Disney Radio. With family-friendly lyrics and an upbeat pop sound, the Jonas Brothers' popularity exploded with the release of *Jonas Brothers*. They had written most of the songs, which included preteen favorites such as "S.O.S." and "Hold On." The album debuted at the fifth position on the Billboard Hot 200 chart and went platinum. In August of the same year, the Jonas Brothers appeared on Miley Cyrus's popular Disney show, *Hannah Montana*, and were invited to open for her next concert tour, increasing their popularity even more.

By 2008 the Jonas Brothers released a third album, *A Little Bit Longer*, which sold 525,000 copies at its release and debuted at the top of the Billboard Top 200 albums chart. They also starred in the Disney Channel movie *Camp Rock* with Demi Lovato, another Disney channel sensation. The highest-ranked program of that year, *Camp Rock* garnered nearly nine million viewers, and the soundtrack went platinum. By the end of 2008 the Jonas Brothers had become the youngest act to date to sign a multimillion-dollar contract with Live Nation. Their success did not go unnoticed by the mainstream media, and *People* magazine devoted a special issue to the trio.

In 2009 the Jonas Brothers released a documentary, *Jonas Brothers: The 3-D Concert Experience*, which gave fans a firsthand look at what the band was like offstage. The brothers also appeared on the Disney Channel series *Jonas* (2009–2010) as themselves. The media exposure continued with an appearance on the June 2009 cover of *Rolling Stone* and a performance with legendary rhythm-and-blues singer Stevie Wonder at the 2009 Grammy Awards. While some fans and critics were confused by the pairing of the Jonas Brothers with Wonder, all three brothers cited Wonder as one of their main musical influences.

While the Jonas Brothers tried to avoid controversy in their public lives, much was made of the purity rings they wore as a pledge to refrain from premarital sex. British comedian Russell Brand poked fun at them when he hosted the 2008 MTV Video Music Awards. The popular animated sitcom *South Park* also satirized both the Jonas Brothers and their purity rings in an episode titled "The Ring." Despite ridicule, the brothers inspired scores of loyal fans to make the same commitment.

After releasing their fourth studio album, *Lines, Vines, and Trying Times*, which debuted at the top of album chart, Nick began writing songs that he felt were not stylistically right for the Jonas Brothers. He established the band Nick Jonas and the Administration, releasing a solo album, *Who I Am*, in 2010. The brothers insisted they were not breaking up and that the band was simply on hiatus. Kevin had married his longtime girlfriend Danielle Deleasa and wanted to spend time with her. In 2011 Joe released a solo album, *Fastlife*, and Nick returned to

Broadway in early 2012, replacing Darren Criss in *How to Succeed in Business without Really Trying.*

Elizabeth Rholetter Purdy

SEE ALSO: Annie Get Your Gun*; Boy Bands; Broadway; Cable TV; Cyrus, Miley / Hannah Montana; Disney (Walt Disney Company); Grammy Awards;* Les Misérables*; MTV;* People*; Rhythm and Blues;* Rolling Stone*;* South Park*; Television; Wonder, Stevie.*

BIBLIOGRAPHY

Debruge, Peter. "Band of 'Brothers' Fans the Frenzy." *Variety,* March 2–8, 2009.

Donahue, Ann. "Nick Jonas." *Billboard,* January 30, 2010.

Gay, Jason. "The Jonas Brothers: The Clean Teen Machine." *Rolling Stone,* August 7, 2008.

Sheffield, Rob. "Big Teenage Kicks with the JoBros." *Rolling Stone,* June 25, 2009.

Jones, Bobby *(1902–1971)*

Golf has changed over the years. Balls fly farther. Clubs are made of space-age materials like graphite and titanium. Courses are longer, more demanding, and come in more shapes and sizes with different types of grass. But no one dominated the game during any era like Bobby Jones did during his, or won so much in so short a time.

From 1923, when he won his first major (the U.S. Open), to his retirement in 1930, Jones won the U.S. Amateur five times, the U.S. Open four times, the British Open three times, and the British Amateur once. In 1930, at age twenty-eight, he accomplished what no one has done since: winning the Grand Slam—the U.S. Open, the British Open, the U.S. Amateur, and the British Amateur—in the same year. After winning his first major, Jones won 62 percent of the major championships he entered. Golf has had its share of greats: Harry Vardon, Walter Hagen, Gene Sarazen, Byron Nelson, Sam Snead, Ben Hogan, Arnold Palmer, Jack Nicklaus, and Tiger Woods. But no one has come close to matching Jones's record or so completely dominated their contemporaries. And Jones did it all for fun, for free, as an amateur.

Robert Tyre Jones Jr. stood out in other ways. Of the top echelon players in golfing history, he was one of the most highly educated, with degrees in mechanical engineering from Georgia Tech, literature from Harvard, and law from Emory. Born in Atlanta in 1902, Jones was the son of attorney Robert Jones and his wife Clara. From an early age it was apparent that the youngster possessed a special talent. He began playing golf at age six; at age nine he won the junior championship at East Lake, his father's club; at age fourteen he won the Georgia State Amateur; at age fifteen he won the Southern Amateur; at age seventeen he was runner-up in both the Canadian Open and the U.S. Amateur.

Jones's early success was so great that public expectations may have hindered him in tournaments; he won no major titles until 1923. However it appears that Jones, a perfectionist prone to bursts of anger, learned to control his emotions over this period. Throughout the rest of his career he was known for his sportsmanship and decorum on the course.

Jones continued to be active in the golf world after his retirement. Although uninterested in endorsements, he produced two series of movie shorts titled *How I Play Golf* (1931, 1933) and helped design a new standard of golf club for Spalding Company. Jones demonstrated his remarkable versatility with his great masterpiece—the Augusta National Golf Club. After raising funds to purchase a plot in Augusta, Georgia, known as Fruitland, Jones codesigned the course with Alister MacKenzie. In 1934 the first annual Invitational tournament was held. By 1938 it was being called the Masters, and it eventually came to be considered as one of the four major tournaments in the world. However, Augusta National later became controversial and subject to boycotts due its policies of not admitting women or blacks.

In 1948 Jones contracted syringomyelia, a rare and crippling spinal disease, and his condition worsened until he was eventually confined to a wheelchair. His greatest tribute came in 1958 when he received the Freedom of the City Award at St. Andrews, Scotland, in what many have called one of the most moving ceremonies in the history of game.

Lloyd Chiasson Jr.

SEE ALSO: *Golf; Hogan, Ben; Nicklaus, Jack; Palmer, Arnold; Spalding, Albert G.; Vardon, Harry; Woods, Tiger.*

BIBLIOGRAPHY

Barkow, Al. *Gettin' to the Dance Floor: An Oral History of American Golf.* New York: Atheneum, 1986.

Davis, Martin. *The Greatest of Them All: The Legend of Bobby Jones.* Greenwich, CT: American Golfer, 1996.

Grimsley, Will. *Golf: Its History, People and Events.* Englewood Cliffs, NJ: Prentice-Hall, 1966.

Jones, Bobby. *Golf Is My Game.* Garden City, NY: Doubleday, 1960.

Miller, Dick. *Triumphant Journey: The Saga of Bobby Jones and the Grand Slam of Golf.* New York: Holt, Rinehart and Winston, 1980.

Rapoport, Ron. *The Immortal Bobby: Bobby Jones and the Golden Age of Golf.* Hoboken, NJ: John Wiley and Sons, 2005.

Rice, Grantland, and O. B. Keeler. *The Bobby Jones Story.* Atlanta, GA: Tupper & Love, 1953.

Jones, George *(1931–)*

George Jones is an American country music singer. He has thrilled audiences with his traditional honky-tonk voice and has remained a steady force in the country music industry throughout his long career. Initially Jones was an improbable star, offering a twangy voice reminiscent of early hillbilly music at a time when rock and roll was making inroads into country music, but he persevered and went on to become a country music icon. Jones has received many awards, including Grammy, Country Music, and Academy of Country Music awards. In 1992 he was inducted into the Country Music Hall of Fame, and in 2008 he was recognized by the Kennedy Center Honors. Country music superstar Garth Brooks once said that Jones has "the greatest voice ever to sing country music."

Jones's early life made him an unlikely candidate for

George Jones. *George Jones began his long career as one of country music's most successful traditionalists in the 1950s, charting hits into the 1990s.* MICHAEL OCHS ARCHIVES/GETTY IMAGES.

stardom. He was the youngest of seven children, born to a poor family in the small town of Saratoga, Texas. His father was a pipe fitter and truck driver. His mother played the piano at church. The entire family listened to country music on the radio, especially the *Grand Ole Opry* broadcast from Nashville, Tennessee, and Jones came of age listening to artists Floyd Tillman, Ernest Tubb, Roy Acuff, and Bill Monroe. In the years during and after World War II, he made his way to dance halls in towns such as Port Arthur and Orange, which were brimming with wartime industrial growth and found the atmosphere intoxicating.

Jones began playing the guitar in high school and from then on focused all of his energies on becoming a recording star. Attempting to sound like his heroes Acuff and Hank Williams Sr., he sought out venues such as local clubs and events such as school dances where he could hone his skills. He joined the marines during the Korean War, served for three years, then returned to Texas, where, beset with doubts that he could ever break into show business, he found employment as a house painter. Nonetheless, he continued to sing and play guitar whenever he could, and over the next few years became a regular of the Texas honky-tonk circuit, performing in small towns throughout the area. Based on his local success, Jones then contacted producer Pappy Daily at Starday Records, located in Beaumont, about making a record. The partnership proved a good one. Starday, as a local record company, was one of the few country music labels that was not moving into the rockabilly style then taking Nashville by storm.

COUNTRY STARDOM

Starday recorded and released Jones's first hit, "Why Baby Why" in 1955, but his first couple of years as a recording musician met with varied results. He was invited to join the Grand Ole Opry in 1956, a lifelong dream come true, and two years later he left Starday for a deal with the more prestigious Mercury label. In 1959 his single "White Lightning" reached number one on the country music charts, and by 1962 he was a country music celebrity, recording two number one hits, "Tender Years" and "She Thinks I Still Care." That year, and again in 1963, the Country Music DJ Convention (which became the Country Music Association Awards in 1967) named him Male Vocalist of the Year. Throughout the 1960s Jones recorded hit after hit, such as "Window up Above," "We Must Have Been out of Our Minds," "Take Me," and "The Race Is On," under a variety of labels, including United Artists, Musicor, and Epic. While dominating the country charts, he also toured ceaselessly, both nationally and internationally, seemingly without rest.

Jones's celebrity status and the exhausting pace of his tours began to take a serious toll. During the 1960s he began drinking heavily, which, periodically, led to his cutting concerts short or canceling them altogether. He appeared drunk onstage regularly, and by the mid-1960s his career seemed to be on the verge of collapse. In 1968, however, it was rejuvenated when he began touring with singer Tammy Wynette, who had recently emerged as a new country music star. The combination was ideal, for both sang ballads in a traditional country style and both were known for their very distinctive voices. Fans were thrilled when Jones and Wynette married in 1969. The relationship proved to be more public than private. Onstage, they sang both solos and duets, generally ending a concert with a song proclaiming their mutual devotion. The marriage proved lucrative, too, as the couple began recording together under the Epic label, churning out hit after hit in the early 1970s, including the 1974 number one hit, "We're Gonna Hold On." At the same time, Jones recorded solo hits such as "The Grand Tour" and "The Door," both of which reached number one in 1974.

Although the public image of his marriage to Wynette bolstered Jones's career, it was not long before he again began to experience hard times. He and Wynette lived in constant pursuit by reporters, and the resultant strain caused their relationship to grow turbulent and destructive. As the situation worsened, Jones began to drink heavily again. Their inevitable breakup added bizarrely to their public appeal, and in 1975, the year they divorced, the couple recorded "Golden Ring" and "Near You," both of which became hits. In the years following the divorce, Jones's career once again seemed to be nearing the end. He missed several show dates, leading to numerous legal entanglements and an eventual declaration of bankruptcy, and in the early 1980s he was in the news more often for his legal problems than his music. He was arrested on a number of occasions relating to his alcohol and drug abuse and was sued by ex-wives and numerous creditors.

A REFLECTION OF COUNTRY MUSIC

Jones continued to perform and record, even during the darkest times. In 1980 he released what is perhaps his best-known single, "He Stopped Loving Her Today," considered by some to be the best country music recording ever. It was a major hit, and Jones received the Country Music Association (CMA) Award for Single of the Year. Jones's personal problems never affected his popularity, and he continued recording a string of hits throughout the

1980s. In 1986 he entered a new phase of his career, winning the CMA Award for Video of the Year for his single "Who's Gonna Fill Their Shoes." In 1991 he signed a new recording deal with MCA Records, and the following year he was inducted into the Country Music Hall of Fame. In the early 1990s, Jones enjoyed further success by incorporating rock and roll into his music with hits such as "I Don't Need Your Rockin' Chair" and the successful album *High-Tech Redneck*.

While these new hits demonstrated Jones's versatility and his willingness to experiment with contemporary styles, he continued to thrive on the music that first brought him success. His album *It Don't Get Any Better than This* (1998) is very much in his traditional style. Jones continued to record into the twenty-first century, with albums such as *The Rock: Stone Cold Country* (2001), which reached number five on the country charts, and *Hits I Missed . . . And One I Didn't* (2005), which climbed to number thirteen. He also filmed music videos such as *The Blues Man* (2005) with singer Dolly Parton and *Country Boy* (2010) with singers Aaron Lewis, Chris Young, and Charlie Daniels. Jones's influence and talent have been honored through numerous awards, including the U.S. National Medal of Arts in 2002 and a Grammy Hall of Fame Award for "He Stopped Loving Her Today" in 2007. He was elected into the Texas Country Music Hall of Fame in 2010 and received the Grammy Lifetime Achievement Award in 2012. In many respects, Jones stands as a reflection of country music itself: open to innovation while rooted in tradition.

Jeffrey W. Coker

SEE ALSO: *Brooks, Garth; Country Music; Daniels, Charlie; Grammy Awards;* Grand Ole Opry*; Monroe, Bill; Parton, Dolly; Williams, Hank, Sr.; World War II; Wynette, Tammy.*

BIBLIOGRAPHY

Allen, Bob. *George Jones: The Saga of an American Singer.* Garden City, NY: Doubleday, 1984.

"Biography." GeorgeJones.com. Accessed May 14, 2012. Available from http://www.georgejones.com/bio/index.php

Brown, Jim. *George Jones: Why Baby Why.* Kingston, ON: Quarry Music Books, 2001.

Jones, George, and Tom Cater. *I Lived to Tell It All.* New York: Villard Books, 1996.

Malone, Bill C. *Country Music U.S.A.*, rev. ed. Austin: University of Texas Press, 1985.

Nash, Alanna. *Behind Closed Doors: Talking with the Legends of Country Music.* New York: Knopf, 1988.

Jones, Jennifer *(1919–2009)*

Actress Jennifer Jones's career was launched by a very public affair with the renowned producer David O. Selznick. He signed her to a long-term contract, changed her name, and prepared her for stardom. Her first screen lead was in *Song of Bernadette* (1943), a film whose popularity earned her an Academy Award. She was nominated for Best Supporting Actress Oscars in *Since You Went Away* (1944), *Love Letters* (1945), and *Love Is a Many Splendored Thing* (1955). Jones played a wide variety of characters, including the innocent and placid as well as the tempestuous and sensuous, although she was not considered a formidable actress. But she undoubtedly captured a mood Americans longed for, ultimately becoming one of the most popular melodramatic actresses of the 1940s. Jones died in Malibu, California, on December 17, 2009, at the age of ninety.

Liza Black

SEE ALSO: *Academy Awards; Movie Stars; Selznick, David O.; Star System.*

BIBLIOGRAPHY

Epstein, Edward Z. *Portrait of Jennifer: A Biography of Jennifer Jones.* New York: Simon & Schuster, 1995.

Green, Paul. *Jennifer Jones: The Life and Films.* Jefferson, NC: McFarland, 2011.

Jones, Leroi

SEE: *Baraka, Amiri.*

Jones, Tom *(1940–)*

Many comparisons have been drawn between Welsh singer Tom Jones and rock legend Elvis Presley. Both appropriated singing styles associated with black rhythm-and-blues music, both became infamous for their sexually charged dancing styles, and both were loved for over-the-top Las Vegas club performances in the 1960s and 1970s. Indeed, Jones and Presley maintained a well-documented admiration for each other and often performed cover versions of each others' songs. However, Jones's diversity and longevity far exceeded Presley's. Throughout the 1980s and 1990s, when many of his contemporaries had devolved into all-but-forgotten lounge lizards, Jones performed pop, rock, country, and dance tunes, often collaborating with a roster of acts half his age for the ears of equally young listeners.

Born Thomas Jones Woodward in Pontypridd, South Wales, on June 7, 1940, Jones grew up in the song-filled atmosphere of a coal-mining community, often putting on performances for his mother in the family living room. His days of youth were relatively short, however, and by age seventeen he was both a husband and father. Having no real training in a trade, Jones bounced between a number of odd jobs to support his growing family, including glove cutting and selling vacuums door-to-door. Nevertheless, he still found the time to sing at night in local dance halls, and after a number of years he had earned a sizable reputation as front man for Tommy Scott and the Senators, a rock and soul outfit influenced by R&B singers Solomon Burke and Jackie Wilson, as well as Presley and Jerry Lee Lewis.

After being discovered by songwriter and manager Gordon Mills in 1963, Jones signed with the Decca label. His debut single was only mildly successful, but the follow-up, "It's Not Unusual," became a giant international hit, as well as Jones's signature tune. At the time the unbridled sexual delivery of Jones's singing, as well as his pelvis-thrusting dance moves, were considered too racy for conservative broadcast companies like the BBC. Moral squeamishness could not restrain public demand, however, and after "It's Not Unusual" was leaked by an off-shore pirate radio station, Jones became a highly visible

Tom Jones. *Tom Jones's powerful voice and sexy stage persona made him a popular entertainer in the 1960s and 1970s.* O'NEILL/ HULTON ARCHIVE/GETTY IMAGES.

sex symbol. Throughout the 1960s many of his singles were major hits, notably the Burt Bacharach–penned "What's New, Pussycat?" and he honed his stage performance touring with world-class acts like the Rolling Stones.

During the 1970s Jones occasionally scored with singles like the up-tempo dance cut "She's a Lady," but his presence on Top 40 charts gradually declined, perhaps due to changing currents in pop music. At the same time, however, his popularity as a live performer grew. Fully the master of his wide-ranging voice, Jones injected such raw passion into his stage shows that adoring fans were often moved to toss their underwear at his feet. He became an essential booking for the top clubs in the Las Vegas circuit and was even given his own television variety show on the ABC network, *This Is Tom Jones* (1969–1971).

For years Jones kept a relatively low profile, but in the late 1980s his career took on an unexpected new breath of life. Beginning with a remake of the Prince song "Kiss" in collaboration with the British electronic innovators the Art of Noise in 1988, Jones worked with many younger acts from diverse musical backgrounds, meeting with a high level of approval from all age groups. In 1992, for example, he masterminded a unique six-part series called *The Right Time* in which he paid tribute to a number of musical genres through intimate performances with acts as wide-ranging as Joe Cocker, Stevie Wonder, the dance groups EMF and Erasure, and pop warblers Shakespears' Sister. Continuing in this vein, in 1994 he signed to the Interscope label, a company devoted almost exclusively to edgy young acts like Nine Inch Nails and Snoop Dogg. As with country legend Johnny Cash, Jones was able to extend his legacy into the generation of the 1990s, largely without the element of irony or kitsch appreciation that tinged the later careers of other 1960s holdovers.

In the twenty-first century, Jones has continued to perform live shows and release albums, including 2008's *24 Hours*, the first album of entirely new material he has issued in the United States in fifteen years. A much-beloved and instantly recognizable figure to several generations of music lovers, Jones appeared on *American Idol* (2002–) in 2011 and was slated to be a judge for the musical talent show *The Voice UK* as of early 2012.

Shaun Frentner

SEE ALSO: American Idol; *Cash, Johnny; Las Vegas; Lewis, Jerry Lee; Pop Music; Presley, Elvis; Rock and Roll; The Rolling Stones; Sex Symbol; Snoop Dogg; Wonder, Stevie.*

BIBLIOGRAPHY

Macfarlane, Colin. *Tom Jones: The Boy from Nowhere.* New York: St. Martin's Press, 1988.

Jonestown

Officially known as the People's Temple, the Jonestown commune of American religious zealots lived in the small South American country of Guyana during the 1970s. This community has become synonymous with fanatical cultism and mass suicide.

The group originated in Northern California under the leadership of pastor Jim Jones. As Jones became increasingly megalomaniac and unstable, he relocated his church and its followers to an isolated jungle compound in a foreign country. There he used brainwashing techniques to break his people's will and force them to comply with his demands.

Government officials in the United States became concerned after hearing reports of church members being held against their will, and a delegation was sent to investigate. After a violent confrontation between cultists and the delegation, Jones ordered his followers to commit suicide by drinking a cyanide potion. Those who refused were shot. When U.S. officials entered the compound on November 18, 1978, they found 913 bodies, including that of Jones himself.

Tony Brewer

SEE ALSO: *Communes; Cults.*

BIBLIOGRAPHY

Chidester, David. *Salvation and Suicide: Jim Jones, the Peoples Temple, and Jonestown*, rev. ed. Bloomington: Indiana University Press, 2003.

Kerns, Phil. *People's Temple, People's Tomb.* Plainfield, NJ: Bridge Logos International, 1979.

Kilduff, Marshall, and Ron Javers. *The Suicide Cult.* New York: Bantam Books, 1978.

Krause, Charles. *Guyana Massacre: The Eyewitness Account.* New York: Berkley Books, 1978.

Jong, Erica *(1942–)*

Erica Jong's first novel, *Fear of Flying* (1973), made her one of the central figures of the sexual revolution of the 1970s. Her frank and explicit depictions of female sexual desire shocked the world and gained her the praise of everyone from *Playboy* editors to author John Updike. Women have given her a more mixed reception, however. Her many works of fiction and poetry that portray women fulfilling their fantasies of sexual abandon played well among the newly liberated generation of women in the 1970s; feminists of the 1980s and 1990s, however, challenged her promotion of anonymous sex for its own sake and her claim to speak for baby boomer women's sexual desires. Nonetheless, she brought women's struggles to balance love, sex, self-development, and creativity to the attention of a mass audience.

Jong grew up in an affluent Jewish family in New York and attended Barnard College. She was a PhD candidate at Columbia University, studying eighteenth-century British literature, when she began her career as a writer. She published two volumes of poetry, and when *Fear of Flying* caught the attention of writer Henry Miller (who compared the book to his *Tropic of Cancer*) and Updike (who compared it to Philip Roth's *Portnoy's Complaint* and J. D. Salinger's *Catcher in the Rye*), her name became a household word. She was repeatedly asked by reporters to help explain women's perspectives on sexual liberation, and her frank, sassy commentary provided good copy for *Playboy* and *Redbook* alike.

Fear of Flying, which opens with the then-shocking intimation that the heroine is not wearing a bra, captured a cultural moment when women were shedding propriety and clothing in an attempt to gain fulfillment and freedom—the moment that gave birth to modern feminism and the sexual revolution. The novel tells the story of Isadora Wing, a writer who accompanies her stiff, cold, psychiatrist husband to a conference in Zurich. There she meets an Englishman who seems to epitomize unrepressed, guiltless sexual fulfillment, which she calls the "zipless fuck," a phrase that became a catchword for her generation an emblem of Jong's popular image. Isadora soon learns, though, that the man who has rescued her from her prosaic life is impotent, and she returns to her husband. The book ends with Isadora convincing herself that her search for empty and meaningless orgasms was no substitute for true self-development.

Jong continued Isadora's story in *How to Save Your Own Life* (1977) and *Parachutes and Kisses* (1984). In the second book Isadora becomes a successful author, leaves her husband, begins life again with a young screenwriter, and has a baby. In the final installment of the trilogy, the baby's father deserts her, and she must learn to be a single mother. In these three books, as well as in her many other novels, short stories, and poems, Jong's message is that sexual freedom is paramount to a woman's self-discovery.

Although her subsequent books never repeated the success of *Fear of Flying*, Jong continued to act as a prominent voice on women's issues throughout the 1980s and 1990s. Pitted against such well-known feminists as Camille Paglia, Katie Roiphe, and Andrea Dworkin on talk shows and in popular magazines, she was accused of upholding the virtues of female heterosexual experimentation in a time when date rape and violence against women were prominent concerns. Other feminists simply consider her recipe for liberation inadequate. Amy Virshup has argued that despite Jong's advocacy of self-empowerment, "It is always Mr. Right who leads [her heroines] onward and upward." Anne Z. Mickelson has charged that her depictions of sex mirror those found in "girlie magazines" and that "by adopting the male language of sexuality, Jong is also fooling herself that she is preempting man's power." In her memoir *Fear of Fifty* (1994), Jong took the counteroffensive, attacking the "puritan feminists" who she feels have tried to silence her for her positive portrayals of heterosexual sex and motherhood.

Jong has called the success of *Fear of Flying* a "curse," explaining, "[It] typecast me in a way that I've been trying to get free of ever since. I'm enormously grateful to it, and yet very eager to be seen as a woman of letters and not just Erica 'Zipless' Jong." Dissatisfied with her reputation as a popular icon, she has attempted to solidify her standing in the literary canon with *The Devil at Large: Erica Jong on Henry Miller* (1993), in which she describes her literary relationship with the prominent writer. In *Fear of Fifty* and *What Do Women Want?: Bread, Roses, Sex, Power* (1998), she portrays herself as a spokesperson for baby boomer women who wanted sexual fulfillment and empowerment in the 1970s and who have aspired to reinvent their relationships with men on the basis of love and mutual respect in the 1990s and the first decade of the 2000s. Her autobiographical writing has continued to broaden her career and perspectives in the twenty-first century. In 2007 Jong's literary archive was acquired by Columbia University, a confirmation of her status as a writer of lasting merit.

Anne Boyd

SEE ALSO: *Baby Boomers; Best Sellers; Bra;* The Catcher in the Rye*; Daytime Talk Shows; Feminism; Miller, Henry; Paglia, Camille;* Playboy; Redbook*; Sexual Revolution; Updike, John.*

BIBLIOGRAPHY

Jong, Erica. *Fear of Fifty.* New York: HarperCollins, 1994.

Jong, Erica. *What Do Women Want?: Bread, Roses, Sex, Power.* New York: HarperCollins, 1998.

Jong, Erica. *Seducing the Demon: Writing for My life.* New York: Tarcher Publishing, 2006.

Jong, Erica. "It Was Eight Years Ago Today (But It Seems Like Eighty)." Huffington Post, January 16, 2008. Accessed January 4, 2012. Available from http://www.huffingtonpost.com/

Mickelson, Anne Z. *Reaching Out: Sensitivity and Order in Recent American Fiction.* Metuchen, NJ: Scarecrow Press, 1979.

Virshup, Amy. "For Mature Audiences Only." *New York*, July 18, 1994, 40–47.

Joplin, Janis *(1943–1970)*

Regarded as the greatest white female blues singer, Janis Joplin is also remembered as a hedonistic, hard-drinking, bra-disdaining, bisexual challenger of social conventions. She often is associated with Jimi Hendrix and Jim Morrison, a trio of dynamic performers who all died within a year of each other between September 1970 and July 1971 and whose "live hard, die fast" philosophy not only epitomized the 1960s but also tolled the end of that spectacular, turbulent epoch.

FROM TEXAS TO SAN FRANCISCO

The young Joplin was an intelligent, creative girl with many interests and talents. Born January 19, 1943, in Port Arthur, Texas, she was raised by liberal parents who encouraged her interests in music, art, and literature. Her favorite author was F. Scott Fitzgerald, and she identified with the glamorous, ruinous lives of Scott and Zelda Fitzgerald and her favorite singers, Billie Holiday and Bessie Smith. She learned to sing the blues as well as play guitar, piano, and autoharp. However, Joplin's main ambition was to become an artist; she drew and painted and majored in art in college.

Joplin's interests drew her to the beatnik scene in San Francisco in 1964, where she met Robert Crumb and other artists. She sold paintings, sang with various blues bands, and developed an amphetamine addiction. In 1965 she made her way back to Texas to withdraw from the temptation of drugs, and she returned to college.

A year later she was invited back to San Francisco to sing with Big Brother and the Holding Company. She returned to find the beatnik scene succeeded by the hippie scene. She partied with the Grateful Dead, Country Joe and the Fish, and Jefferson Airplane. Joplin soon distinguished herself even among these luminaries with her booming, unbridled vocals and the raw, electric blues of Big Brother. They cut several singles, and their growing reputation took them to the Monterey International Pop Festival.

Cashing in on Joplin's new popularity, Mainstream Records repackaged their singles as *Big Brother and the Holding Company, Featuring Janis Joplin* (1967). Released without the band's permission, it is an uneven album wavering between folk, psychedelic, and pop music. Their next album, *Cheap Thrills* (1968), revealed a band that had found its identity in raunchy electric blues. Joplin is at her best in the sultry, sizzling "Summertime" and "Piece of My Heart," which reveal the tortured combination of toughness and vulnerability that became her trademark.

Big Brother was never esteemed by the critics, and Joplin was persuaded to form a new band for her next album, *I Got Dem Ol' Kozmic Blues Again Mama!* (1969), but she never developed a rapport with the Kozmic Blues Band. With two sax players and a trumpeter, they had a brassy sound that smothered Joplin's vocals. Nor was there anything particularly cosmic about their blues style, which was more mainstream than Big Brother's. Joplin recognized the unsuitability of this group and formed the Full Tilt Boogie Band. The brassy sound of the Kozmic Blues Band was discarded, and the two keyboardists—rather than the two aggressive guitarists of Big Brother—allowed Joplin's vocals free rein.

INTENSE PERFORMER

Joplin wrote few of her own songs, but more often turned others' songs into her own through wrenching, probing performances. She chose her songs well, finding a medium through which she could express her soul in all its passion and insecurity. Some feminists are uncomfortable with the sexual desperation Joplin revealed in her recordings, but singing was her catharsis; she was not only rebelling against the double standards of the age but also honestly exploring her soul. In her essay in *The Rolling Stone Illustrated History of Rock & Roll*, Ellen Willis claims that Joplin was compelled to stay in show business because of the limited opportunities that would have awaited her as a woman. The truth is that Joplin sang because she loved and needed it, and she had plans to open a bar after her singing career ended. The "female = victim" equation shows little appreciation for the bold young woman who left her hometown for San Francisco in 1964, relying only on her talents to make it on her own, and announced to the male-dominated rock world that "a woman can be tough."

Joplin's popularity was now at its zenith, and she felt pressured to live up to her hedonistic image, attempting to sustain the intensity of her stage performances in her daily life. She drank constantly and resorted to heroin. She lost contact with the sensitive woman she had been and started rumors that she was unpopular in school and had been estranged from her parents (although letters printed in *Love, Janis* reveal that she was always close to her family). This side of Joplin was exploited in the sensationalistic 1979 Bette Midler film *The Rose*, loosely based on Joplin's life.

On October 4, 1970, after a recording session with Full Tilt, Joplin died from a heroin overdose. "Buried Alive in Blues" was left as an instrumental, but *Pearl* (1971) is otherwise complete. It is Joplin's most polished album, containing the unforgettable "Me and Bobby McGee." It is difficult to listen to Joplin's music without a pang of regret for her tragically wasted talent, but she often said that she would rather live intensely than spend a long life in front of the TV. When friends warned her that she would lose her voice if she kept shrieking, she replied that she would rather give it her all and be a great singer while young instead of a mediocre singer with a long career. Joplin's excess was part of her artistry.

The enduring fascination Joplin commands is testified by many posthumous releases, including *Janis Joplin in Concert* (1972), *Janis Joplin's Greatest Hits* (1973), *Janis* (documentary and soundtrack, 1975), *A Farewell Song* (rarities, 1983), and *Janis Joplin with Big Brother and the Holding Company, Live at Winterland '68* (1998). Joplin was elected to the Rock and Roll Hall of Fame in 1995.

Douglas Cooke

SEE ALSO: *Blues; Crumb, Robert; The Doors; The Grateful Dead; Haight-Ashbury; Hendrix, Jimi; Hippies; Holiday, Billie; Jefferson Airplane/Starship; Midler, Bette; Psychedelia; Smith, Bessie; Woodstock.*

BIBLIOGRAPHY

Dalton, David. *Janis.* New York: Simon & Schuster, 1971.

Friedman, Myra. *Buried Alive: The Biography of Janis Joplin.* New York: William Morrow, 1973.

Joplin, Laura. *Love, Janis.* New York: Villard Books, 1992.

Willett, Edward. *Janis Joplin: Take Another Little Piece of My Heart.* Berkeley Heights, NJ: Enslow Publishers, 2008.

Willis, Ellen. "Janis Joplin." In *The Rolling Stone Illustrated History of Rock & Roll,* 3rd ed., Anthony DeCurtis, James Henke, and Holly George-Warren, eds. New York: Random House, 1992.

Joplin, Scott *(1868–1917)*

As a pioneering African American composer of ragtime music, Scott Joplin took part in a musical revolution in America at the turn of the twentieth century and left an enduring mark on the musical culture of the country. Best known during his lifetime for *Maple Leaf Rag* (1899), Joplin wrote some two dozen compositions in the catchy, syncopated style that served as accompaniment to cakewalk dancing, to new forms of urban sporting life, and to a more generalized revolt against nineteenth-century gentility and restraint. He helped establish the conventional structure of ragtime compositions and successfully blended familiar genres of European music with African American rhythms and melodies into a genuine musical hybrid.

"KING OF RAGTIME WRITERS"

After 1900 ragtime music emerged as the first nationally recognized American music, and Tin Pan Alley publishers flooded the popular sheet music market with thousands of snappy, syncopated songs and piano pieces. Hiram K. Moderwell, one of Joplin's contemporaries, called ragtime the "folk music of the American city," and John Stark, the publisher of *Maple Leaf Rag*, dubbed Joplin the "King of Ragtime Writers."

Although he was unquestionably born with a musical gift, Joplin's genius must be attributed at least partly to childhood influences from the region of his birth. Born near Linden, Texas, in 1868, the second son of sharecroppers Jiles and Florence Joplin, the future composer grew up amid former slaves and their rich musical traditions. As a youngster he heard black work songs, spirituals, and ring shouts, as well as the European waltzes, schottisches, and marches that black musicians like his father performed at white parties and dances.

When the Joplins moved to Texarkana, which had sprung into existence in the early 1870s at the junction of the Texas & Pacific and Cairo & Fulton Railroads, Scott not only attended school but also learned to play the piano belonging to a wealthy family whose house his mother cleaned. As his talent developed, he began studying with a German music teacher (thought most probably to be Julius Weiss) from whom he learned the basic elements of serious European compositions and the rhythms, melodies, and harmonies on which they depended. Joplin began performing as an adolescent, impressing those who heard him with the originality of his music. As one contemporary later recalled, "He did not have to play anybody else's music. He made up his own, and it was beautiful; he just got his music out of the air."

It is not known exactly when Joplin left Texarkana, but sometime in the 1880s he set out to make his living as an itinerant musician. It also is not known where he worked and lived before he gained fame during the 1890s. Oral histories place him at the World's Columbian Exposition in Chicago in 1893, where he tried out some of his arrangements with a newly formed band performing, no doubt, in the city's tenderloin district. He was convinced that his rhythmically daring music had a ready, eager audience. Ragtime's misplaced accents, its complex melodies that flowed from bass to treble and back, and the flurry of its notes invited toe-tapping, knee-slapping, head-bobbing movement from those who heard it; the music was perfect for the flashy strutting of the popular cakewalk. Moreover, the 1890s economic depression, which affected the middle class as well as the underpaid or unemployed working class, sparked a nationwide questioning of the long-held American belief in self-denial and personal restraint. Joplin's music struck a chord with a generation ready to shake off the vestiges of nineteenth-century propriety by kicking up its heels to the exuberant strains of ragtime.

Following the World's Columbian Exposition, Joplin made his way to Sedalia, Missouri, an important railhead in the east-central part of the Show-Me State. More significantly, perhaps, for the black musician, Sedalia was the home of the George R. Smith College for Negroes. Joplin enrolled in music courses at the black institution and began performing in various settings in Sedalia along with other talented African American musicians, earning a reputation as a popular entertainer and composer of ragtime music. He performed with the Queen City Band, an all-black group that provided music for various public entertainments and played in clubs, brothels, and dance halls, as well as at private parties. He also mentored and collaborated with younger black musicians such as Arthur Marshall and Scott Hayden. Marshall remembered his teacher as "a quiet person with perfect manners who loved music and liked to talk about it." He was "a brother in kindness to all."

Undoubtedly the most important association Joplin formed in Sedalia was with a white publisher of sheet music, John Stark. By the time Stark published *Maple Leaf Rag* in 1899, Joplin had published four other compositions: two marches, a waltz, and *Original Rags*. Although skeptical of the marketability of Joplin's work—he viewed the composition as too difficult for local patrons—Stark admired *Maple Leaf Rag* and agreed to put out a limited printing. Very quickly, orders for Joplin's rag began to pour in, and Stark issued several new editions over the next few years.

Stark moved his business to St. Louis in 1900 and continued to publish Joplin works, including *Peacherine Rag* (1901), *Augustan Club Waltz* (1901), *A Breeze from Alabama* (1902), *Elite Syncopations* (1902), *The Entertainer* (1902), and *The Strenuous Life* (1902). Stark also promoted Joplin's career by declaring him the "King of Ragtime Writers," by aggressively marketing his latest works, and by regularly contributing advertising copy and articles about him to the nationally circulated *Christensen's Ragtime Review*. Stark's business sense no doubt contributed to Joplin's decision to write *The Cascades* (1904) as a tribute to the attraction of that name at the Louisiana Purchase Exposition in St. Louis in 1904. As Joplin's fame spread, he, too, moved to St. Louis, where he lived from 1901 to 1907. There he continued composing and performing.

GRANDER AMBITIONS

While writers after his death remembered Joplin principally as the composer of dancehall music, Joplin himself harbored grander ambitions for his art. Even as he relied on sheet music sales, teaching, and performance to make a living, he devoted much of his creative energy to the writing of serious music with syncopated rhythm. His first such effort, a ragtime ballet called *The Ragtime Dance*, featured current African American dance steps choreographed to vocal and piano accompaniment. Although he had composed several profitable rags for Stark in 1901 and 1902, the publisher only reluctantly agreed to publish *The Ragtime Dance* in 1902, but it never sold well. *The Guest of Honor*, a ragtime opera that unfortunately no longer exists, marked Joplin's second venture in the field of serious composition.

In 1903 he formed the Scott Joplin Drama Company in St. Louis and recruited former students to perform in the ambitious work. The cast rehearsed and Joplin rented a theater, but only one dress rehearsal is known to have taken place because Joplin failed to find financial backing for the production. Despite these setbacks, the composer continued his endeavors toward the incorporation of African American and ragtime motifs into serious music, and after 1907 he worked feverishly on his second opera, *Treemonisha*.

Joplin spent the last decade of his life in New York, where he worked on *Treemonisha*; published more than twenty compositions, including such well-known pieces as *Gladiolus Rag* (1907), *Pine Apple Rag* (1908), and *Solace—A Mexican Serenade* (1909); gave private music lessons; and performed on the vaudeville stage. He was an early active member of the Colored Vaudevillian Benevolent Association, whose membership included many of the cultural leaders in black Harlem. His obsession with the seriousness of his work was reflected in *School of Ragtime—Six Exercises for Piano* (1908), which demanded "proper time" and "the supposition that each note will be played as it is written." "The 'Joplin ragtime' is destroyed," he insisted, "by careless or imperfect rendering." He railed publicly against flashy performers who played his, and other, rags too fast and sloppily, and he decried the vulgar lyrics that accompanied many popular ragtime songs.

Joplin finished his second opera in 1911 and began searching diligently for financial backers and a suitable venue to stage a performance. The opera's main theme—the need for education in the African American community to combat the pernicious effects of ignorance and superstition—placed the work squarely in the middle of one of the most serious debates spawned by the "race question." Moreover, in a rare newspaper interview in 1911, Joplin defended *Treemonisha* as serious—not popular—art: "In most of the strains I have used syncopation (rhythm) peculiar to my race, but the music is not ragtime and the score complete is grand opera." The opera was performed only once during Joplin's lifetime, in 1915, and the production suffered from lack of props, costumes, and an orchestra. It was met by utter critical silence and quickly faded from collective memory.

PERSONAL STRUGGLES

The failure of Joplin's second opera coincided with the composer's personal decline. Although reasonably successful as a composer and performer, and widely recognized as the King of Ragtime, his adult life had not been happy. In 1900 he had married Belle Jones, who offered little support for his artistic endeavors and who either died or left him shortly after the death of their only child in 1906. A second marriage ended quickly and tragically with his wife's death. Lottie Stokes, Joplin's third wife, whom he married in New York, cared for her husband during his final battle against the debilitating symptoms of syphilis. Increasingly distracted, frequently unable to play the piano or compose, and grown unreliable as a private music teacher, Joplin spent the final two years of his life in the throes of the disease that eventually took his life on April 1, 1917.

More than fifty years after his death, Joplin became the focus of popular and scholarly attention when Vera Brodsky Lawrence recovered and republished his collected works; Joshua Rifkin recorded many of them; and the hit movie, *The Sting* (1973), featured his music. In the wake of this rediscovery, biographies of Joplin began to appear, and *Treemonisha* was revived by serious opera companies around the country. In his own day, however, the musician faced numerous barriers to his success, only some of which he overcame. Race prejudice, of course, placed severe limits on the kinds of compositions that would garner financial support, while his lack of academic credentials hindered his acceptance as a serious composer among both blacks and whites. Despite these injustices, Joplin was a vital contributor to the cultural shake-up that took place in the United States in the early 1900s, and his classic ragtime pieces helped propel the nation into the modern era.

Susan Curtis

SEE ALSO: *Cakewalks; Dance Halls; Louisiana Purchase Exposition; Vaudeville.*

BIBLIOGRAPHY

Benson, Kathleen, and James Haskins. *Scott Joplin*. Garden City, NY: Doubleday, 1978.

Berlin, Edward. *The King of Ragtime: Scott Joplin and His Era*. New York: Oxford University Press, 1994.

Curtis, Susan. *Dancing to a Black Man's Tune: A Life of Scott Joplin*. Columbia: University of Missouri Press, 1994.

Hubbard-Brown, Janet. *Scott Joplin: Composer*. New York: Chelsea House, 2006.

Janis, Harriet, and Rudi Blesh. *They All Played Ragtime: The True Story of an American Music*. New York: Alfred Knopf, 1950.

Jordan, Louis *(1908–1975)*

One of America's most prominent jazz, blues, and rhythm and blues (R&B) musicians of the 1940s, Louis Jordan was a singer, a baritone and alto sax player, a clarinetist, an actor, and a bandleader. From 1942 to 1951 he had eighteen number one hits on the R&B chart and was one of the biggest African American box-office draws in the country, besides being an important figure and role model in black popular entertainment. His music reflected his African American roots while appealing to both black and white audiences.

His combo, Louis Jordan and the Tympany Five, helped to define the shuffle boogie rhythm, as well as "jump blues." (*Jump* is a term first used in jazz and later in R&B that refers to the instrumentation of trumpet, alto and tenor sax, piano, bass, and drums.) The innovative Jordan was the first jazz musician to make a short film based on one of his popular hit songs (*Caldonia*), an early precursor of the contemporary music video. His influence on rock and roll can be heard in the music of Bill Haley, Chuck Berry, Fats Domino, and James Brown, among others. The Rock and Roll Hall of Fame depicts him as "the Father of Rhythm & Blues" and "the Grandfather of Rock 'n' Roll."

From his earliest years, Jordan was guided and motivated by a strong conviction and desire to become an entertainer. "I wanted to give my whole life to making people enjoy my music. Make them laugh and smile. So I didn't stick to what you'd call jazz. I have always stuck to entertainment," he once said. Jordan blended visual showmanship with a penchant for clowning and rolling his big eyes, impeccable musicianship, and a gratifying original and rhythmic vocal style.

MUSICAL ROOTS

Born Louis Thomas Jordan on July 8, 1908, in Brinkley, Arkansas, Jordan was the son of James Aaron Jordan, a music teacher and bandleader for the Brinkley Brass Band and the infamous Rabbit Food Minstrels, and of a mother who died when he was young. His father was a multi-instrumentalist and a motivational figure in Jordan's life. As a boy, Jordan sang in the local Baptist church, mastered the clarinet and saxophone family of instruments, and toured during the summers, along with his father, with the Rabbit Foot Minstrels and Ma Rainey's TOBA Troupe. These early experiences instilled in Jordan a passion for perfecting his music through disciplined rehearsals and an appreciation for showmanship. He worked as a sideman with Ruby Williams's band in Hot Springs, Arkansas, before moving to Philadelphia.

Once Jordan had arrived in Philadelphia, professional opportunities presented themselves. He met Ralph Cooper, a bandleader and the coordinator of the amateur night at the Apollo Theater in Harlem, New York, who hired him as member of the Apollo house band. Jordan joined Chick Webb's group, playing at the Savoy Ballroom from 1936 to 1938. He left the Webb band confident enough to organize his own group, the Louie Jordan Elks Rendezvous Band (the "Louie" spelling was intentional since people often mispronounced his name as Lewis), which began its engagements at the Elks Club in Harlem. The band's name was later changed to Louis Jordan and His Tympany Five, which remained a constant despite personnel changes. The word *Tympany* was included because drummer Walter Martin actually played that instrument in the group.

A JAZZ SUPERSTAR

Louis Jordan and His Tympany Five became one of the most successful small bands in jazz history. Jordan signed a Decca contract that lasted from 1938 to 1953, recording many compositions in its "Race Series." His recording of "A Chicken Ain't Nothing but a Bird" signaled a pivotal point in the direction and kind of material Jordan would record. This song's novelty lyrics, shuffle and boogie rhythm, and soloing of lead instrumentalists all proved to be a successful formula. The subsequent recording of "I'm Gonna Move to the Outskirts of Town" (1942), a twelve-bar blues tune, launched Jordan as a major recording star.

A string of Top 10 hits on the R&B chart followed, including "What's the Use of Getting Sober" (1942), "Five Guys Named Moe" (1943), "Ration Blues" (1943), "G.I. Jive" (1944), "Is You Is or Is You Ain't (Ma' Baby)" (1944), "Mop Mop" (1945), "Caldonia" (1945), "Don't Let the Sun Catch You Cryin'" (1946), "Choo Choo Ch'Boogie" (1946), "Ain't That Just Like a Woman" (1946), "Ain't Nobody Here but Us Chickens" (1946), "Let the Good Times Roll" (1946), "Open the Door Richard" (1947), "Beans and Corn Bread" (1949), and "Saturday Night Fish Fry (Part I)" (1949). "Saturday Night Fish Fry" presaged rock and roll and the music of Haley. However, when rock and roll came into its own in the 1950s, Jordan's career began to decline and his contract with Decca ended. He signed with Mercury and rerecorded old hits, including "Caldonia." Jordan moved to Los Angeles in the early 1960s and recorded one album with Ray Charles's Tangerine label. He formed Pzazz, his own record label, in 1968.

OTHER ACCOMPLISHMENTS

A number of Jordan's recordings can be classified as blues, which he sang with perfect diction in a sophisticated, cosmopolitan, smooth, and crooning style that attracted both black and white audiences. For a number of his touring engagements, promoters booked his band to play two separate engagements in the same evening, one for a white and one for a black audience. He also led a big band in 1951 and 1952.

Jordan was a competent jazz improviser, and his work on alto sax is memorable. His choices of songs, as well as his own compositions, were based on gospel, blues, jazz, and the vernacular of black speech and African American folk culture. The song texts draw from the black hipster slang of the 1940s. Jordan sang about the subjects of black folk, women ("chicks" and "chickens"), Saturday night fish fries, drinking, love, and partying—in sum, the travails and pleasures of the postwar black urban experience. His compositions "Beware (Brother, Beware)" and "Look Out (Sister)" can be considered precursors to rap music. Jordan also made a number of "soundies," precursors to the music video, and appeared in a number of films.

Jordan's music epitomizes an era of good times, and it paved the way for R&B. He continued to tour until he collapsed and died of a heart attack on February 4, 1975, in Los Angeles. Since his death, there has been a gradual rebirth of interest in his work, with his music being featured in various movie soundtracks, such as *The Blues Brothers* (1980). *Five Guys Named Moe*, a musical that featured Jordan's music, opened on Broadway in 1992 and captured a Tony Award nomination for Best Musical.

Willie Collins

SEE ALSO: *Apollo Theater; Berry, Chuck; Blues; The Blues Brothers; Brown, James; Charles, Ray; Domino, Fats; Haley, Bill; Jazz; Rap; Rhythm and Blues; Rock and Roll; Tony Awards; Top 40.*

BIBLIOGRAPHY

Chilton, John. *Let the Good Times Roll: The Story of Louis Jordan and His Music.* Ann Arbor: University of Michigan Press, 1994.

Jordan, Michael *(1963–)*

Michael Jordan, the most successful and skilled player in the history of professional basketball, first came into the public eye in the early 1980s as a standout freshman for a University of North Carolina team that won a national title in 1982. As a member of the Chicago Bulls, he won six National Basketball Association (NBA) titles, along with six individual scoring championships (1990–1991, 1991–1992, 1992–1993, 1995–1996, 1996–1997, and 1997–1998) and five Most Valuable Player Awards (1987–1988, 1990–1991, 1991–1992, 1995–1996, and 1997–1998). An international sports icon and a role model for youth and adults alike, Jordan helped redefine the male athlete as a figure of sublime grace, technical skill, and ferocious athleticism. His determination, diligence, and fiercely competitive attitude also enhanced the public perception of black masculinity during the 1980s and 1990s. Aside from his professional prowess, as a commercially valuable endorser and an entrepreneur, Jordan became one of the highest-paid sportsmen

Michael Jordan. *Along with a host of achievements and records as an individual player, Michael Jordan won six world championships as a member of the Chicago Bulls.* AL MESSERSCHMIDT/WIREIMAGE/GETTY IMAGES.

of his era. In his postplaying career, Jordan has remained in the public eye as majority owner of the Charlotte Bobcats, while continuing to appear in numerous television appearances and charity events.

YOUNG STAR ATHLETE

Michael Jordan was born on February 17, 1963, in Brooklyn, New York. His father, James Jordan, was a General Electric employee, and his mother, Delores, worked as a supervisor at a local bank. Soon after his birth, the family relocated to Wallace, North Carolina, and then to Wilmington, where the young Jordan was raised. In early childhood as well as adolescence, he showed exceptional skill in all areas of sports, including baseball and football. When he suffered a minor injury while playing football in high school, his parents encouraged him to pursue basketball.

Jordan did not initially make the starting squad for his high school basketball team, but he made the lineup in his junior year, having shot up in height to 6 feet, 3 inches (he would eventually become 6 feet, 6 inches tall). Much of his early skill and training in basketball was derived from playing with his brother Larry in the backyard at home; in his formative years he also idolized and patterned himself after the legendary Julius Erving (aka Dr. J), one of the great basketball players of the 1970s.

After high school, Jordan settled on attending the University of North Carolina at Chapel Hill, where he would play on the basketball team under coach Dean Smith. Although Smith by reputation rarely played his freshmen, Jordan's unique abilities guaranteed him time on the court. The young athlete quickly became known for his incredible agility and dexterity on the court, as well as for his ability to think instinctively and create innovative shots. For his efforts, Jordan was voted ACC (Atlantic Coast Conference) Rookie of the Year.

After bringing his team to the NCAA (National Collegiate Athletic Association) championships, Jordan won nearly every major individual award in college basketball, including the Wooden Award, the Naismith Award, and the Rupp Trophy. He was also voted College Basketball Player of the Year by the *Sporting News*. In 1984, at twenty-one years of age, Jordan made the U.S. Olympic Games basketball team under coach Bobby Knight. Averaging a remarkable 17 points a game, he led the team to a gold medal in eight straight wins. The Olympic win brought Jordan to high visibility in basketball circles and made him a household name in the United States.

After announcing his decision to leave school early and enter the NBA draft in 1984, Jordan was selected by the Chicago Bulls in the first round (third pick overall). Wearing jersey number 23 in his rookie professional season, he averaged 28.2 points a game, third highest in the league. With his outstanding leaping ability and uncanny grace in the air, Jordan seemed to defy the laws of gravity. His spectacular individual efforts were fodder for late-night sports highlight programs and quickly contributed to his renown. For the combination of his high-scoring abilities and stylish acrobatics, the handsome, soft-spoken player was voted Rookie of the Year and was rapidly becoming America's best-loved sports star.

The Nike shoe company (which was struggling at the time) took advantage of Jordan's popularity and signed him to a lucrative endorsement deal that resulted in the Air Jordan shoe, which quickly became the most successful product in sports marketing history. The high sales of the product marked the beginning of a long and commercially rewarding relationship between Nike and Jordan.

EMERGENCE IN THE NBA

Throughout his 1985–1986 season, Jordan continued soaring to new heights. When he fractured his ankle early in the season, the dedicated star ignored doctors' orders and went back to regular play, despite the danger of doing more serious damage. By the end of the season, however, he had led his team to the playoffs against the Boston Celtics. On April 20, 1986, Jordan established a NBA playoff record by scoring 63 points in a single game against the Celtics.

Jordan continued his high scoring rate through the 1987–1988 season and became the first player to win both the Defensive Player of the Year Award and the NBA scoring title in the same year. He also took home the Most Valuable Player (MVP) Award in the All-Star game. Although he again won the scoring title in the 1988–1989 season, Jordan remained personally unsatisfied that he had not yet managed to lead the Bulls past Eastern Conference power (and hated rivals) Detroit and into the NBA finals.

In the 1990–1991 season, his seventh in the NBA and under new coach Phil Jackson, Jordan received increased on-court support from his gifted teammate Scottie Pippen. As a result, the Bulls finally advanced past Detroit to an NBA finals showdown with the Los Angeles Lakers. In the much-publicized on-court matchup between Jordan and the Lakers' legendary Magic Johnson, the Bulls finally prevailed, and Jordan received the title for which he had fought so long. In the following 1991–1992 season, he took home his third consecutive MVP Award and his sixth straight NBA scoring title with a 30.1 point average per game. In the playoffs that year, the Bulls repeated as champions against the Portland Trail Blazers by bouncing back from an 81–78 deficit in the final game. Jordan scored 12 of the Bulls' final 19 points to clinch a 97–93 victory.

The successes continued to rack up for Jordan over the forthcoming seasons. In 1992 he once again joined the U.S. team for the Olympic Games. Supported by Magic Johnson, Larry Bird, and others, the American "Dream Team" won their games by an average of 44 points, securing the gold medal. In the 1992–1993 NBA season, Jordan took home his seventh straight scoring title and won the championship against Charles Barkley and the Phoenix Suns. Jordan averaged 41 points per game in the six-game final series.

By this time Jordan's success had brought him international superstardom, yet his most important role was, perhaps, behind the scenes. In 1989 he had married Juanita Vanoy. Together, the couple would raise three children (Jeffrey, Marcus, and Jasmine) in the Highland Park suburb of Illinois, and the sports star would eventually bring home $45 million a year from endorsement deals that ranged from breakfast cereal to his own line of cologne products. He also purchased a restaurant in Chicago, Michael Jordan's Steak House, which instantly became a popular tourist stop. His profile had risen to such an extent that he even hosted an episode of NBC television's *Saturday Night Live* in 1991.

EARLY RETIREMENT

Although Jordan, well known for his charity work, was widely recognized as an admirable role model, there were persistent rumors that he had become addicted to gambling, and some began to criticize him for overly aggressive behavior on the court. In 1993 his father was shot to death in South Carolina by two local youths who were attempting to steal his automobile. On October 6 of the same year, in the midst of the tragedy surrounding his father, Jordan shocked the world by announcing his retirement from basketball. He was only thirty and at the peak of his game and popularity. Speculation persisted that Jordan's "retirement" was actually a league-ordered suspension of the NBA's brightest star amid substantiated stories that Jordan was wagering hundreds of thousands of dollars on golf games.

Again surprising the public, Jordan took advantage of his retirement to pursue one of his long-lost dreams: to play professional baseball. After signing with the Chicago White Sox, Jordan was assigned to play with the Sox's Birmingham Barons minor-league team, and he asserted that his ultimate goal would be to make the major leagues. Although numerous onlookers took this new career move to be a publicity stunt or a way to stay competitively sharp during his "suspension," many of his fans were intrigued by his daring. Jordan rode the team bus, shared small locker rooms, and received a pittance in comparison to his salary during his tenure with the Bulls.

Unfortunately, in contrast to his performance on the basketball court, Jordan's abilities on the baseball field were limited even on a minor-league standard. Yet, his courage to try and his humility on the baseball field made the larger-than-life sports star seem more human and more vulnerable, further endearing him to his already loyal fans. In the meantime, the Chicago Bulls were suffering without their star player and were quickly eliminated from the playoffs. The NBA as a whole also suffered; sorely missing Jordan's star appeal, the playoffs in 1993 between the New York Knicks and the Houston Rockets drew an uncharacteristically low television audience.

RETURN TO NBA DOMINANCE

Providence intervened for Jordan fans. On March 18, 1995, because of a baseball strike, Jordan returned from his eighteen-month hiatus from the court to rejoin the Bulls. In his return game—against the Indiana Pacers—Jordan posted 19 points, 6 rebounds, 6 assists, and 3 steals in 43 minutes of play. Eventually, however, the Bulls were defeated in the playoffs by the Orlando Magic, which were bolstered by the presence of young and versatile players such as Shaquille O'Neal and Penny Hardaway.

In the 1995–1996 season, Jordan and the Bulls were joined by the outrageous Dennis Rodman, ironically their longtime nemesis from the Detroit Pistons' Bad Boys days. Along with Rodman and Pippen, Jordan once again led the Bulls to the NBA title, their fourth in six years. The star also picked up his eighth scoring championship with an average of 30.4 points per game, as well as another MVP Award; that year he also claimed *Sport Magazine*'s award as the top athlete of the last half of the twentieth century. In 1996 Jordan made his film debut in the half-animation, half-live-action star vehicle *Space Jam*, which was a box-office hit.

In the 1997–1998 season, Jordan was given a $33 million contract for one year's play, and he also earned his fifth MVP Award. He became the first player in history to be selected to the NBA All Defensive First Team nine times, beating Bobby Jones's previous record of eight. Jordan was named MVP of the 1998 All-Star game, and he won his sixth NBA championship after leading the Bulls past the Utah Jazz in the playoffs.

On January 13, 1999, aged thirty-five and at the top of his game, Jordan again announced his retirement, this time on the heels of a protracted labor dispute that saw the league lock out the players. It seemed the proper time for perhaps the greatest basketball player ever to step down. He had risen to the highest level of status and achievement in global popular sports culture. Throughout his professional career, he had been a shining symbol of the American Dream, expanding the very possibilities of human achievement in his field. In the June 1998 issue of *Hoop* magazine, one writer described Jordan's professional career as the new "universal measuring device in appraising greatness."

NEW CAREER PATHS

In 2000 Jordan joined the NBA Washington Wizards as part owner and president of basketball operations. Although past his peak, he still could not extinguish his competitive fire, and in September 2001 he also began to play as a member of the Wizards team. Jordan produced respectable numbers over the 2001–2002 season, averaging 22.9 points per game, along with 5.7 rebounds and 5.2 assists. In the process, however, his personal life was thrown into turmoil.

In January 2002, months after the star player had established a second residence in Washington, D.C., his wife of twelve years filed for divorce. As part of her court filing, Juanita Jordan insisted on having full custody of the couple's three children, while stating that an attempt to repair the marriage was "impractical and not in the best interest" of her family. Although rumors surfaced that Jordan's alleged philandering and excessive gambling may have contributed to the breakup, the NBA player adamantly denied these reports.

Jordan played one more year for the Wizards, appearing in 82 games, 67 as a starter, while averaging 20 points and 6.1 rebounds per game. Following the 2002–2003 season, he retired for the third and final time. Although he was no longer active on the court, he was intent on remaining involved with the league, and in 2006 Jordan became a part owner of the Charlotte Bobcats. His early years with the franchise proved frustrating, primarily because of fellow owner Robert Johnson's questionable personnel moves. A low point for the Bobcats came in 2008, when Johnson laid off the entire community-relations department. Coupled with the team's poor play, the decision inflicted significant damage on the organization's fan base.

Meanwhile, Jordan's reputation as the greatest player of all time remained unchanged. In 2009 he was inducted in the Naismith Memorial Basketball Hall of Fame. Jordan also received some long-awaited vindication in 2010, when Ron Shelton's documentary *Jordan Rides the Bus*, part of the award-winning ESPN series *30 for 30*, demonstrated conclusively that there was no evidence linking Jordan's gambling habits to his retirement from basketball in 1993.

In 2010 Jordan reached a deal to become majority owner of the Bobcats. In discussing his ambitions for the franchise, he cited the success of the city's previous NBA team, the Hornets. "Number one for ten years!" he exclaimed to Mark Price of the *Charlotte Observer*, referring to the Hornets' decade-long streak in leading the NBA in attendance. "I want to duplicate that. I want us to be number one in attendance and number one in the community." Indeed, for Jordan, working to make the team successful went beyond winning on the court. "It's part of my upbringing to give back" to the community, he told Price. "I'm in a position now to use my actions, my team's name, my name, and all my relationships to have an impact."

Jason King

SEE ALSO: *Barkley, Charles; Baseball; Basketball; Bird, Larry; The Boston Celtics; The Chicago Bulls; Divorce; Dream Team; Erving, Julius "Dr. J"; ESPN; Gambling; Golf; Johnson, Earvin "Magic"; Jones, Bobby; Knight, Bobby; The Los Angeles Lakers; National Basketball Association (NBA); National Collegiate Athletic Association (NCAA); The New York Knickerbockers; Nike; Olympics; O'Neal, Shaquille; Pippen, Scottie; Rodman, Dennis;* Saturday Night Live*; Smith, Dean; Sports Heroes; Television; Tennis Shoes/Sneakers.*

BIBLIOGRAPHY

Halberstam, David. *Playing for Keeps: Michael Jordan and the World He Made.* New York: Random House, 1999.

Jordan, Michael. *Rare Air: Michael on Michael.* San Francisco: Collins Publishers, 1993.

Jordan, Michael. *For the Love of the Game: My Story.* New York: Crown Publishers, 1998.

Lawrence, Mitch. "Searching for Michael Jordan." *New York Daily News*, December 3, 2006.

Leahy, Michael. "Gambling Man." *Washington Post*, June 14, 2002.

Price, Mark. "Michael Jordan Seeks to Restore Charlotte Bobcats' Image." *Charlotte Observer*, February 18, 2012.

Joy of Cooking

An 800-page cookbook that begins with a quote from Johann Wolfgang von Goethe's *Faust* seems an unlikely candidate for a spot on a list of the best-selling books of the twentieth century. But Irma S. Rombauer's *Joy of Cooking* (1931) sold more than fourteen million copies before 1997—a record that speaks for itself in terms of the enormous influence the book has wielded on social culture. In 1975 Scribner issued a revised edition. Despite vast changes in American eating habits over the decades, the tome again landed on the best-seller lists. By the end of the twentieth century, it was the top-selling all-purpose cookbook in publishing history, deemed the bible of American culinary customs, from cocktails to custards.

IRMA ROMBAUER

Part of *Joy of Cooking*'s success lies in the way it presents the art of food preparation in simple, concrete terminology. Rombauer was a widowed St. Louis, Missouri, socialite of German birth when she began assembling her wealth of recipes into book form in 1930, partly at the request of her two grown children. Married to a lawyer in 1899, she had had little experience in the kitchen as a young wife. Like other affluent women of the era, she relied on domestic staff to help plan and cook meals for family dinners and social events. Her husband was an avid outdoorsman, however, and he had instructed her in some of the basics of the camp stove.

Over the next few decades Rombauer matured into an accomplished chef and renowned hostess. One of her aims in writing the book was to convince American women that cooking was not a tedious, daily chore, but rather—a "joy." However, the book's title has a tragic tinge. Rombauer's husband, who had long suffered from depression, committed suicide in the family home shortly after the stock market crash of 1929. He left his wife and two children an estate of just $6,000, and Rombauer used half of that sum to put her first edition into print.

The recipes that Rombauer assembled for the original *Joy of Cooking: A Compilation of Reliable Recipes with a Casual Culinary Chat* provided new cooks with the basics. Illustrated by her daughter, Marion Rombauer Becker, the book sold 3,000 copies—out of Rombauer's St. Louis home. The stylized, Art Deco cover depicted a gowned St. Martha of Bethany, the patron saint of cooks, slaying a dragon representing kitchen drudgery. Inside were to be found old European recipes, such as braised heart slices in a sour sauce, adapted for use with American ingredients and kitchen tools. There were several meat dishes that reflected traditional peasant fare and used every part of an animal. On a lighter note, Rombauer told readers about her cook Marguerite's culinary prowess. In a chatty style she explained the mechanics of food preparation. She assumed, for example, that novices in the kitchen did not know how to separate egg whites when a recipe called for it and so guided them through it. Likewise she instructed them in other fundamentals, such as flour sifting and deboning chicken.

THE DEVELOPMENT OF *JOY OF COOKING*

In 1936 Indianapolis publisher Bobbs-Merrill brought out a *Joy of Cooking* edition rewritten and enlarged by the author. This version displayed a unique recipe setup that became the book's most famous feature. Ingredients were listed in bold type so that a recipe could be quickly scanned to determine whether the ingredients were on hand in the pantry or refrigerator. And just what to do with those ingredients was detailed in a step-by-step sequence. This edition was an immediate success, due in part to the fact that, with the Great Depression, many well-to-do households could no longer afford to keep servants, and numerous affluent women had recently entered the kitchen full time. They sorely needed Rombauer's instructions.

Rombauer was far ahead of her time in recognizing the need for a cookbook designed to help working women prepare quick and easy meals. The result was *Streamlined Cooking*, a spin-off of *Joy of Cooking*. The recently invented pressure cooker was a key element in many of the main-dish recipes. It was not as successful as *Joy*, but when she merged the two into a 1943 edition of *Joy of Cooking*, she hit upon the perfect formula. Combining the easy recipes from *Streamlined* with the step-by-step method of *Joy* produced an instant classic. Large numbers of women were working outside the home as a result of labor shortages created by World War II, and Rombauer's recipes took wartime food rationing into consideration. When the third revision of the book appeared in 1951, household help had become a relic of a bygone era for all but the wealthiest of households. Though many women worked outside the home during the 1950s, the image of the competent, attractive homemaker advanced by advertising and television programs became firmly entrenched, and *Joy of Cooking* served as the how-to guide to achieving domestic fulfillment for legions of American women.

JOY OF COOKING'S LEGACY

By the 1960s *Joy* was a perennial best seller, a standard bridal shower gift, and a staple accessory of almost every middle-class household. "Its virtues were its compendiousness, its useful tables and explanations, its pragmatic, clear directions, and a certain sprightly and encouraging tone," declared Diane Johnson in the *New York Review of Books* in 1997. Johnson explained that later food critics of the 1970s and 1980s railed against some the book's more archaic elements and its reliance on processed foods, especially after American culinary tastes grew more daring and gourmet cooking became all the rage. This trend was exemplified by Julia Child's *Mastering the Art of French Cooking*, first published in 1961. By the 1962 edition, Marion Rombauer Becker had taken over the project, though her mother's name remained on the cover. This and successive editions were revised, with certain recipes discarded, to reflect America's increasing culinary sophistication. The quote from Goethe remained, however: "That which thy fathers have bequeathed to thee, earn it anew if thou wouldst possess it."

Irma Rombauer died in 1962. Her October 17, 1962, *New York Times* obituary noted that "the cookbook that brought her fame is considered one of the most lucid and accurate ever written. Mrs. Rombauer wrote charmingly and well about food." The paper also credited her with introducing elegant European recipes in accessible terminology "so they could be prepared with relative speed and ease by the average American housewife." A fifth edition of *Joy of Cooking* published in 1975 became the best selling of all, with an estimated 2.2 million copies sold by 1997, and, despite editorial changes, it still provided many delightful reminders of a bygone era. "Unless you choke your duck, pluck the down on its breast immediately afterward, and cook it within 24 hours, you cannot lay claim to having produced an authentic Rouen duck," begins the recipe for Duckling Rouennaise, a modified version of the genuine article. The recipe instructs readers to roast a 5-pound bird on a spit or rotisserie, and then serve it sliced, in a chafing dish with a sauce prepared from its crushed liver, veal pâté, onion, butter, and burgundy wine. Recipes for veal kidney, blood sausage, lamb head with a rosemary wine sauce, and pig's tails still abounded, and a diagram for skinning a squirrel remained.

Stand Facing the Stove: The Story of the Women Who Gave America the "Joy of Cooking" (1996) is a chronicle of the book by food writer Anne Mendelson, who praised the 1975 edition for its flaws as well as its virtues. "It records," writes Mendelson, "the sheer improbability of twentieth-century American cooking from the Great Depression to the Ford administration, a lawless mélange of blueprints for progress, nostalgic hankerings, gourmet cults, timesaving expedients, media-inspired fads, and unexpected rebellions."

EDITIONS OF 1997 AND 2006

Rombauer's grandson, Ethan Becker, and publisher Scribner revised *Joy* for a 1997 edition, the first new one in more than two decades. Expanded to an exhaustive 1,100-plus pages, it vaulted to the best-seller lists immediately. As always, it had changed with the times: leaner, low-fat recipes prevailed, and a range of new ethnic dishes such as Vietnamese pho was included. Despite its popularity, many critics found the 1997 edition too bland. The new book lacked the unique narrative voice that made *Joy* such a pleasurable book to read and cook with. In response, Scribner brought out a facsimile of the very first edition in 1998, complete with the dragon-slaying St. Martha cover. The seventy-fifth anniversary edition, published in 2006, provided a return to the format of earlier editions, restoring indispensable sections edited out of the 1997 edition, such as "Know Your Ingredients"; chapters on arranging meals and table settings; and recipes for old-style dishes like casseroles and aspic. This new edition was a critical and popular success, praised by cooking professionals and home cooks alike for retaining the charm of Rombauer's original while providing essential new information for the twenty-first-century cook.

Carol Brennan

SEE ALSO: *Best Sellers; Child, Julia; Foodies.*

BIBLIOGRAPHY

"Irma Rombauer: The *Joy of Cooking*." *Notable American Unitarians*. Accessed February 2012. Available from http://www.harvardsquarelibrary.org/unitarians/rombauer.html

Johnson, Diane. "American Pie." *New York Review of Books*, December 18, 1997, 20–23.

Levenstein, Harvey A. *Paradox of Plenty: A Social History of Eating in Modern America*. New York: Oxford University Press, 1993.

Mendelson, Anne. *Stand Facing the Stove: The Story of the Women Who Gave America the "Joy of Cooking."* New York: Henry Holt, 1996.

"Mrs. Irma S. Rombauer Dies; Author of 'Joy of Cooking,'

86." *New York Times*, October 17, 1962, 38.

"No More Simmered Porcupine." *U.S. News & World Report*, January 1, 1997, 10.

Rombauer, Irma S. *Streamlined Cooking; New and Delightful Recipes for Canned, Packaged and Frosted Foods and Rapid Recipes for Fresh Foods.* Indianapolis, IN: Bobbs-Merrill, 1939.

Rombauer, Irma S., and Marion Rombauer Becker. *Joy of Cooking*. New York: Scribner, 1975.

Shepley, Carol Ferring. *Movers and Shakers, Scalawags and Suffragettes: Tales from Bellefontaine Cemetery*. St. Louis: Missouri History Museum, 2008.

The Joy of Sex

Published in 1972, during a period when the English-speaking world was experiencing a rapid relaxation of many of its Victorian-era taboos about the open discussion of sexuality, Dr. Alex Comfort's "lovemaking manual," *The Joy of Sex: A Gourmet Guide to Lovemaking*, caused an immense stir for its frankly nonpuritanical and lighthearted approach to a subject previously shrouded in religious stricture and clinical seriousness. For readers eager to "swing" with the "sexual revolution" or just to perk up a drab marital bed, this volume, as well as its sequels and spin-offs over the next two decades, were the first mass-market books offering graphic text and illustrations designed to help people guiltlessly expand their sexual horizons by experimenting with new techniques and positions.

Although it was welcomed in many progressive circles, *The Joy of Sex* was roundly criticized in others for its gender and cultural bias that singularly describes female organs with vulgar language, its reliance on expressions such as "exotic" and "oriental" to describe some unfamiliar techniques, and its dismissal of same-sex relations as trivial and unfulfilling. Still, the book was considered a breakthrough for the way it brought sexuality to the arena of everyday conversation, leading to the more relaxed approach taken by later sexologists such as Dr. Ruth Westheimer and Dr. Judy Kuriansky.

A BOLD NEW SPIN ON SEX

As published by Crown, *The Joy of Sex: A Gourmet Guide to Lovemaking* (also known in some editions as *The Joy of Sex: A Cordon Bleu Guide to Lovemaking*) is described in the jacket copy as "the first really happy and outstanding new lovemaking manual, a contemporary Western equal to the great Eastern classics of the *Kama Sutra* and the Pillow Books of China." Based on the "experience of happily married people and edited by Dr. Alex Comfort with the advice of doctors and professional counselors," the book offers more than 100 line drawings and several pages of paintings in full color by Charles Raymond and Christopher Foss. Also included are sixteen pages of "oriental exotic art from Japan, India, and China." Although Comfort—a British gerontologist, social activist, and poet-novelist—is listed as the book's editor, he actually researched and wrote the entire manuscript, explaining later that he could not be identified as its author because of restrictions that then prohibited British physicians from writing "popular" books. Although the book claims to be based "on the work of one couple," Comfort later confessed that he employed other "consultants" as source material.

It was Comfort's original intention to illustrate *The Joy of Sex* with actual photographs of couples, but the photos never "caught the proper zest," as he later told literary critic Hugh Kenner. "There was always an expression that asked, 'Am I doing it right?' So two artists [Raymond and Foss] worked from the photographs to produce the illustrations you see. . . . But if the pictures help people turn on, that's part of what the book is for," Comfort explained.

In his introduction, Comfort writes that "one aim of this book is to cure the notion, born of non-discussion, that common sex needs are odd or weird." He adds, "There are, after all, only two 'rules' in good sex, apart from the obvious one of not doing things which are silly, antisocial, or dangerous. One is 'don't do anything you don't really enjoy,' and the other is 'find out your partner's needs and don't balk them if you can help it.'" Comfort wanted couples to be willing to acknowledge a wide "range of human needs" that might include practices and fantasies—aggression and role-playing, for example—that "the last half-century's social mythology pretended weren't there."

SEX AS FOOD

Based on his premise that fine sex is analogous to a cook's finesse in blending ingredients and techniques to create a meal of both "culinary fantasies as well as staple diets," Comfort sets up his table of contents like a menu: "Starters," "Main Courses," "Sauces and Pickles," and "Problems." Among the "sauces and pickles" are several dozen "dishes" that in a more puritanical age would have been called naughty or even perverse. The hodgepodge bill of fare includes items both familiar and obscure: anal intercourse, bondage, "foursomes and moresomes," grope suits, harness, ice, motor cars, pompoir, railroads, rubber, vibrators, and viennese oyster. (Comfort later admitted to curious readers that the "grope suit," a purportedly Scandinavian gadget designed "to induce continuous female orgasm," is really a "joke" he invented.)

Some of the items listed incurred the wrath of critics who objected to Comfort's cultural insensitivity in describing certain sexual techniques using Eurocentric terms such as *Chinese style, Indian style, Japanese style*, and *south Slav style*. Other items, perhaps evocative of an earlier, Anglocentric bias when French postcards were considered the ultimate in naughtiness, are cast in terminology such as *feuille de rose, pattes d'araigné*, and *postillionage*.

THE JOY OF GAY SEX

Besides the expected condemnations by conservative and religious critics, *The Joy of Sex* came under fire from feminists who complained that Comfort used street-slang terms for women's body parts while describing male organs in clinical fashion. Nonmainstream couples who found their lifestyles were demeaned or ignored were also upset. In the 1972 edition, same-sex behaviors are relegated to the "problems" section, under the misleading heading of "bisexuality." Though Comfort generously admits "all people are bisexual: that is to say they are able to respond sexually to some extent towards people of either sex," he made few friends in the gay and lesbian community by declaring, "Being homosexual isn't a matter of having this kind of response, but usually of having some kind of turn-off towards the opposite sex which makes our same-sex response more evident or predominant." Comfort concludes the section on "bisexuality" by writing, "Straight man-woman sex is the real thing for most people—others need something different but their scope is usually reduced, not widened, by such needs."

This heterosexist attitude inspired the 1977 publication of the gay-positive *The Joy of Gay Sex*, written by Dr. Charles Silverstein and Edmund White with illustrations by Michael Leonard, Ian Beck, and Julian Graddon. It was Silverstein who, in 1973, had successfully persuaded the American Psychiatric Association to remove homosexuality from its list of mental disorders. In his introduction, Silverstein writes that *The Joy of Gay Sex* is "by gays, for gays, about the gay subculture that comes equipped with its own rituals, its own agonies and ecstasies, its own argot."

LATER EDITIONS

With the emergence of the AIDS crisis in the 1980s, both *The Joy of Sex* and *The Joy of Gay Sex* underwent revisions. Newer editions promote safer sex, a topic that had been thought relatively unimportant in the 1970s when, for example, Comfort could write, "Sex must be physically the safest of all human activities (leaving out social repercussions)." Safer-sex instruction, together with illustrations of models using condoms, are included in some of the sequels and spin-offs to both series, including Comfort's *The New Joy of Sex* (1992) and *The New Joy of Gay Sex* (1992), on which Silverstein collaborated with Felice Picano with illustrations by Deni Ponty and Ron Fowler.

In 2002, two years after Comfort's death, Crown published a thirtieth-anniversary edition of *The Joy of Sex*, revised by British sexologist Susan Quilliam with updated content for readers coming of age in the new century. Although this revision addresses sex in the digital age, provides a more in-depth look at female sexuality, and includes extensive information on safe-sex practices, it still focuses almost exclusively on the practices of heterosexual couples. Because it contains little information about gay sex, masturbation, or fringe sexual movements such as BDSM, younger generations have largely flocked to writers such as Dan Savage and Tristan Taormino and to newer books such as Nerve.com's best-selling sex guide *The Big Bang* (2003).

Edward Moran

SEE ALSO: *AIDS; Best Sellers; Gay Men; Savage, Dan; Sexual Revolution.*

BIBLIOGRAPHY

Comfort, Alex. *The Joy of Sex: A Cordon Bleu Guide to Lovemaking* (also known as *The Joy of Sex: A Gourmet Guide to Lovemaking*). New York: Crown, 1972.

Comfort, Alex. *More Joy: A Lovemaking Companion to "The Joy of Sex."* New York: Crown, 1987.

Comfort, Alex. *The New Joy of Sex*, ed. by Julie Rubenstein. New York: Crown, 1992.

Comfort, Alex, and John Raynes (illustrator). *Sexual Foreplay.* New York: Crown, 1997.

Kenner, Hugh. "The Comfort behind the *Joy of Sex.*" *New York Times Magazine*, October 27, 1974, 18ff.

Silverstein, Dr. Charles, and Edmund White. *The Joy of Gay Sex.* New York: Crown, 1977.

Silverstein, Dr. Charles, and Felice Picano. *The New Joy of Gay Sex.* New York: HarperCollins, 1992.

Joyner, Florence Griffith *(1959–1998)*

Olympic runner Florence Griffith Joyner, nicknamed "Flo-Jo," was one of the most beloved athletes of the late twentieth century. She inspired legions of young female athletes with her speed, confidence, and winning looks. Almost as famous for her muscular physique and her flamboyant style—particularly her six-inch-long, intricately patterned and polished fingernails—Joyner made the track-and-field establishment sit up and take notice, and officials and fans alike mourned her sudden death of an apparent heart seizure in 1998 at age thirty-eight.

Blazing down the track in brightly colored outfits, including her trademark one-legged tights, Joyner was hailed as the world's fastest woman runner at the peak of her career in the mid-1980s. A phenomenal sprinter who set world records in the 100- and 200-meter dashes (10.49 seconds and 21.34, respectively), she also won three gold medals and one silver at the 1988 Summer Olympics in Seoul, Korea. Although a planned comeback in 1996 failed to materialize due to an Achilles tendon injury, Joyner's presence was still felt in track and field.

Born December 21, 1959, Joyner was raised in the projects of the Watts district of Los Angeles, the seventh of ten children of electronics technician Robert Griffith and his wife, after whom Florence was named. She started to run for sport at age seven and continued with it even when, as a teenager, doctors discovered that she had a heart murmur and advised her to quit. Under the tutelage and encouragement of coach Bobby Kersee, Joyner earned a sports scholarship to the University of California at Los Angeles (UCLA). She ranked as the National Collegiate Athletic Association champion in the 200-meter dash (22.39 seconds) before graduating from UCLA in 1983 with a degree in psychology. After college Joyner continued to develop her phenomenal speed and went on to win the silver medal in the 200 meters at the 1984 Olympics in her hometown of Los Angeles.

Joyner retired briefly from running after the Los Angeles Olympics to pursue work as a bank secretary and beautician, but she was encouraged to return to the track by Kersee. Her records in the 100 and 200 meters in Seoul were unbroken at the time of her death. In October 1987, she married coach and Olympic gold medalist Al Joyner Jr., the older brother of heptathlon world-record-holder Jackie Joyner-Kersee (Bobby Kersee's wife). They made their new home in Mission Viejo, California, and in 1988, Al Joyner took over coaching duties for his wife from Kersee. The couple's daughter, Mary, was born in 1991.

Joyner retired from her career as a sprinter in 1989 and turned her enormous energies to designing sportswear and working toward her cosmetology license. Her determination and desire for perfection drove her in these areas as they had in her running. Joyner also designed uniforms for the National Basketball Association's Indiana Pacers, and she cochaired the President's Council on Physical Fitness as a means of further inspiring young athletes.

Joyner's untimely death was noted by President Bill Clinton, who told reporters, "We were dazzled by her speed, humbled by her talent, and captivated by her style. Though she rose to the pinnacle of the world of sports, she never forgot where she came from." While some in the media speculated that the use of performance-enhancing drugs such as steroids may have contributed to Joyner's death, such rumors had consistently been disproved throughout her career. During her participation in the Olympics, for example, she was tested for drug use eleven times and always came up clean. It was widely known that Joyner had suffered from a number of medical problems throughout her career and had been hospitalized on several occasions.

An autopsy revealed that Joyner died in her sleep of asphyxiation, the result of an epileptic seizure. Left behind to mourn this energetic and inspiring athlete were her husband, her seven-year-old daughter, and legions of fans who considered themselves fortunate to have witnessed the amazing performances of one of the fastest women in the world.

Pamela L. Shelton

SEE ALSO: *Joyner-Kersee, Jackie; Olympics.*

BIBLIOGRAPHY

Moore, Kenny. "Very Fancy, Very Fast." *Sports Illustrated*, September 14, 1988.

Pellegrini, Frank. "FloJo, 1959–1998." *Time*, September 21, 1998.

Stewart, Mark. *Florence Griffith-Joyner*. New York: Children's Press, 1997.

Tresniowski, Alex, et al. "Like Lightning." *People*, October 5, 1998.

Joyner-Kersee, Jackie *(1962–)*

Born in East St. Louis, Illinois, and raised in a house she remembers as "little more than paper and sticks," Jackie Joyner-Kersee eventually became known throughout the world as one of the finest female athletes of all time. Inducted into the U.S. Track & Field Hall of Fame in 2004, Joyner-Kersee won six Olympic medals over the course of her athletic career—including three gold medals—while also becoming a record holder in both the multievent heptathlon (the female version of the decathlon) and the long jump.

In retirement, Joyner-Kersee has dedicated herself to charity work, establishing the Jackie Joyner-Kersee Center in 2000 while also serving as an ambassador for athletic participation throughout the world. Even after leaving the world of competitive track and field, she stands as an example of how strength and determination can triumph over adversity. An African American, she battled racial discrimination and gender bias to triumph in the male-dominated field of athletic competition, all in spite of her personal battle with a debilitating medical condition.

ATHLETIC PROWESS

Jackie Joyner-Kersee was one of four children born to Al Joyner and his wife, Mary. Her brother, Al Jr., is also an athlete who has achieved Olympic greatness, winning the gold in the triple jump in 1984; he married runner Florence "Flo-Jo" Griffith in 1987. An active child, Jackie joined the track team at East St. Louis's Lincoln High School, where she benefited from having some excellent coaches and excelled at the long jump. However, her performance on the basketball court was what got her noticed, and after graduating in 1980, she attended the University of California at Los Angeles (UCLA) on a basketball scholarship.

At UCLA Jackie first met Bob Kersee, a controversial coach who had a great impact not only on her career but on her personal life. Her college years proved to be challenging as, under Kersee's direction, the young athlete perfected her skills and ultimately won the National Collegiate Athletic Association (NCAA) heptathlon two years in a row and walked away with the 1982 USA championship. The injury that would dog her career—a pulled hamstring—first made itself known as she prepared to compete in the 1983 World Championships in Helsinki, Finland, and she was forced to withdraw. She was also diagnosed with an asthmatic condition requiring constant medication.

However, Jackie's medical setbacks were nothing compared to learning of the tragic death of her thirty-seven-year-old mother, Mary, who had been the young woman's inspiration. Though her grief threatened to derail her academic and athletic career, she rallied, as she had from each of her medical setbacks, and went on to pursue her dreams. Graduating with a major in history in the top 10 percent of her class from UCLA, she was also named the school's athlete of the year in 1985 and won the Broderick Cup, a prize awarded to the country's most outstanding female collegiate athlete.

Jackie Joyner-Kersee Wins Olympic Gold. *Jackie Joyner-Kersee waves to crowd after receiving the gold medal for winning the heptathlon event at the 1992 Summer Olympic Games in Barcelona, Spain.* GARCIA/AFP/GETTY IMAGES.

Her first year out of college proved to be a momentous year for Jackie. She married Kersee in January 1986 and won a heptathlon at that year's Goodwill Games in Moscow. Setting the world record of 7,148 points for the event during the Goodwill Games, Joyner-Kersee competed in other events across the country, winning the Jesse Owens Award for outstanding performance in track and field in 1986.

OLYMPIC HEIGHTS

Joyner-Kersee made outstanding performances in a number of events during 1987, including the Mobil Indoor Grand Prix (winner, women's overall); the Pan American Games (winner, long jump); and the World Championships, held in Rome, where she equaled the world record of 24 feet, 5.5 inches in the long jump. She suffered her first major asthma attack after returning from the Rome Games, and doctors prescribed the short, periodic use of prednisone, a steroid banned in athletic competition, in addition to her regular medication. Because Joyner-Kersee resisted becoming reliant upon drugs and stopped taking any medications as soon as she felt better, her condition worsened over the years, and during the 1993 spring games she was forced to compete wearing an allergen-filtering mask. Meanwhile, she won another Jesse Owens Award in 1987 for her outstanding track-and-field performance.

Joyner-Kersee continued to break records over the following decade. In the 1988 Olympic Games she took the gold in both the heptathlon and long jump and equaled the U.S. record for 100-meter hurdles. Sidelined by a painful injury to her right hamstring during the heptathlon's 200-meter run at Tokyo's 1991 World Championships, a resolute Joyner-Kersee worked her way back into top form, taking the gold for the heptathlon and the bronze for the long jump at the following year's Olympic Games at Barcelona.

Joyner-Kersee set the U.S. record for indoor 50 hurdles before losing the heptathlon event at the Olympics for the first time in her career in 1996. Despite the recurrent hamstring injury that forced her to withdraw from the event, she still managed to win the Olympic bronze in the long jump while in Atlanta. She also renewed her love affair with basketball, joining the Richmond Rage (a Virginia team) and playing in the newly formed American Basketball League for women.

Her performance at the 1998 Goodwill Games held in New York City signaled Joyner-Kersee's official retirement from athletic competition. And what a performance it was. Ending the two-day, seven-event heptathlon with an outstanding performance in the 800 meters, she took the title with 7,291 points, breaking her own 1986 world record. Her Goodwill victory was Joyner-Kersee's twenty-fifth win out of the thirty-six multievent competitions she had entered during her career. In December 1999 *Sports Illustrated* named Joyner-Kersee the greatest female athlete of the twentieth century. She briefly emerged from retirement in 2000, when she tried out for the Olympic team in long jump; however, she failed to earn a spot on the U.S. team, thereby ending her comeback bid.

PHILANTHROPY

In the ensuing decade, Joyner-Kersee began to devote her energy to philanthropic work. In 2000 she opened the Jackie Joyner-Kersee Center in her hometown of East St. Louis, with the intent of providing a venue for underprivileged youth to participate in athletic competition. The center was funded by the Jackie Joyner-Kersee Foundation, a charitable organization established by the athlete in 1988, which had raised more than $12 million with the help of corporate sponsors. In 2006 she joined Lance Armstrong, Muhammad Ali, and other celebrated sports figures in forming Athletes for Hope, an organization dedicated to promoting philanthropic activity among athletes from all fields of competition.

Toward the end of the decade, however, the Jackie Joyner-Kersee Center suddenly found itself struggling to stay afloat. In 2009 the organization was forced to shut down amid questions surrounding its financial dealings, particularly a payment of nearly half a million dollars to an association affiliated with Joyner-Kersee's husband. Although the center was nearly seized through foreclosure, Joyner-Kersee managed to solicit enough donations to keep it afloat. In January 2011 the East St. Louis School District agreed to underwrite the organization's lease, and the center was reopened.

Pamela L. Shelton

SEE ALSO: *Ali, Muhammad; Armstrong, Lance; Basketball; Joyner, Florence Griffith; National Collegiate Athletic Association (NCAA); Olympics; Owens, Jesse; Sports Heroes.*

BIBLIOGRAPHY

Blount, Rachel. "Husband's Nudge Is More than a Notion." *Star Tribune*, July 16, 2000.

Harrington, Geri. *Jackie Joyner-Kersee*. New York: Chelsea House, 1995.

Jensen, Sean. "Staying on Track." *Saint Paul Pioneer Press*, February 8, 2004.

Johnson, Lindsey. *A Woman's Place Is Everywhere: Inspirational Profiles of Female Leaders Who Are Expanding the Roles of American Women*. New York: Master Media, 1994.

Joyner-Kersee, Jackie, and Sonja Steptoe. *A Kind of Grace: The Autobiography of the World's Greatest Female Athlete*. New York: Warner, 1997.

Spirn, Michele. *Against the Odds: The Jackie Joyner-Kersee Story*. New York: AMSCO, 2001.

Judas Priest

British rock band Judas Priest gained national recognition in the United States in the 1980s. They were one of the first groups to be associated exclusively with the term *heavy metal*, and their onstage theatrics included motorcycle rides, pyrotechnics, and leather outfits with chain and spike accessories. Their music evoked a dark fantasy world where rugged heroes wandered in ruined landscapes and defeated evil forces. A decade of hard rock was shaped by the image and message of Judas Priest, and their influence permeated new forms of rock in the 1990s.

The band was officially formed in 1969 when the original British Invasion of groups such as the Beatles, the Rolling Stones, and the Yardbirds slowed and made way for American rockers. The original members of Judas Priest hailed from Birmingham in the industrial midlands of England, where Black Sabbath and many other British hard rock groups got their start. Judas Priest's first American record release, 1977's *Sin after Sin*, gained them only a cult following in the United States. It was not until their album *British Steel* appeared in 1980 that the band received significant airplay with the singles "Living after Midnight" and "Breaking the Law"—loud, simple party anthems that showcase vocalist Rob Halford's alternately growling and screaming voice. The 1982 album *Screamin' for Vengeance* features Judas Priest's typical mix of machismo and futuristic doom and was their largest success to date. Its throaty tribute to pride and revenge, the song "You Got Another Thing Comin'," entered the pop charts and was the band's first successful video.

In 1985 Judas Priest was cited in a suit filed by Tipper Gore's Parents' Music Resource Center as being influential in several highly publicized suicide pacts. The secret messages found in their songs "Let's Be Dead" and "Do It" were presented as evidence, and although no direct link was ever established, the case attests to Judas Priest's stature as a figurehead for the heavy metal genre. The band survived this legal onslaught and several lineup shifts during the 1990s, continuing to release new work thirty years after their inception. Younger heavy metal groups expanded, diversified, and absorbed enough mainstream norms to sell records, but Judas Priest remained loud and angry, true to their roots.

Judas Priest's formula for success—aggressive presentation, operatic screams, extended guitar solos, allusions to mythology and apocalypse—would be adopted and adapted by many other acts during the next decade. Their guitarists, K. K. Downing and Glenn Tipton, had long, bleached hair; Halford had impressive biceps to complement his clenched teeth and rode his Harley-Davidson onstage as the last encore for each elaborate concert. The group tapped into a mysterious suburban longing—young record-buying white males seemed particularly attuned to Judas Priest's territorial posing and violent fantasies.

Judas Priest was one of the first heavy metal bands to expand successfully beyond the comfortable realm of mammoth concerts and album sales; they cracked the MTV market in an age where pop and new wave dominated the channel and managed somehow to maintain a reputation as purists and outsiders even at the height of their commercial success. "Breaking the Law" found new cult life when MTV's *Beavis and Butt-Head* air-guitared regularly to the song in the 1990s. Grunge musicians of the next generation often mentioned Judas Priest as a primary influence.

In 1992, lead singer Rob Halford left the band. Six years later, in 1998, he came out publicly as a gay man. This generated both controversy and respect for Halford within the gay community and the aggressively macho heavy metal scene.

Rarely has a musical act so consistently and unabashedly typified a late-twentieth-century style of musical expression, and through the changing composition of the members and various pressures and turmoil, the band managed to make it through the first decade of the twenty-first century, selling as many as fifty million albums worldwide. After a reunion that included Halford's return, a tour through Europe in 2003, and a second popular tour and live album in 2009 (*Touch of Evil: Live*), the band announced their 2011–2012 world farewell "Epitaph Tour" through North and South America, Europe, and Asia.

Colby Vargas

SEE ALSO: *The Beatles;* Beavis and Butt-Head*; Black Sabbath; British Invasion; Electric Guitar; Grunge; Heavy Metal; MTV; New Wave Music; Pop Music; Rock and Roll; The Rolling Stones; Suicide; The Yardbirds.*

BIBLIOGRAPHY

Bukszpan, Daniel. *The Encyclopedia of Heavy Metal.* New York: Barnes & Noble Books, 2003.

Gett, Steve. *Judas Priest, Heavy Duty: The Official Biography.* Port Chester, NY: Cherry Lane Books, 1984.

Judas Priest Official Website. Accessed August 13, 2012. Available from http://www.judaspriest.com

Weinstein, Deena. *Heavy Metal: A Cultural Sociology.* New York: Lexington Books, 1991.

Judge

A flourishing weekly American humor magazine for almost sixty years, *Judge* was renowned during the 1920s for bringing a new generation of sophisticated humor writers and cartoonists to the attention of American readers, including S. J. Perelman, Theodor Seuss Geisel (Dr. Seuss), Ralph Barton, Johnny Gruelle, Ernie Bushmiller, and Harold Ross.

Judge was founded in New York City in 1881. It survived until 1939 in its initial run, offering a mix of jokes, short humor pieces, reviews, and gag cartoons. The humor magazines of the nineteenth century, unlike late-twentieth-century publications such as *MAD Magazine* and *Cracked*, were aimed at adult readers and included topical and political observations as well as broad comedy and ethnic jokes. Created five years after the appearance of one of its chief competitors, *Puck*, *Judge* was similar to that magazine in form and content and also owed something to Britain's well-established *Punch*. A key figure in the early development of *Judge* was cartoonist James Albert Wales, who left *Puck* to put together the group that launched the new magazine.

The next major humor weekly to appear was *Life*, which debuted in 1883. *Puck* folded in 1918, but *Judge* and *Life* remained rivals well into the 1930s. Although it was never quite as slick or sophisticated as *Life*, *Judge* managed to hold its own, and by 1925 it proclaimed on its covers that it had a "larger circulation than any other humorous weekly in the world." One man credited with boosting *Judge*'s circulation was Norman Anthony, who became editor in 1922. He promoted the single-caption cartoon and devised theme issues that focused on such topics as advertising, celebrities, radio, and college.

Among the new contributors Anthony recruited for these issues were cartoonist Jefferson Machamer, Seuss, and Perelman. Initially a cartoonist as well as a writer, Perelman contributed somewhat surreal cartoons as well as humor pieces and magazine parodies; his cartoons were always accompanied by a block of writing in the style that would later feature in his *New Yorker* pieces and in the nonsense dialogue he composed for the Marx Brothers movies. Ross, who later founded the *New Yorker*, worked for Anthony briefly; other eventual members of the *New Yorker* team who produced work for *Judge* included Chon Day, Charles Addams, Gardner Rea, and Whitney Darrow Jr. Milt Gross, Don Herold, William Gropper, Bill Holman (creator of the *Smokey Stover* comic strip), Vernon Grant, and Bushmiller (creator of *Nancy*) also contributed to the magazine. *Judge*'s theater critic in the 1920s and early 1930s was the formidable George Jean Nathan, and movie reviews were provided by Pare Lorentz, an acclaimed documentary filmmaker.

Anthony was lured away to *Life* in 1929 and was replaced by John Shuttleworth. In 1931 Anthony created *Ballyhoo*, a much more raucous magazine that satirized advertising and many other icons of popular culture. *Life*, a monthly by that time trying unsuccessfully to mimic the *New Yorker*, ended its run in 1936 and sold its title to Henry Luce for his new photojournalistic weekly. *Judge* itself had become a monthly, and for awhile it ran a cover line: "Including the humorous tradition and features of *Life*." The magazine lasted until 1939 before folding; it was revived twice but never regained its earlier popularity.

Ron Goulart

SEE ALSO: *Advertising; Celebrity; Comics; Dr. Seuss;* Life; *Luce, Henry;* MAD Magazine; *The Marx Brothers; The* New Yorker; *Radio.*

BIBLIOGRAPHY

Horn, Maurice, ed. *The World Encyclopedia of Cartoons*. New York: Chelsea House Publications, 1980.

Trachtenberg, Stanley, ed. *American Humorists, 1800–1950*. Detroit, MI: Gale Research, 1982.

Judson, Arthur *(1881–1975)*

Between 1930 and 1950 Arthur Judson exerted unprecedented influence in the field of classical music in the United States, acting as unofficial chief adviser to the country's major symphony orchestras. The engagement of both conductors and soloists for symphony concerts depended, to an extraordinary degree, on his recommendations. Officially Judson held dual positions as president of Columbia Concerts Corporation, the country's leading artists' management agency—which came to be known as "the Judson Empire"—and simultaneously managed the New York Philharmonic and Philadelphia orchestras. However, it was not only his powerful status that won the trust of orchestra boards but also his knowledge of music and impeccable judgment of quality. To these virtues were added shrewd business sense and an instinct for what would draw audiences. As artists' manager, he was known to represent only the finest musicians and, accordingly, won their confidence and loyalty. No one person since has taken control of classical music to the same extent as Judson.

Milton Goldin

SEE ALSO: *The Boston Symphony Orchestra.*

BIBLIOGRAPHY

Smith, Cecil. *Worlds of Music*. New York: Lippincott, 1952.

Judy Bolton

Judy Bolton was the protagonist of a popular girls mystery series. Unlike contemporary series produced by syndicates and ghostwriters using pseudonyms, the Judy Bolton series was created and written entirely by Margaret Sutton. Grosset & Dunlap initially published four volumes in 1932, then printed one per year through 1967 for a total of thirty-eight volumes. Many of the stories were based on real events, actual sites, and Sutton's or her acquaintances' experiences. The books appealed to readers because the character of Judy was more realistic than other series sleuths. More than five million copies of Judy Bolton books sold before the series was canceled.

Sutton wrote her first books before the Nancy Drew series was published, but publishers were not interested in her idea. She was told how syndicate books were written, and she declined to write formulaic plots. Because of Nancy Drew's popularity in the early 1930s, however, girl detective stories became marketable, and an editor at Grosset & Dunlap contacted Sutton about publishing the Judy Bolton tales. In 1932 *The Vanishing Shadow*, *The Haunted Attic*, *The Invisible Chimes*, and *Seven Strange Clues* were issued.

PLOTLINES

More interested in literary craft than commercial success, Sutton's writing did not resemble the contents of mass-marketed books sold in other series. Judy differs from other detective heroines in girls series books because she realistically grows up and is not frozen at a specific age. She also is concerned about social issues and is sensitive to members of other socioeconomic classes and cultures. Judy chooses her friends and cases because she is interested in those people and wants to improve their living conditions. Although the Judy character was not as popular as Nancy Drew, she provided a stronger role model for readers.

In the first book, Judy, a doctor's daughter, is a red-haired, fifteen-year-old high school student living in northwestern Pennsylvania during the 1930s. She wants to be a detective, explore the world, and solve problems, but her life remains ordinary, sometimes disappointing, and not spectacular like Nancy Drew's. In the series, Judy ages to twenty-two years old, graduates from high school and college, works, marries, and accepts adult responsibilities. This maturation does not limit her adventures or inquisitiveness and reinforces the reality of her stories, unlike other series in which characters are static and artificial.

Judy travels and meets new people, establishing relationships beyond her family. She confronts social issues and displays tolerance and acceptance of others. Judy is also depicted as sometimes being outspoken, temperamental, and capable of making mistakes, causing her to appear more human to readers, who could identify with Judy more than with flawless detectives such as Nancy Drew. Judy relies on her intellect, not her appearance, and uses her ability to surmount obstacles instead of counting on material goods or family connections. She persistently seeks the truth with the help of her cat, Blackberry; brother, Horace; friend Honey; or romantic partner, Peter Dobbs, an FBI (Federal Bureau of Investigation) agent who considers Judy his equal. They like to solve mysteries together.

The Judy Bolton series successfully endured for three decades. Grosset & Dunlap canceled the series after book thirty-eight, *The Secret of the Sand Castle*, was published in 1967. Sutton believed that the publisher capitulated to pressure from the Stratemeyer Syndicate because Judy Bolton ranked second to Nancy Drew in sales. The monopolistic syndicate disliked competitors and discouraged Grosset & Dunlap from advertising and distributing series books. Sutton also claimed that the syndicate had stolen plots and titles from her books for their series. She had planned a thirty-ninth book, *The Strange Likeness*, set in the Panama Canal Zone where Judy gave birth to twins Peter and Pam, but it was never completed.

CRITICAL PRAISE

Scholars have scrutinized the Judy Bolton books for themes and symbolism, praising the sound plots, thrilling pace, realism, and social commentary. Some critics have labeled Judy as a feminist who was an independent thinker—a confident, capable person who resented restrictions based on gender. They have identified such recurrent themes as the problems of urbanization and the search for identity. Scholars have stressed that Judy's encounters with stereotypes about ethnic and religious groups and awareness of class consciousness address timeless issues that would impact readers of all generations. Judy challenges prejudices and attempts to understand circumstances so that she can change them.

The books also provide commentary about child labor, unsafe work conditions, unemployment, and elitism. For example, Judy cleverly hosts a costume party so that members of different social classes do not know the identity of each other and mingle. Sutton created many of the books during the Great Depression, and, although that catastrophe is not mentioned by name, many of the mysteries are connected to economic conditions, situations, and motivations.

BOLTON FAN BASE

Through the years the Judy Bolton books became nostalgic collectibles for many adult women. Marcia Muller, pioneering author of hard-boiled detective novels featuring the savvy female protagonist Sharon McCone, reveals that Judy was her favorite teenage girl detective because she seemed real and could speak for herself. Muller also states that the Judy Bolton mysteries were interesting and not improbable like other series.

In 1985 author Kate Emberg and a group of collectors formed the Judy Bolton Society, which published the *Judy Bolton Society Newsletter*. This group became the Society of Phantom Friends, named for the thirtieth volume in the series, and its newsletter, *The Whispered Watchword*, discussed Judy Bolton and other series books. The Phantom Friends developed a friendship with Sutton and presented her with its Life Achievement Award.

Emberg wrote and published a new Judy Bolton, *The Whispering Belltower*, with Sutton's permission, and *The Talking Snowman* was cowritten by Sutton and Linda Joy Singleton. Phantom Friends members Melanie Knight, Rosemarie DiCristo, and Linda Tracy compiled the *Guide to Judy Bolton Country*, a comprehensive reference manual about all aspects, major and trivial, of the Judy Bolton books. Judy Bolton Days, held annually in Coudersport, Pennsylvania, Sutton's hometown, enables fans to visit sites mentioned in the series. Judy Bolton admirers also have created websites about the popular character. Because the Judy Bolton series was out of print, Applewood Books and Aeonian Press published facsimile reprints in the late twentieth century. Avid collectors continue to search for original volumes in used bookstores.

Elizabeth D. Schafer

SEE ALSO: *FBI (Federal Bureau of Investigation); The Great Depression; Nancy Drew; Stratemeyer, Edward.*

BIBLIOGRAPHY

Mason, Bobbie Ann. *The Girl Sleuth: A Feminist Guide.* Old Westbury, NY: Feminist Press, 1975.

Rollings, Peter C., and Susan W. Rollings, eds. *Gender in Popular Culture: Images of Men and Women in Literature, Visual Media, and Material Culture.* Cleveland, OH: Ridgemont Press, 1995.

Juke Boxes

Coin-activated automatic record players were one of the earliest methods by which public venues could make money from Thomas Edison's phonograph invention. The juke box really came of age in the 1930s and 1940s when the Great Depression almost eliminated the sale of records to individuals and made the coin-slot record player an important source of musical entertainment. These machines brought specific kinds of music to the public and played a part in the ascent of swing and rock and roll as mass movements of popular culture.

The failure to develop a long-playing record in the first half of the twentieth century put a premium on technology that could automate the process of playing several records one after the other. The first automatic record changer was patented in 1921, and it was followed by many different devices that could pick and play discs; some could even play both sides of a record.

The first coin-slot machine with electronic amplification and a multirecord changer was produced in 1927 by the Automatic Music Instrument Company (AMI). AMI was joined by J. P. Seeburg, Rudolph Wurlitzer, and the Rockola Manufacturing Company in devising coin-slot machines with advanced record-changing mechanisms that could select from twenty or twenty-four discs.

At the end of the 1920s, only around 50,000 of these machines were in use, but the repeal of Prohibition in 1933 brought about a dramatic change in American social life as people flooded back into bars and clubs. No popular drinking establishment was without one. The term *juke box* originated from the lingo of the South, where dancing or "jooking" to records was a popular pastime. Small drinking establishments with only recorded sound for musical entertainment were called "juke joints." Here, patrons would dance to blues or country music that they selected from the discs stored in the juke box.

In the hedonistic atmosphere of these bars, loud dance music, comedy routines, and raunchy songs about sex were popular choices on the juke box. Dancing was a very important part of social life, and swing records on a juke box were the next best thing to attending (and paying for) a live concert. The juke box made the most of the technological development of amplification and speakers. It could project sound to every corner of a bar or soda fountain. The blaring volume of the playback made it possible to hear and dance to the music above the noise of a crowded bar. The juke boxes of the 1930s gave listeners the highest volume of sound reproduction available outside the movie theater.

During the Great Depression, records were considered a luxury good. Radio became a major source of music in the home, but listeners still wanted to choose their music and to hear it when they wanted to. Instead of buying a record for a dollar, they paid a nickel to hear it on a juke box. In the 1930s the number of juke boxes in use rose to a high of 500,000. They could be found in taverns, pool halls, restaurants, hotels, cafés, bus stations, and even beauty parlors. More than half of the nation's juke boxes were in the South. The store of records had to be changed every week, and by 1936 more than half of

Juke Box. A young woman leans against a brightly lit jukebox in the late 1960s. MICHAEL OCHS ARCHIVES/GETTY IMAGES.

all records produced in the country were destined for juke boxes. The demand provided valuable work for Depression-era musicians, especially for jazz and blues artists, whose livelihoods were most threatened by the bad economic times. Many of the classic jazz and blues records of the 1930s were made for juke boxes.

Customers' choice provided valuable information in the marketing of recordings, and juke boxes were fitted with indicators that displayed which discs were the most popular. Returns from juke boxes were an important gauge of the growing popularity of rhythm and blues in the 1940s and of rock and roll in the 1950s. Independent record companies often had to resort to bribery to get juke box operators to use their records, and there were allegations that the lucrative business was in the hands of organized crime. In the post–World War II years, juke boxes became larger and more ornate; the modernistic designs of Wurlitzer made the coin-slot machine stand out in a bar or restaurant. But the days of the juke box were numbered as a booming economy allowed consumers to buy their own records.

Attempts to produce video juke boxes in the 1960s and 1970s were technologically successful but could not return the machine to the dominant place in public entertainment it enjoyed in the 1930s and 1940s.The twenty-first century has seen more and better versions of the DVD juke box, demonstrating a lasting nostalgia for the old technology and the period it evokes.

Andre Millard

SEE ALSO: *Blues; Country Music; Edison, Thomas Alva; The Great Depression; Jazz; Long-Playing Record; Mafia/ Organized Crime; Prohibition; Radio; Rhythm and Blues; Rock and Roll; Soda Fountains; Swing Dancing; World War II.*

BIBLIOGRAPHY

Chapple, Steve, and Rebee Garofalo. *Rock 'n' Roll Is Here to Pay.* Chicago: Nelson Hall, 1977.

Millard, Andre. *America on Record: A History of Recorded Sound.* Cambridge, UK: Cambridge University Press, 1995.

Sanjek, Russell. *American Popular Music and Its Business.* New York: Oxford University Press, 1988.

Segrave, Kerry. *Jukeboxes: An American Social History.* Jefferson, NC: McFarland, 2002.

Julia

Debuting on NBC in September 1968, *Julia* was the first network television series to star an African American in the leading role since *Amos 'n' Andy* and *Beulah* left the air in 1953. The gentle situation comedy featured Diahann Carroll as Julia Baker, a widowed black nurse with a six-year-old son, Corey, living a thoroughly integrated lifestyle in a Los Angeles apartment building. Surrounded by whites, the Bakers encounter only the most innocuous instances of prejudice.

The series reached the airwaves during a particularly incendiary period in American race relations—the aftermath of Martin Luther King Jr.'s assassination; a "long hot summer" of riots and burning in inner-city ghettos and rising Black Power militancy. Inevitably, the series, which ignored all these issues, stirred controversy. The character of Julia was dismissed by some as a "white Negro," and the series was considered irrelevant, if not dangerous, especially because it featured no African American male characters of authority or narrative importance. On the other hand, the series was praised for opening doors for subsequent African American sitcoms and for demonstrating that American audiences, black and white, could enjoy nonstereotyped black characters on prime time. After a successful three-year run, *Julia* left the air in 1971.

Aniko Bodroghkozy

SEE ALSO: The Amos 'n' Andy Show*;* Beulah*; King, Martin Luther, Jr.; Race Riots; Sitcom; Television.*

BIBLIOGRAPHY

Bodroghkozy, Aniko. "'Is This What You Mean By Color TV?': Race, Gender, and Contested Meanings in *Julia*." In *Private Screenings: Television and the Female Consumer*, ed. Lynn Spigel and Denise Mann. Minneapolis: University of Minnesota Press, 1992.

Bodroghkozy, Aniko. *Groove Tube: Sixties Television and the Youth Rebellion*. Durham, NC: Duke University Press, 2001.

Juliá, Raúl *(1940–1994)*

Raúl Juliá was a beloved stage and screen actor who was admired for his work on and off the screen. Due to his fine training and technique, he was one of the few Hispanic actors successful in transcending cultural stereotypes to win a diverse and interesting series of roles in Hollywood and abroad. Juliá broke onto the stage in New York in Hispanic community plays and through Joseph Papp's innovative casting in the New York Shakespeare Festival's production of *Macbeth* in 1966. He continued to appear in Shakespeare Festival productions and made his Broadway debut in 1968. In the early 1970s Juliá broke into film, the medium that led to his greatest popularity.

Born Raúl Carlos Juliá y Acelay in San Juan, Puerto Rico, on March 9, 1940, into a relatively well-off family, Juliá began acting in school plays and, while studying law at the University of Puerto Rico, continued devoting much time to amateur productions. Juliá moved to New York to study acting in 1964 and shortly thereafter made his stage debut in a Spanish-language production of Pedro Calderón de la Barca's classic *La vida es sueño* (*Life Is a Dream*). Soon he was performing in the Hispanic neighborhoods of the city in small theaters and in the open air.

In 1966 famed producer Joseph Papp gave Juliá his first break, disregarding Juliá's ethnicity and casting him in *Macbeth*. Juliá subsequently performed in a number of Papp plays, including William Shakespeare's *Hamlet*, and Hispanic community theater in the late 1960s and early 1970s. He went on to be cast in Broadway roles, to receive rave reviews and four Tony nominations for work in *The Two Gentlemen of Verona*, *Where's Charley?*, *Threepenny Opera*, and *Nine*. His debut on Broadway was as the servant Chan in Jack Gelber's 1968 production of *The Cuban Thing*. A milestone in his career was the success of Papp's *Two Gentlemen of Verona* and Juliá's Tony-nominated portrayal of Porteus in this musical adaptation; the play moved from Central Park's Delacorte Theater to Broadway's St. James Theater.

During the 1980s and early 1990s Juliá created a distinguished career as a film actor, playing a wide variety of roles, from romantic detectives to evil villains. One of his most highly acclaimed parts was that of a revolutionary in the Academy Award–nominated *Kiss of the Spiderwoman* in 1986. Juliá also played some very popular offbeat roles in such highly commercial films as *The Addams Family* (1991) and its sequel, *Addams Family Values* (1993). Among his other noteworthy films are *Eyes of Laura Mars* (1978), *One from the Heart* (1982), *Compromising Positions* (1985), *Tequila Sunrise* (1988), *Moon over Parador* (1988), *Tango Bar* (1988), *Romero* (1989), *The Rookie* (1990), and *Havana* (1990).

When not acting on the stage or screen, Juliá made frequent appearances on *Sesame Street* and donated his services to the Hunger Project, an international organization whose goal is to eradicate world hunger. He also worked with Hispanic community organizations, most notably the Hispanic Organization of Latin Actors (HOLA). Juliá died of a massive stroke on October 24, 1994, but his legacy lives on through a number of annual awards that are presented in his name, including the Raúl Juliá HOLA Founders Award, the National Hispanic Foundation for the Arts' Raúl Juliá Award for Excellence, and the Puerto Rican Family Institute's Raúl Juliá Global Citizen Award, as well as scholarships offered at the prestigious Julliard School and the Joseph Papp Public Theater in New York. One of Juliá's final performances, as the Brazilian rain forest activist Chico Mendes in the HBO movie *Burning Season* (1994), earned him several posthumous accolades, including an Emmy Award, a Golden Globe, and a Screen Actors Guild Award.

Nicolás Kanellos

SEE ALSO: *Academy Awards; The Addams Family; Broadway; Central Park; Community Theater; Emmy Awards; Hollywood;* Sesame Street*; Television; Tony Awards.*

BIBLIOGRAPHY

Carnes, Mark C. *American National Biography, Supplement 2*. New York: Oxford University Press, 2005.

Cruz, Bárbara. *Raúl Juliá: Actor and Humanitarian*. Springfield, NJ: Enslow, 1998.

Mortiz, Charles, ed. *Current Biography Yearbook*. New York: H.W. Wilson, 1982.

Stefoff, Rebecca. *Raúl Juliá*. New York: Chelsea House, 1994.

Tardiff, Joseph T., and L. Mpho Mabunda, eds. *Dictionary of Hispanic Biography*. Detroit, MI: Gale, 1996.

Jurassic Park

Jurassic Park is the title of Michael Crichton's best-selling novel (1990) and the popular film adaptation by Steven Spielberg (1993), which spawned two film sequels, *The Lost World: Jurassic Park* (1997) and *Jurassic Park III* (2001). In the story, Jurassic Park is the name of a theme park placed on a tropical island where millionaire John Hammond plans to exhibit live dinosaurs that have been created from fossilized DNA.

Jurassic Park III. *Sam Neill as Dr. Alan Grant faces off against velociraptors on Isla Sorna in 2001's* Jurassic Park III. AMBLIN/UNIVERSAL/THE KOBAL COLLECTION/ILM (INDUSTRIAL LIGHT & MAGIC).

Following the technophobic discourse first enunciated by Mary Shelley's novel *Frankenstein* (1818), Crichton and Spielberg depict how, inevitably, the supposedly safe environment of the park collapses under the pressure of the dinosaurs' instincts. The attacks by the dinosaurs turn an enjoyable inaugural tour of Jurassic Park into a nightmare for Hammond's team, his family, and his guests, including prestigious scientists. *The Lost World*, also based on a Crichton novel (1995) and directed by Spielberg, was less successful. The plot focuses on another island where the species of the park breed unchecked and on the efforts of a group led by Dr. Ian Malcolm, a victimized guest in *Jurassic Park*, to stop the dinosaurs and the men who want to capture them for commercial purposes. *The Lost World* is, incidentally, a title that connects Crichton's and Spielberg's works to a piece of fiction that made dinosaurs fashionable: Arthur Conan Doyle's novel *The Lost World* (1912) and its silent film adaptation by Willis O'Brien (1925).

A CAUTIONARY TALE

Like *Frankenstein*, *Jurassic Park* examines the ethical dilemmas involved in utilizing technoscience to create life out of dead matter. The targets of Crichton's criticism are biotechnology businesses and the lack of proper controls in laboratories working with human and animal DNA. Crichton is concerned by the dependence of scientific research on business interests. This is shown in the relationship between paleontologist Alan Grant, the main character in *Jurassic Park*, and Hammond. Hammond's funding of Grant's research places the principled scientist at the same level of dependence as his unscrupulous colleagues. Ambitious young scientists and reckless businessmen such as Hammond have the potential to form alliances that lead to dangerous ventures such as Jurassic Park and even to the extinction of human life.

Dr. Malcolm, Crichton's messenger in the novel, emphasizes this technophobic point when he protests that "there is no humility before nature. There is only a get-rich-quick, make-a-name-for-yourself-fast philosophy. Cheat, lie, falsify—it doesn't matter." In the novel, the dinosaurs eventually kill both Hammond and Malcolm (although the latter is brought back in the book's sequel, with the explanation that he was only mistakenly pronounced dead). Hammond's death is presented as an act of poetic justice, whereas Malcolm's unjust demise proves the accuracy of his chaos theory and also drives home Crichton's apocalyptic vision.

SPIELBERG'S SPIN

In Spielberg's *Jurassic Park*, Hammond and Malcolm survive, and it is the dinosaurs that are destroyed. The grim moralizing of Crichton's cautionary tale and his introduction of the chaos theory are thus significantly modified to make way for hope. Beyond its hope for the future—and for a future sequel—Spielberg's film differs from Crichton's novel in another important aspect. The technophobic message of Crichton's novel has to compete with Spielberg's skillful use of special effects for the audience's attention. The film's appeal is largely based on the celebration of the technology behind the animatronics (electronic puppetry designed by Stan Winston) and infographics (computer simulations developed by Industrial Light & Magic) employed to represent the dinosaurs. By endorsing Spielberg's films, Crichton undermines his own message. Nevertheless, this is an ambiguous message. Spielberg's and Crichton's success suggested that if they ever decided to open a real Jurassic Park, people would flock to meet the dinosaurs. In fact, people do go to the Universal Studios theme parks, where the fake dinosaurs of *Jurassic Park* can be seen.

Feminist writers such as Marina Warner have criticized a problematic aspect of both the print and film versions of *Jurassic Park*: the sex of the dinosaurs. They are all created female to ensure that no natural reproduction takes place on the island. Furthermore, as the character Dr. Henry Wu notes, since all embryos are initially female, "from a bioengineering standpoint, females are easier to breed." However, the scientists refer to lethal giants such as the Tyrannosaurus Rex as being male. The upshot, according to feminist commentators, is that the scientists of Jurassic Park believe that females are easier to control. As the plot develops, this belief proves to be radically wrong. After wreaking havoc on the island, some female dinosaurs mutate into males capable of starting sexual reproduction. This is presented by Crichton in ambiguous terms, as a symbol of life's unstoppable drive toward reproduction. The controversial theme of the female monster that threatens human life with uncontrolled reproduction is also the focus of films such as *Aliens* (1986) and *Species* (1995). Godzilla, in contrast, turns out to be a hermaphrodite in the eponymous 1998 film.

A LASTING IMPACT

Audiences of all ages are fascinated with dinosaurs, which helped both the book and movie versions of *Jurassic Park* become enormous hits. The popularity of these creatures is based on their unique status as monsters: Dinosaurs are threatening because of their enormous size, but they are also fragile victims of evolution. The Darwinian fate of dinosaurs sends a message to humans about the thin threads on which life depends. In *Jurassic Park*, genetic engineering, rather than a freak evolutionary occurrence, transforms the dinosaurs from relics of the prehistoric past into a threat for the future akin to that posed by other monsters of science fiction, notably extraterrestrials. Of course, dinosaurs also make wonderful toys for children, as Spielberg and Universal Studios know well.

In 2001 the American Film Institute named *Jurassic Park* the thirty-fifth most thrilling film of all time. The movie is also acknowledged as a highly influential early example of the capabilities of computer imaging in cinema. However, *Jurassic Park*'s true power is the way it allows us to glimpse into the future and wonder whether science will ever make it possible for a real Jurassic Park to open.

Sara Martin

SEE ALSO: *Blockbusters; Crichton, Michael; Doyle, Arthur Conan; Science Fiction Publishing; Spielberg, Steven.*

BIBLIOGRAPHY

Blanco Lucas, Adolfo. *Cinesaurios.* Barcelona, Spain: Royal Books, 1993.

Brode, Douglas. *The Films of Steven Spielberg.* New York: Citadel Press, 1995.

Kinnard, Roy. *Beasts and Behemoths: Prehistoric Creatures in the Movies.* Metuchen, NJ: Scarecrow Press, 1988.

Perry, George. *Steven Spielberg: Close Up; The Making of His Movies.* New York: Thunder's Mouth Press, 1998.

Shone, Tom. *Blockbuster: How Hollywood Learned to Stop Worrying and Love the Summer.* London: Simon & Schuster, 2004.

Juvenile Delinquency

The term *juvenile delinquency*, which refers to law breaking by minors, also includes status offenses such as truancy, homelessness, and the state of being unsupervised by a suitable adult guardian. The term was first used after the American Civil War when criminologists and social reformers began calling attention to the poverty, disease, crime, and inadequate home life often found in urban communities, particularly among immigrants. Jane Addams, Robert Woods, Florence Kelley, and other settlement house leaders in the 1890s lobbied state legislators and private and public charities to eliminate juvenile delinquency by eradicating these social problems. In order to offer increased protection for children, they proposed new laws dealing with mandatory school attendance, public health, and safety. Activists concerned with assisting troubled youth founded recreational organizations (such as the Boy Scouts and Girl Scouts), team sports, Sunday schools, juvenile courts, pediatric medical clinics, and the field of child psychology during the early twentieth century. Juvenile delinquency continued to be a major social problem, however. By the early twenty-first century, street gangs composed predominantly of young minority males had surfaced in almost every major town in the United States.

PARADIGM SHIFT

Sociologists and criminologists, many from the University of Chicago, argued that delinquents were a by-product of poverty, because statistics seemed to indicate that the incidence of crime increased with unemployment. Later studies attributed delinquency to a wide range of environmental conditions associated with poverty, including overcrowded, slumlike dwellings; low-level sanitation; and inadequate recreation. According to research conducted by Sheldon and Eleanor Glueck, by the 1920s the Harvard Law School Crime Survey had begun producing evidence to support this view. Using an interdisciplinary approach to form a multiple-factor theory of juvenile delinquency, researchers gathered evidence to identify the quality of a child's family life as the single most important factor in criminal behavior. Recidivism rates remained high among juvenile delinquents despite professional intervention. After 1950, however, a paradigm shift caused most sociologists to blame delinquency on individual or family dysfunction rather than on low social or economic class.

Adolescent gang wars, although not unheard of in the nineteenth century, became a national concern after World War I and more so after World War II. Many urban streets and parks were unsafe. Despite greater police patrols and an expansion of state reform schools for delinquents, juvenile delinquents continued to avoid school, choosing instead to loiter and make trouble in public spaces. Churches and social workers developed summer camps and other recreation programs to attempt to deal with the problem. They also initiated foster home services. American psychologist G. Stanley Hall, who coined the term *adolescence* in 1901, advocated the scientific study of juvenile delinquency. British American psychiatrist William Healy established the first child guidance clinics in the United States in Chicago (1909) and Boston (1917). He was a pioneer in establishing links between juvenile delinquency and emotional disturbance. Healy and his wife, Augusta Fox Bronner, trained a new generation of social workers, psychologists, and probation officers to treat young offenders on this basis.

During the Great Depression, Hollywood recognized juvenile delinquency as an important urban problem that rendered great material for movie plots. Some of the films that grew out of this recognition were *Angels with Dirty Faces* (1938), *Boys Town* (1938), *Crime School* (1938), and *They Made Me a Criminal* (1939). *Rebel without a Cause* (1955) focused on the alienation felt by middle-class, suburban teenagers. *West Side Story* (1961), a film adaptation of the landmark Broadway musical by Leonard Bernstein, was a modern revision of William Shakespeare's *Romeo and Juliet*, featuring rival gangs in New York City in the 1950s in lieu of feuding families.

Blackboard Jungle (1955), the first film to feature rock-and-roll music, showed the harrowing experience that public school teachers encountered in a New York City high school in the 1950s. The treatment of rebellious middle-class adolescents in modern psychiatric centers was depicted in *Born Innocent* (1974). In contrast, *Boyz N the Hood* (1991) portrayed senseless violence and drug abuse in South Central Los Angeles black teenage gangs. Ironically, by that time Hispanics rather than African Americans had become the dominant force in the street gangs that were terrorizing America.

Much of the violence perpetrated by street gangs in the late twentieth century was connected to drug use, and government estimates placed the number of known drug abusers in the United States at 12.6 million in 1991. School violence was also on the rise. In 1994 Congress passed the Gun-Free School Act that mandated a one-year suspension for students bringing guns to school. By the following year, 28.4 percent of American schools were reporting that gang activity had become a problem. The problem was even more severe in urban areas, where 40.7 percent of schools documented gang activity. Toward the end of the twentieth century, concerns over violence in schools also brought increased attention to the practice of bullying, which was shown to dramatically increase the possibility of gun violence in schools.

In 1999 the worst school shooting in American history to that date took place at Columbine High School in Littleton, Colorado, when twelve students and a teacher were murdered by two students who had been bullied. That same year, the National Youth Gang Survey revealed that 90 percent of all gang members were male and that almost 80 percent were either Hispanic or African American. Some 16 percent were under the age of fourteen. Between 2001 and 2002, gang activity rose an additional 50 percent. By 2009 the National Gang Threat Assessment Report had identified a million gang members in the United States, stating that 80 percent of all crimes that occurred in the United States were being committed by gang members.

Peter C. Holloran

SEE ALSO: *Addams, Jane; Bernstein, Leonard; Boy Scouts of America; Gangs; Girl Scouts; The Great Depression;* Rebel without a Cause*;* West Side Story*; World War I; World War II.*

BIBLIOGRAPHY

Bartollas, Clemens. *Juvenile Delinquency.* New York: Wiley, 1985.

Glueck, Sheldon, and Eleanor T. Glueck. *One Thousand Juvenile Delinquents.* Cambridge, MA: Harvard University Press, 1934.

Hawes, Joseph M. *Children in Urban Society.* New York: Oxford University Press, 1971.

Holloran, Peter C. *Boston's Wayward Children: Social Services for Homeless Children, 1830–1930.* Boston: Northeastern University Press, 1984.

Howell, James C., and John P. Moore. *History of Street Gangs in the United States.* Washington, DC: Department of Justice, 2010.

Sandhu, Harjit S. *Juvenile Delinquency: Causes, Control, and Prevention.* New York: Gregg Division, McGraw-Hill, 1977.

Shoemaker, Donald J. *Theories of Delinquency: An Examination of Explanations of Delinquent Behavior.* New York: Oxford University Press, 2010.

Slobogin, Christopher, and Mark A. Fondacaro. *Juveniles at Risk: A Plea for Preventive Justice.* New York: Oxford University Press, 2011.

Kahn, Roger *(1927–)*

Roger Kahn's 1972 best seller *The Boys of Summer* instantly set the standard for nonfiction baseball writing. The memoir eloquently captured the essence of the 1950s Brooklyn Dodgers, analyzing the courage of Jackie Robinson, Roy Campanella, and teammates both on the diamond and in their post-baseball lives. A former reporter for the New York *Herald-Tribune* and protégé of John Lardner (1912–1960), Kahn established himself as the premier baseball author of his generation with a series of critical and popular successes. His simple, clear prose evokes family and literature and articulates the hold baseball continues to have upon the American consciousness. *Memories of Summer*, which includes poignant profiles of Willie Mays and Mickey Mantle, was published in 1997, the same year Kahn led a failed quest to bring the Dodgers back to Brooklyn.

Kahn's admirers have ranged from Ronald Reagan to Robert Frost, who discussed the fortunes of the Boston Red Sox with Kahn during a 1960 interview. In a 2006 memoir titled *Into My Own*, Kahn describes his friendships with such luminaries as Frost, Robinson, Pee Wee Reese, and Eugene McCarthy, ending the book with a poignant account of the death of his son, Roger Laurence Kahn, who committed suicide in 1987 after years of depression and drug use.

Andrew Milner

SEE ALSO: *Baseball; Best Sellers; Boston Red Sox; The Brooklyn Dodgers; Frost, Robert; Mantle, Mickey; Mays, Willie; Reagan, Ronald; Reese, Pee Wee; Robinson, Jackie; Sports Heroes.*

BIBLIOGRAPHY

Kahn, Roger. *The Boys of Summer*. New York: Harper and Row, 1972.

Kahn, Roger. *How the Weather Was*. New York: Harper and Row, 1973.

Kahn, Roger. *Memories of Summer*. New York: Hyperion, 1997.

Shannon, Mike. "Roger Kahn." In *Baseball: The Writers' Game*. South Bend, IN: Diamond Communications, 1992.

Kaltenborn, Hans von *(1878–1965)*

With his peppery but precise delivery, Hans von Kaltenborn was a familiar voice on the American airwaves for over thirty years. He started his career as a newspaperman, but then moved to radio just as the new medium was beginning to establish itself as a disseminator of news. In the 1920s, when broadcast news was rare and usually consisted of a narrative accounting of current events, Kaltenborn maintained the unorthodox view that newscasters should not only report facts and information, but they should also provide analysis and insight. Generally regarded as the first regular radio news commentator, Kaltenborn had a vast knowledge of foreign affairs and international politics, which amply equipped him for covering crises in Europe and the Far East in the 1930s. His vivid reporting of the Spanish Civil War (1936–1939) and the Czech Crisis of 1938, more than any other feat of broadcasting, firmly established the credibility of radio news and helped to overcome the United States' isolationist sensibilities.

Throughout his life, Kaltenborn was rarely far from the news. He was born on July 9, 1878, to German immigrant parents in Milwaukee, Wisconsin, and when he was old enough, he left his father's building material business to do odd jobs at a local newspaper. His press career began in earnest when, at age nineteen, he joined the Fourth Wisconsin Volunteers Infantry and covered the Spanish-American War (1898) for the *Merrill Advocate* newspaper. In 1902 he moved to New York to work for the *Brooklyn Daily Eagle*, and three years later he entered Harvard University in Massachusetts to attend its journalism program. Always restless, Kaltenborn spent his summers traveling in Europe and lecturing on conditions there when he returned home. It was in this latter capacity that Kaltenborn developed the oratorical skills that would serve him well when he switched to radio.

On April 4, 1922, while working as an *Brooklyn Daily Eagle* editor, Kaltenborn delivered the first current-events analysis in radio history while covering a coal strike for WVP, a government radio station on Bedloe's Island (later called Liberty Island) in New York Harbor. The same year, he broadcast a news summary live from the Statue of Liberty for WYCB, a sister station to WVP. Throughout the 1920s, Kaltenborn's on-air activities were confined largely to the New York area, with a weekly half-hour program of commentary for WEAF and the program *Kaltenborn's Digest* for WOR. In 1923 he became the first "network" newscaster when a Washington, D.C., station decided to link with WEAF and carry his broadcasts. By 1929 he was a national personality and could be heard on nineteen CBS stations.

In 1930 Kaltenborn resigned from the *Brooklyn Daily Eagle* and became a full-time broadcaster. His national radio exposure was given a major boost by his coverage of the 1932 presidential campaign and when his *Kaltenborn Edits the News* program moved to a Friday-evening spot in 1935.

Unlike many of his contemporaries, Kaltenborn understood his radio audience. While spoke rapidly, he was always lucid and rarely employed complex words or long sentences. He quickly overcame the blustering habits he had acquired as a platform speaker and adopted an informal and more conversational vocal style that appealed to listeners. Rather than use a script, he preferred to speak extemporaneously, often making gestures as if his vast audience could see him. His penchant for ad-libbing often brought him into conflict with sponsors and network executives, who expected to review his speech before airtime. In 1948 U.S. president Harry S. Truman delighted the nation when he imitated Kaltenborn's clipped style for the newsreel cameras.

BROADCASTS WAR

In the mid-1930s newscasts were not sponsored, and they attracted few listeners. Signs of conflict in Europe soon increased the American public's interest in radio news. Kaltenborn was quick to recognize this. In 1936 he brought the Spanish Civil War into millions of American living rooms with his live report of the Battle of Irun. With microphone in hand and concealed within a haystack, Kaltenborn gave listeners a complete blow-by-blow account as General Francisco Franco's forces endeavored to drive the Loyalists from the field. His eyewitness report was "punctuated by machine gun fire," and he even managed to remain on the air after exploding shells severed a main cable. With this broadcast (the first live report of a combat action), Kaltenborn gained the admiration of the entire broadcast community and earned a place for his *Headlines and Bylines* program in CBS's coveted Sunday lineup. Kaltenborn's other broadcast achievements in 1936 and 1937 include reports from the League of Nations and the London Economic Conference and interviews with Adolf Hitler and Benito Mussolini.

Kaltenborn achieved many notable on-air triumphs by 1938, and his coverage of the Czech Crisis in September of that year made him a household name. When Hitler's demands for the cessation of the Sudetenland threatened to plunge all of Europe into war, Kaltenborn spent eighteen days in CBS's Studio Nine keeping America informed of every phase of the crisis. Sleeping on a cot and subsisting on a diet of onion soup and coffee, Kaltenborn would rush to the microphone whenever a news flash or bulletin arrived, deliver the news to an anxious public, and immediately comment on it. Every time he performed this ritual, all broadcasts on the 115-station network were instantly interrupted. In addition to reading dispatches and providing commentary, Kaltenborn also acted as the first modern news anchor, coordinating the on-air reports of other network correspondents stationed at points throughout Europe. Fluent in German and French, Kaltenborn was able to provide simultaneous translations of the speeches of Hitler and French premier Édouard Daladier. By September 28, Kaltenborn had made

Hans von Kaltenborn. *Milton Berle, left, sits next to Hans von Kaltenborn as hosts of a cancer fundraiser in 1949.* YALE JOEL./ CONTRIBUTOR/TIME & LIFE PICTURES/GETTY IMAGES.

eighty-five separate broadcasts on the situation. This feat generated more than fifty thousand letters and telegrams of praise, as well as *Radio Daily*'s Most Popular Commentator award. His enormous renown earned him both a sponsor (Pure Oil) and a contract guaranteeing complete editorial freedom (quite unprecedented). The faith Kaltenborn's listeners developed in radio news as a result of his Czech Crisis broadcasts contributed to the widespread hysteria produced by actor Orson Welles's *War of the Worlds* broadcast on CBS. Kaltenborn's reputation for being the first and most reliable man on the air led to a woman's comment on the public panic: "How ridiculous! Anybody should have known it was not a real war. If it had been, the broadcaster would have been Hans."

In the summer of 1939, when Germany signed a nonaggression agreement with the Soviet Union and threatened the integrity of Poland, Kaltenborn mobilized for another crisis. As Europe moved closer to the brink of war, he spent three weeks on the continent interviewing key political and diplomatic figures. When he delivered the news of the outbreak of World War II in September, more than half of all radios in America were tuned to him.

ADVOCATES JOINING THE WAR

In 1940 Kaltenborn found himself immersed in controversy. The United States was officially neutral during the early years of World War II, and Kaltenborn was an outspoken interventionist. His broadcasts in favor of aiding Britain were bitterly criticized by the American First Committee. When this position brought him into conflict with CBS news director Paul White, Kaltenborn relocated to NBC.

In 1941 Kaltenborn's commentaries increasingly focused on the need for American vigilance and defense in the Pacific. He observed the gradual deterioration of U.S.-Japanese relations and warned of an aggressive move by the latter just weeks before Japan attacked Pearl Harbor. With America's entry into the war, Kaltenborn remained an active broadcaster. At age sixty-three, he carried a microphone to every major battlefront (from Guadalcanal to Rome) and interviewed soldiers and statesmen alike. In 1945 he fulfilled a personal mission when he covered the opening of the new United Nations in San Francisco. His wartime accomplishments were recognized with the 1945 DuPont Radio Award and nine other honors in 1946.

Kaltenborn remained at NBC after the war and continued regular news broadcasts until 1953. Thereafter he made several television appearances, but he never developed an affection for the visual medium. Kaltenborn's rich on-air life and his many broadcast achievements are chronicled in his autobiography, *Fifty Fabulous Years* (1950), and in a string of books containing his most well-known radio commentaries—*Kaltenborn Edits the News* (1935), *I Broadcast the Crisis* (1938), and *Kaltenborn Edits the War News* (1942). When he died in June 1965, much of the broadcast industry and many of his former associates attended his funeral in New York City.

Robert J. Brown

SEE ALSO: *Radio;* War of the Worlds*; Welles, Orson; World War II.*

BIBLIOGRAPHY

Brown, Robert J. *Manipulating the Ether: The Power of Broadcast Radio in Thirties America.* Jefferson City, NC: McFarland, 1998.

Fang, Irving E. *Those Radio Commentators!* Ames: Iowa State University Press, 1977.

Kaltenborn, Hans von. *I Broadcast the Crisis.* New York: Random House, 1938.

Kaltenborn, Hans von. *Fifty Fabulous Years.* New York: Putnam, 1950.

McCarthy, Meghan. *Aliens Are Coming! The True Account of the 1938 War of the Worlds Radio Broadcast.* New York: Knopf, 2006.

Kansas City Jazz

During the 1920s and 1930s, jazz flourished in Kansas City, Missouri, which was known as the "fourth capital of jazz" and "Paris of the Plains." It became a key part of a significant happening in American sociopolitical history, as well as evolved into an important musical style. The rapidly spreading popularity of jazz in the 1920s led to the rise of the "territory bands" that were located throughout the Midwest and Southwest. The bands would designate a specific city, often a small one, as home base, and hold dance dates throughout the surrounding territory. Jesse Stone, later the chief producer at Atlantic Records, and Walter Page were among the best known of the territory bandleaders. Other musicians who got their start in the territories included Earl Bostic and Buster Smith.

THE RISE OF KANSAS CITY JAZZ

Kansas City, known as "Tom's Town," became the most important of the territorial centers with the ascension of the political machine run by Tom Pendergast. His high tolerance for corruption led to a wide-open city during the Prohibition era, with Kansas City becoming a center for anyone looking for booze, gambling, prostitutes, or entertainment. As a result, many of the important territory bands, such as Page's (originally from Oklahoma City) made their way to Kansas City, where clubs were open twenty-four hours a day and the music never stopped. It was estimated that in the mid-1920s, in the area centered by Vine Street and bounded by 12th Street to the north and 18th Street to the south, there were at least fifty clubs featuring music at any given time.

The first major Kansas City bandleader was Kansas City native Bennie Moten, whose band included during its run, from 1922 until his death in 1935, such musicians as Walter Page, Hot Lips Page, Eddie Durham, Eddie Barefield, Count Basie, Ben Webster, Buster Smith, and Jimmy Rushing. Moten's band became a model for the Kansas City sound, which was based on ragtime and blues. Kansas City jazz typically featured a full, big-band sound, with simple arrangements that were based on riffs, or two- to four-bar musical phrases, rather than on fully developed melodies. This left a good deal of room for solo work, and some of the most important soloists in jazz developed within the Kansas City bands, including Coleman Hawkins (who left Kansas City early, in 1922); Webster; Herschel Evans; and, most importantly, Lester Young and Charlie Parker.

Other important Kansas City bands included Walter Page's Blue Devils and Andy Kirk's Twelve Clouds of Joy. Page, a bassist, pioneered the "walking" bass style that became the rhythmic underpinning of swing and bebop. The Blue Devils included

Jay McShann Kansas City Orchestra. *The Jay McShann Kansas City Orchestra included saxophonist Charlie Parker, third from left.* FRANK DRIGGS COLLECTION/CONTRIBUTOR/ARCHIVE PHOTOS/GETTY IMAGES.

Young, Smith, Hot Lips Page, Basie and Rushing. After his own group disbanded, Page played with Moten and Basie. Kirk's band, which included Don Byas, Howard McGhee, and Fats Navarro, was noted for the arrangements of piano player Mary Lou Williams. She was one of many significant piano stylists who flowered in Kansas City.

The two great piano influences on the Kansas City players were ragtime (ragtime composer Scott Joplin was a Missourian) and blues. Whereas blues was a prime ingredient in all Kansas City jazz, perhaps the foremost purveyors of Kansas City blues were pianist Pete Johnson and blues shouter Big Joe Turner. Turner was the bartender at the Sunset Club, where Johnson played piano, and he sang from behind the bar, with a powerful voice that needed no amplification. The owner of the Sunset Club and other clubs was Piney Brown, who would come to be the archetype of the Kansas City sound through Turner's "Piney Brown Blues" ("I dreamed last night / I was standin' on 12th Street and Vine / I shook hands with Piney Brown / And I could not keep from cryin'").

COUNT BASIE

The most important piano player and the most important band leader to emerge from Kansas City was William "Count" Basie. Basie, unlike most of the other territory musicians, was not a native midwesterner. Originally from New Jersey, he was stranded in Kansas City when a touring group he was with broke up. He then played for a while as an accompanist in silent movie theaters until he joined the Blue Devils in 1928 and Moten's Kansas City Orchestra in 1929. When Moten's group disbanded in 1932, its core musicians, including Walter Page and drummer Jo Jones, became the core of the Count Basie Orchestra, which also featured Evans, Young, Harry Edison, Dicky Wells, Buck Clayton, and vocalists Rushing and Helen Humes. Turner and Johnson were important in bringing the Kansas City sound to wider recognition when they were included in John Hammond's famous 1938 Spirituals to Swing Concert at Carnegie Hall. But it was primarily Basie who brought Kansas City jazz to nationwide popularity and ultimately international fame through radio broadcasts, touring, and recording.

Although the Kansas City club scene was affected by the Great Depression, it endured through the 1930s. The indictment of Boss Pendergast for income tax evasion in 1939 marked its conclusion. Before its popularity dwindled, however, it produced a mighty harbinger of the future, pianist Jay McShann, who came to Kansas City in 1936, formed a sextet in 1937, and put together his first big band in 1939. McShann's band was solidly blues- and riff-oriented, but it was also known as a breeding ground for new musical ideas. Parker joined McShann's band in 1940. His twelve-bar solo on the band's 1941 recording of "Sepia Bounce" contributed to the bebop revolution of the 1940s.

In the twenty-first century, major renovations have taken place in the area around 18th and Vine, and jazz is again playing an important role in the nightlife of Kansas City. On any night of the week, restaurants, night clubs, and jam sessions cater to visitors who frequent the historic area. The Mutual Musicians Foundation building, which was frequently visited by members Basie and Parker, now hosts lively Saturday night jam sessions. During the day, the history of Kansas City jazz can be relived by visiting the American Jazz Museum or the Horace M. Peterson III Visitor Center. A 17-foot bronze memorial to Parker can be seen at 17th and Vine.

Tad Richards

SEE ALSO: *Atlantic Records; Basie, Count; Blues; The Great Depression; Hawkins, Coleman; Jazz; Joplin, Scott; Parker, Charlie; Prohibition.*

BIBLIOGRAPHY

Abbate, Vincent. "Kansas City, Here I Come." *American History* 37, no. 4 (2002).

Driggs, Frank, and Chuck Haddix. *Kansas City Jazz: From Ragtime to Bebop: A History.* New York: Oxford University Press, 2005.

Pearson, Nathan W., Jr. *Goin' to Kansas City.* Urbana: University of Illinois Press, 1987.

Russell, Ross. *Jazz Style in Kansas City and the Southwest.* New York: Da Capo Press, 1977.

Kantor, MacKinlay *(1904–1977)*

In a literary career spanning nearly fifty years, MacKinlay Kantor grew from a pulp fiction writer who simply sought to earn a living to a highly respected novelist who made significant contributions in several genres. While he is perhaps best known for his 1956 Pulitzer Prize–winning novel *Andersonville,* Kantor also wrote influential works in the areas of detective fiction, Westerns, and social commentary.

An Iowa native, Kantor began his writing career in the early 1920s, working as a reporter and columnist for an increasingly large series of newspapers in his home state and writing pulp fiction for various inexpensive publications. After several years he moved to Chicago, where he sought a larger canvas for his writing. Although he struggled initially, his first book, *Diversey,* which dealt with gang warfare in Chicago, was published in 1928, after which Kantor published a long string of books, articles, and short stories. He served as a war correspondent during World War II from 1943 to 1944 and as a combat pilot for the U.S. Air Force in 1945. The latter experience provided the basis for his writing success that brought him national exposure.

While Kantor had published a number of works prior to the outbreak of World War II, his 1945 novella *Glory for Me,* based on his experiences as an air force gunner, was adapted for the big screen in 1946. The result was the film *The Best Years of Our Lives,* directed by William Wyler, which traces the experiences of three World War II veterans and the difficulty they have adjusting after returning home. The film won several Academy Awards, including an unprecedented double award to veteran Harold Russell, who portrayed a sailor who lost both his hands in the war, for best supporting actor and for bringing hope to returning veterans. Kantor's story also served as the basis for the television movie *Returning Home,* made in 1975.

The publication of the historical novel *Andersonville* a decade later brought Kantor even greater recognition. He had long been fascinated with the Civil War, and the book was the result of the author's renowned diligent and thorough research. *Andersonville* recounts the suffering of Union prisoners in a Confederate prison camp in Georgia. Prominent Civil War scholars such as Bruce Catton and Henry Steele Commager praised Kantor's book as the greatest Civil War novel ever written. The book spawned several made-for-television films, including *The Andersonville Trial* (1970), which portrays the war crime trials of the camp's commanders, including the head official, Henry Wirz, who was the only Civil War soldier executed for war crimes. The book was later adapted into a television miniseries (*Andersonville*) in 1996. Kantor's final novel, *Valley Forge,* published in 1975, was another fictional work based on historical events. It portrays the difficult experiences of the Continental army during the American Revolution.

Although best known for his historical fiction, Kantor drew fans for his works of suspense fiction, which mostly dealt with criminal justice procedure in their plots. Throughout the 1930s he produced a large number of pulp fiction suspense stories,

MacKinlay Kantor. *MacKinlay Kantor won the Pulitzer Prize in 1956 for* Andersonville. © **CORBIS.**

including a series dealing with the exploits of Nick and Dave Glennan, Irish American brothers who are police officers. Kantor frequently rode along with police patrols, partly for research for his stories and partly because he had developed friendships with a number of police officers.

Kantor credited his early experience in writing pulp fiction for his later success:

> I used to write a great deal of stuff for the pulp detective-and-crime story magazines, in the years when I had to make my living that way, and I don't think that my rather complicated talents were harmed in the least. The severe routine of such endeavor stimulated my sense of plot and construction, which needed such stimulation very badly indeed.

Among the awards Kantor won during his career are the O. Henry Award for his short story "Silent Grow the Guns," as well as the Presidential Medal of Freedom for his body of work. He also received honorary doctorates in literature from Grinnell College, Drake University, Lincoln College, and Ripon College. In addition to his work as a war correspondent in World War II, Kantor served as a war correspondent during the Korean War in 1950 and worked as a consultant for the U.S. Air Force for several years. He died of a heart attack on October 11, 1977, in Sarasota, Florida. He and Florence, his wife of more than fifty years, had two children.

Jason George

SEE ALSO: *Academy Awards;* The Best Years of Our Lives*; Best Sellers; Detective Fiction; Gangs; Pulp Magazines; World War II.*

BIBLIOGRAPHY

Eckley, Wilton. "MacKinlay Kantor." In *Dictionary of Literary Biography*, vol. 9. *American Novelists, 1910–1945*, ed. James J. Martine. Detroit, MI: Gale Research, 1981.

Kantor, Tim. *My Father's Voice: MacKinlay Kantor Long Remembered.* New York: McGraw Hill, 1988.

"MacKinlay Kantor." *Contemporary Authors.* Detroit, MI: Gale Literary Databases, 1999.

Zaidman, Laura. "MacKinlay Kantor." In *Dictionary of Literary Biography*, vol. 102: *American Short-Story Writers, 1910–1945*, 2nd series, ed. Bobby Ellen Kimbel. Detroit, MI: Gale Research, 1991.

Karan, Donna *(1948–)*

At the age of twenty-six and a week after giving birth, Donna Karan was catapulted into the national spotlight when she was named chief designer of the Anne Klein women's clothing line upon Klein's death in 1974. Like Klein, Karan projected her personality and lifestyle onto her clothes, creating active, versatile sportswear. She often layered bodysuits with easy, loose wraps. By the 1980s Karan had made blazers a basic for Anne Klein.

In 1984 backers of the company set Karan up in her own business, DKNY, which became one of the first publicly traded fashion houses in 1996. Her designs are idiosyncratic and personal. She designs for herself, certainly for a buxom physical type, and for the New York sensibility identified in her label. Her attire has been worn by celebrities, including Barbra Streisand, which has contributed to making Karan a star of the fashion world. In 2001 Donna Karan International and the brand name DKNY were acquired by LVMH (Moët Hennessy-Louis Vuitton), and since 2002 Karan has had much less direct involvement with the design of the product line. In subsequent years she has suffered attacks over the use of fur in her designs, and in spite of her promise to stop, PETA continues to accuse the brand of using rabbit fur. Through these events the line remains popular and successful.

Richard Martin

SEE ALSO: *Streisand, Barbra.*

BIBLIOGRAPHY

Karan, Donna, and Ingrid Sischy. *The Journey of a Woman: 20 Years of Donna Karan.* New York: Assouline, 2004.

Sischy, Ingrid. *Donna Karan.* New York: Universe/Vendome, 1998.

Kardashian, Kim *(1980–)*

A favorite topic of the American tabloid media, Kim Kardashian is a reality TV star who exemplifies the twenty-first-century culture of celebrity. Not known for any creative talent, such as singing or acting, she is often called a *celebutante*, a term that emerged in the 1930s to describe a debutante cum celebrity. Like Los Angeles socialites Paris Hilton and Nicole Richie, who are famous mostly for being rich, leading a party lifestyle, and appearing on reality television, Kardashian, along with sisters Kourtney and Khloé, launched their reality TV show *Keeping up with the Kardashians* in 2007. Kardashian has used her television persona to become a successful businessperson.

Kardashian became prominent in 2007, when a homemade sex video with singer Ray J was leaked online. Because she was still married to her first husband, music producer Damon Thomas, when she made the video in 2003, the indiscretion caused an enormous amount of publicity, most of it negative. When the video was released, Kardashian brought a lawsuit against the company that published it and eventually won an estimated $5 million settlement.

She used the opportunity to launch her career as a reality television star on the E! network. *Keeping up with the Kardashians* initially depicted a family on the fringes of celebrity society. Kardashian's stepfather, Bruce Jenner, had been an Olympic decathlon champion, and her biological father, Robert Kardashian, was one of former football player O. J. Simpson's defense lawyers in the trial of the twentieth century. In particular, the show focused on the lives of Kardashian and sister Kourtney as they navigated the privileged side of Los Angeles, going to parties, participating in mundane family drama, and chasing celebrity. Famously, the show documented Kardashian's nude photo shoot for *Playboy* magazine.

The series became extremely successful and generated a number of spin-offs, including *Kourtney and Kim Take New York* (2011–). Even Kardashian's brief marriage to professional basketball player Kris Humphries was turned into a reality television spectacle: the 2011 wedding reportedly garnered the couple nearly $18 million, though they divorced three months later. As a result, Kardashian has become one of the best-paid reality TV stars and a constant subject of the celebrity news cycle.

Kardashian seems to welcome the attention, encouraging fans to follow her life through Facebook, Twitter, and her personal website. She has even appeared on scripted television programs, including *90210* (2008–) and *CSI: NY* (2004–), and in the 2008 film *Disaster Movie.* An active businesswoman, she is heavily involved in the branding of products ranging from perfumes to weight-loss formulas. She is also an advocate for the Kiss Away Poverty campaign that funds female entrepreneurs. She has even tried her hand as an author, publishing *Kardashian Konfidential* (2010) with Khloé and Kourtney as a nonfiction account of their eventful lives.

Isabel Istanders

SEE ALSO: *Cable TV; Celebrity;* Dancing with the Stars*; Debutantes; Divorce; Facebook; Hilton, Paris; Media Feeding Frenzies;* Playboy*; Reality Television; Sex Scandals; Simpson, O. J.; Simpson Trial; Tabloids; Twitter.*

BIBLIOGRAPHY

Keveney, Bill. "MTV's *Real World* Launched a Revolution." *USA Today*, December 21, 2007, 1–4.

Kardashian, Kim; Kourtney Kardashian; and Khloé Kardashian. *Kardashian Konfidential.* New York: St. Martin's, 2011.

Kaufman, Gil. "Kim Kardashian Is Highest-Paid Reality TV Star of 2010." *MTV News*. Accessed May 2012. Available from http://www.mtv.com/news/articles/1653687/kim-kardashian-highest-paid-reality-tv-starof-2010.jhtml

Karloff, Boris *(1887–1969)*

One of the most famous horror movie stars of all time, Boris Karloff has become virtually synonymous with Frankenstein. As depicted by Karloff in 1931, Frankenstein was a sympathetic figure, a gentle monster—an image that has remained in the popular psyche for more than seventy-five years. Although he acted in more than 150 films, Karloff will always be associated with his monster.

Karloff was born William Henry Pratt on November 23, 1887, in a London suburb. The youngest of nine children, he never knew his father, a British civil servant who died in India when William was a baby. After the death of his mother a few years later, William was raised by his siblings, one of whom enjoyed a brief career as an actor on the London stage. From boyhood, he was drawn to the theater and attempted to emulate his older brother by appearing in school theatricals. The rest of his family, however, wished him to follow in the footsteps of his father, so William prepared for a career in the civil service.

He graduated from Kings College, London, with the intention of applying to serve in the consulate in Hong Kong. His passion for acting had not waned, however, and he attended the theater every chance he could get. At twenty-two he finally decided to pursue his theatrical ambitions; however, to escape family disapproval, he left England for Canada. William traveled across the country for more than a year, taking odd jobs, before arriving in Vancouver, where he tried to break into the local repertory company. After months of rejections, he spotted an advertisement for an experienced character actor in a company in Kamloops, British Columbia. Deciding to change his name to fit the "role," he remembered an obscure relative on his mother's side of the family named Karloff. Feeling that William also was not quite right, he settled on Boris, and he got the job.

For almost ten years Karloff honed his craft in repertory companies throughout Canada. In 1917 he arrived in Los Angeles, where the fledgling movie industry was booming. After a slow start, the tall, striking actor began to win extra roles and small speaking parts in silent pictures. Because of his strong, dark features, Karloff was usually cast as a villain, appearing in more than forty silent pictures. When Hollywood switched to sound, the actor's theatrical training proved an asset, and he found his niche.

In 1930 Universal Pictures gambled on a film based on Bram Stoker's *Dracula.* Starring Bela Lugosi in the title role, the film was a huge success. Universal decided to capitalize on the public's newfound taste for horror movies with *Frankenstein,* also starring Lugosi. However, the actor did not like the role and wanted to drop out. When the studio informed him that he would be released from his contract only if he could find another actor for the part, Lugosi suggested Karloff.

Directed by James Whale, *Frankenstein* became an immediate classic. Karloff, whose strong features, athletic build, and considerable height were perfect for the role, gave a subtle and sympathetic performance that won over critics and touched the hearts of audiences. Universal immediately cast the versatile ac-

Boris Karloff. *Boris Karloff stars as Byron Orlok in the 1968 thriller* Targets. SILVER SCREEN COLLECTION/CONTRIBUTOR/ MOVIEPIX/GETTY IMAGES.

tor in two more leading roles, in *The Mask of Fu Manchu* (1932) and *The Mummy* (1932). The two films cemented his popularity, and in 1932 the forty-five-year-old Karloff became a star.

Throughout the 1930s Karloff starred in a string of popular horror pictures for Universal, including *The Black Cat* (1934), *Bride of Frankenstein* (1935), *The Raven* (1935), and *Son of Frankenstein* (1939), playing mad scientists and tormented monsters. He was also regularly cast as Asian characters and starred in a series of "Mr. Wong" detective movies. By the early 1940s, however, with the world at war and the United States on the brink of joining in, public interest in horror movies had waned, and Karloff's livelihood was threatened. The veteran actor nevertheless trooped on. In 1941 he starred in the Broadway production of *Arsenic and Old Lace*, and throughout the decade Karloff found work in a wide variety of films, from the occasional horror picture to comedies such as *The Secret Life of Walter Mitty* (1947).

Unlike many Hollywood stars, Karloff never fought his typecasting. He understood that he owed his fame to Frankenstein and thus was good-humored about spoofing his horror image in such films as *Abbot and Costello Meet the Killer, Boris Karloff* (1949). By the early 1960s, with horror movies once again in vogue, the aging actor found himself a cult hero and very much in demand. He appeared with his fellow horror stars Basil Rathbone, Peter Lorre, and Vincent Price in two popular films for American International Pictures, *The Raven* (1963) and *The Terror* (1963). Karloff brought his creepy voice to the role of the Grinch in the television version of Dr. Seuss's children's Christmas tale *How the Grinch Stole Christmas!* (1966). In 1968 the eighty-one-year-old Karloff gave an extraordinary turn as an aging horror-movie star in Peter Bogdanovich's first film, *Targets.*

Karloff loved his profession, and he never stopped acting in movies. Famous for playing monsters, his real-life gentle spirit and gracious demeanor shone through on-screen, no matter how scary the role. He embraced his cult status, becoming in the process one of popular culture's most beloved figures, the man behind the gentle monster.

Victoria Price

SEE ALSO: *Abbott and Costello; Frankenstein; Horror Movies; Lorre, Peter; Lugosi, Bela; The Mummy; Price, Vincent; Silent Movies.*

BIBLIOGRAPHY

Bojarski, Richard, and Kenneth Beale. *The Films of Boris Karloff.* Secaucus, NJ: Citadel Press, 1974.

Jensen, Paul M. *Boris Karloff and His Films.* New York: A. S. Barnes, 1974.

Mank, Gregory William. *Bela Lugosi and Boris Karloff.* Jefferson, NC: McFarland, 2009.

Underwood, Peter. *Karloff: The Life of Boris Karloff.* New York: Drake Publishers, 1972.

Kasem, Casey *(1932–)*

One of the most identifiable voices in radio and television, Casey Kasem is known throughout the world as the original personality behind radio's most successful countdown program, *American Top 40.* Born Kemel Amin Kasem in Detroit, Michigan, in 1932, Kasem dreamed of becoming a baseball player until his broadcasting career began at WJLB Detroit in 1954. While he appeared in several motion pictures, numerous commercials, and television cartoon series (most notably as the voice of Shaggy on the popular *Scooby Doo* series), Kasem did not become a household name until the debut of *American Top 40* on July 4, 1970. He is considered to be the standard-bearer in modern countdown programs, having revolutionized the format with his unique style and warm personality.

Kasem's trademark "teaser-bio" format, which he first employed at an Oakland, California, radio station, became the hallmark of *American Top 40* and influenced countless disc jockeys and similarly themed radio programs. His teaser-bio technique allowed him to essentially "tease" the audience by discussing a recording artist's previous chart singles, biographical information, or any other relevant information before playing the actual song.

In addition, Kasem allowed listeners to send in personal letters with musical requests. These "long-distance dedications" were then read on the air beginning with two words known throughout the world by radio listeners: "Dear Casey." Arguably the most popular and recognized segment of the program, these long-distance dedications became as ingrained in popular culture as the songs ranked on the program.

Kasem's innovative formatting in radio programming would certainly be a sufficient legacy for most on-air personalities, but his most notable and identifiable characteristic is unquestionably his unique vocal delivery. With his warm voice and reliance on active words and phrases (such as "pole-vaulting," "leapfrogging," and "tumbling"), Kasem brought a friendly, sportsmanlike atmosphere to the competitive arena of record sales and airplay statistics that has won millions of fans.

The success of Kasem's *American Top 40* on FM stations around the world resulted in several television series based around the show's format. With the fragmentation of radio formats beginning in the early 1990s, Kasem kept pace with changing musical tastes and trends. In addition to *American Top 40,* he has hosted a variety of countdown programs such as *Casey's Hot 20* (for the adult contemporary market), all using the teaser-bio format. He also piloted an award-winning CD series, *Casey Kasem Presents American's Top 10.*

Kasem gave his last *American Top 40* countdown on January 4, 2004, but continues to make special appearances on awards shows. He remained the voice of Shaggy in the *Scooby Doo* series until 2010, when he was replaced by Matthew Lillard; at that time, Kasem became the voice of Shaggy's father, Colton Rodgers. In his private life, he works as an advocate with the Arab-American Institute, which published his brochure *Arab-Americans: Making a Difference.*

Proof of Kasem's remarkable impact on radio and television is evident not only in his staying power but also in the numerous honors and awards he has amassed. His legendary status was cemented with a star on the Hollywood Walk of Fame; with the *Billboard* Lifetime Achievement Award; and with his induction into several halls of fame, including the National Association of Broadcasters Hall of Fame Radio Division in 1985, the National Radio Hall of Fame in 1992, and the Broadcasting & Cable Hall of Fame in 1998.

Michael K. Chapman

SEE ALSO: *Disc Jockeys; Hollywood; Pop Music; Radio; Saturday Morning Cartoons; Television; Top 40.*

BIBLIOGRAPHY

Durkee, Rob. *"American Top 40": The Countdown of the Century.* New York: Schrimer Books, 1999.

Fong-Torres, Ben. *The Hits Just Keep on Coming: The History of Top 40 Radio.* San Francisco: Miller Freeman Books, 1998.

MacFarland, David T. *The Development of the Top 40 Radio Format.* New York: Arno Press, 1973.

Kate Plus 8

SEE: *Jon & Kate Plus 8.*

Katrina

SEE: *Hurricane Katrina.*

The Katzenjammer Kids

The mischievous brothers Hans and Fritz Katzenjammer were invented by German-born cartoonist Rudolph Dirks in 1897. Along with the Yellow Kid, Happy Hooligan, and Little Nemo, they became pioneering stars of the American newspaper comics that burgeoned in the early 1900s. The Kids—along with their Mama, the Captain, and the Inspector—are also among the very few comics characters ever to have two separate and independent pages devoted to their activities.

The Kids—Fritz was the blond one and Hans the dark-haired brother in the original cartoons—made their debut in William Randolph Hearst's *New York Journal* on Sunday, December 12, 1897. Dirks was twenty when he was asked by his editor to come up with a feature in the vein of the fiendish youths Max and Moritz, created some three decades earlier in Germany by Wilhelm Busch. Much more than imitations, the Brothers Katzenjammer developed distinct personalities of their own. They are brilliant strategists, impressive orators, clever conversationalists, and experts at creating explosions, setting traps, and persuading assorted animals (especially elephants and wildcats) to participate in their schemes. They are dedicated to attacking conformity, pomposity, adult authority, and the traditional values held by society. Combining the best qualities of con men, burglars, guerrilla warriors, and jesters, they elevate prankery to a fine art. The lads, along with the other central characters, speak in a sort of vaudevillian Dutch dialect that is rich with such words as "dollink," "dumbkopf" and "dodgasted."

Dirks broke with Hearst in 1913 and, after protracted legal battles, took his characters to Joseph Pulitzer's rival *New York World* in 1914. The final court decision, however, basically affirmed that both Hearst and Dirks had the rights to the characters. In Hearst papers across the country *The Katzenjammer Kids* again appeared, while in those newspapers using *World* features, the page was eventually called *The Captain and the Kids.* The new artist employed by Hearst to draw its strip was Harold H. Knerr, a talented cartoonist from Philadelphia who had inked a *Katzenjammer* imitation titled *The Fineheimer Twins* for several years. Although he never explained why, Knerr switched the names of the boys, making Hans the fair-haired one and Fritz the darker one.

Both versions began setting the Katzenjammer Kids and the other characters in less urban, more exotic locales. The boys and their Mama—along with their star boarders, the Captain and the Inspector—began taking trips all over the world. By the mid-1920s, Dirks had his crew residing on a tropical island that was ruled over by black royalty. Although the Knerr and Dirks versions were supposed to be completely independent of one another, Knerr soon had his crew settling down on one of the Squee-Jee Islands. Knerr's island had similar rulers, but he added some new characters, such as a spinster school teacher named Miss Twiddle and her two pupils, little blond Lena and the curly-haired and hypocritical Rollo Rhubarb, who equaled the Kids in slyness and plotting. By adding Lena to the mix, Knerr was able to expand the range of Hans and Fritz's activities—for example, both boys suffered through spells of courting Lena.

By the late 1930s, both versions were being reprinted in competing comic books. For several years that decade, the United Feature Syndicate, which had taken over the feature when the *World* folded, offered a daily *The Captain and the Kids* strip. Wacky in the Marx Brothers mode, this mock adventure strip was written and drawn by Bernard Dibble, a former Dirks assistant and ghost artist. Dirks continued to sign his page, but in the mid-1940s, he turned the drawing over to his son John. The senior Dirks died in 1968, and United stopped its version in 1979. Knerr died in 1949, though the Katzenjammers have continued under such artists as Doc Winner, Joe Musial, and Hy Eisman.

Ron Goulart

SEE ALSO: *Comics; Hearst, William Randolph; The Yellow Kid.*

BIBLIOGRAPHY

Goulart, Ron, ed. *The Encyclopedia of American Comics.* New York: Facts on File, 1990.

Marschall, Richard. *America's Great Comic Strip Artists.* New York: Abbeville Press, 1989.

Roberts, Garyn G. *Dick Tracy and American Culture.* Jefferson, NC: McFarland & Company, 2003.

Kaufman, Andy *(1949–1984)*

Andy Kaufman burst onto the national scene as a guest on the very first episode of *Saturday Night Live* in October 1975. Standing in the middle of a bare stage accompanied by an old record player, Kaufman put on a recording of the *Mighty Mouse* theme song. He stood silent until the chorus, when he broadly lip-synched "Here I come to save the day!" He then went mute until the chorus arrived again. This type of perplexing yet hysterical performance became Kaufman's trademark and is his legacy as an original comic force. Despite his untimely death at the age of 35 from lung cancer, Kaufman's impact on popular culture was dramatic.

Kaufman was a comedian who never told a joke; instead he broke the mold by creating a new comic style that was as much

Andy Kaufman. *Andy Kaufman performs his stand-up act in 1978.* PAUL NATKIN/CONTRIBUTOR/WIRE IMAGES/GETTY IMAGES.

performance art as traditional stand-up. Although Kaufman began his career working clubs such as the Improv, he never considered himself a comedian. Steve Allen, in his book *Funny People*, says, "A comedian, quite simply, wants laughs. Andy demands more. He calls for an emotional involvement that runs a fuller gamut. He wants you to feel uncomfortable, uneasy, unhappy, ecstatic, deeply moved, derisive, bored. He wants you to believe his characters are who they claim to be and react accordingly."

Throughout his career, Kaufman challenged his audience. On another *Saturday Night Live* appearance, Kaufman's "joke" was simply to read from *The Great Gatsby*. He could delight an audience with stunts such as taking his Carnegie Hall audience out for milk and cookies and infuriate another audience by bringing a sleeping bag on stage and napping as part of his performance.

Kaufman used a *Saturday Night Live* appearance for another stunt that blurred the line between reality and illusion. After Kaufman was cut from an episode in 1982, he publicly feuded with producer Dick Ebersol. The feud climaxed when a telephone poll was held to determine whether Kaufman should be allowed back on the show. He lost and never appeared on the program again. A similar feud had been displayed on *Saturday Night Live*'s competitor *Fridays* just a year earlier. During a live show in February 1981, Kaufman got into an argument and physical altercation with members of the cast and crew. Again, this hoax perpetuated by Kaufman and the show's producers was perceived as real by many viewers.

The apex of this part of his career was Kaufman's involvement in professional wrestling. A lifelong wrestling fan, particularly of villain wrestler "Nature Boy" Buddy Rogers, Kaufman declared himself the "inter-gender wrestling champion" and began challenging women in his concert audiences to wrestle. His match with *Playboy* model Susan Smith was featured in the magazine's February 1982 issue.

After a match against a woman in Memphis, Kaufman became involved in a pro wrestling feud with local champion Jerry "The King" Lawler, which included Kaufman sending videos mocking the Memphis fans. Kaufman was "injured" by Lawler during a match, and the two appeared for an interview on *Late Night with David Letterman* in July 1982, supposedly to offer apologies. Things got heated and Lawler slapped Kaufman hard across the face, knocking him down. Kaufman responded with an obscenity-laced tirade. All of this was treated as front-page news, as real. It was, like other moments in Kaufman's hoax history and in professional wrestling, merely an elaborate ruse.

Kaufman played the bad guy in the feud with Lawler and delighted in people jeering him. He invented a heel entertainer character called Tony Clifton, the world's most obnoxious performer, who would taunt his audience. Kaufman claimed he was not Clifton, which was somewhat true because his writing partner Bob Zmuda often played Clifton. Kaufman went to great lengths to create the illusion that Clifton was real.

Kaufman's performance as Latka Gravas on the critically acclaimed television series *Taxi* (1978–1983) was his biggest mainstream success. Latka was based on one of Kaufman's most popular characters, "the foreign man," a twitchy immigrant who spoke in a combination of broken English and gibberish. Kaufman's best-known bit was the foreign man telling old jokes, doing horrible impressions, and then launching into a brilliant impersonation of Elvis Presley.

While successful on TV and in concert, Kaufman made only a few movies. *Heartbeeps* (1981) was a critical and commercial dud. Better received were his two wrestling movies: *I'm from Hollywood* (1988), which chronicles the feud with Lawler, and his send-up of the art house hit *My Dinner with Andre* called *My Breakfast with Blassie* (1983), in which Kaufman converses with retired pro wrestler Fred Blassie at a coffee shop.

Most of Kaufman's best moments were captured in NBC's *A Comedy Salute to Andy Kaufman* (1995). Another tribute to Kaufman was the 1992 hit song "Man on the Moon" by R.E.M. The song asks "Andy, are you goofing on Elvis?" *Man on the Moon* was also the title for a 1999 film about Kaufman's life starring Jim Carrey. As with Elvis, there is a persistent rumor that Kaufman is still alive. With his penchant for hoaxes, it was a rumor that spread widely, and faking his own death indeed was something Kaufman had considered. Kaufman was brilliant at defying reality as an entertainer and highlighting irony as a comedian. He was, according to Ron Rosenbaum in a 1998 *Esquire* article about Kaufman, "going where few comedians had dared go before . . . he made comedy dangerous again."

Patrick Jones

SEE ALSO: *Allen, Steve; Carnegie Hall; Letterman, David;* Playboy; *Presley, Elvis; R.E.M.;* Saturday Night Live; *Stand-Up Comedy;* Taxi.

BIBLIOGRAPHY

Allen, Steve. *Funny People.* New York: Stein & Day, 1981.

Boosler, Elayne. "Andy." *Esquire,* November 1984, 70–72.

Hill, Doug, and Jeff Weingard. *Saturday Night: A Backstage History of Saturday Night Live.* New York: Beech Tree Books, 1986.

Keller, Florian. *Andy Kaufman: Wrestling with the American Dream.* Minneapolis: University of Minnesota Press, 2005.

Rosenbaum, Ron. "The Return of Andy Kaufman." *Esquire,* March 1998, 58.

Kaye, Danny *(1913–1987)*

Specializing in tongue-twisting patter songs, Danny Kaye was a consummate entertainer and comic. He is remembered for a string of comedies he made for Hollywood executive Samuel Goldwyn in the 1940s, as well as his persistent and honorable efforts for charities, especially the United Nations International Children's Emergency Fund (UNICEF).

Born David Daniel Kaminsky in Brooklyn, New York, in 1913, he had a mixed entertainment career prior to catching on in films. He was a vaudevillian, a dancer, a singer, and a comedian, though he didn't initially achieve success in any of these disciplines. His first movies were two-reel comedies—such as *Getting an Eyeful* (1938), *Cupid Takes a Holiday* (1938), and *Dime a Dance* (1937)—that were moderately amusing but failed commercially.

Danny Kaye. *Danny Kaye gained success in the 1940s after bringing his singing, dancing, and comic talents to the big screen.* BARON/GETTY IMAGES.

ENTER SYLVIA FINE

Kaye made his Broadway debut in 1939, and his fortunes turned when he met and married his talented lyricist, Sylvia Fine, who provided him with most of his best material. His number "Tschaikowsky" from the musical *Lady in the Dark,* in which he named fifty-four Russian composers in thirty-nine seconds, proved to be a show-stopper.

Goldwyn saw Kaye do a comedy routine in a nightclub and resolved to turn him into a star. Though he was not able to convince Kaye to get a nose job, Goldwyn did persuade him to lighten his hair in order to brighten his features. Goldwyn put Kaye under contract and gave him a starring role in a mediocre wartime musical, *Up in Arms* (1944). "The Lobby Number," a song about waiting in line at the movies and then waiting through an endless parade of meaningless credits, is one of the film's few bright spots.

Wonder Man (1945) is much better, with Kaye in a dual role as twin brothers, one of whom is murdered for fingering a mob boss. The ghost of the murdered brother then inhabits the body of his milquetoast twin. The film's highlight comes when, in trying to evade some killers and alert the police, Kaye assumes the identity of an opera singer and improvises his part.

However, Kaye soon came to feel that he was being treated as a specialty act rather than as an actor. Goldwyn placed him in lackluster remakes such as *The Kid from Brooklyn* (a 1946 rehash of Harold Lloyd's *The Milky Way*), *A Song Is Born* (an off-the-mark 1948 adaptation of James Thurber's *The Secret Life of Walter Mitty*), and *Hans Christian Anderson* (a well-intentioned but failed 1952 musical bio). During this period, Kaye limited himself to one film per year, devoting the rest of his time to performing on radio, on records ("Civilization" with the Andrews Sisters was a highlight), and on the stage.

TAKING CONTROL

Twentieth Century Fox's *On the Riviera* (1951) was yet another dual role for Kaye, as well as a remake of both *Folies-Bergère* and *That Night in Rio.* For Warner Brothers, Kaye appeared in *The Inspector General* (1949), based on the Gogol story. He was determined to take control of his film career, and he and his wife formed their own production company, Dena, named after their daughter. They hired the writing-directing-producing team of Norman Panama and Melvin Frank, who conjured Kaye's two finest films—*Knock on Wood* (1954) and *The Court Jester* (1956)—and fashioned characters for him about whom audiences could really care.

In *Knock on Wood,* Kaye plays a ventriloquist who finds himself caught up in international espionage and, at the climax, eludes his pursuers at a ballet. *The Court Jester* is an even better movie. At a cost of $4 million, it was the most expensive screen comedy ever made to that point. Kaye plays a member of the underground protecting the rightful king of England, an infant who bears the birthmark of the purple pimpernel on his bottom. Unforgettable moments in the film include Sylvia Fine's version of "The Jester's Lament," the witch's warning ("The pellet with the poison's in the vessel with the pestle; the chalice from the palace is the brew that is true!"), and a send-up of swashbuckling scenes.

In between *Knock on Wood* and *The Court Jester*, Kaye appeared in Paramount's *White Christmas* (1954) as Bing Crosby's buddy; together, they seek to boost the popularity of Dean Jagger's winter resort. Despite the film's mediocrity, it proved to be Kaye's biggest hit. Kaye received a special Oscar in 1954 "for his unique talents, his service to the Academy, the motion picture industry, and the American people."

Kaye tried another musical biography in Mel Shavelson's *The Five Pennies* (1959), in which he plays bandleader Red Nichols. However, with Kaye routines written into the story line, it seems as if Red Nichols is impersonating Danny Kaye and not vice versa. The film's one true highlight is Kaye's dynamic duet with Louis Armstrong. Kaye returned to form in *On the Double* (1961), in which he yet again is in a dual role, this time as an American GI asked to impersonate a British military martinet. At the climax, Kaye also impersonates Adolf Hitler and a Dietrich-like chanteuse named Fräulein Lily. A try at slapstick comedy in Frank Tashlin's *The Man From the Diner's Club* (1963) failed to serve Kaye's talents well.

FROM THE BIG SCREEN TO THE SMALL SCREEN

Television beckoned, and Kaye dropped his film career for a variety program, *The Danny Kaye Show*, which ran from 1963 to 1967. He returned to film in 1969 to play the philosophical Ragpicker in *The Madwoman of Chaillot*, and while the "trial" scene—in which Kaye "defends" the knaves of the world—is outstanding, the rest of this adaptation of Jean Giradoux's play is decidedly lackluster. Kaye also tried his hand at conducting during this period. Despite his lack of formal training, he was given comic gigs as a guest conductor with various city orchestras. In 1970 he returned to Broadway to play Noah in the Richard Rodgers musical *Two by Two*.

The last of Kaye's great work was done on television, starting in 1976 when he played Geppetto in *Pinocchio* and Captain Hook in *Peter Pan*. In *Skokie* in 1981, he portrayed a concentration camp survivor who protests street demonstrations by Neo-Nazis. And in Harlan Ellison's "Paladin of the Lost Hour" for the revived *Twilight Zone* series in 1985, he appeared as a mysterious old man who possesses a watch holding Earth's last hour.

Kaye leaves behind a legacy of entertaining performances on Decca Records, several show-stopping comedy routines and songs in various films (in which he usually played shy but lovable schnooks who win the girl at the end), an increased awareness of the aims of UNICEF, and some memorable performances on television.

Dennis Fischer

SEE ALSO: *Broadway; Crosby, Bing; Goldwyn, Samuel; Vaudeville.*

BIBLIOGRAPHY

Adir, Karin. *The Great Clowns of American Television*. Jefferson, NC: McFarland, 1988.

Freeland, Michael. *The Secret Life of Danny Kaye*. New York: St. Martin's Press, 1985.

Gottfried, Martin. *Nobody's Fool: The Lives of Danny Kaye*. New York: Simon & Schuster, 1994.

Maltin, Leonard. *The Great Movie Comedians*. New York: Harmony Books, 1982.

Parish, James Robert, and William T. Leonard. *The Funsters*. New Rochelle, NY: Arlington House, 1979.

Siegel, Scott, and Barbara Siegel. *American Film Comedy*. New York: Prentice Hall, 1994.

Keaton, Buster *(1895–1966)*

With the possible exception of Charlie Chaplin, Buster Keaton stands as the greatest comedian of the silent movie era. Keaton appeared in well more than 100 shorts and features during his fifty-year film career. At the height of his popularity, he played aloof, stone-faced characters (he only smiled once in a film) who fiercely battle both nature and out-of-control machinery to achieve modest goals (usually for the affections of a woman). Much of his best work was lost for decades, only to be rediscovered by an appreciative new generation of filmgoers in the 1950s.

Keaton began learning his craft at an early age. Born Joseph Francis Keaton in Piqua, Kansas, in 1895, he spent his youth traveling the vaudeville circuit with his parents, who staged a mildly popular comedy act. By age five, Buster, who received his nickname from a family friend after he tumbled down a flight of stairs without hurting himself, had become the star attraction of "The Three Keatons." His primary role in the show was to absorb his father's abuse—his dad kicked, punched, and threw Buster around the stage with little regard for his son's well-being. Buster's ability to take this abuse without showing pain or emotion brought roars of approval from packed houses and lifted the act to prominence.

THE BIG SCREEN BECKONS

Keaton's big break came in 1917 when he met comedic film star Roscoe "Fatty" Arbuckle, who was familiar with his vaudeville work. Arbuckle asked him to make a brief appearance in his short, *The Butcher Boy*. Keaton accepted and never returned to the stage. The film was a hit, and Keaton joined Arbuckle's Comique Studio as an actor, a director, and a gag writer. He eagerly studied Arbuckle's filmmaking methods and made them his own. Keaton brought the emotionless demeanor he had affected for his stage act to the screen, and he tried to strike a balance between Arbuckle's slapstick style and his own, more subtle brand of humor. The resulting mix worked, and the two made a number of successful films between 1917 and 1920. When Arbuckle left Comique in 1920, Keaton was put in charge of the studio's comedy unit.

Making the most of his newfound authority, Keaton put together a string of acclaimed two-reel comedies that contain some of the finest moments ever captured on film. Many of his gags have a surrealistic quality. In *The High Sign* (1920), for example, he sits down on a bench and unfolds a newspaper that, when fully exposed, completely engulfs him. He wanders lost through a maze of want ads before escaping through a hole in the paper.

His best work also played on the audience's love-hate relationship with a world that was becoming increasingly mechanized. Sometimes, as in *The Electric House* (1922),

***Buster Keaton in* The General.** *Buster Keaton starred in and directed* The General, *the film he considered as his favorite, in 1926.* HULTON ARCHIVE/STRINGER/ARCHIVE PHOTOS/GETTY IMAGES.

machines go too far. Keaton's elaborately wired house goes haywire, causing his washing machine to throw dishes and his escalator to move so quickly that it hurls people out of a window. At other times, man is clearly the master of machine. In *The Blacksmith* (1922), Keaton (without realizing it) manages to turn a white Rolls-Royce black, one handprint or blowtorch mark at a time. The infernal and filthy machine meets its demise when Buster shatters its windows with a sledgehammer and then crashes an engine into it. Sometimes the laugh is at man's expense, sometimes at the machine's, but the two are always inextricably linked.

Keaton's sense of absurd surrealism and his use of machines as comedic vehicles carried over into his full-length comedies. In 1923 he directed his first feature film, *The Three Ages*, a satire of D. W. Griffith's *Intolerance*. Although it was an admirable debut, he did not really hit his stride until *Sherlock Jr.* (1924), in which he plays a projectionist who, while dreaming, becomes a character in the movie he is showing, a concept that Woody Allen would later use in *The Purple Rose of Cairo* (1985).

Keaton cranked out more films in the next two years, including his hilarious *The Navigator* (1924), before producing his magnum opus, *The General* (1926). In this, his favorite film, he plays a young, southern train engineer eager to enlist in the Confederate Army. The army rejects him, claiming that he is more valuable as an engineer than a soldier. Adding insult to injury, the Yankees steal his beloved locomotive and spirit it across their lines, with Keaton furiously chasing in another engine. He eventually steals back his train, and the film climaxes with a spectacular crash as a bridge collapses under the pursuing bluecoats' train. Besides containing some priceless comedy, *The General* has an epic sweep that is matched by few silent-era films.

RESCUED FROM OBSCURITY

Keaton's work during the 1920s should have been enough to ensure his place among the immortals of film, yet he was in very real danger of being forgotten. Even at the peak of his popularity, he was unfavorably compared to his rival, Chaplin, whom he privately loathed. Critics labeled Chaplin an "intellectual" comedian, while Keaton was viewed merely as an average funnyman who knew how to take a fall.

His sound-era films did little to enhance his reputation. In 1928 Keaton gave up his independence and signed with MGM (Metro-Goldwyn-Mayer). When he made the leap to talking films, he found himself being typecast as an incompetent bumbler. Worse, he had to play second banana to the scene-stealing comic Jimmy Durante. The two combined on several dreary films in the 1930s that effectively ended Keaton's career.

He continued to make mostly forgettable films into the 1960s, highlighted by memorable appearances in *It's a Mad, Mad, Mad, Mad World* (1963) and *A Funny Thing Happened on the Way to the Forum* (1966), and also starred in two short-lived television shows. His silent movies sat in film cans, unwatched and disintegrating, until the 1957 release of *The Buster Keaton Story*, a mostly fictionalized account of his life that renewed interest in his films, which were restored and finally acknowledged as classics. He received a special Academy Award in 1959 for his "unique talents." His body torn by a lifetime of smoking and bouts of alcoholism, Keaton died of cancer in 1966.

David B. Welky

SEE ALSO: *Allen, Woody; Arbuckle, Fatty; Chaplin, Charlie;* The General*;* Intolerance*; Silent Movies; Vaudeville.*

BIBLIOGRAPHY

Blesh, Rudi. *Keaton.* New York: Macmillan, 1966.

Keaton, Buster. *My Wonderful World of Slapstick.* New York: Doubleday, 1960.

Knopf, Robert. *The Theater and Cinema of Buster Keaton.* Princeton, NJ: Princeton University Press, 1999.

Meade, Marion. *Buster Keaton: Cut to the Chase.* New York: HarperCollins, 1995.

Keeping Up with the Kardashians

SEE: *Kardashian, Kim.*

Keillor, Garrison *(1942–)*

The humorist Garrison Keillor is best known as the host of *A Prairie Home Companion* (1974–1987; 1993–) and the *American Radio Company* (1989–1993), both of which have been carried nationally on public radio to up to five million weekly listeners. He has also published stories for the *New Yorker*, novels about radio and small-town life in the Midwest, a book of political essays, and other works. Keillor is the consummate storyteller, whose creation of the small town of Lake Wobegon, Minnesota, where "all the women are strong, all the men are good-looking, and all the children are above average," has won him a large following of listeners and readers drawn to the nostalgic, down-home sentiment of his monologues and stories.

Born Gary Edward Keillor in Anoka, Minnesota, he grew up in rural Brooklyn Park, where he was a devoted listener of popular radio shows such as *Fibber McGee and Molly* and *Gang Busters.* Because his fundamentalist parents banned television until Keillor was in high school, he tended to see television as sinful and radio as a magical doorway to another world far away from his hometown. In 1991 Keillor published *WLT: A Radio Romance*, a novel that recreates the golden days of radio and suggests the nostalgia Keillor feels for the medium. As he told Reed Bunzel, "There's no romance in television: it's just the Wal-Mart of the mind. Radio is infinitely sexier."

WRITER AND RADIO PERSONALITY

Keillor began in radio in 1963 at KUOM at the University of Minnesota, where he was an English major. Simultaneously, he was also honing his writing skills, wanting to follow in the footsteps of the legendary Mark Twain and his favorite writers at the *New Yorker*, E. B. White and James Thurber. He published his first story in the magazine in 1970. Ever since, he has had a dual career as a writer and radio personality.

In the 1970s Keillor created a popular morning show on St. Paul's public radio station that would eventually be called *A Prairie Home Companion.* The show combined many styles of music; humorous spots for made-up commercial sponsors, such as Powdermilk Biscuits (which "help shy persons get up and do what needs to be done") and Jack's Auto Repair; and tall tales that bordered on burlesques of small-town life. Over the years, Keillor would develop his style of storytelling toward local-color realism told from the visitor's point of view. Opposed to the ironic distance maintained by contemporary stand-up comics, he wanted the freedom to poke fun at the provincialism and Lutheran view of life that pervaded small towns in Minnesota, while also creating sympathy for his characters (many of them based on people he knew). The result—his nearly thirty-minute-long monologues on the news from Lake Wobegon—has become the most admired segment of his radio program.

With the publication of his most popular novel, *Lake Wobegon Days* (1985), Keillor solidified the identity of the small Minnesotan town in the nation's imagination and established his own persona as the hometown boy who could never go home again. Two years later he published *Leaving Home: A Collection of Lake Wobegon Stories.* He then left St. Paul, where he had been producing *A Prairie Home Companion*, to move to

Garrison Keillor. *Garrison Keillor performs in Louisville, Kentucky, in 2011.* STEPHEN J. COHEN/CONTRIBUTOR/GETTY IMAGES ENTERTAINMENT/GETTY IMAGES.

Denmark with his new wife and devote himself to his writing. He returned to the United States within a few months, however, and settled in New York City, where he fulfilled his long-time dream of being on staff at the *New Yorker.*

RETURN TO MINNESOTA

In 1989 Keillor returned to radio, producing a program titled *American Radio Company of the Air.* Like *A Prairie Home Companion,* it was a throwback. It drew many well-known musical acts, but it tried to shed the small-town image of its predecessor to become more of a glitzy big-city show. Keillor's new persona was that of a midwestern boy who was wide-eyed and lost amid the wonders of New York City, which had beckoned to him through his radio as a child. Within a few years, though, Keillor's radio company was forced to leave the city because of the exorbitant expense of producing its shows there.

Keillor took *American Radio Company* to Minnesota in 1992 and renamed it *A Prairie Home Companion,* combining many of the elements of his original show with those of his New York show. It continues to be a mainstay of public radio programming nationwide. Keillor and company take the show on the road and broadcast a portion of the season from New York, drawing large audiences wherever they go. The show still features its trademark news from Lake Wobegon and commercial sponsors, which include Bertha's Kitty Boutique and Beboparebop Rhubarb Pie ("Nothing gets the taste of shame and humiliation out of your mouth like Beboparebop Rhubarb Pie"), as well as recurring spots such as Guy Noir, reminiscent of old detective shows.

Keillor's career continued on its dual path throughout the 1990s and into the twenty-first century. He wrote more books set in Lake Wobegon and a number of other works, ranging from the political satire *Me, by Jimmy "Boy" Valente* (1999) to the children's book *Daddy's Girl* (2005). He also published *Good Poems* (2002), *Good Poems for Hard Times* (2005), and *Good Poems, American Places* (2011), anthologies of poems that Keillor has read on his short, daily radio program, *The Writer's Almanac.* He wrote the script for and appeared in the 2006 film *A Prairie Home Companion,* a fictional behind-the-scenes look at the making of his radio show, starring Lily Tomlin, Meryl Streep, and Woody Harrelson.

Keillor underwent heart surgery in 2001 and suffered a small stroke in 2009. He briefly thought about retiring from *A Prairie Home Companion* in 2011 but reconsidered. A member of the National Radio Hall of Fame since 1994, he has received a National Humanities Medal (1999), a Peabody Award (1980), a Grammy Award (1987), and two Cable ACE Awards (1988). Although National Public Radio refused in the 1980s to distribute *A Prairie Home Companion* because it believed the show would have only regional appeal, Keillor has proven that Americans from New York to California cannot get enough of the sentimental nostalgia and good-natured humor that pervade his stories about Lake Wobegon.

Anne Boyd

SEE ALSO: Fibber McGee and Molly*; Grammy Awards; The* New Yorker*; Radio; Streep, Meryl; Television; Thurber, James; Tomlin, Lily; Twain, Mark; Wal-Mart; White, E. B.*

BIBLIOGRAPHY

Bunzel, Reed E. "Garrison Keillor: An American Radio Romance." *Broadcasting,* January 6, 1992, 86-87.

Lee, Judith Yaross. *Garrison Keillor: A Voice of America.* Jackson: University Press of Mississippi, 1991.

Scholl, Peter A. *Garrison Keillor.* New York: Twayne, 1993.

Songer, Marcia. *Garrison Keillor: A Critical Companion.* Westport, CT: Greenwood Press, 2000.

Keitel, Harvey *(1939–)*

The long, prolific career of New Yorker Harvey Keitel comprises more than eighty films that can be roughly divided into three main periods: 1973–1980, the years marked by his collaborations with Martin Scorsese; 1981–1992, a decade that Keitel spent waiting for his breakthrough while he made a long list of films in the United States and Europe; and the period after 1992, when he became a popular actor thanks to Quentin Tarantino's *Reservoir Dogs.* Two biographies about Keitel have included the word *darkness* in their subtitles. Indeed, many audiences have appreciated, above all, Keitel's ability to act out through his roles deep emotional conflicts that seemingly have to do as much with his characters' personalities as with the actor's own allegedly dark personality. Whether this darkness is part of his public or private persona, it has been an essential factor to his status as a star.

Keitel should be seen as a cult star rather than as simply a star, because in his work he has been constantly associated with cult directors working within independent cinema. The first to give him a chance as an actor was Scorsese, who counted on Keitel's talent for roles in *Mean Streets* (1973), *Alice Doesn't Live Here Anymore* (1974), and *Taxi Driver* (1976). The association with Scorsese was later renewed when Keitel played Judas in the controversial *The Last Temptation of Christ* (1988). This film marked the beginning of the end of a long period in which Keitel kept away from Hollywood, apparently embittered by his failure to land the role of Captain Willard in Francis Ford Coppola's *Apocalypse Now* (1979).

It is important to note that during those years of semi-exile, Keitel played roles in European films of diverse nationalities, some of them better known—*Death Watch/Death in Full View* (Germany, 1980) or *La nuit de Varennes* (Italy, 1982)—and others better forgotten. Keitel, however, maintained his links with European filmmaking even into the 1990s, when he became regarded as a well-established star in Hollywood. He played, thus, the main role in the noted Greek *Ulysses' Gaze* (1995), a film very far from the usual Hollywood fare.

At home, Keitel's association with independent cinema finally led to stardom thanks to his roles in Quentin Tarantino's cult hits *Reservoir Dogs* (1992) and *Pulp Fiction* (1994). He also benefited greatly from this association, for Keitel was actively involved in the production of both films. The early 1990s brought Keitel other leading roles, first as the corrupt lieutenant of Abel Ferrara's violent, mystic *Bad Lieutenant* (1992) and then as the unlikely hero of Jane Campion's rereading of Victorian melodrama in *The Piano* (1993), possibly the first film in which Keitel was cast against type in a romantic leading role.

Keitel's definitive entrance into mainstream Hollywood brought him roles in Ridley Scott's *Thelma & Louise* (1991) (he had previously played one of the two duelists in Scott's 1977 television film of Joseph Conrad's story "The Duellists") and the adaptation of Michael Crichton's novel *Rising Sun* (1993).

***Harvey Keitel and Tim Roth in* Reservoir Dogs.** *Harvey Keitel's Mr. White tends to an injured Tim Roth as Mr. Orange in a scene from 1993's* Reservoir Dogs. LIVE ENTERTAINMENT/THE KOBAL COLLECTION.

Keitel's career has also been closely associated with writer Paul Auster. He played Auggie Wren in *Smoke* and *Blue in the Face* (both 1995), films scripted by Auster, and starred in Auster's debut film as a director, *Lulu on the Bridge* (1998). Keitel's successful career developed, thus, on three fronts simultaneously: Hollywood mainstream cinema, American independent films, and European cinema.

Keitel is not easy to classify in the Hollywood categories of leading or supporting actor. His many leading roles in independent films did not receive as much publicity as they deserved. As far as Hollywood is concerned, he is a star supporting actor but not a figure at the same level as his friend Robert De Niro or Al Pacino. Keitel has, however, taken greater risks than may big stars would have assumed when playing, for instance, the tormented policeman of *Bad Lieutenant* or Champion's romantic hero in *The Piano*—not only because of the physical nudity required for both roles but because of the force of the emotional nakedness in his performances.

Keitel's commitment to acting was acknowledged in 2002 at the Moscow International Film Festival, where he was presented with the Stanislavsky Award in recognition of his training in New York with Lee Strasberg and the nuanced and complex acting technique evidenced throughout his career. He has continued to work in a range of national cinemas as well as in television, playing a detective in ABC's version of the British crime drama *Life on Mars* (2008–2009). It might well be that independent cinema affords versatile actors like Keitel more ground on which to test their acting instincts than Hollywood mainstream cinema, hence his fidelity to directors such as Scorsese, Tarantino, and Auster—and theirs to him.

Sara Martin

SEE ALSO: Apocalypse Now*; Crichton, Michael; De Niro, Robert; Hollywood;* Mean Streets*; Pacino, Al;* Pulp Fiction*; Scorsese, Martin; Scott, Ridley; Tarantino, Quentin;* Taxi Driver.

BIBLIOGRAPHY

Caveney, Graham. *Harvey Keitel.* London: Bloomsbury, 1995.

Clarkson, Wensley. *Harvey Keitel: Prince of Darkness.* London: Piatkus Books, 1997.

Fine, Marshall. *Harvey Keitel: The Art of Darkness.* New York: Fromm International, 1998.

Howell, G. "The Gospel According to Harvey." *Vogue,* December 1993, 288–289.

Hunter, Jack. *Harvey Keitel.* London: Creation Books, 1999.

Schnabel, J. "Harvey Keitel, Zoe Lund and Abel Ferrara: The Unholy Trinity That Makes 'Bad Lieutenant' a Religious Experience." *Interview,* December 1992, 138–141.

Tosches, N. "Heaven, Hell, Harvey Keitel." *Esquire,* September 1993, 23.

Kelley, David E. *(1956–)*

With the success of the quirky television show *Ally McBeal* (1997–2002) in the late 1990s, David E. Kelley established himself as a preeminent producer and writer of popular television series. In 1986 Steven Bochco, the executive producer of the television series *L.A. Law* (1986–1992), hired Kelley, a former lawyer, to write for the show, and Kelley demonstrated his aptitude early on for revealing the conflict between interior concerns and external realities, a gift that he can apply to drama and comedy with equal facility. At his best, Kelley creates programming that eschews formulaic plots and neat, tidy endings in favor of three-dimensional characters facing credible ethical dilemmas; these dilemmas are often underscored by unsettling, self-reflexive fantasy commentaries that openly air difficult or controversial issues.

Kelley refined his techniques with some slightly surreal plots on the television shows *Picket Fences* (1992–1996) and *Chicago Hope* (1994–2000) before launching *Ally McBeal* and *The Practice* (1997–2004). After a string of unheralded efforts, including *Snoops* (1999), *Girls Club* (2002), and *The Brotherhood of Poland, New Hampshire* (2003), Kelley once again found success with *Boston Legal* (2004–2008), a spin-off of *The Practice* that won several Emmy Awards and a Golden Globe Award, largely on the strength of the on-screen rapport of actors James Spader and William Shatner. Kelley's next television offering, *Harry's Law* (2011–), starred Kathy Bates and earned fairly positive reviews.

Kelley writes much of every episode for his television shows, which is rare for a producer. His judgment, acumen, and direct involvement has made him something of a television auteur, and in 1999 he became the first television producer to win both the Golden Globe Award for the Best Comedy Series (for *Ally McBeal*) and the Golden Globe Award for Best Drama Series (*The Practice*) in the same year. Kelley is married to actress Michelle Pfeiffer, with whom he has a daughter, Claudia Rose, and a son, John Henry.

Sandra Garcia-Myers

SEE ALSO: Ally McBeal*; Bochco, Steven; Emmy Awards;* L.A. Law*; Pfeiffer, Michelle; Television.*

BIBLIOGRAPHY

Braxton, Greg. "The Man behind the Curtain." *Los Angeles Times Magazine*. November 30, 1997, 15.

Gates, Anita. "From Annie to Ally: Capturing the Insecure Human Condition." *New York Times*, December 20, 1998.

Levine, Josh. *David E. Kelley: The Man behind Ally McBeal.* Toronto: ECW Press, 1999.

Kelly, Gene *(1912–1996)*

A dancer and choreographer of enormous grace and indefatigable vitality, Gene Kelly created a new synthesis of music and dance in American movies. His unique achievement was to expand the range of dancing in the movies. For fellow dancers Fred Astaire and Ginger Rogers, dancing took place in a refined social world; for Kelly, dancing was part of everyday life and the real world. In place of the ballrooms of Astaire and Rogers, Kelly danced on car roofs, tables, and sofas, as well as in streets deluged with rain, thus extending dance to a mundane world that would seem to ordinarily exclude it.

Born in 1912, Kelly at first wanted to be a professional athlete, but his mother stoked his interest in dancing. After graduating from college, he performed in vaudeville and taught dancing. He moved to New York City in 1938 and began appearing in musicals. In 1942 Metro-Goldwyn-Mayer (MGM) enticed Kelly to go to Hollywood, where he made his first film with Judy Garland. In the next decade he appeared in an unprecedented series of lively movie musicals, including *On the Town* (1949), *Summer Stock* (1950), and *An American in Paris* (1951). His work culminated with *Singin' in the Rain* (1952), which Kelly starred in, choreographed, and codirected with Stanley Donen. As movie musicals lost their popularity in the late 1950s, however, Kelly's career began to decline.

Jeffrey Escoffier

SEE ALSO: *Astaire, Fred, and Ginger Rogers; Garland, Judy; MGM (Metro-Goldwyn-Mayer); The Musical;* Singin' in the Rain*; Vaudeville.*

BIBLIOGRAPHY

Singin' in the Rain. Film. Directed by Gene Kelly and Stanley Donen. Culver City, CA: MGM, 1952.

Yudkoff, Alvin, *Gene Kelly: A Life of Dance and Dreams*. New York: Back Stage Books, 2001.

Kelly, Grace *(1928–1982)*

Her icy beauty and regal poise made Grace Kelly one of the most popular movie stars of the 1950s, and when she married into one of Europe's oldest royal families, becoming Her Serene Highness Princess Grace of Monaco, she became the star of a real-life fairy-tale romance that captured the global imagination.

Born into a wealthy Philadelphia family, Grace Kelly was raised in a household that valued achievement. Her father, a former champion Olympic rower, was a successful businessman who encouraged Grace and her siblings to excel in both athletics and academics. Educated at parochial and private schools, she made her debut in Philadelphia society at sixteen. After graduating from high school in 1947, however, she left home for New York City, where she attended the American Academy of Dramatic Arts. She initially found work modeling and acting in small television roles, then made her Broadway debut in 1949. Her strikingly perfect features and exquisite beauty soon took her to Hollywood, where she made her first film appearance in 1951.

A year later Kelly starred as Gary Cooper's wife in *High Noon*. Overnight she became one of Hollywood's most sought-after leading ladies—the quintessential cool blond. Signed by MGM (Metro-Goldwyn-Mayer) in 1953, she starred opposite Clark Gable in *Mogambo*, garnering her first Oscar nomination. She won the 1955 Academy Award for Best Actress for her performance in *The Country Girl* (1954).

Kelly's next three movies, all directed by Alfred Hitchcock, became instant classics: *Dial M for Murder* (1954), *Rear Window* (1954), and *To Catch a Thief* (1955). Although her film career lasted only five years, she was recognized numerous other times for her roles, winning Golden Globes in 1954, 1955, and 1956;

James Stewart and Grace Kelly. *Grace Kelly, right, starred opposite James Stewart in the 1954 Alfred Hitchcock suspense thriller* Rear Window. **SILVER SCREEN COLLECTION/CONTRIBUTOR/MOVIEPIX/GETTY IMAGES.**

a New York Film Critics' Circle Award in 1954; and BAFTA nominations in 1955 and 1956.

By the mid-1950s Kelly was Hollywood's most popular movie star. While attending the Cannes Film Festival in 1955, she captivated one of the world's most eligible bachelors: Prince Rainier, the monarch of the tiny Mediterranean principality of Monaco. She returned to the United States to make what would be her final film, *High Society* (1956), with Bing Crosby and Frank Sinatra. In April that year she married Rainier in a ceremony that her biographer, Robert Lacey, describes as "the first modern event to generate media overkill." Guests included Ava Gardner and Aristotle Onassis.

After her marriage Kelly retired from acting. Because she was still under contract to MGM, however, the wedding was filmed as a movie and shown in the United States, increasing her fame. Images of Princess Grace entertaining Hollywood celebrities at Monaco charity events and appearing around the world with other European royalty enchanted her admirers at home, and she remained one of America's most popular public figures.

After the birth of Kelly's three children—Princess Caroline, Prince Albert, and Princess Stephanie—rumors circulated that she was unhappy and lonely in her marriage. She had hoped to return to acting, and in 1964 Hitchcock offered her the lead in *Marnie*, but negative public opinion in Monaco forced Prince Rainier to decline on her behalf. Even as she grew older and gained weight, the fairy-tale appeal of her life with her children continued to intrigue and delight American audiences. As the children grew and began to lead wild and sometimes problematic lives (particularly her daughters), Americans followed the European soap opera with glee, and when Princess Grace died in a car accident in 1982, they joined Monaco in genuine mourning.

Having given up acting in her twenties, Kelly remains locked in the public imagination at the height of her beauty. Her status as a cultural icon ensured her a star on the Hollywood Walk of Fame when it was founded in 1960. She was the first actress to appear on an American postage stamp and was ranked thirteenth on the American Film Institute's list of all-time great female stars.

Victoria Price

SEE ALSO: *Academy Awards; Broadway; Celebrity; Cooper, Gary; Crosby, Bing; Gable, Clark; Gardner, Ava;* High Noon; *Hitchcock, Alfred; Hollywood; MGM (Metro-Goldwyn-Mayer); Movie Stars;* Rear Window; *Sinatra, Frank; Television.*

BIBLIOGRAPHY

Bradford, Sarah. *Princess Grace.* London: Weidenfeld & Nicholson, 1984.

Conant, Howell. *Grace.* New York: Random House, 1992.

Curtis, Jenny. *Grace Kelly: A Life in Pictures.* New York: Barnes & Noble Books, 2002.

Lacey, Robert. *Grace.* New York: G. P. Putnam's Sons, 1994.

Monaco, James; James Pallot; and Baseline. *Encyclopedia of Film.* New York: Perigee, 1991.

Kelly, Walt

SEE: *Pogo.*

Kelly Bag

The Kelly bag became an American fashion institution in 1956. In September of that year, five months after she married Prince Rainier of Monaco, the former film star Grace Kelly returned to the United States for a two-month visit, clad in fashionable maternity wear and sporting a square, black bag that she had purchased for the journey. The princess was widely photographed carrying the large leather bag in front of her expanding waistline, and a fashion trend was born. Known from then on as the Kelly bag, it was in fact manufactured by Hermès. The chic and expensive Paris design house had been making the pocketbooks—each of which was fashioned by hand—since 1935. The bags were scaled-down models of the Hermès saddlebags, which were made to hold the bridles and riding tack of the European rich.

For many American women the bag symbolized the elegance and style for which Kelly was known both on-screen and off. It did not lose its allure for succeeding generations and became the most popular Hermès handbag ever. In the twenty-first century, it has successfully resisted the trends of mass production and globalization, harkening back to the era in which Kelly made it famous: it is still made by hand in France.

Jennifer Davis McDaid

SEE ALSO: *Kelly, Grace; Movie Stars.*

BIBLIOGRAPHY

Jackson, Jennifer. "Shh! Hermès' Deepest Secrets." *Harper's Bazaar,* September 1998, 234.

Lacey, Robert. *Grace.* New York: G. P. Putnam's Sons, 1994.

"Princess Grace Arrives on Visit." *New York Times,* September 12, 1956.

Rutherford, Abigail. *Warman's Handbags Field Guide: Values and Identifications.* Iola, WI: Krause Publications, 2009.

Kelly Girls

Since the 1960s Kelly Girls has been synonymous with female temporary office workers. Originally a groundbreaking temporary employment service, the name has expanded to a generic term, describing all temporary workers, including those who are neither female nor employees of Kelly Services. Kelly Girls describes not only a company and a type of work but also a cultural and economic phenomenon, the shift from the permanent career employee to the flexible "temp." Even *Forbes* magazine headlined its July 16, 1986, article about the practice of hiring nuclear scientists and technicians on a temporary basis "Sophisticated Kelly Girls."

THE BEGINNING OF THE TEMP WORKER

In 1946 William Russell Kelly opened Russell Kelly Office Services in Detroit, Michigan, to provide inventory, calculating, typing, and copying services to local businesses. When his clients began to ask if Kelly's employees could come to their places of business to work, Kelly was happy to oblige. He began to offer workers who could fill in when needed in a variety of situations due to employee illness or vacations, busy seasons, or special projects. His hiring base was largely female, many of them housewives and students. Kelly had tapped into a genuine employer need, and his business grew. In 1954 he opened his second office in Louisville, Kentucky. In 1957 Russell Kelly Office Services was changed to Kelly Girl Service Inc., and by 1964 there were 169 offices in forty-four states. The Kelly Girl became the perfect prefeminist icon of the working woman—brisk, efficient, and unthreatening. After all, she was not a woman but a girl and only temporary, just filling in.

In 1966 Kelly Girls became Kelly Services, and the company continued to expand the field of temporary employment. Living up to its motto "Tested, Bonded, Insured and Guaranteed," Kelly created specialized computer software for training workers with amazing rapidity to use a wide variety of word processing equipment. With many awards for business achievement and sales of more than $3 billion in 1996, Kelly Services became one of the leaders in the industry, along with employment giant Manpower, the Olsten Group, and newcomers such as MacTemps (later called Aquent).

A MORE DIVERSE TEMP AGENCY

The profit-driven economy of the 1990s dramatically increased the role of the temp worker. When Kelly Girls first began, there were three classifications of workers: clerk, typist, and secretary. By the 1990s Kelly Services had more than 120 classifications. Besides the "pink collar" jobs, such as secretary and teacher, and the industrial jobs, temps were hired in management, technical, professional, and even executive positions. Although temporary work is touted as advantageous to a diverse group of workers because of flexibility and variety, in fact, the majority of temp workers are minority young women who are hired for clerical or industrial jobs. Whereas some are attracted to the flexible hours and training, almost two-thirds would prefer permanent employment if it were available to them.

Corporations are drawn to the use of temps for a variety of reasons. It is a simple way to replace permanent workers who are off the job temporarily or to add extra hands during peak production periods. Sometimes a worker's skills, such as computer programming or consulting, are only needed on a short-term basis. By going through a temp agency, an employer can avoid the interviewing and hiring process, and, often, also avoid paying benefits. Some employers, capitalizing on this advantage, have created a new category of worker, the "permatemp," hired on as a temporary worker but kept on the job for months or even years without the benefits afforded to permanent employees. In response to this, some employee advocates are attempting to organize temporary workers to fight against violations of their rights. One such group in Greenville, South Carolina, the Carolina Alliance for Fair Employment, has been working since 1984 to force employers to comply with state and federal employment laws.

The nebulous status of the temporary worker is chillingly dramatized in Jill and Karen Sprecher's 1997 movie *Clockwatchers*, about four female temp workers. Within a claustrophobic office atmosphere, the temporary workers are portrayed as invisible and powerless. The bosses do not even bother to learn their names or distinguish their faces, and their small acts of rebellion are mostly futile.

Temporary employment has undeniable advantages for both the employee, who may be able to learn a wide variety of skills on an individualized schedule, and the employer, who can inexpensively fill in employees as needed. It can be problematic, however, working in an atmosphere where neither employee nor employer feels responsibility toward the other. The Kelly Girl, trim and brisk in her suit and carrying her steno pad may be out of date, but she initiated the era of the temporary worker. It remains to be seen whether the temp will become the disposable worker.

INTO THE TWENTY-FIRST CENTURY

The economic downturn of the early twenty-first century played havoc with the lives of many temporary workers. It was particularly hard in places such as Silicon Valley, California, where the high salaries made by technological geniuses ran salaries up on everything from groceries to homes. Temps, who find themselves on the low end of employment scales, often find it hard to make ends meet in such situations. An injury or an illness can put some of them on the street. In 2010 government figures showed that the number of temporary employees in the United States had reached two million. There was, however, some good news. Companies were transferring more temps into permanent positions, and some temp agencies, such as Working Partnerships USA, began offering insurance to their employees.

Tina Gianoulis

SEE ALSO: *Feminism; The Great Recession.*

BIBLIOGRAPHY

Cohany, Sharon R. "Workers in Alternative Employment Arrangements." *Monthly Labor Review* 119, no. 10 (1996): 31.

Cook, Christopher D. "Temps Demand a New Deal." *Nation*, March 27, 2000, 270.

Davidson, Paul. "More Temp Workers Are Getting Hired." *USA Today*, March 8, 2010.

Hatton, Erin Elizabeth. *The Temp Economy: From Kelly Girls to Permatemps in Postwar America*. Philadelphia: Temple University Press, 2011.

Henson, Kevin D. *Just a Temp: Expectations and Experiences of Women Clerical Temporary Workers*. Philadelphia: Temple University Press, 1996.

"Kelly Services." Accessed March 2011. Available from http://www.kellyservices.com

Larson, Jan. "Temps Are Here to Stay." *American Demographics* 18, no. 2: 26.

Kennedy Assassination

The images are remarkably familiar. The convertible limousine winds its way through Dallas crowds; John F. Kennedy, America's youngest president, smiles and waves in the backseat; gunfire, three jerks, the limousine slows and then accelerates; Jackie Kennedy shrieks and covers her husband; an emotional Walter Cronkite tells the nation that its president has died, removes his glasses, and wipes his eyes.

TELEVISED TRAGEDY

On November 22, 1963, President Kennedy was shot as he paraded through Dallas, Texas. That same afternoon Dallas police arrested their suspect, Lee Harvey Oswald, an itinerant ex-U.S. marine and self-described Marxist-Leninist who had lived in the Soviet Union. Within days Oswald was also dead, shot by nightclub-owner Jack Ruby on national television in the basement of a Dallas police station.

Sociologist Todd Gitlin has captured the sense of immediacy that televised politics brought to the American social sphere of the 1960s. Kennedy's election to office marked a new age in American political culture. "History with a capital H had come down to earth, either interfering with life or making it possible; and that within History, or threaded through it, people were living with a supercharged density: lives were bound up within one another, making claims on one another, drawing one another into the common project." Americans knew Kennedy as "the television president," and their relationship with the man and his politics was infused with this feeling of intimacy.

It should come as no surprise, then, that Kennedy's violent and sudden death moved the American public so dramatically. His funeral rites were a profoundly public affair, painstakingly arranged by his widow, broadcast on all of the nation's television networks and witnessed in 93 percent of the country's television-viewing households. "America wept tonight," *New York Times* columnist James Reston wrote, "not alone for its dead young President, but for itself. The grief was general, for somehow the worst in the nation had prevailed over the best." Five years later, Kennedy's younger brother and incumbent New York Senator, Robert F. Kennedy, was also assassinated.

CONSPIRACY THEORIES

What is remarkable, however, is the range of responses the Kennedy assassination has elicited in the following decades. The official committee charged with investigating the assassination, the Warren Commission, issued a report confirming that Lee Harvey Oswald was indeed the murderer and asserting that Oswald had acted alone. Almost immediately, critics began to contend that the scenario reconstructed in the Warren Report seemed unlikely at best, dismissing in particular the infamous "single-bullet theory," which proposes that one bullet was responsible for multiple injuries to Texas governor John Connally, who was riding in the front seat of the car, and to the president. For many, Kennedy's death revealed a dark, conspiratorial underside to American politics. It caused a loss of American innocence and became a harbinger for the turbulent decades that lay ahead.

Kennedy Motorcade in Dallas. *President Kennedy's motorcade makes its way through the streets of Dallas, Texas, moments before his assassination on November 22, 1963.* AP IMAGES.

Hundreds of conspiracy theories have attempted to account for Kennedy's killing. Initially, most of these conjectures came from Europe. Soon, however, conspiracy theorizing on the Kennedy assassination became a cottage industry in America, with leftists charging that the assassination was the result of a pact involving American security forces; the Mafia; Cuban dictator Fidel Castro; rightists uncovering plots that involved the Soviet Union, the civil rights movement, and American communists; and even Kennedy's vice president, Lyndon Baines Johnson. This last theory was bolstered in 2011 when tapes from a 1963 interview with Jackie Kennedy revealed her own suspicions about Johnson's involvement.

Those revelations, among many others, were confided to the Pulitzer Prize–winning historian Arthur M. Schlesinger Jr. soon after JFK's death. Schlesinger, who had worked closely with the president and First Lady in the Kennedy White House, meticulously documented the presidency, assassination, and its aftermath in his journals and in interviews with the Kennedy family. Schlesinger's more than 6,000 pages of journal entries were distilled into an 900-page tome published in 2007, which also disclosed that at the time of RFK's death, some believed that he was killed because he planned, if elected president, to reopen the investigation of the death of his brother.

THE MOVIE AND ITS REPERCUSSIONS

One of the most prominent of the Kennedy conspiracy theorists was New Orleans district attorney Jim Garrison. Garrison charged New Orleans businessman Clay Shaw with conspiracy to kill the president and, in 1967, brought him to trial. Shaw was acquitted, but in 1991 filmmaker Oliver Stone gave Garrison's theory a second hearing before the American moviegoing public. Stone's *JFK* is a fast-paced, paranoia movie that mixes Abraham Zapruder's 8-millimeter amateur film of the Dallas shooting and other pieces of historical footage with staged material and describes the assassination plot as "a riddle wrapped in a mystery inside an enigma" (which is precisely what Winston Churchill had said about the Soviet Union). It brought crankish conspiracy theorizing into the American spotlight, rekindled the debate over Kennedy's death and generated a new debate of its own about the popular media's cultural authority and responsibility; it was a booming commercial success. Fifty million people saw *JFK* in movie theaters, and the film brought Stone two Academy Awards.

Most likely as a result of this film and the public discussion around it, the Kennedy assassination narrative questioning the one-bullet theory became so omnipresent in American culture that a 1992 episode ("The Boyfriend") of the television sitcom *Seinfeld* could parody it without scandal and with the assumption that the audience understood. On the political front, the Assassination Records Review Board was formed; from 1992 to 1998 it released more than 60,000 withheld or classified documents associated with the assassination and its aftermath. All remaining documents, which have been challenged by various agencies for security reasons, are scheduled to be released by the year 2017. The creation of the commission seems to have been an effort to quell a renewed wave of mistrust in the public sphere.

The spread of conspiracy theorizing about the Kennedy assassination may be a result, in part, of what historian Richard Hofstadter called "the paranoid style in American politics." Such paranoia even resulted in the 1981 exhuming of Oswald's body, since many doubted that his corpse was entombed there. Largely, however, it seems to stem from a more innocent source. Television beamed the drama of the Kennedy assassination and its repercussions directly into the homes of millions of Americans. It made the Kennedy funeral the most widely watched television event in American history. Most Americans who were alive at the time know where they were when Kennedy was shot. In a sense every American was there with the president as he died.

A magnetic pull continues to attract popular culture to the Kennedy assassination into the twenty-first century. Revelations such as those found in Schlesinger's journals and memorabilia associated with the event still capture the American public's imagination. At an auction in 2010, Oswald's original coffin sold for $87,469. And in 2012 a Colorado real estate developer purchased the hearse that carried the body of JFK for $160,000. That these items could be auctioned for such high prices nearly fifty years after Kennedy's death is proof of a persevering morbid fascination with John F. Kennedy.

Thurston Domina

SEE ALSO: *Academy Awards; Civil Rights Movement; Conspiracy Theories; Cronkite, Walter;* JFK*; Mafia/Organized Crime; Onassis, Jacqueline Lee Bouvier Kennedy;* Seinfeld*; Stone, Oliver; Television.*

BIBLIOGRAPHY

Bugliosi, Vincent. *Reclaiming History: The Assassination of President John F. Kennedy.* New York: W. W. Norton, 2007.

Brown, Thomas. *JFK: History of an Image.* Bloomington: Indiana University Press, 1988.

Garrison, Jim. *On the Trail of the Assassins.* New York: Sheridan Square Press, 1988.

Gitlin, Todd. *The Sixties: Years of Hope, Days of Rage.* New York: Bantam, 1987.

Hofstadter, Richard. *The Paranoid Style in American Politics, and other Essays.* Cambridge, MA: Harvard University Press, 1964, 1996.

Lane, Mark. *Rush to Judgment: A Critique of the Warren Commission's Inquiry in the Murders of President John F. Kennedy, Officer J. D. Tippit and Lee Harvey Oswald.* London: Bodley Head, 1966.

United States Assassination Records Review Board. *Final Report of the Assassination Records Review Board.* Washington, DC: Author, 1998.

Zelizer, Barbie. *Covering the Body: The Kennedy Assassination, the Media, and the Shaping of Collective Memory.* Chicago: University of Chicago Press, 1992.

Kenneth Robeson

Pulp magazine publisher Street and Smith used the house name "Kenneth Robeson" in two of its publications. Kenneth Robeson was credited as the author of most of the novels that appeared in *Doc Savage Magazine* from 1933 to 1949. The first issue carried the byline Kenneth Roberts; then, due to a mistake by an editorial assistant, the March 1944 issue listed on the cover Lester Dent, the true author of the novel. Dent wrote the majority of the *Doc Savage* novels but worked with at least five ghostwriters on about thirty-eight of the stories.

In 1939 Street and Smith launched *Avenger Magazine* with novels by Kenneth Robeson, "the creator of Doc Savage." All twenty-four of the *Avenger* novels were written by Paul Ernst. In the 1960s and 1970s the name Kenneth Robeson appeared on paperback reprints, and in the 1990s it is listed on seven original Doc Savage novels written by Will Murray; they were based on Dent's notes and story fragments.

Randy Duncan

SEE ALSO: *Doc Savage; Pulp Magazines; Street and Smith.*

BIBLIOGRAPHY

Cannaday, Marilyn. *Bigger than Life: The Creator of Doc Savage.* Bowling Green, OH: Bowling Green State University Press, 1990.

McCarey-Laird, Maggie Martin. *Lester Dent: The Man, His Craft, and His Market.* West Des Moines, IA: Hidalgo Publications, 1995.

Kent State Massacre

For thirteen seconds on May 4, 1970, Ohio National Guardsmen opened fire on students protesting the Vietnam War at Kent State University in Kent, Ohio, killing four and wounding nine others. What had merely been a small campus demonstration—one of thousands nationwide—quickly developed into a symbol of the Vietnam era in America. A Pulitzer Prize–winning photograph taken at the shooting shows an anguished young woman kneeling over the body of a dead student with her arms raised in despair and her facial expression asking "why?"; the photo became a significant illustration of the end of the Woodstock era. Any lingering romantic notions of the 1960s ended with the Kent State massacre.

On April 30, 1970, President Richard M. Nixon appeared on national television to announce that U.S. troops were invading Cambodia to strike suspected Vietnamese guerrilla strongholds there. The new policy contradicted his previous plan, which had pledged that a "Vietnamization" of the war would gradually reduce America's involvement in the conflict. Reaction to the escalation of the war effort was immediate and intense, especially on the nation's college campuses, where more than 1.5 million students protested the announcement. Nixon fueled the outrage by labeling the student protesters "bums" who were "blowing up the campuses."

On May 1 a late-night disturbance in downtown Kent fueled by a warm spring evening, students leaving local bars, and a motorcycle gang led Mayor Leroy Satrom to declare the city under a state of emergency. Although the city suffered only minor damages, the next day the mayor requested the presence of the Ohio National Guard to quell the unruliness. Even with the soldiers on campus, student protesters held a rally the next day, and the university Reserve Officers Training Corps (ROTC) building was burned down. The destruction of the ROTC building was a major event leading to the violence at Kent State, but the mystery over who set the fire was never solved. Initially, it

National Guardsmen at Kent State. *National Guardsmen move across the commons on the Kent State University during anti-war protests on May 4, 1970.* © BETTMANN/CORBIS.

was assumed that the fire was started by radical students, but others speculated that it may have been set by government agents to provide a reason for government intervention.

Ohio governor James Rhodes arrived in Kent on May 3 and condemned the student radicals, comparing them to Nazi brown shirts and communists. That evening, protesters gathered on campus but were forced to leave with the assistance of tear gas. A sit-in held on Main Street was also dispersed by the troops.

A rally was scheduled for May 4 and drew approximately 2,000 students, many of whom were curious onlookers and those shuffling between classes. National Guard officers ordered the protesters to leave and shot tear gas into the crowd when the command was not followed. More than 100 fully armed guardsmen then moved against the students. The troops advanced toward the students, over a hill, and then down to a practice football field. When they reached a fence at the far end of the field, some of the soldiers knelt and aimed their weapons at the demonstrators. While the troops massed together, students retreated into a parking lot between several buildings. Others lobbed rocks and tear gas canisters back at the guardsmen.

After ten minutes, the troops moved back up the hill. When they reached the crest, a group of twenty-eight guardsmen wheeled around and fired in the direction of the parking lot. They fired sixty-one rounds of ammunition. Of the thirteen people killed or injured, only two were actively participating in the demonstration. One student was killed while walking to class and another, ironically, was an ROTC student. Many of the injured students were more than 100 yards from the guardsmen.

Kent State was shut down after the shootings and remained closed for the rest of the school year. As news about the incident spread, campus unrest escalated. Nearly 500 colleges were closed or disrupted. Ten days later, another campus shooting occurred at Jackson State University in Mississippi when police and state patrolmen fired into a dormitory at the all-black school, killing two students and wounding at least nine others. The relative lack of attention given to the massacre at Jackson State embittered many African Americans.

The Kent State massacre bookends a generation that began with the assassination of President John F. Kennedy in 1963 and included the murders of his brother Robert F. Kennedy and civil rights leader Martin Luther King Jr. in 1968. Kent State was transformed from a sleepy midwestern college into the symbolic epicenter of student protest in the Vietnam era.

Kent State remains a symbol of antiwar protest and government repression. The incident has been immortalized in countless books and even a television movie, but nothing was more stinging than the Crosby, Stills, Nash, and Young song "Ohio" with its haunting lyrics, "Tin soldiers and Nixon's coming . . . four dead in Ohio!"

Bob Batchelor

SEE ALSO: *Crosby, Stills, and Nash; Kennedy Assassination; King, Martin Luther, Jr.; Protest Groups; Vietnam; Young, Neil.*

BIBLIOGRAPHY

Bills, Scott L., ed. *Kent State/May 4: Echoes through a Decade.* Kent, OH: Kent State University Press, 1982.

Davies, Peter. *The Truth about Kent State: A Challenge to the American Conscience.* New York: Farrar, Straus & Giroux, 1973.

Eszterhas, Joe, and Michael D. Roberts. *13 Seconds: Confrontation at Kent State.* New York: College Notes and Texts, 1970.

Gordon, William A. *The Fourth of May: Killings and Coverups at Kent State.* Amherst, NY: Prometheus Books, 1990.

Heineman, Kenneth J. *Campus Wars: The Peace Movement at American State Universities in the Vietnam Era.* New York: New York University Press, 1993.

Michener, James A. *Kent State: What Happened and Why.* New York: Random House, 1971.

Rosinsky, Natalie M. *The Kent State Shootings.* Mankato, MN: Compass Point Books, 2008.

Kentucky Derby

The oldest continuously run sporting event in the United States, the Kentucky Derby is America's most famous horse race, rich in tradition and celebrated by racing fans throughout the world. In May 1875 Colonel Meriwether Lewis Clark, taking his lead from the English Derby at Epsom Downs, established the race for three-year-old thoroughbreds over a 1.5-mile course (later reduced to 1.25 miles). Attracting an annual crowd of more than 100,000 spectators, the Kentucky Derby has been called the "greatest two minutes in sports." It is also the first leg of racing's most sought-after goal, the Triple Crown, awarded to those rare horses that win at the Kentucky Derby, the Preakness, and Belmont.

HISTORY OF THE DERBY

Although the idea for building a racetrack and attracting the best horses to a rich, classic race originated with Clark, a visionary promoter in his mid-twenties, the business and promotional talents that elevated the Derby to a race of international importance came from a Louisville tailor named Matt Winn, who began managing the failing track in 1902. As a boy, standing on his father's flatbed truck, Winn had seen Aristides win the first Derby at the Churchill Downs racetrack in Louisville; he attended every single Derby after that—seventy-five in all—until his death in 1949.

The Derby received a boost in prestige in 1915 when Harry Payne Whitney agreed to run his filly Regret. She led from the start, becoming the only female thoroughbred to win the Derby until the 1980s, when Genuine Risk and Winning Colors duplicated the feat. After the race, Whitney remarked that he did not care whether Regret ever raced again. "She has won the greatest race in America," he said, "and I am satisfied." Winn was determined to keep the Kentucky Derby at that high level.

Racing historian Joe Estes has divided the Kentucky Derby story into three periods: 1875–1898, 1899–1914, and 1915

2011 Kentucky Derby. *John Velazquez rides Animal Kingdom to victory at the Kentucky Derby in 2011.* AP IMAGES.

onward, with the first period highlighted by the appearance at Churchill Downs of the finest American thoroughbreds from Kentucky and the great stables of the Northeast. Though the purses were not large, owners were motivated to improve the breed of racehorses by competing with the best. One of the racing stars of this early period was Isaac Murphy, an African American jockey who rode Buchanan to victory in 1884, Riley in 1890, and Kingman in 1891. His record of three Kentucky Derby wins was not equaled until 1930, when Earl Sande won on Gallant Fox, and it was not surpassed until 1948, when Eddie Arcaro won the fourth of his five Derbies on Citation.

Murphy has been credited with the highest winning percentage of any jockey, 44 percent. The significance of this phenomenal record is evident when compared with that of Arcaro, the greatest modern era jockey, whose lifetime winning average in a more competitive era was 22 percent. Among the memorable horses of the first years were Hindoo, which had a string of eighteen consecutive race victories that included the 1881 Derby; Ben Brush, which won the first 1.25-mile Derby in 1896; and Plaudit, the winner in 1898.

From 1899 to 1914, the great stables in the Northeast began shipping their horses to the American Derby at Washington Park in Chicago, and the Kentucky Derby became more of a local race. When a horse named Donerail won in 1913 and paid $184.90—the longest odds of any Derby winner in history—the classic race received some beneficial publicity, but it was not until 1915 that the modern era began, signaling the return of America's greatest racehorses to the "run for the roses." Racing fans remember such brilliant thoroughbreds as Exterminator, Sir Barton, Zev, Black Gold, Bubbling Over, Gallant Fox, Twenty Grand, Cavalcade, Omaha, War Admiral, Whirlaway, Count Fleet, Assault, Citation, Swaps, Carry Back, Northern Dancer, Majestic Prince, Riva Ridge, Secretariat, and Seattle Slew.

FAMOUS HORSES

The most famous American racehorse, Man o' War—overwhelmingly voted the greatest horse of the first half of the twentieth century—did not run in the Kentucky Derby but did win the other two Triple Crown races. He raced for only two seasons (1919–1920), but he won twenty of twenty-one races and established speed records at five tracks over various distances. He was such a compelling favorite that he raced at odds as short as one in 100. Retired to stud in late 1920, Man o' War sired sixty-four horses who ran in stakes races, including War Admiral, winner of the 1937 Triple Crown. Gallant Fox, who won the Triple Crown in 1930, raced for two seasons, winning eleven of seventeen starts. His winnings of $308,275 in 1930 held the single-season record for seventeen years until purses escalated after World War II. He sired Omaha, the Triple Crown winner in 1935, and numerous other successful horses. Gallant Fox and Omaha remain the only father-son combination to win the Triple Crown.

Whirlaway, a nervous and erratic animal with an unusually long tail, won the Triple Crown in 1941, ridden by Arcaro, with a record-breaking run in the Derby. Noted for spectacular stretch runs, Whirlaway would either win gloriously or lose badly and compiled a record of thirty-two wins in sixty races, but he was the first horse to earn more than half a million dollars; Citation, the 1948 Triple Crown winner, was the first horse to win a full million. Native Dancer, the first outstanding horse whose major victories were seen on national television, finished second to Dark Star in the 1953 Kentucky Derby, marking his only defeat in a career of twenty-two races. The first televised Derby was won in 1952 by Hill Gail.

In 1973 Secretariat became the first Triple Crown winner since Citation in 1948. An unusually large chestnut, 16 hands in height, he combined size with amazing speed. He was the first horse to run the Derby in less than two minutes, also setting a record for the final half mile and quarter mile. At Belmont he won by 31 lengths while establishing the track record of 2:24. In 1977 a "Cinderella" horse, Seattle Slew, became the first horse that, unbeaten in his racing career, also won the Triple Crown. Slew had been bought as a colt by Mickey and Karen Taylor and Jim and Sally Hill for the bargain-basement price of $17,500 in 1975. They sold him to a syndicate for the then-record sum of $12 million in 1978, the year that Affirmed became the third Triple Crown winner of the 1970s, capping an amazing decade for racing.

FAMOUS JOCKEYS

Jockeys have played a prominent role in the history of the Kentucky Derby. Arcaro and Bill Hartack each won the classic race five times, and Willie Shoemaker rode into the winner's circle four times. Raleigh Colston became the first person to own, train, and ride a Derby runner; he rode Searcher in the first Derby and owned and trained Colston, the third-place finisher in the 1911 race. During a remarkable seven years from 1958 through 1964, Shoemaker was America's leading money-making jockey. In 1970 Diane Crump made history as the first female jockey to ride in the Kentucky Derby. Gary Stevens joined the legendary Isaac Murphy, Earle Sande, and Angel Cordero as a three-time winner in 1997. In 2010 Calvin Borel became the first jockey to win three times in a four-year period, having also won in 2007 and 2009.

Tragedy struck the Kentucky Derby in 2008. The highly ranked filly Eight Belles made a gallant run in the race, coming in second to winner Big Brown. However, moments after crossing the finish line, the filly broke both her front ankles, and went down hard, throwing her rider. She had to be euthanized right away.

More than 135 years after the first Kentucky Derby, the race is still being contested on the same hallowed turf that the first Derby winner trod. The Kentucky Derby has thus entered a third century, firmly entrenched as a celebrated occasion in "the sport of kings." In keeping with that royal association, Queen Elizabeth II of England attended the 133rd running of the race in 2007.

Benjamin Griffith

SEE ALSO: *Gambling; Sports Heroes; World War II.*

BIBLIOGRAPHY

Brodowsky, Pamela K.; Tom Philbin; and Churchill Downs. *Two Minutes to Glory: The Official History of the Kentucky Derby*. New York: HarperCollins, 2009.

Chew, Peter. *The Kentucky Derby: The First 100 Years*. Boston: Houghton Mifflin, 1974.

Kelley, Robert, and John Hervey. *Racing in America, 1937–59*. New York: Jockey Club, 1960.

Longrigg, Roger. *The History of Horse Racing*. New York: Stein & Day, 1972.

Palmer, Joe H. *This Was Racing.* New York: Barnes, 1953.

Plattner, Andy. *Kentucky Derby Vault.* Florence, AL: Whitman Publishing, 2008.

Kentucky Fried Chicken

When Corbin, Kentucky, restaurateur Harland Sanders established a chicken franchise business in the mid-1950s, the pressure-cooking process he had developed twenty years earlier put him at the forefront of the American fast-food revolution. In 1964 he sold the flourishing Kentucky Fried Chicken Corporation for $2 million. The company continued to promote its "finger lickin' good" southern fried chicken by retaining Sanders, dubbed the "Kentucky Colonel," as a roving ambassador and corporate icon.

PepsiCo's $840 million buyout of the corporation in 1986 somewhat compromised the brand's down-home identity. The new owner rebranded the franchise "KFC"—the word *fried* deemed inappropriate in an era of consumer health consciousness—and integrated it with PepsiCo-owned fast-food chains Taco Bell and Pizza Hut. Nevertheless, Colonel Sanders's southern patrician visage continued to decorate thousands of KFCs worldwide.

In 2009 KFC responded to health-conscious consumers by adding grilled chicken to its menu. To promote the new option, company representatives appeared on *The Oprah Winfrey Show*, promising a free meal to customers who downloaded a coupon from the KFC website within two days. The response was overwhelming, and the company, unable to meet demand, withdrew the offer, enraging customers all over the United States.

Martyn Bone

SEE ALSO: *Fast Food; The Internet; Pepsi-Cola; Pizza; Winfrey, Oprah.*

BIBLIOGRAPHY

Cawelti, John G. "'That's What I Like about the South': Changing Images of the South in the 1970s." In *The Lost Decade: America in the Seventies*, ed. Elsebeth Hurup. Aarhus, Denmark: Aarhus University Press, 1996.

Kern, Jerome *(1885–1945)*

American Jerome Kern was one of the most significant composers of the twentieth century. With his string of Princess Theater musicals, the immortal musical *Show Boat* (1927), and his songs for stage and screen, Kern in many ways defined the American popular song.

Through his series of Princess Musicals, such as *Oh, Boy!* (1917), Kern helped to create an intimacy in the musical comedy that helped end the dominance of European imports on Broadway. But it was with *Show Boat* and its cavalcade of songs, such as "Ol' Man River" and "Can't Help Lovin' Dat Man" that Kern achieved his greatest fame. Other popular Kern songs include "Smoke Gets in Your Eyes" from *Roberta* (1933) and "All the Things You Are" from *Very Warm for May* (1939). He wrote songs for the films *Swing Time* (1936) and *You Were Never Lovelier* (1942), among others. He won two Academy Awards for best song: one in 1936 for "The Way You Look Tonight" and the other in 1940 for "The Last Time I Saw Paris." Kern, in his scores for stage and screen, established a standard for popular song that exists well into the twenty-first century.

William A. Everett

SEE ALSO: *Academy Awards; Broadway; The Musical;* Show Boat.

BIBLIOGRAPHY

Banfield, Stephen. *Jerome Kern.* New Haven, CT: Yale University Press, 2006.

Bordman, Gerald M. *Jerome Kern: His Life and Music.* New York: Oxford University Press, 1980.

Davis, Lee. *Bolton and Woodhouse and Kern: The Men Who Made Musical Comedy.* New York: Heineman, 1993.

Ewen, David. *The Story of Jerome Kern.* New York: Holt, 1953.

Freedland, Michael. *Jerome Kern.* London: Robson, 1978.

Lamb, Andrew. *Jerome Kern in Edwardian London.* Brooklyn, NY: Institute for Studies in American Music, 1985.

Kerouac, Jack

SEE: *On the Road.*

Kerrigan, Nancy *(1969–)*

The 1993 U.S. figure skating champion, Nancy Kerrigan, was recognized as an elegant and artistic practitioner of the sport, one of America's premier ice princesses. In 1994 the beautiful Kerrigan was catapulted into much wider and most unwelcome fame through an internationally scandalous incident that brought her archrival, Tonya Harding, into international disrepute and irrevocably altered the image of the sport.

Already the holder of the 1992 Olympic bronze medal, Kerrigan was the favorite for the gold at the upcoming Winter Olympics in Lillehammer, Norway, at the time of the 1994 U.S. Championships in Detroit, Michigan, which doubled as the Olympic Trials that year. On the eve of the championships, while practicing at Detroit's Cobo Arena, Kerrigan received an injurious thwack on her right leg, which put her out of competition. The assailant, Shane Stant, proved to be part of a conspiracy of four men, one of whom was Harding's husband, Jeff Gillooly, and the attack had been planned to put Kerrigan out of action, thus clearing the way for Harding to win the U.S. title and a place at the Olympics. The gifted Kerrigan, granted an exemption from the U.S. trials, won the silver at Lillehammer, finishing only a fraction of a point behind Oksana Baiul, the Ukrainian gold medalist. Harding was allowed to skate at the Olympics, and the final free skate between Kerrigan and Harding drew record television ratings. Kerrigan subsequently endured bad press when she sniped at Baiul, was overheard to complain about her corporate sponsor, and married her agent.

The anti-Kerrigan conspiracy backfired disastrously. The four men involved all served prison sentences, while Harding—put on three years' probation, divorced from Gillooly, and banned from the U.S. Figure Skating Association—has remained covered in ignominy.

Kerrigan took a break from her career to have a baby but returned to the rink as a professional skater, enjoying considerable popularity and financial rewards, while the sport itself, thanks in part to the 1994 scandal, continues to attract major television viewing audiences. Kerrigan was inducted into the U.S. Figure Skating Hall of Fame in 2004.

Mary Hess

SEE ALSO: *Harding, Tonya; Olympics; Skating.*

BIBLIOGRAPHY

Baughman, Cynthia, ed. *Women on Ice: Feminist Essays on the Tonya Harding/Nancy Kerrigan Spectacle.* New York: Routledge, 1995.

Brennan, Christie. *Inside Edge: A Revealing Journey into the Secret World of Figure Skating.* New York: Anchor Books, 1997.

Frey, Jennifer. "Harding, Kerrigan: Another Sad Performance." *Washington Post*, February 8, 1998.

Small, W. J. "Kerrigan Finds Balance on and off Ice." *Philadelphia Inquirer*, September 17, 1998.

Kershaw, Doug *(1936–)*

Doug Kershaw, from Tiel Ridge, on the Gulf Coast of Louisiana, was one of the first to popularize southwestern Louisiana's Cajun sound, an infectious dance music characterized by fiddles and accordions as lead instruments. French is the language of most Cajun music—Hank Williams's "Jambalaya" is essentially an English lyric to the Cajun standard "Grand Texas," and Little Richard's "Keep a-Knockin" is an anglicized rock-and-roll version of "Tu Peut Coupez." Kershaw, however, sang in English from the beginning, and that gave him a quick in-road to a larger musical world.

With his brother Rusty, he went to Nashville in the mid-1950s. They made several records together as Rusty and Doug, culminating in Kershaw's breakout hit, "Louisiana Man," which reached number ten on the country charts in 1961. "Louisiana Man" never reached the Top 100 on the pop charts, but an appearance on Johnny Cash's hit television show made Kershaw a pop phenomenon, and his flamboyant fiddling style and stage presence (he favored velvet Edwardian suits) put him in demand as a solo act. He recorded duets with Hank Williams Jr. and Fats Domino, and in 1960 "Louisiana Man" became the first song broadcast back to earth from the moon during the Apollo 12 mission. In 2009 Kershaw was inducted into the Louisiana Music Hall of Fame.

Tad Richards

SEE ALSO: *Apollo Missions; Cash, Johnny; Country Music; Domino, Fats; Little Richard; Rock and Roll; Williams, Hank, Jr.; Williams, Hank, Sr.*

BIBLIOGRAPHY

Aswell, Tom. *Louisiana Rocks: The True Genesis of Rock and Roll.* New York: Pelican Books, 2009.

Kesey, Ken *(1935–2001)*

Described as a psychedelic outlaw and the "Dr. Strange" of American letters, Ken Kesey's fame as a counterculture luminary was assured by the impact of his novel *One Flew over the Cuckoo's Nest* (1962). Kesey was a champion wrestler who graduated from the University of Oregon and studied creative writing at Stanford, where he discovered the bohemian life he continued to pursue. Over the years he turned that life into the stuff of fiction, traveling across the country in a psychedelic-colored bus (now in the Smithsonian Institution) with his band of Merry Pranksters, whose adventures were chronicled by Tom Wolfe in *The Electric Kool-Aid Acid Test* (1968) and by Kesey himself in *The Further Inquiry* (1990). Kesey fraternized with Timothy Leary; fled to Mexico to avoid prosecution for marijuana possession; and lived in a commune with his wife, Faye (who bore him three children), and others, including Mountain Girl, who bore his fourth child, Sunshine. While embracing this unconventional lifestyle, Kesey wrote several major novels and other fiction, including two charming children's books.

One Flew over the Cuckoo's Nest (1962) was Kesey's first novel. The story of an unlikely redeemer who triumphs over the authoritarian Combine run by Big Nurse Ratched, the work was partly based on Kesey's own experiences as the paid subject of drug experiments at the veterans' hospital in Menlo Park, California. It remains a comedic masterpiece and a cult classic, lent further weight by the 1975 multi-Oscar-winning film version, starring Jack Nicholson. His second novel, *Sometimes a Great Notion* (1964), while less famous than *One Flew over the Cuckoo's Nest*, is considered by many critics to be his true masterpiece. Centered on the Stampers, a family with a logging business in a fictional Oregon town, the novel lays out the family's struggles after the local union loggers go on strike to protest lower wages and reduced employment opportunities in lumber mills after the introduction of the chainsaw. The Stampers, whose company employs only nonunion workers, defiantly decide that they will not only ignore the strike but will supply the local economy with all of the lumber that would have been cut were the workers not on strike.

Kesey died of complications from liver cancer on November 10, 2001, at the age of sixty-six.

Barbara Tepa Lupack

SEE ALSO: *Academy Awards; The Beat Generation; Best Sellers; Cancer; Communes; Hippies; Leary, Timothy; Nicholson, Jack;* One Flew over the Cuckoo's Nest*; Psychedelia; Wolfe, Tom.*

BIBLIOGRAPHY

Christensen, Mark. *Acid Christ: Ken Kesey, LSD and the Politics of Ecstasy.* Tucson, AZ: Schaffner Press, 2010.

Leeds, Barry H. *Ken Kesey.* New York: Ungar, 1981.

Porter, M. Gilbert. *The Art of Grit: Ken Kesey's Fiction.* Columbia: University of Missouri Press, 1982.

Tanner, Stephen L. *Ken Kesey.* Boston: Twayne, 1983.

Wolfe, Tom. *The Electric Kool-Aid Acid Test.* New York: Farrar, Straus & Giroux, 1968.

Ke$ha *(1987–)*

"Fun, unapologetic, rowdy, quirky, humorous, and interesting, but with substance." That is how electro pop superstar Ke$ha has described her music, but one could arguably apply those descriptors to the artist herself. Edgy, brash, and irreverent, Ke$ha came onto the scene in 2005 as an eighteen-year-old songwriter and background singer but scored her big break in early 2009 with an appearance on hip-hop artist Flo Rida's number one single, "Right Round." She then climbed her way to chart-topping success with the release of her first album, *Animal*, which debuted at number one on the Billboard 200 in January 2010 and produced two number one singles and a string of subsequent Top 10 hits.

Kesha Rose Sebert was born in Los Angeles, but her mother, singer-songwriter Pebe Sebert (best known for cowriting the 1978 single "Old Flames Can't Hold a Candle to You"), moved the family to Nashville, Tennessee, in 1991 after inking a songwriting deal. Ke$ha took to songwriting early on and began recording demos that Pebe would hand out to various industry contacts, garnering some interest in the younger Sebert's budding talent. In 2005, at eighteen and on track to study psychology at a prestigious university, Ke$ha answered the call to a career in music: she dropped out of school and returned to Los Angeles, where she was signed to Dr. Luke's record label, Kemosabe Entertainment.

In 2006 Ke$ha signed on with DAS Communications, where she collaborated to co-write "This Love" for the Veronicas, contributed background vocals to Britney Spears's "Lace and Leather," and appeared in the video for Katy Perry's "I Kissed a Girl." On the heels of the success of "Right Round," Ke$ha signed a multialbum deal with RCA records and got to work finishing her debut album, already six years in the making. The album's first single, "Tik Tok," would top the charts in eleven countries, set the weekly record for most digital downloads of a female artist, and eventually become the longest-running number one debut single by a female artist since 1977. The album's second, third, and fourth singles—"Blah Blah Blah," "Your Love Is My Drug," and "Take It Off"—would all achieve similar chart-topping success.

Ke$ha's Nashville upbringing, along with exposure to her mother's original songwriting, lends an unexpected country influence to her pop-driven tunes. She attributes her lyrical storytelling style (often criticized as crass and juvenile for its frivolous tales of partying and relationship reveals) to her appreciation for the honesty inherent in time-honored country lyrics. She credits her older brother with exposing her to hip-hop and punk, which along with 1980s pop and dance round out her musical influences. Her trademark sound is a talky, exaggerated "sing-rap" style.

Ke$ha's devil-may-care attitude and wild performance style struck a chord with legions of fans who identified with her record and its celebration of youth, life, and good (if not exactly clean) fun. Her onstage persona (unkempt, raunchy, wildly sexy) and glitter-heavy glam-rock fashion style (drawing from the likes of Queen and David Bowie) have combined to make Ke$ha a memorable, if polarizing, figure. Some critics have lambasted her unfiltered language and heavily autotuned vocals, whereas fans have flocked to embrace her unique expression of identity. The title track to her debut album, a tune that encourages individuality, has become an anthem of sorts; it is from this song that the multitude of Ke$ha fans have derived their moniker: *animals*. The longevity of Ke$ha's contribution to music has yet to be seen, but it is certain that she has made her mark in the collective consciousness of American pop culture.

Mariel E. Demler

SEE ALSO: *Autotune; Bowie, David; Perry, Katy; Pop Music; Rap; Spears, Britney; Top 40.*

BIBLIOGRAPHY

Day, Elizabeth. "She's a Walking, Talking Living Dollar." *Observer*, November 29, 2009.

Scaggs, Austin. "Party Animal: Behind Ke$ha's Big Debut." *Rolling Stone*, January 26, 2010.

Spitznagel, Eric. "Ke$ha Spends More on Glitter Every Month than Most People Spend on Rent." *Vanity Fair*, February 10, 2011.

Werde, Bill. "Ke$ha: The Billboard Cover Story." *Billboard*, February 19, 2010.

Kewpie Dolls

The creation of Rose O'Neill (1874–1944), Kewpie dolls were one of many crazes that swept America—and the world—in the early years of the twentieth century. Chubby, babylike figures with a tuft of hair (or topknot) similar to very young infants, the figures were popular prizes at carnival and amusement parks and were also sold through retailers. The figures are still popular among doll collectors and continue to be manufactured from the original molds under license by Lee Middleton Original Dolls.

The figures originally appeared in *Ladies' Home Journal* around 1905 as illustrations accompanying stories by O'Neill. At the prompting of her editor, O'Neill expanded the drawings into a series of illustrated verse for children and dubbed her creations *Kewpies* after the god of love, Cupid. In 1910 she moved her characters to *Woman's Home Companion*, and, according to O'Neill, hundreds of letters began to arrive from admirers seeking a doll like the Kewpies in her illustrations. At first O'Neill responded with paper dolls, but in 1912 she filed a design pattern for a doll.

The new dolls were initially manufactured for the Borgfeldt Company of New York by a number of European doll makers, such as the renowned German firm Kestner, and were mostly china, or bisque, dolls. At this time the bulk of dolls sold in the United States were manufactured in Europe. America's entry into World War I altered this arrangement, and domestic manufacturers, such as the Mutual Doll Company, began producing Kewpies. These later dolls were made from a variety of materials. The dolls were probably modeled in clay from O'Neill's drawings by Joseph Kallus, often described as O'Neill's assistant. After O'Neill's death, Kallus controlled the licensing and manufacture of Kewpie dolls until his death in 1984, when manufacturer Jesco acquired the rights.

In the 1910s Kewpies were a hot property, and O'Neill received licensing proposals for a variety of products, including

Kewpie Dolls. *Various Kewpie dolls are displayed at a 2009 exhibition in Tokyo, Japan, celebrating the 100th anniversary of the character's creation.* AP IMAGES.

cutlery, crockery, baby carriages, ice cream molds, and long johns. Many manufacturers simply bypassed O'Neill and appropriated the name and image for use in their products. William Hecht used Kewpies as the name of a line of children's clothing without authorization, and Japanese toy manufacturers turned out unauthorized Kewpies. Kewpie dolls came in a variety of sizes and types. There were cowboys, farmers, bellboys, and firemen. There were also black Kewpies known as Hottentots.

One licensing venture that appealed to O'Neill was a comic strip version of the Kewpies. In 1917 she produced a weekly page for the Sunday comic supplements featuring drawings and verse. It appeared for a year. In the mid-1930s, she revised the feature as a comic strip, with word balloons and a continuous story line, but the strip was short-lived as a result of O'Neill's declining health.

O'Neill's Kewpie dolls packaged cuteness as an item for purchase. It says something about the commercialization of American culture in the twentieth century that the readers of her early stories were not satiated by the illustrations and requested something more tangible. The ubiquitous nature of the dolls is attested to by the appearance of *Kewpie* in standard dictionaries to describe a type of doll rather than a brand-name product.

Ian Gordon

SEE ALSO: *Amusement Parks; Comics;* Ladies' Home Journal*; Toys; Traveling Carnivals; World War I.*

BIBLIOGRAPHY

Armitage, Shelley. *Kewpies and Beyond: The World of Rosie O'Neill.* Oxford: University Press of Mississippi, 1994.

Formanek-Brunell, Miriam. *Made to Play House: Dolls and the Commercialization of American Girlhood, 1830–1930.* New Haven, CT: Yale University Press, 1993.

O'Neill, Rose Cecil, and Miriam Formanek-Brunell. *The Story of Rose O'Neill: An Autobiography.* Columbia: University of Missouri Press, 1997.

Scott, Sharon M. *Toys and American Culture: An Encyclopedia.* Santa Barbara, CA: Greenwood, 2010.

Key West

Located on an 8-square-mile coral island off the southern tip of Florida, Key West is the southernmost city in the continental United States. Its location and environment give the place a mystique as the "Last Resort," the place where mainland North America dribbles to an ambiguous end in the Caribbean. As an artifact of popular culture, Key West generates powerful and often contradictory cultural messages: it is at once a quintessential navy town and a haven for literary figures, beachcombers, cruise ship passengers, and assorted eccentrics. During the Cuban missile crisis in 1962 and thereafter, it served the rhetoric of American presidents as a rugged outpost of democracy vis-à-vis Castro's Cuba with its Russian missiles "just 90 miles from our shores."

Contrary to popular belief, the name Key West has nothing to do with the island's western aspect in the Florida Keys, which drift languorously from the mainland like a strand of seaweed. The name is really a corruption of *Cayo Hueso* (Island of Bones), the moniker given to the island by Spanish explorers after they reputedly found the skeletal remains of native people slaughtered in a fierce battle. Perhaps the coral rock that forms the island suggested bony encrustations to superstitious sailors wary of shipwrecks on the jagged reefs that have long made Key West a nautical graveyard and a refuge for smugglers, salvagers, and castaways.

Hemingway Days in Key West. *Ernest Hemingway look-alikes ride and push fake bulls as they make the turn on Duval Street during the "Running of the Bulls" in Key West in 2011.* **AP IMAGES.**

A NAVAL TRADITION

For much of its history, Key West has been the site of a U.S. Navy base. Commander David Porter established the first navy presence there in the 1820s, imagining he had created the "Gibraltar of the Gulf." Key West prospered as the only Southern city to remain under Union control throughout the Civil War. At the time of the Spanish-American War, the entire Atlantic fleet was based in Key West's harbor. During World War II the island was known rather dubiously as the "Singapore of the West." Resident poet Elizabeth Bishop predicted in 1942 that after the war, a ruined Key West would be "nothing but a naval base and a bunch of bars and cheap apartments." The island regained some of its dignity in 1946 when President Harry Truman procured the naval commandant's headquarters for his "Little White House." Although its presence was much diminished, the navy still owned about a quarter of the town at the beginning of the twenty-first century.

All things nautical contribute to the island's famous ambiance. Winslow Homer discovered Key West in 1885, finding watercolor the perfect medium through which to capture the shimmering cerulean seas and lush green landscapes drowsing under a tropical sun. For twentieth-century poet Wallace Stevens, the essence of Key West was its aqueous ambiguity, its ephemeral substance surrounded by the "ever-hooded, tragic gestured sea." His well-known poem "The Idea of Order at Key West" can be interpreted as a hymn either to order or disorder or to a subjective reality simultaneously negotiating between both. Even the act of withdrawing to the bustling, commercial North and away from sultry Key West, can bring uncertainty, as Stevens laments in the poem "Farewell to Florida." Here, the poet watches from a ship as "Key West sank downward under massive clouds / And silvers and greens spread over the sea. The moon / Is at the mast-head and the past is dead." Yet: "Her mind had bound me round."

ISLAND LORE

More than any other writer, Ernest Hemingway is associated with Key West in the popular mind. After leaving Paris in 1928, he acted on the suggestion of fellow writer John Dos Passos and established residence in a rented house in Key West with his wife, Pauline. In 1931 the Hemingways bought an eighty-year-old limestone villa, where they lived together until they divorced in 1940 and which now serves as one of the island's principal tourist attractions. Hemingway wrote several short stories; many articles; and one novel, *To Have and Have Not* (1937), about Key West, which he portrays as seedy, decadent, and impoverished, "the St. Tropez of the poor."

Hemingway's growing celebrity soon obscured the more prosaic details of his life. Leicester Hemingway writes in *My Brother, Ernest Hemingway* (1962) that his brother's Key West period "begins in the public mind with a picture of a bronzed giant fighting huge fish, then heading inshore for the roughest, toughest bar to celebrate the catch, possibly pausing somewhere to beat out a letter to *Esquire*, using words growled from one corner of the mouth. It was not like that ever." Nevertheless, the Hemingway Days Festival, which began in 1981, celebrates the machismo image of the writer with parodies and pastiches of his works, contests in which white-bearded and barrel-chested men compete in Hemingway look-alike contests, costume parties, arm-wrestling competitions, and drinking bouts at Sloppy Joe's Bar.

A long line of other writers—including Jack London, Tennessee Williams, Robert Frost, John Hersey, Tom McGuane, Truman Capote, Alison Lurie, Bishop, and Annie Dillard—have found Key West congenial. Popular crime and mystery writers such as Laurence Shames and James W. Hall have used the city as the backdrop for their stories, exaggerating its eccentricities. In *Bones of Coral* (1991), Hall describes Key West as an "outpost for the unstable, maladjusted, the just plain insane. If they weren't insane when they came, they turned that way. They became islanders, devolved creatures."

More likely, they were merely inspired to become beachcombers, boozers, and faux marooned mariners awaiting the next tide. Singer Jimmy Buffett and his Coral Reefer Band—with their besotted, erzatz-pirate, parrot-pop anthems—celebrate this offbeat, unfettered Key West attitude, which can be decanted in Buffett's Margaritaville Cafe on the island and purchased in any of the dozens of souvenir shops and T-shirt emporia. Conch Republic Days each year advance this maverick tradition, commemorating the island's ostensible secession from the United States in 1982, with the imaginary Conch Republic surviving as a symbol of Key West's singularity as the Last Resort.

Paul Ashdown

SEE ALSO: *Buffett, Jimmy; Capote, Truman; Dillard, Annie; Frost, Robert; Hemingway, Ernest; Hersey, John; London, Jack; Spring Break; Williams, Tennessee; World War II.*

BIBLIOGRAPHY

Cox, Christopher. *A Key West Companion*. New York: St. Martin's Press, 1983.

Hemingway, Leicester. *My Brother, Ernest Hemingway*. Cleveland, OH: World Publishing, 1962.

Longenback, James. *Wallace Stevens: The Plain Sense of Things*. New York: Oxford University Press, 1991.

Ogle, Maureen. *Key West: History of an Island of Dreams*. Gainesville: University Press of Florida, 2003.

Stevens, Wallace. *Collected Poems*. New York: Knopf, 1954.

Williams, Joy. *The Florida Keys: A History & Guide*, 10th ed. New York: Random House, 2003.

The Keystone Kops

Mack Sennett's Keystone Kops have long been a byword for bungling, absurd, and hilarious incompetency. Icons of the early comedy "flickers" that made Sennett the most significant, famous, and successful pioneer of film comedy, the Kops made their first appearance on the early silent screen in *Hoffmeyer's Legacy* (1912). The Keystone Kops were named for Sennett's Keystone Studios and were featured regularly in the American silent-era slapstick movies pioneered at the studios in 1912.

With the release of *The Bangville Police* (1913), the Kops were established as a much-loved American institution and an integral element of Sennett's production output and comedy style. Sporting handlebar mustaches and ill-fitting uniforms, the conscientious but utterly inept policemen (and sometimes the Keystone Firemen) fell out of cars; under cars; over cliffs; and, more often than not, over themselves—all at artificially high speeds, defining the art of slapstick in which Sennett specialized and which would be refined by the arrival of Charlie Chaplin at Sennett's studio in 1914.

Sennett was blessed from the beginning with a stable of gifted comic practitioners. They were tuned into Keystone's rambunctious style, with its emphasis on sight gags, pratfalls, and the throwing of custard pies (a routine that originated there) and that was enhanced by Sennett's under-cranked

Keystone Kops. *The Keystone Kops appear in a scene from the 1914 silent film* In the Clutches of the Gang. **HULTON ARCHIVE/GETTY IMAGES.**

camera, speeded-up frames, and skillful editing. Among these artists were Ford Sterling and Chester Conklin, the most famous members of the zany police force, whose escapades, in which reality was suspended and subverted to create a world of comic chaos, anchored the hundreds of slapstick comedies and farces made at Keystone.

Renowned for carrying out their own hair-raising—and frequently dangerous—stunts, the original Kops lineup featured actors Charles Avery, Bobby Dunn, George Jesky, Edgar Kennedy, Hank Mann, Mack Riley, and Slim Summerville. Mann, who played Chief Teeheezel, was subsequently replaced by Ford Sterling, and with Sennett using the group as a proving ground for ambitious young actors seeking a career with the studio, the lineup changed frequently. At one time future star Roscoe "Fatty" Arbuckle was among its uniformed members. Despite their considerable success with contemporary audiences, however, the Kops were soon eased out of the regular Keystone roster. Many other Sennett comedies continued to feature the group's chaotic brand of slapstick, and they made a return of sorts when they were paid homage in *Abbott and Costello Meet the Keystone Kops* in 1955.

The influence of the Keystone Kops on the development of comedy in cinema is significant. This influence can be most particularly perceived in the films of Laurel and Hardy and, later, in cruder form, The Three Stooges. And whereas over the decades verbal humor came to either replace or complement visual humor, the preposterously farcical elements that informed the antics of the Kops have survived in variously modified forms to the present day, from Jerry Lewis through Mel Brooks to Robin Williams and Jim Carrey.

David Holloway

SEE ALSO: *Abbott and Costello; Arbuckle, Fatty; Brooks, Mel; Chaplin, Charlie; Laurel and Hardy; Lewis, Jerry; Sennett, Mack; Silent Movies; The Three Stooges; Williams, Robin.*

BIBLIOGRAPHY

Bordwell, David, et al. *The Classical Hollywood Cinema: Film Style and Mode of Production to 1960.* London: Routledge, 1985.

Dyer, Richard. *Stars.* London: British Film Institute, 1979.

Hoffmann, Frank W., and William G. Bailey. *Arts & Entertainment Fads.* New York: Haworth Press, 1990.

Lahue, Kalton C., and Terry Brewer. *Kops and Custards: The Legend of Keystone Films.* Norman: University of Oklahoma Press, 1968.

Langman, Larry. *American Film Cycles: The Silent Era.* Westport, CT: Greenwood Press, 1998.

Ross, Steven J. *Working Class Hollywood: Silent Film and the Shaping of Class in America.* Princeton, NJ: Princeton University Press, 1998.

Sennett, Mack. *King of Comedy.* San Francisco: Mercury House, 1990.

Kill Bill

Director Quentin Tarantino's two-part film *Kill Bill*—consisting of *Kill Bill: Vol. I* (2003) and *Kill Bill: Vol. II* (2004)—fits into several well-known categories: modern Western, revenge drama, martial arts movie, and cult classic. At the same time, it crosses genre boundaries to create a unique film experience. Mixing extreme action with sophisticated layers of ambiguity and irony, *Kill Bill* has both emotional and intellectual appeal. It also offers an iconic portrayal of female self-empowerment, skillfully rendered by the film's cocreator, actress Uma Thurman.

Kill Bill revolves around a character initially known only as "the Bride," who is beaten, shot, and left for dead at her wedding. Through a series of flashbacks and nonchronological scenes, the Bride is revealed to be Beatrix Kiddo, a highly accomplished martial artist; former member of the Deadly Viper Assassination Squad and former lover of their charismatic boss, Bill. After learning she is pregnant with Bill's child, Kiddo flees, hoping to leave the group and its violent lifestyle behind. Bill and the Vipers, however, find her, kill everyone at the wedding, leave her in a coma, and take the baby. When she awakens several years later, Kiddo sets out to eliminate the Vipers—and kill Bill.

In a memorable sequence that features strong visual elements, striking camera angles, and compelling musical accompaniment, the sword-wielding Kiddo defeats a samurai gang in a Japanese nightclub, then bests one of the Vipers in a dramatic duel. The other Vipers are all gruesomely dispatched before Kiddo finds Bill, enjoying a surreally normal home life with their young daughter. In a final, painfully believable conversation, the former couple explore issues of morality, intimacy, and emotional bondage, gathering themes and plot threads that have been woven through the two films.

The intense love-hate relationship between Bill and Kiddo adds complexity to the film, capturing the powerful and potentially destructive attachment of master and protégé. At the beginning of their relationship, Bill had sent Kiddo to be trained by his own teacher, a legendary kung fu master. The fierce old man was eventually so impressed by Kiddo's perseverance that he told her (and only her) his greatest secret: the technique of the Five Point Palm Exploding Heart. In the end Kiddo demonstrates the method on an astonished Bill, and they share a poignant moment before he dies. A victorious, exhausted Kiddo leaves with her daughter.

Although *Kill Bill* is extremely violent throughout, the action is so stylized and contextualized that it seems artistic rather than realistic, which makes the films more acceptable to mainstream audiences. Both volumes enjoyed box-office success and developed a strong fan following—especially among women, many of whom empathized with Kiddo's anger and admired her systematic, remorseless, and determined quest for revenge. Critics also liked the film, praising Tarantino's skillful integration of visual and musical references to a wide variety of classic and modern films, including U.S. and Italian spaghetti Westerns, horror movies, Asian cinema, anime, and even Hollywood extravaganzas.

Cynthia Giles

SEE ALSO: *Animé; Hollywood; Horror Movies; Spaghetti Westerns; Tarantino, Quentin; The Western.*

BIBLIOGRAPHY

Holm, D. K. *Kill Bill: An Unofficial Casebook.* London: Glitter, 2004.

Lavin, Maud. *Push Comes to Shove: New Images of Aggressive Women.* Cambridge, MA: MIT Press, 2010.

McGee, Patrick. *From "Shane" to "Kill Bill": Rethinking the Western.* Malden, MA: Blackwell, 2007.

Kimmel, Jimmy *(1967–)*

Talk show host Jimmy Kimmel has surprised critics more than once by finding an unexpectedly large audience for his particular brand of outrageous humor. A former radio sports commentator, he seemingly came from nowhere to become one of television's most successful late-night personalities. Though some viewers and critics are disgusted by what they consider his smug juvenile comedy, others find his show fresh and contemporary. Kimmel has grown and matured as a performer during his decade of hosting *Jimmy Kimmel Live!* and has been rewarded with such prestigious jobs as speaking at the White House Correspondents' Dinner and hosting the Primetime Emmy Awards.

The eldest of three children of Jim and Joan Kimmel, James Christian Kimmel was born in 1967 in Brooklyn, New York, and moved with his family to Las Vegas, Nevada, when he was nine years old. As a child he idolized CBS talk show host David Letterman, and when he was older he listened to radio shock-jock Howard Stern, forming an ambition to become a provocative entertainer. He gained his first show business experience as a disc jockey on campus radio stations while attending the University of Nevada, Las Vegas, and Arizona State University. He left college without graduating and took a number of radio jobs around the country before landing a position in the mid-1990s as Jimmy the Sports Guy on the *Kevin & Bean* morning show on KROQ radio in Los Angeles.

In 1997 Kimmel moved to television as cohost of the Comedy Central game show *Win Ben Stein's Money*, trading quips with Stein, an actor and a political commentator. Kimmel's quick wit and brash style meshed well with the show's quirky format, and he and Stein shared a 1999 Emmy Award for Best Game Show Host. That same year Kimmel was given his own show on Comedy Central, the highly satiric *The Man Show*. The program extolled all things masculine and politically incorrect with the deadpan irony that would become Kimmel's trademark. Though critics found the show misogynistic, immature, and vulgar, it found a receptive audience among men between the ages of eighteen and thirty-four and remained on the air for six seasons. Also in 1999 Kimmel formed his own production company, Jackhole Industries, and began producing even more juvenile male-oriented shows such as *Crank Yankers*, which featured a cast of puppets, some with purposely offensive names such as Special Ed, the mentally disabled puppet, and Moo Shu, the Chinese rapper.

In 2002, as ABC sought ways to draw in more young viewers, the network took note of Kimmel's success with that demographic and hired him to host a new late-night show to follow the newsmagazine *Nightline*. *Jimmy Kimmel Live!* debuted the night of the Super Bowl in January 2003, featuring rapper Snoop Dogg as cohost and actor George Clooney and rock group Coldplay as guests. One of the notable events of the premier occurred when an audience member vomited after drinking too much at the show's open bar.

Kimmel was a young host seeking to appeal to a young audience, and he approached his show with an informality that set it apart from other late-night shows. A host rather than a comic, he did not deliver a stand-up monologue, and he dressed casually. Critics blasted *Jimmy Kimmel Live!*, calling the program aimless and the host unprepared, and the program lagged unsurprisingly behind late-night giants *The Tonight Show with Jay Leno* and the *Late Show with David Letterman*. His underdog status, however, gave Kimmel the freedom to develop innovative comedy routines, and his unpredictable and often crude humor continued to appeal to the young audiences it was meant to attract.

ABC stood by the show, renewing it through three slow seasons, and by the fourth year ratings began to climb. Kimmel reverted to a more traditional talk show format, eliminating the cohost and dressing in suits and ties, but he retained his earthy sardonic humor. In 2008 Kimmel's then-girlfriend and fellow shock-comic Sarah Silverman surprised him on the show with a homemade music video titled "I'm F—ing Matt Damon." The video delighted the audience and became a viral Internet hit with more than eight million viewers. Kimmel responded with his own video, "I'm F—ing Ben Affleck," which included not only the title actor but a host of A-list celebrities, including Brad Pitt, Cameron Diaz, and Don Cheadle, singing the X-rated lyrics.

As Kimmel's popularity increased, ABC backed the show more enthusiastically with a new ad campaign and more high-profile guests. Kimmel was increasingly acknowledged as an influential talent and was tapped to host the 2012 Primetime Emmy Awards show. His performance at the prestigious 2012 White House Correspondents' Dinner was widely ruled a triumph of hilarity.

Tina Gianoulis

SEE ALSO: *Clooney, George; Coldplay; Damon, Matt; Emmy Awards; Game Shows; The Internet; Leno, Jay; Letterman, David;* Nightline*; Pitt, Brad; Radio; Silverman, Sarah; Snoop Dogg; Stern, Howard; Television;* The Tonight Show.

BIBLIOGRAPHY

Grego, Melissa. "Student of the Game." *Broadcasting & Cable*, February 16, 2009, 10.

Grossman, Ben. "Gimme More Jimmy." *Broadcasting & Cable*, March 3, 2008, 4.

Hibberd, James. "Kimmel's Old-School Shift Wins Following; Ratings Rise as Late-Night Host Bows to Tradition." *TelevisionWeek*, December 18, 2006, 3.

Young, Susan. "Latenight Growth Spurt: After Rough Start, Kimmel Reaches Milestone with Loyal Aud in Tow." *Daily Variety*, April 3, 2008, A1.

King, Albert *(1923–1992)*

Albert King was one of the most distinctive, innovative, and influential blues guitarists of the postwar era. He was also one of the only blues players to sell records and play for white audiences without losing his traditional black following. His years with Stax Records in the 1960s produced a series of albums that blended classic blues with modern rhythm and blues and soul.

King was an imposing figure—standing 6 feet, 4 inches tall and weighing more than 250 pounds—and it could be heard in his music. His muscular guitar tone and economical use of notes was sustained by a raw power nearly impossible to copy. A left-handed player, King played his Gibson Flying-V guitar upside down and backward, so rather than fret notes quickly up and down the neck, he was forced to use his strength to bend notes, producing a strikingly vocal quality. His tone was an inspiration to guitarists Stevie Ray Vaughan and Michael Bloomfield as well as to fellow lefty Otis Rush. British guitarist Eric Clapton, while with the band Cream, played a King solo nearly note-for-note in his 1967 hit "Strange Brew."

King was born in Indianola, Mississippi, not far from fellow blues guitarist B. B. King, who was about twenty-eight months younger. Albert would often joke that they were brothers, but the two did not meet until both were famous. Although they cited the same musicians—Blind Lemon Jefferson, Lonnie Johnson, and Aaron "T-Bone" Walker—as their biggest influences, the two Kings sounded nothing alike. While B. B. danced above the beat with a jazz player's phrasing and a trebly tone, Albert dug deep into the groove with thick, meaty bends. B. B. rose to prominence in the 1950s, yet Albert had to wait until the mid-1960s, when he was more than forty years old, to make his mark.

As a child, King built his own guitar from a cigar box and whisk broom wires. He spent his early years picking cotton, working construction, driving a bulldozer, and developing his beefy musical style. In the early 1950s, while living in Oceana, Arkansas, King formed the In the Groove Boys, his first band, with some friends.

King soon moved to Gary, Indiana, where he began playing drums for Jimmy Reed. In 1953 he cut his first singles, "Bad Luck Blues" and "Be on Your Merry Way," for the Parrot label in Chicago. King's next recordings were in 1959 for the Bobbin label in St. Louis, Missouri, where he adopted a big-band swing style led by Johnnie Johnson, the pianist who played on many of Chuck Berry's greatest recordings. King remained with Bobbin and the King label of Cincinnati, Ohio, which leased some of the Bobbin sides, until 1963, when he made the move to Stax Records in Memphis, Tennessee.

King's union with the Stax house band of Booker T. and the MGs resulted in some of the best and most popular blues records ever produced. Drummer and producer Al Jackson, organist Booker T. Washington, bass player Donald "Duck" Dunn, and guitarist Steve Cropper, plus the Memphis Horns of Wayne Jackson and Andrew Love, provided the perfect foundation for King's career. *Born under a Bad Sign*, released in 1967, was a revelation. Most of the songs strayed from typical twelve-bar blues shuffles, but King was right at home.

"We were, basically, on top of the music scene as far as what we thought the R&B public wanted to hear," Cropper said in *Blues Guitar: The Men Who Made the Music*. "So it was a little more polished, a little slicker than some of the other blues coming out. He had his own unique style, and it still got in the blues rack. But the songs that we picked for him and some of the arrangements we did wound up in the pop and R&B racks, too." Rock critic Robert Palmer writes in the liner notes to *Albert Live*, a double album released in 1977 and available on the Tomato label, that King's impact at the time of the release of *Born under a Bad Sign* "was as inescapable among blues players as John Coltrane's influence was in jazz."

King became popular with young, white audiences in the late 1960s when rock promoter Bill Graham booked him to open a series of shows at the Fillmore Auditorium in San Francisco, sharing bills with Jimi Hendrix and Janis Joplin. King's second album on Stax, *Live Wire/Blues Power*, was recorded at the Fillmore and is regarded by many critics as one the finest recordings of blues in concert.

King continued to push the boundaries of blues into the 1970s by playing with the St. Louis Symphony and becoming the first blues player to appear with full orchestration. His 1972 album, *I'll Play the Blues for You*, built upon *Born under a Bad Sign* with a James Brown funk feel. King's mid- to late 1970s releases took on a disco feel, which was an attempt to update his sound. These albums were overproduced and failed to capture the energy of his previous work. He continued to record for Fantasy Records of Berkeley, California, which had bought out Stax, and returned to form with his album *I'm in a Phone Booth, Baby* in 1984. He continued to tour until his death from a heart attack on December 21, 1992, in Memphis.

Jon Klinkowitz

SEE ALSO: *Berry, Chuck; Blues; Brown, James; Clapton, Eric; Coltrane, John; Graham, Bill; Hendrix, Jimi; Joplin, Janis; King, B. B.; Rhythm and Blues; Rock and Roll; Soul Music; Vaughan, Stevie Ray; Walker, Aaron "T-Bone."*

BIBLIOGRAPHY

DeCurtis, Anthony. "Living Legends." *Rolling Stone*, September 21, 1989, 89–99.

Obrecht, Jas, ed. *Blues Guitar: The Men Who Made the Music.* San Francisco: GPI Books, 1990.

Paul, Alan. "Live Wire." *Guitar World*, July, 1991, 42–47.

Talevski, Nick. *Knocking on Heaven's Door: Rock Obituaries.* London: Omnibus, 2006.

King, B. B. *(1925–)*

To people the world over, B. B. King is the personification of the blues. No blues or rock-and-roll musician in America can escape his influence, either directly or indirectly. His fusion of acoustic country blues with jazz set the stage for half a century of development in African American music. Although he never attained the widespread commercial success enjoyed by others, King rose to his billing as "King of the Blues" without compromising his style or musicianship.

King is credited with bringing vibrato to the electric guitar. The stinging, fluttering sound of his guitar, named Lucille, is totally unique and instantly recognizable. King's story is one of the most amazing in American music. His rise from picking cotton in Mississippi to touring the world has become part of the mythology of the American Dream.

MISSISSIPPI ROOTS

Riley B. King was born September 16, 1925, on a farm near Itta Bena, Mississippi. His parents separated when he was four, and he lived with his mother until her death when he was nine. He then lived with his maternal grandmother (his father was in nearby Lexington) and on his own, supervised by an extended family of aunts, uncles, and caring white plantation owners. His earliest musical memories were the hollers of fellow field workers, and his first exposure to the guitar came in church, where

B. B. King. *B. B. King performs in San Francisco, California, in 2011.* C FLANIGAN/CONTRIBUTOR/WIREIMAGE/GETTY IMAGES.

he heard the Reverend Archie Fair play. He listened to the records of Blind Lemon Jefferson and Lonnie Johnson on an aunt's Victrola.

"Blind Lemon and Lonnie hit me the hardest, I believe, because their voices were so distinct, natural, and believable. I heard them talking to me," King writes in his autobiography, *Blues All around Me* (1996). "As guitarists, they weren't fancy. Their guitars were hooked up to their feelings, just like their voices. . . . No one molded my musical manner like Blind Lemon and Lonnie. They entered my soul and stayed." As a teenager, King fell under the spell of "T-Bone" Walker, the swinging Texan who pioneered the electric guitar along with Charlie Christian. Other key influences were guitarist Django Reinhardt from Belgium and saxophonists Lester Young and Louis Jordan.

King bought his first guitar for $15 when he was twelve and played it while singing tenor with the Elkhorn Jubilee Singers, a gospel group he organized with a cousin and two friends. By the mid-1940s he had moved to Memphis, Tennessee, and sought out his cousin, Bukka White. Already a famous musician, White took King under his wing. King's signature vibrato developed as a result of his failure to master White's slide technique.

EARLY CAREER

King played blues and gospel on street corners around Beale Street and landed a ten-minute show on radio station WDIA sponsored by Pepticon, a cure-all tonic. King was a hit and became a regular disc jockey known as the "Beale Street Blues Boy," later shortened to "B. B." His radio show led to bookings outside Memphis and the recording of his first singles in 1949 on the short-lived Bullet label. King was soon discovered by Ike Turner, who was working at the time as a talent scout for Modern Records. King had a hit with "Three O'Clock Blues," which spent fifteen weeks at the top of Billboard's R&B chart in 1951 and afforded him the opportunity to tour nationwide.

King stayed with Modern Records until 1962 and then went to ABC Records. Through the 1950s and 1960s he maintained a grueling touring schedule, playing as many as 340 dates per year. He recorded *Live at the Regal*, one of the finest examples of live blues, in 1965 at Chicago's Regal Theatre. Still, King remained a star only on the so-called "Chitlin' Circuit" of black clubs. He fell through the cracks when rock and roll came around, unable to cross over like Little Richard, Fats Domino, or Bo Diddley, and he did not fit in with the soul movement of the 1960s like Ray Charles or the Motown Records roster. Furthermore, he was unable to capitalize on the blues revival of the 1960s, during which country-blues artists such as Lightnin' Hopkins and Son House were embraced by white folk-music fans. Academics saw King's electric guitar and swinging horn section as a corruption of the country-blues tradition.

RECOGNITION AND ACCLAIM

King's fortunes changed in 1968 when he hired manager Sidney Seidenberg, who booked him into white rock venues such as the Fillmore Auditorium in San Francisco and on television's *The Tonight Show* and *The Ed Sullivan Show*. Seidenberg's work paid off in 1970: King's biggest hit, "The Thrill Is Gone," reached number fifteen on the Billboard pop chart. Continuing to push for mainstream bookings, Seidenberg opened up Las Vegas and booked tours of the Soviet Union and Africa.

King started to receive numerous career-achievement awards, earning induction into the Blues Foundation Hall of Fame in 1984 and the Rock and Roll Hall of Fame in 1987. Additionally in 1987, he was given the Grammy Lifetime Achievement Award. King's fans had always been older, but he gained exposure with a much younger audience when Bono of the Irish rock group U2 wrote a duet with King, "When Love Comes to Town," in 1988. The song made the U2 concert movie *Rattle and Hum* and won an MTV Video Music Award. King also opened for U2 on the band's North American tour.

His 1993 album *Blues Summit*, consisting of duets with eleven other top blues performers, maintained his reputation as an American institution. That reputation was enhanced when he received the Presidential Medal of the Arts in 1990 and again when his life was celebrated by President Bill Clinton at the Kennedy Center Honors in 1995. In 1997 he received a Lifetime Achievement Award from the Blues Foundation. King continues to record both solo and in collaboration with other artists. His 2000 collaboration with Eric Clapton, *Riding with the King*, won the 2001 Grammy for Best Traditional Blues Album.

King was ranked number three on *Rolling Stone*'s "100 Greatest Guitarists of All Time." After his eighth Entertainer of the Year Award at the Blues Music Awards, King was retired from eligibility, and in 2006 the award was renamed the B. B. King Entertainer of the Year in his honor. He won his fifteenth Grammy (not including his Lifetime Achievement honor) in 2009, receiving the Best Traditional Blues Album for *One Kind Favor* (2008).

King began opening blues clubs in the 1990s, and now the B. B. King Blues Club has numerous locations across the country, including one in his home state of Mississippi. He continues to identify strongly with his roots. In 2008 the B. B. King Museum and Delta Interpretive Center opened in Indianola, Mississippi, celebrating King's career and legacy and offering visitors a musical history of the Delta. He was awarded the Mississippi Medal of Service in 2011. In addition to his work in Mississippi, King is a board member of Little Kids Rock, which provides musical education in the form of free instruments and instruction for public school children.

Jon Klinkowitz

SEE ALSO: *Blues; Charles, Ray; Clapton, Eric; Diddley, Bo; Domino, Fats; Grammy Awards; Jazz; Jordan, Louis; Little Richard; Rock and Roll; Sullivan, Ed;* The Tonight Show*; Turner, Ike and Tina; U2; Walker, Aaron "T-Bone."*

BIBLIOGRAPHY

Danchin, Sebastian. *Blues Boy: The Life and Music of B. B. King*. Jackson: University of Mississippi Press, 1998.

Keil, Charles. *Urban Blues*. Chicago: University of Chicago Press, 1966.

King, B. B., and David Ritz. *Blues All around Me: The Autobiography of B. B. King*. New York: Avon Books, 1996.

Kostelanetz, Richard, and Anson John Pope. *The B. B. King Companion: Five Decades of Commentary*. New York: Schirmer Books, 1997.

Kostelanetz, Richard, and Jesse Reiswig. *The B. B. King Reader: 6 Decades of Commentary*. Milwaukee, WI: Hal Leonard, 2005.

Sawyer, Charles. *The Arrival of B. B. King: The Authorized Biography*. New York: Da Capo Press, 1980.

King, Billie Jean *(1943–)*

Intensely competitive and outspoken in her demand for equality for women athletes, Billie Jean King changed the face of women's sports, paving the way for today's professional women athletes. Holder of a record twenty Wimbledon titles and winner of all four Grand Slam tournaments, King is perhaps best remembered for her defeat of Bobby Riggs during the epic Battle of the Sexes in 1973. Passionately dedicated to tennis, to women's rights, and to being one of the best athletes—male or female—of her day, King's heroic actions redefined what was possible for women, making her a role model for generations to come.

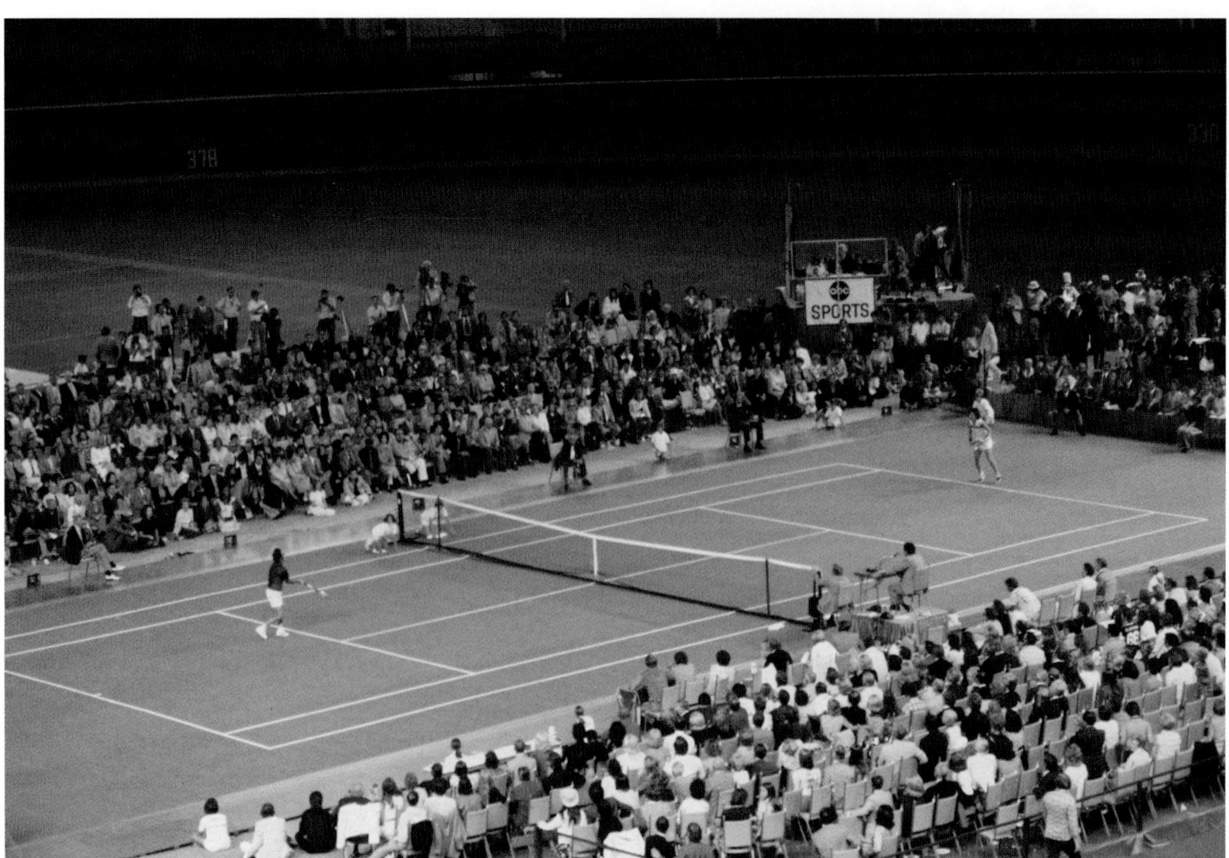

Billie Jean King and Bobby Riggs. *Billie Jean King and Bobby Riggs compete in the Battle of the Sexes at the Houston Astrodome in September 1973.* FOCUS ON SPORT/CONTRIBUTOR/GETTY IMAGES SPORT/GETTY IMAGES.

EARLY LIFE

Billie Jean Moffitt was born in Long Beach, California, on November 22, 1943. The daughter of a fireman and a homemaker, and the sister of future San Francisco Giants relief pitcher Randy Moffitt, Billie Jean was an athletic girl who excelled at softball. At a very young age, she announced to her mother that she planned to do something special with her life, and when she discovered tennis a few years later, she dedicated herself to the sport. Because the family could not afford a membership at the local country club, she learned her sport on the public courts. By the time she was twelve, she was good enough to play in sanctioned tournaments, and her father got a second job while her mother sold Avon and Tupperware so that their daughter could compete. As a teenager, Billie Jean not only fought the elitism of tennis but also was made painfully aware that girls' sports were valued differently than boys' when the boys' team received funding and the girls had to fend for themselves.

In 1961 seventeen-year-old Billie Jean qualified to play doubles at Wimbledon, and she and her partner, Karen Hantze, funded by a local businessman, flew to England to compete. They won, becoming Wimbledon's youngest women's doubles winners ever. But in the early 1960s, winning Wimbledon was not enough to start a career in tennis. In fact, there were no real careers in tennis for women. Tennis was an amateur sport, and the only money to be made was a few hundred dollars under the table for showing up at a tournament. So Billie Jean returned home and enrolled at Los Angeles State College, where she fell in love with a fellow student, Larry King.

The couple married in 1965, and King put her husband through law school by playing tennis, which she continued to do with great success, winning all the big tournaments. In 1968 the major championships were finally opened up to professionals as well as amateurs. But the prize money for the women was dramatically unequal to that awarded to the men—women sometimes earned as little as one tenth of what men did. This infuriated King, who conceived of the idea of starting a women's tour.

TENNIS CAREER

In 1970 King and a group of women players refused to play an important tournament where the prize money was eight to one in favor of the men. Instead, with the aid of Gladys Heldman, the founder of *World Tennis* magazine, they put together a competing tournament in Houston, with $5,000 in prize money. The powers that be in the tennis world threatened to suspend the defecting players, but the women held fast. When Heldman solicited $2,500 more in prize money from Philip Morris, which was marketing a new cigarette for women, the tournament was christened the Virginia Slims International—the first professional women's tennis tournament.

Although some of the players, most notably Chris Evert, refused to sign on, the Virginia Slims women's tour was a success in its first year. And so was King, who continued to do well in the major tournaments, beating Evert in the U.S. Open final that same year and becoming the first woman athlete to win $100,000 in prize money in a single year.

Within two years all the women players joined the tour, and tennis itself was irrevocably changed. King, however, still had more causes for which to fight. Holding her ground against all dissenters, she pushed through the Women's Tennis Association, a union of women tennis players. Women's sports, buoyed by Title IX, which prevented discrimination against women athletes, had begun to change. Then came the event that transformed King into a feminist heroine beyond the boundaries of tennis.

In 1973 fifty-five-year-old former Wimbledon champion Bobby Riggs played the number two woman in the world, Margaret Court, in a tennis match that would prove, Riggs hoped, that men were better athletes than women. In what has been referred to as the Mother's Day Massacre, Riggs beat Court in straight sets. As King later wrote, "My first reaction was, 'Oh no, now I'm going to have to play him.'" Indeed, a match was soon arranged between Riggs and the number one woman on the tour, King.

On September 20, 1973, 30,000 fans filled the Houston Astrodome, and fifty million viewers tuned in on television to watch King take on the self-proclaimed male chauvinist pig, Riggs, in the Battle of the Sexes. Fit, tanned, and ready to play, King won the $100,000 winner-take-all match in three straight sets. More than a sporting event, the King–Riggs match became a defining moment in American popular culture and feminist history, one of the few events that elicits an exact response to the question, "Where were you when . . . ?"

A POWERFUL ADVOCATE

At the end of her career, King was outed as a lesbian, becoming the first woman in professional sports to bear the brunt of a nation's homophobia. Although her admission of her sexuality was clouded by her stated discomfort with being a lesbian and her continued marriage to Larry, King laid the groundwork for women such as Martina Navratilova, Melissa Etheridge, and Ellen DeGeneres to come out of the closet. Now openly lesbian, King lends her outspoken advocacy to gay causes and has been honored for her support by organizations such as the Human Rights Campaign, GLAAD, and Lambda Legal Foundation. She was awarded the Presidential Medal of Freedom in 2009 for championing gender equality in professional sports and for her work on behalf of lesbian and gay rights.

One of *Life* magazine's 100 Most Important Americans of the twentieth century, King is a heroine to countless women who saw, in her defeat of Riggs and in her unqualified success as one of the first professional women athletes, hope for their own dreams. A dedicated activist and coach, she continues to lobby on behalf of the causes in which she fervently believes, from Team Tennis to Elton John's AIDS Foundation, remaining a powerful force for change and a monument to passionate persistence.

Victoria Price

SEE ALSO: *AIDS; Avon; DeGeneres, Ellen; Evert, Chris; John, Elton; Lesbianism; Navratilova, Martina; Outing; Riggs, Bobby; Sports Heroes; Tennis; Tupperware; Wimbledon.*

BIBLIOGRAPHY

Fleming, Anne Taylor. "The Battles of Billie Jean King." *Women's Sports and Fitness* 1, no. 11 (1998): 130–138.

Gitlin, Marty. *Billie Jean King: Tennis Star & Social Activist.* Edina, MN: ABDO, 2011.

Hahn, Lucinda. "The Shots Heard Round the World." *Tennis,* August 1998, 22–25.

Jenkins, Sally. "Billie Jean King." *Sports Illustrated,* September 19, 1994, 60–61.

King, Billie Jean. "I Just Had to Win." *Tennis*, August 1998, 26–30.

King, Billie Jean, and Kim Chapin. *Billie Jean*. London: W. H. Allen, 1975.

King, Billie Jean, and Frank Deford. *The Autobiography of Billie Jean King*. New York: Granada, 1982.

Kort, Michele. "Billie Jean King." *Advocate*, August 18, 1998, 40–43.

King, Carole *(1942–)*

Carole King has had two of the most successful careers in rock history: first as a member of one of rock and roll's best-known songwriting teams, Goffin and King, and then as a top-selling singer/songwriter of the 1970s. Along the way she proved there was a place in rock and roll for pleasant, unpretentious songs and performers who did not rely on stage theatrics, sexuality, or other gimmicks.

Born Carol Klein on February 9, 1942, she began writing songs at an early age. By her teens she was riding the subway from her home in Brooklyn, New York, to Manhattan, where she shopped her tunes on Tin Pan Alley, an area where writers and publishers cranked out pop hits in assembly-line fashion. Under her stage name, Carole King, she made her first recording, "Oh Neil," an answer to "Oh Carol" by Neil Sedaka, and hit the Top 40 in 1962 with "It Might as Well Rain until September."

Carole King. *Carole King performs on NBC's* Today *show in 2011.* AL PEREIRA/CONTRIBUTOR/WIREIMAGE/GETTY IMAGES.

She enjoyed even greater success as a songwriter. She met lyricist Gerry Goffin in 1960; they married soon thereafter but divorced in 1968. During their marriage, they wrote some of the most enduring songs in early rock and roll: "Will You Love Me Tomorrow?" "Take Good Care of My Baby," and "The Loco-Motion" (written for their babysitter, who recorded under the name Little Eva). Like popular songwriting pairs Burt Bacharach and Hal David and Jerry Leiber and Mike Stoller, Goffin and King made standard pop formulas seem fresh.

The duo worked out of a small office around the corner from the Brill Building, a hub of songwriting activity during the late 1950s and early 1960s. Their melodies and lyrics were expansive: simple but original, popular but timeless. Their only brush with controversy came with their 1962 song about domestic violence, "He Hit Me (And It Felt Like a Kiss)." In 1963 Beatles songwriters John Lennon and Paul McCartney stated their ambition to be the British Goffin and King. Ironically, rock groups who wrote their own material, such as the Beatles, ultimately ended Tin Pan Alley's dominance over the pop charts.

After divorcing, King returned to recording her own songs, first as the front woman for a three-piece rock group called the City. The group's one release failed, and she decided to go it alone. Her first solo effort, the 1970 album *Writer*, failed to make a splash, though it would later receive critical acclaim for its treatment of a variety of pop and rock styles with lively, accessible melodies and gentle, unassuming vocals.

In the years that followed, she stuck to a similar formula and achieved multiplatinum record sales. On the heels of the success of soft-rock singer/songwriters such as folksinger James Taylor and supergroup Crosby, Stills, Nash, and Young, King released *Tapestry* (1971), which was an immediate smash. The album was a seemingly endless source of AM radio hits such as "I Feel the Earth Move," "So Far Away," and "It's Too Late" and cover versions of "Will You Still Love Me Tomorrow?" "You've Got a Friend," and "(You Make Me Feel Like) A Natural Woman." The themes of her songs were deep yet easily understood, upbeat but touched with sadness, intelligent but not intellectual. Critics called her a Joni Mitchell for the masses. *Tapestry* sold more than fifteen million copies and for several years was the best-selling album of all time.

Her success continued with *Music* (1971) and *Rhymes & Reasons* (1972), but her ambitious 1973 concept album *Fantasy* met with critical backlash. At the time reviewers disparaged hearing her view on the world's ills, though later they would refer to the album as a remarkably affecting, coherent piece of work. After two hit singles, "Nightingale" and "Jazzman," from 1974's *Wrap around Joy*, King watched her album sales steadily decline. Yet her gentle piano-based approach continued to echo through the works of artists from rock singer Christine McVie to lesbian icon Cris Williamson.

In 1980 King released *Pearls*, an album of songs from her heyday with Goffin. Although "One Fine Day" became a hit single, she could not reverse the trend toward new wave and heavy metal, which virtually swept singer/songwriters off the pop landscape. After 1983's *Speeding Time*, she took a hiatus from professional music.

In the 1990s the music world hailed her as a pioneer. Goffin and King were inducted into the Rock and Roll Hall of Fame in 1990. The 1996 Alison Anders film *Grace of My Heart* was a loose portrayal of King's life. King's sincerity and gift for writing deceptively simple melodies influenced popular singers from Mariah Carey to Alanis Morissette. In 1998 she returned with the single "Anyone At All," the theme from director Nora Ephron's film *You've Got Mail.*

King staged a comeback with her 2004 Living Room Tour and a 2005 live album, which landed at number seventeen on the Billboard 200. In 2010 she teamed up with Taylor for the Troubadour Reunion Tour, named for the West Hollywood, California, nightclub where they had played together in the 1970s. The live album from that tour, a Billboard hit and commercial success, brought her music back into the spotlight for a new generation to enjoy.

David B. Wilson

SEE ALSO: *The Beatles; Brill Building; Carey, Mariah; Crosby, Stills, and Nash; Heavy Metal; Lennon, John; McCartney, Paul; Mitchell, Joni; Morissette, Alanis; New Wave Music; Pop Music; Taylor, James.*

BIBLIOGRAPHY

Perone, James E. *Carole King: A Bio-bibliography*. Westport, CT: Greenwood Press, 1999.

Weller, Sheila. *Girls Like Us: Carole King, Joni Mitchell, Carly Simon—and the Journey of a Generation*. New York: Atria Books, 2008.

King, Freddie *(1934–1976)*

Of the three "Kings of the Blues" (Albert King and B. B. King are the others), Freddie King had arguably the most influence on early rock and roll. The youngest of the three unrelated guitarists, King had hits as early as 1961 that had an enormous impact on the California surf music of Duane Eddy and the Ventures. He was also a key early influence on British band leader John Mayall and young guitarists Eric Clapton and Peter Green.

Born in Gilmer, Texas, on September 3, 1934, King came from the Texas blues tradition of "T-Bone" Walker and "Lightnin'" Hopkins but moved at age sixteen to Chicago, where he fell under the spell of Eddie Taylor and Jimmy Rogers. King joined Magic Sam and others in founding the West Side sound, a more percussive and up-tempo alternative to the blues played on the South Side by older musicians such as Muddy Waters and Howlin' Wolf. King's initial success came on the Federal/King label in Cincinnati, Ohio, where his instrumental recordings, including "Hide Away" (1960)—which reached number twenty-nine on the pop chart, number five on the Billboard R&B chart, and was later covered by Clapton—and "The Stumble," served as a dictionary of licks for aspiring guitarists.

King and King Records parted ways in 1967, and he went on to record two albums for Cotillion: *Freddie King Is a Blues Master* (1969) and *My Feeling for the Blues* (1970). His songs continued to be hits with other musicians, and the success of covers by Clapton and Cream, as well as Mick Taylor of the Rolling Stones, built him an English fan base as well. He went on a series of UK dates in 1969 and came home to a new recording contract with Shelter. The three albums King recorded with the label—*Getting Ready* (1971), *The Texas Cannonball* (1972), and *Woman across the River* (1973)—reflected a new funkier sound and resulted in more touring opportunities.

King signed with Clapton's label, RSO, in 1974 and released two more albums, one featuring Clapton on several songs. However, the years of touring caught up with him, and he died in 1976 at age forty-two. A seven-CD box-set retrospective, *Freddie King: Taking Care of Business 1956–1973*, was released in 2009, which includes previously unreleased demo sessions and early rare tracks. King also was honored by the Rock and Roll Hall of Fame in 2012.

Jon Klinkowitz

SEE ALSO: *Blues; Clapton, Eric; Hopkins, Sam "Lightnin'"; Howlin' Wolf; King, Albert; King, B. B.; Rock and Roll; The Rolling Stones; Walker, Aaron "T-Bone"; Waters, Muddy.*

BIBLIOGRAPHY

Humphrey, Mark. "Freddie King: The Texas Cannonball." *Guitar Player*, August, 1995, 99–106.

Obrecht, Jas, ed. *Blues Guitar: The Men Who Made the Music*. San Francisco: GPI Books, 1990.

Weissman, Dick; Richard Carlin; and Craig Morrison. *Blues*. New York: Infobase, 2005.

King, Larry *(1933–)*

Larry King has been one of the foremost television talk-show hosts in the history of American broadcasting. His distinctive style, at once relaxed and commanding, and his focus on issues of topical interest elevated the talk-show genre to something of national importance. Starting out as a disc jockey on local radio, King worked hard to rise in the world of broadcasting, overcoming self-created reversals of fortune to become a pioneer of the modern phone-in show on both radio and television. CNN's most popular program during the late-twentieth and early twenty-first centuries, *Larry King Live* (1985–2010) transformed its host into one of the most sought-out interviewers in the world, a man who proved that entertainment value need not be sacrificed in order to examine important matters.

EARLY PASSION FOR BROADCASTING

Larry King was born Lawrence Harvey Zieger in Brooklyn, New York, on November 19, 1933, the son of Russian immigrants who a year previously had been devastated by the death of their firstborn son. Larry was nine when his bar-owner father died of a heart attack, leaving his mother to support the boy and his younger brother on welfare. Deeply affected by his father's death, King stopped paying attention to his studies and crippled his chances of entering college. After graduating from high school, he immediately sought work to help support his mother and brother.

Despite his lack of academic dedication, King aspired to a career in radio. In his early twenties, while working for UPS as a delivery man, he frequented broadcasting studios around New

York but grew increasingly despondent about the prospects of getting broadcasting work. Then a CBS staff announcer suggested that if he was serious about getting on the air, he should leave the world's media capital for a smaller but growing media market where more opportunities were available.

This advice led King to Florida, where a lack of immediate success found him sweeping floors at the smallest station in town. He used the opportunity to learn everything he could about the radio business and, at age twenty-three, he got his break as a morning disc jockey on a small Miami AM station. It was the station's manager who suggested he drop the "ethnic" name Zieger in favor of the more American King. By 1961 Larry King was a popular personality in the southern Florida radio market. His success in the medium led him to try his hand in the emerging world of television, and in 1960 he began hosting a program on a Miami station. During this time and through the early 1970s, he maintained shows on both radio and television and wrote newspaper columns in the *Miami Herald* and the *Miami News*, which helped fuel his popularity in Florida.

Larry King. *Larry King is considered the twentieth century's foremost television talk-show host.* EPSILON/CONTRIBUTOR/GETTY IMAGES ENTERTAINMENT/GETTY IMAGES.

OVERCOMING SCANDAL TO ACHIEVE FAME

King's hard-earned success shuddered to an unfortunate halt in the 1970s. During the 1960s he overspent wildly, gambled on horses, and failed to pay his taxes. He also became involved with Lou Wolfson, a shady Florida financier connected to the scandal that led to the resignation of Supreme Court Justice Abe Fortas in 1969. A scheme to bankroll New Orleans, Louisiana, district attorney Jim Garrison's investigation of the John F. Kennedy assassination was Wolfson's brainchild, one in which King became deeply enmeshed. King was the middleman in the arrangement, but skimmed some of the cash intended for Garrison as a means to help get himself out of debt. When Wolfson learned of this, he charged King with grand larceny and, although the charge was eventually dismissed, the damage was done.

King left Florida radio in 1971, taking his talents and his focus to the West Coast, where he rebuilt his career by writing magazine articles and working in radio. By the mid-1970s, time had healed his reputation and image, and he was welcomed back into the market where he had started: southern Florida.

After building up his show in Miami, King was able to take his self-titled radio program, *The Larry King Show*, to a national audience in 1978, making it the first nationwide call-in show. His popularity led to further opportunity in 1985, when the four-year-old Cable News Network (CNN) was looking to expand its programming to temper its image as merely a video wire service. CNN put *Larry King Live* on television as the first international live phone-in television program. He interviewed public figures across a wide spectrum that included athletes, actors, writers, politicians, and foreign dignitaries. The mix of guests and King's unique style found an immediate public response. King projected innate curiosity and an intense interest in his guests that provoked more honest answers than many of them were accustomed to giving before a national audience. Allowing the general public to ask questions (which like King's tended to be uninflammatory softballs) gave the show a friendly feel that contributed to his reputation as "the King of Talk."

King's influence was highlighted on February 20, 1992, when billionaire Ross Perot used *Larry King Live* to announce his intention to run for the presidency. This led other politicians to use King's program as a forum to discuss the issues. The 1992 election became the first in which candidates used talk shows as a major means to reach voters while circumventing traditional channels. They saw King, now dubbed "the Kingmaker," as the number one host for the purpose. The major presidential candidates appeared on King's show seventeen times in the last two weeks of the campaign alone, each of them devoting a full hour to the program during this intense time.

The status of *Larry King Live* rose several more notches on November 9, 1993, when Vice President Al Gore agreed to appear on the air with Perot as King moderated their debate on the controversial North American Free Trade Agreement (NAFTA). In subsequent elections many potential candidates used the program to test the waters before their White House bids.

Throughout these years, King received numerous honors recognizing his leadership in his field, including the Broadcaster of the Year Award from the International Radio and Television Society and the ACE Award for Program Interviewer. He also won the Jack Anderson Investigative Reporting Award and the George Foster Peabody Award for Excellence in Broadcasting. During the 1980s and 1990s, King also authored a number of books, including *Larry King by Larry King* (1982); *Tell It to the King* (1988); *"Mr. King, You're Having a Heart Attack"* (1989); *Tell Me More* (1990); *On the Line: The New Road to the White House* (1993); *How to Talk to Anyone, Anytime, Anywhere: The Secrets of Good Conversation* (1994); and the children's books *Daddy Day, Daughter Day* (1997, with daughter Chaia) and *Powerful Prayers* (1998). In the later part of the decade King also wrote a weekly column for *USA Today*.

NEW CHALLENGES

King continued to helm his acclaimed CNN show throughout the early years of the twenty-first century. During this period he also published several more notable books, among them *Anything Goes! What I've Learned from Politicians, Pundits, and Presidents* (2000) and *Remember Me When I'm Gone: The Rich and Famous Write Their Own Epitaphs and Obituaries* (2004). As the decade progressed, however, King's ratings began to slump, as more and more younger viewers turned to rival cable networks MSNBC and FOX as their primary sources for news and information. Finally, in 2010, King and CNN agreed to discontinue his long-running interview hour. The final episode of *Larry King Live* aired on December 16, 2010. King's last show featured a number of high-profile guests: Bill Clinton and Regis Philbin appeared via live video feed, while Bill Maher and Dr. Phil McGraw visited the studio to wish King farewell.

Soon after leaving his eponymous program, King reflected on his years with CNN in a new book, *Truth Be Told: Off the Record about Favorite Guests, Memorable Moments, Funniest Jokes, and a Half Century of Asking Questions* (2011). Although he had given up his nightly time slot, he remained affiliated with CNN during this time, with a deal to produce special programs four times per year. In December 2011 King hosted an on-air celebrity dinner, *Dinner with the Kings*, which included such diverse guests as Conan O'Brien, Shaquille O'Neal, and Quincy Jones. At the dinner, King confided to his guests that he wanted to be cryogenically frozen when he died, in case he could be brought back to life in the future.

In February 2012 King and CNN agreed to sever ties completely. A month later, he entered into an agreement with Mexican telecommunications magnate Carlos Slim to host a new Internet-based interview program on the start-up network Ora.tv. With a new technological medium at his disposal, King showed no sign of retiring.

Alyssa L. Falwell

SEE ALSO: *Cable TV; Celebrity; CNN; The Internet; Kennedy Assassination; McGraw, Dr. Phil; O'Brien, Conan; O'Neal, Shaquille; Perot, Ross; Radio; Talk Radio; Telephone; Television;* USA Today.

BIBLIOGRAPHY

Harnick, Chris. "Larry King's 'Dinner' Reveal: Freeze Me When I Die." HuffPost TV, AolTV.com. Accessed May 22, 2012. Available from http://www.aoltv.com/2011/12/06/larry-king-reveal-freeze-death/

King, Larry. *Truth Be Told: Off the Record about Favorite Guests, Memorable Moments, Funniest Jokes, and a Half Century of Asking Questions*. New York: Weinstein Books, 2011.

Shales, Tom. "A Star-Studded, but Still Somewhat Muted, Farewell for 'Larry King Live.'" *Washington Post*, December 17, 2010.

Stelter, Brian. "Larry King's CNN Coda Comes to a Close." *New York Times*, February 16, 2012.

Stelter, Brian. "New Internet TV Network to Feature Larry King." *New York Times*, March 12, 2012.

King, Martin Luther, Jr. *(1929–1968)*

Dr. Martin Luther King Jr. was the most popular and effective leader of the African American struggle for civil rights in the United States. His philosophy of nonviolent direct action galvanized thousands of Americans, both black and white, to press for granting the full measure of human and political rights to African Americans. Although he was not personally responsible for mobilizing protest, he was certainly one of the greatest organizers of people the world has ever seen. In the early twenty-first century, a national holiday is named in his honor, and numerous highways, streets, schools, playgrounds, and public buildings display his name.

FROM PRIVILEGE INTO THE FRAY

For a man who would capture the attention of both his country and the world, King's early life was fairly sheltered. Born into the black upper class of Atlanta, Georgia, in the midst of the Great Depression, King felt very few effects of the economic crisis. As the son of a popular Baptist pastor, King was afforded the opportunity of a childhood free from overt racial discrimination. He graduated from Atlanta's all-black, elite Morehouse College at the age of nineteen, then earned a bachelor's degree in theology at Crozer Theological Seminary in Chester, Pennsylvania. While at Crozer, King absorbed the ideas of Christian socialism that would play a tremendous role in his life's work. He built upon these ideas of social justice as he pursued his doctorate in theology at Boston University.

After receiving his degree when he was twenty-six, King was appointed pastor of the conservative Dexter Avenue Baptist Church in Montgomery, Alabama, where he gained notoriety by spearheading the successful 1955 Montgomery Bus Boycott under the auspices of the Montgomery Improvement Association (MIA). The leaders of the MIA chose King as the leader of the protest for several reasons but primarily because he was new to the area and the white power structure had not yet made his acquaintance. The bus boycott emboldened King to form the Southern Christian Leadership Conference (SCLC), which served as a vehicle for mobilizing African Americans to protest discriminatory treatment. Largely made up of ministers, the SCLC's stated goal was "To Redeem the Soul of America."

NONVIOLENCE AS A WEAPON

With the help of the other civil rights organizations—including the Student Nonviolent Coordinating Committee (SNCC), the Congress of Racial Equality (CORE), and the National Association for the Advancement of Colored People (NAACP)—the SCLC initiated several campaigns throughout the South in their pursuit of voting rights and integration. Throughout the civil rights drive, King remained firmly committed to his philosophy of nonviolence. At times both his critics and supporters failed to understand how blacks could remain nonviolent in a country that spoke the language of violence. But King was persistent in following Mohandas K. Ghandi's philosophy, applied in India

Martin Luther King Jr. in Washington, D.C. *Dr. Martin Luther King Jr. delivers his "I Have a Dream Speech" in Washington, D.C., in August 1963.* FRANCIS MILLER/CONTRIBUTOR/TIME & LIFE PICTURES/GETTY IMAGES.

earlier in the twentieth century, that nonviolent resistance was the most potent weapon available to oppressed people in their struggle for freedom.

King's prominence reached new heights during the August 1963 March on Washington for Jobs and Freedom, at the end of which he delivered his "I Have a Dream" speech. Although he had used the phrase many times before, this time it struck a rich chord with blacks and whites alike. On the heels of the dramatic oration, King received the Nobel Peace Prize—he was the youngest recipient and the first African American—for his unwavering dedication to nonviolent social change. The award indicated that although white southerners were defiant in their opposition to the twin goals of voting rights and integration, millions of people across the globe supported King and his movement.

King was continually represented in both the print and broadcast media and soon became an icon. He capitalized on his press coverage by articulating the goals and aims of the civil rights movement to viewers and readers near and far. He also published three popular books, *Stride toward Freedom: The Montgomery Story* (1958), *Why We Can't Wait* (1964), and *Where Do We Go from Here? Chaos or Community* (1967). Throughout the 1960s King toured the country, giving an untold number of speeches and sermons on behalf of the cause he so ardently espoused. He spoke before a packed house in nearly every city. To some activists a local campaign did not seem legitimate unless King gave it his blessing.

A VICTORY AND A TRAGEDY

In 1965 King and other civil rights leaders realized the fruits of their labor when President Lyndon Baines Johnson signed the Voting Rights Act into law. In the words of historian Adam Fairclough, "It was the crowning achievement of the civil rights movement."

King's popularity began to wane when he spoke out against the Vietnam War in May 1966, against the wishes of even some of his close confidants. Many thought that he should stick to civil rights and leave foreign policy to others. He decided, however, that he must publicly protest an unjust and violent conflict. The result was that nearly every major U.S. newspaper condemned his views. King persisted in his domestic struggle, launching the Poor People's Campaign that he hoped would transcend the wide chasm of race, culture, and religion. Tragically, he was assassinated on April 4, 1968, while aiding Memphis sanitation workers in their fight for better working conditions.

Few activists can hope to be as popular or effective as King. The mere mention of his name evokes greatness, commitment, and dedication. He is respected throughout the world, even by his enemies, and his life's work on behalf of the oppressed will long be the standard by which other movements are measured. In recognition of his achievement, President Ronald Reagan set aside the third Monday of January as a federal holiday, Martin Luther King Day, in 1986. It was officially recognized in all fifty states in 2000. King was posthumously awarded the Presidential Medal of Freedom in 1977 and the Congressional Gold Medal in 2004. King's legacy was set in stone, literally, by sculptor Lei Yixin, whose "Stone of Hope" depiction of King sits as the centerpiece of the Martin Luther King Jr. Memorial in the National Mall area of Washington, D.C., which opened to the public in August 2011.

Leonard N. Moore

SEE ALSO: *Civil Disobedience; Civil Rights Movement; March on Washington; Reagan, Ronald; Student Demonstrations; Vietnam.*

BIBLIOGRAPHY

Arsenault, Raymond. *Freedom Riders: 1961 and the Struggle for Racial Justice.* New York: Oxford University Press, 2006.

Carson, Clayborne. *The Autobiography of Martin Luther King, Jr.* New York: Intellectual Properties Management and Warner Books, 1998.

Fairclough, Adam. *Martin Luther King, Jr.* Athens: University of Georgia Press, 1995.

Garrow, David. "The FBI and Martin Luther King, Jr." *Atlantic Monthly*, July–August 2002.

Harding, Vincent. *Martin Luther King: The Inconvenient Hero.* New York: Orbis Books, 1997.

Jackson, Thomas. *From Civil Rights to Human Rights: Martin Luther King and the Struggle for Economic Justice.* Philadelphia: University of Pennsylvania Press, 2006.

King, Martin Luther, Jr. *The Papers of Martin Luther King Jr.*, ed. Clayborne Carson; Peter Holloran; Ralph Luker, et al. Berkeley: University of California Press, 1992.

Ling, Peter. *Martin Luther King, Jr.* New York: Routledge, 2002.

King, Rodney *(1965–2012)*

African American Rodney King became a symbol of racial violence in 1991 when he was brutally beaten by white officers of the Los Angeles Police Department (LAPD). Captured on video by a witness, the incident sparked outrage across the country and launched an investigation that resulted in the arrest of the officers. When an all-white jury acquitted the officers in 1992, violent riots erupted in the predominately black neighborhoods of Los Angeles that lasted for six days. King's beating marked a pivotal moment in the evolution of race relations in America, initiating an intense debate about the lingering

Rodney King. *Rodney King makes a public plea to end rioting in Los Angeles, California, in May 1992.* DOUGLAS BURROWS/CONTRIBUTOR/GETTY IMAGES NEWS/GETTY IMAGES.

problem of prejudice in American society, while calling into question the role of the police in perpetuating racial divisions in African American communities.

The second of five children, Rodney Glen King was born in Sacramento, California, in 1965. King's father, who worked in maintenance and construction, was an alcoholic who beat his children. His mother was a Jehovah's Witness. King did so poorly in high school that the school held him back a grade, and he had to take special education classes. In 1982, at the age of seventeen, he fathered a daughter out of wedlock.

Fed up and frustrated with school, King dropped out in 1984, six months before graduation, and got a job in construction. That same year he married Denetta, who was not the mother of his first child, and the couple soon had a daughter. They later divorced. In 1988 King married Crystal Waters, who had two children of her own. They had one daughter together and divorced in 1996.

In 1989 King robbed a convenience store. He was convicted of attempted robbery and served one year at the California Correctional Center in Susanville. After being paroled, King was unable to find construction work and took a job as a part-time laborer at Dodger Stadium.

When he was not working, King hung out with friends, usually drinking 40-ounce bottles of Olde English 800. On the night of March 2, 1991, he and his friends were doing just that. In fact, there was an open bottle of beer in the car when King saw the flashing lights of a California Highway Patrol (CHP) car behind them. Knowing that he was violating his parole, King initially tried to get away, leading the CHP on a high-speed chase. He finally pulled off the freeway into a community called Lake View Terrace. By then several LAPD squad cars had arrived, and there was a helicopter hovering above.

Resident George Holliday, who was awakened by the commotion, reached for his new Sony Handycam recorder and began recording the activity below his apartment window. The next day television news station KTLA 5 broadcast Holliday's nine-minute amateur videotape, which revealed some eighty-one seconds of King being brutally beaten by at least four police officers. Viewers were appalled to see the police officers stunning King with Taser darts and then pummeling him repeatedly with steel batons. King suffered a fractured eye socket, facial nerve damage, nine skull fractures, and a severe concussion. His injuries led to permanent brain damage, leg numbness, and a permanent limp.

A SYMBOL OF RACIAL DIVISIONS

Four LAPD officers, Stacey Koon, Theodore Briseno, Laurence Powell, and Timothy Wind, were arrested and charged with using excessive force on King. A trial was held in 1992 in the predominately white community of Simi Valley, and the jury found all four officers not guilty. Almost immediately Los Angeles erupted in violence. Rioting and looting lasted for six days, and when it was over, fifty-two people were dead, 2,500 were injured, and the community had suffered $443 million in property damage. Two days after the verdicts, King made his now-famous plea for an end to the rebellion. Facing news cameras outside his attorney's Wilshire Boulevard office, a visibly shaken and tearful King said, "People, I just want to say . . . can we all get along? Can we get along? Can we stop making it horrible for the old people and the kids? . . . We'll get our justice. . . . Please, we can get along here."

Not all of the protesting was violent. Unified Against Genocide, for example, was a San Francisco–based group headed by activist Angela Davis, whose members called for a retrial under California's hate crime law. Most, however, looked to the upcoming federal trial for justice. That trial, which took place in 1993, found Koon and Powell guilty of violating King's civil rights. Both men were ordered to serve thirty-month prison terms.

Although King's first attorney, Steven Lerman, initially stated that he would seek $56 million ($1 million for each blow) in a civil rights suit against the LAPD, the amount went down to around $9 million by the time King and his new lawyer arrived in court. On April 20, 1994, a jury awarded King $3.8 million in damages.

In the following years King attempted to rebuild his life. He earned his general equivalency diploma (GED) and briefly pursued a music career. In spite of these positive steps, however, he was unable to overcome his troubled past. In 1996 he was arrested for a hit-and-run and spent ninety days in jail. A short time later, King was found guilty of abusing his wife and was placed on probation. During these years, he also found himself suffering from financial woes, having spent nearly half of his settlement money on legal fees.

King finally achieved some stability in the early 2000s, working for a construction firm owned by his brother and devoting more time to his children. He endured yet another setback in 2003, however, when he crashed his car into a house at 100 miles per hour, breaking his pelvis. In 2008, after struggling for years with alcoholism, King agreed to appear on the reality television show *Celebrity Rehab*.

More than twenty years after his fateful beating, King appeared to have gained control over his life. He achieved sobriety. He became a grandfather. In 2010 he got engaged to Cynthia Kelley, who had been the only African American on the jury for his civil trial against the City of Los Angeles. He also wrote a memoir, *The Riot Within: My Journey from Rebellion to Redemption* that was published in 2012. However, on June 17, 2012, Rodney King died from—as of this writing—undetermined causes.

As the wounds from his past continued to heal, King remained a vital reminder of the nation's ongoing struggle to reconcile itself with its racist past. For many, the infamous 1991 incident marked the beginning of significant reform. "The main impact that the Rodney King case had is that it accelerated change," reporter Lou Cannon told CNN in 2011. "It's not tenable any longer in the United States of America for a police force of a major city to govern without having the community being a part of that governance."

Kristal Brent Zook

SEE ALSO: *The City of Angels; CNN; Race Riots; Reality Television; Television.*

BIBLIOGRAPHY

Boyer, Peter. "The Selling of Rodney King." *Vanity Fair*, July 1992, 78–162.

Cannon, Lou. *Official Negligence: How Rodney King and the Riots Changed Los Angeles and the LAPD.* New York: Times Books, 1997.

Cooney, Daniel. "Beating Victim Rodney King Reluctant

Symbol Ten Years Later." *Toronto Star*, March 3, 2001.

Gale, Dennis. *Understanding Urban Unrest: From Reverend King to Rodney King*. Thousand Oaks, CA: Sage Publications, 1996.

Gibbs, Jewelle Taylor. *Race and Justice: Rodney King and O. J. Simpson in a House Divided*. San Francisco: Jossey-Bass, 1996.

Gooding-Williams, Robert. *Reading Rodney King/Reading Urban Uprising*. New York: Routledge, 1993.

Jordan, June. "The Truth of Rodney King." *Progressive*, June 1993, 12.

Kavanagh, Jim. "Rodney King, 20 Years Later." CNN.com. Accessed May 2, 2012. Available from http://articles.cnn.com/2011-03-03/us/rodney.king.20.years.later_1_laurence-powell-theodore-briseno-king-attorney-milton-grimes?_s=PM:US

King, Rodney, and Lawrence J. Spagnola. *The Riot Within: My Journey from Rebellion to Redemption*. New York: HarperCollins, 2012.

LeDuff, Charlie. "12 Years after the Riots, Rodney King Gets Along." *New York Times*, September 19, 2004.

King, Stephen *(1947–)*

Stephen King's connections to horror fiction are so compelling that for many, he virtually embodies the genre. He has become, in words echoed by more than one commentator, the unchallenged "king of horror." His reputation is deserved, resting as it does on a strongly colloquial narrative style that has been particularly appropriate to his brand of horror and on a prolific output. King has written at least sixty novels and books of nonfiction, more than 100 published short stories, and more than 200 nonfiction articles ranging from scholarship to fan writing. There have been two dozen theatrical and television adaptations of his works and seemingly endless audiobook, video, and e-book variations. After a serious road accident in 1999, King has been less prolific, but he has continued to add to his canon, acquiring along the way a degree of critical admiration beyond the horror genre.

Stephen King. *Stephen King reads from* 11/22/63: A Novel *at the John F. Kennedy Presidential Library and Museum in Boston, Massachusetts, in November 2011.* MARC ANDREW DELEY/CONTRIBUTOR/GETTY IMAGES ENTERTAINMENT/GETTY IMAGES.

A POP CULTURE PHENOMENON

King's popularity has made him a legitimate "brand-name writer," as evidenced by the many references to him and his creations in cinema, television specials, sitcom episodes, syndicated newspaper cartoons, and elsewhere. As a writer, he has continuously redefined the commercial possibilities of horror fiction, beginning in 1976 with his first appearance on the best-seller lists with *'Salem's Lot* (1975). In August 1981 *Firestarter* (1980), *The Dead Zone* (1979), and *The Shining* (1977) appeared on best-seller lists simultaneously, marking the first time that an American author was represented by three books. During one week in January 1986, King had five titles simultaneously on the national lists: the hardcover editions of *Skeleton Crew* (1985) and *The Bachman Books* (1985) and the mass-market and trade paperback editions of *The Talisman* (1984), *The Bachman Books*, and *Thinner* (1984). For several years, instances of two, three, and four titles appearing simultaneously were frequent enough that they were taken for granted—for King, the exceptional has become the norm.

At the same time, King has used his facility with the conventions of horror fiction to achieve more than base titillation and terror. From the beginning, his books have been built not only on strong narratives and intriguing characters but also on insights into contemporary American society. More than any other author in the field, King speaks for the experiences, expectations, achievements, and disappointments of the baby boomer generation, often coupling his cosmic horrors and monsters with references to the minutiae of daily life. Gypsy curses share the pages with Ding Dongs, and apocalyptic plagues with Payday candy bars.

His novels examine flaws in American education (*Carrie* in 1974 and *Rage* in 1977), the ramifications of America's love-hate relationship with the automobile (*Christine* in 1983), the failure of the American family (*The Shining* and *Roadwork* in 1981; *Christine* and *It* in 1986; *Rose Madder* in 1995), America's obsessive consumption of energy regardless of the cost (*The Tommyknockers* in 1987), and the nation's potentially suicidal flirtation with devastating technology (*The Stand* in 1978). King also reflects a distinctly political/social agenda with what are essentially feminist tracts in *Gerald's Game* (1992) and *Dolores Claiborne* (1992) and more balanced but still socially conscious themes in *Insomnia* (1994), *Rose Madder* (1995), and *Bag of Bones* (1998). In most of his fictional works, however, he constructs an artful balance between story and commentary, rarely allowing theme to overmaster narrative. In this, if in nothing else, King has demonstrated himself to be a master of his art.

BECOMING A WRITER

King's status in the realm of contemporary popular fiction is no accident; rather, it is the result of an innate genius for storytelling and an extraordinary dedication to his craft. Born on September 21, 1947, King began with derivative stories and juvenilia, including self-published chapbooks such as *The Star Invaders*. He had placed his first marketable story by age seventeen and had written major portions of at least three novels, composed nearly eighteen months of weekly columns for his college newspaper, and published eight short stories before graduating from the University of Maine in 1970.

A decade later, King had made his permanent home in Bangor, Maine; completed the first draft for what many consider to be one of his masterworks, *It*; published ten books, with film versions of several; and enjoyed the first of many triple-title entries on the best-seller lists. A further decade later, in 1990, King published the original version of *The Stand*, using his leverage in the industry to restore hundreds of pages cut from the original and to reemphasize his mastery of the horror genre.

In the 1990s King confirmed his stamp on American publishing with the appearance of the six-part novel, *The Green Mile* (1996). He published two novels simultaneously in 1996 under two different names—Stephen King's *Desperation* and Richard Bachman's *The Regulators*—using the same cast of characters as imagined by two distinctly different personalities, with both works verging on an awareness of the numinous nature of human life. As Stephen King, he published *Needful Things* (1991) and further episodes of a decades-long, multivolume tale, *The Dark Tower* series, which promised to solidify his position as heir to the grand traditions of the Renaissance epic, the American Western, apocalyptic fantasy, postapocalyptic science fiction, and mythic romance.

A PROLIFIC OUTPUT

A glance at the list of King's novels suggests his wide-ranging interests and his ability to tell stories about almost every traditional monster or conventional terror associated with horror fiction while also transforming that monster or terror into an emblem for contemporary events, problems, or concerns. *Carrie* blends narrative with pseudo-documentary to detail a naive girl's confrontation not only with menstruation but also with ill-defined and partially understood psychic powers. *'Salem's Lot* revitalizes the vampire tradition by emphasizing the underlying isolation and disintegration of community implicit in the figure of the undead feeding unsuspected on the energy of the living. *The Shining*—one of King's finest, most literary, and most cohesive novels—interweaves sophisticated literary layering with a traditional ghost story while at the same time demonstrating how fragile family bonds can become in times of social upheaval.

In 1977 King published *Rage*, the first of six pseudonymous novels under the name Richard Bachman. *Rage*, partially completed prior to King's enrolling at the University of Maine, depicts a high school student who murders a teacher and holds his class hostage—events perhaps startling in fiction at the time but, as King seems to foreshadow in the novel, occurring only too frequently in real life. Subsequent Bachman books include *The Long Walk* (1979), *Roadwork*, *The Running Man* (1982), *Thinner*, and—after a decade-long hiatus during which the name Richard Bachman surfaced primarily in in-jokes among readers and critics—*The Regulators* (1996). All except *Thinner* and *The Regulators* were early works, more recognizably mainstream than anything King had published until *Gerald's Game* and *Dolores Claiborne*, with appropriately socially oriented themes—the inequity and insanity of a military draft in *The Long Walk*, the 1974 oil crisis in *Roadwork*, the depersonalizing effects of the media in *The Running Man*. These novels frequently suggest horrors, but they remain primarily psychological and evocative rather than physical and explicit, demonstrating once again that King is more capable of subdued and realistic treatments than many of his critics might allow.

THE STAND AND *NIGHT SHIFT*

In 1978 *The Stand* appeared. Although the novel was structurally deformed by editorial deletions amounting to some 400 manuscript pages, this epic fable of technology gone mad, of wholesale death, and of the struggle to restore order from chaos remains one of King's strongest works. The complex web of character and subplot—particularly in the unexpurgated 1990 version—gives the story unusual resonance and demonstrates King's deft hand at characterization. *The Stand* is also central to King's vision of the struggle between lightness and darkness, with its villainous Randall Flagg reappearing as the Magician Flagg in *The Eyes of the Dragon* (1984), as the Man in Black in *The Dark Tower: The Gunslinger* (1982), and as LeLand Gaunt in *Needful Things*. Additionally, there are subtle echoes of the character in *Insomnia* (1994), *Rose Madder*, *The Drawing of the Three* (1987), *The Waste Lands* (1991), and *Wizard and Glass* (1997).

The year 1978 also saw the publication of King's first collection of horror tales, *Night Shift*, which included early versions of materials treated in *'Salem's Lot* and *The Stand* and stories that inspired a number of subsequent films: *Graveyard Shift* (1990), *The Boogeyman* (1982), *Trucks* (2000), *Sometimes They Come Back* (1991), *The Cat's Eye* (1985, based on the stories "The Ledge" and "Quitters Inc."), *The Lawnmower Man* (1992), *Children of the Corn* (1984, and its multiple sequels), and *The Woman in the Room* (1983). The stories established King as a master of short fiction as well as the novel, and pieces such as "Night Surf" and "I Am the Doorway" give play to his occasionally surrealistic, almost poetic imagination.

HORROR AND FANTASY

The Dead Zone, *Firestarter*, and *Cujo*, published between 1979 and 1981, further demonstrate King's ability to meld horror with realism, science fiction with science, fantasy with imagination. Readable, engaging, and ultimately frightening beyond their suggestions of monsters, each attacks a manifestation of contemporary culture: insanity disguised as rationality; uncontrolled science in league with power-hungry politics; and families disintegrating under the internal pressure of selfishness and the external pressure of economics and, again, politics. These books also provide useful background to King's critical assessment of horror in fiction and film, *Stephen King's Danse Macabre* (1981), which describes the evolution of dark fantasy from 1953 through 1978. *Danse Macabre* is both entertaining and enlightening, not only defining a genre but often reflecting the autobiographical and literary impulses behind King's own fiction.

In 1982 King published *Stephen King's Creepshow*, a comic-book anthology of five tales, and *Different Seasons*, a collection of four novellas, including "Rita Hayworth and Shawshank Redemption" (the inspiration for the 1994 Academy Award–nominated film *The Shawshank Redemption*), "The Body" (a semiautobiographical work translated brilliantly into film by Rob Reiner in 1986 as *Stand by Me*), "The Breathing Method" (a traditional ghost story), and "Apt Pupil" (a frightening analysis of reciprocal corruption released as a film of the same name in 1998). The concern for adolescent trauma at the heart of "The Body" and "Apt Pupil" continues in 1983's *Christine*, an oddly disjointed novel in which the narrative stance shifts from the first person, to the third, and back to the first. Nevertheless, the book extends King's concern for anatomizing contemporary society and also provides the backdrop for a chilling ghost story.

Cycle of the Werewolf, published in 1983 and originally conceived as text for an illustrated calendar, is King's first extended treatment of the werewolf. However, the major novel he published that year was *Pet Sematary*, a disquisition on death that remains one of King's darkest and most powerful stories, as it directly confronts the reality of death and its effect on the human personality. The primary characters must confront death and attempt a reconciliation to it. To the degree that they fail, the novel becomes a tragedy verging on desperation, culminating in what is arguably King's most chilling conclusion.

EXPERIMENTATION

King completed a number of experimental works in 1984. The first collection of *Dark Tower* stories, *The Dark Tower: The Gunslinger*, introduces an ongoing quest cycle, incorporating elements of horror but transcending them to touch on genres such as the traditional Western, action-adventure, romance, and alternate-universe science fiction. All of these pieces blend seamlessly into a classic epic. Subsequent volumes in the series—such as *The Drawing of the Three*, *The Waste Lands*, and *Wizard and Glass*—emphasize King's ambitious format, his streamlined style, his interconnecting thematic structures, and his highly imaginative combinations of characters, settings, and plots. Similarly, *The Eyes of the Dragon* (1987), published by King's Philtrum Press, is unique as the writer's major foray into overt fantasy. Telling the story of a dying king, a wronged prince, and an evil magician and set in a mythical kingdom complete with dragons, *The Eyes of the Dragon* touches briefly on one of the alternate worlds of *The Dark Tower* but nevertheless stands alone as an important alternative to horror in King's works.

In 1984 King also published his only collaborative novel to date, *The Talisman*, written with Peter Straub, one of the few writers who could challenge King's preeminence in contemporary horror. An epic quest that parallels the outlines of the *Dark Tower* stories while alluding to writers as disparate as Mark Twain and C. S. Lewis, *The Talisman* balances between the reality of twentieth-century America and the idyllic potential of the Territories and blends horror with an innocent's journey across the face of a modern America populated by monsters both real and illusory, human and inhuman. Readers expecting a combination of King's colloquialism and Straub's meticulous formalism might be disappointed, as it is stylistically and structurally unlike anything either might write individually. It does, however, generate its own movement and power through the synergy of their imaginations. King's pseudonymous work *Thinner* was also published in 1984. Combining a gypsy curse with the hypocrisy of suburban life, *Thinner* is so obviously a King story that it led several researchers to unravel the secret of the Richard Bachman pseudonym.

King's second major collection of short fiction appeared in 1985. *Skeleton Crew* contains such stellar works as "The Mist," "Raft," "Gramma," and "The Reach." The collection was followed in 1986 by *It*, King's magnum opus and the culmination of his years-long concentration on children, childhood, and monsters. Criticized for its scope and length (more than 1,100 pages in the American hardcover edition), the novel attempts a complex, multileveled, encyclopedic look at American culture and society between 1958 and 1985, during which seven children—and their grown-up counterparts—confront the monster in the sewers, the darkness beneath the surface of their lives. King stretches his storytelling powers to create an intricacy of text rivaled only by *The Stand* and the *Dark Tower* saga.

YET ANOTHER CREATIVE TURN

King's next sequence of novels represents another shift in direction. *Misery* (1987), *The Tommyknockers*, *The Dark Half* (1989), and "Secret Window, Secret Garden" from *Four Past Midnight* (1990) show the author turning his imaginative microscope on himself—the writer as public personality and private individual. Ranging from the "realism" of *Misery*, in which the only monster is a grotesquely insane human, to the "horror" of *The Dark Half*, in which the monster is a pseudonym-made-flesh (the novel is appropriately dedicated to Richard Bachman), these stories suggest the fine line between imagination and reality. Although they are unlike much of what might be considered "classic" King, they have been well accepted by readers. The film version of *Misery* (1990) received the Academy Award for Best Actress (Kathy Bates) and increased King's mainstream appeal.

King's 1991 book *Needful Things* also departs radically from his earlier novels. Set in Castle Rock, Maine, his primary fictional landscape, this novel is his version of Twain's "The Man That Corrupted Hadleyburg," complementing themes initiated in *The Dead Zone*, *Cujo*, "The Body," *The Dark Half*, *Christine*, *The Talisman*, and *The Tommyknockers*. When a new store opens, townspeople may find what they believe is their heart's desire and purchase it at a bargain price, contingent on the promise of a small trick. The subsequent interlocking circles of purchases and promises magnify the worst in human nature, driving a powerful tale of sin and redemption through trial and suffering and forgiveness. Concluding with the destruction of Castle Rock itself, *Needful Things* closes out one segment of King's career with a complex and ultimately optimistic fable of good versus evil of the lightness confounding, however momentarily, the darkness.

MOVING AWAY FROM PURE PLOT

Gerald's Game, *Dolores Claiborne*, *Insomnia*, *Rose Madder*, and *Bag of Bones* (1998) suggest King's new focus. In each, theme threatens to overshadow storytelling. The books leave little doubt that in sexual terms, males are monsters—or, as *Rose Madder* states explicitly, men are beasts. *Gerald's Game*, a thin book for King, both in page count and in content, received strong reviews from establishment journals but less favorable responses from readers awaiting further evidence of King's ability to combine commentary with story.

Dolores Claiborne links themes and episodes directly to *Gerald's Game*, though it significantly returns in part to King's earlier focus on story. A literary tour de force, the novel is a single, uninterrupted monologue of more than 300 pages that exploits the multiple possibilities in the title character's name (*Dolores* equals *sorrow* plus *clay-borne*). With *Insomnia*, King moves toward a balance between his desire to examine social problems—specifically, spousal and child abuse—and his compulsion to tell his stories. In a daring move, King makes his protagonist a septuagenarian and simultaneously commits himself to describing the tedium of an insomniac.

By the time *Rose Madder* appeared, King was again writing novels that create their social impact through the medium of the story. His protagonist in this story is an abused woman, but her restoration to power and dignity becomes an integral part of a greater narrative, one that develops fully King's penchant for mythic themes. Much the same might be said for *Bag of Bones*, in which racism and child abuse become elements in a story that becomes larger than the sum of its parts—it is a ghost story side by side with a social indictment, each concern echoed in the other, amplifying the other, and completing the other.

INJURY

On June 19, 1999, King was hit by a van while walking along the side of the road near his home in Lovell, Maine. He suffered serious injuries, including a broken hip and damage to his leg that almost resulted in its amputation. At the time of the accident, he was working on a nonfiction book *On Writing*, which is part memoir and part creative writing textbook. Despite the pain from his injuries, the book was completed and published the following year; it was also serialized in the *New Yorker*. King states on his website that he writes much more slowly since the accident—indeed, his output of novels has been modest compared with earlier years. He has, however, put considerable energy into anthologies, short stories, and even poetry.

In 2000 King became a pioneer of online publishing. With the help of publisher Simon & Schuster, he offered his novella "Riding the Bullet" as an e-book in 2000, making it the first such mass-market offering and the first attempt by an established writer to use the Internet to sell stories. "Riding the Bullet" went on sale for $2.50, though it was available free for a time, eventually being downloaded 400,000 times. Although in some ways the experiment was a success, readers were frustrated by the digital-rights-management software, which in many cases prevented them from reading the book. Later that year, King began serializing a novel called *The Plant* online without the help of his publisher. Although the experiment began well, sales of each successive episode declined, and the project was shelved after five months.

Above all, King is a savvy commercial writer with an interest in new ways of selling his work and reaching his readers. He has continued to pursue digital publishing. In 2009 he sold a horror story about a professor and his pink e-reader exclusively on Amazon's then-new Kindle e-reader platform. The following year, he said to an NPR interviewer, "Ultimately, this sort of thing scares the hell out of me. But it is the way that things are."

Perhaps the most conspicuous of all contemporary horror writers, and certainly the most recognizable, King has been the subject of scores of books—scholarly, academic, biographical, bibliographical, documentary, and fannish. Hundreds of articles have been written about him, ranging from intense analysis to popular appreciation. He has been the object of conferences and symposia, scornful mainstream reviews, fan responses verging on idolatry, and more media attention than perhaps any other living writer. King has altered the face of modern horror and—working along with a handful of other writers of equal stature—has helped to make this once-denigrated genre a respected branch of literature. As further proof of his acceptance by the literary establishment, in 2003 he received the National Book Foundation Medal for Distinguished Contribution to American Letters.

Michael R. Collings

SEE ALSO: *Academy Awards; Best Sellers; E-Readers; Horror Moves; The Internet; Made-for-Television Movies; Science Fiction Publishing; Television; The Western.*

BIBLIOGRAPHY

Badley, Linda. *Writing Horror and the Body: The Fiction of Stephen King, Clive Barker, and Anne Rice*. Westport, CT: Greenwood Press, 1996.

Beahm, George W. *Stephen King: America's Best-Loved Boogeyman*. Kansas City, MO: Andrews McMeel, 1998.

Beahm, George W. *Stephen King from A to Z: An Encyclopedia of His Life and Work*. Kansas City, MO: Andrews McMeel, 1998.

Collings, Michael R. *Scaring Us to Death: The Impact of Stephen King on Popular Culture*. San Bernardino, CA: Borgo Press, 1997.

Dubner, Stephen J. "What Is Stephen King Trying to Prove?" *New York Times*. Accessed March 2012. Available at http://www.nytimes.com/2000/08/13/magazine/what-is-stephen-king-trying-to-prove.html

Hoppenstand, Gary, and Ray B. Browne, eds. *The Gothic World of Stephen King: Landscape of Nightmares*. Bowling Green, OH: Bowling Green State University Popular Press, 1987.

Kaste, Martin. "Is Your E-Book Reading up on You?" NPR. Accessed March 2012. Available from http://www.npr.org/2010/12/15/132058735/is-your-e-book-reading-up-on-you

Kirkpatrick, David D. "A Stephen King Online Horror Tale Turns into a Mini-Disaster." *New York Times*. Accessed March 2012. Available from http://www.nytimes.com/2000/11/29/business/a-stephen-king-online-horror-tale-turns-into-a-mini-disaster.html

Lant, Kathleen Margaret, and Theresa Thompson, eds. *Imagining the Worst: Stephen King and the Representation of Women*. Westport, CT: Greenwood Press, 1998.

Magistrale, Anthony. *The Moral Voyages of Stephen King*. Mercer Island, WA: Starmont House, 1989.

Power, Brenda Miller; Jeffrey D. Wilhelm; and Kelly Chandler. *Reading Stephen King: Issues of Censorship, Student Choice, and Popular Literature*. Urbana, IL: National Council of Teachers of English, 1997.

Punter, David. *Gothic Pathologies: The Text, the Body, and the Law*. New York: St. Martin's Press, 1998.

Stefoff, Rebecca. *Stephen King*. New York: Marshall Cavendish Benchmark, 2010.

Timpone, Anthony, ed. *Fangoria Masters of the Dark*. New York: HarperPrism, 1997.

Winter, Douglas E. *Stephen King: The Art of Darkness*. New York: New American Library, 1984.

King Kong

One of the classic monster movies of all time, the 1933 production of *King Kong* is best remembered for the dramatic scenes of a giant ape climbing the recently erected Empire State Building and batting away airplanes with Ann Darrow in his grasp, though she is universally remembered not with that character's name but as the real-life actress who portrayed her, blond scream queen Fay Wray. That image of Kong and Wray atop a New York skyscraper, along with Dorothy on the Yellow Brick Road and Scarlett returning to the ruins of Tara, ranks among the iconic film scenes of the pre–World War II era. A popular sensation in its day, *King Kong* failed to win a single Academy Award nomination yet has outlived most of its contemporaries to achieve the stature of an enduring myth, as evidenced by the success of the 2005 remake.

A CLASSIC TALE

A modern variation on *Beauty and the Beast*, the screenplay was credited to popular pulp writer Edgar Wallace, though *King Kong* was the brainchild of documentary film pioneer Meriam C. Cooper and his partner in adventurous filmmaking, Ernest Schoedsack. The film's effects, groundbreaking in their day, were the handiwork of stop-motion animator Willis H. O'Brien, whose efforts on the silent film version of Sir Arthur Conan Doyle's *The Lost World* had laid the groundwork for *King Kong*. Promising Wray "the tallest, darkest leading man in Hollywood," Cooper and Schoedsack cast her as Ann Darrow, the petite object of Kong's affection. Rounding out the cast were Robert Armstrong as the headstrong filmmaker, Carl Denham (modeled after Cooper), and Bruce Cabot as the rugged seaman who falls for Darrow even before Kong does. Kong himself was in actuality a small model. O'Brien's genius was that moviegoers not only believed that Kong was a giant but also that he had a soul.

King Kong. *A poster advertises the 1933 release of* King Kong. BUYENLARGE/CONTRIBUTOR/TIME & LIFE PICTURES/GETTY IMAGES.

Like other "jungle" movies of the period, *King Kong* delineates a clash between the "civilized" and the "primitive." Denham's "bring 'em back alive" expedition to remote Skull Island uncovers a living prehistoric world populated by local natives and—on the other side of their great wall—dinosaurs, pterodactyls, and Kong himself. The islanders kidnap Ann to offer her as a bride for the giant gorilla, prompting a struggle in which many men die in the attempt to rescue her from her fate. Eventually Kong is subdued and taken to Manhattan, where Denham exploits the great beast as the "Eighth Wonder of the World." But the love-smitten Kong escapes, rampages across Manhattan, recaptures Ann, and ends up atop the Empire State Building, only to plummet to his death in a dramatic air assault. Denham's rueful obituary: "It wasn't the airplanes—it was beauty that killed the beast."

All of this thrill-packed hokum was made convincing by O'Brien's effects, aided by skillful art direction (Skull Island was a mythical landscape straight out of Gustave Doré); the optical printing of Linwood Dunn; the sound effects of Murray Spivack; and, above all, the almost wall-to-wall musical score by Max Steiner. It has been suggested that Depression-era audiences took a particularly vicarious delight in seeing Kong lay waste to the buildings and subway trains of the cold-hearted Manhattan. *King Kong* has remained a staple of late-night television and of film festivals, chiefly because O'Brien endowed his great brute with an uncanny personality that evoked sympathy from audiences.

THE INFLUENCE OF *KING KONG*

King Kong spawned a modestly budgeted, inferior sequel, *Son of Kong* (1933). O'Brien also worked on one more giant ape movie, *Mighty Joe Young* (1949), aided by his young protégé, Ray Harryhausen, who went on to make many successful screen fantasies of his own, such as *The 7th Voyage of Sinbad* (1958) and *Jason and the Argonauts* (1963), all of which carry echoes of *King Kong*. In truth, there is something of the big hairy ape in every giant-monster movie that has followed, from Japan's *Godzilla* (1954) to Steven Spielberg's *Jurassic Park* (1993) and, of course, in the moderately successful 1976 remake *King Kong*. But no other creature feature seems to have quite caught the public imagination as the original *King Kong* until famed *Lord of the Rings* director Peter Jackson undertook a high-budget remake of the original 1933 film in 2005.

A SUCCESSFUL REMAKE

While Jackson went to great lengths to maintain many of the elements of Cooper's film (even maintaining the original 1930s timeframe), his use of computer-generated imagery (CGI) and motion-capture technology brought the unbridled strength and underlying humanity of Kong, the perilous creatures and pitfalls of Skull Island, and the frantic Manhattan firefight with the doomed ape to life in new and exhilarating ways. The film was well received by critics and audiences and won several Oscars for its sound and visual effects.

The success of Jackson's remake, however, also resurrected a long-standing debate over what film scholars and civil rights leaders have perceived as the racist implications of the King Kong story. In the original film, Skull Island is said to be off the coast of Africa, and critics have suggested that the plot is an allegory for the capture and transport of African slaves, one that plays into the racist stereotypes and fears of white society by portraying Kong as a hulking, dimwitted beast with a threatening lust for blond-haired, fair-skinned maidens. The fact that Jackson changed the location of Skull Island to the South Seas while going to great lengths to maintain the integrity of many other aspects of Cooper's film seemed to suggest that the filmmaker himself recognized the merit of such accusations, and led reviewers, news reporters, scholars, and even casual audience members to view *King Kong* with increased scrutiny.

Nevertheless, the image of Kong and his beloved atop the skyscraper has been continually copied in horror movies and parodied in cartoons, comic books, and countless television commercials. For a period in the 1980s, a pop shrine to the gorilla's memory was created when a giant inflated model of King Kong was hung near the top the Empire State Building. Still, the original black-and-white film has lost none of its power to enthrall. Modern digital technology may have outstripped O'Brien's hands-on puppetry, but it has not replaced the charm and humanity that every great fairy tale requires and that *King Kong* displays in abundance.

Preston Neal Jones

SEE ALSO: *Academy Awards; CGI; Empire State Building; Godzilla;* Gone with the Wind*; The Great Depression;* Jurassic Park*;* Lord of the Rings *Film Trilogy; Spielberg, Steven;* The Wizard of Oz*; World War II.*

BIBLIOGRAPHY

Erb, Cynthia. *Tracking King Kong: A Hollywood Icon in World Culture.* Detroit, MI: Wayne State University Press, 2009.

Goldner, Orville, and George E. Turner. *The Making of King Kong.* New York: Ballantine, 1976.

Gottesman, Ronald, and Harry Geduld. *The Girl in the Hairy Paw: King Kong as Myth, Movie and Monster.* New York: Avon, 1976.

Harryhausen, Ray. *Film Fantasy Scrapbook*, 2nd ed. South Brunswick, NJ: A. S. Barnes, 1974.

Morton, Ray. *King Kong: The History of a Movie Icon from Fay Wray to Peter Jackson.* New York: Applause Theatre & Cinema Books, 2005.

Kingston, Maxine Hong *(1940–)*

Novelist Maxine Hong Kingston was born in the United States to Chinese immigrant parents. Her writing centers on the experiences of Chinese Americans and is part of a multiculturalist critique that challenges the image of the United States as culturally homogenous. Her first book, *The Woman Warrior: Memoirs of a Girlhood among Ghosts* (1976), details her own efforts to integrate the Chinese and American elements in her life and weaves a feminist perspective into the story. In 1981 she won the National Book Award for her novel *China Men*, and in 1997 President Bill Clinton presented her with the National Humanities Medal. Her writing undermines narrative traditions, just as she challenges a unilateral view of culture and history.

Petra Kuppers

SEE ALSO: *Feminism; Multiculturalism.*

BIBLIOGRAPHY

Bloom, Harold, ed. *Asian-American Writers.* New York: Infobase Publishing, 2009.

Kingston, Maxine Hong. *China Men.* London: Picador, 1981.

Lim, Shirley. *Approaches to Teaching Maxine Hong Kingston's "The Woman Warrior."* New York: Lang, 1991

The Kingston Trio

Formed in 1957 in San Francisco, the folk group called the Kingston Trio gained popularity with its three-part harmonies and energetic, humorous approach to folk music. Courting a pop audience and sporting striped shirts, neatly pressed chinos, and an upbeat attitude, the group originally consisted of guitarists Bob Shane and Nick Reynolds and banjoist Dave Guard (he was replaced by songwriter/rock artist John Stewart in 1961). Backed by Guard's five-string banjo, an acoustic guitar, and congas, the Trio's first big hit was "The Ballad of Tom Dooley," a harmonized saga of a condemned man awaiting execution, based on an old song of the Civil War era. The recording sold more than three million copies and won the Kingston Trio its first Grammy Award. Among its numerous albums, several of which now count among the best-selling records of the 1950s and 1960s, five of its first six would make it to the number one spot.

The Kingston Trio began as a casual association between Shane, Reynolds, and Guard. After working up their repertoire at local bars, the group got its first major gig: a one-week stint at the Purple Onion, a favorite nightspot of California's San Francisco college crowd during the late 1950s. (Guard was a student at Stanford University when the group formed.) Quickly signed to Capitol Records, the group released its first record in early 1958 and went on to release numerous others, including a 1962 tribute to the presidency of John F. Kennedy titled *New Frontier.* The Kingston Trio's appearance at the groundbreaking 1959 Newport Folk Festival in Rhode Island was documented in its album *Live at Newport.* Until the British Invasion in the 1960s, the Trio was a mainstay of the U.S. pop charts. In addition to being the first musical group to have sales of LP records outnumber singles, fourteen of the Kingston Trio's albums made it to the Top 10 spot, with five of those reaching number one and several charting for a year or more.

Punctuated by the twang of the banjo, the music of the Kingston Trio had a danceable feel that captured the hearts of pop fans and turned the band into one of the first crossover groups to bridge the folk and pop genres. Because it made three-part harmony and acoustic guitar look so simple, the group sparked a wave of interest in folk music across the country and was later credited with helping usher in the U.S. folk revival of the 1960s.

As strong as its fan base was, however, the Kingston Trio also had its detractors. The group's overt commercialism stood in direct contrast to the back-to-the-earth values associated with folk music and embodied by groups such as the Weavers, and the Kingston Trio was reviled in many folk-music circles. "I don't think we ever took ourselves seriously enough to think that we belonged to folk music," Stewart said in a 1966 interview. Rather than stick to the traditional musical interpretations extolled by purists, the Trio intentionally sought new input

The Kingston Trio. *Bob Shane, left, John Stewart, and Nick Reynolds made up the Kingston Trio, one of the first crossover groups to bridge the folk and pop genres.* MICHAEL OCHS ARCHIVES/STRINGER/GETTY IMAGES.

for its music, adapting such diverse ethnic music traditions as Appalachian mountain melodies and calypso into its own clean-cut, upbeat style.

Children of the Morning (1966) was the last album recorded by the Kingston Trio. Audience musical preferences were changing, and the rock-folk synthesis the Trio catalyzed in the 1950s was, by the late 1960s, the province of groups such as Simon and Garfunkel, the Mamas and the Papas, and the Association. Although the band officially broke up in 1967, Shane received permission to reform it under an altered name, and the New Kingston Trio toured with Jim Connor and Pat Horine until 1973 and then with Roger Gambill and Bill Zorn until 1976.

In 1976 Shane secured the right to use the original name, the Kingston Trio, by relinquishing any rights in and profits from the original corporation. Between 1976 and his retirement in 2004, he toured under that name with a number of different musicians. After his retirement the band continued to tour under the leadership of New Kingston Trio member Zorn. As for other Trio members, Stewart went on to record with Stevie Nicks and Lindsey Buckingham of the rock group Fleetwood Mac. Guard, who had left because of personality clashes with Shane and Reynolds, formed the Whiskeyhill Singers in the early 1960s.

The band received numerous awards over the decades, including a Billboard Music Award for best new singing group (1958), Grammy Awards for "Tom Dooley" (1959) and their album *At Large* (1960), a Grammy Hall of Fame Award for "Tom Dooley" (1998), and a Grammy Lifetime Achievement Award (2010). The Kingston Trio was inducted into the Vocal Group Hall of Fame in 2000 and the Hit Parade Hall of Fame in 2008. "Tom Dooley" was included on the Library of Congress National Registry of Historically Significant Recordings in 2008.

Pamela L. Shelton

SEE ALSO: *British Invasion; Fleetwood Mac; Folk Music; Grammy Awards; The Mamas and the Papas; Newport Jazz and Folk Festivals; Pop Music; Simon and Garfunkel.*

BIBLIOGRAPHY

Blake, Benjamin; Jack Rubeck; and Allan Shaw. *The Kingston Trio on Record.* Naperville, IL: Kingston Korner, 1986.

Cantwell, Robert. *When We Were Good: The Folk Revival.* Cambridge, MA: Harvard University Press, 1966.

Childs, Marti Smiley, and Jeff March. *Where Have All the Pop Stars Gone?* Davis, CA: EditPros, 2001.

Lawless, Ray M. *Folksingers and Folksongs in America: A Handbook of Biography, Bibliography, and Discography.* Westport, CT: Greenwood Press, 1981.

Kinison, Sam *(1953–1992)*

Sam Kinison is remembered as the innovator of rage comedy, a style defined by the punctuation of a comedy routine with seemingly out-of-control fits of screaming and howling. His intense stand-up routines were filled with obscenities, and he often used Jesus Christ as a main character in his jokes.

Kinison was born on December 8, 1953, in Yakima, Washington. He followed in his father's footsteps and began his career as a Pentecostal minister. Soon, however, he drifted into comedy clubs, where he caught the attention of comic Rodney Dangerfield. Dangerfield provided Kinison with showcase bookings in his own nightclub and a role in his movie *Back to School* (1986). The comedian also appeared on *Saturday Night Live*, a Home Box Office (HBO) cable special, and the short-lived TV sitcom *Charlie Hoover*.

Ironically, Kinison had recently completed successful treatment for his well-documented substance abuse when he was accidentally killed on April 10, 1992, by a teenage drunk driver who professed to having been one of his fans. In 2011 Carl La Bove, Kinison's best friend and long-time opening act, released DNA evidence indicating that his daughter was in fact the result of an affair that Kinison had with his wife in the late 1990s.

Barry Morris

SEE ALSO: *Cable TV;* Saturday Night Live*; Sitcom; Stand-Up Comedy; Television.*

BIBLIOGRAPHY

Kinison, Bill, and Steve Delsohn. *Brother Sam: The Short, Spectacular Life of Sam Kinison.* New York: William Morrow, 1994.

Talevski, Nick. *Knocking on Heaven's Door: Rock Obituaries.* London: Omnibus Press, 2006.

Kinsey, Dr. Alfred C. *(1894–1956)*

Although he was in many ways the very model of the "egghead" scientist, complete with crew-cut and bow tie, few academic researchers have had such a widespread impact on American culture as Dr. Alfred C. Kinsey, the founder of the Institute for Sex Research (later renamed for Kinsey) at Indiana University. Kinsey and his colleagues revolutionized the study and understanding of human sexuality through the publication of the two famous *Kinsey Reports*, more accurately titled *Sexual Behavior in the Human Male* (1948) and *Sexual Behavior in the Human Female* (1953). Instant best sellers and cultural touchstones that few people actually read, the reports explicitly divorced moral judgment from the study of sexuality and opened sexual inquiry to professional disciplines beyond the medical sciences. While the aim of Kinsey's work was explicitly to collect quantifiable data, its cultural repercussions could be felt in the ways sexual topics were taught, discussed, and debated in American society throughout the latter half of the twentieth century and into the twenty-first.

Raised in a strict home and trained in zoology and entomology at Harvard, Kinsey began his scientific career by becoming the world's expert on gall wasps, which he collected by the thousands. Among other things, he discovered that they exhibited odd reproductive habits. After being hired by Indiana University in 1920 and asked to coordinate an undergraduate course on marriage, Kinsey discovered how little reliable scientific research was available on human sexuality. He and his colleagues (most notably Wardell Pomeroy, Clyde Martin, and Paul Gebhard) then initiated an elaborate project to collect data, which eventually involved almost 18,000 personal interviews and the accumulation of a vast archive of erotic as well as scientific materials. Though linked to a state university, the institute relied upon independent funding and donations in order to counter regular misperceptions that Indiana taxpayers might be supporting a pornography collection: early on, to demonstrate his techniques, Kinsey even collected the sexual histories of his sponsors at the Rockefeller Foundation and National Research Council.

Adopting a radically empirical stance, Kinsey's institute categorized and cross-indexed sexual information in minute detail, while carefully avoiding the moralizing perspectives that had hampered previous discussions of sexual behavior and expression. In the institute's neutral vision, pornography might be as valuable for research as anthropology. For the first time in American culture, the practice of masturbation was simply taken for granted, though its multiple variations were carefully catalogued. By all accounts, Kinsey and his team were masterful in their ability to put their interviewees at ease while they revealed their most intimate activities and fantasies. The public response to those interviews was, on the other hand, a mixture of shock and fascination that also turned the research scientist into a national celebrity.

HOMOSEXUALITY

Undoubtedly the first report's most controversial revelation, especially in the historical context of servicemen returning to civilian life, was that homosexual activity was common to many American men: 37 percent of Kinsey's sample had experienced

Alfred Kinsey. *Dr. Alfred C. Kinsey authored of the two groundbreaking reports on human sexual behavior.* **HULTON ARCHIVE/STAFF/HULTON ARCHIVE/GETTY IMAGES.**

at least one homosexual encounter leading to orgasm. Adopting a scale from 0 to 6, ranging from exclusive heterosexuality to exclusive homosexuality, Kinsey challenged stereotypes linking homosexuality and effeminate behavior and defined homosexuality as behavioral rather than constitutional. According to his statistical summary, about 4 percent of American men were exclusively homosexual. Although Kinsey's statistics have been the subject of extensive criticism and confusion (he is commonly misquoted as claiming that 10 percent of American men are homosexual), reexaminations of his figures have also frequently affirmed the validity of his findings. Overall, his research argued that homosexuals as a group, and homosexuality as an activity, were much more typical and, therefore, less statistically "deviant" than previously assumed.

FEMALE SEXUALITY

The report on female sexuality was equally controversial, though the press and public downplayed its discovery that, while only 3 percent of Kinsey's sample were exclusively homosexual, the women in the study tended to be better educated than their male counterparts. Instead, attention focused on Kinsey's detailed analysis of the female orgasm and his revealing that almost half of the women interviewed had experienced premarital intercourse, while around 26 percent had enjoyed extramarital sexual relations. Clearly, Kinsey's data challenged beliefs about the prevailing female behavior, which turned out to largely be ideals rather than reality.

More than a half century after the publication of his reports, Kinsey remains a controversial figure, though the most heated debates about his work have generally moved back into the academy where they began. Periodically his objectivity and statistical findings are challenged, and often they are reconfirmed. James H. Jones's 1997 biography revealed many surprising details of Kinsey's own complex sexual life—married and the father of four children, Kinsey was also homosexually active. Appearing just a year later, Jonathan Gathorne-Hardy's biography of Kinsey challenged many of Jones's assertions and revealed how much of what is known about or attributed to Kinsey is simply a matter of public speculation, often put forth in service of various moral or political agendas. For cultural historians, the recurrence of such debates itself provides evidence of Kinsey's ongoing role in American life.

In the early twenty-first century, a period of increasing comfort with the diverse spectrum of sexuality, a flurry of fictional and nonfictional works once again brought Kinsey and his theories into the realm of popular culture. Most notably, the biopic *Kinsey* (2004) was based on Gathorne-Hardy's biography and portrayed Kinsey (played by Liam Neeson) as a devoted scientist but an ultimately troubled man. T. Coraghessan Boyle's novel *The Inner Circle* (2004) is a fictional account of a young research assistant's struggle to reconcile Kinsey's findings with his own relationship experiences. The PBS documentary *Kinsey* (2005) provides revealing interviews with many of Kinsey's colleagues and his earliest readers, who describe the impact that the *Kinsey Reports* had on their sexual attitudes. In addition to literature and film, Kinsey's legacy was examined in the musical *Dr. Sex* (2003) and the radio play *Mr. Sex* (2005).

Responding to Kinsey's reemergence in popular culture, conservative authors such as Judith Reisman published a series of books attacking his theories as junk science tinged with a dangerous tendency toward eugenics and pedophilia, claims that were reinforced by the 2009 documentary *The Kinsey Syndrome.* While the merits of such attacks remain up for debate, it is impossible to deny that the *Kinsey Reports* are directly responsible for making once-taboo topics—masturbation, homosexuality, female orgasm—frequent discussion topics in the media and in the home.

Corey K. Creekmur

SEE ALSO: *Gay Men;* The Joy of Sex*; Public Television (PBS);* Sex and the Single Girl.

BIBLIOGRAPHY

Boyle, T. Coraghessan. *The Inner Circle.* New York: Viking, 2004.

Bullough, Vern L. *Science in the Bedroom: A History of Sex Research.* New York: BasicBooks, 1994.

Christenson, Cornelia V. *Kinsey: A Biography.* Bloomington: Indiana University Press, 1971.

D'Emilio, John, and Estelle B. Freedman. *Intimate Matters: A History of Sexuality in America.* New York: Harper & Row, 1988.

Ditzion, Sidney. *Marriage, Morals, and Sex in America: A History of Ideas.* New York: Bookman Associates, 1953.

Gathorne-Hardy, Jonathan. *Kinsey: Sex the Measure of All Things.* Bloomington: Indiana University Press, 1998.

Irvine, Janice M. *Disorders of Desire: Sex and Gender in Modern American Sexology.* Philadelphia: Temple University Press, 1990.

Jones, James H. *Alfred C. Kinsey: A Public/Private Life.* New York: W. W. Norton, 1997.

Pomeroy, Wardell B. *Dr. Kinsey and the Institute for Sex Research.* New York: Harper & Row, 1972.

Reisman, Judith. *Kinsey's Attic: The Shocking Story of How One Man's Sexual Pathology Changed the World.* Nashville, TN: Cumberland House, 2005.

Robinson, Paul. *The Modernization of Sex: Havelock Ellis, Alfred Kinsey, William Masters and Virginia Johnson.* New York: Harper & Row, 1976.

Kirby, Jack *(1917–1994)*

One of the most prolific and influential comic-book creators, Jack Kirby is deservedly known as "the king of comics." Kirby, born Jacob Kurtzberg, grew up on New York's tough Lower East Side. The brawls and colorful characters of his youth influenced his work—from the explosive fight scenes to the numerous kid-gangs he created (the Newsboy Legion and Boy Commandos, among others). Kirby teamed with Joe Simon beginning in 1940, and they created scores of comic books, including the first romance comic. In March 1941 their most famous creation, Captain America, debuted in *Captain America Adventures.*

Over the next twenty years, Kirby virtually created the visual language of superhero comics. His panels were crammed with dynamic action and visual excitement. Perhaps his best work was in the 1960s, when he and writer-editor Stan Lee transformed faltering Atlas Comics into pop-culture powerhouse Marvel Comics with characters such as the Fantastic Four and the X-Men.

Randy Duncan

SEE ALSO: *Captain America; Comic Books;* The Fantastic Four; *Lee, Stan; Marvel Comics; The X-Men.*

BIBLIOGRAPHY

Evanier, Mark. *Kirby: King of Comics*. New York: Abrams, 2008.

Hatfield, Charles. *Hand of Fire: The Comics Art of Jack Kirby*. Jackson: University Press of Mississippi, 2012.

Ro, Ronin. *Tales to Astonish: Jack Kirby, Stan Lee, and the American Comic Book Revolution*. New York: Bloomsbury, 2004.

Theakston, Greg, Jack Kirby. *The Complete Jack Kirby: 1940–1941*. New York: Pure Imagination Publishing, 1997.

KISS

After four decades in the business and sales in the neighborhood of 100 million albums, KISS can legitimately be placed among the world's great rock and roll bands. Their best-known songs, such as "Rock and Roll All Nite," "Shout It Out Loud," and "Detroit Rock City," stand as true rock anthems. The band can also be credited with inventing the radio-friendly power ballad ("Beth," 1976), though it took nearly ten years before other hard-rock bands to follow suit. Their chart successes notwithstanding, KISS made their greatest contribution to rock and roll on the stage. Their outrageous make-up and over-the-top theatrics radically expanded rock fans' expectations for showmanship.

DONNING THE MAKE-UP

KISS was formed in New York City in 1972 by bass player Gene Simmons and vocalist/guitarist Paul Stanley after their band, Wicked Lester, was dumped by Epic Records. Stanley and Simmons recruited guitarist Ace Frehley and drummer Peter Criss, both of whom who had advertised their availability in music magazines. With the lineup in place, the group devised an ingenious strategy to market its act to fans and record labels. Drawing on precedents set by glam-rock acts such as the New York Dolls and shock rocker Alice Cooper, the members of KISS reinvented themselves as four larger-than-life stage characters by means of elaborate costumes and Kabuki-style make-up. Simmons played a blood-spitting, fire-breathing demon; Stanley masqueraded as a bare-chested, hyper-macho Casanova; Frehley became an outer-space guitar wizard; and Criss played the role of a prowling cat-man. To enhance the effect, the band members did not permit themselves to be seen or photographed in public without their make-up.

In addition to their clever use of theatrical disguises, KISS developed an elaborately choreographed performance that, along with their aggressive self-promotional releases, attracted the attention of television producer Bill Aucoin, who helped the band garner a contract with Casablanca Records. Their first three albums, released in quick succession in 1974 and 1975, sold modestly, and the band was lambasted by critics everywhere. Nevertheless, KISS built up an impressive audience through constant touring, which showcased their groundbreaking use of pyrotechnics, set design, and stage lighting. They also greatly expanded their audience because they were more willing than most bands to schedule dates in smaller-market cities and geographically isolated locales.

KISS. *Gene Simmons, left, Ace Frehley, and Paul Stanley of KISS perform in London, England, in 1980.* **PETER STILL/CONTRIBUTOR/REDFERNS/GETTY IMAGES.**

Recognizing that their musical energy was somewhat lost in the studio setting, KISS released a concert album, *Alive* (1975). Peaking at number nine on the charts, *Alive* catapulted the band to the top of the rock world and relieved it of nagging debt problems. The next studio album, *Destroyer* (1976), marked an important shift in sound and image, as KISS abandoned its simplistic, almost silly, straight-ahead guitar rock for a more polished and radio-friendly sound. This drew in a more diverse fan base. The KISS Army, as the band's fan base is known, was initially peopled almost exclusively by teenage males, but it now was beginning to also include teenage females and a lucrative preteen audience. Perhaps most important in KISS's transition was the release of the pop single "Beth," a ballad penned by Criss as a tribute to his wife. "Beth" reached the Top 10 and became the band's best-selling single. KISS's biggest year was 1977, when several of their albums were on the charts simultaneously and they wound up as Billboard's number two album artist, behind only Fleetwood Mac.

KISS OVERLOAD

Capitalizing on their multiplatinum successes, the group further expanded its multimedia approach to rock. Taking a leaf out of the Beatlemania book, KISS made everything from lunchboxes to action figures available to their adoring fans. In 1977 Marvel comics published a KISS comic book, purportedly printed with ink that had been mixed with blood drawn from the band members. The next year the band was featured in a movie called *KISS Meets the Phantom of the Park*. The October release date was appropriate since KISS Halloween costumes were all the rage. It was rumored that the band even bought nearly 200 acres near Cincinnati, Ohio, in order to build a theme park that never materialized. KISS's widespread popularity and Simmons's demonic stage character prompted concern by parent groups and the nascent religious right. Several youths, trying to copy Simmons's fire-breathing stage act, were badly burned, and objectors suggested that KISS was really an acronym for Knights in Satan's Service, a charge flatly rejected by the band. In Germany, the KISS logo raised concern in Germany because of the resemblance of the last two letters to the swastika that represented the Nazis.

As the more conservative 1980s approached, KISS and their excesses began to seem dated. Beginning with their four "solo" albums, released in 1978, the band hit a slump that would last through the early 1980s. Among the ill-fated releases of this era was *Dynasty* (1979), which featured the peculiar disco-oriented single "I Was Made for Loving You," a song that alienated many longtime fans. KISS deviated even further from their basic formula of teen-friendly hard rock when they recorded *The Elder* (1981), a concept album that was partially co-written by Lou Reed. Neither *The Elder* nor *Dynasty* sold well by the standards that the band had set a few years earlier.

During the 1980s KISS underwent several lineup changes. Criss and Frehley left the band and were replaced by Eric Carr and Vinnie Vincent, respectively. Subsequently, Vincent was replaced by Mark St. John, who in turn gave way to Bruce Kulick. After nearly a decade, Eric Singer took over for Carr, who was terminally ill with cancer.

CHARGING BACK

In 1983 KISS abandoned their make-up and entered headlong into the emerging pop-metal arena, competing with the likes of Def Leppard and Bon Jovi. As metal mania reached a fever pitch in the 1980s and early 1990s, KISS enjoyed a significant resurgence, again reaching platinum status with albums such as *Lick It Up* (1983) and *Animalize* (1984). They never quite regained their former momentum, however, and members of the band ventured into other projects. Both Stanley and Simmons, for example, tried acting.

As the 1990s rolled around, KISS were established as rock legends. Dozens of KISS tribute bands were on the road in the 1980s and 1990s, albeit without the elaborate stage sets, and in 1994 a KISS tribute album was recorded. Titled *KISS My Ass*, it stood as a sarcastic rebuke to all the critics who had scorned the band over the years and featured KISS covers from artists as diverse as Garth Brooks and Lenny Kravitz. Indeed, a number of bands were influenced by KISS, including popular 1980s-era metal bands such as Faster Pussycat, Mötley Crüe, Ratt, DIO, and Twisted Sister. The KISS influence could also be felt, if not heard, in grunge bands of the early 1990s such as Nirvana and Soundgarden, which approached the business of songwriting and rock stardom with the same tongue-in-cheek attitude as KISS.

Interest in KISS was revitalized substantially in the mid-1990s when the original lineup reunited to perform a few numbers for MTV's *Unplugged* program. Reaction from fans was so favorable that a reunion tour was scheduled, replete with make-up, blood spitting, and pyrotechnics. The tour drew huge crowds and brought the band's peculiar brand of live entertainment to a new generation of fans. Years of difficulties and crisis within the band followed, but in 2009 KISS mounted their first tour of Europe in a decade to promote their first album in as long, *Sonic Boom*. In 2012 another album, *Monster*, showed the world that KISS was not ready yet ready to fade into history.

Steve Graves

SEE ALSO: *Brooks, Garth; Cooper, Alice; Grunge; Heavy Metal; Mötley Crüe; Nirvana; Reed, Lou; Rock and Roll.*

BIBLIOGRAPHY

Leaf, David, and Ken Sharp. *KISS: Behind the Mask; The Official Biography*. New York: Warner Books, 2003.

Lendt, C. K. *KISS and Sell: The Making of a Supergroup*. New York: Watson-Guptill, 1997.

Levine, Barry, and Ken Sharp. *The KISS Years*. New York: H. & H. Global, 1997.

Sherman, Dale. *Black Diamond: The Unauthorized Biography of KISS*. London: Collector's Guide Publishers, 1997.

Stevens, Joe. *KISS—Revenge Is Sweet: An Illustrated Biography*. London: Omnibus Press, 1997

Swenson, John. *Headliners: KISS*. New York: Tempo Books, 1978.

Kitsch

The word *kitsch* is perhaps one of the oldest, crudest, and most unclear terms used to describe the popular art of modern societies, though it is also a term that is almost universally understood. First appearing in the writings of cultural and social critics of the late nineteenth century to describe the effects of early industrialism on the common culture of nations in Europe and

North America, the term has evolved and taken on a variety of sometimes quite contradictory meanings throughout more than a century of use. Although the precise etymology of *kitsch* is uncertain, most scholars attribute its origins to the Munich art markets of the 1860s, where the word was used to describe inexpensive paintings, or "sketches" (the English word mispronounced by Germans or elided with the German verb *verkitschen*, to "make cheap"). Kitsch artworks appealed to the naive tastes of the emerging, newly moneyed Munich bourgeoisie who, in typical nouveau riche fashion, desired objects they thought to be typical of high taste, without knowing exactly what high taste was.

Like *pornography, art*, or other slippery terms, kitsch is easier to demonstrate by example than it is to clarify by definition: it tends to apply most easily to ornamental statuary, tchotchkes of different kinds, manufactured sentimental knick-knacks, souvenirs, and decorative objects reflecting a childlike simplicity—things that are simply meant to make people feel good about themselves and the world. What makes an object kitsch, however, is not simply the fact of its being decorative; kitsch artificially inflates the comfort of decoration into a uniquely fake aesthetic statement. Thus, there are two sides of kitsch that require explanation: kitsch is a unique aesthetic style, but it is also the effect of specific social and historical changes. As an effect of historical changes, it is caused by industrialization, urbanization, and the rise of a new middle class. As an aesthetic quality, kitsch combines an emulation of high art forms and styles with a dependence on comfort and very direct expressions of aesthetic pleasure.

HISTORY AND AESTHETICS

By the mid-nineteenth century, improvements in mechanized manufacture, distribution, and commercial retail, together with a trend toward urbanization, made it possible for mass-produced cultural goods to reach vast numbers of people. In Europe and North America, these economic changes opened up clerical and lower-level management positions that helped create a new, largely urban, middle class. Peasants and traditional workers who had previously been content with regional, rural, and traditional forms of culture found themselves buying mass-produced trinkets, decorations, and ornaments for the home. With disposable income and leisure time to kill, this new class of urban professionals sought distractions and amusements, but most importantly it sought to carve out a status for itself as "cultured" and "sophisticated," especially in Europe, by exhibiting its taste for fine things.

These petty professionals swarmed over the new luxury items that were being churned out in mass volume, gravitating especially to the knock-off imitation luxury products, "fine art" items crudely and glibly manufactured to resemble the posh and high art objects of the old aristocracy: gilded furniture, glass-beaded jewelry, highly ornate candelabras, imitation oil paintings, miniature ceramic copies of ancient statues, and other household ornaments meant to produce maximum effect without too much bother or cost. As societies industrialized and more and more people gained access to mass-produced cultural goods, kitsch emerged as the lowest common cultural denominator of modern society, cutting across old class distinctions through the techniques of the new mass consumption. For this reason the rise of kitsch has been widely blamed for the erosion of elite high culture and the uprooting of regional folk cultures, as well as the wider "dumbing down" of modern societies.

The influx of kitsch objects gradually brought with it an overall change in attitudes toward the definition of beauty itself. Unlike the traditional elite classes who exercised refinement and cultivation in their appreciation for the subtleties of true artistic expression, the new classes lacked any taste for subtlety, preferring art that was loud, direct, and excessive. Where true art required strenuous interpretation and a cultivated sensibility, and presented the viewer with personal and ethical challenges, the kitsch of mass-produced art sought to make itself available to the maximum number of people. It took the shortest, easiest, and most direct route, always preferring more intense aesthetic expression through added features and exaggerated effects. On the question of beauty, the purveyor of kitsch reasons according to the "more is better" principle: Why have a chandelier hung only with cut glass baubles when there is one available with cherubs and electric candles? Why be content with a plaster reproduction of the Venus in the foyer when it can be lit from behind, producing a more dramatic effect? Why settle for a simple oil seascape when one can be purchased that includes crashing waves, seagulls, and a partially obscured moon shining right through the towering curl of a cresting wave?

The mass-produced art of the new classes simply declares the effect it intends: "beauty!" "exotica!" "sentiment!" The familiar earmarks of kitsch: exploding fields of flowers, the faces of cute children, etc., deliver aesthetic response with greater intensity and in a more direct manner because of its use of overstatement. However, even while kitsch maximizes aesthetic effect, it remains faithful to its vision of high art: kitsch believes itself to be sincere, graceful, even profound—like high art itself. Thus, this quality of maximized effect in the form of high culture defines an important aspect of kitsch.

THE ATTRACTION TO KITSCH

Even more than simply graceless and overstated techniques, what makes an object kitsch is its dependence on expressions of comfort, happiness, and an artificial sense of well-being. Kitsch expresses a pleasurable experience of everyday comfort, coziness, and easy solace, an artificially simplified and synthetically comfortable image of the world, allowing an easy and gratuitous sense of bliss. Kitsch achieves this in many ways: in Norman Rockwell's paintings of small-town America, for example, kitsch expresses a contrived sense of wonderment at the innocence and folly of everyday people and things, especially children, animals, and old people whose everydayness is raised to the level of an important human virtue. In Rockwell's paintings there is little ambiguity about the people he represents: they are cute, and this fact hits the viewer with immediate and unmistakable force. Kitsch aims for the easiest responses it can get, preferring to deliver the nostalgic comfort of familiar feelings rather than presenting new and uncomfortable challenges. For this reason, kitsch appeals to sentimentality, as also demonstrated in the work of Margaret Keane, well known for paintings of teary-eyed clowns and children with enormous, almond-shaped eyes. The response to Keane's work is a simple, obvious, and direct joy in what is simply and obviously joyful: cute little children.

According to the definition of kitsch, for both Rockwell and Keane, there is a pretentious aspect to their work. Although their subject matter is comfortable and accessible, it is not simply decorative. These are sincere, human expressions of a fundamental human quality, calling for the same respect and admiration reserved for humanity alone. In this way, cute kitsch makes the same appeal as high art does to the higher values of human beauty. And, more importantly for kitsch, the fawning sentimental reactions these images demand from their viewers are made to seem somehow virtuous, profound, and universally human. The viewer is flattered into feeling that the cuteness of one of Rockwell's everyday folks expresses the same essential value of human life that Michelangelo gave to the statue of David. There are no allowances made for tastes that are able to appreciate both for what they are.

The attraction to kitsch is seen as expressing the value of familiarity and comfort itself, raised up to the level of a true artistic statement, amplified through exaggerated effects so as to be easy and accessible to all. In short, kitsch tries to stimulate in a direct and accessible fashion, passing off comfort and sentimentality as expressions of profound human significance or deep personal meaning. Kitsch prefers to show what is already known so as to eschew the discomfort of experiencing something for the first time.

CONNOTATIONS

Kitsch is at once a volatile, flexible, and vague term, infinitely adaptable to the specific historical conditions of its use, conditions where popular culture is thought to be getting out of hand. Comparing a few of the most important uses of the term illustrates how some uses of kitsch emphasize its aesthetic while others focus on its historical and social dimensions.

Austrian writer Hermann Broch has discussed kitsch's development in the nineteenth century, and its connection with romanticism, noting that both kitsch and romanticism promised a uniquely modern flight from reality into a world that was sheltered from the tension and uncertainly of modern life. His essay "Notes on the Problem of Kitsch" points out that kitsch expresses that escape as a dreamy experience of happiness, tranquility, and sugary harmony, and a flight into comfort. Broch's article goes to the heart of that comfort as the product of these historical changes: kitsch comfort has its origins in the rising middle class that invented it. This taste for domestic comfort, Broch writes, became the badge of bourgeois identity, or the marker of their status as a legitimate class, rivaling the elite aspirations of aristocratic art. In this way, the middle-class valuation of comfort was inflated to the pretentious status of high art, as it learned to masquerade as art.

THE CONSCIOUSNESS OF THE MASSES

By the twentieth century, kitsch was being given a new set of meanings by the critics of mass culture, particularly intellectuals of the American Left who used the term to criticize the culture of the new "consumer," or mass society. Dwight MacDonald, Irving Howe, and others no longer blamed kitsch for the erosion of elite or regional culture but for the manipulation of the consciousness of the masses. Kitsch, the critics postulated, controlled people's thoughts and cultural outlooks through a bombardment of comic books, radio, TV shows, and movies expressing manufactured emotional, aesthetic, and social outlooks. Reducing adults to children, the new kitsch made masses easier to manipulate by reducing their cultural needs to the easy gratification offered by Disney cartoons, pulp literature, and romance novels. MacDonald wrote, "The Lords of kitsch, in short, exploit the cultural needs of the masses in order to make a profit and/or to maintain their class rule."

To these commentators of the 1950s, writing at the heyday of the mass culture theory, it seemed as if the same propaganda tactics that had worked so well for fascists and communists were operative in the kitsch of American capitalism and mass culture, draining the minds of consumers and ultimately cultivating subordination to authority. So barbarous was the effect of kitsch that one commentator was inclined to compare the manic and violent behavior of Donald Duck to the sadism of an SS soldier. Kitsch also proved useful for advocates of avant-garde culture, most notably Clement Greenberg, whose classic essay *Avant-Garde and Kitsch* stands as one of the best-known pieces on the topic. Greenberg, bent on making a distinction between the avant-garde and the popular culture of the masses, trashed kitsch for its parasitic quality, drawing its lifeblood from the creative sweat of "real artists," and keeping the masses in a state of cultural imbecility and confusion. For Greenberg, kitsch represented "the epitome of all that is spurious in the life of our times."

FROM KITSCH TO CAMP

Taken together, all these arguments hinge on the assumption of an objective standard of taste of one sort or another. An object cannot be labeled "kitsch" without assuming that there is, somewhere, a universal standard of beauty against which an object can be judged and condemned as kitsch. By the end of the twentieth century, with an increasing emphasis on cultural diversity and a postmodern acknowledgment of the relative standards of beauty in different societies, this objective standard of taste was not so easy to argue. In a climate of multiculturalism and cultural relativism, *kitsch* as a term describing an inherently inferior variety of art and culture, seemed to have no ground left on which to stand. In fact, the tables had turned; and in much cultural criticism of the late twentieth century, the term had fallen out of use. Particularly in the late 1990s, when the charm of camp (an ironic appreciation of kitsch, quite distinct from kitsch itself) defined so much of contemporary taste in popular culture, classical uses of the term *kitsch* seemed more and more difficult to justify. The cultural studies approach to popular culture had largely abandoned the term, at least in the morally charged, pejorative usage given it by nineteenth-century and mass culture theorists.

Nonetheless, kitsch has refused to go away, and it has appeared in some highly innovative commentaries. The closed, artificial world of kitsch and the dreamy sense of pleasantness and well-being it promises still puzzle cultural analysts, even when it was not tied to a strong judgment on the value of aesthetic content or to the control of the masses. Two such commentaries on kitsch stand out: Milan Kundera's *The Unbearable Lightness of Being* (1984) discusses the kitsch of communist society, which trumpets an artificial joy in the spontaneous exuberance of socialist life and the strained comfort of the company of one's comrades. A darker side of kitsch is revealed by Saul Friedlander in his *Reflections of Nazism: An Essay on Kitsch and Death* (1984). Friedlander discloses the ways in which Nazi kitsch, in a manner quite different from standard forms of capitalist "entertainment" kitsch, excites a morbid fascination with death, particularly in the melodramatic image of the tragic death of the soldier. In fact, freed from its elitist underpinnings, kitsch has proven more effective a term for describing the strange euphoria of the synthetic that characterized much of consumer culture at the end of the twentieth century.

The debate over whether or not kitsch is a viable form of art has continued into the twenty-first century. Those who defend it dismiss the negativity of art critics who pan it. Much of the criticism, they say, has been derived from an arrogance that suggests that only those who restrict their tastes to fine art are capable of differentiating true art from kitsch. Betty Spackman writes in *Material Religion* that the most often slammed subgroup of kitsch is Christian kitsch, those religious works of art that exist in a nebulous world somewhere between religion and popular culture. Regardless of the constant criticism, kitsch has become a ubiquitous element of popular culture, and entire websites are devoted to extolling the virtues of contemporary kitsch and/or offering it up for sale.

Sam Binkley

SEE ALSO: *Camp; Comic Books; Consumerism; Disney (Walt Disney Company); Multiculturalism; Pop Art; Postmodernism; Radio; Rockwell, Norman; Romance Novels; Television.*

BIBLIOGRAPHY

Boyers, Robert, ed. "On Kitsch: A Symposium." *Salmagundi*, Winter–Spring 1990, 197–312.

Broch, Hermann. "Notes on the Problem of Kitsch." In *Kitsch: The World of Bad Taste*, ed. Gillo Dorfles. New York: Universe Books, 1969, 49–76.

Calinescu, Matei. "Kitsch." In *Five Faces of Modernity*. Durham, NC: Duke University Press, 1987.

Dorfles, Gillo. *Kitsch: The World of Bad Taste*. New York: Universe Books, 1969.

Friedlander, Saul. *Reflections of Nazism: An Essay on Kitsch and Death*, tr. Thomas Weyr. Bloomington: Indiana University Press, 1993.

Greenberg, Clement. "Avant-Garde and Kitsch." In *Art and Culture: Critical Essays*. Boston: Beacon Press, 1961.

Goodwin, Sarah Webster. *Kitsch and Culture: The Dance of Death in Nineteenth-Century Literature and Graphic Arts*. New York: Garland, 1988.

Kulka, Tomas. *Kitsch and Art*. University Park: Pennsylvania State University Press, 1996.

Kundera, Milan. *The Unbearable Lightness of Being*, tr. M. H. Heim. New York: Harper and Row, 1984.

MacDonald, Dwight. "A Theory of Mass Culture." In *Mass Culture*, ed. B. Rosenberg and D. M. White. Glencoe, IL: Free Press, 1957.

Nemoianu, Virgil. *Postmodernism and Cultural Identities: Conflicts and Coexistence*. Washington, DC: Catholic University of America Press, 2010.

Siraganian, Lisa. *Modernism's Other Work: The Art Object's Political Life*. New York: Oxford University Press, 2012.

Spackman, Betty. "Reconsidering Kitsch." *Material Religion* 1, no. 3 (2005): 405–416.

Kiwanis

In the words of its mission statement, the Kiwanis Club is an international organization dedicated to "service" and the "advancement of individual, community, and national welfare." It promotes a strong spiritual life for its members, a high standard of living, and the idea of citizens' civic obligations to others. The organization was founded on January 21, 1915, in Detroit, Michigan, by Allen Simpson Browne, a Moose (another service association) Lodge organizer, and Joseph Prance, a tailor. The name was drawn from a Native American phrase that can be interpreted variously to mean "we have a good time," "we trade," and "we advertise."

By the late 1990s the Kiwanis had 300,000 members in more than 8,000 clubs in eighty-two countries. Made up predominantly of businesspeople and professional men and women, the organization gives approximately $70 million a year to charitable institutions and individuals and seven million hours of direct community service. Perhaps best known for widely posted signs that feature a circled K, the Kiwanis Club symbolizes a commitment to the biblical Golden Rule—doing onto others as you would have them do unto you.

The Kiwanis began as a networking club for local merchants and salesmen to make contacts with prospective clients. It came to symbolize certain features of modern middle-class life. Cultural critics of the 1920s poked fun at its conformist, self-congratulatory, and boosterist elements. Spurred on by satirist H. L. Mencken's antagonism to the "booboisie," author Sinclair Lewis drew up a scathing portrait of small-town businessmen in his novel *Babbitt* (1922). Lewis mocked his central character's membership in local civic organizations that seemed more concerned with providing stability and making connections than with actually doing good works. In response, *Kiwanis* magazine called for continued "boosting" to counter the negativism of its critics. Nonetheless, Lewis's portrait of simplistic spirituality wedded to pragmatic materialism remained a popular image of the Kiwanis Club.

The Kiwanis Club grew out of a variety of voluntary organizations that French historian Alexis de Tocqueville discussed in *Democracy in America* (1835–1840), his classic analysis of nineteenth-century American culture. Many early members of the club were originally Moose and Elks Lodge members. The Kiwanis became part of a modern set of mainstream service organizations, including the Rotary and Lions clubs. Fostering the belief that citizens can solve social problems through local and voluntary activity, it provides opportunity for and examples of middle-class philanthropy and service for societal good. In his book *Service Clubs in American Society* (1993), Jeffrey Charles argues that the Kiwanis have tried to unite traditional values of community and compassion with the modern system of corporate profit and competitive individualism.

The emphasis on voluntarism, some may argue, symbolizes the more conservative element of the Kiwanis. During the early years of the Great Depression, the volunteer spirit was linked to Herbert Hoover's distrust of the federal government. In the 1950s the Kiwanis Club became closely associated with anticommunist campaigns and the conformist culture that social critics mocked in such books as C. Wright Mills's sociological text *White Collar* (1951) and journalist William Whyte's *The Organization Man* (1956). Not surprisingly, the club was using the 1950s emergence of the United States as a world superpower to spread internationally in larger numbers.

After a Supreme Court ruling barred private clubs from banning women, the Kiwanis began to admit women members in 1987. Nonetheless, like other civic organizations the club experienced a decline in American membership during the mid- to late 1990s. Reporting on the general waning of voluntarism, Harvard University political scientist Robert Putnam has argued that the trend reflects a wider loss of civic engagement in the United States and the demise of Tocqueville's ideal of America as a voluntarist republic. Nonetheless, the club has had a great impact on the civic and social identity of many middle-class Americans and has played a significant role in American culture.

Kevin Mattson

SEE ALSO: *Communism; The Great Depression; Lewis, Sinclair; Mencken, H. L.;* The Organization Man.

BIBLIOGRAPHY

Charles, Jeffrey. *Service Clubs in American Society: Rotary, Kiwanis, and Lions.* Urbana: University of Illinois Press, 1993.

Hines, Thomas. "Echoes from 'Zenith': Reactions of American Businessmen to *Babbitt.*" *Business History Review*, Summer 1967, 123–140.

Kelly, Dan. "Blood and Pancakes: Service Clubs at Century's End." *Baffler* 11 (1998), 35–45.

Putnam, Robert. "Bowling Alone: America's Declining Social Capital." *Journal of Democracy*, January 1995, 65–78.

Taylor, Stuart, Jr. "High Court Rules that Rotary Clubs Must Admit Women." *New York Times*, May 5, 1987.

Klein, Calvin *(1942–)*

More than any other designer, Bronx-born Calvin Klein invaded and conquered popular culture. Long an elite, "trickle-down" phenomenon, fashion was made wholly democratic by Klein, beginning with his success in jeans in the 1970s, continuing through massive advertising, and sustained in such forms as designer underwear. He promoted an austere, reductive, and modern sensibility, becoming the designer fashion students aspired to emulate and whose name appears on innumerable T-shirts and underwear waistbands. Since a memorable 1981 advertising campaign in which Brooke Shields purred seductively, "You wanna know what comes between me and my Calvins? Nothing," Klein's edgy ads have been at the forefront of contemporary visual culture, defining sexual limits, the spirit of youth, and social provocativeness. His ubiquitous name is synonymous with fashion as media and mass culture. In 2002 Calvin Klein Incorporated was sold to shirtmaker Phillips Van Heusen.

Richard Martin

SEE ALSO: *Advertising; Consumerism; Jeans; T-Shirts.*

BIBLIOGRAPHY

Gaines, Steven, and Sharon Churcher, *Obsession: The Lives and Times of Calvin Klein*, New York: Birch Lane Press, 1994.

Marsh, Lisa. *The House of Klein: Fashion, Controversy, and a Business Obsession.* New York: Wiley, 2003.

Klein, Robert *(1942–)*

One of the leading lights of stand-up comedy in the 1970s was New York–born monologist Robert Klein. Often compared to scatological, trailblazing comedian Lenny Bruce, Klein perfected a gentler, more observational form of humor in the same vein as comedian David Brenner and writer/director Woody Allen. After making his initial splash as a stage actor and releasing the 1973 comedy album *Child of the Fifties*, Klein became the darling of the comedy club circuit. He followed up with a series of one-man shows, which he parlayed into a successful second career as a character actor.

In the 1990s he focused almost exclusively on ensemble performance, appearing onstage to positive reviews opposite Jane Alexander in Wendy Wasserstein's *The Sisters Rosenzweig* (1992) and on film in *Primary Colors* (1998), which was directed by his old friend Mike Nichols. Since 1975 Klein has appeared in numerous live HBO specials, which he compiled and released in 2007. His many television and film roles include a much-lauded turn in the 2007 movie *Reign over Me*, starring Adam Sandler.

Robert E. Schnakenberg

SEE ALSO: *Allen, Woody; Bruce, Lenny; Cable TV; Nichols, Mike, and Elaine May; Stand-Up Comedy; Television.*

BIBLIOGRAPHY

Berger, Phil. "The Comedy Class of '73." *M*, August 1992.

"Robert Klein, Still Big Mensch on Campus." *Jewish Exponent*, June 4, 1998.

Kmart

Once the nation's largest retailer, Kmart was an early leader in the discount merchandising game. An offshoot of the venerable S. S. Kresge variety store chain, it came to epitomize the familiar, everyday shopping experience of the late twentieth century: a massive parking lot on the edge of town and a large, boxlike, single-story structure with a bewildering selection of reasonably priced goods. The spontaneous in-store advertising gimmick of a revolving beacon has made "blue light special" part of American society's shared language. Often the object of ridicule and disparaging comments (the *New York Times* described the store as "a caricature of strip mall culture"), it has nevertheless played host to the consumer purchasing power of some seventy million customers. Along with Wal-Mart and Target, Kmart changed the way Americans buy what they need.

The first Kmart opened in a suburb outside of Detroit (Garden City, Michigan) in 1962. It was a watershed year for retailing in United States, as it also witnessed the openings of the first Target and the first Wal-Mart. While many observers were captivated by the charismatic personality of the late Sam Walton and focused on the phenomenal growth of his Wal-Mart empire, Kmart was the first of the discount chains to aspire to a national presence and the first to successfully challenge the department store giants for retail supremacy. It was also the first retail firm to accurately cater to the new suburban lifestyle by offering the type and variety of consumer items that were increasingly in demand.

By 1970 the company had built more than 400 stores and was the undisputed discount store sales leader with more than a billion dollars in sales annually. During the next two decades, Kmart grew enormously, and by 1989 the firm had surpassed Sears to become the nation's leading retailer. The following year, however, Wal-Mart caught up and took over the lead position, which it retained throughout the 1990s. Many analysts felt that

Kmart Opening. *A line of people wait to enter a new Kmart store in 1962.* AMERICAN STOCK/ GETTY IMAGES.

it was simply a matter of age and beauty, because most Kmarts were both older and smaller than the more recently built Wal-Marts. Different location strategies may have played a role also, with Kmart avoiding the smaller towns where its fierce competitor seemed to thrive best. Looking for an edge, the Kmart Corporation took an ill-advised leap into diversification, acquiring several specialty outlets, such as Builders Square and Walden Books, which did not perform as expected.

Long regarded as simply a cheap and convenient place to buy necessities (a larger version of its ancestral five-and-dime), Kmart management strove to change the store's image during the late 1990s. Under the watchful eye of former Target executive Floyd Hall, Kmart embarked on an aggressive program of site renewals. Acting to rectify a public perception of poorly stocked, dark, dirty stores, Kmart executives launched a modernization campaign, remodeling and replacing aging facilities, building brighter, wider aisles and more sophisticated displays. They replicated the computerized warehousing and inventory techniques pioneered by their archrival, Wal-Mart. Adopting a strategy of "lifestyle merchandising," the company acquired celebrity sponsorship of particular collections of specialty clothing and housewares, contracting with Kathy Ireland, Jaclyn Smith, and Martha Stewart to push a more upscale product line. In a radical departure in terms of both market and store design, Kmart opened a four-level outlet in the heart of Manhattan. The company matched innovative online shopping with real-time returns to any of its 2,000 store locations across the country, poising itself to capture a larger market share of the discount retail world.

In 2002, however, Kmart declared bankruptcy. It suffered a radical restructuring, closing 300 stores and laying off more than 30,000 workers. The business merged with Sears Roebuck and Company in 2005, creating the new entity Sears Holding Corporation. A range of new marketing and branding ventures in subsequent years ended with another wave of store closures in 2011. Barring any further failures in managing the company, the familiar loudspeaker announcement "Attention, Kmart Shoppers!" may yet ring in the ears of American consumers for years to come.

Robert Kuhlken

SEE ALSO: *Advertising; Consumerism; The Internet; The* New York Times*; Online Shopping; Stewart, Martha; Wal-Mart.*

BIBLIOGRAPHY

Blackwell, Roger. *From Mind to Market: Reinventing the Retail Supply Chain.* New York: Harper-Collins, 1997.

Drew-Bear, Robert. *Mass Merchandising: Revolution & Evolution.* New York: Fairchild Publications, 1970.

Peterson, Robert A. *The Future of U.S. Retailing.* New York: Quorum Books, 1992.

Saporito, Bill. "Kmart: The High Cost of Second Best." *Fortune,* July 26, 1993.

Turner, Marcia Layton. *Kmart's Ten Deadly Sins: How Incompetence Tainted an American Icon.* Hoboken, NJ: John Wiley and Sons, 2003.

Knievel, Evel *(1938–2007)*

A familiar sight on television in the late 1960s and 1970s, motorcycle stuntman Evel Knievel thrilled and delighted audiences around the world. With reckless abandon, Knievel attempted monumental motorcycle stunts that almost always ended with broken bones and other serious injuries. His legendary exploits were the focus of several movies and television specials and, in many ways, served as a precursor to the extreme sports programming that is so popular in the 2010s, notably the X Games.

Robert Craig Knievel was born in Butte, Montana, on October 17, 1938. At age eight, he witnessed a stunt show featuring Joey Chitwood's Auto Daredevils, and a dream was born. It was also at this early age that Knievel began a series of entanglements with the law that would continue for many years. An outstanding athlete, he won the Northern Rocky Mountain Ski Association Class A state ski jumping championship in 1957 and played professional ice hockey in North Carolina before starting, managing, and playing for his own semiprofessional ice hockey team, the Butte Bombers.

In the early 1960s, Knievel worked for a while as a hunting guide with his own Sur-Kill Guide Service. However, after he discovered that elk were being senselessly slaughtered in Yellowstone National Park, he hitchhiked to Washington, D.C., to advocate for their survival, and his efforts helped stopped this killing. After a motorcycle accident, Knievel moved into insurance sales, and he sold a record 271 policies in just one week. Soon, though, he was back on the wrong side of the law—this time as a safecracker and con man. He finally left this life of crime and opened a Honda dealership in Washington.

Knievel's road to national stardom began in 1965 with the creation of Evel Knievel's Motorcycle Daredevils team. The team quickly became just Knievel, and he supervised every aspect of the stunt show. On New Year's in 1968, he made it to the big time, leaping over the fountains in front of Caesar's Palace in Las Vegas, Nevada, a distance of 141 feet. Though the jump was successful, the landing was not: Knievel spent thirty days in a coma.

He followed this with other record-breaking jumps and his ill-fated attempt to jump the Snake River Canyon in 1974 in Idaho on his "Skycycle." In 1975 Knievel brought his show overseas to Wembley Stadium in London, where he broke his pelvis in an attempt to leap thirteen double-decker buses in front of a crowd of 90,000. He took his antics one bus farther in his next leap at King's Island in Ohio in 1975, going over fourteen greyhound buses on ABC's *Wide World of Sports*. Knievel's last jump was a disaster; he was seriously injured attempting to leap a tank of live sharks at the Chicago Amphitheater in 1976.

During the 1970s Knievel was among the first personalities to license his image for the production of toys. These

Evel Knievel. *Evel Knievel makes a record jump over a row of nineteen cars in February 1971.* RALPH CRANE/CONTRIBUTOR/TIME & LIFE PICTURES/GETTY IMAGES.

motorcycles and action figures sold extremely well and made him millions of dollars. He also was a spokesperson for several products.

Though Knievel achieved great popularity in his lifetime, he was ultimately betrayed by his dark side. His womanizing, abuse of alcohol, and racist attitudes were largely hidden during his heyday in the 1970s. However, after a 1977 incident in which Knievel brutally attacked a critic with a baseball bat, his image suffered a final blow, and he lost his credibility. His role as a pitchman all but disappeared. Knievel died on November 30, 2007, at the age of sixty-nine after suffering for years from diabetes and pulmonary fibrosis.

Jay Parrent

SEE ALSO: *Extreme Sports; X Games.*

BIBLIOGRAPHY

Collins, Ace. *Evel Knievel: An American Hero.* New York: St. Martin's Press, 1999.

Montville, Leigh. *The High-Flying Life of Evel Knievel: American Showman, Daredevil, and Legend.* New York: Doubleday, 2011.

Scalzo, Joe. *Evel Knievel and Other Daredevils.* New York: Grosset and Dunlap, 1974.

Knight, Bobby *(1940–)*

Bobby Knight was a college basketball coach best known for leading the University of Indiana Hoosiers from 1971 to 2000. Fiery, aggressive, and dominating, he often engaged in behavior that overshadowed his team's remarkable championship play. With his incredible personality and passion for the game and his players, he is one of a rare breed in the world of sports who transcends his game and becomes an icon in other worlds. Nicknamed "The General," Knight often threw tirades at officials and the media. Despite his behavior, he was one of the most respected and revered basketball coaches in the United States. Many of his players received high honors for their performances, and six went on to serve on the U.S. men's Olympic basketball team. Knight was Big Ten Coach of the Year in 1973, 1975, 1976, 1980, and 1981 and National Coach of the Year in 1975, 1976, 1987, and 1989.

As a child in Orrville, Ohio, Knight played a number of sports. After graduating from high school, he attended Ohio State University, where he played basketball. Knight teamed with Jerry Lucas and John Havlicek to win the national championship in 1960 and make trips to the final game three times. Although not a star on the court, he was a competent player, and he learned everything Ohio State coach Fred Taylor had to offer. Knight graduated in 1962 and began his coaching career as an assistant coach at Cuyahoga Falls High School in Ohio.

In 1963 Tates Locke, the basketball coach at the U.S. Military Academy at West Point and a close friend of Knight's, offered Knight an assistant coaching position, which he accepted. When Locke resigned, Knight took over as head coach and developed the West Point players into a formidable team, winning 102 games and earning four trips to the National Invitational Tournament finals. One of his players, Mike Krzyzewski, later became the head coach at Duke University, and adopted much of Knight's coaching philosophy.

After six years at West Point, Knight accepted the position of head basketball coach at Indiana University. He achieved success quickly, leading the Hoosiers to the Final Four in 1973. He then went on to coach the team to the National Collegiate Athletic Association (NCAA) championship in 1976, 1981, and 1987. Knight was named Coach of the Year in 1975, 1976, and 1987.

In 1979 Knight coached the U.S. men's basketball team at the Eighth Pan American Games in Puerto Rico. The team won the gold medal. In 1984 he coached the U.S. men's team at the Summer Olympics in Los Angeles. It also won the gold medal. In 1991, with more than 700 career-coaching victories, Knight was inducted into the Naismith Memorial Basketball Hall of Fame in Springfield, Massachusetts.

In 1997 an Indiana University player complained that Knight grabbed him by the neck during a practice, and soon a video of the incident was leaked to the media. For the next three years more allegations of physical confrontations and intimidations emerged, forcing the university to launch an investigation. In mid-2000 the university fined Knight $30,000, suspended him for three games, required that he issue apologies, and established a zero-tolerance policy for inappropriate behavior. Just a few months later a student accused Knight of grabbing him by the arm and verbally berating him. When Knight refused to resign, the university fired him.

In 2001 Knight accepted the job as head basketball coach at Texas Tech University. He rebuilt the basketball program, and the Red Raiders quickly improved. In 2006 Knight was inducted into the National Collegiate Basketball Hall of Fame in Kansas City, Missouri, and in 2007 he became the winningest basketball coach in NCAA men's Division 1 history after winning his 880th game. In 2008 he retired with a total a record of 902 wins and 371 losses.

Jay Parrent

SEE ALSO: *Basketball;* Hoosiers*; National Basketball Association (NBA); National Collegiate Athletic Association (NCAA); Olympics.*

BIBLIOGRAPHY

Delsohn, Steve, and Mark Heisler. *Bob Knight: The Unauthorized Biography.* New York: Simon & Schuster, 2006.

Feinstein, John. *A Season on the Brink—A Year with Bob Knight and the Indiana Hoosiers.* New York: Macmillan, 1986.

Mellen, Joan. *Bobby Knight—His Own Man.* New York: Avon Books, 1989.

Knots Landing

The second-longest-running prime-time drama—after *Gunsmoke*—in television history, *Knots Landing*'s reign lasted from 1979 to 1993. The show's fourteen-season tenure is even more prestigious because it survived both the competition of glitzier prime-time soaps (such as *Dynasty*) and the advent of cable television.

Ironically, this spin-off of the phenomenally popular prime-time drama *Dallas* was created prior to its predecessor. Co-creators David Jacobs and Michael Filerman envisioned a television series modeled after film director Ingmar Bergman's 1973 Swedish miniseries (later edited into an Academy Award–nominated film) *Scenes from a Marriage*. The concept involved a study of neighboring married couples—in various states of contentment—living in a cul-de-sac in Southern California. Though CBS liked the pilot, they wanted something more glamorous and on a larger scale, resulting in Jacobs and Filerman pitching *Dallas*.

Once *Dallas* became a hit, the producers wove in the story of Gary Ewing (Ted Shackelford), the alcoholic and weak-willed younger brother of J. R. (Larry Hagman) and Bobby (Patrick Duffy). A ne'er-do-well, the teenage Gary had married Valene Clemmons (Joan Van Ark) and fathered their child, Lucy. Though circumstances had separated the couple for sixteen years, on a special *Dallas* episode premiering on December 13, 1979, Gary and Valene—who had found each other again—remarry and move to a California town named Knots Landing. The original idea was that if the couple could get on their feet in a place far away from Gary's powerful relatives, they could then send for Lucy and be reunited as a family. But as luck—and the vicissitudes of television drama—would have it, this reunion never took place.

Though *Knots Landing* received only mediocre ratings during its first short season (only thirteen episodes), the producers made three major changes in the second season, which caused ratings to escalate. First, they shifted the format of the show from self-contained episodes to serialization, introducing plotlines that could span the entire season. Second, they created plotlines that would allow for visits from *Dallas* characters to boost ratings. And third, and perhaps most important, they cast television and film actress Donna Mills—known primarily for, as she puts it, "victim roles"—as sultry vixen Abby Cunningham, who is obsessed with both money and power. Thus, upon meeting Gary and learning of his wealthy family, Abby sets her sights on him, and her destructive efforts become the central conflict in the series, as "true lovers" Gary and Valene break up and then struggle to reunite through a succession of lovers and spouses.

As seasons passed, *Knots Landing* continued to hold its own in its Thursday night time slot against stiff competition from the popular dramas *Hill Street Blues* and then *L.A. Law*. Despite the increasing influx of more melodramatic plotlines (such as Valene's twin infants being stolen and then sold by a nefarious baby doctor), the producers of *Knots Landing* contended that the secret of the show's longevity was the emphasis on middle-class characters and relationships, which to some extent mirrored the experiences of its audience. Scenes often depict characters involved in everyday situations, such as

Knots Landing. *Larry Hagman makes a toast with, clockwise from top, Donna Mills, Michele Lee, Ted Shackelford, and Joan Van Ark on the TV soap opera series* Knots Landing *in 1980.* CBS PHOTO ARCHIVE/CONTRIBUTOR/CBS/GETTY IMAGES.

preparing meals and taking out the trash. In addition, the show was often praised by critics for taking on serious subjects such as alcoholism, prescription drug abuse, teen drug abuse, mental illness, child abuse, divorce, and bereavement—issues with which its campier rivals refused to deal.

While former Broadway star Michelle Lee proved to be the show's anchor, appearing in every episode as Valene's neighbor and best friend Karen Fairgate McKenzie, throughout the course of its run *Knots Landing* also featured a series of appearances by veteran Hollywood stars. These celebrities included Ava Gardner, Howard Duff, Ruth Roman, and Julie Harris, who actually became a cast member for several seasons as Valene's mother, receiving an Emmy nomination for her work. But the show could also prove a star-making vehicle, as evidenced by the rise of Alec Baldwin, who later starred in major Hollywood films such as *The Hunt for Red October* (1990) and the popular TV series *30 Rock*. Originally introduced as mild-mannered Joshua Rush, Valene's half brother, Baldwin performs a virtuoso transformation over the ensuing season as the humble preacher's son becomes first a televangelist and then a raving megalomaniac, who marries and batters his wife, Cathy Geary (Lisa Hartman).

As the plotlines grew more outlandish (Karen suddenly becomes a talk show host and is stalked by a crazed fan), ratings slipped dramatically in the thirteenth season. In addition, annual contract renewals of the increasingly large cast rendered the show too costly to produce despite the producer's reducing the number of appearances by regular cast members and even writing out some of the show's long-running characters. As a result, the producers willingly canceled the show in 1993, Jacobs commenting, "I think we all felt rather than continue to amputate limbs, which is really what we were doing, that it was just time to stop."

In 1997 the majority of the cast members reunited for a four-hour miniseries, *Knots Landing: Back to the Cul-de-sac*, which suffered from contrivance and silliness, resulting in its low ratings. In its wake, creator Jacobs went on to create several short-lived series and scored another hit with *Lois & Clark* (1993–1997). Fans of *Knots Landing* have developed a number of websites in remembrance of the show.

Rick Moody

SEE ALSO: *Baldwin, Alec;* Dallas; Dynasty; *Gardner, Ava;* Hill Street Blues; L.A. Law; *Soap Operas; Television.*

BIBLIOGRAPHY

Snauffer, Douglas. *The Show Must Go On: How the Deaths of Lead Actors Have Affected Television Series.* Jefferson, NC: MacFarland, 2008.

Van Wormer, Laura. *Knots Landing: The Saga of Seaview Circle.* Garden City, NY: Doubleday, 1986.

Knowles, Beyoncé *(1981–)*

Singer and actress Beyoncé first rose to prominence as a teenager with Destiny's Child, one of the best-selling female groups of all time. She has since gone on to have an incredibly successful solo career, with a respectable movie career and her 2006 album *I Am . . . Sasha Fierce* winning her six Grammy Awards. She is married to music/media mogul Jay-Z, with whom she has a daughter. The two are regularly referred to as one of the most powerful couples in entertainment.

Beyoncé Giselle Knowles was born on September 4, 1981, to salesman and manager Mathew and stylist/designer Tina. She spent her early life in Houston, Texas. Reportedly a quiet child, she nonetheless began entering talent competitions during her youth, showing off a surprisingly robust voice and a penchant for showmanship. In 1990 the ten-year-old singer successfully auditioned for the female singing group Girl's Tyme, which featured a continually changing lineup of girl singers. When Girl's Tyme faltered, Knowles' father took over as manager for what would become Destiny's Child, including the teenaged Knowles, Kelendria "Kelly" Rowland, LaTavia Roberson, and LeToya Luckett.

After performing locally and rehearsing for several years, the band signed with Columbia Records and released two albums in succession. Their 1998 self-titled debut sold more than a million copies in the United States, and 1999's follow-up *The Writing's on the Wall* was an even bigger hit, launching the girls into the public eye. The album featured three hit singles—"Bills, Bills, Bills," "Jumpin' Jumpin'," and "Say My Name"—sold more than eight million copies, and garnered two Grammy Awards for "Say My Name." Around this time, however, Luckett and Robinson began accusing Mathew Knowles of favoring his daughter in an attempt to generate her solo career, and both left the band. Reforming as a trio, with Knowles, Rowland, and Michelle Williams, the band released two more albums—*Survivor* (2001)—which included the hit singles "Independent Women," "Survivor," and "Bootylicious"—and *Destiny Fulfilled* (2004).

In 2003, while Destiny's Child was on hiatus, Knowles released her first solo album, *Dangerously in Love*, which went platinum several times over. It entered the Billboard chart at number one and featured four best-selling singles—"Crazy in Love" (with Jay-Z), "Me, Myself, and I," "Baby Boy" (with Sean Paul), and "Naughty Girl." She received five Grammy Awards in 2003, including Best Contemporary R&B Album, Best R&B Song, and Best Female R&B Vocal Performance. Her star rising, she spent the summer touring with Missy Elliot and Alicia Keys, performing to sold-out crowds across the country.

Knowles determined that she wanted more freedom to produce her second album and, unbeknownst to Columbia Records or her father, who was still acting as her manager, she began to record and produce tracks on her own and with her own money. Drawing in influential artists such as the Neptunes; Swizz Beatz; and rapper, hip-hop producer, and media mogul Jay-Z, Knowles wrote, recorded, and produced *B'Day*. Released on September 5, 2006, the album shot up to number one, and the single "Déjà vu," a duet with Jay-Z, debuted at the top of the charts. Critics praised the singer's use of hip-hop driven beats, her edgier lyrics and rhymes, and her sexier persona.

Knowles' third album, *I Am . . . Sasha Fierce*, introduced fans to the singer's imaginary alter ego, Sasha Fierce. As she explained on her website, "Sasha Fierce is the fun, more sensual, more aggressive, more outspoken and more glamorous side that comes out when I'm working and when I'm on the stage." *I Am . . . Sasha Fierce* contains the hit "Single Ladies (Put a Ring on It)," a spunky dance/R&B number in which the singer tells an ex-boyfriend, "If you liked it then you should have put a ring on it." The video of "Single Ladies (Put a Ring on It)," featuring Knowles and two of her dancers performing a routine inspired by the 1969 Bob Fosse dance "Mexican Breakfast," was nearly as popular as the song itself. In January 2010 Knowles won six Grammy Awards, including three Grammies for "Single Ladies (Put a Ring on It)."

Knowles is known as an actor as well as a singer. While still in Destiny's Child, she took on the lead role in the MTV film *Carmen: A Hip Hopera*, a modernized version of George Bizet's opera *Carmen*. Her performance was well received, with critics remarking on her sensuality and ability to seduce the audience. She went on to star with Mike Myers in *Austin Powers in Goldmember*, and sang "Hey Goldmember," the film's theme song. She then worked with Cuba Gooding Jr. in *The Fighting Temptations* (2003), starred in *The Pink Panther* (2006), and was featured in *Dreamgirls* (2006). In the latter, a film version of the successful stage musical based on the story of Motown records and the Supremes, she headlined with Jennifer Hudson, Jamie Foxx, and Eddie Murphy, playing one of the members of a 1960s all-girl pop group called the Dreamettes.

Knowles is relatively circumspect about her personal life, despite the fact that she has essentially grown up in the public eye. She is uniformly pleasant to fans and polite and engaging with interviewers, and she is known to be easy and undemanding to work with. While she began dating rap mogul Jay-Z at some point after they first worked together in 2002, they have kept their romantic relationship extremely private, and it was a surprise to both fans and the media when the couple said in early 2008 that they had recently married in secret. In January 2012, several months after announcing Knowles's pregnancy at the 2011 MTV Video Music Awards, the couple welcomed their first child, Blue Ivy Carter.

Jenny Ludwig

SEE ALSO: *Girl Groups; Grammy Awards; Hip-Hop; Jay-Z; Motown; MTV; Murphy, Eddie; Pop Music; Rhythm and Blues; Ross, Diana, and the Supremes; Top 40.*

BIBLIOGRAPHY

Easlea, Daryl. *Crazy in Love: The Beyoncé Knowles Biography.* London: Omnibus Press, 2011.

Knowles, Beyoncé; Kelly Rowland; and Michelle Williams. *Soul Survivors: The Official Autobiography of Destiny's Child.* New York: Harper Entertainment, 2002.

Kodak

The Eastman Kodak Company (Kodak, for short) is the U.S. corporate photo giant whose film and imaging products are recognized worldwide. Headquartered in Rochester, New York, the company was incorporated in 1901 as the successor to the small dry-plate business founded in 1880 by George Eastman (1854–1932). From its modest beginnings in a rented loft space, the original Eastman Dry Plate Company (which became the Eastman Dry Plate and Film Company and then simply the Eastman Company) expanded rapidly, largely because of Eastman's inventive and marketing genius. By 1900 distribution outlets were established in France, Germany, Italy, and other European countries. By the end of the twentieth century, Kodak, one of industry's most readily identifiable trademarks, had operations in Canada, Mexico, Brazil, the United Kingdom, France, Germany, and Australia, and Kodak products were marketed by subsidiary companies to people in more than 150 countries. During the economic downturn of the early twenty-first century, however, the future of Kodak appeared bleak as stock shares plunged below a dollar and rumors of bankruptcy were rife.

An amateur photographer with little formal education, Eastman recognized the technological possibilities of the newly discovered dry-plate method of photography, which, by substituting a dry coat of gelatin emulsion containing silver salts for the wet collodion then in use, allowed plates to be prepared well in advance and developed long after exposure. For three years Eastman worked as a bank clerk and experimented at night in his mother's kitchen. By 1880, having developed both a successful formula for creating gelatin emulsions and a patent for a machine to mass produce the precoated dry plates for sale to other photographers, he began commercial distribution. Devoted unconditionally to the quality of his product, he once recalled and replaced a batch of defective plates already in the hands of dealers. "Making good on those plates took our last dollar," he said, "but what we had was more important—reputation."

KODAK INNOVATIONS

As manager of all phases of the new company's operations, Eastman—assisted by a full-time research scientist—continued pursuing ways to simplify the photographic process. One result was U.S. film (1884), a three-layered strippable negative that eliminated the burdensome glass plate and became the forerunner of all modern film. By 1888 the Kodak camera, the first camera uncomplicated, affordable, and portable enough to be used by large numbers of amateur photographers, was introduced with the slogan "You Push the Button, We Do the Rest"; after use, the camera was mailed back to Rochester for film processing and reloading.

The new camera also marked the initial appearance of *Kodak*, a name coined by Eastman himself. Noting the "strength" and "incisiveness" of his favorite letter K (the first letter of his mother's maiden name, Kilbourn), Eastman had played with it in various combinations. The resulting word, *Kodak*, trademarked in 1888 and today one of the company's most valued assets, was, according to Eastman, "short" and "[in]capable of mispronunciation," and it would not be "associated with anything . . . except the Kodak [camera]."

Other photographic innovations followed, including the first commercial transparent roll film, which made possible Thomas Edison's developments in motion pictures; the pocket (1895) and folding pocket (1898) Kodak cameras, which are considered the ancestors of all modern roll-film cameras; and the inexpensive but revolutionary Brownie camera (1900), which sold for $1 plus fifteen cents for film. Each time a new possibility for the photographic medium arose, Eastman seized the opportunity. For instance, he entered into an agreement to supply plates and paper for Wilhelm Roentgen's newly discovered X-ray process and produced the first film especially coated for motion pictures. (At the beginning of the twenty-first century, more than 90 percent of all motion pictures were shot on Kodak film.)

KODAK PRINCIPLES

Yet Eastman was more than a brilliant inventor; he was also a remarkably shrewd and progressive businessman who followed four modern principles: mass production, low product pricing, foreign and domestic distribution, and extensive advertising. So

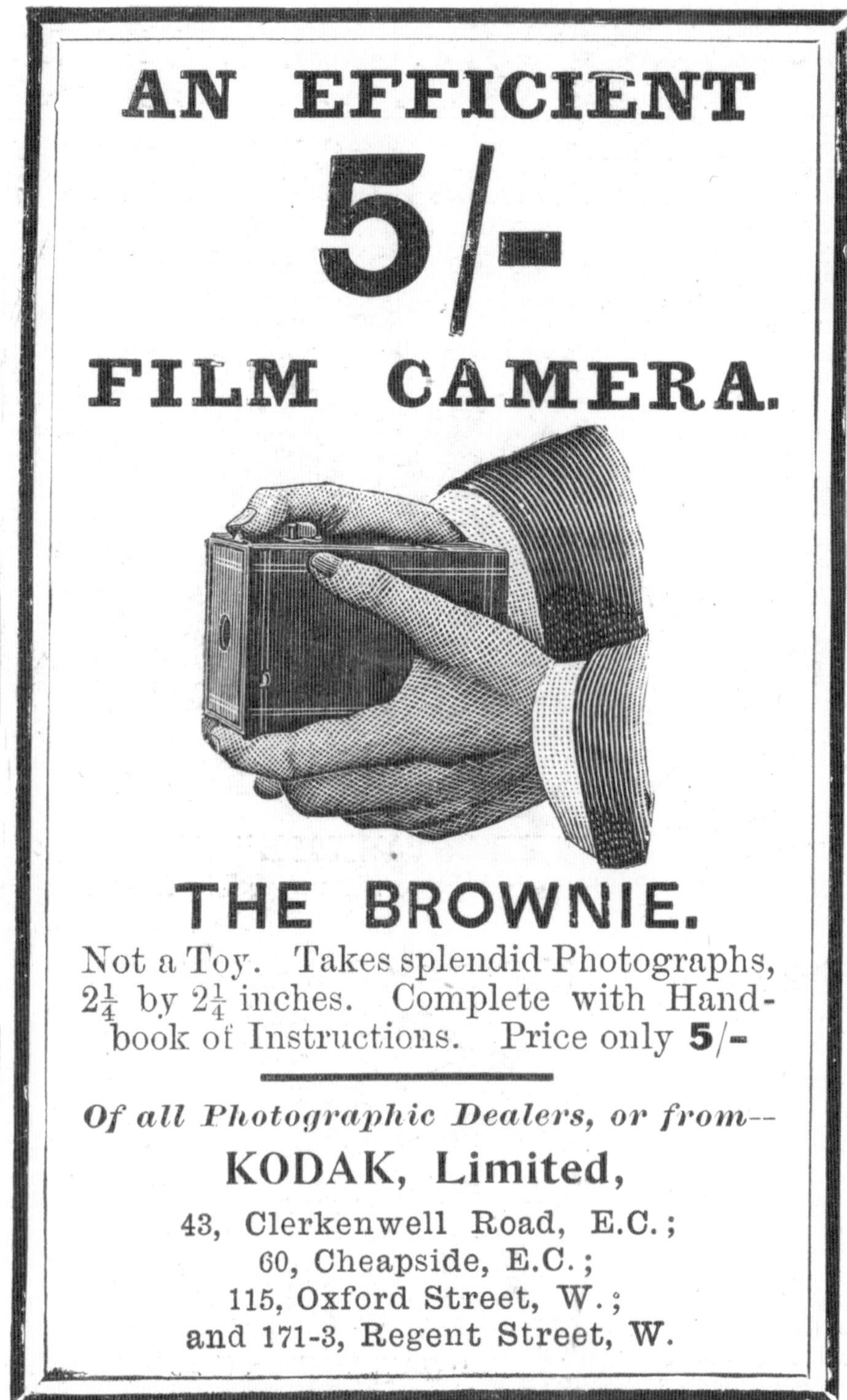

Kodak. *Kodak advertised the Brownie camera in the* Illustrated London News *in August 1900.* UNIVERSAL HISTORY ARCHIVE/GETTY IMAGES.

strong was Eastman's belief in the last principle that he promoted his company's products in the leading papers and periodicals of the day, often writing the ads himself. He inaugurated the use of the Kodak girl to pitch his cameras; instructed his advertising department to embark on ambitious campaigns, such as the installation of 6,000 road signs ("Picture Ahead! Kodak as You Go") on U.S. highways in the early 1920s; linked the marketing of the Brownie camera to Palmer Cox's familiar cartoon characters; and tied in products to particular audiences and events—for example, Boy Scout Brownie Cameras (1932), and Kodak Coquette Cameras, with matching lipstick holders and compacts (1930).

Believing that employees deserved more than just a good wage, Eastman implemented benefit, accident, and pension funds, as well as company reward programs, such as the wage dividend program, in which workers benefitted above their wages in proportion to the yearly dividend on the company stock. Eastman's social philosophy also extended to his personal life: a noted philanthropist who often posed as Mr. Smith, he contributed generously to educational and cultural institutions and to other charities, especially those that supported improving children's welfare. On one day alone in 1924, he gave $30 million to the Massachusetts Institute of Technology, from which he recruited some of his best scientists and engineers; the University of Rochester; the Hampton Institute; and the Tuskegee Institute. In 1932, moments after bequeathing the bulk of his estate to the University of Rochester, an ailing Eastman took his own life. His suicide note was simple and direct: "My work is done. Why wait?"

With the introduction of products such as Kodachrome color film (1935), cartridge-loaded Instamatic still and movie cameras (1960s), the disc camera series (first marketed in 1982), and digital and single-use cameras, as well as with various advances in optics (established as a Kodak department as early as 1912) and imaging technologies, the company that Eastman founded remained on the cutting edge of professional and amateur photography.

Kodak continued to involve itself in innovation in the twenty-first century, focusing chiefly on the field of imagery over a wide spectrum. In 2000 the Health Imaging Division introduced forty-five new products. The following year Kodak partnered with Maytag to offer film and throwaway cameras in vending machines. Other innovations have included the popular EasyShare camera that allows users to take high-quality photographs and upload them to home computers in a matter of seconds and ink-jet printing and photographic papers that make it easy to print high-quality, low-cost photographs at home.

TRANSITION PERIOD

Despite innovative progress, the early twenty-first century proved to be a difficult time for Kodak. Some analysts have traced the beginning of the end of Kodak to 1975 when the company invented digital cameras that provided the technology for twenty-first century smartphones, which have the ability to take photographs. Despite estimated profits of $2.5 billion in 2011, the company continued to report overall losses, and Eastman's home base was hard hit by the company's economic woes. In the 1980s Kodak had employed some 62,000 people; by 2012 there were less than 7,000 employees in the Rochester facility. Company officials instituted a rapid reorganization, announcing that Kodak would henceforth focus on cutting costs and promoting digital imaging, but in January 2012 the company filed for bankruptcy. Whatever the outcome of Kodak, the legacy of Eastman remained strong in his hometown, which boasted the Eastman School of Music of the University of Rochester and the George Eastman House, a museum devoted to the history of photography.

Barbara Tepa Lupack

SEE ALSO: *Brownie Cameras; Smartphones; Suicide.*

BIBLIOGRAPHY

Ackerman, Carl W. *George Eastman.* Boston: Houghton Mifflin, 1930.

Applebome, Peter. "Despite Long Slide by Kodak, Company Town Avoids Decay." *New York Times,* January 16, 2012.

Brayer, Elizabeth. *George Eastman: A Biography.* Baltimore, MD: Johns Hopkins University Press, 1996.

Collins, Douglas. *The Story of Kodak.* New York: Abrams, 1990.

"Kodak." Accessed on March 2012. Available from http://www.kodak.com/ek/US/en/Home.htm

"The Last Kodak Moment?" *Economist,* January 14, 2012.

West, Nancy Martha. *Kodak and the Lens of Nostalgia.* Charlottesville: University of Virginia, 2000.

Kojak

The popular TV series *Kojak* took its name from the character of Lieutenant Theo Kojak, the iconoclastic commander of a detective squad at the Manhattan South precinct in New York City and one of the more memorable characters to appear on 1970s television. With his habitual consumption of lollipops and his trademark line, "Who loves ya, baby?" Lieutenant Kojak earned a loyal TV following that ultimately led to cult status as one of the small screen's most endearing law enforcers.

At first Telly Savalas, the actor who brought Lieutenant Kojak to life, might have seemed an unlikely candidate for a television hero. The fortyish Greek American actor, with his shaved head, substantial nose, and unconventional looks, had generally played villains throughout his career. Among his many portraits of evil men were Pontius Pilate (*The Greatest Story Ever Told*), James Bond's nemesis Ernest Stavro Blofeld (*On Her Majesty's Secret Service*), and redneck psychopath Archer Maggot (*The Dirty Dozen*). But Savalas turned out to be an inspired choice for the role of the tough-but-tender detective.

Kojak's first appearance was in the made-for-TV movie *The Marcus-Nelson Murders,* broadcast in the spring of 1973. Widely regarded as one of the best television movies ever made, the two-hour special won two Emmy Awards (for writing and directing) and generated network interest in producing a series based on it. The series, titled *Kojak,* premiered in the fall of 1973 and ran for five seasons, airing a total of 118 hour-long episodes.

Although the opening title sequence included footage of Kojak firing a pistol, the character rarely engaged in violent action during the weekly episodes. Kojak usually solved crimes by interpreting evidence, persuading reluctant witnesses, playing department politics when necessary, and directing his squad of detectives in conducting an investigation. As an urban crime drama, *Kojak* did not lack for incidents of violence—but these were typically played out either by criminals or by Kojak's detectives while engaged in apprehending the criminals. As such, the principal enforcer on Kojak's squad was detective Bobby Crocker (played by Kevin Dobson). Other regular cast members included Kojak's boss, Captain McNeil (Dan Frazier), Detective Saperstein (Mark Russell), and Detective Stavros (played by Savalas's brother George but billed in the cast credits as "Demosthenes").

Although the show was canceled in 1978, the character of Kojak has been revived several times. He was the protagonist in two made-for-TV movies: *The Belarus File* (1985) and *The Price of Justice* (1987). Then, in 1989, Savalas agreed to portray Kojak in a series of two-hour shows to be part of a "wheel" program, *The ABC Saturday Mystery*. As such, the adventures of Kojak alternated with three other detective shows, including the popular *Columbo*, starring Peter Falk. The new show, which lasted only one season, promoted Kojak to inspector and surrounded him with a new supporting cast—including Andre Braugher, who would later go on to acclaim and an Emmy Award for his work on another cop show, *Homicide: Life on the Streets*. *Kojak* was revived again in 2005, starring Ving Rhames in the lead role (Savalas had died in 1994) and Chazz Palminteri as Captain Frank McNeil. It aired only ten episodes.

Justin Gustainis

SEE ALSO: Columbo; The Dirty Dozen; *Emmy Awards; James Bond Films; Made-for-Television Movies.*

BIBLIOGRAPHY

Myers, Richard. *TV Detectives.* San Diego, CA: A. S. Barnes, 1981.

Kellerman, Jonathan. *True Detectives: A Novel.* New York: Ballantine Books, 2009.

Koontz, Dean R. *(1945–)*

Few writers have labored as long and as hard as Dean R. Koontz has to achieve his reputation as a writer of high-quality commercial suspense fiction. Not only has Koontz produced quality works in a variety of genres, but he has also become a leading advocate for quality writing and creativity, producing two guides for would-be writers of fiction. Clearly one of the more significant trendsetters of the twentieth century when it comes to maintaining integrity in the highly commercialized fiction market, Koontz well deserves his reputation.

Dean Koontz. *Dean Koontz speaks to booksellers and fans at a literary event in 2004.* J. MERRITT/CONTRIBUTOR/FILMMAGIC/GETTY IMAGES.

EARLY LIFE

Born an only child in Everett, Pennsylvania, in 1945, Dean Ray Koontz married his high school sweetheart, Gerda Cerra, in 1966. That same year he published his first story, "Kittens," in the *Atlantic Monthly*, an auspicious beginning for a young writer. After taking a job as a teacher-counselor in the Appalachian Poverty Program, he published his first stories as a professional writer, "Soft Come the Dragons" and "Behold the Sun," both of which appeared in the *Magazine of Fantasy & Science Fiction*. A year later Koontz worked as a high school English teacher in Harrisburg, Pennsylvania, writing after the school day was done. By 1969 he had sold twenty short stories and three short novels, all works of science fiction. That year he left his job as a teacher to write full time. In quick succession, more science fiction stories and novels came into print, with his novella *Beastchild* receiving a 1971 Hugo nomination.

In 1972 Koontz's prolific output and the public's perception of him primarily as a writer of science fiction forced him to adopt the first of several pseudonyms. His goal, as he made clear in various interviews, was to break out of the shell imposed by the science fiction category. Under the watchful eye of Random House editor Lee Wright, Koontz adopted the nom de plume of K. R. Dwyer and wrote his first thriller, *Chase*. Throughout the 1970s and 1980s, alongside fiction that continued to appear under his own name, Koontz wrote thrillers, mysteries, romance novels, horror tales, and even science fiction as Brian Coffey, Anthony North, Richard Paige, Aaron Wolfe, John Hill, David Axton, Leigh Nichols, and Owen West.

WRITING CAREER

Koontz achieved his first successes as a writer with contracts he had landed at major publishers such as Random House, Atheneum, and Bobbs-Merrill. His novels *Demon Seed* (Bantam, 1973) and *Shattered* (Random House, 1973) proved especially auspicious, receiving film treatments in 1977 by MGM (Metro-Goldwyn-Mayer) and Warner Brothers. Film versions of *Watchers* (1987) and other thrillers from the 1980s, however, eventually convinced Koontz to give up on selling movie rights to his work unless he could retain authorial control of the screenplay. His dissatisfaction with film treatments of his work and strong sense of ownership toward it explain in large part why far fewer Koontz novels have been filmed than have those of his counterpart, Stephen King. Koontz has extended this proprietary sensibility to the published editions of his early work, having retrieved the copyright for all of his early and out-of-print science fiction. The avowed intent was either to keep certain works out of print as long as copyright law permitted or republish them in rewritten form. The latter was the case with his 1975 novel *Invasion*, written as Aaron Wolfe; it reappeared completely reworked in 1994 as *Winter Moon* by Dean R. Koontz.

Koontz's critical reception has always been positive. Reviewers recognize that his fiction is no more and no less than high-standard commercial fiction, and, as a consequence, they have scored him well in that regard. Few of his novels have achieved the level of artfulness of contemporaries such as Stephen King and Clive Barker or lesser-known fiction writers such as Ramsey Campbell and T. E. D. Klein. Koontz does not ordinarily like to experiment, with the exception of such rarities as *The Voice of the Night* (1980) and *The Vision* (1977). Certain patterns clearly emerge in most of his mature, later fiction: there is always a love interest; major and important minor characters generally come from dysfunctional families and broken homes (based in part on Koontz's own experiences); an oddball sense of humor infiltrates the occasional banter between characters; and his politics, when revealed at all, incline toward a libertarian, anti-gun control stance, with a strong dose of pro–civil rights liberalism thrown in.

Finally, despite Koontz's abdication of the genre, science-fiction-based premises run throughout the later major fiction: *Watchers, Shadowfires* (1987), and *Midnight* (1989) focus on the threat of genetic engineering; *Night Chills* (1976) offers a disturbing portrait of mind control; the story of *Lightning* (1988) is driven by time travel; and *The Vision, The Bad Place* (1990), *Cold Fire* (1991), and *Dragon Tears* (1993) depend upon the psychokinetic abilities of their protagonists and antagonists.

In 2004 Koontz received a golden retriever, Trixie, as a thank-you for his charitable donations to Canine Companions for Independence, which provides service dogs to the disabled. He proceeded to write two books, *Life Is Good: Lessons in Joyful Living* (2004) and *Christmas Is Good* (2005), under the name Trixie Koontz; both books expound on the canine vision of life's joys. Though Trixie died in 2007, Koontz continued to write posts in her voice on his website, under the name TOTOS (Trixie on the Other Side).

WRITING PHILOSOPHY

Koontz's success can largely be summed up by the attention he has consciously paid to his craft. Unlike many of his commercial peers, Koontz recognized right away that to use a formula for writing commercial fiction means caring deeply about that formula. For evidence of this heartfelt belief, one only needs to look at his nonfiction work. In 1972, owing to his early success, Koontz was tapped by the publishers of *Writer's Digest* to author *Writing Popular Fiction*, a how-to guide for beginning writers. Nine years later, he revisited the topic in *How to Write Best-Selling Fiction*, also published by *Writer's Digest*. In the first guide, the still-novice writer emphasized the profitability of category fiction, offering basic advice about the various genres in which he had written. In the latter guide, his earlier suggestions were turned on their head as the now-seasoned writer admonished would-be writers to avoid all forms of category fiction, instead providing pointers for the creation of high-quality, cross-genre suspense fiction. This 180-degree shift, according to Koontz, reflected his decision in 1973 (a year after publishing *Writing Popular Fiction*) to leave the narrow field of science fiction.

Because he cared about his craft in a way that few commercial writers do, Koontz rose to the top of best-seller lists; he demonstrated how much he cared by keeping his lesser works out of print and protecting his major works from the corrupting influence of television and film producers. Popular fiction is meant to give readers pleasure, and Koontz has not failed in this mission. In *The Dean Koontz Companion* (1994), horror-fiction writer Charles de Lint sums up Koontz's contributions to fiction: "Dedication to his craft, an optimistic belief in the inherent goodness of humankind, a loving partner, and business acumen . . . these have all combined in Koontz to give us an author capable of bringing a reader to tears and laughter, sometimes on the same page, in a manner that no other author has been able to duplicate."

Bennett Lovett-Graff

SEE ALSO: *Barker, Clive; Best Sellers; Horror Movies; King, Stephen; Science Fiction Publishing.*

BIBLIOGRAPHY

Greenberg, Martin H.; Ed Gorman; and Bill Munster, eds. *The Dean Koontz Companion*. New York: Berkley Books, 1994.

Koontz, Dean Ray. *Writing Popular Fiction*. Cincinnati, OH: Writer's Digest Books, 1972.

Koontz, Dean Ray. *How to Write Best-Selling Fiction*. Cincinnati, OH: Writer's Digest Books, 1981.

Munster, Bill, ed. *Sudden Fear: The Horror and Dark Suspense Fiction of Dean Ray Koontz*. San Bernardino, CA: Borgo Press, 1988.

Sharp, Michael D. *Popular Contemporary Writers*. New York: Marshall Cavendish Reference, 2006.

Koresh, David, and the Branch Davidians

The 1993 standoff between federal agents and the people inside the Branch Davidian compound at Waco, Texas, resulted in the deaths of approximately eighty Branch Davidians, including leader David Koresh. The tragedy upset Americans to varying degrees. There was widespread dismay over the deaths of at least twenty children. Blame abounded as federal decision making came under question, and Koresh was denounced for putting children in harm's way. Meanwhile, some used the tragedy at Waco to stoke their antigovernment fervor.

The Waco compound, named Mount Carmel, was referred to in news accounts as "Ranch Apocalypse." Prior to the standoff, an investigation of the Davidians produced evidence of a large illegal weapons stockpile on the property. In addition, reports surfaced that Koresh was molesting children at Mount Carmel, to which a fourteen-year-old girl later testified at a Congressional hearing. Of greater concern was the possibility that Koresh, a self-proclaimed apocalyptic visionary, planned to lead his followers into mass suicide.

On February 28, 1993, an initial raid produced a gun battle that killed five Branch Davidians and four Bureau of Alcohol, Tobacco, and Firearms (ATF) agents. It was the worst loss of life for federal law-enforcement agents in the twentieth century. The standoff that ensued lasted fifty-one days. An estimated 720 lawmen converged on Waco, including 250 Federal Bureau of Investigation (FBI) agents and 150 ATF agents. Many suffered the strain of the lengthy standoff. Waco had a 90 percent occupancy rate, making living quarters scarce; agents were scheduled to shifts that lasted weeks at a time. Koresh's tendency to ramble during negotiations further exacerbated the strain on agents.

One of the negotiating tactics that the FBI employed was to broadcast Koresh's apocalyptic visions on the radio in exchange for the release of Davidian members and Koresh's eventual surrender: "My father, my god who sits on the throne in heaven, has given me a book of seven seals . . . If America could learn these seals they would respect me. I'm the anointed one . . . It's the fulfillment of prophecy." Following the broadcast, however, Koresh turned recalcitrant, unwilling to exchange his "messianic" status in the compound for prison life. He expressed fears of being raped by other inmates, conscious of the fate that child molesters faced in prison.

FBI plans for a tear-gas assault in order to end the standoff circulated in March and were presented to U.S. Attorney General Janet Reno. The plan was to "ease" the residents out of the compound by injecting tear gas, or CS gas, into the compound. Reno withheld approval until assurances were made that the gas would not harm the children, knowing that the gas masks on the compound would not fit their faces. According to Dick Reavis in his 1995 book *The Ashes of Waco*, a civilian expert from the Army Research Laboratory in Maryland told Reno that "although there had been no laboratory tests performed on children relative to the effects of the gas, anecdotal evidence was convincing that there would be no permanent injury." Reno approved the plan on April 17.

The FBI tank and tear-gas assault took place on the morning of April 19. At 6:02 a.m. combat engineering vehicles punched holes in the compound walls to pump the CS gas into the building. The wall openings allowed much of the gas to escape, however, and made the FBI's assumption that the gas would prompt an evacuation invalid. Around 11:40 a.m. the building began to burn, fanned by 30-mile-per-hour prairie winds. Survivors from the compound said that the tanks crushed a pressurized container filled with liquid propane, starting the fire. The FBI maintained that they saw flames erupt in several places, indicating the fire was set deliberately by members of the compound.

In the aftermath of the assault, news reports placed the death toll between seventy-five and ninety-five people, including more than twenty children; all were Branch Davidians. Most died from smoke inhalation, but two dozen were killed by gunshot, either by suicide or by another member in the compound.

Survivor Marjorie Thomas, who suffered third-degree burns on more than 50 percent of her body, described the assault from an inside perspective in Reavis's book: "The whole entire build-

The Burning of the Branch Davidian Compound. *Fire consumes the Branch Davidian compound after a teargas assault by federal agents on April 19, 1993.* TIME LIFE PICTURES/CONTRIBUTOR/TIME & LIFE PICTURES/GETTY IMAGES.

ing felt warm all at once, and then after the warmth, then a thick, black smoke, and the place became dark. I could hear—I couldn't see anything. I could hear people moving and screaming, and I still was sitting down while this was happening."

The incident at Waco became a self-fulfilling prophecy for the Branch Davidians. The more Koresh sized up the standoff for its apocalyptic message, the more the FBI viewed Koresh as engaging in stalling tactics. When the FBI responded with pressure to get Koresh to comply, it only confirmed for Koresh that the end was near, and the cycle repeated itself. Congress, which questioned the wisdom of the plan, would conclude that the FBI had not acted illegally.

As a result of Waco, antigovernment factions regarded the ATF as jackbooted thugs, and a loose network of paramilitary groups sprouted throughout the country, calling themselves citizen militias. Largely composed of white men, the militias conducted training exercises in isolated areas, acting out their own apocalyptic visions of an impending civil war. One militia member told *Time* in 1994: "The Waco thing really woke me up. They went in there and killed women and children." The militia's antigovernment paranoia encouraged wild beliefs, such as foreign soldiers hiding under Detroit in salt mines and highway signs containing secret markings to guide foreign troops. Not all reactions spawned by the incident, however, could be dismissed as easily as the rumors: Timothy McVeigh bombed the Alfred P. Murrah Federal Building in Oklahoma City in 1995 in retaliation for what he considered the government's illegal actions at Waco.

Daryl Umberger

SEE ALSO: *Cults; FBI (Federal Bureau of Investigation).*

BIBLIOGRAPHY

Allen, John L., Jr. "Warning from Waco: The Cultural Bias Can Be Hazardous to Health." *National Catholic Reporter*, October 24, 1997, 19.

Church, Emily. "Waco Probe Focuses on Wisdom, Not Legality of FBI Action." *Congressional Quarterly Weekly*, July 29, 1995, 30–31.

Farley, Christopher John. "Patriot Games." *Time*, December 19, 1994, 48–49.

Gibbs, Nancy. "'Oh, My God, They're Killing Themselves!'" *Time*, May 3, 1993, 26–41.

Rainie, Harrison. "The Final Days of David Koresh: Armageddon in Waco." *U.S. News & World Report*. April 25, 1993, 24–31.

Reavis, Dick J. *The Ashes of Waco*. New York: Simon and Schuster, 1995.

Thibodeau, David, and Leon Whiteson. *A Place Called Waco: A Survivor's Story*. New York: PublicAffairs, 1999.

Thurman, James N. "Criticism Leads ATF to Soften 'Thug' Image." *Christian Science Monitor*, April 17, 1998, 5.

Wagner, Betsy. "Waco: Once Again, the Unexpected." *U.S. News & World Report*, July 31, 1995, 8.

Korman, Harvey *(1927–2008)*

Comic actor Harvey Korman is best known for his work as comedian Carol Burnett's sidekick on *The Carol Burnett Show* from 1967 to 1977. His talent for physical humor and oddball accents made him a master sketch comic. His skills were so versatile that he could entertain as a robust Yiddish mama in one skit and become a comical Rhett Butler in the next. During the series' run he garnered four Emmy Awards and became known as one of television's outstanding supporting players.

He delighted small-screen audiences during the 1983–1984 television season by playing dual roles in *Mama's Family*, a situation comedy about a dysfunctional but funny small-town southern family. He introduced each episode as debonair Alistair Quince and occasionally appeared as Ed Higgins, the husband of loudmouth Eunice (played by Burnett). He also appeared in more than thirty films, including several *Pink Panther* features and farces by writer/director Mel Brooks. Korman was known for his ability to perform in skits without stealing scenes from stars—a gift that kept him working with top comic actors until his death in 2008 at the age of eighty-one.

Audrey E. Kupferberg

SEE ALSO: *Brooks, Mel; Burnett, Carol; Emmy Awards; Lawrence, Vicki; Sitcom; Television.*

BIBLIOGRAPHY

"Harvey Korman of 'Burnett Show' Dies at 81." *New York Times*, May 30, 2008.

Kosinski, Jerzy *(1933–1991)*

Jerzy Kosinski—a Poland-born American who was the author of two sociological studies and nine novels, a survivor of the Holocaust, the husband of a U.S. Steel heiress, an avid sportsman, a college lecturer, and a sex-club connoisseur—lived a life as fantastic as his fiction. After winning critical acclaim for *The Painted Bird* (1965) and *Steps* (1968), Kosinski turned increasingly to popular American culture and to his own life for literary inspiration. The wickedly satirical *Being There* (1971) became a hit film that was also scripted by Kosinski and starred Peter Sellers. Later novels such as *Cockpit* (1975), *Blind Date* (1977), and *Pinball* (1982) did not ring true with critics, though some did make best-seller lists. Controversy surrounding the authorship of his books plagued Kosinski in his last years, and it became the topic of his final, "auto-fictional" novel, *The Hermit of 69th Street* (1988). Nevertheless, Kosinski (who committed suicide in 1991) continues to be regarded as a major force in contemporary American fiction.

Barbara Tepa Lupack

SEE ALSO: *Sellers, Peter.*

BIBLIOGRAPHY

Karolides, Nicholas J. *Censored Books II: Critical Viewpoints, 1985–2000*. Lanham, MD: Scarecrow Press, 2002.

Klinkowitz, Jerome. *Literary Disruptions: The Making of a Post-contemporary American Fiction*. Urbana: University of Illinois Press, 1975.

Lavers, Norman. *Jerzy Kosinski*. Boston: Twayne, 1982.

Lilly, Paul R., Jr. *Words in Search of Victims: The Achievement of*

Jerzy Kosinski. Kent, OH: Kent State University Press, 1988.

Lupack, Barbara Tepa. *Plays of Passion, Games of Chance: Jerzy Kosinski and His Fiction*. Bristol, UK: Wyndham Hall/Rhodes-Fulbright International Library, 1988.

Sloan, James Park. *Jerzy Kosinski: A Biography*. New York: Dutton, 1996.

Kotzwinkle, William *(1938–)*

William Kotzwinkle has published dozens of books of fiction since the 1970s, making his mark in virtually every genre, including mystery, science fiction, social satire, erotica, historical fiction, film novelization, and talking-animal fantasies for children and adults alike. Born in Scranton, Pennsylvania, in 1938, Kotzwinkle told an interviewer in the early 1990s that his original ambition was to be an actor but that he kept coming up with lines in his improvisation class that were much better than his acting, so he became a writer instead. Along the way, he also worked as a sign painter, a shipping clerk in a theatrical supply house, and a department store Santa Claus.

AN EVENTUAL WRITER

As a writer, Kotzwinkle was a late bloomer. He was thirty-three years old when his first book was published in 1971, a collection of short stories titled *Elephant Bangs Train*. From then on, however, he made up for lost time with a steady output, averaging a book a year from the island home off the coast of Maine that he shared with his wife, novelist Elizabeth Gundy.

By the 1990s Kotzwinkle had managed to attract loyal followings in multiple genres. With his long-term collaborator and fellow Penn State graduate, illustrator Joe Servello, Kotzwinkle published *Herr Nightingale and the Satin Woman* in 1978, which earned him a permanent place in the detective-fiction realm. Grief-support networks in France were continuing to recommend his *Swimmer in the Secret Sea*, a novel about the loss of an unborn child, decades after its publication in 1975. *Doctor Rat* (1976), a grim tale of laboratory vivisection as told by its subjects, earned him a World Fantasy Award in 1977.

His science fiction credentials, combined with a willingness to try anything, led Kotzwinkle to novelize several hit films, including *E.T.: The Extra-Terrestrial (1982)*—one of whose spin-offs, *E.T. The Extra Terrestrial Storybook* (1982), won him the 1984 Buckeye Children's Book Award—and *Superman III* (1983). In turn, several of Kotzwinkle's books have been optioned for movie production, including *Jack in the Box* (1980), released as a film in 1990, and *The Bear Went over the Mountain*, whose cinema rights were acquired by the Jim Henson organization shortly after its publication to rave reviews in 1996.

A SATIRICAL POSTMODERNIST

Kotzwinkle's most enduring gift is his satire, and its sharpest tool is a merciless juxtaposition of the sublime and the ridiculous: Chaucerian undercutting in paragraphs that build up a character's world view with a straight face—even a painterly lyricism at the beginning of a paragraph—only to deflate it with a sharp jab in the last sentence. *The Fan Man* (1974) displays a keen ear for dialect (its protagonist, a spaced-out, somewhat-deranged New Yorker named Horse Badorties, speaks appallingly flawless Lower East Side hippy English). *The Midnight Examiner* (1989) hilariously spoofs daily life on a supermarket-tabloid weekly, while *The Bear Went over the Mountain* (reminiscent of both the children's classic *The Bear That Wasn't* and the film *Being There*) is a devastating send-up of the book-publishing world at the end of the twentieth century.

Kotzwinkle has been described as one of the first American postmodern novelists, both because of his eclecticism (a fact reflected in his wide range of publishers) and because of his plots, which are arguably nonpermanent art and, in keeping with the postmodern aesthetic, are less memorable in their sequence of details than in the individual scenes themselves. His scenes have a way of etching themselves indelibly into a reader's memory: the embarrassment of the loose-bowelled suitor at the door of his hot date in *Nightbook* (1974), the primly sublimated sexual desire flickering at tea between the country vicar and his hostess in *Hermes 3000* (1972).

CONTINUED EXPERIMENTATION

In 2001 Kotzwinkle and coauthor Glenn Murray published *Walter the Farting Dog*, the first in what has become a best-selling series of picture books. Illustrated by Audrey Colman, *Walter the Farting Dog* has been published in a dozen languages and spawned an edition of Walter plush toys. Kotzwinkle's wife became the coauthor starting with the third book in the series, *Rough Weather Ahead for Walter the Farting Dog* (2005).

All the while, Kotzwinkle has continued to experiment in the world of adult science fiction. In 2005 he published *The Amphora Project*, his first adult novel since 1996's *The Bear Went over the Mountain*. Featuring mutants, robots, and mercenaries, *The Amphora Project* is a space opera about a consortium of scientists seeking to create immortality and a space pirate who discovers the true evils at the heart of their experiment.

The ease with which Kotzwinkle's books read and the jack-of-all-trades appearance of his booklist belie a concentrated research style. In order to understand Arthur, the rightful author of the book appropriated by Hal Jam, the title character of *The Bear Went over the Mountain*, Kotzwinkle spent several months sleeping in a tent and meditating five hours a day. For the sake of authenticity in *Trouble in Bugland* (1983), a children's mystery tale whose detective is a praying mantis, the author claimed to have spent an entire summer on his knees watching crickets. It is this attention to detail that has assured him a place in American literary history. Even if he falls short of ranking as one of the great modern writers, his books will be read and reread for many years to come for sheer pleasure.

Nick Humez

SEE ALSO: *Best Sellers; Detective Fiction;* E.T. The Extra-Terrestrial*; Postmodernism; Science Fiction Publishing; Superman.*

BIBLIOGRAPHY

Barry, William. "'Bear' Takes Maine Writer over the Top," *Maine Sunday Telegram*, December 15, 1996.

Kotzwinkle, William. *Elephant Bangs Train*. New York: Pantheon Books, 1971.

Kotzwinkle, William. *Hermes 3000*. New York: Pantheon Books, 1972.

Kotzwinkle, William. *The Fan Man*. New York: Harmony Books, 1974.

Kotzwinkle, William. *Nightbook.* New York: Avon, 1974.

Kotzwinkle, William. *Doctor Rat.* Henley-on-Thames, UK: Aidan Ellis, 1976

Kotzwinkle, William. *Herr Nightingale and the Satin Woman.* New York: Knopf, 1978.

Kotzwinkle, William. *E. T.: The Extra-Terrestrial.* New York: Putnam, 1982.

Kotzwinkle, William. *Trouble in Bugland.* Boston: Godine, 1986.

Kotzwinkle, William. *The Hot Jazz Trio.* Boston: Houghton Mifflin, 1989.

Kotzwinkle, William. *The Midnight Examiner.* Boston: Houghton Mifflin, 1989.

Kotzwinkle, William. *The Bear Went over the Mountain.* New York: Doubleday, 1996.

Koufax, Sandy *(1935–)*

As a result of his dominance of the National League from 1962 through 1966, Sandy Koufax is regarded by many baseball historians as the greatest pitcher of all time. He certainly was the most overpowering left-hander ever, striking out record numbers of batters during his run. Koufax added considerably to his mystique by retiring young, at age thirty-one, following the 1966 season, and all but disappearing from public view.

Over the course of his twelve-year career with the Brooklyn/Los Angeles Dodgers (the team moved to LA in 1958), Koufax won 165 games, lost only 87, and collected 2,396 strikeouts. He threw four no-hitters, including a perfect game against the Chicago Cubs on September 9, 1965. With Koufax and hard-throwing right-hander Don Drysdale leading the starting rotation, the Dodgers won three National League pennants and two World Series championships between 1962 and 1966.

Born Sanford Braun in Brooklyn, New York, he eventually assumed his stepfather's last name of Koufax. He played both baseball and basketball in high school, and his strong left arm attracted the interest of the hometown Brooklyn Dodgers, who signed him in 1954. Koufax struggled in his early years with the Dodgers, but he showed enough promise to maintain a spot on the roster every spring. In 1962 he finally put everything together. Only a circulation problem in his index finger—the first in a long line of ailments—kept him from a twenty-win season.

The next season Koufax established himself as baseball's best pitcher. He won twenty-five games and lost only five as the

Sandy Koufax. *A three-time Cy Young Award winner, left-hander Koufax won 165 games (40 of them shutouts) in a career cut short by injury. At the age of thirty-six, he became the youngest player ever to be inducted into the MLB Hall of Fame.* FOCUS ON SPORT/CONTRIBUTOR/GETTY IMAGES SPORT/GETTY IMAGES.

Dodgers roared into the World Series against the New York Yankees. Koufax was dominant against the Yankees, winning two games as Los Angeles swept the four-game series. After the season, Koufax was honored with the National League Cy Young Award, given to the most outstanding pitcher.

Koufax battled arthritis in 1964 but still won nineteen games. The next season he decided to give up throwing between starts in order to preserve his arm, and the results were stunning: he had twenty-six wins against only eight losses and established a major-league record with 382 strikeouts. He won two more games in the World Series as the Dodgers edged the Minnesota Twins. Again, Koufax garnered the National League Cy Young Award.

Fresh off their World Series championship, Koufax and Drysdale used their considerable leverage against the notoriously stingy Dodgers ownership. They held out in tandem from signing new contracts until the club agreed to meet their financial terms. The innovative negotiating ploy sent shockwaves through baseball and foreshadowed the power struggle between players and team owners that would result in the establishment of free agency in the 1970s. Koufax backed up his contract threats by winning his third National League Cy Young Award in 1966. He posted a 27–9 record with a 1.73 earned run average and 317 strikeouts. The Dodgers again reached the World Series, though they lost this time to the Baltimore Orioles.

Despite the disappointing finish to the season, Koufax seemed to be at the top of his game. It was a shock to the baseball world, then, when Koufax announced his retirement. He explained that he did not want to risk permanent damage to his oft-injured left arm. Five years after hanging up his spikes, he became the youngest player ever to be enshrined into the National Baseball Hall of Fame.

Like a baseball version of J. D. Salinger, Koufax shunned the public eye after his retirement. He worked briefly as a commentator on baseball telecasts, but his shy, diffident manner was ill suited for TV. In his rare public appearances since then, his every utterance has been heeded with a gravity normally reserved for retired generals and former presidents. To millions of baseball fans worldwide, he remains one of the game's most enigmatic legends.

Robert E. Schnakenberg

SEE ALSO: *Baseball; The Brooklyn Dodgers; World Series.*

BIBLIOGRAPHY

Giordano, Geraldine. *Sandy Koufax.* New York: The Rosen Publishing Group, 2003.

Shatzkin, Mike. *The Ballplayers: Baseball's Ultimate Biographical Reference.* New York: William Morrow, 1990.

Siegman, Joseph. *Jewish Sports Legends: The International Jewish Sports Hall of Fame.* Washington, DC: Brassey's, 1997.

Kovacs, Ernie *(1919–1962)*

Ernie Kovacs was one of network television's most daring and innovative comedians. From 1950 to 1962 he used the small screen as his personal canvas, challenging all of the medium's early conventions and assumptions. A master of live television and a pioneer in the use of videotape, Kovacs realized the potential of television as a unique art form and paved the way for future experimentation by David Letterman, MTV, and artist Nam June Paik. Kovacs was one of the first stars in television without a preceding career in vaudeville and theater. His sensibility was idiosyncratically attuned to experimenting with video technology and special effects. Although his various series rarely lasted a year, all his programs were marked with a surreal playfulness and inventive use of music. He was, in the words of critic William Henry III, "probably the best mind that has yet been drawn to create television."

EARLY CAREER

Born in Trenton, New Jersey, in 1919, Kovacs worked as a newspaper columnist and radio announcer before his transition to television in 1950. He hosted several programs simultaneously on a local NBC affiliate in Philadelphia, including a fashion and cooking show. Station executives at WPTZ noticed his flair for improvisation and asked him to create the first morning show on television, *For 3 to Get Ready* (named after Channel 3 in Philadelphia). Kovacs created a zany atmosphere to wake up his audience. He ad-libbed with the camera crew and spoke directly with his viewers, even forming a special club, the Early Eyeball Fraternal and Marching Society. He set the pattern for his later comedy by using cheap, offbeat props, including a pair of novelty glasses that inspired the creation of his enduring character, the fey poet Percy Dovetonsils.

Ernie Kovacs. *Ernie Kovacs was one of the first performers to achieve fame based almost exclusively on his work in television.* RALPH MORSE/CONTRIBUTOR/TIME & LIFE PICTURES/GETTY IMAGES.

NBC executives took notice of his success in the morning and formulated the *Today Show*; in May 1951 they also gave Kovacs his first network series, *It's Time for Ernie*. The fifteen-minute afternoon show featured Kovacs alone in the Philadelphia studio, supported by the music of the Tony de Simone Trio. In July Kovacs made his prime-time debut, serving as a summer replacement for *Kukla, Fran, and Ollie*. The new series, appropriately called *Ernie in Kovacsland*, had a regular cast that included singer Edie Adams, who would later become Kovacs's second wife. In January 1952 Kovacs returned to daytime and hosted *Kovacs on the Corner*, a series modeled on a radio sketch of Fred Allen, "Allen's Alley," in which the comedian regularly met a series of oddball characters. His denizens included Pete the cop; Luigi the barber; and a midget, Little Johnny Merkin. This time he asked his fans to come to the studio and wave back to the viewers at home for a segment titled "Yoo-Hoo Time."

NOTHING IN MODERATION: EXPERIMENTING WITH TELEVISION

In April 1952 WCBS lured Kovacs and gang to New York for a weekday afternoon show, *Kovacs Unlimited*. Most of the freewheeling gags and skits were completely unrehearsed. The response to the zany comedian led to a brief prime-time series, opposite Mr. Television, Milton Berle. Unlike most live variety series, Kovacs decided to create his own interior, free associative world without a studio audience. He concocted more and more with visual experiments, often skewering other television shows and commercials in the process. His self-reflexive parodies on the television medium itself provided the inspiration for *Saturday Night Live* (1975–) and *SCTV* (1976–1981), predating these revolutionary series by twenty years.

During the mid-1950s television executives had trouble scheduling Kovacs and his electronic adventures. In 1954 the DuMont network programmed him into the late-night slot. In 1955 he returned to daytime on NBC and, later that year, to prime time as a summer replacement for *Caesar's Hour* (1954–1957). The latter was his most professional series, with a stable of writers and lavish production numbers, garnering the program three Emmy Award nominations. In 1956 Kovacs became a part-time host of the *Tonight Show* (1953–).

For all his series the comedian unleashed a Kovacsian universe of video magic, populated with off-the-wall characters. Most of his creations were insane parodies of familiar television types, including Matzoh Hepplewhite, the inept magician; Uncle or Auntie Gruesome, who recounted macabre fairy tales; Mr. Question Man, who made mockery of the simplest queries; and Wolfgang Sauerbraten, the Bavarian disc jockey. The most bizarre and popular of Kovacs's repertory company was the Nairobi Trio, three instrumentalists dressed in overcoats, bowler hats, and gorilla masks. The trio acted like mechanical toys, miming to the odd tune of "Solfeggio."

Kovacs was at his most outlandish when he produced, wrote, and starred in special presentations. In 1956 he developed a silent character, Eugene, along the lines of Charlie Chaplin's Little Tramp. A year later the Eugene show explored his mute world with only music and sound effects. For this first special done entirely in pantomime, he created an illusory, illogical world with sets and objects confounding gravity.

In the late 1950s Kovacs resettled in Los Angeles. He brought his mustachioed good looks to several comic films, most notably the service high jinks of *Operation Mad Ball* (1957); *Bell, Book, and Candle* with James Stewart and Kim Novak (1958); and the spy spoof, *Our Man in Havana* (1960). While in Hollywood he hooked up with a sponsor, Dutch Masters Cigars, which had total faith in him. Dutch Masters hired Kovacs, an inveterate cigar smoker, to dream up commercials and host the quiz show, *Take a Good Look* (1959–1961).

From 1961 to 1962 Kovacs created eight specials for Dutch Masters and ABC that culminated a decade of video exploration. He wanted to take "sound to sight" and pioneered the music video, conjuring up moody, dreamlike imagery to accompany Pyotr Ilyich Tchaikovsky's *1812 Overture* and Bela Bartok's *Concerto for Orchestra*. Kovacs wanted to communicate comedy in the most economical fashion and used quick blackouts to express his dark humor. He also employed all electronic effects at his disposal—superimposition, matting, reverse polarity, asynchronous sound—to sustain a world that was off-kilter and slightly perverse. The final special aired posthumously, ten days after Kovacs was killed in an automobile accident.

Kovacs's motto was "Nothing in Moderation," and this visionary lived life and created programs at a fever pitch. A true television auteur, he laid the groundwork for future video experimentation, from the mainstream (*Laugh-In* [1967–1973], the *Monty Python* films, and *Pee-wee's Playhouse* [1986–1991]) to the avant-garde (Laurie Anderson, William Wegman). He proved that one man with a singular sensibility could flourish in commercial television; his legacy was spectacular but all too brief.

Ron Simon

SEE ALSO: *Automobile; Berle, Milton; Chaplin, Charlie; Emmy Awards; The Fifties; Hollywood;* Kukla, Fran, and Ollie*; Letterman, David; Live Television;* Monty Python's Flying Circus*; MTV;* Pee-wee's Playhouse*; Radio; Stewart, Jimmy; Television;* The Tonight Show*; Vaudeville; Videos.*

BIBLIOGRAPHY

Horton, Andrew. *Ernie Kovacs & Early TV Comedy: Nothing in Moderation*. Austin: University of Texas Press, 2010.

The Museum of Broadcasting. *The Vision of Ernie Kovacs*. New York: Museum of Broadcasting, 1986.

Rico, Diana. *Kovacsland: A Biography of Ernie Kovacs*. New York: Harcourt Brace Jovanovich, 1990.

Whalley, David. *The Ernie Kovacs Phile*. New York: Simon & Schuster, 1987.

Kraft Television Theatre

From the opening night on May 7, 1947, until its close on October 1, 1958, the *Kraft Television Theatre* produced 650 small-screen dramas of remarkably high quality and consistency. Presenting a range of works, from Shakespeare to original contemporary plays, live on camera using some of America's best actors and directors, *Kraft Television Theatre* helped to bring the television industry out of its infancy. In 1946 the number of television sets manufactured in the United States totaled a mere 225. A year later, when *Kraft Television Theatre* premiered, 8,690 were produced. The numbers began to soar, with Kraft's prestigious series of live theatrical events signaling the advent of television's Golden Age.

Television drama became an important showcase for young writers such as Rod Serling, Paddy Chayefsky, Reginald Rose, and Tad Mosel. The motion picture studios owned the rights to most of the important new plays and were reluctant to permit the works to be aired by their upstart rival, thus television was forced to seek out and buy original drama. During the 1956–57 season, Kraft offered a $50,000 prize for the best original play produced during the year, to be judged by Helen Hayes, Walter Kerr, and Maxwell Anderson. The prize went to William Noble for his television play *Snapfinger Creek*.

Actors who appeared on the *Kraft Theatre*, many in the early stages of their careers, included Jack Lemmon, Art Carney, Joanne Woodward, Paul Newman, Martin Milner, Cloris Leachman, Lee Remick, James Dean, Grace Kelly, Anthony Perkins, Rod Steiger, and E. G. Marshall. Among the memorable productions were *Alice in Wonderland* (1954), starring Robin Morgan as Alice and Art Carney as the Mad Hatter; *Romeo and Juliet* (1954), featuring sixteen-year-old Susan Strasberg; Eugene O'Neill's *The Emperor Jones* (1955), with Ossie Davis in the title role; and a drama about the sinking of the *Titanic* (1956) with a cast of 107. In 1956 James Whitmore starred in *A Profile in Courage*, and the show was introduced by then-senator John F. Kennedy, author of the book from which the script was adapted.

In order to attract a more youthful audience, in the mid-1950s the series presented a number of plays centering on popular music. Singers who acted and sang in these shows included Gisele Mackenzie, Ferlin Husky, and Julius LaRosa. Rock and roll emerged in 1957, with Tommy Sands playing an Elvis Presley–type role in *The Singin' Idol*. A song featured in this telecast, "Teenage Crush," sold one million records. The same year, Sal Mineo introduced his biggest hit, "Start Movin'," in a *Kraft Theatre* production, *Drummer Man*.

An important footnote to the *Kraft Theatre* series was the proof it presented of television's ability to sell products. In early 1947 Kraft decided to give the new medium an acid test, promoting a new product, McLaren's Imperial Cheese—selling poorly at a then-expensive $1 per pound—exclusively on its new dramatic series. By the third week, every package of the new cheese in New York City had been sold.

When the series ended its long run of live television drama, *TV Guide* summarized the astounding statistics: During its eleven and a half years, *Kraft Theatre* had presented 650 plays chosen from 18,845 scripts; starred or featured 3,955 actors and actresses in 6,750 roles; and rehearsed 26,000 hours on 5,236 sets. Costs rose from $3,000 for the debut production in 1947 to $165,000 for one show in 1958. Ed Rice, who was the script editor during the show's complete run, said that the entire studio space used in 1947 was half the size needed to produce commercials alone in 1958. These statistics, however, do not begin to measure the importance the series had in elevating popular culture in America during the Golden Age of Television.

Benjamin Griffith

SEE ALSO: *Advertising; Chayefsky, Paddy; Dean, James; Kelly, Grace; Leachman, Cloris; Movie Stars; Newman, Paul; O'Neill, Eugene; Presley, Elvis; Rock and Roll; Serling, Rod; Television;* TV Guide.

BIBLIOGRAPHY

Brooks, Tim, and Earle Marsh. *The Complete Directory to Prime Time Network TV Shows, 1946-Present*, 9th ed. New York: Ballantine Books, 2007.

Castleman, Harry, and Walter J. Podrazik. *Watching TV: Four Decades of American Television*. New York: McGraw-Hill, 1982.

McNeil, Alex. *Total Television: A Comprehensive Guide to Programming from 1948 to Present*. New York: Penguin, 1991.

Young, William H., and Nancy K. Young. *World War II and the Postwar Years in America: A Historical and Cultural Encyclopedia*. Santa Barbara, CA: ABC-CLIO, 2010.

Krantz, Judith *(1928–)*

American author Judith Krantz achieved astounding commercial success with her debut novel, *Scruples*, in 1978. It set the standard for what came to be called the "money/sex/power" novel and, like many of her subsequent best sellers, was made into a television miniseries. Krantz—and her successors in the genre, Jackie Collins and Barbara Taylor Bradford—in essence re-created the Cinderella story, chronicling a sympathetic heroine's quest toward personal fulfillment and abundant material wealth. Her books have sold millions of copies worldwide,

Judith Krantz. *Judith Krantz began her career as a novelist with the aim of writing fiction that appealed to women readers.* STEVE GRAYSON/STAFF/WIREIMAGE/GETTY IMAGES.

but her spectacular success also signified a great shift in the publishing world: she was one of the first writers of popular fiction to be marketed as a celebrity.

EARLY LIFE

Born Judith Tarcher in the late 1920s, Krantz grew up in affluent surroundings on New York's Central Park West. Her father was an advertising executive who taught her how to write ad copy, and her mother enjoyed a career as an attorney during an era when professional working mothers were a rarity. She graduated from Wellesley College and, after spending two years in France as a fashion publicist, went to work in the Manhattan magazine publishing world in the early 1950s. In 1953 she married a television cartoonist who later turned film producer, Steve Krantz, and they resided in New York until the early 1970s. From both there and in their new Los Angeles home, Krantz, now the mother of two, wrote freelance articles for women's magazines such as *Cosmopolitan* and *Good Housekeeping*. When she began to notice that popular fiction did not seem to offer a lot of titles aimed at female readers that were actually written by a woman—only the late Jacqueline Susann stood out among the roster—she decided to try her hand at a novel.

BEST SELLERS

Scruples was published in early 1978 and hit the top of the *New York Times* best-seller list a few months later; it remained there for one year. The tale—ugly-duckling Boston Brahmin girl Billy Ikehorn spends a college year in Paris; comes back gorgeous; opens a ritzy designer boutique on Rodeo Drive; and becomes a rich and famous film producer with her handsome, adoring European husband—struck a chord with the reading public, especially women. Krantz's Ikehorn was blessed with beauty and some inherited money but had gone to the "school of hard knocks" and ultimately achieved her power and abundant, minutely detailed luxuries through simple hard work. For millions of working women across all income strata, it was a modern-day Horatio Alger tale. In two years *Scruples* sold millions of copies, and Krantz became a household name.

Her second novel, *Princess Daisy* (1980), set a record for reprint bidding even before the hardcover edition appeared on shelves—Bantam's purchase of the paperback rights at $3.2 million was, at the time, the most ever paid for a work of fiction. Establishment critics derided *Princess Daisy*, and many in the publishing industry saw it and Krantz as harbingers of a new style of doing business, marked by a great deal of preprint hype and national tours by the author—now a figure of celebrity—an integral part of the budget. *Mistral's Daughter* (1983), like her previous two novels, featured the requisite Krantz narrative structure: the strikingly beautiful—in an idiosyncratic way—heroine who either inherits her money—after having to prove herself worthy of it—or comes into it through perseverance and hard work; she also shops a great deal and either lives in or travels to some of the world's poshest places (France and Manhattan figure frequently in the plot, naturally). Racy bedroom scenes, long and detailed lists of designer labels and divine food and drink, and actual celebrities from the worlds of fashion and entertainment (always dear friends or colleagues of the heroine's) appear liberally throughout the pages.

In her 1986 book *I'll Take Manhattan*, Krantz's heroine lives in Trump Tower and is a friend of the owner, quintessential 1980s tycoon Donald Trump. As in Krantz's other novels, the heroine's mastery of the city—the ultimate symbol of capitalist success—is a key element in the narrative structure; she is the embodiment of the savvy, sophisticated New Yorker. Mainstream establishment critics for the most part brutally lambasted this and the author's other novels; one described Krantz's talent for characterization as on "the level of advertising copy."

A SUCCESSION OF NOVELS

Krantz's later books never really achieved the fantastic success of her first few. She churned out a steady succession of novels over the next decade—*Till We Meet Again* (1988), *Dazzle* (1990), *Scruples Two* (1992), *Lovers* (1994), *Spring Collection* (1996), and *The Jewels of Tessa Kent* (1998)—that failed to conquer the best-seller lists. Still, they remained a perennial summertime read or airport purchase. "Charming French designers, designing French charmers, conventionally unconventional sculptors, voracious virgins, testy tycoons, flaky fakes, talented directors and kinky knights in tarnished armor bounce about" through Krantz's novels, noted Barbara Raskin of the *New York Times*. Yet Krantz's plots and characterizations also possess a particularly American slant to them: her heroines always exhibit great personal ambition and succeed in business at the uppermost echelons of the once male-dominated executive ranks. While Krantz took a break from novel writing after *The Jewels of Tessa Kent*, she released a moderately successful autobiography titled *Sex and Shopping: The Confessions of a Nice Jewish Girl* in 2000.

In her essay in *Women: A Cultural Review*, scholar Rita Felski compares the Krantz oeuvre to the classic bildungsroman of nineteenth-century European literature that features a young and innocent protagonist who, on his quest toward self-discovery, achieves urban sophistication, maturity, fame, and material success through his willfulness, focused ambition, and high personal moral standards. Krantz made her protagonists quintessentially feminine but with admirably "masculine" traits. Felski notes that most of the best-selling popular fiction of the 1980s came to model itself on Krantz's formulas, and "the Krantzian heroine, furthermore, soon appeared in other media texts and genres, as similar images of striving corporate femininity began to appear in prime-time television drama, advertising, and women's magazines."

In 2012 actress Natalie Portman was developing a soap opera based on *Scruples*, with Krantz's son Tony slated to be executive producer of the show.

Carol Brennan

SEE ALSO: *Best Sellers; Celebrity;* Cosmopolitan*; Made-for-Television Movies; Romance Novels; Television.*

BIBLIOGRAPHY

Broyard, Anatole. "Books of the Times." *New York Times*, December 8, 1982, C29.

Dullea, Georgia. "At a Party for Judith Krantz, Life Imitates Art." *New York Times*, May 2, 1986, A24.

Felski, Rita. "Judith Krantz, Author of *The Cultural Logics of Late Capitalism*." In *Women: A Cultural Review* 8, no. 2 (1997): 129–142.

Lehmann-Haupt, Christopher. "Books of the Times." *New York Times*, September 11, 1986, C23.

Moritz, Charles. "Judith Krantz." *Current Biography Yearbook 1982*. New York: H.W. Wilson, 1983.

Prial, Frank J. "Stick This in Your Mid-Sized Louis Vuitton."

New York Times Book Review, August 28, 1988, 11.

Shapiro, Laura. "From the Little Fur Desk of Maxi Amberville." *New York Times Book Review*, May 4, 1986, 15.

Krassner, Paul *(1932–)*

Paul Krassner was the Alexander Pope, the Dorothy Parker, and the F. Scott Fitzgerald of the 1960s. In his satirical magazine the *Realist*, which began publication in 1958, he revealed himself as a creature very much of his time but somehow separate from it. He was the voice of sardonic, pomposity-deflating laughter, his barbs aimed at the culture and counterculture alike. Here's Krassner describing LSD: "Last week I took my third acid trip. This time I saw God. Otherwise, it was nothing."

Krassner was a fellow traveler in drug exploration with Timothy Leary, in political agitation with Abbie Hoffman, and in comic innovation with Lenny Bruce. The *Realist* was the dark, warped conscience of the 1960s. With a staff of basically two people—Krassner and a great editor, Bob Abel—it attracted writers such as Bruce, Woody Allen, Terry Southern (author of *Dr. Strangelove*, 1964), and Avery Corman (*Kramer vs. Kramer*, 1977).

But its most important writing was done by Krassner himself, in such satirical pieces as "The Parts Left out of the Manchester Book," in which Krassner purports to have discovered a missing chapter from William Manchester's exhaustive study of the John F. Kennedy assassination, *Death of a President* (1967). In the most striking and scandalous part of Krassner's version, a Secret Service agent discovers Lyndon Johnson performing an unnatural sex act on Kennedy's neck wound, in an attempt to confuse investigators by changing the angle of the wound. Incredibly, this satire achieved a sort of underground echo of the Orson Welles/Howard Koch "War of the Worlds" radio broadcast. Nobody quite stormed the White House demanding that Johnson be impeached for sex crimes, but a surprising number of people believed that this story really had been censored from Manchester's book.

Krassner created one of the most amorphous political movements of the 1960s, perhaps of all time: the Youth International Party. It was amorphous in that it didn't exist; it was a political movement in that it became a huge media creation, and by the end of the 1960s nearly everyone had heard of it. In 1968, when the Democratic National Convention in Chicago turned into a free-flowing riot, the police, the media, and many others blamed the uprising on "the Yippies," as Krassner's Youth International Party was known. Krassner, however, was passed over when the group of "Yippie instigators" who became the Chicago Seven were arrested—although if anyone deserved the publicity that Abbie Hoffman, Jerry Rubin, and the rest gained from that media circus, it was Krassner. The cops probably overlooked him because they couldn't figure him out; the FBI, in one report, referred to him as "a raving, unconfined nut." Krassner later titled his memoirs *Confessions of a Raving, Unconfined Nut* (1993).

The *Realist* ceased publication in 1974. Krassner started it up again in 1985, but it no longer had the centrality to the countercultural nervous system that it once had. In addition to his role as a countercultural gadfly, Krassner had his fingers in a number of unlikely pies. One of his most curious jobs was a short-lived stint as editor of *Hustler* in 1978, during the period when *Hustler* publisher Larry Flynt sought to portray himself as a First Amendment defender and counterculture hero. In an unusual foray into the mainstream, Krassner was a writer for the *Ron Reagan Jr.* TV series in the 1980s.

Through the 1980s and 1990s Krassner's primary vehicle for his satiric thrusts was stand-up comedy, which led to his releasing several comedy albums, including *We Have Ways of Making You Laugh* (1996) and *Brain Damage Control* (1997). He has continued to write and perform at a frantic pace. Among later works are a series on drugs—*Pot Stories for the Soul* (1999), *Psychedelic Trips for the Mind* (2001), and *Magic Mushrooms and Other Highs* (2004)—as well as political commentary, including *Who's to Say What's Obscene? Politics, Culture and Comedy Today* (2009).

Tad Richards

SEE ALSO: *Allen, Woody; The Chicago Seven;* Dr. Strangelove or: How I Learned to Stop Worrying and Love the Bomb*; Fitzgerald, F. Scott; Hippies; Hoffman, Abbie;* Hustler*; Kennedy Assassination; Leary, Timothy; Parker, Dorothy; Southern, Terry; Stand-up Comedy;* War of the Worlds*; Welles, Orson; Yippies.*

BIBLIOGRAPHY

Contemporary Authors Online. Detroit, MI: The Gale Group, 1999.

Krassner, Paul. *Confessions of a Raving, Unconfined Nut: Misadventures in the Counter-Culture.* New York: Simon & Schuster, 1993.

Krassner, Paul. *The Winner of the Slow Bicycle Race.* New York: Seven Stories Press, 1996.

Krazy Kat

The newspaper comic strip *Krazy Kat* by George Herriman (1880–1944) concerns a love triangle between Krazy Kat, Ignatz Mouse, and Officer Pupp: Krazy loves Ignatz, Ignatz hates Krazy, Pupp loves Krazy. Ignatz feels compelled to express his hatred of Krazy by tossing a brick at the unoffending cat's head. Krazy longs for the bricks as tokens of the mouse's love. Not realizing that Krazy desires to be pelted by masonry, Pupp pursues Ignatz in order to arrest the mouse before the brick is thrown. One of the strip's major themes is obsession: Ignatz is obsessed with throwing the brick, Krazy with receiving it, and Pupp with stopping it. From this simple premise, Herriman's imagination produced a unique series that many consider the greatest comic strip ever produced.

The action takes place in Coconino County, Arizona, a desert landscape of buttes and mesas. Other residents of Coconino County include Joe Stork ("purveyor of progeny to prince and proletariat"), Kolin Kelly (brick merchant), Walter Cephus Austridge, Mrs. Kwakk Wakk, Gooseberry Sprigg (the Duck Duke), Marihuana Pelona, Don Kiyoti (Mexican bandit), Mock Duck (Chinese launderer), Bum Bill Bee ("pilgrim on the road to nowhere"), Krazy's cousins Krazy Katfish and Krazy Katbird, and Ignatz's wife and three sons.

The strip began as a doodle at the bottom of an episode of *The Dingbat Family*, another Herriman strip, on July 26, 1910.

Krazy and Ignatz continued to frolic along the bottom border of their parent strip until 1913, when they were granted a regular daily strip of their own. *Krazy Kat* premiered on Sunday, April 23, 1916, but not in the color supplement; instead the *Krazy Kat* Sunday page appeared in the drama and art section. The placement of *Krazy* in a different section from the other "Sunday funnies" indicates the strip's appeal to a smaller audience. It was beloved by writers, artists, and intellectuals but did not catch on with the average newspaper reader. Under normal market conditions, the strip might have been canceled early in its run. *Krazy Kat*, however, had a devoted fan in its publisher, William Randolph Hearst, who kept the strip running.

In 1924 respected critic Gilbert Seldes devoted a chapter of his book *The Seven Lively Arts* to praise for *Krazy Kat*, calling it "the most amusing and fantastic and satisfactory work of art produced in America today." The 1946 collection of the strip boasted an introduction by famous poet E. E. Cummings. Few comic strips received such attention from the artistic elite. One element of the strip that attracted this praise was its play with language. Krazy Kat speaks a bizarre and unique dialect, a mixture of a variety of real-life dialects, and creates bizarre puns from what Ignatz says. As Krazy says in a 1918 episode, "lenguage is, that we may mis-unda-stend each udda."

Another unique aspect of the strip was its constantly changing landscape. Even as the characters remain stationary, the background often shifts behind them, creating a surreal effect. Other elements in the strip are as indeterminate as the scenery—Krazy's gender, for one. Sometimes Krazy is a "she," sometimes a "he." When questioned about the inconsistency, Herriman explained that Krazy was "a sprite," a magical being with no gender. A final aspect that often garnered praise was the self-reflexivity of many episodes. Because they live in a world of ink on paper, characters are allowed to redraw their environment.

Krazy Kat died with its creator in 1944. Despite the fact that it has long since passed from the funny pages, the strip has never been forgotten. Scholars often place Herriman in the company of the great modernists. For example, in his book *Comics as Culture*, M. Thomas Inge declares that "to the world of comic art George Herriman was its Picasso in visual style and innovation, its Joyce in stretching the limitations of language, and its Beckett in staging the absurdities of life."

Christian L. Pyle

SEE ALSO: *Comics; Hearst, William Randolph; Modernism; Picasso, Pablo.*

BIBLIOGRAPHY

Herriman, George. *Krazy Kat*. New York: Henry Holt, 1946.

Herriman, George. *The Komplete Kolor* Krazy Kat, ed. Richard Marschall. Abington, PA: Remco Worldservice Books, 1990.

Herriman, George. *Krazy & Ignatz: The Komplete Kat Komics 1925 & 1926*, ed. Bill Blackbeard. Seattle, WA: .Fantagraphics, 2001.

Herriman, George; Patrick McDonnell; Karen O'Connell; et al. Krazy Kat: *The Comic Art of George Herriman*. New York: Abrams, 1986.

Inge, M. Thomas. *Comics as Culture*. Jackson: University Press of Mississippi, 1990.

Seldes, Gilbert. *The Seven Lively Arts*. New York: Harper, 1924.

Yoe, Craig. Krazy Kat *& the Art of George Herriman: A Celebration*. New York: Abrams ComicArts, 2011.

Krupa, Gene *(1909–1973)*

Gene Krupa was perhaps the most famous drummer of the big band era. His work, first with Benny Goodman and later with his own band, defined jazz drumming for generations of percussionists. His flamboyant style and boundless energy made him the center of attention whenever he played. Krupa was the first legitimate superstar of the drum set, and his work on the classic Goodman tune "Sing, Sing, Sing" was the first extended drum solo in recorded music history. His solos combined controlled frenzy and musical genius.

Krupa was born in Chicago in 1909. He started playing the drums as a young boy and by the early 1920s was participating in jam sessions with some of Chicago's best jazz players. His popularity was cemented when he joined Goodman's band in the mid-1930s. After leaving Goodman in 1938, he formed his own band and successfully blended swing and pop music to entertain the public throughout the 1940s.

Although the big band era was rapidly coming to an end, Krupa's battles with addiction also helped stall his career in the early 1950s. Unable to control his cravings, he saw his skills and popularity diminish. He enjoyed a brief revival in 1959 when his life story was made into a film starring young actor Sal Mineo, but he never regained his previous international fame. In 2009 the British magazine *Rhythm* named Krupa the third-best drummer of all time.

Geoff Peterson

SEE ALSO: *Big Bands; Goodman, Benny; Jazz.*

BIBLIOGRAPHY

Crowther, Bruce. *Gene Krupa, His Life & Times*. New York: Universe Books, 1987.

Klauber, Bruce H. *World of Gene Krupa: That Legendary Drummin' Man*. Ventura, CA: Pathfinder, 1990.

Klauber, Bruce H. *Gene Krupa: The Pictorial Life of a Jazz Legend*. Los Angeles: Alfred Publishing, 2005.

Ku Klux Klan

The Ku Klux Klan is America's oldest and most notorious white supremacist organization. Originally formed to combat Reconstruction in the South following the Civil War, it soon became identified with virulent and violent racism, nativism, anti-Semitism, and terrorism. The group has been embedded in the American cultural psyche and political consciousness virtually since its inception, evoking fear for its victims and repugnance among the educated and liberal elements of society, while profoundly influencing the attitudes of those induced to follow its tenets, which are strongly wrapped in a skewed vision of patriotism. The Klan's public behavior and its treatment and exposure in the media have served to keep its presence in the public eye.

The name derived from the Greek *kyklos*, meaning "circle," and a corruption of *clan*, or family, a fanciful idea created by six idle young Confederate war veterans who relieved the tedium of life in Pulaski, Tennessee, by dressing up in ghostly white sheets by night and playing pranks on their neighbors. Although its numbers gradually increased, the Klan was little more than a gang of ruffians until 1867, when Congress passed the Congressional Reconstruction Act. The new law mandated military occupation of the South, invalidated most of the region's existing state governments, and decreed that the rights of the newly freed black slaves would be guaranteed by force, if necessary. The Reconstruction-era South proved fertile ground for opportunists who poured into war-ravaged areas, further heightening existing political and racial tensions.

POST–CIVIL WAR ERA

Confronted with this challenge to the traditional Southern power structure, the Ku Klux Klan turned to terror, dedicating itself to the continuation of white supremacy in the South, a return to black subjugation, and resistance to any attempts to change the traditional Southern way of life. Its weapons were arson, beatings, torture, mutilation, and murder. No one knows how many people were lynched, shot, burned alive, or beaten to death during the Klan's initial reign of terror, but these outrages finally spurred Congress to pass anti-Klan legislation in 1871 and 1872. Federal troops sent to enforce the law failed to wipe out the Klan, but they did succeed in driving it into a period of dormancy. The Klan legend, however, was only beginning.

The next major appearance of the Ku Klux Klan to penetrate the nation's consciousness occurred shortly after the turn of the century. In 1905 a racist former minister from North Carolina named Thomas Dixon published *The Clansman*, a novel depicting the supposed evils of Reconstruction and the alleged heroism of the Klan in resisting it. A year later Dixon produced a sequel, *The Leopard's Spots*, which developed the same themes. Both novels sold well, especially in the South, but their real importance was derived from the influence they exercised on director D. W. Griffith, who used much of the material in his 1915 epic film, *The Birth of a Nation*. Given the viewpoint of Dixon's novels, it is unsurprising that Griffith's classic of the cinema is exceedingly racist. The scenes set during Reconstruction depict blacks as moronic dupes of Northern carpetbaggers and lust-crazed despoilers of white women. The film's main characters, the Stoneman family, are saved from a savage black mob only by the timely intervention of the Ku Klux Klan.

The film was both hugely popular and immensely inflammatory. It was seen by many whites, protested by many blacks, and frequently caused race riots at theaters where it played; it was also very popular with the Klan, which used it as a propaganda device for recruitment. Klan chapters advertised for new members in newspaper ads and would insist that their ads run next to those for local screenings of *The Birth of a Nation*. Robed Klansmen attended showings of the film in several cities and towns, handing out literature to the exiting audiences.

Another positive depiction of the Klan can be seen in the 1918 film *The Prussian Cur*. Directed by Raoul Walsh (who had

Ku Klux Klan. *Ku Klux Klan members rally in New York City in 1999.* JONATHAN ELDERFIELD/CONTRIBUTOR/GETTY IMAGES NEWS/GETTY IMAGES.

worked with Griffith on *The Birth of a Nation*), this production was one of the last of the "hate films" that flourished in America during World War I, designed to support the war effort by inflaming hostility toward the German enemy. Walsh's film concerns a German agent in America who, while on a mission of sabotage, is caught and jailed. A group of disloyal German Americans try to free him but are thwarted by the arrival of robed Klansmen who return the spy to prison and force his would-be rescuers to kiss the American flag.

The original Klan, which had faded away in the 1870s, had been revived in 1915 by William Joseph Simmons, who commemorated the organization's rebirth with a cross-burning ceremony atop Georgia's Stone Mountain, which contains an etched Confederate Memorial to Confederate President Jefferson Davis and Generals Robert E. Lee and Stonewall Jackson. Simmons hired a public relations firm to spearhead recruitment for his new Knights of the Ku Klux Klan. The Southern Publicity Association, formed in 1917 by Bessie Tyler and Edward Clarke to help sell war bonds, was phenomenally successful in attracting members. The new Klan, which opposed the aspirations of blacks, Jews, immigrants, Catholics, labor unions, and suffragettes, had much to offer those concerned about the social changes taking place in the United States. Tyler and Clarke used all the methods of modern public relations to gain favorable publicity for their client: they arranged for journalists to interview Simmons, who charmed them; they secured Klan cooperation in the filming of newsreels designed to show the Klan in a favorable light; and they set up impressive public initiation ceremonies for new Klansmen. They also held rallies designed to attract even more members while garnering publicity for the organization.

The Klan continued to grow during the 1920s, but during the course of the decade it became the subject of controversy in an unlikely place: the pages of *Black Mask*, a popular pulp magazine that was the first publication to introduce "hard-boiled" detective stories into American culture. Beginning in 1923 the magazine began an ongoing feature called "Klan Forum," in which readers were invited to debate the merits of the Klan. At the same time *Black Mask* began running a series of detective stories with plot lines critical of the Klan. Many of these were written by Carroll John Daly, whose hero, the aptly named Race Williams, opposed the Klan and fought to frustrate its racist activities.

POST–WORLD WAR II PERIOD

The Klan appeared in popular culture only sporadically during the next several decades. *The Burning Cross* (1947), a film starring Hank Daniels and Virginia Patton, concerns a returned World War II veteran who confronts the Klan in his hometown. In *Storm Warning* (1951), Ronald Reagan plays a crusading district attorney out to convict a group of Klansmen who have committed murder. *The Cardinal* (1963) contains a segment in which Klansmen of the 1930s try to intimidate a Catholic priest, played by Tom Tryon. A 1975 episode of the made-for-TV film series, *The FBI Story*, was titled "Attack on Terror: The FBI versus the Ku Klux Klan."

In the 1980s, in conjunction with the rise of Far Right extremism, media interest in the Klan was reignited. The 1981 documentary film *Resurgence: The Movement for Equality vs. the Ku Klux Klan* concerns a two-year strike against a chicken processing plant in Laurel, Mississippi. The strikers, mostly black women, eventually triumph over a hostile management, extended unemployment, and threats of violence by the local Klan, who oppose the women because of both their labor activity and their race. Two years later *Twilight Zone: The Movie* premiered, paying homage to Rod Serling's classic television series. The film contains stories of the fantastic and the supernatural. In the first, Vic Morrow plays a vicious bigot who is magically transformed into a victim of oppression in several scenarios, one of which has him as the victim of a Ku Klux Klan lynching.

Perhaps the most prominent of the decade's Klan depictions is Alan Parker's powerful *Mississippi Burning* (1988). Loosely based on actual events, the film follows an FBI investigation into the murders of three civil rights workers by the Klan in 1964. Gene Hackman, Willem Dafoe, and Frances McDormand bring star power and intensity to an unrelentingly grim story of murder, hatred, and betrayal. That same year *Betrayed* offered a gripping look at the ways in which entrenched racism may be passed from one generation to another. The film stars Debra Winger as an undercover FBI agent who reluctantly falls in love with Gary Simmons (Tom Berenger), a widower with two children who is deeply involved in the white supremacy movement.

Television also took its turn at transforming the Klan's history into drama. *Cross of Fire*, a two-part made-for-TV movie directed by Paul Wendkos, was broadcast in November 1989. Set in the 1920s, the film focuses on the rise and fall of Klan leader D. C. Stephenson, an actual Klan Grand Dragon in the decade after World War I. The film is concerned less with the activities of the Klan during this period than it is with Stephenson's personal villainy and eventual comeuppance.

However, the media of the 1980s was not solely the province of the Klan's enemies. Klansmen themselves launched vigorous efforts to spread their message and attract new recruits. Beginning in 1984 a former California Klan leader named Tom Metzger began to use public-access cable television to further his cause of white supremacy. By law, public access channels are open to anyone who submits a videocassette in the proper format, and Metzger's cassettes contained episodes of his talk show, *Race and Reason*. The number of cities in which the show appeared during its six-year run is not precisely known—Metzger claimed fifty, his foes said about twenty. But it was clear that the Klan was still actively spreading its message of hatred and distrust.

Meanwhile, David Duke was busy furthering his political ambitions in Louisiana. Duke, a former Klan leader, had ostensibly tried to put his racist past behind him by claiming that he was not anti-black but rather pro-white. Dubbed "the blow-dried Klansman," he proved adept at modern campaign techniques and learned how to exploit the press for his political purposes. He managed to win election to the Louisiana State legislature in 1989, but he failed in later bids to win elections for governor and a seat in the U.S. Senate. It was a foregone conclusion that he would fail to win the Republican presidential nomination in 1988. However, he has continued his quest for high political office and made another try for the nomination in 2012.

RESURGENCE

The 1990s offered even more exposure, both positive and negative, of the Klan and its message. Daytime talk shows, especially those hosted by Geraldo Rivera, Jerry Springer, and Sally Jesse

Raphael, often invited Klan members as guests—usually to face the scorn of both the host and much of the studio audience. The 1991 documentary *Blood in the Face* presents white supremacists, including Klan members, using their own words. Through interviews, video from Metzger's *Race and Reason* program, and video footage of a white supremacist gathering (including a Klan wedding performed in front of a burning cross), the film provides an unflinching portrait of a side of America that many never see.

Other depictions of the Klan were produced for network television and cable. *Murder in Mississippi* (1990) deals with the same crimes as those depicted in *Mississippi Burning* but from the point of view of African Americans. Another made-for-TV film, *Sophie and the Moonhanger* (1996), involves a woman's discovery of her husband's Klan affiliations and his plans for violence against her black friends. In 1997 HBO premiered Spike Lee's film, *4 Little Girls*, focusing on the 1963 Klan bombing of a Birmingham, Alabama, church that left four children dead.

But the most sinister aspect of the Klan in the 1990s involved the Internet. Klan organizations around the country learned that they could reach greater numbers of people with a website than with leaflets or newspapers—and, unlike an appearance on a talk show such as *Oprah*, there are no jeering crowds. Thus, the Internet allows the Klan to control all aspects of the message of "white power," which has not changed substantially in more than 130 years. During this same period, the federal courts hampered the activities of the Klan to some extent by upholding hate crime laws that allowed racketeering laws to be used against members convicted of hate crimes, with the result that civil rights groups sometimes took over KKK property. White supremacy was far from dead, however. That point was brought home to Americans with a vengeance on the morning of April 19, 1995, when white supremacist and paramilitary member Timothy McVeigh bombed a federal building in Oklahoma City, killing 168 people. Nineteen of those dead were children under the age of six who were in a day care facility in the building.

Detailed information on the inside workings of the Klan surfaced in 2011 when John Matthews, a former FBI mole who had been infiltrating KKK groups for decades, went public with his story. A 2009 report on right extremist groups was withdrawn in 2009 amid conservative protests, but Daryl Johnson, a former domestic terror analyst for Homeland Security, warns that the threat continues to grow in the twenty-first century. According to the Alabama-based Southern Poverty Law Center, the number of right-wing extremist groups climbed from 149 in 2008 when Barack Obama was elected president to 824 in 2012, the year that Obama faced reelection. The link between KKK members and paramilitary groups has continued to strengthen, and the availability of bomb-making instructions and links to other white supremacists via the Internet makes such right-wing extremists as the Klan ever more threatening.

Justin Gustainis

SEE ALSO: *Advertising;* The Birth of a Nation*;* Black Mask*; Cable TV; Civil Rights Movement; Daytime Talk Shows; Equal Rights Amendment; FBI (Federal Bureau of Investigation); Firearms; Griffith, D. W.; Hackman, Gene; Hard-Boiled Detective Fiction; The Internet; Lee, Spike; Lynching; Made-for-Television Movies; Obama, Barack; Pulp Magazines; Race Riots; Reagan, Ronald; Rivera, Geraldo; Serling, Rod; Springer, Jerry; Tabloid Television; Television;* The Twilight Zone*; White Supremacists; Winfrey, Oprah; World War I; World War II.*

BIBLIOGRAPHY

Bartoletti, Susan Campbell. *They Called Themselves the K.K.K.: The Birth of an American Terrorist Group*. Boston: Houghton Mifflin Harcourt, 2010.

Chalmers, David Mark. *Hooded Americanism: The History of the Ku Klux Klan*. New York: F. Watts, 1981.

Cutlip, Scott M. *The Unseen Power: Public Relations, A History*. Hillsdale, NJ: Lawrence Erlbaum Associates, 1994.

Esolen, Gary. "More than a Pretty Face: David Duke's Use of Television as a Political Tool." In *The Emergence of David Duke and the Politics of Race*, ed. Douglas Rose, 136–155. Chapel Hill: University of North Carolina Press, 1992.

Fox, Craig. *Everyday Klansfolk: White Protestant Life and the KKK in 1920s*. East Lansing: Michigan State University Press, 2011.

Greenhaw, Wayne. *Fighting the Devil in Dixie: How Civil Rights Activists Took on the Ku Klux Klan in Alabama*. Chicago: Lawrence Hill Books, 2011.

Jackson, Kenneth T. *The Ku Klux Klan in the City, 1915–1930*. New York: Oxford University Press, 1967.

Quarles, Chester L. *The Ku Klux Klan and Related American Racialist and Antisemitic Organizations: A History and Analysis*. Jefferson, NC: McFarland, 1999.

Riley, Michael. "White and Wrong: New Klan, Old Hatred." *Time*, July 6, 1992, 24–27.

Schneiderman, R. M. "I Was an Undercover White Supremacist." *Newsweek*, November 28, 2011.

Wade, Wyn Craig. *The Fiery Cross: The Ku Klux Klan in America*. New York: Simon & Schuster, 1987.

Kubrick, Stanley *(1928–1999)*

American filmmaker Stanley Kubrick's ambitious and evocative works include widely acknowledged masterpieces such as *Dr. Strangelove or: How I Learned to Stop Worrying and Love the Bomb* (1964), *2001: A Space Odyssey* (1968), and *A Clockwork Orange* (1971). His films have been nominated for thirteen Academy Awards. However, he only won one, the 1969 Oscar for Special Visual Effects for *2001*.

Born in New York City in 1928, Kubrick began his career as a still photographer in high school. *Look* magazine picked up his shot of a newspaper vendor on the day President Franklin D. Roosevelt died and hired him as a freelance photographer at age seventeen. Kubrick began making films in 1951, borrowing money from family and friends to produce a sixteen-minute documentary called *Day of the Fight*. He continued to work on small films, both documentaries and features, and slowly began to make a name for himself.

After directing actor Kirk Douglas in *Paths of Glory* (1957), his big break came when he was brought in by Douglas to replace director Anthony Mann on the set of the Hollywood blockbuster *Spartacus* (1960). The film marked Kubrick's first box-office success, but the experience frustrated him. It would be the last time he worked on a film without total creative control. In the early 1960s he moved from New York to London and began tackling topics of exceptional breadth and cultural concern. Although he would only make eight films over the next twenty-five years, he achieved mythical stature, refusing to give interviews and reportedly requiring actors to sign on to films with no set time limits on their contracts. Often working from novels as source material, he mostly focused on the darker side of humanity, using pessimism and sarcasm as his weapons of choice.

His first feature in the United Kingdom, *Lolita* (1962), was an adaptation of Russian author Vladimir Nabokov's erotic novel. Kubrick followed with the satirical nuclear holocaust comedy *Dr. Strangelove*, featuring actor Peter Sellers in the multipersonality roles of Dr. Strangelove. The movie was a commercial success and gave the director the freedom to choose virtually any project he desired.

However, it would be four years before his next project, *2001*, was released. He collaborated on the film with the author of the book on which it was based, Arthur C. Clarke. In the movie, Kubrick examines human evolution and humankind's place in the universe through a tale of deep-space exploration. The movie became a cult classic, and despite receiving as much critical derision as acclaim, it is considered hugely influential for its cinematic special effects and on the science fiction film genre.

Kubrick continued to explore a variety of dark themes across various subjects. *A Clockwork Orange* focuses on futuristic gang violence. It became controversial for its depiction of carefree brutality, including a rape scene that is deeply disturbing in its playfulness. *The Shining* (1980), which is generally considered a horror film, explores a man's insanity and the violence he wreaks on his family, and the atrocities of Vietnam are depicted in *Full Metal Jacket* (1987). Only his 1975 film *Barry Lyndon*, a period piece following the adventures of an eighteenth-century Irishman, lacked any emphasis on cruelty, sex, or violence; it was also notable for its cinematography, with many scenes lit only by candlelight.

Several of Kubrick's projects were never completed, including a historical costume epic, *Napoleon*, that the director spent three years researching. (The film was dropped by MGM due to the failure of a competing film.) Another project that was never produced, *Waterloo*, written in 1970, was released as a ten-volume special edition package in 2009 containing Kubrick's screenplay, production notes, and research images. Finally, a Holocaust film titled *The Aryan Papers* was shelved after Kubrick learned of director and friend Steven Spielberg's Holocaust project, *Schindler's List* (1993).

In 1997 the Director's Guild of America selected Kubrick for the D. W. Griffith Award for Lifetime Achievement. Shortly thereafter he began working on his last film, *Eyes Wide Shut* (1999), with then-married costars Tom Cruise and Nicole Kidman. The film took fifteen months to shoot, and a few months before its release, Kubrick died of a heart attack. However, his final contribution to cinema came with the 2001 release of Spielberg's *A.I.: Artificial Intelligence*, a project Kubrick had initiated and worked on for a number of years. The film was dedicated to his memory.

As a director, Kubrick put his signature on subjects as varied as the Cold War, the ambiguities of violence, and the limits of human consciousness with his uniquely powerful screen images. Although critics unanimously praise his technical mastery, many remain baffled and outraged by his disturbing narratives. Nevertheless, his films continue to be as compelling and controversial as they were when first released.

John Tomasic

SEE ALSO: *Academy Awards; Clarke, Arthur C.;* A Clockwork Orange*; Cold War; Cruise, Tom;* Dr. Strangelove or: How I Learned to Stop Worrying and Love the Bomb*;* Lolita*;* Schindler's List*;* Spartacus*; Spielberg, Steven;* 2001: A Space Odyssey*; Vietnam.*

BIBLIOGRAPHY

Abrams, Jerold J., ed. *The Philosophy of Stanley Kubrick.* Lexington: University Press of Kentucky, 2007.

Ciment, Michel. *Kubrick*, tr. Gibert Adair. London: Collins, 1983.

Cocks, Geoffrey; James Diedrick; and Glenn Perusek, eds. *Depth of Field: Stanley Kubrick, Film, and the Uses of History.* Madison: University of Wisconsin Press, 2006.

Falsetto, Mario, ed. *Perspectives on Stanley Kubrick.* New York: G. K. Hall, 1996.

Kolker, Robert Philip. *A Cinema of Loneliness.* New York: Oxford University Press, 1988.

Rice, Julian. *Kubrick's Hope: Discovering Optimism from "2001" to "Eyes Wide Shut."* Plymouth, UK: Scarecrow Press, 2008.

Kudzu

Created in 1981 by editorial cartoonist Doug Marlette (1949—2007), the comic strip *Kudzu* reveals the universal aspects of life as depicted in a small town. Marlette used his experiences growing up in the South to develop his characters and situations. "I located it in North Carolina because I was born there," Marlette said, "but it could be anywhere." His main character, Kudzu Dubose, is an awkward teenager in limbo between childhood and adulthood. Kudzu chronically suffers and good naturedly copes with heartbreak, agony, and failure. He is surrounded by characters who depict common human traits such as narcissism, self-indulgence, and greed.

Marlette selected the name Kudzu for his comic strip and protagonist because his character resembled the kudzu vine. Imported to the United States from Japan in 1876, kudzu flourished in the Deep South's warm climate. "Kudzu is a fast-growing oriental creeper. It was introduced years ago in the South to control soil erosion and is now a menace that covers millions of acres," Marlette explained. "My Kudzu is something of a menace, too, or at least his blunderings are." Marlette noted that both the kudzu vine and his character were pests and defined by their ability to grow despite deterrents. "Like Scarlett O'Hara or Dilsey in Faulkner's *The Sound and the Fury*," Marlette stated, "the kudzu plant—and, I hope, the comic strip—endures and prevails."

KUDZU DUBOSE

The cartoon town of Bypass, North Carolina, is a stereotypical small southern town full of eccentrics. The protagonist, Kudzu, is a naïve adolescent whose innocence causes him problems. Poetic and vulnerable, Kudzu is artistic, and the theme of dreams versus reality prevails in his life.

Kudzu lives with his overbearing mother, whom he obeys, but he longs to leave home, escaping the boredom of Bypass to discover the world and acquire personal power in his life. He wants to be a "great writer" and thinks he needs to move to New York City to achieve his dreams. He keeps a journal and has a short story rejected by the *New Yorker* magazine. Kudzu is constantly discouraged, misunderstood, and feels despair, but he determinedly seeks happiness. He also desires romantic love and wears a chest wig in an effort to be more masculine.

Kudzu is oppressed by his mother, who is unwilling to allow her son freedom. Mrs. Dubose is a manipulative woman whose bossy behavior resulted in her husband abandoning her and Kudzu. She is an emotional burden to Kudzu, faking illnesses to control her son by making him feel guilty for not taking adequate care of her. She insists that he wear a beeper so that she can always contact him. She does not appreciate her son's talents, dismissing him when he wins writing contests. Kudzu's closest companion at home is his bird, Doris, who does impressions when she is alone and craves chocolate.

Kudzu's Uncle Dub owns a filling station and cafe where he works part time. Dub is crude, anti-intellectual, and insensitive, exactly Kudzu's opposite. A "good ol' boy" who prefers his hunting dogs to humans, Dub is simple while Kudzu is complex.

Kudzu's best friend, Maurice Stonewall Jackson, is an African American who is Kudzu's touchstone with reality. Maurice is cool and self-assured, and his goal is to leave the suburban middle-class lifestyle for an urban ghetto. His mother works as a maid for the Tadsworths, the richest family in town. She dreams of Maurice attending Harvard and knows exactly how many biscuits she has cooked to earn his tuition. Maurice and Kudzu explore black and white identities and relationships in the New South.

Kudzu's love interest, Veranda Tadsworth, is the daughter of Bubba Tadsworth, who owns the local mill, has a huge estate, and is the most powerful man in the county. Marlette describes Veranda as being the "Southern belle from hell." Materialistic, confident, and self-absorbed, Veranda callously rejects Kudzu's romantic overtures. His unrequited love for her inspires his creativity. Veranda, who takes shop class thinking it means shopping, ridicules Kudzu's moonlight serenades and love poems.

THE REVEREND WILL B. DUNN

Preacher Will B. Dunn is a major character in Bypass. Claiming "human relations is my life," Dunn provides humorous insights about his congregation at Bypass Baptist Church and admits, "Let's face it—the sheep are startin' to get on the shepherd's nerves!" His sermons deal with such topics as the Solid Gold Dancers. Dunn sometimes burps while presiding at wedding ceremonies and falls asleep during his own sermons. He sells videos of his sermons and delivers interesting wedding and funeral services with personal comments.

Dunn is always looking for heavenly signs that he should continue his ministry. He counsels Kudzu about the meaning of life and writes an advice column, "Tell It to the Preacher," for the *Bypass Bugle*, penning pithy and unhelpful replies. He also hosts the televised *The Reverend Will B. Dunn Show*, providing a toll-free number for love offerings. He gossips about his congregants and attends aerobic dance classes. Dunn's goal is to specialize in ministering to the wealthy, and Bubba Tadsworth secures his services. Dunn has a kinder, more reverential side, bringing Christmas gifts to five-year-old Tad Tadsworth when his father makes him work the night shift as a security guard at the mill.

Many American clergy embraced the Dunn character for highlighting that ministers are not perfect. Marlette received the Wilbur Award from the Religious Public Relations Council, and his character's adventures are often printed in church bulletins and religious periodicals.

Marlette introduced some new characters in the 1990s, such as Nasal T. Lardbottom, Kudzu's classmate and the "whitest white boy"; Mr. Goodvibes, a secular humanist and the school's guidance counselor; and Ida Mae Wombat, an aspiring dental hygienist who desires Kudzu. During the 1990 election campaign, Marlette drew Senator Jesse Helms of North Carolina as a character in *Kudzu*. Cartoon Helms waged the Cold War Separation Anxiety campaign against an international artistic conspiracy in response to Helms's real crusade against the National Endowment for the Arts. The strip featured Helms on the reelection campaign trail, nostalgically recalling that when he was younger, "art was sad-faced clowns, big-eyed children, and black velvet Elvises" and culture was "what the veterinarian scraped off the cow's tongue to check for hoof-and-mouth disease." These strips were controversial. Many North Carolina newspapers moved *Kudzu* to the opinion pages, and the *Raleigh News and Observer* canceled it. Readers demanded that the strip be resumed, and after Election Day, the newspaper printed all of the strips.

Kudzu comic strips have been published in numerous book collections. Marlette also adapted the comic strip into *Kudzu: A Southern Musical* in the 1990s. He died in a car accident in 2007, and *Kudzu* ended with his death.

Elizabeth D. Schafer

SEE ALSO: *Comics.*

BIBLIOGRAPHY

Marlette, Doug. *Just a Simple Country Preacher: More Wit and Wisdom of Reverend Will B. Dunn.* Nashville, TN: T. Nelson, 1985.

Marlette, Doug. *Chocolate Is My Life: Featuring Doris the Parakeet.* Atlanta, GA: Peachtree Publishers, 1987.

Marlette, Doug. *I Am Not a Televangelist!: The Continuing Saga of Reverend Will B. Dunn.* Atlanta, GA: Longstreet Press, 1988.

Marlette, Doug. *A Doublewide with a View: The* Kudzu *Chronicles.* Atlanta, GA: Longstreet Press, 1989.

Marlette, Doug. *In Your Face: A Cartoonist at Work.* Boston: Houghton Mifflin, 1991.

Marlette, Doug. *Even White Boys Get the Blues:* Kudzu*'s First Ten Years.* New York: Times Books, 1992.

Marlette, Doug. *Faux Bubba.* New York: Times Books, 1993.

Kuhn, Bowie *(1926–2007)*

A former lawyer, Bowie Kuhn served as Major League Baseball commissioner from 1969 to 1984. His achievements included raising baseball's attendance level, procuring lucrative television contracts, introducing divisional play in both leagues, and sponsoring night baseball in the World Series. Despite baseball's increasing profitability during this time, Kuhn often claimed that rising player salaries would bankrupt the sport. He was reluctant to become involved in the several player strikes that plagued his reign, though he did force owners to scrap plans for a 1976 preseason lockout.

While widely perceived as an "owner's commissioner," he suspended owners Ted Turner and George Steinbrenner for various infractions and feuded with Oakland owner Charlie Finley. When Finley attempted to unload superstars Joe Rudi, Vida Blue, and others for $3.5 million in cash, Kuhn nixed the sale, declaring that it was not in baseball's best interests. The owners did not renew Kuhn's contract, and he was succeeded by Peter Ueberroth. Kuhn died in 2007 and was posthumously inducted into the Baseball Hall of Fame in 2008.

Matt Kerr

SEE ALSO: *Baseball; Steinbrenner, George; Turner, Ted; World Series.*

BIBLIOGRAPHY

Kuhn, Bowie. *Hardball: The Education of a Baseball Commissioner.* Lincoln: University of Nebraska Press, 1997.

Porter, David, ed. "Kuhn, Bowie Kent." In *Biographical Dictionary of American Sports.* Westport, CT: Greenwood Press, 1987.

Kukla, Fran, and Ollie

Outside of Howdy Doody and the Muppets, Kukla and Ollie were probably the most popular and successful puppets ever to appear on television. Unlike Jim Henson's characters, however, they haven't endured or survived beyond the death of their creator.

Burr Tillstrom (1917–1985) first brought his quietly funny and eccentric hand puppets to TV in the autumn of 1947. Accompanied by a personable actress named Fran Allison, the mild-mannered yet egocentric dragon named Oliver and the enthusiastically nice, bald little fellow named Kukla (Russian for *doll*) made their debut on a show originally titled *Junior Jamboree*, which aired on a Chicago station. The title became *Kukla, Fran, and Ollie* early in 1949, and as the coaxial cable spread across the country, so too did the show. By 1951 the popular program was seen nationally at 7 p.m. weeknights. Initially intended for kids, the Kuklapolitans eventually attracted a large and enthusiastic audience of teenagers and adults as well.

For most of its run from 1949 onward, the show was done live and unscripted from the Merchandise Mart studios of NBC's Chicago station WNBQ. The set was simple, consisting of a sort of portable Punch & Judy theater. Allison stood in front of it, her head on a level with the tiny proscenium, and chatted with Ollie, the falsetto-voiced Kukla, and the other regulars in the puppet cast. These included Fletcher Rabbit, Cecil Bill, Beulah Witch (named after Beulah Zachary, the show's producer), and Madame Ooglepuss. Music was provided by pianist Jack Fascinato. Tillstrom did all the voices and manipulated all the puppets.

Kukla, Fran, and Ollie was casual and informal, the humor quiet and personal. It fit in with the aims and attitudes of some of the other early shows of what's been called the Chicago School—such as *Garroway at Large* and *Stud's Place*—in the days when television was very much a unique medium and quite a bit more relaxed than it later became. Now and then, Tillstrom and company would attempt something more ambitious, staging miniature musicals and the like, but for the most part the show concentrated on the conversations between Allison and the various facets of Tillstrom. Watching the show regularly had the effect of leading viewers to believe that the puppets were real. Even Allison was said to have operated under that illusion while she was on stage with them.

Tillstrom became interested in puppetry while still in his early teens. Kukla was one of his earliest puppets; Oliver J. Dragon and the others came later. After performing everywhere from nightclubs to department stores, he moved into television. When the *Junior Jamboree* got under way, Tillstrom added Allison to the mix. She had been active in Chicago radio for several years, singing in a trio, doing comedy with the offbeat Ransom Sherman, and playing the popular Aunt Fanny on the *Breakfast Club* show every weekday morning.

Kukla, Fran, and Ollie remained successful for roughly a decade. In 1950 reports indicated that Tillstrom had signed a million-dollar, five-year contract. Despite the broadcast success the show never managed to inspire much in the way of merchandising. In later years new episodes were done for syndication, and Tillstrom produced an occasional special. Kukla, Ollie, and the rest died with him in 1985; Allison died in 1989.

Ron Goulart

SEE ALSO: *Department Stores; Henson, Jim;* The Howdy Doody Show*; Live Television; The Muppets; Radio; Syndication; Television.*

BIBLIOGRAPHY

Brooks, Tim, and Earle Marsh. *The Complete Directory of Prime Time Network TV Shows.* New York: Ballantine Books, 1979.

Von Schilling, James Arthur. *The Magic Window: American Television, 1939–1953.* New York: Haworth Press, 2003.

Kung Fu

Described as an "Eastern Western," *Kung Fu* was one of the seminal television programs of the 1970s. Starring David Carradine as the character Kwai Chang Caine, a Shaolin priest who wandered about the American West during the mid-1800s, the show deals directly with issues of racism. *Kung Fu* chronicles the experiences of Chinese immigrants in the West and often aligns them with other marginalized communities, such as African Americans and the working class.

During the early 1970s the economic dominance of Hollywood was failing, allowing room for experimentation and the development of new television genres. Inspired by the success of the independently produced *Sweet Sweetback's Baadasssss Song* (1971), directed by Melvin Van Peebles, the mainstream industry co-opted the film's revolutionary aesthetic and politics to create Blaxploitation films—urban action movies featuring African American casts. Also influencing the industry were films by the world's third-largest producer, Hong Kong. Imported martial arts films such as *Five Fingers of Death* (1972) and *Fist of Fury* (1972) shared the top spots with *Super Fly* (1972) and *Coffy* (1973).

Emerging on the heels of the civil rights movement and the struggle for gender equality, these two genres found their biggest audiences with people of color in urban areas, for they featured nonwhite heroes fighting against oppression. In Blaxploitation films, the stars struggled against white domination and racism; in the Hong Kong martial arts films, the protagonists challenged colonialism and the Japanese. The popularity of these films was not lost on the television industry, for on February 22, 1972, a ninety-minute pilot for a new series was aired on the ABC network—*Kung Fu*, created by Ed Spielman and Howard Friedlander. The success of the pilot, which earned a 33 percent share of the prime-time audience, resulted in a one-hour drama series that was to last three seasons.

Kung Fu was an odd show for television because, as producer-writer John Furia Jr. states, it "lacked frantic, frenetic motion. Our characters moved and spoke slowly, and tersely. They used fewer words rather than more." The show also brought to mainstream American audiences precepts of Confucianism, Taoism, and Zen. Stylistically it also differed from other programs, for it made frequent use of flashbacks and used slow motion during its action sequences.

Kung Fu was frequently criticized because of its contradictory nature. Though the character of Caine was depicted as a nonviolent man, every episode features his use of martial arts in a physical altercation. Another problem was the casting. Martial arts star Bruce Lee, master of *jeet kune do*, was considered for the role, but it was given to white actor Carradine. Asian Americans protested the decision, but the show got around the issue by making Caine a person of mixed heritage. He was the son of a white American man and a Chinese woman.

Despite these issues, *Kung Fu* was a favorite among television viewers. The show was commercialized through products such as lunch boxes, and it caused an increase in interest of martial arts and Asian cultures.

Frances Gateward

SEE ALSO: *Blaxploitation Films; Civil Rights Movement; Hollywood; Lee, Bruce; Martial Arts; Television; The Western.*

BIBLIOGRAPHY

Anderson, Marina. *David Carradine: The Eye of My Tornado.* Montreal: Transit, 2010.

Pilato, Herbie J. *The Kung Fu Book of Caine: The Complete Guide to TV's First Mystical Eastern Western.* Boston: Tuttle, 1993.

Kutcher, Ashton *(1978–)*

Actor, producer, and model Christopher Ashton Kutcher was born on February 7, 1978, in Cedar Rapids, Iowa. He has a fraternal twin, Michael, and an older sister, Tausha. Kutcher's parents, Larry and Diane, worked on assembly lines at General Mills and Proctor Gamble, respectively. When Kutcher was thirteen, his parents divorced, and Michael had to have a heart transplant. Kutcher turned rebellious during his final years in high school but straightened out in time to study biochemical engineering at the University of Iowa.

In 1997 Kutcher won a Fresh Faces of Iowa contest, which provided him with a modeling contract in New York City. He garnered attention with ads for Calvin Klein and the Abercrombie and Fitch catalog. The following year, he was chosen to star as the amiable dimwit Michael Kelso in *That '70s Show*, which remained on the air until 2006. During this period he also cocreated the television show *Punk'd* (2003–2007), in which hidden cameras recorded celebrities as the butt of pranks. In 2005 Kutcher married Demi Moore, but the couple split in 2011. Also in 2011, Kutcher replaced bad boy Charlie Sheen in the CBS comedy *Two and a Half Men.*

That '70s Show proved to be important to Kutcher for both professional and personal reasons. It gave him his first real break as an actor, and it also provided him with a cadre of friends that endured past the show's end. He starred in a number of films during the run of *That '70s Show*, including the school comedy *Coming Soon* (1999) and the romantic comedy *Down to You* (2000). He took his first shot at drama with *Reindeer Games* (2000), a crime film starring Ben Affleck. Kutcher achieved leading-man status that same year playing a wacky stoner in the comedy *Dude, Where's My Car?* While critics trounced the film, it turned out to be a box-office success. He topped off a busy 2000 by being included on *People* magazine's "50 Most Beautiful People" list.

SUPERSTARDOM

Kutcher's movie *Texas Rangers* (2001) barely made a ripple, but his star continued to rise. The following year, *Teen People* magazine named him to its "25 Hottest Stars under 25" list. In 2003 he coproduced his first film, *My Boss's Daughter*, in which he also starred opposite Tara Reid. That same year he appeared in *Just Married* with Brittany Murphy. Off-screen Kutcher was romantically linked to Moore, who was fifteen years his senior.

Along with his friend Jason Goldberg, Kutcher became cocreator and producer in 2003 of *Punk'd*. The pranks on the show included scaring singer Justin Timberlake into thinking that he was in danger of losing his possessions to cover back taxes, convincing actress Eliza Dushku that she was being arrested for shoplifting, and persuading singer Pink that she was in trouble because her boyfriend had been running a motorcycle chop shop. Kutcher also created the reality show *Beauty and the Geek* (2005), which paired smart men with beautiful but not-so-intelligent females.

In 2004 Kutcher received a leading dramatic role, playing Evan in *The Butterfly Effect*. The sci-fi film, which focuses on Evan's ability to change traumatic events by traveling into his past, grossed nearly $60 million. In 2005 Kutcher starred in the romantic comedies *Guess Who* with Zoe Saldana and *A Lot Like Love* with Amanda Peet. He married Moore that same year and developed a close relationship with her three daughters, Rumer (born 1988), Scout (1991), and Tallulah (1994), who called Kutcher MOD (My Other Dad).

Kutcher turned to drama again in 2006, starring with Kevin Costner in the coast guard adventure *The Guardian* and appearing in *Bobby*, about the 1968 assassination of presidential candidate Robert F. Kennedy. He also voiced the mule deer Elliot in the animated *Open Season*. Kutcher returned to romantic comedy in 2008, playing opposite Cameron Diaz in *What Happens in Vegas* but also appeared with Michelle Pfeiffer in a drama, *Personal Effects*, about a wrestler caught up in a search for his sister's killer. That same year he produced the television show *Miss Guided*, which lived up to its name and was canceled after one season. In 2009 he appeared as a womanizer in *Spread* with Anne Heche. By 2010 Kutcher had settled back into romantic comedies, appearing in *Killers* opposite Katherine Heigl and *Valentine's Day* with Jessica Alba. His career had blossomed to the point where, in 2010, *Time* magazine included him on its "100 Most Influential People" list.

UPS AND DOWNS

Ever the overachiever, Kutcher continued to spread his wings in different directions. He briefly returned to modeling, serving as the model for Pepe Jeans London in 2008 and appearing on a Brazilian runway for the Colcci label in 2011. He also invested in two Los Angeles restaurants, Geisha House and Dolce. Kutcher and Moore established the Demi & Ashton Foundation to eradicate child sex slavery globally, and he became a creative directive for Ooma, which sells telephone devices, and a cofounder of Katalyst, a studio for social media. Furthermore, Kutcher has been a major presence on Twitter, becoming the first celebrity to reach one million followers.

Although 2011 was a banner year for Kutcher professionally, it brought a major crisis to his personal life. On the positive side, he was chosen to replace Sheen on *Two and a Half Men*, beating out possibilities such as Hugh Grant for the role. Kutcher also appeared in Garry Marshall's ensemble comedy *New Year's Eve* and starred with Natalie Portman in *No Strings Attached*. On the negative side, Kutcher's marriage to Moore unraveled after six years.

Moore went into a downward spiral that culminated with hospitalization in November 2011 and a stint in rehab. Kutcher, meanwhile, was photographed with a new girlfriend in tow, though he remained close to Moore's daughters. *Two and a Half Men* drew an impressive twenty-eight million viewers for Kutcher's debut, but that number wound up dropping to just over fourteen million. Still, the program's ratings were higher than in Sheen's final season. It was another step forward for the overachiever from Iowa.

Elizabeth Rholetter Purdy

SEE ALSO: *Animated Films; Costner, Kevin; Divorce; Marshall, Garry; Moore, Demi; MTV;* Punk'd; *Television; Twitter.*

BIBLIOGRAPHY

Anderegg, David. *Nerds: Who They Are and Why We Need More of Them*. New York: Jeremy P. Tarcher/Penguin, 2007.

Edwards, Gavin. "Ashton Kutcher." *Rolling Stone*, May 29, 2003.

Richardson, Chris. "Ashton Kutcher Replaces Charlie Sheen on *Two and a Half Men*." *Christian Science Monitor*, May 14, 2011.

Weinman, Jaime J. "The Ashton Kutcher Phenomenon." *Maclean's*. August 15, 2011.

Kwan, Michelle *(1980–)*

Michelle Kwan is often called the best all-around figure skater of her generation, with a particular emphasis on artistry. Extremely popular, she most resembles ice queens Peggy Fleming and Kristi Yamaguchi, successfully combining grace and athletic ability as well as achieving artistic and financial success. Her consistent excellence and precocity made her a star; in 1994 a thirteen year-old Kwan stepped easily into the vacuum left by Nancy Kerrigan's turning professional.

Initially, Kwan was presented as an "exotic" but found her stride as an interpreter of classical pieces. She went on to win five World Championships (1996, 1998, 2000, 2001, and 2003); a silver medal at the 1998 Olympic games in Nagano, Japan; and a bronze medal at the 2002 Olympic games in Salt Lake City, Utah. Following a number of injuries, Kwan withdrew from the 2006 Olympic games and has done little competitive skating since then, preferring to focus on her graduate work at the Fletcher School of Law and Diplomacy at Tufts University. She graduated with a master's degree in 2011.

Mary Hess

SEE ALSO: *Fleming, Peggy; Kerrigan, Nancy; Olympics; Skating.*

BIBLIOGRAPHY

Brennan, Christine. *Inside Edge: A Revealing Journey into the Secret World of Figure Skating*. New York: Anchor Books, 1997.

Brennan, Christine. *Edge of Glory: The Inside Story of the Quest for Figure Skating's Gold Medals*. New York: Scribner, 1998.

Downey, Mike. "Real Life Becomes a Short Program." *Los Angeles Times*, February 20, 1998.

Ryan, Joan. *Little Girls in Pretty Boxes: The Making and Breaking of Elite Gymnasts and Figure Skaters*. New York, Doubleday, 1995.

Tresniowski, Alex. "Belle on the Ball." *People*, November, 1997.

L. L. Cool J. *(1968–)*

L. L. Cool J. is a rap singer, an actor, and an author. In 1984, at the age of sixteen, he signed a recording contract with Def Jam Records. Known ever after for his lyrical braggadocio and rap egotism, L. L. Cool J. (Ladies Love Cool James) would go on to split his time between music and acting.

L. L. Cool J. was born James Todd Smith in Queens, New York, in 1968. In 1985, when he was seventeen years old, Def Jam released his first album, *Radio*, and it went platinum. One of the songs on the album, "I Can't Live without My Radio," is featured in *Krush Groove* (1985), a movie in which L. L. makes a cameo appearance. In 1986 he was cast in *Wildcats* and wrote the theme song for the movie.

L. L.'s second album, *Bigger and Deffer* (1987), also went platinum and includes the song "I Need Love," a slow, sexy love song that is credited as rap's first ballad. His third album, *Walking with a Panther*, had less success. One song from the album, "Goin' Back to Cali," is included on the soundtrack for the movie *Less than Zero* (1987), based on the novel by Bret Easton Ellis and starring Andrew McCarthy.

In 1990 Def Jam released L. L.'s fourth album, *Mama Said Knock You Out*, named after his grandmother's advice to "knock out" his critics. It went on to become his best-selling album and made L. L. a phenomenon in the pop world as well as in hip-hop. He released four singles off the album and won the Grammy Award for Best Rap Solo Performance in 1991. Hot off the success of *Mama Said Knock You Out*, L. L. performed at President Bill Clinton's first inauguration in 1993 and was featured on an episode of the television series *Rockumentary* on MTV. He was also the first black recording artist to appear on *MTV Unplugged*, another MTV television series, where he performed an acoustic live set.

In the mid-1990s L. L. began to split his time between music and acting, working on movies and recording albums concurrently. In 1995 he starred in the sitcom *In the House*, while simultaneously releasing his double-platinum album *Mr. Smith*. The sitcom ran for five seasons; the album spawned three Top 10 hits. In 1996 L. L. won his second Grammy Award for "Hey Lover," a duet with the group Boyz II Men. In 1997 he received an MTV Video Vanguard Award and became a published author with the release of his autobiography *I Make My Own Rules*.

L. L. was also busy appearing in movies, including *Halloween H20* (1998), *Any Given Sunday* (1999), *Deep Blue Sea* (1999), *S.W.A.T.* (2003), and *Last Holiday* (2006). In 2009 he took on the role of Sam Hanna, an agent with the Naval Criminal Investigative Service in the television show *NCIS: Los Angeles*, a spin-off of the immensely popular *NCIS*. Musically, he continued to release album after album, all of which appeared within the Top 20 on the Billboard 200 chart and went either gold or platinum. In 2000 he celebrated his fifteen years in the recording industry with the release of *G.O.A.T.: Featuring James T. Smith, The Greatest of All Time*, which debuted at number one. In 2002 he released a children's book, *And the Winner Is*, and in 2007 he published his workout regime in *LL Cool J's Platinum Workout: Sculpt Your Best Body Ever with Hollywood's Fittest Star*. He published a follow-up in 2010 titled *LL Cool J's Platinum 360 Diet and Lifestyle: A Full-Circle Guide to Developing Your Mind, Body, and Soul*.

In 2011 L. L. was honored with an I Am Hip-Hop Icon Award for lifetime achievement at the annual BET (Black Entertainment Television) Awards, as well as winning an NAACP (National Association for the Advancement of Colored People) Image Award for Outstanding Actor in a Drama Series for his role on *NCIS: Los Angeles*. In 2012 he hosted the Grammy Awards and started the show with a prayer for singer Whitney Houston, who had died the day before the ceremony. In addition to being a musician, an actor, and an author, L. L. is a businessman. In 2008 he cofounded Boomdizzle, an online music community that features a virtual studio that allows musicians all over the world to record together in real time. L. L. met his wife, Simone, in 1987, and they married in 1995. The couple has four children.

Nathan Abrams

SEE ALSO: *Ellis, Bret Easton; Grammy Awards; Hip-Hop; Houston, Whitney; MTV; Rap; Sitcom; Television; Top 40.*

BIBLIOGRAPHY

Fernando, S. H., Jr. *The New Beats: Exploring the Music Culture and Attitudes of Hip-Hop*. Edinburgh: Payback Press, 1995.

L. L. Cool J. and Karen Hunter. *I Make My Own Rules*. New York: St. Martin's Press, 1997.

L. L. Cool J. *And the Winner Is*. New York: Scholastic, 2002.

L. L. Cool J.; David Honig; and Jeff O'Connell. *LL Cool J's Platinum Workout: Sculpt Your Best Body Ever with Hollywood's Fittest Star*. Emmaus, PA: Rodale, 2007.

L. L. Cool J.; David Honig; Chris Palmer; et al. *LL Cool J's Platinum 360 Diet and Lifestyle: A Full-Circle Guide to Developing Your Mind, Body, and Soul*. Emmaus, PA: Rodale, 2010.

Nelson, Havelock, and Michael A. Gonzales. *Bring the Noise: A*

Guide to Rap Music and Hip-Hop Culture. New York: Harmony Books, 1991.

Stoute, Steve. *The Tanning of America: How Hip-Hop Created a Culture That Rewrote the Rules of the New Economy*. New York: Gotham Books, 2011.

"La Bamba"

Ritchie Valens (1941–1959) merged traditional Mexican music with rock and roll when he recorded "La Bamba" in 1958. Since then, his version of "La Bamba" has been recorded more than 150 times in the United States. The lasting influence of Valens's music after his tragic death in a plane crash was reinforced by the aptly titled movie *La Bamba* (1987), which chronicles the brief life of the Chicano singer. The film's soundtrack version of "La Bamba," recorded by Los Lobos, rekindled mainstream interest in the song.

"La Bamba" has been recorded by artists ranging from Trini Lopez (1966) and the Plugz (1979) to the Rice University Marching Band and the Mormon Tabernacle Choir. The rhythmic history of "La Bamba" places it as a *son jarocho*, meaning a musical form of the *jarocho*, the mixed race of people from the eastern coastal region of Mexico. "La Bamba" is also the name of a dance that dates back to the Mexican colonial period and stems from a musical tradition merging African, Caribbean, and indigenous cultures from the southern part of the state of Veracruz. The *sones jarochos* are performed on stringed instruments such as a small harp and small eight-string and four-string guitars.

Despite its long history and many different versions, "La Bamba" is inextricably linked to the emergence of Chicano rock in America.

Rafaela Castro

SEE ALSO: *Big Bopper; Holly, Buddy; Los Lobos; Rock and Roll; Valens, Ritchie.*

BIBLIOGRAPHY

Guevara, Ruben. "The View from the Sixth Street Bridge: The History of Chicano Rock." In *The First Rock & Roll Confidential Report*, ed. Dave Marsh, 113–126. New York: Pantheon Books, 1985.

Holscher, Louis M.; Celestino Fernandez; and Laura L. Cummings. "From Local Tradition to International Phenomenon: La Bamba." In *Renato Rosaldo Lecture Series*, vol. 7. Tucson: Mexican American Studies & Research Center, University of Arizona, 1991.

Loza, Steven J. "Origins, Form, and Development of the Son Jarocho: Veracruz, Mexico." *Aztlan, International Journal of Chicano Studies Research* 13, nos. 1, 2 (1982): 257–274.

L.A. Law

A groundbreaking prime-time television series, *L.A. Law* emerged in 1986 from the stable that had brought a new veracity to ensemble series drama with *Hill Street Blues* (1981–1987). Setting his new show in a high-powered law office, trend-setting producer Steven Bochco (and cowriter Terry Louise Fisher), rooted the episodes firmly in character-driven scripts of intelligence, authenticity, and wit, while expanding on the concept of multiple story lines. Gone were the idealized television attorneys of yesteryear such as Perry Mason. This team, played by a large A-grade cast, presented a realistic cross-section of the likable, the insecure, the authoritative, and the downright smarmy. Many of the situations straddled several episodes and involved a seamless blend of office politics, love affairs, or sexual misadventure, played out parallel with the firm's legal concerns, ethical dilemmas, and courtroom appearances. The fundamentally serious approach was leavened with doses of witty dialogue and occasionally outrageous absurdities.

Because the law firm dealt in multiple areas of the law, the cases were able to legitimately range from divorce to murder and to engage a variety of complex contemporary issues, from date rape and child abuse to capital punishment, outing of homosexuals, and voluntary euthanasia. *L.A. Law* ran from 1986 to 1994. It collected twenty Emmy Award nominations in its first season and won four Best Drama Emmys, as well as Golden Globes, Television Critics Association Awards, and a Peabody Award. Most significantly, its approach and narrative style paved the way for the even more compelling relationships and finely honed characterizations of *ER* in the 1990s.

Sandra Garcia-Myers

SEE ALSO: *Bochco, Steven; Emmy Awards;* ER*;* Hill Street Blues*; Outing; Perry Mason; Television.*

BIBLIOGRAPHY

Asimow, Michael, and Shannon Mader. *Law and Popular Culture: A Course Book*. New York: P. Lang, 2004.

Marc, David, and Robert J. Thompson. *Prime Time, Prime Movers: From "I Love Lucy" to "L.A. Law"—America's Greatest TV Shows and the People Who Created Them*. Boston: Little, Brown, 1992.

Thompson, Robert J. *Television's Second Golden Age: From "Hill Street Blues" to "ER"*. New York: Continuum, 1996.

Labor Unions

Throughout much of the twentieth century, the American labor movement has been a dynamic force for social change. The struggle for workplace representation and social equality has reshaped much of the American political landscape. Yet the cultural impact and significance of labor unions goes far beyond the political action of shop-floor organization. Unions, both through their actions and imagery, have deeply influenced American popular culture. At different times and in different ways, workers have used unions to define their own sense of individual and collective identity. Unions have been at the forefront of defining American working-class masculinity. They have struggled with the issues of gender relations both within their organizations and with their imagery and rhetoric. Labor organizations have also served as both standard bearers of racial separation and forces for racial integration.

While the labor movement has helped to create a forum for social action and some union members have been at the forefront of other social movements, unions have also been a force of conservatism and moderation, as well as continuing an identity with whiteness. Thus, the cultural impact of unions on American popular culture is multifaceted and conflicted. Through their own actions and the representations of unions in American film, music, television, and literature, labor organizations have served as a focal point for the construction of a sense of community. While this community provided some with a collective identity and a sense of belonging, it also defined whom the community accepted and who remained outside of it.

OVERCOMING RACIAL DIVISION

Racial and ethnic divisions played a significant role in labor organizing during the nineteenth century. In many ways, ethnic communities and similarities fostered organization within that ethnicity; for instance, Irish American workers were likely to join Irish labor unions. However, such actions opened the door for company managers to play one ethnicity or race off another. Capital broke the postwar strikes of 1919 with such actions. Because of their insulated ethnic and racial communities, workers were not able to transcend the divisions that separated them.

Following 1919, both capital and labor leaders tried to learn from their mistakes. Seeing the strength of ethnic-based organizations, businesses tried to diversify their workforces and combine different ethnicities and races. Such workplace interaction, however, only assisted the development of transethnic and transracial organizing. With the collapse of the economy in 1929, ethnic banks, stores, and other pillars of ethnic cohesion collapsed. As the last vestiges of the ethnic community went bankrupt, workers turned to each other and to their unions to reestablish a sense of community. In 1935 the National Labor Relations Act, also known as the Wagner Act, was put into law. It paved the way for workers to form unions with the federal government overseeing labor relations.

Cesar Chavez and Striking Grape Pickers. *Cesar Chavez, lower left, poses with grape pickers in California in support of the United Farm Workers Union in March 1968.* ARTHUR SCHATZ/CONTRIBUTOR/TIME LIFE PICTURES/GETTY IMAGES.

Such transethnic and transracial organizations proved to be the backbone of the Congress of Industrial Organizations (CIO). The new labor congress based itself on the concept of clear class consciousness. Workers would have standing in the industrial union regardless of skill, trade, ethnicity, race, or gender. Although later developments would prove racism and sexism a persistent problem for the labor movement, the CIO's commitment to transracial organization remains significant. Many CIO members in the late 1930s truly believed that they had overcome racial and ethnic divisions; however, the career of A. Philip Randolph and the struggle of the Brotherhood of Sleeping Car Porters show that the internal conflict over racial identity remained an important part of the American labor movement.

By the first couple of decades of the twentieth century, Pullman sleeping cars had become the epitome of luxury in railroad travel. An essential part of the Pullman experience was the service of the Pullman porter. Always an African American male, the porter's job was to see to every need of the passenger. When these porters tried to organize into the Brotherhood of Sleeping Car Porters (BSCP) beginning in the mid-1920s, they encountered resistance not only from the Pullman Company but also from the predominately white CIO.

The Pullman workers appointed as their leader A. Philip Randolph, a veteran civil rights advocate. As president of the BSCP, Randolph took on much of the leadership of the CIO, pointing out to them the hypocrisy of denying admission to a black union. White unionists' backlash against Randolph and the BSCP showed the persistence of racism within the labor movement. For many white workers, their union jobs helped to define them not only as workers but as whites as well. A white organization that pushed black workers aside reinforced racial identities and hierarchies.

The porters' selection of Randolph to lead their organizing drive demonstrates the important connections that existed between labor and other social movements. Before he joined the BSCP, Randolph worked for the National Association for the Advancement of Colored People (NAACP). Even after becoming the union president, he remained closely tied to the campaign for civil rights. Randolph and other black trade unionists were an important part of the 1941 March on Washington Movement. By threatening a mass demonstration in Washington, D.C., Randolph forced President Franklin Roosevelt to open wartime production jobs to black workers.

Randolph remained a major figure in the civil rights movement and was a prominent figure on the March on Washington in 1963 led by Martin Luther King Jr. Trade union activity helped to define a conservative white identity, and racial minorities used labor organizations to foster racial pride. Thus, when African American garbage men struck in Memphis, Tennessee, during 1968, they walked their picket lines with the simple slogan "I am a man."

Likewise, Chicano farmworkers looked to labor organizations to claim their sense of self-worth and ethnic identity. In the mid-1960s the United Farm Workers (UFW), led by Cesar Chavez, organized in the fields of California, where large producers hired mostly migrant farmworkers to harvest their crops. The farmworkers organized mostly to protect themselves from poor wages, dangerous work, and hazardous chemicals, yet UFW demonstrations were full of references to Chicano culture and racial pride. Much like the Irish or Polish labor unions of the late nineteenth century, Mexican American ethnic cohesiveness fostered labor organization and vice versa.

The response within the AFL-CIO and other trade unions was mixed. Like the campaign of the BSCP, the rise of the UFW threatened the racial identity of many white trade unionists. The International Brotherhood of Teamsters, for example, launched a campaign to both unionize delivery drivers in the California fields and to break the strength of the UFW. In this way, racial divisions and the use of unions to promote racial identity remained a contested aspect of the American labor movement.

CONFRONTING GENDER BIAS

In addition to race, the labor movement has a conflicted past on gender relations and gender identity. For most male workers, union membership defined the nature of working-class masculinity. The campaign for a "family wage" demonstrates how deep this masculinity lies in labor organizations. For most of the twentieth century, a principal demand of labor organizations has been the family wage. This denotes that the company should pay workers enough to support a family, but it also suggests that a man should make enough money to prevent his wife from working. The family wage ideal suggests that work is a masculine space where women should not be present.

Likewise, the imagery of labor and labor organizations revolved around the masculine nature of work. Artists often depicted industrial labor as a muscular man engaged in physical labor. When the AFL and the CIO joined in 1955, their official logo became two very muscular arms shaking hands. The images of Rosie the Riveter and other women working in wartime plants during World War II reinforced the masculine ideal of labor. Propaganda posters show these women as muscular, tough, and "man" enough to do the job. Such masculine imagery conflicted heavily with the reality of female labor. Despite female participation in union activity, however, labor identity remained centered upon an ideal of masculinity.

With the rise of industrial unionism and the decline of ethnically based communities in the 1930s, labor unions came to represent more than just a source of racial and gender identity. In many ways, union membership and union activities became the focal point of communities and provided members with a sense of belonging and camaraderie. Organizations such as union bowling teams and softball leagues, along with activities such as dances at union halls and union picnics, brought union members together outside of the shop floor. Through such actions, the members of the union became a sort of extended family and promoted what historian Liz Cohen calls in *Making a New Deal* a "culture of unity." Such an extension of union activity enhanced labor's impact on American popular culture. Unions began to take part in civic activities that were outside the scope of their particular point of production.

From such civic activities emerged the concept of the "union town." Some cities became known for the strength of their unions as well as the influence that those unions and union members held in that town. Likewise, the culture of solidarity enhanced the impact of the union on family structures. As children attended union picnics or participated in parades, they became deeply aware of being part of a union family. The prospect of growing up and joining the union became, for working-class males, a rite of passage into American masculinity. The songs of Bruce Springsteen perhaps portray this transition best. Springsteen suggests that the moment of entrance into working-class manhood was the day a young man received his first union card. Once a part of the union, he could then enjoy the communal identity that unions provided.

REPRESENTING UNIONS

Springsteen is not the only example of union imagery in American popular culture. On the contrary, the images of labor, workers, and unions have been consistent in American culture. Much like unions themselves, popular culture has been conflicted over the presentation of union themes and union imagery. Many of the representations have focused on unions as organizations devoted to fighting social inequalities and striving for workplace equality. Yet there exists within American popular culture a common depiction of unions and union members as backward-looking conservatives or exploitative, corrupt manipulators. Both images occur with frequency in American popular culture, often present within the same film or other cultural representation.

The first real presence of labor imagery in popular culture was probably the proletarian novel of the twentieth century. Extremely popular for the first few decades of the century, proletarian novels emerged from the traditions of muckraking journalism. Often these novelists used their work to expose the exploitative nature and conditions of the American working class. Because of this purpose, unions commonly held a revered position within the novels as organizations formed by the workers to tackle the problems of large-scale industrial capitalism.

Upton Sinclair presents an excellent example of the proletarian novelist. Arriving in Chicago at the beginning of the twentieth century, Sinclair announced that he intended to write the *Uncle Tom's Cabin* of the labor movement. Sinclair's book *The Jungle* (1906) details the working environment and living conditions in the meat-packing industry in Chicago. Many attribute the creation of governmental regulations and food safety laws to his descriptions of meat packing. Sinclair continued his descriptions of working-class life and union organization in later works such as *King Coal* (1917) and *Oil!* (1927).

In a similar fashion, John Steinbeck details the movement of migrant workers from Oklahoma to the fields of California in *The Grapes of Wrath* (1939). Through his description of the Joad family, Steinbeck presents a family struggling to stay together despite the hardships of the Depression and the exploitation of the California farmers. He also creates the character of Tom Joad, who quickly becomes a symbol of the idealistic union organizer. Like Sinclair, Steinbeck offers—in works such as *The Grapes of Wrath* and *Cannery Row* (1945)—descriptions of working-class life and the struggle of workers to gain, through unionization, a measure of respect.

In his *USA* trilogy (1930, 1932, 1936), John Dos Passos takes a slightly different approach. Several characters within his works are members of the Industrial Workers of the World (IWW), but Dos Passos does not offer detailed descriptions of workers' lives. Rather he uses union members as foils for the rest of his characters. Dos Passos, Steinbeck, and Sinclair have important similarities. Each of them was an advocate and supporter of the labor movement, and their representations of unions in their works portray their politics.

Proletarian novelists aimed their work mostly toward a middle-class audience. Yet in the first several decades of the century, a nationalized consumer economy emerged that was capable of creating mass cultural images through film and music. For the first time, the working class became the audience for much of American mass culture. Thus, as the working class began to receive the images of unions and union activities, labor and labor-related themes came to dominate American culture.

In the genre of film, Hollywood started to create movies about working people and their organizations. These included the film version of Steinbeck's novel *The Grapes of Wrath* (1940), starring Henry Fonda as Tom Joad. However, Hollywood did not always follow the direction of the proletarian novelists. Instead, the movie industry presents conflicted imagery of unions and union organizations. Unions and union members come to represent both social possibility and conservative regression.

In addition to the characterization of Tom Joad, there is the story of corrupt unionism in *On the Waterfront* (1954). In the film, Marlon Brando portrays worker Terry Malloy's fight against a corrupt union boss who rules the organization through violence and fear. Yet the imagery within *On the Waterfront* is conflicted as well. On one hand, the film presents unions and union leadership as a corrupt and dictatorial organization, yet underlying Brando's fight is the notion that a worker's union is something worth fighting for.

For the most part, Hollywood films during the early Cold War were rooted in anticommunism and antiradicalism. The Hollywood blacklist prevented many filmmakers from making sympathetic labor films. The exception is the production of *Salt of the Earth* (1954). Made by a blacklisted crew and starring many amateur actors, *Salt of the Earth* tells the story of Chicano miners in their struggle to maintain their solidarity and bring some measure of safety to their labor. Such a depiction of a successful strike and class-based solidarity was uncommon for its time.

Hollywood soon returned to stories celebrating workers and their desire for union organization, such as *Norma Rae* (1979), starring Sally Field. In the film, Field plays a textile worker who struggles, against seemingly insurmountable odds, to establish a union in her plant. Likewise, *Matewan* (1987) offers a story of a union organizer and the miners who organize transracially to battle the mining company. Even Sylvester Stallone took a spin as a tough but idealistic Teamster organizer in *F.I.S.T* (1978). More recently, films such as *Bread and Roses* (2000) *Live Nude Girls Unite!* (2000), and *North Country* (2005) have explored the impact that women workers have had not only on their individual industries (janitorial services, exotic dancing, and mining, respectively), but on organized labor as a whole.

Yet for every sympathetic representation, there are also films such as *Hoffa* (1992) that offer a darker picture of union activity. As Jimmy Hoffa, Jack Nicholson presents a labor leader who rules the Teamsters through violence, corruption, and absolute power. In *Hoffa*, workers only protest when the leadership tells them to do so. Hoffa himself, however, does remain a semisympathetic character because he suggests that everything he does is in the interest of the membership. Ultimately, though, Nicholson's Hoffa is closer to the representation of the working class in television. From Jackie Gleason in *The Honeymooners* (1955–1956) to Archie Bunker in *All in the Family* (1971–1979) and Homer Simpson in *The Simpsons* (1989–), television has represented working-class males as self-centered conservatives who are lovable yet ignorantly out of touch with the rest of society. The documentary *Class Dismissed: How TV Frames the Working Class* (2005) considers the effect of such depictions on the psyche of middle-class workers, arguing that they serve to temper the enthusiasm and solidarity of union members and to discourage nonunion laborers from organizing.

Beyond movies and literature, the labor movement's greatest cultural legacy is probably the labor troubadour. Many labor organizations have used folksongs and folk music as a way of promoting their cause. From this emerged the tradition of socially conscious folk and rock music. The first well-known labor troubadour of the twentieth century was Joe Hill (1879–1915). As an organizer for the IWW, Hill wrote songs relating the desire for union representation. Convicted for murder on questionable charges, Hill was executed in Utah in 1915. Since then, his name and his songs have become an important part of union mythology.

Taking up where Hill left off, Woody Guthrie (1912–1967) became the voice of the labor movement in the 1930s. Through songs such as "This Land Is Your Land," Guthrie expressed not only the struggles of southern migrant labor but also suggested to his listeners the importance of joining a union and claiming the rights of an American citizen. Similarly, Pete Seeger's (1919–) roots lie in the traditions of the labor union folksinger. Like Guthrie, Seeger sang of the pride of working and the desire for equality and union representation. Yet Seeger and his style of folk music achieved an influential popularity within American culture, eventually leading to socially conscious folksingers such as Bob Dylan (1941–), Joan Baez (1941–), and Billy Bragg (1957–).

Labor's influence on music does not end with folk music. Rather, several rock-and-roll artists explore in their music the impact of working-class origins. Perhaps the best example of this is the music of Springsteen (1949–). Through stories about the acquisition of a union card or the closing down of the local textile mill, labor unions and working-class culture represent a major part of his music. In songs such as "My Hometown" (on *Born in the USA* [1984]) or "Youngstown" (on *The Ghost of Tom Joad* [1995]), Springsteen confronts the meaning of union membership and working-class culture in a deindustrializing society. He even evoked the memory of past labor imagery by titling one of his albums *The Ghost of Tom Joad* after the Steinbeck character.

AN UNCERTAIN FUTURE

Because of such imagery in music, films, and other cultural media, unions and the American working class remain an important aspect of American popular culture. In the twenty-first century, however, unions have faced unprecedented resistance from wealthy capitalists and right-wing activists. What began in 1981, when conservative president Ronald Reagan (who had, ironically, led a strike among Hollywood actors in 1952) emboldened antiunion employers by firing nearly 13,000 striking members of the Professional Air Traffic Controllers Organization (PATCO) and replacing them with workers who were willing to endure longer hours and lower wages, led to a precipitous decline in union membership and activity: unions have gone from representing nearly a third of workers in the 1950s to just 20 percent of workers in 1983, and only around 12 percent in 2012. Such decreases have been exacerbated by the economic downturn of 2008, during which conservative pundits have largely blamed "greedy" unions for high unemployment rates, despite record corporate profits during the same period.

In 2011 Wisconsin governor Scott Walker took such rhetoric to new heights, signing into law a bill that stripped collective bargaining rights from the state's 200,000-plus public employees, citing the 1981 firings as inspiration and calling labor union organization an "expensive entitlement" rather than a right. The law triggered massive protests from workers and left-leaning politicians, and, despite parts of the law being struck down by federal courts, Walker became just the third governor in U.S. history to face a recall election, which he survived. Even in the face of staunch resistance, conservative politicians in Arizona, as well as in Ohio and Indiana, advanced similar laws in 2012.

With middle-class incomes stagnating and more and more workers finding it difficult to make ends meet in the twenty-first century, labor unions are perhaps more important to the future of America than during any other period since the Great Depression. Even in the face of unprecedented resistance, the industrial worker is never far from the American cultural mind, and industrial labor is closely tied to union membership and the forms of communal organizations and identities that unions create.

S. Paul O'Hara

SEE ALSO: All in the Family*; Baez, Joan; Blacklisting; Brando, Marlon; Chavez, Cesar; Civil Rights Movement; Communism; Dylan, Bob; Field, Sally; Folk Music; Gleason, Jackie;* The Grapes of Wrath*; The Great Depression; Guthrie, Woody; Hollywood; King, Martin Luther, Jr.; March on Washington; Nicholson, Jack;* On the Waterfront*; Rock and Roll; Seeger, Pete;* The Simpsons*; Sinclair, Upton; Springsteen, Bruce; Steinbeck, John; World War I; World War II.*

BIBLIOGRAPHY

Asher, Herbert B.; Eric S. Heberlig; Randall B. Ripley; et al. *American Labor Unions in the Electoral Arena.* Lanham, MD: Rowman & Littlefield, 2001.

Cohen, Lizabeth. *Making a New Deal: Industrial Workers in Chicago, 1919–1939.* New York: Cambridge University Press, 1990.

Denning, Michael. *The Cultural Front: The Laboring of American Culture in the Twentieth Century.* New York: Verso, 1996.

Dudley, Kathryn Marie. *The End of the Line: Lost Jobs, New Lives in Postindustrial America.* Chicago: University of Chicago Press, 1994.

Faue, Elizabeth. *Community of Suffering: Men, Women, and the Labor Movement in Minneapolis, 1915–1945.* Chapel Hill: University of North Carolina Press, 1991.

Lichtenstein, Nelson. *Labor's War at Home: The CIO in World War II.* New York: Cambridge University Press, 1982.

Lichtenstein, Nelson. *The Most Dangerous Man in Detroit: Walter Reuther and the Fate of American Labor.* New York: Basic Books, 1995.

Lipsitz, George. *Rainbow at Midnight: Labor and Culture in the 1940s.* Urbana: University of Illinois Press, 1994.

Meier, August, and Elliot Rudwick. *Black Detroit and the Rise of the UAW.* New York: Oxford University Press, 1979.

Milkman, Ruth, ed. *Women, Work, and Protest: A Century of U.S. Women's Labor History.* Boston: Routledge and Kegan Paul, 1985.

Roediger, David R., and Elizabeth D. Esch. *The Production of Difference: Race and the Management of Labor in U.S. History.* New York: Oxford University Press, 2012.

Wagner, Viqi. *Labor Unions.* Detroit, MI: Greenhaven Press, 2008.

Zieger, Robert. *The CIO, 1935–1955.* Chapel Hill: University of North Carolina Press, 1995.

Lacoste Shirts

The Lacoste sports shirt, made of cotton pique and bearing a logo in the shape of an alligator, was named for its creator, tennis pro Rene "The Crocodile" Lacoste. The shirt was worn as a fashion statement in the early 1980s by those sporting the "preppy" look, which sought to duplicate the style favored by those attending the Ivy League schools of the East Coast. In the early 1990s Lacoste shirts enjoyed a brief resurgence of popularity among those who wished to satirize the fashion. Since then, the shirts have continued to sell as a distinctive brand, leaving their preppy identification behind as the company pushes its ecologically oriented logo campaign, "Save Your Logo," in which Lacoste funds efforts in Nepal and Colombia to protect the alligator depicted on the shirts' distinctive logo.

S. Naomi Finkelstein

SEE ALSO: *Advertising; Ivy League; Preppy; Retro Fashion.*

BIBLIOGRAPHY

Flippin, Royce. *Save an Alligator, Shoot a Preppie.* New York: Visual Library, 1981.

Hartmann, Lisa. *The Preppy Handbook.* New York: Workman Publishing, 1980.

Ladd, Alan *(1913–1964)*

A compact tough-guy actor, Alan Ladd arrived at stardom by way of a pair of film noir movies in the early 1940s. After nearly a decade of small parts, he was given the role of Raven in Paramount Pictures' *This Gun for Hire* (1942), a somewhat toned down adaptation of the Graham Greene thriller. Although he didn't get star billing—that went to Robert Preston and Veronica Lake—Ladd stole the picture, playing a sort of existentialist hired assassin. He managed to make the cold, doomed character unsettling and yet appealing. The scenes between him and Lake suggested to the studio that they would make a bankable romantic team, and before his first major film was released, Ladd and Lake were working together again in *The Glass Key* (1942), a dark, violent version of Dashiell Hammett's novel. Brian Donlevy was the ostensible star, but Ladd was again the one who got most of the attention, as well as thousands of fan letters.

Both films, which hit theaters fairly close together, got good reviews and did well at the box office (*This Gun for Hire* grossed $12 million). From 1942 to 1964 Ladd appeared in nearly fifty more movies. Many were run-of-the-mill action pictures, but included on the list were *The Blue Dahlia* (1946), *The Great Gatsby* (1949), and *Shane* (1953).

Born in Arkansas, Ladd grew up in Southern California, where he attended North Hollywood High. He was interested in acting early on and also excelled at track and swimming. His mother committed suicide before his career took off, a fact he kept hidden throughout his lifetime. In 1939 agent Sue Carol, a moderately successful movie actress in the late 1920s and early 1930s and ten years Ladd's senior, became his agent. She began to get him movie work at various studios.

Ladd played small parts in *Rulers of the Sea* (1939) at Paramount, the first *Green Hornet* (1940) serial at Universal, and somewhat larger parts in a string of Poverty Row productions. He also can be heard, though only dimly seen, in the early scenes of *Citizen Kane* (1941), where a group of journalists are viewing the "News on the March" short about the life of Kane. In Disney's *The Reluctant Dragon* (1941), he is in a live-action sequence explaining the *Baby Weems* storyboard to the touring Robert Benchley. He also had a featured role in RKO's *Joan of Paris* (1942), which starred Michele Morgan and Paul Henreid. In 1942, having divorced his first wife, Ladd married his agent.

Alan Ladd as Shane. *Alan Ladd starred as the title character in the hit western* Shane *in 1953.* **SILVER SCREEN COLLECTION/ CONTRIBUTOR/MOVIEPIX/GETTY IMAGES.**

Ladd also had a career at the microphone. A self-trained radio actor, he started getting parts on local Los Angeles broadcasts in 1936, and within two years he was playing small roles on national programs such as *Lux Radio Theater*. After he became famous, he frequently starred on the Lux show, and it was Ladd, not Humphrey Bogart, who appeared as Rick on its 1944 dramatization of *Casablanca*. In 1948 Ladd produced, syndicated and starred in a successful radio mystery series called *Box 13*.

During the 1940s, despite some time out for service in the armed forces, Ladd appeared in several dozen more films. In two of them—*The Blue Dahlia* and *Saigon* (1948)—he again played opposite Lake. His height has been variously reported, but he was apparently about 5 foot 6 inches. That made Lake, at approximately 5 feet, an ideal romantic movie partner for him. Among the other actresses he worked with in the 1940s were Loretta Young, Gail Russell, Dorothy Lamour, and Donna Reed. William Bendix, who became a close friend offscreen, was in several of Ladd's movies, playing his loyal sidekick in *China* (1943), *The Blue Dahlia*, and *Calcutta* (1947). During the 1950s Ladd starred in twenty-three more movies, the majority of them not especially memorable. He did, however, have a starring role in George Stevens's *Shane* in 1953, a Western that has earned the status of a classic and that some critics believe is Ladd's best performance.

Somewhere along the way, however, Ladd had picked up a drinking habit, and his excesses started to show on his face from the middle 1950s onward. In his last picture, *The Carpetbaggers* (1963), he played a supporting role. He died in January 1964 of an overdose of sedatives taken while drinking.

Ron Goulart

SEE ALSO: *Benchley, Robert; Bogart, Humphrey;* Casablanca*;* Citizen Kane*; Disney (Walt Disney Company); Film Noir; Hammett, Dashiell; Lake, Veronica; Lamour, Dorothy; Reed, Donna;* Shane*; Suicide; The Western; Young, Loretta.*

Bibliography

Eames, John Douglas. *The Paramount Story*. New York: Crown Publishers, 1985.

Halliwell, Leslie. *Mountain of Dreams*. New York: Stonehill Publishing, 1976.

Linet, Beverly. *Ladd*. New York: Arbor House, 1979.

Ladies' Home Journal

SEE: *Bok, Edward.*

Lady Gaga *(1986–)*

American pop singer and performance artist Lady Gaga has a star identity that challenges conventional ideas about gender and celebrity. She began her recording career at the age of twenty-two and quickly became a sensation. Known for her outrageous performances, over-the-top fashion sense, and danceable pop hits, she has been lauded by critics, has toured the world, and has gained millions of famously devoted fans. Neil Strauss in

Lady Gaga at the Grammys. *Lady Gaga holds the Grammys she won for Best Female Pop Vocal Performance and Best Pop Vocal Album in 2010.* VALERIE MACON/AFP/GETTY IMAGES.

Rolling Stone in 2010 described Gaga's onstage persona as "a highly personal piece of performance art dressed up as pop spectacle," and *Forbes* has named her one of the most powerful women in the world.

Born Stefani Joanne Angelina Germanotta on March 28, 1986, in New York City, Gaga briefly attended New York University's Tisch School of the Arts before dropping out to make her way in the East Village music scene. There she began performing with artist Lady Starlight, dancing in burlesque shows, and writing lyrics for stars such as Britney Spears. By her own account, Gaga lived close to the edge during this period of hardship and artistic maturation: "All of the things I went through were on my own quest for an artistic journey to fuck myself up like Warhol and Bowie and Mick, and just go for it."

After choosing her performance name from the song "Radio Ga Ga" by rock group Queen, she was signed by Interscope Records and recorded her first album, *The Fame* (2008). It was a massive hit, and she became the first artist to claim four number one songs from a debut album ("Just Dance," "Poker Face," "Lovegame," and "Paparazzi"). *The Fame* also garnered her six Grammy Award nominations and two wins, as well as slew of MTV Video Music Awards nominations and three wins.

Her second album, *The Fame Monster* (2009), garnered three Grammy Awards—one for Best Pop Vocal Album, one for Best Female Pop Vocal Performance, and one for Best Short Form Music Video. Her 2011 album, *Born This Way*, broke records by selling a million copies in five days. The title track won the MTV Video Music Award for Best Video with a Message and Best Female Video.

Gaga has built her career through live performances, promoting each album with a new tour. Her shows combine videos and sophisticated, transgressive costumes. During the Fame Ball tour, she showed a triptych of fifty-seven-second films, "Pop Ate My Brain," "Pop Ate My Heart," and "Pop Ate My Face," collectively titled *Who Shot Candy Warhol?* Some of her most famous fashion choices include a dress made of meat, machine-gun breastplates, and a bubble dress made of transparent orbs. Many of her outfits challenge conventional conceptions about gender. For the 2011 MTV Video Music Awards, for example, she dressed in drag and performed as Jo Calderone. Her personal hair and fashion stylists, deemed Haus of Gaga, design much of what she wears. In 2012 *Time* magazine named her one of the top fashion icons of all time.

Gaga's performance identity is the centerpiece of her star persona, and it elicits intense reactions, both positive and negative. In her essay in *Current Objectives of Postgraduate American Studies*, scholar Katrin Horn observed it as a kind of "feminist camp," which takes the signs of conventional femininity, such as hair and breasts, and makes them outrageous. Horn wrote that through costumes that exaggerate her body parts, Gaga is "a parodic subject and sexy object at the same time." This strategy has elicited its share of critics, such as scholar Camille Paglia, who calls Gaga's performance art "a high-concept fabrication without an ounce of genuine eroticism."

Gaga is unabashed in her pursuit of fame. As she told Strauss, "I want to be a legend. Is that wrong?" Gaga has a unique relationship with her fans, who call her Mother Monster and whom she calls her little monsters. She has even established a social media site, LittleMonsters.com, where her fans can interact. As of early 2012, after three years of touring, she had sold fifteen million albums and fifty-one million singles. With more than twenty million followers on Twitter, thirty-three million likes on Facebook, and a billion views of her videos on sites such as YouTube, the *Guinness Book of World Records* deemed her the Most Searched-for Female on the Internet and the person with the Most Followers on Twitter.

As she ascended to the top, Gaga became increasingly involved in philanthropy. In 2012 she launched the Born This Way Foundation at Harvard University, supporting the needs of underprivileged and abused teenagers. She has been active in her support of LGBT (lesbian, gay, bisexual, and transgender) rights and was one of the featured speakers at the National Equality March in Washington, D.C., in 2009.

Isabel Istanders

SEE ALSO: *Bowie, David; Celebrity; Facebook; Gay Men; Grammy Awards; The Internet; Lesbianism; MTV; Performance Art; Pop Music;* Rolling Stone*; Spears, Britney; Top 40; Twitter; Warhol, Andy; YouTube.*

BIBLIOGRAPHY

Horn, Katrin. "Camping with the Stars: Queer Performativity, Pop Intertextuality, and Camp in the Pop Art of Lady Gaga." *Current Objectives of Postgraduate American Studies* 11, no. 11 (2010).

Paglia, Camille. "No Sex Please, We're Middle Class." *New York Times*, June 26, 2010.

Strauss, Neil. "Lady Gaga Tells All." *Rolling Stone*, July 8, 2010.

Laetrile

Laetrile, alternatively referred to as amygdalin or vitamin B17, has been in use as a healing agent for thousands of years. Claimed by many to be an almost miraculous cure for cancer, Laetrile has been the subject of court battles and controversy for decades. Whereas proponents point to ancient Egyptian and Chinese documents that refer to its therapeutic properties, the medical and pharmaceutical establishment denies that Laetrile has any healing properties and is, on the contrary, a toxic compound that can be dangerous to human health.

In the 1920s a German immigrant doctor in San Francisco, Ernst Krebs, created a curative liquid called amygdalin from the extract of apricot kernels. Authorities stopped him from selling his medicine on the grounds that the cyanide content made it too toxic. Thirty years later Krebs's son, Dr. Ernst Krebs Jr., formulated a less toxic form of the compound, which he named Laetrile. He continued to work on the substance, and by 1970 he had created a derivative compound, which he called vitamin B17.

The theory that Laetrile can cure cancer revolves around B17. Laetrile supporters claim that B17 is a legitimate vitamin. Past societies, and many present ones that have a low incidence of cancer, have regularly consumed foods containing B17 as part of their diet. These foods are the kernels found inside the pit of many fruits—including apricots—and many grains and vegetables—such as millet, buckwheat, and cassava—which are uncommon in modern urban diets. Supporters of Laetrile claim that cancer is a vitamin-deficiency disease caused by a lack of B17 and that supplementing B17 in the diet can prevent cancer and shrink existing tumors. Supporters cite a variety of studies, including several at New York's respected Sloane-Kettering Institute, which prove the efficacy of Laetrile in shrinking tumors and prolonging life in animals with cancer.

Opponents of the use of Laetrile, among them the American Cancer Society, challenge the accuracy of the advocates' experiments, calling their research anecdotal and flawed. They have performed their own studies, which show that Laetrile has virtually no success in treating cancer. Though they admit the danger of toxicity is small, they also point to several cases of sickness and even death in small children who have accidentally ingested Laetrile. Opponents insist that B17 is not a necessary vitamin but merely Krebs's concoction—at best useless, at worst harmful. Whereas Laetrile's supporters point to a "propaganda attack" by multinational pharmaceutical companies to quash their natural and holistic cure, the medical establishment calls Laetrile "quackery."

Laetrile has been the focus of extensive litigation for decades. Since its inception, the U.S. government has fought to keep it out of the country, forcing patients in search of Laetrile therapy to seek it at clinics in Mexico and other countries. In 1977 a U.S. district court ruled that the Food and Drug Administration (FDA) had illegally seized shipments of Laetrile. That decision was overturned in 1979, but from 1977 to 1987 terminally ill patients could legally obtain Laetrile if they had an affidavit from a doctor allowing it. In 1987 that too was overturned, and since the late 1990s it has been illegal to import Laetrile or to transport it across state lines.

As one of the major causes of death in industrialized countries, cancer is greatly feared in modern society. Many environmentalists and health-food advocates blame modern industry with its petrochemical pollutants for causing the upsurge in cancer deaths. Though billions of dollars are spent on research, medical science is still far from prevention or cure of many types of cancer. Because it is used in conjunction with other vitamin therapy and a natural, whole foods diet, Laetrile has great appeal to advocates of holistic health, who have lost faith in the "legitimate" medical establishment. They cite the low cure rates from FDA-approved chemotherapy and radiation cancer treatments and demand the right to seek their own solutions.

Tina Gianoulis

SEE ALSO: *Cancer; Vitamins.*

BIBLIOGRAPHY

Chamberlain, Jonathan. *Cancer: The Complete Recovery Guide.* Syosset, NY: Long Island Press, 2008.

Culbert, Michael L. *Vitamin B17, Forbidden Weapon against Cancer: The Fight For Laetrile.* New Rochelle, NY: Arlington House, 1974.

Griffin, Edward G. *World without Cancer: The Story of Vitamin B17.* Thousand Oaks, CA: American Media, 1974.

Herbert, Victor. *Nutrition Cultism: Facts and Fictions.* Philadelphia: George F. Stickley, 1980.

Lahr, Bert *(1895–1967)*

Vaudeville comedian Bert Lahr devoted most of his six-decade career to portraying hapless, reckless, and uproariously funny characters who came to life through the contortions of his "rubber face" and his exaggerated pantomime. He transformed quizzical mimicry to an art form, preferring the vaudeville stage to both the cinema and serious theater. It is therefore one of the great ironies of American entertainment that Lahr is best remembered for two roles outside his preferred medium. As the Cowardly Lion in the musical film *The Wizard of Oz* (1939), he has captivated generations with his humble search to become the courageous "King of the Forest." In the enigmatic drama *Waiting for Godot* (1956) by Samuel Beckett (1906–1989), Lahr played the tatterdemalion Estragon. In the words of theater critic Brooks Atkinson—in this performance he seemed "to stand for all the stumbling, bewildered people of the earth who go on living without knowing why." While these two roles helped make Lahr a household name, his greatest contributions were on the comic stage as a contemporary of Ed Wynn (1886–1966), Louis Mann (1865–1931), and the irascible W. C. Fields (1880–1946).

Lahr's origins were modest. He was born Irving Lahrheim on August 13, 1895, in the Yorkville section of Manhattan. At the age of fourteen, he began to appear in bit roles in vaudeville. He debuted on Broadway in Harry Delmar's Revels in 1927 and later starred in productions of *Hold Everything* (1928), *Flying High* (1930), *Hot-Cha* (1932), and *Life Begins at 8:40* (1934). A hard worker with a fastidious eye for detail, Lahr

Bert Lahr. *Burt Lahr starred as the Cowardly Lion in* The Wizard of Oz *in 1939.* MGM/THE KOBAL COLLECTION.

capitalized on his bulbous nose and clown mouth to carve out a distinctive niche in a crowded comic market. His onstage trademark was an overstated humility. "Laughter is never too far away from tears," he explained in an interview. "You will cry at a peddler much easier than you would cry at a woman dressed in ermine who had just lost her whole family."

Lahr gained widespread acclaim for *DuBarry Was a Lady* (1939), in which he played a washroom attendant who is drugged and, while unconscious, dreams he is King Louis XV of France. The *New York Times* hailed Lahr as "the most versatile comedian in the business" and argued that he was "not only likeable and funny, which are the primary essentials of a comic, but [also] skillful and accomplished, with extraordinary range." Atkinson compared him favorably to blockbuster stars Wynn, Victor Moore (1876–1962), and Jimmy Durante (1893–1980). Lahr drew similar praise for reinventing the role of Boniface in Georges Feydeau's *Hotel Paradiso* (1957) and for his performance as the title character in *Foxy* (1964), a play based on Ben Jonson's *Volpone.* Critic Walter Kerr, writing in *Life* magazine in 1964, noted "something religious" in Lahr's comedy and attributed his sympathetic humor to a face that had taken on "the contours of a Byzantine cathedral." This "sacred" element became increasingly apparent in Lahr's later roles in *The Fantasticks* (1964), *Thomson's Ghost* (1966), and *The Night They Raided Minsky's* (1968).

Yet *The Wizard of Oz* and *Waiting for Godot* proved to be Lahr's lasting legacy to American entertainment. In *Oz,* he plays a double role: in the opening and closing segments of the film, he portrays a Kansas farmhand who urges Dorothy Gale (Judy Garland [1922–1969]) to have courage. During the main sequence of the movie, he plays the Cowardly Lion, who accompanies Dorothy, the brainless Scarecrow (Ray Bolger [1904–1987]), and the heartless Tin Man (Jack Haley [1898–1979]) on their eventful pilgrimage to the Emerald City of Oz. As the Lion, he dreams of becoming "King of the Forest" and earning the respect of rabbits and chipmunks. Eventually the Wizard presents him with a testimonial—but not before Lahr delivers one of the most celebrated comic soliloquies in cinematic history:

> Courage! What makes a king out of a slave? Courage! What makes the flag on the mast to wave? Courage! What makes the elephant charge his tusk in the misty mist, or the dusky dusk? What makes the muskrat guard his musk? Courage! What makes the Sphinx the Seventh Wonder? Courage! What makes the dawn come up like thunder? Courage! What makes the Hottentot so hot? What puts the ape in apricot? What have they got that I ain't got? Courage.

Beckett's *Godot* offered Lahr another opportunity to test his range. The play itself was a mystery wrapped in an enigma, an absurdist blend of James Joyce (1882–1941) and Marcel Proust (1871–1922) that Atkinson panned as "uneventful, maundering [and] loquacious." The one bright light, according to Atkinson, was Lahr's performance. The critic wrote that "Lahr is an actor in the pantomime tradition who has a thousand ways to move and a hundred ways to grimace in order to make the story interesting and theatrical, and touching, too." Lahr himself believed it was his greatest performance.

When Lahr died on December 4, 1967, he left behind a reputation for painstaking labor and unflagging determination. His efforts helped transform popular comedy from a mode of light entertainment into a widely respected art form. He was a reminder to all that comedy is serious business.

Jacob M. Appel

SEE ALSO: The Wizard of Oz.

BIBLIOGRAPHY

Funk, Lewis, and John E. Booth. *Actors Talk about Acting.* New York: Random House, 1961.

Gilman, Richard. *Common and Uncommon Masks.* New York: Random House, 1971.

Lahr, John. *Notes on a Cowardly Lion: The Biography of Bert Lahr.* New York: Knopf, 1969.

Lake, Ricki *(1968–)*

Billed as an "Oprah Winfrey for Generation X," Ricki Lake has a career and well-publicized personal life that have run parallel to those of rival Winfrey. However, whereas Winfrey has acted in movie adaptations of Toni Morrison and Alice Walker novels, Lake has appeared most memorably in campy John Waters movies, and whereas Winfrey's talk show was perceived as up-market, Lake's was arguably more lightweight, possibly even trashy. Nonetheless, much like Winfrey, Lake's story remains the very stuff of American popular mythology—a narrative that could easily be the subject of one of her talk shows. Her well-documented battle against obesity, her struggle to escape an abusive relationship, and her fluctuating professional fortunes all lend her credibility as a celebrity "agony aunt," as her personal history brings her closer to her audience.

Ricki Lake. *Ricki Lake parlayed her acting career into a stint as a talk show host in the mid-1990s.* JASON LAVERIS/CONTRIBUTOR/ FILMMAGIC/GETTY IMAGES.

FROM ACTRESS TO TALK-SHOW HOST

Trained at stage school, Lake's big break came at the age of nineteen, when she was cast as the lead in cult director Waters's 1988 movie *Hairspray*, a campy take on pre-Beatles American youth culture in which Lake played a bouffanted, overweight teenager who improbably wins both a televised dance competition and the heart of the local heartthrob. Subsequently, Lake appeared in other Waters movies and demonstrated her range in an adaptation of Hubert Selby Jr.'s grim exposé of urban living *Last Exit to Brooklyn* (1990). She also found small-screen fame as nurse Holly Pelegrino in the Vietnam war drama *China Beach* (1988–1991).

Her eponymous talk show debuted in 1993 and rapidly became a ratings success, pushing *The Oprah Winfrey Show* hard for the coveted top spot. In a seemingly ever-expanding generic field, the show aimed to capture a more youthful audience by tackling topics deemed attractive to this demographic. Boston-based journalist Traci Grant christened it "the *Melrose Place* of talk shows." Under the banner of "Talk for Today's Generation," individual show titles in the 1997 season clearly reflected this unashamedly youthful bias—"Ricki's Dating Bootcamp," "Hidden Secret Pregnancies," "Controlling Parents," "Teen Alcoholism," "School Bullies," and "Growing up Gay." As Lake herself has observed, "This show is geared toward a totally different audience, which could not relate to talk shows before we came along. So in that sense I guess we are a voice for younger people."

In the 1998 season Lake revamped the show to include music, more celebrity appearances, and games. Although the show continued with discussion at its core, it also introduced features such as "Fun Fridays," in which the host took a look at news and gossip from the world of TV, movies, and music. Such alterations indicated that the talk-show formula needs constant refreshing to appeal to a notoriously volatile niche market.

Some commentators have argued that with show titles that typically read—as the *Guardian*'s Andy Pietrasik has noted—like "the diary of a nation immersed in self-help lessons," talk shows provide a healthful arena for the airing of previously taboo topics. Lake pointed out that "people do sometimes talk about intimate things which I wouldn't necessarily talk about for the first time on TV, . . . but it's better to get this stuff out than slip it under the rug." Gail Steinberg, executive producer of *Ricki Lake*, has claimed that "talk shows are the community of the nineties," providing a cathartic outlet for millions of ordinary Americans who cannot afford either expensive therapy or access to professional advice. To their supporters, talk shows are the televisual equivalent of the town meeting, enabling ordinary members of the great American public to exercise their constitutional right to free speech and to establish their own agenda (within the parameters demarcated by the show's makers and backers, of course).

A SHIFT IN STYLE

Although all of the above applies to early talk show incarnations such as *Donahue* (1970–1996) or even *The Oprah Winfrey Show* (1986–2011), which tackled issues such as atheism, racism, and political corruption, talk shows of the 1990s sparked controversy for their perceived abandonment of any semblance of constructive debate. As Jane Shattuc points out in *The Talking Cure: TV Talk Shows and Women*, in this respect *Ricki Lake* was typical of talk shows that shifted from a public dimension to "interpersonal conflicts that emphasized the visceral nature of confrontation, emotion and sexual titillation." Here then, Lake's own showbiz background may be taken as symbolic of the shift away from any "serious" journalistic intentions the genre may have previously harbored.

Former Secretary of Education William Bennett famously singled out the *Ricki Lake* show as "cheap, demeaning and immoral," likening it to "the moral equivalent of watching a train wreck." The American Psychotherapy Association called for its members to boycott guesting as "experts" on talk shows, ostensibly because they indulged in potentially harmful pop psychology and meaningless psychobabble. The association argued that talk of the "healing process" and calls to "forgive and get on with your life" simply encourage a victim culture in which people take no responsibility for their own actions.

Detractors claim that talk shows offer studio and TV audiences the dubious and vicarious pleasure of watching others being ritually humiliated, conducting trial-by-television in which hosts like Lake draw more out of their guest/victims in order to whip audiences into a frenzy. For many critics, *Ricki Lake* is responsible for dragging the whole genre down-market, spearheading a new wave of talk shows such as *The Jerry Springer Show* (1991–), which, in their relentless drive for ratings success, have unearthed increasingly outrageous guest/victims and sensationalistic topics.

Combating charges of titillation, Lake is reported to have said, "There's a line we don't cross. We won't put someone on a stage to laugh at them, belittle them, make fun of them, and basically destroy their life." Although this sensitivity is sometimes difficult to discern, the show's ironic, camp aesthetic was more visible. Perhaps, then, viewers are not supposed to take it too seriously. After all, Lake's show was less reverential, more self-consciously driven by the primary desire to entertain rather than to educate, and so ultimately closer to the movies of Waters than many—including perhaps Lake herself—have been prepared to admit. *Ricki Lake* was on the air for eleven seasons until being cancelled in 2004.

POST-SHOW YEARS

Throughout her career as a television host, Lake continued to pursue work as an actor, appearing as a guest on various television shows and starring in the occasional movie (both TV and cinema). In 2006 she served as the host for the CBS limited series *Gameshow Marathon*. The following year, she filmed a pilot for ABC titled *The Middle* but was replaced by Patricia Heaton (*Everybody Loves Raymond*) when the show entered production.

Although her talk show may have been less philanthropic than Oprah's, in her personal life Lake has been a very vocal proponent of several causes that hit close to home for the actress. After going through a thirty-six-hour labor when she had her first child, Lake began to focus her energies on U.S. birth and midwifery practices, and in 2008 she produced a documentary titled *The Business of Being Born* with director Abby Epstein. Called "*An Inconvenient Truth* of obstetrics" by Michael Rechtshaffen of the *Hollywood Reporter*, the film reveals many of the hidden dangers behind Caesarean births. Lake and Epstein went on to publish a book on the subject, *Your Best Birth* (2009), as well as to film a follow-up documentary and start a website devoted to helping women research their birth options. In addition to her focus on childbirth, Lake is also involved in All-Stride, an online community focused on helping parents and children deal with childhood obesity.

Lake returned to national television in 2011, appearing on the celebrity show *Dancing with the Stars*. Despite having some of the highest scores of any of the competitors, she finished in third place. She scored with the viewers, however, and her high-profile return resulted in the planning of a new daily talk show and the writing of a memoir.

Simon Philo

SEE ALSO: *Birthing Practices; Celebrity;* Dancing with the Stars*; Daytime Talk Shows; Donahue, Phil; Hollywood; The Internet; Morrison, Toni; Movie Stars; Reality Television; Sitcom; Springer, Jerry; Television; Walker, Alice; Waters, John; Winfrey, Oprah.*

BIBLIOGRAPHY

Fraser, Nicholas. "The Cheap Triumph of Trash TV." *Guardian*, January 31, 1998, 1–2.

Keller, Teresa. "Trash TV." *Journal of Popular Culture* 26, no. 4 (1993): 195–206.

Nickson, Chris. *Go, Ricki!* New York: Avon Books, 1996.

Pietrasik, Andy. "Go Ricki, Go!" *Guardian*, November 7, 1997, 2–3.

Shattuc, Jane. *The Talking Cure: TV Talk Shows and Women.* New York: Routledge, 1997.

Wasko, Janet. *A Companion to Television.* Oxford: Wiley-Blackwell, 2010.

Lake, Veronica *(1919–1973)*

Remembered for her peekaboo hairstyle in Paramount's 1941 *I Wanted Wings* and for her reputation for being difficult to work with, actress Veronica Lake managed in her relatively short period of stardom to appear in several movies that went on to become classics. Her performances in *Sullivan's Travels* (1941), *This Gun for Hire* (1942), and *The Blue Dahlia* (1946) still hold up.

Born in Brooklyn as Constance Frances Marie Ockleman, Lake was an attractive child, and she began to win beauty contests during her teenage years while her family was living in Florida. When they resettled in Southern California, her mother urged her to try acting. By 1939 she was playing small parts as Constance Keane (her stepfather's last name) in such films as *All Women Have Secrets* and *Sorority House*. She also appeared opposite veteran tipsy comedian Leon Errol in a 1939 RKO comedy short titled *The Wrong Room*. In this bedroom farce set in a resort hotel, Lake played a newlywed who keeps fainting in Errol's vicinity, causing him to have to hide her unconscious body from his wife and other interested parties. In her largest part thus far, the young actress spent most of her screen time pretending to be out cold.

FEMME FATALE

According to Lake, it was as Constance Keane that she introduced "*the* hairstyle of the century." Her hair fell over one eye while she was playing a small part in *Forty Little Mothers*, a 1940 Eddie Cantor comedy. Lake's hair did not attract attention, however, until producer Arthur Hornblow Jr., who rechristened her Veronica Lake, cast her as the femme fatale in *I Wanted Wings*, a movie about three air corps cadets. In her first major movie role, Lake's hair was long and blond, and it kept falling over her right eye. The media referred to her as the girl with the peekaboo hair style, and the tag stuck with her throughout the World War II years, even after she cut her hair.

Although Lake did not have many scenes in her maiden voyage under her new name, she made a very strong impression. Paramount executives were the first to realize her potential impact, and many of the ads for the film were dominated by a large head-and-shoulders glamour shot of Lake. "Blonde Bomber," read a typical headline, "She flew them into the ground!" Despite the gimmickry attached to her debut and the negative responses of some movie critics, Lake was a competent actress, although from the start she had a knack for antagonizing many of the people she worked with. Mitchell Leisen, who directed her in *Wings*, developed a strong dislike for her, commenting, "She was impossible. . . . Every suggestion you made, she fought; you fought with her all day long."

Lake's next film was *Sullivan's Travels*, written and directed by the formidable Preston Sturges and released at the end of 1941. Her character has no name in this satire-melodrama about Hollywood and the place of comedy in a troubled world, and she is simply called "the Girl" in the script. Sturges, who had already turned out three box-office hits for Paramount, was determined to have Lake in the role. The studio was opposed, suggesting everyone from Ida Lupino to Lucille Ball to Claire Trevor, but Sturges got his way, saying of Lake, "She's nothing much in real life—a quiet, rather timid little thing. But the screen transforms her, electrifies her. . . . I think she's the biggest bet in the business."

Veronica Lake. *Veronica Lake, known for her peekaboo hairstyle, starred in several classic movies during her relatively brief career.* SILVER SCREEN COLLECTION/CONTRIBUTOR/MOVIEPIX/GETTY IMAGES.

Lake was several months pregnant during the filming, which added to her usual difficulties. Sturges later complained that she was difficult to handle and often caused production delays. Joel McCrea, who costarred as Sullivan, vowed he would never work with her again. Although the film was not initially as successful as Sturges's earlier ones, it has since come to be considered one of his masterpieces.

RISE AND DECLINE

Lake next helped launch Alan Ladd's career as a star, appearing opposite him in the film noir *This Gun for Hire* early in 1942. The film starred Ladd as a hired killer mixed up with Nazi spies and Lake as a nightclub singer who accidentally gets tangled up with him and befriends him. A diminutive actor, Ladd did not seem short when playing opposite Lake, who was 5 feet, 6 inches tall, and there was a strong screen rapport between them that audiences sensed. "We were a good match for each other," Lake recalled. A hit as a team, they were immediately put into another hard-boiled thriller, *The Glass Key* (1942). That same year Lake also starred in *I Married a Witch*, a fantasy-comedy directed by expatriate Frenchman Rene Clair. After McCrea turned down the role of the politician who weds a reincarnated seventeenth-century witch, Fredric March played it. On the screen they seem compatible, but in her autobiography the actress admitted, "I hated Fredric March. . . . He gave me a terrible time."

In 1943 Lake played a combat nurse in the serious war film *So Proudly We Hail*. She was back opposite Ladd in 1946 in *The Blue Dahlia*, scripted by Raymond Chandler, and she made her final film with him, *Saigon*, in 1948. Between 1943 and 1948 Lake was cast mostly in a series of weak comedies and dramas, playing opposite such actors as Franchot Tone and Eddie Bracken. Her reputation for being difficult to work with and her assorted domestic troubles did not help her career. With her second husband, director Andre De Toth, Lake made a Western, *Ramrod*, in 1947. McCrea, who had apparently overcome his aversion by then, costarred. After being let go by Paramount, Lake appeared opposite Richard Widmark in Twentieth Century Fox's *Slattery's Hurricane* (1949).

Lake's life went into a decline after that. It was filled with a few low-budget films, tours in summer stock, a hostess job on a local television station, bouts of heavy drinking, a stint as a barmaid in New York, and unsuccessful attempts at a comeback. She died of hepatitis in 1973.

Ron Goulart

SEE ALSO: *Ball, Lucille; Chandler, Raymond; Film Noir; Hollywood; Ladd, Alan; Lupino, Ida; Sturges, Preston; Tone, Franchot; Trevor, Claire.*

BIBLIOGRAPHY

Chierichetti, David. *Hollywood Director*. New York: Curtis Books, 1973.

Eames, John Douglas. *The Paramount Story*. New York: Crown Publishers, 1985.

Lake, Veronica, and Donald Bain. *Veronica.* New York: Citadel Press, 1971.

Lenburg, Jeff. *Peekaboo: The Story of Veronica Lake.* Lincoln, NE: IUniverse, 2001.

LaLanne, Jack *(1914–2011)*

"Stop! Look! Listen! It's time for *The Jack LaLanne Show.*" So began Jack LaLanne's daily exercise program, syndicated on television stations nationwide from 1959 to 1985. The muscular man in the jumpsuit led simple exercises, often of his own invention, and urged his audience along with the enthusiasm of an evangelist: "If your back porch is draggin' and your shoulders are saggin' and you have no pep in your step, it's time for a change!"

In this age of fitness gurus, personal trainers, and exercise videos devoted specifically to achieving "buns of steel," it is difficult to imagine a time without health clubs, when weight training and aerobic exercise were viewed by doctors as extreme and potentially dangerous activities. However, in 1936, when LaLanne opened the first fitness club in the United States, many considered him a kook and a fanatic. Though he was arguably a fanatic on the subject of health, his exercise show foreshadowed a national obsession with fitness, and LaLanne himself set many of the current trends by inventing the first weight machines and producing the first exercise video. LaLanne's simple and accessible approach to exercise continued to gain wide popularity until and beyond his death, and his show is seen as a predecessor to nearly all fitness shows, from Wai Lana's yoga program to Jillian Michaels's *The Biggest Loser.*

Jack LaLanne. *Jack LaLanne wears his trademark jumpsuit while leading television viewers in simple exercises in the 1960s.* © EVERETT COLLECTION INC/ALAMY.

EARLY LIFE AND CAREER

Jack LaLanne grew up in California, first in the desert town of Bakersfield, then moving to Berkeley while he was still a child. His father's early death was caused in part by poor nutrition, and the young LaLanne was addicted to sweets. Plagued by headaches, bulimia, and a nasty temper, he was labeled a troublemaker and dropped out of school by age fifteen. That year he attended a lecture at the Oakland Women's City Club that changed his life. The subject of the lecture was health, nutrition, and the evils of meat and sugar, and LaLanne was, in his own evangelical words, "born again." He changed his diet and began to work out daily. He went back to school, made the high school football team, and went on to college, where he studied to become a chiropractor.

Instead, in 1936 LaLanne opened the Jack LaLanne Physical Culture Studio in Oakland, the first fitness club of its kind. He offered clients nutritional advice and supervised exercise programs, including weight training, which was almost unheard of at the time. Doctors advised their patients to stay away from the new health club, warning that LaLanne was an exercise "nut" whose programs would make them muscle-bound and give them hemorrhoids or heart attacks. LaLanne persisted, however, and with the assertive marketing that would become the hallmark of his career, he went out and approached prospective clients, promising that he would help them make the desired changes in their bodies or refund their money.

THE JACK LALANNE SHOW

In 1951 a local health food manufacturer sought someone to host its television fitness show, and LaLanne seemed the natural choice. Often aired in the early morning hours, his exercise program was simple and unaffected. Using no more complicated equipment than a chair, LaLanne—with his broad shoulders and narrow hips encased in a one-piece jumpsuit—led a series of calisthenics, encouraging his audience to jump and pump along with him. Though his set was minimalist and his message simple, LaLanne was not above using tricks to attract his audience. One of these tricks was Happy, the white German shepherd who appeared on the show. Knowing that the most avid early morning television viewers were children, LaLanne introduced the dog to attract children to the show. Then he told the children to go find their mothers, fathers, and grandparents and bring them to exercise with him. It was as clever a ploy to boost ratings as any concocted by network executives.

Another maneuver LaLanne used to attract both viewers to his television show and converts to his cause of fitness was the amazing physical feat. Beginning in 1954, when he swam the length of the Golden Gate Bridge underwater while pulling 140-pound weights, LaLanne performed increasingly astonishing acts of strength and nerve. In 1956, at age forty-two, he swam from Alcatraz to Fisherman's Wharf in San Francisco wearing handcuffs. At forty-five he did 1,000 push-ups and 1,000 chin-ups in one hour and twenty-two minutes. In 1975, when he was sixty years old, he repeated his swim from Alcatraz to Fisherman's Wharf, this time handcuffed, shackled, and towing 1,000 pounds. In 1984 he swam handcuffed and shackled for a mile and a half across Long Beach Harbor, celebrating his seventieth year by towing seventy boats holding seventy people. When asked to explain these Houdini-like performances, he replied, "Now, I'm not comparing myself to Jesus, but why do you think Jesus was such a success? Because he performed miracles. This drew attention to his philosophy, which is why he had this terrific impact on civilization. I just want to help as many people as I can."

The Jack LaLanne Show ran Monday through Friday mornings for thirty-four years in syndication, and even after the end of his program, LaLanne maintained his status as fitness expert by writing books, producing videos, and speaking on his favorite subjects. He continued to appear on television in various commercial spots highlighting his longevity, and there was talk of a new incarnation of his television show at the end of the twentieth century. Determined to maintain his "superman" image as long as possible, LaLanne quipped, "I can't die. It would ruin my image." Nonetheless, he gave into the inevitable on January 23, 2011, dying of pneumonia at his Los Angeles home. His family avers that he continued his exercise routine, despite his week-long illness, until the day he died.

Tina Gianoulis

SEE ALSO: *Advertising; Aerobics;* The Biggest Loser*; Leisure Time; Syndication; Television; Videos; Yoga.*

BIBLIOGRAPHY

"Jack LaLanne." *Current Biography* 55 (1994): 26–30.

LaLanne, Jack. *Revitalize Your Life after 50: Improve Your Looks, Your Health, and Your Sex Life.* Mamaroneck, NY: Hastings House Book Publishers, 1995.

Ottum, Bob. "Look, Mom, I'm an Institution. (Jack LaLanne)." *Sports Illustrated,* November 23, 1981, 64–69.

Lamarr, Hedy *(1913–2000)*

Austrian actress Hedy Lamarr was frequently called the most beautiful woman in motion pictures. Although her acting ability was adequate at best, she became a Hollywood superstar during the 1930s and 1940s. She created a sensation when she appeared nude in the Czechoslovakian film *Ecstasy* (*Ekstase*) in 1933. Then, as a leading lady with Metro-Goldwyn-Mayer (MGM), she became world famous.

Born Hedwig Kiesler, the daughter of a director of the Bank of Vienna, Lamarr had a privileged childhood. As a teenager she was extraordinarily beautiful. Some claim that one of her suitors committed suicide when she refused to marry him. In the early 1930s she became a mildly successful stage and film actress in Germany and Austria, where she mingled with director Otto Preminger. When she appeared as the unfaithful wife in *Ecstasy*, however, she—and the film—sparked international controversy. Religious and government leaders denounced the picture, but critics and the public made it a hit.

After the release of *Ecstasy*, she married munitions millionaire Fritz Mandl, who was so jealous that he tried to buy up every copy of the film so that it could be destroyed. Despite the fact that Mandl was Jewish, he was accepted into the closed world of the Nazi Party. Lamarr was disgusted by his affiliation, and he kept her a virtual prisoner in their castle. Eventually she escaped to Paris, where she obtained a divorce in 1937. That summer she moved to London and met agent Bob Ritchie, who introduced her to MGM mogul Louis B. Mayer. He brought her to Hollywood and renamed her Hedy Lamarr after a silent-film star he admired—Barbara La Marr. Lamarr's first picture in the United States, *Algiers* (1938), quickly elevated her to international stardom.

She followed her debut with appearances in several more successful films, including *Ziegfeld Girl* (1941) and *White Cargo* (1942), in which she sparked a fashion craze by wearing a turban. A popular pinup girl of World War II, she participated in war bond and United Service Organization (USO) tours, as well as received a patent as coinventor of a complex communication system designed to direct torpedoes at moving ships. After the war her popularity quickly declined, although she starred with Victor Mature in the 1949 hit *Samson and Delilah*. In addition to her first marriage, she wed five more times. Among her husbands were actor John Loder and screenwriter Gene Markey.

Lamarr appeared in her last feature film, *The Female Animal*, in 1957, fading from view except for an occasional television appearance. In 1966 she was charged with shoplifting from a department store but was acquitted. A supposed autobiography, *Ecstasy and Me*, appeared in the 1960s, but she later sued her ghostwriters, claiming the story was fiction. On January 19, 2000, Lamarr, who was living alone in Florida, died at the age of eighty-six. Although she was not a movie star for long, she is remembered as one of the most beautiful women to grace the silver screen.

Jill A. Gregg

SEE ALSO: *Hollywood; MGM (Metro-Goldwyn-Mayer); Preminger, Otto; Sex Symbol; War Bonds.*

BIBLIOGRAPHY

Shearer, Stephen Michael. *Beautiful: The Life of Hedy Lamarr.* New York: Thomas Dunne Books/St. Martin's, 2010.

Young, Christopher. *The Films of Hedy Lamarr.* Secaucus, NJ: Citadel, 1978.

LaMotta, Jake *(1922–)*

In the boxing community, Jake LaMotta (born Giacobe LaMotta) is best known for his six-fight series with the man widely recognized as the greatest fighter in the history of boxing, Sugar Ray Robinson. LaMotta handed Robinson his first professional loss on February 5, 1943, and although Robinson won their other five fights, several were closely contested. Outside the boxing community, LaMotta is best known for the Academy Award–winning film about his life, *Raging Bull* (1980). The film focused on LaMotta's stormy personal life, especially his abusive relationship with his second wife, Vickie.

LaMotta fought against mob control of his career throughout the 1940s and early 1950s. A middleweight contender by the early 1940s, he refused to "fix," that is, to purposely lose a fight so that organized crime elements in boxing could make money betting on the fight's outcome. As a result of his refusal to cooperate with the mob, which controlled boxing, LaMotta was denied an opportunity to fight for the middleweight title for the better part of his career. By 1947, frustrated with his failure to secure a title shot, LaMotta finally agreed to lose intentionally to contender Billy Fox in exchange for an opportunity to become middleweight champion of the world. LaMotta made good on the opportunity with a tenth-round technical knockout of world champion Marcel Cerdan.

Max Kellerman

SEE ALSO: *Boxing;* Raging Bull*; Robinson, Sugar Ray.*

BIBLIOGRAPHY

Barratt, Robin. *The Mammoth Book of Tough Guys.* Philadelphia: Running Press Book Publishers, 2011.

LaMotta, Jake; Joseph Carter; and Peter Savage. *Raging Bull: My Story.* New York: Da Capo Press, 1997.

Lamour, Dorothy *(1914–1996)*

The curvaceous brunette actress known as Dorothy Lamour was born Mary Leta Dorothy Slaton in New Orleans, Louisiana. Celebrated for her trademark sarong, which she first wore in her debut film, *The Jungle Princess* (1936), and her combination of sultriness and breezy good humor, Lamour enjoyed a long career under contract (with the usual loan outs) to Paramount. She appeared in numerous South Sea romances, including John Ford's *The Hurricane* (1937) and *Aloma of the South Seas* (1941) but is perhaps best remembered as the bone of contention between Bing Crosby and Bob Hope in six "Road" films, beginning with *Road to Singapore* in 1940 and ending with *Road to Bali* in 1952. She was replaced by Joan Collins in *Road to Hong Kong* (1962) but briefly appeared as herself in the film.

Prior to her movie career, Lamour worked as an elevator operator and was Miss New Orleans (1931). She later became a band vocalist (for her first husband, bandleader Herbie Kaye) and a radio performer. Much loved by audiences and her peers, she made dozens of movies, including Rouben Mamoulian's *High, Wide and Handsome* (1937), in which she played a saloon singer, and *Johnny Apollo* (1940), in which she starred as Tyrone Power's girlfriend. She danced the cancan in *Slightly French* (1949) and donned star-spangled tights for *The Greatest Show on Earth* (1952).

Lamour took to the stage in 1951 and made her Broadway debut in 1958 in *Oh! Captain.* She also made several guest appearances on television shows such as *The Colgate Comedy Hour* and *Damon Runyon Theatre.* In 1961 Lamour toured with her own nightclub act and later with the musicals *DuBarry Was a Lady* (1963) and *Hello, Dolly!* (1967). She published her autobiography in 1980.

Bianca Freire-Medeiros

SEE ALSO: *Broadway; Crosby, Bing; Ford, John; Hope, Bob.*

BIBLIOGRAPHY

Lamour, Dorothy. *My Side of the Road.* Englewood Cliffs, NJ: Prentice-Hall, 1980

Mielke, Randall G. *Road to Box Office: The Seven Film Comedies of Bing Crosby, Bob Hope, and Dorothy Lamour, 1940–1962.* Jefferson, NC: McFarland, 1997.

Nichols, James R. *The Stronger Sex: The Fictional Women of Lawrence Durrell.* Madison, NJ: Fairleigh Dickinson University Press, 2011.

L'Amour, Louis *(1908–1988)*

Louis L'Amour is one of the best-selling authors of all time. From the early 1950s through the 1980s, he wrote more than one hundred Western and adventure novels that have sold a total of approximately two hundred million copies. Decidedly outside of the genteel traditions of the East Coast publishing establishment, L'Amour's works are noted for their spare prose, rugged situations, unambiguous morality, and colorful casts of straight-shooting characters who tame the American West with grit and determination.

Himself a native North Dakotan and an adventurous soul, L'Amour succeeded in capturing the essence of the frontier. Some of his novels have gone into more than twenty printings, and more than two dozen of them have been adapted into films, including *Hondo* (1953), the book that made him famous. He is especially noted for his Sackett family saga, which starts with *The Daybreakers* (1960) and includes such notable books as *Sackett* (1961), *The Sackett Brand* (1965), *Mustang Man* (1966), *Ride the Dark Trail* (1972), *Sackett's Land* (1974), and *Jubal Sackett* (1985). In 1977 the appearance of a novella and a group

Louis L'Amour. *Louis L'Amour wrote more than 100 Western and adventure books.* © ROGER RESSMEYER/CORBIS.

of stories that had been previously unpublished prompted an evaluator in *Kirkus Reviews* to comment: "That's a big, gritty voice at work, lifting melodrama to the heavens of storytelling. . . . As ever, L'Amour's characters distinguish themselves from run-of-the-mill westerners by the hard thud of their boots on soil and the worn leather ease of their dialogue. Awesome immediacy, biting as creosote slapped on a fencepost."

A REAL-LIFE ADVENTURER

Louis Dearborn LaMoore—he changed the spelling of his name in hopes of enhancing the marketability of his fiction—was born in Jamestown, North Dakota, on March 22, 1908, the youngest of seven children of Louis Charles and Emily Dearborn LaMoore. His father was a veterinarian and farm-machinery salesman who also served for a time as the Jamestown police chief; his mother was an amateur writer who had ambitions to be a schoolteacher. His great-grandfather had been a pioneer on the nineteenth-century American frontier. L'Amour credited his success to his ability to absorb family lore and other experiences from real life, as well as his avid reading of such classic writers as Charles Dickens, William Shakespeare, and Zane Grey. Wanderlust overtook him, and for several years after leaving school at age fifteen, he worked as a lumberjack, a longshoreman, and a circus hand before going to sea. After adventures in China and Africa, he returned to the United States and enjoyed a brief career as a semiprofessional boxer before studying creative writing at the University of Oklahoma, though he dropped out before earning a degree. In 1939, Lusk Publishing in Oklahoma City, Oklahoma, issued *Smoke from This Altar*, L'Amour's only book of poetry.

Although his writing career was interrupted by his service as a first lieutenant in World War II, L'Amour began to gain some fame as a storyteller-in-arms, regaling his buddies in the U.S. Army Tank Corps with tales of his exploits. After his discharge in 1945, he moved to Los Angeles and began submitting his stories to Western and adventure magazines. He used the pen name Tex Burns, convinced that his work would not be published under his real name (the spelling of which he had already changed to L'Amour). Editors quickly accepted many of his stories, and before long, he was being published in mainstream periodicals such as the *Saturday Evening Post* and *Collier's*. The first novel that appeared under his own name, *Westward the Tide*, was published in England in 1950. The next year, Doubleday published *Hopalong Cassidy and the Riders of High Rock*, which was written under the Tex Burns moniker and continues the Hopalong Cassidy series originated by Clarence E. Mulford. Over the next three years, he published two more books, *Yellow Butte* and *Utah Blaine*.

HITTING IT BIG WITH *HONDO*

L'Amour achieved his greatest fame with the 1953 publication of the novel *Hondo*, which is set in Arizona in the 1870s and tells the tale of an Indian scout and his relationship with a young wife who was deserted by her husband and her son. It sold millions of copies and was made into a 3-D film with Geraldine Page as the wife and a cast of male "Western" actors led by John Wayne. Notable among L'Amour's other books that have been made into films are *Heller with a Gun* (1960, changed to *Heller in Pink Tights* for the screen and starring Sophia Loren and Anthony Quinn), *Catlow* (1963, starring Yul Brynner), and *Shalako* (1968, starring Sean Connery). L'Amour reversed the book-to-film process in 1962 with one of his most successful novels, *How the West Was Won*. It was adapted from James R. Webb's screenplay for the film, which also came out in 1962.

The success of *Hondo* led to a longstanding contract with Bantam Books, which remained L'Amour's publisher for the rest of his career. *The Daybreakers* was published 1960, beginning a string of eighteen novels tracing the Sackett family from their roots in sixteenth-century England to the Jamestown colony in the New World and, eventually, to the Western frontier. The series also chronicles two pioneer families encountered by the Sacketts, the Irish-born Chantrys and the French Canadian Talons, thus painting a sweeping portrait of the settling of America over the centuries. L'Amour had hoped to write at least fifty books in the series, using Honoré de Balzac's *La Comédie Humaine* as his model. *The Sackett Companion: A Personal Guide to the Sackett Novels*, published the year of L'Amour's death in 1988, offers extensive information on all of the Sackett novels, including a glossary of characters, locales, genealogies, and maps and a key to references and literary allusions.

AN ICONIC AMERICAN

Although disdained by many highbrow readers, L'Amour's work is representative of an important slice of American popular culture, in which the frontier serves as a larger-than-life stage for epic struggles between good and evil. Robert L. Gale, who published a monograph on the author in 1985, summarizes L'Amour's appeal for generations of readers when he describes him as "an anachronism [who] succeeds just the way Mother's Day, apple pie, baseball, Chevys, and Ronald Reagan do in these otherwise dyspeptic times: he extols the old-fashioned American virtues of patriotism, loyalty, unflinching courage, love of family, and a vision of the Old West both as the arena of the famous American second chance and also as mankind's last, best hope."

L'Amour was the first writer to be honored with both the National Gold Medal of the U.S. Congress (1983) and the Presidential Medal of Freedom, bestowed by former *Death Valley Days* host Ronald Reagan in 1984. He died on June 10, 1988, in Los Angeles.

Edward Moran

SEE ALSO: *Best Sellers; Hopalong Cassidy;* How the West Was Won*; Pulp Magazines; The Western.*

BIBLIOGRAPHY

Gale, Robert L. *Louis L'Amour*. New York: Twayne, 1992.

Hall, Halbert W., with Boden Clarke. *The Work of Louis L'Amour: An Annotated Bibliography and Guide*. San Bernardino, CA: Borgo Press, 1995.

Hamilton, Geoff, and Brian Jones. *Encyclopedia of American Popular Fiction*. New York: Facts On File, 2009.

L'Amour, Louis. *The Sackett Companion: A Personal Guide to the Sackett Novels*. New York: Bantam Books, 1988.

L'Amour, Louis. *Education of a Wandering Man*. New York: Bantam, 1989.

Pilkington, William T. *Critical Essays on the Western American Novel*. Boston: G. K. Hall, 1980.

Weinberg, Robert E. *The Louis L'Amour Companion*. Kansas City, MO: Andrews and McMeel, 1992.

Lancaster, Burt *(1913–1994)*

Burt Lancaster was the first, and the biggest, of the new crop of post–World War II stars and the last great survivor of Hollywood's Golden Age. In a career that began late and lasted more than forty years, the former circus acrobat matured from handsome and famously smiling athletic hunk to dignified elder statesman, bowing neither to time nor changing fashion. In his early films there was an almost disturbing disjunction between the tough, grim, often doomed characters he played and his own extraordinary beauty, but over the years his screen image—uniquely for a major box-office star of the time—constantly shifted. Lancaster's formidable determination enabled him to outlast the studio system to whose demise, as the first major producer-star of the modern era, he contributed. He was also a complex and contradictory character who gave many indifferent performances in poor films amid his fine work.

EARLY LIFE

Lancaster was the fourth child of an East Harlem, New York, family headed by a postal clerk. Undersized until his teens, Burton Stephen Lancaster quickly learned to use his fists and developed a love of sports. A more serious and solitary side of his nature responded avidly to books and music, but he dropped out of New York University, where he won an athletic scholarship, to work up an acrobatic act with his friend Nick Cravat.

The pair went on the road as low-paid circus performers during the Great Depression, and in 1935 Lancaster married a circus aerialist, a relationship that lasted barely a year. Needing a break, he joined the Federal Theater Project in New York before returning to circus life with Cravat. In 1939 injury forced him off the high wire, and a succession of stopgap jobs followed, the first as a salesman at Marshall Fields.

Burt Lancaster. *Burt Lancaster won a Academy Award for his acting in* Elmer Gantry *in 1960.* PHOTOSHOT/CONTRIBUTOR/HULTON ARCHIVE/GETTY IMAGES.

In 1942 Lancaster worked as a singing waiter before shipping overseas with the Fifth Army's Entertainment unit. During this time he met Norma Anderson, a war widow who became his second wife in December 1946. The couple had five children; they divorced in 1969. By then Lancaster had launched an acting career that began with a role as a soldier in a Broadway play called *The Sound of Hunting*. This brought him an agent, Harold Hecht, and a Hollywood contract with producer Hal Wallis.

While waiting to start work for Wallis, Lancaster, a self-proclaimed Ernest Hemingway aficionado, talked his way into the part of Swede in *The Killers* (1946). He was already thirty-two years old, unknown and inexperienced, but paired with another newcomer, Ava Gardner, and directed by a master of film noir, Robert Siodmak, he enjoyed instant success and rapidly became bankable, particularly in noir material. Among his best movies was Jules Dassin's powerful prison drama *Brute Force* (1947), in which the actor showed himself to be a leader of men and demonstrated his unique ability to convey suppressed rage simmering beneath a silent and stoic surface.

Having been forced into some poor films by Wallis, and in danger of being typecast in noir, Lancaster sought new directions. Thus, in 1950 he and Hecht, now business partners, sold a property to Warner Brothers, resulting in *The Flame and the Arrow*, a high-spirited swashbuckler in which Lancaster, with Nick Cravat as his pint-sized sidekick, unveiled his athletic skills with breathtaking zest and vigor. He did so again in *The Crimson Pirate* (1952), and the same year he tackled the role of Shirley Booth's alcoholic husband in *Come Back, Little Sheba*. From then on, across seventy-seven films in forty-five years, Lancaster alternated between safety and experimentation, failures both honorable and dishonorable, and high-level successes that have stood the test of time.

AN EXPANSIVE RANGE

Lancaster gained new distinction and his first Oscar nomination for *From Here to Eternity* (1953), in which he notoriously cavorted on the beach with Deborah Kerr, and made an only partially successful foray into directing with *The Kentuckian* (1955). He took to the high wire again in *Trapeze* (1956) and in 1957 expanded his Western filmography with *Gunfight at the O.K. Corral*. In *Sweet Smell of Success* (1957), he scored a notable acting success as the pathologically venomous newspaper columnist J. J. Hunsecker. This was Lancaster's first performance for Hecht-Hill-Lancaster, his own production partnership, which allowed him to dive into the deep waters of his often troubled ambition and come up with winners in which he did not always appear, such as the classic *Marty* (1955).

Lancaster began the 1960s with *Elmer Gantry*, for which he won the Best Actor Oscar for his devilish, barnstorming performance. In 1962 he was the *Birdman of Alcatraz* (another Oscar nomination), and in 1963 he starred in *The Leopard* for Luchino Visconti, a role that took him to Italy and elevated his stature throughout Europe. These were the highlights of his middle age. He worked for Visconti again in *Conversation Piece* (1975) and for Bertolucci in *1900* (1977), but other than the cult experiment *The Swimmer* (1968) and a handful of first-class performances in more predictable films, quality gave way to quantity.

Then, in 1981, aged sixty-eight, white-haired, mustachioed, and dignified, Lancaster put the seal on his extraordinary career with Louis Malle's *Atlantic City*, playing a former petty crook living on dreams and memories and wistfully pursuing a hopeless involvement with a young waitress. He earned several awards and a fourth Oscar nomination for a finely judged performance that is widely considered his most fully realized achievement.

Lancaster continued to work throughout the 1980s, concluding his career with a saintly cameo in *Field of Dreams* (1989). Although something of a loner in his private life, Lancaster spoke publicly for liberal democratic values and worked for many causes, including AIDS (Acquired Immune Deficiency Syndrome) awareness, until his last years. Having recovered from a quadruple bypass operation in 1983, he suffered a stroke in December 1990. Permanently paralyzed on his right side, he remained confined to his apartment, a caged lion raging against his enforced inactivity, cared for by his young third wife until his death on October 21, 1994.

Lancaster transcended the limitations of his talent by the sheer weight and magnetism of his screen presence. As David Thomson writes in *A Biographical Dictionary of Film*, "Brave, vigorous, handsome, and an actor of great range, Lancaster [has] never yielded in his immaculate splendor, proud to be a movie actor. And he has crept up on us, surviving, persisting, often in poor health. He [is] one of the great stars. Perhaps the last."

Robyn Karney

SEE ALSO: *Academy Awards; AIDS; Broadway;* Field of Dreams*; Film Noir;* From Here to Eternity*; Gardner, Ava; The Great Depression; Hemingway, Ernest; Hollywood; World War II.*

BIBLIOGRAPHY

Buford, Kate. *Burt Lancaster: An American Life*. Cambridge, MA: Da Capo Press, 2001.

Crowther, Bruce. *Burt Lancaster: A Life in Films*. London: Robert Hale, 1991.

Karney, Robyn. *Burt Lancaster: A Singular Man*. London: Bloomsbury Publishing, 1996.

Thomson, David. *A Biographical Dictionary of Film*. New York: Alfred A. Knopf, 1994.

Landon, Michael *(1936–1991)*

As an actor, a writer, a director, and a producer, Michael Landon flourished for nearly forty years, mostly in television dramas that reflected old-fashioned, small-town sentiments and traditional family values. He aimed his productions at viewers who were "hungry for shows in which people say something meaningful," he once said. "I want people to laugh and cry, not just stare at the TV."

Landon was born Eugene Maurice Orowitz on October 31, 1936, in Queens, New York. He grew up in Collingswood, New Jersey, where his prowess in sports led to an athletic scholarship from the University of Southern California. After suffering an injury, he turned his attention toward acting. Landon played a number of TV roles and starred in the campy 1957 film *I Was a Teenage Werewolf* and a handful of other "B" movies aimed at the teenage market.

In 1959 Landon began a fourteen-year run as Little Joe on the popular TV Western *Bonanza*. From 1974 through 1982 he produced the family program *Little House on the Prairie*. In addition to his producing duties and playing the lead role, he wrote and directed many of the episodes. The Academy of Television Arts and Science presented him with his only Emmy, the Academy Founders Award, in 1982. Two years later Landon created the program *Highway to Heaven*, an episodic series of stories about the value of love and kindness in overcoming life's adversities. He once again showed his versatility, serving as a writer, director, and producer in addition to being the star actor. Landon was diagnosed with pancreatic cancer in 1991, and he died on July 1 of that year at age fifty-four, leaving behind a wife and nine children from his three marriages.

James R. Belpedio

SEE ALSO: *"B" Movies;* Bonanza*;* I Was a Teenage Werewolf*.*

BIBLIOGRAPHY

Daly, Marsha. *Michael Landon: A Biography*. New York: St. Martin's, 1987.

Brooks, Tim, and Earle Marsh. *The Complete Directory to Prime Time Network and Cable TV Shows, 1946–Present*, 6th ed. New York: Ballantine Books, 1995.

Flynn, Harry, and Pamela Flynn. *Michael Landon: Life, Love, and Laughter: A Tribute to a Beloved Actor by the People Who Knew Him Best*. Universal City, CA: Pomegranate Press, 1991.

Ito, Tom. *Conversations with Michael Landon*. Chicago: Contemporary Books, 1992.

Wilson, Cheryl Landon, with Jane Scovell. *I Promised My Dad: An Intimate Portrait of Michael Landon by His Eldest Daughter*. New York: Simon & Schuster, 1992

Landry, Tom *(1924–2000)*

Tom Landry has become an icon of American football largely due to his tremendous success as the coach of the Dallas Cowboys. His calm demeanor and trademark hat also serve to distinguish his legend from that of other football coaches.

Landry compiled an overall record of 270–178–6 as the head coach of the Dallas Cowboys from 1960 to 1988, the third-most wins of any coach in the history of the National Football League (NFL). Landry was the Cowboys' first and only coach during that time period and helped build them into "America's Team." During his twenty-nine years as coach, Landry led the Cowboys to two Super Bowl titles and five National Football Conference championships. Under his leadership the Cowboys were famous for last-minute comebacks and miracle wins. In spite of Landry's tremendous success, he was unceremoniously dismissed when Jerry Jones bought the Dallas Cowboys in 1989.

Landry was born September 11, 1924, in Mission, Texas. He played quarterback for the Mission High School Eagles and led the team to the regional championship in 1941. In 1942 he enrolled at the University of Texas on a football scholarship. However, World War II interrupted his education and collegiate football career. He began flight training with the army air corps in 1943 and served as a fighter pilot during the war. He was discharged from the air corps in 1945 after flying thirty bombing missions over Europe.

In 1946 Landry reenrolled at the University of Texas. He started at fullback for the 1947 Texas team that won the Sugar Bowl and was named second-team All-Southwest Conference selection. He ended his senior season at Texas in 1949 by rushing for 117 yards in a Texas Orange Bowl victory. After college he signed a professional football contract with the New York Yankees of the All-American Football Conference, where he played as a backup fullback, defensive back, and punter. In 1950 he joined the NFL's New York Giants. As a player he recorded thirty-two interceptions and had a 40.9-yard punting average. He was named a Giants assistant defensive coach in 1954 and, as a player-coach, won All-Pro honors as a defensive back. His last active season as a player was 1955.

In 1959 Landry was named head coach of the NFL expansion franchise in Dallas. Although the Cowboys were 0–11–1 in their inaugural season, Landry was offered a ten-year contract with the Cowboys in 1964. The contract extension paid off for the organization, as Landry turned the team into perennial winners. When Jerry Jones bought the Cowboys, he shocked the city of Dallas, the state of Texas, and Cowboy fans everywhere by firing Landry on February 25, 1989. However, the coach's

Tom Landry. *Tom Landry won 270 games in his twenty-nine-year career as head coach of the Dallas Cowboys.* RONALD C. MODRA/ SPORTS IMAGERY/CONTRIBUTOR/GETTY IMAGES SPORT/GETTY IMAGES.

legacy in professional football and to the city of Dallas was immediately recognized. He was honored by the city of Dallas with Tom Landry Day on April 22, 1989, and was elected to the Pro Football Hall of Fame in 1990. He died February 12, 2000, at the age of seventy-five.

Kerry Owens

SEE ALSO: *The Dallas Cowboys; National Football League (NFL); Professional Football; Super Bowl.*

BIBLIOGRAPHY

Bayless, Skip. *God's Coach: The Hymns, Hype, and Hypocrisy of Tom Landry's Cowboys.* New York: Simon & Schuster, 1990.

Freeman, Denne, and Jaime Aron. *I Remember Tom Landry.* Champaign, IL: Sports Publishing, 2001.

Klein, Dave. *Tom and the Boys.* New York: Kensington, 1990.

Landry, Tom, and Greg Lewis. *An Autobiography: Tom Landry.* New York: Harper-Collins, 1990.

St. John, Bob. *The Landry Legend: Grace under Pressure.* Dallas, TX: Word Publishing, 1989.

Stowers, Carlton. *Dallas Cowboys: The First Twenty-Five Years.* Dallas, TX: Taylor Publishing, 1984.

Lang, Fritz *(1890–1976)*

Fritz Lang fled Nazi Germany in 1932 and eventually settled in Hollywood, where he directed more than twenty films. His crime dramas, including thrillers such as *The Big Heat* (1953), gave rise to the genre known as film noir and spawned generations of imitators.

Lang crafted his distinct visual style in Berlin, Germany, during the 1920s, translating onto film the exaggerated emotions and vivid imagery of German Expressionist painting. He set pivotal scenes in cramped stairways and corridors and employed varying camera angles and starkly contrasting light and shadow for effect. In the silent film *Metropolis* (1926), he created an archetype for the city of the future, complete with a slave class of machinelike workers and a cyborg temptress. *M* (1931), which features Peter Lorre as a child murderer hounded by society, effectively foreshadows the threatening environment fostered in Germany in the years leading up to World War II.

John Tomasic

SEE ALSO: *Film Noir; Lorre, Peter;* Metropolis; *Silent Movies; World War II.*

BIBLIOGRAPHY

Humphries, Reynold. *Fritz Lang: Genre and Representation in His American Films.* Baltimore, MD: Johns Hopkins, 1989.

Kaplan, Ann. *Fritz Lang: A Guide to References and Resources.* Boston: G. K. Hall, 1981.

Lang, Fritz, and Barry Keith Grant. *Fritz Lang: Interviews.* Jackson: University Press of Mississippi, 2003.

Weinberg, Herman. *Fritz Lang.* New York: Gordon Press, 1979.

lang, k.d. *(1961–)*

The voice of singer k.d. lang—rich and powerful and possessing an effortlessly broad range—is the first thing admirers mention about her. Even lang herself talks about her voice and its demands as if it doesn't quite live inside her. It has nonetheless gained her entry into some arenas that might seem unwelcoming for a lanky, country-bred, lesbian performance artist.

COUNTRY ORIGINS

Born Kathryn Dawn Lang on November 2, 1961, in Edmonton, Alberta, lang grew up in the hamlet of Consort, population 650, four hours out into the Canadian countryside. The farming and ranching town gave the singer her country roots as well as a certain self-acceptance that comes from living where "everybody knows you." Her parents were both musical, and lang's mother, determined to nurture her children's cultural development, drove long miles on country roads to take them to piano lessons.

Two events took place in lang's early teens that changed her life forever. When she was twelve, her father deserted the family; at thirteen, she began her first lesbian affair with the wife of one of her teachers. By the time she was fifteen, lang identified herself as a lesbian, and she soon moved to Edmonton

k.d. lang. *k.d. lang performs in Los Angeles in 2011.* DAVID LIVINGSTON/CONTRIBUTOR/GETTY IMAGES ENTERTAINMENT/GETTY IMAGES.

in search of broader horizons. There she joined a crowd who called themselves GOYA (Group of Young Artists), and she began to stage performance art influenced by the punk movement. When she started singing country music, that too became a sort of performance art. Wearing a skirt made of curtains from her mother's house, a pair of men's cowboy boots sawed off above the ankle, a rakish grin, and her hair in spikes, lang pranced onto the stage and filled the theater with her voice.

American country music is a little like a small town, somewhat narrow-minded and limited in scope, yet at the same time accepting of the fact that each family contains its share of eccentricity. Lang's soulful voice and exuberantly emotional renditions earned her a place within the country music family, but her unconventional persona ensured that she would never be quite at ease there. Although she earned her first three Grammy Awards in 1988 and 1989 after having released the country albums *A Truly Western Experience* (1984), *Angel with a Lariat* (1987), and *Absolute Torch and Twang* (1989), she was not able to get radio play for her songs and so was denied popular acceptance.

BREAKING OUT

In 1992, following the dictates of her voice and her own reluctance to be bound by genre, lang branched out with *Ingénue*, an album of mostly original songs with a torchy, old-fashioned feel. One of the singles, "Constant Craving," became her first major radio hit. It articulated a recurrent theme in her work—persistent, unfulfilled need as the human condition. She reiterates this idea in other songs, notably on *Drag* (1997). Every song on the album involves smoking cigarettes—a symbol, lang says, of "rebellion or sexiness" and of "love . . . an elusive thing all of us crave . . . even though it kills us." The desperate, unfulfillable longing that throbs so effectively in lang's voice is perhaps one of the most powerful connections she makes with her young audiences, who are familiar with the roots of addiction. Often still leading emotionally unsatisfying lives despite the fairy-tale promises of technology and with the threat of AIDS adding a terrifying aspect to explorations of intimacy, modern listeners resonate with lang, whether she chooses to sing country; camp; torch ballads; Brazilian-, Beach Boys–, or Tony Bennet–inspired melodies; pop music; or folk.

After taking a decade-long hiatus from recording, lang returned with *Watershed* (2008), the greatest hits album *Recollection* (2010), and *Sing It Loud* (2011). She has been nominated twelve times for Grammy Awards, winning in 1988, 1989, 1990, 1993, and 2004. Whereas critics took little note of her earlier work, her later albums have been much lauded.

DEFYING THE STATUS QUO

Along with transcending genre, lang has made a specialty of transcending gender. Wearing suits and ties as often as skirts and makeup, her hair close cropped, lang has inspired an acceptance of androgyny in a broad audience. In 1993 she posed for the cover of *Vanity Fair* sitting in barber's chair, wearing a pin-striped suit, and sporting a face full of shaving lather; behind her, wearing a bathing suit and heeled boots, superfemme model Cindy Crawford prepares to shave her. Although the titillating cover drew criticism from many quarters, that issue of *Vanity Fair* was the third-biggest seller in the magazine's history. Because she openly acknowledged her homosexuality early in her career, lang's most loyal and consistent fans have been lesbians, though she has sometimes been dismayed by expectations that she represent a certain lesbian image. She has been politically active in gay issues such as the fight against AIDS and has paved the way for other lesbian entertainers, including Melissa Etheridge and Ellen DeGeneres, to be publicly honest about their sexuality.

A vegetarian since 1981, lang has also campaigned for animal rights. In one of the most controversial acts of her career, she appeared in an advertisement sponsored by People for the Ethical Treatment of Animals saying, "Meat stinks." Country audiences who had managed to overlook her butch appearance and irreverent attitude did not tolerate the blow to their livelihood. Even in her hometown in Alberta's beef country, the proud plaque reading "Home of k.d. lang" was angrily removed.

A cornerstone of lang's career has been to challenge traditions, whether the expectations of a disenfranchised lesbian community or the demands of the celebrity system. She has refused to pick a look or a musical genre and stick with it and because of this has carved out a broad niche for her sophisticated voice as a raw-boned pop and country performance artist.

Tina Gianoulis

SEE ALSO: *AIDS; Alternative Country Music; Androgyny; The Beach Boys; Bennett, Tony; Camp; Celebrity; Cigarettes; Country Music; The Cowboy Look; Crawford, Cindy; DeGeneres, Ellen; Folk Music; Grammy Awards; Lesbianism; Outing; Performance Art; Pop Music; Punk; Radio; Supermodels;* Vanity Fair*; Vegetarianism.*

BIBLIOGRAPHY

Appelo, Tim. "Is k.d. lang Really Patsy Cline?" *Savvy*, July 1988, 18.

Bennetts, Leslie. "k.d. lang Cuts It Close." *Vanity Fair*, August 1993, 94.

"Biography: k.d. lang." Warner Brothers Records. Accessed February 2012. Available from http://www.wbr.com/kdlang/cmp/biography.html

Jones, Stacy Linn Holman. *Torch Singing: Performing Resistance and Desire from Billie Holiday to Edith Piaf.* Lanham, MD: AltaMira Press, 2007

Sischy, Ingrid. "k.d." *Interview*, September, 1997, 138.

Stein, Arlene. "Androgyny Goes Pop; But Is It Lesbian Music?" *OutLook*, Spring 1991, 26.

Udovich, Mim. "k.d. lang." *Rolling Stone*, August 5, 1993, 54.

Lansky, Meyer *(1902?–1983)*

Meyer Lansky loomed large in the American imagination, both in his lifetime and afterward. Upon his death he was hailed as "treasurer of the mob," "the Mafia's banker," and "the most influential Godfather in the history of American organized crime." According to the *New York Daily News*, obituaries across the country reported how, under Lansky's supervision, organized crime had penetrated legitimate businesses and moved "from back alleys to executive boardrooms."

Lansky was the inspiration for the Hyman Roth character (played by famed acting teacher Lee Strasberg) in Francis Ford Coppola's *The Godfather: Part II* (1974) and was portrayed in other Mafia films, including *Bugsy* (1991) and *Mobsters* (1991). His life was detailed in the Michael Lasker character in the television miniseries *The Gangster Chronicles* (1981). In *Lansky*, a 1999 HBO cable feature written by acclaimed playwright David Mamet, Richard Dreyfuss played the famed Jewish gangster. But the stories that nurtured the Lansky legend—those that boasted about his leadership of Murder, Inc., a group of killers for hire, and his position as "Chairman of the Board" of the mob's National Syndicate—could not be corroborated by his biographer Robert Lacey. In fact, much of Lansky's life has not been verified; sources differ about his birth name, his birth year, his nationality, how he met his two "best" friends (Salvatore "Lucky" Luciano and Benjamin "Bugsy" Siegel), whether he ordered Siegel's assassination, and whether he died with a fortune of nearly $300 million or with very little money.

The history of Las Vegas, Nevada, is intertwined to some extent with the history of American gangsters, and in 2011 a museum opened with the purpose of allowing visitors to relive the period when gangster activity was at its height. In February of that year the Tropicana Las Vegas Resort introduced the Las Vegas Mob Experience, an interactive experience designed by former Disney Imagineers. After being forced to make decisions as they pass through, visitors, who are addressed by name in their own languages, are faced with being hit, made, arrested, or placed in witness protection when leaving the experience. In addition to life-size holograms of Lansky and other mob figures, authenticity was added by working with surviving family members of mob members and using personal possessions such as Lansky's diary, Siegel's 1933 Packard, and Luciano's Studebaker. A second museum, the Las Vegas Museum of Organized Crime and Law Enforcement, opened on February 14, 2012, in a building that formerly housed a post office and federal court building. The chief draw of this museum is a wall removed from the scene of the Valentine's Day Massacre in 1929 involving a shootout between rival gangs.

SEE ALSO: The Godfather*; Las Vegas; Luciano, Lucky; Mafia/Organized Crime; Mamet, David; Siegel, Bugsy;*

BIBLIOGRAPHY

Block, Lawrence, ed. *Gangsters, Swindlers, Killers, and Thieves: The Lives and Crimes of Fifty American Villains*. New York: Oxford University Press, 2004.

Eisenberg, Dennis; Uri Dan; and Eli Landau. *Meyer Lansky: Mogul of the Mob*. New York: Paddington Press, 1979.

Lacey, Robert. *Little Man: Meyer Lansky and the Gangster Life*. Boston: Little, Brown, 1991.

Messick, Hank. *Lansky*. Berkeley, CA: Medallion, 1971.

Yancey, Kitty Bean. "Tourists Can Play Mobster at Two New Vegas Museums." *USA Today*, February 24, 2011.

Laptops

Since the first room-size computers were introduced during the 1940s, there has been a race among computer engineers to create smaller and more efficient machines. Where once a computer small enough to fit on a desktop was hailed as a modern marvel, by 2012 the market was flooded with compact electronic laptops, notebooks, tablets, and even pocket-size smartphones that brought an increasing variety of computer functions within constant reach.

Laptop computers, so named because they can be placed in the lap while being used, first appeared during the early 1980s. They were initially dismissed as clever but impractical toys that could never effectively compete with desktop models. However, advances in technology helped designers solve such problems as poor screen visibility, limited compatibility with other computers, short battery life, and high prices, and by the 1990s the use of laptops was widespread.

PREDECESSORS

Inventors have long been fascinated by the idea of creating machines to process information. Among the first computing machines were mechanical calculators invented by British mathematician Charles Babbage during the first half of the nineteenth century. The Electronic Numerical Integrator and Calculator (ENIAC) was one of the first digital computers. Invented by J. Presper Eckert and John Mauchly at the University of Pennsylvania during the 1940s, the ENIAC was around 1,800 square feet in size and weighed almost 30 tons. Personal computers appeared during the mid-1970s with the Altair kit for do-it-yourselfers and the first manufactured models from Tandy and Apple.

Almost as soon as computers came into the office and the home, computer engineers began working on portable models. These ranged from models called "transportables" or "luggables"—suitcase-size units just barely more easily moved than desktop computers—to more truly portable briefcase-size models. These early models were known by a variety of terms, including *knee-top computers, lap-sized*, or *lap-top computers*; various brands such as Osborne, Tandy, Gavilon, STM Electronics, and Hewlett Packard vied to perfect them during the early 1980s. By 1985 *laptop* had emerged as the generally accepted term.

Early laptops varied widely in size and price. The IBM Portable Personal Computer (PPC), introduced in 1984 for more than $4,000, was a hefty 30 pounds. The Tandy Radio Shack 100, launched in 1983, weighed less than 4 pounds and cost less than $500. It was useful for journalists who could hook it to a phone using rubber cups and file a story in minutes. Though customers were charmed by the possibilities of laptops, however, few thought they were practical. Many of the early machines had to sacrifice quality for compactness and had awkward keyboards, screens that were difficult to read, limited memory, and other problems. In addition, they cost as much as a desktop computer, leading many to feel there was no reason to invest in the smaller laptop, which had a much higher risk of theft. Salespeople and other traveling workers found them useful, but many others predicted they would never catch on.

However, advances in processing chips and other types of technology made it possible to improve the performance of portable computers. Color screens were introduced in 1989, and manufacturers began creating sleeker, more modern designs. By the 1990s laptop popularity was on the rise and it continued to grow into the first decade of the 2000s. Laptops were used on NASA space shuttle flights and carried by state and government workers as well as all sorts of field workers. Auditors, estimators, and repair people could replace volumes of bulky manuals and information tables with a lightweight computer. Writers and editors could meet deadlines while on the road. Where once industry analysts had scoffed at the idea of using a computer on an airplane, laptops became common sights on planes and in airport lounges, and in 2000 Laptop Lane franchises appeared in a number of airports offering private office spaces for travelers.

FOR WORK AND PLAY

Laptops were flexible and fun, and soon it was not only office workers and students who used laptops but everyone. Pundits began to speculate that the laptop would replace the desktop as the home computer of choice. As software options expanded, laptops were created especially for video gaming, such as the Alienware M17X (2009) and the Qosmio F755-3D (2012), which featured three-dimensional imagery. Musicians and disc jockeys brought laptops onstage and into clubs to mix and play music and create special effects. This laptop music scene is documented in Dustin Morrow's film *Laptop* (2010).

Laptops became not only computers but televisions, radios, and digital recorders as well, as users streamed music, television shows, and films. They also became identified with a youthful rebellious hacker culture, as seen in the David Fincher thriller *The Girl with the Dragon Tattoo* (2011), which features a tough, outlaw heroine whose laptop is an integral part of her identity.

As the use of laptops spread it became a liability not to have one. In 2005, in an effort to spread computer technology and education to the undeveloped world, Nicholas Negroponte, cofounder of the Media Lab at the Massachusetts Institute of Technology, initiated a program he called One Laptop per Child. Negroponte designed a simple and inexpensive laptop computer that he hoped to provide to millions of impoverished children worldwide with the help of grants, donations, and government funds.

The proliferation of laptops brought security and safety issues as well. As predicted, the small computers were easy to steal, risking not only their expensive hardware but their even more valuable data. In 2000 the U.S. State Department investigated a missing laptop that held top secret information; in 2011 a laptop stolen from NASA contained important command codes for the International Space Station. There have been many instances of theft of business laptops with customers' personal information on them.

Laptop use presents a number of potential health threats. Eye strain and back pain are common results of excessive computer use, and the heat from laptop motors resting on the tops of the thighs can cause "laptop thigh" or *erythema abigne*, a discoloration of the skin caused by heat exposure. Some experts believe the heat can lower sperm count and even cause sterility in men.

Tina Gianoulis

SEE ALSO: *Apple Computer; Computer Games; Disc Jockeys;* The Girl with the Dragon Tattoo*; IBM (International Business Machines); The Internet; NASA; Netbooks; Radio; Smartphones; Television; Video Games.*

BIBLIOGRAPHY

"Computers to Go." *Changing Times* no. 40 (1986): 65.

Goldstein, Mark L. "Power to the People: Evolving the Computer Revolution." *Industry Week*, no. 229 (1986): 81.

Martin, James A. "The Pain of Portable Computing." *PC World*. Accessed May 2012. Available from http://www.pcworld.com/printable/article/id,17082/printable.html

Preve, Francis. "Takin' It to the Streets, Part 1—Gigging with a Laptop Is Getting Hot." *Keyboard*, October 1, 2003, 96.

Swedin, Eric G., and David L. Ferro. *Computers: The Life Story of a Technology*. Baltimore, MD: Johns Hopkins University Press, 2007.

Lardner, Ring *(1885–1933)*

Ring Lardner's cynical humor made him one of the most popular writers of the 1920s. Throughout his career, first as a sports writer and columnist and then as the author of short stories, light verse, and plays, Lardner's works received both popular and critical acclaim. He was recognized as a foremost humorist and satirist of the early twentieth century and was noted especially for his memorable use of slang vernacular to characterize and often ridicule his subjects.

Lardner was born in an affluent Michigan family and was educated at home during his early childhood. As a youth he played baseball and enjoyed music. He attended Niles High School, where he played football, sang in a quartet, and wrote the class poem. He then worked in minor capacities in Chicago offices and for the Michigan Railroad before a year of college at the Armour Institute in Chicago to study engineering. He dropped out of college and began his career in 1905, writing for various Chicago newspapers.

By 1910 Lardner's perceptive and entertaining style made him nationally known as a sports journalist and columnist. His sense of humor allowed him to report on even dull games in an engaging manner by including personal anecdotes about the players and winning the favor of fans and the athletes themselves. At the height of his career as a sports writer, his columns were syndicated to approximately 120 newspapers. His enthusiastic and informal style of reporting became a standard for sports journalists and commentators that still exists.

In 1914 the *Saturday Evening Post* published the first of the baseball stories for which Lardner became famous as a fiction writer. His first-person epistolary stories were an instant success. The critics and the public loved his use of slang vernacular and his keen wit. The stories take the form of letters written to a friend back home by a belligerent young pitcher for the Chicago White Sox. They tell of the pitcher's raucous adventures while traveling and playing with the team. What started out as a humorous serial enjoyed by thousands of newspaper readers became, in 1916, the collection *You Know Me Al: A Busher's Letters*. The narrator, Jack Keefe, came to be known as an irrepressibly asinine character whose life, because of his dimwitted pugnacity, bordered on grotesque and tragic. These stories and Lardner's subsequent publications became a standard for later sports fiction in their use of the vernacular and their humorous characterizations of the athlete.

Lardner's tales progressed from stories about baseball to satirical observations of American life overall. He pointed out the stupidity, vapidity, and cruelty of common people, including salespeople, stenographers, stockbrokers, songwriters, athletes, barbers, and actresses—the gamut of middle-class America. When he published *How to Write Short Stories* (1924) and his subsequent collections mocking the commonplace, he received praise from such noteworthy critics as Edmund Wilson, H. L. Mencken, and Virginia Woolf. The nation came to regard him as the new Mark Twain.

In 1933 Lardner died of a heart attack. He had published several plays, light verse, fourteen full-length collections of essays and stories, and more than 4,500 newspaper articles. His career kept him in the literary spotlight through the Roaring Twenties, when Americans were generally looking for excitement and were ready to find fault with humdrum life. His timing as a satirist of the commonplace put him at the forefront of American fiction during the first half of the twentieth century. By the latter half of the century, he had dropped out of the canon of American literature. A few of his stories ("Haircut," "Some Like Them Cold," and "Golden Honeymoon") occasionally appeared in anthologies, but as Jonathan Yardley suggests in his 1977 biography of the writer, "Lardner's literary reputation remains uncertain and his influence is often misunderstood. It is time to give him his due."

Sharon Brown

SEE ALSO: *Baseball; Mencken, H. L.; The* Saturday Evening Post*; Twain, Mark; The Twenties.*

BIBLIOGRAPHY

Elder, Donald B. *Ring Lardner.* Garden City, NY: Doubleday, 1956.

Evans, Elizabeth. *Ring Lardner.* New York: F. Ungar, 1979.

Geismar, Maxwell David. *Ring Lardner and the Portrait of Folly.* New York: Crowell, 1972.

Lardner, Ring. *Letters of Ring Lardner*, ed. Clifford M. Caruthers. Washington, DC: Orchises, 1995.

Lardner, Ring, Jr. *The Lardners: My Family Remembered.* New York: Harper & Row, 1976.

Yardley, Jonathan. *Ring: A Biography of Ring Lardner.* New York: Random House, 1977.

The Larry Sanders Show

The Larry Sanders Show was a dark, hilarious, caustic satire of the behind-the-scenes world of late-night television. Conceived by comedian Garry Shandling, it ran on HBO from 1992 to 1998. With a brilliant premise—the show chronicled the goings-on of a fictional late-night talk show—*The Larry Sanders Show* starred Shandling as Sanders, the self-obsessed host, and the onstage/backstage structure of the thirty-minute weekly comedy provided very provocative, innovative television. The show-within-a-show construct revealed the talk show world as the characters really wanted it seen, while simultaneously showing the backstabbing, ugly showbiz world in which they actually lived. None of the characters on the show ever seemed to learn anything from their mistakes, and there were no happy or moralistic endings anywhere in sight.

The show was groundbreaking on a number of fronts (though it certainly owed a debt to Norman Lear's syndicated 1977–1978 talk show satire *Fernwood 2-Night*). Unlike the major networks' half-hour sitcoms, *Larry Sanders* had no laugh track. The network powers that be had said that the lack of a laugh track was disconcerting to viewers, but HBO apparently had no problem with this. It ultimately served to pull the audience in more, making them a part of the backstage world by letting them in on the joke instead of pointing the joke out to them.

Because the show broadcast on HBO, it could use mature subject matter and language, without which the satire would not have been nearly as biting. HBO also allowed it less ratings pressure than the networks would have been able to, giving it time to build a loyal following while earning numerous Cable Ace Awards and Emmy nominations. There were no sponsors to please or displease, a situation that can make for very edgy television.

As the show's chief plotline, Larry's self-loathing and egomania are alternately fed and assuaged by show staffers, girlfriends, and guests. Throughout the series, a number of characters come and go, but there is not a sympathetic one in the bunch. Larry's ex-wives and girlfriends parade through, each one less likeable than the one before. Emmy Award–winner Rip Torn played Artie, the foul-mouthed, ego-soothing, Machiavellian producer who is perfectly suited to deal with Larry's raging insecurities and paranoid delusions. Jeffrey Tambor played his incredibly mean, stupid, obsequious sidekick Hank ("Hey now") Kingsley. Janeane Garofolo spent a few seasons as Paula, the smart-ass talent booker. Wallace Langham played Phil, the insensitive-pig head writer. Scott Thompson played Hank's terribly efficient gay assistant, Brian. All of them are preoccupied with losing the place in the showbiz food chain that they have scratched out for themselves, and they spend lots of energy trying to reinforce their positions by eliminating any obstacles, real or perceived. Larry and Artie occupy much of their time worry-

Garry Shandling. *Garry Shandling appears at the* Not Just the Best of The Larry Sanders Show *DVD release party in 2007.* MARK SULLIVAN/CONTRIBUTOR/WIREIMAGE/GETTY IMAGES.

ing about the ratings and the network bosses. It sometimes gets very ugly. The characters seem to be human shells, with no morals or consciences.

The show's guests were celebrities played by themselves, though they seemingly played exaggerated, distorted versions of themselves. Dozens of major stars, including Roseanne Barr, Warren Beatty, Jim Carrey, Ellen DeGeneres, Dana Carvey, Sharon Stone, Robin Williams, Barry Levinson, and Carol Burnett, appeared on the program. David Duchovny had a very funny recurring role as a guest. Larry believes that David has a crush on him, and Larry's homophobic discomfort makes it nearly impossible for him to maintain his composure around this A-list star that he cannot afford to lose as a guest.

After the 1997 season, Shandling announced that the next season would be the last. In the first episode of the 1998 season, Larry performs the only brave act of the entire series: after getting pressure from the network bosses to make uncomfortable changes to the show in order to attract more and younger viewers, Larry tells off the bosses and announces that he is quitting. The rest of the final season deals with Larry's unraveling at the realization that the show is ending and he will thus lose his entire identity.

In a brilliant bit of real-life irony, Shandling announced in early 1998 that he was suing his former manager, Brad Grey, a partner in Brillstein-Grey, the production company for *The Larry Sanders Show*. Shandling claimed that Grey made millions of dollars using his association with Shandling as leverage for attracting other clients, and that Shandling should be entitled to money as a result. Grey countersued. The case continued, even as *The Larry Sanders Show* ended and took its place in pop culture history.

Joyce Linehan

SEE ALSO: *Beatty, Warren; Burnett, Carol; Cable TV; Carson, Johnny; DeGeneres, Ellen; Leno, Jay; Letterman, David; Networks;* The Tonight Show*; Williams, Robin.*

BIBLIOGRAPHY

Leverette, Marc; Brian L. Ott; and Cara Louise Buckley. *It's Not TV: Watching HBO in the Post-Television Era.* Hoboken, NJ: Taylor & Francis, 2008.

Shandling, Garry; David Rensin; and Lawrence Sanders. *Confessions of a Late Night Talk Show Host.* New York: Simon & Schuster, 1998.

LaRussa, Tony *(1944–)*

Regarded by his peers as one of baseball's best managers, Tony LaRussa has enjoyed an enviable record of success, earning three manager of the year awards, six pennants, twelve division titles, three league championships, and three World Series titles. A former infielder, LaRussa played professionally for sixteen seasons but never once spent an entire year in the majors. He began his professional managing career in 1978 and accepted his first major-league commission the next year with the Chicago White Sox.

A highly controlling manager, LaRussa developed a reputation as one of the game's most innovative strategists. His promiscuous use of relief pitchers ushered in a new era of specialization in baseball and was widely blamed for lengthening games to almost interminable levels. After leaving Chicago, LaRussa won the World Series with the Oakland Athletics in 1989. He guided the St. Louis Cardinals to three National League Championships and to the 2006 and 2011 World Series titles. Three days after winning the 2011 World Series, on October 31, 2011, LaRussa announced his retirement.

Robert E. Schnakenberg

SEE ALSO: *Baseball; World Series.*

BIBLIOGRAPHY

Bloss, Bob. *Baseball Managers: Stats, Stories, and Strategies.* Philadelphia: Temple University Press, 1999.

James, Bill. *The Bill James Guide to Baseball Managers.* New York: Scribner, 1997.

Rains, Rob. *Tony La Russa: Man on a Mission.* Chicago: Triumph Books, 2009.

Las Vegas

The evolution of Las Vegas, Nevada, is one of the most intriguing of any U.S. city. A desert oasis and water and electricity supplier for most of the Southwest, the legendary gambler's paradise is one of the world's most tantalizing and popular vacation spots. The city has been cast most famously in the spurious, glamorous image of the Mafia. As such, countless novels, movies, and television dramas have contributed to the city's allure.

Las Vegas came of age after World War II, a shining example of the American dream of excess. Its neon-lit casino strip glows on the horizon, a beacon attracting thousands of folks eager to try their luck. An adult Disneyland in southwestern Nevada, the once-dusty tinsel town combines Old West history and futuristic, urban aesthetics. Reviled as often as it is romanticized for its glorious vice, it has earned the nickname "Sin City."

DESERT OASIS

In 1829 Spanish trader Antonio Armijo, traveling to Los Angeles, attempted to shorten the route by going through the desert instead of around it. While traversing the Old Spanish Trail, he discovered water and named the site Las Vegas—"The Meadows." Here, Spanish merchants would ease the rigors of desert travel.

In 1844 explorer John C. Frémont, for whom much of downtown Las Vegas is named, was first to chart the area. Ten years later, religious leader Brigham Young sent Mormon missionaries from Salt Lake City, Utah, to colonize the Las Vegas Valley. The Mormons built an adobe fort and began converting the local Paiute Indians. But desert life proved too harsh and they abandoned their outpost in 1857.

Although Nevada became a state in 1864, it was not until 1904, as America expanded its borders, that Las Vegas saw significant activity. The San Pedro–Los Angeles–Salt Lake Railroad began laying track through the valley. The railroad company bought up prime land and water rights from homesteaders and operated a dusty watering stop. The town soon attracted hotels, saloons, a few thousand residents, and inevitably a red-light district.

Further expansion remained slow until 1928, when the Boulder Dam Project Act was signed into law. The project, an attempt to tame and harness the raging Colorado River, received $165 million in funding under president Herbert Hoover. It became the largest antigravity dam in the world, built 40 miles outside of Las Vegas on the Nevada–Arizona state line.

When construction began in 1931, governor Fred Balzar also approved a "wide open" gambling bill proposed by rancher and assemblyman Phil Tobin. Although gambling had long existed in Las Vegas, it had been outlawed several times. Tobin maintained that regulation of the pastime would increase tourism and boost the state's economy. Thus, gambling was made permanently legal in all of Nevada except for one place—Boulder City. (Hoover, anxious to ensure a return on his investment during the height of the Great Depression, feared gambling and prostitution would undermine progress on the dam.)

By the time the dam was completed in 1935, the economy in southern Nevada was booming. Many of the workers settled in the area. The dam provided a seemingly endless supply of water and electricity to Nevada and the surrounding states. The onset of World War II brought further prosperity to the region when pilots and gunners came to train at the Las Vegas Aerial Gunnery School, which would later become Nellis Air Force Base and the Nevada Test Site for nuclear weapons.

THE MAFIA AND THE STRIP

During the 1930s Las Vegas boasted only a handful of luxury hotels and small but successful casinos. In 1941 developer Thomas Hull opened the first modern casino hotel, El Rancho, just off Highway 91, which connected with Los Angeles. With a Western motif, 100 rooms, a large swimming pool, and massive parking lots, El Rancho opened to almost immediate success. Later that year, the Last Frontier Hotel opened up the road, and the famous Las Vegas Strip was born.

In 1946 Benjamin "Bugsy" Siegel, a New York City mob boss protecting interests on the West Coast, recognized the vast potential for organized crime in Las Vegas. Taking advantage of cheap land, legalized gambling, and friendly police relations—at least initially—Siegel began spending vast amounts of money on building the lavish Fabulous Flamingo casino, which ushered in the neon era that has come to characterize Vegas nightlife. Celebrities frequented the casino, and every night was like New Year's Eve. But not even the Flamingo's glittering façade could hide the fact that the casino was paying out more in winnings than it kept in profits. The situation led to mob dissension, and Siegel was killed six months later in a gangland hit. Ironically, business at the casino boomed thereafter, especially as tourists flocked to see the Fabulous Flamingo, the house that Bugsy built.

Many other gangsters followed Siegel's lead, and several grand casinos sprang up on the Strip. The best-known include the Horseshoe, Sands, Sahara, Riviera, and Tropicana. Each was bigger and brighter than the last, sporting gigantic pools, thousands of rooms, and garish neon signs. Nobody in America

The Bellagio in Las Vegas. *The water show at the Bellagio Hotel and Casino is one of the many spectacles awaiting visitors to Las Vegas.* GEORGE ROSE/CONTRIBUTOR/GETTY IMAGES NEWS/GETTY IMAGES.

would (or could) halt the millions of dollars in laundered money that poured into the desert town in the 1950s, and an ever-increasing number of celebrities, big spenders, and high rollers enjoyed rubbing elbows in the gambling and organized crime mecca.

Eventually, the federal government began weeding out the more visible troublemakers and kingpins. By the 1960s the city's power balance rested between East Coast payola skimmers and wealthy, influential ranchers. In 1966 aviation pioneer and Hollywood mogul Howard Hughes sold Trans World Airlines for nearly $550 million. He was holed up in a Vegas casino when the IRS informed him that he had to spend half the money soon or risk paying taxes on all of it. When asked to leave by the gangster who owned the place, Hughes found the solution to his financial dilemma. Although neither a gambler nor connected to the mob, he bought the casino and went on a spree, snapping up several other hotels, the airport, and much prime real estate.

Overnight, Las Vegas became largely the property of a reputable businessman and began to take on a more positive, corporate image. The city attracted serious jet-setting gamblers and corporate financial investors. In 1970 Hilton became the first hotel chain to establish a branch in the desert oasis. Later Ramada, Holiday Inn, Hyatt, and most notably MGM—with its monumental MGM Grand—followed suit. The Nevada Gaming Commission and the FBI kept close tabs on the new breed of casino. (Even late in the first decade of the twenty-first century, supposedly, Vegas has little mob involvement.)

REINVENTION AND DECLINE

By the mid-1970s Vegas had more than 35,000 hotel rooms and over 400,000 permanent residents. Rooms cost less than in any other major city, and restaurants were cheap and plentiful, encouraging visitors to spend their money in the casinos, where the house makes its highest profits. Ironically, acquiring comps—perks such as free drinks or limousine rides, traditionally a show of respect from the house for heavy gambling—became a status symbol among the nouveau riche.

However, the 1970s brought a lull in tourism due to the legalization of gambling in Atlantic City, New Jersey. The burgeoning, mob-supported East Coast strip and the effects of the recession in the early 1980s discouraged middle-class Americans from journeying to the desert for an extravagant weekend. But Vegas recovered in the late 1980s and 1990s, establishing itself as an international vacation spot for honeymooners (after a quick marriage in one of hundreds of themed chapels), a winter getaway, and a family destination providing scenic Southwest landscapes along with star-studded entertainment and safe, low-stakes gaming.

As Vegas transitioned into a land of campy cabarets, all-you-can-eat buffets, and themed hotels, twenty-first-century developers sought to refashion the city as an upscale luxury destination for the hip and young. Encouraged by the popularity of large-scale casino resorts built in the 1990s, new casino hotels, such as the Bellagio, Mandalay Bay, and the $2.7 billion Wynn Las Vegas helped renew the Strip's high-class status. The structures offer five-star rooms, world-class restaurants and retail shops, and trendsetting nightclubs—alongside the traditional casino experience.

Keeping Vegas in the popular imagination despite its challenges have been its ever-present status as a venue for films. The romantic comedy *Honeymoon in Vegas* (1992), the dark drama *Leaving Las Vegas* (1995), and the popular remake of the fun 1960 "Rat Pack" movie *Ocean's Eleven* are just a few examples of feature films set in the city. NBC also dramatized life within a casino with its series *Las Vegas*, which ran from 2003 to 2008. Las Vegas has also attempted to draw attention as a sports venue. In the aftermath of the University of Nevada–Las Vegas's (UNLV) NCAA men's basketball national championship in 1990, the city has frequently hosted basketball championship tournaments for the Western Athletic Conference (WAC), the Mountain West, and the Big West. Since 1992 Las Vegas has hosted a college football bowl game at UNLV's home field, Sam Boyd Stadium, and in 1994 it was even home to a Canadian Football League team, the Las Vegas Posse, during that league's short-lived American expansion.

Simultaneously, city leaders sought to modernize the downtown area with an aggressive revitalization project aimed at nongaming attractions. An extensive advertising campaign in 2004 made the phrase "What happens in Vegas, stays in Vegas," a nod to the city's seedy history and status as the premiere destination for adult debauchery, the city's unofficial motto. Nevertheless, the economic downturn late in the first decade of the 2000s severely affected the flow of visitors and cash to the area, crippling the local economy. Unemployment skyrocketed to nearly 15 percent, home prices dropped to less than half of what they were in 2006, and development projects such as the $2.9 billion Fontainebleau Las Vegas casino resort and the $4 billion Echelon Place resort complex were indefinitely put on hold.

In 2007 Vegas lost its place as the top gambling destination in the world to the coastal Chinese region of Macau. Despite a modest economic recovery in the 2010s, the city continued to struggle with filling the thousands of hotel rooms built in the boom years of the 1990s. Its 500,000 permanent residents found it difficult to attain long-term employment. Regardless, Las Vegas has never run short on hope or vision, and city leaders remained determined to restore the city to its once-cherished position as the world's leading purveyor of luxury, fantasy, and vice. With the explosion in popularity of high-stakes Texas hold 'em poker, the town remains a focus for gamers. The World Series of Poker, from its inception in 1970 with only a handful of participants, featured almost 7,000 contestants in its main event in 2011. The series even drew live television broadcasts for the first time on ESPN. In 2005 it moved from the smaller Binion's Horseshoe Casino downtown to the newer and larger Rio on the Strip.

Tony Brewer

SEE ALSO: *Advertising; Atlantic City; FBI (Federal Bureau of Investigation); Gambling; The Great Depression; The Great Recession; Holiday Inns; Hoover Dam; Hughes, Howard; Leisure Time; Mafia/Organized Crime; Siegel, Bugsy; Television; World War II.*

BIBLIOGRAPHY

Balboni, Alan Richard. *Beyond the Mafia: Italian Americans and the Development of Las Vegas.* Reno: University of Nevada Press, 1996.

Berman, Susan. *Lady Las Vegas: The Inside Story Behind America's Neon Oasis.* New York: TV Books, 1996.

Kranmar, Ed, and Avery Cardoza. *Las Vegas Guide.* Washington, DC: Passport Press, 1993.

Land, Barbara, and Myrick Land. *A Short History of Las Vegas.* Reno: University of Nevada Press, 1999.

McCracken, Robert D. *Las Vegas: The Great American Playground.* Reno: University of Nevada Press, 1997.

Mullen, Lawrence J. *Las Vegas: Media and Myth.* Lanham, MD: Lexington Books, 2007.

Venturi, Robert; Denise Scott Brown; and Steven Izenour. *Learning from Las Vegas: The Forgotten Symbolism of Architectural Form.* Cambridge, MA: Institute of Technology Press, 1977.

Zook, Lynn M.; Allen Sandquist; and Carey Burke. *Las Vegas: 1905–1965.* Charleston, WV: Arcadia Publishing, 2009.

Lasorda, Tommy *(1927–)*

In an era when the life expectancy for managerial careers in baseball was short, Los Angeles Dodgers' skipper Tommy Lasorda outlasted them all. From his debut in September 1976 until his retirement two decades later, the popular Lasorda was his team's motivational leader as well as its greatest fan. Displaying a youthful exuberance on the field, in the dugout, at press conferences, and in his television commercials, Lasorda's eternal optimism was contagious. His knack for bringing out the best in his players contributed both to his team's success and Lasorda's well-earned reputation as a player's manager.

Tommy Lasorda. *Tommy Lasorda was the manager of the Los Angeles Dodgers from 1977 to 1996 before taking a front-office position with the organization.* JASON LAVERIS/CONTRIBUTOR/FILMMAGIC/GETTY IMAGES.

PLAYING CAREER

Lasorda began his major-league baseball career as a left-handed pitcher with the Brooklyn Dodgers in 1954. As a twenty-six-year-old rookie with poor control on a pitching staff that boasted the likes of Don Newcombe, Carl Erskine, and Johnny Podres—and soon Sandy Koufax and Don Drysdale—Lasorda quickly found himself exiled to the hapless Kansas City Athletics. His major-league career ended there in 1956 with a record of zero wins versus four losses. After returning to the Dodgers' minor-league system, where he toiled for a few more seasons, Lasorda hung up his spikes in 1960 and became a scout and then a minor-league manager for the newly relocated Los Angeles Dodgers.

It was not until 1973 that Lasorda finally made it back to the major leagues, this time as a coach under long-time Dodgers manager Walter Alston. If Dodgers' owner Walter O'Malley was never forgiven for moving his team out of Brooklyn, he was nevertheless credited for his loyalty to his field managers. Alston, who had made his managerial debut the same year Lasorda threw his first pitch for the Brooklyn team, finally retired in September 1976 after having honored twenty-three consecutive one-year contracts. Lasorda was finally given the opportunity for which he had been preparing for almost two decades.

DODGERS MANAGER

With four games left in the 1976 season, Lasorda took over as manager of the Los Angeles Dodgers, a job that he would keep for twenty years. Enjoying instant success, he guided his team to back-to-back pennants in 1977 and 1978, capped by a come-from-behind World Series victory in 1981. Along the way he made himself popular with both the fans and his team. Inspiring his players as much by bumping bellies with umpires in disputes over blown calls as by backslapping, handclapping, and butt-patting his way through game-winning rallies, the animated Dodgers manager enjoyed a rapport with players shared by few of his peers. At the same time, despite the O'Malley family's tradition of one-year contracts for its managers, no major-league skipper was more secure than Lasorda. And Lasorda affirmed his reciprocal devotion to the Dodgers by proclaiming that if cut he would "bleed Dodger blue."

Lasorda's lessons in self-confidence parlayed into a side career as a pitchman for Ultra Slim-Fast, a product that he used to shed some excess pounds in the late 1980s. (He apparently saw little contradiction when he simultaneously marketed his own brand of spaghetti sauce.) Through his commercials and, in the early 1980s, appearances on children's shows, Lasorda became familiar as a television personality to a broader public. His colorful verbal exchanges with umpires on the field, however, would hardly have passed the networks' censors and were decidedly inappropriate for Lasorda's younger admirers.

On the diamond Lasorda reached the pinnacle of his managerial career during the storybook 1988 season, when the weak-hitting Dodgers unexpectedly triumphed over the powerful Oakland Athletics in the World Series. Although the Dodgers experienced some success in the years that followed, the team failed to win another pennant during the balance of Lasorda's tenure, which ended in the middle of the 1996 season when he experienced health problems. Retiring with a record of 1,599 wins (versus 1,439 losses) and six pennants, he moved to the Dodgers' front office and in 1998 became the team's interim general manager; shortly thereafter he was persuaded to give up the position and was named a senior vice president in the organization. In 1997 Lasorda achieved the distinction of being inducted into the National Baseball Hall of Fame as a manager, following his predecessor, Alston (inducted in 1983).

RETIREMENT

After his Hall of Fame induction, Lasorda stayed involved in baseball. In 2000 he managed the U.S. Olympic baseball team, leading it to its first-ever gold medal at the Olympic Games in Sydney. His gregarious personality suited him for his unofficial role as an ambassador for baseball. He traveled the world, including several stops in Japan, to promote the game to which he devoted his life. In 2008 he was awarded the Order of the Rising Sun Gold Rays with Rosette by the emperor of Japan for his contributions to Japanese baseball. His place in pop culture history was solidified when his picture was installed in the National Portrait Gallery of the Smithsonian Institution. But Lasorda was always more suited for the diamond and found himself as honorary coach for the Dodgers in celebration of his eighty-fourth birthday, the majority of those years spent wearing his beloved Dodger blue.

Always careful to defend his players publicly—though rarely hesitant to blast a malcontent in private—Lasorda earned a degree of loyalty enjoyed by few managers. In an era characterized by escalating salaries and labor disputes, his spirited approach to baseball was a breath of fresh air for a sport that was increasingly being recognized as a business. Even long retired from the game, Lasorda has stayed connected with a blog on Major League Baseball's website.

Kevin O'Connor

SEE ALSO: *Advertising; Baseball; The Brooklyn Dodgers; Olympics; Television; World Series.*

BIBLIOGRAPHY

Delsohn, Steve. *True Blue: The Dramatic History of the Los Angeles Dodgers, Told by the Men Who Lived It.* New York: Morrow, 2001.

Lasorda, Tommy, and David Fisher. *The Artful Dodger.* New York: Arbor House, 1985.

McNeil, William F. *The Dodgers Encyclopedia.* Champaign, IL: Sports Publishing, 1997.

Plaschke, Bill, and Tommy Lasorda. *I Live for This!: Baseball's Last True Believer.* Boston: Houghton Mifflin, 2007.

"Tommy Lasorda." In *Notable Sports Figures*, ed. Dana R. Barnes. Detroit, MI: Gale, 2004.

Zimmerman, Tom. *A Day in the Season of the L.A. Dodgers.* New York: Shapolsky, 1990.

Lassie

One of the most popular dog stars in the United States during the mid-1900s, Lassie, an intelligent, brave collie, demonstrated loyalty, compassion, and love toward humans and fellow animals. Lassie appeared in films for MGM (Metro-Goldwyn-Mayer) from 1943 to 1951, in a television series from 1954 to 1974, in an animated Saturday morning program from 1973 to 1975, and in a 1978 feature film update. Lassie's heroics included finding and rescuing lost people, caring for the sick and injured, and warning individuals about impending natural and human catastrophes. Through the Lassie stories viewers gained an appreciation of the strong bond that could be forged between humans and canines.

The character of Lassie originated in a short story titled "Lassie Come Home" by Eric Knight that appeared in a 1938 issue of the *Saturday Evening Post.* Knight had used his own devoted dog Toots as the model for Lassie, and the collie's story touched the emotions of the magazine's readership. He expanded the plot and published the story as a novella in 1940. The novella reached sales of more than one million copies and attracted the attention of MGM, which offered Knight $8,000 for the theatrical rights to the work.

The dog that eventually became Lassie was an eight-month-old collie named Pal who, in 1941, was driving its owner to distraction. The dog chased cars, chewed furniture, barked incessantly, and rejected the idea of being housebroken. In desperation, the owner took Pal to the recently opened kennel and dog-training school operated by Rudd Weatherwax. Weatherwax accepted the challenge of training the rambunctious puppy, and within a week Pal had mastered basic obedience training.

When notified that he could claim the dog, however, the owner hesitated. After enjoying a collie-free household, the owner was reluctant to disturb his family's peace and quiet with the return of the puppy. He struck a deal with Weatherwax by which the trainer would keep the collie in lieu of the training fee. Having trained dogs for Hollywood films, Weatherwax was impressed with Pal's intelligence and recognized that the dog could be groomed for a movie career. Within six months of receiving additional training, Pal's abilities far surpassed those of any other beginner with whom Weatherwax had ever worked.

PAL TO LASSIE

Pal demonstrated those abilities during an audition for the lead in the MGM film *Lassie Come Home*, but he was initially not chosen for the featured role, which went to a pedigreed female collie. As a non-pedigreed male, Pal was selected to be a double dog or stunt dog for the female lead. Once filming began, however, Pal's performance in a pivotal scene—Lassie's struggle to swim the swollen Tweed River between Scotland and England—convinced the director, Fred M. Wilcox, to give the lead dog role to Pal.

Lassie Come Home relates the story of an impoverished family in Yorkshire, England. To sustain his family Sam Carraclough (Donald Crisp) sells his son's beautiful collie, Lassie, to the Duke of Rudling (Nigel Bruce), who brings the animal to his Scotland home and to his daughter Priscilla (Elizabeth Taylor). Still devoted to young Joe Carraclough (Roddy McDowall), Lassie escapes and begins the long journey home to Yorkshire, enduring dangers and hardships as well as the kindness of strangers. Dog and master are reunited finally, and Joe is able to keep his dog.

The scene of high drama in the film is Lassie's struggle to swim the Tweed River. Wilcox selected the flooded San Joaquin River in Northern California as the site for this scene. At a signal from Weatherwax, Pal jumped into the swirling water and swam toward the designated spot on shore. When the collie climbed out of the water, Weatherwax signaled him. Pal put his tail between his legs, his head down, and crawled up the bank looking exhausted. The director was astounded. According to David Rothel in *Great Show Business Animals*, Wilcox later told Weatherwax: "Pal jumped into that river, but it was Lassie who climbed out."

THE SMALL SCREEN

The overwhelming success of *Lassie Come Home* led to other Lassie film adventures: *Son of Lassie* (1945), *Courage of Lassie* (1946), *Hills of Home* (1948), *The Sun Comes Up* (1949), *Challenge to Lassie* (1949), and *The Painted Hills* (1951). Although Pal had earned millions of dollars for MGM, the studio dropped its option on Lassie after the last film and returned all rights to Pal to Weatherwax, allowing the trainer to consider a Lassie television series.

In 1953 Pal's son, named Lassie, shot a pilot for the series, set in the rural U.S. community of Calverton. The Campbell Soup Company agreed to sponsor the half-hour weekly program, and *Lassie* debuted on CBS on September 12, 1954. The human cast included Tommy Rettig as Jeff Miller; Jan Clayton as his widowed mother, Ellen; George Cleveland as Jeff's grandfather George "Gramps" Miller, and Donald Keeler as Jeff's friend Sylvester "Porky" Brockway. The show became an instant hit with viewers as well as with critics. In 1954 *Lassie* won an Emmy Award for best children's program. The following year the show captured another Emmy as well as a prestigious Peabody Award.

Cast and location changes occurred during the nearly two decades of the *Lassie* television series. In September 1957 the Millers sold the farm to a childless couple, Paul and Ruth Martin, played by Jon Shepodd and Cloris Leachman. Jeff gave Lassie to seven-year-old orphan Timmy (Jon Provost), who joined the Martin household. A year later Timmy's parents were being played by June Lockhart and Hugh Reilly. By 1964 the Martins had left the farm to take advantage of free land in Australia. Timmy went with them, but Lassie remained behind because of animal quarantine regulations, so Lassie acquired a new master, U.S. Forest Ranger Corey Stuart, played by Robert

Generations of Lassies. *The family of collies that portrayed Lassie during the show's run included, from left, Pal (the original Lassie), young Laddie, Lassie, old Laddie, and Lassie Jr.* CBS PHOTO ARCHIVE/CONTRIBUTOR/CBS/GETTY IMAGES.

Bray. In 1968, after Ranger Stuart was injured in a forest fire, Lassie was given to two young rangers, Scott Turner (Jed Allan) and Bob Erickson (Jack De Mave). Lassie, however, roamed independently through many of the episodes.

Lassie continued in syndication for three more seasons, from 1971 to 1974. During the first season Lassie wandered the countryside without human companionship. The last two seasons found the collie in a new home on a ranch in California with the Holden family. Throughout the various series the role of Lassie was always played by one of Pal's descendants. From 1973 to 1975 Lassie returned to television in an animated, Saturday-morning adventure, *Lassie's Rescue Rangers*. The story of *Lassie Come Home* was updated and Americanized in the film *The Magic of Lassie* (1978), featuring Jimmy Stewart, Mickey Rooney, Alice Faye, Mike Mazurki, Stephanie Zimbalist, Pernell Roberts, and a sixth-generation descendant of the original Pal as Lassie.

AWARDS

PATSY (Performing Animal Top Stars of the Year) is the animal equivalent of the Academy Award, and between 1958 and 1971 Lassie was honored with nine PATSY Awards, which are given by the American Humane Association. In 1973 Lassie was the first inductee into the American Humane Association's Hall of Fame. Two years later *Esquire* magazine included Lassie among its collection of Great American Things, putting the collie in the company of stars such as Fred Astaire, Walter Cronkite, Marilyn Monroe, Jackie Robinson, and John Wayne. Lassie remained a familiar icon in the pantheon of animal actors in U.S. popular culture, especially to the baby boomer generation who grew up watching the television series in the 1950s.

In the twenty-first century Lassie was still a part of collective memory. The canine hero returned to the screen in 2005. Directed by Charles Sturridge and starring Peter O'Toole as the duke, the film remained true to the original story and was based in England and Scotland. The television incarnation of Lassie was not forgotten either; in April 2005 the cable channel TV Land ran a marathon of the original *Lassie* to celebrate the show's fiftieth anniversary. Lassie's endurance served as a testament to the role of humankind's best friend in U.S. popular culture.

Pauline Bartel

SEE ALSO: *Academy Awards; Astaire, Fred, and Ginger Rogers; Baby Boomers; Cronkite, Walter; Emmy Awards; Hollywood; Leachman, Cloris; MGM (Metro-Goldwyn-Mayer); Monroe, Marilyn; Robinson, Jackie; The* Saturday Evening Post*; Saturday Morning Cartoons; Stewart, Jimmy; Syndication; Taylor, Elizabeth; Television; Wayne, John.*

BIBLIOGRAPHY

Brooks, Tim, and Earle Marsh. *The Complete Directory to Prime Time Network TV Shows 1946–Present.* New York: Ballantine, 1979.

Cregan, Amanda. "Lassie at Home." *Intelligencer*, August 24, 2010.

Edelson, Edward. *Great Animals of the Movies.* Garden City, NY: Doubleday, 1980.

Leder, Jane Mersky. *Stunt Dogs.* Mankato, MN: Crest House, 1985.

Paietta, Ann C., and Jean L. Kauppila. *Animals on Screen and Radio: An Annotated Sourcebook.* Metuchen, NJ: Scarecrow Press, 1994.

Rothel, David. *Great Show Business Animals.* San Diego, CA: Barnes, 1980.

Terrace, Vincent. *Encyclopedia of Television Series, Pilots, and Specials 1937–1973.* New York: Zoetrope, 1986.

Weatherwax, Rudd B., and John H. Rothwell. *The Story of Lassie: His Discovery & Training from Puppyhood to Stardom.* New York: Duell, Sloan & Pearce, 1950.

Weintraub, Joanne. "Lassie Comes Home: TV Land Marks Show's 50th Anniversary with 14-Hour Marathon of Classic Episodes." *Milwaukee Journal Sentinel*, April 22, 2005.

The Late Great Planet Earth

Originally published in 1970, Hal Lindsey's *The Late Great Planet Earth* offers readers a guide to finding the future in the text of the Bible. With fifteen million copies in print, Lindsey's best seller struck a chord with readers, uncovering order in the chaotic close of the twentieth century. The author argued that many of the predictions of the Old and New Testaments had come true, offering hope to many Judeo-Christians and showing that the Bible, and the morality it imposes, has resonance in contemporary life.

After reading the book, many of Lindsey's fans turned to the Bible to predict future events. The work spurred readers to study the Good Book with care and reenergized Christianity. Critics have argued that few of Lindsey's predictions for the 1980s came true and that he preyed on readers' hopes and fears. Regardless, the prophetic rhetoric of the text helped make it the most popular book of the 1970s.

Brian Black

SEE ALSO: *Best Sellers; Welles, Orson.*

BIBLIOGRAPHY

Lindsey, Hal, and C. C. Carlson. *The Late Great Planet Earth.* Grand Rapids, MI: Zondervan, 1970.

Latin Jazz

The blending of Latin music and jazz has occurred in countless forms, under many guises, over much of the twentieth century and into the twenty-first. Cuba, New York City, and Puerto Rico all played key roles in the initial fusion, but the unfolding of this complex musical genre has had worldwide implications.

The fusion began in early 1920s Cuba, where descendants of African slaves brought a song form known as *son* to Havana from the sugar-plantation-filled province of Oriente. They settled in segregated barrios, where their passionate music thrived, despite its rejection by the white Cuban elite, who preferred the *danzon*, music derived from eighteenth-century French court *contradanse*, performed by string-and-flute bands called *charangas*. *Son* had its bands as well, called *conjuntos*, which instead featured trumpets and timbales (stand-mounted drums and cowbells). Both types of music were powered by the conga and bongos, which had found their origins in religious drum rituals but by the mid-1920s were also being used as backing for dancers at a growing number of American-owned tourist nightclubs.

ARRIVAL IN AMERICA

In 1930, after Moises Simon's composition "The Peanut Vendor" sparked rumba mania in the United States, Cuban and Puerto Rican musicians arrived in New York in growing numbers, frustrated with limited work opportunities back home and attracted by the artistic renaissance taking place in Harlem, New York. Immediately their presence was felt in jazz circles, with Cuban flautist Alberto Socarras appearing in *Blackbirds of 1928* and other Broadway shows and Duke Ellington incorporating Latin compositions into his sets. Rumba was still considered a novelty, however, and the majority of Latin music remained segregated in the Harlem barrio. White audiences received a watered-down trickle from bands such as the orchestra led by popular Mexican bandleader Xavier Cugat, who, with his niece, actress Margo, was said to have "introduced the rumba to New York City." Even African American musicians initially blanched at participating in what appeared to be a more primitive (the conga and bongos were hand-beaten) and less respectable form of music.

In 1940 multi-instrumentalist Mario Bauza and singer Frank Grillo (aka "Machito") formed the Afro-Cuban Orchestra, a mixed group of Cubans, Puerto Ricans, and Americans, in New York City. The band tackled head-on the rhythmic, cultural, and financial challenges facing the combining of Latin music and jazz as the decade progressed. Simultaneously, the mambo, another African rhythm refined with jazz inflections by Havana big bands such as the *conjunto* of Arsenio Rodriguez and *charanga* of La Maravilla del Siglo Orchestra, began to gain popularity on American shores in the excitement-starved wake of World War II.

Trumpeter Dizzy Gillespie took fast action. He had been molding his own revolutionary form of jazz, called "bebop," through the 1940s. In 1946 he invited recent Cuban émigré percussionist Chano Pozo into his newly formed big band. The flamboyant Pozo electrified and entranced audiences throughout America and Europe, and together the pair made landmark recordings such as "Manteca" before Pozo's tragic drug-related murder in late 1948. Their work, along with the continued pioneering by the Afro-Cubans, came to be known as "Cubop."

POSTWAR INNOVATIONS

By the 1950s the mambo had become an international sensation through the efforts of populist bands such as Perez Prado's and the Lecuona Cuban Boys. Desi Arnaz performed groundbreaking singer Miguelito Valdes's "Babalu" on the *I Love Lucy* television series. The Afro-Cubans themselves received widespread critical recognition after jazz legend Charlie Parker recorded with them and when, under Machito's guidance, the Palladium, a new club devoted to the Latin sound, opened on Manhattan's 53rd Street, down the block from Birdland. Soon the club was packed nightly with multiracial crowds and celebrities dancing up a storm and be-boppers such as Gillespie sitting in. In addition to the Afro-Cubans, two other orchestras made famous at the Palladium were battling bands led by suave Puerto Rican tenor vocalist Tito Rodriguez and Nuyorican (New York–born Puerto Rican) timbalist Tito Puente. Musicians from these groups formed a core of performers who remained popular into the 1990s.

As the 1950s progressed, the term *Cubop* was supplanted by *Latin jazz*, as Latin rhythms from other countries (the Puerto Rican bomba, the Colombian *cumbia*, the Dominican *meringue*) made their way into repertoires. Cuba, however, was the source of the last American big band rhythm craze, the cha-cha. A simpler, shuffling form of mambo, the cha-cha swept the nation in the late 1950s. *Charanga* bandleader José Fajardo is credited with bringing the rhythm to the United States and performing it in 1959 for John F. Kennedy during his presidential campaign. Shortly afterward, Cuba's communist revolution dramatically curtailed its participation in musical development, although expatriates continued to influence matters.

Meanwhile, hard times were leading many top jazz musicians to form smaller, more economical combos. It became common for many of these combos to include Latin percussion. Successors to Chano Pozo's legacy, including Mongo Santamaria, Patato Valdes, Willie Bobo, and Ray Barreto, found themselves being lured from the Palladium scene to a succession of jazz combos, many led by white musicians such as George Shearing, Cal Tjader, and Herbie Mann. Whether or not they were being exploited, the wider exposure benefited the percussionists, many of whom went on to start their own groups.

Rock music assumed commercial dominance in the early 1960s, spelling an end to the heyday of the Latin big band era. A transitional period for Latin jazz musicians followed with the boogaloo (Latin-spiced rhythm and blues, of which Barreto's "El Watusi" was a popular highlight) and Latin soul trends. Growing inner-city decay left many musicians scrambling for gigs by the end of the decade, but in the 1970s Puente and other veterans found themselves at the fore of the flourishing salsa movement. After maintaining steady popularity in New York, Miami, and Los Angeles through the 1980s (which featured Willie Bobo appearances on *The Cosby Show*), Latin jazz again rose in the national consciousness in the 1990s, through streams as diverse as "bachelor pad" and "exotica" nostalgia, European-imported acid jazz, and the efforts of celebrity devotees such as David Byrne and Andy Garcia.

Latin jazz is still going strong in the United States in the twenty-first century. Despite its long history, Arturo O'Farrill, music director and founder of the Afro Latin Jazz Orchestra at Lincoln Center (2002–2007), believes that it is still considered an infant when it comes to being "codified and recognized." In January 2005 Lincoln Center presented two nights of Latin jazz to American audiences. The show featured Chilean-born Claudia Acuna, Cuban-born Graciela Ferez, and Newark-born Herman Olivera, who had worked closely with Puente. Latin jazz can still be heard throughout New York City, which offers venues ranging from Arthur's Tavern, Birdland, and the Jazz Club to the Museum of Natural History and the Guggenheim.

C. Kenyon Silvey

SEE ALSO: *Arnaz, Desi;* The Cosby Show*; Ellington, Duke; Gillespie, Dizzy;* I Love Lucy*; Jazz; Parker, Charlie; Puente, Tito; Rock and Roll.*

BIBLIOGRAPHY

Bergman, Billy. *Hot Sauces: Latin and Caribbean Pop*. New York: Quill, 1985.

Case, Brian; Stan Britt; and Trisha Palmer. *The Illustrated*

Encyclopedia of Jazz. New York: Harmony, 1978.

Fernandez, Raul A. *From Afro-Cuban Rhythms to Latin Jazz.* Berkeley: University of California Press, 2006.

Reyes, Damasco. "A Celebration of Great Latin Jazz at Lincoln Center." *New York Amsterdam News* 96, no. 4 (2005).

Stewart, Alex. *Making the Scene: Contemporary New York City Big Band Jazz.* Berkeley: University of California Press, 2007.

Sweeney, Philip. *The Virgin Directory of World Music.* New York: Henry Holt, 1992.

Laugh-In

"Sock it to me!" "Here come da judge!" "You bet your sweet bippy!" "Look that up in your Funk and Wagnalls!" For a few years, these and other *Laugh-In* catchphrases circulated promiscuously in the everyday speech of North Americans. During the late 1960s NBC's Monday night comedy series was more than just another television program—it was a cultural event. Holding the top spot in the Nielsen ratings for two seasons, from 1968–1969 to 1969–1970, the show revolutionized the comedy-variety genre and, more than any other prime-time program of the period, signaled the massive social, moral, and generational changes the nation was undergoing. *Laugh-In* was the quintessential television show of the swinging 1960s.

Laugh-In. *Dick Martin, left, and Dan Rowan were the hosts of* Laugh-In, *which ran on television from 1968 to 1973.* LORIMAR/NBC-TV/THE KOBAL COLLECTION.

AN UNCONVENTIONAL VARIETY SHOW

Considering the show's emphasis on youth, left-liberal politics, sexual liberation, and "New Wave" video techniques, the guiding lights behind *Laugh-In* formed an unlikely team. Dan Rowan (1922–1987) and Dick Martin (1922–2008) were aging forty-something veterans of the nightclub and lounge circuit, having polished their act as a tuxedoed comedy duo since 1953. In 1966 they filled in for Dean Martin in his summer variety show. NBC gave the pair a summer special the following year, which proved to be the genesis of *Laugh-In*. Rowan and Martin brought in veteran television producer George Schlatter, whose credits in the industry dated back to the 1950s and Dinah Shore's variety series.

If the show's hosts and its executive producer seemed to have little connection to the burgeoning youth culture of the 1960s, its producer and head writer, Paul Keyes, was even further removed. Keyes's comedy credits dated back to penning jokes for Jack Paar. He was also a close friend of Richard Nixon and a major campaign adviser to the 1968 presidential candidate. Despite their establishment backgrounds, these men produced a show designed to appeal to the sensibilities, tastes, politics, and lifestyles of 1960s youth—as well as those elders who increasingly wanted to be "with it."

Laugh-In (which is also known by its full name, *Rowan and Martin's Laugh-In*) largely dispensed with the conventions of the comedy-variety genre. Rather than showcasing guest stars with extended musical segments, the show featured short cameo appearances of celebrity guests delivering one-liners. Rather than present sketches that developed over five to ten minutes, *Laugh-In* reveled in ten-second blackouts, non sequiturs, and endless rapid-fire one-liners delivered by performers, in printed form on the screen, or on a dancing bikini-clad body. Much of *Laugh-In*'s content harkened back to vaudeville, from its jokes to its penchant for broad slapstick. For instance, every time Cockney-accented Judy Carne, a series regular, happened to utter the famous phrase "Sock it to me girl!" she would invariably get soaked with water, bonked on the head, or dropped through a trap door.

What made the show revolutionary was not its approach to comedy but rather its visual style. With flashes, zooms, breathtakingly quick cuts, and psychedelic colors, *Laugh-In* displayed a kinetic, frantic pace that was unprecedented in television. Not since Ernie Kovacs's self-reflexive use of the television medium for his visual brand of comedy in the 1950s had a television show so overtly drawn attention to the televisual form. *Laugh-In* used hundreds of separate shots per show, requiring the services of four to five full-time video editors to assemble all the myriad tiny segments together. Some shots would be on screen for less than half a second, as when the bikini-clad dancer would stop momentarily as the camera zoomed in on a joke written somewhere on her bare anatomy. Frequently, viewers would not have enough time to speed read through the one-liner (for example, "Forest fires prevent bears") before the camera zoomed back into a full shot of the merry dancer.

ADDRESSING TIMELY ISSUES

Reflecting the "sexual revolution" of the period, in which the easier availability of birth control and the social experimentation of the young were freeing up sexual expression, *Laugh-In* engaged in heavy doses of scatological and risqué humor. Martin played the unrepentant bachelor wholly preoccupied with bedding young women. Ruth Buzzi's beleaguered hair-netted old lady found herself constantly sexually accosted by Arte Johnson's dirty old man on a park bench. The old man would mutter salacious invitations as he slid closer to her on the bench, and Buzzi's old lady would eventually retaliate, using her purse as an effective weapon.

Laugh-In also engaged in highly topical political humor, influenced by other politically tinged television comedies such as *That Was the Week That Was* (1964–1965) and *The Smothers Brothers Comedy Hour* (1967–1969). With one-liners such as "George Wallace, your sheets are ready," the series emphatically took a left-liberal stance. This did not, however, prevent personalities associated with the political right—such as John Wayne—from agreeing to appear in cameos. Most famously, presidential candidate Richard Nixon appeared in 1968 and delivered the line: "Sock it to me?" But by 1969, with Nixon ensconced in the White House, Keyes, who was closely associated with the Nixon administration as an adviser and a speech writer, began lashing out at what he (and the White House) perceived to be the show's penchant for anti-Nixon and anti-Pentagon attacks. Keyes left the series in a huff.

Although *Laugh-In* engaged in many of the same kinds of political critiques that were getting the Smothers Brothers censored and eventually thrown off the air over at CBS, Rowan and Martin's show never suffered the same heavy-handed censorship; the NBC Standards and Practices department tended to worry more about jokes having to do with sex and religion. Also, the blackout, rapid-fire manner of delivery tended to blunt the political implications of much of the humor. By the time the viewer got the message behind the joke, two or three other nonpolitical jokes or blackouts had already whizzed by.

LASTING INFLUENCE

Laugh-In launched the careers of a number of its regular cast members, most notably Goldie Hawn, who played a giggly dumb blond, and Lily Tomlin, who created a number of famous characters, from cheeky little girl Edith Ann to Ernestine the sarcastic and all-powerful telephone operator ("one ringy-dingy, two ringy-dingy . . . "). Other cast members became famous for particular shticks. Johnson played a German soldier, forever peering through bushes and pronouncing something to be "verrrrrry interesting . . . but shtupid!" Earnest-faced Henry Gibson would appear with flower in hand and recite a pathetic poem. Episodes ended with all the cast members and cameo guests behind a joke wall painted in swirly psychedelic colors. They would pop their heads through small doors and deliver yet more one-liners. This joking would continue through the credits, with yet more blackout sketches, until the episode would end with the disembodied sound of one set of hands clapping.

By 1973, with most of its original cast gone, the program ran out of steam. The show's visual style, so cutting edge in the 1960s, quickly became dated. *Laugh-In* remains very much a show of its era (though it was revisited briefly in an unsuccessful 1979 sequel to the series). Although it did not go on to serve as a direct inspiration for subsequent brands of television comedy, the show's frenetic editing pace, so revolutionary in 1968, is now, with the influence of music videos and commercials, quite unremarkable.

Aniko Bodroghkozy

SEE ALSO: *Martin, Dean; Screwball Comedies; The Smothers Brothers; Stand-Up Comedy; Television; Tomlin, Lily; Vaudeville.*

BIBLIOGRAPHY

Erickson, Hal. *"From Beautiful Downtown Burbank."* Jefferson, NC: McFarland, 2000.

Rowan and Martin's Laugh-In: The Burbank Edition (television scripts). New York: World Publishing, 1969.

Lauper, Cyndi *(1953–)*

Singer Cyndi Lauper burst onto the music scene in 1984—just as the music video, now a mainstay of the rock industry, was coming of age. Lauper's unique brand of color, vitality, and sass were a perfect fit for the new video medium, and she made her dynamic songs into vibrant videos full of kitschy, campy energy. Lauper's own appearance was a sort of camp: she wore her hair in an asymmetrical style dyed in bright fuchsias and magentas and wore flamboyant thrift-shop-chic outfits. Her look, along

Cyndi Lauper. *Cyndi Lauper's funky fashions and catchy pop songs made her an icon of the 1980s.* EBET ROBERTS/REDFERNS.

with her nasally New York voice, caused some critics to call her "Betty Boop" or "kewpie doll" and to dismiss her as a novelty act. However, behind the day-glo hair and the bohemian clothing, Lauper is a serious artist with a social conscience and a pragmatic approach to changing the world.

Lauper's first big hit, "Girls Just Want to Have Fun," is a riotous anthem to personal freedom for women that appeals to everyone from middle-aged feminists to girls just entering adolescence. The irrepressible pro-woman lyrics in this and other chart toppers earned Lauper recognition in 1985 as *Ms.* magazine's Woman of the Year for the issues she tackled in her songs as well as her efforts to change the role of women in rock. Los Angeles–based Women in Film also honored Lauper in the mid-1980s for hiring women in all aspects of her music videos, including staging, costumes, design, editing, and casting. "I tried to give women a different face," Lauper said, "a stronger, more independent one, and that's what 'Girls Just Want to Have Fun' was all about."

MISFIT MAKES GOOD

Lauper grew up with a strong, supportive female role model. Born in Queens, New York, to working-class parents who divorced when she was five, Lauper, her brother, and her sister were raised by their mother, Catrine Dominique. Though life was hard raising three children while working as a waitress, Lauper's mother actively encouraged creativity and independent thinking in her children. Struggling through parochial school, Lauper was a lonely child who always felt like a misfit. She escaped into music, feeling a "drive to sing"—first along with her mother's records, then, around age twelve, performing her own folksy compositions while accompanying herself on the guitar. Around the same time she began the wild color experiments on her hair, making the most of her misfit status by becoming an eccentric. She attended four separate high schools, dropping or flunking out of each, until she earned her high school equivalency. After an unhappy year at a Vermont college, she came back to New York to try for a singing career.

In 1977 she released an album with the band Blue Angel. The album was well received by critics but sold poorly, and the band broke up, sending Lauper back to singing in bars and picking up odd jobs. She had just declared bankruptcy in 1983 when she got her own recording contract with Portrait Records. Her first album, *She's So Unusual*, released in 1983, sold almost five million copies. It was the first debut album in history to have four Top 5 hit songs. Lauper's quirky personal style and her high-pitched yet tough singing voice immediately clicked in the bubbly world of 1980s pop. She rocketed to instant popularity, receiving a Grammy, an MTV Music Award, and an American Music Award. *Rolling Stone* named her Best New Artist in 1984.

Although some pundits speculated Lauper would be a "one-hit wonder," more discerning critics heard the quality and flexibility of style and voice in her multioctave range. She released other albums with less dramatic success: *True Colors* (1986) sold a million copies, but *A Night to Remember* (1989) didn't fare as well and only produced one hit, "I Drove All Night." Lauper, however, does not measure her success by sales alone, and she continued to produce albums, exerting increasing control over her own career. Because as many as four years would go by between her albums, she was constantly said to be making a "comeback" during the 1990s. Well respected in the rock music world, Lauper has been grudgingly credited by the most sneering of critics for her range of sound, be it squeaky, earthy, soulful, or sweet. By the end of the 1990s she continued to write "social issue" songs about such topics as incest, domestic violence, abortion, and racism, managing to be passionate without becoming preachy. In "She Bop" she even pulled off a feisty and funny reclamation of female masturbation.

In the first decade of the 2000s Lauper released a number of greatest hits and cover albums, including *At Last* (2003) and *The Body Acoustic* (2005), as well as a Grammy-nominated album of dance music titled *Bring Ya to the Brink* (2008). But it was her 2010 offering, the appropriately titled collection of blues standards *Memphis Blues*, that brought Lauper her greatest share of attention since her early releases. The album was number one on the Billboard Blues Album chart for fourteen weeks and became Lauper's third release to receive a Grammy nomination.

Lauper has also branched out into acting, and critics often herald her as a bright spot in otherwise negligible films, as was the case with *Off and Running* (1991). She has also made guest appearances on television, most notably on the popular 1990s sitcom *Mad about You*, for which she won an Emmy Award in 1995. In 2010 she was a popular contestant on *Celebrity Apprentice*, and in 2012 she began filming a reality television show for the WE network. Lauper has even appeared on Broadway, performing the role of Jenny in a 2006 revival of *The Threepenny Opera*. In 2012 she arranged the music for a theatrical adaptation of the 2005 film *Kinky Boots* alongside Broadway veteran Harvey Fierstein.

SOCIAL OUTREACH

An avid supporter of lesbian, gay, bisexual, and transgender (LGBT) rights, in 2007 Lauper organized the True Colors Tour, featuring a diverse collection of musicians and comedians, to support local and national LGBT organizations. The following year she expanded her charitable outreach by founding the True Colors Fund, and in 2010 the fund initiated its "Give a Damn" campaign, aimed at increasing awareness of LGBT equality efforts among the straight community. In 2011 she oversaw the opening of the True Colors Residence, a homeless shelter and support facility for LGBT youth in New York City. She has also served as a spokesperson for HIV/AIDS awareness campaigns.

Lauper remains down-to-earth and gutsy, continuing to identify with her working-class roots and with other women. Married since 1991 to actor David Thornton, she had her first child, son Declyn, at age forty-four. She lives with her family in New York's Upper West Side and continues to make music while trying to avoid the pitfalls of the superstar lifestyle. "I'm an entertainer," she reflected, "trying to express the fact that you can liberate yourself and say, hell, yes, I can do it. Life is not a prison sentence."

Tina Gianoulis

SEE ALSO: *AIDS; Betty Boop; Blues; Broadway; Emmy Awards; Feminism; Gay and Lesbian Press; Gay Liberation Movement; Kewpie Dolls; Movie Stars; MTV; Pop Music; Reality Television; Rock and Roll;* Rolling Stone*; Teenagers; Television; Top 40; Videos.*

BIBLIOGRAPHY

Burston, Paul. "Cyndi Lauper Is Back and the Girl Still Wants to Have Fun." *Times* (London), August 2, 2008.

Cocks, Jay. "These Big Girls Don't Cry." *Time*, March 4, 1985, 42.

Jerome, Jim. "Cyndi Lauper: Verve and Videos Turn an Outcast Oddball into a Musical Phenomenon." *People*, September 17, 1984, 82.

Kamen, Philip, and Peter Goddard. *Cyndi Lauper*. New York: McGraw-Hill, 1986.

Morreale, Marie, and Susan Mittelkauf. *The Cyndi Lauper Scrapbook*. New York: Bantam Books, 1985.

Laura

Laura (1944) is a classic American film noir directed by Otto Preminger. Critic Pauline Kael calls the movie "everybody's favorite chic murder mystery." Moderately successful when it was released, *Laura* has become a cult favorite and a staple of the classic movie cable channels.

Laura features a superb ensemble cast, including Gene Tierney as the mysteriously disappeared Laura and Dana Andrews as investigating detective Mark McPherson, who falls in love with Laura's portrait. Adding to the complicated yet stylish plot are Clifton Webb as the cynical radio personality Waldo Lydecker, who regards the beautiful Laura as both his creation and his property; Vincent Price as Laura's shallow, southern playboy suitor Shelby Carpenter; and Judith Anderson as Laura's rich spinster aunt and Shelby's would-be lover. Nominated for five Academy Awards, *Laura* won for best cinematography. The haunting score by David Raskins would become one of the most famous movie themes ever written.

Victoria Price

SEE ALSO: *Academy Awards; Cable TV; Film Noir; Hollywood; Preminger, Otto; Price, Vincent; Tierney, Gene.*

BIBLIOGRAPHY

Kael, Pauline. *5001 Nights at the Movies*. New York: Holt, 1991.

Silver, Alain, and Elizabeth Ward. *Film Noir: An Encyclopedic Reference to the American Style*. Woodstock, NY: Overlook Press, 1979.

Laurel and Hardy

The first and, arguably, best of filmdom's famous two-man comedy teams, Stan Laurel and Oliver Hardy were among the great silent-era clowns (along with Charlie Chaplin) who survived and thrived well into the talkie era. The two thrilled audiences with their carefully crafted style of comedy. Their short films, ranging from the pie-throwing apotheosis *The Battle of the Century* (1927) to the Oscar-winning *The Music Box* (1932), in which the boys strain to lug a piano up a steep hill, established their endearing characterizations as loyal friends—often hen-pecked husbands—who keep going from one "swell predicament" to "another fine mess."

EARLY CAREERS

Stan Laurel (real name: Arthur Stanley Jefferson) was born in 1890 in Ulverston, England, and began his show business career when he was only sixteen. By 1910 he was touring America with Fred Karno's London Comedians, not only performing but also working as the understudy to another young up-and-comer named Charles Chaplin. When Chaplin "went Hollywood" the troupe disbanded. He continued to kick around vaudeville until the early 1920s, though he started making films under the Stan Laurel name in 1917 with *Nuts in May*. In all he made some sixty movies before being partnered with Hardy. In a business in which a young stand-up can rise from obscurity to sitcom stardom in a couple of years (and return to anonymity just as quickly), Laurel spent two decades searching for his most apt comedy persona.

Oliver Hardy was born Norvell Hardy in 1892 in Harlem, Georgia. He grew up with a love of music. By 1910 the eighteen-year-old was running a movie theater and thinking to himself that he could probably act as well as the professionals he was watching on-screen. A few years later he had a chance to prove his abilities by working for the Lubin and Vim companies in Jacksonville, Florida. Although he made 100 short films, Hardy's weight typecast him as "the heavy," giving support to the comedians but never taking the lead himself.

TWO MINDS WITHOUT A SINGLE THOUGHT

The fates and their respective theatrical abilities brought Laurel and Hardy to Hollywood pioneer Hal Roach's studio, where the specialty was comedy, the budgets were small, and the talent was big. Laurel signed on with Roach in 1923; three years later the studio hired Hardy. Ace comedy director Leo McCarey had the inspiration to put the duo together. Unlike such latter-day comedy partners as Abbott and Costello or Martin and Lewis, who would hone their comedy personae onstage in front of live audiences before making it big in the movies, Laurel and Hardy grew into a team from film to film. During their series of short films in the 1920s, the derby-wearing duo quickly established their now-famous identities as the skinny one and the fat one: "Two minds," as Laurel described them, "without a single thought."

In 1927 the men made their first movie together, *Putting Pants on Phillip*. *Phillip* was uncharacteristic of what was to come, but the team hit their stride with their next film *The Battle of the Century*. In the 1930s Laurel and Hardy graduated to feature-length films that continued to spread their worldwide popularity. Although the movies eventually suffered a decline in quality when studio conflicts limited comic genius Laurel's ability to carefully plan and develop their vehicles, the stars themselves never wore out their welcome. The original Laurel and Hardy films still have the power to get an audience laughing at the pitfalls and pratfalls of twentieth-century urban living.

BANANA PEELS AND PIE FIGHTS

"Reciprocal destruction" became the phrase used to describe how, in a Laurel/Hardy film, a deceptively simple tit-for-tat escalates into a donnybrook. In *Battle*, one little banana peel pratfall ultimately leads to the biggest pie fight in movie history, encompassing an entire city block of citizens. But Laurel and Hardy didn't need spectacle to be just as hilarious in their subsequent shorts. The situation could be as simple as Stan trying to help Ollie put a radio antenna up on a roof or the two trying to make their dry-docked boat seaworthy. Or—as in their Oscar-winning talkie, *The Music Box*, Laurel and Hardy simply attempting to deliver a piano to a house way up there on top of the hill, with the only access via a narrow set of steps.

For all the brilliance of their slapstick, the comedy of Laurel and Hardy was personality driven, not situational. The characters they developed were two well-meaning but naive child-men—Stan, not too bright, and Ollie, who only *thinks* he's smarter than his pal—trying to cope with the vicissitudes of employment, matrimony, warfare, society, and technology, with the one constant being their friendship. Audiences laughed at the antics of Laurel and Hardy, but more than that, they fell in love with the boys. (No less loveable was a veritable stock company of brilliant supporting players, including James Finlayson and Mae Busch).

So endearing and enduring were the Laurel and Hardy characters that their appeal was only strengthened, not dissipated, by the dawn of sound film. (The early Laurel and Hardy talkies benefited enormously from the delightful underscoring of T. Marvin Hatley, composer of the "Cuckoo," which became the boys' signature tune.) Roach put his star team in feature-length movies, and still they prospered. Perhaps their best such film was *Way Out West* (1937).

Of the two actors, behind the scenes, Laurel was the prime creator, working with the hand-picked Roach production team on the story, gags, production, and even the editing of their films. He actually thought of himself more as a gag writer than a performer. Laurel and Roach did not always see eye to eye, but by and large the studio chief respected his star's talent and allowed it free reign. It is thanks to the work they did at Roach that Laurel and Hardy, the skinny guy and the fatso in their two derbies, became comedy icons recognized and adored wherever in the world movies were shown. And it is a tribute to Laurel and Hardy's appeal that they remained universally loved, even when the films themselves stopped being loveable.

LOSS OF CREATIVE CONTROL

Like other clowns from the golden age of screen comedy, Laurel and Hardy ran into trouble when they found themselves working for a production company that had no understanding of their working methods or an appreciation of how crucial those methods were to the art of their comedy. By the 1940s the duo had left Roach and ended up at Twentieth Century Fox. Seeking to cash in on the new, brash brand of comedy popularized by Abbott and Costello, Fox basically disallowed Laurel's input into the creative process. Gone were the carefully worked out scenarios and the opportunities to improvise on the central gag situations. For fans of the team, the 1940s films represented a mishandling of talent.

Laurel and Hardy. *Stan Laurel and Oliver Hardy appeared in* Babes in Toyland, *directed by Gus Meins and Charles Rogers, in 1934.* JOHN KOBAL FOUNDATION/CONTRIBUTOR/MOVIEPIX/GETTY IMAGES.

For the most part Laurel and Hardy called it quits with the movies after *The Bullfighters* in 1945 and spent the next decade delighting audiences overseas with personal appearances on stage. (In 1951 there was one disastrous comeback film, an international coproduction called *Atoll K*, which is even harder to watch than the 1940s Fox films.) Over the years Hardy would occasionally put in a solo appearance as a character actor in a movie, but these were few and far between. Eventually his health started to fail, and he died in 1957.

In their heyday, for all their international success, Laurel and Hardy were not treated very kindly by most critics. The much-married Laurel spent his last years living quietly in his Santa Monica, California, apartment, corresponding with his many fans and occasionally receiving visits from them. Thanks chiefly to the lobbying efforts of one such fan, comedian Dick Van Dyke, a campaign led to a special honorary Oscar for Laurel in 1961. Laurel was appreciative but also wistful that the honor had not come in time to be shared with Hardy. Probably more gratifying to Laurel was the formation of an international Laurel and Hardy fan club, dubbed The Sons of the Desert (after the fraternal order in their 1934 film of the same name). Even to this day local chapters of this organization gather around the globe to watch the films of the screen's first great comedy duo.

When Laurel died in 1965 he was eulogized as a great artist. It probably would have been nice if Laurel and Hardy had heard such praise in their heyday, but in the final analysis, it couldn't possibly have meant as much to them as the sound of one good belly laugh.

Preston Neal Jones

SEE ALSO: *Abbott and Costello; Academy Awards; Chaplin, Charlie; Silent Movies; Van Dyke, Dick; Vaudeville.*

BIBLIOGRAPHY

Louvish, Simon. *Stan and Ollie: The Roots of Comedy: The Double Life of Laurel and Hardy*. New York: St. Martin's Press, 2002.

Maltin, Leonard. *The Laurel and Hardy Book*. New York: Curtis Books, 1973.

McCabe, John. *Mr. Laurel and Mr. Hardy*. New York: Grosset & Dunlap, 1966.

Mitchell, Glenn. *The Laurel and Hardy Encyclopedia*. London: B. T. Batsford, 1995.

Scagnetti, Jack. *The Laurel and Hardy Scrapbook*. New York: Jonathan David Publishers, 1976.

Skretvedt, Randy. *Laurel and Hardy: The Magic behind the Movies*. Beverly Hills, CA: Moonstone Press, 1987.

Lauren, Ralph *(1939–)*

Bronx-born Ralph Lauren is the great dreamer of American fashion. He launched his fashion empire with wide ties (Polo Neckwear) in 1967. By 1968 Lauren was covering the menswear business, adding women's wear in 1971. He won further fame for designing Robert Redford's wardrobe for the movie *The Great Gatsby* (1974).

Lauren builds on consistent themes: Anglophilia centered around stately homes and rustic luxury, including tweeds, tartans, and Fair Isle sweaters; the heroic American West, celebrating the cowboy but revering Native American crafts; the Ivy League and clubby American elite of the 1920s; Hollywood and movie stars, particularly of the 1930s; and style icons, including the Duke of Windsor. Burnishing these powerful images, visualized in advertising photographed by Bruce Weber, Lauren has communicated a self-confident American style, compounded of aristocracy and adventure. Lauren's New York flagship store is a Madison Avenue mansion that feels more like a historic home than a retail establishment.

In 1997 Lauren took his company, Polo Ralph Lauren, public (as RL), and by 2010 it had annual revenues of more than $5 billion. Lauren was decorated by French president Nicolas Sarkozy as Chevalier de la Legion d'honneur, and in 2011 *Forbes* magazine estimated his wealth at $6.1 billion.

Richard Martin

SEE ALSO: *Hollywood; Ivy League; Movie Stars; Redford, Robert.*

BIBLIOGRAPHY

Gross, Michael. *Genuine Authentic: The Real Life of Ralph Lauren*. New York: Harper-Collins, 2003.

Trachtenberg, Jeffrey A. *Ralph Lauren: The Man behind the Mystique*. Boston: Little, Brown, 1988.

Laver, Rod *(1938–)*

In 1969 "Rocket" Rod Laver did what no other male tennis player had done before or has done since—he won the Grand Slam for the second time. Only one other men's player, American Don Budge, had ever won the Grand Slam—the Australian, the French Open, Wimbledon, and the US Open—even once. Laver is considered by many to have been the best tennis player ever, and his statistics make a good case for the Australian-born Hall of Famer. He was ranked number one in the world in 1961, 1962, 1968, and 1969. He won eleven grand slam events—four Wimbledons, three Australian titles, two French Opens, and two U.S. championships. In addition, in Davis Cup competition he compiled a singles record of 16–4. In 2000 center court at Melbourne Park, Australia, was named the Rod Laver Arena to honor his achievements.

Lloyd Chiasson Jr.

SEE ALSO: *Sports Heroes; Tennis; Wimbledon.*

BIBLIOGRAPHY

Feinstein, John. *Hard Courts: Real Life on the Professional Tennis Tours*. New York: Villard Books, 1992.

Grimsley, Will. *Tennis: Its History, People and Events*. Englewood Cliffs, NJ: Prentice-Hall, 1971.

Laver, Rod, and Bud Collins. *The Education of a Tennis Player*. New York: New Chapter Press, 2009.

Lorimer, Larry. *The Tennis Book: A Complete A-to-Z Encyclopedia of Tennis*. New York: Random House, 1980.

Noel, E., and James O. M. Clark. *A History of Tennis*. Newburyport, MA: Duckworth, 1991.

Schickel, Richard. *The World of Tennis*. New York: Random House, 1975.

Laverne and Shirley

Premiering on ABC in January 1976, *Laverne and Shirley* captured nearly 50 percent of the television-viewing audience, becoming an instant hit. In its first season, the sitcom—set in 1950s Milwaukee, Wisconsin—ranked second only to *Happy Days*, the show from which *Laverne and Shirley* was spun off. The series ended its run in 1983.

The program's success can be attributed to the appeal of its title characters, Laverne DeFazio and Shirley Feeney—played by Penny Marshall and Cindy Williams, respectively—who are single women employed as bottle cappers at the Shotz Brewery. They lack college degrees or promising careers and live in a modest basement apartment, which made them blue collar when working-class comedies such as *All in the Family* reigned and women were entering the workforce in record numbers. In addition, their slapstick comedy recalled *I Love Lucy*, a classic of the 1950s. Unlike Lucy and Ethel, however, Laverne and Shirley did not have husbands. They were, as their theme song asserted, doing it their way.

Belinda S. Ray

SEE ALSO: All in the Family; Happy Days; I Love Lucy; *Marshall, Garry; Sitcom; Television.*

BIBLIOGRAPHY

Brooks, Tim, ed. *The Complete Directory to Prime Time Network and Cable TV Shows 1946–Present*. New York: Ballantine Books, 1995.

McNeil, Alex. *Total Television: The Comprehensive Guide to Programming from 1948 to the Present*. New York: Penguin USA, 1997.

Morreale, Joanne. *Critiquing the Sitcom: A Reader*. New York: Syracuse University Press, 2003.

Law & Order: SVU

Law & Order: Special Victims Unit (*SVU*) was the first spin-off of the legendary long-running procedural crime drama *Law & Order*. Coming out of the success of a show dedicated to the investigation and prosecution of violent crimes (often based on news-making incidents from real life), *Law & Order: SVU* delved into even more lurid subject matter by focusing on sex crimes. With the original *Law & Order* entering its tenth season, creator Dick Wolf, the show's creator, decided to franchise his record-breaking success with the introduction of a new series, which premiered on September 20, 1999. The show was an immediate hit, consistently outperforming its parent show in network ratings despite—or perhaps because of—the public's fascination with its disturbing content. As John Leonard wrote in *New York Magazine*, "It probably doesn't hurt that almost every episode of *SVU* can be counted on to obsess about and drool all over occasions of rape and/or pedophilia."

The show owes much of its popularity to its two lead characters, Detectives Elliot Stabler and Olivia Benson (played by actors Chris Meloni and Mariska Hargitay, respectively). Benson and Stabler are deeply troubled individuals who turn to their work to solve their personal problems: Stabler's troubled family life and Benson's struggle to come to terms with being the child of a rape victim. The ways in which their character flaws complement each other provides a chemistry akin to that of Mulder and Scully in *The X-Files* (1993–2002), who likewise served as foils for each other's shortcomings. The tension built up by Stabler and Benson is often relieved by the comic repartee of the other pair of detectives in the SVU department, Odafin Tutuola (Ice-T) and John Munch (Richard Belzer, who first played this character on *Homicide* from 1993 to 1999), although they carry a certain amount of gravitas as well.

SVU has also drawn in viewers by featuring famous guest stars in many of its episodes. Carol Burnett, Treat Williams, Mario Bello, Serena Williams, Christopher "Ludacris" Bridges, and John Ritter are among the celebrities who have appeared on the show. Ritter, in particular, played against the "nice guy" character he was most known for (Jack Tripper on *Three's Company*) in an episode in which he portrays a very creepy psychiatrist.

Several other spin-offs, including *Law & Order: Criminal Intent* (2001–2011) and *Law & Order: Trial by Jury* (2005–2006) did not fare nearly as well as *SVU*. For a multitude of reasons, including the aforementioned star power and the intensity of the characters, *SVU* has been by far the most successful of Wolf's *Law & Order* franchise.

Daniel Coffey

SEE ALSO: *Ice-T; Television;* Three's Company; *Williams, Venus and Serena;* The X-Files.

BIBLIOGRAPHY

Green, Susan, and Randee Dawn. *"Law & Order: Special Victims Unit": The Unofficial Companion*. Dallas, TX: BenBella Books, 2009.

"*Law & Order* Creator Dick Wolf Talks Casting." *BackStage*, September 16, 2011.

Leonard, John. "The Donk-Donk Dynasty: As *Law & Order* Founders, *SVU* Still Thrives, Thanks to Sex, Sadism, and Two Very Screwed-up Cops." *New York Magazine*, April 29, 2007.

Lawn Care/Gardening

Where the American settler had wilderness at their doorstep, the contemporary American has created the lawn, a buffer of pseudo-nature between the public and private domain. Tending this landscape ornament has grown into an American pastime and supports a multimillion-dollar industry. Its surrounding green turf defines the American home from those in most other nations.

Despite its kitsch embellishments (such as pink flamingos and lawn orbs), the American lawn grows out of a serious tradition in landscape architecture. Andrew Jackson Downing and others who imported garden design and planning from Europe in the mid-1800s determined the green "setting" around homes to be majestic, utilitarian, and unique. The planting of grass defined the leisure household of the upper classes, who had more than enough land on which to situate a home. The grass thus became the background for landowners to incorporate more ornate garden designs.

From this point, the lawn and garden trend becomes entwined with growing suburbanization. As developers and designers in the early twentieth century tried to perfect a form of housing that was simple and cheap, yet dignified, the lawn became part of the basic landscape form of the American home. The design suggests changes in terms of attitudes toward the private and public self: often, the suburban design includes a front, communal green space intended to enhance visual presentation of the home and a rear green space for private playing and other activities. These tendencies became increasingly ubiquitous as the suburban home spread itself throughout the United States.

Home building exploded from 1950 onward, and even the most basic homes came to incorporate lawns, which have quickly become an indispensable part of American culture. For instance, when William Levitt perfected the minimalized version of the prefabricated home (of which thousands can be constructed in only a week) following World War II, a lawn remained integral to the design. While residents appreciate the green space's visual appeal, particularly in the suburban development, tending one's lawn or garden becomes the remnant of a fleeting human connection with nature. Some scholars view it as the American connection with the "pioneer spirit" of westward expansion through a continued proximity with nature—albeit a quite manufactured one.

Whatever the motivation, lawn and garden care became a multimillion-dollar industry after the 1960s. With the growth of the middle class in the twentieth century, males often found themselves with leisure time that could be channeled to activities and hobbies such as tending the garden and lawn. These practices became aesthetically and socially connected to the growing popularity of golf and defined much of middle-class male persona, such as that seen in television's Ward Cleaver or Tim "The Tool Man" Taylor. More recently, efforts have been made to simplify lawn care through the use of chemicals and "lawn management" companies, including ChemLawn and Lawn Doctor. In many suburbs, lawn care is a monthly expense, with charges varying when chemical application is needed a few times a year or, in the case of drought regions, when green coloring is added to the chemicals to achieve the desired aesthetic. This shift to the "industrial lawn" has led some Americans to view this green space as more of a burden than a blessing.

In recent years the image of the lawn has changed, as many Americans refuse to blindly adopt landscape forms not of their own choosing. This is particularly true in arid and semiarid portions of the United States, where lawns require a significant amount of limited water resources. Naturalist Michael Pollan speaks for many environmentalists when he refers to the lawn as "nature under culture's boot." Such sentiment, though, has not altered the American interest in maintaining a natural zone between home and society. Critics of the lawn have often turned to xeriscaping and other alterations that involve regionally native biota and no turf grass.

A minority of homeowners, fed up with the industrial lawn, have turned to organic practices. Drawing lessons from agriculture, organic lawn care prioritizes the replenishment of soil minerals. Because many North Americans were trained to rake up leaves and grass clippings, their lawns have been deprived of the only organic matter that would naturally replenish them and the soil beneath them. Because chemical fertilizers generally supply nutrients without affecting soil structure, they do not improve the soil or its ability to provide what the grass needs. The types of grasses are also partly to blame. In general, organic lawn care begins with two types of maintenance: focusing on natural methods to replace annual or biannual fertilizing or aerating, and shifting weekly care to prioritize watering deep, mowing high, and allowing clippings to lie.

In each of these new examples, homeowners have gone to great lengths to ensure that the setting of their home is not simply concrete. Therefore, whether a vegetable garden, green sward of grass, or a graveled space with cacti, Americans place a unique importance on maintaining some kind of natural environment around their homes.

Brian Black

SEE ALSO: *DIY/Home Improvement; Environmentalism; The Fifties;* Home Improvement*;* Leave It to Beaver*; Leisure Time; Suburbia; Television; World War II.*

BIBLIOGRAPHY

Baker, Sandy. *The Complete Guide to Organic Lawn Care.* Ocala, FL: Atlantic Publishing Group, 2011.

Bormann, F. Herbert; Diana Balmori; Gordon T. Geballe; et al. *Redesigning the American Lawn.* New Haven, CT: Yale University Press, 1993.

Jenkins, Virginia Scott. *The Lawn.* Washington, DC: Smithsonian Institution, 1994.

Pollan, Michael. *Second Nature.* New York: Laurel Books, 1991.

Steinberg, Theodore. *American Green.* New York: Norton, 2006.

Lawrence, Vicki *(1949–)*

Thanks to her resemblance to comedienne Carol Burnett, versatile television personality Vicki Lawrence broke into show business when she was eighteen years old. Burnett was looking for a young comedic actress to play her kid sister in sketches for *The Carol Burnett Show*, a variety program that ran from 1967 to 1978. Born in Inglewood, California, Lawrence had been singing in a group called the Young Americans when she got the part. Soon she was playing an array of skit characters on the show. One of her ongoing roles—the one for which she is best known—was the hilarious, purse-lipped, irascible southern matriarch Thelma Harper. Lawrence's portrayal later evolved into the series *Mama's Family*, which aired from 1983 to 1990.

In 1973 Lawrence topped the charts with her only hit single, "The Night the Lights Went out in Georgia." Three years later she won an Emmy Award for Best Supporting Actress in a Variety Show for her work on the Burnett series. She added to her coterie of fans in the mid-1990s as the hostess of the daytime talk show *Fox after Breakfast*, later renamed *The Vicki Lawrence Show*. In 2007 she revived the character of Mama for her long-running tour *Vicki Lawrence and Mama: A Two-Woman Show*.

In January 2011 Lawrence was criticized for making a video parody of Ted Williams, a homeless man and former radio announcer, whose videos had gone viral on YouTube. Advocates for the homeless objected to her series of jokes about "overnight sensations," and the head of the National Coalition for the Homeless characterized the comments as "some of the most un-Christian things imaginable."

Audrey E. Kupferberg

SEE ALSO: *Burnett, Carol; Daytime Talk Shows; Emmy Awards; Pop Music; Radio; Stand-Up Comedy; Television; Viral Videos; YouTube.*

BIBLIOGRAPHY

Lawrence, Vicki, and Marc Eliot. *Vicki! The True-Life Adventures of Miss Fireball.* New York: Simon & Schuster, 1995.

Lawrence, Vicki, and Monty Aidem. *Mama for President: Good Lord, Why Not?* Nashville, TN: Thomas Nelson, 2008.

Lawrence of Arabia

Lawrence of Arabia (1962) remains one of the most epic, literate, and beautiful films ever made. It brought instant stardom for actors Peter O'Toole and Omar Sharif; O'Toole in particular drew praise for his skillful depiction of Lawrence, a complex antihero beset by inner demons and motivated by a heady mixture of noble purpose, self-aggrandizement, compassion, and brutality and a large dollop of abnormal psychology.

The film is based on the exploits of British scholar and military officer Thomas Edward Lawrence. Born in North Wales in 1888 and educated at Oxford, Lawrence took a walking tour of Syria and Palestine to gather material for a thesis. His time living among the Arabs and learning their language, dialects, and customs proved invaluable to the British Intelligence Service with the outbreak of World War I.

The Turks, who were allied with Germany, ruled most of the Middle East with such brutality that the Arabs revolted, and the British sided with the Arabs. Lawrence knew that Britain and France had plans to divide Arabia between them when the war was over, but he felt if he could help the Arabs unite and defeat the Turks, the British would be unable to overlook the Arabs' moral claim to freedom. Lawrence joined forces with Auda abu Tayi, leader of the Howeitat tribe, and together they captured Aqaba without firing a shot; raided Turkish positions; and blew up sections of the Hejaz Railway, which was vital to the Turks. The Arabs pronounced Lawrence's name "El Aurens," as if he were already a prince, and he finally succeeded in leading the Arab army, under Prince Feisal, into Damascus.

American journalist Lowell Thomas and his cameraman caught many images of Lawrence in the desert, then toured the world with his illustrated lecture series, making Lawrence an international legend. After the war he remained an adviser on Arab affairs until 1922 when he enlisted in the Royal Air Force as a private under an assumed name. In 1926 he published *The Seven Pillars of Wisdom*, a complex and highly regarded blend of history, autobiography, philosophy, and mythmaking. He was killed in 1935 when the motorcycle he was riding struck a tree.

After the success of *The Bridge on the River Kwai*, producer Sam Spiegel approached director David Lean with the idea of making a film about Lawrence. After months of researching Lawrence's life, Lean agreed the story could make a fascinating film, provided a good script could be written. The first screenwriter proved unsatisfactory, and when Spiegel happened to attend the new hit play *A Man for All Seasons*, a historical play about Sir Thomas More and Henry VIII written by Robert Bolt, he hired Bolt for the job. Albert Finney and Marlon Brando were considered for the lead role, but the relatively unknown Peter O'Toole landed the part, and the film was shot in 1961 and 1962 in Jordan, Almeria, Morocco, and England. Lawrence's brother Arnold, who became Lawrence's literary executor upon his death and had permitted Spiegel to make the movie based on *Seven Pillars of Wisdom*, attended a rough cut of the film. When the film ended, Arnold stood up and shouted at Spiegel, "I should never have trusted you!" He then stormed out of the theater.

In O'Toole's first scene in the film, Lawrence does a trick putting a match out between his fingers. When another officer tries the same trick, he winces, "Ooh! It damn well 'urts!"

Lawrence of Arabia. *Peter O'Toole starred as T. E. Lawrence and Omar Sharif as Sherif Ali in* Lawrence of Arabia. COLUMBIA/THE KOBAL COLLECTION.

"Certainly it hurts," Lawrence replies. "What's the trick, then?" the officer asks. "The trick," Lawrence answers, "is not minding that it hurts." When Lawrence says he thinks the burning desert is going to be fun, an officer suggests that he has "a funny sense of fun," and there are suggestions that Lawrence enjoys the extreme tests of endurance that the desert provides. To keep peace among the Arab tribes before entering Aqaba, Lawrence is forced to shoot one of the Arabs, then later confesses, "I enjoyed it." And before Damascus, Lawrence exhibits maniacal glee as he joins in the slaughter of a column of Turks, shouting, "No prisoners!" and shooting at point-blank range one Turk with his hands up in surrender. It is easy to see why Lawrence's brother was so incensed but, as was later revealed, he may have been angered by the fact that the film was uncomfortably close to the truth.

In a 1985 interview, Arnold finally revealed the terrible family secret buried for so long—Lawrence hated the thought of sex and, after immersing himself in medieval literature about characters who quelled sexual longings by enduring beatings, he opted to do the same. A former Royal Tank Corps private admitted to ritually flogging Lawrence, at his request, from 1925 to 1934. A number of historians have hinted at Lawrence's possible homosexuality, and a number of film historians have called the film's homosexual overtones blatant.

Although all of this makes *Lawrence of Arabia* a far cry from *Rambo*, it makes for a more thought-provoking epic—heroic exploits may not always stem from the most heroic of motives—filled with great dialogue, great performances, gorgeous cinematography, and a sense of history. The title character's humanness and faults make the film easier to identify with. *Lawrence of Arabia* won seven Academy Awards, including best film, director, cinematography (Freddie Young), and musical score (Maurice Jarre).

Bob Sullivan

SEE ALSO: *Academy Awards;* The Bridge on the River Kwai*; War Movies; World War I.*

BIBLIOGRAPHY

Brownlow, Kevin. *David Lean.* London: Richard Cohen Books, 1996.

Castelli, Louis P., and Caryn Lynn Cleeland. *David Lean: A Guide to References and Resources.* Boston: G. K. Hall, 1980.

Caton, Steven Charles. Lawrence of Arabia: *A Film's Anthropology.* Berkeley: University of California Press, 1999.

Silverman, Stephen M. *David Lean.* New York: Harry N. Abrams, 1989.

La-Z-Boy Loungers

The La-Z-Boy Lounger, a reclining chair also known as the easy chair, is a heavily padded item of furniture, generally upholstered in Naugahyde or another similarly tough and durable fabric and boasting a built-in ottoman. By pulling a side lever, a person can simultaneously recline the chair back and kick out the attached footrest, arriving at a position somewhere between sitting and lying down.

Businessmen Edwin Shoemaker (c. 1907–1998) and Edward Knabusch (1900–1988) of Monroe, Michigan, made the first loungers in 1927. Combining the science of ergonomics with automobile and airplane seat design, they developed what eventually became the La-Z-Boy. In 1941 Edward Barcalo (1870–1963) licensed the design of Hungarian businessman Anton Lorenz (1861–1964) for a "scientifically articulated" TV chair, which he dubbed the Barcalounger. This chair became La-Z-Boy's largest competitor.

The chairs, which originally sacrificed high style for immediate comfort and versatility, have remained enduring symbols of masculine tastes in the United States. Although many companies produced loungers throughout the century, La-Z-Boy remained the most popular brand and became the generic name for them all. Long associated with sports viewing, in 2011 the company introduced a new recliner for ultimate sports fans, with options to show off favorite logos and mascots from professional and college sports teams.

Wendy Woloson

SEE ALSO: *Leisure Time.*

BIBLIOGRAPHY

"Our History." Accessed on March 2012. Available from http://www.la-z-boy.com/about/history/

Patton, Phil. *Made in U.S.A.: The Secret Histories of the Things That Made America.* New York: Grove Weidenfeld, 1992.

Stern, Jane, and Michael Stern. *The Encyclopedia of Bad Taste.* New York: HarperCollins, 1990.

le Carré, John *(1931–)*

In a review of James Fennimore Cooper's *The Spy* (1821), a critic wrote: "No sympathy can be excited with meanness, and there must be a degree of meanness ever associated with the idea of Spy." Eighty-four years later the *Morning Post* titled its review of Joseph Conrad's *The Secret Agent* "The Real Anarchist" and claimed that "it is a study of real value for the student of contemporary politics." This reveals something about the evolving conception of the spy in society, and the novels of John le Carré further explore and develop this image.

Le Carré was born David John Moore Cornwell in Poole, Dorset, on October 19, 1931. His mother abandoned the family when he was six, and le Carré later learned that his father, Ronnie Cornwell, was a crafty con man who had served a prison term. Betrayal and deception were to become the key themes of his writings. After studying German at Berne University, he completed his national service with the Intelligence Corps in Austria. It is likely that he was recruited into the British Secret Service in Berne, although le Carré has never actually given the exact date of his enrollment, nor has he elaborated upon the exact nature of his work. In 1952 he returned to England, where he completed his German studies, graduating cum laude in 1956 at Lincoln College, Oxford.

THE GEORGE SMILEY NOVELS

Le Carré entered the Foreign Office in 1959 and, in 1961, was posted to the British embassy in Bonn, Germany, as second secretary. That same year he published his first novel, *Call for the Dead*, introducing the antiheroic figure George Smiley of the Circus, the British security service. The critical reception of his debut focuses mainly on the manipulation of the conventional "whodunit" into the spy thriller. This notion of subverting the rules of the genre has become the predominant critical view of his novels. What has been instrumental in the process of canonization of le Carré is the realization that his books could be read as political parables—a "thriller that demands a second reading as a treatise on our times."

In 1963, still working as second secretary at the height of the Cold War, le Carré published *The Spy Who Came in from the Cold*, a grimly realist tale of betrayal and deception, the key theme being that espionage in itself inevitably leads to moral corruption. Its huge success enabled him to resign from the Foreign Office. Critic Graham Greene called it the best spy novel he had ever read. The reactions from the professionals, however, were hostile. "You bastard, you utter bastard," one of his former colleagues yelled at the author at a diplomatic dinner. Richard Helms, sworn in as director of intelligence at the CIA (Central Intelligence Agency) in 1966, resented the climate of despair in le Carré's novel. Thomas Powers writes in his *The Man Who Kept the Secrets* that "it was not just the violence Helms minded, but the betrayal, the mood of defeat, the meanness, the numb loneliness of a man for whom loyalty has become a joke. . . . Le Carré was undermining the very bedrock of intelligence, the faith of men in the meaning of their work."

John le Carré. *Author John le Carré appears at the premiere of the movie adaption of his 1974 book* Tinker, Tailor, Soldier, Spy *in London, England, in 2011.* FRED DUVAL/CONTRIBUTOR/GETTY IMAGES ENTERTAINMENT/GETTY IMAGES.

In the George Smiley trilogy *Tinker, Tailor, Soldier, Spy* (1974; made into a film in 2011), *The Honourable Schoolboy* (1977), and *Smiley's People* (1979)—also published as *The Quest for Karla* trilogy—le Carré not only debates the morality of espionage but also explores the theme of love's betrayal. "But who are the foes? Once upon a time it was clear, but now nothing is certain. The enemy in those days was someone we could point at . . . today all I know is that I have learned to interpret the whole of life in terms of conspiracy," Smiley sighs in *The Honourable Schoolboy*. It therefore comes as no surprise that le Carré's only novel with an unambiguously evil villain, the illegal arms dealer Richard "Dicky" Roper in *The Night Manager* (1993), is also his only novel with a "happy ending."

In the Cold War novels that deal with the Circus and the KGB, the real and the absolute enemy are frequently not the same person or entity. Often the most intense enemy is to be found in the protagonist's own camp (*The Spy Who Came in from the Cold*, *The Quest for Karla*) and sometimes the protagonist turns out to be his own worst enemy (*A Perfect Spy*, 1986).

LATER WORK

After the fall of the Iron Curtain and the end of the Cold War in 1989, the focus of le Carré's fiction shifted away from the world of international espionage to address topical contemporary issues, often involving the shady economical and political realities of the new globalized economy. *The Night Manager* (1993) addresses the smuggling of drugs, money, and arms, depicting the Latin American drug wars, the intricacies of offshore banking in the Caribbean, and the tendency of U.S. and European governments to overlook these crimes unless they begin to affect their own countries. In *The Constant Gardener* (2001), which was made into a critically acclaimed film in 2005, the protagonist discovers his activist wife's death was the result of her discovery of a drug testing scandal involving an international pharmaceutical conglomerate. In *Our Kind of Traitor* (2010), le Carré depicts the global recession through the eyes of a British couple approached by a Russian money launderer who wants to trade information for immunity from prosecution.

As a public figure, the author has had to face the consequences of the strained fact-fiction continuum that characterizes his novels. "My great sin," he said once, "ever since I wrote *The Little Drummer Girl*" (1983), "was suggesting that the state of Israel—that Palestine—was in fact a twice-promised land." When a *New York Times* book review of his novel *The Tailor of Panama* (1996) suggested that the main character "was an anti-Semitic Judas" caricature, le Carré vehemently denied the charge, asking the *Guardian* to publish a speech he had made to the Anglo-Israel Association. This prompted a response from Salman Rushdie, author of *The Satanic Verses*, who has lived under a *fatwa* (death threat) since early 1989 and whom le Carré had publicly criticized. Rushdie pointed out that not only had he suffered from far more rigorous religious intolerance than le Carré but also that le Carré never spoke out against the fatwa, to which le Carré replied, "there is no law in life or nature that says great religions may be insulted with impunity." The first and foremost quality of a good intelligence officer, as former CIA director Allen Dulles said, is to discern between fact and fiction. Le Carré demonstrates that it might be far more important to discern between friend and foe.

Le Carré controversially and publically spoke out against the Iraq War, publishing a 2003 article in the *Times* titled "The

United States of America Has Gone Mad," in which he criticizes President George W. Bush for using the bombing of the World Trade Center as an excuse to invade Iraq. In subsequent years he has given a series of mainstream and liberal media interviews in which his critique of the Iraq War is coupled with a larger concern about the governmental misuse of media as propaganda.

Rob van Kranenburg

SEE ALSO: *Best Sellers; Cold War; Detective Fiction.*

BIBLIOGRAPHY

Bloom, Clive, ed. *Spy Thrillers: From Buchan to le Carré.* Basingstoke, England: Macmillan Press, 1990.

Bold, Alan Norman. *The Quest for le Carré.* London: Vision Press, 1988.

Le Carré, John. *A Perfect Spy.* New York: Alfred A. Knopf, 1986.

Le Carré, John. *The Secret Pilgrim.* London: Hodder and Stoughton, 1991.

Le Carré, John. *The Night Manager.* New York: Alfred A. Knopf, 1993.

Le Carré, John. *Our Game.* London: Hodder and Stoughton, 1995.

Le Carré, John. "Opinion: The United States of America Has Gone Mad." *Times* (London), January 15, 2003.

Monaghan, David. *Smiley's Circus: A Guide to the Secret World of John le Carré.* London: Orbis, 1986.

Powers, Thomas. *The Man Who Kept the Secrets: Richard Helms & the CIA.* London: Weidenfeld and Nicholson, 1979.

Stafford, David. *The Silent Game: The Real World of Imaginary Spies.* London: Viking, 1988.

Le Guin, Ursula K. *(1929–)*

In the introduction to Joe De Bolt's collection of essays about Ursula K. Le Guin, Barry N. Malzberg claims that "Le Guin is probably the first writer to emerge solely within the confines of the genres to win significant literary recognition. . . . She is . . . the most important contemporary writer of science fiction, and this field cannot be understood if she is not." Le Guin's name found a place alongside figures such as H. G. Wells and J. R. R. Tolkien in the National Public Radio 2011 survey of the Top 100 science fiction and fantasy books. Her major works appear on nearly every list of important science fiction and fantasy on popular blogs that feature lists of the "best books" within either genre. Her short fiction has appeared in numerous publications, including *Amazing Science Fiction*, the *New Yorker*, *Playgirl*, and *Playboy*.

Le Guin's success within the genres of speculative fiction has earned her multiple Hugo, Locus, Nebula, and James Tiptree Jr. awards. Her appeal outside that arena has yielded her such honors such as the National Book Award and the Newbery Award. After more than three decades of publishing, Le Guin was honored with various lifetime achievement awards, including the Science Fiction and Fantasy Writers of America's prestigious Grand Master Award. Few authors have been as well received and influential in the span of their own lives as Le Guin.

CENTRAL THEMES

If there were a central metaphor to describe Le Guin's life and work, it might be the interplay of individual and society. Her own interaction with society began in a family of literate intellectuals. Her mother, Theodora Kracaw Kroeber, published *The Inland Whale: Nine Stories Retold from California Indian Legends* in 1959. As biographer Elizabeth Cummins Cogell has claimed, this work suggests the "awareness of the female character," which has become such a force in Le Guin's own tales.

Neither did Le Guin escape the influence of her father, Alfred Kroeber, who wrote prolifically in the field of anthropology. This discipline pokes its way to the surface of many of Le Guin's finest and best-known works, such as *The Left Hand of Darkness* (1969) and "Solitude." Anthropology is, however, more than an overt theme in her stories; it is also the source of some of her greatest strengths: her ability to craft a world, universe, and history with utter believability. One of her father's favorite books, Dunsany's *A Dreamer's Tales*, impressed upon her that the archetypal images evoked by myth and fable could be—and indeed still were being—called forth in literature. Her father also introduced her to the principles of Taoism, forming the foundation for her concepts of balance, equilibrium, and death in many of her worlds. She has even published her own translation of the *Lao Tzu: Tao Te Ching.*

EARLY COMPOSITIONS

Le Guin began writing early, and she recalls submitting her first science fiction story to *Astounding Stories Magazine* around the age of ten. The story was rejected, but Le Guin claims that she was more "delighted to have a genuine rejection slip" than she was dejected. Much later, she read J. R. R. Tolkien's *The Lord of the Rings*, which impressed her so deeply that she claims, "If I'd read it as a kid I might have written bad imitations of it for years. As it was, I already was finding my own voice, and so could just have the joy of reading Tolkien as the creator of the greatest of the fantasy worlds."

Le Guin has constructed an original path that winds through the traditions of science fiction and fantasy as well as mainstream fiction. Writer and critic Orson Scott Card has noted particularly her concept of the ansible, a conceit now commonly used in science fiction, which allows two parties to communicate simultaneously despite their distance. British author Tom Becker has praised her attention to "real world physics," saying that she exceeds even De Camp, "the only other [early science fiction] writer I know of who wasn't violating the law of relativity." Fellow science fiction writer Élisabeth Vonarburg has recognized Le Guin's influence on "non-American, non English-speaking writers," as well as female writers born in the second half of the twentieth century. "I still hear," noted Vonarburg, "from a number of young or less young female readers what I myself have been saying for years: 'I came back to reading SF because of Le Guin.'"

Le Guin's first novel, *Rocannon's World*, was published by Ace Books in 1966. Since then she has explored topics as wide in variety as the influence of gender upon society (perhaps best achieved in *The Left Hand of Darkness*), what it means to be human, and the individual as outcast. Yet it is no great task for an author to speak out on a wide variety of tasks; where Le Guin has made her greatest mark is in her ability to craft a sound narrative with characters who embody the concepts she hopes to explore. Le Guin is above all a deeply talented storyteller, one whom Becker has used to demonstrate the point that feminism is not only a source of ideas but also a source of excellent literature.

POPULAR AND CRITICAL RECEPTION

It is difficult to narrow Le Guin's body of work to just a handful of important titles, but there are a few that have made particular impression on the field. The first of these, *The Left Hand of Darkness*, has crept into the canon's outskirts through women's studies and graduate programs and was the first of her works to receive overwhelming acknowledgment from the writing community. *The Dispossessed*, published in 1974, has likewise gained praise from nearly every quarter. Her *Earthsea* series (1968–2001), marketed as children's books, reached new audiences for Le Guin. Unlike the other two works, this series is a high fantasy series, and it is largely on the strength of *Earthsea* that she has gained notoriety as a fantasy writer. This series became influential on subsequent high fantasy in turn, revising several tropes descended from Tolkien and others.

Le Guin is an active and vocal member of several feminist organizations and has also been active in conservationist groups. As a writer, she has helped shape the ideas of such diverse speculative elements as magic, the power of language, interstellar communication, dragons, and the relationship of people across gender and racial boundaries. Her poetry has also elicited praise from critics, and she brings the poet's sense of language to her fiction. Through various exercises and prompts, Le Guin's 1998 book, *Steering the Craft*, outlines her ideas on writing and challenges the traditional insistence that writers stick to present tense.

Although she pursues different genres and themes, Le Guin has never ventured too far from her passions. She returned to the Hainish Cycle, first visited in *The Left Hand of Darkness*, with 2000's award-winning *The Telling*. In 2001 Le Guin offered a prequel to her critically acclaimed *Earthsea* series with the collection *Tales from Earthsea* as well as the fifth installment, *The Other Wind*, which won the World Fantasy Award for Best Novel. Following the shift made in the fourth book in the series, *Tehanu* (1990), the books are narrated by a decidedly female protagonist.

While admittedly concerned with feminist causes, Le Guin has attempted to write stories that are not heavy-handed with the message. Her work has been recognized for its ability to address sociological issues through its straightforward prose and quotidian exploits. Her 2008 novel, *Lavinia*, is a perfect example. The book gives voice to the princess Lavinia, who never spoke a word in Virgil's *Aeneid*. Departing from Virgil, Le Guin fleshes out the concerns and desires of the minor character, creating a richer and deeper world for both Lavinia and Aeneas. Throughout her career, she has remained an astute social critic in both her novels and public life.

Joe Sutliff Sanders

SEE ALSO: *Feminism; The* New Yorker*;* Playboy*;* Playgirl*; Science Fiction Publishing; Tolkien, J. R. R.*

BIBLIOGRAPHY

Cogell, Elizabeth Cummins. *Ursula K. Le Guin: A Primary and Secondary Bibliography*. Boston: G. K. Hall, 1983.

De Bolt, Joe. *Ursula K. Le Guin: Voyager to Inner Lands and to Outer Space*. Port Washington, NY: Kennikat Press, 1979.

Freedman, Carl, ed. *Conversations with Ursula K. Le Guin*. Jackson: University of Mississippi Press, 2008.

Olander, Joseph D., and Martin Harry Greenberg, eds. *Ursula K. Le Guin*. New York: Taplinger, 1979.

Leachman, Cloris *(1926–)*

An exceptionally good and versatile actress, angular and wistful looking, Cloris Leachman made a striking film debut in *Kiss Me Deadly* (1955). While raising five children, starting in the mid-1950s and continuing for about sixteen years, she frequently appeared in secondary roles. Her identity as an actress remained vague. It was her poignant, exquisitely judged Oscar-winning performance as the lonely and neglected wife in *The Last Picture Show* (1971) that brought her due recognition and led her to two treasurable performances for Mel Brooks: the terrifying Frau Blucher in *Young Frankenstein* (1974) and the deliciously violent nurse in *High Anxiety* (1977).

Leachman joined the acting profession by way of the 1946 Miss America Pageant, in which she was runner-up. Having studied drama at Northwestern University, she worked regularly on Broadway and in live television drama. Her TV career grew substantially from the mid-1970s, bringing her a clutch of Emmy Awards and her own show, *Phyllis* (1975–1977), a spin-off series based on the supporting character she had played in *The Mary Tyler Moore Show* from 1970 to 1975.

In the 1980s Leachman's notable roles included playing the housemother Beverly Ann Stickle in forty-eight episodes of the television series *The Facts of Life* (1986–1988) and ten episodes in the ill-fated Mel Brooks comedy series *The Nutt House* (1989). She won an Emmy Award for her performance in an episode of the television drama *Promised Land* (1997) and provided voices for animated films ranging from *My Little Pony: The Movie* (1986) and Hayao Miyazaki's *Castle in the Sky* (1986) to *A Troll in Central Park* (1994), *Beavis and Butt-Head Do America* (1996), and *The Iron Giant* (1999). She also garnered several Emmy Awards for her occasional appearances as the cantankerous Grandma Ida in the sitcom *Malcolm in the Middle* (2001–2006) and played the mother of Ellen DeGeneres in *The Ellen Show* (2001–2002).

Leachman appeared in a string of films throughout the first dozen years in the twenty-first century, including *Spanglish* (2004), *The Longest Yard* (2005), *Beerfest* (2006), *The Women* (2008), and *The Fields* (2011). She also made history as the oldest contestant on the competition series *Dancing with the Stars* (2008–2009) and had a recurring role in the comedy series *Raising Hope* (2010–), for which she received an Emmy nomination in 2011.

As the winner of more Emmy Awards than any other actor in her six-plus decades in Hollywood, Leachman has had as successful of a career as it has been long. She received a star on the Hollywood Walk of Fame in 1980 and was inducted into the Television Academy Hall of Fame in 2011. As an indication of her beloved status across generations, her 2009 autobiography, *Cloris: My Autobiography*, was a *New York Times* best seller and was warmly received by critics and readers alike.

Robyn Karney

SEE ALSO: *Academy Awards; Animated Films;* Beavis and Butt-Head*; Best Sellers; Broadway; Brooks, Mel;* Dancing with the Stars*; DeGeneres, Ellen; Emmy Awards; Hollywood;* The Mary Tyler Moore Show*; Miss America Pageant; Television.*

BIBLIOGRAPHY

Katz, Ephraim. *The International Film Encyclopedia.* New York: HarperCollins, 1994.

Leachman, Cloris, and George Englund. *Cloris: My Autobiography.* New York: Kensington Books, 2009.

Willsmer, Trevor. "Cloris Leachman." *Who's Who in Hollywood,* ed. Robyn Karney. New York: Continuum, 1993.

Leadbelly *(1885–1949)*

In the pantheon of blues legends, few figures loom as large as Leadbelly, the peripatetic guitar player with the constitution of iron. The gifted composer of such standards as "Goodnight Irene," "Midnight Special," and "Where Did You Sleep Last Night," Leadbelly led a troubled life. Thrice consigned to imprisonment in the Deep South, he had his sentence commuted twice on the strength of his musicianship alone. But his penchant for trouble was inextricably linked to his genius, and like legendary guitarists Robert Johnson and Blind Lemon Jefferson, his hard times became interwoven with his musical abilities. The years of Leadbelly's fame were short and far from remunerative, and he did not live to see his songs become standards and his talent revered.

Leadbelly. *Leadbelly's tumultuous life ended before he was able to see several of his songs become American standards that inspired many artists of the rock era.* MICHAEL OCHS ARCHIVES/STRINGER/ GETTY IMAGES.

EARLY LIFE

Leadbelly was born Huddie Ledbetter in the backwoods of northern Louisiana near Shreveport. His family was relatively affluent, with a fair-sized farm in Harrison County, Texas, that they bought when Ledbetter was five. He was musically precocious from an early age—he began performing on the streets of Shreveport as a teenager—and he soon graduated from windjammer (a rudimentary accordion) to guitar. Ledbetter grew up to be a man of extremes. A veritable John Henry of the cotton fields, he could drink most men under the table and was purported to be the best musician in the area. His appetite for women was of a piece with his other attributes, and he soon married Lethe Henderson.

In what became a pattern of behavior, Ledbetter would work hard for a time, content to remain domestic, but then some deep-seated impulse would send him on the road. He would vanish, then show up months later penniless and bruised. For all his carousing, Ledbetter's ambition to make a living solely from music remained intact. After a stint on the railroad, he vowed to realize his ambition. He became enchanted by the twelve-string guitar, bought one with his scant savings, and took to the streets of Dallas, where he busked for drinks and spare change.

After teaming up with Jefferson, his life slid into a nonstop bacchanal of music, drink, and women until he was convicted of his first serious crime and sentenced to a year on a chain gang. Within three days he had escaped, rejoining his family in Harrison County. His wife located him there, and they moved to De Kalb, Texas, where she later died. Ledbetter careened into a profound depression. Some months later he shot and killed a drunk while playing a local dance, drawing a thirty-five-year sentence.

SECOND CHANCES

Much of Ledbetter's legend revolves around the two gubernatorial pardons he received on the strength of his musical talent. In 1918 Ledbetter was remanded to Huntsville penitentiary, where he acquired a prodigious reputation for work and music. His surname was soon corrupted into Leadbelly, a moniker he took pride in, denoting as it did his iron constitution. While Leadbelly was in prison, he performed for Texas Governor Patrick Neff, who came to see the legendary singing convict. A year after performing for Neff, Leadbelly was free, perhaps the first convict to sing his way to freedom. He won his freedom a second time, having been convicted of assault in his native Louisiana, due to the auspices of John Lomax, an archivist for the Library of Congress. During a tour of the South with his son Alan, Lomax recorded a plea to Louisiana Governor O. K. Allan, and in 1934 Leadbelly was again pardoned.

Leadbelly's time in the limelight was brief and bitter. Following his release, he was employed by Lomax as a driver for him and his son. Leadbelly located musicians in the towns and prisons they visited, and on a northern leg of the journey, Lomax began arranging recitals for his, at times, obstreperous driver. Much to Leadbelly's consternation, he was made to perform in prison stripes. He took the stage at Bryn Mawr College in Pennsylvania and Columbia University in New York, his extensive repertoire and prison record adding to his appeal for the collegiate audiences. He was the toast of the town, a talented curiosity, but Leadbelly missed his wife, who he had married shortly after his release. He also rankled under Lomax's cautious administration, frequently slipping off on drinking sprees. The pair eventually parted company.

For the rest of his life, Leadbelly remembered his brush with fame and strove to recapture the elusive pot of gold. He moved back to Shreveport, where his celebrity could not prevent him from serving more jail time. He then returned to New York, and the years slipped by. In 1939 he stabbed a man at a party and spent a year on Riker's Island. After this prison stint, Leadbelly held a variety of odd jobs while occasionally playing on the radio or in Greenwich Village and Harlem.

In 1949 he was flown to Paris for a string of unsuccessful engagements that ultimately killed his dreams of fame and the good life. By November the mysterious back pains that had plagued him for years had been diagnosed as amyotrophic lateral sclerosis—Lou Gehrig's disease. He died in Bellevue on December 6, 1949, with his guitar by his side. Six months later "Goodnight Irene" had sold two million copies. Meanwhile, Leadbelly's widow was applying for work as a laundress.

Like many first-generation blues musicians, Leadbelly was a man stuck between the antebellum South and the modern age. Part of his problem, certainly, was the record industry, in which black artists were often cheated, but it was Leadbelly's erratic nature that prevented him from capitalizing on his success. By the time he had a chance at fame, he was too set in his ways to turn professional. But for all that, he was a man of intense pride who resented having to play a convict or barefoot country boy to promote himself. When his first collection of songs appeared, it pained him that the cover photo showed him barefoot and sitting on a barrel. Seeing how many artists made the music charts with his songs would likely not have pleased him, when he himself had profited so little.

Michael Baers

SEE ALSO: *Blues; Jazz; Johnson, Robert.*

BIBLIOGRAPHY

Garvin, Richard M., and Edmond G. Addeo. *The Midnight Special: The Legend of Leadbelly.* New York: Bernard Geis Associates, 1971.

Hamilton, Marybeth. *In Search of the Blues.* New York: Basic Books, 2009.

Lomax, John Avery; Alan Lomax; and George Herzog. *Negro Folk Songs as Sung by Leadbelly "King of the Twelve-String Guitar Players of the World," Long-Time Convict in the Penitentiaries of Texas and Louisiana.* New York: Macmillan, 1936.

Wolfe, Charles K., and Kip Lornell. *The Life and Legend of Leadbelly.* New York: HarperCollins, 1992.

A League of Their Own

The 1992 film comedy *A League of Their Own* revitalized interest in and helped memorialize a neglected chapter of sports history: the All-American Girls Professional Baseball League (AAGPBL). With men from the United States leaving to fight in World War II, Chicago Cubs owner Philip K. Wrigley (the chewing gum mogul) thought that women playing baseball might help keep interest in the sport alive until the war was over and the men returned home.

As depicted in the film, the league began in 1943 with four teams: the Rockford Peaches, the Racine Belles, the Kenosha Comets, and the South Bend Blue Sox. When it became evident that the war would not seriously affect the major leagues, Wrigley sold the women's league to Chicago advertising executive Arthur Meyerhoff. However, after the men returned home, instead of fading into oblivion, the AAGPBL prospered because of the women's extraordinary baseball abilities. By 1948 the league had grown to ten teams and attracted 910,000 paid fans. The AAGPBL lasted twelve seasons, until 1954, destroyed in part by television, especially televised professional baseball. During its existence, the league never would have attracted as many fans as it did without the high level of pure athleticism demonstrated by the players.

THE LEAGUE ON FILM

The film *A League of Their Own* is a craftily constructed comedy that gets big laughs, manages an emotional tale of sibling rivalry, and imparts a surprisingly accurate painless history lesson. In addition, the movie has been an inspiration for some young girls, showing them that there is no such thing as a male sport or, for that matter, a male occupation. Much of the film's strength stems from the fact that the actresses playing the athletes seem, themselves, to be athletic, which is absolutely vital to telling the story of a professional women's baseball league able to sustain itself by attracting fans through sheer excellence on the field.

The film, which cost about $50 million to make, went approximately $15 million over budget; however, according to *Sports Illustrated,* if the extra money was spent "for the technical advice, it was money well spent. Thanks to the efforts of Southern Cal coaching legend Rod Dedeaux, the USC coaching staff and AAGPBL alumna Pepper Davis, nobody in *A League of Their Own* throws like a girl. In fact, everybody throws better than John Goodman did in *The Babe.*"

Geena Davis and Lori Petty play the two central characters, rival sisters who move from farm life to the major leagues. Again, according to *Sports Illustrated,* "it's hard to believe that Davis never played baseball before arriving on the set, because in a pickup game you would choose her as your catcher over, say, Tom Berenger, the backstop in *Major League,*" while Petty "displays a nice flair for the mound." Screenwriters Lowell Ganz and Babaloo Mandel (who also wrote the films *Splash* and *City Slickers*) made the sisters a pitcher (Petty) and a catcher (Davis)—perfectly logical positions for two sisters who practiced alone on a farm—and used those positions to maximum effect during the film's climactic game, with the sisters on opposing teams during the league's first World Series. Even comedy relief Madonna and Rosie O'Donnell seem athletic; John Lovitz is hilarious as scout Eddie Capadino; director Penny Marshall's brother, Garry, plays the Wrigley character (here made a candy bar mogul); and David Strathairn portrays the promotional genius who believes that the league has a future beyond the war.

CREATING DUGAN

Actor Tom Hanks, however, steals the film in a career-altering role as an alcoholic, chauvinistic manager named Jimmy Dugan.

The movie *Big* (1988) showed that Hanks could act, but his next few films, including *The 'burbs* (1989), *Turner & Hooch* (1989), and *Joe Versus the Volcano* (1990), were panned by both critics and audiences. Hanks approached Marshall about playing the role of the team manager, and, after working out some issues with the character, she agreed.

The movie script describes the character of Dugan as a fifty-two-year-old broken-down alcoholic, but, as Hanks told Marshall, instead of being made to look older, he was more interested in playing a thirty-six-year-old broken-down alcoholic. He began by figuring out why his character was not still playing ball or joining up to fight in the war. Hanks solved the problem by giving the character a pronounced limp, an injury sustained during a drinking mishap. Another problem, suggested by Marshall, was how to make this character less attractive; if the manager were cute, everybody would be wondering why the girls on the team were not attracted to this handsome guy. Hanks found the solution: "How about if I get fat?"—and, according to Hanks, he has been fat ever since.

Hanks is both funny and touching as Dugan, who begins with the belief that "girls are what you sleep with after the game, not what you coach during the game." He gradually develops a deep respect for the players. Hanks followed up his performance in *A League of Their Own* with highly praised roles in *Philadelphia* (1993), *Sleepless in Seattle* (1993), and *Forrest Gump* (1994). The greatest achievement of *A League of Their Own*, however, remains its reviving, from semi-obscurity, the achievements of the women of the AAGPBL, who definitively demonstrated that America's pastime is not a pastime just for males.

Bob Sullivan

SEE ALSO: *Baseball; Hanks, Tom; Madonna; Marshall, Garry; Movie Stars; O'Donnell, Rosie; World War II.*

BIBLIOGRAPHY

Berlage, Gai Ingham. *Women in Baseball: The Forgotten History.* Westport, CT: Praeger Publishers, 1994.

Browne, Lois. *Girls of Summer: The Real Story of the All-American Girls Professional Baseball League.* New York: HarperCollins Publishers, 1993.

Galt, Margot Fortunato. *Up to the Plate: The All-American Girls Professional Baseball League.* Minneapolis, MN: Lerner Publications, 1995.

Gregorich, Barbara. *Women at Play: The Story of Women in Baseball.* San Diego, CA: Harcourt Brace, 1993.

Hanmer, Trudy J. *The All-American Girls Professional Baseball League.* New York: New Discovery Books, 1994.

Macy, Sue. *A Whole New Ball Game: The Story of the All-American Girls Professional Baseball League.* New York: Holt, 1993.

Madden, W. C. *The Women of the All-American Girls Professional Baseball League: A Biographical Dictionary.* Jefferson, NC: McFarland, 1997.

LeapFrog

LeapFrog Enterprises, based in Emeryville, California, manufactures toys that integrate learning technologies. The company sells its toys globally in more than twenty-five countries and in 2012 was the fourth-largest toy company in the United States after Mattel, Hasbro, and Lego. In 2011 LeapFrog had more than $450 million in revenue and released its latest innovative learning toy, the LeapPad Explorer.

The company began in 1995, when founder and CEO Mike Wood designed Phonics Desk to help his son read. With this new technology, the user slid word cards into the machine and then spelled out the words using plastic letters. The machine spoke, offering feedback and instruction to the user, ultimately helping the child match letters to sounds. It also played stories, music, and rhymes. The use of sight, sound, and touch to teach language comprehension became a hallmark of LeapFrog's products.

Another breakthrough came in 1999, when LeapFrog introduced the LeapPad, which featured Near Touch technology. Near Touch allows children to hear words when they touch them with a pen-like pointer. With this feature LeapPad offered what were called "point-and-press talking books." This new design provided users what technology scholars Yvonne Rogers and Sara Price describe in the 2009 book *Mobile Technology for Children* as the essential component of mobile learning technologies for children: learning experiences that are embodied as a form of play and that are linked to abstract concepts and knowledge. The LeapPad was popular with parents and formed the core of LeapFrog's earnings.

Impressed by the technology, teachers began to ask for a similar learning toy. The company responded by opening a new division, LeapFrog Schoolhouse, devoted entirely to products designed for students. Many of these products, such as the Tag School Reader and the All Around Me storybook series, allow students to listen to stories and interact as they follow along. Others, such as the English Learners Family Involvement Program and the Read-It-All Summer Program, give teachers a way to keep students involved outside the classroom.

By 2000 LeapFrog had sales of nearly $200 million and began to expand into international markets. LeapFrog became a publicly traded company on the New York Stock Exchange in 2002. The next year the company released the popular Leapster, which is a handheld gaming platform that balances educational challenges with the fun of game playing. The Toy Industry Association awarded Leapster the Most Innovative Toy and Best Educational Toy awards in 2004.

In 2005 LeapFrog released another innovative product, the FLY Pentop Computer, which uses an optical eye for input and a speaker to offer feedback. Roughly the size and shape of a traditional pen, the FLY features a number of applications, including a calculator, a writing assistant, and educational games, many of which require a cartridge to be loaded into the pen. Users are given oral instructions to write a word, for example, and they then use the pen to write that word on digital paper. The digital paper is encoded with a pattern of dots that the pen reads to interpret what is written. The pen then offers feedback, correcting or approving the work of the user.

This technology was poised to "unlock the textbook," according to Robert Calfee, dean of the University of California Riverside Graduate School of Education and a LeapFrog advisory board member. Immediately afterward the company continued to fulfill this promise. In 2008 the Tag Reading System, designed for younger students, came out. In 2011 LeapFrog released the LeapPad Explorer, which *Time* magazine described as "a tablet for the younger set." It has a touchscreen, microphone, gaming control pad, and camera. Like many of LeapFrog's educational toys, the Explorer mimicked technology to which children were already exposed, such as tablets, laptops, and smartphones, and sought new pathways for learning and feedback.

Isabel Istanders

SEE ALSO: *Computer Games; Laptops; Smartphones; Toys; Video Games.*

BIBLIOGRAPHY

Druin, Allison, ed. *Mobile Technology for Children: Designing for Interaction and Learning.* Burlington, MA: Morgan Kaufmann, 2009.

Helft, Miguel. "LeapFrog Hopes for Next Hit with Interactive Reading Toy." *New York Times*, January 28, 2008.

Townsend, Allie. "Toy Fair 2011: The 15 Smartest Toys for Young Geniuses." *Time Specials*, February 15, 2011.

Lear, Norman *(1922–)*

Perhaps the most significant of several producers who reshaped American television in the 1970s, Norman Lear brought his particular genius to the situation comedy. Infusing sitcom content with social commentary and earthy language while also updating its visual form with the immediacy of live videotaping, Lear created a string of shows—*All in the Family* (1968–1979), *Sanford and Son* (1972–1977), *Maude* (1972–1978), *The Jeffersons* (1975–1985), *One Day at a Time* (1975–1984), *Mary Hartman, Mary Hartman* (1976–1978)—that captured national audiences as effortlessly as they did the zeitgeist.

Norman Lear. *Normal Lear was the creative force behind several groundbreaking sitcoms in the 1970s, including* All in the Family, Sanford and Son, Maude, *and* The Jeffersons. **AP IMAGES.**

EARLY CAREER

Lear's career began almost by accident. A salesman by day and gag writer by night, he sold a routine to Danny Thomas that resulted in an offer to write for *Ford Star Revue* in 1951. He moved on to work as a writer for Dean Martin and Jerry Lewis on *The Colgate Comedy Hour* (1950–1955), followed by similar jobs with other variety shows. By the end of the 1950s, however, Lear was tired of the weekly grind of television and turned to film writing and producing. In 1959 he and director Bud Yorkin formed Tandem, a production company responsible for a series of light sex comedies—*Come Blow Your Horn* (1963), *Divorce American Style* (1967), *The Night They Raided Minsky's* (1968)—throughout the 1960s.

Although moderately successful, the Tandem films never ended Lear's interest in television. In 1968 he obtained the rights to *Till Death Us Do Part*, a controversial British situation comedy about a Tory bigot and his argumentative family that was a smash hit in Great Britain. The show, Lear said, was appropriate for an American public that was "in the mood to have its social problems and shortcomings analyzed." His first pilot episodes for the American adaptation were rejected by ABC, which found the protagonist too offensive. CBS, however, picked up the third pilot and began broadcasting *All in the Family* in January 1971. By fall, conservative blowhard Archie Bunker and his family were the most popular characters on American television.

PERFECTING THE SITUATION COMEDY

Lear created a comic formula in *All in the Family* that he rapidly replicated in other sitcoms: a loud, insensitive protagonist gets caught up in a social issue and/or family problem that finally reveals both his/her blindness to reality as well as the genuinely good heart beating beneath all the bluster. *Sanford and Son* (NBC, 1972–1977), adapted from the groundbreaking British sitcom *Steptoe and Son*, made the protagonist a crotchety black junkyard dealer in the Watts area of Los Angeles. *Maude* (CBS), a spin-off of *All in the Family*, featured a liberal feminist as the central character. Another spin-off, *The Jeffersons* (CBS), employed Archie Bunker's entrepreneurial ex-neighbor George Jefferson, a bigoted black man, in the focal role. In *Good Times* (CBS, 1974–1979), a spin-off of *Maude* set in the Chicago housing projects, Lear jumped the generation gap, making a callow black youth the source and butt of the series' jokes. *One Day at a Time* (CBS), which presented the comic travails of a working single mother, strayed from the formula a bit, spreading the buffoonery between two teenage daughters and a randy building superintendent. The producer's unabashed liberalism worked its way through the weekly morality plays these series offered, but the lesson of each show was tempered by the revelation of humanity in the most reactionary of characters—or a foolishly closed mind in the most liberal.

Lear augmented the didactic directness of his plots and characters with live, three-camera videotaping that added speed (through quick cuts) and intensity (through extreme close-ups), as well as decibels from the studio audience, to performances and dialogue. The package proved remarkably successful, and numerous other situation comedies adopted the topicality, verbal crudeness, and production style of the Lear series.

The further Lear attempted to move from the *All in the Family* formula, however, the less his efforts worked, at least on the network level. A 1975 adaptation of Lanford Wilson's play *Hot l Baltimore* for ABC lasted only half a season, whereas several other gimmicky sitcoms—*The Dumplings* (1976), *All's Fair* (1976–1977), *A Year at the Top* (1977), *Apple Pie* (1978)—came and went with long notice but little remembrance. The social relevance that Lear rode through the Vietnam-Watergate era was quickly becoming dated, as America moved through the "malaise" of the Carter years and into the happy new morning of the Reagan era.

Lear, however, did have two major successes off of network television. The syndicated *Mary Hartman, Mary Hartman* (1976) savagely parodied soap operas and their commodified worlds while using the genre's continuing story line to present the gripping and tragicomic disintegration of the show's title character. A spin-off of that series, *Fernwood 2-Nite/America 2-Nite* (1978), performed a similar generic deconstruction of the late-night talk show.

POLITICS AND OTHER PURSUITS

As the popularity of his 1970s creations waned, Lear stepped away from television in the early 1980s to work on behalf of People for the American Way, a liberal political organization he helped found as a response to conservative groups such as the Moral Majority. He did occasionally revisit the medium with series—*Sunday Dinner* (CBS, 1991), *The Powers That Be* (NBC, 1992–1993)—that attempted to address contemporary social and political issues with the visual and verbal urgency of his earlier shows. One series even returned to Archie Bunker's old house—*704 Hauser* (CBS, 1994)—now occupied by a black couple trying to deal with their son's interracial relationship. None of those shows, however, lasted beyond thirteen episodes.

For his work, Lear has won numerous awards, including four Emmys, and in 1984 he was among the first inductees into the Television Academy Hall of Fame. He has a star on the Hollywood Walk of Fame, and in 1999 President Bill Clinton bestowed upon him the National Medal of Arts. Various civil liberties groups have lauded Lear as his focus shifted to politics and away from television. He would eventually return to TV—not as a writer or producer—but as an interview subject on various cable shows, such as *All in the Family: The E! True Hollywood Story* (1996); *Carroll O'Connor: All in a Lifetime* (2001); *Inside TV Land: African Americans in Television* (2002); and *Intimate Portrait: Bea Arthur* (2003). In 2003 he served as a consultant to Trey Parker and Matt Stone on several episodes of *South Park* (1997–); he also did some voice work for the show.

Norman Lear occupies a well-earned place in the pantheon of American television. Emerging at the moment when new FCC rules concerning network financing and syndication gave producers unprecedented power in the American television industry, he brought an individual style and mission to the producer's role that few have been able to emulate, much less match. Time has not favored the blunt topicality of most of his work, but the best of that work stands equal to the best of any age. And Lear's influence on the medium as a whole and the sitcom in particular extends far beyond the specific historic moments he chose as the immediate targets of his wit.

Jeffrey S. Miller

SEE ALSO: All in the Family*; Arthur, Bea; Cable TV; Emmy Awards; Feminism;* Good Times*; Hollywood;* The Jeffersons*; Lewis, Jerry; Live Television; Martin, Dean;* Mary Hartman, Mary Hartman*;* Maude*; Moral Majority;* One Day at a Time*; Reagan, Ronald;* Sanford and Son*; Sitcom; Soap Operas;* South Park*; Syndication; Television; Thomas, Danny; Vietnam; Watergate.*

BIBLIOGRAPHY

Marc, David. *Comic Visions: Television Comedy and American Culture.* Boston: Unwin Hyman, 1989.

Marc, David, and Robert Thompson. *Prime Time, Prime Movers.* Syracuse, NY: University of Syracuse Press, 1995.

McCrohan, Donna. *Archie & Edith, Mike & Gloria.* New York: Workman, 1987.

McKinley, Jesse. "Norman Lear Discovers Soul Mates in *South Park.*" *New York Times*, April 10, 2003, E1.

Newcomb, Horace, and Robert S. Alley. *The Producer's Medium: Conversations with Creators of American TV.* New York: Oxford University Press, 1983.

Leary, Timothy *(1920–1996)*

Who was Timothy Leary? Prophet? Charlatan? Mystic? Mephisto? Years after his death, his legacy is still contested, with advocates and detractors both passionately debating his worth.

Timothy Leary. *Timothy Leary's experiments with and advocacy of hallucinogenic drugs made him an icon of the 1960s counterculture.* ANNE FISHBEIN/CONTRIBUTOR/MICHAEL OCHS ARCHIVES/GETTY IMAGES.

The Pied Piper of LSD, the man who coined the phrase "turn on, tune in, drop out," eulogized in song, his image disseminated on posters, Leary was perhaps the most famous academic of the 1960s, ranking with Marshall McLuhan as prophet of the postindustrial age. He began the decade as a Harvard professor and ended it in prison. During his life he was a clinical psychologist doing groundbreaking work in behavioral change, but he became a rebel, guru, fugitive, and prisoner. Leary's life never lacked for adventure, nor his work for controversy, but to this day it remains unclear whether drugs were his salvation or his ruin.

Born to an alcoholic army dentist and a prim New England aristocrat, Leary claimed in his autobiography, *Flashbacks*, that he was conceived the day after prohibition took effect, implying a predestined—or ironic—connection to drug prohibition. His upbringing displayed a classic Irish schizophrenia. His father came from an upper-crust Boston-Irish family—rebellious, irreverent, and idiosyncratic—whereas his mother belonged to a devoutly religious family of conservative gentleman farmers. As a youth Leary was more inclined toward his paternal side; he was kicked out of several colleges before being drafted in 1943. He spent the war stateside working as a clinical psychologist at an army hospital in Virginia, where he met his first wife, Marianne. With a family to support, Leary forswore rebellion, attaining a doctorate at the University of California, Berkeley.

With two small children, a house, and a post at the Kaiser Foundation Hospital in Oakland, California, Leary appeared to have settled into the sedate life of an academic. He might have continued along this path had his wife not committed suicide on the morning of his thirty-fifth birthday. Her death threw Leary's entire world into tumult—in four months his hair turned completely gray—but it also liberated him. Resigning his position, Leary fled with his children to Europe with the vague notion of working up the data he had amassed from his years at Kaiser.

While at Kaiser Leary made a crucial discovery. Using a waiting list of patients at the clinic, Leary and his colleague, Frank Barron, devised a simple way to test the efficacy of therapy: those who received therapy and those on the waiting list were tracked and then compared. "To say they were horrified by what they found is a little strong—amazed, worried, amused, disturbed—you could use any of those," writes Jay Stevens in *Storming Heaven*. "Because what they found was that there was no difference. . . . About a third had stayed the same, a third had deteriorated, and a third had gotten better."

Behavioral change became Leary's obsession; in Florence, where he had settled, it was his intention to work on his findings, but he was unmotivated and at loose ends. Barron, now teaching at Harvard, visited Leary, bringing with him tales of Psilocybe mexicana, a wondrous drug he had recently taken in Mexico. Leary was skeptical. He was more enthusiastic, however, when Barron mentioned that his boss, David McClelland, director of the Harvard Personality Clinic, was vacationing in Florence. Leary paid him a visit, carrying along a backpack full of manuscripts, and walked away with a lectureship.

HARVARD DAYS

Leary's career was back on track, but Harvard would eventually prove his downfall as an academic. When he arrived in the fall of 1959, he was nearing forty and was at the bottom rung of the academic ladder, but he proved to be a popular lecturer, charming his students and faculty members alike. He had forgotten all about Barron's glowing praise of magic mushrooms, but while vacationing with Barron in Mexico that winter, Leary tried Psilocybe mexicana; he returned to Harvard a changed man. With the blessing of McClelland, Leary inaugurated what became the infamous Harvard Psychedelics Research Project, using a synthesized version of the mushroom manufactured by Sandoz Laboratory of Switzerland.

Far from being quixotic, Leary knew exactly what he was after with the Harvard project. He was still searching for that elusive vitalizing transaction—that key to lasting behavioral change—and he had a suspicion that hallucinogens held the key to sloughing off conditioning. Before long the rumors of strange goings-on at Leary's Cambridge house alarmed Harvard authorities, but Leary was able to stave them off for a time.

He had come up with an inspired study to test psilocybin's efficacy in effecting behavioral change: he would give the drug to inmates at Concord State Prison and monitor the change in values and recidivism rates of the test group. The change was miraculous, but it underscored a point of contention between Leary and his superiors: "The prisoners were changing true enough," writes Stevens, "but they were changing in a way that made science uncomfortable: they were getting religion. And if psilocybin could do that to hard-core cons, imagine what it was doing to the members of the psilocybin project." After the *Harvard Crimson* (the school newspaper) published a series of articles in which Leary was taken to task for his sloppy science, the long-brewing conflict came to a head. Before he was asked to leave, Leary resigned.

MILLBROOK COMMUNITY

Psychedelics had accessed a utopian strain in Leary's character, and he became obsessed with forming a psychedelic community to continue his research and train psychedelic guides and disciples. Leary and his coconspirators returned to Mexico, where they hoped to establish a research facility; they were expelled within a few weeks. They then set up shop in the Dominican Republic with similar results. Antigua also evicted them, but upon returning to Cambridge, heiress Peggy Hitchcock volunteered her family's estate in upstate New York. Millbrook was a five-mile-square estate with an enormous mansion and several buildings dotting the property. It was the ideal locale for their project, situated close enough to New York to attract the city's intelligentsia, whose paid attendance offset expenses.

Millbrook evolved into part retreat, part research project, and part conference center. It proved to be the quiet before the storm, for Leary had not yet been dismissed as a menace to society. Participants remember it as an idyllic place. The big house, as the main mansion was called, was covered—inside and out—with psychedelic murals, and visitors were frequently treated to the sight of jazz trumpeter Maynard Ferguson puttering in the garden or society matrons high on one of a variety of controlled substances.

Tumult had become Leary's operating paradigm. He already had the rebel's instinct for jumping into the fray, and his experience at Harvard had reaffirmed his conviction that to buck the authorities was his destiny. Thus, after being busted for marijuana possession while en route to Mexico with his new wife, Rosemary, and his two children, he returned to Millbrook full of plans to further expand the consciousness revolution. He met with McLuhan, who told him to keep a positive profile and use the tools of Madison Avenue to make his case, singing "Lysergic acid hits the spot / Forty billion neurons, that's a lot." Not long afterward, Leary coined his famous phrase, "Turn on, tune in, drop out," which was taken up as a standard in the burgeoning hippie movement. Psychedelic usage was spreading like wildfire, and like the officials at Harvard, the state authorities objected not so much to the danger to life and limb as to the moral changes LSD usage seemed to inspire.

Leary's metamorphosis from drug researcher to counterculture guru was not a pleasant one. By year's end LSD was illegal, with no visible effect on the drug's availability. LSD's illegality only heightened its allure, and incidence of adverse reactions grew to epidemic proportion. The new breed of psychedelic aficionados knew no more about Leary and his theories than that one singular phrase; he was put in the uncomfortable position of being blamed for the hippies while having little authority among them. He continued to lobby for sensible drug policies, but the situation was far beyond his control.

FROM GURU TO FUGITIVE

For the remainder of the decade, Leary would be more or less sidelined in the debate, though as an icon, he was omnipresent. He became a familiar figure in books, on posters, and on the radio. The Moody Blues eulogized him in a song whose opening lines went: "Timothy Leary's dead / no no no / he's outside looking in"—they had little way of knowing how prescient their lyrics were. Leary continued appearing at various events, from the first human Be-In to Altamont, even running for governor of California in 1970, but with the myriad drug cases hanging over his head, he was a man preoccupied. He knew his time was running short.

With the close of the decade, Leary's role as a guru ended, and his new role as fugitive began. In January 1970 he was imprisoned and was facing twenty years. Nine months later he was a fugitive, escaping from jail with the aid of the Weathermen Underground. He fled to uneasy sanctuary in Algeria, where members of the Black Panther Party offered protection. Leary and Rosemary were eventually placed under house arrest by the Panthers before escaping to a temporary asylum in Switzerland. In 1972 Leary was finally apprehended in Afghanistan and remanded to U.S. custody, where he served time in several federal and state prisons before being released in the winter of 1975.

Leary remarried and spent the rest of his life developing interactive software; he was also interested in the Internet and space travel. He continued to lecture, appearing for a time in debates with his ex-nemesis, Watergate conspirator G. Gordon Liddy. Aside from a midnight raid of his Laurel Canyon home, the last years of his life were free of controversy. He died of cancer in May 1996. Fittingly, his final resting place is in orbit; his ashes were shot into space from an island off the coast of Morocco.

Leary holds a paradoxical position in the history of American culture. His confederates blamed him, possibly fairly, for the abrupt cessation of LSD research funding. But for Leary it was a matter of losing the battle and winning the war. In becoming an advocate for hallucinogens on a grand scale, he thought he was goading America's psychological evolution, as opposed to staying in the sterile environment of the laboratory. If ultimately he misjudged the efficacy of his tactics, that, too, is part and parcel of the man himself.

Leary was the first to confess his naïveté. By addressing himself directly to the baby boomers, he lost the support of the scientific establishment and a great deal of his credibility, but for a brief time he was the spiritual leader to a generation. In a way Leary played out the ancient role of the prophet, and he paid the price. History alone will decide whether he was a savant or addled by the very drugs he advocated.

Michael Baers

SEE ALSO: *Black Panthers; Communes; Consciousness Raising Groups; Hippies; The Internet; LSD; Marijuana; McLuhan, Marshall; Radio; Suicide; War on Drugs; Watergate.*

BIBLIOGRAPHY

Kleps, Art. *Millbrook: The True Story of the Early Years of the Psychedelic Revolution.* Oakland, CA: Bench Press, 1977.

Leary, Timothy. *Changing My Mind—Among Others.* Englewood Cliffs, NJ: Prentice-Hall, 1982.

Leary, Timothy. *Flashbacks: An Autobiography.* Los Angeles: Jeremy P. Tarcher, 1983.

Lee, Martin A., and Bruce Shlain. *Acid Dreams: The CIA, LSD, and the Sixties Rebellion.* New York: Grove Press, 1985.

Stevens, Jay. *Storming Heaven: LSD and the American Dream.* New York: Grove Press, 1987.

Lattin, Don. *The Harvard Psychedelic Club.* New York: HarperCollins, 2011.

Least Heat Moon, William *(1939–)*

In 1978 William Trogdon (who writes as William Least Heat Moon) was an obscure English teacher whose job and marriage were falling apart around him. In an effort to cope with his feelings of isolation and alienation, Least Heat Moon set out on a three-month, 13,000-mile journey on the back roads—the blue highways—of America. Tracking his Osage background, he traveled clockwise around the country ("That's the Indian way"), interviewing locals and occasionally photographing them. His record of the journey, issued as *Blue Highways: A Journey into America* (1982), was a surprise publishing sensation, winning several awards and remaining on the *New York Times* best-seller list for thirty-four weeks.

Unlike other famous American "road" books—such as Jack Kerouac's *On the Road* (1957), John Steinbeck's *Travels with Charley* (1962), Tom Wolfe's *The Electric Kool-Aid Acid Test* (1968), and Robert Pirsig's *Zen and the Art of Motorcycle Maintenance* (1974)—*Blue Highways* combines insights into the human experience with a modest, intensely personal tone. Least Heat Moon subsequently published *PrairyErth* (1991), an in-depth study of Chase County, Kansas, its people, and its history; *River Horse* (1999), an account of a journey he took across the United States almost entirely by water; *Columbus in the Americas* (2002), a biography; and *Roads to Quoz: An American Mosey* (2008), in which he returns to the road yet again. He has also contributed to numerous publications as a journalist and photographer.

Samuel I. Bellman

SEE ALSO: *Automobile; Best Sellers; The* New York Times*;* On the Road*; Steinbeck, John; Wolfe, Tom.*

BIBLIOGRAPHY

Least Heat Moon, William. *Blue Highways: A Journey into America.* Boston: Little, Brown, 1982.

"Least Heat Moon, William." *Contemporary Authors New Revision Series,* vol. 47. Detroit, MI: Gale Research, 1995.

Leather Jacket

Few pieces of clothing carry the rich connotations of the leather jacket, especially when it is the personality-laden black motorcycle style. Since the prehistoric era, people have worn leather, but beginning in the twentieth century the black leather jacket became the symbol of the outlaw when it was used as protective outerwear for motorcycle enthusiasts.

Actor Marlon Brando exemplified the criminal or outcast style in the film *The Wild One* (1953), as did James Dean in *Rebel without a Cause* (1955), and the coat became a necessity for Hells Angels and other bikers who emblazoned their club's name on the back. The most famous leather jacket in U.S. history, however, may be the one worn on the television show *Happy Days* (1974–1984) by Arthur "Fonzie" Fonzarelli. It was placed on display at the Smithsonian in 1980 but later removed.

Rock stars and punks later latched on to this bad boy image of black leather, but leather jackets eventually found mainstream favor when manufacturers began creating them in a variety of styles and colors, such as the brown bomber jacket. In the twenty-first century Royal Chie introduced a snake-skin print leather jacket with raccoon trim. Aviator-style jackets also became popular, and runway models began demonstrating that leather jackets for women could be worn with dressy as well as casual clothes. The mystique of the original biker style, however, endures.

Geri Speace

SEE ALSO: *Brando, Marlon; Dean, James;* Happy Days; *Hells Angels.*

BIBLIOGRAPHY

Farren, Mick. *The Black Leather Jacket.* New York: Abbeville Press, 1985.

Fitzpatrick, Catherine. "For the Ultrahip, Skins Have Always Been In." *St. Louis Post-Dispatch,* January 8, 1998.

Giuntini, Parme, and Kathryn Hagen. *Garb: A Fashion and Culture Reader.* Upper Saddle River, NJ: Pearson Prentice Hall, 2008.

Jensen, Jim. "Black Leather Is a Timeless Fashion Statement." *Rocky Mountain News,* August 7, 1998.

Leave It to Beaver

Leave It to Beaver was one of a number of family situation comedies that proliferated on the small screen in the 1950s and 1960s. Along with *Father Knows Best, The Donna Reed Show,* and *Ozzie and Harriet, Leave It to Beaver* portrays the trials and tribulations of everyday life in a U.S. suburb. The difference between *Leave It to Beaver* and the other shows is that it tells its stories (all 234 of them) from the point of view of the youngest family member, Theodore "Beaver" Cleaver. Through the eyes of a child, life in the postwar economic boom is simple and sweet. Problems arise, but they are always resolved by a kind and loving family working together.

Leave It to Beaver debuted in the spring of 1957 as a pilot called *It's a Small World.* When the series premiered in the fall of that year, it starred Jerry Mathers as Beaver, an adorable seven-year-old boy whose actions, no matter how well-intended, always seem to land him in some kind of trouble. Tony Dow played Wally, Beaver's twelve-year-old brother. Wally is the quintessential all-American boy, a popular athlete with a healthy interest in girls. Barbara Billingsley played mother June, the patient, understanding housewife who seems to do all her housework in high heels and pearls. Hugh Beaumont acted the role of Ward Cleaver, the wise and patient father who commutes to work in his business suit but is always home in time for dinner. They represent the perfect American family—devoted parents; well-behaved, polite children; and a beautiful home in Mayfield, USA, complete with white picket fence. No one ever really fights on the show: Ward and June are completely sup-

Leave It to Beaver. *The Cleaver family of television's* Leave It to Beaver *included, from left, Tony Dow as Wally, Barbara Billingsley as June, Hugh Beaumont as Ward, and Jerry Mathers as the Beaver.* AP IMAGES.

portive of each other and of the boys, and the boys learn all their lessons gently.

One of the series' most memorable characters is Eddie Haskell, played by Ken Osmond. Eddie is an obsequious weasel. He is a friend of Wally's who feigns respect and admiration when dealing with parents and adults, while behaving like a rat to young Beaver and his friends. He is not really smart enough to pull it off, though, and most of the adults on the show see through his ruse. His questionable character is explained by the occasional appearance of his family, which proves that the apple never falls far from the tree. Though he is slimy, Eddie never really poses a threat to Wally's good character. Wally and everyone else know what he is and what motivates him.

Leave It to Beaver is perhaps better remembered by the audiences who saw it as reruns in the 1980s and 1990s than by 1950s and 1960s television viewers. Though it did run for five seasons (first on CBS and later on ABC), it was never rated in Nielsen's top twenty for the years it was originally broadcast. Those years belonged to cowboys and pioneers in shows such as *Gunsmoke*, *Wagon Train*, *Bonanza*, and *The Rifleman*. In the same way that the television audiences of 1957 to 1963 seemed to indulge in the nostalgia of the old American West, audiences of the Ronald Reagan years were drawn to the nostalgia of 1950s America. In syndicated reruns, *Leave It to Beaver* became something of a cult phenomenon. The suburban life of a nuclear family in the 1950s and early 1960s seen through the eyes of an innocent appeared to strike a chord with U.S. audiences in the 1980s.

As a testament to its resurgence in popularity, a reunion show was filmed in 1983. The TV movie *Still the Beaver* shows viewers an unemployed, nearly divorced thirty-three-year-old Beaver facing the reality of raising two slightly troublesome sons on his own. Wally, though a successful attorney married to his high school sweetheart, has no children and is dealing with an unscrupulous contractor—none other than Eddie Haskell. June is still around and still trying to help, but she does not have the commanding wisdom of the deceased Ward, who could make everything right with a few words of advice in the 1950s. An idyllic childhood did not ensure that the Cleaver boys would grow up and live unquestionably happy lives. The pleasant, sun-filled days in Mayfield did not foreshadow June's future as a widow, and father did not know best anymore.

Because of the success of the television movie, in 1985 Disney produced a new series with the same name. In the series Beaver is divorced and living at home with June and his two sons. In 1986 the series was bought by WTBS and renamed *The New Leave It to Beaver*. It ran until 1989. In 1997 a Hollywood film based on the original series was released but bombed at the box office.

Joyce Linehan

SEE ALSO: The Adventures of Ozzie and Harriet*;* Bonanza*;* Father Knows Best*;* Gunsmoke*; Reagan, Ronald; Sitcom; Suburbia; Television;* Wagon Train.

BIBLIOGRAPHY

Applebaum, Irwyn. *The World according to Beaver*. New York: Bantam, 1984.

Bank, Frank, and Gib Twyman. *Call Me Lumpy: My "Leave It to Beaver" Days and Other Wild Hollywood Life*. Lenexa, KS: Addax Publishing Group, 1997.

Buccieri, Lisa Rojany. *Leave It to Beaver*. Los Angeles: Price Stern Sloan, 1997.

Mathers, Jerry, and Herb Fagen. . . . *And Jerry Mathers as "The Beaver."* New York: Berkley Boulevard, 1998.

Led Zeppelin

Led Zeppelin is considered by many to be one of the greatest rock bands in the history of music. Formed in June 1968 as the New Yardbirds, the British band included Jimmy Page (formerly of the group the Yardbirds, which broke up in 1968) on guitar, Robert Plant as vocalist, John Bonham on drums, and John Paul Jones on bass/keyboards. For the remainder of 1968 the new band toured Scandinavia, the United Kingdom, and the United States and recorded its first album. In October the band changed its name to Led Zeppelin.

Led Zeppelin released its eponymous first album in the United States in January 1969 and in the United Kingdom in March 1969. It contains heavy blues-driven rock songs that carry a frightening manic edge never before heard in popular music, and it was a huge success. The group's second album, *Led Zeppelin II* (1969), brought further success, buoyed by the Top 10 single "Whole Lotta Love." The old-time blues and acoustic tunes on the group's third album, *Led Zeppelin III* (1970), however, were less popular than earlier efforts. In 1971 the band released *Led Zeppelin IV* (a.k.a. *Zoso*), its most acclaimed work ever. It contains the fiery "Black Dog" and the nostalgic, dreamy epic, "Stairway to Heaven," which remains among the most loved and respected songs in all popular music, routinely voted number one on all-time best lists.

Led Zeppelin maintained its immense success with the well-balanced *Houses of the Holy* (1973), which has a funk and reggae influence and is considered by many to be the band's all-around best album. The double album *Physical Graffiti* (1975) is the band's most diverse album, containing some of its most beautiful acoustic pieces, such as "bron-Yr-Aur," as well driving and powerful epics like "Kashmir." In subsequent years Led Zeppelin released the heavy *Presence* (1976), the live *The Song Remains the Same* (1976), and the melodic *In through the Out Door* (1979). Tragedy struck in 1980 when Bonham died of asphyxiation after a bout of drinking. After his death, Led Zeppelin disbanded.

As the icons of 1970s hard rock, Led Zeppelin is best known for its scorching guitar work, screeching vocals, pounding drums, and the driving beats of its heaviest songs; the band's repertoire includes lilting love songs, traditional folk and blues songs, and standard rock and roll. Some Led Zeppelin songs explore fantasy elements, whereas others show a freewheeling spirit of hippie adventure and fun. Some show a sad, mystic longing for joys gone and times past.

Led Zeppelin albums are innovative not just because of their content but also because of the design of their packaging. The sleeve of *Physical Graffiti* displays various objects and personages who can be made to appear and disappear in various "windows," whereas the sleeve of *Led Zeppelin III* is a moveable psychedelic pinwheel. *Led Zeppelin IV* has no band or title information anywhere on the jacket. *In through the Out Door* was released with six different covers; the album's inner sleeve changes colors when dampened. Mysterious symbols on album covers, mysterious song titles, and a general avoidance of

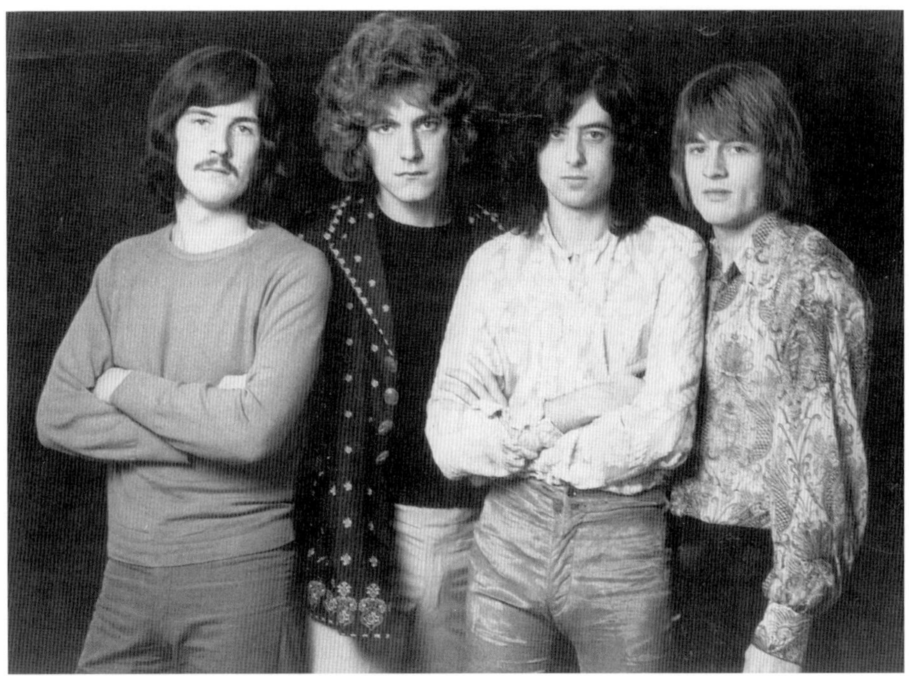

Led Zeppelin. *The members of Led Zeppelin, from left, John Bonham, Robert Plant, Jimmy Page, and John Paul Jones, pose in 1968.* MICHAEL OCHS ARCHIVES/GETTY IMAGES.

interviews all led to a sense that the band and its music were filled with deep, hidden meanings. Some critics feared that these meanings were satanic, leading to the false but widespread rumor that "Stairway to Heaven" contains pro-Satan messages when played backward on a turntable.

Led Zeppelin tours were hugely popular in the mid-1970s and featured powerful drum solos by Bonham, grotesque guitar solos by Page (some of which featured Page scraping his guitar strings with a violin bow), and the sweaty sex appeal of bare-chested Plant. At its peak of popularity, the bandj regularly played to stadium and arena audiences of more than 50,000 people. During its 1973 tour of the United States, the band had its concert at Madison Square Garden in New York filmed and released as the movie *Song Remains the Same* in 1976 alongside the album of the same name. The movie features heavy jamming, extended solos by Page and Bonham, and a quartet of remarkable quasivideos, each of which features one of the band members on a personal adventure, with the band's songs playing in the background.

Led Zeppelin's impact on popular music was tremendous. The band is considered one of the forefathers of blues-based hard rock in general and of heavy metal in particular, and its legacy is apparent in groups that followed, such as KISS, Queen, Rush, Iron Maiden, Metallica, the White Stripes, and Wolfmother. Led Zeppelin is also among the forefathers of 1990s Seattle grunge music, with echoes found in groups such as Nirvana, Pearl Jam, Mudhoney, and Soundgarden. Throughout the 1980s, 1990s, and first decade of the 2000s, Led Zeppelin remained among the most popular rock bands, continuing to sell albums and to receive regular radio airplay. In the 1990s Atlantic Records released remastered versions of all the band's albums, as well as two box sets, a ten-CD set of complete recordings, and various documentary and concert videos, including the DVD set *Led Zeppelin* (2003).

David Elroy Goldweber

SEE ALSO: *Blues; Grunge; Heavy Metal; Hippies; Iron Maiden; KISS; Nirvana; Pearl Jam; Rock and Roll; The Yardbirds.*

BIBLIOGRAPHY

Cross, Charles R. *Led Zeppelin: Shadows Taller than Our Souls.* New York: It Books, 2009.

Davis, Stephen. *Hammer of the Gods: The Led Zeppelin Saga.* New York: Morrow, 1985.

Kendall, Paul, and Dave Lewis, eds. *Led Zeppelin: In Their Own Words.* New York: Omnibus, 1995.

Lewis, Dave. *Led Zeppelin: A Celebration.* New York: Omnibus, 2003.

Wall, Mick. *When Giants Walked the Earth.* New York: St. Martin's, 2010.

Yorke, Ritchie. *Led Zeppelin: The Definitive Biography.* Novato, CA: Underwood-Miller, 1993.

Ledbetter, Huddie

SEE: *Leadbelly.*

Lee, Bruce *(1940–1973)*

Bruce Lee was born Li Jun Fan in San Francisco's Jackson Street Hospital on November 27, 1940, between 6 and 8 p.m.—significant in both the hour and year of the Dragon. The fourth son of Grace Li, a Chinese woman whose ancestry was one-quarter British, and Li Hoi Chuen, a star of the classical Chinese opera, Lee's name means "Protector of San Francisco." The circumstances of his birth are appropriate for a man who spent his career poised between two continents acting as a conduit for cultural exchange. While introducing American audiences to the culture of Chinese martial arts and working to bring Western technology to a nascent Chinese film industry, Lee enjoyed a stellar film career that was cut short by his untimely passing. Fanciful theories about the circumstances of his death added to the martial arts master's imposing mystique and guaranteed his place in the American cultural consciousness.

In addition to his film exploits, Lee was one of the premier martial arts instructors in the United States. Celebrities such as James Garner, Roman Polanski, and Kareem Abdul-Jabbar were among those he taught, and Lee introduced his students to both kung fu (almost entirely unknown in America at the time) and his own martial art of Jeet Kune Do (a combination of styles, including those of kung fu, Thai kickboxing, and American boxing). Early in his career as an instructor, he broke new ground by teaching Kung Fu to non-Asians—a manifestation of his strong desire to spread the Chinese culture to the United States. His efforts proved fruitful: the success of the martial arts schools he founded has resulted in the continued widespread popularity of martial arts instruction in America.

A CHILD STAR

Lee began his screen career at an early age: he was given his first film role at the age of three months, playing a female infant in

Bruce Lee. *Bruce Lee starred in* Enter the Dragon, *directed by Robert Clouse, in 1973.* **SILVER SCREEN COLLECTION/CONTRIBUTOR/MOVIEPIX/GETTY IMAGES.**

Golden Gate Girl (1941), which was shot in San Francisco shortly before his family left the United States to return to their home in Hong Kong. Growing up, he appeared in more than twenty films. It was during this period that he became known to Chinese film audiences as Lee Siu Lung, "The Little Dragon." As a teen, motivated by the desire to defend himself against the assaults of Hong Kong street gangs, he began his education in kung fu under the direction of Yip Man of the Wing Chun school of Kung Fu. His strength and grace were immediately apparent, and by the time he was eighteen, Lee was a champion tournament fighter.

In 1959 Lee's parents, fearing for his safety after he had gotten into a string of street fights, sent him to the United States. He returned to his birthplace in San Francisco and began working odd jobs and studying to earn his high school diploma. He used what little spare time he had to teach martial arts in city parks and from his own backyard. In 1961 Lee enrolled at the University of Washington as a philosophy major. While there, he taught kung fu to other students and wrote an undergraduate thesis on his own fighting style of Jeet Kune Do.

Lee became occupied with efforts to expand the scope of his martial arts instruction, but he did not decisively act upon that desire until he had fallen in love with his future wife, Linda Emery. They met at the University of Washington, where Emery was also a student, and as their relationship progressed, it became apparent to Lee that he needed to consider more seriously the future of his career if they were to be financially secure. Thus, he set out to open his own martial arts school: the Jun Fan Kung-Fu Institute. Although his investment of time and money seemed precarious at the start, his reputation spread quickly. In less than a year he opened a second Jun Fan Kung-Fu school and attracted the attention of television producer William Dozier.

DISILLUSIONMENT, THEN FAME

In 1965 Dozier signed Lee to a one-year option for the series *The Green Hornet*, casting him as the Green Hornet's sidekick, Kato. When the series premiered in 1966, he received wide publicity for the uncommonly graceful and skillful way he performed his stunts. To his chagrin, however, articles on him often contained careless errors (referring to him, for example, as a "karate master") and either ignored or made light of the spiritual significance of the martial arts he practiced. By the time *The Green Hornet* was canceled in 1967, Lee had become somewhat discouraged with such misrepresentations, a feeling only amplified by his difficulty finding acting work thereafter.

A serious injury in 1970 resulted in months of rehabilitation and afforded Lee the time to document his philosophy of martial arts. The next year, disillusioned by rejection and racism in the American movie and television industry, he returned to Hong Kong film with *The Big Boss* (1971, also known as *Fists of Fury*), which broke box-office records in China. Over the next three years, Lee starred in his best-known films, *The Way of the Dragon* (1972, released in the United States under the title of *The Return of the Dragon*) and *Enter the Dragon* (1973).

A MYSTERIOUS DEATH

On July 20, 1973, after complaining of a headache, Lee took a dose of the painkiller Equagesic, lay down in bed, and lost consciousness. When he could not be revived, Lee was rushed to the hospital, where he was pronounced dead. Two funerals were held for Lee—a big event in Hong Kong for his throngs of

Chinese fans and a more intimate ceremony in Seattle, Washington, for his friends and family. Soon reports circulated in the media that he had died of an overdose of illegal drugs. There was even speculation that he had been murdered by gangsters or by an underground society of kung fu devotees angered by his practice of teaching the art to non-Chinese. However, the official coroner's report concluded that he died of a massive allergic reaction to Equagesic.

The rumors, however, never died. Over time the various theories about his death have fallen under the title of "The Curse of the Dragon," adding a tinge of the supernatural to his already legendary status. His mystique has had ample soil in which to grow. The popularity of his films set the stage and the standard for a Hong Kong film industry that has become one the most successful and innovative in the world, and he has been the inspiration for generations of American youth seeking formal training in the martial arts. His fame gave momentum to a dialogue between America and China by which the two cultures have influenced each other and, thus, have been transformed.

Manuel V. Cabrera Jr.

SEE ALSO: *Martial Arts.*

BIBLIOGRAPHY

Bleecker, Tom. *Unsettled Matters: The Life and Death of Bruce Lee.* Lompoc, CA: Gilderoy Publications, 1996.

Block, Alex Ben. *The Legend of Bruce Lee.* New York: Dell, 1974.

Chunovic, Louis. *Bruce Lee: The Tao of the Dragon Warrior.* New York: St. Martin's Griffin, 1996.

Clouse, Robert. *The Making of "Enter the Dragon."* Burbank, CA: Unique Publications, 1987.

Gaul, Lou. *The Fist That Shook the World: The Cinema of Bruce Lee.* Baltimore, MD: Midnight Marquee Press, 1997.

Lee, Bruce. *Words of the Dragon: Interviews, 1958–1973*, ed. John Little. Boston: Tuttle, 1997.

Roensch, Greg. *Bruce Lee.* New York: Rosen Publishing Group, 2002.

Thomas, Bruce. *Bruce Lee.* New York: St. Martin's, 1993.

Lee, Gypsy Rose *(1911–1970)*

Even to those who have never seen and would never consider seeing a strip show, the name Gypsy Rose Lee conjures up a glittering image. Lee invented the intellectual striptease performance and took stripping out of dingy burlesque halls and into the high-toned venues of Broadway. Although she was notorious for her inability to sing or dance, Lee was a natural performer who knew how to control an audience with timing, humor, and sex appeal. In the 1940s *Variety*'s J. P. McEvoy described Lee's act as a "burlesque of burlesque—literally more tease than strip."

Lee was born Rose Louise Hovick in Seattle, Washington, on January 9, 1911 (there is some uncertainty about her birth year, as she claimed to have been born in 1914). Her father was a cub reporter for the *Seattle Post-Intelligencer*, and her mother was an amateur performer with big ambitions. Shortly after the birth of Lee's sister, June, in 1916 (some sources say 1913), Lee's mother took the girls and left their father. By the time Lee was five, both girls were enrolled in dancing school and soon afterward began their careers singing and dancing on the grueling vaudeville circuit. Lee would later spin yarns about studying ballet, sociology, and anthropology at the Imperial School in Moscow, but she actually had little formal schooling. Her mother falsified papers and lied about the girls' ages to stay one step ahead of the truant officer and keep the children on the stage.

June eventually left her controlling mother to go on to a successful Broadway career (using the name June Havoc), leaving her sister to perfect her striptease on the bump-and-grind stages of burlesque. Gypsy, who got her nickname from a fondness for fortune-telling, got her big break in 1936 when she did her strip in the theatrical revue *The Ziegfeld Follies.*

Gypsy Rose Lee. *Famous for its timing, humor, and sex appeal, Gypsy Rose Lee's burlesque act was once described as "more tease than strip."* **PICTORIAL PARADE/STAFF/ARCHIVE PHOTOS/GETTY IMAGES.**

A master of creating image and effect, Lee managed to exemplify the stripper in the public imagination without exposing her naked body for more than a second or two at a time. "Bare flesh bores men," she said, and she went about finding a way to keep audiences interested while keeping her own dignity intact. Considering zippers inelegant, she outfitted her clothes with snaps, used rubber cement to attach her lace stockings to her legs, secured her G-string with unbreakable dental floss, and covered it all with an evening gown, gloves, fur coat, and jewels. By the time Lee had pranced and joked her way down to her underwear, the audience was hers. Leaving nothing to chance, Lee sometimes paid a woman in the audience to scream or a waiter to drop a tray as she dramatically removed her brassiere a split second before the lights went out and the laughter and applause thundered.

When H. L. Mencken dubbed Lee an "ecdysiast" from the Greek word for one who sheds, it inspired Lee to take an intellectual approach to her craft, and she began to sprinkle her act with quotes from the likes of Spinoza and Aldous Huxley, creating the paradoxical "intellectual strip." Audiences loved her. When she performed at the 1939 New York World's Fair, she drew crowds as large as 17,500, more than President Franklin Roosevelt and politician Wendell Wilkie combined.

In 1937 Twentieth Century Fox's Darryl F. Zanuck signed Lee to a $2,000-a-week contract to make movies with her clothes on. Outcries from conservative groups such as the Catholic Legion of Decency forced her to use her real name, Louise Hovick, for her movie roles. She was not skilled as an actor and later believed that going to Hollywood had been a "big mistake." Although Lee projected an elegant, sophisticated image in her act, she was really a hard-boiled trouper from small-town vaudeville stages. Her lowbrow vaudevillian sensibility did not fit in with many of the actors who wanted to be viewed as upper class.

Lee continued to manage her image into a profitable career. In the 1940s she became a best-selling author with *The G-String Murders*, and in 1957 she wrote her own memoirs, which were made into the popular musical *Gypsy*. Her quick wit and salty humor placed her in demand as a panelist on television shows, and she had her own syndicated talk show in the 1960s. She was diagnosed with lung cancer in 1969 and died the next year.

Gypsy Rose Lee was full of contradictions—she was at once the intellectual stripper, the poor glamour girl, and the rich, successful entertainer who cooked on a hot plate in her hotel room to save money. Although she was always a figure of romance, she had three failed marriages. But with faultless showmanship and pure brass, she created a persona that eclipsed the real Louise Hovick and outlived her. She added an icon to American culture that will not be soon forgotten.

Tina Gianoulis

SEE ALSO: *Broadway; Burlesque; Hollywood; Mencken, H. L.; Strip Joints/Striptease; Syndication; Vaudeville; World's Fairs; Zanuck, Darryl F.;* The Ziegfeld Follies.

BIBLIOGRAPHY

Frankel, Noralee. *Stripping Gypsy: The Life of Gypsy Rose Lee.* New York: Oxford University Press, 2009.

Lee, Gypsy Rose. *Gypsy: A Memoir.* New York: Simon and Schuster, 1986.

Preminger, Erik Lee. *Gypsy and Me: At Home and on the Road.* Boston: Little, Brown, 1984.

Lee, Harper

SEE: *To Kill a Mockingbird.*

Lee, Manfred B.

SEE: *Queen, Ellery.*

Lee, Peggy *(1920–2002)*

The adage that "less is more" sums up Peggy Lee's style as a singer and performer of the American popular song. With her assured stage presence and vocal perfectionism, Lee captured a

Peggy Lee. *Peggy Lee, who began her career during the big-band era, is best known for her hit songs "Fever" and "Is That All There Is?"* SILVER SCREEN COLLECTION/CONTRIBUTOR/MOVIEPIX/GETTY.

devoted audience over a career that spanned more than fifty years. During her career she wrote or cowrote more than 200 songs and recorded more than 600. Such songs as "Fever" and "Is That All There Is?" are still instantly identifiable with Lee, even by those who are unfamiliar with the rest of her repertoire.

Lee was born Norma Deloris Egstrom in Jamestown, North Dakota. Her childhood and adolescence were marked by family hardships, including her mother's death when Lee was four, her father's alcoholism, and a stepmother's cruelty and physical abusiveness. Later in life Lee said that she got through this period by escaping outdoors, where she could sing and talk to the trees. This aura of self-sufficiency remained her hallmark throughout her career.

Lee received her first break as a singer on a radio station in Fargo, North Dakota. She and a friend later moved to California, where she tried to break into the music business. She had a number of bad experiences, however, including illness, low-paying jobs, and a near abduction into white slavery. Temporarily beaten down, she returned to the Midwest. In 1941 clarinetist and bandleader Benny Goodman heard Lee sing at the Ambassador West Hotel in Chicago. As luck would have it, singer Helen Forrest was leaving Goodman's band, so he hired Lee as her replacement. Singing with Goodman's band provided Lee with the opportunity she needed to become a successful recording artist. Her hits during the period she spent with Goodman included "My Old Flame," "Why Don't You Do Right?" and "How Deep Is the Ocean?"

In 1943 Lee married Goodman's guitarist Dave Barbour, with whom she cowrote three songs: "It's a Good Day," "Don't Know Enough about You," and "Mañana." She left Goodman the same year and went solo. Lee and Barbour later divorced, after which she married three more times. She acknowledged later that Barbour remained the love of her life, and he continued to be an important musical influence. Other collaborations with Barbour included "Fever" and the albums *Black Coffee* and *Beauty and the Beat*, which were among Lee's most celebrated works.

During the 1950s Lee was active in films, both performing songs and taking on acting roles. She appeared in *The Jazz Singer* (1953), with Danny Thomas; and *Pete Kelly's Blues* (1955), for which she was nominated for an Academy Award as Best Supporting Actress. In Walt Disney's animated *Lady and the Tramp*, Lee provided the voice for several feline characters and wrote the song "He's a Tramp." Performing extensively in concert halls and clubs and on television in the years that followed, Lee appeared with such major entertainers as Nat King Cole, Bing Crosby, and Frank Sinatra. By the 1980s Lee had cut back on personal appearances because of major health problems that included complications from diabetes, lung ailments, and double bypass surgery. Lee's long-awaited, autobiographical Broadway musical, *Peg*, proved a disappointment, opening and closing in one week in 1983. Soon thereafter, her fall on a Las Vegas stage resulted in a broken pelvis, confining her to a wheelchair during future performances.

Nevertheless, Lee continued to perform, albeit on a somewhat more limited scale. A younger audience was becoming aware of her gifts for gesture, nuance, and subtle sexual appeal. *New York Times* writer Stephen Holden described Lee's "pastel shadings," her "air of perpetual dreaminess," and her "heart-tugging fragility and mystical resilience." *Village Voice* columnist Michael Musto referred to "those 'fever all through the night' tones that could turn a gay man straight." In her autobiography, *Miss Peggy Lee* (1989), Lee wrote, "You can bet on it! I plan to do another turn or two . . . and if the body is a little bit reluctant, I *know* the spirit is willing." Her body finally gave out in 2002, but her spirit and her music live on. In 2010 *Billboard* named Peggy Lee's *Come Rain or Come Shine* to its Top 10 Traditional Jazz Albums.

Sue Russell

SEE ALSO: *Academy Awards; Big Bands; Broadway; Cole, Nat King; Crosby, Bing; Disney (Walt Disney Company); Goodman, Benny; Jazz; Pop Music; Sinatra, Frank; Thomas, Danny.*

BIBLIOGRAPHY

Hemming, Roy, and David Hajdu. *Discovering Great Singers of Classic Pop*. New York: Newmarket, 1991.

Holden, Stephen. "Peggy Lee at 67: Still in the Swingtime of Her Life." *New York Times*, January 31, 1988.

Lee, Peggy. *Miss Peggy Lee*. New York: Donald I. Fine, 1989.

Lees, Gene. *Singers and the Song II*. New York: Oxford, 1998.

McGee, Kristin A. *Some Liked It Hot: Jazz Women in Film and Television*. Middleton, CT: Wesleyan University Press, 2009.

Musto, Michael. "La Dolce Musto." *Village Voice*, February 9, 1988.

Richmond, Peter. *Fever: The Life and Music of Miss Peggy Lee*. New York: H. Holt, 2006.

Lee, Spike *(1957–)*

A controversial artist and a wizard at self-promotion, Spike Lee became America's best-known African American filmmaker in the 1980s. By the end of the 1990s, he was widely recognized in critical circles as one of the most important filmmakers in America, period. With a string of provocative films dealing in unprecedented ways with the complexities of contemporary African American urban life, Lee helped to energize the spirit of independent filmmaking in the United States. Over time, he transcended film through his entrepreneurial ventures and his controversial statements in the media.

STARTING OUT

The filmmaker was born Shelton Jackson Lee on March 20, 1957, in Atlanta, Georgia. His parents relocated to Brooklyn, New York, in 1959. During his early childhood in the 1960s, Lee spent many of his summers visiting relatives in the South, where he encountered vicious displays of racial segregation. As he grew older, he borrowed from these experiences to create films that explore the detrimental effects of bigotry on the cultural fabric of American life.

After studying communications at Morehouse College in the mid-1970s, Lee undertook graduate studies at New York University's film school. Upon graduation in 1982, he received the Student Academy Award for his third-year thesis project, *Joe's Bed-Stuy Barbershop: We Cut Heads*. Despite the critical acclaim his film generated, Lee was unable to raise significant money for a feature project. Nevertheless, the budding filmmaker remained determined. In Alex Patterson's biography *Spike Lee*, Lee claims that the experience "cemented in my mind what

Spike Lee. *Spike Lee poses with a poster from his first feature film,* She's Gotta Have It*, in 1986. The success of the movie went on to inspire a new generation of African American filmmakers.* ANTHONY BARBOZA/CONTRIBUTOR/ARCHIVE PHOTOS/GETTY IMAGES.

I always thought all along: that I would have to go out and do it alone, not rely on anyone else."

The director's independent spirit served him well in the years following his graduation from school. By 1986 Lee had amassed the financial and emotional support of his friends in order to write, produce, direct, edit, and costar in his first feature, *She's Gotta Have It*. Inspired by the success of Prince's *Purple Rain* (1984), *She's Gotta Have It* marked a drastic change in the climate of filmmaking in the United States. Financed using creative ingenuity, the movie stands out from other films of the era because of its aggressive cinematic techniques and its portrayal of the subtleties of African American life. It was a huge success for an independent film, drawing lines around the block in New York.

MAJOR SUCCESS

She's Gotta Have It earned Lee a major prize at the prestigious Cannes Film Festival. Yet the movie received equal amounts of glowing praise and stinging criticism, as would most of Lee's work that followed. A number of white critics found the film to be unrealistic in comparison to previous films dealing with African American subject matter. Meanwhile, a handful of African American female critics took issue with Lee's portrayal of the female lead character. Nonetheless, the film demonstrated the commercial clout of African American audiences, which wanted to see realistic portrayals instead of stereotypes.

In addition, a number of African Americans who had been previously been excluded from film jobs were put to work on the project as cinematographers, designers, and the like. Eventually, the success of *She's Gotta Have It* helped launch a black new wave of filmmaking. Often referred to as "New Jack Cinema," this movement showcased many black male artists who wrote screenplays and directed films centered on their personal experiences as African Americans.

Lee followed *She's Gotta Have It* with *School Daze* (1988), a contentious musical comedy dealing with the politics of skin color on a historically black college campus. His next film, *Do the Right Thing* (1989), marked the beginning of Lee's association with Universal Pictures and proved to be a watershed moment in the director's career. An inflammatory tale of racism in Brooklyn's Bedford-Stuyvesant neighborhood, *Do the Right Thing* grossed more than $30 million and was met with critical acclaim, though some reviewers felt the film's dubious message would provoke rather than quell racial violence. *Do the Right Thing* received the L.A. Film Critics Award for Best Picture and Best Director, yet it was virtually ignored at the Academy Awards, earning only a nomination for Best Screenplay. Nevertheless, *Do the Right Thing* lifted Lee to new levels of visibility in American society. In fact, he became known for his flamboyant, off-the-cuff remarks in the media concerning issues of race.

EXPERIENCING A LULL

The sharp-tongued director continued to make movies about African American life. *Mo' Better Blues* (1990) is a tale of a black jazz musician (played by Denzel Washington) and his relationship with two women. The film fared moderately well at the box office but drew sharp criticism for its portrayals of Jews. A cautionary tale of interracial desire, *Jungle Fever* (1991) made a bigger box-office impact, yet it was overshadowed by other films from the New Jack Cinema movement Lee had helped to facilitate, including John Singleton's acclaimed *Boyz 'n' the Hood* (1991).

Lee finally won the rights in the early 1990s to undertake his most ambitious project: a film about Muslim civil rights leader Malcolm X, starring Washington. The project marked the first time a film of such epic scope had employed both a black director and leading actor. Yet even before its release, *Malcolm X* received negative attention from African American critics who felt Lee was only interested in commercializing the civil rights legend for his own personal gain. When the director eventually ran into financial trouble and could not finish the film, he received charitable donations from a number of prominent black celebrities, including Oprah Winfrey and Prince. Upon its release in 1992, the film earned its money back, though it did not garner major awards or much in the way of other critical attention.

After *Malcolm X*, Lee returned to films smaller in scope. Cowritten by his siblings, *Crooklyn* (1994) is Lee's semiautobiographical tale of his childhood in Brooklyn in the 1970s. After fathering his first child with wife Tonya Lewis, Lee filmed *Clockers* (1994) and *Girl 6* (1995). *Get on the Bus* (1995), a low-budget feature about the historic Million Man March, marked Lee's return to independent forms of film production.

ENTREPRENEURIAL EFFORTS

As the commercial viability of his films waned, Lee's skills at self-promotion and his entrepreneurial ambitions kept him in the limelight. By the late 1980s he had launched a self-merchandising store in Brooklyn and had begun to direct music videos for artists such as Tracy Chapman and Public Enemy. He also directed and costarred in a popular series of Nike commercials with Michael Jordan and established a music division within his production company, 40 Acres and a Mule Filmworks.

In the late 1990s Lee authored a book about his love for basketball, and he formed a merger with DDB Needham, a major advertising firm. In 1998 he released *He Got Game* for Disney's Touchstone Pictures. The film centers on the director's central preoccupations in and out of the spotlight: fatherhood, basketball, and celebrities. Featuring another collaboration between Lee and Washington, *He Got Game* became the director's first film to open at number one at the box office. It also received mostly positive reviews.

THE EARLY 2000s

Lee continued to write and direct thought-provoking films in the first decade of the 2000s, including *Bamboozled* (2000), a meditation on race in the entertainment industry centered on a fictional minstrel show, and *She Hate Me* (2004), a comedic look at corporate crime, unemployment, and gay parenting. He also directed several big-budget films, including the stand-up comedy concert film *The Original Kings of Comedy* (2000); the crime dramas *25th Hour* (2002) and *Inside Man* (2006); and *Miracle at St. Anna* (2008), an adaptation of James McBride's story of a group of African American soldiers during World War II. Perhaps his most successful work of the early 2000s is the documentary *When the Levees Broke: A Requiem in Four Acts* (2006), a critical look at the damage caused by Hurricane Katrina and the U.S. government's feeble response to the crisis. It won three Emmys and Image and a Peabody Awards. The 2010 follow-up documentary, *If God Is Willing and da Creek Don't Rise* (2010), was also well received.

Lee's love of sports led him to direct two documentaries on athletes, *Jim Brown: All American* (2002) and a day-in-the-life look at basketball star Kobe Bryant during the 2008 National Basketball Association playoffs titled *Kobe Doin' Work* (2009). He also directed Roger Guenveur Smith's one-man performance of the life of African American activist Huey P. Newton, *A Huey P. Newton Story* (2001). Lee's political beliefs once again came to the fore in 2008, when he became a vocal supporter of Barack Obama in his presidential bid, and in 2012, when he hosted a fund-raiser for President Obama's reelection campaign and even presented him with a personalized pair of Air Jordan shoes.

Although Lee has been criticized for his controversial films and statements in the media, he has helped to change the segregated nature of filmmaking by bringing African American talent into the mix. His films have expanded conversation in American society about racial prejudice, often giving audiences new ways of seeing the plight of black people in the contemporary moment. His movies have been widely praised for providing positive images of black people that have counteracted the history of stereotypes in Hollywood. A visionary artist and a highly visible figure in American popular culture, Lee has left an indelible legacy.

Jason King

SEE ALSO: *Brown, Jim;* Do the Right Thing*; Hurricane Katrina; Jordan, Michael; Malcolm X; Million Man March; Nike; Obama, Barack; Prince; Washington, Denzel; Winfrey, Oprah.*

BIBLIOGRAPHY

Aftab, Kaleem, and Spike Lee. *Spike Lee: That's My Story and I'm Sticking to It.* New York: W. W. Norton, 2005.

Breskin, David. "Spike Lee: The Rolling Stone Interview." *Rolling Stone*, July 11–25, 1991, 64.

Conard, Mark T., ed. *The Philosophy of Spike Lee.* Lexington: University Press of Kentucky, 2011.

Hamlet, Janice D., and Coleman R. R. Means, eds. *Fight the Power!: The Spike Lee Reader.* New York: Peter Lang, 2009.

Jones, K. Maurice. *Spike Lee and the African American Filmmakers: A Choice of Colors.* Brookfield, CT: Millbrook Press, 1996.

Lee, Spike, and Terry McMillan. *Five for Five: The Films of*

Spike Lee. New York: Workman, 1991.

Lee, Spike, and Cynthia Fuchs. *Spike Lee: Interviews*. Jackson: University Press of Mississippi, 2002.

Lee, Stan *(1922–)*

As a comics writer, editor, producer, and promoter, Stan Lee invented pop culture icons and revitalized the comic-book industry, becoming the comic world's first celebrity. After retiring from full-time comic-book making, his various media projects and appearances made him an American legend. Before transforming the comics industry, however, he spent twenty years toiling in obscurity.

CHILDHOOD AND EARLY CAREER

Young Stanley Lieber had visions of becoming a great writer. As a student, he won the *New York Herald Tribune* essay contest three weeks in a row. After graduating from high school at seventeen, he took what he thought would be a temporary job with Timely Comics, a company owned by his cousin-in-law Martin Goodman. At first the job consisted of proofreading, sharpening pencils, and making coffee. A year later Lee wrote his first comic-book piece—a two-page text section in *Captain America* Number 3. He signed the work "Stan Lee," his first use of the pen name that eventually would become his legal name.

A few months later, he wrote his first comic-book script for a short back-up story in *Captain America* Number 5. Although he was realizing his dream of becoming a professional writer, he aspired to more than working in the crude medium of comic books. When editors Joe Simon and Jack Kirby left Timely Comics to work at rival DC Comics, Lee took their place. Although the name of the company would change repeatedly over the next thirty years, he would remain its editor and chief writer.

During his first twenty years as editor, Lee churned out mostly mediocre comics in genres that were popular at the moment, all the while maintaining his ambition to quit comics and move on to "legitimate" writing. By 1960, when the comic-book industry was in a slump, he became tired of following trends and being a hack. Goodman's company, then called Atlas Comics, was on the verge of folding, so he instructed Lee to mimic DC Comic's successful superhero team book, *Justice League of America*. Lee detested the assignment and told his wife, Joan, that he was going to quit. Later, in an interview in *Comic Book Marketplace*, he paraphrased his wife's response: "If you want to quit anyway, why don't you do the book he wants, but do it the way you'd like to do it?" He followed her advice, and the result, which appeared in 1961, was *The Fantastic Four*.

THE MARVEL YEARS

Made in collaboration with Kirby as artist, *The Fantastic Four* was grander, wackier, and more realistic than anything the competition had produced. Although the basic premise of the superhero team was borrowed from DC Comics, the execution was unparalleled. Most of the grandeur came from Kirby's drawings, whereas its strong sense of humanity and fun came from Lee's dialogue and captions. The duo followed this initial success with characters such as the Incredible Hulk and Thor in 1962 and the X-Men in 1963.

Stan Lee. *Stan Lee appears at the New York Comic Con in 2011.* ROB KIM/CONTRIBUTOR/FILMMAGIC/GETTY IMAGES.

Working with artist Steve Ditko, Lee produced his most famous creation, Spider-Man, in 1962. Goodman thought that no one would want to read about a high school science nerd who gained the powers of something as creepy as a spider, so he limited Lee to running the story in *Amazing Fantasy* Number 15, the final issue of that series. The sales figures for the issue were so strong that Spider-Man appeared in his own title the following year.

Before 1961 comic-book superheroes had one-dimensional, virtually interchangeable personalities and lived formulaic lives. Lee created heroes who, when not defending the earth from bizarre menaces, lead lives much like other New Yorkers'. His stories are set in the real world, not in fictional cities such as Superman's Metropolis. His heroes have trouble hailing cabs and are razzed by teenage toughs. They chat with the mailman and lose money in the stock market. Young Peter Parker juggles typical teen problems with his job fighting super villains as Spider-Man, learning that "with great power comes great responsibility."

By the time *The Fantastic Four* Number 1 was published, Atlas Comics had gone out of business. Goodman soon began using Marvel Comics as the name of his company. With the rising popularity of Lee's work, the name became permanent. Lee was quick to trumpet the "Marvel Age of Comics," and the company's innovative characterization and storytelling began to attract older, more sophisticated readers. He became a charismatic pitchman, making radio and television appearances, giving interviews to mainstream magazines, and touring the college lecture circuit.

LATER CAREER

In 1972 he retired from comic-book writing and editing in order to oversee production of animated cartoons and films based on Marvel characters. Although he continues to write the *Amazing Spider-Man* newspaper comic strip, most of his later work has been in nonprint media. He has more than sixty producer credits for his work on feature films and television movies and shows that feature Marvel characters. He also has worked as a voice actor, narrating Marvel animated series and video games. He has appeared as himself in more than 100 documentaries and television shows including *The Simpsons, MADtv, Entourage*, and *Big Bang Theory*. He was the subject of a feature-length documentary, *With Great Power: The Stan Lee Story* (2011), and starred in several reality television shows, including *Who Wants to be a Superhero?* in 2006 and 2007 and *Stan Lee's Superhumans*, which debuted in 2010.

Even after he stopped regularly writing for Marvel, the title page of each of its comic books still carried his name, proclaiming "Stan Lee presents . . . " In 2001 longtime Marvel rival DC Comics enticed him to lend his name to *Just Imagine Stan Lee Creating the DC Universe*, a series of one-shot comic books in which he teamed with various artists to create new versions of Superman, Wonder Woman, and other high-profile DC characters. He has collaborated with entities as diverse as MTV and the National Hockey League to create new superheroes, and Archie Comics created a new imprint, Stan Lee Comics, to produce comic books and animation featuring new characters.

In 2008 Lee was awarded the National Medal of the Arts for his contributions to American culture. Three years later his name appeared on a star on Hollywood's Walk of Fame. In 2012 he received the Producers Guild of America's Vanguard Award. Despite being known to many as a creative genius and the innovator who saved the flagging comic-book industry, he remains a controversial figure. Many critics dismiss him as a self-serving huckster who takes credit for others' work, pointing out that the artists who worked with him, particularly Kirby and Ditko, did much of the storytelling.

One of Lee's most important contributions to the comics industry was his process. While scripting and editing most of the titles in the early days of Marvel, he created what would become known as the Marvel method. First he would hold a story conference with the artist and outline the plot for a particular issue or story line. Then the artist would draw a story and Lee would write the dialogue and captions. Although his exact contribution to any particular comic book will probably never be known, it is clear that Marvel Comics—and comics in general—would not be what they are without Lee's creativity, boundless enthusiasm, and love of the medium that he once intended to outgrow.

Randy Duncan

SEE ALSO: *Animated Films; Archie Comics; Comic Books; Comics; DC Comics;* The Fantastic Four*; The Incredible Hulk; Kirby, Jack; Marvel Comics; MTV; National Hockey League (NHL); Reality Television;* The Simpsons*; Spider-Man; Superman; Television; Wonder Woman; The X-Men.*

BIBLIOGRAPHY

Alexander, Mark. *Stan Lee & Jack Kirby: The Wonder Years.* Raleigh, NC: TwoMorrows Publishing, 2011.

Brodsky, Bob. "Maestro of the Marvel Mythos!" *Comic Book Marketplace.* July 1998, 28–54.

Fingeroth, Danny, and Roy Thomas, eds. *The Stan Lee Universe.* Raleigh, NC: TwoMorrows Publishing, 2011.

Lee, Stan, and George Mair. *Excelsior! The Amazing Life of Stan Lee.* New York: Fireside, 2002.

Mclaughlin, Jeff. *Stan Lee: Conversations.* Jackson: University Press of Mississippi, 2007.

Raphael, Jordan, and Tom Spurgeon. *Stan Lee and the Rise and Fall of the American Comic Book.* Chicago: Chicago Review Press, 2003.

Ro, Ronin. *Tales to Astonish: Jack Kirby, Stan Lee, and the American Comic Book Revolution.* New York: Bloomsbury, 2004.

Leggings

Leggings, footless tights of a heavier weight than nylon stockings, have been worn for centuries by men, women, and children, often as an extra layer under clothes to provide warmth in cold weather. During the 1980s, as fashions became more revealing, ankle- or capri-length leggings worn with an oversized sweater or shirt became an important part of a fashionable young woman's wardrobe. Leggings have made several fashion comebacks, first in the 1980s, when they were supplanted by looser, flowing styles, and again during the mid-1990s, when Paris designers placed them on the runway under sheer evening dresses. By 2005 leggings had returned again, and they have remained in style into the 2010s, remaining fresh with the use of a wide variety of fabrics ranging from Lycra to leather.

A versatile fashion accessory that can be worn by women of varying ages and sizes, leggings offer a compromise of coverage and exposure, by showing leg shape while providing insurance of modesty under ultra-short skirts. Though during the 1980s some young women wore leggings in place of pants, most fashion experts of the twenty-first century agree that they should be covered to at least mid-thigh by skirts, tunics, or long shirts.

Leggings got a boost during the early 2000s when studies began to reveal the dangers of wearing the tight blue jeans that were fashionable at the time. Unnerved by evidence that long-term wearing of very tight denim pants could cause problems such as digestive difficulties, bladder infections, and blood clots, women began to seek fashionable alternatives. Leggings came to the forefront because they were stylishly tight but stretchy enough to allow movement and circulation.

By the twenty-first century leggings came in a variety of fabrics and styles, including *jeggings*, or jean leggings that were either made of denim/Lycra blends or printed to look like denim, complete with printed pockets. Dressy leggings were made of velour or sequined material, and fashion-forward styles were made of leather. Shiny synthetic creations dubbed liquid leggings appeared on celebrities and fashionistas. The leggings trend continued, with the appearance of numerous brands and specialized stores. For example, in 2009 a former buyer for Macy's department store, Beth Gold-Cohen, recognizing that many women could not easily find leggings to fit them, launched Lyssé Leggings, a brand specializing in creating a variety of leggings for all body types.

Tina Gianoulis

SEE ALSO: *Department Stores; Jeans; Macy's; Retro Fashion.*

BIBLIOGRAPHY

"From Fad to Mainstream Fashion: 'Leggings' Emerging as a Growing Segment in World Market." ApparelResources .com. Accessed May 22, 2012. Available from http://www .apparelresources.com/next.asp?cod=arti&type=F&cat=9&msg=11647

Monget, Karyn. "Stores See Big Potential with Fashion Leggings." *WWD*, July 25, 1996, 16.

Monget, Karyn. "Lyssé Leggings Gets Active." *WWD*, April 23, 2012, 6.

Menkes, Suzy. "A Great Pair of Leggings." *New York Times Magazine*, August 27, 2006, L180.

Legos

Legos were certainly not the only building toys on the market during the better part of the twentieth century, but they were the ones that quintessentially represented the culture of the time. Wooden building blocks had been around for thousands of years and symbolized a simple, preindustrial era. Toys such as Erector and Meccano sets, with their nuts and bolts and metal girders, captured the aspirations of the skyscraper era experienced in the 1910s and 1920s. Legos, however, as interlocking plastic bricks 1 1/4 by 5/8 inches with eight knobs on top, combined the concept of a simple toy with newer materials.

The concept for the Lego brick was born in 1932 when Danish carpenter Ole Kirk Kristiansen used scrap material from his furniture-making business to make wooden bricks for children's toys. In 1947 the Lego Company began using plastic and was making all of its bricks out of plastic by 1960. These basic bricks, made of red, yellow, white, blue, and black indestructible plastic and infinitely combinable into all manner of shapes and structures, had not changed in design since their early models. By 2010 more than 300 billion Lego bricks had been sold around the world.

The word *Lego*, from the Danish *leg godt*, or "play well," epitomized the philosophy of the Lego Company, which was to provide a "system" of play: simple, educational toys that allowed children to be creative and use their imaginations. The company manufactured various lines of their signature bricks specifically intended for different age ranges: Primo bricks were larger and meant for infants; Duplo for preschoolers; Technic kits for builders ages nine to eleven; and Freestyle for older children. The bricks themselves combined order with flexibility—one was limited to the rectangular form of the brick but could use it in combination with other bricks to build almost anything from one's imagination. Norman Mailer, for example, used Legos in the 1960s to build his own version of the "city of the future" using 15,000 Lego bricks. In addition, Lego manufactured kits that allowed one to make anything from castles, airplanes, and ships to houses, cars, and bridges.

By the 1980s and 1990s Lego kits became more specialized and less interchangeable, reflecting children's desire to possess things on demand rather than having to use their intellectual skills to get them. These kits came with more prebuilt components that lessened the challenge of original construction. In addition, the parts became more particularized, including things beyond the basic bricks. The Lego "Mindstorms" kits, introduced in 1998 and starting at $200, integrated computer chips in the bricks, allowing for interactive possibilities.

It was estimated that by 1993, 70 percent of American families with children owned at least one Lego product. By 1996 Lego was the world's fifth-largest toymaker, amassing a profit of $79 million in that year. During this era Lego also shifted its focus from creating educational toys for kids to becoming the most familiar brand name among adults with children. To this end, the company expanded its product line to include backpacks and children's clothing. In addition, it expanded its LegoLand theme park. Known as the "Disneyland of Europe," the first LegoLand was built in Billund, Denmark (home to the Lego factory), in 1968. LegoLand California opened near Carlsbad in 1999, Lego Deutschland opened in Germany in 2002, Lego Windsor opened in the United Kingdom in 1996, and Lego Florida opened in Winter Haven in 2011. Lego parks under construction include those in Malaysia (2012) and Japan (2015). A park in the United Arab Emirates has been indefinitely delayed.

These developments epitomized equally the shifts in the nature of children's play and in the formation of corporate identity during the late twentieth century. At one time Lego bricks—as simple and affordable objects of a sturdy material that allowed educational yet creative play—encouraged children to build their own universes. Eventually, however, the bricks were no longer basic structural elements but were instead prebuilt component parts used to create a predetermined object with the help of instructions and expensive computer technology. This reflected both the tendency of parents to steer their children toward more sophisticated play as well as Lego's desire to abandon its original mission of manufacturing sound toys with integrity and become, rather, the embodiment of an identifiable brand name that manufactured mass-media experiences for children (as evidenced by LegoLand) that were worlds away from simply building houses with colored bricks.

Although the main target audience continues to be children, adults have also found uses for Legos. Chain bookstores sell complicated kits for constructing famous architectural landmarks such as the White House and the Empire State Building. The most outlandish use may have been in 2009 when British TV host James May conceived of the notion to build a house made entirely of 3.3 million Legos at a cost of $100,000. Unable to obtain legitimate building permits, May constructed a temporary home on land belonging to a winery, and it was dismantled after one night of residence. The Legos were donated to charity.

Lego continues to make traditional kits that allow children to use their imaginations, but the company is increasingly focusing on sets connected to popular movie series such as Harry Potter, *Star Wars*, Batman, and *Pirates of the Caribbean*. A series of video games based on these popular characters also allows children to use their imaginations while manipulating Lego characters and items on television and computer screens and participating in virtual adventures. Legos have become so ingrained in popular culture that many sets have become collector items, selling for hundreds of dollars on the popular auction site, eBay.

Wendy Woloson

SEE ALSO: *Amusement Parks; eBay; Empire State Building; Erector Sets; Harry Potter; Leisure Time; Mailer, Norman;* Pirates of the Caribbean*;* Star Wars*; Toys.*

BIBLIOGRAPHY

Baum, Dave. *Dave Baum's Definitive Guide to Lego Mindstorms.* London: Apress, 2000.

Bethune, Brian. "A House Made Entirely of Legos." *Maclean's*, September 23, 2010.

Lane, Anthony. "The Joy of Bricks: What Have the Danes Done for Children?" *New Yorker*, April 27/May 4, 1998, 96–103.

Stoddard, Maynard Good. "The Toy That Built a Town." *Saturday Evening Post*, October 1, 1984, 62–66.

Wiencek, Henry. *The World of LEGO Toys.* New York: Harry N. Abrams, 1987.

Lehrer, Tom *(1928–)*

Tom Lehrer, a mathematician/balladeer, grew up in New York City. As a child he received piano lessons, learning classical

Tom Lehrer. *Tom Lehrer performs his offbeat, topical brand of musical humor in Copenhagen, Denmark, in 1967.* JAN PERSSON/CONTRIBUTOR/REDFERNS/GETTY IMAGES.

music until he asked his parents to find a teacher who would teach him to play popular tunes. In 1943, at the age of fourteen, child-prodigy Lehrer became an undergraduate at Harvard, majoring in mathematics. He earned his Bachelor of Arts and Master of Arts within three years. During his undergraduate days he also found time to write song parodies, including a fight song for his alma mater, "Fight Fiercely, Harvard," which became popular at the university and would eventually show up on his first record. Thus marks the beginning of one of the twentieth century's most controversial satirists.

FROM MATH TO MUSIC

With his undergraduate degrees tucked under his belt, Lehrer stayed on at Harvard to work toward a graduate degree in math. His first musical performance came in 1950 when he teamed up with other musically inclined members of the university community to form a quartet that sang at a Harvard Law School function. One item on the repertoire was a Lehrer composition: a song that listed chemical elements (though not necessarily in order) to the tune of Gilbert and Sullivan's "Modern Major General." "The Elements" would later find appreciative audiences beyond Harvard. Lehrer also wrote a parody poking fun at a sculpture on campus that had been designed by Walter Gropius. The poem was published in the *Harvard Crimson*.

In 1953 Lehrer decided to put out a record of the various songs with which he had been entertaining people around Cambridge. He expected *Songs by Tom Lehrer* to sell around 400 copies; it ended up selling 350,000. That same year he decided to leave Harvard to work for the technical firm Baird-Atomic. His work for the company was followed by a stint in the army, a tour of duty that inspired his hilariously nasty song "It Makes a Fellow Proud to be a Soldier." Lehrer then toured the United States and the English-speaking world to entertain his audiences with new songs, interspersed with acerbic commentary. A record based on one of his concerts—*An Evening Wasted with Tom Lehrer*—came out in 1959 and sold almost as well as his first record.

Next Lehrer decided to return to graduate school—he was a graduate student at Harvard for a total of ten years and at Columbia for one year. By 1965 he had completed all the work required for his degree, except for the dissertation, but he decided to stop seeking a doctorate. He began teaching mathematics at MIT's political science department in 1962. He then became a professor at the University of California, Santa Cruz. His work as a math teacher, however, did not stop Lehrer from performing his music; the British magazine the *Spectator* reported in 1998 that Lehrer had made "109 concert appearances" over the course of his career.

In 1964 Lehrer had some topical political songs performed on the NBC program *That Was the Week That Was* (a program taken from England). He put out a record, also titled *That Was the Year That Was*, based on the NBC songs. He wrote some of the songs for the children's television series *The Electric Company* in the early 1970s. In the early 1980s there was a touring show called *Tomfoolery*, in which a four-member cast sang an ensemble of Lehrer's old songs. Although Lehrer helped with the production, he did not sing in it.

A couple of his songs seem to foreshadow future events. In a 1965 song about George Murphy, a now-forgotten actor turned senator, Lehrer mused that many Hollywood actors had become politicians, "from Helen Gahagan to . . . Ronald Reagan." In his song "Pollution" Lehrer anticipated President Bill Clinton in his advice for coping with America's smog: "wear a gas mask and a veil / Then you can breathe, long as you don't inhale."

DARING SUBJECT MATTER AND CONTROVERSY

Lehrer's humor was somewhat daring—at least for its time. In 1982 he wrote: "I was often accused of bad taste in the '50s and '60s, but the songs which prompted that accusation seem positively genial today." At the very least, his humor was unconventional, as evidenced by a word he used to describe President Lyndon Johnson's increasing military involvement in Vietnam—*escallatio*. The song "I Hold Your Hand in Mine" is about a man who holds onto some of the remains of the woman he killed—"still I keep your hand / As a precious souvenir." "The Masochism Tango" combines a catchy dance tune with lyrics about S&M, whereas "Smut" celebrates the joys of porn: "I could tell you things about Peter Pan / And the Wizard of Oz—There's a dirty old man!" And, of course, there is the favorite tune of the American Society for the Prevention of Cruelty to Animals, "Poisoning Pigeons in the Park."

The Lehrer song that caused the most controversy was "The Vatican Rag." Here—in a movie that offended many Catholics—he sings irreverently about the Catholic sacraments. Lehrer later defended the song, arguing that he was making fun of "the Catholic ritual," not "the religion." When he performed "The Vatican Rag" at the hungry i nightclub, Lehrer indicated that the song was simply a logical extension of the liturgical reforms of the Vatican II conference—reforms under which the Mass could be performed in the vernacular. He further disrupted church officials and members when he said that the Vatican II reforms were intended to make the Church "more commercial," implying that Catholicism was being turned into a "product" the Church was selling. In that sense the song can be seen as a satire about the perils of departing from religious orthodoxy (though both Lehrer and his Catholic critics would probably disagree with such an interpretation).

Since 1965 Lehrer has not written new songs for public performance. He explained that "satire was made obsolete when Henry Kissinger got the Nobel Peace Prize." He went on to teach math and music courses at the University of California, Santa Cruz, from 1972 to 2001 but largely disappeared from public view save for two performances in 1998 to honor the producer of *Tom Foolery* and a handful of singles that were included in various retrospective albums. Among these were a 1997 rerelease of his two studio albums titled *Songs & More Songs* and a three-disc box set of his entire catalog titled *The Remains of Tom Lehrer* (2000). The CD/DVD combo *The Tom Lehrer Collection* (2010) was notable for including videos of Lehrer's most famous live performances.

Though he never enjoyed (or perhaps actively avoided) any semblance of celebrity, Lehrer's songs made a lasting impression on American entertainment and paved the way for other satirists such as "Weird Al" Yankovic and the Capitol Steps to combine clever humor and catchy melodies with biting social and political commentary. As a testament to their poignancy and longevity, several of his works have recently been featured on television shows including *Gilmore Girls* (2000–2007), *NCIS* (2003–), and *The Big Bang Theory* (2007–).

Eric Longley

SEE ALSO: *Celebrity; Compact Discs; Hollywood; Pornography; Reagan, Ronald; Television; Vietnam;* The Wizard of Oz; *Yankovic, "Weird Al."*

BIBLIOGRAPHY

Bernstein, Jeremy. "Tom Lehrer: Having Fun." *American Scholar* 53, no. 3 (1984): 295–302.

Feingold, Michael. "Tom Capsule." *Village Voice*, December 16, 1981, 132, 134.

Kercher, Stephen E. *Revel with a Cause: Liberal Satire in Postwar America.* Chicago: University of Chicago Press, 2006.

Lanier, Kristina. "Whatever Happened To . . . " *Christian Science Monitor*, July 16, 1998, 13.

Lehrer, Tom. *Songs by Tom Lehrer.* London: Reprise Records, 1953.

Lehrer, Tom. *An Evening Wasted with Tom Lehrer.* London: Reprise Records, 1959.

Lehrer, Tom. *That Was the Year That Was.* London: Reprise Records, 1965.

Lehrer, Tom. "In His Own Words: On Life, Lyrics and Liberals." *Washington Post*, January 3, 1982, E1, E5.

Lehrer, Tom, adapted by Cameron Mackintosh and Robin Ray. *Tom Foolery: The Words and Music of Tom Lehrer.* New York: Samuel French, 1986.

Phillips, Peter. "A True Eccentric." *Spectator*, May 9, 1998, 50.

Rovner, Sandy. "From Math to Sass: 25 Years of Succulent Satire." *Washington Post*, January 3, 1982, E1, E5.

Leibovitz, Annie *(1949–)*

From her first assignments for *Rolling Stone* in the early 1970s to her defining images of celebrity found in *Vanity Fair* since 1983, Annie Leibovitz changed the way Americans see the twentieth century and beyond. Capturing both the glamorous and the banal sides of celebrity, she has also transformed the way other photographers have captured the twentieth century on film. For four decades, Leibovitz has crafted an image of the twentieth century as the American century, indelibly marked by a fascination with celebrity.

PICKING UP THE CAMERA

Born in Westbury, Connecticut, in 1949, Leibovitz studied painting at the San Francisco Art Institute in the late 1960s, graduating with a degree in fine arts in 1971. She discovered a passion for photography and bought her first camera during that time. Early on, family photographs—her own and others—were strong influences on her work. The power of the camera to encapsulate and communicate family histories drew her to documentary photography and to the work of, among others, the great American photographers Margaret Bourke-White and Robert Frank.

While a student, Leibovitz spent a semester in a work-study program on a kibbutz in Israel. During her stay a friend gave her a subscription to *Rolling Stone* and, upon her return to San Francisco, she met with art director Robert Kingsbury. Kingsbury was especially impressed by pictures of an antiwar demonstration she had shot in San Francisco the day before. In 1970 he published some of Leibovitz's kibbutz images in *Rolling Stone*'s photo gallery. Later in the year he published the antiwar pictures and began to give Leibovitz regular assignments. In 1973 she was named *Rolling Stone*'s chief photographer.

LIFE AS A ROCK PHOTOGRAPHER

Leibovitz learned her greatest lesson about photographing celebrities during her first out-of-town shoot for *Rolling Stone.* The assignment was to photograph John Lennon. She was a young, green magazine photographer with a deadline. He was a legend, a musician whose melodies had given him everlasting fame, but he was also normal, just an everyday guy asking her what she'd like him to do. From that moment on, as Leibovitz remembers in the introduction to her 1990 book, *Portraits*, she got involved with her photos, allowing her own point of view and experiences to shape the picture's gut.

As Lennon shaped Leibovitz's approach to celebrity photography, Leibovitz shaped the public's enduring memory of Lennon. On December 8, 1980, she returned to New York to again shoot Lennon for *Rolling Stone.* She posed him nude, curled up in the fetal position next to his wife, Yoko Ono. His love for Ono and his attachment to her are palpable in the

Annie Leibovitz. *Annie Leibovitz counts among her works many of the iconic celebrity images of the twentieth century.* BEN HIDER/CONTRIBUTOR/GETTY IMAGES ENTERTAINMENT/GETTY IMAGES.

photo. Tragically, just hours after this shoot, Lennon was assassinated outside his apartment building. Suddenly, Leibovitz's picture, published in the January 1981 issue of *Rolling Stone*, became imbued with deeper meaning and resonance.

A year later Leibovitz photographed Ono at Central Park in Manhattan. Dwarfed by trees in a field named after one of the Beatles' most famous songs—Strawberry Field—a black-clad Ono appears small and alone. It is as if Ono and Leibovitz had to create another image together in order to bring closure to the events of December 1980. The photograph is haunting. Moreover, it is haunted by the memory of the picture of Ono and Lennon, perhaps one of the most enduring images of the 1980s.

When the Rolling Stones invited Leibovitz to photograph their concert tour in 1975, she created the original "behind-the-scenes" show-all. Her images revealed the working world of rock and roll: Mick Jagger onstage, so thin as to be nearly transparent (Leibovitz told an interviewer in 1990 that Jagger lost about 10 pounds during each performance and she had wanted to capture not only the onstage energy but also the way spent energy looked); Jagger in makeup; Jagger in a terry cloth robe with his hair wrapped in a turban; Jagger, Keith Richards, and the rest of the band traveling, playing, resting, and working. Rock and roll, the viewers learned, is not all high living. Strenuous efforts are required to produce such massive performances. Seeing the inner workings of a Stones concert enabled readers to see the less glamorous parts of the legendary group's success.

CELEBRITY PORTRAITURE

When Condé Nast Publications reintroduced its glamorous *Vanity Fair* in 1983, Leibovitz became the magazine's first contributing photographer. Her first book was published the same year, and she had her first gallery showing the next, in November 1984. She became one of an elite club—a magazine photographer accepted by the art world, herself a celebrity due to her photographs of celebrities.

In her tenure at *Vanity Fair*, Leibovitz has continued to define celebrity and portraiture. Her images are among the most memorable in the magazine's history, including Whoopi Goldberg in a bathtub full of milk (1984), Diane Keaton dancing around Leibovitz's studio (1987), and the cover that featured Demi Moore in an elegant pose, pregnant and nude (1988). Leibovitz has immortalized Hollywood's stars, often showing their more private side. In her pictures of Arnold Schwarzenegger (June 1997), Leonardo DiCaprio (January 1998), and Brad Pitt (February 1995 and November 1998), for instance, Leibovitz shows vulnerable men and handsome hunks. She has also immortalized other celebrities, including President Bill Clinton (March 1993 and November 1997). Leibovitz's time at *Vanity Fair* has been punctuated by her annual December Hall of Fame, which highlights Americans (celebrities and not) who made the year special. And, each March from 1995 through 2011, she created Hollywood covers and portfolios that were perhaps more eagerly awaited than the Academy Awards they honored.

Leibovitz's celebrity portraiture has also appeared in advertising, first in a campaign for American Express—with unforgettable, seemingly candid shots of Ella Fitzgerald and Sammy Davis Jr., among others—and for the Gap, featuring black-and-white portraits of celebrities wearing their favorite staples from a retailer that defines American popular fashion.

TURNING FROM PUBLIC TO PRIVATE

Leibovitz is a magazine photographer, shooting commissioned photographs on a deadline. She has, unlike some of her contemporaries, worked within the conventions of magazine photography, rarely testing limits, except perhaps those of the imagination. And yet her commercial photography always bears her personal mark, her distinct vision of celebrity and of our world. She is a fan of her subjects, but she is also one of them—a celebrity photographer of celebrities.

Living as a celebrity, however, Leibovitz has guarded her private life and rarely appeared in front of the camera. She rarely photographs herself, saying that she feels so personally defined by the way she sees the world through the camera that she cannot imagine herself on the other side of it. This modesty, settled comfortably amid the power of her art and the fame of her images, makes Leibovitz an uncommon celebrity. That stance toward privacy changed, however, when her longtime partner Susan Sontag—American essayist, novelist, filmmaker, and activist—died of cancer in 2004. A few weeks later, Leibovitz's father died as well. In her attempt to deal with the combined impact of their deaths, Leibovitz made a startling transformation from private to public both in words and in photographs.

The retrospective *Annie Leibovitz: A Photographer's Life 1990–2005* debuted at the Brooklyn Museum in October 2006, and an accompanying book of the same title was published by Random House. For the first time, Leibovitz combined her professional photographs with those of her personal life, featuring photos of Sontag throughout their fifteen-year relationship, including her final battle with cancer; photos of her family and friends; and photos of her three daughters. "I don't have two lives," said Leibovitz in the introduction. "This is one life, and the personal pictures and the assignment work are all part of it."

This new direction in Leibovitz's photography has continued, and in 2011 she released a new exhibit, *Pilgrimage* (and book of the same title), featuring photographs she took of historical sites across the United States. Rather than her usual portraits of celebrities, these are portraits of places that carry meaning within the American cultural landscape, both those of nature—such as Niagara Falls and Walden Pond—and those of a more celebrity-like iconic status—the homes of Elvis Presley and Georgia O'Keefe, for example.

The introduction of Leibovitz's private life to the public has not entirely been due to her photography, however. In 2009 the lending group Art Capital Group filed a $24 million breach-of-contract lawsuit against Leibovitz, claiming she had failed to pay back loans against which she had put up her past and future copyrights as collateral. The loan was taken over by L.A.-based equity firm Colony Capital in 2010, but it is unclear whether Leibovitz's photography rights are secure.

Ilene S. Goldman

SEE ALSO: *Advertising; Cancer; Celebrity; Celebrity Couples; DiCaprio, Leonardo; Fitzgerald, Ella; The Gap; Goldberg, Whoopi; Hollywood; Lennon, John; Moore, Demi; Movie Stars; O'Keeffe, Georgia; Pitt, Brad; Presley, Elvis; Rock and Roll;* Rolling Stone*; The Rolling Stones; Schwarzenegger, Arnold;* Vanity Fair.

BIBLIOGRAPHY

Leibovitz, Annie. *Photographs: Annie Leibovitz, 1970–1990.* New York: HarperCollins, 1991.

Leibovitz, Annie. *A Photographer's Life, 1990–2005*. New York: Random House, 2006.

Leibovitz, Annie. *Pilgrimage*. New York: Random House, 2011.

Leibovitz, Annie, and Sharon DeLano. *Annie Leibovitz at Work*. New York: Random House, 2008.

Leisure Suit

Like bell bottoms, platform shoes, and mood rings, the leisure suit came to symbolize the swinging mid-1970s and its pervasive disco culture. The matching polyester jacket and pants often came in such colors as powder blue or burnt orange and could sport either wide collars and lapels or none at all. Many came adorned with a belt to be worn tunic-style. Originally designed after World War II as resort wear for the wealthy, the early leisure suits were priced handsomely and constructed out of wool gabardine. Though they enjoyed a brief heyday in the 1970s, leisure suits were soon acknowledged as tacky.

Beginning in 1988, however, a 1970s nostalgia revival led to an annual leisure suit convention in Des Moines, Iowa. In the 1990s a series of computer games featuring a sleazy character named Leisure Suit Larry epitomized the garment as the unofficial uniform of the déclassé. A new version of the game, *Leisure Suit Larry: Magna Cum Laude*, was introduced in 2004, featuring Larry's nephew, Larry Lovage, who appears on a television dating show. The game was highly criticized for nudity and sexual themes. The tenth game in the series, *Leisure Suit Larry: Box Office Bust*, premiered in 2009 for the PC, PlayStation 3, and Xbox 360, featuring the two Larrys solving a mystery at a movie studio. It was not well received by critics.

Geri Speace

SEE ALSO: *Computer Games; Disco; Leisure Time; Retro Fashion; Television; Toys; Video Games.*

BIBLIOGRAPHY

Adato, Allison, and David Burnett. "A Leisure Suit Convention." *Life*, February 1996, 18.

Stern, Jane, and Michael Stern. *The Encyclopedia of Bad Taste*. New York: HarperCollins, 1990.

Leisure Time

Despite Americans' persistent complaints about not having enough free time, the twentieth century ushered in an unprecedented age of leisure. In previous centuries leisure time had been at a premium, but even then Americans found time to gather together with family, friends, or church and community groups to spend time according to their own customs, tastes, and morals. In the twentieth century, economic developments such as a shorter work week, increased wages, vacation time, and enhanced productivity resulted in more free time for workers, and changing attitudes toward leisure reflected the greater role that leisure time played in American life. The shift in attitudes was subtle and sweeping, and the significance was barely noticed by most. The free time that allows for "the newfound delight of young fathers in their babies," writes Margaret Mead in her 1958 essay in *Mass Leisure*, represented "another intrinsically rewarding pattern which no large civilization has ever permitted." The observation is at once a measure of the unprecedented role of leisure in everyday life and of how much Americans have changed their definition of leisure. As more workers telecommute from home, work has become less regimented, and the traditional markers between work and free time have become blurred.

Twentieth-century America's preoccupation with leisure time represents an enormous change from the attitudes held by the settlers, who cleared their land and farmed it for subsistence. Primarily agrarian, early nineteenth-century Americans found that most of their time was consumed by agricultural work. Those who loafed beyond what was socially acceptable found themselves ostracized within their small communities. Places of entertainment, such as theaters, were regarded as dens of vice that were populated by drunk actors and prostitutes. But in preindustrial America, leisure and work often commingled. As Roy Rosenzweig observes in *Rethinking Popular Culture*, "the rum barrell (sic) was always near the work—ready for distribution, by this means they kept the men hard at work all day." The prevailing mindset was exemplified by Benjamin Franklin in *Poor Richard's Almanac*: "Leisure, is Time for doing something useful. . . . Trouble springs from Idleness, and grievous Toil from needless Ease."

INDUSTRIALIZATION

Industrialization ushered in major changes to the workplace. Mechanization, the specialization of labor, and regulation made the workplace strictly a place for doing a job. Drinking, for example, was banished to the saloon. These sharp delineations led to the recognition that free time had value and that how one spent one's free time had significance. Middle-class reformers, who took issue with the rowdy, hard-drinking, working-class culture, began to view industrialism as a potential wedge that could come between workers and a more meaningful culture. "When the operation of the machine tends to relieve the operative of all thought, the man or woman who tends it risks becoming a machine, well oiled and cared for, but incapable of independent life," worried industrialist Edward Atkinson. Americans slowly began to realize that overwork could be as destructive as idleness and that a useful pursuit of leisure could be beneficial.

The pursuit of leisure had been defined as an upper-class privilege by Thorstein Veblen in his *The Theory of the Leisure Class*, published in 1899. Veblen introduced the phrase "conspicuous consumption" to describe leisure as "a nonproductive consumption of time." Leisure was associated with pursuits that did not contribute to making a living, and the notion of "culture" tied such pursuits to higher aims—the arts, religion, and higher education. As the middle class grew in the early twentieth century, its definitions of culture and leisure reflected its emphasis on hierarchical order. The polarization between rich and poor gave the growing middle class impetus to create a social role for culture that distinguished the status-seeking middle class from the working and immigrant classes below it.

POSTWAR LEISURE

After World War II, the idea of "earned" pleasure—free time as a reward for hard work—began to break down. According to

Mead, Americans sought to restore an equilibrium that had been disrupted by the hardships of war and the wartime separation of men and women. Soldiers had too little leave time, and war workers had too much disposable income. The desire to get some joy out of life superseded all else, and the home became the place where Americans sought that joy. They began to reconceive the relationship between work and family life. "As once it was wrong to play so hard that it might affect one's work," writes Mead, "now it is wrong to work so hard that it may affect family life."

Around the time of World War I, few considered adolescence a separate stage of life. The term *teenager* was not commonly used until the 1940s. Before the 1950s, teenagers had been expected to work full time, like adults. Most adolescents worked by age fifteen, moving from childhood straight into adulthood. But with the increasing opportunities for secondary education in the 1920s and a lack of available work during the Depression, American children found that their adulthood was postponed. Thus, the emergence of a distinct youth culture during the 1950s helped to define some leisure activities. The postwar prosperity of the 1950s brought fatter allowances to teenagers, and this new demographic group became a target market. Entire industries retooled their operations to meet the needs of these indiscriminate consumers flush with disposable income. This development transformed twentieth-century popular culture, as new icons such as Elvis Presley became cultural phenomena and encouraged the purchase of rock-and-roll concert tickets, trendy clothes, and long-playing records.

In addition to the prosperity of the times, technological changes—such as television and movies—transformed the leisure experience into a consumptive one for adults as well as teenagers. Leisure expenditures in 1950 had increased tenfold from those in 1909, when Americans were likely to make their own music or toys. Correspondingly, the average work week dropped from twelve hours a day in 1900 to seven-and-a-half hours a day in 1960, as increased productivity helped to shrink working time. By the end of the twentieth century, it had become possible to speak of a "leisure industry."

Whereas work was once the primary identifier for individuals, leisure rapidly became more and more central to identity. In the introduction to an issue titled "Americans at Play," *Life* magazine wrote in 1971:

> The weekend is a state of mind, betrayed by a vacant stare that lasts till Tuesday and an anticipatory twitching that begins on Thursday. We talk fishing at the factory, surfing at the store, skiing in the office, and when we make new acquaintances, we identify ourselves less by what we do for a living than by what we do to loaf. . . . Wherever we are, inside our head, we're *out there.*

Nothing could slow Americans' appetite for leisure time activities: "Leisure spending rose on a steady curve through Vietnam, an oil embargo, runaway inflation, an energy crisis, unemployment and a recession," writes Mark Jury in *Playtime! Americans at Leisure.* Leisure spending increased from $58.3 billion in 1965 to $160 billion in 1977. Though fueled by factors such as fewer working hours, higher wages, and earlier retirement, leisure spending also represented a willful reorganization of personal priorities. Jury indicates that leisure products, such as boats, that were once only available to the wealthy could now be purchased, through extended financing, by the middle class. Leisure had become one of the great American levelers.

People not only reorganized their spending priorities according to their leisure activities, but they also reorganized their work to accommodate their desire for leisure time. Though the more prosperous middle-class workers had less time to devote to leisure activities than their working-class counterparts and the income gap between the educated and the uneducated continued to increase, the rise of the service economy provided an alternative work experience for many. The service economy enabled a number of Americans of various levels of education to take on extra jobs whenever they needed extra income. Some could make an above-average income from tips, but for most the service economy offered modest incomes and flexible working hours that provided them with the time and the money needed to pursue leisure activities. In one case, according to Jury, a "leisure freak" named Pete gave up acting to become a hairdresser because he could earn $12,000 a year working three days a week and devote the rest of his time to skydiving, bodybuilding, motorcycle racing, and anything else he chose to pursue.

NEW CONNOTATIONS

As more and more Americans participated in leisure time, the very definition of leisure came into question. Instead of encompassing all time away from work, leisure began to be defined as "doing something" enjoyable. Leisure has evolved into the time in which one is free, apart from others. In the 1990s fewer Americans were married than in the previous generation, and fewer still were parents, as many put off parenthood for longer periods.

Despite these trends, Americans in the early twenty-first century remained largely home-centered. In 2006 Gallup's annual lifestyle poll revealed that staying home with family (32 percent) and watching television (22 percent) were Americans' top two choices for spending an evening. Those two responses had been consistently the most popular since 1960, though the poll reported demographic differences in the responses. For example, watching television is much more popular with those sixty-five and older than with the eighteen-to-twenty-nine segment. Educational differences also prompted different responses: college or postgraduate degree holders were more involved in reading or dining out, while less educated people preferred television. "As our leisure time has increased since 1965," Geoffrey Godbey told the *Christian Science Monitor*, "the gain has been plowed into more TV because it can be sequenced, an hour here, an hour and a half there. TV fits so well now, and it is immediately accessible."

Despite increased free time, Americans complain that they have less of it. Their complaints constitute a healthy debate among those involved in leisure studies (a field of sociological inquiry that in itself indicates the prominence of leisure in American life). One plausible explanation for this discrepancy emerges in the concept of "time-deepening," which "assumes that, under pressure of expanded interest and compulsion, people are capable of higher rates of 'doing'." Godbey and John P. Robinson describe this conception in their book *Time for Life* and base their study on "time diaries," in which study groups recorded how they spent their free time. Time-deepening is the *sense* of being rushed, a sense that is either self-imposed or perceived.

Ironically, in the early twenty-first century, even as the economy floundered, the sale of luxury items skyrocketed. Many of the luxury items purchased were related to leisure activities, including mobile phones, which were used not only for phone calls and texting but also for accessing the Internet and software applications and for enormous flat-screen televisions that provided access to hundreds of channels and live events. In large part the upsurge in luxury spending was fueled by baby boomers nearing retirement age who felt entitled to rewards for all the work put in during their younger years. In a survey of customers with incomes of more than $100,000 conducted by American Express Platinum, 59 percent preferred spending money on experiential luxuries such as dining in restaurants, travel, and entertainment than on objects and gadgets. Unlike younger individuals of affluent means, baby boomers nearing retirement spent money on time-shares in expensive resorts, sophisticated media rooms for their homes, major renovations to existing homes, and luxury travel modes such as private air transportation and mega yachts.

In 2006 *Time* examined the ways in which Americans spent leisure time. Estimates suggested that Americans had at least forty-five minutes a day more of leisure time than did earlier generations. However, the average American spent 2.5 hours a day watching television, and extra time available frequently resulted in watching TV for longer periods. There were differences in the ways in which males and females and marrieds and singles spent their leisure time. For instance, women spent an average of fourteen minutes a day on the telephone as opposed to men, who spent only seven minutes day on that activity. Males watched television for an average of three hours and twenty-eight minutes each day, but women watched for only two hours and forty-one minutes. Marrieds spent one hour and twenty-four minutes eating and drinking in an average day, while singles completed the task sixteen minutes sooner. Studies have continued to link family time spent on leisure activities to increased family bonding and stability, a trend that has continued for several decades. Leisure time has become an integral part of daily life in America and is considered essential for individual and family health.

Daryl Umberger

SEE ALSO: *Baby Boomers; Cell Phones; The Fifties; The Great Depression; Long-Playing Record; Presley, Elvis; Rock and Roll; Teenagers; Television; The Twenties; Vietnam; World War I; World War II.*

BIBLIOGRAPHY

"Americans at Play." *Life*, September 3, 1971, 10–11.

Barney, William L. *The Passage of the Republic: An Interdisciplinary History of Nineteenth-Century America.* Lexington, MA: D. C. Heath, 1987.

Betts, Kate. "Luxury Fever." *Time: Style and Design*, Fall 2004.

Bronson, Po. "How We Spend Our Leisure Time. " *Time*, October 23, 2006.

Butsch, Richard, ed. *For Fun and Profit: The Transformation of Leisure into Consumption.* Philadelphia: Temple University Press, 1990.

Csikszentmihalyi, Mihaly, and Judith LeFevre. "Optimal Experience in Work and Leisure." *Journal of Personality and Social Psychology* 56, no. 5 (1989): 815–822.

Ehn, Billy, and Orvar Löfgren. *The Secret World of Doing Nothing.* Berkeley: University of California Press, 2010.

Franklin, Benjamin. *The Autobiography and Other Writings.* New York: Penguin, 1986.

Holmstrom, David. "Leisure Time in the '90s: TV Soaks up the Hours." *Christian Science Monitor*, June 3, 1997, 13.

Jennings, Peter, and Todd Brewster. *The Century.* New York: Doubleday, 1998.

Jury, Mark. *Playtime! Americans at Leisure.* New York: Harcourt Brace Jovanovich, 1977.

Kando, Thomas. *Leisure and Popular Culture in Transition.* St. Louis, MO: C. V. Mosby, 1975.

Kaplan, Max. *Leisure in America: A Social Inquiry.* New York: John Wiley & Sons, 1960.

Mead, Margaret. "The Pattern of Leisure in Contemporary American Culture." In *Mass Leisure*, ed. Eric Larrabee and Rolf Meyersohn. Glencoe, IL: The Free Press, 1958.

Robinson, John P., and Geoffrey Godbey. *Time for Life: The Surprising Ways Americans Use Their Time.* University Park: Pennsylvania State University Press, 1997.

Rosenzweig, Roy. "The Rise of the Saloon." In *Rethinking Popular Culture: Contemporary Perspectives in Cultural Studies*, ed. Chandra Mukerji and Michael Schudson. Berkeley: University of California Press, 1991.

Veblen, Thorstein, and Stuart Chase. *The Theory of the Leisure Class.* New York: Modern Library, 1934.

LeMond, Greg *(1961–)*

Greg LeMond is one of the most successful professional cyclists in the United States. In 1986 he was the first American to win the Tour de France, the most prestigious race in cycling. He was just twenty-five years old.

In early 1987 LeMond went turkey hunting with his uncle and his brother-in-law and was accidentally shot in the back. He was flown by helicopter to a hospital, where doctors removed approximately thirty shotgun pellets from his body. With thirty-five pellets remaining—three in his heart, five in his liver, and the rest spread throughout his body—LeMond recovered, but his return to cycling was further delayed by an emergency appendectomy in late 1987 and surgery on an infected shin tendon in 1988. In 1989 LeMond returned to the Tour de France, and he won in dramatic fashion, finishing just eight seconds ahead of his nearest rival. It was the closest win in the race's history.

In 1990 LeMond repeated his success, winning the Tour de France for a third time. He also won the World Championship Road Race, another prestigious race, twice, in 1983 and 1989. In 1989, the year in which LeMond won both the Tour de France and the World Championship Road Race, *Sports Illustrated* magazine named him its "Sportsman of the Year" and featured him on the cover of its December issue. A muscle disorder forced him to retire from competitive racing in 1994. In later years LeMond became an outspoken critic against doping in cycling.

Simon Philo

SEE ALSO: *Bicycling; Sports Heroes;* Sports Illustrated*; Tour de France.*

BIBLIOGRAPHY

Abt, Samuel. *LeMond: The Incredible Comeback of an American Hero.* New York: Random House, 1990.

Abt, Samuel. *A Season in Turmoil.* Boulder, CO: Velo Press, 1995.

Wyatt, Edward. "LeMond Returns to Tour, and Likes What He Sees." *New York Times*, July 13, 2008.

L'Engle, Madeleine *(1918–2007)*

Madeleine L'Engle wrote more than two dozen books of poetry, plays, memoirs, and fiction and was credited with bringing science fiction into mainstream young-adult fiction. Often compared to Irish-born author C. S. Lewis, she used science and Christianity to create stories of spiritual quests, battles between good and evil, and an omnipresent God of love. Her well-known young-adult novel, the Newbery Medal winner *A Wrinkle in Time* (1962), is a coming-of-age story that blends science fiction and fantasy. The awkward and intense Meg must travel in time and space to fight "the black thing" on a planet of utter conformity, ruled by an emotionless brain. L'Engle asked all the cosmic questions about morality, religion, love, and identity, and the book found international popularity with children and critics.

L'Engle was born in New York City on November 29, 1918, and had written her first story by the age of five. After a nomadic childhood moving between the United States and Europe, she graduated from Smith College in Northampton, Massachusetts, in 1941 and moved back to New York to begin her adult life as an actor and a playwright. Her first novel, *The Small Rain*, was published in 1945. A second book, *And Both Were Young*, was named one of the *New York Times* ten best books of 1949. L'Engle married actor Hugh Franklin in 1946, and they moved back and forth between New York and Connecticut as they began to raise a family together. While in Connecticut, the couple ran a general store; in New York Franklin pursued his acting career while L'Engle began teaching and writing. It was not until nearly twenty years later that she would truly find fame and success as a writer.

In 1960 L'Engle published her first book about a young girl named Vicky in *Meet the Austins*. This book would evolve into what is known as L'Engle's Chronos series, which concentrates on the Austin family. Two years later the first book in the Kairos series, *A Wrinkle in Time*, was finally published. This series focuses on the families of Meg Murry and Calvin O'Keefe. *A Wrinkle in Time* uses concepts from German-born physicist Albert Einstein's writings on relativity, as well as from German physicist Max Planck's quantum theory, combined with the religious idea of moral purpose. Although the book had been rejected by twenty-six publishers before being accepted at Farrar, Straus & Giroux, it quickly became popular and began earning honors. Of note, the novel won the Newbery Medal for best children's book in 1963, as well as a Sequoyah Book Award and a Lewis Carroll Shelf Award. At the time of L'Engle's death in 2007, *A Wrinkle in Time* had sold eight million copies and was in its sixty-ninth printing.

While the Chronos and Kairos series have some overlapping characters and exist somewhat within the same universe, *A Wrinkle in Time* and its sequels, *A Wind in the Door* (1973) and *A Swiftly Tilting Planet* (1978), combine elements of science, time travel, and extrasensory perception. The Austin books, on the other hand, take place in a more solidly realistic milieu. Both series, however, deal with the battle of good and evil: the battle in the Kairos series is at the mythic cosmos level; in the Chronos series it is the battle within a person's self that is at hand.

Interestingly, L'Engle's books for children were as attacked as they were lauded. She was criticized by secularists for having too much religion in her books and by religious conservatives for having too liberal (or universal) a view of God. *A Wrinkle in Time* has consistently been one of the most banned books in the United States in the fifty years since its publication.

L'Engle continued to write books in both the Chronos and Kairos young-adult series, while simultaneously publishing adult fiction and romance, memoirs, poetry, and essays on writing and religion. She taught courses and gave lectures at various universities over the years, maintaining a vigorous speaking schedule, and served as both librarian and writer-in-residence for the Cathedral Church of St. John the Divine. In 1998 she was awarded the Margaret A. Edwards Lifetime Achievement Award, and she has been given numerous honorary doctorate awards from colleges and universities all across the country. In 2004 she became the second children's author to win the National Humanities Award.

After facing a number of health complications in her later years, L'Engle died on September 6, 2007. A biography in the form of interviews with those who knew her best, *Listening for Madeleine: A Portrait of Madeleine L'Engle in Many Voices*, edited by Leonard S. Marcus, was published in 2012.

Jessy Randall

SEE ALSO: *Best Sellers; Einstein, Albert; Lewis, C. S.; Romance Novels; Science Fiction Publishing.*

BIBLIOGRAPHY

Hettinga, Donald R. *Presenting Madeleine L'Engle*. New York: Twayne, 1993.

L'Engle, Madeleine. *The Crosswicks Journal ("A Circle of Quiet"; "The Summer of the Great-Grandmother"; and "The Irrational Season")*. San Francisco: Harper, 1997.

Marcus, Leonard S., ed. *Listening for Madeleine: A Portrait of Madeleine L'Engle in Many Voices*. New York: Farrar, Straus & Giroux, 2012.

Lennon, John *(1940–1980)*

Rock legend John Lennon is celebrated for being a member of the Beatles as well as for being the co-composer of the Beatles' song catalog, which includes many of the most popular rock songs ever written. He is also, however, notable for his solo career, his enduring status as a celebrity victimized by one of his own fans, and as a celebrity who used his fame to draw attention to various causes. Born in Liverpool, England, and raised in a middle-class home that lacked a father and, eventually, a mother as well (she died in a car accident), Lennon was largely raised by his Aunt Mimi, who warned him that, although playing the guitar was fine, it was unlikely to earn him a living. While attending art school Lennon formed a skiffle group, the Quarrymen, that became the foundation of the Beatles.

Lennon was the initial leader of the Beatles and their most controversial member. At the 1963 Royal Command Performance, he told the audience, "On the next number, would those in the cheap seats clap their hands? The rest of you rattle your jewelry." Upon being made a member of the Most Excellent Order of the British Empire (MBE), Lennon observed, "I

John Lennon. *John Lennon poses during a gig in Hamburg, Germany, in 1962, before the Beatles gained international fame.* TS PRODUCTIONS/CONTRIBUTOR/HULTON ARCHIVE/GETTY IMAGES.

can't believe it. I thought you had to drive tanks and win wars." He prompted even more controversy when on November 25, 1969, he returned his MBE "with love" to the Queen to protest Britain's involvement in Biafra and Vietnam as well as his song "Cold Turkey" slipping in the charts.

In 1966 Lennon told Maureen Cleave in the *London Evening Standard*, "The Beatles are bigger than Jesus Christ," creating a religious backlash in the United States. A similar British backlash was created when he appeared nude on the cover of his *Two Virgins* album. Eight prints were removed from an exhibition of Lennon's erotic lithographs due to threat of possible prosecution under the Obscene Publications Act. (Lennon's lithos were later declared "unlikely to deprave or corrupt" by legal experts and handed back.)

In addition to music and art, Lennon dabbled in literature. He wrote his first book, *In His Own Write* (1964), which subsequently won Foyle's Literary Prize. This was followed a year later by *A Spaniard in the Works* (a pun on the English expression "A spanner [meaning monkey wrench] in the works"). He appeared in films with the Beatles (*A Hard Day's Night* [1964], *Help!* [1965], *Let It Be* [1970]) and also had a minor role in Richard Lester's absurdist black comedy *How I Won the War* (1967). Additionally, he was the subject of the documentary film *Imagine* (1988).

ENTER ONO

Lennon married Cynthia Powell on August 23, 1962, a union that produced a son, Julian, who later became a respected name in the music business. The couple divorced on November 8, 1968, a month after Lennon and his Japanese artist lover Yoko Ono were busted by the drug squad (they were also arrested for possessing cannabis in September 1969). Lennon and Ono became an inseparable couple and were wed on the Rock of Gibraltar on March 20, 1969. For their honeymoon they conducted a "Bed-in for Peace" at the Amsterdam Hilton, and Lennon officially changed his name from John Winston Lennon to John Ono Lennon. It was while trying to console and counsel Julian on his relationship with his new stepmother that Paul McCartney wrote "Hey Jude," which became a major hit for the Beatles. Lennon proceeded to use his celebrity status to bring attention to all kinds of causes, from freeing Angela Davis to giving Ireland back to the Irish.

Lennon also formed his first post-Beatles group, the Plastic Ono Band, which initially consisted of himself, Ono, Eric Clapton, Klaus Voorman, and Alan White, who threw together an under-rehearsed show for a live concert in Toronto that was recorded as an album and on film. His next Plastic Ono Band effort, with Voorman on bass, Ringo Starr on drums, and occasional piano by Billy Preston and Phil Spector, is one of rock's all-time classic albums. Sparse and powerful, the album was an outgrowth of Lennon's involvement in primal scream therapy techniques as he tried to exorcise his personal pain and rejection by tempering them with feelings of love and hope.

Ironically, following the breakup of the Beatles, even Starr had greater initial chart success than Lennon. If *Plastic Ono Band* evoked Lennon's agony, his *Imagine* album celebrated his ecstasy and proved to be another rock classic. This was the most melodic of his solo albums, a quality he subsequently downplayed as his peace rhetoric gave way to rabble-rousing political statements, as on the abrasive *Some Time in New York City* album. Lennon decided to immigrate to the United States, but his political activities brought him under investigation by the FBI, and he was ordered to leave the country by the Immigration Authorities. He was able to successfully fight the deportation, and in January 1974 he asked the queen for a Royal Pardon in connection with his drug conviction in order to travel to and from the United States.

Lennon and Ono suffered a temporary split that found Lennon keeping time with their employee May Pang and getting drunk. He eventually announced that the separation hadn't worked out, and the couple got back together and remained so for the rest of Lennon's life. Their marriage resulted in a son, Sean, who has also embarked on a musical career. Lennon created the albums *Mind Games* (1973), *Walls and Bridges* (1974), and *Rock 'n' Roll* (1975), as well as the best-of compilation *Shaved Fish* (1975), before retiring from music for five years to spend time raising his son and become one of the world's most famous househusbands. He announced in Japan, "We really have nothing to say. We've basically decided, without a great decision, to be with our baby as much as we can until we feel we can take time off to indulge ourselves in creating things outside our family."

After discovering sounds in B-52s albums that reflected that of Ono, Lennon decided that it was time to reenter the musical mainstream. He created a collaborative album with his wife in 980 titled *Double Fantasy*, with the couple trading off songs; the result was a welcome return to form, lacking perhaps the urgency of Lennon's best works but reflecting his personal growth and current perspectives. Sadly, on December 8, 1980, Mark David Chapman, an ex-security guard and an avid Lennon fan, stepped out of the shadows in the courtyard of the Dakota apartment building in New York where Lennon and Ono were living with five-year-old Sean. Chapman fired at least five shots at Lennon, and the first one hit him directly in the chest. He had only recently celebrated his fortieth birthday. With great prescience Lennon told a reporter in 1965—when the Beatles were at the height of their popularity—that they would probably die in a plane crash or be killed by "some loony." He left behind half an album of material that was later released on the posthumous *Milk and Honey* (1984), which, despite some worthwhile Lennon tracks ("Nobody Told Me" and "Borrowed Time"), does not hold up as well as his earlier work.

Lennon's commitment as an artist left a lasting impression, from his passion for political causes to his celebrated love for Ono in the face of public hostility and disdain. His solo music has frequently been repackaged. His demo tapes and home recordings formed the basis of a long-running radio show, "The Lost Lennon Tapes"; a couple of these recordings formed the basis for the two Beatles reunion singles, "Real Love" and "Free as a Bird," and many of these pieces were collected together for release in late 1998 as the *Lennon Anthology* album. They offer a complete portrait of Lennon, encompassing both his happiness and his sadness, his anger and his humor. He had realized years earlier that what people around him were most interested in was Lennon himself, and few artists ever put so much of themselves into their art.

In 2010 Lennon would have turned seventy; the year also marked the thirtieth anniversary of his death. There were numerous tributes, including a box set of all of his solo albums remastered and packaged with personal photographs and home recordings. He had essentially defined his own legacy in an interview given three days before his death, commenting that "our life is our art." Lennon is remembered for his life as well as his art, and both have become part of the essential fabric of American music and celebrity.

Dennis Fischer

SEE ALSO: *The Beatles; Celebrity; Celebrity Couples; Clapton, Eric; Divorce; FBI (Federal Bureau of Investigation); Firearms; Marijuana; McCartney, Paul; Radio; Rock and Roll; Spector, Phil.*

BIBLIOGRAPHY

Cott, Jonathan, and Christine Doudna. *The Ballad of John and Yoko*. Garden City, NY: Dolphin Books, 1982.

Carr, Roy, and Tony Tyler. *The Beatles: An Illustrated Record*. New York: Harmony Books, 1981.

Davies, Hunter. *The Beatles*. New York: McGraw Hill, 1978.

Norman, Philip. *Shout!* New York: Warner Books, 1981.

Romano, Andrew. "Lennon's Other Legacy." *Newsweek*, December 3, 2010.

Schaffner, Nicholas. *The Beatles Forever*. Harrisburg, PA: Stackpole, 1977.

Suddath, Claire. "Lennon Lives." *Time*, October 18, 2010.

Womack, Kenneth, and Todd F. David, eds. *Reading the Beatles: Cultural Studies, Literary Criticism, and the Fab Four*. Albany: State University of New York Press, 2006.

Leno, Jay *(1950–)*

On television, Jay Leno exudes the image of an easygoing, affable comedian. This he is, but he is also one of the hardest-working men in show business. His perseverance, long hours (he claims he sleeps only four hours a night), and sheer determination have brought him to the top of the late-night talk show ladder as host of *The Tonight Show with Jay Leno*, where he is seen by millions of viewers each weeknight.

Born on April 28, 1950, in New Rochelle, New York, Leno grew up in the Boston suburb of Andover, Massachusetts. He graduated from high school in 1968 and from Emerson College in 1972. On March 2, 1977, he made his first television appearance as a guest on *The Tonight Show*, then hosted by Johnny Carson. However, like many television comedians, Leno got his start traveling around the country doing stand-up comedy, performing no less than 250 times a year in every imaginable corner of the United States.

Persistence paid off for Leno. By the mid-1980s, he was guest hosting many talk shows, including *The Tonight Show* starting in September 1987. Following Carson's retirement, Leno became the permanent host of *The Tonight Show* on May 25, 1992. His tenure in one of the most storied positions in television did not begin well. On the advice of his manager, Helen Kushnick, an avowed enemy of Carson, Leno did not mention Carson's name in his first show, an omission that was glaring. Kushnick also forbade Leno's guests to appear on other

Jay Leno. *Jay Leno performs on the set of* The Tonight Show with Jay Leno *in 2011.* KEVIN WINTER/NBCUNIVERSAL/CONTRIBUTOR/GETTY IMAGES ENTERTAINMENT/GETTY IMAGES.

talk shows. Even though Kushnick had engineered Leno's rise from comedy clubs to *The Tonight Show*, Leno and NBC wound up firing the increasingly domineering manager.

The popularity of *The Tonight Show with Jay Leno* increased dramatically following Kushnick's departure. After ninety weeks of trailing *The Late Show with David Letterman* in the ratings, Leno finally won a weekly ratings war with the CBS talk show host in July 1995. By 1996 he was regularly winning in the ratings, and he was widely regarded as the king of late-night talk by the end of the decade.

Much has been made about Leno's feud with Letterman. The subject was even the basis for a book and an HBO movie, *The Late Shift* (1996). In the late 1970s Letterman had served as a guest host for *The Tonight Show*. In 1982 NBC gave him his own show, *Late Night with David Letterman*, which aired directly after Carson's *The Tonight Show*. When Carson retired, Letterman (and many others) hoped to replace him as host. Instead, the job went to Leno, thanks in large part to his manager's intensive lobbying. In 1993 Letterman declined to renew his contract with NBC and moved to CBS, where he was given a show opposite Leno. The ordeal bred ill will between the two, and they reportedly have not spoken to each other since. Nonetheless, Leno still insists that he is on good terms with Letterman.

Leno was involved in another controversy in 2009, the year in which he was scheduled to hand over *The Tonight Show* to late-night upstart Conan O'Brien. Five years earlier, Leno had signed what was to be his final contract extension and named O'Brien, whose *Late Night with Conan O'Brien* had followed *The Tonight Show* since Letterman's departure for CBS, as his successor. In 2008, however, Leno announced that he had changed his mind and would not retire from television but would instead launch a new show, *The Jay Leno Show*, to run in prime time. Both shows faltered in the ratings, as longtime Leno viewers struggled to identify with O'Brien's younger, hipper brand of humor and Leno failed to generate high ratings in his earlier time slot.

Hoping to rectify this problem, NBC announced it would shorten *The Jay Leno Show* to a half hour and broadcast it at 11:35 p.m. (Eastern Standard Time), moving *The Tonight Show* back to a 12:05 a.m. start time. O'Brien publicly voiced his displeasure with the decision, and the network was forced to negotiate a $45 million buyout for him and his staff in January 2010 amid a flurry of criticism from media commentators and fans of O'Brien. Leno was restored as the host of *The Tonight Show*, and O'Brien launched a competing program, *Conan*, on TBS. In May 2012 O'Brien appeared as a guest on *The Late Show*, whereupon he and Letterman shared their mutual distaste for Leno.

Despite such criticism, Leno's appeal as a pop icon is multifaceted. As the successor of the legendary Carson on *The Tonight Show*, he automatically gained prestige and legitimacy. Leno is perceived as a perfectionist, which endears him to other hardworking Americans. In addition, he is not a Hollywood socialite—he is dedicated to his wife, Mavis, to whom he has been married since 1980. Nor is he a Hollywood pretty boy—he is defined by his prominent chin and big, wavy hair. Thus, when people watch him on television every night, many see someone not unlike themselves.

Matt Kerr

SEE ALSO: *Carson, Johnny; Letterman, David; O'Brien, Conan; Stand-Up Comedy; Television;* The Tonight Show.

BIBLIOGRAPHY

Carter, Bill. *The Late Shift: Letterman, Leno, and the Network Battle for the Night*. New York: Hyperion, 1994.

Carter, Bill. *The War for Late Night: When Leno Went Early and Television Went Crazy*. New York: Viking, 2010.

Leno, Jay, and Bill Zehme. *Leading with My Chin*. New York: HarperCollins, 1996.

Walker, Jay. *The Leno Wit: His Life & Humor*. New York: William Morrow, 1997.

Leonard, Benny *(1896–1947)*

Considered by many to be the greatest fighter of American boxing's golden age in the 1920s, Benny Leonard (born Benjamin Leinert) was one of the few white champions of his era to take on all comers, regardless of race. Nicknamed "The Ghetto Wizard," ("Ghetto" for his Lower East Side upbringing; "Wizard" for his cerebral approach to fighting), Leonard is regarded as the greatest Jewish boxer of all time.

In 1917, at the age of twenty-one, Leonard became lightweight champion, and he held the title for nearly eight years, at which point he retired at his mother's request. Because he had invested his boxing earnings wisely, Leonard was financially secure when he called it quits in 1925. However, he was hit hard by the stock market crash of 1929 and made an ill-fated comeback in 1931, eventually losing to Irishman Jimmy McClarnin, who was making a name for himself by knocking out notable Jewish fighters. Despite the inglorious ending to his career, Leonard is remembered as one of the premier fighters of the first half of the twentieth century.

Max Kellerman

SEE ALSO: *Boxing.*

BIBLIOGRAPHY

Liben, Meyer. *Justice Hunger: A Short Novel and Nine Stories*. New York: Dial Press, 1967.

Schulberg, Budd. *Sparring with Hemingway: And Other Legends of the Fight Game*. Chicago: I. R. Dee, 1995.

Shapiro, Michael. *The Jewish 100: A Ranking of the Most Influential Jews of All Time*. New York: Carol Publishing, 1994.

Leonard, Elmore *(1925–)*

American author Elmore "Dutch" Leonard is often mentioned in the same class as Ross Macdonald and Dashiell Hammett as a writer whose work exceeds the expectations of suspense novels. However, though Leonard is praised as a master of the crime novel—with his fast-moving action, hard-boiled characters, and detailed but not flowery descriptions—his writing style does not fall neatly into the crime or detective genre. Many critics, in fact, decline to peg him as a genre writer due to his skillful craftsmanship. Leonard's realistic, contemporary dialogue reads practically effortlessly, and his story lines often interject social commentary without distraction. Often dubbed the "Dickens of Detroit," Leonard began his literary career writing Westerns in the 1950s and has been writing fiction full time since 1967. He chugged along relatively unnoticed until his works *LaBrava* (1983) and *Glitz* (1985) established him as an accomplished novelist. Though at that time he made national news, he did not become a major name until his tale of a starstruck loan shark, *Get Shorty*, was released as a film in 1995.

EARLY LIFE

Leonard was born on October 11, 1925, in New Orleans, Louisiana, and relocated with his family several times before finally settling in the Detroit, Michigan, area. After high school, he served in the U.S. Navy during World War II, then attended college at the University of Detroit, where he graduated with a bachelor's degree in philosophy in 1950. Though he aspired to become a writer, Leonard was concerned about making a living, so he took a job at a Detroit advertising agency and rose early in the morning to work on Western stories, which he chose because he thought they would be the most lucrative. In 1951 he sold his first piece, "Apache Agent," to the magazine *Argosy* and in 1953 sold his first novel, *The Bounty Hunters*. He followed that up with four more over the next eight years.

Elmore Leonard. *Elmore Leonard holds the Peabody Award given to him in 2011 for the television series* Justified, *which is based on his novella* Fire in the Hole. **BENNETT RAGLIN/CONTRIBUTOR/WIREIMAGE/GETTY IMAGES.**

FIRST RECOGNITION

In 1961 Leonard had a major breakthrough with *Hombre*, a book about a white man raised by the Apache Indian tribe. It was later named one of the twenty-five best Western novels of all time by the Western Writers of America in 1977. He quit the ad agency and wanted to begin writing full time but had a family of five children to support, so he took freelance jobs writing for educational and industrial films, as well as advertising. When Twentieth Century Fox bought the rights to *Hombre* in 1967 for $10,000, Leonard finally had the means to pursue fiction as a career. Because Westerns were losing their audience, he switched to crime novels and published his first in this genre, *The Big Bounce*, in 1969.

CRIME AND MYSTERY NOVELS

Throughout the 1970s Leonard wrote more suspense fiction and also worked regularly adapting novels—including a few of his own—for the screen. Though these jobs paid well, Leonard longed to return to books, and in 1983 he published *LaBrava*, for which he earned an Edgar Allan Poe Award from the Mystery Writers of America in 1984. After that, his 1985 work, *Glitz*, became a best seller and Book-of-the-Month Club selection, thrusting him into the mainstream. Leonard's novels became known for their direct focus on plot and characters' actions, rejecting the psychoanalytical aspect prevalent in so many crime tales. His dialogue was fresh and realistic, the characters quirky and intriguing rather than two-dimensional and formulaic, and the stories satisfyingly gripping.

GET SHORTY

Though Leonard's books continued to be popular throughout the 1980s and into the 1990s, the few that were made into films did not meet with much critical or popular success. By the mid-1990s, however, Hollywood had rediscovered Leonard, and director Barry Sonnenfeld was hired to direct the screen adaptation of *Get Shorty*, which was released in 1995. This adaptation had a vein of humor running through it that surprised Leonard at first, since his works are not comical, but the new take delighted critics and moviegoers alike. The story involved a loan shark who goes to California to collect on a debt and becomes entranced with Hollywood.

After *Get Shorty*, hip director Quentin Tarantino in 1997 reworked the novel *Rum Punch* into *Jackie Brown*, starring 1970s Blaxploitation queen Pam Grier as a flight attendant who is involved with a petty gun runner. Following that, Leonard made $2.5 million for the rights to *Out of Sight*, and by 1998 Tarantino had purchased the rights to three more Leonard novels. In the fall of 1998, ABC created a television series based on the 1991 book *Maximum Bob*, about a tough Florida judge and his bizarre wife. Meanwhile, *Touch* was adapted for film as well, and in 1998 Leonard released his first noncontemporary novel in years, *Cuba Libre*, a story of horse smugglers set roughly a hundred years earlier. Filmmakers Joel and Ethan Coen, who made *Raising Arizona* and *Fargo*, immediately showed interest. During this period, Leonard planned a sequel to *Get Shorty*, published in 1999 as *Be Cool* and adapted for film in 2005 under the same title.

THE TWENTY-FIRST CENTURY

In the first decade of the 2000s Leonard published a number of well-received novels, including *Tishomingo Blues* (2002), *The Hot Kid* (2005), *Up in Honey's Room* (2007), and the celebrated *Road Dogs* (2009), a continuation of *Out of Sight*. He also published his first children's novel, *A Coyote's in the House* (2004) during this period. *The Big Bounce* was adapted for film a second time in 2004, as was the short story "3:10 to Yuma" in 2007. His 1989 novel *Killshot* was made into a motion picture in 2009, and his characters from *Out of Sight* and *Fire in the Hole* (2001) served as the basis for the television series *Karen Sisco* (2003) and *Justified* (2010), respectively. Toward the end of the decade, Leonard began to receive serious critical recognition for his seemingly endless string of literary achievements, including the F. Scott Fitzgerald Award in 2008 and the PEN USA Lifetime Achievement Award in 2009. He also earned a Peabody Award in 2011 for his work on *Justified*.

Leonard's knack for creating seedy villains and shopworn heroes does not come from first-hand experience. Living a relatively tame life in an upscale suburb outside of Detroit, the author does not prowl the underworld for material, except for an occasional trip to the police station to listen to speech rhythms of cops and crooks; he has an assistant perform a good deal of his research. Nevertheless, his offbeat hoodlums ring true, and readers have come to enjoy his plot twists and portrayals of people on the other side of the tracks without relying on stereotypes and clichés.

Geri Speace

SEE ALSO: *Advertising; Best Sellers; Coen, Joel and Ethan;* Fargo; *Film Noir; Hammett, Dashiell; Soderbergh, Steven; Tarantino, Quentin; The Western.*

BIBLIOGRAPHY

Challen, Paul. *Get Dutch!: A Biography of Elmore Leonard.* Toronto: ECW Press, 2000.

Elmore Leonard: A Reader's Checklist and Reference Guide. Middletown, CT: CheckerBee, 1999.

Giles, James R., and Wanda H. Giles, eds. *Dictionary of Literary Biography, Vol. 173: American Novelists since World War II. Fifth Series.* Detroit, MI: Gale Research, 1996.

Prial, Frank J. "It's No Crime to Talk Softly." In *New York Times Biographical Service*, 298. Ann Arbor, MI: UMI, 1996.

Yagoda, Ben. "Elmore Leonard's Rogues' Gallery." In *New York Times Biographical Service*, 1649. Ann Arbor, MI: UMI, 1984.

Leonard, Sugar Ray *(1956–)*

Sugar Ray Leonard was the first boxer, and certainly the first non-heavyweight, to cash in on the era of exploding sports salaries ushered in by Muhammad Ali. A baby boomer coming of age in the early 1980s, Leonard seemed to personify his generation: apolitical and corporate, with style superseding but not necessarily precluding substance. An Olympic gold medal winner in the junior welterweight class, Ray Charles Leonard took the name "Sugar Ray" as an amateur. Any fighter adopting this nickname would have an almost impossible act to follow, because the man most boxing experts agree was the greatest pound-for-pound fighter in the history of the sport was Sugar Ray Robinson. Yet by the end of Leonard's career, the name Sugar Ray would conjure an image of Leonard just as soon as one of Robinson, and in the consciousness of many baby boomers and most Generation Xers, the new Sugar Ray even usurped the original.

Leonard first burst into the American consciousness during the 1976 Olympic Summer Games when famed announcer Howard Cosell publicized the fact that Leonard fought with a picture of his girlfriend taped to his socks. Following his Olympic victory, he embarked on a professional boxing career, winning the welterweight title in 1979 and remaining undefeated until 1980, when he lost a fifteen-round decision to Panamanian legend Roberto Durán. Leonard won back his title in a rematch with Durán later that the same year when Durán, frustrated, disgusted, and behind on points, quit in the middle of the eighth round, turning his back on Leonard and uttering the infamous phrase "no mas," which means "no more" in Spanish.

Outside the ring, Leonard became well known for raising public awareness regarding eye-related injury. During his epic welterweight unification bout with Thomas "The Hitman" Hearns in 1981, Leonard suffered a detached retina. The following year he retired from boxing, even though a mega-fight awaited him and the seemingly invincible Marvelous Marvin Hagler. During this retirement, Leonard parlayed his boxing celebrity and infectious smile into a career as a television boxing announcer for the premium cable channel HBO. The specter of the fight-that-could-have-been against Hagler loomed in Leonard's mind, however, and despite the risk to his vision and having fought only once in a five-year span, he came out of retirement to fight Hagler. After twelve rounds of boxing, Leon-ard pulled off one of the unlikeliest upsets in modern sports history. He was awarded Hagler's middleweight title with a split-decision victory. The fight was also significant because it was the first major bout in which thumbless gloves were used (a stipulation Leonard insisted on during negotiations for the fight in order to protect his surgically repaired eye).

The epic battles with Hagler, Hearns, and Durán would take their toll on Leonard, who fought less and less by the mid-1980s. He would participate in only four fights from the time of his 1981 battle with Hearns until the 1989 rematch, which ended in a draw. After defeating Durán again, Leonard fought only twice more, retiring for good after a loss to Héctor Camacho in 1997.

With his boyish good looks and personable, articulate interview style, Leonard was a media hit from the beginning. He worked for various networks as a boxing analyst and appeared in TV ads for Ford, Coca-Cola, and even the makeup company Revlon. He could also be found on TV in guest-starring roles, as a host on Sylvester Stallone's boxing show *The Contender* (2005–2007), and as a contestant on *Dancing with the Stars* in 2011. But behind the nice-guy persona was a warrior always willing to take on the most dangerous opposition for the largest purse available. Leonard proved he was more than the front-runner many initially believed him to be. In 2011 Leonard took another courageous step by penning an autobiog-

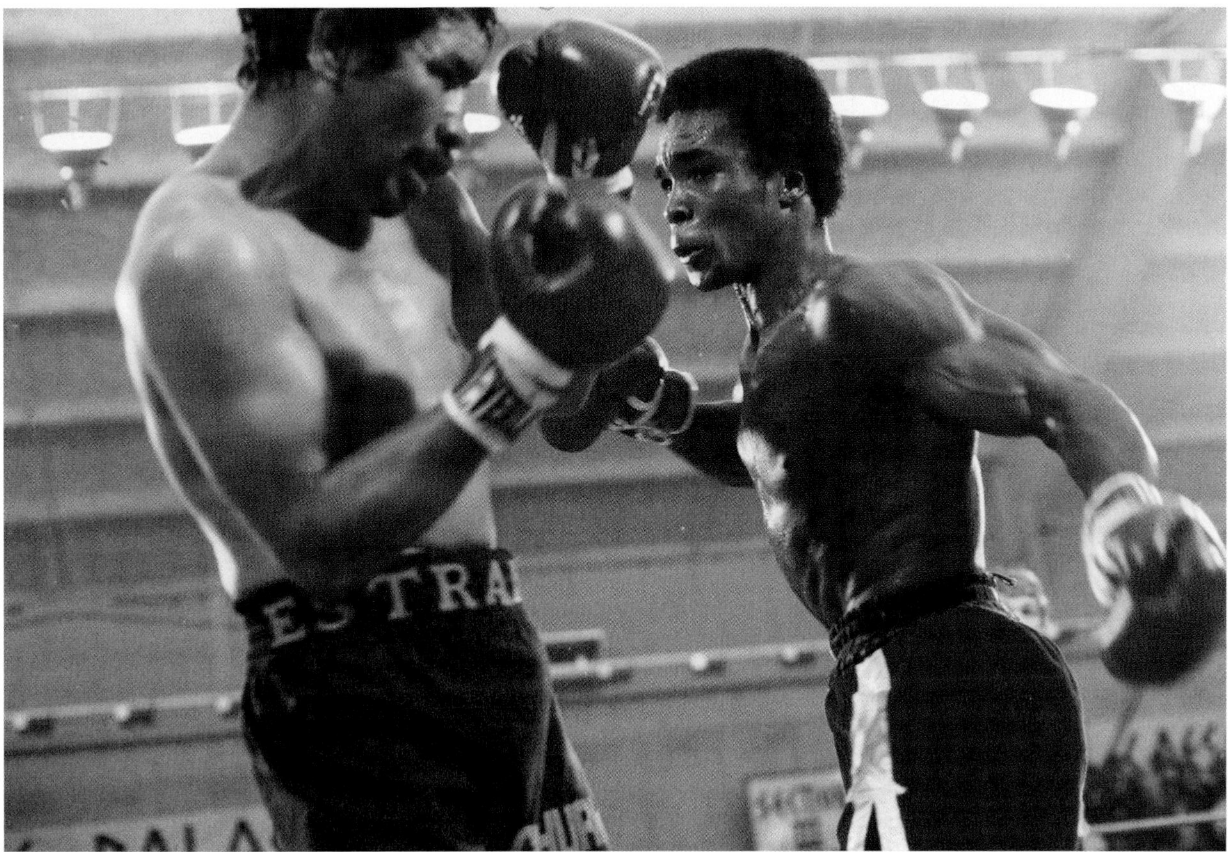

Sugar Ray Leonard. *Sugar Ray Leonard throws a punch at Augustin Estrada in their 1977 bout in Las Vegas.* FOCUS ON SPORT/CONTRIBUTOR/GETTY IMAGES SPORT/GETTY IMAGES.

raphy in which he discussed not only his own substance abuse but also that he had been sexually abused as a young fighter by an unnamed "prominent Olympic boxing coach." Few boxers have lived lives as turbulent, and few were, pound for pound, tougher or more talented than Sugar Ray Leonard.

Max Kellerman

SEE ALSO: *Advertising; Boxing; Cable TV; Camacho, Héctor "Macho"; Coca-Cola; Cosell, Howard;* Dancing with the Stars*; Durán, Roberto; Ford Motor Company; Hagler, Marvelous Marvin; Olympics; Reality Television; Robinson, Sugar Ray; Sports Heroes; Stallone, Sylvester; Television.*

BIBLIOGRAPHY

Araton, Harvey. "Baring His Secret Pain." *New York Times*, May 18, 2011, B12(L).

Barnes, Dana R., ed. "Sugar Ray Leonard." In *Notable Sports Figures*. Detroit, MI: Gale, 2004.

Goldstein, Alan. *A Fistful of Sugar: The Sugar Ray Leonard Story*. New York: Coward, McCann & Geoghegan, 1981.

Leonard, Sugar Ray, and Michael Arkush. *The Big Fight: My Life in and out of the Ring*. New York: Viking, 2011.

Russell, Thaddeus. "Sugar Ray Leonard." In *Encyclopedia of African-American Culture and History*. Detroit, MI: Gale, 2006.

"Sugar Ray Leonard." In *Encyclopedia of World Biography Vol. 24*. Detroit, MI: Gale, 2005.

Summerall, Pat. *Sports in America*. New York: HarperCollins, 1996.

Toperoff, Sam. *Sugar Ray Leonard and Other Noble Warriors*. New York: McGraw-Hill, 1987.

Leone, Sergio *(1929–1989)*

When his first Western, *A Fistful of Dollars*, was released in 1964, Sergio Leone was forced to use the name Bob Robertson to hide his Italian identity due to the widespread belief that only Americans could make successful Westerns. The success of his Westerns as well as of his last movie, *Once upon a Time in America* (1984), which exploited the formula of the gangster movie—another typical American genre—proved this assumption wrong. Leone's choice of pseudonym was in fact deeply ironic: Bob Robertson is the English transposition of the Italian name ("Roberto Roberti") used by Leone's father, himself a film director. The choice points to Leone's lifelong struggle to reconcile his fascination with American culture and mythology with his Italian background, which he was seemingly trying to conceal. The same reconciliation is spelled out by the name given (at first disparagingly) to the genre of films with which Leone has come to be identified, the spaghetti Western.

THE DOLLARS TRILOGY AND OTHER WESTERNS

Leone's reputation as a director was established by the popular success of the so-called "Dollars trilogy," which also helped Clint Eastwood achieve star status: *A Fistful of Dollars* (1964); *For a Few Dollars More* (1965); and *The Good, The Bad, and The Ugly* (1966) ranked among the top-grossing Italian movies at the international box office between 1956 and 1971. These three movies were made outside the Hollywood production system and were not simple carbon copies of traditional Westerns. Perceptive critics have listed diverse works as sources for the trilogy, including (to mention but a few) Sicilian morality and puppet plays, Carlo Goldoni's *The Servant of Two Masters* (first performed in 1746), Akira Kurosawa's samurai film *Yojimbo* (1961), Charles Chaplin's *Monsieur Verdoux* (1947), George Stevens's *Shane* (1953), Robert Aldrich's *Vera Cruz* (1954), and the unusual Westerns by Nicholas Ray and Samuel Fuller. The traditional optimism of the genre is tempered in the Dollars trilogy by the violence pervading the environment in which the characters live without being able to trust each other and to which they conform without trying to change it. Money is, of course, the primary motivation for action. Yet in Leone's early Westerns, money is not meant to be invested or to buy goods, as it was in traditional Westerns; it is simply something to possess or worship.

Although by the end of the trilogy Leone felt he had exhausted the possibilities of the genre (he wanted to shoot a gangster movie instead), he was persuaded by Paramount to make another: *Once upon a Time in the West* (1968). Its all-star cast, including Claudia Cardinale, Henry Fonda, Charles Bronson, and Jason Robards, and its exploitation of the traditional Western theme concerning the impact of technological progress (represented here by the railroads and by the building of the town of Sweet Waters) on the Western frontier made it, in theory, a more appealing movie to American audiences than the Dollars trilogy. Yet the movie flopped badly in the United States, where it was savagely cut by the distributors.

In 1972 Leone released *Duck, You Sucker* (aka *A Fistful of Dynamite*). At first titled *Once upon a Time, the Revolution*, the movie is a pessimistic post-Western on the Mexican Revolution, which was strongly criticized by left-wing intellectuals for its supposedly conservative politics. The most often quoted sentence from the movie is "Revolution is confusion," and Leone himself described the film as being about the friendship between a naive Mexican and an Irish-Catholic intellectual: it is "the story of Pygmalion reversed. The simple one teaches the intellectual a lesson. . . . Finally the intellectual throws away his book of Bakunin's writings. You suspect damn well that this gesture is a symbolic reference to everything my generation has been told in the way of promises."

ONCE UPON A GANGSTER MOVIE

Once upon a Time in America represents a change in genre (the Western is replaced by the urban gangster movie) and in narrative technique. Earlier films were characterized by linear chronological narration with a flashback inserted at a topical moment, but here Leone substitutes a story line that moves continuously between the 1920s, 1930s, and 1960s. Still, the film addresses the same themes and exploits situations similar to those in Leone's Westerns. The plot is structured around the usual two-character confrontation, the problem of friendship and betrayal, the impact of money on human relationships, and the entrapment of the villain at his own hands. The typical close-ups of the characters' eyes, which are a distinctive feature of Leone's Westerns (and which usually precede a gunfight), are developed in Leone's last film in a veritable obsession with images of looking and of meeting glances.

As Robert C. Cumbow points out in *Once upon a Time: The Films of Sergio Leone*, *Once upon a Time in America*, like Leone's Westerns, is a "buddy movie" with a clear homosexual subtext. The two male protagonists (whose first intercourse with the same woman is characterized by premature ejaculation and temporary impotence) have relationships with women that are "never more than a mirror of their relationship with each other." As in the Westerns, the female figures of *Once upon a Time in America* follow the Mary/Eve Catholic dichotomy: they are either sexual objects, prostitutes, or almost spiritual figures.

In spite of their fairy-tale titles and their superficial simplicity, Leone's movies are a powerful and intense exploration of the mythic America he had created in his own mind. More often than not, the myth has to come to terms with, in Cumbow's words, "a dark and complex vision of morality and the psyche." This apparent discrepancy is vividly echoed by Leone himself when he recounts the intrusion, experienced during World War II, of "real-life Americans" into his childhood and adolescent dreams of America: "They were no longer the Americans of the West. They were . . . victorious soldiers . . . who were materialist, possessive, keen on pleasures and earthly goods. [In them] I could see . . . nothing—or almost nothing—of the great prairies, or of the demi-gods of my childhood."

Luca Prono

SEE ALSO: *Bronson, Charles; Chaplin, Charlie; Eastwood, Clint;* A Fistful of Dollars*; Fonda, Henry;* The Good, the Bad, and the Ugly*; Spaghetti Westerns; The Western; World War II.*

BIBLIOGRAPHY

Cumbow, Robert C. *Once upon a Time: The Films of Sergio Leone.* Metuchen, NJ: The Scarecrow Press, 1987.

Frayling, Christopher. *Spaghetti Westerns: Cowboys and Europeans from Karl May to Sergio Leone.* London: Routledge & Kegan Paul, 1981.

Frayling, Christopher. *Sergio Leone: Something to Do with Death.* New York: Faber and Faber, 2000.

Leopold and Loeb

Nathan Leopold and Richard Loeb, the sons of two of Chicago's wealthiest and most prominent German Jewish families, precipitated one of the twentieth century's most sensational mass media events when they kidnapped and murdered a fourteen-year-old neighbor boy, Robert Franks, in May 1924.

At first there was little suspicion that the pair—close friends since childhood—had any involvement in the disappearance of the Franks boy. The nineteen-year-old Leopold, son of a millionaire box manufacturer, was a law student at the University of Chicago and had earned earlier distinction for his pathbreaking studies in ornithology. One year younger than Leopold, Loeb, whose father was a respected executive at Sears, Roebuck and

Leopold and Loeb. *Nathan Leopold, left, and Richard Loeb listen to proceedings at their kidnapping trial in 1924.* ROLLS PRESS/POPPERFOTO/CONTRIBUTOR/GETTY IMAGES.

Company, was also an accomplished student, having become the youngest person ever to graduate from the University of Michigan at the age of seventeen. On May 31, 1924, however, the pair shocked the nation when they abandoned their alibis, turned against one another, and confessed to the Franks murder. For the next three months, the combination of intense public interest in the case and the willingness of the national media to indulge, even encourage, that interest in an effort to increase circulation figures made Leopold and Loeb not only household names but also two of the nation's most notorious criminals.

ROLE OF THE PRESS

Seldom in the history of American journalism had the nation's press played such an instrumental role in the shaping of a news event as it did the story of Leopold and Loeb. Aside from the day-to-day reporting of developments in the case, journalists uncovered pieces of evidence and tracked down material witnesses to the crime that later proved critical to the prosecution's case. When the families of the two young men hired famed attorney Clarence Darrow and a team of expensive psychiatrists to defend their sons in court, the media encouraged the public to question whether justice could be bought. Finally, as the courtroom drama unfolded, the press covered the proceedings in relentless detail, giving extensive coverage to the testimony of the psychiatrists and Darrow's eloquent summation, in which he questioned the merits of capital punishment and called upon the court to spare the lives of his youthful clients.

The story of Leopold and Loeb earned widespread notoriety not only because of the media's efforts to prioritize it as a news event but also because the image of the defendants was one onto which Americans could easily project their own fears and anxieties about modern society. During the initial rush to suggest explanations for the pair's actions, the media, in concert with prosecuting attorney Robert Crowe, depicted Leopold and Loeb as wealthy, overeducated, self-confident daredevils whose plot to commit "the perfect crime" represented a serious threat to the legal and moral foundations of society. Citing factors such as the pair's non-Christian upbringing, their growing interest in atheism, and their exposure to the allegedly subversive world of the university as possible causes for their strange behavior, the newspapers explained the killers' motives in a manner that reinforced nativist sentiments and common religious prejudices. Crowe and the media incited additional public outrage by labeling Leopold and Loeb "perverts," a then widely used euphemism that in this instance gave the public reason to fear that the two boys were not just murderers but also pedophiles, pornographers, and homosexuals.

As the courtroom proceedings unfolded, however, defense attorney Darrow and his expert psychiatrists offered a different and potentially far more unsettling theory to explain why Leopold and Loeb had behaved the way they did. Drawing upon theories of psychoanalysis and child development that had yet to become widely accepted, they recast the defendants as ordinary American youths whose immature crime was the product of inattentive parenting and unresolved childhood insecurities. Such was the effectiveness of the defense strategy that many parents, earlier frightened by the thought that their son or daughter might become another Franks, grew increasingly concerned that their child might become the next Leopold or Loeb, even as they persisted in their demands that the pair receive the death sentence for the crime. In the end, Judge John R. Caverly, acknowledging the young ages of the defendants, spared their lives and sentenced them instead to life plus ninety-nine years in prison.

THE AFTERMATH

The lives of Leopold and Loeb continued to captivate the public's attention and remained an important part of popular culture in the United States throughout the twentieth century. The national media kept close track of the pair's activities in prison, including Loeb's own murder at the hands of another inmate in 1936 and Leopold's efforts to win parole in the mid-1950s. Fictional accounts of the case, such as director Alfred Hitchcock's 1948 film *Rope*, also served to sustain the public's curiosity in the pair by explaining their crime in a manner that addressed the needs and concerns of contemporary U.S. citizens. The most influential of these fictional accounts was novelist Meyer Levin's *Compulsion*. Published in 1956 and remade into a Broadway play and then a motion picture in 1959, Levin's novel resonated with readers for its probing examination of the psychological and sexual motives behind Leopold and Loeb's friendship and criminal activities. Director Tom Kalin's 1992 movie, *Swoon*, similarly recast the story of Leopold and Loeb to suit changing times by examining the pair's likely homosexual bonds.

Late in life Leopold struggled to regain control over his public image. As part of his successful efforts to win parole, he completed his autobiography, *Life Plus 99 Years*, in 1958. Shortly after his release from prison in 1959, Leopold filed suit against author Levin for misrepresentation and invasion of privacy. The suit was not resolved until 1970, when the Illinois Supreme Court decided that Levin's account of Leopold's life was not misleading and that the latter's status as a public figure denied him the right to privacy. Following parole, Leopold moved to Puerto Rico, where he married, conducted research, and died in 1971.

Scott A. Newman

SEE ALSO: *Capital Punishment; Darrow, Clarence; Media Feeding Frenzies.*

BIBLIOGRAPHY

Fass, Paula S. "Making and Remaking an Event: The Leopold and Loeb Case in American Culture." *Journal of American History* 80, no. 3 (1993): 919–951.

Fass, Paula S. *Kidnapped: Child Abduction in America*. New York: Oxford University Press, 1997.

Higdon, Hal. *The Crime of the Century: The Leopold and Loeb Case*. New York: Putnam, 1975.

Leopold, Nathan Freudenthal. *Life Plus 99 Years*. Garden City, NJ: Doubleday, 1958.

Theodore, John. *Evil Summer: Babe Leopold, Dickie Loeb, and the Kidnap-Murder of Bobby Franks*. Carbondale: Southern Illinois University Press, 2007.

Les Misérables

Billed as "the world's most popular musical," *Les Misérables* has been translated into twenty-one languages and performed in theaters all over the world. The first performance was staged in 1980 in a Paris sports arena, with music by Claude-Michel Schönberg, book by Schönberg and Alain Boublil, lyrics by Herbert Kretzmer, and adaptation by Boublil and Jean-Marc Natel. In 1985 Cameron Mackintosh took over as producer, in collaboration with London's Royal Shakespeare Company, creating the show's legacy as one of the most significant musical theater works of the late twentieth century.

Based on writer Victor Hugo's somber and sprawling novel, *Les Misérables* brings to the stage the tale of Jean Valjean, a man determined to survive and do good in the face of vengeful persecution. Freed from prison after doing hard labor for stealing a loaf of bread, he reverts to his old ways, stealing from a bishop who tried to help him. When the bishop protects him from the law, Valjean decides to reform, eventually becoming a successful factory owner.

Valjean befriends one of his factory workers—a young woman named Fantine, who has been forced into prostitution to support her young daughter Cosette. After Fantine dies of tuberculosis, Valjean rescues Cosette from the money-hungry Thenardiers family, with whom she has been living, and raises her as his own. Pursued by the sinister police inspector Javert, Valjean and Cosette arrive in Paris on the eve of the 1832 uprising. Cosette meets Marius, a student, and the couple falls in love.

To complicate matters, Eponine, the Thenardiers' daughter, is also in love with Marius. She dies in the assault on the student barricade along with many young idealists. Marius is seriously injured in the conflict, and Valjean carries him to safety, leaving Cosette to care for him. In an effort to stop the wedding of the couple, the Thenardiers blackmail Marius and threaten to expose the truth about Cosette's father, whom they allege is a murderer. Marius learns that it was Valjean who saved him, and he and Cosette seek out the dying Valjean, finding him moments before he is welcomed into the afterlife by Fantine, Eponine, and the chorus of students.

The characters of Hugo's novel provide the story with its universal appeal. Valjean represents the inherent good in every person, and Javert symbolizes evil. Valjean's wayward soul is redeemed as a single act of mercy helps him to change his ways. The sacrificial deaths of Fantine, Eponine, and the students are among the most emotional moments in the show, without which Valjean's noble death would not have such a dramatic impact. Taken as a whole, *Les Misérables* demonstrates the best and worst of humanity, and each of its various subplots offer a moral lesson.

Schönberg's music for *Les Misérables* is rich and romantic. Recurring melodies are used to enhance the dramatic plot as it develops. Valjean and Javert share much of the same music, which demonstrates their roles as two sides of the human condition. Among the most moving songs are Fantine's "I Dreamed a Dream," the inspiring choral number "Do You Hear the People Sing?" Eponine's "On My Own," Valjean's prayer for Marius "Bring Him Home," and Marius's grief-filled "Empty Chairs at Empty Tables."

Designer John Napier's incredible sets add drama to the show. The student barricade, the two parts of which are joined on stage to intense music, is an integral component of the musical. A rotating center unit was introduced to allow for the innovative staging that characterized the original production.

Les Misérables opened in 1985 at the Royal Shakespeare Company's Barbican Theatre in London. It quickly transferred to the Palace Theatre in London's West End. The original London production starred Colm Wilkinson, Alun Armstrong, and Patti LuPone. The New York production opened in 1987 and featured Wilkinson, Terrence Mann, Frances Ruffelle, and Judy Kuhn.

Les Misérables. *The London cast of* Les Misérables *performs the moving number "Do You Hear the People Sing?" during a production in 2010.* WARNER BROS./HANDOUT/MOVIEPIX/GETTY IMAGES.

The original cast recordings from London and New York and the complete symphonic recording from 1991 are available, as are video recordings of the tenth anniversary concert at London's Royal Albert Hall and the twenty-fifth-anniversary concert at London's O2. In late 2012, a theatrical verion of the musical debuted, starring Hugh Jackman, Anne Hathaway, and Russell Crowe.

William A. Everett

SEE ALSO: *Broadway; LuPone, Patti; The Musical.*

BIBLIOGRAPHY

Behr, Edward. Les Miserables, *History in the Making*. London: Pavilion Books, 1996.

Everett, William A. "The Mega-Musical as Transcultural Phenomenon." In *The New Europe at the Crossroads*, ed. Ursula E. Beitter. Baltimore, MD: Lang, 1998.

Sternfeld, Jessica. *The Megamusical.* Bloomington: Indiana University Press, 2006.

Vermette, Margaret. *The Musical World of Boublil and Schönberg*. New York: Applause Theatre and Cinema Books, 2006.

Lesbianism

Romantic, sexual, and emotional attachment between women was named *lesbianism* after the island of Lesbos, home of Sappho, a Greek poet of the seventh century. Sappho wrote eloquently of her complex passion for her women lovers, and her ancient verses demonstrate the long tradition behind the lesbians of the early twenty-first century. Lesbians come from every nation, ethnic group, and economic class. Though some may feel little sense of community with other lesbians, they are united by, if nothing else, their attraction to women and the stigmatization of that attraction by many modern societies. Because of that stigmatization, many lesbians conceal their sexual identities, making an accurate count of their number difficult, but estimates range from 6 to 10 percent of women. In the early 1990s one study placed the number of lesbians in the United States between six and thirteen million.

Women recognize themselves as lesbians in a wide variety of ways. Some may feel from early childhood that they are "different," and some of these women may act on their attraction to other girls while still quite young. Others may be aware of such attractions at an early age but not act on them until much later. Girls who exhibit tomboyish traits may be labeled as lesbians and ridiculed by parents or peers for being different. Some women may not "come out" until middle age, after long-term

Lesbianism. *Actress Portia de Rossi and comedian Ellen DeGeneres attend the 19th Annual GLAAD Media Awards.* JASON LAVERIS/ CONTRIBUTOR/FILMMAGIC/GETTY IMAGES.

relationships with men. Still others may feel a clear attraction for women but never act on it because of social pressure or isolation.

Lesbians have often been conflicted about what to call themselves, and which term one chooses can be meaningful. Some call themselves "gay women," though many consider this a conservative term and argue that *gay* was invented to describe homosexual men. Many more radical lesbians refer to themselves as "dykes," reclaiming an anti-lesbian epithet. Black lesbians were sometimes contemptuously called "bulldaggers," and that term has been reclaimed as well by black lesbians who argue that the name originated with the Amazon queen Boadicea. Among themselves, lesbians worked out code references to announce their identity. In one of these codes, a woman was described as a "friend of Dorothy" if she was known to have sex with other women.

Because women have traditionally been somewhat less visible in patriarchal society, one or two women living without men have tended to arouse condescension or pity rather than the suspicion of homosexuality in early America. Therefore, lesbians who were financially independent of men were able to live together with relative ease. These relationships, sometimes called "Boston marriages," were socially tolerated. Choices for working-class and poor women were more limited, but some lesbians found a solution by passing as men so that they could marry other women openly.

EARLY TWENTIETH CENTURY

In the early twentieth-century United States, where homosexuality was considered a vice by straight society and was beginning to be considered a mental illness as well, urban lesbians continued to find each other as best they could in backstreet bars and private social clubs. The visibility of lesbians and gays was greatly enhanced during World War II as gays poured out of rural and small-town America to join the military or work in the defense industry. Many did not return home but settled in urban centers such as New York, San Francisco, and Chicago, where they established underground communities that revolved around gay clubs, bars, and, for women, sports teams.

Lesbians began to develop their own subculture. A large part of this culture involved butch and femme, lesbian roles that appeared to be based on traditional definitions of masculine and feminine behavior but were deeply rooted in lesbian culture in their evolution. A butch, for example, often dressed in traditionally male clothes, down to the underwear, and might wear her hair combed in a ducktail, while a femme might wear the same makeup and high heels as a heterosexual woman.

The butch woman's attire, while giving her a certain status within the lesbian community, made her extremely visible and vulnerable walking down the street, where she was liable to be attacked, beaten, or raped. Therefore, assuming a femme identity served a protective function in the straight world, where femmes were viewed as "normal." In the 1940s and 1950s, lesbians pressured each other to assume either the butch or the femme role. Those who did not identify either way were called "kiki" or "sooners" ("just as soon be one as the other"), often with derision.

THE "NEW" LESBIANISM

The women's liberation and gay liberation movements of the 1970s brought revolutionary change to lesbianism. Lesbians were at the forefront of women's liberation. Inspired by the exciting new ideas of feminism, some women who thought of themselves as straight began to question their need to form relationships with men. Women who had never before considered the possibility of same-sex relationships began to wonder if they might be lesbians. Some radical feminists declared that no woman could be a true feminist if she had not renounced men altogether.

These "political lesbians" came out by the thousands and began to demand acceptance from both gay men and straight feminists. They also began to build a visible "women's culture." Lesbian journals, bookstores, and coffeehouses became places to discuss the endless ramifications of lesbian politics. Lesbian musicians recorded on lesbian music labels and played at women's music festivals across the country.

Many lesbians were swept up in a kind of euphoric idealism by this new openness, and the diversity of the lesbian population inevitably led to conflict. The young feminist lesbians alienated many of the older lesbians by criticizing their butch/femme roles. Among feminists, unacknowledged differences of race, class, and ethnicity led to bitter divisions. Lesbians who wanted to create women-only spaces and focus on lesbian issues without men fought with those who wanted to continue to work with gay men or heterosexual feminists. Lesbians who preferred the safety of the closet disliked the blatant visibility of political lesbians, since it drew attention to their existence.

Their visibility, however, was perhaps the biggest contribution of the 1970s lesbians. Young feminist lesbians, while eschewing the butch/femme drag of earlier generations, wore the uniform of the androgynous political dyke: blue jeans, flannel shirt, work boots, and short hair. Utilitarian and counterculture, this manner of dress also allowed lesbians to recognize each other with ease.

The work done by earlier generations of butch and femme bar dykes and lesbian feminists bore fruit in the 1980s and 1990s. While lesbians of the 1970s worked hard to be taken seriously within the feminist and other progressive movements, lesbians of the hedonistic 1980s were more focused on making lesbianism fun. Even the serious political groups were aggressively irreverent. "We Recruit" was the tongue-in-cheek motto of the Lesbian Avengers, a radical group that arose in New York in the early 1990s and quickly spread across the nation.

Another development that shook the lesbian community in the 1980s was the rise of sado/masochism (s/m). Not uncommon in the gay male community, s/m was almost totally unacknowledged among lesbians until the mid-1980s. Then, s/m lesbians, calling themselves sexual radicals, began to speak out publicly, calling many lesbian feminists puritanical and repressive. They claimed the right to define their own sexuality, even if it included pornography, casual sex, and butch/femme roles. These s/m lesbians, or leather dykes, began to reclaim the butch/femme roles that feminists had disparaged, proclaiming them an integral part of lesbian sexuality.

GROWING ACCEPTANCE

The look of young lesbians of the 1980s was heavily influenced by the outrageous hair and clothes of the punks, and lesbian style, with its piercings, spiky hair, and tattoos, was in turn widely imitated by young heterosexual women. This, coupled with the increasing visibility of lesbian celebrities such as musicians k.d. lang and Melissa Etheridge, began to bring lesbianism to the attention of the national media. Captivated by the tough, hip image of "grrl power," establishment organizations such as *Time* magazine and television's *Prime Time* began to explore the new phenomenon of "lesbian chic." Once invisible, lesbians had now become trendsetters. Many lesbians were disgusted with their "discovery" by the press and found the courtship of the media to be opportunistic and artificial. A popular sticker that began to appear at gay events read, "Queer Liberation: A Movement, Not a Market."

In the late 1980s and 1990s, a new movement of "queer power" began to break down the barriers among different sexual minorities. Bisexuals and transgendered people began to demand acceptance within the lesbian and gay communities as well as in the straight world. For lesbians this meant that several new groups had begun to consider themselves members of the lesbian community. Bisexuals and transgendered people, both men and women, claim that they are a part of the definition of *lesbianism* too. Though many lesbians, especially those who came of age before the 1980s, resist these broadening categories, there is no doubt that the "queer" movement has added depth and complexity to questions of sexual identity.

Though some lesbians are childless by choice or necessity, many are mothers. Lesbians who have children from previous marriages with men often worry about losing custody if their sexuality becomes known, and activist groups have organized around the country to fight for the rights of lesbian mothers. Lesbians who want to conceive children without intercourse with a man use alternative insemination. In the 1970s many lesbians made informal arrangements with sympathetic gay men to obtain sperm with which they inseminated themselves, resulting in a "baby boom" of so-called "turkey baster babies." The AIDS epidemic, which devastated the gay male community in the 1980s, drastically curtailed these informal and inexpensive arrangements, forcing lesbians to the far more costly sperm banks to obtain "safe" sperm.

Other lesbians turned to adoption, which is also an expensive option. Because of the red tape involved in traditional adoptions, lesbians often adopt disadvantaged or foreign children. The large number of unwanted girls in China led to a "boomlet" of lesbians adopting Chinese babies in the 1990s, and large cities often boast support groups for lesbian mothers and their Chinese daughters.

INFLUENCE OF LESBIANISM

Though usually hidden, lesbian influence has been felt throughout American history. Whether it is writers like Willa Cather, performers such as Bessie Smith, activists like Angela Davis, or athletes such as Martina Navratilova, lesbians have been an integral part of the fabric of American society. Behind the scenes, lesbians have been at the forefront of movements for societal change and improvement, from the fight for women's suffrage to AIDS activism. Because lesbians are not motivated by male preferences to the degree that heterosexual women are, lesbians have often taken the lead in confronting the damaging unfairness of conventional standards of beauty. The concepts of fat oppression and "looksism" were hotly discussed within the lesbian community long before they reached the talk-show circuit. This work, begun in the iconoclastic 1970s, continues.

Lesbians have also spearheaded reforms in the fields of psychiatry and mental health. Because any deviation from their prescribed societal role often landed women in mental hospitals, many lesbians were forcibly committed and subjected to various brutal "cures." Since the 1960s many have fought against abuses of lesbians and gays by the mental health system. Others have become therapists themselves in an effort to create an alternative mental health care system that is more responsive to the needs of the disenfranchised.

CONTEMPORARY LESBIAN CULTURE

Lesbian culture has permeated American life. Lilith Fair, the popular women's concert tour, has its roots in the women's music festivals that sprang up across the country as lesbianism gathered its strength in the 1970s. And the grrl power of the 1980s continues to empower young women through the dangerous process of coming of age in a male-dominated society. In the 1990s films such as *Bound*, *Chasing Amy*, and *The Incredibly True Life Adventures of Two Girls in Love* placed lesbians in the center of mainstream entertainment.

Lesbians have also found their way onto television, though initially only as peripheral characters. In the late 1990s comedian Ellen DeGeneres made a historical connection by coming out as a lesbian both in real life and on her sitcom, *Ellen*. The fact that her series was cancelled only a few episodes after a coming-out episode that broke ratings records points to the slowness of public acceptance. However, DeGeneres has proved to have considerable staying power, hosting her own talk show since 2003. DeGeneres and her wife, actress Portia de Rossi, are a highly visible couple in the show business community. In *Unbearable Lightness: A Story of Loss and Gain*, de Rossi frankly described the pain involved in acknowledging her homosexuality.

Lesbianism has gained traction on television in the early twenty-first century. *The L Word* was the first television show in

American history centered on lesbian characters and themes. The popular teen show *Glee* has integrated homosexuality into ongoing story lines involving both male and female characters. From the beginning of the show, there was evidence of a lesbian relationship between Brittany (Heather Morris) and Santana (Naya Rivera); Jane Lynch, an out lesbian, plays the androgynous coach Sue Sylvester, who uses males to support her claims of heterosexuality.

Lesbians continue to lay claim to the redefinition of lesbianism that started in the 1970s: being a lesbian doesn't merely mean having sexual attraction for women. It means living a woman-centered life and providing a place where women and girls can take themselves seriously apart from their relation to men. It is perhaps this shift in the worldview of women and girls that is lesbianism's greatest contribution to American culture.

Tina Gianoulis

SEE ALSO: *AIDS; Daytime Talk Shows; DeGeneres, Ellen; Equal Rights Amendment; Gay and Lesbian Marriage; Gay and Lesbian Press; Gay Liberation Movement;* Glee; *lang, k.d.; Navratilova, Martina; Outing; Punk; Safe Sex; Sitcom; Smith, Bessie; Tattoos;* Time; *World War II.*

BIBLIOGRAPHY

Aragon, Angela Pattatucci. *Challenging Lesbian Norms: Intersex, Transgender, Intersectional, and Queer Perspectives.* New York: Harrington Press, 2006.

Bernstein, Robin, and Seth Clark Silberman. *Generation Q: Gays, Lesbians, and Bisexuals Born around 1969's Stonewall Riots Tell Their Stories of Growing up in the Age of Information.* Los Angeles: Alyson Publications, 1996.

Ciasullo, Ann M. "Making Her (In)Visible: Cultural Representations of Lesbianism and the Lesbian Body in the 1990s." *Feminist Studies* 27, no. 3 (2001): 577–608.

Faderman, Lillian. *Odd Girls and Twilight Lovers: A History of Lesbian Life in Twentieth Century America.* New York: Columbia University Press, 1991.

Glazer, Deborah F., and Jack Drescher, eds. *Gay and Lesbian Parenting.* New York: Haworth Medical Press, 2001.

Louis, Valerie. "What It's Like to be a Gay Woman Now." *Cosmopolitan*, March 1989, 228.

Potter, Clare. *The Lesbian Periodicals Index.* Tallahassee, FL: Naiad Press, 1986.

Tully, Carol Thorpe. *Lesbians, Gays, and the Empowerment Perspective.* New York: Columbia University Press, 2000.

Let Us Now Praise Famous Men

A photographic essay published as a Houghton Mifflin book in 1941, *Let Us Now Praise Famous Men* was a collaborative project by writer James Agee (1909–1955) and photographer Walker Evans (1903–1976), who were sent by *Fortune* magazine to document the lives of southern tenant farmers. Whereas the book originated as one of many similar projects within the 1930s documentary tradition, it has come to be seen as an enduring work of philosophy, cultural history, and autobiography, as well as being an acknowledged American literary classic.

In April 1936, *Fortune* magazine, one of the most liberal magazines during the 1930s, asked Agee to contribute an article to its Life and Circumstances series about poor and lower-middle-class Americans. His assignment was to write on the lives of white southern tenant-farm families and to include a photographic essay with his report. Agee requested that Walker Evans, a staff photographer for the Farm Security Administration, accompany him to Alabama, and the government and *Fortune* magazine's parent company, Time, Inc., reached an agreement whereby Evans's work would become government property.

Agee and Evans traveled the rural South and lived with three families in July and August 1936. Agee eventually produced an article deemed unacceptable by *Fortune*, not only because of its length—it was ten times longer than assigned—but because its substance and tone did not comply with *Fortune*'s optimistic and sometimes paternalistic stance. After a year of attempted editing, *Fortune* released the article to Agee, who received a contract from Harper and Brothers to expand the work into a book-length manuscript. When Agee submitted the work in 1939, Harper refused to publish it without substantial revisions, which the author was unwilling to make. Eventually, Agee received a contract from Houghton Mifflin, who published the book in September 1941, an inopportune time for a book on a domestic issue, because the nation's attention was focused on the accelerating war in Europe and Asia.

The book itself did not fit into any accepted category of literature, nor did it compare with the documentary photo-essays popular in the 1930s, such as Margaret Bourke-White and Erskine Caldwell's *You Have Seen Their Faces* (1937) and Dorothea Lange and Paul Taylor's *An American Exodus* (1939). *Let Us Now Praise Famous Men* is at heart an attack on the documentary tradition of the Great Depression. William Stott's *Documentary Expression and Thirties America* and Michael Staub's *Voices of Persuasion: Politics of Representation in 1930s America* both describe the manner in which Agee and Evans's work defied the prevailing trends. As Staub points out: "Agee's text repeatedly and obsessively undermined its author's authority to write the very text we read, rejecting therefore one of the era's most valued documentary conventions." That convention, according to Stott, was that "experience per se became a good."

Agee agonized over his ability to truthfully represent the lives of the three families he and Evans had lived with, and he feared their feelings about and reactions to the intrusion he imposed on their lives. "It is not going to be easy to look into their eyes," he wrote, as he contemplated the exacting and detailed description of the Gudger family home he had just written. Agee realized that his intentions, however noble, were far outside the realm of the Gudgers' everyday, or even occasional, experience. This gap between subject and writer faced Agee like a dark abyss as he desperately tried to build a bridge across it. It is this bridge, or at least the attempt to build it, that makes *Let Us Now Praise Famous Men* different from other documentary works and that led to the cold reception it received upon publication. Since the 1960s, *Let Us Now Praise Famous Men* has grown in estimation among an academic audience that has become more sensitive to the ideas and implications of representation.

Charles J. Shindo

SEE ALSO: *Caldwell, Erskine;* Fortune; *The Great Depression.*

BIBLIOGRAPHY

Bergreen, Laurence. *James Agee: A Life*. New York: Dutton, 1984.

Madden, David, ed. *Remembering James Agee*. Baton Rouge: Louisiana State University Press, 1974.

Rathbone, Belinda, and Walker Evans. *Walker Evans: A Biography*. Boston: Houghton Mifflin, 1995.

Shindo, Charles J. *Dust Bowl Migrants in the American Imagination*. Lawrence: University Press of Kansas, 1997.

Staub, Michael E. *Voices of Persuasion: Politics of Representation in 1930s America*. New York: Cambridge University Press, 1994.

Stott, William. *Documentary Expression and Thirties America*. Chicago: University of Chicago Press, 1973.

Let's Pretend

From the 1930s to the mid-1950s, *Let's Pretend* was one of the most enduring and highly lauded radio programs for children ever broadcast. For more than two decades of Saturday mornings (apart from a few years in a biweekly, early evening slot during the 1938–1939 season), the show presented familiar fairy tales such as "Cinderella," "Rumplestiltskin," "Sleeping Beauty, "The Little Lame Prince," and "Jack and the Beanstalk," along with the occasional original stories, in fully dramatized half-hour segments featuring a large cast of new as well as seasoned radio performers, and accompanied by specially composed musical scores. In the pre- and early-TV era, these imaginatively produced shows nurtured the imaginations of countless American youngsters with a simple but potent fusion of spoken word, music, and sound effects, which together evoked many a magical image in the collective mind of generations as yet unsullied by the literal visualizations of television.

Let's Pretend was originally titled *The Adventures of Helen and Mary* when it was first heard on CBS in September of 1929, the creation of Yolanda Langworthy. In 1934 the title changed to *The Land of Let's Pretend* (and later, simply *Let's Pretend*), and the show became the province of Nila Mack, a vaudeville and Broadway actress, who developed the show's concept to its full potential. Mack wrote the program, adapting her scripts from sources ranging from Hans Christian Andersen and the Brothers Grimm to the Arabian Nights, while also creating original tales (including an annual Christmas show).

Mack also directed the weekly productions, which often included promising child stars, many of whom went on to further success in broadcasting, theater, and movies. Additionally, the casts regularly included adult performers, some of whom had grown up on the show to become "steadies," remaining with *Let's Pretend* until its last broadcasts in the mid-1950s. Performed before a live studio audience of mostly children in CBS's Radio Playhouse 3 in New York City, the show was hosted for most of its run by "Uncle" Bill Adams, who remained with the show until it went off the air.

The weekly format included a musical opening, after which Uncle Bill and cast members decided on some magical mode of transportation to the Land of Let's Pretend. This ritual journey, abetted immeasurably by the assistance of the studio's versatile sound effects man, set the stage for a different tale of fantasy each week.

Though *Let's Pretend* was consistently popular and won many prestigious media awards in its day, its commercial exploitation seems quite mild by twenty-first century standards, being limited mostly to a few storybooks and some children's record albums on the Columbia label. Thus, few collectible artifacts survive to mark the existence of one of radio's most popular shows for young people.

The esteem with which CBS held Mack's award-winning show was exemplified by the fact that, for the first several years of its broadcast, the network chose to carry the show without a commercial sponsor, until, in 1943, Cream of Wheat became the first and only product to garner that honor. The hot cereal also inspired what may have been among the first, and certainly one of the most memorable, examples of the singing commercial. Regular listeners to the show probably still remember the infectious jingle's first few lines:

> Cream of Wheat is so good to eat, Yes, we have it every day.
>
> We sing this song, it will make us strong, And it makes us shout hooray!

Nila Mack died in January 1953, and Johanna Johnston wrote the final episodes of *Let's Pretend*. The last broadcast of one of the most imaginative and well-loved shows of a kinder, gentler era in children's media entertainment was heard on October 23, 1954.

Ross Care

SEE ALSO: *Radio; Radio Drama; Television.*

BIBLIOGRAPHY

Dunning, John. *Tune In Yesterday: The Ultimate Encyclopedia of Old-Time Radio, 1925–1976*. Englewood Cliffs, NJ: Prentice-Hall, 1976.

Lackman, Ron. *Same Time . . . Same Station*. New York: Facts On File, 1996.

Letterman, David *(1947–)*

From 1980 onward, television talk show host David Letterman has entertained viewers with his wry observational humor, zany antics, and refusal to kowtow to celebrities. First aired on the NBC network, his late-night program *The David Letterman Show* evolved into *Late Night with David Letterman* (1982–1993). Then he moved his show to CBS, where it became *The Late Show with David Letterman* (1993–). Throughout the changes, he maintained his reputation as one of the most innovative personalities on television, bringing a playful spontaneity to the well-rehearsed business.

His uncanny ability for ad-libbing and propensity for undertaking creative stunts, has kept the show perennially fresh. What has made his show a leader is its postmodern approach to television. He often zones in on cultural icons and commonly accepted (but nevertheless ridiculous) aspects of society and culture, such as canned ham. Although his notorious penchant for condescension and put-downs during celebrity interviews rankles some, audiences recognize him as a dynamic host who insists that guests work for their spot on his stage.

EARLY LIFE AND CAREER

Letterman was born in Indianapolis, Indiana, on April 12, 1947. His father, Joseph, was a florist, and his mother, Dorothy, served as a church secretary. Letterman, who has one older and one younger sister, has described his upbringing as typical lower-middle class. He ran track in high school, held a paper route, and bagged groceries at a local supermarket in his teens. A rambunctious youth who made mediocre grades, he was nevertheless ambitious. From an early age, he aspired to become a broadcaster, despite his parents' wishes that he pursue a more practical profession. He adored television—perhaps because his parents kept a tight control over their children's viewing—enjoying the variety show *Arthur Godfrey and His Friends* (1949–1959) and idolizing talk show host Johnny Carson.

After high school, Letterman attended Ball State University in Muncie, Indiana, which is known for its outstanding communications program. While in college, he found a summer job as a replacement announcer at a local television station. Eventually he became an announcer and weekend weatherman at the ABC affiliate in Indianapolis. There, he tried out some of his humor on the air and realized he wanted to become a comedy writer.

After graduating from Ball State in 1969, he was hired to work full time at the station where he had worked summers. His job was to announce the weather and to host an occasional children's program or late-night movie. There, he continued cultivating his quirky sense of humor, describing hail as being the size of canned hams and reporting on weather conditions in fictional locales. He left to host a radio talk show at the Indianapolis station WNTS but quickly tired of the callers.

David Letterman. *David Letterman's wry wit and penchant for silly humor have made him a staple in late-night television since 1982.* KEVIN MAZUR/CONTRIBUTOR/WIREIMAGE/GETTY IMAGES.

Next he took a full-time job as host of *Clover Power*, a show about children's agricultural projects, which he later admitted centered on poking fun at the young guests. He also began sending unsolicited scripts to *The Mary Tyler Moore Show* (1970–1977) on a regular basis, hoping that someone would discover his talents. Finally, his wife, Michelle Cook (they divorced in 1977), insisted they move to Los Angeles so that he could devote himself to pursuing his chosen career.

BREAKING INTO SHOWBIZ

In 1975 Letterman arrived in Los Angeles and began performing in stand-up comedy clubs. He cites Jay Leno, a club circuit regular and later the host of *The Tonight Show* (1992–2009, 2010–), as one of his greatest influences at the time. As Letterman became popular in the clubs, he eventually landed a job as a comedy writer.

In 1978 *The Tonight Show*, hosted by Johnny Carson (1962–1992), invited Letterman to appear, a major step in any entertainer's career. At the end of Letterman's routine, Carson invited the comedian to sit and chat with other guests—an honor seldom bestowed on a first-time performer. After just three more appearances, Letterman began filling in for Carson, acting as guest host on more than twenty occasions during 1979. Observers mused that he might take over as permanent host when Carson retired, one of Letterman's lifelong dreams.

In 1980 NBC signed Letterman to a contract, giving him a daytime talk show. *The David Letterman Show* (1980), although short-lived, proved the prototype for his later format. Intended to cover such subjects as household tips and cooking demonstrations, the show was not a ratings hit. Nevertheless, Letterman and Merrill Markoe, who was his female companion for ten years and provided much of his material, used the show to develop the irreverent humor and zany antics that would become his trademark. Sometimes he would take the camera and stroll around the city, looking for funny sights. One time he visited several establishments, each with a sign claiming to have the world's best coffee. Another time, the producers let loose a herd of sheep in the studio.

Letterman even used the show to unveil his famous Stupid Pet Tricks segment, which featured average people and their performing animals. Critics loved the novel format, and the doomed series built a small but loyal audience. Eventually NBC offered him the late-night time slot of 12:30 a.m. to 1:30 a.m. Eastern Standard Time.

LATE NIGHT ON NBC

Late Night with David Letterman first aired on February 1, 1982, broadcasting from the NBC studios in New York City. In addition to the variety-show antics from his former daytime program, Letterman incorporated traditional talk show elements such as an opening monologue; chitchat with his bandleader, Paul Shaffer; and interviews with celebrity guests. However, the show maintained a rough-around-the-edges atmosphere, which set it apart from the slick, showbiz image of other programs.

The program teemed with a sense of wonderment at much of what the rest of society takes for granted, from the ubiquitous canned ham to a duo of recent immigrants selling New York souvenirs out of their Manhattan shop. Drawing regular people onto the program became a trademark, whether Letterman put them in the spotlight for only a few seconds or kept them as recurring characters. One such personality was Meg Parsont, a good-natured woman whose office at Simon & Schuster was across from Letterman's. When he phoned the surprised publishing employee on the air, he enjoyed talking to her so much that she became a recurring feature.

Perhaps one of the show's funniest, best-known, and most enduring segments is the Top 10 list. The popular routine centers on a topic, such as nicknames cabbies give passengers, and ten sometimes silly, sometimes uproarious punch lines. Another of his trademarks is to create bizarre on-screen situations just to see what happens. Some of his signature events include donning a Velcro suit and jumping off a trampoline toward a Velcro wall, wearing a suit covered in Alka-Seltzer tablets and diving into a tank of water, and covering himself with tortilla chips and immersing himself in yogurt dip. His other sight gags include placing various objects, such as a can of pork and beans, into a powerful hydraulic press.

He often has brought the show's behind-the-scenes crew in front of the camera. For example, he had stage manager Biff Henderson drive a Golf Cart of Death through pyramids of everyday objects, including a tower of plastic champagne glasses. Henderson's obvious glee shone during the numerous slow-motion replays Letterman ordered throughout the night's broadcast. Audiences caught Letterman's infectious sense of fun and sent the show to the top of its ratings slot within a few years of its debut.

THE LATE SHOW ON CBS

Much to Letterman's dismay, his goal of taking over *The Tonight Show* was quashed when NBC announced in 1992 that the position would go to Leno. Soon rival network CBS enticed Letterman with a generous salary. After some insider dealings, NBC finally offered Letterman the coveted *Tonight Show* position but with a number of stipulations and with a less attractive pay package than CBS had offered. Letterman left NBC in 1993 and debuted *The Late Show with David Letterman* as a head-to-head competitor of Leno's *Tonight Show*. In spite of legal haggling with NBC over intellectual property, Letterman carried over his goofy personality and most of his stalwart gags, such as the Top 10 list and Stupid Pet Tricks.

But he also faced detractors, who regarded some of his more lunatic antics as puerile and unfunny. He appeared ill at ease hosting the 1995 Academy Awards ceremony, where his humor was, in the opinion of many, out of sync with the occasion. More seriously, he developed a reputation as a difficult host. Rather than sidestepping tough questions and gushing over his guests' accomplishments, he often put people on the spot. He once opened an interview with boxing promoter Don King by asking about King's outrageous hairstyle. He even questioned world's smartest woman Marilyn Vos Savant why she was not doing something important with her life.

Although prone to openly insulting his top-name guests, Letterman has insisted he is not mean-spirited; his wisecracks often slip out. However, many stars have taken offense and have refused to appear on the program. Some, such as singer Cher, musician Courtney Love, and actor Joaquin Phoenix, agreed to appear on the program only to go on the offensive (a tactic that could inspire months of subsequent on-air ribbing from the slighted host). Daytime talk show icon Oprah Winfrey complained of feeling "completely uncomfortable" during her appearances on *Late Night* in the 1980s. However, she put an end to the rumored feud by appearing on*The Late Show* in 2005 and inviting Letterman to appear on *The Oprah Winfrey Show* (1986–2011) in 2007.

His reputation for ridicule notwithstanding, Letterman has managed to reveal a down-to-earth side of celebrities that competing programs often miss. He scored a ratings coup when he booked actor Hugh Grant to appear on the show after Grant was arrested for his much-publicized tryst with a prostitute. He even convinced actress Teri Garr to take a shower during the program and goaded actress Mariel Hemingway into cleaning fish.

REPUTATION AND LEGACY

As the head of the production company Worldwide Pants, Letterman has been responsible for a number of hit shows and movies outside of his work on *The Late Show*. Some of his most notable production credits are the sitcom *Everybody Loves Raymond* (1996–2005) and the off-the-wall *The Late Late Show with Craig Ferguson* (2005–). His assortment of awards includes five Emmy Awards, four American Comedy Awards, and the Johnny Carson Award for Comedic Excellence.

In 2001 he was widely praised for his monologue during the first broadcast after the attacks of 9/11. Critics regarded it as a remarkably earnest and important step toward national recovery. The following year he turned down an opportunity to move to a different time slot on the ABC network, eventually signing a contract with CBS through 2012.

In 2009 he shocked long-standing viewers by revealing that he had conducted a series of affairs with his female employees, including personal assistant Stephanie Birkitt. He also disclosed that he had been subjected to an extortion plot that threatened him with publishing the sordid details of his affairs if he did not pay $2 million. (It was later revealed that the extortionist was a producer at CBS who shared an apartment with Birkitt.) Letterman issued a public apology on his show, directing the bulk of his remarks to his wife, Regina, whom he had married just months before. He managed to calm the firestorm of media criticism by combining his obvious remorse with his quirky, self-deprecating humor. He joked, "I got into the car this morning and the navigation lady wasn't speaking to me."

Despite his public foibles and stormy relationships with certain celebrities, his iconoclastic style has been a hit with viewers who are appreciative of his ironic take on commercialism and late-night television. Even after undergoing quintuple bypass surgery in 2000, he has not seemed to lose his youthful enthusiasm or sense of excitement. Although his hopes of inheriting Carson's show went unfulfilled, his talent for taking ordinary cultural elements and pointing out their inherent humor—and his unshakable poise in the face of tragedy—has ensured his place alongside Carson as one of America's late-show greats.

Geri Speace

SEE ALSO: *Academy Awards; Carson, Johnny; Celebrity; Cher; Consumerism; Daytime Talk Shows; Emmy Awards;* Everybody Loves Raymond*; Leno, Jay; Love, Courtney;* The Mary Tyler Moore Show*; Movie Stars; 9/11; Sex Scandals; Stand-Up Comedy; Television;* The Tonight Show*; Winfrey, Oprah.*

BIBLIOGRAPHY

Adler, Bill. *The Letterman Wit: His Life and Humor.* New York: Carroll & Graf, 1994.

Brownfield, Paul. "The Joke's on Who?" *Los Angeles Times*, February 8, 1998, calendar 4.

Cader, Michael, and Fabienne Marsh. *Dave's World: The Unofficial Guide to "The Late Show with David Letterman."* New York: Warner Books, 1995.

Carter, Bill. *The Late Shift: Letterman, Leno, and the Network Battle for the Night.* New York: Hyperion Books, 1994.

Latham, Caroline. *The David Letterman Story.* New York: F. Watts, 1987.

Lennon, Rosemarie. *David Letterman: On Stage and Off.* New York: Windsor Publishing, 1994.

Timberg, Bernard. *Television Talk: A History of the TV Talk Show.* Austin: University of Texas Press, 2002.

Zehme, Bill. "Letterman Lets His Guard Down." *Esquire*, December 1994, 96.

Zoglin, Richard. "Interview: David Letterman—He's No Johnny Carson." *Time*, February 6, 1989, 66.

Levin, Meyer *(1905–1981)*

Jewish American novelist and filmmaker Meyer Levin contributed several books to the proletarian social fiction movement of the 1930s and early 1940s. His two best-known literary works are the Chicago-based novels *The Old Bunch* (1937), about the Jewish ghetto, and *Citizens* (1940), which deals with the killing of ten steel-mill strikers on Memorial Day in 1937. The latter earned Levin the praise of author Ernest Hemingway, who proclaimed it "a fine and exciting American novel." In his books Levin utilized multiple viewpoints, holding that such a device was in itself an affirmation of democracy and allowed him to carry out a more complete social analysis. After World War II, he directed *My Father's House* (1947), the first full-scale feature film to be produced in Palestine. He then went to Europe, where he filmed the underground Jewish exodus to Israel. In 1956 he published *Compulsion*, one of the first examples of a nonfiction novel. Based on the Leopold and Loeb murder case of 1924, it inspired the 1959 movie *Compulsion*, starring Orson Welles.

Luca Prono

SEE ALSO: *Hemingway, Ernest; Leopold and Loeb; Welles, Orson; World War II.*

BIBLIOGRAPHY

Foley, Barbara. *Radical Representations: Politics and Form in U.S. Proletarian Fiction, 1929–1941.* Durham, NC: Duke University Press, 1993.

Graver, Lawrence. *An Obsession with Anne Frank: Meyer Levin and the "Diary".* Berkeley: University of California Press, 1997.

Klein, Marcus. *Foreigners: The Making of American Literature, 1900–1940.* Chicago: University of Chicago Press, 1981.

Levi's

Levi's is the registered trademark of a kind of blue denim jeans made by Levi Strauss & Company of San Francisco. Other garments and accessories made by Levi Strauss, such as tailored slacks, jackets, hats, shirts, skirts, and belts, are sometimes also referred to as "Levi's," but the trademark is properly applied only to the line of jeans with the designated style number "501." Levi's are distinguished by a fly with metal buttons rather than a zipper, copper rivets on the pocket seams, a leather label sewn on the waistband, a stitched pattern of a double *V* on the back pockets, a red tag with the word *Levi's* sewn into the seam of the right back pocket, and the use of heavyweight cotton denim that will "shrink-to-fit" an inch or so at the waist and legs with the first laundering. After nearly 100 years of steady, though unremarkable, sales—almost entirely wholesale, to cowboys and agricultural workers in the West—the popularity of Levi's flourished after World War II when they became the fashionable attire of middle-class teenagers, spurred by a new marketing thrust in which the company abandoned wholesaling in favor of manufacturing garments under its own name.

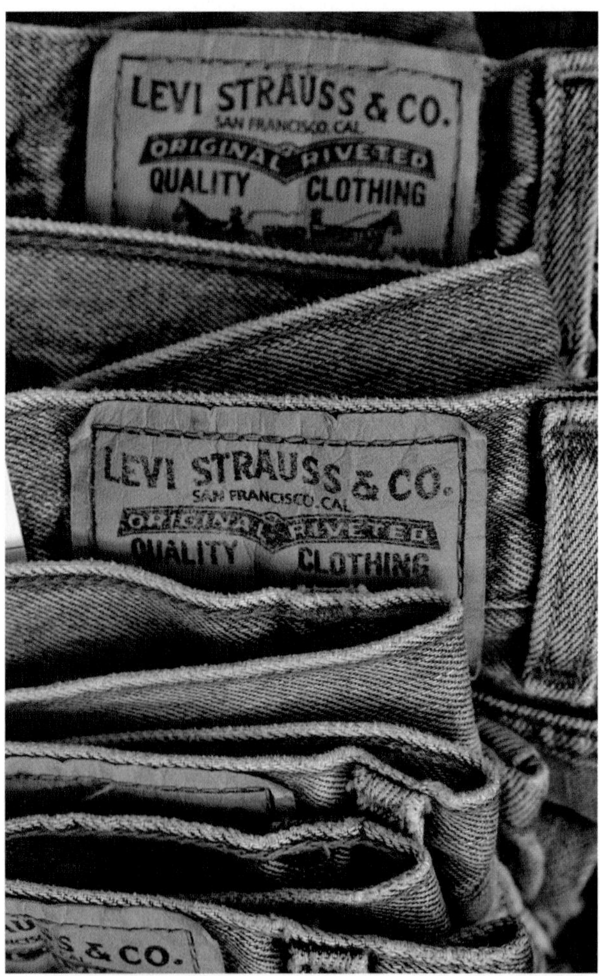

Levi's. *The Levi Strauss brand remains a staple of many wardrobes around the world over 150 years after it was first launched.* BLOOMBERG/CONTRIBUTOR/BLOOMBERG/GETTY IMAGES.

Levi Strauss & Company takes its name from Levi Strauss (1829–1902), a Bavarian who immigrated to San Francisco in 1850 at the height of the California gold rush. He brought a store of dry goods with him in hopes of setting up a business supplying miners and prospectors in the gold fields. Discovering that what these consumers needed above all was a durable pair of trousers, Strauss hired a tailor to design a serviceable pair of pants. The original garment was made of tent canvas, which was changed after a few years to the now world-famous blue denim. The trousers sold so well that Strauss concentrated on their manufacture to the exclusion of all other merchandise.

In 1853 Strauss formed a partnership with his brothers, Jonas and Louis, and they ran their company until his death in 1902, at which time executive control of the firm passed to four nephews. In 1918 the Haas family—part of the Strauss family by marriage—took over. After World War II, at the same time they decided to promote Levi's to retail consumers, the Haases also made a public offering of Levi Strauss stock. During the company's explosive growth in the 1950s and 1960s, the stock's performance matched pace.

Other types of pants—work, casual, and dress—were added to the inventory, as were jackets, shirts, and various items of women's clothing. By 1985, when the Haases and other members of the Strauss family staged a leveraged buyout and returned the company to private hands, Levi Strauss & Company had become the largest manufacturer of pants in the world. In February 1999 the company announced that it was closing down its manufacturing operations in the United States and moving them overseas.

By late 2010 Levi Strauss's brands included Levi's, Red Tab, Signature by Levi Strauss & Co., Dockers, and Denizan. The company employs approximately 16,200 people around the world and sells its products in more than 110 countries. Its net revenue for fiscal 2010 was $4.4 billion, a 7 percent increase over the prior year.

The success of Levi's signals, among other things, the first flexing of the huge economic muscle of baby boomers. How Levi's became *the* brand of blue jeans to wear provides a case study in demographics and aggressive marketing. The Levi's story also reflects the shifting, after 1945, of America's cultural center of gravity to the West Coast. The unchallenged supremacy of Levi's—in which the brand name has become the generic term for all blue jeans—also reflects the penchant of bourgeois youth to adopt the attire and mannerisms of lower social classes.

Gerald Carpenter

SEE ALSO: *Baby Boomers; Jeans; World War II.*

BIBLIOGRAPHY

Cray, Ed. *Levi's.* Boston: Houghton Mifflin, 1978.

Downey, Lynn; Jill Novack Lynch; and Kathleen McDonough. *501: This Is a Pair of Levi's Jeans–The Official History of the Levi's Brand.* San Francisco: Levi Strauss, 1995.

Schoenberger, Karl. *Levi's Children: Coming to Terms with Human Rights in the Global Marketplace.* New York: Grove Press, 2000.

Levittown

In 1946 developer William J. Levitt and his brother Alfred capitalized on the twin circumstances of enormous demand and unequaled opportunity of the post–World War II era by purchasing 1,500 acres of potato fields in Nassau County, Long Island, and then building 6,000 small, boxy houses there in little more than a year. By the time Levitt started building, America had returned to a state of relative normalcy for the first time in more than fifteen years. Although the end of the war produced a massive housing shortage, white working-class Americans began to experience practically unprecedented levels of prosperity, which was fueled in large part by comprehensive government programs designed to allay the social strife that many feared would accompany the war's end. By 1949 Levitt had named the new development after himself and offered what were originally rental units for sale. Potential buyers stood in long lines, hoping for an opportunity to land a Levitt house of their very own. Within the next three years, more than 15,000 homes were built and sold.

The white male soldiers who returned from Europe and the Pacific came back not only to a warm welcome but also to a wide-ranging social program designed to lift them up from the dire economic circumstances so many experienced for so long during the 1930s. The G.I. Bill of Rights offered qualified vets job training, a paid year-long sabbatical, educational funds, and, perhaps most importantly, the opportunity to buy their own inexpensive home, even if they lacked savings. Many minorities were barred from enjoying these benefits due to housing, job, and educational discrimination and because 60 percent of African American veterans were given dishonorable discharges from military service, thus making them ineligible for benefits. The Federal Housing Administration (FHA) also fueled the dual process of empowerment for the white working class and the exclusion of minorities from suburban life by offering developers low-cost loans to build and then encouraging them to write restrictive racial covenants into the deeds of the new homes.

EASY-OPEN, READY-TO-USE HOMES

Using the same methods of mass production that were used to produce so many of the new labor-saving technological devices of the postwar period, Levitt's small, two-bedroom, one-bath homes turned out spare, plain, and boxlike. The large kitchen picture window of the original homes, soon hailed as the central focus of suburban life, faced out to the front lawn, while the bedrooms and other more private areas were arranged toward the back. Eventually, Levitt built new plans that moved the living room to the back of the home. This layout encouraged women to greet one another during the day, while maintaining privacy for the nuclear family when the male breadwinner returned home at night. In this way, homeowners could keep some of the feeling of community that they remembered from their childhoods in the city. Children could play while their mothers watched. When dinner was finished (or when the oven bell clicked to signal that the TV dinners were heated through and bubbling), mother could shout for her children to come in. The spaces for more intimate socializing, arguing, and the harsher 1950s-style discipline of children were designed for a new style of privacy previously unknown to working-class urban dwellers.

Significantly, the homes had no basements but were instead set on concrete slab foundations, a technique Levitt borrowed from ancient Rome. While many had disdain for the technique (one older suburbanite declared simply: "Without a basement, it's not a house!"), the method allowed for extremely rapid methods of construction: after the slabs were laid, crews with specific duties were dispatched to complete their work in assembly-line fashion, using prefabricated building materials. During one period, Levitt was starting and finishing approximately 150 houses a day.

In essence, a Levittown home was the first "easy-open, ready-to-use" home. Each came complete with a washing machine and a television set at a time when these devices were still seen as wonders of technology available only to the upper middle classes. Now women who'd grown up in the poverty of New York City were free to explore new activities called "hobbies," which might include furniture refinishing, cake decorating, or playing mah-jongg with neighbors. Children now played with real baseballs and bats on real playing fields instead of playing stickball on unsafe city streets.

The first residents felt as though they had entered paradise, and in many ways, they had. No longer would these former city dwellers be forced to live in the cramped, unhealthful conditions that characterized urban life in twentieth-century America. The Levittown experiment was certainly the most consequential, long-lasting, and just plain successful result of the G.I. Bill. And it was not the last. Soon other inexpensive and federally subsidized new suburbs appeared in such places as Lakewood, California. Levitt himself followed up with new Levittowns in Pennsylvania and New Jersey.

In the ensuing years, the new suburbanites truly knew the best of both worlds. Children drank clean, fluoridated water in Levittown and awoke in the mornings to the bright hues of sunflowers outside their bedroom windows. There was always someone to play with, and parents did not fear bad associations in the new suburb as they did in the city. Milk and bread were delivered fresh each morning to the side door of the home. Men had shiny, new tail-finned cars with which to drive into the city to work at prosperous factory, trade union, or white-collar jobs. Real wages grew enormously during this time, and everyone in the home soon had plenty of disposable income to spend on big ticket items such as "high-fidelity" equipment on which to play long-playing record albums, pricey bicycles for each child, and elaborate wardrobes for everyone in the family. In the new suburbs, status became very important: "keeping up with the Joneses" was a new catch phrase. If neighbor Jones had a new power mower, neighbor Smith now wanted one too.

IMPACT ON MINORITIES

The original community was not as ethnically homogenous as the more gentrified prewar suburbs; the new residents were freed from the restrictions that had prohibited Jews and other white ethnics from purchasing suburban homes before World War II. Levitt himself was Jewish and clearly saw no reason to bar Jewish and Catholic vets from a chance at this new American Dream. However, with encouragement from the FHA, he did find plenty of reasons to maintain the restrictions barring African Americans and people of Puerto Rican origin from buying a home in Levittown. The deed to each of the original Long Island homes included a covenant barring such families from ever buying the home. If an owner later decided to sell his home to a "Negro family," that owner could be sued by his neighbors.

This was all perfectly legal until 1948, when the U.S. Supreme Court ruled such covenants unconstitutional. Levitt fought the Court's ruling for years afterward, culminating in a titanic battle in the late 1950s. He held a press conference in New Jersey, insisting that his new Levittown would be restricted to whites only. He claimed, perversely, that he did this for the benefit of minorities who had been harassed in the community. He finally had to back down and make provisions for minorities to buy into Levittown, but no new laws specifically criminalized racial covenants until the Fair Housing Act of 1968. Many houses retained such restrictions for decades, and a few deeds still had them in the late 1990s.

As the new housing developments were in the process of rapid construction, the building of highways, expressways, and freeways boomed. Most of the existing interstate highway infrastructure was built after World War II and prior to 1971. This boom in construction, with its attendant urban renewal, facilitated the movement of urbanites out of the working-class and poor neighborhoods in which they'd grown up. Many apartment buildings were simply bulldozed to make way for the new transport corridors. Those left behind—the minorities who were not permitted entrance in the new suburbs—were left with urban environments that were decimated by the construction of roads leading out of the cities and into the countryside. In an effort to house these displaced persons, the federal government financed crowded public housing facilities that soon fell into states of disrepair. These districts were then red-lined by banks as poor risks for home and business loans. Cities became tolerable places to work and inhospitable or downright uninhabitable places in which to live.

At the same time, life in the suburbs flourished. Veterans not only took advantage of the new educational opportunities for themselves but made sure that quality new schools were built in the new suburbs for their children, who would come to be known as baby boomers because so many of them were conceived between 1946 and 1964. The baby boom reached its peak in 1957, just before Levitt built Levittown, New Jersey.

The homes in the newer phases of Levittown, Long Island, and in the new Levittowns were considerably more spacious and carefully designed than the original boxy "Capes." Family and social life moved almost completely toward the back of the home and the picture window moved along with it. Neighbors now spent less time "coffee klatching" in the kitchen and more time on organized, more private socializing in the backyard and in the new family rooms of the homes. The original Levittown homes were also changed and expanded by their owners and came to resemble the newer models. The seemingly limitless creativity of the original and new "Levittowners" gave the lie to the myth of suburban homogeneity so prevalent during the 1950s.

Most of the original, simple Cape-style homes built during the initial phase have been remodeled beyond all recognition; Levitt himself designed the houses with such extensive remodeling in mind. The attics were large and fit for habitation once finished, and many homeowners quickly added dormers, which seemed to jut out from the roofs of the houses. Carports became garages, and backyards were screened in. In the days before homeowners associations, houses were painted all manner of shades and hues. A man's "little box," as the homes were dubbed by a critical popular culture, was truly his castle. It has become difficult to find an untouched original Levittown Cape.

Robin Markowitz

SEE ALSO: *Baby Boomers; Manufactured Homes; Suburbia; World War II.*

BIBLIOGRAPHY

Bennett, M. J. *When Dreams Came True: The GI Bill and the Making of Modern America.* Washington, DC: Brassey's, 1996.

Conrad, P., and Brian Selznick. *Our House: The Stories of Levittown.* New York: Scholastic, 1995.

Gans, H. *The Levittowners: Ways of Life and Politics in a Suburban Community.* New York: Pantheon Books, 1967.

Kunstler, J. H. *The Geography of Nowhere: The Rise and Decline of America's Man-made Landscape.* New York: Touchstone, 1993.

Kushner, David. *Levittown: Two Families, One Tycoon, and the Fight for Civil Rights in America's Legendary Suburb.* New York: Walker, 2010.

Sacks, K. B. "How Did Jews Become White Folks?" In *Race,* ed. R. Sanjek and S. Gregory, 78–102. New Brunswick, NJ: Rutgers University Press, 1996.

Lewinsky, Monica *(1973–)*

In 1998 Monica Lewinsky was at the center of a sordid White House sex scandal that dominated political news in 1998 and culminated in the historic impeachment—only the second in American history—of William Jefferson (Bill) Clinton, forty-second president of the United States. The privileged daughter of affluent Beverly Hills parents, Lewinsky had graduated with a psychology degree from Lewis and Clark College in May 1995 and had taken an unpaid internship at the White House a month later. She met President Clinton that November and became an employee in the White House Office of Legislative Affairs. Around this time she and Clinton began having sexual encounters in the White House; the affair lasted through 1997, even after she left her post to work at the Pentagon.

Monica Lewinsky. *Monica Lewinsky's affair with President Bill Clinton in the mid-1990s earned her a dubious place in American political history.* © UPI/LANDOV.

In late 1997 Lewinsky began to confide the salacious details of the affair to Pentagon coworker Linda Tripp, who secretly tape-recorded many of the conversations. Soon thereafter, attorneys for Paula Jones, who had initiated a sexual harassment suit against Clinton, alerted Lewinsky that she was on the witness list in the Jones case, which sought to establish a pattern of sexual misconduct on the part of the president. Lewinsky provided them with a sworn affidavit denying a sexual relationship with the president. When the story of the affair, the Tripp tapes, and independent counsel Kenneth Starr's expanded investigation into the matter broke to the public on January 20, 1998, a political and media tumult began. Lewinsky's legal jeopardy, based on her affidavit for the Jones attorneys, faded in July when her attorneys negotiated an immunity agreement with the independent counsel's office. She also turned over to Starr's investigators a blue dress stained with what laboratory tests confirmed to be semen that was most likely the president's.

On August 17, 1998, after four hours of videotaped testimony before a federal grand jury, Clinton confessed to the world in a televised address that indeed he had had an "inappropriate relationship with Ms. Lewinsky." A now-famous report written by Starr's office and submitted to the U.S. Congress and the American public gave intimate details of that relationship, which involved no sexual intercourse but did include oral sex. Based on charges of perjury before the grand jury and a pattern of obstruction of justice, the U.S. House of Representatives on December 19, 1998, passed articles of impeachment against Clinton that required a Senate trial for final judgment. The resulting trial began on January 7, 1999, and ended on February 12 with the defeat, largely along partisan lines, of both charges.

In the aftermath of the Clinton impeachment, Lewinsky first had the opportunity to speak publicly about her ordeal in a March 1999 television interview with Barbara Walters for the news program *20/20.* Journalist Andrew Morton published the book *Monica's Story* (1999) based on interviews with her. In March 2002 she appeared on an episode of HBO's *American Undercover* series to answer questions from an audience about her affair with Clinton. Her efforts to build an identity and a livelihood have been wide ranging: selling a line of handbags, appearing on *Saturday Night Live,* serving as a Jenny Craig weight-loss spokesperson, and hosting a short-lived dating show on the Fox Network titled *Mr. Personality.* In 2005 she moved from New York to London. She earned a master's degree in social psychology from the London School of Economics in 2006. Since then she has largely stayed away from the extraordinary media attention given to her and her sensational story.

Philip L. Simpson

SEE ALSO: *Celebrity; Fox News Channel;* Saturday Night Live*; Sex Scandals; Sexual Harassment; Starr, Kenneth; 20/20; Walters, Barbara.*

BIBLIOGRAPHY

Berlant, Lauren, and Lisa Duggan. *Our Monica, Ourselves: The Clinton Affair and the National Interest.* New York: New York University Press, 2001.

Clinton, Bill. *My Life.* New York: Knopf, 2004.

Kalb, Marvin. *One Scandalous Story: Clinton, Lewinsky, and Thirteen Days that Tarnished American Journalism.* New York: Free Press, 2001.

Morton, Andrew. *Monica's Story.* New York: St. Martin's Press, 1999.

The Starr Report. New York: Pocket, 1998.

The Starr Report: The Evidence. New York: Pocket, 1998.

Lewis, C. S. *(1898–1963)*

C. S. Lewis's *The Chronicles of Narnia*, published during the 1950s, are the most widely read Christian fairy tales of the twentieth century. Children devour them, not realizing, in most cases, that they are reading religious morality tales in the guise of pagan fantasy.

C. S. Lewis. *C. S. Lewis wrote the Narnia series as a means of familiarizing children and other readers with the Christian faith.* JOHN CHILLINGWORTH/STRINGER/PICTURE POST/GETTY IMAGES.

LIFE AND WORKS

Clives Staples Lewis (called "Jack") was born on November 29, 1898, in Belfast, Northern Ireland. His mother died when he was nine, devastating him and his brother Warren. As a child, Lewis was bookish and precocious and enjoyed writing of an imaginary world of talking beasts called "Animal-Land." In adolescence he became an atheist; his education at Oxford and experience in the trenches in World War I did little to change his philosophy.

Between 1925 and 1954, Lewis was a Fellow of English Language and Literature at Magdalen College, Oxford. When he was in his early thirties, as a result of his father's death and his intellectual friendships, Lewis's religious beliefs changed drastically and he became a Christian apologist. From then on, Lewis devoted much of his time to writing literary works that might convince others of the merits of Christian thought.

The Chronicles of Narnia, a series of seven children's books, fall into this category. Lewis peopled his imaginary country with fantastic creatures (including fauns, witches, and centaurs) usually associated with paganism—but had the great lion Aslan, a Christ figure, rule them. The author described the Christian meanings of the series thus: the first book, *The Lion, the Witch, and the Wardrobe*, is about "the Crucifixion and Resurrection"; *Prince Caspian* deals with the "restoration of the true religion after a corruption"; *The Voyage of the Dawn Treader*, "the spiritual life"; *The Silver Chair*, "the continued war against the powers of darkness"; *The Horse and His Boy*, "the calling and conversion of a heathen"; *The Magician's Nephew*, "the Creation and how evil entered Narnia"; and *The Last Battle*, "the coming of Antichrist (the ape), the end of the world and the last judgment."

Lewis insisted that the *Chronicles* were not Christian allegories but "supposals." He explained the difference by saying that Aslan "is an invention giving an imaginary answer to the question 'what might Christ become like if there really were a world like Narnia, and He chose to be incarnate and die and rise again in that world as He actually has done in ours?' This is not an allegory at all. . . . Allegory and such supposals differ because they mix the real and the unreal in different ways."

The Narnia books were written, however, to familiarize people, especially children, with the Christian faith. Lewis said he was trying to portray the basic principles of Christianity, or "that which has been believed everywhere, always, by all": ecstatic love for the world. He said he wrote the stories to "set before our imagination something that has always baffled the intellect." They are not at all didactic—Lewis despised religious education as a child. He wanted to recreate the beauty and love he found in Christian stories, not teach about it. By writing in this way, Lewis made Christianity palatable to agnostics and atheists. *The Chronicles of Narnia* appeal to Christians and non-Christians, and in most cases children do not realize these as Bible stories written through a pagan lens.

Lewis also wrote science fiction novels, including the *Space Trilogy*, which consists of *Out of the Silent Planet* (1938), in which the hero, Edwin Ransom, is roughly based on his friend and fellow Inklings member J. R. R. Tolkien; *Perelandra* (1943), a retelling of John Milton's *Paradise Lost* set on Venus; and *That Hideous Strength* (1945). He considered *Till We Have Faces* (1956), a retelling of the Eros and Psyche myth, to be his best novel.

Lewis was an articulate proponent of Christianity, arguably the most important Christian writer of the twentieth century.

His most important theological works are *The Problem of Pain* (1940), a defense of pain and the existence of Hell as evidence of an ordered universe; *The Screwtape Letters* (1942), a correspondence between the demon Screwtape and his nephew Wormwood concerning possession of the soul of an unsuspecting human; and *Mere Christianity*, a published version of the radio addresses he made during World War II as "the apostle to skeptics" in Britain and the United States. His spiritual autobiography, *Surprised by Joy* (1955), is still widely read.

In 1956 Lewis married Joy Davidman, who had converted to Christianity from Judaism partly under the influence of Lewis's books. Soon afterward, Joy became ill from bone cancer, and she died in 1960. Lewis died three years later, on November 22, 1963. In 1993 Anthony Hopkins and Debra Winger starred in *Shadowlands*, a feature-length film about Lewis's life.

NARNIA IN POPULAR CULTURE

The first book in the Narnia series, *The Lion, the Witch, and the Wardrobe*, is the best known. In it, four children—Lucy, Edmund, Susan, and Peter—enter an old wardrobe and emerge in Narnia, a land caught in perpetual winter under the evil rule of the White Witch. Through the sinister influence of some magical Turkish Delight candy, Edmund betrays his brother and sisters; to save the boy, the great lion Aslan must sacrifice his life. Aslan is gloriously reborn through a "deeper magic" and seats the "sons of Adam and the daughters of Eve" on four thrones at Cair Paravel. After many years of benevolent rule, the kings and queens of Narnia return through the wardrobe to find themselves children again.

This book was made into a feature-length television cartoon in 1979 in the United States. The first four books in the series were adapted for the British Broadcasting Company (BBC) in the late 1980s and early 1990s, with Tom Baker playing Puddleglum in *The Silver Chair*. Walden Media produced feature films of the first three books between 2005 and 2010, to mixed critical reception. The first film received unintended press when Andy Samberg and Chris Parnell of *Saturday Night Live (SNL)* created a music video titled "Lazy Sunday," in which they eat cupcakes as they sing and rap their way to a Sunday matinee of *The Chronicles of Narnia*. The film, widely viewed on YouTube during the first year of the website's existence, is credited with bringing a new audience to *SNL*. In 2011 a *Doctor Who* Christmas special titled "The Doctor, the Widow, and the Wardrobe" played with Lewis's themes, sending a child to a magical, snow-covered world.

Lewis's Narnia continues to inspire other writers. Lev Grossman's best-selling novels *The Magicians* (2009) and *The Magician King* (2011) draw heavily upon the Narnia books; Grossman's "Fillory" is a thinly disguised version of Narnia. Laura Miller's *The Magician's Book: A Skeptic's Adventures in Narnia* (2008) relates her experience rereading the Narnia series as an adult, newly aware of the books' Christian themes.

Jessy Randall

SEE ALSO: Doctor Who; Saturday Night Live; *Science Fiction Publishing.*

BIBLIOGRAPHY

Ford, Paul F. *Companion to Narnia*. San Francisco: Harper, 1994.

Lewis, C. S. *C. S. Lewis, Letters to Children*. Edited by Lyle W. Dorsett and Marjorie Lamp Mead. New York: Macmillan, 1985.

Lewis, C. S. *Surprised by Joy: The Shape of My Early Life*. New York: Harcourt Brace Modern Classic, 1995.

Lewis, C. S. *The Collected Letters of C. S. Lewis*. Edited by Walter Hooper. 3 vols. San Francisco: Harper, 2004–2007.

Wilson, A. N. *C. S. Lewis: A Biography*. New York: Fawcett Columbine, 1990.

Lewis, Carl *(1961–)*

The son of two Willingboro, New Jersey, teachers, Carl Lewis went from being an awkward teenager to winning nine Olympic gold medals before he retired in 1997, setting numerous world records along the way. Qualifying in the long jump for the first of his U.S. record five Olympic teams in 1980, Lewis missed the Moscow games because of America's boycott ordered by President Jimmy Carter in response to Soviet aggression in Afghanistan. He then won four gold medals at the 1984 Los

Summer Olympics 1992. *Carl Lewis takes off on the anchor leg of the men's 4X100 meter relay at the 1992 Olympic Games in Barcelona, Spain.* AP IMAGES.

Angeles Games in the 100 meters, 200 meters, 4×100-meter relay, and long jump, matching Jesse Owens's feat at Berlin in 1936. In the process, Lewis not only tied Owens's record for track and field gold medals at a single Olympic Games but also revived popular appreciation for Owens's achievements.

Lewis went on to win gold at the 1988 Seoul games, the 1992 Barcelona games, and the 1996 Atlanta games. In winning the long jump in Atlanta, he became only the second track-and-field athlete (after discus thrower Al Oerter) to win gold in an event in four Olympiads. (He remains the only track-and-field athlete to have qualified for five Olympic teams.) Lewis aggressively controlled his own career and marketing; with his agent, Joe Douglas, he used both his individual success and that of his tremendously popular Santa Monica Track Club to professionalize track and field, making it possible for runners to support themselves through athletics. He also advocated for increased testing to end the use of performance-enhancing drugs in track. (Whereas some observers considered it simple jealousy when Lewis claimed that Canadian sprinter Ben Johnson's victories against him were due to steroid use, Lewis's sentiments were vindicated after Johnson tested positive for steroid use at the 1988 Olympics in Seoul.)

Although Lewis held no individual world records at his retirement in 1997, he had recorded numerous performances that were among the ten best of all time in the 100 meters, 200 meters, 4×100-meter relay, and long jump. Despite never setting the world record in the long jump, with his consistency over seventeen years of competition at the highest level, he is most certainly the greatest long jumper in world track-and-field history.

Regardless of Lewis's success, however, he has failed to win the acclaim and endorsements in the United States that have greeted him elsewhere. While the fact that track and field has long been more popular in Europe and Asia partially accounts for this failure, other factors must be taken into account as well. Media portrayals of Lewis as aloof have most likely contributed to the American public's lukewarm feelings. Of perhaps more significance, though, have been persistent rumors about Lewis's sexuality (which he has refused to address in public). British decathlon champion Daley Thompson's decision, at the 1984 Los Angeles Games, to wear a T-shirt that asked, "Is the World's Second Greatest Athlete Gay?" to a press conference after his victory—a pointed reference to Lewis—brought this controversy into the public eye. Since then Lewis has received less attention than other athletes far less successful, in far less visible sports.

Despite these questions about Lewis's public acceptance, however, he has not only been a successful competitor, but he has also served as an articulate ambassador and advocate for his sport, shown in the 1999 *Sports Illustrated* decision to name him Olympian of the Century and, that same year, the International Olympic Committee vote making him Sportsman of the Century.

C. John Smolenski

SEE ALSO: *Gay Men; Olympics; Owens, Jesse;* Sports Illustrated.

BIBLIOGRAPHY

Coffey, Wayne. *Carl Lewis.* Woodbridge, CT: Blackbirch Press, 1993.

Klots, Steve. *Carl Lewis.* New York: Chelsea House, 1995.

Lewis, Carl, and Jeffrey Marx. *Inside Track: My Professional Life in Amateur Track and Field.* New York: Simon & Schuster, 1990.

Smith, Gary. "I Do What I Want to Do: Carl Lewis." *Sports Illustrated,* July 18, 1984.

Lewis, Jerry *(1926–)*

For more than half a century comedian Jerry Lewis entertained audiences around the world with his unique style of exaggerated mugging and heavy-handed sentimentality. A national presence since the mid-1940s, when he teamed up with crooner Dean Martin to create one of the legendary comedy acts in show business, Lewis is hailed by some as a comic master equal to Charlie Chaplin and Buster Keaton and reviled by others as self-indulgent and grating. In *The Complete Directory to Prime Time TV Stars* (1987), author Tim Brooks best captures the intensity of the contrasting opinions of Lewis: "He is perhaps the most controversial performer in show business; depending on whom you read, he is either the greatest comic genius of the Western world, or the most idiotic no-talent to ever foul the screen."

After a decade as entertainment's hottest comedy team, Martin and Lewis broke up in 1956. Lewis went on to write and direct a number of popular films. After his film work diminished he remained in the public eye as the host of the annual Labor Day Muscular Dystrophy Association (MDA)

Jerry Lewis as the Nutty Professor. *Jerry Lewis performs as one of his most famous characters in* The Nutty Professor *in 1963.* ALAN BAND/KEYSTONE/GETTY IMAGES.

Telethon. Lewis overcame a series of personal problems in the 1980s to enjoy a resurgence of popularity on both film and stage. However, despite his international acclaim, he remains an acquired taste for many Americans.

CHILDHOOD AND EARLY CAREER

Born Joseph Levitch on March 16, 1926, in Newark, New Jersey, Lewis seemed destined for a life in entertainment. His parents, vaudevillian Danny Lewis and pianist Rae Lewis, were veteran performers who encouraged their son to follow in their footsteps. Lewis made his professional debut at the age of five in New York's Borscht Belt singing "Brother Can You Spare a Dime." As a teen the young comic was noted for his manic stand-up routine in which he impersonated popular singers.

His career stalled until 1946, when he formed an act with an Italian singer named Dean Martin. Their partnership began on July 25, 1946, at the 500 Club in Atlantic City when Lewis suggested his friend replace another entertainer who had quit the bill. The pair originally worked separately but later joined forces on the stage, where they traded insults, improvised jokes, and embodied a sense of lunacy. Martin's handsome, romantic persona made him the perfect straight man for the goofy Lewis. Many of their routines revolved around Lewis's attempts to break up Martin's musical numbers with childish antics.

Film producer Hal Wallis discovered the team performing at the famous Copacabana nightclub and signed them to a long-term contract with Paramount Pictures. They made their screen debut in *My Friend Irma* (1949), in which they essentially performed their nightclub routine. Audiences quickly embraced the pair, who went on to star in more than a dozen highly successful comedies. Along with their movie work, Martin and Lewis appeared frequently in nightclubs, on radio shows, and on television. In the mid-1950s their relationship soured, and their decision to break up the act made national headlines. Martin and Lewis made their last regular appearance together at the Copacabana on July 25, 1956: ten years to the day after they became a team.

SOLO SUCCESS AND FILM CAREER

Many believed the split would doom both of their careers, but Martin achieved success and Lewis emerged as a comedy auteur. During the 1960s Lewis produced, starred, and directed a number of successful comedies. His most noteworthy films from this period are *The Bellboy* (1960), *Cinderfella* (1960), *The Patsy* (1964), and *The Nutty Professor* (1963). In this last film, a take-off of Robert Louis Stevenson's *Dr. Jekyll and Mr. Hyde* (1886), Lewis plays a nerdy chemist who transforms himself into a cool lounge lizard named Buddy Love. Some critics interpreted this character as a parody of Martin.

French critics declared Lewis's 1960s films as proof of his comic mastery and deemed *The Nutty Professor* the best picture of the year. Many Americans found his work overly broad and sentimental, but Europeans saw him as the successor to Chaplin and Keaton. In 1984 he was inducted into the French Legion of Honour and praised by the French Minister of Culture for his humanitarian work and comic genius.

Despite his praise from Europe, Lewis's popularity in America declined in the 1970s. He alienated U.S. audiences by mugging through tired plots in self-indulgent films. His career hit a low point with the unreleased film *The Day the Clown Cried* (1972), in which he portrayed a clown named Helmut Doork who tries to entertain Jewish children while imprisoned in a Nazi concentration camp.

CHARITY WORK AND LATER CAREER

While he suffered setbacks in his comedy career, Lewis began raising funds to fight the disease muscular dystrophy. He raised millions of dollars each Labor Day and was nominated for the 1977 Nobel Peace Prize for his efforts. On a 1976 telethon, Lewis was stunned by the surprise appearance of Martin. Frank Sinatra reunited the pair, who had remained distant for decades, in one of TV's most memorable moments. In 1989 Martin and Lewis reunited onstage for the final time in Las Vegas when Lewis made a surprise appearance to present Dean with a birthday cake and to thank him for all the joy he gave to the world. In 2005 Lewis released a memoir titled *Dean & Me: A Love Story*.

Lewis's career took an upswing in the 1980s with his acclaimed dramatic performance as a talk show host kidnapped by Robert De Niro in Martin Scorsese's *The King of Comedy* (1983). He appeared infrequently thereafter in films, but he made strong showings on the TV crime drama *Wiseguy* (1987–1990) and on Broadway in the 1995 revival of *Damn Yankees*.

Lewis remains an influential figure on the American comedy landscape, and several of his 1960s films, like *The Nutty Professor*, have been remade. In 2011 Lewis's forty-five-year run as the host of the MDA Telethon came to an end. He is also still a controversial figure: when asked about the ambivalent feelings he generates, Lewis replied: "People hate me because I am a multifaceted, talented, wealthy, internationally famous genius." Such statements may reveal why Lewis has not been completely embraced by the American public. However, his unique comic style and voluminous charity work have won him a spot in the hearts of millions around the globe.

Charles Coletta

SEE ALSO: *Chaplin, Charlie; De Niro, Robert; Dr. Jekyll and Mr. Hyde; Keaton, Buster; Martin, Dean; Movie Stars; Sinatra, Frank; Stand-Up Comedy.*

BIBLIOGRAPHY

Apter, Michael J., and K. C. P. Smith. "Humour and the Theory of Psychological Reversals." In *It's a Funny Thing, Humour*, eds. Antony Chapman and Hugh Foot. New York: Pergamon, 1977, 95–100.

Brooks, Tim. *The Complete Directory to Prime Time TV Stars.* New York: Ballantine Books, 1987.

Grace, Arthur. *Comedians.* New York: Thomasson-Grant, 1991.

Levy, Shawn. *King of Comedy.* New York: St. Martin's Press, 1996.

Lewis, Jerry, and Herb Gluck. *Jerry Lewis in Person.* New York: Atheneum, 1982.

Lewis, Jerry, and James Kaplan. *Dean & Me: A Love Story.* New York: Doubleday, 2005.

Marx, Arthur. *Everybody Loves Somebody Sometime (Especially Himself): The Story of Dean Martin & Jerry Lewis.* New York: Hawthorn, 1974.

Pomerance, Murray. *Enfant Terrible!: Jerry Lewis in American Film.* New York: New York University Press, 2002.

Lewis, Jerry Lee *(1935–)*

Self-taught pianist, composer, and singer Jerry Lee Lewis is an original artist who, along with Elvis Presley, personifies the popular cultural ethos of the 1950s, when rock and roll emerged and rose to popularity, but Lewis forged his own unique and uninhibited style within the genre. His musical influences included African American blues and gospel, as well as the popular music heard on records and the radio. His early piano style is basically a simple rhythmic boogie left hand, with excessive use of glissando (rapid running of the thumb across the keys) and a distinctive percussive pounding in the right hand; his characteristic vocal style makes use of yodeling, upward bends with occasional falsetto breaks. The combined result is frenetic, entertaining, sometimes moving, and intensely musical.

One of the last surviving pioneers of '50s rock-and-roll music, Lewis has been a pianist and vocal stylist since the age of nine. He began playing professionally at the age of fifteen and rapidly developed into a consummate showman, enjoying a commercially successful career punctuated with a long spell of disfavor arising from the conduct of his personal life. His songs have made both the pop and country singles charts, and his rise to stardom from his humble beginnings is a tribute to his creativity, tenacity, and originality. Lewis's music can be divided into two stylistic periods: the rock-and-roll period, from 1957 to 1968, and country, from 1968 onward (although he also continues to play revival and "oldies" bills, performing numbers from the rock-and-roll repertoire).

Jerry Lewis the Rocker. *Jerry Lee Lewis, one of the pioneers of rock and roll who was known for his flamboyant and uninhibited style, performs in 1980.* DAVID REDFERN/STAFF/REDFERNS/GETTY IMAGES.

FROM HUMBLE BEGINNINGS

Born on September 29, 1935, in the northern Louisiana town of Ferriday, Lewis grew up in grinding poverty, the son of subsistence farmer Elmo Lewis and Mamie Lewis, whose meager living depended on the price of cotton. The family switched from the Baptist denomination to the Assembly of God Church, where the young Jerry Lee sang. He and his cousin, later the notorious evangelist Jimmy Lee Swaggart, would sneak into Haney Big House in the so-called "colored" section of town and listen to the bluesmen play. Lewis, a poor student, attended school only sporadically, and he occasionally shoplifted from the local merchants. The piano became an early focus in his life, and he spent hours practicing on a neighbor's piano and those in the church until his father borrowed against his belongings and bought an upright Starck piano for his ten-year-old son.

The youthful Lewis felt an affinity for the percussive sound of boogie-woogie blues, and his favorite songs during the 1940s were the popular boogie hits "House of Blue Lights" and "Down the Road a Piece." He also sang Jimmie Rodgers and Al Jolson songs that he picked up from listening to his parents' records. In 1948 he first heard Hank Williams on *The Louisiana Hayride*, a radio program patterned after the Grand Ole Opry and broadcast from Shreveport, Louisiana. Lewis idolized Williams and learned his songs from the local radio broadcasts. Thus, Rodgers, Jolson, and Williams, along with boogie-woogie, were the influences that shaped his own style. In 1949 a hillbilly band played at the opening of a Ford dealership in Ferriday. The Lewises were present, and Elmo Lewis urged the owners of the dealership to permit his fourteen-year-old son to sit in on piano. They consented, Lewis performed Stick McGhee's "Drinkin' Wine, Spo-Dee-O-Dee," and the people loved him. Thereafter he quit school entirely to play for the local community on his upright piano that Elmo would load onto a pickup truck.

His religious upbringing in the Assembly of God Church caused conflict for Lewis, whose lifestyle was at odds with the church teachings, and he periodically hesitated at the crossroads of whether to serve God or Mammon. At the age of fifteen he thought he might pursue the ministry and was sent off to attend Southwestern Bible Institute in Texas, but he soon developed a taste for the Dallas nightlife and tired of the institute's routine and discipline. He was eventually expelled from for playing the gospel song "My God Is Real" in a boogie-woogie style. His spiritual struggles tended to resolve themselves in favor of the secular when he needed money, and in 1954 he was hired by Johnny Littlejohn, a local Mississippi disc jockey and bandleader. From time to time, his conflict between God and the so-called devil's music would surface, and Littlejohn would have to plead with him to continue in the band.

SUN RECORDS

Lewis continued to play professionally in Louisiana and Mississippi in "bucket of blood" clubs with the Johnny Littlejohn band. In the course of auditioning for *The Louisiana Hayride* program on KWKH in Shreveport, he recorded two songs, "I

Don't Hurt Anymore," and "I Need You Now." The Memphis-based Sun Records, which had become the premier label of white rock and roll by 1954 with Elvis Presley on their label, was a good prospect for an aspiring performer, and Lewis's family gathered thirty-three dozen eggs and sold them to the local supermarket to finance a trip to Memphis to audition for Sun. He cut a few country and rock-and-roll sides for Sun. On Lewis's second trip to Memphis, he recorded "Crazy Arms," a country hit by Ray Price that convinced Sun owner Sam Phillips that his music was commercially viable. While the record failed to make any charts, the response to "Crazy Arms" was ecstatic.

From 1956 to 1957 Lewis worked as a session pianist for Sun singers Warren Smith and Billy Lee Riley and continued to tour professionally. In 1957 Sun released "Whole Lotta Shakin' Goin' On," which was followed by a long tour with Johnny Cash in Canada, during which Lewis honed his stage act with antics such as kicking back the piano stool and playing the piano with his foot and closed each performance with "Whole Lotta Shakin' Goin' On." He also earned the nickname "Killer" for his knockout performances. "Whole Lotta Shakin' Goin' On" and "Great Balls of Fire" peaked at number one and number two, respectively, on the pop singles chart, and both reached number one on the country singles chart that summer, while "Breathless" reached number seven on the pop chart. Lewis's performance of "Whole Lotta Shakin' Goin' On" triggered a backlash among people who perceived the song and its singer as a pernicious influence on young teenagers.

The power and sway of rock and roll was too strong for the small backlash against Lewis's music, and his popularity surged. He enjoyed a number of important bookings that exposed him to a national audience, including appearances on *The Big D Jamboree* (a country-and-western show from Dallas), the *Steve Allen Show* in New York, Alan Freed's television show *The Big Beat*, and Dick Clark's *American Bandstand*. Lewis also performed at the Apollo Theater in Harlem, New York, for a predominantly black audience and was well received. A twelve-day engagement booked by Alan Freed at the Paramount Theatre in New York, where Lewis shared the headline spot with Fats Domino, broke attendance records.

WOMAN TROUBLES

A number of women came to play a significant role in Lewis's life. At the age of sixteen, while toying with the idea of becoming a minister, he married and divorced Dorothy Barton; in 1953, on the eve of his eighteenth birthday, he married Jane Mitchum and became a father. Before the breakup and divorce of that marriage, he fell in love with his second cousin, thirteen-year-old Myra Gale. Lewis and Gale were married and soon after, accompanied by Myra, Lewis embarked on a tour engagement in England. A media frenzy and public animosity over his child-bride's age ensued, forcing the cancellation of the tour after just three performances. He returned to the United States amid a storm of controversy, and despite issuing an apologetic response to *Billboard* readers upset by his marriage, the media was unrelenting and moral outrage continued. Lewis's career went into decline for ten years.

In addition to concert engagements, he appeared in a handful of movies, including *Jamboree* (1957), a low-budget Warner Brothers excuse for featuring rock-and roll artists, in which he sang "Great Balls of Fire," and *High School Confidential* (1958). He was also in *Be My Guest*, a low-budget pop musical filmed in London in 1965, and played Iago in a Los Angeles production of *Catch My Soul* (1968), a rock opera version of William Shakespeare's *Othello*. While theater critics were negative about the show itself, Lewis's performance as Iago was deemed sensational.

COUNTRY COMEBACK

The musician finally made a comeback, as a country star, in 1968. His contract with Sun Records had ended in 1963, and he signed with Smash Records, a subsidiary of Mercury Records. That year Lewis recorded "Another Place, Another Time" for Smash, and for the first time in ten years found himself with a Top 10 country hit, which crossed over to the pop charts. By 1969 Lewis was one of the hottest country singers in the South. A string of hit records, including "What's Made Milwaukee Famous (Has Made a Loser out of Me)" (1969), "There Must Be More to Love than This" (1970), and "Chantilly Lace" (1972), helped to raise his concert fee to $10,000 per performance. He made a successful appearance at the Grand Ole Opry in 1973, and he recorded the last sides for Mercury and then signed with Elektra.

Controversy and tragedy dogged Lewis throughout his life. Both his sons died, triggering a return to the pills and alcohol that he had been addicted to since his teens. He accidentally shot his bass player in the chest (he miraculously survived) and in 1976 was arrested for waving a gun outside Presley's mansion, Graceland. Lewis wed seven times, the seventh in 2012—to the ex-wife of his cousin, Rusty Brown, who happens to be the brother of Myra, Lewis's bride of 1957. The circumstances surrounding the deaths of his fourth and fifth wives have been viewed with suspicion. His fourth wife died in a swimming pool, and his fifth was found dead at his home following a methadone overdose. By 1979 the IRS took possession of his property in lieu of $274,000 in back taxes. He has been hospitalized several times, reportedly close to death, and was alleged to have suffered a mild heart attack in 1996.

Lewis was one of the first inductees to the Rock and Roll Hall of Fame in 1986 and, despite the shadows hanging over his life, "The Killer" has been performing for more than sixty years, resolutely upbeat in body and spirit as the "last man standing" in the Sun Records dynasty. In 1989 *Great Balls of Fire!*, a biographical movie, was released, starring Dennis Quaid as Lewis and charting the rocky road with Myra (Winona Ryder) in dramatic detail. In September 2006 he released an album titled "Last Man Standing" consisting of duets between Lewis and other top artists, and in 2010 he released *Mean Old Man* to stellar reviews.

Willie Collins

SEE ALSO: *Allen, Steve;* American Bandstand*; Apollo Theater; Blues; Cash, Johnny; Celebrity; Celebrity Couples; Clark, Dick; Country Music; Divorce; Domino, Fats; Gospel Music;* Grand Ole Opry*; Jolson, Al; Media Feeding Frenzies; Pop Music; Presley, Elvis; Radio; Rock and Roll; Rodgers, Jimmie; Sun Records; Swaggart, Jimmy; Television; Williams, Hank, Sr.*

BIBLIOGRAPHY

Bonomo, Joe. *Jerry Lee Lewis: Lost and Found*. New York: Continuum Books, 2009.

Cain, Robert J. *Whole Lotta Shakin' Goin' On: Jerry Lee Lewis*. New York: Dial Press, 1981.

Guterman, Jimmy. *Rockin' My Life Away: Listening to Jerry Lee Lewis.* Nashville, TN: Rutledge Hill Press, 1991.

Lewis, Myra, and Murray Silver. *Great Balls of Fire: The Uncensored Story of Jerry Lee Lewis.* New York: Quill, 1982.

Tosches, Nick. *Hellfire: The Jerry Lee Lewis Story.* New York: Delacorte Press, 1982.

Lewis, Sinclair *(1885–1951)*

A native of Sauk Centre, Minnesota, Sinclair Lewis became one of America's most forceful social critics during the 1920s. Lewis attended Yale, then held an assortment of editorial and journalistic positions through his early twenties, including a stint selling short-story plots to Jack London. Lewis wrote several fairly pedestrian novels, notable for their bourgeois sentiments, before he struck literary gold in 1920 with *Main Street* and the novels of social criticism that followed in its wake: *Babbitt* (1922), *Arrowsmith* (1925), *Dodsworth* (1929), and *Elmer Gantry* (1927). Finally Lewis felt free to express his radical self, his feelings of dissatisfaction with American complacency, mediocrity, and moral narrowness.

In 1930 his honesty earned him the first Nobel Prize in Literature awarded to an American. Sadly, of the ten novels that followed before his death in 1951, only one—*It Can't Happen Here (1935)*—caught further significant attention. He lost his moorings as a writer once the world of the 1920s, about which he had written so searingly, receded behind the Great Depression and World War II.

Bennett Lovett-Graff

SEE ALSO: *The Great Depression; London, Jack; The Twenties; World War II.*

BIBLIOGRAPHY

Bloom, Harold, ed. *Sinclair Lewis: Modern Critical Views.* New York: Chelsea House, 1987.

Hutchisson, James M. *The Rise of Sinclair Lewis, 1920–1930.* University Park: Pennsylvania State University Press, 1996.

Lingeman, Richard R. *Sinclair Lewis: Rebel from Main Street.* St. Paul, MN: Borealis Books, 2005.

Parrington, Vernon. *Sinclair Lewis: Our Own Diogenes.* New York: Haskell House Publishing, 1973.

Liberace *(1919–1987)*

As "The Rhinestone Rubinstein" or the "Las Vegas Liszt," pianist-entertainer Liberace created his own sequined niche in the American popular imagination. He fashioned himself to appeal to the middlebrow masses as a latter-day reincarnation of the nineteenth-century Romantic grand pianist, and he dazzled millions of (mostly female) fans with his flamboyant performances of showy and accessible music. As America's first television matinee idol, Liberace capitalized on the then new technology during the 1950s. His popular appeal brought him appearances in Hollywood films and television series, mentions in songs (the Chordettes' 1954 hit "Mr. Sandman," among others), and he was parodied (as "Loverboynik") in a 1956 episode of Al Capp's comic strip *Li'l Abner*. Liberace's stardom sprang from a highly marketable and carefully packaged conflation of high and low cultural ingredients, and his model of musical spectacle influenced subsequent stars from Elvis Presley to Michael Jackson. Though he was ridiculed for his fey mannerisms, attacked for his closeted homosexuality, and lambasted for his glib and sentimentalized musicianship, Liberace's famous comeback still silences his critics: "I cried all the way to the bank."

Wladziu (called Walter) Valentino Liberace was born on May 16, 1919, near Milwaukee, Wisconsin. His father, a former member of John Philip Sousa's concert band, played French horn in the Milwaukee Symphony Orchestra. His mother, of Polish descent, chose his middle name after her favorite film idol, Rudolf Valentino. Legend has it that in 1923 the young Walter, a child prodigy, met Jan Paderewski, the acclaimed Polish pianist and statesman, who praised his playing. Liberace began performing professionally as a classical pianist during his high school years, but Depression-era hardships prompted him to earn money playing in nightclubs, movie houses, and at social events. Engaged to perform with the Chicago Symphony in 1939, he was persuaded to use the stage name "Walter Bust-

Liberace. *Liberace performs in 1985 with his trademark lavish costume and candelabra.* L. BUSACCA/CONTRIBUTOR/WIREIMAGE/GETTY IMAGES.

erkeys" for his other "low-class" performing ventures. After one recital, audience members called for a rendition of the popular song "Three Little Fishes," which the pianist paraphrased in the style of various classical composers as an encore crowd-pleaser. This "crossover" intersection of classical and popular material became a significant characteristic of his future career.

EARLY CAREER

Escaping military service in World War II because of a back problem, Liberace in 1940 went to New York, where he served as an intermission pianist at fashionable venues such as the Waldorf-Astoria's Persian Room. He later moved to Los Angeles with the hopes of furthering his career. During this period he experimented with various attention-getting techniques such as encouraging audience participation in his act (the "Chopsticks" duet routine, for example), and playing "duets with the masters" by accompanying recordings of the great classical pianists. He also introduced his trademark on-stage candelabra (apparently an idea he took from the 1945 hit Hollywood biopic of Chopin, *A Song to Remember*). When his violinist brother George returned from war service in 1945, the two formed a supper-club act and toured the country under contract with the Statler and Radisson hotel chains. Around this time Liberace was inspired by a motivational self-help book by Claude Bristol, *The Magic of Believing*, and eventually contributed an introduction to the 1955 edition, writing, "To attain success, one must positively think success."

TELEVISION SUCCESS

That success came to Liberace in the 1950s through his innovative television program, *The Liberace Show*, which first aired in 1951 and rapidly became a hit in the Los Angeles area. Through syndication in 1953 the program found a large national audience, rivaling *I Love Lucy* in popularity. At its peak, *The Liberace Show* commanded a weekly audience of 35 million and was carried by 219 television stations in the United States. This recognition generated recording opportunities for Liberace, and in 1953 alone he sold two million records—albums and singles. His 1953 engagement at Carnegie Hall sold out and was followed by a 1954 success at Madison Square Garden. A Hollywood Bowl appearance prompted another important innovation in his presentational style: as the distant audience would be unable to distinguish him, in his black evening clothes, from the similarly clad orchestra, he wore a white tuxedo. From then on his stage outfits only increased in ostentatious flair.

FILM CAREER

Liberace made attempts to translate his television appeal into Hollywood stardom, but his few films were flops. He starred in the syrupy *Sincerely Yours* (1955) as a concert pianist afflicted by deafness who turns to anonymous acts of goodwill to regain his belief in life. The movie was essentially a vehicle for thirty-one of Liberace's renditions at the piano. He also had a minor pianist role in *South Sea Sinner* (1950) and a cameo as a camp casket salesman in *The Loved One* (1965). Guest spots on television series included *Batman* (1966), *Kojak* (1973), and *The Muppet Show* (1976).

LAS VEGAS

Las Vegas was the city most suited to the style and content of Liberace's musical act. During the 1950s and 1960s, Vegas audiences relished the kitsch appeal of his spectacular shows with their outrageous costumes and the star's coy banter, and he was that city's highest-paid entertainer in 1955. In 1956 Elvis Presley joined Liberace for a historic show at the Riviera Hotel, during which the two stars traded outfits and instruments. In 1979 the pianist opened the Liberace Museum, which occupies one corner of a Las Vegas shopping mall and houses his costumes, custom-designed automobiles (including a 1962 Rolls Royce covered with mirrored tiles), antique pianos, and the world's largest rhinestone. During the high-rolling 1980s, Liberace's aristocratic illusions and extravagant style appealed to younger audiences once again, and his shows at New York's Radio City Music Hall in 1984, 1985, and 1986 broke all box-office records in that landmark theater's history.

PRIVATE LIFE

Although he toured abroad extensively, everywhere lionized as a celebrity, Liberace was particularly proud of his three Royal Command Performances in England, but the British tours were problematic for the furor of speculative gossip they unleashed about his private life. In 1957 he successfully sued *Confidential* magazine for libel when it insinuated that he was homosexual. Two years later, he also won a suit against Britain's Mirror newspaper group over an article by columnist "Cassandra" (William Connor), who had written that Liberace was "the summit of sex—Masculine, Feminine, and Neuter . . . the biggest sentimental vomit of all times. Slobbering over his mother, winking at his brother, counting the cash at every second." While men may have scoffed at his exaggerated effeminate mannerisms, women fans defended Liberace, citing in his favor his oft-displayed love and concern for his own mother. Fan disapproval, however, greeted the announcement that he planned to marry actress-dancer Joanne Rio in 1954; in one week, 6,000 letters were received, 80 percent of which opposed the marriage. In 1982 Scott Thorson filed a $113 million "palimony" suit against the entertainer, claiming that he had been not only Liberace's bodyguard and chauffeur but also his long-term lover. Liberace settled out of court for close to $1 million.

Among the enduring images of Liberace's campy appeal are his 1976 Bicentennial red-white-and-blue hot-pants outfit, his extravagantly expensive (and long) fur and bejeweled capes, his on-stage arrival in chauffeur-driven luxury cars decorated with mirrors and rhinestones, and his Peter-Pan-style gimmick of flying across stage at the close of a performance. When asked how he could play with so many large rings on his fingers, Liberace answered, "Very well, thank you." Liberace's showmanship has provided ample material for academic treatments of spectacle, sexuality, and other topics of cultural study. Marjorie Garber regards Liberace's outrageous displays as an example of "unmarked transvestism." Margaret Drewal sees his capes as invoking Bela Lugosi as Count Dracula, and Kevin Kopelson examines the homophobia surrounding his reception in light of the "queer" connotations of his pianism and performance mannerisms. The unique showman-pianist died from AIDS on February 4, 1987, a sad ending that failed to end speculation about his sexuality.

Ivan Raykoff

SEE ALSO: *AIDS; Batman; Carnegie Hall;* I Love Lucy*; Jackson, Michael;* Kojak*; Las Vegas;* Li'l Abner*; Lugosi, Bela; The Muppets; Presley, Elvis; Sousa, John Philip; Valentino, Rudolph.*

BIBLIOGRAPHY

Bristol, Claude M. *The Magic of Believing.* New York: Prentice-Hall, 1955.

Drewal, Margaret Thompson. "The Camp Trace in Corporate America: Liberace and the Rockettes at Radio City Music Hall." In *The Politics and Poetics of Camp*, ed. Moe Meyer. New York: Routledge, 1994.

Faris, Jocelyn. *Liberace: A Bio-Bibliography.* Westport, CT: Greenwood Press, 1995.

Garber, Marjorie. "The Transvestite Continuum Liberace-Valentino-Elvis." In *Vested Interests: Cross-Dressing and Cultural Anxiety.* New York: Routledge, 1992.

Kopelson, Kevin. "Classified Information." In *Beethoven's Kiss: Pianism, Perversion, and the Mastery of Desire.* Palo Alto, CA: Stanford University Press, 1996.

Liberace. *Liberace: An Autobiography.* New York: Putnam, 1973.

Liberace. *The Things I Love.* New York: Grosset and Dunlap, 1976.

Liberace. *The Wonderful Private World of Liberace.* New York: Harper and Row, 1986.

Pyron, Darden Asbury. *Liberace: An American Boy.* Chicago: University of Chicago Press, 2001.

Thomas, Bob. *Liberace: The True Story.* New York: St. Martin's Press, 1987.

Thorson, Scott, with Alex Thorleifson. *Behind the Candelabra: My Life with Liberace.* New York: Dutton, 1988.

Liberty

More than one American magazine since the late nineteenth century has been titled *Liberty.* It was the name appropriately chosen by philosophical anarchist Benjamin Ricketson Tucker (1864–1939) for the journal he published from 1881 to 1908. The most popular *Liberty*, however, was probably the mass-circulation pulp magazine that reached a circulation of more than two million during the 1930s, when it was controlled by the eccentric publisher Bernarr Macfadden. In more recent years, a small libertarian periodical that advocated tax reform and government noninterference in personal freedoms was also called *Liberty.*

The first issue of Tucker's *Liberty* made its appearance in Boston in August 1881; in 1892 the magazine moved to New York, where it was based until a fire put it out of business twenty-seven years later. Its statement of purpose as expressed in the first issue was a militant one: "Monopoly and privilege must be destroyed, opportunity afforded, and competition encouraged. This is *Liberty*'s work and 'Down with Authority' her war-cry." Tucker himself wrote many of the screeds advocating freedom of the individual from domination by the state and promoting radical causes of the day, including birth control, free love, and women's suffrage.

Tucker believed that the state should eventually be dissolved through nonviolent means, which was to him the only way of ending the inequities of the capitalist system; he thus railed loudly against the banking and monetary system for its enslavement of labor. He also urged U.S. citizens to refuse to exercise their right to vote, believing that by participating in elections they were implicating themselves in politics designed to maintain the power structure. In the pages of *Liberty*, Tucker also espoused the self-reliant philosophy of American essayists Ralph Waldo Emerson and Henry David Thoreau and defended Walt Whitman's verse collection *Leaves of Grass* against critics who deemed it obscene. When the magazine's offices were destroyed by fire in 1908, Tucker moved to Nice in the south of France and later to Monte Carlo in Monaco.

Another magazine bearing the name of *Liberty* was ranked as one of the three major weeklies in the United States—along with *Collier's*, *Literary Digest*, and the *Saturday Evening Post*—at the beginning of the 1930s. *Liberty* claimed a large circulation when it was purchased by Macfadden in 1931 from its previous owners, Robert McCormick of the *Chicago Tribune* and Joseph Patterson of the *New York Daily News.* Macfadden, who made a fortune in publishing somewhat seamy pulp magazines of the true-confession and detective variety, was also publisher of the notorious New York *Evening Graphic*, a sensational paper that was a prototype of the later supermarket tabloid. He first placed *Liberty* at the service of Franklin D. Roosevelt's 1932 presidential campaign and then, under editor Fulton Oursler, turned it into a cheap, sensational magazine with a focus on adventure stories, sex, and scandal printed on low-quality newsprint. Each article was accompanied by a reading time note to inform supposedly busy readers how many minutes and seconds they could expect to spend on the piece.

Macfadden's escapist magazines were popular during the Great Depression, reaching a combined circulation of seven million by 1935, but *Liberty* began to decline soon afterward, a victim of its fuzzy editorial focus, its little bit of everything approach, and its failure to define its readership. Even Macfadden's practice of donning a leopard-skin loincloth to lead his employees in morning calisthenics could not save *Liberty*, which folded in 1942. After leaving the publication, Oursler underwent a well-publicized religious conversion and became a senior editor of *Reader's Digest*, to which he contributed inspirational pieces. He was perhaps best known, however, as the author of *The Greatest Story Ever Told*, about the life of Jesus Christ.

Edward Moran

SEE ALSO: *Confession Magazines; The Great Depression; Macfadden, Bernarr; Pulp Magazines; The* Saturday Evening Post*; Tabloids.*

BIBLIOGRAPHY

Reed, David. *The Popular Magazine in Britain and the United States.* London: British Library, 1997.

Tebbel, John. *The American Magazine: A Compact History.* New York: Hawthorn Books, 1969.

Tebbel, John, and Mary Ellen Zuckerman. *The Magazine in America: 1741–1990.* New York: Oxford University Press, 1991.

Wood, James Playsted. *Magazines in the United States.* New York: Ronald Press, 1971.

Young, William H., and Nancy K. Young. *The 1930s.* Westport, CT: Greenwood Press, 2002.

Lichtenstein, Roy *(1923–1997)*

Artist Roy Lichtenstein was one of the foremost members of the Pop Art movement, which challenged traditional definitions of art beginning in the 1960s. Lichtenstein's trademark style, developed by 1962, was painting in the form of a comic-strip frame. In famous works such as *Hopeless* (1963) and *Whaam!* (1963) he borrowed the bright colors, flat forms, simple scenes, and printing processes of the newspaper comic and expanded them to the large canvas, right down to the "Ben Day" dots and dialogue balloons. In the mid-1960s Lichtenstein used the style to depict images from historical art styles such as Abstract Expressionism and De Stijl. Whereas Pop Art in general seemed to critique the vapid world of everyday life and the secularization of high culture, Lichtenstein's remained ambiguous—though he continued to create public sculptures and murals as well as private art until his death in 1997, he never explained whether he was mocking the banality of modern culture or finding beauty in the ordinary.

Dale Allen Gyure

SEE ALSO: *Abstract Expressionism; Comics; Pop Art; Warhol, Andy.*

BIBLIOGRAPHY

Alloway, Lawrence. *Roy Lichtenstein.* New York: Abbeville Press, 1983.

Coplans, John. *Roy Lichtenstein.* New York: Praeger Publishers, 1972.

Lichtenstein, Roy. *Roy Lichtenstein: Pop-Paintings, 1961–1969.* New York: W. W. Norton, 1989.

Mercurio, Gianni. *Roy Lichtenstein: Meditations on Art.* New York: Skira, 2010.

Life

Two of the most prominent magazines ever published in the United States have borne the name *Life*, each vastly different in style and content but a unique mirror of the tastes and images of its era. The first, published from 1883 to 1936, offered polished humor and satire and was renowned for the "Gibson Girl" (and "Gibson Man") illustrations of Charles Dana Gibson that embodied the standards of the turn-of-the-twentieth-century young sophisticate. As this magazine foundered in the 1930s, publishing mogul Henry Luce spent $96,000 to purchase its "name and good will" in order to create his own version of *Life*, a slick, photo-oriented magazine published weekly from 1936 to 1972 and less frequently thereafter. During the peak of its influence from the 1940s through the 1960s, this second *Life*, a visual companion of sorts to *Time*, Luce's weekly newsmagazine, exalted the art of photojournalism to unprecedented levels by offering a graphic snapshot of American manners and morals to millions of readers—and helped shape public opinion on issues ranging from the role of America in world affairs to the role of the "Negro" at home and from the perils of fascism and communism to the realities of an affluent postwar society.

For the first thirty-six years of its existence, Luce's *Life* was arguably America's most influential mass magazine, one whose generalized approach gave it an advantage in successfully negotiating many of the contradictions that more specialized publications could not. It advanced the cult of the celebrity without resorting to tabloid sensationalism or gossip; it extolled the can-do attitude of the homespun war hero without glorifying militarism; it presented an image of a more homogeneous America without neglecting the plight of the poor and racial minorities; it sent a Republican message of order and authority without treading on the Democratic predilection for the common person. *Life* did not aspire to be either as highbrow as the *Saturday Review* or as specialized as the *Literary Digest*, but it did bring to its multifaceted readers a commendable grab bag of visually outstanding articles on everything from medieval architecture to Ernest Hemingway to grand opera, albeit often side by side with pieces depicting amusing farm animals or eccentric folk artisans.

EARLY DAYS

The first of the two *Life* magazines was founded in New York City by John Ames Mitchell, a Harvard graduate, who appointed Edward Martin Sandford, a classmate who had founded the *Harvard Lampoon* in 1876, as its first editor. Combining satire, verse, and criticism with advertisements for luxury products, *Life* became, as Christopher Gray wrote in the *New York Times* on November 5, 1995, "sophisticated and satirical, something like the old *Spy* magazine without the nastiness." Publisher Mitchell later commissioned the architectural firm Carrére and Hastings to erect an elaborate beaux arts headquarters for its editorial offices, helping authenticate New York City's role as the nation's nerve center of publishing and image making. For a while, illustrator Gibson occupied the building's atelier, from which he issued the Gibson Girl—and Gibson Man—illustrations that defined the look of his generation.

By the mid-1930s Luce, who had founded *Time* magazine in 1922 and *Fortune* in 1930, had established a work group within his publishing empire to develop plans for an American "picture magazine" based on the model of European periodicals such as the Parisian *Vu* or the *Illustrated London News*. Working from offices in New York's Chrysler Building, the group included John Stuart Martin, a *Time* editor, researcher Natasha von Hoershelman, and a Yale graduate named Dwight Macdonald, who later achieved renown as an essayist and critic. But much of the concept for the new magazine came from an employee of a rival publisher, Clare Boothe Brokaw, an editorial staffer at *Vanity Fair* magazine who became Luce's second wife in 1935. When the two met for the first time, Brokaw proposed an idea she had been unsuccessfully trying to sell to her own publishers at *Condé Nast*, one that would report "not *all* the news nor, necessarily, the most important news, but the most interesting and exciting news," using photographs. Those photographs were to be interpreted through accompanying articles by capable writers and journalists.

Luce was especially fascinated with what he termed the "picture-magic" capabilities of photography, especially in the new German miniature cameras such as the Leica that enabled photojournalists to expand the limitations of candid photography. The pictures were then featured in articles such as "*Life* Goes to a Party." Luce had already become convinced of the power of the visual image in journalism through his experience as producer of the popular *March of Time* newsreels, which reached millions of American moviegoers. His hiring of Kurt Korff, a German, as picture consultant, underscored his commitment to produce a magazine "designed to capture and occupy the position of No. 1 look-through magazine of America . . . the damnedest best non-pornographic look-through magazine in the United States."

LAUNCH

An early working title for this proposed ten-cents-a-copy "look-through magazine" in its first prospectus was *Dime: The Show-Book of the World*, a designation greeted with derision by colleagues who feared the name would be confused with that of *Time*. Before the first issue of *Life* hit the newsstands, other names considered but rejected for the fledgling periodical included *Album*, *Eye*, *Flash*, *Go*, *Nuze-Vuze*, *Scan*, *See*, *Snap*, and *Wide Awake!* In the meantime, Macdonald had been soliciting dossiers from the world's leading photographers, including Henri Cartier-Bresson, who had to turn down a request for more work due to other commitments.

The original *Life* photographers were Margaret Bourke-White, Alfred Eisenstaedt, Tom McAvoy, and Peter Stackpole. Robert Capa, another early cameraman whose work was often published by *Life*, remained an independent contractor for most of his career. Arguably the most famous and instantly recognizable photograph *Life* ran was Eisenstaedt's shot of an exuberant sailor and nurse lost in a kiss in Times Square during V-J celebrations in the summer of 1945. Loudon Wainwright, who edited *Life* when it became a monthly in the late 1970s, suggested that an interest in the lives of ordinary people like the nurse and the sailor was what made *Life* such a powerful medium. As he wrote in his memoir *The Great American Magazine: An Inside History of Life*: "Whatever its preoccupations with royalty and politics and the high and low jinks of the famous . . . *Life*'s greatest resource for its best picture stories would always be the lives of ordinary people, their work, their pleasure, their follies, their anguish. Such stories touched virtually every reader."

The cover of the first volume of *Life*, published on November 23, 1936, featured Bourke-White's dramatically lit photograph of Fort Peck Dam, a proud artifact of the Works Progress Administration's (WPA) contribution to public works in Depression-era America. Inside, a famous editorial photograph of a doctor in a surgical mask holding the newborn George Story upside down appears with the double-entendre caption "Life Begins." The florid caption encapsulated what the magazine was about and set the style that other captions continued to imitate over the next thirty-six years. "The camera," it read, "records the most vital moment in any life: Its beginning. A few hours ago, the child lay restless in its mother's womb. A second ago, its fetal life was rudely ended when the surgeon snapped its umbilical cord. . . . Suddenly the baby's new and independent life begins. He jerks up his arms, bends his knees and, with his first short breath, gives out a red-faced cry." For *Life*'s twenty-fifth anniversary in 1961, Story was pictured holding his own daughter; he was also featured in *Life's* fiftieth birthday issue in 1986 and in its sixtieth birthday issue in 1996.

A WINNING FORMULA

From the first issue, the magazine's cover bore the familiar red rectangle in the upper-left corner with the word *Life* in white sans-serif capitals, a logo that with notable exceptions appeared on every one of the more than 2,000 issues for the next six decades. The logo was dropped entirely from the cover of the April 26, 1937, issue, which bore a leghorn rooster, and it was printed twice in black instead for issues memorializing slain president John F. Kennedy in 1963 and once in green for an Earth Day cover in 1990. Until 1963, the cover of *Life* also featured a distinctive red border along its bottom.

For the next thirty-six years, until December 29, 1972, *Life* appeared weekly. From 1973 through 1977 it appeared only as a twice-yearly special issue. In 1978 it began monthly publication, with occasional special single issues making it a "fourteenthly" (as in 1989) or even "fifteenthly" (as in 1988 and 1990). In 1991, during the Persian Gulf War, it resumed weekly publication for the duration of the conflict. From its earliest days, *Life* relied on a tried-and-true formula of outstanding photographs presented in a wide variety of departments, ranging from in-depth reportage on breaking news to features that relied on clever juxtapositions of text and image or on photo spreads of children and animals, singly or in tandem.

Despite its generally conservative stance on many social and cultural issues, *Life*, from its earliest days, occasionally published material that made it a target for censors. On April 11, 1938, one of its first issues was banned in many localities for its quite nonprurient portrayal of scenes from the educational film *The Birth of a Baby*. Charges were quickly dropped, with many public figures, including First Lady Eleanor Roosevelt, backing *Life*'s stance. Another controversy erupted in 1955 when *Life* published photographer Lennart Nilsson's images of the human embryo, which some anti-abortionists later used to justify their argument that life begins at conception. "Maybe . . . it starts with a kiss," remarked Nilsson. Also in the early 1950s *Life* published a reproduction of Tom Kelley's 1949 calendar shot of a nude Marilyn Monroe.

WAR COVERAGE

Life quickly sold out its first press run of 250,000 newsstand copies and within a year reached a circulation of 1.5 million, which cost the magazine much revenue because its initial advertising rates were pegged to a smaller circulation. Within four years, it was claiming an audience of nearly twenty million readers each week. Over its thirty-six-year span as a weekly, *Life*, in the words of Loudon Wainwright, became "the most successful weekly the world has ever known," reaching a circulation of 8.5 million at its peak.

Life came into its own with its extensive coverage of World War II, both on the battlefield and on the home front. *Life* photographers sought and found hazardous assignments on the front lines, preferring this direct journalism to the practice of some other publications in accepting staged photographs distributed by the War Department. *Life*'s weekly portrayal of the horrors of war—and of the grit and determination of Americans and their allies—helped create a sense of national unity and purpose far beyond that of earlier eras before spot-news photography had been developed.

Although Mathew Brady pioneered the use of the camera on the battlefield some eighty years earlier, he did not portray the home front as carefully and as craftily as did *Life*. Through its "Day in the Life of . . . " feature, in which photographers and reporters covered simultaneous events in different parts of the country, *Life* helped readers take comfort in seeing a national pattern emerge through the mosaic of local color. This was particularly effective in home-front reporting during World War II, in the feature "American Sunday." Describing the section, Wainwright wrote: "In this somewhat grandiose and typically cornball effort, sixteen photographers from coast to coast took pictures on a single day that would emphasize our sturdy unanimity. . . . What it all added up to was a forgivably dull exercise in patriotism by photography, a sort of Norman Rockwellism in pictures that was supposed to make the readers feel powerfully joined together in a common cause—which, in fact, they already did." In a sense *Life* was using its photographers to replicate what Rockwell was creating with pen and ink for the rival *Saturday Evening Post*: a homespun, motherhood-and-apple-pie version of America whose very guilelessness in the face of militarism and fascism became one of the strongest weapons in its arsenal.

Luce himself, the son of Presbyterian missionaries in China, brought a secular evangelicalism to his role as publisher. On February 17, 1941, when isolationism was in fashion among many American political leaders, Luce reserved five photo-free pages in *Life* for his famous essay, "The American Century," in which he pontificated on the role he believed the United States was destined to play in the world arena. He had earlier warned his *Time-Life* colleagues that "the country is in danger. Danger. Danger," and urged them to "cultivate the Martial Spirit" and to be "hawk-eyed in our observation of Preparedness."

In "The American Century," Luce articulated several points that anticipated the American presence in the postwar world, predicting the nurturing of free enterprise and human progress among its most important national goals. Presaging the Marshall Plan and other examples of American humanitarian and economic aid, Luce declared, "We must undertake now to be the Good Samaritan of the entire world. It is the manifest duty of this country to undertake to feed all the people of the world who as a result of this worldwide collapse of civilization are hungry and destitute." Luce's formative years in Asia gave him a lifelong sympathy for China, and he became an ardent supporter of Chiang Kai-shek, a policy that Americans came to support in part because so many of them learned about Asian affairs through the lens of *Life*.

AFFLUENCE AND DISILLUSIONMENT

Luce's idealistic sermon struck a sympathetic chord with the masses of the American people—many of whom were subscribers to *Life*—who emerged from World War II with a heightened sense of purpose about their national identity. With echoes of "The American Century" in their heads, *Life*'s editors and photographers gave a tacit blessing to the new consumer society being created by newly affluent readers as they moved to the suburbs in the 1950s and 1960s. Luce, a Calvinist at heart, had essentially anointed their affluence as a sign of election and an opportunity for national benevolence. Even in the arena of domestic life, *Life* emerged as a powerful if unconscious player in bridging some of the nation's divisions over class and race.

While Luce and the power elite he represented naturally encouraged a more gradualist approach to social change, the graphic immediacy of the photographs in the pages of *Life* helped call attention to the ills of American society. In the decades following World War II, side by side with its frivolous stories on show business and fads, the magazine gave prominent though dispassionate coverage to the plight of blacks in the South, whites in Appalachia, and Native Americans on reservations. *Life* was not at all a muckraking magazine, but by permitting its camera's eye to rove across the nation's psychic landscape, it played a role in dissolving stubborn sectionalisms and replacing them with a greater sense of national civic purpose.

Photographs in the 1940s and 1950s of black children in dingy and overcrowded segregated classrooms helped fuel the nation's determination to end Jim Crow laws. As early as 1938 *Life* published an in-depth fourteen-page feature titled "Negroes: The U.S. Also Has a Minority Problem" that went beyond what other mass-circulation periodicals had done. Despite a tone that sounds patronizing by later standards, the feature was praised by black leaders, including Duke Ellington, who declared his belief that it was "one of the fairest and most comprehensive articles ever to appear in a national publication." In the 1960s, when Hedley Donovan was editor, *Life* supplemented the role of the television networks in publishing graphic pictures of American casualties in Vietnam. One of its most moving issues, published June 27, 1969, ran thumbnail portraits of most of the 242 Americans killed in Vietnam in the week beginning May 28. The spread personalized the conflict for millions of Americans who recognized their kinfolk and neighbors in those pages.

EVOLVING TO THE END

Always striving for an exclusive scoop, *Life* quickly purchased rights to the classic Abraham Zapruder movie of the Kennedy assassination and published all but the goriest shots in its next available issue. In 1971, however, the magazine was the victim of a hoax when it acquired what it believed was the autobiography of Howard Hughes, purportedly based on a series of interviews that author Clifford Irving had held with the billionaire recluse. Irving's scheme unraveled when Hughes, who had never met Irving, threatened to sue. By that time it was becoming clear that the mass audience that was once *Life*'s mainstay (as well as that of *Look* and the *Saturday Evening Post*) was vanishing, giving way to television and other sources of information and entertainment. Besieged by overwhelming production costs and the withdrawal of some large advertisers, *Life* ceased weekly publication with its December 29, 1972, issue. It reemerged as a semiannual from 1973 through 1977 before being reborn as a monthly in 1978, with occasional special editions each year.

At the dawn of the twenty-first century, *Life* published its last issue. By 2000 circulation had plummeted to a little more than 1.5 million as a result of the Internet and the explosion of information available through an assortment of new technologies. However, *Life* is still considered the most popular magazine ever published in the United States. In addition to Eisenstaedt's photograph of the young couple, *Life* is remembered for such photographic moments as the Beatles cavorting in a Miami swimming pool as caught by John Loengard in 1964 and Bill Eppridge's 1968 photo of Robert Kennedy lying dead on the floor of a Los Angles hotel after being hit by an assassin's bullet. *Life* keeps discovering new energy when there seems to be nothing left: in 2004 the magazine resurfaced as an insert in weekend editions of newspapers, with stories on subjects ranging from celebrities to social issues—an incarnation that lasted until 2007.

Edward Moran

SEE ALSO: *The Beatles; Condé Nast; Earth Day; Ellington, Duke;* Fortune*; Gibson Girl; The Great Depression; Hemingway, Ernest; The Internet; Kennedy Assassination; Luce, Henry; Rockwell, Norman; The* Saturday Evening Post*;* Time*;* Vanity Fair*; Works Progress Administration (WPA) Murals; World War II.*

BIBLIOGRAPHY

Brinkley, Alan. *The Publisher: Henry Luce and His American Century*. New York: Alfred A. Knopf, 2010.

Doss, Erika. *Looking at "Life" Magazine*. Washington, DC: Smithsonian Institution Press, 2001.

Hamblin, Dora Jane. *That Was the Life*. New York: W. W. Norton, 1977.

Reed, David. *The Popular Magazine in Britain and the United States, 1880–1960*. London: The British Library, 1997.

Tebbel, John, *The American Magazine: A Compact History*. New York: Hawthorn Books, 1969.

Tebbel, John, and Mary Ellen Zuckerman. *The Magazine in America: 1741–1990*. New York: Oxford University Press, 1991.

Wainwright, Loudon. *The Great American Magazine: An Inside History of "Life."* New York: Alfred A. Knopf, 1986.

Wood, James Playsted. *Magazines in the United States*. New York: Ronald Press, 1971.

The Life of Riley

The 1950s family television program *The Life of Riley* offered one of situation comedy's original "dopey dads" as a protagonist and was successful in laying the foundation for later working-class sitcoms such as *The Honeymooners* and *Roseanne*. Unlike his counterparts on *Father Knows Best* and *Leave It to Beaver*, the blue-collar family man Chester A. Riley was constantly befuddled by life's minor inconveniences, and his frequently uttered exclamation, "What a revoltin' development this is!" after creating confusion for his long-suffering family, became a catchphrase.

William Bendix had originated the Riley role on radio in 1944, but it was Jackie Gleason who first brought the popular character to the small screen for the DuMont Network in 1949. This initial series lasted only one season, but NBC revived Riley in 1953, starring William Bendix in a return to his signature role. The show ended a successful six-season run in 1958.

Charles Coletta

SEE ALSO: Father Knows Best*; Gleason, Jackie;* Leave It to Beaver*;* Roseanne*; Sitcom; Television.*

BIBLIOGRAPHY

Castleman, Harry, and Walter Podrazik. *Harry and Wally's Favorite TV Shows*. New York: Prentice Hall, 1989.

Mitz, Rick. *The Great TV Sitcom Book*. New York: Perigee, 1983.

Li'l Abner

The *Li'l Abner* comic strip was a child of the Great Depression of the 1930s, a period when country bumpkins, poverty, and rural lifestyles were perfectly acceptable subjects for a comic strip. Its creator, Al Capp, was a raucous and audacious humorist, capable of mixing barnyard humor with increasingly perceptive social satire. He and his assorted assistants were also good at drawing pretty young women. Launched by the United Feature Syndicate in 1934, the newspaper strip was an immediate success, and by the 1940s Capp and his title character, Abner Yokum, were nationally famous and being written up in *Life*, *Time*, and various other popular publications. By that time the strip was appearing in about 900 newspapers. The strip lasted until 1977 and gave the United States an unofficial national holiday and quite a few catchphrases and memorable characters.

Abner, who dwells in the benighted rural community of Dogpatch, remains steadfastly naive and obtuse throughout the long run of the feature. He lives in a cabin with his Mammy, who is the boss of the family and possesses assorted mystical powers; his Pappy; and their pig, Salomey. Clueless when it comes to romance, Abner takes a long time even to realize that he is being pursued by the lovely, blond, and sparsely clad Daisy Mae. In order to give the maiden ladies of Dogpatch a chance with the other obtuse, or just downright reluctant, bachelors, Capp introduced Sadie Hawkins Day in the late 1930s. During this annual ritual the eligible bachelors get a running start, and then the unmarried women take off in pursuit. Any woman who catches a man is allowed to keep him and drag him immediately to the local preacher, Marryin' Sam. This festivity caught on with the public, and high schools and colleges all across the country staged similar events.

Among the many odd and eccentric characters that Capp concocted were Moonbeam McSwine, Earthquake McGoon, Evil Eye Fleagle, Hairless Joe and Lonesome Polecat (brewers of Kickapoo Joy Juice), Lena the Hyena (who lived in the country of Lower Slobbovia, somewhat of an icebound Dogpatch, "where the favorite dish of the natives is raw polar bear and vice versa"), General Bullmoose (the epitome of ruthless and swinish business tycoons), Senator Jack S. Phogbound, the Shmoos, and the Kigmies. These last two creatures represented, respectively, consumer greed and prejudice. The strip made fun of a wide range of contemporary fads and foibles, including Frank Sinatra, zoot suits, beauty contests, and superheroes. Capp spoofed Chester Gould's *Dick Tracy*, too, by making Abner a dedicated fan of an even more brutal and invulnerable sleuth named Fearless Fosdick. Both Fosdick and his creator Lester Gooch were Li'l Abner's "ideels."

Although Abner steadfastly refuses to become any brighter, he does give in and marries Daisy Mae in 1952. The nuptials, commemorated with a *Life* cover featuring Abner, Daisy Mae, and Marryin' Sam, garnered Capp a good deal of publicity. But he eventually came to regret the move, blaming the strip's decline from the 1950s to the 1970s on the fact that a married Li'l Abner did not seem as interesting as a single one.

Equally important, though, to the strip's loss of popularity was Capp's perceived shift from liberal to conservative. "My politics didn't change," he insisted. "I had always been for those who were despised, disgraced and denounced by other people." He also asserted that conservatives hated him right to the end. Be that as it may, readers, especially younger ones, were not especially amused by the attacks on campus demonstrations and the antiwar movement. Caricaturing activist folk singer Joan Baez as Joanie Phonie did not inspire sufficient laughter. An ailing Capp finally decided to shut down the whole operation in November 1977. The circulation of *Li'l Abner* had by then dropped to about 300 papers.

In its prime the strip had branched out into several areas. First came *Li'l Abner* Big Little Books, then the strip was regularly reprinted in *Tip Top Comics* and *Comics on Parade*. There was a short-lived radio show starring John Hodiak, a movie that featured Buster Keaton as Lonesome Polecat in 1940 (and another movie in 1959), and a lackluster series of five animated cartoons out of Columbia Pictures in the mid-1940s.

In November 1956 a *Li'l Abner* musical opened at the St. James Theatre on Broadway with Peter Palmer as Abner, Edie Adams as Daisy Mae, Stubby Kaye as Marryin' Sam, and Tina Louise as Appassionata Von Climax. It ran for just under 700 performances and later became a successful movie musical. Capp died in 1979.

Ron Goulart

SEE ALSO: *Baez, Joan; Broadway; Comic Books; Dick Tracy; The Great Depression; Keaton, Buster; Radio; Sinatra, Frank; Student Demonstrations; Zoot Suit.*

BIBLIOGRAPHY

Berger, Arthur Asa. *Li'l Abner: A Study in American Satire.* New York: Twayne, 1969.

Capp, Al. *The World of Li'l Abner.* New York: Farrar, Straus and Young, 1953.

Capp, Al. *The Best of Li'l Abner.* New York: Holt, Rinehart, and Winston, 1978.

Goulart, Ron. *The Funnies.* Holbrook: Adams Publishing, 1995.

Marschall, Richard. *America's Great Comic Strip Artists.* New York: Abbeville Press, 1989.

Sheridan, Martin. *Comics and Their Creators.* Boston: Hale, Cushman & Flint, 1942.

Theroux, Alexander. *The Enigma of Al Capp.* Seattle, WA: Fantagraphics Books, 1999.

Limbaugh, Rush *(1951–)*

The undeniable king of conservative talk radio since the 1990s, Rush Limbaugh spread his vituperative conservative agenda across the airwaves, making him one of the most controversial and talked-about public figures in the United States. The new era of talk radio was made possible through satellite technology, which allowed an AM radio program to be broadcast live across the United States (or even the world), enabling listeners to call in to a show and participate. Some of these programs were devoted to sports, whereas others practiced a mixture of crude sexual titillation and outrageous social commentary. The most popular genre of talk radio, however, involved political commentary, and the czar of this milieu was undeniably Rush Limbaugh.

Rush Hudson Limbaugh III was born in 1951 in Cape Girardeau, Missouri, where he developed an interest in radio at a young age, working as a deejay at a local station while still in high school. Admitted to Southeast Missouri State College, he dropped out after his freshman year. He then held a number of jobs at small radio stations around the country, followed by five years as a public relations assistant for the Kansas City Royals baseball team. Limbaugh returned to radio in 1983, when a Kansas City station hired him as a talk-show host and commentator. It was in this job that he began to manifest what would become his characteristic style, although neither his audience nor his employer at the time found Limbaugh's approach appealing, and he was fired.

In 1984 Limbaugh got an on-air job at KFBK, a San Diego, California, radio station that was in dire financial trouble

Rush Limbaugh. *Rush Limbaugh's brand of conservative commentary has made him one of the most popular and most controversial media figures on the political scene.* JOHN MEDINA/STRINGER/WIREIMAGE/GETTY IMAGES.

and whose owners were willing to gamble on something new. They gave Limbaugh a three-hour morning show, along with free rein to be as outrageous as he wished. This time, Limbaugh's style, a blend of conservative politics and acid humor directed at liberals, was more successful. Limbaugh's show soon became the most popular radio program in the city.

In 1988 Limbaugh's reputation and ratings came to the attention of Edward McLaughlin, who had just founded the Excellence in Broadcasting Network, a radio syndicate with fifty member stations. Limbaugh relocated to New York City and addressed a national audience for the first time. He was a hit almost instantly. His audience (largely white, male, conservative, and young) delighted in his characterization of liberals as "feminazis," "environmental wackos," and "hustlers for the homeless." Limbaugh took calls from listeners while on the air, and many of his fans began expressing their agreement with him by uttering a single word: *dittoes*.

A MULTIMEDIA PHENOMENON

Limbaugh's popularity stemmed not only from his verbal jabs at the Left but also his use of words with audio effects. A regular segment titled "AIDS Update" featured singer Dionne Warwick's song "I'll Never Love This Way Again" in the background, and a report on liberal efforts to protect endangered species was accompanied by singer Andy Williams's "Born Free," interrupted by automatic weapons fire and the sound of animals screaming. Many critics believe that Limbaugh reached his nadir when he began subjecting the rare hostile phone call to a "caller abortion," in which he responded to the caller with the sound of a vacuum pump and then disconnected the call.

Limbaugh's influence went beyond his ability to bring in vast audiences and big bucks. He is widely believed to have played a role in the 1994 elections, when the Republicans recaptured the majority in the House of Representatives. Limbaugh's on-air advocacy was supplemented by numerous personal appearances at Republican fund-raising events. He also affected legislation. President Bill Clinton's lobby reform bill initially had bipartisan support when he sent it to the House in 1995, but Speaker Newt Gingrich decided at the last moment to oppose it after he faxed his views to Limbaugh, who strongly criticized the plan on the air. The result: members of Congress received a deluge of phone calls opposing lobbying reform, and the bill's support evaporated.

For a period of time during the 1990s, Limbaugh was a multimedia phenomenon. In addition to his three-hour radio show, he had a half-hour television program in syndication around the country. Further, his book, *The Way Things Ought to Be* (1992), was a best seller. Loyal fans could subscribe to a monthly newsletter, *The Limbaugh Letter*, which also told them how to purchase videotapes of their hero's personal appearances.

However, Limbaugh also experienced some setbacks in the mid-1990s as his act wore thin among moderate conservatives and liberal animosity against him mounted. His second book, *See, I Told You So* (1993), sold considerably fewer copies than his first. In 1996 Limbaugh decided to cancel his television show after a four-year run because of declining ratings. At about the same time, a few radio stations stopped carrying his program, just as comedian Al Franken's tongue-in-cheek book, *Rush Limbaugh Is a Big Fat Idiot and Other Observations* (1996) began to climb the best-seller lists.

In 2003 Limbaugh's fortunes would rise again because of his defense of President George W. Bush's decision to send troops into Iraq, launching the Persian Gulf War. As the war progressed, Limbaugh was also a vociferous and extreme critic of the opponents of the war. His visibility and influence as a conservative talk-show host increased, and he eventually became one of the leading voices of the conservative movement in the country. However, the cantankerous commentator also had his share of trouble. He began working as a sports analyst for ESPN in the early 2000s and in 2003 made racially charged comments about quarterback Donovan McNabb on the air. The resulting protests forced Limbaugh to resign. Later that year, he admitted publicly that he was addicted to the painkiller oxycodone and checked himself into a rehab facility. His problem with drugs did not end there. In 2006 he was arrested on charges of doctor shopping, going to multiple doctors to obtain more prescriptions for painkillers than was legal. He and the prosecutor reached a deal in which the prosecutor dropped the charges and Limbaugh agreed to continue treatment for his addiction.

CONSISTENTLY CONTROVERSIAL

Limbaugh's detractors pointed to his troubles as evidence of his hypocrisy, but his fans continued to support him. He has been consistently controversial and, inevitably, insulting to many who opposed his version of political truth. His critics have repeatedly pointed out his errors, but this seems to matter little to the millions of listeners who keep him at the top of the talk-show charts year after year.

In 2012 Limbaugh made remarks that ignited unprecedented levels of outrage. In February Congress held a hearing to determine whether the provision of the 2009 health care law that mandates that health insurers must cover birth control violated the religious freedom of employers who oppose contraception. Many people denounced the hearing because only male religious leaders testified. One witness, a female law student at Georgetown University, a Catholic institution, testified at the hearing, arguing that birth control should be covered by health insurance at religious institutions.

Limbaugh publicly blasted the young woman on his show, calling her a "slut," who was having so much sex that she could not afford her birth control and wanted the government to pay for it. Public anger over the insults was immediate and intense, and Limbaugh issued an apology a week later. Because of his comments, several of his shows advertisers, including Carbonite, LegalZoom, ProFlowers, and Quicken Loans, canceled their ads. A month later, however, Limbaugh claimed that his ratings had actually gone up because of his comments—even as advertisers continued to shun him. As 2012 progressed, it remained to be seen whether the conservative analyst would ultimately survive the controversy.

Justin Gustainis

SEE ALSO: *Cable TV; ESPN; Gulf Wars; Radio; Religious Right; Talk Radio; Television; Williams, Andy.*

BIBLIOGRAPHY

Chafets, Zev. *Rush Limbaugh: An Army of One*. New York: Sentinel, 2010.

Colford, Paul D. *The Rush Limbaugh Story: Talent on Loan from God; An Unauthorized Biography*. New York: St. Martin's, 1993.

Franken, Al. *Rush Limbaugh Is a Big Fat Idiot and Other Observations*. New York: Delacorte Press, 1996.

Haimson, Leonie, et al. *The Way Things Really Are: Debunking Rush Limbaugh on the Environment.* New York: Environmental Defense Fund, 1995.

Limbaugh, Rush. *The Way Things Ought to Be.* New York: Pocket Books, 1992.

Limbaugh, Rush. *See, I Told You So.* New York: Pocket Books, 1993.

Rendall, Steve; Jim Naureckas; and Jeff Cohen. *The Way Things Aren't: Rush Limbaugh's Reign of Error; Over 100 Outrageously False and Foolish Statements from America's Most Powerful Radio and TV Commentator.* New York: New Press, 1995.

Lincoln Center for the Performing Arts

At the inception of its initial fund-raising campaign, President Dwight D. Eisenhower hailed the Lincoln Center for the Performing Arts as the "great cultural adventure" that would transform 16 deteriorated acres on the West Side of Manhattan into a magnificent complex of auditoriums. The idea of bringing the educational and performing arts together in the largest such complex in the world was considered radical for its time. Following its ground breaking in 1959, Lincoln Center served as an unofficial referendum on how the new rich, as well as the masses, perceived the performing arts at the height of America's imperial age.

The center's architecture has been consistently criticized, and complaints that it incorporates all the worst architectural elements of its era and that it seems to turn its back on the city it is there to serve have been common. But the results have been undeniable: by the mid-1960s the media was announcing that a "cultural explosion" was at hand in the United States. *Fortune*'s futurist, Alvin Toffler, argued that "millions of Americans have been attracted to the arts, changing the composition of the audience profoundly."

The other side of the coin was that in the mid-1950s auditoriums in New York City were being demolished in favor of parking lots (Carnegie Hall was to be replaced by a skyscraper), and no opera company, symphony orchestra, or repertory theater company anywhere in the country had a fifty-two-week season. Ballet companies came in and out of existence with bewildering rapidity and based their finances on the whims of wealthy patrons, one of whom, Rebekah Harkness, danced along with the troupe. Loud protests about the overall depressing situation of the performing arts came mainly from performers. The public appeared largely indifferent.

TURNING IDEAS INTO REALITY

The bright, shining example of what *might* be, and the precursor of the Lincoln Center, was the New York City Center of Music, Drama, and Art. In 1943, after the Shriners failed to pay city taxes for a Mecca Temple in Midtown Manhattan, Mayor Fiorello H. LaGuardia encouraged the building's use for artistic purposes. In an amazingly short time, it housed a symphony orchestra led first by Leopold Stokowski and then by Leonard Bernstein, a ballet company directed by Lincoln Kirstein and choreographer George Balanchine, a drama company directed by José Ferrer, and an opera company whose performers included Beverly Sills.

The *New York Times* advised that "with 43 percent of patrons recording annual incomes under $5,000 and another 43 percent with incomes under $10,000, the Center is an undertaking for the 'Common Man.'" Better yet, 40 percent of patrons had college degrees, and more than a third were either working toward a graduate degree or already had one. Many could not afford tickets for Carnegie Hall or the Metropolitan Opera. But regardless of age or circumstance, attendees projected enthusiasm and willingness to support experiments in the arts.

The notion for Lincoln Center originated with LaGuardia in the 1930s when he conceived of a "Municipal Arts Center" near Manhattan's Rockefeller Center. The enormous structure he contemplated was to house the Museum of Modern Art, the Metropolitan Opera, and the New York Philharmonic. John D. Rockefeller Jr. and his sons grasped the value of such an assemblage of world-famous arts organizations near their majestic real estate development. Nelson Rockefeller, who had recently graduated from Dartmouth, volunteered as a fund-raiser. But the Great Depression was a bad time to test public opinion, and the plan was dropped.

Accounts of how Lincoln Center came to be and its significance in America's cultural history usually begin with a chance discussion held by John D. Rockefeller III at a September 1954 meeting of the Council for Foreign Relations in the Poconos. Two other board members brought him news that Carnegie Hall was set to be demolished and suggested that the Metropolitan Opera House should also be demolished. Rockefeller formed an exploratory committee and traveled to Europe for a reconnaissance of concert halls and opera houses.

WEALTHY BENEFACTORS

Fully persuaded that America must have equal or superior auditoriums to those in Europe, Rockefeller announced that he would head a permanent group seeking to construct a New York City arts center. He was not known to have an interest in the performing arts, so his willingness to lead the largest single private-sector fund-raising campaign to date in American history (raising the $184 million needed for completion) was surprising. Some suspected that reasons other than popular yearning for the performing arts had influenced Rockefeller.

In fact, they had. Rockefeller, who had presidential ambitions, wanted to ingratiate himself with the intelligentsia—voters like those who attended City Center performances. Furthermore, William Zeckendorf, a real estate developer, wanted to build a competing version of Rockefeller Center in Manhattan's Lincoln Square area. And not least, Robert Moses, New York's most astute political insider and then a Rockefeller ally, had access to federal and city funds for what promised to be the largest "coordinated Title I [urban redevelopment] project in the country," also earmarked for the Lincoln Square area. Ostensibly to replace the slums, Moses offered the public (and Rockefeller) a package that included the Metropolitan Opera, the New York Philharmonic, Fordham University's Law School, the Juilliard School of Music, and public housing.

The campaign for Lincoln Center proved a great many pundits wrong. Rockefeller family members invested $15 million in the facility and raised another $60 million from their wealthy acquaintances, because no other way could be found to complete the fund-raising effort. The repeated refusals to contribute to the campaign by New York's old and new commercial aristocracies demonstrated that they would attend performances—but not if they had to do more than buy tickets. Unless benefactions were tax deductible and/or immense sums in public funds were invested in the proposed facilities, the very rich preferred hearing performances in existing structures or in Europe.

The most staggering findings of all related to the reactions of the masses to a "cultural explosion." The vast expenditures of time and money did not produce anything near in imagination or appeal to what had been created at the City Center for a fraction of the cost. The masses did not initially flock to Lincoln Center.

COMMITMENT TO THE ARTS

Over the following years, the center expanded by recruiting other venues of New York's performing arts: the New York Philharmonic (1962); the Julliard School of Music and the Metropolitan Opera (1966); the New York City Opera, the New York City Ballet, and the New York Public Library for the Performing Arts (1965); the Chamber Music Society of Lincoln Center (1972); the Film Society of Lincoln Center (1974); Lincoln Center Theater (1985); and the School of American Ballet and Jazz at Lincoln Center (1996). By 2012 five million people were visiting Lincoln Center each year. The 16-acre complex continues to deliver on its promise to promote new artists and bring international artists to American audiences.

Lincoln Center's fiftieth anniversary in 2009 was accompanied by completion of major renovations at Promenade and the West 65th Street Corridor and resulted in the addition of a new street-level glass-walled television studio and a remodeled fountain and plaza. West 65th Street was renamed Street of the Arts. The state-of-the-art Rosemary and Meredith Willson Theater, which is housed in the newly christened Irene Diamond Building, also opened in time for the anniversary celebration. An exhibition, "Lincoln Center: Celebrating 50 Years," provided a display of 400 objects, ranging from photos and costumes to set pieces and records, all chronicling the center's illustrious history. To reach the widest audiences possible, Lincoln Center offers free concerts at special times such as the holiday season and Black History Month.

Milton Goldin

SEE ALSO: *Ballet; Bernstein, Leonard; Carnegie Hall; The Great Depression; Jazz; The* New York Times*; The Rockefeller Family.*

BIBLIOGRAPHY

Goldin, Milton. "'Why the Square?' John D. Rockefeller 3rd and the Creation of Lincoln Center for the Performing Arts." *Journal of Popular Culture*, Winter 1987, 17–30.

Longley, Marjorie; Louis Silverstein; and Samuel A. Tower. *America's Taste 1851–1959*. New York: Simon & Schuster, 1960.

"Lincoln Center Celebrates Itself." *American Theatre* 26, no. 9 (2009).

"Lincoln Center Undergoes a Dramatic Face Lift." *Architectural Record* 197, no. 2 (2008).

Marks, Peter. "It's a Success, but Is That Enough?" *New York Times*, October 27, 1996, 2:1.

Martin, Ralph G. *Lincoln Center for the Performing Arts*. New York: Prentice-Hall, 1971.

Muschamp, Herbert. "Critic's Notebook: Lincoln Center's Enduring Vision." *New York Times*, July 19, 1996, C:1.

Young, Edgar B. *Lincoln Center: The Building of an Institution*. New York: New York University Press, 1980.

Lindbergh, Anne Morrow *(1906–2001)*

Although Anne Morrow Lindbergh catapulted into the headlines after her 1929 marriage to celebrated aviator Charles Lindbergh, she achieved widespread recognition for her own writings in the fields of aviation and conservation. Lindbergh recounted her journey with her husband to China in *North to the Orient* (1935) and told of their 30,000-mile-above-the-ground survey of Atlantic air routes in *Listen! The Wind* (1938). These works attracted critical attention for their sensitive literary style; they also made Anne Lindbergh's travels the subject of public interest.

With the publication of *Gift from the Sea* (1955), Lindbergh became a leading advocate of the nascent environmental movement. The work, often described as a "love letter" to nature, became a national best seller. The awareness generated by *Gift from the Sea* primed the public for the writings of environmentalist Rachel Carson and helped make conservation palatable to mainstream America.

Jacob M. Appel

SEE ALSO: *Environmentalism; Lindbergh, Charles.*

BIBLIOGRAPHY

Herrmann, Dorothy. *Anne Morrow Lindbergh: A Gift for Life*. New York: Ticknor & Fields, 1992.

Hertog, Susan. *Anne Morrow Lindbergh: Her Life*. New York: Nan A. Talese, 1999.

Lindbergh, Anne Morrow. *The Flower and the Nettle: Diaries and Letters of Anne Morrow Lindbergh, 1936–1939*. New York: Harcourt Brace Jovanovich, 1976.

Lindbergh, Anne Morrow. *War Within and Without: Diaries and Letters of Anne Morrow Lindbergh, 1939–1944*. New York: Harcourt Brace Jovanovich, 1980.

Mayer, Elsie F. *My Window on the World: The Works of Anne Morrow Lindbergh*. Hamden, CT: Archon Books, 1988.

Milton, Joyce. *Loss of Eden: A Biography of Charles and Anne Morrow Lindbergh*. New York: HarperCollins, 1993.

Lindbergh, Charles *(1902–1974)*

Charles Lindbergh's 1927 nonstop solo flight across the Atlantic, the first of its kind, instantly transformed the twenty-five-year-old aviator into an international celebrity. The "Lone Eagle," a shy and uncomfortable youth, found himself at the center of history's first media blitz as journalists from across the globe tried to profit from the public's insatiable demand for Lindbergh news and gossip. Although Lindbergh's popularity peaked in the fad frenzy of the 1920s, he continued to be the subject of tabloid headlines throughout his life. He gained public sympathy after the kidnapping and murder of his son in 1932, was widely condemned for his German sympathies in the wake of World

War II, and finally rehabilitated himself as an early voice for the environmental conservation movement.

Lindbergh's diverse accomplishments range from the invention of a prototypic artificial heart to the publication of a Pulitzer Prize–winning memoir. Yet whereas "Lucky Lindy" contributed immensely to the field of aeronautics, his lasting significance is as one of the first—if not the first—popular celebrities whose private life in all its details became a matter of public interest and record.

The future aviation pioneer was born into a wealthy Minnesota family on February 4, 1902. His father, Charles Augustus Lindbergh Sr., represented Little Falls and the surrounding area in the United States Congress, and the young Lindbergh divided his childhood between the family farm and the drawing rooms of Washington's inner circle. He showed exceptional promise as a teenager and enrolled in an engineering program at the University of Wisconsin at the age of eighteen. Two years later, after learning to fly, he dropped out of the school to pursue the rugged, hand-to-mouth existence of an airmail pilot and barnstormer. He attended army flight school (1924–1925), then became a regular on the Robertson Aircraft Corporation's Chicago–St. Louis postal flight route. Here he attracted the attention of a group of Missouri businessmen who agreed to sponsor Lindbergh for the Orteig Prize—a $25,000 bounty offered by New York hotel magnate Raymond Orteig to the first aviator to fly nonstop from New York to Paris.

Charles Lindbergh. *Charles Lindbergh poses with the* Spirit of St Louis, *the plane he used to make the first nonstop solo flight across the Atlantic Ocean in 1927.* GENERAL PHOTOGRAPHIC AGENCY/ STRINGER/HULTON ARCHIVE/GETTY IMAGES.

THE TRANSATLANTIC FLIGHT

The preparations for Lindbergh's flight drew limited media coverage as other aviators had attempted the solo transatlantic voyage without success. Those in the media who took notice dubbed Lindbergh "the flying fool." Meanwhile his backers purchased a specially designed aircraft from the Ryan Aircraft Company of San Diego, California. Lindbergh dubbed it *The Spirit of St. Louis.* The plane itself would later become a celebrated artifact of American lore—the subject of countless books and an immensely popular display at the Smithsonian Institute's National Air and Space Museum. Lindbergh captained the monoplane on a test run from San Diego to New York with an overnight stop in St. Louis; the 20-hour, 21-minute trip set a transcontinental record.

On May 20, 1927, at precisely 7:52 a.m., Lindbergh departed from New York's Roosevelt Field on the 3,600-mile journey that would make him famous. Thirty-three and a half hours later he landed at Le Bourget Field on the outskirts of Paris. More than a hundred thousand Parisians came to welcome him. Similar receptions followed in London and Ottawa as millions of fans struggled to catch a glimpse of the overnight hero.

THE AFTERMATH OF THE FLIGHT: HONOR AND SUCCESS

Lindberg became the darling of governments and the upper class; King George of England presented him with the Air Force Cross and King Albert of Belgium honored him as a Knight of the Order of Leopold. After grand parades in New York City and Washington, President Calvin Coolidge personally pinned the Distinguished Flying Cross to Lindbergh's lapel. Myron Herrick, the United States ambassador to France, expressed the sentiments of millions when he wrote to the president, "Had we searched all America we could not have found a better type than young Lindbergh to represent the spirit and high purpose of our people."

Promoters offered Lindbergh lucrative theatrical and movie contracts worth almost $2 million. He rejected them outright, to popular acclaim. The young pilot instead offered his services to the Daniel Guggenheim Fund for the Promotion of Aeronautics and toured all forty-eight states as part of a campaign to promote aviation. His travels also took him to Latin America, where he fell in love with Anne Morrow, the daughter of American ambassador Dwight Morrow. The couple wed in 1929.

Lindbergh devoted the next five years of his life to various scientific causes. He promoted the research of rocket pioneer Robert Goddard (then a professor at Clark University) and convinced the Guggenheim family to bankroll the physicist's work; Goddard's discoveries later proved to be highly instrumental in the development of space travel and satellite technology. Lindbergh also invented a prototype of the artificial heart with French surgeon Alexis Carrel. Although the device could not yet be implanted in humans, it demonstrated that human tissue could be kept alive outside the body. Despite these accomplishments, Lindbergh quickly tired of incessant media attention and sought to avoid the limelight. He and his wife retreated from the public eye to a 390-acre compound in Hopewell, New Jersey.

THE LINDBERGH KIDNAPPING

Personal tragedy returned Lindbergh to the headlines in 1932 when his twenty-month-old son, Charles Augustus Jr., was kidnapped from the family's New Jersey estate. Ten weeks later, after Lindbergh paid a $50,000 ransom, the boy's body was found in the nearby woods. After a lengthy investigation, suspicion fell upon Richard Bruno Hauptmann, a German-born carpenter with a record of petty criminal offenses, and he was arrested in 1934.

The trial, which began on January 3, 1935, developed into a media circus. Critic H. L. Mencken echoed popular sentiment when he termed the event "the biggest story since the Resurrection." More than 60,000 curiosity seekers and 750 reporters converged on Flemington, New Jersey, in the hope of seeing the kidnapper. Vendors sold models of the ladder used to climb into the child's bedroom and specious "locks of the child's hair." In the courtroom Attorney General David Wilenz capitalized on prevailing anti-German sentiments and depicted the accused as "the filthiest and vilest snake that ever crawled through the grass." The prosecution also pioneered the use of scientific experts: calling on handwriting specialists and even a wood technologist to demonstrate that Hauptmann had written the ransom notes and constructed the ladder discovered near the crime scene.

The jury convicted Hauptmann of kidnapping and felony murder, and he was executed in 1936. In response to the case, Congress passed the "Lindbergh Law" making kidnapping a federal offense. The Lindberghs, now the recipients both of widespread public sympathy and renewed media attention, retreated to Europe to escape from the scrutiny of the press.

WWII CONTROVERSY

While in Europe, Lindbergh toured the aircraft industries of France and Germany. Hitler's Nazi regime feted the aviator and impressed him with the technological superiority of its air force: the Luftwaffe. Lindbergh was reported to claim that "the German air fleet could whip the Russian, French, and British air fleets combined." In 1938 Luftwaffe commander Hermann Goering presented Lindbergh with the Service Cross of the German Eagle. Three weeks later, Hitler's SS perpetrated the *Kristallnacht* massacre of Germany's Jews. Lindbergh refused to return the medal, and he later made anti-Semitic remarks that tarnished his previously untouchable reputation. He attracted additional notoriety when, after his return to the United States in 1939, he advocated American neutrality in World War II. He became a prominent spokesman for the America First Committee, an isolationist lobby, and publicly attacked President Franklin Roosevelt's foreign policy.

Lindbergh halted his antiwar activities following the Japanese attack on Pearl Harbor in 1941. He tried to enlist in Army Air Corps but was rejected. He flew fifty combat missions as a civilian adviser to the United Aircraft Corporation, but this service did little to repair his tarnished image. The aviator retired to Connecticut and Hawaii, where he served as a part-time adviser to several private airlines and the Department of Defense. President Dwight Eisenhower appointed him a brigadier general in the Air Force Reserves in 1954.

LEGACY

The final decades of Lindbergh's life were devoted to travel and environmental causes. He lobbied for the protection of the blue whale and opposed supersonic air travel on the grounds that it might harm the earth's atmosphere. He also devoted himself to the study of indigenous cultures in Southeast Asia and Africa. His memoir, *The Spirit of St. Louis* (1953), won the Pulitzer Prize in 1954. Charles Lindbergh died of cancer on August 26, 1974, at his family retreat on the Hawaiian island of Maui.

The Lindbergh craze continues to influence American culture long after Lindbergh's passing. Prior to the 1920s the press generally honored the privacy rights of public figures. Yet Lindbergh's combination of personal reserve and public celebrity made him the victim of one of the darkest episodes in the history of American reportage. For years after his flight, reporters stalked his home and family to feed the public minor details about his life. The media frenzy surrounding the "Lindbergh Baby" kidnapping paved the way for the sensational trials of Casey Anthony, Sam Sheppard, Candace Mossler, and Melvin Powers.

Although the publicity-shy Lindbergh turned down efforts to exploit his fame financially, other popular figures eagerly capitalized on the new celebrity craze. Lindbergh unwittingly opened the private lives of public figures to mass scrutiny. After 1927 "The Lone Eagle" discovered to his chagrin that America would no longer leave its heroes alone.

Jacob M. Appel

SEE ALSO: *Air Travel; Celebrity; Environmentalism; Lindbergh, Anne Morrow; The Twenties; World War II.*

BIBLIOGRAPHY

Alhgren, Gregory, and Stephen Monier. *Crime of the Century: The Lindbergh Kidnapping Hoax.* Boston: Branden Books, 1993.

Davis, Kenneth Sydney. *The Hero: Charles A. Lindbergh and the American Dream.* Garden City, NY: Doubleday, 1959.

Haines, Lynn, and Dora B. Haines. *The Lindberghs.* New York: Vanguard Press, 1931.

Handleman, Philip. *A Dream of Pilots.* Gretna, LA: Pelican Publishing, 2009.

Kennedy, Ludovic. *The Airman and the Carpenter: The Lindbergh Kidnapping and the Framing of Richard Hauptmann.* New York: Viking, 1985.

Lindbergh, Charles A. *The Spirit of St. Louis.* New York: Scribner, 1953.

Lindbergh, Charles A., and Fitzhugh Green. *We.* New York: Putnam, 1927.

Ross, Walter Sanford. *The Last Hero: Charles A. Lindbergh.* New York: Harper & Row, 1976.

Van Every, Dale, and Morris de Haven Tracy. *Charles Lindbergh: His Life.* New York: D. Appleton, 1927.

Linkletter, Art *(1912–2010)*

For more than sixty years, Art Linkletter performed before radio microphones and television cameras, first becoming widely known for two long-running shows: *House Party* on CBS TV and radio for more than twenty-five years and *People Are Funny* on NBC TV and radio for nineteen years. During his career he received four Emmy nominations and two Emmy Awards, as well as a Daytime Emmy Lifetime Achievement Award. His book, *Kids Say the Darndest Things!* remained number one on the nonfiction best-seller list for two consecutive years and was one of the top fourteen best sellers in U.S. publishing history.

Born in Moose Jaw, Saskatchewan, Canada, on July 17, 1912, Linkletter graduated from San Diego State College in 1934 and became program director at KGB, the local radio station. In 1935 he directed radio activities for the California International Exposition, followed by similar positions with the Texas Centennial Exposition (1936) and the San Francisco World's Fair (1937–1939). From 1940 to 1955 he was president of Linkletter Productions, writing, producing, and starring in West Coast radio shows such as *House Party* and *What's Doin', Ladies?*

Art Linkletter's House Party, which became television's longest-running daytime variety show, began on radio in 1944, originating from the West Coast. In 1952 his blend of audience participation and easygoing conversation made a smooth transition to television, where it remained a popular fixture until 1969. Audiences looked forward to a special daily feature of the show when Linkletter interviewed four young school children. He had a talent for eliciting comical reactions and humorous remarks from the kids, providing material for his series of books, *Kids Say the Darndest Things!*

Art Linkletter. *Art Linkletter turned his interviews with children into a best-selling series of humor books titled* Kids Say the Darndest Things. RON GALELLA, LTD./CONTRIBUTOR/RON GALELLA COLLECTION/GETTY IMAGES.

In 1954 Linkletter began hosting television's *People Are Funny*, one of the earliest audience-participation quiz shows. Contestants were chosen from the studio audience and involved in stunts to prove that people are funny. The stunts were designed to test such things as memory, level of greed, or decision making, with contestants being doused with water or hit with pies as penalties. Others would be asked to complete a task during the following week—for example, trying to cash a check written on a 40-pound watermelon—and report back with the results. A computer-dating segment was added to the show during the 1956–1957 season: a couple matched by a Univac computer became acquainted while answering questions in a quiz-show format.

In 1965 Linkletter became the host of *Hollywood Talent Scouts*, a variety show featuring young unknowns who had been discovered by celebrities. Tom Smothers introduced a young comedian named Pat Paulsen (who later worked on the Smothers Brothers show); actor Bob Crane presented a singer named Marilyn McCoo (later to become lead singer with the Fifth Dimension); and producer Carl Reiner brought along a writer from *The Dick Van Dyke Show*, Garry Marshall, to try his luck as a stand-up comic. Marshall later became producer of two of television's brightest sitcoms, *Happy Days* and *Laverne and Shirley*.

Linkletter did not confine his talents to show business; he became well known in the world of business, serving as chairman of Linkletter Enterprises and on the boards of directors of organizations such as MGM (Metro-Goldwyn-Mayer), Western Air Lines, and Kaiser Hospitals. He crusaded for social security reform as the National Chairman of the United Seniors Association and chairman of the board of UCLA's Center on Aging. In addition, his 1990 book, *Old Age Is Not for Sissies*, was successful, and he made frequent appearances on the public-speaking circuit to discuss the foibles of old age as well as the darn things kids say.

The darn things phenomenon in fact remained so popular that in 1995 CBS revived it in a comedy special hosted by Bill Cosby. It became a running series from 1998 to 2000, with Linkletter occasionally appearing as cohost. As Linkletter frequently told interviewers, "You live between your ears, you can't turn back the clock, but you can rewind it!" He was awarded a 2002 National Humanities Medal, originally known as the Charles Frankel prize, by then-president George W. Bush. In 2003 he was honored with a Daytime Emmy Lifetime Achievement Award and in 2005 was named a Disney Legend after appearing at the fiftieth anniversary of Disneyland's opening—he was the host of Disneyland's first opening day in 1955.

Linkletter continued to write inspirational books, and in 2005 he coauthored an antiaging handbook with Mark Victor Hansen titled *How to Make the Rest of Your Life the Best of Your Life*. In 2008 he suffered a mild stroke and began to curtail his public appearances. He died on May 26, 2010, at his home in Los Angeles.

Benjamin Griffith

SEE ALSO: *Cosby, Bill; Disney (Walt Disney Company); Emmy Awards;* Happy Days; Laverne and Shirley; *Marshall, Garry; MGM (Metro-Goldwyn-Mayer); Radio; Reiner, Carl; Sitcom; The Smothers Brothers; Stand-Up Comedy; Television; World's Fairs.*

BIBLIOGRAPHY

Brooks, Tim, and Earle Marsh. *The Complete Directory to Prime Time Network TV Shows: 1946–Present.* New York: Ballantine, 1981.

Hansen, Mark Victor, and Art Linkletter. *How to Make the Rest of Your Life the Best of Your Life.* Nashville, TN: Nelson Books, 2006.

Lackmann, Ron. *Same Time . . . Same Station: An A–Z Guide to Radio from Jack Benny to Howard Stern.* New York: Facts On File, 1996.

McNeil, Alex. *Total Television: A Comprehensive Guide to Programming from 1948 to the Present.* New York: Penguin, 1991.

The Lion King

The Lion King, the Walt Disney Company's animated feature about a young lion cub in Africa, ranks among the most popular and most profitable films of all time. When it was released in the summer of 1994, the movie set off a craze among young and old alike in the United States, eventually becoming the third-fastest film to earn more than $100 million at the box office. In addition, the movie brought in millions more through creative marketing tie-ins. Several of the film's themes—family responsibility, interconnectedness, and inner direction—seemed to resonate with audiences, making the film one of the most revealing cultural documents of the decade.

STORY LINE

Although Disney presented *The Lion King* as the first original work among its stable of animated features, the script owed artistic debts to numerous classic literary works, including *Hamlet, The Adventures of Huck Finn*, and Disney's own animated film *Bambi*. As in *Bambi, The Lion King* traces the travails and triumphs of a young prince. Simba progresses from birth to mature adulthood, learning valuable lessons about courage and family responsibility along the way. As a youngster, Simba (voiced by Jonathan Taylor Thomas) learns of the delicate balance of predators and prey within his kingdom, the pridelands.

In a Shakespearian turn, the young prince's evil, stereotypically gay uncle Scar (Jeremy Irons) dupes him into believing that his practice roar has caused the death of his father, Mufasa (James Earl Jones). Guilt-ridden, Simba foregoes his royal inheritance in favor of self-exile among a merry bunch of jungle-

The Lion King ***on Stage.*** *A scene from the stage production of* The Lion King *is featured at the 2008 Tony Awards.* THEO WARGO/STAFF/WIREIMAGE/GETTY IMAGES.

dwelling, bohemian misfits, whose motto, *hakuna matata*—meaning "no worries"—became a hit song. Eventually, however, after intense soul-searching, Simba (voiced as an adult by Matthew Broderick) realizes that he, like Huck Finn before him, cannot run from his social obligations. Upon returning to the pridelands, Simba finds that Scar and his hyena followers have upset the delicate circle of life that holds the kingdom together. A climactic struggle with Scar leads to Simba's restoration to the throne as well as to ecological and social renewal. The film concludes as it begins, with the birth of a new heir.

MOVIE COMPARISONS

Comparing *The Lion King* to Disney's 1942 classic *Bambi*, which was also the most profitable film of its decade, illuminates exactly where Disney's father-son story stands in U.S. cultural history. Whereas Walt Disney selected an innocent deer to be king of the predatorless animal realm in *Bambi*, in the 1990s, perhaps reflecting U.S. acceptance of its own power in the post–Cold War world, Disney's heirs make a predatory lion into the ruler of an animal kingdom full of predation.

The Lion King's vision of the family also differs from *Bambi*'s in significant ways. *Bambi*'s parents represented the ideal of mid-twentieth-century parents: he, the classic military father, awesome and aloof yet reliable and protective; she, the consummate feminine nurturer, demure and self-sacrificing. In *The Lion King*, however, Simba's father Mufasa epitomizes the sensitive 1990s dad, the loving, involved father who wakes up early on the weekends to spend quality time with his son. Simba's mother, as many feminist critics have pointed out, barely plays a role in the family. Few audiences missed *The Lion King*'s messages about family and responsibility, which many consider the most vexing issues of the decade.

As in *Bambi*, the world in *The Lion King* divides into two camps—one clearly pure and good, the other conscienceless and wicked. But as opposed to *Bambi*'s gun-toting hunters, in *The Lion King* it is evil gangs of unmannered hyenas from just outside the realm that threaten the security of the pridelands. In the context of the Los Angeles uprisings of 1992, the O. J. Simpson case of 1994, and a decade-long debate over welfare reform, many critics saw a racial subtext to the villainous outsiders. They noted that the racialized voices of the hyenas hewed to hackneyed stereotypes of African American and Hispanic threats to nice kids from the suburbs who stray too far from home.

CRITICS

The Lion King also ignited a lively debate among newspaper columnists, educational pundits, and parents around the nation about the role of violent death in children's films. Whereas some argue that *The Lion King* included no more violence than the 6 p.m. news, other critics, most notably Terrence Rafferty in a much-quoted *New Yorker* article, contends that Disney's film would traumatize those children who could not easily distinguish between fiction and reality. *The Lion King* also received numerous complaints about its representation of nature. As *Bambi* did before it, critics such as Ted Kerasote of *Audubon* magazine notes that the film eliminated any acceptable human role in nature, except perhaps as "passive ecotourists watching an Eden in which we play no part."

Given its popularity despite these criticisms, *The Lion King* was well on its way to becoming the classic family story for a post–Cold War era. In 1998 Disney released a sequel, *The Lion King 2: Simba's Pride*, featuring Simba's daughter, Kiara, as the main character. The plot focuses on Kiara's attempts to bring Simba's pride and the outcasts back together again.

The debut of *The Lion King* as a Broadway musical in 1997 not only ensured the continued popularity of the Disney film, but it also broke ground on Broadway and started a new tradition of Disney musicals. Elton John and Tim Rice, who wrote the music and lyrics, respectively, for the film, wrote three songs for the play, and South African singer/composer Lebo M created the African music for the production. The curtain goes up on a stage that has been transformed into an African jungle. In a review written for the *New York Times*, Ben Brantley described the first ten minutes of the play by noting that it turns the entire audience into four-year-olds who "can only marvel at the exotic procession of animals . . . in balletic flight." Greg Evans of *Variety* called it "a theatrical achievement unrivaled in its beauty," and Linda Winer of *Newsday* labeled it "a jaw-dropping magnificent spectacle."

Director Julie Taymor won two Tony Awards in 1998, one for Best Director of a Musical and the other for Best Costume Design. She also won numerous other awards for directing, costumes, masks, and puppetry. By the early twenty-first century, *The Lion King* was back on Broadway and had launched a national tour. In October 2011 Disney released a two-disc diamond edition Blu-ray/DVD combo set and packed it with special features.

Thomas Robertson

SEE ALSO: *Animated Films; Broadway; Cold War; Disney (Walt Disney Company); John, Elton; Simpson, O. J.; Simpson Trial; Tony Awards.*

BIBLIOGRAPHY

Benshoff, Harry M., and Sean Griffin. *America on Film: Representing Race, Class, Gender, and Sexuality at the Movies.* Malden, MA: Blackwell, 2004.

Brantley, Ben. "Cub Comes of Age: A Twice-Told Tale." *New York Times*, November 14, 1997.

Kerasote, Ted. "Disney's New Nature Myth: *The Lion King*." *Audubon* 96, no. 6 (1994): 132.

Rafferty, Terrence. "The Current Cinema." *New Yorker*, June 20, 1994, 86–89.

Sealey, Kelvin Shawn, ed. *Film, Politics, & Education: Cinematic Pedagogy across the Disciplines.* New York: Peter Lang, 2008.

Ward, Annalee R. "The Lion King's Mythic Narrative: Disney as Moral Educator." *Journal of Popular Film and Television*, 23 (1996): 171–178.

Whitley, David S. *The Idea of Nature in Disney Animation.* Burlington, VT: Ashgate, 2008.

Lionel Trains

For generations of Americans, Christmas just wouldn't be the same without the sight of a Lionel train click-clacking along the tracks beneath the tree. Above all other toy train manufacturers, Lionel stands for genuine quality and craftsmanship. Founded in 1903 by Joshua Lionel Cowen, this New York–based company had assumed dominance of the toy train market by 1926.

Focused almost exclusively on O-gauge electric trains, the firm's carefully painted reproductions of diesel locomotives and earlier metal die-cast models of steam engines have become coveted collector's items. For the cars behind the locomotive, the company made a wide variety of rolling stock, including both passenger and freight cars. Moreover, the trademark Lionel layout was typically an animated affair, with a generous supply of operating accessories.

The company's direction and fortunes were briefly revitalized during the 1990s, when rock musician Neil Young assumed part ownership of Lionel, known at that time as Lionel, LLC. However a series of economic and legal woes throughout the latter half of the 1990s culminated with the closing of the last Lionel, LLC, manufacturing plant in 2001. The company subsequently licensed the Lionel name to numerous other ventures and experienced a brief resurgence in 2004 with the success of *Polar Express*, a kid's Christmas movie in which a young boy takes a harrowing train ride to the North Pole where he meets Santa and receives the year's first Christmas gift. Whereas Lionel trains were inducted into the National Toy Hall of Fame in 2006, and the company showed solid profits, legal battles ultimately led to bankruptcy and a court-approved reorganization of the company's structure in 2008.

Robert Kuhlken

SEE ALSO: *Electric Trains; Toys; Young, Neil.*

BIBLIOGRAPHY

Carp, Roger. *The World's Greatest Toy Train Maker: Insiders Remember Lionel.* Waukesha, WI: Kalmbach Publishing, 1997.

Grams, John, and Terry Thompson. *Legendary Lionel Trains.* Waukesha, WI: Kalmbach Publishing, 2004.

Hollander, Ron. *All Aboard!: The Story of Joshua Lionel Cowen & His Lionel Train Company.* New York: Workman Publishing, 1981.

McComas, Tom, and James Tuohy. *A Collector's Guide and History to Lionel Trains.* Wilmette, IL: TM Productions, 1975.

Lippmann, Walter *(1889–1974)*

Renowned twentieth-century American journalist and political analyst Walter Lippmann championed a responsible press in a time when, beneath the posture of detachment, elite journalists were deeply involved in the mechanics of the government. Lippmann was one of the chief architects of a professional journalism characterized by independence and objectivity. At the same time, however, he renounced the ideals of citizen-based democracy as unfeasible. His column appeared in hundreds of newspapers as a syndicated feature from 1931 into the 1970s. He won two Pulitzer Prizes, the Medal of Freedom, and three Overseas Press Club awards. In addition to authoring several books, he was the founding editor of the *New Republic* and director of the editorial page at the *New York World.*

Lippmann was born in New York City to Jacob and Daisy Baum Lippmann. His father was a successful clothing manufacturer who provided his son with exposure to the high culture of New York and summer travels to European and American resorts. By the time he enrolled at Harvard in 1906, Lippmann had already toured Europe extensively. His privileged upbringing was reflected throughout his career: in his friendships; in his political philosophies; and, perhaps most conspicuously, in his skeptical view of the public.

Set against the soaring rhetoric of democracy flourishing in America at the time, Lippmann's *Public Opinion*, written in 1922, outlines the limitations of the media in performing the function of public enlightenment. In this widely influential tome, Lippmann argues that the vast majority of citizens are unable to comprehend, let alone synthesize, complex national and international political issues, thus an informed and engaged public is an illusion. Journalists, he claims, are of little help because they cannot produce a complete image of the political scene, offering instead an inadequately selective series of glimpses. Describing this limited view of complex subjects, Lippmann borrowed the term *stereotype* for a printer's mold. John Dewey called *Public Opinion* "perhaps the most effective indictment of democracy as currently conceived ever penned."

To relieve the public of the burden of participation in government, Lippmann advocated the establishment of a class of experts, which would shape the public mind and character. The press would serve to transmit the judgments of these well-informed opinion leaders, thereby considerably reducing the role of the public. In addition, news would expose the experts to publicity in order to keep them honest and focused on public rather than private interests.

Throughout his career Lippmann enjoyed prestige, access

Walter Lippmann. *Walter Lippmann delivers a lecture at Cambridge University in 1952.* JOHN CHILLINGWORTH/STRINGER/PICTURE POST/GETTY IMAGES.

to heads of state and royalty, and the confidence of "insiders," whom he decided early on were the truly important people in society. Many believed he helped write Woodrow Wilson's famous Fourteen Points, which shaped the Treaty of Versailles, and he was adviser to numerous political figures, including President John F. Kennedy and his successor, Lyndon Johnson.

Yet he maintained what he felt was a professional distance as a journalist. He criticized the United States–supported invasion of Cuba despite his ties to the Kennedy administration, and he disagreed in his columns with President Johnson's decision to send troops to Vietnam. Offended by Johnson's later attempts to sway his coverage, Lippmann resigned from writing his widely syndicated column.

Although Lippmann's views on the press still reverberate in the writing of mass media scholars and critics, he is often quoted out of context in a way that emphasizes his concerns with professionalism while downplaying his largely elitist opinions. His ideas endure because debates regarding the role of the mass media in democracy remain unsettled. While his views regarding the limitations of the press have profoundly influenced the way journalism is practiced today, Lippmann's powerful work as a columnist, reporter, and philosopher suggests that he neither accepted these restrictions for himself nor imposed them on his readers.

Adrienne Russell

SEE ALSO: New Republic*; Syndication; Vietnam.*

BIBLIOGRAPHY

Childs, Marquis, and James Reston, eds. *Walter Lippmann and His Times*. New York: Harcourt, Brace, 1959.

Steel, Ronald. *Walter Lippmann and the American Century*. Boston: Little, Brown, 1980.

Weingast, David Elliott. *Walter Lippmann: A Study in Personal Journalism*. New Brunswick, NJ: Rutgers University Press, 1949.

Lipstick

Lipstick has become one of the most widely used cosmetics since Cleopatra first stained her lips with carmine in 69 BCE. Made of waxes or oils, lipstick colors and protects the lips. "Even women who don't wear makeup wear lipstick," write Meg Cohen Ragas and Karen Kozlowski in *Read My Lips: A Cultural History of Lipstick*. Often referred to as "hope in a tube," lipstick has captivated women (and men) since the earliest rosy stains forever linked lipstick and women's lips with femininity and sexuality.

First mass-produced in 1915 when American Maurice Levy designed a metal case for the waxy tube, lipstick was one of the few luxuries purchased by Depression-era women. Lipstick hit its stride commercially in the 1950s, and despite the creation of numerous formulations, lipstick trends proved cyclical throughout the twentieth century. Deep red lipstick is associated with the glamour of 1950s Hollywood, and pastels were popular in the 1960s; eventually cosmetic companies began producing lipstick in a variety of colors ranging from frosty lime to black.

Honored in 1997 as one of only twelve objects included in an exhibition titled "Icons: Magnets of Meaning," lipstick has transcended its decorative roots and become culturally indispensable as a quick and affordable way to transform one's image. The common beauty product met with controversy in 2007 when studies showed that many popular brands contained traces of lead; however, it was determined that there was not enough present to cause serious concern, and sales were not affected.

Alison Macor

SEE ALSO: *The Great Depression; Hollywood.*

BIBLIOGRAPHY

Angeloglou, Maggie. *A History of Make-up*. New York: Macmillan, 1970.

De Castelbajac, Kate. *The Face of the Century: 100 Years of Makeup and Style*. New York: Rizzoli, 1995.

Ragas, Meg Cohen, and Karen Kozlowski. *Read My Lips: A Cultural History of Lipstick*. San Francisco: Chronicle Books, 1998.

Scott, Linda M. *Fresh Lipstick: Redressing Fashion and Feminism*. New York: Palgrave Macmillan, 2005.

Wang, J.; A. B. Kay; J. Fletcher; et al. "Is Lipstick Associated with the Development of Systemic Lupus Erythematosus (SLE)?" *Clinical Rheumatology* 27, no. 9 (2008): 1183–1187.

Liston, Sonny *(1932?–1970)*

Charles "Sonny" Liston is best remembered as the man who lost the heavyweight title to Muhammad Ali (then Cassius Clay) in 1964. A fearsome slugger, Liston captured and terrified the American consciousness in the early 1960s. His criminal past and his stint in prison were well publicized, as were his ties to organized crime. However, the single most well-known item about Liston was his baleful stare, which often petrified opponents even before the bell for the first round sounded.

In the early 1960s, the heavyweight champion of the world was clean-cut Floyd Patterson. Patterson's manager and trainer, Cus D'Amato, had spent the better part of his life fighting the influence of organized crime in boxing and was intent on protecting the heavyweight title from the mob. Realizing that his charge would have little chance against the fearsome Liston, D'Amato refused to allow Patterson to defend his title against the man many in boxing were already referring to as the uncrowned champ. Liston, meanwhile, was busy flattening the heavyweight division, waiting for what he hoped would be his inevitable title shot. Eventually, Patterson, a proud champion, relented and took Liston on against the advice of D'Amato. On September 25, 1962, in a fight that was widely seen as good versus evil, Liston knocked Patterson out in one round to win the heavyweight title. Liston then repeated his performance with another one-round demolition of Patterson the following year. At that point there were many among the hard-to-impress boxing media who considered Sonny Liston the best heavyweight ever to lace on a pair of gloves.

Enter Cassius Clay, soon to be known to the world as Muhammad Ali. Clay was the light heavyweight gold medalist in the 1960 Olympic Games in Rome. The outspoken young fighter was fast becoming the sport's number one star, despite the fact that most boxing experts did not envision a world title

Cassius Clay and Sonny Liston. *Sonny Liston, right, takes a blow from Cassius Clay in a 1964 fight for the world heavyweight title in Miami, Florida.* FOCUS ON SPORT/CONTRIBUTOR/GETTY IMAGES SPORT/GETTY IMAGES.

in his future, especially not with the unbeatable Liston sitting on the heavyweight throne. Nevertheless, as the outstanding contender to the title in 1964, Clay earned a try against Liston. Sonny Liston, the overwhelming favorite at 7–1 odds, was totally bewildered by the young challenger's hand and foot speed, and after six rounds of fighting, Liston refused to answer the bell for the seventh, insisting that he had damaged his shoulder during the bout and was unable to continue fighting. The following year, Clay again defeated Liston, this time with a one-round knockout courtesy of a "phantom punch" that many attributed to Clay's faster-than-the-human-eye hand speed but that many others saw as a fraudulent punch in a fixed fight. The controversy surrounding this fight has never been resolved, and the "phantom punch" remains a favorite topic of argument for boxing fans to this day.

Liston's last fight was in 1970 against Chuck Wepner, the fighter who nearly lasted the distance against Muhammad Ali and in doing so inspired a young actor in attendance named Sylvester Stallone to write the screenplay for the movie *Rocky*. Liston won the Wepner fight with a tenth-round technical knockout. Later that year, Liston was found dead in his home, reportedly from a heroin overdose. Those who knew him personally insist that Liston did not use heroin and that his death was actually a mob execution. Charles "Sonny" Liston, a man who did not know where he was born or how old he was, died as he lived—under a shroud of mystery and controversy.

Max Kellerman

SEE ALSO: *Ali, Muhammad; Boxing;* Rocky; *Stallone, Sylvester.*

BIBLIOGRAPHY

Steen, Rob. *Sonny Liston: His Life, Strife and the Phantom Punch.* London: JR Books, 2008.

Young, Andrew Sturgeon. *Sonny Liston: The Champ Nobody Wanted.* Chicago: Johnson Publishing, 1963.

Little Black Dress

The little black dress, a simple yet timeless fashion innovation that was first popular in the 1920s, has been called the foundation of any woman's wardrobe and the one style item that makes her both look and feel great. Author Edna O'Brien has called it "both chic and armor," though the black dress was originally considered something of an antifashion statement when it appeared after World War I with its "less is more" concept, which was inspired by the simple lines of the chemise and the functional uniforms of French shop girls and waitresses.

The little black dress was promoted by many designers throughout the twentieth century, but most couture authorities credit its origin to famed French designer Gabrielle Bonheur "Coco" Chanel (1883–1971). Chanel opened her first dress shops between 1912 and 1914 in Paris and Deauville, France, where she was the first to create women's clothing to be worn without corsets, as well as fashions that emphasized comfort, ease, and practicality with no loss of elegance. She initiated a number of influential and enduring fashion trends, such as the chemise dress, tweed skirts and sweaters, and feminized male items such as trousers and pea jackets. Chanel was advocating the little black dress as a new uniform for afternoon and evening as early as 1915. As fashion writer Caroline Rennolds Milbank noted: "Deceptively simple, these dresses were wizardries of cut and proportion. Chanel used traditional elegant material—lace, tulle, embroideries, or soft, weightless silks—in a newly tailored way. The little black dress made women wearing anything else seem overdressed, and during the first years of her career—the war years—overdressing was severely frowned upon." Countless other designers—including Edward Molyneux, Jean Patou, and Balenciaga—carried Chanel's concept into the future.

Writers on fashion have lauded both the essentiality and versatility of the little black dress. Originally designed for the afternoon cocktail hour, it was soon lauded for the relaxed mood it brought to feminine evening wear. Its basic simplicity made it easily accessorized, and it has been called an entire wardrobe in itself when worked with scarves, purses, and real or faux pearls and other jewelry. Smart working women are still advised to keep a small evening bag at the office for transforming the workaday black dress into instant elegance after hours.

The versatility of the little black dress is key to its enduring success. Appropriate for formal and informal wear in both winter or summer, the dress has been praised by fashion writers for the way it focuses on the face, looks great with a tan, stands out or blends in, and intrigues and seduces. On a purely functional level, it hides stains and, best of all, slims the figure—enthusiasts swear it can appear to take off 10 pounds. The little black dress owes a great deal of its durability to its color. Black soon shook its long association with mourning to become the most basic of fashion colors, by turns elegant, classic, sexy, or funky. Impeccable fashion precedents for basic black include Audrey Hepburn in *Breakfast at Tiffany's* (1961); Anita Ekberg in Federico Fellini's *La Dolce Vita* (1960), in which she wears a clerical variation of the little black sheath dress fashioned after an Italian priest's garb; and nuns, beatniks, and Morticia Addams. In 2006 Christie's auctioned off Hepburn's dress for an astronomical £410,000, or more than $800,000. At that time, it was the highest amount ever paid for a gown used in a film.

The durable fashion staple was further, if bizarrely, immortalized in Richard O'Brien's *Shock Treatment*, a 1981 film sequel to the cult smash *The Rocky Horror Picture Show* (1975). *Rocky Horror*'s now-married and somewhat-taken-for-granted heroine, Janet Majors, performs an aggressive rock number, "Little Black Dress," while in the process of a fashion makeover geared to instantly transform her into the chic and attention-grabbing woman of the hour, courtesy of a "minimal, criminal, cynical Little Black Dress." In 2009 it was used in the title of a memoir, *Mennonite in a Little Black Dress*, by Rhoda Janzen, in which the mention of the fashion staple instantly signals the type of sophisticated woman who is far removed from a strict religious upbringing. The little black dress has never gone out of fashion or lost its iconic status, echoing Chanel's observation that fashion fades but style remains the same.

Ross Care

SEE ALSO: Breakfast at Tiffany's; *Chanel, Coco; Cocktail Parties; Hepburn, Audrey;* The Rocky Horror Picture Show.

BIBLIOGRAPHY

"Black Dress." *In Style*, December 1997, 95.

Edelman, Amy Holman. *The Little Black Dress*. New York: Simon & Schuster, 1998.

Ludot, Didier. *The Little Black Dress: Vintage Treasure*. New York: Assouline Publishing, 2001.

Milbank, Caroline Rennolds. *Couture—The Great Designers*. New York: Stewart, Tabori, & Chang, 1985.

Little Blue Books

Little Blue Books—compact, cheap, and often carrying alluring titles or topics—became immensely successful in the United States in the 1920s and 1930s. Because they cost only a nickel apiece, the books represented the true reading taste of Americans, according to their publisher, Emanuel Haldeman-Julius (1889–1951). He referred to the thousands of titles he published in a small town in southeastern Kansas as "a university in print" and a "democracy of literature." Many of his best-selling books promised frank discussions of sex for an American public that was still deemed bashful about the question. But the chapbooks also gave thrifty readers a broad range of literature at practically no cost: ancient and modern works, essays, fiction, philosophy, humor, biography, self-improvement manuals, and a variety of other works.

Haldeman-Julius, son of a Russian Jewish immigrant bookbinder in Philadelphia, worked at socialist newspapers in New York and elsewhere before marrying (Anna) Marcet Haldeman in 1916. The daughter of a prominent banking family in a small town in Kansas called Girard, and a niece of the prominent social worker Jane Addams, Haldeman supplied him with half of his last name and funds for his purchase of a financially struggling socialist newspaper called the *Appeal to Reason*. Although he eventually was forced to cease publishing the paper, he continued with other journalistic efforts.

Haldeman-Julius said he first thought of printing cheap books for the masses after reading a copy of Oscar Wilde's *Ballad of Reading Gaol* when he was fifteen. In 1919 he introduced his concept with twenty-five-cent paperbacks, beginning with *Reading Gaol* and *The Rubaiyat of Omar Khayyam*. Variously called Pocket Classics, People's Classics, and Pocket Series, they sported covers of different colors. Two years later the publisher spurred sales by cutting the price to a nickel apiece, adopting blue covers (although some later came with covers in yellow and other colors), and naming the series Little Blue Books.

Cheaply bound and printed on inexpensive newsprint, the books measured 3 1/2 by 5 inches and usually contained sixty-four pages, though they could run from thirty-two to 128 pages. Haldeman-Julius advertised them widely in newspapers and magazines at twenty for a dollar postpaid, and they became enormously popular. By 1927 he reported he had sold twenty-one million, and it has been estimated that he sold more than 300 million in his lifetime. The publisher boasted he could provide the information and entertainment found in hardcover books at one-hundredth the price.

NOT TOO SAUCY

Although books with sexy titles or topics became Haldeman-Julius's most popular category, strict laws prohibited distribution of material relating to sexual subjects through the mails. The texts—some by authors such as Margaret Sanger, an early public advocate of birth control—were not as saucy as some readers perhaps hoped. Sex-hygiene manuals employed euphemistic titles to avoid embarrassment to customers, Haldeman-Julius said. *What Every Young Woman Should Know*, *What Every Young Man Should Know*, and *How to Be Happy though Married* were several top sellers.

Although he could be coy about titling the sex manuals he published, Haldeman-Julius did not hesitate to spice up titles of slow-moving books. Sales of Theophile Gautier's novel *Fleece of Gold* jumped from 8,000 copies in 1925 to 50,000 the next year when he retitled it *The Quest for a Blonde Mistress*. Sales of Victor Hugo's drama *The King Enjoys Himself* rocketed from 8,000 to 38,000 after Haldeman-Julius renamed it *The Lustful King Enjoys Himself*.

The entire series catered to Americans' quest for self-improvement and self-education. Although Haldeman-Julius boasted that his reprints included "all the famous authors from Aesop to Zarilla," he also hired freelancers to write original books, including his perennially popular line of self-help chapbooks that promised to make readers smarter, stronger, more attractive, and better in practically every way. His most productive writer, a former priest in London, pumped out 10,000 words a week and seven and a half million words in all. Haldeman-Julius also picked liberally from older works with expired copyrights. He estimated in 1928 that one-quarter of his books fell in the latter category. Authors of the 2,000 titles on his list included Edgar Allan Poe, Clarence Darrow, Will Durant, Upton Sinclair, Bertrand Russell, and William Shakespeare. Books extolling socialism were common.

WRITER AND PUBLISHER

Besides editing the Little Blue Books, Haldeman-Julius wrote many himself, including fiction and essays. One of his favorite themes was atheism (*The Church Is a Burden, Not a Benefit, in Social Life*; *The Meaning of Atheism*; *Studies in Rationalism*; and *Is Theism a Logical Philosophy?*), although he also offered his customers versions of the Bible and other religious material. He claimed he wanted only to provide readers a range of subjects and philosophies and to let them draw their own conclusions. He wrote a number of books with his wife, who also wrote some by herself, including *What the Editor's Wife Is Thinking About*, which jumped from annual sales of 1,000 to 16,000 when it was retitled *Marcet Haldeman-Julius' Intimate Notes on Her Husband* in 1927.

Cheap and portable, the books remained popular even during the Great Depression, but their popularity began to decline after World War II as greater prosperity made the books less appealing. Haldeman-Julius carried on the business until he died in his swimming pool on his ranch outside Girard in 1951, shortly after being sentenced to six months in prison and a $12,500 fine for income tax evasion. (The death was ruled an accidental drowning.) His son, Henry J. Haldeman, continued to publish the books until the late 1970s, tempting readers with titles such as *Your Sex Life after 80*, *Pin-Ups of Now Magazette*, and *Rupture and Hernia*, but they never regained the popularity of their early years.

Daniel Lindley

SEE ALSO: *Big Little Books; Dime Novels; The Great Depression;* Pulp Fiction*; Pulp Magazines; Romance Novels; World War II.*

BIBLIOGRAPHY

Greasley, Philip A., ed. *Dictionary of Midwestern Literature: Volume One: The Authors*. Bloomington: Indiana University Press, 2001.

Green, George, and Mary Green. "Reader, Can You Spare a Dime?" *Biblio*, March 1998, 46–47.

Haldeman-Julius, E. *The First Hundred Million*. New York: Simon & Schuster, 1928.

Haldeman-Julius, E. *The World of Haldeman-Julius*. New York: Twayne, 1960.

Little House on the Prairie

SEE: *Wilder, Laura Ingalls.*

Little League

From its inception in 1939 to the present, Little League has evolved into the primary outlet for youngsters to participate in baseball—America's national pastime. In the early twenty-first century more than two-and-a-half million boys and girls from across the globe between the ages of four and eighteen partake in Little League programs. Those who coach in the league, which is incorporated as a not-for-profit organization, do not simply teach children how to swing a bat, toss a curveball, or steal a base. The essence of Little League is clearly stated in its official pledge: "I trust in God. I love my country and will respect its laws. I will play fair and strive to win. But win or lose, I will always do my best."

INCEPTION

Little League was founded in 1939 in Williamsport, Pennsylvania, by Carl Stotz and brothers George and Bert Bebble. The initial league consisted of three teams; a year later, a second league was added, with ten more coming onboard during World War II. In 1947 the first non-Pennsylvania league—located in Hammonton, New Jersey—became an official Little League, and the initial Little League World Series, the organization's showcase event, was held. The victor was Williamsport's Maynard Little League. By the following year, ninety-four youth baseball programs had become official Little Leagues, and in 1949 there were 307 leagues spanning the United States. Little League went international in 1951, with the establishment of a program in British Columbia, Canada. Six years later a team from Monterrey, Mexico, became the first foreign squad to win a World Series title. When it repeated the following year, Monterrey became the first back-to-back Little League champion.

LITTLE LEAGUE'S GOLDEN AGE

In 1952 the organization had its initial full-time president in Peter J. McGovern, and there were more than 1,500 Little Leagues in and outside the United States. The following year

Little League World Series, 1961. *Baseball teams from Hawaii and Quebec compete in the Little League World Series in Williamsport, Pennsylvania, in 1961.* ROBERT RIGER/GETTY IMAGES.

CBS first televised the Little League World Series, with Howard Cosell behind the microphone. By 1955 there was at least one Little League in all forty-eight of the contiguous United States, and by 1959 the organization had grown to more than 5,000 leagues. That year, which was the twentieth anniversary of Little League, President Dwight Eisenhower announced that the week following the second Monday in June of every year would be designated National Little League Baseball Week.

Throughout the 1960s Little League continued to develop. Senior League Baseball was established for thirteen- to fifteen-year-olds, as was Big League Baseball for those ages sixteen to eighteen (Big League has since expanded to include fifteen-year-olds). A summer camp was inaugurated in Williamsport, and Little League was granted a Federal Charter of Incorporation by the U.S. Congress. The World Series was broadcast on ABC's *Wide World of Sports*. Teams from Spain and Venezuela made it to the series—and one from West Tokyo, Japan, became the first Asian squad to win a championship.

MODERNIZING THE SPORT

The 1970s saw the introduction of the aluminum bat, the evolution of which came in conjunction with the League. Girls began taking part in League softball programs, and Junior League was inaugurated for thirteen- to fourteen-year-olds. By the end of the decade, there were 6,500 Little Leagues, 2,850 Senior Leagues, and 1,300 Big Leagues. In the 1980s the Peter J. McGovern Little League Museum commenced operation in South Williamsport; Vice President George H. W. Bush threw out the first pitch in the League championship contest; and the original 1947 World Series winners, the Maynard Little Leaguers—now well into middle age—were honored on the fortieth anniversary of their triumph. In the 1990s Little League continued evolving as a Challenger Division was established for physically and mentally impaired youngsters. ESPN2 began televising regional championship games in 1997, and the 100th country (Burkina-Faso) began offering Little League programs at the end of the decade.

In the first decade of the 2000s the Little League World Series was increased from eight to sixteen teams. Little League International expanded its TV contracts by signing an eight-year contract with ESPN and entering into agreements with the New England Sports Network and Madison Square Garden Network to televise early round regional tournament games. On a down note, a highly publicized mini-scandal erupted in 2001 after Danny Almonte, pitching for the Rolando Paulino All-Stars of the Bronx, New York, tossed a perfect game in the Little League World Series and led the team to a third-place tournament finish. The team's postseason was erased from the books when it was discovered that Almonte was fourteen years old—two years above the age limit for Little Leaguers.

ROAD TO THE MAJORS

Many major leaguers began their baseball careers in Little League. Boog Powell and Ken Hubbs played in the 1954 Little League World Series. Rick Wise and Hector Torres did so in 1958. In 1971 Lloyd McClendon belted five dingers in five World Series at-bats. Other Little League World Series participants have included Wilson Alvarez and Jason Bay, Derek Bell and Jim Brower, Sean Burroughs and Chen Chin-Feng, Jason Marquis and Lastings Milledge, Guillermo Quiroz and Gary Sheffield, Jason Varitek and Dan Wilson. Tom Seaver, who played in the Spartan Little League in Fresno, California, was the inaugural inductee in the Hall of Excellence, located in the Peter J. McGovern Little League Museum. Other alumni include Carl Yastrzemski—the first Little Leaguer to make the Baseball Hall of Fame—Jim Palmer, Mike Schmidt, Nolan Ryan, Cal Ripken Jr., Wade Boggs, George Brett, Steve Carlton, Gary Carter, Rollie Fingers, Catfish Hunter, Robin Yount, Don Sutton, Dusty Baker, and Dale Murphy.

Yet not all star Little Leaguers were destined to make the major leagues. In 1956 Fred Shapiro, playing for Delaware Township, New Jersey, tossed the first perfect game in the Little League World Series. The hero of the 1964 competition was Danny Yacarino of the Staten Island, New York, Mid Island Little League, who hurled a no-hitter and belted a home run in the championship contest against Monterrey. Another notable Little League graduate is former National Football League quarterback Brian Sipe, who participated in the 1961 Series, with his team, hailing from El Cajon, California, winning the championship. Among the Little League Museum Hall of Excellence honorees are National Basketball Association Hall of Famer Kareem Abdul-Jabbar, a member of New York City's Inwood Little League; NBA star and U.S. Senator Bill Bradley of the Crystal City, Missouri, Little League; George Will, the nationally syndicated columnist and political commentator who played Little League ball in Champaign, Illinois; actor Tom Selleck, a graduate of the Sherman Oaks, California, Little League; and Vice President Dan Quayle of the Huntington, Indiana, Little League. Other notable participants include singer-songwriter Bruce Springsteen; actor Kevin Costner, who starred in the baseball films *Bull Durham* (1988), *Field of Dreams* (1989), and *For Love of the Game* (1999); Joe Biden, vice president and longtime U.S. senator; and President George W. Bush, the first American chief executive to have played Little League. In 2004 pro golfer Cathy Gerring, Olympic ice hockey star Krissy Wendell, and police detective Nancy dosReis became the first women inducted into the Hall of Excellence.

LITTLE LEAGUE'S DECLINE

Despite its historical longevity, Little League, like Major League Baseball, encountered a lull in its popularity. Over the first decade of the twenty-first century, Little League's numbers declined by almost 25 percent. Major League Baseball responded by funding renovation projects, particularly in urban areas where baseball experienced its sharpest drops in participants. As sports such as soccer and lacrosse became more popular, youth baseball's demise stemmed from a variety of causes. Whether due to the pace of the game, increased competition from other sports, or the lack of instant college or professional success, Little League's membership continually dropped.

The official goal of Little League is to "promote, develop, supervise, and voluntarily assist in all lawful ways, the interest of those who will participate in Little League Baseball." Its true purpose, however, is not simply to train youngsters in baseball fundamentals and then send them out on the field to win at all costs. Beyond athletic competition and the enjoyment inherent in learning and playing baseball, the primary objective of Little League is to build within all participants character and loyalty, a solid work ethic, and a sense of identity as a citizen of their home country. Indeed, the emphasis in Little League is not on developing outstanding ballplayers but on developing exemplary world citizens.

Rob Edelman

SEE ALSO: *Abdul-Jabbar, Kareem; Baseball; Bradley, Bill; Carlton, Steve; Cosell, Howard; Costner, Kevin; ESPN;* Field of Dreams*; Golf; Hockey; National Basketball Association (NBA); National Football League (NFL); Olympics; Palmer, Jim; Quayle, Dan; Ripken, Cal, Jr.; Ryan, Nolan; Sports Heroes; Springsteen, Bruce; Teenagers; Television;* Wide World of Sports*; Will, George F.; Yastrzemski, Carl.*

BIBLIOGRAPHY

Broadus, Catherine, and Loren Broadus. *Laughing and Crying with Little League: A Training Manual for Little League Parents.* New York: Harper & Row, 1972.

Brown, Paul B. *My Season on the Brink: A Father's Seven Weeks as a Little League Manager.* New York: St. Martin's Press, 1992.

Burroughs, Jeff, and Tom Hennessy. *The Little Team That Could: The Incredible, Often Wacky Story of the Two-Time Little League World Champions.* Chicago: Bonus Books, 1994.

Dixon, Ramon "Tru," and David Aromatorio. *How Far Do You Wanna Go?: The True Story of the Man Who Turned 16 Inner City Kids into a Team of Champions.* Far Hills, NJ: New Horizon Press, 1997.

Dunow, Henry. *The Way Home: Scenes from a Season, Lessons from a Lifetime.* New York: Broadway Books, 2001.

Fine, Gary Alan. *With the Boys: Little League Baseball and Preadolescent Culture.* Chicago: University of Chicago Press, 1987.

Frommer, Harvey. *Growing up at Bat: 50 Years of Little League Baseball.* New York: Pharos Books, 1989.

Geist, Bill. *Little League Confidential: One Coach's Completely Unauthorized Tale of Survival.* New York: Macmillan, 1992.

Hohenstein, Kurt. *The Rules of the Game: Simple Truths Learned from Little League.* Nashville, TN: Thomas Nelson, 1996.

Katz, Jesse. *The Opposite Field: A Memoir of Love and Little League.* New York: Three Rivers Press, 2009.

Lindenberger, Wade, and Mike Ford. *The Blue Bombers: The True Story of the 2009 Little League World Champions.* San Diego, CA: Pro Management Press, 2010.

Ralbovsky, Marty. *Destiny's Darlings: A World Championship Little League Team Twenty Years Later.* New York: Hawthorn Books, 1974.

Van Auken, Lance and Robin. *Play Ball! The Story of Little League Baseball.* University Park: Pennsylvania State University Press, 2001.

Voigt, David Quentin. *A Little League Journal.* Bowling Green, OH: Bowling Green University Popular Press, 1974.

Little Magazines

The origin of American little magazines can be traced back to the radical pamphlets of the American Revolution, but the oldest literary magazine is the *North American Review* founded in Boston in 1815. Little magazines became an important outlet for literary works. The terms *little magazine* and *literary magazine* are often interchangeable. They describe magazines dedicated to publishing experimental art, creative writing, unconventional social ideas and political theories, and—in general—writing that could find no other home. Little magazines served as an important venue for promising new writers and social and artistic movements. The *little* in little magazines generally refers to small staffs, meager budgets, and low print runs, especially when compared to commercial counterparts.

LITTLE MAGAZINES' HUMBLE BEGINNINGS

Beginning in the 1910s, a combination of new ideas and technologies generated a proliferation of little magazines that made possible the modernist movement. With the publication of *Poetry: A Magazine of Verse* in 1912, guided by luminaries such as Harriet Munroe and Ezra Pound, the little magazine became a key to understanding modernist writing that commercial magazines turned down.

The little magazine's influence was, and still is, targeted to a select group of kindred spirits, generally literary, intellectual, and creative individuals. The magazines may reflect the efforts of a particular editor or publisher or a writer's cooperative, such as the Southern Appalachian Writers Cooperative's *New Ground* magazine. A number of little magazines have been or are associated with a college or university, most often affiliated with an English department—for example, the *American Literary Review* at the University of North Texas. Sometimes a little magazine will serve as a springboard for a small book press. One such magazine is *CALYX: A Journal of Art and Literature for Women,* which engendered CALYX Books.

The exact number of little magazines is difficult to track because of frequent turnover and erratic publication schedules. Promotional budgets are nearly nonexistent, and most have trouble attracting advertising revenue. Many struggle to meet their overhead expenses, and few break even financially. Unlike commercial magazines, which are based on profit, a mass market audience, and large promotional budgets and staffs, little magazines are subsidized with volunteer labor based largely on passion. Little magazine writing is often nonconformist and thought-provoking and, occasionally, disturbing and radical. Little magazines need intellectual freedom and are willing to remain little in order to have this.

PROLIFERATION OF LITTLE MAGAZINES

The 1930s through the 1950s were a vibrant time for little magazines. The content was largely focused in the areas of the arts and literature, with writing that was edgy, peculiar, and asocial. Authors had an independent spirit and idiosyncratic nature and were advocates of free expression and free speech. Many of these little magazines served as a venue for the bohemian; beat; and, later, hippie cultures. The works were eclectic and experimental, such as ethnopoetics; promoted artistic movements, such as cubism or surrealism; or were associated with social movements, such as anarchism or feminism. During this time literary genres expanded into areas of fantasy literature and science fiction.

By 1945 approximately 600 little magazines were said to exist, and by the mid-1970s it was thought there was an additional 1,500. The growth was a result of technology that accelerated the capability of printing and reproduction of inexpensive, easy-to-produce copies. Continued growth came as a result of increased grant money through public and private agencies, which was facilitated by organizations such as the Coordinating Council of Literary Magazines and the Council of Literary Magazines and Presses. As little magazines grew in number, so did the coverage. A subset of little magazines evolved as a result of political unrest during the 1960s, and some went underground, creating the term *underground press*, now a little-used term. Radical, or progressive, magazines began to focus on alternative music and lifestyles, publishing critiques of politics, sociology, culture, and current events. In the 1980s little magazines were sometimes affiliated with the development of university ethnic studies, gender studies, and multicultural studies, and in the first decade of the 2000s little magazines became more amenable to creative nonfiction writing covering topics such as the environment and social justice.

Literary magazines are the core of little magazines, covering a variety of genres, such as poetry, prose, fiction, short stories, plays, photography, collages, satire, and criticism. Magazine examples include *Hammers*, a magazine for Chicago poets emphasizing sociopolitical commentary; the *Connecticut Poetry Review*, a standout among the many poetry magazines; *A&U Magazine*, a forum for creative responses to those living with HIV and AIDS; the *Dirty Goat*, a taste of contemporary artists in the international arts scene; and the *Briar Cliff Review*, an eclectic, cultural, and art magazine focusing on Sioux writers. Annotated indexes of many literary magazines can be found using an Internet search engine.

PUBLISHING ONLINE

From the twentieth-first century on, little magazines have found it increasingly necessary to concentrate on the business end. Many editors and publishers got into the magazine business accidentally, for no other purpose than to edit and distribute good writing that they liked. Few magazines would have been able to survive without institutional or patron support. The twenty-first century has brought new challenges, and the rapid development of communication technologies has forced new business models. Many little magazines have an online presence. Some offer information about the publication, whereas others provide free limited or full access to the content. Some literary magazines have opted out of print and are strictly online, a cost-effective option. Writers and editors have access to publishing platforms and magazines, and completed works can be posted to literary websites. The new communication technologies are challenging traditional literature of the past, for example, by distinguishing self-publishing from editorial and refereed guided publishing.

The purpose of a little magazine is not to compete with commercial magazines but to remain solvent so that ideas and values outside of the commercial mainstream magazines may have a voice. The publishers and editors of little magazines are focused and want to retain editorial control over the content. This ensures that the magazines will stay independent and small. When a little magazine becomes big, something unique is lost.

Byron Anderson

SEE ALSO: *AIDS; The Beat Generation; Environmentalism; Feminism; Free Speech Movement; Hippies; The Internet; Modernism.*

BIBLIOGRAPHY

Anderson, Elliott, and Mary Kinzie, eds. *The Little Magazine in America: A Modern Documentary History*. Yonkers, NY: Pushcart Press, 1978.

Churchill, Suzanne W., and Adam McKible. *Little Magazines & Modernism: New Approaches*. Burlington, VT: Ashgate Publishing, 2007.

Fogarty, Robert S. "Literary Reviews and *Little Magazines*." In *Encyclopedia of American Cultural & Intellectual History, Vol. 3*, ed. Mary Kupiec Cayton and Peter W. Williams. New York: Scribner, 2001

Fulton, Len, ed. *The International Directory of Little Magazines and Small Presses*. Paradise, CA: Dustbooks, 1965–Present.

Scholes, Robert, and Clifford Wulfman. *Modernism in the Magazines: An Introduction*. New Haven, CT: Yale University Press, 2010.

Little Orphan Annie

Little Orphan Annie, the most popular hapless waif in the United States for almost a century, first showed up in newspaper comic sections in 1924. The brainchild of cartoonist Harold Gray, Annie was inspired in part by the sort of feisty orphans America's sweetheart Mary Pickford had been playing on silent movie screens for more than a decade as well as by the pluck-and-luck lads Horatio Alger Jr. had introduced in his novels in the previous century.

The conservative and eccentric Gray sent his redheaded, blank-eyed, little orphan on a relentless odyssey through the United States, commencing in the Roaring Twenties, continuing through the Great Depression of the 1930s, into the grim years of World War II, through the Cold War, and into the restless 1960s. Along the way he created scores of memorable characters, all drawn in his bleak, shadowy, and highly individual cartoon style. Chief among them were the avuncular Daddy Warbucks; the almost supernatural Punjab; and Sandy, one of the most faithful and long-lived dogs in comics history. Sandy's frequent "Arf" became a national catchword and was even quoted in a song about Annie. In 2010 Tribune Media Services finally ended the comic strip's run. By that time it was appearing in less than twenty newspapers.

A former assistant to Sydney Smith on the popular comic strip *The Gumps*, Gray had learned a good deal about melodrama and suspense. He began his own strip in the traditional style for that sort of tale, showing the plucky Annie leaving a bleak orphanage when she was adopted by a wealthy business tycoon named Oliver "Daddy" Warbucks. As novelist Charles Dickens had helped establish nearly a hundred years earlier, an orphan's lot is often not a happy or stable one, and Annie did not remain happily secure in the Warbuck's household for long. Soon she was on the road, unjustly separated from her benefactor and accompanied by the loyal Sandy. The pair roamed the country, encountering both kindly souls who took them in and consummate scoundrels who set them on the run again.

During the Great Depression of the 1930s, Gray was one of the few comic strip artists who dealt directly with life among those who were hard hit by the economic woes of the period. Despite his long-term dislike for President Franklin D. Roosevelt, he was not the sort of conservative who blamed the poor and homeless for their plight. Annie spent considerable time in the lower depths, never losing her belief that hard work and honesty would win the day. Unlike most of the unemployed and homeless she encountered, the admirable orphan was frequently rescued and returned to upper-class comfort by Daddy Warbucks. One of Gray's greatest challenges was to come up with new and plausible ways for the moppet to become parted once more from her surrogate parent.

During World War II, Daddy Warbucks turned his factory over to the government and became a lieutenant colonel in, for some reason, the British Army. On the home front Annie organized the Junior Commandos, who not only kept an eye out for spies and saboteurs but also, more practically, collected waste paper and scrap metal. "This is war, kids," Annie told her young colleagues, "*our* war, just as much, or more maybe, than anybody else's—we're *givin'* all we can to help those who are *givin' ever'thing* for us!"

Little Orphan Annie branched out into other media soon after its inception. The Cupples & Leon Company began issuing hardcover reprint books of the strip in 1926. In the 1930s came Big Little Books and various comic-book appearances. A kids' daily radio serial took to the air in the spring of 1931, broadcast initially out of NBC's Blue Network studios in Chicago. Ovaltine sponsored the show for nearly a decade and sold shake-up mugs for just a dime and the aluminum seal from inside a tin of their product. There were several styles of mugs, but all had a decal of Annie, usually accompanied by Sandy, on the side.

Annie hit the movies in 1932, when RKO made *Little Orphan Annie* with Mitzi Green in the title role and slow-burn comedian Edgar Kennedy as Daddy Warbucks. In all these venues Annie frequently uttered her favorite, and famous, exclamation—"Leapin' lizards!" In 1977 the unsinkable orphan made Broadway in the hit musical *Annie*. The show, which won seven Tony Awards and ran for 2,377 performances, featured stars such as a young Sara Jessica Parker in the title role. *Annie* became a movie in 1982, featuring actor Albert Finney as Daddy Warbucks and comedian Carol Burnett as Miss Hannigan, the orphanage matron.

Gray died in 1968, thus never getting to see his little monster, as he often called her, sing and dance on the stage. His longtime assistant, Bob Leffingwell, carried on the strip for a short time and was then replaced by a series of others. Longest on the job were artist Tex Blaisdell and writer Elliot Caplin. In 1974 reprints of old Gray continuities began running. Finally, at the end of 1979, and because of the popularity of the musical, Leonard Starr was brought in to write and draw a new version. The comic strip, eventually renamed *Annie*, continued into the twenty-first century, although toward the end not as many newspapers carried it as when Gray was in his prime.

Ron Goulart

SEE ALSO: Annie*; Broadway; Burnett, Carol; Cold War; Comic Books; The Great Depression; Pickford, Mary; Radio; Tony Awards; World War II.*

BIBLIOGRAPHY

Conan, Tobias. "Little Orphan Annie (1924–2010)." *Canadian Business*, August 16, 2010.

Goulart, Ron, ed. *The Encyclopedia of American Comics*. New York: Facts On File, 1990.

Gray, Harold. *Arf! The Life and Times of Little Orphan Annie: 1935–1945*. New Rochelle, NY: Arlington House, 1970.

Smith, Bruce. *The History of Little Orphan Annie*. New York: Ballantine Books, 1982.

The Little Rascals

SEE: *Our Gang.*

Little Richard *(1932–)*

Richard Wayne Penniman—better known as Little Richard—was one of the most audacious, seminal, and hysterical performers in rock and roll in the 1950s. With his flamboyant costumes, a 6-inch high pompadour, and feral stage antics, Little Richard's performances unleashed the ecstasy of his gospel roots and, coupled with sexual innuendo, gave rock and roll its first zany artist. Black and gay, Little Richard was uncompromising in his image, which had its roots in drag-queen revues, traveling medicine shows, the church, and clubs.

Little Richard was a symbol of rebellion who became one of the first black artists to have enormous crossover appeal among both American and British pop audiences and to foster the transformation of R&B into rock and roll. His songs became staples of the genre. Little Richard's recording output for Specialty Records in slightly more than a two-year span in the 1950s produced his most noteworthy hits, including three that went to number one on the R&B chart and four that reached the Top 10 on the pop chart.

MUSICAL ROOTS

Little Richard was born December 5, 1932 (some sources give his birth date as 1935), in Macon, Georgia, to Charles and Leva Mae Penniman, a bricklayer and educator, respectively. His upbringing was religious, conservative, and strict, and his effeminacy, along with a physical defect consisting of a right leg

Little Richard. *Rock and roll pioneer Little Richard, performing on stage in 2009, has enjoyed a career spanning six decades.* **SKIP BOLEN/CONTRIBUTOR/WIREIMAGE/GETTY IMAGES.**

that is shorter than his left, set him apart from his peers. Though he was raised as a Seventh Day Adventist, his mother put him in a charismatic Baptist church in Macon in hope of changing his homosexual behavior. At age thirteen, Little Richard was banished from his home because of his homosexuality and became estranged from his parents.

Little Richard's early musical influences were primarily gospel. He wanted to become a gospel singer in the vein of Brother Joe May, one of his early influences, but singing for the Lord proved to be a short-lived goal. By the ninth grade, he had dropped out of school and joined a traveling medicine show, in which he sometimes wore a dress and danced with the chorus girls. In 1951, at age nineteen, Little Richard made several recordings for RCA in the style of bluesman Billy Wright, a mentor. He then moved to Houston, Texas, and recorded with the Tempo Toppers (a vocal group), the Duces of Rhythm (an instrumental backup group), and the Johnny Otis band. At the suggestion of singer Lloyd Price, he sent a demo to Specialty Records, which wound up pairing Little Richard with producer Robert "Bumps" Blackwell, who was conscious of musical trends.

Blackwell was successful in producing a sound that had not been previously heard on records. Little Richard became one of the first rock-and-roll artists to take tunes consisting of senseless sounds and disjointed phrases and images and make them into commercially viable songs. Little Richard also used the technique of scatting (singing wordless syllables to improvised melodies). On "Tutti Frutti" (1955), he whooped and scatted, demonstrating his gospel roots. "Tutti Frutti" has been hailed as the sound of rock and roll's beginning. The song climbed to number two on the Billboard R&B chart and number seventeen on the pop chart. Several seminal hits followed, including "Long Tall Sally" (1956), "Slippin' and Slidin' (Peepin and Hidin')" (1956), "Rip It Up" (1956), "Lucille" (1956), and "Good Golly Miss Molly" (1958). Little Richard also appeared in three films during the 1950s, beginning with *The Girl Can't Help It* (1956).

GOD AND ROCK

In late 1957, at the pinnacle of his career and in the midst of a tour of Australia, Little Richard shocked the musical world by announcing that he was abandoning music to pursue theological studies and that he would never sing rock and roll again. He enrolled in Oakwood College, a Seventh Day Adventist school in Huntsville, Alabama. Intermittently throughout his career, the Reverend Richard Penniman has evangelized in small churches and in large arenas. In 1959 he married his soul mate, Ernestine Campbell, a union that lasted until 1961. In 1962 Little Richard toured the United Kingdom with Sam Cooke; initially singing gospel that did not go over well with the audience, he switched to rock and roll and was a smashing success.

In 1963 Little Richard worked with the Beatles and the Rolling Stones. He recorded rock and roll between 1964 and 1976 on several labels—including Vee Jay, Modern, and OKeh—and with mixed results. He returned to the church in the mid-1970s, becoming an evangelist and bible salesman. He eventually loosened his strict religious adherence again and, in 1986, was inducted into the Rock and Roll Hall of Fame. Ultimately, Little Richard found a way to unite his faith and his celebrity: the Reverend Penniman has been called to perform religious services for many of his famous peers, including officiating the weddings of Tom Petty, Bruce Springsteen, and Cyndi Lauper.

A CULTURAL ICON

Little Richard resumed performing secular music in a more subdued fashion and had a part in the successful film *Down and Out in Beverly Hills* (1986), which includes his song "Great Gosh A'Mighty." He has continued to appear in many films as both himself and as fictional characters, playing a mayor in *Purple People Eater* (1988) and contributing his vocal talents in the animated *The Trumpet and the Swan* (2001). His acting credits even include a spot in an episode of the television soap opera *The Young and the Restless* in 2008.

Little Richard has experienced a resurgence in popularity in the twenty-first century. From advertisements and reality television shows to performing at White House celebrations, he has continued to be a vibrant presence in American popular culture. In recognition of his contributions, he has been given numerous honors. For example, he has a star on the Hollywood Walk of Fame, and a boulevard in his hometown of Macon was named for him. He has also been inducted into numerous halls of fame in addition to rock and roll's hall, which speaks to the breadth of his influence. Simply put, Little Richard is assured a prominent place in the history of modern music.

Willie Collins

SEE ALSO: *The Beatles; Cooke, Sam; Evangelism; Gospel Music; Lauper, Cyndi; Rhythm and Blues; Rock and Roll; The Rolling Stones; Springsteen, Bruce.*

BIBLIOGRAPHY

Gulla, Bob. *Icons of R&B and Soul: An Encyclopedia of the Artists Who Revolutionized Rhythm*. Westport, CT: Greenwood Press, 2008.

Hildebrand, Lee. *Stars of Soul and Rhythm & Blues*. New York: Billboard Books, 1994.

White, Charles. *The Life and Times of Little Richard: The Quasar of Rock*. New York: Da Capo Press, 1994.

Live Television

Unique to television, live broadcasting—the ability to record and broadcast the sounds and images from events as they occur—endures as one of the industry's most debated, inflated, and promoted terms. Although the majority of television programming has been filmed (or taped) since the early 1950s, live broadcasting—from the Superbowl to the Academy Awards, from presidential debates to international coverage of wars and "low-speed" car chases—plays a central role in the identity of the television industry, representing its technological potential if not the essence of the medium.

The prominent role that live broadcasting plays is not surprising when one considers that television as a technology emerged from the interests and investments of corporations responsible for radio, which was itself developed as a form of wireless point-to-point, or live, communication. From the beginning, television producers and critics pointed to live broadcasting as a way of differentiating television from other media. Jack Gould, television critic for the *New York Times* during the 1950s, went so far as to describe the difference between watching a film and viewing a live program on TV as "the difference between looking at somebody and being with somebody." Live programming in the 1950s included the great variety spectaculars such as *The Colgate Comedy Hour*, sporting events, and anthology dramas such as *Studio One* and *The Alcoa Hour*.

THE GOLDEN AGE OF TELEVISION

Still in its infancy from a technological perspective, live television during this period—the Golden Age of Television—consisted of events staged before several large and static cameras. Unlike today's coverage, live broadcasting in the 1950s required a stable physical location and an event that was either scheduled or long enough in duration to justify the movement of studio cameras. This limited the types of event that could be covered live, but the attraction to these broadcasts and their impact on the country was tremendous. In 1949 three-year-old Kathy Fiscus captured the hearts and minds of the country as rescuers in California attempted to free her from the well she had fallen into. In 1951 the Kefauver hearings on politics and organized crime mesmerized a nation that watched the American political process in action on TV.

The routine coverage of breaking stories and international events associated with live broadcasting in the early twenty-first century would not arrive on the airways until technology advanced to allow for more portable cameras. Live television coverage increased during the 1960s as networks recognized the value of broadcasting live events. The list of most-watched programs and events from that decade is dominated by live broadcasts. Coverage of events such as the Nixon-Kennedy debates (viewed by 91.8 percent of all homes with televisions), Kennedy's assassination and funeral (viewed by 96.1 percent of all television homes), and the *Apollo XI* moon landing (viewed by 93.9 percent of all television homes) demonstrated not only the popularity of the medium but also how live television events came to function as defining cultural moments for an entire generation.

Although the presentation of live special events increased during the 1960s, regularly scheduled live programs began to disappear from the prime-time schedule. By the early 1950s television had moved from a real time (9 EST and 6 PST) to a TV time schedule that made the presentation of live programs more difficult. Further complicating the situation was the fact kinescopes of live shows (a copy of the program filmed off the television screen) looked flat, which made them unattractive to viewers in other time zones and limited the programs' usefulness in syndication as reruns. The high cost of producing live television programming also contributed to its gradual disappearance.

NEW MODELS OF LIVE BROADCASTING

The networks nonetheless recognized viewer attraction to this type of broadcast and searched for new models that could incorporate qualities of live broadcasting. During the 1960s and on through the 1970s, networks employed techniques such as "live on tape" in an effort to capture the feeling of live television. Media critics have noted that the ideology of liveness functions to create a feeling of a viewing community that overcomes the physical distance separating viewers. Presenting programs as if they were live suggests a shared experience, with television functioning as a site of national unification. The fact that very few programs actually unite viewers in even the minimal sense of all watching the same thing at the same time is not nearly as important to the networks as the impression of a shared viewing experience.

Morning news programs such as *Good Morning America*, network nightly news, and various talk shows work diligently to create the impression that one is viewing up-to-the-minute news and events along with millions of other viewers around the country. The truth is, of course, that these programs are taped, and though they may indeed be broadcast live for parts of the nation, they are broadcast to most viewers several hours after taping. The sensation of experiencing these programs as a live broadcast is created through the use of stylistic conventions associated with live broadcasting: the placement of graphics—such as the temperature or time of day—by local affiliates on the television screen and the speakers' use of language, in phrasing such as "we take you *now* to. . . . "

The television industry has become increasingly sophisticated in its ability to blur the visible boundaries between live and taped programming while at the same time exhibiting an increased ability to meet the demand for coverage of live events. Occurrences taking place anywhere, at any time, are instantaneously beamed into living rooms and public spaces around the world. Whether it is a bombing in the Gulf War, police pursuit of a celebrity murder suspect moving slowly along the Los Angeles freeway, a bank robbery, or school violence, television brings it to the viewers live. Duration and location are no longer barriers to live coverage, as helicopters and mobile units scour the world in an effort to break the stories that will capture our attention. Once reserved for the occasional and unusual occurrence, live breaking stories have become so commonplace that they appear as mere interruptions. The exception is, of course, the live televising of sporting events. Sports, along with important political speeches and some ceremonies, seem to demand a live presentation, and the coverage and presentation of these types of events has grown dramatically during the last few decades.

With the simplicity of early broadcasting behind us, terms such as *live* have become complicated and difficult to define. In fact, the definition of *live*—"broadcast directly at the time of production instead of from recorded or filmed material"—does not apply to many of the programs that one might generally think of as "live." Contemporary broadcasting practices regularly present news programs as live even though they are primarily produced from taped material and broadcast (for most of the country) hours after they are taped. Live sporting events include filmed segments that are planned to illustrate predetermined points within the broadcast and include pregame and half-time shows constructed from taped materials. Even special events such as the Olympics mix filmed biographies, taped events, and live coverage.

Although the boundaries between live and taped programming remain blurred, and broadcasts often include portions of both, the attraction to witnessing an event live, with millions or even billions of other viewers, has by no means diminished for today's television audiences.

James Friedman

SEE ALSO: *Academy Awards; Apollo Missions; Comic Books; Comics Code Authority; Daytime Talk Shows; EC Comics; Gulf Wars; Kennedy Assassination; Mafia/Organized Crime; The* New York Times*; Olympics; Professional Football; Radio; Simpson, O. J.;* Studio One*; Super Bowl; Syndication; Television.*

BIBLIOGRAPHY

Caldwell, John Thornton. *Televisuality: Style, Crisis, and Authority in American Television.* New Brunswick, NJ: Rutgers University Press, 1995.

Dyan, Daniel, and Elihu Katz. "Performing Media Events." In *Impacts and Influences: Essays on Media Power in the Twentieth Century*, ed. James Curran, Anthony Smith; Pauline Wingate; et al. London: Methuen, 1987.

Feuer, Jane. "The Concept of Live Television: Ontology as Ideology." In *Regarding Television*, ed. E. Ann Kaplan. Los Angeles: American Film Institute, 1983.

Friedman, James, ed. *Reality Squared: Televisual Discourse on the Real.* New Brunswick, NJ: Rutgers University Press, 2002.

John, Hartley. *Television Truths.* Malden, MA: Blackwell, 2008.

L.L. Bean, Inc.

The history of L.L. Bean, Inc., founded in 1912, really begins with the quintessential rags-to-riches story of the company's founder, Leon Leonwood Bean. Born in 1872 to Benjamin and Sarah Bean, L. L. was the fourth of six children. Orphaned at the age of twelve, he was taken in variously by friends and family, although he mainly fended for himself, eventually becoming an avid outdoorsman who loved hunting, fishing, and other outdoor activities. In an effort to create a hunting boot that would allow his feet to remain dry while walking through the woods, Bean stitched a leather shaft to rubber bottoms, creating what he called at the time "Bean Boots." Convinced that other woodsmen would appreciate his footwear, Bean began selling his boots through the mail with a money-back guarantee. As the story goes, however, of the 100 pairs he sold, Bean made good on his guarantee for ninety of them when their stitching gave way.

Undaunted, Bean made improvements to his design and continued selling the boots along with other outdoor equipment and sporting goods, establishing his mail-order business in Freeport, Maine, where it remained headquartered in the 2010s. In 1917 Bean opened a retail store, located next door to the mail-order offices, to accommodate those customers who invariably stopped by his workshop to make purchases. Over the years, a reputation for quality products and good customer service helped the business prosper. It was announced in 1951 that the retail store would stay open around the clock, 365 days a year, and in 1954 the product line was expanded to include women's items.

After Bean's death in 1967 at the age of ninety-four, his grandson Leon Gorman took over leadership of the company. Leon was at the helm in the late 1970s and early 1980s when the preppy fad helped to fuel demand for L.L. Bean products. Preppies were characterized by their style, which incorporated well-tailored and conservative-yet-casual clothing, including their "uniform" of polo shirt, khaki pants, and leather and rubber footwear—all staples in the L.L. Bean catalog.

Although the preppy craze faded, L.L. Bean did not. The trend toward healthier lifestyles that began in the 1980s and lasted into the 2000s boosted sales of the company's outdoor and sporting equipment. In 2001 Gorman moved to the position of chairman of the board, and Christopher J. McCormick became the first nonfamily member to become president and CEO of L.L. Bean, Inc. In 2010 the company's reported annual net sales of $1.44 billion, and, with nearly three million visitors each year, the retail store was one of Maine's most popular tourist attractions.

Staying true to the values of its founder as it moved ahead into the new millennium, L.L. Bean seemed assured of remaining a fixture in its industry. Among its other initiatives, the company made a commitment to construct all its new buildings according to the U.S. Green Building Council's LEED standards. The firm also continued to emphasize customer service. To celebrate its 100th anniversary, L.L. Bean instituted everyday free shipping for all of its U.S. and Canadian customers.

Mia Consalvo

SEE ALSO: *Online Shopping; Preppy.*

BIBLIOGRAPHY

Bean, L. L. *My Story: The Autobiography of a Down-East Merchant.* Freeport, Maine: L.L. Bean, Inc., 1960.

Gorman, Leon A. *L.L. Bean, Inc.: Outdoor Specialties by Mail from Maine.* New York: The Newcomen Society in North America, 1981.

Gorman, Leon A. *L.L. Bean, Inc.: The Making of an American Icon.* Boston: Harvard Business School Publishing, 2006.

Montgomery, M. R. *In Search of L.L. Bean.* Boston: Little, Brown, 1984.

Lloyd Webber, Andrew *(1948–)*

Sir Andrew Lloyd Webber has written some of the most commercially successful musicals of the contemporary era. Among his most popular shows are *Joseph and the Amazing Technicolor Dreamcoat* (1968), *Jesus Christ Superstar* (1971), *Evita* (1978), *Cats* (1981), *The Phantom of the Opera* (1986), and *Sunset Boulevard* (1993). Lloyd Webber's gift for melody has spawned such classic musical theater songs as "Memory" and "Music of the Night."

Lloyd Webber was born in London on March 22, 1948. His father was a faculty member at the Royal College of Music, and his mother was a piano teacher. Lloyd Webber showed musical aptitude at a very young age and, while still a youth, composed short musical entertainments for his family.

EARLY MUSICAL THEATER PRODUCTIONS

Lloyd Webber's first musical was *Joseph and the Amazing Technicolor Dreamcoat.* With lyricist Tim Rice, he created an eclectic score to accompany the Old Testament story of Joseph and his brothers. Musical numbers ranged from Elvis-style rock to calypso and soft rock ballads. *Joseph*'s two big songs, "Any Dream Will Do" and "Close Every Door," became hit singles.

Jesus Christ Superstar, another collaboration with Rice, began life as a double album. Concert tours of the "rock opera" followed, and ultimately a stage version emerged. *Superstar*, the story of the crucifixion of Jesus Christ as seen through the eyes of Pontius Pilate, garnered seven Tony Awards, including Best Musical and Best Score. Mary Magdalene's song "I Don't Know How to Love Him" became a pop standard. The 1973 film version starred Ted Neeley and Carl Anderson.

Evita, based on the life of Eva Perón, also began as a concept album. Patti LuPone and Mandy Patinkin starred in the Broadway version. The show received numerous Tony Awards, including Best Actress (LuPone). For the 1996 film, which starred Madonna and Antonio Banderas, Lloyd Webber wrote a new song, "You Must Love Me." The song earned an Academy Award for the composer.

Cats, based on T. S. Eliot's *Old Possum's Book of Practical Cats*, is Lloyd Webber's longest-running show both in London's West End and on Broadway. Like *Joseph and the Amazing Technicolor Dreamcoat*, *Cats* contains songs written in a variety of musical styles. "Memory," the show's climactic number, is a sentimental ballad that has been championed by singers Elaine Paige and Barbra Streisand, among others.

Song and Dance (1982) consisted of two parts: *Tell Me on a Sunday*, a one-woman show, and *Variations*, a set of variations on Niccolò Paganini's famous caprice for cello and rock band. *Variations* was written for Lloyd Webber's cello-playing brother, Julian.

Starlight Express (1984), a train epic with music, followed. The cast of the high-tech fantasy dash around the ramp-enhanced theater on roller skates. Rock, blues, and country elements are apparent in the amplified score. A ninety-minute version of *Starlight Express* opened in 1993 at the Las Vegas Hilton,

Andrew Lloyd Webber at* Phantom *Anniversary. *Andrew Lloyd Webber, center, appears with* The Phantom of the Opera *stars Sarah Brightman and Michael Crawford at a performance to celebrate the musical's twenty-fifth anniversary in 2011.* DAVE M. BENETT/CONTRIBUTOR/GETTY IMAGES ENTERTAINMENT/GETTY IMAGES.

the first major legitimate stage production to play in the famed gambling city.

CONTINUING SUCCESS

The Phantom of the Opera is perhaps Lloyd Webber's best-known work. Based on Gaston Leroux's novel, the musical includes the songs "Music of the Night," "All I Ask of You," "The Phantom of the Opera," and "Think of Me." Michael Crawford and Sarah Brightman, then Lloyd Webber's wife, starred in the original production. *Phantom* is indicative of a trend in the late 1980s toward a "sung-through" musical—one in which spoken dialogue is limited and often replaced by operatic recitative (speech-singing). The lavish sets, impressive special effects, and hauntingly beautiful musical score have made the show one of the most popular musicals worldwide. The lavish film adaptation starring Emmy Rossum and Gerard Butler appeared in 2004, and in 2006 a ninety-five-minute truncated version opened in Las Vegas as *Phantom—The Las Vegas Spectacular*.

Aspects of Love (1989) launched the career of its male lead, Michael Ball. The sung-through musical was an adaptation of David Garnett's tale of intergenerational love and included the ballad "Love Changes Everything." The show played for more than three years in London, but its 1990 Broadway run lasted only 377 performances.

Sunset Boulevard, based on the film of the same name, included some spectacularly romantic music. Two songs, "With One Look" and "As if We Never Said Goodbye," both of which are sung by the lead character Norma Desmond, have entered the repertoires of singers as diverse as KiriTeKenawa and Barbra Streisand. As did *The Phantom of the Opera*, *Sunset Boulevard* includes elaborate and impressive sets. John Napier's grandiose staircase is as much a character in the musical as are any of the humans. The London production starred LuPone, whereas the Los Angeles and New York productions featured Glenn Close. Betty Buckley succeeded both LuPone and Close in their respective runs.

Whistle Down the Wind (1998), inspired by the film of the same name, is set in Louisiana in 1959. A collaboration with Jim Steinman, the score includes typically romantic love songs and explosive rock music.

The Beautiful Game (2000), a collaboration with Ben Elton, concerns a group of teenagers growing up in 1969 Belfast. The plot centers on members of a soccer team who become overwhelmed by the religious and political violence surrounding them. Lloyd Webber's intimate musical score captures the myriad emotions explored in the politically charged tale. A reworked version, *The Boys in the Photograph*, opened in Winnipeg, Canada, in 2009.

The Woman in White (2004), based on the nineteenth-century Wilkie Collins thriller, boasts a romantic and largely effusive score characterized by an effective use of musical reprises. Charlotte Jones's book alters aspects of the source material, including the ending. William Dudley's original set designs rely heavily on video projections to create a sense of mystery and grandeur that complements the plot's inherent intimacy.

The highly anticipated sequel to *The Phantom of the Opera*, *Love Never Dies* (2010), is set in Coney Island, New York, in 1907. The story is based on elements of *The Phantom of Manhattan* by Frederick Forsyth and an original treatment by Elton. It played less than eighteen months in London. A reworked version opened in Melbourne, Australia, in 2011.

OTHER WORKS

In addition to his musical theater works, Lloyd Webber has written concert works. *Variations* also exists in a version for cello and orchestra. *Requiem* (1985), written for Lloyd Webber's father, includes the memorable duet "Pie Jesu."

With his impressive array of commercially and artistically successful shows, Lloyd Webber is one of the most important composers for the musical theater of his time. His innate gift for melody and his ability to create music, which live up to the dazzling special effects characteristic of so many of his shows, have contributed immensely to his worldwide success.

William A. Everett

SEE ALSO: *Academy Awards; Broadway;* Cats*;* Jesus Christ Superstar*; Las Vegas; LuPone, Patti; Madonna; The Musical; Patinkin, Mandy;* The Phantom of the Opera*; Streisand, Barbra;* Sunset Boulevard*; Tony Awards.*

BIBLIOGRAPHY

Citron, Stephen. *Sondheim & Lloyd Webber: The New Musical.* New York: Oxford University Press, 2001.

Coveney, Michael. *Cats on a Chandelier: The Andrew Lloyd Webber Story.* London: Hutchinson, 1999.

Ganzl, Kurt. *The Complete* Aspects of Love. New York: Viking Studio Books, 1990.

Lloyd Webber, Andrew, and T. S. Eliot. Cats: *The Book of the Musical.* San Diego, CA: Harcourt Brace Jovanovich, 1983.

McKnight, Gerald. *Andrew Lloyd Webber.* New York: St. Martin's Press, 1984.

Nassour, Ellis, and Richard Broderick. *Rock Opera: The Creation of* Jesus Christ Superstar *from Record Album to Broadway Show and Motion Picture.* New York: Hawthorn Books, 1973.

Parker, Alan. *The Making of* Evita. New York: Collins, 1996.

Perry, George C. *The Complete* Phantom of the Opera. New York: Henry Holt, 1991.

Perry, George C. Sunset Boulevard: *From Movie to Musical.* New York: Henry Holt, 1993.

Richmond, Keith. *The Musicals of Andrew Lloyd Webber.* London: Virgin, 1995.

Snelson, John. *Andrew Lloyd Webber. Yale Broadway Masters.* New Haven, CT: Yale University Press, 2004.

Sternfeld, Jessica. *The Megamusical.* Bloomington: Indiana University Press, 2006.

Walsh, Michael. *Andrew Lloyd Webber, His Life and Works: A Critical Biography.* New York: Abrams, 1989, 1997.

Loafers

America has had a love affair with the moccasin-style shoe known as the loafer for many decades. In the 1950s and 1960s, loafers—particularly the Bass brand called "Weejuns"—were all the rage, especially among students, who slipped coins into the slits on the top, creating so-called "penny loafers." Although slip-ons had been around for years, their "preppy" (short for "prep school") style was extolled in a 1960 editorial in the *Daily Tar Heel*, the newspaper of the University of North Carolina, which asked: "What are Bass Weejuns?" The answer was given as "the thing on the feet of those who are with it."

Many firms, including the Italian high-style Gucci company, manufactured slip-on shoes, but it was the Maine-based G. H. Bass & Company that launched the classic penny loafer style in 1936, duplicating a Norwegian design. According to Bass archivist Carol Paolino, the company named their shoes Weejuns from a contraction of Norwegian and *injun*, the crude slang for *Indian.* Soon, the shoes, and all successive makes of a similar design, became known as loafers, a label that signifies their easy-to-wear comfort and casual style. During the 1980s the shoes became an essential part of the popular preppy garb: khakis, oxford shirts, and loafers. Yet they weren't confined to would-be snobs. Pop superstar Michael Jackson wore loafers and white socks when he performed his signature moonwalk, and Don Johnson of the hit TV series *Miami Vice* (1984–1990) wore loafers without socks with his light-colored suits.

Because the shoe design was so closely associated with the 1980s, it fell out of favor for a time afterward. By the 2010s, however, fashion magazines and websites were declaring that loafers had become trendy with college students and fashionistas once again.

Michael L. Posner

SEE ALSO: *Gucci; Jackson, Michael;* Miami Vice*; Movie Stars; Preppy; Retro Fashion; Slang.*

BIBLIOGRAPHY

Banks, Jeffrey; Doria de La Chapelle; and Lily Pulitzer. *Preppy: Cultivating Ivy Style.* New York: Rizzoli, 2011.

Bayles, Fred. "An American Original Has Lost Its Footing." *USA Today*, February 10, 1998, 4A.

McLaughlin, Patricia. "Loafer Love Affair: Walk a Mile in These Shoes, Step into Fashion." *St. Louis Post-Dispatch*, November 19, 1997, 3.

Locke, Alain *(1886–1954)*

In 1925 Alain Locke—a relatively obscure thirty-nine-year-old professor of philosophy at Howard University—transformed the American literary landscape when his special issue of the *Survey Graphic* familiarized the nation with the literati of the Harlem Renaissance. Later expanded into the anthology *The New Negro*, Locke's sampling of the best African American literature of the 1920s helped launch the reputations of poets Countee Cullen and Langston Hughes. After the publication of *The New Negro*, Locke joined James Weldon Johnson as one of the two elders of African American literature.

Locke encouraged black writers to address themes relating to their own culture and history in their works and to strive for artistic perfection. His efforts significantly influenced the leading black authors of the day, including Nella Larsen, Zora Neale Hurston, and Wallace Thurman. Later in life Locke became one of the chief interpreters of the movement he helped to launch. His 1936 publications, *Negro Art—Past and Present* and *The Negro and His Music*, were seminal works in the field of cultural pluralism.

Jacob M. Appel

SEE ALSO: *Cullen, Countee; Harlem Renaissance; Hughes, Langston; Hurston, Zora Neale; Johnson, James Weldon.*

BIBLIOGRAPHY

Buck, Christopher. *Alain Locke: Faith and Philosophy.* Los Angeles: Kalimat Press, 2005.

Linnemann, Russell J., ed. *Alain Locke: Reflections on a Modern Renaissance Man.* Baton Rouge: Louisiana State University Press, 1982.

Locke, Alain LeRoy. *The New Negro: An Interpretation.* New York: Arno Press, 1968.

Locke, Alain LeRoy. *The Philosophy of Alain Locke: Harlem Renaissance and Beyond*, ed. Leonard Harris. Philadelphia: Temple University Press, 1989.

Washington, Johnny. *Alain Locke and Philosophy: A Quest for Cultural Pluralism.* Westport, CT: Greenwood Press, 1986.

Washington, Johnny. *A Journey into the Philosophy of Alain Locke.* Westport, CT: Greenwood Press, 1994.

Lohan, Lindsay *(1986–)*

Much more famous for her troubles with the law than for her talents as a performer, Lindsay Lohan got her start in modeling and acting as a child. At age eleven she starred in a string of successful Disney films, beginning with 1998's *The Parent Trap.* By her nineteenth birthday, however, she had earned a reputation as a party girl, and she was frequently photographed club hopping in Los Angeles with her bad-girl friends singer Britney Spears and socialite Paris Hilton. A series of highly publicized probation violations stemming from her second conviction for driving under the influence in July 2007 pushed Lohan's off-screen antics to the foreground. Her struggles with alcohol and drugs and defiant attitude toward the law generated a media frenzy, and her mug shots, court appearances, and comings and goings from jail were widely documented on newscasts and on the Internet, providing ample fodder for late-night comedy.

Her tailspin also elicited some serious commentary on the nature of celebrity in America. Her story provoked thoughtful exploration of society's role in exacerbating self-destructive behavior. Some questioned the values of a culture that would glorify her wild-child persona and then revel in her downfall. Others denounced Lohan, along with friends Hilton and Spears, for their sense of entitlement and for capitalizing on the publicity surrounding their legal scrapes. All three were scolded for neglecting their responsibilities to their impressionable young fans by glamorizing drinking, drugging, and promiscuous sex.

CHILDHOOD AND EARLY CAREER

Lohan's upbringing, according to many biographical accounts, is at least partially to blame for her personal problems. She is portrayed as the product of divorced parents with a turbulent history of substance abuse and struggles over the direction of their daughter's career. Her mother, Dina, and father, Michael, have been accused of shamelessly promoting themselves at their daughter's expense. Dina, a former actress and dancer, served as Lindsay's manager and was widely criticized for inviting the television newsmagazine *Entertainment Tonight* (1981–) to film her visit with Lindsay at a drug rehabilitation facility. Dina also appeared with Lindsay's younger sister, Ali, in the 2008 reality show *Living Lohan.* Michael has been incarcerated on several occasions on alcohol and related charges, and in 2011, at the height of Lindsay's headline-grabbing travails, he appeared on the fifth season of the reality show *Celebrity Rehab with Dr. Drew* (2008–).

Raised on Long Island, New York, Lohan signed with the Ford Modeling Agency at the age of three and soon began appearing in television commercials, including spots for restaurants Wendy's and Pizza Hut, and for Jell-O desserts opposite actor Bill Cosby. She made her acting debut at the age of ten playing the character Alli Fowler on the NBC network soap opera *Another World* (1964–1999). She left the show after being cast to play identical twins in the remake of the 1961 movie *The Parent Trap* featuring actress Hayley Mills. Lohan was widely praised for her acting abilities in the film. In a *New York Times* review of the movie, Janet Maslin wrote, "Miss Lohan . . . plays the dual role with apparent effortlessness and with so much forcefulness that she seems to have been taking shy violet lessons from Sharon Stone."

The Parent Trap led the actress to additional Disney contracts, including three television movies and the commercially successful feature film *Freaky Friday* (2003), which stars actress Jamie Lee Curtis as a mother who switches bodies with her daughter for a day. Film critic Roger Ebert in the *Chicago Sun-Times* credited Lohan with "that Jodie Foster sort of seriousness and intent focus beneath her teenage persona." Lohan, who signed a five-record contract with producer Emilio Estefan in 2002, showed off her singing voice on the soundtrack of the film as well as on the soundtrack for 2004's *Confessions of a Teenage Drama Queen.*

TABLOID SCRUTINY AND LEGAL TROUBLES

Lohan's triumphs continued into her late teens with the box-office hits *Mean Girls* (2004) and *Herbie: Fully Loaded* (2005) and her debut album, *Speak* (2004), which went platinum. But she soon became a frequent subject in the tabloids for her late-night revelries, and rumors began to circulate about her suddenly thin appearance. In a 2006 *Vanity Fair* interview that fueled more gossip about her fast lifestyle, she admitted to struggling with bulimia and dabbling in drugs. Reports of her erratic behavior and unexplained absences on the set of *Georgia Rule* (2007) overshadowed positive notices for smaller roles in the 2006 ensemble films *A Prairie Home Companion* and *Bobby.*

During part of the filming of the low-budget thriller *I Know Who Killed Me* (2007)—a box-office disaster featuring Lohan in a notorious pole-dancing scene—the actress was living in a rehabilitation facility and attending Alcoholics Anonymous meetings. But with back-to-back DUI arrests involving illegal cocaine possession in May and July of 2007, she was forced to withdraw, or was released, from various record and film contracts. The ensuing probation violations, including positive drug tests, missed court and community service appointments, and the alleged theft of a $2,500 necklace from a Los Angeles jewelry store, protracted her legal woes over a five-year period. Her run-ins with the law appeared to have ended in late March of 2012 when a Los Angeles County Superior Court judge finally released her from supervised probation.

The actress made several attempts to revitalize her sagging career, including photo shoots for *New York Magazine* (2008) and *Playboy* (2012), guest appearances on the television show *Ugly Betty* (2006–2010), and a role in the exploitation film *Machete* (2010). But her fulfillment of the terms of her probation may have had the most positive influence on her professional reputation. On February 21, 2012, she was signed to star in an original Lifetime biopic about actress Elizabeth Taylor, and less than two weeks later she hosted *Saturday Night Live* (1975–).

Janet Mullane

SEE ALSO: *Celebrity; Cocaine/Crack; Cosby, Bill; Disney (Walt Disney Company); Divorce;* Entertainment Tonight*; Hilton, Paris; The Internet; Jell-O; Media Feeding Frenzies; Reality Television;* Saturday Night Live*; Spears, Britney; Tabloid Television; Tabloids; Taylor, Elizabeth; Television;* Vanity Fair.

BIBLIOGRAPHY

Chocano, Carina. "How Tabloid Train Wrecks Are Reinventing Gothic Literature." *New York Times*, September 2, 2011.

Ebert, Roger. Review for *Freaky Friday*. *Chicago Sun-Times*, August 6, 2003.

Heffernan, Virginia. "Party and Punishment." *New York Times*, October 22, 2010.

Maslin, Janet. Review of *The Parent Trap* (1998). *New York Times*, July 29, 1998.

McGrath, Charles. "Why a Fallen Angel Is a Centerfold." *New York Times*, November 5, 2011.

Lolita

Penned by Russian émigré turned American novelist Vladimir Vladimirovich Nabokov (1899–1977), *Lolita* ranks high among twentieth-century fictional works that have achieved literary acclaim as a result of controversy and censorship. Indeed, the initial rejection of this book by international and American readers produced so much focus on *Lolita* that rather than being abandoned as obscene pornography, its ideas and theme have survived and continue to influence American popular culture into the twenty-first century.

The novel details the tragic yet amusing tale of Humbert Humbert, a dubious European émigré who harbors an obsession for young girls. Upon receiving an inheritance from an uncle, he moves to a small New England town to accept an academic position. Seeking lodging, Humbert rents a room from Charlotte Haze after he encounters her twelve-year-old daughter, Dolores. In time, consumed by his secret passion to be near Dolores (or Lolita, as he affectionately calls her), Humbert marries Charlotte. Shortly thereafter Charlotte dies in a car accident after reading Humbert's diary entries revealing his obsession for Lolita. Relieved at this turn of events, Humbert takes Lolita on an extended journey across America, during which time she seduces him and they become lovers. Eventually Lolita becomes weary of Humbert's possessiveness and leaves him for another, whom Humbert later seeks out and murders.

As noted in his essay, "On a Book Entitled *Lolita*," Nabokov was aware that his treatment of incest in Lolita was one of three themes considered taboo by American publishers. In order to maintain his tenured status as a professor at Cornell University, he initially elected to publish the novel anonymously. After being rejected by American publishers Simon & Schuster, Viking Press, New Directions, and others because of its alleged

Lolita. *Sue Lyon starred as the sexually precocious Lolita in Stanley Kubrick's 1962 film adaptation of Vladimir Nabokov's novel.* MGM/THE KOBAL COLLECTION.

pornographic content, *Lolita* was finally published under Nabokov's own name in late 1955 by Olympia Press in Paris.

The initial printing of 5,000 copies sold immediately and brought Nabokov recognition in Europe. A December 1955 article written by Graham Greene in England's *Sunday Times* soon focused international attention on the novel. Greene's praise of the novel as "one of the three best works of 1955" aroused members of the British press to obtain copies and to proclaim alarm about the safety of young girls. The novel subsequently captured the interest of G. P. Putnam & Sons of New York, which published the first American edition in August 1958.

Once *Lolita* became available in American bookstores, its commercial success soared due to book reviews read by a more literate public as well as censorship practiced by a moral, conservative public. Within book reviews the repetitive use of words such as *obscene, immoral, pornography, scandal,* and *incest*, among others, likely nurtured the public's focus on the perceived lurid or immoral theme of the novel. Moreover, in September 1958 the Public Library of Cincinnati, Ohio, banned *Lolita* from its bookshelves, and other libraries and school systems nationwide followed suit. In a much-publicized event, the citizens of Lolita, Texas (named after resident Lolita Reese in 1910), debated whether to change the town's name to avoid the scandal associated with the book. Collectively, these and other incidents focused attention on *Lolita*, such that it maintained the number one position on the *New York Times* best sellers list for the last eleven weeks of 1958 and well into 1959.

In 1962 the Metro-Goldwyn-Mayer (MGM) film version of the novel (screenplay by Nabokov) produced a renewed interest in *Lolita* and subsequently increased its profits from book and movie-ticket sales. A few decades later, in 1997, an updated film version was made that attracted more publicity than the 1962 version due to its purported sexual content. In Sweden, an opera based on the novel was produced, and Lund University's electronic library is named Lolita.

Lolita has been published without interruption since 1958, which provides ample evidence of its longevity and popularity. Its theme, language, and commercial value continue to impact American and international culture. For example, in psychoanalysis, such phrases as the "Lolita Syndrome" and "Lolita Complex" have been used to describe a middle-aged man's secret lust for prepubescent females or the unhealthy desire for young females.

Marlena E. Bremseth

SEE ALSO: *Best Sellers; Media Feeding Frenzies; MGM (Metro-Goldwyn-Mayer); The* New York Times*; Pornography; Public Libraries; Sex Scandals.*

BIBLIOGRAPHY

Baker, George. "Lolita: Literature or Pornography?" *Saturday Review*, June 1957, 18.

Bloom, Harold, ed. *Vladimir Nabokov's* Lolita. New York: Chelsea, 1987.

Bloom, Harold, ed. *Lolita*. New York: Chelsea House, 1993.

De Grazia, Edward. *Girls Lean Back Everywhere*. New York: Random House, 1992.

Pifer, Ellen. *Vladimir Nabokov's Lolita: A Casebook*. New York: Oxford University Press, 2003.

Lollapalooza

The alternative rock traveling circus Lollapalooza began in 1991 as the brainchild of Perry Farrell, then front man of Jane's Addiction. The summer festival brought together seven alternative rock acts and their respective loyal followings for afternoon and evening concerts at large outdoor venues across the United States. Likened to the Woodstock festival of 1969, Lollapalooza expanded each year, with acts playing several stages simultaneously and with circus tents set up on the grounds to house such "sideshow" attractions as tattooing and body-piercing vendors, voter registration tables, free Internet surfing, presentations by proponents of marijuana legalization, exotic foods, and the requisite (and profitable) Lollapalooza merchandising booths. The show grew to include more than thirty bands on three stages, took a hiatus in 1998, toured once again in 2003, and in 2005 reestablished itself as a successful annual multi-stage weekend festival in Chicago's downtown Grant Park.

Lollapalooza's five-year hiatus began when the tour was canceled in 1998, reportedly so planners could regroup and ensure that the next edition of the tour was better integrated. Critics had generally agreed that each new tour seemed less coherent and that the quality of the acts as a packaged whole suffered, with disparate fringe bands taking the place of the 1991 festival's relatively mainstream selection of alternative rock groups. The Lollapalooza tour was revived in 2003, but in 2004 organizers attempted to expand it to two days in each city and, instead, had to cancel all dates due to low ticket sales. In 2005 Lollapalooza was held for one weekend in Grant Park on the lakefront in Chicago and was so successful that by 2008 organizers and the city had agreed it would remain as an annual event at least until 2018. In its new incarnation it embraced the eclectic diversity that had once been criticized, spreading hip-hop, reggae, indie rock, electronica, and modern roots across eight stages, boasting a farmer's market among its vendors, and reserving one stage for Kidzapalooza.

The commercial success of Lollapalooza encouraged the creation of other outdoor rock festivals, including the less esoteric H.O.R.D.E. (Horizons of Rock Developing Everywhere) festival (1992–1998) and the gynocentric Lilith Fair (1997–1999; 2010)—named for Adam's apocryphal first wife—which featured all-female acts. Lollapalooza went international with the creation of Lolla Chile in 2011 and Lolla Brazil in 2012. Though originally conceived by Perry Farrell as a farewell tour for Jane's Addiction, Lollapalooza became a multigenre, multigenerational, and international music festival. Two decades later Farrell was still running the festival, which had, like the band that originated it, survived hiatuses and alterations to continue making music.

Tilney Marsh

SEE ALSO: *Alternative Rock; Body Piercing; Girl Groups; Indie Music; The Internet; Marijuana; Reggae; Rock and Roll; Tattoos; The Windy City; Woodstock.*

BIBLIOGRAPHY

Beck; Courtney Love; Stephen Malkmus; et al. *Online Diaries: The Lollapalooza Tour Journals of Beck, Courtney Love, Stephen Malkmus, Thurston Moore, Lee Ranaldo, and Mike Watt*. New York: Soft Skull Press, 2001.

George-Warren, Holly; Patricia Romanowski Bashe; and John Pareles, eds. *The Rolling Stone Encyclopedia of Rock & Roll*, 3rd ed., rev. and updated. New York: Fireside, 2001.

Lombard, Carole *(1908–1942)*

The quintessential comedienne of the screwball comedy, Carole Lombard starred in many film classics of the 1930s and early 1940s, such as *Nothing Sacred* and *My Man Godfrey*, the latter of which earned her an Oscar nomination. Audiences indulged in the over-the-top antics of the screwball genre partially because of Lombard's likeability and allure. Known for her coarse language offscreen and beauty on-screen, she married two motion picture superstars, William Powell and Clark Gable, during her short life.

Born Jane Alice Peters in Indiana, she was discovered by director Allan Dwan at the age of twelve. She became one of Mack Sennett's bathing beauties and later made the transition to sound films. She was popular with the Hollywood community, particularly on set, and her costar in *Twentieth Century*, legendary actor John Barrymore, called her the greatest actress with whom he had ever worked. She was active in selling war bonds during World War II and died in a plane crash near Las Vegas on the way home from a bond-selling tour in 1942.

Jill A. Gregg

SEE ALSO: *Barrymore, John; Gable, Clark; Powell, William; Screwball Comedies; Sennett, Mack; War Bonds.*

BIBLIOGRAPHY

Harris, Warren G. *Gable and Lombard.* New York: Simon and Schuster, 1974.

Ott, Frederick W. *The Films of Carole Lombard.* Secaucus, NJ: Citadel, 1972.

Rollyson, Carl. *American Biography.* New York: IUniverse, 2006.

Swindell, Larry. *Screwball: The Life of Carole Lombard.* New York: Morrow, 1975.

Lombardi, Vince *(1913–1970)*

No individual meant more to the rise of the National Football League (NFL) during the 1960s (with the possible exception of league commissioner Pete Rozell) than the legendary coach of professional football's most legendary team, Vince Lombardi of the Green Bay Packers. The 1960s ushered in a new era in professional football: armed with its first national television contract and rising attendance, the NFL went from a regional curiosity to a nationwide force in America within a decade.

Lombardi's success coaching the Packers from 1959 to 1967 is unparalleled in pro-football history. In seven seasons, he never had a losing season, and he led the Packers to five NFL championships, including Super Bowls I and II in 1967 and 1968. These achievements, coinciding with the NFL's rising popularity, turned the coach and the Packers into national celebrities. Lombardi, who sometimes used harsh methods to instill discipline, became a beloved but controversial figure, caught in the crossfire of the cultural battles of the late 1960s. To some, his coaching represented the best of American leadership; to others, the worst.

CHURCH AND FOOTBALL

Vincent Lombardi was born June 11, 1913, to the children of Italian immigrants in Brooklyn, New York. His father, Harry, owned a wholesale meat business and was a stern disciplinarian who presided over a proud, close-knit household. The Lombardis' love of family, the Catholic Church, and their Italian ancestry led young Vince to prepare for the priesthood in 1929. But after three years at Cathedral School of the Immaculate Conception, for reasons he never revealed, Lombardi left to attend St. Francis Academy in Brooklyn on a football scholarship. He played both offense and defense, winning both a reputation as a punishing player and a football scholarship to Fordham University.

At Fordham, Lombardi was often injured and did not play much until his senior year. In the meantime, he met Marie Planitz, the New Jersey–born daughter of a Wall Street stockbroker. Planitz was the only girlfriend Lombardi ever had, and they married in 1940. He played both offensive and defensive guard his senior year, and he was an anchor of the famed Seven Blocks of Granite, the team's offensive line.

Despite his reputation as a punishing and emotional player, Lombardi's dreams of a playing career floundered. After two seasons playing semipro football, he began planning for law school. Instead he accepted an offer to teach and coach sports at St. Cecilia High School in Englewood, New Jersey, a decision that would change his life. Coaching eight years of football at

Vince Lombardo. *Vince Lombardi leads the Green Bay Packers to victory over the Kansas City Chiefs in Super Bowl I in Los Angeles, California, in January 1967.* FOCUS ON SPORT/CONTRIBUTOR/ GETTY IMAGES SPORT/GETTY IMAGES.

St. Cecilia, Lombardi found his calling. His system, a rigid, organized style that stressed fundamentals, found success on the field. After St. Cecilia, he became a college football coach, first as an assistant at Fordham for the 1947–1948 season, then at the United States Military Academy at West Point from 1948 to 1954.

Although Lombardi's career thrived, he was passed over for many university head-coaching positions, a fact Lombardi attributed to anti-Italian discrimination. In 1954 he accepted a position as assistant coach with the NFL's New York Giants. In five years as New York's masterful offensive coordinator, he pioneered coaching techniques, especially the use of film to teach players. In 1959, three years after CBS signed the first contract to televise NFL games nationally, Lombardi was named head coach of the Green Bay Packers.

COACHING THE PACKERS

As coach of the Packers, Lombardi inherited a team plagued by a lack of leadership, poor organization, undisciplined players, and eleven consecutive losing seasons. He immediately gained the players' attention when, at his first team meeting, he announced that anyone unwilling to work hard enough to win should leave the team. Talented players who were once either too timid (like Bart Starr) or temperamental (like Paul Hornung) thrived under Lombardi's unchallenged authority, and in his first season the Packers finished 7–5.

The team continued to improve under Lombardi's direction. From 1960 to 1966 it achieved a 73–20–3 record and won four NFL championships. The Packers became a highly disciplined team that won with toughness, not flash. In their signature play, the sweep, offensive linemen pulled away from the line of scrimmage and formed a wall of blockers, smashing open holes for the following ball carrier. The Packers' tough play quickly gained fans across the nation, and their success catalyzed the NFL's advances in the popular consciousness.

During this time, Lombardi became the face of professional football around the world. His book, *Run to Daylight* (1963), was a best seller. He became extremely popular on the lecture circuit, espousing not only his theories on football but also on society and politics. Lombardi was lavished with praise by some, including many in business, for his intelligence, character, leadership, and commitment to God and family. During the late 1960s, when so many institutions and leaders were under fire, Lombardi was perceived as evidence that old notions of authority remained tenable and desirable. But critics condemned the coach as blunt, rude, and dictatorial, an antiquated symbol of an outmoded leadership style. This dual public image followed Lombardi for the rest of his life.

Lombardi, however, was not so easily pigeonholed. Scarred by his experiences with prejudice, he was a strong supporter of the civil rights movement and insisted that all of his players be treated equally while traveling in the South. Lombardi also supported gun control. But the coach found the 1960s counterculture and antiwar activists antithetical to the values of order and loyalty he held dear and spoke out vehemently against them. Like many Americans, Lombardi was trying to make sense of the changing world around him. His complicated evaluation of that world undoubtedly contributed to his popularity across the ideological spectrum, a popularity that had both Vice President Hubert Humphrey and former vice president Richard Nixon considering Lombardi as a running mate for the 1968 presidential election.

In 1968 Lombardi retired as coach of the Packers, but restlessness led him back to football, and he became coach and general manager of the Washington Redskins in 1969. Lombardi soon fell ill, however, and ravaged by cancer, he died with wife, Marie, by his side on September 3, 1970, at the age of fifty-seven. After his death, the NFL renamed its championship trophy after Lombardi, honoring the man whose gridiron success and public persona defined the modern era of professional football.

Alexander Shashko

SEE ALSO: *Civil Rights Movement; The Green Bay Packers; National Football League (NFL); Starr, Bart; Super Bowl.*

BIBLIOGRAPHY

Havel, Chris. *Lombardi: An Illustrated Life.* Iola, WI: Krause Publications, 2011.

Lombardi, Vince, and W. C. Heinz. *Run to Daylight!* Englewood Cliffs, NJ: Prentice-Hall, 1963.

O'Brien, Michael. *Vince: A Personal Biography of Vince Lombardi.* New York: William Morrow, 1987.

Wells, Robert W. *Lombardi: His Life and Times.* Madison, WI: Wisconsin House, 1971.

Lombardo, Guy *(1902–1977)*

For forty-eight years, bandleader Guy Lombardo and his Royal Canadians, featuring the lead saxophone and singing of his brother Carmen and the lead trumpet of brother Lebert, continued the tradition of New Year's Eve broadcasts on radio or television from New York City. They presented programs of easy-listening, low-key dance music that climaxed with "Auld Lang Syne" at the ringing in of the New Year. Jazz music buffs labeled Lombardo "the king of corn," but loyal fans of his music, billed as "the sweetest music this side of heaven," bought more than 250 million of his recordings.

Pop music critic George T. Simon explains in *Simon Says: The Sights and Sounds of the Swing Era* the band's phenomenal success: "It hits superb tempos, and though it doesn't produce a rhythmically inspiring beat, it produces a succession of steady, unobtrusive beats that make it a pleasure to take your girl out on the floor and move around to the best of your ability. If you can dance at all, you can dance to Lombardo's music." He adds that "Lombardo, with his years and years of experience, knows how to select tunes that create a mood, an intimate, cozy mood." In fact, Lombardo claimed to have introduced more than three hundred songs to the public.

From the band's beginning in 1923 in their hometown of London, Ontario, they were a close-knit group, with brothers Guy, Carmen, and Lebert sharing ownership. Two other siblings, Rose Marie and Victor, joined the band later. Although the original three brothers had an equal share in the orchestra's profits, Lombardo was, as Decca Records producer Milt Gabler remarked, the "complete boss. No matter what anybody else says or thinks, if Guy feels strongly about something, that's it." He apparently used his authority tactfully, for Larry Barnett, a top talent agency executive, said, "Guy Lombardo is the nicest man that's ever been in the music business."

Guy Lombardo. *Bandleader Guy Lombardo's music was a staple of many New Year's Eve celebrations for nearly fifty years.* MICHAEL OCHS ARCHIVES/STRINGER/GETTY IMAGES.

One of the band's engagements in Cleveland, Ohio, caught the eye of the then-new Music Corporation of America (MCA), and the career of the Royal Canadians was well launched, leading to their first national broadcast in 1927, from Chicago. By 1929 the orchestra was the winter attraction at Manhattan's Roosevelt Grill, where it was booked perennially for thirty years. When the Grill closed, the band moved to the Waldorf-Astoria, which became the annual site of its famous year-ending broadcasts.

Already selling more recordings than any other band, the orchestra continued through the years to add other superlatives. It played more Presidential Inaugural Balls than any other big-name dance band. It also introduced more hit songs: "Boo Hoo," "Coquette," "Sweethearts on Parade," and "Seems Like Old Times" (all four written by Carmen), as well as "Gimme a Little Kiss," "You're Driving Me Crazy," "Heartaches," "Little White Lies," "Little Girl," "Annie Doesn't Live Here Anymore," and "Everywhere You Go," to name only a few. It also set many all-time attendance marks at various venues, including the Savoy Ballroom in Harlem, New York.

In the 1960s Lombardo turned to other activities. He was a well-known speedboat racer, winning the Gold Cup, the sport's highest honor. He also became immensely wealthy, drawing large royalties from music publishing ventures; opening successful restaurants on Long Island and in Tampa Bay, Florida; and producing popular shows at the Jones Beach Marine Theater on Long Island. His nationwide tours with the Royal Canadians, playing to packed houses, continued into the 1970s.

When asked to explain his phenomenal success, Lombardo answered simply: "Bands happened, musicians happened. And we happened." Others would point to the band's professional, businesslike approach to its work and its persistence in staying with a winning formula. "We really have never changed," Lombardo once said. "We've improved, yes, but we never have changed." He added, "Anything that's popular, I like."

Benjamin Griffith

SEE ALSO: *Big Bands; Jazz; Pop Music.*

BIBLIOGRAPHY

Kressley, Dave, and Charles Garrod. *Guy Lombardo and His Royal Canadians.* Zephyrhills, FL: Joyce Record Club, 1995.

Simon, George T. *Simon Says: The Sights and Sounds of the*

Swing Era, 1935–1955. New Rochelle, NY: Arlington House, 1971.

Simon, George T. *The Big Bands*. New York: Macmillan, 1974.

Walker, Leo. *The Wonderful Era of the Great Dance Bands*. New York: Da Capo, 1990.

London, Jack *(1876–1916)*

In his writing as in his highly publicized personal life, Jack London provided an overture to the complexities of American society in the early years of the twentieth century. Despite a professional career of less than twenty years, London wrote more than fifty novels, 200 short stories, and an additional 400 pieces of nonfictional prose. His various adventures as a South Seas sailor, socialist politician, Alaskan argonaut, Asian war correspondent, California farmer, and general hobo exemplified the wanderlust that characterized both America's roots and its future. Although London's persona invites a comparison with Theodore Roosevelt's philosophy of the strenuous life or Frederick Jackson Turner's vision of frontier regeneration, he reveled in ambiguities beyond the scope of his contemporaries.

London was born in San Francisco, the illegitimate child of Flora Wellman. Before his first birthday, his mother had married John London, a widower with two daughters. The resulting family was plagued by hardship; the specter of poverty would prove to be the strongest feature of London's childhood. The family frequently moved throughout the Bay Area, and Jack entered the working world at age ten. Such a life fostered self-reliance and independence, virtues that later became prominent themes in London's writing. Denied a formal education, the boy compensated with voracious reading; he became a fixture at the public libraries, absorbing the advice of Horatio Alger and the adventures of great explorers.

By age fifteen London had entered the world of the outlaw, staking out an existence by thieving oysters from the commercial beds around San Francisco Bay. His nautical career assumed legitimacy in 1893 when he joined the crew of a sealing vessel working in the North Pacific. Following a seven-month sea voyage, he returned to the Bay Area but quickly embarked on a cross-country odyssey, initially as a member of Joseph Coxney's "Army" of unemployed men who were traveling to Washington in a quest for government assistance in the wake of the Panic of 1893. By the time this group reached Missouri, London was ready to travel alone and panhandled his way to Niagara, New York. These wanderings climaxed with an arrest for vagrancy in June 1894. After serving a thirty-day sentence, he returned to California.

Such youthful experiences became the inspiration for literature. Several of London's short stories dealt with the world of the oyster pirates, and his tenure on the high seas later provided the foundation for *The Sea Wolf* (1904). The autobiographical work *The Road* (1907) recounts his trek across America. Literary scholars generally perceive these adventures as critical in London's emergence as a writer. Close contact with an assortment of sailors and vagabonds instructed the youth in the art of storytelling. Furthermore, these escapades—particularly the humiliation of incarceration—ignited London's sense of social justice and ultimately shaped his political beliefs.

Jack London. *Jack London wrote more than 50 novels and 200 short stories while living a life of adventure in the late 1800s and early 1900s.* **HULTON ARCHIVE/GETTY IMAGES.**

LIMITED FORMAL EDUCATION

By 1895 London was attending Oakland High School and augmenting his class work with impassioned readings of Karl Marx, Charles Darwin, and Herbert Spencer. He had previously dabbled in writing, and an account of his sealing experiences, "Story of a Typhoon off the Coast of Japan," was published in the *San Francisco Morning Call* in November 1893. During his year in high school, London spent more time on this craft, contributing an assortment of writings to the student literary magazine. Despite the haphazard nature of his formal education, he successfully completed the entrance examination for the University of California at Berkeley, but his college experience proved short-lived; at the close of the first semester, he had to leave the university for financial reasons.

London responded to this setback by giving priority to his writing. Aflame with the ideals of socialism (he became an active member of the Socialist Labor Party in 1896), he embarked on a frenzy of composition, experimenting in everything from political tracts to poetry and bombarding San Francisco publishers with the results. Despite his enthusiasm, his efforts were rewarded with little beyond rejection forms, and the aspiring writer eventually became a laundry worker at a private academy for boys. The semiautobiographical novel *Martin Eden* (1909) discusses his difficulties during this time. Although this was a particularly discouraging point in his development, his fortunes soon changed.

In the summer of 1897, London became one of the thousands of hopeful migrants to the gold fields of the Klondike. As a prospector, however, he enjoyed a distinct absence of luck. For much of his mining career, he was constrained by brutal weather or debilitating illness, but these setbacks did not prevent him from realizing the epic and allegorical potential of the world around him. By the summer of 1898, he had returned to San Francisco, financially none the richer for his experience but reeling with ideas. By April 1900 his first novel *The Son of the Wolf* had appeared to a welcoming public. For the next decade London transformed his Yukon adventures into an assortment of successful short stories and novels that have proved to be his most enduring work, particularly the novels *The Call of the Wild* (1903) and *White Fang* (1906).

Despite the enormous popularity of such tales, London's sagas of the Yukon are only one component of a multifaceted career. Shortly after establishing himself as a major American novelist, he embarked on a journalistic mission for the American Press Association. Although originally retained to report on the Boer War in South Africa, the assignment was canceled, and London opted to examine the urban slums of England. During the fall of 1902, he donned a suitable disguise and lived in the squalor of London's East End. The eventual product was his nonfiction study *The People of the Abyss* (1903), a pioneering work in undercover journalism. Such writing provided an outlet for his narrative skills and a vehicle to espouse his political views, and the author later ranked this work as his greatest accomplishment.

Journalistic pursuits continued in 1904 when he traveled to Japan to report on the Russo-Japanese War for the Hearst papers. Although he lived in proximity to the fighting for nearly six months, the Japanese government closely monitored his activities and dispatches, thus thwarting his efforts. Frustrated by this interference, London gave up and returned to California.

THE SEA WOLF

In the period between these adventures, London completed one of his most successful novels, *The Sea Wolf*, in many ways the quintessential Jack London story: a sheltered, inexperienced individual is thrown into a hostile alien world and, through his struggle for survival, emerges a hero. At the same time, however, this contact with the unfamiliar compels the protagonist to confront the possibility of an inherent evil within the human soul. In this case, the hero is Humphrey Van Weyden, a sheltered San Francisco literary critic who, following an accident at sea, is rescued by a sealing vessel bound for Japan. The ship is commanded by the tyrannical Wolf Larsen, who takes delight in forcing Van Weyden to adapt to the rough life of a seaman. Although Van Weyden is repelled by the savage barbarity of the captain, he is also intrigued by Larsen's primitive but pronounced intellect. As the story progresses, Van Weyden must balance the redemptive qualities of a physically demanding life with the moral debaucheries represented by Larsen.

The Sea Wolf is very much a reflection of the literary and cultural atmosphere of the time. The novel's emphasis on random happenings and the weakness of the individual invites a comparison with naturalist writers such as Frank Norris and Theodore Dreiser. One should also consider that Theodore Roosevelt was in the White House, and the president's views on the virtues inherent in physical struggle and the regenerative possibilities of antimodernism were well known to the American public. Furthermore, London was shrewd enough to include a romantic subplot (Larsen rescues another ill-fated traveler who happens to be female) in order to engage a wider audience. The resulting novel, which rivaled *The Call of the Wild* in popularity, has been translated into numerous languages and adapted for movies several times, most successfully in 1941 with John Garfield, Ida Lupino, and Edward G. Robinson.

As London's literary career progressed, he continued his involvement in an assortment of unusual pursuits. During 1905 he stood unsuccessfully as the socialist candidate in the campaign for mayor of Oakland. Later that year he purchased a large tract of land in California's Sonoma Valley to enjoy the life of a country squire. Eventually this project became the primary focus of his energies, but his attention was diverted by one of his most publicized adventures: an attempt to sail around the world in a ship of his own design. Given the nature of his writing, it is understandable that the public was intrigued by this escapade.

The original plan was to depart from San Francisco in the fall of 1906 and spend the next seven years circling the globe. Unfortunately, the voyage was doomed from the start. London's dream ship, *The Snark*, ended up costing five times the initial estimate, and its slow construction delayed the voyage for six months. The resulting vessel proved to be less than seaworthy, and major repairs were required when the party reached Hawaii in May 1907. By the time the ship crawled into the South Seas, London and his crew were demoralized and suffering from an assortment of health problems, some of which would trouble London for the remainder of his life. Forced to confront failure, the voyage was abruptly terminated at the end of 1908.

Despite these setbacks, the sailor continued to write. As had been the case with his Yukon experience, he mined the tropic setting of his ill-fated voyage for an assortment of short stories. Many of these are collected in the volumes *South Sea Tales* (1911) and *The House of Pride, and Other Tales of Hawaii* (1912).

LONDON THE RANCHER

The Sonoma Ranch occupied increasing attention during London's final years. While he was of a distinctly urban origin, he confronted the mysteries of agronomy with the same zeal he had displayed toward education and politics. Accounts of his actual success are contradictory, but he was clearly a pioneer of a scientific approach to farming. Once again, his life was reflected in his writing. In one of his last major novels, *The Valley of the Moon* (1913), London provides an epic account of two members of Oakland's working poor who flee the horrors of the city to find prosperity and happiness in the California countryside.

By contrast, the thematic sequel to this work, *Little Lady of the Big House* (1916), provides a darker vision of agrarian life and can be seen as a reflection of the chaos and unhappiness that confronted London toward the end of his life. The later book concerns a California rancher who is professionally successful but plagued by personal anguish.

The last three years of London's life involved an assortment of medical and economic difficulties. Despite his reputation for ruggedness, he had always been careless about his physical health, and before he reached the age of forty, his body was failing from a combination of abuse and neglect. At the same time, reckless spending and questionable investments drained his finances and forced him to accelerate his work schedule to meet the demands of his creditors. During 1916 he traveled to Hawaii with an eye toward recuperation, but it was too little too late. On November 22, London succumbed to the effects of kidney failure.

Although London's death was a cause for national mourning, his presence in the American literary canon quickly faded. Much of his work went out of print, and he continues to be mistakenly perceived as a writer of adolescent adventure fiction. He seldom enjoyed the critical acclaim given to contemporaries such as Norris or Dreiser, but in terms of popular success, his work far outshone that of his peers. He tackled an astounding array of topics in his writing and delighted the imaginations of millions of readers worldwide. While his overall influence is difficult to assess, it can by no means be dismissed.

J. Allen Barksdale

SEE ALSO: *Dreiser, Theodore; Garfield, John; Norris, Frank; Robinson, Edward G.*

BIBLIOGRAPHY

Kershaw, Alex. *Jack London: A Life*. London: HarperCollins, 1997.

Labor, Earle, and Jeanne Campbell Reesman. *Jack London*, rev. ed. New York: Twayne, 1974.

London, Charmian. *The Book of Jack London*. New York: Century, 1921.

Stasz, Clarice. *American Dreamers: Charmian and Jack London*. New York: St. Martin's Press, 1988.

Stefoff, Rebecca. *Jack London: An American Original*. New York: Oxford University Press, 2002.

Walker, Franklin. *Jack London and the Klondike: The Genesis of an American Writer*. San Marino, CA: Huntington Library, 1994.

The Lone Ranger

The Lone Ranger was the creation of George W. Trendle, a theater manager and former lawyer who in 1930, in partnership with John H. King, purchased radio station WXYZ, a Detroit, Michigan, affiliate of CBS. Hoping to turn greater profits, Trendle severed his affiliation with CBS in 1932 and transformed XYZ into an independent station with its own acting company and its own productions. One of Trendle's ideas, developed with studio manager Harold True and producer James Jewell, was a new show about a Western hero, a larger-than-life Robin Hood of the West, whose personal code of ethics and morals would set him apart from ordinary heroes. In collaboration with Fran Striker, a writer who had previously produced a Western program with a similar theme on a radio station in Buffalo, New York, Trendle's group transformed the idea into the most familiar and enduring fictional legend in American popular folklore.

WHO WAS THAT MASKED MAN?

The Lone Ranger was originally one of six Texas Rangers who were ambushed at Bryant's Gap by the evil Butch Cavendish Gang. Five rangers are killed, but the severely wounded John Reid is discovered by Tonto, a Native American who had been his boyhood friend. Before the ambush, Reid's brother, Dan (the captain of the Ranger squad), says that his wife and son are coming West and that they will need help running their silver mine if anything should happen to him. While nursing the wounded ranger, Tonto prepares six graves, leaving one empty so

The Lone Ranger. *Clayton Moore, left, and Jay Silverheels brought the Lone Ranger and Tonto to life in the television and movie versions of the western tale.* SILVER SCREEN COLLECTION/CONTRIBUTOR/ARCHIVE PHOTOS/GETTY IMAGES.

the Cavendish Gang will believe that they had killed all of the Rangers. After four days the wounded lawman gains consciousness and discovers that he is the only surviving Ranger, the Lone Ranger. He decides to wear a mask to disguise his identity.

As the program evolved over the next few months, the Lone Ranger acquires a great white stallion—his dependable mount, Silver—and together with the ever-faithful Tonto, he journeys about the western United States quashing criminal activities and bringing evildoers, always referred to as owl hoots, outlaws, and low-down coyotes, to justice. Eventually he uses silver bullets from his brother's silver mine not only as ammunition but also as a signature and calling card. On occasion the Lone Ranger's nephew, Dan Reid, rides with the pair.

The program was aimed at juvenile listeners. The Lone Ranger uses perfect grammar and pronunciation and never smokes, drinks, or associates with women, except to save them from evil. He never shoots to kill; bad guys are always "winged" in the arms or shoulder. The exception is Butch Cavendish, whom he eventually kills in self-defense. The program featured classical music as the background theme, because the station did not have to pay royalties on music that was in the public domain. Gioachino Rossini's "William Tell Overture," the musical theme of the program, became, in fact, a part of popular Americana.

The plots were formulaic. The bad guys are always brought to justice, and each show ends with one of the townspeople asking, "Who was that masked man?" An authority figure would announce, "He's the Lone Ranger!" as in the distance the audience heard the Lone Ranger's deep voice intoning, "Hi yo, Silver, awaaaaay!" as he rides off to his next adventure.

The program first aired on January 30, 1933, without a sponsor. After trying out several actors in the role of the Lone Ranger, Trendle settled on law student Earl Graser in May 1933. John Todd, a former Shakespearean actor, played Tonto throughout the program's twenty-two-year run. In 1941 Graser was killed in a car accident and was replaced by the deep-voiced Brace Beemer, who had been the announcer/narrator of the show and who had appeared as the Ranger in public appearances because Graser was too short. Beemer played the part until the show went off the air in 1955. In 1946 the voice of Fred Foy was added as the announcer/narrator. The sponsor of the program for its final fifteen years on radio was General Mills, thus the breakfast cereals Wheaties and Cheerios were indelibly linked with *The Lone Ranger* by schoolboys everywhere.

By 1934 the fame of the Lone Ranger had traveled beyond the lower Michigan area to Chicago. WXYZ contracted with Chicago's WGN to receive the show via telephone. Shortly thereafter New York's WOR joined them. These three stations then formed the Mutual Radio Network and added stations throughout the country. The half-hour show was broadcast on Monday, Wednesday, and Friday at 6:30 p.m. Before tape or wire recording became available, each show had to be broadcast three times, once each for the Eastern, Central, and Pacific time zones.

THE MASKED MAN MOVES TO TELEVISION

Throughout most of its run, the programs were written by Striker and directed by Al Hodge, Charles Livingston, and Fred Flowerday. In 1949 the Lone Ranger came to television. The introduction and closing, by Foy, and the theme music were recorded in Detroit and superimposed on half-hour filmed programs, which were produced in California. Clayton Moore, a former "B" movie actor, and Jay Silverheels, a Mohawk Indian who had played small parts in several films, were the lead actors. The television program lasted from September 15, 1949, through September 12, 1957. The opening episode recounts the Bryant's Gap story of the ambush of the Rangers and the adoption of the name and the mask. Reruns of the show continued well into the 1960s on many independent stations.

In 1937 and 1939 Republic Pictures released fifteen-part Lone Ranger serials, but they varied somewhat from the radio formats. In 1956 Warner Brothers released *The Lone Ranger*, starring Moore and Jay Silverheels; the pair later appeared in *The Lone Ranger and the Lost City of Gold*, a 1958 United Artists feature. In 1981 the ITC/Wrather Corporation released *The Legend of the Lone Ranger*, a big-budget film starring Klinton Spilsbury and Michael Horse in the lead roles, with Jason Robards as President U. S. Grant. It was a pretentious and overblown film, which quickly dropped from circulation. Spilsbury, whose entire spoken dialogue had to be dubbed by another actor, won two Golden Raspberry Awards, one for worst actor and the other for worst new star. The film won an additional award for worst musical score.

A controversy arose when the Wrather Corporation, which by then owned the rights to the Lone Ranger, sought an injunction against Moore, ordering him to stop presenting himself as the Lone Ranger because he was too old and too fat, even though he weighed fifteen pounds less than he did when he was in the TV series. Shortly before Jack Wrather's death in 1985, the court order was suspended. Moore, wearing wraparound sunglasses instead of a mask, continued to tour during the injunction period, and after the suspension, he donned the mask again for personal appearances.

Another Trendle creation, which began on WXYZ on January 31, 1936, was the Green Hornet. Britt Reid, son of the Lone Ranger's nephew Dan Reid, was a big-city newspaper publisher by day. By night he was a masked, caped crusader who fought urban corruption in his super-fast car, "The Black Beauty," which was driven by his Japanese valet Kato. (According to some sources, after December 7, 1941, Kato became a Filipino.) *The Green Hornet* went off the air in 1952. The same production team also created *The Challenge of the Yukon* (1939–1955), WXYZ's other long-running adventure series. The same troupe of actors played various roles on all three programs.

James R. Belpedio

SEE ALSO: *"B" Movies; Radio; Radio Drama; Television; United Artists; The Western.*

BIBLIOGRAPHY

Buxton, Frank, and Bill Owen. *The Big Broadcast, 1920–1950.* New York: Viking Press, 1972.

Dunning, John. *Tune in Yesterday: The Ultimate Encyclopedia of Old Time Radio, 1925–1976.* Englewood Cliffs, NJ: Prentice Hall, 1976.

Harmon, Jim. *Radio Mystery and Adventure: and Its Appearances in Film, Television, and Other Media.* Jefferson, NC: McFarland, 2003.

Lichtman, Jim. *The Lone Ranger's Code of the West.* Palm Desert, CA: Scribbler's Ink, 1996.

Moore, Clayton, and Frank Thompson. *I Was That Masked Man.* Dallas, TX: Taylor Publishing, 1996.

Osgood, Dick. *WYXIE Wonderland: An Unauthorized 50-Year Diary of WXYZ, Detroit.* Bowling Green, OH: Bowling Green University Popular Press, 1981.

Van Hise, James. *Who Was That Masked Man?: The Story of the Lone Ranger.* Las Vegas, NV: Pioneer Books, 1990.

Long, Huey *(1893–1935)*

One of the most skillful orators and successful politicians of the 1920s and 1930s, Hugh Pierce Long was a demagogue, but one with strong populist appeal. Long was elected governor of Louisiana and then a U.S. senator, and, had his life not been cut short by an assassin's bullet, he might have posed a formidable threat to Franklin D. Roosevelt's tenure in the White House. He is immortalized, in a thinly disguised version, in one of America's great political novels: Robert Penn Warren's *All the King's Men* (1946).

Born into a middle-class Louisiana family, Long studied law for a year before gaining admission to the Louisiana bar in 1915. A few years later he was elected to the state's Public Service Commission, which regulated the oil companies that were such an important part of Louisiana's economy. Long became known as a critic of the oil companies' exploitation of the state and its people, and he tried to ride this reputation into the governor's mansion in 1924. He lost that election but won the next, in 1928. He was elected to the U.S. Senate two years later.

Huey Long. *Huey Long delivers an impassioned speech in the early 1930s. His populist appeal was countered by his corruption and abuse of political power.* FOTOSEARCH/STRINGER/ARCHIVE PHOTOS/GETTY IMAGES.

It was in the Senate that Long began to develop a national reputation, much of which grew from his proposed "Share Our Wealth" program. This plan was intended as a solution to the hardships brought on America by the Great Depression, which had begun in 1929; it involved, as its name suggests, a government-directed redistribution of assets—taking from the rich and giving to the poor and middle class. Long proposed confiscation of individual wealth of more than $50 million (an idea he later revised to $5 million) and guaranteed a minimum income of $5,000 per year to the poor (later revised to between $2,000 and $2,500).

Although Long's plan was almost certainly unconstitutional, it found favor with large segments of the public, to whom the Depression had brought hardship, poverty, and hopelessness. At his urging, "Share Our Wealth" societies sprang up all over the country—groups that might well have formed the basis for a Huey Long presidential candidacy. Certainly Long himself entertained that notion, and he had expressed the intent to run against President Franklin Roosevelt in the 1936 election. He never got the chance, however. On September 10, 1935, Huey Long was shot dead in the Louisiana capitol. His assassin was the son of a former political opponent.

In many ways, Long was typical of the southern demagogues who flourished in the region between, approximately, 1870 and 1970. He was a populist in that he claimed to stand for the "little guy" against the power of the established economic and political interests; he professed to have humble origins, although his background was middle class; he identified himself with his cause so thoroughly that it soon became impossible to separate the two in the public mind; he was a powerful and emotional public speaker, with a style that emphasized the "plain folks" appeal; and his rhetoric tended to focus on an enemy—whether the oil companies, the wealthy, or the Roosevelt administration. One difference—making Long virtually unique among southern demagogues—was that he never engaged in race baiting. Rather, whenever he mentioned blacks in his speeches, he claimed that they were victims of the "big interests" as much as poor whites.

Despite the undeniable corruption, political chicanery, and abuse of power that characterized Long's career, he is still revered by many in Louisiana, where he is remembered as the champion of "the little man." And, if Long's life itself was not enough to guarantee the persistence of his legend, then ample assistance was provided by *All the King's Men,* which was made into a popular film in 1949 and remade in 2006. The Pulitzer Prize–winning book chronicles the rise of Willie Stark through the jungles of southern politics, and no one familiar with Long's career is likely to miss the similarities. The character of Stark is written as a great political leader who nonetheless possesses the fatal flaw of hubris. The same could be said of the man who was his inspiration.

Justin Gustainis

SEE ALSO: *Best Sellers; The Great Depression; New Deal.*

BIBLIOGRAPHY

Boulard, Garry. *Huey Long.* Gretna, LA: Pelican, 2003.

Brinkley, Alan. *Voices of Protest.* New York: Alfred A. Knopf, 1982.

Warren, Robert Penn. *All the King's Men.* New York: Harcourt, Brace, and World, 1946.

Williams, T. Harry. *Huey Long*. New York: Alfred A. Knopf, 1969.

Long, Shelley *(1949–)*

In 1982 the sitcom *Cheers* premiered, costarring Shelley Long as the overeducated barmaid Diane Chambers. Diane's on-again/off-again romance with bar owner Sam Malone (Ted Danson) made the show a hit. Long won an Emmy for the role in 1983, but she left the series at the height of its success in 1987 to pursue a film career that quickly fizzled. Her films include *The Money Pit* (1986), *Outrageous Fortune* (1987), *The Brady Bunch Movie* (1995), and *A Very Brady Sequel* (1996). In the early 2000s she starred in several television movies, such as *The Brady Bunch at the White House* (2002), *The Santa Trap* (2002), *Falling in Love with the Girl Next Door* (2006), *Ice Dreams* (2009), and *A Holiday Engagement* (2011).

Christian L. Pyle

SEE ALSO: The Brady Bunch*;* Cheers*; Made-for-Television Movies; Sitcom; Television.*

BIBLIOGRAPHY

Wenger, Mark. *The "Cheers" Trivia Book*. Secaucus, NJ: Carol Publishing Group, 1994.

Long-Playing Record

The long-playing, or LP, format for sound recordings was one of the most important innovations in entertainment technology after World War II. In addition to extending the duration of recordings, the microgroove, long-playing vinyl record brought new levels of fidelity to recorded sound. Its wide acceptance by listeners worldwide ensured that this was to be the primary format for sound recordings from its commercial introduction in the 1940s until the emergence of digital recording in the 1980s.

LP Record Player. *Precision is required to position the needle correctly on a long-playing record.* **NICKY J. SIMS/REDFERNS/GETTY IMAGES.**

The search for a longer-playing format for sound recordings began immediately after the invention of the phonograph in 1877. The technology was aimed at the business user, and the two- to three-minute playback of the cylinder was too short for the phonograph's intended use as a dictating machine. One of the major advantages of the disc over the cylinder format was that it was easier to extend the play of the disc by increasing its size. By the first decades of the twentieth century, the playing time of discs had been extended to seven or eight minutes, but this was still too short to reproduce the classical music and speeches of leading politicians to which owners of talking machines wanted to listen.

The development of a long-playing disc was undertaken by several companies for different reasons. Western Electric's system of synchronized sound for movies was introduced in the early 1920s. It employed oversized 16-inch discs with a playing time of about twenty minutes. This system was improved in the 1930s and 1940s: more and more sound signals were inscribed in the smaller grooves to bring greater fidelity in the playback. During World War II, chemical manufacturers created new plastic materials that were applied to a variety of uses. "Unbreakable" long-playing vinyl records of popular music, the V discs, were sent to American troops overseas during the war, establishing an important precedent for the long player. Vinyl records were more durable and could take longer grooves than the hard shellac discs used for commercial recordings.

COLUMBIA'S CONTRIBUTION

The recorded-sound industry viewed the postwar economy with some apprehension, for it had spent much of the 1930s facing precipitous drops in demand for its products. It hoped to win over the postwar market with technological improvements, such as automatic record changers and exaggerated claims of the fidelity of its recording systems. The Columbia Company developed a long-playing record in its research laboratories under the direction of Dr. Peter Goldmark. Columbia was a long-established company, manufacturing talking machines and records in both cylinder and disc formats since the turn of the twentieth century. It knew that a long-playing record would open up the market for recordings of classical music and attract the attention of audiophiles, encouraging other users to desert the 78 revolutions per minute (rpm) shellac disc for the new format.

Goldmark and his team of engineers brought together many innovations of recorded sound in their long-playing technology, some of them stretching back to the early part of the twentieth century. To achieve a playing time of thirty minutes, the groove in the record had to be nearly half a mile long. Instead of the normal eighty to 100 grooves cut per inch, the 12-inch-diameter long player was cut with between 224 and 260 grooves per inch; hence, the term *microgroove* was used to describe these records. A permanent, jeweled stylus with a synthetic sapphire or diamond was used instead of the usual steel needle—an innovation first introduced by Thomas Edison in 1913. Manufacturing the new long-playing records demanded unprecedented standards of cleanliness and precision, and Goldmark embarked on a crusade to clean up the Columbia record-pressing plants.

When executives of the Columbia Company announced the long-playing record to the press in 1948, they portrayed it as a revolutionary new technology that would take "the musical world by storm." This was more a marketing ploy than an accurate depiction of the development of the technology—most of the innovations in the new product had been made years before. Even the playing speed of 33-1/3 rpm dated from the 1930s, when it was used in long-playing transcriptions of radio programs. Nevertheless, Columbia touted its long-playing record as a major event in the history of sound recording and eagerly expected the rest of the recording industry to adopt it.

Columbia miscalculated the reaction of RCA, long its rival in the record business and a company that prided itself on being the leader in new technology. RCA had developed a long-playing disc in the 1930s, but it had failed to catch on. When RCA heard of the Columbia research project, it hurriedly introduced its own microgroove, 45 rpm, 7-inch disc, and the "Battle of the Speeds" was on. This delayed the introduction of microgrooved discs because the customer had to choose from four speeds of revolving disc: 78, 45, 33-1/3, and 16 rpm.

NEW FORMAT, NEW SOUND SYSTEM

It was not until the mid-1950s that the 12-inch disc established itself as the format for long-playing records, and the introduction of the Westrex stereophonic sound system in 1957 made it the format for high-fidelity recordings. As had been expected, lovers of classical music and audiophiles embraced the new long-playing disc. The record companies were kept busy transferring their recordings of orchestral music from piles of 78 rpm shellac discs to one long player. A new source of music for the long player was found in the Broadway play; the soundtrack for *My Fair Lady* was the best-selling long-playing recording of the 1950s, and it was followed by soundtracks from other plays and films. Artists such as Frank Sinatra moved into the long-playing format in the 1950s, producing thematic albums such as *Come Fly with Me*, which contained songs about travel. Yet pop music—music for teenagers—stayed on the 45 rpm single format. The single was cheap (less than a dollar) and easily carried around, and the three-minute playing time was perfect for AM radio, which wanted lots of time between songs for commercials.

In the 1960s most recording artists released material on long-playing discs, which were now called LPs. (The term *album* came from bound albums of 78 rpm discs, which were the stopgap long players of the 1930s and 1940s.) In popular music, the LP was simply a compilation of 10 to 13 three-minute songs that had been released on singles. The Beatles' *Sgt. Pepper's Lonely Hearts Club Band* of 1967 is acclaimed as the first concept album in which the whole of the recording was more artistically significant than the individual songs. It was followed by numerous concept albums, as rock artists now saw the LP rather than the single as the format for their music. Packaging two LPs in one cover gave even greater length to the concept album and encouraged rock groups to embark on more ambitious projects, such as the Who's rock opera *Tommy*. The LP permitted the length of a song to extend beyond the three-minute limit set by the 45 rpm single and AM radio. In the 1970s some adventurous groups, such as the Allman Brothers, released albums of live music with one track covering a whole twenty-minute side of an LP.

DIGITAL AGE

The introduction of digital recording on the compact disc (CD) in 1982 was supposed to make the vinyl LP obsolete by the end of the decade, but that did not happen. Although the CD had the important advantage of not deteriorating with every play, and it clearly sounded better, millions of consumers chose to stay with the scratches and nicks of their beloved LPs. Although the playing time of the CD was more than seventy minutes, most performers of popular music still made recordings that stayed within the forty-minute duration of the LP. The long-playing record quickly disappeared from the shelves of the major music retailers but continued to be sold from specialist shops that dealt solely in the obsolete recordings. Manufacturers of turntables and styli kept in production throughout the 1990s, supported by record collectors who were loath to move into the digital format, rap and hip-hop performers who sampled and scratched records to make their music, and disc jockeys who still used discs in their shows.

The rise of the MP3 player and the rapid decline of the record industry that sold hard media such as CDs and LPs should have reduced the long-playing record to the status of an antique in the twenty-first century, yet it proved far more resilient than the CD in surviving in a market that had been transformed by downloading music from the Internet. Although vinyl LPs had only a tiny share of the overall market for sound recordings, their sales numbers increased while those of CDs have declined: from 2007 to 2010, the LP was the fastest-growing format for prerecorded music. Older consumers and audiophiles continue to purchase vinyl records for their high-fidelity and nostalgia value, and record companies have discovered a dynamic market in rereleases of classic albums from the 1960s and 1970s. These are packaged with the original artwork, pressed in high-quality (180-gram) vinyl that promises higher fidelity, and often come with coupons that provide a free MP 3 download so that the customer got the best of both old and new technologies.

Many small independent record companies in niche markets such as punk or heavy metal have started to release their music on vinyl and found that young consumers were attracted to the tactile pleasures of handling a disc. With attractive art work and considerable prestige, the 7-inch disc has become as popular in indie music as the 12-inch was in dance and hip hop. The long life of the long-playing record has also helped independent record stores survive, whereas many chains of record and video retailers have disappeared. After being pronounced dead in the 1990s, the vinyl disc not only survived but looked likely to prosper well into the twenty-first century.

Andre Millard

SEE ALSO: *Album-Oriented Rock; The Allman Brothers Band; Atlantic Records; The Beatles; Compact Discs; Concept Album; Edison, Thomas Alva; Eight-Track Tape; MP3; Phonograph; Pop Music; Rock and Roll; Sinatra, Frank; The Who; World War II.*

BIBLIOGRAPHY

Biagi, Shirley. *Media Impact: An Introduction to Mass Media.* Andover, MA: Cengage Learning, 2011.

Gellat, Roland. *The Fabulous Phonograph, 1877–1977.* New York: Macmillan, 1977.

Goldmark, Peter, and Edson Lee. *Maverick Inventor: My*

Turbulent Years at CBS. New York: E. P. Dutton, 1973.

Lewisohn, Mark. *The Beatles Recording Sessions.* New York: Harmony, 1988.

Millard, Andre. *America on Record: A History of Recorded Sound.* Cambridge, MA: Cambridge University Press, 1995.

Read, Oliver, and Walter Welch. *From Tin Foil to Stereo: Evolution of the Phonograph.* Indianapolis, IN: Howard Sams, 1977.

Loos, Anita *(1888–1981)*

Known primarily for authoring more than 200 screenplays between 1912 and 1953, when she retreated from Hollywood, Anita Loos also wrote the acclaimed 1925 novel *Gentlemen Prefer Blondes*, which she adapted for Broadway and motion pictures. Centered on the adventures of gold digger Lorelei Lee, a caricature of writer H. L. Mencken's "stupid little blond," Loo's work evolved from a serial for *Harper's Bazaar* to a novel that was ultimately translated into fourteen languages. The story was produced for the screen in 1928 and again in 1953, with Marilyn Monroe delivering an iconic performance as Lorelei.

As a screenwriter, Loos is generally credited with helping create the Golden Age of Hollywood. She wrote scenarios for D. W. Griffith and helped launch the career of Douglas Fairbanks Sr. Her strength as a writer lay in clever lines and dialogue rather than story and character development.

Steve Hanson

SEE ALSO: *Fairbanks, Douglas, Sr.;* Gentlemen Prefer Blondes*; Griffith, D. W.; Mencken, H. L.; Monroe, Marilyn.*

BIBLIOGRAPHY

Loos, Anita. *A Girl Like I.* New York: Viking, 1966.

Loos, Anita. *Kiss Hollywood Goodbye.* New York: Viking, 1974.

Loos, Anita. *Cast of Thousands.* New York: Grosset & Dunlap, 1977.

Loos, Anita; Cari Beauchamp; and Mary Loos. *Anita Loos Rediscovered: Film Treatments and Fiction.* Berkeley: University of California Press, 2003.

Yeck, Joanne. "Anita Loos." In *Dictionary of Literary Biography, Vol. 26: American Screenwriters*, eds. Robert Morsberger, Stephen Lesser, and Randall Clark. Detroit, MI: Gale Research, 1984.

Lopez, George *(1961–)*

Comic George Lopez had the kind of painful childhood that might have resulted in an angry, thwarted life. However, he also possessed a sense of humor that allowed him to transcend his grief and frustration, and he found a role model. As a teenager watching young Puerto Rican comic Freddie Prinze on the NBC sitcom *Chico and the Man*, Lopez not only learned about disarming pain with humor but also that it was possible for a Latino comic to achieve success. Though Prinze's tortured life ended in a probable suicide in 1977, Lopez was inspired to reach beyond his own poverty and emotional deprivation. When he did achieve success, it was not by leaving his past behind but by making it part of his act and creating a comic persona that combined mordant commentary with a buoyant sweetness that has made him a favorite not only with Latinos but also with a broad television audience.

George Edward Lopez was born in 1961 in the Los Angeles suburban town of Mission Hills. An only child, he was abandoned by his birth parents—his father when he was an infant and his mother when he was ten years old—and raised by his grandmother, a factory worker whose own hard life left her with few resources for nurturing a child. Lonely and unhappy, Lopez found refuge in making people laugh, and he spent the night of his high school graduation on an open mike at a comedy club. By the 1980s he had quit his factory job to perform stand-up comedy full time, getting an occasional film role, such as in Richard Correll's 1990 *Ski Patrol.*

In 2000 well-known actor Sandra Bullock saw Lopez perform at the Los Angeles comedy club La Brea Improv. Bullock was interested in producing a television series that would increase media visibility of the growing Latino community, and she approached Lopez about being part of the project. The resulting show, *George Lopez*, ran from 2002 to 2007, attracting from six to nine million viewers and ranking in the top 100 shows during its run.

Lopez explores episodes in the many-faceted life of a Mexican American family. The father, George, is a factory worker, recently promoted to management; the mother, Angie, is a third-generation Chicana who did not grow up speaking Spanish; the grandmother, Benny, is a critical and exacting woman who works in the factory her son manages. George and Angie have two children, a teenage daughter, Carmen, and a preteen son, Max. As he did in his comedy act, Lopez mined real-life experiences from his difficult childhood for his show, but in the half-hour series they could be developed more fully, allowing for comedy of real depth and poignancy.

After the cancellation of his sitcom, Lopez was offered a talk show on TBS. The late-night time slot of *Lopez Tonight* allowed the comic to use the edgier material that made his stand-up act so popular. In addition to *Lopez Tonight*, which ran from 2009 to 2011, Lopez has appeared in a number of films and comedy specials. He is an avid golfer and hosted the Bob Hope Chrysler Classic from 2007 to 2009, in addition to launching his own George Lopez Celebrity Golf Classic Tournament. In 2010 he and his wife, Ann, a television producer, launched the charitable Ann and George Lopez Foundation to offer support to children who, like young George Lopez, may be growing up without much hope of future success.

Tina Gianoulis

SEE ALSO: *Bullock, Sandra; Prinze, Freddie; Sitcom; Stand-Up Comedy; Television.*

BIBLIOGRAPHY

Diaz, Jaime. "George Lopez Had a Tough Start in Life and in Golf. But Funny How Things Change." *Golf Digest*, February 2008, 104.

Guzman, Lila, and Rick Guzman. *George Lopez: Latino King of Comedy.* Berkeley Heights, NJ: Enslow Publishers, 2008.

Lopez, George, and Armen Keteyian. *Why You Crying?: My Long, Hard Look at Life, Love, and Laughter.* New York: Touchstone, 2004.

Navarro, Mireya. "A Life So Sad He Had to Be Funny; George

Lopez Mines a Rich Vein of Gloom with an All-Latino Sitcom." *New York Times*, November 27, 2002.

Lopez, Jennifer *(1969–)*

Jennifer Lopez began her career as a dancer, but she has become one of the most versatile and bankable performers in show business. Affectionately dubbed "J.Lo" by the press, she has been nominated for multiple Latin, pop, R&B, and hip-hop music awards; launched lucrative perfume and fashion lines; founded TV, film, and digital production companies; and received popular and critical acclaim for her roles in films such as *Selena* (1997) and *Out of Sight* (1998). Lopez's crossover appeal has earned her transnational star status and clout.

Born in the Bronx, New York, in 1969 to Puerto Rican parents, Lopez began dance lessons by age five. After graduating from high school, she appeared in local musical plays and videos until she landed her first break in 1990 as a "Fly Girl" (lead backup dancer) on Fox's *In Living Color*. She moved to Los Angeles and worked with Rosie Perez, who choreographed the "Fly Girls" on the show. Lopez went on to work as a backup dancer for singer Janet Jackson.

Like many Latina actresses before her, Lopez got her start playing a variety of Hispanic/Latina nationalities—a Mexican immigrant in Gregory Nava's critically acclaimed film, *My Family* (*Mi Familia*, 1995), a Cuban nanny in *Blood and Wine* (1996), and a Mexican American in *Anaconda* (1997). Her first major film break came in 1997 when she was chosen from among more than 2,000 actresses to play Tex-Mex music star Selena Quintanilla in Gregory Nava's biopic *Selena*. Lopez's convincing portrayal of the slain singer-songwriter earned her a Golden Globe nomination.

Lopez broke barriers faced by many Latina actresses deemed too "ethnic" to play romantic leads in mainstream Hollywood films. As both Wesley Snipes's and Woody Harrelson's love interest in *Money Train* (1995), Matthew McConaughey's dream girl in *The Wedding Planner* (2001), and Ralph Fiennes's beautiful hotel maid/socialite in *Maid in Manhattan* (2002), Lopez successfully crossed racial and ethnic borders. She became the highest-paid Latina actress in Hollywood when she earned $15 million for her 2005 role in *Monster-in-Law*.

Lopez has scored hits with both English- and Spanish-language songs and earned awards in different music categories. Her debut album *On the 6*, released in 1999, quickly made the Top 10 on the Billboard 200, then went multiplatinum in the United States, Europe, and Canada. She has since been nominated many times for both music videos and albums. This ability to traverse genres and formats is evident in the range of awards she has earned: in 2000, for example, Lopez received MTV's Video Music Award for Best Dance Video ("Waiting for Tonight"), then in 2002 won for Best Hip-Hop Video ("I'm Real"). MTV Europe presented her with the Best R&B Artist Award in 2000—as well as the Best Female Artist Award in 2001 and 2002. In 2003 she earned the American Music Award for Favorite Pop/Rock Female Artist, then won again in both 2007 and 2011 for Favorite Latin Artist. She is the only female to ever have a number one album on billboard charts (*J.Lo*) and a number one film (*The Wedding Planner*) at the same time.

Lopez has successfully capitalized on her multimedia talents, business savvy, work ethic, and beauty, amassing a fortune that in 2007 placed her ninth on *Forbes* magazine's list of the "top twenty richest women in entertainment." But her professional success has not always transferred into her personal life. Her relationship with rapper Sean "P. Diddy" Combs, brief marriage to dancer Cris Judd, engagement to Ben Affleck, and marriage to singer Marc Anthony in 2004 and subsequent divorce in 2011 have all provided tabloid fodder.

Her curvaceous body has also been the object of both adoration and ridicule: from urban legends about her posterior being insured for millions to a host of jokes on late-night television and websites about the size of her butt, Lopez's shape has elicited fascination and scrutiny. London's *Daily Mail* even ran a story that credited "Miss Lopez's rounded posterior" with making curvy bottoms trendy, claiming that it had "created a demand for silicone buttock implants" in America.

But Lopez is currently the only woman voted the "sexiest women in the world" twice by men's entertainment magazine *FHM*'s American readers and the only one to make their sexiest 100 list seven times. She earned "best female body" rank in *Celebrity Bodies Magazine* in 2001, came in second on *Stuff* magazine's 2002 list of 102 Sexiest Women in the World, and fifth in *Maxim*'s Hot 100 list (2003). In 2011 the then forty-two-year-old mother of twins Emme and Maximilian (by Anthony) appeared on the cover of *People* magazine with the headline "World's Most Beautiful Woman."

Lopez has left her mark in American culture, applying her talents in a range of venues and expanding her influence beyond popular music and movies. Her decision to join *American Idol* as a judge and to produce a television reality show that celebrates Latin talent throughout the world (*Q' Viva!: The Chosen*) extends her reach even further, making her a household name not only in the United States but also in the global entertainment industry.

Myra Mendible

SEE ALSO: American Idol*; Combs, Sean "P. Diddy"; Grammy Awards;* In Living Color*;* People*; Pop Music; Selena; Top 40.*

BIBLIOGRAPHY

Medible, Myra. *From Bananas to Buttocks: The Latina Body in Popular Film and Culture.* Austin: University of Texas Press, 2007.

Newling, Dan, and Tony Bonnici. "Does My Bum Look Big in This? In a Figure-Hugging Dress, J-Lo Shows Her Famous Shape to the Full." *Daily Mail* (London), February 27, 2003.

López, Nancy *(1957–)*

In 1978 twenty-one-year-old Nancy López became the first Hispanic to win a Ladies Professional Golf Association (LPGA) tournament. Among the youngest women golfers ever to win at the professional level, she went on to become one of the greatest women's golf champions of all time. Born to Mexican American parents in Torrance, California, in 1957, López was raised in Roswell, New Mexico. She learned golf from her father, and by age eleven she was already beating him.

While López was growing up, her parents struggled to give her the best opportunities possible to perfect her golf game;

however, many doors were shut to the López family because they could not afford to join the country clubs where the best golf was taught and played. Nevertheless, López persevered, and at the age of twelve she won the first of three state women's tournaments, including the New Mexico Women's Open. As a teenager she was the only female member of her high school golf team, and in 1972 and 1974 López won the U.S. Golf Association Junior Girls tournament. As an eighteen-year-old high school senior she placed second in the U.S. Women's Open.

After high school, López attended Tulsa University on a golf scholarship and won the intercollegiate title. This helped her make the decision to drop out of college to become a professional golfer. In 1978, during her first full season as a pro, she won nine tournaments, including the LPGA Championship, which she later won two more times. López was named Rookie of the Year, Player of the Year, and Female Athlete of the Year and won the Vare Trophy—becoming the first LPGA player to ever take home all four honors in the same season. On her first year on the professional tour, she set a new record for earnings by a rookie: $189,813.

After entering the pro circuit, López consistently ranked among the top women golfers in the world. In 1979 she won eight of the nineteen tournaments she entered, which *Sports Illustrated* classified as "one of the most dominating sports performances in half a century." After marrying baseball star Ray Knight, López took a break from her career when she gave birth to daughter Ashley Marie in 1983. Two months later, she began touring again, and by 1987 she had won thirty-five tournaments and qualified to become the eleventh member of the LPGA Hall of Fame.

In all, López has nearly fifty tournament victories on tour. Her most outstanding year was 1985, when she won five tournaments and finished in the top ten at twenty-five others. That year she also won the LPGA Championship and earned more money—more than $400,000—than any other player on the circuit. By 1987 she had earned more than $2 million.

During the 1990s age and injuries began to take their toll on López; she continued to play, albeit on a shorter schedule. During the 1997 U.S. Open, at the age of forty, she became the first woman to shoot four rounds in the sixties, although she finished second in the tournament, losing by a stroke to Alison Nichols. The U.S. Open was one of the only majors she never won; her loss to Nichols marked her fourth second-place finish. López retired in 2002; although she mounted a brief comeback in 2007–2008, she did not make the cut.

López represented the United States in Solheim Cup competition, both as a member of the 1990 team and as captain of the 2005 team, and later served as captain of the 2009 PING Junior Solheim team. She was named the 2011 Memorial Tournament Honoree by Jack Nicklaus—an award given to individuals who have had a profound impact on the game. She continues to be an important figure in the world of golf, both through the Nancy López Award, presented annually to the best female amateur golfer, and through her numerous public appearances and involvement in charity. López sponsors an annual tournament for AIM—Adventures in Movement, an organization supporting people with mental and/or physical challenges. She also runs Nancy López Golf, which not only sells women's clubs and accessories but also serves as a conduit between López and her many fans. She hosts a blog, records video tips for aspiring golfers, offers up favorite recipes, and answers fan questions.

Nicolás Kanellos

SEE ALSO: *Golf; Nicklaus, Jack; Sports Heroes;* Sports Illustrated.

BIBLIOGRAPHY

Kanellos, Nicolás. *Hispanic American Almanac.* Detroit, MI: Gale Research, 1997.

Telgen, Diane, and Jim Kamp. *Latinas! Women of Achievement.* Detroit, MI: Gale Research, 1996.

Lopez, Robert

SEE: *El Vez.*

Lord of the Rings Film Trilogy

The Lord of the Rings trilogy of films, based on J. R. R. Tolkien's three-volume fantasy series (published 1954–1955), were some of the most highly anticipated cinematic products of all time. In 1995 director Peter Jackson, inspired by the 1978 animated adaptation of the novels, set out to produce a modern live-action film that compressed the action of the three volumes into one feature-length film. There were a number of scripts and studios involved before the project fell through. In 1998 New Line Cinema picked up the struggling project and encouraged Jackson to have the script rewritten into a trilogy to more closely match the original three novels.

The production cost more than $640 million and was the first time an entire feature film trilogy was filmed simultaneously with the same director and cast, making it one of the largest film undertakings ever completed. Filming took place over fifteen months in New Zealand, and the rigorous schedule allowed the studio to release the movies with only a year between each installment: *The Fellowship of the Ring* in 2001, *The Two Towers* in 2002, and *The Return of the King* in 2003. The films star Elijah Wood as the hobbit Frodo Baggins; Viggo Mortensen as Aragorn; Sean Bean as Boromir; Ian McKellen as Gandalf; Orlando Bloom as the elf Legolas; John Rhys-Davies as the dwarf Gimli; and Dominic Monaghan, Billy Boyd, and Sean Astin as Frodo's hobbit friends Merry, Pippin, and Sam.

SUCCESSFUL ADAPTATION

From the moment of the announcement of the films' production through the release of trailers and the premiere of each film, the Internet was abuzz with rumors, analysis, and news about the films, actors, special effects, and plot points. Few movies have received such close attention throughout the process. The three films split the plot in roughly the same way as the original novels, following the exploits of the hobbit Frodo and the Fellowship of the Ring as they travel through Middle Earth in a quest to destroy the ancient ring and its creator, the powerful Lord Sauron. Although the movies incorporate much of the source material, Jackson and his writers made some creative changes.

Fans of the books were split on the edits, and many decried Jackson's decision to excise "The Scouring of the Shire" from *The Return of the King,* in which the Hobbits lead the final battle in the War of the Ring against the fallen wizard Saruman.

Additionally, fans were concerned about missing plot points, particularly the first novel's sequences with Tom Bombadil, a favorite minor character from the story, and changes to character motivations or descriptions. Elements of the films were hotly debated, such as the use of chain mail versus armor, or the presence of wings on the Balrog (a monster that attacks the questing heroes). Despite not always accurately following the original written texts, the films were well received by many viewers.

Critics generally applauded Jackson's efforts, paying particular attention to the special effects, casting, and cinematography. Numerous publications have hailed the trilogy as some of the all-time best movies, including *Time*, *Entertainment Weekly*, and *USA Today*. Elvis Mitchell of the *New York Times* commented that the final film is "a meticulous and prodigious vision made by a director who was not hamstrung by heavy use of computer special-effects imagery." Similar to fans of the book, not all critics celebrated the films. Roger Ebert of the *Chicago Sun Times* lamented the slow pacing of the movies and thought that the story line was too far from real-life concerns, while the narrative was lost within the elaborate effects. He did, however, acknowledge that as a whole the trilogy represented "a work of bold ambition at a time of cinematic timidity." As a whole, the movies have outlasted the critics and outgrossed their predecessor *Star Wars*.

All three movies incorporated elaborate, groundbreaking special effects, including the detailed work by Weta Workshops, the maker of many of the props and creatures for the productions. Using computer-generated images, animatronics, motion capture suits, and digital doubling, the films erected a seamless world and its inhabitants. In order to accurately represent the size differences between the characters, the films employed forced perspective, a technique used to create optical illusions, and then layered multiple shots of the same scene. The most notable special-effect was the creature Gollum, which involved a painstaking process of rendering the actor's movements into an animated version and then superimposing this image over the scene.

The trilogy was filmed at more than 150 sites in New Zealand, and the landscape of that country became almost a character within the film. As scholar Robin Anne Reid has argued, the filmic vocabulary of sweeping scenery, dominating the tiny figures of the questing fellowship as they scale mountains and trek across Middle Earth, became a major feature of the trilogy. Perhaps for that reason New Zealand has become a major tourist site for fans of the movies—not only the "Hobbiton" set made for the production but also other sites seen in the background of major moments of the series.

All three films were nominated for Academy Awards, and *The Return of the King* won in all eleven categories in which it was nominated, tying the record for the most wins in one year for a movie. The films remain the highest-grossing trilogy in history and helped solidify Jackson as a major player in Hollywood. According to Janice Bogstad, editor of *Picturing Tolkien* (2011), Jackson has speculated "that the Tolkien novels will be important long after people have forgotten his films and that perhaps they can be made better by someone else when more sophisticated filmic techniques are available." In the meantime Jackson's movies remain the gold standard for cinematic interpretations of Middle Earth. Like the *Star Wars* and Harry Potter films, the *Lord of the Rings* series proved that a blockbuster could appeal to multiple ages at one time—separate films did not need to be made to appeal to children and adults. Although it is hard to imagine another film project undergoing a film schedule similar to Jackson's, *Lord of the Rings* helped to establish fantasy films as a legitimate, box-office genre and to outline a marketing strategy for future movie franchises.

Kim Keeline

SEE ALSO: *Academy Awards; Blockbusters; Hollywood; Science Fiction Publishing; Tolkien, J. R. R.*

BIBLIOGRAPHY

Bogstad, Janice, and Philip E. Kaveny, eds. *Picturing Tolkien: Essays on Peter Jackson's "The Lord of the Rings" Film Trilogy.* Jefferson, NC: McFarland, 2011.

Ebert, Roger. Review of "Lord of the Rings: The Return of the King." *Chicago Sun Times*, December 17, 2003, 31.

Mitchell, Elvis. "Triumph Tinged with Regret in Middle Earth." Review of *The Lord of the Rings: The Return of the King. New York Times*, December 16, 2003, 31.

Sibley, Brian. *"The Lord of the Rings": The Making of the Movie Trilogy.* New York: Houghton Mifflin, 2002.

Stratyner, Leslie, and James R. Keller, eds. *Fantasy Fiction into Film: Essays.* Jefferson, NC: McFarland, 2007.

Lorre, Peter *(1904–1964)*

Often typecast as a menacing figure, Peter Lorre achieved Hollywood fame during the 1930s, first as a featured player and later as a character actor who trademarked his screen performances with a delicately strung balance between good and evil. To villainous parts he added a touch of dark humor, while he shaded comic roles with sinister overtones. Though he deprecated his art as "face-making," Lorre took his work seriously and lamented Hollywood's use of his tricks but not his talent. His globular eyes and diffident whine have inspired comic impersonations and have been widely caricatured in commercials (General Mills' "BooBerry"), cartoons (*Ren and Stimpy*), and literature (*Catcher in the Rye*).

Born in Rozsahegy, Hungary, Ladislav Loewenstein moved to Moedling, Austria, in 1912, where he debuted in a primary school production of *Snow White*. Contrary to reports that he ran away from home to become an actor, after high school graduation he attended business school and landed a job as a bank teller in Vienna, where he juggled a bourgeois vocation by day and a Bohemian life by night, performing on the side in improvisational settings. At Jacob Moreno's Theater of Spontaneity, he learned to act out "the lived out and unlived out dimensions of his private world." Before releasing the talented unknown into the world, Moreno gave him a more suitable professional name, Peter Lorre, which recalled his resemblance to "Struwwelpeter," an unkempt character in German children's literature.

EARLY CAREER

From Vienna, Lorre moved on to the Lobe and Thalia theaters in Breslau, Germany, in 1924. Contracts with Zurich's Schauspielhaus and Vienna's Kammerspiele, where he played comedies, farces, and dramas, brought him to Berlin and to the attention of poet-dramatist Bertolt Brecht, who cast him as a cretinous high school student in Marieluise Fleischer's play *Engineers in*

Ingolstadt in 1928. After that, he was, in his own words, "the hottest thing on the Berlin stage." German director Fritz Lang caught sight of Lorre at a dress rehearsal of Frank Wedekind's *Spring Awakening*, in which he played a sexually frustrated teenager, and knew he had found the star of his first sound film. *M* (1931), which introduced Lorre as a shadow falling across a reward poster and an off-screen voice, catapulted the actor into international fame as a notorious child murderer, forever confusing him in the public eye as a psychotic type.

After fleeing Nazi Germany two days before the Reichstag fire on February 27, 1933, the Jewish actor joined fellow émigrés in Paris, where *M* still played and people recognized him as *le maudit* (the murderer). Later that year Lorre accepted director Alfred Hitchcock's invitation to come to England and appear as a fiendish terrorist in *The Man Who Knew Too Much* (1934). A film contract with Columbia Pictures brought him and his wife, actress Celia Lovksy, to the United States in July 1934. America, he felt, owed him nothing more than a chance to shed his screen past as a villain. "Ever since I came to this country I've been trying to live down my past," explained Lorre. "That picture *M* has haunted me everywhere I've gone."

Peter Lorre. *Peter Lorre played Joel Cairo in the 1941 film* The Maltese Falcon. **WARNER BROS/FIRST NATIONAL/THE KOBAL COLLECTION.**

U.S. CAREER

Despite Lorre's attempts to be and think American—he even tried to lose his accent—Hollywood closed its door on the actor, repeatedly casting him as the outsider who hinted at things better left unknown. He attached no importance to his role as a demented doctor in *Mad Love* (1935), his first American film, which he preferred to call psychological terror instead of horror, a genre he disliked. "I'm associated with horror movies, but I've only done one, *The Beast with Five Fingers* . . . I don't want to go down in history as a monster," Lorre noted. "I've never played a frog that swallowed a city or something like that."

Looking to become a general character actor, Lorre accepted Twentieth Century Fox's invitation to play a variety of parts. A series of Japanese detective films based on J. P. Marquand's *Mr. Moto*, however, threatened an even narrower use of his talents. At Warner Brothers, where he costarred with pal Humphrey Bogart, Lorre hit his personal and professional stride, appearing in vehicles that popularized his sinister image, such as *Casablanca* (1942), and explored his more melancholy, philosophical side, such as *Three Strangers* (1946).

His acting style reflected a change of attitude, away from psychological probing toward what German author Thomas Mann called "perfected naturalness," at the same time causal and comfortable, off center and ironic. He told friends he would play anything—a Martian, a cannibal, even Bugs Bunny—to avoid a suspension. In 1946 Warner Brothers called his bluff, casting him in *The Beast with Five Fingers*, for what turned out to be the requiem for the waning horror genre. Lorre spent the next few years in relative inactivity, which he blamed on "graylisting" by the House Committee on Un-American Activities, a legacy of his friendship with Brecht, that ended in bankruptcy in 1949.

CAREER DISSATISFACTION

Feeling that Hollywood had turned its back on him, the actor left for Europe, where he sought the elusive pivotal role denied him in Hollywood. In Germany he directed, coauthored, and starred in *Der Verlorene* (*The Lost One*) in 1951, which weighed the enormity of Adolf Hitler's state-sponsored mass crimes against the fate of a single human being, a murderer who becomes the victim of murderous times. Lorre denied that he had returned to Europe to remake *M* and chalked up to coincidence any similarities between the stories of compulsive killers told in overlapping realist and expressionist styles. When German audiences, who wanted to put the past behind them, rejected the darkly fatalistic movie, Lorre reluctantly went back to the United States.

After appearing in a summer stock production of *A Night at Mme. Tussaud's*, Lorre found himself cast against type as a comically droll rogue in director John Huston's *Beat the Devil* (1953). The reunion of the "unholy three"—Huston, Bogart, and Lorre—turned the clock back to happier days, when a sense of camaraderie fed the spirit of fun. Such departures, however, failed to arrest the downward spiral of Lorre's career. When Hollywood refused to risk a less commercial use of his talents, he wearily accepted roles that spoofed his sinister movie personality. Ironically, by the end of his life, his appearances in horror-comedies opposite Vincent Price and Boris Karloff (*Tales of Terrors* [1962], *The Raven* [1963], *Comedy of Terrors* [1964]) came to outnumber his performances in the genre they parodied. At age fifty-nine the overweight actor suffered a fatal cerebral hemorrhage on March 23, 1964.

The emblematic personalities of Bogart and Brecht locked Lorre into a choice, which he never made, between celebrity and intellectual respectability. Frustrated by his failure to carve a niche for himself in Hollywood, the erudite actor planned numerous projects tailored to his aptitude and capabilities, most notably film stories with his friend and mentor Brecht, in whose development of epic acting theories he had played a part during the Weimar years (1919–1933). His failure to bridge the gap between person and persona, however, drove the private Lorre deeper into hiding and more sharply defined the seemingly disembodied legacy of his screen image.

Stephen D. Youngkin

SEE ALSO: *Bogart, Humphrey; Hitchcock, Alfred; Hollywood; Horror Movies; Huston, John; Karloff, Boris; Lang, Fritz; Price, Vincent; World War II.*

BIBLIOGRAPHY

Lyon, James K. *Bertolt Brecht in America*. Princeton, NJ: Princeton University Press, 1980.

Youngkin, Stephen D. *The Lost One: A Life of Peter Lorre*. Lexington: University Press of Kentucky, 2005.

Youngkin, Stephen D.; James Bigwood; and Raymond Cabana Jr. *The Films of Peter Lorre*. Secaucus, NJ: Citadel Press, 1982.

Los Angeles

SEE: *The City of Angels.*

The Los Angeles Lakers

The Los Angeles Lakers are perhaps best known for Showtime, an era named for the team's blend of athletic brilliance and crowd-pleasing charisma, which helped transform basketball into one of the most popular sports on the planet. Led by Earvin "Magic" Johnson, the 1980s Lakers were a basketball dynasty and legendary rivals of Larry Bird's Boston Celtics. The Showtime era ushered in an age of superstars such as the inimitable Michael Jordan. Then, in the waning days of Jordan's career with the Chicago Bulls, the Lakers acquired a new superstar, Kobe Bryant, who helped the team dominate in the first decade of the 2000s.

MIDWESTERN ROOTS

Since forming in 1946, the Lakers have qualified for the playoffs more than 90 percent of the time, more often than any other franchise. Yet, in their first year, as the Detroit Gems of the National Basketball League (NBL), they finished with a deplorable record of 4–40, still the worst in modern professional basketball. Their losing streak attracted a group of Minneapolis investors who bought the team for $15,000 and moved it to Minnesota, the "Land of 10,000 Lakes." Owing to their losing record, the newly dubbed Lakers received first pick in the 1947 draft.

The team's general manager was twenty-six-year-old sportswriter Sid Hartman. In an era before basketball scouts, Hartman seemed to know everything and everyone in the basketball world. Signing excellent players from other leagues, including jump shooter Jim "Kangaroo Kid" Pollard and 6-foot-10-inch center George Mikan, Hartman and his investors laid the foundation for basketball's first dynasty. In their first season, the Lakers were 43–17, and they won the league championship.

In 1948 the Lakers and three top competitors joined a new league, the Basketball Association of America (BAA). Two years later the NBL and BAA merged to form the National Basketball Association (NBA). The Lakers, led by Mikan, Pollard, and power forward Vern Mikkelsen, continued to dominate during the early 1950s. In 1956 the team faced its first losing season, and Hartman hatched the idea of finishing in last place in order to get the first draft pick and choose center Bill Russell. The owners balked, Russell went to the Celtics, and the team was eventually sold.

The Lakers continued to lose, finishing in last place in 1958. That year they were rewarded with top draft pick and offensive powerhouse Elgin Baylor, the player who virtually invented hang time—the ability to jump and remain in the air while gliding to the hoop. Even with Baylor's one-man heroics, the team lingered at the bottom of the NBA. In 1959 team owners began discussing relocation to the warmer West Coast.

THE MOVE TO LOS ANGELES

In 1960 the Lakers relocated to California, where they played in Los Angeles Memorial Sports Arena. Securing the second draft pick, they acquired a skinny forward from West Virginia named Jerry West. After picking up splinters on the bench for most of his first season, West finally saw court time. Along with Baylor, who trailed only Wilt Chamberlain of the Philadelphia Warriors in scoring, West helped improve his team's fortunes. At the end of the 1961 season, the Lakers squeaked into the playoffs and pushed the St. Louis Hawks to a fifth game. While in St. Louis, owner Bob Short called local sportscaster Chick Hearn to arrange a live broadcast for Los Angeles fans, and Hearn soon became the voice of the Lakers.

Although the Hawks pulled out a two-point victory in the 1961 championships, Los Angeles fans embraced the Lakers. Celebrities such as actress Doris Day, comedian Danny Thomas, and singer Pat Boone began regularly attending games. Boosted by their glamorous fans, the 1960s Lakers became one of the most successful franchises in NBA history, drawing record crowds and making the playoffs every year. Led by Baylor and West, the team won the Western Division championship six out of nine years. Each time they made it to the finals, however, they lost to their nemesis, Russell's Celtics.

BUILDING THE FRANCHISE

Despite their inability to clinch a world championship, the Lakers were lauded as winners. Jack Kent Cooke, a Canadian millionaire and part owner of the Washington Redskins, saw an opportunity to turn the Lakers into a big-time, money-making franchise. He bought the team in 1965 for $5.2 million and set about transforming it. His first step was to build Los Angeles Forum. His second was to acquire Chamberlain, a perennial scoring leader.

In 1968 and 1969 Baylor, West, and Chamberlain led their team to the playoffs but failed to capture the title of World Champions. In the 1970 Western Division championships, they were nearly stopped by rookie center Kareem Abdul-Jabbar and the Milwaukee Bucks. When the Lakers made it past the Bucks, however, they ran smack into the New York Knicks, who came to dominate the Eastern Division after Russell retired from the Celtics. Led by Willis Reed, Bill Bradley, and Walt "Clyde" Frazier, the Knicks handed the Lakers some of their most frustrating losses at Madison Square Garden.

By the early 1970s the Lakers' star players were in their thirties with not much time left in their careers. Cooke was determined to win, so he assembled a strong lineup that included left-handed guard Gail Goodrich, forward Happy Hairston, and coach Bill Sharman. In 1972 the team won thirty-three straight games—the longest winning streak in professional basketball history. At the end of the season, they once again faced Abdul-Jabbar's Bucks, winning the conference finals in five games. They met the Knicks in the championships and, with Chamberlain's playing brilliant ball playing, captured their first trophy.

The next season, the Lakers made it to the finals but lost. Chamberlain retired and the team floundered as it looked for a new center. Abdul-Jabbar, named MVP in 1971 and 1972, was a natural choice. But in his first few seasons as a Laker, the new recruit had no real supporting players, and despite his daily heroics, the team slid from prominence, missing the playoffs two years in a row.

SHOWTIME

In 1979 investor Jerry Buss bought the Lakers, marking a new era for the team. Having finished in last place, the Lakers once again had the first draft pick. They chose Johnson, a college sophomore from Michigan, who had just led his team to win the NCAA championship over Bird's Indiana State. A 6-foot-9-inch point guard, Johnson had a charismatic smile and the uncanny ability to turn any team to gold. In Johnson, high-flying forward Michael Cooper, guard Norm Nixon, and Jamaal Wilkes of the Golden State Warriors, Abdul-Jabbar finally had a team.

In 1980 the Lakers faced all-star Julius "Dr. J" Erving and the Philadelphia 76ers in the finals. In Game Five of the series, Abdul-Jabbar twisted his ankle. Johnson stepped up to lead the team, dazzling fans and bringing home the trophy. The Lakers of the 1980s became a dynasty shaped around the twin powers of Johnson and Abdul-Jabbar. The era also was marked by the arrival of fresh talent such as Byron Scott, A. C. Green, and the incredible James Worthy, and famous fans such as actor Jack Nicholson, who was known for sitting courtside, wearing his iconic shades. Led by West, now general manager, and dapper coach Pat Riley, the Lakers made it to the playoffs every year.

In 1984 Bird's Celtics beat the Lakers in the finals, inciting one of professional sports' greatest rivalries. Roland Lazenby writes in *The Lakers: A Basketball Journey*, "Showtime was a hoops fairy tale, pro basketball's Age of Camelot, when Magic Johnson and Larry Bird were the boy wonders who pulled the proverbial sword from the stone. Until they came along, the game had struggled to find an identity among American professional sports." The Lakers followed up with championship wins in 1985 and 1987, and in 1988 they beat the bad-boy Detroit Pistons to become the first team since the 1960s Celtics to win back-to-back championships. It seemed like Showtime would continue forever.

By 1989, after twenty years in the NBA, Abdul-Jabbar announced he would retire. The same year the Lakers lost the championship to the Pistons. Some have claimed Abdul-Jabbar's retirement was the end of Showtime; others cite Riley's 1990 departure. Still others point to the following year, when Johnson announced that he was HIV positive and left the game—though he returned to win MVP in the 1992 All-Star Game. Although the young but undeniably talented team continued to make it to the playoffs in the mid-1990s, Johnson's departure clearly signaled that Showtime was over.

A NEW ERA

The team's fortunes began to change in 1996 with the acquisition of Bryant, a rookie from the Charlotte Hornets, and superstar center Shaquille O'Neal from the Orlando Magic. Bryant, whom many saw as the next Jordan, was the second-youngest player in NBA history. Because he and O'Neal were each superstars in their own right, their competitive relationship prevented the team from achieving much success. With the 1999 hiring of coach Phil Jackson—the guru who had won six titles with Jordan's Bulls—the team gelled, winning three consecutive championships from 2000 to 2002.

In 2004 the Lakers traded O'Neal, and Coach Jackson stepped away from the game. During the 2004–2005 season, Bryant became the youngest player to reach the 14,000-point milestone. However, at the end of the season, for the first time since 1994, the team missed the playoffs. The next year, Jackson returned as coach, and in 2008 the team acquired 7-foot Spanish center Pau Gasol, which reunified the team. The Lakers returned to the finals but lost to the Celtics.

The loss did not set them back for long, however, and in 2009 and 2010 they won back-to-back championships. Bryant had five championship rings with no sign of his career waning. Although the team lost in the 2011 semifinals and Jackson retired at the end of the season, the Lakers' undeniable glamour remains. A perpetual contender with a celebrity-riddled fan section, the Lakers constitute one of professional sports' most successful, charismatic teams.

Victoria Price

SEE ALSO: *Abdul-Jabbar, Kareem; AIDS; Basketball; Bird, Larry; Boone, Pat; The Boston Celtics; Bradley, Bill; Celebrity; Chamberlain, Wilt; The Chicago Bulls; Day, Doris; Erving, Julius "Dr. J"; Frazier, Walt "Clyde"; Hollywood; Johnson, Earvin "Magic"; Jordan, Michael; National Basketball Association (NBA); National Collegiate Athletic Association (NCAA); The New York Knickerbockers; Nicholson, Jack; O'Neal, Shaquille; Riley, Pat; Russell, Bill; Thomas, Danny; West, Jerry.*

BIBLIOGRAPHY

Hollander, Zander, and Alex Sachare, eds. *The Official NBA Basketball Encyclopedia*. New York: Villard, 1989.

Johnson, Earvin, and William Novak. *My Life*. New York: Random House, 1992.

Lazenby, Roland. *The Lakers: A Basketball Journey*. New York: St. Martin's Press, 1993.

Lazenby, Roland. *The Show: The Inside Story of the Spectacular Los Angeles Lakers in the Words of Those Who Lived It*. New York: McGraw Hill, 2006.

Los Angeles Times Sports Staff, and Phil Jackson. *The Los Angeles Lakers: 50 Amazing Years in the City of Angels*, rev. ed. San

Leandro, CA: Time Capsule Press, 2010.

Travers, Steven. *The Good, the Bad, and the Ugly Los Angeles Lakers: Heart-Pounding, Jaw-Dropping, and Gut-Wrenching Moments from Los Angeles Lakers History*. Chicago: Triumph Books, 2007.

Los Lobos

The Mexican American band Los Lobos (originally named Los Lobos del Este Los Angeles, or "The Wolves of East Los Angeles") was formed in 1974 by high school friends David Hidalgo, Conrad Lozano, Louis Perez, and Caesar Rosas. In 1984 saxophonist Steve Berlin left his band, the Blasters, to join the original four as the only non-Chicano member. In 1987, with the release of their first hit single "La Bamba," a cover of the Ritchie Valens's classic of the same name, the band was catapulted into the mainstream popular music scene.

As a primarily Mexican American group that has achieved widespread recognition, the band serves as a cultural icon to its multicultural listeners. And like the few other East Los Angeles musicians (such as Valens himself and Lalo Guerrero) who surmounted economic and social adversity to achieve fame, they serve as role models to Chicanos who may fear that their attempts to escape from poverty will be thwarted by prejudice. The group's success and diverse following speak to the accessibility of their music, and the band's self-professed mission to further the cause of intercultural and intergenerational harmony promotes a feeling of a "hip" family reunion at their popular concerts.

STRONG ROOTS

Los Lobos is known for its innovative blending of genres such as jazz, blues, Tex-Mex, country, and even punk. The band's roots, however, lie in rock and roll and in the Mexican music of their heritage. After Hidalgo acquired an accordion from a friend who was stationed in Germany, the group began to explore Tex-Mex and electrified their acoustic sound. Although this change cost them their first full-time restaurant gig, it was this interest in finding common ground among seemingly disparate forms of expression that has since become the band's signature.

The band got their start playing at local weddings and other parties. By the mid-1980s, however, the members of Los Lobos started to compose their own songs and entered the Hollywood music scene, which was then filled with clubs offering small venues for beginning bands to find their footing. After gaining recognition as the opening act for the Blasters, they appeared in clubs such as the Whisky, the Roxy, and the Cathay de Grande. Their second album, *And a Time to Dance* (1983), released under the Slash Records label, earned the group their first Grammy.

By the time Los Lobos released their third album, *How Will the Wolf Survive?* in 1984, the band had answered its own question by adding extensive touring to its repertoire. This heavy roadwork resulted not only in financial security but also in a more distinctive sound, realized in *By the Light of the Moon* (1987), an incorporation of jazz, blues, and country music. With the release of *La Pistola y El Corazōn* (1988), the band revisited its roots by implementing traditional Mexican chord progressions and lyrics. Critics praised the upbeat sounds of*The*

Los Lobos. *Members of Los Lobos appear at a record store in 2002 to promote their album* Good Morning Aztlan. **ALBERT L. ORTEGA/CONTRIBUTOR/WIREIMAGE/GETTY IMAGES.**

Neighborhood (1990); the complexity of *Kiko* (1992); the funk-rock fun of *Colossal Head* (1996); and *This Time* (1999), which is laced with mystical Mexican folklore.

LONG-LIVED SUCCESS

In 2001 Los Lobos was honored with a Billboard Magazine Lifetime Achievement Award. Their 2002 album *Good Morning Aztlán* was a continuation of their diverse brand of rock. In 2004 *The Ride* featured guests Tom Waits, Mavis Staples, Bobby Womack, and Elvis Costello. Also in 2004, Los Lobos released *Live at the Fillmore* on DVD, a full-length live show in San Francisco. They celebrated traditional acoustic Mexican music on *Acoustic en Vivo* (2005). In 2006 Los Lobos's first album of all-new music in four years, *The Town and the City*, was met with high praise and comparisons to the complexity of their 1992 album *Kiko*. With lyrics by Perez portraying his childhood in East Los Angeles, *The Town and the City* is somber and soulful, about uncertain journeys and loss.

In 2010 Los Lobos went home to a rundown neighborhood in East Los Angeles to record *Tin Can Trust* in a studio that did not even have a couch when they arrived. After more than thirty years as a band, they were so full of music that they arrived with little prepared, and an album of richness, depth, and exploration poured out of them. It contains a rhythm-and-blues instrumental, two songs in Spanish, an anthem about the barrio, a piece about the Lady of Guadalupe, and an ambitious attempt to recount the entire story of the Spanish conquest of Mexico in one song. Los Lobos has been praised for continuing to grow increasingly imaginative, straying farther and farther from the well-worn rock beat.

Los Lobos's work as a band has been enhanced and celebrated by many movie soundtracks. In 1987 they shot to the top of popular consciousness and the charts with the soundtrack for *La Bamba* (1987, starring Lou Diamond Phillips as Richie Valens), which earned Los Lobos two Grammy nominations and an MTV Music Video Award. They suddenly found themselves touring the world to open for such bands as U2 and the Clash. But Los Lobos did not allow sudden commercial stardom to hijack their career. Instead, they paid tribute to their Mexican roots with *La Pistola y El Corazōn* the following year. In 1992 the band was featured on the soundtrack for the film *The Mambo Kings*, resulting in Academy Award and Grammy Award nominations for Best Song from a Film for the song "Beautiful Maria of My Soul." Their work on the film *Desperado* (1995) earned them their third Grammy Award. They also contributed to the soundtracks for *Feeling Minnesota* (1996), the HBO hit series *The Sopranos* (1999), and *Nacho Libre* (2006).

COMMITMENT TO COMMUNITY

Commercial success has allowed Los Lobos to pursue their personal interests in family and ethnic harmony through benefit work. In 1990 they played on a compilation album of classic music from Disney movies. They made appearances on the children's television program *Sesame Street* and in 1994 recorded "Elmo and the Lavender Moon" (named after their song "Kiko and the Lavender Moon") for the album *Sesame Street's 25th Anniversary*. The album *Papa's Dream*, recorded with Lalo Guerrero in 1995 and based on Guerrero's dream of visiting Mexico for his eightieth birthday, is similarly dedicated to children. In 2009 Los Lobos made their own album of Disney classics: *Los Lobos Goes Disney*.

Community and political activism are important to Los Lobos. Their first album *Si Se Puede!* (1976) was a benefit for the United Farmworkers. The band regularly performs charity concerts for organizations such as Integrity House, a center for people with disabilities. They attempt to tackle social problems through their song lyrics, many of which treat the destructive effects of substance abuse and domestic violence. In 2008 Los Lobos participated in Music for Democracy's Be the Change voter registration drive.

Despite their success, Los Lobos has not escaped the effects of discrimination on the basis of their Chicano heritage. The Academy Award committee initially rejected the band's song "Cancion del Mariachi" on the grounds that it was "unintelligible," a decision that revealed the American music scene's lingering discomfort with ethnically influenced music. In spite of the band's encounters with obstacles such as these, they remain a source of inspiration for California's Mexican American population in the delicate balancing act of promoting both Chicano pride and intercultural crossover. They have been praised as uniquely and broadly American for their musical range, which runs from funk to flamenco, through rocking guitar solos and soulful tenor melodies, with both boogie and jazz influences, and lyrics in two languages. Los Lobos has certainly proved that they are not, as the title of their first independent release suggests, *Just Another Band from East L.A* (1993).

Carly Andrews

SEE ALSO: *Academy Awards; Blues; Costello, Elvis; Country Music; Disney (Walt Disney Company); Grammy Awards; Hollywood; Jazz; "La Bamba"; Pop Music; Punk; Rhythm and Blues; Rock and Roll;* Sesame Street*;* The Sopranos*; U2; Valens, Ritchie; Waits, Tom.*

BIBLIOGRAPHY

Buckley, Peter. *The Rough Guide to Rock.* London: Rough Guides, 2003.

Stacy, Lee. *Mexico and the United States.* New York: Marshall Cavendish, 2002.

Lost

The television series *Lost* (2004–2010) premiered on ABC during a time when the network was struggling to reinvent its prime-time lineup. Featuring a deceptively simple premise—survivors of a plane crash trapped on a mysterious island—the show's innovative creators (Jeffrey Lieber, J. J. Abrams, and Damon Lindelof) proceeded to weave a complex tapestry of story lines that explored the past, present, future, and even alternate realities of the characters while simultaneously exploring the bizarre history of the island itself. This enigmatic style quickly captured the imagination of audiences, and the show proved both a critical and ratings smash, winning several awards, including the Emmy for Outstanding Drama Series in 2005.

Centering on the survivors of Oceanic Flight 815, the story initially focuses on Jack Shepherd, a doctor with a troubled past, and John Locke, a paraplegic who emerges from the crash magically healed. Uncomfortable with the leaderships roles thrust upon them, they struggle to organize the resistant survivors, who are set on protecting their own respective secrets. Kate is an accused murderer. Charlie is a heroin addict. Sawyer is a con artist. Sayid is a former Iraqi soldier and torturer. And Hurley is a lottery winner whose life seems cursed. Forming an uneasy alliance, they band together with the other survivors to defend themselves from the malevolent inhabitants of the island—known as the "Others"—and determine what happened to the "Dharma Initiative," a group scientists who had been performing experiments on the island in the 1970s.

As the saga unfolds, flashbacks explore the backstory of the characters leading up to the crash, flash-"sideways" explore parallel story lines that assume the crash never happened, and flash-forwards suggest "possible" futures. Despite its complicated plot, the key element of *Lost* is the all-encompassing struggle of good versus evil, which is manifest in the story of the island itself. In the last season the viewers learn that the guardian of good, Jacob, has been battling the forces of evil embodied in his brother—who has become a disembodied entity made of smoke—for thousands of years. Jacob attempts to pass his mantle as protector on to the crash survivors just as the "Smoke Monster" struggles to find disciples to help him to move into the world in human form. Astute viewers of the show have identified a number of literary antecedents to such a theme, ranging from the Bible to William Golding's *Lord of the Flies.*

Though the series continued to explore the intriguing idea of an island and people "lost" in time and space, as seasons passed, an increasing number of viewers began to complain that the show had become simply too complex and convoluted. This resulted in an extremely polarized response to the series finale, when the impossible number of questions and theories were explained away by suggesting that the characters were simply stuck in a form of spiritual limbo between mortality and the afterlife—a concept somewhat reminiscent of *Jacob's Ladder* (1990), in which a dying soldier hallucinates a series of alternate realities.

In addition to its other innovations, the creators of *Lost* created an extremely successful online presence. The show's website, *The Fuselage*, offered hints regarding upcoming plot developments and allowed viewers to interact with the series' creative team. The *Missing Pieces* webisodes, billed as anonymous video diaries made by several of the survivors, offered further information about the characters and their plight. These "transmissions" became so popular and so central to hardcore fans' experience of the show that they were even nominated for an Emmy in the short-format category.

Though the series experienced several fluctuations in viewership and ratings, *Lost* is considered by many to be one of the best television shows of the first decade of the 2000s, and it has become a pop culture touchstone, inspiring a number of parodies and homages in all types of media (exemplified by the rock band Weezer, naming their 2010 album *Hurley*, complete with the character's photo on the cover).

Linda Martindale

SEE ALSO: *Abrams, J. J.; The Internet; Television.*

BIBLIOGRAPHY

Ankerberg, John, and Dillon Burroughs. *What Can Be Found in "Lost"?* Eugene, OR: Harvest House, 2008.

Laist, Randy, ed. *Looking for "Lost": Critical Essays on the Enigmatic Series.* Jefferson, NC: McFarland, 2011.

Oromaner, Marc. *The Myth of "Lost": Solving the Mysteries and Understanding the Wisdom.* New York: iUniverse, 2008.

Piatt, Christian. *"Lost": A Search for Meaning.* St. Louis, MO: Chalice Press, 2006.

Porter, Lynnette; David Lavery; and Hillary Robson. *"Lost"'s Buried Treasures.* Naperville, IL: Sourcebooks, 2007.

Stuart, Sarah C. *Literary "Lost": Viewing Television through the Lens of Literature.* New York: Continuum, 2011.

The Lost Weekend

Released in 1945 by Paramount Studios, *The Lost Weekend*, written by Charles Brackett and Billy Wilder, is considered Hollywood's first film about the ravages of substance abuse. A grim, harrowing, and emotional drama, the film focuses on a struggling writer and his alcoholism. Lobbyists for the liquor industry tried to have the film destroyed before its release—fearing the negative depiction of their product—to no avail. Upon release, the film was widely popular with audiences and critics alike. It received four Academy Awards: best actor for Ray Milland, best director for Billy Wilder, best writing (screenplay) for Charles Brackett and Billy Wilder, and best picture for Paramount.

Frances Gateward

SEE ALSO: *Academy Awards; Hollywood; Wilder, Billy.*

BIBLIOGRAPHY

Denzin, Norman K. *Hollywood Shot by Shot: Alcoholism in American Cinema.* New York: Aldine de Gruyter, 1991.

Lottery

Observe the cash register line at any state lottery agent the days before an unusually large jackpot, and the observer will get some idea of the popularity of this form of government fundraising. Some call it a state-sponsored vice, whereas others believe it is a regressive and voluntary tax on the poor. Still, millions of people across the United States and around the world line up to play Lotto, Quik-picks, Power Ball, Keno, and many other games and purchase a chance to change their lives with a major financial windfall.

Though the current wave of lotteries began in the 1960s, the lottery is not a new method for governments to raise money. In the late eighteenth and early nineteenth centuries, it was common for government and other institutions to sell chances to win prize money in order to fund specific civic projects. In 1767 Boston's Faneuil Hall was refurbished with funds raised by a lottery. When state governments began to hire private companies to administer their lotteries, the doors opened to fraud. It was not long before the lottery seemed to be irretrievably corrupt, and by the late 1800s lotteries were illegal in every state in the union.

Outlawing lotteries did not make them disappear, however. It just sent them underground, where organized crime took over. Numbers games—high-odds betting on an unpredictable series of numbers, such as sports scores—became a regular form of entertainment, especially among the urban poor. In an effort to reclaim some of the income going to the mob, the states of

New York and New Hampshire started their own lotteries in the 1960s. Excited by the prospect of millions of dollars in new revenues voluntarily supplied by citizens, eleven states in 1975 started their own lotteries. By 2012 there were forty-three state lotteries in the United States and more than eighty international lotteries.

PROBLEMS

The justification for holding state lotteries is that lottery profits are intended to be spent on education and other underfunded public services such as parks. However, schools have not seen the windfalls that lottery proponents promised. Indeed, state legislatures approve less general funds to go to education because of a belief that lottery proceeds are sufficient. In addition, some school districts report that education bonds became harder to pass because of the public perception that the schools are getting rich from the lottery. In fact, only thirty-four cents of each dollar spent on a lottery ticket actually goes into the state budget, and in many states very little of that gain benefits education.

One reason for this is lottery advertising. Since the federal ban on advertising state lotteries was lifted in 1975, many states have huge lottery advertising budgets and run aggressive campaigns to sell their lotteries to the public. These ads are run by government agencies, so they are not bound by truth-in-advertising regulations that regulate commercial businesses. A few states, such as Virginia, require that the actual, astronomical odds be stated clearly in each ad. Many lotteries, however, are free to state odds for the smallest prize, such as a free ticket, while advertising the multimillion-dollar jackpot. Though lottery officials like to promote the lottery as entertainment, not gambling, many of their ads are directed to the poor. The Illinois lottery put an ad on a billboard above a poor Chicago neighborhood with the slogan, "This could be your way out." What the sign did not say is that the odds of winning the lottery can be as much as twenty million to one, ridiculously higher than the casino slot machine odds of twenty to one. Media outlets, particularly personal finance advice resources, frequently report on the unlikelihood of winning a big lottery prize, often using colorful comparisons. For example, in 2012 a nationwide lottery promised a $540 million payout, but a commentator on NPR explained that individuals were "100 times more likely to die of flesh-eating bacteria" than to win the half-billion-dollar prize.

Adding to the problems of the state lottery is the fact that most lotteries are being contracted to private companies to run. There are several companies that run the U.S. lotteries, including Gtech, Scientific Games, Automated Wagering International, and Video Lottery Technologies. Of these Gtech is by far the most powerful, with contracts for twenty-six U.S. lotteries and sixty-five international lotteries. Like the private lottery companies of the nineteenth century, Gtech has a reputation for ruthless and corrupt business practices and is constantly the subject of rumors that it uses illegal means to obtain its lottery contracts and break its competition. In 1996 Gtech executive J. David Smith was convicted of fraud, bribery, conspiracy, and money laundering in a New Jersey lottery kickback scheme. None of these behind-the-scenes machinations appear to have an impact on those who play the lottery.

State-run lotteries continue to look for ways to generate excitement and attract new players. One technological advance has been the development of video lottery terminals (VLTs), in which players insert payment, select their number, and pull a lever or push a button to play the games. In some states, such as South Dakota, VLTs provide the main source of lottery income. Another development has been multistate lotteries such as Mega Millions and Powerball. These attract players across the country because of their enormously high payouts; the highest-recorded jackpot so far was $656 million awarded by Mega Millions in 2012. The lottery has also found new avenues through online sales. Both independent and government-run lotteries were available to consumers in the 2010s. Following the precedent set by Liechtenstein, Australia, and the United Kingdom, in 2012 the state of Illinois was the first in the United States to offer its lottery online. Officials hoped that the new access point would boost much-needed revenues, but it was as yet unseen what impact this would have on domestic lottery sales.

There is, perhaps, nothing more American than the desire to get rich, and the many state lotteries seem to offer a chance at this most material pursuit of the American dream. Stories of winners such as the eight Nebraska men who won the biggest single ticket payout ($365 million) in 2011 or the Florida waitress who won $1 million on a scratch ticket and was later featured on ABC's *20/20* become highly publicized and celebrated in the media. Such coverage perpetuates the hope that anyone could be the next big winner. However, many view the lottery as no more than state-sponsored gambling. The profits invite corruption, and the misleading advertisements invite a disproportionate number of poor people to trade their money for a long shot at becoming one of the privileged few. Even lottery winners have their complaints. They often lack experience in dealing with large sums of money, and they encounter envy and hostility from friends and coworkers and are preyed on by swindlers. There are countless cautionary tales of winners who not only lose everything but find themselves deeply in debt, incarcerated, or destitute. Many lottery winners, interviewed years later, reported losing friends, becoming estranged from family, and spending the money too quickly.

Tina Gianoulis

SEE ALSO: *Gambling; Mafia/Organized Crime.*

BIBLIOGRAPHY

Clotfelter, Charles T., and Philip J. Cook. *Selling Hope: State Lotteries in America.* Cambridge, MA: Harvard University Press, 1989.

Elkind, Peter. "The Numbers Crunchers." *Fortune*, November 11, 1996.

Gearey, Robyn. "The Numbers Game—State Lotteries: A Ticket to Poverty." *New Republic*, May 19, 1997.

Sweeney, Matthew. *The Lottery Wars: Long Odds, Fast Money, and the Battle over an American Institution.* New York: Bloomsbury, 2009.

Louis, Joe *(1914–1981)*

Boxer Joe Louis was the first African American "household name" familiar to most white Americans. During his reign as heavyweight boxing champion from 1937 to 1949, Louis did what no other black athlete had done before: he earned the respect and devotion of a mass audience of middle-class whites across the nation. His 1938 victory over Max Schmeling came

Joe Louis. Joe Louis takes to the corner of the ring while the referee prepares to end the fight between Louis and the defeated Max Schmeling in their heavyweight title rematch bout in June 1938. IMAGNO/CONTRIBUTOR/HULTON ARCHIVE/GETTY IMAGES.

to symbolize the conflict between the democratic United States and Nazi Germany while providing African Americans with a national celebrity. According to biographer Richard Bak in *Joe Louis: The Great Black Hope*, "In his day he was the most famous black man in America." Louis's heroics in the ring came to represent the potential ability of African Americans to overcome racism and discrimination. Before Jackie Robinson integrated baseball in 1947, Louis truly was "The Great Black Hope."

Louis was born Joseph Louis Barrow in Lafayette, Alabama, on May 13, 1914. He accompanied his family to Detroit, Michigan, soon thereafter and began his boxing career in the seamy, impoverished Black Bottom section of the city. In his first amateur bout, he was knocked down seven times. Yet with the help of manager John Roxborough, the aspiring athlete soon honed a powerful right cross and a matching left hook—acquiring the distinctive compact style that was his trademark throughout his career. By 1934 Louis had worked his way from the Brewster gym to a victory in the 175-pound championship match at the U.S. Amateur Athletic Union. He turned professional on July 4, 1934.

PROFESSIONAL CAREER

In the three years that followed, Louis defeated a veritable who's who of boxing greats. He won his first twenty-seven fights, twenty-three by knockout. Among his victims were legends Max Baer, Paolino Uzcudun, and Natie Brown. Yet he drew national attention only after trouncing former heavyweight champion Primo Carnera at New York's Madison Square Garden. The Louis-Carnera bout, coinciding with Italian dictator Benito Mussolini's preparations for his attack on Ethiopia, acquired symbolic significance: In an era when nations prided themselves on the performances of their athletes, Louis's victory over the Italian Carnera came to represent, in the American consciousness, the Ethiopian underdogs in their struggle against the technologically superior armies of fascist Italy. The fight also instantly transformed Louis into black America's most famous symbol. Following the victory, thousands of celebrants poured into the streets of Harlem, New York.

Despite a knockout loss to Germany's Schmeling in 1936, Louis earned a shot at heavyweight champion James J. Braddock through subsequent victories over Jack Sharkey and Bob Pastor. Braddock and Louis met on July 22, 1937, at Chicago's Comiskey Park. Tensions ran high as the prospect of an African American heavyweight champion angered many whites. The only previous black boxer to hold the title, Jack Johnson, had been forced to flee the country under threat of imprisonment after having a relationship with a white woman. Yet when Louis delivered a come-from-behind knockout blow in the eighth round to assume the heavyweight title, white America responded with subdued admiration. Black America went wild. From that moment forward, many African Americans came to believe that the future of their struggle for equality depended upon the continued success of the "Brown Bomber." Hundreds of thousands of African Americans followed his every match on the radio; the black press hounded him for his opinions on the issues of the day. He even became the subject of a popular Duke Ellington song. Rather than rest on his laurels, the world's most famous black man returned to the ring to defend the honor of his country.

The second Louis-Schmeling match, at Yankee Stadium on June 22, 1938, was arguably the most celebrated event in the sport's history. It was also one of the shortest. Louis dominated the fight from the first punch, and only two minutes and four seconds had elapsed before Louis knocked Schmeling to the mats with a pair of broken vertebra. Throughout much of the North and Midwest, the new heavyweight champion became the first black celebrity to appeal to people of all races.

WORLD WAR II AND BEYOND

Louis added to his popularity when he put his career on hold to join the war effort against Germany, enlisting in the army as a private and mustering out as a sergeant. During his military service, he also appeared in war propaganda films for the U.S. government and fought exhibition bouts to raise funds for military causes. His return to boxing after World War II was heralded by the media, which derided his opponents as members of "Bum of the Month Club." By 1949, when he retired long enough for Ezzard Charles to acquire the heavyweight title, Louis had earned a reputation as boxing's all-time greatest star. His division record of twenty-five successful title defenses still stands to this day.

Louis returned to the ring briefly in 1950 and 1951. He lost a fifteen-round decision to Charles in his debut and was later knocked out in eight rounds by future heavyweight champion Rocky Marciano. A man who knew when to quit, Louis then retired permanently. He left one of boxing's most impressive career records: seventy-one fights, sixty-eight wins, and fifty-four knockouts. In addition to Baer, Braddock, and Schmeling, his list of unsuccessful opponents included "Jersey Joe" Walcott, Billy Conn, and Jimmy Bivins.

Like many early celebrities, Louis experienced difficulty adjusting to life out of the limelight. Although he had won more than $4 million in purses over the years, poor financial management left the retired boxer deep in debt. In addition, he faced unpaid federal income taxes. "I just don't know where the money went," he lamented. "I wish I did. I got 50 percent of each purse and all kinds of expenses came out of my cut." By the mid-1950s Louis had descended into a sedentary life of emotional trauma and narcotics abuse. He earned his living as a greeter at Caesar's Palace in Las Vegas, Nevada. In the words of Bak, "Joe was battling his own demons during the 1960s, so the civil rights movement passed him by." He died in Las Vegas on April 12, 1981.

Even if Louis did not actively take part in the civil rights movement of the 1960s, he—more than almost any other individual—made it possible. The 1930s were dark days for African Americans. Most paths to achievement, including most professional sports, were off-limits to blacks. Boxing, which Bak terms "a pretty nefarious sport," offered one of society's few arenas for interracial competition. Louis capitalized on the opportunity that boxing afforded and showed black Americans that, given a fair chance, they could equal or better even the most accomplished whites.

Louis also demonstrated to many white Americans that such success didn't have to be hostile or unpalatable. When Brooklyn Dodgers general manager Branch Rickey decided to integrate baseball during the 1940s, he told his scouts to find him "someone just like Joe Louis." Even the popularity of Martin Luther King among Northern white liberals during the mid-1950s was, in part, a consequence of Louis's success in convincing many whites that black Americans could handle publicity and leadership responsibly.

Tributes to the world's greatest boxer now abound, including a sports stadium in Detroit, a postage stamp, and a two-ton monument by sculptor Robert Graham. As reporter Jimmy Cannon once said of him: "Louis was a credit to his race . . . the human race."

Jacob M. Appel

SEE ALSO: *Boxing; Civil Rights Movement; Johnson, Jack; Robinson, Jackie.*

BIBLIOGRAPHY

Adler, David A., and Terry Widener. *Joe Louis: America's Fighter*. Orlando, FL: Gulliver Books, Harcourt, 2005.

Bak, Richard. *Joe Louis: The Great Black Hope*. Dallas, TX: Taylor, 1996.

Barrow, Joe Louis Jr., and Barbara Munder. *Joe Louis: 50 Years an American Hero*. New York: McGraw-Hill, 1988.

Fleischer, Nat. *The Louis Legend*. New York: The Ring, 1956.

Kessler, Gene. *Joe Louis: The Brown Bomber*. Racine, WI: Whitman, 1936.

Louis, Joe, with Edna Rust and Art Rust. *Joe Louis: My Life*. New York: Harcourt Brace Jovanovich, 1978.

Mead, Chris. *Champion: Joe Louis, Black Hero in White America*. New York: Scribner, 1985.

Nagler, Barney. *Brown Bomber*. New York: World Publishing, 1972.

Van Deusen, John George. *Brown Bomber: The Story of Joe Louis*. Philadelphia: Dorrance, 1940.

Van Every, Edward. *Joe Louis, Man and Super-Fighter*. New York: Frederick A. Stokes, 1936.

Louisiana Purchase Exposition

The Louisiana Purchase Exposition, also called the World's Fair, was held in St. Louis, Missouri, in 1904 to celebrate the centennial of the Louisiana Purchase. From the opening ceremonies on April 30 to the final day on December 1, twenty million people attended the daily events and viewed American icons such as Geronimo. At the time, it was the largest world's fair ever.

The Louisiana Purchase Exposition emphasized American prowess in technology, industry, and military leadership. Electricity used to illuminate the Hall of Festivals, Colonnade of States, Palaces of Electricity and Education, and Machinery Hall cost $2 million, an enormous amount of money back then.

The Great Floral Clock, with a seventy-four-foot minute hand, was the centerpiece exhibit. Other exhibits included Abraham Lincoln's private railway coach and a 260-foot-high Ferris wheel. With comparatively little fanfare, the 1904 Olympics took place in St. Louis during the Louisiana Purchase Exposition.

The grandness of the Louisiana Purchase Exposition has had a lasting effect. The movie *Meet Me in St. Louis* (1944), starring Judy Garland, romantically depicts the fair. The 1904 World's Fair Society, established in 1986, publishes the monthly *World's Fair Bulletin* and proposed staging a 2004 world's fair in St. Louis. Additionally, the Missouri Historical Society displayed an exhibit near the Louisiana Purchase Exposition site where people excavated collectibles from landfill rubble.

Elizabeth D. Schafer

SEE ALSO: Meet Me in St. Louis*; World's Fairs.*

BIBLIOGRAPHY

Bennitt, Mark, ed. *History of the Louisiana Purchase Exposition.* St. Louis, MO: Universal Exposition Publishing, 1905.

Birk, Dorothy Daniels. *The World Came to St. Louis: A Visit to the 1904 World's Fair.* Foreword by August A. Busch Jr. St. Louis, MO: Chalice Press, 1979.

Breitbart, Eric. *A World on Display: Photographs from the St. Louis World's Fair, 1904.* Albuquerque: University of New Mexico Press, 1997.

Strait, James; Mark Moran; and Mark Sceurman. *Weird Missouri: Your Travel Guide to Missouri's Local Legends and Best Kept Secrets.* New York: Sterling Publishing, 2008.

Louisville Slugger

The Louisville Slugger, the official bat of Major League Baseball, is synonymous with America's pastime. In 1884 Bud Hillerich—a manufacturer of wooden posts, columns, bowling balls, and pins in Louisville, Kentucky—produced a custom-made bat for major league star Pete Browning. While swinging the new bat, Browning soared out of a slump and initiated demand for Hillerich's bats. By 1894 Hillerich's product was being called the Louisville Slugger, a name that has appeared in an oval on each bat ever since then.

Hillerich began the now-ubiquitous practice of athletes endorsing sporting goods when, in 1905, Honus Wagner gave permission for his autograph to be included on the bats. Since then, the signatures of many other famous players have appeared on Louisville Slugger bats, including those of Ty Cobb, Babe Ruth, Mickey Mantle, Roger Maris, Hank Aaron, Johnny Bench, Jose Cardenal, Derek Jeter, and Alex Rodriguez. These endorsements, as well as the records that have been broken by players while using the bats, firmly established the Louisville Slugger's reputation. Most notably, Ruth hit sixty home runs in 1927 using Louisville Sluggers made to his specifications.

In 1970 the company began producing aluminum Louisville Slugger bats, and five years later, it added Louisville Slugger baseball and softball gloves. To learn about the famous bat's history, baseball fans can tour the company's factory and visit its museum, both of which are in Louisville.

Sharon Brown

SEE ALSO: *Aaron, Hank; Baseball; Bench, Johnny; Cobb, Ty; Mantle, Mickey; Maris, Roger; Ruth, Babe; Wagner, Honus.*

BIBLIOGRAPHY

Arnow, Jan. *Louisville Slugger: The Making of a Baseball Bat.* New York: Pantheon Books, 1984.

Love, Courtney *(1964–)*

One of the most interesting and controversial figures, male or female, of the 1990s and early 2000s, Courtney Love has defiantly challenged assumptions about what is considered acceptable behavior for a woman, always blazing her own trail in the process. Wearing torn baby-doll dresses, with unkempt knotted hair and a guitar strapped around her shoulders, Love caught the attention of Middle America, even becoming the subject of parody on *Saturday Night Live*—the ultimate litmus test of mainstream recognition. As the lead singer/guitarist for the rock band Hole, as an actress, and as the wife of Nirvana front man Kurt Cobain, Love has garnered both critical acclaim and vicious personal attacks on her character.

Love's life has been filled with all the drama of a big budget Hollywood movie. Beginning as an actress who had small parts in a handful of films during the 1980s, she went on to form Hole, a noise-rock band that released one acclaimed record in underground music circles. Love gained a much higher profile when she married Cobain, leader of the archetypal grunge band Nirvana, in 1992. During their brief, stormy marriage, she was

Courtney Love. *Courtney Love performs at a festival in Seattle, Washington, in 2010.* DANNY MARTINDALE/CONTRIBUTOR/WIREIMAGE/GETTY IMAGES.

alternately portrayed in the press as a drug-addicted mother or as a talentless leech, riding the coattails of her husband's fame. After Cobain's suicide, which took place days before the release of Hole's second album (aptly titled *Live through This*), she did her grieving in public, exposing her rage and tears for all the world to see. Constantly the subject of sensational tabloid and mainstream news stories, Love had done an about-face by 1997, resurfacing as a Golden Globe–nominated movie star. In the five years between Cobain's death and her own emergence as a respected Hollywood actress, Love lived through more than most people do in a lifetime.

EARLY LIFE AND CAREER

Born into a hippie family with minor connections to the Grateful Dead, Love's first mass media exposure occurred when she was five years old and appeared in a group photo on the back of the Grateful Dead's 1969 *Aoxomoxoa* album. She had a slightly troubled childhood, getting caught shoplifting at age twelve and being sent to a reform school. After dropping in and out of school and eventually moving all over the world—occasionally earning money as a stripper—Love finally moved back to Los Angeles, where she found her way into two Alex Cox films, *Sid & Nancy* (1986) and *Straight to Hell* (1987).

While in Los Angeles, she formed Hole with guitarist Eric Erlandson, and after a couple 7-inch single releases, the band quickly gained recognition with its 1991 release *Pretty on the Inside*, produced by Kim Gordon of Sonic Youth. Hole quickly became darlings of the British mainstream music press and American independent music magazines. After her courtship and subsequent marriage to Cobain on February 24, 1992, Love reluctantly became associated with another famous female scapegoat, Yoko Ono. Like Ono, who also had a successful career before she met and married rock star icon John Lennon, Love endured sexist and unfounded media speculation that her relationship to Cobain was a scam to further her own career. The fact that Hole signed to the same major label Nirvana belonged to didn't help negate those assumptions.

After a *Vanity Fair* article implied that Love had taken heroin while pregnant with her daughter, Frances Bean Cobain, she and her husband battled child services for the custody of their child—a fight they ultimately won. Interestingly, a similar situation happened to Ono and Lennon, who very briefly lost custody of Sean Ono Lennon after Yoko tested positive for drug use after giving birth to her son. (The case against them was dropped after it turned out the drugs were painkillers given by doctors during childbirth.) In 1993 Love began recording Hole's follow-up album, even as she was dealing with a troubled marriage. The weekend before Hole was to release their second album, prophetically titled *Live through This*, Cobain was found dead, the victim of a self-inflicted gunshot wound. In a rare instance of public mourning by a celebrity, Love read parts of Cobain's suicide note during a tape-recorded message to Cobain's fans, interjecting comments about her guilt, her anger, and her sadness over her husband's death.

A defiantly abrasive, angry, and aggressive album, *Live through This* was universally praised, winning year-end critics polls at *Spin*, *Rolling Stone*, and the *Village Voice*. The sales of the album slowly built steam, and despite the setback of another tragedy—the heroin overdose death of Hole bassist Kristen Pfaff two months after Cobain's death—Love pushed on and began touring to promote her album. *Live through This* eventually went multiplatinum.

That tour and subsequent tours provided fodder for tabloid and mainstream press, as Love drunkenly shouted obscenities from the stage, dove into the audience, and got into scuffles with airline flight attendants, pushy reporters, and other female punk rock singers. During a live televised MTV Awards after-show party, a visibly drunk Love hurled a shoe at Madonna's head, disrupting an interview with the superstar.

A NEW IMAGE

But in 1997 Love began to clean up her media image, replacing the tangled hair and torn baby-doll dresses with a thinner body, designer dresses, and stylishly cut hair. She had been hard at work on her acting career, appearing in minor roles before landing a starring role in *The People vs. Larry Flint*. Her powerful performance earned her a Golden Globe nomination and led to further serious movie offers. In 1998 Hole released another aptly titled album, *Celebrity Skin*, to largely favorable critical response.

Love starred alongside Jim Carrey in the Andy Kaufman biopic *Man on the Moon* (1999), and for a moment it appeared that an aura of calm and stability had finally settled on her tormented life. In the early 2000s, however, Hole entered into a legal dispute with their record label; the band officially broke up in 2002. After a starring role in the thriller *Trapped* (2002), Love released the solo record *America's Sweetheart* (2004) amid numerous financial and legal problems and rumors of renewed drug addictions. The album received mixed reviews, but it was her bizarre behavior in interviews—most notably in a rambling, incoherent appearance on *Late Night with David Letterman* in 2004—that dominated public perception. She was ordered by the court to participate in a ninety-day drug and alcohol rehabilitation in 2006 and published the memoir *Dirty Blonde: The Diaries of Courtney Love* soon after.

Despite claims made by her daughter, who filed a restraining order against her in 2009, Love insists she has been drug free since her court-ordered rehab. She put together a new lineup for Hole in 2009 and released the album *Nobody's Daughter* with the group the following year. She continues to tour the world with the band and announced plans to publish a memoir of her tumultuous relationship with Cobain in 2011. She remains a powerful voice against the exploitation of artists in the music industry and has been called a hero to feminists and gay rights groups for her uncompromising public stance in the face of personal and widespread injustices, as well as for her refusal to be pigeonholed as the former wife of a revolutionary rock star.

Kembrew McLeod

SEE ALSO: *Alternative Rock; Celebrity; Celebrity Couples; Feminism; Gay Liberation Movement; The Grateful Dead; Hippies; Hollywood; Kaufman, Andy; Lennon, John; Letterman, David; Madonna; Movie Stars; MTV; Nirvana; Punk; Rock and Roll;* Rolling Stone*;* Saturday Night Live*; Spin; Suicide; Tabloids;* Vanity Fair.

BIBLIOGRAPHY

Brite, Poppy. *Courtney Love.* New York: S & S Trade, 1997.

Love, Courtney. *Dirty Blonde: The Diaries of Courtney Love.* New York: Faber and Faber, 2006.

Rossi, Melissa. *Courtney Love: Queen of Noise.* New York: Pocket Books, 1996.

The Love Boat

Like its sister series, *Fantasy Island* (1977–1984), ABC's *The Love Boat* was one of television's most reliable barometers of celebrity. Guests on the show, it was said, were either on their way up or on their way down. That they wanted to come on at all was evidence of the program's formidable popularity with viewers. Perfectly ensconced in a Saturday night time slot, when shut-ins and the socially challenged are most apt to be watching TV, this airy seaborne soufflé rode the public's fascination with recognizable performers to ratings success over the course of nine improbable seasons from 1977 to 1986.

Based on a forgettable 1974 novel by former cruise ship director Jeraldine Saunders, the lighthearted series interwove three romantic plots for an hour each week. The show eschewed the book's soapy conventions in favor of romantic comedy like the similarly structured *Love, American Style* (1969–1974). Set onboard the fictional cruise liner *Pacific Princess*, *The Love Boat* featured a cast of regulars playing the roles of the ship's crew, with a new batch of has-beens and up-and-comers introduced as passengers in each episode. Plot complications often involved mistaken identities, bittersweet reunions, and the ever-popular premarital reservations. The sex was suggested rather than shown, although the very concept of a "love boat" reflected the permissive sexual attitudes coming to the fore in American culture at the time.

The Love Boat. The Love Boat *starred, clockwise from left, Lauren Tewes as Julie McCoy, Fred Grandy as "Gopher" Smith, Ted Lange as Isaac Washington, Bernie Koppel as Dr. Adam Bricker, Jill Whelan as Vicki Stubing, and Gavin MacLeod as Captain Merrill Stubing.* AARON SPELLING/LOVE BOAT COMPANY/THE KOBAL COLLECTION.

Producer Aaron Spelling was enlisted to shepherd the program to air after two pilot episodes went down in flames, reportedly because of poor casting. With his keen sense of the likes and dislikes of the American viewing public, Spelling assembled a floating repertory company of genial "B"-list performers. Gavin MacLeod of TV's *Mary Tyler Moore Show* (1970–1977) played the ship's captain, Merrill Stubing. The antic Bernie Kopell, so effective as the evil genius Siegfried on *Get Smart* (1965–1970), provided comic tonics as ship physician Adam "Doc" Bricker. Newcomer Lauren Tewes played perky cruise director Julie McCoy, while Fred Grandy and Ted Lange rounded out the cast as the ship's purser and bartender, respectively.

The *Pacific Princess* sailed to many exotic locations over the course of its nine-year run. Acapulco, Stockholm, Helsinki, and Sydney were only a few of the ports that welcomed the ocean liner of love. Even more exciting were some of the guest stars who booked passage—many of them for multiple engagements. Suzanne Somers, John Ritter, and Loni Anderson were a few of the contemporary stars who dropped in for an episode or two, although game show regulars such as Bert Convy, Fannie Flagg, and the Landers Sisters were more typical of the caliber of star featured recurrently. The show also became a safe haven for old-time Hollywood legends, many of them lured by the promise of a free cruise (the show was often filmed on location). Some of the show business fossils who turned up on the Love Boat decks included Lana Turner, Alice Faye, and Don Ameche.

Perhaps the most bizarre passenger to grace the *Princess*'s poop deck was pop art impresario Andy Warhol, who played himself on the program's 200th episode in 1985. The man who coined the term *fifteen minutes of fame* may have been bemused by the show's celebration of the cult of celebrity, but he showed no emotion as he virtually sleepwalked through his appearance. In a turn of events that surely would have tickled Warhol's fancy, bumbling ship's purser Grandy actually won a seat in the U.S. House of Representatives in 1987, shortly after the show concluded its nine-year voyage.

The Love Boat steamed on unchanged well into the 1980s, although original cast member Tewes was forced to leave the show in 1984 after a well-publicized bout with cocaine addiction. A few format tweaks (including the introduction of the singing, dancing "Love Boat Mermaids") heralded the show's inevitable ratings slide, however, and the *Princess* was finally put into dry dock in 1986. It returned for a series of highly rated televised reunion movies, all featuring the original cast. A new series, *Love Boat: The Next Wave* debuted in 1998 to lukewarm public response.

Richard Kinon, who directed many episodes of *The Love Boat*, once described the show's formula as "romance and pap." Few television historians would disagree with that assessment, although in its own way the program did say something about the mood of the country that watched it so avidly. At its height *Love Boat* was a kind of floating Studio 54 for the mom-and-pop set—a weekly shipboard party filled with famous faces and soft-serve sexcapades. And for a weary post-Watergate populace desperate for any entertainment that did not require hard thinking, this was just what the cruise director ordered.

Robert E. Schnakenberg

SEE ALSO: *Celebrity; Cocaine/Crack;* Fantasy Island*;* Get Smart*; Hollywood;* The Mary Tyler Moore Show*; Movie Stars; Pop Art; Romance Novels; Sexual Revolution; Spelling, Aaron; Studio 54; Television; Turner, Lana; Warhol, Andy; Watergate.*

BIBLIOGRAPHY

Saunders, Jeraldine. *"Love Boat:" Collector's Edition.* St. Paul, MN: Llewellyn Publications, 1998.

Spelling, Aaron, and Jefferson Graham. *Aaron Spelling: A Prime-Time Life.* New York: St. Martin's Press, 1996.

Wallace, David. "Once Slated for Dry Dock, *The Love Boat* Cruises Boozily into Its Ninth Nautical Season." *People Weekly*, April 15, 1985, 130.

Lovecraft, H. P. *(1890–1937)*

H. P. Lovecraft, by some estimates, is the greatest writer of horror fiction since Edgar Allan Poe. His influence on modern horror art has been enormous, despite his pulp fiction origins. The homage that modern horror writers (and filmmakers) continue to pay him emanated largely from the distinctly modern sensibility he brought to his fiction.

Howard Philips Lovecraft was born on August 20, 1890, in Providence, Rhode Island, the only child of Winfield Scott and Sarah Susan Philips Lovecraft. In 1893 Lovecraft's father was declared insane and committed to Butler's Hospital in Providence, where he died five years later. Lovecraft and his mother moved in with his maternal grandparents, where he attended various Providence public schools. After his grandfather's death in 1904, the family's financial status underwent an immediate decline, and Lovecraft had a nervous breakdown in 1908, just prior to his high school graduation. Over the next five years, he would stay home, living the life of a reclusive autodidact and schooling himself in a multiplicity of subjects, including Roman history, chemistry, astronomy, and eighteenth-century life and letters.

EARLY WRITING CAREER

Lovecraft's first foray into writing began at age sixteen with regular contributions of articles on astronomy to various local and statewide publications. In 1914 he joined the United Amateur Press Association, becoming an active member and contributor, self-publishing thirteen issues of his journal, the *Conservative*, from 1915 to 1923.

Lovecraft's first tales circulated among his amateur journalist friends, printed in such ephemeral publications as the *United Amateur*, the *Vagrant*, the *Wolverine*, and the *Tryout*. He abandoned the world of amateur journalism in 1923 when the first and most important of the large-circulation pulps, *Weird Tales*, took notice of his talents. Unlike most other writers discovered while young, Lovecraft broke in at the age of thirty-three, becoming, as a consequence, the old man of fantasy fiction, a distinction he took to heart by encouraging in paternal fashion younger talents such as Robert Bloch, Fritz Leiber, and Frank Belknap Long.

After his discovery by *Weird Tales*, story after story from Lovecraft's pen showed up in its pages, including such trademark tales as "Dagon," "The Tomb," "The Rats in the Walls," "The Call of Cthulhu," "Pickman's Model," "The Colour out of Space," "The Dunwich Horror," and "The Whisperer in the Darkness." He wrote his first novellas, *The Case of Charles Dexter Ward* and *The Dream-Quest of Unknown Kadath*, in 1927.

OUTSIDE INFLUENCES

In addition to the advancement of his career as a fiction writer, Lovecraft's life changed in other significant ways during the 1920s. In 1919 his mother was institutionalized, as his father had been, at Butler Hospital, where she died two years later. Not coincidentally, Lovecraft broke free geographically, traveling beyond the confines of Providence to Boston for his first conference of amateur journalists. His taste for travel and love of New England whetted by this excursion, he began to travel more regularly to Boston, New York, Portsmouth, Marblehead, and Newport. Summer trips took him to even further climes, including Quebec, Montreal, Canada; Charleston, South Carolina; New Orleans, Louisiana; and Saint Augustine, Florida.

One of the more important events of the 1920s that would set the tone for how Lovecraft would wish to live was his short marriage to Sonia Greene, a fellow amateur journalist, with whom he lived in New York City for nearly two years. Her relocation to Cleveland, Ohio, for work and his inability to find any form of gainful employment in New York resulted in the marriage's dissolution and Lovecraft's return to Providence and bachelorhood.

1930s WRITING

In the 1930s two important changes in Lovecraft's life occurred. His fictional output began to slow, while his politics changed from that of the classic conservative to the New Deal Democrat. The few efforts Lovecraft made to write original material in the 1930s produced excellent results. His novellas *At the Mountains of Madness* and *The Shadow over Innsmouth* were written back-to-back in 1931, and "The Shadow out of Time" appeared in *Astounding Stories* in 1936. Unfortunately, his creative powers appeared to ebb as more of his efforts were spent rewriting or cowriting stories with lesser pulp-fiction writers such as Hazel Heald, Duane Rimel, R. H. Barlow, and William Lumley.

On March 15, 1937, Lovecraft died of intestinal cancer at Jane Brown Memorial Hospital in Providence. His passing was noted by the many fans and loyal friends whom he had made in his lifetime. Beyond this small coterie, he remained largely unknown. His reputation as a writer was revived years later by Donald Wandrei and August Derleth, both protégés of the master and founders of Arkham House, a press in Sauk City, Wisconsin, that published the work of fantasy and science fiction writers who had benefited from Lovecraft's influence.

CAREER CRITIQUES

Lovecraft's rise to fame since has been a troubling one for academics and fans alike. For academics, that main source of trouble is the popularity of a writer whose talents were best captured by Jacques Barzun's statement, "How the frequently portentous but unintelligible H. P. Lovecraft has acquired a reputation as a notable performer is explained only by the willingness of some to take the intention for the deed and by a touching faith that words put together with confidence must have a meaning." For fans and supportive scholars, the most difficult obstacle to any appreciation of Lovecraft has been his unbridled racism and classism, both of which are deeply implied in his tales of racial degeneration and miscegenation. On the other hand, many continue to credit Lovecraft with applying a modern sensibility to the world of horror by highlighting in a way that few of his predecessors had—barring Poe—the materialist foundations of modern terror.

Bennett Lovett-Graff

SEE ALSO: *Derleth, August;* Pulp Fiction; *Science Fiction Publishing;* Weird Tales.

BIBLIOGRAPHY

Cannon, Peter H. *H. P. Lovecraft.* Boston: Twayne, 1989.

Joshi, S. T. *H. P. Lovecraft.* West Warwick, RI: Necronomicon Press, 1996.

Joshi, S. T. *Icons of Horror and the Supernatural: An Encyclopedia of Our Worst Nightmares.* Westport, CT: Greenwood Press, 2007.

Lévy, Maurice. *Lovecraft: A Study in the Fantastic.* Tr. by S. T. Joshi. Detroit, MI: Wayne State University Press, 1988.

St. Armand, Barton Levi. *The Roots of Horror in the Fiction of H. P. Lovecraft.* Elizabethtown, NY: Dragon Press, 1977.

Low Riders

A low rider vehicle, which can be a car, a truck, a motorcycle, or even a bicycle, is one that has been altered to ride very low to the road: it almost sits on the ground and has a sleek, streamlined appearance. The word is also applied to the owners or drivers of such vehicles, who might participate in all the activities associated with low riding, such as cruising, caravanning to car shows, or just hanging out and showing off their customizing skills.

The practice of customizing cars was started at least as early as the 1930s in Los Angeles and Sacramento, although the expression "low rider" did not come into usage until the 1960s, after a custom-car subculture had arisen in the Southwest, particularly in California. Low rider cars are commonly identified with Latinos and Chicanos, sometimes negatively in connection to gang activity, but there are also Anglo Americans who indulge in the practice. Traditionally, low riders have often been working-class young men who feel pride in their culture and want to maintain an outward manifestation of it in their vehicles. In doing so, many of them may be following a family tradition of two and three generations.

The customizing culture of 1950s California dictated a lowered look, originally achieved by the inelegant method of placing heavy bricks and cement bags in the trunk of the car. Other customizers began manipulating the chassis of the car by lowering the car's block or cutting the spring coils. Later it was discovered that hydraulic lifts, operated manually by the driver, could be used to lower and raise both the front and rear ends of a car and that the batteries could be stored in the trunk. The most popular cars adapted for low riding are long ones, such as Fords, Buicks, and Chevrolets. Once the car is lowered it is considered to be "lifted" or "juiced up." Some low riders can be rocked from side to side by means of these lifts, creating the "car dancing" effect.

Each low rider is given its own personal style by means of different techniques that are creatively employed by their owners. Interiors are often upholstered in crushed velvet, usually red or black, with wall-to-wall carpeting. The vehicle may also be

Low Rider. *A crowd watches as hydraulic lifts raise a low-rider car off of ground.* **STEPHANIE MAZE/CONTRIBUTOR/NATIONAL GEOGRAPHIC/GETTY IMAGES.**

outfitted with a bar, a chandelier, a stereo, and a television. The car's two-toned body is often painted with a lacquer that contains iridescent flakes. Chrome is important for appearance, and the undercarriage, wheels, bumper, and other parts might be chrome and/or gold plated. The car is often adorned with cultural decorative motifs and designs, such as a fire-lace design, pinstriping, or a mural. Popular mural themes include Aztec or Mayan scenes or Mexican religious icons, such as the Virgin of Guadalupe.

Cruising is an important aspect of the low-riding scene, although an expensively customized car will only be driven to car shows. The objective of cruising is to socialize, to see and be seen; it is sometimes compared to *el paseo*, a "strolling" custom known throughout Latin American and Mexican cities.

Since the 1970s *Low Rider Magazine* has been influential in disseminating information on low rider clubs and happenings throughout the Southwest, and it has even been published in a Japanese edition for car-show organizers in Tokyo and Osaka. A low rider 1969 Ford LTD, called "Dave's Dream," has been displayed at the Smithsonian National Museum of American History in Washington, D.C., the first such vehicle to be exhibited there. The car belongs to three men from Chimayo, New Mexico, who started customizing it in 1975.

Rafaela Castro

SEE ALSO: *Automobile; Ford Motor Company; Smithsonian Institution.*

BIBLIOGRAPHY

Bright, Brenda Jo. "Remappings: Los Angeles Low Riders." In *Looking High and Low: Art and Cultural Identity*, eds. Brenda Jo Bright and Elizabeth Bakewell. Tucson: University of Arizona Press, 1995.

Castro, Rafaela. *Chicano Folklore: A Guide to the Folktales, Traditions, Rituals and Religious Practices of Mexican Americans*. New York: Oxford University Press, 2001.

Marks, Susan Tosaw. "Low Riding: One Road to an Ethnic Identity." *Southwest Folklore* 4, no. 1 (1980): 40–50.

Plascencia, Luis F. "Low Riding in the Southwest: Cultural Symbols in the Mexican Community," 141–175. In *History, Culture, and Society: Chicano Studies in the 1980s*, eds. Mario T. García; Bert N. Corona; National Association for Chicano Studies; et al. Ypsilanti, MI: Bilingual Press/ Editorial Bilingüe, 1983.

Stone, Michael Cutler. "Bajito y Sauvecito (Low and Slow): Low Riding and the 'Class' of Class." *Studies in Latin American Popular Culture* 9 (1990): 85–126.

Trillin, Calvin. "Our Far-Flung Correspondents: Low and Slow, Mean and Clean." *New Yorker*, July 10, 1978, 70–74.

Low-Carb Diets

By 2004 low-carbohydrate diets had become so popular that more than 50 percent of the U.S. public had either tried one or were currently on one, according to Mintel, a London-based market research firm. Although most of these diets proved to be quick fixes and were the subject of disagreement and scrutiny by the medical community, immediate results made this particular fad hard for many people to resist. Low-carb regimens such as Atkins, the South Beach Diet, and the Zone began making headlines in the 1990s as the new way to lose weight.

In 1972 Doctor Robert Atkins published *Dr. Atkins Diet Revolution*, a book that emphasized replacing carbohydrate-rich foods with red meat and other fare high in protein and fat. At that time most people were not really interested in the book or Atkins's claims that one could lose a significant amount of weight by replacing bread and pasta with meat. In 1981 Doctor David Jenkins developed the glycemic index, which classifies foods according to the rapidity of their effect on blood sugar levels. Although not exclusively a low-carb guideline, the glycemic index became the basis of several weight-loss plans, including Jenny Craig and Nutrisystem.

The low-carb craze gained popularity in the late 1990s with celebrity advocates such as Jennifer Aniston. Doctor Atkins republished his famous text as *Dr. Atkins New Diet Revolution* (1992), and the *New York Times* best-seller list was full of similar diet books. At the height of the low-carb craze, Atkins was named *Time* magazine's 2002 Person of the Year for his influence on Americans' diets. Food manufacturers profited from the fad by creating or relabeling products as low carbohydrate. Even foods high on the glycemic index received a low-carb seal of approval; Kellogg's retooled its Special K cereal, Eggo waffles, and Keebler cookies to be more enticing to dieters. According to Mintel, by 2004 about 375 of these new products packed the shelves. The Zone simplified life further by preparing and delivering diet-specific foods, and other plans such as Atkins branded their own meal replacement bars and prepackaged dinners to be sold in grocery stores. Meat, eggs, nuts, and meat-based snacks remained the core of such diets, however, with the meat snacks market increasing 147 percent from 1997 to 2002.

The scientific basis behind these weight-loss plans came from the theory that reducing the amount of carbohydrates in a diet put the human body into a state of ketosis. In this state the body forms ketones, which in effect burn fat rather than carbs for energy since glycogen stores have been depleted. Ketosis was presumed to reduce the feeling of hunger, so a person on a low-carb diet would eat less food, therefore losing weight and experiencing immediate results. Proponents also claimed that low-carb diets could even mitigate chronic diseases such as diabetes, metabolic disease, and epilepsy.

A typical low-carb plan limits the intake of carbohydrates to only 20 to 60 grams per day, or 5 percent of daily food intake, whereas U.S. dietary guidelines recommend that 50 to 60 percent of daily food intake be carbohydrates. Opponents asserted that it was not possible to remain on that kind of diet indefinitely because of its restrictiveness. The medical community also argued that the consumption of such large quantities of proteins and fats led to kidney and liver problems as well as to heart failure. In 2002 Dr. Atkins suffered a nonfatal heart attack, and although he and his physician maintained that it was the result of an infection, many speculated that the dangers of Atkins and other low-carbohydrate diets were to blame. Dr. Atkins died in 2003 from complications due to a head injury.

After 2004 the low-carb craze began to abate. The advent of surgical weight-loss solutions may have contributed to this decline. Also, with lifestyle-related chronic illnesses such as type 2 diabetes and heart disease on the rise, quick-fix diets such as Atkins and South Beach have yet to prove effective in stemming the epidemic. In the twenty-first century most medical and nutrition professionals agreed that a diet rich in fruits and vegetables and low in sugars and fats, combined with moderate exercise, were the keys to longevity and well-being. Although low-carb plans reappeared in the form of the Dukan Diet and the 17-Day Diet, neither generated the same enthusiasm that was seen in the 1990s and early 2000s.

Jill Clever

SEE ALSO: *Dieting.*

BIBLIOGRAPHY

Hellmich, Nanci. "Low-Carb 17-Day, Dukan Diets Disappoint Nutritionists." *USA Today*, April 18, 2011.

McDonald, Kim. "The Skinny on the Low-Carb Craze: Diet and Fatness in America." *Duke Magazine*, September–October 2004.

Scales, Mary Josephine. *Diets in a Nutshell: A Definitive Guide on Diets from A to Z.* Clifton, VA: Apex Publishers, 2005.

Stein, Joel; Dan Cray; Julie Grace; et al. "The Low-Carb Diet Craze." *Time*, November 1, 1999, 54.

Low-Rise Jeans

Blue jeans, once only worn by workers and bohemians, became designer fashions during the late 1970s and have remained a staple wardrobe item for both men and women. Once jeans became chic, designers began to alter their classic silhouette, widening or slimming the leg and raising or lowering the waist as styles changed. Low-rise jeans first became popular during the hippie era of the 1960s and 1970s, when they were dubbed "hip huggers" and imparted a casual, sensual look to the wearer. Although low-cut jeans never completely went out of style and remained on the periphery of the fashion scene, they did not gain wide popularity again until the early 1990s, when New York designer Daryl Kerrigan reintroduced them. In 2000, rock and pop stars such as Britney Spears and Lenny Kravitz popularized revealing fashions such as extremely low-rise jeans, and the fashion reignited once again for both men and women. Although fashion writers have been predicting the end of the low-rise jean since 2005, the belly-exposing pants continue to be worn by the young and the fashionable.

Whereas early hip-hugger jeans rested on the hips, at or just below the navel, modern low-rise jeans, which have a rise from crotch to waistline of 5 to 8 inches, may fall several inches below the waist. Extremely low-cut jeans were called "ultra low rise" or "dangerously low rise." As the style took off in the early 2000s, fashion brands such as True Religion, 7 for All Mankind, Miss Sixty, and Earl Jeans marketed low-rise, boot-cut jeans that ranged in price from $100 to $200 a pair.

Although low-rise jeans were extremely popular with young people, the daring style was not for everyone. Modified low-rise jeans with an 8- to 10-inch rise were created for the older market, and SLL Inc. designed a popular Tummy Tuck Jean that incorporated a girdle into a low-rise silhouette to enable more full-figured women to wear them.

Low-rise jeans were necessarily revealing, and the fashion inspired a number of slang terms. *Muffin top* refers to flesh that hangs over low-slung waistbands; *butt cleavage* describes too much exposure in the back; and a *whale tail* is the exposed back of a woman's thong that rises over the top of the jeans.

School administrators, parents, and others in authority were often unhappy with increasingly revealing low-rise jeans, especially with the fashion of allowing underwear to peek out over the top of low waistbands. Many made rules to limit the fashion, and in 2004 Louisiana state representative Derrick Shepherd introduced a bill to outlaw the wearing of pants below the waist and the exposure of underwear, but the law did not pass.

Tina Gianoulis

SEE ALSO: *Jeans; Pants for Women; Retro Fashion; Spears, Britney.*

BIBLIOGRAPHY

Bermudez, Andrea. "How Low Can You Go?" *Daily News Record*, May 6, 2002, 17.

Brown, Rachel. "Girdle-Style Jeans Become a Hit as Women Want Fashion and Fit." *Los Angeles Business Journal*, August 1, 2005, 1.

Lee, Georgia. "The Great Waist Debate." *WWD*, October 14, 2004, 14.

Malone, Scott. "Legislating the Low-Rise." *WWD*, April 29, 2004, 8.

Tyre, Peg. "Jeans Rising: Hark! The End of the Ultra-Low-Rise Era Nears." *Newsweek*, March 27, 2006, 52.

Loy, Myrna *(1905–1993)*

Actress Myrna Loy is best remembered for her definitive screen depiction of the "Perfect Wife," opposite most of the major leading men of the 1930s and 1940s. Initially a bit player of exotic femme fatales, Loy found a more prominent niche as Nora Charles, the witty, elegant spouse of Nick Charles, played by William Powell, in the 1934 film *The Thin Man*. The movie was so successful that Loy and Powell went on to make five more from 1936 to 1947. Shaping Loy's subsequent parts and the public perception of her, the role of Nora was rather restricted (her sophistication primarily an adjunct to her husband's good taste), but it was one Loy played with understated aplomb and her success reflects its attractiveness more broadly, an indication of women's limited choices during the 1930s and 1940s.

Kyle Smith

SEE ALSO: *Powell, William.*

BIBLIOGRAPHY

Quirk, Lawrence. *The Films of Myrna Loy*. Secaucus, NJ: Citadel Press, 1980.

Kotsilibas-Davis, James, and Myrna Loy. *Myrna Loy: Being and Becoming*. New York: Knopf, 1987.

Leider, Emily Wortis. *Myrna Loy: The Only Good Girl in Hollywood*. Berkeley: University of California Press, 2011.

LSD

LSD is an acronym for lysergic acid diethylamide, also commonly known as acid. It is a powerful psychedelic drug that induces a temporary psychotic state that may include hallucinations and "deep insight" into the nature of things, say its adherents who made it into one of the counterculture's drugs of choice, especially during the 1960s. Developed by the Central Intelligence Agency (CIA) a decade earlier as a counterespionage mind-controlling agent, LSD was initially intended for psychological torture during the Cold War. Psychiatrists later studied the drug as a means of observing their patients' uninhibited anxieties, and it was also used, with some success, to treat schizophrenia and autism in children, as well as chronic alcoholism and heroin addiction. In the 1950s hundreds of subjects, including Hollywood and media celebrities and prominent artists, participated in experimental trips under the direction of Dr. Oscar Janiger, a Los Angeles–area psychiatrist, and other local therapists.

Not until LSD was widely ingested recreationally, though, at the urging of Dr. Timothy Leary and others, did it attain near-sacramental status among the avatars of mind-expansion after about 1965. Dropping acid evolved into a tribal act of civil disobedience, and some of the best minds of the twentieth century dabbled with the drug while seeking spiritual enlightenment. Many who advocate the unrestricted use of LSD charge that Sandoz Laboratories cut off access to the drug for research purposes under pressure from prohibitionists who feared its impact on cultural transformation when it became a drug of choice in the youth community in the late 1960s. Some advocates believe reports of bad trips (psychotic episodes, going blind from staring at the sun, suicides by leaping from tall buildings) are exaggerated urban myths; they claim moderate doses of the drug do not produce such extreme effects and that the draconian prohibition of the drug prevented researchers from devising safer regimens for ingesting it. In the 1980s and 1990s, disco doses of contraband LSD were often distributed via blotter paper, sheets of cartoonlike decals that were chewed and ingested.

Dr. Albert Hoffman first synthesized LSD in 1938 at Sandoz Laboratories in Switzerland while researching ergot, the hallucinogenic rye fungus that is the natural source of lysergic acid. There he stumbled onto a powerful serotonin inhibitor he called LSD-25 (the twenty-fifth in a series of ergot derivatives), which produced intensely vivid hallucinations and altered states of perception. In 1943 he unwittingly absorbed the drug through his fingers, inducing a mild hallucinogenic state that he tried to duplicate several days later by deliberately dosing himself with 250 micrograms. Hoffman published his findings, but Sandoz soon lost interest in his experiments.

GOVERNMENT TESTING

In 1942, however, the OSS (Office of Strategic Services, predecessor of the CIA) assembled a group of military scientists to examine the possibilities of a truth drug for deployment on political prisoners, and they tried a host of increasingly powerful pharmaceuticals throughout the 1940s, often with dubious results. After World War II the CIA consulted academics and psychiatrists as well as police crime labs to help expand its chemical-knowledge base. By the 1950s the CIA had developed an anything goes attitude toward this objective, which eventually led to exploration of the shelved projects at Sandoz.

The CIA first used LSD on human subjects in 1951 and intensified its research, spurred by the growing fear of communist espionage. Researchers found that the effects of LSD could vary wildly according to personal and social expectations (the set) and the physical surroundings (the setting) during the hallucinogenic trip, so agents were directed to dose themselves and each other to become familiar with the drug's potential. In 1953 the CIA launched Operation MK-ULTRA, which authorized surprise tests on civilians and by 1955 had opened a safe house in the Haight-Ashbury district of San Francisco that lured unwitting subjects for a taste of the new drug in real-life situations. Acid's unpredictable nature eventually led to more specialized hallucinogens, and the CIA discontinued the safe-house project in the mid-1960s. However, by then LSD was already turning heads in the academic community.

CELEBRITIES

From the mid-1950s Dr. Janiger carried out his experiments without accepting any funding from the CIA or the military. Instead, he charged subjects $20 per visit and used drugs supplied by Sandoz. Among the 900-odd visitors to his LSD salon were Beat poet Allen Ginsberg; writer Anaïs Nin; Zen philosopher Alan Watts; novelist Christopher Isherwood; actors James Coburn, Dennis Hopper, and Jack Nicholson; and a group of Unitarian ministers who were disappointed that they had not experienced hoped-for spiritual transcendence. Besides Dr. Janiger, other Southern California psychiatrists who dispensed experimental doses to their clients included Dr. Mortimer Hartman, who gave the drug to actor Cary Grant as a treatment for alcoholism, and Dr. Sidney Cohen, who supplied LSD to Henry Luce (of *Time* magazine) and Clare Boothe Luce, his wife and a well-known playwright.

Luce perhaps achieved a better record of transcendence than did the Unitarian ministers when he reported an encounter with God on a golf course; his wife thought that LSD should be given only to the elite, saying, "We wouldn't want everyone doing too much of a good thing." In a 1998 interview, Dr. Janiger offered the drug-induced Eleusinian Mysteries in ancient Greece as a possible model for the creative use of LSD in contemporary culture: "The discussions I had with [Aldous] Huxley and [Alan] Watts and the others in those early years [really] centered on the way our culture might institutionalize LSD . . . and it would be very much like the Greek model."

Psychotropic treatment had caught the eye of Huxley, whose book *The Doors of Perception* exposed the educated public to the possibilities of an intellectual, psychedelic experience. By 1957 experiments with LSD and the creative mind were being conducted by a clinical psychologist at Harvard named Leary, who experienced a shamanic state and beatific visions while on acid. He and his colleagues claimed mass tripping (getting high on a psychedelic drug) could foster a new age of philosophical peace and freedom, and Leary spoke widely about the drug's positive applications, though other researchers dubbed these theories "instant enlightenment."

GOING UNDERGROUND

When the CIA abandoned serious LSD research, the scientific community lost its government supply of the drug, and Leary and others continued their research underground, supplying themselves with acid from a growing black market. There were many self-styled experts on LSD in the mid-1960s, many of whom had first been dosed in military-sponsored tests at Stanford, Harvard, and other universities, and most subscribed to the ideal of a unifying group trip. These communal experiments were tried on the east and west coasts of the United States, and it was author Ken Kesey who mobilized this new wave of positive if absurdist religiosity based largely on the acid trip.

In 1959 Kesey, a recent Woodrow Wilson fellow at Stanford University, had been a $75-a-day guinea pig in LSD experiments at the Veterans' Administration Hospital in Menlo Park, California, where he remained employed as a mental-ward attendant after his part in the experiments were completed. His experiences there formed the basis for his celebrated 1962 novel *One Flew over the Cuckoo's Nest.* Two years after its publication, Kesey and a group of friends who dubbed themselves the Merry Pranksters set off on a cross-country trip (destination: the New York World's Fair) in a garishly painted old school bus, along the way extolling the virtues of psychedelia and hallucinogens as a bridge to harmony and understanding. The trip was itself memorialized in Tom Wolfe's 1968 book, *The Electric Kool-Aid Acid Test.* Kesey tried to unite the mystique of a drug lifestyle with politically conscious activism, and subsequent acid tests encouraged participants to confront the cosmic umbilical cord of the ego while high on LSD.

FOLK REMEDY

Simultaneously, writers and musicians were turning on and psychedelicizing their work—most notably Ginsberg, Hunter S. Thompson, Bob Dylan, the Beatles, and the Grateful Dead—further enhancing LSD's role as a folk remedy of sorts for the hippie nation and a recreational enabler for both deep introspection and outrageous social protest. It had long been supposed by many Beatles fans that the band's 1967 song "Lucy in the Sky with Diamonds" (an acronym for LSD) was inspired by an acid trip, though Paul McCartney told Joan Goodman in a 1984 *Playboy* interview that the song was merely about "a drawing that John's son [Julian] brought home from school" and about one of his classmates named Lucy. Also in that year, Nicholson, one of Dr. Janiger's subjects, included his experiences in his script for a 1967 low-budget film *The Trip*, that starred another subject, Hopper, and Peter Fonda.

The Haight-Ashbury district of San Francisco—site of the government's earlier safe-house projects—became the hub of a psychedelic revolution. There, black market acid was first sold on a mass scale, with acid manufacturers convinced they were performing an important public service. But just as the community began to throb with acid tests, free rock concerts, street theater, and full-blown psychedelia, LSD was made illegal in 1966, and Sandoz ceased its medical research distribution because of the bad press acid was receiving. Many blamed Leary's early outspokenness for the crackdown, but changes in attitude toward LSD research had already demonized the drug.

Although doctors began speaking out publicly against the use of LSD, this dialogue only served to inform more potential users (mostly young, well-educated, white middle-class users) about the drug. By the 1967 Summer of Love, it seemed as if everyone in the United States was turning on or trekking west to San Francisco, where the action was, though the progenitors of acid culture were already burning out. The Haight, once an idyllic nexus, became a psychedelic tourist trap, and soon a pharmacopoeia of designer drugs (of which LSD was one of the weakest) emerged on the scene to bolster the waning euphoria.

CONTEMPORARY CULTURE

In the wake of many highly publicized, violent confrontations with authority, acid culture subsided by the early 1970s into a cabal of psychedelic drug devotees, convinced that they were being denied access to transcendence by fearful guardians of straight society. Much of LSD's early cultural history has been told in Jay Stevens's 1987 book, *Storming Heaven: LSD and the American Dream.* By the 1990s, however, a nonprofit advocacy group called the Multidisciplinary Association for Psychedelic Studies (MAPS) was lobbying the Food and Drug Administration to approve medical studies of LSD as well as marijuana and other drugs, such as the popular Ecstasy. The group, which included a number of prominent research scientists, was founded by Rick Doblin in the hopes of continuing Dr. Janiger's important but aborted research. As Dr. Janiger told an interviewer in 1998:

> LSD didn't pan out as an acceptable therapeutic drug for one reason: Researchers didn't realize the explosive nature of the drug. . . . You can't manipulate it as skillfully as you would like. It's like atomic energy—it's relatively easy to make a bomb, but much harder to safely drive an engine and make light. And with LSD, we didn't have the chance to experiment and fully establish how to make it do positive, useful things.

At the end of the twentieth century, hits of LSD were most frequently available on colorful blotter-paper decals, permitting easy ingestion of disco doses far below those responsible for the well-publicized bad trips of earlier times. Artists such as Mark McCloud compiled a huge archive of these blotter-paper designs, which he considers an example of late-twentieth-century folk art. LSD was no longer tantamount to social defiance but became a metaphor for the search for enlightenment via ritualistic drug use in an urban, industrialized society, as well as for the multifarious waves of cultural experimentation it inspired in the United States of the 1960s. As a gateway to global transcendence at the millennium, LSD still inspired many testimonials on websites, and researchers began to take a new and more favorable look at the once-demonized drug.

In 2011 Swiss researchers announced that they had concluded a study in which carefully controlled doses of LSD were used to treat patients who exhibited anxiety about having life-threatening illnesses. That same year researchers in Berlin reported using LSD to treat cluster headaches, a condition that causes almost unbearable pain. Both studies used very small samples and so were not conclusive. The research, however, represented perhaps the beginning of a trend—at least in Europe—to investigate medical uses of LSD.

Tony Brewer

SEE ALSO: *The Beat Generation; The Beatles; Cold War; Dylan, Bob; Ginsberg, Allen; Grant, Cary; The Grateful Dead; Haight-Ashbury; Hippies; Hollywood; Hopper, Dennis; Kesey, Ken; Leary, Timothy; Luce, Henry; Marijuana; McCartney, Paul; Nicholson, Jack;* One Flew over the Cuckoo's Nest*;* Playboy*; Psychedelia; Rock and Roll; Thompson, Hunter S.;* Time*; Wolfe, Tom; World War II.*

BIBLIOGRAPHY

Grof, Stanislav. *LSD: Doorway to the Numinous: The Groundbreaking Psychedelic Research into Realms of the Human Unconscious.* Rochester, VT: Park Street Press, 2009.

Hofmann, Albert. *LSD My Problem Child: Reflections on Sacred

Drugs, Mysticism, and Science. Santa Cruz, CA: MAPS, 2009.

Jaffe, Jerome H., ed. *Encyclopedia of Drugs and Alcohol*. New York: Macmillan, 1995.

Leary, Timothy; Ralph Metzner; and Richard Alpert. *The Psychedelic Experience: A Manual Based on the Tibetan Book of the Dead*. New York: University Books, 1964.

Lee, Martin A., and Bruce Shlain. *Acid Dreams: The CIA, LSD, and the Sixties Rebellion*. New York: Grove Press, 1985.

Stevens, Jay. *Storming Heaven: LSD and the American Dream*. New York: Grove Press, 1987.

Whalen, John. "The Hollywood Experiment." *L.A. Weekly*, July 3, 1998.

Lubitsch, Ernst *(1892–1947)*

Film director, actor, and producer Ernst Lubitsch rose to fame during the 1910s in Germany and immigrated to Hollywood in 1930. His sophisticated comedies were highly successful in the United States, and he was made director of production at Paramount Pictures in 1935. The "Lubitsch Touch" was a tongue-in-cheek social commentary style full of sexual innuendo, which exposed and ridiculed social conventions. It was evident in films such as *Lady Windermere's Fan* (1925) and the Greta Garbo vehicle *Ninotchka* (1939).

Petra Kuppers

SEE ALSO: *Garbo, Greta.*

BIBLIOGRAPHY

Eyman, Scott. *Laughter in Paradise*. New York: Simon and Schuster, 1993.

Hake, Sabine. *Passions and Deceptions: The Early Films of Ernst Lubitsch*. Princeton, NJ: Princeton University Press, 1992.

Sheunemann, Dietrich. *Expressionist Film: New Perspectives*. Rochester, NY: Camden House, 2003.

Lucas, George *(1944–)*

American filmmaker, screenwriter, and entrepreneur George Lucas has pioneered innovative and technologically advanced filmmaking techniques that have changed the industry. He is the creative mind behind such popular movies as *American Graffiti* (1973), the *Star Wars* franchise (1977, 1980, 1983, 1999, 2002, and 2005), and the *Indiana Jones* series (1981, 1984, 1989, and 2008). Lucas began his film career in the late 1960s while attending the University of Southern California. One of his class projects later became the cult classic *THX-1138* (1971).

In the late 1970s Lucas began work on *Star Wars*. Many industry experts believed Fox Studios had made a huge error in financing the space opera; they predicted that the $10 million budget would bring the financially stricken studio to its knees. But *Star Wars* became one of the most successful movie franchises in film history and helped make Lucas among the most powerful people in Hollywood.

Lucas's use of technology, especially the innovation of wedding cameras to computers, created a cinematic revolution. His technological innovations created a level of cinematic wizardry that made the unbelievable ultra-believable. Following Lucas's lead, the American film industry learned to make special effects more potent while the wizardry behind them became less visible. Lucas introduced another powerful innovation in American filmmaking: merchandising. He traded half his directing fee for the original *Star Wars* movie for merchandising rights, and the subsequent boom in *Star Wars* goods—toys, video games, collectibles—flooded America and made Lucas a very wealthy man. In his many business ventures—Lucasfilm, LucasArts, Industrial Light & Magic—Lucas extended his creative and technical genius to a number of multimedia productions, ranging from television commercials to some of the most popular computer-based video games produced.

Lucas struck another profitable chord with the American movie-watching public in 1999. He rekindled the *Star Wars* franchise with a set of three new films, prequels to the massively successful 1970s trilogy. *Star Wars Episode 1: The Phantom Menace* (1999) and the following two episodes relate the story of how some of the most beloved *Star Wars* characters came to be. Although many critics and fans felt the prequel trilogy was inferior to the older films, all three performed well at the box office; *The Phantom Menace* was ranked in the top ten highest-grossing films of all time as of 2012. Merchandising and promotional tie-ins were again a large part of the film's publicity and helped boost overall revenue.

Lucas's work in the twenty-first century has largely been limited to revisiting and expanding on his first successes. In addition to the new *Star Wars* installments, Lucas also re-upped the *Indiana Jones* franchise with *Indiana Jones and the Kingdom of the Crystal Skull* (2008). Again the new version was perceived to be inferior to its predecessors, but Jones's new adventure was another box-office hit, perhaps due in part to the familiarity of the title character. In recognition of his accomplishments, the American Film Institute awarded Lucas a Lifetime Achievement Award in 2005.

Since 2008 Lucas has produced an animated television series and video games based on his legendary characters. However, he announced his retirement from the film industry—or rather from large-scale blockbuster films—in 2012. Instead, he wishes to focus on small projects. Lucas's influence on American films has been indelible. Not only a pioneer in filmmaking technology, he has also been the creator of some of film's most memorable characters.

Craig T. Cobane

SEE ALSO: American Graffiti*; Blockbusters; Hollywood;* Raiders of the Lost Ark*;* Star Wars*;* Star Wars *Episodes I–III: The Prequel Trilogy; Toys; Video Games.*

BIBLIOGRAPHY

Champlin, Charles. *George Lucas: The Creative Impulse*, rev. ed. New York: Harry N. Abrams, 1997.

Hearn, Marcus. *The Cinema of George Lucas*. New York: Harry N. Abrams, 2005.

Jenkins, Garry. *Empire Building: The Remarkable Real-Life Story of "Star Wars."* Secaucus, NJ: Carol Publishing Group, 1999.

Lucas, George, and Sally Kline, ed. *George Lucas: Interviews*. Jackson: University Press of Mississippi, 1999.

Pollock, Dale. *Skywalking: The Life and Films of George Lucas*. New York: Da Capo Press, 1999.

Rubin, Michael. *Droidmaker: George Lucas and the Digital Revolution.* Gainesville, FL: Triad Publishing, 2005.

Luce, Henry *(1898–1967)*

Editors rarely attract more attention than their publications, but Henry Luce's success in magazine publishing made him a legend in his own lifetime and an enduring influence after his death. Luce's constant articulation of and fight for the United States and its values throughout his life (and particularly during the politically and culturally charged years of the Cold War) ensured that his impact went far beyond mere journalism and established him within the canon of influential American public figures.

Henry Robinson Luce was born on April 3, 1898, to American Presbyterian missionary parents, in Tengchow (now Penglai), China. In 1913 the family returned to the United States, and Luce was quick to take on the values of American society and to become part of its elite. He attended the prestigious Hotchkiss School on a scholarship before proceeding to Yale University, where he was selected to join the Phi Beta Kappa fraternity and Skull and Bones, a famous Yale secret society. Luce had now entered mainstream, if privileged, America, and the aristocratic-elitist philosophy of Yale was one to which he would subscribe all his life. He cemented his relationship with the world of establishment privilege by his first marriage, on December 22, 1923, to the wealthy and well-connected Lila Ross Hotz and furthered his influence and connections with his second marriage, on November 23, 1935, to the rising social and literary star, Clare Boothe Brokaw (famous, as Clare Boothe, for her play, *The Women*).

Henry Luce. *Time Inc. founder Henry Luce was once said to have reached one quarter of the U.S. population with his magazines.* ALFRED EISENSTAEDT/CONTRIBUTOR/TIME LIFE PICTURES/GETTY IMAGES.

Luce's publishing career began shortly after graduation from Yale when he and fellow Yale alum Briton Hadden, whom he had first met at Hotchkiss, discussed plans to start a magazine together. Although Luce saw the world of journalism merely as a stepping-stone into politics, a world which really held his fascination, he agreed to the venture. Hadden proposed an idea for a magazine that, based upon selected newspaper stories in a given week, would condense the news into an easily digestible magazine format. The pair considered the idea further, moved to New York, incorporated their company as Time Inc., and began to hire staff. After a year spent developing the original idea, the first issue of *Time* magazine hit the newsstands on March 3, 1923. The first issue did not sell particularly well, but over the next few years a dedicated staff worked hard to ensure the long-term success of the publication, and by 1926 the magazine had built a solid foundation from which to grow. By 1935 *Time* made a profit of $2,249,823.

Luce started the second Time Inc. publication, *Fortune* magazine, in February 1930. It grew out of the business sections of *Time*, which Luce thought could be expanded into a publication in its own right to create a new kind of business journalism, radically different from existing trade journals. *Fortune* grew steadily, and by 1935, it too was making a profit. A year later, in November 1936, Luce launched *Life* magazine. Breaking new frontiers in photojournalism to tremendous, and ultimately world famous and historically valuable, effect, the magazine aimed to "see life; to see the world; to witness great events . . . to see and take pleasure in seeing, to see and be amazed: to see and be instructed." Like the other Luce publications, *Life* soon became a success. Finally, in 1954, Luce added *Sports Illustrated.* A sports magazine had been his personal project for some time, yet it was born against the advice of many. Luce, however, read the market just right, launching the magazine at the peak of the postwar leisure industry.

EDITOR IN CHIEF, PHILANTHROPIST, AND A REPUBLICAN

As editor in chief of all Time Inc. publications, Luce was technically responsible for all final editorial decisions, although he left the day-to-day decision making to trusted colleagues on each publication, appointing managing editors such as Edward Thompson at *Life*, Hedley Donovan at *Fortune*, and E. Roy Alexander at *Time.* Luce worked from an office on the *Life* editorial floor at the Time-Life building in New York City, from where he observed proceedings, occasionally talked directly with individual editors, and sat in on discussions about subjects for editorials. He had little to worry about in terms of magazine content because, even without his direct daily editorship of each and every publication, his managing editors knew well the kind of magazines he wanted and subscribed to roughly the same ideology. As Thompson explains in his autobiography, *A Love Affair with Life and Smithsonian*, "One could not ignore Luce's strong political opinions, but if I hadn't believed roughly in the kind of world Luce wanted, I couldn't have worked at Time Inc. very long." Even when he was away from New York, Luce would keep in touch by phone or cable, but even so, as Thompson observed, "We knew enough about what he didn't believe in to avoid direct contradiction of his views."

In 1936 Luce established the philanthropic Henry Luce Foundation. It awards grants largely for cultural and educational needs, although the money available was somewhat limited until it received a large bequest from Luce upon his death. In 1955 Yale established the Henry Luce Professorship of Jurisprudence, and the Luce Scholars Program has since promoted and enabled overseas educational exchange. Luce's interests also extended into the world of politics, particularly into the affairs of his spiritual home, China. He was an active member of the China lobby in the United States and campaigned consistently in support of Chiang Kai-shek, the president of Taiwan, and against recognition of Chairman Mao Tse-tung. Not only were these opinions expressed fiercely in his magazines, but they were also brought to bear upon the center of the political world through Luce's friendships and correspondence with political figures, particularly President Dwight D. Eisenhower. The cause of Republicanism always remained close to Luce's heart, and he was never ashamed to admit his political leanings. When asked if his news reporting was in any way biased, he was famously quoted as saying, "I am a Protestant, a Republican and a free enterpriser, which means I am biased in favor of God, Eisenhower and the stockholders of Time Inc." Luce's religious beliefs remained strong throughout his life, providing the moral impetus for much of his life's work, particularly his concern to educate as well as to entertain.

In 1964, three years before he died, Luce passed on his position as editor in chief to his trusted friend and colleague, Hedley Donovan. (Luce's partner and cofounder, Hadden, had died of an illness in 1929.) It was a timely decision, ensuring that the success of the corporation he had nurtured throughout his life would continue after his death, as indeed it did well into the twenty-first century. A memorial service for Luce was held on March 3, 1967 (the same date as the forty-fourth anniversary of the first issue of *Time*), in New York's Madison Avenue Presbyterian Church, where he had worshipped for forty-three years.

Emma Lambert

SEE ALSO: Fortune; Life; Sports Illustrated; Time.

BIBLIOGRAPHY

Baughman, James L. *Henry R. Luce and the Rise of the American News Media*. Boston: Twayne Publishers, 1987.

Brinkley, Alan. *The Publisher: Henry Luce and His American Century*. New York: Knopf, 2010.

Guzzardi, Walter, Jr. *The Henry Luce Foundation: A History, 1936–1986*. Chapel Hill: University of North Carolina Press, 1988.

Herzstein, Robert Edwin. *Henry R. Luce: A Political Portrait of the Man Who Created the American Century*. New York: Scribner's, 1994.

Kobler, John. *Luce: His Time, Life, and Fortune*. Garden City, NY: Doubleday, 1968.

Neils, Patricia. *China Images in the Life and Times of Henry Luce*. Savage, MD: Rowman and Littlefield, 1990.

Swanberg, W. A. *Luce and His Empire*. New York: Dell, 1972.

Thompson, Edward K. *A Love Affair with Life and Smithsonian*. Columbia: University of Missouri Press, 1995.

Luciano, Lucky *(1897–1962)*

Sicilian-born Charles "Lucky" Luciano is renowned for initiating a new era in organized crime in the United States by establishing a national syndicate that aligned the Italian mafia with Jewish and Irish crime organizations in the 1930s. After his family immigrated to the United States, Luciano began his criminal career by bullying schoolchildren into paying him not to beat them up. He reportedly met his lifelong affiliate Meyer Lansky when Lansky refused to pay him. He began dealing narcotics as a teenager, and as a member of the notorious Five Points gang, Luciano is reputed to have participated in numerous beatings and murders. In addition to gambling and drug peddling, he gained power and wealth during the Prohibition era as a successful bootlegger and used a combination of violence and extortion to gain control over prostitution in Manhattan.

In October 1929 Luciano was kidnapped and severely beaten and stabbed by four assailants who left him unconscious on a Staten Island, New York, beach. He was found by a police officer and taken to a hospital, where he was interviewed by detectives. At the time Luciano claimed he had no idea who could have attacked him, but in later years he blamed the incident on "the cops." Two years later, with sufficient loyalty and power behind him, Luciano ushered in a new epoch in organized crime by ordering the murders of two rival gang leaders, "Joe the Boss" Masseria and Salvatore Maranzano, whose families were then engaged in a fierce turf war. With these two old-line leaders out of the way, Luciano consolidated his power among the Italian mobsters and formed a national syndicate with such crime figures as Lansky, Louis "Lepke" Buchalter, Joe Adonis, Dutch Schultz, Albert Anastasia, and a few select others.

From 1932 to 1936 Luciano lived the high life, headquartered in a luxurious suite at the Waldorf-Astoria he occupied under the alias Charles Ross and where he entertained numerous women. However, after the mob assassination of the renegade Schultz, which had been ordered by the syndicate directors, Luciano became the target of an investigation by New York district attorney Thomas E. Dewey. Luciano was convicted on charges of extortion and direction of harlotry and was sentenced to thirty to fifty years in prison.

While serving his sentence, Luciano applied for parole and was twice rejected before winning his freedom in a wartime bargain with the U.S. government. A former luxury liner, the S.S. *Normandie*, exploded in the Hudson River as it was being refitted as a troopship in 1942. When dockworkers refused to cooperate in the investigation into the bombing, naval authorities asked Luciano to use his influence to prevent further incidents along the waterfront. In addition, through Luciano's intercession, the U.S. military gained the cooperation of the Sicilian mafia in the Allied invasion of Sicily in 1943.

In 1946 Luciano was freed from prison and deported to Italy. He immediately resumed his criminal activities in Rome and in February 1947 traveled to Havana, Cuba, to meet with other leaders of the syndicate. When the U.S. press reported his presence in Havana, Luciano was ordered out of Cuba and

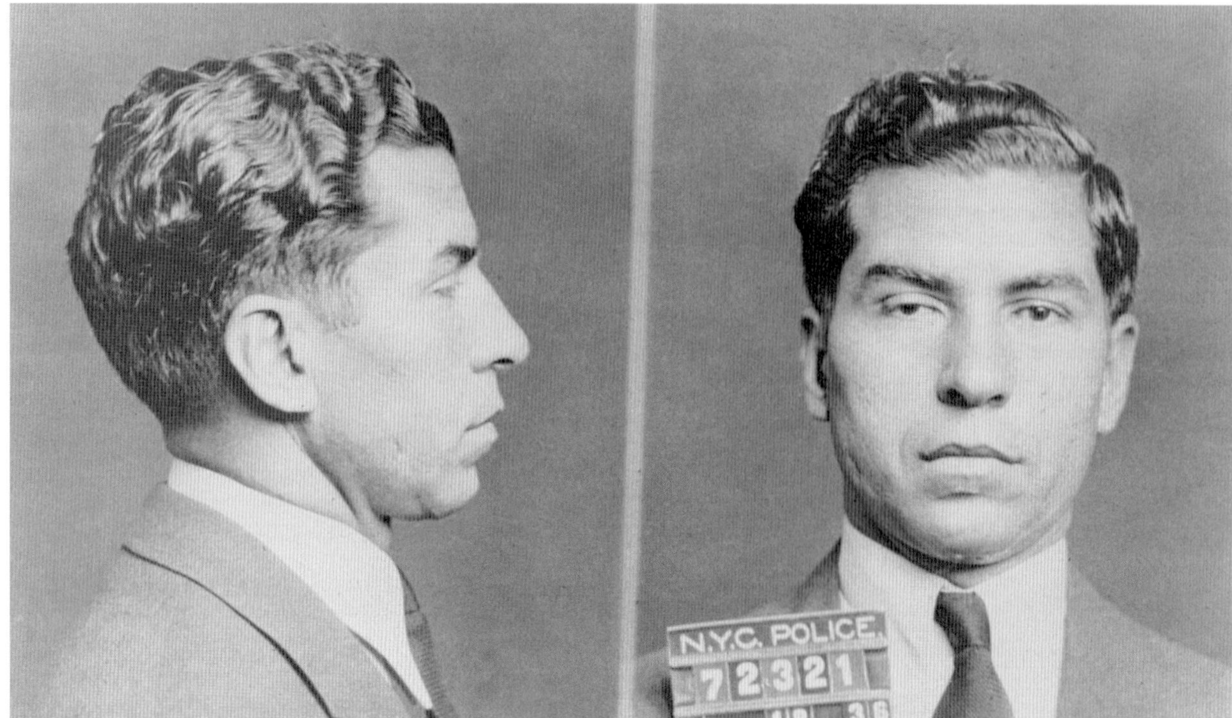

Lucky Luciano. *Crime boss Charles "Lucky" Luciano stands for a police mug shot after his arrest in 1936.* NEW YORK DAILY NEWS ARCHIVE/CONTRIBUTOR/NY DAILY NEWS/GETTY IMAGES.

returned to Italy. He lived thereafter in Naples, where he contemplated such projects as a book of memoirs and a motion picture depicting his career. He died of a heart attack in 1962 at the Naples airport while waiting for movie producer Martin Gosch.

Although not as widely portrayed in the media as the more famous gangster Al Capone, Luciano was depicted in multiple books, movies, and television series after his death. In 1975 Gosch and Richard Hammer adapted Luciano's autobiographical screenplay into the book *The Last Testament of Lucky Luciano.* Films such as *The Cotton Club* (1984), *Billy Bathgate* (1991), and *Bugsy* (1991) cashed in on Luciano's influence and presence during the 1930s and 1940s. Most notably, Christian Slater starred as Luciano in the much maligned 1991 film *Mobsters,* which dramatized Luciano's rise. In 2010 HBO launched the critically acclaimed TV series *Boardwalk Empire,* which portrays the early criminal careers of Luciano, played by Vincent Piazza, and other gangsters.

Laurie DiMauro

SEE ALSO: *Capone, Al; The Cotton Club; Lansky, Meyer; Mafia/Organized Crime; Prohibition; World War II.*

BIBLIOGRAPHY

Feder, Sid, and Joachim Joesten. *The Luciano Story.* New York: Da Capo Press, 1994.

Gosch, Martin, and Richard Hammer. *The Last Testament of Lucky Luciano.* New York: Little, Brown, 1975.

Higgins, Jack. *Luciano's Luck.* New York: Stein and Day, 1981.

Nash, Jay Robert. *Encyclopedia of World Crime, Vol. III.* Wilmette, IL: CrimeBooks, 1990.

Nash, Jay Robert. *World Encyclopedia of Organized Crime.* New York: Da Capo Press, 1993.

Newark, Tim. *Lucky Luciano: The Real and the Fake Gangster.* New York: Thomas Dunne Books, 2010.

Powell, Hickman. *Lucky Luciano: His Amazing Trial and Wild Witnesses.* Secaucus, NJ: Citadel, 1975. First published as *Ninety Times Guilty.* New York: Harcourt Brace, 1939.

Raab, Selwyn. *Five Families: The Rise, Decline, and Resurgence of America's Most Powerful Mafia Empires.* New York: Thomas Dunne Books, 2005.

Sifakis, Carl. *The Encyclopedia of American Crime.* New York: Smithmark, 1992.

Ludlum, Robert *(1927–2001)*

One of the most commercially successful authors of the twentieth century, Robert Ludlum is arguably the most widely read writer of the espionage thriller genre. He was the author of more than twenty best-selling standalone novels, under his own name and the pseudonym Jonathan Ryder, and many series titles, including the Bourne series, which began with *The Bourne Identity* in 1980. His books have sold more than 200 million copies worldwide, and many have been made into films, including the Bourne series.

Born May 25, 1927, in New York City, Ludlum lost his father when he was only seven. By the time he was sixteen, he had decided that he wanted to be an actor. In 1943 he was cast in the Broadway show *Junior Miss,* but two years later he enlisted in the marines. After his stint in the military, Ludlum went to Wesleyan University. By 1951 he had completed his bachelor's degree and married his girlfriend Mary. For much of the 1950s Ludlum worked as an actor, moving between summer stock theaters and Broadway, and by the mid-1950s he began to get regular work on television. He appeared in more than 200 of the plays presented on such shows as *Kraft Television Theatre* and *Studio One*.

By 1956 Ludlum had moved back to Broadway and become a producer, and he later founded the Playhouse-on-the-Mall in Paramus, New Jersey, which did well throughout the 1960s. Among his successes as a producer were *The Owl and the Pussycat* and a revival of *The Front Page*. While he worked on Broadway, Ludlum continued to find steady employment on television, exploiting his deep voice doing voice-overs for television commercials. It was during this time that he found his true calling as an author.

Ludlum started writing books in the late 1960s, and his first novel, *The Scarlatti Inheritance*, was released in 1971. He garnered critical praise for his complex characters and use of tension. He quickly followed his initial success with the publication of *The Osterman Weekend* in 1972 and *The Matlock Paper* and *Trevayne* in 1973. Readers throughout the world snatched up his books, and in the space of only three years, he was catapulted to the status of best-selling author, and he continued to churn out best sellers. Among the many TV and film adaptations of his novels, the Bourne series, starring Matt Damon in the role of Jason Bourne, has been the most successful. Based on the conceit that a man with no memory is trying to discover his true identity from within a conspiracy plot centering on a secret CIA operation, it threatened to develop into a long-running series along the lines of the Bond franchise.

Ludlum's novels are exemplary "airport" novels, generally having extremely complicated plots yet being easy enough to read in the course of a journey. Alongside Tom Clancy, Frederick Forsyth, and others, his conspiracy thrillers helped define a category of novel that is almost a genre in its own right. Most of Ludlum's books revolve around some form of global domination conspiracy. In some novels, such as *The Holcroft Covenant*, he uses the revival of the Nazi movement. In others it is a shadow society of powerful industrialists and politicians. In either case the protagonist is a lone individual who accidentally discovers the conspiracy and must expose it before global domination is achieved. Although the hero often succeeds, some of Ludlum's novels end with the conspiracy moving forward despite the protagonist's efforts.

A further feature of Ludlum's books is that they often include a great deal of factual detail and technical information. Like Forsyth, he was a dedicated researcher, understanding that his largely male audience demanded technical realism even if his plots offered wild fantasy.

In the 1990s, after a heart bypass operation, Ludlum began to work with other writers who fleshed out his plots and shared the credit. He died in 2001, after which his name was registered as a trademark. Apart from five novels posthumously credited to him, many others have been written by other writers under the "Robert Ludlum" brand.

Geoff Peterson

SEE ALSO: *Best Sellers; Blockbusters; Bourne Series; Broadway; Clancy, Tom; Damon, Matt; Forsyth, Frederick; James Bond Films;* Kraft Television Theatre*;* Studio One*; Television.*

BIBLIOGRAPHY

Macdonald, Gina. *Robert Ludlum: A Critical Companion.* Westport, CT: Greenwood Press, 1997.

Williams, John. "Robert Ludlum." *Guardian* (London), March 14, 2001.

Lugosi, Bela *(1882–1956)*

With his aristocratic accent, distinctive profile, slicked dark hair, spidery fingers, and mesmerizing eyes, not to mention his swirling black cape, Hungarian-born actor Bela Lugosi helped create cinema's definitive Dracula, the vampire as sexual and charming as he is villainous. During his career, which spanned more than fifty years, Lugosi became part of cinema folklore and is now recognized as one of Hollywood's greatest horror stars.

Born Béla Ferenc Dezsö Blaskó in Lugos (the town from which he derived his stage name) near Transylvania, Lugosi came to the United States in late 1920 and, over the next few years, appeared in small film and theater parts. His break came with the title role in the play *Dracula*, which ran for thirty-three weeks on Broadway in 1927 and successfully toured the West Coast in 1928 and 1929. This led to the 1931 Universal Studios film, whose romantic settings and sexual undercurrents revolutionized the horror-film genre and established Lugosi's place in Hollywood history.

Bela Lugosi. *Bela Lugosi stars as Count Mora in the 1935 film* Mark of the Vampire. CLARENCE SINCLAIR BULL/CONTRIBUTOR/ MOVIEPIX/GETTY IMAGES.

Lugosi, however, quickly became the victim of his own success. Despite the stardom that *Dracula* brought him, he resisted attempts by both Universal and the media to make him the heir to horror film icon Lon Chaney Sr. Refusing to be typecast, he aspired instead to the romantic leading roles he had performed on the Hungarian stage. Unfortunately, his poor judgment resulted in a series of bad career choices, long periods of unemployment, and perpetual financial problems. Perhaps his single worst mistake was rejecting a major role in *Frankenstein* (1931), Universal's next big film after *Dracula*. Originally slated to play the monster, Lugosi disliked both the heavy makeup and the character's lack of dialogue, and so the part went to Boris Karloff, who soon surpassed Lugosi in salary as well as fame, becoming his lifelong rival. Even years later, when Universal again tried to exploit the public's hunger for horror films by teaming Karloff and Lugosi in such films as *The Black Cat* (1934), *The Raven* (1935), and *The Body Snatcher* (1945), Lugosi received second billing and played a decidedly supporting role to Karloff.

Lugosi himself helped to diminish his star power by taking small, odd roles such as the Apache in *Gift of Gab* (1934) and lead roles in serial and low-budget movies such as *Ape Man* (1943) and *Voodoo Man* (1944). Ironically, some of his most interesting and memorable roles were the types of parts he initially sought to avoid: the mad scientist, Dr. Mirakle, in *Murders in the Rue Morgue* (1932); the zombie master, Murder Legendre, in *White Zombie* (1932); the vampire, both fake (Count Mora the actor in *Mark of the Vampire*, 1935) and real (Armand Tesla in *Return of the Vampire*, 1944); and the sinister servant, Ygor, the broken-necked companion of Frankenstein's monster, in *Son of Frankenstein* (1939), another Karloff-Lugosi collaboration (and, apart from Dracula, probably Lugosi's most memorable screen character).

Yet even within the genre he had helped to create, Lugosi's status eroded rapidly. He was not considered for the lead or offered even a minor role in the 1936 sequels to his classic *Dracula* and *White Zombie*. And in the 1940s, when Universal began producing new horror films such as *The Wolf Man*, Lugosi had to settle for bit parts, such as that of a gypsy, while the title roles went to Lon Chaney Jr. and other actors. Eventually, in films such as the Bowery Boys adventure *Spooks Run Wild* (1941) and *Bud Abbott and Lou Costello Meet Frankenstein* (1948), he took to parodying himself. As a means of financial survival, Lugosi pursued other avenues—stage, vaudeville, radio, and television—usually with limited success. The vagaries of his career contributed to the dissolution of four of his five marriages and to his drug addiction, for which he voluntarily sought help and reportedly beat before his death from a heart attack in 1956.

In his last years Lugosi came to the attention of the notoriously inept director Ed Wood Jr., who cast him in *Glen or Glenda?* (1953) and in the infamous *Plan 9 from Outer Space* (filmed 1956; released 1959), which was built around the few minutes of footage shot before Lugosi's death for a different Wood film. The recognition of Lugosi's talent by Wood and other fans, however, helped to introduce the legendary actor to a new audience of filmgoers and to generate interest in his early work as well. Unfortunately, Lugosi never witnessed the revived popularity of his films. He died impoverished and largely forgotten and was buried, wrapped in his Dracula cape, in Culver City, near Hollywood, California. As bizarre as his screen persona, Lugosi was an actor of limited range but a man of many appetites—for women, reading, Hungarian food, good cigars, stamp collecting, and politics.

Barbara Tepa Lupack

SEE ALSO: *Broadway; Dracula; Frankenstein; Hollywood; Horror Movies; Karloff, Boris; Vaudeville; Wood, Ed.*

BIBLIOGRAPHY

Cremer, Robert. *Lugosi: The Man behind the Cape*. Chicago: Regnery, 1976.

Mank, Gregory William. *Karloff and Lugosi: The Story of a Haunting Collaboration, with a Complete Filmography of Their Films Together*. Jefferson, NC: McFarland, 1990.

Rhodes, Gary Don. *Lugosi: His Life in Films, on Stage, and in the Hearts of Horror Lovers*. Jefferson, NC: McFarland, 1997.

Smith, Ronald L. *Horror Stars on Radio: The Broadcast Histories of 29 Chilling Hollywood Voices*. Jefferson, NC: McFarland, 2010.

Lunceford, Jimmie *(1902–1947)*

In 1940 the swing orchestra led by Jimmie Lunceford won first place in a much-publicized Battle of the Bands with twenty-seven other groups, including those led by Count Basie, Benny

Jimmie Lunceford. *Jimmie Lunceford leads his band in a 1940 performance.* GILLES PETARD/CONTRIBUTOR/REDFERNS/GETTY IMAGES.

Goodman, and Glenn Miller. Known for innovative arrangements, imaginative instrumentation, and full-bodied swinging sound, the Lunceford orchestra exerted a powerful influence over big-band music during the swing era of the late 1930s and early 1940s, as well as on post–World War II dance bands.

James Melvin Lunceford was born in Fulton, Mississippi, and moved to Memphis, Tennessee, where he studied music with Paul Whiteman's father, Wilberforce. In 1926 he earned a bachelor's degree from Fisk University in Nashville. During the 1920s he played in jazz bands led by Elmer Snowden and Wilbur Sweatman. Although he became proficient in all the reed instruments, he seldom played in bands, preferring to conduct. Before beginning his professional career as a bandleader in 1929, Lunceford organized and taught a student orchestra at Memphis Manassas High School, establishing an enduring musical legacy.

Lunceford's first success came in Buffalo, New York, in the early 1930s. In 1933 he took his band to New York City, appearing at the famous Cotton Club. The band made a recording for Victor, but the music selected—"White Heat" and "Jazznocracy"—was written in a racing tempo, unsuited for the band's relaxed, subtle style. From the beginning, Lunceford had molded a highly disciplined orchestra that practiced carefully rehearsed showmanship in their playing. He preferred precise ensemble playing in a medium two-beat swing tempo rather than the exciting solos and upbeat tempos of the Basie and Goodman bands, and he gradually won a wide audience for his unique style.

When Sy Oliver joined the orchestra in 1933, bringing his distinctive "growl" trumpet style as well as his prodigious talents as an arranger, Lunceford found the ideal partner in developing the oddly swinging style that became the band's trademark. Oliver recalls how the two met: "One day in Cincinnati, I heard the Lunceford band rehearsing. I was so impressed, because Jimmie was so careful about every single detail, then I asked him that I could try writing for the band." Oliver, who also arranged some of Tommy Dorsey's best-known numbers, excelled in devising unusual instrumentation. He conceived the arrangement of "Liza," in which Lunceford played the flute, his only recorded appearance playing an instrument with his band.

The greatest boost to the band's fame came in September 1934 when they began a series of great sides for Decca Records. Based on the brilliant scores created by Oliver, their most popular hits included "For Dancers Only," "Organ Grinder's Swing," "My Blue Heaven," "Four or Five Times," "Cheatin' on Me," and "Margie," among others. For some reason, Lunceford did not like one of Oliver's most popular arrangements, "Yes, Indeed!" which became a hit in a Dorsey recording. Although the band featured ensemble playing, it also had individual stars, including Trummie Young, a trombonist and vocalist, and Jimmie Crawford, a drummer with a simple, swinging style that made a perfect engine for the band's rhythms.

By 1942 the band's popularity began to decline as a number of longtime members left for various reasons, including the wartime draft. Lunceford continued his rigorous schedule. On July 12, 1947, he died of a heart attack while on tour in Seaside, Oregon. For several years, pianist Edwin Wilcox and saxophonist Joe Thomas led the band before it finally left the music scene. Jazz critic George Simon wrote: "But what great music it left! For many it remains, pressed in the grooves of all the fine Decca and Columbia records it made. And for those of us lucky enough to have caught the band in person it has also left memories of some of the most exciting nights we ever spent listening to any of the big bands!"

Lunceford's achievements have continued to be recognized. Lunceford and the band's swing arrangements were featured in the Smithsonian Collection of Recording's six-record anthology *Big Band Jazz: From the Beginnings to the Fifties* alongside those of jazz greats Basie, Duke Ellington, Goodman, and countless others. In 2009 he was awarded a note on the Beale Street Walk of Fame in Memphis, and in 2011 a Mississippi Blues Trail marker was dedicated in his name, just outside Fulton. In 2011 Mosaic Records released a limited edition seven-CD box set titled *The Complete Jimmie Lunceford Decca Sessions*. The accompanying booklet includes rare photos from the archives of Lunceford's tenor Joe Thomas, as well as an introduction by Lunceford biographer Eddy Determeyer. Lunceford's music and memorabilia collection is housed in the Special Collections archives at his alma mater, Fisk University.

Benjamin Griffith

SEE ALSO: *Basie, Count; Big Bands; The Cotton Club; Dorsey, Tommy; Ellington, Duke; Goodman, Benny; Jazz; Miller, Glenn; Swing Dancing; Whiteman, Paul; World War II.*

BIBLIOGRAPHY

Determeyer, Eddy. *Rhythm Is Our Business: Jimmie Lunceford and the Harlem Express* Ann Arbor: University of Michigan Press, 2006.

Esposito, Tony, ed. *Golden Era of the Big Bands*. Miami, FL: Warner, 1995.

Fernett, Gene, and Dan Morgenstern. *Swing Out: Great Negro Dance Bands*. New York: Da Capo Press, 1993.

Simon, George T. *The Big Bands*. New York: Macmillan, 1974.

Lupino, Ida *(1918–1995)*

An actress, a director, and a screenwriter of considerable reputation, Ida Lupino was born into a distinguished British theater family. After a less than satisfactory start in Hollywood as a blond ingenue type, Lupino broke through with a strong performance in the drama *The Light That Failed* (1939). Signed by Warner Brothers, she became famous for her roles as a hard-boiled, tough-luck dame, earning the moniker "the poor man's Bette Davis." Lupino worked with the best directors (Raoul Walsh, Fritz Lang) and top costars (Humphrey Bogart, Edward G. Robinson, Olivia de Havilland). A striking brunette with a memorable voice, which she likened to "a fat man who's been drinking a lot," Lupino handled glamorous roles and drab character parts with equal ease. Her pathbreaking career as a director and screenwriter of film and television received favorable critical assessment. Lupino's droll persona and her versatility made her a popular performer with a long career.

Mary Hess

SEE ALSO: *"B" Movies; Bogart, Humphrey; Broadway; Davis, Bette; Hollywood; Lang, Fritz; Robinson, Edward G.*

BIBLIOGRAPHY

Cuthbert, David. "Feminist Femme Fatale." *Times-Picayune*, March 26, 1998.

Donati, William. *Ida Lupino: A Biography*. Lexington: University Press of Kentucky, 1996.

Everitt, David. "A Woman Forgotten and Scorned No More." *New York Times*, November 23, 1997.

Kuhn, Annette, ed. *Queen of the 'B's: Ida Lupino behind the Camera*. Westport, CT: Greenwood Press, 1995.

LuPone, Patti *(1949–)*

Patti LuPone has carved a place in cultural iconography as one of the finest exponents of a great American art form: the Broadway musical. Her voice—at once full and strong, lyrical and smooth—has a distinctive, instantly recognizable steely quality that thrills audiences. Her remarkable vocal technique, combined with her considerable talent as a dramatic actress, enhances her interpretations of the heavyweight roles that come her way.

Trained at the Juilliard School, Lupone rose to Broadway stardom as Evita Peron in *Evita* (1979), winning Tony and Drama Desk awards. Other highlights of her career include creating the role of Fantine in *Les Misérables* (1985) for the Royal Shakespeare Company in London—the city to which she returned in 1993 to create Norma Desmond in Andrew Lloyd Webber's musical version of *Sunset Boulevard*. It was also in London where she played the dramatic role of Maria Callas in Terence McNally's play *Master Class* in 1997.

Her star quality at home in the United States was confirmed with the Lincoln Center revival of *Anything Goes* (1987), as well as the revivals of *Pal Joey* (1995) and *Sweeney Todd* (2005). Additionally, she won Tony and Drama Desk awards for her psychologically challenging portrayal of Mama Rose in *Gypsy* (2008). LuPone's versatility has led to work in film and on television, notably the role of Libby Thatcher in ABC's *Life Goes On* (1989–1993). She is also active as a recording and touring artist.

William A. Everett

SEE ALSO: *Broadway;* Les Misérables*; Lloyd Webber, Andrew; The Musical;* Sunset Boulevard.

BIBLIOGRAPHY

Gans, Andrew. "My Heart Belongs to Patti." *Playbill* 14, no. 1 (1995): 50–53.

LuPone, Patti, and Digby Diehl. *Patti LuPone: A Memoir*. New York: Crown, 2010.

Lynch, David *(1946–)*

Few directors have parlayed their unique style and vision into as much respect and success as David Lynch has earned since the late 1970s. Best known for his highly complex and ambiguous cinema, Lynch's most famous film is the now-classic *Blue Velvet* (1986). This coming-of-age story of the naive but endlessly curious Jeffrey Beaumont (Lynch mainstay Kyle Maclachlan) chronicles the protagonist's nightmarish descent into the underworld of the fictional town of Lumberton, which is run by villain Frank Booth (the menacing Dennis Hopper in a role that resuscitated his career). Although Lynch's previous film (*The Elephant Man*, 1980) had been nominated for a number of Academy Awards, including Best Picture, it was the quirky, independent *Blue Velvet* that paved the way for the iconoclastic director's influence on generations of filmmakers to come—including American directors Quentin Tarantino, Jim Jarmusch, and the Coen brothers and international auteurs such as Jean-Pierre Jeunet and Marc Caro. Lynch's style became his signature, to the point where reviewers, unable to comprehend the assortment of bizarre characters and dialogue of either *Wild at Heart* (1990) or *Lost Highway* (1997), simply claimed that Lynch was being Lynch.

David Lynch was born on January 20, 1946, in Missoula, Montana. The eldest of three children, he spent most of his youth daydreaming in the natural environs of Missoula. Unsatisfied with conventional school (he once referred to it in an interview as "a crime against young people . . . [which] destroyed the seeds of liberty"), Lynch attended high school at the Corcoran School of Art in Washington, D.C., with his best friend, Jack Fiske, where he pursued his original artistic impulse—painting. Both Fiske and Lynch rented a studio in Alexandria to paint, and after graduation both enrolled at the Boston Museum School. However, the two friends eventually dropped out over dissatisfaction with the unimpressive quality of the courses and students.

David Lynch. *Known for his dark, quirky work as a film director, David Lynch promotes his debut solo album* Crazy Clown Time *in 2011.* DAVID BUCHAN/CONTRIBUTOR/GETTY IMAGES ENTERTAINMENT/GETTY IMAGES.

EARLY CAREER

Lynch worked at an assortment of odd jobs (including one at a picture framing shop, where he was fired for not being able to get up in the morning) to pay for his eventual enrollment at the Pennsylvania Academy of Fine Arts in Philadelphia in 1965. It is there that he met his first wife, Peggy, and formulated an aesthetic that would come to influence his work—"film painting": I imagined a world in which painting would be in perpetual motion . . . [and] began to make animated films which looked like moving paintings." During his second year of study at Philadelphia, Lynch produced his first film, called *Six Figures Getting Sick* (1966); it was subsequently shown at a school exhibition and awarded a prize.

In April 1968 Peggy gave birth to their first child, Jennifer. Shortly after *Six Figures Getting Sick*, Lynch completed *The Alphabet* (1968), which generated enough attention to land Lynch an American Film Institute grant for his next film, *The Grandmother* (1970). According to French critic Michel Chion, the director of the American Film Institute "remarked that it was common to class films into categories—fiction, animations and so on—but that *The Grandmother* was in a category all by itself." The director then suggested that Lynch apply for a grant to the Institute of Advanced Film Studies, the AFI's film school in Beverly Hills, California. Consequently, Lynch moved his family to California in 1970 and threw himself strictly into cinema. He and his wife divorced in 1974, and Lynch went on to wed Mary Fisk in 1977, with whom he had a son, Austin, in 1982.

FEATURE FILMS

Lynch's first feature film was the notorious and amazing *Eraserhead* (1977). A surreal study in chiaroscuro and psychology, *Eraserhead* still defies definition and synopsis: Henry, who is "on vacation" in an industrial wasteland, discovers that he has fathered a monstrous offspring. After an affair with his neighbor, Henry is subjected to the snickers of the monster/baby and subsequently assaults it in an unreal and fantastic finale. The film opened to both violent disapproval and ecstatic praise—the latter from distributor Ben Barenholtz, who is credited with creating the midnight cult film circuit.

Gaining a faithful fan base and prizes at various festivals, *Eraserhead* eventually attracted attention from Hollywood, and Lynch was offered the chance to direct *The Elephant Man* by none other than Mel Brooks, who once remarked that Lynch was like "Jimmy Stewart from Mars." As a mainstream film *The Elephant Man* attracted the scorn of Lynch's highbrow critics but was nonetheless a success, earning Oscar nominations and instant Hollywood credibility. Lynch was offered various projects (including George Lucas's *Return of the Jedi*) but settled on the cinematic adaptation of Frank Herbert's classic sci-fi novel, *Dune* (1984). A failure at the box office—and with both critics and die-hard Herbert fans—*Dune* nevertheless showcased some of Lynch's trademark cinema.

ADDING TELEVISION TO THE MIX

After the bombastic budget of *Dune*, Lynch scaled down with *Blue Velvet* and then scaled down even further, venturing into television with the revolutionary cultural phenomenon *Twin Peaks*. Television had never seen anything like *Twin Peaks*, with its unconventional characters; innovative score; and mystical FBI protagonist, Dale Cooper (Kyle Maclachlan, again). Soon the United States was buzzing with anticipation over the next episode; in its first season the series garnered fourteen Emmy nominations. During this period Lynch was everywhere: he made the hugely successful film *Wild at Heart*, which won the Golden Palm at the Cannes Film Festival; he started a television sitcom called *On the Air*; he released the music for *Twin Peaks*, which he cowrote with Angelo Badalamenti (another longtime collaborator); and he scripted a comic strip for the *L.A. Weekly* called *The Angriest Dog in the World*. Lynch even found the time to father a son, Riley, with Mary Sweeney, who served as film editor on *Twin Peaks* and several subsequent projects.

The television public eventually tired of *Twin Peaks*, and it was canceled after its second season. Lynch's cinematic prequel to the series, *Twin Peaks: Fire Walk with Me* (1992), a return to the darker side of the idyllic northwestern town everyone had come to forget during the series' progression to more lighthearted episodes, angered most critics and fans. Lynch returned to the screen in 1997 with *Lost Highway*, another daring cinematic exercise in which a young musician, framed and condemned for the murder of his wife, transforms into a completely different person and is set free, only to discover eerie parallels between his old and new lives. Lynch followed *Lost Highway* with the surprisingly tame and straightforward drama *The Straight Story* (1999), a true story that follows Alvin Straight's 300-mile journey from Iowa to Wisconsin on a riding lawnmower.

Also in 1999 Lynch began work on another television pilot, this time about a woman struggling to recover her identity after a car crash that leaves her to wander through Hollywood in a state of amnesia. Though the pilot was ultimately rejected, Lynch gathered enough funding to release it as a feature film titled *Mulholland Drive* (2001). Despite his return to abstract storytelling and dense symbolism, the film received rave reviews and was hailed as a masterpiece on par with *Blue Velvet*, earning Lynch the Best Director Award at Cannes and an Oscar nomination, among numerous other accolades.

Throughout the early 2000s, Lynch released a series of short and Web-based works, including the Internet series *Rabbits* (2002) and *Dumbland* (2002) and the short horror film *Darkened Room* (2002). He collected many of his early short works in *The Short Films of David Lynch* (2002) before turning his attention to his next full-length film, *Inland Empire* (2006). The well-received film drew on the now-familiar themes of confused identity and the sinister Hollywood underground. Lynch then completed a number of short films, including *Boat* (2007), *More Things That Happened* (2007), *Lady Blue Shanghai* (2010), and *The 3 Rs* (2011).

MUSIC AND MEDITATION

Since the first decade of the 2000s Lynch has increasingly focused on his various interests outside of film. He has contributed music and vocals to a number of collaborative albums, including *BlueBob* (2000), *Polish Night Music* (2008), and the Danger Mouse–produced *Dark Night of the Soul* (2010), to which he also added several of his surreal photographs. His first proper solo album, *Crazy Clown Time*, was released in 2011 to positive reviews. A longtime advocate of transcendental meditation, Lynch created the David Lynch Foundation for Consciousness-Based Education and Peace in 2005, delivering speeches and raising funds to encourage the use of mediation in conflict resolution and creative endeavors. His efforts in this area were captured in the 2010 documentary *David Wants to Fly* and in his book *Catching the Big Fish* (2006). A number of

Lynch's paintings and photographs were displayed in exhibitions held in Paris in 2007 and in New York in 2012. He married long-term girlfriend Mary Sweeney in 2006, though the couple divorced in early 2007. In 2009 he married Emily Stofle, an actress who starred in several of his films.

Scott Thill

SEE ALSO: *Academy Awards;* Blue Velvet*; Brooks, Mel; Celebrity; Coen, Joel and Ethan; Comics; Cult Films; Divorce; Emmy Awards; FBI (Federal Bureau of Investigation); Herbert, Frank; Hollywood; Hopper, Dennis; Horror Movies; The Internet; Lucas, George; Movie Stars; Science Fiction Publishing;* Star Wars*; Stewart, Jimmy; Tarantino, Quentin; Television;* Twin Peaks.

BIBLIOGRAPHY

Barney, Richard A. *David Lynch: Interviews.* Jackson: University Press of Mississippi, 2009.

Chion, Michel, and Robert Julian. *David Lynch.* London: British Film Institute Publishing, 1995.

Kaleta, Kenneth. *David Lynch.* New York: Twayne Publishers, 1993.

Lynch, David. *Catching the Big Fish: Meditation, Consciousness, and Creativity.* New York: Jeremy P. Tarcher/Penguin, 2007.

Mactaggart, Allister. *The Film Paintings of David Lynch: Challenging Film Theory.* Chicago: Intellect, 2010.

McGowan, Todd. *The Impossible David Lynch.* New York: Columbia University Press, 2007.

Nochimson, Martha. *The Passion of David Lynch: Wild at Heart in Hollywood.* Austin: University of Texas Press, 1997.

Olson, Greg. *David Lynch: Beautiful Dark.* Lanham, MD: Scarecrow Press, 2008.

Sheen, Erica, and Annette Davison, eds. *The Cinema of David Lynch: American Dreams, Nightmare Visions.* New York: Wallflower Press, 2004.

Lynching

Rooted in the broader tradition of vigilantism, the word lynching is primarily associated with the killing of African Americans by white mobs during the period from the Civil War to the late twentieth century. At the height of lynchings in the United States, between 1882 and 1956, more than 4,700 men, women, and children were killed, about 80 percent of them black. In particular, lynching became an integral part of social control in the South, where whites sought to maintain their traditional authority and deny African Americans basic political, social, and economic freedoms. Although the practice declined in the face of gains made during and after the civil rights era, occasional lynchings continued up to the turn of the twenty-first century.

Lynching originated in Bedford County, Virginia, around the time of the Revolutionary War when Colonel Charles Lynch and other white males organized informally to apprehend and punish Tories and other lawless elements. The term "lynch law" spread throughout the American frontier as lawbreakers were punished with summary whippings, tarring and feathering, and occasional extralegal hangings or shootings in areas where organized legal systems were scarce. Victims were mostly white and ranged from petty criminals to Catholics and immigrants. After the 1830s lynchings began to assume a more racial tone in the North in the form of race riots and other mob actions staged in opposition to the movement to end slavery.

THE SOUTH

In the South, lynching did not gain its special association with race until after the Emancipation Proclamation. The economic self-interest of white masters made it illogical for them to kill or seriously harm their slaves, especially in light of the rigid system of slave control then in existence. Exceptions were made in the cases of slave rebellions when white mobs actively sought out and killed suspected African American participants.

Beginning in the Reconstruction Era, freed blacks became more common targets of lynch mobs as justification for the protection of white supremacy, for misdeeds from murder to talking back to whites, or for other violations of strict social mores. The mythical desire of African American men to rape white women accounted for less than one-quarter of all lynchings, and that estimate does not take into account the southern definition of rape, which included all sexual relations between the races. Still, white mobs lynched black men accused of rape in such far northern states as Maine, Minnesota, and Washington.

Lynching had become an almost wholly southern phenomenon by the turn of the twentieth century. Most lynchings involved secret hangings and shootings administered by small

Anti-Lynching Rally. *Two African American men in Chicago, Illinois, stop to read a sogm promoting a rally against the practice of lynching in August 1946.* JOHN F. WELD/CHICAGO HISTORY MUSEUM/GETTY IMAGES.

groups of white men in mainly rural areas. Public lynchings in the South came to involve torture and mutilation and frequently included death by being burned alive instead of strangulation. The public ritual included prior notice of the event, selection of a symbolically significant location, and the presence of a large crowd that included women, children, and even photographers. A black school teacher turned journalist, Ida B. Wells-Barnett, began publicizing southern lynchings in her newspaper, the *Memphis Free Speech and Headlight*, beginning in 1892 and continuing until she left the South out of fear for her personal safety.

At least a half-dozen black southern women, including a pregnant Georgia woman named Mary Turner and thirteen-year-old nanny Mildrey Brown, were lynched in the late nineteenth and early twentieth centuries in the South. The *Chicago Tribune* began a tally of lynchings in 1882 that it continued until 1968. It was joined by *Crisis*, the official publication of the National Association for the Advancement of Colored People (NAACP), in 1912, in a list that came to be called "The Shame of America."

TWENTIETH CENTURY

The NAACP began investigating individual lynching cases during World War I. One of the more prominent instances involved Leo Frank, a Jewish factory supervisor who was lynched in 1915 near Marietta, Georgia, for allegedly murdering a thirteen-year-old white Atlanta girl, Mary Phagan. The identities of the real killer and lynch mob participants remained under speculation, and the incident was reexamined in President John F. Kennedy's 1956 Pulitzer Prize–winning book, *Profiles in Courage*, and in the short-lived Broadway musical *Parade* in the late 1990s. In 1986 the Georgia Board of Pardons and Paroles pardoned Frank without addressing the issue of his guilt or innocence, but evidence was later uncovered that seemed to point to the guilt of Jim Conley, a black janitor who had been seen carrying Phagan's body.

Other whites and immigrants were lynched by southern mobs, including eleven Italian immigrants in New Orleans in 1891 and twenty-six Mexicans and Mexican Americans in Texas and New Mexico in 1915. The NAACP's first report, *Thirty Years of Lynching in the United States, 1889–1918*, released in the race riot year of 1919, influenced the U.S. House of Representatives to approve the Dyer Anti-Lynching Bill in 1922 by a vote of 230 to 119. The legislation, introduced by Representative L. C. Dyer of Missouri, asserted the federal government's right to protect individual rights and anticipated the Civil Rights Act of 1964. The U.S. Senate, dominated by southerners such as John Sharp Williams and Pat Harrison of Mississippi, prevented the Dyer Bill from coming to a vote.

Walter Francis White, the NAACP's executive director, published additional lynching research in his 1929 *Rope and Faggot: A Legal Assault on Lynching*. Various congressional efforts were made during the 1930s and 1940s, including the 1934 Costigan-Wagner Anti-Lynching Act. Southern legislators, led by Mississippi's Theodore G. Bilbo, filibustered the bill to death. Meanwhile, nine black youths known as the Scottsboro Nine were legally lynched in Alabama in 1931 after they were convicted of the rape of two white women by an all-white jury. There were more than 3,000 hastily tried "legal" lynchings in which African American defendants were denied the right to a fair trial by all-white juries in the United States between 1880 and 1960 that are not included in the total number of "illegal" lynchings.

LEGAL PROCEEDINGS

The number of lynchings in the South declined after 1935 but never ceased altogether. Southerners were able to prevent serious legislation until the 1960s, but the federal courts, led by the U.S. Supreme Court in the 1951 *Williams v. United States* case, reaffirmed that federal law, including the Civil War–era Fourteenth Amendment, forbid local and state law enforcement officials from depriving citizens of individual rights. Vocal opposition to lynching from inside and outside the South contributed to its decline. Actor Paul Robeson met with President Harry Truman as part of a crusade to end lynching in 1946. Nevertheless, sporadic lynchings continued. A fourteen-year-old Chicago youth, Emmett Till, was murdered in 1955 in Mississippi for allegedly whistling at a white woman, and a black veteran, Mack Charles Parker, was shot to death in the same state in 1959 as he awaited trial for the alleged rape of a white woman.

A Ku Klux Klan member, Henry Francis Hays, was convicted and executed for the random lynching of a nineteen-year-old African American man, Michael Donald, in Mobile, Alabama, in 1981. The victim's mother, Beulah Mae Donald, won a $7 million civil suit against the Klan in 1987 for the wrongful death of her son, the first such case in the Klan's long history. In 1998 a forty-nine-year-old unemployed African American man, James Byrd Jr., was chained and dragged to his death behind a pickup truck in Jasper, Texas, in what authorities termed a "backwoods lynching." And a "Redneck Shop" opened in Laurens, South Carolina, in 1996, specializing in Ku Klux Klan memorabilia such as lynching photographs and T-shirts reading "Original Boys in the Hood." Clearly its root cause, racism, continues to be present in the United States.

Even into the twenty-first century, echoes of this history could still be observed in more subtle methods of silencing or disenfranchising minority groups. Acts of vigilantism such as the killing of black youth Trayvon Martin in 2012 have been likened to lynching. Yet, significant efforts have been made to ensure that this dark part of American history is never forgotten. Academics study the psychology, history, and culture of lynching as a way to understand its legacy in contemporary race politics and as a means to heal. Pictures of lynchings have been compiled into photographic essays and books such as 2000's *Without Sanctuary: Lynching Photography in America* and *Lynching Photographs* (2008), which have made the past feel all too real. In 2003 America's Black Holocaust Museum opened in Milwaukee, Wisconsin. Despite closing its physical facility, as of 2012 the museum operated an interactive website that educated visitors about injustices suffered by African Americans. Although lynching is officially a felony in all fifty states, acts of mob violence persist in the United States and throughout the world.

Richard Digby-Junger

SEE ALSO: *Civil Rights Movement; Ku Klux Klan; Robeson, Paul.*

BIBLIOGRAPHY

Allen, James. *Without Sanctuary: Lynching Photography in America*. Sante Fe, NM: Twin Palms Publishers, 2000.

Apel, Dora and Shawn Michelle Smith. *Lynching Photographs: Defining Moments in American Photography*. University of California Press, 2008.

Brundage, W. Fitzhugh. *Lynching in the New South: Georgia and Virginia, 1880–1930*. Urbana: University of Illinois Press, 1993.

Duggan, Paul. "'That Ain't the Boy I Knew': How Did 'Regular Kid' Become Man Accused in Grisly Race Killing?" *Washington Post*, February 16, 1999, A05.

Edwards, Willard. "Robeson's Talk of Lynch Action Angers Truman." *Chicago Daily Tribune*, September 24, 1946, 5.

Finkelman, Paul, ed. *Lynching, Racial Violence, and Law*. New York: Garland Press, 1992.

Ifill, Sherrilyn. *On the Courthouse Lawn: Confronting the Legacy of Lynching in the Twenty-First Century*. Boston: Beacon Press, 2007.

Kovaleski, Serge F. "South Carolina's Trouble in a Hood: Is Old Cinema Featuring KKK's Past or the Rebirth of a Hateful Nation?" *Washington Post*, May 30, 1996, A3.

Massey, James L., and Martha A. Myers. "Patterns of Repressive Social Control in Post-Reconstruction Georgia, 1882–1935." *Social Forces* 68: 458–488.

McMurry, Linda O. *To Keep the Waters Troubled: The Life of Ida B. Wells*. New York: Oxford University Press, 1998.

Zangrando, Robert L. *The NAACP Crusade Against Lynching, 1909–1950*. Philadelphia: Temple University Press, 1980.

Zuckerman, Dianne. "Murder Stories: Lynchings of Black Women Recounted." *Denver Post*, March 19, 1999, E30.

Lynn, Loretta *(1935–)*

With such feisty hits as "You Ain't Woman Enough" (1966) and "Fist City," (1968) country singer/songwriter Loretta Lynn voiced the concerns of blue-collar women during the 1960s and 1970s. When she came to Nashville in 1960, "girl singers" were still considered risky ventures by record executives and promoters. The first female superstar of the modern country industry, Lynn established herself as a true celebrity, capable of selling Crisco vegetable shortening as well as records and concert tickets. Her success as an entertainer also proved that she could remain true to her rural background and retain her traditional vocal style, even as Nashville and the industry were becoming increasingly sophisticated.

Loretta Lynn. *Loretta Lynn's first hit song, 1960's "I'm a Honky-Tonk Girl," set her on the course to be the first female superstar in modern country music.* MICHAEL OCHS ARCHIVES/GETTY IMAGES.

One of eight children, Loretta Webb was born on April 14, 1935, in the poverty-stricken coal-mining town of Butcher Hollow, Kentucky. She married Oliver V. Lynn, who was known by the nicknames "Doolittle" and "Mooney" (because he made moonshine), in her early teens. The newlyweds moved to Custer, Washington, and over the next four years had four children. Lynn's husband gave her a guitar purchased from Sears and Roebuck for her eighteenth birthday. Within a few years she learned to play the instrument and began composing songs.

Convinced of his wife's talent, Mooney took Lynn to local beer joints and got her a job as a singer with a country band. After winning a talent contest at an area fair, she appeared on a Tacoma television show hosted by rising country star Buck Owens. A former lumberman with an interest in music saw the program and gave Lynn the money to make a record in Los Angeles. Steel guitar virtuoso Speedy West rounded up quality California session players for her debut, and "I'm a Honky-Tonk Girl" was released on the tiny Zero label early in 1960. Whereas Lynn's live performances usually featured current songs popularized by country stars, her first single was an original composition.

EARLY CAREER

Lynn and her husband spent months promoting the record themselves, mailing out 3,500 copies of the record to radio stations and visiting numerous stations in person to ask the disc jockeys to play it. By the summer of 1960 the song had reached number fourteen on the country charts. Lynn traveled to Nashville, the epicenter of the country industry and home of the Grand Ole Opry, where she made her first guest appearance in mid-October. With the help of the Wilburn Brothers, Doyle and Teddy, she obtained a contract with Decca Records (which became MCA in the early 1970s) despite producer Owen Bradley's objection that her voice closely resembled that of Kitty Wells. The Lynns moved to Nashville, and the newcomer became Patsy Cline's protégée, even as other female artists conspired to keep her off the Opry. Though her style demonstrated characteristics of both Wells and Cline, Lynn eventually developed a sound of her own. She resisted efforts to polish her image as a performer, preferring cowboy boots to high-heeled shoes and singing with an accent that belied her rural Kentucky upbringing.

SUCCESS

Two years after her breakthrough hit, Lynn had her first Decca Top 10 single with "Success" (1962). Five years later, "DON'T COME HOME A-DRINKIN' (With Lovin' on Your Mind)," cowritten with her sister Peggy Sue Wells, became the first of sixteen number one records Lynn recorded between 1966 and 1975. During the 1960s Lynn occasionally performed duets with honky-tonk legend Ernest Tubb, and the following decade she and Conway Twitty had several hits together. She became the first female recipient of the Country Music Association's (CMA) Entertainer of the Year award in 1972, and eight years later the CMA named her Artist of the Decade. Her best-selling autobiography, *Coal Miner's Daughter*, appeared in 1976, followed four years later by a film version starring Sissy Spacek and Tommy Lee Jones that brought the story of her career into the popular realm.

Lynn branched out from music, opening a chain of western-wear stores and a dude ranch near her home in Tennessee. At the height of her career during the 1970s, she kept a punishing schedule that took its toll on her health. Although her recording career tapered off during the late 1980s, she continued to tour throughout the 1990s and into the twenty-first century. After taking some time off after the death of her husband in 1996, she followed the less successful *Still Country* with the comeback album *Van Lear Rose* in 2004. A collaboration with Jack White of the White Stripes, the album became a crossover hit, appealing to both longtime fans of Lynn and to a younger generation pulled in by White's name and involvement.

Lynn's success surpassed that of any other female country artist during the 1960s and 1970s, and her immense popularity destroyed industry stereotypes about women performers. Her combination of traditional country styles with lyrics that reflected the modern working-class woman's perspective appealed to a large audience, particularly wives and mothers who faced the same problems she addressed in her songs. Lynn has spoken out against racism and illiteracy, and in the mid-1990s she warned women about the dangers of breast implants. She is not afraid of controversy, and she stood behind songs such as "Rated X," which dealt with the stigma of being a divorced woman, and "The Pill," a paean to birth control.

In *Coal Miner's Daughter*, Lynn notes that she is "not a big fan of Women's Liberation, but maybe it will help women stand up for the respect they're due." Although she may not have considered herself a feminist, many of her songs exhibited a progressive attitude that was seldom found in country music. This assertion of pride in her gender and her working-class culture made Lynn the heir to Kitty Wells's title of "the Queen of Country Music" and one of the genre's female legends.

Anna Hunt Graves

SEE ALSO: *Celebrity; Cline, Patsy; Country Music;* Grand Ole Opry*; Movie Stars; Owens, Buck; Radio; Spacek, Sissy; Wells, Kitty.*

BIBLIOGRAPHY

Bufwack, Mary A., and Robert K. Oermann. *Finding Her Voice: The Saga of Women in Country Music.* New York: Crown, 1993.

Lynn, Loretta, and George Vecsey. *Coal Miner's Daughter.* Chicago: Henry Regnery, 1976.

Malone, Bill C., and Judith McCulloh, eds. *Stars of Country Music: Uncle Dave Macon to Johnny Rodriguez.* Urbana: University of Illinois Press, 1975.

Nash, Alanna. *Behind Closed Doors: Talking with the Legends of Country Music.* New York: Alfred A. Knopf, 1988.

Wolff, Kurt, and Duane, Orla. *Country Music: The Rough Guide.* London: Rough Guides, 2000.

Zanderbergen, George. *Nashville Music: Loretta Lynn, Mac Davis, Charley Pride.* Mankato, MN: Crestwood House, 1976.

Zwisohn, Laurence J. *Loretta Lynn's World of Music: Including an Annotated Discography and Complete List of Songs She Composed.* Los Angeles: Palm Tree Library, 1980.

Lynyrd Skynyrd

After several years as an incendiary but unsigned Florida bar band, Lynyrd Skynyrd emerged in 1973 to supersede the Allman Brothers as the most popular exponents of southern rock. Though Lynyrd Skynyrd's use of the Confederate battle flag ensured that the Stars and Bars became a symbol of the rebellious attitude central to contemporary rock and roll, the group's defiant celebration of a particular southern white cultural identity was inextricably related to the racial politics of the South in the post–Civil Rights period. In 1977 the group disbanded after a plane crash killed two of its members. However, the Lynyrd Skynyrd mythology grew precipitously over the next decade, culminating in an emotional and rapturously received reunion of the remaining bandmates in 1987. Although only one member (Gary Rossington) of the original lineup remained in 2012, the band lives on with concert tours and new recordings, as well as in popular culture in songs such as Kid Rock's number-one hit "All Summer Long," which both mentions and samples the group's hit "Sweet Home Alabama." Skynryd songs have long highlighted movie soundtracks, from 1974's *The Longest Yard* through 2010's *Despicable Me.*

THE BEGINNING

Lynyrd Skynyrd's nucleus of vocalist Ronnie Van Zant, drummer Bob Burns, and guitarists Gary Rossington and Allen Collins came together at a Jacksonville, Florida, high school. Though the influence of the town's black bluesmen was acknowledged in Skynyrd's 1974 song "The Ballad of Curtis Loew," the band's distillation of country, rock and roll, and blues derived largely from England's Muddy Waters acolytes, the Rolling Stones. In 1969 Van Zant, Rossington, Collins, and Burns left high school—though not before a straitlaced gym coach called Leonard Skinner inadvertently inspired the band's lasting moniker—and began to play the club scene in Florida and Georgia. The following year the group was offered a contract with Capricorn Records, the label that had established southern rock as a genre. However, Van Zant refused the deal, not wanting his band to be overshadowed by Capricorn's premier act, the Allman Brothers. Lynyrd Skynyrd remained unsigned until 1973, when Al Kooper acquired them for his fledgling MCA offshoot, Sounds of the South.

The Kooper-produced debut, *Pronounced Leh-nerd Skin-nerd*, was released that year, and its final track, the guitar epic "Free Bird," received extensive radio airplay. On such songs as "Poison Whiskey," "Mississippi Kid," and "Gimme Three Steps," the album introduced the staple character of Skynyrd lyrics, the hard-drinking, gun-toting, and womanizing "good ol' boy." A prestigious support slot on the Who's 1973 U.S. tour was followed by the hit single "Sweet Home Alabama" from the gold-selling follow-up album *Second Helping* (1974). The song was written in response to Neil Young's "Southern Man" (1970) and "Alabama" (1972), in which the Canadian singer-songwriter scathingly criticized the South for the patriarchal racism that had endured beyond the end of slavery. Opening with the image of the rock-and-roll rebel returning "home" to his "kin" in "the Southland," "Sweet Home Alabama" was an attempt to reconcile, to use Paul Wells's terms in his essay in *Dixie Debates*, rock's "codes of the road" with "the conservative notions of family and community championed within a southern ethos." However, by including an overt endorsement of segregationist governor George Wallace, the song invoked and defended a southern white cultural identity constructed upon racism and social inequality.

EVOLUTION AND TRAGEDY

Burns was replaced on drums by Artimus Pyle for the third album, *Nuthin' Fancy* (1975). "Saturday Night Special" and "Whiskey Rock-a-Roller" were further paeans to the good ol' boy's penchant for guns and liquor, but the more problematic politics of southern nationalism were evident on "I'm a Country Boy." Like the earlier "Simple Man" (1973) and "Swamp Music" (1974), "I'm a Country Boy" advocated an agrarian way of life but extended rural romanticism to the extent of depicting cotton picking "on the Dixie line" as a labor of love, conveniently ignoring the actual historical toil of black southerners.

Guitarist Ed King left the group during the 1975 tour, and it was apparent from 1976's predictably titled *Gimme Back My Bullets* that the musical virtuosity of the first two albums had palled. Replacement guitarist Steve Gaines joined the band in early 1976, and with the further addition of a regular female backing group, the Honkettes, the band sounded revitalized on their 1976 tour (captured on the double live set, *One More from the Road*). The sixth album, *Street Survivors*, was released in October 1977. Only days later, the group's private plane plunged into a Mississippi swamp, killing Van Zant, Gaines, and the latter's sister Cassie (a member of the Honkettes), as well as seriously injuring Rossington, Collins, bassist Leon Wilkinson, and keyboardist Billy Powell.

Lynyrd Skynyrd's legacy overshadowed the reunion of Rossington, Collins, Wilkinson, and Powell in the Rossington Collins Band (1979–1982), as well as the plethora of post-Skynyrd southern rock outfits such as .38 Special, Confederate Railroad, Molly Hatchet, and Blackfoot. Led by the initially reluctant Rossington, and with Van Zant's brother Johnny on vocals, Lynyrd Skynyrd rose again in 1987 for a tribute tour that paid moving homage to Ronnie Van Zant and the group's 1970s heyday. The group's neo-Confederate posturings remained unreconstructed, typified by the tacky sleeve art for the 1996 live album *Southern Knights* and "The Last Rebel" (1993), an ode to the heroic warriors of the Lost Cause. Somewhat appropriately, the deification of Van Zant, notably in Doc Holliday's "Song for the Outlaw" (1989), fed into the larger mythology of "Johnny Reb" taking his stand for Dixie.

HONORS FOR THE BAND

Variations of the band continued after the 1987 tour, but death began taking its toll, with Collins dying in 1990, Wilkinson in

Lynyrd Skynyrd. *Lynyrd Skynyrd, featuring from left to right Allen Collins, Ronnie Van Zant, and Gary Rossington, performs in 1976.* RICHARD E. AARON/CONTRIBUTOR/REDFERNS/GETTY IMAGES.

2001, and Billy Powell in 2009. The new century brought great acclaim to the band, with two books published in 2002, being named as one of the 100 greatest artists of all time by *Rolling Stone* magazine in 2004, and induction into the Rock and Hall of Fame in 2006. "Sweet Home Alabama" racked up honors as well, as the song was ranked number 398 on *Rolling Stone*'s list of the "500 Greatest Songs of All Time" in 2004 and number four on the *National Review*'s "50 Greatest Conservative Rock Songs" in 2006; CMT also named it the greatest southern rock song of all time. Perhaps the greatest honor came in 2009 as Alabama adopted "Sweet Home Alabama" as a slogan on the state's license plates.

Martyn Bone

SEE ALSO: *The Allman Brothers Band; Civil Rights Movement; Rock and Roll;* Rolling Stone; *The Rolling Stones; Waters, Muddy; Young, Neil.*

BIBLIOGRAPHY

Brant, Marley. *Freebirds: The Lynyrd Skynyrd Story.* New York: Billboard Books, 2002.

Lynyrd Skynyrd Songbook. Melville, NY: Duchess Music, 1977.

Odom, Gene, and Frank Dorman. *Lynyrd Skynyrd: Remembering the Free Birds of Southern Rock.* New York: Broadway Books, 2002.

Wells, Paul. "The Last Rebel: Southern Rock and Nostalgic Continuities." In *Dixie Debates: Perspectives on Southern Culture*, ed. Richard King and Helen Taylor. London: Bloomsbury, 1996.

M

Ma Perkins

A pioneering soap opera, *Ma Perkins* was heard on daytime radio for close to thirty years. For most of that time it was sponsored by Procter & Gamble's Oxydol soap flakes. The fifteen-minute show began in 1933 and did not leave the air until 1960. For several years it was broadcast on both NBC and CBS. The busy team of Frank and Anne Hummert produced the show, and one of the initial scriptwriters was Robert Hardy Andrews, who also wrote *Jack Armstrong, the All-American Boy* in its earliest radio days.

Ma, dubbed "America's mother of the air," was a feisty widow who ran a lumberyard in the town of Rushville Center. The small town was both folksy and turbulent, and Ma was equal parts maternal figure, therapist, and busybody. Virginia Payne, actually in her early twenties when the show commenced, played the sixty-something Ma for the entire run of the show. The commercials relied on the irritation factor, usually repeating the product name at least two dozen times per episode. It has been estimated that in the lifetime of *Ma Perkins*, the program "helped sell over three billion boxes of Oxydol."

Ron Goulart

SEE ALSO: *Radio; Soap Operas.*

BIBLIOGRAPHY

Cox, Jim. *The A to Z of American Radio Soap Operas.* Lanham, MD: Scarecrow Press, 2009.

Dunning, John. *On the Air: The Encyclopedia of Old-Time Radio.* New York: Oxford University Press, 1998.

Swasy, Alecia. *Soap Opera: The Inside Story of Procter & Gamble.* New York: Random House, 1993.

Mabley, Moms *(1894?–1975)*

When Jackie Mabley was growing up one child of many in a poor southern family, her mother told her she would have to leave North Carolina in order to make something of herself. Mabley took her mother's advice to heart, overcoming great odds to become not only a widely recognized and successful stand-up comic but also the unforgettable "Moms," an African American archetype with too much common sense and sensuality to take herself too seriously. Dressed in her flamboyant signature outfit of Hawaiian shirt over a housedress with bright socks, floppy slippers, and a hat she crocheted herself, Moms Mabley called her audience her "children." She entertained them with raunchy jokes and devilish playfulness, punctuating her act with bulging eyes and a toothless leer. In an entertainment industry where African American women continue to receive little recognition, Mabley's sixty-year career stands as a role model.

Born Loretta Mary Aiken in Brevard, North Carolina, the details of Mabley's youth are vague, but it seems clear she was born into a large, poor family. Early in her life she sought a way out; her father was killed when she was a child, and she had been raped twice before she left home at the age of thirteen to join the traveling performers of a minstrel show. Mabley spent her teenage years singing, dancing, and doing sketch comedy

Moms Mabley. *Jackie "Moms" Mabley took her act from the "chitlin' circuit" to Broadway, television, and movies over the course of her lengthy career.* MICHAEL OCHS ARCHIVES/STRINGER/GETTY IMAGES.

along the "chitlin' circuit," the black-owned clubs and performance halls that offered work to black entertainers. Though a product of segregation, the black clubs were for the most part safe and comfortable places for both black audiences and performers. While traveling with the show, she became involved with fellow performer Jack Mabley. Though they never married, she began to use the name Jackie Mabley, saying, "He took a lot off me, the least I could do was take his name."

HARLEM

With the arrival of the 1920s and the beginning of the Harlem Renaissance, Mabley found her way to New York, where she performed her act in such famous venues as the Cotton Club and the Savoy Ballroom, sharing the bill with the likes of Duke Ellington and Cab Calloway. Later she would incorporate her friendships with these famous performers into her act, hinting broadly at her affairs.

By the 1930s the Depression slowed the entertainment business, and Mabley made ends meet by working at church socials and movie houses. In 1931 she collaborated with renowned Harlem Renaissance writer Zora Neale Hurston, writing and performing a Broadway play called *Fast and Furious: A Colored Revue in Thirty-Seven Scenes*. By 1939 Mabley began to appear regularly at the Apollo Theater in Harlem, where over the next thirty-five years she would perform more than any other entertainer. Here she continued to develop her comic act—the salty old lady with the mobile face and gravelly voice. It was at the Apollo that she acquired the nickname "Moms" from her fellow performers, who appreciated her nurturing sympathy. During her years of performing at the Apollo, Mabley often saw famous white comics in the audience and accused them of stealing her material.

Though Mabley's act may seem stereotypical to some, it was really quite a clever show business ploy. While attractive young women, particularly black women, could show little in the way of intelligence or sexuality without condemnation, "Moms" was safe—a laughable figure of fun. From behind the shabby clothes and mobile toothless grin, Mabley could offer sharp-witted insights and social commentary that would have been unacceptable from a more serious source. Beloved by African American audiences, Mabley's whole persona was an "in" joke among blacks, and she did not hesitate to focus her scathing humor on whites and their ill treatment of other races. She also demonstrated glimmers of an early feminism with her jokes about old men and their illusions of authority. One of her trademark jokes was, "Ain't nothing an old man can do for me but bring me a message from a young man."

THE SIXTIES

It was this sly satirical edge along with the emergence of the civil rights movement that brought Mabley her second surge of fame in the rebellious 1960s. On *The Ed Sullivan Show* and the controversial *Smothers Brothers Comedy Hour*, Mabley brought her bawdy humor to white audiences for the first time. Over the course of her lengthy career, she also appeared in several movies, from small parts in *A Midsummer Night's Dream* (1968) and Eugene O'Neill's *The Emperor Jones* (1933) to a starring role in *Amazing Grace* (1974). The prolific Mabley also made more than twenty-five popular comedy albums and was invited to the White House by President John F. Kennedy. Perhaps one of Mabley's most touching performances is her hoarsely emotional recording of the song "Abraham, Martin, and John" about the deaths of the great civil rights leaders.

Though she had four children and five grandchildren, Mabley lived most of her life as a lesbian. Although she was not "out" in the modern sense, certainly Mabley did break taboos and challenge assumptions throughout her career with her character of an old woman who was sexual, savvy, and irrepressible. The girl who survived childhood rape to carve out a successful career in the inhospitable world of show business grew up to be Moms, who described her television appearances by saying, "I looked at the world as my children."

Modern black comediennes pay tribute to Mabley as a foremother. In 1986 playwright Alice Childress wrote *Moms: A Praise for a Black Comedienne*, which was produced on Broadway in 1987. Respected comic and actress Whoopi Goldberg "does" Mabley as one of her comic characters, and the documentary *I Be Done Been Was Is* names Mabley as an inspiration for the black female comics who followed her.

Tina Gianoulis

SEE ALSO: *Apollo Theater; Broadway; Calloway, Cab; Civil Rights Movement; The Cotton Club; Ellington, Duke; Goldberg, Whoopi; The Great Depression; Harlem Renaissance; Hurston, Zora Neale; Minstrel Shows; O'Neill, Eugene; Savoy Ballroom; The Smothers Brothers; Stand-Up Comedy; Television.*

BIBLIOGRAPHY

Gates, Henry Louis, and Evelyn Brooks Higginbotham. *African American Lives*. New York: Oxford University Press, 2004.

Harris, Trudier. "Moms Mabley: A Study in Humor, Role Playing, and the Violation of Taboo." *Southern Review* 24, no. 4 (1988): 765.

Williams, Elsie A. *The Humor of Jackie Moms Mabley: An African American Comedic Tradition*. New York: Garland, 1995.

Mac, Bernie *(1957–2008)*

African American stand-up comedian and actor Bernie Mac was best known for creating and starring in the popular sitcom *The Bernie Mac Show* (2001–2006). On the show he portrays an excitable surrogate father to his sister's children, who are adorable yet full of mischief and, in the case of the eldest niece, teenage attitude.

Bernard Jeffrey McCullough was born on October 5, 1957, in Chicago. As a small child, he saw a Bill Cosby stand-up routine on television and was immediately inspired to become a comedian. He performed his first show at the age of eight, impersonating his grandparents at the dinner table for their church congregation. During his teens he continued to practice comedy at home and at church on Chicago's South Side. When he was sixteen, his mother died and his grandmother assumed the responsibility of raising him. These two women—and their idiosyncratic methods of raising him—featured prominently in the comedic material he went on to perform throughout his career.

At the age of nineteen, Mac got married, and soon after the couple became the parents of a daughter. Mac then began touring the comedy circuits and performing at amateur nights.

For more than a decade he performed whenever and wherever he could, honing his act by working up to fifty weeks a year while holding various odd jobs to supplement his income.

In the 1990s Mac made the risky decision to pursue comedy full time, and it paid off. He won the Miller Lite Comedy Search, was awarded a part on the popular HBO television series *Def Comedy Jam*, and was cast in numerous movies. His early films included *Mo' Money* (1992), *Who's the Man?* (1993), and *Friday* (1995). His first starring role came in a baseball film, *Mr. 3000*. Meanwhile, his stand-up career flourished. He eventually won a place in *The Original Kings of Comedy*, a hugely successfully tour and film produced by African Americans for black audiences.

In 2001 the Fox network produced *The Bernie Mac Show*, a black sitcom written from the point of view of an affluent, funny, and ultimately angry fictionalized version of Mac. The show chronicles Mac's anguish and joy after taking custody of and rearing his drug-addicted sister's three kids, Bryana (Dee Dee Davis), Jordan (Jeremy Suarez), and Vaness (Camille Winbush). Mac portrays an old-fashioned father figure who practices tough love and values law and order, with the child-rearing practices at the heart of the show based on those of his own upbringing. He often incorporates aspects of his stand-up comedy routine in the TV show and regularly employs the theatrical technique of breaking the fourth wall by speaking directly to the camera and to the audience (who Mac addresses as America). "Now America, tell me again," his character asks in one episode, "why can't I whip that girl?"

The Bernie Mac Show was a hit, with more than ten million viewers tuning in each week until it was canceled in 2006. It was also popular with critics. Mac was lauded for portraying a complex black character and broaching difficult racial issues. He once attributed the success of his to show to having the courage "to touch on subject matters or issues that everyone else is politically scared of."

In 2007 Mac founded the Bernie Mac Foundation, a nonprofit organization dedicated to finding a cure for sarcoidosis, a disease he suffered from that is characterized by the presence of inflammatory cells on vital organs. Additionally, he raised money for Senator Barack Obama's presidential campaign in 2008 and published a memoir titled *I Ain't Scared of You* (2001). On August 9, 2008, Mac died from pneumonia and other complications arising from his disease. His memorial service was attended by more than 6,000 mourners.

Willie R. Collins

SEE ALSO: *Baseball; Cosby, Bill; Hollywood; Obama, Barack; Sitcom; Stand-Up Comedy; Television.*

BIBLIOGRAPHY

Boyd, Todd, ed. *African Americans and Popular Culture: Theater, Film, and Television.* Westport, CT: Praeger, 2007.

I Ain't Scared of You: A Tribute to Bernie Mac. DVD. Directed by Robert Small. Chatsworth, CA: Image Entertainment, 2012.

Mac, Bernie, and Darrell Dawsey. *I Ain't Scared of You: Bernie Mac on How Life Is.* New York: MTV Books, 2001.

Mac, Bernie, and Pablo F. Fenjves. *Maybe You Never Cry Again.* New York: Regan Books, 2003.

MacDonald, Jeanette *(1903–1965)*

Jeanette MacDonald is one of the best-loved singing actresses of early film. The image of the star greeting an earthquake with a song in *San Francisco* (1936) is forever enshrined in the popular consciousness—a moment further immortalized by Judy Garland's 1961 recording of the title song, which recalls how MacDonald "stood among the ruins and sang." MacDonald became equally well-known for her partnership with Nelson Eddy. The couple, universally known as "America's Singing Sweethearts" at the height of their popularity, epitomized the lush romantic world of the 1930s film operetta.

CHILDHOOD AND EARLY CAREER

Born on June 18, 1903, in Philadelphia, Pennsylvania, MacDonald showed promise as a dancer and singer from a very young age. She began her professional career as a chorus girl on Broadway before assuming lead roles in musicals such as *Tangerine* (1922) and *The Magic Ring* (1923). Her film debut could not have been more auspicious. Paramount's most stylish European director, Ernst Lubitsch, cast the blue-eyed, blond-haired soprano opposite debonair Frenchman Maurice Chevalier in *The Love Parade* (1929). The first of four sophisticated, frothy films she made with Chevalier, *The Love Parade* was a major box-office hit that garnered several Oscar nominations and made MacDonald an overnight star. She signed an exclusive contract with RCA Victor Records and cut her first commercial record (songs from *The Love Parade*) on December 1, 1929.

Jeanette MacDonald. *Jeanette MacDonald parlayed her signing and stage popularity in the 1920s into a successful film career in the 1930s and 1940s.* SILVER SCREEN COLLECTION/CONTRIBUTOR/MOVIEPIX/GETTY IMAGES.

She made a few minor forgotten films at other studios, but her career grew at Paramount, where she costarred with Dennis King in *The Vagabond King* (1930). This was the first of her many film adaptations of Broadway operettas, such as with British star Jack Buchanan in *Monte Carlo* (1930), with Chevalier again for *One Hour with You* (1932), *Love Me Tonight* (1932), and Lubitsch's entrancing version of Franz Lehar's *The Merry Widow* (1934).

THE MOVE TO MGM AND NELSON EDDY

MacDonald made successful European concert tours in 1931 and 1933 that enhanced her already tremendous popularity abroad. During the 1933 tour she met Louis B. Mayer, who offered her an exclusive contract with MGM. She accepted the offer, leaving Paramount and the world of high-style, European sophistication for a studio that specialized in wholesome, saccharine American romance. She began her tenure at MGM and her partnership with Nelson Eddy with *Naughty Marietta* (1935), in which MacDonald plays a French princess who journeys to America and falls in love with an Indian scout. The operatically trained baritone and the fetching soprano warbled "Ah, Sweet Mystery of Life" and captivated the public, who later flocked in even greater numbers to *Rose Marie* (1936). The latter film was quintessential operetta nonsense, offering such disparate musical delights as "Some of These Days," "Dinah," and scenes from Puccini's *Tosca*.

The monumental success of *Rose Marie* assured MacDonald's status as a star. The "Singing Sweethearts" continued with the whimsical *Maytime* (1937), *The Girl of the Golden West* (1938), *Sweethearts* (1938, their first in Technicolor and biggest hit), *New Moon* (1940), *Bitter Sweet* (1940), and *I Married an Angel* (1942)—the last, least, and silliest, which spelled the end of the partnership. Together the couple represented the archetypal screen lovers who surmount all obstacles to end up together. MacDonald was invariably cast as some kind of well-born woman caught up in alien circumstances and rescued through the love of the rather wooden Eddy, who matched her perfectly with his beautiful voice and noble profile.

During this successful run, MacDonald also costarred with Clark Gable and Spencer Tracy in *San Francisco* and with Allan Jones in *The Firefly* (1937). She married actor Gene Raymond in 1937 and costarred with him in *Smilin' Through* (1941).

AFTER MGM

Wartime audiences were less interested in the innocent MacDonald-Eddy operettas, and MGM terminated MacDonald's contract in 1942. Between 1939 and 1946 she made numerous cross-country concert tours. She constantly broke attendance records and soon became the biggest box-office draw in the concert world. During World War II she devoted much of her time to entertaining the troops and expanded her range to live opera. She made her operatic debut on May 8, 1943, at His Majesty's Theatre in Montreal, Canada, singing as Juliet in Gounod's *Romeo and Juliet* (later reprising the role at the Chicago Civic Opera House on November 4, 1944). However her voice proved too small to carry adequately in an opera house, and she quickly abandoned the pursuit.

Macdonald's film career essentially ended after the war, although she had a cameo in *Follow the Boys* (1944) for Universal. In 1948 she played the mother in *Three Daring Daughters* (1948), which was not quite a musical but more like a movie with music. She was also in a Lassie film, *The Sun Comes Up* (1949). MacDonald remained active in radio and on television until her death, making numerous appearances on programs such as "Railroad Hour," "The Voice of Firestone," "The Toast of the Town," "Playhouse 90," and "Person to Person." During the 1950s she played in various summer stock theatrical productions, and she made her Las Vegas nightclub debut in 1953.

Jeanette MacDonald died on January 14, 1965, of heart disease. Her husband was with her throughout her prolonged illness. At her memorial service her recordings of "Ave Maria" and "Ah, Sweet Mystery of Life" were broadcast outside the chapel for those who came to pay their respects. She had been a staunch Republican supporter, and her honorary pallbearers included Richard Nixon, former Presidents Dwight Eisenhower and Harry Truman, Chief Justice Earl Warren, and Ronald Reagan.

By the end of the twentieth century MacDonald had become an enduring legend, the memory of her soprano voice and beguiling screen persona kept alive by television. The old-fashioned innocence and corniness of her films with Eddy have become objects of affectionate ridicule, best summed up in a review of *Naughty Marietta* by Judith Crist, who wrote, "When these two profiles come together to sing 'Ah, Sweet Mystery of Life', it's beyond camp, it's in a realm of its own."

William A. Everett

SEE ALSO: *Eddy, Nelson; Gable, Clark; Hollywood; Las Vegas; Lassie; MGM (Metro-Goldwyn-Mayer); Movie Stars; Reagan, Ronald; Tracy, Spencer.*

BIBLIOGRAPHY

Castanza, Philip. *The Complete Films of Jeanette MacDonald and Nelson Eddy*. Secaucus, NJ: Citadel Press, 1978.

Dugan, Eleanor. *The Films of Jeanette MacDonald and Nelson Eddy*. South Brunswick, NJ: A. S. Barnes, 1975.

Parish, James Robert. *The Jeanette MacDonald Story*. New York: Mason/Charter, 1976.

Stern, Lee Edward. *Jeanette MacDonald*. New York: Jove Books, 1977.

Turk, Edward Baron. *Hollywood Diva: A Biography of Jeanette MacDonald*. Berkeley: University of California Press, 1998.

Wayne, Jane Ellen. *The Golden Girls of MGM*. New York: Carroll & Graf, 2003.

MacDonald, John D. *(1916–1986)*

The creator of the best-selling Travis McGee series of detective novels, John D. MacDonald gained most of his fame and fortune by writing paperback originals. Although he initially started out writing stories for the pulps after leaving the service in 1946, he moved into paperbacks in 1950. The pulps were fading away in the postwar years, whereas 25-cent books were burgeoning. The prolific MacDonald was able to take advantage of this growing new market.

Between his first hard-boiled thriller, *The Brass Cupcake*, in 1950 and his first McGee novel, *The Deep Blue Goodbye*, in 1964, he wrote more than forty novels. He went on to publish many more, including a total of twenty-one featuring McGee.

Many of them were best sellers. MacDonald was a good writer—respected by readers, reviewers, and fellow writers alike—and he always managed to inject considerable social criticism into his books. McGee, who owned a boat and lived in Florida, was himself a sort of floating private eye.

Ron Goulart

SEE ALSO: *Best Sellers; Detective Fiction; Hard-Boiled Detective Fiction; Pulp Magazines.*

BIBLIOGRAPHY

Campbell, Frank D., Jr. *John D. MacDonald and the Colorful World of Travis McGee.* San Bernardino, CA: Borgo Press, 1977.

Geherin, David. *John D. MacDonald.* New York: F. Ungar Publishing, 1982.

Hirshberg, Edgar W. *John D. MacDonald.* Boston: Twayne, 1985.

Merrill, Hugh. *The Red Hot Typewriter: The Life and Times of John D. MacDonald.* New York: Thomas Dunne Books/St. Martin's Minotaur, 2000.

Moore, Lewis D. *Meditations on America: John D. MacDonald's Travis McGee Series and Other Fiction.* Bowling Green, OH: Bowling Green State University Popular Press, 1994.

Shine, Walter, and Jean Shine. *A Bibliography of the Published Works of John D. MacDonald with Selected Biographical Materials and Critical Essays.* Gainesville, FL: Patrons of the Library, University of Florida, 1980.

Shine, Walter, and Jean Shine. *Rave or Rage: The Critics and John D. MacDonald.* Gainesville, FL: University of Florida Press, 1993.

Macfadden, Bernarr *(1868–1955)*

Publisher, aspiring politician, and professional eccentric: all of these labels might describe Bernarr Macfadden, one of the characters who populated the American cultural scene of the twentieth century. However, although Macfadden made his fortune publishing the phenomenally successful *True Story*, he requested that his tombstone would read simply, if not modestly, "the father of physical culture." He was in fact very proud of his publishing successes, yet he always hoped that he would be remembered primarily for his advocacy of modern principles for good health (pro-vegetarianism, pro-exercise, antismoking).

Bernarr Macfadden. *Bernarr Macfadden leads an exercise session with six members of the U.S. Senate in 1924.* © CORBIS.

Ironically, in light of the fact that some of his physical health principles do now appear to have been prophetic, Macfadden was always viewed as a quack. His preference for spectacularly ill-conceived cures (ranging from dunking ailing infants in ice cold water, fasting for days, and refusing all conventional medical care), in tandem with his penchant for publicity stunts of dubious taste (such as publishing photographs of himself and his family half-nude), made him a laughing stock in the first half of the century. His antiprudery, pro-sexual liberalization stance merely added to his contemporary disrepute. Thus, ultimately, Bernarr Macfadden has not been remembered for his work as the self-proclaimed guru of "physical culture" but remains famous for the role he played as an enormously successful publisher and infamous as one of the most peculiar popular icons ever to grace the American scene.

During the 1920s Macfadden made a huge name for himself as the publisher, first of *True Story*, then of the whole stable of "True" magazines (*True Romance*, *True Experience*, *True Detective*), and finally, of the doomed daily New York newspaper the *Graphic*. Riding on the waves of these successes, he attempted to further his career in the fields of physical culture and politics. Unfortunately, in these, his favored public arenas, Macfadden's failures proved as grand as his successes. By the 1940s the publisher had not only failed in every one of his various bids for public office but had also lost his publishing empire, his wife and family, and even the support of the many working-class Americans who had once admired him—although they wouldn't vote for him.

The finale to Macfadden's story was not a happy one, but the man himself remained undaunted. In 1949, on his eighty-first birthday, he made a parachute jump in front of his new, forty-two-year-old wife. That same year, as in the years that preceded it and those that followed, millions of Americans continued to buy *True Story*. And, after a fashion that would have very much pleased Macfadden, today we see the realization of his most cherished and personal dream in the cult of the quest for perfect bodies and perfect health that began in late twentieth-century America. The name Bernarr Macfadden may conjure up a comical image, but some of his ideas have endured.

EARLY LIFE

Born in 1868 in the Ozarks, Macfadden was a child of poverty. He spent his early years working at odd jobs and moving from the home of one relative to another. His father died when he was very young, and his mother, who was too ill to care for her child most of the time, died when he was just a boy. A skinny, sickly child, he almost succumbed to tuberculosis in his youth, but after his recovery, he determined that he would never again be weak or ill and thereafter devoted his life to the pursuit of good health.

The young Macfadden started working out at gymnasiums, a hobby which eventually led to jobs as director of athletics at a small college in Missouri, manager of a gym in St. Louis, and eventually to the establishment of his own gym in New York City. In 1898 he began publication of the magazine *Physical Development*. In that publication, Macfadden frequently railed against traditional medicine, a move that would pit him in a permanent battle with the American Medical Association. However, the magazine was modestly successful and enabled him to pursue other dreams.

AN ALTERNATIVE LIFESTYLE

In the early years of the twentieth century, the publisher established a series of cheap vegetarian restaurants in New York City, offering the poor nourishment at a price they could afford, and in 1905 he established an alternative community, a physical culture "city" at Spotswood, New Jersey. The community was a failure. Where Macfadden had envisaged 30,000 healthy Americans, there were merely 200 devotees who lived at subsistence level while working night and day trying to build their "city."

Meanwhile, Macfadden, who rarely lived at the site (leaving his wife and his secretary/mistress to run the venture), continued with his physical culture crusades. He mounted a physical culture exhibition at Madison Square Garden, resulting in his first run-in with Anthony Comstock's Society for the Suppression of Vice. Although Macfadden was released after it became clear that his "obscene" models were actually wearing flesh-colored tights, he was never again free of the anti-vice society's keen attention. Soon after, Macfadden was arrested when he published a serialized story in *Physical Culture* about the dangers of venereal disease (a tragic but entertaining tale of a young man's downfall). This time Macfadden was found guilty on obscenity charges and sentenced to two years of hard labor. In 1909, after years of appeals, he was pardoned, though not exonerated, by President William Howard Taft.

All his life he would declare that his publishing, and other work, was dedicated to the eradication of dangerous prudery. In his time, that stance was increasingly viewed as little more than a cover for the propagation and support of pornography and debauchery. Whatever the case, Macfadden came to be most famous for his exposure of the sexual realities and secrets of American society.

TRUE STORY

In 1919 he achieved his first really great success with the publication of *True Story*. The magazine, which presented first-hand confessions of sex and other sins, was enormously popular with its young working-class audience, and Macfadden earned his first million as his magazine achieved its first million readers. Characteristically, he used the money from *True Story* to pursue a series of other strange ventures. In 1924 he launched his first newspaper, the *Graphic*, which he imagined as a crusading tell-all newspaper "for the people, by the people, and of the people." Walter Winchell got his start as a gossip columnist at the *Graphic*. At first the newspaper, humorously dubbed "the pornographic," was a great success, but financial mismanagement led to its demise in the 1930s.

However, during the 1920s, it seemed as if Macfadden had the Midas touch. Believing his own publicity, he began to imagine himself a great American leader and attempted to enter politics, hoping eventually to run for president. He failed in bids to become the mayor of New York, governor of Florida, and "secretary for health" (a position he hoped Franklin Roosevelt might establish with him in mind). As part of his political image, he trained some of Benito Mussolini's soldiers in the principles of physical culture, almost at the same time that he began publication of a magazine edited by Eleanor Roosevelt titled *Babies, Babies, Babies*. The Roosevelts dumped Macfadden as they became increasingly aware of his embarrassingly peculiar and eclectic interests.

MACFADDEN'S DOWNFALL

Ultimately, all of Macfadden's efforts to enter politics were spectacularly unsuccessful, not to mention personally damaging. Having invested so much money and time in promoting his public ambitions, he lost control of his personal affairs and allowed minority stockholders to gain increasing control of *True Story*. When, in 1941, they accused him of using the magazine's money to fund his campaigns and of fudging circulation figures, he was forced to relinquish his control of the company.

At home, things were even worse. Macfadden had been a strong patriarch, forcing his family (including the many children named in his image, such as Byrne, Braunda, and Byron) to live by strict physical culture principles. Eventually, his wife, Mary, revolted. Although Macfadden claimed that he wished to divorce Mary because she had become too fat for his healthy taste, she cited his refusal to allow her a normal life and his determination that she should continue to bear children, even when her pregnancies were considered life-threatening, as reasons for their divorce. In 1953 Mary wrote what could be considered one of the first celebrity exposés, in which she claimed Macfadden was a bad father, a fraud, a semifascist, and a generally all-round bad guy. Macfadden was devastated by his former wife's betrayal, and in 1955 he died of an attack of jaundice precipitated, ironically, by a three-day fast.

Macfadden died a penniless failure. Yet, in spite of his several reversals of fortune, he managed to place himself permanently on the historical map of American culture. Many of the cultural values he tried to sell have found a market. *True Story* endures today, while the growth of talk shows and reality television suggest an ongoing American penchant for the public confessional. The sexual liberalization of American society, if only in the conservative terms that Macfadden imagined it, is a fait accompli. Many of his key health principles now enjoy widespread support, and there has even been a revival of scholarly interest in Macfadden's work as a publisher, physical health proponent, and spokesperson for the voiceless. Scholars continue to debate the value of his contributions, and where one sees the championing of causes and merits of certain aspects of his particular philosophy of "physical culture," another sees vicious demagoguery or the exploitation of the ignorant and innocent.

Pornographer or sexual liberal, champion of the poor or purveyor of the worst in popular taste—unsurprisingly, there is little room for agreement over the contradictions inherent in his story, and the fact that the debate continues would give Macfadden heart. For, as he once said when questioned about the negative publicity he received, "They're laughing Henry Ford into a greater success the same way." In his heyday, Macfadden saw no need for critical approval. All the affirmation he needed was to watch the circulation figures of *True Story* magazine grow. The popular vote of his readers was Macfadden's confirmation of his own success.

Jackie Hatton

SEE ALSO: *Daytime Talk Shows; Reality Television;* True Story Magazine*; Vegetarianism.*

BIBLIOGRAPHY

Cohen, Lester. The New York Graphic: *The World's Zaniest Newspaper*. Philadelphia: Chilton, 1964.

Ernst, Robert. *Weakness Is a Crime: The Life of Bernarr Macfadden*. New York: Syracuse University, 1991.

Gavreau, Emile, and Mary Macfadden. *Dumbbells and Carrot Sticks*. New York: Henry Holt, 1953.

Hatton, Jacqueline Anne. *True Stories: Working-Class Mythology, American Confessional Culture, and* True Story *Magazine, 1919–1929*. Working Dissertation, Cornell University, 1997.

Hunt, William. *Body Love: The Amazing Career of Bernarr Macfadden*. Bowling Green, OH: Bowling Green State University Popular Press, 1989.

Oursler, Fulton. *The True Story of Bernarr Macfadden*. New York: Lewis Copeland, 1929.

Puskar-Pasewicz, Margaret. *Cultural Encyclopedia of Vegetarianism*. Santa Barbara, CA: Greenwood Press, 2010.

Wood, Clement. *Bernarr Macfadden: A Study in Success*. New York: Lewis Copeland, 1929.

MacMurray, Fred *(1908–1991)*

Though never a first-string actor, Fred MacMurray had a long and successful career that stretched from the 1930s to the 1970s, encompassing both film and television roles. MacMurray made his name playing a particular type of male lead—amiable, upbeat, and anxious to please—that was easily adapted, in later

Fred MacMurray. *Fred MacMurray had a successful movie career in both comedies and dramas before coming to television in 1960 to star in* My Three Sons. **SILVER SCREEN COLLECTION/CONTRIBUTOR/MOVIEPIX/GETTY IMAGES.**

life, to playing father figures on television and in children's films. On a number of occasions, however, the actor was furnished with roles that allowed a questioning and undermining of his more familiar persona.

Likable and pleasant looking, MacMurray appeared regularly in 1930s and 1940s romantic comedies (working nine different occasions for Mitchell Leisen, one of the most expert directors of light farce), playing the affable leading man opposite Hollywood's top actresses. It is perhaps a mark of his percolation into the American consciousness as an exemplification of the ordinary, wholesome American male that made him the perfect physical model for a new comic-book hero of the period: Captain Marvel.

Despite his constant film work throughout World War II, he never rose to star status, appearing in comedies, adventures, and routine melodramas, whose caliber increasingly suggested the decline of his drawing power. Yet it was also during this period that MacMurray sporadically played some of his best roles, markedly against his previous wholesome type. Directory Billy Wilder had already shown the possibilities of this in *Double Indemnity* (1944), a film in which MacMurray plays a salesman giving in to love and greed. The morally inadequate naval lieutenant of *The Caine Mutiny* (1954), the corrupt policeman of *Pushover* (1954), and the serial adulterer of *The Apartment* (1960) also provided MacMurray with interesting roles that gave him the opportunity to stretch as an actor.

MacMurray's career fell into decline until rescued by a series of films for Disney—the best remembered being *The Absent-Minded Professor* (1961)—and the TV series *My Three Sons* (1960–1972), one of television's longest-lasting sitcoms. Both depended on MacMurray's unthreatening bemusement and fatherly trustworthiness.

Through the majority of his films, MacMurray created the persona of a gentle, likable, wholesome, All-American guy who is anxious to please and make something of his life and who, despite setbacks, always succeeds. This is a role he carried off perfectly in light comedy (whether a 1930s Leisen farce or a 1960s Disney film), and it is in this role that he became a familiar face (if not a familiar name) in film and on television.

In more dramatic roles he was less convincing, particularly if called upon to be a tough guy or to show moral fiber. A good example of this can be found in the thriller *Above Suspicion* (1943), in which the persona he had mastered appears too fragile in a harsher, less sympathetic world. However, it is exactly this fragility that Wilder was able to bring out of MacMurray, guiding the veteran actor to his best performances. As an insurance salesman in *Double Indemnity* and an advertising executive in *The Apartment*, MacMurray's characters simultaneously believe in and use the good-guy persona to sell themselves. However, what seemed upstanding and trustworthy at first becomes shifty and rather seedy, and that which was marked by sincerity and integrity reveals itself as mere veneer without moral backbone. Ultimately, it is because MacMurray so successfully made his name playing the charming young salesman or the admirable father figure that, in a tougher environment, he made such an apt fraudster, murderer, and adulterer.

MacMurray made dozens of films over a career spanning forty years, and the majority of these were light fare celebrating romance, the status quo, and the will to succeed in the American male. From callow youth to absentminded professor, from kindly romantic lead to archetypal dad, MacMurray typified a comfortable and undemanding view of American manhood. Yet, on occasion, and exactly because of his familiarity, he gave disturbing performances that questioned the moral depth of his own brand of prepackaged wholesome, All-American sincerity.

Kyle Smith

SEE ALSO: *Captain Marvel;* Double Indemnity; My Three Sons; *Wilder, Billy.*

BIBLIOGRAPHY

Parish, James Robert; Don E. Stanke; and Michael R. Pitts. *The All-Americans.* New Rochelle, NY: Arlington House, 1977.

Shipman, David. *The Great Movie Stars.* London: MacDonald, 1989.

Tranberg, Charles. *Fred MacMurray: A Biography.* Albany, GA: BearManor Media, 2007.

Macon, Uncle Dave *(1870–1952)*

Uncle Dave Macon, singer, songwriter, and banjo player, was one of the earliest pioneers of country music. Born in 1870 in Smart Station, Tennessee, David Harrison Macon grew up in Nashville in the boardinghouse run by his parents that was frequented by traveling vaudeville musicians. From them, Macon learned how to play the five-string banjo and numerous old folk songs. However, he grew up to earn his living in the hauling business and performed solely as an amateur at local events until he was discovered at the age of forty-eight by a talent scout for Loew's theaters. His success brought an invitation to join the new *Grand Ole Opry* radio show in Nashville in 1926, and he quickly became one of its most popular stars, both as a solo performer and with his band, the Fruit Jar Drinkers. "Uncle" Dave was a key link between traditional southern music and modern country music, introducing nineteenth-century folk styles to modern audiences with songs such as "Way down the Old Plank Road" and "Roll down the Line." He played until his death in 1952, and he is honored annually by the three-day festival Uncle Dave Macon Days in Murfreesboro, Tennessee, which features the National Old-Time Banjo Championship.

Timothy Berg

SEE ALSO: *Country Music; Folk Music;* Grand Ole Opry.

BIBLIOGRAPHY

Malone, Bill C. *Country Music U.S.A: A Fifty-Year History.* Austin: University of Texas Press, 1968.

Stambler, Irwin, and Grelun Landon. *Country Music: The Encyclopedia.* New York: St. Martin's Press, 1997.

Macy's

If New York City is the capital of American consumerism, then the Macy's department store is its White House. The self-proclaimed largest store in the world, Macy's has been located on Herald Square at 34th Street in Manhattan since 1902.

Though it now has retail outlets throughout the nation, the New York City store is a national landmark, its windows spectacularly decorated for the holidays. The Herald Square store has made Macy's an American tradition.

The role of Macy's in American culture has evolved remarkably since Zaccheus Macy and his family operated their first store on Nantucket Island. Throughout the late 1700s it filled the general needs of the whalers who shopped there. While the clothing selection has certainly changed, the retail structure that made Macy's work has remained in place.

Macy's obtained an unusual position of prominence among American retailers in 1926 when it began hosting New York City's Macy's Thanksgiving Day Parade. The huge balloons that hover over the Manhattan parade route provide an annual reminder of the store's influence. The events surrounding the parade have taken on lives of their own, from the filling of the mammoth balloons to the holders who have kept the five-story-high Big Bird under control. An episode of the television sitcom *Seinfeld* (1990–1998) was even shaped around the characters' interest in serving as holders in the parade.

Brian Black

SEE ALSO: *Consumerism; Department Stores; Parades;* Seinfeld*; Television.*

BIBLIOGRAPHY

Barmash, Isadore. *Macy's for Sale.* New York: Weidenfeld & Nicholson, 1989.

Grippo, Robert M. *Macy's: The Store, the Star, the Story.* Garden City Park, NY: Square One Publishers, 2009.

Trachtenberg, Jeffrey A. *The Rain on Macy's Parade: How Greed, Ambition, and Folly Ruined America's Greatest Store.* New York: Times Business, 1996.

MAD Magazine

The phenomenon of *MAD* began as a comic book that poked fun at other comic books but soon became a full-fledged magazine that poked fun at anything and everything. Although a product of the conservative, repressive 1950s, *MAD* was unique among contemporaneous periodicals—or any other media, for that matter—in its zeal to skewer sacred cows. Its satire, lampoons, put-ons, and take-offs, presented via phantasmagorically comical artwork, made *MAD* a particular success among younger readers. Between the *MAD* fans who came of age with a jaundiced view of the worlds of advertising, politics, and culture and the *MAD* fans who grew up and actually joined those worlds, the magazine can be said to have become an enormous influence on contemporary American society. Moreover, *MAD*'s influence on entertainment can be seen on everything from the television show *Laugh-In* to music videos on MTV. Unlike many magazines, *MAD* continued to thrive in the first decades of the twenty-first century.

EC COMICS

William M. Gaines (1922–1992), was the son of Max Gaines, publisher of comic books under the banner of "EC" or "Educational Comics." When Max died in a boating accident in 1947, William inherited the family business. Under the younger Gaines's supervision, Educational Comics was rechristened Entertaining Comics and would eventually become known primarily for a line of gritty comics featuring crime, war, science fiction, and—especially—horror.

In the midst of the McCarthy era, Gaines's new grisly books seemed shocking in comparison to other comics. Although there was dark humor in *Tales from the Crypt* and *The Vault of Horror*, EC's war comics—*Two-Fisted Tales* and *Frontline Combat*—distinguished themselves by a seriousness of purpose and a conscious desire to present a deglamorized view of warfare. As traditional comics became darker in tone during the late twentieth century—with Batman evolving into The Dark Knight and the plots and visuals of many comics resembling R-rated movies—such EC titles as *Tales from the Crypt* and *The Vault of Horror* no longer seemed controversial.

THE FIRST ISSUE

Harvey Kurtzman (1924–1993), the writer and editor of *Two-Fisted Tales* and *Frontline*, had been educated at New York's High School of Music and Art. When Kurtzman petitioned Gaines for an increase in income, Gaines, who had noted Kurtz-

MAD Magazine *Publisher William Gaines.* *MAD publisher William Gaines poses with a copy of the magazine in 1970.* **AP IMAGES.**

man's sly wit creeping into stories written for teen and Western titles, offered Kurtzman the opportunity to create a bimonthly humor book—a *comic* comic book. Although no one is certain how it came to be titled, the first issue of *Tales Calculated to Drive You MAD* was published in autumn of 1952. Kurtzman lampooned the comics he himself liked least, the crime and horror titles.

What immediately made *MAD* unique, aside from its irreverent, irrepressible spirit, was the way in which the text and art sparked a comic alchemy that neither could have achieved alone. When Kurtzman's stories were put together with the drawings of Will Elder and John Severin, Jack Davis and Wally Wood, the result resembled a cross between Hieronymous Bosch and the Borscht Belt: The comic frames were littered with visual and verbal non sequitors, and the distinct influence of Jewish humor was found on every page, exposing many impressionable middle-American children for the first time to Yiddish words like *furshlugginer*.

SATIRIZING POP CULTURE

The first issue of *MAD* was far from a success. But by the fourth issue—with its "Superduperman" parody of Superman—*MAD* started to gain popularity. Although Superman's owner, DC Comics, threatened to bring a lawsuit, nothing came of it. Thereafter, *MAD* lampooned and parodied many of the comics with which it shared newsstand rack space. America's typical teen, "Archie," became juvenile delinquent "Starchie." Donald Duck became Darnold Duck, finally wreaking his revenge against archrival, "Mickey Rodent." Wonder Woman became "Woman Wonder," whose boyfriend, Steve Adore, gets a prurient thrill whenever she changes into her super-heroine uniform inside her glass plane. Batman became "Bat Boy," and Robin became "Rubin," who discovered to his peril that his companion was "no furshlugginer ordinary bat boy," he was "a vampire bat boy." And virtually everybody else in comicdom became Melvin—"Melvin of the Apes," "Little Orphan Melvin," "Smilin' Melvin," and so forth.

Ever vigilant for new targets, Kurtzman and company cast a wider net and started giving the *MAD* treatment to television shows, with such parodies as "Dragged Net" and "Howdy Doit"; movies, with "Stalag 18," "Hah! Noon," "Ping Pong," and "From Eternity Back to Here." Classic literature did not escape Kurtzman's wit: he presented the poetry of Edgar Allan Poe and others verbatim but illustrated with incongruous lunacy by *MAD*'s artists. Kurtzman and company even had the audacity to tackle the Army-McCarthy hearings in "What's My Shine," which treated the controversial Senate proceedings as if they were a TV game show.

FROM COMIC BOOK TO MAGAZINE

Soon *MAD* was more popular with children and teens than some of the comics it had spoofed. Its unprecedented and unexpected success led to a host of imitators, none lasting more than a few issues. *MAD*'s popularity would eventually prove a lifesaver for Gaines, who, along with other comics publishers, began to come under fire in 1953 from journalists, social critics, and senators for his line of crime and horror comics. The upshot of all this unwelcome attention on the industry was the formation of the Comics Code Authority, which Gaines refused to join but which enacted a ban against certain words in comics—words such as *horror, terror*, and *crime*—words that provided Gaines's EC with 80 percent of its profits. Pressured by distributors, he eventually abandoned his horror titles. Since *MAD* was just about his only successful title left and since it did not conform to the Comics Code, Gaines came to an inevitable decision: upgrade *MAD* from comic book to magazine.

In 1955 *MAD* became a magazine, and Al Feldstein became its editor, following disputes between Kurtzman and Gaines. (Kurtzman went on to a long and eventually profitable association with Hugh Hefner.) As a magazine, *MAD* proved more popular than ever. Gracing its covers—usually painted by Kelly Freas—was the magazine's gap-toothed mascot, Alfred E. Neuman, aka the "What, Me Worry?" kid. The magazine continued to print comics and movie parodies but added guest contributions from such media notables as Ernie Kovacs, Bob and Ray, Jean Shepherd, and Danny Kaye. Nevertheless, the heart of the magazine was the material contributed by its staff writers, referred to on the masthead as "the usual gang of idiots." Anything on the American scene, from commerce to culture, was fair game. A parody of the latest hit movie might be juxtaposed with a *MAD* visit to the new phenomenon called supermarkets.

The magazine was filled with ads—none of them real, except the ones for *MAD* T-shirts and subscriptions. *MAD*'s policy of never accepting advertising bolstered its position as gadfly and debunker. When Salem Cigarettes, for example, had a slew of magazine and TV ads featuring young lovers in pastel, pastoral settings, *MAD* made its own pastel pastoral, in which a young couple was floating their "Sailem" cigarette packs on the burbling brook; the headline: "Sail 'em—don't inhale 'em!" Peppering each issue of *MAD* would be such nonsense words and catch phrases as *potrzebie*, "I had one grunch but the eggplant over there," and "It's crackers to slip a rozzer the dropsy in snide." When one reader's letter begged *MAD* to explain this last sentence, *MAD*'s editor helpfully replied: "'It's crackers to slip a rozzer the dropsy in snide' is good advice."

CULTURAL INFLUENCE

MAD's general tone of lunacy and irreverence proved infectious. To defend itself against a *MAD*-corrupted generation that had learned to be cynical about marketing ploys, Madison Avenue gradually came to produce more and more ads and commercials that were funny on purpose. It might not be a stretch to consider that those same ad-wary youngsters also grew up to take with a grain of salt the pronouncements of politicians—particularly those politicians who were trying to put those youngsters into uniform and pack them off to Vietnam.

If the *New Yorker* had the dark humor of Charles Addams, *MAD* had its "maddest artist," Don Martin, whose bizarre fantasies with lantern-jawed, flexible-footed figures became a staple of the magazine, as did Sergio Aragones's "Spy vs. Spy," which even became a computer game in the 1980s and was revived for game consoles in 2005. Aragones's creation was also featured in commercials for Mountain Dew. Considering the primacy of cartooning to *MAD*, it is curious and perhaps unfortunate that no attempt has ever been made to replicate the magazine as an animated film. *MAD*'s venture into the movies, *Up the Academy* (1980), was an embarrassing would-be imitation of *Animal House* (1978). On the other hand, an earlier project for the stage, *The MAD Show*, was a success in New York and on tour and has been cited as a precursor to the *Laugh-In* television series. Certainly some of the "mad" spirit has been invested into *Saturday Night Live* and *MAD TV*.

MAD has permeated American popular culture in many unexpected ways, even appearing on one of Fred Astaire's celebrated TV specials, in which Astaire danced a duet with Barrie Chase while wearing an Alfred E. Neuman mask. Even without Kurtzman and Gaines, *MAD* continued to be popular at the end of the twentieth century. Like the *New Yorker*, which made all its issues available on CD-ROM, in 2006 an *Absolutely MAD* DVD gathered more than 600 issues on one disc. In the twenty-first century *MAD Magazine* continues to delight new generations of youngsters around the world. Most of them, of course, eventually grow up—unlike *MAD*, the perpetual adolescent of periodicals.

Preston Neal Jones

SEE ALSO: *Advertising; Archie Comics; Army-McCarthy Hearings; Batman; Comics; DC Comics;* Dragnet*; EC Comics;* The Howdy Doody Show*;* Laugh-In*; The* New Yorker*; Pepsi-Cola;* Saturday Night Live*; Wonder Woman.*

BIBLIOGRAPHY

DeBartolo, Dick. *Good Days, and MAD: A Hysterical Tour Behind the Scenes at "MAD Magazine."* New York: Thunder's Mouth Press, 1994.

Jacobs, Frank. *The Mad World of William M. Gaines.* Secaucus, NJ: Lyle Stuart, 1972.

Jacobs, Frank. *The Incomplete History of MAD Comics.* Reprinted in *Tales Calculated to Drive You MAD.* New York: EC Publications, 1997–1999.

Jacobs, Frank. *MAD: Cover to Cover: 48 Years, 6 Months, and 3 Days of "MAD Magazine" Covers.* New York: Watson-Guptill, 2000.

Kurtzman, Harvey. *My Life as a Cartoonist.* New York: Pocket Books, 1988.

Reidelbach, Maria. *Completely MAD: A History of the Comic Book and Magazine.* Boston: Little, Brown, 1991.

Mad Men

Since its premier in July 2007, *Mad Men* has become one of the hottest and most critically acclaimed dramas on television. Created for the AMC channel by Matthew Weiner (a former writer and producer for the HBO series *The Sopranos*), the series probes the social, cultural, and political climate of mid-twentieth-century America through the lens of a New York advertising agency, the fictional Sterling Cooper (later Sterling Cooper Draper Pryce). In the world of the show, meticulously groomed white men in suits drink scotch and smoke cigarettes inside a high-rise building on Madison Avenue in New York, as they devise marketing campaigns for such corporations as Kodak, Playtex, and Heinz. Meanwhile, the world outside is rapidly changing due to the radical political and cultural upheavals that defined the 1960s—transforming both American society and the way the "Mad Men" appeal to the consumer imagination.

The central protagonist is Don Draper, the handsome, shrewd, and exceptionally talented creative director of a fictional Madison Avenue firm. A Korean War deserter who assumed his dead commander's identity, Draper has essentially conned his way into the 1950s dream: a powerful job in Manhattan, a beautiful and sophisticated wife, two kids, and a house in the suburbs. Still, Draper is a restless and domineering womanizer whose secret past keeps him quietly alienated from his family and the world around him.

Mad Men. *John Slattery, left, and Jon Hamm anchor the stylish period television drama* Mad Men.
AMC/THE KOBAL COLLECTION.

The first season of *Mad Men* immediately drew praise for its meticulous attention to period detail, its complex characters, and its representations of the events and movements of the era. In season one the 1960 presidential election between Richard M. Nixon and John F. Kennedy lurks in the background as Draper is courted by a rival agency. In the third season Draper's marriage to his wife, Betty, reaches a crisis just as President Kennedy is assassinated. And in seasons four and five, the historic influence of the Beatles manifests itself both in the plot (Don's daughter, Sally, wants to see the Fab Four at Shea Stadium) and in the soundtrack ("Tomorrow Never Knows" from Rubber Soul features prominently in one episode). The show has won multiple Emmy Awards for Outstanding Drama Series as well as for writing, hair design, casting, and art direction.

Mad Men is anchored by an outstanding ensemble cast. Draper is played by Jon Hamm, who went from being a struggling actor to a full-fledged star in a matter of months for his nuanced portrayal of a deeply flawed character. Draper's blond, picture-perfect wife, Betty, played by January Jones, is bored with her role as a housewife and is unsure how to cope with her sense of dissatisfaction. Elisabeth Moss plays Peggy Olson, an independent young woman from Catholic, working-class Brooklyn who starts as Draper's secretary but soon proves that she has the talent and drive to become the first female copywriter in the office. Christina Hendricks plays Joan Harris (later Holloway), the voluptuous, kittenish, and at once highly competent office manager, who is undone by the death of Marilyn Monroe in season two, apparently fearing a similar fate for herself. John Slattery plays Roger Sterling, a World War II veteran and wealthy philanderer who inherited his position as partner at the firm and regards the martini as a birthright but is facing his increasing irrelevance in the day-to-day business of handling accounts.

When the series opens, Draper is the rising star at Sterling Cooper, an established but small advertising firm whose most important customer is the Lucky Strike cigarette company. Draper continues working for the agency after it is bought out by a larger British firm, but when it changes hands yet again, he and a few select colleagues create a new agency, Sterling Cooper Draper Pryce. During this same time, Draper's secrets begin to unravel, his marriage crumbles, he develops a drinking problem, and he is forced to build a new life.

Mad Men was AMC's first original scripted series, and its success distinguished the cable channel as an outlet for high-quality series run by creators and producers with an auteur level of vision not typically seen on television. The success of this model led AMC to add other carefully crafted series to its repertoire, including *Breaking Bad*, *The Killing*, and *The Walking Dead*. The cost of producing these shows is higher than that of shows on other networks, leading AMC and the producers of *Mad Men* to become deadlocked in a protracted renewal negotiation that delayed the show's fifth season by more than one year.

The popularity of *Mad Men* has prompted a resurgence of interest in the culture of the early 1960s. The show is almost as well known for its fashion and interior design as it is for its writing and acting, and viewers have embraced the retro aesthetic of the show, even throwing *Mad Men*–themed parties. The program's 1960s setting inspired the settings of such big-budget films as *X-Men: First Class* (2011) as well as such television shows as *Pan Am* and *The Playboy Club*, which have attempted to ride the coattails of *Mad Men*'s success. The show has also encouraged more networks to take risks on high-quality and high-concept shows by demonstrating that a series that asks a lot of its viewers intellectually and emotionally can find an enthusiastic and wide audience.

Adrienne Furness

SEE ALSO: *Advertising; Cable TV; Emmy Awards; Kennedy Assassination; The Martini; Monroe, Marilyn; Television; The X-Men.*

BIBLIOGRAPHY

Gordon, Devin. "The Men of Summer; No *House*? No *Lost*? No Sweat. This Is Basic-Cable Season, and AMC's *Mad Men* Is Its Must-See TV." *Newsweek*, July 16, 2007, 56.

Kaplan, Fred. "Drama Confronts a Dramatic Decade." *New York Times*, August 6, 2009.

Stanley, Alessandra. "Back to Work for *Mad Men*." *New York Times*, July 16, 2010.

Madden, John *(1936–)*

John Madden is easily identifiable to several generations of football fans. To those who grew up watching football in the 1960s and 1970s, Madden is best remembered as the fiery, extremely successful coach of the Oakland Raiders. To those who first began watching football in the 1980s, he is the colorful commentator who can explain the most complicated football in layman's terms. To children of the 1990s and later, Madden is the name behind a popular football video game. But Madden has been more than a coach-turned-broadcaster-turned-promoter: He has literally *taught* the game for several decades.

EARLY LIFE

Born in 1936 in Minnesota, Madden and his family moved to the San Francisco suburb of Daly City, California, when John was five. In high school he excelled in baseball and football. He then played the latter as a two-way tackle at California Polytechnic College, San Luis Obispo (Cal Poly), in 1957–1958, earning all-conference honors. Madden was drafted by the Philadelphia Eagles in the twenty-first round of the 1958 National Football League (NFL) draft, but his playing career ended shortly afterward because of a knee injury. Rather than immediately return to California, Madden remained in Philadelphia, where he learned the basics of football from the Eagles quarterback Norm Van Brocklin.

Madden eventually returned to California, where he earned a bachelor's degree in 1959 and a master's degree in 1961 from Cal Poly. From 1960 to 1963, he coached at California's Hancock Junior College, first as an assistant and then later as head coach. From 1964 to 1966, he worked with famed coach Don Coryell as defensive coordinator for the Aztecs of San Diego State College, then the number-one small-college team in the nation.

COACHING CAREER

In 1967 Madden accepted a job as the linebacker coach for the Oakland Raiders of the American Football League (AFL). Two years later, at the age of thirty-two, he became the Raiders' head coach, the youngest in AFL history. He took his team to the

AFL championship game in his first season but lost to the Kansas City Chiefs. In 1970 the AFL merged into the NFL, with Oakland playing in the Western Division in the new American Football Conference (AFC). During the next nine seasons, Madden's Raiders won the AFC West seven times. In 1977 Madden led his team to a 32–14 victory over the Minnesota Vikings in Super Bowl XI, becoming the youngest coach to win a Super Bowl. For his efforts, he was named Coach of the Year by the Washington (D.C.) Touchdown Club. Following the 1978 season, Madden retired from coaching.

John Madden's ten-year professional coaching career was one of the more notable in football history. He compiled an impressive record of 112–39–7 (.731). His offensive line was replete with Hall of Famers: Jim Otto, Gene Upshaw, and Art Shell are all enshrined at Canton, Ohio. On the sidelines, Madden was easily identifiable. Vocal and emotional, the six-foot-four, 270-pound, redheaded Madden could often be seen ranting, raving, and flailing his arms, often at the referees. Moreover, Madden coached at a time when the AFL/AFC was trying to gain legitimacy in the eyes of the older, more-storied NFL/National Football Conference (NFC). Madden's success contributed to a new respect for the junior conference.

John Madden. *John Madden coaches the Oakland Raiders to victory in Super Bowl XI in January 1977.* **FOCUS ON SPORT/CONTRIBUTOR/GETTY IMAGES SPORT/GETTY IMAGES.**

BROADCASTING CAREER

In 1980 Madden took his enthusiasm for football into the broadcasting booth with CBS Sports. He quickly became one of football's more popular commentator-analysts—and certainly its most animated. Madden also employed a now-famous on-screen chalkboard, on which he explained plays to the viewers. In 1981 Pat Summerall joined the broadcast team; he and Madden ultimately would work together for twenty-one seasons. In 1994 Madden switched networks, inking a four-year, $32 million contract with Fox, a lucrative deal that, at the time, surpassed any NFL player's contract. In 2002 Madden left Fox to become a commentator on ABC's *Monday Night Football*, and in 2005 he began to do color commentary for NBC's *Sunday Night Football.* Madden retired from television sportscasting on April 16, 2009, with the simple explanation, "It's time." However, he continued to do a brief daily chat on KCBS radio in San Francisco each morning.

Madden won sixteen Outstanding Sports Personality/Analyst Emmy Awards between 1982 and 2009. He has also received the Touchdown Club of America's Golden Mike Award, as well as twice being named the Sports Personality of the Year by the American Sportscasters Association. The Pro Football Hall of Fame bestowed upon Madden the Pete Rozelle Radio-Television Award in 2002, and he was inducted into the Hall of Fame in 2006.

MADDEN'S TALENTS

Madden is not just another coach-turned-broadcaster. His unique talent lies in his ability to translate his infinite football wisdom into language intelligible to the average home viewer. While many commentators and pregame shows analyze the details of the game, Madden praised the grimy and gritty hustle of players. He continues to name an annual "All-Madden Team" to honor the roughest, meanest, fiercest, and most competitive players. He also inaugurated the tradition of handing out a "game turkey" to the most deserving player at the annual Thanksgiving Day game. Madden's "just one of the boys" image has contributed in part to his status as a football icon.

Madden is also known for his well-publicized fear of flying. During his coaching career, he flew because practice schedules and time constraints demanded it. His broadcasting career, though, afforded him more time to travel from game to game. Initially he traveled via train, but then Greyhound provided him with a custom-built bus known as the Madden Cruiser. From the Madden Cruiser, the burly broadcaster often held pregame tailgating parties, yet another reason he is a fan favorite.

THE VIDEO GAME

Despite all of these talents and successes, Madden is probably best known to his younger fans for something that happened off the gridiron: EA Sportsline's best-selling football video game. The game was known as *John Madden Football* until 1993, when EA Sportsline received permission from the NFL to use the names of NFL teams and players. The new version of the game, called *Madden NFL*, features players and coaches from actual NFL teams, realistic playbooks and up-to-date player stats, and voice commentary recorded by Madden and other professional NFL commentators. One of the first and most successful sports simulation video games, *Madden NFL* sold more than eighty-five million copies by 2010, amounting to more than $3 billion in sales. In addition to the video game, Madden also endorses several other products, including Ace Hardware, Outback Steakhouse, and Dr Pepper. He has also written several books.

As a coach, commentator, and video game endorser, John Madden has brought football to generations of fans in an entertaining yet highly intelligent manner. He is a proven teacher of athletes and spectators alike. In essence, Madden has been the football coach for the common person.

Matt Kerr

SEE ALSO: *College Football; Computer Games; Greyhound Buses;* Monday Night Football*; National Football League (NFL); The Oakland Raiders; Professional Football; Super Bowl; Video Games.*

BIBLIOGRAPHY

Madden, John, with Dave Anderson. *Hey, Wait a Minute, I Wrote a Book.* New York: Villard, 1984.

Madden, John, with Dave Anderson. *One Knee Equals Two Feet.* New York: Villard, 1986.

Madden, John, with Dave Anderson. *One Size Doesn't Fit All.* New York: Villard, 1988.

Madden, John, with Dave Anderson. *All Madden: Hey, I'm Talking Pro Football!.* New York: HarperCollins, 1996.

Maddow, Rachel *(1973–)*

During the first decade of the 2000s Rachel Maddow emerged as one of America's leading liberal commentators. She first gained recognition as the host of a radio show on Air America in 2004. Four years later Maddow became the first openly gay host of a prime-time news program, *The Rachel Maddow Show* (2008–), a beacon for progressive news that airs on MSNBC.

Maddow has established herself as an anchor in an arena dominated by white men. Her success has helped bring younger views into the news fold. As Julia Baird noted in *Newsweek*, "Maddow seems to have genuinely charmed younger viewers, a Twitter-savvy, podcasting generation that has hankered for someone more like them."

Rachel Anne Maddow was born April 1, 1973, in Castro Valley, California. Her father was a U.S. Air Force captain who became a civilian lawyer, while her mother served as school administrator. Maddow earned a degree from Stanford University in public policy. During her college years she came out as a lesbian and later worked with ACT UP, an AIDS-awareness group. In 1994 she became the first openly gay American to receive a Rhodes scholarship, eventually receiving a doctorate in politics from Oxford University.

While finishing her dissertation in Northampton, Massachusetts, Maddow heard an announcement about open auditions at a local radio station. She won the contest and became the cohost of WRNX-FM's morning show, *Dave in the Morning*. She later hosted *Big Breakfast* on another Northampton radio station. In March 2004 Maddow joined the national Air America network, cohosting the series *Unfiltered* with *Daily Show* cocreator Lizz Winstead and rapper Chuck D. Two weeks after *Unfiltered* was canceled in April 2005, Maddow was given her own program, *The Rachel Maddow Show* (2005–2010), which became a hit for Air America.

In 2005 Maddow added cable television news to her résumé, joining MSNBC as a liberal counterpart to the conservative Tucker Carlson on his show *Tucker* (2005–2008). She also served as a guest commentator on other cable news shows. In 2008 Maddow signed an exclusive contract with MSNBC as a political analyst and was prominent during the channel's election coverage. She appeared regularly on *Countdown with Keith Olbermann* (2003–2011) and, because of their political compatibility, was asked to guest host for him. In July 2008 she successfully filled in when Olbermann was on vacation, connecting especially with younger viewers.

In September 2008 Maddow was given her own time slot on MSNBC at 9 p.m. *The Rachel Maddow Show* followed *Countdown* and provided a two-show lineup for liberal viewers. Maddow's program was an immediate critical and popular success, often beating CNN's iconic Larry King in the ratings. Unlike many cable news personalities, Maddow eschews aggressiveness and hectoring. As Alessandra Stanley of the *New York Times* has observed, "Her program adds a good-humored female face to a cable news channel whose prime time is dominated by unruly, often squabbling schoolboys."

The Rachel Maddow Show is presented live from New York City and is a combination of political analysis and lighter pop-culture reports. She has established continuing segments to bring structure to her nightly news show. In the "Rachel Re" segment the host offers a detailed examination of a given topic and often displays her academic prowess. In "Debunktion Junction" she tries to bring some factual reporting to murky political matters. In "Talk Me Down" she discusses a single troubling issue, inviting an expert to elaborate. Her "Ms. Information" segment presents stories that have been underreported by the mainstream press.

Maddow's show also contains some fun and humorous elements that appeal to her younger viewers. In "Moment of Geek" she explains some puzzling developments in science and math. Her "Just Enough" segments survey the byways of popular culture and entertainment. In the relaxing "Cocktail Moment," Maddow, playing bartender, concocts such drinks as the Sidecar and the Old Fashioned.

Maddow is not a doctrinaire liberal and has been able to build bridges with people who have alternate viewpoints. She has praised and criticized President Barack Obama, especially questioning his war strategy and detention policies. She has also been welcoming of many conservative voices, notably pundit Pat Buchanan and Michael Steele, former chairman of the Republican National Committee. The president of Fox News, Roger Ailes, has even praised Maddow's book *Drift: The Unmooring of American Military Power* (2012).

After the departure of Olbermann from MSNBC in January 2011, Maddow became the channel's leading anchor, attracting more than a million people nightly. In 2011 she received a News and Documentary Emmy for her analysis. Maddow has also been recognized by the GLAAD Media Awards for her reporting. She claims, however, to be uncomfortable with her celebrity and to be more interested in "connecting the dots in a story."

Ron Simon

SEE ALSO: *AIDS; Cable TV; Chuck D; Emmy Awards; Fox News Channel; King, Larry; Lesbianism; Obama, Barack; Radio; Talk Radio; Television; Television Anchors.*

BIBLIOGRAPHY

Baird, Julia. "When Left Is Right." *Newsweek*, November 21, 2008.

Freeman, Hadley. "Rachel Maddow: 'I'm Definitely Not an Autocutie.'" *Guardian* (London), April 24, 2011.

Guthrie, Marisa. "Rachel Maddow: How This Wonky-Tonk Woman Won TV." *Hollywood Reporter*, October 5, 2011.

Maddow, Rachel. *Drift: The Unmooring of American Military Power*. New York: Crown Publishing, 2012.

Stanley, Alessandra. "A Fresh Female Face amid Cable Schoolboys." *New York Times*, September 24, 2008.

Made-for-Television Movies

Conceived in the 1960s as an inexpensive way to fill time in a network's schedule, the made-for-television movie has since grown into a staple of network and cable television programming. More made-for-television movies are broadcast on network television each year than movies are released in theaters, and cable channels such as USA Network, Lifetime, and HBO all rely heavily on their own original movies to attract audiences. Although there are inadequacies inherent in the television movie formula—budgets are lower than for theatrical releases, commercial interruptions are distracting, and the television medium is more likely to restrict content than is the motion picture—made-for-television movies have risen in quality and critical acclaim over the years. A made-for-television movie can be quite prestigious, justifiably attracting large audiences among television viewers who are looking for material they might not find elsewhere.

DEBUT OF THE MADE-FOR-TELEVISION MOVIE

The Killers, a 1964 picture directed by Don Siegel and a remake of the 1946 film noir of the same name, was supposed to be the first made-for-television movie. However, upon completion, the movie was deemed too violent to be shown on television and was released theatrically. Instead, *See How They Run*, a thriller about three children being pursued by hit men, became the first made-for-television film, airing on NBC in October 1964. Both *The Killers* and *See How They Run* were produced by Universal Studios, the company that pioneered the made-for-television concept and initially produced the vast majority of such movies.

The studio saw four advantages to producing made-for-television movies: Many of its television movies also doubled as pilots for future series—*Dragnet* (1951–1959), *Ironside* (1967–1975), *Marcus Welby, M.D.* (1969–1976), *The Outsider* (1968–1969), *The Name of the Game* (1968–1971), *Rod Serling's Night Gallery* (1969–1973), and *Columbo* (1971–1978, 1989–2003) were all introduced by Universal in this way (as were *Hawaii Five-O* [1968–1980] and *Medical Center* [1969–1976], though not by Universal). Made-for-television movies could also be released theatrically in other countries—something Universal frequently did with great financial success. An above-average movie designated for television could easily be diverted to American theaters instead, and some of Universal's television movies were remakes of its older films, which meant the studio could reuse props, costumes, and sets (the second made-for-television movie, for example, *The Hanged Man* [1964], was a remake of *Ride the Pink Horse* [1947]).

By 1969 the television movie had become so popular that ABC scheduled *The Movie of the Week*, a series of films made specifically for television. At that time suspense and comedy films dominated; later, movies about social problems became standard. Male leads were commonplace, usually middle-aged performers who had enjoyed successful television careers in the 1950s and 1960s; performers such as John Forsythe, Robert Stack, and Lloyd Bridges became frequent television movie stars. *The Movie of the Week* itself ran for only ninety minutes, with commercials, meaning that the average ABC made-for-television movie was less than an hour and fifteen minutes long. Two-hour movies were still common, however, and *Vanished*—produced by Universal from Fletcher Knebel's political thriller—ran for two consecutive nights in March 1971 for a total of four hours, the first multipart made-for-television movie.

Other noteworthy television movies of this period include *My Sweet Charlie* (1970), a film about a close friendship between a black attorney and a pregnant white woman—a role that won Patty Duke the first Emmy ever given to a made-for-television movie; *Brian's Song* (1971), about Chicago Bears running back Brian Piccolo and his death from cancer; *That Certain Summer* (1972), a sensitive depiction of homosexuality; and *The Night Stalker* (1972), which starred Darren McGavin as reporter Carl Kolchak, who discovers a vampire is loose in Las Vegas. *The Night Stalker* became the highest-rated made-for-television movie to date when it aired, and it is still one of the highest-rated television movies ever made, as well as being the acknowledged inspiration for *The X-Files* (1993–2002).

ADDING A LITTLE MYSTERY

NBC developed a slight variation of the made-for-television movie in 1971 when it introduced *The NBC Mystery Movie*. This was a rotating series of television movies with recurring characters, meaning that each series would be seen once every three or four weeks. When *The NBC Mystery Movie* began, it consisted of *Columbo*, *McMillan & Wife*, and *McCloud*. All three programs were produced by Universal, and all three had appeared previously as made-for-television movies. NBC added a second *Mystery Movie* the next year with three new rotating series: *Madigan*, *Cool Million*, and *Banacek*. Over the next five years, many other programs appeared as part of the *Mystery Movie* series of television movies, none of them as successful as the original three. The rotating television movie format remained popular and was still in use in the 1990s.

In the late 1970s the content of made-for-television movies changed somewhat; female stars became more common, and movies began to tackle serious social issues. Elizabeth Montgomery emerged as the "Queen of TV movies" with her frequent appearances in the 1970s and 1980s; she starred in twenty-two television movies before her death in 1995. (Montgomery's primary competition for television movie queen is Jane Seymour, who had roles in thirty-nine made-for-television movies or miniseries by 1998; other contenders include Melissa Gilbert with thirty-five, Meredith Baxter with thirty-four, Cheryl Ladd with twenty-seven, and Jaclyn Smith with twenty-five.)

Perhaps the most acclaimed "social problem" made-for-television movie was *Sybil* (1976), the story of a multiple-personality victim for which actress Sally Field won an Emmy. Other television movies addressed spousal abuse (*Battered* [1978], *Intimate Strangers* [1977]); rape (*A Case of Rape* [1974]); and the physically challenged (*Special Olympics* [1978]). One of the most influential of the social dramas was *Walking through the Fire*, a 1979 made-for-television movie about a woman with Hodgkin's disease. The success of this movie inspired many similar television films in the 1980s—sardonically referred to as "disease of the week" movies by some critics. In addition to the social problem films of this period, there were many quality literary adaptations in the late 1970s, among them *The Last of the Mohicans* (1975); *Captains Courageous* (1977); and *Too Far to Go* (1979), based on a series of John Updike stories. Many of the literary adaptations were produced by Hallmark Cards as part of its *Hallmark Hall of Fame* series.

Not all television movies of the late 1970s were serious dramas. A generally escapist air permeated network television during this period, and many television movies of the late 1970s reflected that escapism. Action movies were fairly common; supernatural thrillers appeared occasionally; and the success of *Charlie's Angels* (1976), a television movie before it was a series, led to several "jiggle" movies. Typical movies of the time included *Exo-Man* (1977); *Sex and the Married Woman* (1977); *The Spell* (1977); *The Initiation of Sarah* (1978); *Gold of the Amazon Women* (1979); *Institute for Revenge* (1979); *The Seeding of Sarah Burns* (1979); and the highest-rated made-for-television movie of the 1978–1979 season, *Dallas Cowboy Cheerleaders*, one of the first television movies to generate a sequel. Even some of the social problem dramas relied heavily on sensationalism; *Little Ladies of the Night* (1977), a movie about teen prostitutes that remains one of the highest-rated television movies of all time, spent more time showing its cast in various stages of undress than it did addressing the problem of prostitution.

Another trend emerging in the 1970s was the television series revival. *The Many Loves of Dobie Gillis* (1959–1963), *Gilligan's Island* (1964–1967), and *The Mod Squad* (1968–1973) all were revived as television movies in the 1970s, a practice now quite common. A surprise success in 1979 was the television movie *Elvis*; airing against *Gone with the Wind* and *One Flew over the Cuckoo's Nest*, the dramatization of the life of Elvis Presley drew bigger audiences than either of the other movies. During the 1978–1979 television season, more television movies aired on the three major television networks than were released in theaters. A decade later the ratio of television movies to theatrical movies was almost three to one.

SERIOUS DRAMAS

The increasing trend toward serious drama resulted in two particularly controversial made-for-television movies in the early 1980s. *The Day After* (1983) depicts a nuclear war (and its aftermath) between the United States and the Soviet Union. The film was the subject of much debate before it even aired: some teachers and ministers encouraged families to watch it together and discuss it, nuclear freeze supporters applauded ABC's decision to air the film, and conservative critics feared that it might lead to a relaxed stance toward the Soviets. The movie did become the highest-rated television movie to that date and remains one of the highest-rated movies, television or theatrical, ever broadcast. *Something about Amelia* (1984) focuses on a teenage girl who suffers from an incestuous relationship with her father. The film was rather frank and certainly not innocuous family fare; the casting of *Cheers* star Ted Danson as the father shocked some viewers. Television movies had certainly matured since their introduction in 1964; indeed, some critics argued that one was more likely to find rewarding drama on television than at the movie theater.

As HBO and other cable channels recognized the need for original programming, they also began making television movies. The first cable television movie, *The Terry Fox Story*, was made for HBO in 1983. Today that cable channel makes dozens of television movies each year, as does its rival, Showtime. HBO in particular has undertaken some ambitious projects, including a biography of Joseph Stalin starring Robert Duvall and an adaptation of Randy Shilts's history of AIDS research, *And the Band Played On* (1993). It has also continued the tradition of social-issue movies with productions such as *If These Walls Could Talk* (1996), which chronicles the abortion-related experiences of women from three different generations, and *Temple Grandin* (2010), which is about an autistic woman who becomes a scientist in the humane livestock handling industry.

Among basic cable channels, the USA Network is the largest producer of made-for-television movies. USA has been making original movies since 1989. The Disney Channel found success with the made-for-television movie musical in *High School Musical* (2006), which spawned two sequels, whereas the Lifetime Channel specialized in producing movies for women audiences. Because of the proliferation of cable stations, the television movie remained as ubiquitous in the early twenty-first century as ever before.

Randall Clark

SEE ALSO: *Abortion; AIDS; Cable TV; Cancer;* Charlie's Angels*;* Cheers*; The Chicago Bears;* Columbo*; The Dallas Cowboys; Disney (Walt Disney Company); Dobie Gillis;* Dragnet*; Duvall, Robert; Emmy Awards; Field, Sally; Film Noir; Gay Men;* Gilligan's Island*;* Gone with the Wind*;* Hallmark Hall of Fame*;* Hawaii Five-O*;* High School Musical*;* Holocaust*; Las Vegas; Leisure Time;* Marcus Welby, M.D.*;* The Mod Squad*; Movie Stars; The Musical;* One Flew over the Cuckoo's Nest*; Presley, Elvis; Special Olympics; Television; Updike, John; War Movies;* The X-Files.

BIBLIOGRAPHY

Karol, Michael. *The ABC Movie of the Week Companion: A Loving Tribute to the Classic Series.* New York: iUniverse, 2008.

Marill, Alvin H., and Leonard Maltin. *Movies Made for Television: 1964–2004.* Lanham, MD: Scarecrow Press, 2005.

Madonna *(1958–)*

In late 1983 an unfamiliar, high, piercing female voice emerged on American pop radio with increasing and puzzling frequency. Shortly thereafter, a sexually obsessed, self-involved, and irregularly clad young woman writhed on music video screens in homes and in dance clubs in urban areas across the United States imploring "Everybody" to dance her dance of liberation. The intriguing figure with the jarring voice turned out to be a white neo-disco singer who frequented the bohemian enclaves of Lower Manhattan during the early 1980s, seemingly just trying to make it in show business. When asked her real ambition, the young woman told a stunned Dick Clark: "To rule the world." Madonna Louise Ciccone meant it. Over the course of the next decade, the self-proclaimed "boy toy" fought to dominate every corner of the entertainment world with seductive films, consistently successful music, and disturbingly magnetic public gestures, while at the same time expressing a more generous desire to convert everyone to her cause of personal freedom.

Madonna's rise to world domination did not come in a vacuum. The Bay City, Michigan, native first appeared as a mere aftershock to a series of large and small pop explosions that rocked the music world during the 1980s. After Michael Jackson's thunderous transformation from former child prodigy to Elvis-sized icon, the next tremor came from thirtyish female singer Cyndi Lauper, who couched her broad-based feminism in a cloak of gentle weirdness and cute, cuddly charm. Lauper was soon swept aside by the triumph of the young black musician, writer, producer, and singer from Minneapolis named Prince, who pushed an ethos of sex as salvation in his film *Purple Rain*.

While Prince had been performing and fomenting nervous unrest over his themes of overt sexuality at his Warner Brothers record label for several years, it wasn't until he found his place in the post-Jackson hysteria that he crossed over to the mainstream. Not long after Prince's biggest pop moment, the nearly middle-aged blue-collar rocker Bruce Springsteen found himself sucked into the post-*Thriller* whirlwind. Unlike artists like Prince, Jackson, and Elvis Presley, whose fame appeared to cause them personal strife, Madonna seemed especially capable of handling her own rise to celebrity.

***Madonna in* Desperately Seeking Susan.** *Madonna set a fashion trend with her trademark look in the 1985 movie* Desperately Seeking Susan. **ORION/THE KOBAL COLLECTION/RITTS, HERB.**

EARLY YEARS

Madonna had a bittersweet childhood in a suburban town in Michigan, losing her mother to breast cancer when Madonna was five years old. As a young adult, she left her studies at the University of Michigan to pursue her career with vigor in New York. Apparently impervious to most criticism, Madonna trusted her own instincts as she embarked on her own path.

Madonna's initial acceptance by the critical mainstream of rock was, to say the least, chilly. She originally appeared too glossy, too egocentric for the Left-leaning, humanist rock critical establishment. It was easy for such critics to like Prince—himself a sexually obsessed, egocentric male ex-disco singer. He was described as "daring" and "challenging." He too had a decidedly less than charming voice and was capable of producing glossy records, yet his violence and machismo saved him from the scorn experienced by Madonna. Even his desire to leave R&B behind—in favor of a rock style so whitened that MTV played his videos before they would touch those of the "too black" Jackson—earned him immediate praise as another great barrier smasher in the rock pantheon. Prince was the critics' darling years before he hit it really big.

That Madonna accomplished similar maneuvers from the opposite direction initially earned her derision. When the general music-buying and listening public connected immediately with her, the dissenters wrote her off as a concoction of pure music-biz hype. By early 1985, however, this became an increasingly laborious task. After Madonna's first single, "Everybody," crossed over from the dance charts to the Billboard Hot 100 and her first and second albums, *Madonna* and *Like a Virgin*, had become the latest post-*Thriller* sensations, she demanded some serious attention.

A NEW SENSATION

Madonna is the one performer of all those caught in the mid-1980s pop mania who used it successfully to make her point. She relished the massive attention, knew how to use it to further her personal and artistic interests, and had no other ambition than to dominate popular entertainment for as long as possible. If it meant hiring Jackson's manager, she did that; if it meant creating disconcerting publicity stunts that deliberately subverted religious, sexual, and racial mores, she also did that. "Unlike the others, I'd do anything / I'm not the same; I have no shame," she sang in "Burning Up," a single from *Madonna*. She courted mass attention, and her pursuit of it became an essential part of her presentation. Madonna quickly found her voice, and it was and remained for a long time a dead-on connection with her audience. Her work needed no further justification. Her personal striving, at first glance so redolent of a 1980s Reagan-era ethic, contrasted intriguingly with her clear intent to share this sense of limitless possibility with her largely adolescent female audience.

Even as Madonna achieved sensation status, she continued to have critics. *Rolling Stone* magazine accused her of having "one guiding emotion: ambition." While it is difficult to recall any male rocker taken to task for committing that particular infraction, the magazine leveled a worse claim: that she had "used her boyfriends" in her climb to the top. "The men who have gotten close to her—tough guys a lot of them—have gotten their hearts broken as often as not." Unlike many other women, Madonna seemed aware of and able to use her sexuality to further her own ideas.

As her popularity increased, many tried to find comparisons and influences. Some tried to equate Madonna to Marilyn Monroe, especially given the 1984 "Material Girl" video, with her take on "Diamonds Are a Girl's Best Friend." But Madonna soon made it clear that she was really nothing at all like Monroe. Madonna projected an image of the self-possessed woman who will get out of life exactly what she wants regardless of what any man might want her to be. She conveyed a strength of will rarely matched by any other pop singer, woman or man.

Madonna had the ability to stir violent emotions. As the years progressed, she used this ability in increasingly daring ways. In one particularly audacious episode, she used a 1989 video for the song "Like a Prayer" (also featured in a simultaneously released Pepsi-Cola commercial) to create a firestorm of barely suppressed racial and sexual anxiety. The video depicts a black man being crucified for trying to save a white woman from a gang of white rapists. Catholics were outraged, and Pepsi pulled the more innocuous ad. With 1986's "Papa Don't Preach," she offers an unorthodox pro-choice message rejecting abortion as her personal choice. In another 1986 video, Madonna plays with a more serious taboo, depicting a prepubescent boy lusting after the sexually potent female pop star. In the early 1990s her video for "Justify My Love" was banned from MTV because of its graphic sexual content, leading to an interrogation of sorts on ABC's *Nightline*. People were either attracted to her or violently repulsed by her. Some even felt themselves pulled in both directions at once.

But in her 1991 rockumentary *Truth or Dare*, Madonna seemed to lose her focus and simply tried to create controversy for its own sake. And though her book called, simply, *Sex*, featured a series of sexually explicit and sexually violent photographs, its publication elicited indifference instead of outrage. It wasn't that she went too far, as some thought; it was more that she seemed to be going in circles, trapped in her own idea of her cultural significance.

STAYING POWER

She did recover from the episode and continued to have consistent success during the mid- to late 1990s, a time when many artists were having trouble selling records. By century's end, it was clear for the first time that perhaps Madonna's music was what mattered most of all. It did not take her long to recoup and redouble her efforts in this area. When she made films, she seriously considered the music. Her part in *Evita* (1996) remains a musical triumph before it is anything else. Despite her more controlled public presence after the birth of her first daughter in 1996 and her much-publicized conversion to the mystical Jewish tradition of Kabbalah, Madonna's defiance, her shameless sexuality, her basic honesty of spirit, as well as her ambition, continued to permeate her music. Her seventh studio album, *Ray of Light* (1998), was universally praised and garnered four Grammy Awards, confirming that she had created an indomitable radio presence that, by the late 1990s, never entirely subsided.

In 2000 Madonna released the electronica-inspired album *Music*, which became her most successful offering in more than a decade. She earned another Grammy for *Confessions on a Dance Floor* in 2006, was inducted into the Rock and Roll Hall of Fame in 2008, and performed at the Super Bowl in 2012. Also during this period she published a set of five children's books, adopted a young Malawian child, signed a $120 million contract with concert promoter Live Nation, wrote and directed two full-length films, engaged in commercial ventures ranging from clothing lines to fitness centers, and married and divorced acclaimed film director Guy Ritchie. In short, the Material Girl continued to command the world's attention in the twenty-first century, despite increased competition from her (much younger) imitators such as Lady Gaga, Nicki Minaj, and Ke$ha.

During her rise to fame, Madonna resisted the censure of some traditionalist feminists who insisted her embrace of pure sexuality was counterproductive, and she continued to wear her boy-toy belt buckle beneath her bare navel in the face of resentment on the part of sexists and ultraconservatives. But beginning in the 1990s, Madonna became the new darling of young feminists who found her work to be a sophisticated critique of post-1970s patriarchy. Young academics padded their curricula vitae with their Madonna studies, and this too became a point of controversy among conservative cultural critics. While this is unusual in pop music, it is not unheard of in pop culture; Mae West put across a similar persona in much tougher times. Lauper appealed to a mass audience because she was simply able to cut her feminism with an endearing weirdness and cuddliness. Madonna was never cuddly or weird—merely provocative.

Madonna carried this defiance right into her singing. Although critics always questioned her talent, her longevity proved the cynics wrong. Madonna's singing is not formally soulful, not tasteful, perhaps not entirely pleasant. Her voice cuts right through a song so that the listener is forced to either engage with her words and melodies or be repelled enough to turn her off—the voice's very offensiveness is absolutely essential to its power. In this she has perhaps more in common with punk originator Johnny Rotten than with master vocalists such as Jackson, Sam Cooke, Tammi Terrell, or any of a number of others. The sharp, childlike, high and husky tones communicate all the sexuality, violence, self-possession, and extreme confidence of the image she projects. In her music, the image, the ideas, the voice are all a totality, inseparable.

Madonna sums up her achievement in "Dress You Up," an early single and video in which she clarifies the breadth, contradiction, and ultimate scope of her ambition. In the video we see what at first appears to be typical rockumentary preconcert footage of young fans, dressed as Madonna, excitedly heading for a concert. Unlike similar "live concert" videos that appeared at this time, there is nothing self-congratulatory about this one. Madonna's projection here, as elsewhere, is essentially about freedom—personal freedom, freedom of expression, perhaps most importantly a freedom from fear. Critic Dave Marsh pointed out early on in his *Rock and Roll Confidential* newsletter that while Lauper sang of girls who want to have fun, Madonna was a girl actually having fun without regard for the consequences. The consequences are, of course, of great importance, but even after three decades in the music industry, Madonna had not solved the riddles of all that divides and unites men and women. What she did was to sweep aside some limiting barriers to understanding what such freedoms might be about, and she just so happened to become the top-selling female artist in history in the process.

Robin Markowitz

SEE ALSO: *Clark, Dick; Cooke, Sam; Disco; Feminism; Grammy Awards; Jackson, Michael; Ke$ha; Lady Gaga; Lauper, Cyndi; Monroe, Marilyn; MTV;* Nightline; *Pepsi-Cola; Presley, Elvis; Prince; Rock and Roll;* Rolling Stone*; Springsteen, Bruce; Super Bowl; Videos; West, Mae.*

BIBLIOGRAPHY

Andersen, Christopher P. *Madonna: Unauthorized.* New York: Simon & Schuster, 1991.

Ciccone, Christopher, and Wendy Leigh. *Life with My Sister Madonna.* New York: Simon Spotlight Entertainment, 2008.

Cross, Mary. *Madonna: A Biography.* Westport, CT: Greenwood Press, 2007.

Editors of *Rolling Stone. Madonna: The "Rolling Stone" Files: The Ultimate Compendium of Interviews, Articles, Facts, and Opinions from the Files of "Rolling Stone."* New York: Hyperion, 1997.

Metz, Allan, and Carol Benson, eds. *The Madonna Companion: Two Decades of Commentary.* New York: Schirmer Books, 1999.

Miklitsch, Robert. *From Hegel to Madonna: Towards a General Economy of "Commodity Fetishism."* Albany: State University of New York Press, 1998.

Morton, Andrew. *Madonna.* New York: St. Martin's Press, 2001.

O'Brien, Lucy. *Madonna: Like an Icon.* New York, HarperEntertainment, 2007.

Mafia/Organized Crime

Since the 1920s the Mafia, and organized crime in general, has captured the popular imagination. Bank robbers, bootleggers, and Mafia dons have received considerable press, not all unfavorable. Cast as antiheroes, fictional mobsters such as Vito Corleone and real crime bosses such as Al Capone and John Gotti have often been portrayed in a sympathetic light. Drawn with a romantic touch, literary and cinematic mafiosi have been depicted as honorable men in their own fashion, and their luxurious lifestyles have cast them as anti–Horatio Alger exemplars of the American Dream. Nevertheless, the Mafia's appeal is often ambivalent, as even the greatest dons have met grim fates.

ORIGINS

Organized criminal groups have had a long history in America. Among the most popular following the Civil War were the outlaw bands that ran with the Reno brothers in Indiana or with Jesse James and Cole Younger, who operated out of Missouri. Bandits were immortalized in dime novels of the late nineteenth century and decades later appeared in songs written by folk artists such as Woody Guthrie and films starring actors Tyrone Power and Henry Fonda.

The Mafia, as Stephen Fox contends in *Blood and Power: Organized Crime in Twentieth-Century America*, emerged in New Orleans following the Civil War, led by Sicilian American Joseph Macheca. During the 1880s Sicilian brothers Charles and Tony Matranga wrested control of operations from the powerful Provenzano family, who had dominated the New Orleans docks. Irish, Jewish, and "native American" criminal societies were independently rooted in their own communities during the early twentieth century.

The Godfather. *The 1972 film* The Godfather *and its sequels are the most successful of a variety of film and television dramas that feed the public's fascination with organized crime.* SILVER SCREEN COLLECTION/CONTRIBUTOR/MOVIEPIX/GETTY IMAGES.

In Chicago, mob syndicates controlled criminal activity, led by kingpin Mont Tennes's gambling ring and mobster James "Big Jim" Colosimo's saloons and prostitution dens. In New York, police lieutenant Charles Becker wielded his vice squad to ensure protection payments. Although a national organization had not emerged, talk abounded of conspiratorial fixes, particularly in the wake of the 1919 World Series of Major League Baseball, in which several members of the heavily favored Chicago White Sox cast their lot with gamblers to ensure a loss to the Cincinnati Reds. The "big fixer" responsible for the scheme was reputed to be New York gambler Arnold Rothstein, who was later immortalized as the crooked businessman Meyer Wolfsheim in F. Scott Fitzgerald's *The Great Gatsby.*

PROHIBITION

With the ratification of the Eighteenth Amendment, which officially ushered in Prohibition, criminals for the first time began to distribute illegal commodities on a nationwide basis. The number of syndicates mushroomed. Smuggling, bootlegging, and brewing moonshine thrived. Fascist dictator Benito Mussolini's 1922 rise to power in Italy, and his efforts to rein in the Mafia, further spurred migration of mafiosi such as Joe Bonanno and Joe Profaci to the United States.

Major East Coast syndicates—the "Big Seven"—were led by underworld chieftains such as Charles "Lucky" Luciano, Frank Costello, Benjamin "Bugsy" Siegel, and Meyer Lansky. Most arrived in Atlantic City in 1929, along with Capone and other important syndicate figures from the Midwest, to attend what some call organized crime's first national convention. Others point to a 1928 meeting in Cleveland, Ohio, featuring mobsters from the East, South, and Midwest, as the first major assembly. Ties between organized crime and political machines strengthened, and Italians, Poles, and other groups joined the Irish in establishing such connections.

By the mid-1920s Capone had supplanted crime boss Johnny Torrio as head of a vast syndicate in Chicago. In New York the top underworld figure was Giuseppe "the Boss" Masseria, who ran vice operations in Brooklyn and Manhattan. In 1930 Masseria and rival boss Salvatore Maranzano battled for control of the Italian underworld. Maranzano agreed to end the crime war if Masseria's lieutenants, Lucky Luciano and Vito Genovese, murdered their boss. Luciano not only killed Masseria but orchestrated the killing of Maranzano as well, becoming king of New York's policy, narcotic, and prostitution syndicates.

Throughout the era, organized criminals ran a host of entertainment venues. Gangsters controlled top nightclubs such as Chicago's Grand Terrace, Harlem's Cotton Club, and Kansas City's Twelfth and Eighteenth Streets jazz joints. Mob-connected managers shepherded musical greats such as bandleader Duke Ellington and trumpeter Louis "Satchmo" Armstrong. Mobsters also had a stake in the fight game, including boxing's most prestigious division. Long after legendary Joe Louis captured the heavyweight title in 1937, fixes, real and imagined, plagued professional boxing and such fighters as Jake LaMotta, Sugar Ray Robinson, Rocky Marciano, and Sonny Liston.

Horse racing also fell to the Mafia. In 1934 federal agents discovered that more than 300 horses had received narcotic injections to induce faster performances. Newspaper publisher Moe Annenberg became a powerful organized crime figure, wielding his racing sheets and the Nationwide News Service (which reported on developments at the tracks), before he was imprisoned for tax evasion. *New York Daily Mirror* gossip columnist Walter Winchell constantly received tidbits from mobsters such as Capone and Costello. News magnate William Randolph Hearst's top feature writer, Damon Runyon, penned short stories that portrayed mobsters as amiable in their own fashion (the stories were later adapted for the Broadway musical and Hollywood film *Guys and Dolls*). Entertainers prone to gambling, such as actor George Raft and comedians Joe E. Lewis and Milton Berle, also became associated with mob figures.

THE GREAT DEPRESSION

As organized crime's reach extended into gambling, labor racketeering, loan-sharking, narcotics, and prostitution, criminals invested profits in legitimate or semi-legitimate businesses, including hotels, restaurants, and entertainment enterprises. In Louisiana, Florida, and Nevada, mobsters from the East set up plush gambling casinos. Costello and mobster Dandy Phil Kastel constructed the Beverly Club casino just outside of New Orleans, and in Miami Beach, Costello, Lansky, Siegel, and syndicate leader Joe Adonis financed the Colonial Inn, another gambling showcase. Throughout the Miami Beach area, Costello controlled horse tracks, dog tracks, and bookie joints. He also purchased real estate, bars, hotels, restaurants, a radio station, and other commercial enterprises.

Meanwhile Capone's influence spread through the Midwest to Dallas, Texas, where he promised newly elected sheriff Steve Guthrie an annual income of $150,000 to allow organized crime to thrive (though Guthrie refused the money). Jacob Rubenstein—a Chicago hoodlum who called himself Jack Ruby—remained in Dallas, becoming infamous decades later for shooting Lee Harvey Oswald, the gunman arrested for the assassination of President John F. Kennedy. Las Vegas had even greater allure for mobsters such as Siegel, Lansky, and Capone. Among the hotels that organized crime helped to establish were the Flamingo, the Desert Inn, the Thunderbird, the Sands, the Riviera, the Stardust, the Dunes, and the Tropicana.

In the early 1930s Hollywood released a series of well-received gangster films, some based on true events and real underworld characters. Gangsters appeared in the guise of truck drivers, kids from slums, Italian immigrants, or stockyard laborers in such films as *Quick Millions* (1931) and *The Secret Six* (1931). Other movies depicted the rise and fall of organized crime bosses through such characters as Irish gangster Tommy Powers, played by James Cagney in *Public Enemy* (1931); Capone-like mob lieutenant Tony Camonte, played by Paul Muni in *Scarface* (1932); and Chicago mobster Caesar "Rico" Bandello, performed by Edward G. Robinson in *Little Caesar* (1931). Although the heyday of gangster films was 1930–1932, their impact lingered in movies with a similar cynical, rapid-fire style; sharp dialogue; and a naturalistic approach. Gangsterism remained a popular genre, with more than 900 such films made before 1970.

FEDERAL INVESTIGATION

During the 1920s and 1930s FBI director J. Edgar Hoover denied the existence of organized crime, although some of its top figures faced criminal indictments. In late 1931 prominent Chicago businessmen assisted in the prosecution of Capone for tax evasion, and he was sentenced to eleven years. (According to public lore, Capone was brought down by Prohibition agent Eliot Ness and his Untouchables, who were later immortalized in the television series and movie of the same name.) Five years later Luciano began serving a thirty- to fifty-year sentence after New York City district attorney Thomas E. Dewey secured his conviction. Myths circulated about the crime-fighting prowess of the Bureau of Investigation—renamed the Federal Bureau of Investigation in 1935—and Hoover received considerable positive press as the nation's number one G-man. But his reputation had less to do with the FBI's efforts to rein in organized crime than with tales of agents' encounters with bank robbers such as Charles "Baby Face" Nelson, Pretty Boy Floyd, and John Dillinger.

During World War II and its aftermath, the federal government's response to organized crime proved highly contradictory. In 1945 Dewey, as governor of New York, commuted Luciano's sentence, allegedly because the mob boss had helped to prevent sabotage on the docks. In 1950 Senator Estes Kefauver, chairman of the Special Senate Committee to Investigate Organized Crime in the United States, began holding public hearings. Mobsters' reliance on the Fifth Amendment—"I decline to answer on the grounds that it might tend to incriminate me"—did not serve them well. Televised hearings, watched by an estimated thirty million viewers, captured shifty bosses such as Costello, now head of the family that Genovese and Luciano formerly led.

The Kefauver Committee reported dealings between Costello and top New York City politicians, including former district attorney and mayor William O'Dwyer. Costello was convicted of contempt of Congress and tax evasion. Writing in the *Nation* in early 1957, Sidney Lens compared the Mafia to the American Communist Party: "It is a loose federation, highly centralized in some respects (such as dealing out 'justice' to its traitors), but decentralized in execution of business ventures. . . . It is certainly not a membership organization. It is more of a loosely-knit force with tens of thousands of 'fellow-travelers.'"

THE MAFIA UNCOVERED

Talk circulated about the Mafia developing a more elaborate crime structure. A police raid in Apalachin, New York, in November 1957 resulted in the holding of Genovese, Joe Bonanno, Carlo Gambino, and several other syndicate big shots. Promises of deportation and tax examination proved illusory, though a conspiracy trial of many of the participants at Apalachin began in May 1959.

The issue of ethnicity was not far from the surface. In *The Mafia Mystique*, Dwight C. Smith Jr. cites a 1959 *Newsweek* article about the constitution of organized crime: "The group doesn't call itself the Mafia, but others do, because most of the top executives are Sicilians and other southern Italians." The Senate Permanent Subcommittee on Investigations, led by Senator John McClellan from Arkansas, explored organized crime's ties to labor organizations, particularly the teamsters. (John F. Kennedy was a member of the subcommittee, and his younger brother Robert served as chief counsel.)

Discussion of the Mafia frequently appeared in popular publications, and academic explorations of the subject increased. *The Enemy Within*, by Robert Kennedy, about his involvement with McClellan's subcommittee, was published in 1960 and focused on teamsters Dave Beck and Jimmy Hoffa. In 1963 gangster Joseph Valachi testified before McClellan's subcommittee and traced the evolution of organized crime—which he called the Cosa Nostra. He also discussed the Apalachin meeting, reputedly held by the Mafia's Grand Council or the Commission of the Cosa Nostra, thus seemingly verifying organized crime's existence. Following the assassination of President Kennedy in Dallas on November 22, 1963, talk of organized crime involvement proliferated, including rumors of the participation of Louisiana don Carlos Marcello.

MOBSTERS IN BOOKS AND FILM

Following Valachi's testimony, media interest in the Mafia exploded, and a firestorm arose over publication of *The Valachi Papers*. Charges that the book slandered ethnic groups—particularly Italians and Jews—caused twenty-two publishers to turn it down before Putnam agreed to print it in 1968. It proved to be a best seller, as did another book published that year: Mario Puzo's *The Godfather*. In contrast to crime writer Mickey Spillane's hard-boiled approach, Puzo devised a businessman protagonist who ran a number of illegal enterprises. The novel's antihero controls a Mafia organization by relying on long-standing relationships and family blood ties.

Puzo returned to earlier characterizations of organized crime as ethnically driven. Distinctively Italian, *The Godfather* contained, as Smith notes, the word *Mafia* scores of times, *mafioso* eleven times, and *Cosa Nostra* twice. The novel traces Vito Corleone's rise to organized crime preeminence and the syndicate's subsequent takeover by his son Michael, the reluctant new don, who proves as ruthless as his father. Reviewers perceived the book to be about "America's most powerful and least understood subculture." Smith argues, "Its success was a matter of timing. The public was ripe for a book that would demonstrate the 'reality' of the twenty-year campaign of the law-enforcement community to depict organized crime as an evil, alien, conspiratorial entity comprised of Italians bearing the 'Mafia' label."

Cinematic versions of Puzo's work, *The Godfather* (1972) and *The Godfather Part II* (1974), were huge commercial and artistic successes. Other films of the era took on organized crime, such as Arthur Penn's *Bonnie and Clyde* (1967), which portrayed Depression-era bank robbers Bonnie Parker and Clyde Barrow, played by radiant Faye Dunaway and dashing Warren Beatty. However, the runaway success of *The Godfather* franchise, punctuated with Academy Awards for Best Picture for both movies, resulted in a new spate of gangster films such as *The Untouchables* (1987) and *GoodFellas* (1990).

Also appearing in books and on film were the memoirs of organized crime figures such as Bonanno, Jimmy "the Weasel" Fratianno, and Willie Sutton. Before 1980 only Valachi and Fratianno had reneged on the Mafia code of silence, *omertà*. (Gay Talese's 1971 book *Honor Thy Father* had benefited from a series of interviews with Joe Bonanno's son Bill, a crime figure in his own right.) Soon Sammy "the Bull" Gravano, a onetime lieutenant of the Gambino crime family, and high-ranking members of other families came forward with their stories.

A NEW ERA OF CRIME

In 1970 Congress passed the Racketeer Influenced and Corrupt Organizations Act (RICO), which was designed to prevent proponents of organized crime from profiting from their offenses. Punishment included twenty years to life in prison and forfeiture of all profits. Still, organized crime spread into new areas such as child prostitution, banking, and environmental schemes. However, the Mafia's influence had lessened, thanks to defections by key players turned government witnesses, deadly squabbles, and concerted prosecutorial action.

New bands of organized criminals emerged, including outlaw motorcycle groups, black gangs, and immigrant syndicates. Biker gangs specialized in popular synthetic drugs such as speed, PCP, and LSD. Black hoodlums shifted from gambling to drugs, including heroin and cocaine. Southeast Asian, Caribbean, South American, and Eastern European groups, among others, became involved in the sale of narcotics and arms. Figures from a variety of groups appeared in cinematic guise, played by top actors such as Mel Gibson, Danny Glover, Harrison Ford, and Michael Douglas.

In the twenty-first century, Americans continued their love affair with organized crime antiheroes through popular productions about modern gangsters. The HBO drama *The Sopranos* (1999–2007) starring James Gandolfini as mob boss Tony Soprano and Edie Falco as his wife, won twenty-one Emmys and five Golden Globes. *Boardwalk Empire*, which premiered on HBO in 2010, has also been well received by critics. Set in the 1920s in Atlantic City, the show chronicles the rise to power of mob boss Enoch (Nucky) Thompson during the Prohibition Era. Steve Buscemi plays the lead role. Movie audiences clamored for such neo-gangster films as *Knockaround Guys* (2001) and *The Departed* (2006), as well as period pieces such as *Road to Perdition* (2002), *American Gangster* (2007), and *Public Enemies* (2009).

Real organized crime continues to become more sophisticated and more dangerous as American gangs such as MS-13, the 18th Street Gang, the Latin Kings, the Jamaican Posse, and Hells Angels extend their reach into transnational crime. Drive-by shootings and identity theft have supplemented the standard rap sheet of robbery, money laundering, prostitution, and weapons and drug trafficking.

Although traditional criminal groups are not prone to committing acts of terrorism, individual members frequently take on tasks for international terrorists. Multiple government agencies have responded to these new threats from organized crime, including the National Security Council, the Department of Homeland Security, the Department of Justice, and the U.S. Agency for International Development—hoping to stave off a new era of organized crime.

Robert C. Cottrell

SEE ALSO: *Academy Awards; Armstrong, Louis; Baseball; Beatty, Warren; Berle, Milton;* Bonnie and Clyde*; Cagney, James; Capone, Al; Communism; Dillinger, John; Dime Novels; Ellington, Duke; FBI (Federal Bureau of Investigation); Fitzgerald, F. Scott; Fonda, Henry; Ford, Harrison; Gangs; Gibson, Mel;* The Godfather*;* GoodFellas*; Gotti, John; Guthrie, Woody; Hearst, William Randolph; Hoover, J. Edgar; Kennedy Assassination; LaMotta, Jake; Las Vegas; Liston, Sonny; Louis, Joe; LSD; Luciano, Lucky; Marciano, Rocky; Muni, Paul; Prohibition; Raft, George; Robinson, Edward G.; Robinson, Sugar Ray; Runyon, Damon; Siegel, Bugsy;* The Sopranos*; Spillane, Mickey; Winchell, Walter; World War II.*

BIBLIOGRAPHY

Albanese, Jay S. *Transnational Crime and the 21st Century: Criminal Enterprise, Corruption and Opportunity*. New York: Oxford University Press, 2011.

Albini, Joseph L. *The American Mafia: Genesis of a Legend*. New York: Appleton-Century-Crofts, 1971.

Blumenthal, Ralph. *Last Days of the Sicilians: The FBI's War against the Mafia*. New York: Pocket Books, 1989.

Bonavolonta, Jules, and Brian Duffy. *The Good Guys: How We Turned the FBI 'Round—and Finally Broke the Mob*. New York: Simon & Schuster Trade, 1996.

Breslin, Jimmy. *The Gang That Couldn't Shoot Straight*. New York: Little, Brown, 1997.

Davis, John H. *Mafia Dynasty: The Rise and Fall of the Gambino Crime Family*. New York: HarperCollins, 1993.

Fox, Stephen. *Blood and Power: Organized Crime in Twentieth-Century America*. New York: William Morrow, 1989.

Hamm, Mark, and Cécile Van de Voorde. "Crimes Committed by Terrorist Gangs: Theory, Research, and Prevention." *Trends in Organized Crime* 9, no. 2 (2005): 18–51.

Hess, Henner. *Mafia & Mafiosi: Origin, Power, and Myth*. New York: New York University Press, 1998.

Homer, Frederic D. *Guns and Garlic: Myths and Realities of Organized Crime*. West Lafayette, IN: Purdue University Press, 1974.

Jacobs, James B.; Christopher Panarella; and Jay Worthington. *Busting the Mob: "United States v. Cosa Nostra."* New York: New York University Press, 1994.

Maas, Peter, ed. *The Valachi Papers*. New York: Bantam Books, 1968.

Mintz, Steven, and Randy Roberts. *Hollywood's America: United States History through Its Films*. St. James, NY: Brandywine Press, 1996.

Ryan, Patrick J., and George E. Rush. *Understanding Organized Crime in Global Perspective: A Reader*. Thousand Oaks, CA: Sage Publications, 1997.

Shelley, Louise I., and John T. Picarelli. "Methods and Motives: Exploring Links between Transnational Organized Crime and International Terrorism." *Trends in Organized Crime* 9, no. 2 (2005): 52–67.

Smith, Dwight C., Jr. *The Mafia Mystique*. New York: Basic Books, 1975.

Talese, Gay. *Honor Thy Father*. New York: World Publishing, 1971.

Varese, Federico. *Mafias on the Move: How Organized Crime Conquers New Territory*. Princeton, NJ: Princeton University Press, 2011.

The Magnificent Seven

"They were seven—and they fought like seven hundred!" screamed the posters for *The Magnificent Seven*, a Western that spawned a number of sequels and helped launch the careers of actors Steve McQueen, James Coburn, and Charles Bronson. The movie is a remake of director Akira Kurosawa's Japanese classic film *Seven Samurai*, and its macho élan lifts it above the formulaic and into the high canon of film.

Directed by Hollywood craftsman John Sturges, *The Magnificent Seven* stars Yul Brynner, who plays Chris Adams, the laconic leader of a band of seven gunmen recruited by a Mexican farming village to defend it from an army of 100 bandits. McQueen plays the hotshot marksman of the bunch, and Eli Wallach plays the head bandito, providing the precedent for a similar turn as a Mexican rogue six years later in *The Good, the Bad, and the Ugly*.

Sturges's film has none of the technical wizardry of the Kurosawa original, which used slow motion, a rapidly moving camera, and long-lens photography to capture the spectacular battle sequences. Sturges opted for conventional shoot-'em-up scenes that derive their impact from the audience's empathetic association with the main characters. With his black hat and limited vocabulary, Brynner is the epitome of Western cool, almost iconic in his glacial stoicism. By contrast, McQueen is working on the brash rebel persona he would later perfect in films such as *Bullitt* (1968), *The Cincinnati Kid* (1965), and Sturges's own *The Great Escape* (1963). The latter film is notable in its use of many of the same actors, a large ensemble cast, and the exploration of male bonding to the exclusion of all other themes. *The Magnificent Seven*, to its credit, at least has a few female characters.

Male audiences love *The Magnificent Seven*, especially male filmmakers. The film's visual style and antiheroic iconography clearly influenced director and producer Sergio Leone and the other pioneers of "spaghetti Western" cinema. In its time, however, *The Magnificent Seven* was only a moderate hit, earning just one Oscar nomination for best score. The fact that it did not set the world on fire was perhaps a sign that the days of the big Hollywood Western were over.

The Magnificent Seven spawned three sequels, each one less interesting than the last. Brynner returned as Chris for *Return of the Seven* (1966). He passed on the hero's reins—figuratively and literally—to the less-compelling George Kennedy in *Guns of the Magnificent Seven* (1969). Completing the descent into made-for-TV-style mediocrity was *The Magnificent Seven Ride!* (1972), starring Lee Van Cleef, Mariette Hartley, and a young Gary Busey. No one was surprised when the property was spun into a short-lived television series in 1998.

Robert E. Schnakenberg

SEE ALSO: *Academy Awards; Bronson, Charles; Brynner, Yul;* The Good, the Bad, and the Ugly*; Leone, Sergio; McQueen, Steve; Spaghetti Westerns; The Western.*

BIBLIOGRAPHY

Andreychuk, Ben, ed. *The Golden Corral: A Roundup of Magnificent Western Films*. Jefferson, NC: McFarland, 1997.

Pitts, Michael R. *Western Movies: A TV and Video Guide to 4200 Genre Films*. Jefferson, NC: McFarland, 1997.

Slatta, Richard W. *The Mythical West: An Encyclopedia of Legend, Lore and Popular Culture*. Santa Barbara, CA: ABC-CLIO, 2001.

Magnum, P.I.

The 1980s CBS television series *Magnum, P.I.* was created to take advantage of the Hawaiian facilities built by CBS to produce *Hawaii Five-0* (1968–1980). On the surface, *Magnum* was a standard private eye drama, starring the preternaturally handsome Tom Selleck as Thomas Magnum. The series' early success started a boomlet of crime dramas with good-looking male leads. However, it was the underlying subtext—the Vietnam veteran as hero—that set *Magnum* apart. While it was not the first series to feature Vietnam vets, it was the first to have Vietnam as a subtext, and the show set off a mid-1980s trend of TV shows featuring heroes with Vietnam backgrounds, including *The A-Team* (1983–1987), *Riptide* (1984–1986), *Stingray* (1985–1987), and *Miami Vice* (1984–1990). Vietnam vets had previously been portrayed mostly as victims of post-traumatic stress, and the success of these series changed the way they were viewed, at least in popular culture.

In the pilot, which aired December 11, 1980, former navy lieutenant Thomas Magnum is hired by mysterious millionaire pulp writer Robin Masters (who is never seen on-screen; he is heard only a few times per season in a voice provided by Orson Welles early on) to test the security of his Hawaiian estate, Robin's Nest. When Magnum successfully evades the guard dog Dobermans Zeus and Apollo, as well as the estate's major domo, Higgins, he is hired as the estate's new security chief and moves into the estate's guesthouse. Magnum's presence rankles Jonathan Quayle Higgins (John Hillerman), the very British former military commando, to no end. Higgins, forever writing his memoirs of years in military service in Africa and Asia, regards Magnum as a nuisance. Eventually, however, they bond through their experiences in war.

The Masters estate becomes the base of Magnum's struggling private investigation operation. Magnum is often aided in his investigations, usually unwillingly, by two fellow vets—marines Theodore "T. C." Calvin (Roger E. Mosley) and Orville "Rick" Wright (Larry Manetti). Magnum continually "borrows"

Magnum, P.I. *Tom Selleck starred as Hawaii-based private investigator Thomas Magnum on the hit CBS television series* Magnum, P.I. *from 1980 to 1988.* SILVER SCREEN COLLECTION/CONTRIBUTOR/ARCHIVE PHOTOS/GETTY IMAGES.

T. C.'s chopper, Rick's underworld contacts, and Masters's red Ferrari to solve crimes and protect people on the estate. Higgins eventually becomes another unwilling helper in Magnum's investigations.

Magnum became much more than a standard-issue action drama due to cocreator Donald Bellisario, himself a former marine (who would later create *Quantum Leap* [1989–1993] and *JAG* [1995–2005]). Bellisario turned the series into a meditation on Vietnam and friendship. Glen Larson had originally conceived of Magnum as an ex-CIA agent, a playboy freeloading on the estate, much in the mold of his other successful action series, *Knight Rider* (1982–1986). Bellisario was brought in when Selleck objected to that characterization, and Bellisario changed Magnum into the Vietnam veteran of naval intelligence and added Rick and T. C.

In the first six years of *Magnum*, Vietnam was practically another character. The pilot ties smuggled gold to a member of Magnum's commando team in Vietnam, and introduces Rick and T. C. as members of that team, all marked by their Croix de Guerre rings (the symbol of the French Resistance). In the second season Magnum's long-lost wife Michelle (who wears her croix on a pendant) returns from Vietnam, then goes back as a spy. In various episodes, Magnum has Vietnam flashbacks, which usually ties the past into the present-day plot. These cinematic flashbacks, the other Vietnam references, and Magnum's sometimes-psychic flashes, marked *Magnum* as different, as did Selleck's voice-overs of Magnum's thoughts, one of the few times this has been done in series television. Within those monologues, Magnum often refers to his "little voice," a variation on his conscience, that warns him of danger. The little voice is always counseling him and making the leaps of intuition he needs to escape or solve the crime.

Once Bellisario left the show and Selleck and other producers took over, *Magnum* became a more traditional detective show. The series was to end in 1987, and the finale depicts Magnum dying and going to heaven, complete with cameos by all the recurring characters. However, the series came back for one more year and the death became near-death. The two-hour series finale airing May 1, 1988, was highly rated and wrapped up the series: Magnum gains custody of Lily (his daughter with Michelle), abruptly quits the private eye business, and rejoins the navy. Rick marries, and it is implied that Higgins might be in reality the unseen Robin Masters. Since the series' end, there have been rumors it may be revived in movie form.

Michele Lellouche

SEE ALSO: The A-Team; Miami Vice; *Television; Vietnam; Welles, Orson.*

BIBLIOGRAPHY

Carson, Tom. "Magnum's America: "Nam and Apple Pie." *Village Voice.* October 19, 1982, 65.

Kuehler, Marilyn Kay. "Point Man for the Vietnam Presence on *Magnum P.I.*" *Los Angeles Times,* August 1, 1981, Sec. II, 10.

Manetti, Larry, and Chip Silverman. *Aloha Magnum: Larry Manetti's* Magnum, P.I. *Memories.* New York: Renaissance Books, 1999.

Newcomb, Horace M. "Magnum: The Champagne of TV?" *Channels,* May/June 1985.

Snauffer, Douglas. *Crime Television.* Westport, CT: Praeger, 2006.

Mah-Jongg

Mah-jongg, an ancient gambling game that originated among the Chinese ruling class more than 2,000 years ago, gained widespread popularity in the United States beginning in the 1930s, especially as a leisure pastime among American Jewish women. Recognized the world over by its ritualized play and the satisfying clack of tile against tile, mah-jongg is a complicated four-person game whose rules are similar to the card game rummy. It is played with 152 tiles, colorfully painted with three suits (bamboo, characters, and dots), four winds, eight flowers, and three dragons.

From its aristocratic origins, the game became popular among all classes in China and soon spread throughout Asia and the world, with different versions evolving in Japan, the Philippines, Europe, and the United States. Since 1937 the National Mah-Jongg League has governed the rules of the American game, although enthusiasm for the pastime faded at the end of the 1960s, in part because of the increasing popularity of contract bridge. During the 1980s and 1990s, however, the game began to enjoy a renaissance as nostalgic baby boomers sought to revive the once-favored social pastime of their mothers. One organization even instituted a mah-jongg tournament cruise, an annual event that celebrated its twenty-fifth anniversary in 2010. Classic four-hand mah-jongg should not be confused with mah-jongg computer games, which proliferated in the 1990s and early 2000s. These are actually forms of solitaire that use mah-jongg tiles instead of cards.

Tina Gianoulis

SEE ALSO: *Baby Boomers; Board Games; Bridge; Computer Games; Gambling; Leisure Time.*

BIBLIOGRAPHY

Greene, Susan. *The Mah Jongg Group.* Port Washington, NY: Ashley Books, 1974.

Millington, A. D. *The Complete Book of Mah-Jongg.* London: A. Barker, 1977.

Sandberg, Elaine, and Tom Sloper. *Beginner's Guide to American Mah Jongg: How to Play the Game & Win.* Tokyo: Tuttle Publishing, 2007.

Shiu, Priscilla. *The Mystic Mah-Jongg Game.* New York: Exposition Press, 1973.

Mailer, Norman *(1923–2007)*

With the publication of his brilliant first novel, *The Naked and the Dead* (1948), Norman Mailer established himself as the next important writer of his age. Over the following six decades, he fulfilled that promise many times over. His literary output was extraordinary—more than thirty volumes of fiction and nonfiction. His prolificness was matched only by the prodigiousness of his public persona.

His works aroused controversy and elicited as much scorn as acclaim. Even after garnering numerous literary awards, including the National Book Award and two Pulitzer Prizes, and repeated mentions as a contender for the Nobel Prize, he was relentlessly criticized for his views on sex, violence, and politics. Admirers applauded him for his bold experimentation, yet he remained elusive and a curiosity to many of his critics and readers. Some could not agree on the literary merits of his books, the quality of his ideas, or his ultimate place in American letters.

CRITICISM AND PERSONA

The critical disagreement over his work resulted, in part, from the versatile nature of his writing. Since 1941, the year he won first prize in *Story* magazine's annual college contest, he wrote widely, if not always well. In addition to writing poetry (*Deaths for the Ladies, and Other Disasters*, 1962), drama (*The Deer Park—A Play*, 1967), and screenplays (such as *Maidstone*, 1971, written for one of the experimental films he produced), he explored numerous prose forms, including autobiography, biography, book reviews, essays, interviews, letters, literary criticism (*Genius and Lust*, 1976, on the works of Henry Miller), memoir, newspaper columns, novella (the graphic, erotic *The Time of Her Time*, 1959), political reportage (*St. George and the Godfather*, 1972), short stories (*Short Fiction*, 1967), and sports reportage. Although he considered himself a novelist above all, his versatility defied easy categorization, and his forays outside of high culture occasionally confounded even his strongest supporters.

He admitted to undermining his reputation as a serious writer through his tireless self-promotion and penchant for celebrity. "Every time I get into the newspapers," he once remarked, "I injure myself professionally." Much of his life reads like the stuff of fiction: He had six marriages, the second of which ended after he stabbed his wife Adele (for which he was briefly jailed and committed to Bellevue Hospital). He had numerous legal and financial problems, which were exacerbated by his pugnaciousness and affinity for drugs and alcohol. He was a frequent television talk show guest and once ran a costly campaign for mayor of New York City. And he had odd personal alliances with controversial people such as convicted murderer Jack Henry Abbott (whose prison letters Mailer helped to get published and whose release he facilitated, only for Abbott to kill again), as well as public feuds with, among others, writers William Styron and Gore Vidal (whom he punched out at a party).

Norman Mailer. *In his lengthy and prolific writing career, Norman Mailer served as one of the most outspoken commentators on modern society.* J. KEMPIN/CONTRIBUTOR/FILMMAGIC/GETTY IMAGES.

Mailer transformed his outrageous life into popular essays and fiction. But his melding of life and art led critics to analyze and dissect the figure behind the books rather than the quality of the writing itself. His "crude celebrity," as Vidal dubbed it, made Mailer's name familiar to readers and nonreaders alike, assuring his status as a literary personality. However, he struggled to achieve universal admiration.

EARLY LIFE AND CAREER

Born in Long Branch, New Jersey, in 1923, and raised in Brooklyn, New York, Mailer graduated with honors from Harvard University in 1943 with a degree in aeronautical engineering. Drafted by the army in early 1944, he served as a rifleman with a combat unit in the South Pacific. After his discharge two years later, he returned to Brooklyn, where he began his celebrated first novel. *Naked* is a realistic and naturalistic account of the dialectic contest between authoritarian General Cummings and his liberal aide Lieutenant Hearn (a contest that recurs in much of Mailer's fiction) and of the fates of the other platoon members on the fictional island of Anopopei.

In his next two novels he shifted his artistic focus from the omniscient narrator who probed the consciousness of multiple characters in *Naked* to existential first-person narratives that redefined the role of the hero in an unheroic world. Despite its bold depiction of Cold War American politics and idealism, *Barbary Shore* (1951) was a critical and popular failure. Although *The Deer Park* (1955) received reviews that were more favorable, critics disapproved of its sexual explicitness and cynicism. Several collections of Mailer's prose works, many of which attacked technological society, appeared over the next decade: *Advertisements for Myself* (1959), which included "The White Negro," his Beat-influenced treatise on the hipster-hero; *The Presidential Papers* (1963); and *Cannibals and Christians* (1966).

THE VIETNAM ERA

Mailer returned to fiction in 1965 with *An American Dream*, the compelling story of Stephen Rojack's regeneration through sex and violence, followed by *Why Are We in Vietnam?* (1967), in which a bear hunt serves as a metaphor for America's involvement in the war. He continued his reflections on American values in such nonfictional works as *The Armies of the Night* (1968), a disarmingly passionate and award-winning account of the 1967 march on the Pentagon; *Miami and the Siege of Chicago* (1968), about the tumultuous political conventions of that year; *Of a Fire on the Moon* (1970), an analysis of the first lunar landing; and *The Prisoner of Sex* (1971), a critical examination of the women's movement that incurred the wrath of feminists and launched a series of vitriolic attacks on him and his work. One reviewer dismissed *Prisoner* as "dribble: long and continuous."

Much of Mailer's writing during the 1970s focused on famous—sometimes infamous—Americans, including actress

Marilyn Monroe (*Marilyn*, 1973, and *Of Women and Their Elegance*, 1980), boxer Muhammad Ali (*The Fight*, 1975), and murderer Gary Gilmore, the first prisoner to be executed in the United States in more than a decade (*The Executioner's Song*, 1979). *Ancient Evenings*, the massive and surprisingly successful novel of epistemological adventure in ancient Egypt, which he began in 1971, was published in 1983.

LATER WORKS

The 1980s and 1990s saw spirited works from Mailer, such as the best-selling murder mystery *Tough Guys Don't Dance* (1984), one of several of his books to be adapted to film. *Harlot's Ghost* (1991) is a lengthy novel about CIA operations over two generations. He returned to his "nonfiction fiction" narrative techniques in 1995 with *Oswald's Tale: An American Mystery*, in which he explores the mind of President John F. Kennedy's assassin, Lee Harvey Oswald. He switched genres again in 1997 with *The Gospel According to the Son*, an unconventional "autobiographical" retelling of portions of the Bible. His last novel, *The Castle in the Forest*, imagines Adolf Hitler as the product of incest; the work is generally seen as a companion to *Gospel*.

Ambitious, egotistical, often controversial, and always entertaining, Mailer, until his death in 2007, continued to do what he did so well for more than half a century: challenge and provoke with his unconventional ideas and techniques. In the last five years of his life, he released three cantankerous and provocative essay collections challenging the political and cultural status quo—*Why Are We at War?* (2003), *The Big Empty: Dialogues on Politics, Sex, God, Boxing, Morality, Myth, Poker, and Bad Conscience in America* (2006), and *On God: An Uncommon Conversation* (2007). He was, arguably, as writer Sinclair Lewis (1885–1951) declared, "the greatest writer to come out of his generation"; certainly, he was one of the most astute social observers and literate spokespeople of his time.

Barbara Tepa Lupack

SEE ALSO: *Ali, Muhammad; The Beat Generation; Best Sellers; Celebrity; Cold War; Feminism; Kennedy Assassination; Lewis, Sinclair; Monroe, Marilyn; Styron, William; Vidal, Gore; Vietnam; World War II.*

BIBLIOGRAPHY

Braudy, Leo, ed. *Norman Mailer: A Collection of Critical Essays.* Englewood Cliffs, NJ: Prentice Hall, 1972.

Leeds, Barry H. *The Structured Vision of Norman Mailer.* New York: New York University Press, 1969.

Lennon, J. Michael, ed. *Critical Essays on Norman Mailer.* Boston: G. K. Hall, 1986.

Merrill, Robert. *Norman Mailer Revisited.* New York: Twayne, 1992.

Mills, Hilary. *Mailer: A Biography.* New York: Empire, 1982.

Poirier, Richard. *Norman Mailer.* New York: Viking, 1972.

Major League Baseball

Baseball has long enjoyed a privileged status in American sports culture. Romanticized as the "national pastime" by journalists and authors since the mid-nineteenth century, the game has elicited a range of literary tributes over the decades, inspiring works by such authors as Bernard Malamud, Ernest Thayer, and John Updike. Although numerous writers have idealized professional baseball over the years, the game has also been a lucrative business since the beginning, both for owners and for players. By the twenty-first century, Major League Baseball (MLB) had evolved into a multibillion-dollar corporate entity, with financial interests extending far beyond the playing field into such diverse areas as media, merchandising, licensing, food and beverage concessions, and other related revenue streams.

EARLY HISTORY

Organized competitive baseball in the United States traces its origins to 1842, with the formation of the New York Knickerbocker Base Ball Club. In 1858, as baseball grew in popularity, players and team owners formed the National Association of Base Ball Players (NABBP), the game's first official league. Composed of twenty-two individual teams, the association was instrumental in codifying many of the game's rules, while also establishing a centralized administration to oversee various aspects of the game. Technically, the NABBP was an amateur organization and prohibited payments to participants; however, the game was driven by money from the beginning, and the best players received undisclosed financial rewards in exchange for their services.

After the Civil War the financial possibilities of the game became impossible to ignore. In 1871 nine teams joined together to organize the first professional baseball league, the National Association, with each franchise paying $10 as the cost of membership. From the beginning the National Association was troubled by poor organization and rampant gambling, and the league disbanded five years later. Meanwhile, a group of team owners from the NABBP, led William Hulbert, began to explore the possibility of creating another professional league. After negotiations with several other teams, Hulbert helped launch the National League of Professional Baseball Clubs in 1876; the association would become more commonly known as the National League (NL), widely considered the precursor of modern Major League Baseball. Among the NL's charter franchises included the Chicago White Stockings, which would later become the Chicago Cubs.

From the beginning, the National League was founded on the principle that team owners, rather than players, should exert control over the financial aspects of the game. Star players in the league's early years earned significant monetary rewards, with some earning as much as $4,500 per year. In their efforts to field competitive teams, the National League franchises often engaged in intense bidding wars to try to obtain a player's services; on many occasions, good players left one team for another in the middle of the season, creating a chaotic competitive atmosphere. The National League owners resolved this problem in the 1878–1879 offseason, when they entered into a secret pact aimed at limiting a player's ability to move between teams. Known as the "reserve clause," this new regulation enabled owners to designate five players as "reserved," thereby prohibiting rival owners from offering them contracts. By 1883 this clause was extended to include the entire roster, thereby granting baseball owners complete control over their players. The reserve clause would remain intact for nearly a century, until player challenges to the rule finally forced owners to grant them greater power to pursue their own contracts under what became known as free agency.

Over the remaining two decades of the nineteenth century, other professional baseball leagues continued to form, including the American Association (1882–1891) and the short-lived Players League (1890); however, none would rival the financial and organizational power of the National League. The only threat to the National League's supremacy emerged in 1885, with the founding of the Western League of Professional Baseball Clubs, or Western League. Originally composed of minor-league teams, the Western League was concentrated in the Midwest, where the National League had yet to establish a real presence. Although the Western League failed repeatedly during the late 1880s and early 1890s, it finally achieved stability in 1893, when Ban Johnson, a journalist from Cincinnati, Ohio, was elected league president. Under Johnson's leadership, the Western League evolved into a well-organized and profitable entity and expanded into East Coast markets previously dominated by National League clubs.

In 1899 the Western League was renamed the American League of Professional Baseball Clubs. A year later the American League (AL) designated itself a major league and soon began openly competing with the National League for the country's best players. After two years of contentious battles over talent, the two leagues resolved to coexist, forming the basis of the modern version of Major League Baseball. As part of their pact, the two leagues agreed to compete each year in a series of championship games, known as the World Series, to determine the best baseball team in America. The first World Series took place in 1903, with the Boston Americans (later Red Sox) of the American League defeating the National League Pittsburgh Pirates, five games to three. The victory brought immediate legitimacy to the upstart American League, while ensuring that Major League Baseball would remain a dual-league entity.

THE MODERN ERA

Over the first two decades of the twentieth century, the popularity of major-league baseball grew steadily, as baseball fans developed fierce loyalties to their hometown teams, and early stars such as Ty Cobb, Walter Johnson, and Honus Wagner set new standards for excellence on the field. This era also saw the construction of a number of fabled baseball stadiums; among the notable early venues, Fenway Park (1912) and Wrigley Field (1914) continued to host baseball games into the twenty-first century. During these years major-league baseball games were typically low-scoring contests, driven more by pitching and strategy than by offensive prowess; baseball historians refer to this period as the "dead-ball era." After a series of rule changes came into effect in the early 1920s, the character of baseball changed dramatically, as skilled batters began to earn recognition for their ability to hit the ball out of the park. The most legendary baseball slugger from these years was Babe Ruth, who established several baseball batting records over the course of his career, while helping launch the New York Yankees as the game's first dynasty.

As major-league baseball grew in prestige, the game's capacity to generate revenue increased, both through ticket sales and through new forms of media exposure. On August 5, 1921, KDKA in Pittsburgh, Pennsylvania, became the first station to broadcast a baseball game over the radio. Within four years, the Chicago Cubs became the first team to offer fans regular radio broadcasts of their home games. As more and more teams forged deals with local radio outlets, MLB's earnings steadily increased.

In 1933 MLB held its first All-Star game, a friendly midseason contest between the American and National Leagues; the "Midsummer Classic" would soon become one of the game's most hallowed institutions. During this period the league also began to devote greater attention to preserving and commemorating the accomplishments of its stars. In 1936 MLB created the Baseball Hall of Fame in Cooperstown, New York, in order to recognize the greatest players in the game's history. Meanwhile, the league's media presence continued to grow substantially. A turning point came in 1939, with the first television broadcast of a live baseball game. Televised baseball proved enormously popular; by 1946 the New York Yankees were able to sell local TV rights to their games for $75,000.

Throughout its first several decades, the structure of Major League Baseball remained basically unchanged, with sixteen teams evenly divided between the American and National Leagues. The era following World War II, however, marked a period of tremendous change for the nation's pastime. The most significant shift came in 1947, when Brooklyn Dodgers second baseman Jackie Robinson became the first African American player in the major leagues. Although Robinson's debut sparked fierce resistance from a number of players, owners, and fans, his presence signaled the end of baseball's long history of segregation; by 1959 every major-league team had signed an African American player.

The period of the 1950s and 1960s witnessed major geographical changes for baseball, as the league began to expand to the West Coast. Following the 1957 season, the NL's Giants relocated from New York City, where they had played since 1883, to San Francisco; that same year, the Brooklyn Dodgers moved to Los Angeles. These years also saw an increase in the number of MLB teams. In 1961 both the AL and the NL increased from eight teams to ten. Each league added two more teams in 1969, while dividing into east and west divisions. That same year, the AL and NL played its first league championship series to determine which team would advance to the World Series.

Major League Baseball experienced even more radical changes in the 1970s, when a series of challenges to the reserve clause granted players greater freedom to decide where to play. Greater player movement soon led to massive pay increases. Between 1975 and 2004, the average salary for a major-league player rose from $45,000 to $2.4 million. This growth was accompanied by a comparable rise in revenues, as teams saw average earnings skyrocket from $6.4 million to $119 million over the same span. As money became more and more of a focal point, relationships between players and owners became increasingly strained, leading to work stoppages in 1981 and 1994–1995. The 1994 strike, which resulted in the cancellation of the World Series, proved particularly damaging to the sport's reputation.

In spite of this negative publicity, Major League Baseball soon rebounded. In 1995 the league introduced a new playoff format, featuring three division winners and a "wild card" team from each league; by doubling the number of playoff teams, MLB made the annual pennant races more competitive, as more contenders vied for a chance to play in the postseason. In 1997 baseball also introduced interleague play, allowing teams from the National and American Leagues to face off during the regular season for the first time in the game's history. The late 1990s saw a surge in baseball offense, as home run totals rose throughout the league, attracting legions of new fans. The high point came in 1998, when sluggers Mark McGwire and Sammy Sosa both chased Roger Maris's record for home runs in a single season, with McGwire emerging as the all-time leader with seventy. Three years later, Barry Bonds would establish a new standard when he hit seventy-three home runs during the 2001 season.

These inflated power numbers soon became tied to one of most damaging public relations scandals in baseball history, however, as reports of performance-enhancing drug use among players began to emerge during the first decade of the 2000s. Among those implicated included McGwire, Sosa, and Bonds, as well as pitcher Roger Clemens. Both Bonds and Clemens would later stand trial on perjury charges, after denying they had ever used banned substances; Bonds was ultimately charged with one count of obstruction of justice, while Clemens was completely exonerated. Still, in the wake of these allegations, other major-league hitters (notably Alex Rodriguez) came under suspicion, while many began to question whether players like Bonds and Clemens belonged in the Hall of Fame. Even in the face of this ongoing controversy, however, baseball remained one of the nation's most popular sports. With total earnings exceeding $7 billion in 2010, Major League Baseball was clearly poised to thrive well into its second century.

Stephen Meyer

SEE ALSO: *Aaron, Hank; Baseball; Bonds, Barry; Boston Red Sox; The Brooklyn Dodgers; The Chicago Cubs; Cobb, Ty; The Detroit Tigers; Fenway Park; Maris, Roger; McGwire, Mark; The New York Yankees; Radio; Robinson, Jackie; Ruth, Babe; Sosa, Sammy; Television; Wagner, Honus; World Series; Wrigley Field.*

BIBLIOGRAPHY

Burk, Robert F. *Much More than a Game: Players, Owners, and American Baseball since 1921.* Chapel Hill: University of North Carolina Press, 2001.

Helyar, John. *Lords of the Realm: The Real History of Baseball.* New York: Villard Books, 1994.

Miller, Marvin. *A Whole Different Ball Game: The Sport and Business of Baseball.* New York: Birch Lane Press, 1991.

Sullivan, Neil J. *The Diamond Revolution.* New York: St. Martin's Press, 1992.

Zimbalist, Andrew. *Baseball and Billions.* New York: Basic Books, 1992.

Malcolm X *(1925–1965)*

Born Malcolm Little in Omaha, Nebraska, in 1925, Malcolm X was the son of a freelance Baptist preacher who followed the teachings of black nationalist leader Marcus Garvey. Following threats on his father from the local Ku Klux Klan, Malcolm and his family moved to Lansing, Michigan. There, in the face of similar threats, Malcolm's father defiantly continued to urge African Americans to take control of their lives, a stand that cost him his life when the Klan-like Black Legion murdered him in 1931. Although found with his head crushed and nearly severed from his body, authorities deemed the death a suicide. As a result, the Littles were denied much-needed insurance benefits. The family deteriorated rapidly as welfare workers sought to turn the children against each other and their mother. Ultimately, Malcolm was removed from his mother's care at age six and placed in a foster home. Shortly thereafter, his mother suffered a mental breakdown from which she never recovered.

In 1941 Malcolm moved to Boston to live with his half-sister but soon quit school and drifted into the urban underworld of narcotics, prostitution, gambling, and burglary. Known as "Detroit Red," he was arrested for robbery in 1946 and sentenced to prison. There, he first learned the importance of education, reading and copying the entire dictionary and then moving on to devour works of history, politics, and literature. Later, at the urging of his siblings, Malcolm converted to the Nation of Islam, or Black Muslims, an ascetic sect that brought discipline into the lives of its members, especially those in prison. Upon joining the Nation of Islam, Malcolm abandoned his "slave name" in favor of Malcolm X, with the *X* standing for his lost African name.

After serving six years in prison, Malcolm X was released in 1952 and immediately traveled to Detroit, Michigan, to meet Black Muslim leader Elijah Muhammad. Assigned to Temple No. 7 in Harlem, New York, he quickly emerged as the sect's most dynamic minister. His charisma helped to boost membership in the Nation of Islam to an estimated 40,000 by 1960. The Nation of Islam preached strict moral purity and the superiority of the black race. Like Garvey's followers in the 1920s, Black Muslims denounced whites as "blue-eyed devils." They opposed integration and called for black pride, independent black institutions, and ultimately a separate black nation.

Malcolm X. *Malcolm X appears in London, England, en route to Egypt to meet with African leaders in 1964 after his break with the Nation of Islam.* EXPRESS NEWSPAPERS/STAFF/HULTON ARCHIVE/ GETTY IMAGES.

Only after African Americans were united, Malcolm X insisted, could they contemplate integration with whites.

MILITANCY AND EPIPHANY

In contrast to Martin Luther King Jr.'s advocacy of nonviolence, integration, and interracial harmony, Malcolm X used fiery rhetoric to launch an uncompromising and fearless assault on America's racial hypocrisy at home and abroad. When confronted by a violent white oppressor, he argued, the oppressed must use "any means necessary" to achieve their liberation. "Afro-Americans should not be victims any longer," he declared. "Bloodshed is a two-way street . . . , dying is a two-way street . . . , killing is a two-way street." Militancy was considered better press than nonviolence, and by 1963 Malcolm X rather than King was appearing most often on TV screens, in newspaper interviews, and on public forums. Often surrounded by menacing body guards, speaking with determined confidence, and jabbing his finger in the air to underscore his points, Malcolm X made an unforgettable impression, eliciting admiration among many black Americans and fear among whites. Civil rights leaders committed to nonviolence and integration publicly repudiated his separatist message and his advocacy of armed self-defense.

Malcolm X became restive, as the Nation of Islam failed to join the rising tide of civil rights activity. Convinced that Muhammad was not sincere, a view validated by evidence of corruption within the organization and compounded by Muhammad's mounting jealousy of Malcolm X's blossoming personal influence, Malcolm X's relationship with the Nation of Islam began to falter. His public assertion in 1963 that President John F. Kennedy's assassination amounted to "chickens coming home to roost" gave Muhammad reason to suspend him.

During this suspension, Malcolm X traveled to Mecca and throughout North Africa, where he discovered Orthodox Islam and experienced an epiphany. Upon his return to the United States in 1964, he shifted his ethical stance. Still convinced that racism "corroded the spirit of America" and that only black people could free themselves, he rejected racism of all kinds, spoke of a common bond linking humanity, and conceded that some whites did want to end racism. He also formally broke with the Nation of Islam and changed his name to El-Hajj Malik El-Shabazz, a move that reflected his Mecca pilgrimage. In February 1965, Malcolm X founded the Organization of Afro-American Unity (OAAU), moved increasingly in the direction of socialism, and expressed growing interest in China. Still in transition, on February 21, 1965, he was assassinated by three Black Muslim loyalists as he spoke in a Harlem ballroom.

As Malcolm X had predicted in his autobiography, he would become more important in death than in life. His message profoundly influenced the development of the Student Nonviolent Coordinating Committee, Black Power, the Black Panther Party, and George L. Jackson. The anger that he sought to channel into political action exploded in the 1965 Watts riot and the string of rebellions culminating in Newark, New Jersey, and Detroit in 1967. By the 1990s, Malcolm X had become a folk hero to African Americans living in decaying American cities. Rap artists chanted his words; murals, hats, T-shirts, and posters displayed his piercing gaze; and filmmaker Spike Lee memorialized his life in a 1992 feature film. In death, Malcolm X has come to symbolize racial pride, dignity, self-defense, and human transcendence.

The legacy of Malcolm X has continued to live on into the twenty-first century, and his reach has become global. During his lifetime, he worked to create links between the people of Africa, the Middle East, and the Americas. According to scholar Peniel Joseph, those efforts continue to set off "political, religious, and cultural reverberations." Adding to existing material on the life and philosophy of Malcolm X has been difficult because of a wall of secrecy that extended to his family, his friends and cohorts, government files, and the Nation of Islam. In 2008 his family finally released his personal archives. It is generally accepted that Manning Marable's 2011 biography of Malcolm X is set to become the definitive treatment of his life. Unfortunately, Marable, an expert in black socialism and radicalism, died shortly before the publication of the work, and further explanations of the influence of Malcolm X must henceforth be produced by other scholars.

Patrick D. Jones

SEE ALSO: *Black Panthers; Kennedy Assassination; King, Martin Luther, Jr.; Ku Klux Klan; Students for a Democratic Society (SDS).*

BIBLIOGRAPHY

Breitman, George. *Malcolm X: By Any Means Necessary.* New York: Pathfinder Press, 1971.

Breitman, George. *The Last Year of Malcolm X: The Evolution of a Revolutionary.* New York: Pathfinder Press, 1989.

Breitman, George, ed. *Malcolm X Speaks: Selected Speeches and Statements.* New York: Grove Weidenfeld, 1990.

Carson, Clayborne, and David Gallen. *Malcolm X: The FBI File.* New York: Carroll & Graf Publishing, 1991.

Conard, Mark. *The Philosophy of Spike Lee.* Lexington: University Press of Kentucky, 2011.

Dyson, Michael Eric. *Making Malcolm: The Myth and Meaning of Malcolm X.* New York: Oxford University Press, 1995.

Goldman, Peter. *The Death and Life of Malcolm X.* New York: Harper & Row, 1973.

Haley, Alex. *The Autobiography of Malcolm X.* New York: Grove Press, 1965.

Horne, Gerald. "'Myth' and the Making of 'Malcolm X.'" *American Historical Review* 98, no. 2 (1993).

Joseph, Peniel E. *Dark Days, Bright Nights: From Black Power to Barack Obama.* New York: Basic Civitas Books, 2010.

Joseph, Peniel E. "Still Reinventing Malcolm." *Chronicle of Higher Education,* May 6, 2011.

Marable, Manning. *Malcolm X: A Life of Reinvention.* New York: Viking, 2011.

Perry, Bruce. *Malcolm: The Life of a Man Who Changed Black America.* New York: Station Hill Press, 1991.

Terrill, Robert E., ed. *The Cambridge Companion to Malcolm X.* New York: Cambridge University, 2010.

Wolfenstein, Victor. *The Victims of Democracy: Malcolm X and the Black Revolution.* Berkeley: University of California Press, 1981.

Mall of America

Since its opening in 1992, the 4.2-million-square-foot Mall of America in Bloomington, Minnesota, has reigned as the largest shopping mall in the United States. It is so large, in fact, that it could accommodate the Yankee Stadium seven times over. The mall has emerged as one of the country's most popular tourist destinations, and tourists account for three or four out of every ten visitors. More than forty million people visit the Mall of America annually—a total higher than that for Disney World, the Grand Canyon, and Graceland combined. The mall originally featured four anchor stores: Nordstrom, Macy's, Sears, and Bloomingdale's. However, early in 2012 Bloomingdale's announced it was closing its Mall of America store due to underperformance. Mall officials indicated that Bloomingdale's would be replaced by four "international forward-fashion stores" but elected not to name them.

The mall's popularity is due as much to its entertainment and cultural amenities as to shopping—though with 520 different specialty shops and merchandise kiosks, the Mall of America is certainly a shopper's paradise. Initially Knott's Berry Farm's Camp Snoopy, a theme park with more than thirty rides and amusements—including a roller coaster, a water ride, and a Ferris wheel—was located at the center of the giant four-story structure. That attraction has since been replaced with the Nickelodeon Universe theme park. The mall is also home to Moose Mountain Adventure Golf, the Sea Life Minnesota Aquarium, Amazing Mirror Maze, the A.C.E.S. Flight Simulator, and Lego and American Girl stores/play areas. The mall's top floor is devoted entirely to glitzy nightclubs, restaurants, and a fourteen-screen movie theater that offers such extras as 3-D, D-Box seating, a VIP theater, and a STARBAR lounge. It also houses a wedding chapel and a police substation.

Entertainment and shopping are not the only draws at the Mall of America. In 2011 the Mayo Clinic opened a wellness and health education center in the mall. There is also a focus on education through South Hennepin Adult Programs in Education, which offers basic adult education and English as a second language classes, and through the Metropolitan Learning Alliance, which provides classes in arts and vocational studies for high school students. As Minneapolis architect Richard Varda observes, "The Mall of America is a city inside a piece at the edge of a city."

HISTORY

The mall began as the brain child of Canada's Triple Five Group, the company that built the famous West Edmonton Mall, which is the largest such building in North America. The company's initial 1985 proposal for a billion-dollar "megamall" at the site of the old Twins stadium in the booming Minneapolis suburb of Bloomington envisioned a leisure and shopping complex even larger and more spectacular than the one that was eventually built. However, after failing to secure a long-term loan, Triple Five Group was forced to partner with Melvin Simon and Teachers Insurance and Annuity Association in 1987. The plan was promptly scaled back to its current dimensions. In May 1988—over the objections of many of the city's citizens—the Bloomington Port Authority agreed to contribute $100 million toward improvements in infrastructure for the development. Construction began in June 1989, and the mall opened for business in August 1992. The final price tag for the entire project was more than $680 million.

Designed by architect Jon Jerde and the Jerde Partnership, the Mall of America is laid out as a multistory "rectangular doughnut" with thoroughfares lined by 4.3 miles of storefronts connecting the department stores on the perimeter and Nickelodeon Universe at its center. Without a doubt the mall's most impressive architectural features are the 8 acres of vast skylights that span the entire 7 acres of Nickelodeon Universe.

Jerde gave each side of the rectangle a distinct architectural theme and matching decor. The corridors on the North side of the mall, known as the North Garden, are painted garden green and scattered with gazebos, wooden trellises, and pavilion-like structures as well as airy terraces overlooking the amusement park. With their barrel-vaulted ceilings and industrial green color scheme, the corridors in the West Market area recall European arcades of the late nineteenth century. The thoroughfares in the South Avenue area have an elegant Rodeo Drive feel created by their upscale boutiques, arches, and peach-and-cream color scheme. The East Broadway area is meant to suggest "modernity" through its polished steel railings, neon, and slick black-and-gray floors. The fourth floor's collection of bars and nightclubs, known as The Upper East Side, self-consciously simulates a big city entertainment district. The total effect of the place is more than a little disorienting, which is precisely as the designers had planned. "We want people to get lost in the Mall," confessed Tim Magill of the Jerde Partnership. "We want to tweak your perceptions so you'll be exposed to areas you would regularly pass by."

SO THEY COME

In its first five years of existence, the mall silenced critics who doubted it could consistently draw the crowds necessary to turn a profit. Economists estimate that the mall and the legions of out-of-state tourists it attracts pump about $1.5 billion a year into the local economy. Thanks to its enormous popularity and mind-boggling size, the mall had become something of a cultural icon by the late 1990s. Celebrities from Bruce Willis to Newt Gingrich made regular appearances within the mall's confines, and Camp Snoopy made its film debut in *The Mighty Ducks* in 1992. The mall appeared again in *D3: The Mighty Ducks* (1996), and in 1996 Arnold Schwarzenegger filmed his Christmas movie *Jingle All the Way* there. More recently the mall served as the backdrop for the reality show *Mall Cops of America*, which was filmed in 2009. It has also been featured on the Disney Channel, the Travel Channel, and The Learning Channel (TLC).

Despite its successes, the Mall of America has had its share of both problems and critics. Though it presents its enclosed environs as a safe alternative to city streets, it has been unable to prevent rapes and robberies from occurring on its premises. In addition, because it is a favorite meeting place and hangout for teenagers from around the Twin Cities metro region, youth crime has been an especially nagging problem. In 1996 the mall's managers responded by implementing a policy requiring children aged sixteen or younger to be accompanied by an adult after 4 p.m. on Fridays and Saturdays, a move that brought about a steep decline in youth crimes and consequently increased adult traffic on weekend nights.

In 1996 the Mall of America was thrust into the center of a debate about the public's right to political expression in commercially owned and operated spaces. On May 19 of that year, a group of ten animal rights activists entered the mall and distributed flyers in front of Macy's, urging people to boycott the store because it sold fur. Mall security told the protesters to leave, and four were issued tickets for trespassing. Hennepin County Judge Jack Nordby sided with the protesters in ruling that Minnesota citizens have reasonable rights to free speech and assembly at publicly supported shopping malls. Nordby's decision was reversed on appeal, but the protesters and the Minnesota ACLU vowed to appeal. In 1999 the Minnesota Supreme Court sided with the appellate court in *State v. Wicklund*.

It is hardly surprising that the mall finds itself in the middle of a controversy over whether or not shopping malls are the functional equivalent of city streets, public parks, and town squares. After all, the amazing assortment of activities collected under its roof make the Mall of America the closest thing to a fully enclosed city America has yet seen. Whatever the courts ultimately decide about its status as "public" space, the Mall of America has been and will continue to be a gathering place not simply for Minnesotans but for the whole world.

Steve Macek

SEE ALSO: *Advertising; American Girl Series; Amusement Parks; Christmas; Consumerism; Department Stores; Disney (Walt Disney Company); Graceland; Legos; Macy's; Malls; Movie Palaces; The New York Yankees; Roller Coasters; Schwarzenegger, Arnold; Teenagers; Willis, Bruce.*

BIBLIOGRAPHY

Crawford, Margaret. "The World in a Shopping Mall." In *Variations on a Theme Park*, ed. Michael Sorkin, 3–30. New York: Noonday Press, 1992.

Frazier, Ian. "The Mall of America." *Atlantic Monthly*, July/August 2002.

Gottdiener, Mark. *The Theming of America: Dreams, Visions, and Commercial Spaces*. Boulder, CO: Westview Press, 1997.

"Mall of America: More Ways to Be You." Accessed March 2012. Available from http://www.mallofamerica.com/home

Nelson, Eric. *Mall of America: Reflections of a Virtual Community*. Lakeville, MN: Galde Press, 1998.

Steller, Chris. "Public Funds, Private Mall: Expansion, RNC's Approach May Reopen Free Speech Question at MOA." *Minnesota Independent*, May 20, 2008.

Waters, Jennifer. "It's a Mall World." *Architecture Minnesota*, January/February 1993, 20–24.

Malls

For more than a century, shopping malls have been part of the American landscape. As modern town centers, they provide space for commerce, social interaction, and cultural events. Their careful design goes beyond shopping to articulate a vision of society. In *You Got to Dance with Them What Brung You: Politics in the Clinton Years*, social commentator Molly Ivins proclaims on her first visit to the enormous Mall of America, "Great Caesar's armpit! Sweet suffering catfish! Holy Gamoley! I have been to the pyramids of America. I have seen the cathedral of commerce. Our Parthenon, our Coliseum, our Chartres."

During the late twentieth century, the abundance of mall shoppers and their frequent treasure-seeking visits exuded an almost religious fervor. In 1986 *Consumer Reports* ranked the mall alongside computers and air-conditioning as one of the top fifty wonders that revolutionized the lives of consumers during

Shopping Mall. *Holiday shoppers flock to a busy mall. Malls have moved beyond their role as a place of commerce to become centers of social and community activity.* SEAN GALLUP/STAFF/GETTY IMAGES NEWS/GETTY IMAGES.

the past fifty years. Nevertheless, malls have faced waning popularity and competition from other consumer outlets, such as online and catalog shopping, prompting developers and retailers to evolve the design and scope of modern commercial centers.

EARLY COMMERCIAL CENTERS

Although malls have become one of the most recognizable features of U.S. towns, the mall is not an American invention. One of the earliest was the Kapali Carsi, or Grand Bazaar, in Istanbul, Turkey, built during the fourteenth century. Encompassing sixty-five streets and passages, with more than 4,000 shops and cafés, the giant marketplace is reputed to have had the most shops under one roof anywhere in the world. Throughout the years, commerce has frequently developed in centralized locations. Built around a courtyard, the five-story Palais Royale in Paris opened to the public in 1784 and offered shopping, dining, and entertainment.

In 1896 Roland Park Shopping Center was erected in Baltimore, Maryland, becoming, arguably, the first American strip mall. The center consisted of six stores and a parking area for horses and carriages. The first suburban shopping center, according to the National Register of Historic Places, was Market Square in Lake Forest, Illinois, built in 1916. However, many consider the predecessor of the modern shopping center to be the Country Club Plaza of Kansas City, Missouri, which was designed in 1922 and accessible only by car. Six years later Grandview Avenue Shopping Center in Columbus, Ohio, was built, with thirty stores and parking for 400 cars.

The next step toward the modern shopping center was the construction of the first enclosed mall in 1956. Built in a suburb of Minneapolis, Minnesota, the Southdale Mall had a clear objective: to keep the weather out. Shoppers could stroll year-round in climate-controlled comfort. Compared to its successors, however, the mall was spartan. It had no food vendors, no skylights, no lifelike statues, no fountains, and no neon signs.

EXPANSION AND VARIATION

The growth and significance of the U.S. shopping mall are best explained in the context of post–World War II America. Before 1950 many Americans lived in urban areas and met their needs within their own neighborhood. Fueled by government guarantees for veterans and the vision of real estate developers such as William Levitt, ownership of single-family housing grew rapidly. Developers constructed homes outside city limits, inciting a mass movement out of cities into the new suburbs. By 2000 more than half of all Americans lived in suburban areas.

The suburban exodus permanently altered the consumer landscape, displacing American commercial, cultural, manufacturing, employment, service, financial, entertainment, and recreational activities out of urban areas. Without city neighborhoods to guide the retail structure, new commercial spaces arose to meet consumers' needs. Thus, malls became visionaries' answer to central urban business districts.

Today, shopping centers come in many shapes, sizes, and varieties. The smallest are community convenience centers—retail spaces of 30,000 to 100,000 square feet that house small businesses such as dry cleaners, pizza joints, and frame shops. These centers survive without large tenants, called anchors, which draw large numbers of consumers. At the next level are community centers of 100,000 to 400,000 square feet, where a large grocery, drug, discount, or department store typically serves as an anchor. Regional shopping behemoths, typically more than 400,000 square feet of retail space, have multiple anchors and attract international consumers.

Extreme examples, called megamalls, have 4 million to 5 million square feet of retail space and draw consumers worldwide. Two examples are West Edmonton Mall (5.2 million square feet) in Alberta, Canada, and the Mall of America (4.2 million square feet) in Minnesota. West Edmonton Mall, built in 1981, has 825 specialty stores; 11 department stores; 2 auto dealerships; 132 restaurants; 32 movie screens; a 5-acre water park with 22 slides; the world's largest indoor amusement park (with a roller coaster); an 18-hole miniature golf course; an ice skating rink; a lake; a 355-room hotel; a chapel; and a menagerie of sharks, dolphins, flamingos, jaguars, and alligators, among other attractions. The Mall of America has 520 specialty stores, more than 50 restaurants, 8 nightclubs, 14 movie screens, a 7-acre amusement park with 28 rides, a 1.2-million-gallon aquarium, and 12,550 parking spaces. Opened in 1992, the Minnesota megamall attracts about forty million visitors annually, produces more than 50,000 tons of waste per year, and is five times larger than Red Square in Moscow.

SOCIAL IMPACT

The proliferation of shopping malls has had an indelible impact on the structure of American retailing. In 1960 there were 4,500 malls, which accounted for 14 percent of retail sales. By 1975, 16,400 malls accounted for 33 percent of retail sales. The number of malls grew to 30,000 in 1987 and ten years later reached 42,000 for a combined retail space of 5.1 billion square feet. Between 1995 and 1998 an average of 900 new malls were built each year. By the end of 2009, there were almost 105,000 shopping centers in the United States for a total of more than 7 billion square feet of retail space, or 23.1 square feet for each American.

As the new town centers of the suburbs, malls centralize commerce by providing a wide variety of goods under one roof. At their best, malls represent a utopian vision, promising an environment free of the elements, dirt, and crime. At their worst, malls are crowded, poorly lit havens for loitering teenagers and shoplifters. Often, indoor malls are carefully designed and controlled environments with barren exteriors that encourage shoppers to be inside, not outside. The enclosed mall represents a stage where consumers can live out a fantasy world, with retailers and mall marketers providing the lighting, props, staging, and supporting actors (mall employees).

Mall stores and common areas are designed to appeal to all of the senses, using décor, noise, lighting, and layout to manipulate consumer behavior. However, even the most innovative tactics are grounded in recapturing the town square environment that Americans lost when they moved away from urban centers. In some ways, malls, with their food courts and large center areas for entertainment, resemble old Italian town squares where people went to shop but stayed for the food.

Shopping malls are also some of the most visited tourist attractions in the country. The Mall of America in Minnesota, Tysons Corner Center in Virginia, and Woodfield Mall in Illinois are each the most visited attractions in their states. Each year, the Mall of America receives more visitors than the Magic Kingdom and Hollywood Walk of Fame combined.

CONSUMER UTOPIA OR CULTURAL SWAMP?

Conceptually, tourist attractions such as Disneyland offer a prototype for the modern mall in terms of principle, philosophy, and operation. Opened one year before Southdale Mall, Disneyland boasts Main Street, U.S.A., a shop-lined avenue that some might contend is truly America's first enclosed shopping mall. The geography of the mall, like the geography of Disneyland, is a reflection of American consumer consciousness. Both are areas designed to evoke happiness and a friendly, familiar environment. Like Main Street, U.S.A., which gives visitors a consumer utopia that leads to the Sleeping Beauty Castle, malls create a shopping paradise anchored by a major department store. And like Disney's shopping promenade, which radiates into the various regions of the park, malls often branch off into other anchor and specialty areas.

The abundance of mall offerings can be mesmerizing: child care, doctor and dental services, professional services, fine dining, entertainment, and education. Malls promise everything Americans need to look and feel better and to make their lives easier and more fun, interesting, and rewarding. The walls of the mall, like the walls of a castle, preserve a way of life desired by consumers worldwide. The mall is a version of an imperial and democratic city where anyone is admitted and everything is available.

Despite their utopian aspirations, however, malls often provoke envy, anxiety, and insecurity in consumers, who cannot afford to buy everything they see. Malls are manifestations of, and possibly instigators of, a world defined by commercialization. William Kowinski in *The Malling of America: An Inside Look at the Great Consumer Paradise* posits that malls are an important economic, cultural, social, and psychological identifier of our time:

> Someday it may be possible—if it isn't already—to be born, go from preschool through college, get a job, date, marry, have children, fool around, get a divorce, advance through a career or two, receive your medical care, even get arrested, tried, and jailed; live a relatively full life of culture and entertainment, and eventually die and be given funeral rites without ever leaving a particular mall complex—because every one of these possibilities exists now in some shopping center somewhere.

COMPETITION AND TRANSFORMATION

Malls have survived changing American lifestyles because they meet a variety of consumer needs. In a time of dual-income families and single-parent households, malls save time-impoverished consumers money and effort. They also provide a social venue for senior citizens and teenagers, as well as a place to exercise for walkers. Nevertheless, many consumers have become disenchanted with the mall experience. In the last decade of the twentieth century, mall visits per month decreased by one-third and consumers spent one-third less time per visit. In a 1996 national survey of mall consumers, the Purdue University Retail Institute found that consumers could easily identify their dissatisfaction with their mall experiences. The following is a list of the five most frequently mentioned negative impressions of malls:

Malls were crowded. Ironically, efforts to increase traffic with special events may actually reinforce the notion of malls as crowded places.

Mall parking had poor lighting, required a lengthy walk, and/or required payment.

Loitering teenagers irritated the consumer.

Poor interior layout and climate led to a negative shopping experience. Some malls were reportedly confusing, unkempt, and poorly lit; others played loud music and had "bad" smells.

Poor treatment in stores.

Other negative aspects of shopping at malls included a lack of visible security, an inability to find help in the store, little selection/variety (store and merchandise sameness), paying more than expected, and an inability to find desired merchandise.

Mall managers and developers must pay attention to the nature of the retail experience in stores, common areas, and even the parking lot. Customer satisfaction with the mall experience affects intent to purchase, consumer loyalty, the amount shoppers spend, and the spread of positive word of mouth. Customer satisfaction has become particularly important as malls face competition from other retail outlets, such as home shopping networks, the Internet, catalogs, and freestanding stores.

As the presence of regional malls began to decline around the turn of the twenty-first century, real estate developers began promoting lifestyle centers as the wave of the future. Developers created the new open-air areas to look like small-town main streets, luring shoppers with attractions such as parks, farmers markets, free concerts, and ice-skating rinks. The centers' zigzag design ensures that shoppers will be tempted to spend money along the way to their destination. The design has proved successful, with shoppers spending an average of $80 per visit as compared to $56 at traditional malls In 2008 not a single closed-air shopping center was scheduled to be built.

One of the largest lifestyle centers is Easton Town Center, located in Columbus, Ohio, which draws more than twenty-one million visitors annually. Built in 1999, the center is located in the heart of a 1,300-acre residential, office, and hotel development, which has helped to ensure the longevity and success of the lifestyle mall design. In 2010 Easton raked in $545 per foot in sales, and its developers were making plans to build condominiums and apartment buildings nearby to provide a ready-made base of regular customers.

Richard Feinberg
Cindy Evans

SEE ALSO: *Amusement Parks; Automobile;* Consumer Reports; *Consumerism; Department Stores; Disney (Walt Disney Company); Home Shopping Network/QVC; Levittown; Mall of America; Online Shopping; Pizza; Roller Coasters; Suburbia; Teenagers; World War II.*

BIBLIOGRAPHY

Feinberg, Samuel. *What Makes Shopping Centers Tick.* New York: Fairchild Publications, 1960.

Ivins, Molly. *You Got to Dance with Them What Brung You: Politics in the Clinton Years.* New York: Random House, 1998.

Jacobs, Jerry. *The Mall: An Attempted Escape from Everyday Life.* Prospect Heights, IL: Waveland Press, 1984.

Kowinski, William. *The Malling of America: An Inside Look at the Great Consumer Paradise.* New York: W. Morrow, 1985.

Longstreth, Richard. *The American Department Store Transformed, 1920–1960.* New Haven, CT: Yale University Press, 2010.

Nelson, Eric. *Mall of America: Reflections of a Virtual Community.* Lakeville, MN: Galde Press, 1998.

Rybczynski, Witold. *Makeshift Metropolis: Ideas about Cities.* New York: Scribner, 2010.

Williamson, Thad. *Sprawl, Justice, and Citizenship: The Civic Costs of the American Way of Life.* New York: Oxford University Press, 2010.

Wilson, William. *Constructed Climates: A Primer of Urban Environments.* Chicago: University of Chicago Press, 2011.

Zepp, Ira. *The New Religious Image of Urban America: The Shopping Mall as Ceremonial Center.* Niwot: University of Colorado Press, 1997.

The Maltese Falcon

In his 1930 novel *The Maltese Falcon*, Dashiell Hammett introduced the reading public to the hard-boiled private detective as a central character. Sam Spade, of Spade and Archer Investigations, is a cynical, violent, and socially unattractive man who thinks nothing of having an affair with his partner's wife or taking part in the evils of shabby San Francisco neighborhoods. Because of his criminal associations, the police do not trust him. The district attorney's office periodically calls him in for questioning. Spade, mindful that his environment has tarnished him, uses his reputation to his advantage.

While the authorities often suspect him of complicity, his clients, ranging from the tawdry to the downright evil, take him into their confidence. To Spade life is not a rational, orderly affair but a series of random, often baneful happenings. Aware of, and adjusting to, the decadence around him, he maintains a strong moral awareness and a strict adherence to his own code of professional ethics. He judges people by his standards, not theirs or society's.

Spade is a descendent of the hard-boiled heroes of detective stories in pulp magazines of the 1920s. These private detectives were a new breed. They did not shun violence; they embraced it and used it to their advantage. Their mannerisms were unrefined, their language was pungent. They moved with ease among the lawless. Their reactions to events were instinctive not reasoned. They sacrificed love and sentiment for principle. Like the lone heroes of the Westerns, they adhered to their professional codes and lived by their guns and fists.

The book is written in a sparse, objective narrative eschewing excess verbiage. Not merely a landmark detective novel that profoundly influenced later detective novels, *The Maltese Falcon* stands on its own merits as a quality literary work.

THE PLOT

When a Miss Wonderly retains the Spade/Archer agency to trail the mysterious Thursby, Miles Archer—believing that she might possibly be another sexual conquest—takes the case. When

The Maltese Falcon. The Maltese Falcon *starred, from left, Humphrey Bogart as Sam Spade, Peter Lorre as Joel Cairo, Mary Astor as Brigid O'Shaughnessy, and Sydney Greenstreet as Kasper Gutman.* WARNER BROS/FIRST NATIONAL/THE KOBAL COLLECTION.

Archer is killed, and shortly thereafter Thursby is found shot to death, Spade is propelled into a complex web of mystery occupied by a cast of characters who plumb the depths of moral corruption and betrayal. Shortly after Archer's death, Spade is visited by Joel Cairo, an effeminate, gardenia-scented thief, who retains him to find a jewel-encrusted statuette known as the Maltese Falcon. Spade discovers a connection between Cairo and Miss Wonderly, whose real name is Brigid O'Shaughnessy. This leads, in turn, to the mysterious fat man, Kasper Gutman, a mincing international swindler and crime baron, and his psychopathic hired gun/bodyguard, Wilmer. Gutman reveals that he, too, is after the Falcon, estimating its worth at an enormous fortune.

In searching Cairo's hotel room for information about the bird, Spade notices that the ship arrival schedules have been clipped from the newspaper. After purchasing a paper, he discovers that the steamer *La Paloma* will arrive that day from Hong Kong. Knowing that Brigid has been in the Orient, Spade goes to the dock and discovers that Gutman, Cairo, Brigid, and Wilmer have been to the ship and talked to its skipper, Captain Jacobi, who has since disappeared. Back at his office, Spade and his loyal secretary, Effie, are interrupted by the arrival of Captain Jacobi, who gives Spade a bundle and then drops dead on the floor. The bundle contains the Maltese Falcon.

After attempting to contact Brigid and being sent on a wild goose chase by Gutman's daughter, Spade finally goes to his apartment to find Brigid waiting outside and Cairo, Gutman, and Wilmer waiting for him inside. They all want the Falcon. Spade announces that he has the bird. He wants $10,000 and someone to turn over to the police for the murders. Gutman, who knows that Wilmer killed Captain Jacobi and assumes that Thursby killed Archer, agrees to turn Wilmer over to the cops in exchange for the statuette. After Gutman counts out ten $1,000 bills, Spade calls Effie and tells her to deliver the bird. Gutman then admits that he had tried to bribe Thursby, but Thursby was too loyal to Brigid and would not throw in with them. This revelation points out Archer's killer to Spade.

The Falcon turns out to be only a lead imitation, a fake—a symbol of the cast of characters in the story. After notifying the police, Spade turns to Brigid and forces her to confess that she killed Archer. She picked the agency at random, she explains, believing that Thursby would kill any detective who followed him. When Thursby failed to kill Archer, Brigid killed him with Thursby's gun in hopes that the police would arrest him and she would be free to get the Falcon for herself. But Thursby was killed by Wilmer a short time later, which told Brigid that the fat man was in town. She then used her sexual wiles to get Spade to help her.

In the end, Spade is forced to turn her over to the authorities, knowing that she would have something on him if he did not and that he would never be able to turn his back on her. Besides, killing a detective is bad for the detective business. His moral code will not allow his feelings for Brigid to get in the way of punishing his partner's murderer. His code might allow him to profit from the Falcon, to deceive criminals, and to pretend to throw in with them, even to accept Gutman's bribe; it would even allow him to have an affair with his partner's wife and to have a passionate affair with Brigid while she is a client. But there is a line he cannot and will not cross.

Spade is committed to removing polluting elements from society and to punishing the murderer of a partner he did not respect. His code will not allow him to violate the principles he has established for himself in his profession. He is as fallible as any man, but he will not sacrifice his own code of professional ethics.

THE FILM VERSIONS

Filmed three times by Warner Brothers, the movie versions transformed Spade from a debonair ladies' man in the 1930s versions to a lonely, possessed detective in the early 1940s rendition. In 1931 Roy Del Ruth directed Ricardo Cortez as Spade, a charming, captivating ladies' man. This pre–ratings code film depicts Spade in a suggestive bedroom scene with Bebe Daniels as Brigid. It also includes a silent mouthing of "S.O.B." by Cairo and partial nude scenes of Brigid. Because of these and other explicit scenes, the Motion Picture Production Code office rejected a 1934 rerelease of the film.

In most respects, the film adheres closely to the story line of the novel. It was later retitled *Dangerous Lady* to distinguish it from the 1941 version. It was remade in 1936 as *Satan Met a Lady* with Warren William as a wisecracking Ted Shayne and Bette Davis as Valerie, a mysterious client, who hires Shayne to hunt down a mysterious fat woman who is hunting for a ram's horn filled with jewels (Alison Skipworth). Shayne sets a trap, pitting the various crooks against each other and solves his partner's murder. The film was an attempt to bring humor to the story and to depict the Spade character as a sophisticated, all-knowing, nightclubbing ladies' man, somewhat in the mold of Nick Charles of *The Thin Man* series produced at Metro-Goldwyn-Mayer. Neither version made much of an impact on the critics or the moviegoing public.

The definitive movie version was produced in 1941 by Hal Wallis and written and directed by John Huston. It is a landmark film that has become a classic of modern popular culture. The 1941 version created the hard-boiled screen detective, the prototype for countless detective movies that followed. It also introduced the cinematic genre later termed "film noir," a style that appeared in hundreds of Hollywood films between 1944 and 1958.

This version is a faithful rendition of the book's story line and stars Humphrey Bogart as the dour, obsessed Spade, and Mary Astor as the sinister Brigid. Peter Lorre plays the elusive Cairo; Sydney Greenstreet, in his first film, is the amoral fat man Gutman; and Elisha Cook Jr. plays the psychopathic killer, Wilmer. This film version is as streamlined and as devoid of description as the novel. The characters describe themselves by their actions and their words. In a terse, almost documentary style, the secrets are revealed to the audience at the same time that Spade learns of them.

Cinematically the film was a departure from the standard Hollywood fare of the 1930s. The odd camera angles, the intrusion of light and shadow into scenes at unexpected angles, the dishonorable motivation and expectations of the main characters, including the protagonist Spade, were somewhat jarring to critics and audiences alike. In addition, Astor's portrayal of Brigid was much darker and more menacing than audiences were accustomed to in female antagonists. But by 1944, after millions of people had lost friends and family members in World War II, this style of filmmaking seemed to have some relevance to the moviegoing public. French critics, who had missed seeing American films from 1940 to 1945, originated the "film noir" tag.

As the world plunged into the Cold War and the specter of the atom bomb cast its pall over civilization, the noir style became popular. The confusing, pessimistic plots, the emphasis on alienation and goals gone awry, and the intrusion of the normal clamor of city life into the movies, exposing a dark underside of American life, were accepted as a realistic portrayal of the complexity of modern postwar civilization.

OTHER VERSIONS

Director Roger Corman, under the pseudonym Harry Neil, made a low-budget parody of *The Maltese Falcon* titled *Target Harry* in 1968, and David Giler wrote and directed a similar spin-off, *The Black Bird*, in 1975. Both films were unsuccessful. A radio series, *The Adventures of Sam Spade*, began on CBS on July 12, 1946, as a summer replacement but became instantly popular. In September it moved into the fall lineup, airing on Sunday nights and sponsored by Wildroot Cream-Oil, a popular men's hairdressing. It was directed by William Spier and starred Howard Duff as Spade and Lurene Tuttle as Effie. In 1949 CBS dropped the show when Hammett's name cropped up in the House Un-American Activities Committee investigations, although he was never charged with disloyalty. NBC picked up the show in the fall of 1949 with Steve Dunne as Spade and Tuttle remaining as Effie. The show went off the air in 1951.

James R. Belpedio

SEE ALSO: *Bogart, Humphrey; Cold War; Corman, Roger; Davis, Bette; Detective Fiction; Film Noir; Hammett, Dashiell; Hard-Boiled Detective Fiction; Hollywood; Huston, John; Lorre, Peter; MGM (Metro-Goldwyn-Mayer).*

BIBLIOGRAPHY

Christopher, Nicholas. *Somewhere in the Night: Film Noir and the American City.* New York: Free Press, 1997.

Hammett, Dashiell. *The Maltese Falcon.* New York: Alfred A. Knopf, 1930.

Krutnik, Frank. *In a Lonely Street: Film Noir, Genre, Masculinity.* New York: Routledge, 1991.

Leff, Leonard J., and Jerold L. Simons. *The Dame in the Kimono.* New York: Anchor Books, 1990.

Luhr, William. *The Maltese Falcon.* New Brunswick, NJ: Rutgers University Press, 1995.

Sperber, A. M., and Eric Lax. *Bogart.* New York: William Morrow, 1977.

Wagner, Ole. *Social Criticism in Dashiell Hammett's "Red Harvest" and "The Maltese Falcon."* Munich, Germany: GRIN, 2007.

Winn, Dilys. *Murder Ink*, rev. ed. New York: Workman Publishing, 1984.

The Mamas and the Papas

One of the most commercially successful folk-rock groups of the mid-1960s, the Mamas and the Papas were known for their rich vocal harmonies as well as their unconventional appearance. The group's four founding members only sang together for a few years, but their recordings, which included nine Top 40 hits, made a lasting impact on pop music. Their first single, "California Dreamin'" (1965), established them as part of a new Los Angeles–based hippie music scene, even though they initially came together as a folk act in New York's Greenwich Village. Few pop groups featured a combination of male and female voices, and this rare sound became a factor in the Mamas and the Papas' popularity among adults.

During the early 1960s, pop music was designed primarily for teenagers. With the advent of performers like the Mamas and the Papas, who used their folk background to create complex arrangements for catchy, intelligent songs, older listeners began buying pop albums. By the time the group disbanded due to personal differences in 1968, other artists such as the Beach Boys and the Beatles were also producing more intricate music. In a relatively short time, the Mamas and the Papas managed to earn the appreciation of a substantial audience that endured for decades after they ceased singing together.

COMING TOGETHER

The son of a marine corps officer, John Edmund Andrew Phillips was born in 1935 on Parris Island, South Carolina. He played the guitar in high school, and he began performing at folk clubs in his early twenties. In addition to his interest in folk music, John was intrigued by vocal groups with smooth harmonies such as the Hi-Los. He formed his own folk quartet, which evolved into the Journeymen, a trio that included Scott McKenzie and Dick Weissman. They were successful during the early 1960s as part of the urban folk revival that had begun at the end of the previous decade.

The Mamas and Papas. *One of the most successful folk-rock groups of the mid-1960s, the Mamas and the Papas included from left, Cass Elliot, John Phillips, Denny Doherty, and Michelle Phillips.* MICHAEL OCHS ARCHIVES/STRINGER/GETTY IMAGES.

While performing in San Francisco, John met and fell in love with Holly Michelle Gilliam, a seventeen-year-old California native. They were married on New Year's Eve in 1962, and by 1964 John, Michelle, and Marshall Brickman were singing together as the New Journeymen. As the group toured, John recruited a tenor from Nova Scotia named Denny Doherty, who had previously sung with the Halifax Three. Brickman left the group in 1965, and the three remaining members traveled to St. Thomas in the Virgin Islands to rehearse new songs John had written. There they were joined by a friend of Doherty's named Cass Elliot, born Ellen Naomi Cohen in Baltimore, Maryland. Doherty and Elliot had sung together as part of the Big Three, which became the Mugwumps, a group that included John Sebastian and Zal Yanovsky, future founders of the Lovin' Spoonful. Later, John would mention these and other names in the song "Creeque Alley" (1967), which explained how the Mamas and the Papas came together.

John realized that folk music's popularity was waning and began designing his new compositions for a pop act using electric instruments. After working on this material in the Virgin Islands, John and Michelle, Doherty, and Elliot went to Los Angeles, where they auditioned for producer Lou Adler of Dunhill Records. He offered them a contract, and they decided to call themselves the Mamas and the Papas. Their first single was to be "Go Where You Wanna Go," until Adler changed his mind and released "California Dreamin'," which became a Top 10 record early in 1966. It was followed a few months later by the single "Monday, Monday" and the group's first album, *If You Can Believe Your Eyes and Ears*, both of which went to number one on the Billboard charts. The group developed a hippie image, often wearing long, flowing robes on stage.

Despite their sudden tremendous success as performers, the Mamas and the Papas were not faring well offstage. Shortly after the band was signed, John discovered that Michelle and Doherty were having an affair. In June 1966 Michelle was fired from the group for a few months, until she and John reconciled their differences. During 1967 John and Adler helped organize the Monterey Pop Festival, and John wrote a song for his former bandmate Scott McKenzie titled "San Francisco (Be Sure to Wear Flowers in Your Hair)" that became a pop anthem for young people seeking out the California counterculture. That year the Mamas and the Papas continued recording and performing sporadically, but by the end of the following year they made the decision to split up.

MOVING ON

Mama Cass, as Elliot was commonly known, was the only member of the group to become a successful solo artist, and she performed up until her death in 1974 from heart failure caused by her excessive weight and drug abuse. A false report that she died choking on a ham sandwich became a widely believed myth that persisted for decades after her death. John and Michelle were divorced in 1970, two years after the birth of their daughter Chynna, who became part of the pop act Wilson Phillips in the early 1990s, along with the daughters of Beach Boy Brian Wilson. Michelle took up acting, appearing in various films and on television during the 1970s and 1980s. John continued songwriting and producing while suffering from an increasingly severe drug addiction that lasted until 1980, when he was arrested on federal charges. After serving a very brief sentence, he stopped using narcotics and became an antidrug spokesperson.

John made numerous public appearances, accompanied by his daughter Mackenzie, a star on television's *One Day at a Time* and also a recovering drug addict. In the early 1980s, John and Mackenzie revived the Mamas and the Papas, along with Doherty, who had failed in his efforts to pursue a solo career, and Elaine "Spanky" McFarlane, from the 1960s group Spanky and Our Gang. In the 1990s John received a liver transplant and Doherty, who had returned to Canada and produced and starred in a popular Canadian Broadcasting Company children's show. Doherty died in 2007 at age sixty-six.

John passed away in 2001 at age sixty-five, just before the release of his final album, *Phillips 66* (2001). In 2009 Mackenzie published a memoir, *High on Arrival*, and appeared on *The Oprah Winfrey Show*, claiming that her father had introduced her to drugs and begun a decade-long affair with her when she was nineteen. Several key family members, including Michelle, have disputed this claim, but others have corroborated it. The Mamas and the Papas were inducted into the Rock and Roll Hall of Fame in 1998, the Vocal Group Hall of Fame in 2000, and the Hit Parade Hall of Fame in 2009. Their recordings continue to demonstrate a collective vocal talent rarely found in pop music.

Anna Hunt Graves

SEE ALSO: *The Beach Boys; The Beatles; Folk Music; Greenwich Village; Hippies;* One Day at a Time*; Pop Music; Rock and Roll; Soap Operas; Top 40; Winfrey, Oprah.*

BIBLIOGRAPHY

Gaar, Gillian G. *She's a Rebel: The History of Women in Rock and Roll.* Seattle, WA: Seal Press, 1992.

Phillips, John, and Jim Jerome. *Papa John.* Garden City, NY: Doubleday, 1986.

Phillips, Michelle. *California Dreamin': The True Story of the Mamas and the Papas.* New York: Warner Books, 1986.

Stanton, Scott. *The Tombstone Tourist: Musicians.* New York: Pocket Books, 2003.

Mamet, David *(1947–)*

One of the most important American playwrights of the late twentieth and early twenty-first centuries, David Mamet is the voice of the common man—or even criminal—in the theater. He has been acclaimed for his gritty depictions of con men, thieves, and other morally bereft characters whose language is rife with the kind of stuttering, pausing, and obscenities that occur in real-life conversation. Despite the spartan phrasing and lack of eloquence in the dialogue, the staccato rhythm ends up flowing naturally, making Mamet's dialogue unique, though he is sometimes roughly compared to fellow author Harold Pinter.

Mamet was awarded the Pulitzer Prize for Drama in 1984 for *Glengarry Glen Ross*, the tale of shady salesmen in a cutthroat real estate sales office that received a Broadway revival in 2005. He has also cultivated a career in feature films as a screenwriter, a director, and sometimes producer and has expounded his views on arts, religion, and politics in a series of books. Since 2005 he has contributed to the online news source the Huffington Post.

Mamet has twice been nominated for an Academy Award for his screenwriting, in 1983 for the legal drama *The Verdict* and again in 1998 for *Wag the Dog*, a fictional tale of an American president who concocts a fake war with the help of a Hollywood producer to distract voters from an emerging sex scandal. The film was released just months before the Bill Clinton–Monica Lewinsky sex scandal and subsequent bombing campaigns in Afghanistan and the Sudan. Mamet also adapted *Glengarry Glen Ross* for film in 1992 and received recognition for his screenwriting on *The Spanish Prisoner* (1997), *The Winslow Boy* (1999), and *State and Main* (2000). He adapted his 1982 one-act play *Edmond* into a film of the same name in 2005 and created an Emmy-nominated television show, *The Unit* (2006–2009), in 2006. His play *Race* debuted on Broadway in 2009 to mixed reviews.

Mamet's literary career includes a collection of poetry, *The Hero Pony* (1990), and three novels—*The Village* (1994), *The Old Religion* (1997), and *Wilson: A Consideration of the Sources* (2000). His nonfiction works include a meditation on the teachings of the Torah titled *Five Cities of Refuge: Weekly Reflections on Genesis, Exodus, Leviticus, Numbers and Deuteronomy* (2003); an account of his conversion from liberal to conservative politics titled *The Secret Knowledge: On the Dismantling of American Culture* (2011); and a critique of the film industry called *Bambi vs. Godzilla: On the Nature, Purpose, and Practice of the Movie Business* (2007).

Geri Speace

SEE ALSO: *Academy Awards; Broadway; Emmy Awards; The Huffington Post; Lewinsky, Monica; Television.*

BIBLIOGRAPHY

Bigsby, Christopher, ed. *The Cambridge Companion to David Mamet*. New York: Cambridge University Press, 2004.

Brewer, Gay. *David Mamet and Film: Illusion/Disillusion in a Wounded Land*. Jefferson, NC: McFarland, 1993.

Carroll, Dennis. *David Mamet*. New York: St. Martin's, 1987.

Kane, Leslie. *Weasels and Wisemen: Ethics and Ethnicity in the Work of David Mamet*. New York: St. Martin's, 1999.

Kane, Leslie. *David Mamet in Conversation*. Ann Arbor: University of Michigan Press, 2001.

Mamet, David. *A Whore's Profession: Notes and Essays*. London: Faber & Faber, 1994.

Nadel, Ira B. *David Mamet: A Life in the Theatre*. New York: Palgrave Macmillan, 2008.

Mamma Mia!

When producer Judy Craymer set out to stage a musical based on the songs of Swedish pop group ABBA, no one expected it to be a worldwide mega hit. In fact, no one expected it to happen. But Craymer persevered, and in the first ten years after its premiere in 1999, *Mamma Mia!* was seen by more than forty million people—and grossed nearly $2 billion. Combining high energy with sentimental appeal, the show has become a perennial favorite in the world of musical theater.

Back in the 1970s, when disco music ruled the pop charts, ABBA became a global sensation with hit songs such as "Dancing Queen" and "Take a Chance on Me." After the group quietly broke up in 1983, its four members went in different musical directions, and ABBA was largely forgotten until a twenty-fifth anniversary celebration introduced their music to a whole new generation. Craymer—a longtime ABBA fan—had the idea for a musical tribute to the group and invited British playwright Catherine Johnson to create a story that would weave together some of the group's best songs.

ABBA songs were not noted for their profound lyrics, but Johnson found a starting place with the song "Mamma Mia!" and from there she created a colorful plot that revolves around Sophie, a young bride-to-be. Sophie wants to be given away by her father, but she doesn't know who he is. So, shortly before her wedding, she secretly invites three possible candidates to the Greek island where her mother, Donna, owns a restaurant. Friends from Donna's past also show up, and complications naturally follow. After a series of musical numbers and romantic revelations, Sophie's parentage is still a mystery, but her mother is reunited with one of the former lovers. Sophie and her fiancé decide to travel the world before marrying, and Donna ends up as the bride.

In 2011, after 4,098 performances, *Mamma Mia!* became the tenth-longest-running musical in Broadway history. A 2008 film version starring Meryl Streep as Donna was also a great success, ranking as the fifth-highest-grossing film of the year. Both onstage and on film, *Mamma Mia!* tells a sweet-natured, music-filled story of love, dreams, and growing up.

Cynthia Giles

SEE ALSO: *ABBA; Broadway; Disco; Hanks, Tom; Movie Stars; The Musical; Pop Music; Streep, Meryl.*

BIBLIOGRAPHY

Andersson, Benny; Björn Ulvaeus; Judy Craymer; et al. *"Mamma Mia!" How Can I Resist You?: The Inside Story of "Mamma Mia!" and the Songs of Abba*. London: Weidenfeld & Nicolson, 2006.

Palm, Carl M., and Anders Hanser. *From Abba to "Mamma Mia!": The Official Book*. London: Virgin, 2000.

The Man from U.N.C.L.E.

Conceived as a spoof of the James Bond films, *The Man from U.N.C.L.E.* was American television's most noteworthy nod to the international success of author Ian Fleming's spy hero. Originated by *Dr. Kildare* (1961–1966) producer Norman Felton with initial support and assistance from Fleming, the series introduced audiences to Napoleon Solo (played by Robert Vaughn) and his Russian partner Illya Kuryakin (David McCallum), secret agents for the United Network Command for Law and Enforcement. Their weekly battles against the evil minions of THRUSH (expanded in the late-1960s U.N.C.L.E. novels of David McDaniel as Technological Hierarchy for the Removal of Undesirables and the Subjugation of Humanity) attracted little critical or popular attention when the show made its debut in fall 1964. After NBC moved the airtime from Tuesday to Monday nights in early 1965, however, it rapidly gained a cultish popularity, particularly among young viewers, for whom lines of U.N.C.L.E. toys and books were manufactured.

In 1966 the network even commissioned a spin-off, *The Girl from U.N.C.L.E.*, to take further advantage of the fad; that series ended after twenty-nine episodes. In *The Man from U.N.C.L.E.*'s later years, its outlandish plots and arch humor became too ridiculous to retain sufficiently wide appeal, and despite efforts to refocus the show on straight adventure, it was retired to syndication in 1968. Various episodes were made into feature films that enjoyed a modest success outside of the United States.

Jeffrey S. Miller

SEE ALSO: Dr. Kildare; *James Bond Films; Syndication; Television.*

BIBLIOGRAPHY

Heitland, Jon. *The Man from U.N.C.L.E. Book: The Behind-the-Scenes Story of a Television Classic.* New York: St. Martin's Press, 1987.

"The Man from U.N.C.L.E/The Girl from U.N.C.L.E." In *Encyclopedia of Television*, 2nd ed., ed. Horace Newcomb. New York: Fitzroy Dearborn, 2004.

The Man Who Shot Liberty Valance

Although John Ford made three more films after its release in 1962, *The Man Who Shot Liberty Valance* is generally thought of as his final masterpiece and one of the best-made Westerns of all time. Critics initially derided the film as unoriginal and a seeming rehash of themes Ford had dealt with more successfully in earlier films, but *Liberty Valance* has ultimately come to be recognized as Ford's most self-reflective work, a film in which he examines the loss of the frontier traits that forged America's early identity.

The Man Who Shot Liberty Valance. *John Wayne starred as Tom Doniphon in the 1962 Western* The Man Who Shot Liberty Valance. PARAMOUNT/THE KOBAL COLLECTION.

In the decades since the release of *The Man Who Shot Liberty Valance*, the film has gained a reputation as a seminal revisionist Western—ironically for the very reasons the film was initially dismissed: its derivative nature and seeming reworking of Ford's earlier movies. In referring to his own past works and readdressing his major thematic interests over the course of his half-century film career, Ford creates a film that serves as his final commentary on the conflict between the frontier and civilization that permeates his Westerns.

SYNOPSIS

The story concerns Senator Ransom Stoddard (Jimmy Stewart), his wife, Hallie (Vera Miles), and their relationship with Tom Doniphon (John Wayne). At the outset of the film, the Stoddards, visibly middle-aged, arrive in the town of Shinbone to attend the funeral of Doniphon, ostensibly an old friend. Stoddard has become a senator on the basis of his reputation as the man who shot the outlaw Liberty Valance (Lee Marvin). But shortly after the film begins, Senator Stoddard recounts the actual events of Valance's death to a local newspaper editor. The greater part of the film is a flashback in which Doniphon is revealed as the real killer of Liberty Valance.

Wayne is particularly effective in the role of Doniphon given his screen persona as a Western hero, which confers on the character a melancholic resonance he might not have otherwise had. In the end, Doniphon dies ignominiously, a long-forgotten remnant of Shinbone's frontier past. At the conclusion of the flashback, the editor rips up his story. When Ransom asks if he is going to print it, the editor tellingly replies, "No sir! This is the West, sir. When the legend becomes fact, print the legend."

Whereas in earlier works Ford glorified the legendary aspects of America's Western past, in *Liberty Valance* the glorification is bitingly ironic. As John Baxter observes in his study *The Cinema of John Ford, Liberty Valance* shows "in detail that civilization, though inevitable, destroys everything honest and good in frontier life."

FORD'S EARLY WORK

In Ford's earlier Westerns—*My Darling Clementine* (1946), *She Wore a Yellow Ribbon* (1949), and *Wagon Master* (1950), to name just a few—the conflict between the frontier and encroaching civilization is amicably resolved. Mike Yawn and Bob Beatty observe, "Ford's West was a place where the best—and the noble—traits of the frontier and of civilization could not only coexist, but actually synthesize into a purely American set of values."

Although others made notable contributions to the genre, Ford's Westerns of the 1940s and early 1950s invented the patterns most commonly associated with classical Hollywood Westerns. Accordingly, as Richard Maltby notes, the Western is sometimes dismissed as being simply a wild place that Hollywood turns into a place of beauty, a place in which to cultivate and grow. But in *The Man Who Shot Liberty Valance*, the optimistic reconciliation of the frontier and civilization that characterized Ford's earlier Westerns is no more; instead, Ford questions the Western mythology that he himself had done so much to create.

MOOD AND TONE VARIANCES

In *Liberty Valance,* Ford wanted to create a mood and tone that paralleled his wavering optimism. As a result, Ronald Davis notes, "he insisted on shooting it in black and white, wanting a dark, anachronistic look, since the picture incorporated his diminishing faith in American values. No longer did he feel like celebrating the course of civilization, which he accepted, but did not necessarily see as progress." In addition, Ford's trademark panoramic shots are notably absent. Instead, the majority of the film was shot inside the Paramount studio.

The film begins in the town of Shinbone, which can be seen as a cinematic descendant of *My Darling Clementine*'s Tombstone. But whereas Tombstone was a frontier town on the edge of civilization, Shinbone has long been urbanized, as evidenced by the notable presence of a train, a telephone, and telephone poles and wires in the film's early scenes. The city's streets are cramped and claustrophobic, more reminiscent of film noir than of Westerns. In Shinbone, a city in which frontier values can no longer coexist with civilization, the results of the closing of the frontier and the rise of American urbanization can be seen.

After years of making films that asserted that the West could be civilized without losing its frontier qualities, Ford in *Liberty Valance* abandons his optimism to his realization that progress had ultimately robbed the West of its identity. As a genre, the Western film no longer flourishes as it did during Ford's time. The few serious Westerns that have been made by Hollywood since the release of *Liberty Valance* have most often been ones in which the legends and myths associated with the American West are exposed as hollow.

Robert C. Sickels

SEE ALSO: *Ford, John;* My Darling Clementine*;* She Wore a Yellow Ribbon*; Stewart, Jimmy; Wayne, John; The Western.*

BIBLIOGRAPHY

Baxter, John. *The Cinema of John Ford.* New York: Barnes, 1971.

Darby, William. *John Ford's Westerns: A Thematic Analysis, with a Filmography.* Jefferson, NC: McFarland, 2006.

Davis, Ronald L. *John Ford: Hollywood's Old Master.* Norman: University of Oklahoma Press, 1995.

Maltby, Richard. "A Better Sense of History: John Ford and the Indians." In *The Book of Westerns,* ed. Ian Cameron and Douglas Pye. New York: Continuum, 1996.

Yawn, Mike, and Bob Beatty. "John Ford's Vision of the Closing West: From Optimism to Cynicism." *Film and History* 26, no. 1–4 (1996): 6–19.

The Manchurian Candidate

A best-selling novel published in 1959 and first brought to the screen in 1962, the year before the death of John F. Kennedy, *The Manchurian Candidate* outlines the assassination of a U.S. president. The film's limited availability in the wake of Kennedy's death and its somewhat prophetic story line helped it gain cult status. Yet there is more to *The Manchurian Candidate* than timing. It is one of the earliest direct attacks on the nature of McCarthyism, as well as one of the first successful indigenous spy novels in America. *The Manchurian Candidate*'s characterization of the lone insane gunman would take on iconic meaning, and its cynical representation of the American political machine is another facet to which the public could relate.

The book, written by Richard Condon (1915–1996), is an unusual work for its time, falling into the category of spy fiction. The spy genre, as Clive Bloom terms it in *Spy Thrillers* (1990), is "the genre tied to international political and social tensions," responding "to a need to represent covert activity by state organizations" via works dealing with the questions of espionage at home and abroad. Hardly anything approaching spy fiction appeared in America until the 1940s and in any numbers until the 1960s, perhaps, as some suggest, because of the nature of American democracy and a foreign policy tending toward isolationism. In the 1960s and 1970s—following the lead of Ian Fleming's James Bond books and influenced by the writings of American intelligence "insiders" such as Victor Marchetti and William F. Buckley Jr., as well as by America's ever-increasing involvement in world affairs—the spy thriller came into its own. *The Manchurian Candidate* is a relatively early, and surprisingly successful, attempt to deal with the issues of the spy novel.

The Manchurian Candidate. The Manchurian Candidate *starred, from left, Frank Sinatra as Major Bennett Marco, Janet Leigh as Eugenie Rose Chaney, and Laurence Harvey as Raymond Shaw.* UNITED ARTISTS/THE KOBAL COLLECTION.

PRINT PHENOMENON

The book's popularity may stem from how it draws together many of the traumas in the 1950s. It starts in the Korean War; has a senator who, in tactics and aims, is a dead ringer for Joe McCarthy; and showcases a strong mother figure as a Russian agent, harking back to Ethel Rosenberg and reflecting post–World War II male fears concerning the increased power of women. Underlying the story is the fear that the communists have mastered a technological superiority that could threaten the American nation (in this case, not the bomb but a sophisticated form of brainwashing). The book cleverly taps into a fear of communism, the effects of rationalism and domestic prosperity on American individualism, and many other issues concerning the nature of sexuality and gender roles. Lastly, all these issues feed into the question of nationhood. For America—now of central importance in world affairs, carrying the self-proclaimed mantle of the defender of democracy—every foreign conflict has potentially devastating ramifications.

The Manchurian Candidate also looks into the future. It is suggestive of the more disorientating war narratives of Vietnam, Afghanistan, and Iraq; of controversial and even criminal politicians; and of an enemy growing more amorphous than the melodramatic portrait presented in the 1950s. And, of course, it develops the idea of a presidential assassination. It is a prophetic novel, yes, but it also shows that many of the elements of post-assassination America must already be in place beforehand for the assassination to be explicable at all. The world did not change the day Kennedy died—those changes were already in motion.

FILM ADAPTATIONS

Though the novel faded from public view once it fell off the best-seller list, Condon's cynical political satire has survived through two movie adaptations. Directed by John Frankenheimer, the original film is a tense, dark, and relatively faithful rendition of the novel, maintaining a documentary style with a number of striking and imaginative scenes. Laurence Harvey's stuffy assassin, Frank Sinatra's twitching hero, and Angela Lansbury's Oscar-nominated mother figure manage to put across many of the major themes of the novel, even some of the nuances of the incestuous relationship between mother and son (Lansbury was only three years Harvey's senior).

The film received a mixed reaction from both critics and audiences—it was picketed in Orange County, California, for being left wing and in Paris for being right wing—but its original and gripping delineation of the lone gunman and his preparations for the murder of the president, so close to the actual death of Kennedy, propelled it into a kind of obscurity. Over the next fifteen years, it was difficult to see the film, enhancing its mystique. Furthermore, as the amount of contradictory information mounted regarding the death of Kennedy, the work seemed prophetic—not only in foreseeing the murder of a president but also in predicting a political atmosphere that could make a conspiracy seem imaginable.

In 2004 director Jonathan Demme released a second adaptation of *The Manchurian Candidate*, starring Denzel Washington and Meryl Streep. While it takes several cues from the original film and the novel, it also incorporates contemporary political concerns into the narrative, such as the aftereffects of the Gulf War, rigged election results, the threat of terrorism, and the ever-expanding military-industrial complex. Just as the novel and first film provide thinly veiled commentary on the American political climate in the wake of McCarthyism and the shadow of the Cold War, Demme's offering is a snapshot of the post–9/11 world and a statement against the shadowy machinations of privatized militias funded by corporations.

Condon's story offers a twisted overview of the Cold War period—a reflection on the cynicism of domestic politics, the anxiety and fragility of the individual will, and the nature of paranoia. It also works, most interestingly, as an early American spy novel. Added to this is the force of Frankenheimer's and Demme's films and their successful characterizations of the novel's main strands.

Kyle Smith

SEE ALSO: *Academy Awards; Best Sellers; Buckley, William F., Jr.; Cold War; Fleming, Ian; James Bond Films; Kennedy Assassination; McCarthyism; 9/11; Sinatra, Frank; Streep, Meryl; Washington, Denzel.*

BIBLIOGRAPHY

Bloom, Clive, ed. *Spy Thrillers: From Buchan to LeCarré.* London: Macmillan, 1990.

Condon, Richard. *The Manchurian Candidate.* New York: McGraw-Hill, 1959.

Jacobson, Matthew Frye, and Gaspar González. *What Have They Built You to Do? "The Manchurian Candidate" and Cold War America.* Minneapolis: University of Minnesota Press, 2006.

McCormick, Donald, and Katy Fletcher. *Spy Fiction: A Connoisseur's Guide.* New York: Facts On File, 1990.

Mancini, Henry *(1924–1994)*

Although he was a highly gifted composer-arranger capable of scoring films of any genre, Henry Mancini is probably best known to the general public for the jazzy, lighthearted, cocktail-confection themes from *Peter Gunn* and *The Pink Panther* (1963) and as the melodist behind such wistful songs as "Moon River" and "The Days of Wine and Roses." A product of the big-band era who ended up in Hollywood in the early 1950s, Mancini served his cinematic apprenticeship as a staff composer (mostly for "B" movies) at Universal Studios. His big break came in 1958 when writer-director Blake Edwards offered him the opportunity to score the private-eye series, *Peter Gunn* (1958–1961). Mancini's main-title theme pioneered the use of jazz music in TV background music and became a hit single from one of the best-selling LPs of all time.

Soon Mancini scores were gracing some of Hollywood's most stylish big-screen productions, and his music was almost as much a star of these films as Audrey Hepburn, Cary Grant, and John Wayne. Record albums and concert tours helped make the shy musician from Pennsylvania one of the few film composers whose name had public recognition. Although he died suddenly in 1994 while working on his first Broadway musical, his legacy is a lasting one. The adult, sophisticated comedies and romances graced by Mancini scores are no longer made in modern Hollywood, but his songs have become standards, an indelible contribution to the soundtrack of our lives.

Henry Mancini. *Composer and arranger Henry Mancini gives a performance in 1980.* SUZIE GIBBONS/CONTRIBUTOR/REDFERNS/GETTY IMAGES.

Enrico (Henry) Mancini was born in Cleveland, Ohio, on April 16, 1924, but grew up in West Aliquippa, Pennsylvania. His Italian immigrant father was a steelworker who loved music and insisted that his only child learn the flute and the piccolo. Young Hank played in the school band and also studied piano, but his most important instruction was self-administered: listening to recordings of the popular big bands, young Mancini taught himself how to arrange music. More formal schooling came later from Pittsburgh theater arranger-conductor Max Adkins. Although Adkins created an opportunity for his student to audition an arrangement for the great Benny Goodman in 1942, the famed clarinetist did not think the young man was ready yet for the big time. (Ironically, years later Mancini would arrange the music for the film *The Benny Goodman Story.*)

Mancini spent a fruitful year studying at the Juilliard School of Music in New York, but a draft notice for World War II interrupted his education. A brief encounter with Glenn Miller saved the young man from the perilous duty of a tail-gunner and transferred him into an air force band. Following the war, Mancini became pianist and arranger for the newly formed band of Miller veteran Tex Beneke, a move that proved decisive for Mancini's personal and professional life. He fell in love with Ginny O'Connor, a member of Mel Torme's singing group, the Meltones, and they were soon married. O'Connor eventually joined another group, the Mello-Larks, and when the singers made a short film at Universal, Mancini got the assignment to arrange their music.

WORK AT UNIVERSAL

Joseph Gershenson, head of the studio's music department, offered the young musician a couple of weeks' work on an Abbott and Costello picture, and this assignment stretched into a six-year apprenticeship in the art and craft of film scoring. With his Beneke background, Mancini was a natural to assist Gershenson on 1953's *The Glenn Miller Story*, and their joint work was nominated for an Academy Award—the first of eighteen for Mancini. (He would eventually win four Oscars.)

Mancini's on-the-job training involved composition for virtually every genre at the Universal film factory, from Westerns to Ma and Pa Kettle comedies, from gangster movies and mysteries to such science fiction/horror thrillers (often in collaboration with Herman Stein) as *The Creature from the Black Lagoon* (1954) and *This Island Earth* (1955). Because the budgets often did not allow for complete original scores, Mancini would frequently be assigned to cobble together music from the scores of older pictures. This afforded him another opportunity for self-instruction, studying the work of veteran film composers such as Frank Skinner, Hans J. Salter, and Miklos Rozsa.

WORK WITH WELLES

But Mancini was about to make his own distinctive mark on film scoring. The first sign of the new direction that he would be taking in film music came in 1958 with his score for Orson Welles's *Touch of Evil.* A neglected film in its day but regarded as a cult classic—particularly in the version that restores Welles's original editing—*Touch* featured a most unusual score. For his gritty film noir set in American and Mexican border towns, Welles decided against the customary practice of providing a dramatic underscore. Instead, nearly all the music heard in *Touch* was source music: the music that would realistically be heard coming from radios and jukeboxes. Nevertheless, with his jazz and pop expertise, Mancini managed to make this music suitably menacing. In its way, it was as essential to the film's mood and as memorable as the famous zither source music in Carol Reed's *The Third Man* (which had starred Welles).

Unfortunately for Mancini, the influx of television was causing the movie studios to cut back on their payrolls, and shortly after *Touch of Evil*, the composer was let go. Ironically, it was television that proved to be Mancini's salvation. Writer-director Edwards, who had known Mancini at Universal, was about to start a new private-eye series for NBC, *Peter Gunn*. Bumping into Mancini by chance one day, on the spur of the moment Edwards offered Mancini the job of scoring his upcoming program.

PETER GUNN

Peter Gunn was the breakthrough moment for Mancini and the beginning of the Americanization of film music. Edwards wanted a fresh sound for his series, which often found the detective visiting a jazz club called Mother's. Taking his cue from the milieu, Mancini injected jazz inflections into the dramatic underscore. Distinguished film composers prior to Mancini had pioneered the use of jazz in movie scoring. Chief among these composers were Alex North in *A Streetcar Named Desire* (1951) and Elmer Bernstein in *The Man with the Golden Arm* (1955). But jazz had rarely been given the emphasis Mancini gave it in *Gunn*, and it had never been used on television, which reached a wider audience than the movies. The now-famous main-title theme, with its hard-driving piano base, gained such immediate popularity that RCA commissioned an entire album of Mancini's *Peter Gunn* music. The LP became a runaway best seller, earning a Grammy Award as Album of the Year and generating a follow-up disc, *More Music from* Peter Gunn. Mancini's gift for innovative, pop-oriented orchestration demonstrated itself again with the score (and LP) for Edwards's next TV series, *Mr. Lucky*, whose main theme featured a jazz organ against strings.

RETURN TO MOVIES

It was Edwards who brought Mancini back into the movie-scoring fold with the Bing Crosby comedy *High Time* in 1960. From then on, movies were Mancini's chief occupation, with occasional forays back into television. He was also persuaded to inaugurate a series of "pops" concert tours that proved immensely successful and, coupled with the continued success of his soundtrack recordings, kept Mancini in the public eye more than any film composer until the advent of John Williams. Many of Mancini's most important movies were written and directed by Edwards, chief among them *Breakfast at Tiffany's* (1961), *The Days of Wine and Roses* (1962), and *The Pink Panther*.

The title theme for *Panther*, as well as the "Baby Elephant Walk" from Howard Hawks's *Hatari!* (1962), became popular instrumental hits that are still recognized. The title songs from *Wine and Roses* and *Charade* (1963), with lyrics by Johnny Mercer, also made the hit parade and remain standards. But Mancini's most enduring achievement was written for Hepburn in *Breakfast at Tiffany's*. Having heard her sing George and Ira Gershwin's "How Long Has This Been Going On?" in *Funny Face* (1957), Mancini knew that Hepburn could handle a range of an octave plus a note. Noodling at the keyboard with that range of notes, in the space of half an hour he came up with the melody that, again with Mercer's masterful lyric, has become immortal under the name "Moon River." (After the first preview of *Tiffany's*, the studio executives wanted to cut the song, but Edwards fought for its inclusion; ironically, the same near-disaster once befell "Over the Rainbow" after a preview of *The Wizard of Oz*, 1939.)

Film composers can become as typecast as film actors, and Mancini sometimes had difficulty convincing producers to give him something more weighty than his usual assignments. But with such films as *The Molly Maguires* (1970) and *The Glass Menagerie* (1987), he proved that his range was not limited to frothy romances and comedies. He wrote some delightful songs, with lyrics by Leslie Bricusse, for Julie Andrews and Robert Preston to sing in Edwards's *Victor/Victoria* (1982), perhaps the last original screen musical in the classic tradition. While preparing a Broadway stage version of *Victor* in 1994, Mancini discovered that he had inoperable cancer; before the year was out, the composer had died.

Mancini scored success after success just before the era of American popular music came to an end. His career blossomed fully as rock and roll was taking the stage, but there were still a few years left in which the classic songwriting craft of men such as Mercer and Mancini could produce elegant, touching songs that would become popular and, eventually, stand the test of time. Perhaps one of the greatest songwriters of his generation, Mancini ended his career ranked next to major composers such as Irving Berlin and Jerome Kern.

Preston Neal Jones

SEE ALSO: *Academy Awards; "B" Movies; Berlin, Irving; Big Bands;* Breakfast at Tiffany's*; Broadway; Crosby, Bing; Film Noir; Goodman, Benny; Grant, Cary; Hawks, Howard; Hepburn, Audrey; Hollywood; Jazz; Kern, Jerome; Miller, Glenn; Pop Music;* A Streetcar Named Desire*; Television; Wayne, John; Welles, Orson;* The Wizard of Oz.

BIBLIOGRAPHY

Mancini, Henry. *Sounds and Scores: A Practical Guide to Professional Orchestration.* Miami, FL: Northridge Music, 1986.

Mancini, Henry; Marilyn Berman; Alan Bergman; et al. *Mancini Music: New and Enlarged Songbook.* New York: Northridge Music, 1971.

Mancini, Henry, and Gene Lees. *Did They Mention the Music?* Chicago: Contemporary Books, 1989.

Thomas, Tony. *Film Score: The View from the Podium.* South Brunswick, NJ: Barnes, 1979.

Williams, John. *The Magic of Mancini.* Bridport, UK: Music from the Movies, 1993.

Manhattan Transfer

The Manhattan Transfer are a vocal group whose stylings are rooted in jazz. However, through its showmanship and willing-

The Manhattan Transfer. *The Manhattan Transfer performs in Los Angeles, California, in 2010. From left are Janis Siegel, Alan Paul, Tim Hauser, and Cheryl Bentyne.* DR. BILLY INGRAM/CONTRIBUTOR/WIREIMAGE/GETTY IMAGES.

ness to sing music as diverse as R&B, doo-wop, Brazilian bossa nova, and rock and roll, the band has had an impact beyond jazz. Founding member Tim Hauser notes that the group modeled itself on the saxophone section of the Count Basie Band, using that sound as a model for the Manhattan Transfer's four-part harmonies. The name of the group is derived from a 1925 novel of the same name by John Dos Passos.

The group has kept its core personnel throughout most of its history, namely Hauser, Cheryl Bentyne, Alan Paul, and Janis Siegel. Each is a fine soloist and contributes a unique sound to the overall ensemble. Working as a marketing executive and a New York cab driver in 1972, Hauser never lost sight of his hope to create a vocal group. One of his cab passengers was Laurel Massé, who was familiar with *Jukin'*, an album Hauser had made with an earlier Manhattan Transfer incarnation. Soon after that, Hauser met Siegel at a party and convinced her to leave her current singing group and join him and Massé in the Manhattan Transfer. He was also able to persuade Paul, from the original cast of *Grease*, to join the group.

The group spent three years working around Manhattan, gaining a cult following. It made its debut in 1975 on Atlantic Records with *The Manhattan Transfer*. The Manhattan Transfer enjoyed a string of Top 10 hits from their next two albums, *Coming Out* (1976) and *Pastiche* (1978), and even had their own short-lived television show on CBS.

Massé left the group in 1978 and was replaced by Bentyne. The Manhattan Transfer's first album with Bentyne was a major domestic hit. Titled *Extensions* (1979), it features "Twilight Zone/Twilight Tone" and "Birdland," a vocalese version of the classic Weather Report tune. "Birdland" yielded two Grammys, for Siegel's arrangement and for the band's performance. In 1981 the Transfer won Grammys for pop and jazz performances—for "The Boy from New York City" and "Corner Pocket," respectively—marking the first time a band had garnered an award in both of those categories.

In 1985 the Manhattan Transfer recorded *Vocalese*, which became recognized as their peak effort. Jon Hendricks, the man generally credited with creating the art form that sets jazz lyrics to jazz solos, joined the band on the album, which was nominated for twelve Grammys and won for Best Jazz Vocal Performance and Best Vocal Arrangement for Two or More Voices. The Manhattan Transfer followed this success with albums featuring Brazilian, Christmas, children's, and doo-wop music.

In 2000 the group released *Spirit of St. Louis*, its last album on the Atlantic label. It subsequently signed with the Telarc label, releasing *Couldn't Be Hotter* in 2003 and *Vibrate* in 2004. *The Symphony Sessions* (2006) gave the Manhattan Transfer an opportunity to rerecord some of their earlier music with a full orchestra. The band also released a number of retrospective albums, including *The Definitive Pop Collection* (2006), *The Platinum Collection* (2007), and *The Manhattan Transfer 35th Anniversary Great American Songbook* (2008). Additionally, the Manhattan Transfer released a Christmas album in 2006 (*An Acapella Christmas*) and a tribute to jazz great Chick Corea in 2009 (*The Chick Corea Songbook*).

The Manhattan Transfer continued to tour the world in the twenty-first century to considerable acclaim. In 2011 Margaret Dorn temporarily replaced an ailing Bentyne, and that same year, Hauser began hosting a one-hour nightly program on Sirius XM Radio that pays homage to music of the 1950s and 1960s. Overall, the Manhattan Transfer have issued more than twenty albums and have won scores of Grammys. Their success has also included worldwide sales in the millions and being named the best vocal group for an entire decade (1980–1990) in *Down Beat* and *Playboy* jazz polls.

Frank A. Salamone

SEE ALSO: *Basie, Count; Doo-wop Music; Grammy Awards; Jazz; Rhythm and Blues; Rock and Roll.*

BIBLIOGRAPHY

Bourne, Michael. "Swing." *Down Beat*, November 1997, 42.

Boyd, Herb. "Swing." *Down Beat*, October 1997, 48.

Weber, Carol Banks. "Manhattan Transfer Delivers Another Flawless Performance." *Entertainment Examiner*, October 26, 2010.

Manilow, Barry *(1943–)*

Best known for his romantic and sometimes too-sweet songs, Barry Manilow was a whipping boy for the critics through much of the 1970s, even as he sold millions of albums and gained a huge fan base. He had thirteen number one hits on the adult contemporary charts during that decade. Even when recording works by other artists, Manilow cultivated a lush and melodic musical style that had been popular during the pre-rock era. His style evolved during the early 1980s from tame, string-laden, AM-radio pop to a more classic, jazzy sound that was heavily influenced by swing and 1930s and 1940s Broadway show tunes (many of which he later covered).

Unabashedly embracing a sentimental style that appealed primarily to white middle-class women, it is not surprising that this Brooklyn-born-and-raised songwriter was frequently denounced by the male-dominated world of rock and rock critics. Because forms of entertainment associated with women—such as soap operas and romance novels—have historically been devalued, those who cater to that audience have been routinely dismissed by mainstream critics as well. Unlike many of his ragtag rock-and-roll counterparts, however, Manilow's résumé has "professionalism" written all over it.

After taking up a variety of instruments at an early age, he attended both the New York College of Music and the Juilliard School, and in 1967 he worked as the musical director of a CBS network television show. From there Manilow remained busy writing a successful off-Broadway adaptation of *The Drunkard*, doing musical arrangement work for Ed Sullivan Productions, and writing a number of well-known commercial jingles for Dr Pepper, Band-Aid, and other advertisements. Throughout the 1970s his voice could be heard singing the McDonald's jingle—"You deserve a break today." He even released a medley of his commercials on one of his 1970s albums.

He got his foot in the door of the pop music world while playing piano for the then-unknown Bette Midler, who mainly performed at the gay Continental Baths in New York City. Manilow soon became her musical director and arranger, coproducing and arranging her Grammy-winning debut album and its follow-up. His own debut album, on the other hand, went nowhere, but his second album featured the number one Billboard pop single "Mandy," laying the groundwork for his rise to fame throughout the rest of the 1970s. Many more hit songs—"I Write the Songs," "Looks Like We Made It," "Could It Be Magic," and "Copacabana (At the Copa)"—soon followed, as did a Grammy and a Tony for a Broadway performance.

A MODERN MUSICAL INTERPRETER

In the early 1980s Manilow began to position himself as a modern interpreter of show tunes and pop standards, working with singers Mel Tormé and Sarah Vaughan and veteran jazz instrumentalists Gerry Mulligan and Shelly Manne on 1984's *2:00 AM Paradise Café*. He followed this same path on 1987's *Swing Street* and 1991's *Showstoppers*, on which he sang with Michael Crawford and Barbara Cook. One of Manilow's self-described career highlights was scoring music to a collection of unpublished lyrics by Johnny Mercer, the famed lyricist who penned a multitude of pop standards from the 1930s to the 1950s. From pop music to show tunes, Manilow has captured a devoted audience who continue to maintain his importance to American music and popular culture.

Well aware that he has been stereotyped, Manilow loves to make fun of himself. In 1993 he appeared on the hit sitcom *Murphy Brown* (1988–1998), taking part in the running gag that Murphy's infant son Avery would only go to sleep when hearing Manilow sing. Murphy, on the other hand, despised his music. Undaunted by her disdain, Manilow accompanies himself on the piano while he sings "I Am Your Child" as clips of Avery growing up and Murphy growing older fill the screen.

It could be argued that it was only after Manilow had fizzled as a pop sensation that he came into his own as a master entertainer. He began the twenty-first century by leaving Arista, his record company, and signing with the more jazz-oriented Concord. He released *Here at the Mayflower* in 2001. The following year he was invited to sing "Let Freedom Ring" at the Super Bowl pregame entertainment. In 2003 *Ultimate Manilow* debuted at the number three spot on the charts. The next year he released *Two Nights Live*, filmed at concerts in New Jersey. Manilow finally made it to Las Vegas in 2005, becoming the headliner at the Las Vegas Hilton until 2009, when he signed a new contract with the Paris Hotel Las Vegas. He continues to perform as a regular headliner there.

His move to Las Vegas coincided with his introduction of a new series of albums celebrating music of different eras. The first of those was *Greatest Songs of the Fifties* in 2006, which topped the charts early in the year. By the end of 2006, Manilow had released *Greatest Songs of the Sixties*, which claimed the number one spot. Manilow followed those hits with *Greatest Songs of the Seventies* (2007) and *Greatest Love Songs of the Eighties* (2008). In the interim, he released *In the Swing of Christmas* in 2007 and rereleased it with bonus tracks in 2009. In 2011 Manilow released *15 Minutes*, which he says started out as the story of a fictional pop star and ended up being the story of his own life. Also that year he started the campaign Get Back in Rhythm to promote public awareness of atrial fibrillation, a heart condition with which he has suffered since 1996.

Kembrew McLeod

SEE ALSO: *Academy Awards; Broadway; Grammy Awards; Las Vegas; McDonald's; Midler, Bette;* Murphy Brown*; Pop Music; Sinatra, Frank; Tony Awards; Vaughan, Sarah.*

BIBLIOGRAPHY

Ali, Lorraine. "Barry Hot." *Newsweek*, February 13, 2005.

Clarke, Alan. *The Magic of Barry Manilow*. New York: Proteus, 1981.

Gardner, Elysa. "Ready to Take a Chance Again, Here's Barry Manilow." *USA Today*, June 13, 2011.

Lulow, Kalia. *Barry Manilow*. New York: Ballantine, 1985.

Manilow, Barry. *Sweet Life: Adventures on the Way to Paradise.* New York: McGraw-Hill, 1987.

Peters, Richard. *Barry Manilow: An Illustrated Biography*. New York: Delilah Books, 1983.

The Manning Brothers

The sons of former National Football League (NFL) star Archie Manning, a ten-year starter for a hapless New Orleans Saints franchise, Peyton and Eli Manning continued the family tradition of elite play at the quarterback position. The brothers, in fact, surpassed their father by a wide margin, each achieving far greater individual and team success than Archie, who during his playing days was widely acknowledged as the best player on some of the worst teams in NFL history. While Archie never had a winning season in his thirteen-year career (1971–1984), Peyton won almost 70 percent of the games he played with the Indianapolis Colts over the course of thirteen active seasons with the club, setting numerous passing records and leading the team to a Super Bowl XLI victory over the Chicago Bears in February 2007. For his part, Eli, five years younger than Peyton, won two Super Bowls with the New York Giants in 2008 and 2012, both over the New England Patriots, and built a reputation as one of the best late-game quarterbacks ever to play. Cooper, the eldest of Archie's three sons, was also a talented athlete and appeared headed toward an NFL career as a wide receiver but was forced give up playing football at age eighteen after he was diagnosed with spinal stenosis.

PEYTON: A COACH ON THE FIELD

Their family ties notwithstanding, Peyton and Eli became players of markedly different temperament, and their various strengths and weaknesses led football aficionados across the country to debate which was the better quarterback. Born on March 24, 1976, Peyton became a meticulous student of the game, famous for spending hours watching film to discern the tendencies of his opponents and to discover the ways he could best exploit their weaknesses. Treated as a peer by the Colts' coaches, Peyton worked closely with the team's staff to develop one of the most comprehensive and sophisticated offenses in the history of the game. Rather than calling plays in a huddle, Manning typically chose the play at the line of scrimmage after scanning the defense and communicated to his players through an intricate series of hand signals. His approach led to remarkable success. A four-time Most Valuable Player (MVP), Manning threw 399 touchdown passes for the Colts, third best ever in the NFL; was named to eleven Pro Bowls; and passed for more than 4,000 yards in a season eleven times. In 2004 he threw forty-nine touchdown passes, which at the time was a single-season record.

For all his success, however, Peyton was known to struggle in the most important games. In fact, before he won the Super Bowl to conclude the 2006 season, Manning had the reputation of being what is called a choker, a derogatory term for an athlete who loses when it matters most. The stigma dated all the way back to his college days at the University of Tennessee, where he lost each of his four games against archrival Florida. Concerns about Manning's ability to win big games reemerged at the end of the 2009 season, when he threw an interception that was returned for a touchdown in the waning moments of his second Super Bowl appearance, a 31–17 loss to the New Orleans Saints.

Although he performed well the following year, Peyton's career suffered a major setback in 2011, when a neck injury caused him to miss the entire season. Without him the Colts floundered, amassing the worst record in the league and earning the right to pick first in NFL draft. Rather than take their chances with an aging quarterback—Manning turned thirty-six shortly after the 2011 season—the Colts cut the greatest player in franchise history and in the draft chose Stanford quarterback Andrew Luck, a phenom as highly touted as Manning once was. As he had at every difficult moment of his career up to that point, Peyton epitomized class when he took his leave of the Colts, breaking down in tears as he thanked owner Jim Irsay for the opportunity to play in Indianapolis. Manning signed with the Denver Broncos shortly after his release.

ELI: THRIVING UNDER PRESSURE

By comparison, Eli's career has been charmed. He was born on January 3, 1981, and, like Peyton, starred at Isidore Newman School, a private high school in New Orleans. In 2000 he decided to follow in his father Archie's footsteps rather than Peyton's, attending the University of Mississippi, Archie's alma mater, instead of Tennessee. After four years of standout play there, Eli was selected first in the 2004 NFL draft by the San Diego Chargers. Before taking his first professional snap, Manning made it clear that he was different from his brother, announcing that he would not play for the Chargers and forcing a trade to the New York Giants. While many in the NFL establishment criticized him for speaking in such a way before he had paid his dues in the league, many others were impressed that a young man facing such high standards within his own family would actively seek the pressure that comes with playing in New York.

Unlike his brother, who was a model of hard work and consistency, Eli was erratic and unreliable for much of his first seven years in New York. Nevertheless, he tended to elevate his game in the fourth quarter and showed poise in the game's most tense moments. His signature victory came in Super Bowl XLII, played in February 2008, when he led a dramatic fourth-quarter drive to defeat the New England Patriots 17–14. The Patriots were undefeated at the time and heavy favorites to win the game. Eli's closing drive featured what many agree is the most memorable play in Super Bowl history. On third down and five, with just over one minute remaining, Manning eluded several tacklers before launching a pass deep into New England territory that journeyman receiver David Tyree caught against the top of his helmet while fighting off a Patriot defender. The Giants won the game soon after. Four years later, in Super Bowl XLVI, Manning again completed a difficult pass late in the game, this one to Mario Manningham, which propelled the Giants once again to victory over the Patriots. After this second championship, many football fans concluded that Eli was the better of the two quarterbacks, despite inferior cumulative statistics. Eli and Peyton have never contributed to the debate and have always supported each other publicly.

FUNNY MEN

In addition to the respect they commanded on the field for their passing and leadership, the Manning brothers also became famous for their deadpan sense of humor. Both have appeared in numerous commercials, and each earned praise from critics and viewers when he hosted *Saturday Night Live (SNL)*. The Mannings were also a hit with the show's staff. According to *Sports Illustrated*, Peyton introduced his mother, Olivia, to *SNL* writers by saying, "She never made it to the NFL. She's a real disappointment." Not to be outdone, when Eli brought his wife and four offensive linemen backstage, he told the cast that his blockers come with him everywhere he goes, adding that they were "even in the room . . . when our daughter was born."

Joseph Campana

SEE ALSO: *National Football League (NFL); Professional Football;* Saturday Night Live; *Super Bowl.*

BIBLIOGRAPHY

Battista, Judy. "After an Emotional Farewell, Manning and the Colts Look to Move On." *New York Times*, March 7, 2012.

Freedman, Lew H. *Peyton Manning: A Biography*. Westport, CT: Greenwood Press, 2009.

Lewis, Michael. "The Eli Experiment." *New York Times Magazine*, December 19, 2004.

Lopresti, Mike. "The Other Manning Brother Lives a Life without Regret." *USA Today*, January 30, 2008.

"Oh, Brother." *Sports Illustrated*, May 14, 2012.

Vacchiano, Ralph. *Eli Manning: The Making of a Quarterback*. New York: Skyhorse, 2008.

Manscaping

While the definition of masculinity has always been culturally fluid, heterosexual manliness in the late twentieth century was generally characterized by a lack of attention to enhancing one's appearance. This changed somewhat in the first decade of the 2000s, as TV shows such as *Sex and the City* (1998–2004) and *Queer Eye for the Straight Guy* (2003–2007) showcased men who were not only openly concerned about their looks but were willing to enhance their bodies cosmetically. One of these enhancements, which became a significant trend, was the large-scale removal of body hair, or *manscaping*, a term coined on *Queer Eye*.

Women had long been expected to be hairless, and in the decades before manscaping came into vogue, male hair removal was mostly undertaken by gays and athletes such as swimmers. As male body hair became defined as distasteful, men began to shave or, more painfully, wax their chests, backs, underarms, arms, and hands in order to achieve a more youthful and "clean" look. Manscaping also includes the removal of pubic hair, from the neat trim called "faux natural" to the "Brazilian" waxes in which all hair on and around the genitals is shaved off.

The burgeoning manscaping trend went hand in hand with an increased male interest in manicures, pedicures, and colognes and other cosmetic products. Not surprisingly, manufacturers of cosmetic products reinforced the cultural tendency toward male self-improvement. Brands such as Gillette and Nivea began creating special products for manscaping, and Philips Norelco mounted a hugely successful campaign for its Bodygroom electric razor. A website created by the company, shaveeverywhere.com, featured a number of comical ads, which included numerous thinly veiled references to pubic manscaping and its aesthetic and sensual benefits.

Marketing campaigns such as Philips Norelco's helped form a perception of manscaping as a roguish hallmark of masculinity. After all, body-hair removal highlights sculpted muscles and trendy tattoos. This image was reinforced by the association of such stars as rap musicians Jay-Z and Sean "P. Diddy" Combs with the manly art of body waxing. Manscaping shows up as outrageous comedy in films such as *The 40 Year Old Virgin* (2005) and *She's out of My League* (2010) and receives slightly more serious treatment in *Mansome*, Morgan Spurlock's 2012 documentary about modern masculinity.

Tina Gianoulis

SEE ALSO: *Combs, Sean "P. Diddy"; Gay Men; Jay-Z; Metrosexual;* Queer Eye for the Straight Guy; Sex and the City; *Waxing.*

BIBLIOGRAPHY

Bondy, Renée. "Rhymes with Cubic Pear." *Herizons* 23, no. 4 (2010): 25.

Creamer, Matthew. "Norelco Puts the Man in Manscaping." *Advertising Age*, May 15, 2006, 45.

Daum, Meghan. "Surveying the Cultural Manscape." *Los Angeles Times*, April 8, 2006, B17.

Hilmantel, Robin. "The New Male Grooming Obsession." *Cosmopolitan*, January 2011, 72.

Saint Louis, Catherine. "Do Women Like Men Quite That Cleanshaven?" *New York Times*, July 9, 2009, E3.

Mansfield, Jayne *(1933–1967)*

Although many people have never seen her movies, Jayne Mansfield remains, long after her death, one of the most recognizable icons of 1950s celebrity culture. More so than for her acting ability, Mansfield is remembered as a glamorous, big-busted sex kitten in competition with Hollywood rivals such as Marilyn Monroe and Mamie Van Doren. Because of her hour-glass figure, newspapers in the 1950s routinely published her body measurements, which led evangelist Billy Graham to once exclaim, "This country knows more about Jayne Mansfield's statistics than the Second Commandment."

The peculiar aspect of Mansfield's life is that although she symbolized sex appeal, perhaps more than any other American actress in the 1950s she was never a major box-office attraction. Still, she kept in the limelight because she was skilled at the art of publicity. Mansfield knew the importance of name and face recognition in the development of stardom. She worked to keep the public interested in her life, and she generated daily publicity to keep her name and pictures in the news. Mansfield's movie career was so brief that she would not have obtained cult status had it not been for the countless number of photos and news stories she generated during her lifetime.

EARLY LIFE

Mansfield was born Vera Jayne Palmer on April 19, 1933, in Bryn Mawr, Pennsylvania. Her parents, lawyer Herbert and retired schoolteacher Vera Palmer, moved the family to Phillipburg, New Jersey. When Jayne was three, her father died of a heart attack at age thirty. Upon her father's death, her mother returned to teaching to support the family. When Mansfield's mother remarried in 1939, the family moved to Dallas, Texas. Throughout her childhood, she was fascinated with movie stars, with Shirley Temple being one of her favorites. She avidly collected Hollywood fan magazines and dreamed of being a film star. As she matured, her idol became Marilyn Monroe.

At age seventeen, on May 6, 1950, she married twenty-one-year-old Paul Mansfield in Fort Worth, Texas. In June of that year, she graduated from Highland Park High School, and in November, she gave birth to a daughter, Jayne Marie. Her husband served in the army during the Korean War, and at various times during the early 1950s, both Mansfield and her husband acted in local theater productions in Dallas. By 1954 the couple moved to Hollywood so Mansfield could have a chance at being the movie star she always dreamed of becoming. She initially did a bevy of screen tests, but no studio would sign her. In the meantime, she sold candy in a Los Angeles theater and worked as a part-time model for the agency where Monroe got her start.

ACTING CAREER

Mansfield's first successful acting assignment occurred on October 21, 1954, when she appeared on television in the *Lux Theater* production of "An Angel Went A.W.O.L." This appearance led her to her first film role in *Female Jungle* (1955). After her first taste of stardom, Mansfield began cranking up her publicity machine, adopting the color pink as her trademark.

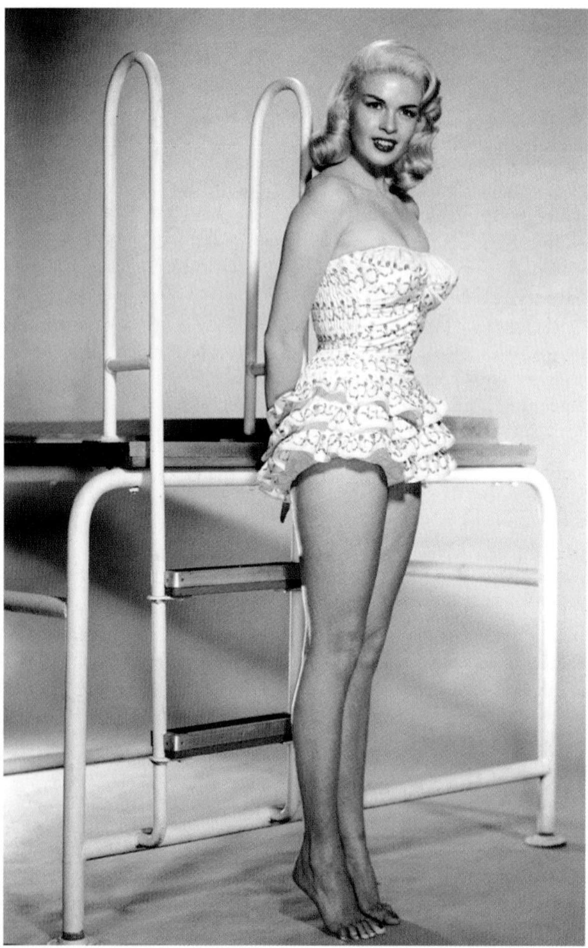

Jayne Mansfield. *Although she did have a brief movie career, Jayne Mansfield's celebrity was mostly based on her sex-kitten image and her ability to keep herself in the public eye.* SILVER SCREEN COLLECTION/CONTRIBUTOR/MOVIEPIX/GETTY IMAGES.

She decorated her house in pink, drove pink cars, and wore pink clothes for the publicity she received from the color.

In January 1955 Mansfield appeared at a Silver Springs, Florida, press junket promoting the film *Underwater!* (1955), which starred Jane Russell and Mansfield. Because Mansfield purposely wore a swimsuit that was too small, her top fell off before an astonished press corps, upstaging Russell's appearance at the junket. This burst of publicity led Warner Brothers to place Mansfield under contract. During this time, Mansfield's marriage fell apart, with the couple separating and then divorcing in 1956. In 1955 Warner Brothers paraded Mansfield through a series of small roles in films such as *Illegal* (1955), *Pete Kelly's Blues* (1955), and *Hell on Frisco Bay* (1955). And although it was rumored that Mansfield would appear with James Dean in *Rebel without a Cause* (1955), that breakthrough vanished when Warner Brothers abruptly dropped her contract.

Mansfield rebounded that same year by landing a larger role in the independent film *The Burglar* (1957). Her agent also insisted that she test for the lead in the Broadway play *Will Success Spoil Rock Hunter?*, which she landed when the play's director liked her exaggerated portrayal of a dumb, blond movie star. Mansfield proved to be a Broadway sensation and won awards in 1956 for her work. Because America became infatuated with the sex-kitten persona she developed in the play, Mansfield appeared in about 2,500 newspaper photographs between September 1956 and May 1957 and had about 122,000 lines of newspaper copy written about her during this time. Because of the successful media blitz, Mansfield was a household name even though few people had seen her perform. While performing in the play, Mansfield also appeared on such New York–based television shows as *What's My Line?*, *Person to Person*, and *Sunday Spectacular*.

By 1957 Twentieth Century Fox had signed Mansfield in hopes of her becoming a new Monroe, who at the time was refusing to make movies unless the studio gave her more money and treated her with respect. Mansfield appeared in two comedy roles for Twentieth Century Fox as a dumb blond—*The Girl Can't Help It* (1956) and the film version of *Will Success Spoil Rock Hunter?* (1957). The studio then cast Mansfield in a dramatic role for the movie version of the John Steinbeck novel *The Wayward Bus* (1957). In the spring of 1957 she received a number of "most promising" awards for her acting on Broadway and on the screen, and later that year she continued to be a focal point for the press and appeared on a number of television variety shows.

Mansfield married former Mr. Universe Mickey Hargitay in Palos Verdes, California, on January 13, 1958. The marriage displeased Twentieth Century Fox because the studio preferred its sex kittens to be unmarried. However, the marriage proved to be a boost for the careers of both Mansfield and Hargitay, with the couple appearing in Las Vegas together on stage. Mansfield and Hargitay became a famous publicity and performing team, with many people watching their performances just to see the pair together. They appeared in nightclub acts from 1958 to 1961, featuring the busty Mansfield and the muscular Hargitay in skimpy costumes.

Although she was a master publicist, Mansfield received her first negative publicity between April and September 1958 when she and Hargitay said they were too poor to pay child support payments being requested by Hargitay's first wife. The press had a field day reporting that the couple, who had just purchased a $76,000 mansion and spent $75,000 to remodel it, were far from being broke. As of 1959 Twentieth Century Fox no longer considered Mansfield star material and instead lent her out for low-budget English and Italian movies. Despite being rejected by American movie studios, Mansfield was still a welcome guest on television, appearing in dramatic parts and on game shows and talk shows.

DECLINE

From 1962 to 1964 Mansfield continued to receive bad press because of ongoing marital problems and a messy divorce with Hargitay, as well as public fights with her third husband, Matt Cimber. By 1965 her career had hit its lowest level, with two movies announced for Mansfield that were never made and her performance in two plays that were critically panned. In 1966 she starred in two low-budget American films, *The Fat Spy* and *The Las Vegas Hillbillys*, and that same year she performed in her last major nightclub appearance at the Latin Quarter. She also spent much of the year touring in small-town productions of the play *Gentlemen Prefer Blondes*.

In 1967 her career descended into lesser nightclub appearances and TV talk shows. She also spent two months touring South Vietnam and entertaining the troops. Her personal life that year was reported to be a living hell, with her fourth marriage to attorney Sam Brody involving physical abuse and a stream of lawsuits. At 2:25 a.m. on June 29, 1967, Mansfield's turbulent life came to an end when she, Brody, and driver Ronnie Harrison were killed instantly in a freak car accident 30 miles outside of New Orleans. Mansfield was decapitated when the car slammed into the rear of a semi truck in a white cloud of fog produced by mosquito-spraying equipment.

Despite the fact that Mansfield was never a major box-office draw, she remains a pop-culture icon because of the massive amounts of publicity she generated, her image as a well-endowed Hollywood sex kitten, and the public's fascination with her gruesome and untimely death. She married four times; had five children; and although her work was rarely lauded by the critics, Mansfield did fulfill her childhood dream of achieving fame.

Dennis Russell

SEE ALSO: *Broadway; Las Vegas; Monroe, Marilyn; Sex Symbol; Tabloids.*

BIBLIOGRAPHY

Faris, Jocelyn. *Jayne Mansfield: A Biobibliography*. Westport, CT: Greenwood Press, 1994.

Mann, May. *Jayne Mansfield: A Biography*. New York: Drake, 1973.

Palmer, Barton R. *Larger than Life: Movie Stars of the 1950s*. New Brunswick, NJ: Rutgers University Press, 2010.

Saxton, Martha. *Jayne Mansfield and the American Fifties*. Boston: Houghton Mifflin, 1975.

Manson, Charles *(1934–)*

A hardened recidivist criminal, Charles Manson sought vengeance on a society he felt perpetuated his vicious cycle of incarceration. With a charismatic litany of love/hate, life/death mind games and heavy drug use, he attracted followers—"the Family"—who beheld him in messianic awe but at the same time were terrified of his brutality. Manson wanted attention, prison psychiatrists would explain, and he would eventually make famous (and infamous) the hippie thrill kill cult that murdered in his name to bring down "the Establishment" at the close of the tumultuous 1960s.

Born Charles Milles Manson on November 12, 1934, in Cincinnati, Ohio, Manson was often left in the care of a religiously strict aunt while his mother committed petty crimes. He was placed in a boys school and, upon escaping, stole to survive, committing his first armed robbery at age thirteen. Described by caseworkers as "aggressively antisocial," Manson was considered a lost cause until he married Rosalie Jean Willis in 1955. Standing trial in Los Angeles for grand theft auto, he was nearly released on probation due to his marriage and newborn son. When he was jailed anyway, Rosalie divorced him and took Charles Manson Jr. away. Manson never saw them again. After a brief probation, during which he was arrested for prostitution, he was returned to prison to serve the remainder of a ten-year sentence.

Though largely illiterate, Manson began studying the Bible, Scientology, and the science fiction of Robert Heinlein, which—combined with his own songwriting aspirations—formed the basis for Manson's concepts of group love and communal living. He was also blown away by Beatlemania, which hit the United States in 1964; he became obsessed with stardom, claiming he could be bigger than the Beatles given the opportunity.

After a transfer to a Los Angeles prison in 1967, Manson was released from the only home he'd ever known. He roamed California, traveling to San Francisco, panhandling, and attracting a cadre of runaways among those flocking to the mecca of the "Summer of Love." Manson also experimented with LSD and encouraged others to do so, spouting his misinformed spiritualism and ingratiating himself into the flower power scene.

GATHERING "THE FAMILY"

"The Family," as they called themselves, were mostly small-time criminals from broken or dysfunctional nuclear homes, and Manson played the role of father, teacher, lover, god, and devil. He was everything they needed, and through emotional manipulation and isolation from a society he claimed had thrown them away, he became everything they wanted as well. Together they cruised California's highways, picking up wayward teenagers, teaching them how to forage, prostitute, and live communally. As the hippie aesthetic became fashionable in Hollywood, the Family was welcomed into the homes of L.A.'s hippest, well-intentioned celebrities: filmmaker Kenneth Anger; producer Terry Melcher; and, significantly, Beach Boy Dennis Wilson, who recorded some of Manson's jangly sociopathic folk tunes and from whom the Family took cash, credit cards, and clothing.

MURDER AND MAYHEM

In 1968 the Family moved to the Spahn movie ranch in Simi Valley, a short drive from downtown Hollywood. Numbering as many as fifty, they worked as ranch hands in exchange for lodging in the dilapidated Western movie sets, scavenged for food in area Dumpsters, and kept a steady stream of runaways flowing toward Manson's already crowded mattress. Meanwhile, he fueled their disenfranchisement with a barrage of synchronicities involving the Bible (specifically the Book of Revelations), Beat-

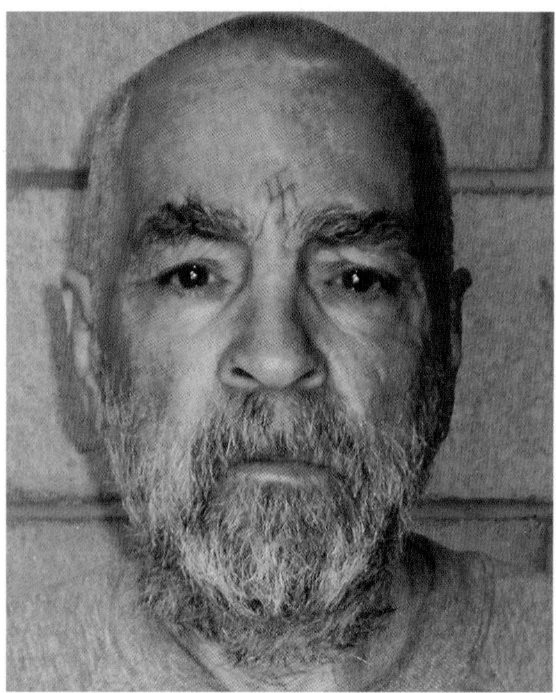

Charles Manson. *Charles Manson appears in 2009 after nearly four decades in prison next to an image from 1970, during his trial for a series of grisly murders in 1969.* AP IMAGES.

les lyrics (specifically the *White Album*), and the sordid events of his own life. He prophesied that a race war would erupt, destroying all major cities and decimating the white population, and that he would rise up from the desert to rule over the remains of the human race. But Manson couldn't wait for his theory of "Helter Skelter" (named after the Beatles song of the same name) to come of its own accord; he and the Family began executing those individuals perceived as threats to this master plan.

The rejection of Manson's music by industry executives who had once befriended him only sparked more murders, the most famous (and grisly) occurring August 9 and 10, 1969, historically known as the Tate-LaBianca murders. Though Manson was not present for these, he incited Family members to slay coffee magnate Abigail Folger, pregnant actress Sharon Tate, and three others in the Hollywood home of director Roman Polanski. By leaving pseudo-political clues—"Piggy" and "Rise" smeared on the wall in the victims' blood and an American flag draped over a couch—the Family hoped to shift blame away from their mission of salvation through murder. The next night Family members killed prominent businessman Leno LaBianca and his wife, Rosemary, in a similar fashion in their home.

Months later Manson's pathology was uncovered due largely to the tenacious investigative work of district attorney Vincent Bugliosi, who reconstructed the events of those August nights and extracted the bizarre motive. After Manson and the murderers were arrested, advocates of the Family held vigils and shaved their heads in a show of solidarity, creating a media circus outside the courthouse. Manson egged on the investigation by claiming he had already been judged and couldn't be punished more than he already had been.

Manson and three Family members were convicted of first-degree murder in 1971. Although Manson was sentenced to death, the death penalty was abolished in California in 1972, and his sentence was reduced to life in prison. He made his first unsuccessful appearance before a parole board in 1978. This opportunity for release comes every seven years and has always been met with stern opposition by the public as well as by the families of the victims. Manson rarely seems disappointed with the prospect of returning to his cell, however, claiming it's safer there than out in society and that his influence is far greater behind bars.

Manson's influence has played out in popular culture in numerous ways. TV crime shows such as *Criminal Minds* have featured Manson-like murders, and numerous documentaries about Manson and the murders have appeared over the years, from 1989's *Charles Manson Superstar* to 2007's *Inside the Manson Gang*. He has been used as a source of parody on TV shows such as *The Ben Stiller Show* (1992–1993), *Saturday Night Live* (1975–), and *South Park* (1997–). Shock rocker Marilyn Manson took his name, and Guns N' Roses even recorded one of Manson's songs on 1993's *The Spaghetti Incident*. Websites dedicated to Manson proliferate the Internet, including charliemanson.com, which includes links to Manson's writing, artwork, and latest news.

The lurid visual appeal of murder scenes; the intricacies of forensic testimony; the demonization of hippies, cults, and communes; and Manson's sinister theories on society's ills have forever changed the public view of "common" criminals and their influence on youth culture. Although the connection between dysfunctional families and crime had always been evident, Manson demonstrated to his followers—and, with media exposure, to the world—that one could become famous through misplaced aggression. Even underground institutions are divided on whether he is a sick symbol of our times or a martyred prophet. Nevertheless, Charles Manson has become one of the most despicable media darlings in popular culture. He was the first, but certainly not the last, sociopath superstar.

Tony Brewer

SEE ALSO: *The Beach Boys; The Beatles; Capital Punishment; Celebrity; Communes; Cults; Divorce; Folk Music; Hippies; Hollywood; LSD;* Saturday Night Live*; Science Fiction Publishing;* South Park*; Teenagers.*

BIBLIOGRAPHY

Bugliosi, Vincent, with Curt Gentry. *Helter Skelter: The True Story of the Manson Murders: 25th Anniversary Edition.* New York: W. W. Norton, 1994.

Emmons, Nuel. *Manson in His Own Words.* Grove Press, NY: 1988.

George, Edward, and Dary Matera. *Taming the Beast: Charles Manson's Life behind Bars.* New York: St. Martin's Press, 1998.

Marynick, Marlin. *Charles Manson Now.* Montreal: Cogito Media Group, 2010.

Sanders, Ed. *The Family: Completely.* New York: Thunder's Mouth Press, 2002.

Watson, Tom. "The Manson Murders at 40." *Newsweek,* August 17, 2009, 38.

Mantle, Mickey *(1931–1995)*

In 1951 nineteen-year-old Mickey Mantle joined the fabled New York Yankees. In the ensuing decade—a time when baseball was still America's pastime, representing all that was good in sports and in the nation—Mantle would evolve into a legend. This innocent boy from Oklahoma became one of the most beloved players in the history of the game. Known as a genuine and humble young man, the kid whose mother had sewn all of his baseball uniforms for him came to evoke the soul of baseball.

Mantle's father, Mutt, directed his son's life toward baseball from the day he was born, naming him after his favorite player, Mickey Cochrane. A natural right-handed hitter, Mantle was taught by his father to become a switch-hitter, making the young man a double threat at the plate. A powerful batter from either side, he switch-hit with great success. By the end of his baseball career, he had racked up 536 home runs, 1,509 runs batted in (RBI), and 2,415 hits, and he had hit .300 or better in ten out of his eighteen seasons. He also, however, struck out a then-record 1,710 times. Three times he was named the Most Valuable Player in the American League—in 1956, 1957, and 1962—and he was unanimously inducted into the Baseball Hall of Fame in 1974. His greatest single-season achievement came in 1956 when he won the triple crown—with 52 home runs, 130 runs batted in, and a .353 batting average.

But Mantle is probably best remembered for just one season—1961—when he and teammate Roger Maris (1934–1985) matched each other homer for homer as they attempted to break Babe Ruth's record of sixty home runs in one season. That Ruth had also been a Yankee added a certain poignancy and excitement to the competition. Ultimately Maris hit a record sixty-one homers that year to Mantle's fifty-four after the Mick was sidelined by injuries—an all-too-frequent occurrence throughout his career.

Television helped make Mantle a figure of popular culture. He joined the Yankees when baseball was at the peak of its popularity: television stations had begun broadcasting games, thus increasing the audience for the sport. Mantle played center field for the New York Yankees at a time when Willie Mays played center field for the New York Giants and Duke Snider played center field for the Brooklyn Dodgers. All three were great players playing in the same city, which also happened to be the media capital of the world. People nationwide could follow their exploits. Those who didn't have television sets in the early to mid-1950s would stand outside appliance store windows in October to watch the World Series—and Mantle was a hero in many of those games.

Mickey Mantle. *Legendary slugger Mickey Mantle, considered by many the best switch-hitter in baseball history, was named the American League's Most Valuable Player three times in eighteen seasons with the New York Yankees.* FOCUS ON SPORT/CONTRIBUTOR/GETTY IMAGES SPORT/GETTY IMAGES.

But being a hero came with a burden. Mantle not only hit with the best, but he also drank with the best. Most of his off-field exploits with alcohol and women never made the sports pages, and so his good-boy image went virtually untarnished. As Tony Castro reports in *Mickey Mantle: America's Prodigal Son*, reflecting on the time one of his sons, then eight years old, fixed a bicycle he had assembled incorrectly, Mantle said, "Even eight-year-olds made excuses for me." He and his wife eventually separated, and the entire family went on to battle alcoholism.

It was not until 1994 that Mantle confronted his alcoholism and checked himself into the Betty Ford clinic, but it was too late—he had damaged his liver beyond repair. He eventually became ill with cancer. A liver transplant buoyed everyone's hopes—family and fans alike—that he had won the latest battle. But the cancer had spread. The soul of baseball died at sixty-three on August 13, 1995, remembered for his innocence, his exploits, his honesty.

R. Thomas Berner

SEE ALSO: *Baseball; The Brooklyn Dodgers; Live Television; Maris, Roger; Mays, Willie; The New York Yankees; Ruth, Babe; Sports Heroes; World Series.*

BIBLIOGRAPHY

Allen, Maury. *Memories of the Mick.* Dallas, TX: Taylor Publishing, 1997.

Castro, Tony. *Mickey Mantle: America's Prodigal Son.* Washington, DC: Potomac Books, 2002.

Faulkner, David. *The Last Hero: The Life of Mickey Mantle.* New York: Simon & Schuster, 1995.

Honig, Donald. *Mays, Mantle, Snider.* New York: Macmillan, 1987.

Mantle, Mickey, and Phil Pepe. *My Favorite Summer, 1956.* New York: Doubleday, 1991.

Mantle Family, The, and Mickey Herskowitz. *A Hero All His Life.* New York: HarperCollins, 1996.

Manufactured Homes

Manufactured homes have become an increasingly attractive and affordable alternative to traditional houses that are built on-site. Factory-built and delivered in one or more sections by tractor-trailer, these structures come in many shapes and sizes, with exteriors of varying styles, textures, and materials. Their interior space and layout approximate those found in more conventional houses—and they cost less. Once considered suitable only for young first-time buyers or retirees, today's manufactured homes appeal to a much larger segment of society. Whether in a designated subdivision or on an individual lot, the modern factory-built home serves America's urgent need for affordable housing.

Since the creation of the first travel trailer, mass-produced transportable shelters have had several identities in America: house trailer, mobile home, and finally manufactured home. Although they are descendants of the mobile home, manufactured homes are no longer considered temporary. Intended to remain in place, they are not merely a stepping-stone to a larger house. Once blocked by institutional barriers, such as local zoning ordinances and impediments to financing and mortgage arrangements, manufactured homes have been allowed to proliferate in many areas of the United States. Yet, one of the main obstacles to greater social acceptance is their association with their trailer predecessors.

PRE–WORLD WAR II

American companies began to produce travel trailers primarily for camping or road trips, taking a cue from the popularity of British motor caravans. During the 1930s inventor Arthur Sherman's covered wagon models rolled off the production line like Henry Ford's automobiles. Sherman advertised his product in popular magazines such as *National Geographic* and *Field and Stream*, and the public responded enthusiastically. Americans began using the wagons as year-round accommodations. In 1936 noted financial analyst Roger Babson, who had foreseen the stock market crash of 1929, predicted that soon more than half of all Americans would be living in trailers.

In fact, several visionaries, including architects Le Corbusier, Walter Gropius, and Buckminster Fuller, had espoused the concept of mass-produced industrialized housing during the early decades of the twentieth century. However, their ideas and designs were never put into production. The first true departure from the towable trailer was the Durham House, a modular unit designed in 1938 by two professors of architecture at the University of Illinois. The structure, with no underlying chassis and presented in a double or single scheme, was designed for permanent or semipermanent placement on a cinder block foundation. However, prospective home buyers did not seem interested in manufactured housing that could not be towed, and the Durham House never caught on. Still, the double-unit Durham House is viewed by many as the precursor of today's double-wide homes.

During the 1930s General Houses Corporation of Chicago tried to sell prefabricated designs, and a few government agencies, such as the Tennessee Valley Authority, had experimented with transportable, sectional housing. Neither caught on. During the 1940s the Lustron House became another failed attempt at marketing mass-produced homes. Instead, it was the combination of mobility and permanent housing that captured consumer consciousness. Thus, the travel trailer industry began billing its products as house trailers.

HOUSE TRAILERS AND MOBILE HOMES

During the 1940s the war created a ready market for the house trailer. The federal government ordered thousands of units to shelter workers for construction and production projects across the country. When hostilities ended and the exodus to the suburbs began, the house trailer provided a competitive alternative to the standardized models in new subdivisions, such as in Levittown, New York.

Trailer parks, once associated with seasonal camps and "tin can tourists," began to offer patrons a sense of permanent community. Moreover, basic designs for house trailers changed, relinquishing those elements symbolically associated with movement. The new designs had features of permanent homes, such as porches that folded out and bay windows. The exteriors became less streamlined and the interiors, less yacht-like. Designers added skirting and suggested landscaping schemes to cover up the hitch and chassis.

In 1954 Marshfield Homes broke the 8-foot-width barrier by introducing a 10-foot-wide model. Manufacturers and trade magazines created a new label for the product, "mobile home." Transportation regulations were modified to allow shipment over public rights of way. Manufacturers made even wider models, and 12- and 14-foot widths became standard. Soon buyers were favoring double-wide homes, designed to be transported in halves and joined together on-site.

Apart from the mobile home industry, deliberate attempts at mass producing industrialized modular housing units were sporadic and unsuccessful. A collaborative effort by several architects exiled from Adolf Hitler's Germany set a course toward production of the Packaged House, an enterprise of much fanfare but little else. During the late 1940s, the General Panel Company turned out a limited quantity of the Packaged House kits from its California plant.

Attempts at marketing manufactured homes by firms such as Uni-Seco Structures, Arcon, and Aluminum Bungalow were equally unsuccessful. Designers saw prefabrication as a way to solve the problem of affordable, available shelter. But consumers were not interested. Even Fuller had labeled his famous Dymaxion house a "theory only." Improvements in design and technological breakthroughs did not improve the commercial success of prefabricated housing. The Marlette Company's sophisticated 1963 industrial design failed to sell. In 1970 a distinctive Frank Lloyd Wright–inspired prairie-style manufactured home was developed but never commercially produced.

In 1975 the mobile home industry changed its named, yet again, to manufactured housing. The change reflected the widening scope of factory-built home designs. The percentage of new houses that were mobile or manufactured rose steadily following the end of World War II, peaking during the late 1960s and early 1970s. For several years manufactured homes constituted about one-third of all housing starts. However, the ratio declined to approximately 20 percent in the late 1990s and fell to around 10 percent late in the first decade of the 2000s and into the early 2010s. A severe economic downturn and tightened lending to low-income buyers discouraged new purchases, and several natural disasters raised concerns about the safety of manufactured homes compared to traditional housing.

GOVERNMENT POLICY

The federal government first recognized the legitimacy of the manufactured home in 1969 when it authorized the Department of Housing and Urban Development (HUD) to grant loans for their purchase, no matter where they were located. However, the local legal landscape remains contested. In a 1982 decision upholding a law restricting manufactured homes to designated parks, the Texas Supreme Court ruled that "mobile homes are different and thus may be classified separately from other residential structures for purposes of regulation." But Michigan's highest court overturned such restrictions as an improper exercise of police power, affirming that "mobile homes today can compare favorably with site-built housing in size, safety, and attractiveness."

In 2000 Congress sought to universalize safety requirements by passing the Manufactured Housing Improvement Act, which stipulated that each state must meet or exceed HUD's installation standards by 2005 or must cede their right to oversee installation to the federal government. Implementation of the law has been spotty. Experts cite the need for increased oversight and regulation of construction and installation.

Although many manufactured homes are virtually indistinguishable from traditional homes constructed on-site, a social prejudice remains, built on the long-term association of trailers with low socioeconomic class and impermanence. Yet, few of today's manufactured homeowners select their houses out of a desire for mobility: nine out of ten placements remain in their original location. As Americans discover that neighborhoods of manufactured homes often look equally as nice as those of traditional homes, the industry continues to expand its target market.

Robert Kuhlken

SEE ALSO: *Bungalow; Camping; Consumerism; Fuller, Buckminster; Industrial Design; Levittown;* National Geographic*; Suburbia; World War II.*

BIBLIOGRAPHY

Bernhardt, Arthur. *Building Tomorrow: The Mobile/Manufactured Housing Industry.* Cambridge, MA: MIT Press, 1980.

Dietz, Albert, and Laurence S. Cutler. *Industrialized Building Systems for Housing.* Cambridge, MA: MIT Press, 1971.

Gianino, Andrew. *The Modular Home.* North Adams, MA: Storey Publishing, 2005.

Herbert, Gilbert. *The Dream of the Factory-Made House: Walter Gropius and Konrad Wachsmann.* Cambridge, MA: MIT Press, 1984.

Johnson, Wes. *The Manufactured Home Buyer's Handbook.* Jefferson, NC: McFarland, 2005.

Reidelbach, John A. *Modular Housing in the Real: A Study of the Industry and the Product, Focusing on the Wood Framed Sectional Unit.* Annandale, VA: Modco, 1970.

Thornburg, David. *Galloping Bungalows: The Rise and Demise of the American House Trailer.* Hamden, CT: Archon Books, 1991.

Wallis, Allan D. *Wheel Estate: The Rise and Decline of Mobile Homes.* New York: Oxford University Press, 1991.

Mapplethorpe, Robert *(1946–1989)*

Robert Mapplethorpe's photography has become overshadowed by the controversy that surrounds much of it. Looking beyond the stir that his images generated reveals a body of work that includes elegant and rich black-and-white photographs of nudes, portraits, still lifes, and flowers. Mapplethorpe's imagery is clear and crisp, with a neutral background. He focuses completely on his subjects, composing everything as a still life. His nudes are reminiscent of classical sculpture, and his flowers are eroticized. The subject matter of some of his photographs is shocking, yet his fresh approach to image making has the power to astonish.

PHOTOGRAPHY AS ART

The man who would shake up the art world grew up in a devoutly Catholic family in Floral Park, New York. Mapplethorpe always felt drawn to art and the power of expression that art could hold. At age seventeen he left home to attend Brooklyn's Pratt Institute, a prominent art school. Originally, he wanted to paint or sculpt; at that time, photography did not hold much credibility as a serious art form. Mapplethorpe, however, found photography by accident and continued to use it because it provided a viable outlet by which to express his ideas and make a statement.

Many of his first artworks were constructions and collages, including pornographic images. As Mapplethorpe began taking his own photographs, he started focusing on the human body as subject, first as a study in form—focusing on contours and tones—and also as portraiture. Some of his earliest portraits are of his friend, and later lover, rock singer Patti Smith. Mapplethorpe photographed Smith over a period of several years in the 1970s and 1980s. Other celebrities who later sat before his camera include Laurie Anderson, David Byrne, Truman Capote, Glenn Close, Richard Gere, Peter Gabriel, Gregory Hines, Roy Lichtenstein, Norman Mailer, Isabella Rossellini, and Arnold Schwarzenegger. Mapplethorpe also photographed some of his sponsors, serious collectors, and prestigious art world personalities, including Andy Warhol and Sam Wagstaff, who later became both his patron and his lover.

Mapplethorpe had a fascination with human form. In the early 1980s he extensively photographed the body builder Lisa Lyon, culminating in the publication of the book *Lady* in 1983. With this project, his interest was not only in the beauty of the body and the structure of musculature but also with gender roles; he wished to document that women could develop—physically—their bodies like men. Exemplifying his other studies of the human form are his images of nude black men. These images are reminiscent of classical sculpture. Mapplethorpe—with his series of photographs *Ajito* (1981), a nude black man seated on a pedestal—reinterpreted the nineteenth-century artist Wilhelm von Gloeden's photograph of a male nude in classical pose. Throughout his career Mapplethorpe also used himself as subject; creating self-portraits with a variety of poses, props, and degrees of makeup, he explored different emotions, personas, and gender distinctions.

Later work includes his studies of still lifes and flowers. He arranged the objects precisely. His approach to this genre was no different than his approach to people. Objectifying all subjects, Mapplethorpe tried to transcend his subjects. He brought lighting, composition, and other elements to a level he considered almost perfection. Critic Emmanuel Cooper states in *Creative Camera*, "For Mapplethorpe, photographing flowers was not very different from body parts. He honed in on the sensual aspects of the flowers, often using them as metaphors for physical contact and the ephemeral nature of beauty."

CONTROVERSY

It is some of his earliest work that brought Mapplethorpe the most notoriety. *Portfolio X*, dating from the mid-1970s, consists of homoerotic and sadomasochistic imagery often depicting graphic sex acts. This work exposed the gay subculture of the 1970s to the mainstream while allowing Mapplethorpe to investigate these areas on his own and to embrace his own homosexuality; he always claimed that he did not "photograph things I've not been involved in myself." Also featured within this grouping of photographs are two images of children, one of

Robert Mapplethorpe. *Although his work often sparked controversy, Robert Mapplethorpe is credited with increasing the appreciation of photography as a viable art form.* LEEE BLACK CHILDERS/CONTRIBUTOR/REDFERNS/GETTY IMAGES.

which, *Rosie* (1976), proved particularly controversial. In this image, Rosie's dress, pulled up by her knee, exposes her genitals.

Included in Mapplethorpe's retrospective *The Perfect Moment* (1989) were these images. Organized by the Institute of Contemporary Art in Philadelphia, this exhibition became the catalyst for a public outcry regarding pornography and obscenity. One of the venues for the show, the Contemporary Art Center in Cincinnati, and its director Dennis Barry had pornography charges brought against them leading to prosecution. Although both were acquitted, the museum continued to deal with repercussions. Similarly, a subsequent venue, the Corcoran Museum of Art in Washington, D.C., experienced withdrawn funding and a shake-up in personnel. Additionally, the sadomasochistic images and the photograph of Rosie became exploited by Jesse Helms, the Republican senator from North Carolina. The publicity generated from the pornography charges emboldened Senator Helms to introduce legislation prohibiting beneficiaries of National Endowment for the Arts (NEA) funding from creating work that "may be considered obscene, including but not limited to depictions of sadomasochism, homoeroticism, [and] the sexual exploitation of children or individuals engaged in sex acts."

The debate surrounding Mapplethorpe's artworks took place a year after his death at age forty-two from an AIDS-related illness. His legacy is far reaching. Previous to his death, he formed the Robert Mapplethorpe Foundation, an organization for funding AIDS-related medical research and the visual arts. Almost single-handedly, he focused the spotlight on photography as a viable art form. After his first major show in 1976, the prices for his images steadily rose, while also bringing other artists' photographic works into the limelight. The largest impact created by Mapplethorpe and his art, however, resulted from the controversy that surrounded his images. The aftermath altered funding for artists and redefined the criteria used to judge whether a work can hold the classification of art.

Smith's 2010 autobiography *Just Kids* tells the story of her friendship with the photographer, shining a humane light on a man whose life, by then, had become overshadowed by the controversy surrounding his work. Mapplethorpe's images continue to be exhibited, discussed, and sold into the twenty-first century, including a major exhibition of his Polaroids at the Whitney Museum of American Art, in New York, in 2008.

Jennifer Jankauskas

SEE ALSO: *AIDS; Capote, Truman; Gay Men; Gere, Richard; Mailer, Norman; Pornography; Schwarzenegger, Arnold; Smith, Patti; Warhol, Andy.*

BIBLIOGRAPHY

Cooper, Emmanuel. "The Photographs of Robert Mapplethorpe." *Creative Camera*, October–November 1996, 40–41.

Kardon, Janet, with essays by David Joselit and Kay Larson and a dedication by Patti Smith. *Robert Mapplethorpe: The Perfect Moment.* Philadelphia: Institute of Contemporary Art, University of Pennsylvania, 1988.

Ripp, Allan, ed., with Carol Squiers and Steven Koch. "Mapplethorpe." *American Photographer*, January 1988, 44–55.

Smith, Patti. *Just Kids*. London: Bloomsbury, 2010.

March on Washington

The first March on Washington was proposed in 1941 by A. Philip Randolph, president of the Brotherhood of Sleeping Car Porters. During the Great Depression, African Americans did not benefit equally from President Franklin Delano Roosevelt's New Deal programs, which sought to bring forth economic relief and industrial reform. As World War II unfolded and industry expanded, racial discrimination continued, as white employers denied black workers access to jobs in war industries. When Roosevelt failed to remedy this situation, Randolph called for 50,000 African Americans to descend on the Capitol in Washington, D.C., to protest.

Roosevelt turned to moderate civil rights leaders, such as National Association for the Advancement of Colored People (NAACP) Executive Director Walter White, for aid in quelling the storm, but Randolph refused to back down. With the help of African American newspapers such as the *Baltimore Afro-American*, the *Chicago Defender*, the *Pittsburgh Courier*, and the *New York Amsterdam News*, which publicized the event, the estimated size of the proposed March on Washington continued to grow. Facing the prospects of an embarrassing march, Roosevelt relented in June 1941 and issued Executive Order 8802, which forbid racial discrimination by defense contractors and established a temporary Fair Employment Practices Committee.

When discrimination persisted in the United States and the promise of the Double V ("victory at home and victory abroad") campaign failed to materialize after the war, the March on Washington group continued to meet annually to discuss African American demands for economic equality. As the civil rights movement emerged and developed further in the wake of the *Brown v. Board of Education* decision, events such as the Montgomery (Alabama) bus boycott, the Little Rock (Arkansas) school desegregation crisis, and the student sit-in wave changed the political climate. In response, black leaders began to discuss and plan a new March on Washington aimed at pressuring the federal government to act on pending civil rights legislation lagging in the Congress.

Chaired by Randolph and organized by Bayard Rustin, the 1963 March on Washington for Jobs and Freedom sought to bring more than 100,000 people to the nation's capital. Significantly, the Southern Christian Leadership Conference and the NAACP put aside their historic differences to support the event. Even so, tensions simmered beneath the seemingly unified surface of the event when moderate leaders and clergymen forced John Lewis of the Student Nonviolent Coordinating Committee to temper criticism of President John F. Kennedy in his remarks.

In the end, however, the March on Washington was a tremendous practical and symbolic success. More than 250,000 black and white Americans stood before the Lincoln Memorial, listening to speeches, songs, prayers, and poetry and registering their demand for racial justice in the United States. A wide variety of civil rights leaders, clergymen, politicians, labor leaders, entertainers, and local civil rights supporters participated in the event, which climaxed with Martin Luther King Jr.'s "I Have a Dream" speech. In the speech, King appealed to the highest ideals of American democracy, stating:

> I still have a dream. It is a dream deeply rooted in the American dream that one day this nation will rise up

March on Washington. *Thousands of civil rights demonstrators assemble around the Lincoln Memorial Reflecting Pool in front of the Washington Monument during the March on Washington in August 1963.* BOB PARENT/CONTRIBUTOR/ HULTON ARCHIVE/GETTY IMAGES.

> and live out the true meaning of its creed: "We hold these truths to be self-evident, that all men are created equal." . . . I have a dream my four children will one day live in a nation where they will not be judged by the color of their skin but by the content of their character. I have a dream today!

The successful 1963 March on Washington represented the culmination of the first phase of the modern civil rights movement and expressed the ideals and aspirations of nonviolent direct action. Following the march, but also due in part to the assassination of Kennedy in 1963 and the efforts of Lyndon Baines Johnson, Congress finally passed the Civil Rights Act of 1964 and, later, the Voting Rights Act of 1965. Since then, numerous groups of varying political stripes, including poor people, women, environmentalists, gays and lesbians, black men, Christian men, and cancer patients, have attempted, none so successfully, to use the March on Washington as a model for delivering demands to the federal government.

In the twenty-first century, disaffected voters have also marched to protest the wars in Iraq and Afghanistan; to voice their displeasure with stagnating employment numbers and wealth inequality; and, in extreme cases, to accuse sitting presidents of espousing fascist, socialist, or communist values. In a jab at the hyperbolic rhetoric and limited effectiveness of such rallies, especially in comparison to the monumental success of the 1963 march, political satirists Jon Stewart and Stephen Colbert staged a "Rally to Restore Sanity and/or Fear" in 2010, during which they held competing demonstrations that poked fun at recent marches' tendency to demonize political opponents without suggesting viable alternatives. While none has achieved the success of the 1963 event, the March on Washington continues to symbolize for many the hopeful possibilities of mass-based protest and nonviolent direct action in the United States.

Patrick D. Jones

SEE ALSO: *Civil Rights Movement; The Great Depression; King, Martin Luther, Jr.; New Deal; Protest Groups.*

BIBLIOGRAPHY

Barber, Lucy G. *Marching on Washington: The Forging of an American Political Tradition.* Berkeley: University of California Press, 2002.

Branch, Taylor. *Parting the Waters: America in the King Years, 1954–1963.* New York: Simon & Schuster, 1988.

Dale, Tim M., and Joseph J. Foy. *Homer Simpson Marches on Washington: Dissent through American Popular Culture.* Lexington: University of Kentucky Press, 2010.

Echols, James. *I Have a Dream: Martin Luther King Jr. and the Future of Multicultural America.* Minneapolis, MN: Fortress Press, 2004.

Euchner, Charles. *Nobody Turn Me Around: A People's History of the 1963 March on Washington.* Boston: Beacon Press, 2010.

Garfinkel, Herbert. *When Negroes March: The March on Washington Movement in the Organizational Politic of FEPC.* Glencoe, IL: Free Press, 1959.

Haskins, James. *The March on Washington.* New York: HarperCollins, 1993.

Reed, Merl. "The FBI, MOWM, and CORE, 1941–1946." *Journal of Black Studies* 21, no. 4 (1991): 465–479.

Marching Bands

From regimental bands parading with soldiers and accompanying them into battle during the American Revolution and Civil War to the halftime spectacles of televised football games seen by millions, pulse-pounding march music rendered by colorful marching bands has been a part of America's heritage since the country's earliest days. Indeed, bands, parades, and John Philip Sousa's famous march "The Stars and Stripes Forever" have all come to symbolize freedom, democracy, and the good old United States of America itself.

The word *band* derives from the Latin *bandum,* meaning "banner," "company," and "crowd." In popular usage, "band" has come to mean any group of instruments, ranging from jug to rock, but its specific meaning derives from the medieval musical ensemble of louder instruments, primarily consisting of brass, reeds, and percussion, geared for outdoor performance. This is in contrast to the softer "orchestra" instruments, including strings and woodwinds, which are better suited for interior settings.

The New Grove Dictionary of American Music comments:

> As with other areas of musical culture, European customs and traditions of band music were brought to America in the 17th century by the colonists. The snare drum was an important and necessary part of colonial life. It served not only to set the cadence for marching men but also to bear orders, warnings, and signals for both military and civilian activities. Whenever possible a fife, bagpipe, or other instrument was used to add melodic interest. These instruments, referred to as the "field music," were used primarily for functional purposes.

Other precursors of the modern marching band include military/regimental bands and the wind ensembles that performed mid-eighteenth-century court and household music throughout Europe.

Over several centuries, the band expanded from a small ensemble of reed instruments to its larger modern counterpart. An interest in Turkish (or janissary) music at the end of the eighteenth century added exotic percussion to the band's instrumentation, of which only the bass drum and cymbals (and sometimes a kettledrum) survive today. As existing instruments were refined and new ones invented (such as Adolphe Sax's saxophones in the mid-1800s), the band eventually grew to the grandiose ensembles of the late nineteenth century. The first all-brass band is thought to be the Boston Brass Band, which was first led by Edward Kendall in 1835. Key figures in the development of the modern band were Patrick S. Gilmore and Sousa; the latter, dubbed America's March King, composed the country's—and the world's—most famous marches. Sousa assumed leadership of the U.S. Marine Band in 1890 and formed his renowned Sousa's Band in 1892.

With the rise of jazz in the 1920s, public interest in traditional bands came to an end. But band music, along with such field music/militaristic traditions as color guards and precision/formation marching, not to mention majorettes and virtuoso baton twirling, soon found a home on American college campuses. Football halftime shows evolved into elaborate spectacles in which colleges vied to create the most unusual, exotic, and fantastic presentations; in a salute to pornography, for instance, the Stanford University formation band spelled out

"SMUT" in huge block letters at the 1972 Rose Bowl. With a few modern touches (such as lightweight, fiberglass sousaphones, throngs of "extras," and perhaps even a celebrity "guest star" added for halftime), the marching band has again secured a place within the schools and universities of the United States.

MARCHING BAND SYMBOLS

Marching bands, parades, stirring marches, and their attendant symbolism have played a recurrent role in signifying American traditions, patriotism, and exuberant emotions. Charles Ives's innovative 1914 arrangement "Three Places in New England" evokes a noisy holiday in the composer's native New England; it features different and overlapping tempi and rhythms to be played simultaneously, creating the effect of marching bands passing each other on the village green. Other modern composers, such as Ralph Vaughan Williams and Samuel Barber, composed works specifically for concert bands, and Frederick Fennell and the Eastman Symphonic Wind Ensemble popularized concert band music with their Mercury "Living Presence" high-fidelity recording in the 1950s.

ON STAGE AND SCREEN

Marching bands have often appeared on the silver screen and the Broadway stage. George Gershwin's 1927 musical *Strike Up the Band* was revamped as a Mickey Rooney/Judy Garland musical in 1940, but other than the spirited title song, little from the satiric Broadway original made it into the screen version. In 1952 Clifton Webb starred as Sousa in *Stars and Stripes Forever*, a film with one of the most unlikely Hollywood subplots ever: the story of invention of the sousaphone, a huge, tuba-like band instrument named after the maestro. Meredith Willson's 1950s Broadway hit *The Music Man* tells the story of a personable con man fraudulently peddling musical instruments in the Midwest by convincing small towns that what they really need to keep their young boys wholesome is a marching band. The hyperbolic imagery of the hit song "Seventy-Six Trombones," the hustler's musical pitch line, was literalized in the finale of the 1962 film version. *The Music Man* was successfully revived on Broadway from 2000 to 2001, demonstrating that Americans still love a band. The movie *Drumline* (2002) tells the fictitious story of a drummer from Harlem recruited to play in the marching band at a historically black college in Atlanta.

Parades as a symbol of all that is thrilling and meaningful in life, and even of the fatalistic progression of life itself, is a motif in several other Broadway songs: *Funny Girl*'s "Don't Rain on My Parade," *Sweet Charity*'s "I'm a Brass Band," and *Hello Dolly!*'s "Before the Parade Passes By." In the 1969 film *Hello, Dolly!*, it took a marching band to accomplish what many film critics had previously deemed impossible: in one of the last and most spectacular production numbers ever staged for a Hollywood studio musical, a mightily expanded marching band, converging down a backlot version of New York's 14th Street, even managed to upstage Barbra Streisand.

Ross Care

SEE ALSO: Hello, Dolly!; *Jazz; Rose Bowl; Sousa, John Philip; Streisand, Barbra.*

BIBLIOGRAPHY

Buyer, Paul. *Marching Bands and Drumlines: Secrets of Success from the Best of the Best.* Galesville, MD: Meredith Music, 2009.

Hitchcock, H. Wiley, and Stanley Sadie, eds. *The New Grove Dictionary of American Music.* New York: Grove's Dictionaries of Music, 1986.

Scuro, Vincent. *Presenting the Marching Band.* New York: Dodd, Mead & Company, 1974.

Marciano, Rocky *(1923–1969)*

Rocky Marciano (born Rocco Francis Marchegiano) is the only champion in the history of boxing to remain officially unbeaten and untied throughout his entire professional career. Heavyweight champion from September 1952 to April 1956, "The Brockton Blockbuster" burst into the American consciousness with a brutal knockout of an aging, twice-retired Joe Louis. Marciano cemented his status as a pop culture icon with championship performances against a triumvirate of dangerous veteran fighters: Jersey Joe Wallcott, Ezzard Charles, and Archie Moore.

Marciano never attempted a comeback after his retirement, but in 1969 he staged a "computer fight" against Muhammad Ali (who was banned from professional boxing at the time). A computer was fed data on both Marciano and Ali and calculated who would win. Marciano and Ali staged the fight according to the computer's projections, and the film was shown in closed circuit theaters throughout the world. Tragically killed in a private-plane crash on August 31, 1969, Marciano never got to see his thirteenth-round "knockout" of Muhammad Ali.

Max Kellerman

SEE ALSO: *Ali, Muhammad; Boxing; Louis, Joe.*

BIBLIOGRAPHY

Cutter, Robert Arthur. *The Rocky Marciano Story.* New York: W. Allen Publishing, 1954.

Skehan, Everett M. *Rocky Marciano: Biography of a First Son.* London: Robson Books, 1977.

Sullivan, Russell. *Rocky Marciano: The Rock of His Times.* Urbana: University of Illinois Press, 2002.

Marcus Welby, M.D.

A popular and groundbreaking medical melodrama, *Marcus Welby, M.D.* aired on the ABC network for seven seasons, from September 1969 until May 1976, with Robert Young in the title role. A star of the silver screen and well-known for his role as Jim Anderson on *Father Knows Best*, the sixty-two-year-old Young returned to television after a seven-year retirement to play Welby.

The plots of the hour-long weekly series revolved around the medical cases of Dr. Marcus Welby, a kindhearted family doctor who runs his office out of his home in Santa Monica, California, and is associated with the Family Practice Center at Lang Memorial Hospital. Welby has an old-school work ethic and treats his patients with respect. After suffering a mild coronary, Welby hires a younger associate, Dr. Steven Kiley (James Brolin), to help him with his workload. Unlike the conservative Welby, Kiley is a handsome ladies' man who rides his motorcycle to make house calls. Although a generation gap exists between Kiley and Welby, the two doctors share the same heart of gold. Receptionist and nurse Consuela Lopez (Elena Verdugo) runs their office.

Much of the appeal of the program surfaced in the way that Welby treated his patients. In 1965 President Lyndon B. Johnson had signed the Medicare bill, raising many questions about the degree and quality of health care offered in the United States. Americans worried they were going to be lost in the bureaucracy of the medical system and that their health would suffer for it. Marcus Welby allayed these fears of depersonalization.

Although Welby was supposed to be a general practitioner, he treated much more than the common cold. The program spearheaded medical issues that raised social, moral, and ethical questions. Welby and Kiley treated conditions such as sickle-cell anemia, autism, drug addiction, organ transplants, leukemia, LSD side effects, and mental retardation. *Marcus Welby, M.D.* even dealt with issues such as abortion and interracial marriage, both controversial topics in the early 1970s.

Little was revealed about Welby's private life, even though much of the show was filmed in his home office. There was no Mrs. Welby. In both the pilot film, which aired in March 1969, and during the first season, Welby has a lady friend, Myrna Sherwood (Anne Baxter); this character was thereafter dropped. It was not until the last season that Welby's married daughter, Sandy (Ann Schedeen), and grandson, Phil (Gavin Brendan), appear on the series. Romance was saved for the dapper Kiley. Kiley finds a love interest in Janet Blake (Pamela Hensley), the public relations director of Hope Memorial Hospital. They were wed on the episode that aired on October 21, 1975.

***James Brolin in* Marcus Welby, M.D.** Marcus Welby, M.D. *co-starred James Brolin as Dr. Steven Kiley, Welby's (Robert Young) assistant.* UNIVERSAL TV/THE KOBAL COLLECTION.

Marcus Welby, M.D. was a popular and highly rated series. Many attribute its success to the fact that for its first two seasons it ran against less appealing programming: a CBS news documentary and often against similar programming on NBC. Nonetheless, *Marcus Welby, M.D.* was ranked the top television show during the 1970–1971 season and continued to win a plethora of awards, including a Golden Globe for Best Television Drama and an Emmy. The character of Marcus Welby was resurrected for the last time in the 1984 television movie, *The Return of Marcus Welby, M.D.* Kiley did not appear in that feature.

Lara Bickell

SEE ALSO: Father Knows Best*; Medicine Shows; Television; Young, Robert.*

BIBLIOGRAPHY

Brooks, Tim, and Earle Marsh, eds. *The Complete Directory to Prime Time Network and Cable TV Shows: 1946–Present*, 9th ed. New York: Ballantine Books, 2007.

Brown, Les. *Les Brown's Encyclopedia of Television.* Detroit, MI: Gale Research, 1992.

McNeil, Alex. *Total Television: A Comprehensive Guide to Programming from 1948 to the Present.* New York: Penguin Books, 1996.

Steinberg, Cobbett S. *TV Facts.* New York: Facts On File, 1980.

Terrance, Vincent. *The Complete Encyclopedia of Television Programs, 1947–1979.* South Brunswick, NJ: A. S. Barnes, 1979.

Mardi Gras

The Mardi Gras festival celebrated in the twenty-first century is the descendant of old fertility rites marking the coming of spring and the rebirth of vegetation. These pagan ceremonies were gradually incorporated into orthodox Christianity, and the pre-Lenten celebration, which begins with the Feast of Epiphany and ends on Ash Wednesday, came generally to be known as Carnival. Derived from the old Italian *carnelevare*, which means taking meat away, Carnival became a kind of festival, or final fling, before a period of fasting. In France, and later in Mobile, Alabama, and New Orleans, Louisiana, the celebration was known as Mardi Gras, or Fat Tuesday. In England it was called Shrove Tuesday, or Pancake Tuesday, because the meat fats were used to make pancakes.

Although Mardi Gras in the United States is generally associated with New Orleans, where half a million people or more gather to celebrate, Carnival actually began in Mobile in 1704, when Nicholas Langlois established the Société de Saint Louis at Fort Louis de la Mobile at Twenty-Seven-Mile Bluff. Later, when the city of Mobile moved to its present site, Michael Krafft, a twenty-three-year-old Pennsylvanian working as a cotton broker, and several of his friends began a celebration on New Year's Eve in 1830 after dining at a local restaurant. They left the restaurant, gathered up rakes, hoes, and cowbells, and initiated a parade through the city. Stopping at the home of the mayor, John Stocking Jr., they were invited in for refreshments. Thus, the society Cowbellion de Rakin was born—and with it the mystic orders of Mardi Gras. From this beginning, New Orleans developed pageants of decorated floats and became famous for its parades.

Mardi Gras had a polarizing focus in New Orleans and Mobile because of its segregation and class participation. Anyone could stand along the parade route, shout "throw me something mister," and gather doubloons (prized aluminum disks with the insignia of the krewe, or organization, etched upon one side and the theme on the other) or moon pies (marshmallow cookies frequently tossed from floats in Mobile). A distinction exists, however, between those who ride the floats and those who lead the balls, between the king, queen, maids, and dukes who dispense the trinkets and those who stand on the streets waiting to catch the beads, plastic cups, doubloons, and toys.

In fact, Mardi Gras has created the ultimate antiestablishment irony, in which a King of Mirth becomes elevated to the establishment whereby the eligible daughters of upper society leaders are presented at a coming-out ceremony. In spite of such pseudo-royal shenanigans, Mardi Gras actualizes a shared experience of joy. It brings people together to experience a time of mystery and magic—and that is perhaps why it has become one of the greatest parties in the world. As they say in New Orleans: *Laissez les bon temps rouler* (Let the good times roll).

The good times of Mardi Gras in New Orleans were put to the test in the early twenty-first century. In August 2005, in the aftermath of Hurricane Katrina, 80 percent of the historic city was flooded as billions of gallons of water poured out from breached levees. The population of the city fell from 500,000 to barely 156,000. The city was deeply divided in 2006 over whether or not to hold Mardi Gras. The deciding factors in continuing with the festivities were based on the need to boost local morale as well as the need to infuse the local economy with added wealth, since Mardi Gras normally generates around a billion dollars for the city.

The number of visitors during Mardi Gras in February 2006 dropped to approximately 360,000, while more than a million people had attended the event the year before. The 2006 celebrations were shortened to eight days, and the number of parades was reduced from thirty-four to twenty-eight. Instead of the usual multiple parade routes, there was only one, which led away from areas still awash in mud-caked debris. The following year attendance rose to 800,000, and by 2011 the number of revelers had returned to pre-Katrina levels. Even though New Orleans was still in the process of rebuilding, the good times were beginning to roll again.

Sue Walker

SEE ALSO: *Hurricane Katrina; Parades.*

BIBLIOGRAPHY

Bagert, Brod, and Charlie Smith. *Throw Me Somethin' Mistuh: The Mardi Gras Book.* New Orleans, LA: Juliahouse, 1995.

Barnes, Judy; J. O. Lane Edwards; Caroline Lee Goodloe; et al. *Coasting through Mardi Gras.* Point Clear, AL: Coasting, 1995.

Finch, Jackie Sheckler. *It Happened in Alabama: Remarkable Events That Shaped History.* Guilford, CT: Globe Pequot Press, 2011.

"Mardi Gras Beats Stronger Post Katrina." *USA Today,* February 5, 2008.

McNulty, Ian. *A Season of Night: New Orleans after Katrina.* Jackson: University Press of Mississippi, 2008.

McNulty, Ian. *Louisiana Rambles: Exploring America's Cajun and Creole Heartland.* Jackson: University Press of Mississippi, 2011.

Patterson, Thom. "Let the Good Times Roll (But Not Too Much)." CNN Online, February 24, 2006. Accessed February 12, 2012. Available from http://articles.cnn.com/2006-02-24/us/different.mardi.gras_1_parades-mardi-gras-guide-zulu-social-aid?_s=PM:US

Schindler, Henri. *Mardi Gras: New Orleans.* New York: Flammarion, 1997.

Mariachi Music

Since its beginnings, mariachi music has been the music of the countryside and its inhabitants—a much-loved local and regional musical genre. But by the late twentieth century this changed, as mariachi music became a significant force in U.S. popular culture. It influenced the Tejano music that arose in the United States and helped to solidify the latter genre as a serious contender in the American music scene. Mariachi music infiltrated into American ceremonies and rituals such as weddings, masses, birthdays, and other festive events that celebrate a rite of passage. Numerous American women of Hispanic descent have joined mariachi groups, in effect keeping this Mexican tradition alive in the United States. As a result, U.S. residents have become aware of Mexican cultural identities and rural traditions that mesh with those indigenous to the United States. Mariachi music conveys stories with which people readily identify. It highlights great moments in people's lives through songs dealing with the rites of courtship, rural life and its people, animals, plants, and other interesting themes.

Popular folk belief has it that mariachi music originated in Mexico in the nineteenth century. Specifically, people have argued that it was born in the Mexican state of Jalisco during the ill-fated reign of the Emperor Maximilian, a Frenchman, in the 1860s. There has always been some dispute regarding the origin of the word *mariachi.* According to legend, mariachi is a variation of the French word *mariage,* which means "wedding." Many people believe that mariachi was a term coined by the French themselves after watching the musicians perform at weddings. A more accurate, scholarly argument maintains that the word and the music associated with it has roots in Mexico itself. Nevertheless, European instruments were adopted by the natives, and despite the ambiguity of the origins of mariachi music, one thing is clear—it was a brand of music that was created by and for the people of the rural areas of Mexico.

The mariachi group as it has been known in the mid-twentieth to early twenty-first centuries, then, began in Jalisco in the nineteenth century. But the genre came into its own and penetrated into American popular culture during the 1950s, when the mariachi group became a kind of musical orchestra and made its own recordings and films. While retaining their traditional base of support, these groups acquired new musical tastes and styles and thereby gained new bases in the process, especially in the United States. Tejano music became very popular in the United States in the late twentieth century, and

Mariachi Music. A mariachi band performs outside a sporting event in Utah. Mariachi music first took hold in the United States in the 1950s. MELISSA MAJCHRZAK/CONTRIBUTOR/MAJOR LEAGUE SOCCER/GETTY IMAGES.

the music of the mariachi had much to do with that success. Popular Tejano singers like Selena used the beautiful harmony of mariachi music.

Mariachis also influenced the Catholic Church in the United States, specifically the Sunday mass. Many Spanish masses in the United States have incorporated mariachis, lending a new musical flavor to the way mass is conducted in the American Catholic Church. The music has also received academic interest. For example, in 2000 Southwest Texas State University (later called Texas State University–San Marcos) began an annual mariachi concert, which expanded over the next ten years to include instructional seminars intended to help pass on mariachi traditions.

A parallel development has been the growing number of American women involved in mariachi music. American women of Hispanic descent have increasingly become a part of mariachi groups since the mid-twentieth century. Women are considered to be on the same musical footing with men with regard to their playing, singing, and dancing and in their overall dedication to expressing Mexican and American folk traditions through the medium of music. The all-female mariachi band the Mariachi Divas, which formed in 1999, is also a multicultural ensemble; in 2009 the group won a Grammy for Best Regional Mexican Album.

Mariachis have performed at many festive occasions in the United States, including weddings, masses, concerts with symphony orchestras, and even funerals. The musical interests of the mariachis have expanded to include both classical and popular music. Because of the growth of mariachi music, Americans have grown aware and appreciative of it and of its themes. The stories told by the mariachis in their music have encouraged Americans of both Hispanic and non-Hispanic descent to look at and enjoy the simpler things in life.

Indeed, the music of the mariachi has had a positive impact, not only on the musical arena of the United States but also on religious and social arenas. The music and lyrics are simple but contain clear-cut depictions of rural life and all the symbols, pleasures, trials, and tribulations that come with that lifestyle. Perhaps it is those themes that best reflect what both Mexicans and Americans long to have—an understanding of the land; nature; and, most importantly, love. All these themes will continue to be represented as long as mariachi music remains dedicated to representing Mexico's fascinating cultural heritage and sharing it with, and in the process enriching, America's popular culture.

David Trevino

SEE ALSO: *Grammy Awards; Multiculturalism; Tejano Music.*

BIBLIOGRAPHY

Greathouse, Patricia. *Mariachi.* Layton, UT: Gibbs Smith, 2009.

Harpole, Patricia W., and Mark Fogelquist. *Los Mariachis!: An*

Introduction to Mexican Mariachi Music. Danbury, CT: World Music Press, 1989.

Rafael, Hermes. *Origen y historia del mariachi*. Mexico City: Katún, 1983.

Sheehy, Daniel. *Mariachi Music in America: Experiencing Music, Expressing Culture*. New York: Oxford University Press, 2005.

Marichal, Juan *(1937–)*

Known for his unorthodox pitching motion and his immaculate control, Juan Marichal won more baseball games in the 1960s (191) than any other pitcher. The "Dominican Dandy" spent fourteen of his sixteen seasons with the San Francisco Giants, accumulating six twenty-win seasons and throwing a no-hitter in 1963. Despite his efforts, he never won a Cy Young Award. Marichal's success did, however, clear the path into major-league baseball for other Latin American players, and he remains influential in Dominican Republic baseball. Marichal was also the all-time leader in wins by a Latin American pitcher (243) until Dennis Martinez eclipsed his record in 1998. Marichal was inducted into the Baseball Hall of Fame in 1983.

Nathan R. Meyer

SEE ALSO: *Baseball; Major League Baseball.*

BIBLIOGRAPHY

Elston, Gene. *A Stitch in Time: A Baseball Chronology.* Houston, TX: Halcyon Press, 2006.

Marichal, Juan. *Juan Marichal: My Journey from the Dominican Republic to Cooperstown.* Minneapolis, MN: MVP Books, 2011.

Marichal, Juan, and Charles Einstein. *A Pitcher's Story.* Garden City, NY: Doubleday, 1967.

Marie, Rose *(1923–)*

Singer and actress Rose Marie has entered the canon of popular entertainers as something of a cultural phenomenon. She flourished in two distinct, widely separated bursts of national popularity, but what set her apart was the sheer longevity of a professional career that began in earliest childhood. Born Rose Marie Mazetta in New York City on August 15, 1923, she began performing on radio when she was three years old, billed as "Baby Rose Marie," singer of current popular songs. She was a child star with her own radio show and then built a career that lasted almost eight decades. Her venues ranged from vaudeville in the Roaring Twenties to television and film in the twenty-first century.

As a child, Marie sang and danced in a number of film shorts, including *Baby Rose Marie, the Child Wonder* in 1929, and she continued on her popular radio show into the early 1930s. She was so famous that when she turned sixteen, her party band was the Glenn Miller Orchestra and she was serenaded by Tony Martin. In the 1940s she sang in clubs from New York City's Copacabana to Las Vegas's Flamingo Hotel and Casino, owned by mobster Bugsy Siegel.

Her acting career on stage, in film, and on television began in the 1940s and spans more than half a century. She appeared occasionally in Broadway revues, which included *Top Banana* with Phil Silvers in 1951. She did some guest shots on television in the 1940s and 1950s and was featured in the television program *My Sister Eileen* in 1960. From 1961 to 1966 she starred on *The Dick Van Dyke Show* as Sally Rogers; this beloved character was a wisecracking, husband-hunting comedy writer, loosely based on the real-life, caustically witty comedy writer Selma Diamond. The role garnered three Emmy Award nominations for Marie, who went on to play Myrna Gibbons on *The Doris Day Show* from 1969 to 1971 and appeared regularly on the *Hollywood Squares* game show for several years in the 1970s.

In 2001 Marie was awarded a star on the Hollywood Walk of Fame. In 2002 she published her memoir, *Hold the Roses*, which is filled with show business stories from as early as the 1920s. She reveals difficulties: for instance, her father was a vaudeville performer who gambled away her child-star earnings. But she remembers playing for President Franklin D. Roosevelt in the Oval Office, and she recalls that "Uncle" Al Capone once gave her a diamond ring and a kiss on the cheek and said to have her father call him if she ever needed anything.

James R. Belpedio

SEE ALSO: *Broadway; Capone, Al; Day, Doris;* Hollywood Squares*; Las Vegas; Miller, Glenn; Radio; Television; The Twenties; Van Dyke, Dick; Vaudeville.*

BIBLIOGRAPHY

Brooks, Tim, and Earle Marsh. *The Complete Directory to Prime Time Network and Cable TV Shows 1946–Present*, 6th ed. New York: Ballantine Books, 1995.

Marijuana

Historically used as a renewable resource and a treatment for minor or terminal illnesses, cannabis (variously called marijuana or hemp) was the harbinger of a contradictory attitude in the United States toward controlled substances. The plant, which may be smoked or eaten as a mild intoxicant, has become the third-most popular recreational drug in America after alcohol and tobacco. Marijuana was once an integral part of early American agrarian society, but advances in synthetic manufacturing eliminated its industrial applications and threatened its highly debated medicinal uses. Modern physicians are intrigued by marijuana's efficacy, but a wave of drug hysteria that started in the 1930s has effectively negated the drug's positive reputation, carrying into the late twentieth and early twenty-first centuries with campaigns labeling the drug as a "gateway" to more dangerous recreational narcotics.

Cannabis generally grows in two forms: hemp and marijuana, the former producing more oil and fiber, the latter producing more of the intoxicating resin whose active ingredient (among 460 other compounds) is tetrahydrocannabinol, or THC. One of the oldest psychoactive plants on the earth, cannabis is native to central Asia and was first cultivated some 10,000 years ago. Many early cultures used hemp to make paper and rope, and some revered marijuana as a sacrament. As early as 2737 BCE in China, written accounts have extolled the use of marijuana as a treatment for malaria, rheumatism, fever, dysentery, or depression; as an appetite stimulant; or as a way to induce sleep. Figures in the classical and Hellenistic eras also noted marijuana as a common remedy.

HISTORY IN THE UNITED STATES

Hemp cultivation in America dates back to colonial Virginia in 1611, when hemp was an important resource for sails, rope, paper, and clothing. King James I ordered colonists to cultivate the plant as an industrial commodity, and some historians contend that Presidents George Washington and Thomas Jefferson advocated a hemp-based economy. Western doctors discovered marijuana in 1839, when W. B. O'Shaughnessey published the results of his experiments with humans and cannabis, lauding marijuana as an effective analgesic.

Soon doctors began studying the drug in earnest and found numerous practical applications, especially in its capacity to subdue restlessness and anxiety in terminal illness. But marijuana use declined in 1850 after the invention of the syringe, which allowed water-soluble drugs such as morphine to be injected intravenously. Also, marijuana preparations were too variable, and other synthetic drugs such as aspirin, chloral hydrate, and barbiturates were far more stable and reliable.

In the 1920s and 1930s, marijuana was increasingly viewed as a catalyst for antisocial behavior, especially among minorities. The Federal Bureau of Narcotics launched a campaign to rid America of "Marijuana, the Devil's Weed," spreading exaggerated and unsubstantiated reports of violent crime, addiction, and psychosis induced by smoking marijuana. The Marihuana Tax Act of 1937 undermined scientific examination of cannabis by heavily taxing and regulating all transactions (medicinal, industrial, and recreational) and linking all forms of the plant with recreational drug use.

Some independent experts tried to dispel the myths but were shouted down by government agencies and the research institutions they supported. Although the purpose of the tax was to discourage recreational marijuana smoking, the measure merely made it difficult or prohibitively expensive to legally procure the drug. Thus, manufacturers eventually switched from hemp to synthetic materials due to financial concerns and the stigma attached to cannabis.

By the 1960s anecdotes of the utility of hemp and marijuana began appearing in popular publications such as *Playboy* and *National Geographic*. These reports originated from a counterculture that equated drug use with social defiance and that considered cannabis prohibition a violation of civil rights. Such attitudes only spurred harsher legislation, and in 1970 Congress passed the Controlled Substances Act, which categorized all psychoactive drugs into five schedules. Cannabis was placed on Schedule I (the most restrictive), prohibiting medicinal marijuana use even under a doctor's supervision.

Legalization March in Oregon. *Supporters of the legalization of marijuana march in Portland, Oregon, in 2012.* © ALEX MILAN TRACY/DEMOTIX/CORBIS.

LEGALIZATION EFFORTS

In 1972 the National Organization for the Reform of Marijuana Laws (NORML) petitioned government agencies to reconsider the industrial applications of hemp and to reclassify marijuana as a Schedule II, permitting its use in a medical setting. In 1980 synthetic THC was placed on Schedule II, but marijuana remained on Schedule I. Marijuana advocates argued that certain other drugs with documented histories of overdose, death, and addiction had been given more lenient categorization. In 1986 hundreds of witnesses and medical experts testified before the U.S. Drug Enforcement Agency (DEA) and produced thousands of pages of documentation supporting marijuana's merits. However, the DEA issued its final rejection of reclassification in 1992.

State governments responded to public outcry, and New Mexico was the first state to legislate in favor of the medicinal use of marijuana in 1978. By 1992 thirty-four states were lobbying for a form of legalization. Only seventeen states were permitted by the federal government to supply patients—mostly those suffering from glaucoma or undergoing chemotherapy to treat cancer—with marijuana. But many states discontinued their programs due to the mountain of paperwork required and the glacial pace at which the federal bureaucracy moved.

A deluge of AIDS cases in the early 1990s reignited demand for medicinal marijuana in order to combat nausea and appetite loss. However, patients often procured the drug by illicit means because the legal application process could take months. Patients even abandoned government supplies of the drug, stating that black market marijuana was more potent and effective, with increased concentrations of THC being attributed primarily to the indoor growing methods illegal growers use to evade aerial surveillance. In 1992 the U.S. government discontinued all medicinal marijuana distribution programs (though the U.S. Department of Health and Human Services applied for and received a patent for medical cannabis in 2003, highlighting its use as an antioxidant and neuroprotectant). Although some imported hemp products are available in the United States, mass production of hemp products remains a legal sticking point for most American manufacturers.

In the first decade of the 2000s the Bush administration and the DEA drew the ire of cannabis proponents by raiding dispensaries and producers in states in which medical marijuana had been legalized. In 2002 two medical marijuana patients in California sued the federal government for violating the Constitution's commerce clause, which restricts the ability of Congress to regulate commerce on the state level. However, in 2005, the Supreme Court ruled in *Gonzales v. Raich* that Congress was within its rights to regulate and disrupt the production and/or sale of cannabis, even in small amounts intended for personal use.

Federal and state initiatives often targeted the medical community to make their point on the matter, as in the case of Tod H. Mikuriya. A California doctor who claimed to have smoked marijuana each morning with his coffee, Mikuriya was fined and placed on probation for writing prescriptions for marijuana to "patients" he never examined. By the time of his death in 2007, he had reportedly written marijuana prescriptions for 9,000 people. The case only solidified the common belief among opponents that the medical argument for marijuana was a thinly veiled attempt to legalize the drug for recreational use.

President Barack Obama used the controversial issue to distance himself from his conservative opponents in 2007, claiming that "federal agents have better things to do" than investigate marijuana production and distribution. Yet a number of federal raids on dispensaries in the early 2010s prompted many to accuse him of a drastic policy reversal.

Public opinion continues to shift on whether to treat cannabis as a controlled substance. Proponents have argued that the historically documented medical applications of marijuana are as real as the suffering it relieves. Others have claimed that the drug is addictive and does not have an acceptable medical application like other specialized, sanctioned, and regulated products legally available to the public. Although classification of marijuana remains a controversial topic in the early twenty-first century, the debate has been largely eclipsed at the federal level by other urgent social and economic issues.

Tony Brewer

SEE ALSO: *AIDS; Cigarettes; Cocaine/Crack;* National Geographic*; Obama, Barack;* Playboy*; War on Drugs.*

BIBLIOGRAPHY

Earleywine, Mitchell, ed. *Pot Politics: Marijuana and the Costs of Prohibition.* New York: Oxford University Press, 2007.

Gerber, Rudolph Joseph. *Legalizing Marijuana: Drug Policy Reform and Prohibition Politics.* Westport, CT: Praeger, 2004.

Goode, Erich, ed. *Marijuana.* New Brunswick, NJ: Aldine Transaction Publishers, 2010.

Grinspoon, Lester, and James B. Bakalar. *Marijuana: The Forbidden Medicine.* New Haven, CT: Yale University Press, 1993.

Herer, Jack, and Leslie Cabarga. *The Emperor Wears No Clothes: The Authoritative Historical Record of Cannabis and the Conspiracy against Marijuana,* 12th ed. Austin, TX: Ah Ha, 2010.

Iversen, Leslie L. *The Science of Marijuana,* 2nd ed. New York: Oxford University Press, 2008.

Jaffe, Jerome H., ed. *Encyclopedia of Drugs and Alcohol,* Vol. 2. New York: Macmillan, 1995.

Shohov, Tatiana, ed. *Medical Use of Marijuana: Policy, Regulatory, and Legal Issues.* New York: Nova Science Publishers, 2003.

Marin, Cheech

SEE: *Cheech and Chong.*

Mario Brothers

Nintendo's Mario Brothers, Mario and Luigi, are among the most iconic video game characters ever created. Recognized by serious gamers and casual fans of electronic entertainment alike, these mustachioed, overall-wearing plumbers from Brooklyn, New York (Mario in the red cap, Luigi in the green), came of age in the 1980s during a wildly creative era that saw the transformation of an industry from the so-called golden age of arcade games to the explosion in popularity of home gaming consoles. Having first appeared in *Donkey Kong*, Mario holds the distinction of playing a leading man in two of the best-selling video games in history. Quite possibly the most popular and identifiable video game character of all-time, Mario still serves as the mascot for Nintendo.

In *Donkey Kong*, which was designed for Nintendo by Shigeru Miyamoto, Mario's mission is to rescue his girlfriend, Pauline, from the titular character, a hostile giant ape that is holding her captive atop a construction site. As Mario attempts to climb a series of girders and ladders to reach Pauline, Donkey Kong hurls barrels and fireballs into his path. Mario must jump over one after another of these dangerous projectiles in order to stay alive; hence his original name, "Jumpman." *Donkey Kong* became an instant sensation when it hit arcades in 1981 and remains one of the most beloved arcade games ever created.

Following the success of *Donkey Kong*, Miyamoto continued to develop the character of Mario, giving him the identity of an Italian American plumber and, most importantly, a game of his own. Released in 1983, *Mario Brothers* finds Mario at large in the treacherous sewers of New York, battling enemy creatures in his quest to find a princess. To adapt the game for two-player mode, Miyamoto created Luigi, who bears a remarkable resemblance to his older brother but is distinguished by his signature green attire. The *Mario Brothers* game was a popular arcade fixture for many years.

With the invention and growth of the home video game business, the popularity of Nintendo and the Mario Brothers grew exponentially. The 1985 release of the Nintendo Entertainment System (NES) was a cultural phenomenon. While Atari, Colecovision, Intellivision, and other game systems were already available to the public, they were quickly eclipsed by the NES, which combined popular characters with better graphics and an easy-to-use controller. The NES invigorated video games at a critical time in their history, immediately after the industry downturn of the early 1980s, which had threatened the future of home electronic gaming.

Since *Mario Brothers* became available on the NES in 1985, games featuring Mario, Luigi, or both brothers have proliferated across gaming systems, from handhelds to three-dimensional platforms. Over the course of a more than thirty-year career, Mario himself has been featured in nearly 200 games. Common elements of all the Mario Brothers games include levels that must be completed as players move from left to right and up and down on the screen. Mushrooms, stars, and other "power-ups" give Mario and Luigi special powers to defeat enemies. In order to complete each level, players must defeat the "boss," a character whose special size, strength, or other ability is difficult to overcome.

Over the years each brother has developed a distinct personality and special skills. Mario, the rough-and-tumble plumber, possesses slightly increased strength and power. Luigi is often portrayed in games as shy and timid but should not be underestimated, due to his superior leaping ability. Their appearances have evolved as well. Originally conceived as nearly identical, Mario has become shorter and stouter, while Luigi has grown taller and leaner. Even though Luigi is often considered as a sidekick or secondary player to his brother, he nonetheless plays an integral role in numerous games, even starring in the popular *Luigi's Mansion*.

In the late 1980s and early 1990s, Mario and Luigi were featured in a cartoon series bearing their name. Episodes included live-action sequences mixed with cartoon segments featuring the brothers and other characters from the Mario universe. Captain Lou Albano, of professional wrestling fame, portrayed Mario in these vignettes and was often joined by friends from the professional wrestling world. In another attempt to dramatize the exploits of the famous duo, *Super Mario Bros.* was released as a live-action film in 1993, with Bob Hoskins in the role of Mario and John Leguizamo in the role of Luigi. Other cast members included Dennis Hopper and Fisher Stevens. Although the film was an overwhelming commercial and critical failure, Nintendo has fared much better with other product tie-ins, such as Mario Brothers' action figures and toys.

Even while technological advances have moved the industry into a new realm of gaming experience, Mario and Luigi continue to win fans among new generations of players and will always hold a unique place in gaming history, as the plumbers from Brooklyn who were there when it all began.

Jay Parrent

SEE ALSO: *Gameboy; Hopper, Dennis; Video Games; Xbox Kinect.*

BIBLIOGRAPHY

Donovan, Tristan. *Replay: The History of Video Games.* East Sussex, UK: Yellow Ant, 2010.

Ryan, Jeff. *Super Mario: How Nintendo Conquered America.* New York: Portfolio Penguin, 2011.

Maris, Roger *(1934–1985)*

Roger Maris holds a significant place in sporting history as the baseball player who broke Babe Ruth's single-season home run record and held that record from 1961 until 1998. He was voted the American League's Most Valuable Player in 1960 and 1961 while playing for the New York Yankees. Maris's pursuit of Babe Ruth's record was the focus of national media attention in 1961—and the attention clearly made him unhappy. The glare of the media spotlight caused Maris, an intensely private person, to lose his hair and gave him insomnia, but he broke Ruth's record by hitting his sixty-first homer in the last game of the season.

Many people were not happy with Maris's achievement, and Commissioner Ford Frick claimed the record was questionable because Maris hit sixty-one homers in 162 games, while Ruth had hit sixty in 154 games. This controversy led to what's known as the "asterisk" controversy—many believed an asterisk belonged after Maris's name in the official record listings, although no real asterisk existed. Maris's record was topped in 1998 by Mark McGwire, who hit seventy home runs, and Barry Bonds, who hit seventy-three in 2001. Controversy struck again as both players were eventually implicated in the steroid controversy that swamped baseball in the first decade of the 2000s. Once again, many baseball fans demanded that the records be noted with an asterisk, and in 2011, Maris's sons stated publicly that they think their late father should still be regarded as the record-holder.

Geoff Peterson

SEE ALSO: *Baseball; Bonds, Barry; Major League Baseball; Mantle, Mickey; McGwire, Mark; The New York Yankees; Ruth, Babe; Sports Heroes.*

BIBLIOGRAPHY

Clavin, Tom, and Danny Peary. *Roger Maris: Baseball's Reluctant Hero.* New York: Touchstone, 2010.

Edwards, C. W. *Maris, Missing from the Hall of Fame.* Annapolis, MD: Corporate Image Publishers, 1992.

Rosenfeld, Harvey. *Roger Maris: Title to Fame.* Fargo, ND: Prairie House Publishers, 1991.

Marlboro Man

Marlboro is America's best-selling cigarette, and a major reason for its popularity can be traced to a cowboy. He is not classically handsome, nor does he wear fancy clothes or a gunbelt cinched around his lean hips. Rather, he is a working man, his face weathered from the sun and wind, his clothing sturdy and functional. He works on a real ranch, and he works hard. And when he wants a smoke, he reaches for a Marlboro.

However, when Marlboro was first marketed in the 1920s, Philip Morris had women smokers in mind, and the Marlboro advertising slogan was "Mild as May." Consequently, Marlboro was a "ladies' smoke" until the 1950s brought the first research linking smoking with lung cancer. This had many smokers searching for a "safer" cigarette. Filters provided that illusion, but many considered filters to be effeminate. Thus, if Philip Morris wanted to sell Marlboro to men, the product's image had to be made more macho. And soon, courtesy of Chicago's Leo Burnett ad agency, the Marlboro man was born.

Justin Gustainis

SEE ALSO: *Advertising; Cigarettes; The Cowboy Look.*

BIBLIOGRAPHY

Felske, Lorry W., and Beverly Jean Rasporich. *Challenging Frontiers: The Canadian West.* Calgary, AB: University of Calgary Press, 2004.

Lohof, Bruce A. *American Commonplace.* Bowling Green, OH: Popular Press, 1982.

Marley, Bob *(1945–1981)*

One of the most important and charismatic champions of human freedoms in the 1970s, Bob Marley emerged from humble beginnings and an early life of austere poverty in his native Jamaica to bring reggae music to international popularity. A rebellious visionary who was unabashedly invested in the Rastafari religion, Marley and his group the Wailers became known the world over for songs of universal love and biblical prophecy, including "No Woman, No Cry" and "Jamming." Although Marley died of cancer in 1981, the singer/songwriter left behind a legacy of socially conscious work that remains popular with audiences worldwide.

BEGINNINGS

Robert Nesta Marley, the man who would become a superstar, was born on February 6, 1945, in St. Ann, Jamaica. After Marley's father died in 1955, Marley spent his childhood being shuffled between the homes of his grandfather; his aunt; and his mother, Cedella, in Kingston. By the late 1950s he was spending much of his time socializing with friends in a government yard (public housing) in Trench Town, a shantytown in western Kingston. His rough, impoverished childhood later became instrumental to his success in songwriting and musical composition. Heavily influenced by the imported sounds of American artists like the Moonglows, the Tams, the Impressions, Elvis Presley, Sam Cooke, and Solomon Burke, Marley developed his adolescent tenor by harmonizing with his friends in the evenings after school.

By 1959 Marley was taking singing lessons, honing his guitar skills, and performing in local talent shows. Along with Peter McIntosh (later known as Peter Tosh), Junior Braithwaite, and two local girls, Marley formed a group called the Teenagers. At age sixteen the singer recorded his first single, "Judge Not," which demonstrated his budding if raspy voice. The song also demonstrated Marley's developing writing skills and his affinity for an emerging sound called ska, which was a mix of calypso, rhythm and blues, and shuffle. In 1962 Marley's mother remarried and relocated to America. Left homeless at age eighteen, he

Bob Marley. *Bob Marley performs in London, England, in 1977.* GRAHAM WILTSHIRE/CONTRIBUTOR/HULTON ARCHIVE/GETTY IMAGES.

began to frequent squatters' camps and learn more about the Rastafari religion, a form vested in contemplative spirituality, philosophy, and asceticism.

In 1964 Marley's musical group renamed itself the Wailing Wailers. "Simmer Down," a politically charged song about Jamaican youth, was released on the Downbeat label and went to number one on Jamaican radio stations. Throughout his career Marley was able to latch on to the social turbulence of the era and channel it into politically charged music. In the 1960s he became a key promoter of "Rude Boy" music, a form of Jamaican music that spread an antiracist, anticolonial, prorevolutionary message. Eventually, Marley became the world's most recognized promoter of the Rastafarian religion and its lifestyles.

SPIRITUALISM AND PROTEST

Over the course of the 1960s, Marley released a series of hit singles in Jamaica, yet his work had little effect outside of his home turf. On February 10, 1966, he married Rita Anderson, a member of the up-and-coming Jamaican singing group the Soulettes. For the rest of his career, Rita performed as his backup singer. The Marleys had five children, though Marley allegedly fathered as many as seven other children with several different women.

By the late 1960s a new form of music was gaining popularity in Jamaica. Reggae was directly influenced by Rasta culture and featured a decidedly slower shuffle than ska. Working with musical producer and reggae mastermind Leslie Kong, Bob Marley and the Wailing Wailers developed a sound that was less polished than their previous recordings—more rough, cutting, and intense. Early in the summer of 1971, Marley released "Trench Town Rock," a socially energized song that topped the Jamaican charts for five months, recasting him as a national folk hero. Soon after, the singer/songwriter began to barter for control of his career, establishing his own recording studio—Tuff Gong Records—at 56 Hope Road in Jamaica. His musical output became more prolific and more openly political, aligned with the People's National Party of Jamaica.

By the early 1970s Marley had gained a significant degree of international recognition. Jamaican music and musicians had gained greater visibility as a result of the work of American artists like Paul Simon and Johnny Nash. After touring and recording with Nash in the early 1970s, Marley gained some popularity in England, where he met Chris Blackwell of Island Records. Blackwell financially backed Marley, allowing him to record an album in Jamaica called *Catch a Fire*. The album was released to great acclaim in the winter of 1973 and marked a milestone in the development of reggae music. Before the release of *Catch a Fire*, reggae had been more concerned with singles rather than the finished product of a full album. Using cutting rock guitars and synthesizers to create an innovative sound, *Catch a Fire* had great appeal to the lucrative rock audience. In its scathing lyrics that sought to indict slavery and colonialism, the album officially launched the era of reggae music.

Marley's follow-up album, *Burnin'*, featured a more folk Jamaican sound and garnered the hit single "I Shot the Sheriff." The singer and his group toured Europe and the United States as an opening act for artists such as Bruce Springsteen, Sly and the Family Stone, and the Jackson Five. By 1974 the old Wailers had disbanded, and Tosh and Bunny Livingston were no longer active members. Already a highly charismatic figure in his native Jamaica and in Britain, Marley became more of a front man. His lead vocals were backed by the I-Threes, consisting of Marcia Griffith, Judy Mowatt, and Rita Marley. He also adopted the management of Marvin Gaye's road manager, Don Taylor.

INTERNATIONAL RENOWN

Marley had not yet attained worldwide popularity by the mid-1970s, yet many of his songs were already being remade by famous artists such as Taj Mahal and Barbra Streisand. Eric Clapton's version of "I Shot the Sheriff" topped the charts, surpassing the earlier success of Marley's own rendition of the song. Clapton's prestige, however, bestowed upon Marley a newfound rock authenticity, and the Jamaican reggae singer eventually rose to visibility in many rock circles as a star on par with Mick Jagger.

In 1975 Marley released the classic *Natty Dread* album, which was inspired by the political warfare that threatened Jamaica in early 1974. The album established him as a preeminent moral authority and a political visionary alongside peers like John Lennon. Marley made public his explicit fondness for the African continent, and he demonstrated an affiliation with African resistance struggles in South Africa and Zimbabwe (then Rhodesia). Sporting long, matted dreadlocks, he became synonymous with the mythical visionary Rasta rebel character of his album's title. The singer/songwriter was undoubtedly recast as not only the prime proponent of reggae but as an international star.

Marley's North American tour was highlighted by a performance at the Los Angeles Roxy Theater in 1975 that was attended by celebrities such as the Grateful Dead, Joni Mitchell, and The Band. Through Marley's attempts at publicity, Jamaican culture and the Rasta religion become more visible to the global masses. More successful albums followed, including *Bob Marley and the Wailers Live* (1976) and *Rastaman Vibration* (1976), his fifth album for Island Records. Although the latter album was something of a disappointment for reggae purists, it brought Marley to new levels of mainstream success.

On December 3, 1976, an assassination attempt on Marley took place two weeks before a well-publicized "Smile Jamaica" concert in Kingston's National Heroes Park. Although he received gunshot wounds to his breastbone and biceps, and Rita was grazed in the head by a bullet, the concert went on as planned. In 1977 Marley released the album *Exodus*, featuring the disco-influenced "Jamming" and the gentle, rocking single "Waiting in Vain." The force of these singles finally brought Marley a significant amount of airplay on black American radio stations, which had previously been unable, or unwilling, to accept his musical style.

On June 15, 1978, Marley was presented with the Third World Peace Medal by all the African delegations to the United Nations for his work on human rights. Soon after the singer made a pilgrimage to Africa. The trip instilled in him new hope for black unity worldwide and brought a militant edginess and explicit Pan-African bent back to his music. This new bent was directly reflected in the lyrics and music for his ninth album for Island Records, *Survival* (1979). His tenth album, *Uprising*, was released in May 1980 and featured the hit singles "Could You Be Loved" and the intensely personal "Redemption Song." By this time, however, Jamaica was rife in political conflict, and because of Marley's political alliances, his return to the island was deemed unsafe. Stranded in exile, he would never again return to the land of his birth.

A STILLED VOICE

After a collapse in 1980, Marley was diagnosed with a cancerous brain tumor that had spread to his lungs and stomach. He played his last concert with the Wailers at the Stanley Theater in Pittsburgh during the *Uprising* tour. While he officially claimed exhaustion as his reason for canceling the remainder of the tour, news of his condition soon became public. The singer relocated to Germany, where he received nontraditional treatment that sustained his strength for a time. After having received the Jamaican Order of Merit under new Prime Minister Edward Seaga, Marley died in Miami on May 11, 1981, surrounded by his family.

Although Marley had often felt a stranger in his homeland, his body was returned to Jamaica for a state funeral, and May 20, 1981, was declared a national day of mourning. Thousands of viewers lined up to see his body as it lay in state at the Kingston National Arena. The words of "Redemption Song" have become his permanent epitaph, and they continue to serve as a rallying cry for people fighting for their freedom.

Marley died without a will, instigating a long struggle over the control of his studios and Tuff Gong empire. According to *Rolling Stone*, it seemed that everyone who was ever close to him sued one another after his death. Ultimately, Marley's family gained control of his songs. As a result, a number of his works have been released in the twenty-first century, including *Live at the Roxy* (2003) and *Live Forever* (2011). Two box sets were also released: *The Complete Upsetter Collection* (2000) and *The Upsetter Singles Box* (2002). Compilation albums, such as *One Love—The Very Best of Bob Marley and the Wailers* (2001), *Feel Alright* (2004), *Gold* (2005), and *Africa Unite: The Singles Collection* (2005), continue to spread Marley's message to old and new fans alike.

A powerful spokesman for human rights and a truly gifted singer/songwriter, Marley remains a vital force in popular music and consciousness long after his tragic death. One of his most memorable songs, "No Woman, No Cry" was remade by the international rap group the Fugees in 1996 and generated mass success. Many of his children became involved as performers in the music industry, and his son Ziggy achieved success beginning in the late 1980s.

Marley brought reggae music and the Caribbean to international visibility as never before, and his courageous and profoundly universal message of the power and dignity of the human spirit made an unforgettable impact on the possibilities for social and political efficacy in the realm of popular music.

Jason King

SEE ALSO: *Clapton, Eric; Cooke, Sam; The Grateful Dead; The Jackson Five; Lennon, John; Mitchell, Joni; Presley, Elvis; Reggae; Rhythm and Blues; Rock and Roll; Simon, Paul; Sly and the Family Stone; Springsteen, Bruce; Streisand, Barbra.*

BIBLIOGRAPHY

Boot, Adrian, and Chris Salewicz. *Bob Marley: Songs of Freedom*. New York: Viking Studio Books, 1995.

Davis, Stephen. *Bob Marley*. Garden City, NY: Doubleday, 1985.

Gilmore, Mikal, and Annie Leibovitz. "Bob Marley: How He Changed the World." *Rolling Stone*, March 10, 2005, 67–78.

Grass, Randall. *Great Spirits: Portraits of Life-Changing World Music Artists*. Jackson: University Press of Mississippi, 2009.

Kisseloff, Jeff. *Voices of Protest from the 1960s: An Oral History*. Lexington: University Press of Kentucky, 2007.

Lazell, Barry. *Marley, 1945–1981*. London: Hamlyn, 1994.

McCann, Ian, and Chris Charlesworth. *The Complete Guide to the Music of Bob Marley*. New York: Omnibus Press, 1994.

Werner, Craig Hansen. *A Change Is Gonna Come: Music, Race, & the Soul of America*. Ann Arbor: University of Michigan Press, 2006.

White, Timothy. *Catch a Fire: The Life of Bob Marley*. New York: Henry Holt, 1996.

Married . . . with Children

From the ashes of television's "happy family" sitcom culture in the late 1980s—epitomized by *The Cosby Show*, *Family Ties*, *Growing Pains*, and their sweater-wearing characters—Fox's unabashedly raunchy *Married . . . with Children* rose up like a dysfunctional phoenix and outlasted almost every competitor. The show was created by Ron Leavitt and Michael Moye (former writers for *The Jeffersons*), who were given the green light by Fox to do something other than the standard TV fare. "We tried to take traditional sitcom clichés and subvert them," Moye said in *Newsweek* in 1996. He and his partner came up with a sexually charged version of the old radio comedy *The Bickersons*. During its run from 1987 to 1997, this cutting-edge show put Fox on the map and gave the network an irreverent identity.

THE ANTI-COSBYS

Married . . . with Children is set in suburban Chicago. The Bundys (named after one of Leavitt and Moye's favorite pro wrestlers, King Kong Bundy) are the anti-Cosbys. Al (Ed O'Neill) is a lowly and chauvinistic shoe salesman with bad breath, armpit stains, and smelly feet. His wife, Peg (Katey Sagal), is a lazy housewife with huge red hair and sleazy clothing who never cleans or cooks but instead spends her days eating bonbons and watching *Oprah*. Fifteen-year-old Kelly (Christina Applegate) is both dim-witted and slutty, and eleven-year-old Bud (David Faustino) is a pervert in the making. The family dog, meanwhile, is Buck, a scruffy beast whose thoughts are sometimes voiced.

Topics for barbs and insults include Al's lack of bedroom prowess and earning power, Peg's lack of sexual satisfaction, Kelly's lack of brainpower and sexual restraint, and Bud's lack of luck with the ladies. Every now and then, they let it slip that they care about each other, though not often. In one episode, a parody of *It's a Wonderful Life*, Sam Kinison plays Al's guardian angel. Al sees how happy his family would have been had he never been born, and he can't allow it. "I want to live!" he cries.

The Bundys' neighbors are the perfect counterpoints to Al and Peg, Steve (David Garrison) and Marcy (Amanda Bearse) Rhoades, insufferable newlywed yuppie accountants who are in love. Al and Peg take glee in bursting their bubble. During the 1988–1989 season, Steve loses his job, indirectly because of Al; after months of unemployment, he leaves Marcy to go to Yosemite to become a park ranger. (In real life, Garrison left the show to be in a play.) Marcy later marries Jefferson D'Arcy (Ted McGinley), thus making her name Marcy D'Arcy. She meets

Married ... with Children. *The cast of the Fox television series* Married ... with Children *included, from left, Amanda Bearse as Marcy D'Arcy, Christina Applegate as Kelly Bundy, Buck the dog, Katey Sagal as Peggy Bundy, Ed O'Neill as Al Bundy, and David Faustino as Bud Bundy.* L. COHEN/CONTRIBUTOR/WIREIMAGE/GETTY IMAGES.

him during a drinking binge at a bankers' convention. Jefferson never works; he lives off Marcy and hangs out with Al.

AN UNLIKELY HIT

The 1988–1989 season was downright magical for *Married . . . with Children.* The ratings improved during the 1988 writers' strike when people started sampling other networks, and they received an additional boost after a Michigan housewife named Terry Rakolta, outraged by a January 1989 episode in which the female characters purchase bras, started a letter-writing campaign encouraging viewers and advertisers to boycott the show. The ironic result was that more people tuned in to see what the fuss was about, as *Married . . . with Children* became Fox's first program to garner double-digit ratings. However, Fox did refuse to air the 1988 season premiere, "A Period Piece," wherein Peg, Marcy, and Kelly all have their periods on a Bundy-Rhoades camping trip. After many tweaks to the content, the episode ran in a later timeslot as "The Camping Show." Another episode, in which Al and Peg are videotaped having sex in a sleazy motel room, was never aired.

In the fall of 1991, Sagal became pregnant, so both Peg and Marcy become pregnant on the show. When Sagal later miscarries, both TV pregnancies are revealed to be a dream of Al's in a homage to *Dallas.* The next year, Seven, the six-year-old son of one of Peg's cousins, moves into the Bundy household. However, the writers couldn't find a way to make the character mesh with the rest of the cast, and he disappears without explanation a few months later.

In other developments, Al and his pals—Griff, Ike, Sticky, and Bob—hang out at a nudie bar (no surprise there), and Al also forms NO MA'AM (the National Organization of Men against Amazonian Masterhood) to preserve their right to drink excessively, act like slobs, and look at porn. As time goes on, Kelly graduates from high school and becomes a model, though she still lives at home. After getting a job as a waitress in a sleazy diner, she later tries TV commercials, first for Pest Boys Exterminating Co. as the Verminator and then as spokesperson for Ice Hole Beer. Bud actually goes to college, but because he has no money, he lives at home and also works part time at the Illinois motor vehicle department as a driving instructor. He finally loses his virginity to Amber, Marcy's aggressive niece.

This blue-collar sitcom tries to reflect a more "normal" American home life, warts and all, harkening back to *All in the Family* while also setting the stage for shows such as *Roseanne. Married . . . with Children* was TV's longest-running network series (not counting news and sports) when it was canceled in 1997. Fittingly, the program's theme song is Frank Sinatra's 1955 recording of "Love and Marriage" with a twist: it is punctuated by the sound of a jail cell slamming shut.

Karen Lurie

SEE ALSO: All in the Family; The Cosby Show; Roseanne; *Sitcom; Television.*

BIBLIOGRAPHY

Brooks, Tim, and Marsh, Earle. *The Complete Directory to Prime Time Network and Cable TV Shows 1946–Present*, 6th ed. New York: Ballantine Books, 1995.

"Fox Unties the Knot." *Mediaweek*, April 28, 1997, 54.

Marin, Rick. "Nuking the Nuclear Family: 'Married . . . with Children' Is Crass, Low Class and the Longest-Running Show on TV. Deal with It." *Newsweek*, April 29, 1996, 70.

McNeil, Alex. *Total Television: The Comprehensive Guide to Programming from 1948 to the Present*. New York: Penguin, 1996.

Nelson, Craig. *Bad TV: The Very Best of the Very Worst*. New York: Delta, 1995.

Marshall, Garry *(1934–)*

New Yorker Garry Marshall (born Marscharelli) named his first memoir *Wake Me When It's Funny: How to Break into Show Business and Stay There* (1995). The title reveals the creative drive behind a man who—as a scriptwriter, producer, and director—became a linchpin in the growth of TV sitcoms from the mid-1960s through the 1980s before focusing his attention on filmmaking. In a career spanning more than half a century, Marshall has directed a long list of movie stars and has earned his own star on the Hollywood Walk of Fame.

A former news reporter, jazz drummer, and stand-up comic, Marshall wrote for several TV shows (*The Joey Bishop Show*, 1967–1969; *The Dick Van Dyke Show*, 1961–1966; *The Lucy Show*, 1962–1968) before presiding over (initially with Jerry Belson) a dozen prime-time series successes. Some of his most notable hits include *The Odd Couple* (1970–1975), *Happy Days* (1974–1984), *Mork & Mindy* (1978–1982), and *Laverne & Shirley* (1976–1983, starring his sister Penny). As an actor, he had a recurring role in *Murphy Brown* (1988–1998).

In the 1980s Marshall turned his talents as a producer and director from television to movies, creating such box-office hits as *The Flamingo Kid* (1984), *Beaches* (1988), *Pretty Woman* (1990), *Frankie and Johnny* (1991), *Runaway Bride* (1999), *The Princess Diaries* (2001), *Raising Helen* (2004), *Georgia Rule* (2007), *Valentine's Day* (2010), and *New Year's Eve* (2011). Though Marshall was criticized for sugarcoating the fundamentally demeaning premise of *Pretty Woman*—a movie about the proverbial prostitute with a heart of gold—he was honored with a Women in Film Lucy Award in 1996 for enhancing the perception of women through television. In 2012 Marshall published his second memoir, *My Happy Days in Hollywood.*

Robyn Karney

SEE ALSO: Happy Days; Laverne and Shirley; Mork & Mindy; Murphy Brown; The Odd Couple; *Sitcom; Television.*

BIBLIOGRAPHY

Katz, Ephraim. *The International Film Encyclopedia*. New York: HarperCollins, 1994.

Karney, Robyn, ed. *Who's Who in Hollywood*. New York: Continuum, 1994.

Marshall, Garry. *Wake Me When It's Funny: How to Break into Show Business and Stay There*. Holbrook, MA: Adams, 1995.

Marshall, Garry. *My Happy Days in Hollywood*. New York: Crown, 2012.

Martha and the Vandellas

Arguably the most soulful of the Motown girl groups, Martha and the Vandellas established themselves as part of "The Sound of Young America" (Motown's company slogan) with the Top 10 single "(Love Is Like a) Heat Wave" in the fall of 1963. Although some of their hits were thought to have political undertones, the songs they made popular during the mid-1960s were, like most Motown singles, African American dance records with a strong backbeat designed to appeal to a white audience.

Martha and the Vandellas emerged as hit makers almost a year before the Supremes began to dominate the charts, but by 1965 the latter group had overtaken the former in popularity. As Motown president Berry Gordy Jr. and the talented songwriting and production team of Holland-Dozier-Holland (brothers Brian and Eddie Holland and Lamont Dozier) focused their attention on the Supremes, they neglected Martha and the Vandellas, as well as other female Motown artists such as the Marvelettes. The success of any 1960s girl group was dependent upon a fragile union of songwriters, musicians, producers, and label executives, giving the female artists themselves very little

Martha and the Vandellas. *Martha and the Vandellas had their first hit in 1963 with "(Love Is Like a) Heat Wave."* MICHAEL OCHS ARCHIVES/GETTY IMAGES.

control over their careers. Like a number of other girl groups, Martha and the Vandellas were unable to sustain their success as recording artists because of their lack of autonomy, in combination with changes in popular music tastes that took place during the mid-1960s.

In 1961 Martha Reeves began working for Motown Records in Detroit, Michigan, as William "Mickey" Stevenson's secretary in the A&R (artists and repertoire) department. She was already a professional singer, having released a single on Check-Mate, a subsidiary of Chess Records, as part of a group called the Del-Phis, which consisted of Reeves, Rosalind Ashford, Annette Sterling, and lead vocalist Gloria Williams. Reeves was hoping to become a Motown artist, and her break came when she was invited to fill in for an absent background singer. This experience gave Reeves the opportunity to bring in Ashford, Sterling, and Williams, and together they provided backing vocals for several of Marvin Gaye's sessions. Having proved themselves to owner Gordy, they were allowed to record a song. Because the Del-Phis were under contract with Check-Mate, the group decided to call themselves the Vels, and the single was released on the Melody label, one of Motown's subsidiaries. When the record failed to become a hit, Williams quit the group and Reeves was chosen to succeed her as the lead singer.

THE HITS

Combining the names of Detroit's Van Dyke Avenue and Della Reese, one of her favorite singers, Reeves renamed her trio Martha and the Vandellas, and the group was signed by Motown's Gordy Records toward the end of 1962. Their first release bombed, while the second made it to number twenty-nine on the pop charts. However, their third single was the smash hit "Heat Wave"—a Holland-Dozier-Holland creation featuring Motown's incomparable session players, including Benny Benjamin on drums and James Jamerson on bass guitar—released in the summer of 1963. Despite the group's success, Sterling dropped out the following year to get married. She was replaced by Betty Kelly, who had belonged to a Motown group known as the Velvelettes. A year after their first hit single, which was followed by several less successful releases, Martha and the Vandellas recorded their signature song, "Dancing in the Street," written by Gaye and Mickey Stevenson. The song became an adolescent anthem that was later covered by a number of artists, including the Mamas and the Papas, David Bowie and Mick Jagger together, and Van Halen.

According to Reeves in Gerri Hirshey's *Nowhere to Run: The Story of Soul Music*, some white listeners interpreted "Dancing in the Street" as "a call [for blacks] to riot." She explains that the song was intended to be nothing more than an up-tempo dance record. The intensity of this record was matched by the group's 1965 hit, "Nowhere to Run," a Holland-Dozier-Holland effort that to some listeners seemed to symbolize the plight of U.S. soldiers fighting in the Vietnam War. At this point in their career, Martha and the Vandellas were being superseded by the Supremes.

The group's last Top 40 single, "Jimmy Mack," had been recorded approximately two years before it was released in 1967; the song was most likely withheld because of its similarity to the Supremes' material. Imitating other Motown acts, the group changed their name to Martha Reeves and the Vandellas that same year. At the beginning of 1968, Reeves's sister Lois replaced Kelly, and two years later Sandra Tilley took Ashford's place. They continued to perform and record until they disbanded in 1972, when Reeves chose to leave Motown and pursue a solo career on other labels.

During the 1970s Reeves released several unsuccessful solo albums. Eventually she decided to resurrect the group for oldies revival performances. During the early 1990s she appeared with the original members of the group and separately with her sisters Lois and Delphine. In 1995 Martha and the Vandellas became members of the Rock and Roll Hall of Fame.

Often described as outspoken, Reeves may have failed to achieve the level of stardom reached by other Motown artists such as Diana Ross because of her reluctance to conform to the label's strict rules of behavior. As she told Hirshey, "Once I used 'damn' in a song and was heavily chastised." Label owner Gordy also played a large role in determining who was worthy of stardom, giving the best songs to acts he favored. While Martha and the Vandellas were able to record a handful of unforgettable pop songs, like many other girl groups they were unable to sustain their careers without the continued support of those who initially helped to create their hit records.

Anna Hunt Graves

SEE ALSO: *Girl Groups; Gordy, Berry; Motown; Ross, Diana, and the Supremes.*

BIBLIOGRAPHY

Betrock, Alan. *Girl Groups: The Story of a Sound.* New York: Delilah Books, 1982.

Gaar, Gillian G. *She's a Rebel: The History of Women in Rock and Roll.* Seattle, WA: Seal Press, 1992.

Hirshey, Gerri. *Nowhere to Run: The Story of Soul Music.* New York: Times Books, 1994.

Reeves, Martha, and Mark Bego. *Dancing in the Street: Confessions of a Motown Diva.* New York: Hyperion, 1994.

Martial Arts

Martial arts are a series of combat systems that follow a traditional code of conduct. Many forms of martial arts are currently practiced worldwide for different reasons, including physical fitness, self-defense, spiritual or religious practices, and sports competitions. Although martial arts are generally associated with East Asia, there are also Indian and South American forms of combat and self-defense. Typical Japanese arts include karate and judo; Chinese forms are composed of kung fu and tai chi; and Korean categories include tae kwon do and hapkido. India's kuttu varisai involves yoga poses, while the Brazilian martial art capoeira includes music and dance combined with combative motions.

The term *martial arts* is derived from Latin and can be traced back to Mars, the Roman god of war. European sword fighting and fencing have also been called arts similar to that of the Japanese shogun swordsmen. Martial arts styles can be broken down into several different categories, such as unarmed combat versus combat with weapons and strike-oriented versus grappling-based. U.S. military forces began the use of different martial arts forms as early as the 1930s, but a major influence on the culture of the Americas and Europe became apparent after the wars in Japan, Korea, and Vietnam.

Martial arts have had a profound effect on arts and culture since as early as 1950, especially in the films of Japanese director Akira Kurosawa, including *Rashomon* (1950), *The Seven Samurai* (1954), and *Ran* (1985)—the last a retelling of William Shakespeare's *King Lear* set in feudal Japan. The TV series *Kung Fu* (1972–1975) starred David Carradine as a U.S. orphan who grows up practicing martial arts in a nineteenth-century Chinese Shaolin monastery. After the death of his master, Po, he returns to the United States in search of his half-brother, thus sparking a series of East-meets-West adventures. One famous line that originated in this series is Master Po's reference to Carradine as "Grasshopper," a word that has since become synonymous with teaching experiences in literature and film.

Other famous martial arts stars include Bruce Lee and Chuck Norris. Lee's acting career began when he played Kato on the cult classic TV series *The Green Hornet* (1966–1967) and *Batman* (1966–1967). He starred in several kung fu movies, including *Enter the Dragon* (1973), before dying of a cerebral edema in 1973. Norris began his martial arts career as a competitor but went on to star in multiple films, including *The Way of the Dragon* (1972) with Lee and the TV series *Walker, Texas Ranger* (1993–2001). His Americanized versions of karate and tae kwon do turned him into an icon, sparking a series of humorous one-liners in 2005 called Chuck Norris facts. One of these exaggerated facts states that "when Chuck Norris goes swimming, he doesn't get wet, the water gets Norris-ed."

Though martial arts films have remained in circulation since their debut in the 1950s, director Quentin Tarantino's *Kill Bill* movies (2003 and 2004) brought the genre back into the spotlight, recasting Carradine as duplicitous kung fu master Bill, who is hunted by his former student and lover Beatrix Kiddo (Uma Thurman). Both movies' soundtracks were produced by rapper RZA from the Wu-Tang Clan, a hip-hop band that has immersed itself in martial arts' culture, likening their hometown of Staten Island, New York, to "the rugged lands of Shaolin" and basing their musical lyrics and philosophy on the 1980s films *Shaolin and Wu Tang* (1983) and *Shogun Assassin* (1980). Indeed, by the twenty-first century martial arts had crossed all societal levels to become an integral part of pop culture, as evidence by the increasing popularity of mixed martial arts competitions around the world.

Ron Horton

SEE ALSO: *Batman; Extreme Sports; Hip-Hop; Hollywood;* Kill Bill*;* Kung Fu*; Lee, Bruce; Tarantino, Quentin; Television; UFC/Mixed Martial Arts; Vietnam; World War II; Yoga.*

BIBLIOGRAPHY

Bolelli, Daniele. *On the Warrior's Path: Fighting, Philosophy, and Martial Arts Mythology*. Berkeley, CA: Frog, 2002.

Green, Thomas A., and Joseph R. Svinth. *Martial Arts of the World: An Encyclopedia of History and Innovation*, 2 vols. Santa Barbara, CA: ABC-CLIO, 2010.

Morgan, Forrest E. *Living the Martial Way: A Manual for the Way a Modern Warrior Should Think*. Fort Lee, NJ: Barricade Books, 1992.

Martin, Dean *(1917–1995)*

Dean Martin remains an example of the consummate popular American entertainer in the post–World War II era. A tremendous influence upon other entertainers of quality, such as Elvis Presley, Martin was equally adept at singing, acting, and live performance. An early pioneer in the entertainment field, Martin saw the development of radio, film, recording, and television as viable options for his varied talents. His eagerness to try these new avenues allowed him to grow beyond nightclubs and other live venues. This resulted in a many-faceted career that functioned on a number of levels for almost fifty years. Additionally, as an entertainer and a member of the hip 1960s Las Vegas "Rat Pack"—along with Frank Sinatra, Sammy Davis Jr., Joey Bishop, and Peter Lawford—Martin created a boozy, brash but lovable onstage character known as Dino who became a part of the vernacular of popular American culture.

Dino Paul Crocetti was born in Steubenville, Ohio, in 1917. Beginning his career as a singer in Ohio in the 1930s, he changed his name to Dean Martin in 1940. Already a local sensation whose romantic, dark Italian good looks and charismatic humor caused female hearts to swoon, Martin signed his first contract with MCA in 1943. This exclusive deal brought him to New York City, where he performed at the Riobamba Room, the same venue as another young singer, Frank Sinatra. Martin's move to the Big Apple allowed him to broaden his horizons considerably.

Dean Martin with Sammy Davis Jr. and Frank Sinatra. *Dean Martin, left, poses with Rat Pack pals Sammy Davis Jr., center, and Frank Sinatra in 1988.* HARRY LANGDON/CONTRIBUTOR/ARCHIVE PHOTOS/GETTY IMAGES.

MARTIN AND LEWIS

Martin broke into radio in 1942, and by 1944 had a fifteen-minute program, *Songs by Dean Martin.* It was during this period that he met his future partner, funnyman Jerry Lewis, via an introduction from friend and singer Sonny King. The team of Martin and Lewis, which became known the world over for its witty patter and seemingly effortless comic style that pitted an attractive straight man against the goofy nerd, was first booked together as an act at Atlantic City's 500 Club in July 1946. Their team act came on the heels of Martin's first recording contract with Diamond Records. While Martin sang, Lewis interrupted, and audiences went wild. Legally teamed together in 1947, Martin and Lewis conquered nightclubs, radio, television, and recordings and made sixteen movies together, including *My Friend Irma* (1949) and *Artists and Models* (1955), before a bitter breakup in 1956.

FILM CAREER

As a solo artist, Martin's film career began with dismal reviews for *Ten Thousand Bedrooms* in 1957. But the following year he redeemed himself with a stunning performance in the 20th Century-Fox production of *The Young Lions*, proving himself as a skilled, serious actor. His work with John Wayne in *Rio Bravo* (1959) heralded Martin's lifelong love affair with Westerns. He also appeared in *4 for Texas* (1963), *The Sons of Katie Elder* (1965), and *5 Card Stud* (1968). Additionally, Martin proved he was capable of high drama, as well as comedy, and everything in between. His films included the Matt Helm series of spy capers, beginning in 1966 with *The Silencers*; Rat Pack films such as *Ocean's Eleven* (1960); and *Airport* (1970), based upon Arthur Hailey's novel of the same name. Martin made his final screen appearance in 1984 in *Cannonball Run II*, his fifty-first film.

MUSICAL CAREER

From early in his career, Martin's influence as a popular singer of note was apparent. Signing with Capitol Records in 1948, he became known for his exquisite vocal treatment of love songs. Yet, like his film career, Martin's music was remarkably varied. He recorded popular standards, jazz, blues, and country-and-western numbers, as well as Italian and Christmas tunes. His many hits at Capitol included "I'll Always Love You" (1950), "That's Amore" (1953), and "Memories Are Made of This." While at Capitol he also first recorded one of the songs for which he is most often associated, "You're Nobody till Somebody Loves You", and a cowboy tune with teen idol Ricky Nelson for the film *Rio Bravo*—"My Rifle, My Pony, and Me" (1959). Martin's ability to transcend genre and style only added to his larger-than-life image. During the course of his recording career, he sang and recorded with Merle Haggard, Nat King Cole, Peggy Lee, Margaret Whiting, Bing Crosby, and members of his beloved Rat Pack.

In 1962 Martin moved his recording career to Sinatra's label, Reprise, and started his own production company, Claude Productions, to ensure that he retained exclusive control over his work. It was at Reprise that Martin recorded albums such as *Dino: Italian Love Songs* (1962), *Dean "Tex" Martin: Country Style* (1963), and *Dino* (1972). He also recorded his signature song, "Everybody Loves Somebody." Using the vocal gymnastics that came so effortlessly to him, Martin's recording session on April 16, 1964, resulted in a number one hit that came in the midst of Beatlemania. This period was a high point in his career, as he was very much an entertainer who had won the hearts of his diverse and ever-expanding audience. His association with the high-living Rat Pack solidified his onstage persona, while his private life became fodder for fan magazines and newspapers.

Adding to his high profile, NBC television premiered *The Dean Martin Comedy Hour* on September 16, 1965. It was one of the highest-rated shows of the 1965–1966 television season. In order to keep Martin, NBC offered him a three-year contract at $283,000 per episode and shares in NBC's parent company, RCA. Because he worked only eight hours a week, Martin still holds the record for being the highest-paid television performer. Again, his breezy, devil-may-care style won over America and his critics. For nine seasons, Martin played up his cocktail-fueled stage persona while remaining a vocal stylist of integrity and substance. It was during the final season that the show's name was changed to *The Dean Martin Comedy Hour* and featured what would eventually be known as "Dean Martin's Celebrity Roasts," a takeoff of the Friars Club roasts.

Following the last season of his television show, Martin continued to perform and record. A highlight of this period was a 1976 reunion with Lewis during one of the annual muscular dystrophy telethons Lewis hosted. Orchestrated by Sinatra, it was a poignant moment, as it had been twenty-two years since the old partners shared a stage. It would be for the last time.

The death of one of Martin's eight children, Dean-Paul Martin, in 1987 severely affected the entertainer. Thereafter he rarely worked or saw even his closest friends, although he remained close with his second wife, Jeanne Biegger Martin, from whom he was divorced. His time was spent watching Westerns on television, playing golf, and dining out. Martin was a sad, frail figure at the end, an image that belied the life he lived to the hilt as the handsome, smiling Italian lover, cocktail in one hand, cigarette in the other, and a "broad" on each arm.

His final performance was at Bally's Las Vegas in June 1990. Martin passed away on Christmas Day 1995, leaving a legacy that epitomizes the ideal of a twentieth-century entertainer and the image of a glamorous, fun-loving, popular icon, who continued to be emulated throughout the world at the end of the twentieth century.

Jana Pendragon

SEE ALSO: *The Big Apple; Las Vegas; Lewis, Jerry; Sinatra, Frank.*

BIBLIOGRAPHY

Martin, Deana, and Wendy Holden. *Memories Are Made of This: Dean Martin through His Daughter's Eyes.* New York: Harmony Books, 2004.

Tosches, Nick. *Dino: Living High in the Dirty Business of Dreams.* New York: Doubleday, 1992.

Martin, Freddy *(1906–1983)*

In 1941 Freddy Martin's dance band recorded *Tonight We Love*, adapted from the well-known opening theme of Pyotr Ilyich Tchaikovsky's Piano Concerto in B-flat Minor. The record sold one million copies by 1946 and inspired sixteen different pop song renditions of the same tune. Martin followed this success with adaptations of other classical works and also made cameo appearances with his band in a few 1940s Hollywood films, including *Stage Door Canteen* (1943). Ohio-born Martin served as music director for Elvis Presley's first Las Vegas appearance, and his tenor saxophone playing elicited the admiration of noted jazz players such as Johnny Hodges, who dubbed him "Mr. Silvertone." Martin's band, famous for its "sweet" sound, played New York's top hotel ballrooms during the 1930s and 1940s and later made its home at the Cocoanut Grove at the Ambassador Hotel in Beverly Hills, California.

Ivan Raykoff

SEE ALSO: *Big Bands; Jazz; Pop Music; Presley, Elvis.*

BIBLIOGRAPHY

Garrod, Charles. *Freddy Martin and His Orchestra.* Zephyr Hills, FL: Joyce Record Club, 1987.

Martin, Quinn *(1922–1987)*

During the 1960s and 1970s it seemed as though all the top television crime dramas carried the weighty introduction "A Quinn Martin Production." From *The Untouchables* and *The FBI* in the 1960s to *Cannon*, *The Streets of San Francisco*, and *Barnaby Jones* in the 1970s, Quinn Martin dominated the crime-action genre on the small screen. At one period the flourishing producer, who got his start as a writer for Desilu Productions, was responsible for more hours of network television programming than any other independent producer or company. In effect he defined the formula for one-hour TV dramas—down to the number of acts; the number of action "beats" per act; and the perfection of the cliffhanger act close, which brought the audience back from each commercial break—leaving a lasting television legacy that continues to pervade popular culture.

Victoria Price

SEE ALSO: *Arnaz, Desi; Ball, Lucille; Television.*

BIBLIOGRAPHY

Brown, Les, ed. *New York Times Encyclopedia of Television.* New York: Times Books, 1977.

Marc, David, and Robert J. Thompson. *Prime Time, Prime Movers: From* I Love Lucy *to* L.A. Law*—America's Greatest TV Shows and the People Who Created Them.* Syracuse, NY: Syracuse University Press, 1995.

Martin, Ricky *(1971–)*

Latino singing sensation Ricky Martin is a crossover artist in many senses of the term. In 1999 he had already achieved success as an actor and an international music star with a million Spanish-language albums sold, when his career ignited in the United States. With his impish good looks and dynamic stage presence, Martin was in the forefront of an enormous upsurge in the popularity of Latin music throughout North America. As American fans began following his every move, Martin's personal life became a topic of speculation as fan sites and tabloids ran articles speculating about the singer's sexuality. In 2010 Martin ended the rumors by openly declaring himself as a gay man. Though his career has slowed since the superstar period at the turn of the twenty-first century, Martin remains a popular and versatile musician, as well as a committed family man and a humanitarian who works to improve the lives of impoverished children around the world.

Martin was born Enrique Martín Morales in 1971 in San Juan, Puerto Rico. His parents divorced when he was only two, but he had a supportive extended family. He learned about music and art from his grandparents. From an early age Martin longed to perform, and he begged his father to let him audition for the Latin boy-band Menudo. Menudo was formed by Puerto Rican music producer Edgardo Diaz, who had the idea of creating a rock group of five male musicians under the age of eighteen. When a member outgrew the band he would leave, and a younger member would replace him. Martin joined Menudo when he was twelve and played with the group until he was seventeen, learning the discipline required for a music career.

After leaving Menudo, Martin spent several years in Mexico, where he acted in serial dramas called *telenovelas*, winning the prestigious Heraldo Award for his work on the show *Alcanzar una Estrella.* He also kept up his singing career and in 1990 signed a contract with Sony Records Latin music division. In 1991 he released *Ricky Martin*, an all-Spanish album, followed by *Me Amarás* in 1993 and *A Medio Vivir* in 1995. "(Un, Dos, Tres) Maria," a single from *A Medio Vivir*, received wide play in the United States and reached number eighty-eight on the Billboard Top 100.

Martin's popularity grew in Latin America, Europe, Australia, and Asia, and he toured the world, playing to enthusiastic audiences. In 1994 and 1995 he took a role on the popular soap opera *General Hospital*, while continuing to record music. In 1998 his song "La Copa de la Vida" was chosen as the theme for the soccer World Cup in France.

In 1999 Martin was invited to play "La Copa de la Vida" at the forty-first Grammy Awards ceremony, where his high-energy performance stopped the show and boosted his career with U.S. audiences. High-profile rock star Madonna asked him to record a duet with her, and Sony and Columbia both offered him contracts. In 1999 he released his first English-language record, *Ricky Martin*, which debuted at number one. The album's biggest hit was "Livin' la Vida Loca," which reached number one on the Billboard singles chart.

Martin's playful sensuality and theatrical performances soon won over American fans. Audiences across the United States were discovering the infectious energy and lively rhythms of Latin music during the late 1990s, and the young and handsome Martin was an accessible Latin performer. As both women and men became enamored with the singer of "Shake Your Bon Bon," fans and journalists began to speculate about his sexual orientation. Martin kept his private life strictly private and refused to answer probing questions, even when Barbara Walters asked him to clear up the mystery on a 2000 episode of *The View*.

However, in 2010, having recently adopted twin sons Matteo and Valentino, Martin came out, announcing on his website, "I am proud to say that I am a fortunate homosexual man." He stated that his new role as a father inspired him to be honest. Martin's openness has not hurt his career. His many fans still profess their love for his music, and his 2011 album *Musica+Alma+Sexo* debuted at number one on the Latin charts and reached number three on the mainstream charts. In 2012 he starred as Che Guevara in *Evita* on Broadway.

In contrast to his effervescent stage persona, Martin is a serious and spiritual man who works on a number of charitable causes. The Ricky Martin Foundation operates programs to help poor, abused, and drug-addicted children, as well as combatting sex slavery and promoting AIDS education.

Tina Gianoulis

SEE ALSO: *AIDS; Boy Bands; The Closet; Coming Out; Gay Men;* General Hospital*; Madonna; Pop Music; Soap Operas; Top 40.*

BIBLIOGRAPHY

Essex, Andrew. "Not So Little Ricky Martin." *Entertainment Weekly*, April 23, 1999, 32.

Griffiths, John. "Ricky Martin Cross Appeal." *Advocate*, July 6, 1999, 26.

Martin, Ricky. *Me*. New York: Celebra, 2011.

Taylor, Chuck. "Ricky Martin Shows That His Musical Timing Isn't So 'Loca.'" *Billboard*, May 29, 1999, 90.

Martin, Steve *(1945–)*

Steve Martin's crazy, off-the-wall, avant-garde brand of humor had major effects on stand-up comedy, television, film, and print. From the 1970s, when his white-suited appearances on the ensemble comedy show *Saturday Night Live* (*SNL*) were widely enjoyed and copied, to the 2010s, when his novels, plays, memoir, and banjo playing were widely acclaimed, Martin brought his wacko bursts of intelligent comedy to millions. Clean-cut yet uninhibited, he rolled with the decades, growing from a novelty act to a respected actor, author, and musician.

Martin was born August 14, 1945, in Waco, Texas. His family moved to California when he was five, and he grew up near Disneyland. He dropped out of college at twenty-one and began writing comedy for the Smothers Brothers in the late 1960s and then for Sonny and Cher in the early 1970s. He appeared on the *Tonight Show* more than forty times and released four comedy albums.

He became known for oddball, surreal stand-up shows without clear beginning or end and for jokes that might be deliberately unfunny and therefore even funnier. He might tension up and up and then deliver an anticlimax rather than a climax, allowing his audience to choose when to laugh. In the early 1970s he could end a show by swimming across his loyal audience in an empty swimming pool or by taking them all to a restaurant. As he put it in an article for the *Smithsonian* in 2008: "My goal was to make the audience laugh but leave them unable to describe what it was that had made them laugh."

His gigs hosting *SNL*, however, made Steve Martin a household name. He appeared on the late-night sketch comedy show as King Tut; Theodoric of York: Medieval Barber; Gilda Radner's dance partner in "Dancing in the Dark"; and, with Dan Aykroyd, as one of the Festrunck brothers, whose catchphrase "We are two wild and crazy guys" never failed to get a laugh. Martin's arrow-through-the-head crazy antics were typical of the early *SNL* era, and he hosted the show more than a dozen times. His sarcastic "well, excuuuuuuuse me" and "naaaaah" became schoolyard mantras. Actor Tom Hanks told an interviewer that Martin had been a pivotal influence on comedy in general: "If you went to Cub Scout meetings in the seventies, they'd do Steve Martin bits," he said. "Everybody was 'Yeah, I'm a wild and crazy guy.' Instantaneously, it just seemed to permeate society."

TRANSITION TO MOVIES AND WRITING

In 1979 Martin had his first starring role in a film: Navin R. Johnson in *The Jerk*, for which he also wrote the screenplay. During the next three decades he made several comedies, including *Dead Men Don't Wear Plaid*, *The Man with Two Brains*, *The Lonely Guy*, *All of Me*, *Three Amigos! Roxanne*, *Dirty Rotten Scoundrels*, *Parenthood*, *L.A. Story*, *The Pink Panther* 1 and 2, *Cheaper by the Dozen* 1 and 2, and *Bowfinger*. He had a cameo in *The Muppet Movie* and took the Spencer Tracy role in a remake of *Father of the Bride*. He also tried his hand at serious acting in *Pennies from Heaven*, *Grand Canyon*, David Mamet's *The Spanish Prisoner*, and his own *Shopgirl*. He hosted the Academy Awards in 2001 and 2003, and he cohosted with Alec Baldwin in 2010.

Martin also had lasting success as an author. His book of comic short stories, *Cruel Shoes*, topped the best-seller list in 1979. His play *Picasso at the Lapin Agile* (set in a bar in 1904 Paris, with characters including Pablo Picasso, Albert Einstein, and Elvis Presley) was performed off-Broadway in 1995 and had a regional run. In 2002 he adapted a German play by Carl Sternheim into an English-language farce, *The Underpants*. In the late 1990s Martin began writing pieces for the *New Yorker*; these were released as a book, *Pure Drivel*, in 1998. He continued writing for the magazine into the 2010s.

His first novel, *Shopgirl*, came out in 2000; in 2005 it was made into a film starring Claire Danes and Martin himself. His other novels are *The Pleasure of My Company* (2003), narrated by an obsessive-compulsive, and *An Object of Beauty* (2010), about the art world. In 2007 he published a memoir of his early years as a stand-up comic and performance artist, *Born Standing Up: A Comic's Life*. In it he describes his process of developing a new form of comedy, one without punch lines. He also published a rhyming children's book, *Late for School*, and an alphabet book with drawings by Roz Chast, *The Alphabet from A to Y with Bonus Letter Z*. In 2012 he published a collection titled *The Ten, Make That Nine, Habits of Very Organized People. Make That Ten: The Tweets of Steve Martin*.

Martin's banjo playing, familiar to fans from his stand-up and his appearance on *The Muppet Show* in 1977, received wider recognition in 2010 when he won a Grammy for his bluegrass album *The Crow*.

Jessy Randall

SEE ALSO: *Academy Awards; Aykroyd, Dan; Baldwin, Alec; Best Sellers; Bono, Sonny; Cher; Einstein, Albert; Grammy Awards; Hanks, Tom; The Muppets; The* New Yorker*; Picasso, Pablo; Presley, Elvis; Radner, Gilda;* Saturday Night Live*; The Smothers Brothers; Stand-Up Comedy; Television;* The Tonight Show*; Tracy, Spencer; Twitter.*

BIBLIOGRAPHY

Lenburg, Greg; Randy Skretvedt; and Jeff Lenburg. *Steve Martin: The Unauthorized Biography*. New York: St. Martin's Press, 1980.

Martin, Steve. *Born Standing Up: A Comic's Life*. New York: Scribner, 2007.

Martin, Steve. "Being Funny." *Smithsonian Magazine*, February 2008. Accessed April 2012. Available from http://www.smithsonianmag.com/arts-culture/funny-martin-200802.html#ixzz1ncNkWyKH

The Martini

The drink that Soviet leader Nikita Khrushchev once called "America's lethal weapon" is easily the most written about cocktail in history. The "lethal" aspect of the recipe is what most Americans know to be the large proportion of gin, or vodka, to a minute flavoring of vermouth. The less one uses of the aromatic dry wine, which takes its name from the German word for "wormwood," the better; this becomes a mark of the martini's degree of dryness. The drink must be served ice cold, so that successive martinis go down with relative ease. The martini owes its staying power to two contradictory elements: its ability to reinvent itself and the martini drinker's fervent exactitude concerning the drink's preparation. The drinker's demonstrated meticulousness has produced a whole culture (or cult) around the drink: the martini is accompanied by its own particular codes, accessories, and literature. This particular cocktail has been praised in the works of such celebrated twentieth-century authors as Ogden Nash, Ernest Hemingway, Jack London, and H. L. Mencken.

The martini is believed to have been invented during the decade following the Civil War. By the 1880s the drink was included in several bartenders' manuals, where it was first referred to as the "Martinez." According to the author of "There Is Something about a Martini," Max Rudin, the current spelling first appeared in 1888 in Harry Johnson's *New and Improved Illustrated Bartender's Manual; or, How to Mix Drinks of the Present Style*. Early recipes for the drink are nothing like the cold, dry cocktail Americans have come to know. Sweetened gin, sweet vermouth, and orange-flavored bitters rendered the nineteenth-century version too sweet to qualify.

***Martini Toast in* After Office Hours.** *Clark Gable, left, and Constance Bennett share a martini toast in a scene from the 1935 film* After Office Hours. © JOHN SPRINGER COLLECTION/CORBIS.

THE MARTINI'S ORIGIN

As with so many other popular cocktails, there are a number of competing claims for the martini's origin; none has been conclusively proven. One theory recounts that the drink was invented in San Francisco by a passing traveler who was bound for Martinez, California. Citizens of Martinez maintain that the traveler, a gold miner who had struck it rich, was leaving their town for San Francisco. A local bartender, lacking the requested champagne, invented the cocktail for him; he liked it and bought a round for the house. Other contenders include the Knickerbocker Hotel in New York, which employed an immigrant bartender in the early 1900s named Martini di Arma di Taggia who was famous for his dry gin and vermouth cocktails.

During Prohibition, when the trade in alcohol became illicit, black market hard liquor commanded large profits. Gin was easier to counterfeit than other liquors, such as whiskey. The hard stuff attained a new status: drinking a martini became a defiant statement against the intolerance of temperance zealots. As speakeasies encouraged the mingling of men and women in a way that saloons previously had not, the martini connoted a new sexuality reflected in these lines from Dorothy Parker:

> I like to have a Martini,
> Two at the very most.
> After three I'm under the table,
> After four I'm under my host.

The drink's image is configured by several codes. The martini's associations are that it is American, modern, sophisticated, upper class, urban, and optimistic; by implication it is therefore not European, old-fashioned, working class, rural, or pessimistic. Rudin writes, "It found its essential form at just about the same time as the skyscraper, the airplane, jazz, and the two-piece business suit. Like them, the martini evoked something essential about twentieth-century America."

Drinking a martini is often a statement of what one is not as much as how one wishes to be perceived. In the 1951 story "Goodbye, My Brother," John Cheever's Pommeroy family makes its annual pilgrimage to their beach house, where they relax by drinking martinis between swims, dinners, and dances. The tone for the story is set when one of the sons, Lawrence (Tifty), displays his ignorance of the family drinking code:

> "Isn't the beach fabulous, Tifty?" Mother asked. "Isn't it fabulous to be back? Will you have a Martini?"
>
> "I don't care," Lawrence said. "Whiskey, gin—I don't care what I drink. Give me a little rum."
>
> "We don't have any *rum*," Mother said. It was the first note of asperity.

Lawrence represents a gloomy, antisocial nature that the rest of his family (and by extension martini drinkers) abhors.

His brother explains, "[Mother] had taught us never to be indecisive, never to reply as Lawrence had. . . . She is deeply concerned with the propriety of her house, and anything irregular by her standards, like drinking straight rum or bringing a beer can to the dinner table, excites in her a conflict."

Cheever's story is also evidence of social drinking's move into the home after the end of Prohibition. A market for martini accoutrements, such as shakers, pitchers, triangle-stemmed glassware, glass stirrers, and even vermouth-infused stones, met the needs of the home bar. The drink that was once so avant-garde had become conservative and suburban by the 1960s. The martini's dark days continued into the 1970s, when the Carter administration used it as a political football by eliminating the tax deduction for the three-martini lunch. Even the conservative swing of the 1980s failed the drink: its reputation for high potency conflicted with anti-drunk-driving sentiments.

RENEWED POPULARITY

As Americans returned to such less healthful indulgences as red meat and cigars during the economic boom of the 1990s, the martini became an obvious companion. Its resurrection was also testimony to its adaptability. Traditional dry martinis gave way to drinks made with flavored vodkas and gins in cocktails that often forgot the vermouth altogether. One version that gained great popularity in the first decade of the 2000s was the appletini, which substituted apple schnapps for gin. This development caused many martini connoisseurs to complain that the new drink was not a martini at all, while others welcomed the variation as a way to save the once-ubiquitous cocktail from oblivion. For many the martini remains an icon of a lost world, according to Rudin, and of a time when "'modern' meant something good—smart, sexy, and pulse-racing, technologically advanced, intelligently made, an example of Americans leading the world."

Daryl Umberger

SEE ALSO: *Cocktail Parties; Hemingway, Ernest; Jazz; London, Jack; Mencken, H. L.; Parker, Dorothy; Prohibition; Skyscrapers.*

BIBLIOGRAPHY

Cheever, John. "Goodbye My Brother." *The Stories of John Cheever*. New York: Ballantine Books, 1980.

Conrad, Barnaby, III. *The Martini*. San Francisco: Chronicle Books, 1995.

Edmunds, Lowell. *The Silver Bullet: The Martini in American Civilization*. Westport, CT: Greenwood Press, 1981.

Haasarud, Kim, and Alexandra Grablewski. *101 Martinis*. Hoboken, NJ: Wiley, 2006.

Regan, Gary. "Shaken and Stirred: When Is a Martini Really a Martini?" *Nation's Restaurant News*, April 14, 1997, 45.

Rudin, Max. "There Is Something about a Martini." *American Heritage*, July/August 1997, 32–45.

Stone, Nannette. *The Little Black Book of Martinis: The Essential Guide to the King of Cocktails*. White Plains, NY: Peter Pauper Press, 2004.

Steinriede, Kent. "Not Your Grandfather's Martini." *Beverage Industry*, September 1997, 24–25.

Marvel Comics

Marvel Comics is one of the two largest publishers of comic books in the United States. It owns many of the most popular characters in comic books, including Spider-Man, the X-Men, the Incredible Hulk, Captain America, and the Fantastic Four. As a major player in the history of the comic-book industry, Marvel's significance is equaled only by its longtime rival and chief competitor, DC Comics. Despite being one of the oldest comic-book companies, Marvel did not emerge as a truly distinctive and influential creative force in the field until the 1960s. Since then, however, the Marvel style has virtually defined the character of mainstream American comic books.

A TIMELY MARVEL

The company that became known as Marvel Comics began its operation in 1939, when a young pulp magazine publisher named Martin Goodman decided to enter the fledgling comic-book business. Taking note of DC Comics' recent success with Superman, Goodman purchased several superhero stories from one of several comic-art studios supplying material to publishers. Soon thereafter Goodman set up his own comic-book production staff under the editorial direction of his teenage nephew Stanley Lieberman, who also wrote comic-book stories under the name of Stan Lee. The company was initially called Timely Comics, but it also referred to itself by the title of its first publication, *Marvel Comics*.

The first issue of *Marvel Comics*, dated November 1939, introduced several original superhero characters, at least two of whom found a lasting audience. The Human Torch, created by Carl Burgos, was actually not a human but an android with the rather terrifying ability to burst into flames and set objects and people ablaze. The Sub-Mariner, created by Bill Everett, was the son of an interracial marriage between an American sea captain and a princess from the undersea kingdom of Atlantis. Possessing superhuman strength and the ability to breathe on land as well as in water, the Sub-Mariner also harbored a fierce antipathy toward the dwellers of the surface world, thereby qualifying him as perhaps the first comic-book antihero.

Neither the Human Torch nor the Sub-Mariner was about to rival the likes of Superman, Batman, or Captain Marvel, but they helped to give Marvel a significant share of the rapidly expanding comic-book market. That share increased in 1941 when Marvel debuted Captain America. The creation of Joe Simon and Jack Kirby, Captain America became the definitive comic-book superpatriot of World War II and Marvel's most popular star. The cover of *Captain America Comics*, issue number one, brashly portrayed the red-white-and-blue-costumed hero socking Adolf Hitler in the mouth. That striking image, appearing more than six months before the United States entered the war, epitomized the staunch anti-Nazi and implicit interventionist tone of this series in particular and of Marvel's output in general. Marvel was among the first comic-book companies to publish anti-Nazi stories. As early as 1939 a Marvel cover showed the Sub-Mariner in battle with the crew of a swastika-flagged submarine, and the Human Torch could be seen burning through the German air force in 1940, more than two years before U.S. air forces would follow suit.

After Pearl Harbor most comic-book publishers enlisted wholeheartedly in the war effort, but few became as completely caught up in it as Marvel did. Marvel responded to the global struggle with a ceaseless barrage of simplified and overstated patriotic stories, in which self-righteously noble American heroes crusaded against viciously caricatured German and Japanese foes. While these comic books did little to inform readers about the real issues and conduct of the war, and some—especially in their depiction of the Japanese—were outright racist, they were hardly unique in wartime American popular culture. Like most of its competitors, Marvel simply worked to bolster the morale of the young people and servicemen who read comic books, while cashing in on wartime patriotism in the process.

POSTWAR DOLDRUMS

The war figured so prominently in Marvel's superhero comic books that sales of these titles plummeted with the return to peace. By the end of the 1940s, Marvel had ceased publication of all its superhero comic books. The company thrived, however, by diversifying its output and exploring new genres such as crime, romance, humor, and horror. Marvel's editorial and publishing strategy during the postwar decade maximized the advantages of Goodman's sizable distribution network. Essentially the company would take note of the most popular current trends in comic books and flood the market with imitations. Typical examples of this approach were *Lawbreakers Always Lose*, Marvel's answer to Lev Gleason Publications' successful *Crime Does Not Pay*, and *Strange Tales*, the latter a pale takeoff on EC's *Tales from the Crypt*. What Marvel's stories lacked in quality the company made up for with quantity, publishing more than 400 comics between 1950 and 1955.

Marvel's conspicuous horror titles garnered the publisher some unfavorable publicity in 1954, when the U.S. Senate Subcommittee on the Judiciary held hearings to investigate the alleged link between comic books and juvenile delinquency. Marvel's business manager testified at the hearings, and although he stood up to the subcommittee's questioning better than EC's publisher William Gaines, Marvel could not escape the public backlash that greeted the comic-book industry in the wake of the investigation. In its defense, Marvel dutifully adopted the industry's new Comics Code governing comic-book content. But declining sales and the bankruptcy of his chief distributor compelled Goodman to drastically curtail Marvel's line. By the end of the 1950s, the company that had published more comic books than any other over the previous two decades had become a marginal player in the field, with only a handful of titles on the market.

Marvel's rapid decline brought the company to the brink of collapse, but the desperate situation inspired a new risk-taking strategy—one that gave Marvel's comic books an edgy quality that they had not possessed in decades. In collaboration with his primary artists, Kirby and Steve Ditko, writer-editor Lee decided to try out a comic-book title featuring superheroes who departed from the conventions of the genre. They would be superheroes who, for all their fantastic powers, talked and acted like believable human characters. In contrast to the impossibly noble and rather bland superheroes then on the market, Marvel's new breed of superhero would display such human weaknesses as jealousy, intemperance, and—most importantly—alienation.

Launched by Marvel in 1961, *The Fantastic Four* marked Lee's initial experiment with this style of characterization. When it proved successful, Lee followed with *The Incredible Hulk* and *The Amazing Spider-Man*, the former in collaboration with Kirby and the latter with Ditko. With Spider-Man, in particular, Lee hit upon the archetypal angst-ridden adolescent superhero so endearing to young readers. When the sales figures and fan mail came in, Lee knew that he had found a formula for success.

NEW HEROES SAVE THE DAY

If the lowly comic book can be said to have experienced a renaissance, then that is what occurred at Marvel Comics during the mid-1960s. In the space of a few years, Marvel introduced a succession of superhero characters who have since become mainstays in comic books. Joining the Fantastic Four, the Incredible Hulk, and Spider-Man were the Mighty Thor, Dr. Strange, the X-Men, Iron Man, the Avengers, Daredevil, and the Silver Surfer. All bore in some way the qualities of the misunderstood outsider, which became the Marvel trademark.

Marvel's rediscovery of the outsider hero marked the comic-book industry's belated recognition of this mythic figure as a compelling force acting on the American imagination. Furthermore, the introduction of ambiguity into the vocabulary of the comic-book superhero spoke to the lingering anxieties underlying Cold War culture—anxieties felt most keenly by the nation's youth. The very notion of a troubled and insecure superhero who could not always accomplish what he set out to achieve indicated the limited scope of his superpowers and suggested also the limitations of the nation as a superpower.

Although these comic books have not held up to the critical eye, they significantly impacted the subsequent history of comic books. Their popularity was undeniable. Marvel became a sensation in the 1960s. By reaching out to a slightly older audience and defying the mainstream conventions epitomized by DC, Marvel garnered a sizable college-aged readership and won approval. In 1965 *Esquire* magazine reported that Marvel had become a phenomenon on campuses nationwide, while characters such as Spider-Man, the Hulk, and Dr. Strange, in particular, had achieved noted status among self-described radicals and the counterculture.

Marvel's popularity and Lee's unabashed and outrageous hucksterism made Lee himself a minor celebrity and an in-demand speaker at college campuses. Marvel's enthusiastic fan base credited Lee and his collaborators with fashioning a new mythology—a complex fictional universe with interlocking characters and themes that involved readers in much the same way as the mythologies of *Star Trek*, J. R. R. Tolkien, and *Dungeons and Dragons* later would. Intentionally or not, Marvel tapped into the escapist, alienated, and anti-mainstream ethos that had always constituted the essence of the comic book's appeal.

Throughout the 1960s and 1970s, Marvel enjoyed a steadily increasing share of the comic-book market. In the early 1970s it surpassed DC, ending that publisher's long era of dominance. Forced to acknowledge the popularity of its rival's approach, DC began to adapt the Marvel style to its own superhero comics—sometimes effectively, often clumsily, and rarely with comparable commercial success. In the booming 1980s Marvel secured its commanding market position even further on the strength of such new hits as the revitalized X-Men and the Punisher, as well as the continuing popularity of its established superheroes. Surveys indicated that Marvel was the top seller in its market. To help ensure its dominance, Marvel returned to its old strategy of flooding the market with titles in the hopes of crowding out the competition. Despite spirited challenges from DC and an array of smaller independent publishers vying for market share, Marvel stayed on top and its characters remained the most popular among comic-book fans.

Marvel's popularity was also boosted by television and film adaptations featuring its heroes. Animated television series introduced Marvel characters to a new and future audience—children. In the 1960s *Fantastic Four* and *Spider-Man* became animated shows and were followed by a string of others, including *The Incredible Hulk*, *Iron Man*, and *X-Men: Evolution*. *Captain America* hit the big screen first in 1944 and again in 1990. In the 1980s the live-action films *Howard the Duck* and *The Punisher* were released.

The company's very success, however, made it a target of criticism from fans and industry insiders. Many charged that Marvel's comic books, once on the cutting edge of the field, had drifted squarely into the predictable mainstream. Longtime fans grew annoyed by Marvel's bewildering multi-issue crossovers and its tendency to spread popular characters such as Spider-Man and the X-Men over too many titles. Some creators complained that a dispassionate and sometimes ruthless corporate atmosphere now pervaded the once intimate company that many had idolized and romanticized as young fans.

Marvel had been a corporate property since 1968 and had changed owners several times. In 1991, under the ownership of billionaire Wall Street investor Ronald Perelman, Marvel Entertainment debuted on the New York Stock Exchange. Shares performed well for several years, despite warnings from market watchers that they were overvalued. Then they declined sharply until 1996, when Marvel was compelled to file for Chapter 11 bankruptcy protection.

ADAPTING TO THE TWENTY-FIRST CENTURY

The company was saved from bankruptcy in 1998 by merging with Toy Biz, a subsidiary of Marvel that had produced action figures based on Marvel superheroes since 1993. That humiliating debacle had more to do with Perelman's unwise investments in other holdings than it did with the popularity of Marvel's comic books, and the publication of the company's comic books continued unabated. But Marvel's troubles also reflected the general crisis the comic-book industry found itself in at the end of the twentieth century, as it struggled to keep its audience in an increasingly crowded, postmodern entertainment industry that catered to youth. Mindful of this predicament, Marvel's advertising campaign in the late 1990s emphasized the characters who had made it the industry's leading publisher.

In the first decade of the 2000s Marvel's renewed focus on its core characters led to the production of several major motion pictures based on popular comic books, including *X-Men* (2000), *Spider-Man* (2002), *Hulk* (2003), *Fantastic Four* (2005), and *Iron Man* (2008). This trend bolstered sales of merchandise such as video games and action figures, but it did not necessarily revive dwindling comic-book sales. In 2009 the Walt Disney Company purchased Marvel Entertainment, the parent company of Marvel Comics, to the dismay of longtime fans and the delight of short-term investors. Marvel and Disney continued to produce big-budget films into the 2010s, including *Thor* (2011) and *The Avengers* (2012). The publishing wing of Marvel struggled under lackluster sales, however, despite the moderate success of the digital subscription service, Marvel Digital Comics Unlimited, which launched in 2007.

In 2011 Marvel Comics underwent a series of layoffs, firing chief operating officer Jim Sokolowski and a number of highly regarded editors and writers, signaling that the company (or more likely their overseers at Disney) continued to grapple with disappointing sales figures. Its characters, however, remained as popular as ever, and in 2012 Disney announced that they would feature a number of Marvel superheroes at their theme parks around the world. As long as Marvel can lay claim to the well-worn, but still appealing, superheroes who do good despite being feared and misunderstood by the public, it should retain its relevant place in the shaping of popular youth culture.

Bradford W. Wright

SEE ALSO: *Captain America; Cold War; Comic Books; Comics Code Authority;* Daredevil, the Man without Fear*; DC Comics; Disney (Walt Disney Company); EC Comics;* The Fantastic Four*; The Incredible Hulk; Lee, Stan; The Silver Surfer; Spider-Man; World War II; The X-Men.*

BIBLIOGRAPHY

Daniels, Les. *Marvel: Five Fabulous Decades of the World's Greatest Comics.* New York: Harry N. Abrams, 1991.

Dougall, Alastair, and Nick Avery. *The Marvel Comics Encyclopedia: The Definitive Guide to the Characters of the Marvel Universe.* New York: Dorling Kindersley, 2006.

Jacobs, Will, and Gerard Jones. *The Comic Book Heroes.* Rocklin, CA: Prima Publishing, 1998.

Lee, Stan. *Origins of Marvel Comics.* New York: Simon & Schuster, 1974.

Lee, Stan. *Son of Origins of Marvel Comics.* New York: Simon & Schuster, 1975.

Weiner, Robert G. *Marvel Graphic Novels and Related Publications: An Annotated Guide to Comics, Prose Novels, Children's Books, Articles, Criticism and Reference Works, 1965–2005.* Jefferson, NC: McFarland, 2008.

Marx, Groucho *(1890–1977)*

The third-born of the performing Marx Brothers, Julius "Groucho" Marx made the most profound contribution to American comedy. His wisecracking stage persona has achieved iconic status akin to Charlie Chaplin's hapless tramp and Buster Keaton's stone face. When teamed with his brothers, Groucho often served as a stand-in for the audience, a reluctant go-between for the more antic Chico and Harpo. Venal, lecherous, and motivated by the desire for money and a life of ease, Groucho's film facade was the male id personified.

When the brothers' movie career had run its course, Groucho evolved into a gentler, more grandfatherly figure as host of the radio and TV quiz program *You Bet Your Life*. Toward the end of his life, he made the talk-show rounds, often appearing in an absurd beret to trade quips with the host.

Robert E. Schnakenberg

SEE ALSO: *Chaplin, Charlie;* Duck Soup*; Game Shows; Keaton, Buster; The Marx Brothers; Vaudeville.*

BIBLIOGRAPHY

Adamson, Joe. *Groucho, Harpo, Chico, and Sometimes Zeppo.* New York: Simon & Schuster, 1973.

Kanfer, Stefan. *The Essential Groucho: Writings by, for and about*

Groucho Marx. New York: Vintage Books, 2000.

Marx, Groucho. *Groucho and Me*. New York: Da Capo Press, 1995.

The Marx Brothers

The Marx Brothers comedy team was made up of three brothers stage-named Groucho, Harpo, and Chico (although two other brothers, Gummo and Zeppo, were included in the act for brief periods), whose madcap antics and semi-slapstick routines earned them a reputation as some of the zaniest performers of their time, with frequent appearances in vaudeville, musical comedy, radio, and film. Two of the brothers, Groucho and Harpo, performed on television in later years: Harpo as a novelty entertainer and, most notably, Groucho as the host of his own game show, *You Bet Your Life*. Though never an enormous hit in their time, the Marx Brothers lived to see their reputation with critics and audiences grow to legendary proportions, and they are especially remembered for their appearances in much-revived films like *Duck Soup* (1933), *A Night at the Opera* (1935), and *A Day at the Races* (1937).

START ON THE STAGE

The five Marx Brothers were born in New York City to Samuel, a tailor, and Minna Schoenberg Marx (the "Minnie" of the musical *Minnie's Boys*), an ambitious stage mother (her brother was Al Shean of the vaudeville comedy team Gallagher & Shean) who thought show business would provide opportunities for her sons. Sources disagree about the brothers' dates of birth, but Groucho's son, Arthur Marx, declares the following order in his 1988 memoir *My Life with Groucho: A Son's Eye View*: "Leonard (Chico) 1887; Arthur (Harpo) 1888; Julius (Groucho) 1890; Milton (Gummo) 1897; Herbert (Zeppo) 1901." Chico died in 1961, Harpo in 1964, Groucho and Gummo in 1977, and Zeppo in 1979.

In musical revues and stage shows throughout the 1910s and 1920s, the Marx Brothers began developing the comic personae they would later immortalize on film. Groucho, often seen as the leader of the group, perfected the persona of a wisecracking finagler with his painted-on mustache, arched

Marz Brothers. *The Marx Brothers included, from left, Harpo, Chico, Zeppo, and Groucho. The comedy team known for its semi-slapstick routines and witty dialogue.* MICHAEL OCHS ARCHIVES/ STRINGER/MICHAEL OCHS ARCHIVES/GETTY IMAGES.

eyebrows, and ever-present cigar. Chico (he pronounced it "Chick-O") donned a silly pointed hat and affected an Italian immigrant's accent. Harpo played the harp, chased pretty girls, honked a toy horn, and erected a legend around the fact that he never spoke. Zeppo, the least known of the quintet, mostly stood around with nothing to do. Gummo performed with his brothers early in the group's career, but he left the act around 1918.

FROM NEW YORK TO HOLLYWOOD

The trademark Marxian style, honed on stage and perfected on film, was marked by a fast pace, absurdist situations, and witty dialogue. Some of the greatest humorists of the period, including George S. Kaufman and S. J. Perelman, would eventually write one-liners for the team. In 1925 the Marx Brothers graduated from music hall obscurity when their Broadway stage production *The Cocoanuts* proved a huge hit. Four years later Paramount Studios signed them to a movie deal. They made the film adaptation of *The Cocoanuts* (1929) at the Kaufman Astoria studio during the day while their second Broadway production, *Animal Crackers*, was running at night. The big-screen *Cocoanuts* is stagy and crudely mounted, although it does contain a number of memorable comic scenes, including the classic "viaduct" (or "why a duck?") routine that relies on fast-paced punning for its humor.

A hit with Marx Brothers' fans and the general public, *The Cocoanuts* established the prototype for all subsequent Marx Brothers films. In it, buxom Margaret Dumont plays a wealthy dowager who must constantly fend off Groucho's advances. There is a sappy musical subplot, and the stolid Zeppo is given little to do. These stock elements were to be incorporated into every film the brothers made for the studio. Next up was *Animal Crackers* (1930), another stage adaptation; its threadbare plot simply let the siblings loose in a rich matron's estate, with predictably antic consequences. Groucho got to warble "Hooray for Captain Spaulding," a Harry Ruby composition that would become one of his trademark songs and the theme for his later television quiz show. The film also provided the pop-cultural lexicon with some of its best-known one-liners, including the chestnut "This morning I shot an elephant in my pajamas. How he got into my pajamas I'll never know."

The success of their first two features prompted the Marx Brothers to leave New York for Hollywood. There they made the three films that purists consider their finest. *Monkey Business* (1931), written by humorist Perelman, placed the foursome as stowaways on an ocean liner. The first Marx Brothers film to be written directly for the screen, *Monkey Business*'s frenetic pace and relative lack of schmaltzy subplot made it one of the team's funniest examples of its formula. Notable scenes include one in which all four Marx Brothers impersonate French crooner Maurice Chevalier in a doomed attempt to buffalo their way past the authorities.

The 1932 follow-up, *Horse Feathers*, was every bit as good. A stroke of screenwriting genius put the brothers on a college campus, with Groucho perfectly (mis)cast as university president. More surreal than *Monkey Business* or any of the group's previous films, *Horse Feathers* (1932) milked much comic mileage out of an anarchic football game staged by the brothers. Songs include Groucho's defining gem "Whatever It Is, I'm against It" and the Woody Allen–inspiring "Everyone Says I Love You."

Duck Soup, another absurdist tour de force, was set in the mythical country of Freedonia, where Groucho got himself elected dictator (probably with the support of the same folks who made him a college president) and promptly declared war on a neighboring nation. Chico and Harpo, as a pair of unscrupulous spies, had some of their finest on-screen moments. The climactic musical numbers alone were worth the price of admission, and its famous "mirror scene" would be reenacted some twenty years later when Harpo appeared on a celebrated episode of TV's *I Love Lucy*.

In the years after its release, *Duck Soup* gained an unwarranted reputation as an antiwar comedy, as if the brothers could see the bellicose aspirations of Adolf Hitler and Benito Mussolini as far back as 1933. The Marxes always denied this, and in fact an antiauthoritarian strain can be detected in all of their comedies of this period. Regardless of its politics, *Duck Soup* flopped at the box office, leading Paramount to jettison the siblings, who chose to carry on without Zeppo.

The three survivors—Groucho, Harpo, and Chico—landed at MGM (Metro-Goldwyn-Mayer), a studio known for its lavish, family-oriented spectaculars. It did not seem like a good fit, and in time would prove not to be, but the first picture the team made there was an undisputed classic. *A Night at the Opera* had all the trademark Marxian elements: rapid-fire comic patter, expert pantomime, and three or four set pieces that were to become landmark scenes in the annals of film comedy. Only the grating presence of a treacly romantic subplot, complete with one too many horrible songs, served as a sign of bad things to come. Nevertheless, the trio was in fine form, having been able to hone their material by road tryouts before the film was shot. With more structure and better production values than previous Marx Brothers films, it won back the mass audience and put the team back on solid commercial footing.

The perils of formula began to catch up with the Marxes in their next release, *A Day at the Races* (1937). Although the film contained a number of funny scenes, it was undermined by an utterly haphazard script and a numbing plethora of excruciating musical numbers. Most disturbingly, MGM—as it would later do with the *Our Gang* kids—tried to recast the brothers as lovable lugs trying to do the right thing for their romantic coleads. "She loves him. Everything's gonna be *all right now*!" the previously cynical Chico is made to say as insufferable lovers Allan Jones and Maureen O'Sullivan play kissy face in front of him. Harpo was even more shamefully abused, forced to front a racist production number with a crowd of dancing "pickaninnies" that is routinely cut from television airings of the film.

LATER YEARS

It was all downhill from there. With the death of MGM titan Irving Thalberg in 1937, the Marx Brothers were assigned to second-tier producers who allowed the quality of their vehicles to slip precipitously. *At the Circus* (1939), *Go West* (1940), and *The Big Store* (1941) all had their share of fine comic moments, but they were dragged down by a kind of cookie-cutter approach normally reserved for lesser comedians. Eventually the team grew tired of the mediocrity and broke up, though they did reunite for the tiresome *A Night in Casablanca* (1946).

After going their separate ways, the "big three" Marx Brothers pursued their individual interests with varying degrees of success. Groucho enjoyed a long career on radio and television as host of the popular quiz show *You Bet Your Life* and cultivated a public persona in later years of a "dirty old man" who craved younger female companionship. Harpo occasionally performed and wrote an autobiography cheekily titled *Harpo Speaks!*, and Chico gambled.

Robert E. Schnakenberg

SEE ALSO: Duck Soup*; Game Shows;* I Love Lucy*; MGM (Metro-Goldwyn-Mayer);* Our Gang*; Television; Thalberg, Irving G.; Vaudeville.*

BIBLIOGRAPHY

Adamson, Joe. *Groucho, Harpo, Chico, and Sometimes Zeppo.* New York: Simon & Schuster, 1973.

Eyles, Allen. *The Complete Films of the Marx Brothers.* Secaucus, NJ: Citadel Press, 1992.

Gardner, Martin A. *The Marx Brothers as Social Critics: Satire and Comic Nihilism in Their Films.* Jefferson, NC: McFarland, 2009.

Louvish, Simon. *Monkey Business: The Lives and Legends of the Marx Brothers.* New York: St. Martin's Press, 2000.

Marx, Arthur. *My Life with Groucho: A Son's Eye View.* London: Robson Books, 1988.

Marx, Harpo, and Roland Barber. *Harpo Speaks!.* New York: B. Geis Associates, 1961.

Marxism

SEE: *Communism.*

Mary Hartman, Mary Hartman

The parody soap opera *Mary Hartman, Mary Hartman* debuted in January 1976 to become the "Bicentennial Soap"—much like *Rocky* became the Bicentennial movie. Yet while *Rocky* hearkened back to a simpler type of hero, Mary Hartman was at once simple—the long-suffering successor to radio's "Mary Noble"—yet complex, for her struggles involved dealing with outlandish crises such as a neighborhood mass murder, the "exposure" of her grandfather as the notorious "Fernwood Flasher," and the basketball coach's drowning in a bowl of her chicken soup. Also, like *Rocky*, the show was an underdog that initially no major network would touch, until producer Norman Lear sold the show to independent stations and produced an unexpected hit, which became a cultural phenomenon. The *Wall Street Journal* deemed it "the funniest show in the history of television."

Mary Hartman, Mary Hartman originated in the mind of sitcom producer Lear, who was riding the wave of success with both *All in the Family* and its spin-off, *Maude*, when he bought the rights to an old radio serial, *The Bickersons*, intending to

Louise Lasser as Mary Hartman. *Louise Lasser played the title character in* Mary Hartman, Mary Hartman, *the soap opera parody series that debuted in 1976.* © LYNN GOLDSMITH/CORBIS.

update and adapt it into a TV sitcom. In the process of development, Lear determined that he wanted to create an unusual hybrid: a straight soap with continuing characters and situations that would simultaneously satirize the medium.

Lear hired a series of veteran comedy writers to develop this concept. The setting would be fictional small town Fernwood, Ohio. The central family would be the Hartmans: blue-collar autoworker husband Tom; his wife, Mary; and their teenage daughter, Heather. Other characters would include Mary's parents and younger sister, the Shumways, as well as neighbors the Haggers, consisting of would-be country singer Loretta and her husband, Charlie.

Whereas this setup was quite workable, Lear wanted to open the show with a series of plot developments that would establish its offbeat nature—but also quite possibly alienate the audience through its breaking of taboos. In the opening episodes, the Hartmans deal with the mass murder of a neighborhood family, the exposure of Mary's grandfather as an exhibitionist, and a frank bedroom discussion between Tom and Mary regarding his long-term impotence.

Although Lear, along with head writers Ann Marcus, Daniel Gregory Browne, and others, struggled to make these crises amusing *and* avoid censorship, the offensive subject matter still worried prospective networks, which contended that either the show needed a live studio audience or a laugh track to point out the humor. Yet Lear resisted, finally selling the show personally, based on his reputation, to approximately ninety independent stations across the country. During the interim the producers went on with the process of casting the project.

According to writer Marcus, the central character of Mary had been written for actress Louise Lasser—ex-wife of Woody Allen and costar in some of his films, such as *Bananas* and *Everything You've Always Wanted to Know about Sex.* Although Lasser was hesitant about the bizarre nature of the project, the producers soon convinced her. Lasser is credited with bringing Mary to life through her deliberate and measured delivery and her creation of Mary's "look"—the wig of braided hair and bangs and the puffy-sleeved housewife minidresses. Lasser seemed to have intuitively captured the unfinished, adolescent/woman nature of Mary, who had not fully integrated as an adult and actually dressed younger than her thirteen-year-old daughter.

THE SHOW DEBUTS

Mary Hartman, Mary Hartman premiered on January 6, 1976. The first episode establishes the anachronistic style, which hearkens to soap operas of the 1950s—complete with corny organ music and the voice of Dody Goodman (who played Mary's mother) calling out "Mary Hartman . . . Mary Hartman!" The opening scenes take place in Mary's kitchen, where much of the action of the series is focused, as she watches soap operas and laments the "waxy yellow buildup" on her own floors (resulting in her climbing underneath the sink and closing the cabinet in depression). Then, upon hearing the report of the death of "the Lombardis, their three kids, two goats, and eight chickens" from neighbor Loretta Haggers (Mary Kay Place), Mary responds—in her now-classic deadpan fashion, "What kind of madman would kill two goats and eight chickens?"

Such black humor in such questionable taste drew an immediate response—both positive and negative. The show was the subject of endless articles in tabloids and highbrow magazines as critics debated its merits. Although *Newsweek* praised it, *Time* magazine found it "silly stupid, silly stupid." Factions of the public found it boring, while others were shocked and revolted, mounting letter-writing campaigns and picketing stations to stop the show, which was broadcast in the afternoon, when their innocent children could be corrupted. Still others found it wildly original, and fan clubs rose as Mary Hartman T-shirts, bumper stickers, and other merchandise began circulating.

For many the show was just plain hysterically funny. The quintessential episode concerns the funeral held for Leroy Fedders, the coach of the Fernwood High basketball team. Ill with a cold, Coach Fedders has been downing shots of bourbon as well as cold medicine when Mary Hartman arrives with a bowl of her chicken soup. As Mary and the coach's wife talk obliviously in the kitchen, Coach Fedders deliriously slumps forward in the bowl of chicken soup and quietly drowns.

Mary, sick with guilt, offers the Fedders family her kitchen for the funeral. Few mourners gather, because, as widow Blanche Fedders concludes, "That's how much people care about you when you never win a game." In delivering the eulogy, Mary pleads, "I do not want any of my friends and neighbors or relatives ever to eat anything I offer them again," then—moments later—invites the mourners to refreshments she's prepared. Loretta Haggers—wheelchair-bound due to an accident involving her car and a carload full of nuns en route to Nashville—then comes forward to sing in her typically upbeat, inappropriately jazzy country style.

Reportedly, Lear himself improvised Coach Fedders's death and took delight in figuring out equally bizarre ways for characters to be eliminated, such as the strange—and somewhat controversial—death of eight-year-old evangelist Jimmy Joe Jeeter, who was electrocuted when a TV set fell into his bathtub. Likewise, partway through the show's run, Martin Mull (later featured on the sitcom *Roseanne*) was introduced as Garth Gimble, a wife beater who is later killed by his wife when she knocks him into a closet and he is impaled by the Christmas tree stored within. Then there was the near-death of Charlie Haggers, who, while defending his wife from the lecherous advances of Jimmy Joe's slimy promoter/father Merle (Dabney Coleman), is accidentally shot in the groin. He subsequently receives a transplant testicle from a German shepherd.

A SHORT RUN

Despite its immense success, the daily grind took its toll on star Lasser. While most soap opera leads appeared in two to three episodes per week, she insisted on being in every one—an especially difficult task because the parodic nature of the show required extensive rehearsal to achieve the right comedic timing. Lasser burned out as the twenty-six weeks of the first season wore on. Her stress was also exacerbated by an incident in her private life involving an arrest for possession of a small amount of cocaine and nonpayment of traffic tickets.

Lasser suggested that this incident, culminating in her nervous breakdown, be written into the show as the season finale. The writers agreed, contriving a scenario in which Mary is chosen as "America's Typical Consumer Housewife" and a film crew is sent to document a week in her life. Subsequently, Mary is flown to New York to appear before a panel of experts on the *David Susskind Show*. These pressures—in addition to Tom's job loss and descent into alcoholism, her sister Cathy's illicit affair with a Catholic priest, Mary being held hostage at a Chinese laundry, and her doomed affair with police Sergeant

Dennis Foley (who has a heart attack the first time they make love)—causes Mary to crack on national TV under scrutiny by experts who are analyzing her life. She eventually ends up in a mental hospital and, upon release, runs off with Foley. Though the show attempted to go on the following season as *Forever Fernwood* without Lasser, its popularity declined, leading to cancellation.

In summary, despite their love or hate for the show, the "something" that seemed to keep disparate factions of viewers watching to the end was *Mary Hartman, Mary Hartman*'s exploration of a character who was a victim of the conflict between television values and reality. Like much of the population, Mary hopes that if she listens to commercials and buys the products, she will have the beautiful life they advertise. Of her character, Lasser herself explained:

> Mary's as sad as any person I've ever heard of in my life, unless they're in a wheelchair somewhere. This is a person who gets up and dresses in pink and blue, thinking it's all going to be fine—and it just falls down on her every single day. She has a daughter that hates her. She has a husband that won't make love to her. And she's just *trying* to figure out what's wrong with *her*. That's not sad? She's a total victim. But what's sweet and sad about her is that she's a survivor. She survives in a world that may not be worth surviving for.

Rick Moody

SEE ALSO: All in the Family*; Lear, Norman;* Maude*; Soap Operas.*

BIBLIOGRAPHY

Craft, Robert. "Elegy for *Mary Hartman*." In *Television: The Critical View*, ed. Horace Newcomb. New York: Oxford University Press, 1979.

Edmondson, Madeleine, and David Rounds. *From Mary Noble to Mary Hartman: The Complete Soap Opera Book*. New York: Stein and Day, 1976.

Gwinn, Alison, ed. *The 100 Greatest TV Shows of All Time*. New York: Entertainment Weekly Books, 1998.

Mary Kay Cosmetics

Mary Kay Cosmetics Inc., a privately held direct selling company, was founded by Mary Kay Ash on September 13, 1963, in Addison, Texas, a suburb of Dallas. The company is the second-largest direct seller of personal care products, behind Avon. Mary Kay carries a line of more than 200 products, including facial skin care products; cosmetics; fragrances; nutritional supplements; sun protection products; hair, nail, and body care products; and men's skin care items. In 2010 the company's estimated wholesale sales were $2.5 billion, up from $1 billion in 1996. Founder Ash, who stepped aside as chairman of the company in 1995, died in 2001.

Mary Kay Cosmetics sells its range of personal care products through approximately 1.8 million independent salespeople worldwide, known as "beauty consultants." These beauty consultants sell the products directly to consumers, often using Mary Kay Cosmetics parties to sell their goods. The company employs and is said to empower many women: several women have attained the position of independent national sales director, with salaries well into the six figures, while others hold the position of independent sales director. They can earn their salary through a combination of retail sales and recruiting new employees.

According to company documents, the vision of Mary Kay Cosmetics is to "provide women with an unparalleled opportunity for financial independence, career and personal fulfillment" and "to achieve total customer satisfaction by delivering the products and services that enhance a woman's self-image and confidence." Ash's original goal was to empower women with personal and financial success opportunities. Her simple philosophy was to have her sales force members prioritize their lives by a simple motto: God first, family second, and career third. Starting a Mary Kay business could cost as little as $100 for the product demonstration kit and educational materials.

Mary Kay now operates in more than thirty-five countries (up from twenty-five in 1998), including Australia, Canada, Argentina, Germany, Malaysia, Mexico, Thailand, the United Kingdom, New Zealand, Guatemala, Taiwan, Spain, Sweden, Bermuda, Brunei, Chile, Norway, Russia, Singapore, Brazil, Japan, the People's Republic of China, Portugal, Finland, the Czech Republic, Ukraine, El Salvador, Hong Kong, Kazakhstan, the Philippines, Slovakia, South Korea, Uzbekistan, Moldova, Poland, India, Fiji, Lithuania, and Armenia. Several other countries are served by a gray market.

The main manufacturing plant is in Dallas. A second plant was opened in Hangzhou, People's Republic of China, to manufacture and package products for East and Southeast Asia. A third plant was opened in La Chaux-de-Fonds, Switzerland, for the European market, including Russia, but later closed in 2003. In 1989 the company stopped animal testing of its products after pressure from animal rights groups. In the early 1990s Mary Kay introduced several makeup products aimed at the growing market for women of color. Its growth in China was affected by a ban on door-to-door selling in April 1998; the company opened negotiations with the Chinese government, which allowed them to sell only to wholesalers and retailers.

Mary Kay is well known for offering cars to its most successful independent beauty consultants and sales directors. First awarded in 1969, this car has typically been a pink Cadillac. The Mary Kay fleet in the United States, which includes some 100,000 cars, is valued at more than $1.5 billion and is the largest commercial fleet of General Motors cars in the world. Over the years the pink Grand Prix, the red Grand Am, and the white GMC Jimmy have been included in the fleet.

In the early 2010s, independent sales directors were offered either $500 a month or a car of their choice, either a silver Toyota Camry or a Chevy Equinox. Top independent sales directors had a cash option of $900 a month or a car (a pink Cadillac DTS or a Cadillac CTS). At the annual sales convention in July 2011, the company announced that the 2011 Ford Mustang would also be available as an incentive to salespeople. In the United Kingdom, Germany, the Netherlands, Spain, and Ukraine, the car was a pink Mercedes-Benz. Argentines received a pink Ford, Taiwanese got a pink Toyota, and Australians got to choose between a Ford Falcon and a Volkswagen Beetle. Successful salespeople in China got a pink Volkswagen Santana, while their counterparts in the Nordic countries received a pink Volvo V50.

The Mary Kay Foundation was founded in 1996 with a twofold mission of funding research to search for cures for breast, uterine, cervical, and ovarian cancers as well as supporting initiatives to prevent violence against women. In 2010 the company gave $1.3 million in cancer research grants to doctors and medical scientists and $3 million to more than 150 women's shelters across the United States.

Abbijit Roy

SEE ALSO: *Automobile; Avon; Consumerism; General Motors.*

BIBLIOGRAPHY

Ash, Mary Kay. *Mary Kay: You Can Have It All.* Rocklin, CA: Prima Publishing, 1995.

Cort, Kathryn T., and William L. Shanklin. "The Wall: How Mary Kay Cosmetics Knocks It Down." *Marketing Management*, Winter 1999.

Glick, Julia. "More Chinese Women Donning Mary Kay Uniforms." Associated Press, August 4, 2006.

Gross, Daniel. "Mary Kay Ash and Her Corporate Culture for Women." In *Forbes Greatest Business Stories of All Time.* New York: John Wiley and Sons, 1996.

Mardenfeld, Sandra. "Mary Kay Ash." *Incentive*, January 1996, 54–60.

"Mary Kay Cosmetics." Accessed April 2012. Available from http://www.marykay.com

"Mary Kay Museum." Accessed January 2012. Available from http://www.marykaymuseum.com

Speedy, Blair. "Mary Kay Survives Retail Slump." *Australian*, March 2, 2011.

Mary Poppins

Vain, brusque, and tart of tongue, Mary Poppins first blew into the Banks home at 17 Cherry Tree Lane, London, in the 1934 book *Mary Poppins* to teach Jane, Michael, and the twins some manners. She also took them on a series of fantastical adventures throughout London, across the globe, and within their own home—all of which she firmly denied had ever taken place (calling it "stuff and nonsense").

The spit-spot governess with the parrot-head umbrella was the brainchild of Australian-born P. L. (Pamela Lyndon) Travers (1899–1996), who more than once declared, "I don't write for children at all. I turn my back on them." Valerie Lawson writes that Travers declared she went by her initials so "people wouldn't bother to wonder if the books were written by a man, woman or kangaroo." Indeed, the books about Mary Poppins are favorites of children and adults, and they show an affinity for the animal world. They have been translated into more than twenty-five languages and sold millions of copies; their tremendous popularity is probably attributable in equal parts to the mythic elements of Mary's character, the boundless universe

Mary Poppins. *Dick Van Dyke (upper left) as Bert, Karen Dotrice as Jane Banks, Matthew Garber as Michael Banks, and Julie Andrews (upper right) as the titular magical nanny appear in a scene from Disney's 1964 feature* Mary Poppins. **SILVER SCREEN COLLECTION/CONTRIBUTOR/MOVIEPIX/GETTY IMAGES.**

she creates, and nostalgia for an illusory coddled British childhood, a notion that strongly influenced the later Disney film and Broadway show.

MARY'S BRISK MAGIC

In the eight Mary Poppins books (four story collections, two single-story books, an alphabet book, and a cookbook) the character of Mary represents unlimited possibility and the magic to be found within the confines of everyday life. As most volumes contain many stories, and as Mary's carpetbag contains many objects (including clothing, furniture, and a bottle of medicine that tastes different according to who swallows it), so does Mary show that an ordinary place or object contains much more than first meets the eye.

She seems to know everyone in London and to be related to a good number of them, but her own origins and history are murky; even Travers claimed not to know where she comes from or goes to between visits. When she arrives at the Bankses' house, Mary enters a neighborhood of upper-middle-class homes in which a child might be more intimate with the servants and eccentric neighbors than with his or her distracted parents. Offering efficient care, insight, and adventure, she is the magic gatekeeper all children wish they knew. With Mary's uncle Mr. Wigg, for example, Jane and Michael laugh until they become weightless and bump against the ceiling, and Mary's favorite shopkeeper breaks off her own fingers and feeds them to the children like candy.

A GODDESS FIGURE

Proud of her relatives and fussy about her appearance, the acerbic Mary of the books has often been compared to a warrior or mother goddess such as the Hindu Kali—Travers herself admitted to an interest in Kali in 1982, noting in the *Paris Review* that her greatest character had some relationship to the all-powerful, sometimes malicious, but ultimately motherly concept known in many cultures simply as The Goddess: "I've only recently come to see that. She is either Mother Goddess or one of her creatures—that is, if we're going to look for mythological or fairy tale origins for *Mary Poppins*." (Perhaps, her last words imply, we are to see Mary Poppins as a creation sprung entirely from the author's imagination.)

Delightfully vain and strict as she often is, Mary's heart is not unreachable. She creates adventures for unfortunates such as the impoverished Match-Man and a Pleiades star who has no money for Christmas gifts. In the books, adventures are episodic, character is static, and conflict is confined to and resolved within individual incidents. But although each magical adventure, like each swallow of medicine, is tailored to the child who enjoys it, Mary makes this world one of fluid relationships. She shows that all sentient beings are of equal worth and capacity: Each resident of Cherry Tree Lane has a relationship to the others and is often blood kin to Mary herself—making her truly a goddess figure who unites everyone.

In the Poppins everyday-fantastical continuum, animals and humans are members of the same kingdom, manifesting the same emotions and intellect. People, many of them from Jane and Michael's neighborhood, are displayed in cages. Similarly, adults often act like children and vice versa. Travers claimed to have "no idea where childhood ends and maturity begins." And even inanimate objects, once examined with the right frame of mind, can turn into active playmates (as in Jane's unsettling adventure within the Royal Doulton Plate) or relatives (as when the plasticine man Jane fashions in the park turns out to be Mary's cousin Sam).

Thus, at the end of each of Mary's visits, the children miss Mary herself as well as her magic world when she disappears with the wind again. Patricia Demers, in her book *P. L. Travers*, summed up the character's appeal: "Mary Poppins seems to come from another world and time, and yet to be also a futuristic model of understanding."

ADAPTATIONS AND A BELOVED MOVIE

Travers was not averse to adapting her work. The dialect in the first book seemed racist to late-century libraries, so she rewrote some scenes. She also served as a consultant on the 1964 Disney film *Mary Poppins*, which starred Julie Andrews and Dick Van Dyke. Combining live action with animation and catchy song-and-dance numbers, the movie dramatizes a few incidents from the first books, invents some of its own, and presents a much gentler Mary. For example, Mary's sympathy for the poor Match-Man is blown into cinematic sweethearthood as Bert and Mary enjoy a date in the park. The movie character likely inspired successors such as Nanny McPhee of early-twenty-first-century films and spawned a hit Broadway musical that began a multiyear run in 2006.

Critics have attacked the hugely popular film for cheapening the magic of the books, and even Travers expressed some disappointment in it. Still, it was her suggestion to set the film in the Edwardian period rather than the 1930s, to which the books belong; she explained that she wanted the images to be "timeless," or well removed from the contemporary scene. Perhaps Travers saw those years just preceding her own childhood as the true location of governess-y coziness, magic, and myth. Or perhaps she wanted to prove that Mary is, as she proclaims at the end of her very last book, "at home . . . wherever I am!"

Susann Cokal

SEE ALSO: *Broadway; Disney (Walt Disney Company); Van Dyke, Dick.*

BIBLIOGRAPHY

Bergsten, Staffan. *Mary Poppins and Myth*. Stockholm: Almqvist & Wiksell International, 1978.

Burness, Edwina, and Jerry Griswold. "The Art of Fiction LXXIII: P. L. Travers." Interview. *Paris Review* 86 (Winter 1982): 210–229.

Commire, Anne, ed. "P. L. Travers." *Something about the Author*, Vol. 54, 148–162. Detroit: MI: Gale Research, 1989.

Demers, Patricia. *P. L. Travers*. Boston: Twayne Publishers, 1991.

Lawson, Valerie. *Mary Poppins, She Wrote: The Life of P. L. Travers*. New York: Simon & Schuster, 2006.

Pérez Valverde, Christina. "Magic Women on the Margins: Eccentric Models in *Mary Poppins* and *Ms Wiz*." *Children's Literature in Education* 40, no. 4 (December 2009): 263–274.

Reckford, Kenneth J. *Aristophanes' Old-and-New Comedy*. Chapel Hill: University of North Carolina Press, 1987.

Westfahl, Gary. *The Greenwood Encyclopedia of Science Fiction and Fantasy: Themes, Works and Wonders*. Westport, CT: Greenwood Press, 2005.

The Mary Tyler Moore Show

The Mary Tyler Moore Show, which aired on CBS from 1970 to 1977, was one of the most influential situation comedies in the history of American television, highly regarded by audiences and critics alike. The show, set in Minneapolis, centers on Mary Richards (played by Mary Tyler Moore), a single career woman in her thirties who works as the associate producer of the six o'clock news at WJM-TV Channel 12, the lowest-rated station in the city. This premise, while seemingly simple, broke new ground for situation comedy by featuring an unmarried, professional woman as the central character and by shifting the setting of the sitcom from the home and the traditional family to the workplace, where a new kind of family was formed—a family consisting of characters in whom audiences felt invested and toward whom they felt a deep affection. In its seven-year run, the show raised the standards for comedy writing, acting, directing, and producing, garnering a record 29 Emmy Awards and thus guaranteeing it a place in the annals of American television programming.

The Mary Tyler Moore Show. The Mary Tyler Moore Show *starred, clockwise from bottom left, Betty White as Sue Ann Nivens, Gavin MacLeod as Murray Slaughter, Ed Asner as Lou Grant, Ted Knight as Ted Baxter, Georgia Engel as Georgette Franklin, and Mary Tyler Moore as Mary Richards.* CBS-TV/THE KOBAL COLLECTION.

THE SHOW IS BORN

The events surrounding the creation and development of *The Mary Tyler Moore Show* are part of television lore. By the late 1960s, Moore was already an established actress, having won two Emmys for her portrayal of Laura Petrie, wife of Rob Petrie, on *The Dick Van Dyke Show* (which ran on CBS from 1961 to 1966). In April 1969, Moore reteamed with Van Dyke for a television musical-variety show titled *Dick Van Dyke and the Other Woman*. The program received high ratings as well as glowing reviews from critics. Impressed with the success of the show, CBS offered Moore a half-hour series, with a commitment to thirteen episodes. Moore accepted under the provision that she and then-husband Grant Tinker would have complete control of the series. CBS agreed, and Moore and Tinker formed their own independent television production company, MTM Enterprises. Tinker then hired a team of young writers, James L. Brooks and Allan Burns, to create the show. As they originally conceived it, the series would revolve around Mary Richards, a thirty-year-old divorcée who had moved to Minneapolis for a job as an assistant to a gossip columnist.

CBS executives balked at the idea, convinced that audiences would think that the "new" Mary had divorced her old television husband, Dick Van Dyke. Ordered to come up with a new premise, Brooks and Burns revised the characters and the plot, and their revision became the famous first episode of *The Mary Tyler Moore Show*, in which Mary Richards moves from a small town in Minnesota—where she and her boyfriend of two years had split up—to the urban environment of Minneapolis in order to start a new life. Within days of moving to the big city, Mary secures a job as associate producer at WJM, a local news station, completely severs ties with her ex-boyfriend, Bill—who comes to Minneapolis to ask Mary to move back home and live with him—not as his wife, but as his mistress—and befriends her upstairs neighbor, Rhoda Morgenstern.

When *The Mary Tyler Moore Show* premiered on September 19, 1970, it was not met with overwhelming critical success, and in its first year it did not rank among the top twenty shows of the season. But over the course of its seven-year run, *The Mary Tyler Moore Show* endeared itself to critics and audiences alike (it placed in the top twenty in every season except the first and the last). The show met with such success in large part due to a talented and diverse cast, all of whom excelled at making their respective characters come to life. Leading the cast was Moore herself, whose portrayal of the lovable, seemingly perfect, somewhat insecure but, over the years, increasingly assertive Mary Richards anchored the show. Though Mary Richards could "turn the world on with her smile," she was not so flawless that audiences could not identify with her. To be sure, Moore's greatest talent was making Mary Richards human: when intimidated by others, Mary would stutter or swallow her words; when exasperated or frustrated at a situation, Mary's arms would fly wildly around her; when upset at work, Mary would sniffle, "Oh, Mr. Grant!" And while, in many ways, Mary Richards was the "girl next door," she was not so innocent or naive that she seemed an anomaly in the early 1970s. She dated many men, had several serious relationships, and—though it was never stated explicitly—had an active sex life.

SUPPORTING CHARACTERS

Mary Richards was the center of the show, but her world would have been a much less interesting place without the supporting characters: Edward Asner in the role of Mary's tough but lovable boss, Lou Grant; Gavin McLeod as Murray Slaughter, the hard-working, wise-cracking WJM news writer; Ted Knight as Ted Baxter, WJM's egotistical, buffoonish anchorman; Valerie Harper as New Yorker Rhoda Morgenstern, Mary's sarcastic neighbor, best friend, and comic foil; and Cloris Leachman as Phyllis Lindstrom, Mary's landlord/friend and resident snob. Harper and Leachman both exited the show (at the end of the fourth and fifth season, respectively) for their own spin-offs—*Rhoda*, which ran from 1974 through 1978, and *Phyllis*, which aired from 1975 through 1977. Around the same time they departed, two new characters were introduced: Georgia Engel as the good-hearted but dim-witted Georgette Franklin, whom Ted dates and, in the sixth season, marries; and Betty White as the manipulative, man-hungry "Happy Homemaker," Sue Ann Nivens.

These characters, just as much as Mary Richards, contributed to the success of *The Mary Tyler Moore Show*. Like Mary, they were likable because they were human; indeed, each character had flaws, but flaws with which the audience could sympathize, if not identify. Over the course of seven years, viewers learned that Lou Grant's toughness masked his inability to be emotionally vulnerable; Murray's self-deprecating comments pointed to his disappointment that he was "just a news writer"; Ted's egotistical boasting belied a real lack of confidence in his abilities; Rhoda's caustic wit served as protection against the deep insecurity she felt about her appearance; Phyllis's political and cultural elitism reassured her that her life was in order, even though she and her husband, Lars, did not have the most exciting relationship; and Sue Ann's aggressive "man-chasing" stemmed from her fear that no man would ever want her. Even soft-spoken Georgette was much more complex than met the eye: As viewers learned in one episode, her good-heartedness provoked others—Ted in particular—to take advantage of her. With the help of Mary and Rhoda, Georgette learned to assert and believe in herself. Every character on the show was both complicated and humane, and even when the characters were at their worst behavior—as Ted, Phyllis, and Sue Ann often were—the viewers were reminded that there was something redeemable about them, something forgivable in each of them.

Though the series was originally conceived as a show about a single working woman, only a few of the 168 episodes dealt directly with Mary's unmarried status. In fact, the show was more concerned with the relationships between Mary and her co-workers and neighbors than with those between Mary and her many dates. Yet whether an episode focused on Mary's love life, home life, or work life, it often addressed—though subtly—relevant social issues of the 1970s: premarital sex, birth control, anti-Semitism, women's liberation, homosexuality, and divorce. It succeeded at incorporating such issues without resorting to preachiness and without employing the polemical style of *All in the Family* (which aired on CBS on the same night as *The Mary Tyler Moore Show* for four seasons). Rather, the humor surrounding these issues softened the controversial nature of them.

There is no better example of the show's ability to combine the serious and the humorous than in its most famous episode: "Chuckles Bites the Dust," from the sixth season. Chuckles the Clown, the host of a children's show produced by WJM, is killed by an elephant in a parade; as Murray explains, Chuckles was dressed as a peanut, and the hungry elephant tried to shell him. The unusual circumstances of his death inspire laughter rather than tears among Mary's co-workers: at the mere mention of Chuckles, everyone—Mr. Grant, Murray, Ted, and Sue Ann—giggles uncontrollably. Mary is outraged at what she perceives to be their lack of decorum and respect for the dead. Murray explains that their laughter is merely their way of coping with the tragedy, but Mary remains indignant. The climax of the plot occurs at Chuckles's funeral: while all of her friends are solemn and composed, Mary, who throughout the episode had righteously denounced the "inappropriate" responses of her co-workers, finds herself unable to control her laughter. "Chuckles Bites the Dust" is still regarded not only as one of the best episodes of *The Mary Tyler Moore Show*, but also as one of the best half-hours of comedy ever produced for television.

At the end of the sixth season, those involved in creating in the show, particularly the writers and producers, decided that the seventh season would be the show's last—not because the quality of the show was suffering, but because they wanted to end the series while the characters, plotlines, and writing were still fresh. Aired on March 19, 1977, "The Last Show" (in which everyone at the news station is fired—except Ted) has since become the exemplar of how to bring a much-loved sitcom to a graceful end. While almost every cast member moved on to other television shows (Ed Asner to *Lou Grant*, Gavin McLeod to *The Love Boat*, Ted Knight to *Too Close for Comfort*, Betty White to *The Betty White Show* and *The Golden Girls*, and Moore herself, who tried her hand at several programs, including *Mary* and *Annie McGuire*), none of them matched the success of *The Mary Tyler Moore Show*.

INFLUENCE ON SOCIETY

Though *The Mary Tyler Moore Show* now belongs to the realm of "classic TV," its influence and impact cannot be underestimated. It changed the face of the situation comedy in innumerable ways. While sitcoms before *The Mary Tyler Moore Show* had featured women in lead roles (*I Love Lucy* in the 1950s and *That Girl* in the 1960s) *The Mary Tyler Moore Show* differed from its predecessors by presenting a female character who was independent, career-oriented, and happily unmarried. Indeed, Mary remained single throughout the seven-year run of the show, and the writers felt no compunction to "marry her off" in the last episode. And while it has been argued that *The Mary Tyler Moore Show*, despite its "career woman" lead, in fact reinforced many stereotypical gender roles—for example, even after seven years, Mary called her boss "Mr. Grant" instead of "Lou," and she often performed "motherly" or "wifely" duties for him such as buying gifts for his wife or doing his laundry—such actions might be better understood as reflecting the insecurity and uncertainty that characterized women's foray into public life in the 1970s. The difficulties that Mary experienced—not knowing how to say "no," having to assert herself in order to be heard, having to draw a line between her professional life and her private life—were no doubt the very same conflicts that real women had to deal with as they entered a male-dominated work force.

Just as *The Mary Tyler Moore Show* reflected the changing role of women in society, so, too, did it reflect changing notions of the family. Whereas popular comedies of the 1950s (such as *Father Knows Best* and *The Adventures of Ozzie and Harriet*) and the 1960s (such as *The Beverly Hillbillies* and *My Three Sons*) centered on the home and the relationships between husband and wife, parents and children, and traditional family structures,

The Mary Tyler Moore Show challenged the definition of family itself, presenting instead a new version of the family, one consisting of friends, co-workers, and neighbors. As Mary tearfully declares in the final episode, "I just wanted you to know that sometimes I get concerned about being a career woman. I get to thinking my job is too important to me, and I tell myself that the people I work with are just the people I work with. And not my family. And last night, I thought what is a family anyway? They're just people who make you feel less alone and really loved. And that's what you've done for me. Thank you for being my family." By redefining the family and resituating the sitcom, *The Mary Tyler Moore Show* paved the way for the dozens of other "workplace comedies" that have followed it, including *Taxi*, *WKRP in Cincinnati*, *Cheers*, and *Murphy Brown*, programs that feature "families" not unlike the family on *The Mary Tyler Moore Show*—people not related by blood or tradition, but drawn together by work, circumstance, and ultimately, affection and love for one another.

Ann M. Ciasullo

SEE ALSO: The Adventures of Ozzie and Harriet; All in the Family; *Asner, Ed;* The Beverly Hillbillies; *Brooks, James L.;* Cheers; *Emmy Awards;* Father Knows Best; *Feminism;* The Golden Girls; I Love Lucy; The Love Boat; Murphy Brown; My Three Sons; *Sitcom;* Taxi; *Van Dyke, Dick; White, Betty;* WKRP in Cincinnati.

BIBLIOGRAPHY

Alley, Robert S., and Irby B. Brown. *Love Is All Around: The Making of "The Mary Tyler Moore Show."* New York: Delta, 1989.

Douglas, Susan J. *Where the Girls Are: Growing Up Female with the Mass Media.* New York: Times Books, 1994.

Feuer, Jane; Paul Kerr; and Tise Vahimagi; eds. *MTM: "Quality Television."* London: BFI Publishing, 1984.

McNeil, Alex. *Total Television: The Comprehensive Guide to Programming from 1948 to the Present.* New York: Penguin, 1996.

Meehan, Diana M. *Ladies of the Evening: Women Characters of Prime-Time Television.* Metuchen, NJ: Scarecrow Press, 1983.

Moore, Mary Tyler. *After All.* New York: Putnam, 1995.

Stark, Steven D. *Glued to the Set: The 60 Television Shows and Events That Made Us Who We Are Today.* New York: Free Press, 1997.

Mary Worth

Mary Worth, the queen of the soap opera comic strips, had a humble beginning in 1934 when she was known as Apple Mary. Martha Orr created the *Apple Mary* feature for the Publishers Syndicate, obviously inspired by the character of Apple Annie in Frank Capra's hit comedy of the previous year, *Lady for a Day*. By 1940, with a new artist and a new writer, Mary was dispensing advice to the lovelorn, and the strip had changed its title to *Mary Worth's Family*. In the early 1940s yet another artist took over, and a few years later the title was shortened to just plain *Mary Worth*.

In its earliest incarnation, the strip dealt with the efforts of a kindly, motherly, street-corner apple peddler to survive the stresses of the Depression; look after her crippled young nephew, Denny; and act as a Good Samaritan to her friends and neighbors. The strip was successful in its original form, picking up a satisfactory list of papers. When Orr retired in 1939, however, the new scriptwriter decided it was time for streamlining. Veteran newspaperman Allen Saunders was already writing *Big Chief Wahoo* (later changed to *Steve Roper*). He took Mary off the streets and moved the continuities closer to those that could be heard on such soap-sponsored daytime radio serials as *Ma Perkins*, *Life Can Be Beautiful*, and *Young Dr. Malone*.

Orr's longtime assistant and sometimes ghost, Dale Conner Ulrey, drew *Mary Worth's Family* in a slicker illustrative style that fit the new, more sophisticated story lines. Mary moved somewhat into the background, acting now as a sort of homespun therapist and occasional catalyst. Saunders wanted her to become "a linking character who provides continuity by tirelessly meeting interesting people." Now and then she also behaved like the classic busybody. The refurbished comic strip prospered. It is probably not a coincidence that Mary Worth was invented in Chicago, the town where many of the early radio soap operas originated.

Ulrey quit in 1942, unhappy with what she considered the tawdry content of the strip and eager to try a feature of her own. Continuing to mastermind the stories, Saunders brought in as artist the gifted Ken Ernst. A prolific comic-book illustrator, using a style inspired by that of his mentors Milton Caniff and Noel Sickles, Ernst had also been ghosting the *Don Winslow of the Navy* newspaper strip. His style was well suited to the ever more worldly stories Saunders was fashioning. Mary Worth was now frequently moving in upper-class circles. "For soap opera suffering," Saunders later explained about the further changes he brought about in the 1940s, "we decided to substitute romantic novelettes about glossy girls in more glamorous professions." He put Mary Worth in contact with actors and actresses, models, and powerful business tycoons, all of them tangled up with complex, and entertaining, romantic problems. Ernst did a good job of illustrating the glossy world that the former Apple Mary began frequenting.

The look and content of *Mary Worth* influenced a whole string of soap opera funnies, including *Rex Morgan, M.D.*, *Judge Parker*, and *The Heart of Juliet Jones*. While almost all of the other story strips have ceased to be, the soapers continue to thrive and *Mary Worth* can still be seen in papers across the country. In the late 1990s it was being written by John Saunders, Allen's son, and drawn by Joe Giella, with Karen Moy taking over the writing following Saunders's death in 2003.

Ron Goulart

SEE ALSO: *Caniff, Milton; Capra, Frank; Comics; The Great Depression; Radio Drama.*

BIBLIOGRAPHY

Goulart, Ron. *The Funnies.* Holbrook, MA: Adams Publishing, 1995.

Waugh, Coulton. *The Comics.* New York: Macmillan, 1947.

*M*A*S*H*

The final episode of *M*A*S*H*, which set a world record with 50,150,000 households watching, aired on February 28, 1983.

The series had little in common with the original novel, save the names of a few characters. Indeed, the TV series was regarded as one of the finest examples of sensitive, socially relevant television, whereas the novel, written by Dr. H. Richard Hornberger under the pseudonym Richard Hooker and published in October 1968, was a black comedy teeming with racist, sexist humor and cruel pranks. Hornberger was a surgeon who worked in a M*A*S*H unit in Korea, and he wrote a realistic novel with characters that were very different from the ones we know today. Lieutenant Colonel Henry Blake is a humorless Regular Army commander. Captain Benjamin Franklin "Hawkeye" Pierce is a crude opportunist who persuades other surgeons to take advantage of their indispensability. Their "mischief" becomes more cruel and extravagant whenever they expect casualties.

Ring Lardner Jr. liked the antiestablishment tone of the novel and adapted it into a screenplay. Twentieth Century Fox gave it to a relatively inexperienced director, Robert Altman, who applied a gritty, quasi-documentary style. The screenplay was a loose adaptation of the novel, but the characters were generally the same. The movie, which was released in 1970, shocked viewers with its graphic operating scenes and morbid humor. But it appealed to the antiwar and antiestablishment sentiments that had been growing throughout the 1960s. Hooker cashed in on the popularity of the film with a series of slapdash sequels to his novel, beginning with *M*A*S*H Goes to Maine* in 1973.

FROM FILM TO TELEVISION

The film was popular enough—and television was becoming sophisticated enough—that Twentieth Century Fox turned *M*A*S*H* into a TV series with producer/director Gene Reynolds, who had previously explored the comedy/drama genre with *Room 222.* Larry Gelbart wrote the pilot episode, and associate producer/casting director Burt Metcalfe procured the actors. The producers planned to show the film to the actors to inculcate them into the roles, but the actors refused to watch it, believing it would be a mistake to try to imitate the original actors. Gelbart approved of their decision to strive for originality and expanded upon it, deciding to embellish each character by observing the actors themselves and encouraging them to invest

M*A*S*H. *The cast of the television series* M*A*S*H*: top row from left, William Christopher as Fr. Francis Mulcahy, Gary Burghoff as Cpl. "Radar" O'Reilly, David Ogden Stiers as Maj. Charles Winchester, and Jamie Farr as Cpl. Max Klinger; bottom from left, Loretta Swit as Maj. Margaret Houlihan, Harry Morgan as Col. Sherman T. Potter, Alan Alda as Capt. Benjamin Franklin Pierce, and Mike Farrell as Capt. B.J. Hunnicut.* **20TH CENTURY FOX/THE KOBAL COLLECTION.**

some of their own personalities into their parts. Throughout the series the cast would examine the script critically to ensure that their lines were true to character. This method contributed to the longevity of the show by allowing the characters to grow and evolve.

HAWKEYE

The Hawkeye of the novel and film is recalcitrant, sneaky, and manipulative—a prankster, comedian, and ladies' man. In the TV series he retains many of these qualities but also becomes a humanitarian with the soul of a poet. Besides getting all the best punch lines, he also gets the best speeches, criticizing the hypocrisy of pompous officers, consoling wounded soldiers at their bedside, or waxing eloquent on any topic that comes along. One remarkable episode, appropriately titled "Hawkeye" (fourth season) is entirely a monologue. After suffering a concussion, Hawkeye is taken in by a Korean family who speaks no English. In order to keep himself awake, he talks aloud to himself and to the uncomprehending family, discoursing on the evils of war, the wonders of the anatomy, and other topics.

Obviously a character with so many admirable virtues could lead to superficiality, monotony, and sanctimony. Alan Alda sought to keep the character interesting by exploring his faults. In "Fallen Idol" (sixth season), Corporal Walter "Radar" O'Reilly is wounded during a trip to Seoul that Hawkeye encourages him to take. Hungover and guilt ridden, Hawkeye is unable to operate on Radar. When the recovering Radar expresses his disappointment, Hawkeye blows up at Radar, sick of the mantle of heroism he is expected to maintain. This episode furthers the growth of Radar's character as well.

The award-winning "Inga," written by Alda, shows Hawkeye reluctant to learn from a female surgeon who upstages him in the O.R. (This episode has an autobiographical element, for as a child Alda was cured of polio by a technique discovered by a woman doctor, who had also met with opposition when proposing her theories.) Later episodes go out of their way to dig up the dark side of Hawkeye. In "C*A*V*E" (seventh season) we discover that Hawkeye is claustrophobic, and in "Bless You, Hawkeye" (ninth season) an allergic reaction to wet clothing awakens Hawkeye's latent but bitter hatred for his best friend and cousin, who had nearly drowned him in a childhood prank. Finally, in the last episode, "Goodbye, Farewell, and Amen" (eleventh season), Hawkeye has a mental breakdown after suppressing a gruesome memory.

HOULIHAN

Margaret Houlihan develops in the opposite direction. Whereas Hawkeye begins as an almost ideal person and writers have to labor to furnish him with faults to create character conflict, Houlihan starts out with few likable qualities. She is an uptight, authoritarian, Regular Army warhorse; an amorous ally of Major Frank Burns; and a fink, always threatening to go over Henry's poor, befuddled head. Of course, there is a passionate side to Houlihan as well. She isn't called "Hotlips" for nothing and seems to have had affairs with various high-ranking officers. However, she soon evolves into one of the most interesting characters in television. The introduction of a fiancé, Colonel Donald Penobscot, contributes to Houlihan's growth as she experiences love, marriage, and divorce.

Houlihan's role as head nurse also provides some touching moments. A breakthrough comes in "The Nurses" (fifth season) when she first reveals her loneliness to her fellow nurses, and in "Temporary Duty" (sixth season) when an old friend from nursing school visits and reminds Houlihan of what a warm, fun-loving person she used to be. These episodes unpeel her camouflage toughness, exposing her more human side. A convergence of Hawkeye's and Houlihan's development occurs in the two-part "Comrade in Arms" (sixth season) when the romantic undercurrent between the two rises to the surface while they are stranded in a hut amid shelling. "Father's Day" (ninth season) introduces Houlihan's father, General "Howitzer" Houlihan, yielding insight into her childhood and motivations. Loretta Swit's performance of Houlihan as she breaks down, opens up, and flowers as a human being throughout the eleven seasons of *M*A*S*H* is one of the greatest achievements of the series.

The humanization of Houlihan reflected the show's tendency to move toward character-oriented stories, and this in turn eroded the irreverent tone of the early years. The show continued to expose the atrocities of war, the inanities of bureaucracy, and the corruption of authority, but it became difficult to sustain convincing characters to represent such evils, and Houlihan was the first to buckle. Frank's character was fundamentally limited and could not evolve in a way that would be both realistic and dramatically effective. The introduction of Houlihan's engagement in the fifth season was intended to develop her character and also put Frank in new, interesting situations (as when he went berserk and arrested an ox). However, this precipitated Frank's decline, and at the end of the fifth season, Linville quit, feeling that his character's dramatic possibilities had been exhausted.

NEW RIVALS, NEW FRIENDS, NEW DRAMATIC POSSIBILITIES

Frank was replaced by Major Charles Emerson Winchester III, a Boston blueblood and Harvard graduate. Intelligent, shrewd, and a formidable surgeon, Charles was a much-needed rival for Hawkeye and Captain B. J. Hunnicut. It had been too easy for them to pick on Frank, who was an incompetent doctor and a petty bigot with no redeeming qualities. Charles brought new dramatic possibilities just when the show might have gone stale. He helped keep the show interesting and funny for another two or three seasons. Writers now had the opportunity to concoct rhetorical, allusive speeches for someone besides Hawkeye. Charles's snobbery and egotism were overplayed in the first few seasons, but this gave him somewhere from which to fall. The humiliations Charles suffered were usually comical, but they could also be quite touching when the character was handled with subtlety and not treated as a mere stereotype of the snob.

Although the villains became less villainous, there was a compromise on the other side as well. When Hawkeye's barely distinguishable sidekick, the irreverent, philandering Trapper John McIntyre, left the show, he was replaced by Hunnicut, a straitlaced, devoted family man. The bumbling, beloved Henry was replaced by no-nonsense Colonel Sherman Potter, a veteran of World Wars I and II. Potter provided a medium between the irreverent doctors and their authoritarian opponents, Frank and Houlihan. Potter partially sympathized with Houlihan, and his presence contributed to her growth.

In each case, the new character—B. J., Potter, and Charles—was intended to contrast with the old character to keep the show interesting. In the long run, however, the cast became one big, happy family once the conflicts between these more moderate characters were exhausted. James H. Wittebols, in *Watching M*A*S*H, Watching America*, argues that these changes reflected the changing mores of the 1970s and 1980s as America moved from 1960s irreverence and hedonism to Reagan-era family values.

The departure of Radar, one of the most popular characters, was a grievous but necessary loss to the show. The teddy bear–toting company clerk, with his rural simplicity and naïveté, was so appealing that the writers did not bother to develop his character significantly until later in the series. The "Fallen Idol" episode discussed above was a major breakthrough, but Radar remained essentially a child. His departure in the two-part "Goodbye Radar" (eighth season) features fine performances and a sensitive script, with just the right balance of drama and subtlety. The story gains poignancy through allusions to Henry's departure five seasons before and is the most dramatic episode since Henry's death. Many viewers must have held their breath, fearing Radar would be killed on the way home, but the dreaded denouement reveals only Radar's teddy bear, left behind in Korea. Radar the person had grown up, and Radar the character had grown stale.

Radar's departure leads to Corporal Maxwell Klinger's promotion as company clerk. Klinger begins as a strictly comic character, providing laughs with his increasingly outrageous women's clothing. After seven seasons of wearing dresses, piling fruit upon his hat, and dressing up as the Statue of Liberty or as a big, blue bird with fuzzy pink feet, Klinger finally becomes a "serious" character and puts away his dresses. The advancement of Klinger and Father Francis Mulcahy as central characters with their own episodes was a sign that the show was running out of steam.

STORYTELLING TECHNIQUES

Sometimes the writers devised new storytelling techniques to alleviate the tedium. Gelbart had decided that each season should feature a few innovations. One of the first involves telling the story through a character's letter to his family, with amusing reminiscences to demonstrate the letter writer's point. This technique is illustrated in Hawkeye's "Dear Dad" episode (first season), followed by Radar's "Dear Ma," Potter's "Dear Mildred," and so forth. Eventually even guest characters such as Sidney Freedman ("Dear Sigmund") are given their turn, and Hawkeye racks up three additional "Dear Dads."

A more original experiment is seen in "The Interview" (fourth season), which features Clete Roberts interviewing the characters on their reactions to the war. Roberts, who was a correspondent in the Korean War, plays himself in this black-and-white episode. This technique is also repeated in the hour-long "Our Finest Hour" (seventh season). "Point of View" (seventh season) is filmed entirely from the point of view of a wounded soldier, from the battlefield to post-op to mess tent, sponge bath, and so on. "Life Time" (eighth season) is filmed in "real time," as a clock in the corner of the TV screen counts down the twenty minutes that the soldier has left until the crucial surgery is performed. Perhaps the most dramatic experiment is the surrealist "Dreams" (eighth season), written by Alda, which peers into the crew's troubled nightmares to expose their deepest fears.

THE LATER YEARS

Although the innovations kept coming, the stories and dialogue grew worse in later years. Episodes were built around trivial plots that would have been barely acceptable as subplots in earlier seasons. Certain tropes—the arrival of wounded just when the gang was having fun and forgetting their troubles, the silent fadeout in the O.R., the dramatic showdown with an unfeeling general—had become cliché. Pathos often sank to bathos or just plain schmaltz. A particularly embarrassing formula in later years was to fade out an episode with a sing-along, as when Potter begins singing "Oh My Darling Clementine" in the O.R. and is gradually joined by everyone else. Other songs recruited for this cheap emotional effect were "Keep the Home Fires Burning" and "Dona Nobis Pacem."

The creators wanted to go out with dignity while they were still on top, but they waited too long. Although the final episode had some fine moments, the show had become unpardonably self-absorbed and was painful to watch. Even the title, "Goodbye, Farewell, and Amen" was suggestive of emotional overindulgence.

But the decline in quality was not entirely due to increasing "seriousness," as is sometimes claimed. The infamous "Abyssinia, Henry" (third season), which reports the death of Henry, is one of the most shockingly dramatic episodes of any comedy and remains a milestone of television history. Grief-stricken viewers sent letters to the show expressing their outrage and indignation; people felt cheated that they had been made to care about a character who was so gratuitously "killed off" at the last minute. McClean Stevenson, who quit the show due to poor working conditions, believed at the time that the character was killed to prevent him from coming back to the show. However, the creators were actually making a radical statement about war that raised viewers' consciousness.

It is doubtful whether the writers of the later seasons could have made such a bold move when they were so immersed in the beauty, the fullness, the roundness of their beloved characters. The original plan to mingle actor and character was at first a fruitful technique that allowed the characters to grow, but it peaked about midway and then degenerated into the common Hollywood malady of narcissism. An episode from the final season, "Hey, Look Me Over," concerning a nurse named Kellye who felt she was being overlooked by Hawkeye, may have reflected an actress (also named Kellye!) who felt she was being overlooked by the producers. The episode was an unintentional parody of what the show had become: a feel-good group for the actors. The success of *M*A*S*H*—its believable, lifelike characters—had become its failure, and the show lingered on too long, like a dying relative on life support.

AFTER M*A*S*H

*M*A*S*H* was followed by a truly wretched sequel, *After M*A*S*H*, which insulted viewers with the grotesquely improbable reunion of Potter, Mulcahy, and Klinger in a stateside hospital. Another sequel of sorts was *Trapper John, M.D.* (1979–1986), which features a balding Trapper righting wrongs in the 1980s in an hour-long drama in the style of *Lou Grant* (another Gelbart show). This Trapper, played by Pernell Roberts, had little in common with the old one, other than his ratings-winning name. Meanwhile, Wayne Rogers, who had played Trapper on *M*A*S*H*, again played a funny doctor on the sitcom *House Calls* (1979–1982), a blatant *M*A*S*H* rip-off. But he was actually closer to the old Trapper than the *Trapper John, M.D.* character, and the show was funnier than later *M*A*S*H* episodes.

At its best, *M*A*S*H* managed to be both relevant in its day and enduring in its syndicated afterlife. The army setting, away from civilian fashions, prevented the show from becoming an eyesore to future viewers. Its 1950s setting prevented the writers from using topical jokes that would become dated—though there were many references to 1940s and 1950s film and radio that went over younger viewers' heads.

The show was not without its ideological anachronisms, however: in "George" (second season), Hawkeye, Trapper, and Henry (all the good guys) show sympathy toward a homosexual soldier whom Frank, predictably, wants to persecute. It seems unlikely that there would have been such liberal understanding toward homosexuality among three out of four doctors back in the Freudian 1950s. This episode might have been less glibly didactic and more dramatically challenging if Henry, Trapper, or Hawkeye had been homophobic rather than the ever-nasty Frank. After all, Hawkeye used the pejorative "fairy" in the first season when the film version still exerted its influence. But things had already changed by the third season.

Although *M*A*S*H* in retrospect seems more modern than its great 1970s rival, *All in the Family*, and has aged better, both shows drunk deep from the well of didacticism, offering liberal platitudes with heavy-handed poetic justice. Plot lines always steered primly toward the moral in twenty-two minutes flat. And this became the long-lasting legacy of these two pioneering shows—drama and didacticism. Every comedy since then would tackle racism, and you always knew who the racist would be; every comedy would have its gay tolerance episode, with an utterly uninteresting gay cousin or neighbor hastily invented for the occasion; every show would kill off, or at least endanger, some character to keep things interesting (as illustrated on *Happy Days* with Richie Cunningham's accident). Even 1990s kingpin *Roseanne* adhered to this hackneyed 1970s format, despite its claims of originality and artistry. Americans found no reprieve from the comedy/drama until the postmodern playfulness of *Seinfeld* and early episodes of *The Simpsons*. These shows' very refusal to be didactic was one of the major innovations in situation comedy since *M*A*S*H*.

Douglas Cooke

SEE ALSO: *Alda, Alan;* All in the Family*; Altman, Robert;* Happy Days*;* Roseanne*;* Seinfeld*;* The Simpsons*; Sitcom; Television; War Movies.*

BIBLIOGRAPHY

Diffrient, David Scott. *M*A*S*H.* Detroit, MI: Wayne State University Press, 2008.

DiMare, Philip C. *Movies in American History: An Encyclopedia.* Santa Barbara, CA: ABC-CLIO, 2011.

Reiss, David S. M*A*S*H: *The Exclusive, Inside Story of TV's Most Popular Show.* Indianapolis, IN: Bobbs-Merrill, 1980.

Wittebols, James H. *Watching* M*A*S*H, *Watching America: A Social History of the 1972–1983 Television Series.* Jefferson, NC: McFarland, 1998.

Mason, Jackie *(1936–)*

One of America's most popular and controversial stand-up comedians, Jackie Mason has entertained audiences on radio and television and in films and one-man shows on Broadway and in London's West End. He has enjoyed two careers, the first being greatly restricted in 1964 after an alleged obscene act on network television, and the second beginning with an award-winning Broadway show in 1987 and continuing, through many award-winning performances, for decades.

After working for several years in resorts in the Catskill Mountains and small nightclubs, Mason caught the eye of Ed Sullivan, who signed him to a $45,000, six-show contract for his network variety hour. In one of these appearances on October 18, 1964, the show was running late, and Sullivan, offstage, raised two fingers to try to speed up Mason's act. Onstage, Mason held up a finger and made jokes about Sullivan's gesture. Although Mason denied it, Sullivan thought it was *the* finger and canceled the comedian's contract. Although Mason claimed he was blackballed in the entertainment industry, he did appear on Sullivan's show in 1967, followed by a few appearances on variety shows hosted by the Smothers Brothers, Dean Martin, and Merv Griffin. After that, his television career ended until he appeared on *Dolly* in 1988 and on *Later with Bob Costas* in 1989. In 1989 he also starred in *Chicken Soup*, one of the highest-rated new sitcoms ever to be canceled in midseason.

Growing up in a family of rabbis on the Lower East Side of Manhattan, Mason was a cantor until the age of twenty-five, when he was ordained as a rabbi, following in the footsteps of four generations of his grandfathers. Three years later he quit the synagogue to become a comedian because, he said, "someone in the family had to make a living." From the beginning of his

Jackie Mason. *Jackie Mason performs his comedy routine on stage in 2009.* GEORGE PIMENTEL/CONTRIBUTOR/WIREIMAGE/GETTY IMAGES.

comic career, Mason's Yiddish accent and tortured New York sentence structure were controversial. Some in his audiences thought him "too Jewish"; others found his material anti-Semitic. The controversy continued, and in 1994 the NAACP (National Association for the Advancement of Colored People) condemned "a set of racist and stereotypical statements about African Americans" made by Mason on the network program *Pat Buchanan and Company*. Still, his comedy is most often applauded for its ironic insights about life's contradictions as well as for Mason's on-target barbs aimed at current follies in politics and life in general.

In 1986 Mason entered a new phase of his show-business career when he took his one-man show, *The World According to Me*, to Broadway. The playbill for the show stated that "Mr. Mason's material will be selected from the following subjects: U.S. Politics, World Affairs, Hollywood Producers & Celebrities, Dating, Communism, Sex Education, Psychiatry, Hookers, Health Hazards, the Army, the Weather, and, of course the ever popular Gentiles and Jews." The freewheeling formula worked well, and the comic continued to sell out theaters on Broadway and in London with such shows as *Jackie Mason: Brand New* (1990), *Jackie Mason: Politically Incorrect* (1994), *Love Thy Neighbor* (1996), *Much Ado about Everything* (1999), and *Prune Danish* (2002). In 2003 he tried a different format in which he hosted a musical comedy revue interspersed with his usual stand-up. Called *Jackie Mason's Laughing Room Only*, it received poor reviews and closed after just fourteen performances. After that he returned to his original format and success with *Freshly Squeezed* (2005), *The Ultimate Jew* (2008), and *Jackie Mason: No Holds Barred* (2009). As one London reviewer remarked, "One man in a black suit on a black stage with black scenery. When the man is Jackie Mason, sparks fly and the stars of the show quickly become Mason's personality, his ideas, and his ability to connect with an audience."

Mason has won numerous awards, including a Tony and an Emmy for his first Broadway show *The World According to Me* and Emmy Awards for the HBO special *Jackie Mason on Broadway* and for his work on *The Simpsons*. His Warner Brothers comedy album was nominated for a Grammy and became a smash hit, as did his autobiography, *Jackie, Oy!* (1988). In 1991 he received the highest honor bestowed by the Israeli government for his support during the Gulf War. He also received an honorary degree from the Oxford University Union, an honor shared with Mohandas K. Gandhi and U.S. presidents Jimmy Carter and John F. Kennedy.

Other books Mason has written include *How to Talk Jewish* (1991); *Jackie Mason & Raoul Felder's Survival Guide to New York* (1997); and, also with Raoul Felder, *Schmucks!: Our Favorite Fakes, Frauds, Lowlifes, Liars, the Armed and Dangerous, and Good Guys Gone Bad* (2007). After the publication of *Schmucks!*, Felder, who was chairman of the New York State Commission on Judicial Conduct, was asked to step down by Governor Eliot Spitzer because of comments in the book considered potentially offensive to certain ethnic groups. In 2010 Mason began a new phase of his career with films titled *One Angry Man* (2010) and *Jackie Goldberg, Private Dick* (2011).

Benjamin Griffith

SEE ALSO: *Broadway; Costas, Bob; Emmy Awards; Griffin, Merv; Gulf Wars; Martin, Dean; Parton, Dolly;* The Simpsons; *The Smothers Brothers; Sullivan, Ed; Television; Tony Awards.*

BIBLIOGRAPHY

Epstein, Lawrence J. *The Haunted Smile: The Story of Jewish Comedians in America.* New York: Public Affairs, 2001

Inman, David. *The TV Encyclopedia.* New York: Perigee, 1991.

Mason, Jackie. *Jackie Mason's America.* Secaucus, NJ: Stuart, 1983.

Mason, Jackie, and Ken Gross. *Jackie, Oy!* Boston: Little, Brown, 1988.

Mass Market Magazine Revolution

Before the nineteenth century, few Americans read newspapers or magazines or engaged in public entertainment. By 1900 these habits had changed, and a small but growing number of magazines had circulations in excess of half a million copies. Americans were becoming increasingly dependent upon these magazines to define important aspects of their lives.

There were many reasons for the transformation of American society from isolated regional communities into a single national culture. Significant among them was the emergence of national mass market magazines beginning in the 1890s. With titles such as *Munsey's*, *McClure's*, *Ladies' Home Journal*, and *Cosmopolitan*, these new magazines provided information on society, fashion, literature, entertainment, celebrities, sports, and current events. The mass market magazine revolution made possible the development of twentieth-century culture, from sound recordings to the rise of the Information Age.

BEFORE MASS CULTURE

For most of civilization, people depended upon each other for information and entertainment. Talking, gossiping, singing, storytelling, dancing, and playing homemade musical instruments were basic forms of amusement, combined with informal competitions such as athletic contests for males and domestic activities for females. Quieter pleasures such as walking, riding, boating, or skating were augmented by rougher pastimes such as gambling, drinking, or gaming. Even centuries after the invention of moveable printing type in 1453, the overwhelming majority of people still entertained themselves in local societies, within a few miles of their birthplaces. The only respites from such homemade amusements were visits by traveling professionals, musicians, jugglers, acrobats, exotic animal trainers, and wagon shows (the ancestor of the circus). Additional public entertainment came via civic and religious ceremonies, church activities, public lecturers, elections, court days, holidays, and similar events.

Printed "mass" communications such as books, newspapers, and magazines played relatively minor roles in most people's lives even in the early years of the United States. With the exception of the Bible, John Bunyan's *The Pilgrim's Progress*, and a handful of other texts, most books were discourses on religion and politics that were meant for only a few. There were ninety-two newspapers and seven magazines in 1790, all supported by small readerships in highly localized settings. The early Federalist Party attempted a national newspaper, the *Gazette of the United States*, but Thomas Jefferson's Anti-Federalists championed the Postal Act of 1792, which based postage rates on the distance a newspaper or magazine had to be delivered through the mail. The result discouraged the development of national publications well into the nineteenth century, except at subscription prices that only the upper class could afford. The Federalists were more successful in efforts to standardize American English. Federalist Noah Webster's dictionary, first published in 1784 and eventually selling more than sixty million copies, helped ensure that all educated Americans read and wrote the same language even if they did not communicate with each other.

COMING TOGETHER

The character of entertainment changed in the early nineteenth century, as people began to experience some of the characteristics of mass culture. For the first time, thousands who did not know each other came together to witness events such as the first major horse race in the United States, which attracted 100,000 spectators to a Long Island, New York, racetrack in 1823, or a well-publicized 10-mile human foot race at the same track in 1835, which attracted thousands of people. Boston's "Peace Jubilee" concert of 1869 featured an orchestra of five hundred, a chorus of 10,000, and an audience of 50,000 and helped define "classical" music. These events were not formally organized or regulated in the way that professional baseball would be after 1876. Instead, they were more like spectacles, emphasizing the extraordinary or the unique.

Showman Phineas T. Barnum's American Museum, which opened in New York in 1842, was the same kind of attraction, showcasing more than 600,000 exhibits and acts, from giants and white elephants to George Washington's nurse. The only unifying theme of Barnum's exhibits was their oddity, but they attracted thousands of paying customers each year and provided nearly everyone else in the country with something to talk about. Barnum also staged midcentury traveling exhibitions, such as midget Tom Thumb and singer Jenny Lind, who played to sold-out audiences in cities and towns across America, along with celebrity actors and actresses such as Edmund Kean, the Kembles, and the Booths.

Even during the age of Barnum, most books, newspapers, and magazines did not represent mass culture. Influential books and pamphlets such as *Uncle Tom's Cabin* had massive readerships but were few in number. Cheap books were available, including pirated novels by Charles Dickens and other European authors; popular "dime novels"; and romance stories by belles lettres authors such as Elizabeth Stuart Phelps, Lydia H. Sigourney, and Mrs. E. D. E. N. Southworth. These popular volumes sold thousands of copies, but their publishers lacked organizational and mass marketing techniques and often operated more for a love of books than for profit.

Penny newspapers appeared in New York, Philadelphia, and other cities, boasting unheard of circulations, but they still spoke mainly to their respective urban areas. A select few newspapers circulated more widely. So-called Family House magazines—*Harper's Monthly*, *Century*, *Scribner's*, and *Atlantic Monthly*—were produced by the major book publishing houses. These had many readers and reached their peak in influence between 1865 and 1893. However, their costs, twenty-five to thirty-five cents per issue, were prohibitive for anyone outside the upper class, and their "gospel of culture" mission to replace the waning influence of religion with high culture failed to capture the imagination of the middle class. A few women's magazines—*Delineator* and *Woman's Home Companion*—built up mass circulations after the Civil War, but they were specialized in their viewpoints, featured editorial content strongly influenced by advertisers, and were overlooked by many other advertisers and the rest of the magazine industry because women had not yet been recognized as a viable national mass market.

A CULTURAL SHIFT

The urbanized and suburbanized later-nineteenth-century America was the breeding ground for the magazine revolution and the first mass culture. Even though the percentage of urban residents did not surpass the percentage of people living in rural areas until 1910, American cities mushroomed during the second half of the nineteenth century. Most major cities doubled in size between 1865 and 1900—in fact, 100 U.S. communities doubled in the 1880s alone. As this happened, the walking cities of the early nineteenth century, such as New York City or Chicago, disappeared. No single resident could have a tangible grasp of all the precincts, processes, or citizens in such large cities. As the inner portions of cities filled with working-class inhabitants, a new American social class, the professional-managerial class, began to collect in homogeneous neighborhoods outside the centers of these metropolises. Professionals, physicians, managers, prosperous merchants, and other businesspeople were attracted to the modern comforts of the suburbs—such as large lots, good streets, quality schools, and public utilities—and they could afford the more expensive housing and transportation costs.

The new suburban homes reflected the growing status of the professional-managerial class, but they imposed previously unknown demands upon their occupants. Ownership was a new development for a population that had previously been urban renters. Beyond rudimentary concerns such as plumbing and heat, owners struggled to define what was appropriate and necessary for the proper exterior images of their homes. Individuality was prized, but exhibitionism was not, and a degree of uniformity came to be considered a virtue. Front yards, unknown in center cities, presented new and daunting decorative challenges. Interior housing spaces represented places to make statements to visitors while also preserving the individuality, utility, and privacy of their owners. Parlors, also known as best rooms or sitting rooms to Victorians, were especially important. Theologian Henry Ward Beecher's dictum that a house was "the measure of [a man's] social and domestic nature" was put to the test in the design and decoration of a parlor. Furnishings needed to display a family's tastes in design and art while simultaneously revealing its history through judicious display of portraits, photographs, and other personal mementos.

These new surroundings and the development of a unique social sphere for the professional-managerial class contributed to reconfigured standards of social decorum as well. For example, traditional Victorian society depended upon the strict ritual of calling cards—printed slips of paper that were used to express condolences, congratulations, friendship, courtship, and so on. By the 1880s the emerging professional-managerial class began to view such scripted behaviors as confining and unnecessary—informality became more socially acceptable.

Social clubs helped ease the process of interaction, but home ownership in the suburbs was often enough to signal respect and suitability to neighbors. In turn, the character of families changed. High school and college education became more common, and family members were encouraged to express their own interests and tastes in socializing, reducing the once-strong influence of the nuclear family upon its individual members. Even children were allowed to develop their own spheres of friends, activities, and tastes.

MUNSEY'S SPARKS THE REVOLUTION

All of these factors contributed to a new need for ready answers to the challenges of everyday life. The mass market magazine revolution did not come about to serve a previously unknown type of magazine reader, for the professional-managerial class already existed in American society. Instead, the demise of the closely monitored circles of local acquaintances that had traditionally provided information to the professional-managerial class left a void that was filled by the mass market magazines, the so-called educators of the late-nineteenth-century's "whirlpool of real life," as it was described by *Cosmopolitan*'s John Brisben Walker.

Munsey's Magazine was the first and most popular of the mass magazines. Founded in New York City in 1889 by Frank Munsey—a Maine farm boy who departed Philadelphia's Centennial World's Fair in 1876 determined to possess his own version of a high-speed rotary printing press that he had seen there—*Munsey's Magazine* lost money for years before, in 1893, it dropped its cover price from twenty-five to ten cents or $1 per annual subscription. *Munsey's* circulation zoomed from 40,000 before the price change to 500,000 in 1895 and 700,000 in 1897. Combined with three of his other titles, Munsey sold more than two million magazines in March 1906, an unthinkable feat only a few years earlier.

Munsey's was joined in the magazine price war by Samuel S. McClure. An Irish immigrant who once taught the social gospel, *McClure's* was founded in 1893 and grew to a circulation of 60,000 by 1894 with a cover price of fifteen cents. The circulation climbed to 250,000 by 1895 following a price cut to a dime. McClure boasted the most expensive advertising rates in America, charging as much as $400 for a single-page display ad in 1905. One issue that year had 200 pages of advertising and a circulation of 450,000. It was said that *McClure's* carried more advertising than any other magazine in the world.

Munsey's and *McClure's* were challenged by John Brisben Walker's *Cosmopolitan*. Walker was a speculator and businessman who applied aggressive techniques to the then-genteel industry of magazines. In 1891, to promote his newly purchased magazine, Walker hired a railroad coach filled with subscription canvassers and had it transported across different parts of the country. He also offered college scholarships to successful *Cosmopolitan* salespeople. Walker broke the fifteen-cents-per-copy barrier in 1893, dropping his price to twelve and a half cents in 1893, only to be eclipsed by Munsey. *Cosmopolitan* rivaled *McClure's* in circulation but never approached that of *Munsey's*, even after the magazine was purchased by William Randolph Hearst in 1905.

Founded in 1883, *Ladies' Home Journal* reached a circulation of more than one and a half million by the turn of the twentieth century and was the first to cut its price to ten cents. Edited for thirty years by Edward Bok, a Dutch literary writer who became the highest-paid editor of the day, the *Journal* called itself the "Bible of the American home," a claim journalist Mark Sullivan said had "a measure of allegorical truth."

A LITTLE BIT OF EVERYTHING

The mass market magazines were characterized by their eclectic content, living up to the literal definition of the word *magazine* as a storehouse of odd and notable information. They all had a great number of illustrations. *Munsey's* specialized in halftone photo engravings, the first real published pictures that many readers had ever seen. Paging through an issue provided the eye with a blur of images that had not existed in earlier magazines. *Munsey's* had topical separations called "departments"—from "Artists and Their Works" (which, for a time, featured reproductions of classical nude paintings) and "In the Public Eye" (a gossipy column on celebrities) to "Storiettes" (brief fiction) and sections on music, poetry, literature, and theater. *Cosmopolitan* had similar cultural departments, as well as features on science and England. *Ladies' Home Journal* had so many departments that some appeared together on the same page.

McClure's, on the other hand, did not have departments—instead, it organized its stories by theme or topic depending on the issue. Advertisements filled each mass market magazine with news of brand-name goods and services that often became like part of the family. For the first time, ads went beyond simple product announcements to make emotional pitches toward health, social status, and even sexuality. As a result, the mass market magazines provided domestic, decorating, and cultural information for women; fashion and sporting news for teenagers; economic and current events information for men; and consumption information that promised to help all the family members buy the "right" products and succeed within their individual and collective spheres of life.

However, mass market magazines did not offer something for everyone. The working class and poor were conspicuously absent from the magazines' portrayal of "real life," except as objects of moral reform who were waiting to be civilized and uplifted by their social betters. They would have to wait for movies and other publications such as confession magazines to experience mass culture. The state of race relations, especially the debased social status of African Americans living under Jim Crow racism, was ignored by the mass market magazines. Editors did not want to cloud the sunny optimism of early twentieth-century whites—who had a "commonsense" assumption of racial supremacy—because it would be disruptive to the commercial messages of their magazines. Women represented a majority of the readership, but they were trivialized, dismissed, and stigmatized in the magazines, especially the New Woman movement of the late nineteenth century. Celebrities were excused, as were selected high-achieving women, but the remainder of females were permitted only traditional social roles in articles and advertisements.

THE MUCKRAKERS

Despite such omissions, *McClure's*, *Cosmopolitan*, and *Ladies' Home Journal* did engage in what was initially called "civic consciousness" but later labeled "muckraking." Beginning in 1893, the same year cover prices were dropped to ten cents, *McClure's* and *Cosmopolitan* printed accounts of conditions among working women and the urban poor and the efforts to revamp the nation's educational system. From that beginning, *McClure's* came to epitomize muckraking in the nation's consciousness, especially in seminal series such as Lincoln Steffen's "Shame of the Cities," Ida M. Tarbell's "The History of the Standard Oil Company," and Ray Stannard Baker's anti-union "The Right to Work," all published after 1900. McClure was not a radical reformer and preferred a middle-of-the-road approach—he refrained from direct assaults against big businesses and encouraged his writers to support their accusations with documented facts.

In contrast, *Cosmopolitan* took a more sensationalistic approach to its muckraking, especially after the magazine was purchased by Hearst in 1905. Socialists Jack London, Upton Sinclair, and Charles Edward Russell wrote extensively for *Cosmopolitan*. David Graham Phillips's "The Treason of the Senate," which was published in *Cosmopolitan* in 1906, provoked an angry President Theodore Roosevelt to apply the term *muck raker* to mass market magazines. *Ladies' Home Journal* was ahead of the better-known muckraking titles. It stopped accepting patent medicine advertisements in 1892, holding that many of the medicines were harmful to their female and child readers. The magazine attacked the entire patent medicine industry in 1904 and 1905, which led to the passage of the first federal Food and Drug Act in 1906. It also published a seminal article on venereal disease in 1908 that encouraged public discussion on a previously forbidden subject. Although *Munsey's* almost never muckraked, it maintained high levels of circulation and profitability.

Muckraking diminished in popularity after 1906, and most of the mass market magazines either changed their editorial focus (usually toward fiction) or perished (as *McClure's* and *Munsey's* did) before 1930. However, mass culture continued to grow in scope and influence through other magazines, as well as through motion pictures, radio, paperback novels, television, national newspapers, cable and satellite television, and the Internet. The advent of the Information Age in the last part of the twentieth century, with its emphasis on knowledge as a salable commodity, became only the most recent manifestation of the unquenchable demand for information ignited by the mass market magazine revolution. Mass culture and society have become inseparable, as historian Richard Ohmann observes in his 1996 book, *Selling Culture: Magazines, Markets, and Class at the Turn of the Century*: "Asking whether we want the mass culture we have is almost the same as asking whether we like the social relations of advanced capitalist society."

Richard Digby-Junger

SEE ALSO: *Baker, Ray Stannard; Bok, Edward; Confession Magazines;* Cosmopolitan*; Dime Novels; Hearst, William Randolph; London, Jack; Muckraking;* Munsey's Magazine*; Sinclair, Upton; Steffens, Lincoln; Suburbia; Tarbell, Ida.*

BIBLIOGRAPHY

Bennion, Sherilyn Cox. "Reform Agitation in the American Periodical Press, 1920–29." *Journalism Quarterly* 48, no. 4 (1971): 645–651.

Gans, Herbert J. *Popular Culture and High Culture: An Analysis and Evaluation of Taste.* New York: Basic Books, 1974, 67–93.

Gordon, Lynn D. "The Gibson Girl Goes to College: Popular Culture and Women's Higher Education in the Progressive Era, 1890–1920." *American Quarterly* 39, no. 2 (1987): 211–230.

Ohmann, Richard. *Selling Culture: Magazines, Markets, and Class at the Turn of the Century.* London, Verso, 1996.

Radway, Janice A. *A Feeling for Books: The Book-of-the-Month Club, Literary Taste, and Middle-Class Desire.* Chapel Hill: University of North Carolina Press, 1997.

Ryan, Susan M. "Acquiring Minds: Commodified Knowledge and the Positioning of the Reader in *McClure's Magazine*, 1893–1903." *Prospects* 22 (1997): 211–238.

Scanlon, Jennifer. *Inarticulate Longings: The* Ladies' Home Journal*, Gender, and the Promises of Consumer Culture.* New York: Routledge, 1995.

Schneirov, Matthew. *The Dream of a New Social Order: Popular Magazines in America, 1893–1914.* New York: Columbia University Press, 1994.

Scholnick, Robert J. "The *Galaxy* and American Democratic Culture, 1866–1878." *Journal of American Studies* 16, no. 1 (1982): 69–80.

Smith, James Steel. "America's Magazine Missionaries of Culture." *Journalism Quarterly* 43, no. 3 (1966): 449–458.

Taylor, Steve. *100 Years of Magazine Covers.* London: Black Dog Publishing Limited, 2006.

Mass Murders

SEE: *Serial Killers.*

The Masses

The *Masses* was a radical magazine published in New York between 1911 and 1917. Its contributors primarily were Greenwich Village intellectuals and artists who sought to develop a culturally based radicalism that emphasized free expression and modernistic styles of art and literature. Edited by Max Eastman during its heyday, the circular met its demise after only six years, having been deprived of access to the mails under the Espionage Act for its antiwar position. The *New Masses* (1926–1947), under the editorship of Mike Gold, developed a more political tone and became more closely tied to the Communist Party. Continuing as *Masses & Mainstream* until 1956, the magazine published writings by several well-known literary figures, such as poet Langston Hughes and novelists Theodore Dreiser and Erskine Caldwell.

Jeffrey W. Coker

SEE ALSO: *Caldwell, Erskine; Communism; Dreiser, Theodore; Greenwich Village; Hughes, Langston; Modernism; World War I.*

BIBLIOGRAPHY

North, Joseph, ed. *The "New Masses": An Anthology of the Rebel Thirties.* New York: International Publishers, 1969.

O'Neill, William, ed. *Echoes of Revolt: "The Masses, " 1911–1917.* Chicago: Ivan R. Dee, 1989.

Zurier, Rebecca. *Art for "The Masses": A Radical Magazine and Its Graphics, 1911–1917.* Philadelphia: Temple University Press, 1988.

Masterpiece Theatre

Masterpiece Theatre, rebranded as *Masterpiece* in 2008, has become synonymous with high-quality television since it began showcasing literary adaptations and biography on the Public Broadcasting Service (PBS) on January 10, 1971. The program has imported British television serials from the outset, more often than not based on British novels that unfold against an English backdrop. For twenty-two years, *Masterpiece Theatre* was hosted by Englishman Alistair Cooke on a set recalling a posh London club. Cooke's refined Oxbridge accent and the show's upscale British fare have been lovingly parodied by *Sesame Street* ("Monsterpiece Theatre" with Alistair Cookie Monster) and *Saturday Night Live* (Dan Aykroyd as snobbish host Leonard Pinth-Garnell).

Masterpiece Theatre was the brainchild of Boston's public television station, WGBH, and was inspired by the success of *The Forsythe Saga*, a twenty-six-episode British television adaptation of John Galsworthy's Edwardian novels shown on PBS in 1969. It was then made possible by financial support from the Mobil Corporation. The first season established the literary emphasis of the show, with serials based on Thomas Hardy's *Jude the Obscure*, Honoré de Balzac's *Père Goriot*, and Fyodor Dostoyevsky's *The Possessed*. The first season likewise presaged the show's Anglophile aspect via such serials as *The First Churchills*, *The Six Wives of Henry VIII*, and *Elizabeth R*. All of the serials aired during the first season were produced by the British Broadcasting Corporation (BBC).

In its original conception *Masterpiece Theatre* was not meant to be a U.S. clearinghouse for British television. Christopher Sarson, the first executive producer, planned for a transition after three years. "The huge disappointment to me is that it didn't turn to American serial dramas," he stated in Terrence O'Flaherty's twenty-fifth-anniversary volume. Lack of finances, however, engendered a reliance on British imports and consequently exposed U.S. audiences to programming unlike typical network products. Only in 1998—more than two decades behind schedule—did PBS announce plans to produce original U.S. content beginning in 1999, complementing its recycled British products under the banner of *Mobil Masterpiece Theatre's American Collection*.

Masterpiece Theatre has consistently attracted older, college-educated viewers and is vaunted by critics as prestigious, quality television. Sales for books adapted on *Masterpiece Theatre* inevitably swell, and the show has scored notable successes. The chronicles of the Bellamy family and their servants throughout the Edwardian era ensured the long-term existence of *Masterpiece Theatre*; sixty-eight episodes of *Upstairs, Downstairs* were broadcast between 1974 and 1977, regularly attracting a worldwide audience of approximately one billion people. *I, Claudius*, a thirteen-episode saga depicting the lives of four Roman emperors, subsequently riveted large audiences during 1977 and was recognized as a television classic. In 1984 and 1985 the fourteen episodes of *The Jewel in the Crown* transported a mass viewership back to colonial India with a hefty budget adapting Paul Scott's tetralogy, *The Raj Quartet*.

In 2008 *Masterpiece Theatre* became *Masterpiece* and spun off into three separate series: *Masterpiece Contemporary*, *Masterpiece Mystery!*, and *Masterpiece Classic*. A modern-day reboot of the world's most famous detective, Sherlock Holmes, was a notable success for *Masterpiece Mystery!* in 2010, whereas 2011 proved to be a banner year for *Masterpiece Classic*, with the first season of the acclaimed hit *Downton Abbey* and BBC Wales' miniseries continuation of *Upstairs, Downstairs*. The Masterpiece imprimatur remains a bulwark of quality television that attracts both discerning viewers and critical acclaim.

Neal Baker

SEE ALSO: *Aykroyd, Dan; Leisure Time; Public Television (PBS);* Saturday Night Live*;* Sesame Street*; Television;* Upstairs, Downstairs.

BIBLIOGRAPHY

Cooke, Alistair. *Masterpieces: A Decade of "Masterpiece Theatre."* New York: Knopf, 1981.

Jarvik, Laurence A. *"Masterpiece Theatre" and the Politics of Quality*. Lanham, MD: Scarecrow Press, 1998.

O'Flaherty, Terrence. *"Masterpiece Theatre": A Celebration of 25 Years of Outstanding Television*. San Francisco: KQED Books, 1996.

Treble, Patricia. "Intelligent Viewers Have Spoken." *Maclean's*, July 28, 2011.

Masters and Johnson

The research team of obstetrician and gynecologist William Masters (1915–2001) and psychologist and sex therapist Virginia Johnson (1925–) pioneered the study of human sexual response. The duo's research helped debunk myths concerning male and female sexual performance, redefine society's definition of "normal" sexual behavior, change both male and female expectations for sexual performance and satisfaction, spark the development of the sex therapy profession, and coin much of the descriptive language used in modern discussions of sexual behavior and response. Masters and Johnson also pioneered the use of direct observation as a technique for studying sexual behavior.

ALTERING ATTITUDES ABOUT SEX

Masters and Johnson's discoveries led to numerous changes in attitudes about sex. For example, their research focused attention on vaginal lubrication as a source of pleasure in intercourse and oral-genital activity, pinpointed the source of that lubrication, and identified its role in reproduction. As couples became more concerned with foreplay activities that produce vaginal lubrication, sex play became more acceptable. Because of the team's determination that female orgasms resulting from nonintercourse stimulation are more intense than those from intercourse, many females were encouraged to explore the pleasures of masturbation, oral-genital stimulation, sexual touch, and the use of mechanical devices such as vibrators. Masters and Johnson's findings also increased emphasis on tactile exploration of the entire body as a sexual activity, helped women understand and appreciate their capabilities in bed, and assisted both men and women in understanding the sexual response cycle and the control they each have over it.

Much of what Masters and Johnson concluded contradicted the prevailing myths concerning pregnancy, breastfeeding, premature ejaculation, homosexual behavior, and numerous other social and cultural impositions associated with sexual dysfunction. Their research helped trigger the sexual revolution of the 1960s and 1970s and significantly altered the relationship between men and women. These changes quickly found their way into literature, film, and television; plot themes now emphasized increased experimentation in sexual behavior, frank discussion and depiction of sexual dysfunction, and the quest for female sexual satisfaction.

Because of Masters and Johnson's research, sex therapy techniques were revolutionized. The team's emphasis on tactile exploration led to the use of assigned "homework," or sexual behavior exercises, in sex therapy that first concentrated on touching experiences (sensate focus), followed by genital exploration (the sexological exam). According to Masters and Johnson, sexual dysfunction is more the result of social and cultural taboos than physical problems; consequently, the breakdown of these taboos was encouraged.

In addition, the team's discoveries concerning multiple orgasms and orgasms from nonintercourse stimulation hastened the development of the sexual aids and "sex toys" industries. Masters and Johnson's four-phase response cycle provided focus points for evaluating sexual response and timing the application of therapeutic efforts, and it gave couples a way to evaluate their own sexual responses. As a result of the team's research, a variety of sex therapies were developed to reduce sexual dysfunction, including squeeze techniques to prevent premature ejaculation and digital insertion exercises to reduce vaginismus (involuntary muscle contractions that make coital penetration difficult and painful).

REVOLUTIONARY RESEARCH

In their most acclaimed piece of work, Masters and Johnson studied 382 college women and 312 college men in more than 10,000 completed sexual response cycles, which provided the material for *Human Sexual Response* (1966). They recorded responses in a variety of scenarios, including masturbation, coitus with a partner, artificial coitus, and breast stimulation. Included in the research were sixty-one females ages forty-one to seventy-eight, making it the first study of sexual response in menopausal and postmenopausal women.

Other research by the team included a study of sexual response in male and female prostitutes, completed before the work was done for *Human Sexual Response*; a study of the rationale, methods, and success of various treatments for sexual problems, published as *Human Sexual Inadequacy* (1970); and a fifteen-year study of homosexual behavior, which compared sexual responses between homosexual and heterosexual subjects and evaluated treatment strategies for improving homosexual sexual performance or reducing homosexual orientation, published as *Homosexuality in Perspective* (1979).

Instead of relying on questionnaires, surveys, and interviews, as most researchers had done to gather data on sexual behavior, Masters and Johnson used direct observation in a laboratory setting to produce the findings in *Human Sexual Response*. In addition to observation to chart changes in the

Masters and Johnson. *The findings of research team of William Masters, left, and Virginia Johnson debunked myths and broadened the definition of "normal" sexual behavior in a way that greatly impacted the modern view of human sexuality.* JOHN CHIASSON/CONTRIBUTORGETTY IMAGES NEWS/GETTY IMAGES.

primary and secondary sex organs, they used photographic equipment and physiological response instruments to record muscular and vascular changes throughout the body during sexual arousal and sexual release, as well as an ingenious phallus-shaped artificial coition machine that photographed changes in the vagina and lower portions of the uterus during artificial coitus. Many of the same research methods were used in their 1979 study of homosexual behavior and response.

CRITICS CHIME IN

Masters and Johnson's research methods and findings have been scrutinized by social scientists. Critics of the *Human Sexual Response* study contest the validity of placing and observing subjects in a laboratory setting, and they also cite a demographic bias in the research, noting that most subjects were white, middle class, and of above-average intelligence. Masters and Johnson's 1970 study of treatment strategies for sexual dysfunction is criticized for a variety of problems in methodology, inadequate measurable definitions for many of the variables in the study, a low response rate in follow-up studies, and the inability of subsequent research teams to replicate the findings. The team's 1979 study of homosexuality is criticized for methodological and definition problems, the choice of research subjects, the laboratory research setting, and differences in interpretation of the findings. Critics claim some of the 1979 subjects were actually bisexual or heterosexuals engaged in homosexual behavior due to temporary sexual dysfunction.

SEX WILL NEVER BE THE SAME

Despite these criticisms, Masters and Johnson made several breakthrough discoveries, including identifying the source of and process for vaginal lubrication and identifying myotonia (increased muscle tension and spasms in various parts of the body) during the sexual response cycle. They also provided evidence that whereas a male's emission phase of arousal cannot be interrupted once it has started, a female's orgasm can be constrained, interrupted, delayed, and postponed by various psychosensory stimuli. Through experimentation, the team additionally determined that there is no difference in sexual response or sensitivity between circumcised and uncircumcised males.

The list of Masters and Johnson's breakthroughs does not end there. The team determined that female orgasms resulting from nonintercourse sexual stimulation are more locally intense and less diffused than those that come from intercourse, and they also found that the female multiple orgasm is common, especially with nonintercourse actions such as breast stimulation. Females, the team discovered, experience increased sexual desire in latter phases of pregnancy, and coital activity during pregnancy is not harmful. After childbirth, breastfeeding speeds the return of sexual desire in mothers. Masters and Johnson's also noted that postmenopausal women experience the same sexual response cycle as younger women, though it is less intense.

Masters and Johnson's description of the four phases in the sexual response pattern became the model for many forms of sex therapy. Those four phases are: excitement (increased muscle tension and tissue engorgement throughout the body), plateau (sustained excitement leading to the orgasmic platform), orgasm (release), and resolution followed by a refractory period (recovery) in the male cycle. Masters and Johnson formed the Reproduction Biology Center and later the Masters and Johnson Institute in St. Louis, Missouri.

Gordon Neal Diem

SEE ALSO: The Joy of Sex*; Sexual Revolution.*

BIBLIOGRAPHY

Belliveau, Fared, and Lin Richter. *Understanding Human Sexual Inadequacy*. New York: Bantam Books, 1980.

Brecher, Edward. *The Sex Researchers*. San Francisco: Specific Press, 1979.

Bullough, Vern L., ed. *The Frontiers of Sex Research*. Buffalo, NY: Prometheus Books, 1979.

Masters, William H., and Virginia E. Johnson. *Human Sexual Response*. Boston: Little, Brown, 1966.

Masters, William H., and Virginia E. Johnson. *Human Sexual Inadequacy*. Boston: Little, Brown, 1970.

Masters, William H., and Virginia E. Johnson. *The Pleasure Bond: A New Look at Sexuality and Commitment*. New York: Bantam, 1976.

Masters, William H., and Virginia E. Johnson. *Homosexuality in Perspective*. Boston: Little, Brown, 1979.

Masters, William; Virginia Johnson; and Robert Kolodny, eds. *Ethical Issues in Sex Therapy and Research*. Boston: Little, Brown, 1980.

Parker, Richard, and John Gagnon, eds. *Conceiving Sexuality: Approaches to Sex Research in a Postmodern World*. New York: Routledge, 1995.

Zilbergeld, Bernie, and Michael Evans. "The Inadequacy of Masters and Johnson." *Psychology Today*, August 1980, 29–43.

The Masters Golf Tournament

Founded by famed golfer Bobby Jones and his friend Clifford Roberts in 1934, the Masters Golf Tournament has become one of the PGA (Professional Golfers' Association) Tour's four major competitions. It is held in Georgia at the Augusta National Golf Club course, which Jones and Roberts designed to be pleasurable and challenging for both the average and the champion golfer. Since 1949 the winner of the event has received a green jacket, which has since become one of the best-known and respected "trophies" in golf. Three-time Masters winner Gary Player has described the significance of the jacket:

> That green jacket stands for a lot more than just winning the Masters. It stands for a gentleman like Bobby Jones and his legacy to the game. It stands for a man like Clifford Roberts, who gave his heart and soul to Augusta National and the tournament itself. It stands for a great golf tournament, it stands for the greatest golf course in the world, and it stands for great men and great achievements. The Masters jacket epitomizes perfection in golf.

Jack Nicklaus has been awarded the green jacket more times than any other golfer, winning six Masters Tournaments between 1963 and 1986—the last when he was forty-six years old. Spaniard Severiano Ballesteros was the youngest champion, winning in 1980 at age twenty-three, until twenty-one-year-old Tiger Woods shattered Ballesteros's record in 1997. Woods also set the tournament record that year with a score of 270 (eighteen under par) while tying six other records, including the largest margin of victory: twelve strokes. In the first decade of the twenty-first century, Woods nabbed the green jackets three more times—in 2001, 2002, and 2005. Perennial fan favorite Phil Mickelson won his first major at Augusta in 2004; he went on to repeat in 2006 and 2010.

D. Byron Painter

SEE ALSO: *Golf; Jones, Bobby; Nicklaus, Jack; Sports Heroes; Woods, Tiger.*

BIBLIOGRAPHY

Eubanks, Steve. *Augusta: A Revealing Look inside America's Most Intriguing Golf Club.* New York: Broadway Books, 1997.

Green, Ron, Sr. *The Masters: 101 Reasons to Love Golf's Greatest Tournament.* New York: Stewart, Tabori & Chang, 2008.

Official Site of the Masters Tournament. Accessed February 27, 2012. Available from http://www.masters.com

Owen, David. *The Making of the Masters: Clifford Roberts, Augusta National, and Golf's Most Prestigious Tournament.* New York: Simon & Schuster, 1999.

Palmer, Arnold. "Augusta Then and Now." *Golf Magazine,* April 1998, 84–88.

Sampson, Curt. *The Masters: Golf, Money, and Power in Augusta, Georgia.* New York: Villard Books, 1998.

Mathers, Marshall

SEE: *Eminem.*

Mathis, Johnny *(1935–)*

Blessed with a superior tenor voice, Johnny Mathis has made a career out of caressing romantic ballads with magical and vital qualities. An accomplished and trained musician with credentials in opera and jazz, Mathis reigns as a true artist. He has earned numerous distinctions in nearly six decades as a professional musician, including being one of the best-selling recording artists of all time. His 1958 album, *Johnny's Greatest Hits,* remained on the Billboard pop album chart for an astounding 490 weeks. This was the first time the term *greatest hits* was used in an album title, and it is now employed throughout the industry. All told, he has placed more than sixty entries onto the pop album chart.

Mathis was born September 30, 1935, in Gilmer, Texas, and was raised in San Francisco. His father, Clem Mathis, had worked briefly as a vaudeville performer, playing piano and singing back in Texas. When Mathis was eight, his father bought an upright piano and taught his son many songs and routines. Mathis also sang in the church choir and at school functions and community events, winning a local amateur contest at age fourteen. He studied with Connie Cox, a music teacher based in Oakland, California, who trained him in opera.

Music was not Mathis's only talent. He was also an exceptional student, holding the offices of student body president at Roosevelt Junior High School and treasurer at George Washington High School. In addition, he was a high school and college athlete in track and field and basketball. Mathis passed on the chance to try out for the 1956 U.S. Olympic team in the high jump, instead choosing a musical career.

While a student at San Francisco State College, Mathis heard famous jazz musicians at the renowned Blackhawk nightclub in San Francisco. He began singing in local nightspots with a sextet led by Virgil Gonsalves, a local baritone saxophone player and fellow student. At a performance with Gonsalves's sextet at the Blackhawk, Mathis attracted the attention of the club's co-owner, Helen Noga, who was so impressed that she was determined to make him a success. George Avakian, a well-known jazz producer, discovered Mathis in 1955 and convinced Columbia Records to sign him. Mathis went to New York and performed at the Village Vanguard and the Blue Angel.

Mathis's first album for Columbia, *Johnny Mathis* (1956), featured jazz arranger Gil Evans and pianist John Lewis of the Modern Jazz Quartet. Containing jazz standards such as "Angel Eyes" and "Easy to Love," it did not click commercially. After Columbia teamed Mathis with Mitch Miller, who wisely steered him toward singing romantic ballads, his career as a pop singer was secured. Mathis released his first big hit, "Wonderful!

Johnny Mathis. *Johnny Mathis, known for a string of hit romantic ballads in the 1950s and 1960s, performs in 2011.* STEVE THORNE/ CONTRIBUTOR/REDFERNS/GETTY IMAGES.

Wonderful!" in 1957, followed by "It's Not for Me to Say" and the romantic "Chances Are." In 1959 he recorded "Misty," his signature song, and quickly became a major concert attraction and mainstay on television shows. His film credits during this period included singing the title song for *Lizzie* (1957) and *A Certain Smile* (1958). In 1964 Mathis launched two companies: Jon Mat to produce his records and Rojon Productions to handle his concert, theater, club, and television appearances.

Mathis's music had been marketed primarily to a white audience, although "Misty" peaked at number ten on the Billboard R&B singles chart. In 1978 his duet with Deniece Williams, "Too Much, Too Little, Too Late," charted at number one on both the R&B and pop charts, cementing his popularity with black listeners. Mathis has recorded numerous other duets, including with Lena Horne, Dionne Warwick, Gladys Knight, Patti Austin, and Take 6. He has been open to a number of diverse album projects, including *Olé* (1965), a Latin American–flavored outing with songs in Portuguese and Spanish, as well as *Johnny Mathis Sings the Music of Bacharach & Kaempfert* (1970). He has also recorded albums of music by Michel Legrand and Duke Ellington, and in 2010 he ventured into country and western with *Let It Be Me: Mathis in Nashville.*

As a testament to his influence, three of his songs ("It's Not for Me to Say," "Misty," and "Chances Are") have been inducted into the Grammy Hall of Fame, and the National Academy of Recording Arts and Sciences honored him with a Lifetime Achievement Award in 2003. Mathis's resonant tenor continues to command the attention and admiration of both fans and critics. Since his recording career began in 1956, he has sold more than 350 million records, and he remains an international superstar who has performed throughout the world. When the jazz producer George Avakian first heard Mathis, he sent a telegram to Columbia Records, stating, "Have found phenomenal nineteen-year-old boy who could go all the way." Mathis has indeed gone all the way, carving out a unique niche in popular music with a distinct style and voice.

Willie Collins

SEE ALSO: *Country Music; Ellington, Duke; Grammy Awards; Horne, Lena; Jazz; Pop Music; Rhythm and Blues.*

BIBLIOGRAPHY

Jasper, Tony. *The Authorised Biography of Johnny Mathis.* London: W. H. Allen, 1983.

LaBlanc, Michael, ed. *Contemporary Musicians: Profiles of the People in Music.* Detroit, MI: Gale Research, 1990.

Larkin, Colin. *Guinness Encyclopedia of Popular Music.* Middlesex, UK: Guinness Publishing, 1995.

The Matrix

The Matrix is a science fiction franchise composed of three feature films (*The Matrix*, 1999; *The Matrix Reloaded*, 2003; *The Matrix Revolutions*, 2003), a collection of short animated films (*The Animatrix*, 2003), several video games, and a series of comic books. There is also an extensive assortment of unofficial books devoted to analysis and interpretation of the Matrix series, including its philosophical and religious dimensions, science fiction associations, and artistic or intellectual influences. The original film introduced innovative cinematic techniques and established a fictional universe that has become an enduring part of popular culture.

In the Matrix universe, the year is approximately 2199, and sentient machines have taken over Earth. They draw bioelectric energy from large numbers of human beings, whose bodies are maintained in liquid-filled pods while their brains experience a virtual reality simulation ("the Matrix") that looks and feels like urban life in 1999. However, some humans have managed to elude the Matrix and operate in the real world, helping imprisoned humans wake up from the virtual simulation and escape to a real-life refuge called Zion.

The film trilogy presents a story arc organized around several characters: Neo, who lives inside the Matrix as a computer programmer and underground hacker; Morpheus, a leader of the free humans; Trinity, a female hacker who has escaped from the Matrix; and "Agent Smith," an artificial intelligence that works inside the Matrix to disable elements causing instability. Smith and other agents appear within the Matrix as real people, but they can occupy the forms of human characters and defy the ordinary rules (such as time and gravity) of material reality. Other entities, such as the Oracle and the Architect—

The Matrix. *The success of* The Matrix *in 1999 spawned two popular sequels as well as a comic-book series.* WARNER BROS/THE KOBAL COLLECTION.

who represent mysterious forces related to the mathematical foundations of the Matrix—become important players as the story unfolds over all three films.

In the first film, Neo leaves the Matrix and learns about its true nature, then rescues a captured Morpheus; gets killed by Agent Smith; and is revived by Trinity, who has fallen in love with him. In the end he is back in the Matrix, but he has acquired an ability to manipulate the conditions there and dedicates himself to liberating other humans confined to the Matrix. The second and third films, which were released just a few months apart, delve into the backgrounds and deeper meanings of the Matrix universe, introducing a number of new elements. After a series of complex interactions between the machines and the humans, the trilogy ends somewhat ambiguously. Neo, who has been revealed as "The One" who is destined to restore order, sacrifices himself and is seemingly (though perhaps not permanently) dead. Although the Matrix is preserved, it appears that humans who resist its virtual reality will be freed.

The first Matrix film was not only praised by critics but also performed well at the box office. Although it opened modestly, *The Matrix* went on to gross $463 million worldwide, and in 2001 it was rated sixty-six on the American Film Institute's list of the "100 Most Thrilling American Films." Two years later, intense anticipation—along with an aggressive marketing campaign—produced a strong opening weekend for *The Matrix Reloaded* and good overall box-office performance, despite some reservations among both critics and fans. Although many reviewers saw the film as a significant achievement, others regarded it as overly cerebral or unnecessarily obscure, and *Entertainment Weekly* included *Reloaded* in its 2007 list of "The 25 Worst Sequels Ever Made." Although audience reception was sharply diminished for the third and last film, which grossed significantly less than its predecessors, the trilogy went on to sell well in a variety of DVD packages, including the ten-disc "Ultimate Matrix Collection."

The popularity of the first Matrix film derived in part from its use of innovative cinematic techniques such as "bullet time" (an effect that slows down an event while the viewpoint moves around the action) and its clever references to ideas from science fiction literature and new technologies. *The Matrix* was essentially a sophisticated blend of martial arts movie; dystopian fable; and quest tale, in which the hero journeys to another reality, awakens to his true nature, and returns to help his community. The sequels ventured further into complex concepts of reality, made greater use of references to esoteric ideas, and introduced new layers of symbolism. For some fans these explorations deepened interest in the story, but for others the increasingly abstract plot arc was too much of a challenge, and the conclusion was ultimately unsatisfying. Nonetheless, the original concepts presented in *The Matrix* not only captured an important moment in the evolution of cyberculture but also introduced a new level of storytelling in science fiction cinema.

Cynthia Giles

SEE ALSO: *Blockbusters; Comic Books;* Entertainment Weekly; *Martial Arts; Science Fiction Publishing.*

BIBLIOGRAPHY

Faller, Stephen. *Beyond the Matrix: Revolutions and Revelations.* St. Louis, MO: Chalice Press, 2004.

Kapell, Matthew, and William G. Doty. *Jacking In to the Matrix Franchise: Cultural Reception and Interpretation.* New York: Continuum, 2004.

Lawrence, Matt. *Like a Splinter in Your Mind: The Philosophy Behind the "Matrix" Trilogy.* Malden, MA: Blackwell, 2004.

Mattingly, Don *(1961–)*

New York Yankees first baseman Don Mattingly was arguably the best player in baseball from 1984 to 1987. Christened "Donnie Baseball" by Minnesota Twins slugger Kirby Puckett, Mattingly won the admiration of his peers with a dogged work ethic and an unwavering respect for the integrity of the game. Named Most Valuable Player in 1985, Mattingly became the New York Yankees captain in 1991, the tenth man so entrusted in the team's illustrious history. Chronic back problems put a premature end to his career after the 1995 season. The Yankees retired Mattingly's number and erected a plaque in his honor on August 31, 1997.

After he left the playing field, Mattingly joined the Yankees coaching staff, first as an instructor in spring training, then as a hitting coach in 2003. After being passed over as the Yankees manager in 2007, he followed former Yankees boss Joe Torre to Los Angeles, where he became the Dodgers hitting coach. In 2011 Mattingly finally achieved his goal of managing, although wearing Dodgers blue and not Yankees pinstripes. As of 2012 he had not been elected to the Baseball Hall of Fame. His voting peaked his first year on the ballot, but with such a short career, his chances of achieving that honor are slim.

Robert E. Schnakenberg

SEE ALSO: *Baseball; The New York Yankees.*

BIBLIOGRAPHY

Crouse, Karen. "Mattingly Takes the Reins of the Troubled Dodgers." *New York Times*, February 17, 2011, B9(L).

Shalin, Mike. *Donnie Baseball: The Definitive Biography of Don Mattingly.* Chicago: Triumph Books, 2011.

Shatzkin, Mike. *The Ballplayers: Baseball's Ultimate Biographical Reference.* New York: William Morrow, 1990.

Maude

Norman Lear's sitcom *Maude* (1972–1978) features one of the most outspoken female characters in television history. The character Maude Findlay (played by Bea Arthur, who also went on to star in the hit series *The Golden Girls*) first appeared on *All in the Family* as Edith Bunker's cousin. She was upper-middle class, educated, liberated, witty, and domineering, the perfect counterpoint for *All in the Family*'s strong-willed and opinionated Archie Bunker. Frances Lear, Norman's ex-wife and the inspiration for Maude, told *People* in 1975 that "a great deal of Maude comes from my consciousness being raised by the [women's] movement—and from Norman's being raised by me." Maude's gutsy approach to life gave her the strength to deal with some of life's most difficult experiences, and Lear's skill enabled her to do so while also maintaining the show's comedic air.

Maude lived in Tuckahoe, New York, with her fourth husband, Walter Findlay (Bill Macy) of Findlay's Friendly Ap-

Maude. *Stars of the sometimes controversial situation comedy* Maude *included, from left, Conrad Bain as Dr. Arthur Harmon, Bill Macy as Walter Findlay, and Bea Arthur as Maude Findlay.* CBS-TV/THE KOBAL COLLECTION.

pliances; her twenty-seven-year-old divorced daughter, Carol Traynor (Adrienne Barbeau); and Carol's nine-year-old son, Phillip (Brian Morrison, Kraig Metzinger). Dr. Arthur Harmon (Conrad Bain), a widower, was the Findlays' next-door neighbor and Walter's best friend. He started dating Maude's best friend, recent divorcée Vivian Cavender (future *Golden Girl* Rue McClanahan). The characters married during the 1974 season.

Maude may have been a model for independent women, but she still had a female servant in the house; in fact, she ran through three of them. Her first maid was Florida Evans (Esther Rolle), a straight-shooting black woman who got a spin-off of her own in 1974, *Good Times* (which aired until 1979). On both *Maude* and *Good Times*, John Amos plays Florida's husband, though he is called Henry on *Maude* and James on *Good Times*. Maude's next maid was Mrs. Nell Naugatuck (Hermione Baddeley), a hard-drinking English woman. Even though Baddeley won a Golden Globe Award for her role as supporting actress in 1976, her character was soon married off and sent back to the British Isles. Victoria Butterfield (Marlene Warfield) joined the show in 1977.

Maude was controversial from the very beginning; during its second month on the air, it seized headlines as the first sitcom to deal with abortion. On November 14, 1972, forty-seven-year-old Maude announced she was pregnant. During the next episode, at the suggestion of Carol and with the support of Walter, she decided to have an abortion, which was legal in New York at the time but not yet nationally. The episode aired two months before the Supreme Court handed down the *Roe v. Wade* decision.

After those two episodes, *Maude* shot up from thirteenth to fifth place in the Nielsen ratings, and CBS received hundreds of calls and 7,000 letters protesting the episodes. The tumult started up again when "Maude's Dilemma" was rerun. Twenty-five CBS affiliates refused to air the show; the network received 17,000 letters; and, as a result of pressure on advertisers by antiabortion groups, only one 30-second commercial was sold.

Nevertheless, *Maude* continued to explore controversial issues. Maude had a face lift and went through menopause. Walter dealt with a serious bout of alcoholism, saw his store go bankrupt, and had a nervous breakdown. The show remained popular despite these sometimes depressing themes until the last season, when the audience started declining. Major changes were planned for the 1978–1979 season: the Harmons and Carol were to leave town, a new supporting cast was to be added, Walter was to retire, and Maude would begin a career in politics. Nevertheless, Arthur announced early in 1978 that she'd be leaving the series. Replacing her was not an option; the producers admitted that no one could play the role as Arthur could and decided to end the show. The political career that Maude was supposed to have was the basis for a brief, odd, and failed Bill Macy vehicle called *Hanging In*.

Karen Lurie

SEE ALSO: All in the Family*; Arthur, Bea;* The Golden Girls*;* Good Times*; Lear, Norman;* People*;* Roe v. Wade*; Rolle, Esther; Sitcom; Television.*

BIBLIOGRAPHY

Brooks, Tim, and Earle Marsh. *The Complete Directory to Prime Time Network and Cable TV Shows 1946–Present*, 6th ed. New York: Ballantine Books, 1995.

Campbell, Sean. *The Sitcoms of Norman Lear*. Jefferson, NC: McFarland, 2007.

Davidson, Casey. "Maude's Choice." *Entertainment Weekly*, November 12, 1993, 76.

Lipton, Michael A. "Queen Lear: After Torment and Tumult, the Impetuous Model for 'Maude' Leaves Life with Unaccustomed Serenity." *People Weekly*, October 14, 1996.

McNeil, Alex. *Total Television*. New York: Penguin, 1996.

Maupin, Armistead *(1944–)*

Armistead Maupin is a novelist most famous for his *Tales of the City* series set in San Francisco in the 1970s. He was born in Washington, D.C., and grew up in Raleigh, North Carolina. After graduating from the University of North Carolina, he served in the U.S. Navy, including a tour of duty in Vietnam. He moved to San Francisco in 1971 as an Associated Press reporter, and in 1974 he began writing vignettes about life in the city's gay community for metro newspapers, including, in 1976, the *San Francisco Chronicle*.

Just as readers a century earlier eagerly awaited the next installment of a story by Charles Dickens, a growing cadre of readers followed the developments among Maupin's diverse family of friends and acquaintances, though he has described his own experiences as merely a "jumping off point" for the stories. *Tales of the City* first appeared in book form in 1978. Five additional books followed in the original series, taking readers from the joyously hedonistic pre-AIDS era to the first stirrings of fear in the face of the epidemic. Famously, Maupin has stated that he came out as gay to his parents through *Tales of the City*.

The first two books were adapted for television by British television company Channel 4 in 1993, airing in the United States the following year. They feature, among others, Olympia Dukakis as Mrs. Madrigal, the landlady with a mysterious allure and a ready stash of marijuana to share with her tenant charges, and Laura Linney in her career's "breakout" role as Mary Ann Singleton. Two further miniseries followed, *More Tales of the City* (1998) and *Further Tales of the City*, which was produced by Showtime and first aired in 2001. In 2011 the series was adapted as a musical.

Maupin's first nonseries novel, *Maybe the Moon*, was published in 1992, and his second, *The Night Listener*, was released in 2000. After the turn of the twenty-first century, he involved himself in adapting his work for TV and film and continued to write novels, including *Michael Tolliver Lives* (2007) and *Mary Ann in Autumn* (2010), both of which feature characters from *Tales of the City* in middle age.

Sue Russell

SEE ALSO: *AIDS; Gay and Lesbian Press; Gay Men; Television.*

BIBLIOGRAPHY

Carman, John. "'More Tales': A Celebration of the City." *San Francisco Chronicle*. June 5, 1998.

Maupin, Armistead. *Tales of the City*. New York: Harper & Row, 1978.

Maupin, Armistead. Personal website. Accessed March 16, 2012. Available from http://www.armisteadmaupin.com

Maus

Swedish American author and artist Art Spiegelman won acclaim in the 1980s with his two-part graphic novel *Maus*, an account of his parents' experiences as Jews in concentration camps during the Holocaust. The work brought respect to the comic art world, fully transforming the genre from "funnies" or superhero stories into a new medium for literature. Spiegelman was awarded a Pulitzer Prize special citation for *Maus* in 1992.

Formerly known as a driving force in the quirky world of self-published and underground comics, Spiegelman was also responsible for many of the offbeat ideas and artwork for Topps Chewing Gum's Wacky Packages and Garbage Pail Kids—trading cards and stickers that featured irreverent pokes at popular culture. In 1980, he and his wife started the avant-garde graphic magazine *Raw*, and in 1992 Spiegelman began serving as a contributing editor for the *New Yorker*, stirring controversy with his cover designs because of what some considered offensive themes. In 1997 he published a children's book titled *Open Me, I'm a Dog*.

Spiegelman was born on February 15, 1948, in Stockholm, Sweden, to Vladek and Anja (Zylberberg) Spiegelman. His parents and older brother were imprisoned in concentration camps at Auschwitz during World War II; the couple survived, but their first son did not. Afterward they moved to Sweden, where Spiegelman was born. The family immigrated to New York City when Spiegelman was two. Though Spiegelman's father wanted him to become a dentist, the young artist was passionate about drawing. He excelled at the High School of Art and Design in New York, and his art was published in alternative and local publications. While still a high school student, Spiegelman turned down an offer to draw comics for United Features Syndicate, deciding that he did not want to tone down his oddball style for a family readership.

Instead, Spiegelman continued writing for underground comics, which were often self-published, printed in small anthologies, or picked up by minor companies. Unlike traditional comics, which usually feature superhero action-adventure or silly humor, underground comics often deal with social issues or taboos, feature black humor or no humor at all, and have been known to contain adult and offensive material.

WORK AT TOPPS

After his freshman year in college, Spiegelman went to work for Topps Chewing Gum Company in 1966, where he stayed for more than twenty years. At Topps, he created the Wacky Packages and Garbage Pail Kids series of trading cards and stickers. Wacky Packages were spoofs of typical supermarket items, such as "Fright Guard" deodorant; "Bustedfingers" candy bars; and, even mocking itself, "Wormy Packages." Later, in a spoof of the popular Cabbage Patch Kids craze, Spiegelman came out with "Garbage Pail Kids" cards, featuring unkempt children with names like Acne Annie and Wrinkled Rita.

In 1968 Spiegelman suffered a nervous breakdown; shortly thereafter his mother committed suicide. The artist then moved to San Francisco, where underground comics were flourishing thanks to such artists as Robert Crumb. Spiegelman's cartoons were published in a number of periodicals, including *Real Pulp*, and in the early 1970s, he produced a number of his own titles. In 1972 he developed the idea for his later masterpiece, *Maus*, when he produced a short cartoon for *Funny Animals* using the idea of Jews in the Holocaust as mice. He taught for a short time at the San Francisco Academy of Art (1974–1975). Also around this time, he banded together with Bill Griffith, creator of Zippy the Pinhead, to form the comic anthology *Arcade* in order to showcase new material.

Later in the 1970s Spiegelman returned to New York, where he met Francoise Mouly, an editor. The two married on July 12, 1977, and joined creative forces, publishing *Raw*, an underground comics anthology magazine. The publication featured a smorgasbord of works from underground and up-and-coming comic artists. Meanwhile, Spiegelman began interviewing his father about his experiences at Auschwitz. The first book of the oral history was published in 1986 as *Maus: A Survivor's Tale, My Father Bleeds History*. Jews are drawn as mice, the Nazis are cats, Poles are pigs, Americans are dogs, and Auschwitz is Mauschwitz.

REACTION TO *MAUS*

Initially people were stunned that someone would dare make a cartoon out of such a serious issue as the Holocaust, perhaps not realizing that *Maus* was a graphic novel, not a funny comic book. In fact, Spiegelman had a difficult time finding a publisher. Pantheon eventually came around, and the book became a sensation. Spiegelman followed this volume in 1991 with *Maus: A Survivors Tale II, and Here My Troubles Began*. The volumes were overwhelmingly praised, especially for their ability to make the reader deal with the events through the use of animals instead of humans (not unlike George Orwell's *Animal Farm*). Spiegelman also noted that Adolf Hitler even used the word *extermination*, typically used only in the context of ridding vermin and pests, to refer to his plan of genocide.

Spiegelman was undoubtedly one of the most integral forces in underground comics throughout the 1970s and started to make his mark in the 1980s with *Raw*. He was also perhaps the most effective artist in changing the image of comic books, thanks to *Maus*. After its publication, the graphic novel finally took its place as a legitimate form of literature and brought the horrors of the Holocaust to another generation of readers in a provocative medium.

Geri Speace

SEE ALSO: *Comic Books; Crumb, Robert; Graphic Novels; The* New Yorker*; Suicide; Underground Comics; World War II;* Zippy the Pinhead.

BIBLIOGRAPHY

Chapman, Jeff, and John D. Jorgenson, eds. *Contemporary Authors, New Revision Series*, vol. 55. Detroit, MI: Gale Research, 1997.

Graham, Judith, ed. *Current Biography Yearbook*. New York: H.W. Wilson, 1994.

Witek, Joseph. *Art Spiegelman: Conversations*. Jackson: University Press of Mississippi, 2007.

Young, James E. "The Holocaust as Vicarious Past: Art Spiegelman's *Maus* and the Afterimages of History." *Critical Inquiry*, Spring 1998, 666.

Max, Peter *(1937–)*

German-born artist Peter Max's work visually captured the flavor of the 1960s and hippie culture. Its cartoonlike, brightly colored, psychedelic images were inspired by a number of styles, including Art Nouveau, pop art, and op art. Max's style had a pronounced effect on subsequent graphic art. His popularity exploded in the late 1960s when his mod motifs were featured on a wide range of products—from clothing to shower curtains—printed with his signature stars, flowers, rainbows, birds, butterflies, and human figures. His poster designs were hotly pursued by admirers, leading to a million-dollar industry by the end of the decade and turning the artist into a cultural hero.

Max's career buzzed along well into the 1990s, as he designed an MTV logo, murals for the 1992 World's Fair, and posters for Bill Clinton's 1993 presidential inauguration and the 1994 Super Bowl and World Cup. Strongly associated with music, his style garnered him a commission from the Rock and Roll Hall of Fame, and he provided art for several Grammy Awards ceremonies. An inhabitant of Manhattan, Max demonstrated his love for the city with a series of fund-raising posters he created in response to the 9/11 terrorist attacks. In the new century he has mostly worked in the mainstream, far from the 1960s counterculture he helped create and celebrate. He produced artwork for the 2002 Olympics, opened a store and gallery at Yankee Stadium, and painted a portrait of President Barack Obama.

Geri Speace

SEE ALSO: *Advertising; Grammy Awards; Hippies; MTV; 9/11; Obama, Barack; Olympics; Op Art; Pop Art; Psychedelia; Rock and Roll; Super Bowl; World Cup; World's Fairs; Yankee Stadium.*

BIBLIOGRAPHY

Charles, Riley A. *The Art of Peter Max*. New York: Harry N. Abrams, 2002.

Houpt, Simon. "Reborn in the USA." *Toronto Globe & Mail*, April 11, 2002, A1.

Staatliche Kunsthalle Berlin. *Peter Max Retrospektive 1963–1993*, ed. Peter Max. Berlin: Edition Q, 1993.

May, Elaine

SEE: *Nichols, Mike, and Elaine May.*

Mayer, Louis B. *(1885–1957)*

Arguably the most influential motion picture executive of the twentieth century, Louis B. Mayer presided over the studio that claimed to have "more stars than there are in heaven," Metro-Goldwyn-Mayer (MGM). In 1938 Mayer was the highest-paid

Louis B. Mayer. *Louis B. Mayer formed his own movie company in 1917 after earning his fortune owning nickelodeons and theaters, eventually building the most successful motion picture studio of its era.* NEW YORK DAILY NEWS ARCHIVE/CONTRIBUTOR/NY DAILY NEWS/GETTY IMAGES.

person in America, earning more than, for example, Franklin D. Roosevelt and Henry Ford. All this was rather impressive for a former junk man.

He was born Lazar Mayer in Russia. In 1888 his family moved to Canada, where his father started a scrap metal business, J. Mayer and Son. Mayer joined his father in the business right after high school, but he always had larger ambitions. In 1904 he married Margaret Shenberg; they had two daughters, Edith and Irene.

Believing that "movies are the one thing you can sell and still own," Mayer got into the nickelodeon business. Distributing the huge hit motion picture *Birth of a Nation* in 1915 made him a very wealthy man. By 1918 he had become the biggest movie theater owner in Massachusetts. Mayer decided that the next step in his career was to make his own films.

In 1918 he formed the Mayer Company. When he began producing films he had only one star under contract, the popular Anita Stewart. He featured her in his first production, *Virtuous Wives* (1918). When Mayer hired Irving Thalberg to become his production chief in 1923, a successful partnership was born. A 1924 merger with Sam Goldwyn and Marcus Loew formed MGM, with Mayer as head of operations for the West Coast. The first project Mayer and Thalberg tackled after moving to the new company was Goldwyn's unwieldy project *Ben Hur* (1925). After they did some recasting and budget cutting, the picture was released to acclaim and became MGM's first big hit.

Mayer, who could be generous and protective but also ruthless and tyrannical, thought of himself as a father figure to his stars. His vision of motion pictures was as wholesome family entertainment, and he refused to believe the audience wanted realism. For a long time he was correct. During the Great Depression, people wanted escapist fare, such as musicals and comedies, to forget the real world. Series motion pictures, such as *The Thin Man* (1934) and the Andy Hardy series, were also popular.

When Thalberg died in 1936, Mayer became the absolute ruler of MGM's West Coast operations. Unfortunately, he had a powerful enemy in company executive Nicholas Schenck. Schenck had long wanted to get rid of Mayer, but he could not do that as long as the company was doing well. After World War II, however, the public had grown hardened and jaded by war and wanted more realism in their movies. Mayer would not accept this, and his longtime feud with the MGM East Coast office grew as the studios' bottom line began to shrink. In the late 1940s Dore Schary was brought to MGM and began producing more realistic films, but they were hardly the big hits for which MGM was famous.

As Mayer began to spend more time away from MGM, the studio's luster continued to fade. The long era of the studio system was ending. Mayer was fired in 1951. He attempted to return to MGM several times, always unsuccessfully. He died of leukemia in 1957. Louis B. Mayer is remembered as a temperamental tyrant who was loved by some who worked for him and hated by others. He will forever be the man who steered the greatest motion picture studio of the time through its golden years.

Jill A. Gregg

SEE ALSO: *Andy Hardy;* The Birth of a Nation*; Goldwyn, Samuel; The Great Depression; Hollywood; MGM (Metro-Goldwyn-Mayer); Movie Stars; The Musical; Studio System; Thalberg, Irving G.; World War II.*

BIBLIOGRAPHY

Altman, Diana. *Hollywood East: Louis B. Mayer and the Origins of the Studio System.* New York: Carol Publishing Group, 1992.

Carey, Gary. *All the Stars in Heaven: Louis B. Mayer's MGM.* New York: Dutton, 1981.

Eyman, Scott. *Lion of Hollywood: The Life and Legend of Louis B. Mayer.* New York: Simon & Schuster, 2005.

Marx, Samuel. *Mayer and Thalberg: The Make-Believe Saints.* New York: Random House, 1975.

Mayfield, Curtis *(1942–1999)*

A talented and prolific songwriter, guitarist, producer, and singer, Curtis Mayfield was one of the most significant pioneers of soul and rhythm-and-blues music in the United States during the 1960s and 1970s. He was perhaps the first black musician to overtly address the indignities of being an African American during America's system of racial apartheid, and many of his songs became closely associated with the civil rights movement of the 1960s. As a producer, an arranger, and a writer, Mayfield was at the center of the so-called Chicago sound, a loose-knit amalgamation of Chicago-area solo artists and groups that suc-

Curtis Mayfield. *Curtis Mayfield performs "Superfly" on an episode of* The Midnight Special *in 1973.* NBCU PHOTO BANK/GETTY IMAGES.

cessfully rivaled Motown's hit-making machine during the first half of the 1960s. As the leader of the musical group the Impressions, Mayfield provided another example of how black music can cross over to the pop mainstream without compromising itself, and as a solo artist he released a series of classic funk albums. Mayfield survived paralysis from the neck down in 1990 and continued to make music into the late 1990s, releasing *New World Order* in 1997.

Beginning as a gospel singer in the 1950s, Mayfield met Jerry Butler while singing in the Northern Jubilee Singers, and the two (along with Sam Gooden and Arthur Brooks) formed the Impressions in 1957. They had a huge hit in 1958 with "Your Precious Love," but Butler soon left to pursue a solo career, though he and Mayfield remained lifelong friends. During the late 1950s and early 1960s, Mayfield wrote, produced, and played guitar on a number of hit songs released by Chicago-area musicians such as Butler, Major Lance, the Five Stairsteps, Cubie, the Fascinations, Billy Butler, and Gene Chandler. At the end of the 1950s, the Butler-less Impressions drifted apart, but in 1961 a re-formed Impressions hit big with "Gypsy Woman." This began a string of Mayfield-written Impressions hits, including "I'm So Proud," "Amen," "People Get Ready," "Keep on Pushing," "We're a Winner," and "We're Rolling On." Not only was he a pioneer as a session musician, producer, arranger, and writer within soul music, but he also started his own successful label, Curtom.

Many of Mayfield's songs with the Impressions, such as "We're a Winner," "I'm So Proud," and "People Get Ready," were veiled and not-so-veiled proclamations of black pride, and during his solo career in the 1970s his songs became even more critical and socially aware. His 1970 self-titled solo debut's first cut contained the long, powerful, and outspoken "(Don't Worry) If There's a Hell Below We're All Gonna Go," which critiqued a white United States and took some of the members of his own race to task. Other songs from that album—"We People Who Are Darker than Blue," "Move on Up," and "Miss Black America"—never let the listener forget the subject of race in the United States, nor did his many other solo albums such as *Roots, Back to the World, Superfly, Sweet Exorcist, Got to Find a Way,* and the sarcastically titled *There's No Place Like America Today.* He moved to Atlanta, Georgia, in the 1970s, and it was there that he wrote his best-selling soundtrack to the film *Superfly* (1972), which contained the hits "Freddie's Dead" and "Superfly," setting the standard for the many blaxploitation albums that followed.

Like many great soul, funk, and R&B stars of the 1970s, Mayfield's career stalled in the 1980s, though he still maintained a respectable output with some minor hits and still-exciting live performances. It was during one of the performances on August 14, 1990, that a lighting rig fell on him, almost killing him and paralyzing him from the neck down (including his vocal chords). After many years of professional physical therapy and voice training, he returned in 1997 with his first solo album since the accident, *New World Order.*

Mayfield died in 1999 at the age of fifty-seven. Nine years later a documentary of his life and career was released. *Movin' on Up: The Music and Message of Curtis Mayfield and the Impressions* contains twenty-two songs and numerous interviews with the people who knew Mayfield best. His widow, Altheida, was present in Atlanta in July 2010 when the National Black Arts Festival honored her husband. She says that many people misunderstood the message he was trying to convey in songs such as "Freddie's Dead." She insists that he was saying that those who lived by the gun were sure to die by the gun. A number of music critics agree, maintaining that racial reconciliation is a ubiquitous theme in much of Mayfield's music.

Kembrew McLeod

SEE ALSO: *Blaxploitation Films; Civil Rights Movement; Funk; Motown; Pop Music; Rhythm and Blues; Soul Music.*

BIBLIOGRAPHY

Friskics-Warren, Bill. *I'll Take You There: Pop Music and the Urge for Transcendence.* New York: Continuum, 2005.

Holtzberg, Maggie. *Portrait of Spirit: One Story at a Time.* Oakville, ON: Disability Today Publishing Group, 1996.

Newfield, Jack, ed. *American Rebels.* New York: Nation Books, 2003.

Vincent, Rickey. *Funk: The Music, the People, and the Rhythm of the One.* New York: St. Martin's Griffin, 1996.

Werner, Craig Hansen. *Higher Ground: Stevie Wonder, Aretha Franklin, Curtis Mayfield, and the Rise and Fall of American Soul.* New York: Crown Publishers, 2004.

Werner, Craig Hansen. *A Change Is Gonna Come: Music, Race,*

& the Soul of America. Ann Arbor: University of Michigan Press, 2006.

Mayfield, Percy *(1920–1984)*

Singer/songwriter Percy Mayfield has been widely described as "the poet laureate of the blues." Armed with a dry baritone, Mayfield sang blues ballads that pondered worlds of trouble, melancholy, pain, and suicide. He was one of the most creative songwriters and performers of California blues.

"I'm a poet, and my gift is love" explained Mayfield to an interviewer in *Living Blues*. Some of his themes dealt with subjects not generally associated with the blues. His biggest hit, "Please Send Me Someone to Love," was a prayer for understanding and peace of mind among all humans. Mayfield's songs have been recorded by performers as diverse as Sade, Dale Evans, and Robert Nighthawk. As staff writer for Ray Charles, he wrote four Top 10 hits.

Mayfield was born in Minden, Louisiana, 30 miles from Shreveport, on August 12, 1920. His mother was a singer who instilled in her son a love for music. As a child Mayfield wrote poems and set them to music. At age fifteen he left Minden, riding the rails before settling in Houston, Texas, for a brief stay. In 1941 he arrived in Los Angeles, where he lived with his older sister. Several orchestras featured Mayfield as a guest singer, and he subsequently landed an engagement with the George Como band. While he honed his songwriting, Mayfield supplemented his income by working as a taxi driver and a dry-cleaning presser. He was a woman's man—handsome and stylish, he could attract women with just a look or a smile.

In 1949 Mayfield approached the Supreme record company about using some of his songs for their artist Jimmy Witherspoon. The surprising outcome was a chance for Mayfield to record himself. He recorded "Two Years of Torture," which gained some attention on the local charts. In 1950 he recorded "Please Send Me Someone to Love" for Specialty Records; this hit secured his fame as a songwriter. "Please Send Me Someone to Love" was followed by several other hits, including "Strange Things Happening," "Lost Love," "What a Fool I Was," "Prayin' for Your Return," "Cry Baby," and "Big Question." After leaving Specialty, his subsequent singles on other labels were not as successful.

Mayfield considered himself above all a balladeer and not a blues singer. His early influences were Al Hibbler and Billy Eckstine. Mayfield's pensiveness and religious leanings set him apart from a number of blues singers. "I promised God I wouldn't write and sing a lie," he once said; Mayfield consistently acknowledged God for his songwriting talents. He epitomized sadness in his songs, and perhaps the lyrics of his own "My Blues" best explain his aesthetic: "Someone may ask the question, why are you so sad? / I would answer quite correctly, the blues is all I've had."

In September 1952 Mayfield was involved in a catastrophic automobile accident, which acutely disfigured his face, changed his voice, and gravely affected his self-esteem. After this setback he became staff writer for Ray Charles, penning at least four Top 10 hits. These include the familiar "Hit the Road Jack," "But on the Other Hand Baby," "Hide nor Hair," and "At the Club." Mayfield also recorded what is considered his best work on an album titled *My Jug and I*. A spirited "River's Invitation," arranged by Charles, placed at twenty-five on the rhythm-and-blues chart in 1963; it was Mayfield's first Top 40 entry in eleven years and also his last. "River's Invitation" is clearly one of the most profound songs of Mayfield's oeuvre. It invokes the river in a metaphysical dialogue, which personifies a peaceful home and death. The river, in turn, invites Mayfield to give up his search for his lost love and join the waters: "You look so lonely / you look full of misery / and if you can't find your baby / come and make your home with me."

Mayfield recorded infrequently in subsequent years, completing an album for Brunswick and three for RCA Victor. In later years companies were not interested in recording him, and he had to pay for his own recording sessions. Mayfield's baritone, however, continued to embrace most songs and convincingly made them his own. As his wife, Tina, recalled, "his music was more or less about sadness." His death from a heart attack came on the eve of his sixty-fourth birthday: August 11, 1984. Mayfield's death signaled the loss of one of the most creative and distinctive poets of rhythm and blues.

Willie Collins

SEE ALSO: *Automobile; Blues; Charles, Ray; Eckstine, Billy; Rhythm and Blues.*

BIBLIOGRAPHY

Santelli, Robert. *The Big Book of Blues: A Biographical Encyclopedia.* New York: Penguin Books, 2001.

Shurman, Dick. "Songs of Inspiration: Living Blues Interview: Percy Mayfield." *Living Blues,* January 1981, 12–25.

Mays, Billy *(1958–2009)*

Growing up in Pittsburgh, Pennsylvania, Billy Mays's future as the bombastic "As Seen on TV" spokesperson was not obvious in his youth. After dropping out of West Virginia University and moving to Atlantic City, New Jersey, in 1983, Mays worked in sales and supplemented his income by selling such products as "The Ultimate Chopper" to tourists on the boardwalk. After moving to Dunedin, Florida, in the late 1990s and establishing his own company, Mays Promotions, Mays's focus shifted to developing a new style of on-air television advertisements in which he could offer the same products that he had sold on the streets.

Before long his recorded sales pitches found a national audience on the Home Shopping Network. Although these commercials began as thirty-second spots, they would eventually expand to thirty-minute programs in which Mays expounded upon the merits of the advertised products with his larger-than-life persona and clear, recognizable voice. Upon his death on June 28, 2009—attributed to heart disease aggravated by cocaine use—the industry lost not only a star but also a pioneer of the medium.

Mays made his name as the spokesperson for such products as OxiClean, Orange Glo, and Kaboom! wearing his signature blue-collared shirt and khaki pants in each appearance. His sincerity and belief in the products were evident in his every word and in his animated demeanor. Televised pitches had previously consisted of subdued, clinical product descriptions, but Mays brought his eye-catching street corner and fair-ground performance style to television, infusing every infomercial with unprecedented entertainment value, capturing the attention of even those viewers who had no intention of buying the product. Of course, the truest mark of success is imitation, and Mays found himself copied by many but not surpassed.

In 2009 the Discovery Channel introduced the series *Pitch-Men* (2008–2011), which teamed Mays with fellow product spokesperson Anthony Sullivan. Featuring new products from individual inventors in the "as seen on television" style, the series tried to assist newcomers in their business ventures. Upon Mays's death, the series aired a tribute to the man who made the technique a success. Mays also realized that his in-your-face technique often elicited complaints from unfamiliar viewers, and he poked fun at himself and other pitchmen in a series of ads for cable network ESPN's online project, ESPN360, in late 2008.

Although many have copied Mays's style and format, few have matched his success. His sincerity and apparent belief in the products he endorsed gave him an air of credibility with his vast audience, and his eagerness to demonstrate the product's benefit helped people find a reason to buy it, whether they needed it or not.

Linda Martindale

SEE ALSO: *Advertising; Cable TV; Cocaine/Crack; Consumerism; ESPN; Home Shopping Network/QVC; The Internet; Popeil, Ron; Television.*

BIBLIOGRAPHY

"Billy Mays, the Infomercial King." *Economist*, January 13, 2012.

Harry, Lou, and Sam Stall. *As Seen on TV: 50 Amazing Products and the Commercials That Made Them Famous.* Philadelphia: Quirk Books, 2002.

"Pitchmen." Discovery Channel. Accessed June 2012. Available from http://www.dsc.discovery.com/tv/pitchmen/

Mays, Willie *(1931–)*

One of the best baseball players ever, Willie Mays dazzled baseball fans with his amazing hitting, base stealing, and fielding. The first true all-around player, he considered the baseball diamond his "stage," and by the time he retired in 1973, he had earned himself a place in the hearts of the American people.

Born in Westfield, Alabama, in 1931, Mays broke into the professional ranks at age sixteen with the Birmingham Black Barons of the Negro National League. On a $250 a month salary, he played two years with the Barons before being signed by the New York Giants of Major League Baseball in 1951. In spite of a disappointing one for twenty-five start, Mays lived up to expectations by capturing Rookie of the Year honors that season.

Nicknamed "Say Hey" because he often forgot the names of his teammates, the center fielder quickly became a crowd favorite due to his spectacular play and his engaging personality. Because he was playing in the media capital of the world, his on-the-field exploits became legend overnight. After serving two years in the army, Mays's popularity reached new heights when he returned to baseball in 1954. That year baseball fans witnessed "the catch," an over-the-shoulder basket catch made by Mays in the World Series against the Cleveland Indians. A photo of him catching the ball made headlines in virtually every major newspaper and sports publication in the country.

En route to leading the Giants to the World Series championship that year, Mays captured the major-league batting title and subsequently was named Most Valuable Player for the 1954 season. For his efforts the Giants rewarded him with a $30,000 contract, the highest in baseball at that time. With his popularity increasing, Mays was featured on the cover of *Time* and the *Saturday Evening Post*, and he also made appearances on the popular *Ed Sullivan Show* (1948–1971) and *Colgate Comedy Hour* (1950–1955). This media coverage brought Mays into the homes of millions of Americans.

Mays remained in the media spotlight throughout his career as he continued to excel. In 1955 he batted .319 with a major-league-leading fifty-one homers and 127 runs batted in (RBIs). Beginning in 1956 he would lead the league in stolen bases for four consecutive years. In 1958 the Giants shocked the baseball world by moving to San Francisco. In spite of the change of venue, Mays continued to delight fans with his extraordinary talent. In the early 1960s he went on a home run hitting barrage by averaging forty-five home runs per season between 1961 and 1965.

When Mays retired in 1973, his career numbers were astounding: .302 average, 660 home runs, and 1,903 RBIs. With these unbelievable numbers, the nineteen-time All-Star became only the ninth player in history to be elected to the Baseball Hall of Fame on his first try. In an era when many great players possessed only one strength, Mays's multidimensional ability earned him a place in the hearts of the American people and legendary status in the annals of America's favorite pastime.

Mays was in the news again in 2007 as his godson Barry Bonds neared his home run record of 660 runs, the third highest on the all-time hit list. In 2010 the state of California declared May 6, Mays's birthday (he turned seventy-nine that year), Willie Mays Day throughout the state. The following year sports writers across the country paid homage to him in celebration of the fiftieth anniversary of 1961, his most productive year. On April 30, 1961, while still recovering from a bout of food poisoning, Mays hit four home runs and batted in eight runs in a single game, going on to hit forty home runs total for the 1961 season.

Leonard N. Moore

SEE ALSO: *Baseball; Bonds, Barry; The Fifties; Leisure Time; Negro Leagues; The* Saturday Evening Post*; Sports Heroes;* Time*; World Series.*

BIBLIOGRAPHY

Hirsch, James S. *Willie Mays: The Life and Legend.* New York: Scribner, 2011.

Mays, Willie, and Lou Sahadi. *Say Hey: The Autobiography of Willie Mays.* New York: Simon & Schuster, 1988.

Shannon, Mike. *Willie Mays: Art in the Outfield.* Tuscaloosa: University of Alabama Press, 2007.

McBain, Ed *(1926–2005)*

Evan Hunter, writing under the pseudonym Ed McBain, established himself as an amazingly prolific author in a number of different genres. He is best known for his gritty "87th Precinct" detective series, which grew to include nearly fifty volumes, beginning with *Cop Hater*, published in 1956. Hunter also published a number of other works under his real name, as well as the pseudonyms Curt Cannon, Hunt Collins, Ezra Hannon, and Richard Marsten.

Hunter first became interested in writing during World War II while serving in the navy. After the war, he attended Hunter College in New York City, studying to become a teacher and graduating Phi Beta Kappa in 1950. After graduation, he taught at a vocational school in New York City. He soon left teaching and then held a series of diverse jobs, including selling lobsters and answering telephones for the American Automobile Association. A turning point for the author came in the early 1950s, when he secured a job as an editor at the Scott Meredith Literary Agency in New York, during which time he began to write and sell short stories, including science fiction and Westerns.

Hunter's experience teaching in the New York schools provided the basis for his first book. *The Blackboard Jungle*. The story of teachers in New York's vocational schools who attempt to deal with unruly, unmotivated students, *The Blackboard Jungle* achieved great popularity upon its release in October 1954. The following year, Metro-Goldwyn-Mayer adapted the book for the screen, and the film, starring Glenn Ford and Sidney Poitier, received four Academy Award nominations. Ten other feature films have been made based on Hunter's books. He also wrote several screenplays, including one for Alfred Hitchcock's 1963 movie *The Birds*, based on a Daphne du Maurier short story.

While the publication of *The Blackboard Jungle* in October 1954 and the subsequent release of the movie based on the book gained Hunter a certain amount of fame, it also proved a mixed blessing for the author. As he told literary critic Roy Newquist in an interview in the 1960s, recorded in Newquist's book *Conversations*, he was not attempting to provide an exposé of the New York schools in the book but was simply writing about his time as a teacher, which he considered to be the most meaningful experience in his life up to that time. Reviewers and interviewers expected him to be an expert on the problems of juvenile delinquency and urban schools, but he refused to play that role. Hunter also noted that the critical reception of his subsequent novels, including *Strangers When We Meet*, *Mothers and Daughters*, and *Paper Dragon*, was not as positive as he hoped it would be.

While the publication and success of *The Blackboard Jungle* did not lead to Hunter's achieving the critical success he felt he deserved, it did create the opportunity for him to launch the

Ed McBain. *Evan Hunter wrote many successful crime and mystery books under the name Ed McBain as well as other pseudonyms.* ULF ANDERSEN/CONTRIBUTOR/GETTY IMAGES ENTERTAINMENT/GETTY IMAGES.

highly successful 87th Precinct series. When Pocket Books issued a reprint of *The Blackboard Jungle*, Hunter decided to send the publisher a mystery he had written under a pseudonym (not McBain). One of the editors at Pocket Books recognized Hunter's style and told him that the publisher needed someone to take over the niche occupied by Erle Stanley Gardner, whose mysteries were recycled every several years under new jackets to enthusiastic popular reaction but who was getting too old to continue to produce as prolifically as he had in the past. Pocket Books offered Hunter a contract to produce three books under the McBain pseudonym, with an opportunity to renew if the series was success, and the 87th Precinct was launched.

McBain has noted that the "nice thing about the '87th Precinct' is that I can deal with any subject matter so long as it's criminally related. With the Ed McBain novels, I only want to say that cops have a tough, underpaid job, and they deal with murder every day of the week, and that's the way it is, folks." The series is set in the fictional city of Isola, clearly patterned after New York City, and deals with the experiences of a consistent set of about a dozen characters, including detectives Steve Carella, Meyer Meyer, and Bert Kling, all of whom deal with various personal issues while generally tackling several cases in each novel.

In addition to the 87th Precinct novels, McBain produced thirteen entries in the popular Matthew Hope series of crime novels, which deal with a Florida attorney who becomes involved in solving mysteries. Despite his great success as McBain, the author continued to produce work as Hunter. His 1994 novel *Criminal Conversation*, about a district attorney whose wife ends up having an affair with a mob boss he is attempting to indict, was a best seller and was purchased by actor Tom Cruise's production company for a potential movie.

In 1986 McBain was given the Grand Master Award by the Mystery Writers of America. While he published no novels under his own name between 1984 and 1994, *Candyland* (2001) is attributed to both McBain and Hunter. The first half of the book is presented in the personal narrative voice associated with Hunter and the second half in the police procedural style associated with McBain. The author died in 2005 in Westport, Connecticut, at the age of seventy-eight.

Jason George

SEE ALSO: *Academy Awards; Best Sellers;* The Blackboard Jungle*; Detective Fiction; Ford, Glenn; Hard-Boiled Detective Fiction; Poitier, Sidney.*

BIBLIOGRAPHY

Dove, George N. *The Boys from Grover Avenue: Ed McBain's 87th Precinct Novels.* Bowling Green, OH: Bowling Green State University Popular Press, 1985.

Ellroy, James, and Otto Penzler. *The Best American Noir of the Century.* Boston: MarinerBooks, 2011.

Newquist, Roy. *Conversations.* New York: Rand McNally, 1967.

McCaffrey, Anne *(1926–2011)*

It is often overlooked that in the late 1960s novelist Anne McCaffrey became the first woman to win the Hugo Award (best novella, *Weyr Search*, 1967) and the Nebula Award (best novella, *Dragonrider*, 1967), the two highest honors of the science fiction/fantasy field. She went on to win fame for her international best-selling series of novels, the Dragonriders of Pern.

Beginning with *Dragonflight* (1968), the Dragonriders series spans more than twenty books and includes the Harper Hall trilogy beloved by young adults—*Dragonsong* (1976), *Dragonsinger* (1977), and *Dragondrums* (1979). In the early twenty-first century she began to collaborate with her son and together produced more books for the series, including *Dragon's Fire* (2006) and *Dragon's Time* (2011).

The series revolves around the world of Pern, a lost Earth colony inhabited by humans who saddle telepathic dragons in order to combat Threads, lethal spores that can only be eradicated by dragon fire. In her study of McCaffrey, Robin Roberts identifies such recurrent themes as the heroine as outsider, the importance of living harmoniously with nature, and the value of art. Other works by McCaffrey include the Killashandra series, the Pegasus series, the Petaybee series, and the Rowan books.

Neal Baker

SEE ALSO: *Best Sellers; Science Fiction Publishing.*

BIBLIOGRAPHY

"Anne McCaffrey." *Contemporary Authors Online.* Detroit, MI: Gale, 2008.

Nye, Jody Lynn, and Anne McCaffrey. *The Dragonlovers' Guide to Pern*, 2nd ed. New York: Ballantine Books, 1997.

Roberts, Robin. *Anne McCaffrey: A Critical Companion.* Westwood, CT: Greenwood Press, 1996.

Roberts, Robin. *Anne McCaffrey: A Life with Dragons.* Jackson: University Press of Mississippi, 2007.

McCall's Magazine

McCall's Magazine dates back to 1873, when James McCall, a Scottish tailor who had recently immigrated to the United States, created a publication called the *Queen: Illustrating McCall's Bazaar Glove-Fitting Patterns* as a vehicle for disseminating his stock of dressmaking patterns. Following McCall's death in 1884, the magazine was continued by his widow. George Bladworth and his wife later took over the management of the magazine and at first renamed it the *Queen of Fashion*, then, in 1897, *McCall's Magazine.*

During the first forty years of its existence, the publication evolved from being exclusively a pattern book to a more general but fairly obscure magazine; a century later *McCall's* still published separate pattern and sew-it-yourself magazines, both in print and online. The magazine's purchase in 1913 by White, Weld & Co., which became the McCall Corporation under the direction of president Edward Alfred Simmons, signaled a dramatic change for the publication. In 1922, a year after national women's suffrage had been achieved, Harry Payne Burton became editor of the new *McCall's Magazine*, vowing to make it a substantial national monthly by raising its editorial standards and publishing high-quality fiction and nonfiction for a new generation of enlightened women.

In 1928, when twenty-three-year-old Otis Wiese became its editor, *McCall's Magazine* came into its own as a major player in the arena of the home- and family-oriented magazines that were then competing for the attention of the more affluent and educated "modern" woman. Wiese reorganized the magazine into three distinct sections—"Fiction and News," "Home Making," and "Style and Beauty"—and developed "youth conference" articles to attract a younger readership. During Wiese's tenure as editor, *McCall's* maintained its strong text-oriented identity with the publication of full-length novels in its pages as well as contributions from such celebrity authors as Eleanor Roosevelt, the Duchess of Windsor, Alfred Kinsey, and Norman Vincent Peale.

During and after World War II, architectural and interiors editor Mary Davis Gillies invited architects and designers to present their concepts for gracious and efficient living in the postwar home through such features as "the kitchen of tomorrow." In 1949 *McCall's* advocated the "Yardville Plan" through a five-part article that encouraged homeowners in cities to create semipublic commons by combining their backyard plots; the idea was reportedly adopted by civic-minded groups in more than 350 American cities.

In the 1950s, in the face of stiff competition from other women's service magazines, Wiese tried to position *McCall's* as a magazine for the entire family under the theme of "togetherness," but the concept was relatively ineffective in helping the magazine maintain its market share, and it was jettisoned entirely by Herbert Mayes, who assumed the editorship in 1958. Mayes effected a bold redesign of the magazine's layout and identity to solidify its position as "The First Magazine for Women" with colorful, vivid layouts and more high-quality fiction by such writers as John Steinbeck, Phyllis McGinley, Anne Morrow Lindbergh, and Herman Wouk. Circulation and advertising revenues quickly improved, and *McCall's* solidified its position as one of the trade-designated "Seven Sisters" of women's service magazines. In 1966 *McCall's* hired twenty-three-year-old Lynda Bird Johnson, the president's oldest daughter, as a contributor in an effort to appeal to young, college-age readers.

Several years later the corporation that owned *McCall's* was absorbed by Norton Simon, and the publication later became part of the women's magazine group at the New York Times Company. Robert Stein, who served as editor during the late 1960s, put heavy emphasis on research organizations to supplement the editorial staff with in-depth information. In 1994 the Times women's group, which also included *Family Circle*, *Child*, and other publications, was sold to Gruner + Jahr USA Publishing, a part of the German media giant Bertelsmann AG. Soon afterward, Kate White, who had been *McCall's* editor-in-chief since 1991, left to become editor of *Redbook* and was replaced by Sally Koslow.

By the mid-1990s *McCall's* was reporting a monthly circulation of around 4.6 million. Among the online services being offered by the publication at the end of the 1990s was Parents.com, a joint online resource that drew on the editorial expertise of *McCall's* and three other national publications: *Child*, *Family Circle*, and *Parents*. In 2000 actress Rosie O'Donnell became the editor of *McCall's*, and in 2001 the magazine was renamed *Rosie's McCall's*, commonly known as *Rosie*. O'Donnell ceased publication of the magazine in 2002, citing artistic differences with Gruner + Jahr. After a long legal battle, Gruner + Jahr gave up its American magazine interests, but it was too late for *Rosie* and its much-beloved predecessor.

Edward Moran

SEE ALSO: Family Circle; *Kinsey, Dr. Alfred C.; Leisure Time; Lindbergh, Anne Morrow; O'Donnell, Rosie; Peale, Norman Vincent;* Redbook; *Steinbeck, John; World War II.*

BIBLIOGRAPHY

Reed, David. *The Popular Magazine in Britain and the United States*. London: British Library, 1997.

Tebbel, John. *The American Magazine: A Compact History*. New York: Hawthorn Books, 1969.

Tebbel, John, and Mary Ellen Zuckerman. *The Magazine in America: 1741–1990*. New York: Oxford University Press, 1991.

Wood, James Playsted. *Magazines in the United States*. New York: Ronald Press, 1978.

McCarthyism

Despite the fact that Americans pride themselves on constitutional protections for free speech, there have been many attempts to limit speech in the United States. Beginning in 1798 with the First Sedition Act, Congress has passed laws banning diverse kinds of speech: criticism of the government, speaking out against war, associating with the Communist Party, obscenity, slander, libel, "fighting words," and seditious speech that attempts to overthrow the government. None of these limits has been so controversial or so damaging as the attempt by Senator Joseph McCarthy in the 1950s to purge the United States of anyone remotely connected with the Communist Party. His unsubstantiated charges led to wrecked lives and careers in all walks of life.

The inherent irony of McCarthyism—the name given to the attempts to seek out and criminalize those suspected of sympathizing with communism—was that by the time of his "Red Scare," American communism was all but dead. The lesson to be learned from his hysteria and the ensuing witch hunt is that even when speech is protected to the extent that it is in the United States, it is still vulnerable to attacks from those who wish to limit the right of others to disagree with them. Those lessons attained new relevancy after the terrorist attacks on the United States on September 11, 2001. On the grounds of fighting terrorism, the U.S. government made major inroads on American rights to privacy, taking particular aim at Arab Americans, academia, and the press.

THE RISE OF AMERICAN COMMUNISM

During the early days of industrialization in the United States, the country played host to a large, active Socialist Party. American workers began to join labor unions and engage in strikes. The surge of immigrants who brought with them a tradition of radicalism influenced native workers who felt exploited by low wages and long working hours to protest against the factory owners. By the 1930s the American Communist Party was in full swing; it came to be known as "the red decade," and author Daniel Aaron dubbed it "a time of 'smelly orthodoxies.'"

The 1930s began with worldwide depression and ended with storm clouds of war around the world. In the throes of economic famine, the country was vulnerable to differing visions and ideologies created by upheaval and despair. American intellectuals—introspective, disillusioned, and articulate—

McCarthy Testifies. *Wisconsin senator Joseph R. McCarthy appears before a Senate foreign relations subcommittee on March 8, 1950, in Washington, D.C., to testify about his allegations that communists had infiltrated the State Department.* AP IMAGES.

became the voice of a people whose world had ceased to be the expected bulwark against want, instability, and insecurity. American communists believed that Soviet communism could provide a model for economic stability and social justice. The heyday of the American Communist Party began with a party that was 70 percent foreign-born and ended with a party that was 44 percent professional and white-collar natives.

A large number of Americans joined the Communist Party for social as well as ideological reasons. Clubs, such as the John Reed Clubs, provided a home for fledgling writers and artists and for those who needed to belong to something in which they could believe. Speeches by Communist Party officials, which frequently focused on the defeat of fascism, had mass appeal to the disillusioned portion of the American population. Richard Crossman writes in *The God That Failed* that such individuals "had lost faith in democracy and were willing to sacrifice 'bourgeois liberties' in order to defeat Fascism. Their conversion, in fact, was rooted in despair—a despair of Western values."

THE DECLINE OF AMERICAN COMMUNISM

However, as the 1930s progressed, many Americans began to reexamine their attraction to communism. A number of events influenced the decline in its popularity, including Joseph Stalin's purges within the Soviet Union and the Non-Aggression Pact he signed with Adolf Hitler in 1939. Alfred Kazin spoke for American communists as a whole when he cried: "It was wrong to make common cause with Hitler, wrong to expose the world to war." Following World War II, the fear of communism became an entrenched element in American society as the Soviet-American alliance slowly deteriorated. In 1947 President Harry Truman signed an executive order that barred communists, fascists, and other totalitarians from the national payroll. Also included in the ban were individuals who were guilty of "sympathetic association" with undesirables or their organizations. The stage was set for McCarthy.

JOSEPH McCARTHY

Joseph McCarthy (1908–1957) was born near Appleton, Wisconsin. He received a law degree in 1935 but was not a success as a lawyer. He handled only four cases in his nine months of practice, bragging that he supported himself by playing poker. While practicing law, McCarthy was accused of destroying judicial records. He won his first election by claiming that his sixty-six-year-old opponent was "seventy-three" or "eight-nine" and was too old to govern. He joined the marines during World War II but left early to launch an unsuccessful bid for the Senate. He would later falsely claim that he had been wounded in action.

After winning an election to the Senate, McCarthy paid little attention to the early days of the so-called Red Scare. But as the Cold War escalated, Americans felt more vulnerable to the threat of communism. China fell to the communists, the Soviet Union exploded its first atomic bomb, and Alger Hiss and Julius and Ethel Rosenberg were accused of spying for the enemy. After being identified as the worst U.S. senator in a 1949 poll, McCarthy mentioned to supporters that he needed a cause to improve his image. He found it with the threat of communism and erroneously stated that 284 communists were employed by the State Department. Despite the fact that none of these individuals remained at the State Department, McCarthy declared on the floor of Congress that he had "proof" of widespread communist activity in the government of the United States.

THE RED SCARE

Throughout the Red Scare, McCarthy never documented a single communist in a government job. However, he amassed enormous power with his false claims. He insisted that the past twenty years of democratic government had been "a conspiracy so immense, an infamy so black, as to dwarf any in the history of man." In 1950 Congress passed the McCarran Internal Security Act, virtually outlawing communism in the United States. This was followed in 1954 with the Communist Control Act, forbidding communists from running for political office. Constitutional scholars acknowledge that both laws were clearly in violation of the First Amendment's protection of freedom of association. Limiting access to the ballot is always a distinctive threat to democracy.

Nonetheless, in *Barenblatt v. United States* in 1959, the Supreme Court insisted that its repeated refusal to view the Communist Party as an ordinary political party left it without First Amendment protections. Mandated loyalty oaths for government employees, including teachers, also violated protected freedom of association. Following the example of Congress, many states passed their own loyalty oaths. In New York State, hundreds of educators lost their jobs. Approximately 20 percent of those eventually called to testify before state and congressional investigating committees were college teachers and graduate students.

By 1954 a blacklist was in place in both the fields of education and entertainment. Few who lost their jobs in either field were ever reinstated. The political witch hunt promoted by McCarthy in the 1950s caused great harm and suffering. Beloved entertainers, such as Charlie Chaplin, were forced out of the United States because of the hysteria. Producers, actors, and writers were blacklisted. Without jobs, many were unable to support their families. Most of the people who McCarthy injured were just people who dared to question the capitalist status quo. Many scholars believe that McCarthy, motivated by a desire for personal recognition, was trying to overthrow the New Deal programs of Franklin D. Roosevelt and establish the Republicans as the majority party. In such an environment, policy makers of both parties were afraid to suggest alternatives to both foreign and domestic policy for fear of being charged with subversion.

McCARTHY'S DOWNFALL

McCarthy's tactics proved successful, and in 1952 Dwight D. Eisenhower was elected president, bringing with him a Republican-controlled Congress. Out of 221 Republicans in the House of Representatives, 185 asked to serve on the House Un-American Activities Committee. Richard Nixon used his Senate seat to fight communism and ended up with the vice presidency in 1952 and 1956. Once the Republican Party was in control, McCarthy could no longer rail against communist conspiracies in the government. So he turned his attention to the army, and that proved to be his downfall. Outraged Americans joined with the military and Johnny-come-lately politicians to denounce McCarthyism. McCarthy was censured in 1954 and died three years later, a bitter outcast. Despite this, he has become a cult hero to the New Right and would have felt vindicated by the renewed articulation of the communist threat under Ronald Reagan in the 1980s.

The U.S. Constitution and the First Amendment can only protect the rights of American citizens when they are willing to stand up for the right to engage in free speech, to openly criticize the government and its policy makers, and to demand the inherent democratic right to disagree with others. McCarthyism was able to gain a foothold in the United States only because people were afraid to challenge the loud voices who claimed that democracy was most vulnerable to outside forces. Democracy in the United States has always been most vulnerable to forces within who do not accept the right of dissent. This is the lesson to be learned from McCarthy and his cohorts.

Elizabeth Rholetter Purdy

SEE ALSO: *Blacklisting; Chaplin, Charlie; Communism; Debs, Eugene V.; Hiss, Alger; The Hollywood Ten; 9/11; Reagan, Ronald; Red Scare; Rosenberg, Julius and Ethel.*

BIBLIOGRAPHY

Adams, John G. *Without Precedent: The Story of the Death of McCarthyism.* New York: W. W. Norton, 1983.

Alwood, Edward. *Dark Days in the Newsroom: McCarthyism Aimed at the Press.* Philadelphia: Temple University Press, 2007.

Carvalho, Edward J., and David B. Downing, eds. *Academic Freedom in the Post-9/11 Era.* New York: Palgrave Macmillan, 2010.

Crossman, Richard. *The God That Failed.* Chicago: Regnery Publishers, 1983.

Diggins, John Patrick. *The Rise and Fall of the American Left.* New York: W. W. Norton, 1992.

Fried, Albert, ed. *McCarthyism: The Great American Red Scare; A Documentary History.* New York: Oxford University Press, 1997.

Fried, Richard M. *Nightmare in Red: The McCarthy Era in Perspective.* New York: Oxford University Press, 1990.

Heale, M. J. *McCarthy's Americans: Red Scare Politics in State and Nation, 1935–1965.* Athens: University of Georgia Press, 1998.

Klingaman, William K. *Encyclopedia of the McCarthy Era.* New York: Facts On File, 1996.

Lately, Thomas. *When Angels Wept: The Senator Joseph McCarthy Affair—A Story without a Hero.* New York: William Morrow, 1973.

Reeves, Thomas C. *The Life and Times of Joe McCarthy: A Biography.* New York: Stein and Day, 1982.

Schrecker, Ellen. *The Age of McCarthyism: A Brief History with Documents.* Boston: Bedford Books of St. Martin's Press, 1994.

Schrecker, Ellen. *Many Are the Crimes: McCarthyism in America.* Boston: Little, Brown, 1998.

McCartney, Paul *(1942–)*

Born to a musical family in Liverpool, England, Paul McCartney taught himself to play guitar and in 1957 joined John Lennon's Quarrymen, which later became the Beatles. In 1961 McCartney took up the bass to distinguish himself from the two guitarists. As the Beatles grew musically, he produced an astonishing series of beautiful compositions, including "Yesterday," "Eleanor Rigby," "Penny Lane," and "Let It Be." In addition to being one of the most innovative and melodic bass players in rock and a great singer, McCartney is also an accomplished guitarist and pianist.

Of all the former Beatles, McCartney has enjoyed the most successful solo career. In albums such as *Ram* (1971), recorded with his wife Linda, he managed to maintain a freshness and creativity that was sometimes missing in the solo work of Lennon and George Harrison. In the mid-1970s McCartney continued his success with the band Wings; their celebrated album *Band on the Run* earned the group a Grammy Award and was reissued in 1999 and again in 2010. McCartney also experimented with electronic music in a project known as the Fireman and has released several albums of classical music, including *Liverpool Oratorio* (1991) and *Ecce Cor Meum* (2006). His albums *Flaming Pie* (1997) and the Nigel Godrich–produced *Chaos and Creation in the Backyard* (2005) are generally considered the strongest of his recent traditional pop records.

Often maligned as the "soft" and "commercial" half of the Lennon-McCartney duo, and jealously cited as the richest man in show business, McCartney will be remembered in history as one of the greatest talents of twentieth-century popular music. After the breast cancer–related death of his wife, Linda, in 1998, McCartney married former model Heather Mills in 2002. The couple divorced in 2008, and McCartney married Nancy Shevell in 2011. He received a Grammy Lifetime Achievement Award in 1990, was knighted by Queen Elizabeth II in 1997, and was awarded the Gershwin Prize and Kennedy Center Honors in 2010.

Douglas Cooke

SEE ALSO: *The Beatles; Cancer; Divorce; Grammy Awards; Lennon, John; Pop Music; Rock and Roll.*

BIBLIOGRAPHY

Blake, John. *All You Needed Was Love: The Beatles after the Beatles.* New York: Perigree Books, 1981.

Carlin, Peter Ames. *Paul McCartney: A Life.* New York: Simon & Schuster, 2009.

Miles, Barry. *Paul McCartney: Many Years from Now.* New York: Henry Holt, 1997.

Sounes, Howard. *Fab: An Intimate Life of Paul McCartney.* Cambridge, MA: Da Capo Press, 2010.

McCay, Winsor *(1867–1934)*

When discussing the greatest names in the fields of comic strip art and animation, none demands more respect and admiration than Winsor McCay, who is generally regarded as the first artistic genius of the comic strip medium. Only a decade after the inception of the comic strip in 1895, McCay produced the form's first masterpiece—*Little Nemo in Slumberland*—which ran from 1905 to 1914. The comic involves a young boy's nightly adventures in the fantastic realm of Slumberland. Each episode concludes with the child being shocked back into reality as he wakes up or falls out of bed. Within this simple framework McCay provided his reader with amazingly beautiful artwork, including breathtaking panoramas, elegant colors, and touches of Art Nouveau decoration. The strip's success allowed the artist to branch out into animation. In 1914 he crafted what is arguably a famous and influential cartoon short—*Gertie, the Trained Dinosaur.* Ultimately, McCay was recognized as one of the giants of American twentieth-century art.

Born in Spring Lake, Michigan, shortly after the Civil War, Zenas Winsor McCay displayed a talent for art from early childhood. In 1897 he began a newspaper career in Cincinnati, Ohio, and by 1903 had created his first comic strip, *Tales of the Jungle Imps.* Other strips, such as *Little Sammy Sneeze* and *Dream of the Rarebit Fiend,* soon followed. McCay was fascinated by the juxtaposition of "real life" and the worlds created by the unconscious mind, and the world of dreams became a recurring theme in his work. The real and dream worlds were depicted in a similar style, thus creating a sense of ambiguity for readers, who were unsure which drawings depicted the characters' "true" reality.

McCay's most celebrated exploration of the dream state came on October 15, 1905, with the publication of *Little Nemo in Slumberland.* The weekly color page presents the sleeping boy, who was modeled on McCay's son, Robert, and his colorful companions—Flip, a green dwarf; Impy the cannibal; and Slivers the dog—as they wander through the increasingly bizarre dreamland. Slumberland was bound only by McCay's vivid imagination. In his book *The Comics,* author Jerry Robinson describes the realm this way: "There were sky bombs, wild train and dirigible rides, exotic parades, bizarre circuses, and festivities of all kinds in Byzantine settings and rococo landscapes. Just the dreams a small boy would like to have." The most celebrated feature in Slumberland is Nemo's own bed, which can walk and fly.

Many of the episodes revolve around the boy's meetings with Morpheus, the kingdom's ruler, and his beautiful daughter. The character of Nemo, whose name means "no one" in Latin, is rather nondescript and displays little personality. Often he is a passive figure who allows the events in Slumberland to overwhelm him. McCay did, however, allow the character to be more active in one 1908 episode set in "Shantytown." Nemo becomes a Christ figure as he heals the sick, transforms the earth into paradise, and resurrects the dead. The strip was an immediate success and one of the medium's first titles to spawn a line of merchandise. It was even the basis of a Broadway musical, with a score written by Victor Herbert.

Little Nemo's adventures continued until 1914, when it ended its run. McCay eventually returned to his most famous creation and produced more Nemo stories from 1924 to 1927. These later strips, however, are not as highly regarded as the initial Nemo series.

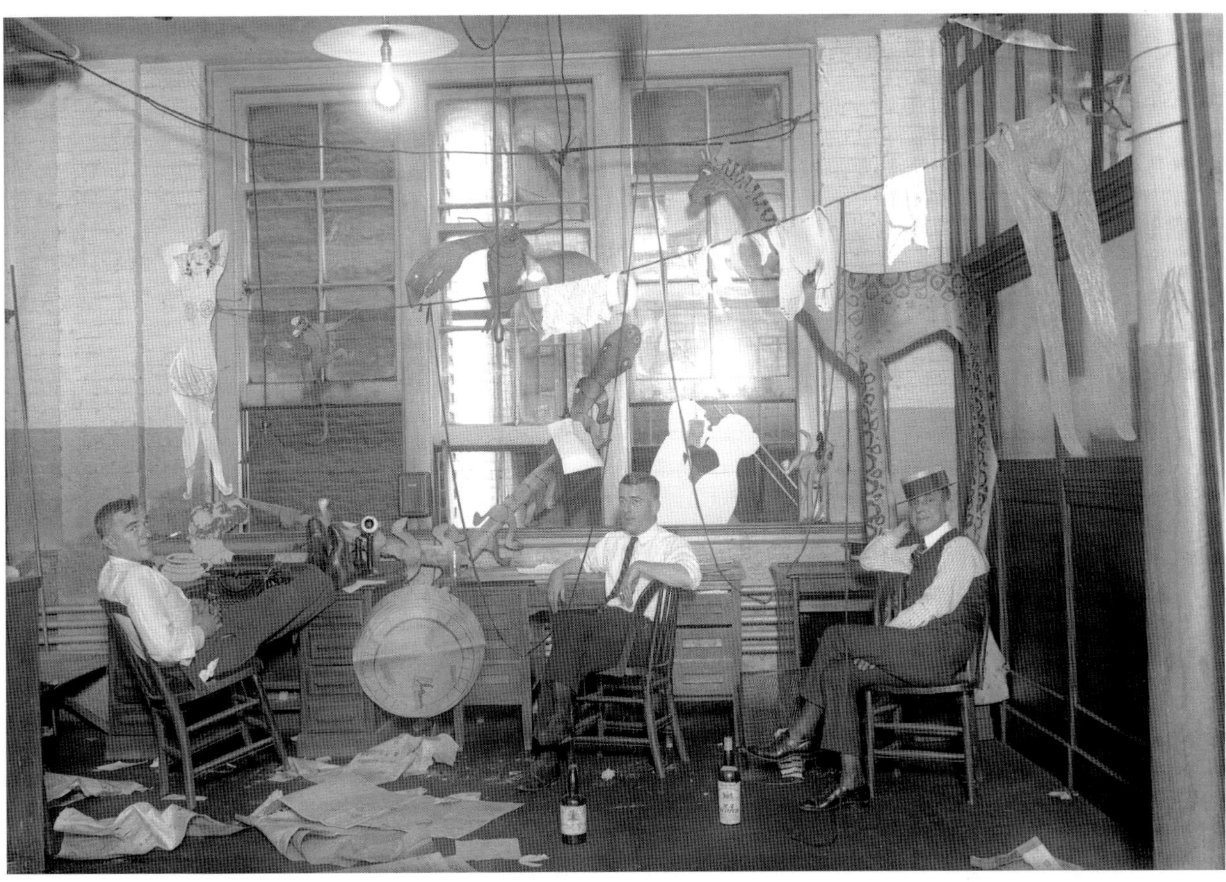

Winsor McCay. *Winsor McCay, right, poses in the Hearst newspaper offices with other cartoonists in the early 1920s.* © BETTMANN/CORBIS.

The popularity of *Little Nemo in Slumberland* allowed McCay the opportunity to begin a career in animation. In 1911 a cartoon short based on the Nemo strips was released. Like his newspaper work, McCay's animation was known for its ambitious nature. His short film *The Sinking of the Lusitania* combines animation and live action to describe the British liner's sinking by a German submarine.

McCay's most lasting contribution to animation is *Gertie, the Trained Dinosaur*. The innovative film depicts a trained dinosaur that performs tricks at the command of McCay, who stands beside the movie screen dressed as a lion tamer. He speaks to Gertie and appears to toss objects to her. The film was a sensation, and McCay was soon presenting it throughout the vaudeville circuit. His act also consisted of "chalk talks," where he drafted quick drawings of the audience and presented illustrated sermons on paper such as "The Seven Ages of Man." By the early 1920s McCay left animation, complaining of its overcommercialization. His later years were spent as an editorial cartoonist for the conservative Hearst newspapers.

Winsor McCay is credited with raising the comic strip to a great American art form. His continual experimentation with perspective, detailed pencil work, and proportion dazzles readers to this day. The dream world of Slumberland allowed him to constantly push the bounds of his imagination. *Little Nemo in Slumberland* is a visual feast that transports even contemporary readers to a land where anything is possible. In 1995 the United States Postal Service honored McCay by placing Little Nemo on one of its stamps to commemorate the comic's centennial. Maurice Horn in *The World Encyclopedia of Comics* perhaps best summarized McCay's legacy when he said the artist deserves the title "primus inter pares," the first among his peers in the history of cartoons.

Charles Coletta

SEE ALSO: *Comics; Hearst, William Randolph; Vaudeville.*

BIBLIOGRAPHY

Horn, Maurice. *The World Encyclopedia of Comics*. New York: Avon Books, 1976.

Marschall, Richard. *America's Great Comic Strip Artists*. New York: Abbeville Press, 1989.

Robinson, Jerry. *The Comics*. New York: Berkley Publishing, 1974.

Walker, Brian. *The Comics before 1945*. New York: H. N. Abrams, 2004.

McCoy, Horace *(1897–1955)*

Sometime newspaper sports editor, pulp magazine story writer, "hard-boiled" novelist, screenwriter, and actor, Horace McCoy is best known for his first novel, *They Shoot Horses, Don't They?* (1935), set during a marathon dance contest in the 1930s and made into a film of the same name in 1969 (directed by Sydney Pollack). He wrote a number of uncompromising novels (one published posthumously) on themes such as civic corruption, Hollywood, the Depression, and the plight of the individual caught in the capitalist machine. His many credits as a screenwriter include *The Trail of the Lonesome Pine* (1936) and *Gentleman Jim* (1942).

Chris Routledge

SEE ALSO: *The Great Depression; Hollywood; Pulp Magazines.*

BIBLIOGRAPHY

Fine, David, ed. *Los Angeles in Fiction: A Collection of Original Essays.* Albuquerque: University of New Mexico Press, 1984.

Madden, David, ed. *Tough Guy Writers of the Thirties.* Carbondale: Southern Illinois University Press, 1968.

Wilt, David E. *Hardboiled in Hollywood.* Bowling Green, OH: Bowling Green State University Popular Press, 1991.

McCrea, Joel *(1905–1990)*

Although he liked doing Westerns best, Joel McCrea appeared in some of the best comedy films of the early 1940s, such as *The Palm Beach Story* (1942), *Sullivan's Travels* (1941), and *The More the Merrier* (1943). The versatile actor also excelled in dramas and thrillers, including *These Three* (1936), *Dead End* (1937), and Alfred Hitchcock's *Foreign Correspondent* (1940). Not a flashy actor, McCrea was a tall, attractive, somewhat self-effacing man who conveyed a sort of rough-hewn honesty and patience that served him well in both serious and comedic roles.

Born in Pasadena, California, McCrea was nine years old when his family moved to Hollywood. Back then it was "all open country"—he and the movie business grew up together. McCrea got his start working as an extra in silent films in the early 1920s; he was initially hired because he was an excellent horseman. By the early 1930s he was starring in talkies such as *Bird of Paradise* (1932), *The Lost Squadron* (1932), and *The Most Dangerous Game* (1932). McCrea switched almost exclusively to Westerns in the mid-1940s, appearing in *Ramrod* (1947), *Four Faces West* (1948), and *Colorado Territory* (1949), along with nearly two dozen others. McCrea's final major Western was Sam Peckinpah's *Ride the High Country*, which has been considered a classic since its release in 1962.

Ron Goulart

SEE ALSO: *Hitchcock, Alfred; Hollywood; Screwball Comedies; Silent Movies; The Western.*

BIBLIOGRAPHY

Katz, Ephraim. *The Film Encyclopedia.* New York: Perigee Books, 1982.

Kobol, John. *People Will Talk.* New York: Alfred A. Knopf, 1985.

McDaniel, Hattie *(1895–1952)*

Although Hattie McDaniel was a performer for most of her life—onstage, in film, and on radio and television—her career was largely defined by the racism of American culture and the limitations it placed on her achievements. Despite her talent as a singer, a dancer, and an actress, Hollywood cast her in more than 300 movies, most often as a cook, a maid, or a mammy. Like many black performers of the time, McDaniel was anxious to succeed in an industry controlled by whites, and she built a successful career from the parts that were offered to her. White audiences familiar with McDaniel only because of her Oscar-winning role as Scarlett's mammy in *Gone with the Wind* are probably unaware of the criticism other African Americans heaped on her (and others) for perpetuating racist stereotypes.

Most of McDaniel's roles involved playing southerners, but she did not come from the South. Born in Wichita, Kansas, and raised in the relatively liberal city of Denver, Colorado, she attended integrated schools. The youngest of thirteen children, McDaniel loved to perform from an early age. In 1910 her father started his own minstrel show, with two of her brothers as performers. When she joined them soon afterward, her career onstage began. She travelled with the show, singing, dancing, and writing songs for almost ten years. After the death of her father in 1922, she found a job on the new Denver radio station KOA, singing jazz songs with a band. She continued to work the vaudeville circuit until the 1930s, when jobs dried up with the arrival of the Great Depression.

McDaniel got another big break while working as a restroom attendant at the Club Madrid near Milwaukee, Wisconsin. When the management needed a singer to fill in, customers recommended the talented woman they had heard singing to herself in the washroom, and McDaniel was offered a new job. At the urging of her brothers, who had gone to find work in California, she finally moved to Los Angeles to try her luck in the movie business. She landed many small roles, often without appearing in the credits. The pay was low, and McDaniel had to work as a maid while she was portraying maids in the movies. Continuing to work hard at her acting, she learned a southern accent that she often used in her stereotypical maid roles, and she began to get more significant parts in larger movies. She received good reviews for her acting in a remake of *Showboat* (1936) and appeared in other films with Marlene Dietrich, Mae West, Katharine Hepburn, and Barbara Stanwyck.

It was her powerful performance as Scarlett's mammy in the 1939 film *Gone with the Wind* that won McDaniel prominent status among white audiences. She made history by becoming the first black woman to win an Academy Award (the second was Whoopi Goldberg, for her role in *Ghost* almost fifty years later). McDaniel's work on *Gone with the Wind*, however, was seen as controversial in the African American community. Her performance was excellent, but Hollywood would not acknowledge the fact that McDaniel was called Mammy by the cast even when not in character or that the black cast members had not been permitted to attend the feted premiere of the movie in segregationist Atlanta, Georgia. Shortly after the movie was released, the National Association for the Advancement of Colored People (NAACP) mounted a campaign against the racist stereotypes of blacks in movies. "Mammyism" and "Uncle Tomism" were decried as harmful to all African Americans. Such actors as Ethel Waters and Stepin Fetchit were loudly

Hattie McDaniel. *Hattie McDaniel was the first African American performer to receive an Academy Award, earning Best Supporting Actress honors for her role as Mammy in* Gone with the Wind. **SILVER SCREEN COLLECTION/CONTRIBUTOR/MOVIEPIX/GETTY IMAGES.**

criticized. As the most famous mammy of the moment, McDaniel received the most hostile censure of all.

Although McDaniel did accept other mammylike roles in film and played the maid on the sitcom *Beulah* (1945–1954)—first on radio from 1947 to 1952 and then on television from 1951 to 1952—she and other black actors formed the Fair Play Committee to try to change Hollywood from within. She had been successful in having the word *nigger* removed from the screenplay of *Gone with the Wind,* and she refused to speak in dialect in *Beulah*. Many African Americans considered these victories too small, however, and the continuing criticism greatly upset McDaniel. This, combined with the pressure of problems in her fourth marriage, contributed to the actress's depression and health problems.

McDaniel died of breast cancer at the Motion Picture Country Home and Hospital in California in 1952. In recent years audiences and critics have recognized that if McDaniel had refused to play the roles available for black women in her era, the world would most likely never have heard of her. She was honored for her strength of character and work in fighting for the advancement of African Americans in the AMC made-for-television movie *Beyond Tara: The Extraordinary Life of Hattie McDonald* (2001), which won a Daytime Emmy for the 2001–2002 season. In 2006 she became the first black Oscar winner to appear on a U.S. postage stamp.

Tina Gianoulis

SEE ALSO: *Academy Awards;* Beulah*; Cancer; Depression; Dietrich, Marlene; Emmy Awards; Fetchit, Stepin; Goldberg, Whoopi;* Gone with the Wind*; The Great Depression; Hepburn, Katharine; Hollywood; Jazz; Made-for-Television Movies; Minstrel Shows; Radio; Stanwyck, Barbara; Television; Vaudeville; Waters, Ethel; West, Mae.*

BIBLIOGRAPHY

Bogle, Donald. *Toms, Coons, Mulattoes, Mammies and Bucks: An Interpretive History of Blacks in America.* New York: Viking Press, 1973.

Cripps, Thomas. *Slow Fade to Black: The Negro in American Film, 1900–1942.* New York: Oxford University Press, 1977.

DiMare, Philip C. *Movies in American History: An Encyclopedia.* Santa Barbara, CA: ABC-CLIO, 2011.

Jackson, Carlton. *Hattie: The Life of Hattie McDaniel.* Lanham, MD: Madison Books, 1990.

McDonald's

From its humble beginnings in 1948 as a drive-in restaurant in Southern California, McDonald's grew by the start of the twenty-first century into the world's largest food service organization, having served more than 100 billion hamburgers in half a century of operation. In 2011 the chain claimed 33,000 restaurants in 119 countries, where sixty-four million customers a day were served, twenty-seven million of them in the United States alone. In six decades the golden arches, Big Macs, and Ronald McDonald have become among the most internationally recognized and controversial icons of American popular culture. Over the company's objections, the prefix "Mc-" has been used informally in English to describe any person or situation whose essential qualities are seen in terms of homogenization, predictability, or banality.

THE BIRTH OF FAST FOOD

It all started in the late 1940s on the crest of the postwar automobile boom when brothers Richard and Maurice McDonald were searching for a way to improve their little octagonal barbecue drive-in business in San Bernardino, California. The concept they created was a revolutionary one that would become the keystone of the nascent fast-food industry: an emphasis on efficiency, low prices, big volume, and speedy self-service and a jettisoning of anything that would slow down the transaction, such as carhops, plates, forks, knives, glassware, dishwashers, tipping, and less popular menu items. When the brothers reopened their restaurant with their "McDonald's New Self-Service System" in 1948, confusion at first reigned, but soon the fifteen-cent McDonald's hamburger that came with ketchup, pickle, and onion became extremely successful. Within a few months customers were lining up to buy the nine available menu items: hamburger, cheeseburger, french fries, potato chips, pie, coffee, milk, soft drinks, and milk shakes.

In 1952 McDonald's sold more than one million hamburgers and 160 tons of french fries, which were becoming famous for their "perfect fry" due to the proper aging of potatoes. The brothers planned to franchise their self-service system and designed, with architect Stanley Meston, the prototype restaurant with its two giant golden arches. The first McDonald's franchise opened in May 1953 in Phoenix, Arizona. In 1954 there were nine franchise restaurants in operation and several others already sold. That same year, intrigued by the 20,000 milk shakes sold every month by the McDonald's business, Ray Kroc (1902–1984), the exclusive distributor of the "Multimixer" milk shake

Ray Kroc's First McDonald's Store. *The first McDonald's restaurant opened by Ray Kroc in Des Plaines, Illinois, in 1955 is now a museum run by the restaurant chain.* © RALF-FINN HESTOFT/CORBIS.

machine, went to San Bernardino to see the McDonald's operation firsthand. Immediately he foresaw the gigantic potentialities of the concept and became the exclusive franchising agent for the McDonald brothers in the United States. In 1955 Kroc formed the new franchising company under the name of McDonald's System Inc. and opened his first McDonald's restaurant in Des Plaines, Illinois. In 1961 Kroc bought out the McDonald brothers for $2.7 million.

Kroc did not invent McDonald's, but he transformed and developed it into a leading institution that has revolutionized the food service industry and altered traditional eating habits throughout the world. The astounding popular success of McDonald's and its unprecedented growth, first in the United States and later in foreign countries, became a commercial legend. Cleanliness, friendly service, and predictability—the capability to deliver consistent products anywhere in the world—have remained a hallmark of McDonald's. Throughout, Kroc's brilliant strategy called for a heavy investment in advertising and public relations. The theme "Look for the Golden Arches" started in 1960.

By 1963 McDonald's restaurants were selling one million hamburgers a day, and the company decided to launch a television advertising campaign. In 1966, three years after his first public appearance in Washington, D.C., Ronald McDonald, portrayed by Willard Scott, made his national television debut. The happy clown became the McDonald's mascot who would attract millions of children and their families to McDonald's restaurants. Kids had long been a target group for the chain's marketing: beginning with the opening in 1971 of the first McDonald's Playland in Chula Vista, California, McDonald's invested millions in playgrounds and ads directed primarily at children, for whom it introduced the Happy Meal in 1979.

BUILDING AN EMPIRE

In 1966, the year after its advertising started to claim that "McDonald's Is Your Kind of Place," McDonald's became a public company listed on the New York Stock Exchange. After almost twenty years of price stability, the hamburger rose from fifteen to eighteen cents, and international expansion began. The first McDonald's restaurant located outside of the United States opened in Canada on June 1, 1967, in Richmond, British Columbia. In 1968 the 1,000th restaurant in the chain opened, and the most popular burger, internationally known as the Big Mac, was added to the menu. In 1972 the Quarter Pounder was introduced, and the McDonald's corporation achieved the $1 billion sales mark. By 1970 McDonald's was represented by 1,600 restaurants in all fifty United States and in four other countries. The 1970s saw an expansion of the restaurant's locales from brightly lit roadside stands surrounded by parking lots to smaller, "townhouse" establishments in urban settings.

During the 1970s, such slogans as "You Deserve a Break Today," "We Do It All for You," and "Nobody Can Do It Like McDonald's Can" permeated the everyday life of millions of customers. Meanwhile, McDonald's entered the breakfast trade with the highly successful introduction of the Egg McMuffin in 1973. By 1980 thirty-five billion hamburgers had been sold, and in 1985 McDonald's became one of the thirty companies that make up the Dow Jones Industrial Average. By 1990, when the eighty billion burger milestone had been reached, the company's 11,800 restaurants in fifty-four countries accounted for $18.7 billion in sales.

With its aggressive expansion into the global market, McDonald's has come to epitomize North American culture, especially the United States and its brand of capitalism. In 1971 the corporation entered the Asian, Australian, and European markets. While the Dutch McDonald's restaurant failed, "Makadonaldo" on the Ginza in Tokyo became an immediate success. In 1979 McDonald's started doing business in South America. With the collapse of Soviet-style communism in the late 1980s, the emergence of McDonald's in socialist or postsocialist societies attracted extensive media coverage and increased the brand's notoriety. The opening of the first McDonald's restaurant in Moscow on January 31, 1990, attracted 30,000 customers and was billed by the media as an important symbolic event, as if the Russians had conceded in the famous "kitchen debate" between Richard Nixon and Nikita Khrushchev in the 1950s. The opening of the first McDonald's restaurant in Africa in 1992 (in Casablanca, Morocco) was not much noticed, but on April 23 of that year, 40,000 Chinese lined up in front of the first outlet in Beijing. The popularity and prosperity of McDonald's in the Czech Republic, East Germany, Hungary, Poland, and Slovenia have been the focus of numerous documentaries and articles.

Not surprisingly, such extraordinary success has also generated protests and criticisms from very different groups, ranging from the Far Left to the Far Right and including environmentalists, nutritionists, religious fundamentalists, cultural critics, and heritage preservationists, among others. McDonald's has taken a stance of being responsive to many of these concerns. Responding to civil rights activists in the 1970s who faulted the chain's hiring practices, the corporation developed training programs for minorities and women. In 1990 McDonald's USA launched the McRecycle program, and in 1991 the company initiated a waste reduction action plan to recycle its packaging products. When the outbreak of mad cow disease across Europe caused McDonald's to post an unprecedented quarterly loss in late 2002, the company began to enforce some of the most stringent rules of any fast-food chain regarding meat sourcing.

In response to demands from increasingly health-conscious customers (beginning in the 1990s, but particularly after the release of the 2004 documentary *Super Size Me*, in which a filmmaker eats nothing but McDonald's food for thirty days and records the negative effects on his health), the restaurants started to offer more dietetic meals by using trans-fat-free oil in the cooking of french fries and adding salads, low-fat parfaits, reduced-fat ice cream, grilled chicken sandwiches, and fruit smoothies to their menus, even going as far as to remove the option to "super size" meals with extra-large drinks and fries from their menus in 2009. In India, McDonald's restaurants serve vegetable McNuggets and a mutton-based Maharaja Mac. In Israel, kosher hamburgers are available, and in Muslim countries, menus are certified as halal. McDonald's has also designed buildings and signs respecting the local architecture. In Miami's Little Havana, a McDonald's restaurant evokes a hacienda, while on Long Island, New York, a restored 1860s house accommodates the fast-food outlet.

ADAPTING TO THE GLOBAL MARKET

McDonald's has borne the brunt of American and European intellectuals who fault it for being an agent of cultural imperialism and globalization responsible for homogenizing indigenous cultures and destroying local traditions. In the United States the rising popularity of franchised fast-food restaurant chains in the 1950s coincided with the steady decline of traditional mom-and-pop eateries and the subsequent homogenization of the roadside landscape. In the early 1970s most of the old stainless-steel "railcar" diners, which offered regional cooking and atmosphere, could not compete with the fast-food chains and were demolished or abandoned, though diners did experience a resurgence of sorts by the 1990s. In 1990 in Hartsville, Tennessee, McDonald's opened its own Golden Arch Cafe as an outlet resembling a traditional 1950s-style diner; the café offered sit-down service from a menu that included lasagna, Salisbury steaks with two vegetables, and grilled chicken platters, with only the french fries a vestige of the fast-food concept.

Close attention to consumption practices reveals more complex interaction patterns. While McDonald's has affected some influential changes in consumer habits, local cultures and identities have constrained McDonald's to adapt to place and reveal local idiosyncrasies. Some obvious examples of this have included changes in menu items, such as the Teriyaki McBurger in Japan or Kiwi Burgers in New Zealand; the provision of beer with meals and large smoking sections in Belgium, France, and Germany; or nomenclature changes to adapt to the metric system. These changes, however, often mask the fact that the process of production and distribution of the food has changed considerably from traditional methods.

For most customers outside the United States, McDonald's offers an altered cultural and social experience that starts when the threshold is crossed. In eastern Asia, writes James L. Watson in *Golden Arches East: McDonald's in East Asia*:

> consumers have quietly, and in some cases stubbornly, transformed their neighborhood McDonald's restaurant into local institutions. . . . In Beijing, Seoul and Taipei, for instance, McDonald's restaurants are treated as leisure centers, where people can retreat from the stresses of urban life. In Hong Kong, middle school students often sit in McDonald's for hours—studying, gossiping, and picking over snacks. . . . One surprise was the discovery that many McDonald's restaurants in East Asia have become sanctuaries for women who wish to escape male-dominated settings.

In Europe the facades of the restaurants are designed to conform to the local architecture, and the interior design varies depending on the city, with references made to the local culture such as modernism in Barcelona, Art Nouveau in Brussels, and Art Deco in Paris. Design quality compensates for the lack of space and higher densities of European McDonald's restaurants. Contrary to the situation in North America, fast food in Europe does not mean fast consumption. Numerous McDonald's restaurants in Paris (where they are known as "McDo") have become afternoon meeting places for elderly women who enjoy chatting while drinking a coffee and eating an apple pie. French teenagers have adopted McDonald's restaurants as headquarters where they can spend hours socializing with their friends, making France the second-largest consumer of McDonald's behind the United States, despite the fierce protests upon the chain's arrival in the 1970s.

Eating in Europe is a social and often familial event that takes time, and people like to share it in a pleasant atmosphere. Consequently, comfortable, individual chairs and real plants had to replace the original fixed chairs and plastic foliage. Some McDonald's restaurants in Europe supply free daily newspapers and dress their tables with cotton tablecloths and small vases of dried flowers. Thus, while McDonald's captured the spirit of postwar America and built its national fame on the rationalization of the fast-food concept, the international success of McDonald's restaurants relies on their ability to sell the American myth through a pseudo-American experience exotic enough to fit local imaginations and expectations about America but flexible enough to be adapted to local customs.

Despite the global economic turbulence of the late 1990s and again late in the first decade of the 2000s, the international division of the McDonald's Corporation achieved continuous growth and success, whereas simultaneously in the United States it faced dramatic difficulties under competition from other restaurant concepts. In 1998 the company decided to adapt the lessons learned abroad to the United States and made a radical cultural, operational, and strategic turn in the management of its domestic market. The company's domestic operations were decentralized and streamlined into five divisions based on geographic regions. Like their international counterparts, independent franchises in the United States have become collaborators in marketing and advertising, with a say in the menu. The company began to experiment with new products such as the Cajun Chicken Sandwich and the McFlurry to respond better to local competitive situations.

After four decades of success based on perfect uniformity and predictability, McDonald's entered the twenty-first century with decentralization, flexibility, and pluralism as its new mantra. In the first decade of the 2000s the company made a public commitment to focus less on expanding its already massive empire and more on providing improved service and a better eating experience at its existing locations. Since having its least successful year on record in 2002, McDonald's has rebounded on the success of its "dollar menu" (introduced in 2003) and specialty items such as angus beef burgers and the McCafe line of espresso drinks, once again making it the largest and most profitable fast-food chain on the planet.

Catherine C. Galley
Briavel Holcomb

SEE ALSO: *Advertising; Environmentalism; Fast Food; French Fries; Hamburger; Leisure Time; Modernism; Multiculturalism;* Super Size Me*; Television.*

BIBLIOGRAPHY

Alfino, Mark; John S. Caputo; and Robin Wynyard, eds. *McDonaldization Revisited.* Westport, CT: Praeger, 1998.

Boas, Max, and Steve Chain. *Big Mac: The Unauthorized Story of McDonald's.* New York: Dutton, 1976.

Fishwick, Marshall, ed. *Ronald Revisited: The World of Ronald McDonald.* Bowling Green, OH: Bowling Green University Press, 1983.

Gilbert, Sara. *The Story of McDonald's.* Mankato, MN: Creative Education, 2009.

Kroc, Ray, and Robert Anderson. *Grinding It Out: The Making of McDonald's.* Chicago: Contemporary Books, 1977.

Leidner, Robin. *Fast Food, Fast Talk: Service Work and Routinization of Everyday Life.* Berkeley: University of California Press, 1993.

Love, John F. *McDonald's: Behind the Arches.* New York: Bantam, 1995.

Ritzer, George. *The McDonaldization of Society: An Investigation into the Changing Character of Contemporary Social Life.* Thousand Oaks, CA: Sage Publications, 1993.

Ritzer, George. *The McDonaldization Thesis: Explorations and*

Extensions. London: Sage Publications, 1998.

Robison, Richard, and David Goodman, eds. *The New Rich in Asia: Mobile Phones, McDonald's, and Middle-Class Revolution*. London: Routledge, 1996.

Spurlock, Morgan, and Jeremy Barlow. *Supersized: Strange Tales from a Fast-Food Culture*. Milwaukie, OR: Dark Horse Books, 2011.

Watson, James L., ed. *Golden Arches East: McDonald's in East Asia*. Stanford, CA: Stanford University Press, 1997.

McEnroe, John *(1959–)*

Famously dubbed "Superbrat" by the British tabloid press, John McEnroe is doomed to have his remarkable athletic accomplishments overshadowed by the media perception of him as a whining, petulant crybaby. But the achievements of one of the most talented male players to ever step on a tennis court cannot be separated from the renewed buzz about the sport generated by his infuriating on-court antics. Simply put, if McEnroe had not come along, tennis in the 1970s would have had to invent him.

John McEnroe. *John McEnroe raises the victor's trophy after his win at Wimbledon in 1981.* GETTY IMAGES/STRINGER/GETTY IMAGES SPORT/GETTY IMAGES.

The son of a U.S. Air Force officer, McEnroe grew up in the Gold Coast of Long Island, New York. But McEnroe was no ordinary suburban tennis brat. He impressed his instructors with his ability to make difficult shots at a young age. Schooled at an elite tennis academy (he was eventually thrown out for bad behavior), McEnroe later attended Stanford University and made his initial splash at Wimbledon in 1977, becoming the youngest man ever to reach the semifinals. He turned pro the following year.

Men's tennis at that time was in a period of transition, as the popular favorite Jimmy Connors saw his run at the top coming to an end. Björn Borg was the king of Wimbledon, having won five titles in a row from 1976 through 1980. But the icy Swede failed to capture the imagination of the public with his mechanical, ground-stroking game. When McEnroe defeated fellow American Vitas Gerulaitis in the U.S. Open final in 1979—becoming the youngest winner since Pancho Gonzalez—a page in tennis history seemed to have been turned. The following year, McEnroe surged into the finals at Wimbledon, where he met Borg in an epic match many consider the greatest of all time. The upstart American fought off five match points in a grueling fourth-set tiebreaker but was defeated in the fifth set. The next year, McEnroe finally broke through, ending the Swede's five-year reign at the All-England Club.

In the six-year span from 1979 through 1984, McEnroe captured the Wimbledon and U.S. Open titles a total of seven times. He became the first man since Bill Tilden in the 1920s to win three straight U.S. Open crowns, from 1979 through 1981. Ranked number one in the world in 1981, 1983, and 1984, McEnroe also was a mainstay of the U.S. Davis Cup team, leading the squad to victory in international competition on five separate occasions. As a doubles player, he usually paired up with fellow American Peter Fleming.

A left-hander, McEnroe possessed unparalleled shot-making ability. He used his skills to his advantage by playing with a ferocious, attacking serve-and-volley style. On fast surfaces, such as the grass at Wimbledon or the hard courts of the U.S. Open, he could often overwhelm plodding baseline opponents like Ivan Lendl. The McEnroe approach put him at a disadvantage on clay, however, or when faced with an opponent who could match him in tenacity, like Connors or Borg.

McEnroe's volatile temperament did him in on more than one occasion as well. Berating chair umpires, arguing line calls, and bickering with spectators were all part of the McEnroe repertoire. Often, he claimed, he used his anger as a way to fire himself up to win points or get back into a match emotionally. But there is no denying that his histrionics cost him at times, as when a meltdown at the 1984 French Open finals allowed Lendl to storm back from a two-set deficit to win the championship.

"Johnny Mac" was not the first tennis player to act in an irregular fashion, of course. Before him, there had been Evonne Goolagong's bizarre "walkabouts" and Ilie Nastase's eternally upthrust middle finger. But something about McEnroe's unique mix of bad sportsmanship and spoiled rich boy arrogance made him the special darling of the tennis press. Newspapers, especially in Britain, invariably caricatured him as a sobbing child braying for attention. The cartoonists and reporters were the ones left crying, however, when McEnroe retired from the professional circuit in 1992, leaving no dynamic successor to take up his crowd-rousing mantle.

After retirement, McEnroe tried to stay in the spotlight. He divorced his wife, actress Tatum O'Neal, in 1994, and married rock singer Patty Smyth in 1997. The musical connection led McEnroe toward a new goal: rock star. That didn't work out; nor did a short-lived television show on MSNBC in 2004. In tennis, he coached Davis Cup teams and served as television commentator. He often appears on television, both as a guest on talk shows and in cameos in shows including *30 Rock* (2006–) and *Curb Your Enthusiasm* (2000–).

McEnroe still competes in the APT, a tennis tour of retired players. His enthusiasm for tennis helped land him in the International Tennis Hall of Fame in 1999. His Hall of Fame biography noted that McEnroe was "as ferocious a competitor as tennis has ever produced, steely in his resolve, unwavering in his convictions . . . who played with singular verve and sparkle. A New Yorker with rare talent, his imagination knew no boundaries."

Robert E. Schnakenberg

SEE ALSO: *Connors, Jimmy; Television; Tennis;* 30 Rock*; Wimbledon.*

BIBLIOGRAPHY

Adams, Tim. *On Being John McEnroe.* New York: Crown Publishers, 2003.

Burchard, S. H. *John McEnroe.* New York: Harcourt Brace Jovanovich, 1979.

Evans, Richard. *McEnroe, a Rage for Perfection: A Biography.* New York: Simon & Schuster, 1982.

Mallozzi, Vincent M. "The View at 50: He Can Be Serious." *New York Times*, March 14, 2009, 10(L).

McEnroe, John, and James Kaplan. *You Cannot Be Serious.* New York: Putnam, 2002.

Tignor, Stephen. *High Strung: Bjorn Borg, John McEnroe, and the Untold Story of Tennis's Fiercest Rivalry.* New York: Harper, 2011.

McEntire, Reba *(1955–)*

Reba McEntire has sold more than fifty-seven million albums, scored more than thirty number one hits, and joined the company of those recognized worldwide by merely their first names. Although she has earned scores of honors, including Grammy Awards and People's Choice Awards, the major contribution of the feisty redhead may be that she has shattered stereotypes within and beyond the country music industry. She has demonstrated to the country community that female singers can play with the big boys and to the music industry at large that a country singer can be as glamorous and as successful as any pop diva.

A WOMAN'S STORY

Because she has diversified into movies and assorted business interests, McEntire is frequently compared to Dolly Parton. A more accurate comparison, however, may be to Loretta Lynn, who earned her fame singing songs about women's lives. McEntire has sung of women surviving on their own, women refusing to be used, and women suffering from AIDS. The defining song of her career may be "Is There Life out There?" The video shows McEntire as a young woman struggling to balance home and children with a low-paying job and college classes. The happy ending on graduation day suggests that there is a life for women beyond the domestic sphere, a reality McEntire and thousands of her listeners have discovered for themselves.

McEntire is not alone in selecting material clearly crafted for a female audience, but no other woman in country music has yet achieved her level of success. Her first charting record came in 1978, and her accomplishments increased over the next three decades as her album sales and concert revenues placed her in competition not merely with the men of country music but also with major artists in other music genres. Like many successful women, McEntire has been the target of criticism for her ambition, but she remains undeterred by these attacks.

FINDING HER VOICE

McEntire credits her determination and pragmatism to her stable middle-class rearing in Chokie, Oklahoma. The daughter of a teacher and a rodeo champion/cattle rancher, she grew up tending cattle, barrel racing, and singing with her siblings. Discovered while she was singing "The Star-Spangled Banner" at the 1974 National Finals Rodeo, she signed with Mercury in 1975. Her early efforts, however, were mediocre, due to a pop veneer that muted her distinctive sound and minimized her

Reba McEntire. *Reba McEntire is one of the top-selling female country music artists of all time.* ED RODE/CONTRIBUTOR/GETTY IMAGES ENTERTAINMENT/GETTY IMAGES.

emotional range. The 1980s brought a change of direction with a more mature McEntire assuming control of her career. She signed on as the opening act for established artists such as the Statler Brothers and Conway Twitty, a move that gave her expert tutelage in the profession and exposure to core country audiences. By the time she signed with MCA in 1984, two of her songs for Mercury had reached number one, including "Can't Even Get the Blues," an upbeat tune that reverses the woman-as-victim stereotype. McEntire was beginning to understand what she had to offer.

In Jimmy Bowen, president of MCA's Nashville, Tennessee, division, she had someone secure enough to encourage artist involvement and smart enough to allow her to return to her distinctive voice and style. The first result of their collaboration was *My Kind of Country* (1984), which included "Somebody Should Leave," a Harlan Howard tune that showcases the emotional power of McEntire's voice. The song became a number one hit.

MADE FOR VIDEO

Not only did *My Kind of Country* fit seamlessly into the wave of new traditionalism that was capturing country audiences in the 1980s, but it also hit as The Nashville Network (TNN) and Country Music Television (CMT) were becoming established venues for country artists. McEntire's sassy persona and down-home accent had immense appeal for TNN and CMT audiences, and she proved to have a deft touch with videos. Country music's audience was also changing. Baby boomers dissatisfied with pop lyrics were searching for a new musical format and discovering the appeal of country. Thus, the country audience became more diverse and, in significant ways, more sophisticated. A real cowgirl, McEntire had the credentials to satisfy traditional country audiences, but she was also part of a college-educated, television-addicted generation that saw past regional barriers. She was poised to take advantage of the changes.

In 1986 her career exploded. With "Whoever's in New England," she had a crossover hit in both audio and video. The album (by the same title) went gold and later platinum, and McEntire was inducted into the Grand Ole Opry. Both the Country Music Association (CMA) and the Academy of Country Music named her female vocalist of the year, and CMA added the coveted Entertainer of the Year trophy. The redhead from Oklahoma had arrived, but this was only the beginning. Determined to control all aspects of her career, she created Starstruck Entertainment in 1988, a corporation that expanded as she saw fit. Starstruck soon encompassed everything from music production, publishing, booking, management, and publicity to film production, construction, and a charter jet service started after McEntire lost seven of her band members in a 1991 plane crash.

NEW FIELDS TO CONQUER

The album that followed the crash, *For My Broken Heart* (1991)—in part an act of public grieving—went double platinum. Her stage show, which during the 1990s required five buses and thirteen trucks to transport, rivaled even Garth Brooks's in its dazzle. Recent tours, however, have involved fewer costume changes and staging gimmicks and more time for conversations with her audience.

Following *For My Broken Heart*, McEntire's platinum-plus record sales continued, her concert revenues and film credits increased, and her music and humanitarian awards mounted. In 2001 she won critical acclaim, including awards from the Drama Desk, the Outer Critics Circle, and Theater World, for her performance as Annie Oakley in Broadway's *Annie Get Your Gun*. That same year, she took up the starring role in the situation comedy *Reba* on the WB network (later renamed CW). The show ran for six years. In 2005 she played the role of Ensign Nellie Forbush in a special concert version of Rodgers and Hammerstein's *South Pacific*, which was filmed for a PBS special and recorded as an album the following year.

McEntire's musical endeavors were put on the back burner during the *Reba* years, but she came back strong after the show went off the air. Her initial album for the label Valory, *Keep on Loving You* (2009), became her first solo album to debut in the top spot on the Billboard country chart. The album generated three hits, including "Consider Me Gone."

McEntire's philanthropic work has also been considerable. She has been an active supporter of Habitat for Humanity since 1994, and her concerts have raised more than $4 million for four projects at the Texoma Medical Center in Denison, Texas: Reba's Ranch House, a state-of-the-art nursery, a mobile mammography unit, and a rehabilitation center. McEntire continues to extend her business ventures, as well. She launched a line of signature clothing in 2005 that has since expanded to include footwear, tableware and dinnerware, bedding, and luggage.

Of course, regardless of whatever else McEntire accomplishes, she will always be best known for her music. She won *Billboard*'s inaugural Woman of the Year award in 2007, was one of only four recipients of the National Artistic Achievement Award in 2010, and was an inductee into the Country Music Hall of Fame in 2011. More than forty years after Tammy Wynette's "Stand by Your Man" defined a female's place in a relationship and on a country stage, McEntire has proved that a woman can challenge heavy-hitting male music stars and win. In the process, she has changed the face of country music.

Wylene Rholetter

SEE ALSO: *Broadway; Country Music;* Grand Ole Opry*; Lynn, Loretta; Parton, Dolly; Rodgers and Hammerstein; Sitcom;* South Pacific*; Television; Wynette, Tammy.*

BIBLIOGRAPHY

Bufwack, Mary A., and Robert K. Oermann. *Finding Her Voice: The Saga of Women in Country Music*. New York: Crown, 1993.

Cusic, Don. *Reba McEntire: Country Music's Queen*. New York: St. Martin's, 1991.

McEntire, Reba. *Comfort from a Country Quilt*. New York: Bantam, 2000.

McEntire, Reba, and Tom Carter. *Reba: My Story*. New York: Bantam, 1994.

Miller, Holly G. "Reinventing Reba." *Saturday Evening Post*, September 1, 2007, 44–90.

McG *(1968–)*

The film director known simply as McG is responsible for some of the most evocative and memorable music videos of the late

1990s and early in the first decade of the 2000s. He has since become a director of prominent films, to which he brings his distinctive, color-saturated style and penchant for placing the viewer right in the middle of the action.

Joseph McGinty Nichol was born on August 9, 1968, in Kalamazoo, Michigan, and grew up in Newport Beach, California. In high school he was the lead singer in a band called the Q Tips with Mark McGrath, the future singer of the popular 1990s band Sugar Ray. McG soon tired of the role of front man, but he continued to help McGrath write songs while studying psychology at the University of California at Irvine, and signed Sugar Ray to a record label that he funded with money he had saved from a job as a delivery driver. He produced the band's first album and cowrote a number of hits on its second and third albums, including "Fly" and "Every Morning." He also directed Sugar Ray's first music video and went on to direct videos for a number of chart-topping bands in the late 1990s and the first decade of the 2000s, including the Offspring, Smashmouth, Cypress Hill, Sublime, Everclear, and Korn. He became such a prominent figure in the music video world that the vice president of music programming at MTV once quipped that the station had become "McG TV."

On the strength of his music video credits, as well as his work on commercials for companies such as the Gap, McG was tapped to direct a feature film remake of the 1970s-era television show *Charlie's Angels*, starring Cameron Diaz, Drew Barrymore, and Lucy Liu. A critical and financial success, the film earned McG the 2002 Hollywood Breakthrough Award at the Hollywood Film Festival and led to a job directing the sequel, *Charlie's Angels: Full Throttle* (2003), and the founding of his production company, Wonderland Sound and Vision. As head of Wonderland, McG served as executive producer of the television shows *Fastlane* (2002–2003), *The Mountain* (2004–2005), *Supernatural* (2005–), and *The O.C.* (2003–2007) and directed another major film, *We Are Marshall* (2006).

In 2007 McG rejoined *The O.C.* creator Josh Schwartz to produce the long-running crime drama *Chuck* (2007–). He then worked on two ill-fated television shows, *Pussycat Dolls Present: Girlicious* (2008) and *Sorority Fever* (2008) before he was offered a chance to direct the fourth film in the *Terminator* franchise, *Terminator Salvation* (2009). Despite mostly negative reviews, the film grossed well over $350 million worldwide and solidified McG's reputation as a moneymaking director. He went on to produce the action series *Nikita* (2010) and to direct the spy comedy *This Means War* (2012), which, despite mostly negative reviews, grossed more than $135 million worldwide. McG continues to be a highly sought-after director, even in the face of his much-publicized battle with agoraphobia and fear of flying, which led to his departure from the film *Superman Returns* (2006).

Jake Schmitt

SEE ALSO: Charlie's Angels*; MTV; Superman; Television;* The Terminator.

BIBLIOGRAPHY

Boehm, Mike. "Behind the McMusic: McG, Director of Hip Videos for MTV and VH1, Started Rolling Credits as a Kid Back in Newport." *Los Angeles Times*, March 19, 1999.

Boucher, Geoff. "McG, the Machine behind 'Terminator Salvation.'" *Los Angeles Times*, May 17, 2009.

McGraw, Dr. Phil *(1950–)*

Oprah Winfrey first called Phil McGraw "America's therapist" when he was a regular on her syndicated talk show. The burly Oklahoman has lived up to the nickname, dispensing folksy analysis and down-to-earth counsel to those who ask him for help with life's problems, first on *The Oprah Winfrey Show*, then on his own long-running talk show, *Dr. Phil.* A savvy motivational speaker with a doctorate in psychology, McGraw introduced a practical, no-nonsense approach to therapy that combined tough love with avuncular compassion. Audiences responded to his straight talk and to his contagious optimism and made his show one of the most successful on television.

Phillip Calvin McGraw was born in 1950 and grew up in Oklahoma and Texas, obtaining his PhD in psychology at North Texas State University. After a short stint in private practice, McGraw found that he preferred the larger stage of motivational work, and in the early 1980s he launched a successful life-coaching business called Pathways. In 1989 he branched out into legal psychology, founding Courtroom Sciences Inc., where he used his skills to advise lawyers on choosing jurors and to help those involved in legal action cope with the stresses of litigation.

In 1995 Oprah Winfrey enlisted McGraw's firm, Courtroom Sciences Inc., to assist in her defense against a lawsuit filed by Texas beef ranchers for warning her talk-show audience about mad cow disease in U.S. cattle. The case did not go to trial until 1998, and in February of that year the jury found that Winfrey's comments did not constitute libel against the ranchers. She was impressed with McGraw's insight and positive approach and invited him to appear on her show. The one-time performance led to a regular Tuesday "Dr. Phil" segment, and soon McGraw was such a popular guest that ratings spiked whenever he was on. Winfrey backed McGraw to launch his own syndicated show, and *Dr. Phil* debuted in September 2002 to audiences so large they drew comparisons to Winfrey's own early shows.

On *Dr. Phil*, McGraw continued the format he had employed so successfully on *Oprah*. Guests with a wide range of life issues would discuss their problems with the therapist and receive hard-headed advice in this vein: "You are not a victim. You are creating the situations you are in." *Dr. Phil*'s popularity grew season after season; in 2005 he signed a contract to host the show until 2014. In addition to his daily television appearances, McGraw became a successful author, with a monthly advice-column in *O: The Oprah Magazine* and a number of best-selling books, such as *Life Strategies: Doing What Works, Doing What Matters* (1999) and *Family First: Your Step-by-Step Plan for Creating a Phenomenal Family* (2004).

In 2008 the self-assured life strategist made one of his few public missteps when he visited troubled rock star Britney Spears while she was being held in a mental ward. McGraw came under intense criticism for the visit, which was seen as a publicity grab, and for public comments he made about Spears's condition. These were condemned by other psychologists as inappropriate. McGraw made a public apology for his role in the incident.

In 2008 McGraw, with his son Jay, helped launch a *Dr. Phil* spin-off called *The Doctors*, which featured a panel of medical specialists. Like *Dr. Phil*, the show featured a wide variety of guests seeking medical support and advice. Popular with audiences, *The Doctors* won an Emmy for Outstanding Talk Show/ Informative in 2010.

Tina Gianoulis

SEE ALSO: *Best Sellers; Daytime Talk Shows; Popular Psychology; Spears, Britney; Television; Winfrey, Oprah.*

BIBLIOGRAPHY

Albiniak, Paige. "After Oprah, It's Phil in the Void." *Broadcasting & Cable*, September 26, 2011, 13.

Dembling, Sophia, and Lisa Gutierrez. *The Making of Dr. Phil: The Straight-Talking True Story of Everyone's Favorite Therapist.* Hoboken, NJ: John Wiley & Sons, 2004.

"Dr. Phil's Home Remedy for Syndication Success." *Television Week*, December 10, 2007, 17.

Karlin, Susan. "Lights, Camera . . . Dr. Phil!" *O: The Oprah Magazine*, September 2002, 66.

McGwire, Mark *(1963–)*

Mark McGwire is known by some as the man who saved baseball and by others as the face of the game's nefarious steroid era of the late 1990s and early in the first decade of the 2000s. His 1998 fight for the single-season home run record with Chicago Cubs outfielder Sammy Sosa recaptured the hearts of a generation of fans lost during the 1994 labor dispute. Subsequent revelations about his and Sosa's use of steroids and other performance-enhancing drugs (PEDs) have since tarnished the accomplishment. The record seventy home runs put McGwire's name in the record books ahead of greats such as Roger Maris and Babe Ruth, making his admitted steroid use all the more controversial among baseball purists.

Born in 1963, McGwire spent much of his youth with his four brothers at either the basketball court, baseball field, or golf course. Their father, John, a dentist, was a dedicated Little League coach. After briefly considering a future in golf during high school, McGwire decided to dedicate himself solely to baseball, attending the University of Southern California. He began his collegiate career as a pitcher, relying on an 85-mile-per-hour fastball to accumulate a 4–4 record and 3.04 earned run average (ERA) in his freshman year. But the powerful 6-foot, 5-inch McGwire marveled coaches with his swing, and he was promptly switched to first base. Over the next two seasons, McGwire hit fifty-one home runs, shattering the previous school record. At the end of his junior year, McGwire married his college sweetheart, Kathy; reentered the draft; and was chosen tenth overall by the Oakland Athletics.

After a stint with the U.S. Olympic team and a couple years in the minor leagues, McGwire made his much anticipated debut as Oakland's everyday first baseman in 1987. Using his remarkably quick and compact swing, McGwire hit forty-nine homers, breaking the rookie record. But even as an impressionable rookie, family came first; McGwire skipped the final game of the season to witness the birth of his son, missing a chance to reach the coveted fiftieth home run plateau. He later told reporters, "That was my fiftieth home run."

ATHLETICS DOMINATE

Led by McGwire, fellow "Bash Brother" Jose Canseco, pitchers Dave Stewart and Dennis Eckersley, and manager Tony LaRussa, the powerful Athletics appeared in the next three World Series, sweeping the San Francisco Giants in the infamous 1989 series marred by a Northern California earthquake. McGwire became one of baseball's most feared hitters, and he was a good defensive first baseman with a tremendous appreciation for the game. In the early 1990s the home runs kept coming, but his batting average dropped, and he struggled through a divorce and a variety of injuries. In 1993 and 1994 he appeared in only seventy-four games combined, due to a nagging left heel problem.

Frustrated by claims that he had become a soft, one-dimensional player, McGwire returned with newfound confidence and an improved swing, hitting an incredible ninety-one home runs over the 1995 and 1996 seasons combined, despite playing in only 234 games combined due to another nagging heel injury. But by 1997 the once-powerful A's had sunk to the bottom of the Western Division, and McGwire, in the midst of another phenomenal season, was the only tradable commodity. So on July 31 he was dealt to the St. Louis Cardinals, reuniting him with former manager and good friend LaRussa. McGwire

Mark McGwire. *St. Louis Cardinals slugger Mark McGwire acknowledges the standing ovation from the crowd as he heads for home after tying Roger Maris's long-standing major league record of sixty-one home runs on September 7, 1998.* AP IMAGES.

became a fan favorite, finishing the season with fifty-eight home runs, just three shy of Maris's single-season record set in 1961. And for perhaps the first time, the fans got a true glimpse of the man behind the 500-foot home runs. After signing a new contract with the Cardinals, McGwire established a charitable foundation for sexually and physically abused children, to which he would annually donate $1 million. At the press conference, the 250-pound McGwire broke into tears.

In 1998 the entire baseball world expected McGwire to once again challenge the single-season home run record. But no one expected Cubs outfielder Sammy Sosa to join him in the quest. Together their crowd-pleasing home runs became larger than the game itself, to the dismay of some purists but to the delight of fans jaded by the ugly 1994 labor dispute. People across the country were fascinated by the camaraderie of the two down-to-earth players, who from different teams and vastly different backgrounds were chasing a piece of history and dealing with enormous media pressure. The incredible season was not free of scandal, however; it was revealed in a 1998 Associated Press (AP) story that the powerful McGwire regularly used androstenedione, or andro, a muscle-building substance banned in many other sports but legal in Major League Baseball (which it was until 2004, when it was added to the federal government's list of controlled substances). In response to the AP story, McGwire raised eyebrows by proclaiming that "everybody that I know in the game of baseball uses the same stuff I use." Sosa, however, denied using andro.

BREAKING THE RECORD

Fittingly it was against Sosa's Cubs on September 7 that McGwire hit a pitch over the wall in left field to break Maris's thirty-seven-year-old record. Hollywood could not have written a better script. After touching home plate, McGwire hugged his ten-year-old son, Matt, the Cardinal's batboy, and received congratulations from fans, teammates, Maris's children, and Sosa himself. But the race was not over; Sosa kept pace with McGwire until the final weekend of the season. McGwire finally pulled ahead for good, hitting four home runs over the final two games and setting the new single-season standard of seventy. It was even more astounding that he shattered the home run record despite a National League record 162 walks.

McGwire's record invigorated casual fans of the game, with ticket sales and television ratings skyrocketing throughout the late 1990s and early in the first decade of the 2000s despite rumblings about PED use. When aging San Francisco Giants slugger Barry Bonds managed to surpass McGwire's record in 2001 with seventy-three home runs, however, the rumblings about widespread steroid use in baseball became outright accusations, and investigative reporters around the country published story after story outlining the incredible statistical jump that a number of players made around the turn of the twenty-first century. In 2003 Major League Baseball instituted a stringent drug-testing policy, and a district attorney in California began investigating a supplement company known as the Bay Area Laboratory Co-Operative (BALCO) for their involvement in the scandal. McGwire's former teammate Canseco then published the tell-all book titled *Juiced: Wild Times, Rampant 'Roids, Smash Hits, and How Baseball Got Big* (2005), in which he admitted to using steroids during his career and named a number of other players that he had introduced to the substances, including McGwire.

McGwire, Sosa, Canseco, Commissioner Bud Selig, and several other players and officials were called before the House Government Reform Committee in 2005 to testify about the prevalence of steroid use in baseball, though McGwire refused to testify on the advice of his lawyers. The accusations persisted, however, and in 2010 he issued a statement to the Associated Press in which he admitted to using a range of steroids and PEDs for a ten-year period culminating in his record-breaking 1998 season. He issued personal apologies to Commissioner Selig; his former coach; and to Roger Maris's wife, Pat, saying, "I wish I had never played during the steroid era."

Responses to McGwire's confession were varied; some argued that his name should be stricken from the record books, whereas others found his honesty refreshing in comparison with other, less forthcoming players' treatment of the issue. He became eligible for induction into the National Baseball Hall of Fame in 2007, and the rapid decline in votes cast for him after the announcement of 2010 is seen by many as a referendum on the accomplishments of the steroid era in general. McGwire took a position as the St. Louis Cardinals' hitting coach in 2010, and when he leaves the game for good, he will leave behind an ambiguous legacy as the man who gave the sport some of its most exciting moments in recent memory but also whose superhuman physique perhaps drove young athletes toward steroid use and ultimately helped destroy the credibility of America's pastime.

Simon Donner

SEE ALSO: *Baseball; Bonds, Barry; Canseco, Jose; Major League Baseball; Maris, Roger; Sosa, Sammy; Sports Heroes.*

BIBLIOGRAPHY

Assael, Shaun. *Steroid Nation: Juiced Home Run Totals, Antiaging Miracles, and a Hercules in Every High School: The Secret History of America's True Drug Addiction.* New York: ESPN Books, 2007.

McGwire, Jay. *Mark and Me: Mark McGwire and the Truth behind Baseball's Worst-Kept Secret.* Chicago: Triumph Books, 2010.

McGwire, Mark. "Where Do I Go from Here?" *Sports Illustrated*, September 21, 1998.

Reilly, Rick. "The Good Father." *Sports Illustrated*, September 7, 1998, 32–40.

Stein, Joel. "Long Live the King." *Time*, September 21, 1998.

Verducci, Tom. "The Greatest Season Ever." *Sports Illustrated*, October 5, 1998.

McHale's Navy

Running for four seasons, from 1962 to 1966, on ABC, *McHale's Navy* remains one of the longest-running military comedies on television. Set for the first three seasons on an island base in the South Pacific and for the last season in Italy, it was a classic wartime farce that pitted a fun-loving crew of misfits against an incompetent commander who wants to see them put behind bars. The plots are standard fare, often involving the crew of the *PT73* trying to get away with something and being saved, just when trouble looms, by an opportunity to sink an enemy sub and emerge as heroes. The three central characters are Commander McHale and Ensign Parker, who are continually engaged in fending off Captain Binghamton, or "Old Leadbottom."

They were played by Ernest Borgnine, Tim Conway (at his bumbling best), and Joe Flynn, respectively.

The show spawned two TV movies during its run—*McHale's Navy* (1964) and *McHale's Navy Joins the Air Force* (1965)—the first with the original cast and the second with Conway and Flynn only. The characters were resurrected for a 1997 feature film of the same title, with Tom Arnold playing McHale.

Frank Clark

SEE ALSO: *Conway, Tim; Made-for-Television Movies; Sitcom; War Movies.*

BIBLIOGRAPHY

Castleman, Harry, and Walter J. Podrazik. *Harry and Wally's Favorite Shows: A Fact-Filled Opinionated Guide to the Best and Worst on TV.* New York: Prentice Hall, 1989.

McNeil, Alex. *Total Television: The Comprehensive Guide to Programming from 1948 to the Present,* 4th ed. New York: Penguin, 1996.

McKay, Claude *(1890–1948)*

While scholar Alain Locke and novelist James Weldon Johnson attempted to make the Harlem Renaissance palatable to white audiences, Claude McKay rose to prominence as the most militant voice in the African American literary movement. The Jamaican-born poet and author blended Marxist ideals with his belief in racial solidarity to produce *Home to Harlem* (1928) and *Banjo* (1929), vivid accounts of black urban life in the United States and Europe. Both volumes championed ordinary people and testified to the health of the African diaspora community.

McKay lived in the Soviet Union and North Africa during most of the 1920s and drew criticism from mainstream black intellectuals and white liberals for his avowed communism. He returned to the United States in 1934, eventually abandoned left-wing politics to follow his interests in the Roman Catholic religion, and penned his popular autobiography, *A Long Way from Home* (1937). While never as famous as contemporaries Countee Cullen and Langston Hughes, McKay was the foremost left-wing black intellectual of his age. His writings foreshadowed and influenced those of Richard Wright and James Baldwin.

Jacob M. Appel

SEE ALSO: *Baldwin, James; Cullen, Countee; Harlem Renaissance; Hughes, Langston; Johnson, James Weldon; Locke, Alain; Wright, Richard.*

BIBLIOGRAPHY

Bronz, Stephen H. *Roots of Negro Racial Consciousness: The 1920s, Three Harlem Renaissance Authors.* New York: Libra, 1964.

Cooper, Wayne F. *Claude McKay, Rebel Sojourner in the Harlem Renaissance: A Biography.* Baton Rouge: Louisiana State University Press, 1987.

Giles, James R. *Claude McKay.* Boston: Twayne Publishers, 1976.

McKay, Claude. *A Long Way from Home.* New York: Arno Press, 1969.

Tillery, Tyrone. *Claude McKay: A Black Poet's Struggle for Identity.* Amherst: University of Massachusetts Press, 1992.

McKuen, Rod *(1933–)*

At his apex, Rod McKuen was the unofficial poet laureate of America. Penning best-selling songs; composing classical music and film scores; and, in his own right, enjoying a certain stature as a recording artist (mixing his poetry and lyrics in a series of well-received albums delivered in a reedy voice fractured by years of singing in nightclubs), McKuen was adored by his legions of fans. "In the sad, minimal world of Rod and his eager know-nothing millions," as one critic has described the poet's rapport with his audience, life exists in an ineffable mist of kittens and sheepdogs and chance encounters in parks and on public transportation. The poet of foggy afternoons and postcoital introspection, McKuen was, in the words of critic David Harsent, a poet with "a formula likely to appeal to the groupies and the grannies alike" with a "neoplastic pleonasm rooted in his universal proposition of the world."

Rod McKuen. *Rod McKuen performs in the Netherlands in 2009.* PAUL BERGEN/CONTRIBUTOR/REDFERNS/GETTY IMAGES.

THE EARLY YEARS

Born in an Oakland, California, charity hospital, McKuen grew up not knowing his father, a fact that left a deep wound but would later serve to stimulate his endless productivity. He was truly a child of the Depression: after his mother married, her husband took a job with a Works Progress Administration road gang, which kept the family moving from state to state for much of McKuen's childhood. As a result, his schooling was spotty. He also suffered a steady stream of physical abuse inflicted upon him by his stepfather. In his later years McKuen would become a spokesman for children's rights. After several failed attempts at escaping from his family, at age eleven he finally succeeded, fleeing to Elko, Nevada, where he found work as a ranch hand, spent three years in a Nevada reformatory, and later joined the rodeo circuit as a trick rider. He also began keeping a journal in this period, describing the events of the day, the weather, and scraps of dialogue in an earnest tone that reveals shades of his later development.

Returning to Oakland after a freak injury ended his rodeo career, he was reunited with his mother and half-brother for a time, then volunteered for the draft in 1953, first serving in Tokyo as a "public information specialist" (McKuen's words), or, as he later described it, a "psychological warfare scriptwriter." Evenings often found McKuen polishing his voice at various Tokyo nightclubs, an activity that resulted in his reassignment to Korea. Also during this time, his first book of poetry was published, a volume titled *And Autumn Came* (1954).

Mustered from duty in 1955, he returned to the Bay Area, where he secured a job singing at a San Francisco nightclub. With his chiseled features and blond hair, he was a natural for Hollywood, and it was around this time that Cobina Wright Sr. of Universal Pictures discovered him and invited him to be her guest in Los Angeles. McKuen spent the next two years as a contract player at Universal, taking supporting roles and starring in a few Westerns until a dispute over a script left him summarily suspended. He impetuously moved to New York, focusing exclusively on his musical career with occasional unsuccessful forays into the world of theater until, in 1962, his throat gave out and he returned to the Bay Area.

POPULAR ACCLAIM

In San Francisco McKuen recovered his voice and began a gestation period in which he traveled, wrote poetry, and collaborated with French composers such as Jacques Brel. Having already developed a cult following, in 1966 he self-published his second book of poetry, *Stanyan Street and Other Sorrows*, selling it through a classified advertisement. Despite this primitive arrangement, the book sold briskly and was picked up by Random House. The 1967 follow-up, *Listen to the Warm*—perhaps McKuen's most famous work—was a runaway success. With the publication of *Lonesome Cities* in 1968, McKuen could boast of finishing the year with three books on the *Publishers Weekly* year-end Top 10 list, making him the first author in seventy years to accomplish this.

McKuen is the poet critics love to hate, and through the years his books have drawn uniformly unkind reviews. In fact, criticism of his poetry is vituperative across the board, as if his popular success was a direct affront to the academy at large. McKuen reacts to his critics' distaste evasively—"the people who find it easy to criticize my work more often than not haven't even read it"—or with hurt: "I would be dishonest if I said it didn't bother me." In the *Journal of Popular Culture*, Andrew Hirt posed the conundrum: "Why the commercial success with poetry of such poor quality?" McKuen's figurative answer—"It just happens I've said something at a time when people need to be talked to"—was occasion for Hirt to suggest, "Maybe great masses have latched on to his poetry because it satisfies a desire in them to feel intellectual."

The brief liner notes from one of McKuen's albums sum up his appeal to the masses: "Rod McKuen speaks to those who've lost them for those who seek them." His poetry, rich with themes of ineffable yearning to be loved, stem from the trauma of his attenuated childhood, particularly the absence of his natural father. In 1976 McKuen wrote *Finding My Father*, a book about his unsuccessful quest to find this phantom. Ironically, the presumptive father, an ice-man in Santa Monica, only a few short miles from McKuen's house, died before the book's publication.

In 1978 McKuen's friend and collaborator Brel died. McKuen was so devastated by his friend's death that he was unable to finish their uncompleted songs until years afterward. In 1981 he stopped touring for an extended period, spending his time doing voice-overs, narrations, and charity work. By the twenty-first century he had resumed touring, appearing all over the world. He also served as the president of the American Guild of Variety Artists. Remastered versions of his music continue to appear, including *Rod McKuen: Greatest Hits* (2003) and *If You Go Away: The RCA Years 1965–1970* (2007). He also continues to write poetry, releasing *Rusting in the Rain: New and Selected Poems* in 2004.

While the period when critics actively loathed him is long over, in the arena of poetry, the gates have long since been barred against any serious consideration of his work. Despite this, McKuen remains a seminal figure in the annals of publishing, where his massive popular success may never be equaled again.

Michael Baers

SEE ALSO: *Best Sellers; The Great Depression; Hollywood; The Western.*

BIBLIOGRAPHY

Boekkooi, Paul. "A Short Interview with Rod McKuen." Artslink.co.uk. Accessed January 2010. Available from http://www.artlink.co.za/news_article.htm?contentID=7628

Hartill, Lane. "Poet, Singer Rod McKuen." *Christian Science Monitor*, September 10, 1998.

Hirt, Andrew J. "Rod McKuen: America's Questionable Poet Laureate." *Journal of Popular Culture* 3, no. 4 (1970): 704–711.

McKuen, Rod. *Finding My Father*. New York: Coward, McCann & Geoghegan, 1976.

Nykoruk, Barbara, ed. *Authors in the News*. Detroit, MI: Gale Research, 1976.

Riley, Carolyn, ed. *Contemporary Literary Criticism*, vol. 3. Detroit, MI: Gale Research, 1975.

Stanley, Debra. *Contemporary Authors*, vol. 40. Detroit, MI: Gale Research, 1987.

McLish, Rachel *(1958–)*

Rachel McLish earned immortality by becoming the first woman to win the Ms. Olympia bodybuilding contest, in 1980. (The Mr. Olympia contests for men, begun in 1965, had quickly became the sport's most prestigious title.) The graceful McLish was the clear choice of the judges. After her victory and the attendant publicity, she became a role model for aspiring young women who wanted to reshape their bodies by training with weights.

McLish, who was of Hispanic descent and was raised in southern Texas and trained in ballet, became well known outside of the subculture of bodybuilding with the release of the feature film *Pumping Iron II: The Women* (1985). A pseudo-documentary, *Pumping Iron II* concentrated on the differences between the lithe McLish and the heavily muscled Beverly Francis, a power-lifting champion. McLish went on to work in other films and in television, and was seen in *Getting Physical* (1984), *Aces: Iron Eagle III* (1992), and *Raven Hawk* (1996).

Jan Todd

SEE ALSO: *Bodybuilding.*

BIBLIOGRAPHY

Goode, Paul B. *Physique: An Intimate Portrait of the Female Fitness Athlete.* New York: Thunder's Mouth Press, 1997.

McLuhan, Marshall *(1911–1980)*

As an audience of millions watched the first television appearance of the Beatles in America, a scant few months after the assassination of John F. Kennedy, one person thought to connect these two events. If the new rhythms, the lyrics, and the haircuts of the Liverpool four brought the first genuine distraction for some from the senselessness of Dallas, Texas, for media analyst Marshall McLuhan it brought confirmation of his view that the medium is the message. McLuhan was about to publish his *Understanding Media*, a book that staked a place for itself amid the turbulent events of the 1960s, explaining them in terms of the effects of electronic technology on the physical senses and sensibilities of mankind.

UNDERSTANDING MEDIA

Born in Edmonton, Alberta, Canada, McLuhan spent most of his youth in Winnipeg. He attended the University of Manitoba, receiving a BA and then an MA, with a thesis on nineteenth-century English novelist George Meredith, before going to Cambridge University, where he earned a PhD in 1942 for his dissertation on the work of sixteenth-century dramatist and satirist Thomas Nashe. When McLuhan achieved international renown in the 1960s and 1970s, many people assumed that somewhere between completing the Nashe dissertation and publishing *Understanding Media* he had quietly dropped the study of English literature. But in McLuhan's earliest days at Cambridge, and in the earliest days of his teaching career in the United States, literary studies and media analysis were already complementary for him and remained so.

There are at least two suitable metaphors for McLuhan's life. The first, the title of Edgar Allan Poe's story "A Descent into the Maelstrom," McLuhan himself used for more than thirty years in evoking the effects of technology on our bodies, clothes, homes, cities, jokes, toys, words, weapons, and more. The second metaphor is related to the solution that Poe's sailor finds for surviving the deadly waters of the Maelstrom, but it is McLuhan's own phrase: "escape into understanding."

The phrase is an injunction, the injunction at the center of all McLuhan's teaching and teasing, an invitation to join him on a voyage of discovery. Applied to McLuhan himself, to his life and his legacy, the phrase also summons individuals to escape from the misunderstandings that surrounded and still surround his teachings. Though it was television that he likened to bacteria and poison (prescribing the antidote of reading), journalists confidently reported that he condemned print. Looking carefully at what McLuhan taught, it is clear that he believed that as new media develop, they do not so much replace older ones as complicate them. In an age of online encyclopedias and dictionaries, McLuhan's contentions may be taken for granted. However, in 1964 few others besides him understood this, and only a few reported his percepts with accuracy.

MEDIA AND THE NATURE OF LANGUAGE

Even casual inspection of McLuhan's writings makes it apparent that the rich variety of his sources includes fields as diverse as anthropology, economic theory, psychology, philosophy from antiquity to the twentieth century, literary criticism, and English and European literatures spanning four centuries. McLuhan said in *Understanding Media* that language was the first technology by which humans let go of their environment in order to grasp it in a new way. The same book devoted one early chapter to the spoken word (conjuring French symbolist poet Charles Baudelaire but discussing philosopher Henri Bergson) and another to the written word (subtitle: "An Eye for an Ear"). McLuhan's posthumously published *Laws of Media* transformed the ancient rhetorical device of chiasmus into the dynamic vectors of tetrad structures for describing semiotics, slang, cliché, and symbolist poetry and advanced the notion that all man's artifacts are structurally linguistic and metaphoric. Clearly, probing the nature of language and fully understanding its role in human affairs was a central concern for McLuhan.

McLuhan knew nothing about galvanic skin response technology, terminal node controllers, or the Apple iPad. He did not know what a biomouse was. But he pointed the way to understanding all of them—not in themselves but in their relation to each other, to older technologies, and above all in relation to ourselves: our bodies, our physical senses, our psychic balance. He was disturbed about European and American societies moving toward the twenty-first century with nineteenth-century perceptions. His writings continue to challenge us to escape into understanding.

Decades after his death, McLuhan is still considered one of the most influential thinkers of modern times. His greatest contributions evolved from his understanding of historic patterns that continue to influence the present and his knowledge that visual media continues to exert a great impact on individuals within modern societies. Scientific studies have substantiated the latter impact by demonstrating the passivity of brain wave patterns in television viewers. McLuhan was the first person to visualize the concept of the global village that has been realized in the late twentieth and early twenty-first centuries through the presence of e-mail, the Internet, instant messaging, social networks, video conferencing, and other sophisticated technologies.

W. Terrence Gordon

SEE ALSO: *Apple Computer; The Beatles; The Internet; iPad; Kennedy Assassination; Social Media; Television.*

BIBLIOGRAPHY

Gordon, W. Terrence. *Marshall McLuhan: Escape into Understanding. A Biography.* New York: HarperCollins, 1997.

Gordon, W. Terrence. *McLuhan for Beginners.* New York: Writers & Readers Publishing, 1997.

McLuhan, Marshall. *Understanding Media: The Extensions of Man.* New York: McGraw-Hill, 1964.

McLuhan, Marshall. *Understanding Me: Lectures and Interviews,* ed. Stephanie McLuhan and David Staines. Cambridge, MA: MIT Press, 2003.

McLuhan, Marshall, and Eric McLuhan. *Laws of Media: The New Science.* Toronto: University of Toronto Press, 1988.

McLuhan, Marshall, and Harley Parker. *Through the Vanishing Point: Space in Poetry and Painting.* New York: Harper & Row, 1968.

McLuhan, Marshall, and Bruce R. Powers. *The Global Village: Transformations in World Life and Media in the 21st Century.* New York: Oxford University Press, 1989.

McLuhan, Marshall, and Wilfred Watson. *From Cliché to Archetype.* New York: Viking, 1970.

McLuhan, Eric, and Frank Zingrone, eds. *Essential McLuhan.* New York: Basic Books, 1995.

McNamara, Eugene, ed. *The Interior Landscape: The Literary Criticism of Marshall McLuhan 1943–1962.* New York: McGraw-Hill, 1969.

Molinaro, Matie; Corinne McLuhan; and William Toye, eds. *Letters of Marshall McLuhan.* Toronto: Oxford University Press, 1987.

Stahlman, Mark D. "The Place of Marshall McLuhan in the Learning of His Times." *Renascence* 64, no. 1 (2011): 5–17.

McMurtry, Larry *(1936–)*

A prolific writer of rare lyrical gifts, Larry McMurtry has enjoyed a reputation as the most eloquent voice of the contemporary American West. Born and raised in rural Texas, McMurtry published his first several novels to critical kudos, but these initial literary efforts won him few homegrown fans. Some Texans were offended by the author's irreverent and unsentimental treatment of his home state, as he exposed the limits of Texas mythology and portrayed small towns such as Thalia (the fictional equivalent of Archer City, where McMurtry graduated from high school) as desiccated and stifling. In *Larry McMurtry's Texas: Evolution of the Myth,* scholar Lera Patrick Tyler Lich describes McMurtry's dusty Thalia as "a place to go insane, a place to be lonely," noting that "a vast expanse around the town and a wind that blows into it seem to choke out life." In later works, McMurtry did equal justice to Texas's sprawling, rowdy cities as crass, commercial meccas of philistinism.

Though he continually dismissed his own work as being without merit, McMurtry has offered a gallery of indelible images from a region of America caught between a sylvan past and a spiritless urban and suburban future. In addition to winning a Pulitzer Prize for *Lonesome Dove* in 1986, in 2006 McMurtry won an Academy Award, a Golden Globe, and a British Academy of Film and Television Arts (BAFTA) Award for his 2005 screen adaptation (with Diana Ossana) of the short story "Brokeback Mountain" by Annie Proulx. The movie, which starred Jake Gyllenhaal and Heath Ledger as cowboys in an unacknowledged love affair, also was nominated for the Academy Award for Best Picture.

TEXAS ROOTS

McMurtry was a popular high school student, active in sports and on the staffs of student publications, but an ambivalence for his western Texas environs was taking hold in the well-read young writer. After graduating from Rice University with an MA in English and winning a prestigious Wallace Stegner Fellowship at Stanford University, McMurtry published *Horseman, Pass By* (1961) when he was just twenty-six years old. This novel about the decline of the Western way of life is essentially a

Larry McMurtry. *Larry McMurtry holds the award he won for Best Screenplay for* Brokeback Mountain *at the Golden Globe Awards in 2006.* **J. VESPA/CONTRIBUTOR/WIREIMAGE/GETTY IMAGES.**

coming-of-age story, as the young Lonnie Bannon surveys two opposing—and unappetizing—models of male possibility: his rancher grandfather Homer, whose diseased cattle represent a dying era, and Lonnie's uncle Hud, a callous, cynical lady-killer whose only allegiance is to his own appetites. "Hud had made terms with the twentieth century," McMurtry notes in *In a Narrow Grave*, his volume of essays, "whereas Homer was unwaveringly faithful to the nineteenth." McMurtry deals Western pride a death blow as he documents the cowboy cliché's passing into anachronism, as the "horsemen" either race their fancy Cadillacs or else fold up and die. His auspicious debut invited comparisons to Thomas Wolfe and James Jones and became the basis for a widely respected film, *Hud* (1963), with Paul Newman in the title role.

Throughout the 1960s McMurtry taught English and creative writing and continued to publish compelling novels. The offbeat love story *Leaving Cheyenne* appeared in 1963 (it was filmed in 1974 as *Lovin' Molly*), and in 1966 he published perhaps his best-known work, *The Last Picture Show*, a bleak evocation of the isolation and emptiness of small-town life. In it he paints a forbidding landscape—"miles of lonesome country" and "a few sandscraped ranch houses." This world is so lacking in opportunity and ambition that middle-aged town denizens can find little to do but worship high school athletes and prom queens as if they were movie stars and prey upon them as sex objects. As the new urban frontier lures the talented and the energetic away, and as Thalia's storefronts are boarded up one by one under vast, empty skies, the author depicts "a place's loss of its only coherent tradition," according to scholar Raymond L. Neinstein in *The Ghost Country: A Study of the Novels of Larry McMurtry*.

With the publication of *The Last Picture Show*, the *New York Times* praised McMurtry as "an alchemist who converts the basest materials to gold." The director Peter Bogdanovich's gritty black-and-white film adaptation emerged as one of the most admired films of 1971, a contemporary classic contributing, in the words of Pauline Kael in *For Keeps: 30 Years at the Movies*, to "a legendary period in movies."

The perceptive and frank *In a Narrow Grave: Essays on Texas* appeared in 1968, followed by the 800-page mega-novel of displacement and ennui, *Moving On* (1970). *Terms of Endearment* (1975) tells the moving story of a complex mother-daughter relationship. When the film version of *Terms of Endearment* reached screens, it equaled or surpassed the success of previous movie adaptations of McMurtry's work, winning the Academy Award for Best Picture in 1984.

A PROLIFIC WRITER

In *Somebody's Darling* (1978) and *The Desert Rose* (1983), McMurtry explores other milieus, but his favorite themes—tradition versus modernity, country versus city—are evident; the former novel depicts the often mindless vagaries of the Hollywood movie industry, and the latter tells of a sweetly vapid Las Vegas stripper named Harmony and her beautiful but calculating daughter. McMurtry regards Harmony as sort of a distaff cowboy, part of "a dying breed" of buxom, lacquered showgirls. As in his male-dominated works, *The Desert Rose* demonstrates an older generation's innocence and helplessness in an increasingly complicated and ravening world. Horsemen are not the only ones passing by, into obscurity.

Other McMurtry novels of note include *Cadillac Jack* (1982); the prize-winning nineteenth-century epic, *Lonesome Dove* (1985), which spawned a popular television miniseries; *Texasville* (1987), an ambitious and satirical sequel to *The Last Picture Show*; and the elegiac sequel to *Terms of Endearment*, *The Evening Star* (1992). McMurtry revisited the Last Picture series with *Duane's Depressed* (1999), *When the Light Goes* (2007), and *Rhino Ranch* (2009).

In the twenty-first century, McMurtry has continued his love affair with the American West and with writing, turning out both fiction and nonfiction at an amazing pace. In 2000 he edited *Still Wild, Short Fiction of the American West, 1950 to the Present*, cowrote the screenplay for *Johnson County War*, and wrote the memoir *Roads: Driving America's Great Highways* and the novel *Boone's Lick*. In 2001 he published a second memoir, *Paradise*. He began the Berrybender Narrative series in 2002 with the release of *Sin Killer* and followed it up with *The Wandering Hill* (2003), *By Sorrow's River* (2003), and *Folly and Glory* (2004). In 2003 McMurtry and Don Graham coedited *Lone Star Literature: A Texas Anthology*.

For McMurtry, 2005 was a particularly prolific year. In addition to his work on *Brokeback Mountain*, he published *Oh What a Slaughter: Massacres in the American West, 1846–1890* and *The Colonel and Little Missie: Buffalo Bill, Annie Oakley, and the Beginnings of Superstardom in America* and wrote the novel *Loop Group*. The following year he released *Missouri River* and *Telegraph Days*. Combining his love of writing with his tendency to revisit his past, McMurtry released *Books, a Memoir* (2008), *Literary Life: A Second Memoir* (2009), and *Writers: A Memoir* (2009). In 2011 he published yet another memoir, *Hollywood: A Third Memoir*, about his adopted home base.

Drew Limsky

SEE ALSO: *Academy Awards; Hollywood; Newman, Paul; Television; The Western; Wolfe, Tom.*

BIBLIOGRAPHY

Kael, Pauline. *For Keeps: 30 Years at the Movies*. New York: Dutton, 1994.

"Larry McMurtry." *Contemporary Authors Online*. Detroit, MI: Gale, 2010.

Lich, Lera Patrick Tyler. *Larry McMurtry's Texas: Evolution of the Myth*. Austin, TX: Eakin Press, 1987.

McMurtry, Larry. *The Last Picture Show*. New York: Penguin, 1986.

McMurtry, Larry. *In a Narrow Grave*. New York: Simon & Schuster, 1989.

Neinstein, Raymond L. *The Ghost Country: A Study of the Novels of Larry McMurtry*. Berkeley, CA: Creative Arts Book Company, 1976.

Peavy, Charles D. *Larry McMurtry*. Boston: Twayne Publishers, 1977.

Reilly, John M. *Larry McMurtry: A Critical Companion*. Westport, CT: Greenwood Press, 2000.

McPherson, Aimee Semple *(1890–1944)*

A charismatic and gifted Pentecostal preacher, Aimee Semple McPherson gained fame as a barnstorming evangelist in the era of Billy Sunday (depicted so tellingly by Sinclair Lewis in *Elmer Gantry*). In every respect, she was a pioneer and an original—

Aimee Semple McPherson. *Aimee Semple McPherson found celebrity as a charismatic evangelist in the 1920s and 1930s.* APIC/CONTRIBUTOR/HULTON ARCHIVE/GETTY IMAGES.

her flamboyant style and colorful personal life guaranteed that she was good press, and her radio broadcasts from the Angelus Temple in Los Angeles drew her flock from coast to coast to hear "Sister Aimee." Her Church of the Foursquare Gospel was a hybrid of show business and Bible-based simplicity. As a minister, she endeavored "to bring sinners to Jesus." Renowned for her stirring sermons and for healing by the laying on of hands, McPherson drew such a following that her personal appearances resembled those of movie stars. Charlie Chaplin, an admirer, remarked that "You give your drama-starved people who absent themselves through fear, a theater which they can reconcile with their narrow beliefs. . . . Whether you like it or not, you're an actress."

The first woman to hold a broadcast license, McPherson was shrewd and farsighted in seeing the potential in a media ministry, and as a healer and a media personality, she laid the groundwork for such preachers as Oral Roberts, Katherine Kuhlman, and Jim and Tammy Bakker. Always well and expensively dressed, she created a persona that withstood controversy and sustained her ministry; the Church of the Foursquare Gospel and the L.I.F.E. Bible College (now Life Pacific College) she founded remain active in 144 countries and claim 8.4 million members.

EARLY LIFE AND MINISTRY

McPherson was born Aimee Kennedy in 1890 in Salford, Ontario; at the age of six weeks she was "consecrated to God and the Salvation Army" by her mother, Minnie, a fervent convert to "the Army," which was making considerable inroads in conservative Canadian towns with "Jubilee services"—music and prayer. With this beginning, Aimee, a child her mother believed to be destined to be a religious leader, found the inspiration for her services. Her marriage to Robert Semple, a missionary, led her to accompany him to China, and his death became the impetus for her to pursue her own calling as an evangelist. She married Harold McPherson and unsuccessfully tried to be a conventional wife and mother. By the time her second marriage had disintegrated, she had found her calling and was touring the country in her "Full Gospel Car"—first with her husband and their son, Rolf, and then with her irrepressible mother.

Wherever McPherson went, she was an immediate success. The novelty of a woman preacher brought out the crowds, but McPherson's power as a speaker and her reputation as a formidable "soul-saver" and healer built her reputation. Her early campaigns were conducted in tents, but finally in 1919 McPherson found her home base in the rapidly expanding city of Los Angeles, where the movie business boomed. She frequently recalled that she arrived there with "ten dollars and a tambourine," and her ministry quickly grew from a simple storefront to large auditoriums. "Sister" did not promote herself as a healer, but the crowds came in hope of miracles. She herself said, "Jesus is the healer. I am only a little office girl who opens the door and says, 'Come in.'"

McPherson loved music, and she is credited with bringing popular music, especially jazz, into the church. She later composed operas, a natural outgrowth of her performances in the pulpit, which were elaborate spectacles featuring Sister in costume, props (which included animals), and a supporting cast of followers. In just four years she opened the 5,300-seat Angelus Temple, built by the contributions of her faithful, "entirely debt-free," as she proudly asserted.

FAME AND SCANDAL

McPherson continued to travel the world, always grabbing headlines. A 1927 New York appearance requested by the notorious Texas Guinan ("Queen of the Nightclubs") was reported as "Evangelist Preaches at Speakeasy." McPherson's appearance became increasingly glamorous as her fame swelled the congregation. Now as blond-haired as any movie queen, Sister preached the gospel while controversy swirled about her personal life. The most notorious incident, which significantly affected her reputation, was the sensational 1926 "kidnapping" from a California beach. McPherson always insisted she had been snatched, drugged, and held captive in Mexico, and later escaped. Upon her triumphant "return from the dead" (after being believed drowned), Sister greeted a cheering crowd of 50,000 people and led a procession to the Angelus Temple. Subsequent attempts to prove she was actually holed up in a "love nest" with Kenneth Ormiston, her radio operator and a married man, were not enough to destroy her popularity. The press, previously friendly, were now her inquisitors. Squabbles (primarily financial) with her mother, her daughter, Roberta, and other temple officials made news and landed her in court on a regular basis, yet McPherson continued to insist that she wanted nothing more than to preach "that old-time religion." She married a third husband, David Hutton, despite her own doctrine that a divorced person should not remarry during the life of a former partner. This marriage ended disastrously, and McPherson's health, always fragile, began to give way. Her death in 1944 at the age of fifty-three gave rise to speculation that she had committed suicide, and the evidence remains inconclusive, like so much in McPherson's life.

What is evident is that McPherson's celebrity allowed her a considerable platform both to preach and to administer her extensive social welfare programs during the Great Depression. She remained popular until the end: 60,000 mourners passed by her funeral bier to pay respects to her. Her legacy is the Church of the Foursquare Gospel, which became headed by her son, Rolf, until 1988; Rolf died in 2009. Her example helped women gain a place as ministers in a patriarchal religion. While relatively little scholarly attention has been given to McPherson, journalists and filmmakers have retold her story with relish. Faye Dunaway played her in a well-received 1976 television film, *The Disappearance of Aimee.*

Mary Hess

SEE ALSO: *Bakker, Jim, and Tammy Faye; Evangelism; Sunday, Billy.*

BIBLIOGRAPHY

Blumhofer, Edith L. *Aimee Semple McPherson: Everybody's Sister.* Grand Rapids, MI: William B. Eerdmans, 1993.

Epstein, Daniel Mark. *Sister Aimee: The Life of Aimee Semple McPherson.* New York: Harcourt Brace Jovanovich, 1993.

McPherson, Aimee Semple. *Aimee: Life Story.* Los Angeles: Foursquare, 1979.

Sutton, Matthew Avery. *Aimee Semple McPherson and the Resurrection of Christian America.* Cambridge, MA: Harvard University Press, 2007.

Thomas, Lately. *Storming Heaven: The Lives and Turmoils of Minnie Kennedy and Aimee Semple McPherson.* New York: William Morrow, 1970.

McQueen, Butterfly *(1911–1995)*

As Scarlett O'Hara's slave Prissy in *Gone with the Wind* (1939), Thelma "Butterfly" McQueen probably did more than any other entertainer to typecast African American actors and actresses in menial roles. Yet, as one of the most widely recognized black actresses of her era and a lifelong advocate for racial equality, McQueen did much to end discrimination in Hollywood. Her decision to abandon cinema in 1947, as well as her outspoken criticism of the film industry, helped change the long-standing practice of relegating African Americans to subservient roles. Still, throughout her six-decade career, she was plagued by her most celebrated on-screen line—Prissy's admission to Miss Scarlett, "I don't know nothin' 'bout birthing babies."

Born on January 8, 1911, in Tampa, Florida, to a stevedore and a domestic, McQueen began her acting career at the suggestion of a teacher. Lacking the professional experience of her peers, she could cite only one previous performance, the "Butterfly Ballet" in a school play, which would earn her the nickname "Butterfly." In 1934 she joined Venezuela Jones's Negro Youth Theatre Group and made one of her first stage appearances in director George Abbott's *Brown Sugar* (1937). While performing in another of Abbott's plays, *What a Life* (1938), she auditioned for the role of Prissy in David O. Selznick's *Gone with the Wind.*

It was as the whiny, comic, and tearful house slave that the actress gained instant acclaim at twenty-eight. Although the part was a minor one and McQueen was originally turned down for the role, she transformed it into one of the most memorable character performances of all time. She stole scenes from stars Vivien Leigh and Clark Gable with her careful blend of the sassy and obsequious. Prissy's admission to Scarlett (Leigh) that she did not know how to deliver Melanie Wilkes's (Olivia de Haviland) child became one of the most often quoted lines of the film.

Yet McQueen regretted her contribution to black stereotyping. "It wasn't a very pleasant part to play," she observed. "I didn't want to be that little slave. . . . However, I did my best. My very best." Late in life she came to terms with the part. "Now I am happy I did *Gone with the Wind,"* she said on the fiftieth anniversary of the film. "I wasn't when I was twenty-eight, but it's part of black history. You have no idea how hard it is for black actors, but things change, things blossom in time." In the years following her film debut, she played bit parts as Lulu, a cosmetics counter assistant, in *The Women* (1939) and as maids in *Mildred Pierce* (1945) and *Flame of the Barbary Coast* (1945).

In 1947 she left Hollywood to work as a real-life maid, taxi dispatcher, and Macy's salesgirl. Although she briefly returned to acting as one of television's first black stars, the maid Oriole on *The Beulah Show* (1950–1953), the proud actress publicly declared her refusal to be typecast in demeaning parts and her

Butterfly McQueen. *Butterfly McQueen left her acting career behind for several years when she became frustrated by the menial roles offered to African American actresses in the 1940s and 1950s.*

frustration with racial attitudes in the film industry. Her plight as an actress paralleled that of many African Americans in the era before the civil rights movement. Forced to choose between minor, often subservient parts and complete exclusion from film, she came to believe that taking no role was better than accepting a regressive one.

McQueen devoted the remainder of her life to a variety of causes, including the Freedom from Religion Foundation and the Humane Society. She earned a bachelor's degree in political science from the City College of New York at the age of sixty-four. When she finally returned to cinema, playing Clarice in *Amazing Grace* (1974) and Ma Kennywick in *Mosquito Coast* (1986), African American actors ranked among the largest box-office draws in the nation. She died on December 22, 1995, after suffering burns sustained in a house fire.

Jacob M. Appel

SEE ALSO: Beulah; *Gable, Clark;* Gone with the Wind; Mildred Pierce; *Selznick, David O.*

BIBLIOGRAPHY

Bourne, Stephen. *Butterfly McQueen Remembered.* Lanham, MD: Scarecrow Press, 2008.

Cameron, Judy, and Paul J. Christman. *The Art of* Gone with the Wind: *The Making of a Legend.* London: W. H. Allen, 1989.

Lambert, Gavin. *The Making of* Gone with the Wind. Boston: Little, Brown, 1973.

Molt, Cynthia Marylee, and Butterfly McQueen. Gone with the Wind *on Film: A Complete Reference.* Jefferson, NC: McFarland, 1990.

Pyron, Darden Asbury, ed. *Recasting "Gone with the Wind" in American Culture.* Miami: University Press of Florida, 1983.

McQueen, Steve *(1930–1980)*

Steve McQueen was the highest-paid movie actor of the 1960s and early 1970s and was perhaps the most popular star of his generation. The essence of early 1960s cool, he established his reputation as America's heroic antihero in films such as *The Magnificent Seven* (1960) and *The Great Escape* (1963). The charismatic and macho McQueen went on to become one of the decade's most sought-after leading men, helping to forever define the qualities expected of cinematic action heroes. Despite his untimely death at age fifty, he has remained an enduring pop culture icon—that rare performer whose work transcends the era in which he lived.

EARLY LIFE

The early life of Terence Steve McQueen reads like a movie script—a single mother raises her only child during the Depression after being abandoned by her husband, and young Steve grows up a troubled boy with little interest in schooling. When his mother remarried, his stepfather beat him and the teenager rebelled by getting into trouble with the law. At age fifteen McQueen was sent to a reform school called Boys Republic in Chino, California. A year and a half later he left the school and hit the road, working as a sailor, as a lumberjack, and later in the oil fields of Texas. At age seventeen McQueen joined the marines and served for three years. Although he did forty-one days in the brig for going AWOL (absent without leave), he received an honorable discharge. He then decided to move to New York City, where he experienced a revelation that transformed his life.

Twenty-year-old Steve McQueen loved Manhattan. He would later say, "For the first time in my life, I was really exposed to music, culture, a little kindness, a little sensitivity. It was a way of life where people talked out their problems instead of punching you." When he was introduced to famed drama coach Sanford Meisner by one of his girlfriends—an aspiring actress—McQueen became intrigued with acting and decided to audition for a play. Thanks to his ruggedly handsome blond good looks, he was cast in a bit part and fell in love with the theater. He enrolled in Meisner's Neighborhood Playhouse and began to work earnestly at learning the craft of acting. With his tuition paid by the GI Bill, McQueen went on to study with Uta Hagen; Herbert Berghof; and finally Lee Strasberg, where he was one of five students out of 2,000 applicants selected to join the prestigious Actors' Studio. A student of the classics, he honed his craft in summer stock and in touring companies before finally making it to Broadway.

Offstage, however, McQueen remained a rebel—riding motorcycles, having serial affairs with women, and generally living the bohemian life in Greenwich Village—before meeting and falling in love with dancer Neile Adams. He was smitten with the beautiful and talented Adams, and the couple moved

Steve McQueen. *Steve McQueen starred as Carter "Doc" McCoy in* The Getaway *in 1972.* SILVER SCREEN COLLECTION/ CONTRIBUTOR/MOVIEPIX/GETTY IMAGES.

in together almost immediately. Not long thereafter the twenty-six-year-old actor was cast in his first movie. Originally hired as an extra in *Somebody up There Likes Me* (1956), the story of Rocky Graziano starring Paul Newman, McQueen was noticed by director Robert Wise, who gave him a small speaking role.

FILM CAREER

Initially, McQueen seemed content to find acting work in New York. But when Adams was cast in Robert Wise's next film, which was to be filmed in California, he reluctantly agreed to head west. After a difficult period of adjustment, McQueen and Adams decided to get married, and while his wife was making pictures, he began to find steady work in television. In 1958 he landed his first supporting role in a film, *Never Love a Stranger*, playing a lawyer. His next film, the cult classic *The Blob*, starred McQueen as a handsome high-school loner. Both films were only moderately successful, but six weeks after their release, McQueen became a household name as the star of television's *Wanted: Dead or Alive* (1958–1961), playing bounty hunter Josh Randall.

Capitalizing on his newfound fame, McQueen began to receive above-title billing in his films. But it was not until he was cast in the 1960 Western *The Magnificent Seven* that he found his niche, playing Vin, a quiet but deadly gunslinger. Inspired by Akira Kurosawa's *Seven Samurai* (1954) and featuring an all-star cast that included Yul Brynner, Eli Wallach, James Coburn, Charles Bronson, and Robert Vaughn, *The Magnificent Seven* became a huge hit, and McQueen, playing the second lead, began to mold his public image.

Although the handsome McQueen would continue to be cast in romantic leads, film audiences particularly loved him as the defiant antihero in films such as *Hell Is for Heroes* (1962) and *The Great Escape* (1963), which catapulted him to international stardom. As Judith Crist wrote in her review for the *New York Herald Tribune*, "Steve McQueen plays a familiar American war-movie type—brash, self-interested, super-brave emoter. For sheer bravura, whether he's pounding a baseball in his catcher's mitt in solitary or stumping cross-country on a motorcycle with scores of Germans in pursuit, Steve McQueen takes the honors." His likable machismo captured the public imagination and landed him on the cover of *Life* magazine.

For the remainder of the 1960s and well into the 1970s, McQueen was one of Hollywood's most popular leading men. As Ephraim Katz notes in *Film Encyclopedia*, "He was one of that rare breed of film stars who didn't have to act or do anything else to mesmerize a screen audience. He could dominate the screen and fill the box-office coffers on the force of his personality alone." Starring opposite some of Hollywood's most beautiful actresses—from Natalie Wood in *Love with the Proper Stranger* (1963) to Candice Bergen in *The Sand Pebbles* (1966) and Ali McGraw (whom he would later marry) in *The Getaway* (1972)—his rugged good looks made him a top leading man. But still it was in his role as action hero that McQueen continued to carve out a unique niche for himself, in films such as *The Cincinnati Kid* (1965) and *Bullitt* (1968).

LAST YEARS

Throughout his career McQueen continued to surprise fans and critics alike with the depths of his acting ability. Nominated for an Academy Award for *The Sand Pebbles*, he later more than held his own costarring with Dustin Hoffman in *Papillon* in 1973. But after appearing in *The Towering Inferno* in 1974, McQueen decided that he wanted to act only opposite his new wife, McGraw. When no offers surfaced for the couple, he hoped to begin directing. His efforts, however, were thwarted, and a disgruntled McQueen began to let himself go, gaining more than 30 pounds and refusing to cut his hair or beard. One of Hollywood's most popular movie stars for more than a decade, he did not make another movie until 1978, and when he finally reappeared on-screen, it was in an unlikely role. Longing to return to his theatrical roots, McQueen brought Henrik Ibsen's classic play, *An Enemy of the People*, to the screen. Unfortunately, staying out of the public eye had caused his popularity to wane, and even a return to an action role in *The Hunter* (1980) did little to restore his stardom.

Diagnosed with cancer in 1979, McQueen, who had long been afraid of doctors, refused to consent to ordinary medical treatment and instead sought out questionable alternative therapies in Tijuana, Mexico. Hounded by the press, he eventually succumbed to his illness in November 1980. Despite his early death, McQueen has remained one of Hollywood's most enduring stars. His influence on film and popular culture helped to jump-start the action movie craze of the 1980s and 1990s.

Victoria Price

SEE ALSO: *Academy Awards; Bergen, Candice;* The Blob*; Broadway; Bronson, Charles; Brynner, Yul; Disaster Movies; Greenwich Village; Hoffman, Dustin;* Life; The Magnificent Seven*; Media Feeding Frenzies; Newman, Paul; Wood, Natalie.*

BIBLIOGRAPHY

Katz, Ephraim. *The Film Encyclopedia*. New York: Harper Perennial, 1994.

St. Charnez, Casey. *The Films of Steve McQueen*. Secaucus, NJ: Citadel Press, 1984.

Stone, Matthew L. *McQueen's Machines: The Cars and Bikes of a Hollywood Icon*. St. Paul, MN: Motorbooks, 2007.

Me Decade

The 1970s have been referred to as many things but are often remembered as a decade of selfish and self-indulgent behavior. In *Habits of the Heart*, one of the most influential books about the decade, Joseph Veroff is quoted as saying that "there has been a shift from a *socially* integrated paradigm for structuring well-being, to a more *personal* or *individuated* paradigm for structuring well-being." This description was less critical of the era's overt selfishness than the term used by novelist Tom Wolfe. Following the stereotypical homogeneity of the 1950s and the tumult of the 1960s, many American institutions had broken down and Americans were left with very little holding them together. In lieu of such common fabric, Wolfe called the era of the 1970s the "me decade."

For Wolfe, the me generation grew out of personal greed. In his infamous 1976 article in *New York Magazine*, he wrote of Americans:

> Once the dreary little bastards started getting money in the 1940s, they did an astonishing thing—they took their money and ran. They did something only aristocrats (and intellectuals and artists) were supposed to do—they discovered and started doting on

> *Me*! They've created the greatest age of individualism in American history! All rules are broken! The prophets are out of business! . . . Neither arguments nor policies nor acts of the legislature have been any match for them in the past. And this one has the mightiest, holiest roll of all, the beat that goes . . . *Me* . . . *Me* . . . *Me* . . . *Me* . . .

Later scholars refer to this change as a "new narcissism." Within cultural studies there has been a recent proliferation of accounts of the rise of narcissism in analyses of consumer culture, celebrity culture, and new media. Why would society suddenly take this turn in the 1970s? Scholars have easily itemized some possible explanations.

The political crises of Vietnam and Watergate, coupled with record high inflation, forced many Americans to retreat from social concerns in order to think more singularly about personal growth and success during the 1970s. Self-help books proliferated and offered advice far different from the "work hard and succeed" mantra that had guided previous generations. Best sellers such as Wayne Dyer's *Your Erroneous Zones* (1976) and Thomas Anthony Harris's *I'm OK, You're OK* (1969) urged readers to know and accept themselves and to celebrate who they were, and Werner Erhard's "est" seminars used strict training within a group format to build self-awareness and offer individual fulfillment.

George and Nena O'Neill's *Open Marriage: A New Life Style for Couples* (1972) advised couples to take their newfound self-knowledge and share it with others within the context of a marriage that allowed multiple sexual partners. Those who sought self-knowledge without the touchy-feely psychologizing took part in some of the many health and fitness fads that blossomed during the 1970s, including the jogging craze and the growth of interest in healthy cooking and vegetarianism.

Though individuals seemed bent on pursuing personal growth, social and economic changes in the 1970s brought a new homogeneity to American culture. Business growth generated massive mergers and the formation of conglomerates that would lay the framework for an economic shift toward service industries. Many such enterprises expanded globally, creating multinational companies that soon exceeded the power of the nations in which they operated. McDonald's, for instance, erected 4,000 new outlets during the 1970s. What McDonald's did for hamburgers, Holiday Inn did for travel, Kmart for retailing, and 7-Eleven stores for neighborhood groceries. Every American city of any size had a "miracle mile" or "strip" nearly identical to that of every other. And, as more white Americans left the troubled inner cities for the safer suburbs, the homogeneity of community life increased as well.

Rick Moody's 1994 novel *The Ice Storm* (made into a film in 1997 by director Ang Lee) dissected the sense of anomie that lay at the heart of those living in the me decade. Moody depicts a set of bored middle-aged adults whose search for happiness in drink, in work, or with their neighbor's spouse leaves them blind to the collapse of their family life. Moody captured the stereotype of the decade; like all stereotypes, it contained more than a grain of truth.

In clear contrast to the communitarianism of the 1960s, the me decade reinforced individualism. It was socially acceptable to be most concerned with your own welfare—no apologies were necessary. Many scholars point to this sensibility, which has been called a fracture with past patterns by some observers, to understand the intellectual foundations of many of the economic patterns of the decades that followed.

Brian Black

SEE ALSO: *Consumerism; est; Holiday Inns; Kmart; McDonald's; Vietnam; Watergate; Wolfe, Tom.*

BIBLIOGRAPHY

Bellah, Robert N.; Richard Madsen; William M. Sullivan; et al. *Habits of the Heart.* Berkeley: University of California Press, 1985.

Chafe, William H. *The Unfinished Journey.* New York: Oxford University Press, 1995.

Cowie, Jefferson. *Stayin' Alive.* New York: Free Press, 2010.

Fox, Richard W., and T. J. Lears. *The Culture of Consumption.* New York: Pantheon, 1983.

Moody, Rick. *The Ice Storm.* Boston: Little, Brown, 1994.

Rodgers, Daniel T. *Age of Fracture.* New York: Belknap Press, 2011.

Stein, Judith. *Pivotal Decade.* New Haven, CT: Yale University Press, 2010.

Wolfe, Tom. "The 'Me' Decade and the Third Great Awakening." *New York Magazine*, August 23, 1976.

Meadows, Audrey *(1924–1996)*

Actress Audrey Meadows was born Audrey Cotter in 1924 (though her birthdate is listed in other sources between 1921 and 1926) to Episcopal missionary parents in Wuchang, China. She intended to become a journalist, but her sister, Jayne, persuaded her to pursue a career in show business. Meadows had an on-again, off-again career on television, radio, and the Broadway stage when she happened upon her most famous, and memorable, role as Alice Kramden on *The Jackie Gleason Show* in 1952.

At first considered too young and pretty for the role of the long-suffering wife of Ralph Kramden—loud-mouthed bus driver and perennial hatcher of get-rich-schemes—Meadows submitted photos to Gleason of herself dressed in dowdy dresses with her hair askew. He hired her for the role, which had originally been created by Pert Kelton on "Honeymooners" sketches on Gleason's *Cavalcade of Stars.* When Gleason brought the show to CBS in 1952, he replaced Kelton with Meadows. She performed in "Honeymooners" sketches on his hour-long show from 1952 to 1955 and then in the classic thirty-nine episodes of *The Honeymooners* from October 1955 to September 1956. She played Alice as strong but practical and understanding in her constant crusade to better the Kramdens' life while opposing her blustering husband's relentless pursuit of crack-brained schemes to get rich.

Meadows was nominated for four Emmys as Best Actress in a Supporting Role from 1954 through 1957, winning the coveted award in 1955. She made some guest appearances on television dramas and panel shows, and she had a featured role in the Cary Grant–Doris Day film *That Touch of Mink* (1962). After marrying Continental Airlines chairman Robert Six, she retired from show business. In 1977 she returned to television for a *Honeymooners* reunion and followed with guest shots on

The Love Boat and other shows, as well as a recurring role on *Too Close for Comfort* in 1982–1983. Meadows died of lung cancer on February 3, 1996.

James R. Belpedio

SEE ALSO: *Emmy Awards; Gleason, Jackie; Grant, Cary;* The Honeymooners*;* The Love Boat.

BIBLIOGRAPHY

Brooks, Tim, and Earle Marsh. *The Complete Directory to Prime Time Network and Cable TV Shows 1946–Present*, 6th ed. New York: Ballantine Books, 1995.

Karol, Michael. *Funny Ladies*. Lincoln, NE: iUniverse, 2004.

McCrohan, Donna. *The Honeymooners' Companion: The Kramdens and the Nortons Revisited*. New York: Workman Publishing, 1978.

Mean Streets

Made in twenty-seven days on a very modest budget, *Mean Streets* is arguably director Martin Scorsese's first significant film. A hit at the 1973 New York Film Festival, important popular critics such as Pauline Kael and Vincent Canby were taken with its freshness and rough, documentary quality, comparing it to French new wave films such as Jean-Luc Godard's *Breathless* (1959) or François Truffaut's *400 Blows* (1959) or American John Cassavetes's intimate, improvisational *Faces* (1968) and *Husbands* (1970). Reviewer Joseph Kanton even saw the film as part of an indigenous American new wave that, along with films such as director George Lucas's *American Graffiti* (1973), Ralph Bakshi's *Heavy Traffic* (1973), and Lamont Johnson's *The Last American Hero* (1973), brought a new "energy and originality" to American cinema.

Scorsese, however, claims that the film's visual quality, both documentary-like and expressionistic at the same time, derives as much from budgetary limitations as it does from aesthetic choices. Whatever the source of the film's style, it was greeted as a breath of stylistic fresh air and as a breakthrough movie for a promising young director who eventually became one of the most significant American filmmakers of his generation.

Like much of Scorsese's early work, *Mean Streets* is about "the neighborhood." Scorsese argues that "*Mean Streets* was an attempt to put myself and my old friends on the screen, to show how we lived, what life was like in Little Italy. It was really an anthropological or a sociological tract." As in many Scorsese films, Catholicism and the Italian American experience are at the heart of his thinking, and the film can be seen as a continuation of his earlier *Who's That Knocking at My Door* (1968), with some real-life experiences and family legends added in.

Mean Streets is also the first of Scorsese's four important gangster films—the others being *GoodFellas* (1990), *Casino* and (1995), and *The Gangs of New York* (2002)—and he has argued that he meant *Mean Streets* as a homage to the Warner's gangster cycle of the 1930s and 1940s. The title is taken from Raymond Chandler's famous 1950 essay on crime fiction, "The Simple Art of Murder." In this essay Chandler defines the honorable hero of the American hard-boiled school of fiction, with which the film's hero shares many qualities.

The plot of *Mean Streets* is a loosely woven series of episodes in the life of Charlie Cappa Jr. (Keitel), a small-time gangster who works for his uncle Giovanni, a powerful and respected Mafia don. Charlie is a street kid who is caught between his childhood friends and his demanding uncle, and he is obsessed

Mean Streets. *Harvey Keitel, left, and Robert De Niro starred in Martin Scorsese's 1973 film* Mean Streets. TAPLIN-PERRY-SCORSESE/THE KOBAL COLLECTION.

with religion, guilt, and the need to do penance—but not the simple penance prescribed by the church. As Charlie says, "You don't make up for your sins in the church. You do it in the streets." A born peacemaker, Charlie is a good but rather ineffectual man—a saint, Scorsese argues—who lives on the margins in a world of violent gangsters and petty thugs.

Charlie's struggle to survive is set against a soundtrack of rock-and-roll songs popular in his time. This use of popular music is a significant Scorsese stylistic flourish. Unlike other films where the use of rock and roll has become a cliché, Scorsese carefully chose the songs for their thematic and atmospheric relevance to both plot and character development.

Mean Streets is set in a small, self-contained society, a closed world where the rules of behavior are strictly enforced. Charlie's main problem is his relationship with Johnny Boy (Robert De Niro), a free spirit who violates social convention with humorous abandon. Johnny Boy is an obsessive, over-the-top gambler who owes everyone in the neighborhood money—money that he never pays back. This leads him into conflict with both Giovanni and Michael (Richard Romanus), a small-time loan shark who ultimately takes his revenge on both Charlie and Johnny Boy. In some sense Johnny Boy is Charlie's ultimate penance, and in the end Charlie cannot redeem him—or himself. But the lively Johnny Boy also has the joy of life so lacking in the conventional and obsessed Charlie. It is exactly this complex character development and story line that make *Mean Streets* a classic Scorsese film.

Jeannette Sloniowski

SEE ALSO: American Graffiti; *De Niro, Robert; Ford, John;* GoodFellas; *Keitel, Harvey; Lucas, George; Scorsese, Martin;* Taxi Driver.

BIBLIOGRAPHY

Bliss, Michael. *Martin Scorsese and Michael Cimino.* Metuchen, NJ: Scarecrow Press, 1985.

Cashmore, Ellis. *Martin Scorsese's America.* Cambridge, UK: Polity Press, 2009.

Ebert, Roger. *Scorsese by Ebert.* Chicago: University of Chicago Press, 2008.

Kelly, Mary Pat. *Martin Scorsese: The First Decade.* Pleasantville, NY: Redgrave Publishing, 1980.

Kelly, Mary Pat. *Martin Scorsese: A Journey.* New York: Thunder's Mouth Press, 1991.

Keyser, Les. *Martin Scorsese.* New York: Twayne, 1992.

Kolker, Robert. *A Cinema of Loneliness: Penn, Kubrick, Scorsese, Spielberg, Altman,* 2nd ed. New York: Oxford University Press, 1988.

Lee, A. Robert. *Gothic to Multicultural: Idioms of Imagining in American Literary Fiction.* New York: Rodopi, 2009.

Lourdeaux, Leo. *Italian and Irish Filmmakers in America.* Philadelphia: Temple University Press, 1990.

Raymond, Marc. "The Multiplicity of Generic Discourses and the Meaning and Pleasure of *Mean Streets.*" *Canadian Journal of Film Studies* 15, no. 2 (2006): 62–80.

Thompson, David, and Ian Christie, eds. *Scorsese on Scorsese.* London: Faber and Faber, 1989.

Media Feeding Frenzies

Sharks tend to be solitary creatures, but blood in the water can draw them from a long distance away. Sometimes, when a number of sharks are consuming the same prey, they can be gripped by a kind of hysteria in which they frantically attack their food, each other, and anything else that may happen by. Such a display of mindless bloodlust is known as a "feeding frenzy." According to William Safire in *Safire's New Political Dictionary,* this expression was first applied to reporters in 1977 in a speech given by Gerald L. Warren, editor of the *San Diego Union.* Warren compared the overly aggressive tactics of some journalists to "sharks in a feeding frenzy." Today, the term usually refers to the covering of a story by a large number of reporters, who do their work aggressively; intrusively; persistently; and, in some cases, recklessly.

MAIN INGREDIENTS

A media feeding frenzy usually stems from two elements: a celebrity and a scandal. *Celebrity* can be used to describe anyone well known to the public, such as an actor, a politician, or a star athlete, for example. *Scandal* usually involves allegations of immoral behavior—often, but not always, of a sexual nature. Two of the biggest scandals to attract the American media's attention in the 1990s were President Bill Clinton's relationship with White House intern Monica Lewinsky and athlete-turned-sportscaster O. J. Simpson's trial for the murder of his ex-wife, Nicole, and her friend, Ron Goldman. In the new millennium, celebrity-related feeding frenzies occurred over such diverse events as the contested Florida vote during the 2000 presidential election; the murder trial of Dr. Conrad Murray after singer Michael Jackson's death; and the child sex-abuse scandal involving Jerry Sandusky, a former Pennsylvania State University football coach—who, while not a celebrity himself, was a close friend and associate of coaching legend Joe Paterno.

Political figures who have provoked a media feeding frenzy through scandals include Zoe Baird (hiring an illegal alien as a nanny), Joe Biden (plagiarism), Rod Blagojevich (corruption), Robert Bork (allegations of racism and sexism), President Clinton (the Lewinsky affair and, earlier, Gennifer Flowers), Thomas Eagleton (mental health), Newt Gingrich (extramarital affairs), Gary Hart (Donna Rice), Ted Kennedy (Chappaquiddick), Wilbur Mills (stripper Fanne Foxe), Richard Nixon (Watergate), Bob Packwood (infidelity), Dan Quayle (allegations of draft dodging), Mark Sanford (extramarital affair), Clarence Thomas (sexual harassment charges by Anita Hill), John Tower (allegations of drunkenness and womanizing), and Anthony Weiner (sexting). Major sports scandals include Barry Bonds (steroids), Kobe Bryant (allegations of rape), Pete Rose (gambling), Sandusky (child abuse), and Mike Tyson (rape). Movie stars and pop stars have generated more than their fair share of scandals: Hugh Grant (solicitation), Eddie Murphy (solicitation), Mel Gibson (anti-Semitism), Lindsay Lohan (drunk driving), and Chris Brown (domestic violence), to name but a few.

Plenty of feeding frenzies have taken place even when celebrity involvement was lacking. In 1992 teenager Amy Fisher, dubbed the "Long Island Lolita," was accused of attempting to murder the wife of Joey Buttafuoco, her considerably older boyfriend. The salacious elements of the story (including details from the police that the seventeen-year-old Fisher had been working as a call girl) were enough to create a frenzy—first in the New York City media market and, eventually, nationwide—

despite the fact that none of those involved were public figures. Four years later, Atlanta, Georgia, security guard Richard Jewell was accused of involvement in the Olympic Park bombing that killed one person and injured several others at the 1996 summer games. The media frenzy, which all but convicted Jewell in the court of public opinion, began with a leaked FBI report saying that Jewell was the "focus" of the investigation. Jewell was ultimately cleared of any involvement in the bombing, and he successfully sued several media outlets for defaming his character.

In the first decade of the 2000s, two separate murder trials—those of Casey Anthony and Amanda Knox—produced feeding frenzies even though neither young woman had been famous before her trial. Each of the defendants was young, white, attractive, and accused of a heinous crime, which was all it took to provoke the press into nonstop coverage.

Although the terminology may be of relatively recent origin, media feeding frenzies are not new phenomena. One of the worst frenzies of the twentieth century took place in 1935. It stemmed from the trial of Bruno Hauptmann for the kidnapping and murder of Charles Lindbergh's twenty-month-old son. In this case the celebrity (Lindbergh, who in 1927 had been the first to cross the Atlantic Ocean in an airplane) was a victim, not the alleged perpetrator, but that did not stop the Hauptmann trial from turning into a three-ring circus. Reporters declared Hauptmann guilty before the trial had even begun; drunken journalists caroused in the streets of Flemington, the small New Jersey town where the trial was held; and reporters in the packed courtroom were able to pass notes to both the prosecutors and defense lawyers as the trial took place. So egregious was the conduct of the press on this occasion that it prompted the American Bar Association to pass its Canon 35, which led to the banning of cameras and radio microphones from all courtrooms. It was a restriction that lasted for fifty years, and even then it was only amended, not abolished. Judges were given discretion about allowing television cameras into their courtrooms, as well as complete control over the ways the cameras were used when their presence was permitted.

THE INSATIABLE APPETITE FOR NEWS

According to Professor Larry Sabato of the University of Virginia, several developments in modern society underlie the rash of feeding frenzies noted in the twenty-first century. A major factor is the changing nature of the news business, especially its greatly increased scope, speed, and competitiveness. There is much more news coverage today than ever before. This is certainly true of television, the source for much of the news that Americans receive. Although the half hour of network news at dinnertime remains a staple, even the networks have added to their coverage of feature stories by offering a plethora of prime-time "magazine shows," such as *60 Minutes*, *20/20*, *48 Hours*, and *Dateline NBC*. Additionally, cable television offers a wide variety of news programming, much of it available twenty-four hours a day. Cable News Network (CNN) was the first to provide this service and was successful enough to spin off a second channel, Headline News. This has led to such ventures as CNBC, MSNBC, and Fox News Channel, with more still to come. In addition, sports networks like ESPN offer news coverage of athletes both on and off the field; entertainment channels, such as E!, present news focusing on films, television, and popular music; and specialized "ethnic" cable networks provide news programs geared toward blacks, Latinos, and other ethnic or racial groups. There is, in short, an immense amount of news being offered to the American (and international) viewer every day. That void has to be filled somehow, which places heavy demands upon those who find, report, and package the news.

In addition to the proliferation of television channels, many Americans now get their news from online sources. By 2010 some 41 percent of Americans reported getting most of their news from the Internet. Online sources included web versions of newspapers; websites affiliated with television, such as CNN.com; media outlets focused exclusively on the Internet, such as the Huffington Post; and blogs written by journalist, columnists, and private individuals. This new platform for news coverage has only increased the push to provide instantaneous, nonstop, and groundbreaking coverage of hot stories.

As a result of the sheer amount of news programming that is available, and the rapidity with which it can be collected and presented to the public, competition between news organizations has reached a new level of intensity. This is one of the prime reasons behind media feeding frenzies. When a "newsworthy" story breaks, a large number of journalists will descend on the scene of the story, driven to find material to fill the many hours of news broadcasting and eager to outdo the competition in discovering new angles to pursue. If the story has elements that make it especially newsworthy (i.e., celebrities and scandal), then the feeding frenzy will begin in earnest.

Another important reason for the increase in the number and intensity of feeding frenzies derives from the way that both journalists and the public have come to view news. For instance, there has been a marked decrease in civility in the behavior of reporters. This manifests itself in such practices as reporters swarming around a public figure, cameras running and microphones extended, as well as the practice called "ambush interviewing," wherein a reporter, usually with a minicam operator in tow, will attempt to surprise an interview subject who has already shown a disinclination to talk to the media. In some cases, the coverage of the news becomes a news story in itself, as in 2012 when Sandusky's wife was videotaped nearly running down a reporter who was filming a news segment in the family's driveway.

But the largest difference in terms of civility in the late twentieth and early twenty-first century is that, for journalists, nothing is considered off limits anymore. For instance, President John F. Kennedy is known today to have been a chronic womanizer, and his weakness was no secret to most White House correspondents during the Kennedy administration. But there were no exposés in the media about his many affairs, because journalistic conventions of the day held that private sexual conduct was not newsworthy unless it affected public behavior. Those who followed the frantic media coverage of President Clinton's sexual involvement with a White House intern in the 1990s or the 2011 story that Representative Weiner had texted sexually explicit photos to several women can easily discern how much media ethics have changed since the early 1960s.

CYNICISM AND PRURIENCE

The way in which journalists approach the gathering of news has also been affected by an increased cynicism within the profession. It is doubtful that experienced reporters were ever given to wide-eyed naïveté, but events over the last several decades have done much to prompt the Fourth Estate to expect the worst of the public figures they cover. President Lyndon Johnson's rhetoric justifying American involvement in Vietnam eventually led journalists to coin the term *credibility gap*—which meant that many people thought that Johnson had engaged in deliberate deception in his relations both with reporters and the American people. A few years later, the Watergate scandal revealed the lengths to which a president could go to deceive the press, manipulate public opinion, and attack his political enemies. In the following decade, reporters covering the Iran-Contra scandal learned how an uninvolved president, "plausible deniability," and the judicious use of paper shredders could combine to violate the law and undermine the nation's foreign policy.

At times, journalistic cynicism seems to be matched by public prurience. As is shown by the ready market for such "tabloid television" programs as *Inside Edition* (as well as their print counterparts, which are available at any supermarket checkout lane), there is a substantial appetite for sleaze in this country. Many Americans are loath to admit their taste for such programs, perhaps out of embarrassment, but the numbers speak for themselves. At the height of the media feeding frenzy over the Simpson criminal trial, a network anchor was asked for his reaction to polls that showed a large percentage of Americans claiming to be disgusted with the media's obsessive coverage of every aspect of the case. "They may say that," the anchorman replied, "but look at the ratings. Our evening news numbers are up since trial coverage started, and every *Special O.J. Report* we do in prime time pulls in bigger audiences than our regular programming usually gets. . . . People may say they don't like this stuff," he concluded, "but they still watch it—they watch it a lot."

Apart from whatever media feeding frenzies may say about American culture, they pose other concerns as well. One involves journalistic objectivity. Journalists involved in the excitement of a scandal story soon begin to take sides, whether they recognize it or not. If a president is accused of sexual misconduct, reporters know that the audience interest is usually in what he did and with whom, not in an evenhanded sifting of the evidence, with full weight given to the denials by the accused. Thus, sides are taken, and objectivity falls by the wayside.

If objectivity is endangered by feeding frenzies, accuracy may not be far behind. A reporter who finds a new angle to a story or an undiscovered bit of evidence knows that the competition is not far away. The glory, acclaim, and fame come from being first with the story. This leaves precious little time to double check information or to ponder the credibility of those providing it. Of course, one can always issue a retraction for a mistake, but retractions never seem to be accorded the same audience attention as allegations, and there is often no way a retraction can wipe out the harm that may have been done.

THE PROFIT MOTIVE

News programs (or publications) are subject to zero-sum logic. That means that for every minute (or column inch, in print) devoted to Story A, there is correspondingly less time or space available for Stories B, C, and D. The subject of a media feeding frenzy will almost always be given considerable air time—such a story generally guarantees good ratings, competing stations will almost certainly feature it, and news editors have to be able to justify the resources allocated to the covering of the story. The result is that the "frenzy" story will take up a significant portion of the newscast, and other stories, regardless of their import, will likely receive short shrift—and short segments. And this practice will probably be repeated, day after day, for as long as the story remains current.

The principal fact to keep in mind about the news business is that it is a business. Although the Constitution says that the news media have a public service obligation, in practice public service today is considered far less important than the bottom line. Feeding frenzies take place because the result of all this frenetic news coverage, to use an old phrase, "sells papers." And the future does not appear to offer hope for much improvement. Competition between news outlets is likely to increase in intensity, and the technology of information transmission will only become faster. As a result, the media feeding frenzies of the future may make the coverage of recent scandals look like a model of good taste and self-restraint.

Justin Gustainis

SEE ALSO: *Anita Hill–Clarence Thomas Senate Hearings; Bonds, Barry; Cable TV; Celebrity; College Football;* Dateline*; ESPN; Fox News Channel; Gibson, Mel; The Huffington Post; The Internet; Iran Contra; Jackson, Michael; Lewinsky, Monica; Lindbergh, Charles; Lohan, Lindsay; Movie Stars; Murphy, Eddie; Olympics; Rose, Pete; Sex Scandals; Simpson Trial;* 60 Minutes*; Sports Heroes; Tabloid Television; Tabloids; Television; Television Anchors;* 20/20*; Tyson, Mike; Vietnam; Watergate.*

BIBLIOGRAPHY

Garment, Suzanne. *Scandal: The Culture of Mistrust in American Politics.* New York: Times Books, 1991.

Sabato, Larry J. *Feeding Frenzy: Attack Journalism and American Politics.* Baltimore, MD: Lanahan, 2000.

Safire, William. *Safire's New Political Dictionary.* New York: Random House, 1993.

Walls, Jeannette. *Dish: How Gossip Became the News and the News Became Just Another Show.* New York: HarperCollins, 2000.

Walsh, Kenneth T. *Feeding the Beast: The White House versus the Press.* New York: Random House, 1996.

Medicine Shows

From about 1870 until the early 1900s, medicine shows were a major form of entertainment in the United States, rivaling the traveling circus in popularity. Typically featuring "doctors" who pitched various products with supposedly medicinal value, these shows toured the country and were performed on small, temporary stages. Musicians, circus acts, jugglers, conjurers, and comedy players were also part of many shows, helping to draw potential customers for the products being offered for sale.

By the early 1700s street performers were plentiful in Britain's colonies in the New World. Quacks and peddlers, working alone or with a few assistants, soon allied themselves with these performers. Selling from the back of a wagon or from a tripod set up on a street, these salesmen gathered a crowd, entertained it, and then peddled fake panaceas. Their remedies and potions were generally harmless concoctions, usually herb compounds mixed with liniment, oil, alcohol, and sugar.

Medicine shows grew in number, size, and popularity as the young country grew, and when the United States industrialized after the Civil War ended in 1865, the shows became advertising vehicles for manufacturers that craved a national market. The largest companies sent out their own shows to sell their line of products. Medicine shows were most popular in small cities and towns where they were often the only live professional entertainment available. A parade down the main street of town heralded their arrival. Since their goal was to sell their products, medicine shows charged little or no admission.

The type of entertainment often changed nightly to encourage repeat business and featured popular acts of the time, such as trick shooters, banjo artists, and minstrelsy. Performers had to be skilled in presenting a mélange of songs, dances, and skits, as well as the traditional afterpiece, an extended sketch that involved violent clowning, unfeeling stereotypes (often a blackface character), and a sheeted ghost. Shows were typically two hours long. The entertainment was offered first for a little more than an hour, and the remainder of the show was devoted to pitches for soaps, tonics, and gadgets such as liver pads that contained a spot of red pepper and glue, which, when melted, provided a sense of warmth and good health.

Ersatz doctors delivered the medical pitches, exalting the miraculous powers of the products. The prestige of German universities provided the inspiration for German "doctors," while the mystery of the Far East provided interest in Oriental healers and remedies. The culture of American Indians inspired the most famous of all shows. As Native Americans were pushed farther West, confined to reservations, and ultimately eliminated from the life of the burgeoning nation, popular culture seized on them as a symbol of natural health and fitness. The Kickapoo Indian Medicine Company sent out the biggest and most elaborate of the touring shows. Founded in 1881, the company, which had no connection to the Kickapoo Nation, promoted a full range of cures, including cough syrups, Indian oils, and worm expellers, as well as, most famously, Kickapoo Indian Sagwa, advertised as a cure to dyspepsia, rheumatism, and other ailments. Members of the Iroquois, Sioux, Cree, and Pawnee tribes, whose services were often leased from Indian agents on reservations, pitched and promoted these products from a traveling "Indian village" and presented war dances, marriage ceremonies, lectures, and in some instances Irish and blackface comedy as entertainment.

By the early twentieth century medicine shows faced government regulation for the first time along with competition from other forms of entertainment. In 1906 the U.S. Congress passed the Pure Food and Drug Act, which made it illegal to make, transport, or sell mislabeled or harmful products. This largely curtailed the types of products offered for sale by medicine shows. By 1920 increasing modernization, the mobility brought about by the automobile, and the rise of motion pictures had altered the nature of small-town life and eliminated the lure and excitement of medicine shows. In 1938 Congress passed the Food, Drug, and Cosmetics Act, which mandated harsher penalties for fake medicines, further impacting medicine shows. They sputtered on into the 1950s, and the last medicine show abandoned the road in 1964.

Louis Scheeder

SEE ALSO: *Advertising; Automobile; Blackface Minstrelsy; Circus; The Indian; Minstrel Shows; Parades.*

BIBLIOGRAPHY

Anderson, Ann. *Snake Oil, Hustlers and Hambones: The American Medicine Show.* Jefferson, NC: McFarland, 2000.

Armstrong, David, and Elizabeth Metzger Armstrong. *The Great American Medicine Show.* New York: Prentice Hall, 1991.

Gioia, Ted. *Delta Blues.* New York: Norton, 2008.

McNamara, Brooks. *Step Right Up.* Garden City, NY: Doubleday, 1976.

Meet Me in St. Louis

Meet Me in St. Louis, one of the greatest movie musicals ever made, was directed by Vincente Minnelli and released in 1944 by Metro-Goldwyn-Mayer (MGM). The film was a smashing success with audiences and critics alike and went on to delight viewers for decades. Set in 1903, the movie mixes family melodrama with light comedy, whimsical romance, and engaging musical numbers and stars Judy Garland in her first significant film role since she played Dorothy in *The Wizard of Oz* (1939). Filmed in brilliant Technicolor, the film glows with extravagant warmth both visually and thematically and evokes nostalgia for turn-of-the-twentieth-century domestic tranquility and pre–World War II innocence.

Meet Me in St. Louis presents a year in the life of the Smith family in St. Louis, Missouri. The patriarch, Alonzo Smith (Leon Ames), is a hardworking lawyer often oblivious to the comings and goings of his own family, even as he sounds the voice of familial authority. His wife, Anna (Mary Astor), is a traditional maternal figure, in charge of the home but willing to concede to her husband's wishes. The romantic angst of her two older daughters, Rose (Lucille Bremer) and Esther (Garland), concerns her as much as does the quality of ketchup the family housekeeper, Katie (Marjorie Main), busily brews in the opening scene. The home is her domain, while the public sphere belongs to Alonzo. Rounding out the Smith family are Princeton-bound Lon Jr. (Henry H. Daniels Jr.), young daughters Agnes (Joan Carroll) and Tootie (Margaret O'Brien), and Grandpa Prophater (Harry Davenport).

As the year in the life of the family progresses, oldest daughter Rose desperately attempts to prompt a marriage proposal from her beau who is away in New York. Seventeen-year-old Esther develops a crush on new neighbor, John Truett (Tom Drake), giving rise to one of the film's lasting songs, "The Boy Next Door." The younger daughters play mock-morbid games with dolls they have deemed terminally ill or already dead and collude with a gang of fellow Halloween hooligans to "kill" Mr. Brokauff, a neighbor with ethnic, middle-European physical features. Five-year-old Tootie's mission to throw flour in his face forms a dark xenophobic edge to the film's depiction of a prosperous, midwestern town wanting for nothing. Each family member takes a turn humming or singing the tune "Meet Me in St. Louis" as evidence of the family's contentment with their grounded sense of place and time.

Then one night Alonzo drops a bomb—he has been promoted and transferred to New York, so the family will be moving. Everyone is devastated by the news. Rallied by Anna, the family gathers around the piano as she and Alonzo sing, "You and I," and they all reluctantly accept the decision. On Christmas Eve, however, Alonzo witnesses Tootie bludgeoning all the snowmen in the backyard because she cannot take them with her to New York. As he sits alone in a darkened room surrounded by packing boxes and bare walls, Alonzo changes his mind and vows to stay in St. Louis "until we rot." The film ends as the family attends the 1904 Exposition.

Meet Me in St. Louis. *Judy Garland, center, performs a number with Tom Drake in the 1944 film* Meet Me in St. Louis. **MGM/THE KOBAL COLLECTION.**

Of all the songs in *Meet Me in St. Louis*, one in particular, "Have Yourself a Merry Little Christmas," sung by Garland, enjoyed a long afterlife. Written by composer and lyricist Hugh Martin, who also wrote "The Boy Next Door" and "The Trolley Song" for the film, "Have Yourself a Merry Little Christmas" became a standard Christmas classic. After Martin wrote the song, Minnelli and Garland objected to some of the lyrics because they were too depressing, so Martin rewrote the song to make it more upbeat. He revised it again in 1957 upon the request of Frank Sinatra, who subsequently recorded the revised version. Both versions of the song have been recorded by numerous artists over the years, and both versions are heard every year at Christmastime.

Meet Me in St. Louis premiered in St. Louis in November 1944 and opened in New York later that same month. It broke box-office records all over the country, becoming MGM's second-biggest moneymaker behind *Gone with the Wind* (1939). It garnered four Academy Award nominations, and O'Brien received a special Academy Award (a miniature statuette) for Outstanding Child Actress of 1944. The success of *Meet Me in St. Louis* encouraged other studios to create imitations, including Twentieth Century Fox's *Centennial Summer* (1946), a musical set against the background of the Philadelphia Great Exposition of 1876.

Meet Me in St. Louis also lived on in yearly appearances on television at Christmastime and in a special video release on its fiftieth anniversary in 1994. The film established Garland as a star and earned her unprecedented clout at MGM. Many people consider her performance to be the best of her career. The film also cemented Minnelli's career in only his third outing as director. Minnelli and Garland married on June 15, 1945, and divorced in 1951. They had one daughter, Liza Minnelli, who became an accomplished performer herself.

Elizabeth Haas

SEE ALSO: *Academy Awards; Christmas; Garland, Judy;* Gone with the Wind*; Halloween; MGM (Metro-Goldwyn-Mayer); Minnelli, Liza; Minnelli, Vincente; The Musical; Sinatra, Frank;* The Wizard of Oz*; World War II.*

BIBLIOGRAPHY

Green, Stanley, and Elaine Schmidt. *Hollywood Musicals Year by Year.* Milwaukee, WI: Leonard, 1999.

Kaufman, Gerald. *Meet Me in St. Louis.* London: British Film Institute, 1994.

Naremore, James. *The Films of Vincente Minnelli.* Cambridge, UK: Cambridge University Press, 1993.

Megachurches

A "megachurch" is any church with a sustained weekly congregation of 2,000 or more headed by a charismatic minister who creates a strong congregational identity. Such churches typically employ a large staff and maintain activities throughout the week, with services that often utilize technologically advanced media systems, and they frequently develop a variety of retail enterprises. Often evangelical, the churches typically espouse a fundamentalist Protestant doctrine and call for strict adherence to "family values," which often includes adopting traditional gender roles, abstaining from sex before marriage, forswearing intoxicants, and eschewing anything that could be construed as homosexual behavior.

A WORLDWIDE PHENOMENON

As of 2012, more than 1,300 megachurches existed in the United States, with approximately 60 percent located in the southern United States; the highest concentrations were in California, Texas, Georgia, and Florida. Megachurches are typically established in suburban areas outside rapidly growing newer cities such as Atlanta, Dallas, Houston, Los Angeles, Orlando, and Phoenix.

Although much of the reporting on megachurches has focused on the U.S. institutions, megachurches are a worldwide phenomenon, with Brazil, Korea, and several African countries claiming thousands of churches with huge weekly attendance. Although the largest megachurch in America averaged 35,000 in attendance, churches in Korea boasted over 250,000 members in their congregations. Membership consists primarily of young, middle-class, conservative people. Researchers have found that most members are under 40 and that the congregations were composed of about 55 percent women and 45 percent men, with 52 percent having college degrees.

WHAT MAKES A MEGACHURCH?

Although megachurches are primarily defined by the weekly attendance of their congregations, there are several other characteristics that mark the phenomenon, and not every large church can be accurately called a megachurch. For example, there are thousands of Roman Catholic parishes in North America in which at least 2,000 people attend mass each week, but they are not considered megachurches as they lack most or all of the other attributes.

Perhaps the most distinctive characteristic of a megachurch, other than the size of its congregation, is the nature of the service. At times referred to as "McChurches," megachurches tend to rely upon show-business elements in their services, with pop music replacing hymns and organs, comfortable contour armchairs replacing pews, multimedia presentations replacing the subdued lighting and shadowed hush of historical Protestant services, and the softening or removal of traditional religious symbols such as the cross. Additionally, they can receive exponentially greater amounts of cash donations, compared with the smaller amounts donated to rural churches and many Catholic parishes.

The pros and cons of a megachurch's visual and technological appeal, as well as other aspects, such as the sometime use of punk and alternative rock inspirational songs, may be debated on both religious and political grounds. However, their services may also be discussed pragmatically. In many ways, megachurches are attempting to attract members that mainstream churches have lost over the years. Fearing that people will be drawn to the trappings of popular culture and will no longer hear the word of God on a regular basis, the large churches attempt to lure potential churchgoers with a performance the congregation is likely to find relevant.

The combination of hip spectacle and traditional message has worked for many churches. Pastor Joel Osteen, leader of Houston's Lakewood Church (with attendance in excess of 44,000, the largest church in the United States), stated that "other churches have not kept up, and they lose people by not changing with the times." Donations to Osteen's church have amounted to as much as $55 million. Osteen, and many of his like-minded brethren and rivals, preach "the gospel of prosperity" and insist that God wants his followers to be rich.

TAX-EXEMPT STATUS

Although this prosperity doctrine may be difficult to reconcile with Jesus's well-established antipathy to money, it also poses challenges to society at large as these well-funded organizations can acquire clout with politicians. Taken collectively, megachurches raise billions of dollars in tax-exempt money. Also, although Section 501(c)(3) of the Internal Revenue Service code—which grants tax-exempt status—tightly limits "how much political and legislative (lobbying) activities they may conduct," these churches endorse politicians and have the capacity to donate large sums to their campaigns.

Megachuches also have the funds to donate to political action committees (PACs) and can therefore influence the legislative process in the United States. In other words, the positions a megachurch takes on broad social issues can impact society as a whole because the churches have the power to help certain candidates and influence legislators. For example, a 2008 investigation by NBC found that the pastor of Without Walls Central Church, a Tampa Bay, Florida, megachurch, directed his congregation to donate funds to Republican gubernatorial candidate Charlie Crist, who had won the election in 2006.

Megachurches have not been free of scandal over the years. In 2006 Ted Haggard, an adviser to President George W. Bush, resigned from the New Life Church after allegations surfaced that he engaged in a sexual relationship with a male prostitute. Archbishop Earl Paulk of the suburban Atlanta–based Cathedral at Chapel Hill was subject to a criminal investigation after it was revealed in 2007 that he had fathered a son through an adulterous relationship with his sister-in-law. In 2010 four young men accused New Birth Missionary Baptist Church pastor Eddie Long of coercing them into sexual acts. However, megachurches do not have a monopoly on such scandals, as numerous stories about Catholic priests who have had criminal sexual relationships with young boys have also come to light.

As the fortunes of megachurches have grown, their pastors have come to resemble CEOs. In 2007 the *New York Times* reported that megachurches held business interests in a variety of areas, constantly branding and rebranding their faith by forming partnerships with shopping malls, sports arenas, and coffee companies. *Business Week* estimated that the average megachurch accumulated $4.8 million per year, leading to enormous salaries for their leaders. Like their corporate counterparts, these churches spend millions of dollars a year in attempts to entice adolescents and children to their congregations.

Gerald Carpenter

SEE ALSO: *Evangelism; Fundamentalism; Televangelism.*

BIBLIOGRAPHY

Allitt, Patrick. *Religion in American since 1945: A History.* New York: Columbia University Press, 2003.

Baylor Institute for Studies of Religion. Accessed June 2012. Available from http://www.isreligion.org

Henriques, Diana B., and Andrew W. Lehren. "In God's Name: Megachurches Add Local Economy to Their Mission." *New York Times*, November 23, 2007.

Loveland, Anne, and Otis B. Wheeler. *From Meetinghouse to Megachurch: A Material and Cultural History.* Columbia: University of Missouri Press, 2003.

"Megachurches." Hartford Institute for Religion Research. Accessed June 2012. Available from http://hirr.hartsem.edu/megachurch/megachurches.html

Symonds, William C. "Earthly Empires: How Evangelical Churches Are Borrowing from the Business Playbook" *Businessweek*, May 23, 2005.

Thumma, Scott, and Dave Travis. *Beyond Megachurch Myths: What We Can Learn from America's Largest Churches.* San Francisco, CA: Jossey-Bass, 2007.

Mellencamp, John *(1951–)*

Viewed through the majority of his career as a poor man's Bruce Springsteen, John Mellencamp was haunted by his record-company-imposed moniker Johnny Cougar and all the shallow pop boy-toy imagery associated with it. Since the release of his first album in 1976, the Indiana-born rock artist made the transformation from Johnny Cougar, the tight-jeans-wearing pretty boy, to John Mellencamp, a serious artist who still did not always get respect. Nonetheless, since the release of *Scarecrow* in 1985, he carved out a niche for himself as one of the great, unpretentious songwriters in the United States, who could accurately reflect the social moods of the time, though he would be the last to acknowledge that label. If music critics were harsh, then Mellencamp was even harder on himself—once going so far as countering an interviewer's claim that he was a great songwriter by saying, "But don't forget, I'm the f—ker who wrote 'Hurts So Good,'" referring to one of his early hits in the 1980s.

Mellencamp was born on October 7, 1951, in Seymour, Indiana. He started his musical life at the age of fourteen playing around his hometown, as well as in other midwestern towns (in wretchedly named bands such as Snakepit, Banana Barn, and Crepe Soul). After his girlfriend, Priscilla Esterline, became pregnant, the two teenagers married, and Mellencamp worked a number of blue-collar jobs to support his new family before attempting to start a music career in New York City. His effort led to a recording contract with MCA, which—to his dismay—dubbed him Johnny Cougar for his first album, *Chestnut Street Incident* (1976).

After his debut album and follow-up, *Kid Inside* (1977), sold poorly, Mellencamp was dropped from the label. He went on to record three insignificant albums for the Riva, though he did score a hit in 1979 with the single "I Need a Lover." Picked up by Mercury Records, he recorded the uneven commercial flop *Nothin' Matters & What if It Did* (1980) before releasing his breakthrough album, *American Fool* (1982). Containing two of his biggest hits, "Hurts So Good" and "Jack and Diane," it still only hinted at the more artistically credible material he would produce by the end of the decade.

Mellencamp finally hit his artistic stride—while never losing his commercial clout—with *Scarecrow* (1985), which dealt with the plight of the American farmer, the decay of American social institutions, and government neglect of its poorest citizens. The political messages that were implicit in his music were made more explicit when he shunned the more trendy Live Aid concert, where he was invited to play, and helped Neil Young and Willie Nelson organize the long-running Farm Aid concerts, which raised money for noncorporate, family farmers.

Mellencamp's next albums, *The Lonesome Jubilee* (1987) and *Big Daddy* (1989), expanded his sound and explored darker lyrical territories that reflected the gloominess he felt when his marriage failed and he lost faith in his songwriting ability. This loss of faith resulted in his not being heard from for nearly two years after the release of *Big Daddy* as he spent time at home painting and contemplating his career. An explicit indication of the self-doubt that plagued Mellencamp throughout his career is the title of his 1997 greatest hits collection, *The Best That I Could Do 1978–1988*.

The 1990s found Mellencamp dropping the Cougar moniker for good and trying on a variety of musical styles that never strayed far from his rock-influenced roots. His albums sold respectably, some better than others, and he still enjoyed

John Mellencamp. *John Mellencamp performs at the New Orleans Jazz & Heritage Festival in 2011.* TIM MOSENFELDER/CONTRIBUTOR/GETTY IMAGES ENTERTAINMENT/GETTY IMAGES.

the occasional hit single. In 1998 he severed his long-standing ties with Mercury, releasing a well-received self-titled album on Columbia in 1998.

Mellencamp began the twenty-first century by releasing *Cuttin' Heads* (2001) with Sony, his new record producer. The album, which some critics consider to be Mellencamp at his peak, continued in the socially conscious vein that had come to represent his style. *Trouble No More* (2003) was a collection of covers that ranged from Skeeter Davis's "End of the World" to Wilson Pickett's "Teardrops Will Fall." In 2007 *Freedom's Road*, which Mellencamp recorded with country superstars Little Big Town, brought him a new kind of notoriety. After he licensed the song "Our Country" for use in a commercial for Chevrolet trucks, the song became his first hit single in years. He next released *Life, Death, Love, and Freedom* (2008), which some critics consider the unhappiest album of his career. Mellencamp recorded *No Better than This* (2010) at sites that were of significance in musical history. Throughout his career he has continued to explore new ways to grow musically, and he credits his fans with being loyal enough to allow him to express himself in new ways.

Kembrew McLeod

SEE ALSO: *Farm Aid; Nelson, Willie; Rock and Roll; Springsteen, Bruce; Young, Neil.*

BIBLIOGRAPHY

Eddy, Chuck. *Rock and Roll Always Forgets: A Quarter Century of Music Criticism*. Durham, NC: Duke University Press, 2011.

Greene, Andy. "John Mellencamp Brings His Raw New Sound to Radio City." *Rolling Stone*, March 4, 2011, 24.

Harshfield, David. *Manchild for Real: The Life and Lyrics of John Cougar Mellencamp*. New York: Vantage Press, 1986.

Holmes, Tim. *John Cougar Mellencamp*. New York: Ballantine Books, 1986.

Torgoff, Martin. *American Fool: The Roots and Improbable Rise of John Cougar Mellencamp*. New York: St. Martin's, 1986.

Mencken, H. L. *(1880–1956)*

From the 1920s through the 1950s, H. L. Mencken was one of the best-known and most feared writers in the United States. Professionally, Mencken was a newspaperman (for the *Baltimore Evening Sun*), a literary and social critic who debunked pompous politicians and simple-minded Americans as belonging to the "booboisie," a magazine editor (of the *American Mercury*), and a philologist (as author of the unscholarly but esteemed *The American Language*). Temperamentally, he was a curmudgeon, an iconoclast, a satirist, a cynic, and a writer provocateur. Known for his acid wit, he spared no one and pilloried everyone. He was both ruthless and rigid, Edmund Wilson once said, and also courageous and fearless. Mencken did not suffer fools gladly, if at all, although he was probably glad for their presence because they provided fodder for his newspaper and magazine columns. He has been compared with Thomas Paine, Jonathan Swift, and Mark Twain.

NEWSPAPER CAREER

The comparison with Twain would no doubt make Mencken proud. As a child, he read voraciously; Twain was his favorite author and *The Adventures of Huckleberry Finn* his favorite book. The idiosyncratic intellectual who become known as the "Sage of Baltimore" never went to college but gave no evidence of being unlettered. Mencken started his newspaper career at the age of eighteen in 1899 at the *Morning Herald* in his native Baltimore, Maryland. He got the job through persistence by offering to work for free and was hired when he quickly showed his talent as a reporter. His first published story was about the theft of a horse, buggy, and several sets of harnesses.

Within a year he was pontificating on subjects far and wide in his own weekly column on the editorial page, in which he also published some of his own poetry. He brought to the page an original and fresh point of view and also began to contribute to national magazines such as *Frank Leslie's Popular Monthly*, which helped expand his audience from local to national.

H. L. Menken. *Essayist, journalist, magazine editor, and satirist H. L. Mencken was known as the "Sage of Baltimore."* AP IMAGES.

In 1906 Mencken joined Baltimore's *Evening Sun*, and he would remain affiliated with the *Sun* papers for most of his lifetime. Later he became a literary reviewer for the *Smart Set*, a second-tier but important magazine. He rejoined the *Sun* in 1920 and resumed his weekly commentary. In 1924 he became coeditor of a new magazine, the *American Mercury*, over which he had total editorial control in a year.

As the editor of the *Mercury*, Mencken went to Boston to sell an issue of the magazine so he could be arrested for selling material that was considered indecent by the standards of the day. The judge threw out the case, and Mencken's star rose because he had thumbed his nose at the bluenoses. By then he was widely known and discussed. He was an intellectual who rose to the top at a time when the written word was supreme, not yet in competition with radio and television. The written word was the medium for conveying ideas, and Mencken's blunt and fresh prose set him off from many other writers of the day.

A SHARP TONGUE

During the culture wars of the 1920s, Mencken was clearly on the side of the modernists; he coined such phrases as "the Bible Belt" and "the Monkey trial" to refer derisively to the 1925 trial of John Scopes, the Tennessee school teacher who had been arrested for teaching evolution. The trial pitted Clarence Darrow, defending Scopes, against William Jennings Bryan. When Bryan died as the trial ended, Mencken wrote: "There was something peculiarly fitting in the fact that his last days were spent in a one-horse Tennessee village, beating off the flies and gnats, and that death found him there."

Mencken was hard on religion of any stripe and once referred to an unnamed evangelist as a "Presbyterian auctioneer of God." He said that Puritans had "the haunting fear that someone, somewhere, may be happy." Politicians were also among his targets. Of the long-winded 1932 convention that nominated Franklin Delano Roosevelt, who went on to become a four-term president, Mencken wrote of speaker after boring speaker: "More than once weary delegates objected that the Niagara of bilge was killing them and along toward four in the morning Josephus Daniels went to the platform and protested against it formally."

As was often the case with Mencken, the phrase "Niagara of bilge" was original. He did not write that patriotism is the last vestige of a scoundrel—that phrase is rightly credited to Samuel Johnson—but he did say: "Whenever you hear a man speak of his love for his country it is a sign that he expects to be paid for it." Displaying his contempt for the masses, Mencken once said: "Democracy is the theory that the common people know what they want, and deserve to get it good and hard."

PERSONAL POLITICAL LEANINGS

Mencken spent the early part of his life in effect disavowing his German roots but was later accused of being soft on Adolf Hitler, anti-Semitic, and racist. His diary, published about thirty-five years after his death, resulted in an anti-Mencken backlash. The reaction is somewhat surprising given that his equally pointed letters had been published twenty years earlier but is less surprising when it is understood that the diary appeared as a politically incorrect document in a generation that valued political correctness.

It is sometimes difficult reconciling the private Mencken with the public Mencken. During his lifetime and after his death, several prominent Jews and African Americans came to his defense. Shortly before a cerebral thrombosis in 1948 ended his public career, he wrote a piece for the *Evening Sun* condemning the Baltimore Park Board for a law that forbade blacks and whites from playing tennis together on municipal courts. Even if the board had the right to make the law, Mencken argued that such a law reflected neither common sense nor common decency.

THE AMERICAN LANGUAGE

Mencken was a prodigious writer. In addition to his essays, he wrote (counting subsequent editions) more than fifteen books. The most enduring of them is *The American Language*, whose first edition appeared in 1919. By the time the fourth edition was published in 1936, it was believed to be a significant if unscholarly contribution to the field of philology. Unlike much of what Mencken wrote, *The American Language* was a book in praise of something, although he jabbed at anyone who was pretentious, including real-estate agents who wanted to be known as "Realtors" and who insisted that the word was protected by trademark and should therefore be capitalized.

Mencken wrote *The American Language* to lay out the differences between the "English" spoken in Great Britain and the "American" spoken in the United States, and so it was for three editions. When the fourth appeared, however, he noted that American had begun to subsume English, a sign not only of the growing U.S. influence after World War I but also an indication that the British had become more accepting of American English. The book is heavily footnoted, for Mencken was profuse in acknowledging the many tips that came his way from readers of earlier editions.

PERSONAL LIFE AND LEGACY

A handsome man, Mencken parted his hair down the middle. Photographs almost always show him with a cigar in his mouth, no doubt a habit he acquired because his father was a cigar manufacturer. In describing the journalist in 1927, Elizabeth Shepley Sergeant, a contemporary, wrote that she "saw a rather short, stocky figure of a man whose blue eyes shone ahead of him like a sort of searchlight. He leaned a little forward, stooping his shoulders, as if to hasten his pace, and he was strongly careened to the right: a boat under full sail." He did not marry until 1930, after his mother died. The marriage was childless and was cut short by his wife's death in 1935. He never remarried. Mencken died in 1956, at the age of seventy-five.

Mencken's scathing wit and keen observations of the world around him continue to hold a place in American culture well into the twenty-first century through the continued use of his neologisms and witticisms, as well as through the establishment of several Mencken Libraries around the country. Collections of "Menckenia" (papers, letters, contributions, and memorabilia) can be found at several universities, including Yale, Harvard, and Goucher College in Baltimore. However, it is perhaps Mencken's coverage of the infamous Scopes trial that has proved to be his most enduring work. A compilation of his articles following the trial were republished in 2006 in *A Religious Orgy in Tennessee*.

R. Thomas Berner

SEE ALSO: American Mercury*; Darrow, Clarence; Modernism; Niagara Falls; Radio; Scopes Monkey Trial; Television; Twain, Mark; World War I.*

BIBLIOGRAPHY

Bode, Carl, ed. *The New Mencken Letters*. New York: Dial Press, 1977.

Bode, Carl. *Mencken*. Baltimore, MD: Johns Hopkins University Press, 1986.

Cooke, Alistair, ed. *The Vintage Mencken*. New York: Vintage Books, 1955.

Hobson, Fred. *Mencken: A Life*. New York: Random House, 1994.

Hobson, Fred C.; Vincent Fitzpatrick; and Brandford Jacobs; eds. *Thirty-five Years of Newspaper Work*. Baltimore, MD: Johns Hopkins University Press, 1994.

Mencken, H. L. *The American Language*. New York: Knopf, 1919.

Mencken, H. L. *A Religious Orgy in Tennessee: A Reporter's Account of the Scopes Monkey Trial*. Brooklyn, NY: Melville House Publishing, 2006.

Stenerson, Douglas C. *Critical Essays on H. L. Mencken*. Boston: G. K. Hall, 1987.

Mendoza, Lydia *(1916–2007)*

Lydia Mendoza, known as the "Meadowlark of the Border," was the first great Mexican American recording star, the first to sing in the vernacular rather than the cultivated operatic style, and the first to appeal to a broad section of working-class Mexican Americans. Born in 1916, Mendoza began singing and playing guitar with her family's band at age eleven. By the early 1930s she was giving live performances on the radio.

In 1934 she released her first solo single, a tango titled "Mal Hombre." Her career as a recording star and performer spanned decades, and her fame extended throughout the Southwest, Mexico, Central America, and northern South America. Her experiences as a performer included performing in the open marketplace in San Antonio and in rural southern Texas during the Depression. Massive parades were organized in her honor in northern Mexico, and her discography contains approximately 200 entries for a diverse list of labels. Mendoza continued to perform until suffering a stroke in 1988. She won numerous awards, culminating with the National Medal of Arts in 1999. She died in 2007 at the age of ninety-one.

Nicolás Kanellos

SEE ALSO: *The Great Depression; Parades; Radio; Tejano Music.*

BIBLIOGRAPHY

Broyles-González, Yolanda. *Lydia Mendoza's Life in Music/La historia de Lydia Mendoza: Norteño Tejano Legacies*. New York: Oxford University Press, 2001.

Strachwitz, Chris, and James Nicolopulos. *Lydia Mendoza: A Family Autobiography*. Houston, TX: Arte Público Press, 1993.

Men's Movement

Prior to the men's movement of the 1970s, few American men thought consciously (or at least publicly) about what it meant to be a man. Masculinity seemed to be a solid (if not precisely defined) social construct. Masculine norms were defined by a loose constellation of characteristics rooted in Judeo-Christian traditions and scriptural stories and transmitted to all children through such codes as the Boy Scout Law; stories emphasizing the importance of strength, endurance (physical and psychological), and competitiveness; and acceptance of and support for the gender status quo. Deviating from these norms, or failing to live up to them, was regarded as—depending on the era—tantamount to being a heathen, a communist, a sissy, or any number of other terms reflecting individual failure.

SPURRED BY OTHER MOVEMENTS

This fairly uniform view of gender was severely fractured by the cultural changes of the 1960s and 1970s, specifically the growth of the counterculture, the rise of the women's liberation and gay liberation movements, and the ongoing "sexual revolution," all of which openly challenged and rejected previously accepted standards for gender-appropriate conduct, expectations, and values. Writing in the journal *Liberation* in the autumn of 1970, in one of the first public statements made concerning what would become known as the men's movement, Jack Sawyer in "On Male Liberation" challenged men to "free themselves of the sex role stereotypes that limit their ability to be human." The stereotypes included the ways men related to women, questions of power and dominance in both private and public life, and freedom for full emotional expression. Sawyer and colleague Joseph Pleck would later expand this discussion in their 1974 work *Men and Masculinity*.

The year 1970 also saw the foundation of the Men's Center in Berkeley, California, which became the base for the discussions that would coalesce into the first men's liberation groups. More groups were soon formed in other parts of the country. In 1971 educator Warren Farrell helped form the National Task Force on the Masculine Mystique within the National Organization for Women, an idea that provided a framework for the further development of the men's movement. Farrell's more lasting contribution to the growth of men's awareness of their culturally limited options was his influential 1975 book *The Liberated Man: Beyond Masculinity*, which quickly assumed for men the place occupied in women's liberation by Betty Freidan's *The Feminine Mystique*. Its publication sparked the beginning of a separate men's literature concerned with offering theories of and solutions to male oppression. Two viewpoints characterized this body of writing: acceptance of feminist criticism of masculine status and behaviors, and calls for the restoration of "traditional" masculine social roles. Among the more important works produced at this time were Herb Goldberg's antifeminist *The Hazards of Being Male: Surviving the Myth of Masculine Privilege* (1976) and the anthologies *The Forty-Nine Percent Majority: The Male Sex Role* (1976) and *For Men against Sexism: A Book of Readings* (1977).

Many of these early debates took place within the structure of consciousness-raising groups, enabling like-minded men to begin the redefinition of their identities, a process that became more formally institutionalized after the first annual Men and Masculinity Conference in 1975, held in Knoxville, Tennessee, and sponsored by the National Organization of Men against Sexism. While useful as forums for increasing awareness, these conferences did little to spark local political organizing on men's issues. Instead, they allowed men to formulate philosophical responses to culturally entrenched sexism and male class privilege, responses that would identify them as the men's liberation, pro-feminist segment of the diverse men's movement. Basic to the men's liberation philosophy was the renunciation of racist, sexist, and homophobic attitudes and behaviors. It was this branch that heavily influenced the content of the academic field of men's studies and much of the formal literature prior to the rise of the popular mythopoetic approach in the 1980s.

Although discussions of men's issues continued in small group meetings at community centers and private homes throughout the 1970s, it was not until the early 1980s that the men's movement expanded significantly as an institutionalized cultural phenomenon in the United States. This decade witnessed a major cultural preoccupation with appropriate role models for male life; the appearance of men's periodicals such as *M*, *Gentle Men for Gender Justice*, and the *Men's Studies Review*; and the emergence of several major organizations centered on various men's issues. While earlier bodies such as the Male Liberation Foundation had existed since 1968, these new groups, such as the National Organization for Men (formed by Sidney Siller in New York in 1983), developed in the midst of the emergence of a "New Age" view of men that emphasized the development of such qualities as sensitivity and vulnerability. Readily identifiable and traditionally masculine behaviors were questioned in favor of more "sensitive" masculine traits (which critics called "wimpiness"). This last issue created a dilemma for men: how did they give up their negative masculine traits without losing what they knew as their masculinity? It was a dilemma that the next wave of the men's movement sought to resolve, by defining and reclaiming a valid masculinity that was not reliant on male aggression and dominance.

THE MYTHOPOETIC APPROACH

A recognition of the diverse male psyche and the validity of male spiritual needs and values, drawn from the lore of many cultures (but especially Native American cultures), characterized a second major branch of the men's movement, the mythopoetic. Due to its popularity and the frequent media appearances of some of its prominent writers and philosophers (especially Robert Bly and Sam Keen), it became identified in the public mind during the early 1990s as the standard image of how the men's movement thought and functioned. Its signature events were weekend or weekly retreats featuring the use of social forms such as the sweat lodge, the medicine wheel, public councils and giveaway ceremonies, and the use of drumming. The mythopoetic men's movement emphasized the reclamation and revitalization of structured ceremony as a vehicle for the definition of essential qualities of manhood and the conscious generation of a contemporary male-centered mythology suited to modern society. The best known writings to emerge from this stage of the men's movements were Bly's widely read 1990 book *Iron John*, which stimulated a whole genre of mythic writings and interpretations during the following decade, and Keen's *Fire in the Belly: On Being a Man* (1991).

Another kind of men's organization, modeled on the twelve-step programs of Alcoholics Anonymous, approached masculinity by examining individual relationships with the father, using such concepts as "woundedness" and "toxic masculinity." The idea of man as victim was also promoted by the fourth major division of the movement, the men's rights and father's rights groups, which centered their sometimes militant attention on issues of child support and custody, the rights of unmarried fathers, and abortion issues. Organizations such as Men's Rights Inc., based in Cambridge, Massachusetts, centered their lobbying activities on equitable treatment of male rights in divorce and opposition to an all-male draft. The rhetoric of this small but vocal segment of the movement was characterized by reversing the logic of many arguments used by feminists, particularly on such topics as sexual harassment.

The major differences between the men's movement and the other social movements emphasizing consciousness raising and role explorations lie in its scope, participants, and leadership. In contrast to the women's movement, whose message was readily understandable and many of whose issues were valid for women from every social class and background, the men's movement appealed primarily to middle-aged white men. Moreover, group leaders emerged either from the academic or religious communities or from a segment of the community of hurt men. Movement leadership was thus perceived as offering limited intellectual and emotional perspectives, which hampered the ability to appeal to the majority of American men. Popular reaction to the men's movement has ranged from confusion over the concerns that stimulated its existence and the archetypal figures being offered in the new male-centered mythology to snickering at the spectacle of middle-class men participating in weekend sessions of chanting and male bonding.

LEGACY OF THE EARLY MOVEMENT

Though the men's movements never achieved the kind of organizational momentum or public profile that allowed the women's and gay liberation movements to achieve many of their aims, they did set the stage for other social actions that focused on recognizing the needs and issues facing American men. The Million Man March, held in Washington on October 16, 1995, centered on reaffirming the spiritual needs, authority, and duties of African American men. A similar emphasis on parental responsibility and obligations to family and spouse was a central principle of the Promise Keepers, a controversial Christian men's political, religious, and cultural organization founded in 1990 as a spiritual reaction against the perceived decline of the secular men's movement and fueled by unease with the faintly pagan flavor of mythopoetics. These events reflected a maturation in the American men's movement, for they indicated that concern for the character and content of the cultural education of men had become a central concern of many social groups by the 1990s.

The established priority of revising socially acceptable definitions of masculinity continued to evolve into the early twenty-first century, although the idea of a men's movement remained very much limited to the developed world, with the bulk of research and writing produced in the United States. The three branches of the movement continued to exist but underwent significant changes in structure and issue priorities. The mythopoetic approach waned in popularity in the late 1990s, and the lack of a vision of social change or a social justice agenda was reflected in the gradual closing of most of its major publications. The self-help focus did maintain itself through American and international chapters of groups such as the Mankind Project and in men's organizations in some U.S. cities. In contrast, the men's rights focus of the movement continued to be effective through a deft use of the Internet by its main advocacy organizations. The pro-feminist school of male thought had a lasting impact through the strengthening of local anti–domestic violence and was engaged with the debates over the definition and future of feminism.

Robert Ridinger

SEE ALSO: *Bly, Robert; Boy Scouts of America; Bromance; Communism; Feminism; Gay Liberation Movement; Metrosexual; Million Man March; National Organization for Women (NOW); New Age Spirituality; Promise Keepers; Sexual Revolution.*

BIBLIOGRAPHY

Bly, Robert. *Iron John: A Book about Men.* Reading, MA: Addison-Wesley, 1990.

David, Deborah S., and Robert Brannon, eds. *The Forty-Nine Percent Majority: The Male Sex Role.* Reading, MA: Addison-Wesley, 1976.

Farrell, Warren. *The Liberated Man: Beyond Masculinity; Freeing Men and Their Relationships with Women.* New York: Random House, 1974.

Fox, John. "How Men's Movement Participants View Each Other." *Journal of Men's Studies* 12, no. 2 (2004): 103–118.

Goldberg, Herb. *The Hazards of Being Male: Surviving the Myth of Masculine Privilege.* New York: Nash, 1976.

Harding, Christopher, ed. *Wingspan: Inside the Men's Movement.* New York: St. Martin's Press, 1992.

Keen, Sam. *Fire in the Belly: On Being a Man.* New York: Bantam Books, 1991.

Kimmel, Michael S., ed. *Changing Men: New Directions in Research on Men and Masculinity.* Newbury Park, CA: Sage Publications, 1987.

Kimmel, Michael S. *Manhood in America: A Cultural History.* New York: Free Press, 1996.

Pleck, Joseph H., and Jack Sawyer, eds. *Men and Masculinity.* Englewood Cliffs, NJ: Prentice-Hall, 1974.

Snodgrass, Jon, ed. *For Men against Sexism: A Book of Readings.* Albion, CA: Times Change Press, 1977.

Menudo

SEE: *Martin, Ricky.*

Merton, Thomas *(1915–1968)*

One of the most highly acclaimed writers of the twentieth century, Thomas Merton is best known in literary circles for his autobiographical novel of religious conversion, *The Seven Storey Mountain*, published in 1948. In the same decade, Merton became a Trappist monk, entering the monastery of Our Lady of Gethsemani, in Kentucky. Continuing to write and produce books of poetry, spiritual meditations, and journals (many of which have been published posthumously), Merton found himself at lifelong odds with both the order's plans for him and his own belief that writing was keeping him from achieving his full spiritual potential.

Merton was never able to completely resolve the conflict between his vocations as writer and as contemplative. He was also never able to reconcile his moral outrage at the state of America and the world, particularly during the Vietnam War era, with his desire to live a simple, quiet life. His protests and friendships with counterculture luminaries like Bob Dylan and Joan Baez earned him the admiration and respect of many young people in the 1960s, who saw in Merton the possibility to find spiritual nourishment while rejecting the perceived immorality of the establishment.

Dan Coffey

SEE ALSO: *Baez, Joan; Dylan, Bob; Vietnam.*

BIBLIOGRAPHY

Cunningham, Lawrence S., ed. *Thomas Merton: Spiritual Master.* New York: Paulist Press, 1992.

Hart, Patrick, ed. *Thomas Merton/Monk: A Monastic Tribute.* New York: Sheed and Ward, 1974.

Kountz, Peter. *Thomas Merton as Writer and Monk: A Cultural Study, 1915–1951.* New York: Carlson Publishing, 1991.

Merton, Thomas, and M. Basil Pennington. *Thomas Merton: I Have Seen What I Was Looking For: Selected Spiritual Writings.* Hyde Park, NY: New City Press, 2005.

Mott, Michael. *The Seven Mountains of Thomas Merton.* Boston: Houghton Mifflin, 1984.

Metalious, Grace *(1924–1964)*

Grace Metalious is best known as the author of the infamous *Peyton Place*, a book that caused a social upheaval even before it was published in 1956. She was born Marie Grace DeRepentigny in Manchester, New Hampshire, in 1924. Her father deserted his wife and three daughters when she was eleven years old. At that time divorce was unusual in a French Canadian family, and she and her sisters felt stigmatized. Discovering the pleasure of writing as an adolescent, she wrote many stories that featured a romantic heroine who gets her hero in the end. She also enjoyed acting in school plays. These activities seemed to offer her an escape from a generally unhappy family.

In high school, she met George Metalious, who was neither Catholic nor of French Canadian background and, thus, was highly unacceptable to her family. Nevertheless, they married in 1943. A few years later, with one child already, the Metalious family moved to Durham, New Hampshire, where her husband attended the University of New Hampshire. It was here that Metalious began writing seriously, neglecting both her house and, eventually, her three children, despite the condemnation of her neighbors.

After graduation, her husband was offered a position as a principal at a school in Gilmanton, New Hampshire. By now the family had three children, all dependent upon his meager salary. While Metalious was living in Gilmanton, Julian Messner, a New York publisher, agreed to publish *Peyton Place*. The book was a best seller by the fall of 1956, and Metalious became a wealthy woman overnight. Eventually, tens of millions of copies were sold in hardcover, along with another twelve million Dell paperbacks. Metalious became famous as the housewife who wrote a best seller; she was referred to as "Pandora in Blue Jeans," the simple small-town woman who opened the box of sins.

Peyton Place ***Author Grace Metalious.*** *Author Grace Metalious's first novel,* Peyton Place, *became a best seller in 1956.* AP IMAGES.

Peyton Place is the story of a small New England town that, beneath its calm exterior, is filled with scandals and dark secrets. The novel contains sex, suicide, abortion, murder and a subsequent trial, and rape. The citizens of Gilmanton were outraged, certain that Metalious was describing real people in the book and sure that she had brought shame and unwarranted notoriety to their town. After *Peyton Place* was published, the whole image of the small town in America was forever changed. From then on, the very phrase "Peyton Place" was used to describe a town that is rife with deep secrets and rampant sex beneath the veneer of picturesque calm.

Peyton Place was banned in many communities; in fact, the Gilmanton public library refused to purchase a copy of the book and did not have one until 1976, when newswoman Barbara Walters donated one to them. In Gilmanton, there were threats of libel suits against Metalious. Ministers and political leaders all over the country condemned the novel, claiming that it would corrupt the morals of young people who read it. The novel was banned altogether in Canada and several other countries.

Despite its notoriety and the large amounts of money it earned her, the book led to the ruination of Metalious. She purchased a house that she had long admired in Gilmanton, then had it extensively remodeled. Meanwhile, her husband's contract with the Gilmanton school was not renewed. Officially, he was not fired, but the rumor was that the dismissal was because of his wife's book. At any rate, it made good publicity for the book. Her husband eventually got a new job in Massachusetts, but Metalious did not join him. Eventually, the two divorced, and Metalious, who had begun drinking heavily, married a local disc jockey.

Metalious went on to write three other novels: *Return to Peyton Place* (1959), *The Tight White Collar* (1960), and *No Adam in Eden* (1963). None of them achieved the same kind success as *Peyton Place*, though there are critics who feel that *No Adam in Eden*, a gritty book about the lives of mill workers in Manchester, is her best. By 1960 the Metaliouses had reconciled and remarried, only to separate again in 1963. She died in 1964 of cirrhosis of the liver and is buried in Gilmanton.

After she died, her first husband wrote his own book, *The Girl from "Peyton Place."* The book offers a husband's view of how Metalious was exploited after the publication of the book but also of how she was responsible for bringing unhappiness to herself and to others. A whole series of other "Peyton Place" books were produced after Metalious's death, with titles like *The Evils of Peyton Place* and *Temptations of Peyton Place*. None of them was a commercial success.

Peyton Place was made into a movie starring Lana Turner and Hope Lange in 1957. It was filmed in Camden, Maine, a location totally unlike any rural mill town. A television series, starring Mia Farrow and Dorothy Malone, was produced and lasted from 1964 to 1969. Both the film and the television show were cleaned up and did not contain the language or sexual specificity of the novel.

Peyton Place is still well known for its depiction of a certain kind of small-town society with many hidden secrets, but its popularity has waned. Although it was scandalous in its time, it no longer has the same shock value it did when it was published.

Robin Lent

SEE ALSO: Desperate Housewives; *Peyton Place; Sex Scandals.*

BIBLIOGRAPHY

Dodson, James. "Pandora in Blue Jeans." *Yankee* 54, no. 9: 92–97, 132–137.

Friedrich, Otto. "Farewell to Peyton Place." *Esquire* 76, no. 12 (1971): 160–168, 306.

Kohn, George C. *The New Encyclopedia of American Scandal.* New York: Infobase Publishing, 2001.

Metalious, George, and June O'Shea. *The Girl from "Peyton Place": A Biography of Grace Metalious.* New York: Dell, 1965.

Toth, Emily. *Inside Peyton Place: The Life of Grace Metalious.* Garden City, NY: Doubleday, 1981.

Metropolis

Made at UFA Studios in Germany, director Fritz Lang's visionary silent film *Metropolis* (1927) was inspired by a visit to New York, on whose skyline Lang based his massive and impressive sets. The movie's pioneering special effects were created by Eugen Schüfftan, who, like Lang, would later flee the Nazis and eventually settle in Hollywood. His Schüfftan process combined live action with miniature sets to produce the film's futuristic effects.

Despite criticism of the weakness of the plot and the naïveté of the resolution, *Metropolis* remains a potent allegory against totalitarianism. The film explores political conflicts, hopes, and fears, as well as enthusiasm for technology and the American way. With its powerful architectural metaphors, gallery of contemporary visions, technological experimentation, and political philosophy, *Metropolis* marks an influential turning point in the development of film art. Although it was admired around the world, the film's huge production costs brought UFA to the brink of bankruptcy. In 1984 music producer Giorgio Moroder edited the film's original 153 minutes down to 83, adding tinted sequences and a rock score.

Anna Notaro

SEE ALSO: *Lang, Fritz; Silent Movies.*

BIBLIOGRAPHY

Kniesche, Thomas W., and Stephen Brockmann, eds. *Dancing on the Volcano: Essays on the Culture of the Weimar Republic.* Columbia, SC: Camden House, 1994.

Kracauer, Siegfried. *From Caligari to Hitler.* Princeton, NJ: Princeton University Press, 1947.

Minden, Michael, and Holger Bachmann. *Fritz Lang's* Metropolis: *Cinematic Visions of Technology and Fear.* Rochester, NY: Camden House, 2000.

Von Harbou, Thea. *Metropolis.* Berlin: Scherl, 1926.

Metropolitan Museum of Art

Among the largest, richest, most famous, and most comprehensive art museums in the world, New York City's Metropolitan Museum of Art boasts collections spanning virtually all periods and cultures. The millions who pass through its handsome and expertly arranged galleries each year—paying a voluntary sum for admission—to view the permanent collection and the special exhibitions are testament to the museum's democratic founding ideal that art exists not just for the cultured few but for the benefit of many. Originally chartered in 1870 and opened in 1872, the Met, as it is commonly known, moved in 1880 to its present handsome building on Fifth Avenue.

By the early twentieth century the museum had established itself as one of the world's major centers for the arts and antiquities. In 1938 its medieval branch, the Cloisters, opened at Fort Tryon Park in Upper Manhattan. By 2010 the Met had burgeoned to more than 2 million square feet of gallery space, with seventeen curatorial departments and a permanent collection of more than two million objects. Besides paintings and sculptures, outstanding treasures include collections of arms and armor, costumes, musical instruments, Tiffany glass, baseball cards, and an entire Egyptian temple.

Craig Bunch

SEE ALSO: *The Big Apple; Conceptual Art; Op Art; Pop Art.*

BIBLIOGRAPHY

Hoving, Thomas. *Making the Mummies Dance: Inside the Metropolitan Museum of Art.* New York: Simon & Schuster, 1993.

Metropolitan Museum of Art. Accessed February 23, 2012. Available from http://www.metmuseum.org

Tomkins, Calvin. *Merchants and Masterpieces: The Story of the Metropolitan Museum of Art.* New York: E. P. Dutton, 1970.

Metrosexual

Simply defined, the term *metrosexual,* a neologism combining the words *metropolitan* and *heterosexual,* refers to an urban straight man with a well-groomed and highly stylized appearance. At the turn of the twenty-first century, *metrosexual* became a buzzword and a lightning rod in American culture, as it represented a new masculine aesthetic that called into question what it really meant to be a "man." While some observers have suggested the term was first used in the 1980s, it is generally accepted that author Mark Simpson coined it in a 1994 magazine article published in the *Independent.* The word caught on in the late 1990s as it was applied to celebrities such as British soccer star David Beckham and American actor Brad Pitt, among others. Furthermore, the surprise success of the Bravo network's reality show *Queer Eye for the Straight Guy* (2003–2007), featuring five gay men giving style tips to a straight man, made the concept of metrosexuality hip in American culture.

As the term was incorporated into the American lexicon, marketers found that metrosexual males constituted a new—and profitable—demographic. Makers of personal care products and high-fashion menswear capitalized on this new market, which seemed to be interested in their products and was willing to pay top dollar to look stylish. Advertisers used hip sports stars such as Beckham and Derek Jeter to promote their products, including fragrance lines named after the athletes. However, critics asserted that the marketing strategy was more effective at targeting women who wanted men to be interested in such products.

Because of its emphasis on grooming and style, activities and interests long considered to be feminine, metrosexuality seemed to blur the line between gay and straight maleness. Many observers maintained that "real" men would and should have no interest in products marketed to the metrosexual demographic. Conservative groups were among those most upset by the gender-bending implications of metrosexuality and claimed that men were becoming feminized. Such critics held that men should maintain traditional rough-and-tumble roles, while fashion and hair care belonged in the traditional woman's domain. Others argued that masculinity is composed of a complex set of characteristics; for example, some men engage in stereotypically masculine behaviors such as home repair and at the same time enjoy art and maintain a sense of fashion. Interestingly, what Americans have come to call metrosexual was already a part of the masculine look throughout Europe and in other parts of the world.

In 2006 the morning news show *Good Morning America* reported on the demise of the metrosexual man. It was true that the term was used less frequently, perhaps due to the backlash against the underlying concept or merely its overuse. However, metrosexual men were still visible in advertising, particularly for grooming products, and a softening of features in male models and young actors also suggests the lasting effects of this trend. Indeed, the question of what makes a man "manly" remains relevant in popular discourse. Aspiring to be a metrosexual may have been a passing fad, but the fact that the term no longer sparks such animated debate may also mean that the look has been absorbed into the contemporary American idea of masculinity.

Jill Gregg Clever

SEE ALSO: *Advertising; Consumerism; Gay Men; Pitt, Brad;* Queer Eye for the Straight Guy.

BIBLIOGRAPHY

Ervin, Margaret. "Politics, Marketing, and the Metrosexual: The Eloquence of a Marketing Tool." Americana: The Institute for the Study of American Popular Culture. Accessed June 2012. Available from http://www.americanpopularculture.com/archive/style/metrosexual.htm

Van Bree, Marc C. M. "The Metrosexual Defined: Narcissism and Masculinity in Popular Culture." Accessed June 2012. Available from http://mcmvanbree.com/metrosexual.htm

MGM (Metro-Goldwyn-Mayer)

"More Stars than There Are in the Heavens." Perhaps no movie-studio tagline in Hollywood's golden age was more recognizable—or descriptive—than this one by Metro-Goldwyn-Mayer (MGM). With its Leo the Lion mascot, MGM was arguably the king of the Hollywood studios, boasting an impressive roster of stars who were exhibited in glossy productions that were enormously popular.

A PRODUCER-DRIVEN STUDIO

MGM was formed in 1924 as the corporate brainchild of Marcus Loew. Its name was derived from a combination of the monikers of the three subsumed companies: Goldwyn Pictures Corporation, formerly owned by Samuel Goldwyn; Louis B. Mayer Pictures; and Metro Pictures Corporation, which had been in business since 1915. In a move that foreshadowed the corporate mergers of the 1980s and 1990s, Metro-Goldwyn-Mayer Corporation was formed as a subsidiary of Loew's, Inc., one of the largest theater chains in North America. Under the Loew's corporate umbrella and the financial leadership of Loew's executive Joseph Schenk, MGM soon became the most fiscally successful Hollywood studio, with production, distribution, and exhibition arms throughout the world. It was known as the "Tiffany" studio, reflected in films such as *Grand Hotel* (1932)—classy, often highbrow productions combining lavish production values and star power with audience-pleasing stories.

Unlike Paramount, a director-driven studio, MGM was producer-driven. MGM was initially headed by two very different men: studio head Mayer and production chief Irving Thalberg. Mayer, a Russian immigrant with a flair for histrionics and storytelling, started in the film business as an exhibitor/theater owner. By the early 1910s he was a successful film producer. Mayer's lowbrow tastes and despotic demeanor contrasted sharply with the sensibilities of the more intellectual Thalberg, who preferred high-toned films, often adaptations of literary classics. Thalberg began his producing career at Universal Pictures when he was barely into his twenties. In 1923 he moved to Metro Pictures, where he became head of production and the creative force behind many of that studio's early successes. Thalberg maintained a strong personal involvement in almost all of MGM's projects, as Darryl F. Zanuck would later do at Twentieth Century Fox. Thalberg is credited with masterminding MGM's hallmark look, glossy photography, expensive Cedric Gibbons–supervised sets, and glamorous Adrian gowns.

During its first decade, MGM established its image with the production of a number of big-budget films. To cast its glamorous productions, the studio maintained a stable of popular and impressive contract players, including Greta Garbo, Lillian Gish, John Gilbert, John Barrymore, Ramón Novarro, Joan Crawford, and Buster Keaton. MGM's formula met with both financial and critical success. One of the most profitable films of the 1920s and 1930s was MGM's Fred Niblo–directed adaptation of *Ben-Hur* (1925). The King Vidor–directed antiwar drama *The Big Parade* also met with financial success that same year. Equally impressive, though far from profitable, was Erich von Stroheim's drastically edited masterpiece *Greed* (1924). In 1929 MGM's popular "all talking—all singing—all dancing" musical *The Broadway Melody* brought the studio the Oscar for Best Picture.

THE GLORY YEARS

The 1930s were the studio's most successful years. Throughout this decade, MGM nurtured the careers of stars who remain icons to this day, including Clark Gable, Crawford, Myrna Loy, Jean Harlow, William Powell, Mickey Rooney, Judy Garland, Spencer Tracy, and Garbo. The star power of the studio is perhaps even more significant when one considers its second-level stars, such as Robert Montgomery, Eleanor Powell, and Robert Taylor. The studio also maintained an impressive list of "B" actors who could easily carry the studio's more pedestrian features, such as Robert Young, George Murphy, and Walter Pidgeon.

MGM rolled out a string of hits in the 1930s. The most noteworthy included comedies such as *The Thin Man* (1934) and *A Night at the Opera* (1935); musicals such as *Dancing Lady* (1933), *Naughty Marietta* (1935), *Rosalie* (1937), and the Oscar-winning *The Great Ziegfeld* (1936); and dramas such as *Fury* (1936), *Anna Christie* (1930), *The Sin of Madelon Claudet* (1931), and *Romeo and Juliet* (1936).

Thalberg's power at MGM remained relatively unchecked until the early 1930s. Despite his enormous capacity for work, the producer was hampered by physical frailty from early childhood. A massive heart attack in December 1932, coupled with struggles with Mayer and Schenk, necessitated a lengthy leave from the studio. During this period, Mayer's son-in-law, David O. Selznick, joined the studio as an executive producer, a move that prompted the oft-repeated Hollywood joke, "The son-in-law also rises." In many ways, Selznick was on the same plane as Thalberg, specializing in high-class dramas such as *A Tale of Two Cities* (1935) and *David Copperfield* (1935) and also overseeing sophisticated comedies such as *Dinner at Eight* (1933). However, following some frustration at MGM, Selznick left the studio in 1935 to become an independent producer through his company Selznick International Pictures.

THALBERG'S PASSING

Upon returning to MGM in mid-1933, Thalberg had much less power and increasingly came into conflict with Mayer. Nevertheless, he continued to be an important producing force, fostering such prestige projects as *The Good Earth* (1937) and *Goodbye, Mr. Chips* (1939), both of which had been on the MGM production schedule for many years. Thalberg's health eventually failed, and he died in September 1936 at the age of thirty-seven. Studio personnel, as well as most of the Hollywood community, were stunned by his death.

All MGM productions stopped for several days, and when filming resumed, the studio shifted away from Thalberg's (and Selznick's) classy, literary-oriented films in favor of Mayer's vision of family entertainment, epitomized by titles such as *Love Finds Andy Hardy* (1938). Many producers who had had close ties to Thalberg were no longer as prominent, as several films either under his direct or indirect supervision were temporarily shelved. In fact, for *Maytime*, a Nelson Eddy–Jeanette MacDonald picture released in 1937, MGM scrapped all the footage shot prior to Thalberg's death and resumed production with a new producer, director, and supporting cast.

THE 1940s AND 1950s

As the studio tried to establish its new image under Mayer's supervision, it also tried to accommodate new technology and World War II. When three-strip Technicolor began to take hold in Hollywood, MGM was the last studio to jump on the bandwagon, preferring to release some of its prestige pictures in glistening sepia prints. MGM's first Technicolor feature was *Sweethearts* (1938). The studio soon used color to its advantage, however, and many prestige productions of the 1940s were filmed in color, among them the highly successful *National Velvet* (1944), starring Elizabeth Taylor and Rooney. Despite the change in production philosophies and the introduction of color, the studio's most memorable efforts in the early 1940s—such as *Mrs. Miniver* (1942), *Meet Me in St. Louis* (1944), and *Woman of the Year* (1942)—retained the glossy MGM look.

During the war years, several of MGM's top stars went into the armed services, including James Stewart, Montgomery, and Gable. Nevertheless, MGM quickly found replacements. Actors such as Van Johnson and Gene Kelly became stars, and Hedy Lamarr, Esther Williams, Garland, Greer Garson, and Lana Turner emerged as the new queens of the studio, supplanting Crawford and Loy.

Though Mayer had imposed his vision on the various production units at the studio following Thalberg's death, this changed dramatically upon the hiring of Oscar-winning screenwriter and producer Dore Schary in 1948. Preferring socially conscious films, Schary soon altered the course of the studio. While musicals featuring stars such as Kelly and Garland remained mainstays, Schary promoted a number of gritty films, including *Battleground* (1949) and *The Next Voice You Hear* (1950). Such starkly realistic offerings incurred the ire of Mayer, but he ultimately lost the power struggle with Schary and was forced into retirement in 1951.

Despite the enormous success of some MGM films in the 1950s—most notably *An American in Paris* (1951), *Singin' in the Rain* (1952), *Gigi* (1958), and a remake of *Ben-Hur* (1959)—the encroachment of television, runaway productions, and rising costs led to a reconsideration of many of the longtime contract players. Gable, Taylor, and Williams, among others, were let go as the studio became increasingly cost-conscious.

A LONG DECLINE

This emphasis on the bottom line took a toll on the studio's image. The look of MGM productions in the 1960s and 1970s could barely be distinguished from those of the other Hollywood studios. In 1970, the company was purchased by financier Kirk Kerkorian, who sold off the fabled back lot and auctioned off most of the studio property. He combined the company with United Artists (UA), creating a new entity, MGM/UA. Meanwhile, the hits were few and far between. With the exception of UA's long-running James Bond series, the combined company's products did poorly at the box office and Kerkorian decided to cut his losses. In 1986 media mogul Ted Turner purchased MGM from Kerkorian, promising in many newspaper articles to return the studio to its glory days. The plan was either short-lived or nonexistent, as Turner soon sold the studio back to Kerkorian while retaining the library for television and cable purposes.

This led to the virtual collapse of the studio. The Culver City lot was sold to Lorimar (and ultimately to Sony, the parent company of Columbia Pictures), and MGM's facilities consisted primarily of offices in various parts of West Los Angeles and Culver City. MGM was sold to Italian producer Giancarlo Parretti, who mortgaged it to pay off his purchase expenses. In the 1990s, the studio was taken over by the French bank Crédit Lyonnais, which hired experienced executive Mark Canton to restore it to enough prominence to be able to put it on the market once again. In 1996 Canton and a group of the studio's executives put together a financial package backed by Kerkorian's Tracinda Corporation and purchased the company from the bank. MGM bought the Polygram library in 1998 and once again had the distinction of owning the largest film library in Hollywood. The studio boasted a few modest financial and critical successes in the 1990s and the first decade of the 2000s.

In late 2010 MGM filed for Chapter 11 bankruptcy as part of a plan worked out with its creditors. Lenders exchanged the its outstanding debt for equity in the studio, which was then transferred to the control of Gary Barber and Roger Birnbaum, the chief executive officers of Spyglass Entertainment. MGM emerged from bankruptcy with $500 million to finance new projects. The legendary studio is, it seems, still breathing.

Steve Hanson

SEE ALSO: *Andy Hardy; Barrymore, John;* Ben-Hur*; Crawford, Joan; Eddy, Nelson; Gable, Clark; Garbo, Greta; Garland, Judy; Gish, Dorothy; Goldwyn, Samuel;* Greed*; Harlow, Jean; Hollywood; James Bond Films; Keaton, Buster; Kelly, Gene; Lamarr, Hedy; Loy, Myrna; MacDonald, Jeanette; Mayer, Louis B.;* Meet Me in St. Louis*; The Musical; Powell, William; Selznick, David O.;* Singin' in the Rain*; Stewart, Jimmy; Studio System; Taylor, Elizabeth; Taylor, Robert; Thalberg, Irving G.; Tracy, Spencer; Turner, Lana; Turner, Ted; United Artists; Zanuck, Darryl F.*

BIBLIOGRAPHY

Bingen, Steven; Stephen X. Sylvester; and Michael Troyan. *MGM: Hollywood's Greatest Backlot.* Solana Beach, CA: Santa Monica Press, 2011.

Eames, John Douglas. *The MGM Story.* New York: Crown Publishers, 1976.

Gabler, Neal. *An Empire of Their Own: How the Jews Invented Hollywood.* New York: Crown Publishers, 1988.

Hay, Peter. *MGM: When the Lion Roars.* Atlanta, GA: Turner Publishing, 1991.

Mordden, Ethan. *The Hollywood Studios: House Style in the Golden Age of Movies.* New York: A. A. Knopf, 1988.

Schatz, Thomas. *The Genius of the System: Hollywood Filmmaking in the Studio Era.* New York: Pantheon Books, 1988.

Vieira, Mark A. *Hollywood Dreams Made Real: Irving Thalberg and the Rise of M-G-M.* New York: Abrams, 2008.

Miami Vice

No television series represented the style or dominant cultural aesthetic of the 1980s as fully or indelibly as *Miami Vice.* A popular one-hour police drama that aired on NBC from 1984 to 1989, *Miami Vice* was in one sense a conventional buddy-cop show—not unlike *Dragnet, Adam 12,* or *Starsky and Hutch*—featuring an interracial pair of narcotics detectives who wage a weekly battle against an urban criminal underworld. But the look and feel of the series—a mixture of flashy production values, music-video-style montages, and extensive use of Miami's beachfront locales and Art Deco architecture—elevated *Miami Vice* from standard cops-and-robbers fare to bona fide television phenomenon in the middle part of the decade. In its insistence that a TV show's style, sound, and attitude mattered more than its substance, *Miami Vice* spawned a host of imitators; sparked trends in the fashion, recording, and tourism industries; and helped transform the traditional face of broadcast television by appealing to a young, urban viewership that was, according to one of the show's directors, becoming "more interested in images, emotions, and energy than plot and character and words."

MTV COPS

Miami Vice's exploitation of the quick-cut visual style of rock music videos both reflected and consolidated the burgeoning influence of MTV (Music Television) on television and popular culture in the 1980s. Tellingly, the show originated in a short memo jotted down by NBC executive Brandon Tartikoff: "MTV Cops." Created by Anthony Yerkovich, a former writer and producer for NBC's more realistic law enforcement show *Hill Street Blues,* and executive produced by Michael Mann, who would go on to become one of Hollywood's most respected auteurs, *Miami Vice* was filmed on location in Miami at a cost of $1.3 million per episode—one of television's priciest productions at the time.

Miami Vice. *Don Johnson, left, and Philip Michael Thomas became stars as well as fashion icons playing cool detectives on NBC's* Miami Vice. RON GALELLA/CONTRIBUTOR/GETTY IMAGES.

Under Mann's exacting creative vision, the show's production team selected locations, buildings, and cars with a keen eye for detail, and scenes were composed in a painterly mode more akin to cinema than television. Tropical pastels—pink, turquoise, and lime green—dominated the show's color scheme, and Mann decreed early on that there would be "no earth tones." Music was also an integral part of the *Miami Vice* aesthetic: each episode featured contemporary pop songs that often served as critical commentaries on the plots (NBC paid up to $10,000 per episode for the rights to the original songs) as well as instrumental scores by Czech-born composer Jan Hammer, whose synthesizer-driven music supplied the show with its moody atmosphere. Hammer's theme song hit number one on the pop charts, as did a *Miami Vice* soundtrack album (one of several released during and after the show's run).

The show's slick depiction of Miami as a mecca for the international drug trade, an American Casablanca teeming with cocaine cowboys and drug runners, initially met with resistance from local city officials, who balked at the show's glamorization of Miami's chronic crime problems. Their fears were soon allayed, however, when it became apparent that *Miami Vice*'s emphasis on the city's striking architecture, gleaming beaches, and cultural exoticism was actually a civic virtue, enhancing Miami's public image and focusing international attention on the South Beach area. The program's opening title sequence—a montage of palm trees, pink flamingos, and bikini-clad women—played like a promotional spot for Miami's tourist industry, and by the late 1980s *Miami Vice* had contributed to the revitalization of once-decrepit Miami Beach and helped the city reclaim its image as a trendy resort playground for the wealthy and fashionable.

SEX APPEAL

At the heart of *Miami Vice*'s popularity were its two charismatic stars, Don Johnson and Philip Michael Thomas, who played hip undercover detectives Sonny Crockett and Ricardo Tubbs. The series rocketed both actors to international sex-symbol status, landing them on the covers of *Time* and *Rolling Stone* in the same year (1985). As an interracial police duo with a cool, easygoing buddy chemistry that seemed to transcend racial differences (on *Miami Vice,* skin color could double as just another fashion accessory), Crockett and Tubbs were perhaps the most recognizable of the numerous black-white male pairings that populated film and television in the 1980s.

The trendy, expensive clothes worn by the two detectives also formed a key element of the show's appeal. Crockett sported a casual-chic look consisting of pastel-colored Italian sport jackets paired with T-shirts, baggy linen pants, and slip-on shoes with no socks, while Tubbs wore dark double-breasted suits, silk shirts with slender neckties, and a diamond earring. The *Miami Vice* "look" soon infiltrated clothing lines in department stores across America. One company even marketed a special electric razor with a "stubble device" designed to leave a Crockett-like five o'clock shadow. To round out the effect, each detective drove a flashy car: Crockett cruised the streets in a black Ferrari, while Tubbs drove a vintage Cadillac convertible. Although such high-end amenities were explained as part of the detectives' cover (Crockett and Tubbs used cars and clothes seized from busted criminals to serve as props in their own masquerade as drug dealers), many critics faulted the show for a lack of realism, pointing out that Crockett and Tubbs's lavish gear would hardly have been affordable on a cop's meager salary. Moreover, the detectives' tendency to dress in ultra-modish attire even when conducting routine, non-undercover police work served as one of many indications that *Miami Vice* generally favored visual style over logical dramatic exposition.

In addition to a supporting cast that included Edward James Olmos as the brooding Lieutenant Castillo (the role earned the actor an Emmy Award in 1985), *Miami Vice* featured a high-profile parade of unusual guest stars—rock musicians, politicians, professional athletes, and corporate magnates—whose appearances were a testament to the show's initial "hotness"; it finished number nine in the 1985–1986 Nielsen ratings. In its third season, the show's popularity dipped when executive producer Mann ordered a dramatic shift to "darker" tones. Blues and blacks replaced the earlier pastels, the plots became murkier, and NBC scheduled the series unsuccessfully against CBS's long-running soap *Dallas*. By its final season, *Miami Vice* had slipped in the Nielsens, finishing last in its time slot among the three networks, and was no longer the "hot" property it had once been. Production values declined, and the show's original visual flair grew muted. As one *TV Guide* critic noted of the show's rapid rise and fast fall, "That's the thing about cutting edges. They're the first things to get dull."

SUBSTANCE BEHIND THE STYLE

Despite its faddishness, however, *Miami Vice* did contain a marked moralistic component. Many episodes hinged on the problem of "cops who'd gone bad" and on the fact that Crockett and Tubbs, undercover vice detectives posing as drug dealers, blended in most smoothly with the criminals they were supposed to apprehend. Absorbing the world-weary fatalism and moral ambiguity of film noir, the series rarely afforded its heroes an unambiguous "triumph" over their adversaries; often what victories they did achieve were pyrrhic or outside the conventional channels of the "system."

Miami Vice was also one of the era's few shows to pay explicit attention to contemporary political controversies—the dubious efficacy of the "war on drugs," the messy contradictions of U.S. political involvement in Central America and Southeast Asia, hidden Wall Street complicity in the Latin American drug trade, and others—that highlighted the difficulties of legislating local justice in a world of competing multinational political and economic interests. The fact that this serious social commentary was often at odds with the show's more obvious worship of Reagan-era wealth and materialism (the clothes, the cars, the money) made *Miami Vice* both an interrogation and an endorsement of the dominant conservative political and cultural ideology of the 1980s.

The show's formal characteristics and its ambiguous politics made it a popular "text" among postmodern academic theorists and cultural critics who found in its pastel sheen both an ironic critique of the 1980s worship of glamour and money and a wholehearted participation in that fetishization. This so-called complicitous critique of 1980s culture prompted Andrew Ross, writing in the journal *Communication*, to dub *Miami Vice* "TV's first postmodern cop show," while other critics, such as Todd Gitlin, in his book *Watching Television*, derided the show's "studied blankness of tone" and saw in its stylized "emphasis on surface" the same techniques of enticement used to lure consumers in car commercials. Despite, or perhaps because of, its relatively short-lived popularity and brief vogue in academia, *Miami Vice* remains an illuminating artifact for scholars interested not only in the history of television but also in the visual, aural, and political texture of the 1980s.

The show's profile in the popular memory underwent a makeover of sorts in 2006 when Mann wrote and directed a big-screen, R-rated version of *Miami Vice* that amplified the dark, anti-glamorous style of the show's third season and, for many critics, stripped away much of the personality and sense of humor of the original series. Starring Colin Farrell and Jamie Foxx as a terse, grimly serious Crockett and Tubbs, the movie showcased Mann's arresting visual style but earned mixed reviews and underperformed at the box office. This tepid reception, coming some two decades after *Miami Vice* first aired, seemed to exemplify the challenges of updating a groundbreaking TV series whose influence and popularity were so closely tied to a specific—and fleeting—cultural moment.

Andrew Sargent

SEE ALSO: Dallas*;* Dragnet*; Emmy Awards; Hollywood; MTV; Olmos, Edward James; Reagan, Ronald;* Rolling Stone*; Sex Symbol;* Starsky and Hutch*; Television;* Time*;* TV Guide*; War on Drugs.*

BIBLIOGRAPHY

Benedek, Emily. "Inside *Miami Vice.*" *Rolling Stone*, March 28, 1985, 56–62, 125.

Buxton, David. *From "The Avengers" to "Miami Vice": Form and Ideology in Television Series.* New York: Manchester University Press, 1990.

Feeney, F. X., and Paul Duncan. *Michael Mann.* Los Angeles: Taschen, 2006.

Feuer, Jane. *Seeing through the Eighties: Television and Reaganism.* Durham, NC: Duke University Press, 1995.

Gitlin, Todd, ed. *Watching Television.* New York: Pantheon, 1986.

Lyons, James. *"Miami Vice."* Wiley-Blackwell Studies in Film and Television. Chichester, UK: Wiley-Blackwell, 2010.

McNeil, Alex. *Total Television: A Comprehensive Guide to Programming from 1948 to the Present*, 4th ed. New York: Penguin Books, 1996.

Ross, Andrew. "*Miami Vice*: Selling In." *Communication* 9, nos. 3–4 (1987): 305–334.

Sanders, Steven M. "*Noir et Blanc* in Color: Existentialism and *Miami Vice.*" In *The Philosophy of TV Noir*, ed. Steven M. Sanders and Aeon J. Skoble, 95–114. Lexington: University Press of Kentucky, 2008.

Seewi, Nurit. *Miami Vice: Cashing In on Contemporary Culture?* Heidelberg: Carl Winter University, 1990.

Zoglin, Richard. "Cool Cops, Hot Show." *Time*, September 16, 1985, 60–63.

Michener, James *(1907–1997)*

With the passing of James Michener in 1997, one of twentieth-century America's most prolific novelists and outstanding philanthropists was lost. Michener's career spanned fifty years, and his often-lengthy books were eagerly consumed by the public. His works explore locales as diverse as the South Pacific,

South Africa, Spain, Afghanistan, Poland, Japan, Israel, the Caribbean, Hungary, the American West, the Chesapeake Bay, Alaska, and outer space. Millions of people worldwide were introduced to these places via dramatic narratives that are tied to geographical and historical events.

Michener's real-life experiences, gained from years of wandering the globe and absorbing the lives and cultures of ordinary people, inspired his writing. In his autobiography, *The World Is My Home* (1992), he explains that writing is a mental discipline, and the strength of his books is their ability to capture a reader's interest and hold it with a good narrative. Often referred to as "America's Storyteller," Michener wanted people to see the diversity of human life and understand and accept individual differences. He argued for the universal ideals of religious and racial tolerance, the value of hard work and discipline, and self-reliance. His books are rich in characters who reflect the history of the countries in which the stories take place.

Each of Michener's works was a commercial success, beginning with his first published book, *Tales of the South Pacific* (1947), which won the Pulitzer Prize. This collection of stories about people in the South Pacific during World War II is based upon the author's own experiences as a soldier posted in the region. *Tales of the South Pacific* depicts the tedium, anxiety, and frustrations of individuals as they wait for fighting to break out. A 1949 adaptation for the stage by Richard Rodgers and Oscar Hammerstein was titled *South Pacific* and starred Mary Martin and Ezio Pinza. It was a major hit on Broadway, becoming one of the longest-running musicals with 1,925 performances. In 1958 the story was made into a blockbuster Hollywood film.

James A. Michener. *James Michener sits for an interview to promote his book* The Novel *in 1991.* **AP IMAGES.**

James Albert Michener was born on February 3, 1907, in New York City. An orphan, he was rescued by Mabel and Edwin Michener of Doylestown, Pennsylvania—the place that became his home during his formative years. His childhood was spent in poverty, which, as he writes in his autobiography, led to his liberal ideals. At age thirteen he and a friend hitchhiked to New York City with only a few cents between them, thus beginning Michener's love of travel. He enjoyed meeting new people and finding out about cultures that were vastly different from his Quaker upbringing. His second major work of fiction, *The Fires of Spring* (1949), deals with a character much like the young Michener: a poor Pennsylvania schoolboy who hitchhikes across America, encountering many different characters and experiences that later become the basis for a writing career.

After graduating with honors from Swarthmore College in Philadelphia in 1929, Michener became an English teacher. In 1933 he received the Joshua Lippincott fellowship to travel and study abroad, and he visited Spain for the first time. His book *Iberia* (1968) depicts his intense interest in the people and places of Spain. Michener returned to teaching in 1936 and became an associate professor at Colorado State College of Education, completing his master of arts in 1937. Over the course of his career, he was awarded more than thirty honorary doctorates.

Although Michener's two early marriages, to Patti Koon and Vange Nord, ended in divorce, his third marriage in 1955 to Mari Yoriko Sabusawa was not only successful but also influential in his continuing commitment to the arts in America. As a result of her guidance and his success, Michener was able to devote time and financial support to the arts. In fact, after her death in 1994, Michener pledged millions of dollars to art museums in Doylestown, Pennsylvania, and in Texas, which had become his home after his epic *Texas* (1985). His wealth was enhanced by the many works of his that were adapted for films and television. Among the most memorable was *Centennial* (1976), an epic tale of the history of Colorado that became the longest-ever miniseries on television with twenty-six hour-long episodes.

Michener was outspoken in his beliefs and often took action on them. In 1950, just after the Korean War had begun, he visited Japan. This led to his books *The Voice of Asia* (1951), *The Bridges at Toko-Ri* (1953), and *Sayonara* (1954). During the Hungarian revolt in 1956, Michener was in Austria, and he assisted dozens of Hungarians to safety. He wrote of this experience in *The Bridge at Andau* (1957). In 1971 Michener wrote sympathetically about the tragic student protests at Kent State University in *Kent State: What Happened and Why*. He was a John F. Kennedy supporter in the 1960s, and he ran unsuccessfully for Congress in 1962 as a Democrat. In 1972 he visited China and Russia as a correspondent traveling with President Richard Nixon. As a result of his efforts for world peace, Michener received the Presidential Medal of Freedom in 1977 from President Gerald Ford. That same year he launched a television series, *James Michener's World*.

In 1996, a year before he died, *Fortune* magazine ranked him among the nation's top philanthropists. The publication estimated that he had donated $24 million in that year alone to charities, art museums, and institutions of learning.

Joan Gajadhar

SEE ALSO: *Kent State Massacre;* South Pacific.

BIBLIOGRAPHY

Becker, George. *James A. Michener.* New York: Frederick Ungar, 1983.

Grobel, Lawrence. *Talking with Michener.* Jackson: University Press of Mississippi, 1999.

Michener, James. *The World Is My Home.* New York: Random House, 1992.

Severson, Marilyn S. *James A. Michener: A Critical Companion.* Westport, CT: Greenwood Press, 1996.

Mickey Mouse

SEE: *Disney (Walt Disney Company); The Mickey Mouse Club; Steamboat Willie.*

The Mickey Mouse Club

Mickey Mouse began as Mortimer Mouse in 1927, drawn by the imaginative Walt Disney. In 1928 the Walt Disney Company released *Steamboat Willie*, a seven-minute cartoon starring Mickey Mouse, and audiences loved it. By the 1930s Disney's mouse was well established as part of American culture, and Mickey Mouse Clubs had sprung up across the country. Every Saturday children and their parents hurried to department stores, where they sang and watched cartoons. The clubs, boasting several million members, eventually disbanded, but in 1955 *The Mickey Mouse Club* debuted. It was a variety television show produced by Walt Disney Productions, which aired on ABC until 1959. The show quickly became a staple in the lives of preteens, who watched the show every afternoon after school.

The show starred twenty-four young people, called Mouseketeers. Disney conducted a nationwide search for personable, unknown youth who would come together for an hour each weekday to entertain America's children. The young stars ranged in age from nine to fourteen. Annette Funicello, the last of those cast, would prove to be the most popular, and after the show ended, she went on to a successful career in the movies. The cast was told that getting along was more important than talent. Those who could not get along, or whose parents were too aggressive, were quietly replaced.

A core group of the most talented and charismatic emerged: Funicello, Sharon Baird, Darlene Gillespie, Karen Pendleton, Sherry Alberoni, Lonnie Burr, Bobby Burgess, Tommy Cole, and Cubby O'Brien. Other Mouseketeers who would go on to television fame were Don Grady, who later costarred in *My Three Sons*; Paul Petersen of *The Donna Reed Show*; and Johnny Crawford of *The Rifleman*. In her autobiography, Funicello writes that profanity was forbidden on *The Mickey Mouse Club* set and that respect for adults was promoted by the Mouseketeers calling them "uncle" and "aunt." "Uncle Walt" was obvious, of course, but the cast carried the command further by labeling the crew by names such as "Aunt Hairdresser" and "Uncle Makeup." The adults who appeared on the show were Jimmie Dodd, a deeply religious actor, songwriter, and dancer, and Roy Williams, a longtime Disney animator.

The Mickey Mouse Club offered consistency to young viewers, along with enough diversity to keep them from becoming bored. The established elements were simple: attractive young stars performing before a live audience, clowns, magicians, cartoons, guest stars, educational elements, and music written for the show. Each day of the week was devoted to a specific theme: Monday was Fun with Music Day; Tuesday was Guest Star Day; Wednesday was Anything Can Happen Day; Thursday was Circus Day; and Friday was Talent Round-Up Day.

Education was promoted by the regular appearance of Jiminy Cricket, a character from Disney's animated film, *Pinocchio*, who walked children through the encyclopedia. Newsreels brought events around the world to the attention of young viewers. Notable guest stars were actors James Cagney, Fess Parker, and Buddy Ebsen and singers Judy Canova and the Lennon Sisters. The show also had various series featuring the regulars or other young stars. The most popular of these series was *The Hardy Boys*, starring Tim Considine and Tommy Kirk as Frank and Joe Hardy; *The Adventures of Spin and Marty*, with Considine as Spin and David Stollery as Marty; and *Annette*, which ultimately led to a recording contract for Funicello.

When the show ended unexpectedly in 1959, it was still rated the top children's show of the day. In 1980 thirty-one members of the cast came together to celebrate the twenty-fifth

Mickey Mouse Club, 1955. *The original Mouseketeers appeared on* The Mickey Mouse Club *beginning in 1955.* **WALT DISNEY PICTURES/THE KOBAL COLLECTION.**

anniversary of *The Mickey Mouse Club*. They danced and sang with as much enthusiasm and a lot more poise than they had at the show's debut. Most still retained some connection to show business. Funicello, who was the only Mouseketeer retained by Disney after the show ended, went on to make a series of movies with actor Frankie Avalon, wrote an autobiography that became a made-for-television movie, and became a spokesperson for muscular dystrophy. Burgess became a regular dancer on *The Lawrence Welk Show*, spending twenty years with the popular television show. O'Brien became a noted drummer, Baird and Alberoni moved on to cartoons and commercial voice-overs, and Burr became a playwright. Cole established a career as an award-winning makeup artist, and Petersen became a major voice in the battle to protect the financial rights of child stars.

The Mickey Mouse Club provided children of the 1950s with positive role models while entertaining them and promoting self-esteem. America's young people tuned in every day to watch the show because they believed the Mouseketeers when they ended each show with the promise to return again and again, "because we like you." *The Mickey Mouse Club* was briefly revived in 1977 and 1989, the latter having the distinction of launching the careers of more Mouseketeers: singers Christina Aguilera, Britney Spears, and Justin Timberlake; and actors Ryan Gosling and Keri Russell. But it is the original show that lives on in the hearts of baby boomers and in late night reruns on the Disney channel.

Elizabeth Purdy

SEE ALSO: *Aguilera, Christina; Avalon, Frankie; Canova, Judy; Disney (Walt Disney Company); The Fifties; Funicello, Annette; The Hardy Boys;* My Three Sons; *Spears, Britney; Television; Timberlake, Justin; Welk, Lawrence.*

BIBLIOGRAPHY

Armstrong, Jennifer. *Why? Because We Still Like You: An Oral History of the Mickey Mouse Club*. New York: Grand Central Publishing, 2010.

Bowles, Jerry. *Forever Hold Your Banner High! The Story of the Mickey Mouse Club and What Happened to the Mouseketeers*. Garden City, NY: Doubleday, 1976.

Browne, Pat. *The Guide to United States Popular Culture*. Bowling Green, OH: Bowling Green State University Popular Press, 2001.

Funicello, Annette, and Patricia Romanowski. *A Dream Is a Wish Your Heart Makes*. Thorndike, ME: Thorndike Press, 1994.

Keller, Keith. *The Mickey Mouse Club Scrapbook*. New York: Grosset & Dunlap, 1975.

Santoil, Lorraine, and Annette Funicello. *The Official Mickey Mouse Club Book*. New York: Hyperion, 1995.

Microsoft

Microsoft, a computer software corporation founded in 1975, has become synonymous in the minds of many with the computer age and its high-speed advances in technology and communication. Often called the General Motors of the computer industry, Microsoft enjoys a mystique in the public imagination that stems from many sources, not the least of which is that favorite American myth of unlimited opportunity: the rags-to-riches story. From its beginnings in the minds of two computer-obsessed students to its status as a $23-billion-a-year industry giant on a sprawling campus in a Seattle, Washington, suburb, Microsoft seems to fulfill that archetypal American promise.

This is perhaps most appropriately reflected in a satirical computer game called "Microshaft's Winblows '98," in which players compete to rise from Penniless Nerd to Supreme Ruler of the Galaxy. The nerd in question is William Henry Gates III, usually referred to as Bill, the CEO of Microsoft. Though never exactly penniless, Gates's lanky, bespectacled appearance fit the stereotype of the "computer nerd," and many have cheered his success for just this reason. Many others have expressed disgust for the other side of the stereotype, the Supreme Ruler, charging Gates as self-congratulatory, self-aggrandizing, and simply too rich.

GATES AND ALLEN'S EARLY PARTNERSHIP

Gates and Paul Allen were upper-middle-class Seattleites, both attending the exclusive private Lakeside School in the late 1960s, when they were introduced in eighth grade to the use of computers and programming languages. Their mutual fascination with the new technology drew them together, and by 1972 they had developed their first software and formed their first company. Traf-o-Data offered city and state traffic departments computerized equipment for counting and analyzing traffic information. Slow-moving government bureaucracies were not quick to adopt the new technology, and Gates and Allen continued to search for more popular applications for their product. In their work on Traf-o-Data, they had incorporated a new invention—the microprocessor chip. Sensing a revolution in technology, they continued designing software for use with the new microprocessors.

It was their work on a programming language for an early personal computer, the MITS Altair, that resulted in the forma-

Microsoft Founder Bill Gates. *Bill Gates stepped down as the head of Microsoft in order to focus his energies on the charitable works of the Bill and Melinda Gates Foundation.* BOSTON GLOBE/ CONTRIBUTOR/GETTY IMAGES.

tion of Allen and Gates's next company, Micro-Soft (later Microsoft). Gates was attending Harvard but dropped out in his sophomore year to focus on his work with Allen in Albuquerque, New Mexico. There, over the course of the next few years, they developed computer programming in languages BASIC, FORTRAN-80, and COBOL 80. In 1978 they worked on developing software for the new Apple II personal computer, and by 1979 Microsoft had acquired fifteen employees and moved back to Gates and Allen's hometown, Seattle.

Microsoft's giant leap into public awareness and business history came in 1980 when IBM (International Business Machines) approached the little software company, seeking operating software for its upcoming line of personal computers. In a brilliant entrepreneurial double-play, Gates and Allen bought an existing operating system that they could quickly modify for IBM's use and began planning to make that operating system the most widely used system in the industry. Seattle Computer had a disk operating system called QDOS that Microsoft bought for $50,000, carefully concealing IBM's interest in the product. Then, recognizing the inevitable rise of "clones" or copies of the IBM-PC, Allen and Gates began to lobby for other software companies to write applications for their operating system, then called MS-DOS. Manufacturers of the IBM clones began to bundle the Microsoft software with their computers, and soon MS-DOS was the industry-standard operating system. Microsoft's place at the head of the industry had been established.

Soon after, Allen was diagnosed with Hodgkin's disease, a form of lymphatic cancer. Though his illness was controlled with treatment, he no longer felt driven to keep a business at the cutting edge of the technological revolution. Though he and Gates remain friends, Allen retired in 1983 to live a more relaxed life on his vast lakeside estate near Seattle, playing music in a band, purchasing sports teams, and managing his investments.

WINDOWS DEBUTS

Gates continued to run the rapidly expanding Microsoft. In the mid-1980s the company developed the revolutionary graphical user interface (GUI) for Apple Computer's Macintosh. The GUI made the computer much more accessible, since commands were delivered by pointing to pictures, or icons, with a lightweight movable attachment called a "mouse," thus eliminating the need to learn complex DOS codes to tell the computer what to do. In late 1987 Microsoft introduced its own GUI, called Windows, so that the DOS-based IBM machines could make use of the "user-friendly" features attracting customers to the Apple Macintosh.

The next year, in the first of many lawsuits that would be brought against Microsoft, the company was taken to court by Apple for copyright violations in the creation of its Windows operating system. Four years later, the suit was dismissed without a trial. Many consider that Microsoft's actions regarding Apple are consistent with a tradition of ruthless, even unscrupulous, business practices. Some in the industry accuse the company of following a policy of "build, buy, or crush" with its competition; that is, what it cannot build, it will buy and resell at enormous profit, and what it cannot buy, it will destroy. While some competitors simply accuse Microsoft of lack of innovation, others have more dramatically compared its tactics to those of the Mafia.

MICROSOFT UNDER ATTACK

In the late 1990s the U.S. Justice Department brought an antitrust lawsuit against Microsoft. The suit accused the software giant of violating antitrust laws by bundling too much of its software into its Windows operating system, thereby giving its own software, particularly its Internet browser, an unfair advantage over the browsers of competing companies. While the court initially deemed Microsoft a monopoly and stipulated that the company separate its software and hardware manufacturing divisions into two separate companies, a federal appeals court eventually overturned the decision, and Microsoft reached a settlement with the Department of Justice that allowed third-party manufacturers of Microsoft-based personal computers (PCs) to include software from competitors such as Apple.

Several similar cases were brought against Microsoft in Europe during the first decade of the 2000s, and in 2007 a European Union court upheld a previous ruling that found Microsoft to be a monopoly and ordered the company to pay nearly $690 million in penalties in 2004. Then, in 2008, the European Union imposed another fine, this time totaling $1.3 billion, for Microsoft's apparent failure to adhere to the rules imposed after earlier sanctions.

NEW TERRITORY FOR MICROSOFT

Microsoft continues to expand, updating its Windows systems and other software and entering vigorously into the new world of Internet and mobile phone communications, as well as the video game console market. In 1996 Microsoft and NBC joined to create MSNBC, a twenty-four-hour news channel on cable television that openly acknowledges its Left-leaning, progressive viewpoint. In 2001 the company launched the Xbox, the first video game system to feature an internal hard drive. Its successor, the Xbox 360, was released in 2005 and allowed users to compete against each other via the Internet and the Xbox Live subscription service.

Microsoft also began developing Windows-based operating systems for Internet-enabled smartphones in the early 2000s. In 2011 the company announced a partnership with mobile phone manufacturer Nokia in the hope of challenging the Apple iPhone for supremacy in the mobile phone market. Microsoft also took aim at another one of its chief competitors, the search engine and Internet technology giant Google, by launching a competing search engine named Bing in 2009. Microsoft also acquired the popular Internet-communication company Skype in 2011.

Gates continues to be driven as a businessman and as a computer advocate, even after his resignation from the positions of chief executive officer in 2000 and chief software architect in 2006. He has written two books focusing on the role of the computer in daily life, *The Road Ahead* (1995) and *Business @ the Speed of Thought* (1999), which concentrates on the business uses of the Internet. Since then, Gates has worked closely with his wife, Melinda, on their humanitarian efforts through the Bill & Melinda Gates Foundation. Meanwhile, his youthful goal of "a computer on every desk and in every home, all running Microsoft software" has seemed to come closer each day. Though certainly a computer in the home is most often a middle-class acquisition, computer courses in public schools and libraries have put more computers than ever within reach of poor and working-class people. Late in the first decade of the 2000s, researchers estimated that 97 percent of the world's PCs were run on Microsoft software.

Perhaps it is Microsoft's embodiment of the rags-to-riches dream that causes the controversy that swirls around it. From two high school computer whiz kids holed up in a room together with computer magazines and ambitious ideas, Microsoft grew into the world's most valuable company. In 1986 it moved to a mammoth complex in Redmond, Washington, just across the lake from Seattle, and in 2006 it announced plans to spend more than a billion dollars in expanding the Redmond campus. The company currently employs more than 93,000 people worldwide, more than 55,000 in the United States alone, and rakes in $23 billion a year.

Former CEO Gates, worth more than $60 billion, has the world's second-largest personal fortune. Many of the early employees of the firm have also earned huge profits from stock options, causing Seattle residents to coin the term *Microsoft millionaires* and to blame rapidly rising local housing costs on the out-of-proportion incomes of software executives. The other side of the rags-to-riches story is the hostility and jealousy of those still left in rags. Both individuals and the media have snarled at the excessive wealth of both Microsoft and Gates, though Gates has managed to temper such animosity by becoming one of the world's foremost philanthropists. There is no doubt that Microsoft has played a monumentally significant role in the popularization of the PC. And if Microsoft is the General Motors of the computer world, computers themselves seem—for better or worse—to have changed American society irrevocably, much as the automobile itself once did.

Tina Gianoulis

SEE ALSO: *Apple Computer; Computer Games; IBM (International Business Machines); The Internet; Smartphones; Xbox Kinect.*

BIBLIOGRAPHY

Andrews, Paul. *How the Web Was Won: Microsoft, from Windows to the Web: The Inside Story of How Bill Gates and His Band of Internet Idealists Transformed a Software Empire.* New York: Broadway Books, 1999.

Edstrom, Jennifer and Marlin Eller. *Barbarians Led by Bill Gates: Microsoft from the Inside, How the World's Richest Corporation Wields Its Power.* New York: Henry Holt, 1998.

Foley, Mary Jo. *Microsoft 2.0: How Microsoft Plans to Stay Relevant in the Post-Gates Era.* Indianapolis, IN: John Wiley, 2008.

Gatlin, Jonathan. *Bill Gates: The Path to the Future.* New York: Avon Books, 1999.

Manes, Stephen, and Paul Andrews. *Gates: How Microsoft's Mogul Reinvented an Industry—and Made Himself the Richest Man in America.* New York: Doubleday, 1993.

Phelps, Marshall, and David Kline. *Burning the Ships: Intellectual Property and the Transformation of Microsoft.* Hoboken, NJ: John Wiley, 2009.

Rivlin, Gary. *The Plot to Get Bill Gates: An Irreverent Investigation of the World's Richest Man . . . and the People Who Hate Him.* New York: Times Business, 1999.

Wallace, James. *Overdrive: Bill Gates and the Race to Control Cyberspace.* New York: John Wiley, 1997.

Wallace, James, and Jim Erickson. *Hard Drive: Bill Gates and the Making of the Microsoft Empire.* New York: John Wiley, 1992.

Middletown

Robert and Helen Lynd set out to study the spirituality in a representative American town in the late 1920s, but instead wound up studying the inhabitants' entire culture. Their work, one of lasting impact and the first "functionalist" study in American sociology, combined sociology and anthropology and considered society on a holistic level. *Middletown: A Study in Modern American Culture*, published in 1929, was a work of both critical and popular acclaim, changing traditional disciplinary attitudes about sociological studies and exposing the public to the shifts in the social fabric brought about by burgeoning consumerism. The "Middletown" of the title was the authors' pseudonym for the place studied—Muncie, Indiana.

Interestingly, neither Robert Lynd (1892–1970) nor his wife, Helen Merrell Lynd (1894–1982), were formally trained sociologists. Robert Lynd, a graduate of the Union Theological Seminary, began his work as a Christian minister but soon became disenchanted by his own admitted agnosticism. Helen Lynd was a graduate of Wellesley College and later completed a master's degree in philosophy from Columbia University. Their collaborative work grew out of John D. Rockefeller Jr.'s Committee on Social and Religious Surveys (CSRS) organization, which conducted field surveys on people's religious practices. In 1923 the CSRS became the Institute for Social and Religious Research, which commissioned new studies; the group's ultimate goal was to unite all Protestant churches in the country in order to create a national network geared toward social service.

Eventually, the directors decided to conduct a more in-depth study of one town, and they considered many small cities in the Midwest. They settled on Muncie, Indiana, because of its manageable population (38,000 in 1924) and its relative homogenization: at the time, the city was made up of 92 percent native-born whites and housed few blacks, immigrants, Catholics, and Jews. Although the institute commissioned a study that focused on the religious practices of Middletown, the Lynds were more inclusive in considering what constituted a community's "spirituality." They believed that "cultural change" could better be measured without a racial component, and also that social progress resided in the efforts of people living in the "Heartland"—midwestern, native-born Protestants. The Lynds gathered their information from many sources, including participant-observation studies, documentary materials, statistics, interviews, and questionnaires; they also studied many details of ordinary life, such as what time people got out of bed, how the car was used, who went to the movies, how the laundry got done, who went to church, what was taught in school, and so on.

The study began in 1924 and lasted fifteen months. Robert Lynd himself stated that his goal was "to define and measure the changes in the life (i.e., habits or behavior) of a small city over the critical period since 1890 as those changes affect the problem of the small city church," and to conduct "a straight fact-finding study." In reality, the Lynds' goals went beyond this—they not only studied Middletown culture but also critiqued it, especially in light of the changes brought about by consumer culture. Rockefeller's institute did not approve of the focus of the study and refused to publish it. Harcourt, Brace, and World published the work, *Middletown*, in 1929, and it went on to become one of the most popular and influential books of the twentieth century. It sold more than 32,000 copies during the eight years of the Great Depression alone and was both a study of and an addition to the growing self-consciousness of consumer society.

As historian Richard Wightman Fox has said, "That book had such an enormous and immediate impact on its thousands of readers because it caught the subtle tensions and confusions of the early years of consumer society in America."

Significantly, the Middletown study, tinged with the irony of the Lynds' own critical voices, exposed small-town America's increasing preoccupation with money and consumption. The townspeople embodied contradictions in that "they showed signs both of possessing the capacity to organize their own lives and of succumbing to the emergent national agencies of 'pecuniary' culture," according to Fox. Robert Lynd returned to Muncie by himself in 1935 for a follow-up study, later published as *Middletown in Transition: A Study in Cultural Conflicts*, an even more personally critical work that exposed Lynd's growing biases against advertising and small-town thinking. In this second work, Lynd contended that people were, in fact, not rational at all, and powerless and passive in the face of advertising.

While Robert Lynd's career foundered after this second major work, he had already left an indelible impression on American culture—he studied a population, unearthed the inner workings of people's daily lives, and exposed this to a vast readership. More significantly, he also established Muncie specifically, and midwestern towns generally, as places characterized by the stereotypically provincial, conservative, and largely ignorant groups of people who inhabited them.

Wendy Woloson

SEE ALSO: *Consumerism; The Rockefeller Family.*

BIBLIOGRAPHY

Caccamo De Luca, Rita. *Back to Middletown: Three Generations of Sociological Reflections*. Stanford, CA: Stanford University Press, 2000.

Fox, Richard Wightman. "Epitaph for Middletown: Robert S. Lynd and the Analysis of Consumer Culture." In *The Culture of Consumption: Critical Essays in American History, 1880–1980*, ed. Richard Wightman Fox and T. J. Jackson Lears, 103–141. New York: Pantheon, 1983.

Hoover, Dwight W. *Middletown Revisited: A Study in Cultural Conflicts*. Muncie, IN: Ball State University, 1990.

Lynd, Robert S. *Middletown in Transition*. New York: Harcourt Brace and Company, 1937.

Lynd, Robert S., and Helen Merrell Lynd. *Middletown: A Study in Contemporary American Culture*. New York: Harcourt, Brace and World, 1929.

Midler, Bette *(1945–)*

One of the brightest and most versatile performers of the last decades of the twentieth century, Bette Midler has conquered every entertainment medium: movies, television, recordings, and the concert stage. Candid, intelligent, and supremely talented, Midler, who burst upon the scene with her ability to shock and provoke, eventually assumed her place as one of America's most beloved entertainers. She continues to perform, appearing in Las Vegas, singing, and acting. She has also become a major force in cleaning up New York City through her New York Restoration Project.

Named after actress Bette Davis (though Midler's first name is pronounced "bet") by a starstuck mother, Midler was born in Honolulu, Hawaii. A white, Jewish outsider in a mostly Asian environment, Midler caught the performing bug in high school, which helped to overcome some of her social anxieties. After filming a bit part in George Roy Hill's *Hawaii* in 1966, Midler left her home for New York City, where she quickly landed a role in the chorus—and later a supporting role—in the Broadway sensation *Fiddler on the Roof.* She remained in the show for three years, all the while honing an inventive stage act composed of torch songs, upbeat novelty numbers, and risqué chatter; her raunchy stage persona, "The Divine Miss M," emerged from engagements at a number of popular New York nightspots. Of all her performances during this fecund early period, she is perhaps best remembered for her legendary two-year run at the Continental Baths, a gay bathhouse. Word of mouth about this newcomer—part Judy Garland, part Mae West—was strong enough to attract a noticeable straight following to this unlikely venue full of towel-clad patrons.

The early 1970s brought continued interest in Midler's career as she drew critical accolades for her first album, *The Divine Miss M*, and for concerts at New York's Carnegie Hall and Palace Theater. To many, her mix of soulful ballads and campy humor was irresistible; she was not above flashing her

Bette Midler. *Bette Midler's versatility as an entertainer has taken her from bawdy, campy stage performer to a respected dramatic actress.* STEVE MACK/CONTRIBUTOR/FILMMAGIC/GETTY IMAGES.

breasts and delivering outrageous sexual banter—for example, "Did you hear that Dick Nixon bought a copy of *Deep Throat*? He's seen it ten or twelve times. He wanted to get it down Pat." Her wonderfully irreverent wit never obscured her genuine musical craft, as she branded her signature on songs such as "Do You Wanna Dance?" and "Friends." Guided by the management of her sometime lover Aaron Russo, Midler turned down a number of high-profile movie projects during this time (including *King Kong* [1976], *Nashville* [1975], and *Rocky* [1976]), but her *Clams on the Half-Shell Review* proved a triumph on Broadway in 1975, and her 1977 television special, *Ol' Red Hair Is Back*, earned her an Emmy Award.

The Rose (1979), a thinly disguised biography of Janis Joplin, was Midler's film debut, catapulting her to a new level of stardom. In it she was able to display both her musical talents and considerable dramatic ability; for what *New Yorker* film critic Pauline Kael called a "passionate, skilled performance," Midler earned an expanded following and an Oscar nomination. She capitalized on that accomplishment with the release of *Divine Madness* (1980), a film version of her stage show of the same name, and soundtrack albums for both movies followed. The title track to *The Rose* became Midler's trademark song and a favorite of her fans.

Despite her achievement in *The Rose*, which was a box-office as well as a critical success, the fledgling film actress was cold-shouldered by the film industry, according to Midler biographer George Mair. The reasons remain mysterious, for the similarly heralded movie debut a decade earlier of another unconventional upstart, Barbra Streisand, had garnered the actress her choice of roles and lucrative contracts. Not so for Midler, who admitted, "I was nominated for an Oscar, but the fact is that I never got another offer." The failure of the caper comedy *Jinxed* (1982)—a dubious project, but the only one Midler could get off the ground during this troubled time—sent the performer into an emotional and professional tailspin. During her late 1982 return to the concert stage in "De Tour," she sang to cheering crowds, which helped to heal some of those wounds.

Decidedly underappreciated but always resourceful, Midler was able to revive her movie career with a string of profitable Disney comedies in the mid-1980s, of which *Down and out in Beverly Hills* (1986), directed by Paul Mazursky, was the subtlest and most interesting. *Ruthless People* (1986) and *Outrageous Fortune* (1987), though broad in humor, showed Midler at her comic best. To movie critics it seemed she could do no wrong: in a review of *Big Business* (1988), Kael found Midler's skills comparable to Charlie Chaplin's.

The comforts of marriage (to Martin Von Haselberg) and motherhood coincided with commercial success, and Midler's newfound stability in Hollywood enabled her to form her own production company. She wielded considerable control over the making of such films as *Beaches* (1988) and *For the Boys* (1990), although she never found a vehicle approaching the artistic merit of *The Rose*. Her comeback in films spurred a renewed appreciation for her singing, and pop ballads such as "Wind beneath My Wings" (from *Beaches*) and "From a Distance" enhanced her reputation as a unique song stylist. Midler's career thrived in the mid-1990s: her television remake of the musical *Gypsy* (1993) was much admired; her film *The First Wives' Club* (1996) was a surprise box-office bonanza; and her concert dates, most notably at New York's Radio City Music Hall, were sold out.

Midler began the twenty-first century by appearing in her own short-lived television show *Bette* for CBS. She has guest-starred on a number of TV shows, including *American Idol* (2002–) and *Dancing on Ice* (2006). As a vocalist she has acknowledged the strong influence of big-band singer Rosemary Clooney. She paid tribute to Clooney with *The Rosemary Clooney Song Book* (2003) and released a studio album tribute to Clooney's contemporary Peggy Lee in 2005. Midler made a Christmas album, *Cool Yule*, in 2006. She has also released two compilation titles: *Jackpot: The Best of Bette* (2008) and *Memories of You* (2010).

During this period, Midler's acting career was less active than in the past, and she received only lukewarm reviews for the film *Isn't She Great* (2000), in which she played writer Jacqueline Susann. She was also a headliner at Caesars Palace in Las Vegas, performing in the typically outrageous "The Showgirl Must Go On." Each year Midler has hosted an event called the Hulaween Gala to raise money for the New York Restoration Project, and in 2011 she auctioned off hundreds of her personal treasures to make additional money for the cause. Midler's ability to delight audiences has never waned.

Drew Limsky

SEE ALSO: *Academy Awards;* American Idol*; Broadway; Camp; Carnegie Hall; Chaplin, Charlie; Clooney, Rosemary; Crystal, Billy; Davis, Bette; Emmy Awards;* Fiddler on the Roof*; Garland, Judy; Hollywood; Joplin, Janis;* King Kong*; Las Vegas; Lee, Peggy; Movie Stars; The* New Yorker*; Pop Music;* Rocky*; Streisand, Barbra; Susann, Jacqueline; Television; West, Mae.*

BIBLIOGRAPHY

Kael, Pauline. *For Keeps: 30 Years at the Movies.* New York: Dutton, 1994.

Mair, George. *Bette: An Intimate Biography of Bette Midler.* Secaucus, NJ: Carol Publishing Group, 1995.

Midler, Bette. *A View from a Broad.* New York: Simon & Schuster, 1980.

Poniewozik, James, and Jeanne McDowell. "Bette Midler." *Time*, October 16, 2000, 106–109.

Steelman, Ben. "Life Is Gong Divinely Again for Miss M." *Orlando Sentinel*, September 1, 1989.

Stockwell, Anne. "Winning Bette." *Advocate*, March 25, 2008, 28–34.

Waldman, Allison. *The Bette Midler Scrapbook.* Secaucus, NJ: Carol Publishing Group, 1997.

Midnight Cowboy

New York Times film critic Vincent Canby may not have thought *Midnight Cowboy* "a film for the ages" when it first appeared in 1969, but the movie represents a particular cultural instance of how Hollywood catered to a new youth market and attempted to bring into the mainstream the underground culture of the late 1960s. A bleak tale made poignant by the tender friendship between a naive Texas stud and the petty con who at first hustles him, *Midnight Cowboy* follows the pair as they struggle to survive the unforgiving streets of New York, dreaming of a better life in Florida.

Directed by British filmmaker John Schlesinger, *Midnight Cowboy* is based on the novel by James Leo Herlihy and was adapted for the screen by Waldo Salt. While Herlihy's story focuses predominantly on Joe, the rather dim country boy turned big-city hustler, Salt's screenplay draws out the character of Ratso Rizzo, the limping con artist who befriends Joe. Another notable difference between the novel and the screenplay involves the sexual politics of a number of scenes. In particular, a sexual encounter between Joe and a pickup in the film is played out violently, while in the novel the exchanges between Joe and the man are situated within the larger context of the growing S and M culture of the 1950s and 1960s.

While many critics of the time read the relationship between Joe and Ratso as nonsexual, others (particularly openly gay reviewers) argued that they were missing the film's subtext. As Michael Moon wrote in his 1993 article in *Quarterly Review of Film & Video*, "Despite its apparent concession to the desire of many of its viewers to believe that Joe Buck . . . and Ratso Rizzo . . . are 'really' and ultimately 'innocent,' *Midnight Cowboy* suggests something much more complicated, and much more perverse, about its protagonists and the masses of men they represent."

THE FILM'S STARS

Midnight Cowboy was released in 1969, two years after Dustin Hoffman's appearance in Mike Nichols's *The Graduate*. This film catapulted the young actor to stardom for his performance as Benjamin Braddock, a disenchanted yet sympathetic college graduate desperately seeking a life different from that of his parents. Hoffman's turn as Ratso in *Midnight Cowboy* was vastly different from his previous work on screen, and the two performances hinted at the versatility of the talented actor.

Midnight Cowboy. Midnight Cowboy *starred Jon Voight as a naive hustler and Dustin Hoffman as his sickly friend trying to survive on the streets of New York City.* UNITED ARTISTS/THE KOBAL COLLECTION.

Midnight Cowboy was Jon Voight's first starring role, but the actor was not Schlesinger's original choice to play Joe. Michael Sarrazin, a Canadian actor who had starred in films such as *The Flim-Flam Man* (1967) and *The Sweet Ride* (1968), was Schlesinger's first pick for the role. When a contractual obligation required Sarrazin to film *They Shoot Horses Don't They?* (1969) during the time when shooting for *Midnight Cowboy* was scheduled, Voight stepped into the role that audiences would remember for years to come.

Midnight Cowboy was shot during a hot summer in 1968 for about $3 million, an average budget for a Hollywood feature made during the 1960s. The film marked the American directorial debut of Schlesinger, a member of the British New Cinema who got his start in filmmaking as a documentarian for the British Broadcasting Corporation (BBC). Schlesinger's previous films were influenced by Italian neorealism, Britain's Free Cinema documentary movement, and the French New Wave, influences found in many of the films of his contemporaries, such as Tony Richardson and Lindsay Anderson. Schlesinger achieved commercial success with *Darling* in 1965, which introduced Julie Christie to audiences and showcased the director's eye for detail, ear for dialogue, and fascination with interpersonal relationships.

Hoffman has said that in previews of the film blocks, people in the audiences would get up and walk out, yet the movie set records upon its release in May 1969. Given an X rating by the newly formed ratings system for its graphic depiction of violence and sexuality, *Midnight Cowboy* played for more than a year at both the Baronet Theater in Manhattan and the Mann Bruin in Los Angeles, eventually grossing more than $20 million. Two years earlier audiences had been stunned and seduced by the almost lyrical depiction of violence in Arthur Penn's *Bonnie and Clyde*. Stanley Kubrick's *2001: A Space Odyssey* (1968) and Sam Peckinpah's *The Wild Bunch* (1969) also made an impression on audiences hungry for a new kind of cinema. As a group these films heralded the beginning of New Hollywood, and *Midnight Cowboy* continued the trend of American films influenced by social and cultural changes as well as European film movements.

CRITICISM AND PRAISE

Midnight Cowboy received mixed critical reviews upon its release. Although Canby doubted the film's timelessness, he described it as "brutal but not brutalizing" and wrote that some of the scenes were "so rough and vivid it's almost unbearable." Characteristically market-conscious, *Variety* commented on Joe Buck's fashions: "Whether fringed leather coats of the kind he wears on screen will hereafter come into, or go out of fashion around town is one of the provocative questions that the film poses." The reviewer was prescient, however, when predicting that *Midnight Cowboy* would be "both hailed and denounced" by audiences and critics alike. Many reviewers praised the surprisingly tender relationship between Joe and Ratso while criticizing Schlesinger's heavy reliance on self-conscious stylization popular in films of the time.

Despite an uneven critical reception, *Midnight Cowboy* was recognized by the international film community with seven

Academy Award nominations and numerous British Academy Awards as well as the New York Film Critics Award for Best Actor and a Golden Globe for Most Promising Newcomer, both awarded to Voight. Of all the awards and accolades the film received, the most notable was its Academy Award for Best Picture. Although its rating was commuted from an X to an R after its Oscar win, *Midnight Cowboy* is the only X-rated film in Hollywood's history to have received the prestigious award.

In 1994, twenty-five years after its controversial explosion onto movie screens and into the collective cultural consciousness, *Midnight Cowboy* was rereleased into theaters. The reissue of the film was tied to the reemergence of the film's distributor, United Artists, after a six-year hiatus. Commenting on his film twenty-five years later, Schlesinger predicted that the same film pitched to a studio executive in the 1990s would not get made. Noting that the tenderness between the male characters would still resonate for contemporary audiences, Schlesinger sadly acknowledged that in a climate of political correctness, the depiction of this relationship would have to change. "Lack of knowledge is awfully freeing," a wistful Schlesinger told the *New Yorker*.

Midnight Cowboy may seem tame compared to contemporary cinema, but when it appeared in 1969 it represented changes not simply in American culture but, as Moon noted, in how the culture conceived of the "real" America. Released during the cinematic heyday of the New Hollywood, *Midnight Cowboy* illustrates the narrative and stylistic elements of that period while foreshadowing what one writer called "the antiheroic bleakness of the Seventies films to come."

Alison Macor

SEE ALSO: Bonnie and Clyde*; Gay Men;* The Graduate*; Hoffman, Dustin;* 2001: A Space Odyssey*;* The Wild Bunch.

BIBLIOGRAPHY

Canby, Vincent. *"Midnight Cowboy." New York Times*, May 26, 1969, 54.

Friend, Tad. "John Schlesinger, Joe Buck, and Ratso." *New Yorker*, February 28, 1994, 41–42.

Landry, Robert J. *"Midnight Cowboy." Variety*, May 14, 1969.

Levy, Emanuel. *And the Winner Is—: The History and Politics of the Oscar Awards*. New York: Ungar, 1987.

Moon, Michael. "Outlaw Sex and the 'Search for America': Representing Male Prostitution and Perverse Desire in Sixties Film (*My Hustler* and *Midnight Cowboy*)." *Quarterly Review of Film & Video* 15, no. 1 (1993): 27–40.

Mildred Pierce

The complex film *Mildred Pierce* (1945) commented on the appropriate roles for women in the post–World War II era. One of the top-grossing films of the 1940s, *Mildred Pierce* provides a dark composite view of postwar suburban America and suggests that society prefers women to stay in the home. Nevertheless, the film offers strong female characters and reverses the gender roles of the typical film noir, ensnaring the lead female in a series of inescapable calamities provoked by the men in her life. The film was based on James M. Cain's 1941 novel of the same name and in 2011 was made into an award-winning HBO miniseries.

Mildred Pierce has been compared to the Greek legend of Medea, the story of a woman who seeks to win the favor of her children but who destroys them in the process. Mildred tries to create a life for herself and her two daughters apart from her unfaithful husband. After leaving her eleven-year marriage, she succeeds as a business owner, but she neglects her daughters and becomes involved with Monte Beragon, a financially irresponsible, lecherous man who woos Mildred's older daughter, Veda. The more voraciously Mildred pursues her career, the more distant she becomes toward her daughters, eventually losing one to pneumonia and the other to Monte. Although Mildred appears to have control of the men in her life—marrying Monte for his name only and verbally dominating her accountant—she is duped by both of them when they sell her business out from under her.

The film differs from the book by adding a murder mystery to the plot, which in turn highlights the villainous, opportunistic aspects of Veda's and Monte's characters. Veda's murder of Monte becomes the focal point of the film and provides a framework for the flashback technique. *Mildred Pierce* is one of the few noir films that has flashback sequences narrated by a female. In addition, when Mildred confesses to the murder of Monte to save her daughter, she takes the place of the typical male film noir protagonist who will defend the femme fatale, even to the death. Directed by Michael Curtiz, the 1945 film features a tour-de-force performance by Joan Crawford in the title role, winning her an Oscar for Best Actress. Ann Blyth, playing Veda, and Eve Arden, as Ida Corwin, were nominated for Oscars for their supporting roles.

In the end, both the book and the film suggest that women cannot and should not compete with men in business. Mildred loses her daughters, her business, and her new husband, but she is given a chance at redemption: she can return to her original husband, the original domestic purpose for her life. Reflecting the anxiety in 1945 over the number of married women in the workplace, the film reinforces the idea that women could not be successful mothers and work outside the home.

In 1996 the U.S. Library of Congress National Film Registry selected the 1945 film version of *Mildred Pierce* for preservation due to its cultural, historical, and aesthetic significance. The 2011 HBO television miniseries version, starring Kate Winslet and Guy Pearce, with Evan Rachel Wood as Veda, won five Emmy Awards and four Golden Globes. Unlike the 1945 film, the miniseries employed younger actresses to portray younger versions of Veda. The miniseries is somewhat truer to the novel than was the 1945 film—the story is recounted in chronological order, without flashbacks or voice-overs, and it omits the murder subplot in the 1945 feature.

James R. Belpedio

SEE ALSO: *Academy Awards; Cable TV; Crawford, Joan; Emmy Awards; Feminism; Film Noir; Made-for-Television Movies; Winslet, Kate; World War II.*

BIBLIOGRAPHY

Behlmer, Rudy, ed. *Inside Warner Bros. (1935–1951)*. New York: Viking Press, 1985.

Crowther, Bruce. *Film Noir: Reflections in a Dark Mirror*. New York: Continuum Publishing, 1988.

Haskell, Molly. *From Reverence to Rape: The Treatment of Women in the Movies*, 2nd ed. Chicago: University of Chicago Press, 1987.

Krutnik, Frank. *In a Lonely Street: Film Noir, Genre, Masculinity*. London: Routledge Press, 1991.

Rosenzweig, Sidney. *"Casablanca" and Other Major Films of Michael Curtiz*. Ann Arbor, MI: UMI Research Press, 1982.

Sochen, Jane. "Mildred Pierce and Women in Film." In *Hollywood's America: United States History through Its Films*, ed. Steven Mintz and Randy Roberts. St. James, NY: Brandywine Press, 1993.

Militias

Militia activism has been a part of the American political and social landscape since the colonial period. Throughout the country's history, various groups of Americans have felt obligated to guard their liberties against what they have perceived as an increasingly autocratic and potentially corrupt federal government. Although the names of these citizen groups have changed over the years—revolutionaries, Minutemen, militias—their belief in a government with limited powers has remained the same. Militias were brought under the scrutiny of popular opinion and academic analysis during three periods in the late twentieth century and early twenty-first century: the 1960s, when groups such as the Posse Comitatus formed amid the turmoil of the civil rights movement and Cold War narratives; the 1990s, which saw events such as the Ruby Ridge standoff in Idaho and the bombing of the federal building in Oklahoma City; and the first decade of the 2000s, following the start of the war on terrorism in the wake of the September 11, 2001, attacks.

EARLY HISTORY

Militia members claim their legitimacy from the Second Amendment to the Constitution—"A well regulated militia being necessary to the security of a free state, the right of the people to keep and bear arms shall not be infringed"—and from an institutionalized historical tradition under which militias have operated at various times in American history. In the colonial period the militia played an integral role in protecting the colonists during the conflict with Native Americans. With ties to Old World governments all but severed, militias became the main line of local defense in colonial communities and isolated settlements. It is this fear of government corruption that convinced many Americans to restrict the size and role of the professional army, which was seen as necessary only to guarantee secured seacoasts and to tame the frontier. The role of citizen militias in defending the United States, however, was short-lived. Those who favored building an American empire began to cite the Militia Act of 1792 as validation of their argument for establishing a professional army solely under the control of the federal government. They criticized the militia as ineffective in the War of 1812 and pressured politicians to dissolve the militia or to place it under federal control.

In the mid- and late 1800s there was both positive and negative reinforcement for the continued existence of militias. Following the Civil War, racially charged paramilitary groups such as the Ku Klux Klan (KKK) emerged. Although they were only loosely derived from the militia tradition, these groups have commonly been considered a part of it. Meanwhile, with western expansion reaching its apex, groups derived more directly from the militia tradition were being sanctioned by the U.S. government as components of cavalry regiments, many of which were eventually folded into the professional military's infrastructure.

The United States emerged from the Spanish-American War as a world power, and it soon became clear that a standing army would play an increasingly important role in maintaining the empire. By performing especially well during the war, the

Michigan Militia Recruitment Poster. *A recruitment poster for the Michigan Militia circa 1995 details the group's philosophy and purpose.* © **CORBIS.**

National Guard, which began as a series of state government-sanctioned militias, secured its place in the American defense machine. Citizen militias were factored out of the American defense equation with the Militia Act of 1903, which segregated the militia into two classes: the organized militia (the National Guard) and the reserve militia (nonenrolled citizen militias). The National Defense Act of 1916, however, sealed the fate of militias as a remnant of a bygone era. The act placed the National Guard more firmly under federal control as the primary reserve force and created an enlisted reserve to supply the professional army, which was enlarged. As the push toward professionalization grew, those involved in militias came to be looked upon as weekend warriors and gun-toting extremists eager to play war games. Militia groups in the twentieth century have been characterized in similar ways. While those opposed to militias view them as a threat to the government, militia members tend to view themselves as the original protectors of American liberty who have been relegated to the position of delinquents and aliens on their own soil.

TWENTIETH-CENTURY MILITIAS

The first significant moment in the twentieth century that spurred paramilitary groups into action was the civil rights movement in the 1960s, which sparked the resurgence of racially motivated pseudo-militias such as the KKK. The strength of the Left during this time disturbed the Far Right, and Cold War narratives, driven by widespread fear of a communist takeover, provided further impetus for groups such as the Minutemen and militias to mobilize. Militia groups were convinced that the nation was being attacked by a communist conspiracy, internally and externally. Even as most Americans ceased to fear an imminent invasion from an external power, paramilitary groups shifted to the "enemy within." As social critic Harry Johnson notes in *The Minutemen*, "The emphasis shifted to the threat of an internal take-over of the country by the 'Communist-Socialist' conspiracy." Groups such as the Posse Comitatus, founded in Portland, Oregon, in 1969, demanded that public officials be arrested by citizens and lynched for their failure to defend the groups' image of the American way of life.

In the 1990s the Ruby Ridge standoff in northern Idaho; the showdown at the Branch Davidian compound in Waco, Texas; and the Oklahoma City bombing focused public attention on militia activity. The Waco compound in which David Koresh and the Branch Davidians lived contained large stores of firearms and ammunition, which the FBI and the Bureau of Alcohol, Tobacco, Firearms and Explosives (ATF) cited as a primary reason for their attempt to seize the property on February 28, 1993. The siege lasted fifty days and ended when a fire devastated the compound, killing the seventy-five civilians residing inside. Despite claims that the FBI did not start the fire, sympathizers of the militia movement perceived the siege, and its outcome, as yet another example of an autocratic government infringing on Second Amendment rights by means of sanctioned violence. Timothy McVeigh, a former member of the U.S. Army who had won a Bronze Star for bravery, was just such a sympathizer, even visiting the Waco compound during the siege in a show of support for the Branch Davidians. In retaliation for Waco, and in protest of the government policies McVeigh felt were behind the incident, McVeigh chose to bomb a federal building in Oklahoma City. The bomb, which McVeigh detonated on April 19, 1995, killed 168 people, including 19 children in a day care center on the second floor.

Given the violent tendencies of people like McVeigh and Koresh, government officials and the media have portrayed militias as fringe groups with a penchant for violence that threatens to disrupt domestic tranquility. In the wake of these events, members of such groups as the Militia of Montana and the Michigan Militia were called to testify before the Senate about their activities. Although a direct link never was established between specific militia groups and either Ruby Ridge or Oklahoma City, it is widely perceived that these are the types of activities that militia organizations sponsor. Militia members claim that it has not been uncommon for them to be arrested for plotting to attack the federal government without actually having carried out any such activities. Extremists of the Far Right were identified as the major threat within America in the late twentieth century.

Analysts often link militia activism to groups such as the Freemen and the Posse Comitatus, the latter of which has an openly racist agenda. The Posse Comitatus—Latin for "the power [or force] of the county"—believes that government at the county level is the only legitimate form of government. Although some of the more extreme militia activists believe that the sheriff of a county is the ultimate authority figure in that jurisdiction, most are taxpaying citizens who believe in the need for a federal government and recognize its authority.

TRACKING TWENTY-FIRST CENTURY MILITIAS

Because of the loose-knit organization of militias for strategic and philosophical purposes, it is difficult to estimate the number of people involved in them. A report compiled by the Anti-Defamation League in early 1995 stated that "militias are operating in at least forty states, with membership reaching some 15,000." In 1996 the Southern Poverty Law Center reported that it had identified 440 self-proclaimed antigovernment militias distributed throughout all fifty states. Membership in militias has seen several periods of resurgence, despite the fact that many analysts characterize militia activism as a passing fad.

In the wake of the Oklahoma City bombings, membership in militia groups began to decline. Some individuals wished to disassociate themselves from McVeigh, and there was considerable dissension within militia groups. Some of the more extreme members were asked to leave when their views did not coincide with those of other members. Some of the furor attached to the Y2K scare had attracted members to militia groups; when the century changed with no major catastrophes, numbers declined. The government also began going after hate groups, with white supremacy groups such as the KKK and Aryan Nation proving generally easy targets. Several states also targeted tax resistors who claimed they had no responsibility to pay taxes to a government they did not support.

Well aware of their mistakes of judgment at Ruby Ridge and Waco, federal officials softened their tactics. The major change, however, occurred after September 11, 2001, when the government instituted a major crackdown on domestic terrorism. The Southern Poverty Law Center estimates that, despite the crackdown, more than a hundred domestic terrorism plots had taken place in the United States in the sixteen years following the Oklahoma City bombing in 1995. Although membership in militia groups did indeed decline following the 2001 attacks, the numbers began to rise again toward the end of the decade, particularly after the election of Barack Obama, whom militia movement sympathizers feared would actively seek to hinder, if not eliminate, their Second Amendment rights. The number of so-called patriot groups climbed from 149 (in 42 militias) in 2000 to 512 (in 127 militias) in 2009 and 824 (in 330 militias) in 2010.

Tim Seul

SEE ALSO: *Civil Rights Movement; Cold War; FBI (Federal Bureau of Investigation); Koresh, David, and the Branch Davidians; Ku Klux Klan; 9/11; Obama, Barack; Y2K.*

BIBLIOGRAPHY

Anti-Defamation League. "ADL Special Report: The Militia Movement in America," *Anti-Defamation League Newsletter*, 1995.

Center for Democratic Renewal. "An Analysis of Militias in America." *Center for Democratic Renewal Newsletter*, April 1995.

Dees, Morris, and James Corcoran. *Gathering Storm: America's Militia Threat.* New York: HarperCollins, 1996.

Duncan, Christopher M. "Men of a Different Faith: The Anti-Federalist Ideal in Early American Political Thought." *Polity* 26 (1994): 387–415.

Jones, J. Harry. *The Minutemen.* New York: Doubleday, 1968.

Klanwatch Project of the Southern Poverty Law Center. "False Patriots: The Threat of Antigovernment Extremists." Montgomery, AL: Southern Poverty Law Center, 1996.

Knickerboker, Brad, and Warren Richey. "A McVeigh Legacy: Militias Wane." *Christian Science Monitor*, June 11, 2001, 137.

Mulloy, D. J. *American Extremism: History, Politics, and the Militia Movement.* New York: Routledge, 2004.

Snow, Robert L. *The Militia Threat: Terrorists among Us.* New York: Plenum Trade, 1999.

Stern, Kenneth S. *A Force upon the Plain: The American Militia Movement and the Politics of Hate.* New York: Simon & Schuster, 1996.

Vinyard, JoEllen McNergney. *Right in Michigan's Grassroots: From the KKK to Today's Michigan Militia.* Ann Arbor: University of Michigan Press, 2011.

"Waco: The Inside Story." *Frontline.* PBS. Accessed February 2012. Available from http://www.pbs.org/wgbh/pages/frontline/waco/timeline.html

Milk, Harvey *(1930–1978)*

The first openly gay man to be elected into a position as a city supervisor, Harvey Milk (affectionately remembered as "the mayor of Castro Street") was assassinated just eleven months

Harvey Milk and Jane Fonda. *Harvey Milk attends a political rally opposing Proposition 6 with actress Jane Fonda in October 1978.* © ROGER RESSMEYER/CORBIS.

after he took office. Although he was cut down at the height of his career, Milk has become even more famous in death—a martyr to the progress of gay rights. Indeed, his political struggles during the 1970s were emblematic of the first major backlash against the gay rights movement of the late 1960s and early 1970s and established the terms by which political clashes over issues of sexuality have subsequently been fought.

A CIVIC LEADER

Born in Long Island, New York, on May 22, 1930, Harvey Bernard Milk was raised in a middle-class Jewish family in Woodmere. In 1951 he graduated from Albany State College, where he had majored in math. Soon after leaving college he joined the U.S. Navy, where he rose to the status of chief petty officer before being dishonorably discharged when his homosexuality was uncovered. After living a fairly closeted life in New York in the 1950s and 1960s, he moved to San Francisco in 1972. At the time, San Francisco's reputation as the gay capital of the United States was forming; after the Stonewall Rebellion, lesbians and gay men in rural locations and small towns began to migrate toward major cities. By the mid-1970s it was estimated that 20 percent of the population of San Francisco was homosexual.

In San Francisco Milk opened a camera store on Castro Street. Following an alleged extortion attempt against him, he decided to run for council office in 1973. In doing so, he challenged the city's more conservative gay establishment—including Jim Foster's Society for Individual Rights (SIR)—who believed that San Francisco would not be able to cope with a gay councilor. Milk, however, garnered populist support—including that of several of the toughest unions—by presenting himself as a "man of the people," fighting for democratic American values: life, liberty, and the pursuit of happiness. He portrayed himself as someone who just happened to be gay; when talking of sexuality, he argued for acceptance of homosexuals as human beings.

Milk's popularity grew; after two unsuccessful campaigns, he was elected city supervisor in 1977. At this time, anti-gay sentiment was starting to build in the United States. Political sympathies were moving to the Right, and television evangelism was beginning to grow in popularity. Opponents of gay rights championed the threatened nuclear family and claimed that homosexuals were "unnatural" and "perverted," recruiters of heterosexuals to their cause, and molesters of children. Individuals such as Anita Bryant—pop singer, born-again Christian, orange juice publicist, and head of the anti-gay organization Save Our Children, Inc.—campaigned and sometimes won; for example, several states repealed gay rights legislation. The Briggs Initiative, or Proposition 6, suggested that openly gay individuals should be prevented from teaching in California's public schools; at the last moment, however, it was defeated.

ASSASSINATION

Dan White, a former police officer, was also elected as a city supervisor for the first time in 1977. White's allegiances made him almost the political opposite of Milk: he represented a more conservative, Irish, working-class constituency. The San Francisco media were fascinated by the two men, and they often appeared on talk shows together. Initially Milk and White courted each other's support, but after disagreements over juvenile offenders and a gay rights bill, their relationship became one of enmity. In the fall of 1978, White resigned from his post; days later, he appealed to Mayor George Moscone to reinstate him. Under pressure from White's political opponents, Moscone refused. On November 27, 1978, White entered City Hall with a .38 Smith and Wesson and killed both Moscone and Milk.

In court, in front of a jury composed mostly of white, working-class Catholics, the defense argued that White had been suffering from depression and that he had been eating a great deal of junk food, which, by causing alterations in blood sugar levels, can cause antisocial behavior; this tactic would later be known as "the Twinkie defense." The case for the prosecution was weak; it made no attempt to outline White's motivations. On May 21, 1979, White was found guilty of two counts of voluntary manslaughter; after the announcement, a crowd besieged city hall, and police stormed the Castro. One hundred homosexual protestors and sixty-one police officers were hospitalized; the evening's events were subsequently termed the "White Night Riots." White was paroled in 1984; unable to obtain employment, he committed suicide a year later.

LASTING IMPACT

In the years following his death, Milk's legend continued to grow in American pop culture. The first major film portrayal of his career, the documentary *The Times of Harvey Milk*, was released in 1984. More than a decade later, he was celebrated in a musical opera, *Harvey Milk* by Stewart Wallace and Michael Korie, which premiered in Houston in January 1995. Milk's inspiring story finally reached a global audience in 2008, with the release of Gus Van Sant's feature film *Milk*. Sean Penn earned a Best Actor Oscar for his portrayal of the gay rights activist, while writer Dustin Lance Black received the Academy Award for Best Original Screenplay. The movie played a critical role in increasing public awareness of Milk's achievements. In 2009 the state of California voted to designate May 22 Harvey Milk Day in honor of the slain gay rights hero.

Decades after his death, Milk still serves as a model example of how integrationist politicians can intelligently and sensitively handle issues of sexuality to their advantage. But to define him solely as a gay rights activist is a disservice to his memory; he was a champion of minorities, of the working person's interests, in a patchwork city of segregated communities. His version of "American values," and its contrast with those espoused by the Right, established the field for similar battles in subsequent decades.

Glyn Davis

SEE ALSO: *Academy Awards; The Castro; Gay Liberation Movement; Gay Men; Stonewall Rebellion; Televangelism.*

BIBLIOGRAPHY

Bello, Marisol. "Cities across the USA to Observe Harvey Milk Day." *USA Today*, May 21, 2010.

Shilts, Randy. *The Mayor of Castro Street.* New York: St. Martin's Press, 1982.

Steinhauer, Jennifer. "Bill Saluting Harvey Milk Brings California Fight." *New York Times*, September 4, 2009.

Teeman, Tim. "The Joyous Ghost of San Francisco." *Times* (London), January 17, 2009.

Weiss, Mike. *Double Play: The San Francisco City Hall Killings.* Reading, MA: Addison-Wesley, 1984.

Millay, Edna St. Vincent *(1892–1950)*

The quintessential romantic American poet of the 1910s and 1920s, Edna St. Vincent Millay became a popular heroine to an entire generation of girls who grew up dreaming of becoming modern women writers. Millay's family was an unconventional one. After her parents separated, Millay's mother, a nurse, reared her children alone, making sure to encourage their creativity.

A published poet at twenty, Millay became a popular literary figure while still in college at Vassar. There she developed a reputation as a free spirit whose romantic and sexual liaisons with women were recorded in her lyric verse. After graduating and moving to avant-garde Greenwich Village, New York, Millay came to epitomize the modern bohemian lifestyle. A woman who "burned the candle at both ends," she took many lovers of both sexes, even as she continued to write popular and award-winning poetry and plays.

After marrying feminist Eugen Boissevain in 1923, Millay's poetry and personal life gradually became more conservative. But she continued to write and tour the country reading her poetry. Wearing only scarlet, Millay attracted overflow audiences of women who looked to the poet as a heroine whose life exemplified the myriad hopeful possibilities for women in the twentieth century.

Victoria Price

SEE ALSO: *Feminism; Lesbianism.*

BIBLIOGRAPHY

Brittin, Norman A. *Edna St. Vincent Millay.* Boston: Twayne, 1982.

Cheney, Anne. *Millay in Greenwich Village.* Montgomery: University of Alabama Press, 1975.

Gould, Jean. *The Poet and Her Book: A Biography of Edna St. Vincent Millay.* New York: Dodd, Mead, 1969.

Milford, Nancy. *Savage Beauty: The Life of Edna St. Vincent Millay.* Waterville, ME: Thorndike Press, 2002.

Miller, Arthur *(1915–2005)*

For most of the twentieth century and into the early days of the twenty-first century, Arthur Miller was probably America's most famous living and most enduring playwright. From the production of his first play in the 1930s through the 1990s, Miller continually sought to explore and demystify the foundations upon which American power was built. During the 1950s in particular, Miller risked his artistic career in order to expose the lies and hysteria that underpinned the McCarthy era. As a symbol of artistic integrity and resistance, his plays contain universal themes that have transcended their American origins; few other American playwrights have been so heavily and consistently produced throughout the world. Miller wrote more than fifty plays, stories, and novels, and he has continued to fascinate because of his marriage in the 1950s to the Hollywood icon Marilyn Monroe.

Born October 17, 1915, in New York, Miller was raised in a middle-class Jewish household in Harlem, supported by his father's coat-manufacturing business. The impact of the Depression, however, forced the family to move to Brooklyn. After high school Miller enrolled at the University of Michigan, then a hotbed of leftist activity. He began to write his first plays while still at college. Miller's origins and experiences heavily influenced these early plays, as Jewish themes coexisted with a socialism that was a product of the Depression. After college Miller briefly worked for the Federal Theatre Project, and following its closure by Congress, he wrote radio plays for the Columbia Broadcasting System (CBS) and the National Broadcasting Company (NBC). Miller tried to enlist during World War II, but a school football injury kept him out of the armed forces. It was not until the end of the war that Miller began to make a name for himself.

EARLY WORKS

In 1947 Miller's *All My Sons* was produced in New York; *Death of a Salesman*, his major achievement, followed in 1949. Both of these plays introduced Miller to the New York theatergoing community as a controversial young playwright, unafraid to expose the negative effects of capitalism and wartime corruption on typical American families and the "common man." Several awards, including the 1949 Pulitzer Prize for Drama and the New York Drama Critics' Circle Award for best play of the year for *Death of a Salesman*, and positive critical reception signaled

Arthur Miller. *Arthur Miller's canon of plays, stories, and novels are known for their skill in dissecting American life and power.* TIME & LIFE PICTURES/CONTRIBUTOR/TIME LIFE PICTURES/GETTY IMAGES.

Miller's arrival on the American dramatic scene. Despite his new fame and unlike many of his colleagues, he chose to remain within the theater industry rather than adopting Hollywood as his new home.

It was during the period of McCarthyism, at the height of the domestic Cold War in the United States, that Miller wrote his best plays and became an international figure. The deleterious effects of U.S. foreign policy and McCarthyism on artistic freedoms concerned Miller. His most famous play, *The Crucible* (1953), takes witch-hunting as an analogy for the contemporary situation. It has since become an enduring metaphor not only for McCarthyism but also for any system of domestic repression and hence is still produced all over the world. This work was followed by *A View from the Bridge* (1955), which attacks the 1950s vogue for informing and naming names before the various Senate and House investigating committees to prove political loyalty. These anti-McCarthy plays, together with Miller's support for many leftist causes, led many to label the playwright as subversive.

On the pretext of a misuse of his passport, the House Committee on Un-American Activities subpoenaed Miller in 1956 to account for his various actions. He refused to name names during his hearing and was thus cited for contempt of Congress. It was this "unfriendly" stance that set Miller apart from many of his colleagues in the film and theater industries and that contributed to his international reputation as a man of integrity. While many other liberal intellectuals were diving for cover or actively cooperating with the McCarthy witch hunts, Miller stood out as symbol of uncompromising resistance at a time when most forms of cultural creativity were steadily being destroyed.

PRIVATE LIFE AND LATER WORKS

Miller's fame increased further as a result of his private rather than public life. In 1955 he announced his engagement to Monroe. Miller—the nerdy, Jewish intellectual from Brooklyn—had inexplicably attracted the most desired woman in America. He wrote *The Misfits* for his new wife, and she starred in the film of the same name in 1960. They divorced the following year. Their marriage was, in part, the subject of Miller's first play in nine years, *After the Fall* (1964), and he reflects upon their relationship in his autobiography, *Timebends* (1987).

In 1962 Miller's life entered a new phase. He married his third wife, the professional photographer Inge Morath. Following his experience of Nazi trials in 1964, Miller openly turned to very personal issues in his work. *After the Fall, Incident at Vichy* (1964), *The Creation of the World and Other Business* (1972), *Playing for Time* (1980), and *Broken Glass* (1994) all deal with the universal issues of the Holocaust and "man's inhumanity toward man." These plays continued Miller's lifelong fascination with the problem of evil and the responsibility of the individual. He also wrote other plays concerned with family, identity, and memory. In addition, he wrote many articles and short stories, and he continued to be politically active, becoming the president of PEN (an association of writers) in 1965 and an anti-Vietnam campaigner.

Miller's last critical and commercial success came with *The Price*, which played on Broadway during the 1968–1969 season. The plot of the play focuses on two estranged brothers who are abruptly reunited upon the death of their father. Although Miller turned his attention to other things in later life, this author of more than twenty plays told an interviewer that, after his death, he wanted to be remembered as a playwright. After a bout with cancer, he died of congestive heart failure at the age of eighty-nine in February 2005. He continues to be remembered as one of America's most enduring playwrights.

Nathan Abrams

SEE ALSO: *Broadway;* Death of a Salesman*; McCarthyism; Monroe, Marilyn; World War II.*

BIBLIOGRAPHY

Berger, Marilyn. "Arthur Miller Moral Voice of American Stage Dies at 89." *New York Times*, February 11, 2005.

Bigsby, Christopher. *Arthur Miller, 1915–1962*. Cambridge, MA: Harvard University Press, 2009.

Bigsby, Christopher. *Arthur Miller, 1962–2005*. Ann Arbor: University of Michigan Press, 2011.

Bigsby, Christopher, ed. *The Cambridge Companion to Arthur Miller*. Cambridge, UK: Cambridge University Press, 1997.

Martin, Robert, ed. *The Theatre Essays of Arthur Miller*. London: Methuen, 1994.

Miller, Arthur. *Timebends: A Life*. London: Methuen, 1987.

Polster, Joshua E. *Reinterpreting the Plays of Arthur Miller*. Lewiston, NY: Edwin Mellen Press, 2010.

Welland, Dennis. *Arthur Miller: The Playwright*. London: Methuen, 1983.

Miller, Glenn *(1904–1944)*

A bandleader, trombonist, composer, and arranger, Glenn Miller was one of America's most prominent musical figures during the big band era in the 1930s and first half of the 1940s. Though his career as a bandleader was brief, lasting only seven years, it was highly productive. Recordings by Glenn Miller and his orchestra sold in the millions, eclipsing marks previously established by Benny Goodman. Miller's lyrical instrumentals, with their distinct groupings of the clarinet and saxophones, ushered in a unique sound in popular dance-band music. His theme song was "Moonlight Serenade," while other notable recordings included "In the Mood," "Tuxedo Junction," and "Pennsylvania 6-5000," all of which symbolized the swing era for millions of people around the world.

EARLY YEARS

Born Alton Glenn Miller on March 1, 1904, in Clarinda, Iowa, Miller moved with his family to Fort Morgan, Colorado, where he spent his formative years. His early musical exposure included listening to his mother play a pump organ at home and playing trombone with the local Boyd Senter Orchestra. Miller enrolled briefly at the University of Colorado and later studied orchestral arranging with Joseph Schillinger. He did extensive work as a sideman with various groups, including stints with Ben Pollack in 1926 and 1927, Paul Ash in 1928, Red Nichols in 1929 and 1930, and the Dorsey Brothers in 1934. Miller was much in demand as a studio musician in New York City in the 1930s and, thus, was paid well. Along with bandleader Tommy Dorsey, he was also a frequent sideman with jazz clarinetist Benny Goodman. By 1935 Miller was the de facto leader, coorganizer, and sideman for Ray Noble's American band. He also admired the Jimmie Lunceford and Count Basie bands.

Glenn Miller. *Glenn Miller and his orchestra were one of the most prominent icons of the big-band era.* MICHAEL OCHS ARCHIVES/ STRINGER/GETTY IMAGES.

In 1937 Miller decided to form his own orchestra, but it disbanded when its recordings sold poorly, as did a 1938 successor that suffered the same commercial fate. In 1939 his third band obtained work at the prestigious Glen Island Casino in the suburbs of New Rochelle, New York. The band's next date was at the Meadowbrook in New Jersey. Both venues featured the orchestra in radio broadcasts, and by midsummer it had achieved a national following. That same year the band began a series of radio broadcasts for Chesterfield cigarettes, reaching phenomenal peaks of popularity with a series of hit records and winning the *Down Beat* poll for top "sweet" band in 1940 and 1941. The band also made two films, *Sun Valley Serenade* (1941) and *Orchestra Wives* (1942).

HITTING HIS STRIDE

The recordings by Glenn Miller and his band were not strong on jazz improvisation. Only a few soloists were featured on each release, although more appeared at live dance dates. An important addition to the band was the Modernaires, an excellent vocal quartet that performed on such hits as "Chattanooga Choo Choo," which sold a million records within six months of its release in 1941. Ray Eberle was featured on ballads such as "At Last" and "Serenade in Blue." In his seminal study *The Swing Era*, Gunther Schuller observes, "The essence of Miller's formula was a kind of smoothed-out jazz: reliable, consistent, sufficiently predictable not to disturb but colorful enough to retain a mild element of surprise, and, above all, not too emotional or deeply expressive, i.e. an attractive patina rather than the real thing." Although Miller rarely played or arranged in later years in order to concentrate on achieving the widest public appeal for his orchestra, he employed the best in the business to do it, including Bill Finegan (who arranged "Little Brown Jug") and Jerry Gray ("Pennsylvania 6-5000").

The band's first recordings in 1939 were eclectic; these were followed with songs that incorporated a swing beat. Several hits came after the Glen Island Casino booking, including "Moonlight Serenade" (a Miller composition), "Sunrise Serenade," and "Little Brown Jug." "In the Mood," released in 1939, was Miller's most monumental hit.

The Miller sound permeated the popular music of the time, and it remains the most nostalgically evocative of the swing era. While not a style or genre, the Miller sound is distinctive, thanks to its unique and skillful use of the band's reed section, which features Wilbur Schwartz's fervent and throbbing clarinet over four saxes. Another Miller trademark is the repetition of a riff until it softly fades away, only to suddenly return at full volume. Each contrasting texture (reeds or brass) is tied to a dynamic level.

AIR FORCE YEARS

In September 1942, in an act of patriotism, Miller joined the air force, leaving behind an extremely lucrative career as a bandleader. His earnings had been estimated at $100,000 per month from recordings alone. In a public statement that shocked the music world, he said, "I, like every American, have an obligation to fulfill. . . . It is not enough for me to sit back and buy bonds." Once in uniform, he proceeded to form the war's most famous service band, which consisted of forty-two pieces, including a nineteen-person jazz component comparable to his civilian band (plus one French horn) and a twenty-piece string ensemble. The band was based in New Haven, Connecticut, and in the spring of 1943, it initiated a series of weekly coast-to-coast air force recruitment radio broadcasts. A year later, orders came for the band to go to England. The band was augmented with three arrangers, a copyist, and five singers, and its performances in England were broadcast over the BBC.

On December 15, 1944, Miller boarded a small plane in London and headed to Paris, which had been liberated that summer, to make arrangements for the band's arrival there. The plane disappeared in flight. Miller's death was mourned internationally, and he was honored as a war hero. His band played in Paris under the direction of Jerry Gray and Ray McKinley for a six-week engagement that was extended to six months because of its popularity.

After the band returned to the United States, Tex Beneke kept its legacy alive with a new group called the Glenn Miller Band with Tex Beneke. In 1954 the *Glenn Miller Story*, a film vaguely based on his life, was released. Beginning in 1956 and for a decade thereafter, a band sanctioned by the Miller estate toured the United States and internationally under his name and under the direction of McKinley.

Miller's short but rich career produced a legacy that evokes the lively musical style of the late Depression and World War II years. During the 1970s the lines "Boy, the way Glenn Miller played / Songs that made the hit parade . . . " were heard by millions each week, sung by Archie and Edith Bunker as the theme song to the sitcom *All in the Family*. Those words resonated with a generation that believed American popular music had lost its way in the raucous years following World War II. Three of Miller's songs—"Moonlight Serenade," "In the Mood," and "Bluebird B-10416-A"—have been inducted into the Grammy Hall of Fame, and he posthumously received a Grammy Lifetime Achievement Award in 2003.

Willie Collins

SEE ALSO: All in the Family*; Basie, Count; Big Bands; Dorsey, Jimmy; Dorsey, Tommy; Goodman, Benny; Grammy Awards; The Great Depression; Swing Dancing; World War II.*

BIBLIOGRAPHY

Schuller, Gunther. *The Swing Era: The Development of Jazz, 1930–1945*. New York: Oxford University Press, 1989.

Simon, George T. *The Big Bands*. New York: Macmillan, 1967.

Simon, George T. *Glenn Miller and His Orchestra*. New York: Da Capo Press, 1980.

Snow, George, and Jonathan Green. *Glenn Miller and the Age of Swing*. London: Dempsey and Squires, 1976.

Miller, Henry *(1891–1980)*

Henry Miller was an American-born bohemian writer whose works, with D. H. Lawrence's, are the first respected books of the twentieth century containing explicit sex. His first and most famous book is *Tropic of Cancer* (1934), an autobiographical novel portraying Miller's promiscuous Paris lifestyle. His subsequent works—including *Tropic of Capricorn* (1939); *The World of Sex* (1940); and the trilogy *Sexus*, *Plexus*, and *Nexus* (1949–1960)—are similarly explicit and autobiographical, while also rich with brilliant commentary on the nature and meaning of being a freethinking artist-writer in the modern world.

Though personal and nonpolitical, Miller's work is often considered obscene and as such has often been censored in the United States and the United Kingdom. Nevertheless, Miller has always been widely read and is the key precursor to the 1950s Beat writers and to the sexually frank hippie writers of the 1960s. Miller is also known for his paintings, his 1941 travel narrative on Greece, and his relationship with diarist and critic Anaïs Nin.

David Elroy Goldweber

SEE ALSO: *The Beat Generation; Best Sellers; Ginsberg, Allen.*

BIBLIOGRAPHY

Brassai, and Timothy Bent. *Henry Miller: The Paris Years*. New York: Arcade, 2011.

Ferguson, Robert. *Henry Miller: A Life*. New York: W. W. Norton, 1993.

Gordon, William A. *The Mind and Art of Henry Miller*. Baton Rouge: Louisiana State University Press, 1967.

Kersnowski, Frank L., and Alice Hughes, eds. *Conversations with Henry Miller*. Jackson: University Press of Mississippi, 1994.

Miller, Roger *(1936–1992)*

Songwriter and singer Roger Miller is best known for his humorous novelty songs that topped the country music charts in the mid-1960s. Miller was born in Fort Worth, Texas, in 1936, but after the death of his father, his mother underwent a serious illness, and Miller went to live with his aunt and uncle in Erick, Oklahoma, a small farming community. Leaving school at the end of the eighth grade, Miller worked as a ranch hand and rodeo rider. During these years, he taught himself to play guitar, banjo, fiddle, piano, and drums. Leaving Oklahoma to join the army, Miller was stationed in Korea, where he worked as a jeep driver. Displaying his musical skills on the side, he was soon transferred to the army's special services division, where he became part of a hillbilly band entertaining the troops. His success there encouraged him to pursue a musical career after leaving the army in 1957.

Miller went to Nashville in 1957, where he worked as a bellhop while writing songs on the side. His success in getting established Nashville singers to record his songs was limited until Ray Price recorded Miller's "Invitation to the Blues." The song became a hit, and Miller went to work as a songwriter in country singer Faron Young's music company. He wrote a number of hit songs there, including "That's the Way I Feel" for Faron Young, "Half a Mind" for Ernest Tubb, and "Billy Bayou"

Roger Miller. *Singer and songwriter Roger Miller is best known for his country-tinged novelty songs of the 1960s.* **SILVER SCREEN COLLECTION/CONTRIBUTOR/MOVIEPIX/GETTY IMAGES.**

for Jim Reeves. His success in songwriting renewed his interest in becoming a recording artist himself. He had a hit with "You Don't Want My Love" and "When Two Worlds Collide" on the RCA label in 1961.

Miller took his newfound success as a performer to Hollywood, where he briefly studied acting and became a regular guest on such popular shows as *The Jimmy Dean Show* and *The Merv Griffin Show.* In Hollywood, Miller developed a new style that became his hallmark sound. Instead of the straightforward country-pop sound popular in Nashville at the time, Miller developed a rather goofy and humorous persona showcasing novelty songs.

In "Dang Me," a Top 10 hit in 1964, Miller sang about a standard country music theme—a man out honky-tonking and drinking his paycheck away while his wife and month-old baby sat at home alone—but he did so in a humorous style. "Dang me, dang me," he sang, "they oughta take a rope and hang me." The bouncy country beat and Miller's country-scat style of singing put a brighter tone on this story of a man feeling guilty about his actions but not enough to do anything about it. That same year Miller scored a hit with "Chug-a-Lug," a song about discovering alcohol on a Future Farmers of America/Four-H field trip. Miller's slurred speech and funny noises added to the novelty effect of the song.

In 1965 Miller scored his biggest hit with "King of the Road," a lighthearted song about a hobo singer. It spent five weeks in the Top 10 of the country music charts. That year became Miller's most successful year. Along with "King of the Road," he scored Top 10 hits with "Engine, Engine No. 9," "One Dyin' and Buryin'," and "Kansas City Star." In 1966 he had a Top 10 hit with "England Swings" and enjoyed a brief run on NBC television as the star of his own weekly show.

After these successes, Miller's career declined. Some of his songs continued to be hits for other artists, including Andy Williams's cover of "In the Summer Time" and Eddy Arnold's rendition of "The Last Word in Lonesome Is Me." He also had a few hits with his recordings of songs by other writers, including Bobby Russell's "Little Green Apples" in 1968 and Kris Kristofferson's "Me and Bobby McGee" in 1969. In the 1970s he turned his attention more to business concerns such as his "King of the Road" hotel chain. He did, however, write songs for Walt Disney's animated film *Robin Hood,* and he had hits with "Open Up Your Heart" and "Tomorrow Night in Baltimore." Miller's last major work was music he wrote for *Big River,* a 1985 Tony Award–winning Broadway musical based on the works of Mark Twain. Miller died in 1992 after a brief battle with throat cancer.

Timothy Berg

SEE ALSO: *Country Music; Twain, Mark; Williams, Andy.*

BIBLIOGRAPHY

The Country Music Foundation, eds. *Country: The Music and the Musicians.* New York: Abbeville Press, 1994.

Malone, Bill C. *Country Music U.S.A.: A Fifty Year History,* rev. ed. Austin: American Folklore Society/University of Texas Press, 1985.

Miller, Roger. *Best of Roger Miller: His Greatest Songs.* CD. Curb Records, 1991.

Miller, Roger. *Super Hits.* CD. Epic Records, 1996.

Stambler, Irwin, and Grelun Landon. *Country Music: The Encyclopedia.* New York: St. Martin's Press, 1997.

Miller Beer

In 1855, when Frederick J. Miller purchased the abandoned Plank Road Brewery in Wisconsin for $3,510, he could not have imagined the success his enterprise would achieve. By the 1990s the Miller Brewing Company had become the second-largest brewery in the United States, and its top brands—Miller High Life and Miller Lite—were household names. Miller's feat can be attributed to the phenomenally successful marketing campaign started when Philip Morris purchased the company in 1969. Using former athletes and other celebrities to promote their products, Miller's marketers coined snappy catchphrases that entered everyday language. Slogans such as "Welcome to Miller Time" successfully transformed Miller High Life from an upscale to a popular product, while "Less Filling, Tastes Great" and "Everything you always wanted in a beer . . . and less" convinced men that Miller Lite was not just for weight-conscious women. These successes sent the company's profile and profits soaring, and the beer was established as a staple ingredient of American life by the end of the twentieth century.

In 2003 Miller's attempts to promote the sale of light beer to college students ran afoul of the National Collegiate Athletic Association (NCAA), which vetoed a commercial proposed for broadcast during March Madness (the men's division college basketball tournament). The ad depicted two well-endowed women catfighting over whether the most important characteristic of the beer was that it tasted great or that it was less filling. The NCAA maintained that the commercial could promote alcohol abuse on college campuses, where it was already a problem. Instead, Miller aired ads showing males trading "yo mamma" jokes and women dreaming of pulverizing wayward boyfriends. In 2008 Miller joined forces with Coors, formerly its chief rival, as MillerCoors, in order to coordinate American production and distribution of their combined products.

Alexander Shashko

SEE ALSO: *Advertising; Basketball; Beer; Celebrity; Consumerism; Coors; National Collegiate Athletic Association (NCAA).*

BIBLIOGRAPHY

Apps, Jerry. *Breweries of Wisconsin.* Madison: University of Wisconsin Press, 1992.

Deford, Frank. *Lite Reading.* New York: Penguin, 1984.

"Tastes Great, but Less . . . Decorum?" *Chronicle of Higher Education* 49, no. 32 (2003).

Milli Vanilli

The popular music group Milli Vanilli rose to worldwide fame on the strength of their hit singles and compelling stage presence but will be remembered most for their inauthenticity. Established in 1988, the pop duo consisted of the attractive and charismatic Rob Pilatus (1965–1998) and Fabrice Morvan (1966–), who—unbeknownst to the audience—danced and lip-synched to the songs of the unattractive U.S. studio band Numarx.

The Milli Vanilli hit "Girl You Know It's True" reached number two on the U.S. pop charts in 1989, and the group's next releases ("Baby Don't Forget My Number," "Blame It on the Rain," and "Girl I'm Gonna Miss You") all reached number one. Not until after Milli Vanilli won the 1989 Grammy Award for Best New Artist, however, did the public find out that Pilatus and Morvan did not actually sing on their records or onstage. The two sported a trendy, marketable look—wearing body-contoured bike shorts and T-shirts and having shoulder-length dreadlocks—but they apparently possessed no musical talent. The record producer Frankie Farian had offered them $4,000 each plus royalties to dance and lip-synch to "Girl You Know It's True" on European television, and after the song became a worldwide hit, the duo continued the scam on television and onstage.

Pilatus and Morvan alleged that Farian promised them studio time but never delivered, and, after their song became a hit, the two were so enamored of the celebrity lifestyle that they preferred not to give up the illusion and continued to lip-synch. When the world learned the duo was mere window dressing, the Grammy committee rescinded their award. Twenty-seven lawsuits alleged fraud against Arista Records, BMG (Arista's parent company), and several concert promoters. More than 80,000 rebates of up to $3 each were given to all individuals who could prove they purchased a Milli Vanilli record or concert ticket.

In 1991 Farian released an album by the real Milli Vanilli (that is, Numarx), but the public ignored it. Two years later Pilatus and Morvan, under the name Rob & Fab, recorded a self-titled album that failed commercially and critically. A cable television documentary on the lives of the duo revealed a post-scandal downhill trajectory into debt, depression, drugs, and suicide attempts on the part of Pilatus (with a premature death from heart failure at the age of thirty-two) and a relatively low-profile life of ignominy on the part of Morvan. He worked as a disc jockey, motivational speaker, and record producer and eventually released a solo album in 2003. In 2011 it was announced that he would be involved with a film based on the duo to be produced by the Kennedy/Marshall Company.

The tragicomedy of Milli Vanilli reinforced the cynicism in popular culture that had begun as a backlash to the rigging of *The $64,000 Question* and other quiz shows in the late 1950s. The duo's legacy lives on whenever someone is revealed lip-synching, such as Ashlee Simpson on her *Saturday Night Live* appearance in 2004. Even when musicians Yo-Yo Ma, Itzhak Perlman, Gabriela Montero, and Anthony McGill performed to a prerecorded track at President Barack Obama's 2009 inaugural, the Associated Press headline read "Just don't call it the inaugural Milli Vanilli."

Tilney Marsh

SEE ALSO: *Grammy Awards; Obama, Barack; Pop Music; Quiz Show Scandals;* Saturday Night Live.

BIBLIOGRAPHY

George-Warren, Holly; Nina Pearlman; Jordan M. Mamone; et al., eds. *The Rolling Stone Encyclopedia of Rock & Roll.* New York: Rolling Stone Press, 1995.

Shriver, Jerry. "Milli Vanilli, 20 Years Later." *USA Today,* January 26, 2010.

Million Man March

On October 16, 1995, approximately 1.2 million African American men converged on the nation's capital to participate in the historic Million Man March, spearheaded by Louis Farrakhan, the controversial head of the Nation of Islam. The march was a call for black men to "look inward at ourselves, what we are, what we have become . . . and what we can do to be better people and help build black communities."

Men from all over the country traveled by bus, plane, train, and automobile to take part in the fifteen-hour event, in what would become the largest gathering of African Americans in the nation's history. Those who could not attend were asked to stay away from work in honor of the march and watch it on television, where all the major networks carried live extensive coverage. Millions watched the monumental event on television, witnessing black men from diverse backgrounds make a pledge to reclaim their communities. In the aftermath of the march there was no question that Farrakhan was, according to author Michael H. Cottman, "now one of the most influential leaders in black America."

Leonard N. Moore

SEE ALSO: *Black Panthers; Civil Rights Movement.*

BIBLIOGRAPHY

Cottman, Michael H., and Deborah Willis. *Million Man*

March. New York: Crown Trade Paperbacks, 1995.

Smith, Robert C. *Encyclopedia of African American Politics*. New York: Facts On File, 2003.

Milton Bradley

Milton Bradley is well known as the producer of such popular American games as Chutes and Ladders, Parcheesi, The Game of Life, and Yahtzee. The company was founded in 1860 by a lithographer named Milton Bradley who, during the Civil War, purchased a game called The Checkered Game of Life from an inventor. By 1868 Bradley had established himself as the leading manufacturer of games in the United States. In the 1950s the company was the first to market home versions of popular television game shows. The first of these was Concentration, followed by Password and Jeopardy. On the hundredth anniversary of the company, Bradley's original game was reissued as The Game of Life. Hasbro, the second leading toy producer after Mattel, purchased Milton Bradley in 1984. In the twenty-first century, Hasbro has continued to attract new audiences to classic Milton Bradley games by rereleasing updated editions of Battleship, Candyland, Chutes and Ladders, Connect 4, The Game of Life, Hungry Hungry Hippos, Operation, Scattergories, and Twister.

Robin Lent

SEE ALSO: *Board Games; Game Shows;* Jeopardy!*; Toys; Twister.*

BIBLIOGRAPHY

Miller, Raymond H. *Milton Bradley*. Detroit, MI: KidHaven Press, 2005.

Shea, James J., Jr. *It's All in the Game*. New York: Putnam, 1960.

Shea, James J., Jr. *The Milton Bradley Story*. New York: Newcomen Society, 1973.

Minimalism

"Less is more," proclaimed the architect Ludwig Mies van der Rohe, echoing the words of Robert Browning in *Andrea del Sarto* (1855) and the gist of Hesiod (c. 700 BCE), who advised "how much more is the half than the whole." In its broadest sense minimalism refers to any form of human expression whose elements have been reduced, simplified, or even eliminated altogether. More specifically, the term has come to denote movements in painting, sculpture, architecture, and music—largely American—that flowered in the 1960s and were still influential at the beginning of the twenty-first century. While many of its best examples have provided viewers or listeners with genuinely moving aesthetic experiences, minimalism is also notable for the degree to which it has tested artistic limits and the patience of audiences. In twentieth-century popular culture, minimal forms from the highway billboard to the sixty-second sound bite have exemplified Mies's dictum.

The quintessential minimalist painting of the 1960s was a monochrome square and its sculptural counterpart a simple geometric solid. Kazimir Malevich's *Suprematist Composition: White on White* (1918) and Aleksandr Rodchenko's *Black on Black* of the same year prepared the way for Robert Rauschenberg's all-white paintings of the early 1950s and Ad Reinhardt's all-black paintings of the 1960s. Barnett Newman, Ellsworth Kelly, Robert Ryman, Frank Stella, Brice Marden, and Agnes Martin are other names associated with minimalist painting of the 1960s. Influential early-twentieth-century precursors of 1960s minimalist sculpture include Marcel Duchamp's found objects or "readymades" and Constantin Brancusi's elegant and highly simplified forms such as *Bird in Space*. Donald Judd, Carl Andre, Robert Morris, and Tony Smith are among the leading figures of 1960s sculptural minimalism. Much minimalist art shares an anonymous impersonality and formal simplicity, but motives behind the pieces have undoubtedly ranged from the purely aesthetic to dadaist playfulness, from expressionism to reactionism and philosophical point making.

Minimal music (also called system or repetitive music) downplays or eliminates certain elements such as melody or harmony while emphasizing others, especially repetition and gradual change, sometimes to the point of alienating new audiences, but other times with beautiful and hypnotic effects. Best known of the minimal composer/performers who came of age in the 1960s are La Monte Young, Terry Riley, Steve Reich, and Philip Glass, all classically trained but variously influenced by eclectic sources including the music of non-European cultures, jazz, and ambient sounds. Glass, who has composed the music for operas such as *Einstein on the Beach* (1976) and films such as *Koyaanisqatsi* (1983), has enjoyed the most commercial success of this group. Brian Eno, David Byrne, Kraftwerk, and a variety of new age musicians have been influenced by minimal music.

Among the most interesting examples of minimalism are those that have severely tested its limits. John Cage's "4' 33"," a 1952 composition in which the musician performs nothing for four minutes and thirty-three seconds, is capable of uniquely attuning the listener to ambient audience sounds. Cage was greatly entertained and impressed with the dramatic interplay of dust particles in Nam June Paik's otherwise imageless sixty-minute film *Zen for Film* (1964). Andy Warhol produced a number of intentionally boring films, including *Sleep* (1963), in which a man is seen sleeping for six hours. At another extreme are certain truly massive, though formally minimal, works of architecture and sculpture. In 1998 Richard Serra oversaw the temporary installation of his nine steel sculptures weighing a total of 750 tons at a Los Angeles museum.

While the lines of influence are not always clear, minimalism in its broadest sense has been at work or play in an intriguing range of twentieth-century contexts: the unadorned, rectilinear glass and steel architecture of Mies and Philip Johnson; the sound bite, the short attention span, and the fifteen minutes of fame predicted for all by Warhol; billboards, television commercials, and advertisements in general; the message of Simon and Garfunkel's "The Sound of Silence" and the cover of *The Beatles* (better known as *The White Album*); the smiley face, the peace sign, and the corporate logo; the hula hoop and the pet rock; the miniskirt and the Volkswagen Beetle; E. F. Schumacher's *Small Is Beautiful*; and the comic strip and the cartoon. *Seinfeld*, the enormously popular television series of the 1990s sometimes described erroneously to be "a show about nothing," often had much to say about the minutiae of daily life. *Art*, Yasmina Reza's drama featuring an all-white painting, won the 1998 Tony Award for Best Play.

Whatever its motives, minimalism played a role in late-twentieth-century America that was far from minimal. In the twenty-first century minimalism continues to influence architecture, but its most recognizable manifestation in popular culture is in technology, in particular the designs of computers and portable devices by Jonathan Ive for Apple Inc.

Craig Bunch

SEE ALSO: *Apple Computer; The Beatles; Hula Hoop; Pet Rocks;* Seinfeld*; Simon and Garfunkel; Tony Awards; Volkswagen Beetle; Warhol, Andy.*

BIBLIOGRAPHY

Baker, Kenneth. *Minimalism.* New York: Abbeville Press, 1988.

Battcock, Gregory, ed. *Minimal Art: A Critical Anthology.* New York: E. P. Dutton, 1968.

Cage, John, in conversation with Joan Retallack. *Musicage: Cage Muses on Words, Art, Music.* Hanover, CT: Wesleyan University Press, 1996.

Colpitt, Frances. *Minimal Art: The Critical Perspective.* Seattle: University of Washington Press, 1993.

Mertens, Wim. *American Minimal Music: La Monte Young, Terry Riley, Steve Reich, Philip Glass*, tr. J. Hautekiet. London: Kahn & Averill, 1983.

Obendorf, Hartmut. *Minimalism: Designing Simplicity.* London: Springer, 2009.

Strickland, Edward. *Minimalism: Origins.* Bloomington: Indiana University Press, 1993.

Zelevansky, Lynn. *Sense and Sensibility: Women Artists and Minimalism in the Nineties.* New York: Museum of Modern Art, 1994.

Miniskirts

SEE: *Hemlines.*

Minivans

Associated in the minds of some demographers with baby boomers and soccer moms, minivans are a type of automotive vehicle that largely replaced the family station wagon in the 1980s and 1990s as a "kid hauler," though they shared that title by end of the 1990s with sport utility vehicles (SUVs). The most popular early versions of the boxy vehicles, which were manufactured by Chrysler Corporation and introduced by its media-savvy chairman Lee Iacocca, are even credited with saving Chrysler from automotive extinction. In *Behind the Wheel at Chrysler*, Doron P. Levin points out the connection between Chrysler's development of the minivan and its economic health, noting, "Rarely had a company so close to bankruptcy sprung back to health with the vigor of Chrysler." Brock Yates went even further in *The Critical Path: Inventing an Automobile and Reinventing a Corporation*, describing minivans as "the true salvation of the Chrysler product line" and positing that the Dodge Caravan and Plymouth Voyager "created an entire new market category for Chrysler and the automobile industry as a whole." The enthusiastic Yates then hailed minivans as one of "a handful of legitimate milestone vehicles [that] turned and expanded the market in new directions due to their revolutionary qualities."

Indeed, their impact was revolutionary, as the 1980s saw minivans quickly replace station wagons in shopping malls around the country as well as in carpool lines and at Little League games. As one of the first vehicles that was deliberately designed with the growing number of female drivers in mind, the minivan was also a clear response to the women's liberation movement, and many of its characteristic features were clearly targeted to women: low step-up height, carlike feel and handling, and built-in child seats. Moreover, several manufacturers deliberately placed female engineers in charge of their design teams to make sure that no appealing family-oriented innovations were missed.

Chrysler Minivan. *The Chrysler minivan became immediately popular with families when it first hit showrooms in 1984.* AP IMAGES.

The immediate popularity of the minivan, which first appeared in automotive showrooms in January 1984, probably stems from both the way it was designed (although associated with Iacocca, minivans are actually the brainchild of Hal Sperlich, a design engineer who also played a key role in developing the popular Ford Mustang in the late 1960s) and from the fact that Chrysler undertook careful research to figure out what potential drivers wanted in a vehicle. In fact, the manufacturer continued to do so—as Yates enthusiastically points out about the innovative 1996 redesign of the minivan. Instead of designing the vehicle from the outside in (Detroit's usual practice), the Chrysler design team "defied convention by first establishing rigid interior dimensions and then wrapping them in a boxlike structure. They decided on an interior height of four feet with a width of five feet—including a full four feet between the rear wheels in order to accommodate what had become an industry storage benchmark: a 4x8-foot sheet of plywood." Yates also observes that Chrysler employed a polling firm that learned potential customers wanted a vehicle that handled like a car and had flexible seating, easily removable seats, and room for as many as seven passengers.

While Chrysler had introduced a product in the 1980s that clearly met the practical needs of drivers, minivans seemed to also meet an emotional need of baby boomers who remembered the vans of their youth, including the Volkswagen Microbus, which was introduced in 1949 and became a primary means of transportation for 1960s flower children and California surfers, and the Corvair Greenbriar, introduced eleven years later. Although Volkswagen continues to manufacture vans, their poor handling prevents them from achieving the popularity of Chrysler's products, and the Greenbriar was a victim of anti-Corvair publicity.

Chrysler held a near monopoly on minivan sales for five years and introduced a total redesign in 1996 that received *Motor Trend* magazine's coveted "Car of the Year" award—the first minivan to be so honored. Chrysler was quickly joined by competition from Ford, General Motors, Toyota, Honda, and Mazda, which introduced their own versions of the popular vehicle. However, by the late 1990s, as their children left the nest, baby boomers no longer needed a vehicle that would seat seven people. As sales collapsed, many manufacturers dropped their minivans altogether, and the vehicle of choice at suburban malls at the end of the millennium became equally boxy SUVs. Meanwhile, industry leaders upgraded their minivan offerings with ever-increasing levels of sophistication, particularly in terms of convenience and entertainment electronics, such as the ubiquitous backseat DVD screens. As a result, the vehicle that harkens back to the colorfully painted Volkswagen bus of the 1960s has remained a familiar sight on the highways and suburban streets of America.

Carol A. Senf
James Farlow

SEE ALSO: *Baby Boomers; Ford Motor Company; General Motors; Hippies; Iacocca, Lee; Sport Utility Vehicles (SUVs).*

BIBLIOGRAPHY

Levin, Doron P. *Behind the Wheel at Chrysler: The Iacocca Legacy.* New York: Harcourt Brace, 1995.

Warner, Mark. *How to Keep Your Minivan Alive!* New York: HPBooks, 2004.

Yates, Brock. *The Critical Path: Inventing an Automobile and Reinventing a Corporation.* Boston: Little, Brown, 1996.

Minnelli, Liza *(1946–)*

In a career that has spanned more than five decades in movies, music, theater, and television, Liza Minnelli has proven herself to be among the nation's most versatile and resilient entertainers. Exemplified by her electrifying debut as a teenage nightclub singer, her starring turns on camera as Kit Kat Klub performer Sally Bowles in *Cabaret* (1972) and shoplifting waitress Linda Marolla in *Arthur* (1981), and her triumphant return to Broadway in her one-woman show *Liza's at the Palace* (2008) after a debilitating case of viral encephalitis, Minnelli has entertained a wide and enduring audience.

As of 2012 she was one of only six women to have won Emmy, Grammy, Oscar, and Tony awards. Yet she is also well known for a turbulent personal life that has included four marriages (to songwriter Peter Allen, director Jack Haley Jr., sculptor Mark Gero, and promoter David Gest), tabloid romances with former child star Desi Arnaz Jr. and comic Peter Sellers, and accusations of alleged violence against her personal staff. In her later years she has enjoyed recognition as a campy icon among the homosexual community while engaging in serious philanthropic work on behalf of AIDS research.

Minnelli was born on March 12, 1946, in Hollywood, California, the daughter of actress Judy Garland and director Vincente Minnelli. Garland and Minnelli's tempestuous relationship ended in 1951, and Garland married producer Sidney Luft, the father of Minnelli's half-siblings John, Joey, and Lorna. Minnelli also has a half-sister, Nina, from her father's second marriage (to Georgette Magnani). The collapse of her parents' marriage, and their subsequent relationships—the two were married a combined nine times—formed the backdrop of a turbulent childhood marked by extremes of glamour and suffering. As a young girl, Minnelli accompanied her father to shoots at Metro-Goldwyn-Mayer's (MGM) studios and watched stars Fred Astaire and Gene Kelly in rehearsal. Yet as a teenager, she also had to manage the household as Garland descended into the throes of addiction and depression; she once had to grab her mother's feet to keep her from jumping from a hotel window. By the time of Garland's death in 1969, Minnelli was largely estranged from her troubled mother.

Although two-year-old Minnelli made a brief appearance in her mother's film *In the Good Old Summertime* in 1949, her entertainment career began in earnest with her debut in the off-Broadway revival of the musical *Best Foot Forward* in 1963. Two years later she won a Tony Award for Best Actress in a Musical for her role in the Broadway premiere of librettist George Abbott's *Flora the Red Menace*. However, it was as a tireless nightclub singer and recording artist during the 1960s that Minnelli first garnered a national fan base. Her first album with Capitol Records, *Liza! Liza!* (1964), sold half a million copies, and before the age of twenty-one, Minnelli was reportedly earning $400,000 a year. Although following albums *It Amazes Me* (1965) and *There Is a Time* (1966) did not sell as well as her first, they received positive acclaim from critics.

Film roles soon followed, including the quirky romance *The Sterile Cuckoo* (1969) with Wendell Burton, and director Otto Preminger's disturbing *Tell Me That You Love Me, Junie Moon* (1970). By the time she won an Academy Award for her performance across from Joel Grey in *Cabaret*, Minnelli had earned a reputation as one of Hollywood's most durable and driven stars, and she found herself frequently compared to fellow singer Barbra Streisand, whose career she had helped jump-start by getting her booked on *The Judy Garland Show* in 1963.

Minnelli need this stamina, as the next decade was filled with a series of box-office disappointments and critical setbacks, including *Lucky Lady* (1975); *A Matter of Time* (1976); and *New York, New York* (1977), although the title song in the last of these failures has become a theme for the singer. She made the first of her unexpected comebacks in *Arthur*, for which she received a Golden Globe nomination, and followed up with a Drama Desk Award nomination for the musical *The Rink* (1984).

Now a veteran performer with an international following, Minnelli scored with hit albums *Results* (1989) and *Gently* (1996), and a Top 20 dance single, "Losing My Mind" (1988). When she replaced Julie Andrews as the lead in *Victor/Victoria* in 1997, it was the culmination of what had become a chronic story of setbacks and surpassed expectations. Even a bout of viral encephalitis in 2000 that left Minnelli temporary wheelchair-bound and unable to sing—and led to numerous, premature professional obituaries—proved unable to derail her career permanently. As of 2012, Minnelli continues to make appearances on television and has served as a guest judge on *Australian Idol* (2009), proof of her international popularity.

No modern American entertainer has managed to create a reputation for herself as a perpetual underdog as effectively as Minnelli, whose alluring blend of frailty and optimism have made her a crowd favorite over three generations.

Jacob M. Appel

SEE ALSO: *Academy Awards; AIDS; Astaire, Fred, and Ginger Rogers; Broadway; Camp; Emmy Awards; Garland, Judy; Grammy Awards; Hollywood; Kelly, Gene; Live Television; MGM (Metro-Goldwyn-Mayer); Minnelli, Vincente; The Musical; Pop Music; Preminger, Otto; Reality Television; Sellers, Peter; Streisand, Barbra; Television; Tony Awards.*

BIBLIOGRAPHY

Clarke, Gerald. *Get Happy*. New York: Delta, 2001.

Mair, George. *Under the Rainbow: The Real Liza Minnelli*. Secaucus, NJ: Carol Publishing, 1996.

Petrucelli, Alan W. *Liza! Liza!: An Unauthorized Biography of Liza Minnelli*. Bromley, UK: Columbus Books, 1983.

Minnelli, Vincente *(1903–1986)*

Hollywood's preeminent director of movie musicals during the 1940s and 1950s, Vincente Minnelli was a master stylist. Characterized by a bold use of color and movement, an elegant sense of visual design, and imaginative development of surreal fantasy sequences, Minnelli's directorial style is epitomized in his masterworks *Meet Me in St. Louis* (1944); *An American in Paris* (1951); *The Band Wagon* (1953); and *Gigi* (1958), the film for which he won an Academy Award for Best Director.

While critics suggested Minnelli's work was more decorative than substantive, they praised his nonmusical films *The Bad and the Beautiful* (1952) and *Lust for Life* (1956) and agreed that the tasteful modernism he brought to his celluloid canvases lent sophistication to the art of film entertainment. Minnelli figured prominently in celebrity gossip, due to his marriage to screen star Judy Garland in 1945 and the fame of their daughter, entertainer Liza Minnelli.

Lisa Jo Sagolla

SEE ALSO: *Academy Awards; Celebrity Couples; Garland, Judy; Hollywood;* Meet Me in St. Louis*; Minnelli, Liza; The Musical.*

BIBLIOGRAPHY

Casper, Joseph Andrew. *Vincente Minnelli and the Film Musical*. New York: A. S. Barnes, 1977.

Harvey, Stephen. *Directed by Vincente Minnelli*. New York: Harper & Row, 1989.

Hischak, Thomas S. *The Oxford Companion to the American Musical: Theatre, Film, and Television*. New York: Oxford University Press, 2008.

Minnelli, Vincente, and Hector Arce. *I Remember It Well*. London: Angus & Robertson, 1974.

Minoso, Minnie *(1922–)*

A former player in the Negro Leagues, Cuban-born Minnie Minoso made his major-league debut with the Cleveland Indians in 1949. In 1951 the *Sporting News* named him Rookie of the Year for leading the American League in steals and triples. That same year he became the Chicago White Sox's first black player. A three-time stolen-base champion, Minoso hit for power and average. He spent most of his career with the Indians and White Sox as an outfielder, but he also had stints in St. Louis, Missouri, and Washington, D.C.

A seven-time All-Star and three-time Gold Glove winner, Minoso retired in 1964 with a .298 career batting average. He briefly returned to the White Sox in 1976 and at fifty-three became the oldest player to collect a hit. In 1980 he became the second major leaguer to bat in five different decades. His appearances with the Northern League's St. Paul Saints in 1993 and 2003 made him the only professional baseball player to compete in seven different decades. A fan favorite, Minoso also served as a goodwill ambassador for the White Sox.

Matt Kerr

SEE ALSO: *Baseball; Major League Baseball; Negro Leagues; The* Sporting News*; Sports Heroes.*

BIBLIOGRAPHY

Minoso, Minnie. *Extra Innings: My Life in Baseball*. Chicago: Regnery Gateway, 1983.

Minoso, Minnie, and Herb Fagen. *Just Call Me Minnie: My Six Decades in Baseball*. Champaign, IL: Sagamore, 1994.

Minstrel Shows

Originating around 1830 and peaking in popularity twenty years later, the minstrel show used blackface comedy to appeal primarily to the average American. Especially prominent in urban centers in the northeastern United States, minstrel shows had a profound impact on nineteenth-century Americans, including Mark Twain, who remarked in his *Autobiography*: "If I could have the nigger show back again . . . I should have but little further use for opera." Although its popularity declined by 1900, the minstrel show continued to shape American popular entertainment. Today it remains a topic of intense historical and political debate, reviled for its racism—including its exploitation of black culture—and remembered as the first indigenous form of American popular culture.

MINSTRELSY IN ANTEBELLUM AMERICA

Thomas D. Rice, an itinerant blackface performer, helped create the minstrel show in approximately 1830 when he saw an elderly black man performing a strange dance and singing, "Weel about and turn around and do jus so; / Ebery time I weel about, I jump Jim Crow." Rice borrowed the man's clothes and dance and launched a successful tour in New York City. Over the next decade, ensembles, rather than solo performers, began to dominate the industry. In 1843 one of the first minstrel show troupes, the Virginia Minstrels (which included blackface entertainer Dan Emmett), formed in New York City, the birthplace and hub of minstrel productions.

Minstrel Show Poster. *A poster promotes a minstrel show circa 1900.* © CORBIS.

As an early expression of American identity in defiance of European aristocracy, the blackface minstrel stood alongside the Yankee (the independent, honest patriot) and the backwoodsman (such as the hearty, uneducated Davy Crockett). In literature and onstage, these stock characters used comedy to subvert pretentious and immoral elites. White male performers put on blackface using burnt cork or greasepaint to offer comic commentary on a variety of topics, including women's rights and slavery; to undermine experts and authority figures; and to make fun of immigrants, Native Americans, and African Americans. The burlesque of William Shakespeare's major plays—with their exuberant physical comedy and transvestite heroines—was a regular feature of minstrelsy. The show also was the first form of American commercial entertainment to draw on black culture, prompting some scholars to approach the study of minstrelsy—often viewed as nothing more than racial stereotyping—as an example of complex intercultural exchange.

Although the minstrel show underwent many transformations in the nineteenth century, the basic structure included three distinct parts. In the first section, a pompous interlocutor stood in the center of a semicircle of performers in blackface. At either end of the semicircle were the unruly Brudder Tambo and Brudder Bones, whose names referred to the instruments they played. These "musicians," dressed in grotesque costumes and, while gesturing wildly on stage, were usually the stars of the show. They exchanged malapropisms, riddles, and one-liners, often deflating the interlocutor with their comic barbs. The second part of the show featured variety acts. The final segment was a one-act skit, usually depicting plantation life.

As tensions surrounding slavery in the United States grew, the political status of African Americans became an inescapable topic for minstrel performers. The minstrel show emerged around the time of the first publication of William Lloyd Garrison's abolitionist newspaper, the *Liberator*, and Nat Turner's slave rebellion, both of which occurred in 1831. Songs and dialogue in the minstrel show sometimes featured grotesque portrayals of the northern black dandy (Zip Coon) and the happy, errant slave (Jim Crow). Famed American songwriter Stephen Foster, who sold many of his songs to minstrel show performer E. P. Christy, depicted peaceful southern plantation life and emotional and sympathetic slaves in tunes such as "Old Folks at Home."

By evoking a sentimental image of the South and the idea of the rebellious, incompetent free black, the minstrel show unquestionably denigrated African Americans. But its depiction of slavery was also ambivalent, particularly before 1850. Black tricksters outwitted masters and, at times, criticized the cruelty of slavery, especially the breakup of slave families. Although minstrel shows, which began in the North, tended to support the Union during the Civil War, they did not support abolition, portraying the end of slavery as neither necessary nor desirable.

The place of women was also a popular topic of minstrel shows, and blackface often served as a medium of misogyny. Overwhelmingly dominated by men, particularly in the antebellum period, the minstrel show jeered at independent women and attacked women's supposed moral superiority. Performances often included songs that ridiculed women's rights:

When woman's rights is stirred a bit
De first reform she bitches on
Is how she can wid least delay
Just draw a pair ob britches on.

One of the show's stock characters was a grotesque black woman, or the "funny ole gal," who stood in contrast to the "plantation yellow girl," an attractive, well-dressed mulatto performed by a man. When portraying the "funny ole gal," female impersonators emphasized her unattractiveness, using mismatched clothes and a shrill voice.

EMANCIPATION AND TRANSFORMATION

After the war the minstrel show underwent substantial changes. The troupes became much larger, and the productions became plush and more elaborate. J. H. Haverly, an experienced manager, increased his profits dramatically when he enlarged his minstrel show companies and advertised their glamour. Producer M. B. Leavitt offered an all-female cast in his minstrel show in 1870, sending the novel female minstrels to flirt with the audience and show off their bodies in skimpy costumes.

Although minstrel performers usually remained in blackface, they also parodied immigrants, including Chinese newcomers, and American business elites. White minstrels began to expand their repertoire, in part because of competition from black performers. Beginning in the 1860s African American minstrels became increasingly successful by advertising their authentic portrayals of black life. Blues and jazz singers such as Bessie Smith and Ida Cox got some of their early show business training in minstrel shows.

The professional minstrel show declined around 1900, but its racial tropes and masks live on in American culture. Vaudeville and musical comedies became the primary sites of blackface entertainment, and minstrelsy helped shape radio and Hollywood films. Two white men, Freeman Gosden and Charles Correll, established a successful radio show, *Amos 'n' Andy*, using African American characters with racial dialect.

CRITICAL RESPONSE

Some historians have argued that the minstrel show was popular among working-class northern men—the show's primary audience in the antebellum period—because it was key to the formation of their identity. It helped workers unite as whites and as superior to blacks, gave them tools to challenge their subordinate status, and offered routes of escape through fantasy. The image of the libidinous, carefree black provided an outlet for spectators' longing for a preindustrial, rural past and a way to counter the discipline and dislocation of urban, industrial life.

In an influential study of the antebellum minstrel show, *Love and Theft: Blackface Minstrelsy and the American Working Class*, Eric Lott states that working-class audiences enjoyed the denigration of African Americans while still identifying with them as a subjugated class, attracted to the childish fun that the black caricatures represented. In *Raising Cain: Blackface Performance from Jim Crow to Hip Hop*, W. T. Lhamon takes a different approach by arguing that the minstrel show was a revolt by young working-class men against bourgeois expectations of thrift and responsibility. Considerable debate remains about the extent to which minstrelsy served the politically progressive goals of the American working class.

In *Blackface, White Noise: Jewish Immigrants in the Hollywood Melting Pot*, Michael Paul Rogin discusses the importance of blackface to twentieth-century Hollywood movies and the Americanization of immigrants. Jewish film stars in blackface, such as Al Jolson in *The Jazz Singer* (1927), displaced African Americans onstage and on-screen to construct new American identities, creating a melting pot for white immigrants. Today scholars continue to locate echoes of minstrelsy, America's first form of mass entertainment, in more recent forms of entertainment such as hip hop, stand-up comedy, and rock and roll.

M. Alison Kibler

SEE ALSO: The Amos 'n' Andy Show; *Blackface Minstrelsy; Cox, Ida;* The Jazz Singer; *Jolson, Al; Smith, Bessie; Stand-Up Comedy; Twain, Mark; Vaudeville.*

BIBLIOGRAPHY

Gubar, Susan. *Racechanges: White Skin, Black Face in American Culture.* New York: Oxford University Press, 1997.

Lhamon, W. T. *Raising Cain: Blackface Performance from Jim Crow to Hip Hop.* Cambridge, MA: Harvard University Press, 1998.

Lott, Eric. *Love and Theft: Blackface Minstrelsy and the American Working Class.* New York: Oxford University Press, 1995.

Mahar, William. *Behind the Burnt Cork Mask: Early Blackface Minstrelsy and Antebellum American Popular Culture.* Urbana: University of Illinois Press, 1998.

Roediger, David. *The Wages of Whiteness: Race and the Making of the American Working Class.* London: Verso, 1991.

Rogin, Michael Paul. *Blackface, White Noise: Jewish Immigrants in the Hollywood Melting Pot.* Berkeley: University of California Press, 1996.

Sweet, Frank W. *A History of the Minstrel Show.* Palm Coast, FL: Backintyme, 2000.

Toll, Robert. *Blacking Up: The Minstrel Show in Nineteenth-Century America.* New York: Oxford University Press, 1974.

Twain, Mark. *The Autobiography of Mark Twain*, ed. Charles Neider. New York: Harper & Row, 1959.

Miranda, Carmen *(1909–1955)*

Singer and actress Carmen Miranda, nicknamed the Brazilian Bombshell, exploded onto the American scene in the 1940s with her lyrically unintelligible songs, her excess, and her exoticism. After arriving in the United States in 1939, she gained almost instant success, helped by the publicity from being dubbed the Franklin D. Roosevelt administration's "Ambassadress of the Good Neighbor Policy." She became the highest-paid actress in the world during World War II as well as the first Latin American to carve her name, handprints, and footprints on the Hollywood Walk of Fame.

Miranda's U.S. films include *Down Argentine Way* (1940), her American debut; *The Gang's All Here* (1943), the first of the "banana series" movies, in which she performs "The Lady with the Tutti-Frutti Hat" amid tropical scenery replete with gigantic—and erotic—bananas; and *Copacabana* (1947), a low-budget comedy with Groucho Marx. Although she experienced a decline in her last years, after her death Miranda was turned into an icon of "kitsch" and continues to be one of the most powerful symbols of Latin American culture.

Bianca Freire-Medeiros

SEE ALSO: *Kitsch; Marx, Groucho.*

BIBLIOGRAPHY

Dahl, Linda. *Come Back, Carmen Miranda: Stories of Latin America*. Bloomington, IN: Xlibris, 2002.

Gellman, Irwin F. *Good Neighbor Diplomacy: United States Policies in Latin America, 1933–1945*. Baltimore, MD: Johns Hopkins University Press, 1979.

Gil-Montero, Martha. *Brazilian Bombshell: The Biography of Carmen Miranda*. New York: Donald I. Fine, 1989.

Roberts, Shari. "The Lady in the Tutti-Frutti Hat: Carmen Miranda, a Spectacle of Ethnicity." *Cinema Journal* 32, no. 3 (1993): 3–23.

Miss America Pageant

Since its inception in 1921, the Miss America pageant has prompted a fierce debate over gender and the qualities of ideal femininity. What began as a "bathing beauty" contest on the Atlantic City Boardwalk soon became a prime target for social reformers who attacked the pageant for its exploitation of young women. In the 1930s and 1940s the pageant added a talent contest and began awarding academic scholarships, hoping to improve its image by uniting attractiveness with intelligence and strength of character. However, it still drew criticism for its emphasis on physical appearance. In spite of the controversies, few critics have demanded that the pageant be discontinued, and it has consistently drawn hundreds of thousands of participants and television viewers each year. With all its faults, the Miss America pageant remains a deeply ingrained tradition in American culture, an annual ritual providing an escape into a fantasyland of rhinestone tiaras and glittering dreams.

INCEPTION OF THE BEAUTY PAGEANT

Although the pageant advertised itself in 1987 as "the greatest scholarship program for girls in the world," the founders of the pageant held far less lofty ideals. Hoping to keep tourists in town past the Labor Day weekend, Atlantic City businessmen in 1921 decided to hold a beauty contest featuring young women from several East Coast cities. The first pageant, which drew thousands of spectators, was a success. Many civic leaders, though, were opposed to it. In the early years of the pageant, contestants were judged solely on their appearance in a bathing suit. Even more upsetting was the discovery that some contestants were married, which disturbed reformers bent on keeping Miss America a symbol of chastity.

Despite the pageant's declaration in 1924 that it would accept only unmarried women as contestants, the sponsors grew tired of complaints against the pageant and in 1928 discontinued their financial support. City officials eager to revive the pageant hired Lenora Slaughter in 1935 to "clean up" the pageant's image. Slaughter immediately enacted rules prohibiting contestants from talking to men during the week of the contest; she also introduced a required talent competition. At last, it seemed, the pageant had become respectable among the general public.

At the same time, the image of Miss America herself was gradually changing. In the 1940s and 1950s Miss America was transformed from a "bathing beauty" into an icon of wholesome young womanhood. During World War II, Miss America sold war bonds and began advertising such domestic products as shampoo, dress patterns, and vitamins for the pageant's corporate sponsors. Moreover, whereas Miss Americas in the 1920s and 1930s typically set their sights on Hollywood careers, winners after 1945 received scholarship money to attend college.

Many Miss Americas of the late 1940s and early 1950s used their prominent public position to extol the virtues of "clean living." Barbara Jo Walker, the 1947 winner, spoke out against smoking and drinking and told reporters that she was not interested in Hollywood contracts, but only in "the marriage contract." By 1954, the year the pageant made its television debut, Miss America had become a symbol of the perfect American young woman. As the pageant's theme song, inaugurated in 1955, declared, "There she is, Miss America; there she is, your ideal. The dreams of a million girls who are more than pretty may come true in Atlantic City, for she may turn out to be the queen of femininity!"

EVOLUTION OF THE BEAUTY QUEEN

In the late 1960s the concept of Miss America as a national ideal—in particular, her endorsement of commercial products and support of the military—did not sit well with many feminists, and in 1968 protesters descended on Atlantic City, carrying signs reading, "Not my ideal," "We shall not be used," and, "Miss America sells it." This was only the first of many controversies over Miss America's image that erupted during the next three decades. In 1984 pageant officials discovered that Vanessa Williams, the first black Miss America, had appeared nude in *Penthouse* magazine, sparking a national wave of debate. Williams, pressured by officials, eventually gave up her crown, but the incident lingered in the public mind as an example of the pageant's hypocrisy: the pageant proclaimed itself a guardian of sexual purity, yet it continued to run a swimsuit competition. The heated debate over the swimsuit contest finally culminated in a 1995 "phone-in vote," in which television viewers were urged to call in and vote on whether the contest should be retained. In the end, tradition carried the day, and the swimsuit contest won by a margin of four to one.

The pageant has also not been immune to behind-the-scenes controversy. Longtime host Bert Parks was fired from the pageant in 1979 and has been followed by a revolving line of hosts, from former title holders Bess Myerson, Phyllis George, and Mary Ann Mobley to entertainers Regis Philbin, Kathie Lee Gifford, Donny and Marie Osmond, Tony Danza, and Mario Lopez. The new hosts, however, were not enough to keep viewers' interest—even with the retained swimsuit competition. In 1998, 33 million viewers watched the pageant. By 2004, that number had fallen to 9 million. As a result, ABC dropped the show, and the Country Music Channel (CMT) picked it up. The pageant was moved from Atlantic City to Las Vegas in 2006. CMT also dropped the show, and it was temporarily picked up by the Learning Channel. The pageant returned to network television in 2011, with ABC reporting a 47 percent increase in viewers over the previous year.

For all its traditional trappings, the Miss America pageant has been a firm advocate of women's higher education and professional achievement: among its alumni are judges, attorneys, physicians, teachers, and several well-known actresses. Most contestants are working on either undergraduate or undergraduate degrees. Others use their prize money to pay off college loans.

The pageant has also stressed the importance of community service. Since 1989 contestants have been required to prepare a "platform" detailing a program of social work that they would enact if chosen Miss America. For many Americans, the paradox of swimsuits and social reform may be too much. But for those who set their sights on the crown, the pageant is serious business. And for the spectators who simply keep an eye on the television, the Miss America pageant offers a chance to compare one's vision of the "perfect woman" against the most known icon of them all, Miss America.

Samantha Barbas

SEE ALSO: *Atlantic City; Beauty Queens; Hollywood; World War II.*

BIBLIOGRAPHY

Banet-Weiser, Sarah. *The Most Beautiful Girl in the World: Beauty Pageants and National Identity.* Berkeley: University of California Press, 1999.

Bivans, Ann-Marie. *Miss America: In Pursuit of the Crown.* New York: MasterMedia, 1991.

Deford, Frank. *There She Is: The Life and Times of Miss America.* New York: Viking, 1971.

Dworkin, Susan. *Miss America 1945: Bess Myerson's Own Story.* New York: Newmarket, 1987.

Riverol, Armando. *Live from Atlantic City.* Bowling Green, OH: Bowling Green State University Press, 1992.

Supernaw, Susan. *Muscogee Daughter: My Sojourn to the Miss America Pageant.* Lincoln: University of Nebraska Press, 2010.

Watson, Elwood, and Darcy Martin, eds. *"There She Is, Miss America": The Politics of Sex, Beauty, and Race in America's Most Famous Pageant.* New York: Palgrave Macmillan, 2004.

Mission: Impossible

The television show *Mission: Impossible* was one of the most widely recognized in broadcast history. The theme music, the burning fuse used to open the credits, the convoluted plots, and the self-destructing tape machine all became widely recognized icons of popular culture, satirized and mimicked on a routine basis. Although the show never reached the top of the television ratings, it had a profound impact on both the television industry and its viewers. Catchphrases from the show, including "Good morning, Mr. Phelps" and "Your mission, should you choose to accept it," became an accepted part of popular vocabulary in the United States. Despite the fact that the original *Mission: Impossible* ended some forty years ago, the show remains one of the most groundbreaking and innovative series in television history.

Mission: Impossible debuted in 1966. Although it fared poorly in the ratings, critics were impressed with the complicated stories, excellent acting, and constant air of suspense. The basic plot of virtually all the episodes, however, was the same: the Impossible Missions Force (IMF), using a variety of disguises and deceptions, fools the enemy into destroying itself. The group often frames one member of the opposition or attempts to convince the enemy that the information they hold is false when it is not. The idea was to create the perfect con so that the enemy would never even realize it had been deceived.

The individual IMF agents were intentionally anonymous. The viewer knew little about the personal backgrounds of any of the agents, and this allowed the writers and producers to introduce new characters with little disruption in the flow of the show. Over the course of the program several agents came and went, including the replacement of the IMF team leader after the first season.

At the beginning of most of the episodes, the group leader (played by Steven Hill in the opening season and Peter Graves until the show's cancellation) receives his instructions through a self-destructing tape. The leader then plans an elaborate deception with his team of agents. The excitement of watching the show was not to see what would happen; the plan is outlined by the team at the beginning of the episode. Rather, the excitement of watching *Mission: Impossible* was to see how the elaborate plan was carried out and what pitfalls might occur during the course of the mission.

One of the most memorable parts of *Mission: Impossible* was the wonderful theme song composed by Lalo Schifrin. When he was asked to compose the theme, he knew nothing about the show except its title. Despite this lack of knowledge, he created a theme that fit the show using a hard-swinging jazz band. The music he wrote remains one of the most recognized television themes of all time.

The popularity of *Mission: Impossible* has waned little since its cancellation in 1973. The show won four Emmy Awards, including Best Dramatic Series; two Golden Globes; and two

Mission: Impossible. *TV's* Mission: Impossible *cast included, clockwise from top left, Greg Morris as Barney Collier, Peter Lupus as Willy Armitage, Peter Graves as Jim Phelps, Barbara Bain as Cinnamon Carter, and Martin Landau as Rollin Hand.* CBS PHOTO ARCHIVE/CONTRIBUTOR/CBS/GETTY IMAGES.

Grammy Awards for Schifrin. Over the life of the series it would be nominated for dozens of awards and gain international respect as one of the best shows on television. It has remained in near-constant syndication since 1974, and dozens of new shows using the *Mission: Impossible* formula have come and gone.

In 1996 the *Mission: Impossible* franchise was brought to new life on the silver screen by Tom Cruise (both acting in, and serving as producer for, the film) and famed thriller director Brian De Palma. The film version of *Mission: Impossible* earned more than $400 million worldwide and generated millions more in video rentals and sales. *Mission: Impossible II,* released in 2000, paired Cruise with a new director—Hong Kong's John Woo, known for his highly choreographed action flicks. The film was a hit and surpassed the first movie's box office with more than $550 million in worldwide gross. *Mission: Impossible III,* released in 2006 and directed by J. J. Abrams of TV's *Lost* and *Alias,* did not fare as well, but many directed the blame at Cruise's offscreen antics rather than at the film itself.

The series rebounded strongly in 2011, however, with the fourth installment, *Mission: Impossible—Ghost Protocol.* This time Cruise recruited Brad Bird, director of such successful animated features as *The Incredibles* (2004) and *Ratatouille* (2007), to take the helm and signed on rising star Jeremy Renner of *The Hurt Locker* (2008) and *The Town* (2010), reportedly to groom him to potentially take over the franchise going forward. *Ghost Protocol* surpassed the previous films in revenue and became Cruise's highest-grossing picture globally; it had already garnered $626 million in worldwide cumulative gross by February 2012. The success of these movies only served to reaffirm the strong affinity the public had for the members of the IMF force.

Geoff Peterson
Julie Peterson

SEE ALSO: *Abrams, J. J.;* Alias*; Blockbusters; Cruise, Tom; Emmy Awards; Grammy Awards;* The Incredibles*;* Lost*; Television.*

BIBLIOGRAPHY

Snauffer, Douglas. *Crime Television.* Westport, CT: Praeger, 2006.

White, Patrick J. *The Complete "Mission: Impossible" Dossier.* New York: Avon Books, 1991.

Mister Ed

Mister Ed was television's mischievous talking horse, who from 1961 to 1966 led his frustrated owner, architect Wilbur Post, through various misadventures in the weekly CBS television fantasy/situation comedy, *Mister Ed.* The role of Wilbur Post was played by Alan Young, and the voice of Mister Ed was supplied by former Western film star Allan "Rocky" Lane. The series was a smash hit with viewers—both children and adults—who tuned in to watch the antics of a palomino that not only talked but also had more horse sense than most people. Mister Ed was network television's first noncartoon talking animal and was inspired by film precursor Francis the Talking Mule.

BRINGING MISTER ED TO THE SCREEN

The concept of a talking horse named Mister Ed was the brainchild of writer Walter Brooks, whose short stories about the eloquent equine appeared in the *Saturday Evening Post* and *Liberty* magazine. These stories were brought to the attention of director Arthur Lubin, who had directed for Universal Pictures all but the last of seven films featuring Francis the Talking Mule. In 1957 Lubin secured an option on the Mister Ed concept with the idea of bringing the talking horse to television. The following year Lubin obtained financial backing from McCadden Productions, the production company owned by comedian George Burns, to produce a pilot. The episode starred Scott McKay and Sandy White as the leads and featured a horse other than the one that eventually appeared in the series as Mister Ed. However, the pilot failed to attract either a network or a sponsor.

Eventually the pilot was brought to the attention of Al Simon, president of Filmways TV Productions. Simon recognized many weaknesses in the production but believed that the pilot had the potential for a hilarious television situation comedy. The Mister Ed concept was resurrected, and the leading roles were recast with Young, Connie Hines, and another horse as Mister Ed. A fifteen-minute presentation film was prepared, containing the funniest bits from the original pilot and an introduction of the new cast. Filmways pitched the show to the Studebaker Corporation, which was interested in aligning itself with an unusual television program. The automobile company agreed to sponsor the show in syndication, and production of *Mister Ed* was scheduled to begin in October 1960.

A TALKING HORSE?

The horse that appeared as Mister Ed in the second pilot had been sold by the time the Studebaker deal came through. With only a month remaining before the start of production, trainer Lester Hilton was dispatched to find another horse to star in the series. Hilton found his star, a golden palomino named Bamboo Harvester, on a San Fernando Valley farm. Filmways paid $1,500 to acquire the horse, which stood 15 hands high and weighed 1,100 pounds. Hilton brought Bamboo Harvester to his ranch to train him. Using hand signals and voice commands, he trained the highly intelligent horse for stunts such as unlatching the stable door, opening a file cabinet, and dialing the telephone. Bamboo Harvester responded to commands of twenty to twenty-five words and took only fifteen minutes to learn a scene. However, as Mister Ed, Bamboo Harvester's most amazing behavior was his ability to talk.

Because Hilton had worked with Francis the Talking Mule, the trainer used the same technique for making Mister Ed appear to speak. Hilton fashioned the horse's bridle with a nylon fishing line that fed into the horse's mouth. When the trainer tugged on the line, Bamboo Harvester tried to dislodge it by moving his lips, so Mister Ed appeared to talk. The deep, baritone voice of Mister Ed belonged to one of the most popular film cowboys of the late 1940s and early 1950s, Lane. Lane and his horse, Black Jack, made thirty-eight Westerns for Republic Pictures, and twice Lane was ranked among the top ten Western moneymakers. Lane took over Wild Bill Elliott's role in the *Red Ryder* series, playing the comic strip cowboy in seven films, then landed his own series of "Rocky" Lane films. When the "B" Western declined in the 1950s, he fell on hard times, finding only minor parts until he won the role of Mister Ed's voice. Embarrassed to be playing the voice of a horse, Lane preferred not to be listed in the show's credits, so Mister Ed was billed as "Himself," which contributed to the illusion that the horse really talked.

The first of twenty-six *Mister Ed* episodes premiered on 115 stations across the country in January 1961. The show was

Mister Ed. *Alan Young as Wilbur Post prepares to marry Mister Ed the talking horse and his equine bride on an episode of* Mister Ed. CBS PHOTO ARCHIVE/CONTRIBUTOR/CBS/GETTY IMAGES.

a hit during its first year, and its ratings attracted the attention of CBS, which acquired the series for the fall 1961 Sunday lineup, where it debuted that October 1. Bamboo Harvester's talents and outstanding performances during *Mister Ed* were honored by PATSY Awards every year from 1962 to 1965. Given by the American Humane Association, the Performing Animal Top Stars of the Year (PATSY) is the animal equivalent of the Academy Award.

CBS canceled *Mister Ed* in midseason 1966, and the show went into immediate syndication. Bamboo Harvester retired to Lester Hilton's ranch, where the horse lived out his days until his death in 1968. The mischievous Mister Ed has left his hoof prints on American popular culture. Not only did he show that animals are smart, but his endearing antics also influenced Americans to recognize the talents and star power of movie and television animal actors. A remake of the series was planned in 2004, and a pilot episode was even filmed, but the show never appeared on TV. As of 2011 no other horse has taken Bamboo Harvester's iconic place, but a new generation can welcome Mister Ed into their living rooms through free Internet episodes and a collection of the series released on DVD.

Pauline Bartel

SEE ALSO: *Academy Awards; Automobile; "B" Movies; Burns, George, and Gracie Allen; Comics; Francis the Talking Mule; The Internet; Leisure Time;* Liberty; *The* Saturday Evening Post; *Sitcom; Syndication; Television; The Western.*

BIBLIOGRAPHY

Edelson, Edward. *Great Animals of the Movies.* Garden City, NY: Doubleday, 1980.

Javna, John. *Cult TV: A Viewer's Guide to the Shows America Can't Live Without!!* New York: St. Martin's Press, 1985.

Nalven, Nancy. *The Famous Mister Ed: The Unbridled Truth about America's Favorite Talking Horse.* New York: Warner Books, 1991.

Rothel, David. *The Great Show Business Animals.* San Diego, CA: A. S. Barnes, 1980.

Terrace, Vincent. *Encyclopedia of Television Series, Pilots, and Specials 1937–1973.* New York: Zoetrope, 1986.

Mister Rogers' Neighborhood

"Won't you be my neighbor?" Fred McFeely Rogers asked television viewers this question for more than three decades on *Mister Rogers' Neighborhood*, a children's show that helped create an entire genre of educational television with a focus on nurturing children's self-worth. Few series have come close to maintaining the continuity and moral tenor of Rogers's long-running PBS series. Lacking the commercial development of nearly all the network's other children series, Rogers's program maintained an unwavering commitment to education.

Born in Pennsylvania in 1928, Rogers began work in television with variety programs such as *The Voice of Firestone* (1949–1959) and *The Lucky Strike Hit Parade* (1950–1959). In November 1953 he moved back to his roots in western Pennsylvania, where he began working at WQED, the nation's first community-supported public television station. Rogers began experimenting with children's programming while at WQED, including the award-winning *Children's Corner*, which contained the puppets and other details that would later been seen on *Mister Rogers' Neighborhood*. During this period, he also began studying child development and became an ordained Presbyterian minister. Each of these sensibilities infused his on-air persona.

After the 1966 release of Fred Rogers's *MisteRogers Neighborhood*, he renamed the program *Mister Rogers' Neighborhood* and it was released nationally in 1968. That same year he was appointed chairman of the Forum on Mass Media and Child Development of the White House Conference on Children and Youth. Rogers had become a leading spokesman on American education and, particularly, how the television medium would be used to help develop it. He steered the programming toward a noncommercial format that could be easily coordinated with classroom use. By 1971 he had created Family Communications, Inc., a company dedicated to children and providing educational support to the families and people who care for them.

Until his death in 2003, Rogers resisted the flamboyant staging of some children's programs for a conservative, unchanging appearance. Each show begins and ends in the living room of his "television house." At the opening of each show, Mister Rogers invites the television viewer to be his neighbor and to enter his house. Then he hangs up his coat in the closet, slips into his cardigan sweater, and changes into his sneakers. From his living room, Rogers introduces the viewer to a new idea or object that becomes the focus of the show for the day or week. After the brief introduction, Mister Rogers visits other people in his neighborhood or places where everyday things are made—a balloon factory or a crayon factory, for example.

Aside from Mister Rogers's seemingly intimate conversations with the viewers—his "television neighbors"—the most engaging action of the program centered on the "Neighborhood

Mister Rogers' Neighborhood. *Mister Rogers poses on the set of his popular children's television show,* Mister Rogers' Neighborhood. **FOTOS INTERNATIONAL/CONTRIBUTOR/ARCHIVE PHOTOS/GETTY IMAGES.**

of Make-Believe," a puppet kingdom ruled by puppets King Friday XIII and Queen Sara Saturday and inhabited by several other puppets as well as humans. To help children make a distinction between real and pretend, none of the characters in the Neighborhood of Make-Believe ever appear in Mister Rogers's "real" world. Despite advances in visual technology, the conveyor between the "real" world of Mister Rogers's living room and the imaginary world of make-believe remained a mechanical trolley.

The themes in the "Neighborhood of Make-Believe" often revolved around the management of feelings, and they were always consistent with the theme introduced by Mister Rogers at the beginning of the show. Puppets and humans used cooperative and constructive problem-solving in the Neighborhood of Make-Believe. While the puppets tried to understand and resolve their emotional troubles, the humans would mediate and help console them, often in song. Some of the songs included "What Do You Do with the Mad that You Feel When You Feel So Mad You Could Bite?" and "There Are Many Ways to Say I Love You." Through his resistance to more modern technologies, supporters often said Rogers created a timeless program that appeals to any viewer from any era.

While many comedians have parodied *Mister Rogers' Neighborhood* (most memorably Eddie Murphy on *Saturday Night Live*), educators backed up Rogers's claim that consistency is crucial for young viewers. Despite remaining out of the marketing loop, *Mister Rogers' Neighborhood* reached almost eight million households and child-care settings each week during the 1990s.

Brian Black

SEE ALSO: *Murphy, Eddie; Public Television (PBS);* Saturday Night Live*;* Sesame Street*; Television.*

BIBLIOGRAPHY

Barcus, Francis Earle. *Images of Life on Children's Television: Sex Roles, Minorities, and Families.* New York: Praeger, 1983.

Collins, Mark, and Margaret Mary Kimmel. *"Mister Rogers' Neighborhood": Children, Television, and Fred Rogers.* Pittsburgh, PA: University of Pittsburgh Press, 1996.

Hendershot, Heather. *Saturday Morning Censors: Television Regulation before the V-Chip.* Durham, NC: Duke University Press, 1998.

Hollingsworth, Amy. *The Simple Faith of Mister Rogers.* Brentwood, TN: Integrity Publishers, 2005.

Pecora, Norma Odom; John P. Murray; and Ellen Ann Wartelle, eds. *Children and Television: 50 Years of Research.* Mahwah, NJ: Lawrence Erlbaum, 2007.

Mitchell, Joni *(1943–)*

Joni Mitchell is one of the most talented female singer-songwriters of the late twentieth and early twenty-first centuries.

Joni Mitchell. *Joni Mitchell rose to fame in the late 1960s as one of the most talented singer-songwriters of her generation.* JACK ROBINSON/HULTON ARCHIVE/GETTY IMAGES.

Her work inspired such diverse musicians as Prince, Thomas Dolby, Madonna, Suzanne Vega, and Shawn Colvin. These artists and many others have endeavored to follow in her footsteps, although few songwriters have matched the virtuosity of her work.

Born Roberta Joan Anderson on November 7, 1943, in Fort McLeod, Alberta, Canada, Mitchell studied art in Calgary. In 1964 she moved to Toronto, where she married folksinger Chuck Mitchell in 1965. One year later, the couple divorced, and Mitchell moved to New York to become a singer and songwriter. In 1967 she met folksinger Judy Collins through a mutual friend who thought that Collins would really like "Both Sides Now," one of the songs Mitchell wrote. Collins did, and she recorded it and another of Mitchell's songs, "Michael from Mountains," on her album *Wildflowers* (1967). Collins's version of "Both Sides Now" became a worldwide hit.

In 1968 Mitchell released an album of her own, *Song to a Seagull*, and it set the tone for the two albums that followed: *Clouds* (1969) and *Ladies of the Canyon* (1970). On these early albums Mitchell sings her own songs, mainly accompanying herself on the guitar and supported by only a few musicians. The suppleness of her voice adds to the complexity of the feelings analyzed within her texts. Most of them are love songs, dramatic and terse, sung in Mitchell's distinctive style: cool yet emotional; lucid yet compassionate.

Clouds not only contains Mitchell's own version of "Both Sides Now" but also the much applauded "Chelsea Morning," which is rumored to have inspired the name of President Bill Clinton's only daughter. *Ladies of the Canyon* presents two other Mitchell classics: "Big Yellow Taxi," an ecological pamphlet that became a hit in the United Kingdom and was later recorded by Bob Dylan on his album *Dylan* (1973), and "Woodstock," which was also recorded by the band Matthews Southern Comfort as a single in 1970 and by Crosby, Stills, and Nash on the album *Déjà Vu* (1970).

Mitchell's next album, *Blue* (1971), featuring James Taylor, is her first real masterpiece. Her songs, both musically and lyrically, are more personal and complex and the result of Mitchell coming to terms with several past love affairs. In 1972 she released *For the Roses*, on which she abandons her familiar terrain of folk music for an approach that is more melodious and poplike. The change of sound is continued on *Court and Spark* (1974), Mitchell's first fully electric album. On this album, featuring Robbie Robertson of the Band, she is backed by Tom Scott's L.A. Express, a group of studio musicians schooled in jazz rock.

Mitchell's 1975 album, *The Hissing of Summer Lawns*, is considered a masterpiece, even though *Rolling Stone* labeled it the "Worst Album of the Year." The result of the singer's growing interest in jazz and world music (one track features the Burundi Drummers), the album shows Mitchell at her least introspective. Taken as a whole, the songs on *The Hissing of Summer Lawns* form an extensive comment on life in the 1970s, in which economic relationships have taken the place of personal relationships. Possession, both of money and of other human beings, is a constant theme of the album.

Mitchell's next album, *Hejira* (1976), reflects her need for musical exploration and adventure. Prominently present on the album is jazz musician Jaco Pastorius, whose fretless bass also dominates the double album *Don Juan's Reckless Daughter* (1977), a recording that reveals Mitchell's interest in Latin American rhythms. The album impressed jazz legend Charles Mingus, who invited Mitchell to work with him on a new project. Unfortunately, Mingus, who had Lou Gehrig's disease, died before the project was completed. Mitchell later produced *Mingus* (1979), a tribute to the musical giant.

In the 1980s and 1990s the quality of Mitchell's work remained impressive, even though she did not maintain the steady pace of her earlier work. She released *Wild Things Run Fast* in 1982, *Dog Eat Dog* in 1985, *Chalk Mark in a Rainstorm* in 1988, *Night Ride Home* in 1991, and *Turbulent Indigo* in 1994. In 1997 she was inducted into the Rock and Roll Hall of Fame and Museum in Cleveland, Ohio, and in 1998 she embarked on a brief U.S. tour with Dylan and Van Morrison.

In 2002 Mitchell announced her retirement, and it appeared that her 1998 album, *Taming the Tiger*, would be her last album of new songs. She discovered, however, that she was not ready to be retired and that she had more songs to write. Mitchell emerged from retirement in 2007 with the release of *Shine*, an album of all new music. That same year she also collaborated with the Alberta Ballet on *The Fiddle and the Drum*, which features her music from the 1980s and 1990s and two new antiwar songs, "If"—based on Rudyard Kipling's poem—and "If I Had a Heart, I'd Cry." Also in 2007, jazz giant Herbie Hancock won Album of the Year at the Grammy Awards for his tribute to Mitchell, titled *River: The Joni Letters*, featuring performances by Norah Jones, Tina Turner, Leonard Cohen, and Mitchell herself.

Jurgen Pieters

SEE ALSO: *Crosby, Stills, and Nash; Dylan, Bob; Folk Music; Gehrig, Lou; Jazz; Madonna; Morrison, Van; Prince;* Rolling Stone*; Taylor, James.*

BIBLIOGRAPHY

Fleischer, Leonore. *Joni Mitchell.* New York: Flash Books, 1976.

Mitchell, Joni. *Joni Mitchell: The Complete Poems and Lyrics.* New York: Crown, 1997.

Whitesell, Lloyd. *The Music of Joni Mitchell.* New York: Oxford University Press, 2008.

Mitchell, Margaret *(1900–1949)*

Atlanta-born author Margaret Mitchell was an unknown in 1936 when her novel *Gone with the Wind* hit bookshelves across the country. The phenomenal success of the book altered her life dramatically. Mitchell's publishers, Macmillan, were convinced that they had a hit on their hands—so convinced that they invested more than $10,000 promoting the novel. But even they were unprepared for sales that numbered more than half a million in a scant three months and more than two million by the time the book ended its twenty-one-month run on the best-seller list. These figures are rendered even more astounding when one recalls what the $3 cost of *Gone with the Wind* represented to many Depression-plagued consumers.

Certainly Mitchell's chronicle of the American Civil War and its aftermath offers compelling material. Additionally, contemporary audiences may have seen themselves reflected in the tale of devastation and struggle, and Scarlett's vow to never go hungry again resonated with audiences who knew the reality of her hunger. Neither explanation, however, serves to account for the sustained popularity of a book that continues to sell hundreds of thousands of copies a year more than seven decades after its publication.

MITCHELL'S NOVEL STRIKES A CHORD

Critics and ordinary readers alike praised the authenticity of Mitchell's work. Even the harshest critics noted, sometimes reluctantly, the author's powerful storytelling and historical accuracy. The reaction of readers, from university professors to laborers, was more visceral; the dramatic background and the vivid characterization engaged readers' emotions as well as their attention. Neither critics nor readers, however, realized the immediacy the Civil War experience held for Mitchell: she had played on land where relics from Sherman's siege could be picked up by curious children, and she had traced with her own fingers the bullet scars, souvenirs of Antietam, on her grandfather Mitchell's head. Her South was a storied land where an oral tradition was still strong. Like William Faulkner, she knew that the past is never truly past.

But Mitchell had no desire to create a sentimental tribute to the glories of the Old South. The daughter of a suffragist mother and a history-buff father, she was too much of a rebel and too aware of the realities of southern experience to belong to the moonlight and magnolias school. She had proved herself willing to challenge aristocratic southern sensibilities long before she began writing *Gone with the Wind.* She scandalized polite Atlanta during her debut year with her public declaration that she would seek work rather than be auctioned off in marriage. No less shocking to her genteel world was the job she did secure writing for the *Atlanta Journal Sunday Magazine*, especially since by the time Peggy Mitchell's byline was appearing, she was the wife of Berrien "Red" Upshaw.

Margaret Mitchell. *Margaret Mitchell was an unknown until her best-selling novel* Gone with the Wind *was published in 1936.* MONDADORI PORTFOLIO/GETTY IMAGES.

Mitchell's *Atlanta Journal* pieces were standard fare for the magazine's largely female readers; fairs, faith, and fashion were frequent topics. But in these articles Mitchell honed her gift for capturing memorable characters and evocative details, skills she would use to powerful effect in *Gone with the Wind.* Her Sunday features also reveal an avid interest in strong-willed women, particularly those who struggled to achieve financial independence. Mitchell wrote for the *Atlanta Journal* for four years, the period of her brief marriage to Upshaw and her years of independence following their divorce. Beset by ill health and frustrated with the limits of journalism, she left the *Atlanta Journal* in 1926, shortly after her marriage to John Marsh.

Soon thereafter she began the manuscript that would become *Gone with the Wind.* Obsessed with privacy, Mitchell hid her writing even from close friends. Because of her secrecy and because her family, honoring her wishes, destroyed most of her papers after her death, little is known about the composition of the novel. We do know that the final chapter was the first written, and the heroine's name was originally Pansy Hamilton. The change to Scarlett O'Hara came only a few months before publication.

HOLLYWOOD'S TAKE ON MITCHELL'S VISION

While Mitchell was waffling on her character's name, Hollywood was already pursuing film rights to the novel. Major studios competed for rights, but David O. Selznick—an independent producer—won with an offer of $50,000, an impressive sum at the time. It soon became clear that Selznick's romanticized vision of the South was quite different from Mitchell's rawer, more diverse, and less pretentious reality. Her aristocrats, the Wilkes clan, are the blandest characters in the 1,037-page novel. The strongest, most colorful characters do not fit popular, sentimental images. Mitchell insists that Scarlett is her father's daughter, and Gerald O'Hara is an Irish immigrant with only the thinnest veneer of gentility. The rogue Rhett Butler, far from playing the cavalier, left genteel Charleston, disgusted with its hypocrisies.

Selznick simplified Scarlett's complexity and ignored the issue of mother-daughter relationships, which figures prominently in the novel. His concern was with the romance of the characters and the region, and for those who saw his 1939 film, Vivien Leigh and Clark Gable became Scarlett O'Hara and Rhett Butler. The white-columned, plantation South of the film became the backdrop for *Gone with the Wind*, however false it may have been to Mitchell's novel. Few people even realize that the words that roll across the screen paying tribute to the "land of Cavaliers" and the last bow of the "Age of Chivalry" are a Hollywood addition that made Mitchell cringe.

Mitchell died in Atlanta on August 16, 1949, the victim of a speeding car. She was aware in the years before her death that the critical reputation of her epic work was declining, a decline that only intensified as the South itself changed radically. *Gone with the Wind* became an embarrassment to a region and a nation confronting its racist heritage. But even as critics first attacked and later ignored Mitchell's novel, *Gone with the Wind* survived. More than seventy-five years after she wrote the novel, it remains one of the best-selling books of all time. Its success is not limited to American audiences: *Gone with the Wind* has been translated into thirty-five languages. In addition, Mitchell and *Gone with the Wind* websites proliferate on the Internet, and scholars continue to examine the literary value of her opus.

Flannery O'Connor, another Georgia writer, once said, "There is something in us, as storytellers and listeners to stories . . . that demands that what falls at least be offered the chance to be restored." Mitchell wrote of a character and a place that believed in that chance. Perhaps therein lies the success of Margaret Mitchell and *Gone with the Wind*.

Wylene Rholetter

SEE ALSO: *Best Sellers; Gable, Clark;* Gone with the Wind*; McDaniel, Hattie; McQueen, Butterfly; Selznick, David O.*

BIBLIOGRAPHY

Brown, Ellen Firsching, and John Wiley. *Margaret Mitchell's* Gone with the Wind: *A best seller's Odyssey from Atlanta to Hollywood.* Lanham, MD: Taylor Trade Publishing, 2011.

Edwards, Anne. *Road to Tara: The Life of Margaret Mitchell.* New Haven, CT: Ticknor & Fields, 1983.

Hanson, Elizabeth I. *Margaret Mitchell.* Boston: Twayne, 1991.

Mitchell, Margaret. *Gone with the Wind.* New York: Macmillan, 1936.

Pyron, Darden Asbury. *Southern Daughter: The Life of Margaret Mitchell.* New York: Oxford University Press, 1991.

Shavin, Norman, and Martin Shartar. *Million Dollar Legends: Margaret Mitchell and "Gone with the Wind."* Atlanta, GA: Capricorn, 1986.

Mitchum, Robert *(1917–1997)*

With his athletic build, heavy lidded eyes, insolent smirk, and bad-boy charm, Robert Mitchum was one of the most popular and enduring actors of the twentieth century. With roles in more than 125 films throughout his career, Mitchum played unforgettable characters, such as the murderous preacher in *The Night of the Hunter* (1955) and the vengeful and sadistic ex-con in *Cape Fear* (1962). He also starred as a leading man opposite some of the most popular and successful actresses of his day, including Ava Gardner, Jane Russell, Deborah Kerr, and Marilyn Monroe. A durable icon, he continued working into his seventies. Upon Mitchum's death in 1997, film critic and movie historian Richard Schickel noted that he "helped define cool for postwar America."

Robert Charles Durman Mitchum was born in Bridgeport, Connecticut, on August 16, 1917, the second child of James and Ann Mitchum. After he was born, the family moved to South Carolina, where James got a job as a railroad worker. In February 1919, when Mitchum was eighteen months old, his father was killed in an accident at work. Ann, who was pregnant with the couple's third child, returned to Connecticut with her children and moved in with her parents. After giving birth, Ann went to work full time to support her family. In 1923, when Mitchum was seven years old, she remarried, but the marriage ended in divorce within a year. Ann married for a third time in 1927 and soon had another child.

In 1929 the stock market crashed, plunging the United States into the Great Depression, and the family, like so many others, struggled to survive. Amid all this instability, Mitchum had a difficult childhood. He was a bright but defiant boy, who was often involved in pranks and fights. He ran away from home more than once and at times was sent to live with relatives in Delaware and in Philadelphia. At fourteen years old, he left home for good.

TRAVELING THE COUNTRY

Lying about his age, Mitchum first worked as a sailor. When the captain found out the boy was underage, he was fired. Hopping trains, Mitchum traveled the country, taking odd jobs where he could find them. After making it to the West Coast, he continued to ride the rails, seeking adventure. Shortly before his sixteenth birthday, he found more than he bargained for in Savannah, Georgia, where he was arrested for vagrancy. Forced to serve on a chain gang, Mitchum managed to escape after only a week. But his ankles were covered with infected wounds from the manacles, and it took the sixteen-year-old, who almost succumbed to starvation, months to return to his mother's home, which by then was in Delaware. Mitchum finally made it to a hospital, where doctors wanted to amputate one of his legs. He was determined to save it and hobbled around on crutches for months. While recuperating, Mitchum's younger brother, John, introduced him to a pretty thirteen-year-old girl named Dorothy. The two fell in love, and even after Mitchum left home again, he promised Dorothy he would return for her.

For the next two years, Mitchum again traveled the country,

***Robert Mitchum in* The Night of the Hunter.** *Robert Mitchum starred as minister Harry Powell in the 1955 thriller* The Night of the Hunter. SILVER SCREEN COLLECTION/CONTRIBUTOR/MOVIEPIX/GETTY IMAGES.

going from job to job, even briefly earning a living as a boxer. He finally ended up in California, where his older sister, Annette (who later changed her name to Julie), was working on the stage as a performer. She encouraged her brother to audition for her company, and soon he was acting, writing, and directing. Mitchum did all three well, but it was his writing that first caught the attention of Hollywood. With the promise of steady work writing for movies, Mitchum proposed to Dorothy. They married in 1940 and permanently settled in Southern California. They eventually had three children together and remained married until Mitchum's death nearly sixty years later. When Mitchum proved unable to support his family with his writing, he took a job as a sheet-metal worker at Lockheed, continuing to act on the side.

A VARIETY OF ROLES

In 1943 a Hollywood producer of Westerns heard that Mitchum could break horses and called the actor in for an audition. Mitchum, who had only helped out with horses on his grandfather's farm, bluffed his way into the job and ended up on the set of a Hopalong Cassidy movie. But first he had to break a bucking bronco that had killed the last actor who had tried to ride it. After three tries, Mitchum tamed the horse and played his first movie role—a minor villain killed by Cassidy. In 1943 he acted in seven Hopalong Cassidy pictures, as well as nine other movies, in a variety of character roles. A year later he was signed by RKO Radio Pictures.

In 1945 Mitchum had a lead role in *The Story of G.I. Joe.* His superb performance led to an Academy Award nomination, and he became Hollywood's newest leading man. In 1948, however, he suffered a setback when he was arrested for marijuana possession. Mitchum told the press, "I'm ruined. I'm all washed up in pictures now, I guess." But Dorothy, RKO, and fans all stood by him, and after serving jail time, the popular actor returned to work.

Throughout the 1950s Mitchum consistently found work in RKO's top pictures, and his reputation as an actor continued to grow. He always seemed to attract rumor and innuendo, however, and the press would dog him throughout his life, alleging infidelities, brawls, and drug charges. But Mitchum's bad-boy persona only added to his audience appeal. In 1962 he starred opposite Gregory Peck in *Cape Fear*, a film that would become his most famous. Although the actor continued to work steadily throughout the 1960s, the roles he was offered varied in quality.

During the 1970s, Mitchum underwent a kind of renaissance, turning in superb performances in *Farewell, My Lovely* (1975), *The Last Tycoon* (1976), and *The Big Sleep* (1978). In the 1980s he appeared on television for the first time, starring in the well-received miniseries *Winds of War* (1983) and its sequel *War and Remembrance* (1988), both based on novels of the same names by author Herman Wouk. He also made cameo appearances in the films *Scrooged* (1988), the 1991 remake of *Cape Fear*, and *Tombstone* (1993).

As his biographer, Mike Tomkies, writes, "Robert Mitchum is probably the most complex character in the entire international film world. He has always seemed to be engaged in perpetual battle with himself. It has produced a fascinating iconoclast." The embodiment of Hollywood cool, Mitchum was a man of many faces—a sensitive poet, a discerning intellectual blessed with a photographic memory, a practical joker, a rebel unwilling to subdue his spirit, and a talented actor devoted to his profession. In 1989 the American Film Institute named him one of the twenty-five greatest actors in the first 100 years of film, and in 1992 he was awarded a Golden Globe Lifetime Achievement Award. Mitchum died in July 1997 at the age of seventy-nine at his home in Santa Barbara, California, from emphysema and lung cancer.

Victoria Price

SEE ALSO: The Big Sleep*; Gardner, Ava; The Great Depression; Hollywood; Hopalong Cassidy; Marijuana; Monroe, Marilyn; Peck, Gregory; Russell, Jane; The Western.*

BIBLIOGRAPHY

Clooney, Nick. "Mitchum's Act Was Quiet Thunder." *Cincinnati Post*, July 4, 1997.

Eels, George. *Robert Mitchum: A Biography*. New York: Franklin Watts, 1984.

Parish, James Robert. *The Tough Guys*. New York: Arlington House, 1976.

Roberts, Jerry. *Robert Mitchum: A Biobibliography*. Westport, CT: Greenwood Press, 1992.

Roberts, Jerry, ed. *Mitchum: In His Own Words*. New York: Limelight Editions, 2000.

Schickel, Richard. "Eternally Cool: Robert Mitchum, 1917–1997." *Time*, July 14, 1997, 73.

Tomkies, Mike. *The Robert Mitchum Story: "It Sure Beats Working."* Chicago: Regnery, 1972.

Mix, Tom *(1880–1940)*

Tom Mix, hero of the silent Western, and his "wonder horse" Tony revolutionized both the style and content of the genre. Whereas earlier Westerns had depicted an austere (and fairly accurate) West and had emphasized character and unembroidered sentiment, Mix introduced a fast-paced and lighthearted version of the West, with a cowboy hero who offered youth, showmanship, and adventurousness. Mix films emphasize the hero's riding and stunting abilities and feature the spectacular natural backdrops of many of America's national parks.

Although he invented a nearly mythic past for himself—one that supposedly included service with Teddy Roosevelt's Rough Riders and military action in the Boxer Rebellion—Mix was actually born and raised in Pennsylvania and moved west to Oklahoma during the early 1900s. He joined the Miller Brothers' 101 Real Wild West Ranch in 1905 and eventually toured with various Wild West shows before returning to the Miller Ranch in 1910.

Mix began working in film in 1911, when he served as an adviser and a stunt double in a William Selig studio documentary about the Wild West. Quickly moving into larger roles, he started making numerous films. In 1914 he graduated to feature films in *In the Days of the Thundering Herd.* He moved to the Twentieth Century Fox studio in 1917 (for which he made more than seventy films). By the mid-1920s, Mix was making $17,000 per week, starring in profitable films that enabled Fox to make other prestigious but unprofitable films. In the late 1920s and 1930s, he appeared in films for FBO (later RKO) and Universal Studios.

Tom Mix. *Tom Mix and his wife and daughter arrive in Great Britain to greet his fans in 1925.* TOPICAL PRESS AGENCY/STRINGER/HULTON ARCHIVE/GETTY IMAGES.

Mix's West was theatrical, adventurous, and glamorous, as was the man himself. Wearing his signature ten-gallon hats (black or white), silk shirts, and round-top boots, Mix and his films appealed to a young audience. An expert horseman and crack shot, he performed almost all his (often-perilous) stunts himself. His fancy rope work and riding stunts always saved the day, along with the help of his trusty horse, Tony. Mix described his screen persona this way: "I ride into a place owning my own horse, saddle, and bridle. It isn't my quarrel, but I get into trouble doing the right thing for somebody else. When it's all ironed out, I never get any money reward. I may be made foreman of the ranch and I get the girl, but there is never a fervid love scene."

Although Mix occasionally appeared in non-Western features, his signature films were all Westerns, including *Chip of the Flying U* (1914), *Sky High* (1922), *Riders of the Purple Sage* (1925), and *The Rainbow Trail* (1925). When the talkies came to Hollywood, an aging Mix left town and joined a traveling circus. Although he did return to Hollywood to make a few films in the 1930s, his heyday had passed. His final film, *The Miracle Rider*, was a fifteen-chapter serial that appeared in 1935. Most of his silent features are unavailable today, due to a fire at the Fox studios that destroyed almost all the prints. In 1940 Mix died in a car accident in Arizona.

Mix's cowboy image lived on well past his death in several ways. NBC radio and later television aired *The Tom Mix Show* from 1933 into the 1950s. Portrayed by various actors, the Mix character ended his shows with such messages as "be a straight shooter," "crime never pays," and "fight on the side of the law and you'll never regret it." He also appeared in various comic-book series, including the Tom Mix Ralston Comics and the Tom Mix Western series, in the 1940s and 1950s. Finally, Mix's good-time cowboy, with his unrealistic and glamorous image, spawned the singing and dancing cowboys and the Western spectacles of 1930s film, and his own lavish lifestyle helped pave the way for the high-living flamboyance of many 1930s and 1940s movie stars' off-screen lives.

Deborah M. Mix

SEE ALSO: *Comic Books; The Cowboy Look; Hollywood; Movie Stars; Rodeo; Silent Movies; The Western.*

BIBLIOGRAPHY

Jensen, Richard, D. *The Amazing Tom Mix: The Most Famous Cowboy of the Movies.* New York: iUniverse, 2005.

Mix, Paul E. *The Life and Legend of Tom Mix.* South Brunswick, NJ: A. S. Barnes, 1972.

Nye, Douglas, E. *Those Six-Gun Heroes: 25 Great Movie Cowboys.* Spartanburg, SC: ETV Endowment of South Carolina, 1982.

Mizer, Bob

SEE: *Athletic Model Guild.*

Mobil Masterpiece Theatre

SEE: *Masterpiece Theatre.*

Mockumentaries

A blend of the words *mock* and *documentary*, a mockumentary presents fictitious characters or events in a documentary-style television show, film, or webcast. Also called faux or pseudo documentaries, they often spoof sociopolitical and cultural issues. Most are comic, but even the more serious depictions of fictitious events, called "docufictions," intend to entertain.

Emerging from a rich satirical tradition, the term *mockumentary* gained cultural traction with Rob Reiner's *This Is Spinal Tap* (1984), which follows fictitious metal band Spinal Tap on a hilariously unsuccessful tour and satirizes the hedonism and hubris common among many rock-and-roll musicians. Christopher Guest, who played a member of the band in *Spinal Tap* went on to direct mockumentaries such as *Waiting for Guffman* (1997), *Best in Show* (2000), and *A Mighty Wind* (2003), which provide farcical looks into small-town theater, dog shows, and folk music, respectively.

Considered one of the most extreme mockumentaries, Sacha Baron Cohen's *Borat* (2006) follows an abrasive and inept Kazakh reporter who tours the United States conducting interviews and provokes outrage due to his sexist and politically incorrect behavior. A box-office hit, the film sparked controversy when participants in the film reported that they had been duped by the film's producers. Similarly, in 2010, actor-director Casey Affleck released the equally enigmatic *I'm Still Here*, which follows Joaquin Phoenix after his purported retirement from acting in order to pursue a career as a hip-hop artist. Phoenix maintained the ruse during the entire filming of the movie, and Affleck did not reveal that the movie was a hoax until after it was released.

Between 2000 and 2010 the popularity of the genre has been manifest in both horror films and on television. *The Blair Witch Project* (1998), *Cloverfield* (2008), *Paranormal Activity* (2009), and *The Devil Inside* (2012) were rendered more disturbing by incorporating purported found footage to enhance their authenticity. Likewise, sitcoms such as *The Office* (2005–), *Parks and Recreation* (2009–), and *Modern Family* (2009–) have used the "fly on the wall" trope to great success. In addition to having characters comment on other characters and the action of the show as if they were talking about real events and real people, television programs re-create the feel of documentary film by shooting such episodes with handheld cameras—or with equipment that lends a handheld camera feel to the filming.

While such self-referencing challenges the myth that the camera does not lie, mockumentaries also comment on the film-going audience at least as much as they do on the subjects they examine. For example, in addition to satirizing aging musicians, *This Is Spinal Tap* pokes fun at rock-and-roll fans. Ostensibly every joke in the film exposes the folly of the band, but it is also true that many people who enjoy the film also admire musicians who are not dissimilar to the stars ridiculed in the movie. If documentaries are, in the words of film scholar Bill Nichols, "fiction (un)like any other," then mockumentaries can show how easily we accept the realities packaged for our consumption and how readily we can be made to laugh, without always realizing that we are the butt of the joke.

Stephen P. Davis

SEE ALSO: Borat*; Folk Music; Guest, Christopher; Heavy Metal; Hip-Hop;* Modern Family*;* The Office*; Reality Television; Spinal Tap; Television.*

BIBLIOGRAPHY

Rhodes, Gary D., and John Parris Springer, eds. *Docufictions: Essays on the Intersection of Documentary and Fictional Filmmaking.* Jefferson, NC: McFarland, 2006.

Roscoe, Jane, and Craig Hight. *Faking It: Mock-Documentary and the Subversion of Factuality.* New York: Manchester University Press, 2001.

Mod

Of the many youth subcultures that developed from pop music, few have endured as long as mod, a culture based on 1960s British youth that involves an almost religious commitment to style as a way to transcend class distinctions. It is a perennial culture with a well-defined set of mannerisms, chief among them an almost fetishlike attachment to mass-produced objects—such as Italian scooters and army-surplus parkas—and a devotion to certain types of music—such as rhythm and blues and ska. Over time, the original catalyst for mod, a subversive sort of working-class dandyism, has fallen away, and mod has become a quaint type of revivalism. American mods are more apt to be suburban and middle class instead of urban and working class.

MOD'S BEGINNINGS

The emergence of the mod subculture began in London in the 1950s, when West Indian immigrants began to settle in the city's neighborhoods. This was an unsettling development for the traditionally xenophobic British, especially for the working class, because it was the working-class neighborhoods where the West Indians settled. Their presence did not go without response. The teddy boys, young thugs who wore Edwardian-style clothes to shock their parents, were hostile to the black immigrants, but mods idolized black singers; black styles; and above all, the indefinable cool of the rude boys, who were young, dapper West Indian delinquents. It was "an affinity which was transposed into style," according to Dick Hebdige, author of the book *Subculture: The Meaning of Style.* Hebdige explains that the black man served "symbolically as a dark passage down into an imagined underworld . . . situated beneath the familiar surfaces of life where another order was disclosed: a beautifully intricate system in which the values, norms and conventions of the 'straight' world were inverted."

In working-class London neighborhoods in the early 1960s, these various elements were percolating. A style of dress was evolving that eschewed the churlish vulgarity of the teddy boys. Its proponents numbered among the hoards of teenage office workers the British educational system set loose on employers. The mods chose to fit into work environments, unlike the petulant hoodlum-worshipping teddy boys, but they suffered no illusions about the strictures of class. Tom Wolfe, author of *The Pump House Gang,* writes, "There is hardly a kid in all of London who harbors any sincere hope of advancing himself in any very striking way by success at work. Englishmen at an early age begin to sense that the fix is in, and all that work does is keep you afloat at the place you were born into."

In response to this manifest truth, the mods developed a covert form of rebellion. They made themselves into visual masterpieces, every detail in place on their person, often wearing hand-tailored clothing. They lived for weekends and bank holidays, for seeing and being seen in the right gear, at the right places, and preferably under the influence of the right drugs—chiefly amphetamines (which tended to exacerbate their maniacal neatness). In short, mods lived a whole style of life that had very little to do with jobs and futures and everything to do with a temporary form of emancipation from an oppressive society.

Being a mod was another instance of teenagers creating a ritualized world to evade the grown-up one. There was a hierarchy ("faces" were the trendsetters, and "tickets" were the followers), a set of rituals, and a value system. Ironically, all this energy was expended in the service of a most ephemeral of styles. Mod was a stylized version of planned obsolescence with fashions changing from month to month or even week to week, which tended to consume a large chunk of the average mod's paltry salary and often led to petty larceny and male prostitution as a means of subsidizing visits to the tailor. In a way, mod was very much like the cargo cults and other religious rituals that aped colonialism, mimicking the dominant ideology in a stylized buffoonish manner where the authorities, be it colonial officials or office managers, could not help but see the asinine picture being painted of them.

Such movements can only exist in a vacuum for so long, and in the spring of 1964, a series of bank holiday riots between mods and teddy boys catapulted the mods into national prominence in England. Then came the first mod band, The Who, whose members had grown up with the style, were of its milieu, and were thus able to voice the mods' disjointed beliefs in song. With the heightened profile came the magazines, the clothing stores, and the marketing efforts that turned the mods from idiosyncratic rebels into the originators of yet another fashion craze. By the time mod became visible it had already begun to break into factions: excessive protohippie dandyism and the skinhead, a "kind of caricature of the model worker," as Phil Cohen, the director of the Centre for New Ethnicities Research and Reader in Cultural Studies at the University of East London, describes them in Hebdige's book.

MOD'S RESURGENCE

Mod lay dormant for nearly ten years before being resurrected in the late 1970s, partly due to the 1979 release of *Quadrophenia*, a film chronicling the mod-rocker bank holiday riots of 1964, and partly as a consequence of punk rock, which as a side effect led to revivals of mod and two-tone, a rude boys–inflected ska music. The movements in England might still retain vestiges of the class antagonisms at the root of the original subculture, but in America, divorced from the particulars of class, time, and place, mod was stripped of its rich array of signifiers, a style revival movement among many others. Without the milieu of working-class social dynamics, the latter-day mods had about them the still, airless quality of a museum exhibit.

The original mods developed in response to specifics of 1960s Britain, such as the rigidity of the class system, the economy, and educational opportunities. Mod was a secret dissent, but in America it was stripped of its class signifiers. American mods were more likely to be college students than blue-collar workers. It was a style cult divorced from its origination by the vast difference in cultures. Mod was a market choice, one alternative among many, meant to convey the very American trait of individualism and not class. This is perhaps the biggest irony of mod's international success; it came to exist as a consequence of the consumerism it initially lampooned.

Michael Baers

SEE ALSO: *Cults; Pop Music; Rhythm and Blues; The Who.*

BIBLIOGRAPHY

Cohen, Stanley. *Folk Devils and Moral Panics: The Creation of Mods and Rockers*. London: MacGibbon & Kee, 1972.

Hall, Stuart, and Tony Jefferson, eds. *Resistance through Rituals: Youth Subcultures in Post-War Britain*. London: Hutchinson, 1976.

Hebdige, Dick. *Subculture: The Meaning of Style*. London: Routledge, 1979.

Laing, David. *The Sound of Our Time*. London: Sheed & Ward, 1969.

Marsh, Dave. *Before I Get Old: The Story of the Who*. New York: St. Martin's Press, 1983.

Mungham, Geoff, and Geoff Pearson, eds. *Working Class Youth Culture*. London: Routledge, 1976.

Perone, James E. *Mods, Rockers, and the Music of the British Invasion*. Westport, CT: Praeger Publishers, 2009.

Wolfe, Tom. *The Pump House Gang*. New York: Farrar, Straus & Giroux, 1968.

The Mod Squad

"One black, one white, one blonde." That was one way to describe the three members of *The Mod Squad*, executive producer Aaron Spelling's enormously successful late-1960s "hippie-oriented" cop drama. Broadcast on ABC from September 1968 to 1973, the series was part of an attempt by the networks to lure baby boomers back to prime time during a period when it seemed this lucrative demographic had abandoned the medium for cinema, rock music, and social protest. The show's premise tried to bridge the generation gap: take three rebellious, disaffected young social outcasts and persuade them to work as unarmed undercover detectives for the Los Angeles Police Department. Producers hoped younger viewers would identify with the lead characters, while the older generation would find comfort in the law-and-order nature of the series.

While this premise seemed terribly calculated, even cynical, the show managed to work. *The Mod Squad* team, Pete Cochran (Michael Cole), a long-haired youth disowned by his Beverly Hills family; Julie Barnes (Peggy Lipton), a willowy "hippie chick"; and Linc Hayes (Clarence Williams III), an Afroed and angry black man busted during the Watts Riots, all displayed continual discomfort about their roles as cops. Their missions usually involved infiltration of some area of the youth counterculture, from underground newspapers to campus antiwar organizations, to ferret out the inevitably grown-up villains who preyed on the idealistic young. This approach proved to be the show's winning formula: the bad guys were almost always short-haired establishment types. During the first year of its run, Spelling gushed, "We're telling it like it is. Somebody has to help adults understand young people. They've got so many hang-ups and nobody seems to care. Love is the answer. Those hippies are right. Those kids are so totally involved with life[,] they've involved me."

The Mod Squad developed a reputation for handling socially relevant issues while so much of prime-time fare focused on the inanities of suburban witches, nuns who could fly, bumbling secret agents who talked into their shoes, and the rural adventures of the gentle folk in Hooterville and Mayberry. *The Mod Squad* was a harbinger of inevitable change in prime-time programming philosophies as the tumultuous 1960s raged on into the early 1970s. The series didn't deal with politically and socially troubling issues every week, but it was noteworthy for tackling such issues at all. One 1970 episode, for example, explored the My Lai massacre in thinly fictionalized form. American public opinion was still quite raw over whether American troops in Vietnam had engaged in war crimes around that action. This episode of *The Mod Squad* provided a complex, sensitive examination of soldier psychology and racism. Another 1970 episode dealt with draft resistance, portraying a draft resister as sympathetic and principled.

The success of *The Mod Squad*, along with its formula of presenting the rebellious and idealistic young as heroes, led prime time to begin a wholesale shift in its approach to programming in the early 1970s. The 1970–1971 network season was ballyhooed as the "Season of Social Relevance." All around the dial, new dramas appeared using *The Mod Squad*'s formula.

The Mod Squad. The Mod Squad *starred, from left, Clarence Williams III as Linc Hayes, Peggy Lipton as Julie Barnes, and Michael Cole as Pete Cochran.* THOMAS/SPELLING/THE KOBAL COLLECTION.

Storefront Lawyers featured idealistic, rebellious young lawyers wanting to use the law to change the Establishment. *The Interns* presented idealistic, rebellious doctors-in-training who fought authority to change the system. Even *Ironside*, an established series, found itself grappling with socially relevant issues such as the draft. However, none of the *Mod Squad* clones ended up a ratings winner. The networks would not get their social relevance approach right until they shifted away from dramas to comedies such as *All in the Family* and *M*A*S*H*, both of which let viewers take in countercultural values and social protest along with spoonfuls of laughter.

By 1973, with the 1960s over, *The Mod Squad* quickly became dated, obviously a product of its time. Its basic formula proved powerful, however, for a new generation of television viewers. When the upstart Fox network wanted to lure young viewers—Generation Xers this time—to its offerings, one of the network's early hits proved to be *21 Jump Street*, a youth-oriented cop show thoroughly modeled on *The Mod Squad*. MGM attempted to cash in on the show's cult success by adapting it into a 1999 film starring Claire Danes (Julie), Giovanni Ribisi (Peter), Omar Epps (Lincoln), and Dennis Farina (Captain Greer). The film flopped at the box office and was assailed by critics.

Aniko Bodroghkozy

SEE ALSO: All in the Family*; Baby Boomers; Generation X; Hippies;* M*A*S*H*; MGM (Metro-Goldwyn-Mayer); Spelling, Aaron; Television.*

BIBLIOGRAPHY

Bodroghkozy, Aniko. *Groove Tube: Sixties Television and the Youth Rebellion.* Durham, NC: Duke University Press, 2001.

Spelling, Aaron, and Jefferson Graham. *Aaron Spelling: A Prime-Time Life.* New York: St. Martin's Press, 1996.

Model T

The Model T was the first car aimed at, and affordable to, a mass market. It was also the first car to be a true American sensation at a time when the United States was transforming from the rural, more craft-based and agrarian economy of the nineteenth century to the urban mass market of the twentieth century. By the post–World War II era, most Americans owned a car, and much of where and how they lived, shopped, and worked had been altered by the ability to travel long distances at a faster rate. Mass production, mass marketing, and mass use of automobiles contributed to this shift. From its debut in 1908, the Model T was America's most popular car.

Henry Ford, along with his team at the Ford Motor Company in Detroit, Michigan, designed the Model T for durability and ease of maintenance. Ford aimed to produce an inexpensive, utilitarian car and eschewed a lot of the "trimmings" featured in those cars aimed at the luxury consumer. Even its name was simply functional, having no significance other than to indicate that the car was the twentieth iteration in Ford's succession of alphabetically designated development and retail models. The car was so standardized that, most years, it was available only in black.

1916 Ford Model T. *The 1916 Model T was one of a long line of Ford cars that dominated the U.S. automobile market in the early twentieth century.* SCIENCE & SOCIETY PICTURE LIBRARY/CONTRIBUTOR/SSPL/GETTY IMAGES.

Sales of the Model T were spectacular. In the early 1920s Ford was selling more than a million Model Ts each year, and over half of the cars sold in the country were Fords. When the price of the Model T was cut, as it was nearly every year from 1911 to 1925, newspapers coast-to-coast reported the news. The car sold so well that the company bought no advertising between 1917 and 1923. Ford's aggressive price cuts created an entirely new market for cars—the mass market. Whereas cars were formerly a luxury of the rich, the workmanlike Model T, by virtue of its low price, was a new product for a new auto consumer, the middle class everywhere.

Consumer demands of this magnitude required a new type of production. Ford worked with his team to make a number of cumulative refinements to the production process, culminating in 1913 with the assembly line. Model T production required division of labor and massive planning coordination to link the efforts of tens of thousands of workers laboring on the assembly lines.

The Model T was a part of the greatest opening of the country since the railroads, allowing rural citizens to travel further, more often, and in the manner once only available to the moneyed leisure class. The explosion in the number of cars on the road led to increased investments in highways, and farmers transferred their production from hay to consumer crops. The phenomenon of the newly affordable Model T replacing horses was part of a larger change in America, in which formerly homemade or locally available commodities as simple as soap or flour were suddenly mass produced and branded.

The Model T had a cultural impact like no car before it, and few after. It was soon popularly referred to by its own nicknames. One was "Tin Lizzie," because of a widespread, somewhat willful misconception that it was so cheap as to be made out of tin; another was "flivver," possibly a reference to its easily wrinkled and bent fenders. The car was also celebrated in songs such as "Ford March & Two-Step," performed at William Howard Taft's inaugural ball of 1909, and the "Flivver Ten Million," performed by the Boston Symphony Orchestra and the New York Philharmonic Orchestra. Between 1915 and 1920 an entire genre of cheap books were published made up solely of jokes about Model Ts and the combination of private pride and public chagrin their owners felt at possessing such durable, utilitarian, somewhat homely vehicles.

The more than ten million low-priced Model Ts sold by Ford created the mass market for automobiles. Although production ceased in 1927, the cultish devotion of Americans to cars was just beginning, and the Model T started it all. Model T Fords have become valuable collectors' items, and the massive market, industry, and culture they spawned are inextricably woven into the fabric of American life.

Steve Kotok

SEE ALSO: *Automobile; The Boston Symphony Orchestra; Ford, Henry; Ford Motor Company; Highway System.*

BIBLIOGRAPHY

Casey, Robert H. *The Model T Turns 100!: Henry Ford's Innovative Design Suited the Nation to a T.* New York: American Heritage, 2009.

Clymer, Floyd. *Henry's Wonderful Model T, 1908–1927.* New York: McGraw-Hill, 1955.

Collier, Peter, and David Horowitz. *The Fords: An American Epic.* New York: Simon & Schuster, 1992.

Lewis, David L. *The Public Image of Henry Ford: An American Folk Hero and His Company.* Detroit, MI: Wayne State University Press, 1976.

McCalley, Bruce. *Model T Ford: The Car That Changed the World.* Iola, WI: Krause Publications, 1994.

Nevins, Allan, and Frank E. Hill. *Ford: The Times, the Man, the Company.* New York: Scribner, 1954.

Strasser, Susan. *Satisfaction Guaranteed: The Making of the American Mass Market.* New York: Pantheon Books, 1989.

Modern Dance

Modern dance was born at the beginning of the twentieth century out of the need to disengage the medium from the formal rigor of ballet, as well as from the image of varied forms of dance as lightweight, sordid entertainment. One of the first dance artists associated with the movement was Isadora Duncan, whose insistence on dance as self-expression and high art paved the way for the more sustained schools of Mary Wigman, Martha Graham, Doris Humphrey, and the Denishawn dance troupe. In Germany and the United States, these founders worked on movement systems that focused on the grounding of the body, natural dance, harmony, creative expression, and feeling. Their techniques continue to shape contemporary theatrical dance.

In the twenty-first century, modern dance has evolved into postmodern and contemporary dance, drawing on the techniques of ballet, jazz, African dance, yoga, gymnastics, martial arts, improvisation, and body mapping. Critics bemoan the fact that no leading innovators have emerged, but attention has focused on choreographers Christopher Wheeldon (British), who left the New York City Ballet to form Morphoses, and Alexei Ratmansky (Russian), who works with the American Ballet Theatre. Trey McIntyre has also shown the potential to play a major role in redefining modern dance for the new century.

Petra Kuppers

SEE ALSO: *Ailey, Alvin; Balanchine, George; Ballet; Cunningham, Merce; Denishawn; Duncan, Isadora; Graham, Martha; Gymnastics; Jazz; Martial Arts; Morris, Mark; Yoga.*

BIBLIOGRAPHY

Brown, Jean Morrison, ed. *The Vision of Modern Dance.* London: Dance Books, 1980.

Segal, Lewis. "Dance: The 21st Century Awaits Its Next Cue." *Los Angeles Times,* December 20, 2009.

Modern Family

Modern Family is a popular and critically acclaimed comedy television series. The debut episode, which aired September 23, 2009, on ABC, drew 12.7 million viewers and was met with overwhelmingly positive reviews. The half-hour show focuses on the awkward, intertwined relationships of an extended family. It is filmed in a mockumentary, or a mock documentary, style so that its characters seem to be the subjects of a documentary.

Three individual families, each representing a modern family of the early twenty-first century, make up the extended family featured in the show. One is a traditional family that has heterosexual married parents, Claire and Phil Dunphy (played by Julie Bowen and Ty Burrell), and their three kids. Another is Claire's father, Jay Pritchett (Ed O'Neill), and his second wife, Colombian-born Gloria (Sofia Vergara), who is much younger than Jay and has a son from a previous relationship. The third family is Claire's brother, Mitchell Pritchett (Jesse Tyler Ferguson), who is gay, and his committed partner, Cameron (Cam) Tucker (Eric Stonestreet), with whom he has an adopted Vietnamese daughter.

Jokes are frequently made at the expense of the differing family units, sometimes in obvious ways. The gay couple and Ed and his much younger wife are often mined for laughs, but always in a tactful manner. *Modern Family* has received acclaim for its candid portrayal of Mitchell and Cam's relationship. The two are sometimes shown in bed together, and they kiss in one episode. While plotlines occasionally address the unique challenges or circumstances of gay couples, typically their spats and difficulties as parents differ little from the other couples and parents on the show.

Another feature of the show that emphasizes how modern the modern families are is their use of contemporary technology. Keeping pace with real-life trends, the characters wait in line for the newest iPad, show one another funny YouTube clips, and embarrass their kids by joining a social network. *New York Times* writer Bruce Feiler noted that "the characters . . . are so immersed in technology that nearly every scene is refracted through a digital funhouse."

The subtle use of mockumentary techniques is another important ingredient in the success of *Modern Family*. This stylistic framing creates a sense that the family is being observed, but it only becomes obvious when characters break from their roles to directly address the camera. Such scenes occur early in each episode to set up the plot and at intervals throughout the episodes when characters often confess that what they have said or done in a given situation was not a true representation of their feelings. Many of the episodes end with a concluding remark or reflection told in the same manner.

Modern Family has been well received since its premiere. It won the 2010 and 2011 Emmy Award for Outstanding Comedy Series. In its 2010–2011 season, it was the highest-rated show for eighteen to forty-nine year olds. Critics praised all of the actors' performances, and together the cast has received numerous awards, including the 2012 Golden Globe Award for Best Television Series, Musical or Comedy. The show's creators, Steven Levitan and Christopher Lloyd, have been credited with reviving the scripted sitcom on U.S. television.

Jeff Merron

SEE ALSO: *Emmy Awards; Gay Men; iPad; Mockumentaries; Sitcom; Television; YouTube.*

BIBLIOGRAPHY

Feiler, Bruce. "What 'Modern Family' Says about Modern Families." *New York Times*, January 23, 2011. Accessed May 31, 2012. Available from http://www.nytimes.com/2011/01/23/fashion/23THISLIFE.html?pagewanted=print

Snierson, Dan. "Family Business." *Entertainment Weekly*, October 1, 2010, 42–47.

Villarreal, Yvonne. "Thank 'Modern Family' for the Revival of the Sitcom." *Los Angeles Times*, October 30, 2011. Accessed May 31, 2012. Available from http://articles.latimes.com/2011/oct/30/entertainment/la-ca-modern-family-20111030

Modern Maturity

From modest beginnings, *Modern Maturity*, the original title of the magazine of AARP (formerly the American Association of Retired Persons), grew into the largest average circulation magazine in the nation—without being available on newsstands. The *Time*-sized publication, a glossy bimonthly, has been sent through the mail to some twenty-three million households that included more than thirty-three million AARP members who received it as part of their annual dues.

The rise of *Modern Maturity* coincided with the growth of AARP, which could trace its roots to a meeting in a Washington, D.C., hotel of its three founding directors: Dr. Ethel Percy Andrus, who came up with the idea for the organization, and two of her associates, Grace Hatfield and Ernest Giddings. According to minutes of that meeting, it was decided to incorporate a nonprofit, nonpartisan membership organization in Washington on July 1, 1958. At the time, Andrus was a seventy-two-year-old California educator and activist who earlier had founded the National Retired Teachers Association.

The start-up money for the organization came from a young Poughkeepsie, New York, insurance broker, Leonard Davis, whom Andrus had persuaded to come to her house in Ojai, California, while he was on a trip to Disneyland with his family. Davis and Andrus sat at her kitchen table discussing her plans for AARP while she showed him a mock-up of the proposed magazine *Modern Maturity*. "There was contagious excitement in flipping through those pages," noted an AARP article discussing the group's history. "Around her kitchen table final copy was written for the magazine." Andrus asked Davis for help in raising the seed money, and the go-getting Davis put up $50,000 to start the ball rolling. He also persuaded Continental Casualty of Chicago to offer insurance for the AARP group. At the time, most insurers would not sell insurance to people older than sixty-five, but Davis saw the opportunity to open doors to a vast new market.

The first issue of *Modern Maturity* was sent in late 1958 to members of Andrus's other organization, the National Retired Teachers Association—members were asked to join AARP for $2 a year. That sum would include benefits associated with membership as well as an annual subscription to *Modern Maturity*. The broad goals of the magazine were "to create a showcase for the achievements of our people; to build many bridges between the world of our needs and the powers that can answer those needs; to open the door to all the various human adventures we can picture for you; and to serve as a forum for the discussion of subjects of interest to retired persons." The first mass mailing was a marketing hit, and membership in AARP grew rapidly, along with readership in *Modern Maturity*. By the time Andrus died in 1967, the circulation was well over a million readers. By the late 1990s AARP had become a powerhouse lobbying organization in Washington, its group health insurance program had become the biggest in the nation, and its pharmacy services the second-largest mail-order drug firm.

FOR MORE THAN JUST RETIREES

From the $2 initial dues for membership, years later the fee rose to $8 a year, which included a $2.40 price for *Modern Maturity* and 85¢ for the AARP *Bulletin* newsletter. Although the group's name contained the phrase "Retired Persons," membership was open to anyone fifty or older, and many who joined were not retired. From its meager beginnings, AARP—by the end of the twentieth century—had become a huge nonprofit industry with an annual budget of more than $200 million, and it boasted businesses generating a cash flow of more than $10 billion that netted some $100 million. Advertising in AARP's publications alone produced more than $30 million. In a 1988 story on AARP, *Money* magazine correspondents reported: "We discovered a loosely knit and paradoxical group, neither as politically threatening as it is often perceived nor as benign as it portrays itself to members. . . . It is an undeniably effective lobby—and yet its membership is so fragmented and random that it lacks a specific shared interest or philosophy." Its lobbying influence on behalf of Medicare and other issues affecting the elderly, combined with a grassroots force of millions of people behind it, made AARP one of the most potent lobbying forces in Washington.

The reader demographics of *Modern Maturity* in 1997 showed a population that was moderately well-off with a median household income of $34,408, nearly two-thirds of its audience having attended or graduated from college, and most owning their own home. Women outnumbered men nearly two to one, and the median age was 65.2 years.

A glance at the magazine shows why it achieved widespread acceptance, ranking with other best-selling magazines of the day. It put on a bright face in the late 1990s, a makeover from an earlier staid image. Its popular style appealed to a wide audience, not just the elderly. It covered topical subjects in well-edited articles. For example, the final issue of 1997 featured popular singer Tony Bennett on a glitzy, full-color cover. "Red Hot and Cool—Tony Bennett: Singing from the Heart," shouted the headline. In a box below the image of Bennett (dressed to kill in a tan suit and open white shirt) was a teaser focusing on a hot health topic: "Managed Care, Can We Learn to Love It?" Inside, articles featured an interview with national television newsman Sam Donaldson; a travel piece about offbeat beaches; a pictorial on notable figures who had turned fifty called "The Big Five Oh"; tips for consumers; food and drink recipes; and a plethora of advertisements ranging from cold and flu medicines to automobiles and promotions for AARP services such as insurance, credit cards, and pharmacy service.

In short, *Modern Maturity* matured into a widely read magazine and a pioneering influence on the American scene in the last part of the twentieth century because of the foresight of an activist woman, Andrus, who refused to be considered elderly and who had the vision to capture an audience of Americans that was growing older. As that demographic became even larger in the first decade of the twenty-first century, the magazine modernized to reflect the different life experiences of the so-called boomer generation as it aged. The title *Modern Maturity* was dropped in 2002, and it became *AARP The Magazine*, maintaining its position as the magazine with the highest circulation in the United States, perhaps even worldwide.

Michael Posner

SEE ALSO: *AARP (American Association of Retired Persons); Bennett, Tony; Gray Panthers;* Time.

BIBLIOGRAPHY

American Association of Retired Persons. "The Story of AARP." Washington, DC: American Association of Retired Persons, 1971.

Schurenberg, Eric, and Lani Luciano. "Special Report: The Empire Called AARP." *Money*, October 1, 1988.

Modern Times

The final cinematic appearance of Charlie Chaplin's Little Tramp character is also the legendary filmmaker's first talkie, though he uses sound sparingly and with predictable artistry. Made at the height of the Depression, in 1936, the film explores the dehumanization and dislocation that accompanied the advent of the industrial age. It provided modern film with some of its most iconic images and a song, "Smile," that became an instant pop standard.

The film's theme is spelled out in the foreword that runs after the opening credits: "'Modern Times.' A story of industry, of individual enterprise—humanity crusading in the pursuit of happiness." The film then opens with an overhead shot of a flock of sheep rushing through a chute. The sheep quickly dissolve into a similar shot of industrial laborers surging out of a subway station on their way to the factory.

A long sequence set on the factory floor follows. The Little Tramp, Chaplin's impish everyman, is shown without his traditional baggy pants, derby hat, and cane. Instead he wears the gray coveralls of a common assembly-line worker. The modern industrial laborer's predicament is symbolized by a scene in which the Tramp is sucked inside a huge machine while oiling it, passing through its myriad gears like just another part in the mechanism. Although he escapes that jam, the Tramp is soon driven mad by the dull routine of factory life. He goes berserk and is hauled off to an asylum. Thus ends the second reel.

The rest of the film continues in episodic fashion. The Tramp is jailed after he inadvertently becomes part of a pro-union march. Released, he meets up with the Gamin (a ravishing Paulette Goddard), an orphan girl who has run away from home to avoid being placed in an orphanage. The two tramps fall in love, and Chaplin's character vows to get them a home "even if I have to work for it." He fails at a series of jobs before the police, inevitably, come looking for the runaway girl. Forced to flee, the pair return to the open road, where they join hands and pledge to "get along" somehow.

Modern Times was promoted as Chaplin's first sound film, but that is something of a misnomer. Chaplin uses sound only to serve the film's theme of technology and dehumanization: spoken voices are heard emanating from mechanical devices, the factory boss is heard urging the Tramp to get back to work, and so on. Chaplin's actual voice is heard only briefly, singing a nonsense song. Special sound effects and an original musical score enhance the pantomime.

A number of the images from *Modern Times*—the Tramp caught up in the machinery, waving the red flag at the head of a labor demonstration, and the final poignant shot of the Tramp and the Gamin walking uncertainly off into the sunset—have become indelibly imprinted on the pop cultural consciousness. As the final undeniable masterwork of one of the twentieth century's greatest directors, it continues to generate criticism and commentary within the world film community. Fittingly, in 1989, *Modern Times* was entered into the National Film Registry, a program created by the Library of Congress to preserve films deemed "culturally, historically, or esthetically important."

Robert E. Schnakenberg

SEE ALSO: *Chaplin, Charlie; The Great Depression;* The Masses; *Silent Movies.*

BIBLIOGRAPHY

Flom, Eric L. *Chaplin in the Sound Era: An Analysis of the Seven Talkies*. Jefferson, NC: McFarland, 1997.

Kamin, Dan, and Scott Eyman. *The Comedy of Charlie Chaplin: Artistry in Motion*. Lanham, MD: Scarecrow Press, 2008.

Mitchell, Glenn. *The Chaplin Encyclopedia*. London: B. T. Batsford, 1997.

Modernism

In its broadest sense, modernism represents the associated and often competing ideas and artistic expressions that surfaced in the wake of the technological and cultural changes of the late nineteenth and early twentieth centuries, up until World War II. Although each artist and thinker projected a different vision of modernism, the modernist aesthetic challenged the perceived unity celebrated by the rationalist thought of the Enlightenment and Victorian culture. By the end of the nineteenth century, many of the modern nation states had taken shape, and a second industrial revolution occurred, leading to a mass migration into urban centers. Rapidly changing technological advances such as the telephone, the automobile, and the radio provided an increased sense of connectedness. However, they also signaled an upheaval of traditional notions of time and space because they provided for increased speed in mobility and communication.

In a way, the increased connectedness led to a growing sense of unease as traditional notions of community and culture were challenged by the fast-paced urban environments, leaving people at once exhilarated by the new set of possibilities and frightened by the uncertainty. Initially, the technological advancements were embraced for their limitless potential. At the onset of World War I, however, artists were more guarded in their acceptance of the rapid changes. The same technology that had produced such elation and promised unbridled progress increased the brutality of war, decimating populations and landscapes. The vast amount of resources and people consumed by the war produced a profound sense of alienation as modernist artists and thinkers attempted to reconcile themselves with a world that had somehow been led astray by the emancipatory promises of the new century. After World War I, artists became more pessimistic about the possibility of the ability of the masses to transcend the limitations brought on by capitalism, socialism, nationalism, etc., and sought refuge deeper within the world of art.

Modernism encompasses a spectrum of thought that viewed the individual as the maker of the world. Universal scientific and religious explanations were contested by thinkers such as Karl Marx, Friederich Nietzsche, Albert Einstein, Charles Darwin, and Sigmund Freud. Coupled with the horrors experienced during World War I, their revolutionary thoughts profoundly influenced the political, social and artistic perspectives reflected in the works of modernist artists, such as James Joyce, T. S. Eliot, Virginia Woolf, Ezra Pound, Marcel Duchamp, and Pablo Picasso.

However it is defined, it is clear that modernism was a celebration of a technological age, the so-called Age of the Machine, and a condemnation of it, a faithful acceptance of any new, exciting cultural expression and the excuse for fearful and anxious reactions in the face of it. The term has often included many artistic movements that originated mostly in Europe (impressionism, expressionism, futurism, cubism, symbolism, and imagism, for example) but soon became truly international, often sharing a tendency toward abstraction and a refusal of realism. The modernist tendency expressed itself as antirepresentationalism in painting, free verse in poetry, and stream-of-consciousness narrative in fiction, to name just a few examples. Most critics agree that the peak of the modernist period was the first quarter of the twentieth century, but some place it as early as the 1890s, as did Frank Kermode in a famous study aptly titled *The Sense of an Ending*.

URBANIZATION AND MODERNISM

Understandably, the impact of the modern times was most visible in the urban areas. Cities such as New York started growing upward, from their pre-elevator six stories to the thirty stories of the skyscraper by the end of the nineteenth century. Daniel Burnham's triangular Flatiron Building (built in 1903), the tallest building of its time, became a symbol of such times. Photographers such as Alfred Stieglitz, Alvin Langdon Coburn, and Edward Steichen started to immortalize these tall buildings as aesthetic objects. However, the skyscrapers soon acquired a different role: performing an advertising function for the commercial interests that had built them in the first place. These structures became icons of the modern age and, above all, of modern industrial civilization.

In New York City the very names of streets such as Broadway, Wall Street, and Madison Avenue reflected those structures of mass communication and persuasion, finance, capitalism, and popular culture that were defining the new modern way of life. New York was to become the modernist metropolis par excellence, but it should be stressed that modernism transformed and embraced not just one city, but many.

The city and the machine became the subject matter of modernist art. In a way, art was perceived as a defense against the ever-changing world of bridges, skyscrapers, steam engines, and railroads. American modernism was characterized by an attempt to connect the new age of the machine with a native cultural tradition. It was as if in order to look at the future one first had to look backward, especially at the century that had just come to a close. This is perhaps one of the most interesting paradoxes of modernity: that the projection into the future and the emergence of a popular modernism also coincided with a deepening traditionalism. This tendency is detectable in literature—in writers as diverse as William Faulkner, William Carlos Williams, and F. Scott Fitzgerald—and in the visual arts with adherents of the precisionist movement. This movement consisted of a handful of young painters and photographers, including Edward Hopper (1882–1967) and Paul Strand (1890–

1976), who employed a combination of realism and cubism, and it would represent one of the most innovative American contributions to international modernism.

ARCHITECTURE

Perhaps no art form represented the modernist aesthetic as prevalently as architecture. Specialized industrial processes had been in effect since the 1880s, but with electricity mechanization was much accelerated. In 1910 one in ten urban homes had electricity, but by 1930 most homes did. The consumer, especially the woman of the house, was surrounded with new machines: irons, sewing machines, vacuum cleaners, toasters, washing machines, refrigerators—in brief, the household was transformed into a wholly new, exciting, mechanized environment. The increased availability of building materials gave rise to a host of new building techniques. In the early twentieth century, architects sought to complement the increased urbanization by constructing purely functional buildings and, by extension, cityscapes.

In a sense, modernist design attempted to restore a fragmented society by assembling a harmonious unity between structures and the surrounding landscape. Prior to World War I, modernists expressed a certain jubilation over the mechanical nature of industrial landscapes. In *The Futurist Manifesto* (1909), Filippo Tommaso Marinetti called for an all-out rejection of the past and for artists to embrace the new machine age by incorporating the speed and youth of the new culture into their designs. By focusing on the structural components of buildings, futurists sought to highlight the simple lines of the steel and other materials that went into fabricating the urban environment. In his influential series of design drawings, Antonio Sant'Elia created an intricate city with towering buildings and bridges, which would highlight the efficient modes of the new industrial metropolis.

The enthusiasm for all things mechanical and industrial lost much of its zeal after World War I. Faced with a daunting number of deaths, many at the hands of "improved" machines such as tanks and cannons, many of the modernists focused their attention on reconciling the relationship human beings had to nature. Designers such as Le Corbusier and Frank Lloyd Wright stripped away ornamentation, such as columns and domes, in order to create buildings that were geometrical in form, typically including glass facades or stark brick or granite exteriors. Le Corbusier's Villa Savoye (completed in 1931) in France and Wright's Falling Water (completed in 1939) in southwestern Pennsylvania are perhaps the most emblematic of this style. Villa Savoye's white, rectangular structure is elevated by a series of pillars, which, for Le Corbusier, allowed for the building and land to coexist in a seemingly harmonious relationship, but it also elevated the construction over nature. The stark whiteness contrasts with the green grass and trees, and the rooftop garden serves to extend the natural landscape the structure exists upon.

Wright attempted to incorporate nature into his buildings plans in more organic ways than Le Corbusier. Developing from his earlier styles, Wright's Falling Water fully immersed the residential home within its surrounding environment. The house is built on top of a waterfall, which pours out from beneath the structure. The window-filled rooms provide an illusory link between the inside and outside, as do the constant sounds of the water that permeates the house. In all, it serves as a testament to technology's triumph over nature, seemingly offering a harmonious unity in the face of an ever-changing and chaotic world.

MUSIC AND PAINTING

Like architecture, music found its inspiration in the scientific and technological progress of the early part of the twentieth century. Where architecture found its smoothness in the geometric shapes and facades of its buildings, music conceptualized this by creating new tonalities and patterns. Arnold Schoenberg epitomized this with his twelve-tone system, which focused on a strict system of organization. Similarly, Igor Stravinsky invented new harmonies through repetition. In the United States, jazz artists including Louis Armstrong and Charlie Parker incorporated the chaotic hustle of urban life into their elaborate compositions.

Painting in the early twentieth century branched out into a wide range of schools, including cubism, expressionism, dadaism, and surrealism. Although each movement had a variety of goals and was influenced by a complex set of circumstances, perhaps the two most compelling influences on modernist painting were Freud's groundbreaking work in psychoanalysis and the technological advances in photography. In his "Manifeste du Surrealisme" (1924), André Breton argued that rationalism hindered creative expression, and artists could truly express themselves only by exploring the deep recesses of the subconscious. The influence of Freud's dream theories are readily apparent in the work of Salvador Dali, who created vivid canvases of seemingly unrelated parts. Picasso's forays into cubism rejected the representational images of realism and romanticism by trying to capture the very act of seeing the object. His *Les Demoiselles d'Avignon* (1907) signaled a break from the traditional modes of painting as he manipulated perspective and depth of field. Perhaps, pushed by the camera, modernist paintings moved further away from representation. The later cubists such as Marcel Duchamp and František Kupka attempted to transcend the technological apparatus by offering paintings that provided for a multitude of perspectives combined into a single image.

NOVELISTS AND POETS

In literature, European writers such as James Joyce, W. B. Yeats, and Virginia Woolf offered various representations of the struggle of the modern person within the increasingly industrialized world. One of modernism's lasting legacies can be found in Joyce's *Ulysses* (1922), which upends traditional narrative structures through its narration of the life of Leopold Bloom. *Ulysses* situates the everyday, mundane issues of Bloom's life within a complex reinterpretation of *The Odyssey*. Virginia Woolf's *Mrs Dalloway* (1925) and William Faulkner's *Absalom, Absalom!* (1936) utilized the stream of consciousness technique by traveling through the minds of various characters, sometimes in such complex ways that it is difficult to discern who is speaking, in order to construct a representation of the protagonist's life.

Poetic explorations followed similar modes of thought; however, the shift from an almost utopian spirit to an overwhelming sense of despair is, perhaps, more readily noticeable within poetry. One of the most influential poets was Yeats, whose writings portrayed one of modernism's most perplexing problems: how to represent the unrepresentable. Large concepts such as truth, beauty, good, and evil had been torn asunder by the work of Nietzsche, who proposed that such knowledge can only be ascertained through multiple perspectives and, at best, only indirectly. Yeats and the poets attempted to construct complex metaphors that would serve to reveal the truth—but only to the truly discerning reader or thinker. Eliot's *The Waste*

Land (1922) and Pound's *The Cantos* (1925) project an undeniable sense of loss and dismay. Both writers offer pondering treatises on how, to paraphrase Eliot, one can shore the fragments against their ruins. Hilda Doolittle (commonly known as H. D.), Mina Loy, Marianne Moore, and Gertrude Stein were among the leading female voices of the modernist movement. Similar to Pound, H. D. attempted to remove sentimentality from poetry by constructing poems through precise language.

AN ONGOING PROJECT

Compared to those in Europe, the American artists were more critical and, in many respects, more worried about the consequences of mechanical civilization. The dangers of robotization deriving from matching the man to the machine and the machine to the man found perhaps their best expression in Charlie Chaplin's *Modern Times* (1936). However, Waldo Frank had already voiced, in his 1919 book *Our America*, the concern of many Americans who feared that the dehumanizing forces of technology would lead to psychic fragmentation and spiritual deprivation. Even so, there was an abiding sense that there was nothing that could be done to check the advance of technological innovation.

As historian Raymond Williams puts it, "Out of an experience of the cities came the experience of the future." In addition to this concern, there is the question of whether modernism has actually ended. Austrian-born U.S. critic Marjorie Perloff, for example has argued that modernism is not a period that has ended but a project in progress. What is certain is that although modernism was not to everybody's taste, the divergent interpretations and expressions of modernism attempted to address the growing concerns of living in a modern world, and it is the movement that has best described and shaped our modern consciousness.

Anna Notaro

SEE ALSO: *Armstrong, Louis; Chaplin, Charlie;* Cosmopolitan*; Einstein, Albert; Faulkner, William; Fitzgerald, F. Scott; Freud, Sigmund; Jazz; Parker, Charlie; Picasso, Pablo; Skyscrapers; World War I; World War II.*

BIBLIOGRAPHY

Bradbury, Malcolm, and James McFarlane, eds. *Modernism, 1890–1930.* Harmondsworth, England: Penguin, 1991.

Britt, George. *Forty Years—Forty Millions: The Career of Frank A. Munsey.* Port Washington, NY: Kennikat Press, 1972.

Covert, Catherine L., and John D. Stevens, eds. *Mass Media Between the Wars: Perceptions of Cultural Tensions, 1918–1941.* Syracuse, NY: Syracuse University Press, 1984.

Czitrom, Daniel J. *Media and the American Mind: From Morse to McLuhan.* Chapel Hill: University of North Carolina Press, 1982.

Fox, Richard Wightman, and T. J. Jackson Lears, eds. *The Culture of Consumption: Critical Essays in American History, 1880–1980.* New York: Pantheon Books, 1983.

Gans, Herbert J. *Popular Culture and High Culture.* New York: Basic Books, 1974.

Garvey Gruber, Ellen. *The Adman in the Parlor.* New York: Oxford University Press, 1996.

Giedion, Sigfried. *Mechanization Takes Command: A Contribution to Anonymous History.* New York: Oxford University Press, 1948.

Kern, Stephen. *The Culture of Time and Space, 1880–1918.* Cambridge, MA: Harvard University Press, 1983.

Lears, T. J. Jackson. *No Place of Grace: Antimodernism and the Transformation of American Culture, 1880–1920.* New York: Pantheon Books, 1981.

Lipsitz, George. *Time Passages: Collective Memory and American Popular Culture.* Minneapolis: University of Minnesota Press, 1990.

Marchard, Roland. *Advertising the American Dream: Making Way for Modernity, 1920–1940.* Berkeley: University of California Press, 1985.

Pells, Richard H. *Modernist America: Art, Music, Movies, and the Globalization of American Culture.* New Haven, CT: Yale University Press, 2011.

Perloff, Marjorie. *21st-Century Modernism: The "New" Poetics.* Malden, MA: Blackwell, 2002.

Schleifer, Ronald. *Modernism and Popular Music.* New York: Cambridge University Press, 2011.

Schoenbach, Lisi. *Pragmatic Modernism.* New York: Oxford University Press, 2012.

Singal, Daniel Joseph, ed. *Modernist Culture in America.* Belmont, CA: Wadsworth, 1991.

Tallack, Douglas. *Twentieth-Century America: The Intellectual and Cultural Context.* London: Longman, 1991.

Werheim, Arthur Frank. *The New York Little Renaissance: Iconoclasm, Modernism, and Nationalism in American Culture, 1908–1917.* New York: New York University Press, 1976.

Momaday, N. Scott *(1934–)*

N. Scott Momaday, winner of the 1969 Pulitzer Prize for Fiction with his first novel, *House Made of Dawn* (1968), achieved international attention as an author of Native American literature. In 2007 Momaday also received a National Medal of Arts honoring his work. Through his poetry, fiction, criticism, and essays—especially *The Way to Rainy Mountain* (1969), the story of the Kiowa people, whose dominance on the American plains ended with the European American expansion—Momaday introduced Native American culture into the canon of American literature. Among his other well-known works are "The Bear," for which he won the Academy of American Poets prize in 1962, and his second novel, *The Ancient Child* (1989), a fictionalized autobiography about an Indian artist in search of his racial identity. As Momaday's popularity increased, so did interest in Native American cultural heritage, economic needs, and legal claims.

Sharon Brown

SEE ALSO: *Best Sellers.*

BIBLIOGRAPHY

"N. Scott Momaday, Ph.D., The Writer Warrior." Academy of Achievement. Accessed November 2011. Available from http://www.achievement.org/autodoc/page/mom0bio-1

Schubnell, Matthias. *N. Scott Momaday: The Cultural and Literary Background.* Norman: University of Oklahoma Press, 1985.

Monday Night Football

Monday Night Football appeared on the American pop-cultural landscape at a time when professional football was becoming the nation's preeminent televised sport. As conceived by National Football League (NFL) commissioner Pete Rozelle, *Monday Night Football* was to be a weekly prime-time showcase for the fast-growing game. ABC Sports, itself an aggressive innovator in the production and marketing of televised athletics under the stewardship of Roone Arledge, was the NFL's partner in this bold endeavor. Together, the NFL and ABC created a ratings behemoth.

A RATINGS SUCCESS

Monday Night Football debuted September 21, 1970, with a game matching Joe Namath's New York Jets against the Cleveland Browns. Keith Jackson provided the play-by-play that first season, with color commentary from the unlikely duo of Don Meredith and Howard Cosell. Meredith, a folksy former quarterback, was soon nicknamed "Dandy Don" by the acerbic Cosell, a one-time lawyer whose pomposity was matched only by his verbosity. The oil-and-water team became a mainstay of the Monday night telecasts. When ex-Giants great Frank Gifford replaced Jackson in 1971, the crew that would dominate the program's glory years was in place.

The Monday night broadcast was an instant ratings success, in no small part thanks to the uniqueness of the concept. By covering only one game a week, ABC could devote sufficient resources to *Monday Night Football* to make it into a prime-time extravaganza. The production used nine cameras instead of the four or five used for other NFL telecasts. Other technical innovations included the deployment of handheld cameras to capture sideline action and the regular use of the Goodyear blimp to provide aerial views of the stadiums. "We approached every game as if it was the Super Bowl," commented NFL senior vice president Dennis Lewin, a one-time *Monday Night Football* staffer.

However innovative the concept and execution, *Monday Night Football* could not have succeeded without the interpersonal dynamics of its broadcast crew. Eschewing the two-man approach used on most sports telecasts, *Monday Night Football* became the first national sports program to place three men in the enclosed space of the play-by-play booth. The mostly male audience found much to hate in the bewigged, professorial Cosell, but that was just the point. He was the man Everyman loved to hate, and his constant needling of the good-natured Meredith and the mush-mouthed Gifford provided some great theater-of-the-absurd exchanges. Even blowouts and mismatches drew huge audiences, as viewers tuned in to hear what "Humble Howard" would say each week.

SURVIVING THE LOSS OF COSELL

The show took a hit when Cosell retired from the *Monday Night Football* booth after the 1983 season. It lost much of its unique claim on the viewers' attention and reaped a harvest of bad press when the outspoken former analyst refused to go quietly. After taking every opportunity to gloat publicly over the show's precipitous ratings decline following his departure, in 1985 Cosell produced a scathing memoir, *I Never Played the Game*, in which he lambasted his former boothmates. Grammatically challenged ex-jocks O. J. Simpson and Joe Namath gamely tried to fill Cosell's analyst's chair, with predictably stupefying results.

For the 1986 season, ABC shunted Gifford to the color commentator's chair and brought in veteran play-by-play man

Monday Night Football *Hosts.* *Frank Gifford, Howard Cosell, and O. J. Simpson prepare to call a* Monday Night Football *game between the Minnesota Vikings and San Francisco 49ers in 1983.* MICHAEL ZAGARIS/CONTRIBUTOR/GETTY IMAGES SPORT/GETTY IMAGES.

Al Michaels to call the action. The facile Michaels quickly established himself as a strong presence in the booth, though Gifford seemed a bit uncomfortable in his new role. The following season, former NFL lineman Dan Dierdorf was added as the inevitable third wheel. Although the garrulous Dierdorf did not seem to mesh well with Gifford, ratings picked up, and ABC did not make a change in the booth (but for the brief addition of Lynn Swann in 1988) for the next eleven years.

During that time, ABC saw its franchise grow into even more of a ratings powerhouse. Young viewers were coming back to *Monday Night Football* in droves, enticed in part by a rollicking Hank Williams Jr. theme song. "Are you ready for some footbaaaaaallll?" the scruffy country-and-western scion wailed in the opening number beginning in 1991. The song went on to invite "all [his] rowdy friends" over for a "Monday night party."

Monday Night Football was thrown for a loop in 1997 when color man Gifford was caught on film by a supermarket tabloid in the arms of a buxom flight attendant who bore no resemblance to his wife, perky TV chat show hostess Kathie Lee Gifford. Although "Giff" later claimed he was set up by the paparazzi, it was an enormous public relations hit for a man whose appeal largely rested on his squeaky clean football hero image. Gifford's indiscretion was only one of many reasons he was ushered out of the broadcast booth in time for the 1998 season. The on-air chemistry between him and Dierdorf was dreadful, and Michaels too often had to play traffic cop between two blabbermouths instead of calling the action. Worst of all, viewers began tuning out this pigskin McLaughlin Group in ever-increasing numbers. Ratings for the 1997 season were down significantly from the year before.

In need of a fresh face, ABC turned to Boomer Esiason, a genial former quarterback with little broadcasting experience. To make room in the booth, the suits moved Gifford into a nebulous cohosting role on a new twenty-minute pregame show, *Monday Night Blast*. Start time of the games was moved up to 8:20 p.m. eastern standard time, to the consternation of many viewers out West. An obvious attempt to inject some energy into the wheezing *Monday Night* franchise, *Monday Night Blast* was a raucous sports bar party hosted by loud-mouthed ESPN anchor Chris Berman. The push was on to recapture the attention of younger viewers—at the risk of alienating older ones with its high-decibel puffery—but at the end of the twentieth century, football ratings continued to decline across the board.

CHANGE AFTER CHANGE AFTER CHANGE

During the first decade of the 2000s the only thing constant about *Monday Night Football* was change. For the 2000 and 2001 seasons, the program experimented with an unusual booth lineup: Michaels was joined by Hall of Fame quarterback Dan Fouts and acerbic comedian Dennis Miller. The combination never quite gelled; Miller annoyed viewers with his long-winded rants, and Fouts failed to provide the authoritative player's voice that fans had come to expect. In 2002 legendary broadcaster and former coach John Madden teamed up with Michaels, and the two quickly developed a smooth and enjoyable chemistry that vastly improved the broadcast.

Then came perhaps the biggest switch of all. After the 2005 season, the NFL ended its thirty-six-year relationship with ABC and moved *Monday Night Football* to ESPN. Michaels and Madden migrated to the Sunday night game, which had shifted from ESPN to NBC, so ESPN had to put together a new *Monday Night Football* announcing team. They chose veteran sportscaster Mike Tirico to do the play-by-play announcing and analyst Tony Kornheiser and former player Joe Theismann to provide the color commentary. The new team proved disastrous. Kornheiser and Theismann did not get along; Theismann spent too much time talking about his glory days as a Washington Redskins quarterback, while Kornheiser continually interrupted him to make sarcastic wisecracks that often fell flat.

After just one year, ESPN replaced Theismann with former Eagles quarterback Ron Jaworski, popularly known as "Jaws," who proved a competent analyst of the nuts and bolts of the game. Kornheiser left the program in 2009, to be replaced by Super Bowl–winning coach Jon Gruden. Controversy struck *Monday Night Football* again in 2011 when Williams, who had performed the "Rowdy Night" opening song for twenty years, was publicly quoted comparing President Barack Obama to Adolf Hitler. In response to the ensuing publicity storm, ESPN dropped Williams's song from the broadcast—although he claimed the decision was his own. In 2012 ESPN announced that Jaworski was leaving the program but would remain with the network. In spite of all the turmoil and the revolving door of the broadcast booth, as of 2012 *Monday Night Football* had been the highest-rated cable program for six years in a row.

Robert E. Schnakenberg

SEE ALSO: *Arledge, Roone; Cable TV; Cosell, Howard; ESPN; Gifford, Frank; Live Television; Madden, John; Namath, Joe; National Football League (NFL); Professional Football; Sex Scandals; Simpson, O. J.; Sports Heroes; Super Bowl; Swann, Lynn; Tabloids; Television; Television Anchors; Williams, Hank, Jr.*

BIBLIOGRAPHY

Cosell, Howard, and Peter Bonventre. *I Never Played the Game.* New York: William Morrow, 1985.

Gunther, Marc, and Bill Carter. *Monday Night Mayhem*. New York: Beech Tree Books, 1988.

Hyatt, Wesley. *Kicking off the Week: A History of Monday Night Football on ABC Television, 1970–2005.* Jefferson, NC: McFarland, 2007.

The Monkees

On September 8, 1965, Los Angeles's *Daily Variety* ran an advertisement calling for "Folk & Rock Musicians-Singers" and "4 Insane Boys, Age 17–21" for "Acting Roles in a New TV Series." The 437 young hopefuls who auditioned for producers Bob Rafelson (*Five Easy Pieces*) and Bert Schneider included Paul Williams, Harry Nilsson, and Stephen Stills (but not Charles Manson, despite the urban legend to the contrary). The goal was to find four lads who embodied the joie de vivre the Beatles displayed in their early celluloid romps, *A Hard Day's Night* (1964) and *Help!* (1965). That Liverpool quartet was already reinventing itself, but many wished that the moptops would stay giddy and innocent forever.

That is what the creators of the Monkees (even the name was similar to the Beatles) were banking on. The television show/rock band consisted of Micky Dolenz, Davy Jones, Peter Tork, and Mike Nesmith, who were prepped, drilled, and rehearsed, in both music and improvisational techniques, until they could pass as a group. Dolenz (drums and lead vocals) was a child actor under the name Micky Braddock, of *Circus Boy* fame. The British-born Jones (assorted handheld percussion instruments), an ex-jockey, played the Artful Dodger on Broadway in *Oliver!* He was also why another British musician named David Jones took the stage name Bowie. Tork (rhythm guitar) was a folk singer. Rounding out the manufactured band was Nesmith (lead guitar), who also had some musical chops. Nesmith, rarely seen without his wool hat in those days, was heir to the Liquid Paper fortune. His mother Bette invented the office product.

EXPERIMENTS IN SYNERGY

In what has been called the precursor to music videos, *The Monkees* featured the wacky adventures of these four freewheeling musicians who lived together in a California beach house. The fluffy surrealistic plots, complete with non sequiturs, sound effects, one-liners, and slow- and fast-motion camera tricks, usually consisted of the boys running afoul of villains and rescuing maidens. It was probably the first show that could be described as "trippy," but it was all good clean fun. A typical plot: The boys throw a party without a chaperone who will please the father of Davy's new girlfriend, so Micky dresses up as a female chaperone. All would wrap up in time for a song at the end, in a format that would be borrowed by another fabricated television show band, *The Partridge Family*.

The Monkees. *The members of the made-for-television band the Monkees were, clockwise from left, guitarist Mike Nesmith, singer Davy Jones, bassist Peter Tork, and drummer Micky Dolenz.* SILVER SCREEN COLLECTION/CONTRIBUTOR/MOVIEPIX/GETTY IMAGES.

With Don Kirshner as music supervisor, the producers brought in the decade's best pop tunesmiths, such as Boyce and Hart and Neil Diamond, to pen the Monkees' songs, which included "Last Train to Clarksville" (which Dolenz claims is an antiwar song), "I'm a Believer," and "Girl." Six of their singles made it to the Top 10, and *The Monkees* won an Emmy for Outstanding Comedy Series in their first season. The albums sold millions and were cross-promoted with the television show every Monday night on NBC at 7:30 p.m. from 1966 to 1968. It was a match made in consumer heaven.

GAINING CONTROL

But Pygmalion was bound to rebel against its creator. The Monkees were not allowed to play instruments on the early records; they were just supposed to provide the vocals. This annoyed the boys and proved embarrassing when they toured, which they did, to throngs of screaming fans. One leg of their tour featured a little-known guitarist named Jimi Hendrix as their opening act; Dolenz recalls, "He'd be in the middle of 'Purple Haze' and kids would be going 'We want Da-vy!'" At a 1967 press conference, Nesmith, the most financially secure Monkee, complained that they were being passed off as something they were not. After a showdown with the producers, the Monkees were allowed more creative freedom. Monkee-penned songs appeared on their third album, the first without Kirshner at the helm.

The television show aired opposite the popular Western *Gunsmoke* and was canceled in 1968. Despite the setback, the group released a number one album, *The Birds, the Bees—the Monkees* (1968) after the announcement. The group made their movie debut that year in the unwatchable *Head*. Written by Jack Nicholson and Bob Rafelson, *Head* featured cameos by Nicholson, Dennis Hopper, Frank Zappa, and boxer Sonny Liston. The band has acknowledged that the film's soundtrack was one of their best accomplishments. Soon after, however, they would begin to splinter.

Tork left the group first, in 1969, citing exhaustion. He pursued a solo career, primarily through contributing to others' albums. He recorded many demos but did not release his own solo single until 1982. Nesmith was the next to leave in 1970. He also stayed in the music business, writing the hit "Different Drum" for Linda Ronstadt's early group, Stone Poneys. After Nesmith's departure, the group had decidedly broken up. Dolenz and Jones teamed up with Boyce and Hart in 1975, but it did not last long. Dolenz continued to write and release singles throughout the 1970s and 1980s. Jones made a cottage industry out of playing "Himself" or "Teen Idol" on several sitcoms, as well as *The Real Brady Bunch*'s theater run (Marcia Brady was president of his fan club; he appeared on an original episode of that show) and the two Brady Bunch movies.

RETURN TO THE SPOTLIGHT

The Monkees enjoyed a revitalization in 1986 with a highly publicized concert tour (mostly without Nesmith, who was still distancing himself from the group), reissues of their albums, and MTV running reruns of the television show. The star-maker machinery thought it was the right time for some new Monkees, and in 1987 another heavily promoted nationwide talent hunt was staged. That hunt produced Larry Saltis, Dino Kovas, Jared Chandler, and Marty Ross, the *New Monkees*. This time the boys lived in a big gothic mansion, with Manford, a stuffy butler, and Helen, a sarcastic pair of disembodied lips, who provided constant commentary on the many television screens throughout the residence. It did not work, the cross-promoted album did not sell, and the search for the New Monkees ended up having taken longer than the resulting show actually ran.

It turned out that people were still interested in the old Monkees. In the 1990s the group got together to record new material and released the eleventh album bearing the group's name, 1996's *Justus*. A tour in 1996 and a television special were welcomed by the masses but criticized by the press. Old conflicts reemerged, and Nesmith abandoned the tour's second leg. Future tours never included all four members at once, and each ended acrimoniously.

Nesmith recorded and released music into the 2010s. He became an innovative video producer, winning the first-ever video Grammy for *Elephant Parts*, and was the executive producer of the cult film *Repo Man* (1984) and others. Author and philanthropist are titles he has also added to his resume. Dolenz has dabbled in acting, producing, and writing; he most recently went on tour with his sister in 2010. Jones recorded music into the first decade of the 2000s, and his last album was released in 2009. Jones died in 2012 after a severe heart attack.

The first and arguably the best of pop's fabricated bands, the Monkees were a 1960s synergy of music, television, and marketing. The band has served as fodder for academic analysis; they were one of the groups analyzed in Hugh Barker and Yuval Taylor's *Faking It: The Search for Authenticity in Popular Music*.

Karen Lurie

SEE ALSO: *The Beatles;* The Brady Bunch*;* Gunsmoke*; Hendrix, Jimi; MTV;* The Partridge Family*; Television.*

BIBLIOGRAPHY

Baker, Glenn A. *Monkeemania: The True Story of the Monkees.* New York: St. Martin's, 1986.

Barker, Hugh, and Yuval Taylor. *Faking It: The Quest for Authenticity in Popular Music.* New York: W. W. Norton, 2007.

Bronson, Harold, ed. *Hey, Hey, We're the Monkees.* Los Angeles: General Publishing Group, 1996.

Dolenz, Micky, and Mark Bego. *I'm a Believer: My Life of Monkees, Music, and Madness.* New York: Hyperion, 1993.

Lefcowitz, Eric. *The Monkees Tale.* Berkeley, CA: Last Gasp, 1985.

Massingill, Randi L. *Total Control: The Michael Nesmith Story.* Mesa, AZ: FLEXquarters, 1997.

Smith, Ethan H. "Chimp off the Old Block: 10 Stupid Questions." *Entertainment Weekly*, November 18, 1994, 104.

Monopoly

Invented, ironically, during the Great Depression of the 1930s, the game of Monopoly symbolizes and exploits the capitalist ethic. It was an immediate success, becoming the quintessential American board game. By the late 1990s it was still the world's biggest-selling copyrighted game, licensed in forty-three countries and published in twenty-six different languages.

Monopoly was inspired by The Landlord's Game, which began as a nonproprietary Quaker folk game. Having been taught how to play by Quaker friends, Charles B. Darrow (1889–1967) developed his own game for public release, using the street names from Atlantic City, New Jersey. In 1935 he sold it for a royalty to the game manufacturer Parker Brothers. It became a worldwide phenomenon, leading to the creation in 1973 of the National and World Monopoly Championships.

The game is based on the working principles of capitalism and real estate. The objective is to become the wealthiest player, "bankrupting" all others through buying and selling properties; building houses; charging rents; and handling mortgages, utilities, and interests. Numerous editions and variations have been developed. In the twenty-first century, there are electronic versions that allow players to make purchases with debit cards rather than with traditional Monopoly money. Special adaptations continue to celebrate popular cultural icons such as Pixar's *Cars* franchise, and Monopoly is available for all the major video gaming systems and for computers and android phones.

Catherine C. Galley
Briavel Holcomb

SEE ALSO: *Atlantic City; Board Games; Computer Games; The Great Depression; Parker Brothers; Smartphones; Video Games.*

BIBLIOGRAPHY

Anspach, Ralph. *The Billion Dollar Monopoly Swindle.* Bloomington, IN: Xlibris Corporation, 2010.

Brady, Maxine. *The Monopoly Book: Strategy and Tactics of the World's Most Popular Game.* New York: D. McKay, 1974.

"Cleaning Up in 2003." *Strategic Finance* 84, no. 8 (2003).

Darzinskis, Kaz. *Winning Monopoly: A Complete Guide to Property Accumulation, Cash Flow Strategy, and Negotiating Techniques When Playing the Best-Selling Board Game.* New York: Perennial Library, 1987.

Monroe, Bill *(1911–1996)*

Seldom can a particular genre of music be credited to the vision and influence of a lone individual as is the case with Bill Monroe and bluegrass. In a career spanning more than half a century, the father of bluegrass created, popularized, and trained numerous practitioners in this distinctly American style of music. While sobriquets such as Creator of the Blues lavished on W. C. Handy or King of Rock and Roll bestowed upon Elvis Presley are gleefully denounced by musicologists, few, if any, scholars challenge Monroe's supremacy in the development of the "high and lonesome sound," a blending of Anglo-Scottish-Irish fiddle tunes, southern gospel singing, and the stylings of African American blues. Born in the isolated community of Rosine, Kentucky, Monroe combined these elements of his local culture into a new form of music, which would attract fans worldwide.

For many people in rural areas, music served a dual function of preserving a heritage and providing entertainment. Monroe was clearly a product and eventually a practitioner of this aesthetic. As the youngest child in a noticeably musical family, Monroe was reared in a world of melodies and ballads. His mother sang and played the accordion and the fiddle. His

Bill Monroe. *Bill Monroe blended elements of many traditional and ethnic musical styles to create the uniquely American genre of bluegrass music.* SYLVIA PITCHER/CONTRIBUTOR/ REDFERNS/ GETTY IMAGES.

siblings developed similar skills on an assortment of stringed instruments. From his own explanation, Monroe identified his greatest influence as his mother's brother, Pendleton Vandiver. Monroe was orphaned during his adolescence, and Vandiver functioned both as guardian and teacher, instructing his nephew in the intricacies of old-time fiddle music. Years later, "Uncle Pen" would be commemorated in one of Monroe's most endearing songs. An additional influence during Monroe's formative years was Arnold Schultz, an African American railroad worker who exposed the youth to country blues guitar.

MONROE BROTHERS

Although Monroe initially played mandolin behind Uncle Pen's fiddling at local dances during the mid-1920s, his emergence as a professional musician coincided with his switch to the mandolin and the formation of a band with brothers Charlie (on guitar) and Birch (on fiddle) in 1927. By 1930 the trio was performing on the radio in Indiana, and by 1936 the Monroe Brothers (sans Birch) had secured a recording contract with Bluebird Records. Possessing a repertoire of sacred and secular material, the duo recorded sixty songs between 1936 and 1938. Although this partnership enjoyed a notable popularity with titles such as "What Would You Give in Exchange for Your Soul?" stylistically there was little to set the Monroes' apart from their peers. Brother acts, a format characterized by limited instrumentation and an emphasis on vocal harmonies, were commonplace among country music practitioners during the 1930s. By late 1938 the Monroe brothers had gone their separate ways.

BLUE GRASS BOYS

In 1939 Monroe assembled a new band he named the Blue Grass Boys. During the same year he joined the staff of the Nashville-based radio show the *Grand Ole Opry*, which resulted in a greater degree of commercial exposure. During this period Monroe's music was clearly undergoing a transformation—moving from the old-time string band and the brother duos into something new but not fully defined. The definition arrived in 1945 when Earl Scruggs, a twenty-year-old banjo player from North Carolina, joined the Monroe organization. Scruggs's pioneering approach to his instrument provided the Blue Grass Boys with a relentless tempo and driving complexity that immediately distinguished the outfit from any of its contemporaries.

The band that emerged in 1945—Scruggs, Lester Flatt (guitar and vocals), Cederic Rainwater (bass), Chubby Wise (fiddle), and Monroe (vocals and mandolin)—would be revered by aficionados as the ultimate bluegrass outfit. During the next three years this version of the Blue Grass Boys created the sound that would remain the model for generations of imitators. By the late 1940s other artists were beginning to record cover versions of Monroe's compositions, and bluegrass was a recognizable genre within country music. The music of Monroe and his associates was multifaceted and far more complex than a casual listen suggests. The most immediately audible characteristic was the emphasis on breathtaking musicianship. On recordings such as "Bluegrass Breakdown" and "Bluegrass Special," the mandolin, banjo, and fiddle all function as lead instruments, soloing in a modernistic fashion that emphasizes not only speed and dexterity but also emotion and composure.

Titles such as "Little Cabin Home on the Hill" and "Kentucky Waltz" were nostalgic remembrances of a past simplicity of time and place. The production of such pastorals coincided with the wartime migration of many Appalachian families into the urban centers of America. For displaced mountaineers, the music of the Blue Grass Boys and subsequent artists provided a comforting link with a life they had left behind.

FLATT AND SCRUGGS

In 1948 Flatt and Scruggs left Monroe to form their own band, the Foggy Mountain Boys. Ironically, their popularity greatly outshone their mentor. During the next twenty years Flatt and Scruggs fronted their own radio program, frequently guest starred on the television show *The Beverly Hillbillies*, provided music for the Hollywood film *Bonnie and Clyde*, and even dabbled in creating bluegrass versions of rock-and-roll songs. Their recordings of "The Ballad of Jed Clampett" and "Foggy Mountain Breakdown" became perhaps the most widely known standards in the bluegrass songbook throughout the rest of the twentieth century.

Although Monroe retained a contract with Decca Records and a permanent spot on the *Grand Ole Opry*, during the 1950s and much of the 1960s his position as a performer was largely overshadowed by that of Flatt and Scruggs. Despite this lack of recognition, Monroe persevered. A prolific composer, he authored dozens of songs and instrumental pieces. Perhaps more important, Monroe kept his vision of bluegrass alive via an endless schedule of live performances. While financial constraints conspired against maintaining a permanent touring band, Bill Monroe and His Blue Grass Boys were an enduring institution. Meticulously attired in matching suits, the Monroe group navigated the highways and backroads of America, graciously performing for fans.

Such determination eventually paid off. As the audiences for folk music expanded during the 1960s, bluegrass enjoyed an increased popularity. Monroe's role in the music's creation was reexamined, and his persona as the father of bluegrass assumed a deeper meaning with each passing year. Despite advancing age and periodic health problems, Monroe remained a dedicated showman well into his eighties. Although often remembered as a fiercely competitive musician, his career is best summarized by his role as a teacher. Regardless if he were training the latest bluegrass boy or jamming with amateurs after a performance, Monroe played an active role in transmitting his music to countless fans, thereby insuring its permanence in American culture. Monroe died in Nashville shortly before his eighty-fifth birthday.

J. Allen Barksdale

SEE ALSO: The Beverly Hillbillies; *Bluegrass; Blues;* Bonnie and Clyde; *Country Music; The Foggy Mountain Boys; Gospel Music;* Grand Ole Opry; *Handy, W. C.; Presley, Elvis; Scruggs, Earl.*

BIBLIOGRAPHY

Ewing, Tom, ed. *The Bill Monroe Reader.* Champaign: University of Illinois Press, 2000.

Malone, Bill C. *Country Music USA.* Austin: University of Texas Press, 1968.

Rooney, Jim. *Bossmen: Bill Monroe and Muddy Waters.* New York: Dial Press, 1971.

Rosenberg, Neil V., comp. *Bill Monroe and His Blue Grass Boys.* Nashville, TN: Country Music Foundation Press, 1974.

Rosenberg, Neil V. *Bluegrass: A History.* Urbana: University of Illinois Press, 1985.

Monroe, Earl "The Pearl" *(1944–)*

From the playgrounds of South Philadelphia in the early 1960s, through a thirteen-year career in the National Basketball Association (NBA), Earl "The Pearl" Monroe earned renown for his artistry on the court. Widely considered one of the greatest guards in basketball history, Monroe is best known for entertaining individual moves such as hesitation fakes and 360-degree spins. Monroe's discipline and intense dedication to winning led to the crowd-pleasing displays of flashy brilliance that earned him the nicknames "The Pearl," "Black Jesus," and "Magic." As part of the generation of African American ballplayers who transformed major college and professional basketball in the 1960s and 1970s, Monroe helped popularize the one-on-one style of offense now common at all levels of play.

Monroe did not begin seriously playing basketball until he was fourteen. Introduced to the game by a junior high school coach, Monroe's basketball education occurred primarily on the playgrounds. As he put it: "All my style came from the Philadelphia schoolyards." At that time African American basketball in Philadelphia centered on the Baker League, a summer program that featured playground legends, experienced pros, college stars, and promising teenagers. Largely self-taught,

Earl "The Pearl" Monroe. *Baltimore Bullets guard Earl "The Pearl" Monroe scrambles after the ball while being guarded by New York Knicks' Walt Frazier in a 1970 playoff game.* AP IMAGES.

Monroe learned the finer points of the game by closely observing the Baker League players, imitating their moves, and inventing his own.

HIGH SCHOOL AND COLLEGE YEARS

At Philadelphia's John Bartram High School, Monroe mostly played center and averaged 21.7 points his senior year. After a year working in a factory and attending Temple Prep School, Monroe enrolled at Winston-Salem State University in North Carolina. At the all-black Winston-Salem, Monroe came under the tutelage of Basketball Hall of Fame coach Clarence "Big House" Gaines. Despite clashes over Monroe's freewheeling playground style, the coach became a kind of surrogate father to the young ballplayer, aiding his maturation both off and on the court. Gaines made an impression on Monroe with cautionary tales about flamboyant, talented African American ballplayers (especially Cleo Hill, a guard with a style similar to Monroe) whose professional opportunities were limited by the racism of owners, coaches, and fans.

Monroe flourished at Winston-Salem. His scoring average climbed from 7 points per game as a freshman to 41.5 points per game in his senior year, breaking the National Collegiate Athletic Association (NCAA) Division II record for most points in a season (1,329) and helping Winston-Salem become the first all-black school to win the NCAA Division II championship.

On breaks from college Monroe returned to the playground courts of Philadelphia, where his skills and style generated an almost religious devotion from his fans. In his book *Giant Steps* (1983), future all-time NBA scoring champion Kareem Abdul-Jabbar recalls two busloads of Philadelphians coming to New York to cheer on the Monroe-led 1965 Baker League champions in the legendary Rucker tournament: "They set up a continuous wail that seemed to be coming from everywhere. 'Where's Jesus?' 'Black Jesus!'" On the first play of the game Monroe delighted his fans with a stop-and-go hesitation dribble that developed into a leaping 360-degree spin, culminating in a pinpoint pass for an assist. Abdul-Jabbar—at that time a nationally known prep star and seasoned veteran of New York's playgrounds—had never seen anyone play like Monroe.

Monroe was a unique player with a distinctive style. He played with finesse, mostly below the rim, and he scored using quickness and rhythmic deceptions. His herky-jerky moves and off-balance shots appeared awkward but were very effective. Monroe's tendency towards individual improvisation prompted more than one writer to compare his playing to a great jazz solo. The flair and obvious joy he displayed while individually dominating his opponents made him a fan favorite. So many young players emulated Monroe that the moves that once made him unique—360-degree spins, double-pump fakes, one-on-one play, stop-and-go dribbles—became common. The style Monroe brought from the playground has, as *Village Voice* writer Clayton Riley put it, become "institutionalized."

PROFESSIONAL CAREER

In 1967 Monroe was selected as the Baltimore Bullets' number one draft choice (second overall in the NBA draft). In his first season he averaged 24.3 points per game and was named rookie of the year. The Bullets made the playoffs in each of his four seasons in Baltimore, while he averaged 23.7 points per game. In 1971, after a disagreement with Bullets management, he was traded to the New York Knicks.

The move to New York raised Monroe's profile immensely; the Knicks had become media darlings after winning the NBA championship in 1970. Basketball was growing in popularity overall, in part due to the ways African American players were changing the game. The civil rights movement opened up opportunities in the NBA for exciting players like Monroe. To some fans, and many in the media, basketball's appeal became tied up with a romanticized image of African American culture. Ironically Monroe's inner-city background now enhanced his appeal to basketball's largely white audience.

Initially some doubted that Monroe's individualistic style could mesh with the team-oriented Knicks, but these opinions were more reflective of misgivings about the style of play that African Americans were bringing to the game. After his first year Monroe learned to integrate his individual brilliance into the Knicks' framework, and he led the team to the NBA championship in 1973.

Summing up Monroe's contribution to basketball in *Elevating the Game: Black Men and Basketball* (1992), Nelson George wrote: "he ushered in a jazzy, exciting, demonstrative approach, that old-school NBA observers hated." This approach, pioneered by Monroe and his contemporaries, is largely responsible for basketball's continued global popularity.

Thomas J. Mertz

SEE ALSO: *Abdul-Jabbar, Kareem; Basketball; National Basketball Association (NBA); National Collegiate Athletic Association (NCAA); The New York Knickerbockers.*

BIBLIOGRAPHY

Abdul-Jabbar, Kareem, and Peter Knobler. *Giant Steps*. New York: Bantam, 1987.

Bradley, Bill. *Life on the Run*. New York: Quadrangle, 1976.

George, Nelson. *Elevating the Game: Black Men and Basketball.* New York: HarperCollins, 1992.

Goudsouzian, Aram, and Harry Edwards. *King of the Court: Bill Russell and the Basketball Revolution*. Berkeley: University of California Press, 2010.

Hoffman, Anne Byrne. *Echoes from the Schoolyard: Informal Portraits of NBA Greats*. New York: Hawthorne Books, 1977.

Jackson, Robert B. *Earl the Pearl: The Story of Earl Monroe.* New York: H. Z. Walck, 1969.

Monroe, Marilyn *(1926–1962)*

In 1962, at age thirty-six and after completing only twenty-nine films, Marilyn Monroe died, leaving a legacy as one of the most recognizable movie stars and powerful cultural images in American history. White-blond hair, seductively lowered eyelids, skin-tight glittery gowns clinging to her hourglass shape, and a cultivated habit of purling her shoulders just as her face broke into a demure smile constituted the inimitable Monroe presence, one exuding idealized femininity and sexual thrill. The epitome of desirability, Monroe was a sex symbol who also suggested vulnerability and a childlike desire to please.

After working with her in 1949's *Love Happy*, Groucho Marx declared, "It's amazing. She's Mae West, Theda Bara, and

Bo Peep all rolled into one." Novelist Norman Mailer, who never met her but penned a book-length tribute titled *Marilyn*, described her as "fed on sexual candy." This mixture of carnal allure and naïveté emanating from a voluptuous woman with the whispery voice of a girl created the distinctive contradiction integral to Monroe's success and the force of her image. She claimed she never cared about money, saying, "I just want to be wonderful."

Monroe's death increased her popularity by incalculable measure, and in her untimely end lies another key to her iconic status. Her screen personality suggested a "bad girl" in the bedroom but also a weak child-woman requiring protection from male predators. When she died from a self-administered barbiturate overdose, it seemed an unlikely and unjust finish for a star of her magnitude. Her shocking death only reinforced the vulnerable aspect of Monroe's appeal. The gossip surrounding her death and the famous men then involved with her—including President John F. Kennedy and his brother Robert F. Kennedy—only whetted the public appetite to know more of her, to see more of her, to feel as if it understood who she really was.

She shared this afterlife with other celebrities who died tragically. Actor James Dean was killed in an automobile crash in the desert in the 1950s after famously proclaiming he aimed to "die young and leave a beautiful corpse." Like Monroe's, his image continues to haunt poster shops and postcard stands decades later. The mythos of a dazzling life burning at both ends until finally extinguishing itself has proven endlessly fascinating to an American culture obsessed by youth. Also like Dean, Monroe was a natural before a photographer's lens. Although movie acting frightened her, and she developed the unconscionable work habits of arriving hours late to a set and requiring countless takes to deliver even minimal lines, she was magic in front of a still photographer. Her face appeared transparent to mood and yet managed to withhold something too, making each picture of her unique.

Marilyn Monroe. *Marilyn Monroe starred as the Girl in Billy Wilder's 1955 film* The Seven Year Itch. **20TH CENTURY FOX/THE KOBAL COLLECTION/SHAW, SAM.**

NORMA JEANE: THE EARLY YEARS

Monroe was born Norma Jeane Mortenson in 1926 in Los Angeles to a single mother struggling with mental illness and a traveling salesman who would not claim her. Traded in and out of orphanages and foster homes, her early childhood was defined by emotional neglect; she became the victim of sexual abuse at the age of eight. She would later lie about her childhood, claiming she was an orphan to hide the fact of her mother's institutionalization. As her own insecurities and episodes of severe depression mounted in nearly direct proportion to her fame, the image of her mother's instability haunted her. She never met her father and pretended that he was movie star Clark Gable.

Monroe's inauspicious roots may not have signaled her future celebrity, but her early experiences being shuffled off to the movies did. As many other film stars from the studio system era in Hollywood would report, moviegoing cultivated in Monroe a driving desire to join the privileged, shining faces and outsized personalities of the silver screen. As she later put it, "I told myself a million times that I was an actress because that seemed to me something golden and beautiful."

In 1942, at age sixteen, Norma Jeane (now going by Norma Jean Baker) agreed to marry Jim Dougherty, a man a few years her senior. Marriage spared her further sexual abuse at the hands of older men and alleviated the obligation of family friends to care for her. Dougherty joined the merchant marines and departed for the war. Norma Jean found employment at the Radio Plane munitions plant, where a photographer discovered her during a shoot to promote women working for the war effort. Her then-brunette good looks so struck him that he helped her win a modeling contract. Shortly after establishing her modeling career, she peroxided her hair, divorced Dougherty, and set her sights on movie stardom at age twenty.

THE CREATION OF MARILYN

In 1946 the head of new talent at Twentieth Century Fox rewarded her with her first contract and renamed her Marilyn. She chose Monroe after her grandmother's last name. Norma Jean's transformation from hardworking plant employee to model and then starlet Marilyn Monroe—dependent on the connections and business acumen of men to further her career—would prove representative of further struggles. Just as her celebrity connoted a contradiction between naive and assertive sexuality, Monroe also represented a woman who, freed from domesticity by World War II, did not know how best to exploit her own raw talents and fierce ambition. She was shrewd and helpless both, involving herself repeatedly with men, such as talent agent Johnny Hyde, to score movie auditions, then turning down studio-offered scripts in search of better parts.

As her career evolved, Monroe became a committed student of the "Method," a theory of acting she learned at the hands of

Lee Strasberg, head of the famous Actors Studio in New York, where other acting luminaries such as Marlon Brando and Montgomery Clift also honed their craft. Her longing to step out of the mold the studios forced upon her and her use of the Method to do so positioned her stardom in a time of limbo. The studio system was eroding, yet its imprint on Monroe's image remained intact. She both fought for attention any way she could get it and resented the static and demeaning stereotype of her movie roles, saying, "A sex symbol becomes a thing. I just hate to be a thing. But if I'm going to be a symbol of something, I'd rather have it be sex."

After appearing in small parts in films including *Love Happy* (1949) and *All about Eve* (1950), Monroe broke through to celebrity status with starring roles in three 1953 features—*Niagara*, *Gentlemen Prefer Blondes*, and *How to Marry a Millionaire*. By the end of the year, American film distributors voted Monroe the top star of 1953. She also won *Photoplay* magazine's Gold Medal Award for the fastest-rising new star, and fan letters poured in at the rate of 5,000 a week. Although her fame ultimately transcended the 1950s, its birth was firmly rooted in conventions of that postwar period. Monroe compares to 1950s stars Lana Turner, Kim Novak, and Janet Leigh. Their round and shapely figures exemplified the 1950s sex symbol and contrasted significantly with the more streamlined and diminutive style of the 1940s star, represented by Barbara Stanwyck and Claudette Colbert, or the slim, statuesque figures of Gene Tierney and Lauren Bacall.

Breasts shaped like missiles—also a dominating aspect of the image of Monroe's *Gentlemen Prefer Blondes* costar Jane Russell—announced themselves in the 1950s style of dress: tight sweaters, cinched waistlines, poofed skirts, and soft-shouldered jackets. Dubbed the "New Look" by *Life* magazine, late 1940s and 1950s women's fashions reacted against war-time clothing by accentuating women's secondary sex characteristics, thereby reinstating prewar images of femininity. Halter tops such as the one Monroe made famous in 1955's *The Seven Year Itch* helped signify the more revealing era. In a famous scene, she stands atop a subway grate while the train whooshes beneath her, blowing up her full skirt around her waist while she tries in vain to hold it down. Bending over, she flashes her cleavage as the halter top both harnesses her chest and allows its exposure. Though the final version of the Billy Wilder–directed classic includes only a brief shot of this sequence, film footage of the shoot resurfaced after the movie's release and has been memorialized in countless billboards and shop windows throughout the world.

PUBLIC IMAGE, PRIVATE TORMENT

Monroe's voluptuousness placed her in a league with female stars of the late 1930s such as West and Jean Harlow. Her exuberant style of femininity and sex appeal descend directly from the screen image of Clara Bow, who also displayed a combination of sexual aggressiveness and wide-eyed, harmless energy in her embodiment of the 1920s flapper. In 1958 Monroe posed for a series of photos relating her to previous screen sirens, including Bow, 1910s Hollywood vamp Theda Bara, and 1940s exotic Marlene Dietrich. Unlike these screen images of daring sexuality, Monroe's image also depended on affability. She represented maternal availability and plentitude to a country recovering from the horrors of war, whereas her comic personality represented harmlessness, a mother who would not exact punishment or even hold men to any standard other than the limits of their own desire.

Her role as Sugar Kane in 1959's *Some Like It Hot* is one of her most definitive. In it she plays a sexy woman so bubbleheaded she doesn't notice that costars Jack Lemmon and Tony Curtis are men pretending to be women to escape from the mob. Monroe's ability to portray "dumb" while also projecting awareness of her effect on audiences was part of her acting style. She laughed at herself in these "dumb blond" parts, but as former roommate Shelley Winters reportedly said of her, "If she'd been dumber, she'd have been happier."

Her two marriages subsequent to Dougherty reflected her battle to define herself on her own terms. In 1954, her fame incipient, she wed American baseball legend Joe DiMaggio, uniting two American figures of growing mythic stature. Lasting only nine months, the marriage collapsed in the face of Monroe's continued hunger for acting success and DiMaggio's possessiveness and inability to accept her Hollywood image as sex symbol to millions of other men. In 1956 she married esteemed playwright Arthur Miller in the wake of the 1955 birth of her own company, Marilyn Monroe Productions, founded to provide her the serious, dramatic parts Hollywood studios refused her. Marrying the intellectual Miller appeared to stem from her deep-seated need to be taken seriously, to be valued for more than her comic portrayals as an empty-headed vessel for male sexual fantasies. As she implored one reporter toward the end of her life, "Please don't make me a joke."

The marriage to Miller failed under the weight of her enormous psychological and emotional needs and her increased reliance on prescription drugs and alcohol to ease the pain of miscarriages, insomnia, and crippling stage fright. Miller wrote *The Misfits*, the 1961 John Huston–directed film that led to box-office disappointment but offered Monroe the last serious role of her career.

CASHING IN ON THE IMAGE

In 1948 Monroe's film contract was not renewed, and she returned to modeling to support herself. During this time she agreed to pose nude for a photographer who had long pestered her to do so. She claimed to have made $50 from the shoot. As would recur frequently in her professional tenure, the photographer made thousands of dollars from the initial sale of the pictures, and the company that produced the calendar made millions. Threatened with scandal after their later release in the early 1950s, Monroe confessed to posing for them, explaining that she needed the money. The public embraced her honesty, rewarding her calculated risk.

The nude calendar photos later appeared in the December 1953 debut issue of *Playboy* magazine. Exploitation of this type was a constant in her career. Laurence Olivier, her costar in 1957's Marilyn Monroe Productions–backed *The Prince and the Showgirl*, said of her death: "Popular opinion and all that goes to promote it is a horribly unsteady conveyance for life, and she was exploited beyond anyone's means."

By the early 2000s hundreds of books had been published about Monroe, from novels such as Joyce Carol Oates's *Blonde* to countless biographies. Major figures of pop culture—such as singers Madonna and Lady Gaga and actress Lindsay Lohan—continued to pay tribute to Monroe by aping her iconic look. In 2011 nearly fifty years after her death, actress Michelle Williams portrayed Monroe in the movie *My Week with Marilyn*, a performance that brought her rave reviews and awards for her ability to convey both Monroe's star power and troubled inner life. Monroe's likeness has retained astounding staying power to sell consumer goods: Marilyn Monroe dolls, plates, ashtrays, magnets, T-shirts, ties, life-sized cutouts, paintings, posters, martini glasses, coffee cups, postcards, lingerie, and songs proliferated in the consumer realm, including an appearance on an official U.S. government–issued stamp in the mid-1990s.

In a famous modified rendition of Edward Hopper's 1941 painting, *Nighthawks*, three indistinct figures at a café counter at night are replaced, in defiance of history, by Hollywood icons Humphrey Bogart, James Dean, and Marilyn Monroe. Post-modern artist Andy Warhol also immortalized Monroe in his famous silk screen of her image duplicated to evoke a negative strip of film. Her serialized face captures the essence of Monroe as the star turned commodity. In 2011 a 26-foot-tall sculpture of Monroe's famous subway grate scene was erected in Chicago for a yearlong exhibit—an installation that immediately aroused controversy over whether it was "fun" or exploitive of female sexuality. Somehow the very debate seemed a fitting part of Monroe's legacy.

Elizabeth Haas

SEE ALSO: All about Eve; *Bacall, Lauren; Bara, Theda; Baseball; Billboards; Bogart, Humphrey; Bow, Clara; Brando, Marlon; Celebrity; Celebrity Couples; Clift, Montgomery; Colbert, Claudette; Dean, James; Dietrich, Marlene; DiMaggio, Joe; Divorce; The Fifties; Flappers; Gable, Clark;* Gentlemen Prefer Blondes; *Harlow, Jean; Hollywood; Hopper, Edward; Huston, John; Lady Gaga;* Life; *Lohan, Lindsay; Madonna; Mailer, Norman; The Martini; Marx, Groucho; Miller, Arthur; Movie Stars; Olivier, Laurence;* Photoplay; Playboy; *Postcards; Russell, Jane;* The Seven Year Itch; *Sex Symbol;* Some Like It Hot; *Stanwyck, Barbara; Tierney, Gene; T-Shirts; Turner, Lana; Warhol, Andy; West, Mae; Wilder, Billy; World War II.*

BIBLIOGRAPHY

Baty, S. Paige. *American Monroe: The Making of a Body Politic*. Berkeley: University of California Press, 1995.

Haspiel, James. *Marilyn: The Ultimate Look at the Legend*. New York: Holt, 1991.

Mailer, Norman. *Marilyn: A Biography*. New York: Grosset & Dunlap, 1973.

Monroe, Marilyn. *My Story*. New York: Stein and Day, 1974.

Monroe, Marilyn. *Marilyn—Her Life in Her Own Words: Marilyn Monroe's Revealing Last Words and Photographs*, ed. George Barris. Secaucus, NJ: Carol Publishing Group, 1995.

Morley, Sheridan, and Ruth Leon. *Marilyn Monroe*. Stroud, UK: Sutton Publishing, 1997.

Smith, Matthew. *The Men Who Murdered Marilyn*. London: Bloomsbury, 1996.

Spoto, Donald. *Marilyn Monroe: The Biography*. New York: HarperCollins, 1993.

Steinem, Gloria. *Marilyn*. New York: Henry Holt, 1986.

Wills, David, and Stephen Schmidt. *Marilyn Monroe: Metamorphosis*. New York: IT Books, 2011.

Monster Trucks

The term *monster truck* can describe everything from surface-mine loaders, armored drug-cartel cars, and various other kinds of outsized vehicles; however, it most often refers to enormous trucks that are designed to crush cars and race around dirt tracks in American arenas, to the delight of their many fans. The most conspicuous feature of monster trucks are the enormous wheels, which are typically quite a bit taller than the average adult human. These monster trucks, their shows, and their audiences coexist across three, interrelated spheres: live rallies or "jams," video games, and toy tie-ins.

The monster truck phenomenon emerged, ironically, from the energy-conscious 1970s, and it has found its most extreme expression in over-the-top twenty-first-century trucks. One of the biggest of these was the Team Hot Wheels vehicle that was entered in the 2012 Monster Jam. It was 17 feet long and 11 feet tall, weighed 10,000 pounds, and was set on 60-inch wheels. Technically, though, monster trucks are not even trucks; rather, they are oversized dune-buggy-style frames that sit on gigantic tires. The shell of a truck is then perched on top of this frame.

With colorful names like Grave Digger and Bigfoot, monster trucks are popular with children and adults alike. Promoters of Monster Jam, one of the largest annual monster truck rallies, describe their event on Dennis Taft's Monster Truck Photo Album website as "one of the largest and most successful touring family shows in the world." In addition to crushed cars and over-the-top trucks, it features such events as a fan vote for Arena Wheelie of the Year and a thirtieth anniversary celebration of Grave Digger, one of the most enduringly popular monster trucks in history. Claiming more than four million fans per year, Monster Jam gives some sense of the extraordinary popularity of this mechanized spectacle today.

Monster trucks often live second and third lives as video game avatars and as toys. Video game titles include *Monster Jam: Urban Assault* and *Monster Jam: Maximum Destruction*. Hot Wheels, a hugely popular line of toy cars, makes a number of monster-truck-inspired toys, including a remote-controlled thirtieth anniversary edition of the Grave Digger.

Isabel Istanders

SEE ALSO: *Automobile; Toys; Video Games.*

BIBLIOGRAPHY

"Hot Wheels and Monster Jam Roar into 2012 Season with New Team Hot Wheels Monster Truck." Press release. December 20, 2011. Accessed May 23, 2012. Available from http://investor.shareholder.com/mattel/releasedetail.cfm?releaseid=634450

Morr, Tom, and Ken Brubaker. *Monster Trucks*. St. Paul, MN: Motorbooks, 2003.

Taft, Dennis. "Monster Truck Photo Album." Accessed May 23, 2012. Available from http://www.monsterphoto.iwarp.com/presrls.htm

Montalbán, Ricardo *(1920–2009)*

With a film and television acting career that spanned a half century, Ricardo Montalbán is one of the most well-known and popular actors of Hispanic heritage. Although he had a distinguished career in feature films, he is best known for his starring role in the *Fantasy Island* television series and for his years of commercials promoting Chrysler automobiles.

Montalbán was born on November 25, 1920, in Mexico City to Spanish immigrant parents. After moving to Los Angeles to attend Fairfax High School, he discovered the theater and began acting in high school plays. In 1940 he moved to New York to pursue a career in acting and made his debut on Broadway in *Her Cardboard Lover*. Afterward he returned to Mexico, making more than two dozen movies. The 1945 film *La casa de la zorra* brought him to the attention of Hollywood, which was turning out an increasing number of films with Latin American themes in support of the Good Neighbor Policy during World War II.

In Hollywood, Montalbán was cast in a series of stereotypical "Latin lover" roles at MGM (Metro-Goldwyn-Mayer) studios, where he signed a contract in 1946. His appearance in *Neptune's Daughter* (1949) was a breakthrough in that it was the first major film to portray a Hispanic character who romantically pursued and married an Anglo woman. Montalbán's Spanish accent and Hispanic looks, however, frequently caused him to be cast in stereotypical roles such as the Latin lover lead, the sidekick or friend to the romantic lead (*Battleground*, 1949), or other non-white or non-American characters. This continued through the 1960s, when he was cast as a Native American (*Across the Wide Missouri*, 1951), as a Japanese warlord (*Sayonara*, 1957), as a French duke (*Love Is a Ball*, 1963), and as an Italian lover (*Sweet Charity*, 1969). In 1969 Montalbán helped found Nosotros, the first organization to promote equal opportunities for Hispanic actors and actresses in Hollywood, in part by its sponsorship of the Golden Eagle Awards to recognize outstanding performances by Hispanic actors.

Among the most important films of Montalbán's career were *Cheyenne Autumn* (1964), *Madame X* (1966), *Escape from the Planet of the Apes* (1971), *Conquest of the Planet of the Apes* (1972), *Return to Fantasy Island* (1978), *Star Trek II: The Wrath of Khan* (1982), and *The Naked Gun: From the Files of Police Squad* (1988).

Montalbán began acting for television productions in the late 1950s, often appearing on *The Loretta Young Show* (1953–1961). From then on, he made numerous guest appearances on various series through the 1970s, many of them Westerns or police dramas. From 1978 to 1984 he starred in his most famous role, that of Mr. Rourke on *Fantasy Island*. In the 1980s he began serving as a spokesperson for the Chrysler Cordoba, a model named for a city in Spain. He also did voice work for television programs, including *Dora the Explorer* (2000–), the popular bilingual children's cartoon starring a Mexican girl. Montalbán died in his Los Angeles home on January 14, 2009.

Nicolás Kanellos

SEE ALSO: *Broadway;* Dora the Explorer; Fantasy Island; *Hollywood; MGM (Metro-Goldwyn-Mayer);* Planet of the Apes; Star Trek; *Television; Young, Loretta.*

BIBLIOGRAPHY

Montalbán, Ricardo. *Reflections: A Life in Two Worlds*. New York: Doubleday, 1980.

Otfinoski, Steven. *Latinos in the Arts*. New York: Facts On File, 2007.

Richard, Alfred Charles, Jr. *Censorship and Hollywood's Hispanic Image*. Westport, CT: Greenwood Press, 1993.

Tardiff, Joseph T., and L. Mpho Mabunda, eds. *Dictionary of Hispanic Biography*. Detroit, MI: Gale, 1996.

Montana, Joe *(1956–)*

A third-round pick in the 1979 draft, Joe Montana became one of the best quarterbacks in National Football League (NFL) history. He retired in 1995 after playing sixteen seasons, during which he compiled four Super Bowl victories; the highest quarterback rating (92.3) of any nonactive passer in history; 273 touchdowns; 3,409 completions; and 40,551 passing yards—an astonishing career record. Described by 49ers broadcaster Wayne Walker as "cooler than the other side of the pillow," Montana was best known for his ability to perform under pressure.

Born in western Pennsylvania—the same region that produced other NFL quarterbacks such as George Blanda, Johnny Unitas, Joe Namath, Jim Kelly, and Dan Marino—Montana played baseball, basketball, and football in high school; however, despite being offered a basketball scholarship to North Carolina State, he chose Notre Dame and football. He left high school a *Parade* All-American and began his collegiate career as one of nine quarterbacks for Notre Dame.

Montana got his first look at playing time in the third outing of his sophomore year in a game against Northwestern. The

Joe Montana. *Joe Montana rolls out to pass during Super Bowl XIX in January 1985. Montana was named the game's Most Valuable Player (MVP) as the 49ers beat the Miami Dolphins 38–16.* FOCUS ON SPORT/CONTRIBUTOR/GETTY IMAGES SPORT/GETTY IMAGES.

starting quarterback left the game injured with Notre Dame trailing 7–0. Montana came off the bench to lead the team to a 31–7 victory. Two games later, against North Carolina, he drove the offense 73 yards to tie the game 14–14 in the fourth quarter and then threw the game-winning touchdown pass with a minute remaining. A week later, against Air Force, he entered the game as a relief quarterback for the last time and overcame a 30–10 deficit in the fourth quarter, leading Notre Dame to a 31–30 victory and securing his spot as the starting quarterback.

By his second year in college, Montana had earned the nickname "Captain Comeback." In 1978, after finishing the season 8–3, Notre Dame faced Houston in the Cotton Bowl. Behind 20–12, Notre Dame was in trouble, and Montana was on the bench with a severe flu. By the fourth quarter, when Montana entered the game, Notre Dame was losing 34–12. After Notre Dame scored on a blocked punt and a two-point conversion to make the score 34–20, Montana ran for a touchdown and completed another two-point conversion. With less than two minutes remaining in the game and his team still behind by six points, he fumbled the ball. Houston could not score to put the game out of reach, however, and Montana gained one last chance. With no time left, he threw to Kris Haines in the end zone, tying the game. Notre Dame won the game after scoring the extra point.

Despite his 25–4 record at Notre Dame, Montana was not highly regarded by the pro scouts. Selected in the third round of the 1979 draft, he had taken over the San Francisco 49ers offense by the end of his second year. In 1979 the 49ers finished with a record of 2–14. In 1981 Montana led them to a 13–3 record, and they went on to defeat the New York Giants in the first round of the playoffs and the Dallas Cowboys in the National Football Conference (NFC) title game, when Dwight Clark made "the Catch"—a leaping, fingertip 6-yard grab at the back of the end zone that sent the 49ers to their first Super Bowl, where they beat the Cincinnati Bengals.

Another glorious year for Montana and the 49ers came in 1984, when the team finished 15–1 and Montana passed for more than 3,600 yards, completing twenty-eight touchdown passes. The same year, however, Miami Dolphins quarterback Dan Marino set two single-season records, throwing for forty-eight touchdowns and 5,084 yards. Montana and Marino were to meet in Super Bowl XIX. Although that game began with the 49ers and the Dolphins trading points, the 49ers scored three consecutive touchdowns in the second quarter, going on to win 38–16. In 1989, a difficult year for the 49ers, they faced the Bengals in Super Bowl XXIII in a rematch of Super Bowl XVI. With less than four minutes left in the game, Montana drove the 49ers offense 92 yards to win the team's third Super Bowl championship of the 1980s. In 1989 the 49ers repeated, defeating the Denver Broncos 55–10 in Super Bowl XXIV, and Montana was named Super Bowl Most Valuable Player for the third time.

After a somewhat bitter split from the 49ers, Montana finished his career with the Kansas City Chiefs. His debut was a success—he led the Chiefs to a 27–3 victory—but injuries kept him out for much of the year. In 1994, against the Denver Broncos, he proved himself "super Joe" once again. With less than two minutes remaining, the Broncos led 28–24. Montana drove the Chiefs 75 yards, and with only eight seconds to go, he hit Willie Davis to give the Chiefs a 31–28 victory. Montana was enshrined in the Pro Football Hall of Fame in 2000. He even has a small town named after him: Joe (formerly Ismay), Montana.

After retiring, Montana briefly tried sportscasting but was unhappy being away from his family. He became involved in wine making, horse breeding, and real estate development. He also served as consultant to his son's high school football team. In the early twenty-first century, Montana finally found an outlet for his love of sport with cutting horse competitions.

Austin Booth

SEE ALSO: *College Football; National Football League (NFL); Professional Football; Sports Heroes; Super Bowl.*

BIBLIOGRAPHY

Montana, Joe, and Bob Raissman. *Audible: My Life in Football.* New York: Morrow, 1986.

Montville, Leigh. "An American Dream: What Kid Doesn't Want to Grow Up to Be Quarterback Joe Montana?" *Sports Illustrated,* December 24, 1990, 90–108.

Steele, Michael R. *The Fighting Irish Football Encyclopedia,* 3rd ed. Champaign, IL: Sports Publishing, 2003.

Wulf, Steve. "The Passing of an Era." *Time,* April 24, 1995.

Zimmerman, Paul. "Born to Be a Quarterback." *Sports Illustrated,* August 6, 1990, 62–75.

Zimmerman, Paul. "The Ultimate Winner." *Sports Illustrated,* August 13, 1990, 72–84.

Montana, Patsy *(1914–1996)*

In 1935 Patsy Montana became a pioneer for women in country music when her recording of "I Want to Be a Cowboy's Sweetheart" sold one million copies, proving to the recording industry that female country singers could achieve commercial success. Featuring her exuberant yodel, the song reveals her desire to experience a cowboy's life firsthand, "to learn to rope and to ride" as his sweetheart and sidekick. When the record was released, Montana, born Rubye Blevins, was singing with a group known as the Prairie Ramblers on *The National Barn Dance,* a country radio show on Chicago's WLS. With "I Want to Be a Cowboy's Sweetheart," Montana established herself as a solo artist with a new nontraditional image: the independent cowgirl. Although her subsequent records were never as popular as her signature song, Montana's career as a performer and recording artist lasted for six decades.

Anna Hunt Graves

SEE ALSO: *Country Music.*

BIBLIOGRAPHY

Bufwack, Mary A., and Robert K. Oermann. *Finding Her Voice: The Saga of Women in Country Music.* New York: Crown, 1993.

Montana, Patsy, and Jane Frost. *Patsy Montana: The Cowboy's Sweetheart.* Jefferson, NC: McFarland, 2002.

Monty Python's Flying Circus

That a British comedy series dealing with, among other things, the Upper-Class Twit of the Year Contest, the Ministry of Silly Walks, and a public argument clinic would become a cultural phenomenon in the United States during the 1970s was, as comedian Eric Idle has said, the last thing in the world one would expect. Nonetheless, *Monty Python's Flying Circus*, the show Idle helped create, became a significant part of American culture in the years immediately following the Watergate scandal, creating a large cult following among young, college-educated viewers and influencing American comedy and television for decades to come.

HATCHING A PYTHON

The roots of *Monty Python's Flying Circus* can be found in the satirical comedy boom occurring in America and Britain during the late 1950s and early 1960s. While satire in the United States was the province of nightclub comics and a few improvisation workshops, in Britain it was centered at the Oxbridge hub of higher education. The Cambridge Footlights Club and similar groups at Oxford entertained their university communities and theatergoers around the nation with revues of topical sketches, impersonations, and song parodies. Oxbridge satire made its way to British television in 1962, with the BBC's *That Was the Week That Was* (*TW3*). Featuring a number of revue veterans, including interlocutor David Frost, *TW3* offered a weekly collection of topical skits, songs, and interviews presented in a bare-bones open studio that allowed viewers to see the mechanics of the show's production as it was going on. Though phenomenally popular, the show's barbed humor quickly ran afoul of the Tory government and the BBC, which canceled the series at the end of 1963 in order to avoid political problems with upcoming elections.

After a failed effort to revisit the *TW3* format, Frost called on his Oxbridge connections to staff his 1966 BBC show, *The Frost Report*. John Cleese and Graham Chapman had written and performed for Footlights Club shows and tours, including one that played in New York in 1964. Idle had followed Cleese and Chapman to Cambridge, where he became familiar to Frost. Terry Jones and Michael Palin, meanwhile, were working in various Oxford revues offering a more zany, absurdist humor than the topical sketches of the Footlights Club. The work that the five of them did together on *The Frost Report* began a series of creative relationships that culminated in 1969, when they rejoined as a group for a BBC series that would come to have a global effect on television comedy.

The first episode of *Monty Python's Flying Circus*, broadcast on October 5, 1969, featured sketches including a television show devoted to famous deaths, a parody of a BBC interview show, and a documentary on the weapon that won World War II: the funniest joke ever told. The sketches were interspersed with cutout animation created by Minneapolis-born artist Terry Gilliam, with whom Cleese had worked during his time in New York. The remaining twelve shows in the first *Python* series continued to develop the group's comedic style, one that was far less satiric, in terms of addressing topical issues and figures, than it was absurd, but one that was also relentlessly and at times viciously antiauthoritarian.

Sketches that hilariously overturned familiar norms—a transvestite lumberjack, a pet shop owner who sells dead parrots—were joined with increasing frequency by comic attacks on the British government; the military; the Church of England; the landed aristocracy; and the legal, medical, and business communities. No institution was more ridiculed, however, than the television industry itself, both in numerous parodies of individual programs and genres and in the group's self-reflexive dismantlings of production conventions: the intrusion of opening and often phony closing credits at inappropriate places, the sudden appearance of "BBC officials" to comment on or complain about the show, the shortening of sketches by characters who decide that they are not funny.

FINDING A U.S. AUDIENCE

Despite regional scheduling difficulties, the first series of *Monty Python's Flying Circus* attracted a substantial late-night audience, strong critical praise, and a firm BBC commitment for more shows. A second series of thirteen episodes ran in fall 1970, and a third series was broadcast in the winter of 1971–1972. Meanwhile, word of the show was beginning to spread beyond its homeland. The Canadian Broadcasting Corporation picked up the first series in 1970, making it available to American viewers near the border. The troupe turned a number of sketches from the first series into an eponymous record album in 1970, followed by three more albums in 1971 through 1973. Copies of the albums, as well as collections of *Python* material in book form, began to make their way into the United States during the early 1970s.

Sketches from the first two series of the show were collected in a film, *And Now, for Something Completely Different*, that was released with less than overwhelming results in 1971. The group itself, touring Canada to take advantage of its popularity there, even went to Los Angeles to make an appearance on *The Tonight Show* with Johnny Carson in 1973. Immediately afterward, however, Cleese left the troupe. The remaining members went on to produce one more six-episode series for the BBC in fall 1974, and that seemed to be the final voyage for *Monty Python's Flying Circus*.

The end of the show in Britain, however, was merely its beginning in the United States. The BBC, having found an American audience for its documentaries and its dramatic serialization of literary works on PBS in the early 1970s, was working to develop the market further. While the often absurd, often savage humor of *Monty Python's Flying Circus* lacked the comfort and the cultural cachet of *Civilization* and the various BBC serials presented under the *Masterpiece Theatre* rubric, PBS affiliate KERA-TV in Dallas, Texas, began to run the show in the summer of 1974. Its immediate success there led PBS affiliates across the country, as well as a few commercial stations, to pick up the show.

By spring 1975, *Monty Python's Flying Circus* was on the air in more than sixty markets, attracting sizable and fanatically devoted audiences from New York to Iowa to Sacramento, California. The show's success was augmented by the 1975 American release of the film *Monty Python and the Holy Grail*, a comic retelling of the Arthurian legends involving dismemberment, orgies, the military use of excrement, and a vicious killer rabbit as well as a typical *Python* ending that ridiculed the conventions of filmmaking as thoroughly as the film did the conventions of the epic.

The American popularity of *Monty Python's Flying Circus* in the mid-1970s can be attributed to several factors. Just as the Oxbridge satire movement in Britain and the nightclub satire comedy scene in America were concomitant developments, the shift from pointed topical satire to a more absurd and archetypal form of humor occurred simultaneously. During the period in which *Python* ascended in Britain, American comics such as George Carlin and Richard Pryor and comedy groups including the Firesign Theatre and the Committee found critical and commercial success by infusing the barbs of their predecessors with the political anger and the broad countercultural "us vs. them" sentiments of the late 1960s.

The political and countercultural elements of their work also spoke to the audience they were priming for *Python*—college-age baby boomers. A group rich in educational and cultural capital, it was an audience that could get what critics called the "overgraduate humor" of *Python* sketches involving contests to summarize Marcel Proust, debates about Sartrean philosophy, and parodies of Pier Paolo Pasolini films. It was also, more importantly, an audience that had grown up under the authority of television and that was innately familiar with the conventions comically demystified by *Python*.

EXTREME REACTIONS

The absurdity of *Python* sketches was matched at times, however, by their reception in America. A 1975 ABC broadcast of three episodes of the final six-episode *Python* series, which had not been released for syndication, led to a historic legal battle culminating in a U.S. Court of Appeals ruling that ABC had infringed on the troupe's copyright by cutting material in order to include commercials. In a landmark settlement, the troupe regained all distribution rights from the BBC and took back the episodes purchased by ABC. It would control its own destiny—at least as far as American television was concerned. Movies, though, were a different matter. The 1979 *Python* film *Life of Brian*, a mock biblical epic in which a poor sap called Brian Cohen is named the Christ, was condemned by numerous religious groups, picketed in many communities, and not distributed to others. The controversy failed to keep *Python* fans away—the film made $10 million in its initial American release.

The American popularity of *Monty Python's Flying Circus* led to mobbed live performances in New York in 1976 and Los Angeles in 1980 (the latter recorded on film) at which audiences recited sketches line for line along with the comedians. Meanwhile, projects by individual members of the group found a ready market in the United States. Cleese's *Fawlty Towers* became almost as popular as *Python* when it was imported to PBS stations in the late 1970s; Palin's *Ripping Yarns* also achieved critical and popular success during its syndicated PBS run; and Idle's *Meet the Rutles*, a documentary spoof on a faux-Beatles pop band, was aired on NBC. At the same time, Gilliam began a prolific career as a film director with *Jabberwocky* and *Time Bandits*, both of which featured *Python* members in the cast.

THE LEGACY ENDURES

The most important legacy of *Monty Python's Flying Circus* in American culture, however, was the development of late-night sketch comedy series that sought to capture the vitality, if not all of the savagery and absurdity, of the British original. Both *Saturday Night Live*, whose creator, Lorne Michaels, idolized *Python* and used it as a model for his own show, and the Canadian *SCTV*, which itself became an imported cult favorite in the late 1970s, owed their existence to the success of *Monty Python*'s comic attacks on authority and television culture.

Since 1980, the original *Monty Python's Flying Circus* has remained a part of the American television landscape, with runs of the series on the MTV and Comedy Central cable networks as well as continued airings on local PBS stations. The group reformed for a film, *The Meaning of Life*, in 1983, while numerous individual projects—Gilliam's films *Brazil* and *The Fisher King*, Palin's BBC travel documentaries, Cleese's film *A Fish Called Wanda* and his guest appearances on American situation comedies—have continued to receive critical and popular acclaim. Chapman's death in 1989 seemed to end any hope for any further group projects; in 1998, however, the remaining members of the troupe announced that they planned to reunite for future film and live projects.

In late 2004 a musical called *Spamalot*, loosely based on *Monty Python and the Holy Grail*, opened in Chicago. The play went on to Broadway, and as of 2012 it was still being performed at various venues around the country. *Monty Python: Almost the Truth—The Lawyer's Cut*, a six-part tribute to and documentary about the comedy team, aired in 2009. The fact that U.S. audiences were still interested in what the comic purveyors of upper-class twits, silly walks, and argument clinics might have to say forty years after their first appearance suggests the lasting hold *Python* has had on American culture.

Jeffrey S. Miller

SEE ALSO: *Broadway; Cable TV; Carlin, George; Carson, Johnny;* Fawlty Towers*; Firesign Theatre;* Masterpiece Theatre*; MTV; Pryor, Richard; Public Television (PBS);* Saturday Night Live*; Second City; Stand-Up Comedy; Syndication; Television;* The Tonight Show.

BIBLIOGRAPHY

Chapman, Graham; Michael Palin; John Cleese; et al. *The Pythons: Autobiography.* New York: Thomas Dunne Books, 2003.

Hewison, Robert. *Monty Python: The Case Against.* London: Methuen, 1981.

Life of Python. Directed by Mark Redhead. London: BBC/DevillierDonegan Enterprises, 1989.

Miller, Jeffrey S. *Something Completely Different: British Television and American Culture, 1960–1980.* Minneapolis: University of Minnesota Press, 1999.

Neale, Steve, and Frank Krutnik. *Popular Film and Television Comedy.* London: Routledge, 1990.

Perry, George. *The Life of Python.* Boston: Little, Brown, 1983.

Wilmut, Roger. *From Fringe to Flying Circus.* London: Eyre Methuen, 1980.

Moonies/Reverend Sun Myung Moon

An unlikely messiah to emerge from the youth movement of the mid–twentieth century, the Reverend Sun Myung Moon (1920–) was a Korean immigrant who addressed his American followers in rambling two-hour sermons, filtered through an interpreter. Although shadowed by a history of matrimonial troubles and conflicts with the law on two continents, he preached family values and obedience to authority. Moon attracted millions of youth who had become dissatisfied with the status quo in their own nations. He made the United States his base of operations in the 1970s and collected followers largely from among the advantaged sons and daughters of mainline Christian and Jewish families. By the end of the twentieth century, the Unification Church controlled a fortune in U.S. property, and Moonies, as his followers were known, were frequently seen on U.S. streets, selling flowers and recruiting new members.

Much of Moon's background is shrouded in secrecy and controversy. He appears to have been born in a province that later became part of North Korea. Although his parents were Presbyterian, he became identified with a charismatic sectarian group that taught that Korea was a promised land destined for apocalyptic events. At age sixteen he allegedly experienced his first vision, one in which his own divine calling was revealed to him. He then changed his first name from Yong to Sun, so that his full name meant "Sun Shining Moon." As he rose to prominence, so did his problems with the North Korean government, resulting in part from his strong stand against communism. In the United States, he was accused of bigamy, draft and tax evasion, and immigration violations.

SPREADING THE MESSAGE

The doctrines of the Unification Church were outlined in *the divine principle*, the movement's basic scripture, credited to Moon but widely believed to have been written by one of his lieutenants. Unification theology was a blend of concepts from Christianity, Buddhism, and Taoism, echoing the eclectic Asian background of Moon himself. The stated goal of his church was the unification of humanity and its salvation in both body and soul.

In his publications and sermons Moon elevated marriage to a cosmic sacrament. Adam and Eve fell from divine favor, he taught, because of lustful self-indulgence, thus bringing forth their children in sin. Christ, he said, came as a second Adam, and although he enlightened the race spiritually, his Crucifixion cut short his full mission of physical as well as spiritual redemption because he did not live to marry and beget perfect children. Moon argued that a third Adam was essential to mankind. This new messiah would succeed precisely where Adam and Jesus had failed: He would marry a perfect woman. Together with God the couple would form a divine trinity; through themselves and their progeny, humanity would at last be fully redeemed.

Though Moon, and the woman (apparently his fourth wife) always at his side, made no special claims for themselves, their followers were free to reach their own rather obvious conclusions about the fulfillment of Moon's prophecy. The most publicized feature of the Unification Church was the mass marriage ceremonies that Moon conducted, first in Korea and later in the United States. In 1988 he rented Madison Square Garden in New York, where he officiated in the mass wedding of more than 6,500 couples. Many of the new spouses had just met at the altar, chosen for one another by church leaders. Races and nationalities were specifically blended in these mega ceremonies.

PARENTAL CONCERN AND LOSS OF MOMENTUM

Moon and his Unification Church soon caused widespread social and parental concern in the United States. Although a disciplined life for otherwise disoriented young people was commendable, parents worried that their children were being exploited. Within the church, conduct was carefully controlled. Smoking and drinking were taboo, and austere standards of sexual conduct were enforced. Members were encouraged to live communally in the church's urban centers or on church-owned ranches.

Fund-raising teams traveled about in vans, selling flowers on street corners or otherwise soliciting contributions, but even as the church itself became wealthy from these efforts, personal wealth was discouraged. There was high turnover in the church, with an estimated one-third of the newer members leaving each year. With a constant supply of postulants therefore required, additional groups were assigned to recruiting new members.

Recruiting techniques were refined and effective. Moonies targeted college campuses, where they showered students with honor and affection. They invited these potential new members to special seminars and retreats and subjected them to long sermons on how to create a better world. Critics of the church accused Moonies of depriving attendees of food and sleep, comparing the indoctrination to Asian prison camp brainwashing. Critics also alleged a dire political agenda, but this was never proved. Young people who joined the Unification Church usually distanced themselves from their families, and a number of concerned parents hired "deprogrammers" to separate their sons and daughters from the church.

By the end of the twentieth century, the Unification Church seemed to lose its momentum, yet Moonie efforts toward gaining full acceptance into American life had produced some results. Leading politicians accepted large sums of money to address Unification-sponsored gatherings, and actor Sir Laurence Olivier starred in *Inchon* (1981), a movie financed by the church. It was a critical and box-office catastrophe in part because of scenes in which the General Douglas MacArthur character is affected by divine guidance during the Korean War.

In 1982 Moon was imprisoned for conspiracy to avoid paying taxes. Upon his release, the billionaire continued to wield power through his newspaper, the *Washington Times*, and control of the United Press International (UPI) news service.

In one of the most bizarre and least well-known events to take place in any federal government building in U.S. history, the Interreligious and International Peace Council, a Moon front group, received permission to honor Moon and his wife with a "Crown of Peace" award at the Dirksen Senate Office Building on March 23, 2004. Several members of the House of Representatives and Senator Mark Dayton, a friend of Moon's who was responsible for giving the group access to the building, attended the ceremony. Dayton later insisted that he had been duped by Moon's supporters and had no idea of what would take place. Declaring himself the Messiah, Moon, adorned in medieval-like robes and a crown, announced in part, "I am God's ambassador, sent to earth with His full authority. I am sent to accomplish His command to save the world's six billion people, restoring them to Heaven with the original goodness in which they were created."

Allene Phy-Olsen

SEE ALSO: *Communism; Cults; Olivier, Laurence.*

BIBLIOGRAPHY

Cohen, Daniel. *The New Believers; Young Religion in America.* New York: Ballantine Books, 1976.

Gorenfeld, John. "Hail to the Moon King." Salon, June 21,

2004. Accessed February 2012. Available from http://www.salon.com/2004/06/21/moon_7/

Mather, George A., and Larry A. Nichols. *Dictionary of Cults, Sects, Religions, and the Occult.* Grand Rapids, MI: Zondervan, 1993.

Moon, Sun Myung. *Divine Principle.* New York: Holy Spirit Association for the Unification of World Christianity, 1977.

Rossi, M. L. *What Every American Should Know about Who's Really Running the World: The People, Corporations, and Organizations That Control Our Future.* New York: Plune, 2005.

Sontag, Frederick. *Sun Myung Moon and the Unification Church.* Nashville, TN: Abingdon, 1977.

"Sun Myung Moon Crowned 'King of America' at U.S. Senate Building." *Church and State* 57, no. 5 (2004).

Moonlighting

Moonlighting's creator and executive producer Glenn Gordon Caron once described the program as "the show that knows it's on television." The 1985–1989 ABC hit was stylish, sophisticated, and clearly aimed at pop culturally hip grownups. It was also plagued with tension, both on and off the set.

Ex-model Maddie Hayes (played by ex-model Cybill Shepherd) learns that her accountant has embezzled from her. Surveying what's left, Hayes finds she owns the unsuccessful Blue Moon detective agency in Los Angeles. She's about to dump it when the guy who's been running it, David Addison (a then-unknown Bruce Willis), cons her into holding onto it to save his job. He proceeds to get her involved in the cases as they get involved with each other. Flighty and sincere Agnes Dipesto (Allyce Beasley) and nerdy Herbert Viola (Curtis Armstrong) work at the agency too and often act as counterpoints for Hayes and Addison. Maddie, the ice princess, and David, the king of the smirking smart asses, forge a partnership that is really just a platform for their burgeoning sexual chemistry. Sure, they solve mysteries, but will they hit the sheets this week?

At the end of the 1985–1986 season, David and Maddie kiss in the parking garage, but it isn't until the end of the next season that they have sex. That episode, called "The Big Bang," drew an estimated sixty million viewers, beating that week's Academy Awards broadcast. Because Shepherd was pregnant at the time, the love scenes had to be filmed standing up with the bed propped against a wall and the camera turned sideways.

People who believe that the best part of a relationship is the part before the relationship actually starts had their point proven with *Moonlighting*, partly because the story line was mishandled. Besides consummating her relationship with David, a suddenly promiscuous Maddie had sex with Sam Crawford (Mark Harmon) and married a nerdy guy named Walter (Dennis Dugan), whom she met on a train; the marriage was soon annulled. She was also pregnant with David's baby, which she then miscarried. Fans were not pleased with any of this.

There was also the widely publicized behind-the-scenes tension. In 1987 Shepherd announced that she was pregnant with twins. This created problems with the show's shooting schedule. When she was available for filming, Willis was off making movies; when he returned, she was gone for medical reasons. Willis, who set the tone for the show, was annoyed that during Shepherd's pregnancy he was working a lot more than she was. Furthermore, after making the successful movie *Die Hard* in 1988, he wanted to make more films. For her part, Shepherd was dissatisfied with the formulaic bitchiness of her character (though she didn't seem to mind being filmed through gauze). Only fourteen episodes were made that season (only twenty episodes were made in 1985–1986; the normal number is twenty-two), few of which had she and Willis together; one episode focused entirely on Agnes and Herbert's romance.

Cost overruns and delays also plagued the series. Some shows couldn't be promoted because they were delivered a day or two before air time, or reruns were substituted at the last minute. This caused *Moonlighting* to lose about 20 percent of its audience, though its ratings were still holding. One reason for the delays was the length of the scripts. The writing was so filled with retorts, references, puns, and rhymes that the scripts were 50 percent longer than those of other hour-long series. With all of this tension, soon there was a running three-way battle between Willis, Shepherd, and Caron, who was forced off the show in the final season in 1989. Caron took three writers with him. By the time *Moonlighting* was over, the ratings had sunk very low. "Can you really blame the audience?" David and Maddie were asked by a silhouetted producer in the true-to-form final episode. "A case of poison ivy is more fun than watching you two lately."

The problems were sometimes used to their advantage, and the *Moonlighting* team produced some inventive, if gimmicky, shows. One episode ran short, so the stars broke the fourth wall and talked to the camera to fill in the gap. They sometimes made in-jokes about the episode to each other; they once referenced winning one out of the sixteen Emmys for which they were nominated for one year. One episode was a reenactment of William Shakespeare's *Taming of the Shrew* with David as Petruchio and Maddie as Kate. Another episode was shot entirely in black and white. In fact, *Moonlighting* owed its existence to classic black-and-white films such as the 1940 film *His Girl Friday*, starring Cary Grant and Rosalind Russell, with their fast-talking banter, as well as Alfred Hitchcock's guy-woos-icy-blond-with-mystery-as-backdrop genre. As such, *Moonlighting* broke new ground in American television, firmly establishing its place in TV and pop culture history.

Karen Lurie

SEE ALSO: *Grant, Cary; Russell, Rosalind; Willis, Bruce.*

BIBLIOGRAPHY

Brooks, Tim, and Earle Marsh. *The Complete Directory to Prime Time Network and Cable TV Shows 1946–Present*, 6th ed. New York: Ballantine Books, 1995.

Dougherty, Margot; Lois Armstrong; and Jack Kelley. "Cybill Shepherd and Bruce Willis Are Named as Prime Suspects in Moonlighting's Untimely Death." *People Weekly*, May 29, 1989, 112.

Karger, Dave. "Making It on 'Moonlighting.'" *Entertainment Weekly*, April 5, 1996, 96.

Longworth, James L. *TV Creators: Conversations with America's Top Producers of Television Drama*, vol. 2. Syracuse, NY: Syracuse University Press, 2002.

Moonlighting. *Cybill Shepherd, left, and Bruce Willis starred as private detectives in the ABC comedy/drama* Moonlighting. **ABC-TV/THE KOBAL COLLECTION.**

McNeil, Alex. *Total Television: The Comprehensive Guide to Programming from 1948 to the Present.* New York: Penguin, 1996.

Pearlman, Cindy. "Moonlighters." *Entertainment Weekly,* June 9, 1995, 14.

Moore, Demi *(1962–)*

Irrespective of her professional accomplishments, film actress Demi Moore rocketed into international controversy in 1991 when she appeared—nude, radiant, and heavy with child—on the cover of *Vanity Fair.* She thus became an iconic symbol of female liberation to those who admired the exposure and a figure of shameless immodesty to those who were offended by the gesture. Either way, her fame was assured, and she went on to produce as well as star in a series of largely successful films, some of which served to fan the flames of disapproval while making her a rich woman. Moore's offscreen life as part of a famous couple, first with actor Bruce Willis, then with actor Ashton Kutcher, have gained her almost as much fame as her film roles, and to many she has become a symbol of the overexposed celebrity.

HOLLYWOOD'S BRAT PACK

Born Demetria Gene Guynes on November 11, 1962, in Roswell, New Mexico, she moved frequently with her family before she went to Los Angeles at the age of fifteen and found work in modeling and television. An ongoing role on the popular daytime soap *General Hospital,* in which she appeared from 1982 to 1983, led her into feature films; however, her first four attempts on the big screen gave her little to do and made no impression. She won her first lead in *No Small Affair* (1984), as an aspiring singer performing in tacky clubs who becomes the love object of teenager Jon Cryer. Moore came across as an attractive, girl-next-door brunette, with a pleasingly husky voice and the ability to invest in a role with matter-of-fact conviction.

Demi Moore. *Former Brat Packer Demi Moore has transitioned to adult roles as well as ventures as a producer and director.* STEVE GRANITZ/CONTRIBUTOR/WIREIMAGE/GETTY IMAGES.

The film led to a role in the following year's ensemble piece about college graduates, *St. Elmo's Fire* (1985). She gave a standout performance as the glamorous, wealthy, and suicidally unhappy member of the group, and Moore became identified as one of a number of youthful actors dubbed the Brat Pack by the Hollywood press. Though the nickname was somewhat dismissive, the Brat Pack actors and their films made a significant contribution to 1980s youth culture, exploring important issues such as class differences, family abuse, and the deep yearning to belong that are common to youth of every generation. Moore also honed her craft in live theater during the 1980s, and she won a Theatre World Award in 1987 for her performance in the off-Broadway show *The Early Girl.*

ADULT ROLES

Moore graduated to full adult status in 1990, costarring with Patrick Swayze and Whoopi Goldberg in the hit romance *Ghost.* By 1991, married to star Willis, she became not only a mother but also a producer, costarring with her husband in her own production, *Mortal Thoughts.* During the next few years she performed respectably in the military courtroom drama *A Few Good Men* (1992) with Jack Nicholson and Tom Cruise and, brilliantly, as Woody Allen's sister in *Deconstructing Harry* (1997). She also gave the voice to Esmeralda in Disney's animated feature *The Hunchback of Notre Dame* in 1996. The same decade, however, marked the emergence of a different direction for Moore.

It became clear that the actress was developing a sharp sense for profitably controversial material. She enhanced her bank balance and raised her profile—though not necessarily the esteem in which she was held—by starring in highly successful but faintly dubious films such as Adrian Lyne's *Indecent Proposal* (1993) and Barry Levinson's *Disclosure* (1994). In the former she was the young wife who, when she and her husband (Woody Harrelson) lose their money in Las Vegas, Nevada, sells her sexual favors for one night to a millionaire (Robert Redford) in exchange for $1 million; in Levinson's film, based on author Michael Crichton's best seller, she was a driven, manipulative, and scheming executive who sexually harasses her subordinate (Michael Douglas).

In the same controversial vein, the movie *Striptease* (1996) lured millions of voyeuristic cinemagoers worldwide with the promise of seeing Moore as they had never seen her before. Their expectations were disappointed, but the movie made its star a rich woman. Attempts to redeem her growing image as a sex symbol by playing the title role in *G.I. Jane* (1997) misfired; Ridley Scott's film was a failure, and Moore took much of the critical flak.

ROMANCING THE SOCIAL NETWORK

Though some commentators believed that Moore's success rested on her exploitation of her body, by the late 1990s she had proven her credentials as an intelligent and talented actress. In 2000 her notoriously stormy marriage to Willis ended in divorce, and in 2003 she once again aroused controversy by dating Kutcher. An actor sixteen years younger than Moore, he was best known for his role as a clueless high school student on Fox Television's *That 70's Show* and as the producer and host of MTV's hidden camera practical joke show, *Punk'd.* Though fans censured and columnists ridiculed the pair, they married in 2005 and developed several joint projects, including a charitable foundation called the Demi and Ashton Foundation (DNA) that worked to raise awareness about such issues as sex trafficking.

In 2009 Moore and Kutcher became known for their extensive use of the new social networking service Twitter. With millions of followers each, Moore and Kutcher brought their fans into the heart of their relationship with intimate tweets such as "race u to the bedroom," which was written on Moore's hand and photographed and posted for all to see. They even discussed press allegations of Kutcher's infidelity on Twitter, and, when Moore announced their breakup in 2011, Kutcher responded with a tweet, "I will forever cherish the time I spent with Demi." In early 2012 Moore sought professional help after landing in the hospital for reported substance abuse.

Moore continued to make films, such as the independent Derrick Borte film *The Joneses* (2009), an examination of consumerism and hidden advertising. She also stayed active behind the camera, producing a talk show for the Lifetime network called *The Conversation* and directing "Charlotte," one segment of a 2011 Lifetime movie series called *Five* showcasing women and breast cancer.

Sara Martin

SEE ALSO: *Advertising; Allen, Woody; Brat Pack; Broadway; Celebrity; Celebrity Couples; Crichton, Michael; Cruise, Tom; Disney (Walt Disney Company); Divorce;* General Hospital*; Goldberg, Whoopi; Hollywood; Kutcher, Ashton; Made-for-Television Movies; MTV; Nicholson, Jack;* Punk'd*; Redford, Robert; Scott, Ridley; Soap Operas; Strip Joints/Striptease; Twitter;* Vanity Fair*; Willis, Bruce.*

BIBLIOGRAPHY

Bennetts, L. "Demi's State of Grace." *Vanity Fair*, December 1993, 176–181.

Collins, N. "Demi's Big Moment." *Vanity Fair*, August 1991, 96–101.

Conant, J. "Demi's Body Language." *Vanity Fair*, August 1992, 112–119.

Franich, Darren. "Aston Kutcher and Demi Moore: A Marriage Made (and Unmade?) on Twitter." *Entertainment Weekly*, November 17, 2011. Accessed April 20, 2012. Available from http://popwatch.ew.com/2011/11/17/ashton-kutcher-demi-moore-divorce-twitter/

Friend, T. "Demi-tough." *Vogue*, October 1995, 278–287.

Gora, Susannah. *You Couldn't Ignore Me if You Tried: The Brat Pack, John Hughes, and Their Impact on a Generation*. New York: Crown, 2010.

Heller, Z. "Demi: One of the Boys." *Harper's Bazaar*, August 1997, 148–155.

Udovitch, M. "Demi Moore." *Rolling Stone*, February 9, 1995, 38–41.

Moore, Michael *(1954–)*

Michael Moore burst onto the American cultural scene in the late 1980s as a chubby, extroverted rabble-rouser who hitched his political message to the medium of satirical comedy in a crusade to spur the national conscience against corporate injustice. A genuine subversive, he made an impact with his debut film, *Roger & Me* (1989), a satirical documentary feature that chronicles his attempts to interview the CEO of General Motors (GM), Roger Smith. Moore wrote, directed, and starred in the film, which became the highest-grossing American documentary up to that time. He has continued his career for three decades of frenzied activity, during which he has published numerous books, produced television shows, and made five more feature-length documentary films. Always an activist as well as an artist, Moore became an outspoken supporter of the Occupy Wall Street movement for economic justice that spread across the United States in 2011.

Moore's comedy and politics emerged from his roots in Michigan in working-class communities in Davison and neighboring Flint. Flint enjoyed a boom from manufacturing automobiles at a dozen General Motors factories until the company abandoned the town, as chronicled in *Roger & Me*. Moore had been a staunch opponent of GM and local Flint politics since founding the *Flint Voice* at the age of twenty-two He partially funded the newspaper through the showing of alternative movies and promoted it through work on the local public radio station, where he hosted a show called *Radio Free Flint*. He also wrote essays for National Public Radio. Outspoken from early on, Moore was elected to his local school board at age eighteen and successfully fought to have its meetings open to the public.

FIRST FILMS

Roger & Me was creatively financed by Moore and his friends through bingo games and other fund-raising efforts and through an out-of-court settlement Moore made with *Mother Jones* magazine over his dismissal from the publication a few months after he had been hired as editor in 1986. Critical opinion about *Roger & Me* was high but divided. The *Washington Post* described *Roger & Me* as a "hilariously cranky bit of propaganda," and critics such as Roger Ebert gave it rave reviews. Others, including the doyenne of the *New Yorker*, Pauline Kael, attacked Moore for rearranging the narrative events of the movie. The critical controversy notwithstanding, the film was voted Best Documentary by the National Board of Review, the New York Film Critics Circle, the Los Angeles Film Critics Association, and the National Society of Film Critics, as well as Best Film at the Toronto, Vancouver, and Chicago film festivals. It was included on several critics' "best of the decade" lists, but it conspicuously failed to be nominated for an Academy Award.

Moore followed up *Roger & Me* with a sequel, *Pets or Meat: A Return to Flint* (1992), a short film shown on PBS. The second documentary repeated the narrated style of the first and seemed more of a continuation than a sequel. In it, Moore caught up on the lives of people from the first film, including "the Rabbit Lady," who sold rabbits as pets or meat. The film was also an update on Moore himself, containing snippets from his appearances on television talk shows such as *Donahue*. He made an unlikely movie "star"—he is heavyset with a goofy grin and has a preference for baseball caps and untucked shirts—yet there is no doubt that the "star" of all of Moore's films is Michael Moore.

Moore's next project was a narrative film, *Canadian Bacon* (1995), starring John Candy, Rhea Perlman, Kevin Pollak, Alan Alda, and Rip Torn. Alda plays a liberal U.S. president who decides to invade Canada in order to boost his popularity in the polls. A cross between *Dr. Strangelove* (there's a similar Doomsday device) and *Wag the Dog* (the invasion of a foreign country for shabby domestic reasons), the film never received wide release nor were the reviews particularly enthusiastic.

TV NATION

Moore's next move was to take the basic *Roger & Me* idea—good guy Mike harasses evil corporate America—to television. His political comedy show, *TV Nation*, was a summer replacement on NBC in 1994, winning the Emmy for Outstanding Informational Series. The show featured weekly, off-the-wall poll results, such as that 16 percent of Perot voters believe that "if dolphins were really that smart they could get out of those nets," and showcased memorable events such as a day of picnicking with "Doctor Death" Jack Kevorkian.

The first episode featured the "CEO Challenge," in which he asked executives to perform menial tasks—for example, getting the head of IBM to format a computer disk. Although not all the stories had a political bent, *TV Nation* was an eclectic mix of news magazine and sketch comedy. Only on *TV Nation* would you see a guy in a Detroit Tigers baseball cap attempting to end the conflict in Bosnia by getting leaders from the warring factions to share a pizza together.

NBC passed on *TV Nation*, but Fox picked it up for eight episodes in the summer of 1995. It was more of the same, including a segment that featured Moore performing maneuvers with the Michigan Militia. He also introduced Crackers, the corporate crime-fighting chicken, alongside featured guests such as Merrill Markoe (David Letterman's former chief writer), actress and stand-up comedian Janeane Garofalo, former MTV presenter Karen Duffy, and filmmaker Rusty Cundieff. Moore chronicled his experiences with the show in a book, *Adventures in TV Nation* (1998), written with his wife, Kathleen Glynn.

The book was not Moore's first. He had published *Downsize This!: Random Threats from an Unarmed American*, an unlikely best seller, in 1996. The book began with two photos: one of the bombed-out federal building in Oklahoma City, the other of a pile of rubble that used to be an automobile factory in Flint. The point of that piece, and the book, is to expose—through satire, irony, and poke-in-the-eye comedy—corporate America's war on working-class families. With chapters such as "Would Pat Buchanan Take a Check from Satan?" "Why Doesn't GM Sell Crack?" and "Why Are Union Leaders So F#!@ing Stupid?" the book is part stand-up comedy in printed form, part political manifesto, and part *Spy* magazine-like pranks.

Moore embarked on an unconventional book promotion tour, refusing to sign books at certain chain stores and seeking out independent booksellers. After a few stops, he was joined by a film crew, which led to the making of *The Big One* (1997). The film features tactics familiar to those of Moore's fans, including the presentation of "Downsizer of the Year" awards to company bigwigs. It opened in selected cities in benefits for local charities, unions, and leftist political groups. Moore would answer questions, promote local causes, tell some jokes, and then inspire the audience to political action. Despite excellent reviews, *The Big One* failed to achieve commercial success; an angry film about corporate America seemed out of synch when the Dow Jones Industrial Average was at an all-time record high.

As the twentieth century ended, Moore continued to pitch his political message to a larger audience. In conjunction with Britain's Channel 4, he negotiated another incarnation of *TV Nation*, which launched in early 1999 under the title *The Awful Truth* and was nominated for Emmys in 1999 and 2001.

TWENTY-FIRST CENTURY

In 2002 Moore made headlines again with his provocative documentary *Bowling for Columbine*, which explored the larger societal causes behind the deaths of thirteen people in a 1999 school shooting in Littleton, Colorado. The film used a lively mix of animation, interviews, and Moore's personal style of antic confrontation to examine the U.S. culture of guns and violence and the fear and social injustice at its core. Though the film's strong leftist political agenda drew mixed reviews, it won a number of awards, including, finally, an Academy Award for Best Documentary Feature in 2003. Never one to waste an opportunity in the spotlight, Moore used his acceptance speech to denounce U.S. society; the war in Iraq; and the 2000 presidential election as "fictitious," declaiming to the president, "Shame on you, Mr. Bush!" before being cut off.

During the first decade of the 2000s, Moore began touring with Rolling Thunder, a traveling Chautauqua-style fair of music and politics devoted to education and the building of a progressive coalition. He also traveled on a solo speaking tour, titled *Michael Moore—Live*. A prolific writer, he continued to advance his agenda for political change with more books, publishing three best sellers in 2004 alone. In Moore's usual style of comic vehemence, *Dude, Where's My Country?* mourns the U.S. rush to intolerance and war and places the blame on corrupt corporate politicians. *Will They Ever Trust Us Again: Letters from the War Zone* is a collection of letters from members of the military and their families who question the policies that control their lives, and *Stupid White Men* is a condemnation of a power elite out of touch with the issues of working people.

In 2004 Moore released his scathing analysis of the September 11, 2001, attacks in New York City and Washington, D.C., and the U.S. government's response. *Fahrenheit 9/11* revealed the Bush administration's disregard of clear information that had existed about an upcoming attack and the troubling evidence of undisclosed ties between high government officials and members of the Saudi royal family. Although *Fahrenheit 9/11* is peppered with Moore's sharp wit, he is off-camera for most of the film, which won the Palme d'Or at the 2004 Cannes Film Festival.

Moore followed *Fahrenheit 9/11* with the powerful documentary *Sicko* in 2007. An indictment of the for-profit health care system, *Sicko* uses the stories of real people to outline the failures of private insurance while exploring the success of government-funded insurance systems in other countries. Even those critical of Moore's over-the-top style of filmmaking could not help admitting that he made his point. In his 2009 documentary, *Capitalism, a Love Story*, Moore returned to the subject matter of the exploitation of the working class by a greedy corporate elite. *Capitalism* was the product of the economic turndown of 2008, when people across the country were experiencing the same desperate financial pressures that Moore had documented in Flint, Michigan, two decades before.

In 2011, as a wave of popular democratic movements swept the Arab world, hard economic times prompted a similar movement for democracy and economic justice in the United States. Largely led by the young and the disenfranchised, the movement, which had started in New York City under the name Occupy Wall Street, soon spread throughout the country as the Occupy movement. A Manhattan resident, Moore became a strong supporter and a frequent speaker at Occupy events. Always controversial on both the Right and the Left, he has faced challenges from some advocates of economic justice who see the successful filmmaker as part of the wealthy elite whom they oppose.

Patrick Jones

SEE ALSO: *Academy Awards; Alda, Alan; Automobile; Cable TV; The Chautauqua Institution; Daytime Talk Shows; Donahue, Phil;* Dr. Strangelove or: How I Learned to Stop Worrying and Love the Bomb*; Emmy Awards; General Motors; Gulf Wars; Labor Unions; 9/11; Perot, Ross; Public Television (PBS); Siskel and Ebert; Television.*

BIBLIOGRAPHY

Bernstein, Matthew, ed. *Michael Moore: Filmmaker, Newsmaker, Cultural Icon.* Ann Arbor: University of Michigan Press, 2010.

Hamm, Theodore. *The New Blue Media: How Michael Moore, MoveOn.org, Jon Stewart and Company Are Transforming Progressive Politics.* New York: The New Press, 2008.

Hinson, Hal. "Roger & Me." *Washington Post,* January 12, 1990.

Jacobson, Harlan. "Michael & Me." *Film Comment,* November–December, 1989.

Kael, Pauline. "Roger & Me." *New Yorker,* January 8, 1990, 51–52.

Moore, Michael. *Here Comes Trouble: Stories from My Life.* New York: Grand Central Pub., 2011.

Scott, A. O. "Open Wide and Say 'Shame.'" *New York Times,* June 22, 2007.

Moore, Sam

SEE: *Sam and Dave.*

Moral Majority

Starting in the mid-1970s, a resurgence of political activity began to develop among conservative Christians in the United States. Alarmed by what they perceived to be the moral decline of American society, they sought to introduce into U.S. politics a new social agenda aimed at fighting the forces of secularization. They subsequently established a number of organizations to promote this agenda, the most prominent of which was the Moral Majority. Founded in 1979 by Jerry Falwell, an influential Baptist minister and televangelist, the Moral Majority joined with other political conservatives to promote the restoration of traditional moral values. Falwell and his followers played a significant role in the election of Ronald Reagan to the presidency in 1980 and, in the following years, sought to focus national attention on the controversial topics of abortion, gay rights, pornography, the exclusion of prayer from public schools, and the Equal Rights Amendment. The Moral Majority also advocated conservative positions on a variety of more secular issues, such as a balanced budget and increased defense spending. In 1989 Falwell disbanded the group, claiming that it had fulfilled its original mission of introducing support for social reform into American politics. Since then, it has continued to serve as a model for political activism among religious conservatives in the United States.

A GROWING COALITION

The Moral Majority was established with the support of various religious and political groups who wished to counter the liberal trends that had emerged within American society during the 1960s and 1970s. By mobilizing conservative Christians, they hoped to produce a rightward shift in the balance of power in American politics. To strengthen the influence of the Moral Majority, Falwell also attempted to expand its constituency beyond its original core within the fundamentalist Protestant community. The group thus came to include a diversity of other religious groups, including Mormons, conservative Roman Catholics, and Orthodox Jews. Falwell purposely avoided initiating official connections between the Moral Majority and any specific political party, on the grounds that the organization's agenda focused primarily on moral issues rather than political positions. In its status as an independent organization, not tied to any party or religious denomination, the Moral Majority represented an extension of existing fundamentalist strategies in the United States, which since the 1920s had concentrated on creating new institutions rather than reforming existing ones.

MASS MEDIA AND GRASS ROOTS

The Moral Majority proved to be very successful in building its coalition of like-minded conservatives. By the 1980 election it included more than two million members, perhaps twice that many during its peak years in the mid-1980s. In spreading its message to potential members, the Moral Majority used two distinct strategies, again following the approaches adopted by earlier fundamentalist Christian movements. First, it made extensive use of the mass media, particularly the broadcast media. Falwell himself had gained considerable experience in the media as the host of the *Old-Time Gospel Hour,* a syndicated religious radio and television program dating from the 1950s. The rapid growth of televangelism during the 1970s and 1980s provided a natural platform for the Moral Majority's message and helped it to find a sizable audience. The Moral Majority also benefitted from the attention of the mainstream news media, who saw in Falwell an articulate and readily accessible spokesman for the Religious Right. Through the extensive news coverage that Falwell received, particularly during the national political campaigns of the early 1980s, the Moral Majority became the leading symbol of the Religious Right's new political influence.

The other strategy adopted by the Moral Majority in spreading its message focused on the development of an extensive grassroots network. The key elements of this network were the many local chapters established across the country. These organizations sought to implement the agenda of the Moral Majority at the local level through their involvement in political races and community issues, and they represented the primary vehicle through which the movement's followers became involved in its activities. Although their impact was not as conspicuous as that of the movement's national leaders, the local chapters had a lasting influence on religious conservatives by demonstrating the effectiveness of community political action. Local strategies were widely adopted by former members as they continued the work of the Moral Majority after it was disbanded.

THE FALL

Although Falwell asserted that the decision to disband the Moral Majority derived from its success in achieving its goals, a number of factors had contributed to a decline in the group's influence by the end of the 1980s. The Moral Majority faced extensive criticism from political liberals and moderates, who accused the group of trying to impose its own moral and religious views on America's pluralistic society. At the same time some conservative Christians faulted the Moral Majority for its involvement in secular political issues, arguing that it should focus on its core religious message. Scandals involving televangelists Jim Bakker and Jimmy Swaggart during the late 1980s did much to discredit conservative Christian institutions; and the failure of televangelist Pat Robertson in the 1988 Republican presidential primary cast doubt on the continuing political strength of religious conservatives, at least at the national level.

Despite its relatively brief history as a formal organization, the Moral Majority had a major impact on America's political landscape and, more broadly, its popular culture. It played a key role in reintroducing religion to the realm of public debate, not only by addressing explicitly religious issues, such as school prayer, but also in asserting the validity of religious belief as the foundation for public policy decisions, as in the controversy over abortion. Its stand on certain issues, however, produced a strong counterreaction among Americans who supported feminism, reproductive choice, gay rights, and other liberal social trends, and it pushed them to pursue a more active defense of their views. The Moral Majority thus helped to expand the debate between liberals and conservatives in American politics to include a broad range of social issues.

FALWELL AND HIS LEGACY

From the beginning an aggressive spokesperson for the Right, Jerry Falwell was a controversial and divisive public figure. His targets were many and various; two of his favorites were Bill and Hillary Clinton. Even other conservatives objected to a video Falwell produced in which he labeled Bill Clinton a drug addict. Hillary Clinton, an unabashed spokesperson for the rights of women and children, was rewarded with Falwell's epithet "Satan." He even attacked the PBS children's show *Teletubbies*, insisting that it was a front for gay rights. After September 11, 2001, Falwell announced that advocates of liberal causes—such as separation of church and state, gay rights, and reproductive freedom—were responsible for the attacks. Falwell's death on May 15, 2007, generated a massive wave of discussions about his legacy. Many conservatives praised him for his positive impact on American politics; others called him an enemy of the American people.

Roger W. Stump

SEE ALSO: *Abortion; Bakker, Jim, and Tammy Faye; Equal Rights Amendment; Evangelism; Feminism; Fundamentalism; Gay Liberation Movement; 9/11; Pornography; Public Television (PBS); Radio; Reagan, Ronald; Religious Right; Robertson, Pat; Swaggart, Jimmy; Syndication; Televangelism; Television.*

BIBLIOGRAPHY

Dochuk, Darren. *From Bible Belt to Sunbelt: Plain Folk, Religion, Grassroots Politics, and the Rise of Evangelical Conservatism.* New York: W. W. Norton, 2011.

Fackre, Gabriel J. *The Religious Right and Christian Faith.* Grand Rapids, MI: Eerdmans, 1982.

Georgianna, Sharon. *The Moral Majority and Fundamentalism: Plausibility and Dissonance.* Lewiston, NY: Edwin Mellen Press, 1989.

Hale, Grace Elizabeth. *A Nation of Outsiders: How the White Middle Class Fell in Love with Rebellion in Postwar America.* New York: Oxford University Press, 2011.

Hedges, Chris. *American Fascists: The Christian Right and the War on America.* New York: Free Press, 2007.

Lambert, Frank. *Religion in American Politics: A Short History.* Princeton, NJ: Princeton University Press, 2008.

Phillips-Fein, Kim. *Invisible Hands: The Making of the Conservative Movement from the New Deal to Reagan.* New York: W. W. Norton, 2009.

Shupe, Anson D., and William A. Stacey. *Born Again Politics and the Moral Majority: What Social Surveys Really Show.* New York: Edwin Mellen Press, 1982.

Moreno, Rita *(1931–)*

Puerto Rican singer, dancer, and actress Rita Moreno lives in the collective memory of moviegoers as Anita, dancing up a storm and singing "I like to be in America, OK by me in America" in the 1961 screen version of *West Side Story*. She won the Best Supporting Actress Oscar for her performance, the first Hispanic actress to do so, and the film brought this uniquely dynamic, fiery, and talented performer wide recognition. It led to a greater awareness of the talent that existed in the Hispanic community.

Born Rosita Dolores Alverio in Humacao, Puerto Rico, in 1931, Moreno was raised in a New York City tenement by her divorced mother, a seamstress. Despite not having much money, the child was able to take dance lessons with Paco Cansino, uncle of Rita Hayworth, who soon had her performing in the children's theater at Macy's department store and at weddings and bar mitzvahs. Initially using the name Rosita Moreno, she first worked on Broadway at age thirteen in a musical called *Skydrift*. After that she performed in nightclubs in Boston, Las Vegas, and New York. At fourteen she went to Hollywood and had a tiny role in a movie called *A Medal for Benny* (1945). Louis B. Mayer put her under contract, but her film career lay dormant until 1950 when she made appearances in *So Young, So Bad*; *The Toast of New Orleans*; and *Pagan Love Song*.

Most of the film roles offered were stereotypical and sometimes demeaning. Between film roles she returned to the stage, where she hoped for better opportunities to use her substantial gifts. Moreno played several distinguished roles onstage, including a dramatic role in Arthur Miller's *A View from the Bridge*, and she was the first Hispanic actress to win a Tony Award—for Best Supporting Actress—presented for her performance in the Broadway production of the musical *The Ritz*, which ran for more than 400 performances in 1975.

With its score by Leonard Bernstein and lyrics by Stephen Sondheim, *West Side Story* (1957) broke new ground in the development of the Broadway musical—not least in being the first mainstream production with a Hispanic theme and showcasing the talents of Hispanic actors and dancers. Some of them, notably Chita Rivera, went on to make important contributions to stage and film. Moreno had originally been offered, and had turned down, the role of Maria in the stage production, but she got her chance to shine in a role more suited to her strong personality when the film was made.

Several of the films in which Moreno played prominent roles indicate Hollywood's stereotyped perception of Hispanics, including *The Ring* (1952), a low-budget programmer about a young Mexican prizefighter attempting to win respect for his people, and *Popi* (1969), an ethnic comedy-drama set in New York's Puerto Rican ghetto. Throughout her career Moreno fought against typecasting to get roles commensurate with her talent—she was touching as the Siamese slave girl Tuptim in *The King and I* (1956), and among many other less distinguished films she had featured roles in *Summer and Smoke* (1961), *Carnal Knowledge* (1971), the film version of her stage success *The Ritz* (1976), and Alan Alda's *The Four Seasons* (1981).

Moreno has also left her mark on television, acting in a variety of series and shows. She won her first Emmy Award for her guest appearances on *The Muppet Show* in 1977 and her second for an episode of *The Rockford Files* in 1978. Her vocalizations for the *Electric Company* television program's album for children won her a Grammy Award in 1972. She was the first female artist to win Tony, Emmy, Grammy, and Academy Awards. Moreno continued to act into her seventies, guest starring on shows such as *Law and Order*, *Ugly Betty*, and *The George Lopez Show*. She has also undertaken ongoing roles, including playing Dori, mother to Fran Dreschler's character in the show *Happily Divorced* in 2011–2012. Moreno reflected on her life in the autobiographical play *Rita Moreno: Life without Makeup*, which she developed with playwright Tony Taccone.

Nicolás Kanellos

SEE ALSO: *Academy Awards; Alda, Alan; Bernstein, Leonard; Broadway; Emmy Awards; Grammy Awards; Hayworth, Rita; Hollywood; Macy's; Mayer, Louis B.; Miller, Arthur; The Muppets; Rivera, Chita; Sondheim, Stephen; Television; Tony Awards;* West Side Story.

BIBLIOGRAPHY

Kanellos, Nicolás. *Hispanic American Almanac.* Detroit, MI: Gale Research, 1997.

Telgen, Diane, and Jim Kamp. *Latinas! Women of Achievement.* Detroit, MI: Visible Ink Press, 1996.

Rita Moreno. *Showing the versatility of her talent, Rita Moreno was the first actress to be awarded an Emmy, a Tony, a Grammy, and an Oscar.* JOE KOHEN/CONTRIBUTOR/WIREIMAGE/GETTY IMAGES.

Morissette, Alanis *(1974–)*

Singer Alanis Morissette was the first pop artist to successfully commercialize the anger of young white women. It had taken surprisingly long for pop music to find its spokeswoman: thirty years after Bob Dylan snarled out "Positively Fourth Street" and nearly twenty years after punk's standard-bearer Sid Vicious of the Sex Pistols fame murdered his girlfriend Nancy Spungen, rage in mainstream music was still just for guys. The breakthrough came in the 1990s when Morissette—who transformed herself from a Canadian perky pop singer à la Debbie Gibson to an angst-ridden Everywoman—generated the top-selling album ever by a female solo artist.

Morissette was born in Ottawa, Canada, on June 1, 1974, twelve minutes after her twin brother, Wade. Her father was French-Canadian, and her mother was a Hungarian refugee. As a child, she wanted to perform in front of people, and by the age of ten she had landed a role on the Canadian children's show *You Can't Do That on Television* (later shown in the United States on Nickelodeon).

Morissette also pursued a singing career, releasing her first single, *Fate Stay with Me*, in 1987 and appearing on television's reality talent show *Star Search* in 1989. Two years later her album *Alanis* was a hit in Canada. Using her first name only, her enthusiastic dancing; big hair; mismatched clothing; and synthetic, bubble-gum dance music placed her solidly in the mall-pop category with Gibson and Tiffany. Morissette lived up to her role as Canadian teen idol, belting out "O Canada" at hockey games and at the 1988 World Figure Skating Championships. Musical tastes had changed, however, and her next album, *Now Is the Time* (1992), was less successful. In order to survive as an artist, Morissette realized she would have to reinvent herself.

RIOT GRRL MOVEMENT

Meanwhile, in the early 1990s U.S. punk rock had given birth to the Riot Grrl movement, a loosely defined school of women playing underground rock and roll in the name of women's empowerment. Following in the uppity women tradition extending from Bessie Smith through Patti Smith to Sonic Youth's Kim Gordon, Riot Grrl bands such as Bikini Kill and Seven Year Bitch went further, venting outrage and confusion as they tackled feminist themes from date rape to incest to war. Though the movement stimulated excitement and discussion among many in the fragmented punk mini-scenes, none of those bands ever found significant commercial acceptance: their music was simply too confrontational and political for the era.

Female anger was purveyed somewhat more successfully by more mainstream acts that were favorites of the critics, such as P. J. Harvey, Tori Amos, and Liz Phair; Phair's 1993 debut album, *Exile in Guyville*, with its acrimony toward past lovers and its graphic discussion of oral sex, closely parallels Morissette's breakthrough. Finally, the stage was set by Hole's 1994 smash success *Live through This*, helped along by the massive publicity surrounding the suicide of Nirvana leader Kurt Cobain, Hole frontwoman Courtney Love's husband. Hole blended Nirvana's grunge rock with a watered-down Riot Grrl sensibility and found wide acceptance. (Love very publicly expressed her dislike of Morissette, who supplanted her as rock's premier Angry Woman.)

Alanis Morissette. *Since bursting onto the charts with the release of* Jagged Little Pill *in 1995, Alanis Morissette continues to write, record, and perform.* X FACTOR/CONTRIBUTOR/GETTY IMAGES ENTERTAINMENT/GETTY IMAGES.

REVAMPING THE MOVEMENT

Morissette moved to Los Angeles in the early 1990s, hooked up with cowriter/producer Glen Ballard, and set about recycling the Riot Grrls' energy while dropping their feminist politics. Released in 1995 on Madonna's Maverick label, *Jagged Little Pill* was an immediate success behind the hit single "You Oughta Know," a diatribe against a former lover and his new girlfriend (an antiwoman attack no self-respecting Riot Grrl would have tolerated). The lyrics pushed the envelope just far enough (MTV edited the line "Are you thinking of me when you fuck her?" but allowed "Would she go down on you in a theater?"). Suddenly, Morissette was a star, not only in Canada but also around the world. Other singles—less cathartic but equally evocative of a sixteen-year-old girl dressed in black writing in her journal—followed, including "Ironic" (which hinges on a popular though incorrect use of the title word), "Head over Feet," and "One Hand in My Pocket."

Unlike many of the women who preceded her, Morissette did not limit her audience by being too ambitious or too clever. She did not express any interest in changing the world, only in complaining about it, and she was not redefining male-female relations, she just wanted her ex to hurt like she did. Audiences looked at Morissette and saw themselves: her voice never soared so high a fan could not sing along; she was not pretty enough to be threatening; she was never hard to understand. To the extent that art is about expressing the thoughts and feelings of a mass audience, *Jagged Little Pill* was as effective a piece of art as rock had produced. In 1996 Morissette won four Grammy Awards: Best Album, Best Rock Album, Best Rock Song, and Best Female Rock Vocal Performance.

LATER CAREER

Jagged Little Pill sold some sixteen million copies in the United States and twenty-eight million worldwide. While Morissette toured and then took time off, a group of similar acts emerged and followed in her wake, among them Fiona Apple and Natalie Imbruglia. The second album of Morissette's second singing career, *Supposed Former Infatuation Junkie*, was released in late 1998, debuting at the top of the charts but falling below expectations. Unable to create further shock with her lyrics, she caused a mild stir by appearing nearly nude in the disc's first video, "Thank You." Morissette's single "Uninvited" was used in the movie *City of Angels* (1998) and won two Grammys. Later albums—*Under Rug Swept* (2002) and *So-Called Chaos* (2004)—were not nearly as popular or commercially successful as her earlier work, and in 2005 the musician returned to *Jagged Little Pill*, shaping an acoustic album and tour.

Although Morissette's twenty-first-century studio recordings were not as successful as her earlier releases, she retained a stable fan base. She opened for the Rolling Stones for a portion of their record-breaking *A Bigger Bang* tour in 2005 and recorded "Wunderkind" for the soundtrack to *The Chronicles of Narnia: The Lion, the Witch and the Wardrobe*. In 2008 she recorded *Flavors of Entanglement*, her final studio album for Maverick Records.

Morissette also appeared in a handful of films and critically acclaimed television shows. In 1999 she played the role of God for Kevin Smith's *Dogma* and then appeared in the cable television series *Sex and the City*, *Curb Your Enthusiasm*, and *Weeds*. Whether history viewed Morissette as a canny self-exploiter (the new Madonna) or as an accidental superstar (the new Tiny Tim), her tremendous commercial success spoke for itself.

David B. Wilson

SEE ALSO: *Cable TV; Feminism; Grammy Awards; Love, Courtney; Madonna; MTV; Nirvana; Pop Music; Punk; Rock and Roll; The Rolling Stones;* Sex and the City*; The Sex Pistols; Smith, Bessie; Smith, Patti; Television; Tiny Tim; Top 40;* Weeds.

BIBLIOGRAPHY

Cantin, Paul. *Alanis Morissette: A Biography*. New York: St. Martin's Press, 1998.

Tomashoff, Craig. *You Live, You Learn: The Alanis Morissette Story*. New York: Berkley Publishing Group, 1998.

Mork & Mindy

In 1978 the ABC comedy *Mork & Mindy* hit the air. The show—about a naive, human-looking alien from the planet Ork—and its star, Robin Williams, quickly became hits. Expressions from the show, such as "nanu nanu" and "shazbat," and Mork's striped suspenders became overnight cultural icons. The frantic pace and inspired lunacy of its first season made it a wonderful addition to television history, especially in the tradition of Williams's hero Jonathan Winters and the show's sitcom ancestor *My Favorite Martian*. During its four seasons on the air, *Mork & Mindy* would change and drop in the ratings, but it will forever be a milestone in television and comedy.

Mork and Mindy. Mork and Mindy *starred Robin Williams, left, and Pam Dawber and ran from 1978 to 1982.* PARAMOUNT TV/THE KOBAL COLLECTION.

The character of Mork first appeared in a February 1978 episode of *Happy Days*, in which Mork tried to kidnap Richie Cunningham. The popular response to the character led to *Mork & Mindy*, which was produced by Garry Marshall, producer of *Happy Days*. In the series, Mork is sent to Earth from the planet Ork in an egg-shaped ship to observe and report on Earth's customs. He meets Mindy McConnell (Pam Dawber) and returns to her house to live in her attic. Mindy plays the straight man to Mork and tries to hide or avoid the complications of his sometimes strangely inhuman methods, such as sitting on his head or drinking through his finger.

The biggest trouble that faces Mindy is that Mork does not know the fundamentals of human interaction. Most importantly, he does not know what not to do or say in "society." In sometimes subtle or not-so-subtle ways, Mork points out many cultural hang-ups that he sees around him. In traditional sitcom approach, each show has a message—obvious to Mork—and he has to report weekly findings to his superior, Orson, on his home planet. This conveniently allows the show to present weekly homilies on topics such as love and greed. Although the approach became a bit tiresome, it did occasionally allow for humorous anecdotes or quips.

In the episodes, commentary comes in the form of broad satire, touching on the melodramatic. Mork takes all earthly events and words literally, allowing for some funny interchanges. *Mork & Mindy* sometimes drifted—especially in later seasons—into commentary over comedy, a move that ultimately hurt its appeal. Williams, however, is a master of improvisation, and his ability to bounce off topics, draw from an endless supply of pop culture asides, and adopt voices and personalities at will kept audiences watching despite sometimes weak story lines. This frantic pace and "never-know-what-to-expect-next" feeling marked the first season but sadly disappeared in subsequent seasons.

Though *Mork & Mindy* was an initial success, the network made major cast changes and the store where Mindy worked disappeared, along with a bunch of minor characters. Second, in an effort to bolster ABC's traditionally weak Sunday lineup, the show was removed from its dominant Thursday slot. *Mork & Mindy*'s worst nemesis, it seemed, was a network set on ruining the show. The sitcom continued to drop dramatically in the ratings, losing almost half its audience over the course of a single season. *Mork & Mindy* plunged from third in the national Nielsen ratings to twenty-sixth. The network attempted to undo some of the changes and return it to its original time slot, but it was too late.

During the final season, in typical sitcom fashion, the pair got married and had a baby. Depending on perspective, the last season offers either a high or low point when Winters took on the role of the baby, Mearth (Orkans are born older and get younger over time). This was either the supreme paring of comics or a mark of the depths to which the show would go to survive. In any event, it was canceled at the end of the season. In 1982 Mork, Mindy, Mr. McConnell, and Orson would all pop up again in one season of animated cartoons also titled *Mork & Mindy* (with the original cast providing voices).

Mork & Mindy represents many of the high and low points of 1970s television comedy. It was one of many spin-offs from successful shows that managed to outdo its parent. It was also one of the many shows that marked ABC's golden period of television comedy at this time, with a lineup of successes such as *Three's Company, Laverne & Shirley*, and *Happy Days*. In addition, it brought national attention to a major star, Williams. Finally, the show also became a major player in the popular culture of the era, introducing catchphrases, a look, and an attitude that continued decades later. In the end, however, the energy and talent of Williams and other cast members were not able to maintain the show, either from bad decision making by the network or perhaps from a lack of steam.

Frank Clark

SEE ALSO: Happy Days*;* Laverne and Shirley*; Marshall, Garry; Sitcom; Television;* Three's Company*; UFOs (Unidentified Flying Objects); Williams, Robin; Winters, Jonathan.*

BIBLIOGRAPHY

Castleman, Harry, and Walter J. Podrazik. *Harry and Wally's Favorite Shows*. New York: Prentice Hall Press, 1989.

Marc, David, and Robert J. Thompson. *Prime Time, Prime Movers: From* I Love Lucy *to* L.A. Law*—America's Greatest TV Shows and the People Who Created Them*. Syracuse, NY: Syracuse University Press, 1995.

McNeal, Alex. *Total Television: A Comprehensive Guide to Programming from 1948 to the Present*. New York: Penguin Books, 1996.

Morris, Mark *(1956–)*

The most important new choreographer to emerge since the mid-1970s, Mark Morris has created a bold synthesis of ballet, folk, and modern dance. Morris has built on his early training and experience as performer of folk dancing by incorporating both modern dance and ballet movements within a framework of folklike ensemble dancing. In 1988 Morris and his company took up residence at Brussels's Royal Opera House. In three tumultuous and controversial years, while local critics and audiences rejected Morris's aesthetically and often sexually provocative work, he produced several of his most important dance pieces, including the evening-length *L'Allegro, Il Penseroso, ed Il Moderato*, based on George Frideric Handel's oratorio, and the *Hard Nut*, his parody of Pyotr Ilyich Tchaikovsky's *Nutcracker*, set in the suburban home of a dysfunctional family.

Morris has continued to produce significant works into the twenty-first century, such as the Gertrude Stein/Virgil Thomson opera *Four Saints in Three Acts*, the *Mozart Dances*, and *Falling Down Stairs* with cellist Yo-Yo Ma, of Johann Sebastian Bach's Third Suite for Unaccompanied Cello. In 2001 the Mark Morris Dance Group established its permanent headquarters in Brooklyn. Dance critic and Morris biographer Joan Acocella, like many other critics, sees Morris as a true "classical" choreographer—and the leading successor to George Balanchine—because his dance pieces issue directly from the music.

Jeffrey Escoffier

SEE ALSO: *Ailey, Alvin; Balanchine, George; Cunningham, Merce; Graham, Martha; Modern Dance.*

BIBLIOGRAPHY

Acocella, Joan. *Mark Morris*. New York: Farrar, Straus & Giroux, 1993.

Escoffier, Jeffrey, and Matthew Lore, eds. *Mark Morris' L'Allegro, Il Penseroso, ed Il Moderato: A Celebration*. New York: Marlowe & Company, 2001.

Morrison, Toni *(1931–)*

Born Chloe Anthony Wofford in 1931, Toni Morrison is one of the most important authors of contemporary American literature. From the late 1970s and well into the twenty-first century, she—along with such acclaimed authors as Alice Walker and Ntozake Shange—helped revise the white, male-dominated literary canon. Her work has placed on all the major best-seller lists and is increasingly taught on college campuses across the nation. Known primarily for her novels—*The Bluest Eye* (1970), *Sula* (1973), *Song of Solomon* (1977), *Tar Baby* (1981), *Beloved* (1987), *Jazz* (1992), *Paradise* (1998), *Love* (2003), *A Mercy* (2008), and *Home* (2012)—Morrison is also prolific in the area of nonfiction. She has authored literary criticism, such as the well-received *Playing in the Dark: Whiteness and the Literary Imagination* (1992), and is also the editor of anthologies, including *Race-ing Justice, En-gendering Power: Essays on Anita Hill, Clarence Thomas, and the Others on the Constructing of Social Reality* (1992), *Birth of a Nation'hood: Gaze, Script, and Spectacle in the O. J. Simpson Case* (1997), and *Burn This Book: Essay Anthology* (2009). Her nonfiction output was collected by Carolyn C. Denard in *What Moves at the Margin: Selected Nonfiction* (2008). Morrison has also written a play, *Desdemona* (2011), composed the libretto for an opera titled *Margaret Garner* (2005), and has collaborated with her son, Slade, on two children's books: *The Big Box* (1999) and *The Book of Mean People* (2002). Although Morrison's work varies in terms of subject, place, and time—and, in the case of her fiction, characters and story—it is always complex and compelling, tackling such subjects as sexism, racism, and class in the United States.

In 1988 Morrison won the Pulitzer Prize for fiction for *Beloved*, a historical novel on the enslavement of Africans and African Americans, which was adapted to a feature film starring Oprah Winfrey in 1998. In 1993 she was awarded the Nobel Prize in Literature, becoming the first African American woman to do so. Other honors include the National Book Critics Circle Award (1977), the American Academy and Institute of Arts and Letters Award (1977), the Robert F. Kennedy Book Award (1988), the National Book Foundation's Medal of Distinguished Contribution to American Letters (1996), the National Humanities Medal (2000), and the Norman Mailer Prize for Lifetime Achievement (2009).

Frances Gateward

SEE ALSO: *Best Sellers; Civil Rights Movement; Feminism; Simpson, O. J.; Walker, Alice; Winfrey, Oprah.*

BIBLIOGRAPHY

Butler-Evans, Elliott. *Race, Gender, and Desire: Narrative Strategies in the Fiction of Toni Cade Bambara, Toni Morrison, and Alice Walker*. Philadelphia: Temple University Press, 1991.

Fultz, Lucille. *Toni Morrison: Playing with Difference*. Urbana: University of Illinois Press, 2003.

Kubitschek, Missy Dehn. *Toni Morrison: A Critical Companion*. Westport, CT: Greenwood Press, 1998.

Li, Stephanie. *Toni Morrison: A Biography*. Santa Barbara, CA: Greenwood Press, 2010.

McKay, Nellie Y. *Critical Essays on Toni Morrison*. Boston: G. K. Hall, 1988.

Page, Philip. *Dangerous Freedom: Fusion and Fragmentation in Toni Morrison's Novels*. Oxford: University Press of Mississippi, 1996.

Peterson, Nancy J., ed. *Toni Morrison: Critical and Theoretical Approaches*. Baltimore, MD: Johns Hopkins University Press, 1997.

Morrison, Van *(1945–)*

Irish singer and songwriter Van Morrison is considered one of the most gifted performers in the history of popular music. Even though he hasn't ever had any really great hits—apart perhaps from the early "Brown Eyed Girl"—he is known by many as the author of "Have I Told You Lately," rated one of the most performed songs of the year in 1994. Nevertheless, Morrison's legacy and influence spans decades. Artists such as Bruce Springsteen, Elton John, Tom Petty, Rod Stewart, Sinead O'Connor, and Jim Morrison have all acknowledged him as a profound influence on their music.

Born George Ivan Morrison on August 31, 1945, in Belfast, Northern Ireland, he left school at the age of fifteen to join the rock-and-roll band the Monarchs on a tour through Europe. From 1963 to 1966 he led Them—a successful British rhythm-and-blues band—whose best-known song, "Gloria," was written by Morrison. In 1967 he embarked on a solo career that resulted in some thirty high-quality albums. *Astral Weeks* (1968), his second, is often cited as one of the best records ever, together with *Sergeant Pepper's Lonely Hearts Club Band* by the Beatles, *Blonde on Blonde* by Bob Dylan, and *Pet Sounds* by the Beach Boys. While the album's sound retained a unique position within Morrison's oeuvre, it nevertheless contained all the ingredients of his later work.

As the 1990s progressed, Morrison experienced commercial success; however, in spite of releasing some of his most profitable albums, he received tepid reviews from critics. In 2000 he created his own record label, Exile Productions, giving him full creative control. He carried his commercial success into the next decade, and the critics eventually warmed to the material.

The prolific and multifaceted Morrison was inducted into the Rock and Roll Hall of Fame in 1993, the Irish Music Hall of Fame in 1999, and the Songwriters Hall of Fame in 2003. He won Grammy Awards for "Have I Told You Lately" and "Don't Look Back." In addition, the albums *Astral Weeks* and *Moondance* and the songs "Gloria" and "Brown Eyed Girl" were all inducted into the Grammy Hall of Fame.

Jurgen Pieters

SEE ALSO: *The Beach Boys; The Beatles; Dylan, Bob; Grammy Awards; John, Elton; Rhythm and Blues; Rock and Roll; Springsteen, Bruce.*

BIBLIOGRAPHY

DeWitt, Howard A. *Van Morrison: The Mystic's Music*. Fremont, CA: Horizon Books, 1983.

George-Warren, Holly; Patricia Romanowski; and Jon Pareles, eds. *Rolling Stone Encyclopedia of Rock and Roll: Revised and Updated for the 21st Century*, 3rd ed. New York: Fireside, 2001.

Heylin, Christopher. *Can You Feel the Silence?: Van Morrison*. Chicago: Chicago Review Press, 2003.

Rogan, Johnny. *Van Morrison: No Surrender*. London: Random House, 2006.

Turner, Steve. *Van Morrison: Too Late to Stop Now*. London: Bloomsbury, 1993.

Yorke, Ritchie. *Van Morrison: Into the Music*. London: Charisma Books, 1975.

Morse, Carlton E. *(1901–1993)*

Carlton E. Morse was a unique figure in the world of old-time radio—a writer, director, and producer who managed to navigate the often opposing worlds of popular success and critical accolade while creating works of enduring dramatic depth on the one hand and blood-and-thunder adventure on the other. Like Steven Spielberg more recently, Morse was one of those very few creators of popular entertainment whose name above the title was as instantly recognizable as any leading actor or famous character.

His principal creations—*One Man's Family* ("radio's preeminent serial," according to historian Gerald Nachman in *Raised on Radio*) and *I Love a Mystery* ("the most respected show of its type")—spanned the entire heyday of radio drama; crossed over into the media of film, television, and comics; and helped establish genre conventions in all these forms, which would continue to delight contemporary audiences throughout the rest of the century. No one familiar with Morse can see Spielberg's cozy suburban families without recalling the Barbours in *One Man's Family* or watch Indiana Jones without thinking of the globetrotting adventures of Jack, Doc, and Reggie in *I Love a Mystery*.

Morse was a legend in the world of old-time radio not only due to the long-standing popularity of his creations but also because of the herculean work habits that enabled him to churn out daily episodes of *I Love a Mystery* and weekly installments of *One Man's Family*, as well as to produce and direct both of his creations while also writing short stories, novels, and philosophical essays in his spare time.

FROM FARM TO FAME

Morse's diligence has invariably been attributed to his early upbringing on a farm in Oregon, to which his family moved five years after his birth in Jennings, Louisiana, on June 4, 1901. His early life milking cows helped establish his lifelong habit of rising at 4 a.m. to begin work, and even after marrying and finding employment as a newspaper columnist in San Francisco, he continued to meet his writing deadlines for the rest of his life by getting up every day at the same time and, by his own accounts, "sitting in front of the typewriter, lost to the world, for as much as two and a half hours." After the newspaper was absorbed by the Hearst syndicate in 1929, Morse began hanging around the NBC studios and, in true Horatio Alger fashion, seized his moment by offering to rewrite another scribe's unusable scripts. Morse's quick work earned him a job penning everything from Westerns to sports dramas to the mysteries that became his early trademark and that were usually based upon his experiences covering the newspaper crime beat.

Morse's early radio experience brought him into contact with a group of performers who would ultimately form an acting company that provided the core cast of both *One Man's Family* and *I Love a Mystery* and the inspiration for many of the characters as well—"writing fictional characters," he later recalled, "but also writing something of each of the actors into the part." The calm authority of Michael Raffetto, for example, could serve equally well as the voice of eldest son, Paul, providing solutions to knotty ethical dilemmas in *One Man's Family* or dishing out the two-fisted realism of Jack Packard against the ghouls and vampires of *I Love a Mystery*. Morse was shrewd enough to exploit the close relationship of all his central actors and characters to lend a unique reality to a medium beset by short rehearsal and writing times. He even allowed his *One Man's Family* clan to age right along with the actors who portrayed them over the nearly thirty-year run.

ONE MAN'S FAMILY AND *I LOVE A MYSTERY*

The genre trappings of each of Morse's two principal creations often obscure the range of his unique contributions to the world of popular entertainment. *One Man's Family* may be accurately termed a "soap opera" and *I Love a Mystery* branded an "adventure serial," but each offers a depth and complexity belied by such labels. *One Man's Family* debuted on May 13, 1932, and from its inception, describes Nachman, "it was an experimental concept, the first radio show to depict the day-to-day lives of a fairly normal family." As the extended Barbour family made its way through the trials of the Great Depression and World War II, Morse rarely resorted to the sensational plot devices associated with soaps operas and instead told small, sometimes uneventful, stories that nonetheless touched on profound issues of love and marriage, birth and death.

While *One Man's Family* represented Morse's contribution to the tradition of American domestic drama, his *I Love a Mystery* embodied the opposite form—a rip-roaring, take-no-prisoners adventure yarn celebrating the American faith in (male) individual freedom and regeneration through violence. Rarely has a single writer-creator produced classic works of enduring popularity in both these quintessentially American forms.

One Man's Family and *I Love a Mystery* were Morse's most important contributions to the world of popular culture, and although he also wrote and directed several other programs during his long career, most were merely lesser imitations of his two masterworks—such as *His Honor, the Barber*, exploiting Barry Fitzgerald's homespun wisdom to dispense the same sort of advice son Paul was dishing out daily in *One Man's Family*, and *Adventures by Morse*, placing Captain Friday and his loyal sidekick Skip Turner in *I Love a Mystery* perils.

Writing and directing so many programs at the same time often prevented Morse from knowing himself exactly how his stories would resolve themselves, a situation that Morse turned to his advantage to highlight the day-to-day doings of his domestic clans and keep things unpredictable on his adventure offerings. Such characteristics were unique to radio's golden age, however, and when that era came to an end in the early 1950s, so did the period of Morse's significance as a preeminent figure on the cultural stage. Images could add nothing to *One Man's Family's* world of gentle talk, and no special effect ever invented was capable of conveying the outlandish horror and spectacle of *I Love a Mystery.*

Although recordings of his two leading creations remained highly prized commodities, Morse lived virtually in isolation for the remainder of his life in a rambling rustic mansion near Redwood City in Northern California. He died in 1993, surrounded by the hundreds of bound volumes of radio scripts that had once excited the American public to dream daily of both living room hugs and vampire shrieks.

Kevin Lause

SEE ALSO: *Radio; Radio Drama; Soap Operas.*

BIBLIOGRAPHY

Blue, Howard. *Words at War: World War II Era Radio Drama and the Postwar Broadcasting Industry Blacklist.* Lanham, MD: Scarecrow Press, 2002.

Dunning, John. *On the Air: The Encyclopedia of Old-Time Radio.* New York: Oxford University Press, 1998.

Harmon, Jim. *The Great Radio Heroes.* Garden City, NY: Doubleday, 1967.

Maltin, Leonard. *The Great American Broadcast: A Celebration of Radio's Golden Age.* New York: Dutton, 1997.

Nachman, Gerald. *Raised on Radio.* New York: Pantheon Books, 1998.

Morton, Jelly Roll *(1890–1941)*

Born Ferdinand Joseph, American jazz musician Jelly Roll Morton is best known for his songs "Jelly Roll Blues" (1905), "King Porter Stomp" (1906), and "Kansas City Stomp" (1919). A composer and pianist, he first found success touring with his band the Red Hot Peppers and then later as a recording artist. Raised in the ragtime and Dixieland musical tradition of New Orleans, Morton went beyond the formal structure of those forms and developed many of the central characteristics of later jazz music. In 1938 folklorist Alan Lomax recorded an interview with and songs by Morton as part of the Library of Congress's Folklore Archives. During the interview Morton elaborates on the development of jazz music from its birth in New Orleans.

Charles J. Shindo

SEE ALSO: *Dixieland; Jazz.*

BIBLIOGRAPHY

Lomax, Alan. *Mister Jelly Roll: The Fortunes of Jelly Roll Morton, New Orleans Creole and Inventor of Jazz.* Berkeley: University of California Press, 1973.

Schafer, William John. *The Original Jelly Roll Blues: The Story of Ferdinand Lamothe, A.K.A Jelly Roll Morton, the Originator of Jazz, Stomps and Blues*. London: Flame Tree Publishing, 2008.

Mosley, Walter *(1952–)*

With the publication of *Devil in a Blue Dress* in 1990, African American novelist Walter Mosley—and his Easy Rawlins mysteries—changed the face of American detective fiction and became one of the United States' best mystery writers. The hero of the series, Easy (Ezekiel) Rawlins, is a black detective operating in a white conservative world. Roger A. Berger notes that Mosley, with his black characters and black-centered settings or locations, "breaks with the traditional white detective story through the oppositional use of black subject matter." Through his black characters and exploration of concerns such as race and sexuality, Mosley joins Rudolph Fisher and Chester Himes as the three most prominent black writers of detective fiction. Mosley became a more familiar name in American popular culture with the release of the film *Devil in a Blue Dress*, starring Denzel Washington, in 1995.

EASY RAWLINS MYSTERIES

Devil in a Blue Dress is the story of Easy Rawlins, a black war veteran who has lost his job at a defense plant in 1948 Los Angeles. While drinking in a bar, he meets DeWitt Albright, who hires him to find Daphne Monet, a woman whom Albright says enjoys "the company of Negroes" and likes "jazz and pigs' feet and dark meat." Albright shows Easy a photo of Daphne, a light-skinned, blue-eyed woman.

A scene where Easy is confronted by Albright's guard introduces the reader to how Easy deals with racism and how he behaves with white people. Easy stutters and squints and even forgets Albright's name. He informs the reader that as a boy he developed the defensive habit of emptying his head of everything whenever he was caught off guard by "a white man of authority," in keeping with the motto "The less you know, the less trouble you find." His habit brings with it a hatred of self and of people in general, both white and black, whom he holds responsible for his feelings: whites for accepting his seemingly dumb behavior as a fact of life, blacks for reminding him that he has to play dumb in front of whites.

Ironically, Easy fails to live up to his motto; the more he learns about the case, the more deeply involved in the story he becomes. When several people start showing up dead, the police suspect that Easy knows who did it, and he is given a deadline to find the killer. More surprises emerge when Easy finally finds Daphne Monet and learns that she is Creole and that Albright is looking for her so that he can blackmail Todd Carter, a white businessman who was supposed to marry Monet, thus ruining

Walter Mosley. *Walter Mosley addresses an audience at Boston University in 2011.* BOSTON GLOBE/CONTRIBUTOR/GETTY IMAGES.

Carter's political career. It is worth noting Easy's manipulative talents, especially in persuading the police to believe his story about the murders and their perpetrators.

SUBJECT OF RACE

While maintaining certain traditional aspects of detective fiction, Mosley explores the issues of race and interracial relations that have remained outside the province of his white counterparts. For example, Mouse—Easy's longtime friend—explains everything in terms of race. Easy's everyday interactions also show the realities of contemporary race relations: Once, a young white woman begins talking to Easy until the boys she is with warn him about talking to "their women." Easy himself relates how the U.S. Army reflects the segregation of the South, having confined him to a typewriter for three years despite his having been trained as "a foot soldier, a fighter." For Easy, the worst kind of racism is when a white person like Todd Carter fails to see a black person in human terms. But most of all, Easy believes that "justice for Negroes" can never be achieved without money to grease the system.

Mosley continued to explore his themes, in various plot guises, in ten more Easy Rawlins mysteries, including *A Red Death* (1991), *White Butterfly* (1992), *Black Betty* (1994), *Little Scarlet* (2004), and *Blonde Faith* (2007), the last in the series. In *A Red Death*, for example, Easy is in the housing business when a racist IRS agent nails him for tax evasion. In exchange for a better deal to pay off his IRS debt, an FBI agent asks him to infiltrate the First African Baptist Church, which is suspected of communist activities.

OTHER WORK

By the late 1990s Mosley was a highly respected, best-selling novelist on both sides of the Atlantic. He did not play it safe and stick solely to the Easy Rawlins series, however. In 1995 Mosley displayed his versatility by publishing a non-detective novel called *RL's Dream*. In 1997 he introduced the character Socrates Fortlow, a new leading man for his new mystery novel, *Always Outnumbered, Always Outgunned*. Socrates, like his ancient Greek philosopher namesake, tries to find answers to "philosophical questions of morality" in a world warped by crime, racism, and poverty.

Another series follows boxer-turned-private investigator Leonid McGill (or LT), who is based in post-9/11 New York City. In 2012 Mosley published the fourth novel featuring McGill, *All I Did Was Shoot My Man*. A complicated hero, LT is often impelled by a sense of atonement to accomplish his investigative work.

By 2012 Mosley's body of work covered the gamut of genres, ranging from hard-boiled crime fiction to science fiction, memoir, political treatise, drama, young adult fiction, graphic novel, and even erotica. Over his career, Mosley has averaged two books per year—truly an impressive output. While the settings of his works have spanned centuries and crossed the globe, the focus remains the same: the African American experience. In fact, the author made headlines in the late 1990s when he sacrificed a book advance with W. W. Norton to instead publish a manuscript with the independent African American publisher Black Classic Press.

While Mosley's crime fiction works, especially the Easy Rawlins novels, remain must-reads for any fan of detective stories, the author's entire body of work is esteemed for its contribution to contemporary American letters. Literary critics attempting to understand the complexities of issues such as race, power, or sexuality increasingly turn to Mosley's rich texts as objects of study.

Pierre-Damien Mvuyekure

SEE ALSO: *Chandler, Raymond; Detective Fiction; Hard-Boiled Detective Fiction; Himes, Chester; Washington, Denzel.*

BIBLIOGRAPHY

Berger, Roger A. "'The Black Dick': Race, Sexuality, and Discourse in the L.A. Novels of Walter Mosley." *African American Review* 31, no. 2 (1997): 281–294.

Wilson, Charles E., Jr. *Walter Mosley: A Critical Companion.* London: Greenwood Press, 2003.

Moss, Kate *(1974–)*

Breastless, hipless, and strikingly skinny, in the 1990s England's Kate Moss brought in the "waif," or "heroin chic," look and temporarily changed the shape of modeling. When the fourteen-year-old Kate was "discovered" by an agent in an airport, her skinny figure was in stark contrast to curvier models such as then-queen Cindy Crawford. Moss catapulted to fame with a reported $1.2 million contract with American designer Calvin Klein. The ad campaign, which showed the waiflike model in seminude photographs, incited controversy. Nonetheless, Moss became one of the top models of the 1990s, and for many people her lifestyle of all-night parties with famous boyfriends exemplified a life of fame and excess.

Although many 1990s supermodels floundered at the turn of the twenty-first century, Moss's fame increased. She gave birth to a daughter in 2002. Soon after, she became the face and figure for brands such as Rimmel cosmetics, Louis Vuitton, and Dior, and she designed clothes for the United Kingdom's Topshop chain. For a while, she was best known for the "cocaine scandal" of 2005, when tabloids ran a photo showing her with lines of white powder. Moss lost her contracts with high-profile brands such as Chanel and Burberry, but the charges were eventually dropped, and (perhaps ironically) the scandal made her even more successful. In 2007 her modeling income was second in the world; in 2010 her agent claimed that, as a direct result of the drug story, Moss's annual earnings had doubled from £2 million to £4 million—proving that party chic will never die.

Susann Cokal

SEE ALSO: *Celebrity; Celebrity Couples; Crawford, Cindy; Feminism; Gossip Columns; Klein, Calvin; Supermodels; Tabloids.*

BIBLIOGRAPHY

Blakeley, Kiri. "The World's Top-Earning Models." *Forbes*, July 19, 2007. Accessed December 9, 2011. Available from http://www.forbes.com/2007/07/19/models-media-bundchen-biz-media-cz_kb_0716topmodels.html

Buttolph, Angela. *Kate Moss: Style.* London: Century, 2008.

Gross, Michael. *Model: The Ugly Business of Beautiful Women.* New York: William Morrow, 1995.

Petreycik, Caitlin. "Kate Moss's Cocaine Scandal Doubled Her Salary." *New York*, October 2010. Accessed December 9, 2011. Available from http://nymag.com/daily/fashion/2010/10/kate_mosss_cocaine_scandal_dou.html

Testino, Mario. *Kate Moss*. New York: Taschen, 2011.

Mother's Day

A day of celebration and commemoration, Mother's Day has occupied a place on America's calendar since the early twentieth century. The woman responsible for its inception was American Anna Jarvis (1864–1948), who wanted to memorialize her own mother and as a result saw the value in honoring all American mothers.

Having grown up in West Virginia, Jarvis moved to Philadelphia in 1892,where she began an extended correspondence with her mother back in her home town. When Jarvis's mother died in 1905, Jarvis not only wanted to keep the memory of her mother alive but also wanted to immortalize what she considered to be the qualities of all mothers: piety, domesticity, maternal purity, loyalty, and love.

Perhaps inspired by other well-established days of remembrance such as Children's Day and Memorial Day, Jarvis set out to make Mother's Day a "holy day" to be celebrated in local churches on the second Sunday in May. The first public memorial service for her own mother took place in 1907, and one year later churches across the United States held official Mother's Day services.

Mother's Day became increasingly popular. People liked the idea of honoring the traditional role of women in the family home, and it reassured those who were uneasy about the "new womanhood" that emerged as a result of World War I. More importantly, various businesses realized it could be a profitable holiday and, therefore, widely publicized it as an important event.

Jarvis, who never married and did not have children, thought Mother's Day should be celebrated simply and solemnly. The symbol of her sentiments was a white carnation, to be worn as an emblem in honor of one's mother. To her consternation, however, the floral industry seized upon her idea and used the carnation in promotions. Thanks to Victorian sentimentality, flowers had long been associated with femininity and domesticity; the American floral trade merely capitalized on this fashion.

As early as 1910, the Florists' Telegraph Delivery Service (FTD) had encouraged sons and daughters to send flowers to their mothers, and in 1917 the floral industry began a national promotion of Mother's Day. By 1918 its famous "Say It with Flowers" campaign had been launched. During the 1920s confectioners, jewelers, and stationers, among others, boosted sales by successfully promoting their own goods as appropriate gifts for Mother's Day, indicating just how popular the day had become.

Jarvis, however, was not happy about the rampant commercialism. Her personal *holy day*, whose identity and observance she had wanted to manage herself, had become a commerce-driven *holiday*. In the hands of the professional florists, her simple white carnation symbol had also become more complicated: white carnations, the florists advocated, should symbolize the memory of mothers no longer living, while red ones should be used for those still alive. Later, these simple floral badges blossomed into full-blown bouquets of more expensive and showy arrangements. Furthermore, due to the FTD's aggressive advertising campaign, face-to-face visits and personal correspondence between mothers and children, which Jarvis considered paramount, were being replaced with impersonal, commercially delivered messages. This trend was further advanced by the greeting card industry, which encouraged people to send their mothers commercially prepared sentimental messages.

In 1920 it was clear that business interests had won the fight over Mother's Day. While previously they had always acknowledged Jarvis as the holiday's founder and described her as a woman of pluck and sound moral values, by the late 1910s her increasing outspokenness about what she saw as the erosion of Mother's Day rituals forced trade associations to distance themselves from her. By 1920 their relationship was severed and Jarvis' version of the origins and proper ceremony of Mother's Day were disavowed.

While Jarvis's efforts to pay tribute to the memory of mothers may have continued to happen on a local level in churches uninfluenced by commercial interests, the promotion of Mother's Day by businesses helped turn it into a nationwide holiday that everyone celebrated in very similar ways, part of what historian and author Leigh Eric Schmidt calls the "commercial management of the calendar" in his book *Consumer Rites: The Buying and Selling of American Holidays*. The success of Mother's Day also spawned other similarly contrived holidays, most notably Father's Day (the third Sunday in June in the United States), which had been advocated in churches since 1910 by Sonora Smart Dodd but not nationally observed until 1972.

Mother's Day, with all its commercial connotations, spread to other countries, such as the United Kingdom, South Africa, and Australia, but each has its own date for the celebration. Other, less popular offshoots that appeared were Sweetest Day, Bosses' Day, Grandparents' Day, and Professional Secretaries' Day, among others. By the twenty-first century Mother's Day was deeply embedded in the American psyche and social fabric and had become a $14 billion industry.

Wendy Woloson

SEE ALSO: *Father's Day; Greeting Cards; World War I.*

BIBLIOGRAPHY

Hatch, Jane M. *American Book of Days*, 3rd ed. New York: Wilson, 1978.

Klebanow, Barbara, and Sara Fischer. *American Holidays: Exploring Traditions, Customs, and Backgrounds*. Brattleboro, VT: Pro Lingua Associates, 1986.

Livingston, Joyce. *Mother's Day*. Uhrichsville, OH: Heartsong Presents, 2005.

Myers, Robert. *Celebrations: Complete Book of American Holidays*. New York: Doubleday, 1972.

Santino, Jack. *All around the Year: Holidays and Celebrations in American Life*. Urbana: University of Illinois Press, 1995.

Schmidt, Leigh Eric. *Consumer Rites: The Buying and Selling of American Holidays*. Princeton, NJ: Princeton University Press, 1995.

Motley, Willard *(1912–1965)*

The publication of Willard Motley's first novel, *Knock on Any Door*, in 1947 established the African American writer and former Works Progress Administration worker among the leading American naturalist novelists, together with Richard Wright, James T. Farrell, and Nelson Algren. The book, which chronicles the progressive corruption of Italian American teenager Nick Romano by Chicago slum life, was in its third printing five days after its publication and remained on the *New York Times* bestseller list for nearly one year. The novel was condensed and published in popular magazines such as *Look* and *Omnibook*. A movie version was directed in 1949 by Nicholas Ray, starring Humphrey Bogart and introducing John Derek as Nick. Motley wrote a sequel to *Knock on Any Door*, along with three other novels, but he was never able to repeat the commercial success of his first book.

Luca Prono

SEE ALSO: *Best Sellers; Bogart, Humphrey; Wright, Richard.*

BIBLIOGRAPHY

Fleming, Robert E. *Willard Motley*. Boston: Twayne, 1978.

Parini, Jay. *American Writers: A Collection of Literary Biographies. Supplement XVII. Max Apple to Franz Wright*. Farmington Hills, MI: Thomson Gale, 2008.

Mötley Crüe

Mötley Crüe, the Los Angeles–based heavy metal quartet whose quadruple-platinum album *Dr. Feelgood* hit the top spot on the Billboard charts in 1991, paved the road to the Top 40 and MTV's video countdown for other big-haired, glam-rock bands of the mid-1980s. As well known for its offstage behavior as for its onstage pyrotechnics, Mötley Crüe enjoyed a heyday that lasted for more than a decade. The band has produced little new music since the 1980s; however, it continues to tour, and the band produced its own "Crüe Fest" ventures in 2008 and 2009.

The foursome came together in early 1981. Drummer Tommy Lee (Thomas Lee Bass) and bassist Nikki Sixx (Frank Carlton Serafino Feranna) were in a band called Christmas when they answered a classified ad placed by guitarist Mick Mars (Robert "Bob" Alan Deal), who was looking for some "lude" and crude band mates. In April the three recruited front man Vince Neil (Vince Neil Wharton), who was then singing for a local band called Rock Candy. Seven months later Mötley Crüe (as Mars christened the band) recorded its first LP, *Too Fast for Love*, for $7,000. The Crüe's pentagram-and-hellfire-saturated sophomore effort, *Shout at the Devil*, was released in 1983; one track, "Bastard," made it onto Tipper Gore's Parents' Music Resource Center's "Dirty Dozen" list of obscene songs, thereby sealing Mötley Crüe's reputation as the Band That Our Mothers Warned Us About.

In 1985 *Theater of Pain* was released to great fanfare. Shortly thereafter, Neil spent a surprisingly lenient twenty-day sentence in a Los Angeles prison for vehicular manslaughter after his drunk driving led to the death of Hanoi Rock's drummer, Nicholas "Razzle" Dingley. Meanwhile, Sixx battled a heroin addiction, but the Crüe's popularity never waned. That same year the band's cover of Brownsville Station's "Smokin' in the Boys' Room" climbed up the Billboard Top 40 chart, and the single "Home Sweet Home" became MTV's most requested music video of all time that November. It would later be named the twelfth-greatest power ballad of all time by VH1.

Lee married *Dynasty* star Heather Locklear in 1986 and introduced his 360-degree revolving drum kit the following year on the "Girls, Girls, Girls" world tour. Only months after the

Mötley Crüe. *From left, Mick Mars, Vince Neil, Tommy Lee, and Nikki Sixx promote a Mötley Crüe concert in Mexico in 2011.* VICTOR CHAVEZ/CONTRIBUTOR/WIREIMAGE/GETTY IMAGES.

Crüe's greatest hits album, *Decade of Decadence*, was released in 1991, Neil was fired from the band for allegedly prioritizing his car-racing hobby over his music career. John Corabi, former vocalist of the Scream, replaced Neil, but the band's renown never again reached that of its earlier days.

The media attention the Crüe received after 1992 centered almost exclusively on Lee's personal life: an intimate home video of Lee and his second wife, *Baywatch* star Pamela Anderson, was mass produced and sold over the Internet, and the couple's three-year marriage ended in 1998 with Lee serving a four-month sentence in a Los Angeles prison for spousal abuse.

Mötley Crüe was a larger-than-life band both onstage and off, and it was the first band to erase the line between heavy metal music and commercial success. Large-market radio stations, once afraid that heavy metal would alienate listeners, discovered that listeners were anything but alienated. By the early 1990s, however, Mötley Crüe's heavy-handed, over-stylized music gave way to the new sound of Seattle grunge bands such as Nirvana and Pearl Jam. MTV's all-metal video program, *Headbanger's Ball*, had faded into oblivion, whereas the grunge/alternative-rock *120 Minutes* had all but been put on a permanent loop.

After being dropped by their label, Mötley Crüe members struggled with more lawsuits, substance abuse, and ego clashes, including Lee leaving the band in 1999. But the publication of the book *The Dirt*, which labeled Crüe "the world's most notorious rock band," was the start of a comeback. A 2005 reunion tour to promote a new album was a huge success, and the band has been on the road ever since, including shows in 2011 to celebrate its thirtieth anniversary. Crüe was a breakthrough band responsible for putting metal front and center, including establishment recognition with Grammy and American Music Award nominations and even a star on the Hollywood Walk of Fame. With album sales of more than eighty million worldwide as of 2012, Mötley Crüe appeared destined to find "home sweet home" in the Rock and Roll Hall of Fame.

Daryna M. McKeand

SEE ALSO: Baywatch*;* Dynasty*; Grammy Awards; Grunge; Heavy Metal; Hollywood; MTV; Nirvana; Pearl Jam; Rock and Roll; Top 40.*

BIBLIOGRAPHY

Handleman, David. "Money for Nothing and the Chicks for Free: On the Road with Mötley Crüe." *Rolling Stone*, August 13, 1987, 34–41, 59.

Lee, Tommy, and Anthony Bozza. *Tommy Land*. New York: Atria Books, 2004.

Neil, Vince, and Mike Sager. *Tattoos & Tequila: To Hell and Back with One of Rock's Most Notorious Frontmen*. New York: Grand Central Publishing, 2010.

Simmons, Sylvie, and Malcolm Dome. *Lüde, Crüde, and Rüde: The Story of Mötley Crüe*. Chessington, UK: Castle Communications, 1994.

Sixx, Nikki, and Ian Gittins. *The Heroin Diaries: A Year in the Life of a Shattered Rock Star*. New York: VH1 Books, 2008.

Strauss, Neil. *The Dirt*. New York: Regan Books, 2001.

Motown

Motown is a record company, a musical style, and a corporate conglomerate with several subsidiary labels. The company was founded in Detroit, Michigan, in 1959 by Berry Gordy Jr. A black entrepreneur and songwriter, Gordy built a successful, independent company that became a formidable phenomenon in the music business. Motown racked up an enviable number of releases that posted on both pop and rhythm and blues (R&B) charts.

At the company's height, an overwhelming 75 percent of Motown's releases charted, compared to the industry average of about 10 percent. By Gordy's estimation, 70 percent of the buyers of a million-seller Motown record were nonblack. Between 1960 and 1970 Motown issued a total of 535 singles, 357 of which became hits. Motown issued fifty-six number one pop and R&B songs in a decade. But the most important Motown asset was its talented and diverse artists, songwriters, producers, and musicians, not the solid gold records or the millions earned in revenue.

Motown derived its name from a popular slang contraction of *motortown*, a nickname for Detroit. Detroit, which was known for its automobile production, also spawned a number of fine musicians, among them rock-and-roll stars Hank Ballard and the Midnighters, distinguished jazz artists such as Milt Jackson

Motown Founder Berry Gordy. *Berry Gordy speaks at a gala celebrating Motown's fiftieth anniversary in 2009.* PAUL WARNER/CONTRIBUTOR/WIREIMAGE/GETTY IMAGES.

and Yusef Lateef, bluesman John Lee Hooker, soul singer Little Willie John, gospel diva Aretha Franklin, and many others who became Motown artists. But prior to Motown, Detroit had no major recording company.

ORIGINS

One of eight children, Berry Gordy Jr. was born in Detroit on November 28, 1929. His father, Berry "Pops" Gordy Sr., and mother, Bertha Gordy, owned several businesses. A high school dropout, Gordy Jr. became an average boxer who fought in the bantamweight class. He abandoned boxing and after serving in the army decided to pursue a musical career. In 1953 an infatuation with jazz prompted Gordy and singer Marv Johnson to open the 3-D Record Mart, a retail store dedicated to jazz. The store folded in 1955, and Gordy went to work for Lincoln-Mercury. While installing upholstery in cars, he began humming tunes and writing lyrics. Gordy's work for the auto manufacturers, learning assembly-line production values, would profit him later in the recording studio.

Gordy developed an instinct for recognizing what made a hit song and became a master tunesmith. When he heard that Jackie Wilson's manager was looking for new material, he proceeded to write four hits for Wilson. His first song, "Reet Petite," hit the charts in 1957, and several other hits followed. Gordy married Raynoma Liles in 1959. Their union was short-lived, though Liles continued to work for Gordy after the divorce. Her musical and technical skills were critical in helping Gordy to refine his songwriting craft, and she convinced him to produce his own records, thus taking control over all aspects of production.

In 1958 Gordy formed a song publishing company, Jobete Music. He also formed Berry Gordy Jr. Enterprises and purchased the buildings that would house Hitsville, U.S.A., and the Motown Record Corporation. In 1959 he created Tamla Record Company using an $800 loan from "Ber-Berry," a family fund earmarked for real estate purchases. In addition to the Motown and Tamla labels, he developed other prominent subsidiary labels, including Gordy in 1962; Soul in 1964; Mowest in 1971;, Tamla-Motown, UK, in 1965; and Hitsville in 1976. Motown also distributed other labels and established several labels to get around the fact that radio stations limited the amount of airplay given to the any one label.

Gordy developed several self-serving policies that ensured Motown would have the upper hand in the manager-artist relationship. For example, if an artist signed as a performer and a writer, any costs incurred in preparing his or her records could be charged against the artist's songwriting royalties. In addition, Motown served as the artists' booking agent. Gordy exercised total control over his talent. In addition to his songwriting abilities, he was a natural leader who knew how to inspire artists. He initially fostered healthy competition among his artists, and after a meeting and the singing of the company song, "Hitsville, U.S.A."—"Oh, we have a very swinging company working hard from day to day"—they would be charged up and ready to set the world on fire.

DISTINCTIVE MOTOWN STYLE

While the Motown musical sound was evolving, artists were groomed to exhibit a distinctive Motown "style." Gordy, with the help of writer and producer Mickey Stevenson, set up an artist development program and recruited teachers to educate artists on showmanship and performance. Maurice King, who had worked with Billie Holiday, became the executive musical director. Gil Askey, who had worked with Billy Eckstine, was the orchestral conductor for Diana Ross and the Supremes and assisted with stage concepts. Cholly Atkins of the famous dancing duo Coles and Atkins became the chief choreographer. Maxine Powell, who had managed a finishing and modeling school, was in charge of dress and grooming. Mandatory classes were held for the artists.

Motown attracted a large, diverse pool of artists, from the pop balladeer Lionel Richie to the funky Rick James. Singer-songwriter Smokey Robinson, leader of the Miracles and a vice president of Motown, was a principal player on the team. Robinson had not refined his songwriting skills before meeting Gordy. Gordy taught Robinson how to write successful songs, and Robinson urged Gordy to go national distributing the company's releases.

In 1959 the company issued singles by the Miracles, Marv Johnson, and Barrett Strong. The Miracles' "Bad Girl" (1959), originally released on Chess Records, was rerecorded at Motown and became the Motown label's first single. "Shop Around" (1961), a Miracles recording on Tamla, became the company's first hit, topping the R&B chart and posting at number two on the pop chart. The Miracles were big record sellers, and during the 1960s they had twenty-one Top 10 R&B hits, including the memorable "Shop Around," "Tracks of My Tears" (1965), and "The Tears of a Clown" (1970). Robinson continued to produce commercial hits for numerous Motown artists, including Mary Wells, the Temptations, and Marvin Gaye.

In January 1959 Johnson recorded "Come to Me" and "Whisper" on the Tamla label, signaling the genesis of the Motown empire. In 1960 Strong recorded "Money" (cowritten by Gordy); although it was a Tamla release, the record was leased to Anna Records (a label Gordy's sister Anna started in 1958) and rose to number two on the R&B charts. Wells became Motown's first superstar. A teenage vocalist, she signed with Motown in 1960, and her self-penned single "Bye Bye Baby" (1960) climbed to number eight on the Billboard R&B chart. Gordy then placed Wells's creative development into the hands of Robinson, with Robinson writing and producing the majority of her hits between 1960 and 1964; the pairing was merely the first display of Gordy's lauded ability to match performers with songwriter-producers.

STAR ACTS

In 1960 the Primes, a vocal quintet, later named the Elgins (not to be confused with the Motown group of the same name) and then rechristened the Temptations, signed with Motown. This legendary group became the most successful vocal group in R&B history, as evidenced by their prolific hit-making abilities and by the popularity of the NBC-TV special *The Temptations* (1998). The Temptations scored forty-three Top 10 R&B singles during their decades-long career. In 1961 the Marvelettes, a female vocal quintet from the Detroit suburb of Inkster, Michigan, released "Please Mr. Postman" and became the first group to score a number one hit for the young—Gordy invented the phrase "The Sound of Young America" as a marketing hook for Motown music—record company.

In 1960 the Primes' "sister" group, the Primettes, composed of Diana Ross, Mary Wilson, Florence Ballard, and Barbara Martin, signed with Motown. Upon Ballard's suggestion, the group's name was changed to the Supremes; Martin left the group shortly after the name change. After several unsuccessful releases, the Supremes paired with the songwriting team of Eddie Holland, Lamont Dozier, and Brian Holland and scored a number one R&B hit with "Where Did Our Love Go" (1964), followed by eleven number one hits. Ballard was fired from the group after seven years, and Ross left the trio in 1970 to pursue a successful solo career, giving Motown its biggest hit single with "Endless Love" (1981), a duet with Richie. Ross left the company in 1981 but returned eight years later. The Supremes went through several personnel changes and disbanded in the late 1970s.

The Motown Revue was one of Motown's successful marketing strategies. Several Motown artists would tour under the company's name for thirty to forty days with a band. The revue was a cost-saving measure and an excellent promotion for the company. In 1962 the first Motown Revue trekked through the South in cars and buses. The 1963 show featured Stevie Wonder at the Regal Theater in Chicago. Motown recorded Wonder singing "Fingertips (Part 2)" (1963), which became the first live recording to reach number one on the R&B and pop charts.

Born Steveland Morris, Wonder has remained with the company since he signed to the Tamla label in 1961. Blind since birth, he is a multitalented artist, a fine vocalist, multi-instrumentalist, songwriter, and producer who has had twenty number one R&B hits and has won twenty-two Grammy Awards. Wonder—along with Gaye—eventually gained complete artistic control, shunning Motown's assembly-line production style in favor of music that mirrored his personal philosophy.

HIT MAKERS

Gaye also signed with Motown, first recording "Let Your Conscience Be Your Guide" in 1961; he married Anna Gordy in 1963. Initially Gaye provided backup vocals and served as a drummer for other company artists. His fourth single for Tamla, "Stubborn Kind of Fellow" (1962), was a commercial success. Many memorable songs followed, including "I Heard It through the Grapevine" (which rose to number one on both the R&B and pop charts in 1968). While his duets with Wells and Kim Weston were moderately received, it was his pairing with Tammi Terrell that really jelled. "Your Precious Love" (1967) and "Ain't No Mountain High Enough" (1967), among other songs, scored in the R&B Top 10.

The 1971 album *What's Going On*, a profound and visionary cycle of songs, lushly orchestrated and exploring sociopolitical and environmental themes, struck to the heart of human existence. It remains Gaye's masterpiece. Gaye altered the face of Motown with this artist-produced album, which was unprecedented at the company at that time. He had many other hits, including "Let's Get It On" (1973) and "Got to Give It Up (Part 1)" (1977), before leaving Motown in the early 1980s.

The Four Tops signed with Motown in 1963, although the group first started in 1954. They enjoyed a string of hits produced by Holland-Dozier-Holland, including "I Can't Help Myself" (1965) and "Reach Out, I'll Be There" (1966), both of which topped the R&B and pop charts. The Jackson Five signed with Motown in 1969 after Gordy learned of them through Gladys Knight and Bobby Taylor; their initial single, "I Want You Back" (1969), rose to the top of the R&B and pop charts, ensuring the Jacksons international stardom. Over the next five years, a total of ten of their singles for Motown posted in the R&B Top 10; two of them, "Never Can Say Goodbye" (1971) and "Dancing Machine" (1974), reached number one on the R&B chart. Motown made solo recordings of Michael, Jackie, and Jermaine Jackson. The group left Motown and signed with Epic in 1976.

Gladys Knight and the Pips joined Motown in 1966 and enjoyed twelve Top 10 R&B hits on Motown's ancillary Soul label. Other artists that recorded for Motown were the Commodores, whose Motown single "Machine Gun" (1974) charted and was followed by a string of hits. Singer-songwriter Richie left the group in 1982 and became a successful solo act. Singer-songwriter Rick James signed with Motown in 1978, scoring a number of hits on the Gordy label, including "Mary Jane" (1979) and "Super Freak (Part I)" (1981). Other Motown artists include Junior Walker and the All Stars, Martha and the Vandellas, Brenda Holloway, Edwin Starr and the Contours, Teena Marie, the Dazz Band, DeBarge, Boyz II Men, Brian McKnight, Erykah Badu, and Johnny Gill.

MOTOWN EVOLVES

The Motown sound was never one style but a number of styles that were created by the producer/writer teams. Motown had a coterie of exceptional writers and producers, beginning with Gordy himself and including Robinson, Norman Whitfield, Ashford and Simpson, and Wonder. The Motown sound evolved over a period of years, beginning with the strong sonic identity imparted by the songwriting team Holland-Dozier-Holland. "Their three-minute soul symphonies managed to take the gospel-rooted sounds of black America to unprecedented levels of universal acceptance and yet retain enough ghetto grit to still appeal to the music's core audience," notes author and critic Lee Hildebrand in *Stars of Soul and Rhythm & Blues*. The Motown sound was also influenced by the Atlantic songwriting team of Jerry Leiber and Mike Stoller, who created orchestral string arrangements for the Drifters.

In the 1960s Gordy established offices in New York and Los Angeles, staffed by executives whose chief responsibility was to scout for TV and film possibilities. In addition, Motown's artists frequently appeared on various talk and variety shows. *T.C.B.—Taking Care of Business* (1968) was Motown Productions' first television endeavor and featured the Supremes, primarily spotlighting Ross, and the Temptations. Motown's attempt to establish itself as a force in the film and television industry saw more failures than triumphs. Several television specials followed, featuring prominent Motown artists, including the Jackson Five, the Supremes, and the Temptations. *Motown 25—Yesterday, Today, and Forever* (1983), an NBC anniversary special, not only garnered top ratings but also was the most-watched variety special in the history of the medium.

The Motown-produced film *Lady Sings the Blues* (1972), staring Ross in a fictionalized account of jazz singer Billie Holiday's life, won several awards but received mixed reviews. Several other films followed with mixed reviews, including *The Bingo Long Traveling All-Stars & Motor Kings* (1976), *Scott Joplin* (1977), *Almost Summer* (1978), and *Thank God It's Friday* (1978). The biggest failure was the 1978 all-black remake of *The Wizard of Oz*, called *The Wiz*. Some Motown artists also scored films, including Robinson's soundtrack for *Big Time* (1988) and Gaye's score of *Trouble Man* (1972).

TROUBLED TIMES

In 1972 Motown's Detroit offices closed and the company relocated to Hollywood, California. All divisions of Motown were restructured under the auspices of Motown Industries. Gordy became chairman of the board, with Ewart Abner II taking over as president. *Black Enterprise* in 1973 listed Motown as the biggest black-owned company in America, grossing $40 million. Motown's reputation as "one big, happy family" was part myth and part fact. Gordy was not only a CEO but also a father figure to many of the young artists, and his roster of talented artists were touted as the Motown family. By the mid-1960s the Gordy family constituted a considerable portion of the Motown payroll. Yet this family slowly became dysfunctional, and its artists were treated as orphans.

With the exception of Ross and Robinson, the artists whose talents and performances made Motown and Gordy rich and famous were the least appreciated and most mistreated element of Motown Records. Artists' royalty statements were substandard, and when they fought for their own interests they were considered insubordinate. As Motown's talent became its enemy, the company was flooded with lawsuits and bitter feelings. Rumors that Motown was controlled by underworld figures began to surface as more whites came to work for the company. These rumors were never substantiated but led to widespread gossip. There also were a number of Motown artist tragedies: Ballard's termination from the Supremes and eventual death of cardiac arrest; the Temptations' Paul Williams's suicide; the murder of Gaye by his father; Motown studio drummer Benny Benjamin's stroke; and the casting aside of bassist James Jamerson Sr. In 1988 Gordy sold Motown to MCA for a reported $61 million.

NEW BEGINNINGS

The company's legend rests on its impressive list of classic hit songs and on the enormous influence that Motown artists, producers, songwriters, and musicians have had on contemporary music. This legend is preserved at the Motown Historical Museum, founded in 1985 in Detroit due to the efforts of Gordy's sister Esther, who once headed up the company's International Talent Management division. The museum provides a retrospective view of the evolution of both the Motown company and the Motown sound, including Studio A, where so many artists recorded hit songs.

Motown's legacy is a monument to the principles of capitalism. Gordy stuck to his credo and succeeded in making a better product than his competition, even though it was often at the expense of his artists, songwriters, and producers. Motown Records merged with Universal Records, forming Universal Motown Records in 2005. The group later divided, and Motown Records became a part of the Island Def Jam Motown Music Group in 2011. In February 2011 Motown artists, among others, were invited to the White House for "The Motown Sound: In Performance at the White House," a concert celebrating Black History Month and the legacy of Motown Records.

The early twenty-first century saw the death of many Motown legends. Rick James died of pulmonary and cardiac failure in 2004; Harry McGilberry of the Temptations died of a drug overdose in 2006; the Commodores' Milan Williams lost his battle to cancer in 2006; Levi Stubbs, lead singer of the Four Tops, passed away in 2008; Teena Marie, the Ivory Queen of Soul, died in her sleep in 2010; and Nick Ashford of the legendary songwriting duo Ashford and Simpson died in 2011. In 2009 Motown lost one of its most iconic figures when Michael Jackson died from respiratory arrest. The Motown Hitsville U.S.A. Museum in Detroit held a vigil, and executives and artists, including Gordy, Wonder, and Robinson, celebrated Jackson's legacy and influence.

Motown attempted to regain its relevance by signing acts such as Black Joe Lewis and the Honeybears, India Arie, and Erykah Badu. Badu's success pushed Motown to develop a neo-soul sound. Following its corporate restructuring, Motown Records enlisted Grammy Award–winning writer and performer Ne-Yo to lead its Artist and Repertoire department in 2012. Ne-Yo has sought to reinvigorate the label by signing and developing talented young acts.

Willie Collins

SEE ALSO: *A&R Men/Women; Ballard, Hank; Blues; Boxing; The Commodores; The Drifters; Eckstine, Billy; Franklin, Aretha; Funk; Gaye, Marvin; Gordy, Berry; Gospel Music; Grammy Awards; Holiday, Billie; Hooker, John Lee; Jackson, Michael; The Jackson Five; Jazz; Martha and the Vandellas; Pop Music; Radio; Rhythm and Blues; Robinson, Smokey; Rock and Roll; Ross, Diana, and the Supremes; Soul Music; Television; The Temptations; Walker, Junior, and the All Stars; Wells, Mary; Wonder, Stevie.*

BIBLIOGRAPHY

George, Nelson. *Where Did Our Love Go? The Rise and Fall of the Motown Sound.* New York: St. Martin's Press, 1985.

Gordy, Berry. *To Be Loved: The Music, the Magic, the Memories of Motown.* New York: Warner Books, 1994.

Hildebrand, Lee. *Stars of Soul and Rhythm & Blues.* New York: Billboard Books, 1994.

Singleton, Raynoma Gordy; Bryan Brown; and Mim Eichler. *Berry, Me, and Motown: The Untold Story.* Chicago: Contemporary Books, 1990.

Taraborrelli, J. Randy. *Motown: Hot Wax, City Cool & Solid Gold.* Garden City, NY: Doubleday, 1986.

Waller, Don. *The Motown Story.* New York: Scribner, 1985.

Mount Rushmore

America, "the land of the free and home of the brave," has many national monuments. Possibly none, though, so unabashedly celebrates American expansionism as the piece of sculpture 23 miles southwest of Rapid City, South Dakota. Completed in stages during the 1920s and 1930s, the Mount Rushmore National Memorial, which is visited by nearly three million tourists annually, celebrates the spirit of America through huge carvings of the faces of four presidents: George Washington, Thomas Jefferson, Abraham Lincoln, and Theodore Roosevelt. While the memorial was intended simply as a tribute to these great leaders, changes in the cultural climate have begun to alter its interpretation. Particularly through the influence of Native American groups, some Americans have begun to question just what kind of symbol this is for their nation. Such is the fate of any landscape that attempts to serve as a sacred symbol for a number of different constituents.

For generations, this mountain was known to the Lakota Sioux as Six Grandfathers. It served as the site for their spiritual

Mount Rushmore. *The Mount Rushmore National Memorial is visited by 40 million tourists each year.* IOFOTO/SHUTTERSTOCK.COM.

journeys, which typically culminated at Harney Peak. The area was disputed after the 1868 Treaty of Fort Laramie, and military campaigns occurred in 1876–1877. Afterward, white settlers referred to the site variously as Cougar Mountain, Sugarloaf Mountain, Slaughterhouse Mountain, and Keystone Cliffs. During an 1885 prospecting expedition, the well-known New York attorney Charles E. Rushmore and others gave the mountain its current name.

The idea for carving the mountain is credited to historian Doane Robinson in 1923. Gutzon Borglum, who had been involved with carving Stone Mountain in Georgia, began work in 1924. As a sculpture, Borglum's Mount Rushmore is one of the world's largest. It is certainly one of the most impressive works of man: it erupts out of the Black Hills, and surrounding mountains roll off endlessly into the horizon. The granite faces tower 5,500 feet above sea level, seeming to peer out over the nation that they helped to foster. President Calvin Coolidge was so impressed with the project that he arranged federal funding to support it. At the project's dedication in 1927, Coolidge stated that he believed the project was "decidedly American in its conception, magnitude, and meaning. It is altogether worthy of our country." In 1933 the National Park Service took control of the project, and federal funds were used for its construction.

The project proceeded briskly, though this is a relative term when reducing the face of a mountain to sculpture. After three years of blasting, chiseling, and drilling, Washington's head emerged. Franklin D. Roosevelt was present at the dedication of the Jefferson portrait in 1936. Lincoln's head was dedicated in 1937 and Theodore Roosevelt's in 1939. Between 1927 and 1941, Borglum worked with 400 workers at the site. He died during the final years of his shrine's construction, and his son Lincoln took over the project.

The project was never truly completed; in fact, the artist intended another giant carving—a memorial to the Sioux Indians—to be located in the Pine Ridge country of Nebraska. Instead, his heirs have taken up the project on a nearby mountain in South Dakota. The creation of the Crazy Horse sculpture continues to unfold, but already it attracts thousands of visitors. Work has been slowed, at least partly, because federal support of the project has been rejected.

Mount Rushmore has proved a lasting image for the nation since 1939. The exact meaning, however, appears to be different for each viewer. Sacred landscapes are defined by ongoing contestation, or debate, over meaning. The situation is particularly acute in the Black Hills, where Sioux and American settlers had a history of armed conflict. To some visitors, as with Coolidge, the towering sculpture in the Black Hills signifies the power and fortitude of the American nation as it followed "Manifest Destiny" westward and then became a global power unlike any other civilization. As Sioux and other Native Americans watch millions of tourists arrive at Mount Rushmore each year, they cannot help but view the creation and celebration as sacrilege. As one Sioux bitterly observed, "This is what conquering means. They could just as well have carved this mountain into a huge cavalry boot standing on a dead Indian."

An icon of American popular culture, Mount Rushmore is memorably used as the location for the climactic chase scene in Alfred Hitchcock's 1959 film *North by Northwest.* The National Park Service refused, however, to allow filming to be done on this sacred landmark, and the scene was actually shot on a studio model of the monument.

Brian Black

SEE ALSO: *Hitchcock, Alfred; National Parks;* North by Northwest.

BIBLIOGRAPHY

Brown, Dee. *Bury My Heart at Wounded Knee.* New York: H. Holt, 2007.

Lame Deer, John, and Richard Erdoes. *Lame Deer: Seeker of Visions.* New York: Simon & Schuster, 1972.

Mathiessen, Peter. *In the Spirit of Crazy Horse.* New York: Viking, 1983.

Taliaferro, John. *Great White Fathers.* New York: Public Affairs, 2004.

Worster, Donald. *Under Western Skies.* New York: Oxford University Press, 1992.

Mountain Biking

In the late 1960s, near San Francisco, Gary Fisher and Charles Kelly began riding their bicycles on trails that no ordinary Schwinn could handle. With Joe Breeze, these two riders set up a group called Clunkers, and they began making their own bikes, specifically designed for off-road, rough-terrain riding. Organizing races throughout the 1970s, the Clunkers watched the popularity of mountain biking sweep the United States.

Fisher perfected bike manufacturing to an art, and by the late 1990s his handcrafted bikes sold for thousands of dollars. Other bike shops and manufacturers followed suit, and mountain bikes became the most common variation of the bicycle by the end of the twentieth century. The popularity of mountain bikes can be attributed to the abundant opportunities for off-road riding in most areas and the ease and comfort of riding mountain bikes when compared to road bikes with skinny tires. Whether in cities or rural areas, riders found compelling reasons to adopt a mountain bike.

Bike manufacturers have always sought to appeal to Americans through the indulgence of luxury. Rarely purchased as a necessity, bicycles are usually acquired as a luxury item. The first great wave of bicycle popularity in the 1870s saw the high-wheel bicycle enjoyed by young men traveling about town. When companies, such as Mead, Sears, Montgomery Ward, and Schwinn, developed bicycles for Americans after World War I, bicycling became most associated with the young. The younger generation almost exclusively rode on pavement or sidewalks in neighborhoods or suburban developments. During the late 1970s, riders perfected new modes of riding and varied designs in order to accommodate the new uses.

Some of these new riders sought to explode the limitations of traditional riding and design. Mountain or dirt biking would take place off of trails and roads, free of pavement. To a generation of young Americans breaking the bounds of many traditional activities, mountain biking offered a more intense experience, potentially full of danger and excitement. The design variations in bicycles included fat, knobby tires; suspension; and new, straight handlebars with a complicated gearing that allowed riders much more flexibility (usually offering twenty speeds). The newer bikes could be adjusted for use in the deep woods or on roadsides, reflecting the younger generation's desire for versatility.

Mountain bikes are strikingly different from the very reserved, ten-speed bikes of the 1970s, and the new bikes broadened the appeal of bicycling. During the late twentieth century, more people were mountain biking than during any other period in biking. More riders were also seeking out experiences that pushed the limits of safety. Mountain biking, for instance, is a major component of ESPN's popular X Games, an event held twice a year (winter and summer) that allows participants to tempt fate and pursue games, such as a mountain bike races that offer the possibility of serious injury—a necessary "edge" to make activities interesting to many young people.

In the twenty-first century, more and more American commuters are following the lead of Europeans and getting to work by bike. Although "city" bikes have evolved as a hybrid of road and mountain bikes, many city cyclists—including bike messengers—often still favor the sturdy frame and knobby tires of the mountain bike.

Brian Black

SEE ALSO: *Bicycling; ESPN; Extreme Sports; Leisure Time; Suburbia; World War I; X Games.*

BIBLIOGRAPHY

Berto, Frank. *The Birth of Dirt.* New York: Vand der Plas Publications, 2008.

Brimner, Larry Dane. *Mountain Biking.* New York: Franklin Watts, 1997.

Howard, John. *Dirt!: The Philosophy, Technique, and Practice of Mountain Biking.* New York: Lyons Press, 1997.

Wilson, David Gordon. *Bicycling Science.* Boston: MIT Press, 2004.

The Mouseketeers

SEE: *Disney (Walt Disney Company); Funicello, Annette;* The Mickey Mouse Club.

Movie Palaces

Epitomizing the greatness of Hollywood and the glorious excess of the Roaring Twenties, movie palaces were opulent movie theaters with plush carpeting, gilded ceilings, glass staircases, Wurlitzer organs, stylized decor, uniformed ushers, and as many as 6,000 seats. Movie palaces of yesteryear remain a nostalgic reminder of the greatest days of Hollywood and the United States.

THE FIRST MOVIE THEATERS

It was not always thus. When Hollywood was young, and films silent, moviegoing was considered entertainment for the lower classes. Exhibition of early cinema reflected the stark class division of movie audiences. The earliest venues for projected movies were converted storefronts. In 1905 Harry Davis and John Harris, store owners and two of the hundreds of local entrepreneurs who shaped movie history, charged five cents for admission to the movies they showed in their converted store in McKeesport, Pennsylvania. Combining the price of the ticket with the Greek word for "theater," they called their theater the Nickelodeon.

It took another ten years for exhibitors to upgrade their theaters to attract the upper and middle classes. In 1914 exhibitors Moe (1872–1932) and Mitchell (1868–1918) Mark surmised that an upscale exhibition venue would attract an upscale audience. Further, they gambled that this new audience would pay more for the spectacle. On April 11, 1914, the Mark brothers opened the Strand Theater on Broadway in New York City. While not a full-fledged movie palace, the Strand set new standards in movie theater design and ticket prices. With its crystal chandeliers, plush carpet, gold-leafed ceiling, art-hung lobby, and uniformed ushers, the Strand commanded twenty-five cents for admission to its gracious chambers. Built on the eve of World War I, the Strand led the way in increasingly ornate and larger picture houses.

World War I set the backdrop for the arrival of movies and for Hollywood's consolidation as the most powerful center of film production in the world. With the rest of the world at war, the United States experienced the beginnings of unsurpassed industrial and economic growth. The world's other filmmaking countries reallocated their resources to pay for munitions and other wartime needs. Hollywood pumped its films onto screens around the world. For its increasingly opulent films, Hollywood needed suitable venues at home—theaters that would showcase its stars, complement its excess, and provide its patrons with a complete experience of affluence and leisure.

CONSTRUCTING DREAM PALACES

Many people contributed to the boom in movie theater construction, but one man can be credited with setting the standard. Samuel Lionel Rothafel (1882–1936), known as Roxy, began his movie exhibition career with a small family theater in Forest City, Pennsylvania. Turning an old theater into Rothafel's Family Theatre, Roxy discovered his vocation. Soon he was called upon by theater owners across the Northeast to renovate their spaces.

But Roxy was not just redoing these spaces; he reinvented the experience of going to a movie. He moved the orchestra out of a pit and onto the stage and put his ushers in impeccable uniforms. Insisting that the music accompanying a film had to

Moviegoers at the Roxy, 1935. *Moviegoers gather at the entrance of the Roxy Theatre in New York City to see* Charlie Chan in Shanghai *in 1935.* CHARLES PETERSON/GETTY IMAGES.

relate to the film's story, he scored the music for his theaters himself. Between 1913 and 1920 Roxy turned four of New York City's theaters into movie palaces. In the twenty-first century their names—the Strand, the Realto, the Capitol, and the Rivoli—still resonate with the glory of Roxy's vision.

Roxy's movie palaces, like all the others, offered a complete program of entertainment, including vaudeville acts, live music, animal tricks, and finally a newsreel and film. With their eclectic decor and larger-than-life entertainment, the movie palaces did not always present the movie as the main attraction. Often the setting or the vaudeville acts were the draw. Roxy's imprint of excess and his formula for complete entertainment were copied, though never rivaled, across the nation. Two of the smaller gems, the Castro Theater (1922, San Francisco) and the Music Box Theatre (1929, Chicago), were still in operation in the twenty-first century, restored to their original state complete with Wurlitzer and organist.

Roxy fulfilled his dream of building his own theater in 1925. The Roxy defined the movie palace: its rococo-style rotunda, trimmed in gold filigree and supported by twelve marble columns, opened into a theater seating 6,214 people. The five-story structure included six box offices, a hospital, a musical library with more than 50,000 scores, washroom facilities to accommodate 10,000, dressing rooms for stars, a radio broadcast facility, and Roxy's private health club and box. It cost an astounding $300,000 to renovate. When it opened on March 11, 1927, in New York City, the Roxy instantly became the biggest star of all movie palaces.

RADIO CITY MUSIC HALL

In 1930 industrialist John D. Rockefeller and the Radio Corporation of America looked to Roxy to direct their new theater. Resigning his position at his own theater, Roxy went uptown to build the enduring Radio City Music Hall. He toured Europe, looking for inspiration in its most famous theaters and opera houses. The greatest inspiration came on his transatlantic cruise home, when he saw the fiery sun set on the horizon. The stage and coves in Radio City Music Hall look like a sun setting over red velvet. Designed by Donald Deskey (1894–1989), this Art Deco masterpiece features a 60-by-150-foot grand foyer decorated with mirrors, marble, gold leaf, bronze trim, and a mural. It cost more than $7 million to build and seated 6,200.

Radio City Music Hall opened on December 27, 1932. Roxy invited Hollywood stars and political celebrities, and he scheduled nineteen vaudeville acts. Even as he built his dream castle, however, he had lost faith in the movies, believing that vaudeville and radio would replace them. This miscalculation cost Roxy his directorship and broke his spirit. He died on January 13, 1936. Ironically, since its 1979 renovation, Radio City Music Hall has functioned as Roxy himself had imagined—almost exclusively showcasing live entertainment, including the world-famous Rockettes.

GRAUMAN'S CHINESE THEATRE

While Roxy reinvented the movie experience and built the most extravagant of movie palaces, on the West Coast another man was building ornate palaces all around the seat of movie royalty—Hollywood. Sid Grauman (1879–1950) owned and operated Hollywood's most glamorous picture palaces—among them the Million Dollar (1918); the Egyptian (1922), designed after the great tomb of King Tut; and the Metropolitan (1923). He drew attention to his theaters by placing huge searchlights on the sidewalk.

The apex of Grauman's career, and arguably the most famous of all movie palaces, was the Chinese Theatre, opened on May 18, 1927, in ceremonies emceed by pioneer director D. W. Griffith. Built in the style of a Chinese pagoda, Grauman's masterpiece was capped by a 60-foot ceiling sculpture of silver dragons. For all its grandeur, however, the Chinese is best known for its sidewalk, where for more than eighty years Hollywood's brightest stars have signed their names and left their footprints in the cement. One legend has it that this ultimate walk of fame was accidentally conceived when Norma Talmadge stepped in wet concrete during a tour of the construction site. Grauman asked her to sign her name next to her footprint, and the tradition began—a tradition that continued into the 2010s, with stars such as Cher, Robert Duvall, and Helen Mirren leaving their prints.

As the movie palace grew into the standard version of a theater, two architectural trends emerged. One, the atmospheric theater, was pioneered by Austrian-born John Eberson (1875–1954). In an atmospheric theater a Brenograph projected moving images onto a concrete ceiling, creating, for instance, the illusion of a starry night with lights embedded in the cement and moving clouds projected across the ceiling. Eberson used this technology to bring nature inside. Also known for exoticism, he built the Avalon in Chicago, a Persian temple complete with handmade tile and luxuriously draped tents. Scotsman Thomas W. Lamb (1871–1942) led another architectural trend, the hard-top, a variation of an opera house or vaudeville theater. Working frequently for theater magnate Marcus Loew (1870–1927), Lamb at first designed ornate but traditional palaces that featured symmetric, classical styles. As the 1920s grew increasingly flamboyant, so did Lamb's palaces, inspired by Hindu, Persian, Chinese, and Spanish art.

THE END OF AN ERA

The 1930s and the Great Depression brought a slow death to the movie palace. The failure of Roxy's Radio City Music Hall may not have been completely due to his mistaken vision. The U.S. public had less money to go to the movies, especially to the more expensive venues. Most of the major studios declared bankruptcy and stopped building theaters. Only Warner Brothers, Columbia, and United Artists, the three smallest studios, survived the Great Depression with theaters.

The post–World War II period saw the renaissance of the surviving movie palaces and reconstruction of Hollywood studios. The heyday of Hollywood and her movie palace-temples, however, was over. By the end of the 1940s all the studios had agreed to divest their theater holdings as part of a settlement in the Supreme Court case *U.S. v. Paramount, et al.* Television and the suburbs helped cut the movie audience in half, from an average of eighty-five million a week in the 1940s to about half that in the 1950s.

Most of the movie palaces that survived were converted for other use, from community centers to bowling alleys, and in the residential building boom of the 1990s, many were torn down to make way for condominiums and multiplexes. In some communities, however, civic groups formed to save the palaces, and there is a small movement to restore these quintessential U.S. treasures. For example, in 1986 the Chicago Theater in downtown Chicago was saved from demolition and restored to its former glory to be used as an auditorium for prestigious live entertainment. Similarly, in 2007 developers bought the ruined Fox Theater in Pomona, California, and embarked on a $10 million restoration and reconstruction project. The theater had its grand reopening in April 2009. In 2010 a developer in New York City signed a deal to renovate Loew's Kings Theatre in Brooklyn. Through such efforts, some of the movie palaces of yesterday survive to wow new generations with their opulent grandeur.

Ilene S. Goldman

SEE ALSO: *Cher; Duvall, Robert; The Great Depression; Griffith, D. W.; Hollywood; The Rockefeller Family; The Rockettes; Television; Vaudeville; World War I; World War II.*

BIBLIOGRAPHY

Berger, Robert, and Anne Conser. *The Last Remaining Seats: Movie Palaces of Tinseltown (Architecture and Film).* Santa Monica, CA: Hennessey & Ingalls, 2004.

Endes, Stacey, and Robert Cushman. *Hollywood at Your Feet: The Story of the World-Famous Chinese Theatre.* Los Angeles: Pomegranate Press, 1992.

Hall, Ben. *The Best Remaining Seats: The Story of the Golden Age of the Movie Palace.* New York: Potter, 1961.

Margolies, John, and Emily Gwathmey. *Ticket to Paradise: American Movie Theaters and How We Had Fun.* Boston: Little, Brown, 1991.

Melnick, Ross, and Andreas Fuchs. *Cinema Treasures: A New Look at Classic Movie Theaters.* St. Paul, MN: MBI, 2004.

Pildas, Ave. *Movie Palaces: Survivors of an Elegant Era.* New York: Potter, 1980.

Valentine, Maggie. *The Show Starts on the Sidewalk: An Architectural History of the Movie Theater, Starring S. Charles Lee.* New Haven, CT: Yale University Press, 1994.

Movie Stars

The United States is a country with no aristocracy, no landed gentry, and ostensibly no barriers to rising in society. Of course, the paradox of American culture is that the above is true while at the same time being utterly false. If social differences are more fluid than in, say, Great Britain, they are still undeniably real. Yet even the most egalitarian of societies needs its heroes, as it needs the pageant of history to provide context, and starting in the twentieth century, movie stars fulfilled that vital function.

"Once there were no film stars," writes film historian Ronald L. Davis in *The Glamour Factory: Inside Hollywood's Big Studio System.* "In the early days of silent pictures studio heads didn't advertise the names of actors, realizing that fame would bring pressure for higher salaries. For the first year or two [actress] Mary Pickford was known simply as 'The Girl with the Golden Curls.'" Studios continued to suppress the identities of their actors even after the public clamored for their names. With the second generation of filmmakers in the 1910s, this situation changed rapidly.

The men who created Hollywood, and with it, the institution of the movie star, were, for the most part, immigrants, and more often than not they were also entrepreneurs. Many of them came to the movies from some part of the fashion industry, where the ability to anticipate public tastes was indispensable. Adolph Zukor, the first film producer to judge the market potential of feature-length films, was also among the first to use a film's star to market a movie. For his 1912 silent film, *Queen Elizabeth*, he built the publicity campaign for the film around the film's star, Sarah Bernhardt, who was, at the time, the most famous actress in the world.

By the 1915 release of director D. W. Griffith's epic *The Birth of a Nation* (prominently featuring Lillian Gish), the movie star had become the linchpin of film marketing. The new film moguls saw the advantage in mimicking Broadway, where the presence of certain name actors could ensure the success of a play, but they also perceived that film was a medium of broad, simple gestures. It was not enough to merely present an actor and hope for the best. Actors had to be easily recognizable and their characters consistent from one film to the next, to avoid confusing audiences. Studio executives tailored an actor's image around a few easily recognizable features and having once established their identity, repeatedly cast them in similar roles. Hence, Theda Bara always played an exotic seductress; Rudolph Valentino, an Arab prince; and John Gilbert, a Latin lover. It was a frustrating situation for any serious actor but lucrative for the studios.

A NEW BREED OF ROYALTY

In addition to creating screen personas for their actors, the studios furnished their actors with new names and, often, new biographies. In the early 1920s, for example, Fox Studios transformed Theodesia Goodman, a Jewish woman who was born in Ohio to a local tailor and his wife, into exotic Theda Bara, the daughter of an artist and an Arabian princess. Publicists said her name was an anagram for "Arab Death."

Many stars, John Gilbert for one, resented being typecast. But most movie stars of the time were not trained actors and were content just to have the work. Many relished their newfound notoriety. Tom Mix, the star of cowboy serials, lived up to his cowboy image on-screen and off, furnishing his mansion with a wealth of garish Western memorabilia and wearing his trademark white sombrero wherever he went. Rudolph Valentino, however, used his considerable wealth to hide from a prying public, buying the property around Falcon Lair, his Benedict Canyon estate, in order to ward off importuning fans. And from all accounts, Valentino saw acting as a means to an end, taking little pleasure from it.

While many silent movie stars were ambivalent about their careers, they were devoted to the lifestyle that acting afforded them. They lived by the credo propounded by Gloria Swanson, who, shortly after buying razor-blade millionaire King C. Gillette's Beverly Hills mansion, announced, "I have decided that while I am a star, I will be every inch and every moment a star." The new elite built veritable monuments to their celebrity, palaces befitting their status as pseudoroyalty. Very few exercised the modesty of Clark Gable, whose modest ranch house sat amid a working ranch, but followed instead the lead of husband and wife actors Douglas Fairbanks Sr. and Mary Pickford—whose converted hunting lodge, Pickfair, with its bowling alley, screening room, acres of landscaping, swimming pool, and ponds for canoeing—became a yardstick of accomplishment for the nouveaux riche. John Barrymore converted a modest mission-Spanish dwelling into a 7-acre ode to bad taste, with sixteen separate buildings, a Japanese garden, an aviary, and a tower built above his bedroom to which he could retire via trap door when the demands of public life grew too heavy for him to take.

The movie star's extravagance was grist for the mill of the slew of magazines and newspaper columns devoted to this new breed of royalty. In the 1920s no fewer than twenty-six fan magazines, such as *Motion Pictures*, *Picture Play*, *The New Movie*, *Screenland*, and *Photoplay*, appeared to fulfill this vital function. The nation hungered for news about the movie stars, but not just news. All the details of their daily lives—their clothes, their hobbies, who they entertained for dinner, their secret hopes and aspirations—were all assiduously reported, and a movie star who was hostile to the press played a dangerous game with his or her career. Often the stars took pains to appear ordinary or underscore the sacrifices of show business. According to author Martin Levin in his book, *Hollywood and the Great Fan Magazines*, actress Norma Shearer once said, "I love to go to my friends' houses for an evening. I love to have them come to my house. . . . I don't care for huge parties. I seldom go to them and never, never give them."

PUBLICITY AND GOSSIP

In the early twentieth century, movie studios managed publicity for their stars, arranging interviews and appearances. They also orchestrated the stars' offscreen lives as carefully as their filmed performances, including who they were seen with in public and who they married. A star's reputation had a direct effect on the success of their movies, and studio publicists went to profound lengths to shield a valuable star from the potentially disastrous effects of their private missteps.

The reigning—and rival—queens of Hollywood gossip in the early twentieth century were newspaper columnists Hedda Hopper and Louella Parsons. At the peak of their careers in the late 1930s and early 1940s, the two had a combined readership of seventy-five million readers, and each wielded her power ruthlessly, nursing grudges for years, sometimes going to great lengths to scuttle a career. Hopper, for example, had a well-known and deep dislike of actor and director Charlie Chaplin.

Although she denied it, Hopper was anti-Semitic, and she thought Chaplin was Jewish (he was not). She disapproved of the British-born Chaplin living in the United States for years and never becoming a U.S. citizen, and she thought he should donate some of his immense wealth to charity, specifically her favorite charities. When fifty-four-year-old Chaplin married for the fourth time to eighteen-year-old Oona O'Neill in 1943, Hopper was appalled at the difference in their ages and set about helping to bring a paternity suit against Chaplin on behalf of another young woman. Blood tests revealed the child was not his, but by then Chaplin's reputation was already damaged.

In 1941 Parsons heard that the movie *Citizen Kane* (1941), which was about to be released, was based on her boss, newspaper publisher William Randolph Hearst. Given her clout in the industry, she demanded and got a private screening, which she attended with Hearst's lawyers. She reportedly left before the movie was over, convinced that it was about her boss. She then launched a concerted effort to stop the film's release and have it destroyed. Even though Orson Welles, the film's director and star, denied that the movie was based on Hearst, it was still banned from some theaters and initially lost money because of Parsons's efforts.

Star status was a tricky thing to maintain. Some stars, including Chaplin and Pickford, had the business savvy and the talent to endure, but the exception proved the rule. When a familiar profile fell out a favor, the public could be as cold as they had been adoring. "So what?" ran the summation of a piece by columnist Faith Service. "A newer star appears and to you, Fickle Public, our heroine becomes—the Forgotten Face."

Most actors were so thrilled with the amounts of money they made that they spent lavishly, only to find themselves inexplicably out of favor with the public or the studios or both. The tragedy of stardom (luridly documented in Kenneth Anger's *Hollywood Babylon* series) was that success so blinded young, marginally talented performers that despite the object lessons of their fellows, they rarely thought that their star, having ascended, would plummet. This became part of the allure of star-watching, the schadenfreude of seeing the mighty fall. And a fall from grace was a deceptively simple thing. It might be due to the caprices of a restless public, or a too-public display of arrogance, but once you were out, as so many found, the road back into public favor was more often a cul-de-sac. "Looking back on Hollywood," wrote Joan Fontaine, "I realized that one outstanding quality it possesses is . . . *fear*. Fear stalks the sound stages, the publicity departments, the executive offices. Since careers often begin by chance, by the hunch of a producer or casting director, a casual meeting with an agent or publicist, they can evaporate just as quixotically."

DE HAVILLAND'S LAW

In 1945 the movie studio system of contracting actors and actress came to an end as a result of a lawsuit brought by actress Olivia de Havilland against her studio, Warner Brothers. Until that time, contracts between studios and its actors allowed studios to "suspend" an actor for refusing a part that the studio wanted him or her to play and for time the actor spent serving in the military. The length of the suspension was then added to the length of the actor's contract. Under this system, studios could repeatedly suspend their actors, preventing or delaying them from switching studios or from simply renewing their contracts under different terms. De Havilland's lawsuit went all the way to the U.S. Supreme Court, and the decision, known as "de Havilland's law," is the one of most significant legal rulings ever made in Hollywood.

De Havilland's law, combined with a 1948 Supreme Court antitrust ruling that forced the major studios to divest themselves of their theaters, opened the movie industry to independent producers. The locus of power began to shift away from the studios and into the hands of the actors themselves, who became responsible for their own image. They soon discovered, however, that in order to make any money, they would also have to be involved in packaging and producing their films. "Stars discovered that working for the major companies meant they couldn't hold on to most of their earnings," says publicist Arthur Mayer in *The Glamour Factory*. "Each star thereupon sought to establish his own company. . . . If you own a company, you can arrange your taxes quite differently. . . . So the stars all went out for themselves." Many started production companies, such as actress Rosalind Russell and her husband, director Frederick Brisson, who formed Independent Artists, and actor Burt Lancaster and actor and producer Harold Hecht, who formed Norma Productions, named after Lancaster's wife.

As movie stars assumed control of their career and public image, the public's perception of them gradually changed. Prior to the 1950s, all stars appeared to be nearly perfect and eternally glamorous thanks to their studios. By the 1950s the public began to see that movie stars were people too and that they were not always perfect. If an actor was particularly popular or especially skilled, the public often forgave any personal transgressions.

The public's changing perception of movie stars was also affected by changing technology, changing society, historic events, and the passage of time. The perception of the movie star didn't change overnight, but in increments. By the 1950s, the cult of the movie star became the cult of the actor. A pretty face could still excite, but more and more it was an actor's skills that brought him or her fame. And because they were no longer studio employees, the stars were no longer beholden to publicity departments to smile and nod and give interviews to reporters.

Montgomery Clift, Marlon Brando, Paul Newman, and James Dean disdained the careful choreography of studio publicists, guarding their privacy and independence. Marilyn Monroe and Elizabeth Taylor were still sex symbols, but they no longer were forced to hide their personal strife. No longer were the stars demigods or demigoddesses residing in unearthly splendor. Now they were perceived as frail and human—sharing the attributes of lesser mortals. A marijuana-possession conviction failed to tarnish Robert Mitchum's allure, nor did the marital strife of Monroe detract from her star appeal. Maybe it was the general prosperity of the times. In the 1920s, for example, movies and the people who were featured in them were novelties because movies were so new. In the 1930s and 1940s, moviegoers, affected by the Great Depression and two world wars, were seeking an escape from real life and needed heroes. Starting in the 1950s, movies became just a form of entertainment, and the movie stars were simply entertainers.

A NEW GENERATION

By the late 1960s, Hollywood had a new generation of stars, and many of them were not merely actors but also rebels. In varying degrees, stars, such as Peter Fonda, Dennis Hopper, Warren Beatty, and Jane Fonda, were part of the brewing antiwar, counterculture rebellion, and they took aim at society both on-screen and off. British actress Julie Christie was notorious for both her radical politics and her lack of concern with money. Fonda drew scorn and forever became known as "Hanoi Jane" for visiting North Vietnam during the Vietnam War.

The new Hollywood movie stars also did not make any efforts to hide their ethnic origins, unlike their predecessors. Nor were they as classically handsome or beautiful. The public's appreciation and approval of stars was based more and more on their acting ability rather than on their looks. Also, for the first time, African Americans, such as Sidney Poitier, achieved mainstream success. Poitier made history in 1963 when he became the first African American to win an Academy Award for Best Actor.

As the film industry grew and time passed, some of the children of movie stars became movie stars themselves. Jane Fonda and Peter Fonda, for example, are the children of Academy Award–winning actor Henry Fonda. Siblings often became movie stars too. Warren Beatty and Shirley MacLaine are brother and sister, as are Jake and Maggie Gyllenhaal.

Many movie stars of the early twenty-first century had relatives who were in the movie industry before them. George Clooney is the son of actor Nick Clooney and the nephew of singer and actress Rosemary Clooney. Angelina Jolie is the daughter of actor Jon Voight, and Gwyneth Paltrow is the daughter of actress Blythe Danner and producer Bruce Paltrow. Drew Barrymore comes from a family of actors. She is the daughter of John Drew Barrymore, the granddaughter of John Barrymore, and the grandniece of Ethel Barrymore and Lionel Barrymore. They are the product of one or two generations of selective breeding and what Joan Didion calls in *The White Album* "the last extant stable society." In this society the role of the movie star is a well-known commodity, and its pitfalls well-known pitfalls. If today such things as same-sex relationships, black leading men and women, feminists, and miscegenation are accepted, the game itself has changed very little. The same could be said of the public's relationship to movie stars, one of adoration and enduring fascination.

In retrospect, the late 1960s and early 1970s appears as a short aberration in an otherwise uninterrupted, continuous stream of manufactured gods and goddesses, sex symbol selling an idealized version of the masculine and feminine. In today's age of diminished expectations, movie stars still hold out the promise that a pot of gold does exist at the end of the rainbow, and this pot is on display to the public who live out a dream of wealth and physical charms vicariously.

Screenwriter Budd Schulberg once observed that "Hollywood, after all, was only a picture of America run through the projector at triple speed. . . . Hollywood [has] always been an excessive, speeded-up, larger-than-life reflection of the American Way." It is the movie stars who play out these excessive, larger-than-life visions of America, and in so doing, they embody America. Despite the passage of time and changes in image, movie stars remain America's royalty.

Michael Baers

SEE ALSO: *Academy Awards; Bara, Theda; Barrymore, John; Beatty, Warren;* The Birth of a Nation*; Celebrity; Celebrity Couples; Chaplin, Charlie;* Citizen Kane*; Clooney, George; Clooney, Rosemary; Fairbanks, Douglas, Jr.; Fonda, Henry; Fonda, Jane; Gable, Clark; Gish, Lillian; The Great Depression; Griffith, D. W.; Hearst, William Randolph; Hollywood; Hopper, Dennis; Jolie, Angelina; Lancaster, Burt; Mix, Tom; Pickford, Mary; Poitier, Sidney; Russell, Rosalind; Silent Movies; Valentino, Rudolph; Welles, Orson; World War I; World War II.*

BIBLIOGRAPHY

Anger, Kenneth. *Hollywood Babylon.* San Francisco: Straight Arrow, 1975.

Anger, Kenneth. *Hollywood Babylon II.* New York: Dutton, 1984.

Davis, Ronald L. *The Glamour Factory: Inside Hollywood's Big Studio System.* Dallas, TX: Southern Methodist University Press, 1993.

Didion, Joan. *The White Album.* New York: Simon & Schuster, 1979.

Hozic, Aida A. *Hollyworld: Space, Power, and Fantasy in the American Economy.* New York: Cornell University Press, 2001.

Hutchinson, Tom. *Screen Goddesses.* New York: Exeter Books, 1984.

Kobal, John. *Gods and Goddesses of the Movies.* New York: Crescent Books, 1973.

Levin, Martin. *Hollywood and the Great Fan Magazines.* New York: Arbor House, 1970.

Niven, David. *The Moon's a Balloon.* New York, Putnam 1971.

Niven, David. *Bring on the Empty Horses.* New York: Putnam, 1975.

Schneider, Jay. *501 Movie Stars: A Comprehensive Guide to the Greatest Screen Actors.* Hauppauge, New York: Barron's Educational Series, 2007.

Sommer, Robin Langley. *Hollywood: The Glamour Years (1919–1941).* New York: Gallery Books, 1987.

Turner Classic Movies. *Leading Men: The 50 Most Unforgettable Actors of the Studio Era.* San Francisco: Chronicle Books, 2006.

MP3

MP3 is an encoding format for compressing digital audio. It is at the core of the digital recording process, which converts sound into digital files that can be saved in magnetic memory, copied indefinitely, and transmitted over the Internet. The worldwide acceptance of the MP3 encoding standard has given millions of listeners access to a vast range of prerecorded music and spoken word that would have been unimaginable before the introduction of home computing and the Internet. MP3 was part of a revolution in sound recording that made it so easy to access and save music that it threatened to undermine the popular music industry and the protection of copyright.

The MP3 algorithm compresses digital audio files by picking out the sounds that are most easily perceived by the human ear and concentrating on their faithful reproduction; other sounds are not sampled and reproduced with such precision. Thus, MP3 compression can save and reproduce only a tiny fraction of the original sound, and the size of this fraction is determined by other factors, such as the sampling rate. As soon as MP3 was published, other groups developed more efficient formats for encoding digital audio, but none has ever reached the level of acceptance of MP3.

MP3 was a small part of the work done by the International Organization for Standardization (ISO/IEC), a group that sets international standards for commercial and industrial use. A subgroup of ISO/IEC, the Motion Picture Experts Group (MPEG), addressed the problems of standardizing the creation and transmission of digital data that carried sound and images—the music and pictures streaming into televisions, computers, and audio systems. The MPEG-1 standard covered audio layers I, II, and III. When it was published in 1993, the standard hardly attracted any notice, but it was to have a significant effect on the entertainment industry. In the early 1990s it might have taken as long as thirty minutes to download a single song from the Internet, and one would have to wait until the whole file was downloaded before listening to the music. By speeding up the downloading process and requiring far less space in digital memory, MP3 brought digital audio within the reach of anyone with a home computer and a modem.

Music lovers joined with software engineers to devise programs that could decode MP3-formatted music and then made these MP3 players available on the Internet at no charge. Justin Frankel produced one of the first widely used software MP3 players, Winamp, in 1997. This program attracted millions of users and brought about an explosion of websites that provided or exchanged music, often without the permission of its owners or creators. One of these sites, Shawn Fanning's Napster, made peer-to-peer exchange of MP3 digital audio files so popular that it threatened to replace the old system of buying compact discs with freely shared music on the Internet. Soon after Napster's brilliant start in 1999, the company was challenged in the courts and was reduced to a brand name of legal downloading operations; however, Napster had opened the floodgates, and music retailers, record companies, and computer concerns rushed to set up sites to market music on the Internet in MP3 format.

While Internet entrepreneurs and pioneers were posting free music on the Internet in MP3 format, manufacturers of audio equipment were also incorporating MP3 into physical devices that could save and play digital audio. Diamond Multimedia produced the first MP3 hardware, the Rio PMP300 MP3 player, in 1998. It was soon followed by scores of other manufacturers that rushed to produce MP3 players for the portable audio devices market. At first the digital memory of these devices was small in scale, much like the flash cards used in digital cameras, but the introduction of tiny hard discs made it possible to load hours of music onto a device much smaller than the highly popular Sony Walkman.

When the Apple computer company introduced its iPod in 2001, it was one of the many MP3 players on the market, but its eye-catching design and the ease of acquiring legal downloads from its iTunes store made the iPod the standard in portable audio at the beginning of the twenty-first century. iTunes competed successfully with other sites, such as Pressplay and Rhapsody, to become the major source of downloaded music and video on the Internet and a popular alternative to actually buying a compact disc in physical form. The MP3 players that were introduced to compete with the Walkman grew progressively smaller in size, and the technology was soon incorporated into the second and third generation of mobile phones, such as Apple's iPhone, first introduced in 2007.

Andre Millard

SEE ALSO: *Apple Computer; Cassette Tape; Compact Discs; Eight-Track Tape; File Sharing; iPod / iTunes; Napster; Smartphones; Walkman.*

BIBLIOGRAPHY

Alderman, John. *Sonic Boom: Napster, MP3 and the New Pioneers of Music.* Cambridge, MA: Perseus, 2001.

Kot, Greg. *Ripped: How the Wired Generation Revolutionized Music.* New York: Scribner, 2009.

Sinnreich, Aram. *Mashed Up: Music Technology and the Rise of a Configurable Culture.* Amherst: University of Massachusetts Press, 2010.

Sterne, Jonathan. *MP3: The Meaning of a Format: Sign, Storage, Transmission.* Durham, NC: Duke University Press, 2012.

Mr. Dooley

"Mr. Dooley" was a product of the 1890s, a time when a memorable fictional character was likely to come not only from the pages of a novel or play but also from a column in the newspaper. Chicago-born newspaper writer Finley Peter Dunne (1867–1936) created "Mr. Martin J. Dooley" as his satirical mouthpiece. Dooley was a saloon-keeper whose pronouncements on current events, both local and international, couched in a vivid, albeit questionable "Irish" dialect, were as humorous as they were pointed. Not until the country discovered a genuine "cracker-barrel philosopher" in cowboy Will Rogers was there a more popular commentator on war and peace, politics, and the passing parade.

By devising Mr. Dooley to express his thoughts and opinions, Dunne also managed to give voice to the disenfranchised blue-collar population of Irish immigrants who were beginning to form an important part of Chicago life at the turn of the twentieth century. Although his own father, a carpenter, was an immigrant from Ireland, Dunne himself did not live a working-class existence. As Paul Green pointed out in his introduction to a 1988 edition of *Mr. Dooley in Peace and in War*, "[Dunne was] more interested in writing about his people than living with them."

Dunne was born in Chicago in 1867 and grew up comfortably middle class. In 1884 the *Chicago Telegram* hired Dunne as an office boy and reporter. With this job, the young man began a fifteen-year stretch of journalism that would see him employed at half a dozen Windy City newspapers. It was not until 1892 that Dunne started experimenting with Irish dialect, because, he later explained, "It occurred to me that while it might be dangerous to call an alderman a thief in English no one could sue if a comic Irishman denounced the statesman as a thief." Nevertheless, it was not until a year later, after failing to create much of a stir with two other Irish characters, that Dunne hit upon the brainstorm of Martin J. Dooley, middle-aged bartender and commentator on matters both local and national. A self-described saloon keeper and Doctor of Philosophy, Mr. Dooley proved instantly popular with Dunne's readers, and the writer supplied them with his best Dooley columns over the next seven years.

The down-to-earth Mr. Dooley looked with a clear eye at social conditions in his Bridgeport neighborhood, and he saw what was going on all around him in Chicago as a microcosm of larger world events. Dunne's columns would range from poking fun at politics—as when Dooley ran for mayor with the campaign slogan "Rayform th' Rayformers"—to letting Dooley bear witness to vignettes illustrating the harsh life of the marginalized immigrants who frequented his establishment. The columns proved so successful that over the years they were frequently collected in book form.

Although Dunne's unauthentic dialect usage was criticized in Ireland, where his books were never popular, the satirical message was most important in his columns. Dunne eventually wrote more than 300 columns, but those generally considered the best were the ones he wrote while he was still close to his ethnic roots in Chicago. The first Dooley book, published in 1898, was *Mr. Dooley in Peace and in War*. Its success was immediate and so pronounced that it enabled Dunne to relocate to Manhattan—where he reached a wider readership and attain greater national attention—but Mr. Dooley seemed to lose something of the spirit that had first sparked his success.

Nevertheless, Dunne enjoyed lasting popularity, not only with Mr. Dooley but also with other articles, columns, and books, until his death in New York in 1936. He continued to affect popular culture posthumously, albeit indirectly, by having sired successful screenwriter Philip Dunne, whose distinguished credits include the Oscar-winning *How Green Was My Valley* (1941).

"The past," Finley Dunne once wrote, "always looks better than it was because it isn't here." Although very much a product of his era, Dunne's writings stand the test of time, in part because, for better or worse, the topics that are worth poking fun at rarely change or disappear. To cite just one example, Dunne once defined a fanatic as "a man that does what he thinks the Lord would do if He knew the facts of the case."

Preston Neal Jones

SEE ALSO: *Comics; Rogers, Will; The Windy City.*

BIBLIOGRAPHY

Bander, Edward J. *Mr. Dooley & Mr. Dunne: The Literary Life of a Chicago Catholic.* Charlottesville, VA: Michie, 1981.

Dunne, Finley Peter. *Mr. Dooley Remembers: The Informal Memoirs of Finley Peter Dunne.* Boston: Little, Brown, 1963.

Dunne, Finley Peter. *Mr. Dooley in Peace and in War.* Urbana: University of Illinois Press, 1988.

Dunne, Finley Peter, and Robert Hutchinson. *Mr. Dooley on Ivrything and Ivrybody.* New York: Dover, 1963.

Fanning, Charles, and Finley Peter Dunne. *Finley Peter Dunne & Mr. Dooley: The Chicago Years.* Lexington: University Press of Kentucky, 1978.

Taubenfeld, Aviva F. *Rough Writing: Ethnic Authorship in Theodore Roosevelt's America.* New York: New York University Press, 2008.

Mr. Smith Goes to Washington

Mr. Smith Goes to Washington (1939) is one of director Frank Capra's most critically acclaimed films and is considered by many to be his most memorable and enduring work. *Mr. Smith* tells the story of Jefferson Smith, who goes to Washington, D.C., to serve as a U.S. senator. Smith was appointed to the position by the governor of his state due to the untimely death of Senator Foley. The governor, who is controlled by a corrupt media magnet, selects Smith because he is a naive young man likely to be overwhelmed by the job and because the governor believes Smith will neither notice nor understand how the government works. Smith's lack of knowledge and experience, however, are more than offset by his keen sense of moral integrity.

In traditional Capra fashion, the hero is a common man who, although intellectually overmatched, prevails by virtue of his unshakable understanding of right and wrong. Capra presents Smith as a man who cannot be bought, cajoled, or threatened and suggests that these are the qualities that represent the greatest threat to political corruption. In what is now seen as his most patriotic moment, Capra offers a powerful illustration of American mythology through his presentation of Smith, a seemingly powerless man with the ability to take on the entire U.S. Congress.

While *Mr. Smith* is essentially a simple tale of morality, its formal presentation and the social moment in which it was produced make it far more complex. Capra, an Italian immigrant who cherished the United States, was an intelligent man who favored simple tales. A champion of American populist values, Capra often worked with left-wing intellectual writers. For *Mr. Smith* he chose screenwriter Sidney Buchman, who was later named as a communist sympathizer during the hearings conducted by the House Un-American Activities Committee

Mr. Smith Goes to Washington. *James Stewart starred as Jefferson Smith in Frank Capra's 1939 film* Mr. Smith Goes to Washington. SILVER SCREEN COLLECTION/CONTRIBUTOR/MOVIEPIX/GETTY IMAGES.

(HUAC), to write the movie's screenplay. The combination of Capra's ultrapatriotism and Buchman's liberal political and social beliefs generated complicated meanings in *Mr. Smith*. The film is further complicated by Capra's use of montage, previously developed by Russian filmmaker Sergei Eisenstein, whom Capra admired. During two key moments in the film—the opening explanation of the vacant Senate seat, and Smith's filibuster—Capra uses montage to create intellectual and emotional tension.

CAPRA'S ODE TO DEMOCRACY

With a potential world war on the horizon, Capra created in *Mr. Smith* a not-so-subtle response to the activities in Europe by focusing on the mythic qualities of American democracy. While later critics of Capra's work have referred to the film as simplistic fluff, or "Capracorn," the film had unquestionable impact when it was released. *Mr. Smith* was treated to one of the grandest openings of its time, as the film premiered at the DAR (Daughters of the American Revolution) Constitution Hall in Washington, D.C., on October 16, 1939. The screening was hosted by the Press Club and was attended by Supreme Court justices, cabinet officers, congressmen, generals, and the city's social aristocracy.

By the time the film had ended, the controversy surrounding it had begun, as individuals from the press and the government railed against what they saw as a dangerous anti-American motion picture. During a politically unstable time, the idea of America's most popular film director showcasing corruption, drunkenness, and downright incompetence in the U.S. government and press was considered misguided, if not subversive. Had the film been a comedy or more clearly a farce, the intelligentsia may have been more forgiving, but for this project Capra strove to faithfully re-create the look and feel of the Senate. In fact, he had an exact replica of the Senate Chamber built, right down to the inkwells on the desks, and included more than 186 speaking parts in an effort to portray a realistic atmosphere both on the Senate floor and in the surrounding galleries.

NEGATIVE REACTIONS

Following the film's premiere, politicians and newswriters around the country, and indeed around the world, argued against the film's release and threatened retribution against Columbia Pictures and the rest of Hollywood. According to Capra in his autobiography, *The Name above the Title*, the publisher of *Harrison's Reports*, a weekly publication that reviewed films for movie theater operators, sought to promote legislation "that would permit theater owners to refuse to play films that were 'not in the best interests of our country'—meaning, of course, *Mr. Smith*." And according to author Joseph McBride in his book, *Frank Capra: The Catastrophe of Success*, the *Washington Star* reported that *Mr. Smith* depicts "the democratic system and our vaunted free press in exactly the colors [Adolf] Hitler, [Benito] Mussolini, and [Joseph] Stalin are fond of painting them."

In addition, senators publicly spoke about the ridiculous representation of the U.S. Congress, and Joseph P. Kennedy, the U.S. ambassador to Britain, reportedly sent Columbia a telegram asking it to suppress the European release of the film. Kennedy felt that *Mr. Smith* ridiculed democracy, that it would be a crushing blow to U.S. allies in Europe, that it would damage American prestige abroad, and that it would be construed as propaganda for Germany.

Rather than caving in to industry threats and pleas from respected politicians, Capra and Harry S. Cohn, the president of Columbia Pictures, held their ground. Far from anti-American propaganda, *Mr. Smith* is an ode to American patriotism. Capra's Smith does not go to Washington, D.C., looking for a fight, but in the end he risks his career, reputation, and physical well-being to help those who are being bullied and taken advantage of by the fascistic political boss Jim Taylor. Like so many of Capra's heroes, Smith momentarily turns his back and considers running home to his isolated rural community. But when confronted with the words and ideals of Thomas Jefferson and Abraham Lincoln, the hope of a child, and the support of his savvy assistant (played by Jean Arthur), Smith finds the inner strength necessary for fighting a "war" to protect his constituents.

The moral of *Mr. Smith* may have been missed by some in the press and the government, but it did not elude the viewing public. Like all Capra films of this period, *Mr. Smith* was critically and commercially successful. Capra's greatest vindication, however, would not come until several years later when, on November 4, 1942, the *Hollywood Reporter* noted that *Mr. Smith* had been selected by movie theaters in occupied France as the final English-language film to be shown prior to the Nazi ban on American films. Indeed, one theater chose to play *Mr. Smith* continuously during the final thirty days before the ban.

During World War II, Capra demonstrated his own patriotism by enlisting in the service and producing the classic documentary series *Why We Fight*. He used *Mr. Smith Goes to Washington* to express his patriotism, to extol the virtues of his adopted country, and to suggest American commitment to the principles of freedom and democracy.

James Friedman

SEE ALSO: *Academy Awards; Capra, Frank; Communism; Hollywood; McCarthyism; Stewart, Jimmy; World War II.*

BIBLIOGRAPHY

Capra, Frank. *The Name above the Title: An Autobiography.* New York: Macmillan 1971.

Carney, Raymond. *American Vision: The Films of Frank Capra.* Cambridge, UK: Cambridge University Press, 1986.

McBride, Joseph. *Frank Capra: The Catastrophe of Success.* New York: Simon & Schuster, 1992.

Poague, Leland A., ed. *Frank Capra: Interviews.* Jackson: University Press of Mississippi, 2004.

Mr. Wizard

For nearly fifty years, Mr. Wizard dispensed science lessons on television the way most teachers wished they could. Mr. Wizard was the creation of Don Herbert (1917–2007), a radio writer and performer who wanted to make science interesting to children. His first live television program, *Watch Mr. Wizard,* aired in 1951 and featured Herbert using household items to teach the wonders of science. Over the next fourteen years he performed more than 4,500 science demonstrations and became an American institution. According to Stuart Fischer, the author of *Kids' TV: The First Twenty-Five Years,* "This show proved to be one of television's most successful educational programs." It garnered numerous honors, including two Emmy nominations.

Though *Watch Mr. Wizard* went off the air in 1965, Mr. Wizard lived on. Herbert returned to the airwaves in 1972 with a series of thirty-second science lessons called *Mr. Wizard Close-Ups.* In 1979 Herbert and his wife, Norma, helped to create touring science assemblies that visited schools across the United States. And beginning in 1983—amid the boom in nostalgia for pop culture from the 1950s and 1960s—an updated *Mr. Wizard's World* began to appear on the Nickelodeon cable network. The Nickelodeon programs were used widely in American schools to help hook yet another generation of children on science.

Although the new *Mr. Wizard's World* ceased production in 1990, it was shown in reruns on Nickelodeon through the mid-1990s. Since 2005 the programs have been re-aired frequently on The Science Channel. In addition to his television work, Herbert wrote several Mr. Wizard–themed books, including *Mr. Wizard's Science Secrets* (1952) and *Mr. Wizard's Supermarket Science* (1980).

Frank Salamone

SEE ALSO: *Emmy Awards; Television.*

BIBLIOGRAPHY

Fischer, Stuart. *Kids' TV: The First Twenty-Five Years.* New York: Facts On File, 1983.

McCray, Nancy. "Teacher to Teacher." *Booklist* 92, no. 11 (1996).

Mr. Wizard Studios. Accessed May 2012. Available from http://www.mrwizardstudios.com

Ms.

Ms. is a quarterly magazine that features articles about women's issues. Founded in the early 1970s as a monthly magazine by female journalists who were active in the women's liberation movement, it was the first national glossy publication to emerge from the movement. Eschewing articles on homemaking, fashion, and "pleasing your man" that were the mainstays of traditional women's magazines that preceded it, *Ms.* presents articles about who women are and what matters to them. Its debut was greeted with great enthusiasm by women and with outright hostility by the traditional media. ABC News anchor Harry Reasoner opined, "I'll give it six months before they run out of things to say." He went on to complain, "There isn't an article in *Ms.* that wouldn't look perfectly normal in one of the standard women's magazines, and has probably already been there, only better written." The immediate success of *Ms.* soon proved Reasoner and other critics wrong.

Criticisms of the pundits aside, however, American women just awakening to the notion of women's rights must have been hungry for what a popular feminist journal had to offer. *Ms.* was first published on December 20, 1971, as a forty-page preview issue inserted in *New York* magazine. *New York* sold out its 300,000 copies in eight days, and the *Ms.* insert generated 26,000 subscription orders and more than 20,000 letters from readers. The preview issue included articles such as "Welfare Is a Women's Issue," "Can Women Love Women?" and "Heaven Won't Protect the Working Girl."

One of the most influential articles was "The Housewife's Moment of Truth," written by Jane O'Reilly. It describes the sudden moment of awareness when a woman realizes she is being dismissed or oppressed by attitudes and actions she once accepted without question. O'Reilly calls this sudden realization a "click! of awareness." This "click!" became a catch phrase in readers' letters as they wrote in to share their own experiences and sudden insights.

The first full edition of *Ms.*, featuring Wonder Woman on the cover, appeared on newsstands in July 1972. It offered equally provocative and thought-provoking articles, such as "Women Voters Can't Be Trusted," in which writer and feminist Gloria Steinem analyzes the role of women in the electorate. In another article, Margaret Sloan-Hunter deconstructed beauty parlors in "The Saturday Morning Nap-Conversion."

Named for the title that feminists of the time thought should replace *Mrs.* and *Miss*, the conventional titles of courtesy for women, *Ms.* had a distinguished and enthusiastic debut staff. Some staff members, such as Rita Waterman, who had worked at *McCall's* magazine, and Bea Feitler from *Vanity Fair* and *Rolling Stone* magazines, were experienced in the world of magazine publishing. Others, such as Suzanne Levine, Sloan-Hunter, and Letty Cottin Pogrebin, were writers, lecturers, and activists who brought their movement experience and zealous energy to the magazine.

In an effort to work in a way that was consistent with feminist politics, the staff attempted to organize itself without traditional corporate hierarchies, and even salaries were allocated by taking into account the individual needs of a staff person as well as experience and value to the magazine. These efforts to equalize power and money reflected a common trend in progressive organizations of the 1960s and 1970s, though they were often only successful in masking power differences.

FINANCIAL CHALLENGES

In seeking financing for *Ms.*, the founders were insistent that control of the magazine remain in the hands of the women who created it. They reached an agreement with Warner Communications, which invested a million dollars in the fledgling magazine without demanding a controlling interest. *Ms.* was also supported by advertisers, which presented continual challenges since the advertisers often tried to influence the magazine's content, and sometimes they pulled their advertising if their demands were not met.

From the beginning both editorial staff and readers had questioned the contradictions implicit in challenging the status quo while courting advertisers whose interest was served by maintaining the status quo. Advertisers insisted on content that complemented and did not criticize their products. In one situation, Revlon Cosmetics was upset that an issue featured women on the cover who were not wearing makeup, and the company pulled its advertisements from the issue. In 1986 African American writer Alice Walker quit her editorial job with *Ms.*, citing her disappointment in the dearth of people of color in the magazine, especially on the cover, a lack that was, at least partially, mandated by advertisers. A lack of coverage of lesbians, radical feminism, and labor and environmental issues was also due to advertisers' demands.

As *Ms.* bowed to pressure from advertisers, it lost credibility with many of its readers and began to lose subscribers. Staggering under its problems, the magazine stopped publishing for about six months in order to reorganize and reinvent itself. In the summer of 1990, *Ms.* began publishing again as a bimonthly rather than a monthly magazine, with longtime feminist writer-activist Robin Morgan as editor.

The new *Ms.* had a higher newsstand price, a higher subscription rate, and no advertising. The glossy pages were gone, and the magazine featured a more serious and intellectual look. The new magazine also offered expanded international coverage and more in-depth analysis. No longer forced to bow to advertising pressure, the first issue of the new *Ms.* contained both criticism of advertisers' attempts to control media content and pointed apologies for advertisements the magazine regretted running in the past.

The advertisement-free format was a success, winning back many of the serious feminist readers that had abandoned the journal during the years of compromising with advertisers, and *Ms.* has continued its moves toward independence. Though woman-owned for its first fifteen years, the journal has since been owned by several different publishers, and it has always chafed at being forced to remain under mostly male ownership. In the late 1990s, Steinem again led the journal toward a new definition by seeking female investors with the aim of placing control of *Ms.* totally in the hands of women once again.

Born almost at the beginning of the women's liberation movement, *Ms.* has always been a very public representation of that movement. As such, it has drawn both kudos and reproach from both supporters and critics of feminism. Nonfeminist detractors often stereotyped the magazine with the same epithets used for feminists themselves, calling it shrill, petty, and humorless. Feminists have also always been quick to take *Ms.* to task when the magazine has fallen short of their expectations. Conservative feminists have questioned the magazine's liberal bias, while radicals have consistently complained that *Ms.* does not go far enough.

One of the most unique features in *Ms.* is the letters section. The magazine receives hundreds of letters a month, some laudatory, some critical, and many simply telling the reader's story. It is this very personal interaction among its readers that sets *Ms.* apart from other magazines, just as the principle "the personal is political" gave the feminist movement its unique perspective.

GLORIA STEINEM

There is no name more commonly associated with *Ms.* magazine than Gloria Steinem's. An early proponent of women's liberation, Steinem was born in 1934 in Ohio. She learned early about the difficulties that women face when her parents divorced when she was twelve. Steinem was then raised by her mother, a journalist who struggled with depression and societal attitudes about single mothers. She began to earn her flamboyant reputation as a feminist writer and personality in 1963, when she wrote the article "I Was a Playboy Bunny," about her experiences working undercover in a Playboy Club. After cofounding *Ms.* in 1971, she edited the magazine until 1987, then rejoined the staff as consulting editor in 1990. The first issue of the woman-financed *Ms.*, in April 1999, included a letter from Steinem in which she reviewed the magazine's history. She ends ebulliently, "I can't wait to see what happens now."

In the early twenty-first century *Ms.* continued to undergo change. On December 31, 2001, the Feminist Majority Foundation purchased the magazine through the female consortium Liberty Media for Women, of which. Steinem is a member. While continuing to offer popular features, such as "Backtalk" and "No Comment," the publication extended its focus to include the international community of women. For instance, the 2012 winter issue includes a wide range of topics, such as women and technology, international political leaders, same-sex marriages, and the current status of feminism. While other feminist magazines exist and traditional women's magazines are more supportive of women's issues, *Ms.* was there first to articulate and define feminism at a time when it mattered most.

Tina Gianoulis

SEE ALSO: *Advertising; Feminism;* McCall's Magazine*;* Rolling Stone*; Steinem, Gloria;* Vanity Fair*; Wonder Woman.*

BIBLIOGRAPHY

Bean, Kellie. *Post-Backlash Feminism: Women and the Media since Reagan-Bush.* Jefferson, NC: McFarland, 2007.

Farrell, Amy Erdman. *Yours in Sisterhood: "Ms." Magazine and the Promise of Popular Feminism.* Chapel Hill: University of North Carolina Press, 1998.

Pogrebin, Abigail. "How Do You Spell Ms.?" *New York,* November 2011. Accessed April 2, 2012. Available from http://nymag.com/news/features/ms-magazine-2011-11/

Sigerman, Harriet. *The Columbia Documentary History of American Women since 1941.* New York: Columbia University Press, 2007.

Thom, Mary. *Inside "Ms.": 25 Years of the Magazine and the Feminist Movement.* New York: Holt, 1997.

Van Gelder, Lindsy. "Chronicle and Crucible." *Nation,* August 11, 1997, 27.

MTV

MTV (Music Television) is one of the most important pop culture phenomena developed in the late twentieth century. As a medium, it united the two most important popular culture developments of the post–World War II era: rock-and-roll music and television. In the decades since its birth in 1981, MTV has defined an international youth culture centered on the rebellious spirit of rock music and the ceaseless consumption of goods. To

MTV VJs. *The original MTV VJs were, from top left, Nina Blackwood, Mark Goodman, and from bottom left, Alan Hunter, Martha Quinn, and J.J. Jackson.* MARK WEISS/WIREIMAGE/GETTY IMAGES.

many millions of youthful viewers scattered across the globe MTV is the preeminent medium of global youth culture, offering an intoxicating mix of music, postmodern imagery, consumer goods, and original programming. To its owner, cable television giant Viacom, MTV is a highly profitable channel that offers advertisers unparalleled access to a youthful audience. But to its many critics MTV is a corrupter of youth, a purveyor of mindless consumerism, and a degrader of all that is authentic about music.

A MODEST START

Though its reach is now global, MTV had humble beginnings. The channel was born at midnight on August 1, 1981, a NASA rocket launch countdown preparing viewers for the sudden appearance of a blank screen, a succession of moon shots, and the image of astronaut Neil Armstrong planting an MTV flag in the lunar dust. A male baritone voice dramatically proclaimed, "Ladies and gentlemen, rock and roll," and the Buggles' "Video Killed the Radio Star" became the first in a string of music videos to appear in the homes of 800,000 Warner Amex Satellite Entertainment Company (WASEC) subscribers.

The idea of the video itself was not new. African American performers Count Basie, Louie Armstrong, and Bessie Smith appeared in video clips of their songs in the late 1940s; Dick Clark's *American Bandstand* dance show offered "live" (lip-synched) musical performances to a national television audience beginning in 1957; the Beatles released their song "Strawberry Fields Forever" on video in 1967; and other 1970s television shows—*Soul Train, In Concert, Midnight Special,* and *Rock Concert*—offered live or recorded musical performances. But MTV gambled that the viewing audience in 1981 was ready for an around-the-clock music channel. It was a gamble that soon paid off.

The brain behind MTV was Robert Pittman, a former radio disc jockey who had become an executive at WASEC. Pittman hoped that MTV—along with the premium channels Nickelodeon and the Movie Channel—would give his company an edge in gaining subscribers in the highly competitive cable market. The company's $20 million investment soon proved worthwhile. MTV's audience grew from just over two million to twenty-two million in 1984 alone, and advertising revenues kept pace. Though the channel had pulled in just $7 million in advertising revenue within eighteen months, by 1984 it was earning $1 million a week.

In many ways MTV had an ideal cable product: its content cost the channel nothing because recording companies provided the videos free of charge in order to promote their bands, and advertisers, eager to reach MTV's demographic of consumers between the ages of twelve and thirty-four, offered everything from food to clothes to other youth-oriented products. Through the early 1980s MTV viewers were fed a steady diet of videos and ads; in a 1983 piece for *Film Comment*, Richard Gehr described the format as "ersatz commercials punctuated by 'real' ones."

"I WANT MY MTV"

The first videos to air on MTV appear rudimentary and awkward compared to current efforts. The total video rotation during the channel's initial months was a scant 125 videos. The common denominator for the videos was their slipshod production, nonexistent special effects, minimal cost, crude narratives, and home-movie-type appearance. A favorite in the first months was Chris de Burgh's "Don't Pay the Ferryman," a moody Greek myth–inspired narrative about a boat trip across the river Styx with the Grim Reaper as companion.

The quality of videos improved fairly rapidly thanks in no small part to the "King of Pop." Michael Jackson's 1982 release *Thriller* featured three videos—"Thriller," "Billie Jean," and "Beat It"—that revolutionized the art form and galvanized public attention. The video for "Thriller," for example, began with a long introduction by horror film guru Vincent Price, was filmed in a graveyard, and cost an estimated $1.1 million. Hyped for weeks before its release, then debuting in select theaters before it came to MTV, "Thriller" was the first of many videos to generate a buzz of anticipation.

MTV's innovative format and seamless blend of content and advertising drew much attention from academics eager to document the emergence of a postmodern frame of mind. David Tetzlaff observed in a 1986 issue of the *Journal of Communication Inquiry* that "MTV denies the existence of all but the moment, and that moment exists only on the screen"; in *Monopoly Television*, Jack Banks writes that MTV "repudiates linear conceptions of history, rejecting conventional distinctions between past, present, and future, instead placing itself in a timeless present." The result is an experience that encourages viewers to identify more with the products and images on-screen than with historically significant communities of meaning such as families, political parties, or social classes. Even after MTV changed to a more traditional format in the mid-1980s, even after so many advertisements and television programs began to mimic MTV's visual style, the perception remains that MTV leads the postmodern cultural vanguard.

EARLY CRITICISM

MTV's rapid emergence as both a profitable cable channel and a cultural force immediately drew critics. Some African American artists accused MTV of racism for what they felt was a real underrepresentation of nonwhite musicians, though MTV defended itself with the claim that it merely mirrored trends in album-oriented rock. Jackson's mid-1980s dominance as king of the video also served to temper claims of racism. Surgeon General C. Everett Koop, who served under President Ronald Reagan, charged that the heady brew of video clips—which he characterized as racy montages of violence, scantily clad women, and surreal images—could be dangerous to normal or healthy emotional relationships between the sexes. And media mogul Ted Turner accused MTV of producing a nation of "Hitler Youth" (though his hyperbole may have been influenced by the failure of his competing music channel, Cable Music Channel, in 1984).

These were merely the first times that MTV was accused of undermining the morals of America's youth; they were far from the last. But it was difficult to tell if such concerns were legitimate responses to real increases in the amount of sex and violence on the screen or ongoing anxiety felt by members of older generations about the music that makes their children dance. MTV might be truly dangerous, or old folks might just be scared of rock and roll.

MTV experienced growing pains during the mid-1980s. On the one hand all was going well: MTV and other video channels proved to be such a lucrative way to market music that fully 75 percent of singles released were backed by a video.

Moreover, MTV was acquired in 1986 by cable giant Viacom, a move that got MTV into more American homes than ever before. On the other hand, MTV's Nielsen ratings declined from their *Thriller*-induced highs, the channel's coverage of the Live Aid music festival was harshly criticized, and the British art rockers like Duran Duran, the Eurhythmics, and Boy George, who helped MTV establish an identity, were going out of style. Ad revenues declined during the first half of 1987, prompting *Time* magazine to wonder if MTV was "an idea whose time has already gone?" The concern was premature—the one thing MTV has never done is fail to meet the ever-changing demands and interests of its youthful audience.

ORIGINAL PROGRAMMING

In its second phase, MTV devised the radical strategy of downplaying music videos and inventing its own programs. In this way MTV hoped to become a more traditional television channel, breaking with its most postmodern elements. MTV's original programming included *Club MTV* (dance), *The Week in Rock* (news related to the world of rock and roll), and *Remote Control* (a parody of a traditional game show in which contestants were strapped into La-Z-Boy recliners, fed pork rinds and cheese puffs, and asked moronic questions). Most innovative was the program *Yo! MTV Raps*, a compilation of rap videos. Although MTV executives were hesitant about this show's potential, viewer response was tremendous and the show quickly became one of the most popular summer programs on the air. By the mid-1990s, rap and hip-hop had become MTV mainstays.

MTV realized another breakthrough in the early 1990s with its *Unplugged* shows, which showcased top rock bands playing acoustic instruments before a small audience. With this show MTV achieved 1990s media synergy: the *Unplugged* shows generated singles for radio play, videos that could be plugged elsewhere in the channel's lineup, and albums that could be sold in record stores. By allowing the spirit of rock and roll to seep into news and comedy, and by showcasing the innovative music that was coming out of the predominantly African American rap and hip-hop community, MTV gave viewers a reason to stick around.

MTV continued its experiments with content into the 1990s, offering such shows as *Beavis and Butt-Head*, a cartoon about two completely amoral teenage slackers. These antisocial characters set fire to houses; use frogs for batting practice; obsess about women and farts; and are, all in all, mind-numbingly stupid. The show, which was an instant success, became a lightning rod for public fears about the amorality of youth and, not coincidentally, launched its creator, Mike Judge, to fame. (Judge left MTV to produce the cartoon series *King of the Hill* for Fox TV, but returned to relaunch *Beavis and Butt-Head* on MTV in 2011.) MTV's mid-1990s dating show, *Singled Out*, also proved a launching pad for ex–Playboy Playmate and show cohost Jenny McCarthy. McCarthy's combination of California surf babe beauty and bad girl antics—gross jokes and goofy faces—soon landed her an NBC sitcom.

REALITY TELEVISION

The Real World, MTV's original reality program, debuted in 1992 with thirteen episodes set in New York. In *The Real World*, a group of college-age strangers are thrown together in a beautiful house and a camera films every moment of their attempts to learn to live together. Editors cull the mass of footage down to hourly episodes that combine the authenticity of real emotion with the narrative hooks of daytime soap operas. The show was an instant hit, and the experiment has been repeated again and again—more than twenty-five years after its debut, *The Real World* continues in ever more exotic locations.

In the late 1990s MTV sought to diversify its offerings and expand its influence over the youth market. The increasing popularity of reality shows like *The Real World* and *Road Rules* led to a gradual transfer of music-based programming to MTV's sister network, MTV2, which launched in 1996. Soon, even musicians themselves were lining up to take part in the reality TV craze, and in the first decade of the 2000s shows such as *The Osbournes, Carmen and Dave: An MTV Love Story, Meet the Barkers, Newlyweds: Nick & Jessica*, and *Run's House* offered fans a glimpse of the private lives of current and former music video stars.

By the end of the decade, reality shows such as *The Hills* and *Laguna Beach: The Real Orange County* began to depict MTV's target audience—teenagers and early twenty-somethings—living glamorous, carefree (though thoroughly melodramatic) lives in some of the most coveted ZIP codes in America. Viewers eventually tired of these unrealistic and highly stylized portrayals of the teen experience, and by the 2010s a new wave of reality series began to focus on real-life issues concerning teenagers and young adults, including teen pregnancy (*16 and Pregnant, Teen Mom*), health issues (*I Used to Be Fat*), cliques and bullying (*If You Really Knew Me*), and problems with the law (*Busted*). One major exception to this trend was *Jersey Shore*, which like *The Real World* centered on a group of young adults living together, this time a group of Italian Americans who embody the loud-mouthed, over-gelled, artificially tanned, and leopard-printed stereotype of young New Jerseyans. First aired in 2009, the show is something of a cultural phenomenon and has attracted more viewers than any other MTV show in history.

CULTURAL INFLUENCE

While MTV's programming echoes the channel's trademark irreverent and youthful attitude, its popularity and its crossover into movies and mainstream television mean that MTV's attitude is embraced more readily by the larger culture (which has itself been influenced by MTV). By 1990 MTV was available in more than fifty million American homes as part of many providers' basic cable packages. Its growing influence and the channel's desire to awaken a political consciousness in its youthful audience led MTV to campaign against the Gulf War in 1991 and to promote voter registration through such devices as "Rock the Vote" commercials starring rock stars and sponsoring registration drives at college campuses and rock concerts. MTV's most visible early entry into the political arena was its 1992 interview with Democratic presidential candidate Bill Clinton. For nearly ninety minutes Clinton fielded questions from a handpicked audience of earnest young people. Clinton discussed his first rock-and-roll experience—"going nuts over Elvis Presley"—and promised to come back to MTV as president (a promise he kept).

At the same time that MTV was becoming a pillar of American pop culture it was spreading across the globe. MTV debuted in Europe in 1987, offering as its first European video the Dire Straits tune "Money for Nothing," with its hypnotic chant, "I want my MTV." MTV Europe began with more than

1.6 million subscribers in fourteen different countries and became especially popular in Eastern European countries hungry for the baubles of Western capitalist culture that MTV proved so adept at displaying. MTV Brazil was launched in 1990 and MTV Latino followed in 1993; both channels quickly became popular with Spanish-speaking audiences accustomed to far fewer choices in their cable programming. On MTV Latino in 1995, viewers from Mexico to the tip of Chile watched the birth of a new language—"Spanglish"—as VJs used terms such as *Chequenos* (pronounced CHE-kay-nos), meaning "check us out."

MTV viewers the world over love rock and roll, but it is clear that they love different rock and roll at different times: in 1996 the hottest tracks on MTV Latino were by Madonna, Queen, and the Rolling Stones; on MTV Brazil the favorite was Silverchair; while on MTV Europe Jackson and Tina Turner dominated play lists. For their part, MTV's corporate officers enjoyed the music of money rolling in, as the channel brought in $2 for every dollar it spent in 1996.

Jorge Asis, Argentine writer and former minister of culture, commented about the cultural impact of MTV: "The world changed in a very short time. . . . Suddenly, one world fell, and it was absolutely seduced by the world that imposed itself, that won. . . . In a world without utopias, the market becomes a new utopia." Not surprisingly, MTV executives took a more optimistic view of their global distribution. MTV's Sara Levinson claimed, "Music is the global language. We want to be the global rock 'n' roll village where we can talk to the youth worldwide." By the mid-1990s MTV had largely succeeded at reaching that goal, and it promoted its vision of youth culture to 270 million households in more than 125 countries scattered across five continents.

CONTINUING EVOLUTION

The MTV vision is thoroughly rooted in consumerism, for the common language of viewers across the world is music and goods: Justin Timberlake and McDonald's, Britney Spears and Pepsi, Beyoncé Knowles and L'Oréal. To some critics, MTV's global reach seems like an Orwellian Big Brother nightmare, with rock-and-roll attitude providing the cover for multinational corporations to push their products to a world of consumers. But the actual picture is more complex, with a majority of MTV's programming produced locally to coincide with differing regional tastes.

As one of the most watched and most criticized networks on cable television, MTV is the epitome of American pop culture: loud, brash, provocative, opportunistic, and ever changing. For better or worse, no other cable network has wielded greater influence over international trends in music, fashion, or language. A pioneer in many aspects, MTV has helped curb discrimination based on gender, race, and sexual preference as much as it has perpetuated and celebrated America's obsession with sex, drugs, money, and the elusive fountain of youth. Part authentic expression of youth culture, part corporate marketing machine, the phenomenon that is MTV has captured all the contradictions and all the energy that have fueled pop culture since the 1980s.

Arthur Robinson

SEE ALSO: *Album-Oriented Rock;* American Bandstand*; Armstrong, Louis; Basie, Count; The Beatles;* Beavis and Butt-Head*; Boy George; Cable TV; Clark, Dick; Disc Jockeys; Game Shows; Gulf Wars;* The Hills*; Hip-Hop; Horror Movies; Jackson, Michael; Knowles, Beyoncé; La-Z-Boy Loungers; Madonna; McDonald's; NASA; Osbourne, Ozzy; Pepsi-Cola; Presley, Elvis; Price, Vincent; Rap; Reagan, Ronald;* The Real World*; Reality Television; Rock and Roll; The Rolling Stones; Smith, Bessie; Soap Operas;* Soul Train*; Spears, Britney; Teenagers; Television; Timberlake, Justin;* Time*; Turner, Ted; Videos; World War II.*

BIBLIOGRAPHY

Banks, Jack. *Monopoly Television: MTV's Quest to Control the Music.* Boulder, CO: Westview Press, 1996.

Buckley, William F., Jr. "Some Dare Call It Music." *National Review,* October 10, 1994, 87.

Denisoff, R. Serge. *Inside MTV.* New Brunswick, NJ: Transaction Books, 1988.

Gehr, Richard. "The MTV Aesthetic." *Film Comment* 19 (1983), 40.

Goodwin, Andrew. *Dancing in the Distraction Factory: Music Television and Popular Culture.* Minneapolis: University of Minnesota Press, 1992.

Kaplan, E. Ann. *Rocking around the Clock: Music Television, Postmodernism, and Consumer Culture.* New York: Methuen, 1987.

Lewis, Lisa A. *Gender Politics and MTV: Voicing the Difference.* Philadelphia: Temple University Press, 1990.

McGrath, Tom. *"Video Killed the Radio Star": How MTV Rocked the World.* New York: Villard Books, 1994.

McGrath, Tom. *MTV: The Making of a Revolution.* Philadelphia: Running Press, 1996.

Pegley, Kip. *Coming to You Wherever You Are: MuchMusic, MTV, and Youth Identities.* Middletown, CT: Wesleyan University Press, 2008.

Pozner, Jennifer. *Reality Bites Back: The Troubling Truth about Guilty Pleasure TV.* Berkeley, CA: Seal Press, 2010.

Scheurer, Timothy. *Born in the USA: The Myth of America in Popular Music from Colonial Times to the Present.* Jackson: University Press of Mississippi, 1991.

Walker, Chip. "Can TV Save the Planet?" *American Demographics,* May 1996, 42–49.

Muckraking

In 1906, his irritation with the popular press growing, President Theodore Roosevelt coined a new term for the journalists who had helped make, but were beginning to plague, his administration. As he laid the cornerstone for the new House of Representatives office building, he excoriated these *muckrakers* who, instead of respecting and enjoying America's turn-of-the-century prosperity, "continued to rake the filth on the floor." The term stuck, the word entered the language, and the period in U.S. history loosely dating from 1903 to 1912 became known as the muckraking era.

MCCLURE'S MAGAZINE

Muckraking, the investigative journalistic style pioneered by *McClure's* magazine and imitated by scores of U.S. periodicals, had its roots in late-nineteenth-century scandal mongering and yellow journalism. It differed from its precursors, however, in two important regards. Twentieth-century muckrakers aimed their rhetorical cannons strictly at the institutions of power in contemporary society, unlike the yellow journalists of the previous century who had taken sensationalist material from wherever they could find it. Furthermore, muckraking differed from yellow journalism in scope. While journalists regularly exposed local scandals in daily newspapers long before 1903, few such exposés treated national themes for a national audience until the early 1900s. In the single decade of the muckraking era, however, nearly 2,000 muckraking articles ran in U.S. periodicals, and magazines that specialized in muckraking sold an average of three million copies per month.

Historian David Chalmers argues that the muckraking era was born in the January 1903 issue of *McClure's*. Three important articles appeared in that single issue of the monthly magazine: Ida Tarbell weighed in on the economic might of the Standard Oil Trust; Ray Stannard Baker exposed corruption in the ranks of organized labor; and Lincoln Steffens unveiled "The Shame of Minneapolis"—the second chapter in his *The Shame of the Cities* series on municipal graft. In his editorial introduction to the issue, publisher S. S. McClure tied those three articles together and issued a manifesto for the muckraking era: "Capitalists, workingmen, politicians, citizens—all breaking the law, or letting it be broken. Who is left to uphold it? . . . There is no one left: none but all of us."

In "The Muckrake Man," an essay that appeared in the September 1908 issue of the *Independent*, Upton Sinclair, author of one of muckraking's few novelistic endeavors, *The Jungle* (1906), expounded on McClure's theme and attempted to further define muckraking. Sinclair claimed that he knew, "more or less intimately, nearly every man who is at present raking muck in America," and he set out "to speak from the standpoint of the group." Writing, then, for the movement as a whole, Sinclair explained that muckraking's social role was like that of "the particular nerve cell in the burned child which cries out to the child, 'Do not put your finger into the fire again!' [Sinclair's Muckrake Man] represents the effort of the race to profit by experience, and to do otherwise than repeat indefinitely the blunders which have proved fatal in the past."

MUCKRAKING'S INFLUENCE

It is difficult, of course, to assess the extent to which muckraking succeeded in its stated social mission. The instances in which it directly contributed to the breakup of a monopolistic trust or the reform of a corrupt municipal government are depressingly few, although Richard Hofstadter suggests that President Franklin Delano Roosevelt's New Deal sprang indirectly from the muckrakers' political critiques. Several contemporary commentators maintain that muckraking did little besides expand capital's influence in U.S. society by bringing advertisements for mass-produced goods to a new market of rising middle-class readers.

Still, muckraking exerted a seminal influence on U.S. popular culture. Indeed, although the muckraking era is said to have come to an end in 1912 in the wake of the expansion of U.S. newswire services and the rise of professional journalism, its techniques, if not always its moral spirit, continued to reign in the investigative press. Its anecdotal and personal style is echoed in current magazine journalism, and, at the end of the twentieth century, the fruits of the muckraker's nose for scandal continued to animate the front pages of U.S. newspapers.

CONTEMPORARY MUCKRAKING

Muckraking, or investigative journalism as it is more frequently known in the twenty-first century, has become accepted as a legitimate source of journalism and is considered an essential element in the public's right to know about social and political issues. Examples of contemporary muckraking range from the WikiLeaks website, on which tens of thousands of classified government documents were made available online, to former Vice President Al Gore's warnings about environmental destruction (*An Inconvenient Truth: The Planetary Emergency of Global Warming and What We Can Do about It*, 2006) to filmmaker Michael Moore's exposés (*Fahrenheit 9/11*, 2004; *Sicko*, 2007). The activities of Rupert Murdoch and his media empire in the first decade of the 2000s were not muckraking; many were performed with the cooperation of the UK government.

In a series of reports on contemporary muckraking in 2009, *Nieman Reports* suggested that the field is changing rapidly in the twenty-first century as print journalism loses financial backing and legal protections and as the scope of government interference has continued to expand post-9/11. In 2009 Russell Tice, a former analyst for the National Security Agency, admitted to MSNBC that the Bush administration regularly spied on journalists without obtaining warrants as part of the war on terror. In 2011 during civil unrest in Egypt, CNN correspondent Anderson Cooper and other journalists were beaten up by protesters, and a Belgian journalist was beaten, arrested, and accused of spying by unidentified civilians.

Around the world, journalists are being spied on, beaten, arrested, and even murdered. Technology is also having a major impact because journalists are able to locate information online and reach sources they would never find otherwise. The Internet also allows a higher level of anonymity for whistleblowers that was totally out of reach in the days when "Deep Throat" was supplying inside information on the Watergate scandal to *Washington Post* reporters Carl Bernstein and Bob Woodward.

Thurston Domina

SEE ALSO: *CNN; Global Warming;* An Inconvenient Truth*; The Internet; Mass Market Magazine Revolution; Moore, Michael; New Deal; Sinclair, Upton; Steffens, Lincoln; Tarbell, Ida; The* Washington Post*; Watergate; WikiLeaks.*

BIBLIOGRAPHY

Bernstein, Matthew H., ed. *Michael Moore: Filmmaker, Newsmaker, Cultural Icon.* Ann Arbor: University of Michigan Press, 2010.

Chalmers, David Mark. *The Social and Political Ideas of the Muckrakers.* New York: Citadel Press, 1964.

Feldstein, Mark. "The Challenges and Opportunities of 21st Century Muckraking." *Nieman Reports* 63, no. 2 (2009).

Keefe, Patrick Radden. *Chatter: Dispatches from the Secret World of Global Eavesdropping.* New York: Random House, 2005.

Merriner, James L. *Grafters and Goo Goos: Corruption and Reform in Chicago, 1833–2003.* Carbondale: Southern Illinois Press, 2004.

Miraldi, Robert. *Muckraking and Objectivity: Journalism's Colliding Traditions.* New York: Greenwood Press, 1990.

Serrin, Judith, and William Serrin. *Muckraking!: The Journalism That Changed America.* New York: New Press, 2002.

Sinclair, Upton. *The Jungle.* New York: Viking Press, 1906.

Steffens, Lincoln. *The Shame of the Cities*. New York: Hill & Wang, 1904.

Tichi, Cecelia. *Exposés and Excess: Muckraking in America, 1900/2000*. Philadelphia: University of Pennsylvania Press, 2004.

Multiculturalism

Multiculturalism is a catchall term that refers generally to a set of related cultural movements and trends that emphasize the diversity of U.S. culture and society. Its various projects seek to recognize, encourage, and affirm the participation of ethnic minorities in all aspects of American life. They tend to celebrate the contributions made by diverse groups and to consider those contributions as vital to the economic, social, and cultural fabric of the United States. In higher education, multiculturalism began to assume definitive shape during the 1980s as universities revised their programs, textbooks, and curricula to reflect a more inclusive view of American culture.

This change in focus toward inclusion of women, minorities, and non-Western texts and perspectives generated heated debate among academics and sparked the so-called culture wars of the 1980s and 1990s. On one side of the debate, critics argued that multiculturalism promoted factionalism and undermined the foundations of Western culture; proponents claimed that it advocated tolerance and equality. In any case, multiculturalism's impact has extended well beyond academe. It has shaped fashion trends, advertising campaigns, television programming, even corporate slogans, and continues to influence popular tastes in everything from music to food, home decor to literature.

ORIGIN OF MODERN MULTICULTURALISM

Multiculturalism can be said to resonate from the cultural eruptions of the 1960s, when civil rights, Native American, "new ethnicity," and women's liberation movements in the United States shattered images of a coherent national identity. The force and urgency of these protests challenged the authority and credibility of the establishment and shook the public's confidence in the social and political structures that validated it. Students marched in protest against America's involvement or intervention not only in Vietnam but also in Latin America and the Caribbean. In addition to questioning social conformity, economic inequality, and political legitimacy, voices rose in defiance against long-held cultural assumptions and myths.

As thousands of demonstrators across the nation expressed their defiance of U.S. policies and systems, Americans struggled to redefine their roles, values, and allegiances. Many strove to foster some sense of communal belonging, to forge a place for themselves within a more pliant cultural framework. Others questioned the desirability of aspiring to a unified national identity in an increasingly transnational world. The ensuing crisis of identity—on both the national and the personal level—paved the way for a number of institutional and social changes. In the aftermath of Vietnam and Watergate, America's collective self-image changed inexorably, slowly transforming itself to reflect shifting demographic and social realities.

During the 1970s and 1980s, Americans began catching glimpses of this emerging self-image on their television screens as sitcoms and TV dramas integrated their casts. Popular programs such as *Good Times* (1974), *Chico and the Man* (1974), *The Jeffersons* (1975), *Sanford and Son* (1972), and *CHiPS* (1977) featured blacks, Latinos, and other minorities as starring cast members. During the 1974–1975 season, *Sanford and Son* and *Chico and the Man* earned top five ratings.

Alex Haley's best-selling book *Roots* (1976) achieved tremendous success when it aired as a made-for-television movie in 1977. The six-part miniseries, which chronicled several generations of the author's family from their African origins through slavery, fueled a popular trend to discover and adopt formerly repressed ethnic identities. Seeking one's "roots" became fashionable, as did changing one's wardrobe, name, or hairstyle to reflect one's ancestry. In some cases these external transformations reflected a genuine attempt to build ethnic pride; in others it was simply a new fad, a hollow display of ethnic style without political substance. The melting pot ideology that had endorsed an assimilation ethic gradually gave way to new metaphors (such as the "salad" or "stir-fry"), which promoted the retention of discrete cultural traits. This celebration of difference (identified with postmodernist theory and art) found its niche in the popular imagination, adding dashes of color to a post-1960s American canvas.

MULTICULTURALISM ON THE BIG SCREEN

For the first time in America's history, being visibly "different" (belonging to a racial or ethnic subculture group) held commercial appeal. Hollywood responded to this appeal with several films (and sequels) with black leads. Movies such as *Superfly* (1972), *Shaft* (1971), and *The Mack* (1973) exploited images of black (mostly male) defiance of white authority and power. The 1970s saw the emergence of these mass images of blacks as pimps, drug dealers, or shady police officers. Elements of black street culture exploited and popularized in these early films reappeared a decade later, when a variation of these blaxploitation film images formed the impetus for the white music industry's marketing campaign for gangsta rap in the late 1980s and 1990s. Throughout much of that decade, hip-hop music outsold rock among white teens, and the clothing that accompanied it—baggy pants and oversize polo shirts—infiltrated middle America.

Other historically oppressed groups also gained audiences. The commercial appeal of "difference" led to the release of a slew of movies in the 1990s such as *Dances with Wolves* (1990), *Thunderheart* (1992), and a remake of *The Last of the Mohicans* (1992). These films reformulated the standard "cowboys and Indians" genre and offered a different perspective of Native American cultures and histories. Native American perspectives, virtually invisible in history books and films until the late twentieth century, gained status and recognition, Hollywood style. Mainstream audiences across America lined up to see Native Americans depicted, not as savages bent on murdering innocent white women and children, but as a people staunchly defending their way of life. Too often, however, even in these films, the protagonist was either a white person or a Native American portrayed by a white actor.

These twists in Hollywood image-making gradually reconstituted the public's collective memory of historical events and personages. In most cases, these films recycled conventional plots, simply adapting the point of view or integrating the cast. Even so, they did help refashion the sensibilities of a generation of Americans. In part, they helped to prepare general audiences for a multiculturalist reexamination of U.S. history—including a reinterpretation of such grand historical narratives as Manifest

Destiny, the Great Frontier Myth, and egalitarian democracy. Documentary filmmakers have also taken a critical look at Hollywood's version of multicultural awareness: *Images of Indians* (1979) and *The Media Show: North American Indians* (1991) examined Hollywood film stereotypes of Native Americans; *From Here, from This Side* (1988) envisioned cultural domination from the Mexican point of view; *Slaying the Dragon* (1987) explored the imaging of the "docile Asian female" type; and *Color Adjustment* (1991) chronicled the history of black representation on TV. But these critiques did not for the most part impinge on the popular mind-set, as the heightened visibility of minorities fueled both complacency ("they are making progress") and discomfort ("they are taking over").

MULTICULTURALISM IN ADVERTISING

The reimaging of America did foster new images of blacks, Latinos, Asians, and other ethnic group members as middle-class consumers. Recognizing the potential buying power represented by the largest minority groups in the country—African Americans, Latinos, and Asian Americans—advertisers began targeting these long-ignored segments of the U.S. population. Major retailers such as Sears introduced "ethnic" clothing lines—with *ethnic* broadly defined as the use of bright colors and patterns. Cosmetic companies began catering to darker skin tones, using Latina and African American models to promote their products. New interest in regional cultures influenced architecture and interior design, so that Hopi Indian art, Mexican pottery, and southwest crafts might be seen vying for prominence in any suburban home.

In the emerging global economy, multiculturalism translated into multinationalism as American corporations targeted foreign markets. Businesses responded to an increasingly polyglot multicultural environment by offering employee training programs aimed at teaching foreign languages and customs or heightening awareness of diversity issues. Similarly, European companies climbed on the multicultural bandwagon, some using indigenous people as models or spokespersons. The Italian multinational corporation Benetton ran one of the most successful ad campaigns in history by capitalizing on the diversity theme. The slogan "United Colors of Benetton," featured along with the faces of Latino, African, and Asian "types," established the company's multiculturalist image and helped market its high-end clothes worldwide.

MULTICULTURALISM IN EDUCATION

While the "crossover" success of television shows, movies, music, and ads featuring minorities suggested that popular audiences were increasingly receptive to social change, critics continued to point out the contrast between mass-mediated images of successful minorities and their social realities. The heightened visibility of blacks and other minorities on TV and in films signaled progress to some, but to others it fell short of the mark. Critics argued that education must reflect its constituency and serve as the catalyst for a profound change in national consciousness. This required a revamping of an educational system that traditionally excluded or undervalued the contributions of blacks and other minorities within a pluralist U.S. society. Classroom teachers, after all, were not dealing with images but with an increasingly heterogeneous student population. By 1990, minority youngsters accounted for about 32 percent of total enrollment in U.S. public schools—a figure that has continued to rise. Multiculturalists argued that course materials and content scarcely registered this demographic reality.

Subsequent curriculum changes sought to provide a broader knowledge base, extending beyond what has been referred to as a "Eurocentric" approach to education. Such an approach tends to assume the centrality of European thought, history, and culture, relegating all others to a peripheral or even a subordinate role. Standard core courses in schools and universities traditionally stressed the achievements and merits of Western civilization, often reducing the rest of the world to irrelevance. Multiculturalists insisted that exposure to a variety of ethnic perspectives and traditions was both intellectually enriching and socially responsible.

As its influence spread throughout U.S. colleges and universities, multiculturalism generated considerable controversy. In history and English departments, particularly, multiculturalism led to the reevaluation of standard texts that had formed the basis of Western culture. In some cases, this reevaluation revealed gaps, contradictions, and inconsistencies that raised questions about significant events or offered competing versions of history. As more and more voices claimed their right to be heard, "official" accounts were increasingly challenged or revised. Newly minted textbooks and anthologies referenced Native American folktales, testimonials, and cosmologies; diaries and journals by Spanish explorers in the New World; slave narratives and spirituals; women's histories and political essays.

While examining these varied texts and contexts, students might explore the relative worth of ideas and artifacts, sometimes dismantling their own cultural assumptions in the process. They might consider the links between social grouping and status or power, question existing hierarchies, or explore their conceptual and economic frameworks. Critics claimed that multicultural readings gave rise to identity politics—politics based on notions of identity defined by race, gender, sexual orientation, ethnicity, or religion. They accused multiculturalists of politicizing education, of turning the classroom into a political soapbox for professors with their own agendas or gripes. Advocates of the new pedagogy countered with claims of their own: They argued that education had *always* been political, as its institutional goals and methods traditionally served a dominant ideology. They questioned why selectively excluding women and minorities from the canon was not deemed "political" but intentionally including them was. Both cases, advocates reasoned, reflected underlying power struggles and tensions. These issues stirred vigorous debate among academics, often dividing departments into pro- and anti-multiculturalism camps.

MULTICULTURALISM IN LITERATURE

During the 1980s and 1990s, advocates of multiculturalism waged war on the literary canon, introducing new works into their courses and discarding others deemed outdated or irrelevant. As some administrators and faculty members moved to institute a multicultural curriculum, others voiced opposition, often criticizing not only the revised content but also the methods by which it was implemented. By the late 1980s, many university English departments had begun redefining themselves and their function in relation to the broader cultural landscape. In the process, challenging questions presented themselves: What disciplinary boundaries, if any, should delineate the critical study of literary texts? Should English departments broaden their focus to include major works written by non-English-speaking authors in their core curricula? Should they integrate poetry and fiction by women, U.S. minorities, and minoritarian cultures into existing courses or develop special program areas such as women's or ethnic studies?

Most literature by non-Europeans traditionally fell under the rubric of "world literature," a category that conflated Latin America, the Caribbean, Africa, Asia, and other areas into one indistinct cultural mass. Multiculturalists maintained that these diverse cultures not only produced art and literature worthy of recognition, but also offered valuable insights and perspectives on philosophical, religious, ethical, and social questions. Some argued that rather than being peripheral, the study of non-Western civilizations and traditions was integral to understanding the complex interconnectedness of the human experience. English studies programs progressively changed their parameters, becoming increasingly interdisciplinary in content and methodology. This trend toward interdisciplinary study spread across programs, breaking down the traditional boundaries between history and literature, psychology and sociology, or philosophy and science.

Literature written by people of color, however, had successfully infiltrated the mainstream by the 1980s, with novels by Toni Morrison, Leslie Marmon Silko, and Alice Walker among the best sellers. Walker's Pulitzer Prize–winning novel *The Color Purple* was made into a critically acclaimed film directed by Steven Spielberg. Morrison, the first black woman to receive the Nobel Prize in Literature, had already established an international reputation by the time her novel *Beloved* (1987) won a Pulitzer Prize in 1988 and was made into a major motion picture in the late 1990s. In 1993 Amy Tan's best seller *The Joy Luck Club* was also made into a popular film, along with Oscar Hijuelos's *The Mambo Kings Play Songs of Love*. These and many other successful "crossover" books suggested that multiculturalism—whatever its putative flaws or disputed benefits—had already moved into the popular arena.

MULTICULTURALISM IN SOCIETY

The influence of multiculturalism was also felt in personal, professional, and social relationships. Couples grappled with issues of equality, friends and teachers with questions of tolerance and respect, managers with the challenges of communicating with their multicultural clientele. As more women and minorities asserted their rights in the workplace and in the classrooms, individuals faced new legal, professional, and social questions: What constitutes sexual harassment or discrimination? Which words or behaviors are considered racist or sexist? What actions are considered breaches of racial etiquette? What hiring practices need to be instituted to ensure equity, and when are those practices discriminatory against formerly privileged white males?

The ensuing race, gender, and ethnic politics led to a backlash among those who objected to multiculturalism's methods or goals. The epithet "political correctness" (PC) was coined to describe what some considered a dictatorial, restrictive new code of conduct. In some cases, it merely served as a means to dismiss actual abuses or offences. Multiculturalists, portrayed as the "PC Patrol," became a favorite target of conservative talk show hosts, comedy shows, and radio disc jockeys. Just as nineteenth-century caricatures of suffragettes had ridiculed and trivialized women's efforts to gain the right to vote, so do these contemporary images of "Feminazis" and PC enforcers often distort multiculturalism's principal aims and effects.

At the onset of the twenty-first century, America's demographics mirrored in fact what was still debated in theory. Multiculturalism had made tremendous inroads, but it also confronted emerging challenges. On the one hand, the tragic events of September 11, 2001, roused nativist sentiments in American society, fueling the backlash against multiculturalism and reigniting debates about its meanings and effects. On the other hand, the new millennium also marked the election of the first African American president of the United States. Given America's racial history, Barack Obama's election suggested that the walls that kept African American men and women out of the higher echelons of political power were, if not obliterated, at least crumbling. Embodied in this mixed-race, cosmopolitan American president some saw a bellwether of multiculturalism's triumphant progress, while others took the view that Obama personified its deficient or even threatening effects. To still others, Obama's election signaled America's emergence as a "post-racial" culture in which the old hierarchies of race and ethnicity had become irrelevant.

Post-racial discourse represents yet another roadblock in multiculturalism's path to legitimacy, as it bolsters calls for the elimination of race-based affirmative action programs or initiatives aimed at increasing minority representation. Identified by its opponents as a form of regressive tribalism or condemned to irrelevancy by a presumably color-blind post-racial American culture, multiculturalism has yet to settle into a complacent middle age. Instead, in a world grown progressively more interconnected by technological, economic, and political cross-currents, multiculturalism is neither a panacea for social injustice nor the bane of so-called Western culture. It reflects seismic shifts in social attitudes, and just as importantly, registers trends that have been transforming global interrelations for decades.

Myra Mendible

SEE ALSO: *Blaxploitation Films; Feminism; Gangsta Rap;* Good Times*; Haley, Alex; Hip-Hop; Hippies; Hollywood;* The Jeffersons*; Made-for-Television Movies; Morrison, Toni; 9/11; Obama, Barack; Political Correctness; Protest Groups;* Roots*;* Sanford and Son*;* Shaft*; Spielberg, Steven; Student Demonstrations; Television; Walker, Alice; Watergate.*

BIBLIOGRAPHY

D'Souza, Dinesh. *Illiberal Education: The Politics of Race and Sex on Campus*. New York: Free Press, 1991.

Gates, Henry Louis, Jr. *Loose Canons: Notes on the Culture Wars*. New York: Oxford University Press, 1993.

Goldberg, David Theo, ed. *Multiculturalism: A Critical Reader*. Cambridge, MA: Blackwell Publishers, 1994.

Gutmann, Amy, ed. *Multiculturalism: Examining the Politics of Recognition*. Princeton, NJ: Princeton University Press, 1994.

Hoy, Jocelyn. *Reflections on Political Correctness: A Collection of Student Papers on Multiculturalism, Speech Codes, and "The Canon."* Santa Cruz: University of California Press, 1992.

Lott, Bernice E. *Multiculturalism and Diversity: A Social Psychological Perspective*. New York: John Wiley, 2010.

Shohat, Ella, and Robert Stam. *Unthinking Eurocentrism: Multiculturalism and the Media*. New York: Routledge, 1994.

The Mummy

The ancient Egyptians' tradition of preserving the bodies of their dead has fascinated historians and travelers for centuries, and perhaps it is only natural that such preserved corpses have found their way into the U.S. film industry's lexicon of horror.

A near-perfect synthesis of Dracula and Frankenstein, the mummy is a supernatural (as opposed to a medico-scientific) representative of the living dead class of horror film monsters.

Acclaimed cinematographer Karl Freund (*Metropolis, Murders in the Rue Morgue*) made his directorial debut with Universal's *The Mummy* (1932), otherwise known as *Cagliostro* and *Imhotep*. Originally conceived as a vehicle for English actor Boris Karloff, screenwriter John Balderston (*Dracula*) rewrote the film after the 1922 discovery of King Tut's tomb. Accidentally brought back to life when some archaeologists read from a sacred Egyptian scroll, the mummy (Karloff) goes on a mission to claim the soul of a young Englishwoman who turns out to be his beloved but forbidden princess reincarnated. Attempting to thwart him is Doctor Muller (Edward Van Sloan, reprising his role as Van Helsing in *Dracula*). At least ten *Mummy* spin-offs and even more zombie movies followed, including a 1955 comedy titled *Abbott and Costello Meet the Mummy.*

In 1989 gothic novelist Anne Rice published *The Mummy, or Ramses the Damned: A Novel*, and in 1999 a new film series began with director Stephen Sommers's film *The Mummy*, starring Arnold Vosloo as the title monster. Rather than an old-style horror movie, the new film was an action-adventure romp, and computer-generated special effects replaced the spirit gum and distressed bandages that had transformed Karloff. *The Mummy* opened to record profits, prompting at least two sequels, *The Mummy Returns* in 2001 and *The Mummy: Tomb of the Dragon Emperor* in 2008.

Steven Schneider

SEE ALSO: *Abbott and Costello; Dracula; Frankenstein; Horror Movies; Karloff, Boris.*

BIBLIOGRAPHY

Guran, Paula. "The Mummy." In *Icons of Horror: An Encyclopedia of Our Worst Nightmares, Vol. 1.*, ed. S. T. Joshi. Westport, CT: Greenwood Press, 2007.

Rice, Anne. *The Mummy, or Ramses the Damned: A Novel.* New York: Ballantine Books, 1989.

Robertson, Barbara. "Bad to the Bone." *Computer Graphics World*, May 1999, 34.

Twitchell, James B. *Dreadful Pleasures: An Anatomy of Modern Horror.* New York: Oxford University Press, 1985.

Muni, Paul *(1895–1967)*

Paul Muni was considered the foremost serious character actor of 1930s cinema. He came to prominence with a number of contemporary-issue movies, including *Scarface* (1932) and *I Am a Fugitive from a Chain Gang* (1932). He maintained his success through biographical pictures such as *The Story of Louis Pasteur* (1936), *The Life of Emile Zola* (1937), and *Juarez* (1939). He approached each of his roles with unprecedented research into makeup, character, dialect, and background. Although his professionalism is to be admired, even by the 1940s his style was considered by many to be overstated, trite, and dated. A major source of his unprecedented success was, perhaps, a Depression-era audience in dire need of uplifting through simple stories about larger-than-life heroes.

Kyle Smith

SEE ALSO: *The Great Depression.*

BIBLIOGRAPHY

Druxman, Michael B. *Paul Muni: His Life and His Films.* New York: Barnes, 1974.

Lawrence, Jerome. *Actor: The Life and Times of Paul Muni.* New York: Putnam, 1974.

Munsey's Magazine

In 1893 a former telegraph operator named Frank A. Munsey made his namesake the first nationally distributed and mass-read magazine. Munsey, who had grown up poor in rural Maine, recognized that most of the growing middle class in the United States could not afford magazines, so he dropped the cover price of his failing literary monthly from twenty-five to ten cents per copy. Advertisers made up the difference by paying more for and increasing the number of their ads. Munsey also proved that sex sold magazines, publishing a regular page called "Artists & Their Work," which featured a halftone photograph of a draped or undraped female in an artistic setting. *Munsey's Magazine* jumped in readership overnight, becoming the world circulation leader by 1907, and came to be recognized as the prototype of the modern popular magazine. As he made his magazine universally available, Munsey also paved the way for what is now called the Information Age.

EARLY MAGAZINES

The first two U.S. magazines, published by Andrew Bradford and Benjamin Franklin, appeared in 1741, but the periodical industry grew slowly over the next century. Thousands of titles appeared, but all but a few were financial failures with low circulations, little or no advertising, and poor revenue. None could claim a wide national readership. Several "quality" literary journals—*Harper's, Atlantic Monthly*, and *Century*—began to appear and prosper around 1850, but they were much too expensive for the newly emerging educated middle class, especially by yearly subscription. A few women's magazines—*Ladies' Home Journal, Delineator*, and *Woman's Home Companion*—built mass circulations after the American Civil War, but they were specialized in their viewpoint, featured editorial content strongly influenced by advertisers, and were overlooked by most advertisers and the magazine industry because women had not yet been recognized as a viable national mass market.

Munsey was born on August 21, 1854, and grew up on a series of struggling farms near Augusta, Maine. He began making his own way in the world at the age of seven, but it was a visit to the 1876 World's Fair that inspired him to build the first magazine and newspaper publishing empire. At Philadelphia's Centennial Exposition, Munsey saw one of a new breed of R. Hoe & Company's stereotype plate rotary presses spewing out thousands of newspapers per hour and resolved that he would be the proprietor of such an impressive machine one day. To make his dream come true, he wrote freelance articles for local newspapers and saved the money he earned as a telegraph operator. He also convinced several Augusta businesspeople of his prospects and was able to raise enough capital to move to New York City on September 23, 1882. There he founded *Golden Argosy: Freighted with Treasures for Boys and Girls.* The first issue featured several articles, including "Do and Dare, or a Brave Boy's Fight for a Fortune," a short story written by self-success advocate Horatio Alger Jr. that could have been Munsey's own story.

The market for juvenile magazines in the United States was crowded in the late nineteenth century, and Munsey was often broke and always in debt for the first five years of *Argosy*. He began changing the direction of the magazine away from children and more toward teenage boys and men by 1885, but his periodical still failed to capture the public's imagination. Frustrated, Munsey used his own writings and the contributions of the small *Argosy* editorial staff to fill the inaugural issue of the adult literary magazine, *Munsey's Weekly*, on February 2, 1889. The magazine seemed inexpensive at ten cents per copy, but a yearly subscription was still too expensive for most potential middle-class readers, and it lost thousands of dollars over the next two years, even though it built a circulation of 40,000.

MUNSEY'S REVAMPED

In October 1891 Munsey took a gamble. He changed his namesake to a monthly, gave it the same size and look as *Harper's* and the other profitable literary monthlies, and raised its price to twenty-five cents per copy. To differentiate himself from his competitors, he concentrated on light, easy-to-read articles and novelettes, "a complete novel in each number," instead of serious literature and criticism. He also featured the cutting-edge publishing technology of halftone photographs instead of the fine-line wood engravings featured in most other magazines. Still, *Munsey's* lost money. The depression of 1893 made it even more difficult for Munsey to borrow money to keep his floundering magazine business afloat, so he took yet another gamble, dropping *Munsey's* cover price to ten cents per copy and the cost of a subscription to $1 a year.

Munsey's was neither the first magazine to sell at ten cents nor even the first to make a dramatic price cut. *Ladies' Home Journal* built its circulation by selling for a nickel before it raised its price to ten cents in the early 1890s. S. S. McClure dropped the price of his soon-to-become famous magazine to fifteen cents an issue in June 1893, and in response, John Brisben Walker cut the price of his new general-interest monthly, *Cosmopolitan*, from twenty-five to twelve and a half cents in July. *Munsey's* did not fall to ten cents until September. But in lowering his price, Munsey made his periodical the first that was truly affordable to the nation's middle class. To help build circulation at such a cheap price, he bypassed the expensive wholesale magazine distribution monopoly then in existence and advertised to readers directly, using mailed circulars and newspaper advertising.

The result revolutionized the magazine industry. *Munsey's* monthly circulation climbed from 40,000 before its price change to 100,000 in late 1893, 500,000 in 1895, and 700,000 by 1897. His four magazines—*Munsey's*, *Argosy*, *Scrap Book*, and *All-Story*—peaked in March 1906, with a combined circulation of 2.1 million. An average turn-of-the-twentieth-century *Munsey's* featured 160 pages of text and as many as 100 pages of ads, unprecedented figures for the day. Advertising revenues alone averaged $25,000 to $35,000 per issue and more. Munsey toned back the nudity in his "Artists & Their Work" section beginning in 1895 but not before a reputation and market had been created. He featured a monthly section on famous personalities long before celebrities became a magazine mainstay. He solicited fiction and nonfiction writings from well-known authors and public men such as Theodore Dreiser, William Dean Howells, Arthur Conan Doyle, and Theodore Roosevelt, but most of his contributors were modestly paid unknowns. Munsey produced his magazine cheaply on his own printing equipment. Even his signature halftone photographs were acquired cheaply, reproductions of artworks, theatrical pictures, or portraits.

MUNSEY'S PRINCIPLES

One aspect of magazines at the turn of the twentieth century that Munsey never embraced was muckraking. The January 1900 *Munsey's* featured two articles critical of industrial trusts and monopolies, the basic fodder of muckraking, but that was all. While *McClure's*, *Cosmopolitan*, and other muckrake periodicals built their fame and circulations with exposé-style journalism, Munsey stayed with lighter, less critical fare. "*Munsey's Magazine* has never been committed to the muck-raking theory, and never will be," Munsey explained in 1910. "Muck-raking is one thing, and progress is quite another." He was a strong political supporter of progressive Theodore Roosevelt, becoming the primary financier of Roosevelt's ill-fated third-party bid in 1912, but he never considered his magazines a platform for the crusading reforms that marked progressivism.

Munsey admired millionaires, especially J. Pierpont Morgan, the prime financier of U.S. industrial monopolies at the turn of the twentieth century. Like Morgan, Munsey resolved to knit the disparate United States together into one mass marketplace for his product—information—using the newest technology. Beyond halftones and high-speed presses, he used two other recent innovations to make his magazines a success. The telephone allowed quick contact with faraway distributors, eliminating the need for middleman news agencies. Improved railroad shipping services, especially to the untapped markets of the West, made timely distribution of a national magazine such as *Munsey's* possible for the first time in U.S. history.

The profits from his magazines gave Munsey capital to branch out into the newspaper industry, and at one time or another he owned some of the best-known papers in the country, including the *New York Daily News*, *New York Sun*, *New York Herald*, *Washington Times*, *Philadelphia Evening Times*, and *Boston Journal*. As with magazines, Munsey tinkered with his newspapers, reducing and raising prices; using red ink for headlines and other typographical innovations; and adding more photographs, human interest, and other magazine-style features. Some of his changes pleased readers, but they infuriated his newspaper employees, who considered him ignorant of the newspaper business.

Munsey's most irritating business practice, however, was the constant purchase, merging, or elimination—often in a bizarre manner—of what he considered to be superfluous or competitive publications. He likened his newspaper and magazine acquisitions to a grocery store chain he owned. The *New York World* insulted him as "one of the ablest retail grocers that ever edited a New York newspaper." Others, many of them his own employees, considered him the "Grand High Executioner of Journalism."

DECLINE OF AN EMPIRE

Munsey's Magazine and its publisher's empire declined after 1907, more so after Roosevelt's defeat in 1912. *Munsey's* set a then record of 265 pages in one 1918 issue. The magazine became an all-fiction pulp in 1921 but never achieved the circulation it had known in its earlier years. When he was not merging or killing publications, Munsey would make impossible demands, such as ordering politically unpleasant information withheld, firing entire editorial departments, eliminating pages or sections, or punishing uncooperative employees. He paid $4 million for the *New York Herald* in 1920 in part so he could fire the paper's editorial cartoonist for an unflattering drawing of Munsey in 1916. He never married, had no family, lived most of his life alone in hotels, and claimed he did not care for money except for what he could accomplish with it.

Munsey died of appendicitis on December 12, 1925. Other great publishers founded schools of journalism or at least insisted that their publications continue after their death. Munsey, however, ordered that all his properties, magazines and newspapers included, be sold for cash, although much of the profits were used to found New York City's Metropolitan Museum of Art. Ironically, its new publisher combined *Munsey's Magazine* with *Argosy All-Story* in October 1929, eventually dropping the Munsey name altogether. Meanwhile, Munsey, the founder of mass media and the precursor of the Information Age, was eulogized by journalist William Allen White as such: "Frank Munsey contributed to the journalism of his day the talent of a meat packer, the morals of a money changer, and the manners of an undertaker. He and his kind have about succeeded in transforming a once-noble profession into an eight percent security. May he rest in trust!"

Richard Digby-Junger

SEE ALSO: Argosy*;* Atlantic Monthly*; Doyle, Arthur Conan; Dreiser, Theodore;* Harper's*; Mass Market Magazine Revolution; Metropolitan Museum of Art; Muckracking.*

BIBLIOGRAPHY

Britt, George. *Forty Years—Forty Millions: The Career of Frank A. Munsey.* Port Washington, NY: Farrar & Rinehart, 1972.

Filler, Louis. *Crusaders for American Liberalism.* Yellow Springs, OH: Antioch Press, 1950.

Mott, Frank L. "The Magazine Revolution and Popular Ideas in the Nineties." *Proceedings of the American Antiquarian Society,* Spring 1954, 195–214.

Mott, Frank L. "Munsey's Magazine." In *A History of American Magazines.* Cambridge, MA: Harvard University Press, 1957.

Paulsson, Martin. *The Social Anxieties of Progressive Reform: Atlantic City, 1854–1920.* New York: New York University Press, 1996.

Peterson, Theodore. *Magazines in the Twentieth Century.* Urbana: University of Illinois Press, 1964.

Summer, David E. *The Magazine Century.* New York: Peter Lang Publishing, 2010.

Villard, Oswald G. *Some Newspapers and Newspaper-Men.* New York: Knopf, 1923.

Wood, James Playsted. *Magazines in the United States,* 3rd ed. New York: Ronald Press, 1971.

Zuckerman, Mary Ellen. *A History of Popular Women's Magazines in the United States, 1792–1995.* Contributions in Women's Studies 65. Westport, CT: Greenwood Press, 1998.

The Muppets

From their modest beginnings as the stars of TV commercials and children's programming, Jim Henson's Muppets rose to worldwide fame, rivaling Walt Disney's Mickey Mouse and Warner Brothers' Bugs Bunny. Henson (1936–1990) coined the term *Muppets* by combining the words *marionette* and *puppet,* which pretty much describes these sock puppets with arms that are usually operated by a single puppeteer. Henson felt that since the medium of television was more intimate, it demanded of puppets a greater flexibility and expressiveness than the usual painted wooden faces such as Charlie McCarthy or Howdy Doody could provide. It was not only his puppets' faces, however, that were flexible: the loose and loopy sense of humor of the Muppets offered TV viewers a refreshing brand of comedy that, from the beginning, set Henson's work apart from that of his contemporaries.

Jim Henson and Kermit the Frog. *Muppet creator Jim Henson brings Kermit the Frog to life for an episode of* The Muppet Show.

In the 1950s, fresh out of high school, Henson secured a job as a puppeteer at the local NBC TV station in Washington, D.C. All through his college years, his first Muppet prototypes appeared in a five-minute show called *Sam and Friends*, which aired immediately before *The Tonight Show*. In 1958 the program won a local Emmy Award, but, curiously, Henson had until then never taken puppetry very seriously. As he later explained, "It didn't seem to be the sort of thing a grown man works at for a living." A trip to Europe exposed him to a wide tradition of puppetry he had never encountered in the United States. The experience inspired him to pursue puppetry in earnest, and at the same time it convinced him that he wanted to bring something fresh and innovative to the craft.

TELEVISION AND MOVIES

After his graduation from the University of Maryland, Henson earned much of his living by producing TV commercials. One character, Rowlf the Dog, created for a TV dog food ad, ended up as a featured player on *The Jimmy Dean Show* in the 1960s. The talkative, philosophical hound charmed viewers and put a national spotlight on Henson. His Muppets began doing specialty appearances on *The Tonight Show* and *The Ed Sullivan Show*. In one memorable bit, Kermit the Frog, who had not yet made a name for himself, sat idly humming "Glow Worm" and devouring each unfortunate worm that inched his way. The payoff came when one of the tiny worms turned out to be the tip of the snout of a great hairy beast, which then in turn gulped down the frog (and belched). Not limiting himself to puppetry, Henson tested his creativity in other venues, such as *Time Piece*, a 1965 short film (nominated for an Oscar), which he wrote, directed, and starred in.

The turning point for Henson's Muppets came in 1969 with the debut of public television's innovative children's show *Sesame Street*. The program's runaway success made stars out of not only the befuddled Big Bird, the ravenous Cookie Monster, trash-can-dwelling Oscar the Grouch, and roommates Bert and Ernie (named after the cop and cabbie in Frank Capra's *It's a Wonderful Life*) but also the gentle puppeteer's alter ego, Kermit the Frog. For the first time in broadcast history, an educational program started drawing ratings comparable to those of commercial networks, and the Muppets were given their share of the credit and glory for this feat. Millions of three-to-five-year-olds were falling in love with Henson's creations and begging their parents for Muppet merchandise. Henson, providing the singing voice for Ernie and Kermit, even had hit single records with the songs "Rubber Duckie," which was just for fun, and "It's Not Easy Being Green," a subtle plea for racial tolerance. Eventually, such was the Muppets' stature in showbiz that Kermit filled in one night for Johnny Carson as the guest host on *The Tonight Show*. To this day Muppets are starring on the still-running *Sesame Street*.

In the 1970s a series of Muppet TV specials inevitably led to the weekly half-hour *The Muppet Show*. Premiering in 1976, this show featured the puppets in a variety-show format in which they interacted with a different human star each week. But none of these celebrities outshone the Muppets themselves, nor did their stellar performances eclipse the public's interest in the ongoing, one-sided courtship between shy Kermit and the boisterous, short-tempered coquette, Miss Piggy. The phenomenal success of *The Muppet Show*, which has been called the most popular TV show ever, led in turn to *The Muppet Movie* (1979) and other big screen follow-ups, including *The Muppets Take Manhattan* (1984), *The Muppet Christmas Carol* (1992), *Muppet Treasure Island* (1996), and *Muppets from Space* (1999).

DIVERSIFICATION

The continued success of his Muppets in a variety of ventures enabled Henson to branch out into other areas of show business artistry. Henson Associates, a multimedia organization that far outstripped its humble origins with a frog, provided creatures for various filmmakers, such as cinematic realizations of the famous characters from *Alice in Wonderland* for the 1985 movie *Dreamchild*. One of Henson's own special projects, *The Dark Crystal* (1982), was an elfin fantasy in the J. R. R. Tolkien manner, populated entirely by beasts and fairies of Henson's devising.

The Henson influence could be witnessed in the *Star Wars* films in the presence of Yoda, a puppet given voice by longtime Henson associate Frank Oz. TV series continued to issue forth from Henson Associates, including the children's program *Fraggle Rock* and the sophisticated fairy-tale presentations of *The Storyteller*. Henson was responsible for the creature effects in *The Witches*, a film based on a story by Roald Dahl, which turned out to be the last project on which the puppeteer turned media mogul would be involved. In 1990 the tall, bearded, gentle genius suddenly died after a brief illness. His organization continued to produce innovative work in the field of fantasy and creature creation, and, of course, his Muppets proved that they had a life of their own.

During the early years of the twenty-first century, the Muppets continued to be a media presence chiefly through television, videos, and DVDs. *The Muppet Christmas Carol* had become a holiday tradition, and new holiday offerings such as *It's a Very Merry Muppet Christmas Movie* (2002) and *A Muppet Christmas: Letters to Santa* (2008) appeared periodically. In 2003 *Muppets Magic from "The Ed Sullivan Show"* was released as a DVD box set. A new television show, *Muppets TV*, appeared briefly in 2006. In 2011, however, the Muppets were back on the big screen through the efforts of actor Jason Segel, a longtime Henson fan. The movie, which starred Segel and Amy Adams, centers on the Muppets' efforts to save their old theater from a tycoon who wants to destroy it in order to drill for oil.

In trying to explain the fact that the Muppets have endured to become iconic within U.S. culture, Michelle Ann Abate suggests in her 2009 article in the *Journal of Popular Culture* that Henson was able to tap into a long tradition of Anglo-American silliness that was first evident in eighteenth-century nursery rhymes as a way of combating the Age of Reason. That silliness exhibited by the Muppets strikes a spark in adults as well as in children, allowing them all to escape, if only briefly, into the magical world created by Henson, the master puppeteer of the twentieth century.

Preston Neal Jones

SEE ALSO: *Advertising; Bugs Bunny; Capra, Frank; Carson, Johnny; Charlie McCarthy; Disney (Walt Disney Company); Henson, Jim;* It's a Wonderful Life*; Public Television (PBS);* Sesame Street*;* Star Wars*; Sullivan, Ed; Television;* The Tonight Show.

BIBLIOGRAPHY

Aaseng, Nathan. *Jim Henson: Muppet Master.* Minneapolis, MN: Lerner, 1988.

Abate, Michelle Ann. "Taking Silliness Seriously: Jim Henson's *The Muppet Show*, the Anglo-American Tradition of Nonsense, and Critical Critique." *Journal of Popular Culture* 42, no. 4 (2009).

Bacon, Matt. *No Strings Attached: The Inside Story of Jim Henson's Creature Shop*. New York: Macmillan, 1997.

Durrett, Deanne. *Jim Henson*. San Diego, CA: Lucent Books, 1994.

Finch, Christopher. *Jim Henson: The Works, the Art, the Magic, the Imagination*. New York: Random House, 1993.

Garlen, Jennifer C., and Anissa M. Graham, eds. *Kermit Culture: Critical Perspectives on Jim Henson's Muppets*. Jefferson, NC: McFarland, 2009.

Gikow, Louise. *Meet Jim Henson*. New York: Random House, 1993.

Inches, Alison. *Jim Henson's Designs and Doodles: A Muppet Sketchbook*. New York: Abrams, 2001.

Murder, She Wrote

Murder, She Wrote is the longest-running detective drama series in television history. It premiered on CBS in September 1984 and ended in May 1996, after 264 episodes. The program was the highest-rated drama on television for nine of its twelve seasons, and while it was nominated for an Emmy Award for Best Drama three times, it never won.

Murder, She Wrote was created by Peter S. Fischer and the writing and producing team of Richard Levinson and William Link. Levinson and Link created, wrote, and produced several successful television programs, including *Mannix* (1967–1975), *McCloud* (1970–1977), and *Columbo* (1971–1977 and 1989–1990). *Murder, She Wrote* features the character of Jessica Fletcher, a widow, former high school teacher, mystery novelist, and amateur sleuth, who lives in the small, fictional, seaside town of Cabot Cove, Maine. Played by Angela Lansbury, an established film and stage actress, Fletcher becomes involved in the investigation of a murder in each episode and, after following a series of clues, solves the murder by the end of each episode. Lansbury, who was fifty-eight years old when the series began, made television history as the only older woman to ever hold a sole leading role in a drama series. She was nominated for an Emmy Award for her performance every year for twelve years—every year that the series was on the air. She never won.

The role of Jessica was originally offered to stage, film, and television actress Jean Stapleton, who is best known for her role as Edith Bunker on the popular television comedy *All in the Family*, which aired from 1968 to 1979. Stapleton turned down the role. The creators then approached Lansbury, who had played Mrs. Salome Otterbourne, a novelist involved in a murder, in the 1978 movie *Death on the Nile* and Miss Marple, an elderly, unmarried amateur sleuth, in the 1980 movie *The Mirror Crack'd*. Both movies are based on novels by well-known mystery writer Agatha Christie. Lansbury, who was interested in the challenge of a television series, liked the *Murder, She Wrote* script and the character of Jessica. She accepted the role and signed a five-year contract.

Lansbury was born in London on October 16, 1925. Her father, Edgar Lansbury, was a businessman, who died from stomach cancer in 1934. Her mother, Moyna MacGill, was an actress. In 1940 Lansbury, her mother, her twin brothers, and her half sister immigrated to the United States to escape World War II. She immediately enrolled in the Feagin School of Drama and Radio in New York City and studied acting there until 1942.

Lansbury's first movie role was as the devious maid in *Gaslight* (1944), for which she earned an Academy Award nomination for Best Supporting Actress. She received another Academy Award nomination in the same category the very next year for her role as Sibyl Vane in *The Picture of Dorian Gray* (1945). Lansbury went on to appear in many movies throughout her career. Her most acclaimed movie role, and one for which she received her third Academy Award nomination for Best Supporting Actress, was Eleanor Shaw Iselin, the evil mother of the main character, in the Cold War thriller *The Manchurian Candidate* (1962). In later years she provided her voice for characters in the animated movies *The Last Unicorn* (1982), *Beauty and the Beast* (1991), *Anastasia* (1997), and *Fantasia 2000* (1999).

Murder, She Wrote. *Angela Lansbury holds the Golden Globe Award she won for her performance as the sleuthing Jessica Fletcher in* Murder, She Wrote *in 1987.* MAUREEN DONALDSON/ CONTRIBUTOR/ARCHIVE PHOTOS/GETTY IMAGES.

A STAR ON THE STAGE

While Lansbury achieved some success in the movies, she really became a star on the stage. She first appeared on Broadway in 1957 in the comedy *Hotel Paradiso*. Her breakthrough role, however, was the title role in *Mame* in 1966. She received a Tony Award for her performance. She went on to earn four more Tony Awards for *Dear World* (1969), the revival of *Gypsy* (1975), *Sweeney Todd* (1979), and *Blithe Spirit* (2009). She was also nominated for but did not win a Tony for *Deuce* (2007) and *A Little Night Music* (2010).

Murder, She Wrote debuted on September 30, 1984, with the two-hour pilot episode "The Murder of Sherlock Holmes." Jessica was newly widowed and had just published her first book. Over time the character evolved, trading in her manual typewriter for a computer and writing more books. She began to dress with more sophistication and travel the world, where she was usually recognized as a famous mystery author. Throughout the series' twelve years, however, the formula remained the same: at least one murder occurred in each episode that Fletcher solved with her persistent sleuthing.

Regular characters on *Murder, She Wrote* include the Cabot Cove sheriff, first played by Tom Bosley and later Ron Masak; Doctor Seth Hazlitt, played by William Windom; and Fletcher's nephew Grady, played by Michael Horton. The show also features a number of reoccurring characters, such as Cabot Cove realtor Eve Simpson, played by Julie Adams; insurance investigator Dennis Stanton, played by Keith Michell; retired spy Michael Hagarty, played by Len Cariou; and private investigator Harry McGraw, played by Jerry Orbach.

The immediate and enduring popularity of the show and its notable star enabled it to attract many well-known, veteran actors to be guest stars, including Theodore Bikel, Vicki Lawrence, Cesar Romero, Doris Roberts, Shirley Jones, Leslie Nielson, Mike Conners, Jean Simmons, Connie Stevens, Doug McClure, Roddy McDowell, Shirley Knight, Dean Jones, Chuck Conners, Chad Everett, Jackie Cooper, Florence Henderson, Kathryn Grayson, Gloria DeHaven, and Van Johnson. Many young actors and actresses who later became stars also appeared on the show, including Cynthia Nixon, Neil Patrick Harris, Courteney Cox, Megan Mullally, and George Clooney.

During the show's fifth season, Lansbury decided that she was ready to leave the show at the end of the season and not renew her contract. Being the sole lead on a weekly television show required very long workdays, sometimes sixteen to seventeen hours, and Lansbury decided she wanted more time for herself and for other projects. CBS convinced her to stay, agreeing to shorter workdays and to her making only brief appearances in several episodes. So during season six, she appears only to introduce and narrate the murder mystery in several episodes, and various guest stars set about investigating and solving the murders.

FANS, CRITICS, AND ADVERTISERS

Fans did not react well to the changes in season six and ratings dropped. Lansbury continued to narrate episodes in season seven, but in response to fan criticism she narrated fewer of them. In season eight she returned to appearing in all episodes, and ratings improved. In 1992, beginning with season nine, she became an executive producer.

By this time, production of the show had become a bit of a family affair. Lansbury's son, Anthony Pullen Shaw, was one of the many directors. He worked on the series from 1987 until it ended in 1996. Her brother, Bruce Lansbury, wrote several scripts from 1991 to 1996 and served as a supervising producer from 1992 to 1996. Her stepson, David Shaw, was a production manager and then a producer from 1993 to 1996, and her nephew, actor David Lansbury, appeared in three episodes from 1991 to 1993. Lansbury's husband, Peter Shaw, was her manager.

From its first season *Murder, She Wrote* was a hit with audiences, and it found favor with the majority of critics, who praised its cleverness and sophistication, its lack of violence, and Lansbury's polished portrayal. Detractors attacked the solve-it-yourself plotting as patronizing and objected to the mostly older characters. Yet the show's high ratings and longevity attested to its strengths, as did the modest merchandising that evolved from it, such as a computer jigsaw puzzle, a cookbook, and numerous books of fiction.

In the series' later years, its appeal to older viewers became a problem as advertisers sought to target a younger market. Decreasing advertisers coupled with increasingly expensive production costs weakened the network's confidence and support, and in 1995 CBS moved the show without warning from its longtime Sunday night slot to Thursday opposite the immensely popular *Friends*. *Murder, She Wrote* sank in the ratings. The final episode, "Death by Demographics," served as a subtle but pointed reference to the show's situation. A television movie appeared in 1997, and the original episodes went into syndication. In an article in *TV Guide*, Lansbury thanked her fans and expressed the hope that Jessica Fletcher would be remembered as courageous, independent, and "a champion of the wrongfully accused." Additional television movies appeared in 2000, 2001, and 2003.

Stephen L. Thompson

SEE ALSO: *Academy Awards;* All in the Family*; Christie, Agatha; Clooney, George;* Columbo*; Emmy Awards;* Friends*; Lawrence, Vicki; Made-for-Television Movies;* The Manchurian Candidate*; Romero, Cesar; Television; Tony Awards;* TV Guide*; World War II.*

BIBLIOGRAPHY

Collins, Max Allan, and John Javna. *The Best of Crime and Detective TV: "Perry Mason" to "Hill Street Blues," "The Rockford Files" to "Murder, She Wrote."* New York: Harmony Books, 1988.

Edelman, Rob, and Audrey E. Kupferberg. *Angela Lansbury: A Life on Stage and Screen.* New York: Carol Publishing Group, 1996.

Law, John William. *Murder on the Boob Tube.* San Francisco: Aplomb Publishing, 2010.

Parish, James Robert. *The Unofficial "Murder, She Wrote" Casebook.* New York: Kensington Books, 1997.

Riggs, Karen E. "The Case of the Mysterious Ritual: Murder Dramas and Older Women Viewers." *Critical Studies in Mass Communication* 13, no. 4 (1996): 309–323.

Murphy, Eddie *(1961–)*

As a stand-up comedian and a cast member of *Saturday Night Live* (1980–1984), Eddie Murphy rose quickly from obscurity to stardom. In the movies *48 Hrs.* (1982), *Trading Places* (1983), and *Beverly Hills Cop* (1984), he played street-smart characters forced into unusual situations. A stand-up comedian as a teenager, he has reinvented himself numerous times, from action movie star to lead actor in multiple-personality family films to his Golden Globe–winning performance as James "Thunder" Early in *Dreamgirls* (2006).

EARLY COMEDY WORK

Edward Regan Murphy was born in Brooklyn, New York, on April 3, 1961. His parents split up when he was young, and shortly thereafter his father was killed and his mother was hospitalized. During this period he and his brother spent a year in foster care with a woman he has described as a "Black Nazi"—and as the reason he ultimately became a comedian. His mother returned to health and remarried, and they moved to Roosevelt, Long Island, a predominantly African American suburb. Murphy had his stage debut at age fifteen as the emcee at a talent show in 1976. He was only nineteen when he was hired as an extra on *Saturday Night Live* (*SNL*), where he would be one of only two cast members asked to return the following season. He stayed with *SNL* for four seasons, developing many memorable characters, including the popular Mister Robinson, a street-smart urban version of Mr. Rogers.

Midway through his *SNL* stint, his first big break came with a role in Walter Hill's *48 Hrs.* (1982) opposite Nick Nolte. The film was a box-office success, and Murphy received his first Golden Globe nomination. He released his first comedy album that year as well; combining the styles of two of his idols, he mixed the global appeal of Bill Cosby with the raunchy stylings of Richard Pryor. In 1983 he recorded a comedy special for HBO, *Delirious*. His film career continued with follow-up hit *Trading Places* (1983), and Paramount Pictures signed Murphy to a $25 million, six-movie deal.

His real commercial breakthrough came with box-office smash *Beverly Hills Cop* (1984). Murphy also launched a music career in 1984 with the album *How Could It Be*, and he left *SNL* after the 1984 season. Murphy's 1987 live concert film *Raw* is still ranked as the top-grossing stand-up concert, bringing in a lifetime gross of $50 million.

For the next ten years, however, Murphy would struggle to replicate the success of his early films; his 1988 performance in *Coming to America*, playing multiple roles versus costar Arsenio Hall, was a huge success, grossing more than $128 million domestically, and the sequel *Beverly Hills Cops II* (1987) performed well at the box office despite a lack of critical acclaim. Most of his other performances during this time, however, were failures both critically and commercially, including the Murphy-directed *Harlem Nights* (1989), *Boomerang* (1992), sequels *Another 48 Hrs.* (1990) and *Beverly Hills Cop III* (1994), and *Vampire in Brooklyn* (1995).

FAMILY-FRIENDLY SUCCESS

Murphy was able to reinvent himself by leaving behind adult themes and turning to family-oriented fare with his 1996 *The Nutty Professor*, a remake of Jerry Lewis's 1963 hit. In a tribute to Murphy-idol Peter Sellers's multipersonality performance in *Dr. Strangelove* (1964), Murphy took on the roles of seven different characters and earned his second Golden Globe nomination. Since then, his career has seen numerous box-office hits with family-friendly live-action films such as *Doctor Dolittle* (1998) and the sequel *Nutty Professor II: The Klumps* (2000), as well as a string of voice roles in animated films such as *Mulan* (1998) and the hit *Shrek* (2001), with its string of sequels.

It seems paradoxical that Murphy's more recent successes are his most PG outings, as his early reputation was built on raunchy, obscenity-laced comedic performances and his personal life has seen its share of scandalous moments—pulled over in 1997 with a transvestite prostitute in his car, a contentious divorce and custody battle in 2005, sued for paternity in 2007 by Melanie "Scary Spice" Brown (a case she would win after a DNA test), and a two-week marriage to Tracey Edmonds in 2008. Murphy's attempts at more adult-oriented fare during this time—including *Holy Man* (1998), *Life* (1999), and *The Adventures of Pluto Nash* (2002), which received three Razzie nominations—were all considered box-office failures and were generally critically panned.

Murphy reinvented himself once again with a supporting role in the adaptation of the Broadway musical *Dreamgirls* (2006), which starred Jennifer Hudson, Beyoncé Knowles, and Jamie Foxx and was nominated for eight Oscars. Not only would the film gross $150 million worldwide, but Murphy won the Golden Globe and Screen Actors Guild (SAG) awards for best supporting actor and received his first Academy Award nomination as well. In 2007 Murphy finally received an invitation to join the Academy of Motion Picture Arts and Sciences. His next cinematic outings, however—including *Norbit* (2007); *Meet Dave* (2008); *Imagine That* (2009); and *A Thousand Words*, which was shot in 2008 but not released until 2012, and received a rare 0 percent rating on Rotten Tomatoes—were disappointments, and Murphy has been unable to capitalize on his *Dreamgirls* success.

Despite the ups and downs of his film career, Murphy has long been considered the preeminent comedian of the 1980s, and he was the inaugural recipient of the Stand-up Icon Award at the 2011 Comedy Awards. He was scheduled to be the host of the 2012 Academy Awards with producer Brett Ratner, who directed Murphy's 2011 film *Tower Heist*, but when Ratner stepped down after uttering a gay slur on Howard Stern's radio show, Murphy stepped down as well. Reports of *Beverly Hills Cop 4* continue to surface periodically but have yet to come to fruition, and Murphy has also been discussed as the star of a possible cinematic remake of *Fantasy Island*, as well as reportedly signing on to play former Washington, D.C., mayor Marion Barry in a Spike Lee film for HBO.

Christian L. Pyle

SEE ALSO: *Academy Awards; Animated Films; Cosby, Bill; Foxx, Jamie; Knowles, Beyoncé; Pryor, Richard;* Saturday Night Live*; Sex Scandals;* Shrek*; Stand-Up Comedy; Television.*

BIBLIOGRAPHY

Eberwein, Robert. *Acting for America: Movie Stars of the 1980s.* Piscataway, NJ: Rutgers University Press, 2010.

Sanello, Frank. *Eddie Murphy: The Life and Times of a Comic on the Edge.* New York: Carol Publishing, 1997.

Wilburn, Deborah A. *Eddie Murphy.* New York: Chelsea House, 1993.

Murphy Brown

Created, produced, and written by Diane English, *Murphy Brown* debuted in 1988 during a period when women had been nearly eliminated from television by all-male "buddy" shows. One of the only series to focus on a female character that year, it was among the most popular shows of the 1980s and 1990s and even entered the platform of a presidential campaign.

The main character, Murphy Brown (Candice Bergen), was one of the best developed characters to appear on a sitcom. At the beginning of the series, Murphy, a highly competitive journalist, has just returned from the Betty Ford Clinic, where she overcame the drinking and smoking addictions honed during her years as an ambitious journalist. Included in the ensemble cast are her "family" of coworkers on the fictitious television newsmagazine *FYI* and Eldin Bernecky (Robert Pastorelli), house painter turned permanent fixture at home.

Murphy's coanchor is Jim Dial (Charles Kimbrough), a newsman created in the image of Edward R. Murrow, who for twenty-five years had been a respected peer of such luminaries as Walter Cronkite and Dan Rather. Corky Sherwood (Faith Ford) is the naive former Miss America who was brought onto *FYI* to add youth and energy to the "aging" program by covering human interest stories of dubious value. Rounding out the team is Frank Fontana (Joe Regalbuto), Murphy's best friend and *FYI*'s insecure investigative reporter. For the first eight years of the show's run, Miles Silverberg (Grant Shaud) played the neurotic boy wonder who is foisted on the experienced triumvirate as the newsmagazine's producer. In 1996 he was replaced by Kay (Lily Tomlin), a no-nonsense veteran who could be as abrasive as Murphy.

Murphy Brown dealt frankly and intelligently with topical issues such as homelessness; political correctness and oversensitivity; celebrity; ecology and the environment; First Amendment protections; single motherhood; and "family values." Not only did the series readily address issues of substance, but it also often reflected a strong viewpoint on an issue, as when Brown went to jail rather than reveal the source of a story.

It was the series' willingness to take a stand on divisive topics that propelled Murphy Brown into the center of the controversy over contemporary morality. During the 1991–1992 season, the unmarried Murphy becomes pregnant, although the baby is given a quasi legitimacy as the child of Murphy's ex-husband. In part because of the popularity of the character and the show, Murphy became the topic of heated debate within the media and the target of conservative politicians and religious groups. In speeches during the 1992 presidential campaign, Vice President Dan Quayle criticized Murphy for being an unwed mother and a symbol of declining family values. The argument quickly spread to a variety of national magazines, from *U.S. News & World Report* to *Christian Century*. In an episode from the 1992 season, Murphy replies to Quayle's comments in a segment of *FYI* that features real-life nontraditional families.

During the show's final season, Murphy learns that she has breast cancer. In addition to typically comedic plots, many episodes chronicle her battle and the way in which she deals with this new crisis in her life. At the end of several episodes, Bergen made some public service announcements concerning breast cancer awareness. At last, in the final episode, Murphy learns that she is cancer-free. After questioning her priorities and lifestyle, she decides that there is nothing she would rather do than continue her work on *FYI*. For many viewers the most satisfying scene of all is when she returns home to find Eldin, who had left several years earlier to "paint" in Spain, at her town house planning the "masterpiece" he is going to create on her den ceiling.

Murphy Brown. *The cast of* Murphy Brown *included, from left, Joe Regalbuto as Frank Fontana, Candice Bergen as Murphy Brown, Faith Ford as Corky Sherwood, Grant Shaud (standing) as Miles Silverberg, and Charles Kimbrough as Jim Dial.* CBS PHOTO ARCHIVE/CONTRIBUTOR/CBS/GETTY IMAGES.

While Murphy was in many ways a feminist role model, her character was not without the typical conflicting signals and symbols of female characters who find success on nontraditional terms. She flourished in her work, but the traits that aided in her success were those generally ascribed to males in our society—independence, bluntness, excessive self-confidence, courage, and ambition. In addition, her private life, the traditional realm of the female, was a disaster. The implicit message was that to be successful, a woman must be masculinized and lose her femininity, resulting in an empty personal life. Yet, through it all, Murphy was depicted as a survivor—not only of cancer and criticism but also of a dysfunctional childhood and a professional journey replete with "hard knocks." For the viewing audience, her resiliency and persistence may have been the most positive and beneficial aspects of her character.

Denise Lowe

SEE ALSO: *Bergen, Candice; Cancer; Cronkite, Walter; Feminism; Murrow, Edward R.; Political Correctness; Quayle, Dan; Rather, Dan; Sitcom; Television; Tomlin, Lily.*

BIBLIOGRAPHY

Alley, Robert S., and Irby B. Brown. *Murphy Brown: Anatomy of a Sitcom.* New York: Delta, 1990.

Spangler, Lynn C. *Television Women from Lucy to Friends: Fifty Years of Sitcoms and Feminism.* Westport, CT: Praeger, 2003.

Murray, Anne *(1945–)*

Juxtaposing fresh-faced country girl innocence with practical business sense, Anne Murray is a Canadian national treasure who, from the early 1970s, became a singing star throughout North America. By the late 1990s her velvety contralto voice and personable delivery had taken her from her simple beginnings as a ukulele-strumming folk singer to a high profile as one of the most highly paid Canadian entertainers. Though ultracool music critics sometimes sneered at her efforts to broaden her genre (one called her disco album "Madonna of Sunnybrook Farm"), even they found it difficult to fault Murray within the folk-pop-country niche that she made her own.

Murray was born in the Nova Scotia mining town of Springhill to a Scottish Presbyterian surgeon and a coal miner's daughter, just in time to grow up to the smooth pop sounds of the pre-rock-and-roll 1950s. As a toddler, she sang along with her parents' albums, and she gave her first public singing performance at age fifteen, yet Murray had never considered singing as a career choice. "Singing was something you did in the bathtub and around bonfires," she said. "I felt there was no security in singing."

Always a tomboy, who enjoyed playing ice hockey with her five brothers, Murray got a physical education degree from the University of New Brunswick and taught the discipline on Prince Edward Island. As a sideline, she regularly performed on a CBC-TV show called *Singalong Jubilee,* playing a baritone ukulele as she sang folk songs from the maritime provinces and rapidly gained popularity across Canada. Then, in 1970 a recording Murray made of a song called "Snowbird" became an immediate hit, both in Canada and in the United States, launching a singing career that lasted more than thirty years and yielded thirty hit singles, nearly forty albums in three decades, and many awards, as well as television specials in Canada and America.

During the 1970s Murray moved to Toronto and married Bill Langstroth, who had been her associate producer and host on *Singalong Jubilee.* After a brief, difficult period from 1976 to 1978, when she tried but failed to fit into the glitzy American rock scene, she opted to prioritize her family over stardom and placed strict limitations on her touring concert schedule to ensure that she spent sufficient time at home with her children. Whatever income she might have sacrificed as a result was well compensated for by the adroit management of the enterprise that is Anne Murray. The careful investments made by trusted financial advisers, combined with Murray's own hardheaded business sense, turned the singer's sales and royalties into something of an empire. Her company, Balmur Ltd., is a successful talent agency that handles not only her own career but also a handful of other Canadian singers, including her brother Bruce.

When Murray was a child, listening to the girl singers of the 1950s, she aspired to be "just like Doris Day." In a way, she succeeded. Her public persona, like Day's, has always been

Anne Murray. *Anne Murray was honored with the Howie Richmond Hitmaker Award by the Songwriters Hall of Fame in 2008.* G. GERSHOFF/STAFF/WIREIMAGE/GETTY IMAGES.

friendly and likable, fresh and wholesome—sometimes to her dismay. "It's a real pain in the ass, having to read all that crap about me being goody-two-shoes next door," she has complained. Also like Day, she has been pursued through her career by rumors that she is gay. The rumors have been hotly denied, but she has always attracted a large lesbian following, drawn perhaps to her tomboyish appearance, casual manner, and cello-deep voice. Within the gay community stories have circulated of Murray sightings in lesbian bars and of possible affairs with well-known lesbians such as fellow Canadian singer k.d. lang.

Though an internationally known star who has made recordings in phonetically learned French and Spanish and commercials on Japanese TV, Murray has maintained a simple and thrifty lifestyle. While perhaps staying in elite hotels with posh service on tour, at home in Toronto she remained a housewife and mother. Though she separated from her husband in the late 1990s after twenty-three years of marriage, she continued to live with her children and give priority to her personal life over her public career. In 1997 Murray's daughter Dawn Langstroth was diagnosed with anorexia nervosa, and Murray took time away from touring to get Dawn treatment. She returned to touring in 1999 in support of her platinum album *What a Wonderful World* and followed with the highly successful tribute album *Country Croonin'* in 2002. Murray took a small break from touring in 2004 but continued to release studio albums. In 2005 she launched into a series of retrospective events that celebrated her career, including the dual disc *All of Me*, which climbed to thirteen on the Billboard country album charts. Her 2007 studio album, *Anne Murray Duets: Friends and Legends*, went platinum in both Canada and the United States.

Over the course of her prolific career, Murray has won numerous Grammy, Country Music Association (CMA), and Juno awards. In 1989 the Anne Murray Center, a museum devoted to her life and career, opened in her home town of Springhill. In 2006 the Canadian Songwriters Hall of Fame honored her and Leonard Cohen with the Legacy Award for their roles in promoting Canadian artists, and Canada Post acknowledged her iconic status in 2007 by releasing a limited-edition postage stamp. In 2008 she received the Howie Richmond Hitmaker Award as part of the Songwriters Hall of Fame induction ceremony. Murray has published an autobiography, *All of Me* (2009) and has championed numerous causes, including the Anne Murray Charitable Golf Classic.

Tina Gianoulis

SEE ALSO: *Country Music; Day, Doris; Folk Music; lang, k.d.; Pop Music; Top 40.*

BIBLIOGRAPHY

Chin, Paula, and Giovann Breu. "Emotional Rescue." *People*, November 8, 1999, 128.

Grills, Barry. *Snowbird: The Story of Anne Murray*. Kingston, ON: Quarry Press, 1996.

Livingstone, David. *Anne Murray: The Story So Far*. New York: Collier Books, 1981.

Rasky, Frank. "Managing Anne Murray's Millions." *Canadian Business*, May 1983, 32.

Murray, Arthur *(1895–1991)*

The logo of Arthur Murray International Dance Schools is the stylized silhouette of a man and woman dancing. Drawn with broad and sweeping lines, it suggests movement, elegance, and romance—the very qualities that have been associated with the name of Arthur Murray for more than eight decades. Combining his love of dance with a canny business sense and a shrewd perception of human nature, Murray first began giving dancing lessons to earn some extra money. By the time he retired, there were hundreds of studio franchises bearing his name—a name that had become synonymous with ballroom dancing itself.

EARLY LIFE

Born Moses Teichman, the son of Austrian immigrants, Murray grew up on the Lower East Side of Manhattan. He was a shy, hardworking youth who attended high school by day, studied draftsmanship by night, and worked as an errand boy in between. To overcome his shyness, he asked a girlfriend to teach him to dance, and by the time he was seventeen, he was giving lessons himself. In the next few years he studied with the famous

Arthur Murray. *Arthur Murray, right, and his partner demonstrate a dance step in 1943.* AP IMAGES.

performers and dance instructors Irene and Vernon Castle and, through them, got a job in the resort town of Marblehead, Massachusetts, teaching dance to upper-class vacationers. It was 1914 and World War I was imminent; a Germanic (not to mention Jewish) name like Moses Teichman might have made the customers nervous, and at Irene's suggestion, the young man changed his name to Arthur Murray. Following his introduction to elite society in Marblehead, he went to college in Georgia, where he continued to supplement his income by giving dance lessons.

Before 1900 there was little ballroom dance in the United States beyond the fox trot and the polka, but the advent of jazz and ragtime in the early decades of the twentieth century brought a wave of new dances that swept the nation. The Kangaroo Dip, the Chicken Scratch, and the Turkey Trot were just a few of the new dances Americans were anxious to learn. With an acute sense of business timing and strategy, Murray rode the new wave of dance popularity, teaching lessons, organizing dances, and even tapping into the new mail-order market to sell lessons by mail. His success prompted *Forbes* magazine to feature an article about him, headlined "This College Student Earns $15,000 a Year."

Murray owed the success of his mail-order campaign to his innovative approach to dance instruction—his famous "footsteps." Rather than merely describing the movements of a particular dance, he invented the concept of diagrams, with silhouetted footprints illustrating the movements. His advertisement, under the banner "How I Became Popular Overnight," has remained a Madison Avenue classic. The combination of accessible learning techniques and their appeal to the socially insecure made lessons "the Arthur Murray way" wildly popular.

ARTHUR MURRAY STUDIOS

Another trademark of Arthur Murray's approach had originated perhaps that first summer in Marblehead. Perceiving that social dancing was associated with both romance and refinement, Murray promoted those associations in his lessons. When he opened his first franchise studios in 1938, he continued the tradition of providing elegant instructors who would adhere to his philosophy of teaching dance "not as isolated feet or step movements, but as an integral part of social life and an expression and celebration of it."

From those first studios, Murray went on to build an ever-expanding dance empire. There was a dip in business during the Depression, but there were seventy-two Arthur Murray Studios nationwide by 1946, and in the 1950s he graduated from sponsoring early television shows to having his own. *The Arthur Murray Party* ran from 1950 to 1960 and ushered in a new boom in ballroom dancing to accompany the country's new prosperity. At its height, the show brought 2,000 new students a week to Arthur Murray Studios around the country. Many celebrities, from Elizabeth Arden and Katharine Hepburn to Enrico Caruso and the Duke of Windsor, learned to dance in an Arthur Murray studio.

ARTHUR MURRAY INTERNATIONAL

Also in the 1960s, Philip Masters and George Theiss, former students of Murray's, joined the organization. Though their names would never be as famous as their mentor's, they would eventually take the helm of the organization that became known as Arthur Murray International (AMI). The studio remained on the cutting edge of new trends, sending instructors to study in Cuba and bringing back the latest in Latin dance. It was Arthur Murray instructors who introduced the Lambada to the United States in the 1980s, having discovered it in Paris, where it was fast becoming the rage.

When Murray retired in 1964, there were more than 350 franchise studios internationally, pulling in a gross annual income of more than $25 million, but the "no-touch" individualistic style of dancing that became popular in the 1960s decreased the demand for ballroom dancing. AMI persevered, however, capitalizing heavily on the skilled disco-style dancing of the late 1970s as popularized by John Travolta in *Saturday Night Fever* (1977). Happily, all fashion is cyclical, and the "retro" culture of the 1980s and 1990s once again came to admire the elegance, romance, and agility associated with social ballroom dance. By the end of the century in which it was born, AMI was still there, holding out the promise of grace, style, and popularity in its pricey packages of instruction.

The AMI statement of purpose calls dancing "the art that brings people together." With hundreds of franchise studios in the United States, Europe, the Middle East, Canada, Puerto Rico, South America, Australia, and Israel, the organization spreads that art, teaching waltz, fox trot, tango, samba, rumba, and cha-cha to students of widely varying skill and diverse reasons for learning. Whether they are among the thousands who join to find a social life at the Arthur Murray dancing parties or the few who continue the efforts to make ballroom dancing a competitive Olympic event, all are a realization of a shy, young New Yorker's dream. In learning to overcome his own shyness, Murray found a magic solution to the universal problem of social insecurity—and, in true American fashion, he turned it into a multimillion-dollar business.

Tina Gianoulis

SEE ALSO: *Arden, Elizabeth; Castle, Vernon and Irene; The Great Depression; Hepburn, Katharine; Jazz;* Saturday Night Fever*; Television; Travolta, John.*

BIBLIOGRAPHY

Arthur Murray Franchised Dance Studios. Accessed January 17, 2012. Available from http://www.arthurmurray.com

Dannett, Sylvia G. L.; Frank R. Rachel; and Arthur Murray. *Down Memory Lane: Arthur Murray's Picture Story of Social Dancing*. New York: Greenberg, 1954.

Murray, Kathryn. *My Husband, Arthur Murray*. New York: Simon & Schuster, 1960.

Travis, Doris Eaton, et al. *The Days We Danced: The Story of My Theatrical Family from Florenz Ziegfeld to Arthur Murray and Beyond*. Seattle, WA: Marquand Books, 2003.

Murray, Bill *(1950–)*

Despite actor Bill Murray's national success as a screwball comic on television's *Saturday Night Live* and in films such as *Caddyshack* (1980) and *Ghostbusters* (1984)—and his later, more nuanced, performances in independent films such as *Lost in Translation* (2003)—perhaps his most enduring contribution to popular culture was his portrayal of the smug, arrogant weatherman in *Groundhog Day* (1993). The transformation of weatherman Phil into a loving, caring human being by living the same day over and over until he gets it right has become a widely understood symbol of the frustrations of modern life. Murray rendered Phil's redemption with a nonchalant depth that revealed him as much more than a sketch comedian and set his career on a more serious path.

When the network executives of NBC's *Saturday Night Live* (*SNL*) first saw Murray, they wrote him off as an Irish Catholic street fighter. He was no Chevy Chase, and this perception of his quality almost cost him a job with the network and the stardom it brought him. Over the years, however, Murray churned through a succession of images, from slick Las Vegas nightclub singer, through con artist scientist turned ghostbuster, to the suave weatherman of *Groundhog Day*, always with an offhand irony that brought the audience with him into the joke. As film critic Pauline Kael has said of Murray's work in *Ghostbusters*, "He has a genuine outré gift: he makes you feel that his characters are bums inside—unconcerned and indifferent—and he makes that seem like a kind of grace."

EARLY LIFE AND *SNL*

The fifth of nine children of a Chicago lumber salesman, Bill Murray dropped out of a Jesuit college and into arrest on charges of marijuana possession. While on probation, he did a series of manual jobs before following his older brother Brian Doyle Murray into Chicago's famous improvisational comedy theater company, Second City. This led to his joining a cast that included John Belushi, Dan Aykroyd, and Gilda Radner for the *National Lampoon Radio Hour* in 1975 and the subsequent New York cabaret revue, the *National Lampoon Show*. The timing of Murray's move to New York was fortuitous, coinciding with the period when producer Lorne Michaels was developing a new television show, *Saturday Night Live*.

Bill Murray. *Bill Murray's career has taken him from sketch comedian in the early days of* Saturday Night Live *to critically acclaimed actor in films such as* Lost in Translation *and* Rushmore. KEVIN MAZUR/CONTRIBUTOR/WIREIMAGE/GETTY IMAGES.

Murray auditioned for the original cast of *SNL*, portraying a sleazy nightclub singer. He was not hired, however, because he lost out to John Belushi. When Chase left *SNL* after its first season, Michaels sought out Murray despite the network's reservations, and Murray joined the show in 1977. At first, the newcomer remained in the shadows of *SNL* stars Belushi and Aykroyd. When the duo left, Murray was designated the new male star, and during the show's fifth season the majority of the male roles fell to him. He was a particular hit as Nick, a smarmy Las Vegas lounge singer, and as a clueless movie critic who never saw the movies he reviewed but panned them anyway.

FILM ACTOR

Murray's success on *SNL* led him into movies, beginning with *Meatballs* (1979), a puerile adolescent comedy made in Canada, directed by Ivan Reitman, and written by a team of writers and actors including comedian Harold Ramis. Murray left *SNL* after the fifth season and played a variety of roles, large and small, in movies of variable quality, including the semi-delusional greenskeeper in the golf classic *Caddyshack* with Chase and the dramatic lead in a failed remake of *The Razor's Edge* (1984). Also in 1984, Murray was reunited with Ramis, Aykroyd, and Reitman for the hugely successful box-office hit, *Ghostbusters*. His performance as Dr. Peter Venkman—brash, confident, cool, and seemingly unaffected by the cataclysmic events surrounding him—seemed tailor-made for Murray. His persona, and the sardonic wink and roll of the eyes that became a trademark mannerism, appealed as much to movie audiences as it had to fans of *SNL*.

Murray graduated to solo-star status with *Scrooged* (1988), a contemporary take on Charles Dickens's *A Christmas Carol*. He played Scrooge in the guise of a New York television company executive who is forced to confront the hollowness of his life. A more vulnerable, three-dimensional aspect of Murray's acting abilities was mined and revealed, and it was evolved further in *Groundhog Day*. These roles evidenced a new thoughtfulness in his approach to his career, and he sought to continue challenging his abilities by playing characters of substance.

Although established as a popular and successful leading man in the 1990s, he still took supporting roles in movies such as *Mad Dog and Glory* (1993), *Ed Wood* (1994), and *Rushmore* (1998). His performances in all of these movies brought critical acclaim, and he won a Los Angeles Film Critics Association Award for Best Supporting Actor for *Rushmore*. Though still taking the occasional role in studio blockbusters such as the 2000 McG film *Charlie's Angels*, Murray began more and more to focus on quirky independent comedies, such as Wes Anderson's *The Royal Tenenbaums* (2001). As Anderson's career progressed, Murray became one of the idiosyncratic filmmaker's regular cast members, his most prominent role being his turn as the oceanographic explorer Steve Zissou in *The Life Aquatic with Steve Zissou* (2004). In 2003 he earned a new level of professional respect for his work in Sofia Coppola's bittersweet romantic comedy *Lost in Translation*. Murray's portrayal of a jaded actor on the downhill side of fame gained him rave reviews, a number of awards, and an Oscar nomination for Best Actor.

After *Lost in Translation*, Murray withdrew from the conventional Hollywood system. He fired his agents and his publicist, replacing them with an 800 number he answered (or, more often, did not answer) himself. Though he still took film roles that interested him, he became famously inaccessible, though still much in demand as an actor. Besides voice-over work in the forgettable *Garfield* (2004) and *Garfield: A Tale of Two Kitties* (2006), much of Murray's work in the first decade of the 2000s was in independent films, such as the 2009 Aaron Schneider film *Get Low*. Murray appeared as himself in an iconic cameo in the apocalyptic comedy *Zombieland* (2009). In 2012 the prolific actor was slated to appear in several films, including Anderson's *Moonrise Kingdom*, in which he portrays the father of a runaway child. Murray brings his wry sense of humor not only to the roles he plays but also to his assessment of his performances. For example, when asked about his life's regrets, he once replied, "Garfield."

John J. Doherty

SEE ALSO: *Academy Awards; Aykroyd, Dan; Belushi, John;* Charlie's Angels*; Chase, Chevy; Golf; Hollywood; Las Vegas; Marijuana;* National Lampoon*; Radner, Gilda;* Saturday Night Live*; Second City; Television.*

BIBLIOGRAPHY

Karlen, Neal. *Slouching toward Fargo: A Two Year Saga of Sinners and St. Paul Saints at the Bottom of the Bush Leagues with Bill Murray, Darryl Strawberry, Dakota Sadie, and Me.* New York: Spike, 1999.

Labrecque, Jeff. "Bill Murray: Curious Case of Hollywood's White Whale." *Entertainment Weekly*, July 1, 2010, 48.

Murray, Bill, and George Peper. *Cinderella Story: My Life in Golf.* New York: Doubleday, 1999.

Thomas, Mike. *The Second City Unscripted: Revolution and Revelation at the World-Famous Comedy Theater.* New York: Villard, 2009.

Murray, Lenda *(1962–)*

Bodybuilder Lenda Murray became the second black Ms. Olympia in 1990. An outstanding athlete in high school, Murray was an all-city sprinter and a cheerleader at her Detroit, Michigan, high school. She continued cheerleading at Western Michigan University, where she earned a degree in political science and became the second African American to be chosen as the university's homecoming queen. Murray has been a televangelist for exercise on various cable television shows, and she has done color commentary on bodybuilding events for ESPN. She has also been featured in national magazines such as *Vanity Fair, Ebony, Mademoiselle,* and *Sports Illustrated.*

Murray won the Ms. Olympia title in consecutive victories from 1990 until 1995. She finished second in 1996 and 1997, then retired from professional bodybuilding. Her retirement signaled a shift in the sport as judges began to base the award on muscle mass rather than on symmetry and shape. Murray returned to professional bodybuilding in 2002 with a dramatically more muscular physique, and she won the Ms. Olympia title again in 2003 and 2004. She retired permanently in 2004 as the all-time winningest woman in the sport. Murray is married to Urel McGill; the couple started their fitness business, Operation Boot Camp, in 2000 and opened Lenda Murray Bodybuilding, Figure and Bikini Championships in 2004.

Jan Todd

SEE ALSO: *Bodybuilding; Cable TV; Cheerleading;* Ebony*; ESPN;* Sports Illustrated*;* Vanity Fair.

BIBLIOGRAPHY

"Is Women's Bodybuilding Dead?" *Muscleweek*, June 21, 2011.

Lowe, Maria R. *Female Bodybuilders and the Struggle for Self Recognition.* New York: New York University Press, 1998.

Murrow, Edward R. *(1908–1965)*

Edward R. Murrow was one of the preeminent journalists in U.S. broadcasting, having defined the standards of excellence and social responsibility for the news media. He was the guiding force for the development of news and public affairs on radio during the 1930s and 1940s as well as television during the 1950s. He almost single-handedly created a tradition that distinguished the broadcast journalist from the newspaper reporter while embodying the ideals of courage and integrity for the entire profession.

Murrow was one of the few giants of the industry to live up to his legend. He had both the style and substance to incarnate the quintessential roving correspondent. With his rich, resonant voice and penetrating eye, he documented some of the most profound events of the twentieth century. He also looked

Edward R. Murrow. *Edward R. Murrow served as a war correspondent for CBS radio during World War II before embarking on a career in television journalism.* HULTON ARCHIVE/STRINGER/ ARCHIVE PHOTOS/GETTY IMAGES.

the part of the slightly world-weary reporter who was impelled by conscience to set the record straight. A Hemingwayesque figure with brooding good looks and invariably draped in a worn raincoat, Murrow was described as "the only foreign correspondent who could play a foreign correspondent in the movies and give the role all the glamour Hollywood wants."

STUMBLING INTO JOURNALISM

Murrow's rise to fame was even more astounding because he never aspired to a reportorial career. Unlike his contemporaries in radio, who almost exclusively came from a newspaper background, Murrow was trained as an educational administrator. Born Edward Egbert Roscoe Murrow in Greensboro, North Carolina, on April 25, 1908, he graduated from Washington State University with majors in political science, speech, and international relations. He served as president of the National Student Federation, organizing international travel for students and debates between U.S. and European universities. He also was assistant director of the Institute of International Education, where he supervised offices in London, Berlin, and Vienna. He was hired by CBS in 1935 for his executive ability, not his journalistic skills.

His first responsibility was as director of talks and special events, where he secured personalities to appear on the CBS radio network. In 1937 he was sent to London to schedule European speakers and oversee shortwave cultural programming. In March 1938 he was on his way to Poland to arrange for a *School of the Air* broadcast when Adolf Hitler's German forces invaded Austria. Murrow chartered a passenger airliner and, out of necessity, reported the occupation from Vienna. He followed up with reports from London, describing Prime Minister Neville Chamberlain's negotiations with the Germans and the eventual annexation of Czechoslovakia a year later.

In the late 1930s there was no network tradition of reporting international crises. With another major war almost inevitable, Murrow was instructed to staff correspondents in all the major European capitals. His team, known as the Murrow Boys, was radio's first professional corps of journalists and reported daily on CBS's *World News Roundup*. The members, whose ranks included William Shirer, Eric Sevareid, Charles Collingwood, and Howard K. Smith, were imbued with their leader's unflagging dedication and would have an impact on broadcast news for years to come.

WORLD WAR II BROADCASTS

More than anyone else, Murrow was able to bring the war into U.S. homes. During the bombing of London in the fall of 1939 and throughout 1940, his impressionistic prose captured the anxiety and resolve of the British people. Often speaking from the rooftops, Murrow commenced each broadcast with a somber gravity, saying, "This . . . is London." His graphic description, called "metallic poetry" by one critic, gave an eyewitness account of the horror and devastation of the Blitz. Poet Archibald MacLeish stated that Murrow "burned the city of London in our houses and we felt that flame. . . . [He] laid the dead of London at our doors." Because of Murrow's intimate broadcasts, the United States no longer seemed thousands of miles away from the conflict.

In his long career Murrow was never an impartial anchorman. He emerged from the tradition of the radio commentator, who did not shy away from expressing an opinion. During World War II he wove his editorial views subtly into the broadcasts, not trying to be objective about the war against Hitler. As he often said, there is no reason to balance the values of Jesus Christ with those of Judas Iscariot. After World War II Murrow had hope that the media would engage other less defined issues, such as injustice and ignorance.

During the mid-1940s Murrow was a national celebrity but had trouble finding a forum for his pursuit of truth. He was dissatisfied as a CBS vice president in charge of news and public affairs. He deliberately avoided television, proclaiming "I wish goddamned television had never been invented." In 1948 he found peace of mind by producing a series of record albums with Fred W. Friendly, a former radio producer at a Rhode Island station. The *I Can Hear It Now* albums interwove historical events and speeches with Murrow narration and, surprisingly, became a commercial success. The Murrow/Friendly partnership clicked, and the team developed a radio series, *Hear It Now*, which featured the sounds of current events, illuminated, of course, by the wisdom of Murrow.

TRANSFER TO TELEVISION

In 1951 the team agreed to modify the *Now* concept again, this time emphasizing the visual dynamic of television. They called the effort *See It Now*. Murrow did not want the medium's first documentary series to be a passive recap of daily events but an active engagement with the issues of the day. To implement this vision, Murrow and Friendly formed the first autonomous news unit in television. With Murrow as host and editor in chief and Friendly as managing editor, *See It Now* hired its own camera crews and reporters. As he did with radio, Murrow changed the fundamental structure of gathering news in television.

"This is an old team trying to learn a new trade," proclaimed Murrow on the premiere of *See It Now*, which aired on November 18, 1951. Murrow, as in all the programs that followed, was seated in Studio 41 amid the television technology—the monitors and microphones, as well as the supporting technicians. To underscore this breakthrough in instantaneous coverage, he relayed the first live coast-to-coast transmission, summoning up a split screen of the Brooklyn Bridge in New York City and the Golden Gate Bridge in San Francisco.

See It Now achieved many firsts during its early run. Reaching an audience of three million homes, Murrow presented the first broadcast from a submerged submarine. The program also simulated coverage of a mock bomb attack on New York City, with Murrow reporting from an F-94 fighter jet. During the 1952 Christmas season, *See It Now* featured a one-hour report on the realities of the ground war in Korea. The special surveyed the frustrations and anxieties of everyday soldiers and was described by the *New Yorker* as "one of the most impressive presentations in television's short life, . . . [picturing] for us a tragic living legend of our own time . . . with great piety and understanding."

PROVOKING CONTROVERSY

Impelled by the accolades, Murrow and Friendly wanted to report on the anticommunist hysteria that was beginning to envelop the country. The team searched for what Friendly called "the little picture," a story that could symbolize this wrenching issue. In October 1953 Murrow and reporter Joe Wershba produced "The Case of Milo Radulovich," a study of a U.S. Air Force lieutenant who was branded a security risk because his family subscribed to subversive newspapers. In "Argument in

Indianapolis," broadcast one month later, *See It Now* investigated an American Legion chapter that refused to rent its meeting hall to the American Civil Liberties Union, a potent metaphor for how the demagogic tactics of Senator Joseph McCarthy penetrated the Midwest.

On March 9, 1954, *See It Now* decided to expose the architect of this paranoia, McCarthy himself. Murrow used documentary material, "told mainly in his own words and pictures," to refute the half-truths and misstatements of the junior senator of Wisconsin. In his tailpiece Murrow explicitly challenged his viewers to confront their fears: "this is no time for men who oppose Senator McCarthy's methods to keep silent." The McCarthy program produced tensions in the relationship between Murrow and the network. CBS did not assist in promoting the broadcast and questioned whether Murrow had overstepped the boundaries of editorial objectivity.

See It Now continued to provoke controversy. Murrow interviewed J. Robert Oppenheimer, the physicist who was removed as adviser to the Atomic Energy Commission because he was suspected of being a Soviet agent. The series also documented issues of desegregation, the Cold War, and governmental scandal. Beginning in October 1953 Murrow counterbalanced his grave image by hosting a celebrity talk show, *Person to Person*. Each week he electronically visited the homes of personalities from the arts, sports, politics, and business. Critics worried about the show's lack of depth, particularly the interviews with movie stars such as Marilyn Monroe and Marlon Brando. In the late 1950s Murrow hosted a discussion series of greater depth, *Small World*, where he moderated an unrehearsed conversation among intellectuals and world leaders situated in studios and homes around the globe.

A PARTNERSHIP ENDS

Murrow received numerous honors for his work on *See It Now* and *Person to Person*, but his relationship with CBS deteriorated. He complained about the increasing commercialism of television. He lambasted the industry at a 1958 convention for radio and television news directors by stating the medium insulated the viewer from "the realities of the world in which we live." His crusades and jeremiads were accepted in times of war and national hysteria, but in the late 1950s they seemed out of place in a prosperous nation. After the cancellation of *See It Now*, CBS split up the esteemed team of Murrow and Friendly. Friendly became executive producer of *CBS Reports*, for which Murrow occasionally hosted investigative reports such as *Harvest of Shame*, a trenchant examination of the migrant workers' plight.

In 1961 President John F. Kennedy persuaded Murrow to leave CBS to become director of the U.S. Information Agency. Murrow remained in that post until 1964, when he resigned because he was suffering from lung cancer. Always a heavy smoker, he had investigated the connection between cigarettes and cancer for *See It Now*. Murrow died on April 27, 1965, and was saluted by the *New York Times* as "broadcasting's true voice."

ACCOLADES

The New York University School of Journalism placed three of Murrow's reports—*Battle of Britain*, the McCarthy investigation, and *Harvest of Shame*—on its list of best U.S. journalism of the twentieth century. His legacy can be studied at the Edward R. Murrow Center of Public Diplomacy created by Tuft University's Fletcher School of Law and Diplomacy. The university's digital library makes information about the Murrow collection available online. Murrow's abiding importance to journalism was underscored by the 2005 film *Good Night, and Good Luck*, directed and cowritten by actor George Clooney. Clooney hoped that his film about the confrontation between Murrow and McCarthy would spur conversation about journalism's role during such crises as the Iraq War.

Murrow remained one of the most dominant individuals in broadcast news for decades. During his twenty-five-year career, he made more than 5,000 reports, many of which were considered journalistic classics, probing into the twentieth century's most troubling issues with poetry and insight. Murrow and Friendly invented the magazine news format, which became the major documentary form on network television. Shaping the form and content of television news, they also tested the limits of editorial advocacy. Murrow became the exemplar of free speech and democratic ideals in a commercial media. As the *Columbia Journalism Review* notes, Murrow's "spirit is still invoked . . . whenever the glories, the depredations, and the promise of television news come up for argument."

Ron Simon

SEE ALSO: *Brando, Marlon; Cold War; McCarthyism; Monroe, Marilyn; The* New Yorker*; Radio; Shirer, William L.; Television; World War II.*

BIBLIOGRAPHY

Barnouw, Erik. *Tube of Plenty: The Evolution of American Television*. New York: Oxford University Press, 1990.

Bliss, Edward J., ed. *In Search of Light: The Broadcasts of Edward R. Murrow, 1938–1964*. New York: Knopf, 1967.

Bliss, Edward J. *Now the News: The History of Broadcast Journalism*. New York: Oxford University Press, 1975.

Boyer, Peter J. *Who Killed CBS?: The Undoing of America's Number One News Network*. New York: Random House, 1988.

Cloud, Stanley, and Lynne Olson. *The Murrow Boys*. Boston: Houghton Mifflin, 1996.

Edwards, Bob. *Edward R. Murrow and the Birth of Broadcast Journalism*. Hoboken, NJ: Wiley, 2004.

Friendly, Fred W. *Due to Circumstances beyond Our Control . . .* New York: Vintage Books, 1967.

Gates, Gary Paul. *Air Time: The Inside Story of CBS News*. New York: Harper & Row, 1978.

Halberstam, David. *The Powers That Be*. New York: Knopf, 1979.

Kendrick, Alexander. *Prime Time: The Life of Edward R. Murrow*. Boston: Little, Brown, 1969.

Murrow, Edward R., and Fred W. Friendly, eds. *See It Now*. New York: Simon & Schuster, 1955.

O'Connor, John E., ed. *American History/American Television: Interpreting the Video Past*. New York: Ungar, 1983.

Paley, William S. *As It Happened*. Garden City, NY: Doubleday, 1979.

Persico, Joseph E. *Edward R. Murrow: An American Original*. New York: McGraw-Hill, 1988.

Smith, Sally Bedell. *In All His Glory*. New York: Simon & Schuster, 1990.

Sperber, A. M. *Murrow: His Life and Times.* New York: Freundlich, 1986.

Muscle Beach

Muscle Beach is a gymnastics training area on Santa Monica Beach, located south of the Santa Monica Pier in Santa Monica, California. The area was established in 1939 with a simple platform and evolved over time to include a padded gymnastics area, chinning bars, parallel bars, rings, and a small jungle gym for children. At the height of its popularity in the 1940s and 1950s, the area drew tumblers, acrobats, weight lifters, and thousands of spectators. Muscle Beach greatly contributed to the image of a carefree, sun-filled Southern California lifestyle and helped launch a physical fitness craze.

There were, to be sure, other locations where, for a time, physical fitness boomed, albeit under the more precise label of physical culture. John Harvey Kellogg's Sanitarium in Michigan, Bernarr Macfadden's Physical Culture Hotel in Florida, and Robert (Bob) Hoffman's York Barbell Club in Pennsylvania were among the spots where people went hoping to improve their strength, health, and appearance. Two things elevated Muscle Beach over these earlier meccas of strength and health: first, it did not depend on the personal force of one man, and second, the location was unbeatable.

American photography, art, advertising, television, and film have traded on the image of a magical Southern California lifestyle since the beginning of the twentieth century. "California dreamin'" is, in a way, the logical extension of the American dream, and names such as Hollywood, Beverly Hills, and Sunset Boulevard evoke glamour, youth, and good vibrations throughout America. All that was needed to ignite an explosion of interest in the beach lifestyle was a group of insouciant young folks who, by their own example, showed Southern Californians and the world how to have fun in the sun.

In the summer of 1939 Abbye "Pudgy" Evile and her boyfriend, Les Stockton, began to meet with a small group of tumblers and hand balancers at a platform on the Santa Monica Beach. Soon they were joined in the long summer afternoons by others who liked acrobatics. By 1940 the beach was bustling, and Evile and Stockton had been joined by accomplished tumbler-balancers, such as Glenn Sundby, Bruce Conner, and Wayne Long. The weekend crowds who came to see the free, circuslike performances grew, often reaching several thousand spectators.

Soon barbells appeared on the beach, brought by weight trainers who were drawn by the jolly camaraderie of the acrobats, most of whom used weights to strengthen their bodies for the rigor of their stunts. The open use of heavy weights by men and women who were such marvelous athletes had a significant effect on American culture. The nimbleness of these weight-trained athletes went a long way toward convincing anyone who saw them lift and tumble that the use of barbells and dumbells, contrary to the opinion of almost every coach and sports scientist in the country, would not make a person "muscle bound." In 1940 it was believed that the lifting of heavy weights would make a person slow and inflexible, even though there was no scientific evidence to support the belief. But no one who watched Evile and Stockton lift weights and then perform their stunts could still believe in the myth of the muscle-bound lifter. Such weight training would later be universally accepted by coaches and athletes in all sports.

GROWING POPULARITY

Spectators to Muscle Beach during this time gawked at the big, muscular people lifting weights and at the acrobats flipping and twisting through the air. One of the most crowd-pleasing stunts was the human pyramid, performed by Muscle Beach regulars. Stunts of this sort, as well as adagio (in which people are thrown and caught), require careful cooperation among the participants. They fostered, and built on, a sense of fellowship in a noncompetitive atmosphere. Harold Zinkin, who years later would help to invent the Universal weight machine, said the acrobats "shared everything we knew. It was a happy atmosphere, like a jam session with everyone playing his part."

The burgeoning activities at Muscle Beach were significantly disrupted after Japan bombed Pearl Harbor in December 1941 and the United States entered World War II. After the war ended in 1945, activity alongside the pier reached a higher level than ever before. In addition, the city of Santa Monica elevated the platforms so visitors to the increasingly famous Muscle Beach weekends had a better view. By this time bodybuilders had arrived, and their extravagant physiques also drew crowds, like fully fanned peacocks at a zoo. The city soon built a weight pit where the competitive lifters and bodybuilders could pump iron and work on their tan all at the same time, cooled by winds off the Pacific Ocean.

From 1946 through the late 1950s, Muscle Beach lacked the sweetness and purity of the past, but it featured ever-larger crowds and even more bodybuilders. Some of the bodybuilders later made major contributions to the world of weights. One was Jack LaLanne, who was at Muscle Beach almost every weekend to lift and do stunts with his friends. In 1951 he began a pioneering fitness television show that aired for thirty-four years. Steve Reeves, whose bodybuilding titles include Mr. America (1947), Mr. World (1948), and Mr. Universe (1950), was also a regular at the weight pit, and those who were there say that no one ever drew crowds like he did. He went on to enjoy a long and successful career as an actor in movies, such as *Hercules* (1958) and *Hercules Unchained* (1959).

Other regulars at Muscle Beach were Vic Tanny and his younger brother Armand, an outstanding lifter. In the 1950s Vic founded a nationwide chain of modern health clubs that bore his name. They were the first of their kind, and although the chain grew large and unwieldy and eventually failed, Vic's influence was felt by millions of Americans who had their first taste of progressive resistance exercise in his glittering, chrome-filled clubs. Joe Gold developed his muscles as well as his famous tan at Muscle Beach before opening Gold's Gym, which became the training headquarters of the leading bodybuilders in the world during the 1960s and 1970s. Eventually, Gold sold his legendary gym and opened a new place, called World Gym. It attracted so many of the top bodybuilders that Gold was able to successfully franchise it around the United States.

DECLINE AND RESTORATION

By the late 1950s Muscle Beach began to draw some unsavory characters, and after a series of incidents, some of which were criminal in nature, the city closed Muscle Beach and hauled away the weights. Some observers at the time believed that the city, while genuinely worried by the sorts of people who had been joining the throng, was primarily motivated by a desire for more parking for shoppers and tourists. Whatever the reason, Muscle Beach ceased to exist in its original fabled form.

Unwilling to be without a place to train by the beach, however, a dedicated group of bodybuilders convinced the city of Venice to put in a small weight pit on Venice Beach, 2 miles south of the former Muscle Beach. In time, Venice Beach began to draw a regular crowd, and it was often the location chosen by magazine publisher Joe Weider for photo shoots of bodybuilder Arnold Schwarzenegger for *Muscle & Fitness*, the leading magazine in the field. These photographs helped both Weider and Schwarzenegger, and they perpetuated the legend of Southern California as the *terminus ad quem* for bodybuilders everywhere.

In 1977 Schwarzenegger was featured in the remarkable documentary film, *Pumping Iron*, as he and other bodybuilders prepared for and competed in the 1975 Mr. Olympia and Mr. Universe contests. Schwarzenegger won Mr. Olympia, the premier title in the sport, for the sixth time in a row. Conceived and scripted by Charles Gaines and directed by George Butler, the film was a huge critical success. It introduced bodybuilding to a wider public, and weight training became an acceptable way to develop a leaner, healthier body. Schwarzenegger became a celebrity because of *Pumping Iron*, and he went to have an extremely successful movie career. He later entered politics and served two terms as governor of California in the early 2000s.

As bodybuilding gained greater popularity, Venice Beach, which officially adopted the name, "Venice Muscle Beach" in 1986, finally decided to expand the weight training area, and a much larger facility was built with a stage that can accommodate bodybuilding competitions. In the late 1990s, in a major change of heart, the city of Santa Monica also built a new facility on the site of the old Muscle Beach platform, complete with an open-air weight pit, a place for children to exercise, and a sign that reads, "The Original Location of Muscle Beach. The Birthplace of the Physical Fitness Boom of the Twentieth Century."

Since the 1930s Muscle Beach has seen many changes, and the changes have not all been good ones. Drugs now play a major and sinister role in competitive bodybuilding, and they have allowed bodybuilders to develop a combination of muscle mass and definition that the health-conscious bodybuilders of earlier decades could not have imagined. The men and women who were first drawn to Muscle Beach trained hard in the fresh air, ate carefully, and were healthy as horses. Good health was at the heart of their lifestyle. Many later bodybuilders made a Faustian bargain and sacrificed health for appearance. Some of the bodies at Muscle Beach in the twenty-first century might only look healthy.

Jan Todd
Terry Todd

SEE ALSO: *Bodybuilding; LaLanne, Jack; Macfadden, Bernarr; Reeves, Steve; Schwarzenegger, Arnold; Stockton, "Pudgy"; World War II.*

BIBLIOGRAPHY

Chowder, Ken. "Muscle Beach." *Smithsonian*, November 1998, 124–137.

Matzer, Marla. "The Venus of Muscle Beach." *Los Angeles Times Magazine*, February 22, 1998, 20–22.

Rose, Marla Matzer. *Muscle Beach: Where the Best Bodies in the World Started a Fitness Revolution*. New York: St. Martin's Press Griffin, 2001.

Todd, Jan. "The Legacy of Pudgy Stockton." *Iron Game History*, January 1992, 5–7.

Zinkin, Harold. *Remembering Muscle Beach: Where Hard Bodies Began*. Santa Monica, CA: Angel City Press, 1999.

Muscle Cars

Muscle cars were a special breed of automobile that were born in the 1950s, grew throughout the 1960s, and—for the most part—died in the early 1970s. They remain a cultural symbol of style, mild rebellion, and a personal statement of independence. The concept was based upon the simple engineering idea of placing the largest possible engine into the lightest possible chassis. Using this measurement, the muscle cars initially emerged from the factories of a small handful of car manufacturers. Chevrolet was among the first, bringing out a 265-cubic-inch V-8 configuration engine in its lighter, sportier 1955 Bel Air range. Chrysler, meanwhile, offered the awesome hemi-head engine in its full-sized 300-series vehicles.

THE BEGINNINGS

Moving into the 1960s, the formula began to take root. The Chevy 409 became available, followed by the first Pontiac GTO, which featured a 389-cubic-inch displaced motor, with three two-barrel carburetors in a light Tempest body. Other American manufacturers followed suit: Ford with the Fairlane and Galaxie 500, and Chrysler with the Dodge Polara and Plymouth Belvedere.

As with most cultural phenomena, muscle cars began as unique specialist models hidden within the mainstream. In appearance, they were little different from their sedate, mass-produced, assembly-line cousins. As their popularity spread, however, they became more visible entities and—for car enthusiasts—very nearly replaced that much older personal automotive expression, the hot rod.

"HOT" CARS BECOME WIDELY AVAILABLE

By the end of the 1960s the muscle car was commonplace across virtually all manufacturers' model lineups. Virtually all car lines had a "hot" version that was affordable, more powerful, and, above all, faster. Engine sizes exceeded 400-cubic-inch displacements, with General Motors (GM) muscle cars having their largest performance engines in all of their midsized cars. Ford's ultimate performance engines were the 427-, 428-, and 429-cubic-inch varieties and were available in many Ford cars. Chrysler developed 426- and 440-cubic-inch engines as its standard bearers. Many of these engines came equipped with large, four-barrel carburetors or combinations of three two-barrel or two four-barrel carburetors. Horsepower ratings went to more than 400, while gas mileage often fell into the low teens or even single digits. Hood-scoops, bright paint, stripes, graphics, and spoilers helped to define the breed, as did the aggressive model names such as Charger, Cobra, Cyclone, Road Runner, and Challenger.

Muscle cars did not corner or brake well by modern standards, but they did go fast. The standard of performance

Shelby Cobra Roadster. *The Shelby Cobra Roadster, named for creator Carroll Shelby, is one of several types of muscle cars that symbolized freedom and style for car enthusiasts.* RACINGONE/CONTRIBUTOR/ISC ARCHIVES/GETTY IMAGES.

was judged by how fast a car could cover a quarter mile from a standing start. The 14-second bracket seemed to define the breed, but a few exceptional models could go even faster. Drag racing, and the much more dangerous street racing, were very much part of the muscle car phenomenon. The obvious racing tie to muscle cars was usually drag racing, but both Chrysler and Ford also were heavily involved in stock-car racing.

A subset of the muscle car was the "pony" car, a genre that started with the 1964 Ford Mustang. The Mustang's early successful combination of style and performance led to the creation of the Chevrolet Camaro, Pontiac Firebird, Dodge Challenger, Plymouth Barracuda, and American Motors Javelin. All came to populate the Sports Car Club of America's popular Trans-Am road-racing series. Pony cars were even lighter than their muscle car cousins but were frequently available with the same larger displacement engines of their muscle car kin.

MUSCLE CARS AND THE YOUTH CULTURE

Muscle cars were marketed to young people. The design styles, colors, advertising, and price were all aimed at the first-time new-car buyer. Chrysler promoted its performance cars with advertising campaigns that urged consumers to "join the Dodge Rebellion" and launched a line of cars it dubbed the Plymouth Rapid Transit System. Pontiac connected its popular GTO with TV's *Laugh-In*, and Ford openly tied its performance cars to its racing programs and its association with legendary racer and designer Carroll Shelby.

The successful mass-marketing and consequent popularity of the cars were reflected by their appearances in high-profile television series and movies. The eponymous hero of *Mannix* drove Plymouth Barracuda convertibles, among others. Even Jim Rockford of *The Rockford Files* had a Pontiac Firebird. Muscle cars were also prominently featured in films such as *Bullitt* (1968), *Two-Lane Blacktop* (1971), *Dirty Mary Crazy Larry* (1974), and *Vanishing Point* (1971), all of which focused on antisocial or rebellious heroism expressed through cars and the open road. Popular music of the 1960s, too, was laced with muscle-car-oriented tunes such as "Little GTO" and "409."

While not exactly representing the counterculture, muscle cars were certainly a visible accessory of the 1960s youth movement. Muscle cars represented the kind of car parents did not drive and would likely be offended by. How far did the muscle car evolution go? Dodge sold a virtual Grand National Stock Car called the Daytona to the public in 1969. It featured wild aerodynamic pieces and the famous 426-cubic-inch hemi engine; Chevrolet had the massive 454-cubic-inch Chevelle SS in 1971, and Ford had the 428-cubic-inch Mach 1 Mustang in 1970. Even relatively sedate American Motors promoted its Javelin and its racing heritage. In 1972 the company even built and sold the Gremlin X, a subcompact car with a V-8.

BEYOND THE 1970s

Ultimately, early antipollution controls, high insurance costs, and the gas crisis of the early 1970s doomed the muscle cars. Consumer taste shifted toward personal luxury cars, and economics dictated a demand for fuel-efficient domestics and imports. By the 1980s there were but a few survivors of the muscle-car breed. Pontiac was still making the Firebird Trans-Am, Chevrolet the Camaro Z-28, and Ford the Mustang. While each of these models offered a better level of general performance than their 1960s ancestors, they paled in comparison to the raw power available a few years earlier. Many standard cars of the 1990s, meanwhile, were taking their styling clues from the old muscle cars. Spoilers; custom wheels; fat, raised white letter tires; and bulged or scooped hoods are all examples of the performance images first seen thirty years earlier.

By the end of the twentieth century, muscle cars had begun to experience a renaissance of sorts, with restorers and collectors seeking out selected models and reliving the heady days of the 1960s with cheap gas and a lot of horsepower. Even auto manufacturers got back into the act with the rebirth of a few classic muscle-car nameplates. Dodge brought back the Charger as a sedan, complete with hemi engine and a Super Bee option. The Challenger came back—with a 392-engine option. Chevrolet introduced a fully modern 427 Camaro, and Ford produced both a Boss 302 Mustang and a Shelby GT 500. All offered more than 400 horsepower. The main difference is that today these are high-dollar, premium cars that are fully equipped with big brakes, good handling, electronic stability controls, and many options.

Muscle cars represent an era when a mass-produced automobile could make a bold, personal statement in sharp contrast to the average automobile. They might have seemed primitive, but their purpose was pure and, for a certain person, remains a powerful lure today: horsepower—and lots of it.

Sean Evans

SEE ALSO: *Automobile; Drag Racing; Ford Motor Company; Hot Rods;* Laugh-In*; Stock-Car Racing.*

BIBLIOGRAPHY

Campisano, Jim. *American Muscle Cars.* New York: MetroBooks, 1995.

Consumer Guide. *The Great Book of Muscle Cars.* Lincolnwood, IL: Publications International, 1990.

Farr, Donald. *Mustang Boss 302: From Racing Legend to Modern Muscle Car.* Minneapolis, MN: Motorbooks, 2011.

Frumkin, Mitch. *Muscle Car Mania: An Advertising Collection 1964–1974.* Osceola, WI: Motorbooks International, 1981.

Frumkin, Mitch. *Son of Muscle Car Mania: More Ads 1962–74.* Osceola, WI: Motorbooks International, 1982.

Holmstrom, Darwin. *Hemi Muscle Cars.* Minneapolis, MN: Motorbooks, 2011.

Mueller, Mike. *Fifties Muscle: The Dawn of High Performance.* Osceola, WI: Motorbooks International, 1996.

Muscle Cars: American Thunder. Lincolnwood, IL: Publications International, 1997.

Newbery, J. G. *Muscle Cars.* San Diego, CA: Thunder Bay Press, 1994.

Muscular Christianity

Simply defined, muscular Christianity is masculine, or "manly," Christianity. Since the nineteenth century, Christian men in the United States have responded to the so-called feminization of American religion. From the seventeenth century through the end of the Victorian era, approximately two-thirds of America's Christian parishioners were women, and beginning in the 1850s, males began to challenge this dominance by making religion a manly endeavor. Organizations such as the Young Men's Christian Association (YMCA); Men and Religion Forward Movement; Boy Scouts of America; Christian Service Brigade; and, most recently, Promise Keepers sprang from this movement. These groups have emphasized a uniquely masculine expression of Christian faith, American nationalism, citizenship, chivalrous behavior, and even skills in outdoor activities. Today people often use the term *muscular Christianity* to refer to any type of male-dominated, outdoor, virile, or sports-oriented activity that has a specifically Christian or evangelistic purpose.

THE "GREAT REVIVAL"

In addition to its general connotation, muscular Christianity is a specific movement, originating in England and finding voice in the United States beginning with the Great Revival of 1857–1858. The term *muscular Christianity* originated as a literary device in a review of English novelist Charles Kingsley's *Two Years Ago* (1857), written by T. C. Sanders for the *Saturday Review* (February 21, 1857). Sanders recognized Kingsley as the most important and visible representative of this new movement, which valued "a man who fears God and can walk a thousand miles in a thousand hours—who, in the language which Mr. Kingsley has made popular, breathes God's free air on God's rich earth, and at the same time can hit a woodcock, doctor a horse, and twist a poker around his finger." Fellow advocate of Christian masculinity Thomas Hughes, the author of *Tom Brown's Schooldays* (1857) and *Tom Brown at Oxford* (1860), wrote that "muscular Christians has hold of the old chivalrous and Christian belief, that a man's body is given him to be trained and brought into subjection, and then used for the protection of the weak, the advancement of all righteous causes, and the subduing of the earth which God has given to the children of men."

The ideal of muscular Christianity celebrated physical exertion, comradeship, and determination, and it emphasized manliness, morality, health, and patriotism. In these writings, the male human body is a metaphor for social, national, and religious bodies. A man must discipline his body physically and morally to become healthy and influential; in the same way, a country must assert control over socially disruptive forces in order to become a great and holy nation. Therefore, the goals of muscular Christians were not primarily individual but communal—their task was to subdue culture and render it more Christian. Inspired by this movement, Victorian urban revivalists sought to evangelize the nation, spreading the gospel and the accompanying civilizing values of middle-class culture.

A NATIONAL AWAKENING

During the Great Revival of 1857–1858, the United States began to express its own version of masculinized religion; by the 1860s, the term *muscular Christianity* had become commonplace in denominational publications, as well as major periodicals such as the *New York Times.* The revival, perhaps the closest thing in American history to a truly national awakening, differed from previous revivals in three key ways: (1) the leadership was lay instead of clerical; (2) its setting was urban instead of rural; and (3) its participants were primarily male instead of female. The middle-class white men who participated in this "businessmen's revival" formed prayer meetings in the nation's major metropolises and devoted their energies to soul-saving and social reform.

The most lasting institution to emerge from this revival was the YMCA. Although the organization was founded in England in 1844 and transplanted to Montreal and Boston in 1851, it did not gain cultural importance until 1857 when urban revivalists such as D. L. Moody in Chicago joined and championed the movement. Made up primarily of white, middle-class men, the YMCA sought to promote a masculinized Christianity consistent with middle-class businessmen's culture. It also sought to "civilize" the immigrant masses flooding into America's cities.

The idea of muscular Christianity arose in the United States alongside postmillennial ideals of evangelical cultural dominance, manifest destiny, and worldwide mission. Evangelicals argued that the United States held the sympathy of all the nations of the world, and, as Tony Ladd and James A. Mathisen explain in *Muscular Christianity: Evangelical Protestants and the Development of American Sport*, "God could not do without America." If the United States was to hasten the return of Jesus Christ, it had to reform its cities, Christianize the masses, and serve as a beacon of Christian culture for the rest of the world. Spiritual and national aims converged as muscular Christians came to see the United States as the world's savior.

MAKING FAITH MANLY

Muscular Christianity, however, was more than Christianized manifest destiny. In addition to revealing the longing for Christian culture and middle-class dominance, it reflected gender tensions inherent in Victorian America. Antebellum Americans, somewhat fearful of the moral dangers of the open market but also seeking its maximum potential, placed men in the public sphere of economic activity and women in the private sphere of religion and moral nurture. Women would keep their husbands and children moral, men would become entrepreneurs and provide for their families, and together they would form godly homes—the backbone of a Christian nation. The ideal of muscular Christianity challenged this gendered version of Protestantism by making the evangelical faith manly.

During the 1857–1858 revival, leaders aimed all the advertising at men and organized prayer meetings in urban business districts—public spaces accessible almost exclusively to men. Businessmen looked with suspicion upon women who challenged social boundaries and came downtown to participate in prayer meetings. Thus, muscular Christianity can be said to be an attempt by religiously marginalized men to recapture evangelical Christianity as a male endeavor.

In 1911 leaders of the interdenominational and lay-led Men and Religion Forward Movement sought to bury feminized religion for good and replace it with a Protestant faith that was manly as well as friendly to a growing consumer-driven economy. Accompanying American Protestants' affirmation of vertically integrated, corporate capitalism was a new gender ideology. Evangelical men argued that religion should no longer be dominated by women somewhat leery of burgeoning capitalist growth; rather, it should become a manly pursuit fully consistent with consumer capitalism and a culture of leisure. Feminized religion's restraint of commerce had become stifling, and middle-class Protestants eventually replaced Victorian sentimentalism with a more muscular Christianity that buttressed their growing economic prosperity.

Although women continue to hold considerable sway in North America's churches, American religion is no longer perceived as effeminate or female-dominated. The sea changes in the American economy, the reorientation of gender coding at end of the Victorian era, and the ideal of muscular Christianity help to explain this shift from feminine to masculine Christianity. Both now exist alongside one another as the number of gender-focused religious groups grow, among them the Council on Biblical Manhood and Womanhood, Christians for Biblical Equality, Promise Keepers, the "Re-Imagining" Conference, and scores of other denominational groups. The ideal of muscular Christianity is a key element in the centuries-long debates regarding gender's role in defining Christian practice and the relationship between religion and commerce—debates Americans will continue for centuries to come.

Kurt W. Peterson

SEE ALSO: *Boy Scouts of America; Evangelism; Promise Keepers; Religious Right.*

BIBLIOGRAPHY

Bederman, Gail. "'The Women Have Had Charge of the Church Work Long Enough': The Men and Religion Forward Movement of 1911–1912 and the Masculinization of Middle-Class Protestantism." *American Quarterly* 41, no. 3 (1989): 432–465.

Bendroth, Margaret Lamberts. "Men, Masculinity, and Urban Revivalism: J. Wilbur Chapman's Boston Crusade, 1909." *Journal of Presbyterian History* 75 (1997): 235–246.

Hall, Donald E. *Muscular Christianity: Embodying the Victorian Age.* New York: Cambridge University Press, 1994.

Ladd, Tony, and James A. Mathisen. *Muscular Christianity: Evangelical Protestants and the Development of American Sport.* Grand Rapids, MI: Baker Books, 1999.

Long, Kathryn T. *The Revival of 1857–58: Interpreting an American Religious Awakening.* New York: Oxford University Press, 1998.

Mangan, J. A., and James Walvin, eds. *Manliness and Morality: Middle-Class Masculinity in Britain and America, 1800–1940.* New York: St. Martin's Press, 1987.

Putney, Clifford. *Muscular Christianity: Manhood and Sports in Protestant America, 1880–1920.* Cambridge, MA: Harvard University Press, 2003.

Van Leeuwen, Mary Stewart. "Weeping Warriors: The Changing Message of Manly Religion." *Books and Culture: A Christian Review* 3, no. 6, (1997): 9–11.

Vance, Norman. *The Sinews of the Spirit: The Ideal of Christian Manliness in Victorian Literature and Religious Thought.* Boston: Cambridge University Press, 1985.

The Musical

Contemporary American musical theater is a widely diverse genre that encompasses a variety of styles. From traditional operettas and musical comedies by composers such as Sigmund Romberg and George Gershwin in the early part of the twentieth century, through mid-twentieth-century dramatic works by Richard Rodgers and Oscar Hammerstein II and their contemporaries, to shows that expand the boundaries of the genre by creators such as Stephen Sondheim and Andrew Lloyd Webber, the musical has been immensely popular with audiences

A Chorus Line. *The cast of* A Chorus Line *performs the show's signature number "One" at the Tony Awards in 2008.* MAZUR/ CONTRIBUTOR/WIREIMAGE/GETTY IMAGES.

worldwide for more than one hundred years. A work in which music and drama are combined in various ways, the Broadway musical adds dance, costumes, sets, orchestration, and musical style to the basic duality of music and drama to create a singular contribution to both American and global popular culture.

Musical works for the stage appeared in the United States prior to the twentieth century, thus establishing important precedents for the Broadway musical. Genres, all of which could be considered popular entertainment in some way, included European-style opera, ballad opera, minstrel shows, burlesque, variety shows, extravaganzas, pantomimes, melodramas, and vaudeville. Among the first especially important Broadway musicals is *The Black Crook* (1866). This show was significant for two reasons: it established New York City as a center for musical theater; and it played for 475 performances, instituting a defining goal of the successful Broadway musical—a long commercial run.

EARLY TWENTIETH-CENTURY MUSICALS

During the first third of the twentieth century, three distinct types of musical theater coexisted on Broadway stages: revue, musical comedy, and operetta. Revue was a performer-based genre that included comic skits and songs, often on a central topic. *The Ziegfeld Follies*, Shubert's *Passing Shows*, *George White's Scandals*, and *Irving Berlin's Music Box Revues* were among the most popular series of revues. Significant composers for revues included Irving Berlin and George Gershwin. Fanny Brice, Marilyn Miller, Will Rogers, and Al Jolson were just a few of the stars whose fame was established in the genre.

Musical comedy was similar to revue but included a dramatic plot. These productions featured everyday characters in everyday, albeit comic, situations. The emphasis was on individual musical numbers and star performers. George M. Cohan, Jerome Kern, Gershwin, Vincent Youmans, Cole Porter, and the collaborative team of Richard Rodgers and Lorenz Hart were important contributors to the genre. Among Gershwin's most important shows were *Lady, Be Good!* (1924), *Oh, Kay!* (1926), and *Girl Crazy* (1930). These works, along with Youmans's *No, No, Nanette* (1925), Porter's *Anything Goes* (1934), and Rodgers and Hart's *A Connecticut Yankee* (1927), *Babes in Arms* (1937), and *Pal Joey* (1940), virtually defined the musical comedy. Ethel Merman, Fred and Adele Astaire, and Gertrude Lawrence were but three of the many stars associated with the genre.

The third style of musical theater, operetta, consisted of works that were set in a time and place other than the present. The genre was dominated by the entire musical score, rather than by individual musical numbers and star performers. Sigmund Romberg and Rudolf Friml were the principal composers of operetta during the 1920s. Romberg's *The Student Prince* (1924), *The Desert Song* (1926), and *The New Moon* (1928); and Friml's *Rose-Marie* (1924) and *The Three Musketeers* (1928) were among the era's most popular Broadway shows. After the stock market crash of 1929, the operetta generally lost favor—

audiences in the 1930s preferred the brash musical comedy to the sentimental operetta. They preferred laughter to tears.

THE MODERN MUSICAL

The era of the modern musical began with *Show Boat* (1927, music by Kern, book and lyrics by Hammerstein). In this seminal work, character development and dramatic plot took precedence over music and performers. Music, superb as it was, was intended to serve the plot. Songs such as "Ol' Man River," "Can't Help Lovin' Dat Man," and "You Are Love" were integral to the story line of *Show Boat*; they were not mere decoration or entertainment. In their plot the creators of *Show Boat* addressed serious issues such as racial intolerance, alcoholism, and desertion. No longer was the musical theater merely the domain of effervescent musical comedy and revue and romantic operetta.

The "mature" musical, in which music and lyrics were integrated into the plot, continued in the work of Rodgers and Hammerstein. Their historic collaboration began with *Oklahoma!* (1943) and ended with *The Sound of Music* (1959). Their nine shows included *Carousel* (1945), *South Pacific* (1949), and *The King and I* (1951). Rodgers and Hammerstein used song as a means of defining a character. Numbers such as "Oh, What a Beautiful Morning" from *Oklahoma!*, "Soliloquy" from *Carousel*, "Wonderful Guy" from *South Pacific*, and "Something Wonderful" from *The King and I* humanized and personalized the characters who sang them in ways that were virtually unprecedented in the Broadway musical. These songs revealed the emotions and situations of the characters rather than those of the songwriter.

Rodgers and Hammerstein were often criticized for being "preachy" in their shows. They addressed serious social concerns in their work, including racial prejudice, the role of children in society, and the victory of good over evil in war. In addition to an emphasis on dramatic content, the team established a form for the musical—a long first act, which culminated in a dramatic climax, followed by a much shorter second act in which the dramatic conflict was resolved as quickly as possible.

Contemporaries of Rodgers and Hammerstein who adopted their basic approach to the musical included Alan Jay Lerner and Frederick Loewe, who penned *Brigadoon* (1947), *My Fair Lady* (1956), and *Camelot* (1960); and Frank Loesser, who created *Guys and Dolls* (1950), *The Most Happy Fella* (1956), and *How to Succeed in Business without Really Trying* (1961). Other popular shows from the mid-twentieth century that followed the general plan established by Rodgers and Hammerstein included *Finian's Rainbow* (1947, music by Burton Lane, lyrics by E. Y. Harburg), *Kiss Me, Kate* (1948, music and lyrics by Cole Porter), *Damn Yankees* (1955, music and lyrics by Richard Adler and Jerry Ross), *West Side Story* (1957, music by Leonard Bernstein, lyrics by Stephen Sondheim), *The Music Man* (1957, music and lyrics by Meredith Willson), *Gypsy* (1959, music by Jule Styne, lyrics by Sondheim), *Hello, Dolly!* (1964, music and lyrics by Jerry Herman), *Fiddler on the Roof* (1964, music by Jerry Bock, lyrics by Sheldon Harnick), and *Man of La Mancha* (1965, music by Mitch Leigh, lyrics by Joe Darion). The creators of these shows took the Rodgers and Hammerstein model and expanded it in a variety of ways. William Shakespeare provided the inspiration for *Kiss Me, Kate* (a show that incorporated *The Taming of the Shrew*) and *West Side Story* (a transformation of *Romeo and Juliet*), while his Spanish contemporary Cervantes actually appeared as a character in *Man of La Mancha*. Myth and legend materialized on stage in *Brigadoon*, *Camelot*, and *Finian's Rainbow*.

The mid-twentieth century produced a number of significant musical theater stars. Among the most famous female performers were Julie Andrews, Carol Channing, Mary Martin, Ethel Merman, Chita Rivera, and Gwen Verdon. Male stars included Alfred Drake, Zero Mostel, Robert Preston, and John Raitt. Occasionally, male stars on Broadway were true opera singers, as in the cases of Ezio Pinza and Robert Weede.

CONTEMPORARY MUSICAL THEATER

During the final third of the twentieth century, creators for the Broadway stage made attempts to expand the boundaries of the musical theater in various ways. The concept musical, developed by Sondheim in works such as *Company* (1970) and *Follies* (1971), was a type of show in which narrative plot in the traditional sense did not exist. Composer Marvin Hamlisch, lyricist Edward Kleban, and director-choreographer Michael Bennett chose this approach for *A Chorus Line* (1975), a show in which each person auditioning for a chorus line tells his or her life story. John Kander and Fred Ebb also used the general principle of the concept musical in *Cabaret* (1966) and *Chicago* (1975). In these shows, the duo used song to comment on plot developments rather than to present the narrative in a purely linear fashion. *Cabaret* featured the song "Willkommen" (originally performed by Joel Grey), and *Chicago*'s opening number was "All That Jazz" (originally performed by Gwen Verdon).

Musicals that have eschewed the traditional lyrical style of Broadway song and replaced it with rock numbers include *Hair* (1968, music by Galt MacDermot), *Godspell* (1971, music and lyrics by Stephen Schwartz), *Jesus Christ Superstar* (1971, music by Andrew Lloyd Webber, lyrics by Tim Rice), *The Who's Tommy* (1993), and *Rent* (1996, music, lyrics, and book by Jonathan Larson). This trend has continued with such shows as *Spring Awakening* (2006, music by Duncan Sheik, lyrics by Steven Sater), *Bloody Bloody Andrew Jackson* (2010, music and lyrics by Michael Friedman, book by Alex Timbers), and *Spider-Man: Turn Off the Dark* (2011, music by The Edge and Bono of the band U2). Rock-inspired scores have become increasingly commonplace in musical theater.

Catalog musicals, or jukebox musicals—those that feature the music of a particular composer or performer—are another type of Broadway musical that does not include typical Broadway music. Some shows based on this formula are *Ain't Misbehavin'* (1978, based on Fats Waller), *Sophisticated Ladies* (1981, based on Duke Ellington), *Five Guys Named Moe* (1992, based on Louis Jordan), and *Jelly's Last Jam* (1992, based on Jelly Roll Morton). The popularity of this approach increased in the early 2000s with shows such as *Mamma Mia!* (2001, featuring ABBA songs), *Jersey Boys* (2005, telling the story of Frankie Valli and the Four Seasons), and *American Idiot* (2010, music by Green Day).

MUSICAL INSPIRATIONS

Since the 1970s, composers have continued to write traditional-style shows but have taken inspiration from a range of sources. *Annie* (1977, music by Charles Strouse, lyrics by Martin Charnin) was adapted from comic-book stories. The world of 1940s spies was adapted for *City of Angels* (1989, music by Cy Coleman, lyrics by David Zippel); a Caribbean island provided the inspiration for *Once on This Island* (1990, music by Stephen Flaherty, lyrics by Lynn Ahrens); and the circus provided the backdrop for *Barnum* (1980, music by Cy Coleman, lyrics by Michael Stewart). Literature was musicalized in the cases of *Big River* (1985, music and lyrics by Roger Miller), based on Mark Twain's *The Adventures of Huckleberry Finn*; *The Secret Garden* (1991, music by Lucy Simon, book and lyrics by Marsha Norman), based on the novel by Frances Hodgson Burnett; *Ragtime* (1998, music by Flaherty, lyrics by Ahrens), based on the novel by E. L. Doctorow; and *Wicked* (2003, music and lyrics by Stephen Schwartz, book by Winnie Holzman), based on Gregory Maguire's imaginative reworking of characters from L. Frank Baum's *The Wizard of Oz.*

Film has become an important source for contemporary musical theater works. Musicals based on motion pictures include *42nd Street* (1980, music by Harry Warren, lyrics by Al Dubin), *The Goodbye Girl* (1993, music by Marvin Hamlisch), *Sunset Boulevard* (1994, music by Andrew Lloyd Webber, lyrics by Don Black and Christopher Hampton), and *Passion* (1994, music and lyrics by Stephen Sondheim). Perhaps the most significant shows in this genre, however, are the Disney productions of *Beauty and the Beast* (1994, music by Alan Menken, lyrics by Howard Ashman and Tim Rice) and *The Lion King* (1997, songs by Elton John and Tim Rice).

Earlier genres have also made their reappearance on Broadway either through original works or bona fide revivals. The revue reasserted itself in *Cats* (1982, music by Andrew Lloyd Webber, lyrics based on poems by T. S. Eliot) and *The Will Rogers Follies* (1991, music by Cy Coleman, lyrics by Betty Comden and Adolph Green). Significant revivals during the 1990s included *Guys and Dolls* (1992), *Show Boat* (1994), *Carousel* (1994), *Damn Yankees* (1994), *How to Succeed in Business without Really Trying* (1995), *The King and I* (1996), *A Funny Thing Happened on the Way to the Forum* (1996), and *Chicago* (1996). Revivals have come to be so important on Broadway that the Tony Awards now include the category Best Revival.

Many of these new productions of classic works are better described as "revisals," for they differ substantially from the originals. Some feature innovative approaches, such as British director John Doyle requiring singers to also play instruments, as in his versions of Sondheim's *Sweeney Todd* (2005) and *Company* (2006), while others showcase well-known actors in an effort to generate audiences and thereby revenue.

EVOLUTION OF THE MUSICAL

Other changes in the overall concept of the Broadway musical took place during the final decades of the twentieth century. Chief among these was a move toward a totally sung musical. Drama was no longer to be exclusively in the domain of spoken language. Plot could be advanced largely through music, as in opera. Although shows such as *The Most Happy Fella* were groundbreaking in this approach, it became much more mainstream in works such as Lloyd Webber's *Evita* and Sondheim's *Sweeney Todd: The Demon Barber of Fleet Street* (1979).

When the sung-through (or nearly so) musical was infused with spectacular sets, stage effects, and costumes, the so-called mega-musical emerged. These shows are meant to dazzle the audience with visual effects, which match, or even surpass, the aural ones. Theatricality is paramount. Shows such as *Cats*, *Les Misérables* (1987, music by Claude-Michel Schönberg, lyrics by Alain Boublil and Herbert Kretzmer); *The Phantom of the Opera* (1988, music by Lloyd Webber, lyrics by Charles Hart and Richard Stilgoe); *Miss Saigon* (1991, music by Schönberg, lyrics by Richard Maltby Jr. and Boublil); and *Sunset Boulevard* are prime examples of this approach. Sets are as important as the characters. The tire in *Cats* (as well as the entire theater), the barricade in *Les Misérables*, the ghostly candelabra and huge chandelier in *The Phantom of the Opera*, the helicopter in *Miss Saigon*, and the staircase in *Sunset Boulevard* are as central to each of the shows as are the human characters. These mega-musicals have their roots in London's West End (the British equivalent of Broadway, which has a fascinating heritage of its own), where directors such as Cameron Mackintosh apply their lavish treatment to the genre.

The last quarter of the twentieth century and first decade of the twenty-first have produced a number of significant musical theater stars. Kristin Chenoweth, Christine Ebersole, Sutton Foster, Judy Kuhn, Angela Lansbury, Rebecca Luker, Idina Menzel, Patti LuPone, Donna Murphy, and Bernadette Peters have achieved tremendous accolades for their work on Broadway, as have Norbert Leo Butz, Michael Cerveris, Michael Crawford, Nathan Lane, Brian Stokes Mitchell, and Mandy Patinkin.

LASTING INFLUENCE

The Broadway musical has developed from an entertainment, whether comic (musical comedy and revue) or romantic (operetta), into a substantial artistic genre. Shows from as early as 1927 (*Show Boat*) included moral and social messages, a trend that continued through the middle part of the twentieth century with Rodgers and Hammerstein—and beyond. Many shows from the 1980s and 1990s included a "song of social injustice" in which there is a call for popular response to a particular issue. "Do You Hear the People Sing?" from *Les Misérables*, "Anthem" from *Chess* (1988, music by Benny Andersson and Björn Ulvaeus, lyrics by Tim Rice); "Bui Doi" from *Miss Saigon*; and "The Day after That" from *Kiss of the Spider Woman* (1993, music by John Kander, lyrics by Fred Ebb) are significant examples of such songs.

The Broadway musical has contributed to both the popular music and film industries. Many songs from Broadway shows have gone on to achieve popularity outside of the theater. Broadway was tied closely to Tin Pan Alley (the American popular music style) until World War II. Gershwin standards such as "Embraceable You" and "But Not for Me" were introduced in Broadway shows, as were many Porter and Rodgers and Hart songs. This trend continued with Sondheim's "Send in the Clowns" (from *A Little Night Music*); Schönberg and Boublil's "I Dreamed a Dream" and "Empty Chairs at Empty Tables" (from *Les Misérables*, the latter of which became an anthem for AIDS research); and Lloyd Webber's "The Music of the Night" (from *The Phantom of the Opera*). Performers ranging from opera stars Kiri TeKanawa and Bryn Terfel to popular singers Barbra Streisand (who got her start on Broadway), Judy Collins, and Frank Sinatra have included Broadway songs in their repertoires. Conversely, pop singers such as Paula Abdul appeared on Broadway musical stages during the 1990s.

The Broadway musical is not limited to Broadway, however. Film versions of Broadway musicals have been produced since the late 1920s. *The Desert Song* (1929, Warner Brothers) was the first in a long line of film adaptations that continued through the mid-twentieth century with a string of Rodgers and Hammerstein films. A resurgence of the film musical genre began in the late 1990s, with notable examples being *Evita* (1996, Cinergi Pictures), the Oscar-winning *Chicago* (2002, Miramax), *Hairspray* (2007, New Line Cinema), and *Sweeney Todd: The Demon Barber of Fleet Street* (2007, Dreamworks).Touring productions, resident companies, and amateur and school productions of Broadway musicals have also done much to promote the genre outside of New York City. The musical is certainly one of the popular forms of theatrical entertainment with the American—and world—public.

American musical theater is a widely diverse form of popular entertainment. Its many guises range from pure entertainment to tales with strong moral messages. The Broadway musical has had a dramatic impact on American popular culture not only because of the shows themselves but also because of the individual hit songs that were introduced in the shows. Furthermore, a number of popular musical personalities have established their professional careers on Broadway's musical stages.

William A. Everett

SEE ALSO: Annie*; Astaire, Fred, and Ginger Rogers; Berlin, Irving; Bernstein, Leonard; Brice, Fanny; Broadway; Burlesque;* Camelot*;* Cats*; Cohan, George M.; Doctorow, E. L.; Ellington, Duke;* Fiddler on the Roof*;* 42nd Street*; Green Day;* Hair*;* Hello, Dolly!*;* Jesus Christ Superstar*; Jolson, Al; Jordan, Louis; Kern, Jerome;* Les Misérables*;* The Lion King*; Lloyd Webber, Andrew; LuPone, Patti; Morton, Jelly Roll;* My Fair Lady*;* Oklahoma!*; Patinkin, Mandy;* The Phantom of the Opera*; Porter, Cole;* Rent*; Rivera, Chita; Rodgers and Hammerstein; Rodgers and Hart; Rogers, Will;* Show Boat*; Sinatra, Frank; Sondheim, Stephen;* The Sound of Music*;* South Pacific*; Stock Market Crashes; Streisand, Barbra;* Sunset Boulevard*; Tony Awards; Twain, Mark; Vaudeville;* West Side Story*;* The Ziegfeld Follies.

BIBLIOGRAPHY

Block, Geoffrey. *Enchanted Evenings: The Broadway Musical from "Show Boat" to Sondheim and Lloyd Webber*, 2nd ed. New York: Oxford University Press, 2009.

Bordman, Gerald. *American Operetta*. New York: Oxford University Press, 1981.

Bordman, Gerald. *American Musical Comedy*. New York: Oxford University Press, 1982.

Bordman, Gerald. *American Musical Revue*. New York: Oxford University Press, 1985.

Bordman, Gerald. *American Musical Theatre: A Chronicle*, 4th ed. New York: Oxford University Press, 2010.

Everett, William A. *The Musical: A Research and Information Guide*, 2nd ed. New York: Routledge, 2011.

Everett, William A., and Paul R. Laird, eds. *The Cambridge Companion to the Musical*, 2nd ed. New York: Cambridge University Press, 2008.

Flinn, Denny Martin. *Musical! A Grand Tour*. New York: Schirmer Books, 1997.

Gänzl, Kurt. *Gänzl's Book of the Broadway Musical*. New York: Schirmer Books, 1995.

Gänzl, Kurt. *The Musical: A Concise History*. Boston: Northeastern University Press, 1997.

Green, Stanley. *The World of Musical Comedy*, 4th ed. San Diego, CA: A. S. Barnes, 1980.

Green, Stanley. *Broadway Musicals Show by Show*, 6th ed., revised and updated by Kay Green. New York: Applause Theatre & Cinema Books, 2008.

Hischak, Thomas. *The Oxford Companion to the American Musical: Theatre, Film, and Television*. New York: Oxford University Press, 2008.

Jones, John Bush. *Our Musicals, Ourselves: A Social History of the American Musical Theatre*. Hanover, NH: Brandeis University Press, 2003.

Kirle, Bruce. *Unfinished Show Business: Broadway Musicals as Works-in-Progress*. Carbondale: Southern Illinois University Press, 2005.

Knapp, Raymond. *The American Musical and the Formation of National Identity*. Princeton, NJ: Princeton University Press, 2005.

Knapp, Raymond. *The American Musical and the Performance of Personal Identity*. Princeton, NJ: Princeton University Press, 2006.

Knapp, Raymond, Mitchell Morris, and Stacy Wolf, eds. *The Oxford Handbook of the American Musical*. New York: Oxford University Press, 2011.

Larkin, Colin, ed. *The Guinness Who's Who of Stage Musicals*. Enfield, CT: Guinness, 1994.

Lerner, Alan J. *The Musical Theatre: A Celebration*. New York: McGraw-Hill, 1986.

Mandelbaum, Ken. *Not since Carrie: Forty Years of Broadway Musical Flops*. New York: St. Martin's Press, 1991.

Mast, Gerald. *Can't Help Singin': The American Musical on Stage and Screen*. Woodstock, NY: Overlook Press, 1987.

McMillin, Scott. *The Musical as Drama: A Study of the Principles and Conventions behind Musical Shows from Kern to Sondheim*. Princeton, NJ: Princeton University Press, 2006.

Miller, Scott. *Strike Up the Band: A New History of Musical Theatre*. Portsmouth, NH: Heinemann, 2007.

Stempel, Larry. *Showtime: A History of the Broadway Musical Theater*. New York: Norton, 2010.

Sternfeld, Jessica. *The Megamusical*. Bloomington: Indiana University Press, 2006.

Suskin, Steven. *Opening Night on Broadway*. New York: Schirmer Books, 1990.

Suskin, Steven. *More Opening Nights on Broadway*. New York: Schirmer Books, 1997.

Swain, Joseph P. *The Broadway Musical: A Critical and Musical Survey*. New York: Oxford University Press, 1990.

Wolf, Stacy. *Changed for Good: A Feminist History of the Broadway Musical*. New York: Oxford University Press, 2011.

Wollman, Elizabeth L. *The Theater Will Rock: A History of the Rock Musical, from "Hair" to "Hedwig."* Ann Arbor: University of Michigan Press, 2006.

Mutiny on the Bounty

In 1932 Charles Nordhoff and James Norman Hall became best-selling authors with the publication of *Mutiny on the Bounty*, based upon the true story of mutiny onboard an English naval vessel in the late eighteenth century. They followed their success with sequels, *Men against the Sea* (1934) and *Pitcairn's Island*

Mutiny on the Bounty. *Marlon Brando as Fletcher Christian, right, and Trevor Howard as Captain Bligh, left, starred in the 1962 film* Mutiny on the Bounty. SILVER SCREEN COLLECTION/CONTRIBUTOR/MOVIEPIX/GETTY IMAGES.

(1934). The books tell of exciting nautical adventures, idyllic life on Pacific islands, romantic affairs between sailors and native girls, and power struggles in which good ultimately triumphs over evil. These were the topics, exotic fantasies of long ago and far away, that offered Americans an emotional escape from the throes of economic depression during the 1930s.

FROM PAGE TO SCREEN

In 1933 *In the Wake of the Bounty*, the story of the mutiny, was filmed as a documentary starring Errol Flynn. Some of the film was shot on location on Pitcairn's Island, where, in 1788, the *Bounty* mutineers found a haven from Captain Bligh and the court martial and death that would have met them had they returned to England. This documentary was followed, in 1935, by the hit Metro-Goldwyn-Mayer (MGM) film, *Mutiny on the Bounty*, starring the popular actor Clark Gable. It received Academy Award nominations for its score, film editing, screenplay, director, and three of its actors and won the award for Best Picture of 1935.

The film tells of the H.M.S. *Bounty*, which left England in 1787 to obtain breadfruit plants from Tahiti and transport them to the West Indies, where they could be established as a plantation food source for slaves. Clark Gable played Fletcher Christian, the hero who leads a mutiny against the tyrannical Captain Bligh, portrayed by Charles Laughton. In the beginning of the film, Captain Bligh immediately reveals his sadistic nature. Before the ship sets sail, he has a dead man flogged to show his crew that he will carry out punishment to the letter. The journey includes many similar incidents in which Bligh's harsh discipline establishes his tyranny and kindles the inclination for rebellion by the crew.

After the ship arrives in Tahiti, the crew enjoys a six-month reprieve from Bligh's punishments while the men collect breadfruit plants. During this time they enjoy the island paradise and the company of the native women. When the project is finished, the crew leaves reluctantly. Five of them try to desert ship to return to the island, but they are caught and flogged. Captain Bligh orders all hands on deck to observe the flogging, even though one crew member, the ship's elderly doctor, is too ill to move. Bligh demands that he come to the deck, and the effort kills the old doctor. As Christian watches the doctor die and the flogging begin, he rallies the crew to mutiny. He orders the men to spare Bligh's life. Bligh and some crew members who are still loyal to him travel in a lifeboat for forty-nine days until they reach the Dutch East Indies. Meanwhile, the mutineers return to their paradise, where they marry their Tahitian lovers.

A year later, Bligh, onboard a new ship, the *Pandora*, returns to arrest the mutineers and bring them to justice in the English court. But Christian and some others escape on the *Bounty* to Pitcairn's Island, where they are safe from Bligh forever. Bligh's new ship is wrecked on the reefs surrounding the island, and though he returns to England, testimony against him by one loyal member of the crew who was wrongly charged with mutiny brings condemnation upon Bligh by his peers. This Hollywood ending, in which Bligh's inhumanity is noted and Christian's gentleness and bravery earn him an island paradise, made the movie a great success at a time when Americans clung to hope for escape from their own dilemmas during the financial crises of the Great Depression.

REMAKING A CLASSIC

In 1962 Nordhoff and Hall's novels were republished and the movie remade, this time starring Marlon Brando as Fletcher Christian. Another generation of Americans learned the story of the *Bounty*. Though the film was praised for its score and South Seas cinematography, it did not succeed as well as the classic Gable film. It fell short of the unanimous popularity enjoyed by its predecessor, perhaps because of an uneven performance by Brando, or possibly as a result of the country's preference for contemporary American issues over British naval history. The romances between the sailors and the Tahitian women were exotic and appealing during the 1930s, but American viewers of the 1960s were not entranced. Though the film was not a box-office or critical hit, it was nominated for a share of Academy Awards (seven, though it did not win any), and it did rekindle an interest in Captain Bligh and the H.M.S. *Bounty*. In yet another remake, Anthony Hopkins starred as Captain Bligh and Mel Gibson as Fletcher Christian in a version titled *The Bounty* (1984), in which Captain Bligh is presented less harshly and Christian less favorably than in the novel and earlier films.

The replica of the *Bounty* from the 1962 movie, a full-rigged sailing ship, was donated in 1993 by its owner, Ted Turner, to a nonprofit educational foundation called Tall Ship Bounty. The H.M.S. *Bounty*'s crew trains teen cadets and teaches maritime history to elementary school students. The ship sails between Canada and the Caribbean, docking for public tours and participating in tall-ships festivals. This activity has kept the history of the *Bounty* alive. Several novels also have added to the topic's popularity: *The Journal of Fletcher Christian* (2005), *The Grave Tattoo* (2007), and *Mutiny: A Novel of the Bounty* (2009). More than 2,000 articles, books, and documentary films have been produced, which—in addition to the interest generated by Tall Ship Bounty, the motion pictures, and the novels—have made the Mutiny on the Bounty one of the best-known maritime adventures.

Sharon Brown

SEE ALSO: *Academy Awards; Best Sellers; Brando, Marlon; Flynn, Errol; Gable, Clark; Gibson, Mel; The Great Depression; Hollywood; MGM (Metro-Goldwyn-Mayer); Movie Stars; Turner, Ted.*

BIBLIOGRAPHY

Alexander, Caroline. *The Bounty: The True Story of the Mutiny on the Bounty.* New York: Penguin, 2003.

Boyne, John. *Mutiny: A Novel of the Bounty*. New York: Thomas Dunne Books, 2009.

Collett, Bill. *The Last Mutiny: The Further Adventures of Captain Bligh*. New York: W. W. Norton, 1995.

Corris, Peter. *The Journal of Fletcher Christian*. Sydney: Vintage, 2005.

Denig, Greg. *Mr. Bligh's Bad Language: Passion, Power, and Theatre on the Bounty*. Cambridge, UK: Cambridge University Press, 1992.

H.M.S *Bounty* Organization. Accessed November 2011. Available from http://www.tallshipbounty.org

McDermid, Val. *The Grave Tattoo.* New York: St. Martin's Minotaur, 2007.

Nordhoff, Charles, and James Norman Hall. *The Bounty Trilogy: Comprising the Three Volumes, "Mutiny on the Bounty," "Men against the Sea," and "Pitcairn's Island."* Boston: Little, Brown, 1962.

Mutt & Jeff

Mutt was the tall one, Jeff the short one. They were a funny-paper team for more than seventy years. Though often credited with being the first daily newspaper strip, *Mutt & Jeff* had a few predecessors. It was, however, the first truly successful one.

Cartoonist Harry "Bud" Fisher invented Mutt first, in 1907, introducing him solo in a comic strip that ran daily on the sports page of the *San Francisco Chronicle*. Fisher originally used his strip to recount Augustus Mutt's misadventures in betting on the ponies. He also tossed in racing tips. In 1908, while spending some time in a lunatic asylum, Mutt encountered Jeff and the two teamed up.

Popular from the beginning, *Mutt & Jeff* eventually moved from the *San Francisco Chronicle* to William Randolph Hearst's *San Francisco Examiner*. Eventually the shrewd Fisher acquired ownership of his feature and, with the aid of the Bell Syndicate, became the first millionaire cartoonist in America. A large list of papers all across the country helped, as did extensive merchandising. There were *Mutt & Jeff* reprint books from 1910 on, as well as toys and animated cartoons.

Fisher involved his pair in various contemporary activities, including the fracas with Pancho Villa, World War I, and Prohibition. His basic aim, however, was to get across a joke a day. Mutt was married, henpecked, and the father of an ageless son named Cicero. He and Jeff tried any number of professions but were never able to hold down a job for long. For decades the two of them operated pretty much like a movie or stage comedy team, daily delivering many a tried-and-true joke borrowed from vaudeville. It is safe to say that there was not a single variation of the classic "waiter, there's a fly in my soup" gag that did not appear in *Mutt & Jeff* at least once. Fisher and his staff were very much given to slapstick elements and brickbats; clubs and other weapons were frequent props.

Mutt, although not the brightest of men, was the more practical partner. Jeff was the zany one, often not too well grounded in reality. When one of their innumerable get-rich-quick schemes went awry, Mutt was not above doing violence to his little top-hatted sidekick. Jeff, however, often got the last laugh and, almost always, the pretty girls who frequented the strip. Their basic relationship was akin to that of such screen comedians as Laurel and Hardy or Abbott and Costello.

The life of a millionaire for Fisher was one filled with such upper-class distractions as a racing stable and chorus girls, which did not leave much time for his comic strip. Fairly early in his career, he hired others to produce *Mutt & Jeff.* Ken Kling was the first ghostwriter, and he went on to do comic strips of his own, including a racing tip one called *Joe & Asbestos*. Next came Eddie Mack and then, in the early 1930s, the long-suffering Al Smith. A much better cartoonist than his boss or any of his predecessors, Smith wrote and drew the strip, daily and Sunday, for more than twenty years without any credit and not too much in the way of a salary; he eventually created the Sunday companion strip *Cicero's Cat*. After Fisher's death in 1954, Smith was allowed to sign his name to the strip. He stayed with it, gradually mellowing the tone and putting more emphasis on Mutt's home life, until 1981. For its final two years *Mutt & Jeff* was drawn by George Breisacher.

Ron Goulart

SEE ALSO: *Abbott and Costello; Comics; Hearst, William Randolph; Laurel and Hardy.*

BIBLIOGRAPHY

Goulart, Ron, ed. *The Encyclopedia of American Comics*. New York: Facts On File, 1990.

Horn, Maurice. *100 Years of American Newspaper Comics: An Illustrated Encyclopedia*. New York: Gramercy Books, 1996.

Walker, Brian. *The Comics before 1945*. New York: Abrams, 2004.

Muzak

The seeds of the all-enveloping background sound of music in public places that evolved into Muzak were sown in the early decades of the twentieth century. By the 1950s the concept had developed into a commercial reality that invaded the American way of life, its presence only increasing as the century wore on. The trademarked name "Muzak" has become generic, referring not only to that company's own proprietary mix of piped-in background music but also to any such music in public spaces and the workplace. It is sometimes called "wallpaper" or "elevator" music—a mild pejorative that distinguishes its contrived and synthetic quality from "real" music, which is listened to actively and intentionally, and signifies its role as ambient sound to be experienced subliminally.

MUZAK THEORY

The aesthetic concept of music as an environmental component rather than an artistic abstraction of sound important for its content was consciously advanced in the first decades of the 1900s by French composer Erik Satie in what he called *musique d'ameublement* (furniture music). Workplace music, however, goes much further back to folk genres, such as the songs sung by British textile handworkers and their seagoing counterparts, the chanty men. In the early factories of the Industrial Revolution, workers sang on the job for their own amusement and that of their coworkers, falling silent in the mid-1800s only when the noise of increasingly powerful industrial machinery drowned their voices. (Even then, some factories encouraged glee clubs and hired bands in an attempt to make the workplace less austere.)

Early in the twentieth century, however, the new science of industrial efficiency management was electrified by the discovery made at an indoor bicycle race in 1911 at the old Madison Square Garden in New York. A brass band was part of the entertainment, and statisticians clocking the race discovered that cyclists' average speeds shot up by about 10 percent during the band's sets. Five years later, a commercial laundry experimented with playing ragtime records; productivity increased dramatically when ironing was done in time to the music. In 1922 the Minneapolis post office tried playing records in its night sorting room and found that sorting errors fell.

By 1930 many American factories provided some sort of music, either live or phonograph, and the number of workplaces where music was supplied increased steadily. During World War II one researcher found that recorded music was in seventy-six out of 100 factories visited and that more than half of management stated music increased production. Despite some uncertainty about fitting the rhythm of the music to the actual tasks (one wartime factory in Britain had to withdraw "Deep in the Heart of Texas" because workers stopped what they were doing to clap in time to it), factory music came to be favored both for its cheering effect on morale and for the relief it offered employees obliged to perform monotonous tasks.

SELLING MUZAK TO BUSINESS

Muzak was the creation of General George Owen Squier, who had invented both a high-speed telegraph and telephone-line multiplexing during his rise to the command of the U.S. Army Signal Corps. He took his inspiration from *Looking Backward* (1887), Edward Bellamy's utopian novel featuring a "musical telephone" that brings music programming—rousing in the morning, soothing in the evening—to every house in a futuristically posited dawning of the twenty-first century. In the 1920s Squier entered an agreement with the North American Company, an Ohio utilities conglomerate, to produce a service called Wired Radio that would offer subscribers a choice of three program channels over telephone lines to homes or retail shops. Shortly before his death in 1934, Squier's efforts to come up with a catchier name for his company resulted in the term *Muzak*, a blend of the word *music* with the final syllable from George Eastman's universally pronounceable synthetic trade name Kodak.

In 1936 Muzak moved to New York from its studios in Cleveland. In-house engineers recorded such popular artists as the Dorsey Brothers Orchestra and two members of Benny Goodman's original sextet, Fats Waller and Teddy Wilson, using the cutting-edge technology of 33-1/3 revolutions per minute (rpm) vinylite disks, the forerunner of the long-playing records that would render 78 rpm shellac platters obsolete in the decade following World War II.

Postwar consumer culture spawned suburban sprawl, including the supermarket and, later, the ubiquitous shopping malls, and recorded music contributed to the subnormal eye-blink rate of daydreamy grocery shoppers (although it did not stop them, as sociologist Vance Packard notes in *The Hidden Persuaders*, from a sharp increase in blinking and, presumably, anxiety as they approached the cash registers). Music in the office environment came more slowly, but by the late 1950s the Muzak corporation could boast that its programming was being heard by fifty million Americans daily.

Sequencing was the key to Muzak's success. In response to psychological research showing that workdays started with high energy that fell off sharply after an hour or so until the approach of lunch, Muzak provided programming that offered catchier, cheerier rhythms at midmorning and whose arrangements were laced with woodwinds and occasional brass (in contrast to the subtler and more subdued strings preferred, for example, by restaurants for their early evening trade).

MUZAK EVERYWHERE

Although worker response tended to be highly favorable to judiciously programmed environmental music, not everyone cared for it. When the Washington, D.C., transit system contracted Muzak to supply its vehicles in 1948, disgruntled riders brought a lawsuit. The hearing eventually went all the way to the U.S. Supreme Court (as *Public Utilities Commission v. Pollak*), which ruled in 1951 that the Constitution did not guarantee a passenger on a federally regulated vehicle "a right to privacy substantially equal to the privacy to which he is entitled in his own home." Thus, the court implicitly affirmed the right to play wallpaper music willy-nilly as a form of First Amendment expression.

Since the late 1950s, the recording industry has profitably offered mood-music recordings from artists such as Mantovani, with his sweeping strings that are soothingly romantic and mystical, to arrangements of show tunes to Brian Eno's *Ambient 1: Music for Airports*. Meanwhile, Muzak and its two main competitors, Audio Environments and 3M Sound Products, have thrived on a formula of what former Muzak music designer Christopher Case has defined as "music artfully performed in a manner to uplift, not to intrude." By the 2010s Muzak reported that its products were being played at 335,000 client locations and being heard by more than 100 million people each day.

Nick Humez

SEE ALSO: *Consumerism; Goodman, Benny; Malls; Suburbia.*

BIBLIOGRAPHY

Bellamy, Edward. *Looking Backward: 2000–1887*. Boston: Bedford Books, 1995.

Cardinell, Richmond L. *Music in Industry: Principles of Programming*. New York: ASCAP, 1944.

Husch, Jerri A. *Music of the Workplace: A Study of Muzak Culture*. Ann Arbor, MI: University Microfilms International, 1984.

Lanza, Joseph. *Elevator Music: A Surreal History of Muzak, Easy-Listening, and Other Moodsong*, rev ed. Ann Arbor: University of Michigan Press, 2004.

Packard, Vance. *The Hidden Persuaders*. New York: Pocket Books, 1957.

Satie, Erik. *Écrits*. Paris: Champ Libre, 1977.

Sundstrom, Eric D., and Mary Graehl Sundstrom. *Work Places: The Psychology of the Physical Environment in Offices and Factories*. New York: Cambridge University Press, 1986.

My Darling Clementine

The film *My Darling Clementine* (1946), based on Stuart Lake's novel *Wyatt Earp, Frontier Marshal*, was a remake of the 1939 film *Frontier Marshal*. Its director, John Ford, had built a reputation on directing Westerns, and *My Darling Clementine* is considered by many to be his best and most poetic Western. Ford used the story of the O.K. Corral to create the image of a triumphant postwar America.

The film centers on Wyatt Earp (Henry Fonda) and Doc Holliday (Victor Mature) and their shoot-out with the Clantons at the O.K. Corral. Tombstone, the town over which Earp presides as sheriff, rids itself of evil and thus transforms itself from a wilderness into a garden. Holliday struggles to overcome his sullied past, while Clementine Carter (Cathy Downs) brings a future of innocence to Tombstone. The film ends with a triumphant ushering in of the new church with a social dance at which Earp accompanies Clementine.

Liza Black

SEE ALSO: *Fonda, Henry; Ford, John; The Western.*

BIBLIOGRAPHY

Bogdanovich, Peter. *John Ford*. Berkeley: University of California Press, 1978.

Davis, Ronald L. *John Ford: Hollywood's Old Master*. Norman: University of Oklahoma Press, 1995.

Kalinak, Kathryn Marie. *How the West Was Sung: Music in the Westerns of John Ford*. Berkeley: University of California Press, 2007.

My Fair Lady

My Fair Lady, written by Alan Jay Lerner and Frederick Loewe, was one of the most popular musical plays of the 1950s. Its initial New York run, which began on March 15, 1956, lasted six and a half years for a total of 2,717 performances. The story of phonetician Henry Higgins, who transforms the Cockney flower girl Eliza Doolittle into a society lady through teaching her correct speech, was based on the George Bernard Shaw play *Pygmalion*. It includes musical numbers such as "I Could Have Danced All Night," "On the Street Where You Live," "The Rain in Spain," and "Get Me to the Church on Time."

British actors Rex Harrison and Julie Andrews, who was making her American debut, created the roles of Higgins and Doolittle. The musical won Tony Awards for Best Musical, Actor (Harrison), and Director (Moss Hart). The 1964 film version starred Harrison and Audrey Hepburn, whose vocals were dubbed by Marni Nixon. The film won Academy Awards for Best Picture, Actor (Harrison), Score, and Costume Design.

William A. Everett

SEE ALSO: *Academy Awards; Broadway; Hepburn, Audrey; The Musical; Tony Awards.*

BIBLIOGRAPHY

Block, Geoffrey. *Enchanted Evenings: The Broadway Musical from* Show Boat *to Sondheim*. New York: Oxford University Press, 1997.

Harrison, Rex. *Rex: An Autobiography*. New York: William Morrow, 1975.

Lerner, Alan J. *The Street Where I Live*. New York: W. W. Norton, 1978.

Shaw, George Bernard, and Alan Jay Lerner. Pygmalion *and* My Fair Lady. New York: Signet Classics, 2006.

My Family, Mi Familia

Filmmaker Gregory Nava crafts a multigenerational epic in *My Family, Mi Familia*, a film that follows nearly sixty years in the life of a Latino family whose roots in the United States date back to the 1920s. Released in 1995, Nava's film addresses themes central to the immigrant experience. The financial success of *My Family, Mi Familia* demonstrated that audiences—specifically Latino audiences—were hungry for positive

My Family/Mi Familia. *From left, Maria Canals-Barrera as Irene, Esai Morales as Chucho, and Constance Marie as Toni play one of several generations followed in* My Family, Mi Familia. ZOETROPE/NEW LINE/THE KOBAL COLLECTION.

cinematic representation. Nava's insistence that an entirely Latino cast play his characters (as opposed to bankable Anglo stars) was a victory not only for independent filmmakers working within the Hollywood system but, more importantly, for greater verisimilitude and diversity in filmmaking.

Although he was born and raised in San Diego, California, Nava's own family tree has its roots in Tijuana. Nava has said that he was raised in a border world that experienced a "tremendous clash between the cultures." It is this culture clash that dominates many of his films, such as the acclaimed *El Norte* (1983), a story of a brother and sister who flee Guatemala during a military coup and move northward, first to Mexico and then to California. Their struggle to adapt to a new culture provides the film with its moving drama and conflict. Nava gained much of his filmmaking experience while a student at the University of California at Los Angeles (UCLA) film school, where he made his promising first feature, *Confessions of Aman* (1973). Nearly all of his films have been collaborations with his wife and partner, Anna Thomas, who acted as coscreenwriter and producer on *My Family, Mi Familia.*

FAMILY STORY

Narrated by writer Paco (Edward James Olmos), one of José and María Sánchez's five children, *My Family, Mi Familia* begins when a teenage José (Jacob Vargas) leaves his remote Mexican village in the 1920s to seek out his last surviving relative, an old man known as El Californio (Leon Singer), one of the state's original settlers. José finds work in Beverly Hills as a gardener for a wealthy family. There he meets and falls in love with their housekeeper María (played as a young woman by Jennifer Lopez). By the 1930s the couple has made a life for themselves in California, which includes two children and a third baby on the way. When the pregnant María (Jenny Gago) is mistaken for an illegal immigrant during a routine sweep, she is deported to Mexico and separated from José and their two children for nearly two years.

Once they are reunited as a family, the Sánchez's story jumps to the late 1950s, when their third child, Chuco (Esai Morales)—who has grown into a troubled and rebellious young adult—gets involved in a fight, kills a man, and is shot by the police in front of his younger brother Jimmy (played by Jonathan Hernandez and as an adult by Jimmy Smits). The family's story continues into the 1980s, tracing the lives of the individual family members as they struggle with more sorrow and celebrate life's successes.

Masterfully photographed by cinematographer Edward Lachman, *My Family, Mi Familia* interweaves elements of magical realism (or dream realism, as Nava prefers to call the surreal stylization of films such as *Like Water for Chocolate*) within the epic story coscripted by Nava and Thomas. Partly autobiographical and partly based on Nava's research of families living in East Los Angeles, the film also features mythical references including the pre-Columbian motif Ometeotl, or the creator couple, who are reflected in the characters of José and María. Bridges figure largely in the film as well, serving as literal and metaphorical images uniting different cultures, spaces, and characters.

MIXED REVIEWS

My Family, Mi Familia received mixed critical reviews upon its release in 1995. The multigenerational story often was praised for its ambition but not always for its execution. The *San Francisco Chronicle* called it a "haunting, poignant, and joyful memoir," whereas *Sight & Sound* said, "Although three decades are covered . . . there is little sense of the complexities of the American immigrant experience." Similarly, the *New York Times* review called the film "wildly uneven" but "grandly ambitious" and "warmhearted." Some critics argued that the film's themes are raised but never adequately addressed, and others suggested that the film reinforces Latino stereotypes of the patriarchal family and, through its narrative and stylistic choices, deprives the female characters of agency and action. Nearly all who wrote about *My Family, Mi Familia*, however, praised the film for its positive Latino portrayals. Nava's film received many accolades from community groups and national Latino organizations and won the prize for outstanding feature film at the National Council of La Raza Bravo Awards in 1995.

The film's bilingual title reflects both the filmmakers' desire to appeal to a broad audience and distributor New Line Cinema's fears that Anglo audiences would be disinterested in a film titled only in Spanish. In a rather bold marketing move, New Line launched an entirely Latino promotion that targeted specific cities and regions throughout the country. Traditionally members of the Latino market are younger than average moviegoing audiences and are avid consumers of mass-market entertainment. Perhaps this statistic influenced the film's financial success: in its first week, *My Family, Mi Familia* had the number one per-screen average across the country, earning more money during its opening weekend than any other film playing at that time. With a modest budget of $5.5 million, the film had grossed $7 million by the end of 1995.

During an interview to promote the release of *My Family, Mi Familia*, Nava was quoted as saying, "We have to look to our roots to find our strength." The strengths of *My Family, Mi Familia* lie in its fictional exploration of one family's multicultural roots and each member's struggles to preserve their Latino heritage while making a better life for themselves within the often rigid culture of the United States. Nava believes the immigrant experience is one of great drama and conflict, and the story (and backstory) of *My Family, Mi Familia* reflects this experience.

Alison Macor

SEE ALSO: *Lopez, Jennifer; Multiculturalism; Nava, Gregory; Olmos, Edward James; Smits, Jimmy.*

BIBLIOGRAPHY

Chabram-Dernersesian, Angie. *The Chicana/o Cultural Studies Reader.* New York: Routledge, 2006.

Huaco-Nuzum, Carmen. "Mi Familia/My Family." *Aztlan: A Journal of Chicano Studies* 23, no. 1 (1998): 141–152.

James, Caryn. "My Family." *New York Times*, May 3, 1995, B2.

McCarthy, Todd. *"My Family/Mi Familia." Variety* 358, no. 1 (1995): 74.

O'Brien, Lucy. "My Family." *Sight & Sound* 5, no. 10 (1995): 53–54.

West, Dennis. "Filming the Chicano Family Saga." *Cineaste* 21, no. 4 (1995): 26–29.

My Lai Massacre

On March 16, 1968, in the wake of the Tet Offensive, American soldiers committed perhaps the most brutal—and certainly the most infamous—atrocity of the Vietnam War. The tragedy occurred in My Lai, one of several hamlets located in Song My village in Quang Ngai Province, a historic stronghold of the National Liberation Front.

In the weeks preceding the event, a number of members of Charlie Company had been killed or maimed by the North Vietnamese, and there was a lot of built-up anger among the men who entered My Lai on March 16. During an uneventful search-and-destroy mission, members of Charlie Company, First Battalion, 20th Infantry Division, commanded by Lieutenant William Calley Jr., massacred from 300 to 500 unarmed, unresisting Vietnamese women, children, and elderly men. They raped, sodomized, and mutilated many of their victims. Once the full story of My Lai became public, it reshaped how Americans viewed the war and, in no small way, how they understood their own hallowed history. My Lai seared America's collective memory with seemingly indisputable proof that the nation's behavior often failed to live up to its self-righteous rhetoric.

UNCOVERING THE TRUTH

Remarkably, initial press reports presented the "battle" of My Lai in a positive light. Misled by the military publicity apparatus, one news agency even spoke of an "impressive victory" by American soldiers. The military's misinformation represented only part of a systematic cover-up. The entire chain of command related to the massacre—from Captain Ernest Medina of Charlie Company through the division commander, Major General Samuel Koster—imposed neither corrective nor punitive measures despite their awareness of the events at My Lai. There was a feeling in the military that inequities in the draft were responsible for a college dropout such as Calley even being in charge of Charlie Company. Not until a year after the massacre, in the spring of 1969, when former GI Ronald Ridenhour requested the House Armed Services Committee to explore rumors of mass killings, did the army initiate an investigation. Even then, the army conspired to play down the massacre.

If not for Seymour Hersh, a freelance investigative reporter, the army's indictment of a single soldier would have been the last that Americans ever heard about My Lai. Pursuing the army's low-key announcement of Calley's indictment, Hersh uncovered the full story of the massacre, which the *New York Times* published on November 13, 1969. For weeks thereafter, My Lai dominated news reports across the nation. CBS and other networks aired confessions by soldiers who had participated. *Life* magazine, calling My Lai "a story of indisputable horror," published ten pages of gut-wrenching photographs of the massacre.

Although it had taken over a year and a half, the massacre of My Lai, in all its graphic detail, was a household topic of conversation. Never before had ordinary Americans directly confronted the brutality of their own soldiers. For some, My Lai confirmed their worst fears about America's war in Vietnam. For others, My Lai contradicted not just their vision of the war but also a long-standing American tradition of depicting the enemy—whether it be Indians, Nazis, Japanese, or Vietnamese—as the perpetrators of heinous atrocities.

THE AFTERMATH

Hersh's story set off a maelstrom of controversy, as Americans responded with both denial and outrage. Despite the evidence, many people refused to accept that American soldiers—and by extension, America itself—could commit such barbarous crimes. A December 1969 poll, for instance, found that 49 percent of Minnesotans felt the story was false. Congressman John R. Rarick, a Democrat from Louisiana, dubbed My Lai a "massacre hoax." Even President Richard Nixon referred to My Lai as an "isolated incident." Others, however, charged that My Lai typified a brutal war of muddled tactics and flawed strategy. Many veterans of the war, welcoming the opportunity that My Lai presented, came forward with similar stories, suggesting that civilian killings typified the fighting. Spurred by this controversy, the army appointed Lieutenant General William R. Peers to head a full-scale investigation of My Lai. The Peers Commission indicted twenty-five Americans: thirteen, including Calley, for war crimes and twelve for the cover-up. Sentenced to life imprisonment for murder, Calley was the only one convicted. Legal appeals on his behalf lasted for years afterward.

Much of the cultural response to My Lai cut across ideological lines, focusing more on how the war had corrupted typical American "boys" than on the massacre's real victims. A *Time* poll showed that events such as My Lai concerned only 35 percent of Americans. Calley insisted that he had acted under orders from Medina. Thus, Calley's plight became a cause célèbre, especially among those who saw him as a scapegoat for the army and U.S. government. Veterans groups called for leniency; state legislatures passed resolutions of support; "Free Calley" bumper stickers appeared; and a pro-Calley song, "The Battle Hymn of Lt. Calley," sold 200,000 copies in three days. Sensing the political winds, President Nixon intervened on Calley's behalf.

THE CULTURAL IMPACT

The public sympathy for Calley, who was released on parole in 1974, epitomized Americans' obsession with what the war had done to them, as well as their general disregard for the pain the United States had inflicted upon Vietnam. The theme of the exploited or psychologically scarred Vietnam veteran became a narrative fixture in later cinematic treatments of the war, common both to antiwar films such as *The Deer Hunter* (1978) and *Coming Home* (1978) and conservative offerings such as *First Blood* (1982) and its sequels.

My Lai and American war tragedies in Vietnam also found their way into popular culture, but at first only through analogy. Films such as *Little Big Man* (1970) and *Soldier Blue* (1970) recreate U.S. Army massacres of Native Americans during the nineteenth century. While such movies clearly emerged in response to the war in Vietnam, they seemed to open up all of American history to reinterpretation. Eventually, more direct treatment of American atrocities became a common, if often secondary, feature of Vietnam films. Not until Brian De Palma's *Casualties of War* (1989) did a My Lai–type atrocity become the driving story of a movie. The film, which refueled the debate on the legacy of the war, recounts the story of an American platoon that kidnaps, gang-rapes, and murders a Vietnamese woman during a search-and-destroy mission. The movie is perhaps best understood as a rebuke to the conservative revisionism of the Ronald Reagan era, calling into question the president's claim that the war should be considered a "noble crusade." After My Lai, Americans had to work harder to convince themselves that they were indeed the same shining "City upon a Hill" that John Winthrop had spoken of in 1630 as he led anxious Puritans toward life in the new world.

The Peers Commission, which interviewed 398 witnesses and produced 20,000 pages of testimony, concluded that a lack of leadership was the chief reason for the My Lai massacre. Contributing factors were a lack of training, racist attitudes toward the Vietnamese, a failure to enforce rules and regulations, psychological and organizational problems, and the position taken by local officials that every resident within My Lai was either a Viet Cong or a sympathizer. In the aftermath of the terrorist attacks on the United States on September 11, 2001, the American military became actively involved in the war on terror, waging military campaigns in Afghanistan and Iraq and taking on assignments at prisoner-of-war camps. Military experts such as Lieutenant Colonel Robert Rielly contend that understanding the mistakes that set the stage for the My Lai massacre may help to prevent similar occurrences in the future.

Tom Robertson

SEE ALSO: The Deer Hunter*; 9/11; Rambo; Vietnam; War in Afghanistan; War Movies.*

BIBLIOGRAPHY

Anderson, David L., ed. *Facing My Lai: Moving beyond the Massacre.* Lawrence: University Press of Kansas, 1998.

Bilton, Michael, and Kevin Sim. *Four Hours in My Lai.* New York: Viking, 1992.

Cotkin, George. *Morality's Muddy Waters: Ethical Quandaries.* Philadelphia: University of Pennsylvania Press, 2010.

Engelhardt, Tom. *The End of Victory Culture: Cold War America and the Disillusion of a Generation.* New York: Basic Books, 1995.

Hersh, Seymour. *My Lai 4.* New York: Random House, 1970.

Hunt, Michael H. *A Vietnam War Reader: A Documentary History from American and Vietnamese Perspectives.* Chapel Hill: University of North Carolina Press, 2010.

Oliver, Kendrick. *The My Lai Massacre in American History and Memory.* New York: Manchester University Press, 2006.

Peers, William R. *The My Lai Inquiry.* New York: W. W. Norton, 1979.

Rielly, Robert. "The Inclination for War Crimes." *Military Review* 89, no. 3 (2009).

"Vietnam Online." *American Experience.* PBS. Accessed March 2012. Available from http://www.pbs.org/wgbh/amex/vietnam/trenches/my_lai.html

My So-Called Life

Network television programming has often been criticized for being collectively shallow, insipid, and fashioned to appeal to the mentality of an ill-educated preadolescent. One refreshing exception was *My So-Called Life*, an original and intelligent dramatic portrayal of the world of contemporary teenagers that aired briefly in the mid-1990s. The show is set in Three Rivers, a fictional Pittsburgh suburb. Its heroine, Angela Chase (Claire Danes), is a fifteen-year-old sophomore at Liberty High School. The show follows her as she attempts to deal with her "so-called life"—her adolescent anxieties, quest for identity, relationships with peers, and views of parents and authority figures. Patty and Graham Chase, Angela's mom and dad, are not the one-dimensional adults that are staples in teen-oriented Hollywood movies and television shows. Instead, they are a realistically depicted couple in their forties who face their own problems and crises. It is just this sort of realism that made the show popular with a small group of fans during the cynical 1990s.

My So-Called Life, produced by Marshall Herskovitz and Edward Zwick, premiered on ABC on August 25, 1994. It earned positive reviews and quickly developed a cult following. Unfortunately, its ratings were unimpressive, and *My So-Called Life* had come to television at a time when new shows were axed if they did not immediately earn big ratings. In December ABC announced that the show would be canceled. Had the network allowed it to gestate and build an audience, however, its ratings may have possibly improved. After all, numerous classic television shows of an earlier time—including *M*A*S*H*, *All in the Family*, *Hill Street Blues*, and *Cheers*—started out with low ratings. But *My So-Called Life* would not be so lucky; reruns of its nineteen episodes began airing on MTV the following April.

Rob Edelman

SEE ALSO: All in the Family; Cheers; Hill Street Blues; M*A*S*H; *MTV; Suburbia; Teenagers; Television.*

BIBLIOGRAPHY

Clark, Catherine. *My So-Called Life Goes On*. New York: Random House, 1999.

"My So-Called Life." Accessed August 16, 2012. Available from http://www.mscl.com

My Three Sons

One of the longest-running and most popular situation comedies in television history, *My Three Sons* (1960–1972) offered a cultural anodyne to the turbulent events that characterized the United States during the 1960s, presenting wholesome family entertainment. One of television's first single-parent sitcoms, the series revolves around an all-male household facing the trials and tribulations of life in suburbia in the 1960s.

BACKGROUND

The show starred Fred MacMurray as Steve Douglas, a widowed aeronautical engineer raising his three boys in a motherless household. When the series began the boys were Mike (eighteen), Robbie (fourteen), and Richard, or "Chip" (seven). Also in the home was the kids' gruff but lovable grandfather, Michael Francis "Bub" O'Casey, who moved in to cook and clean for the family. He was played by veteran character actor William Frawley, best known for his portrayal of Fred Mertz on *I Love Lucy*. In the course of its long run, the series' structure changed several times as members of the Douglas clan were added or subtracted. Its tone, however, always remained comfortingly "square."

According to authors Harry Castleman and Walter Podrazik in *Harry and Wally's Favorite TV Shows*, MacMurray came to symbolize the classic idealized television father. They write, "[MacMurray] exudes, revels in, and virtually defines bland TV fatherhood in the role of Steve Douglas. He stands as an edifice, a monument to an age of simplicity, both on TV and in our pristine national image of ourselves." Ironically, this man who played television's most attentive father had no interest in a TV career. He had been a popular and successful movie actor, whose career had begun in the 1930s and included roles in several classic movies, notably the lead in *Double Indemnity* (1944) and the cause of Jack Lemmon's troubles in *The Apartment* (1960). MacMurray also gained pop culture immortality as the facial model for *Captain Marvel*, the 1940s comic-book superhero who exclaimed the magic word "Shazam."

SHOOTING SCHEDULE

Upon being approached to headline a series called *The Fred MacMurray Show*, the star refused, saying he did not wish to devote his time to the medium. To persuade him to reconsider,

My Three Sons. My Three Sons *starred, from left, Stanley Livingston as Chip, Barry Livingston as Ernie, Don Grady as Robbie, and Fred MacMurray as father Steve Douglas.* DON FEDDERSON PRODUCTIONS/THE KOBAL COLLECTION.

the producers altered the show's name to *My Three Sons* to reflect the increased emphasis on the children. When he accepted, they accommodated his contractual requirements by implementing the unique "MacMurray System" shooting schedule. MacMurray agreed to work only for sixty-five days in any one season of the show, so all episodes were written far in advance and filmed out of sequence. MacMurray would then, for example, tape all the year's scenes set in the family kitchen in one afternoon. The cast would then shoot their scenes around the absent MacMurray months later.

Despite its chaotic shooting schedule, the series always portrayed a stable and loving family whose problems were usually minor. All the lead characters had backgrounds in "family entertainment," emphasizing the show's approach and increasing its audience appeal. MacMurray and his eldest TV son, Tim Considine (Mike), had starred in several Disney productions; Don Grady (Robbie) had been a Mouseketeer in the 1950s *Mickey Mouse Club*; and even little Stanley Livingston (Chip) had appeared in several episodes of *The Adventures of Ozzie and Harriet.*

The boys were good kids who never caused serious difficulties for their dad, and the story lines centered on their growing pains and their father's occasional romances. The series' tone was always kept light, with barely a mention of the family's late wife and mother. Furthermore, references to such 1960s strife as political assassinations, Vietnam, and increased drug use among the nation's youth were completely avoided. When the imperfect reality of the outside world was allowed to intrude on the Douglas family, it was generally as a benign acknowledgment of changing trends, demonstrated by such innocuous events as Chip's decision to wear a Beatles' haircut.

SHOW CHANGES

During its run the series underwent several important cast and format changes. The ailing Frawley left the show in 1964 and was replaced by the even grouchier Uncle Charley, played by William Demarest, and in 1965 Considine asked to leave his role as the eldest son. When he departed the show, the plot had MacMurray adopting a local orphan named Ernie—played by Barry Livingston, the real-life brother of Stanley—to keep the series title accurate.

Eventually the entire family moved to California, where father Steve and sons Robbie and Chip all got married. In 1968 Robbie's wife, Katie, gave birth to triplets, named Steve, Charley, and Robbie II. Once again, there were three Douglas boys. Even the all-male family format that served as the series' original basis was abandoned as Steve's new wife moved in with her own daughter, Dodie. The strangest twist of the show occurred in 1972 when MacMurray took on a second role as Lord Fergus McBain Douglas, a Scottish cousin in search of a wife. With such an extended cast, episodes could feature only selected members of the growing Douglas family each week. The show was canceled in 1972 but returned in 1977 for a reunion special.

Few television programs have better represented the perfect family ideal. In *My Three Sons* the kids were decent, the father dependable, and even the grandfather had a soft heart beneath his crusty exterior. MacMurray and company presented good, clean entertainment suitable for the entire family throughout an increasingly troubled era. Along with programs like *Bachelor Father* and *The Andy Griffith Show*, it paved the way for later domestic comedies featuring single-parent households and demonstrated that sitcom audiences would accept a program without a traditional nuclear family as its center. The Douglas family may not have physically fit the "Ozzie and Harriet" mold, but they held the same values, ideals, and gentle good humor.

Charles Coletta

SEE ALSO: The Adventures of Ozzie and Harriet*;* The Andy Griffith Show*; The Beatles; Captain Marvel; Disney (Walt Disney Company); Frawley, William; MacMurray, Fred;* The Mickey Mouse Club*; Sitcom; Television.*

BIBLIOGRAPHY

Bianculli, David. *Dictionary of Teleliteracy*. New York: Continuum, 1996.

Brooks, Tim. *The Complete Directory to Prime Time TV Stars*. New York: Ballantine Books, 1987.

Castleman, Harry, and Walter Podrazik. *Harry and Wally's Favorite TV Shows*. New York: Prentice Hall, 1989.

Mitz, Rick. *The Great TV Sitcom Book*. New York: Perigee, 1988.

N

Nader, Ralph *(1934–)*

Activist Ralph Nader became twentieth-century America's prime crusader in matters of serious public concern. Since the mid-1960s his name has been synonymous with consumer protection, and although he did not originate the consumer rights movement, he publicly expanded, publicized, and legitimized it. Nader elected a broad focus for his cause with the basic goal of protecting the individual citizen from corporate might, concentrating not merely on one issue of public concern but seeking out the effects of profit-motivated industry on the public in many different arenas, from water pollution and automobile and airline safety to insurance, free trade, and law.

Born the son of Lebanese immigrants and raised in Winsted, Connecticut, Nader graduated from Princeton University in 1955 and obtained his law degree from Harvard in 1958. While in law school, his studies of auto injury cases sparked his interest in unsafe automobile designs. He practiced law in Connecticut until 1963, when he moved to Washington, D.C., and began working as a consultant with the U.S. Department of Labor. In 1965 he published his landmark work, *Unsafe at Any Speed*, a critique of the American automobile industry. Using the Chevrolet Corvair as his prime example, Nader cited low safety standards and the failure of car manufacturers to devote a sufficient amount of their profits to safety research as the cause of many accidents.

The publication of Nader's research and results led directly to the passage of the National Traffic and Motor Vehicle Safety Act of 1966, which gave the government the power to set safety standards for all vehicles sold in the United States. Nader then turned his attention to other consumer issues. Working with a team of committed lawyers who were soon known as "Nader's Raiders," he published dozens of studies calling for government regulation of a wide-ranging list of disturbing consumer issues. These included baby food, insecticide, mercury poisoning, and banking. In 1969 Nader founded the Center for Responsive Law for the continuing investigation of many aspects of modern life, including the health hazards of mining and nursing home abuse. Nader's Raiders put their investigative noses into every corner of the industrial and corporate world, highlighting injustices, illegalities, and dangers and incurring the enmity of many captains of industry and commerce.

In the mid-1970s Nader sponsored the "Critical Mass" conferences about the dangers of nuclear power, which produced the ongoing Critical Mass Energy Project. In 1988 he helped to secure the passage of a California initiative to reduce the cost of automobile insurance. In the 1990s he took on the computer industry, fighting the monopolistic practices of many big corporations. The work of Nader and his colleagues is responsible for the creation of such concerned consumer groups as Congress Watch, Public Citizen, Commercial Alert, the Center for Auto Safety, the National Insurance Consumer Organization, and the Health Research Organization.

PRESIDENTIAL CAMPAIGNS

Though he said, "The most important office in America for anyone to achieve is full-time citizen," in 1996 Nader ran for the presidency of the United States. He did not expect to win, but he allegedly wished to call attention to the lack of real debate between the major party candidates, labeling them "a Corporate Party with two heads wearing different makeup." Running on a platform that expounded on the need to fight corporate crime and oppose multinational corporations "whose only allegiance is to profit," Nader was not permitted to participate in the nationally televised candidate debates. Despite Democratic fears that his candidacy would draw votes away from Bill Clinton, the Democratic incumbent won handily. Some traditional Democratic supporters did vote for Nader, however, if only to express their dissatisfaction with the party's lack of response to the concerns of working people.

Nader's next run for the presidency, in 2000, is notable for its role in one of the worst fiascos in American political history. Vice President Al Gore carried the popular vote 51,003,926 to George W. Bush's 50,460,110. Nader received only 2,883,105 votes, but the defection of some Democrats coupled with flawed voting machines and methods in the key state of Florida, in which Bush's brother Jeb was governor, eventually threw the decision into the conservative Supreme Court. In *Bush v. Gore*, the court by a five-to-four decision upheld the votes in Florida that ultimately delivered an advantage to Bush in the electoral college. All five affirmative votes were cast by Republican-appointed justices; only David Souter deserted party ranks to vote with the minority. Nader ran again in 2004 and 2008 but received little attention.

Nader's landmark work for the rights of consumers has made his name a household word throughout the United States and abroad. Even those who disagree with his politics acknowledge him as a sharp watchdog on industry. His methodology, which includes undertaking fact-finding investigations, publishing reports, filing lawsuits, and lobbying for change, has become a model for action in the public interest movement. A deeply committed activist, he has eschewed a celebrity lifestyle in favor of legendary thriftiness, living in a tiny apartment in the town where he grew up and refusing to own a car. Describing his work, Nader has said he wishes to promote "citizen action against the growth of the corporate state and its political and economic disenfranchisement of the public."

Tina Gianoulis

SEE ALSO: *Automobile;* Bush v. Gore *(2000); Consumerism.*

BIBLIOGRAPHY

Ackerman, Bruce, ed. *"Bush v. Gore": The Question of Legitimacy.* New Haven, CT: Yale University Press, 2002.

Celsi, Teresa Noel. *Ralph Nader: The Consumer Revolution.* Brookfield, CT: Millbrook Press, 1991.

Crusz, Rienzi W. G. *Ralph Nader: A Bibliography—1960–1982.* Waterloo, ON: University of Waterloo Library, 1982.

Holsworth, Robert D. *Public Interest Liberalism and the Crisis of Affluence: Reflections on Nader, Environmentalism, and the Politics of Sustainable Society.* Boston: G. K. Hall, 1980.

Isaac, Katherine. *Ralph Nader's Practicing Democracy 1997: A Guide to Student Action.* New York: St. Martin's Press, 1997.

Nader, Ralph. *Crashing the Party: Taking on the Corporate Government in an Age of Surrender.* New York: Dunne Books/St. Martin's, 2002.

Nader, Ralph. *The Ralph Nader Reader.* New York: Seven Stories Press, 2000.

Nagel, Patrick *(1945–1984)*

Painter, illustrator, and graphic artist Patrick Nagel came to prominence around 1980 with works influenced by fashion photography, Art Deco poster art of the 1920s and 1930s, and Japanese wood-block prints. Born in Dayton, Ohio, Nagel grew up in the Los Angeles area, where he spent most of his life. He studied art at the Chouinard Art Institute, and in 1969 he received a bachelor of fine arts degree from California State University at Fullerton. After first working as a freelance artist he joined ABC-TV in 1971, where he produced television graphics for promotion and news broadcasts. After a year he returned to freelance assignments, accepting commissions from major corporations and magazines, including IBM, ITT, United Artists, MGM (Metro-Goldwyn-Mayer), Universal Studios, *Architectural Digest, Rolling Stone, Oui,* and *Harper's.* From 1976 he illustrated the *Playboy* column "The Playboy Advisor."

Although he produced more than sixty different graphic editions during his lifetime, he was best known for the "Nagel women," idealized portraits of fashionable young women who exuded both a sense of style and an alluring mystery. Perhaps inspired by Nagel's wife, the model Jennifer Dumas, these silk-screened limited-edition prints quickly won him an international reputation. Often used in advertisements, they marked a decided turn away from the visual trends of the late 1960s and 1970s. Nagel's crisp lines and flat, cool colors were quite unlike that period's busy, neo-Baroque "psychedelic" poster art. Nagel attempted to depict the new, confident woman of the 1980s, one secure with her sexuality yet simultaneously slightly distanced and aloof. Almost always shown with ghostly white skin, red lipstick, and short black hair, this "Nagel woman" proved a narrow but extremely popular vision.

Nagel's first solo show of painted works sold out in fifteen minutes. In 1982 the pop band Duran Duran invited Nagel to design the cover for its number-one-selling album, *Rio.* Many celebrities, including Joan Collins, posed for Nagel's paintings, attracted perhaps by his rare sense of an almost austere glamour. After his untimely death in 1984, *Playboy* published in its January 1985 issue an homage to Nagel as an artist and a man. His work can be found in the permanent collections of the Library of Congress, the Smithsonian Institution, and the Musée des Arts Décoratifs and the Musée de l'Affiche in Paris.

Vance Bell

SEE ALSO: Playboy; *Pop Art.*

BIBLIOGRAPHY

Nagel, Patrick. *Nagel: The Art of Patrick Nagel.* New York: Perennial Library, 1989.

Patrick Nagel Collection. Accessed December 2011. Available from http://www.patricknagel.com

Reed, Walt, and Society of Illustrators. *The Illustrator in America, 1860–2000.* New York: Society of Illustrators, 2001.

Naismith, James *(1861–1939)*

Dr. James Naismith would no doubt be astounded to see the degree to which the game he invented in the late nineteenth century (not to mention its players) has changed and evolved. As it was, Naismith lived to see the game transformed from one in which people tried to throw a ball into a peach basket hung on the wall to one in which athletic players competed at an extremely high level. As Glenn Dickey notes in his book *The History of Professional Basketball since 1896,* basketball is "the only true American game," as there had existed nothing even remotely resembling it until Naismith invented it in 1891 in Springfield, Massachusetts.

Naismith's invention grew out of a need to help fulfill a curriculum requirement at the Young Men's Christian Association (YMCA) Training School where he taught; students there were required to exercise for an hour a day. While the students could play football in the fall and baseball in the spring, they had no wintertime sport and had to resort to doing an hour of calisthenics every day, which was extremely unpopular. Little did Naismith know that he would not only fill that hour with a more enjoyable activity but would also create what would become one of the world's most popular sports.

EARLY LIFE

Naismith's life prior to going to Springfield was a rather bumpy one. He was born in Ontario, Canada, and dropped out of high school in his midteens, believing that further education was not necessary for his future. He began working as a lumberjack to help support his brother and sister, who with Naismith had been raised by an uncle after their parents died of typhoid fever in 1870. After five years of working, Naismith decided that he needed to continue his education after all, so in 1881 he reentered high school, enrolling as a sophomore. After graduating he decided to go to college, despite opposition from his uncle, who wanted James to stay home and help run the family farm.

Naismith enrolled at McGill University in Montreal, where he became involved in athletics, particularly rugby. He also excelled in academics, graduating in 1887 in the top 10 percent of his class with a degree in philosophy and Hebrew. Following his graduation, Naismith decided to pursue a theological education at Presbyterian College, a school affiliated with McGill. In 1890, upon finishing his theological work, he moved to Springfield, Massachusetts, to take part in the recently founded International Young Men's Christian Association Training School, established to train laypeople in the promotion of Christian values.

As Bernice Larson Webb notes in her book *The Basketball Man: James Naismith*, the guiding ideas of the YMCA Training School were the classical ones of building "a sound mind in a sound body" and using athletics to build character. According to Webb, Naismith wholeheartedly agreed with this philosophy and ardently wanted to be one of the men who spread it. He took a position as a physical education instructor in Springfield, where he taught until the summer of 1895, after which he moved to Denver, Colorado, to serve as physical education director for the Denver YMCA.

INVENTING BASKETBALL

Naismith first began to formulate the principles of basketball in an attempt to help satisfy the curricular needs of a group of students in the Springfield training school's Secretarial Department. Many of the older students in the department had become bored with the exercises they were forced to do to fulfill the school's physical education requirement. Because the activity had to take place indoors, Naismith had to create an activity that did not need a lot of space and did not entail rough contact with other players, as in football and baseball. To solve this problem, he came up with the idea of a game in which two competing teams try to score points by throwing a ball into a peach basket hung on the wall. The players would pass the ball to each other until one of them could put the ball into the basket. While the rules of this game evolved to a greater extent as time went on, Naismith had come up with the basic principles of the game of basketball.

Following his YMCA career in Springfield and Denver, Naismith became the first in a long line of famous basketball coaches at the University of Kansas (KU), which has since had one of the most successful basketball programs in the country. When Naismith arrived in 1898 as the university's physical education and religious director, the school did not yet have a basketball program. He coached the Jayhawks in the game from 1898 to 1907, achieving the dubious honor of being the only coach in KU history to compile a losing record; his teams won fifty-five games and lost sixty.

Because he had an interest in helping to promote other sports programs at KU and never became solely focused on basketball, Naismith handed the basketball coaching reins over to F. C. "Phog" Allen in 1907. Additionally, according to biographer Webb, Naismith was "noticeably uninterested" in coaching basketball and was more concerned with building the character and physical fortitude of his students than in winning games. He was apparently also unhappy with some of the changes that had taken place in the game he had invented. For example, in Rob Rains and Hellen Carpenter's book *James Naismith: The Man Who Invented Basketball*, he is quoted as saying "Oh, my gracious, they are murdering my game" in response to the physical style of play he witnessed in a 1910 game between rivals KU and the University of Missouri.

In addition to inventing the game of basketball, Naismith created the football helmet. When playing the contact sport in Springfield, he frequently complained of receiving ear bruises. To help prevent this, he cut a football lengthwise and began wearing it on his head to cover his ears. The innovation not only prevented such injuries but, more significantly, fostered the further development of the game of football.

Naismith and his wife, Maude, whom he married in June 1894, had three daughters. He retired from the KU faculty in 1937 and died in 1939 at the age of seventy-eight. The Naismith Memorial Basketball Hall of Fame in Springfield is named for him, and he was inducted into the hall in 1959.

Jason George

SEE ALSO: *Basketball; National Basketball Association (NBA); National Collegiate Athletic Association (NCAA); National Football League (NFL).*

BIBLIOGRAPHY

Dickey, Glenn. *The History of Professional Basketball since 1896.* New York: Stein and Day, 1982.

Franzblau, Matt. "James Naismith's Legacy." University of Kansas Men's Basketball Webpage. Accessed September 9, 2011. Available from http://www.kuathletics.com/sports/m-baskbl/spec-rel/091611aag.html

Rains, Rob, and Hellen Carpenter. *James Naismith: The Man Who Invented Basketball.* Philadelphia: Temple University Press, 2009.

Webb, Bernice Larson. *The Basketball Man: James Naismith.* Lawrence: University Press of Kansas, 1973.

Namath, Joe *(1943–)*

"I guarantee it!" Joe Namath's outlandish promise, made poolside in the days preceding the 1969 Super Bowl, angered his own head coach, infuriated his opponents, and helped bring the spirit of the 1960s counterculture into sports. When the New York Jets backed up their twenty-five-year-old quarterback's "guarantee" with a 16–7 upset over the highly favored Baltimore Colts, the new American Football League (AFL) gained credibility and sealed the success of the upcoming merger between the AFL and the National Football League (NFL).

While "Broadway Joe" never challenged "establishment" social structures in the manner of the draft-resisting, poetry-spouting boxer Muhammad Ali, his hedonistic "make love, not war" lifestyle infused the straitlaced atmosphere of professional football with an entirely alien cultural attitude. An openly promiscuous user of adults-only substances (he preferred Johnnie Walker Red Label) who partied all night, Namath simply admitted to behavior usually indulged in secrecy by more clean-cut (and married) athletes. While he apparently never smoked pot and his tastes in music (Glen Campbell and the Fifth Dimension) were decidedly not hip, his abhorrence for hypocrisy was a lightning bolt that shattered the value system of professional sports.

YOUNG ATHLETE

Born Joseph William Namath in the steel mill town of Beaver Falls, Pennsylvania, on May 31, 1943, the young athlete excelled

Joe Namath. Joe Namath prepares for a handoff in Super Bowl III in January 1969. VERNON BIEVER/CONTRIBUTOR/GETTY IMAGES SPORT/GETTY IMAGES.

in many different sports from a very early age. He played high school basketball and was offered a professional baseball contract upon graduation. He decided to play football instead, and he applied to Penn State. However, he failed to attain the minimum score on his college entrance exams and had to settle for the University of Alabama, which was interested in the young quarterback and was less academically demanding.

Initially Namath disliked Alabama, disliked most of the people, disliked the prevailing attitudes about skin color, and generally felt alien and isolated. Not only was he a swarthy-complexioned son of Hungarian immigrants, but he also maintained close friendships with African Americans. The Alabama classmates who referred to him as a "nigger-lover" had noted these associations, while some of Namath's teammates were also resentful because the legendary head coach Paul "Bear" Bryant seemed to take Namath under his wing.

PROFESSIONAL CAREER

By 1964, when Namath finished his final and successful senior year at Alabama, the old New York Titans of the new AFL had a new owner and a new name, the New York Jets. The entertainment mogul Sonny Werblin had purchased the team, promptly deciding that sports should be considered a glitzy form of entertainment; thus he needed a star. Namath left a rather checkered career behind him at Alabama. At one point he was suspended from the football squad for directing traffic in downtown Tuscaloosa while intoxicated. Known as something of a rogue, Namath was also a superb and fearless quarterback who liked to take chances both on and off the field. Werblin had found his star. He gave Namath a record-breaking $427,000 contract, including a lavish signing bonus and jobs for the player's brothers, making him the first true bonus baby in sports. Despite his questionable athletic future—the quarterback underwent knee surgery immediately after his senior season—Werblin offered him lavish terms.

Namath's first few years with the Jets were more notable for his off-the-field activities than for his quarterbacking. His hair was alarmingly long, he had numerous girlfriends, and he spent many nights drinking and hobnobbing with sportswriters and celebrities in New York City. On one occasion he got into a fistfight with a writer at a club and was fined by the team. On another he and his African American teammate Winston Hill tried unsuccessfully to room together during an exhibition game in Birmingham, Alabama, in the mid-1960s. Namath appeared utterly unconcerned with whatever accepted standards of propriety he considered hypocritical, no matter where or to what they applied.

In 1966 the old NFL negotiated a deal with the new AFL; each year the champions of each league would face off in a game that in later years would be called the "Super Bowl," and the leagues agreed to cooperate in matters of drafting and signing players. They planned on an eventual merger, but many were skeptical as to whether the new AFL teams were seriously competitive. The legendary Green Bay Packers, an NFL team, captured the first two Super Bowls. In 1968 Namath and his New York Jets won the AFL title and earned the right to play in the third Super Bowl.

The Jets' shocking victory over the NFL's Colts on January 12, 1969, along with the enormous publicity accorded Namath's outlandish and entertaining pregame behavior and comments, secured the merger. The NFL absorbed the AFL, along with many of the new attitudes toward the sport exemplified by Namath. Then, in the summer of 1969, just as the two leagues were about to merge, Namath stunned the sports world by announcing his retirement from football at age twenty-six. By then he had bought his own club, the "Bachelors III," and NFL Commissioner Pete Rozelle had offered Namath an ultimatum: sell the nightclub, which Rozelle claimed was frequented by "undesirables," or face indefinite suspension. At a much-publicized press conference held at his club, Namath tearfully said that he had to follow his conscience and leave the game behind. Before the beginning of the new season, though, he reconsidered, sold the club, and went to training camp. He later said that a compromise plan worked out between Rozelle and his own attorneys went against his instincts.

Namath continued to play for the Jets through the 1976 season, when chronic injuries and age convinced the team to place him on waivers. The Los Angeles Rams picked him up for one more season, and he retired in 1977 at the age of thirty-four.

Outside football Namath enjoyed a brief career in entertainment. In 1969 he starred in *The Joe Namath Show*, which lasted only one season. He followed up with guest appearances on such television shows as *The A-Team* (1983–1987), *The Love Boat* (1977–1986), and *Fantasy Island* (1977–1984). He also had minor roles in several films. In the early 1970s, Namath was featured in two television commercials that won him a good deal of notoriety. In an ad for Hanes Beauty Mist pantyhose, he appeared on camera wearing pantyhose. In the other ad, which was for Noxzema shaving cream, Namath received an on-air shave by the actress and pinup queen Farrah Fawcett.

Namath has spent his post-football years in the shadow of his glory days. In 1999 he was ranked ninety-sixth on the *Sporting News* List of 100 Greatest Football Players of all time. In addition to serving as a goodwill ambassador for the Jets, Namath does promotional work for the NFL, ESPN Classic, and CBS Sports Line. He also promotes Vestin Group, an investment firm. Namath was diagnosed with arthritis at the age of twenty-three, and he continues to serve as a spokesperson for the Arthritis Huddle Program and for Boehringer Ingelheim Pharmaceuticals. He has lived in Florida since 1966, and he continues to keep in shape by fishing, golfing, and working out.

Robin Markowitz

SEE ALSO: *Advertising;* The A-Team*; Bryant, Paul "Bear";* Fantasy Island*; Fawcett, Farrah;* The Love Boat*; National Football League (NFL); Professional Football; Sports Heroes; Super Bowl; Television.*

BIBLIOGRAPHY

Allen, Maury. *Joe Namath's Sportin' Life.* New York: Paperback Library, 1969.

Kriegel, Mark. *Namath: A Biography.* New York: Viking, 2004.

Namath, Joe, and D. Schaap. *I Can't Wait until Tomorrow . . . 'Cause I Get Better Looking Every Day.* New York: Random House, 1969.

Ralbovsky, M. *The Namath Effect.* Englewood Cliffs, NJ: Prentice-Hall, 1976.

Sanford, William R., and Carl Green. *Joe Namath.* New York: Crestwood House, 1993.

Shamsky, Art, and Barry Zeman. *The Magnificent Seasons.* New York: T. Dunne Books, 2004.

Nancy Drew

Debuting in 1930, the Nancy Drew mysteries are the longest-running American series of girls' books. They were created by Edward Stratemeyer, an author and businessman whose book production company, the Stratemeyer Syndicate, used ghostwriters to complete his outlines for dozens of children's series. Each series was published under a pseudonym; the Nancy Drew books were published under "Carolyn Keene." Intended as a girls' counterpart to the syndicate's popular Hardy Boys mysteries, which began in 1927, Nancy Drew quickly became the best-selling juvenile series in the country. Nancy Drew books went on to be a hit internationally and have now been published in more than two dozen languages. With this girl detective, Stratemeyer created not only a popular series of books but also an enduring cultural icon.

Stratemeyer employed ghostwriter Mildred Wirt, a young journalist from Iowa who had already worked on other series for him, to inaugurate the Nancy Drew books. Wirt developed Nancy as self-reliant and courageous, traits she felt were too rare in girls' fiction at that time. Her books feature a forthright teenager (sixteen at first and later eighteen) who is determined to right wrongs and has a sharp intellect that surpasses those of the local police officers.

Stratemeyer died shortly after Nancy Drew's debut, and he left the syndicate to his two adult daughters, Harriet Stratemeyer Adams and Edna Stratemeyer. Between their outlines and Wirt's compelling prose, the characteristics that made Nancy Drew so popular took shape.

ELEMENTS OF THE SERIES

Nancy is an only child living with her widowed father, attorney Carson Drew, and a motherly housekeeper named Hannah. Nancy's friends assist her with solving mysteries but are never quite as smart or capable as she is. Alone or with her friends, Nancy has the freedom to drive around her hometown of River Heights and the surrounding regions, pursuing criminals and bringing justice to victims. The most remarkable aspect of her character, at least in the early years of the series, is her combination of ladylike femininity and skills that are usually considered "masculine": she can drive expertly, fix flat tires and broken machines, and handle herself in physical fights with criminals—all while wearing fashionable dresses and high heels. A local celebrity, Nancy commands the respect of adults and is praised in newspapers for her amazing crime-fighting feats. This portrayal of female youth was unusual in the early 1930s, which is part of why the series quickly became a best seller among girls and was even read by many boys.

Readers also responded to Nancy's endearing mixture of youth and maturity. Although merely a teenager, she is treated like a near-equal by her father, who seeks her advice on his legal cases and entrusts her with total freedom. With no mother in the way, Nancy is the lady of the house and the master of her own identity. However, she also enjoys the protections of childhood. She never accepts money for her sleuthing, and her father handles all her financial concerns, supplying her with everything she could need or want. Thus, Nancy—and her readers—can enjoy the best of both the youth and the adult worlds.

Nancy was less popular with librarians and schoolteachers, many of whom refused to give these books to children because of the series' literary shortcomings. However, if any flaw has dampened the experience of reading Nancy Drew for some children, it is the protagonist's utter perfection. Nancy represents the ideal balance between the extremes of her friends Bess (a plump "girly girl") and George (a tomboy who is Bess's cousin). Every volume shows her performing a combination of feats that no real girl could manage.

As Bobbie Ann Mason observes in *The Girl Sleuth*, "Nancy is so accomplished that she can lie bound and gagged in a dank basement or snowed-in cabin for as much as twenty-four hours without freezing to death or wetting her pants." While millions of girls have loved the vicarious thrills of identifying with Nancy, some have found her inhuman perfection off-putting and have preferred to read about more realistic heroines. Nancy's impossible accomplishments, unfailing luck, and ever-cheerful attitude have also made her the target of satirists. She has sometimes been skewered in the press, in fiction, and in stage plays such as *Trixie True, Teen Detective*, which premiered off-Broadway in 1980.

CHARACTER REVISIONS

The Nancy Drew series underwent many changes after its initial heyday in the 1930s and 1940s. After ghostwriting nearly all the original volumes, Wirt left the series in 1953, and Adams wrote several subsequent volumes herself. Starting in the late 1950s, Adams also began revising and rewriting the older titles to make them more relevant to younger readers and to remove overt racism (though a fair amount of implied racism remains). The combined effects of the revisions and the loss of the original ghostwriter altered the flavor of the series. In one notable change, Nancy is stripped of some of her independence. She is more submissive to authority and travels more often in a group of friends, thus minimizing the courage and risk taking that highlighted her solo escapades.

The biggest changes came after Adams's death in 1982. The syndicate's properties were purchased by its publisher, Simon & Schuster, which updated Nancy and her adventures. Nancy regains some of her independence while, as an example of real-life girlhood, also appearing more normal and less exceptional. This round of revisions was partly due to the changing times: after the rise of feminism in the 1960s and 1970s, it became more common for young females to be seen as active, intelligent, and capable members of society.

During the 1980s and 1990s, Simon & Schuster also added more ethnic diversity to the books. Whereas minorities previously appeared mostly as villains (or occasionally as victims of crime), they now are police officers, local businesspeople, and even members of Nancy's social circle. Such characters are not numerous, but their presence has made the series more inclusive. This, too, reflects general changes in American society.

SPIN-OFFS

While continuing the core Nancy Drew mysteries, Simon & Schuster created several spin-off series aimed at different age groups. In the 1930s the series was aimed at readers between ages ten and fifteen; by the 1980s the readership was between eight and twelve. The first spin-off series *The Nancy Drew Files* (1986-1997) reclaimed the early-teen audience with a somewhat "sexier" version of Nancy. Interested in trendy clothes and cute boys, this Nancy is a departure from the earlier characterization. The stories are also more sophisticated, including murders for the first time. Critics who fondly remembered the original Nancy disliked these changes and published scathing reviews. However, the series appealed to contemporary "tweens" and yielded more than 120 volumes.

The Nancy Drew Notebooks (1994–2005) targeted younger readers, as Nancy and her friends are in grade school. This series was later revamped as *Nancy Drew and the Clue Crew*. For older teenagers, Simon & Schuster launched the *Nancy Drew on Campus* series (1995–1998), which places Nancy at a university, where she solves crimes related to date rape, drug abuse, and the like. This series was less popular, lasting for only twenty-five volumes. The least successful of the spin-offs was the *River Heights* series (1989–1992), which does not include the same cast of characters. Since the 1980s Simon & Schuster has also combined its two major teen-detective series in several different cross-over books and series, including *Nancy Drew/Hardy Boys Super Sleuths*, *Nancy Drew/Hardy Boys Be-a-Detective*, and *Nancy Drew/Hardy Boys Super Mysteries*.

Throughout all these spin-offs, the core series continued to grow, reaching 175 volumes by 2003. The publisher then made a historic decision: it ended *Nancy Drew Mysteries*, which had been continuous since 1930, and replaced it in 2004 with the new *Nancy Drew, Girl Detective*. This series is similar to the original, except that Nancy now narrates her adventures in the first person. The facelift has proved to be effective, as *Nancy Drew, Girl Detective* has grown steadily. In 2005 the publisher PaperCutz added Nancy Drew to the burgeoning genre of graphic novels. There are more than twenty Nancy Drew graphic novels, and PaperCutz further expanded the franchise in 2010 with the *New Case Files* series.

MEDIA AND MERCHANDISING

Despite the popularity of the Nancy Drew character, she was not widely capitalized upon in other media before the 1970s. In 1938 and 1939 Warner Brothers released four Nancy Drew movies starring Bonita Granville. At only slightly more than sixty minutes apiece, these are "B" movies that were shown with bigger films as part of double features. The films depart significantly from the books, particularly in their comic tone. Nancy Drew did not appear again in a nonbook form until the late 1950s, when Parker Brothers released a Nancy Drew board game. In 1967 the Madame Alexander company produced a Nancy Drew doll, which did not meet with the syndicate's approval. Quickly withdrawn from circulation, this doll is now one of the rarest and priciest Nancy Drew collectibles.

Nancy reappeared on-screen in 1977, this time on television, with ABC's *The Hardy Boys/Nancy Drew Mysteries*, starring Pamela Sue Martin as Nancy. The Nancy Drew episodes alternated weekly with those featuring the Hardy Boys and garnered lower ratings than their counterparts, partially because teen idols Shaun Cassidy and Parker Stevenson played the Hardy Boys characters. Thus, the network canceled the Nancy Drew series and used Nancy only as a recurring character in Hardy Boys episodes. Disliking this arrangement, Martin quit and was briefly replaced by Janet Louise Johnson before Nancy's character was eliminated altogether. During the series' run, a plethora of tie-in Nancy Drew merchandise appeared, including a jigsaw puzzle, a Halloween costume, a lunchbox, a fan-club kit, posters, and T-shirts.

Nearly twenty years passed before the character appeared on TV again: in 1995 Canadian production company Nelvana introduced a syndicated Nancy Drew series, as well as one featuring the Hardy Boys. After conducting a cast search on the Internet, as well as through more conventional channels, the producers hired Tracy Ryan to play Nancy. Both series aired in the United States on the UPN network and were canceled after one season. In 2002 a made-for-TV Nancy Drew movie aired on ABC starring Maggie Lawson.

Somewhat more successful was a theatrical release, *Nancy Drew* (2007), starring Emma Roberts. Aimed at a youth audience, the film presents Nancy as a tween rather than as a mature teen. Older fans of the character had a lukewarm reaction to the film, as did movie critics. Nonetheless, the film made a modest profit and was nominated for some children's film awards. Merchandise related to the film includes movie posters, a soundtrack CD, paperback books sporting Roberts's likeness, and a video game.

As merchandising goes, Nancy Drew has fared best in the video-game format. Several companies have released games, and the most popular and critically acclaimed have been produced by Her Interactiv. Various types of other products have been produced in recent years to capitalize on the iconic status of Nancy Drew with older fans, such as a party game, address books, postcard collections featuring vintage cover art from older volumes, stationery, calendars, and fashion accessories. In the first decade of the 2000s the Tonner company released a Nancy Drew doll, which was marketed with several different outfits and was aimed more at collectors than children. The doll was available for only a limited time. There are also websites devoted to the Nancy Drew phenomenon.

A CULTURAL ICON

Indeed, the Nancy Drew character remains popular with adults who remember the books fondly. This phenomenon began in the 1970s with two simultaneous social trends: the hobby of collecting pop culture memorabilia and the rise of the feminist movement. Numerous newspapers and magazines in the 1970s published articles about the Nancy Drew books of yore, celebrating them both as vintage collectibles and as an influence on a generation of young female readers, many of whom were inspired by the character's example to pursue professional careers.

Adams became a popular subject in the press, particularly after the premiere of the 1977 television series. By then, Adams was writing Nancy Drew volumes by herself, and she told reporters that she was the series' sole author. This statement obscured the work done by numerous ghostwriters, especially that of Wirt. Because the Stratemeyer Syndicate created the characters and provided all the outlines, Adams felt that those ghostwriters were not "authors." Although serious researchers knew the whole story, the general public did not learn about Wirt's role until the University of Iowa hosted a Nancy Drew conference in 1993 and invited her to appear. The conference received national press coverage, and its proceedings were published in *Rediscovering Nancy Drew* (1995), thus making accurate information about Nancy Drew's history readily available. When Wirt died in 2002, obituaries crediting her as the original Nancy Drew author appeared all over the world.

Ghostwriters for Simon & Schuster continue to write Nancy Drew books under the name Carolyn Keene, who presumably would be more than 100 years old by now if she were real. As the subject of a thriving book series, graphic novels, and popular video games, Nancy Drew herself seems likely to reach her 100th birthday. She is no longer as strikingly unique as she once was, as children's books with active, smart, and adventurous heroines are now common. However, Nancy Drew made such offerings possible. Her status in popular culture has been ensured by the millions of readers she has influenced.

Ilana Nash

SEE ALSO: *Best Sellers; Board Games; Consumerism; Detective Fiction; Feminism; Graphic Novels; The Hardy Boys; Made-for-Television Movies; Parker Brothers; Stratemeyer, Edward; Teenagers; Television; Toys; Tweens.*

BIBLIOGRAPHY

Billman, Carol. *The Secret of the Stratemeyer Syndicate: Nancy Drew, the Hardy Boys, and the Million Dollar Fiction Factory.* New York: Ungar, 1986.

Caprio, Betsy. *The Mystery of Nancy Drew: Girl Sleuth on the Couch.* Trabuco Canyon, CA: Source Books, 1992.

Dyer, Carolyn Stewart, and Nancy Tillman Romalov. *Rediscovering Nancy Drew.* Iowa City: University of Iowa Press, 1995.

Kismaric, Carole, and Marvin Heiferman. *The Mysterious Case of Nancy Drew & the Hardy Boys.* New York: Simon & Schuster, 1998.

Mason, Bobbie Ann. *The Girl Sleuth.* Athens: University of Georgia Press, 1995.

Nash, Ilana. *American Sweethearts: Teenage Girls in Twentieth-Century Popular Culture.* Bloomington: Indiana University Press, 2006.

Plunkett-Powell, Karen. *The Nancy Drew Scrapbook.* New York: St. Martin's Press, 1993.

Prager, Arthur. *Rascals at Large, or, the Clue in the Old Nostalgia.* Garden City, NY: Doubleday, 1971.

Rehak, Melanie. *Girl Sleuth: Nancy Drew and the Women Who Created Her.* Orlando, FL: Harcourt, 2005.

Napster

Napster was a groundbreaking file-sharing program that allowed users freely to exchange digital music files, typically in MP3 format, over the Internet. Founded by Sean Parker, Shawn Fanning, and John Fanning, Napster was introduced in June 1999 and quickly transformed the way in which people acquired music and other forms of prerecorded entertainment The program was immensely popular with fans, who did not have to pay for their music, and was reviled by bands, who did not get paid for the music they had made. The music industry brought numerous suits and eventually won the ensuing court battles. Napster was shut down soon after, but the company had already opened the floodgates to free online file sharing and had irrevocably changed the structure of the music industry. Although Napster was later revived as an online music store, it never regained its original popularity or influence.

PERSONAL COMPUTERS AND THE INTERNET

Napster emerged from the rise of the personal computer in the 1980s. The company's employees were drawn from the world of computers, and the ethic of freely sharing digital content came from the community of computer enthusiasts and hackers. One of these enthusiasts was Shawn Fanning, then a Northwestern University student who developed software for the peer-to-peer (P2P) exchange of digital files. Fanning spent a lot of his time in Internet chat rooms, and he imagined a network of music lovers who could share their libraries of recordings with one another. If a server could be created to hold the indexes of numerous websites, each user could access any other site and its content of recordings. Fanning joined with his uncle, John Fanning, an Internet entrepreneur, and Sean Parker, a high school friend who raised the company's initial capital, to create Napster.

As personal computing became more popular, more users used digital encoding systems to record music on their home computers. During the 1990s home computers came with a means to record (or "burn") digital music files onto a hard drive or to a recordable compact disc. At the same time, the growing advances in digital encoding made it possible to transmit digital music over the Internet. In the early 1990s the encoding systems were in their infancy, and it took inordinate amounts of time to transmit information along existing phone lines to relatively slow modems attached to the computer. As MP2 evolved into the far superior MP3, as glass fiber cable replaced phone lines, and as faster modems were built into personal computers, downloading and saving music became easier and easier.

Many free programs were made available to locate, play, and save digital music files. At the same time, the sales of personal computers and the number of users connected to the Internet rose sharply. In 1992 only about two million Americans were connected to the Internet; by 1996 as many as twenty-three million were. Cable companies were connecting Americans to advanced digital networks at work, at home, and at school.

Napster offered a simple and efficient way to access a library of sound recordings so large that it was previously unimaginable. A user searched for a song, and Napster connected the user to that song in the libraries of all of the users currently online. When Fanning and his colleagues at Napster introduced the service in 1999, they hoped to engage about 150,000 users. By the end of the year, more than 500,000 were connected. In 2000 Napster had ten million users and made its first forays into the Internet. Although there had been illegal recording booms in the past, such as the one enabled by the rise of tape cassettes in the 1980s, Napster was unprecedented in its size and scope. The company had well over fifty million users in 2001 and as many as seventy million users by 2002.

The Napster boom had an immediate and damaging effect on the recording industry. The industry had staked its future on the compact disc, which it hoped would be the dominant form of recorded music in the twenty-first century. However, as fast as connections to Napster rose, CD sales fell. The artistic community was divided. Many performers sympathized with the illegal downloaders, for the service articulated a freedom that they had praised in their songs. However, free music for fans meant reduced income for artists. Band royalties declined, artists' livelihoods were threatened, and label profits shrank.

LEGAL CHALLENGES

The music industry's immediate response was to treat Napster and the whole process of downloading as theft of intellectual ownership and breach of copyright. Led by the Recording Industry Association of America (RIAA), a trade association, bands such as Metallica and artists such as Dr. Dre challenged Napster in the courts and pursued selected members of the vast community of downloading pirates. However, when some of these pirates turned out to be sympathetic senior citizens or young children, it was the RIAA and the musicians who looked bad.

Although downloading of copyrighted content was illegal, the people who did it, and the public at large, did not think of it as stealing. To many, the Internet was a social gathering place rather than a commercial exchange, and Napster was considered part of the Internet's ethic of free sharing. While the record industry complained about the millions of dollars of lost sales to Napster, the people busy downloading songs argued that the service was actually helping sales by promoting records and increasing their visibility to millions of Internet browsers. (Even some bands, such as Radiohead, were sympathetic to this argument.)

The court case against Napster lasted from 2000 to 2002. In the end, Napster was deemed illegal and was shut down. While the decision was considered a victory for the RIAA and the entertainment industry, there were plenty of other free shareware programs available online; the absence of Napster hardly made a dent in Internet music piracy.

After the company's 2002 bankruptcy, Napster's name and logo were purchased by Roxio, a software company, and were applied to its legal online music store, which became Napster 2.0. In 2008 the electronics retailer Best Buy purchased the company, and it became a small player in an increasingly large business of online music stores. After leaving the company, Shawn and John Fanning continued to develop various Internet technologies and companies, while Parker became the first president of Facebook and an early investor in numerous other successful Web ventures, including Spotify.

Andre Millard

SEE ALSO: *Compact Discs; Facebook; File Sharing; The Internet; MP3; Radiohead; Social Media.*

BIBLIOGRAPHY

Alderman, John. *Sonic Boom: Napster, MP3 and the New Pioneers of Music.* Cambridge, MA: Perseus, 2001.

Kot, Greg. *Ripped: How the Wired Generation Revolutionized Music.* New York: Scribner, 2009.

Menn, Joseph. *All the Rave: The Rise and Fall of Shawn Fanning's Napster.* New York: Crown, 2003.

NASA

Whether it be through film or print, Americans have always been fascinated with space travel. Stories range from the more mainstream exploration of space to "far-out" depictions of alien abductions and other encounters with creatures from another world. Much of our fascination with space has come out of the work of the National Aeronautics and Space Administration (NASA), which was established in 1958 as an agency of the U.S. government. With ten facilities—including the Lyndon B. Johnson Space Center in Houston, Texas, and the main launch facilities at Cape Canaveral, Florida—NASA's purpose is to coordinate and conduct aeronautical and space research.

THE SPACE RACE

With the Soviet launch of *Sputnik 1*, the first artificial satellite, in October 1957, Americans became concerned about the apparent "technological gap" between the two world powers. In an attempt to bridge this gap, America launched its own satellite and established NASA. NASA quickly brought the "space race" to national attention as it sought to fulfill President John F. Kennedy's challenge to reach the moon before 1970.

Americans watched these events with a childlike fascination. A new frontier was about to be conquered. Cowboys, soldiers, and sports figures were replaced by America's new heroes, the seven astronauts chosen for the first manned space program, Project Mercury. NASA's work ignited tremendous excitement in the nation. Children played with spaceships, wore space helmets, and fired ray guns. Indeed, families even made trips to Cape Canaveral, making it clear that our fascination with space was not just a fleeting one.

The world of popular culture would eventually catch up with, and profit from, this fascination. Television programs such as *Men into Space* became popular as Americans anticipated the first manned flight, not knowing exactly what to expect. Science fiction movies and comic books, already popular since the days of Buck Rogers and Flash Gordon serials, became even more popular. They pictured astronauts traveling into space, landing on hostile worlds, battling aliens, and encountering dangers that threatened mankind. Even Disneyland had its own World of Tomorrow. NASA sparked America's imagination by opening a frontier that had been only a dream.

Excitement was also mixed with fear. Some people who knew the families of astronauts wondered how they could let

***Space Shuttle* Columbia.** *The first manned space shuttle,* Columbia, *was launched from the Kennedy Space Center in April 1981.* SSPL/GETTY IMAGES.

their sons go into space and bring back a deadly disease. Others objected because they believed that God never intended for people to leave Earth. But NASA launched two successful suborbital flights and then placed John Glenn into orbit. In the early years, though, NASA always seemed to be one step behind the Soviet space program. Americans wondered whether NASA would win the ultimate prize of the space race—the first moon landing.

SETBACKS

NASA enjoyed overall success until the deaths of the *Apollo 1* astronauts in early 1967. The three prime candidates for the first moon landing were killed when their spacecraft caught fire on the launchpad. This proved a setback to the program, but NASA would reach its goal on July 20, 1969, when the Apollo Project resulted in the first successful moon landing. The image of Neil Armstrong walking on the lunar surface is permanently impressed upon the memories of Americans who watched it on television. The astronauts were immediate celebrities, and NASA's popularity soared. The *Apollo* spacecraft toured American cities, and it became clear that the successful Apollo program was the ultimate sign of American prestige and technological superiority. NASA's popularity, however, began to wane as Americans grew weary of moon landings. Reruns of *The Howdy Doody Show* achieved higher ratings than NASA's later lunar voyages, and people complained to television stations that their soap operas had been interrupted by these space missions.

In 1973, NASA launched Skylab, the first U.S. manned space laboratory. The Apollo-Soyuz project was a later joint American-Soviet mission, but it took the first manned space shuttle, launched in 1981, to rekindle NASA's popularity. The rise in popularity, however, would be short-lived as a series of failures changed the way Americans looked at NASA.

Christa McAuliffe, the schoolteacher who trained with NASA astronauts for the *Challenger* shuttle mission, made Americans everywhere believe that space travel was possible for the average person. The vision of *Challenger* exploding on the television screen on January 28, 1986, is indelibly burned into the memories of millions of Americans. Many Americans became critical of NASA and the space shuttle program, questioning the safety of space travel and research. After a two-year hiatus, shuttle launches resumed when *Discovery* blasted off in September 1988.

While the agency made successful shuttle launches, it also sent unmanned probes to other planets and placed the Hubble space telescope into orbit, supplying detailed pictures of other worlds. NASA also captured the imagination of the public when it successfully launched the *Mars Pathfinder* in July 1997—the Mars rover sent photographs back to Earth, and the public once again discussed the possibility of life on the Red Planet.

After the *Challenger* tragedy, space shuttle flights became so routine they were only briefly mentioned in the news. Former astronaut and senator John Glenn changed that when he came out of retirement to join the crew of the *Discovery* in 1998, becoming the oldest person to ever travel into space. After thirty years and 135 missions, the shuttle program terminated in 2011. It sent more than 300 astronauts into space, experienced two disasters (*Challenger* in 1986 and *Columbia* in 2003), worked in cooperation with other countries on the International Space Station, conducted medical research, and assisted in environmental studies.

NASA INSPIRES FANS AND SKEPTICS ALIKE

Over the years, NASA has provided inspiration for many science fiction writers and movie makers. The television series *Star Trek* (1966–1969) and the movie *2001: A Space Odyssey* (1968) were released during the "space race" era. NASA has been featured in many popular movies, including *Apollo 13* (1995), which popularized astronaut Jim Lovell's announcement "Houston, we have a problem." Decades after the moon missions, NASA's influence on popular culture could still be seen in such blockbuster movies as *Armageddon* (1998), *Deep Impact* (1998), and *Space Cowboys* (2000). Other features such as *The Right Stuff* (1983), the HBO miniseries *From the Earth to the Moon* (1998), *NASA 360* (2008), and *When We Left Earth: The NASA Missions* (2008) have attempted to document NASA's work.

NASA has even been the source of speculation for conspiracy theorists. Some authors believe NASA covered up unidentified flying object (UFO) sightings by early astronauts. They also accuse NASA of hiding the truth about an alleged monument on Mars supposedly caught on film in 1976. Some groups believe that no moon landing ever took place and that the lunar landing was staged on a movie set. In 2011 movies such as *Super 8*, *Apollo 18*, and *Transformers 3* continued to play on an underlying current of NASA conspiracy theories in American culture.

The history of NASA is a mixture of tragedy and triumph. Over the years, the American public has had mixed feeling regarding the success and usefulness of NASA. With ongoing speculation regarding life on other planets, Americans will continue to be intrigued with NASA's efforts to explore outer space.

James H. Lloyd

SEE ALSO: *Apollo Missions;* Challenger *Disaster;* Sputnik*;* Star Trek*;* 2001: A Space Odyssey*; UFOs (Unidentified Flying Objects).*

BIBLIOGRAPHY

Ferguson, Robert G. *NASA's First A: The First Fifty Years of Aeronautics at NASA*. Washington, DC: NASA, 2012.

Gray, Mike. *Angle of Attack: Harrison Storms and the Race to the Moon*. New York: Norton, 1992.

Launius, Roger D., and Bertram Ulrich. *NASA and the Exploration of Space: With Works from the NASA Art Collection*. New York: Stewart, Tabori, and Chang, 1998.

McCurdy, Howard E. *Inside NASA*. Baltimore, MD: Johns Hopkins University Press, 1993.

Wolfe, Tom. *The Right Stuff*. New York: Bantam Books, 1983.

NASCAR

SEE: *Patrick, Danica; Stock-Car Racing.*

The Nation

The United States' oldest continuously published weekly magazine, *The Nation* has maintained a consistent liberal/radical outlook since its founding by a group of abolitionists at the end of the Civil War in 1865. The causes it has championed over the years include labor unionism in the late 1800s, the formation of the National Association for the Advancement of Colored People (NAACP) in the early 1900s, anti-McCarthyism in the 1950s, and the civil rights and antiwar movements in the 1960s. Furthermore, it opposed the convictions of anarchists Ferdinando Nicola Sacco and Bartolomeo Vanzetti in a murder case in the 1920s and countered Reaganomics in the 1980s.

The Nation's contributing writers have been some of the most prominent figures in politics, the arts, education, and literature, such as W. E. B. Du Bois, H. L. Mencken, Willa Cather, Eleanor Roosevelt, James Baldwin, Jean-Paul Sartre, Cesar Chavez, Ralph Nader, E. L. Doctorow, and Toni Morrison. By the end of the twentieth century, columnists such as Alexander Cockburn, Katha Pollitt, Christopher Hitchens, and Calvin Trillin were offering readers commentary on public policy and cultural issues. Since 1966 the periodical has sponsored The Nation Institute, an independently funded public charity "committed to the creation of a just society and an informed public, as well as to the preservation of rights protected under the First Amendment." Some historians have credited *The Nation* with keeping alive the tradition of muckraking and advocacy journalism in the United States.

DEVELOPING A MISSION

According to *The Nation*'s original prospectus in 1865, the publication was defined as strictly independent and not "the organ of any party, sect or body." Hoping to heal the rifts of the bloody Civil War that had just ended, the founders of the weekly periodical—early backers included Henry Wadsworth Longfellow, James Russell Lowell, William James and his brother Henry James, Henry Adams, and William Dean Howells—further declared that its purpose would be to "make an earnest effort to bring to the discussion of political and social questions a really critical spirit, and to wage war upon the vices of violence, exaggeration and misrepresentation by which so much of the political writing of the day is marred." Its first editor, the Anglo Irish journalist E. L. Godkin, raised $100,000 to launch the magazine, which published its first issue on July 6, 1865, just weeks after General Robert E. Lee's surrender at Appomattox.

Radical abolitionists dominated *The Nation*'s earliest issues. Its major financial backer, George Luther Stearns, was a Boston lead-pipe manufacturer who had supplied John Brown with the munitions for the raid at Harpers Ferry in 1859. The first literary editor was Wendell Phillips Garrison, the son of abolitionist William Lloyd Garrison. Still, although *The Nation* supported most of the Reconstruction program and civil rights legislation, its middle-of-the-road stance disappointed supporters who advocated more radical reforms. In the interests of stabilizing the publication, Godkin distanced himself from what he called "too close identification with a factional or partisan cause." On labor-versus-capital issues, *The Nation* adopted a generally "liberal capitalist" stance, criticizing the excesses of business and supporting unions while steering clear of more ideological socialist solutions. When investors threatened to withdraw support, landscape architect Frederick Law Olmsted helped reorganize the periodical to guarantee its editorial independence.

In 1881, when *The Nation* became an insert in Henry Villard's *New York Evening Post*, Godkin turned over the editorship to Wendell Phillips Garrison. Circulation shrank, and the publication became little more than a book review section for the newspaper. After Garrison retired, several editors followed in quick succession: Hammond Lamont, who died within three years; Sanskrit scholar Paul Elmer More, who added more literary criticism to the publication; and Harold deWolf Fuller. Finally, in 1918, with World War I straining public discourse and threatening civil liberties, Oswald Garrison Villard, Henry's son, took over as editor and turned it into the more radical publication that it has since remained.

TAKING ITS MODERN FORM

Under Oswald Villard's guidance, circulation increased fivefold in just two years, from 7,200 in 1918 to 38,000 in 1920. Villard had earlier helped to found the NAACP and was active in controversial causes, advocating clemency for conscientious objectors, opposing American colonial expansion as in the annexation of Hawaii and Panama, and backing self-determination for the Philippines and Ireland. The U.S. government seized the magazine's September 14, 1918, issue on the grounds that it was seditious. *The Nation* gave extensive coverage to the Bolshevik Revolution in Russia and was the first American publication to publish the new Soviet Constitution. During the 1920s it helped galvanize public opinion in favor of a retrial for Sacco and Vanzetti.

With the resurgence of liberal ideology during the Great Depression, circulation of *The Nation* had increased to 36,000 by the time Villard retired in 1932. He was succeeded by Freda Kirchwey, who remained editor until 1955. Villard continued writing for the publication until 1940, when he broke with Kirchwey in the Stalinist-versus-Trotskyist controversy that had seriously divided American leftists. By the late 1930s, after Kirchwey assumed ownership of the publication, *The Nation* was breaking new ground in American journalism by publishing more articles on the Spanish Civil War and on women's issues, birth control, and sexual freedom. During World War II it staunchly opposed Nazism and fascism in Europe.

In the postwar period, the publication stood firmly against the communist witch hunts by Senator Joseph McCarthy and advocated the peaceful use of atomic energy and the establishment of the state of Israel. Kirchwey angered many leftists, however, by refraining from endorsing the Progressive candidacy of Henry A. Wallace for president in 1948. Faced with financial difficulties, Kirchwey transferred ownership of the magazine in 1943 to The Nation Associates, a network of subscribers that was asked to enroll members. The publication seriously considered a merger with its amicable rival, the *New Republic*.

Carey McWilliams succeeded Kirchwey as editor in 1955 and, with George Kirstein as publisher, continued to question Cold War policies, the growth of the military-industrial complex, Central Intelligence Agency (CIA) involvement in Guatemala, and the events that led to the Vietnam War. *The Nation* also broke new ground in consumer advocacy in the 1950s and 1960s, publishing the first serious article that linked cigarette smoking to cancer, as well as early articles by Nader on car safety. At the same time, *The Nation* took a strong stance on behalf of desegregation and other aspects of the growing civil rights movement and published with greater frequency the views of revisionist American historians such as Walter LaFeber, Gabriel Kolko, Barton Bernstein, H. Stuart Hughes, and Howard Zinn. Kirstein helped stabilize the always precarious financial position of the publication before turning the reins over to James J. Storrow Jr. in the mid-1960s. Storrow's expertise in print technology further bolstered the periodical's fiscal viability.

"A MAVERICK MAGAZINE"

McWilliams was briefly succeeded as editor in 1975 by Blair Clark, who had worked for CBS and the *New York Post* and who had earlier been campaign manager for Senator Eugene McCarthy's presidential campaign in 1968. Within two years, *The Nation* was purchased by a consortium organized by Hamilton Fish III, which selected Victor Navasky as editor. Under the new structure, the editor and publisher became general partners and the investors were limited partners with no editorial voice. Fish was succeeded as publisher by Arthur Carter. After 1994 Katrina vanden Heuvel served as editor, with Navasky becoming publisher and editorial director.

Reflecting on the history of the publication on its 125th anniversary in 1990, Navasky wrote: "A maverick magazine, it has attracted maverick proprietors, which may be one of its survival secrets." He added, "We will continue to fight for causes, lost and found . . . someone once described *The Nation* as a magazine for the permanent minority. . . . A magazine shouldn't come to power. It can nourish, it can prod, it can hector, it can educate, it can cajole, wheedle, expose, embarrass, inform, illuminate and inspire. And if it does all these things . . . the laws of capitalism notwithstanding, it will survive."

Edward Moran

SEE ALSO: *Baldwin, James; Chavez, Cesar; Cigarettes; Civil Rights Movement; Cold War; Doctorow, E. L.; Du Bois, W. E. B.; Feminism; The Great Depression; Labor Unions; McCarthyism; Mencken, H. L.; Morrison, Toni; Muckraking; Nader, Ralph;* New Republic; *Vietnam; World War II.*

BIBLIOGRAPHY

Alpern, Sara. *Freda Kirchwey: A Woman of the Nation.* Cambridge, MA: Harvard University Press, 1987.

Armstrong, W., ed. *The Gilded Age Letters of E. L. Godkin.* Albany: State University of New York Press, 1974.

McWilliams, Carey. *The Education of Carey McWilliams.* New York: Simon & Schuster, 1979.

Tebbel, John. *The American Magazine: A Compact History.* New York: Hawthorn Books, 1969.

Vanden Heuvel, Katrina, ed. *The Nation, 1865–1990: Selections from the Independent Magazine of Politics and Culture.* New York: Thunder's Mouth Press, 1990.

National Basketball Association (NBA)

One of three sports developed in America (lacrosse and volleyball are the others), basketball dates to 1891, the year Young Men's Christian Association instructor James Naismith first hung two peach baskets on the track railing around his gym and encouraged his charges to pitch balls into them. The first professional leagues began operating around the turn of the twentieth century, with the first true national league, the American Basketball League (ABL), established in 1925. A casualty of the Depression, the ABL's demise left the midwestern-based National Basketball League (NBL) as the only major professional basketball league. That monopoly lasted until 1946, when the Basketball Association of America (BAA) was formed by an alliance of arena owners in the major eastern cities. The New York Knickerbockers and the Toronto Huskies played in that league's inaugural game on November 1, 1946.

CREATING THE NBA

Despite staging its games in the nation's best venues, such as New York's Madison Square Garden and the Boston Garden, the BAA had trouble attracting top-flight players. By a fortuitous coincidence that just so happened to be the NBL's strong suit, paving the way for a league merger that resulted in the creation of the National Basketball Association (NBA) in 1949. The new league fielded seventeen clubs in its inaugural season, although the absorption of NBL franchises left the NBA a curious agglomeration of large (New York, Boston) and small (Sheboygan, Wisconsin; Syracuse, New York) markets. As a consequence, six of the league's less competitive teams had folded by the start of the 1950–1951 season.

The contraction actually helped the NBA by dispersing the talent more generously among the surviving franchises. But professional basketball still suffered in comparison to the college game, then all the rage in hoops hotbeds like New York City. Only a point-shaving scandal that rocked the college game in January 1951 allowed the NBA a chance to grab the attention of basketball fans nationwide. The incorporation of African American players, beginning in 1950 with Earl Lloyd and Nate ("Sweetwater") Clifton of the Washington Capitols and Chuck Cooper of the Boston Celtics, further enhanced the level of play and improved the league's image in progressive circles.

Still, professional basketball had trouble captivating the national imagination. Its marquee player in those early years, 6-foot, 10-inch Minneapolis Laker center George Mikan, seemed an unapproachable hero whose massive size drew a host of less talented imitators to the league. The NBA became dominated by big men, and games were slowed down by constant fouling designed to impede their scoring. Public disenchantment was crystallized by a nationally televised contest between the Knicks and the Boston Celtics in 1954, from which the network cut away in the final minutes because the action was so enervating. The NBA quickly adopted rule changes to speed up play and encourage athleticism.

The principal beneficiaries of the new rules were the Boston Celtics. They built a team around two players—center Bill Russell and guard Bob Cousy—who excelled at the fast-break style of play that the new regulations encouraged. With the athletic, intimidating Russell blocking shots out to the agile, propulsive Cousy, the Celtics won five straight NBA championships between 1959 and 1963 and set a standard of excellence in the sport akin to that set by the New York Yankees in baseball. Upon Cousy's retirement, the Celtics added five more titles in the ensuing six years to bring their total to eleven championships in a thirteen-year span. By the end of Boston's remarkable run, the NBA had overcome its early doldrums and established a foothold on the national sports scene.

RIVALRIES AND COMPETITION

The 1970s began with great promise for the NBA. The rivalry between Bill Russell and the league's other dominant center, Wilt Chamberlain of the Los Angeles Lakers, gave professional basketball the first of the compelling mano-a-mano matchups it would successfully market over the ensuing decades. The New York Knicks teams that won the NBA championship in 1970 and again in 1973 attracted many new fans with their cerebral, team-oriented style of play. Passing and shooting became the order of the day, as the league's highly skilled black players came increasingly to dominate the action.

But there were warning signs on the game's horizon as well. A rival league, the American Basketball Association (ABA), seduced away some of the pro game's best young players, including Rick Barry; George "the Iceman" Gervin; and Julius Erving, known popularly as "Dr. J." Though financially unstable, the ABA offered a freewheeling brand of basketball—symbolized by its use of a red, white, and blue ball—that held some appeal for fans in the 1970s. Unwilling to change its own game to emulate the upstart league, the NBA instead entered into prolonged negotiations for a merger that was finally consummated in 1976. Four ABA teams were allowed to join the NBA, and a special draft was arranged to disperse ABA players throughout the consolidated league. Once again, the NBA had established itself as America's sole professional basketball association.

While the merger relieved some of the NBA's financial difficulties, it did not address the league's most pressing underlying problems. A series of violent incidents, capped by Kermit Washington's life-threatening assault on Rudy Tomjanovich—in which a single punch shattered Tomjanovich's jaw and skull—severely tarnished the image of professional basketball. Increasingly, there was talk that substance abuse was rampant around the league. While the NBA implemented programs to remedy this problem, the image of the NBA as a "drug league" persisted into the 1980s.

The NBA reached its nadir in the early part of that decade. A paucity of compelling players and few intriguing rivalries, coupled with the negative press coverage engendered by the drug and violence scandals, prompted many league sponsors to back away from television advertising. As a consequence, the deciding game of the 1980 finals was not even aired live but relegated to late-night tape delay. By 1981 a majority of NBA teams were losing money, and the league itself seemed at a loss for a solution to the crisis.

SAVED BY SUPERSTARS

Salvation came in the form of two young players, Larry Bird and Earvin "Magic" Johnson, who would go on to dominate the game during the 1980s. Rivals in college, they continued their competition in the pros as the focal points of the NBA's two most prestigious franchises, the Boston Celtics and the Los Angeles Lakers, respectively. When they met in the finals for the first time in 1984, it marked an important step in the NBA's return to prominence. The series went seven games and attracted the largest viewing audience in NBA history. To the delight of the league, championship rematches were staged in 1985 and 1987, with the high-flying Lakers winning two out of three from the bruising Bostonians.

A second factor in the NBA's revival was the appointment of a new commissioner, David Stern, in 1984. A league attorney who had helped negotiate the NBA/ABA merger, Stern brought a strong marketing orientation to his new post. Building on the Magic/Bird rivalry, he negotiated a new television contract with NBC prior to the 1990–1991 season, with instructions to the network to promote the league's emerging stars. The result was a decade of expansion in the NBA's popularity fueled by the rise of its brightest star, Michael Jordan of the Chicago Bulls. At first just another prolific scorer, Jordan became an international symbol of competitive fire after capturing three straight championships between 1991 and 1993.

Jordan's ascension to international icon status helped turn NBA basketball into one of the most profitable entertainment properties in the world. Merchandising of team and player logos exceeded the $1 billion mark, while the worth of the average franchise increased threefold from the dark days of the early 1980s. New teams were added in Florida, Minnesota, and North Carolina in 1988 and 1989, allowing the NBA to enter new markets and disperse lucrative franchise fees to the other clubs (it later expanded to Canada as well, in 1995). While Jordan's departure from the league to pursue a baseball career briefly derailed the NBA juggernaut in 1993, his return two years later only seemed to raise his mystique to another level. With a record of 72–10, the Bulls set an all-time single-season record in 1995–1996 en route to the first of three more consecutive world championships. Not since the Celtics of the 1960s had one team so dominated the world of professional basketball—to the delight of the game's fans and the consternation of the other twenty-eight teams.

THREATENED BY LOCKOUTS

In 1998 Jordan retired—for good this time. His departure from the scene raised the obvious questions about the NBA's ability to sustain its growth absent its most compelling international star. Even more troublesome was the public relations disaster caused by a lengthy labor dispute that cut short the 1998–1999 season. Most of the public ire was directed at the NBA players, who made a series of bafflingly intemperate public statements and inexplicably failed to point out that the league was locking them out of the arenas. A new collective bargaining agreement ponderously favorable to the league was signed in January 1999, further solidifying Stern's status with league owners and paving the way for sustained profits ad infinitum.

From the mid-1990s on, the NBA has been searching for the next Jordan—that one superstar who would carry the league on its back and galvanize the fans. Two players, both drafted right out of high school, have contended for that position. The first was Kobe Bryant, drafted by the Charlotte Hornets in 1996 but almost immediately traded to the Los Angeles Lakers. Led by Bryant and former Bulls coach Phil Jackson, the Lakers won five championships in little more than a decade: in 2000, 2001, 2002, 2009, and 2010.

The other young player pegged to fill Jordan's shoes was LeBron James, who was drafted by the Cleveland Cavaliers in 2003. James, often called "King James," proved to be a phenomenal scorer, becoming the youngest player ever to reach 10,000 points. However, the Cavs perennially fell short of the goal of winning a championship, leading many sports analysts to doubt James's status as a team leader. When James became a free agent in 2010, he signed with the Miami Heat in hopes of winning a title with a team that already had two All-Star players (Dwyane Wade and Chris Bosh). The powerhouse team made it to the finals that year but lost to the Dallas Mavericks. However, James proved his worth the following year when his Miami Heat defeated the Oklahoma City Thunder four games to one for the NBA championship.

That summer, the NBA faced its worst crisis of the new century. The National Basketball Players Association and the team owners failed to reach a collective bargaining agreement after negotiating for eighteen months. In response to the stalemate, management instituted another lockout that stretched into the fall, past the date that the 2011–2012 season was due to start. The two sides reached a deal in late autumn, and a shortened sixty-six-game season began on Christmas Day of 2011. Many observers feared that the compressed schedule, which required teams to play at least one stretch of three consecutive games, would lead to increased player injuries, but in general both players and owners were relieved to have the season salvaged. No one wanted to take the risk that fans might discover they could live without the NBA.

Robert E. Schnakenberg

SEE ALSO: *Advertising; Basketball; Bird, Larry; The Boston Celtics; Boston Garden; Chamberlain, Wilt; The Chicago Bulls; Erving, Julius "Dr. J"; James, LeBron; Johnson, Earvin "Magic"; Jordan, Michael; Labor Unions; The Los Angeles Lakers; Naismith, James; The New York Knickerbockers; Russell, Bill; Sports Heroes; Television.*

BIBLIOGRAPHY

Bird, Larry; Earvin Johnson Jr.; and Jackie MacMullan. *When the Game Was Ours.* New York: Houghton Mifflin Harcourt, 2009.

Bjarkman, Peter C. *The Encyclopedia of Pro Basketball Team Histories.* New York: Carroll & Graf, 1994.

Decourcy, Mike. *Inside Basketball: From the Playgrounds to the NBA.* New York: MetroBooks, 1996.

Fox, Stephen R. *Big Leagues: Professional Baseball, Football, and Basketball in National Memory.* New York: William Morrow, 1994.

Minsky, Alan. *Kings of the Court: Legends of the NBA.* New York: Metro Books, 1995.

Peterson, Robert. *Cages to Jump Shots: Pro Basketball's Early Years.* New York: Oxford University Press, 1990.

Salzberg, Charles. *From Set Shot to Slam Dunk: The Glory Days of Basketball in the Words of Those Who Played It.* New York: Dutton, 1987.

Simmon, Bill, and Malcolm Gladwell. *The Book of Basketball: The NBA According to the Sports Guy.* New York: ESPN, 2009.

Vancil, Mark, ed. *NBA at 50.* New York: Random House, 1996.

National Collegiate Athletic Association (NCAA)

One of the world's most influential governing bodies for intercollegiate sports was founded in America in the early 1900s when President Theodore Roosevelt set out to make football less dangerous. Now, in the twenty-first century, more than 1,000 American educational institutions are members of the National Collegiate Athletic Association (NCAA), an organization that establishes rules for the recruiting and eligibility of student athletes, governs athletic conferences, sets the playing rules for twenty-three intercollegiate sports, and conducts eighty-nine national championships in three competitive divisions. In 2010 the NCAA welcomed its first Canadian school, Simon Fraser University, as a member. The move was part of a pilot program.

REGULATING SPORTS

In 1905 the primary offensive weapon in football was the kick return, in which the ball carrier was protected behind a fast-moving, wedge-shaped formation of his teammates. The blocking and gang-tackling resulted in a multitude of injuries and even some deaths, causing many colleges and universities to discontinue the sport. Roosevelt invited college athletics leaders to two White House conferences to discuss possible reforms, and a meeting of thirteen institutions was held in early December 1905 to make changes to the rules of football. To enforce the new rules, the Intercollegiate Athletic Association of the United States was founded later that month, with sixty-two members. Five years later the name of the association was shortened to the National Collegiate Athletic Association.

For several years, the NCAA was primarily a discussion group and rule-making body, but in 1921 it organized its first national championship, in track and field. Gradually, more championships were held, more legislative bodies formed, and more institutions admitted. To be an active member of the NCAA, a college or university must be accredited academically; maintain at least four intercollegiate sports for men and four for women (except for single-gender institutions); agree to comply with the association's rules concerning financial aid, recruiting, playing seasons, and postseason competition; and respect the penalties imposed by infractions of those rules.

After World War II there was a renewed interest in sports, and college athletics became a lucrative business on campuses throughout the country. Reports of rules violations involving the recruiting of student athletes led the NCAA to adopt a "sanity code," with guidelines to regulate practices in financial aid as well as recruitment. The association was also concerned with the proliferation of postseason football games and with the lack of rules regarding televising games, particularly in football. With membership increasing and the problems becoming more complex, the NCAA recognized the need for a full-time professional staff. In 1951 Walter Byers was named executive director.

Recruiting abuses continued, however, and in 1952 the NCAA put in place a mechanism to implement the regulations. The enforcement program voted in by the membership called for cooperation among the athletic conferences, institutions, and the NCAA to delve into reports of violations and determine appropriate penalties. A staff was employed by the association to investigate allegations and determine whether an official inquiry was necessary. Universities found guilty of inappropriate payoffs to student athletes appeared before the committee on infractions, and the resulting penalties ranged from a reduction in the number of athletic scholarships to an institution's being banned from postseason competition. That same year, a national headquarters for the NCAA was established in Kansas City, Missouri, and the membership voted at its annual convention to control the televising of football games and also passed legislation to govern postseason bowl games.

SUBDIVISION AND EXPANSION

In 1973, in the first special convention of the NCAA ever held, member institutions were divided into three legislative and competitive divisions. Division I (made up of the sports programs in the major colleges and universities) and Division II were allowed to offer scholarship grants to athletes, and Division III (made up of smaller institutions) would operate without such grants. Further classification occurred five years later when Division I members voted to create subdivisions I-A and I-AA in the sport of football.

Women became a part of NCAA sports activities in 1980 when ten championships for female athletics were established for 1981–1982 in Division II and Division III. The historic 75th NCAA Convention in 1981 adopted an all-encompassing governance plan to include women's sports programs, service, and representation. The delegates also expanded the women's national championship program by adding nineteen events. Today's women athletes can now participate in basketball, bowling, cross country, fencing, field hockey, golf, gymnastics, ice hockey, indoor and outdoor track, lacrosse, rifle, rowing, skiing, soccer, softball, swimming and diving, tennis, volleyball, and water polo.

The president's commission was created in 1984, and a year later it called a landmark special convention to address continuing problems in the areas of compliance and enforcement. Another special convention was called in June 1987 to launch an eighteen-month national forum on critical problems in college athletics. In the late 1990s the national staff of 300 NCAA employees, by then based in Overland Park, Kansas, was led by president Cedric W. Dempsey.

GUARDING THE INTEGRITY OF SPORTS

A major change came to NCAA football after 1984, when the Universities of Oklahoma and Georgia sued the governing body because of its rule that college football teams were limited to six television appearances over a two-season period. The U.S. Supreme Court ruled that limiting the supply of college games on television stifled competition by taking away schools' freedom to compete in the marketplace. As a result, each college conference gained the freedom to negotiate its own TV deals instead of taking whatever the NCAA negotiated. The ruling led directly to the proliferation of college football games on TV, which caused a massive increase in athletics-related revenues.

The phenomenal success of sports in America—both at the box office and in television ratings—has created problems for the NCAA in its attempts to uphold the integrity of college athletics. Among the most popular sports on television is the annual NCAA men's basketball tournament for Division I, otherwise known as "March Madness." This tournament began in 1939 with an attendance of 5,500 people at Evanston, Illinois, but crowds for the championship games have grown to more than 60,000 and television ratings have rivaled those of the National Football League's Super Bowl.

March Madness also attracts billions of dollars of illegal sports wagering annually. The breadth of the NCAA's gambling problem was demonstrated by a 1996 University of Cincinnati study involving Division I basketball and football players. Of the 648 respondents in the survey, 25.5 percent had gambled on other college sporting events, while 3.7 percent had bet on a game in which they played and 0.5 percent had received payment for not playing well in a game. Because wagering has the potential to undermine the integrity of athletic events, the NCAA opposes all forms of legal and illegal betting on sports and has taken steps to declare athletes ineligible for competition if found guilty of participating in any gambling activity. Some institutions have discontinued their participation in basketball because of this problem.

The NCAA has also grappled with the problem of declaring a national champion in Division I-A football. In Division I-AA, Division II, and Division III, the championship is won in a postseason playoff, but scheduling and postseason bowl bids have made it difficult to use the same method in the major division. Since 1998 the Bowl Championship Series (BCS) has been used to determine the Division I-A national champion. There are five BCS bowl games each year, one of which is for the national championship. The participants in the national championship game are determined through records, polls, and other criteria such as difficulty of schedule. The system is not perfect, but many college football analysts see it as a step in the right direction.

SCANDALS AND CHANGE

As the NCAA entered the twenty-first century, a number of scandals came to light, showing just how difficult it is to regulate such a huge and vastly profitable enterprise. Even during the recession that began in late 2007, college sports earned big bucks. In 2010 the Southeastern Conference (SEC) pulled in a billion dollars from athletic receipts. Increasingly during the early 2000s, allegations abounded that college athletes at big-name programs such as Ohio State and the University of Southern California (USC) were receiving illicit benefits from alumni, boosters, and corporate sponsors. These perks included cash, personal services, merchandise, cars, homes, and airfares. In one highly publicized case in 2010, the NCAA ruled that because former USC running back Reggie Bush and his family had taken money from agents while he was in college, he was ineligible for 2005, the season he won the Heisman Trophy as college football's best player. By the time of the ruling, Bush was in the NFL, but he had to forfeit the prestigious award. In 2012 more than a dozen educational institutions were on NCAA probation because of violations.

Furthermore, the NCAA has had to weather charges of not adequately protecting the safety of its young people. In 2011, for example, a former Penn State assistant football coach was charged with committing sexual abuse. The year before that, a Notre Dame student died when the lift on which he was videotaping football practice collapsed in a windstorm. As of 2011 the NCAA had a staff of fifty-six employees charged with investigating violations of the organization's rules. Some critics wonder if that staff is large enough to monitor the behemoth that is now college athletics.

As part of the 2004 reform effort, the NCAA instituted an academic performance rate, commonly referred to as the APR, that established a formula for measuring academic standards for college athletic programs. In 2008–2009, the punishments for falling below the APR minimum threshold included a loss of scholarships and potentially a ban from postseason appearances. While it is still questionable if this ban includes the college football bowls, as these are not run by the NCAA, several college basketball teams have been banned from the playoffs, including Southern University and the University of Connecticut.

The 2010s also saw changes to some of the NCAA's major football conferences. As part of an ongoing effort to improve competition, Nebraska joined the Big Ten (ironically, bringing the conference up to twelve members), Boise State moved to the Mountain West, and Colorado and Utah were added to the Pac-12. Furthermore, the Big Ten was divided into two divisions, the Legends and the Leaders, whose top teams square off in an annual playoff game to determine the conference champion. This system is similar to that used in the SEC, which has the Eastern and Western divisions. As with so much regarding modern college athletics, the decision to add a championship to a conference's football schedule is made in part because of the extra television revenue such a game provides.

Benjamin Griffith

SEE ALSO: *Basketball; College Football; Gambling; National Basketball Association (NBA); National Football League (NFL).*

BIBLIOGRAPHY

Falla, Jack. *NCAA: The Voice of College Sports.* Kansas City, MO: National Collegiate Athletic Association, 1981.

Finebaum, Paul. *I Hate the NCAA: 303 Reasons Why You Should, Too.* New York: Crane Hill Press, 1996.

Luchs, Josh, and James Dale. *Illegal Procedure: A Sports Agent Comes Clean on the Dirty Business of College Football.* New York: Bloomsbury USA, 2012.

Porto, Brian. *The Supreme Court and the NCAA: The Case for Less Commercialism and More Due Process in College Sports.* Ann Arbor: University of Michigan Press, 2012.

Sack, Allen L., and Ellen J. Staurowsky. *College Athletes for Hire: The Evolution and Legacy of the NCAA's Amateur Myth.* Westport, CT: Praeger, 1998.

Salter, David F., and Thomas M. Jones. *Blueprint for Success: An In-Depth Analysis of NCAA Division III Athletics, and Why It Should Be the Model for Intercollegiate Reform.* Dumont, NJ: F. Merrick, 1993.

Weissberg, Ted. *Breaking the Rules: The NCAA and Recruitment in America's High Schools.* New York: Franklin Watts, 1995.

The *National Enquirer*

As reinvented by Generoso Pope in 1952, and then again in 1968, the *National Enquirer* became the archetype and model of the "supermarket tabloids" of the 1980s and 1990s. The *Enquirer*, with regular sales in excess of four million copies, has the largest circulation of any weekly serial publication in the United States. In the late 1990s it was owned by MacFadden Holdings Inc., which also publishes the tabloids the *Weekly World News* and the *Star* (while the other three principal tabloids—the *Globe*, the *Sun*, and the *National Examiner*—are all owned by Globe Communications). Although, in fact, the *Star*'s coverage led the tabloid pack in some of the sex-and-politics scandals of the 1990s, it was the *National Enquirer*'s photo spread of the Gary Hart/Donna Rice imbroglio (June 2, 1987) that shaped all future coverage. To talk about the *National Enquirer* is to talk about American popular culture at the end of the twentieth century.

Calling a newspaper a "tabloid" is, in the first place, only to say that it is, as Donald Paneth expressed in 1982, "half the size of a standard newspaper, therefore easier to carry and read on subway and bus in the big-city rush hour. It is plentifully illustrated. News is presented tersely, compactly." For most readers, however, the word *tabloid* implies a qualitative, as well as quantitative, judgment, as Paneth goes on to explain: "The tabloid's style usually runs to sensationalism, a 'stoop to conquer' technique—crime and sex, exploitation of piety, sentiment and patriotism, money contests, comic strips, heart-stopping headlines." Up to this point, Paneth is right on the money. But then he makes the mistake of fixing too rigidly the parameters of a popular cultural phenomenon: He defines an "age of the tabloids"—basically, the 1920s—and then says that it is over (an erroneous prediction echoed in 1984 by Edwin and Michael Emery in the book *The Press and America*). How they must have cringed at the title of a *Newsweek* feature by Jonathan Alter, published December 26, 1994: "America Goes Tabloid." Had Paneth quit while he was ahead, had he not tried to trim his story, arbitrarily, into a discrete historical "period," Paneth might have answered Alter with a sneer: "America went 'Tabloid' in 1919, with the founding of the *New York Daily News*!"

EARLY YEARS

Launched smack in the middle of the first great "age of the tabloids," the original *Enquirer* bore no resemblance to the supermarket weekly of today (or to the mutilation-and-weird-romance rag of the 1950s and 1960s). It was not, at first, even a tabloid, but a full-size paper, although it was published from the start as a weekly, on Sunday afternoon. William Griffin, a former advertising executive of the Hearst papers, started the *Enquirer* in 1926 with money he borrowed from William Randolph Hearst. The loan had certain conditions: Hearst was to try out new ideas in the *Enquirer*. This worked out fine for Hearst, since according to an unsigned piece in *Newsweek* (September 8, 1969), "the good ideas carried over into Hearst's own papers; the *Enquirer* was stuck with the bad ones." Still, Griffin continued to publish the *Enquirer* for twenty-six years of eroding circulation. He opposed America's entry into World War II, and he used his paper to attack President Franklin D. Roosevelt's

***Anna Nicole Smith reads* National Enquirer.** *Anna Nicole Smith, a frequent tabloid target herself, reads a copy of the* National Enquirer *at a party celebrating the publication's relaunch in 2005.* SHANE GRITZINGER/CONTRIBUTOR/FILMMAGIC/GETTY IMAGES.

foreign policy. The attacks became so violent that Griffin was indicted for undermining troop morale. The charges were later dropped, but his assaults on Roosevelt lost him yet more readers. By the time the Hearst Corporation sold the *Enquirer* to Pope for $75,000 in 1952, its circulation had dwindled to 17,000. Except for consistently and flamboyantly backing the wrong horses, the paper had made no impression on American journalism.

All of that was about to change. Pope was twenty-five when he bought the moribund *Enquirer*, but he had grown up in the newspaper business (his father had founded the New York–published Italian-language daily, *Il Progresso*). He also knew a thing or two about mass psychology, having served for a year in the Central Intelligence Agency as an officer in its psychological warfare unit. Pope did not immediately plunge his new paper into the murky depths of sensationalism. He tried out several formats. Then, "I noticed how auto accidents drew crowds," he told *Time* magazine in 1972, "and I decided that if it was blood that interested people, I'd give it to them." It was not long after this decision that headlines such as "MOM USES SON'S FACE FOR AN ASHTRAY," "MADMAN CUT UP HIS DATE AND PUT HER BODY IN HIS FREEZER," and "STABS GIRL 55 TIMES" began to grab the attention of people passing by newsstands, and the circulation began to edge upward for the first time in decades—helped a lot, Pope claimed, by a 1958 newspaper strike that removed many of his competitors from the stands for a crucial period of time. Murder was the mainstay of this version of the *Enquirer*—murder mixed with sex and mutilation, although the sex was never explicit. Some of the stories approach the surrealist nuttiness of the "black humor" novelists of the 1960s: "Eva Fedorchuk battered her husband's face to a bloody pulp with a pop bottle. Then she told the police he'd cut himself while shaving."

Another staple of this *Enquirer* was the "consumer" story, which was almost always slanted toward a latent sadism in the reader, a horrific tale, posing as a warning, of an over-the-counter product causing mayhem—as in "HAIR DYE HAS MADE ME BALD FOR LIFE." Celebrity gossip was featured as well, but seldom the sex-based gossip of the late 1990s, and it was always a relatively small part of each issue. Typically, there would be a snickering report of the spectacular public drunkenness of a famous rich person, or movie stars who stripped themselves naked, or crashed their car into a swimming pool, or beat up their date. These reports, according to *Enquirer* insiders who have since come clean, were generally made up out of whole cloth. If a celebrity had ever misbehaved in public—all it took was one incident, no matter how remote from the present—that celebrity was considered fair game. The *Enquirer* gossips would report some similar, if entirely fictional, embarrassment, as if the one true incident had established a pattern of behavior and, for the rest of the hapless famous person's life, any remotely similar faux pas could be legitimately and plausibly attributed to them. But most people who bought the *Enquirer* from 1955 to 1965 seemed to have been attracted by the lurid accounts of violent death and perverse mutilation. During this period, in any case, Pope's formatting innovations built up the *Enquirer's* circulation from 17,000 to more than a million—a formidable achievement, especially since the tabloids, unlike other newspapers, make the bulk of their income from sales of copies, rather than advertising. To the many media pundits and professional scolds who found the *Enquirer* too disgusting to contemplate, Pope shrugged and replied, "Every publication starts out by being sensational."

THE *ENQUIRER*'S MAKEOVER

After 1969, however, *National Enquirer* sales leveled off around $1.2 million and would not budge further. Pope was hardly the sort of publisher who would let a bad trend develop very far before attending to it. Making a study, he concluded that his death-and-dismemberment format had reached some kind of saturation point. "There are only so many libertines and neurotics," he said. More to the point, he noted a precipitous decline in the number of newsstands—the essential platform from which the *Enquirer*'s grisly headlines trolled for "libertines and neurotics." At the same time, he followed with intense interest the success of *Woman's Day* magazine in moving into the then-uncharted territory of the United States' 50,000 supermarkets. Pope made up his mind to follow where *Woman's Day* had led. As Elizabeth Bird noted, he had his eye on a readership that was "more direct and consistent through national supermarket and drugstore chains than through conventional newsstands and other publishing outlets."

At the same time, it seemed obvious to Pope that headlines on the order of "PASSION PILLS FAN RAPE WAVE" and "DIGS UP WIFE'S ROTTING CORPSE AND RIPS IT APART" would not work quite the same magic on grocery shoppers as they had on newsstand passersby. So, he decided to make over the *National Enquirer* once again, as radically as he had in the early 1950s—only this time the tabloid would emerge as wholesome and as golly-gee clean as the *Reader's Digest* of the 1930s (reportedly his model). Gore was gone, as were the kinky "personals," and in their place, Bird says, "features on household repair, pop psychology, unusual human-interest stories, and frequently flattering celebrity stories." The paper also began to cater to the public's burgeoning interest in the occult and mystical, with predictions by noted psychics and regular contributions from astrologers. Pope hired a public relations firm to repackage the public image of his tabloid, and to establish the transition in his writers' minds, he moved the *Enquirer*'s offices from the urban pressure-cooker of New York City to the sleepy tropicality of southern Florida. At first, according to Pope, the circulation dropped by a quarter million, but it soon picked up, and by the early 1980s it was one of the ten most profitable supermarket items.

When the *National Enquirer* began to publish in color, in 1980, Pope founded the *Weekly World News* so he would not have to sell his one-color press, and the *News* revived some of the outrageousness of the old *Enquirer*—although lunatic headlines such as "MAN CUTS OFF OWN HEAD WITH CHAINSAW—AND LIVES" no longer referred to actual bloody incidents, but now sprang from the vivid imaginations of staff members. The *News*, too, found a niche, and it became trendy in college dormitories. By the time it ceased publication (it still exists as a website), the *Weekly World News* had achieved and largely maintained a circulation in excess of a million. The *News* also enabled the *Enquirer* to devote more space to celebrity stories—very much a contested area in the 1970s duel between Pope and Rupert Murdoch, who founded the *Star* in 1974. The duel was resolved after Pope died in 1988, when McFadden Holdings Inc. bought both the *National Enquirer* and the *Weekly World News* ($412 million) and the *Star* ($400 million). This was also the year in which the tabloids began to have a material influence on the political process. The story of Gary Hart's dalliance with Donna Rice aboard the S.S. *Monkey Business* was broken by a mainstream daily, the *Miami Herald*, but it was the *Enquirer*'s full-color cover photo of Hart—sporting a "Monkey

Business" T-shirt with Rice sitting on his lap—that inaugurated the era of "gotcha!" political reportage.

THE TWENTY-FIRST CENTURY

In the first decades of the twenty-first century, the *Enquirer* has continued to publish scandalous accounts of the private lives of politicians and celebrities such as John Edwards, Sarah Palin, Cameron Diaz, Kate Hudson, Mel Gibson, and Billy Joel—though the tabloid has been frequently, and often successfully, sued for libel.

It is, perhaps, more than sheer coincidence that embarrassing tabloid revelations of politicians' private lives have mainly, with the sole exception of Palin, benefited conservative politicians. The *Enquirer* and its competitors are deeply conservative in their reinforcement of every kind of social and psychological norm. They are like Cecil B. DeMille movies, allowing readers/viewers to ogle every sort of lascivious behavior while maintaining an attitude of shocked disapproval. It is entirely appropriate that D. Keith Mano, writing in the February 18, 1977, *National Review*, should propose that, "Given its circulation, the *National Enquirer* is probably the second most important conservative publication in America" (the most important being the *National Review* itself).

On January 19, 2010, reversing many decades of hostility and contempt, the Pulitzer Prize Board announced that the *Enquirer* would now be eligible for a Pulitzer Prize in the categories of Investigative Reporting and National News Reporting.

Gerald Carpenter

SEE ALSO: *Celebrity; DeMille, Cecil B.; Gibson, Mel; Gossip Columns; Hearst, William Randolph; Palin, Sarah;* Reader's Digest.

BIBLIOGRAPHY

Alter, Jonathan. "America Goes Tabloid." *Newsweek*, December 26, 1994/January 2, 1995, 34–39.

Bird, S. Elizabeth. *For Enquiring Minds: A Cultural Study of Supermarket Tabloids*. Knoxville: University of Tennessee Press, 1992.

Emery, Edwin, and Michael Emery. *The Press and America: An Interpretive History of the Media*. Upper Saddle River, NJ: Prentice-Hall, 1984.

"From Worse to Bad." *Newsweek*, September 8, 1969, 79.

"Goodbye to Gore." *Time*, February 21, 1972, 64–65.

Greenberg, Gerald S. *Tabloid Journalism: An Annotated Bibliography of English-Language Sources*. Westport, CT: Greenwood Press, 1996.

Hogshire, Jim. *Grossed-Out Surgeon Vomits inside Patient!: An Insider's Look at Supermarket Tabloids*. Venice, CA: Feral House, 1997.

Hume, Ellen. *Tabloids, Talk Radio, and the Future of News: Technology's Impact on Journalism*. Washington, DC: Annenberg, 1995.

Jossi, Frank, and S. Elizabeth Bird. "Who Reads Supermarket Tabs?" *American Journalism Review*, September 1993, 14–15.

Klaidman, Stephen. "Upbeat *Enquirer* Thrives on Supermarket Sales." *Washington Post*, August 17, 1975, G1–G2.

Mano, D. Keith. "Arts & Manners: The Gimlet Eye." *National Review*, February 18, 1977, 209–10.

Paneth, Donald. *The Encyclopedia of American Journalism*. New York: Facts on File, 1983.

Peer, Elizabeth, with William Schmidt. "The Enquirer: Up from Smut." *Newsweek*, April 21, 1975, 62.

Vitek, Jack. *The Godfather of Tabloid: Generoso Pope Jr. and the "National Enquirer."* Lexington: University Press of Kentucky, 2008.

National Football League (NFL)

Professional football in America dates back to 1892, the year that Yale's All-America guard—William "Pudge" Heffelfinger—accepted $500 to appear in a game for the Allegheny Athletic Association. Despite betting and recruitment scandals, the game enjoyed robust growth during the early decades of the pay-for-play era. But there was no organized league until George Halas and a group of forward-thinking gridiron scions convened in Canton, Ohio, in 1920 to form the American Professional Football Association (APFA). Within two years, this fledgling alliance officially changed its name to the National Football League (NFL).

FINDING A FOOTBALL AUDIENCE

As public relations director for the new league, Halas was charged with the unenviable task of convincing the public of professional football's legitimacy. Few believed the NFL would succeed, given the competition of the "purer" and more tradition-driven college game. Halas's solution to the problem of legitimacy came down to two words: Red Grange. The "Galloping Ghost" was a college legend whose signature on a professional contract would give instant credibility to the pay-for-play enterprise. A shrewd businessman, Grange made sure to ask for a portion of the gate receipts in case the league took off. He made his NFL debut on Thanksgiving Day 1925, inaugurating an association of football and drumsticks that continues to this day.

The Grange-led Chicago Bears became the marquee attraction in the early years of the NFL. Some 73,000 spectators crowded into New York's Polo Grounds that first season to watch the Galloping Ghost lead his team into battle against the New York Giants. Doubts that the NFL could make it outside football's traditional hotbeds in the East and Midwest were soon quashed when the barnstorming Bears played to a house of 75,000 fans at the Los Angeles Memorial Coliseum. And though many expected the NFL to fold when Grange briefly left to join a rival league in 1926, it remained viable and even developed some new stars to replace him. By the time the Galloping Ghost retired in 1934, the league had expanded to ten clubs and was unchallenged as the national forum for professional football.

The 1930s saw the emergence of the Green Bay Packers as the NFL's dominant team. Led by coach Earl "Curly" Lambeau, the Wisconsin-based franchise won three straight league titles to open the decade. A series of rules changes adopted in league meetings helped systematize the pro game and differentiate it from the college variety. Further enhancing the NFL's popularity was a 1934 exhibition game between the Chicago Bears and a team of college All-Stars. The event drew 79,432 fans to Chicago's Soldier Field and resulted in a scoreless tie. Later that year the NFL took another huge step in its development into a national institution when the CBS radio network broadcast the Thanksgiving Day game between the Bears and the Detroit Lions to a national audience.

INSTITUTING A CHAMPIONSHIP GAME

The innovation of a national championship game, begun in 1933, resulted the following season in one of the NFL's first legendary games. In the so-called sneaker game, the New York Giants donned basketball sneakers at halftime to gain an edge over the Bears in a game played on icy turf at the Polo Grounds. The switch from spikes to sneaks spurred a second-half rally that propelled New York to a 30–13 victory.

Perhaps sensing that large-market clubs like the Bears and the Giants were gaining an unfair competitive advantage through their ability to recruit college players, the NFL instituted a draft system the following season. Under the rules, teams with poor records would select first from the available pool of undergraduate talent. University of Chicago halfback Jay Berwanger, recipient of the first Heisman Trophy, became the first man chosen in the first-ever NFL draft on February 8, 1936—though he eventually declined to join the league entirely.

Pro football attendance surpassed the one million mark in 1939, the same year that a contest between the NFL Brooklyn Dodgers and the Philadelphia Eagles was telecast in New York City by NBC. The NFL thus entered the 1940s primed for a decade of growth. Manpower shortages brought on by American involvement in World War II, however, forced a number of teams to merge and others to suspend operations entirely. The Washington Redskins emerged as one of the league's elite teams of the war years, though the Chicago Bears remained the class of the pro circuit. Their 73–0 drubbing of the Redskins in the 1940 championship game is remembered as one of the signature routs in sports history.

In 1950 the NFL took in three teams from a now-defunct rival league, the All-America Football Conference (AAFC), establishing a pattern of "ignore and absorb" that it would follow with subsequent challengers to its hegemony. The Cleveland Browns, perennial champions of the AAFC, went on to become one of the dominant NFL teams of the 1950s. The decade also saw the debut of a new all-star Pro Bowl played at the end of the season. In 1951 the DuMont Network broadcast the first nationally televised NFL game, between the Browns and the Los Angeles Rams. In a further sign of the league's growth—and the expectation that there was more money to be made—the National Football League Players Association formed in 1956 to represent the players' interests.

GAINING FANS THROUGH TELEVISION

By 1958 the NFL's popularity was at an all-time high. The championship game that season, pitting the New York Giants against the Baltimore Colts, attracted a record number of television viewers, reaching more American households than any other sporting event to date. And the contest did not disappoint, as the Colts won a thrilling 23–17 victory in sudden-death overtime in what many consider the greatest game ever played. The pro football landscape looked so promising as the 1960s dawned that yet another rival league, the American Football League (AFL), was formed for the new decade.

To keep the league on course and meet the challenge of the AFL, the NFL selected a new commissioner, Pete Rozelle, in 1960. He was to be the architect of the league's greatest growth and expansion of popularity. His signal achievement of the 1960s was the negotiation of a merger between the NFL and AFL in 1966. The two leagues maintained separate schedules for the first three years of the arrangement, though they agreed to meet in an annual championship game (not called the Super Bowl until 1969) beginning in 1967. Green Bay won the first two such contests, reinforcing the prejudice that the AFL upstarts did not belong on the same field as the "real" NFL pros. But Super Bowl III saw New York Jets quarterback Joe Namath—a college standout whose decision to join the AFL had been a major coup for the fledgling league—boldly predict an upset win over the heavily favored Baltimore Colts. The Jets' remarkable 16–7 victory helped legitimize the merger, solidify the primacy of the Super Bowl as sports' preeminent championship, and spur the NFL on to even greater national prominence.

In the 1970s professional football became a national powerhouse. Rozelle negotiated new national television contracts favorable to the league, including a deal with ABC to televise a Monday night "game of the week" during the regular season. *Monday Night Football* became an instant ratings hit and a venerable weekly showcase for the NFL's best teams. The AFL merger swelled the league to twenty-six teams, but business was so good it expanded even further in 1976 with new franchises in Tampa Bay, Florida, and Seattle, Washington. The Pittsburgh Steelers became the decade's dominant team, winning four Super Bowls in six years. The World Football League (WFL) flourished in 1974–1975, then folded. Nothing, it seemed, could compete with the allure of the NFL.

NEGOTIATING CONFLICTS

In the 1980s it became increasingly clear that the only threat to the NFL's golden goose came from the NFL itself. Players' strikes in 1982 and 1987 forced the league to cancel games and briefly experiment with replacement players, to the consternation of fans who now paid high prices for tickets. The United States Football League (USFL), a spring/summer alternative to the NFL, lasted only three seasons (1984–1987) but managed to drain away some high-profile players. In 1986 it filed an antitrust lawsuit against the NFL and won but was awarded only $1 in damages. More damaging to the league's prestige was the ongoing feud between Rozelle and Oakland Raiders owner Al Davis, who in 1982 sued successfully for the right to move his team to Los Angeles, where an NFL team already existed; he later moved it back to Oakland in 1995.

Despite these distractions, the NFL continued to flourish throughout the 1980s and 1990s. The San Francisco 49ers, and later the Dallas Cowboys, inherited the mantle of Super Bowl dominance from the Steelers. The league expanded globally, first with the World League and later with the more discretely focused NFL Europe. "Super Bowl Sunday" became an unofficial national holiday, with advertising fees for thirty-second commercials during its telecast ranging into the millions of dollars. Even the 1989 retirement of Rozelle, the league's highly effective leader for almost thirty years, could not slow the NFL juggernaut. New commissioner Paul Tagliabue quickly established his authority and continued along Rozelle's expansionist path.

In 1993 pro football entered the age of free agency, as players won the right to negotiate for their services on the open market. But this change, which had proved so problematic for Major League Baseball, caused little disruption for the NFL because of wise fiscal guidelines agreed to by the league and its players. The league continued to expand, adding franchises in Jacksonville, Florida, and Charlotte, North Carolina, in 1995 and allowing expansion teams to locate in Cleveland, Ohio, in 1999 and Houston, Texas, in 2002 to replace teams that had moved. That made a total of thirty-two NFL teams. In August 2006 Roger Goodell succeeded Tagliabue as NFL commissioner. Goodell immediately took a proactive role by pursuing such initiatives as harsher disciplinary measures for rules infractions and player misconduct, efforts to increase the sport's popularity overseas, and the passage of new rules to promote player safety. While those moves were not universally popular, they clearly demonstrated that the NFL was under new and assertive leadership.

The sport also continued to gain fans at an amazing clip. In 2011 *USA Today* reported that a Harris poll showed football to be the most popular sport in America for the ninth year in a row. In spite of its coveted position at the top of the American sports pyramid, the NFL nearly alienated its fans in 2011 as team owners and the NFL Players Association failed to reach a collective bargaining agreement. The protracted disagreement resulted in a lockout that began in March. The impasse was resolved, however, by July, and the 2011 season opened as planned with the only casualty being the preseason game that would have been played to honor inductees into the NFL Hall of Fame. With a new long-term collective bargaining agreement in place, Americans were assured of watching their favorite sport for many years to come.

In 2012 a new scandal that directly related to the league's new player-safety initiatives rocked the NFL. In early March, the league announced that, after a lengthy investigation, it had determined that the New Orleans Saints had instituted a program in violation of league rules to award "bounties" of money to defensive players who knocked opponents out of games. Even more troubling were reports that the team had targeted specific players for injuries. The program allegedly took place from 2009 (the season that ended with a Saints Super Bowl victory) to 2011. In response to the findings, Commissioner Goodell said, "It is our responsibility to protect player safety and the integrity of our game, and this type of conduct will not be tolerated. We have made significant progress in changing the culture with respect to player safety, and we are not going to relent."

The league came down hard on the team, suspending head coach Sean Payton for a year, general manager Mickey Loomis for eight games, and assistant coach Joe Vitt for six games. Former defensive coordinator Greg Williams, who had moved to a new team, was suspended indefinitely. The Saints appealed the length of the punishments, but in April the NFL announced that the suspensions would not be reduced. One reason for the severity of the discipline was that team officials had lied to the NFL during the investigation. Early reports claimed that more than twenty Saints players were also involved. In early May the league suspended four players without pay: linebacker Scott Fujita for three games, defensive end Will Smith for four games, defensive lineman Anthony Hargrove for eight games, and linebacker Jonathan Vilma for the entire season. All four players appealed their punishments; the players' union filed grievances on their behalf; and Vilma filed a defamation lawsuit against Roger Goodell, alleging that the commissioner made erroneous and damaging statements about him.

Two prominent deaths in recent years have intensified the focus on player safety. Within a fifteen-month period, two well-known former players committed suicide. In February 2011 former Chicago Bears safety Dave Duerson committed suicide after complaining of deteriorating mental abilities; he shot himself in the chest and left a note requesting that his brain be used in an ongoing study into the high incidence of chronic traumatic encephalopathy (CTE), a disease caused by repeated damage to the brain due to concussions. Symptoms include dementia, depression, and poor impulse control. The autopsy showed that Duerson did indeed have the disease and fueled suspicions that many former NFL players suffer from CTE because of the repeated hits they take during their careers. The findings added more urgency to the league's ongoing attempts to clean up the game and protect players.

Then, in May 2012, former San Diego Chargers linebacker Junior Seau shot himself in the chest after struggling with depression that many suspected may have been linked to CTE. Seau was beloved in San Diego for his leadership and his extensive charity work—his foundation has raised millions of dollars for youth activities—and his suicide shocked not only his community but also the entire NFL. A few weeks after his death, two separate lawsuits were filed against the NFL charging that the league has not done enough to prevent the long-term damage caused by concussions. As of late May 2012, eighty-one concussion-related lawsuits had been filed on behalf of some 2,240 players. Perhaps more than any other development in league history, this issue calls into question the very nature of the game, and it may take years for the NFL to find an appropriate balance between the ingrained violence of the sport and the well-being of the men who play it.

From its beginnings, the NFL has benefited greatly from the astute management of a handful of visionaries, from Halas to Rozelle to Goodell. This sound stewardship has enabled a league once derided by purists and largely ignored by the masses to expand exponentially, decade by decade, until it stood as the preeminent sports league in America. The NFL's leadership will have to draw upon all its collective experience and wisdom to guide the league through the challenging issues that emerged in the 2010s.

Robert E. Schnakenberg

SEE ALSO: *The Chicago Bears; College Football; The Dallas Cowboys; The Green Bay Packers; Halas, George "Papa Bear"; Labor Unions;* Monday Night Football*; Namath, Joe; The Oakland Raiders; The Pittsburgh Steelers; Professional Football; Radio; Sports Heroes; Super Bowl; Television;* USA Today*; World War II.*

BIBLIOGRAPHY

Dunnavant, Keith. *America's Quarterback: Bart Starr and the Rise of the National Football League.* New York: Thomas Dunne Books, 2011.

Fox, Stephen R. *Big Leagues: Professional Baseball, Football, and Basketball in National Memory.* New York: William Morrow, 1994.

Harris, David. *The League: The Rise and Decline of the NFL.* New York: Bantam Books, 1986.

McDonough, Will. *The NFL Century: The Complete Story of the National Football League, 1920–2000.* New York: Smithmark Publishing, 1999.

Neft, David S.; Richard M. Cohen; and Richard Korch. *The Football Encyclopedia: The Complete History of Professional Football from 1892 to the Present.* New York: St. Martin's, 1994.

Peterson, Robert W. *Pigskin: The Early Years of Pro Football.* New York: Oxford University Press, 1997.

Ross, Charles Kenyatta. *Outside the Lines: African Americans and the Integration of the National Football League.* New York: New York University Press, 1999.

Willis, Chris, and James A. Carr. *The Man Who Built the National Football League: Joe F. Carr.* Lanham, MD: Scarecrow Press, 2010.

National Geographic

For more than a century, the words *National Geographic* have conjured up images of natural wonders, bold exploration, and fascinating foreign cultures. Generations of Americans have looked to the National Geographic Society for information about the wider world, and millions of readers have paged through the familiar yellow-clad *National Geographic* magazine to make contact with a world far beyond their immediate experience. Likewise, the editorial choices of the magazine have shaped the American vision of the outside world, whether via the exhibits in the Explorers' Hall at the society's museum in Washington, D.C., or through its colorful magazine or countless books and television documentaries.

THE SOCIETY

The National Geographic Society was founded in January 1888 when thirty-three members of the elite Cosmos Club in Washington, D.C., gathered there with the goal of founding a "society for the increase and diffusion of geographical knowledge." The end of the nineteenth century was a dynamic period of industrial revolution, immigration, discovery, and change. Curiosity about the world was much in evidence, and the founders of the National Geographic Society sought to feed that hunger for knowledge.

Though the men themselves were from the upper classes—lawyers, bankers, educators, and military officers—the society they formed was more democratic in philosophy than similar royal societies in Europe. Rather than posing restrictive requirements for members, the founders wished to attract a broad base of supporters. The first president of the society, Gardiner Greene Hubbard, was a lawyer and financier who felt that his leadership would demonstrate to the public that membership in the society was not limited to scientists or explorers.

THE MAGAZINE

Within the year, the society published the first issue of *National Geographic* magazine. Supporting the effort to gain a broad base of subscriber-members, the magazine was a departure from the dry, academic journals of other scientific societies in that it used dramatic color photographs to illustrate its stories. *National Geographic* became a pioneer in color photography techniques and eventually became the first U.S. magazine to use an all-color format. For the first time in a scientific journal, photographs of bare-breasted native women were printed in an 1896 issue of *National Geographic*. For decades to follow, youngsters would seek the pages of the magazine for titillation and sex education as well as maps and exploration. Never a purely geographical publication, it offered a sweeping view of the world's wonders, whether geological, plant, animal, or human.

The society also campaigned to attract public interest by funding several high-profile expeditions, which were then extensively reported in the magazine. In 1909 the society funded Commodore Robert Peary's exploration of the North Pole and Hiram Bingham's expedition to Machu Picchu. In later years, the National Geographic Society would fund thousands of expeditions, including the work of such famous naturalists as Jacques Cousteau, Dian Fossey, and Jane Goodall, as well as anthropologists like Louis Leakey. Lavishly illustrated articles in *National Geographic* and, in more recent years, television shows and documentary films have documented each study and exploration.

Through the years *National Geographic* has been accused by social critics of portraying a romanticized view of the world, free of controversy and conflict. The magazine has been slow to respond to such criticism, but in the socially aware era of the 1970s, it finally began to offer reportage on some of the less savory aspects of the world and its people by covering such issues as war, poverty, and pollution.

Founded by an elite group of philanthropists, the National Geographic Society remained very much a family affair. Hubbard's successor as president was his son-in-law, Alexander Graham Bell, whose own son-in-law, Gilbert H. Grosvenor, likewise succeeded him. The next three leaders through the 1990s were also Grosvenors, sons following fathers, including Gil M. Grosvenor, who retired as chairman in 2011, and was succeeded by a nonfamily member. Continuing the tradition of a popular rather than a scientific control over the society, the board of directors largely consists of corporate executives, educators, lawyers, and environmentalists. From its roots as a broad-based society to encourage geographical study, the society has expanded to become the largest nonprofit scientific and educational society in the world.

The society has also expanded its publications far beyond a little monthly journal with beautiful pictures. It is one of the world's largest producers of atlases and maps, turning out maps that were used by the military in both world wars as well as Vietnam. It is the second-largest producer, after the British Broadcasting Corporation, of documentary films for television and has its own cable channel, as well as the National Geographic Kids Network, a closed-circuit network for use in schools.

Along with *National Geographic*, which is also published in Spanish and Japanese editions, the society publishes *National Geographic Kids* for children and *Traveler Magazine*. It also produces a large variety of educational and teaching aids and in the 1990s offered computer programs on many nature-related topics. Also in the 1990s it began to publish geographical books and children's books, plus the first fiction release in its history. Since the turn of the twenty-first century, the National Geographic Society has developed a major presence online, with specialist areas showcasing travel, photography, the environment, and other areas in which it is famous. In 2011 it ranked in the top 1,000 websites worldwide, with more than six million unique users and seventy-one million page views each month.

PHILANTHROPY

In the late 1980s the leadership of the National Geographic Society was horrified to learn that adult Americans had little practical knowledge of geography. Inspired by statistics showing that 17 percent of U.S. citizens could not locate the United States on a world map and that 25 percent could not find the Pacific Ocean, society executives created the National Geographic Society Education Foundation, with the aim of improving geography education. Called the society's 100th anniversary present to the American people by society chairman Grosvenor, the foundation sponsored local geography organizations, offered in-service training for teachers, and promoted geography in the schools through a National Geography Bee and Geography Awareness Week.

Notwithstanding such philanthropic gestures, the society is an extremely wealthy organization. Because of the its nonprofit status, none of the income generated from its many projects is taxable, and the same is true for the real estate owned by the society. Its competitors in the cartographical and educational publishing fields have frequently protested, challenging its legitimacy as a nonprofit organization. However, the society is a venerable Washington institution, well connected in the very government circles that make the decisions about its status, and so far, its tax-free designation is secure.

Alexander Graham Bell, the second president of the National Geographic Society, once wrote, "The world and all that is in it is our theme." True to Bell's vision, the society and its many publications and productions have made every aspect of the earth and its inhabitants a legitimate subject of study, wonder, and appreciation. From military cartography to computer atlas programs that play the language and music of different regions, National Geographic has mapped the planet. From the tops of the highest mountains to the sea floor, scientists funded by National Geographic have explored it. Even the cosmos has come under scrutiny as the society has funded and reported on expeditions into the universe that surrounds us. The National Geographic Society and its publications are beloved American institutions because they have allowed many explorers who may never get far from their hometowns to savor the whole world.

Tina Gianoulis

SEE ALSO: *AT&T;* Life; *NASA; National Parks.*

BIBLIOGRAPHY

Bryan, C. D. B. *The National Geographic Society: 100 Years of Adventure and Discovery.* New York: Harry N. Abrams, 1987.

Cook, James. "The World Is Our Theme." *Forbes,* January 21, 1991, 42.

National Geographic. Accessed February 24, 2012. Available from http://www.nationalgeographic.com

Patterson, Carolyn Bennett. *Of Lands, Legends and Laughter: The Search for Adventure with "National Geographic."* Golden, CO: Fulcrum Press, 1998.

National Hockey League (NHL)

When the National Hockey League (NHL) formed in 1917, it was dominated by Canadians, who were the greatest players in the world. They hailed from the Canadian prairies, and most of the franchises were housed in Canada and the northern United States. Canadian hockey dominance continued until the 1950s, when the Soviets emerged as a postwar powerhouse. The Soviets' speed and brilliant passing revolutionized the game on an international level. The rest of Europe, especially Czechoslovakia and Sweden, followed the lead of the Soviets, developing fast, skilled players. In America, growth at the collegiate level in the 1970s, an Olympic gold medal in 1980, and NHL expansion into several more cities converted the country into a hockey power. Moreover, with the fall of communism and the accompanying blurring of amateur and professional status, the NHL became a hockey melting pot in the 1990s. When the Olympics were held in Nagano, Japan, in 1998, there was not just a single dominant team that was laced with NHL talent—instead, there were several.

The NHL's beginnings were more humble. From 1917 through 1941 the league went through a series of growing pains. The rival Pacific Coast Hockey Association (PCHA), run by Frank and Lester Patrick, was much more progressive and innovative than the NHL. It was the first league to allow goalies to flop to the ice to make saves, allow forwards to pass the puck ahead in the offensive zone, tabulate assists on goals, place blue lines on the ice, and put numbers on players' jerseys. The PCHA folded in 1926, but its innovations, along with the Patricks, crossed over to the NHL. In the 1920s and 1930s, the Patricks led the New York Rangers to three championships with the help of star players Bill Cook, Bun Cook, and Frank Boucher. There were, of course, other stars of this period, including tough, hard-nosed Boston Bruins defenseman Eddie Shore; flashy Montreal Maroons forward Howie Morenz (better known as the "Babe Ruth of hockey" or the "Stratford Streak"); and Fred "Cyclone" Taylor, winner of five PCHA scoring titles.

However, despite the excitement and grit of the game, franchises struggled to survive. By the 1938–1939 season, three of the ten NHL franchises had been claimed by the Great Depression. Following the 1941–1942 season and the death of the New York Americans, the NHL became a six-team league for the next twenty-five years.

A CLASH IN CANADA

The NHL took on a deeply Canadian texture from 1942 to 1967, as the league was dominated by the Montreal Canadiens and the Toronto Maple Leafs, which each won ten Stanley Cup titles. The "two solitudes" of Canada were divided around these two rivals; French-Canadian Catholics rooted for the Habs (the nickname for the Canadiens), and the Presbyterian Scots and other Anglophones cheered on the Leafs. The two teams represented Canada's culture clash. The Leafs played a reserved, defensive style of hockey, whereas the Habs featured a wide-open brand that had fast skating and was crisp and explosive. The battles between these two proud rivals were always bitter and intense. The Leafs were led by such stalwart defensive players as Syl Apps; Teeder Kennedy; George "Chief" Armstrong; slick-skating Davey Keon; and Johnny Bower, who was known as the "China wall." The Canadiens had the fiery Maurice "Rocket" Richard, the innovative Jacques Plante (the first goalie to roam from his crease, play the puck behind the net, and don a mask), Jean Beliveau (a classy player who was considered to be hockey's Joe DiMaggio), and perennial Norris Trophy winner Doug Harvey.

The conflict between English and French Canada was most fully realized in 1955. That year, Richard, who had never won a scoring title, was leading the league in that category with a few games remaining. However, following a scrap with the Bruins' Hal Laycoe, in which Richard slugged a linesman, NHL president Clarence Campbell suspended the superstar for the remainder of the season and the postseason. Fans of the Canadiens regarded Campbell's actions as unjust and yet another form of oppression from Anglo-Canada. In late March of that year, when the president attended a Canadiens game, he was slapped by a fan, and then a tear-gas bomb exploded in the Forum. The Habs forfeited the contest, and the "Richard riot" ensued on St. Catherine's Street. Richard went on radio asking for the riot to be quelled. Though the rioters heeded his plea, the right winger eventually lost the scoring title. Moreover, without him, the Habs lost the Stanley Cup to a Detroit Red Wings team featuring Gordie Howe, Red Kelly, and Terry Sawchuk.

BEYOND THE ORIGINAL SIX

Following the 1966–1967 season, the NHL expanded from six teams to twelve; by 2000 the league had thirty teams. Bobby Orr of the Bruins was a dominant figure in this transition period. Orr revolutionized the defenseman position with his fast skating and rushing style. His play brought the Bruins two NHL titles and helped further expand the game into the United States. Wayne Gretzky was another key figure in the rise of the NHL. His trade from the Edmonton Oilers to the Los Angeles Kings in 1988 was a decisive turning point for the league, bringing its greatest player to a huge entertainment market.

The expansion of the NHL was largely brought about by a host of corporate synergies: the rapid growth in marketing and advertising, the five-team merger with the World Hockey Association (WHA) in 1979, the signing of major television contracts with ESPN and ABC, and an increase in the game's popularity in the United States. In 1980 there were 100,000 U.S. youngsters playing organized hockey, compared to 400,000 Canadians. By 2010 the organizing body for youth hockey in the United States reported that the number of young people playing the sport had passed 500,000. Part of hockey's growing appeal lies in its combination of football-like violence, graceful speed, and nuanced skill. Hockey players across Canada and the United States are admired for their toughness. A player might suffer a nasty gash but go back into the game after being stitched up because, as broadcasters quip, "he's a hockey player." Perhaps an oft-seen bumper sticker best defines the sport's absurdly rugged appeal: "Give Blood. Play Hockey." One of the more extreme examples of this attitude occurred in 2010, when Chicago Blackhawks defenseman Duncan Keith lost seven teeth when he was hit by a puck but returned to the ice to finish the game.

LEARNING FROM THE RUSSIANS

The NHL also is noteworthy for being the most cross-cultural of the major sports leagues. In 1967, 97 percent of hockey players were Canadian. By 2010, 54 percent were Canadian; 24 percent were American; and another 22 percent hailed from other dominant hockey countries, including Finland, the Czech Republic, Slovakia, Sweden, and Russia. In addition, African American players such as Dustin Byfuglien and Wayne Simmonds were also making inroads in what had been a traditionally white sport. The growth in European talent came about through the Summit Series between Canada and Russia in 1972. Since the late 1950s, Canadians complained that their amateurs were not their best players and that the country should be able to send NHL talent to the Olympics. The International Olympic Committee refused, and Canadians groused that the Soviets were really professionals disguised as amateurs. The Summit Series, showcasing Canadian superstars from the NHL, was supposed to give that country the chance to reclaim its hockey supremacy, but what happened instead changed the sport for the next twenty years.

The Summit Series was watched by more than twelve million Canadians, as schoolchildren were marched to the gyms and libraries to watch the afternoon games from Moscow. The Canadians, led by the timely heroics of Phil Esposito and a series of clutch goals by Paul Henderson, won the final game 6–5 and the series 4–3–1. Although victorious, the NHL and Canadians were impressed by the Soviet brand of tactical "firewagon" hockey, with forwards playing a series of set, positional systems and firing the puck with tic-tac-toe passing while slashing through the offensive zone with blazing speed and crackerjack shooting. Following the series, power-skating lessons popped up across the United States and Canada, and the NHL's dump-and-chase, brutal style of play gave way to an approach featuring greater finesse and speed.

The WHA's Winnipeg Jets were actually the first North American team to evolve out of the Soviet model. Bobby Hull and Swedes Ulf Nilsson and Anders Hedberg, with their speed and passing, helped the Jets win three Avco Cups. Later in the NHL, the Oilers perfected the Soviet model, bringing speed, style, and a deadly offensive game to the ice with the likes of Gretzky, Mark Messier, Jari Kurri, and Paul Coffey. The Oilers won five Stanley Cups in the 1980s.

GROWING PAINS

NHL contracts increased in value 400 percent in the 1970s because of the rival WHA. As the players and the game became richer through expansion and major television contracts, hockey seemed headed for a golden period in which it might even seriously compete with baseball, basketball, and football for market share. However, the growth of the fan base was slower than anticipated. In the late 1990s the game still needed to change as fans were bored with 3–1 games and desired the wide-open scoring of the Oilers' era.

The Soviet speed game had disappeared, and in its place teams employed a series of defensive systems, including neutral-zone traps that bottled up the ice surface and halted cross-ice passes. Meanwhile, the players were bigger than ever. In 1967 the average hockey player was 5 foot, 11 inches and weighed 175 pounds; in 1994 he was 6 foot, 2 inches and weighed 204 pounds. This increase in size created less room on the ice for plays to develop and offensive stars to make moves. Furthermore, while the rapid expansion of the game improved revenues, it diluted the talent pool. In the 1940s Hall-of-Famer Max Bentley was a third-line center with the Maple Leafs. In the 1990s it was hard to find quality second-line depth on any team.

Hockey was originally Canada's game: it started in Halifax, and the NHL was formed in Windsor, Ontario. However, by the turn of the twenty-first century, Canadians felt alienated by the NHL's treatment of their national pastime. NHL commissioner Gary Bettman, the first American to serve in that capacity, was not trusted in Canada because he allowed franchises such as the Quebec Nordiques and the Jets to move to the United States and become the Colorado Avalanche and Phoenix

Coyotes, respectively. In the United States, team owners received breaks on taxes, cities agreed to pay stadium leases, and the dollar was stronger than Canada's. If Canadian markets were to survive and remain competitive, the NHL, Bettman, and the Canadian government would need to create some type of compensation for the differences in the worth of the $2 and find a revenue-sharing plan to benefit all of the league's franchises.

DISPUTES OVER EQUITY AND SALARIES

This issue contributed to a labor dispute in the mid-1990s. Negotiations broke down over the league's idea to implement a salary cap and a revenue-sharing program that would help small-market teams compete for talent. The players' union wanted a less aggressive "payroll tax" than the league was proposing and was threatening a strike. In 1994 the owners responded with a preemptive lockout, which lasted until mid-January of the next year. By then, nearly half the season had been lost. The owners had given up the payroll tax idea, but they did obtain a salary cap for rookies and limitations on free agency.

The owners appeared to learn little from the experience, and soon after the dispute was settled, they began to award huge salaries to players. From the 1993–1994 season to the 2003–2004 season, the average annual salary rose from $558,000 to $1,830,000, an increase of 228 percent during a period when U.S. inflation went up 27 percent. Early in the first decade of the 2000s the owners were demanding a salary cap that applied to all players. When the union balked, the owners instituted another lockout, on September 15, 2004. This one set several unenviable records. When the stalemate ended in July 2005, the NHL had become the first professional sports league to lose an entire season to a work stoppage. The league had canceled 1,230 games, also a record.

The owners did obtain a salary cap and new free-agency rules, and players took pay cuts and agreed to drug testing. In addition to these labor-related changes, several rules of play were altered to make the game more offense-oriented and, in turn, more appealing to fans. In 2008, to further captivate fans and increase TV ratings, the NHL instituted an annual outdoor game called the Winter Classic, which was to be played in early January.

THE ROAD AHEAD

In the years following the labor agreement of 2005, the league seemed to reach its goal of more parity among the teams. However, as with the other major professional sports, the NHL has had to address the seriousness of head injuries. With players growing ever stronger and faster, collisions have been causing concussions with alarming frequency. One incident that highlighted the problem involved young superstar Sid "the Kid" Crosby of the Pittsburgh Penguins. After suffering a concussion from a hit in January 2011, Crosby managed to play only eight games during the next twelve months, and some observers feared that he would never play hockey again. One way the league was exploring improving safety was to test lighter-weight shoulder pads, because the hard plastic models the players had been wearing were thought to inflict more harm.

The need to protect its players was just one of the issues facing the NHL as it entered the 2010s. In traditional—meaning cold-weather—hockey markets, television ratings were on the rise. The Sun Belt teams, however, continued to struggle to attract both live and TV audiences. Some analysts believed that if the franchises with little support were allowed to fold, it would be better for the league overall. In the meantime, the NHL was also still trying to figure out how to lift itself to the same level as the National Football League, Major League Baseball, and the National Basketball Association, the three most popular sports leagues in the United States.

Grant Tracey

SEE ALSO: *Gretzky, Wayne; Hockey; Howe, Gordie; Hull, Bobby; Orr, Bobby; Sports Heroes.*

BIBLIOGRAPHY

Bass, Alan. *The Great Expansion: The Ultimate Risk that Changed the NHL Forever.* Bloomington, IN: iUniverse, 2011.

Diamond, Dan, ed. *Hockey Hall of Fame: The Official Registry of the Game's Honour Roll.* Toronto: Doubleday, 1996.

Gardner, Andrew. *Legends of Hockey*, 5 vols. VHS. Directed by Derik Murray. Toronto: Hockey Hall of Fame & Museum, TSN, and Opus Pictures, 1996.

Greig, Murray. *Big Bucks & Blue Pucks: From Hull to Gretzky, an Anecdotal History of the Late, Great World Hockey Association.* Toronto: Macmillan, 1997.

Leonetti, Mike. *Hockey's Original 6: Great Players of the Golden Era.* Vancouver, BC: Greystone Books, 2011.

MacSkimming, Roy. *Cold War: The Amazing Canada-Soviet Hockey Series of 1972.* Vancouver, BC: Greystone, 1996.

Pincus, Arthur; David Rosner; Len Hochberg; et al. *The Official Illustrated NHL History: The Official Story of the Coolest Game on Earth.* London: Carlton Books, 2010.

National Lampoon

Although Great Britain has enjoyed a long tradition of looking to its colleges for humor, in America the crossover from collegiate to professional humorist has for the most part been much less conspicuous. A notable exception, however, was a group of students at Harvard University in the late 1960s who went on in 1970 to found *National Lampoon*, which enjoyed two decades of circulation before effectively ceasing publication in April 1992.

Without the astonishing success attained by Harvard undergraduates Henry Beard and Douglas Kenney, staff members of the venerable *Harvard Lampoon*, the college's century-old humor magazine, it is quite possible that *National Lampoon* might never have come into existence. The two collaborated on parodies of *Time* and *Life* magazines, which went into national distribution and sold well, followed by a J. R. R. Tolkien spoof, *Bored of the Rings*, which was published by Signet in 1969.

BIRTH OF THE BRAND

After graduation Beard and Kenney found a backer for their proposal for a national humor magazine—Matty Simmons, who had just served seventeen years as executive vice president of the pioneering credit card company Diner's Club and was eager to find new areas of investment. In 1967 Simmons had created a company called 21st Century Communications, which later became National Lampoon Inc., with Simmons as its chairman of the board and Leonard Mogel, from Simmons's *Weight Watchers Magazine*, as its publisher. Beard was installed in the magazine's midtown Manhattan office as executive editor; Kenney as editor-in-chief; and Robert Hoffman, fellow *Harvard Lampoon* alum, as managing editor. The art department was run by Peter Bramley, a cartoonist fresh from Massachusetts College of Art, who had moved to Manhattan from Boston in the late 1960s, and Bill Skurski, Bramley's partner in Cloud Studio, which was located in a storefront on Manhattan's Lower East Side. Collaborating with them was photographer Mike Sullivan, who set up and shot the pictures for Cloud Studio's photonovellas.

The first issue rolled off the press in April 1970. It was irreverent and funny, appealing to the burgeoning baby-boom market of college-educated youth now old enough to be entry-level professionals. It was also a magnet for emerging talent: Beard, Kenney, and Hoffman were soon joined by their friends and fellow *Harvard Lampoon* alumni Christopher Cerf and George Trow, as well as a host of New York humorists including Chris Miller, a former advertising copywriter who had also written material for Al Goldstein's unabashedly sexually oriented magazine, *Screw*, and Michael O'Donoghue, whose previous credits included contributions to the *East Village Other* and the *Evergreen Review*.

The freewheeling informality of the early days made for some cliffhanger administration, in no small part due to the erratic lifestyles (and recreational drug habits) of key players. Kenney once simply disappeared for over a month; Beard, running the whole show in his absence, was under such stress that during an interview with one of his art directors, he bit his pipe stem clean through. Burnout and management shakeups were frequent: Hoffman left as managing editor after a year, his job being given to former associate editor Mary Martello. Bramley and Skurski were replaced in 1971 by an in-house art editor, Michael Gross, who in turn lasted only a year. Kenney and Beard were reshuffled into new positions in 1972.

EXPANDING THE BRAND

Although staff volatility was a way of life at the company in its early days, it was all of a piece with the exuberant creativity of the enterprise. O'Donoghue and Tony Hendra, Martello's successor in the managing editor's slot, collaborated on *National Lampoon*'s first comedy album, *Radio Dinner*, issued in 1972. Composed primarily by Christopher Guest, it was a commercial success—it included the classic "Deteriorata" parody, as well as withering spoofs of Bob Dylan; Joan Baez; and former Beatles Paul McCartney, George Harrison, and John Lennon. Hendra followed that up in 1973 with a *National Lampoon* off-Broadway stage review, *Lemmings*, also with music by Guest, and a cast featuring John Belushi and Chevy Chase; it too turned a respectable profit.

That same year, O'Donoghue and P. J. O'Rourke, now the magazine's executive editor, put together *The National Lampoon Encyclopedia of Humor*—the first issue of the magazine devoted entirely to new material and without any advertisements. It included pieces by Beard, Kenney, and O'Donoghue himself, plus cartoons and writing by Ann Beatts, Vaughn Bode, Frank Frazetta, Edward Gorey, B. Kliban, Brian McConnachie, Charles Rodrigues, Ed Subitzky, and a dozen other contributors.

Not everything the National Lampoon team touched turned to gold, however. Flush with the success of *Radio Dinner* and *Lemmings* (the first of several profitable *National Lampoon* stage shows), Simmons bankrolled a weekly syndicated radio show called *The National Lampoon Radio Hour*, which first aired in December 1973. It was cut from an hour to a half hour after several episodes and withdrawn altogether the following summer, having lost money almost from the start, but it provided the material for an album of excerpts, called *National Lampoon/Gold Turkey (Radio Hour/Greatest Hits)*, released in 1975. By this time O'Donoghue had left *National Lampoon* to begin a seven-year stint as the chief writer for a new NBC television comedy show called *Saturday Night Live*, which premiered in 1975 with much of the flavor (and several key cast members, notably Chase and Belushi), of the earlier *National Lampoon* reviews.

When negotiating their original contract with Simmons, Kenney, Beard, and Hoffman had agreed to a five-year buyout option, which they exercised at the end of 1974, receiving a total of $10 million between them. Beard departed immediately (Hoffman had already left to return to graduate school when he ceased to be managing editor in 1971), resurfacing after spending several years as a prolific writer of more conventional humor, sometimes in partnership with Cerf—the two coauthored several books, including *The Official Politically Correct Dictionary and Handbook*. Kenney remained until 1977 and was one of the three scriptwriters for *National Lampoon's Animal House* (the other two were Miller and Harold Ramis), starring Belushi—the highest-grossing (probably in both senses) comedy film of the twentieth century.

FILM PRODUCTION

With the release of *Animal House* in 1978, Simmons began to concentrate more on film production and less on publishing. Other *National Lampoon* films followed, including *National Lampoon's Vacation* (1983), which starred Chase as the paterfamilias of the feckless Griswold household, and its sequels *National Lampoon's European Vacation* (1985), *National Lampoon's Christmas Vacation* (1989), and *National Lampoon's Vegas Vacation* (1997).

Meanwhile, the magazine began a long, slow decline—punctuated by occasional book releases—to its last scheduled issue in May 1992, though it continued thereafter to appear in an annual edition produced by a subcontractor of the new owners of National Lampoon Inc.—J2 Communications. Headed by former Disney executive James P. Jimirro, J2 bought what was left of the National Lampoon in 1990, primarily for its film rights. Indeed, the yearly publication of *National Lampoon* was not for profit in its own right but rather dictated by the founders' original contract, which stipulated that unless the magazine was published at least once a year in a run of at least 50,000 copies, all rights to the National Lampoon name would revert to the *Harvard Lampoon*. Although J2's modest staffing (three full-time and three part-time workers as of the end of 1997) precluded any in-house production, the firm continued throughout the 1990s to license independent producers making *National Lampoon* films and to distribute them to theaters and through cable television channels such as Showtime and The Movie Channel.

Hendra, in his book *Going Too Far*, chronicles the rise and fall of so-called boomer humor beginning with "sick" comic Mort Sahl in the early 1960s and ending with *Saturday Night Live*. *National Lampoon* rode the crest of the wave, and during its heyday in the 1970s was the training school and laboratory for many humorists, including stars such as Beard, Kenney, Belushi, and O'Donoghue as well as a host of lesser lights whose work graced the magazine's pages. That the *National Lampoon* name retained considerable cachet at the end of the twentieth century, enough to be a major selling point for movies to a generation of viewers unborn at the time *Animal House* was released, is testimony to the durability of its contributors' iconoclastic brand of humor in the American popular consciousness.

Nick Humez

SEE ALSO: Animal House*; Baez, Joan; The Beatles; Belushi, John; Cable TV; Chase, Chevy; Dylan, Bob; Guest, Christopher; Lennon, John; McCartney, Paul; Radio;* Saturday Night Live*; Screwball Comedies.*

BIBLIOGRAPHY

Beard, Henry, and Christopher Cerf. *The Official Politically Correct Dictionary and Handbook.* New York: Villard Books, 1993.

Beard, Henry, and Douglas Kenney. *Bored of the Rings: A Parody of J. R. R. Tolkien's "The Lord of the Rings."* New York: New American Library/Signet, 1969.

Bendel, John, comp. *The "National Lampoon" Presents True Facts: The Book.* Chicago: Contemporary Books, 1991.

Hendra, Tony. *Going Too Far: The Rise and Demise of Sick, Gross, Black, Sophomoric, Weirdo, Pinko, Anarchist, Underground, Antiestablishment Humor.* Garden City, NY: Doubleday, 1987.

Karp, Josh. *A Futile and Stupid Gesture: How Doug Kenney and "National Lampoon" Changed Comedy Forever.* Chicago: Chicago Review Press, 2006.

O'Donoghue, Michael, ed. *The National Lampoon Encyclopedia of Humor.* New York: National Lampoon, 1973.

O'Rourke, P. J., ed. *"National Lampoon" Tenth Anniversary Anthology, 1970–1980.* New York: Simon & Schuster, 1979.

Perrin, Dennis. *Mr. Mike: The Life and Work of Michael O'Donoghue: The Man Who Made Comedy Dangerous.* New York: Avon Books, 1998.

Simmons, Matty. *If You Don't Buy This Book, We'll Kill This Dog: Life, Laughs, Love and Death at the "National Lampoon."* New York: Barricade Books, 1994.

National Organization for Women (NOW)

Established in 1966, the National Organization for Women (NOW) was born out of frustration at the lack of progress on women's issues following John F. Kennedy's 1961 formation of the President's Commission on the Status of Women in the United States. Similar commissions had been set up in all fifty states, but their failures to achieve their goals provoked a core group of activists at a national convention in 1966. Gathering in Betty Friedan's hotel room and writing their guidelines on a paper napkin, the activists laid the groundwork for NOW, which was formally launched that October at a convention that attracted 300 men and women. Friedan was elected the group's president. By the end of the twentieth century, NOW had grown into the largest and most organized of the women's groups. It boasts more than 550 local chapters in all fifty states and has more than half a million active members.

In the early years of the organization, Friedan continued to be the motivating force, and now she is considered to be the "mother" of the modern women's movement. She was a logical choice for the first president since she had almost single-handedly aroused the nation's consciousness with her landmark book *The Feminine Mystique* (1963). Pointing out that existing institutions had perpetuated "the problem that has no name," Friedan demanded that women be treated as equals and be allowed to develop their talents while pursuing their own individual goals. She was also instrumental in the formation of the National Women's Political Caucus (NWPC) in 1971, a bipartisan support group that promotes the election of women to public office. As the women's movement grew and attracted media attention, Friedan insisted that she be relieved of her position as NOW's president in favor of more photogenic leaders, such as Gloria Steinem.

On October 29, 1966, NOW issued a statement of purpose, detailing its agenda and establishing itself as the voice of the women's movement. The chief points of that statement read as follows:

> A recognition that the time had come for women to take full partnership in American society; a call to action to claim inherent rights; the insistence that women not be forced to choose between marriage and motherhood or careers; a continuation of the revolution started at Seneca Falls in 1848; and a commitment to use the powers of education, the law, and political office to attain these goals.

Throughout its history, NOW has promoted a group of core issues: abortion and reproductive rights, economic equality, helping women get elected to political offices, and ending discrimination against women. In response to the evolving social environment, other issues have been added, such as affirmative action, an end to sexual harassment and domestic violence, fighting the political right, advancing global and youth feminism, and the advancement of women in the military. The issue of lesbian rights has long been controversial for NOW. A bitter break occurred in the organization over this issue in the early 1970s, but by the 1980s promoting lesbian rights had become a permanent part of NOW's agenda. However, controversy still continues over this issue since many moderates believe that championing it has hurt the women's movement as whole.

The early years of the movement centered on the needs of white, middle-class women. In an effort to broaden its base of support, NOW has also reached out to minority women and pledged support for racial and ethnic diversity. To achieve its political goals, NOW has successfully engaged in such activities as mass mailings and the picketing of certain businesses and politicians. It has been most effective in its class-action suits, public demonstrations, promotion of legislation that is favorable to women, and ability to call attention to the concerns of women around the world.

Less than three decades after the birth of the modern women's movement in the early 1960s, many females believed that the battle had been won, and support for NOW began to wane. This trend was abruptly halted in 1989 when the United States Supreme Court handed down a decision in *Webster v. Reproductive Health Services* that curtailed access to abortion. Membership in NOW rose dramatically. Feminist and journalist Susan Faludi noted that a 1989 poll revealed that women as a whole believed that neither Democrats nor Republicans were responsive to their needs. The three groups most responsive, they insisted, were NOW, the leaders of the women's movement, and feminists.

Despite a claim by *Time* magazine in 1998 that the success of the popular television show *Ally McBeal* signaled the end of feminism, the continued presence of the NOW indicates that women remain aware of the ongoing need for an advocacy group. In recognition of the loss of leaders such as Friedan, who died in 2006, and former president Molly Yard, who died in 2005, NOW launched the 40th Anniversary Oral History Project in 2006. Its purpose was to record NOW's past while simultaneously creating an ongoing oral history of the evolving women's movement. NOW continues its battle to protect abortion rights and safe methods of birth control, and in response to the aging of the baby boomers, the organization has also worked to safeguard the Social Security program.

Elizabeth Rholetter Purdy

SEE ALSO: *Abortion;* Ally McBeal*; Feminism; Gay Liberation Movement; Steinem, Gloria.*

BIBLIOGRAPHY

Barakso, Maryann. *Governing NOW: Grassroots Activism in the National Organization for Women.* Ithaca, NY: Cornell University Press, 2004.

Bellafante, Ginia. "Who Put the Me in Feminism?" *Time*, June 29, 1988: 23–26.

Faludi, Susan. *Backlash: The Undeclared War against American Women.* New York: Doubleday, 1992.

Friedan, Betty. *The Feminine Mystique.* New York, Dell, 1963.

National Parks

America's national park system includes hundreds of areas covering millions of acres in nearly every state and U.S. possession. The national parks include natural wonders, historical and cultural landmarks, and recreational areas as varied as Massachusetts' Cape Cod National Seashore, Hawaii's Volcanoes National Park, New York's Statue of Liberty, and Pennsylvania's Gettysburg National Battlefield. The National Park Service has designed the parks so that they interlock to tell the natural and cultural history of the United States and of humanity's presence there. The National Park Service functions as the parks' primary custodian, preserving natural and historic sites as well as guiding the continued growth of tourism and public education.

The idea of establishing natural and historic areas as national parks developed in the United States during the nineteenth century and evolved to fulfill a perceived cultural need for a strong national identity that could be found in America's monumental scenery. The popular media was essential in the drive to sustain this idea in a country largely dedicated to material progress at any expense. Magazines, newspapers, and paintings promoted the parks as places where any citizen could grow mentally, physically, and spiritually through communion with nature. Because the parks are owned by all citizens, they came to exemplify America's democratic ideal, and they remain national symbols of pride. The rise of the environmental movement in the mid- to late twentieth century has also made the national parks symbols of American environmental consciousness.

IMPETUS

Alfred Runte's *National Parks: The American Experience* states that "gentlemen adventurers, artists, and explorers" had created the national park idea by the second half of nineteenth century. Soon after the American Revolutionary War of the late eighteenth century, intellectuals in the newly created United States were hurt by comments implying that they had no sense of patriotism or appreciation for the past. A new country of limited cultural achievements forced these people to turn to nature to find unique national symbols that they could proudly proclaim to the world. Runte believes that this cultural desire to break with Europe, rather than a deep commitment to ecological preservation, was the catalyst for the development of America's national park system. The founders of the idea of the national park were also spurred by the example of the privately owned land around Niagara Falls, on which promoters, souvenir stands, and ugly fences joined with admission charges to create a national embarrassment.

Yellowstone's Old Faithful. *Tourists gather to watch the eruption of the Old Faithful geyser at Yellowstone National Park in Wyoming.* MARK RALSTON/AFP/GETTY IMAGES.

The world's first national park system began with an 1864 bill, signed by President Abraham Lincoln, that set aside the Yosemite area in California for public use and preservation, and the 1872 designation of the Yellowstone area in Wyoming, Montana, and Idaho as a national park. Yellowstone was the world's first area to be officially designated as a national park.

Private citizen Stephen T. Mather had an idea for a specialized park service to properly manage the new parks around the year 1915 and enlisted the head of the influential National Geographic Society to help him promote the cause. This was the beginning of an invaluable friendship between the society and the park system that aided in park promotion. Renowned environmentalist John Muir and renowned Central Park designer Frederick Law Olmsted also lent their prominent voices to the national park idea. The popular press, however, was the most instrumental voice in the public promotion of the national parks, as it had the power to attract the public support and attendance so essential to the park system's survival. Popular magazines such as Horace Greeley's *New York Tribune*, *National Geographic*, the *Saturday Evening Post*, *Collier's*, and *Harper's Weekly* played on the public's patriotic sentiment to help raise support.

Mather's efforts met with success in 1916 when President Woodrow Wilson created the National Park Service as a bureau within the Department of the Interior with the stated goals of conserving park resources while providing for the public's enjoyment. The Park Service would quickly discover the difficulties inherent in managing the fine balance between preservation of America's finite natural resources and catering to the needs of tourists whose revenues helped support the new agency, a tension that continues to present challenges into the twenty-first century.

The Park Service has had to face the difficulties of maintaining such an extensive system in difficult economic times, such as the prolonged recession that struck the United States in late 2007. Between the loss of tax revenues due to the economic slowdown and the high costs of fighting two wars, the U.S. government piled up unprecedented levels of debt in the the first decade of the 2000s. In the 2010s the National Park Service experienced the effects of those spiraling government deficits. In an effort to rein in federal debt, in 2011 Congress cut $101 million from the $2.75 billion budget for the National Park Service. With a sluggish economy and an out-of-control federal budget continuing to dominate the news, there was no guarantee that legislators would not slash the budget for national parks even more deeply in future years. In order to mitigate economic impact on parks, initiatives to privatize park services were introduced in the first decade of the 2000s. At the time, private companies were already partnered with the national park system to provide concessions, lodging, and specialized activities such as white-water rafting. However, new proposals endeavored to grant private companies control of additional park departments such as maintenance.

PRESERVATION

Until the early twentieth century, the national parks existed mainly among the spectacular scenery of the American West, as the U.S. government created the early parks from lands in the public domain, few of which existed in the East. The West's grand and monumental scenery also served as a primary catalyst for the national park movement, as popular culture glorified the area in magazines, paintings, and dime novels. A move for eastward expansion did not begin until the 1920s due to the major obstacle of obtaining land. Congress would not use taxpayer money to purchase the necessary private lands, forcing the Park Service to rely on private donors to gain eastern parklands. Donors such as the wealthy Rockefeller family provided for the creation of eastern parks such as the Great Smoky Mountains National Park and the Appalachian Trail.

The Park Service acquired more than fifty additional sites in 1933, including those areas previously controlled by the War Department and the Forest Service, as well as the Washington, D.C., National Capital Parks. The 1960s saw the addition of wild and scenic free-flowing rivers, national lakeshores, national trails, and urban national recreation areas; the 1980 Alaska National Interest Lands Conservation Act more than doubled the system's size. The Park Service also branched out into public education when it greatly increased its participation in historical interpretation in the late twentieth century, making it one of the country's leading educators in the areas of American history and environmental values as they relate to the development of the nation's parks.

A third of the areas that constitute the national park system are primarily scenic in nature. Americans prize these areas for their clean air and natural beauty as well as their abundance of bears and other exotic wildlife. Famous examples of scenic national parks include Arizona's Grand Canyon and Petrified Forest, South Dakota's Badlands, and Wyoming's Grand Tetons. The magnificent natural features of these areas are what first spurred the idea of creating national parks to promote American culture and preserve its natural beauty. The Park Service has attempted to return the scenic parks under its care to their primitive appearance before the European settlers' arrival for both aesthetic and ecological purposes. The popular image of these areas is that of a place where the urbanite can go to escape noisy, crowded, industrial city life in nature's tranquility.

The parks dedicated to preserving natural and monumental scenery increased in popularity and importance with the mid- to late-twentieth-century rise of environmental awareness in the United States. The 1963 Leopold Report, which evaluated the National Park Service's environmental policies, led directly to the restructuring of natural resource management to be more in line with ecological preservation. The Park Service continued to face pressures for resortlike development with the increasing popularity of outdoor recreation activities in the late twentieth century.

The Park System also preserves areas of national historic interest. These parks represent a link to the country's past and exemplify the continuity between past and present. They promote the values of American history and are highly patriotic, often drawing comparisons to shrines. Famous examples include Philadelphia's Independence National Historic Park, as well as many famous battlefields of the American Revolutionary and Civil Wars. Prehistoric Native American areas such as the Casa Grande Ruins in Arizona and Mesa Verde National Park in Colorado were preserved to protect them from plundering scavenger hunters.

The 1906 Antiquities Act marked a great step forward in the National Park Service's move into historic preservation. This act gave presidents the power to set aside areas of historic interest by designating them National Monuments. President Theodore Roosevelt effectively used this act and remained closely associated with the park movement well into the twentieth century. The National Park Service moved into historic preservation in the 1920s as the park system expanded eastward. It received control over nearly fifty sites that included many popular Revolutionary War and Civil War battlefields. The Park Service increased its role in historical interpretation when it entered the increasingly popular "living history" movement of the late twentieth century.

IDEOLOGICAL GOALS

One of the national park system's main ideological goals has been the promotion of national enthusiasm for a certain view of America's cultural heritage. The national parks symbolize the virtues that the United States promotes and with which it wishes to be associated. The existence of national parks epitomized the American ideals of altruism, statesmanship, and philanthropy at their best. Park service guidebooks and publications inform readers about how the various parks embody these cultural values. The early parks represented America and effectively served as cultural exemplars to which Americans could point with great pride. The parks also functioned in the nineteenth century as popular moral and religious affirmations of America's manifest destiny to the ownership of this great land, an ownership seemingly sanctioned by nature and nature's God.

Ironically, however, the historical context surrounding the creation of the national parks system came under fire in the late twentieth century. Historians and Native American scholars brought to national attention a less commendable narrative about this treasured part of American identity. The establishment of many national parks had deprived many Native American tribes of their lands. In his text *Dispossessing Wilderness* (2000), Mark Spense examines the removal of Native Americans from what would become Yosemite, Yellowstone, and Glacier National Parks. The establishment of those and other parks, while significant for environmental conservation, are also representative of long-standing tensions between the U.S. government and Native American communities, tensions that have persisted from the time of the first European explorers through the twenty-first century.

In its early stages, supporters thought that national parks would help promote robust health and good citizenship through the rigors of outdoor life. Freeman Tilden, quoted in former Park Service head Conrad Wirth's introduction to *America's Wonderlands*, vividly captured these beliefs when he avowed that "a consummate expression of this ultimate wealth of the human spirit . . . is to be found in the National Park system. . . . Many a man has come to find merely serenity or scenic pictures—and has unexpectedly found a renewal and affirmation of himself." Quiet contemplation among nature's grandeur would both soothe the weary city resident and boost his or her love of the country.

The National Park Service's founding mission was to hold America's natural wonders in public trust for all Americans, past, present, and future. This mission expanded in the mid- to late twentieth century as the Park Service adopted a more ecological focus with the rise of the environmental movement. The national parks and environmental preservation have become synonymous in the United States. Some critics feel that it is precisely the efforts to preserve wilderness areas that will lead to their demise; such is the conclusion put forth in Roderick Nash's seminal text *Wilderness and the American Mind*, first published in 1967. Intense debates over the ecological future of the parks mirror the environmental debates rife in American society. An ongoing debate over utilitarian versus preservationist aims began with the very inception of the national park movement and seem to reignite as opinions of wilderness areas evolve.

The famous nineteenth-century environmentalist Muir valued the country's natural beauty as an asset and national treasure but realized that the general public instead ranked scenery by its size and grandeur. The visiting public also wished to see these great wonders in relative comfort. Concessions to tourists were necessary to increase needed popular support of the parks. Total preservation was therefore an impractical idea. The National Park Service instead marketed its scenery through a "See America First" campaign. In 1956 "Mission 66" demonstrated the Park Service's recognition of the public's role in its creation and continued success with the largest budget allotment for improvement in its history. This money provided for the construction and renovation of roads, trails, hotels, campgrounds, and visitor centers to add to the public's comfort and enjoyment.

The late-twentieth-century growth of environmental awareness, however, also encouraged public support of parks that represented sound ecological units, such as the Florida Everglades, even if the scenery was not as spectacular. Ongoing scientific studies were present in almost all of the parks at the turn of the twenty-first century, reaping the benefits of abundant research subjects. Interest groups formed for park preservation and protection as urbanites and suburbanites took up the environmental cause and used the popular press to gain support, as had their nineteenth-century predecessors. Also serving to publicize the parks was a six-part Ken Burns documentary titled *The National Parks: America's Best Idea*, which aired on PBS in 2009.

Increased environmental awareness and a number of increased threats to wildlands sparked further public debate over how best to manage national parklands. Critics such as Richard Sellers have pointed out that policies governing national park management have vacillated according to who occupies the White House rather than focusing on ecological sustainability. Encroaching development threatened national parks in the early twenty-first century, as did climate change and increased park traffic. Few could agree how to best address these concerns in the 2010s.

A hallmark example of the persistent debates over national parklands is the use of fire suppression. Once a mandated rule in the parks, this policy came under attack in the 1960s when ecologists proposed that forested areas benefitted more from controlled burning, which more authentically mimicked natural occurrences. At the outset of the 2010s, suppression was still practiced but remained under review and continued to provide fodder for land management groups, illustrating the difficult task of arriving at a consensus when it comes to national park policy making.

ATTRACTING VISITORS

The national park movement's proponents heavily marketed the national parks in the popular media in order to attract a variety of visitors. Railroads were the most influential early promoters and played a large role in early development, building rustic hotels to house the guests their trains carried to the parks. The 1916 creation of the National Park Service was inextricably linked with changes designed to increase badly needed tourist revenues. Popular magazine articles promoted the idea of the national parks as economically valuable tourist destinations.

While *sagebrushing* became a popular 1920s term for those visitors who chose to do without creature comforts as they camped among nature's spectacular scenery, automobiles were most instrumental in raising public support. The decision to allow automobiles to enter the parks for the first time provided the biggest boost to tourist numbers. The majority of the American people desired inexpensive and comfortable vacations, an observation not lost on park promoters.

The parks were now more physically and monetarily accessible. Publicity stunts such as tunneling roadways through huge redwood trees and staging bear feeding shows also attracted an increasing number of visitors. The National Park Service branched out into other avenues of public interest with the addition of museums, publications, and other educational activities designed to aid the visiting public.

The popular image of the national parks remains that of breathtaking beauty amid a quiet, almost spiritual atmosphere. Popular images of Park Service employees continue to picture them as rugged men and women who roam the great outdoors and come to the dramatic rescue of stranded visitors. Many Americans cherish fond memories of vacations spent hiking in the sweet air, glimpsing a moose or a bear from the car window or marveling at the timely eruption of Yellowstone's famous Old Faithful geyser. The next generation of park visitors can add a trip to a museum or a talk with a costumed living history interpreter to the list of things to do at a national park. All of the National Park Service's activities combine with the national parks' reputation as monumental tributes to the American spirit to make them powerful cultural and educational forces.

The parks have also enjoyed a steadily increasing popularity among the American public since their nineteenth-century inception. The National Park Service has consistently ranked among the most popular federal agencies in public opinion surveys even late in the twentieth century, when Americans became ever more distrustful of their government. The parks and their employees carry an enduring reputation for excellence into the twenty-first century. America's national parks are truly a unique and monumental cultural legacy.

Marcella Bush Trevino

SEE ALSO: *Environmentalism;* National Geographic*; Yellowstone National Park.*

BIBLIOGRAPHY

Duncan, Dayton, and Burns, Ken. *The National Parks: America's Best Idea.* New York: Alfred A. Knopf, 2009.

Everhart, William C. *The National Park Service.* Boulder, CO: Westview Press, 1983.

Foresta, Ronald A. *America's National Parks and Their Keepers.* Washington, DC: Resources for the Future, 1984.

Harmon, David, ed. *Mirror of America: Literary Encounters with the National Parks.* Boulder, CO: Roberts Rinehart Publishing, 1989.

Meyer, Judith L. *The Spirit of Yellowstone: The Cultural Evolution of a National Park.* Lanham, MD: Rowman & Littlefield, 1996.

Muir, John. *Our National Parks.* Madison: University of Wisconsin Press, 1981.

Nash, Roderick Frazier. *Wilderness and the American Mind,* 4th ed. New Haven, CT: Yale University Press, 2001.

National Geographic. *National Geographic Guide to National Parks of the United States,* 7th ed. Des Moines, IA: National Geographic Books, 2012.

Runte, Alfred. *National Parks: The American Experience,* 4th ed. Lanham, MD: Taylor Trade, 2010.

Sax, Joseph L. *Mountains without Handrails: Reflections on the National Parks.* Ann Arbor: University of Michigan Press, 1980.

Sellers, Richard. *Preserving Nature in the National Parks: A History.* New Haven, CT: Yale University Press, 1999.

Sontag, William H., ed. *National Park Service: The First 75 Years.* Philadelphia: Eastern National Park and Monument Association, 1990.

Spence, Mark David. *Dispossessing the Wilderness: Indian Removal and the Making of the National Parks.* New York: Oxford University Press, 2000.

Tilden, Freeman. *Interpreting Our Heritage.* Chapel Hill: University of North Carolina Press, 1977.

Watkins, T. H., and Dyan Zaslowsky. *These American Lands: Parks, Wilderness, and the Public Lands.* Washington, DC: Island Press, 1994.

Natural Born Killers

The $34 million film *Natural Born Killers* (*NBK*), directed by Oliver Stone, was released in August 1994 amid expectations that its story line, about a serial-killing young couple named Mickey and Mallory Knox, would create another media furor similar to or even greater than the one that centered on Stone's 1991 conspiracy epic, *JFK.* Critics and opinion-page writers proved, rather unexpectedly, to be less antagonistic toward *NBK* than *JFK.* Nevertheless, the former managed to spark a lively critical debate over the merits of its boldly experimental visual design, as well as a series of high-profile condemnations from public figures such as Senator Bob Dole and popular writer John Grisham regarding its high level of on-screen violence. Several "copycat" murders in at least two different countries have also been blamed on the film's supposed detrimental influence on unstable viewers, including the Columbine High School massacre in 1999.

The controversy was nothing new or intimidating to director Stone, who had demonstrated in the past his willingness to tackle politically and culturally volatile material in films such as *Salvador* (1986), *Platoon* (1986), *Wall Street* (1987), *Talk Radio* (1988), *Born on the Fourth of July* (1989), *The Doors* (1991), *JFK,* and *Heaven & Earth* (1993). Undaunted, Stone would go on from *NBK* to direct *Nixon* (1995) and *W.* (2008)—two politics biopics about, respectively, Presidents Richard M. Nixon and George W. Bush. These films' supposed liberties with the historical record landed Stone back in many pundits' ill graces. Though not as overtly political as much of his work, *NBK* does illustrate that Stone, unlike many of his big-name Hollywood contemporaries, was at this stage of his career more interested in antagonizing his mainstream audiences than comforting them.

PART ONE

The plot of *NBK* is divided into two main parts. Part One of the film opens in a southwestern diner, where Mickey and Mallory Knox, in the midst of a cross-country murder spree, massacre all of the employees and patrons except one, who is left behind "to tell the tale of Mickey and Mallory" to investigators. A lengthy flashback then follows, wherein details of Mallory's incestuous abuse by her father and her first meeting with delivery-boy Mickey are revealed in a segment titled "I Love Mallory," patterned after a situation comedy. It is further revealed that Mickey was arrested and imprisoned for grand theft auto but then escaped from prison via what seems like the divine intervention of a desert cyclone. He next returned to Mallory's home to rescue her by killing her parents. The couple took to the road, killing randomly as they went and attracting the frenzied attention of the media and the law.

Having established this back story, the film introduces tabloid television reporter Wayne Gale and serial-killer expert Jack Scagnetti, both of whose destinies are intertwined with Mickey and Mallory's. As these two men chase them down, Mickey and Mallory are sidetracked into the desert, where they encounter a Native American medicine man who sees their true demonic natures and at least temporarily compels Mickey to confront his traumatic past. Terrified, Mickey kills the medicine man—an act that seemingly brings forth the desert rattlesnakes to strike and poison Mickey and Mallory. Desperately fleeing the desert to search for antivenin in a small-town drugstore, the couple are finally apprehended and beaten into submission by a police force led by celebrity-cop Scagnetti.

PART TWO

Part Two of the film resumes a year later, after Mickey and Mallory have been tried, convicted, and then imprisoned in separate wings of the same facility. To forestall execution, Mickey has been finding ways to kill prisoners and guards so that he must be reluctantly spared to stand for yet more trials. Frustrated by his strategy, the prison warden, a petty tyrant named McClusky, conspires with Scagnetti to transport Mickey and Mallory away from the prison where they can then be "shot while trying to escape." Before their plan can take effect, however, Mickey agrees to a post–Super Bowl live television interview with Gale. Mickey's dynamic interview drives his fellow inmates into a spontaneous riot, which in turn allows Mickey to kill his captors and take Gale hostage. He then uses the chaos of the prison riot to rescue (again) Mallory from her cell, where Scagnetti, revealing his true intentions, has been attempting to seduce her. Mickey and Mallory kill Scagnetti and use Gale, now a willing accomplice in Mickey's acts of murder, as a human shield to leave the prison grounds; the prisoners kill and dismember McClusky. Safely away from the prison and reunited, Mickey and Mallory kill Gale and then resume their lives as outlaws.

THE SCREENPLAY

The film evolved out of an original script written by a then-obscure Quentin Tarantino, now famous as writer/director of *Reservoir Dogs* (1992) and *Pulp Fiction* (1994). The script had been reviewed but rejected by many Hollywood studios by 1991, when producers Don Murphy and Jane Hamsher read the script, talked to Tarantino, and agreed to develop it as a project. Murphy and Hamsher then met with Stone. Stone, though unsatisfied with the sketchy development of the Mickey/Mallory relationship, liked parts of the script well enough to commit to the project. Along with screenwriter David Veloz, he began to rework Tarantino's script to provide more background for the serial-killing lovers. Another screenwriter, Richard Rutowski, added a more metaphysical component (the recurrent "demon" imagery and dialogue). Even with the additional writers and revisions, however, most of the finished film's highlights were present in Tarantino's script, such as the opening slaughter of the patrons of a roadside diner, the killer-couple-on-the-road central plot, and the law enforcement and tabloid journalism obsessive pursuit of Mickey and Mallory. Some of Tarantino's other scenes, such as one where Mickey acting as his own lawyer at his trial kills a witness against him, were filmed but never included in the film's theatrical release version.

THE CAST

Woody Harrelson, best known up until that point for his role as the dense but kindhearted bartender Woody on television's long-running series *Cheers* (1982–1993), was cast as Mickey, while Juliette Lewis, a young standout in the 1991 remake of Cape Fear, was cast as Mallory. In other key roles, Robert Downey Jr. was chosen for Gale, Tom Sizemore for Scagnetti, and Tommy Lee Jones for McClusky. All of the main actors (especially Jones) played their roles as over-the-top as possible in order to match the extreme, often cartoonish nature of the film itself.

According to coproducer Hamsher's behind-the-scenes account, the shooting of the film in its desert and prison locales over fifty-three days was a nerve-jangling process. Director Stone drove his actors to ever more excessive performances and made many artistic and technical decisions spontaneously on set. If the film's prison scenes seem more authentic than many, that is because the scenes were shot in Stateville Prison in Illinois, using real-life prisoners as extras under stringent security precautions. The Hollywood actors and production crew mingled with hundreds of hard-time prisoners to film a make-believe riot that, at times, seemed to be a little too realistic for the comfort of the guards and non-prisoners.

When principal photography was finished, editing the film took almost a full year. The end result is flashy, disorienting, and almost unheard of in mainstream Hollywood cinema. Stone, director of photography Robert Richardson, and editors Hank Corwin and Brian Berdan create in *NBK* a hyperkinetic and avant-garde visual style. No one camera angle is maintained for more than a few seconds, and most are much shorter. The film is a feature-length exaggeration of the destabilizing cinematic techniques Stone employed in certain scenes in *Platoon*, *Born on the Fourth of July*, and *JFK*. Different film formats (color, black and white, video, Super 8) and camera lenses, unusual lighting (particularly the use of neon green), deliberately obvious rear projection, variable film rate, jarring and nearly subliminal inserts of main characters transformed into demons and monsters—all contributed to the film's dizzying rush of nearly 3,000 separate images. Ironically enough, in light of the controversy surrounding the film's violence, several violent scenes were dropped during the editing process so that *NBK* would receive an R and not an NC-17 rating from the Motion Picture Association.

The film became a modest hit upon its release, in spite or probably because of the controversy, knocking that summer's long-running box-office champion *Forrest Gump* from the number one position the opening weekend. *Natural Born Killers* remains an interesting if flawed experimental film in Stone's canon of work.

Philip L. Simpson

SEE ALSO: *Downey, Robert, Jr.;* Forrest Gump*; Grisham, John;* JFK*;* Platoon*;* Pulp Fiction*; Stone, Oliver; Tarantino, Quentin.*

BIBLIOGRAPHY

Hamsher, Jane. *Killer Instinct.* New York: Broadway Books, 1997.

Hamsher, Jane, and John August. *"Natural Born Killers": The Strange, Wild Ride of Mickey and Mallory Knox.* New York: Signet, 1994.

Kagan, Norman. *The Cinema of Oliver Stone.* New York: Continuum, 1995.

Kunz, Don, ed. *The Films of Oliver Stone.* Lanham, MD: Scarecrow Press, 1997.

Salewicz, Chris. *Oliver Stone.* New York: Thunder's Mouth Press, 1998.

Toplin, Robert Brent, and Oliver Stone. *Oliver Stone's USA: Film, History, and Controversy.* Lawrence: University Press of Kansas, 2000.

Nava, Gregory *(1949–)*

In the mid-1980s Gregory Nava emerged as a leading Hispanic film writer and director. His third feature film, *El Norte* (1984), was highly acclaimed, earning Nava an Academy Award nomination in screenwriting—the first such nomination for a Latino. Like his later work, the subject of the movie was specifically Hispanic: the story of young peasants, a brother and sister, who emigrate from rural Guatemala to the United States. Nava's next film, *My Family* (1995), was also praised and had high per screen average revenue ($5,241). This figure is important because it brought Hollywood closer to recognizing the value of producing Hispanic-content films with real Hispanic actors.

In 1997 Nava followed up with another box-office smash hit, *Selena*, the screen biography of the Tejano music star. The film helped to launch the career of Latina singer and actress Jennifer Lopez, who portrayed the title character and earned a Golden Globe nomination for the role. The film also earned Nava his first American Latino Media Arts (ALMA) Award for Outstanding Latino Director. His second ALMA was awarded for the Frankie Lymon biopic *Why Do Fools Fall in Love?* (1998). Nava wrote the screenplay for *Frida* (2002), a depiction of the life of Mexican artist Frida Kahlo starring Salma Hayek. He also produced a PBS television series, *American Family: Journey of Dreams* (2002–2004), which illustrates the life of a fictional Latino family in Los Angeles. In 2007 Nava wrote, produced, and directed the crime film *Bordertown*, about unsolved murders in the volatile city of Juarez, Mexico.

Nava's works emphasize themes salient to contemporary Hispanic American life. His films have increased the visibility of Latino issues and have promoted positive and dynamic images of this culture. For these reasons, Nava represents an important voice in the changing composition of the American population.

Nicolás Kanellos

SEE ALSO: *Academy Awards; Lopez, Jennifer;* My Family, Mi Familia*; Public Television (PBS); Selena; Tejano Music.*

BIBLIOGRAPHY

Behar, Henri. "Gregory Nava on *Selena*." Film Scouts Interviews. Accessed May 2012. Available from http://www.filmscouts.com/scripts/interview.cfm?File=gre-nav

Tardiff, Joseph T., and L. Mpho Mabunda, eds. *Dictionary of Hispanic Biography.* Detroit, MI: Gale, 1996.

Navratilova, Martina *(1956–)*

With her unrivaled athleticism, aggressive style, and emotional intensity, Martina Navratilova transformed women's tennis into a power sport. Born and raised in Prague, Navratilova became the Czech national champion at fifteen. In 1975 the eighteen-year-old made international headlines when she defected to the United States. She quickly became one of the top players in the world. Navratilova radically changed her appearance and style of play—becoming the most physically fit and athletically aggressive woman on the tour—and began to dominate the sport.

A multiple winner of the four major tournaments, Navratilova reigned at Wimbledon, winning nine singles and seven doubles championships. She initially retired in 1994 but returned to the game briefly in 1995 and launched a full comeback in 2000. Navratilova played doubles until her final retirement in 2006. By the end of her career she had won more singles titles than any other tennis player, male or female, and was the oldest player to win a Grand Slam title, taken in 2006 when she won the U.S. Open mixed doubles match with her partner Bob Bryan, just one month shy of her fiftieth birthday. She is considered by many to be the greatest woman tennis player of all time and has remained a high-profile public figure since her retirement. Navratilova was welcomed into the International Tennis Hall of Fame in 2000.

At the peak of her success, acting on a naive belief in "American honesty," Navratilova shocked the world by coming out as a lesbian. An outspoken activist for many causes, she has capitalized on her fame in order to raise awareness for issues ranging from gay and lesbian rights to vegetarianism, democracy, and the benefits of an active lifestyle. Among her various humanitarian activities, she often speaks on LGBT (lesbian, gay, bisexual, and transgender) matters and has taken legal action to protect the rights of gays and lesbians in the United States. She has acted as a spokeswoman for AARP and was featured in promotions for animal rights group PETA (People for the Ethical Treatment of Animals).

Despite a breast cancer diagnosis in 2010, Navratilova remains active in the tennis world as a commentator and proactive in her humanitarian endeavors. For example, after she was treated for breast cancer in 2010, she set out to climb Tanzania's Mount Kilimanjaro to raise money for the Laureus Sport for Good Foundation, a nonprofit organization that seeks to fund projects that promote health and well-being through sports, and to show other cancer patients what could be done by those fighting the disease. Unfortunately, she was forced to abandon her trek due to altitude-induced pulmonary edema, from which she recovered quickly. Navratilova is involved in numerous charities and social causes, especially those that encourage fitness for the elderly, sports involvement for children, vegetarianism, and gay and lesbian rights.

Victoria Price

SEE ALSO: *AARP (American Association of Retired Persons); Cancer; Gay and Lesbian Marriage; Gay Liberation Movement; Lesbianism; Tennis; Wimbledon.*

BIBLIOGRAPHY

Blue, Adrianne. *Martina: The Life and Times of Martina Navratilova.* New York: Birch Lane Press, 1995.

Bunsch, Iris. *Three Female Myths of the 20th Century: Garbo, Callas, Navratilova.* New York: Vantage, 1991.

Navratilova, Martina, and George Vecsey. *Martina.* New York: Knopf, 1985.

Naylor, Gloria *(1950–)*

Gloria Naylor is one of the most influential African American women writers of the late twentieth and early twenty-first centuries. She came to prominence in 1982, when her book, *The Women of Brewster Place,* was published. The novel won the National Book Award for Best First Novel in 1983 and was later adapted into a miniseries for television. In his book, *Gloria Naylor: Critical Perspectives Past and Present,* African American scholar and literary critic Henry Louis Gates Jr. notes that the *The Women of Brewster Place* "boldly returns to and rejuvenates naturalism as a mode of narration and plot development."

Gifted with an innovative mind, Naylor is known in American literary circles for her relentless search for her own female voice; she pursues the search by rewriting canonical writers, such as William Shakespeare, Dante Alighieri, and Geoffrey Chaucer in novels like *Linden Hills* (1985), *Mama Day* (1988), and *Bailey's Cafe* (1992). A number of critics maintain that the two latter novels evolved from Naylor's attempts at biblical revisionism, as she seeks to express the African American voice that was left out of the original telling. Heavily criticized for the absence of strong males in *The Women of Brewster Place,* Naylor wrote *The Men of Brewster Place* (1998), a response to her first novel from a black male perspective.

With her fictionalized memoir, *1996* (2005), Naylor created considerable uproar. In it she claims that U.S. government agents have been following her since 1996. Concerned about the lack of privacy in the United States, particularly since the terrorist attacks of September 11, 2001, Naylor contends that the government is employing sophisticated technologies that allow officials to discover what people are thinking and to input words into the minds of selected individuals. Acknowledging that some people may think she is having a nervous breakdown, Naylor maintains that she is only telling her own story and cannot worry about the reactions of others.

Pierre-Damien Mvuyekure

SEE ALSO: *Feminism; 9/11.*

BIBLIOGRAPHY

Gates, Henry Louis, Jr., ed. *Gloria Naylor: Critical Perspectives Past and Present.* New York: Amistad, 1993.

Montgomery, Maxine, ed. *Conversations with Gloria Naylor.* Jackson: University Press of Mississippi, 2004.

"'1996': Under the Watchful Eye of the Government." NPR, January 23, 2006. Accessed January 21, 2012. Available from http://www.npr.org/templates/story/story.php?storyId=5168026

Naylor, Gloria. *The Women of Brewster Place.* New York: Viking Press, 1982.

Naylor, Gloria. *Mama Day.* New York: Vintage Books, 1988.

Naylor, Gloria. *The Men of Brewster Place.* New York: Hyperion, 1998.

Neckties

As an essential accessory of male business and formal wear, a sign of social connections and status, the necktie has been in general use since the 1830s. Its earliest origins, however, are to be found in the more practical neck-warming and face-protecting scarves worn by Croatian troops, dubbed *cravats* by the French in the 1630s. Adapted into voluminous swatches of lace or linen, these gained popularity with the expansion of Parisian fashion influence in the seventeenth and eighteenth centuries, and by the mid-nineteenth century, cravats had become largely ornamental.

ADDING SOME COLOR

During conservative and conventional times, such as the first two decades of the twentieth century, the 1950s, and the 1980s, neckties have often been among the few sources of color and pattern in men's wardrobes. They have allowed their wearers to express individual tastes and even whimsy, but they have also reflected contemporary cultural and regional influences. In the American South and West during the late nineteenth century, the earlier neck cloth evolved into the vestigial string or ribbon tie, while the bandanna soon diverged to serve practical ends for cowboys and other manual workers and became the Boy Scout uniform's neckerchief in the early twentieth century. Finally, the leather-thonged bola emerged in 1949 to become the emblematic male neckwear of choice in at least the traditionally minded areas of the Southwest.

After the American Civil War, throughout most of the rest of the United States, a "four-in-hand" style of knotting ever-narrowing neck scarves became the enduring standard until the 1930s, when it found competition from the Windsor knot. A fuller variation with a triangular knot, intended for wide-collar shirts, it was introduced by the Duke of Windsor and won some loyal adherents beginning in the 1930s. *Neckties*—a term accepted by the fashion industry circa 1912—came to vary in width, design, and fabric according to the vogue. Made exclusively of natural materials, primarily silk and wool, and relatively understated before the 1930s, ties then began to appear in cotton as well as the newer synthetics of rayon, acetate, polyester, and even plastic. The 1930s also witnessed wider ties that complemented the larger lapels of double-breasted jackets.

Countess Mara, one of the first exclusive designers of limited quantity neckties for men who wished to distinguish themselves from the crowd, found the market viable enough to set up her first shop in 1938. Another sign that wearing the correct necktie might bode well for one's chances of upward mobility was the preference of some twentieth-century American men for British club or regimental neckwear. The original intention of this tie was to identify the wearer as an alumnus of an exclusive educational or social establishment or a military veteran. After the rationing of the World War II years ended, a bold look characterized by "loud" neckties took hold from approximately 1945 to 1952. Neckwear was often colorful and whimsical, adorned with animals or geometric patterns or sporting motifs. They were sometimes also idiosyncratic, with artists such as Salvador Dali hand painting designs on individual ties (although silk-screening mass-produced a similar look). Novelty ties such as those whose designs glowed in the dark also burst forth in the 1940s and found cultural echoes in the fish tie motifs of the late 1980s.

The more conservative Cold War decade of the 1950s saw a regression to skinny ties with relatively little space for elaborate decorations. Lasting until the mid-1960s, ties designed to meet this trend became so minuscule that it was hardly a surprise when they literally disappeared from the majority of male necks at that decade's conclusion. They were replaced, even on formal occasions, by turtlenecks and accompanying medallions. But the counterculture's sensibilities during that era also stigmatized neckties as representations of the social conformity espoused by prep school students, establishment politicians, and businesspeople.

The subsequent Peacock Revolution in men's fashions, however, ushered neckwear back into style. The British Carnaby Street influence even popularized fleeting returns to the lace neckwear of previous centuries. By the mid-1970s, ties were again wide enough (at a regulation 5 inches compared to an average width of 2 inches at one point during the previous decade) that they could sport many of the design elements that had appeared during the 1940s.

The return to a conservative, businesslike temperament during the 1980s witnessed the advent of the entrepreneur's "power tie." This was first solid yellow, then red, and later of intricate designs from exclusive European fashion houses such as Gucci, Versace, Ferragamo, Hermès, or Sulka. Finally, the postmodern eclecticism that emerged in the 1990s saw the resurgence of several competing retro looks as young men in particular returned to the late Art Deco styles of the 1930s or to the skinny ties of the later 1950s. Tastes in clothing seemed to be dictated considerably less by the sense of the current era than by a nostalgic desire to return to a favorite decade of the past.

NO LONGER COMPULSORY

Necktie sales hit a high of $1.3 billion in 1995, but they gradually fell in the ensuing years as business-casual attire became more acceptable for many workplaces. For those men who chose to wear a tie in the first decade of the 2000s, neckties grew wider again, with a variety of colors and patterns: stripes, dots, and designs. Perhaps signaling the end to days when ties were compulsory, business attire gave men more freedom to express their own preferences.

Long neckties have also occasionally appeared on women throughout the years, especially as accessories of sporty female apparel during the 1890s and in the 1970s "Annie Hall" look, popularized by Diane Keaton in the Woody Allen film of the same name. Usually, however, women were more inclined to wear variations of a bow tie rather than a necktie. The bow tie has been an alternative for men as well, especially during the 1920s and 1930s. Although larger versions made their mark in the 1970s, John Molloy, touting fashion advice in *Dress for Success*, advised against them lest one not be taken seriously or be thought not quite honest.

Frederick J. Augustyn Jr.

SEE ALSO: *Allen, Woody;* Annie Hall; *Boy Scouts of America; The Fifties; Gucci; Retro Fashion; The Twenties; Versace, Gianni.*

BIBLIOGRAPHY

Baclawski, Karen. *The Guide to Historic Costume.* New York: Drama Book Publishers, 1995.

Chaille, François. *La grand histoire de la cravate.* Paris: Flammarion, 1994.

Eelking, Baron von. *Bilanz der Eitelkeit: Die Geschichte der Krawatte.* Frankfurt: Musterschmidt Göttingen, 1976.

Ettinger, Roseann. *Popular and Collectible Neckties, 1955 to the Present.* Atglen, PA: Schiffer Publications, 1998.

Ettinger, Roseann. *Popular and Collectible Neckties, Pre-1955.* Atglen, PA: Schiffer Publications, 2007.

Gibbings, Sarah. *The Tie: Trends and Traditions.* Hauppage, NY: Barron's, 1990.

Goldberg, Michael Jay. *The Ties That Blind: Neckties, 1945–1975.* Atglen, PA: Schiffer Publications, 1997.

Molloy, John T. *Dress for Success.* New York: Warner Books, 1976.

Negro Leagues

When Jackie Robinson and Branch Rickey brought about the integration of Major League Baseball in 1947, they sounded the death knell of the Negro Leagues. Like many players in the old Negro Leagues, Kansas City Monarchs first baseman Buck O'Neil was too old to play in the majors in 1947, and thus the demise of black baseball shortened his playing career. But no one was happier with baseball integration than O'Neil, who later recalled, "as to the demise of the Negro Leagues—it never should have been, a Negro League. Shouldn't have been." Given the history of race relations in the United States in the late nineteenth and twentieth centuries, O'Neil was sadly wrong—racial segregation in baseball probably could not have been avoided.

EARLY ALL-BLACK BASEBALL

On September 18, 1869, the Pythian Baseball Club of Philadelphia became the first recorded all-black team to play an exhibition game against an all-white team, the City Items. Although it defeated the City Items, the Pythian Club's bid for membership was rejected by the National Association of Base Ball Players, which declared itself against the admission of any clubs composed of, or even including, African Americans. But despite official and unofficial opposition to integrated play, more than fifty African Americans played alongside whites in organized baseball during the 1870s and 1880s.

The year 1887 signaled the beginning of the end for blacks in organized white baseball. First the St. Louis Browns refused to play an exhibition game against an all-black club. Then Cap Anson, the most powerful player in the game, discovered that the New York Giants were about to hire an African American ballplayer, and Anson made it clear that neither he nor any of his white teammates would ever play a team with black players. The late nineteenth century saw the passage of the Jim Crow segregation laws in the South, and at the end of the century in the landmark *Plessy v. Ferguson* case, the Supreme Court accepted the notion of separate but equal public facilities. In the face of a growing player's revolt against integrated play, the major-league owners made a gentleman's agreement to sign no more blacks. The minor leagues followed suit, and soon

Josh Gibson of the Homestead Grays. *Josh Gibson runs to first base on a ground ball during a game in Washington, D.C., in 1940.* TRANSCENDENTAL GRAPHICS/CONTRIBUTOR/GETTY IMAGES SPORT/GETTY IMAGES.

thereafter African Americans disappeared from organized white baseball.

African American baseball fans could still follow a number of independent professional teams such as the Chicago Unions, the Louisville Fall Cities, the Cuban X-Giants, the Indianapolis ABCs, and the New York Lincoln Giants. The best black baseball team at the turn of the twentieth century was the Chicago American Giants, which compiled a remarkable 123–6 record in one barnstorming season, led by pitcher-manager Andrew "Rube" Foster.

After World War I black nationalist Marcus Garvey urged African Americans to adopt self-help as their watchword, to build up their own cultural institutions and their own business enterprises. Foster heard Garvey's call, and in 1919 he began putting together the Negro National League in an effort to provide the North's new black citizens, products of the black migration from the South, with professional baseball of their own. Foster's league had eight teams, including the Kansas City Monarchs, the Detroit Stars, the Dayton Marcos, the Indianapolis ABCs, the Chicago and St. Louis Giants, the Chicago American Giants, and the barnstorming Cuban Giants. By 1923 the league was a huge success, drawing a season's total of some 400,000 fans.

White businessmen, drawn by the potential profits of black baseball, formed a rival organization, the Eastern Colored League. This league had six teams, including the Brooklyn Royal Giants, the Baltimore Black Sox, the Philadelphia Hilldales, the New York Lincoln Giants, the Atlantic City Bacharach Giants, and the barnstorming Cuban Stars. With the establishment of bifurcated black baseball, a Black World Series was played in 1924 between the Kansas City Monarchs and the Philadelphia Hilldales. Whereas Major League Baseball, led by Babe Ruth, turned toward the home run during the 1920s, the Negro Leagues kept alive the type of "scientific baseball" inspired by Ty Cobb, with an emphasis on base hits, stolen bases, defensive strategies, and guile.

SURVIVING THE DEPRESSION

The Great Depression hit black baseball even harder than the white major leagues. The white-owned Eastern Colored League collapsed in 1928, and the Negro National League went bankrupt in 1931. Black baseball relied on barnstorming to survive after 1931. The strongest of the barnstorming teams was the Homestead Grays, an all-star team owned by Cumberland "Cum" Posey. His rival Gus Greenlee, who ran the numbers racket in Pittsburgh's black neighborhoods, bought a semipro team, the Crawford Colored Giants, in 1930; renamed the team the Pittsburgh Crawfords; and began raiding Posey's roster with offers of better pay.

The Crawfords roster included James "Cool Papa" Bell, a smooth-fielding center fielder who may have been the fastest man in baseball history and later made the Hall of Fame. But the team's greatest star, and black baseball's biggest home-run hitter, was catcher Josh Gibson. Gibson hit more than seventy home runs in the final Negro National Leagues season of 1931, and his lifetime total may have approached 1,000. Major-league scouts who saw Gibson play referred to him as "the black Babe Ruth," while fans of the Negro Leagues thought that Ruth should have been called "the white Josh Gibson."

Gibson was a product of the black migration to the North. His father was a sharecropper from rural Georgia who moved to Pittsburgh to work in the steel mills. Gibson had initially trained to be an electrician, but he went into baseball when he realized that he could earn more money. Unlike Ruth and the other power hitters of the "rabbit-ball" era, Gibson had a short, compact swing at the plate, relying on his massive arms and torso for his power, making it difficult to slip a breaking pitch past him. In 1943 the Pittsburgh Pirates sought permission from the commissioner's office to sign Gibson to a contract, but Commissioner Kenesaw Mountain Landis refused. Gibson, perhaps baseball's greatest home run hitter, died a broken man.

Greenlee built a $60,000 stadium for the Crawfords, and in 1933 he took steps to revive the defunct Negro National League. The league now contained six teams, all of them under the control of his fellow racketeers—among the only members of the black community with enough capital in the midst of the Great Depression to finance a league.

The most popular star in black baseball was a tall, gangly pitcher named Leroy "Satchel" Paige. Anytime a team got into financial trouble, it would hire Paige, and the crowds would pour in. Paige was born in the rural south, just outside Mobile, Alabama. He began in the Southern Negro League, playing for the New Orleans Pelicans, the Birmingham Black Barons, the Nashville Elite Giants, and the Cleveland Cubs, always searching for the best money, a pattern he would follow in the Negro National League.

Because black baseball was played in so many places and under so many auspices, no one knows precisely how many games Paige won. But Paige once struck out Rogers Hornsby five times in a barnstorming game, and after he beat the Dizzy Dean All-Stars in 1934, Dean pronounced him the greatest pitcher he had ever seen. Paige became best known for his humorous aphorisms, such as his prescription for how to stay young: "avoid fried meats, which angry up the blood; if your stomach disputes you, lie down and pacify it with cool thoughts; keep the juices flowing by jangling around gently as you move; . . . don't look back—something might be gaining on you." Despite his sleepy appearance, Paige had a shrewd sense of how to sell himself. His showmanship kept the Negro Leagues alive during the hard times of the 1930s.

THE ROAD TO INTEGRATION

By the late 1930s there was growing pressure to integrate baseball. At the 1936 Olympics in Berlin, Jesse Owens triumphed in track and field, winning four gold medals and representing American defiance of Nazi racial theories. In 1937 Joe Louis knocked out Jim Braddock to win the heavyweight championship, leading a small number of black sportswriters to begin actively campaigning for baseball's integration. The Congress of Industrial Organizations and the Communist Party of the USA also began to advocate integration in their official publications.

But America's participation in World War II did the most to advance the cause of baseball's integration. In 1941 A. Philip Randolph, president of the Brotherhood of Sleeping Car Porters, warned that he would lead 50,000 blacks in a march on Washington if defense industries were not immediately opened to blacks as well as whites. President Franklin Roosevelt issued Executive Order 8802, making racial discrimination in federal hiring illegal. Black workers migrated in ever-greater numbers to northern cities seeking employment in the defense industries, causing a boom in attendance at Negro League games. But at the same time the hypocrisy of the United States fighting Nazi racism abroad, while "America's pastime" practiced overt racism at home, became more and more self-evident.

For twenty-five years Landis had worked ceaselessly to enforce the old gentleman's agreement against the hiring of blacks, but he died in 1944. Landis's replacement, Albert Benjamin "Happy" Chandler, was quoted as saying: "If a black boy can make it on Okinawa and Guadalcanal, hell, he can make it in baseball." Rickey, the president and general manager of the Brooklyn Dodgers, had long believed that both fair play and big profits argued in favor of integration: "The greatest untapped reservoir of raw material in the history of the game is the black race. The Negroes will make us winners for years to come, and for that I will happily bear being called a bleeding heart and a do-gooder and all that humanitarian rot." Rickey only needed the right man to break the color line.

Robinson was that man. The grandson of a slave, he was born in Cairo, Georgia, in 1919. His family moved to California, where at Pasadena Junior College and the University of California at Los Angeles, Robinson excelled at every sport. In 1944, when he left the army, Robinson joined the Kansas City Monarchs, playing shortstop for $400 per month. He hit .387 for the Monarchs his first season, and he had a tryout with the Boston Red Sox. Although Boston manager Joe Cronin was impressed with Robinson, the Red Sox passed on the opportunity to be the first team to integrate (instead they would be the last). Rickey's Dodgers announced on October 23, 1945, that Robinson had been signed to play for their AAA team in Montreal.

Just as 1887 had signaled the beginning of the end for blacks in organized white baseball, 1945 signaled the beginning of the end for the Negro Leagues. But few mourned its final official passing in 1955. After Robinson's debut with the Dodgers in 1947, at the beginning of the civil rights movement, African Americans took their rightful place in the national game, redeeming America's pastime.

In the years since, American society has gradually paid more respect to those who played in the Negro Leagues. In 2008 Hall-of-Fame player Dave Winfield organized a tribute in which Major League Baseball teams drafted thirty surviving members of the Negro Leagues. The draftees accepted the honor of finally becoming major leaguers with gratitude. In 2010 the U.S. Postal Service issued commemorative stamps honoring the Negro Leagues.

Todd Anthony Rosa

SEE ALSO: *Baseball; Boston Red Sox; The Brooklyn Dodgers; Cobb, Ty; Garvey, Marcus; The Great Depression; Louis, Joe; Major League Baseball; Olympics; Owens, Jesse; Paige, Satchel; Robinson, Jackie; Ruth, Babe; Sports Heroes.*

BIBLIOGRAPHY

Holway, John B. *Black Diamonds: Life in the Negro Leagues*

from the Men Who Lived It. New York: Stadium Books, 1991.

O'Neil, Buck; Steve Wulf; and David Conrads. *I Was Right on Time.* New York: Simon & Schuster, 1996.

Peterson, Robert. *Only the Ball Was White: A History of Legendary Black Players and All-Black Professional Teams.* New York: Oxford University Press, 1992.

Ribowsky, Mark. *A Complete History of the Negro Leagues, 1884 to 1955.* Secaucus, NJ: Carol Publishing Group, 1995.

Rogosin, Donn. *Invisible Men: Life in Baseball's Negro Leagues.* New York: Kodansha International, 1995.

Withers, Ernest C. *Negro League Baseball.* New York: Harry N. Abrams, 2005.

Neighborhood Watch

Neighborhood watch programs began as a citizen-based response to a rise in crime during the late 1960s. By 1972 they had won approval from the National Sheriffs' Association as an important crime-prevention method. Thousands of these organized community groups exist throughout the United States, working in conjunction with local police stations to help report suspicious behavior in neighborhoods. Perhaps best known for suburban street signs that depict a sinister-looking thief and the word *WARNING* in capital letters, neighborhood watch represents a long-held faith in local neighborhoods as the cradle of community and safety among middle-class Americans.

The trend toward community policing that began in the 1990s lent new urgency to the establishment of neighborhood watch groups. They have been particularly successful in assisting police departments in dealing with the upsurge of street gang activity that is besieging the United States. In 2009 the U.S. Department of Justice stated in the National Gang Threat Assessment report that there were approximately one million gang members operating throughout the United States. Neighborhood watch groups also work closely with law enforcement to maintain neighborhoods and provide opportunities for local young people that help steer them away from gang activity.

Kevin Mattson

SEE ALSO: *Gangs.*

BIBLIOGRAPHY

Bennett, Trevor. *Evaluating Neighbourhood Watch.* Aldershot, UK: Gower, 1990.

Mann, Stephanie, and M. C. Blakeman. *Safe Homes, Safe Neighborhoods.* Berkeley, CA: Nolo Press, 1993.

Sklansky, David Alan. *New Perspectives in Policing.* Cambridge, MA: Harvard Kennedy School of Government, 2011.

Nelson, Ricky *(1940–1985)*

Decades before MTV, the synergy between television and the music industry was manifested by the career of Ricky Nelson. The first rock-and-roll star created by television, Nelson was the youngest and most precocious member of the Nelsons on the long-running *The Adventures of Ozzie and Harriet.* For fourteen years Ricky virtually grew up in front of American television audiences. To viewers coast to coast, he was a surrogate son, brother, and friend. When he began to sing, he became a fantasy boyfriend and one of the leading teen idols of the 1950s and early 1960s. If being a member of "America's favorite family" had made his music career possible, however, it also became a burden—as did the teen idol designation. As a result, Nelson's artistry and status as a musical innovator has long been overlooked.

In fact, Nelson was startlingly versatile, equally at home with rock and roll, rockabilly, rhythm and blues, ballads, and country-and-western music. A devotee of the breakthrough sounds that emanated from Sam Phillips's Sun Records, he aggressively sought to collaborate with the era's most creative talents. Early on, he worked with rockabilly greats Johnny and Dorsey Burnette and with legendary guitarist James Burton. Later, Nelson assembled the Stone Canyon Band; their country rock helped pave the way for what came to be known as the California sound. Not coincidentally, Stone Canyon member Randy Meisner went on to found the group that perfected that sound—the Eagles.

THE NELSON FAMILY

Born Eric Hilliard Nelson, he grew up in a musical family. His father, Ozzie, was a former bandleader; his mother, Harriet Hilliard Nelson, had been the band's singer. During the 1940s their married life became the impetus for the radio show *The Adventures of Ozzie and Harriet.* Ricky Nelson was just nine when he and his older brother, David, joined the cast, playing themselves. They moved onto the big screen with the 1952 movie *Here Come the Nelsons.* It inspired the television series, which debuted on ABC on October 3, 1952.

As depicted by the Nelsons, Dwight Eisenhower–era family life was one of quiet complacency. Ozzie had no discernible job, Harriet was usually in the kitchen, and the boys' most frequent line of dialogue was "Hi, Pop. Hi, Mom." As a youngster, Nelson was known for his bristly crew cut, wisecracks, and panache with punch lines. As a teenager, he became known for his good looks, including heavy-lidded blue eyes and pouty mouth.

RECORDING CAREER

Ozzie helped arrange the session that resulted in Nelson's first record, a rendition of Fats Domino's "I'm Walkin'." Nelson performed the song in an April 1957 *Ozzie and Harriet* episode titled "Ricky the Drummer." Released one week later on Verve Records, it made it to the Top 10 and sold a million copies. Ozzie liked to point out that *Ozzie and Harriet* helped make rock and roll respectable. He also recognized the potential of a television-music tie-in. At the time, the series was being watched by an estimated ten million teenagers a week; Nelson's performances became powerful marketing tools—as did the young star, who became a favorite of teenage fan magazines.

Under contract by Imperial Records, Nelson also became a consistent chart topper. During a five-year period he had thirty-six songs on the charts, with many of them in the Top 10—among his most recognizable tunes were "Poor Little Fool," "Lonesome Town," "It's Late," "Teenage Idol," "Hello Mary Lou," and "Travelin' Man." "Hello Mary Lou," his biggest hit, sold more than seven million copies. As presented on *Ozzie and Harriet,* the song also predated the music videos of the MTV era. Conceived by Ozzie, it was performed in a segment in which the singing Nelson was superimposed over travelogue footage. As he grew older, he understandably attempted to discard his teen idol image, dropping the "y" from his name to become Rick Nelson and appearing in nonmusical movies, such as the Howard Hawks–directed *Rio Bravo* (1959). He also became less interested in the family series.

A NEW BEGINNING

When the series ended in 1966, Nelson attempted new musical directions. Exploring the Nashville sound, he cut a pair of critically lauded albums. In 1969 his interest in literary-oriented artists such as Bob Dylan and Tim Hardin, as well as the country-folk movement of Los Angeles, led to his formation of the Stone Canyon Band, with whom he delivered an evocative version of Dylan's "She Belongs to Me."

But Nelson could not shake his past. At a 1971 Madison Square Garden revival concert, his changed look—including long hair—caught the audience off guard. When he moved from vintage tunes to newer ones, the crowd erupted in boos. A visibly shaken Nelson later wrote and recorded "Garden Party," in which he declared that he would rather drive a truck than perpetually sing his old songs. Nelson's final Top 10 hit, ironically, revived interest in his teen idol past.

LAST PERFORMANCE

The consummate performer eventually returned to singing golden oldies, and by 1983 he was again being booked as "Ricky Nelson." His final performance took place at P.J.'s Alley, a small, dark bar in Guntersville, Alabama, on December 30, 1985. Nelson was killed the next day in a plane crash while traveling to a New Year's Eve show. The death of America's favorite television son made front-page headlines.

The Nelson name has continued, however, as a third generation of Nelsons joined show business. During his marriage to Kris Harmon, daughter of football star Tom Harmon, Nelson fathered four children. Daughter Tracy Nelson is an actress. Twin sons Matthew and Gunnar, billed as the singing duo Nelson, enjoyed a number one hit in 1990. Meanwhile, Nelson's life, including his television and singing personas, remained a source of fascination for die-hard fans even after his untimely death. He was the subject of many books and tributes, with some portraying the perfect son from the perfect family as less than perfect. Since his death, friends and relatives have come forward to admit that there were numerous discrepancies between the television and real-life Nelsons. In truth, they were just as dysfunctional as most families. Far from being perfect, Nelson was just as human as anyone else.

Pat H. Broeske

SEE ALSO: The Adventures of Ozzie and Harriet*; Domino, Fats; Hawks, Howard; MTV; Rhythm and Blues; Rock and Roll; Sun Records; Television.*

BIBLIOGRAPHY

Bashe, Philip. *Teenage Idol, Travelin' Man: The Complete Biography of Rick Nelson.* New York: Hyperion, 1992.

Davidson, Sara. "The Happy, Happy, Happy Nelsons." *Esquire*, June 1971, 97–101, 157–168.

Flythe, Starkey, Jr. "Eric Hilliard Nelson (Alias Ricky) Celebrates Twenty-Five Years in Show Business." *Saturday Evening Post*, April 1976, 52–53, 87–88.

Harrington, Richard. "The Boy Next Door." *Washington Post*, January 2, 1986, B1–B2.

Selvin, Joel. *Ricky Nelson: Idol for a Generation.* Chicago: Contemporary Books, 1990.

Sumrall, Harry. *Pioneers of Rock and Roll: 100 Artists Who Changed the Face of Rock.* New York: Billboard Books, 1994.

Nelson, Willie *(1933–)*

Singer, songwriter, and guitarist Willie Nelson is a legendary name in U.S. country music and a popular promoter of the more eclectic Texas sound that draws liberally on rock, blues, and folk motifs. In the early 1970s he helped lead the revolt against the domination of orthodox country music that was taking place in Nashville, Tennessee. In a career that began in the 1950s, Nelson recorded more than 100 albums and many hit singles in numerous genres and styles, making him a significant crossover artist. He has also starred in several movies and is

Willie Nelson. *After over sixty years in the music business, Willie Nelson continues to perform and record.* GARY MILLER/CONTRIBUTOR/FILMMAGIC/GETTY IMAGES.

known as the founder of Farm Aid, an annual outdoor music festival to benefit struggling farm owners.

EARLY LIFE

Nelson was born on April 30, 1933, in Abbott, Texas, a small farming community near Waco. His parents had recently moved there from Arkansas in search of work. The Nelsons were poor migrant farmers, and the youngster spent much of his childhood picking cotton alongside sharecroppers during the Great Depression. His parents grew weary of their meager existence and left Nelson and his sister Bobbi to be raised by their grandparents, who surrounded the children with music. When Nelson was six, his grandfather bought him his first guitar. By the time he was in high school he was playing in a band alongside his sister.

Nelson's early musical hero was Bob Wills, whose western swing was sweeping the Southwest in the 1940s. Elements of Wills and his Texas Playboys' upbeat dance music found their way into Nelson's music. After a short and unsuccessful attempt at college and a brief stint in the military during the Korean War, he traveled throughout the western United States looking for work in the music business.

While Nelson had always planned to become a performer, his entry into the industry came through his songwriting talents. He had begun writing songs, both lyrics and melodies, as a child, and in the early 1950s he sold his first song, "Family Bible," which became a hit when Pappy Daily recorded it. The song's success brought Nelson to Nashville, where fellow Texan Ray Price hired him to write for Pamper Music. Nelson began to churn out a series of hits for several singers. In 1961 his song "Crazy," recorded by Patsy Cline, reached number one on the country charts and helped vault Cline into the national spotlight. Other successes followed, including Ralph Emery's recording of "Hello Fool" and Faron Young's renditions of "Hello Walls" and "Three Days."

Nelson's successful songwriting led to a recording contract with Liberty Records. His first album produced one hit, "Touch Me," but his own recordings were not as well received as those performed by other artists. In the mid-1960s he started appearing on the Grand Ole Opry regularly. He signed a contract with Victor and recorded hits "The Party's Over" and "Little Things" and wrote "Night Life," a successful song recorded by Price.

BREAKING WITH NASHVILLE

By the late 1960s Nelson was an established figure in Nashville, but his career seemed to be stagnating. On a fateful day in 1971 his Nashville house burned down. He saw the disaster as an omen to head back to Texas. Over the past few years he had begun to associate with new writers and performers, including Kris Kristofferson, Billy Joe Shaver, and Waylon Jennings, who were outside the country music establishment. Back in Texas, Nelson started cultivating a new style of country that borrowed from these outsiders and played upon the image of outlaws in the industry—a harsh, edgy style more reminiscent of the honky-tonk music of Bakersfield, California, singers such as Merle Haggard.

In 1972 Nelson organized an outdoor music festival in Dripping Springs, Texas, just outside Austin, where he promoted new artists—Kristofferson, Jennings, and Tom T. Hall—along with established Nashville figures such as Tex Ritter and Roy Acuff. The festival, which became an annual event, drew on Austin's substantial counterculture and became legendary for its combination of country, rock, and folk music, also combined with drugs and alcohol. Nelson and others used the festivals to promote their outlaw image, with long hair, shaggy beards, and a rough edge that appealed to rock enthusiasts as much as to country music fans.

While most country artists who had crossover success did so in either pop or gospel, Nelson's 1975 album *Red-Headed Stranger* performed well on the rock charts. The following year Nelson and others of the outlaw group recorded *Wanted: The Outlaws!* which stressed their departure from the Nashville sound. Several songs from this album became hits, including Jennings's "Suspicious Minds" and Nelson's "Good-Hearted Woman." The album went platinum, an unprecedented feat for a country record.

Meanwhile, Nelson's albums *Shotgun Willie* (1973) and *Phases and Stages* (1974), recorded on the Atlantic label, met with great success, and his ballad "Blue Eyes Crying in the Rain" (1975) was a hit on the pop and country charts. In the late 1970s he recorded an album of pop songs, *Stardust*, that spent years on the country charts, blurring the lines between musical genres even more.

Nelson's recording success allowed him to launch yet another career, that of a motion picture star. Throughout the 1970s and 1980s he starred in several films, including *The Electric Horseman* (1979), *Honeysuckle Rose* (1980), *Barbarosa* (1982), and *Red-Headed Stranger* (1987). He also began recording with other stars in a wide variety of musical genres, including Bob Dylan, Ray Charles, Neil Young, and Julio Iglesias. Yet at the same time Nelson never forgot his roots. He continued to record with county music legends such as Faron Young and Webb Pierce, and he produced several albums that herald back to Wills's western swing. As one of the Highwaymen (the others were Jennings, Kristofferson, and Johnny Cash), Nelson released two more albums that reinforced the outlaw image.

EXPANDED INFLUENCE

In the mid-1980s Nelson revived the spirit of his outdoor festivals to help generate financial support for struggling U.S. farmers. These Farm Aid gatherings, which attract scores of musicians and thousands of fans, continued to be a regular part of Nelson's work, along with his busy recording and touring schedule. In 2011 he was inducted into the National Agriculture Hall of Fame for his efforts.

Nelson overcame highly publicized legal problems, including a huge debt to the Internal Revenue Service and a drug possession arrest, to continue his pursuit of music. His album *Spirit* (1996), recorded by Island Records, features veteran performers such as Texas Playboys' fiddler Johnny Gimble. The recording offers tunes drawn from pop, rock, swing, and gospel.

For more than five decades Nelson's eclecticism made him a country-music sensation. Teaming up with country icon Emmylou Harris, he recorded the critically acclaimed *Teatro* in an old movie theater, and he continued to perform with various artists, including Toby Keith, Phish, and Ray Charles.

Nelson eventually settled into an elder statesman role, and his status as an icon landed him television spots on *The Simpsons* and *The Colbert Report*. He reflected on his life in several autobiographical books, and in 2010 Graeme Thomson examined his life in *Willie Nelson: The Outlaw*. Nelson also became involved in many social causes, supporting Habitats for

Horses, the biodiesel movement, and the legalization of marijuana. Known for his iconic braids as much as his music, he had them cut in 2010. Nelson was inducted into the Country Music Hall of Fame in 1993.

Jeffrey W. Coker

SEE ALSO: *Blues; Cash, Johnny; Charles, Ray; Cline, Patsy; Country Music; Dylan, Bob; Farm Aid; Folk Music; Gospel Music;* Grand Ole Opry; *The Great Depression; Haggard, Merle; Jennings, Waylon; Pop Music; Rock and Roll;* The Simpsons; *Wills, Bob, and His Texas Playboys; Young, Neil.*

BIBLIOGRAPHY

Byworth, Tony. *The History of Country & Western Music.* New York: Bison Books, 1984.

Carr, Patrick, ed. *The Illustrated History of Country Music.* Garden City, NY: Doubleday, 1979.

Malone, Bill C. *Country Music U.S.A.*, rev. ed. Austin: University of Texas Press, 1985.

Nelson, Willie; Bud Shrake; and Edwin Shrake. *Willie: An Autobiography.* New York: Simon & Schuster, 1988.

Nelson, Willie. *The Facts of Life and Other Dirty Jokes.* New York: Random House, 2002.

Thomson, Graeme. *Willie Nelson: The Outlaw.* London: Virgin Books, 2007.

Nerd Look

The nerd, a distillation of awkward male characteristics of the 1950s, was a social victim and outcast, although usually brainy. In 1985 *Life* magazine listed nerd traits as including adhesive-tape repaired glasses, high-waisted and high-water (that is, too short) geezer pants, a goofy smile, and a nerdpak (a plastic pocket protector with pencils, pens, slide rule or calculator, etc.). Well equipped but vulnerable, the nerd manifested physical awkwardness and adolescence. The hapless figure is famously portrayed by Jerry Lewis in *The Patsy* (1964). By the 1980s the nerd had turned into an unlikely hero. The movie *Revenge of the Nerds* (1984) and its sequels and the Broadway play *The Nerd* (1987), as well as many Woody Allen films, valorized the nerd. His image ranged from the hero in Italian menswear magazines to the assumed persona of Steve Urkel on the long-running television show *Family Matters* (1989–1998). The nerd's triumph is an endearing brain-over-brawn, tortoise-over-hare victory.

As the computer continued to gain prominence in the twenty-first century, the popularity of the nerd exploded. Popular nerd icons included computer entrepreneurs Bill Gates of Microsoft and Steve Jobs of Apple. Popular culture conventions such as Comic Con—for comic-book fans—drew celebrity nerds from all over the world, including New Zealand director Peter Jackson, who is known as the Lord of the Nerds in homage to his successful Lord of the Rings movie trilogy. Nerds also blossomed on television in shows such as *Lost* (2004–2010) and *The Office* (2005–).

Nerd watchers have proclaimed that it has never been so cool to be a nerd as it is in the twenty-first century. Celebrities such as world-renowned singer Josh Groban agree. Groban regularly appeared on camera sporting the nerd look, which he says is similar to the way he looked during the 1990s when the nerd look began to grow steadily more popular. Female nerds, sometimes referred to as nerdettes, have also entered the scene. In 2000, San Jose, California, began holding an annual Sexiest Geek Alive contest in parody of *People* magazine's Sexiest Man Alive annual issue. In the first year, approximately 10,000 males and females entered the contest.

Richard Martin

SEE ALSO: *Allen, Woody; Broadway; Comic Books;* Family Matters; *Lewis, Jerry;* People; *Sitcom; Television.*

BIBLIOGRAPHY

Aspinwall, Cary. "Revenge of the Nerds." *Tulsa World*, August 26, 2007.

Bennett, Jennifer, and Jennie Yarbroff. "Revenge of the Nerdette." *Newsweek*, June 16, 2008.

Bowles, Scott. "Peter Jackson Is Back to Basics on Low-Budget 'District 9.'" *USA Today*, August 5, 2009.

Martin, Richard, and Harold Koda. *Jocks and Nerds: Men's Style in the Twentieth Century.* New York: Rizzoli, 1989.

Netbooks

Netbooks, which entered the personal computer market late in the first decade of the 2000s, are the smaller, sleeker cousin of the laptop. As indicated by its name, the netbook is primarily (though not solely) intended for working and playing on the Internet and can connect online through a variety of wired and wireless methods. It typically offers a smaller hard drive, less powerful processor, and fewer ports for peripheral devices than traditional laptops. It also encourages users to save disk space by using a number of web-based cloud applications, which allow a network to run processes rather than the individual computer. Netbooks are also smaller in size, featuring screens ranging from 7 to 12 inches diagonally, making them significantly more portable than laptops. The netbook's relative lack of factory-installed hardware and software makes it far less expensive to produce than an add-on-laden laptop and, as a result, significantly cheaper for consumers.

While the origins of the netbook are up for debate (slimmed-down laptops known as notebooks have been available since the 1990s), most point to the One Laptop per Child (OLPC) initiative as the catalyst for its emergence as a viable consumer product. OLPC is a nonprofit organization that set out in 2005 to create a durable, $100 laptop for use by students in developing nations. It introduced a working prototype, the XO-1, in early 2006. Seeing the commercial possibilities for inexpensive, highly portable computers, Taiwanese manufacturer Asus introduced its Eee line of netbooks in 2007, and other manufacturers such as Dell, Hewlett-Packard, Lenovo, and Acer followed. Hardware companies such as Intel began producing smaller, less expensive processors, and software giant Microsoft retooled its Windows XP operating system for use on a wide range of netbooks (though that was later replaced by Windows 7). By 2009 netbooks accounted for almost 12 percent of the portable computer market, with 7.5 million devices sold in the United States alone.

With the rise of tablet computers such as Apple's extremely popular iPad, netbooks began to lose ground in the portable computer market. By mid-2011 tablets were outselling netbooks around the world, and netbook sales had stalled or significantly declined in most countries save for developing regions such as South America, leading many experts to declare the technology dead. The vastly less expensive netbooks, however, remain a popular option for educators seeking to introduce their students to twenty-first-century productivity tools.

Jacob Schmitt

SEE ALSO: *Apple Computer; The Internet; iPad; Laptops; Microsoft.*

BIBLIOGRAPHY

Case, Loyd. "Are Netbooks Dead? The Prognosis is Grim." *PCWorld.com*, February 21, 2012.

Lohr, Steve. "From Rising Star to Wallflower, the Netbook Tells a Tale." *New York Times*, February 14, 2011, B1.

Nicolaisen, Nancy. *Getting StartED with Netbooks*. New York: Friends of ED, 2009.

Netflix

Founded in 1997 by Reed Hastings and Marc Randolph and headquartered in Los Gatos, California, Netflix is a movie rental service that has a subscriber base located in the United States as well as Canada, Latin America, the Caribbean, the United Kingdom, and Ireland. Based on the simple premise that movie viewers do not always have time to drive to a video store to rent a movie, Netflix delivers DVDs by mail and streams movies and television shows to homes over the Internet. In 2011 the company split its mail delivery and online streaming functions into two separate plans.

Netflix offers subscribers to its mail service unlimited use of a DVD with no time limits and without the fear of late charges. Individual subscribers can keep the DVD for as long as they wish and return it for a new selection from their queue when they are ready. Other options allow multiple DVDs at a time for higher subscription fees. Netflix does not charge postage for returning the movie in the provided prepaid lightweight return envelope.

The other monthly subscription option, streaming, allows subscribers to use computers, dedicated streaming devices (such as Roku), and game systems like the Nintendo Wii and Sony PlayStation to view available content. In recent years, the company has also made applications for streaming movies and shows available for devices such as the Apple iPad and even smartphones. Heavy users also have the option of using both the streaming and delivery options, at a combined subscription rate. Both services offer a wider selection of movies and shows than a traditional video store, including not only recent releases but also classic movies, foreign and independent films, and classic and new television shows. As a result, many people credit Netflix with putting major video rental chains such as Blockbuster out of business.

Another advantage that Netflix offers subscribers is the option to place a popular film in their queue weeks before its release on DVD. The company's queue system allows subscribers to maintain a list of choices in their chosen priority and know that they can receive a film when the movie becomes available. If a Netflix subscriber's movie is on a waiting cycle, the queue will notify the customer so that the customer may adjust his or her selections accordingly. By using the queue, Netflix allows subscribers to adjust their choices to suit their mood or to account for delays due to a long wait.

Netflix. *Netflix CEO Reed Hastings sits in a cart full of ready-to-be-shipped DVDs at the company's DVD distribution center in San Jose, California, in 2002.* JUSTIN SULLIVAN/GETTY IMAGES.

When Netflix joined the marketplace, the company represented an innovative, twenty-first-century model for business that capitalized on the Internet's ability to eliminate the need for brick-and-mortar storefronts. Using only warehouse shipping centers with no physical showroom, Netflix was able to significantly cut the overhead costs associated with the video rental industry. Its Internet-only philosophy also means that new offerings are made available to a wider group of viewers more quickly, which makes the process appealing to production companies such as Weinstein Company, Fox, DreamWorks, and Sony, which have agreements with Netflix that allow the company not only to acquire the movies first but also to keep greater numbers in stock.

One of Netflix's newest innovations made possible by its low overhead costs is the production of original series available to subscribers through streaming. On February 6, 2012, *Lily Hammer*, an eight-episode series starring Steven Van Zandt, was unveiled for streaming customers to positive reviews. The company has announced plans for other shows, including a series, produced by David Fincher and Kevin Spacey, titled *House of Cards*; the horror series *Hemlock Grove*; and a comedy series *Orange Is the New Black*, based on Piper Kerman's memoir detailing her year in a women's prison. Netflix has also entered into discussions with producers of popular but discontinued television shows such as *Arrested Development* about the possibility of producing Web-only episodes or movies based on the original series, much to the delight of fans who feel slighted by major television networks' decisions to cancel their favorite shows. As more viewers gravitated to watching television on digital platforms, Netflix became a major component for smaller networks, such as the CW, which were struggling to compete in traditional formats.

For all the success Netflix has had (the company boasts 24.4 million subscribers in the United States alone), the company has still met with opposition from its subscribers from time to time. During July 2011, for example, Netflix increased the pricing of its movie plans and in September 2011 announced a plan to separate its streaming and DVD movie rental services and to rename the DVD service Qwikster. Subscribers did not approve of the plan and voiced their concerns on various Internet message boards and social networks, which led to the abandonment of the plan and some embarrassment for the company. Though it occasionally runs afoul of customers' confidence, Netflix has a proven business model that has eliminated much of its competition and has encouraged many start-ups to pursue a similar strategy.

Linda Martindale

SEE ALSO: Arrested Development*; Hulu; The Internet; Video Games; Videos.*

BIBLIOGRAPHY

Elgohary, Wagih R. *Netflix: Striving for Customer Satisfaction.* Monterey, CA: Elgohary House, 2011.

Lüsted, Marcia A. *Netflix: The Company and Its Founders.* Edina, MN: ABDO, 2013.

Network

The black comedy film *Network* (1977) explores a brief period of populist indignation presided over by President Jimmy Carter during which distrust of big government and multinational corporations pervaded America's post-Watergate consciousness. A crazed television talk show commentator's weekly battle cry that he's "mad as hell and not going to take it anymore" captured a crisis of public confidence in American business and political leaders that was fueled by economic recession, Arab oil cartel price fixing, and poor health and safety standards in industry.

Written by television industry veteran Paddy Chayefsky and directed by socially conscious filmmaker Sidney Lumet, the film also indicts the television news business as a profit-driven enterprise that compromised the public interest by sacrificing prestige-driven, hard news reporting for ratings-driven, lurid tabloid sensationalism. Far ahead of their time, the creators of *Network* anticipated the negative impact television's role as an entertainment medium had on the quality of news reporting and public discourse in an age of "reality" television and "personality-driven" political salesmanship.

The parallel themes of how corporate profiteering can subvert the public service potential of a powerful mass communication technology and how a gullible public can be seduced by pseudo-populist personalities were also explored in earlier Hollywood offerings such as *Meet John Doe* (1941) and *A Face in the Crowd* (1957). Both films are cautionary tales about the mass media's co-optation by power-hungry corporate magnates and about the American public's willingness to vest faith in barefoot political messiahs (a Will Rogers–inspired radio personality in the former, a guitar-strumming folk musician in the latter). However, both films' endings also suggest that the mass media's political integrity remained intact and that the American public was capable of distinguishing a celebrity from a hero.

Anticipating the rise of a 200-channel cable universe as the public's window to the world, *Network* jettisons from its outset any residual faith in television news's integrity and the people's ability to distinguish between reality and televisual fiction. Veteran television news anchorman Howard Beale (Peter Finch) appears on-camera drunk during his final six o'clock newscast after being told he had been fired for poor ratings. After denouncing the state of the world as "bullshit" while bordering on a nervous breakdown, the aging journalist's overnight ratings soared. The following week, the new chairman of the network (Robert Duvall) transfers control over its news programming from an Edward R. Murrow–inspired network news executive (William Holden) to a baby boomer entertainment executive raised on television (Faye Dunaway).

The latter performs a makeover of the newscast, transforming it into a three-ring circus featuring Sybil the Soothsayer, the gossip Mata Hari "and her skeletons in the closet," and a "Vox Populi" segment starring the "mad prophet of the airwaves" himself, Howard Beale. As *The Howard Beale Show* takes off in overnight ratings, the network follows it up with *The Mao Tse-Tung Hour*, during which it broadcasts home movies of a communist "revolutionary" group's (modeled on the Symbionese Liberation Army) weekly bank robberies and kidnappings. A particularly hilarious send-up of television network deal making occurs when the Afro-coiffed leader of the group warns network lawyers during negotiations not to "fuck with my distribution costs."

Ironically, the weekly mantra of *The Howard Beale Show* (announcer cue: "How do you feel?" Audience: "We're mad as hell!") became a real-life bumper sticker slogan in 1978 for supporters of Jimmy Carter's successor, California Governor Ronald Reagan. In many ways Reagan's election to the presidency proved a watershed in television's evolution as an entertainment medium. His deregulation of the television industry hastened the rise of ratings-driven news and talk show programming. A former film and television actor, Reagan also successfully sold himself as a "little guy" railing against the system while drawing support from wealthy, politically powerful Southern California business leaders.

Chris Jordan

SEE ALSO: *Baby Boomers; Chayefsky, Paddy; Duvall, Robert; Holden, William; Murrow, Edward R.; Reagan, Ronald; Reality Television; Television.*

Networks

Communications media networks were born with the 1926 radio sign-on of the National Broadcasting Company (NBC), signaling the dawn of a new era of both communications and culture in the United States. The network concept is purely abstract: in its practical form, it is nothing but a series of wires or satellite connections. Yet the history and influence of the broadcast networks became one of the great stories of the twentieth century. Even though they did not create twentieth-century culture, the networks did cement the process of homogenizing the U.S. culture of the period. By 1930, for the first time in history, people were whistling to the same tunes, laughing at the same comedians, and hearing the same politicians' speeches.

Such phenomena happened almost instantaneously. The tastes and judgments of a relatively few urban, northeastern network executives set national standards for everything from dialect and language to fashion and behavior. Only by the end of the twentieth century, when the influence of the old-line networks had faded to a large degree, was it truly possible to grasp the power that they had held over the nation for so long. Though the number of networks grew exponentially over the decades, with the technology of their distribution methods improving by light-years, the concept remained the same. A

First NBC Radio Broadcast. *Chief engineer O. B. Henson, standing, gives the signal to put the first NBC radio show on the air on November 15, 1926.* NBC/NBCU PHOTO BANK/GETTY IMAGES.

network continues to be simply a set of affiliate stations that receive programming from one central source and then beam that programming either by broadcast wave or cable wire to devices that allow them to reach the eyes and ears of a waiting public.

NBC AND CBS

The first major radio network, the National Broadcasting Company, debuted in November 1926 with a glittering, distinctly highbrow, multicity broadcast. Parent company RCA announced that the new network would "provide the best program available for broadcasting in the United States." Although General David Sarnoff is sometimes wrongly identified as the founder of both RCA and NBC, he negotiated RCA's foundational agreement with AT&T in 1926 and it was his vision and marketing savvy that paved the way for NBC's growth. In those early days network broadcasting wore the cloak of dignity. Announcers appeared in evening wear, and there were no commercials. The practice of using only indirect advertising shrouded the for-profit intentions of network executives. A rousing success, NBC was soon running two separate chains, the Red network and the Blue network. Each beamed its own programs to its own set of affiliate stations, though the networks sometimes combined efforts to carry an important speech or news event. Meanwhile, the indirect advertising rule quickly gave way to the common commercial announcement.

By late 1927 NBC was faced with competition. William S. Paley was the restless but ambitious twenty-seven-year-old heir to his family's cigar fortune. Having already seen radio's potential as a medium for advertising cigars, he jumped at the chance to enter the exciting new business of broadcasting. He bought out the struggling Columbia Broadcasting System (CBS; previously known as the United Independent Broadcasters chain, then the Columbia Phonograph Broadcasting System when that company invested heavily). After signing up affiliates, CBS was ready to offer real, albeit impoverished, competition to NBC.

The first genuine fad of the network age hit in 1929, when a pair of Chicago radio performers came to the NBC airwaves in a fifteen-minute nightly comedy serial called *Amos 'n' Andy*. The series, which portrayed African Americans in stereotypical roles, had been a smash in Chicago and in syndication, but it took national exposure on the NBC network to propel the series' popularity into the stratosphere. Stores and theaters piped in the broadcast to keep customers from fleeing homeward at the appointed hour. The broadcast could be heard while walking down any street on a warm night. Many people could do their own imitations of such *Amos 'n' Andy* catchphrases as "I'se regusted" and "Ooh Wah! Ooh Wah!" Both local and national leaders debated whether the program was harmless comedy or racial bigotry. That such scenes were playing themselves out simultaneously in every city, village, and hamlet across the land was the first real testament to the power of the broadcast network as a new cultural force.

The Mutual Broadcasting System came next, formed in 1934 as a loosely organized co-op of major independent stations such as WGN in Chicago and WOR in New York. Though it eventually found itself with the most affiliates of any of the networks, Mutual never really competed with NBC or CBS in terms of ratings or budget. Attempts at launching new national chains such as comedian Ed Wynn's Amalgamated network in 1933 were notorious failures. Smaller regional networks such as Intercity on the East Coast and Don Lee on the West Coast, however, did operate with limited success.

GROWING IMPACT

By 1930 the old notion of radio as a purely local force was gone forever. Network programming soon stretched from morning until midnight, and the networks assumed ironclad contractual control over much of their affiliates' airtime. This practice guaranteed maximum clearance for advertisers' commercials while coincidentally ensuring that people shared a common experience each time they sat before their radios. When vaudevillians such as Jack Benny and Eddie Cantor debuted on the networks in the early 1930s, they found themselves playing to a bigger audience in a single half hour than they would have faced in a lifetime of stage work. Likewise, listeners in Idaho or Alabama who would never have been able to see Benny or Cantor perform live soon took for granted their appearing for free in their homes each week. When President Franklin Roosevelt took to the network air upon his inauguration in 1933, his efforts at calming a Great Depression–panicked populace succeeded in large measure because his words were heard instantaneously by millions of people.

The Big Three networks continued to thrive, settling into the routines and traditions that exist into the twenty-first century. The broadcast schedule consisted of news in the morning; soaps and talk shows in the daytime; more news in the evening; then big-time, big-budget entertainment at night. The September to May broadcast season became a tradition. Tired shows fell by the wayside; new favorites quickly took their places. Another wave of popular entertainers and programs that included *Fibber McGee and Molly*, Bob Hope, Red Skelton, and Edgar Bergen took hold in the late 1930s. It was an incident that occurred on the night of October 30, 1938, however, that provided the clearest demonstration yet of the power of broadcast networks over the people.

While it was actually a dramatization, it was later estimated that more than one million panicked U.S. citizens believed an alien attack was imminent when Orson Welles and his *Mercury Theatre on the Air* presented a modern-day version of H. G. Wells's *The War of the Worlds*. The dramatization had been made more realistic by a series of staged news bulletins. Throughout the country people ran for their lives. Police and radio station switchboards were flooded with frantic calls. *War of the Worlds* was a sensation, and the panic became front-page news. Ironically, it was the recent coverage of the European war crisis by CBS that had conditioned the radio audience to respond when somebody said, "We interrupt this program." By the time the Japanese attacked Pearl Harbor in December 1941, radio's real-time news capability had become commonplace.

NATION AT WAR

Radio networks had a great effect on the wartime psyche of the United States. Entertainment programs never doubted the righteousness of the country's cause or the skill of its leaders. Indeed, wartime events served as a creative jump-start for many series. Meanwhile, the broadcast journalism of the period successfully walked a fine line between patriotism and jingoism. People heard scant criticism of war aims or military leadership; however, in terms of simple reporting of facts, the networks' news departments were in top form, managed by dedicated professionals who vowed to treat their audience equally seriously. The notion that the entire nation of people could gather round their radios and hear a status report on the latest battle or campaign was an incredible innovation, a revolution of both journalism and its public consumption.

By this time there was a new national network, after a government antitrust decision in 1941 forced NBC to sell one of its two chains. The network had been accused of using its decidedly second-string Blue network to stifle competition in cities that were just getting their second or third radio station. In 1943 the Blue network was sold to Life Savers candy magnate Edward Noble, becoming the Blue Network of the American Broadcasting Company, then simply the American Broadcasting Company (ABC).

The early postwar years were some of the grandest in network history; prime-time entertainment programs were at their slickest, big-budget best. CBS chief Paley returned from wartime service determined to take his chain to first place. Those results resounded for decades. Previously, advertising agencies had exercised complete control over the programs broadcast on the network air, but CBS began producing many of its own shows, then selling the advertising time. The result was a set of series that included *Our Miss Brooks*, *My Friend Irma*, and *My Favorite Husband*. These forerunners of the modern-day sitcom later transported the genre to television.

Meanwhile, having apparently despaired of developing his own big-name talent, Paley also managed to steal away many NBC favorites in the legendary 1948–1949 talent raids known as Paley's Comet. Benny, Bing Crosby, George Burns and Gracie Allen, Groucho Marx, Bergen, and others defected during this period for various reasons. CBS ruled the ratings chart for the first time in its history. While NBC managed to hang on to such favorites as Hope, *Fibber McGee and Molly*, and *One Man's Family*, the damage was done. CBS, purposely or not, had also managed to put itself into the best competitive position for television, which was becoming the wave of the future.

A NEW MEDIUM

Television experimentation by the networks had started nearly a decade and a half before the networks transitioned in earnest. NBC had even begun a pattern of regular broadcasts with an extravaganza from the 1939 New York World's Fair. Audience numbers were limited, however, and the war put a halt to most of the experimenting. But by 1947 the networks were back at full steam. Although initially CBS stubbornly held out for color TV, featuring a system that would have rendered every current black-and-white set useless, the network finally relented when consumers proved unwilling to abandon existing sets. Meanwhile, the fledgling DuMont network, founded and managed by the electronics manufacturer of the same name, seemed to be in a good position to overtake ABC as the third network in the new medium. Without its own radio chain to provide talent and financial support, however, that goal proved unattainable.

None of the big radio stars was willing to take the plunge at this early date, but advertisers began testing the television waters. Even as the papers were full of stories about Benny's switch of radio networks, a definite trend developed. In cities where viewers could choose between radio and TV, the latter won easily. NBC television found its first bona fide hit in Milton Berle's *Texaco Star Theater* in 1948. Viewing outpaced radio listening in city after city by 1949.

Radio ratings did not collapse all at once. Instead, the sun set agonizingly slowly over the networks' glory days. A Korean War freeze on some forms of manufacturing put the brakes on the spread of television during the early 1950s. Even as television ruled the nation's cities, outlying areas were still totally dependent on radio. Even so, Benny, Hope, Burns and Allen, Skelton, and others made the jump to television early in the new decade. Jackie Gleason and Lucille Ball joined Berle as the first genuine sensations that the new medium had produced on its own. To be sure, network radio enjoyed a creative resurgence during this period, with daring new series such as *Dragnet* and *Gunsmoke* offering a breath of fresh air to listeners.

Even so, the radio advertising market soon collapsed. The city audience deserted the medium in droves, and most remaining listeners joined the exodus when mass manufacturing of televisions resumed in 1953. By 1955, of the legendary comedians who had ruled the airwaves for twenty-five years, only Bergen remained on the radio. Nighttime drama was all but dead. NBC, in particular, began experimenting with the long-form news/talk format, and network news on the hour surfaced during this period. November 25, 1960, is often referred to as the last day of network radio; on that Friday after Thanksgiving, CBS broadcast the final installments of everything from *Ma Perkins* to *Amos 'n' Andy*. The last network drama, *Yours Truly, Johnny Dollar*, came to an end in 1962. Broadcast network television thereafter became the unchallenged king, a position it held for another two decades.

GLORY DAYS

The mid-twentieth century was a remarkably stable era for the industry. The DuMont network folded in 1956, but NBC, CBS, and ABC thrived. During this period their access into the nation's homes and consciousness was unparalleled. The networks and their products influenced fashion, encompassing everything from coon-skin caps to Capri pants and bouffant hairdos; language, with expressions as familiar as "And away we go" and "Here comes the judge" becoming common catchphrases; and politics, as television news led the way in questioning the country's involvement in Vietnam. While few people had access to the *Washington Post*, network coverage of the Watergate scandal was available on every home television set in the nation.

As NBC and CBS spent the decades fighting it out for first place in the ratings, the networks became adept at turning public fancy into inescapable fads. Westerns gave way to the rural comedies of the early 1960s. In turn, series such as *The Beverly Hillbillies* surrendered to the popularity of *All in the Family* and other socially relevant comedies of the early 1970s. At mid-decade ABC, which had been derogatively nicknamed "Almost a Broadcasting Company," was catapulted to its first-ever reign at the top on the strength of series such as *Charlie's Angels* and *Three's Company*, which were often criticized for their portrayals of beautiful and scantily clad females. As late as 1979, the three networks managed to draw nearly 100 percent of the available viewing audience on any night of the week.

The Big Three networks maintained their dominance of public television for another decade. The addition of several new broadcast networks, however, challenged their rule over the airwaves. Australian media magnate Rupert Murdoch launched the Fox Broadcasting Company in 1986. The station quickly gained a name for itself with scathing comedy series such as *Married . . . with Children*, but it was not until the animated series *The Simpsons* debuted in 1989 that a Fox program ranked relatively high in the Nielsen ratings (indicating popularity).

This fourth station was not considered to be competition until the mid-1990s when Fox signed a contract to air National Football League games and when the Fox programming schedule produced a string of breakout successes such as *Beverly Hills, 90210* and *The X-Files*. Finally, in the 2007–2008 television season, Fox earned the title of the most popular network, once and for all asserting itself as a viable alternative to the three main networks. Several other broadcast networks were launched in the 1990s, including UPN, WB, and Pax, but none met with the meteoric success of Fox or has significantly challenged the prominence of the Big Three networks.

CABLE TV

In 1975 the Home Box Office pay channel took to the air via satellite, with its signal beamed into homes via local cable systems that were able to provide services offering clear signals from faraway broadcast stations. The idea of receiving unedited, recent theatrical films via cable, for a small fee, proved both popular and profitable. Other entrepreneurs quickly followed suit. Atlanta businessman Ted Turner was soon uplinking the signal of his UHF independent station, later named TBS. He called the new channel the Superstation because it could reach audiences throughout the United States. His twenty-four-hour news channel, Cable News Network (CNN), debuted in 1980.

The success of HBO and CNN was instrumental in ending the domination of the Big Three networks over the U.S. airwaves. By the mid-1980s dozens of cable networks had carved out profitable niches for themselves. The television audience that had once contented itself with three or four channels suddenly had ten times that many from which to choose: everything from evangelist Pat Robertson's Christian Broadcasting Network to the all-sports ESPN to the all-music MTV, which was perhaps the first cable network to spark its own generational and cultural revolution. Into the twenty-first century, dozens of channels have become hundreds. From Animal Planet to the Food Network, the Travel Channel to SyFy, there seems to be a television network for any proclivity or area of interest.

The audience for each of these cable networks was initially tiny, the barest fraction of the audience for even the lowest-rated traditional network program. The combined weight of cable viewership, however, sent the old-line network ratings into an irreversible downward spiral by the mid-1980s. It was a great paradox that even though audiences for network programming comprised larger numbers of viewers compared to those for cable programming, the networks had effectively ceded their long-standing role as a guiding cultural force by continuing to program for a mass, homogenous audience in the age of niches and demographic targeting.

The networks' decline had no lesser consequences than their rise. The audience became so fragmented, the number of viewing choices so great, that the concept of the great national audience simply vanished: no more universally understood catchphrases, no more monster-hit series, at least not in the old sense. Another consequence of this fragmentation was the increased polarization of audiences. New networks and television channels not only catered to niche tastes but also to particular viewpoints. For example, the twenty-four-hour news channel, inaugurated by CNN, was a format quickly imitated by numerous networks, which launched their own cable news stations. Among the most popular were Murdoch's Fox News and NBC's MSNBC. Each of these channels provided a political bent that reflected the perspective of their audience; Fox was heralded as a conservative bastion, while MSNBC prided itself for its liberalism. The same pattern of imitation and diversification occurred in any number of genres. Once a source of commonality for people in the United States, networks in the twenty-first century emphasized individuated rather than shared experience.

NEW TECHNOLOGIES, NEW CHOICES

As technology rapidly advances, cable, too, has been threatened. Suddenly, it was possible for consumers to bypass the network setup entirely and have their own individual choice of program services beamed directly into their homes by satellite. The technology had existed for years, in bulkier and more expensive form: in the 1980s and 1990s, a large satellite dish in the front or back of a house indicated to neighbors that the owner possessed this technology. The direct-satellite industry, however, exploded in the late 1990s. Suddenly there were 500 or more channel choices, available through much smaller and more discreet hardware, and eventually just a black box connected to the television set.

The progression of more streamlined and affordable options served to further fragment the viewing audience. Many cable networks even launched second (or third or fourth) satellite-carried program services, carving their audience into even smaller pieces. A formerly monolithic network, HBO encompassed at least seven satellite channels as of 2012, each serving a special interest—such as family or comedy programming—or a particular demographic, such as the Spanish-language HBO Latino channel. Networks such as MTV and ESPN followed in the same model.

Meanwhile, the booming satellite industry was the greatest threat yet to the traditional broadcast networks. Most satellite systems originally bypassed the local network affiliates entirely, but local channels were still available for a small fee. When audiences began demanding greater access to local programming, they became standard fare within satellite consumer packages. While cable and later satellite and digital technologies offering hundreds of unique channels became a new normal for U.S. television audiences, such options remained paid-for services and were thus often inaccessible to those who could not afford the luxury.

THE FUTURE OF NETWORK TV

In the early twenty-first century many changes took place in the way people consumed television. These had an indelible impact on network television and on the entire television industry. Some of the most significant changes included the development of digital recording technology, a device that electronically records and digitally saves television programs. Digital video recorders, or DVRs, further propelled the move toward more fragmented television viewing since the devices enabled viewers to watch shows at any time of the day or week instead of being limited to the time of broadcast. Not only could viewers use DVRs to record entire slates of programming for future viewing, but they could also access network programs through computers, cell phones, tablet computers, eBook readers, and video gaming systems. This broad range of access has enabled networks to continue to reach disparate audiences, particularly through Internet-based streaming services such as Netflix and Hulu, which provide clearinghouse access to television programming on-demand. Additionally, these recordings allowed viewers to fast-forward through commercials, a further subversion of the original network structure.

Another significant shift in the network television format came in 2005, when Congress passed the Digital Transition and

Public Safety Act. The act mandated a switch from analog to digital television broadcast technology for all network channels. It was set to take effect on February 17, 2009, but new televisions or a converter box for older sets were necessary to access the new format, thus the move placed a large burden on economically disadvantaged people. After a six-month delay and the distribution of coupons, the federal mandate went into effect on June 12, 2009.

Commentators have been forecasting the demise of network broadcasting since the first major shift in medium from radio to television. As time has shown, however, the networks have kept pace with every new technological evolution. The Big Three networks have managed to maintain some sense of relevancy by creating new cable channels, purchasing networks, or partnering with owners of existing networks to create a large presence across the range of television offerings. Networks have also created sophisticated websites that provide schedules, background information, photographs, and videos to users of computer and other electronic devices in order to maintain a presence as television viewership shifts into a largely Internet-based format. While the youngest generation might not remember the days of radio, or even of three or four TV channels, in the early twenty-first century networks remain the standard for television viewing in its many and varied iterations.

Chris Chandler

SEE ALSO: *Advertising;* All in the Family*;* The Amos 'n' Andy Show*; Ball, Lucille; Benny, Jack; Bergen, Edgar; Berle, Milton;* The Beverly Hillbillies*;* Beverly Hills, 90210*; Burns, George, and Gracie Allen; Cable TV; Cantor, Eddie; Cell Phones;* Charlie's Angels*; CNN; Community Media; Crosby, Bing; Daytime Talk Shows;* Dragnet*; DVRs; E-Readers; ESPN;* Fibber McGee and Molly*; Foodies; Fox News Channel; Gleason, Jackie; The Great Depression;* Gunsmoke*; Hairstyles; Hope, Bob; Hulu; The Internet;* Ma Perkins*;* Married . . . with Children*; Marx, Groucho; MTV; National Football League (NFL); Netflix; Paley, William S.; Radio; Radio Drama; Robertson, Pat;* The Simpsons*; Sitcom; Skelton, Red; Soap Operas; Syndication; Television;* Three's Company*; Turner, Ted; Vaudeville; Video Games; Vietnam;* War of the Worlds*; The* Washington Post*; Watergate; Welles, Orson; The Western; World's Fairs;* The X-Files.

BIBLIOGRAPHY

Barfield, Ray E. *Listening to Radio, 1920–1950.* Westport, CT: Praeger, 1996.

Berke, Sally. *When TV Began: The First TV Shows.* New York: CPI, 1978.

Brooks, Tim, and Earle Marsh. *The Complete Directory to Prime Time Network and Cable TV Shows*, 6th ed. New York: Ballantine Books, 1995.

Burns, Eric. *Invasion of the Mind Snatchers: Television's Conquest of America in the Fifties.* Philadelphia: Temple University Press, 2010.

Campbell, Robert. *The Golden Years of Broadcasting: A Celebration of the First 50 Years of Radio and TV on NBC.* New York: Scribner, 1976.

Douglas, George H. *The Early Days of Radio Broadcasting.* Jefferson, NC: McFarland, 1987.

Dunning, John. *On the Air: The Encyclopedia of Old-Time Radio.* New York: Oxford University Press, 1998.

Edgerton, Gary R., and Peter C. Rollins, eds. *Television Histories: Shaping Collective Memory in the Media Age.* Lexington: University Press of Kentucky, 2001.

Hilmes, Michele. *Radio Voices: American Broadcasting, 1922–1952.* Minneapolis: University of Minnesota Press, 1997.

Hilmes, Michele. *NBC: America's Network.* Berkeley: University of California Press, 2007.

Johnson, Victoria E. *Heartland TV: Prime Time Television and the Struggle for U.S. Identity.* New York: New York University Press, 2008.

New Age Music

The genre of calm, tranquil music known as New Age emerged from several conflicting trends in popular music in the 1960s and 1970s. It originated on one level from the electronic music (sometimes referred to as "space music") of the late 1960s. Itself a nascent musical form, electronic music was embraced by groups such as Tangerine Dream and incorporated into the music of progressive rock groups such as Pink Floyd and Yes. On another level, and slightly after the popularization of electronic music, New Age music grew out of the dissatisfaction of some musicians with the pervasive influence of technology in contemporary music. These musicians made an attempt to return to simpler ways of making music and began writing and recording peaceful, unobtrusive pieces, mainly for acoustic guitar and piano. These two trends, paradoxically, combined to form what would be known as New Age music.

In addition, the style was informed by other established genres, such as jazz and classical music, and by various forms of ethnic music, particularly Celtic. As a result of New Age's disparate roots, listeners, fans, and critics have always had difficulty in defining it, and record company executives have had similar difficulties in labeling and merchandising New Age recordings. Nevertheless, the genre became very popular in the final two decades of the twentieth century, with many successful record labels devoted solely to releasing New Age music.

SPIRITUALITY OF NEW AGE MUSIC

Much of the draw of New Age music lies in its functionality; it may be the only form of music to have a purpose beyond that of the enjoyment of the music itself. With the advent of all manner of self-awareness and higher-consciousness trends and fads floating about in the 1970s, and the increasing popularity of nontraditional ideas regarding health and well-being, this music, because of its characteristic placidity and lack of dissonance, became the soundtrack for the emerging New Age lifestyle. By the 1980s New Age shops were quite common, and customers could buy healing crystals as well as books on diverse topics relating to concepts such as "inner harmony" and "cosmic consciousness." Cassette tapes of relaxing music were also offered as aural companions for whatever New Age program the browser had embarked upon. This function, then, was what provided New Age music with its single unifying aspect: the ability to provide an appropriate relaxing soundscape for meditation or other restful, pensive pursuits.

The initial thrust of New Age was electronic, and the interest in it was mostly due to pioneering FM radio shows such as *Inner Visions* and *Music from the Hearts of Space*, which began in

1967 and 1973, respectively. These programs showcased the synthesized music known then as space music and only later dubbed New Age. In the mid-1970s the confusion began when guitarist Will Ackerman started the infamous Windham Hill record label as a means of distributing his own music. Ackerman and the other artists who were signed to his label felt their music had little in common with the highly produced, highly synthesized music being recorded in the late 1970s and sought to bring about a revival of acoustic music. It is ironic that Windham Hill, a record label with an aesthetic so opposed to that of the "space" and electronic music movement, ended up sharing the same shelf and record bin space with that very genre.

Music released on Windham Hill albums was homogeneous in structure, if not instrumentation, and even the strikingly austere cover art was always identifiable as a Windham Hill cover. This meant that, when Windham Hill was widely recognized as a New Age label, all the artists who recorded with the label were considered, by extension, New Age artists, regardless of their classical, jazz, folk, or bluegrass backgrounds. New Age recordings became very commercially lucrative, even if consumers and marketers were unsure of what actually constituted New Age music.

ETHNIC INFUSION

The profit margins and confusion increased with the introduction of ethnic music into the equation, a process that began to take place in the late 1980s. Celtic music (itself a very broad and vague category) was the most successful ethnic music to be affiliated with the New Age genre, an assimilation made possible by the success of Irish pop musicians Enya and Clannad, the group she occasionally performed with, who specialized in a breezy, ethereal type of music. The particular instruments used in traditional Celtic folk music appealed to the Windham Hill acoustic aesthetic, and the mythology associated with the Celtic culture and history fit well with the mystical and spiritual characteristics of New Age music. Windham Hill and other New Age record labels, such as Narada and Hearts of Space, started releasing albums with "Celtic" in the title with the (well-founded) assumption that sales would increase even more. Other ethnic music that found a home under the New Age firmament included Native American and Indian music, highlighted respectively by Douglas Spotted Eagle and U. Srinivas.

By the mid-1990s the category of New Age music had exploded in countless different directions, making a once-confusing genre now impossible to define. British singer/songwriter Peter Gabriel's Realworld record label specialized in bringing together musicians from disparate cultures; more often than not, the results were similar to what had become known as traditional New Age music, but without the underlying ethos that initially defined it. Another parallel genre, spearheaded by Brian Eno, was ambient music, which also had its roots in early 1970s electronic experimentation. The difference between ambient and New Age was more subtle and, perhaps, academic. Ambient did not necessarily share New Age's lofty ideals and had no extra-musical function. By the late 1990s, however, New Age music had changed from a musical genre whose practitioners saw themselves as part of a larger spiritual movement to a marketing and merchandising tool for record company executives and music store owners who were not sure where to place recordings by artists who defied easy categorization.

BACKLASH

Critics were generally dismissive of New Age music, calling it "aural wallpaper" and claiming that it was devoid of content. Nevertheless, fans of the genre, mainly people who had bought into the corresponding New Age lifestyle, were undeterred in their appreciation of the music. While record stores, bookstores, and spas were airing the music frequently, many other people responded less than enthusiastically to it. By the 1990s the music became the butt of many widely circulated jokes, to the extent that the genre began to gain significance not only as an artistic expression of the entire New Age phenomenon but also as a cultural barometer indicative of the opinions shared by people who were not part of this group.

Due to the ambiguous marketing of New Age music, and the haphazard labeling of musicians as "New Age," many performers resisted the tag. The popular keyboardist Suzanne Ciani told *Billboard* magazine in a 1995 article that she prefers to be recognized "as a contemporary classical composer and performer" instead of a New Age artist, because "there was so much debris attached to the term, and I didn't want to spend half my day explaining what I wasn't."

Many Celtic and other ethnic musicians are also unhappy with the tendency for their music to be viewed as New Age, which they feel devalues the tradition and importance of their work. Others, however, such as ex–Jefferson Starship guitarist Craig Chaquico, are perfectly content to be acknowledged as New Age artists. The trend toward disavowal of the New Age genre extends to record company executives as well. Ackerman was never comfortable with Windham Hill's New Age image and preferred terms such as *Contemporary Impressionism* or *New Acoustic Music*. Neither of these, apparently, were as catchy as New Age, and the term, with all its cultural implications, stuck.

Since the end of the 1990s, New Age music had become a victim of its own cannibalization of other forms of music, to the extent that the term no longer had any relevance in contemporary culture, and in fact the term began to be reviled by discerning music consumers. As Ryan Hibbett noted in his 2010 essay in *Journal of Popular Music Studies*, "Within the glut of professional and consumer reviews servicing online music providers the following claim is reproduced to no end: 'This is *not* new age music.' That basic assertion, worded in a variety of ways, appears in defense of particular recordings spanning a very wide range of instrumental genres, supplying in each instance a firm point of distinction." The role that New Age music played in massage therapy offices, in clinics, and in meditation was still being filled by the same type of music, but it was now called any number of other names ranging from the aforementioned Celtic and ambient to electroacoustic music, and *New Age music* became a pejorative term that referred to music that was bland and lifeless.

Dan Coffey

SEE ALSO: *Folk Music; Jefferson Airplane/Starship; New Age Spirituality.*

BIBLIOGRAPHY

Bergman, Billy, and Richard Horn. *Recombinant Do Re Mi: Frontiers of the Rock Era.* New York: Quill, 1985.

Diliberto, John. "New Age Matures." *Billboard*, April 1, 1995, 60–63.

Diliberto, John. "Navigating the Shifting Terrain of New Age

Music: The Evolution of a Genre, from World to Folk, Classical to Space." *Billboard*, April 6, 1996, 44–48.

Hibbett, Ryan. "The New Age Taboo." *Journal of Popular Music Studies* 22, no. 3 (2010): 283–308.

Schaefer, John. "ECM and Windham Hill: A Tale of Two Labels." *New Sounds: A Listener's Guide to New Music*. New York: Harper & Row, 1987.

Toop, David. *Ocean of Sound: Aether Talk, Ambient Sound and Imaginary Worlds*. London: Serpent's Tail, 1996.

Werkhoven, Henk. *The International Guide to New Age Music*. New York: Billboard Books, 1998.

Zrzavy, Helfried C. "Issues of Incoherence and Cohesion in New Age Music." *Journal of Popular Culture*, Fall 1990, 33–53.

New Age Spirituality

New Age spirituality blends ancient occult practices with a religious eclecticism made possible by the global village and the information age. California historian of religions Robert Ellwood has described the movement as a "build-your-own-religion kit," where attractive ideas old and new come together in creative patterns designed by each individual. New Age unveiled a kaleidoscope of devotional exercises from East and West, alternative medicines from traditional societies and urban healing cults, psychotherapeutic techniques from the self-realization movement, science fiction fantasies, witchcraft, and earth worship.

ORIGINS

While numerous practices of New Age spirituality claim origins in antiquity, the movement at the end of the twentieth century sprang from the youth revolutions of the 1960s. The alternative culture's experimentations, particularly the use of mind-altering drugs to attain higher states of awareness, gave character to the lifestyle and arts of even the broader culture. As the twentieth century was coming to an end, the customary fin de siècle mood was intensified by the awareness that the end of a millennium was also approaching. Even within the lives of the maturing flower children of the 1960s, enormous changes had taken place. Computers had become essential tools of work and personal management in what was often referred to as the third industrial revolution. Old fears of nuclear holocaust had been replaced by threats of global warming, the destruction of the ozone layer, and the claustrophobic crowding from overpopulation. Popular entertainment fed the apprehensions with its tales of microbes and meteorites attacking the earth and the theory that the ancient Maya prophesied that the world would end in 2012. New Age spirituality addressed these fears.

The liberation movements of the last half of the twentieth century also had their impact on New Age spirituality. Feminism was attentive to a revival of goddess worship, Wicca cults, and gender-blending ceremonies. The shaman or witch doctor of

Medicine Wheel Meditation. *A man meditates in a medicine wheel made of rocks in California.* AP IMAGES.

traditional societies was sought out for his or her ancient wisdom. Aboriginal Australian and Native American religions were studied for what they could reveal about dream states and natural harmonies. While the white Anglo-Saxon ethos was denigrated, any practice or art form labeled "Celtic" was heralded. With the ease of travel and swiftness of communication that the twentieth century brought, the wise and mysterious East seemed suddenly accessible. New Agers were skeptical of Western religions but open to the ancient faiths of India, China, and Japan. Zen meditation, Taoist doctrines of Yin and Yang, Buddhist quietism and nonviolence, and Hindu beliefs in karma and reincarnation were freely adapted.

The high priest of New Age was the guru, the meditation master, and the healer. Maharishi Mahesh Yogi, Indian-born teacher of transcendental meditation, attracted attention in the West in the 1960s, when the Beatles became his followers. Science fiction writer L. Ron Hubbard was the guru of Scientology, though in his later years he became an elusive figure, traveling the seven seas in his private vessel and communicating only through his writings. New Age gurus included Philadelphia activist Ira Einhorn, widely known as the Unicorn, who operated a communication network financed by AT&T. He sought to save the world from destruction through love and the evolution of superior consciousness, even as he came to speak more and more about negative influences coming from the CIA, KGB, and UFOs. After the mummified body of his paramour was discovered in his closet, he fled to Europe to escape trial. A more benign guru, respected worldwide for his political courage and humanitarianism, was the Dalai Lama.

A flourishing market in books by New Age teachers emerged in the last decades of the twentieth century. In many bookstores, the shelves devoted to New Age outnumbered those given to established religion. Some of the most successful writers were Shakti Gawain; M. Scott Peck; Louise Hay; Carlos Castaneda; Clarissa Pinkola Estes; and, possibly the most celebrated of all, Deepak Chopra. Actress Shirley MacLaine became somewhat of a New Age guru herself with the publication of several books on New Age spirituality, including *Out on a Limb* and *Dancing in the Light*, both published in the 1980s. Even the books of orthodox Christians such as C. S. Lewis and J. R. R. Tolkien were appropriated by the New Age, their fantasies taken much more literally than the two authors had intended.

Ecological concern was a central focus of New Agers. The earth deserved to be cherished; rain forests and oceans were to be protected; animals were entitled to respect. The earth, perceived as a female force, remained the best mother, teacher, and healer; ecofeminist theology reached even established theological seminaries. Personified, even deified as Gaia, the earth was attended with animistic ceremonies, affirming the spirits in all creatures. Healing from the earth's natural herbs, crystals, and aromas was preferred to the ministrations of high-tech medicine.

Monotheistic religions were linked in many minds with the despoiling of the earth, while devotion to a multiplicity of gods, it was believed, would reawaken forces that restore equilibrium. Even a venerable institution such as the Unitarian Church, with its origins in New England Puritanism, found itself debating the admission of practicing pagans into its fellowship in the last decade of the twentieth century.

BEYOND SPIRITUALITY

The New Age was an arts and crafts as well as a spiritual movement. Weaving, pottery, jewelry making, and quilting experienced revivals, along with traditional methods of preparing organically grown foods. Carpentry, a craft often associated with divinity in ancient times, was especially honored by the New Age. The Whole Earth Catalog, which was published regularly from 1968 to 1972 and then sporadically until 1998, was intended for those hoping to live a spiritual and sustainable lifestyle. The artistic expression of even Western mysticism was welcome. Jewish Hasidic and Sufi dervish dances and chants intrigued New Agers. Gregorian chants by monks and electronic adaptations of the music of Abbess Hildegard von Bingen were commercially recorded and outsold the compact discs of Native American and Tibetan musicians.

A tragic incident from 2009 highlighted the dangers of blindly following self-appointed gurus. At a personal growth seminar in Arizona, New Age author James Arthur Ray led attendees in a sweat-lodge ceremony modeled on a Native American tradition—fifty-six people packed into a four-foot-tall structure warmed by superheated rocks. Two of the participants died of heat stroke, and a third died days later of massive organ failure. Ray was convicted of negligent homicide.

Inevitably the excesses of New Age spirituality sparked satire. The Reformed Druids of North America (RDNA) organized as a joke and soon had serious inquirers. The Hasidic Druids, formed in 1976, were also tongue in cheek. But New Age spirituality was a serious matter, delivering to its adherents the perpetual comforts and assurances of religion. It provided an outlet for those disenchanted with Christianity and Judaism but unready to accept the secular worldview. Moreover, its music and crafts and the frequent joyfulness of the movement enriched the surrounding mainstream culture.

Allene Phy-Olsen

SEE ALSO: *The Beatles; Feminism; Hubbard, L. Ron; Lewis, C. S.; New Age Music; Tolkien, J. R. R.;* The Whole Earth Catalog.

BIBLIOGRAPHY

Lesser, Elizabeth. *The Seeker's Guide.* New York: Villard Books, 1999.

Melton, J. Gordon; Jerome Clark; and Aidan A. Kelly. *New Age Encyclopedia.* Detroit, MI: Gale Research, 1990.

Needleman, Jacob. *The New Religions.* New York: Doubleday, 1970.

Occhiogrosso, Peter. *The Joy of Sects.* New York: Doubleday, 1994.

Pike, Sarah M. *New Age and Neopagan Religions in America.* New York: Columbia University Press, 2004.

Wilber, Ken. *Eye to Eye: The Quest for the New Paradigm.* Garden City, NY: Anchor Books, 1983.

New Deal

The New Deal was implemented in 1933, just days after the inauguration of President Franklin Delano Roosevelt (FDR). The program encompassed a vast array of legislation designed to relieve the homelessness, unemployment, and failed economy of the Great Depression; to bring about recovery for America's farms and industry; and to reform the economic and social problems that precipitated the Depression. More than just an attempt to get the economy back on track, the New Deal sought to reinvigorate American ideals, traditions, and expression through a series of cultural programs designed to elevate folk art and bring the elite arts to the masses. In doing so, the New Deal left a legacy of public art, literature, music, theater, and photography, while also influencing the popular media of radio and film.

FDR established the Works Progress Administration (initially referred to as WPA and later renamed the Works Projects Administration) in 1935 as an attempt to further boost economic recovery. This vast and complex body sponsored the construction of roads, bridges, parks, sidewalks, airports, sewage systems, water systems, levies, and public buildings such as post offices and schools. Like earlier relief efforts, the WPA was created to provide jobs for the unemployed, but in a departure from other employment programs, it developed several projects designed to employ artists, writers, musicians, and actors. When asked why the government would concern itself with unemployed actors and artists, WPA administrator Harry Hopkins retorted: "Hell, they've got to eat just like other people."

The WPA arts projects grew out of a set of conditions unique to 1930s America. First and foremost, FDR believed that support of the arts by the government would not only employ starving artists but would also help uplift the American spirit by creating beautiful art, plays, and music. Second, many artists (befitting their liberal, or even communistic, tendencies) felt it was a public right to have access to good art—a "cultural right." Third, many in Roosevelt's administration hoped their work would bring about "cultural democracy," the logical sequel to political and economic democracy. And finally, the Depression had made Americans aware of their own uniqueness, even in the arts.

Several of the arts projects were small, and their accomplishments remain obscure, such as the WPA Dance Theater, with its accompanying Young Choreographers Laboratory, and the Composers Forum-Laboratory of the Federal Music Project. Although these various projects differed in direction and purpose, they all shared an overriding concern to discover America and define what it means to be American.

FEDERAL ART PROJECT

To direct the Federal Art Project, Hopkins selected a museum curator, Holger Cahill. Cahill set out the project's objectives in an operating manual in which he argued:

> Through employment of creative artists, it is hoped to secure for the public outstanding examples of contemporary American art; through art teaching and recreational art activities to create a broader national art consciousness and work out constructive ways of using leisure time; through services in applied art to aid various campaigns of social value; and through research projects to clarify the native background in the arts.

Cahill concluded that "the aim of the project will be toward an integration of the arts with the daily life of the community, and an integration of the fine arts and practical arts." To this end, thousands of artists and art teachers were employed by the art project, creating more than 2,500 murals and 18,000 sculptures for public schools, hospitals, libraries, and post offices. These murals, suggesting the works of great Mexican muralists such as Diego Rivera, centered on the theme of hardworking American men and women. They showed Americans at work and at play, employing Native American art styles and emulating some Art Deco techniques, as well as regional artists such as Grant Wood and Thomas Hart Benton.

The result was more than 100,000 paintings and more than 100 community art centers, many of which became permanent community fixtures. Another project, the Index of American Design, sought to catalog and reproduce items illustrating a uniquely American style, such as weather vanes, decoys, ships' figureheads, cigar store Indians, and other regional and ethnic arts. By the mid-1960s it was estimated that the works created under this project were worth more than the cost of the project itself. Several artists who developed their talent in the arts project, including Jackson Pollock and Willem de Kooning, became famous later in their careers. For the most part, however, the products of the arts projects were not masterpieces but rather locally unique arts and crafts projects, art classes for kids, and art appreciation lectures.

FEDERAL THEATER PROJECT

The director of the Federal Theater Project was Hallie Flanagan, from the Vassar College Experimental Theatre. She envisioned the creation of a vast new audience for the theater by sponsoring community theater groups. The *Living Newspaper* became one attempt to mold theater to the documentary drama of everyday concerns by having actors recreate local events in a theater setting. The project also sponsored programs of everything from Shakespeare to modern farce, Gilbert and Sullivan, children's plays, and folk plays.

The Federal Theater Project was perhaps the most controversial of the arts projects because many of the people involved were known to have radical and even communist sympathies. In addition, the theater industry was centered in New York City and left many states out of the project altogether. In total, thirty-one states saw the effects of the Theater Project. Roosevelt's adversaries in Congress used the radical tendency of the program as a way to attack the New Deal. Ultimately they were able to shut down the project altogether in 1939, with arguments reminiscent of more recent battles over funding for the National Endowment for the Arts.

FEDERAL WRITERS' PROJECT

More utilitarian in its creations, the Federal Writers' Project employed more than 10,000 people in various projects. Favoring nonfiction over poetry, novels, and short stories, the writers' project produced guides and pamphlets describing America. Under the direction of Henry Alsberg, a former editorial writer, the project produced the American Guide Series, which generated guides for each state modeled after the European Baedeker guidebooks. The guides were composed of three parts: essays on a variety of subjects, including history, people, arts, economy, politics, and religions of each state; information on the state's cities; and motor tours of the state with descriptive information. These guides were intended to stimulate travel and tourism, encourage conservation of resources by arousing local pride, and broaden scholarly interests by making historical facts readily available.

The Writers' Project also created regional and specific guides, including *The Berkshire Hills* and *U.S. Highway One: From Maine to Florida*, as well as the Life in America series with such volumes as *The Armenians in Massachusetts, The Hopi*, and *Who's Who in the Zoo.* Other projects included a volume titled *American Stuff*, which featured American short stories such as "Uncle Tom's Children" by Richard Wright. The Federal Writers' Project also concerned itself with the collection of folklore. Under the direction of America's two premier folklorists, John A. Lomax and Benjamin A. Botkin, the project recorded the stories of more than 2,000 ex-slaves and collected stories of local customs and folklore.

While not a part of the WPA or any of the arts projects, folk music collecting was also a concern of the government. Based out of the Library of Congress, the Archive of Folk Song (later renamed the Archive of Folk Culture), collected the songs of slaves, Appalachian mountain folk, cowboys, lumberjacks, sailors, and Dust Bowl migrant workers. Under the direction of John Lomax and his son Alan, the Archive of Folk Song "discovered" the music of Huddie Ledbetter, better known as Leadbelly, and Woody Guthrie and recorded their songs as well as conversations with them. Two young folklorists, Charles Todd and Robert Sonkin, traveled to California to record the songs of the migrants in the Farm Security Administration camps.

FARM SECURITY ADMINISTRATION

Perhaps the most influential of the cultural projects of the New Deal grew out of the Farm Security Administration (FSA). Headed by Roy Stryker, the photographic division of the FSA sought to document the living and working conditions of Americans during the Depression. Stryker was able to assemble the best photographers of the day, including Walker Evans, Dorothea Lange, Ben Shahn, Russell Lee, Arthur Rothstein, and Margaret Bourke-White. Many of the photographers produced works of their own, such as Bourke-White's *You Have Seen Their Faces* (with Erskine Caldwell), Lange's *An American Exodus* (with Paul Taylor), and Evans's *Let Us Now Praise Famous Men* (with James Agee). These photographers and their photographs publicized the plight of mainly rural people, from the Dust Bowl migrants to southern tenant farmers and Cajuns in Acadiana.

The photo collection of the FSA also illustrates the main impulse behind the federally sponsored cultural activities of the New Deal: documentation. In all aspects of these various projects, New Deal reformers sought to document the lives of Americans in order to understand, and eventually change, their behavior. Employing the methods of social science, these reformers tried to both preserve and destroy regional, ethnic, occupational, and religious differences in the name of modernization and reform.

Much of the work produced by these projects centered on the themes of rural life or work in the outdoors. This was due, in large part, to the idea that Americans were most clearly American on the frontier of the nineteenth century. Or, more precisely, the frontier created the American character. Writers as far back as Ralph Waldo Emerson and Walt Whitman felt that a uniquely American literature would have to come from areas where nature imposed itself on the everyday life of Americans. John and Alan Lomax felt they found an American art form in the songs of cowboys, lumberjacks, miners, and farmers, and photographers went to the rural areas of California, the South, and the northern plains in search of the real America.

Yet for all of the cultural production that came out of the New Deal, most people's cultural activities were confined to listening to big bands play swing music on the radio or watching the newly developed sound films from Hollywood. Americans had discovered mass popular culture, and in turn, the mass culture industries of radio and motion pictures discovered that they could benefit from mimicking the same themes of "searching for America" as the New Deal programs. Radio shows such as *America's Town Meeting of the Air* and films such as *The Grapes of Wrath* clearly exhibit the influences of government-sponsored art programs.

Charles J. Shindo

SEE ALSO: *Big Bands; Caldwell, Erskine; Communism; Community Theater;* The Grapes of Wrath*; The Great Depression; Guthrie, Woody; Hollywood; Leadbelly; Pollock, Jackson; Radio; Rivera, Diego; Works Progress Administration (WPA) Murals; Wright, Richard.*

BIBLIOGRAPHY

Hobson, Archie. *Remembering America: A Sampler of the WPA American Guide Series.* New York: Columbia University Press, 1985.

Hurley, F. Jack. *Portrait of a Decade: Roy Stryker and the Development of Documentary Photography in the Thirties.* Baton Rouge: Louisiana State University Press, 1972.

Mathews, Jane deHart. *The Federal Theatre, 1935–1939.* Princeton, NJ: Princeton University Press, 1967.

McDonald, William Francis. *Federal Relief Administration and the Arts; The Origins and Administrative History of the Arts Projects of the Works Progress Administration.* Columbus: Ohio State University Press, 1969.

Park, Marlene, and Gerald E. Markowitz. *Democratic Vistas: Post Offices and Public Art in the New Deal.* Philadelphia: Temple University Press, 1984.

Shindo, Charles J. *Dust Bowl Migrants in the American Imagination.* Lawrence: University of Kansas Press, 1997.

Young, William H., and Nancy K. Young. *The Great Depression in America: A Cultural Encyclopedia,* Vol. 1. Westport, CT: Greenwood Press, 2007.

The New Kids on the Block

At the peak of their success, the New Kids on the Block became one of the most celebrated teenage pop musical acts since Menudo and the Jackson Five. Modeled after these precursors, the New Kids on the Block consisted of five young white men from Boston who sported a squeaky clean image and whose eclectic musical styles and slick dance routines borrowed heavily from black performance traditions. By 1989 the group was the most successful act of its kind in the United States, but their popularity seriously waned only two years later, prompting the members to disband in 1994 and pursue solo careers. The act, however, still maintained a sizable fan base, and their long-lasting effect on popular music became evident in 1997 and 1998 when copycat groups such as Hanson, the Backstreet Boys, N'Sync, and 98 Degrees ruled the pop charts. The New Kids on the Block came back together for a reunion tour in 2008 and joined forces with the Backstreet Boys to create NKOTBSB in 2011.

New Kids on the Block. *The members of New Kids on the Block, from left, Jordan Knight, Joey McIntyre, Danny Wood, Donnie Wahlberg, and Jonathan Knight, were a sensation among teenage girls in the late 1980s.* EBET ROBERTS/REDFERNS/GETTY IMAGES.

The five young men who composed the New Kids on the Block were all raised in Boston, Massachusetts. Four of the five members—Donnie Wahlberg, Danny Wood, and brothers Jonathan and Jordan Knight—grew up in the same neighborhood and attended elementary school together. The four friends became aware of each other's performing talents from talent shows and school chorus. By high school Danny and Donnie had even formed their own rap group, appearing at local parties and events.

PROMOTING THE GROUP

By 1985 the young men had met African American producer Maurice Starr. A slightly off-the-wall but extremely gifted song composer, he had already achieved success in the early 1980s by creating and producing the work of an enormously popular black teen act, New Edition. New Edition had hit the charts with bubblegum pop tunes such as "Candy Girl" and "Mr. Telephone Man." After this group's popularity waned by the mid-1980s, Starr walked away from his creation. The members of New Edition each went on to successful solo careers, and the group eventually performed a reunion tour in 1996.

Vying for an even wider racial audience than the one he had generated for New Edition, Starr planned to promote the New Kids on the Block as an all-white teen group modeled after earlier acts such as the Osmonds. He signed the four friends from Boston and, for added effect, brought onboard twelve-year-old Joey McIntyre for his youthful tenor sound. The boys dressed in regular, nondescript styles, including tattered, ripped jeans; teased hairdos; and stylish hats. Sensing the potential to capitalize on an untapped adolescent and preadolescent female fan base, Columbia Records signed the group in January 1986.

The group's first album, titled *New Kids on the Block*, spun off three singles that failed to ignite the charts. Apparently, the record company had promoted the group exclusively to black audiences. For its second album, Columbia focused on Starr's plan to promote the group to a larger, Top 40 audience, more inclusive of white people. Even before the second album was released, the group tried to generate a supportive fan base by touring shopping malls and performing at local concert venues and telethons. In 1988 the group toured the country as the opening act for teenage star Tiffany, and in 1989 their second album, *Hangin' Tough*, was released. It went on to become a multiplatinum best seller.

By 1990 the group was on a grueling touring schedule. Songs such as "The Right Stuff," "Please Don't Go Girl," and "I'll Be Loving You Forever" were firmly planted at the top of the charts. The group's success even spun off a cartoon series on ABC television. Although the New Kids on the Block had secured a decidedly loyal teenybopper audience, the group was derided by many critics, especially because of their practice of lip-synching in live performances and their attempts to promote themselves as hip in the style of black urban musical acts.

Although the Christmas album *Merry Merry Christmas* helped sustain the group's already luminous success in 1989, their third release, *Step by Step* (1990), failed to generate the record sales of previous albums. A 1991 remix album, *No More Games*, similarly failed to gain radio airplay. Apparently, the female teen audience for New Kids on the Block had begun to mature, and other harder forms of music such as gangsta rap were taking center stage, supplanting the formulaic quality of groups such as the New Kids and Vanilla Ice.

NKOTB

In the early 1990s, in order to bolster its waning street credibility, the quintet changed its name to the initialism NKOTB. After releasing a final album, *Face the Music*, to poor reviews, the group finally split up. Although their long-term impact on the popular music scene is not generally considered to have been significant, the blueprint of their success has become familiar: an entrepreneurial producer forms and manages a group of young white teenagers performing black musical and dance styles. This formula became a surefire routine by the late 1990s, with hugely popular groups such as the Backstreet Boys and N'Sync.

After breaking up, the members of NKOTB initially went their separate ways. Wahlberg became an actor, appearing in films such as *The Sixth Sense* (1999). Jordan Knight and McIntyre developed solo singing careers and appeared on reality television. Then in 2008 the group launched a reunion tour, their first in fifteen years, and released the album *Block.* Three years later NKOTB and the Backstreet Boys merged—minus Kevin Richardson, who had left the Backstreet Boys in 2006—to form the new group NKOTBSB.

The nine members of the newly formed group, which included Nick Carter, Howie Dorough, Brian Littrell, and A. J. McClean in addition to the five members of NKOTB, continued to sell out tours in which they performed new tunes as well as old hits. Their audiences predominately consisted of former fans who grew up playing the records of the two bands and were introducing their children to their youthful idols. The group also appeared on television shows, including the *American Music Awards*, *The Today Show*, and *Dancing with the Stars*. Their self-titled album was released in May 2011.

Jason King

SEE ALSO: *Boy Bands;* Dancing with the Stars*; Gangsta Rap; The Jackson Five; Pop Music; Television; Top 40.*

BIBLIOGRAPHY

Abney, Andrea. "Neither New nor Kids, but They're Welcome Back to the Block." *San Francisco Chronicle*, October 13, 2008.

Bauknecht, Sara. "Where the Boys Are: New Kids on the Block and the Backstreet Boys Team Up on Tour." *Pittsburgh Post-Gazette*, June 14, 2011.

Greenberg, Keith Elliot. *New Kids on the Block*. Minneapolis, MN: Lerner Publications, 1991.

New Left

A diverse international movement that sought to reformulate traditional left-wing politics in the 1960s, New Left activism culminated in the widespread upheavals of 1968, "the year of the barricades," when political dissent erupted around the developed world against the backdrop of a major escalation of American activity in Vietnam, the assassinations of Martin Luther King Jr. and Robert Kennedy, and the Soviet invasion of Czechoslovakia. The May 1968 demonstrations in France, which briefly united students and workers in a series of direct confrontations with French government authority, have acquired a near-legendary status in popular historical assessments of the New Left. Throughout the decade, however, it was the United

States that formed the epicenter of New Left politics, largely because of the war in Vietnam and the struggle for civil rights.

Never a cohesive movement as such, the American New Left was a loose, largely student-based coalition of dissenting activist groups. Many of those groups had been born out of the civil rights struggles of the early 1960s, led by the Student Nonviolent Coordinating Committee (SNCC). The need for a rebirth of left-leaning politics seemed particularly acute in the United States, where a combination of the postwar economic boom, the threat of nuclear annihilation, and Joseph Stalin's appropriation of Soviet politics had convinced many that older models of Marxist class struggle were anachronistic. By the time of the Cuban missile crisis in 1962, it had also become clear that moves to reform the Democratic Party into a mass left-liberal alliance had collapsed into wranglings over internal party procedures.

The year 1962 marked the emergence of a recognizably new left-wing agenda as a small cadre of student activists, Students for a Democratic Society (SDS), convened at Port Huron, Michigan. If SNCC and southern civil rights provided the major catalyst for the 1960s movement, it was SDS and its initially northern, white middle-class student constituency that became the driving force behind the first generation of the New Left.

INFLUENCES

Directly influenced by the writings of 1950s intellectuals such as Paul Goodman and C. Wright Mills, SDS announced itself in the formative "Port Huron Statement" of 1962, a document that developed the political and intellectual precepts of Mills's "Letter to the New Left" (1960) into a broad and influential statement about the "values" and "goals" that came to shape the early years of the movement. The statement's author, Tom Hayden, may have preserved some of the language of radical Marxism (not least in his emphasis upon the "alienation" of life lived in the advanced capitalist West), but the document as a whole distanced itself decisively from any analysis grounded exclusively in economics or the politics of class, a kind of analysis that Mills had denounced as "the labor metaphysic." Announcing proudly that SDS would have "no sure formulas, no closed theories," the Port Huron Statement stressed what later became a characteristic New Left openness to a diverse platform of oppositional politics extending well beyond class struggle.

Hayden's thinking about alienation, and New Left thinking in general, owed more to the influence of Jean-Paul Sartre and Albert Camus than it did to orthodox Marxism. The antidote offered was a politics based on "participatory democracy," an activism that sought personal fulfillment through civic participation. As an activist strategy, participatory democracy was most notably espoused in the Economic Research and Action Project (ERAP) of 1963–1965, which sent students into the black ghettos and working-class neighborhoods of nine northern cities, including Chicago; Newark, New Jersey; and Cleveland, Ohio, and in the Northern Student Movement, which conducted literacy programs and assisted in the Harlem, New York, rent strikes of 1964–1965.

VIOLENCE AND SURVEILLANCE

SDS was also instrumental in organizing a number of mass demonstrations, notably the first major protest against the Vietnam War—the August 1965 March on Washington—an event that in certain respects proved to be a watershed for New Left politics. American intervention in Vietnam had escalated dramatically in 1964, and when the United States introduced ground troops in late 1965, the ranks of SDS swelled with new members. SDS membership rose from around 1,000 in 1964 to around 4,300 in 1965 and had expanded to encompass around 100,000 by 1969. Thousands of nonmembers also participated in direct action and demonstrations across the country. In the days immediately following President Richard Nixon's announcement of the invasion of Cambodia in 1970, more than 400 campuses were disrupted, most notoriously at Kent State University, where the National Guard killed four students, and at Jackson State in Mississippi, where two more students died.

The climate became more militant as the stakes rose, and the recruitment of so many to the campaign against the war increased the variety of dissenting positions accommodated within the New Left. Sooner or later it was inevitable that political discord would erupt within the ranks of SDS itself. When the organization was infiltrated by the Maoist PL (Progressive Labor Party) in 1967, SDS was forced into a sharper definition of its own political agenda than the Port Huron Statement had ever intended should be the case—SDS had always been strong on what the statement called "values" but relatively short on what it termed "goals," or on practical steps that might be taken to realize those goals. Holding together so diverse a movement with so unsystematic a political program proved impossible.

By the end of the decade, with a Republican once more in the White House and the Vietnam War continuing, SDS had split into a number of competing factions, each with a different agenda. Others had drifted back toward the Democratic Party. New Left activism did play an important part in bringing the conflict in Vietnam to a halt. But when U.S. involvement in the war ended in 1973 (the war did not end until 1975), the one common cause that had bound so pluralist a "movement" together vanished. Having drifted so far from Marxist orthodoxy, most of the movement lacked the economic analysis that might have turned the oil crisis of 1973 to its advantage, and the New Left soon subsided with the withdrawal of troops from Vietnam.

The existential flavor of early New Left thinking lent the movement a commitment to individual liberation that calls into question its "newness" as such. The specific relation between individual and society stressed in "participatory democracy" can be traced in a number of American political and intellectual traditions of the eighteenth and nineteenth centuries, and as 1960s activist Stanley Aronowitz has put it, the Port Huron Statement was "remarkable for its continuity with traditional American ideas of popular self-government, egalitarian ethics, and social justice." Traditional or not, a further consequence of these commitments was the rise of a countercultural wing of the movement (including hippies and, from 1967 to 1968, the Yippies), which increasingly represented the face of the New Left in the second half of the decade.

In 1971 the fact that the FBI had engaged in illegal covert activities against American citizens for the purposes of bringing down the New Left and stymied their efforts to form coalitions with Black Power groups finally became public knowledge. The outcry that followed shut down the Counterintelligence Programs (COINTELPRO) that had been common during the 1960s. Such programs involved surreptitious entries, electronic surveillance, anonymous phone calls, and the use of paid informants to keep Congress, elected officials, the media, law enforcement, and the Internal Revenue Service appraised of minute details about the lives of individuals involved in the New Left and the civil rights movement. COINTELPRO also went much further. The FBI printed fake brochures, newsletters, and cartoons that purported to be from New Left groups in order to tarnish the group's image and thwart recruitment and coalition efforts. The FBI also used homophobia to portray male group leaders as effeminate and promoted an overall image of perversion and violence.

The Senate Intelligence Commission finally held hearings into the matter in 1975, but it was not until 2007 that a full investigation took place as Congress began gathering information on the constitutional violations of rights carried on by the FBI and the CIA in light of the war on terror that had been spawned by the terrorist attacks of September 11, 2001.

David Holloway

SEE ALSO: *Black Panthers; FBI (Federal Bureau of Investigation); Hippies; Hoffman, Abbie; King, Martin Luther, Jr.; Student Demonstrations; Students for a Democratic Society (SDS); Vietnam; Yippies.*

BIBLIOGRAPHY

Albert, Judith Clavir, and Stewart Edward Albert, eds. *The Sixties Papers: Documents of a Rebellious Decade.* New York: Praeger, 1984.

Ali, Tariq, and Susan Watkins. *1968: Marching in the Streets.* London: Bloomsbury, 1998.

Caute, David. *Sixty-Eight: The Year of the Barricades.* London: Paladin, 1988.

Cohn-Bendit, Gabriel, and Daniel Cohn-Bendit. *Obsolete Communism: The Left-Wing Alternative.* London: Penguin, 1969.

Dabble, John. "Fighting Black Power-New Left Coalitions: Covert FBI Media Campaigns and American Cultural Discourse." *European Journal of American Culture* 27, no. 2 (2008): 65–91.

DeBenedetti, Charles, and Charles Chatfield. *An American Ordeal: The Antiwar Movement of the Vietnam Era.* New York: Syracuse University Press, 1990.

Gosse, Van. *Rethinking the New Left: An Interpretative History.* New York: Palgrave Macmillan, 2005.

McMillian, John, and Paul Buhle, eds. *The New Left Revisited.* Philadelphia: Temple University Press, 2003.

Roussopoulos, Dimitrios, ed. *The New Left: Legacy and Continuity.* New York: Black Rose Books, 2007.

Sayres, Sohnya, et al. *The 60s without Apology.* Minneapolis: University of Minnesota Press, 1984.

Steigerwald, David. *The Sixties and the End of Modern America.* New York: St. Martin's Press, 1995.

New Look

The New Look was a line of women's clothing that debuted in France in February 1947. The line was a smashing success and catapulted French designer Christian Dior to the top of the French fashion industry. Originally named "Corolle," the line was called the "New Look" by *Harper's Bazaar* editor Carmel Snow, and the name stuck.

The New Look line, Dior's first, was his most famous collection, and it featured long, full skirts; small waistlines; and deep necklines. Given the line's debut following the end of World War II, most women were delighted with the extremely feminine garments. Feminists, however, were critical of them and argued that they returned women to a merely decorative role in society and were impractical in the workplace. Others were disapproving of the amount of material needed to manufacture the clothing. It seemed wasteful and opulent so soon after the required rationing during the war.

Dior said of his most famous fashion line, as quoted by Shirley Miles O'Donnel in her book *American Costume, 1915–1970*: "We were emerging from a period of war, of uniforms, of women-soldiers built like boxers. I drew women-flowers, soft shoulders, flowering busts, fine waists like liana and wide skirts like corolla. . . . I wanted my dresses to be constructed, molded upon the curves of the feminine body whose sweep they would stylize."

Nickianne Moody

SEE ALSO: *Feminism;* Harper's*; World War II.*

BIBLIOGRAPHY

O'Donnel, Shirley Miles. *American Costume, 1915–1970: A Source Book for the Stage Costumer.* Bloomington: Indiana University Press, 1982.

Pochna, Marie France. *Christian Dior: The Man Who Made the World Look New.* New York: Arcade Publishing 1996.

Sladen, C. *The Conscription of Fashion.* Brookfield, VT: Ashgate Publishing, 1995.

New Orleans Rhythm and Blues

New Orleans is identified most vividly with jazz, but its rhythm-and-blues tradition is no less distinctive and has resulted in a unique and important body of work. As rhythm and blues began to develop in the 1940s as an American form, New Orleans musicians were listening to the records of people such as Louis Jordan, though they were putting them into their own contexts. The style flowered in the rock-and-roll era of the 1950s and the soul era of the 1960s. The city's music scene then went through a period of commercial stagnation, overlooked for most of the 1970s, but skillful local promotion and the continuing vitality of New Orleans musicians restored it to prominence, if not to the top of the charts, by the end of the twentieth century.

JAZZ ROOTS

By the 1940s New Orleans had long since been passed by as a jazz center, but music was still a powerful force, especially in the black community. The jazz-flavored street bands were still a tradition, and they created the New Orleans phenomenon of the "second line," a disorganized but rhythmically dynamic group of dancers who would follow the bands.

The New Orleans style is piano-based, blues-oriented music. Its emphasis on the piano can be linked to the influence of jazz pioneers in the 1920s such as Jelly Roll Morton, who had been one of the first piano "professors"—originally a term describing conservatory-trained piano players but used in jazz for any piano virtuoso. The style is marked by its "lazy" feel, which comes from rhythms played slightly behind the beat to give the music a "sway." No matter what the subject of the song, the music conveys an easy, pleasant mood. Lyrics can be sung in a bluesy tradition or a raucous gospel shout, but the singing is softened by a contrastingly smooth backdrop of horn lines. The New Orleans style, like jazz, also incorporates Latin and Caribbean rhythmic influences, which do not affect other blues traditions (all true jazz has a Latin tinge, according to Morton). Three figures dominated, and set the tone for, New Orleans rhythm and blues in the 1940s: Professor Longhair (Henry Roeland Byrd), Fats Domino, and Dave Bartholomew.

1940s AND 1950s

Longhair, born in 1918, became the godfather of rhythm and blues in New Orleans. His piano style was built on a mixture of boogie-woogie; New Orleans second line; and Caribbean rhythms, chiefly rumba and calypso. His loose, rolling beat has never been successfully imitated, though it is almost universally thought to be the most profound influence on the New Orleans sound. Longhair was signed by Atlantic Records in 1950, but his style was too idiosyncratic to produce major national hits. Nevertheless, some of his songs, such as "Mardi Gras in New Orleans" and "Tipitina," became classics. Longhair continued to perform in and around New Orleans before giving up music by the 1960s.

Fats Domino. *Fats Domino parlayed his New Orleans R&B roots into superstardom in the early days of rock and roll in the 1950s.* MICHAEL OCHS ARCHIVES/GETTY IMAGES.

Bartholomew, born in 1920, was a trumpet player, bandleader, and producer who turned the New Orleans brass band sound into funky rhythm and blues. Bartholomew's band, which included master instrumentalists such as Lee Allen, Herbert Hardesty, Alvin "Red" Tyler, Earl Palmer, and Frank Fields, provided the musical basis for the most popular R&B and rock and roll of the 1940s and 1950s.

Domino, born in 1928, was the first big R&B star to come out of New Orleans. Influenced by the popular R&B sounds of Jordan and by the country lilt of Western swing, Domino was signed by the Los Angeles independent record label Imperial in 1949. His first record, "The Fat Man" (a reworking of blues great Champion Jack Dupree's "Junker's Blues") was a rhythm-and-blues hit. By the mid-1950s, Domino was a rock-and-roll superstar with hits such as "Ain't That a Shame" and "Blueberry Hill." Domino brought national attention to New Orleans as a source of the emerging rock-and-roll sound.

While Imperial also signed Roy Brown ("Good Rockin' Tonight") and Smiley Lewis ("I Hear You Knockin'"), another Los Angeles label, Specialty, came to New Orleans looking for talent. Specialty found Little Richard, who would electrify rock and roll like no other performer, and others, including Lloyd Price ("Lawdy Miss Clawdy," "Stagger Lee"). The vocal group Shirley and Lee brought sinuous New Orleans rhythms to doo-wop. Shirley and Lee's "Let the Good Times Roll" became an anthem not only of the city but also of rock and roll. The same can be said about "Rockin' Pneumonia and Boogie Woogie Flu," by Huey "Piano" Smith and the Clowns.

1960s

If Bartholomew was the master producer of the rock-and-roll era, Allen Toussaint became the shaper of the soul sound of the 1960s. Born in 1938, Toussaint began his career playing piano on a Shirley and Lee tour, then became part of Bartholomew's studio group. His producing talent became evident when he was called in to supervise a hopelessly disorganized recording session and came out of it with Lee Allen's instrumental "Walkin' with Mr. Lee," which became a national hit. Toussaint's studio perfectionism and New Orleans honky-tonk training were behind the early 1960s hits that moved the sound from rough-and-ready R&B to funky but sophisticated soul: Ernie K-Doe's "Mother In Law," Jessie Hill's "Ooh Poo Pah Doo," and Chris Kenner's "I Like It Like That."

However, Toussaint's masterpieces—"It's Raining" and "I Done Got Over"—came with one of the two greatest New Orleans soul singers, Irma Thomas. Thomas's voice was every bit as good as those of her famous contemporaries, Aretha Franklin and Gladys Knight, though she never achieved their fame. What might have been her breakout hit, "Time Is on My Side," was covered in 1964 by the Rolling Stones, whose version eclipsed hers on the charts.

DECLINE

The last great New Orleans soul song of the 1960s was "Tell It Like It Is," a breakout national hit in 1966 by Aaron Neville, another spectacular soul voice. By that time, however, the British Invasion was eroding the popularity of the New Orleans sound. Many soul greats, including Thomas, lost their careers at this point. The domination of American music by British acts such as the Rolling Stones spelled the demise of many independent soul labels. By 1969 the recording scene in New

Orleans was essentially over. Neville was working as a stevedore on the docks; Thomas was a sales clerk at Montgomery Ward in Oakland, California; and many other local musicians had left town.

Throughout the 1970s, New Orleans was almost a musical ghost town, though the seeds of a revival were planted. In 1970 the first New Orleans Jazz and Heritage Festival attracted an audience of only a few hundred, but its producers plucked Professor Longhair out of obscurity and began the revival of his reputation. He continued to play and record to increasing critical acclaim and cult stardom until his death in 1980.

In 1976 George "Big Chief Jolly" Landry, a New Orleans folk legend for his leadership of the Wild Tchoupitoulas, a "Mardi Gras Indian" unit, recruited his nephews Aaron, Charles, Art, and Cyril Neville for a recording of the Caribbean-flavored rhythm and blues that was the hallmark of the black Mardi Gras sound. The brothers, all New Orleans musical veterans, were to become the internationally famous torchbearers for the revival of New Orleans R&B, as was Mac "Dr. John" Rebennack. With the growing popularity of Jazzfest (by the 1990s, attendance for the six-day festival was measured in the hundreds of thousands) and the resurgence of music tourism in New Orleans, the city established its world dominance as a center for archival rhythm and blues.

HURRICANE KATRINA

When New Orleans was decimated in 2005 by Hurricane Katrina, one of the deadliest and costliest disasters in U.S. history, the effect on the music scene was dramatic. At first, many musicians were missing and feared dead. Graffiti on Domino's home in the heavily hit Lower Ninth Ward read, "R.I.P. FATS/You will be missed," but he was eventually rescued by boat. Instruments, studios, and historic music venues were gone, and musicians set to work making music to fund aid for survivors and to rebuild their homes and the city. Though the suffering and losses were immense and tragic, they redoubled determination to honor and protect New Orleans' great musical history.

Thus, through countless benefit concerts and albums, the music of New Orleans saved itself and was reborn. Domino gamely responded to rumors of his death by making his first album in thirteen years, *Alive and Kickin'* (2006), the proceeds from which he donated to Tipitina's Foundation to help rebuild school music programs, replace instruments, and aid musicians in need. The foundation thanked him with a charity tribute album titled *Goin' Home: A Tribute to Fats Domino* (2007), featuring tracks by Dr. John, Art Neville, Thomas, Toots and the Maytals, B. B. King, and other performers.

Meanwhile, Toussaint, Dr. John, Thomas, and other greats released *Our New Orleans: Benefit Album for the Gulf Coast* (2005). Toussaint, whose career had experienced a resurgence since the renewed interest in New Orleans music in the 1990s, collaborated with Elvis Costello on another benefit album, *The River in Reverse* (2006), and a subsequent tour. Katrina inspired the prolific Dr. John to release a protest album titled *City That Care Forgot* (2008). Thomas credits Hurricane Katrina with reviving her career. After more than a half century as a singer, she won her first Grammy (for Best Contemporary Blues Album) with *After the Rain* (2006).

Tad Richards

SEE ALSO: *Blues; British Invasion; Costello, Elvis; Domino, Fats; Hurricane Katrina; Jazz; Jordan, Louis; King, B. B.; Little Richard; Rhythm and Blues; Rock and Roll; The Rolling Stones; Soul Music.*

BIBLIOGRAPHY

Abrahams, Roger D.; Nick Spitzer; John Szwed; et al. *Blues for New Orleans: Mardi Gras and America's Creole Soul.* Philadelphia: University of Pennsylvania Press, 2006.

Berry, Jason; Jonathan Foose; and Tad Jones. *Up from the Cradle of Jazz.* Athens: University of Georgia Press, 1986.

Broven, John. *Rhythm and Blues in New Orleans.* Gretna, LA: Pelican, 1978.

Hannusch, Jeff. *I Hear You Knockin': The Sound of New Orleans Rhythm and Blues.* Ville Platte, LA: Swallow, 1985.

Otis, Johnny. *Upside Your Head!: Rhythm and Blues on Central Avenue.* Hanover, NH: Wesleyan University Press, 1993.

Piazza, Tom. *Why New Orleans Matters.* New York: HarperCollins, 2005.

Spera, Keith. *Groove Interrupted: Loss, Renewal, and the Music of New Orleans.* New York: St. Martin's Press, 2011.

New Republic

Known as the magazine read aboard Air Force One, the *New Republic* was born a journal of "the collective opinion of the editors," mainly liberal and occasionally radical, and has remained a leading neo-liberal voice in the early twenty-first century. Beginning with its first editor, Herbert Croly, the magazine has sought to arouse in its readers "little insurrections." The successes of the 1930s New Deal and the rise of communism induced Croly's successors to adopt a more pragmatic political philosophy, but the magazine remained left of center. The conservatism of the 1950s, along with an acute financial problem, pulled the magazine from its pure philosophizing to criticism of the arts, books, and mass. However, its ultimate circulation success was grounded in aggressive national political journalism. During most of its history, the "T.R.B." column has been one of the most popular forecasters of the shifting political winds in the nation's capital.

Magazines have always been made for cultural minorities, especially the well educated and politically involved. The *North American Review* was the most influential intellectual journal for much of the nineteenth century, but after the Civil War it was pressed by newer productions such as *Harper's*, *Scribner's*, *Atlantic Monthly*, and the *Nation*. The latter was founded by Irish journalist E. L. Godkin in 1865 and quickly became the country's leading liberal weekly for its support of labor, African American rights, and other liberal causes. The heady years of the early twentieth century produced a number of challengers to the *Nation*, including the socialist *Masses*, but the *New Republic* was the most endearing and successful.

HISTORY

Croly launched the weekly *New Republic* on November 7, 1914, as a "journal of opinion which seeks to meet the challenge of the new time." A political philosopher who had edited *Architectural Record*, Croly received encouragement and financial support from Willard and Dorothy Straight, who in turn had discovered Croly, as did many other liberals, through his 1909

The Promise of American Life, a book that argued that traditional economic individualism was no longer possible in the industrialized early twentieth-century United States.

Joining Croly on the *New Republic*'s first editorial board were Walter Weyl, a prominent economist, and the brilliant Walter Lippmann, a scholar and author who would become the first nationally syndicated political columnist a decade later. The board featured other learned and articulate voices, but Croly predominated in their decisions through his position as editor and his sense of fair play. The Straights' support for the *New Republic* was so strong that H. L. Mencken once referred to the editors as "kept idealists."

The *New Republic* has always been decidedly intellectual and elitist. Croly explained his purpose was "less to inform or entertain readers than to start little insurrections in the realm of their convictions," and he marketed the magazine for a group of readers roughly equivalent to W. E. B. Du Bois's "Talented Tenth." Under Croly the magazine opposed monopolies, entry into World War I, and fascism and favored child labor laws and other workers' reforms, civil liberties, and liberal third-party movements. Circulation climbed from 875 for the first issue to 43,000 during the height of World War I but settled in the range of 37,000 in 1945. In 1926 a new column, "T.R.B.," first appeared, written by Frank Kent of the *Baltimore Sun*. The column's political gossip and commentary came to be coveted by readers in part because it was written anonymously and it was used by politicians to test the popularity of new ideas. The title and pseudonym were adopted by subsequent writers, and the column remained one of the best read features of the magazine.

FINANCIAL CHALLENGES

Surviving the Great Depression, the magazine faced an unprecedented financial challenge in 1953 when support from a trust fund set up by Willard and Dorothy Straight finally ended. It attracted some advertising but could only boast of a paid circulation of 30,000 or less, which was not enough to support itself. It had first published original poetry in 1915 but turned to cartoons and serious criticism of literature and music as both it and the *Nation* struggled to survive in the 1950s political atmosphere. The *New Republic* turned a circulation corner when it began featuring political journalism, going "from shaping events to commenting upon them," as magazine historian Theodore Peterson explains in *Magazines in the Twentieth Century*. The circulation climbed to more than 100,000 in the 1960s.

Seen in the hand of President John F. Kennedy as he boarded Air Force One, the *New Republic* actively supported the civil rights movement in the 1960s and began criticizing Lyndon Johnson's Vietnam policies as early as 1965. Reporter John Osborne provided a humane portrait of Richard Nixon, at one point counting himself as one of Nixon's "silent majority." Ironically, Osborne's investigative reporting of Watergate helped bring about Nixon's resignation as president in 1974. The magazine abandoned Jimmy Carter and the Democratic Party in 1980, supporting Congressman John Anderson's failed third-party presidential candidacy, just as it had backed earlier third-party bids by Theodore Roosevelt, Robert La Follette, and Henry Wallace.

CHANGING FACES OF LEADERSHIP

The *New Republic* found a renewed sense of leadership in Martin H. Peretz, a Harvard University professor. Peretz and his wife, Anne, heir of the Singer Sewing Machine Company, bought the magazine in 1974. Peretz engineered what he termed a "politically balanced," pragmatic liberalism for the magazine, disillusioning many of its traditional readers." The editors of the *Nation* still thrill to the word revolution," Peretz commented in 1992, "and we don't." Peretz regained credibility with liberals when he fired editor Michael Kelly for being an "obsessive right-winger" in 1997, but the magazine was heavily criticized the following year when it was revealed that reporter Stephen Glass had fabricated more than two dozen stories. Beginning in the 1990s Peretz came under fire for anti-Arab rhetoric, noting in 2010, "Vociferousness is my business."

Peretz sold the magazine to CanWest, a Canadian media company, in 2007 but bought it back in 2009 when CanWest almost went bankrupt. A blog version of the *New Republic* called the Plank was started in 2005, and the magazine began charging for premium content in 2010. The print edition underwent major changes in 2007, including a new design, more pages, a larger format, and a twenty issues per year rather than weekly publication schedule. Its website received more than one million monthly visits in 2010, helping to support the struggling print edition. Circulation declined by about one-half between 2000 and 2010, to around 53,000, or about one-third of its liberal rival, the *Nation*, and one-quarter of its traditional conservative competitor, the *National Review*.

Richard Junger

SEE ALSO: *Advertising;* Atlantic Monthly*; Blogging; Civil Rights Movement; Communism; Du Bois, W. E. B.; The Great Depression;* Harper's*; Lippmann, Walter;* The Masses*; Mencken, H. L.;* The Nation*; New Deal;* Scribner's*; Vietnam; Watergate; World War I.*

BIBLIOGRAPHY

Alterman, Eric. "My Marty Peretz Problem—and Ours." *American Prospect*, June 2007.

Bissinger, Buzz, "Shattered Glass." *Vanity Fair*, September 1998.

Kastor, Elizabeth. "Hailing *The New Republic*: Left, Right and Points between at the Magazine's 70th." *Washington Post*, November 28, 1984, F1.

Mott, Frank Luther. *A History of American Magazines, Vol. 5*. Cambridge, MA: Harvard University Press, 1968.

Nourie, Alan, and Barbara Nourie. *American Mass-Market Magazines*. New York: Greenwood Press, 1990.

Peterson, Theodore. *Magazines in the Twentieth Century*. Urbana: University of Illinois Press, 1964.

Seiderman, David. *The New Republic: A Voice of Modern Liberalism*. Westport, CT: Praeger, 1986.

Shafer, Jack, "In Praise of Marty Peretz." Slate, September 14, 2010.

Wallace-Wells, Benjamin. "Peretz in Exile." *New York Magazine*, December 26, 2010.

New 3-D

Filmmakers have experimented with three-dimensional (3-D) video since the early twentieth century, but the technology reached new heights of popularity following the release of James

Cameron's blockbuster movie *Avatar* in 2009. Whereas 3-D films were once considered something only major studios could produce, recent technological developments have placed them within the realm of possibility for even amateur filmmakers.

Most 3-D films rely on a process called polarization, in which two separate projectors transmit slightly different two-dimensional images onto a screen using filters that allow only certain kinds of light to pass though. Polarized 3-D glasses then filter the resulting image so that each eye perceives only one of the two superimposed images. Finally, the brain combines both images back into a single picture that gives the effect of three-dimensional depth. However, the first wave of polarized 3-D had its limitations: viewers could see 3-D images only when their heads were at right angles, and the technique caused eye strain leading to headaches. Thus, many filmmakers regarded it as a gimmick unfit for serious cinema.

Early in the first decade of the 2000s, a company called RealD developed a new, digital method of projecting polarized images that required only a single projector and significantly reduced the amount of eye strain on viewers. Filmmakers also found a way of making 3-D films more lifelike by "shooting in 3-D" using a special dual-lens high definition digital camera or, in the case of animated films, new 3-D animation software such as InTru3D. Among the first films to combine digital 3-D filmmaking and the new projection technology were *Monster House* (2006); *Monsters vs. Aliens* (2009); *My Bloody Valentine 3-D* (2009); and, most notably, *Avatar*. The runaway success of such films led filmmakers to scramble to convert existing films to the 3-D format, and some even rereleased classic films in 3-D, such as Cameron with *Titanic 3-D* (2012).

In the 2010s, 3-D technology entered the home entertainment market when television manufacturers began producing 3-D-ready televisions to accommodate the influx of 3-D content. Camera companies also released dual-lens handheld cameras that can create homemade 3-D movies. While the craze has its detractors—including film purists who decry the loss of color and focus that occurs when a 2-D film is converted to 3-D—the increasing number of 3-D-enabled devices and accompanying media seems to indicate that that technology will not disappear any time soon.

Jacob Schmitt

SEE ALSO: *Animated Films;* Avatar*; Blockbusters; CGI.*

BIBLIOGRAPHY

Mendiburu, Bernard. *3-D TV and 3-D Cinema: Tools and Processes for Creative Stereoscopy*. Oxford, UK: Focal, 2011.

Prince, Stephen. *Digital Visual Effects in Cinema: The Seduction of Reality*. New Brunswick, NJ: Rutgers University Press, 2012.

New Wave Music

If one were to produce a soundtrack album of the 1980s, most of the tracks would probably be labeled "new wave." Much of what passed for new wave fit well with the overall cultural and political milieu of the 1980s. New wave was the type of music most popular among fans of MTV during its early years, and the musicians who specialized in it are best remembered for their angular haircuts, brightly colored costumes, and heavy reliance on synthesizers. Moreover, new wave is the music of 1980s Brat Pack films, such as *The Breakfast Club* (1985), *Valley Girl* (1983), and *Sixteen Candles* (1984).

Figuring out which artist or song fits into a genre is always a difficult proposition, but new wave presents a particular challenge because of the multiple definitions and the music industry's response to the movement. Bands with a variety of sounds and visual styles have been lumped together under the general umbrella offered by new wave. Consider that the rockabilly Stray Cats and the techno-geek Devo are both considered new wave. Part of the problem stems from the fact that punk rock, which was the "first" wave, was very easily hybridized with other forms of music (reggae, rockabilly, disco, Eurodisco) to produce many "second" wave varieties and styles. Complicating matters, virtually every band that did not have long hair was categorized by its record company as new wave, regardless of its sound.

Ultimately, the faddishness of new wave prompted many acts and their fans to rebel against it. Dozens of subgenres were invented to better define acts, though most of these distinctions

Elvis Costello. *Elvis Costello was the first new wave rocker whose music made a major impact on the music charts.* **ESTATE OF KEITH MORRIS/REDFERNS/GETTY IMAGES.**

quickly blurred. Alternative, post-punk, progressive, synthpop, power pop, alternarock, and Eurobeat were among the subgenres that were invented.

BEGINNINGS

The term *new wave* was first applied to acts that emerged in the late 1960s and early 1970s. Though their music may have had little in common, artists from Britain, the United States, and continental Europe were all tagged as new wave. On the European continent, German groups, particularly Kraftwerk, were slowly forging a new style of music that was heavily reliant upon synthesizers. The danceable forms of European synthesizer music, along with the Philadelphia-based sounds of Gamble and Huff, laid the twin foundations for disco in the 1970s. In England, rock music musicians and fans, fed up with the excesses of hard rock bands such as Led Zeppelin and art-rock bands such as Pink Floyd, turned to a simpler form of rock and roll, a new wave sound sometimes called pub rock. Among the most popular acts in this new category were Elvis Costello, Nick Lowe, and Dave Edmunds. Costello was signed by Columbia Records and, in 1978, became the first of the new wavers to make a significant chart impact.

In the United States, there was a similar backlash against the excesses of mainstream rock and roll. In Manhattan, inspired by Lou Reed and the Velvet Underground, Jonathan Richman founded the Modern Lovers. From the suburbs of Cleveland and Akron, Ohio, similar music began to emerge from other youths who had grown tired of the overblown nature of arena rock. Pere Ubu and, later, Devo established a second new wave hearth in the industrial Midwest.

Sonically, the music of each of these new wave movements shared little, except that it could be played by those lacking great skill or extensive training. It was rock and roll played by enthusiastic amateurs and produced by tiny record companies, often owned by friends or by the band. As such, new wave music had much in common with the indie ethos that propelled punk rock forward, except it was never committed to any particular political movement. New wave was not dangerous or anarchic as punk had traditionally been; it was danceable, romantic, and fun.

THE EVOLUTION FROM PUNK

When punk rock became popular in London in the mid-1970s, it gave a new impetus to new wave music. Punk was too dangerous for most fans in Britain and far too much for most Americans. However, its visual style and spirit was infectious, and the democratization of punk rock generated thousands of new bands. Many of the bands established in the immediate aftermath of punk that did not share punk's belligerence were labeled new wave. These bands found some favor among record companies that recognized the potential market for bare-bones rock music but feared the public relations disaster that might accompany "the next Sex Pistols."

In England, the leading edge of post-punk, new wave was led by bands that borrowed the indie ethos, musical simplicity, and some of the visual elements of punk rock, along with the sonic characteristics of other established genres of music. Perhaps the first of these hybrids to emerge was the reggae/punk of bands such as the Clash and the Police. Other hybrids were forged that wedded punk to a beat of 1950s-style R&B and rockabilly. The Pretenders, which featured Akron-born singer Chrissie Hynde, were one of the more notable no-frills rock acts to be classified as new wave. Some bands formed in the 1970s, such as the Human League, did not really become popular until the new wave sound caught up with what they were doing with synthesizers and the like. The Human League's "Don't You Want Me" (1981) became one of the biggest new wave hits.

In the United States, where punk had less impact, there was not the same explosion of do-it-yourself garage rock and indie record labels that occurred in Great Britain in the late 1970s. In America, disco and arena rock continued to dominate the charts throughout much of the period. Thus, when the market for disco collapsed in late 1978, there was little in the pipeline for record companies to fill the void. Many of the punk and new wave acts that were established on the East Coast and in the Midwest had disbanded during the disco era. The few surviving punk/new wave acts came to the fore and sparked American interest in this new genre. Out of New York's CBGB's club scene came Blondie. Fronted by sexy lead singer Deborah Harry, Blondie was far more flexible politically than their punk brethren. This enabled them to cross over into the pop and disco markets in 1979, the breakout year for new wave. That year, the Cars and the Talking Heads, both with ties to the New York punk scene, also entered the charts. The Knack, a beat revival act from Los Angeles, also made a big splash on the charts in 1979 with their single "My Sharona."

THE ELECTRONICA/SYNTHPOP INFLUENCE

Gary Numan's 1979 album *The Pleasure Principle* marked the arrival of British new wave on the North American pop charts. Numan's synthesized dance music set down a template that would come to characterize a broad subgenre within new wave. The heavy reliance on synthesizers and the stark minimalism of Numan suggested influences ranging from Kraftwerk to Brian Eno to Mike Oldfield. Numan's breakout album not only produced an eminently danceable cut, "Cars," but also popularized synthesizer-produced dance music, which became known in some circles as synthpop.

Some of the more notable synthpop acts following Numan onto the American charts included Ultravox, Orchestral Manoeuvres in the Dark, Depeche Mode, the Human League, Howard Jones, a-ha, New Order, Soft Cell, Erasure, and the Pet Shop Boys. New Order, in particular, stands out among this bunch. In 1980 Ian Curtis, the enigmatic lead singer of the band Joy Division, committed suicide, and his band members reformed under the name New Order. They would become one of the most influential bands in new wave.

Numan's rejection of arena rock musical traditions extended to his stage persona, and many new wavers followed suit. These acts adopted his robotic, technological, futuristic persona, which echoed David Bowie's Ziggy Stardust character. Gone was the ultra-macho hard rock poseur, and in its place was a character without definable gender characteristics—metallic and emotionally detached from his audience. The futuristic motif was carried to extremes by bands such as Devo and Flock of Seagulls and contributed substantially to notions of fashion during the early 1980s. The stage persona of synthpop, with its cool detachment, also set it quite apart from punk music, whose purveyors were interested in destroying the boundary between the audience and performer. U.S. audiences were only too happy to preserve the critical distance between themselves and their pop music gods.

VISUALS OVER POLITICS

New wave's impact was increased significantly by the arrival of MTV into the mainstream during the early 1980s. Because many of the indie-label new wave acts from Britain recognized the value of music videos early, they were better prepared to take advantage of the medium than many American acts. The striking visual appeal of British new wave attracted legions of MTV viewers to the genre, though critics were quick to condemn many of these bands on the grounds of their shallow musicality. Culture Club, featuring the outrageously androgynous Boy George, were particularly adept at using music videos to augment suspect musical talent. Other groups, such as Duran Duran, who preferred the term *new romantic* to new wave, were regularly accused of maintaining their popularity through videos.

The heavy emphasis on visual style, combined with a lack of musical depth, doomed the long-term careers of most of the MTV new wave bands. Many were relegated to one-hit-wonder status and did not make it past the first half of the 1980s. Nevertheless, it was one of the most democratic periods in the history of popular music. The clever use of MTV allowed many new wave bands, even those on the tiniest of labels and with the smallest of budgets, to upstage major-label acts that had massive marketing campaigns.

New wave has been both criticized and praised for its lack of an overt political stance. With few exceptions (R.E.M. and the Clash stand out), new wave offered little rebuttal to the policies of Reaganism and Thatcherism. Many new wave acts were clean-shaven, wore their hair short, and even dressed in ties and jackets. In addition, the more outlandish new wave acts, such as Culture Club, were not viewed as a serious threat to the status quo. Instead, they were considered to be campy but harmless self-parodic personae constructed to appeal to the MTV audience. For many, new wave was hopelessly white, middle class, and safe.

CULTURAL INFLUENCE

On the other hand, new wave acts did push the envelope on several fronts. Certainly, the sexual ambiguity, androgynous appearances, and/or overt homosexuality of many of the acts offered something new to popular music. New wave's indie-label orientation also made many artists exempt from charges of co-optation by the corporate entertainment industry. Some new wavers, particularly R.E.M., carried the indie ethos to extremes, rejecting far more lucrative careers on major labels for many years.

There were also a number of bands that could be grouped with Joy Division/New Order on the darker, moodier side of the new wave movement, such as the Cure, the Smiths, and Tears for Fears. Robert Smith of the Cure and Morrissey of the Smiths were cut from the Ian Curtis mold of smolderingly enigmatic and depressed lead singers, and Tears for Fears had a louder, more aggressive sound than most new wave bands. Some acts that became popular in the early 1980s were considered new wave momentarily but quickly lost identification with the movement, such as U2 and INXS, both of which ultimately moved toward traditional rock sounds.

LASTING IMPACT

Although the MTV brand of new wave was a fleeting moment in popular music, the legacy of genre is impressive. The synthesizer-heavy dance sounds of the English and European new wave influenced the development of many of the popular dance genres of the 1990s, including Chicago-based house music; the techno of Detroit, Michigan; and Europe's various incarnations of Eurodisco. Latter-day new wave acts, particularly R.E.M. and Hüsker Dü, have had a lasting impact on the musical climate in the United States. The indie-rock ethos of these acts proved to be a crucial component of the alternative or college-rock era that bloomed during the later 1980s, which, in turn, gave way to the grunge sound that emerged in Seattle, Washington, in the early 1990s and the splintering of the music market in the later 1990s.

Although grunge and new wave would not seem to have many similarities, the influence of both could be clearly seen on a number of groups that emerged in the first decade of the 2000s. English bands such as Franz Ferdinand, the Arctic Monkeys, and even Coldplay carried the new wave sounds into the twenty-first century. (Chris Martin of Coldplay was reportedly inspired to start the band after listening to a-ha.) American bands such as the Strokes, the Yeah Yeah Yeahs, and the Killers also carried on the punk and new wave traditions, as translated through a grunge microscope.

The combination of the indie aesthetic of punk and grunge and the melodic, dance-friendly sounds of new wave has driven much of the pop and rock music in the twenty-first century. Some new wave bands have also found new life, as their songs have been sampled by hip-hop and R&B artists such as Rihanna. In addition, some new wave hits have found their way into other genres, such as Soft Cell's "Tainted Love" (1981), which was covered by heavy metal's Marilyn Manson in 2001. Decades after first being heard, the eclectic new wave beat goes on.

Steve Graves

SEE ALSO: *Alternative Rock; Blondie;* The Breakfast Club*; The Cars; Costello, Elvis; Devo; Disco; Grunge; Indie Music; MTV; Pop Music; Punk; R.E.M.; Rock and Roll; Stadium Concerts; Talking Heads; U2.*

BIBLIOGRAPHY

Arnold, Gina. *Route 666: On the Road to Nirvana.* New York: St. Martin's Press, 1993.

Belsito, Peter, and Bob Davis. *Hardcore California: A History of Punk and New Wave.* Berkeley, CA: Last Gasp, 1983.

Bianco, David, ed. *Who's New Wave in Music: An Illustrated Encyclopedia, 1976–1982.* Ann Arbor, MI: Pierian Press, 1985.

Cateforis, Theo. *Are We Not New Wave? Modern Pop at the Turn of the 1980s.* Ann Arbor: University of Michigan Press, 2011.

Heylin, Clinton. *From the Velvets to the Voidoids: A Prepunk History for a Post-Punk World.* New York: Penguin, 1993.

Kozak, Roman. *This Ain't No Disco: The Story of CBGB.* Boston: Faber and Faber, 1988.

Marcus, Greil. *Lipstick Traces: A Secret History of the Twentieth Century.* Cambridge, MA: Harvard University Press, 1989.

McNeil, Legs, and Gillian McCain, eds. *Please Kill Me: The Uncensored Oral History of Punk.* New York: Penguin, 1997.

Palmer, Myles. *New Wave Explosion: How Punk Became New Wave, Became the 1980s.* New York: Proteus, 1981.

Robbins, Ira A., ed. *The Trouser Press Guide to New Wave Records.* New York: Scribner, 1983.

New York

SEE: *The Big Apple.*

The New York Knickerbockers

New York's professional basketball team, known popularly as the Knicks, has been a vital part of the city's sports landscape since 1946. Winners of two National Basketball Association (NBA) titles, the Knicks are one of basketball's best-known and most prestigious franchises.

An original member of the Basketball Association of America—forerunner of the NBA—the club played its first game in Canada against the Toronto Huskies on November 1, 1946. The first home game took place ten days later at Manhattan's Madison Square Garden. In those early years the Knicks fielded a team of mostly white Jewish and Catholic players drawn from the city's public university system. That began to change in 1950 with the signing of Nat "Sweetwater" Clifton, one of the first black players in the NBA. The team enjoyed only mixed success through its first two decades, consistently making the playoffs but failing to capture even one world championship.

The team's fortunes took a turn for the better in 1968 when Red Holzman took over as head coach. The no-nonsense Holzman preached a philosophy of aggressive defense, fluid passing, and team-first self-abnegation. This approach would have produced results even with mediocre players, but Holzman was blessed with some of the great performers of his era. Center Willis Reed, guard Walt "Clyde" Frazier, and forwards Dave DeBusschere and Bill Bradley were all destined for the Hall of Fame. Together they led the team to a world championship in 1970. The crowning moment came in the seventh game of the finals, when Reed, who had missed the sixth game because of an injury, limped onto the court and scored the game's first basket to the delight of the Madison Square Garden faithful.

The Knicks of this period captured the imagination of the city. The cerebral Bradley, a one-time Princeton standout who went by the somewhat unbefitting appellation "Dollar Bill," helped bring an intellectual patina to the pro game that appealed to the city's *New York Times*–reading cognoscenti. He would later cement his reputation as an intelligent jock by being elected U.S. senator from the state of New Jersey and serving for eighteen years. By contrast, the high-living Frazier was the walking apotheosis of the sports star as man-about-town. With his luxurious Afro, feathered hat, and long leather coat, Clyde was the embodiment of uptown cool. Like Joe Namath before him, he brought a style and sex appeal to his team that attracted the attention of fans and non-fans alike.

For the next several seasons, the Knicks remained one of the NBA's elite teams. The addition of sharpshooting guard Earl "The Pearl" Monroe in 1971 gave the squad an explosive backcourt complement to Frazier. Finalists in 1972, the New Yorkers won the NBA crown for the second time in 1973. Then a slide into dormancy began. Frazier was traded to the Cleveland Cavaliers in 1977, and the team's other great players retired. Holzman himself then gave up the coaching reins, signaling the end of an era in New York basketball.

RETURN TO RESPECTABILITY

A new era dawned in 1985 when now-general manager DeBusschere drafted Patrick Ewing of Georgetown University to be the team's franchise player. A towering, physically gifted center, Ewing battled injuries in his first few seasons but finally blossomed under head coach Rick Pitino, who stressed an up-tempo, pressing attack. The Knicks regularly made the playoffs but could not win a championship. When Pitino left to coach the University of Kentucky in 1990, the organization began to drift again. Only the hiring of former Los Angeles Lakers coach Pat Riley in 1991 returned the club to marquee status.

The fiery, dictatorial Riley, who was recognized as much for his impeccably moussed coiffure as his coaching prowess, harnessed the mercurial talents of such temperamental players as Ewing; Anthony Mason, a former Turkish league cast-off; and John Starks, a supermarket grocery bagger. Playing a suffocating brand of defense, the team made the Eastern Conference finals in 1993 and the NBA Finals the following year. There they fell by turns to the Chicago Bulls and the Houston Rockets, establishing a precedent for failing in big games that infuriated the team's fans throughout the decade.

The Knicks traded Ewing in 2000 and suffered a string of losing seasons after his departure. In 2003 the team hired former all-star point guard Isiah Thomas as president. This move failed to rejuvenate the franchise; the team suffered from a series of scandals, including a sexual-harassment conviction of Thomas that led to his firing and $11.6 million in damages being awarded to the defendant, a former Knicks executive.

After hiring Mike D'Antoni as coach in 2008, the front office embarked on a rebuilding process that included signing star players Amar'e Stoudemire and Carmelo Anthony. In the lockout-shortened 2011–2012 season, the team got off to a miserable 8–15 start. Things changed when D'Antoni inserted point guard Jeremy Lin—a player who had done little his first two years as a pro—into the lineup. Lin immediately went on a tear, leading the team to a winning streak that put it back into playoff contention. While no one could predict how far Lin could carry the Knicks, the resulting excitement over his play (dubbed "Linsanity" by the press) gave Knicks fans a reason to be excited about their team again.

Robert E. Schnakenberg

SEE ALSO: *Basketball; Bradley, Bill; The Chicago Bulls; Frazier, Walt "Clyde"; The Los Angeles Lakers; Monroe, Earl "The Pearl"; Namath, Joe; National Basketball Association (NBA); The* New York Times*; Riley, Pat; Thomas, Isiah.*

BIBLIOGRAPHY

Araton, Harvey. *When the Garden Was Eden: Clyde, the Captain, Dollar Bill, and the Glory Days of the New York Knicks.* New York: Harper, 2011.

Benson, Michael. *Everything You Wanted to Know about the New York Knicks: A Who's Who of Everyone Who Ever Played on or Coached the NBA's Most Celebrated Team.* Lanham, MD: Taylor Trade Publishing, 2007.

Jackson, Kenneth T. *The Encyclopedia of New York City.* New Haven, CT: Yale University Press, 1995.

Kalinsky, George. *The New York Knicks: The Official Fiftieth Anniversary Celebration.* New York: Macmillan, 1996.

The New York Mets

New York's National League baseball franchise, the New York Mets, rose to take the place of two teams that departed for

California in the 1950s. Attired in blue and orange—colors borrowed from the Dodgers and Giants, respectively—the club began play in 1962 at the Polo Grounds in Manhattan. Their new home, Shea Stadium, opened in Queens two years later. In contrast to the corporate-run Yankees, the Mets positioned themselves as scrappy, lovable underdogs, and their Keystone Kops style of play was excused as endearing ineptitude. When the team won its first world championship, improbably, in 1969, the "Miracle Mets" took blue-collar New York by storm. The stars of that era, particularly pitchers Tom Seaver and Tug McGraw, became folk heroes.

The club fell on hard times in the late 1970s, but in the 1980s the Mets boasted a new generation of stars led by pitcher Dwight Gooden and outfielder Darryl Strawberry. The 1986 team won an astonishing 108 games and went on to beat the Boston Red Sox in the World Series to win the franchise's second championship. Both Gooden and Strawberry began to struggle with substance abuse, however, and the team was unable to reach the World Series again for the rest of the 1980s or the entire 1990s. In 1993 the team had its worst season in almost thirty years, losing 103 games.

Gradually, however, the team improved enough to return to the World Series in 2000, dubbed the "Subway Series" as the Mets played their crosstown rivals the New York Yankees. The Yankees won in five games. In 2007 and 2008 the Mets suffered the indignity of being eliminated from the playoffs by losing their final regular-season game at home two years in a row. The team opened a new ballpark, Citi Field, in 2009 but promptly turned in losing seasons their first three years in the stadium. At the end of the 2011 season, the team looked into making alterations to the park to make it more friendly to hitters.

Robert E. Schnakenberg

SEE ALSO: *Baseball; Boston Red Sox; The Brooklyn Dodgers; Gooden, Dwight; The New York Yankees; Sports Heroes; Strawberry, Darryl; World Series.*

BIBLIOGRAPHY

Honig, Donald. *The New York Mets: The First Quarter Century.* New York: Crown, 1986.

Jackson, Kenneth T. *The Encyclopedia of New York City.* New Haven, CT: Yale University Press, 1995.

New York Daily News; Andy Martino; and Anthony McCarron. *The Mets: A 50th Anniversary Celebration.* New York: Stewart, Tabori & Chang, 2011.

Silverman, Matthew. *New York Mets: The Complete Illustrated History.* Minneapolis, MN: MVP Books, 2011.

The *New York Times*

Few family institutions have endured for more than a century and maintained their reputation as has the *New York Times*. While other newspapers used sensationalism to gain as many readers as possible, the *Times* established high standards for journalism not found in other papers and thus created for itself an audience of international newsmakers and government officials. If people wanted to know what their leaders were thinking, they turned to the *New York Times*

When Adolph Ochs purchased the *New-York Daily Times* (as it was named when it was founded in 1851) on August 13, 1896, he promised to produce a newspaper without fear or favor, a newspaper of record, one that published, as the motto on page one has said since February 10, 1897, "All the News That's Fit to Print." The *Times*, which leads all newspapers with more than 100 Pulitzer Prizes, entered the twenty-first century still owned by the descendants of Ochs. The *Times* won its first Pulitzer Prize in 1918 "for its public service in publishing in full so many official reports, documents and speeches by European statesmen relating to the progress and conduct of the war." Fifty-four years later the *Times* won another Pulitzer Prize for publishing, in effect, official reports and documents relating to a war, but that Pulitzer was for the publication of the "Pentagon Papers," and the *Times* had to go to the U.S. Supreme Court to maintain its right to publish what the Nixon administration claimed was classified information.

Despite several high-profile scandals, the *Times* continues to be the most respected newspaper in the United States. As it did for all forms of media, readership began to decline in the 1990s, and the newspaper responded by establishing itself as a major online presence. By the 2010s, the online version of the *Times* was the most widely read American newspaper website. As a means of raising revenue, the paper announced the creation of a paywall, meaning that after accessing a designated number of articles for free, readers would be required to pay a fee to read the paper online. Subscribers to the paper's hard copy were exempt. The *Times* also initiated digital subscriptions for frequent online readers.

GOVERNMENTAL REPORTING

The early *New York Times* avoided the sensational journalism of its day and invested heavily not just in reporting on the federal government but also on international news. It was so thorough, such a paper of record, that one army official reportedly said that the *Times* was "too big to read, too important not to." A former U.S. Navy radio operator recalled delivering the daily secret intelligence report and having one officer say, "Ah, the front page of the *New York Times*."

The *Times* carried a story in 1961 that the United States was planning to invade Cuba. Much to the dismay of reporters and editors, the publisher at the time ordered that the story be toned down so as not to give away government secrets. The story was toned down, the invasion was a failure, and President John F. Kennedy later said he wished the *Times* had published the entire story so he might have canceled the invasion and avoided embarrassment. Although it was not the last time that the *Times* took its cue from Washington, it did signal a shift in how the newspaper responded to government pressure.

One of the paper's biggest breaking stories was the publication of the Pentagon Papers, but there were indications of the increasing depth of the *Times*'s reporting before that. One such signal came in 1966 when a *Times* reporter, Harrison Salisbury, who had won a Pulitzer Prize in 1955 for his reporting on the Soviet Union, managed to report on the Vietnam War from behind the North Vietnamese lines. Salisbury reported, among other things, that U.S. bombs were hitting civilian targets, which had not been made clear by the U.S. government. Until Salisbury's report, most Americans had been led to believe that military targets were bearing the brunt of U.S. bombs.

When the *Times* began publishing a series on the Pentagon Papers in 1971, few realized what a tremendous step it was for the paper as well as for the practice of journalism. A government-

"All the News That's Fit to Print."

The New York Times.

LATE CITY EDITION
Fair, slowly rising temperature today. Tomorrow cloudy, moderately cold, occasional snow.

Copyright, 1941, by The New York Times Company.

VOL. XCI. No. 30,638. NEW YORK, FRIDAY, DECEMBER 12, 1941. THREE CENTS

U.S. NOW AT WAR WITH GERMANY AND ITALY; JAPANESE CHECKED IN ALL LAND FIGHTING; 3 OF THEIR SHIPS SUNK, 2D BATTLESHIP HIT

BLOCKED IN LUZON

But Japanese Put Small Force Ashore in South of Philippine Island

SABOTEURS ARE HELD

Some in Manila Seized for Spreading Rumor About City Water

By H. FORD WILKINS

MANILA, Friday, Dec. 12—The United States Army Far East headquarters announced today that a small Japanese invasion force was reported to have pushed ashore at Legaspi, Southern Luzon, and "the enemy has improved his strength in Northern Luzon," where, however, the situation remains unchanged materially.

Line-Up of World War II

THE ALLIES

Australia	Haiti
†Belgium	*Honduras
Canada	Netherlands Indies
China	New Zealand
Costa Rica	Nicaragua
Cuba	†Norway
†Czecho-Slovakia	*Panama
Dominican Republic	†Poland
*El Salvador	South Africa
Free France	†Soviet Union
Great Britain	United States
†Greece	†Yugoslavia
Guatemala	

THE AXIS

Finland	Japan
Germany	Manchukuo
Hungary	Rumania
Italy	Slovakia

*Have declared war on Japan only.

†At war only with Germany, Italy and their European allies.

CITY CALM AND GRIM AS THE WAR WIDENS

Loyalty and a Determination to Win Are Evident in Every Class and National Group

U. S. FLIERS SCORE

Bombs Send Battleship, Cruiser and Destroyer to the Bottom

MARINES KEEP WAKE

Small Force Fights Off Foe Despite Loss of Some of Planes

By CHARLES HURD

WASHINGTON, Dec. 11—A Japanese battleship, a cruiser and a destroyer have been sunk in the Pacific and a second battleship badly damaged by bomb hits, the United States forces announced in communiqués today recording their first major victories in the war-fare that began last Sunday with surprise Japanese attacks.

Continued on Page Six

Left: The President set his signature to the act against Germany. Center: He checked the time with Senator Tom Connally. Right: After that he placed the United States officially at war with Italy.

WAR OPENED ON US

Congress Acts Quickly as President Meets Hitler Challenge

A GRIM UNANIMITY

Message Warns Nation Foes Aim to Enslave This Hemisphere

By FRANK L. KLUCKHOHN

WASHINGTON, Dec. 11—The United States declared war today on Germany and Italy, Japan's Axis partners.

Continued on Page Five

The International Situation

FRIDAY, DECEMBER 12, 1941

AXIS TO GET LESSON, CHURCHILL WARNS

He Announces Replacement of Libyan General—Upholds Phillips's Judgment

Text of Mr. Churchill's speech will be found on Page 16.

By CRAIG THOMPSON

Continued on Page Seventeen

Our Declaration of War

Special to THE NEW YORK TIMES.

WASHINGTON, Dec. 11—Following are the texts of the documents wherein the President asked a war declaration against Germany and Italy, and Congress acted:

The President's Message

To the Congress of the United States:

On the morning of Dec. 11 the Government of Germany, pursuing its course of world conquest, declared war against the United States.

The long-known and the long-expected has thus taken place. The forces endeavoring to enslave the entire world now are moving toward this hemisphere.

Never before has there been a greater challenge to life, liberty and civilization.

Delay invites great danger. Rapid and united effort by all of the peoples of the world who are determined to remain free will insure a world victory of the forces of justice and of righteousness over the forces of savagery and of barbarism.

Italy also has declared war against the United States.

I therefore request the Congress to recognize a state of war between the United States and Germany, and between the United States and Italy.

FRANKLIN D. ROOSEVELT.

The War Resolution

Declaring that a state of war exists between the Government of Germany and the government and the people of the United States and making provision to prosecute the same.

Whereas the Government of Germany has formally declared war against the government and the people of the United States of America:

Therefore, be it

Resolved by the Senate and House of Representatives of the United States of America in Congress assembled, that the state of war between the United States and the Government of Germany which has thus been thrust upon the United States is hereby formally declared; and the President is hereby authorized and directed to employ the entire naval and military forces of the United States and the resources of the government to carry on war against the Government of Germany; and, to bring the conflict to a successful termination, all of the resources of the country are hereby pledged by the Congress of the United States.

(An identic resolution regarding Italy was adopted)

Secretary Knox Visits Honolulu; Bases There Were Raided 5 Times

Special to THE NEW YORK TIMES.

WASHINGTON, Dec. 11—The Navy Department announced tonight that Secretary Frank Knox had arrived in Honolulu this afternoon.

"Civilian defense measures are working without a hitch," he added.

Continued on Page Eleven

CONGRESS KILLS BAN ON AN A. E. F.

Swift Action Without Debate—Service Terms Are Extended to Six Months After War

Continued on Page Thirty-four

New York Times *Front Page, December 12, 1941. The headline on the front page of the* New York Times *on December 12, 1941, announces the United States' entry into World War II.*

sponsored secret account of the Vietnam War, the papers showed that many of the war's public supporters had private doubts about the involvement of U.S. troops. While the papers showed the administration of President Lyndon Johnson in a bad light, the incumbent president, Richard Nixon, ordered the Justice Department to seek an injunction keeping the *Times* from publishing more of the Pentagon Papers. This was the first time that the federal government attempted prior restraint—an unconstitutional practice. The *Times*, joined by the *Washington Post*, was forced to go to the U.S. Supreme Court to preserve the right to publish without censorship.

A STANDARD BEARER

While winning the right to publish the Pentagon Papers was a historic legal victory, the *Times* has won other legal decisions that have strengthened the practice of journalism. Prominent among those was *New York Times v. Sullivan*, a case decided by the U.S. Supreme Court in 1964. This case was triggered when the *Times* published an advertisement that contained several factual errors about public officials and police in Montgomery, Alabama. The *Times* lost the case in Alabama state courts and appealed to the Supreme Court, which ruled that because the people mentioned in the advertisement were public officials, they would have to prove that the advertisement was published with a reckless disregard for the truth or with knowledge that it contained false statements. By establishing such a high standard for defamation of public officials, the court strengthened the atmosphere for robust debate on public matters necessary to democratic self-government. The case established a federal defamation standard, which created consistent ground rules for publications, particularly those that are distributed in thousands of different jurisdictions.

The *Times* published more than news sections. The paper established a book review section that eventually became a Sunday magazine. During World War II a list of best sellers was added. In the 1980s one author, feeling slighted because his novel was not listed when he felt it should have been, sued the *Times* for $3 million but lost in state court and could not get the decision reversed in the U.S. Supreme Court. By the twenty-first century, the *New York Times* best-seller list was a well-recognized sign of a texts' quality.

Around the same time as the arrival of the best-seller list, the *Times* began publishing a crossword puzzle, one that was so challenging that people would brag if they were able to do it with a pen instead of a pencil. However, the newspaper has resisted publishing editorial cartoons or comics. The *Times* uses the honorifics "Mr." and "Mrs.," whereas many newspapers use a person's surname on second reference, though it was slow to adopt "Ms." because the publisher did not want it.

The *Times* has weathered economic challenges throughout its history. Under the leadership of one of Ochs's grandsons, the paper began advertising itself as "*The New New York Times*" during the 1970s. The paper went from two sections to four, with some of those sections changing daily and thus providing readers with different magazines within the newspaper. Of course, the different sections were aimed at attracting specific advertisers and thus had themes such as food, the home, the arts, and weekend entertainment. One of the most successful sections was "Science Times," which attracted profitable computer advertising, leading the *Times* to create a weekly computer section called "Circuits." Special slick Sunday magazines devoted to fashion or travel also appeared regularly and helped boost the paper's bottom line. During these changes, the reporting improved and the topics diversified as the *Times* went from a paper of record focusing only on policy to one that focused on policy and people. Some have said that when the *Times* covers a topic, it is sociology not journalism—an indication of the depth and breadth of many of its stories.

As with many other print news sources, the *New York Times* was faced with significant financial difficulties at the outset of the twenty-first century. Flagging advertising revenue and decreased circulation had already distressed its position, which was further hindered by economic downturn in 2008. In 2009 the Times Company accepted a $250 million loan from Mexican investor Carlos Slim Helu to pay off mounting debts; the loan was repaid before its deadline thanks to a slight upswing in revenue in 2011. Amid such challenges, the *Times* made what many critics believe to be questionable business decisions. The nearly $24 million severance package that accompanied CEO Janet Robinson's 2011 dismissal was met with much disapproval, particularly by employees who faced cut backs and possible layoffs. In another highly criticized move, it was reported that owners, the Ochs-Sulzberger family, pressured the Times Company to reinstate dividend payouts. Again outcry arose from employees and readers who opposed such executive benefits in a time when the paper was doing all it could to say afloat.

CONTINUING EVOLUTION

Although not perfect, the *Times* has tried to be a dignified newspaper, befitting Ochs's motto. In the 1950s it ran a photograph of Joe DiMaggio and Marilyn Monroe kissing open-mouthed, and the picture editor was removed from his post—although he remained on the payroll—as a result of the criticism. When U.S. Vice President Nelson Rockefeller, a former governor of New York, was photographed raising his middle finger to a group of protesters, the *Times* did not publish the photo and merely said: "After protesters showed they were able to drown out his speech, Mr. Rockefeller then gestured three times with his finger." Another time, a reporter turned in a story quoting someone as saying "chicken shit," and the desk changed it to a "barnyard epithet."

Early in the first decade of the 2000s, the *Times* hired Jayson Blair, a young reporter with almost no experience who subsequently plagiarized and fabricated facts. His misdeeds were exposed beginning on April 26, 2003, when his story about the family of a missing soldier was proved to have been lifted from a previous article in the *San Antonio-Express News*. Blair was immediately fired, and the *Times* began a major investigation into the matter. During the aftermath, several major executives were fired, including executive editor Howell Raines.

The paper has had a playful side at times. When Latin was dropped as a New York public school course, the *Times* ran an editorial with the headline: "Quatenus Mortua Lingua Latina?" The accompanying 105-word editorial was written in Latin with no accompanying translation. While the *Times* has been faulted for being slow to change, it has been a journalistic leader in other areas and often able to do things other newspapers could not.

Perhaps the evolution of the *Times* can be summed up in one short anecdote: in 1976 the paper adopted a six-column format, bringing it in line with the appearance of other newspapers. Its story announcing the change concluded: "The *Times* used a six-column format when the newspaper first appeared on Sept. 18, 1851." In other words, the more the newspaper changed, the more it stayed the same.

R. Thomas Berner

SEE ALSO: *Google; Vietnam; The* Wall Street Journal*; The* Washington Post*; World War I; World War II.*

BIBLIOGRAPHY

Blair, Jayson. *Burning Down My Master's House: My Life at the "New York Times."* Beverly Hills, CA: New Millennium, 2004.

Diamond, Edwin. *Behind the Times: Inside the "New New York Times."* New York: Villard Books, 1994.

Halberstam, David. *The Powers That Be.* New York: Alfred A. Knopf, 1979.

Kraus, Jerelle. *All the Art That's Fit to Print (And Some That Wasn't): Inside the "New York Times" Op-Ed Page.* New York: Columbia University Press, 2009.

Mnookin, Seth. *Hard News: The Scandals at the "New York Times" and Their Meaning for American Media.* New York: Random House, 2004.

Salisbury, Harrison E. *Without Fear or Favor: "The New York Times" and Its Times.* New York: Times Books, 1980.

Shepard, Richard F. *The Paper's Papers: A Reporter's Journey through the Archives of "The New York Times."* New York: Times Books, 1996.

Talese, Gay. *The Kingdom and the Power.* New York: World Publishing Company, 1969.

The New York Yankees

Like Cadillac or BMW, the New York Yankees' brand name is respected the world over, a badge of excellence in the realm of professional baseball. That a hit Broadway play called *Damn Yankees* could play off the antipathy generated in rival cities by the franchise's unmatched success is a testament to the powerful associations the team conjures up in the popular mind. Known for its reverence for tradition, the Yankee organization need do little to market itself to prospective ticket buyers. The mere presence of the club's stately eponymous stadium in the South Bronx, with its wall of plaques commemorating some of the game's greatest players, is enough to keep tourists, baseball aficionados, and loyal fans flocking to see the "Bronx Bombers" play.

LARGER-THAN-LIFE STARS

The team began life as the New York Highlanders in 1903. They were renamed the Yankees in 1913 and began playing in Manhattan's Polo Grounds that same year. Millionaire brewer Jacob Ruppert bought the team with a partner in 1915 for $460,000. His most significant contribution to baseball history was the purchase of Babe Ruth's contract from the Boston Red Sox in 1919, a sale that altered the fortunes of both franchises. The Red Sox became a symbol for futility, beloved by New Englanders but bereft of any luck, common sense, or winning tradition. The Yankees, by contrast, evolved into, well, the Yankees.

With Ruth leading the way, the Yankees won their first World Series in 1923. The team would add two more world championships and six American League pennants in the decade. A magnificent new ballpark, Yankee Stadium, opened in 1923 and was home to a "Murderers' Row" lineup through the late 1920s and into the 1930s. Feared sluggers Lou Gehrig, Earle Combs, and Tony Lazzeri ably complemented the protean Ruth, who swatted sixty home runs in 1927 to lead the team to a 110-win season. Ruth also became America's first national sports icon, a figure so revered he commanded no less than half a dozen nicknames: the Sultan of Swat, the Caliph of Clout, the Wazir of Wham, and so on. Once, asked what he thought about being paid more than President Herbert Hoover, Ruth cracked: "I had a better year than he did." Tethered to the Babe's balloon, the Yankees rose in prominence to become America's preeminent sports franchise.

When the aging of its first generation of stars threatened to end the Yankees' run at the top, the club merely brought in new faces. Joe DiMaggio spearheaded a squad that won six World Series between 1936 and 1943. His fifty-six-game hitting streak in 1941 captured the nation's attention at a time when America stood on the brink of world war. Almost the polar opposite of Ruth in his approach to life and disdain for the limelight, DiMaggio nevertheless became almost as luminous a figure. Certainly his marriage to national sex kitten Marilyn Monroe in 1954 had something to do with that apotheosis as well. Ernest Hemingway immortalized DiMaggio's "grace under pressure" by repeatedly referencing the Yankee Clipper in his 1952 novel *The Old Man and the Sea.*

After DiMaggio retired in 1951, the Yankees filled the void with another altogether different matinee idol. Mickey Mantle, a brawny farm boy from Oklahoma, became the team's new centerfielder. The blond-haired, blue-eyed "Mick" seemed carved out of someone's ideal of what a ballplayer should look like. He could run and hit with power from both sides of the plate. And while he was prone to injury over the course of his seventeen-year career, he would secure a place in the Hall of Fame and a legacy as one of the game's greatest players.

Mantle and his Yankees bestrode the 1950s baseball landscape like a colossus. From 1950 to 1958 the team won six world championships. The 1961 squad led by Mantle and Roger Maris, who broke Ruth's record of sixty home runs in a season, was widely cited as the equal of the 1927 edition. It was during this dynastic period that a vehement hatred of the Yankee organization took hold in a number of cities, as teams like the Brooklyn Dodgers and Cleveland Indians found their championship hopes repeatedly dashed by the free-spending cosmopolites from Gotham.

DECLINE AND REBUILDING

Those rivals would yet see the tables turned, beginning in 1964 when broadcasting behemoth CBS bought the Yankees for a reported $14 million. It was the beginning of a steep decline for the franchise. The team's best players, most notably Mantle, were past the prime of their careers, and the club was slow to recruit African American and Latino players to replace them, as many other organizations were doing. The Yankee front office, it seemed to many, was living in a world of the past. The club sank to tenth place in 1966, posting the worst record of any Yankee squad in fifty-three years. Attendance plummeted. Most galling of all, the Yankees' crosstown rivals, the New York Mets, graduated from bumbling novelties to world champions in 1969.

Slowly, the Yankees began to rebuild. Their new catcher, Thurman Munson, won the Rookie of the Year Award for 1970.

Shrewd trades brought them the likes of Graig Nettles and Chris Chambliss, infielders who would play a prominent role in the club's resurgence. And CBS, seemingly disinterested in the team's fortunes and the desires of its fans, finally sold out from under its losses in 1973. The Yankees' new principal owner was George M. Steinbrenner III, a shipbuilding magnate from Cleveland, Ohio. Steinbrenner vowed to take a hands-off approach, leaving the day-to-day operation of the club to his chief lieutenant, Gabe Paul.

Under new leadership, the Yankees returned to the front ranks of the American League. They competed for a division title in 1974, despite playing their home games in the Mets' own Shea Stadium. A two-year renovation of crumbling Yankee Stadium was completed in time for the 1976 opener. That season was to be flush with renewal for the Bronx Bombers, as they surged to their first American League pennant in twelve years. First baseman Chambliss's dramatic ninth-inning home run in the fifth game of the playoff series against the Kansas City Royals sealed the victory. The exultation felt by legions of long-suffering Yankee fans was to be short-lived, however, as the club was trounced in the World Series by the Cincinnati Reds, four games to none.

Over the next five years, the Yankees reestablished themselves as baseball's elite team, capturing three pennants and two world championships. Their back-to-back World Series wins in 1977 and 1978 were capped by a thrilling come-from-behind divisional pennant race with the Boston Red Sox in the latter year. Controversy and conflict also marked these years of winning. Outspoken slugger Reggie Jackson was added as a free agent in 1977, to the consternation of the team's cantankerous manager, Billy Martin. Together with the increasingly meddlesome Steinbrenner, the three men formed a veritable death grip of sorts, as their public spats were splashed all over the pages of the New York City tabloids. Reliever Sparky Lyle later labeled the team's poisonous clubhouse "The Bronx Zoo." Nevertheless, the Yankees kept on winning, and the fans loved the roller derby atmosphere.

THE MOST SUCCESSFUL FRANCHISE

The Yankees' run of disco-era dominance ended with a 1981 World Series loss to the Los Angeles Dodgers, an embarrassing coda to a strike-shortened season that prompted Steinbrenner to issue an ostentatious public apology to the citizens of New York. The 1980s saw the imperious owner struggle to cover up the team's deficiencies in player development with his checkbook. Steinbrenner signed high-priced players with seemingly little regard for their adaptability to the pressures of playing in New York. Managers were put under intense pressure to succeed, subject to dismissal at any time according to the owner's whims. Three men were hired and fired during the 1982 season alone. Billy Martin returned for three more engagements as the club's skipper, in 1983, 1985, and 1988. Only the presence of Don Mattingly, the club's dignified captain, prevented Yankee fans from being thoroughly alienated by the whole charade.

Yankee fortunes improved only after Steinbrenner's 1990 exile from baseball following allegations he had hired a professional gambler to spy on one of his players. "The Boss" remained locked away from running team affairs for three years, during which time general manager Gene "Stick" Michael effectively ran the club. Freed from Steinbrenner's tyranny, Michael returned the organization to its roots, emphasizing player development at the minor-league level. Future stars Bernie Williams, Derek Jeter, and Mariano Rivera, who would have been traded away in years past, were nurtured until they were ready to take their places in the starting lineup. A few key trades and the judicious use of free-agent signings helped the Yankees recapture first place in the strike-shortened 1994 campaign.

By that time, Steinbrenner was back on the job but in no position to tamper with the interim regime's formula. Some said he had mellowed. Certainly he came back from exile with a renewed willingness to let his "baseball people" run the team. Other than pointlessly firing manager Buck Showalter in 1995 after a loss in the playoffs, he did little to slow the development of a new baseball juggernaut. Under new manager Joe Torre, the team capped a stellar 1996 season with a come-from-behind upset victory over the Atlanta Braves in the World Series. Two years later, the Yankees posted the best record in American League history, going 114–48. They then completed an impressive playoff run by sweeping the San Diego Padres in the World Series. Baseball pundits promptly began arguing over whether this was the greatest team of all time. And when the Yankees' record twenty-fifth world championship banner was raised onto the facade at Yankee Stadium on April 11, 1999, there was no doubt which was the most successful franchise in baseball's first full century. The Yankees added a twenty-sixth championship in 2000.

In the new millennium, the aging Steinbrenner gradually yielded his duties to his sons Hank and Hal. Hal was given control of the team in 2008, even though his father retained the title of chairman. Also in 2008 the Yankees came under the leadership of new manager Joe Girardi, a former major-league catcher who had spent the previous year managing the Florida Marlins. In 2009 the team opened a new $1.5 billion ballpark, still under the name Yankee Stadium. That same year Girardi led the team to its twenty-seventh World Series championship. George Steinbrenner, who had owned the team for thirty-seven years, died in 2010.

Robert E. Schnakenberg

SEE ALSO: *Baseball; Boston Red Sox; Broadway; The Brooklyn Dodgers; DiMaggio, Joe; Gehrig, Lou; Hemingway, Ernest; Jackson, Reggie; Mantle, Mickey; Mattingly, Don; Monroe, Marilyn; The New York Mets; Ruth, Babe; Sports Heroes; Steinbrenner, George; World Series; Yankee Stadium.*

BIBLIOGRAPHY

Anderson, Dave. *The Yankees: The Four Fabulous Eras of Baseball's Most Famous Team.* New York: Random House, 1980.

Chadwin, Dean. *Those Damn Yankees: The Secret History of America's Greatest Sports Franchise.* New York: Verso, 1999.

Frommer, Harvey. *The New York Yankee Encyclopedia.* New York: Macmillan, 1997.

Gallagher, Mark. *The Yankee Encyclopedia.* Champaign, IL: Sagamore Publishing, 1996.

Honig, Donald. *The New York Yankees: An Illustrated History,* rev. ed. New York: Crown, 1987.

Krantz, Les. *Yankee Stadium: A Tribute: 85 Years of Memories: 1923–2008.* New York: It Books, 2008.

Madden, Bill. *Steinbrenner: The Last Lion of Baseball.* New York: HarperCollins, 2010.

Mead, William B. *The Official New York Yankees Hater's*

Handbook. New York: Putnam, 1983.

Stout, Glenn, and Dick Johnson. *Yankees Century: 100 Years of New York Yankees Baseball.* New York: Houghton Mifflin Harcourt, 2002.

Sullivan, George, and John Powers. *The Yankees: An Illustrated History.* Philadelphia: Temple University Press, 1997.

Torre, Joe, and Tom Verducci. *The Yankee Years.* New York: Doubleday, 2009.

Weinberger, Miro, and Dan Riley, eds. *The Yankees Reader.* Boston: Houghton Mifflin, 1991.

The *New Yorker*

The first issue of the *New Yorker* magazine arrived on newsstands in February 1925. The brainchild of Harold Ross, who was viewed as an unlikely genius, the periodical weathered a rocky start but soon established itself as a bastion of literacy, wit, and sophistication. A mix of fact, fiction, poetry, and cartoons, the *New Yorker* set high standards in all four fields, despite the fact that founder/editor Ross had never completed high school. The first writers to set the tone for the magazine were E. B. White and James Thurber. Their sly, elegant wordplay enabled Ross to achieve his vision of a magazine that—unlike the popular *Saturday Evening Post*—would "not be edited for the old lady from Dubuque." With its deliberately cosmopolitan focus, the *New Yorker* found unexpectedly wide favor across the country.

Over the next decades stories and cartoons from the *New Yorker* became the basis for successful plays, films, and television series, ranging from Clarence Day's *Life with Father* and Sally Benson's *Meet Me in St. Louis* to Thurber's *The Secret Life of Walter Mitty* and Charles Addams's cartoon *The Addams Family.* Among the leading literary lights who contributed humor and serious fiction to the *New Yorker* were Robert Benchley, Dorothy Parker, S. J. Perelman, Ring Lardner, Eudora Welty, John Cheever, John O'Hara, Truman Capote, and Woody Allen.

Upon the death of Ross in 1951, William Shawn took over the editorship with equal success until his abrupt dismissal in 1987 after a change in ownership. In later years the periodical went through rough periods, but it has maintained the status of its "snob appeal." It may have smacked of hubris when the *New Yorker* courted new subscribers by touting itself as "the best magazine that ever was," but the people at the periodical knew that, in the eyes of many longtime readers, the hubris was completely justified.

BEGINNINGS

Harold Ross was born in Aspen, Colorado, in 1892. His family later moved to Salt Lake City, Utah, where Ross dropped out of high school during his sophomore year. After itinerant work on a score of newspapers, he enlisted in the army upon America's entry into World War I. Once overseas young Ross went AWOL to Paris, where he managed to get assigned to the staff of the army's new journal for soldiers, *Stars and Stripes.* Before long he was running the paper and turning it into a great success.

As a civilian after the armistice, Ross ended up in Manhattan, where old army buddy Alexander Woollcott invited him to join the legendary Algonquin Round Table—a daily gathering of writers and wits at the hotel of the same name whose avowed purpose was to drink, play cards, and best each other at bons mots (not necessarily in that order). The wits of the Algonquin crowd included Benchley, Parker, Lardner, George S. Kaufman, and Edna Ferber. Together they provided Ross with much of the inspiration to start the new magazine. It was a latecomer to the Round Table, bakery heir Raoul Fleischmann, who provided Ross with the wherewithal that enabled him to realize his dream. Journalist Gigi Mahon has described the odd couple thusly: "Fleischmann was calm and diplomatic, Ross was crude and obstreperous. . . . If one tried to guess which was the baker and which the editor, one would likely have got it wrong."

LAUNCHING A MAGAZINE

Their differences notwithstanding, Ross and Fleishmann formed F-R Publishing Corp., for Fleischmann-Ross. The majority of the money was Fleischmann's, and the concept for the magazine was all Ross's. Public relations man John Peter Toohey christened the publication the *New Yorker*, and artist Rea Irvin created the monocled dandy regarding a butterfly that graced the cover of the first issue and most subsequent issues. Eventually the dandy was given a name, Eustace Tilley. Prior to publication, Ross had set down his vision for the *New Yorker* in a position paper, describing the contents and standards of excellence with which he planned to imbue his magazine. Eventually, as Mahon puts it, "The *New Yorker* could boast the rarest of achievements: It became exactly what it set out to be."

But that first step out of the gate was a stumble. The magazine's tone was arch, and its humor was not funny. Fortunately Fleischmann kept putting money into the enterprise long enough for the *New Yorker* to find its unique voice and a loyal readership. With the valuable editorial assistance of Katharine Angell, who later married White), Ross's magazine began to resemble the one he had always had in mind. Readers started to look forward to such features as the lighthearted "Talk of the Town" and the insightful "Profiles" of prominent people. The first sell-out issue was the result of a piece by Ellin MacKay, who later became the wife of Irving Berlin; "Why We Go to Cabarets: A Post Debutante Explains" contrasted the gay nightlife at cabarets with the stuffy doings at debutante balls. Regardless, the *New Yorker* itself cultivated a definite snob appeal, courting advertisements from only the poshest and ritziest of Manhattan emporiums.

Because his magazine was just starting out, Ross could not afford to publish articles and stories by famous writers. Consequently, he welcomed new talent, and the magazine and its writers grew famous together. White, who is best known for the children's classic, *Charlotte's Web*, contributed greatly to the early success of the *New Yorker* by editing the "Talk of the Town" column and writing its "Notes and Comments" preface. Another prime White contribution to the magazine was his encouragement and support of his friend James Thurber, who soon became known not only for his humorous stories and reminiscences but also for his uniquely artless style of cartooning (a famous Thurber cartoon showed a seal leaning against the headboard of a couple's bed. In the caption the wife says to the husband, "All right, have it your way. You heard a seal bark!"). Other regular *New Yorker* contributors included Ross's friend Woollcott (the "Shouts and Murmurs" column); Wolcott Gibbs (whose brilliant parody of rival *Time* magazine included the famous line, "Backward ran sentences until reeled the mind"); Alva Johnston, author of many of the well-received "Profiles"; and Clifton Fadiman and Lewis Mumford, who wrote about books and art, respectively.

For all the excellence of its prose, the *New Yorker* took a special pride of place among periodicals for its presentation of excellent cartoons. Although not an artist, White supplied the caption for a classic Carl Rose cartoon: A mother at the dinner table says to her child, "It's broccoli, dear." The kid replies, "I say it's spinach, and I say the hell with it." Peter Arno was one noted cartoonist whose gags usually poked fun at the upscale businessmen and matrons of Manhattan. One such cartoon depicted a distinguished-looking gentleman kneeling at his bedside in prayer: "Harrison J. Endicott speaking." The characters created by Charles Addams, on the other hand, inhabited a world all his own, a macabre, fantastic pastiche of horror-movie haunted house and twisted suburbia. Decades later his prime creations would find fame on television—and, still later, in films—as *The Addams Family*.

SUCCESS AND CHANGES

The *New Yorker* ultimately became one of the most successful magazines in the country. However, despite its carefully crafted cosmopolitan image, 70 percent of its readership lived well outside the greater Manhattan area. With the coming of World War II, the periodical inevitably grew more sober in its content, and the *New Yorker*—like a lot of less prominent publications—suffered from wartime paper shortages. Remembering his own military days on *Stars and Stripes*, Ross produced a stripped-down "pony" edition of the *New Yorker* for the armed forces that ended up outselling the original, even gaining new readers who eventually made the postwar *New Yorker* more successful than ever.

Fleischmann had been gaining increasing financial control over the *New Yorker* since its inception, but there was no question that in matters editorial Ross was still at the helm. There was something of the stumblebum about the profane Ross, who reportedly once asked a writer, "Is Moby Dick the whale or the man?" But there was no denying his knack for hiring exceptional talent and then worrying, fretting, questioning, and in general pushing it to the limits of its capability. In his affectionate memoir, *The Years with Ross*, Thurber relates that journalist/financier John Duncan Miller had this impression upon meeting the legendary figure: "During the first half hour, I felt that Ross was the last man in the world who could edit the *New Yorker*. I left there realizing that nobody else in the world could."

Inevitably, however, somebody else had to take over as editor. Ross died in December 1951, and the following month it was announced that his successor would be Shawn. A member of the editorial staff since 1933, Shawn had convinced Ross to devote an entire 1946 issue of the magazine to John Hersey's devastating chronicle, *Hiroshima*. Whereas Ross had been blustery, Shawn was quiet, well spoken, and shy. However, his rule was every bit as absolute as his predecessor's. The years with Shawn at the helm altered the *New Yorker* in subtle ways. There were fewer humorous covers and a tendency toward more serious and political literature, but the magazine continued to be successful.

By the mid-1950s, although ranking seventy-second of all magazines in circulation, the *New Yorker* was running third in terms of advertising pages. As Mahon points out in *The Last Days of the "New Yorker,"* "[The magazine] was . . . virtually alone in catering to people with intelligence and wealth. It was . . . the only literary publication that consistently made money." The *New Yorker* continually proved that seriousness of purpose was not inconsistent with commerce. It was the *New Yorker* that published such groundbreaking works as Rachel Carson's *Silent Spring*, marking the beginning of the environmental movement; James Baldwin's impassioned examination of race relations in *The Fire Next Time*; and Truman Capote's "fact-novel" about murder, *In Cold Blood*. Controversial critic Pauline Kael came to dominate her field, and Roger Angell was considered an outstanding sportswriter.

The institution of the *New Yorker*, commensurate with its high-tone image, has always had about it an air of insularity. Since the magazine's first days with Ross, the masthead has never listed the editor's name. Within that special enclave, a family feeling has always been fostered, frequently reinforced by marriages between personnel. As with most families, there have been squabbles. Such a clear line of demarcation was drawn between the editorial and business branches that they might almost have been working for two different magazines. It was clearly understood that the latter was not to interfere in the doings of the former.

LEADERSHIP IN LATER YEARS

Business had a decisive impact on editorial in the mid-1980s when the *New Yorker* was purchased by media emperor S. I. Newhouse and his Condé Nast corporation. Within a year Shawn was forced into retirement—an action that had a singularly demoralizing effect on the *New Yorker* family. Tina Brown of *Vanity Fair* magazine became the first female editor of the *New Yorker* in 1992. The following year her selection of Art Spiegelman's Valentine's Day cover sparked a national controversy over its depictions of a Jewish man and a black woman kissing. During her tenure Brown focused on photography, added color to the layout, and increased the magazine's circulation. Under her editorship the *New Yorker* won multiple rewards, including its first General Excellence Award in 1995.

When Brown departed Manhattan for Hollywood in 1998, David Remnick took over. He proved to be less concerned with making changes to the magazine, but he oversaw the magazine during the terrorist attacks on September 11, 2001; the cover he created with Françoise Mouly silhouetted the towers against a black background and was highly celebrated. Spiegelman resigned from the magazine in February 2003, citing his belief that the American media became increasingly timid in the wake of the attacks. He later authored an essay that supported the invasion of Iraq in 2003 and endorsed John Kerry for president in 2004. In 2008 he defended the controversial cover, "The Politics of Fear," by Barry Blitt. The cover depicted presidential hopeful Barack Obama dressed in traditional Muslim clothing and Michelle Obama in military fatigues with an AK-47. The couple is standing in the Oval Office with a picture of Osama bin Laden in the background and an American flag burning in the fireplace. Intended as a satirical comment on the rhetoric surrounding Obama's presidential campaign, the cover was criticized by both political parties and sparked debates among journalists.

CHANGING TIMES, CHANGING TECHNOLOGIES

Like many print publications, the *New Yorker* experienced a decline in subscriptions and a loss in advertising sales in the face of the Internet. The proliferation of technology and media forced the entire print industry to scramble to find ways to remain relevant and viable sources of information. The *New Yorker* launched its website in 2001, and although some content is available to every user, the magazine established a subscription-based service for access to the entire current issue as well as to the complete archive of back issues. It has also released iPad and iTunes applications to broaden access for its readers. Sales and subscriptions had stabilized by 2010, and although the advances in technology provided some constancy in readership and subscriptions, the *New Yorker*, like all news brands, faced a growing concern over how companies such as Google, Yahoo!, and Apple were consolidating ad revenue and controlling the platforms on which news was disseminated.

The magazine may never see another long-running editorial dynasty such as Ross's or Shawn's, but it is still a going concern—its reputation a bit battered, perhaps, but still largely intact—and it is still an influential component of contemporary culture. Television's *Seinfeld* aired an episode in which Elaine manages to get a job on the *New Yorker* staff purely because she does not get the joke in one of the cartoons and wishes to confront the editor. Many readers continue to regard the *New Yorker* as "the best magazine that ever was"—whether or not it remains the best magazine that is.

Preston Neal Jones

SEE ALSO: *The Addams Family; Advertising; Allen, Woody; Apple Computer; Baldwin, James; Benchley, Robert; Berlin, Irving; Capote, Truman; Comics; Environmentalism; Google; Hersey, John; Hollywood; Horror Movies; The Internet; iPad; iPod / iTunes; Lardner, Ring; Leisure Time;* Maus*; Meet Me in St. Louis; Obama, Barack; Parker, Dorothy; The* Saturday Evening Post*;* Seinfeld*; Suburbia; Television; Thurber, James;* Time*; Valentine's Day;* Vanity Fair*; White, E. B.; World Trade Center; World War I; World War II.*

BIBLIOGRAPHY

Gambone, Robert L. *Life on the Press: The Popular Art and Illustrations of George Benjamin Luks*. Jackson: University Press of Mississippi, 2009.

Gill, Brendan. *Here at the "New Yorker."* New York: Random House, 1975.

Hamburger, Philip. *Friends Talking in the Night: Sixty Years of Writing for the "New Yorker."* New York: Alfred A. Knopf, 1999.

Lazare, Daniel. "The *New Yorker* Goes to War." *Nation*, June 2, 2003.

Lee, Judith Yaross. *Defining "New Yorker" Humor*. Jackson: University Press of Mississippi, 2000.

Mahon, Gigi. *The Last Days of the "New Yorker."* New York: McGraw-Hill, 1988.

Mehta, Ved. *Remembering Mr. Shawn's "New Yorker": The Invisible Art of Editing*. Woodstock, NY: Overlook Press, 1998.

Mitchell, Amy, and Tom Rosentiel. "State of the News Media 2012: Annual Report on American Journalism." Pew Research Center's Project for Excellence in Journalism, March 19, 2012.

Ross, Lillian. *Here but Not Here*. New York: Random House, 1998.

Silverman, Jonathan, and Dean Rader. *The World Is a Text: Writing, Reading, and Thinking about Visual and Popular Culture*. Boston: Prentice-Hall, 2012.

Thurber, James. *The Years with Ross*. Boston: Little, Brown, 1958.

Newhart, Bob *(1929–)*

Bob Newhart is one of the rare television performers to have starred in two tremendously successful shows. From his early days as a thriving stand-up comedian to his sustained run on popular sitcoms of the 1970s and 1980s, Newhart managed to keep audiences laughing. Most closely identified with *The Bob Newhart Show* (1972–1978) and the later *Newhart* (1982–1990), he played a man who calmly weathered the storms that constantly raged in the lives of his friends and family. Newhart's comedic talent stems from his use of a sense of quiet desperation and a stutter to create his own unique version of the "straight man": not boastful or self-righteous but the quintessential "normal" person.

After serving in the Korean War from 1952 to 1954, Newhart worked as an accountant and an advertising copywriter. He and his friend at the ad agency, Ed Gallagher, amused themselves by making long, antic phone calls to each other, which they recorded as audition tapes for comedy jobs. When Gallagher dropped out, Newhart developed his now famous one-man, two-way telephone conversation stand-up routine. In 1959 he was introduced to the head of talent at Warner Brothers Records. *The Button-Down Mind of Bob Newhart*, released in 1960, was the first comedy album to reach number one on the charts. Newhart set records for comedy album sales through the early 1990s.

Based on this success, Newhart was approached by NBC to host a variety show. The first *Bob Newhart Show* (1961–1962)

Bob Newhart. *Bob Newhart's career in show business has spanned more than fifty years in which he brought his deadpan humor to the stage, television, and screen.* © MARK SULLIVAN/WIREIMAGE/GETTY IMAGES.

won both an Emmy and a Peabody Award but was canceled in the first season. The comedian subsequently appeared in a number of movies, playing small but memorable roles, including Dr. Mason Hume in *On a Clear Day You Can See Forever* (1970), Major Major in *Catch-22* (1970), a cigarette company pointman in *Cold Turkey* (1971), and the president of the United States in *First Family* (1980). He also supplied the voices of Bernard the Mouse (*The Rescuers*, 1977; and *The Rescuers Down Under*, 1990) and Leonard the Polar Bear (*Rudolph the Red-Nosed Reindeer: The Movie*, 1998).

TELEVISION HITS

Newhart is perhaps most famous for the second *Bob Newhart Show*, which debuted in 1972 on CBS and ran for six years. He played Dr. Robert "Bob" Hartley, an almost deadpan Chicago psychiatrist surrounded by friends and family with assorted problems and neuroses. The show costarred Suzanne Pleshette as Bob's wife, Emily, and one of the finest casts of feature players on television, including Bill Daily as the addled neighbor Howard Borden, Peter Bonerz as Bob's friend and office colleague Jerry Robinson, Marcia Wallace as the smart-mouthed secretary Carol Kester, and Jack Riley as the eternally neurotic patient Mr. Elliot Carlin.

The first hit to come out of MTM Enterprises, *The Bob Newhart Show* ushered in a new phase of television comedy. It joined a roster that included such family-focused shows as *All in the Family* (1968–1979), *The Mary Tyler Moore Show* (1970–1977), and others that tried to capture a modern perspective on gender at home and in workplace; and comedy-drama shows such as *M*A*S*H* (1972–1983). By 1978, however, the show faced declining ratings, and Newhart left to go back to live performance.

In 1982 the actor returned to CBS with *Newhart*, playing a New York how-to book author turned Vermont innkeeper and eventual host of a local talk show, *Vermont Today*. Newhart's Dick Loudon had essentially the same temperament as Bob Hartley but was surrounded by a heightened level of insanity. After the end of the first season, the show had assembled most of its main characters: Dick's wife, Joanna; handyman George; the maid Stephanie (the rich and snooty cousin of the show's first maid); and Michael, the producer of the local talk show whose money-consciousness and odd quirks meshed perfectly with Stephanie's. For further comic relief the show added three brothers: Larry, Darryl, and the other brother Darryl, who would do anything for a buck.

Newhart ended in 1990 against the wishes of the network because its star preferred to put the show to rest while it was at its peak. Television fans remember the classic final episode in which Loudon "awoke" in his old bedroom from *The Bob Newhart Show*—with Pleshette next to him—proclaiming that he had had the strangest dream. Critics and fans alike have called this the single best and most surprising episode in television comedy history.

COMEDY COMEBACK

In 1992 Newhart made a comeback when the Showtime cable channel approached him to do the comedy special *Off the Record*. He subsequently starred in two new productions, ready to deploy the formula that had worked so well in his past shows. *Bob* (1992–1993) featured him as a 1950s comic-book creator who is saddled with a new young, brash partner. In *George and Leo* (1997–1998), he played a flustered bookstore owner on Martha's Vineyard who cannot shake the obnoxious father (performed by Judd Hirsch) of his son's wife. Neither won the hearts of viewers in the way that his previous shows had.

Newhart continued his varied career in the twenty-first century. In 2003 he played opposite Will Ferrell as Papa Elf in the box-office topper *Elf*. He appeared on three 2003 episodes of *ER* (1994–2009), for which he earned a 2004 Emmy Award, and in 2005 he had a recurring role on *Desperate Housewives* (2004–2012). Comedy Central listed him as number fourteen on the 2004 *100 Greatest Stand-ups of All Time*. He was nominated for another Emmy in 2009 for a reprisal of his role on the television movie series *The Librarian* that starred Noah Wyle.

The human flaws Newhart displayed in his characters—his quiet, almost meek, manner; his stammering; and the appearance of letting others push him around—may be the very reasons that he became such a significant actor. His characters represent many people's feelings of frustration with a seemingly crazy world.

Frank E. Clark

SEE ALSO: *Advertising;* All in the Family*;* Catch-22*; Daytime Talk Shows;* Desperate Housewives*; Emmy Awards;* ER*;* The Mary Tyler Moore Show*;* M*A*S*H*; Networks;* Rudolph the Red-Nosed Reindeer*; Sitcom; Stand-Up Comedy; Telephone; Television.*

BIBLIOGRAPHY

Castleman, Harry, and Walter J. Podrazik. *Harry and Wally's Favorite Shows: A Fact-Filled Opinionated Guide to the Best and Worst on TV.* New York: Prentice Hall, 1989.

Kercher, Stephen E. *Revel with a Cause: Liberal Satire in Postwar America.* Chicago: University of Chicago Press, 2006.

Marc, David, and Robert J. Thompson. *Prime Time, Prime Movers: From "I Love Lucy" to "L.A. Law"—America's Greatest TV Shows and the People Who Created Them.* Boston: Little, Brown, 1992.

McNeil, Alex. *Total Television: A Comprehensive Guide to Programming from 1948 to the Present*, 3rd ed. New York: Penguin Books, 1991.

Putterman, Barry. *On Television and Comedy: Essays on Style, Theme, Performer, and Writer.* Jefferson, NC: McFarland, 1995.

The Newlywed Game

Short-sighted TV viewers might believe the airing of couples' dirty laundry on television started with the talk show craze of the 1990s, with Jerry Springer as the ultimate ringmaster. But it actually began back in the 1960s in the realm of game shows, courtesy of Springer's spiritual forefather, veteran producer Chuck Barris.

The Newlywed Game ran on and off, daytime and nighttime, between 1966 and 2010. It featured four couples who had been married less than a year, competing against each other. After the wives were "safely secured offstage," the husbands were asked questions such as: "Would your wife say she sleeps with her toes pointing toward the wall, ceiling, or floor?" "What animal would you compare your mother-in-law to?" "If your wife were a car, what would need to be repaired most, her fenders or transmission?" The husbands guessed how the wives would answer, then the wives came back and answered the same questions, and couples got points for matching answers. Then the husbands were sent out, and the process repeated. The couple with the most points won some sort of domestic "newlywed" prize, such as a dishwasher.

Presiding over the festivities was Bob Eubanks, an unctuous, pompadoured host. He got to ask the prying questions and provided deadpan reactions to the wackiness. Sometimes he took it on the road, staging the game in shopping malls all over the country. Eubanks hosted the day and nighttime incarnations of the show until 1989, when he was replaced by Latino comic Paul Rodriguez for a season; the show was canceled soon after that.

The real idea behind *The Newlywed Game* and its slightly older cousin, *The Dating Game* (also from Barris and hosted by the oily Jim Lange), was to see how much sex talk could be gotten away with without getting in trouble with the network's Standards and Practices division. America's puritan/voyeuristic dichotomy was never more apparent than in the loaded questions; the coy yet revealing answers; and, most of all, the titters in the audience—members of which seemed almost shocked at the mere idea that these married people had sex. In fact, those who thought *The Dating Game* ("Bachelor Number One: If I were an ice cream cone, would you lick my cream or bite my cone?") was sleazy were often surprised to learn that, although the contestants were married, *The Newlywed Game* was somehow even sleazier.

This was a time, after all, when jokes about the rabbitlike sex lives of newlyweds still made sense. Couples seldom lived together before marriage, and convention still dictated that no one was really having premarital sex. Of course the word *sex* was not used on the show. It was "whoopee" that the audience was imagining the couples feverishly making, not love. Against the backdrop of the burgeoning sexual revolution, it's almost laughable and somehow more trashy with the euphemism, which became ingrained in the American consciousness.

Legend has it that Howard Hughes was planning to buy ABC, but after catching *The Newlywed Game* one afternoon, he was so disgusted that he immediately called off the deal. The show is also the stuff of urban myth: in response to a question from Eubanks about the "most unusual place you've ever made whoopee," amid responses such as "on the kitchen table" or "the bathroom of a 747," a female contestant supposedly responded, "That would be in the butt, Bob." There has been much speculation as to whether or not this ever happened, and even it if had, network censors would never have allowed in on the air. Barris claims it happened in his book *The Game Show King*; however, he admits he didn't witness it himself. Eubanks, who should know, has repeatedly offered a $10,000 reward to anyone who provides him with a video of the incident.

The later, 1980s versions of the show, such as *The New Newlywed Game*, were a little more explicit and mean-spirited ("If your sex life were made into a movie, which part of the video store would it be found in—horror, fantasy, or XXX-rated weirdo?" "Which of your wife's friends would most likely be harpooned if she were floating in the ocean?"). Reviewing the series in 1987, *TV Guide* called it "the worst piece of sleaze on television today."

Barris, who later spawned *The Gong Show*, once noted that if a newlywed couple loved and respected each other, they probably would never have thought about appearing on *The Newlywed Game*; if they had, they probably wouldn't have been chosen, because they wouldn't have made good contestants. If that opinion doesn't seal the connection between *The Newlywed Game* and the talk show expose-a-ramas, consider the contestant who accused her husband, on the air, of having an affair, saying "I knew about it, but I wanted to wait until we got on national TV to tell everybody."

The Newlywed Game was rebroadcast in syndication in the 1990s and early in the first decade of the 2000s. In 2009 the Game Show Network (GSN) revived *The Newlywed Game* on its cable channel, altering the format slightly and allowing some same-sex couples. Carnie Wilson hosted the show from 2009 to 2010; she was then succeeded by *The View* cohost Sherri Shepherd.

Karen Lurie

SEE ALSO: *Cable TV; Daytime Talk Shows; Game Shows; Hughes, Howard; Malls; Moore, Michael; Springer, Jerry; Syndication; Tabloid Television; Television;* TV Guide*;* The View.

BIBLIOGRAPHY

Barris, Chuck. *The Game Show King: A Confession*. New York: Carroll & Graf, 1993.

Brooks, Tim, and Earle Marsh. *The Complete Directory to Prime Time Network and Cable TV Shows 1946–Present*, 6th ed. New York: Ballantine Books, 1995.

Dougherty, Margot. "Dreaming Up Questions to Choke on, the "New Newlywed Game" Writers Never Quit Making Whoopee." *People Weekly*, August 3, 1987, 44.

McNeil, Alex. *Total Television*. New York: Penguin, 1996.

Nelson, Craig. *Bad TV: The Very Best of the Very Worst*. New York: Delta, 1995.

Newman, Paul *(1925–2008)*

Paul Newman was one of the most respected actors in film history, as well as a noted director and philanthropist. He was involved in more than sixty movies, but he was perhaps best known for his portrayal of the title character in *Cool Hand Luke*. Film buffs saw him neither as a Marlon Brando–like tough guy nor as a "sensitive" lead but as someone who took chances on "ugly" roles. "No star who looked as heroic as Newman ever [portrayed] more losers, cads . . . and beaten men, or played them with more understanding," wrote Mark Harris in *Entertainment Weekly*'s cover story on Newman after the actor's death in 2008. Film critic David Ansen of *Newsweek* added that Newman "played heels whom everyone fell in love with." Despite his renown as an actor, Newman is perhaps best known by younger generations as the face of Newman's Own, the philanthropic food company he cofounded in the 1980s and ran for the rest of his life. Newman died of lung cancer on September 26, 2008.

Newman attributed his stardom to his many early advantages in life, plus his inherited good looks. Blue eyes were his signature: he joked that he would lose his fame and fortune if they ever changed color. Confidence and charisma were reflected in his "King Cool" nickname, but he came from plain, middle-class beginnings.

Born on January 26, 1925, in the Cleveland suburb of Shaker Heights, Ohio, he was the son of a sporting goods store owner. After serving in World War II as a navy radioman/gunner on carrier-based airplanes, he attended Ohio University before being kicked out for unruly behavior. He finished school at Kenyon College, married the aspiring actress Jacqueline Witte, and briefly managed his father's store. He decided to take a chance on an acting career and enrolled in Yale University's School of Drama. He sold sets of *Encyclopaedia Britannica* to support his family, and he later attended the New York Actors Studio.

Actress Joanne Woodward and Newman became close while filming *The Long, Hot Summer* (1958). Despite some feelings of guilt, he divorced Witte (with whom he had fathered three children) and married Woodward. During their half century together, they had three children of their own and lived primarily in Westport, Connecticut.

AN ACCLAIMED CAREER

Newman's early career included Broadway plays, his film debut in the flop *The Silver Chalice* (1954) that he later regretted, and a TV production of Thornton Wilder's *Our Town*. He won praise as a gangster-turned-boxer in *Somebody up There Likes Me* (1956), and he was nominated for an Oscar for playing a repressed alcoholic opposite Elizabeth Taylor in *Cat on a Hot Tin Roof* (1958). He was also cast in *Exodus* (1960), a drama about the Arab-Israeli conflict.

Acclaimed as a lowlife pool shark in *The Hustler* (1961) and a vicious, modern cowboy in *Hud* (1963), Newman's most famous role may be as the nonconforming title character in *Cool Hand Luke* (1967), a prison movie (based on Donn Pearce's book of the same title) that is regarded as one of the best films of its time, with its famed catchphrase, "What we've got here is failure to communicate." He was a top draw by the time he and Robert Redford costarred in the iconic Western, George Roy Hill's tragicomic *Butch Cassidy and the Sundance Kid* (1969). Redford and Newman also headlined the multi-Oscar-winning film *The Sting* (1973). Later, Newman brightened up director Robert Altman's parodic *Buffalo Bill and the Indians* (1976) and a variety of other films, including *The Towering Inferno* (1974) and *Slap Shot* (1977).

In the 1980s Newman delivered "wrenching, emotionally specific performances" in films such as *Absence of Malice* (1981) and *The Verdict* (1982) that "cemented his status . . . as an actor who was interested in the frailty, flaws, and humanity of every character he portrayed," according to Harris. *The Color of Money* (1986), a sequel to *The Hustler*, won Newman a long-elusive Oscar for portraying "Fast Eddie" Felson, an aging pool-hall hustler mentoring another rogue (played by Tom Cruise) with quips like "You gotta have two things to win. You gotta have brains and you gotta have balls. Now, you got too much of one and not enough of the other."

After playing the spirited Louisiana governor Earl K. Long (brother to Huey P. Long) in *Blaze* (1989), he took on projects as diverse as *The Hudsucker Proxy* (1994) and *Nobody's Fool* (1994). Newman created a chillingly murderous mob boss in the Oscar-winning *Road to Perdition* (2002). Offscreen, one of his final roles was as the stage manager of an award-winning 2003 production of *Our Town*.

Newman also worked as a director. His directorial debut, *Rachel, Rachel* (1968), won Oscar nominations for Woodward (Best Actress) and Estelle Parsons (Best Supporting Actress) and won Golden Globes for Best Actress (Woodward) and Best Director. He went on to direct *Sometimes a Great Notion* (1971), which starred Henry Fonda and earned Richard Jaeckel an Oscar nomination for Best Supporting Actor, and *Harry & Son* (1984).

OTHER INTERESTS

Newman became a race-car driver after training for the film *Winning* (1969) and hosting the TV special *Once upon a Wheel* (1971). A serious competitor, he placed as recently as 2005 at the Daytona raceway. Newman, who counted actor and racing buff Steve McQueen among his friends, narrated the 1996 racing season in IMAX film *Super Speedway* and voice acted (as Lightning McQueen's friend) in the animated film *Cars* (2006).

Newman's sense of ethics pushed him well beyond racing and acting, contrary to his renderings of underworld killers and shifty, self-serving cowboys like Hud, whose mantra was "You don't look out for yourself, the only helping hand you'll ever get is when they lower the box." In real life, Newman rejected egotistically limited worldviews and advocated instead for gun control, nuclear disarmament, and progressive politics. He supported the civil rights movement and related causes, including protests against the Vietnam War and efforts to end discrimination against gays. When he was placed on President Richard Nixon's "enemies list," he said that it was one of his greatest distinctions.

Feelings of guilt over the 1978 overdose death of his son Scott only pushed Newman to donate more of his time and effort to social causes. In 1982 Newman and writer A. E. Hotchner founded a line of salad dressings that became Newman's Own, a natural foods–oriented company. The company became famous for donating all of its after-tax profits to philanthropic causes. Despite some controversial partnerships (for example, distributing its salad dressings through Burger King and then, years later, through the McDonald's Corporation), Newman's Own became a unique and enduring legacy. It had donated more than $330 million to charity by 2012.

Stephen P. Davis

SEE ALSO: *Academy Awards; Altman, Robert; Brando, Marlon; Broadway; Burger King;* Butch Cassidy and the Sundance Kid*; Fonda, Henry; Hollywood; McDonald's; McQueen, Steve; Organic Food; Redford, Robert; Taylor, Elizabeth; Wilder, Thornton.*

BIBLIOGRAPHY

Ansen, David. "The Verdict: A Legend." *Newsweek*, September 26, 2008.

Dherbier, Yann-Brice, and Pierre-Henri Verlhac, eds. *Paul Newman: A Life in Pictures*. San Francisco: Chronicle Books, 2006.

Harris, Mark. "Paul Newman, 1925–2008." *Entertainment Weekly*, October 4, 2008.

Levy, Shawn. *Paul Newman: A Life*. London: Aurum, 2010.

Newman, Paul, and A. E. Hotchner. *In Pursuit of the Common Good*. New York: Broadway Books, 2008.

Newman's Own. "Our Story." Accessed May 2012. Available from http://newmansown.com/ourstory.aspx

Newport Jazz and Folk Festivals

Jazz critic Leonard Feather once said that when the Newport Jazz Festival debuted in 1954 in Newport, Rhode Island, it initiated the "festival era" in American music. Though there had been other jazz festivals in Europe, the Newport Jazz Festival—and the Newport Folk Festival, which began a few years later—did indeed popularize a new style of concert giving, creating a music-filled community for several days of performances. In the process, the festivals made live music accessible to a large number of people and gave a huge promotional boost to two of the most truly American forms of music, jazz and folk.

In July 1954 musician and impresario George Wein organized and presented the first Newport Jazz Festival in the beautiful Rhode Island seaside town of Newport. The festival became famous for showcasing jazz greats such as Count Basie, Ella Fitzgerald, Thelonious Monk, Dave Brubeck, and Miles Davis, advancing the careers of those jazz greats by offering them exposure to mainstream audiences. It also gave a stage to new, even radical, voices in jazz: in 1969 the rock group Led Zeppelin played there, in 1998 Liquid Soul brought acid jazz to the venerable New England stage, and in 2011 the festival showcased the irreverent anarchy of innovative quartet Mostly Other People Do the Killing.

Because the festival's cutting-edge music attracted many counterculture and radical fans, it became a natural site for the eruption of political demonstrations. Riots in 1960, 1969, and 1971 resulted in cancellation, and in 1972 the Newport Jazz Festival moved to New York City, where it acquired an urban energy and vitality that had never been present in the sleepy town of Newport. Venues varied, with one of the most inventive being the Staten Island Ferry, aboard which Ray Charles gave a concert. In 1991 the Newport Jazz Festival returned home to Rhode Island, where it celebrated its fiftieth anniversary in 2004.

One of the major innovations introduced by Wein—an energetic organizer with many festivals and concerts to his credit—was to expand the role of corporate sponsorship. Wein was the first to offer sponsors naming rights to concerts, and thus, in 1981, the Newport Jazz Festival became the Kool Jazz Festival when Kool Cigarettes took over sponsorship. In 1986 JVC Electronics became the sponsor, and the festival name changed again to the JVC Jazz Festival. The festival also began to broaden its approach to music and to include performers more representative of rhythm and blues or soul than pure jazz. This approach brought popular stars such as Aretha Franklin and Patti Labelle to the festival's stage. JVC also introduced a series of JVC Newport Jazz Festivals across the United States and in many places abroad, as well as Newport Jazz Cruises between festivals.

Wein sold his interest in the festival in 2007 but returned in 2009 when JVC dropped sponsorship and it appeared as though the festival might not happen. Since then, he has continued to run the festival, juggling sponsorships and turning both the Newport Jazz and Folk Festivals into registered nonprofit organizations to ensure their survival into the future.

Tapping into a new and exciting movement in American folk music, the Newport Folk Festival debuted in 1959 with such soon-to-be famous stars as Joan Baez, who arrived in a converted hearse for her performance. The festival was a perennial draw for the leftover bohemians of the 1950s as well as for the hippies of the 1960s, many of them musical purists who booed Bob Dylan at the 1965 festival for playing an electric

Bob Dylan and Newport Folk Festival. *Bob Dylan performs at the Newport Folk Festival in 1964.* DOUGLAS R. GILBERT/REDFERNS/GETTY IMAGES.

guitar. In 1967 Arlo Guthrie introduced his famous song, "Alice's Restaurant," at the Newport Folk Festival. By 1969, however, the increasing popularity of rock music and the volatile political times brought about the end of the festival, and there was no major folk music venue in Newport for more than fifteen years. Then, in 1985, Wein, continuing to do what he did best, brought the folk festival back to Newport. His reunion of old-time festival mainstays such as Baez, Guthrie, Judy Collins, and Doc Watson brought in crowds of thousands of fans each day. Continuing his tradition of sponsor partnership, he initiated the annual Ben & Jerry's Newport Folk Festival, adroitly tying together the festival and the New England counterculture image of the Vermont ice creamery.

The 1990s saw a new take on festival culture with touring music festivals, such as Lollapalooza and Lilith Fair, and in 1998 the Newport Folk Festival Tour was launched. The tour showcased long-time "folkies" such as Baez, along with newer voices in American folk-rock-country such as Lyle Lovett, Alison Krauss, and Suzanne Vega, thus ensuring itself a wide and ongoing following. In its Rhode Island home, the Folk Festival continued to present both the traditional and the vanguard of the folk genre. In 2005, alternative rock band the Pixies reversed Dylan's controversial move and gave up their amps and cords to play an acoustic set.

The Newport Jazz and Folk Festivals have had an impact far beyond their New England roots. Pioneers of the music festival scene, which by 2012 included hundreds of annual events around the United States, the Newport festivals have not only survived but have also remained vibrant and fresh, still the standard by which music festivals are judged.

Tina Gianoulis

SEE ALSO: *Baez, Joan; Basie, Count; Brubeck, Dave; Charles, Ray; Davis, Miles; Dylan, Bob; Fitzgerald, Ella; Folk Music; Franklin, Aretha; Guthrie, Arlo; Jazz; Led Zeppelin.*

BIBLIOGRAPHY

"After 16 Years, Folk Music Triumphs Again in Newport." *People*, August 26, 1985, 84.

Agostinelli, Anthony J. *The Newport Jazz Festival, Rhode Island, 1954–1971: A Significant Era in the Development of Jazz.* Providence, RI: Agostinelli, 1978.

Goldblatt, Burt. *Newport Jazz Festival: The Illustrated History.* New York: Dial Press, 1977.

Ward, Geoffrey C. "The City of Jazz." *Town & Country*, June 2005, 123–125.

Newsweek

One of America's "big three" weekly newsmagazines, *Newsweek* was founded in 1933, the same year that saw the launch of its rival *United States News* (later merged with *World Report*) and just ten years after the newsweekly genre had been established with the appearance of Henry Luce's *Time* in 1923. The magazine was originally named *News-Week* by founder Thomas J. C. Martyn, *Time*'s first foreign news editor. *News-Week*'s first issue, on February 17, 1933, featured seven photographs of current events on its cover. Four years later, in 1937, the publication merged with Raymond Moley's *Today* magazine and, with Vincent Astor as its president, changed its name to *Newsweek*.

Moley had been a member of President Franklin D. Roosevelt's "Brain Trust," and the editorial slant of the fledgling publication became generally more liberal than that of *Time*, though the two publications resembled each other in format and general appearance. *Newsweek* tried to distinguish itself from its older rival by introducing signed columns and avoiding the breezy language that had come to characterize the Luce publication. The magazine was sold to the *Washington Post* company in 1961, and the *Post*'s liberal-leaning publisher Katharine Graham added journalists and features designed to further distinguish *Newsweek* from its two rivals.

MID-TWENTIETH CENTURY

By the 1950s *Newsweek* had already been taking a leading role among American magazines by devoting more serious coverage to the issue of racial diversity in the United States through in-depth coverage of the "Negro issue" and the struggle for desegregation in the South. By the mid-1960s, when the national consensus was strained by urban unrest and concern over the war in Vietnam, editor Osborn Elliott helped to make the publication a vehicle for advocacy journalism. Without compromising its reportage of weekly news events, an issue in November 1967 included a twenty-three-page section titled "What Must Be Done." In the article, Elliott was quoted as saying, "The reason for this marked change of approach is that the editors have come to believe that at this particular time, on this particular subject, they could not fulfill their journalistic responsibility as citizens by simply reporting what X thinks of Y, and why Z disagrees." Public-policy experts and even rival newsmagazines applauded Elliott's approach, and it encouraged a new breed of advocacy journalists who questioned traditional notions of journalistic "objectivity."

LATE TWENTIETH CENTURY

Two incidents in the early 1980s were profoundly embarrassing to *Newsweek*. In 1981 an account that the magazine published featuring "Jimmy," an eight-year-old heroin addict in Washington, D.C., won a Pulitzer Prize for its reporter, Janet Cooke. She was forced to return the award when she admitted she had embellished details in the story. The second incident occurred on May 2, 1983, when *Newsweek* devoted twelve pages to what were purported to be "Hitler's Secret Diaries" but was later forced to admit that the story was a hoax.

In the mid-1980s, when Richard M. Smith was editor, *Newsweek*—always seeking to distinguish itself from *Time*—underwent a major redesign led by Roger Black. Its first foreign-language edition was published in Japanese in 1986; Korean (1991) and Spanish/Latin American (1996) editions followed. Also in 1996 *Newsweek* entered into a licensing agreement with the Most Group, a Russian publisher, by which it provided material from current issues of the magazine for a Russian language newsweekly called *Itogi* (summing up), with a circulation of 50,000. Maynard Parker, then editor of *Newsweek*, was quoted as saying "it is the first news magazine in Russia and I'm sure it will be challenging because we are in a country where democracy is a new form and where the free press does not have that long a history."

Newsweek further distinguished itself during this period by publishing special issues that offered comprehensive coverage of important news items, historical events, and contemporary ideas. Regular columnists such as Meg Greenfield, Jane Bryant Quinn, George Stephanopoulos, and George Will continued *Newsweek*'s tradition of printing expert opinion side-by-side with its news stories. Its long-running "Periscope" column presented background perspective on the week's news, and its "My Turn" column—the only one of its kind among the newsweeklies—became a vehicle for readers to present their own views on important issues. The magazine was praised for the depth of its reportage and for its journalistic restraint during the investigation of President Bill Clinton by Special Prosecutor Kenneth Starr in 1998.

In the 1990s *Newsweek* was in the vanguard of publications that began disseminating themselves via new digital technologies. It was the first newsweekly to introduce a quarterly CD-ROM version, a move that *Wired* magazine declared "Big Media's most valuable accomplishment to date." In 1994 the magazine was available online and, in 1998, newsweek.com became available on the Internet with extensive archival material and daily updates. At the end of the twentieth century, *Newsweek* also had four regional editions (Atlantic, Asia, Latin America, and Australia), four foreign-language editions (Japanese, Korean, Russian, and Spanish), and twenty-two bureaus around the world. Its circulation in 1999 was reported as 4.4 million worldwide and 3.27 million in the United States.

INTO THE TWENTY-FIRST CENTURY

The early twenty-first century has been a period of changing priorities for *Newsweek*. On June 19, 2000, the magazine entered into a partnership with NBC, MSNBC, and MSNBC.com to offer online access but opted to return to a stand-alone website in 2007. The new site offered improved design and technology. That same year, *Newsweek*'s multimedia team was nominated for an Emmy Award for Best News and Documentary. In 2011 traditional circulation plunged 31.6 percent, down to 1.6 million. Other newsmagazines were also suffering as more and more Americans began to access magazines through computers, smartphones, and other forms of electronic media. There was some doubt as to whether rival *U.S. News & World Report* would even survive.

Edward Moran

SEE ALSO: *Emmy Awards; Starr, Kenneth;* Time; *Vietnam; War on Drugs; The* Washington Post.

BIBLIOGRAPHY

Carew, Michael G. *The Power to Persuade: FDR, the Newsmagazines, and Going to War, 1939–1941.* Lanham, MD: University Press of America, 2005.

Graham, Katharine. *Personal History.* New York: Alfred A. Knopf, 1997.

Landers, James. *The Weekly War: Newsmagazines and Vietnam.* Columbia: University of Missouri Press, 2004.

Tebbel, John. *The American Magazine: A Compact History.* New York: Hawthorn Books, 1969.

Newton, Helmut *(1920–2004)*

Born in Berlin in 1920, Helmut Newton bought his first camera at age twelve. Fleeing Nazi Germany for Singapore, he eventually wound up in Australia, where he married June Freeman—who would become a photographer in her own right under the pseudonym Alice Springs—and took up fashion photography. Newton joined French *Vogue* in 1961, but his big breakthrough to fame came in the 1970s: in May 1975, his *Vogue* fashion spread, "The Story of Ohhh . . . ," shocked America with its explicit eroticism. For taking risks with the conventions of fashion photography, he was labeled by *Time* magazine "a rake, a roué, and a libertine" and by *Newsweek* as "the King of Kink." Other critics were not so kind, and eventually Newton was censored by both British and Italian *Vogue*.

In the ensuing two decades, Newton rose from censored to cherished, earning a reputation as both an art photographer and a fashion photographer. In response to charges of misogyny in a 1998 interview with *Newsweek*, he replied: "Would I spend my life photographing something I hate?" In the late 1990s Newton was best known for his probing images of celebrities and his compelling travel photographs. His photographs speak of his love of women, of romance and sexuality, of artifice, and of consumer culture. In 1999 a book of Newton's photographs, *Sumo*, was released in an edition so large it came with a Philippe Starck stand to hold it up. Although they had declined to play host to an exhibit years earlier, in 2000 the German Centre for Photography hosted a retrospective of his work in Berlin at the Mies van der Rohe Neue Nationalgalerie.

In 2004, after a history of cardiac problems, Newton had a heart attack while at the wheel and fatally crashed his car into a wall across the street from Chateau Marmont, Helmut and June's winter residence in Los Angeles. He was eighty-three years old. A philanthropist as well as a photographer, Newton had donated the rights to sixty of his images to the nonprofit organization Reporters sans Frontières (Reporters without Borders) a few months before his death. In the years since, his work has continued to be celebrated and posthumously published.

In 2004 June, Newton's wife of fifty-six years, published *Mrs. Newton*, her story of their marriage told in a combination of new writings, excerpts from old diaries, and photographs she took both personally and professionally. She followed this up with a 2007 documentary titled *Helmut by June*, which was shown on Cinemax Reel Life and later released on DVD. The film, made with the assistance of film director Brett Ratner, is a series of video snippets from the 1990s, taken during Newton's photo shoots with models and actresses, as well as clips from their private life. While most critics and students of photography consider Newton one of the world's greatest contemporary photographers, some continue to debate the violent sexuality, objectification, and fetishization of women in his photographs.

Ilene S. Goldman

SEE ALSO: *Supermodels;* Vogue.

BIBLIOGRAPHY

Fahey, David. "Interview with Helmut Newton." *Photo Bulletin*, December 1980.

Haskell, Molly. "Helmut Newton—The Theater of Shock." *Vogue*, October 1974, 639.

Newton, Helmut. *Helmut Newton.* Introduction by Karl Lagerfeld. Paris: Centre National de la Photographie, 1986.

Newton, Helmut. *Helmut Newton: New Images.* Bologna, Italy: Galleria d'art Modern, 1989.

Newton, Helmut, and Karl Lagerfeld. *Big Nudes.* New York: Xavier Moreau, 1982.